Henriksen (HM Inspector of Taxes) v Grafton Hotel Ltd [1942] 1 All ER 678, [1942] 2 KB 184

Glasgow and District Restaurateurs' and Hotel-keepers' Association v Dollan [1941] SC 93

Hotel Regina (Torquay) Ltd v Moon [1940] 2 KB 69

R v Liverpool Justices, ex p Liverpool Corpn [1934] 2 KB 277

Davis v Parker [1931] 2 KB 210

Lorden v Brooke-Hitching [1927] 2 KB 237

Smith, Appellant v Fennell, Respondent [1924] 1 KB 556

R v Wandsworth Licensing Justices, ex p Whitbread and Co Ltd [1921] 3 KB 487

Waller and Son Ltd v Thomas [1921] 1 KB 541

R v The Compensation Authority for the County of West Suffolk, ex p Hudson's Cambridge and Pampisford Breweries, Ltd; Same v Same, ex p Same [1919] 2 KB 374

Cassel v Inglis [1916 C 1058] [1916] 2 Ch 211 ICLR: Chancery Division 1 June 1916

Wootton v Lichfield Brewery Co [1914] W 2834 [1916] 1 Ch 44

R v Licensing Justices and Compensation Authority for the City of Chester; ex p Bennion [1914–15] All ER Rep 1186; All ER Reprints 18 May 1914

R v The Licensing Justices and Compensation Authority for the City of Chester, ex p Bennion [1914] 3 KB 349

Jones, Appellant v Jones, Respondent [1910] 2 KB 262

R v Shann [1910] 2 KB 418

Pennington, Appellant v Pincock, Respondent [1908] 2 KB 244

Tower Justices v Chambers [1904] 2 KB 903

Igoe, Appellant; Shann and Ors, Justices for the County and City of Manchester, Respondents [1902] 2 KB 467

R v Thornton, Justices, ex p Lacon & Co Ltd [1899] AC 222, [1898] 1 QB 334

Paterson's Licensing Acts 2012
Volume 2

Editors of previous editions

First to Tenth Editions: James Paterson, MA (Barrister-at-Law)

Eleventh to Twenty-First Editions: William W Mackenzie, MA (subsequently Lord Amulree KC, GBE, PC, LLD)

Twenty-Second to Twenty-Fifth Editions: Gerard R Hill, MA (Barrister-at-Law)

Twenty-Sixth and Twenty-Seventh Editions: Gerard R Hill, MA (Barrister-at-Law) and S E Major (Solicitor)

Twenty-Eighth to Forty-Fourth Editions: H B Hemming, LLB (Barrister-at-Law) and S E Major (Solicitor)

Forty-Fifth to Forty-Ninth Editions: Sir John Pedder, KBE, CB and E J Hayward, OBE (Solicitor)

Fiftieth Edition: E J Hayward, OBE and E R Raymond Boyd (Solicitors)

Fifty-First to Fifty-Fourth Editions: J Whiteside (Solicitor)

Fifty-Fifth to Sixty-Ninth Editions: F Morton Smith, BA (Solicitor)

Seventieth to Ninety-Sixth Editions: J N Martin, OBE (Solicitor)

Ninety-Seventh to One Hundred and Second Editions: Matthew Pink (Solicitor)

One Hundred and Third to One Hundred and Fifth Editions: Lawrence Stevens (Solicitor), Leslie Green (Solicitor) and Simon Mehigan (Barrister)

One Hundred and Sixth to One Hundred and Eighth Editions: Leslie Green (Solicitor), Simon Mehigan (Barrister), Jeremy Phillips (Solicitor, Partner) and Lawrence Stevens (Solicitor)

One Hundred and Ninth to One Hundred and Eleventh Editions: Simon Mehigan QC (Barrister) and Jeremy Phillips (Solicitor, Partner)

One Hundred and Twelfth Edition: Simon Mehigan QC (Barrister), Jeremy Phillips (Solicitor, Partner) and John Saunders QC (Barrister)

One Hundred and Thirteenth Edition and One Hundred and Fourteenth Editions: Simon Mehigan QC (Barrister), Jeremy Phillips (Barrister) and HH Judge John Saunders QC (the Recorder of Birmingham)

One Hundred and Fifteenth Edition to One Hundred and Twentieth Editions: Simon Mehigan QC (Barrister), Jeremy Phillips (Barrister) and The Honourable Mr Justice John Saunders

Paterson's Licensing Acts 2013

One hundred and twenty-first edition

Volume 2

Simon Mehigan QC
Bencher of Lincoln's Inn

Jeremy Phillips
Barrister, of Inner Temple

The Honourable Mr Justice Saunders

LexisNexis®

Members of the LexisNexis Group worldwide

United Kingdom	LexisNexis, a Division of Reed Elsevier (UK) Ltd, Halsbury House, 35 Chancery Lane, London, WC2A 1EL, and RSH, 1–3 Baxter's Place, Leith Walk Edinburgh EH1 3AF
Argentina	LexisNexis Argentina, Buenos Aires
Australia	LexisNexis Butterworths, Chatswood, New South Wales
Austria	LexisNexis Verlag ARD Orac GmbH & Co KG, Vienna
Benelux	LexisNexis Benelux, Amsterdam
Canada	LexisNexis Canada, Markham, Ontario
Chile	LexisNexis Chile Ltda, Santiago
China	LexisNexis China, Beijing and Shanghai
France	LexisNexis SA, Paris
Germany	LexisNexis Deutschland GmbH, Munster
Hong Kong	LexisNexis Hong Kong, Hong Kong
India	LexisNexis India, New Delhi
Italy	Giuffrè Editore, Milan
Japan	LexisNexis Japan, Tokyo
Malaysia	Malayan Law Journal Sdn Bhd, Kuala Lumpur
Mexico	LexisNexis Mexico, Mexico
New Zealand	LexisNexis NZ Ltd, Wellington

Published by LexisNexis

A CIP Catalogue record for this book is available from the British Library.

ISBN 978-1-4057-7034-7

9 781405 770347

Printed and bound by CPI Group (UK) Ltd, Croydon, CR0 4YY

Visit LexisNexis at http://www.lexisnexis.co.uk

Preface

Since the last edition of *Paterson's* there have been a number of significant developments in the gambling field.

First, the ambit of s 19 of the Gambling Act 2005 was discussed in *R (on the application of Camelot UK Lotteries Ltd) v The Gambling Commission* [2012] EWHC 2391 (Admin), a decision of the Divisional Court. In this rolled-up hearing of Camelot's application to proceed with its claim for judicial review, it was claimed that the Commission had erred in law in granting lottery licences to 51 non-commercial societies set up as Community Interest Companies ('CICs') which had common directors and to an external lottery manager ('ELM') which promoted the Health Lottery on behalf of the CICs. Each week at least one CIC ran a lottery draw with additional CICs joining in as more tickets were sold. Matters were arranged to prevent any CIC from exceeding the £4 million threshold for a single lottery set out in s 99(3)(a). The matters central to Camelot's claim were that the CICs were established and conducted for the purpose of private gain to the ELM in breach of s 19 and, further, that the Health Lottery was in reality a breach of the restrictions set out in s 99. The court rejected each of these claims (and, indeed, found that Camelot had inexcusably delayed bringing its claim for a period of thirteen months). It found that s 19 'focuses on the non-commercial society and not on those who work for it or who are employed by it or contracted by it to provide services . . . '. Accordingly the payments it makes to its officers and employees is not a private gain within s 19(1) as is recognised by s 19(3). An ELM is not required by the Act to be non-profit making although its profits are controlled under s 254. The fact that it makes profits does not cause the non-commercial society which contracts with it to be in breach of s 19(1). It also found that each weekly lottery was separate from others and that there was no basis for aggregating their proceeds. The thresholds in s 99(3) had not been exceeded.

Second, the following SIs are worth noting:

- 2012/1633, The Gambling Act 2005 (Amendment of Schedule) Order 2012 changes Sch 6 to the Gambling Act 2005 by deleting and adding to the list of enforcement/regulatory and sports governing bodies with whom the Gambling Commission may exchange information;
- 2012/1851, The Gambling (Licence Fees) (Miscellaneous Amendments) Regulations 2012 substitute new amounts for payments on account of gaming duty;
- 2012/1900, The Remote Gambling (Double Taxation Relief) Regulations 2012 provide for relief in relation to general betting, pool betting and remote gaming duty;
- 2012/829, The Gambling (Operating Licence and Single Machine Permit Fees) (Amendment) Regulations 2012 create new fee categories and add to the list of ancillary remote operating licences.

Whilst the latter might be viewed as a relatively non-controversial document it, *inter alia*, introduced a new so called 'sub-category of remote general betting (standard) operating licence'. The potential problems caused by this new licence arise as a result of the effect of s 65(4), which provides the Secretary of State with power to amend s 65(2) so as to add or remove or vary a kind of operating licence. However, no use having yet been made of this power it is worth asking whether this new licence category and indeed others, such as the trading room licence which became available in August 2008 (see para **6.2167** below), have been validly introduced. Whilst this new licence is described by DCMS and the Gambling Commission as a 'new sub-category' of licence it remains a matter of considerable debate whether such a description achieves avoidance of the need to comply with s 65(4). We are very doubtful whether these new licences have a valid foundation under the Gambling Act.

Among recent publications from the Gambling Commission the following are noteworthy:

- LCCP: a consolidated version of this was published in December 2011 (para **6.2060** below) and a supplement in respect of personal licences in May 2012 (para **6.2712** below);
- The Prevention of Money Laundering and Combating the Finance of Terrorism (2nd Edition), December 2011 (para **6.2241** below);
- Revised Machine Standards for categories A and B1, B2, B3 and B4, C and complex category D, June 2012 (paras **6.2525–6.2540A** below);
- Gaming machine manufacturing, supply maintenance, installation and repair, December 2011 (para **6.2634.4** below);
- Is a licence needed to repair circuit board /PCs used in gaming machines?, August 2012 (para **6.2634.5** below);
- Promoting multiple society lotteries: Advice for society lotteries and external lottery managers promoting individual lotteries under one brand, August 2011;
- Offering lottery, gaming and gaming products under common branding, June 2012 (para **6.2540.1** below);
- Code of practice for equal chance gaming in clubs and premises with an alcohol licence, March 2012 (para **6.2673** below);
- Indicators of betting as primary gambling activity, November 2011 (para **6.2172** below).

The last document calls for particular discussion. It appears that, despite the Commission having made its position clear, difficulties continue to arise on the primary use requirement particularly in the case of betting shops. These stimulated it to publish the above detailed document. What follows is a brief summary of some of its principal points.

It sets out six indicators of whether betting is taking place as the primary gambling activity; they derive from the LCCP requirements and what is said to be 'accepted as typical of commercial betting shop provision in the British market' partly based on gambling industry statistics. These indicators are of general application and it seems that an operator who cannot fulfill them will bear the burden of explaining why his operation is licence compliant.

The first indicator: offering established core products. The Commission expect to see broadcast live betting opportunities for horseracing, greyhound racing, football, numbers and other sports such as golf, tennis and cricket. Taking horseracing as an example, typically regular daily betting would be offered on races in GB and Ireland at two or more meetings together with foreign racing. Live pictures would usually be provided and single, multiple and ante-post bets offered, together with forecast and tricast options and the ability to bet at the starting price or to take the current price.

The second indicator; the provision of information on products/events. This will usually include customer information screens giving all relevant details of events including times and locations, conditions, runners, riders and odds. In addition, form guides and some of the sort of information found in the *Racing Post* would be made available.

The third indicator; promotion of gambling opportunities and products, typically by advertising.

The fourth indicator; the actual use made of betting facilities. The Commission understands that gaming machines are becoming more popular in betting shops but it still expects to see significant betting activity and will consider profits from betting, slippage and staking against industry averages together with business plans which set out the expected use of the premises for betting.

The fifth indicator; the size of the premises must be sufficient to provide betting facilities as the primary gambling activity.

The sixth indicator; the delivery of betting facilities. If the shop offers betting solely by machine it must have more of those than gaming machines. If the shop has a greater number of gaming machines than betting machines then it must also have a permanent manned counter for taking bets in order to fulfill the requirement of a betting licence.

The Commission has further reiterated its views in an information document and issued a special bulletin to licensing authorities in August 2012 on primary gambling activity. These, in particular, address the fourth indicator referred to above. See paras **6.2173–6.2174** below.

Finally, although the changes to the Gambling Act—in particular to s 36—in order to require all offshore operators who have a UK facing business to be licensed, have not yet been published there has been a further call for amendments to the law. In July 2012 the Commons Culture, Media and Sport Select Committee published a report in which it made a number of radical suggestions. These include allowing any local authority to decide whether or not it wishes to have casinos in its area rather than the current designation of areas. It also calls for an increase in the maximum number of B2 gaming machines in casinos and in betting shops in certain cases. It must be doubtful whether any such changes will be enacted in the near future.

The law is stated as at 1 September 2012 although later developments have been included where possible.

Simon Mehigan QC	Jeremy Phillips	The Honourable Mr Justice Saunders
Francis Taylor Building	Francis Taylor Building	Royal Courts of Justice
Inner Temple	Inner Temple	Strand
London EC4Y 7BY	London EC4Y 7BY	London WC2A 2LL
simon@netherbury.demon.co.uk	clerks@ftb.eu.com	

Simon Mehigan QC	Jeremy Phillips	The Honourable Mr Justice Saunders
Francis Taylor Building	Francis Taylor Building	Royal Courts of Justice
Inner Temple	Inner Temple	Strand
London EC4Y 7BY	London EC4Y 7BY	London WC2A 2LL
[illegible].co.uk	clerks@ftb.eu.com	

Table of Contents

Table of Statutes

Paragraph references printed in bold type indicate where the Act is set out in part or in full. Please note all references to paragraphs in Parts 9, 10 and 11 can be found on the CD that accompanies this edition.

C

U

Table of Statutory Instruments

Paragraph references printed in bold type indicate where the SI is set out in part or in full. Please note all references to paragraphs in Parts 9, 10 and 11 can be found on the CD that accompanies this edition.

Table of Other Documents

Please note all references to paragraphs in Parts 9, 10 and 11 can be found on the CD that accompanies this edition.

Table of Cases

Please note all references to paragraphs in Parts 9, 10 and 11 can be found on the CD that accompanies this edition.

C

D

R

S

T

V

W

Y

Z

Part 6

Gambling Act 2005

Section 1

Commentary

INTRODUCTION

6.1 After a tortuous path through Parliament with much last minute horse-trading[1] (partly caused by a lack of parliamentary time before a general election) the Gambling Act emerged in April 2005. The Act to some extent gives effect to proposals in the White Paper 'A Safe Bet for Success' (Cm 5397) published in March 2002. What follows is a commentary on the Act although it is of somewhat tentative nature. Its lack of certainty arises from a number of sources not least that the Act, its copious secondary legislation and the many publications from both the DCMS and the Gambling Commission have not yet been the subject of much judicial scrutiny. It is of fundamental importance that the reader is aware of the documents which are included herein under Section 4 'Additional Material' (para **6.2000** ff below). They contain the current views of the regulatory authorities on many important topics.

In any event it is now clear that the Commission is not merely a rebranded Gaming Board. Unlike the latter it has a comprehensive ability to regulate all gaming, betting and lotteries save for spread betting and the National Lottery. Having a regulator has already proved to be a shock for betting operators; hitherto they had been mercifully free of such an interloper.

The primary functions of the Commission are to:

- issue operating licences to authorise the licensee to provide facilities for gambling;
- issue personal licences to authorise the licensee to perform the functions of a specified management office or a specified operational function;
- specify general licence conditions for each type of licence, and any individual licence conditions it considers appropriate;
- issue codes of practice about how facilities for gambling are provided;
- monitor licence holders;
- investigate and prosecute illegal gambling and other offences under the Gambling Act;
- issue guidance to local authorities on their role under the Gambling and the principles to be applied by them; and
- advise the Secretary of State on the incidence of gambling and how it is carried out, on the effects of gambling, and on its regulation, partly by carrying out regular prevalence studies.

We have included in the additional materials (para **6.2000** ff below) the very extensive Explanatory Notes published with the Act. We take the view that, whilst we do not always agree with their contents, they generally have particular importance; unlike the Notes attached to the Licensing Act 2003 which merely provide a précis of that Act these Notes in many cases give a distinct steer towards the legislative intent of a particular provision or clarify what may appear to be ambiguities or areas of doubt in the mind of the reasonable reader. For example, when looking at s 36(3) on the complex topic of territorial application of the Act and in particular the impact of s 33 (which creates a number of offences) an unlicensed or non-exempted provider of remote gambling facilities will understand that he will only face criminal liability if at least one relevant piece of remote gambling equipment (as defined in s 36(4) and (5)) is situated in Great Britain. Even if no piece of such equipment is so situated he may prefer to have some comfort if he is providing remote facilities for gambling from, say Gibraltar, to punters based in Great Britain. Explanatory Note 139 provides him with precisely that comfort. It informs him that even if punters in Great Britain can 'receive the gambling he is providing' (sic) he is not in breach of the Act. However it also points out that a person commits an offence if any part of his remote equipment is located in Great Britain and he does not have the required authorisation or is not covered by an exception. It emphasises that this is so regardless of whether the gambling facilities are provided to people in Great Britain or (wholly) outside.

However what is the status of such Notes? In our view there is considerable confusion among (dare we say it) lawyers as to the use which can be made of them in the construction of statutory provisions.

Perhaps the most helpful guidance on this topic is to be found in the speech of Lord Steyn in *R (Westminster City Council) v National Asylum Support Service*[2]. His Lordship offered the following advice, all of which appears to be relevant and which is therefore quoted in full:

> 'Brief explanatory memoranda used to be printed at the front of a Bill. Such a document was a précis and did not provide background. In addition ministers were provided with Notes on Clauses, which did by and large explain what a clause in a Bill was meant to do. Later, in an era of greater transparency, Notes on Clauses were made available to backbenchers.
>
> In 1999 a new system was introduced. It involves publishing Explanatory Notes alongside the majority of public bills introduced in either Houses of Parliament by a Government minister: see Christopher Jenkins QC, First Parliamentary Counsel, "Helping the Reader of Bills and Acts" (1999) 149 NLJ 798. The texts of such notes are prepared by the Government department responsible for the legislation. The Explanatory Notes do not form part of the Bill, are not endorsed by Parliament and cannot be amended by Parliament. The notes are intended to be neutral in political tone: they aim to explain the effect of the text and not to justify it. The purpose is to help the reader to get his bearings and to ease the task of assimilating the law. This new procedure has the imprimatur of the House of Commons Select Committee on Modernization and the House of Lords Procedure Committee. The Explanatory Notes accompany the Bill on introduction and are updated in the light of changes to the Bill made in the parliamentary process. Explanatory Notes are usually published by the time the legislation comes into force. Unlike Hansard material there are no costly researches involved. Explanatory Notes for both Bills and Acts are published by Her Majesty's Stationery Office. The notes are also available on the internet at: http://www.parliament.uk for Bills and http://www.legislation.hmso.gov.uk for Acts. [See para **6.2000** ff for the GA 2005 Explanatory Notes.]
>
> The question is whether in aid of the interpretation of a statute the court may take into account the Explanatory Notes and, if so, to what extent. The starting point is that language in all legal texts conveys meaning according to the circumstances in which it was used. *It follows that the context must always be identified and considered before the process of construction or during it.* It is therefore wrong to say that the court may only resort to evidence of the contextual scene when an ambiguity has arisen. In regard to contractual interpretation this was made clear by

Lord Wilberforce in *Prenn v Simmonds* [1971] 1 WLR 1381, 1384–1386, and in *Reardon Smith Line Ltd v Yngvar Hansen-Tangen* [1976] 1 WLR 989, 995–996. Moreover, in his important judgment in *Investors Compensation Scheme Ltd v West Bromwich Building Society* [1998] 1 WLR 896, 912–913, Lord Hoffmann made crystal clear that an ambiguity need not be established before the surrounding circumstances may be taken into account. The same applies to statutory construction. In *River Wear Commissioners v Adamson* (1877) 2 App Cas 743, 763, Lord Blackburn explained the position as follows:

"I shall . . . state, as precisely as I can, what I understand from the decided cases to be the principles on which the courts of law act in construing instruments in writing; and a statute is an instrument in writing. In all cases the object is to see what is the intention expressed by the words used. But, from the imperfection of language, it is impossible to know what that intention is without inquiring farther, and seeing what the circumstances were with reference to which the words were used, and what was the object, appearing from those circumstances, which the person using them had in view; for the meaning of words varies according to the circumstances with respect to which they were used."

Again, there is no need to establish an ambiguity before taking into account the objective circumstances to which the language relates. Applied to the subject under consideration the result is as follows. Insofar as the Explanatory Notes cast light on the objective setting or contextual scene of the statute, and the mischief at which it is aimed, such materials are therefore always admissible aids to construction. They may be admitted for what logical value they have. Used for this purpose Explanatory Notes will sometimes be more informative and valuable than reports of the Law Commission or advisory committees, Government green or white papers, and the like. After all, the connection of Explanatory Notes with the shape of the proposed legislation is closer than pre-parliamentary aids which in principle are already treated as admissible: see Cross, Statutory Interpretation (3rd edn, 1995), pp 160–161. If used for this purpose the recent reservations in dicta in the House of Lords about the use of Hansard materials in aid of construction are not engaged: see *R v Secretary of State for the Environment, Transport and the Regions, ex p Spath Holme Ltd* [2001] 2 AC 349, 407; *Robinson v Secretary of State for Northern Ireland* [2002] UKHL 32, (2002) Times, 26 July, in particular per Lord Hoffmann, at paragraph 40. On this basis the constitutional arguments which I put forward extra-judicially are also not engaged: '*Pepper v Hart*: A Re-examination' (2001) 21 Oxford Journal of Legal Studies 59.

If exceptionally there is found in Explanatory Notes a clear assurance by the executive to Parliament about the meaning of a clause, or the circumstances in which a power will or will not be used, that assurance may in principle be admitted against the executive in proceedings in which the executive places a contrary contention before a court. This reflects the actual decision in *Pepper v Hart* [1993] AC 593. What is impermissible is to treat the wishes and desires of the Government about the scope of the statutory language as reflecting the will of Parliament. The aims of the Government in respect of the meaning of clauses as revealed in Explanatory Notes cannot be attributed to Parliament. The object is to see what is the intention expressed by the words enacted.'

Although these remarks are strictly *obiter*, they must carry considerable weight having regard to their source. The other four members of the Appellate Committee remained silent on the point, restricting themselves to a discussion of the substantive question then before the House. Researches have not produced a subsequent case in which this reasoning or conclusion is disapproved. Indeed it would seem to have been applied in several cases including:

- *R (S & Marper) v Chief Constable of South Yorkshire*[3] in which Notes were used to help identify the mischief at which section 65(1A) Police and Criminal Evidence Act 1984 was directed.
- *Wilson v First County Trust Ltd*[4]:

  'The courts, similarly, must be able to have regard to information contained in explanatory notes prepared by the relevant government department and published with a Bill. The courts would be failing in the due discharge of the new role assigned to them by Parliament [under the Human Rights Act 1998] if they were to exclude from consideration relevant background information whose only source was a ministerial statement in Parliament or an explanatory note prepared by his department while the Bill was proceeding through Parliament. By having regard to such material the court would not be 'questioning' proceedings in Parliament or intruding improperly into the legislative process or ascribing to Parliament the views expressed by a minister. The court would merely be placing itself in a better position to understand the legislation.' (per Lord Nicholls of Birkenhead).
- *P v National Association of Schoolmasters/Union of Women Teachers*[5] in which Lord Hoffmann made reference to notes accompanying the Employment Relations Act 1999 in an attempt to discern the intended function of section 232A. Although he concluded that they are not helpful his Lordship cited with approval the remarks of Lord Steyn in *R (Westminster City Council) v National Asylum Support Service* (quoted above).

It would seem that 'Explanatory Notes' are, quite independently of the rule in *Pepper v Hart*, admissible as part of the 'enacting history' of legislation, presumably as an exercise of the court's inherent jurisdiction to consider all relevant material in attempting to discern the meaning of the statute.

---

1 Evidenced by the almost total emasculation of the original provisions concerning casinos: see in particular ss 166 and 175.

2 [2002] UKHL 38, [2002] 4 All ER 654, [2002] 1 WLR 2956.

3 [2004] UKHL 39, [2004] 4 All ER 193.

4 [2003] UKHL 40, [2003] 4 All ER 97.

5 [2003] UKHL 8, [2003] All ER (D) 384 (Feb). See also *Chief Constable of Cumbria v Wright and Wood* [2006] EWHC 3574 (Admin), [2007] 1 WLR 1407, [2006] All ER (D) 265 (Nov); *Sunlife Assurance Co of Canada (UK) Ltd v HMRC* [2009] EWHC 60 (Ch); *Homeserve Membership Ltd v HMRC* [2009] EWHC 1311 (Ch) and *The Law Debenture Trust Corp plc v Elektrim SA* [2009] EWHC 1801 (Ch).

Transitional provisions

6.2 Schedule 18 sets out a number of powers in respect of the continuation of pre-2005 Act licences. Various statutory instruments (in particular, SIs 2006/1038, 2006/1758 and 2006/3272, as amended by SI 2006/3361 and by SIs 2007/1157 and 2007/1527) set out detailed transitional rules. In December 2006, the DCMS published a very helpful guide on the topic. Given that these arrangements are now likely to be of historical interest only, no further comment is made about them here.

PART 1: GENERAL CONCEPTS

Section 1 *The Licensing objectives*

6.10 Content of the objectives The Act sets out three such objectives.

The first objective is based on attempting to ensure that there is no link between gambling and criminal activities. Gambling must not be a source of crime or disorder nor must it be associated with crime or disorder nor must it be used to support crime.

The second objective is based on fairness: gambling must be conducted fairly and openly.

The third objective is based on protection of the vulnerable; gambling must not be used to harm or exploit children and 'other vulnerable persons'. No doubt the latter category will include those for whom gambling has become an addiction or whose gambling conduct has had significant detrimental effect on their lives or the lives of their families[1].

1 See, for example GA 2005, s 23(5)(f), s 24(10)(d) and s 25(4)(f) where persons who have knowledge of social problems relating to gambling are to be consulted by the Gambling Commission before it publishes its statement of principles, codes of practice and guidance to local authorities. The importance of 'social responsibility' as a concept which must be adhered to by operators is demonstrated by the Gambling Commission document 'Licence Conditions and Codes of Practice' (see para **6.2060** below).

6.11 The relevance of the objectives It seems, despite their (necessarily) general content, that the objectives are intended to play a central role in the functions of the Commission in relation to operating and personal licences and are to be used by those local authorities which are designated under s 2 as 'licensing authorities'.

In particular the Commission must:

- aim to pursue and if appropriate have regard to the objectives when carrying out any function under the Act[1].
- in its Statement of principles for licensing and regulation prepared under s 23, explain how the principles to be applied are expected to assist it in its pursuit of the objectives[2]. In September 2009 the Commission published an updated version of 'Statement of Principles for Licensing and Regulation' (see para **6.2040** below). Notwithstanding that this is a general statement of intent it describes a number of specific stances. For example it states that there will be a presumption in favour of refusing an application or reviewing a licence should relevant offences have been committed.
- in considering an application for an operating licence and a personal licence have regard to the objectives[3].

A licensing authority must in exercising its functions:

- under Part 8 (Premises Licences), aim to permit the use of premises for gambling in so far as the authority thinks it reasonably consistent with the objectives[4].
- under Sch 12 (club gaming permits and club machine permits) have regard to any Commission guidance issued under s 25 and (subject to that) to the objectives[5].
- under Sch 13 (licensed premises gaming machine permits) have regard to the objectives[6].

Moreover the authority has a power (but not a duty) in exercising its functions under Sch 10 (Family Entertainment Centre Gaming Machine Permits) and Sch 14 (Prize Gaming Permits) to have regard to the objectives[7].

---

1 GA 2005, s 22.
2 GA 2005, s 23(2).
3 GA 2005, ss 70(1)(a) and 128.
4 GA 2005, s 153(1)(c).
5 GA 2005, Sch 12, para 27.
6 GA 2005, Sch 13, para 4.
7 GA 2005, Sch 10, para 7(3), Sch 14, para 8(3).

Section 2 *Licensing authorities*

6.12 Some local authorities are designated as licensing authorities[1]; the most numerous are district councils and county councils. Licensing authorities exercise a number of powers; in particular they will decide whether or not to issue premises licences applications, club gaming, club machine, licensed premises gaming machine, family entertainment centre gaming machine and prize gaming permits. They will also have the power to review premises licences already granted. They are also the recipients of temporary use notices under s 219. They may also resolve not to issue casino licences under s 166. They are under a duty to publish a three-year licensing policy setting out a statement of the principles which they propose to apply in exercising their functions under the Act[2]. Secondary legislation published in 2007 sets out the maximum fees chargeable by licensing authorities for applications and annual and other fees for premises licences under Part 8[3]. Further, provision is made in respect of the procedures of licensing committees and sub committees where a hearing is required to be held in respect of premises licence applications. This is unsurprisingly uncontroversial. The DCMS and the Commission have recently published a number of documents concerning licensing authorities. See Gambling Act 2005 Permits: Training Materials for Licensing Authorities, March 2007 (see para **6.2635** below), the more general Training Materials for Licensing Authorities, the April 2007 revised version of the August 2006 document (see para **6.2645** below), and the Guidance to Licensing Authorities on Setting Premises Licence Fees, dated May 2007 (see para **6.2650** below). Further, see the Commission's publication 'Advice to licensing authorities on information exchange with the Gambling Commission', the second edition of which was published in December 2007 and updated in April 2008 (see para **6.2640** below). This identifies five categories of information which will be exchanged between the Commission and licensing authorities. Moreover in September 2012 the Commission produced the fourth edition of its 'Guidance to Licensing Authorities' (see para **6.2655** below). This covers, inter alia, the following topics:

- Principles to be applied by licensing authorities
- Licensing authority statements of licensing policy
- Premises licences
- Definitions of 'responsible authorities' and 'interested parties'
- Premises licence conditions
- Reviews of premises licences by licensing authority
- Provisional statements

- Rights of appeal and Judicial Review
- Information exchange between the commission and licensing authorities.
- Temporary use notices
- Occasional use notices
- Gaming machines
- Casinos
- Bingo
- Betting premises
- Tracks
- AGCs
- FECs (both licensed and unlicensed)
- Permits
- Club gaming permits and club machine permits
- Alcohol-licensed premises
- Prize gaming and prize gaming permits
- Non-commercial gaming
- Permitted and exempt gaming in alcohol-licensed premises
- Travelling fairs
- Crown immunity and excluded premise
- Territorial application of the Gambling Act 2005
- Door supervision
- Small society lotteries
- Chain gift schemes
- Compliance and enforcement of the 2005 Act.

1 Cf GA 2005, s 25(6) and Sch 11, para 41 which define local authorities under the Act. Such local authorities are distinct from licensing authorities under the Act: they have, for example, a specific role to play as registrars of Small Societies Lotteries under Sch 11.

2 GA 2005, s 349. The three-year period will run from 31 January 2007: the Gambling Act 2005 (Licensing Authority Policy Statement) (First Appointed Day) Order 2006, SI 2006/637. The form of the statement and procedures to be followed in preparing and publishing the policy and any revision of it are addressed in the Gambling Act 2005 (Licensing Authority Policy Statement) (England and Wales) Regulations 2006, SI 2006/636. See para **6.1510** below.

3 Gambling (Premises Licence Fees) (England and Wales) Regulations 2007, SI 2007/479.

6.13 Definitions of key concepts Sections 3–18 and s 235 contain a number of provisions which are of fundamental importance to an understanding of the Act. In particular they set out various critical concepts and in so doing enable the following questions to be applied to the relevant facts.

(1) Do those facts constitute gambling as defined in s 3? If not, the regime of the Act will not apply.

(2) If they do, with what type of gambling are we concerned? Is the gambling

  (a) gaming within s 6?
  if so, is it
    (i) casino gaming[1] under s 7; or
    (ii) equal chance gaming (such as bingo[2]) under s 8; or
    (iii) machine gaming[3] under s 235;

  (b) betting[4] under ss 9–13?

or

(c) a lottery[5] under s 14 and Sch 2?

In deciding, in those cases which appear to involve cross-category activities, whether gaming, betting or a lottery exists ss 16–18 provide assistance.

(3) Does the activity involve remote gambling[6]?

(4) Is any person providing facilities for gambling (or making a machine available for use)?

When these questions have been answered it will then be possible to decide whether a licence is required under the Act and, if it is which type of operating licence is relevant under Part 5 of the Act.

---

1 See the Gambling Commission publications at paras **6.2180–6.2244.1**.

2 See the Gambling Commission publications at paras **6.2265–6.2297**.

3 See the Gambling Commission publications at paras **6.2360**, **6.2520–6.2634.5**, **6.2657**, **6.2660–6.2671**, **6.2673–6.2674** and **6.2685–6.2686** below.

4 See the Gambling Commission publications at paras **6.2100–6.2177** and **6.2674** below.

5 See the Gambling Commission publications at paras **6.2300–6.2359B** below.

6 See the Gambling Commission publications at paras **6.2395–6.2513** below.

6.14 Gambling Gambling comprises gaming, betting and the participation in a lottery.

(a) Gaming, defined in s 6, means playing a game of chance for a prize. Such a game does not include a sport, but does include a game which involves both chance and skill (even if the chance element can be eliminated by superlative skill). Moreover it encompasses a game which is 'presented' as involving an element of chance. Presumably with the emphasis on presentation it is irrelevant that the game in fact does not involve chance. It is clear that the concept of 'chance' is closely modelled on the definition found in s 52 Gaming Act 1968.

The concept of 'playing' is defined so as to include a sole participant in a game and even if a computer represents the actions of other players[1].

'Prize' is defined as including money or its worth including a stake and anything provided by the organiser of the gaming.

Playing for a prize encompasses acquiring a chance of winning a prize as a result of playing a game of chance whether or not the player risks losing anything.

Once it has been determined that gaming exists it is necessary to examine which type of gaming is relevant. Sections 7 and 8 distinguish (as does, for example, s 65) between casino gaming and equal chance gaming. A casino is defined as 'an arrangement whereby people are given an opportunity to participate in one or more casino games' ie a game of chance which is not equal chance gaming. Section 8(4) makes it clear that it is possible to provide casino gaming via remote means.

Equal chance gaming exists if it does not involve playing or staking against a bank (however described and whether controlled or administered by a player) and if the chances are equally favourable to all participants.

'Participants' in relation to a game of chance is defined in s 353(1), to include 'a person who discharges an administrative or other function in relation to the game'. The width of these words taken with the definition of equal chance gaming produces the result that a bingo caller (no doubt as agent for his employer) must have as equal a chance of winning the game as those who are normally described as players. This is patently absurd; however that is what the Act appears to say. If common sense is applied one would reject such a conclusion. In legalistic terms one surely here needs to apply that canon of statutory construction which excludes absurdity.

(b) Betting is generally defined by s 9[3]. Its primary meaning is the making or acceptance of a bet[3] on the outcome of an event, or likelihood of anything occurring or not, or whether anything is true or not. It is not relevant that the event has already occurred at the time when the bet is entered into or that one party is then aware of the result. Nor, in relation to a bet placed on the likelihood of anything occurring or not that the thing has already occurred or failed to occur and that one party is aware of that. Clearly betting under the Act will encompass many prize competitions which had hitherto been regulated by s 14 of the Lotteries and Amusements Act 1976.

(c) A lottery is defined in s 14(2) as a 'simple' lottery if (a) payment is required in order to participate, (b) one or more prizes are allocated to one or more members of a class and (c) the allocation of prizes relies wholly on chance. The legislation which the Act replaces provided no definition of lottery although the common law definition[4] now appears to have been adopted but extended in respect of certain skill requirements; see s 14(5). A 'complex' lottery exists if in addition to (a) and (b) above the prizes are allocated by a series of processes and the first of these relies wholly on chance. This definition clearly brings within the ambit of a lottery those events which subsequent to the initial process contain an element of skill.

The three basic elements (a) payment to participate[5], (b) prizes and (c) chance are further examined in the Act. Schedule 2 sets out detailed provisions as to what constitutes a payment to enter. Apart from including within payment obvious matters such as paying money or its worth it is noteworthy that paying a price for goods which reflects the opportunity to participate is sufficient. Presumably if it can be shown that the goods and the opportunity to win a prize sold at £X were previously sold at £X there will be no lottery. Moreover payment of more than a 'normal rate' for making a telephone call will amount to a payment to enter. Whether using a premium rate line to enter will cause a relevant payment to be made is not at all clear because of the definition of 'normal rate' set out in para 5(2)(a). This states that a rate is normal if it does not reflect the opportunity to enter a lottery. It could be that the premium rate charged is no more than a standard premium rate and has not been enhanced to include the entry fee.

Further payments which are caught are those made to discover whether a prize has been won and to claim a prize. However in some instances giving all participants a genuine choice of a free entry can avoid the lottery label even if, in the event, any (or even most) participants do pay to play[6].

'Prize' is specifically stated in s 14(4) to include any money, articles or services howsoever described.

Further provision as to the meaning of the element of chance and the contrast between it and skill is made by s 14(5). This has the effect of treating an allocation of prizes as relying wholly on chance even if there is a requirement to exercise skill or judgement or to display knowledge if the requirement cannot reasonably be expected to prevent a significant proportion of persons who participate from receiving a prize and if the requirement cannot reasonably be expected to prevent a significant proportion of persons who wish to participate in that arrangement from doing so.

1 GA 2005, s 6(3).

3 Spread betting is excluded from the definition of betting. See GA 2005, s 10 which cross refers to FSMA 2000, s 22. The Commission has no jurisdiction over spread bets. Sections 11–13 and Sch 1 make specific provision for betting in respect of prize competitions, pool betting and betting intermediaries.

3 'Bet' is not defined in GA 2005 but apart from in the case of pool betting, it usually comprises a contract in which a stake is placed/agreed to be placed by the parties, which stake (or a multiple thereof) becomes payable to whichever party has successfully forecasted the outcome of a future uncertain event. Accordingly, to place a bet is to hazard a stake in such circumstances. See also *A-G v Luncheon and Sports Club Ltd* [1929] AC 400 at 406 (Lord Dunedin); *Ellesmere v Wallace* [1929] 2 Ch 1 at 49 (Russell LJ).

4 See *Readers Digest Association Ltd v Williams* [1976] 1 WLR 1109.

5 See 'Prize Competitions and Free Draws' published by the Gambling Commission in 2009 (see paras (**6.2089** and **6.2090** below).

6 GA 2005, Sch 2, para 8.

6.15 Cross-category activities Although in some cases it will be obvious whether betting or gaming is taking place or whether there is participation in a lottery and accordingly which type of operating licence is required under s 65, many instances will arise in which an activity appears to straddle two distinct categories. The Act seeks to come to the rescue in such cases by consigning certain activities to a specific berth. Whether its mechanisms for so doing are reasonable is a moot point; see the final sub-paragraph below.

Section 16 informs us that if a transaction satisfies both the definition of betting in s 9 and the definition of gaming in s 6 then if it is also pool betting under s 12 it shall be treated as betting under the Act. However all other cases which appear to be both betting and gaming are to be considered as gaming.

Section 17 makes complex provision for an arrangement which satisfies both the definition of a game of chance (s 6) and a lottery under s 14. If a person who pays in order to join the class amongst whose members prizes are allocated is required to participate in, or to be successful in, more than three processes before becoming entitled to a prize then the Act will treat the arrangement as a game of chance and not a lottery. Moreover, if it satisfies various parts of Sch 11, as listed in s 17(3) or is promoted in reliance on a lottery operating licence, it will be treated as a lottery. However any other arrangement will be treated as a game of chance.

Section 18 is concerned with activities which satisfy the definition of lottery in s 14 and the definition of pool betting in s 12, or the definition of betting in s 9 because it is a prize competition falling within s 11. In such a case if the transaction falls within those parts of Sch 11 identified in s 18(2) it will be treated as a lottery. Otherwise it will qualify as betting under the Act[1].

The designation of an activity as gaming rather than betting or a lottery is likely in some cases to cause serious difficulty in that the only types of gaming operating licences available under s 65 are for casinos and bingo. Unlike the case of betting, the Act does not make provision for the grant of a general gaming licence. In many instances an activity which is neither an unlawful lottery nor betting (such as many forms of commercial poker) will not be contrary to the gaming provisions but will be unlicensable other than in a casino. Was this intended? Why was the opportunity to regulate commercial poker not taken? It seems that the point was not considered.

1 GA 2005, s 18(3).

6.16 Remote gambling If participation in gambling uses the internet, telephone, television, radio or any technology for facilitating communication that will constitute remote gambling under s 4 with the consequence that a remote operating licence under s 67 will be required by the provider of the gambling facilities.

The effect of this provision is likely to be quite far-reaching. For example, a bookmaker who runs a betting office at which he accepts bets from those who are physically present on the premises and from punters who phone in their bets will require two types of licence under the Act; both a general betting operating licence under s 65(2)(c) and a remote operating licence under s 67[1]. Others, such as betting exchanges, which only provide gambling by remote communication will only require the latter type of operating licence.

1 In fact the Commission has avoided the full burden of an operator having to have two licences in some cases by introducing ancillary remote licences. For example the owner of a non-remote general betting operating licence can obtain authorisation to take telephone bets in this way. See, for example, its publication 'Typical Licence Conditions and Codes of Practice for Ancillary Remote General Betting Operators (August 2007) (*Paterson 2009*, para **6.2420**).

6.17 Facilities for gambling Whether or not a person provides facilities for gambling is critical in the Act. For example, criminal liability under s 33 only initially arises if a person has been providing such facilities. Section 5 sets out when such facilities are being provided. In particular s 5(1) states that such provision takes place if a person

(a) invites others to gamble in accordance with arrangements made by him
(b) provides, operates or administers arrangements for gambling by others, or
(c) participates in the operation or administration of gambling by others

Subsection (3) brings within the net remote communication facilities in certain circumstances; sub-s (2) excludes various matters from the definition of facilities for gambling.

It seems that the most controversial part of the definition is likely to be (a) simply because Explanatory Note 751 states that 'both parties to a bet . . . are capable of providing facilities for betting' and states specifically that a punter may be providing facilities for gambling. In most cases (maybe all) this seems an absurd claim; how is a punter who merely bets at the displayed price making any invitation (as required by s 5(1)(a)) to anyone and how can any punter be concerned with making the type of arrangement which is necessary under s 5(1)(a)[1]?

1 See also paras **6.31–6.46** below.

PART 2: THE GAMBLING COMMISSION

6.20 On 1 October 2005[1] the Gaming Board metamorphosed into the Gambling Commission under s 21 of the Act. The Commission regulates all commercial gambling in Great Britain (other than spread betting and the National Lottery). Schedules 4 and 5 to the GA 2005 set out a number of fundamental rules which, inter alia, relate to the Commission's constitution, the tenure of its chairman and of the other commissioners, its powers to appoint staff and the financial arrangements which are necessary for it to function. Like the Board it will have to produce an annual report[2]. Moreover it will have the power to delegate any of its functions to a committee of commissioners or to a single commissioner or to an employee[3].

In May 2005 'An Introductory Guide to the Gambling Commission' was published by the Commission. It has since produced a large number of very useful publications. The current editions of the majority of those are indexed at the beginning of, and reproduced in, Section 4 below.

Part 2 of the Act sets out a number of duties of the Commission, together with various powers which are allied to those duties; it also enables the Commission to carry on a number of functions (for example, under s 28, to investigate and prosecute offences) should it choose to do so.

1 See Gambling Act 2005 (Commencement No 2 and Transitional Provisions) Order 2005, SI 2005/2455.
2 GA 2005, Sch 4, para 16.
3 GA 2005, Sch 4, para 8.

The duty to promote the licensing objectives

6.21 Section 22 mandates the Commission to 'aim' (a) to pursue the licensing objectives[1] and if appropriate to have regard to them and (b) to permit gambling in so far as it thinks it reasonably consistent with the pursuit of those objectives.

Accordingly the Commission's 'statement of principles for licensing and regulation'[2], its Code of Practice[3] and its guidance to local authorities[4] must each aim to pursue the objectives as must the exercise by it of its powers to issue operating and personal licences under Parts 5 and 6 of the Act. This type of enjoinder is only to be expected; however the duty to aim at permitting gambling to take place is rather unusual.[5] It appears to indicate that the Commission's approach should be rather more permissive than has been that of the Gaming Board. This shift in emphasis is understandable given that the Act itself is permissive in nature and is to that extent entirely distinguishable from the 'we don't like it but we will (just) allow it to exist' approach of some of the legislation which the Act replaces.

1 As set out in GA 2005, s 1; see para **6.501** below.
2 GA 2005, s 23; see para **6.2040** below.
3 GA 2005, s 24; see para **6.2060** below.
4 GA 2005, s 25; see para **6.2655** below.

5 However see also s 153 in respect of licensing authorities and premises licences.

The primary functions of the Gambling Commission

6.22 Preparation and publication of a statement of principles for licensing and regulation Section 23 requires the Commission to produce a document which sets out the principles to be applied by it in exercising its functions under the Act. It first did so in December 2006[1]. It is very general in nature and was updated in September 2009.

1 See 'Statement of Principles for Licensing and Regulation', at para **6.2040** below.

6.23 Publication of Codes of Practice Section 24 requires the Commission to publish at least one code of practice; a social responsibility code[1]. The Commission has now issued Codes on a number of topics, most important among these is the recently revised Licence Conditions and Codes of Practice (October 2008 and published in consolidated form in March 2011 and then updated in December 2011) (see para **6.2060** below). These are generally applicable; however the Commission published typical sector specific codes in August 2007 (see paras **6.2100** ff below) and updated them in December 2008.

Any code may be revised or revoked[2]. Before it is first published or revised various bodies must be consulted. These include trade associations and those likely to be affected by the code or revision. Section 24(11) provides the Commission with wide power to consult other bodies and members of the public. The status of any code is addressed in s 24(8) and (9). A failure to comply with a code affords no automatic basis for civil or criminal liability however the proviso in s 24(8) states 'this subsection is subject to any provision of or by virtue of this Act making an exception to an offence dependent on compliance with a code'. A relevant example is to be found in s 33(2) which excludes criminal liability under s 33(1) if a person holds an operating licence authorising the activity in question *and* the activity is carried on in accordance with the Terms and Conditions of the licence. Section 82(1) states that in all cases an operating licence is subject to the condition that the licencee ensures compliance with any relevant social responsibility provision of a code of practice. Moreover, the Commission has power to insist on compliance with the terms of any other code[3]. Accordingly in all cases a breach of the social responsibility code will result in a failure to comply with the terms and conditions of the licence which in turn will cause the statutory defence (in our example, under s 33(2)) to fail. Criminal liability will ensue. The same result will be reached in those cases in which an operator has breached any other code, compliance with which has been made a condition of his licence. It therefore seems that the initial comfort offered by s 24(8) is more apparent than real. Further, s 24(9) expressly provides that a code is admissible in evidence in all legal proceedings, and is to be taken into account in any proceedings in which a court or tribunal deems it to be relevant or by the Commission in the exercise of its functions under the Act.

1 GA 2005, s 24(2).
2 GA 2005, s 24(4).
3 See GA 2005, s 82(3) and ss 75, 78 and 79.

6.24 Publication of guidance to licensing authorities Section 25(1) states that the Commission is under a duty to issue guidance to licensing authorities as to the manner in which they are to exercise their functions under the Act and the principles to be applied by them in so doing. The fourth edition of the guidance was published in September 2012. In particular, the new edition includes changes/updated expressions of the Commission's views on split premises and primary gambling activity (see Part 7 thereof at para **6.2655** below) as well as additional guidance on the meaning of making gaming machines 'available for use'. It also sets out some general principles as to when it is appropriate for the Commission to take action or when the licensing authority should do so.

It is briefly described at para **6.12** above and is reproduced at para **6.2655** ff below.

The local authority[1] must have regard to the guidance. Before issuing the guidance the Commission must have consulted the various bodies set out at s 25(4); these include persons who represent local authorities. Section 25(5) gives the Commission a power to consult persons who represent chief constables and members of the public.

In contrast to ss 23 and 24, s 25 contains no specific reference to the power to revise the guidance, however this is to be deduced from the duty to issue guidance 'from time to time' as set out in s 25(1). The wording used in s 25(4) and (5) also seem to make it clear that any revision will necessarily be preceded by appropriate consultation by the Commission with the bodies referred to therein.

---

1 Defined at GA 2005, s 25(6).

6.25 Operating and personal licences The most important functions of the Commission in practice are likely to be the consideration of applications for operating licences under Part 5, the imposition of conditions attached to such licences, the power to review, suspend and revoke such licences or to demand a financial penalty for their breach and its largely parallel powers in respect of personal licences under Part 6. These are discussed in detail below.

6.25A Miscellaneous duties and powers of the Commission

- Duty to advise the Secretary of State (under s 26) on the incidence of gambling, the manner in which it is carried on, its effects and the regulation of gambling
- Compliance; s 27 gives the Commission power to undertake activities for the assessment (a) of compliance with the provisions of the Act or with any relevant secondary legislation or other matters such as codes or guidance and (b) of whether an offence is being committed under or by virtue of the Act.
- Investigation and prosecution of offences; s 28 gives such powers to the Commission.
- Requiring a licensing authority[1] to provide information; a power to issue such a requirement is contained in s 29. The authority is under a duty to comply with it.
- Exchange of information and consultation.

Under s 30 the Commission may provide information to various bodies[2] for use in the exercise of their functions or a function of the Commission. A more restricted list of bodies[3] may provide information to the Commission. Further the Commission is under a duty to consult the National Lottery Commission and Customs and Excise if it becomes aware of any matter on which that body is likely to have an opinion[4].

1 Defined in GA 2005, s 25(6).
2 Listed in GA 2005, Sch 6 and s 30(3) and (4).
3 Listed in GA 2005, Sch 6, Pts 1 and 2.
4 GA 2005, ss 31 and 32; see also GA 2005, Explanatory Note 118.

PART 3: GENERAL OFFENCES

6.30 Part 3 of the Act is divided into three categories of offences: the provision of facilities for gambling, the use of premises, and miscellaneous offences.

Provision of facilities for gambling

6.31 By s 33 of the Act it is an offence to provide facilities for gambling, unless one of the listed exceptions applies. A person convicted under this provision faces a term of imprisonment not exceeding 51 weeks, a fine, or both[1].

1 GA 2005, s 33(4). Note, s 33 is modified by the Gambling Act 2005 (Horserace Totalisator Board) Order 2007, SI 2007/2102, art 3 re the Tote.

6.32 What constitutes 'providing facilities for gambling'? Section 5(1) of the Act states that a person provides facilities for gambling if he:

(a) invites others to gamble in accordance with arrangements made by him;
(b) provides, operates or administers arrangements for gambling by others; or
(c) participates in the operation or administration of gambling by others.

According to the relevant Explanatory Notes[1], subsection (a) is aimed at people and companies offering the opportunity for people to gamble; subsection (b) 'carries a general flavour of causing facilities to be available'; and subsection (c) 'is concerned with those people who are directly involved in the gambling operation itself'. The examples given in this latter category are a croupier at a gaming table or a person handing out betting slips for the completion of a betting transaction.

In common with many other provisions in the Act, the term 'providing facilities for gambling' has been drafted in broad terms. Indeed, the breadth of the definition in s 5(1) is evident from one of the Explanatory Notes in Part 14 of the Act dealing with 'private gaming and betting'[2], which states that both parties to a bet (the backer and layer) are capable of providing facilities for gambling. This suggests that a person, by simply entering into a wager, may be providing facilities for gambling.

However, it seems very strongly arguable that use of the word 'arrangements' in subsections (a) and (b) of s 5(1) implies more than simply being party to a bet. If the interpretation in Explanatory Note 751 is accurate, surely something like 'on terms proposed' instead of 'arrangements' would have sufficed. The operator of the betting platform is clearly involved in making 'arrangements', but are any of its customers? It is suggested that they are not, unless the language of s 5(1)(a) is to be ignored[3]

1 GA 2005, Explanatory Notes 40–42.

2 GA 2005, Explanatory Note 751.
3 Nor is s 296(3) capable of causing s 5(1)(a) to be rewritten/overridden.

6.33 The exceptions to the 'provision of facilities for gambling' offence. The offence in s 33(1) does not apply to a person holding an operating licence under the Act which authorises the activity in question[1]. Nor does the offence apply to a person acting in the course of a business of another person who holds a licence authorising the relevant activity[2]. In each case, exemption from the offence requires that the licensable activity is carried on in accordance with the terms and conditions of the licence.

Separately however there are number of specific exceptions to the offence provided for in s 33(1)(b). These exceptions are worth examining in turn.

1 GA 2005, s 33(2).
2 GA 2005, s 33(3).

Lotteries and gaming machines

6.34 The offences capturing the provision of unlicensed lottery facilities[1] and making gaming machines available for use without authorisation[2], are excluded from the s 33 offence. They are instead dealt with separately in the Act.

Section 258 in Part 11 of the Act provides that a person commits an offence if he promotes a lottery (other than an exempt lottery) without an operating licence. The four categories of 'exempt lotteries' are defined in Sch 11 to the Act. These are: incidental non-commercial lotteries; private lotteries; customer lotteries; and small society lotteries. Each of these lotteries must fulfill specific conditions to come within the exemption as set out in Sch 11. Those conditions are, in each case, a combination of at least some of the following: that the lottery involve no private gain; that it be open to a limited class of potential participants; that it provide for no rollover; and that restrictions on how the lottery can be advertised be followed. Pursuant to Part 6 of Sch 11, the Secretary of State has the power to vary existing conditions or impose additional restrictions as to what constitutes an 'exempt lottery'. This power has not been exercised yet.

Sections 242 to 245 in Part 10 of the Act provide four categories of offences in connection with gaming machines[3]. Those categories are: making machines available for use; manufacturing, supplying, installing, adapting, maintaining or repairing a machine; making a machine available for use where the amount or value of a prize available through the machine is determined by reference to use made of another gaming machine; and making a machine available which permits money to be paid by means of a credit card.

The penalties applicable to the unlawful provision of lotteries or gaming machines contained in Parts 10 and 11 of the Act are the same as those which apply for a breach of s 33(1). That is, a term of imprisonment not exceeding 51 weeks, a fine, or both.

1 GA 2005, s 34.
2 GA 2005, s 35.
3 The term 'gaming machine' is defined in GA 2005, s 235.

Clubs and miners' welfare institutes

6.35 Section 269 of the Act (in Part 12, which deals with Clubs, pubs, fairs etc) exempts the provision of equal chance gaming by certain categories of clubs from the ambit of s 33, subject to certain conditions.

Equal chance gaming is defined in s 8 of the Act as gaming that does not involve playing or staking against a bank, and where the chances are equally favourable to all participants. The distinction between games of equal and unequal chance is one drawn in s 2 of the Gaming Act 1968 and as the relevant Explanatory Note states:

> 'The Act maintains this distinction, and offers different degrees of regulation and control depending on which types of facilities for gaming are being offered'[1].

---

1 GA 2005, Explanatory Note 56.

To what form of clubs does the exemption for 'equal chance gaming' apply?

6.36 The clubs to which the exemption applies are respectively: members' clubs, commercial clubs, and miners' welfare institutes. These are defined in s 266 to 268 of the Act.

There are five conditions that equal chance gaming offered by each of these social clubs must follow (which are set out in s 269(2) to (6)), to come within the exemption. Those conditions are that:

- the arrangements for the gaming must satisfy any requirements prescribed (if any) by the Secretary of State in relation to the amounts staked or the value of any prizes;
- no amount may be deducted or levied from sums staked or won;
- the participation fee must not exceed such maximum as prescribed (if any) by the Secretary of State;
- a game played on one set of premises may not be linked with a game played on another set of premises; and
- each person participating in the gaming must be a member of the club offering the gaming (or have applied for membership of the club) at least 48 hours before he participates, or is a guest of person who has been a member (or has applied for membership) for at least 48 hours.

Explanatory Note 680 points out that the conditions are similar to those set out in s 40 of the Gaming Act of 1968.

Separately, by s 271 a members' club or miners' welfare institute (but not a commercial club) can provide facilities for gaming in accordance with a club gaming permit issued by a licensing authority. Such a permit allows the provision of games of equal chance, games of unequal chance and up to three gaming machines. Schedule 12 to the Act outlines the process for the grant and maintenance of a club gaming permit.

Premises with an alcohol licence

6.37 The provision allowing gaming facilities to be made available on alcohol licensed premises, subject to the conditions described below, repeals s 6 of the Gaming Act 1968.

Section 278 of the Act states that s 279 which provides the exemption, applies to premises in respect of which: an 'on-premises alcohol licence[1] or relevant Scottish licence'[2] has effect; a bar at which alcohol is served for consumption is provided; and alcohol is served at a time permitted under the alcohol licence. The relevant Explanatory Note states that:

> 'Premises such as restaurants which do not have a bar for serving drinks to customers will fall outside the scope of the premises to which sections 279 to 284 apply'[3].

The conditions which the qualifying premises must fufill to take advantage of the exemption are as follows:

- the facilities must be limited to equal chance gaming[4];
- stakes and prizes must not exceed any limits as to value or amount prescribed by the Secretary of State;
- no amount may be deducted or levied from amounts won;
- no participation fees may be charged (including membership subscriptions pursuant to s 344(3));
- there may not be linking of games between premises[5] and
- persons under the age of 18 must be excluded from the gaming.

Separately, by s 282 and 283 an alcohol licensed premises can, subject to conditions therein provide gaming machines.

The Commission will be conscious that the government's intent is that gaming should not become the main inducement to attend alcohol licensed premises. To this end, s 284 allows a licensing authority to make an order disapplying s 279 or s 282(1) to specified premises. Additionally, there are further conditions in relation to the provision of facilities for bingo contained in s 281, which are primarily designed to prevent what is described as 'high turnover bingo' within that provision, being facilitated on alcohol licensed premises. In short, the gaming should be incidental to the main function of the premises – ie serving alcohol.

1 The term 'on-premises alcohol licence' is defined in GA 2005, s 277(b).
2 The term 'relevant Scottish licence' is defined GA 2005, s 277(c).
3 GA 2005, Explanatory Note 703.
4 See para 6.35 above for details of what constitutes 'equal chance gaming', a term which is defined in GA 2005, s 8.
5 Linked games are defined in GA 2005, s 280(2).

Prize gaming

6.38 A person does not commit an offence under s 33, by providing prize gaming[1] in premises authorised for the purpose, or in accordance with a prize gaming permit, subject to the four conditions listed in s 293.

1 See further para **6.270** ff below.

What is prize gaming?

6.39 The term 'prize gaming' is defined in s 288 as gaming where neither the nature nor the size of a prize played for is determined by reference to the number of persons playing, or the amount paid for or raised by the gaming. The relevant Explanatory Notes provide helpful clarity in this respect, stating that:

> 'This is a type of gaming where the organiser puts up the prizes in advance, as distinct from gaming where the stakes of the participants make up the winnings. Prize gaming is intended to permit low level gaming, for small participation fees, and modest prizes. Bingo played at seaside amusement arcades is a typical venue for such gaming'[1];

and that,

> 'The effect of the definition is that in prize gaming the prizes available will be determined by the operator of the gaming before play commences, and the payment

he receives from the players will not be put directly to any prize on offer. This does not stop operators from estimating what money will be raised from gaming, or predicting the numbers who will take part. Its purpose is to stop the actual amounts raised in a particular game being used to determine the prize in that particular game. Prize gaming can cover both money and non-money prizes'[2].

The four conditions described in s 293, which prize gaming much fulfill are that:

- amounts charged to players for participating must not exceed any amounts prescribed by the Secretary of State;
- the prizes offered in the prize gaming must not exceed any value set by the Secretary of State;
- the prize gaming must take place on the relevant premises, in the course of one day only, and the results must be announced on the premises as soon as possible after the game ends; and
- participation in a game must not entitle the player to participate in any other gambling.

By s 290 and s 292, the authorised premises in which prize gaming may be offered, are gaming and entertainment centres[3] and at travelling fairs[4]. Separately, by s 291, prize gaming may be offered in premises in respect of which a bingo licence has effect[5].

For other types of premises, Sch 14 provides further information in relation to the grant and maintenance of a prize gaming permit.

A machine providing prize gaming will be subject to this part of the Act (and not Part 10, dealing with gaming machines) providing one of the exemptions in s 235(e), (f) or (g) to Part 10 of the Act applies[6].

1 GA 2005, Explanatory Note 725.
2 GA 2005, Explanatory Note 731.
3 Defined in GA 2005, s 290.
4 Defined in GA 2005, s 286.
5 GA 2005, s 291.
6 GA 2005, Explanatory Note 729.

Private gaming and betting

6.40 Section 296(1) of the Act states that a person does not commit an offence under s 33 by providing facilities for private betting or private gaming. The relevant Explanatory Note states that the section enables people:

> 'To participate in and offer facilities for betting and gaming, including on premises, without committing any offence under the Act, provided their activity meets the various conditions for private gaming and betting'[1].

1 GA 2005, Explanatory Note 750. See also the Gambling Commission advice note on non-commercial and private gaming and betting of January 2010 at para **6.2095** below.

What is private gaming?

6.41 Schedule 15 to the Act sets out the conditions for gaming to constitute 'private gaming', which are as follows:

- that no charge can be made for participation in the gaming[1]. (It is immaterial how a charge is described or whether a charge is in money or money's worth. However a stake is not a charge for participation);

- that the gaming must be equal chance gaming[2], unless it is either domestic[3] or residential[4] private gaming[5].
- that gaming must not occur in a place to which the public have access (whether or not on payment)[6].

1 GA 2005, Sch 15, para 3.
2 See para **6.35** above for details of what constitutes 'equal chance gaming', a term which is defined in GA 2005, s 8.
3 More particularly described in GA 2005, Sch 15, para 2(1).
4 More particularly described in GA 2005, Sch 15, para 2(2).
5 GA 2005, Sch 15, para 4.
6 GA 2005, Sch 15, para 5.

What is private betting?

6.42 For the purposes of private betting, Part 2 of Sch 15 states that betting is 'private betting' if it is domestic betting or workers' betting[1].

A betting transaction is domestic betting if it is made on premises in which each party to the transaction lives or habitually resides, whether or not there are other premises in which he also habitually resides[2].

A betting transaction is workers' betting if made between persons each of whom is employed under a contract of employment with the same employer[3].

1 GA 2005, Sch 15, para 6.
2 GA 2005, Sch 15, para 7.
3 GA 2005, Sch 15, para 8.

Betting in the course of a business

6.43 Separately, s 296(3) of the Act states that a person does not commit an offence by making or accepting a bet, or by offering to make or accept a bet, if he acts otherwise than in the course of a business.

This provision in the Act was scrutinised closely during the pre-legislative period and while the Bill was in Parliament. Undoubtedly some traditional bookmakers would like to have seen at least some betting exchange customers specifically singled out for licensing herein. This agenda was given succour by a recommendation of the Parliamentary Joint Scrutiny Committee on the draft Gambling Bill, that so-called 'non-recreational layers' on exchanges should be licensed under the Act[1]. In a written submission of December 2003 to that Committee, William Hill plc argued:

> 'Should there be a case for excluding "recreational" layers on bet exchanges we believe this has to be achieved by defining what is meant by "private and non-commercial betting".'

In other words, as far as William Hill was concerned, there was no doubt that people making lay bets in a non-recreational manner on exchanges should be licensed. The only question was what should be done with people making lay bets in a *recreational* manner.

Ignoring the definitional difficulties of separating recreational from non-recreational activity, any attempt to focus on one side of a betting transaction (the lay side in this case) ignores the reality that a betting exchange is not the only betting platform where an outcome can be opposed. The option of 'selling' an outcome has been available with spread betting firms since the inception of spread betting[2], and traditional bookmakers are increasingly offering markets on outcomes 'not to happen'. For example, England 'not to qualify' for the next soccer world cup.

1 This recommendation of the Committee was rejected by the government.

2 Note that spread betting does not constitute 'gambling' under s 3 of the Act and will continue to be regulated by the Financial Services Authority, as opposed to the Commission.

Is a party to a bet 'providing facilities for betting'?

6.44 Given that the offence under consideration is that contained within s 33 – ie the unauthorised provision of facilities for betting – the first point that needs to be considered is whether a person entering into a bet could be deemed to be providing facilities for betting. Explanatory Note 751 to the Act states:

> 'The definitions set out in Part 1 of the Act means that both parties to a bet (sometimes known as the "backer" and the "layer") are *capable* [emphasis added] of providing facilities for betting.'

It is interesting to note that the final printed draft of the Explanatory Notes to the Bill did not contain the word 'capable' in the equivalent note. It is not clear from this whether the intention of the draughtsman was that a party to a bet is always engaged in providing facilities for betting, or is merely doing so in some circumstances. Perhaps the change to the Explanatory Notes suggests that the latter of those two scenarios is the DCMS view.

The breadth of the drafting in the s 5 provision dealing with 'facilities for gambling' and the question of under what circumstances a person can be deemed to be 'providing facilities', has already been considered above[1].

Another subtle (but potentially more far-reaching) change between the final printed draft of the Explanatory Notes to the Bill and the Notes to the Act, is contained in Explanatory Note 752 which states:

> 'If someone is using betting as a way of earning a living, so that it renders it a business activity, that too *may* [emphasis added] require a licence.'

The equivalent note to the final printed draft of the Bill used the word 'will' where 'may' now appears. This amendment would appear to give the Commission more discretion to determine who may be providing facilities for betting 'in the course of a business', and consequently require licensing. The idea that someone earning a living from gambling 'will' require a licence, would potentially have provided a new class of persons for the Commission to address, namely the class of professional gamblers.

In any event, it is worth noting that whilst an aid to interpretation, Explanatory Notes do not prevail over what the legislation itself states. The Commission is likely to focus on the regulatory objectives contained within s 1 of the Act to determine whether any given betting activity requires licensing.

1 See para **6.32** above.

Non-commercial gaming

6.45 Subject to conditions described below, both non-commercial gaming and betting are excluded from the ambit of the s 33 offence.

Pursuant to s 297, gaming is non-commercial if it takes place at a non-commercial event. A non-commercial event is one where no part of the proceeds generated by the event is to be appropriated for private gain[1]. The 'proceeds' of an event are defined by s 297(3) as all sums raised by the organisers (including directly for the gaming and for admission and any sponsorship of the event etc) minus amounts deducted for expenses reasonably incurred.

A person does not fall foul of s 33 if he provides facilities for either non-commercial prize-gaming or non-commercial equal-chance gaming[2], subject to certain conditions. The conditions that apply to both of these forms of non-commercial gaming are that[3]:

- the players are informed that the purpose of the gaming is to raise money for a specified purpose other than that of private gain;
- the non-commercial event of which the gaming is a part does not take place on premises (other than a track) in respect of which a premises licence has effect, or on a track at a time when activities are being carried on there in reliance on a premises licence, or on premises at a time when activities are being carried on in reliance on a temporary use notice; and
- the gaming must not be remote gaming[4].

In addition, non-commercial equal-chance gaming must comply with regulations introduced by the Secretary of State limiting stakes, participation fees and prize values[5]. See Gambling Act 2005 (Non-Commercial Equal-Chance Gaming) Regulations 2007[6] at para **6.1819** below.

In relation to the restriction on the location at which the gaming can take place, the relevant Explanatory Note states that:

> 'There is nothing to stop such premises [premises with a premises licence or a temporary use notice] running charitable or other gambling events to raise money for good causes, but they should do so using the gambling permissions granted to them by their premises licence or use notice. They cannot rely on any of the allowances granted in Part 14 [of the Act]'[7].

Section 301 of the Act creates the offence of 'misusing profits of non-commercial prize gaming'. This involves using funds raised by the gaming for a purpose other than that specified. This offence carries a penalty of a term of imprisonment not exceeding 51 weeks, a fine, or both.

---

1 The term 'private gain' is defined in GA 2005, s 19(3).

2 See para **6.35** above for details of what constitutes 'equal chance gaming', a term which is defined in GA 2005, s 8.

3 These conditions are set out in GA 2005, s 299 and 300.

4 'Remote gambling' (a term which includes gaming) is defined in GA 2005, s 4(1).

5 Pursuant to s 300(4) of the Act.

6 SI 2007/2041.

7 GA 2005, Explanatory Note 760.

Non-commercial betting

6.46 Section 302 of the Act ('non-commercial betting') provides the basis for exceptions to liability under ss 46, 48, 50 and 51 (offences in relation to children, etc) although not to ss 33 and 37. Non-commercial betting is where neither party to the bet is acting in the course of a business. This provision would appear to cover bets placed between friends.

Territorial application

6.47 Section 36 is a complex and hugely significant piece of the Act. The purpose of this provision is to establish whether an operator is within the jurisdiction of the Commission for the purpose of the s 33 offence. Whilst s 36 will remain in force for some time it will eventually be replaced following an announcement by DCMS in July 2011 that it proposes to introduce licensing for all operators providing gambling facilities to the British market even if they are based abroad.

For non-remote gambling s 33 applies only if something done in the course of the provision of the facilities for gambling, is done in Great Britain[1]. For remote gambling[2] s 33 applies only if at least one piece of 'remote gambling equipment' used in the provision of the facilities is situated in Great Britain[3]. The meaning of 'remote gambling equipment' is considered in detail in para **6.48** below.

The relevant Explanatory Note states:

> 'This means that, where gambling takes place remotely, the person providing the facilities for gambling will not fall within the scope of the offence if he does not have relevant equipment within Great Britain. This is so even if people within Great Britain can receive the gambling he is providing (eg over the internet). On the other hand, where at least one piece of remote gambling equipment is located in Great Britain, a person providing facilities for remote gambling will come within the scope of the offence. Therefore, a person commits the offence if any part of his remote equipment is located in Great Britain and he does not have the required authorisation or is not covered by one the exceptions. This is so regardless of whether the gambling facilities are provided to people in Great Britain or outside'[4].

So, if any part of a gambling operation is located in Great Britain, then the operator needs to be licensed accordingly, unless the activity fits within one of the exceptions described in s 33.

Until the Act was fully implemented, it was unlawful to offer remote gaming from within the UK. As a consequence, UK operators offered remote gaming (primarily in the form of on-line casinos and poker) through subsidiary or related companies based outside the UK. This provision dealing with territorial application was the subject of considerable debate prior to the Act receiving Royal Assent, with particular concern among operators that their non-UK gaming businesses might require licensing in the UK as a consequence of the provision. At the root of this concern was the fact that some functions of these apparently non-UK businesses are provided by equipment located in the UK, which could be deemed to be 'remote gambling equipment' under the extremely broad definition given to that term by s 36(4).

In addition, non-UK operators who believed that their businesses were based wholly outside the UK and should not be subject to a UK licensing regime (and consequently 'potentially' taxation), expressed fears that the definition of 'remote gambling equipment' in the Bill might capture some of their operations. These fears were described in December 2004 in a written submission to the Parliamentary Joint Scrutiny Committee on the draft Gambling Bill by CryptoLogic Inc, the Canadian manufacturer of gaming software, in the following terms:

> 'Internet gaming is a global business, and as such, the Operator, Software Provider, the online gaming infrastructure and many pieces of "remote gambling equipment" that make up the network are often located in different jurisdictions.'

Exacerbating these concerns was the so-called 'all-in all-out' test contained in s 89(2). This requires a licensee to locate all equipment used by it to provide the remote gambling facilities, in Great Britain. So, not only might the broad definition given to 'remote gambling equipment' mean that a UK licence was required for a business which the operator believed was to all intents and purposes being run from outside of Great Britain, but as a consequence of that UK licence, under s 89(2) all equipment used to run that business would need to be located in Great Britain.

Section 89(3) did however grant a discretion to the Commission to exclude certain pieces of equipment used by a UK licensed remote gambling operator from the requirement to be located in Great Britain, if it believed that doing so is reasonably consistent with the licensing objectives. The fact that this discretion was a late addition to the Act (not having appeared in the final printed version of the Bill) suggests that in 2005 there was some sympathy within the DCMS for concerns raised by operators. Those concerns were translated, in 2007, into the repeal of s 89(2) and (3) before they ever came into force[5].

1 Pursuant to s 36(2) of the Act.
2 'Remote gambling' is defined in GA 2005, s 4(1).
3 Pursuant to GA 2005, s 36(3).
4 GA 2005, Explanatory Note 139.
5 See the Gambling Act 2005 (Repeal) (Remote Operating Licence and Credit) Regulations 2007, SI 2007/2321.

6.48 What constitutes 'remote gambling equipment'? Section 36(4) defines the term 'remote gambling equipment'. This definition is however subject to s 36(5) which states that 'remote gambling equipment' does not include equipment: which is used by a person to take advantage of remote gambling facilities provided by another person, and is not provided by that other person. In other words equipment used to access remote gambling facilities does not constitute 'remote gambling equipment', as long as the equipment used to access the facilities is not provided by the operator of the remote gambling facilities. The example cited in the Explanatory Note is a computer keyboard and screen used by a person to access remote gambling facilities[1].

Section 36(4) defines 'remote gambling equipment' as electronic or other equipment used by or on behalf of a person providing facilities for remote gambling to perform any one of four functions. Given the broadly defined nature of at least 2 of these 4 functions, the accompanying Explanatory Notes are likely to prove among the most widely thumbed of all the notes to the Act.

By s 36(4)(a) the first function of 'remote gambling equipment' is that the relevant piece of equipment stores information relating to a person's participation in the gambling. The Explanatory Note states:

> 'Subsection (4)(a) captures equipment which stores information eg a computer database or server, about a person's participation in gambling. This includes the "game history" of a player, including the player's identity and records of their wins and losses. Equipment used for storage of information for general promotional purposes would not be caught by the definition, unless the information relates to someone's participation in gambling'[2].

In accordance with s 36(4)(b) the second function of 'remote gambling equipment' is that the relevant piece of equipment presents to participants in the gambling, a virtual event or process, by reference to which the gambling is conducted. The Explanatory Note states:

> 'Subsection (4)(b) captures equipment used for generating and presenting virtual gambling'[2].

By s 36(4)(c) the third function of 'remote gambling equipment' is that the relevant piece of equipment determines all or part of a result or the effect of a result. The Explanatory Note states:

> 'Subsection (4)(c) captures equipment used by the person providing the gambling (or on his behalf) for determining the result or the effect of the result of the particular transaction. This covers random number generators used in virtual gaming, or the equipment for calculating whether someone has won or lost a bet on a real event.'[2]

By s 36(4)(d) the fourth and final function of 'remote gambling equipment' is that the relevant piece of equipment stores information in relation to a result. The Explanatory Note states:

> 'Subsection (4)(d) captures equipment used to store information relating to a result. This is different to equipment under subsection 4(c) which covers the act of generation of a result, not its subsequent retention.'[2]

It is worth noting that representations made by operators prior to Royal Assent in relation to the scope of the definition of 'remote gambling equipment' were successful in part at least. The definition of 'remote gambling equipment' provided respectively by subsections 36(4)(a) and (d) of the Act, replaced text from the final printed version of the Bill which had defined 'remote gambling equipment' as equipment used to either: 'register information relating to a person's participation in the gambling'; or 'accept payment in respect of gambling'. Those registration and payment functions do not appear to be captured by the 'remote gambling equipment' definition in s 36(4).

Moreover, in March 2008 the Commission published the second edition of a helpful Guidance Note 'Remote Gambling Equipment' (see para **6.2511** below). This sets out the Commission's interpretation of what constitutes such equipment. It is a highly technical document which it is pointless to summarise; suffice it to say that in the case of sports betting it includes bet settling and gambling transaction recording equipment within s 36(4) but otherwise excludes applications, data stores and interfaces to external and/or third party systems.

1 GA 2005, Explanatory Note 141.
2 GA 2005, Explanatory Note 140.

Use of premises

6.49 This part of the general offences revolves around the use of premises to provide facilities for gambling without authorisation.

By s 37(1), subject to certain exceptions or unless authorised under the Act, a person commits an offence if he uses premises or causes premises to be used to: operate a casino, provide facilities for the playing of bingo, make a gaming machine available for use, provide other facilities for gaming or provide facilities for betting as defined in s 37(1)(e).

Section 38 gives the Secretary of State the power by making an order to add to, remove or vary the gambling activities covered in s 37(1). This has not been exercised yet. Clearly the DCMS wish to future-proof the premises offence. Indeed the relevant Explanatory Note refers to the possibility of bringing within the scope of the offence:

> 'Any gambling activities which may be invented in the future, but which are not covered by the list in subsection (1) [to s 37])'[1].

Specific mention is given in s 38(3) to the possibility of an order extending s 37(1) to spread betting. Spread betting is regulated by the Financial Services Authority in accordance with the Financial Services and Markets Act 2000 and is generally excluded from the scope of the Act. Under s 10(1) of the Act a 'bet' does not include a spread bet and therefore spread betting does not constitute 'gambling' under s 3. In the short term the Commission may be relieved to have one less part of the gambling sector for which to create a regulatory framework. However the DCMS has indicated that the exclusion of spread betting from the new regime will remain under review. Indeed, the May 2003 DCMS position paper dealing with the licensing of betting operators, included a statement that the Department 'continues to regard spread betting as a form of gambling', and the exclusion of spread betting from the Act does present certain anomalies (including those described in para **6.63** below, in relation to the cheating offence in s 42(1)).

Section 38(4) permits an order made by the Secretary of State pursuant to s 38(1), to make consequential amendments to other provisions of the Act, in particular those within Part 8. For example, if spread betting were added to the list of gambling activities as envisaged by s 38(3), then this form of activity would almost certainly be added to the list of activities for which a premises licence can be granted subject to s 150, within Part 8.

The penalties applicable to the premises offence in s 37 are the same as those which apply to the 'provision of facilities' offence contained in s 33 – ie a term of imprisonment not exceeding 51 weeks, a fine, or both.[2]

1 GA 2005, Explanatory Note 151.
2 GA 2005, s 37(8).

6.50 The exceptions to the 'use of premises' offence The offence in s 37(1) does not apply to a person holding a licence under the Act which authorises the activity in question[1]. Nor does the offence apply to a person acting in the course of a business of another person when that other person holds a licence authorising the relevant activity[2]. In each case, exemption from the offence assumes that the licensable activity is carried on in accordance with the terms and conditions of the licence.

In addition, the offence does not apply to a person using a track for accepting bets, if the use is authorised by a premises licence (whether or not held by that person)[3]. A 'track' is defined as: 'a horse-race course, dog track or other premises on any part of which a race or other sporting event takes place or is intended to take place'[4]. Most obviously this means that a racecourse bookmaker would not need to obtain a premises licence to accept bets at the course.

Nor does the s 37(1) offence apply to the use of casino for the provision facilities for bingo or betting in accordance with an authorisation under s 174(3)[5].

Again, the offence does not apply to the use of premises to provide facilities for use only by persons who are acting in the course of a business, or who are not on the premises[6]. An example of the former would be the offices of a remote gambling operator and an example of the latter would be premises for housing a server used for remote gambling.

Separately there are a number of specific exceptions to the offence provided for in s 37(7), which allow premises to be used for the provision of specified facilities for gambling without a licence or permit. A number of these exceptions are identical to some of those which are exceptions to the s 33 'provision of facilities for gambling' offence described above. Those exceptions are provided in the following categories: clubs and miners' welfare institutes; premises with an alcohol licence; prize gaming; private gaming and betting; and non-commercial gaming.

There are additional exceptions provided for in s 37(7) as follows:

- occasional use notice;
- football pools;
- temporary use notice;
- gaming machines; and
- travelling fairs.

1 GA 2005, s 37(2).
2 GA 2005, s 37(3).
3 GA 2005, s 37(4).
4 GA 2005, s 353(1).
5 GA 2005, s 37(5).
6 GA 2005, s 37(6).

6.51 Occasional use notice By s 39 an 'occasional use notice' can be served in respect of a track[1] to authorise the provision of facilities for betting, for no more than 8 days per year. Subsections (2)–(6) of s 39 set out the procedure which needs to be followed to serve an occasional use notice. Any person providing facilities for betting pursuant to the notice must also hold the necessary authorisation to act as a betting operator. For a discussion of such notices see 'Guidance to Licensing Authorities – 4th Edition' at para **6.2655** below, Part 15.

The accompanying Explanatory Note states:

> 'The purpose of the section is to ensure that point-to-point racecourses which are used for only a few days a year, and tracks such as golf courses where betting facilities are provided for major competitions, but not otherwise, do not have to obtain a full premises licence in order to avoid the main offence in this Part'[2].

A select number of British racecourses[3] are allocated less than 8 fixtures per year, which would seem to give them the option to serve a temporary use notice, instead of applying for a premises licence as described in Part 8 of the Act.

1 'Track' is defined in GA 2005, s 353(1).
2 GA 2005, Explanatory Note 153.
3 For example, Cartmel and Fakenham.

6.52 Football pools By s 40, a person does not commit an offence under s 37 if he uses premises to do anything permitted in accordance with a pool betting licence under s 93(3). Section 93 allows the holder of a pool betting licence to authorise collectors to dispense and collect coupons, pay winnings etc on behalf of the pools operator. These collectors may operate from door to door, or from ordinary retail premises. As the relevant Explanatory Note states:

> 'Collectors can therefore use premises to accept football pools entries, or pay out winnings without committing that [the s 37] offence'[1].

[1] GA 2005, Explanatory Note 157.

6.53 Temporary use notice Part 9 of the Act allows the holder of an operating licence to serve notice that he intends to offer facilities for gambling from premises which are not licensed to provide gambling, on a temporary basis. Explanatory Note 541 to the Act cites hotels, exhibition centres or entertainment venues as examples of premises in respect of which a temporary use notice might apply.

The gambling activity that the person serving the notice wishes to provide, must be that for which he is already authorised under the terms of his operating licence. The notice can only authorise such gambling activities that the Secretary of State may specify in regulations[1] and which are set out in the notice. A premises cannot be subject to a temporary use notice for more than 21 days (a period which applies to all gambling carried on pursuant to temporary use notices, not just one form of gambling) in any 12 month period[2].

The form which the notice must take is described in s 216 and the procedure involved in giving notice (and for registering objections to the notice) is described from s 219 to s 228 of the Act.

[1] GA 2005, s 215(2) and SI 2007/3157.
[2] GA 2005, s 218.

6.54 Gaming machines In certain circumstances, a person does not commit an offence under s 37 by making gaming machines available for use. The first of these circumstances is where a person makes a gaming machine available for use in accordance with a family entertainment centre gaming machine permit[1].

Nor does a person commit an offence by making a gaming machine available for use where a person using the machine has no opportunity to win a prize, whether or not he pays for use of the machine[2].

Finally, a person does not commit an offence by making a gaming machine available for use where an individual playing the machine does not acquire, by using the machine, an opportunity to win a prize the value of which exceeds any payment made for use of the machine[3].

[1] GA 2005, s 247.
[2] GA 2005, s 248.
[3] GA 2005, s 249.

6.55 Travelling fairs Section 287 allows for an unlimited number of Category D gaming machines[1] to be provided at a travelling fair, provided any facilities for gambling offered at the fair are no more than an ancillary amusement.

The term 'travelling fair' is defined in s 286 as: a fair consisting wholly or principally of the provision of amusements; which is provided by persons who travel from place to place for the purpose of providing fairs, and at a place no part of which has been used for the provision of a fair on more than 27 days in that calendar year.

1 'Category D gaming machines' are defined by the Categories of Gaming Machine Regulations 2007, SI 2007/2158, reg 3.

Miscellaneous offences

6.56 The miscellaneous offences in Part 3, cover: gambling software, cheating at gambling, chain-gift schemes, and the provision of unlawful facilities abroad. With the exception of the cheating offence, each of these categories is a creation of the modern age.

6.57 **Gambling software** Section 41 recognises a new class of persons who may pose a risk of harm and consequently require licensing under the Act. The class of persons is those providing gambling software to be used in connection with remote gambling, and the licensing objective which would appear to underpin this provision is that: 'gambling is conducted in a fair and open way'[1].

To ensure that this objective is not undermined, the activities of software providers may need to be conducted in a regulated environment. The Commission will issue gambling software operating licences in accordance with Part 5 of the Act.

1 GA 2005, s 1(b) and see Explanatory Note 159.

The gambling software provision

6.58 By s 41(1) it is an offence to 'manufacture, supply, install or adapt gambling software, in the course of a business', without holding an operating licence. The penalty for breaching the provision is a prison term not exceeding 51 weeks, a fine, or both[1]. 'Gambling software' is defined as 'computer software for use in connection with remote gambling'[2], but does not include anything for use solely in connection with a gaming machine[3].

The relevant Explanatory Note points out that software designed for use in a gaming machine is covered by the very detailed definition of a 'gaming machine' contained in s 235 of the Act[4]. Section 243 makes it an offence to manufacture, supply (etc) a gaming machine without a licence and s 246 applies the same penalties for breaching s 243 as those applicable to breaching this gambling software provision.

1 GA 2005, s 41(4).
2 'Remote gambling' is defined in GA 2005, s 4(1).
3 GA 2005, s 41(2).
4 GA 2005, Explanatory Note 161.

Who will be caught by the gambling software provision?

6.59 The provision will capture software providers who are dealing directly with the public and separately those who have no dealings with the public, but instead provide software used by remote gambling operators. An example of the first type of software provider might be the manufacturer of software used by gamblers to access gambling sites to place multiple bets at once, or to scan gambling sites to search out arbitrage opportunities. The second type of software provider could include casino or poker software manufacturers whose products are made available to the public by remote gambling operators.

Undoubtedly many gambling operators who manufacture their own software will, in addition to applying for an operating licence, also need to apply for a gambling software licence under s 65(2)(i). Section 97 makes provision for the Commission to establish standards for such software.

Subsection 41(3) states that a person does not supply or install gambling software by reason only of him making facilities for remote communication or non-remote communication available to another person, and those facilities are used by the other person to supply or install gambling software. The accompanying Explanatory Note states that:

> 'Subsection (3) ensures that a communications service provider, who enables someone to download or send gambling software to another person, is not treated as himself supplying or installing that gambling software. This is an exception for "mere carriers" of the software'[1].

This subsection 41(3) of the Act did not appear in the final printed draft of the Bill, so it would seem that the DCMS realised prior to Royal Assent that the pool of people who could have been captured by the provision was wider than that necessary to fulfill the regulatory objectives.

1 GA 2005, Explanatory Note 162.

6.60 The cheating offence The provision in the Act dealing with 'cheating at gambling' provoked much pre-legislative comment. This was in part due to a number of on-going British Horseracing Authority (formerly the Jockey Club) inquiries and a major police investigation into alleged corruption in British horseracing. However, a consequence of the proliferation of betting on other sports has been recent high profile scandals involving alleged corruption, or the misuse of privileged information for betting gain by insiders, in each of: tennis, cricket, snooker, and rugby league.

Possibly as a consequence there was a move from within government that sporting regulators should engage with betting operators to ensure channels of communication were opened and that information in relation to irregularities on relevant betting markets was shared by betting operators with the regulators. During evidence sessions before a Parliamentary Committee considering the impact of betting on the integrity of sport at the end of 2004, the sporting regulators who appeared unanimously endorsed the principle of information sharing. This principle had been pioneered by Betfair's agreement with the Jockey Club of June 2003. Consequently one of the recommendations of that Committee was that all sports should look to enter into information sharing agreements (so-called 'memoranda of understanding' or 'MoU's') with betting operators.

The most obvious result of this can be seen in condition 15 (Information requirements) of the Gambling Commission's 'Licence Conditions and Codes of Practice' document. In addition to requiring UK licensed betting operators to provide information to the Commission, this condition imposes an obligation on those operators to provide the UK sporting regulators listed in Part 3 of Schedule 6 to the Act, with 'any information the licensee suspects may: lead the commission to consider making an order to void a bet; or relate to a breach of a rule applied by that sport governing body'. Such information would logically include personal data in relation to those placing bets.

Separately between 2005 and 2007 a British Horseracing Authority panel of inquiry defined 'inside information' and the circumstances in which its use was acceptable, in the context of horseracing[1]. There is a recognition across a range of sports that controls should be put in place (to the extent that they are not already) to deal with how participants in those sports act on inside or privileged information. The view expressed to the Parliamentary Joint Scrutiny Committee on the draft Gambling Bill by the former British Horseracing Board chairman, that the lifeblood of betting on horses: 'is inside information and what you do with it'[2],[3] seems at this stage to have come from a bygone era.

1 http://www.britishhorseracing.com/inside_horseracing/media/releaseDetail.asp?item=084224.

2 Oral evidence from Peter Savill to the Parliamentary Joint Scrutiny Committee on the draft Gambling Bill, 20 January 2004.

3 See para **6.2060** below.

How cheating at gambling has been dealt with to date

6.61 The new cheating provision repeals s 17 of the Gaming Act 1845 (winning by cheating)[1]. Historically, however, prosecutors have dealt with cheating at gambling through a variety of charges. In August 2005 a group of gamblers who dropped chips onto a gaming table once the roulette ball had come to rest (so-called 'top-hatting'), by creating a distraction at a crucial moment, were convicted of 'cheating at play' under s 17 of the 1845 Act in Middlesex Guildhall Crown Court. However, a gambler similarly engaging in 'top-hatting' was acquitted in Southwark Crown Court of charges of 'obtaining property by deception' in 1993. Likewise (at Southwark Crown Court) in 2000 five gamblers were cleared of charges of 'conspiracy to defraud through horse-doping with a performance-inhibiting drug.'

The common law offence of cheating was abolished by s 32(1) of the Theft Act 1968 and clearly there has not been an obvious or consistent approach in dealing with cheating offences. In any event, deception is not straightforward to prove and any conspiracy charge relies on showing an agreement between at least two persons. Hopefully the new offence will bring some clarity and consistency to this area of the law.

1 GA 2005, s 42(6).

The new cheating provision

6.62 Section 42(1) of the Act provides that a person commits an offence if he cheats at gambling or does anything for the purposes of enabling or assisting another person to cheat at gambling. It is immaterial whether the person who cheats either improves his chance of winning anything, or actually wins anything[1]. The draughtsman was no doubt aware of the authority which held that under the provision which has been repealed[2], an essential ingredient of that offence was that there should be profits from the cheating which are actually obtained[3].

Section 42(3) states that cheating may consist of actual or attempted deception or interference in connection with: the process by which gambling is conducted[4], or a real or virtual game, race or other event or process to which gambling relates[5].

By s 42(5), the penalty for conviction on indictment under the new offence will be a term of imprisonment not exceeding two years[6]; and for a summary conviction a term of imprisonment not exceeding 51 weeks. In either case a fine may be imposed on conviction in addition to, or instead of, a term of imprisonment.

The relevant Explanatory Note states that:

> 'Although "cheating" is not defined, it should be given its normal, everyday meaning'[7].

So, the Commission has been given significant scope to determine what may constitute an offence of cheating, though s 42(3) does (as described above) give some guidance on the matter. Except in the most serious cases, it is likely that sports regulators will deal with those subject to their rules (for example 'licensed persons' under the British Horseracing Authority's Orders and Rules of Racing), without recourse to the Commission. However, although it is conceptually difficult to envisage cheating through betting without the cooperation of a 'licensed person' (or the equivalent in other sports), there may be persons involved in the cheating who are not subject to the regulator's rules. For example those placing bets in collusion with an insider. Those persons will be subject to the new criminal sanctions of the cheating provision.

1 GA 2005, s 42(2).
2 Gaming Act 1845, s 17.
3 *R v Harris, R v Turner* [1963] 2 QB 442, [1963] 2 All ER 294, 127 JP 357.
4 GA 2005, s 42(3)(a).
5 GA 2005, s 42(3)(b).
6 This is the only indictable offence in the GA 2005.
7 GA 2005, Explanatory Note 163.

What behaviour will be captured by the cheating offence?

6.63 Clearly, cheating will cover malpractice involving not just betting, but also gaming. Examples might include an attempt to: fix a roulette wheel, place a bet on an event which has been concluded, or to manipulate a random number generator which determines results on virtual events. The use of a mechanical aid in a casino is not so clear cut. A high profile police investigation involving a group of gamblers who accumulated huge roulette profits in a London casino in March 2004, supposedly with the aid of a concealed mechanical device which predicted where the ball would land, was dropped purportedly because the device did not interfere with the ball or the roulette wheel. Card counting at blackjack[1], which requires considerable skill and discipline, is almost certainly not cheating.

Although the National Lottery is for the most part, excluded from the system of regulation provided for in the Act, pursuant to s 15(2)(a) the offence of cheating can be committed in relation to lotteries forming part of the National Lottery.

Separately, because the definition of 'gambling'[2] excludes spread betting, it would seem that the Financial Services Authority rather than the Commission will be charged to deal with any cheating activity effected through spread betting[3].

Historically, gambling operators taking market risk (ie all operators with the exception of pool betting operators and some betting intermediaries) have in many cases treated cheats and skillful gamblers as equally undesirable. Both represent a drain on the operator's profits and accordingly are quickly excluded. It is to be hoped that the Commission can bring some transparency and fairness to an industry in which a punter using a clever system and a card counter in a casino are perceived as the moral equivalents of a corrupt insider and a roulette wheel fixer.

1 Card counting at blackjack involves estimating the values of the cards still to be dealt, based on the values of the cards already dealt. The card counter will increase his staking when there is a high proportion of high value cards yet to come, because the casino's advantage is reduced in proportion to the number of high value cards not yet dealt.

2 GA 2005, s 3.

3 The exclusion of spread betting from the ambit of the Act is discussed in more detail in para **6.49** above.

Voiding bets

6.64 Pursuant to s 336(1) of the Act the Commission will have the power to void a bet, but only if satisfied that the bet was 'substantially unfair'[1]. In considering whether a bet was unfair, the Commission shall take into account a number of factors pursuant to s 336(4), including the fact that either party to the bet: believed or ought to have believed than an offence under s 42 had been or was likely to be committed in respect of anything to which the bet related, or was convicted or was likely to be convicted of an offence under s 42 in relation to the bet.

The Commission can only make an order to void a bet within 6 months from the date on which the result of the bet is determined[2], unless a party to the bet has been convicted of an offence under s 42, in which case no limitation period applies[3].

In the cash betting environment in particular, the power to void bets is likely to be of limited use other than in cases where betting operators have suspended settlement of a market immediately after the conclusion of an event. This is only a plausible scenario in cases where there has been a manifest irregularity in the event in question. Even if that is the case, the operator will be aware that freezing all bets on the market (or on a specific outcome) which is the subject of investigation, is likely to inconvenience many innocent punters.

1 GA 2005, s 336(3).

2 GA 2005, s 336(5).

3 GA 2005, s 336(6).

6.65 Chain-gift schemes Those organising or having the misfortune to participate in a chain-gift scheme may not necessarily believe that they are engaging in gambling, but the DCMS has decided otherwise by shoe-horning a specific provision criminalising these schemes into the Act. During the pre-legislative period the issue of chain-gift schemes was another live topic, with Tessa Jowell MP, the Culture Secretary, describing the schemes as 'an absolute menace'.

What is a chain-gift scheme?

6.66 A chain-gift scheme is a scheme relying on pyramid contributions. Typically the scheme requires an investor to make a financial contribution and offers a return based on the number of recruits which the investor can provide for the scheme. Investors are often misled about the likely financial returns and although some of the scheme's early members may make money, the scheme is doomed to failure as there are never enough recruits to sustain the pyramid, which will eventually collapse. The most notorious chain-gift scheme of recent years was a scheme called 'women empowering women', which as its name implies, was a scheme aimed exclusively at women. The women investing in this scheme paid a significant joining fee and were then required to recruit other women to join the scheme, in order to sustain the pyramid. True to the form of all pyramid schemes it proved an expensive adventure for many who joined.

The new provision

6.67 Section 43(1) of the Act states that a person who either invites another to join a chain-gift scheme, or knowingly participates in the promotion, administration or management of a chain-gift scheme, commits an offence. A person convicted under this provision faces a term of imprisonment not exceeding 51 weeks, a fine, or both[1]. Unlike most of the remainder of the Act, this provision extends to Northern Ireland[2].

According to s 43(2) of the Act, an arrangement is a chain-gift scheme if: in order to participate a person must pay a joining fee to at least one other participant; and each person who joins is encouraged to invite others to participate and is encouraged to believe that he will receive the joining fees (or part of the joining fees) of other participants, to an amount in excess of the joining fee paid by him. The joining fee must be a payment of money or money's worth, but does not include goods or services and it is immaterial whether payment is made directly to other participant(s) or through a person managing the scheme[3].

There is a degree to which 'participation' in the scheme must be active rather than passive, with the relevant Explanatory Note stating that:

> 'People who participate unwittingly in the promotion of a chain-gift scheme, such as the host of an internet discussion forum upon which a posting promoting a chain-gift scheme has been made, will not commit an offence, provided they are unaware that the posting promotes a chain-gift scheme'[4].

1 GA 2005, s 43(4).
2 GA 2005, s 43(5).
3 GA 2005, s 43(3).
4 GA 2005, Explanatory Note 168.

6.68 Provision of unlawful facilities abroad Section 44(1) of the Act makes it an offence to do anything in Great Britain, or to use remote gambling equipment situated in Great Britain, for the purpose of inviting or enabling a person in a 'prohibited territory' to participate in remote gambling. The Secretary of State has the authority to make an order designating any country or place a 'prohibited territory'[1], and any such order must also prescribe the mode of trial and maximum penalty for the offence[2].

There are many jurisdictions which for the purposes of the Act would like to be designated 'prohibited territories' and have undoubtedly lobbied the DCMS to this end. The prohibitionist stance taken by the US Department of Justice on all matters pertaining to remote betting and gaming will make it a particularly keen observer of whether the Secretary of State's powers are used here.

For other jurisdictions, state-owned monopoly gambling operators provide funding for sport and charitable causes. A written submission to the Parliamentary Joint Scrutiny Committee on the draft Gambling Bill in December 2003, from the relevant departments within several Nordic governments, summarised concerns (which other jurisdictions would claim to share) that access to their markets from UK licensed operators would impact on:

> 'The need to uphold legitimate interests with regard to public policy and order as well as to limit damaging social consequences such as problem gambling and fraud . . . and that betting and lotteries may make a significant contribution to the financing of benevolent or public interest activities such as social or charitable undertakings, sport or culture.'

That submission neatly summarised social policy concerns and the potentially adverse impact on funding for good causes that a proliferation of gambling opportunities may provide. Of course these monopoly gambling operators also provide valuable tax revenue for the states in question.

The relevant Explanatory Note dealing with this provision states that:

> 'The Secretary of State's decision whether or not to exercise this power could depend on matters such as: the development of the global gaming market; the laws which other countries establish to permit, constrain or prohibit the use of remote gambling; the practical measures employed by those countries to secure compliance with such laws; and the extent to which it is possible to reach international agreements about the cross-border use of the internet for gambling'[3].

That guidance, whilst not fettering the Secretary of State's discretion, suggests that no sympathy will be shown to countries offering remote gambling opportunities to their own citizens when they are simultaneously trying to keep out UK licensed operators.

The government will no doubt recognise that a certain way of undermining efforts to make the UK an attractive location for remote gambling operators is to impose restrictions on the territories from which operators can accept customers. Therefore it is expected that the powers conferred on the Secretary of State by this part of the Act will only be used in extreme cases, if at all. They have not been used to date.

1 GA 2005, s 44(2).
2 GA 2005, s 44(3).
3 GA 2005, Explanatory Note 171.

PART 4: PROTECTION OF CHILDREN AND YOUNG PERSONS

Introduction

6.70 Part 4 of the Act (ss 45–64) creates a number of offences relating to children, young persons and gambling. For the purposes of the Act, a 'child' is anyone aged 15 or less and a 'young person' is anyone aged 16 or 17[1].

The Government has stated that it is 'unwavering in its belief that gambling is for adults only. The minimum age to take part should generally be 18. This is because of the risks that children may be damaged by losses that they cannot afford and by exposure to pressures and temptations that they cannot handle'[2]. At the same time, it must be recognised that: '[g]ambling is a widely accepted social practice . . . The current generation of children and young people grow up in an environment where gambling is not only routine, but also accessible and promoted by the government (for example, the National Lottery)'[3]. The statement that people under 18 should not gamble is, therefore, subject to certain exceptions in relation to forms of gambling presently considered to be relatively low risk.

The protection of children and other vulnerable persons from being harmed or exploited by gambling is the third licensing objective (s 1(c)). The pursuit of this objective is evident in the Gambling Commission's Statement of Principles for licensing and regulation of September 2009 at para 2.10–2.11 (see para **6.2040** below), its Codes of Practice (see the LCCP of December 2011 at para **6.2060** below) and its Guidance to licensing authorities[4]. These provisions are underlined by Part 4, which creates three categories of offence: (1) principal offences of inviting young persons to gamble or to enter certain gambling premises and analogous offences committed by young persons who gamble, enter such premises or who provide facilities for gambling themselves (ss 46 to 50); (2) employment offences targeted at those who employ children or young persons in connection with gambling and at young persons who work in these circumstances (ss 51 to 55); and (3) miscellaneous offences such as inviting a child to participate in a lottery or football pools (ss 56 to 58).

1 GA 2005, s 45(1) and (2).
2 DCMS, Draft Gambling Bill: Policy document, Cm 6014 – IV, November 2003, para 6.23.
3 DCMS, Young People and Gambling in Britain: A systematic and critical review of the research literature relating to game machine, lottery and pools coupons practice by children and young people under 18, Technical Paper No 8, November 2004, page 6.
4 GA 2005, ss 23 to 25 (and see 'Guidance to Licensing Authorities – 4th Edition', September 2012 at para **6.2655** below).

General points

6.71 The Gambling Commission may investigate and bring prosecutions in respect of Part 4 offences[1]. All offences in this part of the Act are summary only. However, the time limit for laying an information is raised from the normal six months to twelve months from the date of the offence[2].

Those offences which are expressed as being committed by a 'person' should include in these circumstances 'a body of persons corporate or unincorporate'[3]. Further, where an offence is committed by such a body and it is shown to have been committed with the consent or connivance of an officer of the body or as a result of his negligence, then the officer as well as the body may be guilty of the offence[4].

A person does not escape liability for a Part 4 offence merely because the alleged offence took place at premises operating under a temporary use notice or occasional use notice, rather than a premises licence[5]. For these purposes a temporary use notice is to be treated as the equivalent of a premises licence and an occasional use notice as if it were a betting premises licence[6].

A person charged with an offence of doing anything in relation to a child or young person may rely on the general defence in s 63. He must prove both that he took all reasonable steps to determine the individual's age and that he reasonably believed that the individual was not a child or young person, as the case may be.

Special provision is also made in Part 4 for the use of children in enforcement operations[7].

1 GA 2005, s 28. However, the power to prosecute does not apply in Scotland.
2 GA 2005, s 347.
3 Interpretation Act 1978, s 5 and Schs 1 and 2, Pt 1, para 4(5).
4 GA 2005, s 341.
5 GA 2005, Part 9 and s 39.
6 GA 2005, s 60.

7 GA 2005, s 64.

Principal offences

6.72 Invitation to gamble and gambling Section 46(1) makes it an offence to invite, cause or permit a child or young person to gamble. There is no express requirement of mens rea in the offence (in contrast with the requirement of intention in s 46(3), see para **6.73** below). The offence is subject to the exceptions listed in sub-s (2) and the reasonable belief defence[1].

By virtue of s 46(2), the offence does not apply in relation to a number of forms of gambling:

- participation in private or non-commercial gaming or betting[2];
- participation in a lottery or football pools (but see ss 56 and 57);
- the use of a Category D gaming machine[3]; and
- participation in equal chance gaming in accordance with a prize gaming permit issued under Part 13 of the Act or at a licensed family entertainment centre and participation in prize gaming at a non-licensed family entertainment centre or at a travelling fair in accordance with s 292.

1 GA 2005, s 63.
2 See GA 2005, Part 14, ss 295–302.
3 See GA 2005, s 236.

6.73 Advertising Specific provision is made in s 46(3) to (5) regarding the advertising of gambling to under 18-year-olds. By s 46(3), the offence in sub-s (1) of inviting a child or young person to gamble is stated 'in particular' to include intentionally:

- sending him 'any document which advertises gambling', or
- bringing to his attention 'information about gambling with a view to encouraging [him] to gamble'.

An 'advertiser' is defined as a person whose name or contact details appear in such a document or information as someone to whom payment may be made or from whom information may be obtained. 'Contact details' are defined widely to include an address or other location, a telephone number, an internet site, or an email address. An advertiser is treated as having committed the s 46(1) offence unless he proves that the document was sent or the information was brought to the attention of the child or young person without the advertiser's consent and authority[1].

The government has stated that the aim of these advertising provisions is to make it an offence to target information at under 18-year-olds but not to criminalise every activity which may bring information about gambling to their attention[2]. Section 46(5)(b) makes it a further defence for an advertiser to prove that information about gambling was brought to the attention of a child or young person only incidentally to it being brought to the attention of adults, and with no intention of encouraging the child or young person to gamble.

A responsibly operated billboard campaign by a person advertising on-line poker to adults is therefore unlikely to be caught by the s 46(1) offence. Although information about gambling is likely in this way to be brought to under 18-year-olds' attention, a prosecutor would find it difficult to prove that the information was intentionally brought to the attention of a child or young person with a view to encourage him to gamble. The advertiser would further be able to avail himself of the defence in sub-s (5)(b), if necessary.

Less clear is the situation in which email or mobile telephone 'spam' containing information about gambling is sent out to very many recipients and with no effort on the part of the advertiser to establish their age. Inevitably, under 18-year-olds will be amongst those who receive these messages. In such circumstances, it may be possible for a prosecutor to prove that the advertiser has thereby intentionally brought information about gambling to the attention of a child or young person (s 46(3)(b)). It could also make it difficult for an advertiser, in reliance on the s 46(5)(b) defence, to assert that any gambling information received by an under 18-year-old was so received only incidentally to the information being brought to the attention of adults. But was the spam disseminated with a view to encouraging its young recipient to gamble (s 46(3)(b))? That question will depend on the evidence in each case, including the nature of any notice confining the gambling services in question to adults.

Further provisions in relation to advertising are to be found in Part 16 of the Act.

By s 48(1) a young person commits an offence if he or she gambles. The Government took the policy decision not to extend the s 48 offence to children but held that it should rightly apply to young persons, who are 'able to appreciate that gambling activities of the sort included in the offence are for adults only'[3]. The offence is subject to the exceptions listed in s 48(2), which are identical to those in s 46(2).

1 GA 2005, s 46(4)–(6).

2 Joint Committee on the Draft Gambling Bill, Report Vol 1, Hl 63-I/Hc 139-I, 7 April 2004, Annex 1.

3 Joint Committee on the Draft Gambling Bill, Report Vol 1, Hl 63-I/Hc 139-I, 7 April 2004, Annex 1.

6.74 Invitation to enter premises and entering premises There is a criminal sanction for those who fail to keep under 18-year-olds out of certain premises offering facilities for gambling. Young persons who enter such premises also commit an offence.

It is an offence to invite or permit a child or young person to enter premises in respect of which a casino, betting or adult premises licence has effect (s 47(1), (4) and (5), respectively). The offence is only committed if the invitation or permission to enter is at a time when the premises is being used in reliance on its licence.

The s 47(1) offence in relation to casinos does not apply where a child or young person is permitted to enter the part of a regional casino that is not being used for gambling[1]. The rationale for this exception is that 'the non-gambling areas of regional casinos are likely to be large – perhaps even larger than the gaming area – including restaurants, theatres and other leisure activities', whereas the non-gambling areas of small and large casinos would be too small to offer a suitable range of non-gambling facilities and to ensure that a suitable distance is maintained from the gambling area[2]. Access to casino premises for children and young persons will also be regulated by code of practice[3].

Special considerations apply to the entry of an under 18-year-old to a track[4]. The s 47(4) offence in relation to betting premises does not apply in these circumstances. However, s 47(6) makes it an offence to invite or permit a child or young person to enter an area from which he is required to be excluded by virtue of s 182. That section requires that a premises licence in respect of a track is subject to the condition that children and young persons are excluded:

- from any area where facilities for betting are provided (other than a dog track or a horse racecourse on any day on which racing takes place), and
- where a gaming machine is situated (other than one of Category D).

Finally, s 47(7) makes it an offence to invite or permit a child or young person to enter any part of a licensed family entertainment centre in which he has access to a Category C gaming machine which is being used or is available for use at the time of entry.

The s 47 offences are subject to the reasonable belief defence[5].

A young person (but not a child) commits an offence under s 49 if he enters premises in circumstances in which it would be an offence under s 47 for a person to invite or permit him to enter them.

---

1 GA 2005, s 47(2); regulations made under s 47(3) may make provision for distinguishing between different parts of a premises for these purposes.

2 Richard Caborn (Minister for Sport), Standing Committee (B) debate on Gambling Bill, House of Commons, 30/11/04.

3 GA 2005, ss 24 and 176 and see the LCCP of December 2011 Part II at para **6.2060** below.

4 See definition in GA 2005, s 353.

5 GA 2005, s 63.

6.75 Provision of facilities for gambling Section 50(1) makes it an offence for a young person to provide 'facilities for gambling', which are defined in s 5. The offence is subject to the exceptions in s 50(2) and does not apply to:

- private or non-commercial gaming and betting (see ss 295 to 302);
- lotteries or football pools;
- prize gaming at a travelling fair pursuant to s 292.

Employment offences

6.76 The general rule is that the minimum age for employment in connection with the provision of facilities for gambling is 18, except for lotteries and football pools where the minimum age is 16. The rule is subject to certain exceptions in relation to forms of gambling presently considered to be relatively low risk or where those under 18 are not actually involved in the conduct of gambling.

'Employment' is given a wide definition for the purposes of Part 4, with the clear intention of covering all of the circumstances in which a child or young person may come to work at relevant premises. A reference to employing a person includes 'employing or engaging [him] whether or not under a contract of employment' and 'causing or permitting [him] to be employed or engaged'[1]. This should include employment of children and young persons on a temporary basis, whether they are employed directly or through an employment agency. Where an employment offence is proved, it is deemed to have been committed 'on each day during any part of which the employment continues'[2]. In other words, a new offence is committed on each day of the employment; this may have important implications for sentencing.

---

1 GA 2005, s 61(1)(a) and (b).

2 GA 2005, s 61(2).

6.77 Employment to provide facilities for gambling It is an offence, under s 51(1), to employ a child or young person to provide facilities for gambling. This offence is subject to the exceptions in s 51(2), which are identical to those in s 50(2), and to the reasonable belief defence[1].

As already stated, there is a minimum age of 16 for employment to provide facilities for gambling in connection with a lottery or football pools and a person commits an offence under s 52 if he employs a child in this regard. Section 52 does not apply to the National Lottery. However, it is an offence under existing National Lottery legislation for a child to sell a National Lottery ticket[2].

1 GA 2005, s 63.
2 National Lottery Act 1993, s 13 and reg 3 of the National Lottery Regulations 1994, SI 1994/189.

6.78 Employment otherwise than in the conduct of gambling According to Explanatory Note 185: '[r]estrictions are imposed on the ways in which children and young people can be employed to work on premises where facilities for gambling are provided, even if they are not engaged to perform any gambling activities themselves. This is to ensure that children and young people are not afforded undesirable exposure to gambling.'

Section 53 therefore makes it is an offence to employ a child to perform any function on premises where, and at a time when:

- facilities are provided for the playing of bingo, or
- facilities for gambling are provided in accordance with a club gaming permit or a club machine permit.

The control of gaming machines is considered to be an adult responsibility. It is an offence under s 54(1) to employ a child or young person to perform any function on premises where a gaming machine of any category is situated[1], if he is or may be required as part of his job 'to perform a function in connection with the gaming machine'. Exactly what this means in practice is as yet unclear. Explanatory Note 187 provide some guidance, suggesting that, for example, a child or young person 'may be employed in a family entertainment centre to undertake non-gambling activities, although he may not operate or handle the machine or pay customers prizes in the event that the machine has insufficient money in it . . . '. It has also been suggested that the under 18-year-old 'should be able to man a change desk, for example, in an arcade or family entertainment centre', but should not be involved in the 'supply, maintenance or operation' of any game machine[2].

By virtue of s 54(2), a young person (but not a child) employed in contravention of s 54(1) commits an offence himself.

In a provision that is analogous to s 47, s 55 makes it an offence to employ a child or young person to perform any function on premises where a casino, betting or adult gaming centre premises licence has effect (s 55(1)(a), (b) and (c), respectively). An offence is only committed if the employment is at a time when an activity is being carried out in reliance on the premises licence in question[3]. The law does not prevent under 18-year-olds from entering these premises at other times so that, for example, 'a 16-year-old apprentice joiner may undertake improvement works on the structure of a bar in a casino when it is closed'[4]. The s 55(1)(a) offence in relation to casinos does not, in any event, apply to employment in the non-gambling part of a regional casino[5].

The employment offences of ss 53, 54(1) and 55(1) are all subject to the reasonable belief defence[6]. By virtue of s 55(2), a young person (but not a child) employed in contravention of s 55(1) commits an offence himself.

1 This includes all categories and sub-categories of category B. See the Categories of Gaming Machine Regulations 2007, SI 2007/2158, reg 6.
2 Richard Caborn (Minister for Sport), Standing Committee (B) debate on Gambling Bill, House of Commons, 30/11/04.
3 GA 2005, s 55(2)(a).
4 Explanatory Note 188.
5 GA 2005, s 55(2)(b); regulations made under s 55(3) may make provision for distinguishing between different parts of a premises for these purposes.
6 GA 2005, s 63.

Miscellaneous offences

6.79 Invitation to participate in lottery or football pools It is an offence to invite, cause or permit a child to participate in a lottery or football pools (ss 56(1) and 57(1) respectively). The s 56 offence is subject to exceptions in relation to incidental non-commercial and private lotteries (as defined in s 258 and Sch 11, Pts 1 and 2)[1]. These are forms of lottery considered to be of relatively low risk to under 16 year-olds. Nor does s 56 apply to the National Lottery[2]. However, it is an offence under existing National Lottery legislation for a National Lottery ticket to be sold to a child[3].

The advertising provisions of s 46(3) to (6) apply also in relation to an invitation to a child to participate in a lottery or football pools[4]. Sections 56 and 57 are subject to the reasonable belief defence[5].

1 GA 2005, s 56(1)(a) and (b).
2 GA 2005, s 56(1)(c).
3 National Lottery Act 1993, s 13 and reg 3 of the National Lottery Regulations 1994, SI 1994/189.
4 GA 2005, ss 56(2) and 57(2).
5 GA 2005, s 63.

6.80 Return of stake A licensee must return any stake, fee etc where he becomes aware that it has been paid to him by a child or young person in order to gamble; and he may not give out any prize in these circumstances. A condition to this effect must be attached to all operating licences[1]. Failure to comply with the condition without reasonable excuse is an offence, under s 58. This rule does not apply to the use of a Category D gaming machine or participation in equal chance gaming at a licensed family entertainment centre[2]. Where a lottery or football pools are concerned, the rule applies only to children, and not to young persons[3].

1 GA 2005, s 83(1).
2 GA 2005, s 83(2).
3 GA 2005, s 83(4)(b).

6.81 Category D gaming machines The failure of the GA 2005 to ban the use of Category D gaming machines[1] by children has been controversial. While the government has pointed to an absence of clear research demonstrating a risk of harm from such activity, others have expressed concern. The Joint Committee on the Draft Gambling Bill heard evidence that

> 'Britain is alone in allowing children to play certain types of gaming machine and the Government's Gambling Review Body expressed unease about it . . . The Government is therefore in danger of acting irresponsibly by proposing that the anomaly of juvenile gaming machine playing be allowed to continue and thereby of failing to protect young people and their families'[2].

Section 59(1) seeks to address concerns of this nature by giving the Secretary of State power at some future date to create an offence of inviting, causing or permitting a child to use Category D machines. This provision is itself controversial. Its existence has been referred to as a 'sword of Damocles' hanging over family entertainment centres and other parts of the gambling industry where children frequently play on machines. The industry will take some comfort in the fact that the Secretary of State must enter into consultation, including with 'one or more persons who appear . . . to represent the interests of persons carrying on gambling businesses', before acting[3]. The government has also stated that it would require evidence of harm from prevalence studies and other research in order to trigger the use of this power[4]. Furthermore, any offence created pursuant to s 59 may discriminate between different types of machine; so that 'penny pushers', 'crane grabs' and other relatively harmless machines can be excluded from its ambit[5].

---

1 Defined in the Categories of Gaming Machine Regulations 2007, SI 2007/2158, reg 3.
2 Evidence of Professor Orford, Joint Committee on the Draft Gambling Bill, Report Vol 1, HL 63-I/HC 139-I, 7 April 2004, para 268.
3 GA 2005, s 59(3).
4 Richard Caborn (Minister for Sport), Standing Committee (B) debate on Gambling Bill, House of Commons, 30/11/04.
5 GA 2005, s 59(4).

Penalties

6.82 A person convicted of a Part 4 offence is liable on conviction to a sentence of imprisonment of up to 51 weeks in England and Wales (six months in Scotland), a maximum fine of level 5 on the standard scale, or both[1]. Where the offence is committed by a young person, the maximum sentence is a level 3 fine[2]. A court may also order forfeiture of any article, such as a gaming machine, that appears to relate to the offence in question[3].

---

1 GA 2005, s 62(1) and (3).
2 GA 2005, s 62(2).
3 GA 2005, s 345.

Table of offences under Part 4 of the Gambling Act 2005

6.83 Notes:
(1) A level 3 fine is currently £1,000 and a level 5 fine is £5,000[1].
(2) The maximum sentence of imprisonment in Scotland is six months, not the 51 weeks applicable in England and Wales[2].

Section	Description of offence	Offender	Exceptions/ Defences	Penalty
46(1)	To invite, cause or permit child or young person to gamble	Any person	Exceptions in s 46(2) Reasonable belief about person's age (s 63)	51 weeks imprisonment and/or Level 5
47(1), (4)–(7)	Invitation to enter certain premises offering gambling facilities	Any person	Exceptions: does not apply [1] when no facilities for gambling being offered or [2] in relation to non-gambling part of regional casino (s 47(1)(b) etc and s 47(2)) Reasonable belief about person's age (s 63)	51 weeks imprisonment and/or Level 5
48(1)	Gambling	Young person	Exceptions in s 48(2)	Level 3
49	Entering certain premises offering gambling facilities	Young person	Exceptions: see s 47	Level 3
50(1)	Provision of facilities for gambling	Young person	Exceptions in s 50(2)	Level 3
51(1)	Employment of child or young person to provide facilities for gambling	Any person	Exceptions in s 51(2) Reasonable belief about person's age (s 63)	51 weeks imprisonment and/or Level 5
52	Employment of child to provide facilities for gambling in connection with lottery/football pools	Any person	National Lottery exception (s 52(a); but see National Lottery legislation in this regard) Reasonable belief about person's age (s 63)	51 weeks imprisonment and/or Level 5

Section	Description of offence	Offender	Exceptions/ Defences	Penalty
53	Employment of child to perform any function on premises where and when facilities provided for playing bingo or gambling in accordance with club gaming/ machine permit	Any person	Reasonable belief about person's age (s 63)	51 weeks imprisonment and/or Level 5
54(1)	Employment of child or young person on premises where a gaming machine is situated, if required to perform a function in connection with it	Any person	Reasonable belief about person's age (s 63)	51 weeks imprisonment and/or Level 5
54(2)	Employment in contravention of s 54(1)	Young person.		Level 3
55(1)	Employment of child or young person to perform any function on premises in respect of which a casino/betting/ adult gaming centre premises licence has effect	Any person.	Exceptions: does not apply [1] when no facilities for gambling being provided or [2] in relation to non-gambling part of regional casino (s 55(2)) Reasonable belief about person's age (s 63)	51 weeks imprisonment and/or Level 5
55(4)	Employment in contravention of s 55(1)	Young person		Level 3.

Section	Description of offence	Offender	Exceptions/ Defences	Penalty
56(1)	To invite, cause or permit a child to participate in a lottery	Any person	Does not apply to forms of lottery specified s 56(1)(a) to (c) Reasonable belief about person's age (s 63)	51 weeks imprisonment and/or Level 5
57(1)	To invite, cause or permit a child to participate in football pools	Any person	Reasonable belief about person's age (s 63)	51 weeks imprisonment and/or Level 5
58	Failure to return stake to child or young person	Any person	Offence is only committed without reasonable excuse Reasonable belief about person's age (s 63)	51 weeks imprisonment and/or Level 5

1 Criminal Justice Act 1982, s 37(2).
2 GA 2005, s 62(3).

PART 5: OPERATING LICENCES

Introduction

6.90 Under the Act the licensing function is split into three distinct categories; namely operating licences, personal licences (both to be issued by the Gambling Commission) and premises licences which are to be issued by the local authority where the premises are situated.

The Gambling Commission is the responsible body for the grant of operating licences and subsequent regulation of those who are licensed. The Commission has already said that it will be guided by the following principles:

(1) it will regulate gambling in the public interest and it will do so vigorously;
(2) it will regulate in a transparent, accountable, proportionate, consistent and targeted manner;
(3) its approach to regulation will be risk-based;
(4) its assessment of risk will be led by evidence and where there is no evidence then it will take a cautious approach;
(5) it will consult widely;
(6) It will use its resources effectively.

See an Introductory Guide to the Gambling Commission; this can be found on its website on http://www.gamblingcommission.org.uk.

The Gambling Commission and the role that it plays through operating licences will be central to the success of the Act in satisfying the determination of the government that consumer choice will only be extended where protections can be established to balance the risks of new products.

For every class there will be two types, remote and non remote operating licences. Those operators who want non remote facilities will also need a premises licence for the specific premises. An operator wanting the facility to offer both remote and non remote will need two operating licences, although in some cases as pointed out at para **6.16** above, this requirement has been mitigated in some cases.

Categories of licences

6.91 Section 65(2) creates categories of operating licences as follows:

(a) Casino operating licence
(b) Bingo operating licence
(c) General betting operating licence
(d) Pool betting operating licence
(e) Betting intermediary operating licence
(f) Gaming machine general operating licence (for adult gaming centres)
(g) Gaming machine general operating licence (for family entertainment centres)
(h) Gaming machine technical operating licence
(i) Gambling software operating licence
(j) Lottery operating licence[1].

An operator may make application for more than one of the above. The above categories are applicaple, mutatis mutandis, to remote gambling.

A separate application will have to be made if the operator wishes to offer such gambling[2].

Section 65(4) provides the Secretary of State with power to amend s 65(2) so as to add or remove or vary a kind of operating licence. However, no use having yet been made of this power, it is worth asking whether various new licence categories have been validly introduced. For example, a trading room licence was introduced in August 2008 (see para 6.2167 below) and in April 2012 a general betting (standard) (remote platform) operating licence (see SI 2012/829). The latter is described by DCMS and the Gambling Commission as a 'new sub-category' of licence. Whether such a description achieves avoidance of the need to comply with s 65(4) must surely be a matter of considerable debate.

1 GA 2005, s 65(2) and see SI 2008/1803 which introduces fees for certain new sub categories of licence as explained in the Commission's document 'Changes to licence categories from 1 August 2008'. Trading rooms comprise one of the new categories. See para **6.2167** below).
2 GA 2005, s 67.

General principles and procedure

6.92 The application is made to the Gambling Commission; it needs to specify which activities are to be authorised by the licence and be in a format specified by the Gambling Commission, be accompanied by such other information as the Commission may direct and by the appropriate fee[1]. Demand for the facilities is expressly excluded as a factor for the Commission to take into account[2].

Those with relevant convictions will not secure a licence, nor minors or groups that include them. An annual fee is payable.

In determining any application the Gambling Commission shall have regard to the licensing objectives and make such investigations as are necessary to ensure that the applicant is suitable to carry on the licensed activities. The Commission must also enquire into the suitability of any gaming machine or any other equipment to be used in connection with the licensed activities[3].

In December 2006 the Commission published its Statement of Principles for Licensing and Regulation, the second edition of which is dated September 2009 (see para **6.2040** below). This sets out, inter alia, the general principles which it will apply to applications and covers various procedural matters under s 73. In summary, the Commission will:

- assess integrity by requiring relevant individuals to undergo criminal records checks and, in some cases, seek information about the person from public agencies. Integrity will only be assumed in the case of local authorities which apply to run lotteries;
- assess the competence of applicants particularly with reference to social responsibility matters;
- enquire about the financial position of applicants, including directors and partners of applicants.

Whilst electronic application procedures will be used the Commission reserves the right, in certain cases, to interview applicants.

Further, in January 2008 the Commission published 'Licensing and Regulatory Decisions: Procedures and Guidance'. The second edition is dated November 2010. Part 2 thereof sets out the general principles which the Commission will apply in determining applications for operating licences[4].

---

1 GA 2005, s 69. See also the Gambling (Operating Licence and Single Machine Permit Fees) Regulations 2006, SI 2006/3284.
2 GA 2005, s 72.
3 GA 2005, s 70.
4 See para **6.2088** below.

Conditions to be attached to operating licences

6.93 The Commission has the discretion to specify conditions to be attached to all operating licences or for those falling within a specified class. These conditions will only be lawful and relevant if they are necessary to uphold the licensing objectives.

Conditions may restrict the nature of the activities, the circumstances in which they are carried on, or their extent. To achieve the desired effect the conditions may make provision about facilities that may or must be provided and the manner in which they are provided in connection with the licensed activities. They can specify the number of persons that may or must be employed and the financial resources that must be made available. The Commission are given a wide discretion and far reaching powers as to how they will regulate operating licences through conditions. This is demonstrated by s 79(4)(e) which states that they can attach conditions about 'any other matter.' They can even specify the maintenance of financial reserves in respect of any potential liabilities[1]. In October 2008 the Commission published a number of documents concerned with Licence Conditions and Codes of

Practice ('LCCP'). These were subsequently supplemented. A consolidated version was published in March and December 2011. See para **6.2060** below. The current LCCP is a detailed document of over 50 pages. In brief it sets out:

- the general conditions to be attached to operating licences;
- the general conditions to be attached to personal licences;
- the principal codes of practice, distinguishing between social responsibility provisions and other provisions;
- the code of practice to be attached to casino premises licences concerning access for children and young persons.

Helpfully, in December 2008 the Commission published individual documents which set out typical LCCP for different types of operator. These are set out in the index at the beginning of Section 4 and are reproduced at para **6.2100** ff below.

These take into account the specific powers given to the Commission in ss 89–93 and ss 98–99 in respect of remote gambling, casino, bingo, general betting, pool betting operators and lottery operators. Additionally, in July 2008 the Commission issued a new version of 'Bingo and Casino Equipment Technical Requirements'; see para **6.2244.1** below) pursuant to s 85, has published 11 documents pursuant to s 96 in respect of technical standards to be applied to machines together with a machine standards definition document and a policy statement in respect of legacy machines[2]. These are to be found at para **6.2520** ff below. Further, under s 97 the Commission has published a document dealing with the technical standards which are to be applied to remote gambling software: see (see 'Remote Gambling and Software Technical Standards, August 2009' at para **6.2410** below).

The Commission may subsequently amend or revoke a condition attached to the operating licence. Before doing so they will consult those representing the interests of operating licensees who may be affected by the condition, and such persons specified in s 23(5) as they think appropriate. Any changes that are made must be published as soon as is reasonably practicable. The Commission will continue to monitor operating licences once they have been issued and will make changes that are necessary to reflect operational styles and practices.

In addition the Secretary of State reserves the right to attach specified conditions to operating licences, which gives central government the ability to have direct impact into operational licences should they feel there is a need[3].

The Act makes specific provision for the attachment of conditions about the giving of credit in connection with the licensed activities, or the giving of inducements to people to gamble[4]. One sector for which particular provision is made in respect of these matters is that of the traditional land based casino or bingo operating licence. These categories of licences will not permit the operator to give, participate in, allow or knowingly facilitate credit in connection with gambling. However, the operator will be allowed to site ATM machines in the premises as long as the operator has no commercial connection with the credit provider[5].

---

1 GA 2005, ss 75–79.

2 Legacy machines are category B3, B4, C or D machines which were lawfully in use on premises in Great Britain on 31 August 2007 which comply with the regulations made under s 240 and certain details of which have been notified to the Commission.

3 GA 2005, s 78. An example is to be found in the Gambling Act 2005 (Operating Licence Conditions) Regulations 2007, SI 2007/2257.

4 GA 2005, s 81(1).
5 GA 2005, s 81(2).

Interaction between operating and personal licences

6.94 For each operating licence there will need to be a personal licence holder who occupies a specified management office within the organisation. The Commission can impose a condition on the operating licence stating that the person holding this personal licence is authorised to perform the management function as described and in accordance with any condition attached to the personal licence, which will also be issued by the Commission[1].

This will give a direct route for the Commission when exercising its regulatory control through the operating licence. A management office includes a director in a limited company, a partner in a partnership and in any other organisation, anyone who exercises an operational function. This seems to be very loosely defined and would include anyone capable of influencing the outcome of gambling, receiving or paying money in connection with gambling, manufacturing, supplying, installing, maintaining or repairing a gaming machine.

1 GA 2005, s 80.

Social responsibility

6.95–6.103 One of the key areas of operating licences is to ensure that the licensing objectives are upheld and that all operators conduct their businesses in a socially responsibly way. A condition is placed on each operating licence to ensure that all licensees comply with the codes of practice created under GA 2005, s 24.

There will be specific monitoring of the position with regard to minors and if a licensee becomes aware that a child is using their facilities then they must return any money paid and may not give any prizes to children[1]. The only sectors where children will be permitted to play under an operating licence will be where category D gaming machines are licensed or equal chance gaming takes place at a licensed family entertainment centre.

To this end the Commission can require information to be made available to it from the operator as to the use of the gambling facilities. In particular information will be requested by the Commission if it believes that an offence under GA 2005 has been committed or if the Gambling Commission is carrying out investigations that could lead to a bet being declared void under GA 2005, s 336.

1 GA 2005, s 83.

Maintenance, regulation and duration

6.104 Licensees will have to pay an annual fee for their licences as prescribed by the Secretary of State[1].

If an operator changes their licensed activities or structure of the organisation it is under a positive duty to notify the Commission once regulations are made under s 101[2].

Where the licensee is a limited company and there is a change to the controller of the company (as defined by s 422 of the Financial Services and Markets Act 2000) there is a positive duty under s 102 for the licensee to either surrender the licence or to ask for the licence to continue. If there is no compliance with this duty within five weeks of it arising then the Commission is under a duty to revoke the licence, although it has power to extend this period at its discretion as long as the licence has not been revoked. If, however an application to continue the licence has been made and is accompanied by relevant information then after close scrutiny the Commission can make a positive determination if the new operating licence would have originally been granted with the new 'controller' in situ. If not then the licence will be revoked. The Commission has wide powers but must inform the licensee of its decision and give reasons[3].

Obviously operators may change their style of operation and therefore the Act has had to be drafted so as to allow operating licences to be varied on application.

A licensee can apply to the Commission to vary the licence so as to:

(1) add, amend or remove a licensed activity;
(2) amend another detail of the licence;
(3) add, amend or remove a condition attached to the licence.

The application procedure is the same as that for a new licence and must be accompanied by a statement of the variation sought and the original licence. These provisions build in some flexibility for the operator whilst maintaining the ability of the Commission to retain ultimate control[4].

This is further exhibited by the provisions giving the Commission the ability to require licensees to submit their licences for variations, amendments to any general conditions attached by the Commission or to reflect any operational change in circumstances. This obviously gives the Commission the ability to attach additional conditions should it believe them to be necessary when judged against the licensing objectives[5].

The Commission will maintain a central register of licensees and members of the public will have the right to inspect it and ask for a copy of entries on it. A fee will have to be paid for copy entries. Licensees will also be able to request a copy should a licence be lost or damaged on payment of a fee[6].

Obviously the licence will be something of tangible value as it authorises the holder to operate in a highly regulated industry. Powers are given within the GA 2005 for a police officer to require a licensee to produce the licence, creating a criminal offence should the licensee fail to do so without a reasonable excuse[7].

A further criminal offence is committed if a licensee is convicted of any criminal offence before a court in Great Britain or any relevant offence before a court abroad and does not as soon as is reasonably practicable inform the Commission of that fact. In circumstances where a licensee is convicted of a relevant offence in Great Britain he must inform the court that he holds an operating licence and the convicting court can order forfeiture of that licence which will immediately cease to have effect. As part of this process the court has the power to suspend the licence for a designated time. The court must notify the Commission after it has ordered forfeiture[8].

A licence will have an indefinite duration unless expressly restricted and under s 111 the Commission appears to have a wide discretion as to how it can so restrict the licence. However, in its statement of Principles for Licensing and

Regulation (December 2006, see para **6.2040** of Paterson 2008 and 2009) at para 3.18 the Commission stated that it did not currently intend to exercise this power. The licence will cease to have effect if the licensee surrenders the licence or it lapses[9].

The latter would be occasioned if the licensee dies, is incapable of carrying out the licensed activities or becomes bankrupt. A licence will also lapse if a corporate licensee ceases to exist or goes into liquidation[10].

The Commission's regulatory powers are further enhanced by the ability for a licence to be called in to be reviewed[11]. The powers of investigation are to ensure that conditions are being complied with or where the Commission has fears that a licensee has been convicted of a relevant offence. These powers are wide ranging in that the Commission has the power to hold a review if it takes the view that the licensee is unsuitable to continue to keep the licence or simply that it thinks that a review is appropriate. The Commission may also commence its investigations if it receives a complaint about a particular operator. If the infraction is modest then the licensee should receive nothing more than a warning. As the infringements become more serious so do the powers of sanction with the Commission able to attach additional conditions to licences, suspend or revoke the licence and impose penalties.

In the case of suspension the Commission must specify from when it commences and its duration in terms of time or that it should cease when some future event is performed[12]. The Commission can revoke a licence after a review if it feels that the circumstances are such that a suspension is insufficient[13]. There are curbs on the Commission's powers to suspend or revoke, in that any of the following conditions must apply:

(1) the licensed activity is being or has been undertaken in breach of the licensing objectives;

(2) a condition of the licence has been breached;

(3) the licensee has failed to cooperate with a review;

(4) the licensee is unsuitable to carry on the licensed activities. This could be in circumstances where the integrity, competence or financial standing of the licensee is established[14].

The Commission also has these powers when a licensee has failed to comply with the requirement of regulations under section 101 and section 105.

The Commission is given a wide discretion regarding financial penalties that can be imposed. The licensee needs to be informed that the Commission is considering a financial penalty, the amount it is proposing and reasons why it is proposing such a penalty. This notice will also inform the licensee of the time frame for any representations against the imposition of a financial penalty. Any penalty can be enforced as a civil debt and the Commission will then deduct its direct enforcement costs and pay the balance into the Consolidated Fund[15]. In June 2007 the Commission published a Statement of Principles for Determining Financial Penalties; this was updated in September 2009. (See para **6.2076** below).

All licensees must keep records of their licensed activities and provide the Commission with a written or electronic copy. If a licensee fails to comply with such a request then another criminal offence will have been committed[16].

---

1 See the Gambling (Operating Licence and Single-Machine Permit Fees) Regulations 2006, SI 2006/3284 as amended by SIs 2007/269 and 2007/1791.

2 None have been made.

3 GA 2005, s 102 and 115.
4 GA 2005, s 104.
5 GA 2005, s 105.
6 GA 2005, s 106.
7 GA 2005, ss 108 and 103. The fee payable under the latter is set out in the Sis referred to in fn 1 above.
8 GA 2005, s 109.
9 GA 2005, ss 113–114.
10 GA 2005, s 110.
11 GA 2005, s 116 and see Guidance on regulatory decision making after a licence review, November 2009 at para **6.2088.1** below.
12 GA 2005, s 118.
13 GA 2005, s 119.
14 GA 2005, s 120. Note that ss 116–120 are modified under the Gambling Act 2005 (Horseracing Betting Levy) Order 2007, SI 2007/2159, art 3 in respect of non-payment of levy to the Levy Board.
15 GA 2005, s 121.
16 GA 2005, s 122.

6.105 Levy The Secretary of State may make (but has not yet made) regulations which would require holders of operating licences to pay an annual levy. The timing and system of collection is maintained in a flexible format and any request made would be treated in the same way as the annual fee. The levy fund can then be used to provide financial assistance by way of loan or grants for projects related to assisting those with an addiction to gambling or other licensing objectives. It is anticipated that there will be detailed consultation between the Commission and the Secretary of State to ensure that any monies collected by any such levy will be used effectively[1].

1 GA 2005, s 123.

PART 6: PERSONAL LICENCES

Introduction

6.110 The scheme of the Act is to ensure that gambling is regulated by a combination of operating, personal and, where appropriate, premises licences. In general, while the operating licence authorises an individual, partnership, association or company to operate a particular type of gambling undertaking, those responsible for the overall management of the undertaking, for the compliance function and for the actual control of gambling – for example croupiers will require a personal licence[1].

Specifically, by virtue of a mandatory condition of all operating licences there must be at least one personal licence holder responsible for the management of the licensed undertaking[2]. Where an operating licence is held by a company, partnership or association, at least one holder of a 'specified management office'[3] must hold a personal licence authorising the performance of the management function[4]. There are however two exceptions. The first relates to a club or institute governed by Part 12 which requires a bingo operating licence. No condition may be attached to that operating licence requiring a person to hold a personal licence[5]. The second relates to a 'small scale operator'[6]. This term is defined by regulations[7], which state that the holder of an operating licence will qualify as a small-scale operator if he satisfies the conditions that, in relation to the relevant licensed activities, there are no more than three 'qualifying positions' in his organisation which are occupied by a 'qualified person'. The quoted phrases are defined in reg 2(2) and (3) of SI 2006/3266.

In addition the Commission or the Secretary of State may impose additional conditions[8] requiring that the holder of any designated management function, involving responsibility for those conducting operational activities and/or compliance with the terms of the licence[9] shall be the holder of an appropriate personal licence[10]. Further, conditions may require that those conducting operational functions – any function enabling them to influence the outcome of gaming, payment or receipt of money or manufacturing, supplying, installing, maintaining or repairing a gaming machine[11] – must hold an appropriate personal licence[12].

---

1 GA 2005, s 80.
2 GA 2005, s 80(1).
3 A director, partner or office-holder respectively: s 80(5).
4 GA 2005, s 80(1).
5 GA 2005, s 80(9).
6 GA 2005, s 129.
7 GA 2005, s 129(2) and see the Gambling Act 2005 (Definition of Small-Scale Operator) Regulations 2006, SI 2006/3266.
8 The Commission may impose general conditions under s 75, and individual conditions under s 77. The Secretary of State may impose general conditions under s 78. For general conditions see 'Conditions and Codes of Practice applicable to: Personal Management Licences; Personal Functional Licences', October 2010, at para **6.2710** below. See also two quick guides on PMLs and PFLs published by the Gambling Commission in August 2012 and available on its website.
9 GA 2005, s 80(5)(d).
10 GA 2005, s 80(3).
11 GA 2005, s 80(6).
12 GA 2005, s 80(4).

Definition

6.111 A personal licence is defined[1] as a licence authorising a person to perform the functions of a specified management office or to perform a specified management function[2]. In general the provisions of Part 5 (ie those which are relevant to operating licences) apply[3]. However they have been modified in the case of personal licences by The Gambling (Personal Licences) (Modification of Part 5 of the Gambling Act 2005) Regulations 2006, SI 2006/3267 (and see also, re fees, SI 2006/3285). The intention is to ensure that the criteria and conditions of personal licences should be the same, mutatis mutandis, as those for operating licences, without reproducing the provisions[4]. The terms of the relevant operating licence will specify which posts will require the holder to have a personal licence[5].

---

1 GA 2005, s 127.
2 As defined in GA 2005, s 80. The Secretary of State may by order amend these definitions: s 80(8).
3 GA 2005, s 128.
4 GA 2005, Explanatory Note 357.

5 See s 80.

Criteria for grant and licence conditions

6.112 Personal licences are issued by the Commission[1]. Applicants must be at least 18[2]. The application must specify what functions the applicant is applying for, be made in such form as the Commission requires and be accompanied by the prescribed fee and such supporting documentation as the Commission requires[3]. The Commission may require that the applicant's employer (in the broad sense of the person for whom the applicant provides or intends to provide services[4]) countersign the application or provide additional information[5]. However a person who is not employed may apply for a personal licence, and these powers may not be used to frustrate such an application[6].

In principle the criteria for consideration of the grant of a personal licence are the same as for the grant of an operating licence[7]. However the relevant considerations are likely to be primarily the suitability of the applicant[8] in particular his integrity[9] and competence[10]. A licence can be refused where the applicant has a relevant conviction[11]. The Commission may seek further information from the applicant, and obtain information from any other person[12].

A licence may be issued subject to conditions. These may be general conditions applying to all licences or to those of a specified class (eg for croupiers or cashiers) or they may be specific[13]. In December 2008 (updated October 2010) the Commission published the current typical LCCP for personal licences (see 'Conditions and Codes of Practice applicable to: Personal Management Licences; Personal Functional Licences' at para **6.2710** below). This applies to all personal licence holders. It places a duty on them to report suspicion of offences, to report 'key events' (as defined therein in para 15.2) and to provide certain regulatory information in response to a request from the Commission.

One individual may only hold one personal licence[14], but a licence may authorise more than one function[15]. Additional functions may be added by way of a variation[16].

1 GA 2005, s 65.
2 GA 2005, s 69(3).
3 GA 2005, s 69.
4 GA 2005, s 130(3).
5 GA 2005, s 130(1) and (2).
6 GA 2005, s 130(4).
7 GA 2005, s 70.
8 GA 2005, s 70(1)(b).
9 GA 2005, s 70(2)(a).
10 GA 2005, s 70(2)(b).
11 GA 2005, s 71 and Sch 7.
12 GA 2005, s 73.
13 GA 2005, ss 75–79. See commentary on Part 5 (para **6.90** ff above).
14 GA 2005, s 133(1).
15 GA 2005, s 133(2).

[16] GA 2005, s 104.

Appeals

6.113 Appeals against refusal of a licence in whole or part, the imposition of conditions and other decisions of the Commission in relation to personal licences lie to the First-tier Tribunal under Part 7 of the Act.

Duration

6.114 Once granted a licence will be of indefinite duration[1]. It is however subject to surrender[2], lapse on death, incapacity or bankruptcy[3], forfeiture on conviction of a relevant offence[4] by a court in Great Britain[5], or revocation[6].

1 GA 2005, s 131.
2 GA 2005, s 113.
3 GA 2005, s 114 and see Commission letter 11.11.08 (para **6.2711** below).
4 GA 2005, Sch 7.
5 GA 2005, s 115.
6 GA 2005, s 119.

Fees

6.115 The Secretary of State has power to specify periodic fees to be paid by a Personal Licence holder to the Commission but unlike operating licence fees they will not necessarily be on an annual basis. The Secretary of State may prescribe the amount and period for which the fees must be paid. A Personal Licence may be revoked for non-payment of the periodic fee[1].

1 GA 2005, s 132 and the Gambling (Personal Licence Fees) Regulations 2006, SI 2006/3285.

Review

6.116 The Commission may undertake a review of the activities of an individual personal licence holder,[1] but not a general review of personal licence holders as a class[2]. The review may follow a complaint[3], but in effect the Commission has a very broad discretion to undertake a review[4]. The affected licence holder must be informed of the review[5] and is entitled to make representations[6]. A review may result in regulatory enforcement action in the form of: a warning, adding or varying a condition, suspension or revocation of the licence[7].

1 GA 2005, s 116(2) and see Guidance on regulatory decision making after a licence review, November 2009 at para **6.2088.1** below.
2 GA 2005, s 135 disapplies s 116(1) in the case of personal licence holders.
3 GA 2005, s 116(3)(a).
4 GA 2005, s 116(2).
5 GA 2005, s 116(4).
6 GA 2005, s 116(5).

7 GA 2005, s 117.

Suspension and revocation

6.117 Suspension may be imposed as a penalty[1], or on a precautionary basis pending the completion of a review[2]. Revocation may only be imposed as a penalty. The grounds for suspension and revocation are the same[3], namely that activities are being carried on inconsistently with the licensing objectives, breach of a condition of the licence, the licence holder has failed to co-operate with a review, or is not a suitable person to carry on the licensed activities[4]. Suitability is, in particular, a matter of integrity and competence[5]. A licence may also be suspended or revoked[6] if the holder does not notify the Commission of a relevant change in circumstances[7] or produce the licence for amendment on demand[8].

1 GA 2005, s 118(1).
2 GA 2005, s 118(2).
3 GA 2005, s 120.
4 GA 2005, s 120(1).
5 GA 2005, s 120(3).
6 GA 2005, s 120(2).
7 GA 2005, s 101.
8 GA 2005, s 105.

Financial penalties

6.118 The Commission may impose a financial penalty where the holder of the licence has been guilty of a breach of a licence condition[1]. The notification of intention to impose a penalty must be given within two years of the date when the breach came to the notice of the Commission[2]. The licence holder must be given the opportunity to make representations[3].

1 GA 2005, s 121(1) and see 'Statement of Principles for Determining Financial Penalties, September 2009' at para **6.2076** below.
2 GA 2005, s 121(3).
3 GA 2005, s 121(2).

Offences generally

6.119 Where a licence holder is convicted of a relevant offence[1] the court may, whether or not it imposes forfeiture of the licence, disqualify the licence holder from holding a personal licence for a period of up to ten years[2].

Where the holder of a personal licence is convicted of a relevant offence[3] he must notify the Commission[4] and so must the holder of any operating licence for whom that person is providing services[5]. Failure to do so is an offence in each case[6].

The Commission will, following the suspension or revocation of a personal licence, or notification of the making by a court of a forfeiture or disqualification order notify the holder of an operating licence for whom the Commission believes the personal licence holder to be providing services of the occurrence of the relevant event[7].

Where an operating licence requires a Personal Licensee under s 80 of the Act and the Personal Licence holder acting in the course of, or in connection with any activity authorised by the Operating Licence does so contrary to the terms and conditions of the Personal Licence[8], such an individual commits an offence[9]. This offence may be prosecuted irrespective of whether the operating licence holder is also prosecuted[10].

A personal licence must be produced to a constable or enforcement officer immediately[11] if the individual is carrying on a licensed activity or is on premises for which a premises licence is in force[12]. In any other case it must be produced within a specified time[13]. Failure to do so is an offence[14]. Ordinarily an operating licence need only be produced within a specified time[15]. Note however that in the case of a small scale operator who is not required to hold a personal licence, the operating licence must be produced immediately if required by a constable or enforcement officer while the operator is carrying on a licensed activity[16].

1 GA 2005, Sch 7.
2 GA 2005, s 136.
3 GA 2005, Sch 7.
4 GA 2005, s 109.
5 GA 2005, s 138(2) and (5).
6 GA 2005, s 109(4) and s 138(3) respectively. The penalty in each case is a fine not exceeding Level 2.
7 GA 2005, s 137.
8 Ie the activities undertaken are not those which he is licensed for.
9 GA 2005, s 139. The penalty is imprisonment for up to 51 weeks and/or a fine not exceeding Level 5.
10 GA 2005, s 139(3). The operator offence is under s 33.
11 Ie there is an obligation to carry it on the person in these circumstances.
12 GA 2005, s 134(1)(b) and (c).
13 GA 2005, s 134(1)(a).
14 GA 2005, s 134(2). The penalty is a fine not exceeding Level 2.
15 GA 2005, s 108(1).
16 GA 2005, s 129(4).

PART 7: APPEALS IN RESPECT OF OPERATING AND PERSONAL LICENCES AND WHEN BETS HAVE BEEN VOIDED

The First-tier Tribunal

6.130 With effect from 18 January 2010 the Gambling Appeals Tribunal, established under GA 2005, s 140 was abolished and had all its functions transferred to the First-tier Tribunal, a newly constituted body which derives its existence and powers from the Tribunals, Courts and Enforcement Act 2007, Pt 1 (see the Transfer of Tribunal Functions Order 2010, arts 2 and 3[1]).

Part 7, GA 2005 and related provisions have been substantially amended by that statutory instrument and the previous legislation concerning Gambling Appeal Tribunal procedure have been replaced by new rules; see the Tribunal Procedure (First-tier Tribunal) (General Regulatory Chamber) Rules 2009[2] and a new fees regime is now in place (see the First-tier Tribunal (Gambling) Fees Order 2010[3]). A brief summary of some of the Tribunal Rules is as follows:

- a written notice, within 28 days must be filed with the Tribunal. This must include the grounds of appeal;

- the notice is provided to the Commission by the Tribunal;
- within 28 days of receipt the Commission must file its response, setting out its grounds for opposing the appeal. Time can be extended;
- within 14 days of receipt of the Commission's statement of case the appellant may file a written reply and copies of documents relied upon. Time can be extended;
- in every case there are likely to be detailed directions given by the Tribunal in respect of the disposal of the case (see rr 5–9, 14–18) and there may be a pre-hearing;
- costs; these will be awarded against a losing party only if bringing or defending the appeal or its conduct was unreasonable; see r 10;
- the Tribunal has the power, under r 41, to set aside its own decision and a limited power to review it under r 44; the latter only arises if there exists an application for permission to appeal.

---

1 SI 2010/22.
2 SI 2009/1976 as amended by SI 2010/43.
3 SI 2010/42 as amended by SI 2010/633.

Cases which are appealable

6.131 Sections 141, 144 and 337 set out the decisions from which all appeals can be made. In each case the decisions is that of the Commission[1]. An applicant for a licence can appeal:

(a) where the Commission determines an application under s 69 or s 112 for the issue or renewal of an operating licence or under s 128 for the issue or renewal of a personal licence
(b) where the Commission attaches a condition to an operating licence under s 77 or to a personal licence under s 128[2].
(c) where the Commission determines an application under s 102(2)(b), relating to the continuance in effect of an operating licence where there has been a relevant change of corporate control.
(d) where the Commission determines an application to vary an operating licence under s 104 or s 128 (in the case of a personal licence) a Licensee can appeal,
(e) where the Commission gives a notice under s 114(1)(b) which causes an operating licence (or a personal licence, by reason of s 128) to lapse if in the Commission's opinion the licensee is physically or mentally incapacitated from carrying on the licensed activities.
(f) where the Commission takes action, or determines to take action[3], under s 117[4], following a review under s 116 of an operating licence (or, under s 128, a personal licence).
(g) where the Commission takes action, or determines to take action under s 118[5] to suspend an operating licence following a review under s 116 (or a personal licence by application of s 128).
(h) where the Commission takes action or determines to take action under s 119[6] to revoke an operating licence following a review under s 116 (or personal licence by application of s 128).

(i) where the Commission gives a notice imposing a financial penalty on the holder of an operating licence under s 121(4)[7] (or a personal licence holder by application of s 128).

Further, if a Tribunal remits a matter to the Commission under s 144(1)(e) the subsequent decision or action of the Commission is itself appealable[8].

Moreover, if the Commission makes an order under s 336 to void a bet[9] a party to the bet or to any contract or other arrangement in relation to the bet may appeal[10]. In fact it seems, from the wording of s 336(2) that as the only relevant order which the Commission can make is to void the bet only the party whose bet has been voided can appeal. It appears that an unsuccessful applicant to have a bet voided has no right of appeal.

1 Appeals in respect of premises licences are governed by ss 206 and 209. See the commentary on Part 8, para **6.150** ff below. Appeals in respect of temporary use notices are covered by the commentary on Part 9, see para **6.190** ff below.
2 Note that there can be no appeal against conditions imposed under other provisions, such as, for example, s 75.
3 The phrase 'determines to take action' is also found in s 117(2); this requires that a licensee is notified as soon as is reasonably practicable of the action and the Commission's reasons for it.
4 Such action can vary from giving a warning to the licensee to revocation of the licence.
5 There is a clear overlap/duplication between this paragraph and (f) above in that s 117 cross refers to ss 118, 119 and 120.
6 There is a clear overlap/duplication between this paragraph and (f) above in that s 117 cross refers to ss 118, 119 and 120.
7 There is a clear overlap/duplication between this paragraph and (f) above in that s 117 cross refers to ss 118, 119 and 120.
8 GA 2005, s 144(5).
9 See the commentary on Part 17.
10 GA 2005, s 337(1).

The timing of appeals

6.132 An appeal must be instituted before the period of 28 days of the date on which the appellant was sent 'the act or decision' appealed against[1], although the Tribunal may permit an appeal to be instituted after the end of that period[2]. It does not seem that the extension must be sought or determined within the primary period. An applicant for permission to appeal out of time will need to give reasons in his notice of appeal for the failure to observe the primary limitation period[3]. A potential source of difficulty is applying the 28 day period to those cases in which the Commission must give notification of the action it proposes to take and its reasons for doing so. As can be seen from s 117(2) this duty arises in almost all cases in which an appeal can be pursued. If there is an interval between notification and action does the period run from the former date or only from the latter?

1 SI 2009/1976, r 22(1)(b).
2 SI 2009/1976, r 5(3)(a).
3 SI 2009/1976, r 22(4)(a).

Stay pending appeal

6.133 Section 145(1) states that a decision/action which is appealable will generally have no effect until the period of 28 days in which an appeal can be brought has elapsed or in those cases where an appeal has been brought it has not been abandoned or determined. The section specifically excludes from this automatic stay an appeal which is sought to be brought out of time[1] although it seems that if an application to appeal out of time is successful then so long as that appeal is pursued the stay attaches until its abandonment or disposal. However this is capable of producing a rather unsatisfactory result; it looks as if, for example, a licence will not be suspended during the primary limitation period of 28 days, will then become suspended once that is over and will then cease to be suspended if the licensee has obtained leave to appeal out of time if he pursues his appeal to determination or having started it abandons it. Section 145(1) does not appear to give the Tribunal the power to allow an appeal to be brought out of time on condition that, in our example, the suspension remains in place.

Moreover, it is possible that a stay under s 141(1) will be disapplied by the Commission. The Act provides no assistance as to when this might happen. Explanatory Note 384 suggests that the power is provided so that the Commission can apply the licensing objectives. Given that the Commission has a duty to promote the licensing objectives under s 22 the Explanatory Note appears not to be at all illuminating.

It seems from the drafting of s 145 that the normal position will be that a stay will usually apply but that in certain (no doubt exceptional) circumstances the Commission will disapply it. The decision to disapply is not itself susceptible to an appeal to the Tribunal; it will surely, however, be capable of being judicially reviewed in the High Court. No doubt in such a case the applicant will be anxious to obtain a stay; however this appears to be only directly obtainable, under CPR 54.10, once permission has been given. In some (very urgent and exceptional) cases it may be that an application for an interim injunction under CPR Part 25 can be made.

Moreover, perhaps as a legislative 'belt and braces' approach, The Tribunal Procedure (First-tier Tribunal) (General Regulatory Chamber) Rules 2009[2], r 19A(1) makes provision for the Tribunal to suspend the effect of any decision made by the Commission if an appeal could be brought within the 28 day period or until an extant appeal has been finally determined or withdrawn. The relevant procedure is to be found in r 20.

1 GA 2005, s 145(1)(a).
2 SI 2009/1976.

The powers of the Tribunal

6.134 In determining an appeal the Tribunal must have regard to any relevant provision of any code of practice issued by the Commission under s 24[1]. Moreover it seems clear that the appeal hearing is not merely a review of the Commission's decision but is a rehearing of all matters relevant when the appeal itself is heard. This appears to result from the power of the Tribunal to take into account evidence 'not available to' the Commission[2]. Although the quoted phrase is ambiguous in that it could be said to amount to a power to hear evidence which was not then available because, say, the appellant was not aware of it through no fault of his own it seems unnecessary to adopt such a narrow approach. Accordingly the said phrase can encompass any evidence, whether new or not, which was not placed before the Commission. Does it allow the Commission itself to rely on evidence at the appeal which it did not utilise previously?

Having made its decision the Tribunal can, in respect of the decision or action of the Commission[3]:

(a) affirm it;
(b) quash it in whole or in part;
(c) substitute for all or part of it another decision or action of a kind which the Commission could have taken[4];
(d) add to it a decision or action of a kind which the Commission could have taken[5];
(e) remit the matter to the Commission (generally or on specific grounds).

Additionally it can also reinstate a lapsed or revoked licence[6]. It is clear however that the power to reinstate a lapsed licence can only arise if that came about under s 114(1)(b) but not on any other basis set out in s 114. Further, it is difficult to understand why specific provision has been made in respect of revoked licences; surely if an appellant is successful in his appeal against revocation an inevitable result is that the revocation is quashed and the licence is revived?

Finally, s 144(2) provides the Tribunal with additional powers to make any order which it thinks appropriate in those cases where the appeal has been brought out of time under Tribunal Procedure Rules or in which the Commission exercised its power under s 145(2) to disapply a stay pending appeal. The need for this provision is puzzling; unless it is intended to relate to costs or compensation.

---

1 GA 2005, s 144(3).
2 GA 2005, s 144(4). For the difference between a review and a rehearing see CPR 52.11(1) and (2).
3 GA 2005, s 144(1)(a)–(e).
4 This could include handing out a stiffer penalty: see GA 2005, Explanatory Note 379.
5 This could include handing out a stiffer penalty: see GA 2005, Explanatory Note 379.
6 GA 2005, s 144(1)(f).

Appeals from the Tribunal

6.135 Appeals on points of law only from the First-tier Tribunal can be made to the Upper Tribunal under the 2007 Act, s 11 and in accordance with the Tribunal Procedure (Upper Tribunal) Rules 2008[1]. Section 11(5) lists matters which cannot be appealed. Section 12 is concerned with the general appellate powers of the Upper Tribunal. Permission to appeal is required either under SI 2009/1976, r 42 or SI 2008/2698, r 21.

There is also a very limited right of appeal from the Upper Tribunal to the Court of Appeal, under the 2007 Act, s 13. This also requires permission and is restricted solely to a point of law which, in the view of the Upper Tribunal or the Court of Appeal, would raise some important point of principle or practice or because another compelling reason exists. See s 13(6) and SI 2008/2834.

1 SI 2008/2698.

PART 8: PREMISES LICENCES

Introduction

6.150 A premises[1] licence is a licence granted by the relevant local authority under Part 8 GA 2005 for premises in their area authorising the use of the premises for one or more specified forms of gambling. The premises licence is the third major form of control over gambling provided by the GA 2005, the first being the operating licence and second the personal licence. It replaces the betting office licence authorising use of premises as a betting office under the Betting, Gaming and Lotteries Act 1963 and the gaming licence authorising use of premises as a casino or licensed bingo club under Gaming Act 1968. It also replaces permits authorising the use of premises as amusement centres and amusement arcades under the Gaming Act 1968, Sch 9 and Lotteries and Amusements Act 1976, Sch 3. However, the new regime differs in a number of respects from these licence and permit regimes. There is in particular an absence of any detailed policy steer in the GA 2005 itself to clarify the purposes underlying the premises licence or to establish what criteria should be adopted in granting or refusing a licence.

1 Premises are defined in s 353(1) and (2)(g). See also *Majorstake Ltd v Curtis* [2008] 1 AC 787; [2006] EWCA Civ 1171 and also the Commission document at para **6.2655** below which addresses what constitutes premises generally and in specific instances.

Purpose of the premises licence

6.151 The legislation which the GA 2005 replaces sets out detailed grounds for the grant or refusal of a licence. In the case, for example, of a betting office licence the legislation provided both mandatory[1] and discretionary[2] grounds for refusal. Mandatory grounds were that the applicant was not the holder of a bookmaker's permit, that the premises were not enclosed and that there had to be access to the proposed betting office from the street otherwise than through other premises which were used for non-betting transactions. The discretionary grounds were that the premises were not suitable to be a licensed betting office having regard to their layout, character, condition or location; that the grant would be inexpedient having regard to the demand in the locality for licensed betting offices and that (in the case of a renewal) the premises had not been properly conducted. From these grounds it is possible to deduce that the basic purpose of betting office licensing was to prevent proliferation and to ensure that the premises and the location were suitable for such an office and that the applicant was fit to run a betting business there. Broadly comparable discretionary grounds for refusing a casino licence or a bingo club licence were contained in the Gaming Act 1968[3]. Although the legislation relating to amusement centres and amusement arcades did not spell out criteria in detail nonetheless in practice demand and the impact of the premises on the neighbourhood were usually the principal foci.

1 BGLA 1963, Sch 1, para 19(a).

2 BGLA 1963, Sch 1, para 19(b).
3 GA 1968, Sch 2, para 18, 20(1).

6.152 In their report the Gambling Review Body concluded that the demand test for casinos, bingo premises and licensed betting offices was outdated and should be abolished[1]. This recommendation was accepted by Government and, as noted below, is given effect to by the GA 2005. The GRB then considered what role, in the absence of a need to prove demand, remained for premises licensing. They concluded that it was not the principal function of licensing to consider the suitability of the location or of the premises: these would be determined by planning controls[2]. They saw the primary function of premises licensing as first, to provide a means of preventing the proliferation of gambling venues, and, second, as providing a means whereby local residents could help to shape the communities in which they wanted to live[3]. Noting the provisions of the Local Government (Miscellaneous Provisions) Act 1982 providing for the licensing of sex establishments they recommended that the local authority should have the power to impose a blanket ban on all, or particular types of, gambling premises in a specified area (either the whole of their area or some part of it)[4]. This power would, they considered, allow the local authority to prevent over-concentration of gambling premises in particular areas in a way which might change their character[5]. In addition they recommended that in determining whether the location of the premises for which a licence application was made would be appropriate the local authority should have regard to the general character of the locality and the use to which buildings nearby were put[6]. They also recommended that the Gambling Commission should be required to provide advice to local authorities as to the criteria to be adopted in determining licence applications[7].

The Government broadly accepted the Committee's recommendations, though it rejected the proposal to give to local authorities the power generally to impose blanket bans on gambling premises[8]; this power has been introduced in the GA 2005 only in respect of casino premises. Otherwise the Government concluded that the local authority should consider each application for a licence on its own merits subject to national criteria and guidance from the Gambling Commission and subject to the principles contained in their own licensing policy[9]. An attempt to reintroduce the demand criterion at the Committee stage of the Bill having been rejected[10], this is the format that has been adopted (see para **6.158** below).

---

1 Gambling Review Report CM 5206 2001 paras 20.28; 20.31.
2 Gambling Review Report para 21.1.
3 Gambling Review Report para 18.19.
4 Gambling Review Report para 21.9.
5 Gambling Review Report para 21.10.
6 Gambling Review Report para 21.13.
7 Gambling Review Report para 21.13.
8 DCMS: 'A Safe Bet for Success — Modernising Britain's Gambling Laws' Cm 5397 2002 para 3.10.
9 'A Safe Bet for Success' Appendix B recommendation 44.

10 House of Commons Standing Committee B Thursday 2 December 2004 Cols 353–355.

Requirement for a premises licence

6.153 The premises licence is the principal, though not the only, means by which use of premises for gambling may be authorised under the GA 2005. It is an offence to use premises, or to cause or permit premises to be used, to operate a casino, to provide facilities for bingo, to make a gaming machine available for use, to provide other facilities for gaming, or to provide facilities for betting unless such use is authorised by a premises licence, or one of a number of other forms of authorisation provided by the Act applies[1]. These latter forms of authorisation are set out in para **6.154** below. There are five types of premises licence, namely:

- a casino premises licence authorising premises to be used for the operation of a casino;
- a bingo premises licence authorising premises to be used for the provision of facilities for the playing of bingo;
- an adult gaming centre premises licence authorising premises to be used for making Category B gaming machines available for use;
- a family entertainment centre premises licence authorising premises to be used for making Category C gaming machines available for use;
- a betting premises licence authorising premises to be used for the provision of facilities for betting, whether by making or accepting bets, by acting as a betting intermediary or by providing other facilities for the making or accepting of bets[2].

A premises licence is not required in order to provide facilities for gambling on premises if the facilities are to be used only by persons who:

- are acting in the course of a business, or
- are not on the premises[3].

The Explanatory Notes give as an example of the first case, a telephone call centre set up by a betting operator to accept telephone bets, and, as an example of the second case, the use of premises to house a server which is used for the purposes of remote gambling[4]. Thus, for example, a betting exchange business which uses premises to house its server, and which bases staff at the premises, will not require a premises licence for the premises, provided (as would be the usual case) all the betting exchange business was carried on remotely and customers did not attend at the premises.

The basic rule is that premises may only be subject to one premises licence at a time, with the result that the type of gambling permitted will be limited to the particular type authorised by the licence[5]. That rule is subject to the following exceptions:

- tracks: a betting track may be subject to more than one premises licence at a time provided each licence relates to a different area of the track. Where a track, or part of a track, is subject to a premises licence any application for a premises licence to authorise another type of gambling there must be accompanied by an application to vary the existing licence so that it will no longer have effect if and when the new licence is granted[6];
- licensed Adult gaming centres: these may provide any number of Category C and D gaming machines as well as up to 4 Category B gaming machines[7];

- licensed Family entertainment centres: these may provide any number of Category D gaming machines as well as any number of Category C gaming machines[8];
- licensed Casinos: small, large and regional casinos (as to which see paras **6.160** and **6.161** below) may provide Category B, C or D gaming machines subject to limits on numbers specified in the Act. A regional casino using at least 40 gaming tables may also use Category A machines subject to limits on numbers set out in the Act[9];
- licensed Bingo premises: these may provide up to 4 Category B gaming machines and unlimited numbers of Category C and D machines[10];
- licensed Betting premises may use up to a total of 4 gaming machines of Category B, C or D[11], except where the licence is granted in respect of a track[12]. In such a case the licence will only authorise use of gaming machines if the holder also holds a pool betting operating licence[12].

---

1 GA 2005, s 37.
2 GA 2005, s 150.
3 GA 2005, s 37(6).
4 GA 2005, Explanatory Note 149.
5 GA 2005, s 152. See however below at para **6.158A** below.
6 GA 2005, s 152.
7 GA 2005, s 172(1).
8 GA 2005, s 172(2).
9 GA 2005, s 172(3), (4), (5).
10 GA 2005, s 172(7).
11 GA 2005, s 172(8).
12 GA 2005, s 172(8), (9).

Exceptions to the requirement for a premises licence

6.154 Gambling may be provided on premises without a premises licence in the following cases:

- bets may be accepted on a track under an 'occasional use notice': s 39;
- written authority may be given which has the effect of authorising premises to be used for the collection of pool bets and stakes etc: s 40;
- premises may be used for gambling under a temporary use notice having effect under Part 9 GA 2005;
- certain gaming machines may be used in premises if a family entertainment centre gaming machine permit exists for the premises, or if either no prize, or a limited prize only, may be won;
- equal chance gaming may be provided in a members' club, a commercial club or a miners' welfare institute (s 269); gaming may be provided in accordance with a club gaming permit (s 271); and gaming machines may be provided in accordance with a club machine permit (s 273);
- facilities for equal chance gaming may be provided, and no more than two Category C or D gaming machines may be provided, on premises for which an on-premises alcohol licence has effect: sections 278, 279 and 282. A Category C or D gaming machine may also be provided on such premises in accordance with a licensed premises gaming machine permit: s 283;

- one or more Category D gaming machines may be made available for use at a travelling fair: s 287;
- 'prize gaming' may be provided, subject to specified conditions, on premises for which a prize gaming permit exists (s 289), in an adult gaming centre or a licensed family entertainment centre (s 290), in premises for which a bingo premises licence has effect (s 291), and at a travelling fair (s 292).

In addition no premises licence is required where the gaming or betting provided is private gaming or betting (s 296), nor where facilities are provided for non-commercial prize gaming or non-commercial equal chance gaming (s 298).

The licensing authority

6.155 In England the licensing authority will be the district council, the county council (in the case of a county where there are no district councils), the London borough council, the Common Council of the City of London or the Council of the Isles of Scilly[1]. In Wales the licensing authority will be the county council or the county borough council[1]. Application for a licence is made to the licensing authority in whose area the premises are wholly or partly situated[2]. The licensing authority have a number of duties and powers in addition to their function of granting or rejecting applications for premises licenses. They must prepare, consult on and publish a three-year statement of the principles they will apply in exercising their functions under the Act[3]; they may resolve not to issue casino premises licences in their area[4]; and they must determine the amounts of the licence fees they will charge[5]. The Act delegates the authority's functions to the licensing committee of the authority established under the Licensing Act 2003[6] with the following exceptions: first, neither their duty to publish a three-year licensing statement nor their power to resolve not to grant casino licences is automatically delegated, nor may the authority themselves delegate these functions[7]; second, their duty to fix fee levels is not automatically delegated, but they themselves may delegate it to the licensing committee[8]. The licensing committee may itself sub-delegate functions to a sub-committee or to an officer[9] though delegation to an officer is not permitted so as to enable him to determine an application for a premises licence, or an application to vary a premises licence, where representations (presumably usually objections) have been made and not withdrawn[10] nor to determine an application for a transfer following representations by the Commission[11] nor to determine an application for a provisional statement where representations have been made and not withdrawn[12].

1 GA 2005, s 2.
2 GA 2005, s 159. 'Premises' includes any place and in particular a vessel and a vehicle: s 353(1). However no premises licence may be issued for a vehicle as defined by s 353(1): s 211(1)(a). A premises licence may be issued for certain vessels (ie basically a boat or hovercraft — see definition in s 353(1)): s 211(1)(b)–(d). Provision is made by s 211 about the place where a vessel is taken to be situated and also the parties who will be treated as responsible authorities in relation to the application.
3 GA 2005, s 349.
4 GA 2005, s 166.
5 GA 2005, s 212 which must not exceed the maximum set out in the Gambling (Premises Licence Fees) (England and Wales) Regulations 2007, SI 2007/479.
6 GA 2005, s 154.

7 GA 2005, s 154(2).
8 GA 2005, s 154(2).
9 GA 2005, s 154(3).
10 GA 2005, s 154(4).
11 GA 2005, s 154(4).
12 GA 2005, s 154(4).

Making an application for a premises licence

6.156 An application for a premises licence is made to the licensing authority in whose area the premises are wholly or partly situated[1]. The applicant must either hold, or have applied for, an operating licence authorising him to carry on the type of gambling for which the licence is sought[2], though this requirement does not apply in the case of a track to be used only for accepting bets[3] a provision enabling a track occupier to obtain a premises licence to allow betting, and in particular bookmaking, on his track without himself holding a betting operating licence. The applicant must have a right to occupy the premises to which the application relates[4]. The Explanatory Notes state that this requirement will be satisfied where the applicant occupies under a legal right to be in occupation whether by way of a freehold or leasehold interest or by holding the premises on a tenancy agreement[5]. Regulations provide for the form of the application and the information to be supplied[6], and for the publication of notice of the application and the giving of notice to specified bodies and persons[7].

1 GA 2005, s 159.
2 GA 2005, s 159(3).
3 GA 2005, s 159(4).
4 GA 2005, s 159(5).
5 GA 2005, Explanatory Notes, paras 427 and 734.
6 GA 2005, s 159(6). See the Gambling Act 2005 (Premises Licences and Provisional Statements) Regulations 2007, SI 2007/459, regs 3–5, 12–14 and 16.
7 GA 2005, s 160.

Responsible authorities and interested parties

6.157 Where an application is made to a licensing authority for a premises licence an 'interested party' or 'responsible authority' may make representations in writing to the licensing authority[1]. It must do so within 28 days[2]. In practice this limits the right to make objections to such parties or authorities. The 'responsible authorities' are as follows:

(a) a licensing authority in whose area the premises are wholly or partly situated,
(b) the Gambling Commission,
(c) the chief officer of police for a police area in which the premises are wholly or partly situated,
(d) the fire and rescue authority for an area in which the premises are wholly or partly situated,
(e) the local planning authority for an area in which the premises are wholly or partly situated,

(f) the authority having functions in minimising or preventing the risk of pollution of the environment or of harm to human health in an area in which the premises are wholly or partly situated,

(g) a body designated by the licensing authority for an area in which the premises are wholly or partly situated as competent to advise the authority about the protection of children from harm,

(h) HMRC, and

(i) any other person prescribed by regulations[3].

An 'interested party' is a person who, in the opinion of the licensing authority:

(a) lives sufficiently close to the premises to be likely to be affected by the authorised activities,

(b) has business interests that might be affected by the authorised activities, or

(c) represents persons who satisfy para (a) or (b)[4].

Responsible authorities and interested parties not only have the right to make representations on an application for a new premises licence, but also the right to make representations on various applications which may be made in respect of an existing premises licence (eg for variation of a licence, see para **6.171** below), though in the case of some applications (eg to transfer a premises licence, see para **6.172** below) responsible authorities will be able to make representations but interested parties will not. In addition both responsible authorities and interested parties may apply for a review of a premises licence (see para **6.178** below) and are entitled to make representations on a review of a premises licence initiated by the local authority itself (see para **6.180** below).

The definition of 'responsible authority' calls for no comment. As to 'interested parties' some questions may be posed. There are four types of 'interested party': first, residents living close enough to the premises to be likely to be affected by the authorised activities (who could, perhaps, be called 'resident interested parties'); second, persons (eg an official of a residents association or an ad hoc spokesperson) representing such residents; third, persons having business interests that might be affected by the authorised activities ('business interested parties'), and fourth, persons (eg an officer of a Chamber of Commerce) representing such business interested parties.

As to resident interested parties there may, no doubt, be guidance from licensing authorities in their licensing statements issued under s 349 as to the tests to be applied in determining whether a person lives sufficiently close to premises to qualify as a resident interested party. Any test will, however, need to be flexibly formulated and applied as some gambling premises will impact on much wider areas than others: a large casino, for example, or a large family entertainment centre is likely to be much wider in its effects than a modestly sized betting office or even a large betting office. Some assistance as to the approach which should be taken by licensing authorities in deciding whether a particular person is an interested party or not is to be found in the fourth edition of the Commission's Guidance to Licensing Authorities, September 2012 (see para **6.2655** below) at Part 8.

There appears to be nothing in the definition of resident interested party (or of business interested party) to suggest that it is a requirement that the resident or business be actually located within the area of the licensing authority (though this is likely to be the usual case) provided the authorised activities are likely to affect the residential or business interests in question. See a discussion of this matter and the contrast between the provisions of the Act and s 13 of the Licensing Act 2003 in *R (on the application of 4 Wins Leisure Ltd) v The Licensing Committee for Blackpool Council*[5].

More fundamentally, however, the following question must be posed: once the persons who qualify as resident interested parties have been identified, what kinds of representation will they be entitled to make? The definition of 'interested party' uses the test of living sufficiently close to the premises to be affected by them as a means of defining the expression 'interested party'. Does this definition have the consequence that such resident interested parties (and any persons representing them) will be limited to making representations about the impact of the premises on the surrounding area (including their own places of residence) or may they make representations about any and all aspects of the proposal which may be relevant to the licensing objectives and to any other matters which the licensing authority are obliged to consider (in particular under s 153, see para **6.158** below), even though these are matters which will not directly affect them and will not or may not affect residents living within the premises' footprint? If the former, then not only is there a limit on the number of residents living within the licensing authority's area who may be permitted to make representations, but there will also be a limit on the representations that they can make since these will be confined to representations about the immediate impact of the premises on its footprint area. Accordingly, in many cases, there will be little scope for premises licensing to fulfil the role envisaged by the Gambling Review Body of enabling local residents to help shape the communities in which they want to live (see para **6.152** above). If, on the other hand, resident interested parties can deal with broader issues such as the impact of another set of gambling premises on the character of the area, or the possibly damaging social effects of further gambling premises within the area of the licensing authority, one is prompted to ask why the power to make such representations should be limited to this specific group. It is surely possible that many people who reside within the licensing authority's area but who will not be directly affected by activities on the premises, and who will not therefore qualify as 'interested parties', may have relevant and well informed observations to make on such broader issues. Why should they be denied a hearing? The anomaly becomes even starker when one considers that in some cases residents and businesses from outside the licensing authority's area will qualify as interested parties and will be able to make representations. The strict wording of the provision may perhaps suggest that the former interpretation is correct, but it is nonetheless suggested that for the following reasons the latter interpretation is to be preferred notwithstanding the anomalies it produces. First, the debates in Standing Committee B suggest that this was the Government's intention. An attempt was made to extend the definition of 'interested party' to include any person who had concern about or responsibility for addressing social well-being in the community from which the authorised gambling activities might draw custom. The Government opposed the amendment (which was withdrawn) but in the course of the debate Mr Richard Caborn, the Minister for Sport and Tourism, stated that 'Evidence from persons who have responsibility for social well-being might well form part of an individual representation, but we consider it important that there should be a clear link between the premises and the person making the representation'[6]. This seems to imply that an individual resident (or business) interested party could make representations about the social impact of the proposal on the authority's area or could allow his representations to be used as a platform for such representations by others. Of equal significance perhaps is the fact that, as has been noted, interested parties will be entitled to make representations on various applications relating to an existing licence and to apply for, or to make representations on, a review. In this connection they will no doubt often be invited to make representations as to matters which go well beyond the impact of the licensed premises on its immediate area. For example the licensing authority may institute a review of a licence if they think that the premises have been used in breach of a licence condition (see para **6.180** below). A resident interested party may be wholly unaffected by such a breach of condition but will still be entitled to make representations. This supports the view that they are also intended to have a broad power to make representations on all relevant issues on the first application for a licence.

In the case of business interested parties, or their representatives, a similar though not identical question arises. A business interested party is a person who has business interests that may be affected by the authorised activities at the premises. This would cover the case where a business is sufficiently close to the premises to be directly affected by the activities there, but it is not, it seems, limited to that case; a business interest could be affected even though the business was itself outside the area of the premises' immediate impact. Suppose, for example, a radio taxi business is located in offices a mile away from a town centre. Most of its business is derived from trips into the town centre in the evenings to pick up customers who have been enjoying the cinemas, pubs and restaurants there. An application is made to obtain a licence for a large adult gaming centre in the centre of town. The proposals give rise to widespread apprehension that the presence of the centre will create a threatening atmosphere driving people out of the town centre and damaging trade there. The taxi business's offices are too far away from the town centre to be directly affected, but it clearly has business interests in ensuring that a plentiful supply of potential patrons continue to frequent the town centre and it should therefore qualify as a business interested party.

However this raises the same question as arises in the case of resident interested parties: once a person has qualified as a business interested party is he limited in the representations he can make to matters directly relating to the impact which the activities on the licensed premises may have on his business interests, or may he deal with any and all of the broader issues that may arise? For the same reasons as apply in the case of a resident interested party it is suggested that the latter interpretation is to be preferred. This seems consistent with the views expressed in the Committee debate, and it is consistent with the fact that a business interested party will be able to deal with a range of issues when making representations in respect of applications and reviews relating to an existing licence which may go well beyond the impact of the premises on his business interests.

There is an additional question that arises in connection with business interested parties. Where an application for a premises licence is made to provide gambling facilities of a type that are already provided within the locality by existing traders those traders will be likely to want to oppose the application as trade objectors. The position that will then arise seems curious. Such traders will undoubtedly have business interests that might be affected by the proposal since the proposal will result in competition for their businesses so they will qualify as business interested parties under s 158. However, s 153(2) provides that in determining whether to grant a premises licence the licensing authority may not have regard to the expected demand for the facilities which it is proposed to provide. Accordingly the authority will not be entitled to take into account representations to the effect that there is no sufficient demand to warrant the grant of a further premises licence and they will be obliged to refuse to entertain representations from trade objectors on those grounds. However, provided (as has been suggested above) business interested parties are entitled to make representations relating to broader matters it will it seems be open to trade objectors to make representations relating to any other relevant considerations that arise in relation to the licensing objectives and under s 153.

1 GA 2005, s 161.
2 The Gambling Act 2005 (Premises Licences and Provisional Statements) Regulations 2007, SI 2007/459, regs 13–15 and 17.
3 GA 2005, s 157. See SI 2007/459, regs 12–16.
4 GA 2005, s 158. See SI 2007/459, regs 12–16.
5 [2007] EWHC 2213 (Admin), [2007] All ER (D) 185 (Aug), Sullivan J.
6 Standing Committee B, Thursday, 2nd December 2004 (Afternoon) Col 359.

Determination of application

6.158 In determining an application the licensing authority must hold a hearing[1] if:

- representations have been made by an interested party or responsible authority and have not been withdrawn;
- the authority intend to use their discretion under s 169(1) to attach a condition to a licence; or
- the authority intend to use their discretion under s 169 to exclude a default condition (ie a condition automatically attached to the licence under s 168 unless excluded by the authority in its discretion)[2].

A hearing may, however, be dispensed with if the applicant and any interested party or responsible authority who have made representations consents to this course[3], or the authority think that the representations are vexatious or frivolous or will certainly not influence their determination of the application[4]. If the authority do propose to dispense with a hearing on these latter grounds they must as soon as is reasonably practicable notify the person who made the representations[5], presumably to enable him to seek a remedy by way of judicial review if so advised.

Where the applicant for the premises licence is an applicant for an operating licence[6] the authority cannot determine the application until the relevant operating licence has been issued[7].

On considering an application for a premises licence (whether at a hearing or not) the licensing authority must either grant it or reject it[8]. In making that determination the licensing authority will be subject to the provisions of s 153 which sets out the principles to be applied by the authority in exercising all their functions under Part 8 GA 2005 (ie including, but not limited to, the grant or refusal of an application for a premises licence). Section 153(1) provides as follows:

'In exercising their functions under this Part a licensing authority shall aim to permit the use of premises for gambling in so far as the authority think it—

(a) in accordance with any relevant code of practice under s 24,
(b) in accordance with any relevant guidance issued by the Commission under s 25,
(c) reasonably consistent with the licensing objectives (subject to paras (a) and (b)), and
(d) in accordance with the statement published by the authority under s 349 (subject to paras (a) to (c)).'

The subsection starts by imposing a general duty on the authority to 'aim to permit the use of premises for gambling' and then sets out a series of four factors which may, in any individual case, qualify or override the general duty. The first point to note is that the provision imposes a duty on the licensing authority: it must, subject to the qualifying factors, aim to permit the use of premises for gambling. What is the scope of this duty? It is suggested that there are two elements: first, it creates a presumption in favour of granting the premises licence since it is only if the licence is granted that the premises may lawfully be used for gambling. But the duty seems to go further than that. The verb 'to aim' is defined by the OED[9] as meaning: '5. To calculate one's course with a view to arriving (at a point); to direct one's course, to make it one's object to attain. Hence figTo have it as an object, to endeavour earnestly'. The Shorter OED[10] defines it as: '3. Direct one's course, make it one's object to attain, intend, try'. A person who 'aims' to achieve a result will usually take active steps to bring it about. The provision appears to place a duty upon the licensing authority to exercise their powers so far as is lawfully possible to achieve a position in which they can grant the premises licence and thus permit the premises to be used for gambling. The most obvious way in which the authority will be able to exercise their powers in this way will be by an imaginative use of their power to frame and impose conditions (see para **6.159** below) so as to overcome objections to the application which might, in the absence of suitable conditions, lead to the application being rejected. No doubt the authority could also, in a case where a licence application gave rise to issues which could not be addressed by suitably drafted conditions, seek to consider with the applicant whether amendments to the application might overcome the objections and enable it to be granted. However, it is also necessary to recognise that the language of s 153(1) stops short of being mandatory; 'aim to permit' provides a strong steer to look favourably on an application, but no more.

As to the list of qualifying factors, these are set out in s 153(1)(a)–(d). Section 153(1)(a) qualifies the duty to aim to permit use of premises for gambling to the extent that such use must be in accordance with any relevant code of practice issued by the Gambling Commission under s 24. That section requires the Gambling Commission to issue codes of practice about the manner in which facilities for gambling are to be provided (whether by the holder of a licence or by another person). In issuing a code of practice the Gambling Commission will be subject to a duty under s 22 to promote the licensing objectives. Accordingly any code of practice should be consistent with those objectives. Section 153(1)(b) qualifies the licensing authority's duty to aim to permit the use of premises for gambling to the extent that such use must be in accordance with any relevant guidance issued by the Gambling Commission under s 25. This section requires the Gambling Commission to issue guidance to local authorities[11] as to the manner in which they are to exercise their functions under the Act and the principles that they should apply in exercising those functions. Again the effect of s 22 is that in issuing such guidance the Commission will be under a duty to promote the licensing objectives, so again such guidance should be consistent with those objectives. The effect of all this is that any code of practice and any guidance to local authorities ought to promote the licensing objectives and no inconsistencies between the two should arise. On that basis codes of practice and guidance are placed (by s 153(1)(a) and (b)) as enjoying equal importance at the top of the hierarchy of factors set out in s 153(1)(a)–(d).

Next comes s 153(1)(c): this provides that the duty of the licensing authority to aim to permit the use of premises for gambling is qualified to the extent that such use must be reasonably consistent with the licensing objectives, but it goes on to provide that this condition is 'subject to paras (a) and (b)'. In principle there should, of course, be no conflict between (a) and (b) (which will both reflect the Gambling Commission's duty to promote the licensing objectives) and (c) (which will reflect the licensing authority's view of what the licensing objectives require). However the effect of the legislation appears to be that should there be any conflict between the two then the guidance set out in codes of practice or guidance emanating from the Gambling Commission will 'trump' any factors which the licensing authority themselves would otherwise have taken into account as relevant to the licensing objectives under s 153(1)(c).

Finally, s 153(1)(d) provides that the duty of a licensing authority to aim to permit the use of premises for gambling is qualified to the extent that such use must be in accordance with the authority's own statement issued under s 349. In preparing that statement the authority are not themselves expressly required to have regard to the licensing objectives, but they are obliged to have regard to guidance issued by the Gambling Commission under s 25 and such guidance deals, amongst other things, with the formulation by the authority of their licensing policy (see para **6.2655** below). Since the s 25 guidance must itself promote the licensing objectives the effect should be that the authority's licensing policy will itself be consistent with those objectives so that it should not conflict with any code of practice or guidance issued by the Commission nor with the licensing objectives themselves. However, s 153(1)(d) provides that consideration of the licensing authority's own policy is 'subject to paras (a) to (c)' which appears to mean that in the case of an inconsistency a relevant Commission code of practice, relevant guidance or the licensing objectives themselves would 'trump' the authority's licensing policy.

In determining the application the authority may not have regard to the expected demand for the facilities which it is proposed to provide[12], nor may they have regard to the question whether or not the proposal is likely to be granted planning permission or building regulation approval[13]. Where the authority have resolved under s 166 not to issue casino premises licences an application for such a licence will, of course, necessarily fail and be rejected[14].

Where the application is granted the authority must as soon as reasonably practicable give notice of the grant in the form prescribed to the applicant, the Commission, any person who made representations, the chief officer of police for any area in which the premises are wholly or partly situated and HMRC[15] and must issue the licence to the applicant and must give him a summary of the terms and conditions in the prescribed form. If they have attached a condition to the licence under s 169(1)(a) or have excluded a default condition[16] they must give their reasons[17]. If representations were made by an interested party or a responsible authority they must give their response to the representations[18].

Where the application is rejected the authority must as soon as reasonably practicable give notice of the rejection in the form prescribed to the applicant and to the same parties as are entitled to be notified of a grant[18]. The notice must give the authority's reasons for rejecting the application[19].

1 As to procedure at hearings in relation to applications see SI 2007/173.
2 GA 2005, s 162. See further para **6.159** below.
3 GA 2005, s 162.
4 GA 2005, s 162(3).
5 GA 2005, s 162(4).
6 Ie under GA 2005, s 159(3)(b).
7 GA 2005, s 163(2).
8 GA 2005, s 163(1).
9 The Oxford English Dictionary 2nd Edition Oxford 1989.
10 OUP 5th Edition.
11 See 'Guidance to Licensing Authorities – 4th Edition, September 2012' at para **6.2655** below.
12 GA 2005, s 153(2).
13 GA 2005, s 210.
14 GA 2005, s 153(3), 166.
15 GA 2005, s 164 and see SI 2007/459, regs 17 and 19.
16 Ie a condition under GA 2005, s 168.
17 GA 2005, s 164(2)(b).
18 GA 2005, s 164(2)(c).
19 GA 2005, s 165 and SI 2007/459, regs 18 and 19.

Division of premises

6.158A Since the 2008 edition of *Paterson's Licensing Acts* the extent to which premises can be divided, with the consequence that each created set of premises is capable then of being licensed has become an important topic for debate. It has arisen chiefly in connection in the context of machines; some operators have concluded that instead of, for example, having a single AGC licence which authorises the holder to make up to four Category B gaming machines available for use, why not double that capacity by dividing the premises in two, each having its own licence? The topic was first addressed by the Commission in paras 7.11–7.20 and 21.6 of its Guidance to Licensing Authorities of June 2007. It further examined the point in respect of bingo premises in a document published on 17 April 2008.

This stated that licensing authorities must be satisfied that each area is a separate set of premises in order to grant more than a single premises licence.

The issue was further addressed by the Commission in a document published on 25 April 2008. The Commission concluded that paras 7.11–7.12 of its Guidance required strengthening and announced that it would publish a consultation document on the topic. This it did in June 2008; this was concerned with both split premises (para 2) and primary use of premises (see paras **6.158B–6.158C** below). In respect of split premises the current views of the Commission are expressed in Part 7 of the Guidance to Licensing Authorities, 4th Edition, September 2012 (para **6.2655** below). In particular at paras 7.13–7.26 the Commission states

(1) a single building should in most cases be the subject of a single premises licence application;
(2) however if different parts of a building can properly be regarded as separate premises then more than one such application can be made;
(3) dividing a building in an artificial or temporary manner by, for example, using ropes or moveable partitions is an improper attempt to obtain more than a single premises licence.

The primary use of premises

6.158B Another topic of recent importance is whether an applicant for, say, a betting premises licence is actually required, if successful, to provide betting facilities or whether he can simply take advantage of the authorisation contained in s 172(8) ie make up to four category B2 gaming machines available for use without offering any betting facilities? The Commission first addressed the matter in a letter dated 12 March 2008 and concluded, in the case of both betting and bingo premises, that an operator must provide the principal activity authorised by its operating and premises licences before taking advantage of any entitlement to make gaming machines available on those premises. In the case of bingo, however, it conceded that gaming machines at bingo premises could be made available for use at times when bingo was not being played there so long as bingo facilities were generally offered at those premises. On 26 March 2008 the Commission published another letter on the topic, which in particular concerned betting facilities. Unfortunately this was not nearly as clear as the earlier letter. It stated that providing the 'barest minimum' of eg betting facilities was not consistent with the Act and that such facilities should be a 'core element' of that the operator offered. It then muddied the waters by stating that 'it would be *undesirable* for betting premises to offer only or predominantly gaming machines' (emphasis added). It threatened legislation to deal with the problem.

Next, on 17 April 2008 it published a document concerning bingo premises addressed to licensing authorities. Finally, in June 2008 the Commission published a consultation paper; at para 3 therein it posed a number of questions on the topic. The final views of the Commission on this subject were published in January 2009.

6.158C The final views of the Commission were originally set out in LCCP supplement 4: Primary Gambling Activity. This has since been incorporated in the consolidated version of the LCCP at para 16 ff, Part I (see para **6.2060** below), the latest version of which was published in December 2011. This document makes it a general condition of a licence that an operator of bingo, casino and betting premises must make genuine provision of core facilities (eg betting in a betting shop); to which the provision of gaming machines must be subordinate. In particular, in the case of betting for example, facilities which must be offered include the provision of information to enable customers to access details of the events on which bets can be made, the ability to place bets, obtain results of relevant events, calculate wins/losses and be paid out if successful. It acknowledges that proper betting machines are sufficient to satisfy the requirement so long as they outnumber gaming machines. Codes of Practice at para 9 of Part II of the consolidated LCCP additionally set out factors to which the operator should have regard in order to demonstrate that such genuine provision is being made. For example, in the case of a betting shop these are:

- the ratio of the space available to customers allocated to betting, to that allocated to gaming machines;
- the extent to which betting is promoted on the premises and by way of external advertising compared to gaming machines;
- the use, either expected or actual, to be made of betting/gaming machines;
- the range and frequency of events on which bets can be made.

However it is clear that this list does not preclude other factors being relevant in a particular case nor is it always necessary for all the factors to be fulfilled in order to demonstrate compliance.

6.158D It appears that, despite the Commission having made its position clear, difficulties continue to arise on the primary use requirement particularly in the case of betting shops. These stimulated it to publish, in November 2011, a detailed document 'Indicators of betting as primary gambling activity'. The full text of this can be found at para **6.2172** below. What follows is a brief summary of some of its principal points.

It sets out six indicators of whether betting is taking place as the primary gambling activity; they derive from the LCCP requirements and what is said to be 'accepted as typical of commercial betting shop provision in the British market' partly based on gambling industry statistics. These indicators are of general application and it seems that an operator who cannot fulfill them will bear the burden of explaining why his operation is licence compliant.

The first indicator: offering established core products. The Commission expects to see broadcast live betting opportunities for horseracing, greyhound racing, football, numbers and other sports such as golf, tennis and cricket. Taking horseracing as an example, typically regular daily betting would be offered on races in GB and Ireland at two or more meetings together with foreign racing. Live pictures would usually be provided and single, multiple and ante-post bets offered, together with forecast and tricast options and the ability to bet at the starting price or to take the current price.

The second indicator; the provision of information on products/events. This will usually include customer information screens giving all relevant details of events including times and locations, conditions, runners, riders and odds. In addition form guides and some of the sort of information found in the Racing Post would be made available.

The third indicator; promotion of gambling opportunities and products, typically by advertising.

The fourth indicator; the actual use made of betting facilities. The Commission understands that gaming machines are becoming more popular in betting shops but it still expects to see significant betting activity and will consider profits from betting, slippage and staking against industry averages together with business plans which set out the expected use of the premises for betting.

The fifth indicator; the size of the premises must be sufficient to provide betting facilities as the primary gambling activity.

The sixth indicator; the delivery of betting facilities. If the shop offers betting solely by machine it must have more of those than gaming machines. If the shop has a greater number of gaming machines than betting machines then it must also have a permanent manned counter for taking bets in order to fulfill the requirement of a betting licence.

The Commission has further reiterated its views in an information document and issued a special bulletin to licensing authorities in August 2012 on primary gambling activity. These, in particular, address the fourth indicator referred to above. See paras **6.2173–6.2174** below.

Conditions

6.159 There are three types of condition which may be attached to a premises licence, 'mandatory conditions' under s 167, 'default conditions' under s 168 and conditions attached by the licensing authority in their discretion under s 169. The Secretary of State may make regulations requiring that a specified condition or conditions ('mandatory conditions') be attached to premises licences generally, or to licences for premises in a specified class or in specified circumstances[1]. This power has now been exercised in the Gambling Act 2005 (Mandatory and Default Conditions) (England and Wales) Regulations 2007[2] in respect of:

- all premises licences;
- casinos;
- bingo premises;
- adult gaming centres;
- family entertainment centres;
- betting premises;
- tracks.

He may also make regulations prescribing for a specified condition or conditions ('default conditions') to be attached to any premises licence unless excluded by the licensing authority who issue the licence; the regulations may provide for such conditions to apply to premises licences generally or only to a specified class of premises licence or in specified circumstances[3]. This power has now been exercised in the Gambling Act 2005 (Mandatory and Default Conditions) (England and Wales) Regulations 2007[4] in respect of:

- casinos;
- bingo premises;
- betting premises;
- tracks.

Where a licensing authority propose to exclude a default condition they must hold a hearing of the application unless the applicant and any interested party or responsible authority who have made representations agree to dispense with a hearing[5]. The licensing authority may themselves attach a condition or conditions to a premises licence[6]. Such a condition may address a matter which would have been catered for by a default condition which the licensing authority have decided to exclude[7], thus enabling the licensing authority to attach conditions which they consider are better framed to deal with the circumstances than the default condition would be. However, the discretionary power to attach conditions is not limited to this situation and the licensing authority have a wide discretion (subject to the controls noted below) to attach conditions to licences. Such conditions may apply to the premises generally or to a specified part of the premises[8]. A licensing authority may not, however, attach a condition in their discretion which prevents compliance with a condition of the operating licence which authorises the holder to carry out the activity in respect of which the premises licence is granted[9].

No mandatory condition, default condition or discretionary condition may be applied to a premises licence requiring all or part of the premises, or any activity taking place there, to be operated or carried on as a club or other body with membership or restricting use of any part of the premises wholly or partly by reference to membership of a club or other body[10], nor may any such condition be attached which imposes limits on stakes, fees, winnings or prizes[11] though a mandatory condition dealing with fees for admission to a track is permitted[12].

If a mandatory condition, default condition or discretionary condition is attached requiring door supervision of the premises, then if the person carrying out the guarding is required to hold a licence under the Private Security Industry Act 2001 that condition is treated as if it were also a condition of the premises licence[13].

A premises licence must be subject to the condition that the premises shall not be used to provide facilities for gambling on Christmas Day[14].

1 GA 2005, s 167(1), (2).
2 SI 2007/1409.
3 GA 2005, s 168(1), (2); s 169 (1)(b).
4 SI 2007/1409.
5 GA 2005, s 162(1)(c); s 162(2).
6 GA 2005, s 169(1)(a). These can include, for example, restricting the use of the premises to only part of the year: see SI 2007/479, art 9.
7 GA 2005, s 169(2).
8 GA 2005, s 169(3).
9 GA 2005, s 169(4).
10 GA 2005, s 170.
11 GA 2005, s 171(1).
12 GA 2005, s 171(2).
13 GA 2005, s 178.
14 GA 2005, s 183.

Particular types of premises

6.160 Casinos The GA 2005 defines a casino as 'an arrangement whereby people are given an opportunity to participate in one or more casino games'[1]. A 'casino game' means a game of chance which is not equal chance gaming[2]. The definition applies both to traditional casinos located physically in buildings in which players play casino games, and to online casinos offering casino games by means of remote communication[3], though only the former will be required to hold a premises licence[4]. The Government's proposals for the licensing of premises for casinos (which were modelled closely on the recommendations of the Gambling Review Body) proved to be highly contentious and the provisions of the GA 2005 represent a substantial dilution of the original proposals. The Gambling Review Body concluded that the demand test for casinos (as for all gambling premises) should be abolished[5] together with the rule confining casinos to permitted areas[6] and the rule requiring casinos to be run as clubs[7]. The risk that casinos (and especially small casinos) might proliferate could, the Committee thought, be prevented by giving to local authorities the power to impose blanket bans on casino premises (as on all other gambling premises)[8] and by empowering the Gambling Commission to give guidance which local authorities should be obliged to follow on the minimum floorspace for gaming areas in casinos. The Committee themselves recommended a minimum floor space of 2,000 square feet for the gaming floor devoted to table games in any casino[9]. The Government agreed with these recommendations in principle[10] except for the proposal to allow local authorities a general power to impose blanket bans, a proposal which was later revived for casinos only. In a Statement 'Future Set Out For UK Casinos'[11] the Government proposed that there be two categories of casino, namely 'small' (with a total table gaming area of between 5,000 and 10,000 square feet) and 'large' (with a total table gaming area of above 10,000 square feet). Many existing casinos have table gaming areas of less than 5,000 square feet, and these would be permitted to continue. The Statement also alluded to the probability of large leisure developments incorporating casinos (variously called 'resort' or 'regional' casinos) which would be of very substantial size, though no separate category for these was proposed. By the time the Gambling Bill was published in October 2004 the categories of casino had been expanded to four, namely 'regional casinos', 'large casinos', 'small casinos' and 'below the minimum size for a licensed casino'[12] (the latter to accommodate casinos existing at the date of the passing of the Act). The Bill also included a clause[13] enabling a local authority to resolve not to issue casino premises licences. Subject to that, however, the Government's view was that there should be no statutory limit to the number of casinos but that the number and location of casinos of all three types for which licences could be granted under the Act should be determined by market forces.

This approach, however, encountered formidable opposition in the course of Parliamentary debate and in a document 'Casinos: Statement of National Policy'[14] published in December 2004 the Government announced that it proposed to limit the number of premises licences for small, large and regional casinos to eight each. However, even this concession was insufficient to allay concerns especially regarding regional casinos, and the Government finally agreed to limit the number of regional casinos to one in the first instance in order to secure Opposition co-operation in getting the Bill enacted. Thus the GA 2005 in its final form provides:

- that a casino may be one of four types namely a regional casino, a large casino, a small casino or below the minimum size for a licensed casino[15];
- that premises licences may be granted by local authorities for casinos of the first three types[16]. No licence may be granted for a casino of the fourth type; such casinos will be casinos of below the relevant floor size which are in existence when the Act comes into force and will be permitted to continue in operation as casinos under the transitional provisions of Sch 18;
- that a licensing authority may resolve not to issue casino premises licences[17];
- that there may only be one casino premises licence in force for a regional casino, eight casino premises licences in force for large casinos and eight in force for small casinos[18]. The Secretary of State may, however, by order revise these limits so as to substitute a new maximum number of casino premises licences[19].

During 2007 before the Act came into force it was announced that the Government was unhappy about the venue of the single regional casino in Manchester and that this would not be permitted there (or anywhere?) without further consultation. However in 2008 three statutory instruments revived what some had thought was a terminally-ill patient, the 2005 Act casino at least in respect of all categories save the regional casino[20]. Further, SI 2009/1970 defines what is not a gaming table under s 172(3) and sets out the circumstances in which a gaming table is treated as being used under s 172(3)–(5).

1 GA 2005, s 7(1).
2 GA 2005, s 7(2).
3 GA 2005, s 7(4).
4 GA 2005, s 37(1)(a); s 37(6).
5 Gambling Review Report CM 5206 2001 paras 20.16–20.25; 20.28.
6 Gambling Review Report 20.10 Recommendation 36.
7 Gambling Review Report 22.7 Recommendation 49.
8 Gambling Review Report 21.9.
9 Gambling Review Report 20.11, 21.5.
10 DCMS 'A Safe Bet for Success' Appendix B Recommendations 36, 37, 38, 41 and 43.
11 Office of the Deputy Prime Minister and DCMS 7.8.03.
12 Gambling Bill 2004, cl 7(5).
13 Gambling Bill 2004, cl 157.
14 DCMS 'Casinos: Statement of National Policy' 16.12.04.
15 GA 2005, s 7(5).
16 GA 2005, s 174(1).
17 GA 2005, s 166.
18 GA 2005, s 175(1), (2), (3).
19 GA 2005, s 175(8).
20 See SIs 2008/469, 2008/1327, 2008/1330.

6.161 Casinos for which premises licence applications can be made are classified as large or small in accordance with regulations[1]. Current proposals[2] from Government are that:

- **Large casinos** A casino falls within this category if the combined floor area of those parts used for providing gambling facilities is at least 1,500 sq m but does not exceed 3,500 sq m[3]. They will be permitted five gaming machines (of up to Category B1) for each gaming table available for play, up to a maximum of 150 machines, and will also be permitted to provide betting and bingo[4];
- **Small casinos** A casino falls within this category if the combined floor area of those parts used for providing gambling facilities is at least 500 sq m but does not exceed 1,500 sq m[5]. They will be permitted 2 gaming machines (of up to Category B1) for each gaming table available for play, up to a maximum of 80, and will also be permitted to provide betting, but not bingo[6].

A casino is below the minimum size under the 2005 Act if the combined floor area of those parts used for providing gambling facilities is less than 500 sq m[7].

1 GA 2005, s 7(5).
2 DCMS 2005: 'Gambling Act: Regulatory Impact Assessment' para 4.15.
3 See SI 2008/1330, reg 2(2).

4 GA 2005, s 172(4); s 174(3). All sub-categories of B are allowed save B3A: see SI 2007/2158, reg 6(3).
5 See SI 2008/1330, reg 2(3).
6 GA 2005, s 172(5); s 174(3), (4). All sub-categories of B are allowed save B3A: see SI 2007/2158, reg 6(3).
7 See SI 2008/1330, reg 2(4).

6.162 In addition to authorising the operation of a casino, a casino premises licence will authorise the holder to make facilities available for betting on the outcome of a virtual game, race, competition or other event or process[1]. The licence will also authorise the holder to make available any number of games of chance other than casino games (eg equal chance card room games)[2]. Regulations will provide for conditions to be imposed on casino licences to control the provision of automated table games such as Touchbet Roulette (where a real game of roulette is played with a wheel which is automatically spun without a croupier). Such conditions may limit the number of such machines and the number of players that can be accommodated on any one machine[3]. Conditions may also be imposed requiring the provision on the casino premises of recreational facilities or other specified facilities[4].

A casino premises licence will be subject to a condition requiring compliance with Part II of the LCCP issued by the Gambling Commission (see para **6.2060** below) relating to access to the casino premises of children or young people. The code requires specified steps to be taken to ensure that children and young people do not enter the areas of the casino where gaming takes place[5] and lays down requirements relating to door supervision by a physical presence, not merely CCTV cameras, and the provision of evidence of age by persons seeking to enter such areas[6].

A casino premises licence will also be subject to a condition prohibiting the licensee from giving credit in connection with gambling authorised by the licence and from participating in, arranging, permitting or knowingly facilitating the giving of credit in connection with such gambling. Such a condition will not prevent the installation of a machine enabling cash to be obtained on credit from an independent credit provider, but the licensee must have no commercial connection with the credit provider and may receive no payment or reward in connection with the machine[7].

1 GA 2005, s 173.
2 GA 2005, s 174(2).
3 GA 2005, s 174(6).
4 GA 2005, s 174(7).
5 GA 2005, s 176(1), (2).
6 GA 2005, s 176(2).
7 GA 2005, s 177.

Competing applications for casino premises licences

6.163 The statutory cap on the number of premises licences that may be issued for regional, large and small casinos creates the need for a procedure to ensure that the power to award them is fairly distributed across the different licensing authorities throughout the country. It also makes necessary a mechanism by which such authorities may determine who is to receive a licence in cases where demand for licences exceeds the permitted supply. The Secretary of State has determined the geographical distribution of casino premises licences and specified which licence authorities may issue premises licences of a specified kind and the number of licences which may have effect[1]. Neither an application for a casino premises licence nor an application for a provisional statement[2] relating to a casino may be made to a licensing authority if the authority would have no authority to grant it under the Order[3]. The Gambling Act 2005, Sch 9, para 2 requires a licensing authority to invite applications where a limit is specified in relation to the relevant category of casino premises licence under s 175. The Gambling (Inviting Competing Applications for Large and Small Casino Premises Licences) Regulations 2008[4] set out the rules about such invitations.

Regulation 3 provides that, before considering an application, a licensing authority must:

- publish an invitation calling for applications that accords with regs 4 and 5; and
- make arrangements for the provision, free of charge, of information about an invited application to be provided to a person on request until the latest date by which an application must be made in order to be considered by the licensing authority. The application pack must accord with reg 6.

Regulation 4 provides for the manner in which an invitation must be published. Regulation 5 sets out the information that must be included in an invitation. This information includes the closing date.

Regulation 6 sets out the information that must be included in an application pack.

Regulation 7(1) and (2) provides that:

- a licensing authority may not consider an application before the closing date stated in the invitation to which the application relates; and
- a licensing authority is not required to consider an application that is made after the relevant closing date.

Regulation 7(3) provides that an application that is made before the relevant closing date shall be treated, for the purposes of the Act and regulations made under it, as if it were made on the relevant closing date. This will mean, for example, that the period within which a person may make representations in relation to an application (prescribed by reg 15 of the Gambling Act 2005 (Premises Licences and Provisional Statements) Regulations 2007[5]) will begin from the relevant closing date rather than the date that the application was actually made.

Where a licensing authority which is authorised to issue one or more casino licences of a specified kind receives applications for licences in excess of the number which they could grant they must adopt a two-stage approach in determining the applications as laid down in GA 2005, Sch 9. First, they must consider each application individually to determine whether they would grant the application on its merits under s 163[6] if they had a free hand and the cap imposed by s 175 and the Order did not exist[7]. In deciding this question the licensing authority must not have regard to whether any of the other competing applications is more deserving of being granted[8], but each competing applicant is an 'interested party' in relation to any other competing application[9] and so may make representations as to the merits of that application. Where the licensing authority decide that they would not grant the application on its merits under s 163 then the application is rejected and the applicant has a right of appeal to the magistrates' court[10]. Where the authority decide that they would grant the application on its merits under s 163 they will make a 'provisional decision to grant an application'[11]. Any person who made representations in relation to the application and the applicant may appeal against that decision[12]. Where the authority provisionally decide to grant a number of licences in excess of the number they have the power to award under s 175 and the Order they must determine which of the competing applications they will grant[13]. For that purpose they must determine which of the competing applications would in their opinion be likely if granted to result in the greatest benefit to their area[14]. They may secure such anticipated benefits by entering into a written agreement with an applicant for the provision of services in their area, or otherwise[15], and may attach conditions to the licence to give effect to such an agreement[16]. Having determined to grant one or more applications the licensing authority must then grant those applications and reject any other competing applications[17]. The Secretary of State has now issued issue a code of practice to guide licensing authorities in the decision making process under Sch 9[18]. As noted an appeal lies to the magistrates' court in respect of a decision under Sch 9, para 4 to make a provisional decision to grant an application or a decision to reject an application on its merits[19] but no appeal may be brought in respect of a decision made under Sch 9, para 5 to grant or refuse one of a number of competing applications[20]. No doubt a disappointed applicant could seek to challenge the decision by way of an application for judicial review if grounds existed.

The places in which 2005 casinos may be situated are listed in SI 2008/1327.

1 GA 2005, s 175(4).
2 For provisional statements see para **6.183** below.
3 GA 2005, s 175(5), (6).
4 SI 2008/469.
5 SI 2007/459.
6 For GA 2005, s 163 see para **6.158** above.
7 GA 2005 Sch 9, para 3, 4.
8 GA 2005 Sch 9, para 4(2)(a).
9 GA 2005 Sch 9, para 4(2)(b).
10 GA 2005 Sch 9, para 4(2)(c); s 206(1).
11 GA 2005 Sch 9, para 4(2)(c).
12 GA 2005 Sch 9, para 4(2)(c); s 206(2).
13 GA 2005, Sch 9, para 5.
14 GA 2005, Sch 9, para 5(3)(a).
15 GA 2005, Sch 9, para 5(3)(b).
16 GA 2005, Sch 9, para 5(3)(c).
17 GA 2005, Sch 9, para 5(4).
18 See the DCMS Code of Practice published on 26 February 2008. (See para **6.2242** below).
19 GA 2005, Sch 9, para 8(1).
20 GA 2005, Sch 9, para 8(4).

Resolution not to issue casino premises licences

6.164 As has been noted the Gambling Review Body recommended that local authorities should have the power to institute a blanket ban on all, or particular types of, gambling premises in their area or any specified part of it[1]. The Government rejected this proposal as too sweeping, but introduced it in the case of casinos only. A licensing authority may resolve not to issue casino premises licences[2]. The exercise of this power by the licensing authority is one that may not be delegated to the licensing committee[3]. No criteria for the exercise of the power are set out in the Act; rather the Act states that in passing such a resolution a licensing authority 'may have regard to any principle or matter'[4] a provision which appears designed to confer a virtually unlimited and unfettered discretion on the authority. In practice the local authority would be subject to the usual principles of public law in exercising their discretion to make such a resolution reasonably and in good faith, for proper purposes only, and in accordance with the spirit as well as the letter of the Act. The Act does not provide for the exercise of the discretion to be conditional upon any form of consultation, but here again public law principles would, at least in some circumstances, be likely to impose a duty to engage in some degree of consultation particularly if there were parties who could claim to have a legitimate expectation to be consulted.

A resolution must apply to the issue of casino licences generally[5], so it would not be possible for a licensing authority to resolve, for example, against granting casino premises licences for regional and large casinos but to leave their discretion intact in the case of small casinos. The resolution must specify the date on which it takes effect[6]; it lapses at the end of the period of three years beginning with that date[7], though it may be revoked before then by a further resolution[8]. A resolution may be passed whether or not the licensing authority have already issued casino premises licences[9], but a resolution will not have any effect on licences issued before it takes effect[10], nor on provisional statements relating to the operation of a casino in force at that time[11], nor on licences converted into casino premises licences under Sch 18, or casino premises licences issued in accordance with a requirement of that Schedule[12]. A resolution not to issue casino premises licences may not be taken into account in carrying out a review of a casino premises licence[13]. The Secretary of State may by order require a licensing authority to consider, either once or at specified intervals, whether or not to pass a resolution not to issue casino premises licences[14]. Such an order may be directed to one or more licensing authorities, may require the licensing authority to consult persons or classes of persons likely to be affected by the resolution, may require other procedural steps and may specify a period within which the consideration must take place[15].

1 Gambling Review Report DCMS 2001, para 21.9.
2 GA 2005, s 166.
3 GA 2005, s 154(2)(a).
4 GA 2005, s 166(2).
5 GA 2005, s 166(3)(a).
6 GA 2005, s 166(3)(b).
7 GA 2005, s 166(3)(d).
8 GA 2005, s 166(3)(c).
9 GA 2005, s 166(4)(a).
10 GA 2005, s 166(4)(b).
11 GA 2005, s 166(4)(c).
12 GA 2005, s 166(4)(d) and (e).
13 GA 2005, s 166(4)(f).
14 GA 2005, s 166(7); s 166(8)(e).
15 GA 2005, s 166(8)(a)–(d).

Mandatory and default conditions which attach to casino premises licences

6.164A Regulation 3 of the Gambling Act 2005 (Mandatory and Default Conditions) (England and Wales) Regulations 2007[1] attaches to all such premises licences the following mandatory conditions:

(1) The summary of the terms and conditions of the premises licence issued under s 164(1)(c) of the GA 2005 shall be displayed in a prominent position within the premises.
(2) The layout of the premises shall be maintained in accordance with the plan.
(3) The premises shall not be used for
(a) the sale of tickets in a private[2] or customer[3] lottery or
(b) the sale of tickets in any other lottery in respect of which the sale of tickets is otherwise prohibited[4].

Regulations 4–9 additionally attach the following conditions to casino premises licences, some have general and others specific application.

---

1 SI 2007/1409.

2 See GA 2005, Sch 11, paras 10 and 11.

3 See GA 2005, Part 3, Sch 11.

4 See the National Lottery Regulations 1994 (SI 1994/189) which prohibit the sale of National Lottery tickets in specified premises licensed for gambling activities (see para **11.1593** on the accompanying CD).

Mandatory conditions attaching to all casino premises licences

1 —
(1) The principal entrance to the premises shall be from a street.
(2) No entrance to the premises shall be from premises that are used wholly or mainly by children, by young persons, or by both.
(3) No customer shall be able to enter the premises directly from any other premises in respect of which a licence issued under Part 8 of the Act, or a permit issued under Schedule 10, 12 or 13 to the Act, has effect.

2 A gap of at least 2 metres shall be maintained between any ordinary gaming table and any other equipment, apparatus or structure used by a person to gamble on the premises.

3 No more than 40 separate player positions may be made available for use in relation to wholly automated gaming tables at any time.

4
(1) The rules of each type of casino game that is available to be played on the premises shall be displayed in a prominent place within both the table gaming area and other gambling area of the premises to which customers wishing to use facilities for gambling have unrestricted access.
(2) The condition in sub-paragraph (1) may be satisfied by—
(a) displaying a clear and legible sign setting out the rules; or
(b) making available to customers leaflets or other written material containing the rules.

5 Any ATM made available for use on the premises shall be located in a place that requires any customer who wishes to use it to cease gambling at any gaming table, gaming machine or betting machine in order to do so.

Default conditions attaching to all casino premise licences

No facilities for gambling shall be provided on the premises between the hours of 6am and noon on any day.

Mandatory conditions attaching to converted casino premises licences

1 A notice shall be displayed in a prominent place at every entrance to the premises stating that no person under the age of 18 years is permitted to enter

the premises.

2 —

(1) This paragraph shall apply to premises which have a gambling area the floor area of which is no less than $200m^2$.

(2) In determining the floor area of the gambling area, all areas in which facilities for gambling are provided on the premises shall be taken into account.

(3) The premises shall contain a non-gambling area, the floor area of which is no less than 10% of the floor area of the gambling area.

(4) The non-gambling area may consist of one or more areas within the premises.

(5) Lobby areas and toilet facilities may be taken into account in calculating the non-gambling area; but the non-gambling area shall not consist exclusively of lobby areas and toilet facilities.

(6) Facilities for gambling shall not be provided in the non-gambling area.

(7) At any time during which facilities for gambling are being provided on the premises, each separate area comprising the non-gambling area, other than the lobby areas and toilet facilities referred to in sub-paragraph (5), shall contain recreational facilities that are available for use by customers on the premises.

Mandatory conditions attaching to regional casino premises licences

1 A notice shall be displayed in a prominent place at every entrance to the gambling area of the premises stating that no person under the age of 18 years is permitted to enter that part of the premises.

2 The gambling area of the premises shall not be capable of being seen from any part of the premises to which children, young persons, or both, have access.

3 —

(1) The premises shall contain a table gaming area the floor area of which is no less than $1000m^2$.

(2) Subject to sub-paragraph (3), in determining the floor area of the table gaming area, any number of separate areas within the premises may be taken into account.

(3) Any separate area that comprises less than 12.5% of the minimum required table gaming area shall not be taken into account in determining the table gaming area.

(4) No gambling shall be permitted in the table gaming area of the premises other than gambling by way of table gaming.

4 —

(1) The premises shall contain a non-gambling area the floor area of which is no less than $1500m^2$.

(2) The non-gambling area may consist of one or more areas within the premises.

(3) Lobby areas and toilet facilities may be taken into account in calculating the non-gambling area; but the non-gambling area shall not consist exclusively of lobby areas and toilet facilities.

(4) Facilities for gambling shall not be provided in the non-gambling area.

(5) At any time during which facilities for gambling are provided on the premises, each separate area comprising the non-gambling area, other than the lobby areas and toilet facilities referred to in sub-paragraph (3), shall contain recreational facilities that are available for use by customers on the premises.

5 A notice shall be displayed in a prominent place in each part of the premises used for providing facilities for betting, setting out the terms on which persons

are invited to bet on the premises.

6 —

(1) A notice setting out the information in sub-paragraph (2) shall be displayed in a prominent place at the main point on the premises where payment for the charge is to be made for a game card (or set of game cards) in respect of a game of bingo.

(2) The notice in sub-paragraph (1) shall include the following information—

(a) the cost (in money) of each game card (or set of game cards) payable by an individual in respect of a game of bingo;

(b) in respect of each game card (or set of game cards) referred to in paragraph (a), the maximum amount that will be charged by way of a participation fee for entitlement to participate in that game; and

(c) a statement to the effect that all or part of the participation fee may be waived at the discretion of the person charging it.

(3) The notice may be displayed in electronic form.

(4) A reference in this paragraph to a charge in respect of gaming does not include an amount paid for an opportunity to win one or more prizes in gaming to which section 288 of the 2005 Act (meaning of "prize gaming") applies.

(5) The rules of each type of bingo game that is available to be played on the premises shall be made available to customers in each part of the premises used for providing facilities for bingo.

(6) The condition in sub-paragraph (5) may be satisfied by—

(a) displaying a sign setting out the rules,

(b) making available leaflets or other written material containing the rules, or

(c) running an audio-visual guide to the rules prior to any bingo game being commenced.

7 No more than 40 separate betting positions may be made available for use in relation to betting machines at any time.

Mandatory conditions attaching to large casino premises licences

1 A notice stating that no person under the age of 18 years is permitted to enter the premises shall be displayed in a prominent place at every entrance to the premises.

2 —

(1) The premises shall contain a table gaming area, the floor area of which is no less than $1000m^2$.

(2) Subject to sub-paragraph (3), in determining the floor area of the table gaming area, any number of separate areas within the premises may be taken into account.

(3) Any separate area that comprises less than 12.5% of the minimum required table gaming area shall not be taken into account in determining the table gaming area.

3 No gambling shall be permitted in the table gaming area of the premises other than gambling by way of table gaming.

4 —

(1) The premises shall contain a non-gambling area which comprises no less than $500m^2$.

(2) The non-gambling area may consist of one or more areas within the premises.

(3) Lobby areas and toilet facilities may be taken into account in calculating the non-gambling area; but the non-gambling area shall not consist exclusively of lobby areas and toilet facilities.

(4) Facilities for gambling shall not be provided in the non-gambling area.

(5) At any time during which facilities for gambling are being provided on the premises, each separate area comprising of the non-gambling area, other

than the lobby areas and toilet facilities referred to in sub-paragraph (3), shall contain recreational facilities that are available for use by customers on the premises.

5 A notice shall be displayed in a prominent place in each part of the premises used for providing facilities for betting, setting out the terms on which persons are invited to bet on the premises.

6 —

(1) A notice setting out the information in sub-paragraph (2) shall be displayed in a prominent place at the main point on the premises where payment for the charge is to be made for a game card (or set of game cards) in respect of a game of bingo.

(2) The notice in sub-paragraph (1) shall include the following information—

(a) the cost (in money) of each game card (or set of game cards) payable by an individual in respect of a game of bingo;

(b) in respect of each game card (or set of game cards) referred to in paragraph (a) the maximum amount that will be charged by way of a participation fee for entitlement to participate in that game; and

(c) a statement to the effect that all or part of the participation fee may be waived at the discretion of the person charging it.

(3) The notice may be displayed in electronic form.

(4) A reference in this paragraph to a charge in respect of gaming does not include an amount paid for an opportunity to win one or more prizes in gaming to which section 288 of the 2005 Act (meaning of "prize gaming") applies.

(5) The rules of each type of bingo game that is available to be played on the premises shall be made available to customers in each part of the premises used for providing facilities for bingo.

(6) The condition in sub-paragraph (5) may be satisfied by—

(a) displaying a sign setting out the rules,

(b) making available leaflets or other written material containing the rules, or

(c) running an audio-visual guide to the rules prior to any bingo game being commenced.

7 No more than 40 separate betting positions may be made available for use in relation to betting machines at any time.

Mandatory conditions attaching to small casino premises licences

1 A notice stating that no person under the age of 18 years is permitted to enter the premises shall be displayed in a prominent place at every entrance to the premises.

2 —

(1) The premises shall contain a table gaming area, the floor area of which is no less than 500m^2.

(2) Subject to sub-paragraph (3), in determining the floor area of the table gaming area, any number of separate areas within the premises may be taken into account.

(3) Any separate area that comprises less than 12.5% of the minimum required table gaming area shall not be taken into account in determining the table gaming area.

3 No gambling shall be permitted in the table gaming area of the premises other than gambling by way of table gaming.

4 —

(1) The premises shall contain a non-gambling area which comprises no less than 250m^2.

(2) The non-gambling area may consist of one or more areas within the premises.

(3) Lobby areas and toilet facilities may be taken into account in calculating

the non-gambling area; but the non-gambling area shall not consist exclusively of lobby areas and toilet facilities.

(4) Facilities for gambling shall not be provided in the non-gambling area.

(5) At any time during which facilities for gambling are being provided on the premises, each separate area comprising the non-gambling area, other than the lobby areas and toilet facilities referred to in sub-paragraph (3), shall contain recreational facilities that are available for use by customers on the premises.

5 A notice shall be displayed in a prominent place in each part of the premises used for providing facilities for betting, setting out the terms on which persons are invited to bet on the premises.

6 No more than 40 separate betting positions may be made available for use in relation to betting machines at any time.

Bingo premises licences

6.165 In addition to authorising the provision of facilities for the playing of bingo a bingo premises licence[1] authorises the holder to make available for use Category B gaming machines, as long as the number of these does not exceed 20% of the total number of machines on the premises[2], and an unlimited number of Category C and Category D gaming machines[3]. Such a licence will also be subject to a condition prohibiting the holder from giving credit in connection with the gambling authorised by the licence in the same terms as apply in the case of a casino premises licence (see para **6.162** above)[4]. As in the case of a casino a machine may be installed on the premises enabling cash to be obtained on credit from an independent credit provider if the licensee has no commercial connection with the credit provider and derives no benefit from the provision of the machine[5].

1 GA 2005, s 150(1)(b).
2 This includes only sub-category B3 and B4 machines: see SI 2007/2158, reg 6(3).
3 GA 2005, s 172(7) as amended.
4 GA 2005, s 177(1) and (2).
5 GA 2005, s 177(3).

Mandatory and default conditions which attach to bingo premises licences

6.165A Regulation 3 of the Gambling Act 2005 (Mandatory and Default Conditions) (England and Wales) Regulations 2007[1] attaches to all such premises licences the following mandatory conditions:

(1) The summary of the terms and conditions of the premises licence issued under s 164(1)(c) of the GA 2005 shall be displayed in a prominent place within the premises.

(2) The layout of the premises shall be maintained in accordance with the plan.

(3) The premises shall not be used for
(a) the sale of tickets in a private[2] or customer[3] lottery or
(b) the sale of tickets in any other lottery in respect of which the sale of tickets is otherwise prohibited[4].

Regulations 10–11 additionally attach the following conditions to all bingo premises licences.

1 SI 2007/1409.
2 See GA 2005, Sch 11, paras 10 and 11.

3 See GA 2005, Part 3, Sch 11.

4 See the National Lottery Regulations 1994 (SI 1994/189) which prohibit the sale of National Lottery tickets in specified premises licensed for gambling activities (see para **11.1593** on the accompanying CD).

Mandatory conditions

1 A notice stating that no person under the age of 18 years is permitted to play bingo on the premises shall be displayed in a prominent place at every entrance to the premises.

2 No customer shall be able to enter the premises directly from any other premises in respect of which one of the following permissions has effect—

(a) a casino premises licence;

(b) an adult gaming centre premises licence;

(c) a betting premises licence other than a track premises licence; and

3 —

(1) This paragraph shall apply where children or young persons or both are permitted by the licence holder to enter the premises, and Category B or C gaming machines are made available for use on the premises.

(2) Any area of the premises to which category B and C gaming machines are located—

(a) shall be separated from the rest of the premises by a physical barrier which is effective to prevent access other than by an entrance designed for the purpose;

(b) shall be supervised at all times to ensure children or young persons or both do not enter the area; and

(c) shall be arranged in such a way that ensures all parts of the area can be observed by the persons mentioned in sub-paragraph (3).

(3) The reference to supervision in this paragraph means supervision by—

(a) one or more persons whose responsibilities include ensuring children or young persons or both do not enter the area; or

(b) closed circuit television which is monitored by one or more persons whose responsibilities include ensuring that children or young persons or both do not enter the area.

(4) A notice stating that no person under the age of 18 years is permitted to enter the area shall be displayed in a prominent place at the entrance to any area of the premises in which Category B or C gaming machines are made available for use.

4 —

(1) In the case of a charge for admission to the premises, a notice of that charge shall be displayed in a prominent place at the principal entrance to the premises.

(2) In the case of any other charges in respect of gaming, a notice setting out the information in sub-paragraph (3) shall be displayed at the main point where payment for the charge is to be made.

(3) The notice in sub-paragraph (2) shall include the following information—

(a) the cost (in money) of each game card (or set of game cards) payable by an individual in respect of a game of bingo;

(b) in respect of each game card (or set of game cards) referred to in paragraph (a) the amount that will be charged by way of a participation fee for entitlement to participate in that game; and

(c) a statement to the effect that all or part of the participation fee may be waived at the discretion of the person charging it.

(4) The notice may be displayed in electronic form.

(5) A reference in this paragraph to a charge in respect of gaming does not include an amount paid for an opportunity to win one or more prizes in

gaming to which section 288 of the 2005 Act (meaning of "prize gaming") applies.

5 —

(1) The rules of each type of game that is available to be played [on] the premises other than games played on gaming machines shall be made available to customers within the premises.

(2) The condition in sub-paragraph (1) may be satisfied by—

(a) displaying a sign setting out the rules,

(b) making available leaflets or other written material containing the rules, or

(c) running an audio-visual guide to the rules prior to any bingo game being commenced.

6 Any ATM made available for use on the premises shall be located in a place that requires any customer who wishes to use it to cease gambling in order to do so.

Default conditions

1 Subject to paragraph 2, no facilities for gambling shall be provided on the premises between the hours of midnight and 9am.

2 The condition in paragraph 1 shall not apply to making gaming machines available for use.

Adult gaming centre premises licences

6.166 An adult gaming centre premises licence[1] authorises the holder to make available for use Category B gaming machines as long as the number of these does not exceed 20% of the total number of machines on the premises, together with an unlimited number of Category C and Category D gaming machines[2].

---

1 GA 2005, s 150(1)(c).

2 GA 2005, s 172(1) as amended. Note that category B machines can only be sub-category B3 and B4 machines: see SI 2007/2158, reg 6(3).

Mandatory conditions which attach to adult gaming centre premises licences

6.166A Regulation 3 of the Gambling Act 2005 (Mandatory and Default Conditions) (England and Wales) Regulations 2007[1] attaches to such premises licences the following mandatory conditions:

(1) The summary of the terms and conditions of the premises licence issued under s 164(1)(c) of the GA 2005 shall be displayed in a prominent place within the premises.

(2) The layout of the premises shall be maintained in accordance with the plan.

(3) The premises shall not be used for

(a) the sale of tickets in a private[2] or customer[3] lottery, or

(b) the sale of tickets in any other lottery in respect of which the sale of tickets is otherwise prohibited[4].

Regulation 12 additionally attaches the following mandatory conditions to all AGC premises licences:

1 A notice stating that no person under the age of 18 years is permitted to enter the premises shall be displayed in a prominent place at every entrance to the premises.

2 No customer shall be able to access the premises directly from any other

premises in respect of which a licence issued under Part 8 of the Act, or a permit issued under Schedule 10, 12 or 13 to the Act, has effect.

3 Any ATM made available for use on the premises shall be located in a place that requires any customer who wishes to use it to cease gambling at any gaming machine in order to do so.

4 —

(1) No alcohol shall be permitted to be consumed on the premises at any time during which facilities for gambling are being provided on the premises.

(2) A notice stating the condition in sub-paragraph (1) shall be displayed in a prominent place at every entrance to the premises.

---

1 SI 2007/1409.

2 See GA 2005, Sch 11, paras 10 and 11.

3 See GA 2005, Part 3, Sch 11.

4 See the National Lottery Regulations 1994 (SI 1994/189) which prohibit the sale of National Lottery tickets in specified premises licensed for gambling activities (see para **11.1593** on the accompanying CD).

Family entertainment centre premises licences

6.167 A family entertainment centre premises licence[1] authorises the holder to make an unlimited number of Category C and Category D gaming machines available for use on the premises[2].

---

1 GA 2005, s 150(1)(d).

2 GA 2005, s 172(2).

Mandatory conditions which attach to family entertainment centre premises licences

6.167A Regulation 3 of the Gambling Act 2005 (Mandatory and Default Conditions) (England and Wales) Regulations 2007[1] attaches to such premises licences the following mandatory conditions:

(1) The summary of the terms and conditions of the premises licence issued under s 164(1)(c) of the GA 2005 shall be displayed in a prominent position within the premises.

(2) The layout of the premises shall be maintained in accordance with the plan.

(3) The premises shall not be used for:

(a) the sale of tickets in a private[2] or customer[3] lottery or

(b) the sale of tickets in any other lottery in respect of which the sale of tickets is otherwise prohibited[4].

Regulation 13 additionally attaches the following mandatory conditions to all FEC premises licences:

1 No customer shall be able to access the premises directly from any other premises in respect of which one of the following premises licences has effect—

(a) a casino premises licence;

(b) an adult gaming centre premises licence;

(c) a betting premises licence other than a track premises licence.

2 Any ATM made available for use on the premises shall be located in a place that requires any customer who wishes to use it to cease gambling at any gaming machine in order to do so.

3 —

(1) Where Category C gaming machines are made available for use on the

premises, any area of the premises in which those machines are located—
(a) shall be separated from the rest of the premises by a physical barrier which is effective to prevent access other than by an entrance designed for the purpose;
(b) shall be supervised at all times to ensure children or young persons or both do not enter the area; and
(c) shall be arranged in such a way so as to permit all parts of the area to be observed by the persons mentioned in sub-paragraph (2).
(2) The reference to supervision in this paragraph means supervision by—
(a) one or more persons whose responsibilities include ensuring children or young persons or both do not enter the area; or
(b) closed circuit television which is monitored by one or more persons whose responsibilities include ensuring that children or young persons or both do not enter the area.
(3) A notice stating that no person under the age of 18 years is permitted to enter the area shall be displayed in a prominent place at the entrance to any area of the premises in which Category C gaming machines are made available for use.

4 —
(1) No alcohol shall be permitted to be consumed on the premises at any time during which facilities for gambling are being provided on the premises.
(2) A notice stating the condition in sub-paragraph (1) shall be displayed in a prominent place at every entrance to the premises.

---

1 SI 2007/1409.
2 See GA 2005, Sch 11, paras 10 and 11.
3 See GA 2005, Part 3, Sch 11.
4 See National Lottery Regs 1994 (SI 1994/189) which prohibit sale of National Lottery tickets in specified premises licensed for gambling activities (para **11.1593** on accompanying CD).

Betting premises licences

6.168 As well as authorising premises to be used for the provision of facilities for betting[1] a betting premises licence[1] authorises the holder to make available for use up to four gaming machines each of which must be of Category B, C or D[2], though this provision only applies to a betting premises licence in respect of a track if the holder also holds a pool betting operating licence[3]. A betting premises licence authorises the holder to make facilities available for betting on the outcome of a virtual game, race, competition or other event or process[4] such as the bets on virtual races like Portman Park (virtual horses) and Millersfield (virtual greyhounds) currently offered in many licensed betting offices.

A betting premises licence in respect of a track may only authorise the acceptance of bets by way of pool betting if those bets are on horse-racing or dog-racing and the bets are accepted by the holder of the betting premises licence or in accordance with arrangements made by him[5]. A betting premises licence in respect of premises which are not a dog track is subject to the condition that pool bets on dog-racing may not be accepted in reliance on the licence except in accordance with arrangements made with the occupier of the dog-track on which the racing takes place[6].

As has been noted above a betting premises licence authorises use of up to four gaming machines on the premises. Betting premises may also make available betting machines which can be used to bet on future real events, and such machines do not qualify as gaming machines[7]. Conditions may, however, be attached to a betting premises licence relating to the number and nature of betting machines to be used on the premises and the circumstances in which they may be made available for use[8].

A betting premises licence in respect of a track must be subject to a condition that the licensee must ensure that children and young persons are excluded from any area where facilities for betting are provided and any area where a gaming machine (other than a Category D machine) is situated[9]. However, the requirement to exclude children and young persons from betting areas does not apply to a dog track or to a horse-race course on days when dog-racing or horse-racing or a race or other sporting event take place or are expected to take place there[10].

1 GA 2005, s 150(1)(e).
2 GA 2005, s 172(8). Only sub-categories B2, B3 and B4 are included: see SI 2007/2158, reg 6(3).
3 GA 2005, s 172(9).
4 GA 2005, s 173.
5 GA 2005, s 179.
6 GA 2005, s 180.
7 GA 2005, s 235(2)(c).
8 GA 2005, s 181(1).
9 GA 2005, s 182(1).
10 GA 2005, s 182(2) as amended by SI 2007/1410.

Mandatory and default conditions which attach to non-track betting premises licences

6.168A Regulation 3 of the Gambling Act 2005 (Mandatory and Default Conditions) (England and Wales) Regulations 2007[1] attaches to all such premises licences the following mandatory conditions:

(1) The summary of the terms and conditions of the premises licence issued under s 164(1)(c) of the GA 2005 shall be displayed in a prominent place within the premises.

(2) The layout of the premises shall be maintained in accordance with the plan.

(3) The premises shall not be used for:
(a) the sale of tickets in a private[2] or customer[3] lottery or
(b) the sale of tickets in any other lottery in respect of which the sale of tickets is otherwise prohibited[4].

Regulations 14 and 15 additionally attach the following conditions to all non-track betting premises licences.

1 SI 2007/1409.
2 See GA 2005, Sch 11, paras 10 and 11.
3 See GA 2005, Part 3, Sch 11.
4 See the National Lottery Regulations 1994 (SI 1994/189) which prohibit the sale of National Lottery tickets in specified premises licensed for gambling activities ((see para **11.1593** on the accompanying CD).

Mandatory conditions

1 A notice stating that no person under the age of 18 years is permitted to enter the premises shall be displayed in a prominent place at every entrance to the

premises.

2 —

(1) Access to the premises shall be from a street or from other premises with a betting premises licence.

(2) Without prejudice to sub-paragraph (1), there shall be no means of direct access between the premises and other premises used for the retail sale of merchandise or services.

3 Subject to anything permitted by virtue of the 2005 Act, or done in accordance with paragraphs 4, 5, 6 and 7 below, the premises shall not be used for any purpose other than for providing facilities for betting.

4 Any ATM made available for use on the premises shall be located in a place that requires any customer who wishes to use it to leave any gaming machine or betting machine in order to do so.

5 No apparatus for making information or other material available in the form of sounds or visual images may be used on the premises, except for apparatus used for the following purposes—

(a) communicating information about, or coverage of, sporting events, including—

(i) information relating to betting on such an event; and

(ii) any other matter or information, including an advertisement, which is incidental to such an event;

(b) communicating information relating to betting on any event (including the result of the event) in connection with which betting transactions may be or have been effected on the premises.

6 No publications, other than racing periodicals or specialist betting publications, may be sold or offered for sale on the premises.

7 No music, dancing or other entertainment shall be provided or permitted on the premises, save for entertainment provided in accordance with paragraph 5.

8 —

(1) No alcohol shall be permitted to be consumed on the premises at any time during which facilities for gambling are being provided on the premises.

(2) A notice stating the condition in sub-paragraph (1) shall be displayed in a prominent place at every entrance to the premises.

9 A notice setting out the terms on which customers are invited to bet on the premises shall be displayed in a prominent place on the premises to which customers have unrestricted access.

Default conditions

No facilities for gambling shall be provided on the premises between the hours of 10pm on one day and 7am on the next day.

Mandatory and Default conditions which attach to all track premises licences

6.168B Regulation 3 of the Gambling Act 2005 (Mandatory and Default Conditions) (England and Wales) Regulations 2007[1] attaches to all such premises licences the following mandatory conditions:

(1) The summary of the terms and conditions of the premises licence issued under s 164(1)(c) of the GA 2005 shall be displayed in a prominent place within the premises.

(2) The layout of the premises shall be maintained in accordance with the plan.

(3) The premises shall not be used for:

(a) the sale of tickets in a private[2] or customer[3] lottery or

(b) the sale of tickets in any other lottery in respect of which the sale of tickets is otherwise prohibited[4].

Regulations 16 and 17 additionally attach the following conditions to all track premises licences.

---

1 SI 2007/1409.

2 See GA 2005, Sch 11, paras 10 and 11.

3 See GA 2005, Part 3, Sch 11.

4 See the National Lottery Regulations 1994 (SI 1994/189) which prohibit the sale of National Lottery tickets in specified premises licensed for gambling activities (see para **11.1593** on the accompanying CD).

Mandatory conditions attaching to all types of track premises licences

1 No customer shall be able to access the premises directly from any other premises in respect of which one of the following premises licences has effect—
(a) a casino premises licence;
(b) an adult gaming centre premises licence.

2 A notice stating that no person under the age of 18 is permitted to bet on the premises shall be displayed in a prominent place at every public entrance to the premises.

3 The terms on which a bet may be placed must be displayed in a prominent place within the premises to which customers wishing to use facilities for betting have unrestricted access.

4 The premises licence holder shall make arrangements to ensure that betting operators who are admitted to the premises for the purpose of accepting bets—
(a) will be operating under a valid operating licence; and
(b) are enabled to accept such bets in accordance with—
(i) the conditions imposed under sections 92 (general betting operating licence) or 93 (pool betting operating licence) of the 2005 Act, or
(ii) an authorisation under section 94 (horse-race pool betting operating licence) of that Act.

5 The premises licence holder shall make arrangements to ensure that reasonable steps are taken to remove from the premises any person who is found to be accepting bets on the premises otherwise than in accordance with the 2005 Act.

6 Any ATM made available for use on the premises shall be located in a place that requires any customer who wishes to use it to cease gambling in order to do so.

Default conditions attaching to all track premises licences

1 Subject to paragraph 2, no facilities for gambling shall be provided on the premises between the hours of 10pm on one day, and 7am on the next day.

2 The prohibition in paragraph 1 does not apply on days when a sporting event is taking place on the premises, in which case gambling transactions may take place at any time during that day.

Mandatory conditions attaching to horse-race courses

1 —
(1) This paragraph shall apply to converted track premises licences in respect of premises that are horse-race courses.
(2) The licence holder shall ensure that in respect of any part of the track, which immediately before 1st September 2007 was made available for the purposes of complying with a condition imposed under section 13(2) of the 1963 Act (which provides for conditions to be imposed on a certificate under section 13 relating to the places which are to be provided for

enabling betting to take place on the track), that part shall continue to be made available for the purposes of enabling betting operators and betting operators' assistants to use it for carrying on business in connection with providing facilities for betting.

(3) Sub-paragraph (2) is without prejudice to any application under section 187 of the 2005 Act (application to vary a premises licence) to change the location of the part of the track to which that sub-paragraph applies.

(4) Where such an application is granted, sub-paragraph (2) is to have effect as if it required the licence holder to ensure that the part of the track identified in the application as the new location for the area referred to in that sub-paragraph is made available for the purposes of enabling betting operators and betting operators' assistants to carry on business in connection with providing facilities for betting.

(5) References in this paragraph to an "existing betting area" are to any part of the track which is required to be made available in accordance with the preceding provisions of this paragraph for the purposes of enabling betting operators and betting operators' assistants to carry on business in connection with providing facilities for betting.

(6) The charge for admission to an existing betting area for the purposes of carrying on business in connection with providing facilities for betting shall not exceed—

(a) where payable by a betting operator, five times the cost of the highest charge paid by members of the public who are authorised to enter that part of the track; and

(b) where payable by a betting operator's assistant, the cost of the highest charge paid by members of the public who are authorised to enter that part of the track.

(7) A betting operator or betting operator's assistant shall not be charged, for admission to an existing betting area, an amount which differs from that charged to any other betting operator or betting operator's assistant for admission to that part of the track.

(8) No charges may be made to betting operators and betting operators' assistants who are admitted to the existing betting areas of the track, other than—

(a) the charge for admission in accordance with sub-paragraphs (6) and (7), and

(b) charges levied to cover costs reasonably incurred in connection with enabling betting operators and betting operators' assistants to operate in the existing betting area.

(9) This paragraph shall not apply after 31st August 2012.

2 —

(1) This paragraph shall apply to all track premises licences in respect of premises that are horse-race courses.

(2) The licence holder shall provide a place on the premises where betting operators and betting operators' assistants, including small-scale operators, may carry on business in connection with providing facilities for betting and to which the public may resort for the purpose of betting.

(3) The reference in this paragraph to "small-scale operators" shall have the same meaning as prescribed in The Gambling Act 2005 (Definition of Small-scale Operator) Regulations 2006.

(4) This paragraph shall not apply to converted track premises licences before 1st September 2012.

3 In this Part "converted track premises licence" means a premises licence issued in respect of a track where—

(a) the holder of the licence held a certificate under section 13 of the

1963 Act, in respect of the same or substantially the same premises (referred to below as "the 1963 Act permission");

(b) the 1963 Act permission had effect immediately before 1st September 2007; and

(c) the holder of the licence was granted the premises licence, under transitional provisions made under paragraph 9 of Schedule 18 to the 2005 Act, by reason of his holding the 1963 Act permission.

Mandatory conditions attaching to dog racing tracks

1 A totalisator on the premises shall only be operated—

(a) while the public are admitted to the premises for the purpose of attending dog races and no other sporting events are taking place on the premises; and

(b) for effecting with persons on the premises betting transactions on dog races taking place on the premises.

2 —

(1) At any time during which the totalisator is being lawfully used on the premises—

(a) no betting operator or betting operator's assistant shall be excluded from the premises by reason only of the fact that he proposes to accept or negotiate bets on the premises; and

(b) there shall be made available on the premises space for betting operators and betting operators' assistants where they can conveniently accept and negotiate bets in connection with dog races run on the premises on that day.

(2) This paragraph is without prejudice to section 180 (pool betting on dog races) of the 2005 Act.

3 For the purposes of this Part, "totalisator" means the apparatus for betting known as the totalisator or pari mutuel, or any other machine or instrument of betting of a like nature, whether mechanically operated or not.

Duration of premises licence

6.169 Unless brought to an end by one of the provisions of the GA 2005 (eg surrender, lapse) premises licences will be of unlimited duration subject to the power of the Secretary of State to make regulations providing that premises licences, or a class of premises licences, shall expire at the end of a prescribed period[1]. Such regulations may have retrospective effect and may make provision about renewals[2]. None have yet been published.

---

1 GA 2005, s 191(1), (4).

2 GA 2005, s 191(2), (3).

The licence

6.170 A premises licence must specify the name of the person to whom it is issued together with a home or business address for him, specify the premises to which it relates and the activities permitted and specify any condition attached under s 169(1)(a) and any default condition excluded under s 169(1)(b). It must also include a plan of the premises and if a period has been prescribed for the expiry of the licence it must specify the period[1]. Regulations have been made imposing additional requirements about the form and contents of a premises licence[2]. A licensing authority must maintain a register of premises licences issued by it and must make arrangements for public inspection of the register and for copies of entries on the register to be provided to the public[3]. Regulations may be made about the form of such registers and the manner in which they are to be maintained[4]. Regulations may also be made requiring licensing authorities to give to the Gambling Commission specified information about premises licences issued by them, and for the Gambling Commission to maintain a register of such information and to make it available for public inspection and for copies of the entries to be supplied[5].

On the grant of a premises licence the holder will have to pay a first annual fee, and he will have to pay an annual fee before each anniversary of the issue of the licence[6]. Regulations made by the Secretary of State prescribe the maximum amount of such fees (which may differ depending on the type of gambling authorised and the circumstances of the licence)[7]. The regulations provide for the amount of the fee to be determined by a licensing authority[8]. Section 212 lays down the procedure to be followed by the licensing authority in fixing fees[9]. A premises licence must be kept on the premises to which it relates[10], and must be made available on request to a constable, an enforcement officer or an authorised local authority officer[11]. Where a premises licence or a summary of the licence[12] is lost, stolen or damaged the licensee may apply to the licensing authority for a copy[13] and the licensing authority must, on payment of the prescribed fee, grant the application and issue a certified copy of the licence or summary if it is satisfied that the original has been lost, stolen or damaged and that the loss or theft (where that is the basis of the application) has been reported to the police[14]. The copy is to be treated as if it were the licence or summary[15].

If the holder of a premises licence ceases to reside or attend at the address specified in the licence he must as soon as reasonably practicable notify the licensing authority and inform them of a home or business address at which he resides or attends[16]. Regulations may be made requiring the holder of a premises licence to notify the licensing authority of other specified changes of circumstances[17]. Where a change of circumstances notified to the licensing authority falsifies information contained in the premises licence the notification must be accompanied by the licence (or an application for a copy) and the prescribed fee, and the licence must be altered by the licensing authority, or any copy issued on the application must be issued by the authority in a form, so as to reflect the change in circumstance[18].

---

1 GA 2005, s 151(1).
2 GA 2005, s 151(2). See SI 2007/459, regs 20–21 and 24.
3 GA 2005, s 156(1).
4 GA 2005, s 156(3). There are no regulations yet.
5 GA 2005, s 156(4).
6 GA 2005, s 184(1).
7 GA 2005, s 184(3), (4). See SI 2007/479.
8 GA 2005, s 212(1).
9 GA 2005, s 212(2)-(6).
10 GA 2005, s 185(1).
11 GA 2005, s 185(1).
12 Ie given under GA 2005, s 164.
13 GA 2005, s 190(1).
14 GA 2005, s 190(2), (3) and (4) and SI 2007/459, reg 13.
15 GA 2005, s 190(5).
16 GA 2005, s 186(1).
17 GA 2005, s 186(2).

18 GA 2005, s 186(3), (4), (5).

Variation of premises licence

6.171 The holder of a premises licence may apply to the licensing authority to vary the licence by adding, amending or removing an authorised activity, amending another detail of the licence, excluding a default condition or adding, amending or removing a discretionary condition.[1] A licence may not, however, be varied so as to apply to premises to which it did not previously relate.[2] The Gambling Act 2005 (Premises Licences and Provisional Statements) Regulations 2007[3] make provision for variation applications. Regulation 7 states that an application to vary must be in the form specified in Sch 2 and if it is an application to vary the premises plan it must be accompanied by a plan which must show the matters required by an application for the issue of a premises licence. See also regs 12–16 which set out to whom notice of the application must be given, its publication, the period within which representations may be made by an interested party or responsible authority and the manner of making and giving applications/notices. An application for a variation must be accompanied by a statement of the variation sought[4] and also by the licence to be varied or a statement explaining why this is not reasonably practicable and an application for a copy[5]. In granting an application for variation the licensing authority must specify a time when the variation will begin to have effect, and it may make transitional provisions[6].

1 GA 2005, s 187(1).
2 GA 2005, s 187(2).
3 SI 2007/459.
4 GA 2005, s 187(5).
5 GA 2005, s 187(6).
6 GA 2005, s 187(7).

Transfer of premises licence

6.172 A person may apply to a licensing authority for a premises licence to be transferred to him[1]. The application is made in the same way as an application for a new licence except as is provided by GA 2005, ss 188 and 189 and by SI 2007/459, regs 8 and 11 and Sch 3[2]. The differences are noted below. The application must specify the time when the transfer is to take effect and be accompanied by a written statement by the licensee consenting to the transfer[3] though the licensing authority have a discretion to dispense with the latter requirement and to proceed to determine the application without the licensee's consent if the application states that the applicant has failed to contact the licensee having taken all reasonable steps to do so[4]. If the licensing authority decide to dispense with the requirement of the licensee's consent they must themselves take all reasonable steps to notify the licensee[5]. The application for transfer must be accompanied by the licence or a statement explaining why this is not reasonably practicable and an application for a copy[6]. Where the application for transfer is made by an applicant who states that he has failed to contact the licensee any application for a copy of the licence must be made by that applicant and a reference to the licence being lost, stolen or damaged is to be treated as a reference to the licence being unavailable to the applicant for transfer[7]. Notice of the application for transfer need only be given to those responsible authorities mentioned in s 157(a)–(c) and (h)–(i)[8]. Although those responsible authorities will be able to make written representations to the licensing authority on the transfer application no such representations will be able to be made by interested parties[9].

A licensing authority must grant the application for transfer unless they think it would be wrong to do so having regard to representations made by one or more responsible authorities[10]. On granting the application the authority must alter the licence to show the applicant as the licensee and must specify the time when the transfer takes effect (which will be either the time specified in the application or, if later, the time when the application is granted)[11]. The authority may also make such other alterations as appear to be required[12].

An application for transfer of a premises licence may include a request that the licence shall have effect as if the applicant for transfer were the licensee during the period between the receipt of the transfer application by the licensing authority and the determination of the application, and if such a request is made the licence will have effect in those terms[13].

Where, following a competition under GA 2005, Sch 9 (see para **6.163** above), a casino premises licence has been granted subject to a condition which gives effect to a written agreement between the licensee and the licensing authority, the licence may not be transferred unless the transferee enters into an agreement which appears to the licensing authority to have substantially the same effect as the original agreement and the condition is altered to give effect to the new agreement[14].

1 GA 2005, s 188(1).
2 GA 2005, ss 188(2), 189(4).
3 GA 2005, s 188(3).
4 GA 2005, s 189(1).
5 GA 2005, s 189(1)(a).
6 GA 2005, s 189(2).
7 GA 2005, s 189(3).
8 SI 2007/459, reg 12(2).
9 GA 2005, s 189(5).
10 GA 2005, s 188(4).
11 GA 2005, s 188(5)(a), (b).
12 GA 2005, s 188(5)(c).
13 GA 2005, s 189(6).
14 GA 2005, s 188(6).

Termination of premises licences

6.173 As noted (see para **6.169** above) premises licences will be of unlimited duration unless future regulations provide otherwise. A licence may, however, be determined in a number of ways.

Surrender

6.174 The licensee may surrender the licence by notifying the licensing authority of his intention to surrender it and by giving to the authority either the licence or a written statement explaining why it is not reasonably practicable to produce it[1]. The licensing authority must as soon as reasonably practicable after receipt of the notification inform the Gambling Commission, the chief officer of police for any area in which the premises are wholly or partly situated and HMRC[2].

[1] GA 2005, s 192(1).
[2] GA 2005, s 192(2).

Revocation

6.175 Where the licensee fails to pay the annual renewal fee the licensing authority must revoke the licence unless they think that the failure to pay is attributable to administrative error[1].

[1] GA 2005, s 193.

Lapse and reinstatement of premises licence

6.176 Where a premises licence has been issued to an individual the licence lapses if the licensee dies, becomes in the opinion of the licensing authority (as notified to the individual) incapable of carrying on the licensed activities by reason of mental or physical disability, or becomes bankrupt within the meaning of s 381 of the Insolvency Act 1986[1]. In other cases (ie in practice where the licence has been granted to a company) the licence lapses if the licensee ceases to exist or goes into liquidation within the meaning of s 247(2) of the Insolvency Act 1986[2]. Where a licensing authority becomes aware that a premises licence issued by them has lapsed they must as soon as is reasonably practicable notify the Gambling Commission, the chief officer of police for any area in which the premises are wholly or partly situated and HMRC[3]. During the period of six months beginning with the date of the lapse of the premises licence a person may apply to the licensing authority for the licence to be reinstated with the applicant as licensee[4]. The person seeking reinstatement will have to hold a relevant operating licence except in the case of betting premises licences in respect of tracks. The application is made in the same way as is an application for a new licence subject to the differences noted below[5]. The application for reinstatement must be in the form set out in Sch 4 to SI 2007/459[6] and must request that the reinstatement take effect upon the application being granted[7]. It must be accompanied by the licence or by a statement explaining why it is not reasonably practicable to provide the licence, and an application for the issue of a copy of the licence[8] made by the applicant for reinstatement[9]. Any reference in such an application to the licence being lost, stolen or damaged is to be treated as a reference to the licence being unavailable to the applicant for reinstatement[10]. Regulations requiring notice of the application for reinstatement to be given provide that notice need not be given to all responsible authorities but only those set out at s 157(a)–(c) and (h)–(i)[11]. Although responsible authorities will be able to make written representations to the licensing authority on the reinstatement application no such representations will be able to be made by interested parties[12].

The licensing authority must grant the application for reinstatement unless they think it would be wrong to do so having regard to representations made by one or more responsible authorities[13]. On granting the application the licensing authority must alter the licence so that the applicant for reinstatement becomes the licensee, must specify in the licence that the reinstatement takes effect at the time when the application is granted and must make any other alteration of the licence that appears to be required[14]. Where an application for reinstatement is granted the licence has effect as if the applicant for the reinstatement were the licensee during the period beginning with the receipt of the application for reinstatement and ending with the determination of the application[15].

---

1 GA 2005, s 194(1).
2 GA 2005, s 194(2).
3 GA 2005, s 194(3).
4 GA 2005, s 195(1), (2).
5 GA 2005, s 195(3).
6 SI 2007/459, reg 9.
7 GA 2005, s 195(4).
8 GA 2005, s 196(1).
9 GA 2005, s 196(2)(a).
10 GA 2005, s 196(2)(b).
11 GA 2005, s 196(3). See SI 2007/459, reg 12(2).
12 GA 2005, s 196(4).
13 GA 2005, s 195(5).
14 GA 2005, s 195(6).
15 GA 2005, s 196(5).

Review of a premises licence

6.177 The power conferred on the licensing authority to review a premises licence is designed to provide a means by which the authority may, where appropriate, monitor the use made of the premises and may, if necessary, take steps to control that use or even bring the use to an end by revoking the licence. A licensing authority may carry out a review in response to an application for review made to it by a third party who is qualified to apply, or it may carry out such a review on its own initiative.

Application for review

6.178 A responsible authority or an interested party may apply to the licensing authority for a review by the authority of a premises licence[1]. Curiously the statutory provisions do not in terms specify that the premises licence to which the application relates must be one which was granted by the licensing authority to whom the application is made, but this is clearly to be implied. A responsible authority which applies for a review may often be part of the same local authority as the licensing authority, and this raises the prospect of a licensing authority sitting in judgment on an application to review a premises licence which was brought at the instigation of another section of the same local authority. Although the licensing authority would not be an independent and impartial tribunal for the purpose of Article 6 ECHR that requirement should be satisfied by the right of appeal to a magistrates' court so that the procedure as a whole should be Convention compliant. An application must be made in the form and manner prescribed by SI 2007/2258, reg 3 and Sch 1[2] specifying the grounds on which the review is sought and containing or being accompanied by prescribed information or documents[2]. Regulations require the applicant to give notice of the application to the licensee and to the responsible authorities in relation to the premises, and require the local authority to publish notice of the application[3]. The regulations may, inter alia, require a notice to specify a time (28 days) within which the licensee, a responsible authority or an interested party may make representations about the application to the licensing authority[4].

1 GA 2005, s 197(1).
2 GA 2005, s 197(2).
3 GA 2005, s 197(3), (4). See SI 2007/2258, regs 4 and 5.
4 GA 2005, s 197(6). See SI 2007/2258, reg 5(5).

Grant or rejection of application

6.179 A licensing authority may reject an application for review of a premises licence if they think that the grounds on which the review is sought

- do not raise an issue relevant to the principles to be applied in accordance with s 153. This (see para **6.158** above) is the section which lays down the principles to be applied generally by the licensing authority in the exercise of their functions[1];
- are frivolous or vexatious[2];
- will certainly not cause the authority to wish to take action of a kind open to them following a review (ie to revoke or suspend the licence or modify one or more conditions)[3];
- are substantially the same as the grounds specified in an earlier application for review[4];
- are substantially the same as representations made in relation to the application for the grant of, or a variation of, the premises licence.[5].

In the case of the two latter grounds for rejection of the application the licensing authority must consider the length of time that has elapsed since the making of the earlier application for review or since the making of the representations[6]. Where the licensing authority consider that grounds for rejection of the application apply to some but not all of the grounds on which the application for review is made they may reject the application so far as it relates to those grounds but allow it to proceed on the other grounds[7]. If and in so far as the licensing authority do not reject the application for review they must grant the application and proceed to carry out the review[8].

1 GA 2005, s 198(1)(a).
2 GA 2005, s 198(1)(b), (c).
3 GA 2005, s 198(1)(d).
4 GA 2005, s 198(1)(e).
5 GA 2005, s 198(1)(f), (4); s 187(3); s 161.
6 GA 2005, s 198(2).
7 GA 2005, s 198(3).
8 GA 2005, s 199; s 201(1)(a); (2).

Initiation of review by licensing authority

6.180 A licensing authority may carry out two types of review on its own initiative, namely

- a general review of the use made of premises which trade under premises licences of a particular class[1]
- a specific review of the use made of a particular set of premises in reliance on a premises licence.[2]

Again, curiously, the statutory provisions do not specify that these powers may be exercised by the licensing authority only in relation to premises licences which they have themselves granted; this is to be implied. Although the power to conduct both types of review is conferred by GA 2005, s 200 they are very different in their effects. The general review appears designed to authorise the licensing authority to review the functioning of a particular sector of the gambling industry (eg the casino sector, the adult gaming centre sector, the licensed betting office sector) within their area. The authority may review the use made of the premises and in particular the arrangements made by licensees to ensure compliance with conditions attached to the licence[3]. The authority is not obliged to give notice of its intention to conduct such a review and there is no provision for the licensee or anyone else to make representations about it or for any hearing to be held, though in most, if not in all, cases a review of this kind is likely to involve the authority in seeking information from licence holders. The authority is not obliged to publish any findings on completing the review nor is there any power to take any specific steps in the light of the review. Rather the purpose of such a general review appears to be to enable the authority to obtain information. No doubt if a licensing authority concluded that further investigations or steps were required they would consider whether to exercise their powers either to initiate a specific review or reviews of particular premises, or to carry out inspections through their inspectors, who are 'authorised persons' for the purposes of carrying out inspections of gambling premises under Part 15 GA 2005.

As to the second type of review which a licensing authority may initiate, an authority may review any matter connected with the use of premises in reliance on a premises licence if they have reason to suspect that the premises may have been used in purported reliance on a licence but not in accordance with a condition of the licence, or if for any reason (which may relate to the receipt of a complaint about the use of the premises), they think that a review would be appropriate[4]. Before reviewing a premises licence the authority must give notice of their intention to hold the review to the licensee, and they must publish notice of their intention to hold the review[5]. Regulations have been made about the giving and publishing of notice[6], and these in particular require a notice to specify a time (28 days) within which the licensee, a responsible authority or an interested party may make representations about the review to the licensing authority[7].

1 GA 2005, s 200(1).
2 GA 2005, s 200(2).
3 GA 2005, s 200(1).
4 GA 2005, s 200(2)(a), (b).
5 GA 2005, s 200(3).
6 SI 2007/2258, reg 8 and Schs 4 and 5.
7 GA 2005, s 200(5).

Review

6.181 Where the licensing authority have granted an application for a review (see para **6.179** above) or have given notice of their intention to hold a review (see para **6.180** above) they must, as soon as reasonably practicable after the expiry of any period for representations by the licensee, a responsible authority or an interested party[1], review the premises licence[2]. The purpose of the review is to consider whether to take in relation to the licence action of a kind specified in s 202(1) (ie revocation or suspension of the licence or modification of one or more conditions)[3]. The licensing authority is required to hold a hearing unless the applicant for the review (if there is one) and each of the persons who have made representations about the review[4] have consented to the conduct of the review without a hearing[5], or the licensing authority think that each representation made about the review[4] is frivolous or vexatious or will certainly not influence the review[6]. As to the procedure at review hearings, see SI 2007/173.

1 Ie under GA 2005, s 197(6) or s 200(5).
2 GA 2005, s 201(1)(2).
3 GA 2005, s 201(3).
4 Ie under GA 2005, s 197(6) or s 200(5).
5 GA 2005, s 201(4)(a).
6 GA 2005, s 201(4)(b).

Action following the review

6.182 As a result of a review of a premises licence the licensing authority may:

- revoke the licence;
- suspend the licence for a period not exceeding three months;
- exclude a default condition attached to the licence under s 168 or amend an exclusion;
- add, remove or amend a discretionary condition attached to the licence under s 169[1].

The fact that the authority 'may' take one of the above steps shows that a discretion is conferred on them to act or not to act as they see fit. Accordingly a fifth possibility exists, namely that the authority decide not to take any steps at all. In considering whether to take action of one of the four specified kinds following the review the licensing authority must have regard to:

- the matters specified in s 153 (ie the general principles to be applied by the licensing authority in the exercise of their functions under Part 8 GA 2005 – see para **6.158** above);
- any representations made by the licensee, a responsible authority or an interested party;[2]
- any representations made at the hearing of the review (if there is one); and
- where the review is being held in response to an application by a responsible authority or an interested party any grounds specified in the application (apart from any which have been rejected)[3].

A licensing authority may in particular take one of the steps authorised under s 202(1) on the grounds that the licensee has not used the licence[4]. If they do decide to take one of the authorised steps the licensing authority must specify the time at which the action is to take effect.[5]

As soon as possible after completion of a review of a premises licence under s 201 a licensing authority must give notice, which must be in the prescribed form and must give the authority's reasons for their decision,[6] to the licensee, the applicant for review (if any), the Gambling Commission, any person who made representations,[7] the chief officer of police for any area in which the premises are wholly or partly situated and HMRC[8].

1 GA 2005, s 202(1).
2 Ie under GA 2005, s 197(6) or s 200(5).
3 GA 2005, s 201(5).
4 GA 2005, s 202(3).
5 GA 2005, s 202(2).
6 GA 2005, s 203(2). See SI 2007/2258, regs 13 and 14 and Sch 6
7 Ie under GA 2005, s 197(6) or s 200(5).

8 GA 2005, s 203(1).

Provisional statement

6.183 Sections 204–205 of the GA 2005 provide that in certain circumstances a person may apply for a 'provisional statement' from the licensing authority. A provisional statement is not the same as a premises licence but if granted it will in the words of the Explanatory Notes 'offer a degree of certainty to the applicant when he comes to apply for a premises licence'[1]. Despite the fact that there are a number of significant differences the provisional statement in the Gambling Act 2005 is clearly modelled on the 'provisional statement' introduced by the Licensing Act 2003, ss 29–32, though this is widely considered to be one of the least satisfactory innovations of the 2003 Act. For a discussion and critique of the 2003 Act provisions see para **1.334** of this work above. The central criticism of the provisional statement arrangements in the 2003 Act is that they fail to give to a person who is about to engage in construction or development work a sufficient degree of assurance that they will be granted a premises licence under the Act once the works are completed, and are a very poor substitute for the 'provisional licence' provided for by the previous legislation[2] where it was mandatory to declare a provisional licence final provided the works as specified in the deposited plan were satisfactorily completed and the applicant was a 'fit and proper person' to hold a Justices' licence. There is no certainty under the Licensing Act 2003 that the grant of a provisional statement will ensure that a premises licence will be obtained in due course, and the equivalent provisions of the GA 2005 are subject to the same criticism.

A person may apply under the Gambling Act 2005 for a provisional statement in respect of premises that:

- he expects to be constructed;
- he expects to be altered; or
- he expects to acquire a right to occupy[3].

The first two grounds mirror the grounds on which a provisional statement may be granted under the Licensing Act 2003; the third is specific to the Gambling Act 2005.

The application must include such plans and other information in relation to the construction, alteration or acquisition as are prescribed[4]. The Gambling Act 2005 (Premises Licences and Provisional Statements) Regulations 2007[5]set out particular rules in respect of provisional statements. The application is in the form set out in reg 10 and Sch 5. It must be accompanied by a scale plan in accordance with reg 4(2)–(9) as applied by reg 5(3) and (4). Notice of the application must be given to all responsible authorities under s 157 (see reg 12, note the Explanatory Note is incorrect on this point) within seven days; it must contain the information set out in Part 6 of Sch 7. The notice must be published/displayed under reg 12(6) as applied by (7) and (8); the form of the notice must comply with Part 8 of Sch 6. Thereafter, representations by interested persons/the responsible authorities must be made within 28 days (reg 15). Conditions can be attached to any grant (reg 17(3) and (6)). The form and content of a statement must comply with regs 23–26. Otherwise, the provisions of Part 8 of the GA 2005 apply except in the following respects[6]. First, the general rule that a premises licence may not be issued in respect of premises if a premises licence already has effect in relation to the premises (see para **6.153** above)[7] does not apply in relation to an application for a provisional statement[8]. Thus an application for a provisional statement for premises to be used for a casino could be made and granted for premises which currently have a bingo premises licence, though any subsequent application for a casino premises licence would have to be on terms that the bingo premises licence would be surrendered if the casino premises licence was granted. The requirement that an applicant for a premises licence must either hold, or have applied for, an operating licence authorising him to carry on the activity for which the premises licence is sought[9] does not apply to an application for a provisional statement[10], nor does the requirement[11] that the applicant for a premises licence must have a right to occupy the premises apply to an application for a provisional statement[12]. Indeed one of the grounds on which an application for a provisional statement can be made is that the applicant does not have, but expects to acquire, a right to occupy.

No specific direction is made as to the matters which the licensing authority is to take into account in considering whether to grant a provisional statement, but the provisions of s 153 (requiring the licensing authority to aim to permit the use of premises for gambling in so far as they think it in accordance with various stated factors, and requiring them not to have regard to the expected demand for facilities for gambling) will apply to the exercise of this function as it does to the exercise of all their functions under Part 8 GA 2005[13]. The provisions of Part 8 relating to the attachment to premises licences of mandatory conditions (s 167), default conditions (s 168), the exclusion of default conditions (s 169) and the attachment of discretionary conditions (s 169) apply to provisional statements as they do to premises licences[14]. Where a provisional statement is issued in respect of premises and an application is subsequently made for a premises licence in respect of the premises the licensing authority must disregard any representations made in relation to that application unless they think that the representations:

- address matters that could not have been addressed in representations in relation to the application for the provisional statement, or
- reflect a change in the applicant's circumstances[15].

The first ground is potentially wide in scope and would seem capable of applying in particular where there has been a change in circumstances relating to the premises or to the area in which the premises are located[16]. The second ground applies only where there has been a change in the applicant's circumstances (as distinct from a change in the premises or its location). The Explanatory Note gives as an example of such a change the case where the applicant has been convicted of a relevant offence following his application for a provisional statement such that he is now unable to obtain an operating licence[17].

There is likely to be plenty of scope for responsible authorities and interested parties who wish to make representations on the premises licence application to maintain that their representations ought to be admitted under one or other of these heads. The licensing authority may only refuse the application, or may only grant it on terms and conditions not included in the provisional statement,

- by reference to matters which the licensing authority have considered on the basis that they could not have been addressed in representations relating to the application for the provisional statement, or
- by reference to matters which in their opinion reflect a change in the applicant's circumstances[18].

However these limits on the matters which the licensing authority may take into account for the purpose of rejecting the application or changing the terms and conditions on which the provisional statement was granted only apply if the premises have been constructed or altered in accordance with the plans and information included with the application for the provisional statement[19]. Any departure from the plans or information will render the provisional statement irrelevant and will allow the licensing authority to entertain any representations by responsible authorities or interested parties on the licence application, and to consider the application with a discretion wholly unfettered and uncoloured by the grant of the provisional statement. Curiously ss 204–5 make no provision for an application to be made to the licensing authority for consent to modifications of the plans or information lodged with the original application[20] so that where (as is likely to happen often) modifications become necessary after the grant of a provisional statement it appears that a fresh application for a new provisional statement will be required if the applicant wishes to continue to secure the benefits of a provisional statement.

In the case of the Licensing Act 2003 the unattractive features of the provisional statement procedure may well drive applicants to seek to acquire a full premises licence even though the premises are not yet constructed, extended or changed, a course of action which the statutory Guidance issued under s 182 of that Act recognises as possible, at least where clear plans of the proposed structure exist and a clear description can be given of the activities and arrangements proposed there[21]. In the 2008 edition of *Paterson* we made the comment that

> 'Commission Guidance to licensing authorities (see "Guidance to Licensing Authorities –2nd Edition" at para **6.2655**) does not, at Part 11, appear to offer applicants a means of obtaining a premises licence without having to rely upon the provisional statement procedure'.

However the High Court on 14 January 2008 in *R (on the application of Betting Shop Services Ltd) v Southend on Sea Borough Council*[22] ruled that a licensing authority had acted incorrectly in refusing to consider an application for a premises licence even though the relevant premises were incomplete. It rejected a claim that in such a case an applicant could only apply for a provisional statement.

In that case the applicant held an operating licence, had a right to occupy the premises and otherwise complied with s 159. However the premises were not fully constructed (they had walls and a certain amount of the outer structure but were not equipped for gambling) and although it was in possession of a provisional statement as it desired the greater certainty of a premises licence it had decided to apply for such. Trade rivals of the applicant objected and the matter was dealt with as a preliminary issue by the authority. It rejected the application on the basis of paras 7.55–7.57 of the then current Commission's Guidance to licensing authorities and in particular the following words:

> 'The intention behind part 8 of the Act is that the references to "the premises" are to the premises in which gambling may now take place. Thus a licence to use premises for gambling should only be issued in relation to premises that are ready to be used for gambling. This is why the Act allows an operator to apply for a provisional statement if the building is not yet complete, needs alteration, or he does not yet have a right to occupy it.'

Prior to the judicial review hearing the Commission made written submissions to the High Court. In those it conceded that the relevant part of the Guidance might not be correct. The High Court ruled that it was not and that so long as an applicant complied with s 159 he was entitled to apply for a premises licence; that the premises had not been completed did not take away that right. The licensing authority could, if it deemed it appropriate, grant the licence subject to conditions (under s 169) which took account of the fact that at the time of application the premises were incomplete. The Commission has now revised its Guidance in the light of that ruling: see para **6.2655** below, paras 7.61–7.67.

1 GA 2005, Explanatory Note 522.
2 Ie s 6 of the Licensing Act 1964.
3 GA 2005, s 204(1).
4 GA 2005, s 204(3). See SI 2007/459, reg 10 and Sch 5.
5 SI 2007/459.
6 GA 2005, s 204(3). See SI 2007/459, reg 10 and Sch 5.
7 GA 2005, s 152(1)(b).
8 GA 2005, s 204(4).
9 GA 2005, s 159(3).
10 GA 2005, s 204(4).
11 Ie under GA 2005, s 159(5).
12 GA 2005, s 204(4).
13 GA 2005, s 204(2); s 153.
14 GA 2005, s 204(2), s 205(3).
15 GA 2005, s 205(2).
16 Compare Licensing Act 2003, s 32(3)(b).
17 GA 2005, Explanatory Note 523.
18 GA 2005, s 205(3)(a)(b).
19 GA 2005, s 205(4).
20 Contrast Licensing Act 1964, s 6(3).
21 DCMS Guidance issued under s 182 of the LA 2003, para 5.85.
22 [2008] EWHC 105 (Admin).

Appeals

6.184 Where a licensing authority reject an application relating to a premises licence the applicant may appeal to a magistrates' court[1]. Where they grant such an application any person who made representations in relation to the application, or the applicant, may appeal[2]. The right of appeal conferred on the applicant in a case where the application is granted is presumably designed to enable him to appeal against a grant made on terms (eg as to conditions) which he wishes to challenge. The applications in respect of which appeal will lie are applications for a premises licence[3], applications to vary a premises licence[4], applications for transfer of a premises licence[5], applications for reinstatement[6], applications for review of a premises licence[7] and applications for a provisional statement[8]. In addition where a licensing authority takes action as a result of a review[9] by revoking or suspending a premises licence or by modifying conditions attached to it[9] then the licensee, any person who made representations in relation to the review, the person (if any) who applied for the review and the Gambling Commission may appeal to the magistrates' court[10]. In addition where a licensing authority, as the first stage of the two-stage process for determining competing casino premises licence applications under Sch 9 (see para **6.163** above), decides whether it would grant an individual licence application on its merits[11] an appeal lies to the magistrates' court:[12] if the application is rejected the applicant may appeal and if it is granted then any person who made representations in relation to the application and the applicant may appeal[12]. No appeal however may be brought against a determination made by a licensing authority at the second stage[13] of the process to grant one competing application in preference to another or others[14].

GA 2005, Sch 9 also provides for the two stage process applicable to casino premises licences to apply to applications for provisional statements in respect of premises for which it is intended to apply for a casino premises licence[15] if the Schedule would apply to the premises licence application (ie if there would be more applications for premises licences than the licensing authority would have authority to grant[15]). On granting such a provisional statement the licensing authority may provide for it to cease to have effect at the end of a specified period[16] and it may extend that period on the application of the holder of the provisional statement[17]. Where the authority reject an application for extension, or grant such an application, the applicant may appeal to the magistrates' court[18]. There is no provision for the making of representations on such an application and so no appeal lies on the part of any other person[18].

1 GA 2005, s 206(1).
2 GA 2005, s 206(2); s 207(1).
3 GA 2005, s 159.
4 GA 2005, s 187.
5 GA 2005, s 188. In the case of a transfer application an appeal lies both on the grant or rejection of the application and, by the licensee or the applicant for transfer, on the exercise by the licensing authority of its powers to alter the licence on granting the application: GA 2005, s 188(4)(5); s 206(4).
6 GA 2005, s 195.
7 GA 2005, s 197.
8 GA 2005, s 204.
9 Ie under GA 2005, s 202.
10 GA 2005, s 206(3).
11 Ie under GA 2005, Sch 9, para 4(1).
12 GA 2005, Sch 9, para 8; s 206(1)(2).
13 Ie GA 2005, Sch 9, para 5.
14 GA 2005, Sch 9, para 8(4).
15 GA 2005, Sch 9, para 9.
16 GA 2005, Sch 9, para 10(3).
17 GA 2005, Sch 9, para 10(4).
18 GA 2005, Sch 9, para 10(4)(b).

Procedure

6.185 An appeal is instituted by giving notice of appeal to the designated officer of the magistrates' court for a local justice area in which the premises are wholly or partly situated[1]. The appeal must be instituted within 21 days beginning with the day on which the appellant receives notice of the decision against which the appeal is brought[2]. The licensing authority will be the respondent[3] but in appeals brought under s 206 the licence holder (or the applicant in the case of an appeal against the grant of an application for a premises licence) must also be a respondent unless he is the appellant[4].

The magistrates' court may:

- dismiss the appeal;

- substitute for the decision appealed against any decision that the licensing authority could have made;
- remit the case to the licensing authority to decide in accordance with a direction from the court;
- make an order about costs[5].

Where the magistrates' court remit the case to the licensing authority to decide in accordance with their direction any subsequent determination by the licensing authority will be subject to the same appeal process[6]. Any determination or action made by the licensing authority has no effect while an appeal under s 206 could be brought or where such an appeal has been brought and has not yet been either finally determined or abandoned[7]. However a licensing authority making a determination or taking any other action may direct that this suspending provision shall not apply[8] so that the determination or action will have immediate effect; however the magistrates' court determining an appeal against the determination or action may make any order that it thinks appropriate[9] and so may reinstate the suspension in whole or in part for such period as it thinks fit.

The Act gives no guidance as to the procedure to be adopted on the hearing of an appeal or as to the type of appeal which is to be conducted. It does not (in contrast with s 144(4)) provide that in determining an appeal account may be taken of evidence which was not available to the body from whom the appeal lies. Nevertheless it is anticipated that the appeal will take the form of a complete rehearing of the application originally made to the licensing authority with all parties being entitled (and indeed expected) to call evidence on the appeal, including evidence which may differ from, or be additional to, evidence and material put before the licensing authority. Reference to the Committee Debates suggests that this was the Government's intention. Dealing with the powers of the now defunct Gambling Appeal Tribunal, and the magistrates' court on appeal Mr Richard Caborn, Minister for Sport and Tourism, said as follows:

> 'All appeals to the gambling appeals tribunal can be based on law and fact. When a person appeals to the tribunal against a decision taken by the gambling commission, the commission will already have heard the facts of the case. The tribunal will hear those facts again and will also be able to consider any additional evidence that may not have been available to the commission. That means that there are always two opportunities for the facts to be heard. Any onward appeal from the tribunal to the High Court . . . . may be permitted on a point of law only. That is standard practice. Likewise, for appeals to the magistrates' court . . . the court will hear the facts again and will be able to consider any additional evidence that may not have been available to the licensing authority'[10].

Moreover, many licensing decisions will depend on findings of fact and an appeal would probably need to be a re-hearing so that the procedure as a whole can comply with Article 6 of the ECHR. The licensing authority will not constitute an 'independent and impartial' tribunal for the purposes of Article 6. Accordingly a re-hearing on the facts and merits would seem to be required. Any doubts as to whether an appeal to magistrates is by way of rehearing have surely been conclusively answered by the *Hope and Glory* case (see para 8.2 below).

A party to an appeal under s 206 may appeal on a point of law to the High Court[11].

1 GA 2005, s 207(1)(a), (b).
2 GA 2005, s 207(1)(c).
3 GA 2005, s 207(2).
4 GA 2005, s 207(2).
5 GA 2005, s 207(3)(a)–(d).
6 GA 2005, s 207(4).
7 GA 2005, s 208(1).
8 GA 2005, s 208(2).
9 GA 2005, s 208(2).
10 Standing Committee B, 2.12.04 Afternoon Col 346.
11 GA 2005, s 209(a).

PART 9: TEMPORARY USE OF PREMISES

Limited alternative to premises licence

6.190 If the holder of an Operating Licence wishes to use premises for only a temporary period he may, instead of seeking a Premises Licence, use premises to carry on equal chance gaming of a limited nature under the Temporary Use provisions of Part 9 of the Act and the Gambling Act 2005 (Temporary Use Notices) Regulations 2007[1]. Such a notice and the relevant rules are not to be confused with the concept of the occasional use notice exception relevant only to tracks to be found in s 39.

1 SI 2007/3157; GA 2005, s 214.

6.191 Limitations A temporary Use Notice can only currently apply to the following actiivities; the provision of facilities for any form of equal chance gaming where the participants take part (other than by means of a gaming machine) in a competition which is intended to produce a single, overall winner[1]. A Temporary Use Notice is given by the holder of an Operating Licence[2] and must be in the prescribed form[3]. It must specify the activity to be carried on in reliance of the Notice, the premises and the period of time during which the Notice is to have effect as well as the times of day during which the activities will be conducted, any period during the previous twelve months during which a Temporary Use Notice has been in effect at (any part of) the premises, the date on which the Notice is given and any other information to be prescribed by regulations to be made by the Secretary of State[4].

Premises may be the subject of a Temporary Use Notice for no more than twenty-one days in any twelve month period[5]. More than one Temporary Use Notice may be applied for during a twelve month period provided that the aggregate of periods of temporary use do not exceed twenty-one days[6]. If the maximum permitted period will be contravened under a Notice served on the licensing authority, then the licensing authority must serve a counter-notice nullifying the effect of such a Temporary Use Notice[7]. Where a Temporary Use Notice would contravene the maximum permitted period but could have effect for some part of the specified period without such contravention, the licensing authority (in consultation with the person who served the Notice) should give a counter-notice excluding the offending period[8].

1 SI 2007/3157, reg 2.

2 GA 2005, s 215 (cf the much wider class of applicants for a Temporary Event Notice under the Licensing Act 2003).
3 GA 2005, s 216.
4 GA 2005, s 216. Two forms are prescribed depending on whether the premises are part of a vessel or not: reg 3, above.
5 GA 2005, s 218(1). See SI 2007/3157, Sch 1.
6 GA 2005, s 218(2).
7 GA 2005, s 218(3).
8 GA 2005, s 218(4)–(6).

Giving notice

6.192 A Temporary Use Notice (plus a copy) must be served by the holder of the Operating Licence on the licensing authority for the area in which the premises are situated[1] and must be served before the period of three months ending with the day before that on which the Temporary Use Period is due to start[2]. The Notice must be accompanied by the prescribed fee[3] and copies must be provided to the Gambling Commission, the Police and HM Customs within seven days of the date the Notice is given[4].

Where premises are situated in the area of more than one licensing authority, the Notice may be given to either authority, with a copy to the other[5].

The functions of the licensing authority are, under s 232, delegable.

1 GA 2005, s 219(1) (that authority must acknowledge it in writing as soon as is reasonably practicable: GA 2005, s 220).
2 GA 2005, s 219(2).
3 GA 2005, s 219(3). Not to exceed £500 (SI 2007/3157, reg 7).
4 GA 2005, s 219(4).
5 GA 2005, s 219(6).

Objections

6.193 If the licensing authority, or any of the authorities receiving a copy of the Temporary Use Notice, thinks that the Notice should not have effect or should only have effect subject to modification, it may serve a Notice of Objection to the person serving the Temporary Use Notice[1]. This must be in the form prescribed in SI 2007/3157, reg 4, Sch 2. An objector other than the licensing authority, must provide a copy of its objection to the licensing authority[2]. A Notice of Objection and any copy must be served within the period of fourteen days beginning on the date on which the Temporary Use Notice is given and must state the reasons for objecting[3]. A Notice of Objection may be withdrawn, in which case it shall be disregarded[4].

1 GA 2005, s 221(2).
2 GA 2005, s 221(3).
3 GA 2005, s 221(4).
4 GA 2005, s 221(6).

6.194 Hearing objections Where a Notice of Objection is served, the licensing authority must hold a hearing at which representations may be made by the person who gave the Temporary Use Notice, the person who gave the Notice of Objection and any other person entitled to receive a copy of the Temporary Use Notice, unless all those entitled to make representations agree in writing that a hearing is unnecessary[1]. In circumstances where a Notice of Objection has been served, and a hearing has neither taken place nor been dispensed with, the objector may by notice in writing to the person who gave the Temporary Use Notice propose a modification. If the person who served the Temporary Use Notice accepts the modification he may serve a new Notice incorporating the modification and the objection will be treated as withdrawn[2] without prejudice to the right of the other authority upon whom the revised Notice is served to object[3].

1 GA 2005, s 222.
2 GA 2005, s 223(2).
3 GA 2005, s 223(3).

6.195 Counter-notice In circumstances where a Notice of Objection has been given and a hearing has taken place, or been dispensed with, the licensing authority may serve a counter-notice providing that a Temporary Use Notice shall not have effect or shall have effect only in respect of a specified activity and/or during a specified period of time or at specified times of the day, or shall have effect subject to compliance with a specified condition[1]. Such a counter-notice must be in the form to be prescribed by the Secretary of State. It must state the reasons for giving it and contain the relevant prescribed information. It must be given as soon as reasonably practicable. Copies of such a counter-notice must be given by the relevant authority as soon as reasonably practicable to all those persons entitled to receive a copy of the Temporary Use Notice.

1 GA 2005, s 224.

6.196 Dismissal of objections and appeals Where a Notice of Objection has been served and the licensing authority has decided not to serve a counter-notice, the authority must as soon as reasonably practicable give notice of its determination to the giver of the Temporary Use Notice and to the Gambling Commission, the Police and HMRC[1]. In the circumstances where the authority has either given a counter-notice or a determination in response to a Notice of Objection, the person who gave the Temporary Use Notice, or any person entitled to receive a copy of it, may appeal to the magistrates' court for the area in which the premises are situated (or partly situated) by serving a Notice of Appeal within fourteen days beginning on the day in which the appellant receives the Notice on which the appeal is based[2].

Where the licensing authority has determined to allow a temporary use without serving any counter-notice, any appeal should include the person serving the Temporary Use Notice as a respondent together with the licensing authority[3].

On appeal, the magistrates' court may dismiss the appeal or direct the licensing authority to take action of a specified kind or remit the case to the licensing authority with a direction. The court may also make an order as to costs[4]. A party to an appeal may make a further appeal to the High Court on a point of law only[5].

1 GA 2005, s 225.
2 GA 2005, s 226.
3 GA 2005, s 226(5).
4 GA 2005, s 226(6).

[5] GA 2005, s 226(8)

6.197 Endorsement of notice Where a Temporary Use Notice is served on a licensing authority and no objection is received within the fourteen day period, the authority shall endorse the copy and return it to the person giving the Notice as soon as reasonably practicable[1]. If a Notice of Objection has been served then, as soon as reasonably practicable after proceedings on the Temporary Use Notice are concluded and the licensing authority determines not to issue a counter-notice, the authority shall endorse a copy and return it to the person serving the Temporary Use Notice as soon as possible.

[1] GA 2005, s 227.

PART 10: GAMING MACHINES

Introduction

6.210 Part 10 of the Act contains the main gaming machines[1] provisions. However, it interlocks with critical provisions regarding operating, premises and personal licences under Part 5 and Part 8 so must be read in conjunction with those key sections. Part 10 defines 'gaming machine' together with the offences relevant to illegal use or manufacture of a gaming machine.

Manufacture, supply, maintenance, repair, installation and adaptation of a gaming machine (including software) are all regulated activities under this Part.

Part 10 applies to any gaming machine situated in Great Britain, or anything done in Great Britain in relation to a gaming machine, wherever that machine is situated[2]. For example, a gaming machine manufactured in Great Britain, for export to another country, will be covered by the provisions in Part 10. Accordingly, a gaming machine technical operating licence under Part 5 of the Act will be available to manufacturers and suppliers who wish to cater for the overseas market. Such machines need not comply with the categorisation regulations under s 236 if the machines are for export. Machines supplied for use in Great Britain will need to comply with the requirements of Part 10, even if manufactured abroad.

[1] A useful overview of the categories of gaming machines and the numbers permitted in each type of premises is to be found in Part 16 of the Commission's Guide to Licensing Authorities, September 2012 at para **6.2655** below. See also the publications concerning gaming machines at para **6.2520** below.

[2] GA 2005, s 251.

Gaming machine – definition

6.211 Section 235 provides a definition of a gaming machine for the Act. It is significantly broader than the definition of gaming machine in s 26 of the Gaming Act 1968, which the Act repeals and which proved so problematic in the Gaming Board's attempt to address fixed odds betting terminals (FOBTs) and 'internet roulette'. Under the 1968 Act the following machines were regulated under s 26: any machine which was constructed or adapted for playing a game of chance and which had a slot or other aperture for the insertion of money or money's worth.

The new definition accommodates developments in technology which have taken place since the 1968 Act. It also covers a wide range of gambling activities which can take place on a machine, and includes betting on virtual events.

Section 235(1) defines a gaming machine as a machine that is designed or adapted for use by people to gamble (whether or not it can be used for other purposes). The wide definition should be read in conjunction with the broad power of the Secretary of State (under s 6) by regulation to specify that a specific activity shall be treated as a game of chance or a sport[1]. However, the Secretary of State's new powers should mean that, for practical purposes, activities can be caught in the regulatory net simply by the means of further regulations. Subsection (3)(b) contains further detail about how the words 'designed or adapted' are to be interpreted, particularly in relation to a computer.

The ambit of s 235(1) has been recently examined by the High Court[2] when it had to consider whether particular poker machines available for use in public houses were gaming machines.

The only difference between the machines and conventional slot machines was that they had no facility for awarding a prize, the existence and administration of any awarded prize being entirely dependent upon human intervention. Moreover, none of the machines in question informed the player of the potential prize before the game was played or indicated that any prize other than the award of additional credit was available. The machines, further, did not have any means of delivering a prize or documentation that a player was entitled to a prize or of freezing the screen to display any entitlement to a prize before making a claim.

Mr Bird had been convicted of making gaming machines available for use and for maintaining such machines contrary to s 242(1) and s 243(1). The Gambling Commission's case against Mr Bird was that he supplied machines to licensed premises. Customers could play games of chance on the machines and a successful player would receive credits from the machine permitting him to play further games free. Customers in some of the licensed premises to which Mr Bird supplied machines were permitted by the bar staff or the licensee to cash in the credits and were paid prize money from the bar till. Mr Bird denied being aware of these practices and further denied receiving any financial benefit from such arrangements. He appealed to the crown court and, on a preliminary issue his appeal was allowed. The matter then proceeded to the High Court by case stated on the basis of two questions. Firstly, had the crown court been correct to conclude that although the machines were designed or adapted to play a game of chance, they were not designed or adapted to play a game of chance and thereby acquire a chance of winning a prize because:

(a) the machine itself did not inform the player that he would be able to claim a prize; and
(b) the machine did not have a mechanism to deliver a prize or to provide a document evidencing the right to claim a prize and therefore was not a gambling machine within the meaning of the Act;

and second, on the facts found were the machines gaming machines within the meaning of the Gambling Act 2005.

The court rejected the Crown Court reasoning for allowing the appeal; it said that the lower court had mistakenly attached importance to the fact that the machines:

(a) did not deliver a prize;
(b) nor a piece of paper or a certificate to be exchanged for a prize;
(c) did not indicate that a prize might be awarded.

It had also thought it important that 'the prize was dependent on human intervention'. The High Court pointed out that the statutory question did not require any of those elements. It decided that the machines were designed for use to play a game of chance for a prize. They were 'recognisably capable of being used to generate a chance upon which a prize might be awarded'. In reaching that decision the Court laid down a number of principles and made observations which should help in a wider context. First 'the machines in question . . . are gaming machines because they were designed with a view to use in playing a game of chance for a prize.That characteristic derives from the nature of the game, the way in which the machine enables it to be played and the nature of the outcome, whose only likely possibility was the awarding of some prize'. Second, it was stated that 'also' in the phrase 'whether or not it can also be used for other purposes' in s 235(1) had the effect 'that although the machine may be used for other purposes, its design or adaptation is in the first instance directed to gaming . . .'.

Finally, it considered an argument that the ambit of that subsection was, if literally applied, so wide that it would encompass an iPhone or even a pinball machine. Re the iPhone, it rejected any claim that it might be a gaming machine as it is not designed or adapted to be used 'in games of chance for a prize'. Although software can be uploaded onto an iPhone so that such a game as Joker Poker can be played, the machine itself was not designed with a view to that use and loading software does not amount to adapting it.

It also expressed a non-conclusive view that an ordinary pinball machine would not fall within s 235(1) because it is designed with a view to amusement.

---

1 GA 2005, s 6(6).

2 *R (Gambling Commission) v Bird* [2010] EWHC 995 (Admin).

Skill machines

6.211A Skill machines are not gaming machines under the Act. Skill machines are unregulated by the Act's provisions. No gambling under s 3 occurs on such a machine, accordingly it is not used by people to gamble as required by s 235(1). However, if a machine advertises itself as offering a skill game but in fact is designed to look and offer recognised games of chance, such as roulette or bingo, then the element of chance will cause the machine to fall within s 235(1). Moreover, it seems that if a compensation or control mechanism operates in such a way that an element of chance is introduced into the way the game is played, that can cause what would otherwise be a skill machine to become a gaming machine; see para **6.2634** below for a Commission document of July 2009 discussing these issues.

Exceptions

6.212 Subsection (2) of s 235 sets out a number of exceptions to sub-s (1) which ensure that the gaming machine definition does not capture certain specified types of machine.

Unlike requirements under the 1968 Act, the definition at sub-s (1) does not depend on any concept of players depositing payments into the machine via a slot, or on the gambling activity being generated from within the machine itself (as opposed to being transmitted to the machine from other equipment, such as a remote number generator).

The following are not gaming machines:

- **A domestic or dual-use computer which can be used for participating in remote gambling.** These are defined in the Gambling Act 2005 (Gaming Machines) (Definitions) Regulations 2007[1] (and see also the Gambling Commission publication on dual-use computers at para **6.2634.2** below). A domestic computer is one which is capable of being used for a purpose that is not related to gambling, is located in a private dwelling and is used on a domestic occasion. The definition of a dual use computer is much more complex. It must be capable of being used for a purpose not related to gambling and either (i) it is not knowingly adapted or presented by or on behalf of its owner or a person connected with him in such a way as to facilitate or to draw attention to the possibility of its use for gaming or (ii) if it is so adapted or presented (a) its availability is restricted to private use or is intended to be so or (b) it is being adapted, maintained or repaired but its use is restricted to persons using it in connection with its adaptation, maintenance or repair in certain circumstances which are too complex/opaque to summarise here.
- **Remote gambling (other than a computer).** The fact that a telephone or interactive television can be used to participate in gambling will not of itself render the equipment a gaming machine[2]. This exception does not apply to computers.
- **A machine which is designed or adapted for betting only on future real events.** This exemption is designed to prevent equipment, such as automated betting terminals, through which people place bets on real, not virtual, events, from being counted as gaming machines. The event must be a future event at the time the machine is used, meaning that betting on pre-recorded activities, where the result is already known, is not exempt. The exempt equipment is not unregulated. Explanatory Note 581 makes it clear that making it available as part of a business will be providing facilities for betting, and will require the relevant operating licences under the Act. However, in regulatory terms, these machines are not to be treated as gaming machines[3].
- **A machine upon which someone enters a lottery.** If a machine only dispenses lottery tickets or vends lottery paper scratchcards, then the machine is outsides the definition of a gaming machine so long as the machine does not (a) determine the result of the lottery, and (b) does not announce that result unless the prescribed interval (at least 1 hour[4]) has elapsed between the sale of the ticket and the announcement of the result. In no circumstances can the machine determine the result of the lottery[5].

- **A machine for playing bingo which is used by the holder of a bingo operating licence, in accordance with conditions attached by the Commission**[6]. This is designed to exempt what is known as 'mechanised cash bingo' equipment which is used for playing real bingo games, but whose degree of computerisation or mechanisation means that it would otherwise be caught by the definition of gaming machine.
- **A machine for playing bingo prize gaming which is used by the holder of a gaming machine general operating licence** (for an adult gaming centre or a family entertainment centre), in accordance with conditions attached to those licences by the Commission[7]. This is designed to exempt equipment used for playing real prize bingo, in accordance with the terms of Part 13 of the Act. Note, however, that a question mark remains over the effectiveness of the drafting of Part 13.
- **A machine for playing bingo prize gaming which is used by an unlicensed family entertainment centre or pursuant to a prize gaming permit, in accordance with any Commission code of practice.** This exemption is similar to that at sub-s (2)(g), but applies to different types of operator who have prize gaming rights under Part 13[8].
- **A machine which is used for playing manual games of chance.** This is a machine which:
  - — is controlled or operated by someone employed to do so (eg a croupier spinning a roulette wheel); or
  - — is used in connection with a real game of chance which is controlled or operated by an individual (eg a computer terminal for staking on the outcome of a roulette wheel that is spun by a croupier)[9].

  In these situations the equipment could be characterised as a gaming machine under the definition, but the fact that it is operated as part of a real game of chance means that it is not to be regulated under the gaming machine provisions. Such equipment and activities will be regulated under Parts 5 and 6 of the Act by the Gambling Commission and under Part 8 by Local Authorities.
- **A machine which is used for playing automated games of chance in a casino**[10]. This was one of the Government's concessions to the UK casino industry made at the last minute of the Parliamentary session in order to facilitate the Act's passage. This is equipment used for playing a real game of chance, pursuant to a casino operating licence, but which has no human involvement from the organisers of the casino game, and which is not linked to a game which does have such human involvement. For example, apparatus such as a roulette wheel which is completely mechanised, and works without the need for any croupier to rotate the wheel, spin the ball or accept stakes. This equipment is not a gaming machine provided it is used in accordance with Commission licence conditions[11].

These various exemptions seek to prevent the broad definition of gaming machine from unintentionally capturing equipment. The definition in sub-s (1) is intended to cover a gaming machine that is used for taking part in virtual gaming, virtual betting or a virtual lottery (where the draw is part of the activity determined by the machine).

Subsection (3) provides clarification about the characteristics of a gaming machine. Reference to part of a gaming machine includes computer software to be used in a gaming machine, but does not include a component of a gaming machine which does not influence the outcome of the gambling[12]. This means that where a gaming machine technical operating licence is required for the manufacture, installation etc of gaming machines, computer software intended for use in the machine is included within the licensing requirement. However, the machine casing material such as chip board and glass in which the machine mechanism is contained is not included in this requirement. References to installing part of a gaming machine include installing computer software[13]. This is required because machines can be configured or changed by the downloading of gambling software, without any need to physically interfere with the machine.

Under s 235(5), the Secretary of State has made regulations[14] which state that if a single piece of apparatus is a gaming machine and is made available for use to more than one person at a time then it is to be treated as the number of gaming machines equal to the number of people able to use it at that time. This position is of some significance. Using bingo premises as an example, we know[15] that the operator can make up to a certain number of category B machines (in sub-categories B3 and B4 only) available for use. Should a machine be playable by two players at the same time it will count as two machines, thereby restricting how many other machines can be lawfully in place (the number is no more than 20% of all machines on the premises).

---

1 SI 2007/2082.
2 GA 2005, s 235(2)(b).
3 GA 2005, s 235(2)(c).
4 SI 2007/2495.
5 GA 2005, s 235(2)(d), and see also the Gambling Commission publication of August 2012 'Comparing lottery ticket dispensers and category B3A gaming machines' available on the Commission's website.
6 GA 2005, s 235(2)(e).
7 GA 2005, s 235(2)(f).
8 GA 2005, s 235(2)(g).
9 GA 2005, s 235(2)(h).
10 GA 2005, s 235(2)(i).
11 GA 2005, s 174(6).
12 GA 2005, s 235(3)(c).
13 GA 2005, s 235(3)(d).
14 The Gaming Machine (Single Apparatus) Regulations 2007, SI 2007/2289.
15 See s 172(7)(a) as amended and SI 2007/2158, reg 6(3).

Gaming machines: Categories A to D

6.213 The Categories of Gaming Machines Regulations 2007[1], made under s 236, define the four machine categories (and divides category B into five sub-categories) by reference to maximum charges for use and maximum prize values.

Further provisions are contained in the Gaming Machine (Circumstances of Use) Regulations 2007[2], made under s 240. These set out detailed rules about the display of certain types of information on machines, methods of payment, the nature of prizes available, payment limits, autoplay, residues and delivery of prizes.

When considering the limits placed by either set of regulations on prizes, it is also important to take into account s 343, particularly s 343(3); this permits exchange of prizes so long as the final prize value does not exceed the aggregate of those prizes given in exchange.

1 SI 2007/2158, as amended by SI 2009/1502, effective 10 June 2009.
2 SI 2007/2319.

6.214–6.219 In June/July 2007, the Commission issued a number of detailed machine standards documents together with machine standards definitions: see paras **6.2520–6.2580** below.

Offences

6.220 Making machine available for use The primary offence of making a gaming machine available for use unlawfully is set out in s 242[1]. An offence is committed if a person makes any gaming machine available for use unless:

- He holds an operating licence which permits such use;
- He holds a family entertainment centre permit;
- He holds a club gaming permit or a club machine permit under Part 12;
- He has appropriate permission for alcohol licensed premises under Part 12;
- He makes gaming machines available at a travelling fair as permitted by Part 12, or;
- The machine offers no, or a limited, prize (as defined in Part 10).

Under Part 3 of the Act it is a separate offence for a person to use premises for making a gaming machine available for use without the necessary authorisation or exemption, such as a premises licence or a Category D gaming machine permit. It will also be an offence under this section to make a gaming machine available for use if the machine does not comply with regulations made by the Secretary of State under s 240.

1 According to a Commission publication of December 2007 a machine is only made available for use if it can be played. See para **6.2632** below and para 16.25–16.30 of the Guidance to Licensing Authorities, September 2012 at para **6.2655** below.

6.221 Manufacture, supply etc Section 243 stipulates that various activities concerning the manufacture or supply[1] of a gaming machine must also be regulated. Under Part 5 of the Act, gaming machine technical operating licences are available for those wishing to manufacture, supply, install, adapt, maintain or repair a gaming machine. Failure to hold such an operating licence, when undertaking any of these activities, is an offence under this section.

Exceptions apply:

- for those holding a single machine supply and maintenance permit;
- for machines exempted by regulations under s 248(2) (no prize);
- where the activities relate to a gaming machine that is for scrap; or
- where the supply is incidental to the sale or letting of a property.

This means that no operating licence is required where a machine is being broken up and no further use is made of it for gaming machine purposes, and where the machines are ancillary to the sale of a business which uses gaming machines. Any use, after sale, will continue to be subject to the other requirements of the Act.

The supply or installation of gaming machines is currently subject to the restriction that it is unlawful if the machine is designed or adapted to permit money to be paid by means of a credit or debit card[2].

---

1 No exchange occurs when a machine is part exchanged, according to advice published by the Commission in December 2007.

2 The Gaming Machine (Supply etc) Regulations 2007, SI 2007/2320. Note, SI 2007/2321 has repealed s 245.

6.222 Linked machines It is an offence, under s 244, for gaming machines to be linked[1] so that they operate together, and the value of the prize available on one machine is determined to any extent by use of the other machine. There is one exception to this, which is that sub-s (2) permits machines to be linked at licensed casino premises provided that all of the machines are situated on the same premises. Linkage of gaming machines in this way does not authorise casino licensees to offer maximum prizes in excess of those allowed for the category of machine being used.

No linking between licensed casino premises is permitted, but sub-s (3) gives the Secretary of State power to lift this prohibition, subject to appropriate Parliamentary approval.

---

1 See also the Commission's publication 'Machine Standards Linked Progressives', June 2007: see para **6.2560** below.

Exceptions to offences

6.224 Family entertainment centre permits (Category D only) Section 247 provides an exception to ss 37 and 242 in respect of machines which are made available for use under a FEC gaming machine permit. Such permits allow gaming machines to be made available for use without an operating or premises licence. They relate only to the lowest category of machine ie D. If an FEC wished to use Category C and D machines, it would require an appropriate operating and premises licence, under Parts 5 and 8 of the GA 2005.

Only premises which are wholly or mainly used for making gaming machines available for use may hold an FEC gaming machine permit. This is a change from the position prior to the Act, when any premises could apply for a permit allowing them to use an 'amusements with prizes' gaming machine (the nearest equivalent to a Category D machine). The intention is that gaming machines in certain non-gambling premises, like those previously sometimes located in, for example, fish and chip shops, should be removed. This is consistent with the Government's attempt to do away with 'ambient gambling'. Schedule 10 sets out the procedures for the application for and grant of an FEC gaming machine permit by licensing authorities, ie local authorities. It also regulates the permit's form[1] and maintenance. Provision is made for the licensing authority to maintain a register of permits issued. Permits cannot be issued to vessels or vehicles.

Under paragraphs 6–10, the authority may prepare a statement of its principles in respect of the issue of these permits, and this can include matters which they propose to take into account in considering the suitability of an applicant. In exercising its functions under Sch 10, including determining any application, the authority may have regard to the licensing objectives but must have regard to any guidance issued by the Commission. There is clearly scope for inconsistency between discretion exercised by the Commission and local authorities. The authority must consult the local police prior to granting an application.

Paragraph 11 concerns the form and content of permits. Under paragraphs 12 to 21, permits will normally last 10 years, but will lapse if the holder ceases to occupy the premises, dies, becomes unfit to hold the licence or becomes bankrupt or insolvent. The notes relating to prize gaming permits under Part 14 expand upon the meaning of 'occupy' for these purposes. Lapsed permits may, however, remain in force for up to six months. This is to allow an orderly transfer of the affairs of the licence holder, and the maintenance of the business (with its machines) while a new permit is obtained. Permits cannot be transferred, but must be re-applied for if there is a new occupier of the premises to which the permit relates.

Holders may surrender their permits voluntarily, and a court may order forfeiture of a permit if the holder is convicted of any relevant offence (see s 126). Permits can be renewed[2], and a licensing authority may only refuse the application for renewal if access to the FEC by an authorised officer has been refused without reasonable excuse, or renewal would not be reasonably consistent with pursuit of the licensing objectives.

There is an appeal mechanism provided for those who wish to contest a decision of a licensing authority under this Schedule.

1 See SI 2007/454, reg 4 and Sch 1.
2 See SI 2007/454, reg 3(c).

6.226 No and limited prizes Even if a gaming machine is made available for use where no relevant licence or permit exists, this does not invariably mean than an offence has been committed, for ss 248 and 249 state that:

- where a person using a machine has no opportunity to win a prize, whether or not he pays for use of the machine (s 248), no offence is committed. However, if a prize (as defined in s 239) is available, a machine is a gaming machine, even if there is no payment required to use it;
- where a person (whether they pay for use of the machine or not) has the opportunity to win only a limited prize as follows:
  - — solely another opportunity to play the machine (ss 248 and 239); or
  - — a prize whose value does not exceed any payment made for use of the machine (s 249),

  no offence is committed.

The definition of such a payment is broad (s 249(2)), and this includes payments which entitle someone to use a machine eg entrance charges to premises where machines are located. Section 343 contains powers for the Secretary of State to make rules about how to determine the value of a prize[1].

The Secretary of State may make regulations which exempt certain gaming machines from the licensing requirements for manufacture, supply, etc (s 248(2))[1].

1 None have been made yet.

6.227 Single-machine supply and maintenance permits Under s 250 an exception exists to the general rule that a person who supplies, etc, a gaming machine must hold a gaming machine technical operating licence. The Commission may issue a permit in relation to a specific gaming machine that authorises its supply, repair, installation, or maintenance without an operating licence. A fee is payable for the permit[1].

The Commission can only grant a single-machine permit if it believes that the supply etc, of the machine will not have any impact on the licensing objectives. This permit procedure replaces the permits issued by the Gaming Board under s 27 of the Gaming Act 1968, to individuals outside the gaming business who have single machines which they wish to dispose of, or repair.

Regulations under s 248(2) could also be used to deal with circumstances where obtaining a permit was considered an onerous obligation for the particular activity concerned, and the gaming machine was not designed or expected to be used in a manner which permitted it to deliver prizes.

1 See SI 2006/3284.

PART 11: LOTTERIES

Introduction

6.240 A lottery[1] is defined in Part 1 of the Act[2].

Under the provisions of s 14 an arrangement is either a simple lottery (if persons are required to pay in order to participate in the arrangement in the course of which one or more prizes are allocated by a process which relies wholly on chance) or a complex lottery (if persons are required to pay in order to participate in the arrangement in the course of which one or more prizes are allocated but where there are a series of processes to determine the outcome and the first of these relies wholly on chance). Schedule 2 makes provision about the circumstances in which an arrangement is or is not to be treated as requiring payment to participate. These circumstances include paying money, transferring money's worth and paying for goods or services at a price or rate which reflects the opportunity to take part in the arrangement. Schedule 2 also identifies circumstances in which sending a letter by post, or making a telephone call or using any other method of communication, does not constitute making a payment. The Schedule confirms that requiring a payment to discover whether a prize has been won, or requiring a payment to take possession of a prize also constitutes payment to participate in the arrangement.

Section 14(5) identifies processes which, in relation to a lottery arrangement, are to be treated as relying wholly on chance even if some exercise of skill or some display of knowledge is involved.

It should be noted that, notwithstanding the foregoing definitions, s 14(7) empowers the Secretary of State by Regulations (approved by both Houses of Parliament under the provisions of s 355(4)) to provide that any kind of arrangement is or is not to be treated as a lottery. The Secretary of State is also empowered (by such Regulations) to amend both s 14 and Sch 2.

Part 11 of the Act (in conjunction with Schs 2 and 11) sets out the arrangements for regulating lotteries in Great Britain.

Section 98 sets out the ground rules for the grant of a lottery operating licence and s 99 the mandatory conditions attached to such a licence.

1 See the Commission's publications Lotteries and the Law', May 2007 at para **6.2300** below), 'Lotteries – What do we mean by 'lotteries'?' at para **6.2350** below and 'Prize Competitions and Free Draws' and 'Running prize competitions and free draws', May and December 2009, at paras **6.2089–6.2090** and **6.2094** below.

2 GA 2005, s 14 and see para **6.14** above.

Promoting a lottery

6.241 A person promotes a lottery if he makes, or takes part in making, arrangements for a lottery[1]. In particular a person is deemed to be promoting a lottery if he makes arrangements for the printing of lottery tickets or for the printing of promotional material or if he arranges for the distribution or publication of promotional material or if he possess promotional material with a view to its distribution or publication. A person also promotes a lottery if he makes any other arrangements to advertise it or if he invites participation in it, or sells or supplies (or offers to sell or supply) lottery tickets, or if he possesses a lottery ticket with a view to its sale or supply or indeed if he does or offers to do anything by which a person becomes a members of a class among whom lottery prizes are to be allocated[2]. A person is also deemed to be promoting a lottery if he uses premises for the purposes of allocating prizes in, or for any other purposes connected with the administration of, a lottery[3]. For the purposes of these prohibitions 'promotion material' is defined as any document which advertises or invites participation in, or contains information about how to participate in, a specified lottery or which lists winners in a specified lottery[4].

An external lottery manager is defined as one who makes arrangements for a lottery on behalf of a society or authority of which he is not a member or an officer or an employee[5]. Where arrangements for a lottery are made by such an external lottery manager on behalf of a society or authority then both that manager and the society or authority are deemed to be the promoters of the lottery[6].

A lottery ticket may be either a document or an article so long as it confers, or can be used to prove membership of a class for the purposes of allocating prizes in a lottery[7]. A lottery ticket is deemed to be sold or supplied if something is done as a result of which a person becomes a member of a class among whom prizes in a lottery are to be allocated; thus it is not always necessary for there to be a physical lottery ticket in the hands of the participant[8].

It can therefore be seen that promoting a lottery is very widely defined, as is the concept of a lottery ticket. This is clearly deliberate and is intended to include electronic tickets and other arrangements which may not be in the traditional format.

1 GA 2005, s 252(1).

2 GA 2005, s 252(2).

3 GA 2005, s 252(2).

4 GA 2005, s 252(3).

5 GA 2005, s 257.
6 GA 2005, s 252(4).
7 GA 2005, s 253(1)
8 GA 2005, s 253(3).

Interpretation

6.242 The 'proceeds' of a lottery are defined as the total amount paid for tickets. Its 'profits' are the proceeds less deductions for prizes less both any funds which are 'rolled over' to another lottery and also any other costs reasonably incurred in organising the lottery[1]. The Act allows rollovers to certain lotteries (other than the National Lottery) and defines a rollover as an arrangement under which a prize not allocated or claimed in one lottery will increase the value of prizes available for allocation in another lottery[2]. As a consequence it is necessary to identify the two lotteries in question, especially where a single lottery may operate with more than one draw. Thus if prizes are to be allocated by means of more than one draw those draws together will constitute a single lottery only if the class of entrants among whom prizes can be allocated remains the same for both draws. If not then each draw is a separate lottery[3]. 'Draw' is in turn defined as the process by which a lottery prize is allocated, even if not a draw in the traditional sense[4].

1 GA 2005, s 254.
2 GA 2005, s 256(1).
3 GA 2005, s 256(2).
4 GA 2005, s 255.

Offences

6.243 The promotion of a lottery is unlawful unless it is specifically permitted under the Act. So to be lawful a lottery must either be one which is promoted in accordance with an operating licence issued under ss 98 and 99[1] or the lottery must be an exempt lottery[2].

No offence is committed by anyone who acts on behalf of the holder of an operating licence and in accordance with the terms and conditions of that licence and it is also a defence for a person charged with the unlawful promotion of a lottery to show that he reasonably believed that it was an exempt lottery or that it was being promoted pursuant to an operating licence[3]. Of course, if the defendant is able to show that the arrangement was not a lottery at all that also provides a defence[4]. Although the National Lottery as such is not regulated by the Act, the Act does provide that no offence is committed if a defendant shows that he reasonably believed that arrangements in which he was involved related to a lottery forming part of the National Lottery[5].

It is also an offence to *facilitate* a lottery not permitted under the Act[6]. The concept of 'facilitating' is wider than that of promotion but only covers a situation where a person prints lottery tickets for a specified lottery or where he prints promotional material for a specified lottery or where he advertises a specified lottery and that lottery is not permitted, ie it is neither exempt nor is it promoted in accordance with an operating licence[7]. Again 'promotional material' is widely defined to cover a document which advertises a specified lottery or which invites participation in a specified lottery or which contains information about how to participate in, or lists winners in, a specified lottery[8]. But since the offence of facilitating a lottery applies only to a specified lottery no offence is committed by someone who, for example, prints draw tickets which could be used in lotteries generally.

The same defences discussed above in relation to the promotion of a lottery are also available to a defendant accused of unlawfully facilitating a lottery, namely that the lottery was exempt or was being promoted pursuant to an operating licence, that there was no lottery at all or that the arrangements to which the charge relates form part of the National Lottery[9].

The Act introduces the offence of misusing the profits of a lottery which is being promoted lawfully under the Act[10]. Where a lottery is being promoted under an operating licence and the promoter has advertised or stated on the lottery tickets, that the proceeds will be used for a particular purpose an offence is committed if the proceeds are used for something else[11].

For these purposes 'advertisement' specifically includes, but is not limited to, any written notice which announces that the lottery will take place or which invites participation[12]. In those exempt lotteries where there are restrictions on the purposes for which the lottery can be promoted (which are discussed below but which comprise incidental non-commercial lotteries, private society lotteries and small society lotteries) an offence is also committed if the proceeds are wrongly used[13].

A non-commercial society (defined in s 19[14] as a society established and conducted for charitable purposes or for purposes enabling participation in, or for the purposes of supporting, sport, athletics or a cultural activity, or which is established and conducted for any other non-commercial purpose other than private game) commits an offence if it promotes a small society lottery without the necessary registration with the local authority or if it does not comply with the procedures for submitting returns to that authority[15].

1 GA 2005, s 258(2).
2 GA 2005, s 258(1).
3 GA 2005, s 258(4).
4 GA 2005, s 258(4)(b).
5 GA 2005, s 258(4)(c).
6 GA 2005, s 259(1).
7 GA 2005, s 259(2).
8 GA 2005, s 259(5).
9 GA 2005, s 259(4).
10 GA 2005, ss 260 and 261.
11 GA 2005, s 260(2).
12 GA 2005, s 260(5).
13 GA 2005, s 261(2).
14 See also the Commission's publication, December 2007, 'Lottery guidance for charity trading companies and sporting clubs: Gambling Act 2005' (para **6.2351** below).
15 GA 2005, s 262.

6.243A The ambit of s 19 was discussed in *R (on the application of Camelot UK Lotteries Ltd) v Gambling Commission*[1], a decision of the Divisional Court. In this rolled-up hearing of Camelot's application to proceed with its claim for judicial review, with the substantive hearing to follow if permission were granted, it was claimed that the Commission had erred in law in granting lottery licences to 51 non-commercial societies set up as Community Interest Companies ('CICs') which had common directors and an external lottery manager ('ELM') which promoted the Health Lottery on behalf of the CICs. Each week at least one CIC ran a lottery draw with additional CICs joining in as more tickets were sold. Matters were arranged to prevent any CIC from exceeding the £4 million threshold for a single lottery set out in s 99(3)(a). The matters central to Camelot's claim were that the CICs were established and conducted for the purpose of private gain to the ELM in breach of s 19 and further that the Health Lottery was in reality a breach of the restrictions set out in s 99. The court rejected each of these claims (and, indeed, found that Camelot had inexcusably delayed bringing its claim for a period of thirteen months). It found that s 19 'focuses on the non-commercial society and not on those who work for it or who are employed by it or contracted by it to provide services . . . ' Accordingly the payments it makes to its officers and employees is not a private gain within s 19(1) as is recognized by s 19(3). An ELM is not required by the Act to be non-profit making although its profits are controlled under s 254. The fact that it makes profits does not cause the non-commercial society which contracts with it to be in breach of s 19(1). It also found that each weekly lottery was separate from others and that there was no basis for aggregating their proceeds. The thresholds in s 99(3) had not been exceeded.

1 [2012] EWHC 2391 (Admin).

Territorial application

6.244 Section 265 provides that Part 11 of the Act only applies to anything done in relation to a lottery in Great Britain or by means of remote gambling equipment[1] which is itself situated in Great Britain. Section 265 further limits the territorial application of Part 11 by providing that it does not regulate any lottery if the only participants are outside Great Britain and there is no person in Great Britain possessing tickets for the lottery with a view to selling or supplying them to a person, thereby causing him to become a participant[2]. Section 265(3) provides a defence to ss 258/259 where the defendant can show that he reasonably believed that Part II did not and would not apply by reason of s 265(3).

1 Defined in GA 2005, s 36(4) and (5).
2 GA 2005, s 265(1) and (2).

Permitted lotteries

6.245 A lottery promoted in Great Britain will be unlawful unless it is either run in accordance with an operating licence issued under Part 5 of the Act or it is an exempt lottery under Sch 11. The arrangements for the issue of operating licences for the promotion of lotteries are discussed above. However Sch 11 identifies the categories of exempt lotteries as being incidental non-commercial lotteries, private lotteries, customer lotteries and small society lotteries (that is to say, society lotteries which are small in that they do not generate sufficient proceeds to require to be promoted under an operating licence but can be promoted pursuant to the registration of the society in question with a local authority; it is the lottery which is small, not the society).

These exempt lotteries, which may well be of significant charitable and commercial importance, are addressed in turn.

6.246 Incidental non-commercial lotteries A lottery is exempt if it is promoted incidentally to a non-commercial event which event is itself not run for, and at which nothing is raised for the purposes of, private gain[1]. Nothing can be deducted from the proceeds other than amounts (prescribed by the regulations[2] made by the Secretary of State) for the cost of prizes and for the cost of organising the lottery. It is only these prescribed sums which can be deducted regardless of the actual cost of the prizes or the actual cost of organising the lottery[3]. The incidental non-commercial lottery must, as with the non-commercial event to which it is incidental, be run other than for private gain, and there can be no rollover, and tickets must only be sold, and the results announced, at the connected event and only while that event is taking place[4].

It is this exemption which will allow the traditional raffle or draw to be held at events such as a traditional village fete or a charitable dance, but it will be necessary to ensure that the strict rules are observed and that nothing is raised by way of private gain (either during the connected event or in the promotion of the lottery itself), and also that the prescribed limits on the cost of prizes and amount of expenses are observed.

There is nothing to require that the ticket must be a physical document (as may be customary) and the wide definition of a lottery ticket[5] would permit non-documentary tickets to be sold.

1 GA 2005, Sch 11, paras 1 and 2.
2 See SI 2007/2040: a maximum of £500 is allowed for the cost of prizes and £100 for organising costs.
3 GA 2005, Sch 11, paras 3 and 4.
4 GA 2005, Sch 11, paras 5—7.
5 GA 2005, s 253.

6.247 Private lotteries Under Part 2 of Sch 11 private lotteries are further sub-divided into 'private society lotteries', 'work lotteries' and 'residents' lotteries'. Thus:

- **A private society lottery** is one promoted only by authorised members of a society (defined to mean any group or society established and conducted for purposes not connected with gambling)[1] in which tickets are sold only to members of the society itself or are sold on premises wholly or mainly used for the administration of the society or the conduct of its affairs[2].

  Advertisements for a private society lottery may only be displayed or distributed on the society's own premises and must not be sent to any other premises. Tickets must be in documentary form and can be sold or supplied only by or on behalf of the promoters and no such ticket (nor the right to take part in the lottery which it confers) is transferable[3]. Furthermore all tickets must be sold at the same price for payment in full (no credit is allowed) and must state the name and address of each of the promoters and must specify those to whom the tickets can be sold or supplied and must explain that the tickets (and the chances represented by them) are not transferable[4]. The promotion of a private society lottery must be authorised in writing by the society, or, if it has one, by its governing body[5]. Where a society has branches or sections each is deemed to be a 'society' for the purposes of operating a private society lottery[6].

A private society lottery must be promoted only for one of the purposes which the society is conducted[7] and there can be no rollover[8].

- **A work lottery** is one where the promoters work on a single set of premises and where tickets are sold or supplied only to those who also work on those premises. However an individual is deemed to work on premises if he is employed to work at or from the premises or if he undertakes work at or from the premises, or conducts a business at or from the premises, even if he is not physically there[9]. The reference to a 'single set of premises' would seem to indicate that it is not necessary that the promoters and the entrants are all working at (or from) the same physical building or address. A work lottery must be organised in such a way as to ensure that no profits are made and this would prohibit the promotion of a work lottery for the purpose of giving the profits to a charitable cause[10]. Advertisements for a work lottery may only be displayed or distributed on the work premises themselves and must not be sent to any other premises[11]. The restrictions on, and the requirements as to, tickets and the prohibition of rollovers which apply to a private society lottery apply equally to a work lottery.
- **A residents' lottery** can be promoted by those who live (or habitually reside, even if there are other premises where they also habitually reside) in the same residential premises[12]. A residents' lottery must be promoted to ensure that no profits are made and again this would prohibit the promotion of a residents' lottery for the purpose of giving the profits to charity[13]. No advertisement of a residents' lottery can be displayed other than on the residential premises themselves and such advertisements cannot be sent to other premises[14]. The restrictions on, and the requirements as to, tickets and the prohibition of rollovers which apply to private society lotteries and to work lotteries also apply to a residents' lottery.

---

1 GA 2005, Sch 11, para 10(2).
2 GA 2005, Sch 11, para 10(1).
3 GA 2005, Sch 11, para 14 and para 15 and para 16.
4 GA 2005, Sch 11, para 17 and para 18.
5 GA 2005, Sch 11, para 10(3).
6 GA 2005, Sch 11, para 10(4).
7 GA 2005, Sch 11, para 13(1).
8 GA 2005, Sch 11, para 19.
9 GA 2005, Sch 11, para 11.
10 GA 2005, Sch 11, para 13(2) and see also GA 2005, s 254.
11 GA 2005, Sch 11, para 14(2).
12 GA 2005, Sch 11, para 12.
13 GA 2005, Sch 11, para 13(2).
14 GA 2005, Sch 11, para 14(3).

6.248 Customer lotteries For the first time the Act introduces a new concept of a customer lottery. This is a lottery where the promoter occupies business premises in Great Britain and where tickets (which must be in documentary form)[1] are sold or supplied only to a customer who is physically present on those business premises[2].

No profits can be made in a customer lottery[3] and since no advertisement for it can be displayed or distributed outside the business premises (or sent to any other premises)[4] it is clear that the purpose of the customer lottery is solely to encourage loyalty among and to reward customers of the promoter.

As with a private lottery, tickets in a customer lottery cannot be transferred[5]. Each ticket must state the name and address of the promoter as well as specifying those to whom the promoter is willing to sell or supply tickets and that it is not transferable[6]. The price must be shown on the ticket and must be paid in full, so no credit can be given[7]. For each customer lottery the maximum prize (in money or money's worth or partly in one and partly in the other) cannot be more than £50 and there can be no rollover[8]. At any one business premises there can only be one draw during each seven day period but there is no reason why more than one customer lottery cannot be operated at the same time from those premises so long as this restriction is observed[9].

1 GA 2005, Sch 11, para 23.
2 GA 2005, Sch 11, para 20.
3 GA 2005, Sch 11, para 21.
4 GA 2005, Sch 11, para 22.
5 GA 2005, Sch 11, para 24(2).
6 GA 2005, Sch 11, para 25.
7 GA 2005, Sch 11, para 26. This would prohibit the sale of tickets by credit card.
8 GA 2005, Sch 11, paras 27 and 28.
9 GA 2005, Sch 11, para 29.

6.249 Small society lotteries Part 4 of Sch 11 sets out the procedure under which a small society lottery is exempt and can therefore be promoted without the need for the promoter to hold an operating licence.

A small society lottery can only be promoted wholly on behalf of a non-commercial society[1] and it must satisfy all of the following conditions[2]:

- the arrangements must be such that the proceeds cannot exceed £20,000;
- the society must not raise proceeds of more than £250,000 from society lotteries promoted by it wholly or mainly in any one calendar year;
- the arrangements for the promotion of the lottery must ensure that there is no potential that the promoting society raises proceeds of more than £250,000 in a calendar year;
- the promoting society cannot already have promoted a large lottery (ie one which does not meet these requirements) during the same calendar year or during any of the preceding three calendar years;
- the lottery must be promoted only for the purposes for which the promoting society is conducted;
- at least 20% of the proceeds must be applied for those purposes[3];
- no participant must win (in money or money's worth or partly in one and partly in the other) more than £25,000[4].

The arrangements for a small society lottery may include a rollover from one such small society lottery to another so long as both are promoted by the same society and so long as the maximum prize limit of £25,000 is maintained[5].

Paragraph 36 of Sch 11 requires that a ticket in a small society lottery must be in documentary form, identifying the promoting society, stating the price of the ticket and the name and address of the society member designated by the society to have responsibility for the promotion of the lottery or, if there is one, the name and address of the external lottery manager. The ticket must also state the date of the draw (or of each draw) or must be worded so that the participant can determine the date on the which the draw will take place[6]. Despite the requirement that the small society lottery ticket must be in documentary form it is permissible for such ticket to be sold electronically so long as the participant can either retain the message electronically (for example by saving it on his personal computer) or it can be printed[7]. Thus a ticket in a small society lottery could be purchased on a personal computer so long as there are facilities enabling the participant to print it, but entry through a shared use personal computer from which there can be no printing, or on which the participant cannot retain the ticket electronically, would not qualify.

The price for each ticket must be the same and, since no credit can be given, it must be paid at the time it is allocated[8]. There can be no hidden charge for entry into a small society lottery other than payment of the price[9].

To promote a small society lottery the non-commercial society must register with a local authority in accordance with Part 5 of Sch 11 and must remain registered throughout the period during which the lottery is promoted[10]. The registration procedure is discussed below[11] and in addition the society must adhere to the requirements for the filing of records (which are set out in para 39 of Sch 11) and it must do this within the strict time limits provided.

Paragraph 55 of Sch 11 sets out the obligations of the local authority in relation to information which is supplied to it by societies registering and the rights of members of the public to inspect that information.

1 Defined in GA 2005, s 19.
2 GA 2005, Sch 11, para 31 and para 32.
3 GA 2005, Sch 11, para 33.
4 GA 2005, Sch 11, para 34.
5 GA 2005, Sch 11, para 35.
6 GA 2005, Sch 11, para 36(1).
7 GA 2005, Sch 11, para 36(2). This would prohibit the sale of a ticket by credit card.
8 GA 2005, Sch 11, para 37(1).
9 GA 2005, Sch 11, para 37(2).
10 GA 2005, Sch 11, para 38.
11 See para **6.250** below.

6.250 Registration with local authority Although the Act permits the promotion of a small society lottery without the need for the issue of an operating licence by the Gambling Commission, it sets out in Part 5 of Sch 11 the procedure by which a promoting society must be registered with the local authority. In England the authority in question is the District Council, County Council (where there is no District Council) or London Borough Council (or the Common Council of the City of London or the Council of the Isles of Scilly) for the area in which the principal premises of the society are located. In Wales it means the County Council or the County Borough Council and in Scotland the Licensing Board established under s 1 of the Licensing (Scotland) Act 1976[1].

The Secretary of State has prescribed the form in which the application for registration must be made, including the purposes for which the society is conducted[2]. Once the application is lodged, the local authority must enter the name of the society (along with such information as the Secretary of State may also prescribe) in a register to be kept for this purpose and the authority must notify the society that it is registered. It is also required to notify the Gambling Commission of such registration[3]. The Gambling Commission is also obliged to record such registration[4].

The local authority may only refuse an application for registration if, in the preceding five years:

- an operating licence held by the applicant society has been revoked under s 119(1) of the Act; or
- an application for an operating licence by the society has been refused[5].

However the local authority also has a discretion (after allowing the society an opportunity to make representations)[6] whether or not to grant an application for registration if it considers that:

- the application for registration is not made by a non-commercial society; or
- somebody who will, or may, be connected with the promotion of the lottery has been convicted of one of the offences listed in Sch 7 of the Act (or a similar offence committed outside the United Kingdom); or
- the applicant society has provided false or misleading information.

Once registration is granted the society must pay an annual fee of such amount as the Secretary of State will prescribe[7].

The local authority is empowered to revoke a registration if it considers that it would be obliged or permitted to refuse an application for that registration were it being made anew, so long as the authority first gives to the society an opportunity to make representations[8].

An appeal to the magistrates' court lies from the decision of the local authority to refuse to register a society or to revoke a registration. Notice must be given within 21 days from the day on which the society is notified of the refusal or revocation[9]. On the appeal the magistrates' court may affirm or reverse the local authority's decision or make any other order (including a transitional provision)[10].

1 GA 2005, Sch 11, para 41.
2 GA 2005, Sch 11, paras 42 and 56, and see SI 2007/2328.
3 GA 2005, Sch 11, para 44.
4 GA 2005, Sch 11, para 45.
5 GA 2005, Sch 11, para 47.
6 GA 2005, Sch 11, paras 48 and 49.
7 GA 2005, Sch 11, para 54.
8 GA 2005, Sch 11, para 50.
9 GA 2005, Sch 11, para 51.
10 GA 2005, Sch 11, para 51(3).

6.251 Additional restrictions In addition to the requirements for the operation of exempt lotteries set out in Part 5 of Sch 11, the Act (in Part 6 of Sch 11), gives to the Secretary of State wide power to impose new obligations in relation to the delivery of tickets in exempt lotteries, as well as power to impose conditions or limitations in respect of rollovers[1]. The Secretary of State is also empowered to impose additional restrictions on those who may sell or supply exempt lottery tickets, on those who may buy them, on the circumstances in which they are permitted to be sold or supplied, on the nature of the lottery tickets themselves and as to the information to appear on them, as well as the arrangements for advertising exempt lotteries and the deductions which promoters may lawfully make from the proceeds[2]. The Secretary of State is given an even more sweeping power to restrict, by order, the extent to which activities may be carried on in reliance on the exemptions set out in Sch 11 and in particular is given power to restrict the number of lotteries (whether incidental non-commercial lotteries, private society lotteries, work lotteries, residents' lotteries, customer lotteries or small society lotteries) which any one individual or society can promote within a specified period[3]. The Secretary of State can also prescribe a minimum interval between the promotion of any one lottery and another but before making any such order the Secretary of State must first consult the Gambling Commission[4]. Finally the Secretary of State is given power, by order, to vary any of the monetary amounts or percentages provided for in Sch 11 so that any of the figures or percentages set out above can be varied[5].

1 GA 2005, Sch 11, paras 57 and 58
2 GA 2005, Sch 11, para 59.
3 GA 2005, Sch 11, para 59(3) and (4).
4 GA 2005, Sch 11, para 59(5).
5 GA 2005, Sch 11, para 60.

6.252 Interpretation Part 7 of Sch 11 to the Act includes, in relation to the promotion of exempt lotteries, a very wide definition of advertisements specifically extending them to include any document or electronic communication announcing that a lottery will take place or inviting the public to take part[1].

1 GA 2005, Sch 11, para 61.

PART 12: CLUBS, PUBS AND FAIRS

6.260 Part 12 of the GA 2005 regulates gaming and gaming machines in clubs and alcohol licensed premises, and also at travelling fairs. It does not extend to betting[1] or lotteries.

1 See the Commission's document of April 2008 re betting in pubs and clubs at para **6.2672** below.

Clubs; gaming and gaming machines

6.261 There are three categories of club: members' clubs; commercial clubs; and miners' welfare institutes[1]. The latter are treated separately because they are subject to a specific management regime.

Both members' and commercial clubs must have at least 25 individual members, and be established permanently[2]. A members' club must also be managed by and for the benefit of the members[3]. While clubs must ordinarily be 'established and conducted wholly or mainly for purposes other than the provision of facilities for gaming' it is possible for a club to be established wholly or mainly for conducting gaming of a prescribed kind (bridge and whist) so long as no other gaming is carried on (a 'gaming club')[4]. This is intended, according to the explanatory notes[5] to allow for a bridge or whist club where the game is played for stakes, but there seems no reason why it should not extend to other games such as backgammon or mah-jongg.

Equal chance gaming as defined in Part 1 of the Act[6] is permitted in clubs and miners' welfare institutes subject to prescribed limitations on the amount of stakes (generally £10 maximum)[7], prizes (up to £250 for poker)[8] and entry fees (these vary from £1–£20)[9]. The club may not take any part of the stake[10]. In the case of members' clubs, a person must have been a member for 48 hours before participating in gaming, or be a bona fide guest of a member[11]. The gaming must be confined to one set of premises, so there can be no linked games.[12]

For the purposes of the Act, a member must have had a previous acquaintance with their guest and must not invite the guest to the club or institute only to enable the guest to use the gambling facilities provided[13].

A game is linked if it is played partly on one set of premises and partly on another. Two games will also be linked if the result of one game is or may be wholly or partly determined by reference to the result of the other game, or the amount of winnings in one game is or may be wholly or partly determined by reference to the amount of participation in the other game[14].

The exemption for equal chance gaming in clubs and institutes is also subject to regulations which prescribe different limits on stakes, prizes and participation fees dependent upon the different types of club or institute, types of game and types of fee[15].

A members' club or miners' welfare institute may apply for a club gaming permit (although again a gaming club will be limited to its specific gaming activity)[16]. The effect of a permit is to allow up to three gaming machines of classes B (sub-categories B3A and B4 only), C or D[17], and also additional gaming, in the form of unlimited stakes equal chance gaming and also prescribed games of chance[18]. Under the previous legislation pontoon and chemin de fer were prescribed. This has been continued under the Act[19]. The general public, and children and young persons, must be excluded from those parts of the premises where such gaming is carried on[20], and no participation fee may be charged, or levy or deduction made from stakes by or on behalf of the operator of the club or the provider of the gaming facilities except in accordance with regulations made for the purpose[21]. The maximum daily net fee is £3[22].

Any club gaming permit which is granted must be made subject to three conditions. The first condition requires that persons participating in gaming in reliance on the permit must have been members of the club or institute, or applied or have been nominated for membership, at least 48 hours before participating[23]. Alternatively persons may be guests of such a member[24]. The second condition prohibits persons under 18 years of age from using a category B or C machine[25] and the third condition stipulates that the holder of the club gaming permit must comply with any relevant Gambling Commission code of practice made under s 24 of the Act, concerning the location and operation of a gaming machine[26].

A club machine permit may be obtained by a members' club, commercial club or miners' welfare institute[27] again authorising up to three machines of categories B (sub-categories B3A and B4 only), C or D[28], but not allowing the high stakes equal chance gaming or any other facilities for gaming authorised by a club gaming permit. In a members' club (but not a commercial club) or a miners' welfare institute any club machine permit which is granted must be made subject to the condition that persons may only use gaming machines if they have been members of the club or institute, or were nominated for membership, at least 48 hours before use, or are guests of such a person[29]. In all three types of club, a club machine permit must also be granted subject to the conditions that no person under 18 years of age shall use a category B or C machine[30] and that the holder of the permit must comply with any relevant code of practice made under s 24 of the Act, relating to the location and operation of a gaming machine[31].

Club gaming permits and club machine permits are granted in accordance with Sch 12 by the licensing authority[32]. The application must be made in prescribed form to the licensing authority, together with prescribed supporting information and a fee[33]. A copy of the application must be sent to the Commission and the chief officer of police within 7 days; they can object in accordance with the procedure set out in SI 2007/1834, reg 9[34]. A permit must be refused if the applicant is not a qualifying club or miners' welfare institute[35], or if the premises are mainly used by children or young persons[36]. An application may also be refused if the applicant has a previous gaming related conviction, has breached a condition of a permit, or a previous permit has been cancelled within the past 10 years or there are objections from the Commission or the police[37]. Where the applicant holds a club premises certificate for the sale of alcohol there is a fast track procedure under which the Commission and police may not object save in limited cases[38] A permit lasts for 10 years, unless it lapses, is surrendered, cancelled or forfeited[39]. A fast track permit lasts indefinitely as long as the club premises certificate remains in force[40]. Permits are subject to the payment of a £50 annual fee[41]. Failure to pay the annual fee will result in a Permit being cancelled unless due to an administrative error[42].

Where a Permit requires renewal the application for renewal must be made not earlier than three months and not later than six weeks before the date on which the Permit is due to expire[43]. It should be noted that there is no provision for a renewal application to be made after the latest date due to inadvertence equivalent to the procedure relating to registration under Part III of the Gaming Act 1968[44]. Variation of a permit can be obtained[45].

---

1 GA 2005, ss 266–268. See also the Gambling Commission publication of October 2010 on members' clubs and commercial clubs at para **6.2569** below.

2 GA 2005, s 266(1)(c), (d) and s 267(1)(b), (c).

3 GA 2005, s 266(1)(b).

4 GA 2005, s 266(2) and s 267(2). See SI 2007/1942.

5 GA 2005, Explanatory Note 676.

6 GA 2005, s 8 and see the Commission's Code of Practice on equal chance gaming in clubs and pubs, March 2012 (para **6.2673** below).

7 GA 2005, s 269(2)(a). See SI 2007/1944, reg 2.

8 GA 2005, s 269(2)(b). See SI 2007/1944, reg 3.

9 GA 2005, s 269(4). See SI 2007/1944, regs 4 and 5.

10 GA 2005, s 269(3).

11 GA 2005, s 269(6).

12 GA 2005, s 269(5).

13 GA 2005, s 270(6).

14 GA 2005, s 270(5).

15 GA 2005, s 270. See SI 2007/1944.

16 GA 2005, s 271(2)(a). See also 'Gaming Machine Permits Code of Practice – Club Gaming Permits and Club Machine Permits – Alcohol Licensed Premises Permits and Permissions, June 2007' at para **6.2660** below.

17 GA 2005, s 271(3)(a). See SI 2007/2158, reg 6(4).
18 GA 2005, s 271(3)(b), (c).
19 GA 2005, Explanatory Note 684. See SI 2007/1945 (blackjack is not included).
20 GA 2005, s 271(4)(c), (d).
21 GA 2005, s 271(4)(a), (b).
22 SI 2007/1945.
23 GA 2005, s 271(6)(a).
24 GA 2005, s 271(6)(b).
25 GA 2005, s 271(7)(a).
26 GA 2005, s 271(7)(b) and see fn 16 re Commission Code of Practice.
27 GA 2005, s 273(2)(a).
28 GA 2005, s 273(2). See SI 2007/2158, reg 6(4).
29 GA 2005, s 273(3).
30 GA 2005, s 273(4)(a).
31 GA 2005, s 273(4)(b) and see fn 16 re Commission Code of Practice.
32 See SI 2007/1834, regs 4, 5, 8(1), 12 and 17.
33 GA 2005, s 274(1).
34 GA 2005, Sch 12, para 3(1). See SI 2007/1834, reg 7.
35 GA 2005, Sch 12, para 6(1)(a).
36 GA 2005, Sch 12, para 6(1)(b).
37 GA 2005, Sch 12, para 6(1)(c)–(e).
38 GA 2005, Sch 12, para 10. See SI 2007/1942, reg 3.
39 GA 2005, Sch 12, paras 17–19 and 21–23.
40 GA 2005, Sch 12, para 17(2).
41 GA 2005, Sch 12, para 14. See SI 2007/1834, regs 12–14.
42 GA 2005, Sch 12, para 22.
43 GA 2005, Sch 12, para 24 (2)(a), (b). See SI 2007/1834, regs 6 and 8(2).
44 GA 1968, Sch 7, para 4 (2)(a).
45 GA 1968, Sch 7, para 15.

Alcohol licensed premises; gaming and gaming machines.[1]

1 See the Commission's Code of Practice at para 6.2660 below.

6.262 Premises (other than a vehicle)[1] with an on-premises alcohol licence[2] and containing a bar at which drinks are served to customers may conduct permitted gaming at the times when alcohol is authorised to be sold[3]. Restaurants with no bar facility are therefore excluded.

Equal chance gaming for stakes (no more than £5) and prizes (maximum £100 for poker), with no levy on or deduction from stakes or prizes by or on behalf of the operator of the premises, with no participation fee or linking to other premises and where children and young persons are excluded from participation is automatically permitted[4]. Under the 1968 Act dominoes and cribbage were automatically permitted, and other games, such as backgammon, could be specifically authorised; these are now, in principle, within the automatic permission[5].

Alcohol licensed premises are automatically entitled to two category C or D gaming machines[6], provided that written notice is given to the licensing authority and the prescribed fee of £50 paid[7].

Application may also be made pursuant to Sch 13 for a licensed premises gaming machine permit in order to provide additional Category C or D gaming machines. There is no statutory limit on the number which may be applied for[8]. There is an application fee and an annual fee for the permit[9]. The application is made in the prescribed form to the licensing authority[10]. The authority may grant the application as made, or for a lesser number of machines, or reject it[11]. No conditions may be attached[12]. In considering whether to grant the permit the licensing authority must take into account the licensing objectives[13], any guidance issued by the Commission under s25, and such other matters as they consider relevant[14].

If the licensing authority is minded to refuse a permit, or to grant it otherwise than as applied for it must give notice to the applicant (unless the refusal is on the grounds that the applicant does not hold an on-premises alcohol licence[15]) and give the applicant the opportunity to make representations, which may be written or oral[16].

The permit will be in a prescribed form[17], and must be kept on the premises[18] and produced on demand by an authorised person[19]. It is an offence to fail to do so[20]. The licensing authority may issue a replacement for a lost, stolen or destroyed permit[21].

The permit will cease to have effect if the premises and/or the holder cease to have an on-premises alcohol licence[22], or the holder surrenders it[23].

The permit may be cancelled if the annual fee is not paid[24], and may be cancelled or varied if the licensing authority considers that it is not reasonably consistent with the licensing objectives for the permit to remain in effect[25], gaming has been undertaken otherwise than in accordance with the permit[26], the premises are mainly used or to be used to make gaming machines available[27], or an offence under the Act has been committed on the premises[28]. The Schedule appears to indicate that the power also arises in relation to gaming in breach of a condition of the permit[29], but this is inconsistent with para 5(1) which prevents the imposition of conditions. If the licensing authority is minded to cancel or vary a permit it must give notice to the holder and give the holder the opportunity to make representations or hold a hearing, in accordance with procedures to be prescribed[30].

There is a right of appeal to the magistrates' court against refusal, grant otherwise than as applied for, cancellation or variation of a permit[31]. A cancellation or variation shall not take effect until the time for appeal has expired, or the dismissal of the appeal, whichever is later[32].

Where a permit holder or the officer of a permit holder is convicted of a relevant offence[33] the convicting court may forfeit the permit and order its delivery up[34]. Forfeiture takes effect from the date of the order[35].

A permit may be transferred if application is made at the time that a transfer of the on-premises alcohol licence is applied for[36].

All gaming machines provided in alcohol licensed premises must be operated in accordance with any code of practice issued by the Gambling Commission under s 24 of the Act concerning the location and operation of gaming machines[37]. Where a club gaming permit or a club machine permit is in force for the premises, it will regulate the availability and use of gaming machines rather than the provisions applying to alcohol licensed premises[38].

There is power for a licensing authority to withdraw the automatic entitlements on defined grounds and subject to an obligation to grant a hearing[39]. There is a right of appeal to a magistrates' court[40].

1 GA 2005, s 278(1).
2 GA 2005, s 278(1)(a).
3 GA 2005, s 278 (1)(c).
4 GA 2005, s 279. See SI 2007/1940, regs 2 and 3 and the Commission publication of July 2009: Poker in Pubs (para **6.2674** below).

[5] GA 2005, Explanatory Note 708.
[6] GA 2005, s 282(1).
[7] GA 2005, s 282(2). See SI 2007/1832.
[8] GA 2005, Sch 13, para 15(1).
[9] GA 2005, Sch 13, para 9(1)(b). For fees see SI 2007/1833, regs 3, 5 and 7.
[10] GA 2005, Sch 13, paras 1, 2.
[11] GA 2005, Sch 13, para 4(2).
[12] GA 2005, Sch 13, para 5(1).
[13] GA 2005, Sch 13, para 4(1).
[14] GA 2005, Sch 13, para 4(1).
[15] GA 2005, Sch 13, para 6(1).
[16] GA 2005, Sch 13, para 6(2)(b)–(3).
[17] GA 2005, Sch 13, para 7(1). See SI 2007/1833, reg 4.
[18] GA 2005, Sch 13, para 8.
[19] GA 2005, Sch 13, para 10(1).
[20] GA 2005, Sch 13, para 10(2).
[21] GA 2005, Sch 13, para 11. See SI 2007/1833, reg 9.
[22] GA 2005, Sch 13, para 13.
[23] GA 2005, Sch 13, para 14.
[24] GA 2005, Sch 13, para 17(1).
[25] GA 2005, Sch 13, para 16(1)(a).
[26] GA 2005, Sch 13, para 16(1)(b).
[27] GA 2005, Sch 13, para 16(1)(c).
[28] GA 2005, Sch 13, para 16(1)(d).
[29] GA 2005, Sch 13, para 16(1)(b).
[30] GA 2005, Sch 13, para 16(2).
[31] GA 2005, Sch 13, para 21(1)–(2)(a).
[32] GA 2005, Sch 13, para 16(4).
[33] GA 2005, Sch 13, para 18(1).
[34] GA 2005, Sch 13, para 18(4).
[35] GA 2005, Sch 13, para 19(1).
[36] GA 2005, Sch 13, para 18(3).
[37] GA 2005, ss 282(3) and 283(3).
[38] GA 2005, s 282(4).
[39] GA 2005, s 284(1)–(3).
[40] GA 2005, s 284(5)–(6)(a).

Bingo

6.263 There are special rules for bingo, which apply *mutatis mutandis* both to clubs[1] and alcohol licensed premises[2]. While small scale bingo is permitted under the automatic entitlement[3], if 'high turnover bingo' is offered, then a bingo operating licence[4] under Part 5 is required[5], although there is no requirement to have an officer or manager who is a personal licence holder[6].

'High turnover bingo' is bingo where the stakes or prizes exceed £2,000 in a seven-day period[7]. One such occurrence triggers a 'high turnover period' lasting for 12 months (inclusive of the seven day trigger period)[8], and if high turnover bingo is offered in the high turnover period an offence is committed if a bingo operating licence has not been obtained[9]. It should be noted that the first, or triggering, occurrence is not an offence, although it does create an obligation to notify the Commission[10]. This obligation does not arise if a bingo operating licence is already held[11]. In principle therefore a club or alcohol licensed premises could offer an annual high turnover bingo event (eg at Christmas) without needing a bingo operating licence, although the obligation to notify the Commission would arise.

1 GA 2005, s 275.
2 GA 2005, s 281.
3 GA 2005, ss 269, 271 and 279.
4 GA 2005, s 65(2)(b).
5 GA 2005, ss 275(1) and 281(1).
6 GA 2005, s 80(9).
7 GA 2005, ss 275(2) and 281(2).
8 GA 2005, ss 275(3)–(4) and 281(3)–(4).
9 GA 2005, ss 275(7) and 281(7).
10 GA 2005, ss 275(6) and 281(6).
11 GA 2005, ss 275(6) and 281(6).

Travelling fairs

6.264 A travelling fair is one held on a site which has been used in whole or part for the provision of a fair on no more that 27 days during the current calendar year[1], consists wholly or principally of the provision of amusements[2] and is provided wholly or principally by persons who travel from place to place to provide fairs[3].

Gaming machines of category D[4] may be made available at travelling fairs[5]. There is no explicit restriction on the number permitted, but the provision of facilities for gambling (including but not limited to gaming machines) must amount to no more than an ancillary amusement at the fair[6].

1 GA 2005, s 286(b)(ii).
2 GA 2005, s 286(a).
3 GA 2005, s 286(b)(i).
4 GA 2005, s 236 and see SI 2007/2158, reg 3.
5 GA 2005, s 287(a).
6 GA 2005, s 287(b).

PART 13: PRIZE GAMING

Introduction

6.270 The provisions of Part 13 of the 2005 Act (ss 288–294) relate to prize gaming. Prize gaming is defined at s 288 as gaming in which neither the nature nor the size of the prize played for is determined by reference to the number of players or the amount paid for or raised by the gaming. This means that the operator must determine the prize *in advance* of the game, although '[t]his does not stop operators from estimating what money will be raised from gaming, or predicting the numbers who will take part. Its purpose is to stop the actual amounts raised in a particular game being used to determine the prize in that particular game'[1].

Where there is already in place an appropriate authority for gaming generally, there is no need to seek further authority for prize gaming under Part 13[2]. Part 13 has its origins in s 21 of the Gaming Act 1968 and s 16 of the Lotteries and Amusements Act 1976. Its provisions, together with regulations made under them, ensure that prize gaming is confined to gaming which is considered to be relatively harmless and, consequently, requires less stringent regulation than gaming generally.

The scheme of Part 13 is to set out the circumstances in which prize gaming may take place legally, and therefore without the commission of an offence under either s 33 or 37 of the 2005 Act (providing facilities for gambling or using premises for gambling). The flowchart below provides an overview of the provisions of Part 13.

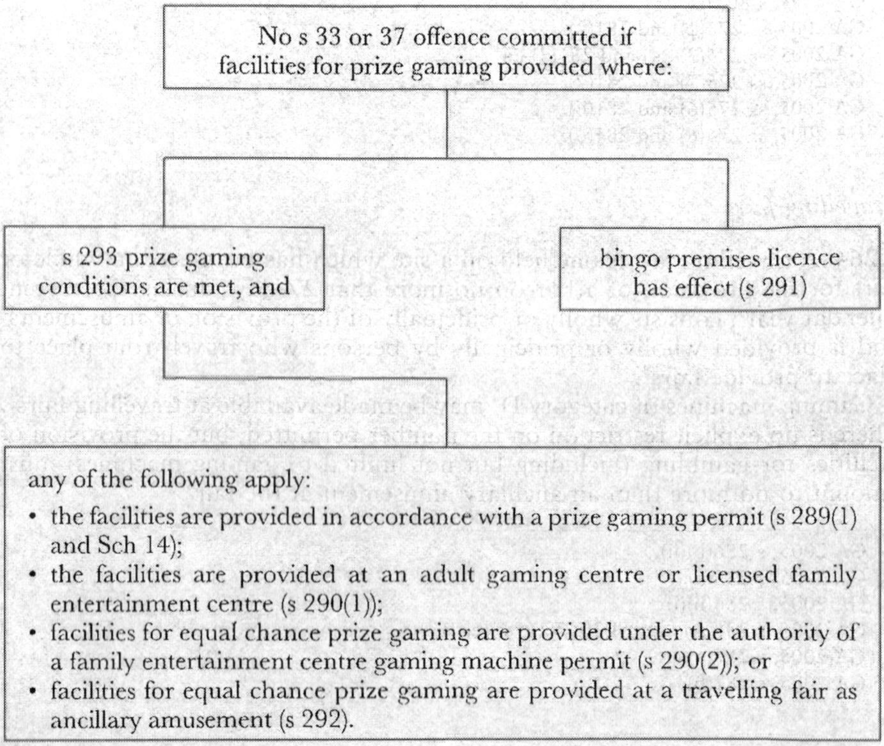

[1] GA 2005, Explanatory Note 731.
[2] See GA 2005, Explanatory Note 726.

Prize gaming conditions

6.271 Section 293 provides the basis for the conditions that must be met before facilities for prize gaming may be provided legally under Part 13 (other than in the case of bingo halls, which are considered below). Section 293 and regulations to be made pursuant to s 293 prescribe four conditions for prize gaming. The first condition limits the level of the participation fees that may be charged to £1 individually and £500 in total in a single game[1]. The second condition ensures that facilities for a particular game are provided, the game in question is played and its results are announced all on the same premises and in the course of a single day. The third condition limits the value of prizes (whether monetary or non-monetary) that may be offered to £70; the aggregate for a game cannot exceed £500[2]. Finally, the fourth condition prohibits any link from the gaming in question to further gambling of any description. 'In other words, the prize gaming must be free-standing and self-contained'[3].

1 SI 2009/1272, reg 2.
2 SI 2009/1272, reg 3.
3 GA 2005, Explanatory Note 746.

Prize gaming permits

6.272 No s 33 or 37 offence will be committed where facilities for prize gaming are provided at specified premises under the authority of a prize gaming permit issued by a licensing authority under s 289 and Sch 14. Such gaming will also have to be in compliance with the prize gaming conditions. No prize gaming permit may be issued to a child or young person (ie those under 18)[1] although a child or young person may participate in equal chance prize gaming (but not other forms of prize gaming)[2].

Schedule 14 sets out the procedures governing prize gaming permits, which are similar in certain respects to those governing family entertainment centre gaming machine permits[3].

An application for a prize gaming permit must be made to the licensing authority in whose area the specified premises are wholly or partly located, by the person who occupies or proposes to occupy them[4]. The form of the application will be set by the authority, in compliance with the relevant provisions of Sch 14[5]. A licensing authority may prepare a statement of principles governing the exercise of its functions in respect of prize gaming permits. Whilst the authority need not have regard to the licensing objectives when dealing with such permits, it must take account of the Gambling Commission Guidance, issued to local authorities under s 25[6].

There will be little point in applying for a prize gaming permit for a venue in respect of which a premises licence or club gaming permit has effect because the licence or permit should already authorise prize gaming. In any event, the Schedule prohibits such applications from being made[7]. For different reasons, permits may not be issued in respect of vehicles or vessels[8].

The licensing authority may grant or refuse the application but it may not attach conditions to any permit granted[9]. The authority must consult the police before it may grant a permit[10]. It may not refuse an application unless it has notified the applicant of its intent to do so and has given him an opportunity to make representations. The authority must give the applicant reasons for any subsequent refusal[11].

The permit must be in the prescribed form and will have effect for ten years[12]. This is unless before that time it either lapses or, in accordance with the provisions of Sch 14, is surrendered by its holder or forfeited by a court after its holder is convicted of a relevant offence[13]. A prize gaming permit will lapse if its holder ceases to occupy the specified premises[14]. It will also lapse in the circumstances specified in Sch 14, para 15(1) and (2) (for example, if its holder dies, becomes bankrupt or becomes mentally or physically incapable of carrying on). There is a six month period of grace following the lapse of a permit, during which prize gaming may continue in the circumstances specified in para 15(3) (for example, where business is continued at the specified premises by the personal representatives of a holder who has died).

An application to renew a prize gaming permit must be made to the licensing authority not more than six months and not less than two months before its expiry. The procedures for renewal mirror those for the initial application. A permit may continue to have effect beyond ten years if an application for renewal is still pending at the time it would ordinarily expire or if at that time an appeal against an authority's refusal to renew is pending[15].

A failed applicant for a prize gaming permit may appeal to the magistrates' court for the local justice area in which the premises in question are wholly or partly situated. He must do so within 21 days of receipt of the notice of decision. The magistrates may dismiss the appeal, substitute any decision which the licensing authority could have initially made or remit the case to the authority to decide it in accordance with any direction of the court. The magistrates may also make an order as to costs.

A permit holder must keep his permit on the premises and must produce it to a constable, enforcement officer or authorised local authority officer. Failure to produce the permit without reasonable excuse is an offence, punishable by a level 2 fine[16].

Schedule 14 also requires a licensing authority to keep a register of permits it has issued. Members of the public must be allowed to inspect the register on request and to obtain copies of entries upon payment of a reasonable fee[17].

---

1 GA 2005, Sch 14, para 3(2).
2 GA 2005, Part 4 (ss 46 and 48). 'Equal chance gaming' is defined at s 8.
3 GA 2005, s 247 and Sch 10.
4 GA 2005, Sch 14, paras 3(1) and 5. 'The reference to "occupy" in this context means a legal right to be in occupation of the premises. This can either be by having a freehold or leasehold interest in the property, or holding it on a tenancy agreement' (GA 2005, Explanatory Note 734).
5 GA 2005, Sch 14, para 6. For application and renewal fees, see SI 2007/455, reg 3.
6 GA 2005, Sch 14, para 8.
7 GA 2005, Sch 14, para 4.
8 GA 2005, Sch 14, para 24.
9 GA 2005, Sch 14, para 9(1) and (2).
10 GA 2005, Sch 14, para 10.
11 GA 2005, Sch 14, para 9(4) and 11.
12 GA 2005, Sch 14, paras 12 and 13 and see SI 2007/455, reg 4 and Sch 1.
13 GA 2005, Sch 14, paras 16 and 17. For relevant offences, see s 126 and Sch 7.
14 GA 2005, Sch 14, para 14(1). Note also that a prize gaming permit does not take effect if its holder does not actually occupy the specified premises on its start date (para 14(2)).
15 GA 2005, Sch 14, para 18.
16 GA 2005, Sch 14, paras 19 and 20.
17 GA 2005, Sch 14, para 23.

Adult gaming centres, family entertainment centres and travelling fairs

6.273 Section 290(1) stipulates that no s 33 or 37 offence will be committed where facilities for prize gaming are provided at an adult gaming centre or a licensed family entertainment centre, so long as there is in each case compliance with the prize gaming conditions.

Similarly, under ss 290(2) and 292, the offences will not be committed where facilities for equal chance prize gaming (but not other forms of prize gaming) are provided pursuant to a family entertainment centre gaming machine permit or at a travelling fair[1]. Again, in each case there must be compliance with the prize gaming conditions.

Where travelling fairs are concerned, there is an additional requirement that the provision of facilities for gambling must amount to no more than an ancillary amusement at the fair[2]. 'Ancillary amusement' is not defined in the

Act. It is submitted that in this context it refers to gambling that is 'subservient or subordinate' to the non-gambling amusements provided at the fair. A comparison of the relative importance of the gambling to those other amusements should therefore be made in deciding whether it is truly ancillary[3].

Section 294 gives the Secretary of State power to remove by order the exemptions in relation to prize gaming conferred by ss 289, 290 and 292 (in respect of prize gaming permits, adult gaming centres, family entertainment centres and travelling fairs). This is apparently a contingency in case, for example, an additional class of operating licence dealing with prize gaming is added to Part 5 of the Act, which would render those sections superfluous[4].

1 'Equal chance gaming' is defined at GA 2005, s 8; 'travelling fair' is defined at GA 2005, s 286.
2 GA 2005, s 292(c).
3 See *Young v O'Connell* [2001] LLR 158, per Glidewell J at 162–163.
4 According to GA 2005, Explanatory Note 747.

Bingo halls

6.274 Special provision is also made in Part 13 for premises in respect of which a bingo premises licence has effect. Section 291 operates to extend to holders of bingo premises licences opportunities to provide facilities for prize gaming analogous to those that were available to their predecessors under the Gaming Act 1968[1].

By virtue of s 291, prize gaming may lawfully take place at such venues without the need for further authority; no s 35 or 37 offence will be committed in these circumstances. However, conditions under the Gambling Act 2005 (Operating Licence Conditions) Regulations 2007[2] reg 3 (as amended in 2010), attached to a bingo operating licence restrict the way in which prize gaming facilities may actually be provided at bingo halls[3]. In particular, participation fees that may be charged are limited to £1 per chance (maximum total for a game is £500) and the value of any single prize that may be offered is capped at £100 (or £70 in some cases) with a maximum overall total per game of £500.

1 Gaming Act 1968, s 21.
2 SI 2007/2257.
3 GA 2005, s 291(2)–(4) and Part 5, ss 75, 78 and 91.

PART 14: PRIVATE AND NON-COMMERCIAL GAMING AND BETTING

6.280 Sections 295–302 and Sch 15 set out the requirements for such gaming and betting; the provision of facilities for those activities and the use of premises for them is neither a breach of s 33 nor s 37. The relevant provisions are analysed in the commentary on Part 3; see para **6.30** ff above.

PART 15: INSPECTION

6.290 Part 15 (Inspection)[1] deals with the powers of entry to and inspection of premises.

The powers of entry and inspections are given to three categories of person:

- Constables

- Enforcement officers. These are employed or appointed by the Commission[2].
- Authorised persons. These are listed in s 304 and include authorised officers of the local authority in whose area the premises are situated; authorised officers of an authority which has statutory functions for environmental and human health protection, fire officers and health and safety inspectors.

Not all three categories enjoy the same powers. For example whilst each can enter premises, with other persons[3] not all can use reasonable force to gain entry in all cases. A constable can generally use such force; an enforcement officer can only such force under s 306 (suspected offence) and s 307 (inspection of gambling) whilst an authorised person can only do so in respect of s 307[4]. The Gambling Act 2005 (Inspection) (Provision of Information) Regulations 2007[5] place a number of obligations upon those carrying out inspections. These relate to evidence of identity, the right for persons on the premises to request a written record of the visit, the duty to provide such record and the requirement that inspectors inform persons they are questioning of their power to question (should they remain silent) together with the existence of the offence of obstruction under s 326.

1 See the Commission's publication 'Compliance and Enforcement Policy Statement', September 2009 at para **6.2075** below.

2 See also GA 2005, s 312 for similar powers in relation to clubs and miner's welfare institutes but note that these are not exercisable by an authorised person.

3 GA 2005, ss 309(1), 310(1), 311(1), 312(4) and 313(1).

4 GA 2005, s 315(1).

5 SI 2007/319.

Permitted activities

6.291 Section 305 of the GA 2005 is concerned with such activities. Although it appears under the heading 'Kinds of Inspection' this is misleading as it is drafted in much wider terms. Clearly 'activities' are not so limited. It gives power to all three categories of inspector to undertake activities so long as they are concerned with assessing:

- Compliance with any provision made by or under the Act; or
- Whether an offence under or by virtue of the Act 'is being committed'. The limiting use of the present tense here should not give rise to any significant difficulty in respect of offences already committed as the earlier power to assess compliance should be sufficient, although, as noted below entry in respect of past offences will require a warrant.

Suspected offence

6.292 A constable or an enforcement officer (but not an authorised person) may enter premises either without a warrant or with a warrant.

- **Entry without a warrant.** Such an entry can be made to a non-dwelling[1] if the constable or enforcement officer reasonably suspects that an offence under the Act may be (a) being committed on the premises or (b) about to be committed on the premises. If entry to a dwelling is in question or the suspicion relates to an offence which has already been committed a warrant will be required.

- **Entry with a warrant.** An application for a warrant must be made by the constable or officer to a justice of the peace. He can only issue the warrant (which has a life of 28 days[2]) if at least one of the following matters are fulfilled
  (a) he is satisfied that there are reasonable grounds for suspecting that an offence under the Act has been committed on the premises;
  (b) he is satisfied that there are reasonable grounds for suspecting that evidence of the commission of the offence may be found on the premises and
  (c) either that admission to the premises has been refused or is likely to be refused unless a warrant is produced;
  (d) that the purpose of entry may be frustrated or seriously prejudiced unless immediate entry can be secured;
  (e) that there is likely to be nobody at the premises capable of granting admission.

Section 306(4) further provides that in order for grounds (a) and (b) above to be met the JP must further be satisfied that notice of intent to apply for the warrant has been given to a person occupying the premises or having responsibility for their management or that the purpose of entry may be frustrated or seriously prejudiced by giving such notice.

Section 318 makes similar (but not identical) provision for the need to obtain a warrant in any case where entry to a dwelling is sought.

1 GA 2005, s 306(1) and s 318.
2 GA 2005, s 306(5).

GA 2005, s 307 Inspection of gambling.[1]

1 See also GA 2005, s 312 for similar powers in relation to clubs and miner's welfare institutes but note that these are not exercisable by an authorised person.

6.293 If a constable, enforcement officer or authorised person reasonably suspects that facilities for gambling (other than private or non-commercial betting or gaming[1]) may be being provided, about to be provided or have been provided on premises which are not a dwelling he may enter without a warrant so long as he does so.

(a) to discover whether such facilities are being provided, are about to be provided or have been provided there or
(b) to determine whether an operating licence or premises licence is held in respect of provision of those facilities there or
(c) to determine whether facilities are being, will be or have been provided in accordance with the terms and conditions of any operating or premises licence.

1 See paras **6.40–6.46** above.

The power to enter premises in respect of which an application for a licence has been made (but not yet determined)

6.293A A number of provisions[1] in Part 15 enable an enforcement officer and in some cases a constable, an authorised local authority officer or an authorised person to enter such premises for a purpose connected with consideration of the application. The provisions encompass family entertainment centres, premises licenced for alcohol for which an application for a gaming machine permit has been made under Schedule 13, prize gaming permits, club gaming and machine permits and any premises for which a licence has been applied.

Moreover, a similar power exists in respect of premises for which a temporary use notice has been served[2].

1 GA 2005, ss 309(1), 310(1), 311(1), 312(4) and 313(1).
2 GA 2005, s 315(1).

The power to enter premises when a licence has already been granted

6.294 A constable or enforcement officer may enter premises which he reasonably believes to be used by the holder of an operating licence for purposes connected with the licensed activities solely to determine whether those activities are being carried on in accordance with the terms and conditions of the licence[1]. According to Explanatory Note 773 this provision is wide enough to allow entry into premises where gambling itself is not being conducted; such as the head office of a casino business.

Similar provisions, some of which allow entry by an authorised local authority officer, apply in respect of family entertainment centres[2], premises licensed for alcohol[3], and premises for which a prize gaming permit exists[4]. Further provisions specifically give the power to enter any premises licensed under the Act for a purpose connected with a review under s 201[5] or to inquire whether a registered society lottery is being promoted. Section 315(2) enables entry to be made to premises for which a temporary use notice has effect to determine whether an activity there is being carried on otherwise than in accordance with the notice.

1 GA 2005, s 308.
2 GA 2005, s 309(2).
3 GA 2005, s 310(2).
4 GA 2005, s 311(2).
5 GA 2005, s 313 (2).

Section 316: Production of authorisations on demand

6.295 A constable or enforcement officer (but no other person) may require the holder of an operating licence to produce a copy of any authorisation in respect of the acceptance by his agent of a pool bet under s 93(2), various activities in respect of football pool bets under s 93(3), horse-race pool bets under s 94(2) and in respect of casino premises[1]. Parallel provision is made in respect of the production of such an authorisation by an agent[2]. A failure to comply with a request without reasonable excuse is an offence[3].

1 GA 2005, s 316(3).
2 GA 2005, s 316(2) and (4).

3 GA 2005, s 316(5).

Powers exercisable on entry

6.296 A person who has the power to enter under Part 15 can then[1]:

(a) inspect any part of the premises and any machine or other thing on the premises;
(b) question any person on the premises;
(c) require access to any written or electronic record which is kept on the premises[2];
(d) require to be supplied with a copy, in such form as he directs, of an entry in a written or electronic record which is kept on the premises;
(e) remove and retain anything if he reasonably believes that it constitutes or contains evidence of—
   (i) the commission of an offence under the Act, or
   (ii) the breach of a term or condition of a licence issued under the Act;
(f) remove and retain anything if he reasonably believes that it is being used or has been used in the commission of an offence under the Act.

However s 317 does not override the qualifications contained in s 9(2) of the Police and Criminal Evidence Act 1984 relating to legally privileged material, excluded material or certain special procedure material[3].

1 GA 2005, s 317.
2 See also GA 2003 s 319; unless a justice of the peace grants a warrant under s 319(2) and (3) the records must relate entirely to the matters to which the power of entry relates.
3 See also ss 10, 11 and 14 of PACE. Moreover the Codes of Practice under PACE are relevant to Part 15: see GA 2005, s 317(6).

Miscellaneous provisions

6.297

- A power under Part 15 may only be exercised at a reasonable time[1]. Unless the circumstances warrant it dawn raids would not appear to be permitted.
- An enforcement officer or authorised person (but not a constable) is under a duty to produce evidence of his identity and authority to any person who appears to be occupying or to have responsibility for the management of the relevant premises[2].
- Obstruction or failure to cooperate with a person exercising a power under Part 15 is an offence if no reasonable excuse exists for such behaviour[3].

1 GA 2005, s 320.
2 GA 2005, s 321.

[3] GA 2005, s 326.

PART 16: ADVERTISING

Note

In September 2010, the Commission published the third version of a Guide to Advertising Codes relevant to gambling: see para **6.2086** below.

6.310 The advertising of gambling is to be heavily regulated. However the Gambling Act 2005 itself does not make complete provision for such. Although it does set out some detailed rules it also leaves much to secondary legislation (which is currently awaited). Accordingly, only a fragmented view of the overall picture is now available. Advertising[1] bears a wide meaning in the Act; it encompasses: (1) any action which encourages a person to take advantage of facilities for gambling; (2) or if with a view to increasing the use of such facilities a person brings[2] them or information about them to the attention of anyone; (3) if a person participates in or facilitates an activity knowing or believing it is designed to encourage a person to take advantage of gambling facilities or increase the use of such facilities by bringing[3] them to the attention of any person.

Section 330 states that the advertisement of unlawful gambling is an offence. Such gambling is defined as unlicensed gambling (where a licence under the Act is required) or gambling which does not enjoy any exception set out in the Act.

Moreover, in all cases, save that of a lottery[4] the advertisement of 'foreign gambling' is prohibited[5]. Such gambling is: (a) non-remote gambling which is to take place in a non-EEA State; (b) remote gambling where none of the arrangements for which are subject to the law about gambling of an EEA State or Gibraltar, the Isle of Man, Alderney, Tasmania or Antigua and Barbuda[6]. The sufficiency of such law is fulfilled even if it prohibits remote gambling. Bizarrely it seems that the prohibition only bites if the EEA State has no law at all applicable to remote gambling; it does not apply if there is an outright ban of it.

Section 332 and s 333 are concerned with non-remote and remote advertising and the difficult issue of territorial application. Section 332 makes it clear that the regulations (which are awaited) and the provisions of ss 330 and 331 can only apply to non-remote advertising which takes place wholly or partly in Great Britain. Section 333 makes similar provision in respect of remote advertising although this necessarily takes into account the potentially complex nature of such advertising.

[1] Defined in GA 2005, s 327.

[2] Bringing facilities to the attention of a person has an extended meaning: see GA 2005, s 327(2).

[3] Bringing facilities to the attention of a person has an extended meaning: see GA 2005, s 327(2).

[4] GA 2005, s 330(3). Advertising of lotteries is however regulated in Part 11, ss 258 and 259.

[5] GA 2005, s 331.

[6] See SI 2007/2329 (as amended) and the DCMS publication 'White Listing' DCMS, January 2007: see para **6.2055** below.

PART 17: LEGALITY AND ENFORCEABILITY OF GAMBLING CONTRACTS

6.320 Section 334 repeals all the law which from the eighteenth century sought to make void gaming and wagering contracts and arrangements associated with them. The repeal however only relates to those contracts which are effective after it occurs; gaming etc contracts prior to 31 August 2007 are subject to the full rigour of the old statutes.

The fact that a contract post-31 August 2007 concerns gambling will not, on that ground, prevent its enforcement[1]; it will however inevitably be subject to all the general rules which apply to contracts.

[1] GA 2005, s 335.

Power of Gambling Commission to void bets

6.321 Section 336 sets out the power of the Commission to declare a bet void on the ground that it was 'substantially unfair'. The power to do so however only arises if the bet is accepted by or through the holder of a general operating betting or pool betting operating licence[1].A remote operator within those categories will also be included. In April 2011 an order was made under this section by the Commission in respect of bets made on the results of the X Factor television programme.

In deciding whether the bet was substantially unfair the Commission must take account of the following (if they arise)

(a) the fact that either party to the bet supplied insufficient, false or misleading information in connection with it,

(b) the fact that either party to the bet believed or ought to have believed that a race, competition or other event or process to which the bet was related was or would be conducted in contravention of industry rules[2],

(c) the fact that either party to the bet believed or ought to have believed that an offence under s 42 had been or was likely to be committed in respect of anything to which the bet related, and

(d) the fact that either party to the bet was convicted of an offence under s 42 in relation to the bet.

As Explanatory Note 833 points out, a bet where one of the above factors applies will not be automatically voided. If both parties were aware of the matter at the time the bet was entered into it is very unlikely that unfairness will arise.

The power to void a bet is circumscribed by a general limitation period[3] of 6 months beginning on the day on which the result of the bet is determined.

The result of a declaration of voidness is that any money paid in relation to the bet is to be repaid[4].

Section 337(3) allows the Commission to make 'incidental provision'; this rather vaguely phrased but apparently wide power is to some extent particularised by two examples. These relate to the consequences of the Commission's order to void a bet for bets connected with that bet[5] and further to the consequences of the primary order for other parts of a 'betting transaction' one part or aspect of which has been ruled to be void. It appears[6] that this power would enable the Commission to rule that all bets successive to a void bet in an accumulator also be made void.

It is noteworthy that in order to make its role in this area more effective than it would otherwise have been the Commission has been given two specific powers:

- it can order disclosure of information or documents in relation to the relevant bet from a person by or through whom the bet was made or accepted[7]. A failure without reasonable excuse to comply with a request for disclosure is an offence[8].
- under s 338 it can order that an interim moratorium be imposed; this has the effect of negating an obligation to pay money under the bet Such an order is effective for an initial period of 14 days, although this can be extended by further periods of 14 days. After 14 days the Commission can impose a moratorium if it has reason 'to suspect' that it may wish to make an order to void the bet. This is likely only to arise in those cases in which the claim for a declaration of voidness is very likely to be upheld. Moreover, given the nature of cash betting it is unlikely that in such cases the Commission will be able to take any meaningful action of this nature. Further, s 338(8) imposes a duty on the Commission if it has ordered an interim moratorium to rescind it if it ceases to entertain the suspicion.

---

1 Note, ss 336–338 are modified in respect of a number of operations, including the Tote: see SI 2007/2102.

2 Defined in s 337(7) as rules established by an organisation having by virtue of an agreement, instrument or enactment, responsibility for the conduct of races, competitions etc.

3 This does not apply in the cast of a conviction under s 42: GA 2005, s 336(6).

4 GA 2005, s 336(2).

5 GA 2005 s 337(3).

6 See GA 2005, Explanatory Note 836.

7 GA 2005, s 337(4).

8 GA 2005, s 337(5) and (6).

Section 2

Statutes

GAMBLING ACT 2005

(2005 c 19)

Arrangement of Sections

PART 3
GENERAL OFFENCES

PART 4
PROTECTION OF CHILDREN AND YOUNG PERSONS

PART 5
OPERATING LICENCES

An Act to make provision about gambling

[7 April 2005]

Commencement details for individual provisions appear below them.

Extent

See s 361.

Parliamentary Debates

House of Commons:

2nd Reading 1 November 2004: 426 HC Official Report (6th series) col 25.

Committee Stage 9 November 2004, 11 November 2004, 16 November 2004, 30 November 2004, 2 December 2004, 7 December 2004, 9 December 2004, 14 December 2004, 16 December 2004, 11 January 2005: HC Official Report, SC B (Gambling Bill).

Remaining Stages 24 January 2005: 430 HC Official Report (6th series) col 46.

Consideration of Lords Amendments 7 April 2005: 432 HC Official Report (6th series) col 1623.

House of Lords:

2nd Reading 22 February 2005: 669 HL Official Report (5th series) col 1136

Committee Stage 10 March 2005: 670 HL Official Report (5th series) col 920; 6 April 2005: 671 HL Official Report (5th series) col 822.

Remaining Stages 6 April 2005: 671 HL Official Report (5th series) col 822.

Consideration of Commons Reasons 7 April 2005: 671 HL Official Report (5th series) col 947.

PART 1
INTERPRETATION OF KEY CONCEPTS

Principal concepts

6.501 1 The licensing objectives

In this Act a reference to the licensing objectives is a reference to the objectives of—

(a) preventing gambling from being a source of crime or disorder, being associated with crime or disorder or being used to support crime,

(b) ensuring that gambling is conducted in a fair and open way, and

(c) protecting children and other vulnerable persons from being harmed or exploited by gambling.

Commencement

Brought into force by the Gambling Act 2005 (Commencement No 2 and Transitional Provisions) Order 2005, SI 2005/2455, art 2 and Schedule, as from 1 October 2005.

The licensing objectives

For the duty of the Gambling Commission to promote the licensing objectives, see s 22.

The statement under s 23 must explain how the principles to be applied by the Gambling Commission in exercising its functions under this Act are expected to assist the Commission in pursuit of the licensing objectives; see s 23(2).

In considering an application under s 69, the Commission must have regard to the licensing objectives; see s 70(1)(a).

In exercising their functions under Pt 8 of this Act a licensing authority must aim to permit the use of premises for gambling in so far as the authority think fit reasonably consistent with the licensing objectives; see s 153(1)(c).

In exercising their functions under Sch 10 or Sch 14 a licensing authority need not (but may) have regard to the licensing objectives; see Sch 10, para 7(3), Sch 14, para 8(3).

In exercising a function under Sch 12 a licensing authority is to have regard to any relevant guidance under s 25, and (subject to that) the licensing objectives; see Sch 12, para 27.

A licensing authority to whom an application is made under Sch 13 are to consider it having regard to the licensing objectives; see Sch 13, para 4.

Definitions

'child': ss 45(1), 353(1)
'gambling': ss 3, 353(1)

Explanatory Notes

30 [para **6.2004** below]

6.502 2 Licensing authorities

(1) For the purposes of this Act the following are licensing authorities—

(a) in relation to England—

(i) a district council,

(ii) a county council for a county in which there are no district councils,

(iii) a London borough council,

(iv) the Common Council of the City of London, and

(v) the Council of the Isles of Scilly,

(b) in relation to Wales—

(i) a county council, and

(ii) a county borough council, and

(c) in relation to Scotland, a licensing board [continued in existence by or established under section 5 of the Licensing (Scotland) Act 2005 (asp 16)] [1].

(2) For the purposes of Schedule 13, the Sub-Treasurer of the Inner Temple and the Under-Treasurer of the Middle Temple are licensing authorities.

Commencement

Brought into force by the Gambling Act 2005 (Commencement No 2 and Transitional Provisions) Order 2005, SI 2005/2455, art 2 and Schedule, as from 1 October 2005.

Sub-s (1): Licensing authorities. For the power of the Gambling Commission to require the provision of information by a licensing authority, see s 29. For the requirement on licensing authorities to prepare and publish a three-year licensing policy, see s 349.

Explanatory Notes

31–33 [para **6.2004** below]

[1] Sub-s (1): in para (c) words from "continued in existence" to "the Licensing (Scotland) Act 2005 (asp 16)" substituted by SSI 2009/248, art 2(1), Sch 1, Pt 1, para 12(1), (3).

6.503 3 Gambling

In this Act 'gambling' means—

(a) gaming (within the meaning of section 6),

(b) betting (within the meaning of section 9), and

(c) participating in a lottery (within the meaning of section 14 and subject to section 15).

Commencement

Brought into force by the Gambling Act 2005 (Commencement No 2 and Transitional Provisions) Order 2005, SI 2005/2455, art 2 and Schedule, as from 1 October 2005.

Explanatory Notes

34 [para **6.2004** below]

6.504 4 Remote gambling

(1) In this Act 'remote gambling' means gambling in which persons participate by the use of remote communication.

(2) In this Act 'remote communication' means communication using—

(a) the internet,

(b) telephone,

(c) television,

(d) radio, or

(e) any other kind of electronic or other technology for facilitating communication.

(3) The Secretary of State may by regulations provide that a specified system or method of communication is or is not to be treated as a form of remote communication for the purposes of this Act (and subsection (2) is subject to any regulations under this subsection).

Note

See the Gambling Commission publications at paras **6.2395–6.2513** below.

Commencement

Brought into force by the Gambling Act 2005 (Commencement No 2 and Transitional Provisions) Order 2005, SI 2005/2455, art 2 and Schedule, as from 1 October 2005.

Regulations under this section

At the time of going to press no regulations had been made under this section.

As to regulations under this Act generally, see s 355.

Definitions

'gambling': ss 3, 353(1)

Explanatory Notes

33–37 [para **6.2004** below]

6.505 5 Facilities for gambling

(1) For the purposes of this Act a person provides facilities for gambling if he—

(a) invites others to gamble in accordance with arrangements made by him,

(b) provides, operates or administers arrangements for gambling by others, or

(c) participates in the operation or administration of gambling by others.

(2) But a person does not provide facilities for gambling for the purposes of this Act by virtue only of—

(a) providing an article other than a gaming machine to a person who intends to use it, or may use it, in the course of any of the activities mentioned in subsection (1)(a) to (c),

(b) providing, otherwise than in the course of providing, operating or administering arrangements for gambling or participating in the operation or administration of gambling, an article to a person who intends to use it, or may use it, for gambling, or
(c) making facilities for remote communication available for use by—
(i) persons carrying on any of those activities, or
(ii) persons gambling in response to or in accordance with any of those activities.

(3) A person provides facilities for gambling (despite subsection (2)(c)) if—
(a) he makes facilities for remote communication available for use,
(b) the facilities are adapted or presented in such a way as to facilitate, or to draw attention to the possibility of, their use for gambling, and
(c) the nature, adaptation or presentation of the facilities is such that—
(i) they cannot reasonably be expected to be used for purposes other than gambling, or
(ii) they are intended to be used wholly or mainly for gambling.

(4) The Secretary of State may by order, for the purposes of subsection (3)(c)—
(a) provide that facilities of a specified nature, or adapted or presented in a specified way, cannot reasonably be expected to be used for purposes other than gambling;
(b) provide that facilities of a specified nature, or adapted or presented in a specified way, can reasonably be expected to be used for purposes other than gambling;
(c) specify criteria by which it is to be determined whether facilities can reasonably be expected to be used for purposes other than gambling;
(d) provide that facilities of a specified nature, or adapted or presented in a specified way, shall be taken as being intended to be used wholly or mainly for gambling;
(e) provide that facilities of a specified nature, or adapted or presented in a specified way, shall be taken as not being intended to be used wholly or mainly for gambling;
(f) specify criteria by which it is to be determined whether facilities are intended to be used wholly or mainly for gambling.

Commencement

Brought into force by the Gambling Act 2005 (Commencement No 2 and Transitional Provisions) Order 2005, SI 2005/2455, art 2 and Schedule, as from 1 October 2005.

Sub-s (4): Secretary of State. See the note to s 4.

Orders under this section

At the time of going to press no orders had been made under this section.

As to orders under this Act generally, see s 355.

Definitions

'gambling': ss 3, 353(1)
'gaming machine': ss 235, 353(1)
'remote communication': ss 4(2), (3), 353(1)

Explanatory Notes

38–45 [para **6.2004** below]

Gaming

6.506 6 Gaming & game of chance

(1) In this Act 'gaming' means playing a game of chance for a prize.
(2) In this Act 'game of chance'—

(a) includes—
(i) a game that involves both an element of chance and an element of skill,
(ii) a game that involves an element of chance that can be eliminated by superlative skill, and
(iii) a game that is presented as involving an element of chance, but
(b) does not include a sport.

(3) For the purposes of this Act a person plays a game of chance if he participates in a game of chance—
(a) whether or not there are other participants in the game, and
(b) whether or not a computer generates images or data taken to represent the actions of other participants in the game.

(4) For the purposes of this Act a person plays a game of chance for a prize—
(a) if he plays a game of chance and thereby acquires a chance of winning a prize, and
(b) whether or not he risks losing anything at the game.

(5) In this Act 'prize' in relation to gaming (except in the context of a gaming machine)—
(a) means money or money's worth, and
(b) includes both a prize provided by a person organising gaming and winnings of money staked.

(6) The Secretary of State may by regulations provide that a specified activity, or an activity carried on in specified circumstances, is or is not to be treated for the purposes of this Act as—
(a) a game;
(b) a game of chance;
(c) a sport.

Commencement

Brought into force by the Gambling Act 2005 (Commencement No 2 and Transitional Provisions) Order 2005, SI 2005/2455, art 2 and Schedule, as from 1 October 2005.

Sub-s (1): Gaming. As to the treatment of participating in a lottery which forms part of the National Lottery as gaming, see s 15(3).

As to the treatment of transactions which satisfy the definition of gaming in this section and the definition of betting in s 9, see s 16.

Sub-s (2): Game of chance. As to the treatment of arrangements which satisfy the definition of a game of chance in this section and the definition of lottery in s 14, see s 17.

Sub-s (6): Secretary of State. See the note to s 4.

Sub-s (6): May by regulations, etc. Ss 16, 17 are subject to regulations under sub-s (6) above; see ss 16(4), 17(5).

Regulations under this section

At the time of going to press no regulations had been made under this section.

As to regulations under this Act generally, see s 355.

Definitions

'gaming machine': ss 235, 353(1)
'participant': s 353(1)
'winnings': s 353(1)

Explanatory Notes

46, 47 [para **6.2004** below]

6.507 7 Casino

(1) For the purposes of this Act a casino is an arrangement whereby people are given an opportunity to participate in one or more casino games.

(2) In this Act 'casino game' means a game of chance which is not equal chance gaming.

(3) But the Secretary of State may by regulations provide that a specified activity, or an activity carried on in specified circumstances, is to be or not to be treated as a casino game for the purposes of this Act (and subsection (2) is subject to regulations under this subsection).

(4) For the purposes of this section it is immaterial—

(a) whether an arrangement is provided on one set of premises or on more than one;

(b) whether an arrangement is provided wholly or partly by means of remote communication.

(5) The Secretary of State shall make regulations by reference to which any casino may be classified as—

(a) a regional casino,

(b) a large casino,

(c) a small casino, or

(d) below the minimum size for a licensed casino

(6) Regulations under subsection (5) may make provision by reference to—

(a) the number of gaming tables used or designated for the playing of specified casino games or classes of casino game,

(b) the location of gaming tables used or designated for the playing of specified casino games or classes of casino game,

(c) the concentration of gaming tables used or designated for the playing of specified casino games or classes of casino game,

(d) the floor area used or designated for a specified purpose,

(e) any combination of the matters listed in paragraph (a) to (d), or

(f) any other matter.

(7) Regulations under subsection (5) may—

(a) include provision for determining what floor area is to be treated as being used or designated for a purpose;

(b) include provision for determining what activities do or do not amount to the playing of a specified casino game or class of casino game;

(c) include provision for determining what is or is not to be treated as a gaming table (and, in particular, in what circumstances a number of tables are to be treated as if they were a single gaming table);

(d) provide that a gaming table is to be treated as being used or designated only if specified conditions (which may, in particular, relate to purpose of use, extent of use or circumstances of use) are satisfied.

Note

See the Gambling Commission publications at paras **6.2180–6.2244.1**.

Commencement

Subsections (1)–(4) brought into force by the Gambling Act 2005 (Commencement No 2 and Transitional Provisions) Order 2005, SI 2005/2455, art 2 and Schedule, as from 1 October 2005. Subsections (5)–(7) brought into force by the Gambling Act 2005 (Commencement No 6 and Transitional Provisions) Order 2006, SI 2006/3272, art 2, Sch 2 as from 30 April 2007; for transitional provisions see art 6, Sch 4 thereto (as amended by SI 2007/1157, arts 7–12). Sub-ss (5)(b)–(d), (6), (7): brought into force by the Gambling Act 2005 (Commencement No 8) Order 2008, SI 2008/1326, art 2, Schedule as from 20 May 2008.

Sub-s (3): Secretary of State. See the note to s 4.

Subordinate Legislation

Categories of Casino Regulations 2008, SI 2008/1330 (made under sub-ss (5)–(7)).

As to regulations under this Act generally, see s 355.

Definitions

'equal chance gaming': ss 8, 353(1)
'game of chance': ss 6, 353(1)
'premises': s 353(1), (2)(g)
'remote communication': ss 4(2), (3), 353(1)

Explanatory Notes

48–55 [para **6.2004** below]

6.508 8 Equal chance gaming

(1) For the purposes of this Act gaming is equal chance gaming if—

(a) it does not involve playing or staking against a bank, and
(b) the chances are equally favourable to all participants.

(2) For the purposes of subsection (1) it is immaterial—

(a) how a bank is described, and
(b) whether or not a bank is controlled or administered by a player.

Note

See the Gambling Commission publications at paras **6.2265–6.2297**.

Commencement

Brought into force by the Gambling Act 2005 (Commencement No 2 and Transitional Provisions) Order 2005, SI 2005/2455, art 2 and Schedule, as from 1 October 2005.

Definitions

'gaming': ss 6, 353(1)
'participant': s 353(1)

Explanatory Notes

56, 57 [para **6.2004** below]

Betting

6.509 9 Betting: general

(1) In this Act 'betting' means making or accepting a bet on—

(a) the outcome of a race, competition or other event or process,
(b) the likelihood of anything occurring or not occurring, or
(c) whether anything is or is not true.

(2) A transaction that relates to the outcome of a race, competition or other event or process may be a bet within the meaning of subsection (1) despite the facts that—

(a) the race, competition, event or process has already occurred or been completed, and
(b) one party to the transaction knows the outcome.

(3) A transaction that relates to the likelihood of anything occurring or not occurring may be a bet within the meaning of subsection (1) despite the facts that—

(a) the thing has already occurred or failed to occur, and
(b) one party to the transaction knows that the thing has already occurred or failed to occur.

Note

See the Gambling Commission publications at paras **6.2100–6.2177** and **6.2674** below.

Commencement

Brought into force by the Gambling Act 2005 (Commencement No 2 and Transitional Provisions) Order 2005, SI 2005/2455, art 2 and Schedule, as from 1 October 2005.

Sub-s (1): Betting. As to the treatment of transactions which satisfy the definition of betting in this section and the definition of gaming in s 6, see s 16.

Sub-s (1): Making . . . a bet. See further s 10 as to the meaning of 'bet' in sub-s (1) above, and s 11 and Sch 1 as to the meaning of 'makes a bet' in that subsection.

Definitions

'accepting a bet': s 353(2)(a)

Explanatory Notes

58–60 [para **6.2004** below]

6.510 10 Spread bets, &c

(1) For the purposes of section 9(1) 'bet' does not include a bet the making or accepting of which is a regulated activity within the meaning of section 22 of the Financial Services and Markets Act 2000 (c 8).

(2) An order under section 22 of that Act which has the effect that a class of bet becomes or ceases to be a regulated activity may, in particular, include transitional provision relating to the application of this Act to that class of bet.

(3) This section is subject to section 38(3).

Commencement

Subsections (1) and (2) brought into force by the Gambling Act 2005 (Commencement No 2 and Transitional Provisions) Order 2005, SI 2005/2455, art 2 and Schedule, as from 1 October 2005. Subsection (3) brought into force by the Gambling Act 2005 (Commencement No 6 and Transitional Provisions) Order 2006, SI 2006/3272, art 2, Sch 2 as from 1 September 2007; for transitional provisions see art 6, Sch 4 thereto (as amended by SI 2007/1157, arts 7–12).

Definitions

'accepting a bet': s 353(2)(a)

Explanatory Notes

61, 62 [para **6.2004** below]

6.511 11 Betting: prize competitions

(1) For the purposes of section 9(1) a person makes a bet (despite the fact that he does not deposit a stake in the normal way of betting) if—

- (a) he participates in an arrangement in the course of which participants are required to guess any of the matters specified in section 9(1)(a) to (c),
- (b) he is required to pay to participate, and
- (c) if his guess is accurate, or more accurate than other guesses, he is to—
  - (i) win a prize, or
  - (ii) enter a class among whom one or more prizes are to be allocated (whether or not wholly by chance).

(2) In subsection (1) a reference to guessing includes a reference to predicting using skill or judgment.

(3) Schedule 1 makes further provision about when a person is to be or not to be treated for the purposes of subsection (1)(b) as being required to pay to participate in an arrangement.

(4) In subsection (1)(c) 'prize' includes any money, articles or services—

- (a) whether or not described as a prize, and
- (b) whether or not consisting wholly or partly of money paid, or articles or services provided, by the members of the class among whom the prizes are allocated.

Commencement

Brought into force by the Gambling Act 2005 (Commencement No 2 and Transitional Provisions) Order 2005, SI 2005/2455, art 2 and Schedule, as from 1 October 2005.

Sub-s (1): Makes a bet. Participating in a lottery which forms part of the National Lottery is not to be treated as betting for the purposes of this Act where it would satisfy the definition of betting in s 9 by virtue of this section; see s 15(4).

As to the treatment of transactions which satisfy the definition of participating in a lottery in s 14 and also the definition of pool betting in s 12 or the definition of betting in s 9 by virtue of this section, see s 18.

Definitions

'betting': ss 9, 353(1)
'participant': s 353(1)
'prize': ss 6(5), 353(1) (and sub-s (4) above)
'stake': s 353(1)

Explanatory Notes

63, 64 [para **6.2004** below]

6.512 12 Pool betting

(1) For the purposes of this Act betting is pool betting if made on terms that all or part of winnings—

(a) shall be determined by reference to the aggregate of stakes paid or agreed to be paid by the persons betting,

(b) shall be divided among the winners, or

(c) shall or may be something other than money.

(2) For the purposes of this Act pool betting is horse-race pool betting if it relates to horse-racing in Great Britain.

Commencement

Brought into force by the Gambling Act 2005 (Commencement No 2 and Transitional Provisions) Order 2005, SI 2005/2455, art 2 and Schedule, as from 1 October 2005.

Sub-s (1): Pool betting. Participating in a lottery which forms part of the National Lottery is not to be treated as betting for the purposes of this Act where it would satisfy the definition of pool betting in this section; see s 15(4).

As to the treatment of transactions which satisfy the definition of participating in a lottery in s 14 and also the definition of pool betting in this section or the definition of betting in s 9 by virtue of s 11, see s 18.

Definitions

'betting': ss 9–11, 353(1)
'stake': s 353(1)
'winnings': s 353(1)

Explanatory Notes

65 [para **6.2004** below]

6.513 13 Betting intermediary

(1) In this Act 'betting intermediary' means a person who provides a service designed to facilitate the making or acceptance of bets between others.

(2) For the purposes of this Act acting as a betting intermediary is providing facilities for betting.

Commencement

Brought into force by the Gambling Act 2005 (Commencement No 2 and Transitional Provisions) Order 2005, SI 2005/2455, art 2 and Schedule, as from 1 October 2005.

Definitions

'accepting a bet': s 353(2)(a)
'betting': ss 9–11, 353(1)

Explanatory Notes

66 [para **6.2004** below]

Lottery

6.514 14 Lottery

(1) For the purposes of this Act an arrangement is a lottery, irrespective of how it is described, if it satisfies one of the descriptions of lottery in subsections (2) and (3).

(2) An arrangement is a simple lottery if—

(a) persons are required to pay in order to participate in the arrangement,

(b) in the course of the arrangement one or more prizes are allocated to one or more members of a class, and

(c) the prizes are allocated by a process which relies wholly on chance.

(3) An arrangement is a complex lottery if—

(a) persons are required to pay in order to participate in the arrangement,

(b) in the course of the arrangement one or more prizes are allocated to one or more members of a class,

(c) the prizes are allocated by a series of processes, and

(d) the first of those processes relies wholly on chance.

(4) In this Act 'prize' in relation to lotteries includes any money, articles or services—

(a) whether or not described as a prize, and

(b) whether or not consisting wholly or partly of money paid, or articles or services provided, by the members of the class among whom the prize is allocated.

(5) A process which requires persons to exercise skill or judgment or to display knowledge shall be treated for the purposes of this section as relying wholly on chance if—

(a) the requirement cannot reasonably be expected to prevent a significant proportion of persons who participate in the arrangement of which the process forms part from receiving a prize, and

(b) the requirement cannot reasonably be expected to prevent a significant proportion of persons who wish to participate in that arrangement from doing so.

(6) Schedule 2 makes further provision about when an arrangement is to be or not to be treated for the purposes of this section as requiring persons to pay.

(7) The Secretary of State may by regulations provide that an arrangement of a specified kind is to be or not to be treated as a lottery for the purposes of this Act; and—

(a) the power in this subsection is not constrained by subsections (1) to (6) or Schedule 2, and

(b) regulations under this subsection may amend other provisions of this section or Schedule 2.

Note

See the Gambling Commission publications at paras **6.2300–6.2359B** and its 'Guidance on Prize Competitions and Free Draws', May and December 2009 (see paras **6.2089–6.2090** below).

Commencement

Brought into force by the Gambling Act 2005 (Commencement No 2 and Transitional Provisions) Order 2005, SI 2005/2455, art 2 and Schedule, as from 1 October 2005.

Sub-s (1): Lottery. As to the treatment of arrangements which satisfy the definition of a game of chance in s 6 and the definition of lottery in this section, see s 17; and as to the treatment of transactions which satisfy the definition of participating in a lottery in this section and also the definition of pool betting in s 12 or the definition of betting in s 9 by virtue of s 11, see s 18.

Sub-s (7): Secretary of State. See the note to s 4.

Sub-s (7): May by regulations, etc. Ss 17, 18 are subject to regulations under sub-s (7) above; see ss 17(5), 18(4).

Regulations under this section

At the time of going to press no regulations had been made under this section.

As to regulations under this Act generally, see s 355.

Explanatory Notes

67–74 [para **6.2004** below]

6.515 15 National Lottery

(1) Participating in a lottery which forms part of the National Lottery is not gambling for the purposes of this Act (despite section 3(c) but subject to subsections (2) and (3) below).

(2) Participating in a lottery which forms part of the National Lottery is gambling for the purposes of—

(a) section 42, and

(b) section 335.

(3) Where participating in a lottery which forms part of the National Lottery would also constitute gaming within the meaning of section 6, it shall be treated as gaming for the purposes of this Act if and only if a person participating in the lottery is required to participate in, or to be successful in, more than three processes before becoming entitled to a prize.

(4) Participating in a lottery which forms part of the National Lottery shall not be treated as betting for the purposes of this Act where it would—

(a) satisfy the definition of pool betting in section 12, or

(b) satisfy the definition of betting in section 9 by virtue of section 11.

(5) Schedule 3 shall have effect.

Commencement

Subsections (1)–(4), and subs (5) in so far as it relates to para 2 of Sch 3, brought into force by the Gambling Act 2005 (Commencement No 2 and Transitional Provisions) Order 2005, SI 2005/2455, art 2 and Schedule, as from 1 October 2005. Subsection (5) brought into force for remaining purposes by the Gambling Act 2005 (Commencement No 6 and Transitional Provisions) Order 2006, SI 2006/3272, art 2 as from 1 September 2007; for transitional provisions see art 6, Sch 4 thereto (as amended by SI 2007/1157, arts 7–12).

Definitions

'gambling': ss 3, 353(1)
'lottery': ss 14, 353(1)
'the National Lottery': s 353(1)
'participating in a lottery': ss 14, 353(2)(c)
'prize': ss 14(4), 353(1)

Explanatory Notes

75 [para **6.2004** below]

Cross-category activities

6.516 16 Betting and gaming

(1) This section applies to a transaction which satisfies—

(a) the definition of betting in section 9, and

(b) the definition of gaming in section 6.

(2) A transaction to which this section applies which is pool betting (within the meaning of section 12) shall be treated for the purposes of this Act as betting (and not as gaming).

(3) Any other transaction to which this section applies shall be treated for the purposes of this Act as gaming (and not as betting).

(4) This section is subject to regulations under section 6(6).

Commencement

Brought into force by the Gambling Act 2005 (Commencement No 2 and Transitional Provisions) Order 2005, SI 2005/2455, art 2 and Schedule, as from 1 October 2005.

Explanatory Notes

76 [para **6.2004** below]

6.517 17 Lotteries and gaming

(1) This section applies to an arrangement which satisfies—

(a) the definition of a game of chance in section 6, and

(b) the definition of a lottery in section 14.

(2) An arrangement to which this section applies shall be treated for the purposes of this Act as a game of chance (and not as a lottery) if a person who pays in order to join the class amongst whose members prizes are allocated is required to participate in, or to be successful in, more than three processes before becoming entitled to a prize.

(3) An arrangement to which this section applies shall, subject to subsection (2), be treated for the purposes of this Act as a lottery (and not as a game of chance) if—

(a) it satisfies paragraph 1(1)(a) and (b) of Schedule 11,

(b) it satisfies paragraph 10(1)(a) and (b) of Schedule 11,

(c) it satisfies paragraph 11(1)(a) and (b) of Schedule 11,

(d) it satisfies paragraph 12(1)(a) and (b) of Schedule 11,

(e) it satisfies paragraph 20(1)(a) and (b) of Schedule 11,

(f) it satisfies paragraph 30(1)(a) and (b) of Schedule 11, or

(g) it is promoted in reliance on a lottery operating licence.

(4) Any other arrangement to which this section applies shall be treated for the purposes of this Act as a game of chance (and not as a lottery).

(5) This section is subject to regulations under section 6(6) or 14(7).

Commencement

Brought into force by the Gambling Act 2005 (Commencement No 2 and Transitional Provisions) Order 2005, SI 2005/2455, art 2 and Schedule, as from 1 October 2005.

Sub-s (3): Lottery operating licence. As to the nature, etc of operating licences, see s 65 and the note 'Operating licences' thereto. As to lottery operating licences, see, in particular, s 98.

Definitions

'operating licence': s 353(1)
'prize' (in relation to a lottery): ss 14, 353(1)
'prize' (in relation to gaming): ss 6(5), 353(1)
'promoting a lottery': ss 252, 353(2)(h)

Explanatory Notes

77 [para **6.2004** below]

6.518 18 Lotteries and betting

(1) This section applies to a transaction which satisfies the definition of participating in a lottery in section 14 and also—

(a) satisfies the definition of pool betting in section 12, or

(b) satisfies the definition of betting in section 9 by virtue of section 11.

(2) A transaction to which this section applies shall be treated for the purposes of this Act as participating in a lottery (and not as betting) if—

(a) it satisfies paragraph 1(1)(a) and (b) of Schedule 11,

(b) it satisfies paragraph 10(1)(a) and (b) of Schedule 11,
(c) it satisfies paragraph 11(1)(a) and (b) of Schedule 11,
(d) it satisfies paragraph 12(1)(a) and (b) of Schedule 11,
(e) it satisfies paragraph 20(1)(a) and (b) of Schedule 11,
(f) it satisfies paragraph 30(1)(a) and (b) of Schedule 11, or
(g) it is promoted in reliance on a lottery operating licence.

(3) Any other transaction to which this section applies shall be treated for the purposes of this Act as betting (and not as participating in a lottery).

(4) This section is subject to regulations under section 14(7).

Commencement

Brought into force by the Gambling Act 2005 (Commencement No 2 and Transitional Provisions) Order 2005, SI 2005/2455, art 2 and Schedule, as from 1 October 2005.

Sub-s (2): Lottery operating licence. As to the nature, etc of operating licences, see s 65 and the note 'Operating licences' thereto. As to lottery operating licences, see, in particular, s 98.

Definitions

'operating licence': s 353(1)

Explanatory Notes

78 [para **6.2004** below]

6.519 19 Non-commercial society

(1) For the purposes of this Act a society is non-commercial if it is established and conducted—

(a) for charitable purposes,
(b) for the purpose of enabling participation in, or of supporting, sport, athletics or a cultural activity, or
(c) for any other non-commercial purpose other than that of private gain.

(2) In subsection (1) 'charitable purposes' means—

(a) in relation to England and Wales, [purposes which are exclusively charitable purposes (as defined by section 2 of the Charities Act 2011)], and
(b) in relation to Scotland, purposes which are charitable purposes only (that expression having the same meaning as in the Income Tax Acts).

(3) The provision of a benefit to one or more individuals is not a provision for the purpose of private gain for the purposes of this Act if made in the course of the activities of a society that is a non-commercial society by virtue of subsection (1)(a) or (b).

Note

See comments on *R (on the application of Camelot UK Lotteries Ltd) v Gambling Commission* [2012] EWHC 2391 (Admin) at para **6.243** above.

Commencement

Brought into force by the Gambling Act 2005 (Commencement No 2 and Transitional Provisions) Order 2005, SI 2005/2455, art 2 and Schedule, as from 1 October 2005.

Sub-s (2): England; Wales. See the note to s 2.

Amendment

Sub-s (2): in para (a) words from 'purposes which are' to 'Charities Act 2011)' in square brackets substituted by the Charities Act 2011, s 354(1), Sch 7, Pt 2, para 105.

Definitions

'society': s 353(1)

Explanatory Notes

79–82 [para **6.2004** below]

PART 2
THE GAMBLING COMMISSION

6.520 20 Establishment of the Commission

(1) There shall be a body corporate to be known as the Gambling Commission.

(2) Schedule 4 (which makes provision about the constitution and proceedings of the Commission) shall have effect.

Commencement

Brought into force by the Gambling Act 2005 (Commencement No 2 and Transitional Provisions) Order 2005, SI 2005/2455, art 2 and Schedule, as from 1 October 2005.

Sub-s (1): Gambling Commission. For further provisions of this Act relating to the Gambling Commission, see s 21 and Sch 5 (Gaming Board: transfer to the Commission); s 22 (duty to promote the licensing objectives); s 23 (statement of principles for licensing and regulation); s 24 (codes of practice); s 25 (guidance to local authorities); s 26 (duty to advise Secretary of State); s 27 (compliance); s 28 (investigation and prosecution of offences); s 29 (licensing authority information); s 30 and Sch 6 (other exchange of information); s 31 (consultation with National Lottery Commission); and s 32 (consultation with Commissioners for Her Majesty's Revenue and Customs).

Explanatory Notes

92 [para **6.2005** below]

6.521 21 Gaming Board: transfer to Commission

(1) Section 10 of and Schedule 1 to the Gaming Act 1968 (c 65) (Gaming Board for Great Britain) shall cease to have effect.

(2) The functions, rights and liabilities of the Gaming Board for Great Britain shall on commencement become functions, rights and liabilities of the Gambling Commission.

(3) The persons who immediately before commencement are the members of the Gaming Board for Great Britain shall be treated as if on commencement they were appointed as commissioners of the Gambling Commission under paragraph 1 of Schedule 4 to this Act.

(4) The person who immediately before commencement is the chairman of the Gaming Board for Great Britain shall be treated as if on commencement he were appointed as the chairman of the Gambling Commission under paragraph 1 of Schedule 4 to this Act.

(5) In this section 'commencement' means the coming into force of this section.

(6) Schedule 5 (which makes supplementary provision in relation to the transfer of functions and property from the Gaming Board to the Gambling Commission) shall have effect.

Commencement

Brought into force by the Gambling Act 2005 (Commencement No 2 and Transitional Provisions) Order 2005, SI 2005/2455, art 2 and Schedule, as from 1 October 2005.

Sub-s (2): Gambling Commission. As to the establishment, etc of the Gambling Commission, see s 20, Sch 4, and the note 'Gambling Commission' to that section.

Sub-s (5): Coming into force of this section. At the time of going to press no order had been made under s 358 bringing this section into force.

Explanatory Notes

93 [para **6.2005** below]

6.522 22 Duty to promote the licensing objectives

In exercising its functions under this Act the Commission shall aim—

(a) to pursue, and wherever appropriate to have regard to, the licensing objectives, and

(b) to permit gambling, in so far as the Commission thinks it reasonably consistent with pursuit of the licensing objectives.

Commencement

Brought into force by the Gambling Act 2005 (Commencement No 2 and Transitional Provisions) Order 2005, SI 2005/2455, art 2 and Schedule, as from 1 October 2005.

The Commission.

Ie the Gambling Commission; see s 353(1). As to the establishment, etc of the Gambling Commission, see s 20, Sch 4, and the note 'Gambling Commission' to that section.

Definitions

'the Commission': s 353(1)
'gambling': ss 3, 353(1)
'the licensing objectives': ss 1, 353(1)

Explanatory Notes

94 [para **6.2005** below]

6.523 23 Statement of principles for licensing and regulation

(1) The Commission shall prepare a statement setting out the principles to be applied by it in exercising its functions under this Act.

(2) The statement under this section shall, in particular, explain how the principles to be applied are expected to assist the Commission in its pursuit of the licensing objectives.

(3) The Commission shall—

(a) review the statement from time to time, and

(b) revise the statement when the Commission thinks it appropriate.

(4) The Commission shall as soon as is reasonably practicable publish—

(a) the statement, and

(b) any revision.

(5) Before issuing or revising a statement under this section the Commission shall consult—

(a) the Secretary of State,

(b) Her Majesty's [Commissioners for Her Majesty's Revenue and Customs] [1],

(c) one or more persons who appear to the Commission to represent local authorities (including, in Scotland, licensing boards),

(d) one or more persons who appear to the Commission to represent chief constables of police forces,

(e) one or more persons who appear to the Commission to represent the interests of persons carrying on gambling businesses,

(f) one or more persons who appear to the Commission to have knowledge about social problems relating to gambling, and

(g) to such extent and in such manner as the Commission thinks appropriate, members of the public.

Note

In December 2006 (updated in September 2009) the Commission published a Statement under s 23 (see para **6.2040** below).

Commencement

Brought into force by the Gambling Act 2005 (Commencement No 2 and Transitional Provisions) Order 2005, SI 2005/2455, art 2 and Schedule, as from 1 October 2005.

Sub-s (1): The Commission. Ie the Gambling Commission; see s 353(1). As to the establishment, etc of the Gambling Commission, see s 20, Sch 4, and the note 'Gambling Commission' to that section.

Sub-s (1): Shall prepare a statement. The statement maintained under this section must specify the principles to be applied by the Gambling Commission in considering applications under s 69; see s 70(4) (and see further s 70(5)–(8)). The statement must also specify the Commission's practice in relation to the delegation of functions in relation to such applications, the holding of oral hearings of applications, and evidence required or accepted in connection with applications; see s 73(4).

The Gambling Commission must publish any determination under ss 111(1), 112(7) as part of a statement (or revised statement) under this section; see ss 111(4), 112(7)(c).

Sub-s (5): Secretary of State. See the note to s 4.

Definitions

'chief constables of police forces': s 353(1)
'the Commission': s 353(1)
'gambling': ss 3, 353(1)
'the licensing objectives': ss 1, 353(1)

Explanatory Notes

95–99 [para **6.2005** below]

---

1 Words in square brackets substituted by virtue of the Commissioners for Revenue and Customs Act 2005, s 50(1), (7).

6.524 24 Codes of practice

(1) The Commission shall issue one or more codes of practice about the manner in which facilities for gambling are provided (whether by the holder of a licence under this Act or by another person).

(2) In particular, a code shall describe arrangements that should be made by a person providing facilities for gambling for the purposes of—

(a) ensuring that gambling is conducted in a fair and open way,

(b) protecting children and other vulnerable persons from being harmed or exploited by gambling, and

(c) making assistance available to persons who are or may be affected by problems related to gambling.

(3) A code may include provision about how facilities for gambling are advertised or described.

(4) A code may be revised or revoked by the Commission.

(5) A code, and any revision, must state when it comes into force.

(6) The Commission shall publish a code and any revision in a manner which the Commission thinks likely to bring it to the attention of those whose activities it concerns.

(7) The Commission may make different provision under this section for different cases or circumstances (whether or not by way of separate codes of practice).

(8) A failure to comply with a provision of a code shall not of itself make a person liable to criminal or civil proceedings; but this subsection is subject to any provision of or by virtue of this Act making an exception to an offence dependent on compliance with a code.

(9) But a code—

(a) shall be admissible in evidence in criminal or civil proceedings,

(b) shall be taken into account by a court or tribunal in any case in which it appears to the court or tribunal to be relevant, and

(c) shall be taken into account by the Commission in the exercise of a function under this Act.

(10) Before issuing or revising a code under this section the Commission shall consult—

(a) the Secretary of State,

(b) Her Majesty's [Commissioners for Her Majesty's Revenue and Customs] [1],

(c) one or more persons who appear to the Commission to represent the interests of persons who—

(i) carry on gambling businesses, and

(ii) are likely to be affected by the code or revision,

(d) one or more persons who appear to the Commission to have knowledge about social problems relating to gambling, and

(e) in the case of a code including provision by virtue of subsection (3), one or more persons who appear to the Commission to have a relevant responsibility for regulating the advertising industry.

(11) Before issuing or revising a code under this section the Commission shall also consult, if and to the extent that the Commission thinks appropriate having regard to the nature of the code or revision—

(a) one or more persons who appear to the Commission to represent local authorities (including, in Scotland, licensing boards),

(b) one or more persons who appear to the Commission to represent chief constables of police forces,

(c) one or more persons who appear to the Commission to represent the interests of persons carrying on gambling businesses (apart from those consulted under subsection (10)(c)), and

(d) in such manner as the Commission thinks appropriate, members of the public.

Note

The Commission has issued Codes of Practice under this section (consolidated December 2011): see para **6.2060** below.

Commencement

Subsections (1)–(8), (10) and (11) brought into force by the Gambling Act 2005 (Commencement No 2 and Transitional Provisions) Order 2005, SI 2005/2455, art 2 and Schedule, as from 1 October 2005. Subsection (9) brought into force by the Gambling Act 2005 (Commencement No 6 and Transitional Provisions) Order 2006, SI 2006/3272, art 2 as from 1 September 2007; for transitional provisions see art 6, Sch 4 thereto (as amended by SI 2007/1157, arts 7–12).

Sub-s (1): The Commission. Ie the Gambling Commission; see s 353(1). As to the establishment, etc of the Gambling Commission, see s 20, Sch 4, and the note 'Gambling Commission' to that section.

Sub-s (1): Codes of practice. As to compliance with particular provisions of a code of practice issued under this section, see s 82. In determining an appeal the Gambling Appeals Tribunal must have regard to any relevant provision of a code of practice issued under this section; see s 144(3).

In exercising their functions under Pt 8 of this Act a licensing authority must aim to permit the use of premises for gambling in so far as the authority think fit in accordance with any relevant code of practice under this section; see s 153(1)(a).

The Gambling Commission must issue one or more codes of practice under this section about access to casino premises for children and young persons; see s 176.

A club gaming permit, a club machine permit and a licensed premises gaming machine permit are subject to the condition that the holder comply with any relevant provision of a code of practice issued under this section about the location and operation of a gaming machine; see ss 271(7)(b), 273(4)(b), 283(3).

Compliance with any relevant provision of a code of practice issued under this section about the location and operation of a gaming machine is a condition which must be satisfied of the purposes of s 282; see s 282(3).

Sub-s (1): Person. See the note 'Persons' to s 23.

Sub-s (10): Secretary of State. See the note to s 4.

Sub-s (10): Commissioners for Her Majesty's Revenue and Customs; persons. See the notes to s 23.

Definitions

'chief constables of police forces': s 353(1)
'child': ss 45(1), 353(1)
'the Commission': s 353(1)
'gambling': ss 3, 353(1)
'providing facilities for gambling': ss 5, 353(2)(i)

Explanatory Notes

100–106 [para 6.2005 below]

---

1 Words in square brackets substituted by virtue of the Commissioners for Revenue and Customs Act 2005, s 50(1), (7).

6.525 25 Guidance to local authorities

(1) The Commission shall from time to time issue guidance as to—

(a) the manner in which local authorities are to exercise their functions under this Act, and
(b) in particular, the principles to be applied by local authorities in exercising functions under this Act.

(2) A local authority shall have regard to guidance issued under subsection (1).

(3) The Commission shall publish guidance issued under subsection (1).

(4) Before issuing guidance under subsection (1) the Commission shall consult—

(a) the Secretary of State,
(b) Her Majesty's [Commissioners for Her Majesty's Revenue and Customs] [1],
(c) the Scottish Ministers,
(d) one or more persons who appear to the Commission to represent local authorities,
(e) one or more persons who appear to the Commission to represent the interests of persons carrying on gambling businesses, and
(f) one or more persons who appear to the Commission to have knowledge about social problems relating to gambling.

(5) Before issuing guidance under subsection (1) the Commission shall also consult, if and to the extent that the Commission thinks appropriate having regard to the nature of the guidance—

(a) one or more persons who appear to the Commission to represent chief constables of police forces, and
(b) in such manner as the Commission thinks appropriate, members of the public.

(6) In this section 'local authority' means—

(a) in relation to England—
  (i) a district council,
  (ii) a county council for a county in which there are no district councils,
  (iii) a London borough council,
  (iv) the Common Council of the City of London,
  (v) the Sub-Treasurer of the Inner Temple and the Under-Treasurer of the Middle Temple, and
  (vi) the Council of the Isles of Scilly,
(b) in relation to Wales—
  (i) a county council, and

(ii) a county borough council, and

(c) in relation to Scotland, a licensing board [continued in existence by or established under section 5 of the Licensing (Scotland) Act 2005 (asp 16)] [1].

Note

A copy of the third edition of the guidance published in May 2009 is at para **6.2655** below.

Commencement

Brought into force by the Gambling Act 2005 (Commencement No 2 and Transitional Provisions) Order 2005, SI 2005/2455, art 2 and Schedule, as from 1 October 2005.

Sub-s (1): The Commission. Ie the Gambling Commission; see s 353(1). As to the establishment, etc of the Gambling Commission, see s 20, Sch 4, and the note 'Gambling Commission' to that section.

Sub-s (1): Guidance. In exercising their functions under Pt 8 of this Act a licensing authority must aim to permit the use of premises for gambling in so far as the authority think fit in accordance with any relevant guidance under this section; see s 153(1)(b).

In exercising their functions under Sch 10 or Sch 14 a licensing authority must have regard to any relevant guidance under this section; see Sch 10, para 7(3), Sch 14, para 8(3).

Sub-s (4): Secretary of State. See the note to s 4.

Sub-s (4): Commissioners for Her Majesty's Revenue and Customs; persons. See the notes to s 23.

Sub-s (6): England; Wales; district council; county council; London borough council; Common Council of the City of London; Isles of Scilly; county borough council. See the notes to s 2.

Definitions

'chief constables of police forces': s 353(1)
'the Commission': s 353(1)
'gambling': ss 3, 353(1)

Explanatory Notes

107–111 [para **6.2005** below]

---

[1] Sub-s (6): in para (c) words from "continued in existance" to "the Licensing (Scotland) Act 2005 (asp 16)" in square brackets substituted by SSI 2009/248, art 2(1), Sch 1, Pt 1, para 12(1), (3).

6.526 26 Duty to advise Secretary of State

(1) The Commission shall give advice to the Secretary of State about—

(a) the incidence of gambling,

(b) the manner in which gambling is carried on,

(c) the effects of gambling, and

(d) the regulation of gambling.

(2) Advice under this section shall be given—

(a) in response to a request from the Secretary of State, and

(b) on such other occasions as the Commission thinks appropriate.

(3) The Commission shall send a copy of any advice under this section to the Scottish Ministers.

Commencement

Brought into force by the Gambling Act 2005 (Commencement No 2 and Transitional Provisions) Order 2005, SI 2005/2455, art 2 and Schedule, as from 1 October 2005.

Sub-s (1): The Commission. Ie the Gambling Commission; see s 353(1). As to the establishment, etc of the Gambling Commission, see s 20, Sch 4, and the note 'Gambling Commission' to that section.

Sub-s (1): Secretary of State. See the note to s 4.
Sub-s (3): Scottish Ministers. See the note to s 25.

Definitions
'the Commission': s 353(1)
'gambling': ss 3, 353(1)

Explanatory Notes
112 [para **6.2005** below]

6.527 27 Compliance

The Commission may undertake activities for the purpose of assessing—

(a) compliance with provision made by or by virtue of this Act;

(b) whether an offence is being committed under or by virtue of this Act.

Commencement
Brought into force by the Gambling Act 2005 (Commencement No 6 and Transitional Provisions) Order 2006, SI 2006/3272, art 2 as from 1 September 2007; for transitional provisions see art 6, Sch 4 thereto (as amended by SI 2007/1157, arts 7–12).

The Commission.
Ie the Gambling Commission; see s 353(1). As to the establishment, etc of the Gambling Commission, see s 20, Sch 4, and the note 'Gambling Commission' to that section.

Definitions
'the Commission': s 353(1)

Explanatory Notes
113 [para **6.2005** below]

6.528 28 Investigation and prosecution of offences

(1) The Commission—

(a) may investigate whether an offence has been committed under this Act, and

(b) may institute criminal proceedings in respect of an offence under this Act.

(2) The power in subsection (1)(a) may be exercised whether in response to information received by the Commission or otherwise.

(3) Subsection (1)(b) shall not apply in relation to the institution of proceedings in Scotland.

Commencement
Brought into force for certain purposes as from 1 January 2007, for remaining purposes as from 1 September 2007 by the Gambling Act 2005 (Commencement No 6 and Transitional Provisions) Order 2006, SI 2006/3272, art 2, Sch 1; for transitional provisions see art 6, Sch 4 thereto (as amended by SI 2007/1157, arts 7–12).

Sub-s (1): The Commission. Ie the Gambling Commission; see s 353(1). As to the establishment, etc of the Gambling Commission, see s 20, Sch 4, and the note 'Gambling Commission' to that section.

Definitions
'the Commission': s 353(1)

Explanatory Notes
114 [para **6.2005** below]

6.529 29 Licensing authority information

(1) The Commission may require a licensing authority to provide information that—

(a) forms part of a register maintained by the authority under this Act, or

(b) is in the possession of the authority in connection with a provision of this Act.

(2) A requirement under subsection (1) may include a requirement for information to be—

(a) compiled or collated in a specified manner;

(b) provided in a specified form.

(3) A licensing authority shall comply with a requirement under this section.

Note

See 'Information exchange between the Gambling Commission and Licensing Authorities' (December 2007) (see para **6.2640** below).

Commencement

Brought into force by the Gambling Act 2005 (Commencement No 6 and Transitional Provisions) Order 2006, SI 2006/3272, art 2 as from 1 September 2007; for transitional provisions see art 6, Sch 4 thereto (as amended by SI 2007/1157, arts 7–12).

Sub-s (1): The Commission. Ie the Gambling Commission; see s 353(1). As to the establishment, etc of the Gambling Commission, see s 20, Sch 4, and the note 'Gambling Commission' to that section.

Sub-s (1): Licensing authority. For the licensing authorities for the purposes of this Act, see s 2.

Subordinate Legislation: See the Gambling Act 2005 (Licensing Authority Policy Statement) (England and Wales) Regulations 2006; SI 2006/636, art 5(c).

Definitions

'the Commission': s 353(1)
'licensing authority': ss 2, 353(1)

Explanatory Notes

115 [para **6.2005** below]

6.530 30 Other exchange of information

(1) The Commission may provide information received by it in the exercise of its functions to any of the persons or bodies listed in Schedule 6—

(a) for use in the exercise of the person's or body's functions, or

(b) for the purpose of a function of the Commission.

(2) Any of the persons or bodies listed in Part 1 or 2 of Schedule 6 may provide to the Commission, for use in the exercise of its functions, information received by the person or body in the exercise of his or its functions.

(3) The Commission may provide information received by it in the exercise of its functions to the Comptroller and Auditor General for use in the exercise of his functions under Part 2 of the National Audit Act 1983 (c 44).

(4) The Commission may provide information received by it in the exercise of its functions to a person if the provision is for the purpose of—

(a) a criminal investigation (whether in the United Kingdom or elsewhere), or

(b) criminal proceedings (whether in the United Kingdom or elsewhere).

(5) Note 2 to Schedule 6 shall not apply to the provision of information under subsection (3).

(6) Provision of information in reliance on this section may be subject to conditions (whether as to use, storage, disposal or otherwise).

(7) The Commission may charge a fee for the provision of information under subsection (1)(a).

(8) This section is subject to section 352.

Commencement

Brought into force by the Gambling Act 2005 (Commencement No 2 and Transitional Provisions) Order 2005, SI 2005/2455, art 2 and Schedule, as from 1 October 2005.

Sub-s (1): The Commission. Ie the Gambling Commission; see s 353(1). As to the establishment, etc of the Gambling Commission, see s 20, Sch 4, and the note 'Gambling Commission' to that section.

Subordinate Legislation: see the Gambling Act 2005 (Licensing Authority Policy Statement) (England and Wales) Regulations 2006; SI 2006/636, Art 5(c).

Definitions

'the Commission': s 353(1)

Explanatory Notes

116 [para **6.2005** below]

6.531 31 Consultation with National Lottery Commission

(1) If in the course of the exercise of its functions the Gambling Commission becomes aware of a matter about which the National Lottery Commission is likely to have an opinion, the Gambling Commission shall consult the National Lottery Commission.

(2) The Gambling Commission shall comply with any direction of the Secretary of State (which may be general or specific) to consult the National Lottery Commission.

Commencement

Brought into force by the Gambling Act 2005 (Commencement No 2 and Transitional Provisions) Order 2005, SI 2005/2455, art 2 and Schedule, as from 1 October 2005.

Sub-s (1): Gambling Commission. As to the establishment, etc of the Gambling Commission, see s 20, Sch 4, and the note 'Gambling Commission' to that section.

Sub-s (2): Secretary of State. See the note to s 4.

Explanatory Notes

117, 118 [para **6.2005** below]

6.532 32 Consultation with [Commissioners for Her Majesty's Revenue and Customs][1]

(1) If in the course of the exercise of its functions the Gambling Commission becomes aware of a matter about which the [Commissioners for Her Majesty's Revenue and Customs][1] are likely to have an opinion, the Gambling Commission shall consult the [Commissioners for Her Majesty's Revenue and Customs][1].

(2) The Gambling Commission shall comply with any direction of the Secretary of State (which may be general or specific) to consult the [Commissioners for Her Majesty's Revenue and Customs][1].

Commencement

Brought into force by the Gambling Act 2005 (Commencement No 2 and Transitional Provisions) Order 2005, SI 2005/2455, art 2 and Schedule, as from 1 October 2005.

Sub-s (1): Gambling Commission. As to the establishment, etc of the Gambling Commission, see s 20, Sch 4, and the note 'Gambling Commission' to that section.

Sub-s (1): Commissioners for Her Majesty's Revenue and Customs. See the note to s 23.

Sub-s (2): Secretary of State. See the note to s 4.

Explanatory Notes

119 [para **6.2005** below]

[1] Words in square brackets substituted by virtue of the Commissioners for Revenue and Customs Act 2005, s 50(1), (7).

PART 3
GENERAL OFFENCES

Provision of facilities for gambling

6.533 33 Provision of facilities for gambling

(1) A person commits an offence if he provides facilities for gambling unless—
- (a) an exception provided for in subsection (2) or (3) applies, or
- (b) an exception provided for by any of the following provisions applies—
  - (i) sections 34 and 35,
  - (ii) sections 269 and 271 (clubs and miners' welfare institutes),
  - (iii) section 279 (premises with alcohol licence),
  - (iv) sections 289 to 292 (prize gaming),
  - (v) section 296 (private gaming and betting), and
  - (vi) section 298 (non-commercial gaming).

(2) Subsection (1) does not apply to any activity by a person if—
- (a) he holds an operating licence authorising the activity, and
- (b) the activity is carried on in accordance with the terms and conditions of the licence.

(3) Subsection (1) does not apply to any activity by a person if—
- (a) he acts in the course of a business carried on by a person who holds an operating licence authorising the activity, and
- (b) the activity is carried on in accordance with the terms and conditions of the licence.

(4) A person guilty of an offence under this section shall be liable on summary conviction to—
- (a) imprisonment for a term not exceeding 51 weeks,
- (b) a fine not exceeding level 5 on the standard scale, or
- (c) both.

(5) In the application of subsection (4) to Scotland the reference to 51 weeks shall have effect as a reference to six months.

Commencement

Brought into force by the Gambling Act 2005 (Commencement No 6 and Transitional Provisions) Order 2006, SI 2006/3272, art 2 as from 1 September 2007; for transitional provisions see art 6, Sch 4 thereto (as amended by SI 2007/1157, arts 7–12).

Sub-s (1): Person. See the note 'Persons' to s 23.

Sub-s (1): Offence. For the power of the Gambling Commission and other specified persons to undertake activities for the purpose of assessing whether an offence is being committed under or by virtue of this Act, see s 27 and s 305; for the power of that Commission to investigate and prosecute offences, see s 28; as to offences committed by a body, see s 341; and for the time limit on prosecutions, see s 347. See also s 306 for powers of entry as respects a suspected offence, and s 345 as respects forfeiture of an article relating to an offence. For territorial limitations on offences under this Part of this Act, see ss 359, 360.

For the territorial application of this section, see s 36.

Neither a premises licence nor any provision of Pt 8 of this Act disapplies or provides a defence to the offence under this section; see s 150(3).

Sub-s (2): Operating licence. As to the nature, etc of operating licences, see s 65 and the note 'Operating licences' thereto.

An authorisation under s 93(3) is to be treated for the purposes of this section as if it were a pool betting operating licence, but has no effect in relation to any activity, entry or payment that relates partly to a football pool and partly to another form of gambling; see s 93(4). An authorisation under s 94(2) is to be treated for the purposes of this section as if it were a pool betting operating licence authorising the provision of facilities for horse-race pool betting; see s 94(3).

Subordinate Legislation: various modifications to s 33 are made in the Gambling Act 2005 (Horserace Totalisator Board) Order 2007, SI 2007/2102, Art 3).

Definitions

'act which is authorised by a licence': s 353(5)
'gambling': ss 3, 353(1)
'operating licence': s 353(1)
'providing facilities for gambling': ss 5, 353(2)(i)

Explanatory Notes

134–137 [para **6.2006** below]

6.534 34 Exception: lotteries

Section 33 shall not apply to the provision of facilities for a lottery.

Commencement

Brought into force by the Gambling Act 2005 (Commencement No 6 and Transitional Provisions) Order 2006, SI 2006/3272, art 2 as from 1 September 2007; for transitional provisions see art 6, Sch 4 thereto (as amended by SI 2007/1157, arts 7–12).

Definitions

'lottery': ss 14, 353(1)
'providing facilities for gambling': ss 5, 353(2)(i)

Explanatory Notes

134–137 [para **6.2006** below]

6.535 35 Exception: gaming machines

Section 33 shall not apply to making a gaming machine available for use.

Commencement

Brought into force by the Gambling Act 2005 (Commencement No 6 and Transitional Provisions) Order 2006, SI 2006/3272, art 2 as from 1 September 2007; for transitional provisions see art 6, Sch 4 thereto (as amended by SI 2007/1157, arts 7–12).

Definitions

'gaming machine': ss 235, 353(1)

Explanatory Notes

134–137 [para **6.2006** below]

6.536 36 Territorial application

(1) For the purposes of section 33 it is immaterial whether facilities are provided—

(a) wholly or partly by means of remote communication;
(b) subject to subsections (2) and (3), inside the United Kingdom, outside the United Kingdom, or partly inside and partly outside.

(2) Section 33 applies to the provision of facilities for non-remote gambling only if anything done in the course of the provision of the facilities is done in Great Britain.

(3) Section 33 applies to the provision of facilities for remote gambling only if at least one piece of remote gambling equipment used in the provision of the facilities is situated in Great Britain (but whether or not the facilities are provided for use wholly or partly in the United Kingdom).

(4) In this Act 'remote gambling equipment' means, subject to subsection (5), electronic or other equipment used by or on behalf of a person providing facilities for remote gambling—

(a) to store information relating to a person's participation in the gambling,
(b) to present, to persons who are participating or may participate in the gambling, a virtual game, virtual race or other virtual event or process by reference to which the gambling is conducted,

(c) to determine all or part of a result or of the effect of a result, or
(d) to store information relating to a result.

(5) In this Act 'remote gambling equipment' does not include equipment which—
(a) is used by a person to take advantage of remote gambling facilities provided by another person, and
(b) is not provided by that other person.

Note

What constitutes key equipment under s 36 is discussed in the Gambling Commission Guidance Note 'Remote Gambling Equipment' (March 2008) (see para **6.2511** below).

Commencement

Brought into force by the Gambling Act 2005 (Commencement No 6 and Transitional Provisions) Order 2006, SI 2006/3272, art 2 as from 1 September 2007; for transitional provisions see art 6, Sch 4 thereto (as amended by SI 2007/1157, arts 7–12).

Sub-s (2): Great Britain. See the note to s 12.

Sub-s (4): Person. See the note 'Persons' to s 23.

Definitions

'gambling': ss 3, 353(1)
'providing facilities for gambling': ss 5, 353(2)(i)
'remote communication': ss 4(2), (3), 353(1)
'remote gambling': ss 4, 353(1)
'virtual game, race or other event or process': s 353(3)

Explanatory Notes

138–143 [para **6.2006** below]

Use of premises

6.537 37 Use of premises

(1) A person commits an offence if he uses premises, or causes or permits premises to be used, to—
(a) operate a casino,
(b) provide facilities for the playing of bingo,
(c) make a gaming machine available for use,
(d) provide other facilities for gaming, or
(e) provide facilities for betting (whether by making or accepting bets, by acting as a betting intermediary or by providing other facilities for the making or accepting of bets).

(2) Subsection (1) does not apply in relation to the use of premises by a person if the use is authorised by a premises licence held by him.

(3) Subsection (1) does not apply in relation to the use of premises by a person if he acts in the course of a business carried on by another person who holds a premises licence authorising the use.

(4) Subsection (1) does not apply in relation to the use of a track by a person for accepting bets if the use is authorised by a premises licence (whether or not held by him).

(5) Subsection (1) does not apply in relation to the use of a casino for the provision of facilities for bingo or betting in accordance with an authorisation under section 174(3).

(6) Subsection (1) does not apply in relation to the use of premises to provide facilities which are to be used only by persons who—
(a) are acting in the course of a business, or
(b) are not on the premises.

(7) Other exceptions to subsection (1) are provided in—
(a) sections 39 and 40,
(b) section 214 (temporary use notice),
(c) sections 247, 248 and 249 (gaming machines),
(d) sections 269, 271 and 273 (clubs and miners' welfare institutes),
(e) sections 279, 282 and 283 (premises with alcohol licence),
(f) section 287 (travelling fairs),
(g) sections 289 to 292 (prize gaming),
(h) section 296 (private gaming and betting), and
(i) section 298 (non-commercial gaming).

(8) A person guilty of an offence under this section shall be liable on summary conviction to—
(a) imprisonment for a term not exceeding 51 weeks,
(b) a fine not exceeding level 5 on the standard scale, or
(c) both.

(9) In the application of subsection (8) to Scotland the reference to 51 weeks shall have effect as a reference to six months.

Commencement

Brought into force by the Gambling Act 2005 (Commencement No 6 and Transitional Provisions) Order 2006, SI 2006/3272, art 2 as from 1 September 2007; for transitional provisions see art 6, Sch 4 thereto (as amended by SI 2007/1157, arts 7–12).

Sub-s (1): Person. See the note 'Persons' to s 23.

Sub-s (1): Offence. For the power of the Gambling Commission and other specified persons to undertake activities for the purpose of assessing whether an offence is being committed under or by virtue of this Act, see s 27 and s 305; for the power of that Commission to investigate and prosecute offences, see s 28; as to offences committed by a body, see s 341; and for the time limit on prosecutions, see s 347. See also s 306 for powers of entry as respects a suspected offence, and s 345 as respects forfeiture of an article relating to an offence. For territorial limitations on offences under this Part of this Act, see ss 359, 360.

For the power of a licensing authority to institute criminal proceedings in respect of an offence under this section, see s 346.

Sub-s (8): Summary conviction; standard scale. See the notes to s 33.

Power to amend

For the power of the Secretary of State to amend sub-s (1) above, see s 38.

Saving

The issue of an operating licence does not affect the application of this section; see s 65(3).

Definitions

'accepting a bet': s 353(2)(a)
'act which is authorised by a licence': s 353(5)
'acting as a betting intermediary': s 13(2)
'betting': ss 9–11, 353(1)
'betting intermediary': ss 13(1), 353(1)
'bingo': s 353(1)
'casino': ss 7, 353(1)
'gaming': ss 6, 353(1)
'gaming machine': ss 235, 353(1)
'premises': s 353(1), (2)(g)
'premises licence': s 353(1)
'providing facilities for gambling': ss 5, 353(2)(i)
'track': s 353(1)

Explanatory Notes
144–152 [para **6.2006** below]

6.538 38 Power to amend section 37

(1) The Secretary of State may by order amend section 37(1) so as to—
(a) add a gambling activity,
(b) remove a gambling activity, or
(c) vary the entry for a gambling activity.

(2) In subsection (1) 'gambling activity' means an activity that is—
(a) a kind of gambling, or
(b) the provision of facilities for a kind of gambling.

(3) In particular, an order under subsection (1) may have the effect of applying section 37(1) to betting of the kind referred to in section 10(1) (subject to any specified exceptions).

(4) An order under subsection (1) may, in particular, make consequential amendment of—
(a) section 150;
(b) another provision of Part 8;
(c) any provision of this Act, or of another enactment, that relates to Part 8.

Commencement

Brought into force by the Gambling Act 2005 (Commencement No 6 and Transitional Provisions) Order 2006, SI 2006/3272, art 2 as from 1 September 2007; for transitional provisions see art 6, Sch 4 thereto (as amended by SI 2007/1157, arts 7–12).

Sub-s (1): Secretary of State. See the note to s 4.

Sub-s (3): In particular, etc. Section 10 is subject to sub-s (3) above; see s 10(3).

Sub-s (4): Part 8. Ie Pt 8 (ss 150–213 and Sch 9) of this Act.

Orders under this section. At the time of going to press no orders had been made under this section.

As to orders under this Act generally, see s 355.

Definitions
'gambling': ss 3, 353(1)
'providing facilities for gambling': ss 5, 353(2)(i)

Explanatory Notes
144–152 [para **6.2006** below]

6.539 39 Exception: occasional use notice

(1) A person who accepts bets on a track, or who causes or permits premises to be used for the acceptance of bets, does not commit an offence under section 37 if—
(a) a notice has been given under this section in respect of the track, and
(b) the activity is carried on in accordance with the notice.

(2) A notice under this section (an 'occasional use notice') in respect of a track may be given only by a person who is—
(a) responsible for the administration of events on the track, or
(b) an occupier of the track.

(3) An occasional use notice must—
(a) be given in writing to the licensing authority for any area in which the track is wholly or partly situated, and
(b) be copied to either—
(i) in England and Wales, the chief officer of police for any area in which the track is wholly or partly situated, or
(ii) in Scotland, the chief constable of the police force maintained for the police area comprising that area.

(4) An occasional use notice must specify a day on which it has effect.

(5) An occasional use notice may not be given in respect of a track for a day in a calendar year if eight occasional use notices have been given in respect of that track for days in that year.

(6) In this section—

(a) 'chief officer of police' has the meaning given by section 101(1) of the Police Act 1996 (c 16), and

(b) a reference to a chief officer's area is a reference to the area in respect of which he has responsibility under that Act.

(7) The Secretary of State may by order amend subsection (5) so as to substitute a different maximum number of occasional use notices for a calendar year.

(8) An order under subsection (7) increasing the maximum number of occasional use notices for a calendar year may also make provision prohibiting the giving of a temporary use notice in a calendar year in respect of premises if a specified number of occasional use notices have been given in respect of the premises in that year.

Commencement

Brought into force by the Gambling Act 2005 (Commencement No 6 and Transitional Provisions) Order 2006, SI 2006/3272, art 2 as from 1 September 2007; for transitional provisions see art 6, Sch 4 thereto (as amended by SI 2007/1157, arts 7–12).

Sub-s (1): Person. See the note 'Persons' to s 23.

Sub-s (1): Notice. See further, in connection with a requirement under this Act to give a notice, s 353(4).

Sub-s (3): Licensing authority. For the licensing authorities for the purposes of this Act, see s 2.

Sub-s (3): England; Wales. See the note to s 2.

Sub-s (7): Secretary of State. See the note to s 4.

Orders under this section

At the time of going to press no orders had been made under this section.

As to orders under this Act generally, see s 355.

Definitions

'accepting a bet': s 353(2)(a)
'licensing authority': ss 2, 353(1)
'premises': s 353(1), (2)(g)
'track': s 353(1)

Explanatory Notes

153–155 [para **6.2006** below]

6.540 40 Exception: football pools

(1) A person does not commit an offence under section 37 if he uses premises to do anything in accordance with an authorisation under section 93(3).

(2) The Secretary of State may make regulations disapplying subsection (1) to specified classes of premises.

Commencement

Brought into force by the Gambling Act 2005 (Commencement No 6 and Transitional Provisions) Order 2006, SI 2006/3272, art 2 as from 1 September 2007; for transitional provisions see art 6, Sch 4 thereto (as amended by SI 2007/1157, arts 7–12).

Sub-s (1): Person. See the note 'Persons' to s 23.

Sub-s (2): Secretary of State. See the note to s 4.

Regulations under this section

At the time of going to press no regulations had been made under this section.

As to regulations under this Act generally, see s 355.

Definitions

'premises': s 353(1), (2)(g)

Explanatory Notes

156,157 [para **6.2006** below]

Miscellaneous offences

6.541 41 Gambling software

(1) A person commits an offence if in the course of a business he manufactures, supplies, installs or adapts gambling software unless he acts in accordance with an operating licence.

(2) In this Act 'gambling software'—

(a) means computer software for use in connection with remote gambling, but

(b) does not include anything for use solely in connection with a gaming machine.

(3) A person does not supply or install gambling software for the purposes of subsection (1) by reason only of the facts that—

(a) he makes facilities for remote communication or non-remote communication available to another person, and

(b) the facilities are used by the other person to supply or install gambling software.

(4) A person guilty of an offence under this section shall be liable on summary conviction to—

(a) imprisonment for a term not exceeding 51 weeks,

(b) a fine not exceeding level 5 on the standard scale, or

(c) both.

(5) In the application of subsection (4) to Scotland the reference to 51 weeks shall have effect as a reference to six months.

Commencement

Brought into force by the Gambling Act 2005 (Commencement No 6 and Transitional Provisions) Order 2006, SI 2006/3272, art 2 as from 1 September 2007; for transitional provisions see art 6, Sch 4 thereto (as amended by SI 2007/1157, arts 7–12).

Sub-s (1): Person. See the note 'Persons' to s 23.

Sub-s (1): Offence. For the power of the Gambling Commission and other specified persons to undertake activities for the purpose of assessing whether an offence is being committed under or by virtue of this Act, see s 27 and s 305; for the power of that Commission to investigate and prosecute offences, see s 28; as to offences committed by a body, see s 341; and for the time limit on prosecutions, see s 347. See also s 306 for powers of entry as respects a suspected offence, and s 345 as respects forfeiture of an article relating to an offence. For territorial limitations on offences under this Part of this Act, see ss 359, 360.

Sub-s (1): Operating licence. As to the nature, etc of operating licences, see s 65 and the note 'Operating licences' thereto.

Sub-s (4): Summary conviction; standard scale. See the notes to s 33.

Definitions

'act which is authorised by a licence': s 353(5)
'gaming machine': ss 235, 353(1)
'installing computer software': s 353(2)(d)
'operating licence': s 353(1)
'remote communication': ss 4(2), (3), 353(1)
'remote gambling': ss 4, 353(1)
'supply': s 353(1)

Explanatory Notes

158–162 [para **6.2006** below]

6.542 42 Cheating

(1) A person commits an offence if he—

(a) cheats at gambling, or

(b) does anything for the purpose of enabling or assisting another person to cheat at gambling.

(2) For the purposes of subsection (1) it is immaterial whether a person who cheats—

(a) improves his chances of winning anything, or

(b) wins anything.

(3) Without prejudice to the generality of subsection (1) cheating at gambling may, in particular, consist of actual or attempted deception or interference in connection with—

(a) the process by which gambling is conducted, or

(b) a real or virtual game, race or other event or process to which gambling relates.

(4) A person guilty of an offence under this section shall be liable—

(a) on conviction on indictment, to imprisonment for a term not exceeding two years, to a fine or to both, or

(b) on summary conviction, to imprisonment for a term not exceeding 51 weeks, to a fine not exceeding the statutory maximum or to both.

(5) In the application of subsection (4) to Scotland the reference to 51 weeks shall have effect as a reference to six months.

(6) Section 17 of the Gaming Act 1845 (c 109) (winning by cheating) shall cease to have effect.

Commencement

Brought into force by the Gambling Act 2005 (Commencement No 6 and Transitional Provisions) Order 2006, SI 2006/3272, art 2 as from 1 September 2007; for transitional provisions see art 6, Sch 4 thereto (as amended by SI 2007/1157, arts 7–12).

Sub-s (1): Person. See the note 'Persons' to s 23.

Sub-s (1): Offence. For the power of the Gambling Commission and other specified persons to undertake activities for the purpose of assessing whether an offence is being committed under or by virtue of this Act, see s 27 and s 305; for the power of that Commission to investigate and prosecute offences, see s 28; as to offences committed by a body, see s 341; and for the time limit on prosecutions, see s 347. See also s 306 for powers of entry as respects a suspected offence, and s 345 as respects forfeiture of an article relating to an offence. For territorial limitations on offences under this Part of this Act, see ss 359, 360.

Sub-s (1): Gambling. Participating in a lottery which forms part of the National Lottery is gambling for the purposes of this section; see s 15(2).

Sub-s (4): Summary conviction. See the note to s 33.

Definitions

'gambling': ss 3, 353(1)

'real': s 353(1)

'virtual game, race or other event or process': s 353(3)

Explanatory Notes

163–165 [para **6.2006** below]

6.543 43 Chain-gift schemes

(1) A person commits an offence if he—

(a) invites another to join a chain-gift scheme, or

(b) knowingly participates in the promotion, administration or management of a chain-gift scheme.

(2) An arrangement is a 'chain-gift' scheme if—

(a) in order to participate in the arrangement a person must make a payment to one or more other participants (a 'joining fee'), and

(b) each person who participates in the arrangement—

(i) is required or invited to invite others to participate, and

(ii) is encouraged to believe that he will receive the joining fees, or part of the joining fees, of other participants, to an amount in excess of the joining fee paid by him.

(3) For the purposes of subsection (2)—

(a) 'payment' means a payment of money or money's worth, but does not include the provision of goods or services, and

(b) it is immaterial whether a payment is made directly or through a person responsible for managing or administering the scheme.

(4) A person guilty of an offence under this section shall be liable on summary conviction to—

(a) imprisonment for a period not exceeding 51 weeks,

(b) a fine not exceeding level 5 on the standard scale, or

(c) both.

(5) In the application of subsection (4) to Scotland or Northern Ireland the reference to 51 weeks shall have effect as a reference to six months.

Commencement

Brought into force by the Gambling Act 2005 (Commencement No 6 and Transitional Provisions) Order 2006, SI 2006/3272, art 2 as from 1 September 2007; for transitional provisions see art 6, Sch 4 thereto (as amended by SI 2007/1157, arts 7–12).

Sub-s (1): Person. See the note 'Persons' to s 23.

Sub-s (1): Offence. For the power of the Gambling Commission and other specified persons to undertake activities for the purpose of assessing whether an offence is being committed under or by virtue of this Act, see s 27 and s 305; for the power of that Commission to investigate and prosecute offences, see s 28; as to offences committed by a body, see s 341; and for the time limit on prosecutions, see s 347. See also s 306 for powers of entry as respects a suspected offence, and s 345 as respects forfeiture of an article relating to an offence. For territorial limitations on offences under this Part of this Act, see ss 359, 360.

Sub-s (4): Summary conviction; standard scale. See the notes to s 33.

Explanatory Notes

166–169 [para 6.2006 below]

6.544 44 Provision of unlawful facilities abroad

(1) A person commits an offence if he does anything in Great Britain, or uses remote gambling equipment situated in Great Britain, for the purpose of inviting or enabling a person in a prohibited territory to participate in remote gambling.

(2) In subsection (1) 'prohibited territory' means a country or place designated for the purpose of this section by order made by the Secretary of State.

(3) An order under subsection (2) shall prescribe the mode of trial and maximum penalty for an offence under subsection (1).

Commencement

Brought into force by the Gambling Act 2005 (Commencement No 6 and Transitional Provisions) Order 2006, SI 2006/3272, art 2 as from 1 September 2007; for transitional provisions see art 6, Sch 4 thereto (as amended by SI 2007/1157, arts 7–12).

Sub-s (1): Person. See the note 'Persons' to s 23.

Sub-s (1): Offence. For the power of the Gambling Commission and other specified persons to undertake activities for the purpose of assessing whether an offence is being committed under or by virtue of this Act, see s 27 and s 305; for the power of that Commission to investigate and prosecute offences, see s 28; as to offences committed by a body, see s 341; and for the time limit on prosecutions, see s 347. See also s 306 for powers of entry as respects a suspected offence, and s 345 as respects forfeiture of an article relating to an offence. For territorial limitations on offences under this Part of this Act, see ss 359, 360.

Sub-s (1): Great Britain. See the note to s 12.

Sub-s (2): Secretary of State. See the note to s 4.

Orders under this section

At the time of going to press no orders had been made under this section.

As to orders under this Act generally, see s 355.

Definitions

'remote gambling equipment': ss 36(4), (5), 353(1)

Explanatory Notes

170–172 [para **6.2006** below]

PART 4
PROTECTION OF CHILDREN AND YOUNG PERSONS

Interpretation

6.545 45 Meaning of 'child' and 'young person'

(1) In this Act 'child' means an individual who is less than 16 years old.

(2) In this Act 'young person' means an individual who is not a child but who is less than 18 years old.

Commencement

Brought into force by the Gambling Act 2005 (Commencement No 6 and Transitional Provisions) Order 2006, SI 2006/3272, art 2 as from 1 September 2007; for transitional provisions see art 6, Sch 4 thereto (as amended by SI 2007/1157, arts 7–12).

Explanatory Notes

174 [para **6.2007** below]

Principal offences

6.546 46 Invitation to gamble

(1) A person commits an offence if he invites, causes or permits a child or young person to gamble.

(2) But subsection (1) does not apply in relation to—

(a) participation in private or non-commercial gaming,

(b) participation in private or non-commercial betting,

(c) participation in a lottery,

(d) participation in football pools,

(e) the use of a Category D gaming machine,

(f) participation in equal chance gaming in accordance with a prize gaming permit,

(g) participation in equal chance gaming at a licensed family entertainment centre,

(h) participation in prize gaming at a non-licensed family entertainment centre, or

(i) participation in prize gaming at a travelling fair in accordance with section 292.

(3) In subsection (1) a reference to inviting a child or young person to gamble includes, in particular, a reference to intentionally—

(a) sending to a child or young person any document which advertises gambling, or
(b) bringing to the attention of a child or young person information about gambling with a view to encouraging the child or young person to gamble.

(4) If a document which is sent to a child or young person and which advertises gambling gives the name or contact details of a person to whom payment may be made or from whom information may be obtained, that person shall be treated as having committed the offence under subsection (1) unless he proves that the document was sent—

(a) without his consent, and
(b) without his authority.

(5) If information about gambling is brought to the attention of a child or young person and includes the name or contact details of a person to whom payment may be made or from whom information may be obtained, that person ('the advertiser') shall be treated as having committed the offence under subsection (1) unless he proves that the information was brought to the attention of the child or young person—

(a) without the advertiser's consent or authority, or
(b) as an incident of the information being brought to the attention of adults and without a view to encouraging the child or young person to gamble.

(6) In subsections (4) and (5) 'contact details' means—

(a) an address or other location,
(b) a telephone number,
(c) an internet site, or
(d) an email address.

Commencement

Brought into force by the Gambling Act 2005 (Commencement No 6 and Transitional Provisions) Order 2006, SI 2006/3272, art 2 as from 1 September 2007; for transitional provisions see art 6, Sch 4 thereto (as amended by SI 2007/1157, arts 7–12).

Sub-s (1): Person. See the note 'Persons' to s 23.

Sub-s (1): Offence. For the power of the Gambling Commission and other specified persons to undertake activities for the purpose of assessing whether an offence is being committed under or by virtue of this Act, see s 27 and s 305; for the power of that Commission to investigate and prosecute offences, see s 28; as to offences committed by a body, see s 341; and for the time limit on prosecutions, see s 347. See also s 306 for powers of entry as respects a suspected offence, and s 345 as respects forfeiture of an article relating to an offence. For territorial limitations on offences under this Part of this Act, see ss 359, 360.

For the penalties for offences under this section, see s 62, and for a defence, see s 66.

Sub-s (2): Category D gaming machine. As to the categories of gaming machine, see s 236.

Application

Sub-ss (3)–(6) above are applied with modifications by ss 56(2), 57(2).

Definitions

'adult': s 353(1)
'advertising gambling': ss 327, 353(2)(b)
'Category D gaming machine': s 353(1)
'child': ss 45(1), 353(1)
'equal chance gaming': ss 8, 353(1)
'football pools': s 353(1)
'gambling': ss 3, 353(1)
'licensed family entertainment centre': ss 238, 353(1)
'lottery': ss 14, 353(1)
'non-commercial betting': ss 302, 353(1)
'non-commercial gaming': ss 297, 353(1)

'participating in a lottery': ss 14, 353(2)(c)
'private betting': ss 295, 353(1), Sch 15, Pt 2
'private gaming': ss 295, 353(1), Sch 15, Pt 1
'prize gaming': ss 288, 353(1)
'prize gaming permit': ss 289(2), 353(1)
'travelling fair': ss 286, 353(1)
'young person': ss 45(2), 353(1)

Explanatory Notes
175–177 [para 6.2007 below]

6.547 47 Invitation to enter premises

(1) A person commits an offence if he invites or permits a child or young person to enter premises if—

(a) a casino premises licence has effect in respect of the premises, and

(b) the premises are being used in reliance on that licence when the child or young person is invited or permitted to enter.

(2) But subsection (1) does not apply where—

(a) a child or young person is permitted to enter a part of premises which are being used for a regional casino, and

(b) that part is not being used for the provision of facilities for gambling when the child or young person is permitted to enter.

(3) The Secretary of State may for the purposes of subsection (2) by regulations make provision for—

(a) distinguishing between one part of premises and another;

(b) determining when use is being made of a part of premises.

(4) A person commits an offence if he invites or permits a child or young person to enter premises other than a track if—

(a) a betting premises licence has effect in respect of the premises, and

(b) the premises are being used in reliance on that licence when the child or young person is invited or permitted to enter.

(5) A person commits an offence if he invites or permits a child or young person to enter premises if—

(a) an adult gaming centre premises licence has effect in respect of the premises, and

(b) the premises are being used in reliance on that licence when the child or young person is invited or permitted to enter.

(6) A person commits an offence if he invites or permits a child or young person to enter an area from which children and young persons are required to be excluded by virtue of section 182.

(7) A person commits an offence if he invites or permits a child or young person to enter part of premises if—

(a) the premises are a licensed family entertainment centre,

(b) a person entering that part of the premises has access to a Category C gaming machine, and

(c) at the time when the child or young person is permitted or invited to enter, a Category C gaming machine is being used or is available for use.

Commencement

Brought into force by the Gambling Act 2005 (Commencement No 6 and Transitional Provisions) Order 2006, SI 2006/3272, art 2 as from 1 September 2007; for transitional provisions see art 6, Sch 4 thereto (as amended by SI 2007/1157, arts 7–12).

Sub-s (1): Person. See the note 'Persons' to s 23.

Sub-s (1): Offence. For the power of the Gambling Commission and other specified persons to undertake activities for the purpose of assessing whether an offence is being committed under or

by virtue of this Act, see s 27 and s 305; for the power of that Commission to investigate and prosecute offences, see s 28; as to offences committed by a body, see s 341; and for the time limit on prosecutions, see s 347. See also s 306 for powers of entry as respects a suspected offence, and s 345 as respects forfeiture of an article relating to an offence. For territorial limitations on offences under this Part of this Act, see ss 359, 360.

For the penalties for offences under this section, see s 62, and for a defence, see s 63.

Sub-s (2): Regional casino. As to the classification of casinos, see s 7(5)–(7).

Sub-s (3): Secretary of State. See the note to s 4.

Sub-s (7): Category C gaming machine. As to the categories of gaming machine, see s 236.

Application

Sub-s (6) above is applied by s 60(2).

Regulations under this section

At the time of going to press no regulations had been made under this section.

As to regulations under this Act generally, see s 355.

Definitions

'Category C gaming machine': s 353(1)
'child': ss 45(1), 353(1)
'licensed family entertainment centre': ss 238, 353(1)
'premises': s 353(1), (2)(g)
'premises licence': s 353(1)
'providing facilities for gambling': ss 5, 353(1)
'track': s 353(1)
'young person': ss 45(2), 353(1)

Explanatory Notes

178–182 [para **6.2007** below]

6.548 48 Gambling

(1) A young person commits an offence if he gambles.

(2) But subsection (1) does not apply to—

(a) participation in private or non-commercial gaming,
(b) participation in private or non-commercial betting,
(c) participation in a lottery,
(d) participation in football pools,
(e) the use of a Category D gaming machine,
(f) participation in equal chance gaming in accordance with a prize gaming permit,
(g) participation in equal chance gaming at a licensed family entertainment centre,
(h) participation in prize gaming at a non-licensed family entertainment centre, or
(i) participation in prize gaming at a travelling fair in accordance with section 292.

Commencement

Brought into force by the Gambling Act 2005 (Commencement No 6 and Transitional Provisions) Order 2006, SI 2006/3272, art 2 as from 1 September 2007; for transitional provisions see art 6, Sch 4 thereto (as amended by SI 2007/1157, arts 7–12).

Sub-s (1): Offence. For the power of the Gambling Commission and other specified persons to undertake activities for the purpose of assessing whether an offence is being committed under or by virtue of this Act, see s 27 and s 305; for the power of that Commission to investigate and prosecute offences, see s 28; and for the time limit on prosecutions, see s 347. See also s 306 for powers of entry as respects a suspected offence, and s 345 as respects forfeiture of an article relating to an offence. For territorial limitations on offences under this Part of this Act, see ss 359, 360.

For the penalties for offences under this section, see s 62.

Sub-s (2): Category D gaming machine. As to the categories of gaming machine, see s 236.

Definitions

'Category D gaming machine': s 353(1)
'equal chance gaming': ss 8, 353(1)
'football pools': s 353(1)
'gambling': ss 3, 353(1)
'licensed family entertainment centre': ss 238, 353(1)
'lottery': ss 14, 353(1)
'non-commercial betting': ss 302, 353(1)
'non-commercial gaming': ss 297, 353(1)
'participating in a lottery': ss 14, 353(2)(c)
'private betting': ss 295, 353(1), Sch 15, Pt 2
'private gaming': ss 295, 353(1), Sch 15, Pt 1
'prize gaming': ss 288, 353(1)
'prize gaming permit': ss 289(2), 353(1)
'travelling fair': ss 286, 353(1)
'young person': ss 45(2), 353(1)

Explanatory Notes

175–177 [para **6.2007** below]

6.549 49 Entering premises

A young person commits an offence if he enters premises in circumstances where a person would commit an offence under section 47 if he invited or permitted the young person to enter.

Commencement

Brought into force by the Gambling Act 2005 (Commencement No 6 and Transitional Provisions) Order 2006, SI 2006/3272, art 2 as from 1 September 2007; for transitional provisions see art 6, Sch 4 thereto (as amended by SI 2007/1157, arts 7–12).

Offence

For the power of the Gambling Commission and other specified persons to undertake activities for the purpose of assessing whether an offence is being committed under or by virtue of this Act, see s 27 and s 305; for the power of that Commission to investigate and prosecute offences, see s 28; and for the time limit on prosecutions, see s 347. See also s 306 for powers of entry as respects a suspected offence, and s 345 as respects forfeiture of an article relating to an offence. For territorial limitations on offences under this Part of this Act, see ss 359, 360.

For the penalties for offences under this section, see s 62.

Definitions

'premises': s 353(1), (2)(g)
'young person': ss 45(2), 353(1)

Explanatory Notes

178–182 [para **6.2007** below]

6.550 50 Provision of facilities for gambling

(1) A young person commits an offence if he provides facilities for gambling.

(2) But subsection (1) does not apply to the provision of facilities in connection with—

(a) private or non-commercial gaming,
(b) private or non-commercial betting,
(c) a lottery,
(d) football pools, or
(e) prize gaming at a travelling fair in accordance with section 292.

Commencement

Brought into force by the Gambling Act 2005 (Commencement No 6 and Transitional Provisions) Order 2006, SI 2006/3272, art 2 as from 1 September 2007; for transitional provisions see art 6, Sch 4 thereto (as amended by SI 2007/1157, arts 7–12).

Sub-s (1): Offence. For the power of the Gambling Commission and other specified persons to undertake activities for the purpose of assessing whether an offence is being committed under or by virtue of this Act, see s 27 and s 305; for the power of that Commission to investigate and prosecute offences, see s 28; and for the time limit on prosecutions, see s 347. See also s 306 for powers of entry as respects a suspected offence, and s 345 as respects forfeiture of an article relating to an offence. For territorial limitations on offences under this Part of this Act, see ss 359, 360.

For the penalties for offences under this section, see s 62.

Definitions

'football pools': s 353(1)
'lottery': ss 14, 353(1)
'non-commercial betting': ss 302, 353(1)
'non-commercial gaming': ss 297, 353(1)
'private betting': ss 295, 353(1), Sch 15, Pt 2
'private gaming': ss 295, 353(1), Sch 15, Pt 1
'prize gaming': ss 288, 353(1)
'providing facilities for gambling': ss 5, 353(1)
'travelling fair': ss 286, 353(1)
'young person': ss 45(2), 353(1)

Explanatory Notes

183 [para **6.2007** below]

Employment offences

6.551 51 Employment to provide facilities for gambling

(1) A person commits an offence if he employs a child or young person to provide facilities for gambling.

(2) But subsection (1) does not apply to the provision of facilities in connection with—

(a) private or non-commercial gaming,
(b) private or non-commercial betting,
(c) a lottery,
(d) football pools, or
(e) prize gaming at a travelling fair in accordance with section 292.

Commencement

Brought into force by the Gambling Act 2005 (Commencement No 6 and Transitional Provisions) Order 2006, SI 2006/3272, art 2 as from 1 September 2007; for transitional provisions see art 6, Sch 4 thereto (as amended by SI 2007/1157, arts 7–12).

Sub-s (1): Person. See the note 'Persons' to s 23.

Sub-s (1): Offence. For the power of the Gambling Commission and other specified persons to undertake activities for the purpose of assessing whether an offence is being committed under or by virtue of this Act, see s 27 and s 305; for the power of that Commission to investigate and prosecute offences, see s 28; as to offences committed by a body, see s 341; and for the time limit on prosecutions, see s 347. See also s 306 for powers of entry as respects a suspected offence, and s 345 as respects forfeiture of an article relating to an offence. For territorial limitations on offences under this Part of this Act, see ss 359, 360.

See further s 61(2). For the penalties for offences under this section, see s 62, and for a defence, see s 63.

Definitions

'child': ss 45(1), 353(1)
'employing a person': s 61
'football pools': s 353(1)
'lottery': ss 14, 353(1)
'non-commercial betting': ss 302, 353(1)
'non-commercial gaming': ss 297, 353(1)
'private betting': ss 295, 353(1), Sch 15, Pt 2
'private gaming': ss 295, 353(1), Sch 15, Pt 1
'prize gaming': ss 288, 353(1)
'providing facilities for gambling': ss 5, 353(1)
'travelling fair': ss 286, 353(1)
'young person': ss 45(2), 353(1)

Explanatory Notes

184–189 [para **6.2007** below]

6.552 52 Employment for lottery or football pools

A person commits an offence if he employs a child to provide facilities for gambling in connection with—

(a) a lottery (other than a lottery which forms part of the National Lottery), or
(b) football pools.

Commencement

Brought into force by the Gambling Act 2005 (Commencement No 6 and Transitional Provisions) Order 2006, SI 2006/3272, art 2 as from 1 September 2007; for transitional provisions see art 6, Sch 4 thereto (as amended by SI 2007/1157, arts 7–12).

Person. See the note 'Persons' to s 23.

Offence. For the power of the Gambling Commission and other specified persons to undertake activities for the purpose of assessing whether an offence is being committed under or by virtue of this Act, see s 27 and s 305; for the power of that Commission to investigate and prosecute offences, see s 28; as to offences committed by a body, see s 341; and for the time limit on prosecutions, see s 347. See also s 306 for powers of entry as respects a suspected offence, and s 345 as respects forfeiture of an article relating to an offence. For territorial limitations on offences under this Part of this Act, see ss 359, 360.

See further s 61(2). For the penalties for offences under this section, see s 62, and for a defence, see s 63.

Definitions

'child': ss 45(1), 353(1)
'employing a person': s 61
'football pools': s 353(1)
'lottery': ss 14, 353(1)
'the National Lottery': s 353(1)
'providing facilities for gambling': ss 5, 353(1)

Explanatory Notes

184–189 [para **6.2007** below]

6.553 53 Employment on bingo and club premises

A person commits an offence if he employs a child to perform any function on premises where, and at a time when—

(a) facilities are provided for the playing of bingo, or
(b) facilities for gambling are provided in accordance with a club gaming permit or a club machine permit.

Commencement

Brought into force by the Gambling Act 2005 (Commencement No 6 and Transitional Provisions) Order 2006, SI 2006/3272, art 2 as from 1 September 2007; for transitional provisions see art 6, Sch 4 thereto (as amended by SI 2007/1157, arts 7–12).

Sub-s (1): Person. See the note 'Persons' to s 23.

Sub-s (1): Offence. For the power of the Gambling Commission and other specified persons to undertake activities for the purpose of assessing whether an offence is being committed under or by virtue of this Act, see s 27 and s 305; for the power of that Commission to investigate and prosecute offences, see s 28; as to offences committed by a body, see s 341; and for the time limit on prosecutions, see s 347. See also s 306 for powers of entry as respects a suspected offence, and s 345 as respects forfeiture of an article relating to an offence. For territorial limitations on offences under this Part of this Act, see ss 359, 360.

See further s 61(2). For the penalties for offences under this section, see s 62, and for a defence, see s 63.

Definitions

'bingo': s 353(1)
'child': ss 45(1), 353(1)
'club gaming permit': ss 271(2), 353(1)
'club machine permit': ss 273(2), 353(1)
'employing a person': s 61
'premises': s 353(1), (2)(g)
'providing facilities for gambling': ss 5, 353(1)

Explanatory Notes

184–189 [para **6.2007** below]

6.554 54 Employment on premises with gaming machines

(1) A person commits an offence if—

(a) he employs a child or young person to perform any function on premises where a Category A, B, C or D gaming machine is situated, and

(b) the child or young person is or may be required in the course of his employment to perform a function in connection with the gaming machine.

(2) A young person commits an offence if he is employed in contravention of subsection (1).

Commencement

Brought into force by the Gambling Act 2005 (Commencement No 6 and Transitional Provisions) Order 2006, SI 2006/3272, art 2 as from 1 September 2007; for transitional provisions see art 6, Sch 4 thereto (as amended by SI 2007/1157, arts 7–12).

Sub-s (1): Person. See the note 'Persons' to s 23.

Sub-s (1): Offence. For the power of the Gambling Commission and other specified persons to undertake activities for the purpose of assessing whether an offence is being committed under or by virtue of this Act, see s 27 and s 305; for the power of that Commission to investigate and prosecute offences, see s 28; as to offences committed by a body, see s 341; and for the time limit on prosecutions, see s 347. See also s 306 for powers of entry as respects a suspected offence, and s 345 as respects forfeiture of an article relating to an offence. For territorial limitations on offences under this Part of this Act, see ss 359, 360.

See further s 61(2). For the penalties for offences under this section, see s 62, and for a defence, see s 63.

Sub-s (1): Category A, B, C or D gaming machine. As to the categories of gaming machine, see s 236 and the Categories of Gaming Machine Regulations 2007, SI 2007/2158.

Definitions

'Category A gaming machine': s 353(1).
'Category B gaming machine': s 353(1).
'Category C gaming machine': s 353(1).

'Category D gaming machine': s 353(1) and see SI 2007/2158, reg 6.
'child': ss 45(1), 353(1).
'employing a person': s 61.
'premises': s 353(1), (2)(g).
'young person': ss 45(2), 353(1).

Explanatory Notes

184–189 [para 6.2007 below]

6.555 55 Employment in casino, &c

(1) A person commits an offence if he employs a child or young person to perform any function on premises in respect of which any of the following have effect—

(a) a casino premises licence,

(b) a betting premises licence, and

(c) an adult gaming centre premises licence.

(2) But subsection (1) does not apply—

(a) to employment at a time when no activity is being carried on in reliance on the premises licence, or

(b) to employment on a part of premises which are being used for a regional casino at a time when that part is not being used for the provision of facilities for gambling.

(3) The Secretary of State may for the purposes of subsection (2) by regulations make provision for—

(a) distinguishing between one part of premises and another;

(b) determining when use is being made of a part of premises.

(4) A young person commits an offence if he is employed in contravention of subsection (1).

Commencement

Brought into force by the Gambling Act 2005 (Commencement No 6 and Transitional Provisions) Order 2006, SI 2006/3272, art 2 as from 1 September 2007; for transitional provisions see art 6, Sch 4 thereto (as amended by SI 2007/1157, arts 7–12).

Sub-s (1): Person. See the note 'Persons' to s 23.

Sub-s (1): Offence. For the power of the Gambling Commission and other specified persons to undertake activities for the purpose of assessing whether an offence is being committed under or by virtue of this Act, see s 27 and s 305; for the power of that Commission to investigate and prosecute offences, see s 28; as to offences committed by a body, see s 341; and for the time limit on prosecutions, see s 347. See also s 306 for powers of entry as respects a suspected offence, and s 345 as respects forfeiture of an article relating to an offence. For territorial limitations on offences under this Part of this Act, see ss 359, 360.

See further s 61(2). For the penalties for offences under this section, see s 62, and for a defence, see s 63.

Sub-s (2): Regional casino. As to the classification of casinos, see s 7(5)–(7).

Sub-s (3): Secretary of State. See the note to s 4.

Regulations under this section

At the time of going to press no regulations had been made under this section.

As to regulations under this Act generally, see s 355.

Definitions

'child': ss 45(1), 353(1)
'employing a person': s 61
'premises': s 353(1), (2)(g)
'premises licence': s 353(1)
'providing facilities for gambling': ss 5, 353(1)
'young person': ss 45(2), 353(1)

Explanatory Notes
184–189 [para **6.2007** below]

Miscellaneous offences

6.556 56 Invitation to participate in lottery

(1) A person commits an offence if he invites, causes or permits a child to participate in a lottery other than—

(a) an incidental non-commercial lottery that is exempt for the purposes of section 258 by virtue of Part 1 of Schedule 11,

(b) a private lottery (whether a private society lottery, a work lottery or a residents' lottery) that is exempt for the purposes of section 258 by virtue of Part 2 of Schedule 11, or

(c) a lottery which forms part of the National Lottery.

(2) Subsections (3) to (6) of section 46 shall have effect in relation to subsection (1) of this section as they have effect in relation to subsection (1) of that section; and for that purpose—

(a) references to a child or young person shall be treated as references only to a child, and

(b) references to gambling shall be treated as references to participation in a lottery.

Commencement

Brought into force by the Gambling Act 2005 (Commencement No 6 and Transitional Provisions) Order 2006, SI 2006/3272, art 2 as from 1 September 2007; for transitional provisions see art 6, Sch 4 thereto (as amended by SI 2007/1157, arts 7–12).

Sub-s (1): Person. See the note 'Persons' to s 23.

Sub-s (1): Offence. For the power of the Gambling Commission and other specified persons to undertake activities for the purpose of assessing whether an offence is being committed under or by virtue of this Act, see s 27 and s 305; for the power of that Commission to investigate and prosecute offences, see s 28; as to offences committed by a body, see s 341; and for the time limit on prosecutions, see s 347. See also s 306 for powers of entry as respects a suspected offence, and s 345 as respects forfeiture of an article relating to an offence. For territorial limitations on offences under this Part of this Act, see ss 359, 360.

For the penalties for offences under this section, see s 62, and for a defence, see s 63.

Definitions
'child': ss 45(1), 353(1)
'lottery': ss 14, 353(1)
'the National Lottery': s 353(1)
'participating in a lottery': ss 14, 353(2)(c)

Explanatory Notes
190, 191 [para **6.2007** below]

6.557 57 Invitation to participate in football pools

(1) A person commits an offence if he invites, causes or permits a child to participate in football pools.

(2) Subsections (3) to (6) of section 46 shall have effect in relation to subsection (1) of this section as they have effect in relation to subsection (1) of that section; and for that purpose—

(a) references to a child or young person shall be treated as references only to a child, and

(b) references to gambling shall be treated as references to participation in football pools.

Commencement

Brought into force by the Gambling Act 2005 (Commencement No 6 and Transitional Provisions) Order 2006, SI 2006/3272, art 2 as from 1 September 2007; for transitional provisions see art 6, Sch 4 thereto (as amended by SI 2007/1157, arts 7–12).

Sub-s (1): Person. See the note 'Persons' to s 23.

Sub-s (1): Offence. For the power of the Gambling Commission and other specified persons to undertake activities for the purpose of assessing whether an offence is being committed under or by virtue of this Act, see s 27 and s 305; for the power of that Commission to investigate and prosecute offences, see s 28; as to offences committed by a body, see s 341; and for the time limit on prosecutions, see s 347. See also s 306 for powers of entry as respects a suspected offence, and s 345 as respects forfeiture of an article relating to an offence. For territorial limitations on offences under this Part of this Act, see ss 359, 360.

For the penalties for offences under this section, see s 62, and for a defence, see s 63.

Definitions

'child': ss 45(1), 353(1)
'football pools': s 353(1)

Explanatory Notes

192 [para **6.2007** below]

6.558 58 Return of stake

A person commits an offence if without reasonable excuse he fails to comply with a condition attached to an operating licence by virtue of section 83.

Commencement

Brought into force by the Gambling Act 2005 (Commencement No 6 and Transitional Provisions) Order 2006, SI 2006/3272, art 2 as from 1 September 2007; for transitional provisions see art 6, Sch 4 thereto (as amended by SI 2007/1157, arts 7–12).

Person. See the note 'Persons' to s 23.

Offence. For the power of the Gambling Commission and other specified persons to undertake activities for the purpose of assessing whether an offence is being committed under or by virtue of this Act, see s 27 and s 305; for the power of that Commission to investigate and prosecute offences, see s 28; as to offences committed by a body, see s 341; and for the time limit on prosecutions, see s 347. See also s 306 for powers of entry as respects a suspected offence, and s 345 as respects forfeiture of an article relating to an offence. For territorial limitations on offences under this Part of this Act, see ss 359, 360.

For the penalties for offences under this section, see s 62, and for a defence, see s 63.

Operating licence

As to the nature, etc of operating licences, see s 65 and the note 'Operating licences' thereto.

Definitions

'operating licence': s 353(1)

Explanatory Notes

193 [para **6.2007** below]

6.559 59 Age limit for Category D gaming machines

(1) The Secretary of State may by order create an offence of inviting, causing or permitting a child or young person below a specified age to use a Category D gaming machine.

(2) An order under subsection (1) may, in particular—

(a) apply (with modifications) or include provision similar to section 46(3) to (6);

(b) make consequential amendments of this Act.

(3) Before making an order under subsection (1) the Secretary of State shall consult—

(a) the Commission,

(b) one or more persons who appear to the Secretary of State to represent the interests of persons carrying on gambling businesses, and

(c) one or more persons who appear to the Secretary of State to have knowledge about social problems relating to gambling.

(4) An order under subsection (1) may apply to a class of Category D gaming machine determined by reference to—

(a) the nature of the facilities for gambling which are made available on the machine,

(b) the nature or value of a prize offered by the machine,

(c) the manner in which the machine operates, or

(d) any other matter.

Commencement

Brought into force by the Gambling Act 2005 (Commencement No 6 and Transitional Provisions) Order 2006, SI 2006/3272, art 2 as from 1 September 2007; for transitional provisions see art 6, Sch 4 thereto (as amended by SI 2007/1157, arts 7–12).

Sub-s (1): Secretary of State. See the note to s 4.

Sub-s (1): May by order. Section 64(1) (use of children in enforcement operations) applies to an order under this section; see s 64(2).

Sub-s (1): Category D gaming machine. As to the categories of gaming machine, see s 236.

Sub-s (3): The Commission. Ie the Gambling Commission; see s 353(1). As to the establishment, etc of the Gambling Commission, see s 20, Sch 4, and the note 'Gambling Commission' to that section.

Sub-s (3): Persons. See the note to s 23.

Orders under this section

At the time of going to press no orders had been made under this section.

As to orders under this Act generally, see s 355.

Definitions

'Category D gaming machine': s 353(1)
'child': ss 45(1), 353(1)
'the Commission': s 353(1)
'gambling': ss 3, 353(1)
'prize': ss 239, 353(1)
'young person': ss 45(2), 353(1)

Explanatory Notes

194, 195 [para **6.2007** below]

General

6.560 60 Temporary use notice

(1) For the purposes of this Part—

(a) a temporary use notice in respect of the use of premises to carry on an activity shall be treated as if it were a premises licence authorising that activity, and

(b) an occasional use notice in respect of premises shall be treated as if it were a betting premises licence.

(2) Sections 47(6) and 182 shall apply in relation to a notice treated as a premises licence by virtue of subsection (1) above.

Commencement

Brought into force by the Gambling Act 2005 (Commencement No 6 and Transitional Provisions) Order 2006, SI 2006/3272, art 2 as from 1 September 2007; for transitional provisions see art 6, Sch 4 thereto (as amended by SI 2007/1157, arts 7–12).

Sub-s (1): This Part. Ie Pt 4 (ss 45–64) of this Act.

Definitions

'act which is authorised by a licence': s 353(5)
'premises': s 353(1), (2)(g)
'premises licence': s 353(1)
'temporary use notice': ss 215(1), 353(1)

Explanatory Notes

196 [para **6.2007** below]

6.561 61 Employment

(1) In this Part a reference to employing a person includes a reference to—

(a) employing or engaging the person whether or not under a contract of employment, and

(b) causing or permitting the person to be employed or engaged.

(2) Where a person commits an offence under this Part by employing a person or by being employed, he shall be treated as committing the offence on each day during any part of which the employment continues.

Commencement

Brought into force by the Gambling Act 2005 (Commencement No 6 and Transitional Provisions) Order 2006, SI 2006/3272, art 2 as from 1 September 2007; for transitional provisions see art 6, Sch 4 thereto (as amended by SI 2007/1157, arts 7–12).

Sub-s (1): This Part. Ie Pt 4 (ss 45–64) of this Act.

Explanatory Notes

197, 198 [para **6.2007** below]

6.562 62 Penalty

(1) A person guilty of an offence under this Part shall be liable on summary conviction to—

(a) imprisonment for a term not exceeding 51 weeks,

(b) a fine not exceeding level 5 on the standard scale, or

(c) both.

(2) But in relation to an offence committed by a young person subsection (1) shall have effect as if—

(a) paragraphs (a) and (c) were omitted, and

(b) in paragraph (b) the reference to level 5 were a reference to level 3.

(3) In the application of subsection (1) to Scotland the reference to 51 weeks shall have effect as a reference to six months.

Commencement

Brought into force by the Gambling Act 2005 (Commencement No 6 and Transitional Provisions) Order 2006, SI 2006/3272, art 2 as from 1 September 2007; for transitional provisions see art 6, Sch 4 thereto (as amended by SI 2007/1157, arts 7–12).

Sub-s (1): Person. See the note 'Persons' to s 23.

Sub-s (1): This Part. Ie Pt 4 (ss 45–64) of this Act.

Sub-s (1): Summary conviction; standard scale. See the notes to s 33.

Definitions

'young person': ss 45(2), 353(1)

Explanatory Notes

199 [para **6.2007** below]

6.563 63 Reasonable belief about person's age

(1) Where a person is charged with an offence under this Part of doing anything in relation to an individual who is a child it is a defence for the person charged to prove that—

(a) he took all reasonable steps to determine the individual's age, and
(b) he reasonably believed that the individual was not a child.

(2) Where a person is charged with an offence under this Part of doing anything in relation to an individual who is a young person it is a defence for the person charged to prove that—

(a) he took all reasonable steps to determine the individual's age, and
(b) he reasonably believed that the individual was not a young person.

Commencement

Brought into force by the Gambling Act 2005 (Commencement No 6 and Transitional Provisions) Order 2006, SI 2006/3272, art 2 as from 1 September 2007; for transitional provisions see art 6, Sch 4 thereto (as amended by SI 2007/1157, arts 7–12).

Sub-s (1): Person. See the note 'Persons' to s 23.

Sub-s (1): This Part. Ie Pt 4 (ss 45–64) of this Act.

Definitions

'child': ss 45(1), 353(1)
'young person': ss 45(2), 353(1)

Explanatory Notes

200 [para **6.2007** below]

6.564 64 Use of children in enforcement operations

(1) Nothing in this Part renders unlawful—

(a) anything done, in the performance of his functions, by a constable, an enforcement officer or an authorised person, or
(b) anything done by a child or young person at the request of a constable, enforcement officer or authorised person acting in the performance of his functions.

(2) Subsection (1) applies to an order under section 59 as to the provisions of this Part.

Commencement

Brought into force by the Gambling Act 2005 (Commencement No 6 and Transitional Provisions) Order 2006, SI 2006/3272, art 2 as from 1 September 2007; for transitional provisions see art 6, Sch 4 thereto (as amended by SI 2007/1157, arts 7–12).

Sub-s (1): This Part. Ie Pt 4 (ss 45–64) of this Act.

Sub-s (1): Enforcement officer. As to enforcement officers, see, generally, s 303.

Definitions

'authorised person': ss 304, 353(1)
'child': ss 45(1), 353(1)
'enforcement officer': s 353(1)
'young person': ss 45(2), 353(1)

Explanatory Notes

201 [para **6.2007** below]

PART 5
OPERATING LICENCES

Introductory

6.565 65 Nature of licence

(1) The Commission may issue operating licences in accordance with the provisions of this Part.

(2) An operating licence is a licence which states that it authorises the licensee—

(a) to operate a casino (a 'casino operating licence'),

(b) to provide facilities for playing bingo (a 'bingo operating licence'),

(c) to provide facilities for betting other than pool betting (a 'general betting operating licence'),

(d) to provide facilities for pool betting (a 'pool betting operating licence'),

(e) to act as a betting intermediary (a 'betting intermediary operating licence'),

(f) to make gaming machines available for use in an adult gaming centre (a 'gaming machine general operating licence' for an adult gaming centre),

(g) to make gaming machines available for use in a family entertainment centre (a 'gaming machine general operating licence' for a family entertainment centre),

(h) to manufacture, supply, install, adapt, maintain or repair a gaming machine, or a part of a gaming machine (a 'gaming machine technical operating licence'),

(i) to manufacture, supply, install or adapt gambling software (a 'gambling software operating licence'), or

(j) to promote a lottery (a 'lottery operating licence').

(3) The issue of an operating licence does not affect the application of section 37.

(4) The Secretary of State may by order amend subsection (2) so as to—

(a) add a kind of operating licence,

(b) remove a kind of operating licence, or

(c) vary a kind of operating licence.

(5) An order under subsection (4) may, in particular, make consequential amendment of this Part (or a provision of this Act or another enactment that relates to this Part).

Commencement

Subsections (1), (3)–(5) brought into force for certain purposes as from 1 January 2007, for remaining purposes as from 1 September 2007 by the Gambling Act 2005 (Commencement No 6 and Transitional Provisions) Order 2006, SI 2006/3272, art 2, Sch 1; for transitional provisions see art 6, Sch 4 thereto (as amended by SI 2007/1157, arts 7–12). Subsection (2) brought into force by the Gambling Act 2005 (Commencement No 2 and Transitional Provisions) Order 2005, SI 2005/2455, art 2 and Schedule, as from 1 October 2005.

Sub-s (1): The Commission. Ie the Gambling Commission; see s 353(1). As to the establishment, etc of the Gambling Commission, see s 20, Sch 4, and the note 'Gambling Commission' to that section.

Sub-s (1): Operating licences. See further s 66 (form of licence); s 67 (remote gambling); s 68 (combined licence); ss 69–74 (issue); ss 75–88 (conditions); ss 89–99 (rules for particular kinds of licence); ss 100–109 (maintenance); ss 110–115 (duration); ss 116–122 (regulation); and ss 123–126 and Sch 7 (general).

For offences in connection with the provision of facilities for gambling, see ss 33–36, for offences in connection with the use of premises, see ss 37–40, and for miscellaneous offences, see ss 41–44. Provisions for the protection of children and young persons are contained in Pt 4 of this Act.

For powers of entry in connection with operating licences, see ss 307, 308, 310.

For the power of the Gambling Commission to void a bet, see s 336.

Sub-s (1): This Part. Ie Pt 5 (ss 65–126 and Sch 7) of this Act.

Sub-s (2): Casino operating licence. See the note 'Operating licences' above, and see, in particular, as respects casino operating licences, s 90. The unauthorised use of premises as a casino is an offence under s 37, and for offences in connection with the employment of a child or young person in a casino, see s 55.

Sub-s (2): Bingo operating licence. See the note 'Operating licences' above, and see, in particular, as respects bingo operating licences, s 91. The unauthorised use of premises for providing facilities for the playing of bingo is an offence under s 37, and for offences in connection with the employment of a child on bingo premises, see s 53.

Sub-s (2): General betting operating licence. See the note 'Operating licences' above, and see, in particular, as respects general betting operating licences, s 92. The unauthorised use of premises for providing facilities for betting is an offence under s 37.

Sub-s (2): Pool betting operating licence. See the note 'Operating licences' above, and see, in particular, as respects pool betting operating licences, s 93. The unauthorised use of premises for providing facilities for betting is an offence under s 37.

Sub-s (2): Betting intermediary operating licence. See the note 'Operating licences' above. The unauthorised use of premises for providing facilities for betting is an offence under s 37.

Sub-s (2): Gaming machine general operating licence. See the note 'Operating licences' above. The unauthorised use of premises for making a gaming machine available for use is an offence under s 37, and for offences in connection with the employment of a child or young person on premises with gaming machines, see s 54.

Sub-s (2): Gaming machine technical operating licence. See the note 'Operating licences' above, and see, in particular, as respects gaming machine technical operating licences, s 96.

Sub-s (2): Gambling software operating licence. See the note 'Operating licences' above, and see, in particular, as respects gambling software licences, s 97. It is an offence to manufacture, supply, etc gambling software unless in accordance with an operating licence; see s 41.

Sub-s (2): Lottery operating licence. See the note 'Operating licences' above, and see, in particular, as respects lottery operating licences, ss 98, 99. For offences in connection with an invitation to a child to participate in a lottery, see s 56.

Sub-s (4): Secretary of State. See the note to s 4.

Application

This Part of this Act is applied, with modifications, in relation to an application for the variation of an operating licence by s 104(3), (4), and in relation to an application for renewal of an operating licence by s 112(2), (5).

This Part of this Act is also applied, with modifications, to personal licences by s 128.

Orders under this section

At the time of going to press no orders had been made under this section.

As to orders under this Act generally, see s 355.

Definitions

'acting as a betting intermediary': s 13(2)
'adult gaming centre': ss 237, 353(1)
'betting': ss 9–11, 353(1)
'betting intermediary': ss 13(1), 353(1)
'bingo': s 353(1)
'casino': ss 7, 353(1)
'the Commission': s 353(1)
'family entertainment centre': ss 238, 353(1)
'gambling software': ss 41(2), 353(1)
'gaming machine': ss 235, 353(1)
'installing computer software': s 353(2)(d)
'licensee': s 126(1)
'lottery': ss 14, 353(1)
'operating licence': s 353(1)
'pool betting': ss 12, 353(1)
'promoting a lottery': ss 252, 353(2)(h)
'providing facilities for gambling': ss 5, 353(2)(i)
'supply': s 353(1)

Explanatory Notes

202–209 [para 6.2008 below]

6.566 66 Form of licence

(1) An operating licence must specify—

(a) the person to whom it is issued,

(b) the period during which it is to have effect, and

(c) any condition attached by the Commission under section 75 or 77.

(2) The Secretary of State may by regulations require the Commission to ensure that an operating licence—

(a) is issued in such form as the regulations may specify, and

(b) contains, in addition to the matters specified in subsection (1), such information as the regulations may specify (which may, in particular, include information about conditions attached to the licence by virtue of section 78).

Commencement

Brought into force for certain purposes as from 1 January 2007, for remaining purposes as from 1 September 2007 by the Gambling Act 2005 (Commencement No 6 and Transitional Provisions) Order 2006, SI 2006/3272, art 2, Sch 1; for transitional provisions see art 6, Sch 4 thereto (as amended by SI 2007/1157, arts 7–12).

Sub-s (1): Operating licence. As to the nature, etc of operating licences, see s 65 and the note 'Operating licences' thereto.

Sub-s (1): Person. See the note 'Persons' to s 23.

Sub-s (1): The Commission. Ie the Gambling Commission; see s 353(1). As to the establishment, etc of the Gambling Commission, see s 20, Sch 4, and the note 'Gambling Commission' to that section.

Sub-s (2): Secretary of State. See the note to s 4.

Application

See the note to s 65.

Regulations under this section

At the time of going to press no regulations had been made under this section.

As to regulations under this Act generally, see s 355.

Definitions

'the Commission': s 353(1)

'operating licence': s 353(1)

Explanatory Notes

210 [para 6.2008 below]

6.567 67 Remote gambling

(1) An operating licence is a 'remote operating licence' if it authorises activity to be carried on—

(a) in respect of remote gambling, or

(b) by means of remote communication.

(2) A remote operating licence may not also authorise activity which is neither—

(a) in respect of remote gambling, nor

(b) carried on by means of remote communication.

(3) An operating licence must state whether it is a remote operating licence or not.

Commencement

Brought into force for certain purposes as from 1 January 2007, for remaining purposes as from 1 September 2007 by the Gambling Act 2005 (Commencement No 6 and Transitional Provisions) Order 2006, SI 2006/3272, art 2, Sch 1; for transitional provisions see art 6, Sch 4 thereto (as amended by SI 2007/1157, arts 7–12).

Sub-s (1): Operating licence. As to the nature, etc of operating licences, see s 65 and the note 'Operating licences' thereto.

Sub-s (1): Remote operating licence. See the note 'Operating licences' to s 65, and see, in particular, as respects remote operating licences, s 89.

Application

See the note to s 65.

Definitions

'operating licence': s 353(1)
'remote communication': ss 4(2), (3), 353(1)
'remote gambling': ss 4, 353(1)

Explanatory Notes

211–213 [para **6.2008** below]

6.568 68 Combined licence

(1) An operating licence may be a licence of more than one of the kinds described in section 65(2).

(2) Subsection (1) is subject to the following provisions of this section.

(3) A casino operating licence authorises the holder, by virtue of this subsection, to provide facilities—

(a) for betting on the outcome of a virtual game, race, competition or other event or process, subject to any exclusion or restriction provided for by way of condition under section 75 or 77;

(b) for any game of chance other than bingo (and this paragraph does not prevent the combination of a casino operating licence and a bingo operating licence in reliance on subsection (1)).

(4) A general betting operating licence authorises the holder, by virtue of this subsection, to provide facilities for betting on the outcome of a virtual race, competition or other event or process other than a game of chance, subject to any exclusion or restriction provided for by way of condition under section 75 or 77.

(5) The following kinds of operating licence authorise the holder, by virtue of this subsection, to make one or more gaming machines within Categories A to D available for use (in addition to authorising the activities specified in accordance with section 65(2))—

(a) a non-remote casino operating licence,

(b) a non-remote bingo operating licence,

(c) a non-remote general betting operating licence, and

(d) a non-remote pool betting operating licence.

(6) No other kind of operating licence (other than a gaming machine general operating licence) may authorise the holder to make a gaming machine available for use.

Commencement

Brought into force for certain purposes as from 1 January 2007, for remaining purposes as from 1 September 2007 by the Gambling Act 2005 (Commencement No 6 and Transitional Provisions) Order 2006, SI 2006/3272, art 2, Sch 1; for transitional provisions see art 6, Sch 4 thereto (as amended by SI 2007/1157, arts 7–12).

Sub-s (1): Operating licence. As to the nature, etc of operating licences, see s 65 and the note 'Operating licences' thereto.

Sub-s (5): Categories A to D. As to the categories of gaming machine, see s 236.

Application

See the note to s 65.

Definitions

'betting': ss 9–11, 353(1)
'bingo': s 353(1)
'Categories A to D gaming machines': s 353(1)
'game of chance': ss 6, 353(1)
'gaming machine': ss 235, 353(1)

'holder': s 126(1)
'operating licence': s 353(1)
'providing facilities for gambling': ss 5, 353(2)(i)
'virtual game, race or other event or process': s 353(3)

Explanatory Notes

214–221 [para **6.2008** below]

Issue

6.569 69 Application

(1) A person may apply to the Gambling Commission for an operating licence to be issued authorising him to provide facilities for gambling.

(2) An application must—

(a) specify the activities to be authorised by the licence,

(b) specify an address in the United Kingdom at which a document issued under this Act may be served on the applicant,

(c) be made in such form and manner as the Commission may direct,

(d) state whether the applicant has been convicted of a relevant offence,

(e) state whether the applicant has been convicted of any other offence,

(f) contain or be accompanied by such other information or documents as the Commission may direct, and

(g) be accompanied by the prescribed fee.

(3) An application may not be made by—

(a) a child or young person, or

(b) a group that includes a child or young person.

(4) The Secretary of State may by regulations—

(a) require an applicant for an operating licence to notify specified persons within a specified period (which may be wholly or partly before the application is made), and

(b) provide for the consequences of failure to comply with a requirement under paragraph (a) (which may, in particular, include provision for an application to be disregarded or for a licence to lapse).

(5) In subsection (2)(g) 'prescribed' means prescribed by regulations made by the Secretary of State; and the regulations may, in particular, make different provision for—

(a) applications for the authorisation of different classes of activity, or

(b) different circumstances.

Commencement

Brought into force for certain purposes as from 1 January 2007, for remaining purposes as from 1 September 2007 by the Gambling Act 2005 (Commencement No 6 and Transitional Provisions) Order 2006, SI 2006/3272, art 2, Sch 1; for transitional provisions see art 6, Sch 4 thereto (as amended by SI 2007/1157, arts 7–12).

Sub-s (1): Person. See the note 'Persons' to s 23.

Sub-s (1): May apply. As to the consideration of an application, see ss 70–72, for the procedure, see s 73, and as to determination, see s 74. As to appeals to the Gambling Appeals Tribunal, see s 141.

Sub-s (1): Gambling Commission. As to the establishment, etc of the Gambling Commission, see s 20, Sch 4, and the note 'Gambling Commission' to that section.

Sub-s (1): Operating licence. As to the nature, etc of operating licences, see s 65 and the note 'Operating licences' thereto.

Sub-s (2): United Kingdom. See the note to s 36.

Sub-s (2): Be accompanied by the prescribed fee. The Gambling Commission may disregard an irregularity or deficiency in or in relation to an application under this section, other than a failure to pay the fee required by sub-s (2)(g) above; see s 73(5).

Sub-s (4): Secretary of State. See the note to s 4.

Sub-s (4): Notify. See further, in connection with a requirement under this Act to give a notice, s 353(4).

Application

See the note to s 65.

As to regulations under this Act generally, see s 355.

Subordinate Legislation: see SIs 2006/3284, 2006/3285 and 2008/1803.

Definitions

'child': ss 45(1), 353(1)
'conviction': s 126(1)
'operating licence': s 353(1)
'providing facilities for gambling': ss 5, 353(2)(i)
'relevant offence': ss 126(2), (3), 353(1), Sch 7
'young person': ss 45(2), 353(1)

Explanatory Notes

222–223 [para **6.2008** below]

6.570 70 Consideration of application: general principles

(1) In considering an application under section 69 the Commission—

(a) shall have regard to the licensing objectives,

(b) shall form and have regard to an opinion of the applicant's suitability to carry on the licensed activities,

(c) shall consider the suitability of any gaming machine to be used in connection with the licensed activities, and

(d) may consider the suitability of any other equipment to be used in connection with the licensed activities (by reference, in particular, to any relevant provision of standards established under section 89).

(2) For the purpose of subsection (1)(b) the Commission may, in particular, have regard to—

(a) the integrity of the applicant or of a person relevant to the application;

(b) the competence of the applicant or of a person relevant to the application to carry on the licensed activities in a manner consistent with pursuit of the licensing objectives;

(c) the financial and other circumstances of the applicant or of a person relevant to the application (and, in particular, the resources likely to be available for the purpose of carrying on the licensed activities).

(3) In considering an application for a non-remote casino operating licence the Commission shall have regard, in addition to the matters specified in subsection (1), to the applicant's commitment to—

(a) protecting vulnerable persons from being harmed or exploited by gambling, and

(b) making assistance available to persons who are or may be affected by problems related to gambling.

(4) The statement maintained by the Commission under section 23 must specify the principles to be applied by the Commission in considering applications under section 69.

(5) The statement must, in particular, specify the kind of evidence to which the Commission will have regard when assessing integrity, competence and financial or other circumstances; and that evidence may include—

(a) interviews conducted by or on behalf of the Commission;

(b) references provided to the Commission at the request of the applicant;

(c) information or opinions provided to the Commission (whether or not on request) by other persons;

(d) information sought by the Commission as to solvency in general and financial reserves in particular;

(e) the completion of training (whether provided in accordance with arrangements made by the Commission or otherwise);

(f) the possession of qualifications (whether awarded in accordance with arrangements made by the Commission or otherwise).

(6) The statement must also, in particular, specify the kind of evidence to which the Commission will have regard in considering the suitability of a gaming machine or of other equipment; and that evidence may include—

(a) the result of a test carried out by a person at the request of the Commission;

(b) the opinion of any person.

(7) The statement may specify a class of applicant or other person in relation to whom the Commission will or may assume integrity for the purpose of subsection (2)(a).

(8) The statement may specify a class of gaming machine or other equipment in relation to which the Commission will or may assume suitability; and—

(a) a class may, in particular, be defined by reference to standards under section 89 or 96 or by reference to regulations under Part 10, and

(b) subsection (1)(c) and (d) shall not apply to the consideration of an application in so far as it specifies that a gaming machine or other equipment falling within a class specified under this subsection is to be used in connection with the licensed activities.

(9) For the purposes of this section—

(a) in relation to an application, a reference to the licensed activities is a reference to the activities which will be the licensed activities if the application is granted, and

(b) a person is relevant to an application if, in particular, he is likely to exercise a function in connection with, or to have an interest in, the licensed activities.

(10) For the purposes of this section 'equipment' includes—

(a) a computer,

(b) a device for the playing of a casino game, and

(c) any other piece of equipment;

(but a gaming machine is not equipment for the purposes of this section).

Note

See the Gambling Commission's 'Statement of Principles for Licensing and Regulation', September 2009 (see para **6.2040** below).

Commencement

Brought into force for certain purposes as from 1 January 2007, for remaining purposes as from 1 September 2007 by the Gambling Act 2005 (Commencement No 6 and Transitional Provisions) Order 2006, SI 2006/3272, art 2, Sch 1; for transitional provisions see art 6, Sch 4 thereto (as amended by SI 2007/1157, arts 7–12).

Sub-s (1): The Commission. Ie the Gambling Commission; see s 353(1). As to the establishment, etc of the Gambling Commission, see s 20, Sch 4, and the note 'Gambling Commission' to that section.

Sub-s (2): Person. See the note 'Persons' to s 23.

Sub-s (3): Operating licence. As to the nature, etc of operating licences, see s 65 and the note 'Operating licences' thereto.

Saving

Section 71 does not prejudice the generality of this section; see s 71(2).

Application

See the note to s 65.

6: Gambling Act 2005: Statutes

Definitions

'casino game': ss 7(2), (3), 353(1)
'the Commission': s 353(1)
'gambling': ss 3, 353(1)
'gaming machine': ss 235, 353(1)
'the licensed activities': s 126(1) (and sub-s (9)(a) above)
'the licensing objectives': ss 1, 353(1)
'operating licence': s 353(1)

Explanatory Notes

224–229 [para **6.2008** below]

6.571 71 Consideration of application: criminal record

(1) The Commission may refuse an application under section 69 if the applicant or a person relevant to the application has a conviction for a relevant offence.

(2) This section does not prejudice the generality of section 70.

(3) The reference in subsection (1) to a person who is relevant to an application shall be construed in accordance with section 70(9)(b).

Commencement

Brought into force for certain purposes as from 1 January 2007, for remaining purposes as from 1 September 2007 by the Gambling Act 2005 (Commencement No 6 and Transitional Provisions) Order 2006, SI 2006/3272, art 2, Sch 1; for transitional provisions see art 6, Sch 4 thereto (as amended by SI 2007/1157, arts 7–12).

Sub-s (1): The Commission. Ie the Gambling Commission; see s 353(1). As to the establishment, etc of the Gambling Commission, see s 20, Sch 4, and the note 'Gambling Commission' to that section.

Application

See the note to s 65.

Definitions

'the Commission': s 353(1)
'conviction': s 126(1)
'relevant offence': ss 126(2), (3), 353(1), Sch 7

Explanatory Notes

230 [para **6.2008** below]

6.572 72 Consideration of application: demand

In determining whether to grant an operating licence the Commission may not have regard to—

(a) the area in Great Britain within which it is proposed to provide facilities, or

(b) the expected demand for facilities which it is proposed to provide.

Commencement

Brought into force for certain purposes as from 1 January 2007, for remaining purposes as from 1 September 2007 by the Gambling Act 2005 (Commencement No 6 and Transitional Provisions) Order 2006, SI 2006/3272, art 2, Sch 1; for transitional provisions see art 6, Sch 4 thereto (as amended by SI 2007/1157, arts 7–12).

Operating licence

As to the nature, etc of operating licences, see s 65 and the note 'Operating licences' thereto.

The Commission

Ie the Gambling Commission; see s 353(1). As to the establishment, etc of the Gambling Commission, see s 20, Sch 4, and the note 'Gambling Commission' to that section.

Great Britain

See the note to s 12.

Application

See the note to s 65.

Definitions

'the Commission': s 353(1)
'operating licence': s 353(1)
'providing facilities for gambling': ss 5, 353(2)(i)

Explanatory Notes

231 [para **6.2008** below]

6.573 73 Procedure

(1) For the purpose of considering an application under section 69 the Commission may—

(a) require the applicant to provide information;
(b) consult, and have regard to information provided by or an opinion stated by, any person.

(2) In subsection (1) 'information' and 'opinion' mean information or an opinion about—

(a) the applicant,
(b) a person relevant to the application, or
(c) the licensed activities.

(3) In particular, the Commission may require the production of an enhanced criminal record certificate under section 115 of the Police Act 1997 (c 50) relating to—

(a) the applicant, or
(b) a person relevant to the application.

(4) The statement maintained by the Commission under section 23 must, in particular, specify the Commission's practice in relation to—

(a) the delegation of functions in relation to applications,
(b) the holding of oral hearings of applications, and
(c) evidence required or accepted in connection with applications.

(5) The Commission may disregard an irregularity or deficiency in or in relation to an application, other than a failure to pay the fee required by section 69(2)(g).

(6) For the purposes of this section a reference to the licensed activities or to a person relevant to an application shall be construed in accordance with section 70(9).

Note

See the Gambling Commission's 'Statement of Principles for Licensing and Regulation', September 2009 (see para **6.2040** below).

Commencement

Brought into force for certain purposes as from 1 January 2007, for remaining purposes as from 1 September 2007 by the Gambling Act 2005 (Commencement No 6 and Transitional Provisions) Order 2006, SI 2006/3272, art 2, Sch 1; for transitional provisions see art 6, Sch 4 thereto (as amended by SI 2007/1157, arts 7–12).

Sub-s (1): The Commission. Ie the Gambling Commission; see s 353(1). As to the establishment, etc of the Gambling Commission, see s 20, Sch 4, and the note 'Gambling Commission' to that section.

Sub-s (1): Person. See the note 'Persons' to s 23.

Application

See the note to s 65.

Definitions

'the Commission': s 353(1)
'the licensed activities': s 126(1) (and sub-s (6) above)

Explanatory Notes
232, 233 [para **6.2008** below]

6.574 74 Determination of application

(1) On considering an application under section 69 the Commission shall—

(a) grant it,

(b) reject it, or

(c) grant it in respect of one or more of the activities specified in accordance with section 69(2)(a) and reject it in respect of the others.

(2) Where the Commission grants an application in whole or in part it shall as soon as is reasonably practicable—

(a) notify the applicant of the grant, and

(b) issue an operating licence to the applicant.

(3) Where the Commission rejects an application in whole or in part it shall as soon as is reasonably practicable notify the applicant of—

(a) the rejection, and

(b) the reasons for it.

Commencement

Brought into force for certain purposes as from 1 January 2007, for remaining purposes as from 1 September 2007 by the Gambling Act 2005 (Commencement No 6 and Transitional Provisions) Order 2006, SI 2006/3272, art 2, Sch 1; for transitional provisions see art 6, Sch 4 thereto (as amended by SI 2007/1157, arts 7–12).

Sub-s (1): The Commission. Ie the Gambling Commission; see s 353(1). As to the establishment, etc of the Gambling Commission, see s 20, Sch 4, and the note 'Gambling Commission' to that section.

Sub-s (2): Notify. See further, in connection with a requirement under this Act to give a notice, s 353(4).

Sub-s (2): Operating licence. As to the nature, etc of operating licences, see s 65 and the note 'Operating licences' thereto.

Application
See the note to s 65.

Definitions
'the Commission': s 353(1)
'operating licence': s 353(1)

Explanatory Notes
234 [para **6.2008** below]

Conditions

6.575 75 General conditions imposed by Commission

(1) The Commission may specify conditions to be attached to—

(a) each operating licence, or

(b) each operating licence falling within a specified class.

(2) For the purposes of subsection (1)(b) a class may be defined wholly or partly by reference to—

(a) the nature of the licensed activities;

(b) the circumstances in which the licensed activities are carried on;

(c) the nature or circumstances of the licensee or of another person involved or likely to be involved in the conduct of the licensed activities.

(3) Where the Commission issues an operating licence it shall attach to the licence any condition specified under subsection (1) as a condition to be attached to operating licences of a class within which the licence falls.

Note

See 'Licence Conditions and Codes of Practice' published by the Gambling Commission in December 2011 (see para **6.2060** below).

Commencement

Subsections (1) and (2) brought into force by the Gambling Act 2005 (Commencement No 2 and Transitional Provisions) Order 2005, SI 2005/2455, art 2 and Schedule, as from 1 October 2005. Subsection (3) brought into force by the Gambling Act 2005 (Commencement No 6 and Transitional Provisions) Order 2006, SI 2006/3272, art 2, Sch 1 as from 1 January 2007; for transitional provisions see art 6, Sch 4 thereto (as amended by SI 2007/1157, arts 7–12).

Sub-s (1): The Commission. Ie the Gambling Commission; see s 353(1). As to the establishment, etc of the Gambling Commission, see s 20, Sch 4, and the note 'Gambling Commission' to that section.

Sub-s (1): May specify conditions. Any condition attached by the Gambling Commission under this section must be specified in the operating licence; see s 66(1)(c).

See further as to conditions under this section, s 76 (general conditions: procedure); s 79 (scope of powers to attach conditions); s 80 (requirement for personal licence); s 81 (credit and inducements); s 82 (compliance with codes of practice); s 84 (premises); s 85 (equipment); s 86 (gaming machines); s 87 (membership); and s 88 (information).

See also, as respects the attachment of conditions under this section to particular kinds of operating licence, s 89(5)(a), (d), (7) (remote operating licence); s 90 (casino operating licence); s 92(3) (general betting operating licence); s 93(6)–(8) (pool betting operating licence); s 94(5)–(7) (horse-race pool betting operating licence); s 96(4)(a), (d), (6) (gaming machine technical licence); s 97(2)(a), (d), (4) (gambling software operating licence: standards); s 98(3), (5), (6) (lottery operating licences); s 99 (mandatory conditions of lottery operating licence); and s 291(2) (bingo halls).

The Gambling Commission may require the holder of an operating licence to submit it to the Commission for the purpose of amendment to reflect a general variation of conditions under this section; see s 105. For the power of the Commission to review arrangements made by licensees to ensure compliance with condition attached under this section, see s 116(1).

Sub-s (1): Operating licence. As to the nature, etc of operating licences, see s 65 and the note 'Operating licences' thereto.

Sub-s (2): Person. See the note 'Persons' to s 23.

Application

See the note to s 65.

Definitions

'the Commission': s 353(1)
'the licensed activities': s 126(1)
'licensee': s 126(1)
'operating licence': s 353(1)

Explanatory Notes

235–238 [para **6.2008** below]

6.576 76 General conditions: procedure

(1) The Commission may amend or revoke a condition specified under section 75; and a reference in this section to the specification of a condition includes a reference to the amendment or revocation of a condition.

(2) Before specifying a condition the Commission shall consult—

(a) one or more persons who in the Commission's opinion represent the interests of operating licensees who may be affected by the condition, and

(b) such of the persons specified in section 23(5) as the Commission thinks appropriate (if any).

(3) The Commission shall publish any specification as soon as is reasonably practicable.

(4) Where the Commission proposes to specify a condition—

(a) at least three months before making the specification the Commission shall give notice of it to the holder of each licence which—

(i) has effect at that time, and
(ii) is within a class affected by the specification,

(b) if the Commission issues, after that time but before the specification is made, an operating licence of a class affected by the specification, the Commission shall give the licensee notice of the proposed specification, and

(c) on the making of the specification an existing licence shall by virtue of this paragraph be subject to the condition specified.

(5) If the Commission thinks it necessary by reason of urgency to make a specification without giving the notice required by subsection (4)(a)—

(a) the Commission shall give as much notice as it thinks possible in the circumstances to the persons mentioned in that provision,

(b) subsection (4)(b) shall have effect after the time when notice is given under paragraph (a) above, and

(c) subsection (4)(c) shall have effect.

(6) Subsection (4)(c), in its application to the amendment or revocation of a condition (by virtue of subsection (1)), shall be treated as—

(a) making existing licences subject to the condition as amended, or

(b) relieving existing licences from the condition revoked.

Commencement

Subsections (1)–(3) brought into force by the Gambling Act 2005 (Commencement No 2 and Transitional Provisions) Order 2005, SI 2005/2455, art 2 and Schedule, as from 1 October 2005. Subsections (4)–(6) brought into force by the Gambling Act 2005 (Commencement No 6 and Transitional Provisions) Order 2006, SI 2006/3272, art 2, Sch 1 as from 1 January 2007; for transitional provisions see art 6, Sch 4 thereto (as amended by SI 2007/1157, arts 7–12).

Sub-s (1): The Commission. Ie the Gambling Commission; see s 353(1). As to the establishment, etc of the Gambling Commission, see s 20, Sch 4, and the note 'Gambling Commission' to that section.

Sub-s (2): Persons. See the note to s 23.

Sub-s (4): Notice. See further, in connection with a requirement under this Act to give a notice, s 353(4).

Sub-s (4): Operating licence. As to the nature, etc of operating licences, see s 65 and the note 'Operating licences' thereto.

Sub-s (4): Shall . . . be subject to the condition. Sub-s (4)(c) above is saved by s 105(5).

Application

See the note to s 65.

Definitions

'the Commission': s 353(1)
'holder': s 126(1)
'licensee': s 126(1)
'operating licence': s 353(1)

Explanatory Notes

235–238 [para **6.2008** below]

6.577 77 Individual condition imposed by Commission

Where the Commission issues an operating licence it may attach a condition to the licence.

Commencement

Brought into force by the Gambling Act 2005 (Commencement No 6 and Transitional Provisions) Order 2006, SI 2006/3272, art 2, Sch 1 as from 1 January 2007; for transitional provisions see art 6, Sch 4 thereto (as amended by SI 2007/1157, arts 7–12).

The Commission

Ie the Gambling Commission; see s 353(1). As to the establishment, etc of the Gambling Commission, see s 20, Sch 4, and the note 'Gambling Commission' to that section.

Operating licence

As to the nature, etc of operating licences, see s 65 and the note 'Operating licences' thereto.

May attach a condition

Any condition attached by the Gambling Commission under this section must be specified in the operating licence; see s 66(1)(c). See further as to conditions under this section, s 79 (scope of powers to attach conditions); s 80 (requirement for personal licence); s 81 (credit and inducements); s 82 (compliance with code of practice); s 84 (premises); s 85 (equipment); s 86 (gaming machines); and s 87 (membership).

See also, as respects the attachment of conditions under this section to particular kinds of operating licence, s 89(5)(a), (d), (7) (remote operating licence); s 90 (casino operating licence); s 92(3) (general betting operating licence); s 93(6)–(8) (pool betting operating licence); s 94(5)–(7) (horse-race pool betting operating licence); s 96(4)(a), (d), (6) (gaming machine technical licence); s 97(2)(a), (d), (4) (gambling software operating licence: standards); s 98(3), (5), (6) (lottery operating licences); and s 99 (mandatory conditions of lottery operating licence).

As to applications to add, amend or remove a condition attached to an operating licence under this section, see s 104.

For the power of the Gambling Commission to review arrangements made by licensees to ensure compliance with condition attached under this section, see s 116(1), and for the power of the Commission to attach an additional condition to a licence under this section, or remove or amend a condition attached to a licence under this section, following a review under s 116(1) or (2), see s 117.

As to appeals to the Gambling Appeals Tribunal, see s 141.

Application

See the note to s 65.

Definitions

'the Commission': s 353(1)
'operating licence': s 353(1)

Explanatory Notes

235–238 [para **6.2008** below]

6.578 78 Condition imposed by Secretary of State

(1) The Secretary of State may by regulations provide for a specified condition to be attached to operating licences falling within a specified description.

(2) Transitional provision of regulations under this section (made by virtue of section 355(1)(c)) may, in particular, apply a condition (with or without modification) to licences issued before the regulations are made (or come into force).

Commencement

Brought into force by the Gambling Act 2005 (Commencement No 6 and Transitional Provisions) Order 2006, SI 2006/3272, art 2, Sch 1 as from 1 January 2007; for transitional provisions see art 6, Sch 4 thereto (as amended by SI 2007/1157, arts 7–12).

Sub-s (1): Secretary of State. See the note to s 4.

Sub-s (1): Specified condition. See further as to conditions under this section, s 79 (scope of powers to attach conditions); s 80 (requirement for personal licence); s 81 (credit and inducements); s 82 (compliance with code of practice); s 84 (premises); s 85 (equipment); s 86 (gaming machines); s 87 (membership); and s 88 (information).

See also, as respects the attachment of conditions under this section to particular kinds of operating licence, s 89(7) (remote operating licence); s 90(1) (casino operating licence); s 92(3) (general betting operating licence); s 93(6)–(8) (pool betting operating licence); s 94(5)–(7) (horse-race pool betting operating licence); s 96(6) (gaming machine technical licence); s 97(4) (gambling software operating licence: standards); s 98(5) (lottery operating licences); and s 291(2), (3) (bingo halls).

For the power of the Commission to review arrangements made by licensees to ensure compliance with condition attached under this section, see s 116(1).

Sub-s (1): Operating licences. As to the nature, etc of operating licences, see s 65 and the note 'Operating licences' thereto.

Application

See the note to s 65.

As to regulations under this Act generally, see s 355.

Subordinate Legislation:

The Gambling Act 2005 (Operating Licence Conditions) Regulations 2007, SI 2007/2257).

Definitions

'operating licence': s 353(1)

Explanatory Notes

235–238 [para 6.2008 below]

6.579 79 Scope of powers to attach conditions

(1) Without prejudice to the generality of the powers conferred by sections 75, 77 and 78, a condition attached under any of those sections may, in particular, do any of the things specified in this section.

(2) A condition may have the effect of restricting the activities that may be carried on in reliance on the licence by reference to—

(a) the nature of the activities,

(b) the circumstances in which they are carried on, or

(c) their extent.

(3) A condition may make provision wholly or partly by reference to—

(a) the nature of the licensed activities;

(b) the circumstances in which the licensed activities are carried on;

(c) the nature or circumstances of the licensee or of another person involved or likely to be involved in the conduct of the licensed activities.

(4) In regulating the licensed activities a condition may make provision about—

(a) the facilities that may or must be provided in connection with the licensed activities;

(b) the manner in which facilities are provided;

(c) the number of persons that may or must be employed in the provision of facilities;

(d) the financial resources available for particular purposes to the person providing facilities;

(e) any other matter.

(5) A condition may relate to the financial circumstances of the licensee or of another person involved or likely to be involved in the conduct of the licensed activities; in particular, a condition may make provision about the maintenance of reserves in respect of potential liabilities.

(6) A condition of a remote operating licence may restrict the methods of communication that may be used in the course of the licensed activities.

(7) A condition may make provision about how facilities for gambling are advertised or described.

(8) A condition may make provision about the provision of assistance to persons who are or may be affected by problems related to gambling.

(9) A condition may make provision about—

(a) establishing the identity of users of facilities;

(b) recording the identity of users of facilities;

(c) restricting facilities to persons registered in respect of the facilities in advance.

Commencement

Brought into force, in so far as it relates to section 75(1) and (2) and section 76(1) to (3), by the Gambling Act 2005 (Commencement No 2 and Transitional Provisions) Order 2005, SI 2005/2455, art 2 and Schedule, as from 1 October 2005. Brought into force for remaining purposes by the Gambling Act 2005 (Commencement No 6 and Transitional Provisions) Order 2006, SI 2006/3272, art 2, Sch 1 as from 1 January 2007; for transitional provisions see art 6, Sch 4 thereto (as amended by SI 2007/1157, arts 7–12).

Sub-s (1): A condition attached, etc. Section 101 does not prevent the imposition of a requirement to notify the Gambling Commission of a specified change of circumstances by way of the attachment of a condition to an operating licence; see s 101(8).

For the power of the Gambling Commission to review any matter connected with the provision of facilities for gambling as authorised by an operating licence if the Commission has reason to suspect that activities may have been carried on in purported reliance on the licence but not in accordance with a condition of the licence, see s 116(2)(a); and for the powers of the Commission following such a review, see ss 117–120. See also s 121 for the power of the Commission to require the holder of an operating licence to pay a penalty for breach of a condition, and s 122 for the power of the Commission be provided with information for the purpose of determining whether activities have been carried on in purported reliance on the licence but not in accordance with a condition of the licence.

Sub-s (3): Person. See the note 'Persons' to s 23.

Sub-s (6): Operating licence. As to the nature, etc of operating licences, see s 65 and the note 'Operating licences' thereto.

Application

See the note to s 65.

Definitions

'advertising gambling': ss 327, 353(2)(b)
'gambling': ss 3, 353(1)
'the licensed activities': s 126(1)
'licensee': s 126(1)
'operating licence': s 353(1)
'providing facilities for gambling': ss 5, 353(2)(i)

Explanatory Notes

240, 241 [para **6.2008** below]

6.580 80 Requirement for personal licence

(1) The Commission shall use its powers under sections 75 and 77 to ensure that in respect of each operating licence at least one person—

(a) occupies a specified management office in or in respect of the licensee or in connection with the licensed activities, and

(b) holds a personal licence authorising the performance of the functions of the office.

(2) A condition under either of those sections may impose requirements which relate to a management office and are in addition to any required by subsection (1).

(3) A condition attached to an operating licence by virtue of section 75, 77 or 78 may, in particular, provide that if a specified management office is held in or in respect of the licensee or in connection with a licensed activity (whether or not in pursuance of another condition)—

(a) it must be held by an individual who holds a personal licence authorising the performance of the functions of the office, and

(b) anything done in the performance of the functions of the office must be done in accordance with the terms and conditions of the personal licence.

(4) A condition attached to an operating licence by virtue of section 75, 77 or 78 may, in particular, provide that if a specified operational function is performed in connection with a licensed activity it must be performed—

(a) by an individual who holds a personal licence authorising performance of the function, and

(b) in accordance with the terms and conditions of the personal licence.

(5) In this section 'management office' in relation to a licensee means—

(a) if the licensee is a company, the office of director,

(b) if the licensee is a partnership (including a limited liability partnership), the office of partner,

(c) if the licensee is an unincorporated association, any office in the association, and

(d) in any case, any position the occupier of which is required, by the terms of his appointment, to take or share responsibility for—

(i) the conduct of a person who performs an operational function in connection with a licensed activity, or

(ii) facilitating or ensuring compliance with terms or conditions of the operating licence.

(6) In this section 'operational function' means—

(a) any function which enables the person exercising it to influence the outcome of gambling,

(b) receiving or paying money in connection with gambling, and

(c) manufacturing, supplying, installing, maintaining or repairing a gaming machine.

(7) Provision by virtue of subsection (1) may be general or may relate only to specified—

(a) kinds of operating licence,

(b) cases, or

(c) circumstances.

(8) The Secretary of State may by order amend the definition of 'management office' or 'operational function' for the purposes of this section.

(9) In relation to a bingo operating licence issued to a members' club, a commercial club or a miners' welfare institute—

(a) subsection (1) shall not apply, and

(b) a condition attached by virtue of section 75, 77 or 78 may not—

(i) require that a person hold a personal licence, or

(ii) operate by reference to whether a person holds a personal licence.

Commencement

Brought into force, in so far as it has effect to define 'management office' and 'operational function' for the purposes of s 127, by the Gambling Act 2005 (Commencement No 2 and Transitional Provisions) Order 2005, SI 2005/2455, art 2 and Schedule, as from 1 October 2005. Brought into force for remaining purposes by the Gambling Act 2005 (Commencement No 6 and Transitional Provisions) Order 2006, SI 2006/3272, art 2, Sch 1 as from 1 January 2007; for transitional provisions see art 6, Sch 4 thereto (as amended by SI 2007/1157, arts 7–12).

Sub-s (1): The Commission. Ie the Gambling Commission; see s 353(1). As to the establishment, etc of the Gambling Commission, see s 20, Sch 4, and the note 'Gambling Commission' to that section.

Sub-s (1): Operating licence. As to the nature, etc of operating licences, see s 65 and the note 'Operating licences' thereto.

Sub-s (1): Personal licence. As to the nature of personal licences, see s 127.

Sub-s (8): Secretary of State. See the note to s 4.

Application

See the note to s 65.

Orders under this section

At the time of going to press no orders had been made under this section.

As to orders under this Act generally, see s 355.

Definitions

'commercial club': ss 267, 353(1)
'the Commission': s 353(1)
'director': s 353(1)
'gambling': ss 3, 353(1)
'gaming machine': ss 235, 353(1)
'the licensed activities': s 126(1)
'licensee': s 126(1)
'members' club': ss 266, 353(1)
'miners' welfare institute': ss 268, 353(1)
'operating licence': s 353(1)
'personal licence': ss 127, 353(1)
'supply': s 353(1)

Explanatory Notes

242–251 [para **6.2008** below]

6.581 81 Credit and inducements

(1) A condition attached to an operating licence by virtue of section 75, 77 or 78 may, in particular, restrict or otherwise make provision about—

(a) the giving of credit in connection with the licensed activities;

(b) the making of offers designed to induce persons to participate, or to increase their participation, in the licensed activities;

(c) participation in arrangements for inducing, permitting or assisting persons to gamble.

(2) A non-remote casino operating licence or a non-remote bingo operating licence shall by virtue of this subsection be subject to the condition that the licensee may not—

(a) give credit in connection with gambling, or

(b) participate in, arrange, permit or knowingly facilitate the giving of credit in connection with gambling.

(3) But the condition in subsection (2) shall not prevent the licensee from permitting the installation and use on the premises of a machine enabling cash to be obtained on credit from a person (the 'credit provider') provided that—

(a) the licensee has no other commercial connection with the credit provider in relation to gambling,

(b) the licensee neither makes nor receives any payment or reward (whether by way of commission, rent or otherwise) in connection with the machine, and

(c) any conditions about the nature, location or use of the machine attached by virtue of section 75, 77 or 78 are complied with.

(4) In this section 'credit' includes—

(a) any form of financial accommodation, and

(b) in particular, the acceptance by way of payment of a fee, charge or stake of anything other than—

(i) cash,

(ii) a cheque which is not post-dated and for which full value is given, or

(iii) a debit card payment which is not post-dated and for which full value is given.

(5) In subsection (4)(b)(iii) 'debit card payment' means a payment—

(a) debited against a person's banking account, and

(b) made by means of a card which is not a credit-token within the meaning of section 14 of the Consumer Credit Act 1974 (c 39).

Commencement

Brought into force by the Gambling Act 2005 (Commencement No 6 and Transitional Provisions) Order 2006, SI 2006/3272, art 2, Sch 1 as from 1 January 2007; for transitional provisions see art 6, Sch 4 thereto (as amended by SI 2007/1157, arts 7–12).

Sub-s (1): Operating licence. As to the nature, etc of operating licences, see s 65 and the note 'Operating licences' thereto.

Sub-s (3): Person. See the note 'Persons' to s 23.

Application

See the note to s 65.

Definitions

'gambling': ss 3, 353(1)
'the licensed activities': s 126(1)
'licensee': s 126(1)
'machine': ss 235(3)(a), 353(1)
'operating licence': s 353(1)
'premises': s 353(1), (2)(g)
'stake': s 353(1)

Explanatory Notes

252–255 [para **6.2008** below]

6.582 82 Compliance with code of practice

(1) An operating licence shall by virtue of this section be subject to the condition that the licensee ensures compliance with any relevant social responsibility provision of a code of practice issued under section 24.

(2) In subsection (1)—

(a) the reference to a licensee includes a reference to anyone employed or engaged by a licensee to perform an operational function within the meaning of section 80, and

(b) the reference to a social responsibility provision of a code is a reference to a provision identified by a code as being included in pursuance of section 24(2).

(3) This section does not prevent compliance with a provision of a code, other than a social responsibility provision, from being made the subject of a condition under section 75, 77 or 78.

Note

See Part II LCCP, December 2011 (see para **6.2060** below).

Commencement

Brought into force by the Gambling Act 2005 (Commencement No 6 and Transitional Provisions) Order 2006, SI 2006/3272, art 2 as from 1 September 2007; for transitional provisions see art 6, Sch 4 thereto (as amended by SI 2007/1157, arts 7–12).

Sub-s (1): Operating licence. As to the nature, etc of operating licences, see s 65 and the note 'Operating licences' thereto.

Application

See the note to s 65.

Definitions

'licensee': s 126(1) (and sub-s (2)(a) above)
'operating licence': s 353(1)

Explanatory Notes

256 [para **6.2008** below]

6.583 83 Return of stakes to children

(1) An operating licence shall by virtue of this section be subject to the condition that if the licensee becomes aware that a child or young person is using or has used facilities for gambling provided in reliance on the licence, the licensee—

(a) must return any money paid in respect of the use of those facilities (whether by way of fee, stake or otherwise) by the child or young person as soon as is reasonably practicable, and

(b) may not give a prize to the child or young person.

(2) But subsection (1) does not apply to—

(a) the use of a Category D gaming machine, or

(b) participation in equal chance gaming at a licensed family entertainment centre.

(3) The condition in subsection (1)—

(a) shall have effect despite any contract or other agreement and despite any rule of law, and

(b) shall not enable a licensee to demand repayment of, and shall not require a child or young person to return, a prize paid before the licensee becomes aware that the participant is a child or young person.

(4) In this section—

(a) a reference to a licensee includes a reference to anyone employed or engaged by a licensee to perform an operational function within the meaning of section 80, and

(b) in relation to participation in a lottery or football pools a reference to a child or young person shall be treated as a reference only to a child.

(5) In this section 'prize' includes both a prize provided by a person organising gambling and winnings of money staked.

Commencement

Brought into force by the Gambling Act 2005 (Commencement No 6 and Transitional Provisions) Order 2006, SI 2006/3272, art 2 as from 1 September 2007; for transitional provisions see art 6, Sch 4 thereto (as amended by SI 2007/1157, arts 7–12).

Sub-s (1): Operating licence. As to the nature, etc of operating licences, see s 65 and the note 'Operating licences' thereto.

Sub-s (1): Subject to the condition. A person commits an offence if without reasonable excuse he fails to comply with a condition attached to an operating licence by virtue of this section; see s 58.

Sub-s (2): Category D gaming machine. As to the categories of gaming machine, see s 236.

Sub-s (5): Person. See the note 'Persons' to s 23.

Application

See the note to s 65.

Definitions

'Category D gaming machine': s 353(1)
'child': ss 45(1), 353(1)
'equal chance gaming': ss 8, 353(1)
'football pools': s 353(1)
'gambling': ss 3, 353(1)
'licensed family entertainment centre': ss 238, 353(1)
'licensee': s 126(1) (and sub-s (4)(a) above)
'lottery': ss 14, 353(1)
'operating licence': s 353(1)
'providing facilities for gambling': ss 5, 353(2)(i)
'stake': s 353(1)
'winnings': s 353(1)
'young person': ss 45(2), 353(1)

Explanatory Notes

257–259 [para **6.2008** below]

6.584 84 Premises

(1) An operating licence—

(a) may not include a condition (whether attached by virtue of section 75, 77 or 78)—
   (i) requiring that the licensed activities be carried on at a specified place or class of place,
   (ii) preventing the licensed activities from being carried on at a specified place or class of place, or
   (iii) specifying premises on which the licensed activities may be carried on, but
(b) may include a condition about—
   (i) the number of sets of premises on which the licensed activities may be carried on;
   (ii) the number of persons for whom facilities may be provided on any premises where the licensed activities are carried on.

(2) An operating licence of any kind may authorise activities carried on in more than one place.

Commencement

Brought into force by the Gambling Act 2005 (Commencement No 6 and Transitional Provisions) Order 2006, SI 2006/3272, art 2, Sch 1 as from 1 January 2007; for transitional provisions see art 6, Sch 4 thereto (as amended by SI 2007/1157, arts 7–12).

Sub-s (1): Operating licence. As to the nature, etc of operating licences, see s 65 and the note 'Operating licences' thereto.

Application

See the note to s 65.

Definitions

'the licensed activities': s 126(1)
'operating licence': s 353(1)
'premises': s 353(1), (2)(g)

Explanatory Notes

260, 261 [para **6.2008** below]

6.585 85 Equipment

(1) A condition attached to an operating licence by virtue of section 75, 77 or 78 may make provision about equipment used in connection with the licensed activities.

(2) In particular, a condition attached by virtue of this section may—
(a) make provision about the number of pieces of equipment, other than equipment for playing bingo, that may be used to provide facilities for gambling;
(b) make provision about the specification of equipment used to provide facilities for gambling.

(3) For the purposes of this section 'equipment' includes—
(a) a computer,
(b) a device for the playing of a casino game, and
(c) any other piece of equipment.

(4) But a gaming machine is not equipment for the purposes of this section.

Note

See the Gambling Commission's 'Bingo and Casino Equipment Technical Requirements', July 2008 (see para **6.2244.1** below).

Commencement

Brought into force by the Gambling Act 2005 (Commencement No 6 and Transitional Provisions) Order 2006, SI 2006/3272, art 2, Sch 1 as from 1 January 2007; for transitional provisions see art 6, Sch 4 thereto (as amended by SI 2007/1157, arts 7–12).

Sub-s (1): Operating licence. As to the nature, etc of operating licences, see s 65 and the note 'Operating licences' thereto.

Application

See the note to s 65.

Definitions

'bingo': s 353(1)
'casino game': ss 7(2), (3), 353(1)
'gaming machine': ss 235, 353(1)
'the licensed activities': s 126(1)
'operating licence': s 353(1)
'providing facilities for gambling': ss 5, 353(2)(i)

Explanatory Notes

262–264 [para **6.2008** below]

6.586 86 Gaming machines

(1) An operating licence may not include a condition (whether attached by virtue of section 75, 77 or 78)—

(a) about the number or categories of gaming machine that may be made available for use in accordance with the licence,

(b) that contradicts a provision of regulations under section 236, 240 or 241, or

(c) of a kind prohibited by regulations under any of those sections.

(2) An operating licence may be subject to a condition (whether imposed by virtue of section 75, 77 or 78) that a specified gaming machine may not be made available for use in reliance on the licence if the Commission has notified the licensee in writing that the manufacture, supply, installation, adaptation, maintenance or repair of the machine—

(a) was not carried out in reliance on a gaming machine technical operating licence, or

(b) did not comply with standards established under or by virtue of section 96.

Commencement

Brought into force by the Gambling Act 2005 (Commencement No 6 and Transitional Provisions) Order 2006, SI 2006/3272, art 2, Sch 1 as from 1 January 2007; for transitional provisions see art 6, Sch 4 thereto (as amended by SI 2007/1157, arts 7–12).

Sub-s (1): Operating licence. As to the nature, etc of operating licences, see s 65 and the note 'Operating licences' thereto.

Sub-s (2): The Commission. Ie the Gambling Commission; see s 353(1). As to the establishment, etc of the Gambling Commission, see s 20, Sch 4, and the note 'Gambling Commission' to that section.

Sub-s (2): Notified. See further, in connection with a requirement under this Act to give a notice, s 353(4).

Sub-s (2): Writing. See the note to s 39.

Application

See the note to s 65.

Definitions

'the Commission': s 353(1)
'gaming machine': ss 235, 353(1)
'licensee': s 126(1)
'operating licence': s 353(1)
'supply': s 353(1)

Explanatory Notes

265–267 [para **6.2008** below]

6.587 87 Membership

An operating licence may not be subject to a condition (whether by virtue of section 75, 77 or 78)—

(a) requiring facilities to be provided by, or used in the course of the activities of, a club or other body with membership, or

(b) restricting the provision or use of facilities wholly or partly by reference to membership of a club or other body.

Commencement

Brought into force by the Gambling Act 2005 (Commencement No 6 and Transitional Provisions) Order 2006, SI 2006/3272, art 2, Sch 1 as from 1 January 2007; for transitional provisions see art 6, Sch 4 thereto (as amended by SI 2007/1157, arts 7–12).

Operating licence

As to the nature, etc of operating licences, see s 65 and the note 'Operating licences' thereto.

Application

See the note to s 65.

Definitions

'operating licence': s 353(1)

Explanatory Notes

268 [para **6.2008** below]

6.588 88 Information

(1) A condition attached to an operating licence by virtue of section 75 or 78 may require the provision of information of a specified kind to—

(a) the Commission, or

(b) another specified person or class of person.

(2) A condition attached by virtue of this section may, in particular—

(a) relate to information about the use made of facilities provided in accordance with the operating licence;

(b) require a person to provide any information that he suspects may—

(i) relate to the commission of an offence under this Act,

(ii) relate to a breach of a rule applied by a sporting or other body, or

(iii) lead to the making of an order under section 336.

Commencement

Brought into force by the Gambling Act 2005 (Commencement No 6 and Transitional Provisions) Order 2006, SI 2006/3272, art 2, Sch 1 as from 1 January 2007; for transitional provisions see art 6, Sch 4 thereto (as amended by SI 2007/1157, arts 7–12).

Sub-s (1): Operating licence. As to the nature, etc of operating licences, see s 65 and the note 'Operating licences' thereto.

Sub-s (1): The Commission. Ie the Gambling Commission; see s 353(1). As to the establishment, etc of the Gambling Commission, see s 20, Sch 4, and the note 'Gambling Commission' to that section.

Sub-s (1): Person. See the note 'Persons' to s 23.

Application

See the note to s 65.

Definitions

'the Commission': s 353(1)

'operating licence': s 353(1)

Explanatory Notes

269 [para **6.2008** below]

Rules for particular kinds of licence

6.589 89 Remote operating licence

(1) This section applies to a remote operating licence.

. . .

(4) The Commission may establish, or provide for the establishment of, standards in respect of—

(a) a system used for the generation of results in a virtual game, virtual race or other virtual event or process used in the course of remote gambling;

(b) any other aspect of the process of remote gambling.

(5) In particular, the Commission may—

(a) provide for the enforcement of standards by the attachment of conditions under section 75 or 77;

(b) make arrangements with any person for the establishment of standards;

(c) make arrangements with any person for the administration of tests of compliance with standards;

(d) for the purpose of considering whether a condition under section 75 or 77 has been complied with, require the licensee under a remote licence—

(i) to submit to a test in accordance with arrangements made under paragraph (c) above, and

(ii) to produce specified evidence of the result of the test;

(e) for the purpose of considering whether to grant an application under this Part, require a licensee under a remote licence or an applicant for a remote licence—

(i) to submit to a test in accordance with arrangements made under paragraph (c) above, and

(ii) to produce specified evidence of the result of the test.

(6) Standards established under subsection (5) may, in particular, be expressed—

(a) by reference to the opinion of a specified person or class of persons;

(b) by reference to a specified process or piece of equipment.

(7) This section is without prejudice to the generality of sections 75, 77 and 78.

Note

See 'Remote Gambling and Software Technical Standards' published by the Gambling Commission in August 2009 (see para **6.2410** below) and see the Note to s 85 above.

Commencement

Subections (1), (4)–(7) brought into force by the Gambling Act 2005 (Commencement No 6 and Transitional Provisions) Order 2006, SI 2006/3272, art 2, Sch 1 as from 1 January 2007; for transitional provisions see art 6, Sch 4 thereto (as amended by SI 2007/1157, arts 7–12). Subsections (2) and (3) brought into force as from 1 September 2007 by the Gambling Act 2005 (Commencement No 6 and Transitional Provisions) Order 2006, SI 2006/3272, art 2; for transitional provisions see art 6, Sch 4 thereto (as amended by SI 2007/1157, arts 7–12).

Sub-s (1): Operating licence. As to the nature, etc of operating licences, see s 65 and the note 'Operating licences' thereto.

[Sub-s (2) and (3) repealed by SI 2007/2321, reg 2(a)]

Sub-s (5): Person. See the note 'Persons' to s 23.

Sub-s (5): This Part. Ie Pt 5 (ss 65–126 and Sch 7) of this Act.

Application

See the note to s 65.

Definitions
'the Commission': s 353(1)
'the licensed activities': s 126(1)
'licensee': s 126(1)
'the licensing objectives': ss 1, 353(1)
'operating licence': s 353(1)
'remote gambling': ss 4, 353(1)
'remote gambling equipment': ss 36(4), (5), 353(1)
'virtual game, race or other event or process': s 353(3)

Explanatory Notes
270–273 [para **6.2008** below]

6.590 90 Casino operating licence

(1) A casino operating licence may be subject to a condition (whether imposed by virtue of section 75, 77 or 78) restricting the class of casino game that may be made available.

(2) A casino operating licence may be subject to a condition imposed by virtue of section 75 or 77 specifying rules for the playing of—
(a) a casino game;
(b) another game of chance.

Commencement
Brought into force by the Gambling Act 2005 (Commencement No 6 and Transitional Provisions) Order 2006, SI 2006/3272, art 2, Sch 1 as from 1 January 2007; for transitional provisions see art 6, Sch 4 thereto (as amended by SI 2007/1157, arts 7–12).

Sub-s (1): Operating licence. As to the nature, etc of operating licences, see s 65 and the note 'Operating licences' thereto.

Application
See the note to s 65.

Definitions
'casino game': ss 7(2), (3), 353(1)
'game of chance': ss 6, 353(1)
'operating licence': s 353(1)

Explanatory Notes
274, 275 [para **6.2008** below]

6.591 91 Bingo operating licence

(1) Regulations under section 78 may provide for the attachment to a bingo operating licence of a condition—
(a) limiting amounts that may be staked;
(b) limiting the amount that may be charged by way of participation fee;
(c) limiting the amount or value of a prize or class of prize;
(d) requiring that at least a specified proportion of stakes be paid out by way of prizes;
(e) imposing requirements that are specific to games of bingo played on more than one set of premises (whether facilities for the game are provided in accordance with one bingo operating licence or more than one).

(2) But subject to subsection (1) a bingo operating licence may not be subject to a condition—
(a) limiting the amount that may be accepted or charged by way of stakes,
(b) limiting the amount that may be charged by way of participation fee,
(c) restricting the nature, amount or value of prizes,
(d) controlling the proportion of stakes paid out by way of prizes,

(e) preventing the provision of prizes funded other than out of stakes,
(f) preventing or limiting an arrangement whereby the fact that a prize is not won or claimed in one game of bingo increases the value of the prizes available in another game of bingo,
(g) requiring a game of bingo to be played entirely on one set of premises, or
(h) imposing requirements that are specific to games of bingo played on more than one set of premises (whether facilities for the game are provided in accordance with one bingo operating licence or more than one).

(3) Regulations by virtue of subsection (1)(b) may, in particular, make different provision for different kinds of fee.

(4) Provision made by virtue of subsection (1)(c) may define a class of prize—
(a) by reference to a game or a number of games,
(b) by reference to a period of time, or
(c) in any other way.

Commencement

Brought into force by the Gambling Act 2005 (Commencement No 6 and Transitional Provisions) Order 2006, SI 2006/3272, art 2, Sch 1 as from 1 January 2007; for transitional provisions see art 6, Sch 4 thereto (as amended by SI 2007/1157, arts 7–12).

Sub-s (1): Operating licence. As to the nature, etc of operating licences, see s 65 and the note 'Operating licences' thereto.

Application

See the note to s 65.

Definitions

'bingo': s 353(1) and see the Commission's publication of June 2009'Key Characteristics of Bingo' at para **6.2297** below.
'operating licence': s 353(1)
'participation fee': ss 344, 353(1)
'premises': s 353(1), (2)(g)
'providing facilities for gambling': ss 5, 353(2)(i)
'stake': s 353(1)

Explanatory Notes

276–279 [para **6.2008** below]

6.592 92 General betting operating licence

(1) A general betting operating licence shall, by virtue of this section, be subject to the condition that bets may be accepted on behalf of the licensee only by—
(a) the licensee,
(b) a person employed by the licensee under a written contract of employment, or
(c) the holder of another general betting operating licence.

(2) A general betting operating licence shall, by virtue of this subsection, contain an implied term permitting the use of postal services for the making of bets.

(3) The effect of the term implied by subsection (2) may not be disapplied or restricted by a condition attached under section 75, 77 or 78.

Commencement

Brought into force by the Gambling Act 2005 (Commencement No 6 and Transitional Provisions) Order 2006, SI 2006/3272, art 2, Sch 1 as from 1 January 2007; for transitional provisions see art 6, Sch 4 thereto (as amended by SI 2007/1157, arts 7–12).

Sub-s (1): Operating licence. As to the nature, etc of operating licences, see s 65 and the note 'Operating licences' thereto.

Sub-s (1): Written. See the note 'Writing' to s 39.

Application

See the note to s 65.

Definitions

'licensee': s 126(1)
'operating licence': s 353(1)
'postal services': s 353(2)(f)

Explanatory Notes

280–283 [para 6.2008 below]

6.593 93 Pool betting operating licence

(1) A pool betting operating licence shall, by virtue of this section, be subject to the condition that bets may be accepted on behalf of the licensee only—

(a) by the licensee,

(b) by a person employed by the licensee under a written contract of employment,

(c) by the holder of another pool betting operating licence, or

(d) in accordance with subsection (2) or (3).

(2) A bet is accepted by a person ('the agent') on behalf of a licensee in accordance with this subsection if—

(a) the agent is authorised by the licensee in writing to accept bets on behalf of the licensee,

(b) the agent is an adult,

(c) at the time of accepting the bet the agent is on a track,

(d) the bet is accepted in reliance on an occasional use notice, and

(e) the bet is in connection with a horse-race or a dog race.

(3) The holder of a pool betting operating licence that authorises (whether expressly or impliedly) the provision of facilities for football pools may in writing authorise an adult or young person—

(a) to make documents or other facilities available in connection with the licensed activities;

(b) to receive entries on behalf of the licensee;

(c) to receive payments on behalf of the licensee;

(d) to make payments of winnings on behalf of the licensee.

(4) An authorisation under subsection (3)—

(a) shall be treated for the purposes of section 33 as if it were a pool betting operating licence, but

(b) shall have no effect in relation to any activity, entry or payment that relates partly to a football pool and partly to another form of gambling.

(5) An authorisation under subsection (3) may be issued on terms and conditions which may, in particular, include—

(a) provision for payment by the person issuing the authorisation;

(b) provision for commission.

(6) A condition of a pool betting operating licence (whether attached by virtue of section 75, 77 or 78) may make provision regulating or restricting the activities of persons authorised under subsection (3).

(7) A pool betting operating licence shall, by virtue of this subsection, contain an implied term permitting the use of postal services for the making of bets.

(8) The effect of the term implied by subsection (7) may not be disapplied or restricted by a condition attached under section 75, 77 or 78.

(9) The Secretary of State may by order—

(a) amend or repeal subsection (2)(e);

(b) amend subsection (3) so as to permit authorisation in relation to betting of a specified kind that relates to a sport but is not a football pool.

Commencement

Brought into force by the Gambling Act 2005 (Commencement No 6 and Transitional Provisions) Order 2006, SI 2006/3272, art 2, Sch 1 as from 1 January 2007; for transitional provisions see art 6, Sch 4 thereto (as amended by SI 2007/1157, arts 7–12).

Sub-s (1): Operating licence. As to the nature, etc of operating licences, see s 65 and the note 'Operating licences' thereto.

Sub-s (1): Written. See the note 'Writing' to s 39.

Sub-s (2)(a): under Part 1, para 13 LCCP, October 2008 (see para **6.2065** below) the operator must inform the Commission in writing within 14 days of such authorisation.

Sub-s (2)(d): Occasional use notice. As to such notices, see s 39.

Sub-s (3): May . . . authorise, etc. A person does not commit an offence under s 37 if he uses premises to do anything in accordance with an authorisation under sub-s (3) above; see s 40(1) (but see also s 40(2)).

Sub-s (9): Secretary of State. See the note to s 4.

Production of authorisations on demand

See s 316.

Application

See the note to s 65.

Orders under this section

At the time of going to press no orders had been made under this section.

As to orders under this Act generally, see s 355.

Definitions

'adult': s 353(1)
'betting' ss 9–11, 353(1)
'football pools': s 353(1)
'gambling': ss 3, 353(1)
'holder': s 126(1)
'the licensed activities': s 126(1)
'licensee': s 126(1)
'occasional use notice': ss 39(2), 353(1)
'operating licence': s 353(1)
'postal services': s 353(2)(f)
'providing facilities for gambling': ss 5, 353(2)(i)
'track': s 353(1)
'winnings': s 353(1)
'young person': ss 45(2), 353(1)

Explanatory Notes

284–288 [para **6.2008** below]

6.594 94 Horse-race pool betting operating licence

(1) This section applies to a pool betting operating licence which provides for this section to apply.

(2) The holder of a licence to which this section applies may in writing authorise a person to provide facilities for horse-race pool betting.

(3) An authorisation under subsection (2) shall be treated for the purposes of section 33 as if it were a pool betting operating licence authorising the provision of facilities for horse-race pool betting.

(4) An authorisation under subsection (2) may be issued on terms and conditions which may, in particular, include—

(a) provision for payment to or by the person issuing the authorisation;

(b) provision for agency or commission.

(5) A condition of a pool betting operating licence to which this section applies (whether attached by virtue of section 75, 77 or 78) may make provision regulating or restricting the activities of persons authorised under subsection (2).

(6) A pool betting operating licence to which this section applies shall, by virtue of this subsection, contain an implied term permitting the use of postal services for the making of bets.

(7) The effect of the term implied by subsection (6) may not be disapplied or restricted by a condition attached under section 75, 77 or 78.

(8) The Secretary of State may by order repeal this section.

Commencement

Brought into force by the Gambling Act 2005 (Commencement No 6 and Transitional Provisions) Order 2006, SI 2006/3272, art 2, Sch 1 as from 1 January 2007; for transitional provisions see art 6, Sch 4 thereto (as amended by SI 2007/1157, arts 7–12).

Sub-s (1): Operating licence. As to the nature, etc of operating licences, see s 65 and the note 'Operating licences' thereto.

Sub-s (2): Writing. See the note to s 39.

Sub-s (2): Person. See the note 'Persons' to s 23.

Sub-s (8): Secretary of State. See the note to s 4.

Production of authorisations on demand. See s 316.

Application

See the note to s 65.

Orders under this section

At the time of going to press no orders had been made under this section.

As to orders under this Act generally, see s 355.

Definitions

'holder': s 126(1)
'horse-race pool betting': ss 12, 353(1)
'operating licence': s 353(1)
'postal services': s 353(2)(f)
'providing facilities for gambling': ss 5, 353(2)(i)

Explanatory Notes

289, 290 [para **6.2008** below]

6.595 95 Betting on the National Lottery

(1) This section applies to—

(a) a general betting operating licence,
(b) a pool betting operating licence, and
(c) a betting intermediary operating licence.

(2) A licence to which this section applies shall, by virtue of this subsection, be subject to the condition that nothing may be done in reliance on the licence in relation to a bet on the outcome of a lottery which forms part of the National Lottery.

Commencement

Brought into force by the Gambling Act 2005 (Commencement No 6 and Transitional Provisions) Order 2006, SI 2006/3272, art 2, Sch 1 as from 1 January 2007; for transitional provisions see art 6, Sch 4 thereto (as amended by SI 2007/1157, arts 7–12).

Sub-s (1): Operating licence. As to the nature, etc of operating licences, see s 65 and the note 'Operating licences' thereto.

Application

See the note to s 65.

Definitions

'lottery': ss 14, 353(1)
'the National Lottery': s 353(1)
'operating licence': s 353(1)

Explanatory Notes

292 [para **6.2008** below]

6.596 96 Gaming machine technical operating licence: standards

(1) The Commission may establish, or provide for the establishment of, standards in respect of the manufacture, supply, installation, adaptation, maintenance or repair of gaming machines or parts of gaming machines.

(2) Standards under subsection (1)—

(a) may operate by reference to regulations under Part 10, and

(b) may not make provision which is inconsistent with a provision of regulations under Part 10.

(3) Standards under subsection (1) may, in particular, make provision (which may include provision designed to discourage repetitive play or to protect children or other vulnerable persons from harm) about—

(a) the nature of a game that a machine is designed to be used to play;

(b) the way in which the results of a game are to be determined or presented;

(c) the nature of images or information displayed by or on a machine.

(4) In particular, the Commission may—

(a) provide for the enforcement of standards by the attachment of conditions under section 75 or 77;

(b) make arrangements with any person for the establishment of standards;

(c) make arrangements with any person for the administration of tests of compliance with standards;

(d) for the purpose of considering whether a condition under section 75 or 77 has been complied with, require the holder of a gaming machine technical operating licence—

(i) to submit to a test in accordance with arrangements made under paragraph (c) above, and

(ii) to produce specified evidence of the result of the test;

(e) for the purpose of considering whether to grant an application under this Part, require the holder of or an applicant for a gaming machine technical operating licence—

(i) to submit to a test in accordance with arrangements made under paragraph (c) above, and

(ii) to produce specified evidence of the result of the test.

(5) Standards established under subsection (1) may, in particular, be expressed—

(a) by reference to the opinion of a specified person or class of persons;

(b) by reference to a specified process or class of machine.

(6) This section is without prejudice to the generality of sections 75, 77 and 78.

Note

The Gambling Commission in June 2007 published many Machine Standards and other relevant documents (see paras **6.2520–6.2580** below).

Commencement

Brought into force by the Gambling Act 2005 (Commencement No 6 and Transitional Provisions) Order 2006, SI 2006/3272, art 2, Sch 1 as from 1 January 2007; for transitional provisions see art 6, Sch 4 thereto (as amended by SI 2007/1157, arts 7–12).

Sub-s (1): The Commission. Ie the Gambling Commission; see s 353(1). As to the establishment, etc of the Gambling Commission, see s 20, Sch 4, and the note 'Gambling Commission' to that section.

Sub-s (2): Part 10. Ie Pt 10 (ss 235–251 and Sch 10) of this Act.

Sub-s (4): Person. See the note 'Persons' to s 23.

Sub-s (4): Operating licence. As to the nature, etc of operating licences, see s 65 and the note 'Operating licences' thereto.

Sub-s (4): This Part. Ie Pt 5 (ss 65–126 and Sch 7) of this Act.

Application

See the note to s 65.

Definitions

'child': ss 45(1), 353(1)
'the Commission': s 353(1)
'gaming machine': ss 235, 353(1)
'holder': s 126(1)
'machine': ss 235(3)(a), 353(1)
'operating licence': s 353(1)
'supply': s 353(1)

Explanatory Notes

293–295 [para **6.2008** below]

6.597 97 Gambling software operating licence: standards

(1) The Commission may establish, or provide for the establishment of, standards in respect of the manufacture, supply, installation or adaptation of gambling software.

(2) In particular, the Commission may—

(a) provide for the enforcement of standards by the attachment of conditions under section 75 or 77;

(b) make arrangements with any person for the establishment of standards;

(c) make arrangements with any person for the administration of tests of compliance with standards;

(d) for the purpose of considering whether a condition under section 75 or 77 has been complied with, require the holder of a gambling software operating licence—

(i) to submit to a test in accordance with arrangements made under paragraph (c) above, and

(ii) to produce specified evidence of the result of the test;

(e) for the purpose of considering whether to grant an application under this Part, require the holder of or an applicant for a gambling software operating licence—

(i) to submit to a test in accordance with arrangements made under paragraph (c) above, and

(ii) to produce specified evidence of the result of the test.

(3) Standards established under subsection (1) may, in particular, be expressed—

(a) by reference to the opinion of a specified person or class of persons;

(b) by reference to a specified process or description of software.

(4) This section is without prejudice to the generality of sections 75, 77 and 78.

Note

See 'Remote Gambling and Software Technical Standards' published by the Gambling Commission in August 2009 (see para **6.2410** below).

Commencement

Brought into force by the Gambling Act 2005 (Commencement No 6 and Transitional Provisions) Order 2006, SI 2006/3272, art 2, Sch 1 as from 1 January 2007; for transitional provisions see art 6, Sch 4 thereto (as amended by SI 2007/1157, arts 7–12).

Sub-s (1): The Commission. Ie the Gambling Commission; see s 353(1). As to the establishment, etc of the Gambling Commission, see s 20, Sch 4, and the note 'Gambling Commission' to that section.

Sub-s (2): Person. See the note 'Persons' to s 23.

Sub-s (2): Operating licence. As to the nature, etc of operating licences, see s 65 and the note 'Operating licences' thereto.

Sub-s (2): This Part. Ie Pt 5 (ss 65–126 and Sch 7) of this Act.

Application

See the note to s 65.

Definitions

'the Commission': s 353(1)
'gambling software': ss 41(2), 353(1)
'holder': s 126(1)
'installing computer software': s 353(2)(d)
'operating licence': s 353(1)
'supply': s 353(1)

Explanatory Notes

296 [para **6.2008** below]

6.598 98 Lottery operating licences

(1) A lottery operating licence may be issued only to—

(a) a non-commercial society,
(b) a local authority, or
(c) a person proposing to act as external lottery manager on behalf of a non-commercial society or a local authority.

(2) A lottery operating licence may authorise—

(a) promotion generally or only specified promoting activities;
(b) the promotion of lotteries generally or only the promotion of lotteries of a specified kind or in specified circumstances;
(c) action as an external lottery manager (in which case it is known as a 'lottery manager's operating licence').

(3) In issuing a lottery operating licence to a society or authority the Commission—

(a) may attach a condition under section 75 or 77 requiring that the society or authority ensure that all the arrangements for the lottery are made by the holder of a lottery manager's operating licence, and
(b) may, if they attach a condition under paragraph (a), issue the lottery licence to the society or authority without consideration of the matters specified in section 70(1)(b).

(4) A lottery operating licence shall, by virtue of this subsection, permit the delivery of lottery tickets by.

(5) The effect of the term implied by subsection (4) may not be disapplied or restricted by a condition attached under section 75, 77 or 78.

(6) In issuing a lottery operating licence the Commission may attach a condition under section 75 or 77 preventing, restricting or controlling the use of a rollover.

(7) In this section 'local authority' means—

(a) in relation to England—
  (i) a district council,
  (ii) a county council,
  (iii) a parish council,
  (iv) a London borough council,
  (v) the Common Council of the City of London, and
  (vi) the Council of the Isles of Scilly,
(b) in relation to Wales—
  (i) a county council,
  (ii) a county borough council, and
  (iii) a community council, and
(c) in relation to Scotland, a council constituted under section 2 of the Local Government etc (Scotland) Act 1994 (c 39).

Commencement

Brought into force by the Gambling Act 2005 (Commencement No 6 and Transitional Provisions) Order 2006, SI 2006/3272, art 2, Sch 1 as from 1 January 2007; for transitional provisions see art 6, Sch 4 thereto (as amended by SI 2007/1157, arts 7–12).

Sub-s (1): Operating licence. As to the nature, etc of operating licences, see s 65 and the note 'Operating licences' thereto.

Sub-s (1): Person. See the note 'Persons' to s 23.

Sub-s (3): The Commission. Ie the Gambling Commission; see s 353(1). As to the establishment, etc of the Gambling Commission, see s 20, Sch 4, and the note 'Gambling Commission' to that section.

Sub-s (7): England; Wales; district council; county council; London borough council; Common Council of the City of London; Isles of Scilly; county borough council. See the notes to s 2.

Application

See the note to s 65.

Definitions

'the Commission': s 353(1)
'external lottery manager': ss 257, 353(1)
'holder': s 126(1)
'lottery': ss 14, 353(1)
'lottery ticket': ss 253(1), 353(1)
'non-commercial society': ss 19, 353(1)
'operating licence': s 353(1)
'promoting a lottery': ss 252, 353(2)(h)
'rollover': ss 256, 353(1)

Explanatory Notes

297–303 [para **6.2008** below]

6.599 99 Mandatory conditions of lottery operating licence

(1) In issuing a lottery operating licence to a non-commercial society or to a local authority the Commission shall attach conditions under section 75 or 77 for the purpose of achieving the requirements specified in this section.

(2) The first requirement is that at least 20% of the proceeds of any lottery promoted in reliance on the licence are applied—

(a) in the case of a licence issued to a non-commercial society, to a purpose for which the promoting society is conducted, and

(b) in the case of a licence issued to a local authority, for a purpose for which the authority has power to incur expenditure.

(3) The second requirement is that—

(a) the proceeds of any lottery promoted in reliance on the licence may not exceed [£4,000,000], and

(b) the aggregate of the proceeds of lotteries promoted wholly or partly in a calendar year in reliance on the licence may not exceed £10,000,000[1].

(4) The third requirement is that it must not be possible for the purchaser of a ticket in a lottery promoted in reliance on the licence to win by virtue of that ticket (whether in money, money's worth, or partly the one and partly the other) more than—

(a) £25,000, or

(b) if more, 10% of the proceeds of the lottery;

and any rollover must comply with this subsection.

(5) The fourth requirement is that where a person purchases a lottery ticket in a lottery promoted by a non-commercial society in reliance on the licence he receives a document which—

(a) identifies the promoting society,

(b) states the name and address of a member of the society who is designated, by persons acting on behalf of the society, as having responsibility within the society for the promotion of the lottery, and

(c) either—

(i) states the date of the draw (or each draw) in the lottery, or

(ii) enables the date of the draw (or each draw) in the lottery to be determined.

(6) The fifth requirement is that the price payable for purchasing each ticket in a lottery promoted in reliance on the licence—

(a) must be the same,

(b) must be shown on the ticket or in a document received by the purchaser, and

(c) must be paid to the promoter of the lottery before any person is given a ticket or any right in respect of membership of the class among whom prizes are to be allocated.

(7) For the purpose of subsections (5) and (6) a reference to a person receiving a document includes, in particular, a reference to a message being sent or displayed to him electronically in a manner which enables him, without incurring significant expense or delay, to—

(a) retain the message electronically, or

(b) print it.

(8) The sixth requirement is that membership of the class among whom prizes in any lottery promoted in reliance on the licence are allocated may not be dependent on making any payment (apart from payment of the price of a ticket).

(9) Where—

(a) conditions are attached to a lottery operating licence in accordance with this section, and

(b) the lottery operating licence is also subject to a condition under section 98(3)(a) requiring arrangements for the lottery to be made by the holder of a lottery manager's operating licence,

the conditions specified in paragraph (a) above shall, by virtue of this subsection, attach to the lottery manager's operating licence in so far as it is relied upon in pursuance of the condition specified in paragraph (b) above.

(10) Nothing in this section prevents the Commission from attaching a condition to a lottery operating licence of a kind similar to but more onerous than a requirement of this section.

(11) The Secretary of State may by order vary a monetary amount or a percentage in this section.

Commencement

Brought into force by the Gambling Act 2005 (Commencement No 6 and Transitional Provisions) Order 2006, SI 2006/3272, art 2, Sch 1 as from 1 January 2007; for transitional provisions see art 6, Sch 4 thereto (as amended by SI 2007/1157, arts 7–12).

Sub-s (1): Operating licence. As to the nature, etc of operating licences, see s 65 and the note 'Operating licences' thereto.

Sub-s (1): The Commission. Ie the Gambling Commission; see s 353(1). As to the establishment, etc of the Gambling Commission, see s 20, Sch 4, and the note 'Gambling Commission' to that section.

Sub-s (11): Secretary of State. See the note to s 4.

Application

See the note to s 65.

Orders under this section

At the time of going to press no orders had been made under this section.

As to orders under this Act generally, see s 355.

Definitions

'the Commission': s 353(1)
'holder': s 126(1)
'lottery': ss 14, 353(1)
'lottery ticket': ss 253(1), 353(1)
'non-commercial society': ss 19, 353(1)
'operating licence': s 353(1)
'prize' (in relation to a lottery): ss 14(4), 353(1)
'proceeds' (in relation to a lottery): ss 254(1), 353(1)
'promoting a lottery': ss 252, 353(2)(h)
'rollover': ss 256, 353(1)

Explanatory Notes

304–307 [para **6.2008** below]

Amendment

Sub-s (3): in para (a) sum "£4,000,000" in square brackets substituted by SI 2009/207, art 2. Date in force: 4 February 2009: see SI 2009/207, art 1.

---

1 See para **6.243A** above for a discussion of these thresholds in the *Camelot* case.

Maintenance

6.600 100 Annual fee

(1) The holder of an operating licence—

(a) shall pay a first annual fee to the Commission within such period after the issue of the licence as may be prescribed, and

(b) shall pay an annual fee to the Commission before each anniversary of the issue of the licence.

(2) In this section—

'annual fee' means a fee of such amount as may be prescribed, and

'prescribed' means prescribed by the Secretary of State by regulations.

(3) Regulations under this section may, in particular, make different provision for—

(a) different kinds of operating licence, or

(b) different circumstances.

(4) Subsection (1)(b) does not apply in relation to an anniversary of the issue of a licence on or immediately before which the licence ceases to have effect by virtue of section 111.

Commencement

Brought into force by the Gambling Act 2005 (Commencement No 6 and Transitional Provisions) Order 2006, SI 2006/3272, art 2, Sch 1 as from 1 January 2007; for transitional provisions see art 6, Sch 4 thereto (as amended by SI 2007/1157, arts 7–12).

Sub-s (1): Operating licence. As to the nature, etc of operating licences, see s 65 and the note 'Operating licences' thereto.

Sub-s (1): Annual fee. For the power of the Gambling Commission to revoke an operating licence if the licensee fails to pay the annual fee in accordance with this section, see s 119(3).

Any sum due by way of levy by virtue of s 123 is to be treated for the purposes of this Act as if it were due by way of annual fee under this section; see s 123(4).

Sub-s (1): The Commission. Ie the Gambling Commission; see s 353(1). As to the establishment, etc of the Gambling Commission, see s 20, Sch 4, and the note 'Gambling Commission' to that section.

Sub-s (2): Secretary of State. See the note to s 4.

Application

See the note to s 65.

Subordinate Legislation

Gambling (Operating Licence and Single-Machine Permit Fees) (Amendment) Regulations 2007, SI 2007/269 (made under sub-ss (2), (3)). See also SI 2007/1791, SI 2006/3284 and SI 2008/1803.

As to regulations under this Act generally, see s 355.

Definitions

'the Commission': s 353(1)

'operating licence': s 353(1)

Explanatory Notes

308 [para **6.2008** below]

6.601 101 Change of circumstance

(1) The Secretary of State may make regulations requiring the holder of an operating licence—

(a) to notify the Commission of any change of circumstance of a prescribed kind in relation to him or to a licensed activity, and

(b) to give the Commission prescribed details of the change.

(2) If a change of circumstance notified under subsection (1) falsifies information contained in the operating licence in accordance with section 66 the notification must be accompanied by—

(a) the prescribed fee, and

(b) either—

(i) the licence, or

(ii) an application to the Commission for the issue of a copy of the licence under section 107.

(3) Where notification is accompanied by the licence, the Commission shall—

(a) make such alteration to the information contained in the licence as appears to it to be required by the change in circumstance, and

(b) return the licence to the licensee.

(4) Where the notification is accompanied by an application for a copy of the licence, the Commission shall, if it grants the application, issue the copy in a form which appears to the Commission to reflect the change in circumstance.

(5) In this section 'prescribed' means prescribed by regulations under this section.

(6) The holder of an operating licence commits an offence if he fails without reasonable excuse to comply with regulations under this section.

(7) A person guilty of an offence under subsection (6) shall be liable on summary conviction to a fine not exceeding level 2 on the standard scale.

(8) This section does not prevent the imposition of a requirement to notify the Commission of a specified change of circumstance by way of the attachment of a condition to an operating licence.

Commencement

Brought into force by the Gambling Act 2005 (Commencement No 6 and Transitional Provisions) Order 2006, SI 2006/3272, art 2, Sch 1 as from 1 January 2007; for transitional provisions see art 6, Sch 4 thereto (as amended by SI 2007/1157, arts 7–12).

Sub-s (1): Secretary of State. See the note to s 4.

Sub-s (1): Operating licence. As to the nature, etc of operating licences, see s 65 and the note 'Operating licences' thereto.

Sub-s (1): Notify. See further, in connection with a requirement under this Act to give a notice, s 353(4).

The Gambling Commission may require the holder of an operating licence to submit it to the Commission for the purpose of amendment to reflect a change notified under this section; see s 105.

Sub-s (1): The Commission. Ie the Gambling Commission; see s 353(1). As to the establishment, etc of the Gambling Commission, see s 20, Sch 4, and the note 'Gambling Commission' to that section.

Sub-s (6): Offence. For the power of the Gambling Commission and other specified persons to undertake activities for the purpose of assessing whether an offence is being committed under or by virtue of this Act, see s 27 and s 305; for the power of that Commission to investigate and prosecute offences, see s 28; as to offences committed by a body, see s 341; and for the time limit on prosecutions, see s 347. See also s 306 for powers of entry as respects a suspected offence, and s 345 as respects forfeiture of an article relating to an offence.

Sub-s (7): Summary conviction; standard scale. See the notes to s 33.

Application

See the note to s 65.

Regulations under this section

At the time of going to press no regulations had been made under this section.

As to regulations under this Act generally, see s 355.

Definitions

'the Commission': s 353(1)
'holder': s 126(1)
'licensee': s 126(1)
'operating licence': s 353(1)

Explanatory Notes

309, 310 [para **6.2008** below]

6.602 102 Change of corporate control

(1) This section applies where the holder of an operating licence is a company limited by shares ('the company').

(2) If a person becomes a controller of the company ('the new controller'), within the meaning of section 422 of the Financial Services and Markets Act 2000 (c 8), the company shall inform the Commission and either—

(a) surrender the operating licence under section 113, or

(b) apply to the Commission under this section for a determination that the operating licence shall continue to have effect.

(3) An application under subsection (2)(b) must be accompanied by such information as the Commission may direct about—

(a) the new controller,

(b) his interest in the company, and

(c) his interest in any company of which the company is a subsidiary (within the meaning of [section 1159 of the Companies Act 2006]).[1]

(4) On considering an application under section (2)(b) the Commission shall—

(a) make the determination sought, if satisfied that the Commission would have granted the operating licence to the licensee had the new controller been a controller of the company when the application for the operating licence was made, and

(b) otherwise, revoke the operating licence.

(5) If the Commission becomes aware that a company has failed to comply with the duty under subsection (2) within the period of five weeks beginning with the day on which the duty began to apply to the company, the Commission shall revoke the relevant operating licence.

(6) But the Commission may extend the period under subsection (5)—

(a) before it expires, or

(b) after it expires (if the relevant operating licence has not yet been revoked).

Commencement

Brought into force by the Gambling Act 2005 (Commencement No 6 and Transitional Provisions) Order 2006, SI 2006/3272, art 2, Sch 1 as from 1 January 2007; for transitional provisions see art 6, Sch 4 thereto (as amended by SI 2007/1157, arts 7–12).

Sub-s (1): Operating licence. As to the nature, etc of operating licences, see s 65 and the note 'Operating licences' thereto.

Sub-s (2): The Commission. Ie the Gambling Commission; see s 353(1). As to the establishment, etc of the Gambling Commission, see s 20, Sch 4, and the note 'Gambling Commission' to that section.

Sub-s (2): Apply . . . for a determination. As to appeals to the Gambling Appeals Tribunal, see s 141.

Supplemental provisions

See s 103.

Application

See the note to s 65.

Definitions

'the Commission': s 353(1)
'holder': s 126(1)
'licensee': s 126(1)
'operating licence': s 353(1)

Explanatory Notes

311–316 [para **6.2008** below]

1 Sub-s (3): in para (c) words 'section 1159 of the Companies Act 2006' in square brackets substituted by SI 2009/1941, art 2(1), Sch 1, para 247.

6: Gambling Act 2005: Statutes

6.603 103 Section 102: supplemental

(1) The Secretary of State may by regulations provide for section 102 not to apply to the holder of a specified description of operating licence.

(2) An application under section 102(2)(b) must be accompanied by the prescribed fee.

(3) An application may be made under section 102(2)(b) in respect of a person who is expected to become a controller of a company.

(4) The Commission shall as soon as is reasonably practicable inform an applicant under section 102(2)(b) of—

(a) the Commission's decision, and
(b) the reasons for it.

(5) In giving a direction under section 102(3) the Commission shall have regard to normal commercial practices in relation to the confidentiality of information.

(6) Regulations under subsection (2) above may, in particular, provide for a reduction of fee where the application is a result of—

(a) the merger of more than one company, or
(b) the division of a company.

(7) Revocation of an operating licence under section 102 shall be treated for all purposes (including the application of section 119) as revocation under section 119.

Commencement

Brought into force by the Gambling Act 2005 (Commencement No 6 and Transitional Provisions) Order 2006, SI 2006/3272, art 2, Sch 1 as from 1 January 2007; for transitional provisions see art 6, Sch 4 thereto (as amended by SI 2007/1157, arts 7–12).

Sub-s (1): Secretary of State. See the note to s 4.

Sub-s (1): Operating licence. As to the nature, etc of operating licences, see s 65 and the note 'Operating licences' thereto.

Application

See the note to s 65.

Subordinate Legislation:

SI 2006/3284, 2007/269, 2007/1791, 2008/1803.

As to regulations under this Act generally, see s 355.

Definitions

'holder': s 126(1)

'operating licence': s 353(1)

Explanatory Notes

311–316 [para **6.2008** below]

6.604 104 Application to vary licence

(1) The holder of an operating licence may apply to the Commission to vary the licence by—

(a) adding, amending or removing a licensed activity,

(b) amending another detail of the licence, or

(c) adding, amending or removing a condition attached to the licence under section 77.

(2) A licence may not be varied under this section so as to authorise anyone other than the person to whom it was issued to provide facilities for gambling.

(3) The provisions of this Part shall apply in relation to an application for variation as they apply in relation to an application for a licence—

(a) subject to the provisions of this section, and

(b) with any other necessary modifications.

(4) Regulations under this Part which relate to an application for an operating licence may make—

(a) provision which applies only in the case of an application for variation;

(b) provision which does not apply in the case of an application for variation;

(c) different provision in relation to an application for variation from that made in relation to an application for an operating licence;

(d) different provision in relation to applications for variations of different kinds.

(5) An application for variation must (in addition to anything required by section 69) be accompanied by—

(a) a statement of the variation sought, and

(b) either—

(i) the licence to be varied, or

(ii) a statement explaining why it is not reasonably practicable to produce the licence.

(6) In granting an application for variation the Commission—

(a) shall specify a time when the variation shall begin to have effect, and

(b) may make transitional provision.

Commencement

Brought into force by the Gambling Act 2005 (Commencement No 6 and Transitional Provisions) Order 2006, SI 2006/3272, art 2, Sch 1 as from 1 January 2007; for transitional provisions see art 6, Sch 4 thereto (as amended by SI 2007/1157, arts 7–12).

Sub-s (1): Operating licence. As to the nature, etc of operating licences, see s 65 and the note 'Operating licences' thereto.

Sub-s (1): May apply, etc. The Gambling Commission may require the holder of an operating licence to submit it to the Commission for the purpose of amendment to reflect the grant of an application for variation under this section; see s 105.

As to appeals to the Gambling Appeals Tribunal, see s 141.

Sub-s (1): The Commission. Ie the Gambling Commission; see s 353(1). As to the establishment, etc of the Gambling Commission, see s 20, Sch 4, and the note 'Gambling Commission' to that section.

Sub-s (2): Person. See the note 'Persons' to s 23.

Sub-s (3): This Part. Ie Pt 5 (ss 65–126 and Sch 7) of this Act.

Application

See the note to s 65.

Subordinate Legislation:

SI 2006/3284, 2006/3285, 2007/269, 2007/1791, 2008/1803.

Definitions

'the Commission': s 353(1)
'holder': s 126(1)
'the licensed activities': s 126(1)
'operating licence': s 353(1)
'providing facilities for gambling': ss 5, 353(2)(i)

Explanatory Notes

317–319 [para **6.2008** below]

6.605 105 Amendment

(1) The Commission may require the holder of an operating licence to submit it to the Commission for the purpose of amendment to reflect—

(a) a general variation of conditions under section 75,
(b) a change notified under section 101,
(c) the grant of an application for variation under section 104,
(d) the attachment of an additional condition, or the amendment of a condition, under section 117,
(e) the grant of an application for renewal under section 112, or
(f) anything done in relation to a personal licence under Part 6.

(2) A licensee shall comply with a requirement under subsection (1) within the period of 14 days beginning with the day on which he receives notice of the requirement.

(3) A person commits an offence if he fails without reasonable excuse to comply with a requirement imposed under subsection (1).

(4) A person guilty of an offence under subsection (3) shall be liable on summary conviction to a fine not exceeding level 2 on the standard scale.

(5) Subsection (1)(a) is without prejudice to section 76(4)(c).

Commencement

Brought into force by the Gambling Act 2005 (Commencement No 6 and Transitional Provisions) Order 2006, SI 2006/3272, art 2, Sch 1 as from 1 January 2007; for transitional provisions see art 6, Sch 4 thereto (as amended by SI 2007/1157, arts 7–12).

Sub-s (1): The Commission. Ie the Gambling Commission; see s 353(1). As to the establishment, etc of the Gambling Commission, see s 20, Sch 4, and the note 'Gambling Commission' to that section.

Sub-s (1): Operating licence. As to the nature, etc of operating licences, see s 65 and the note 'Operating licences' thereto.

Sub-s (2): Notice. See further, in connection with a requirement under this Act to give a notice, s 353(4).

Sub-s (3): Offence. For the power of the Gambling Commission and other specified persons to undertake activities for the purpose of assessing whether an offence is being committed under or

by virtue of this Act, see s 27 and s 305; for the power of that Commission to investigate and prosecute offences, see s 28; as to offences committed by a body, see s 341; and for the time limit on prosecutions, see s 347. See also s 306 for powers of entry as respects a suspected offence, and s 345 as respects forfeiture of an article relating to an offence.

Sub-s (4): Summary conviction; standard scale. See the notes to s 33.

Application

See the note to s 65.

Definitions

'the Commission': s 353(1)
'holder': s 126(1)
'licensee' s 126(1)
'operating licence': s 353(1)

Explanatory Notes

320, 321 [para **6.2008** below]

6.606 106 Register of operating licences

(1) The Commission shall—

(a) maintain a register of operating licences containing such details of and relating to each licence as the Commission thinks appropriate,
(b) make the register available for inspection by members of the public at all reasonable times, and
(c) make arrangements for the provision of a copy of an entry in the register to a member of the public on request.

(2) The Commission may refuse to provide access to the register or to provide a copy of an entry unless the person seeking access or a copy pays a fee specified by the Commission.

(3) The Commission may not specify a fee under subsection (2) which exceeds the reasonable cost of providing the service sought (but in calculating the cost of providing a service to a person the Commission may include a reasonable share of expenditure which is referable only indirectly to the provision of that service).

Commencement

Brought into force by the Gambling Act 2005 (Commencement No 6 and Transitional Provisions) Order 2006, SI 2006/3272, art 2, Sch 1 as from 1 January 2007; for transitional provisions see art 6, Sch 4 thereto (as amended by SI 2007/1157, arts 7–12).

Sub-s (1): The Commission. Ie the Gambling Commission; see s 353(1). As to the establishment, etc of the Gambling Commission, see s 20, Sch 4, and the note 'Gambling Commission' to that section.

Sub-s (1): Operating licences. As to the nature, etc of operating licences, see s 65 and the note 'Operating licences' thereto.

Application

See the note to s 65.

Definitions

'the Commission': s 353(1)
'operating licence': s 353(1)

Explanatory Notes

322 [para **6.2008** below]

6.607 107 Copy of licence

(1) The Commission may make arrangements to issue to a licensee on request a copy of an operating licence which has been lost, stolen or damaged.

(2) The arrangements may, in particular, include a requirement—

(a) for the payment of a fee not exceeding such sum as may be prescribed for the purposes of this subsection by the Secretary of State by regulations;

(b) in the case of a licence being lost or stolen, that the licensee has complied with specified arrangements for reporting the loss or theft to the police.

(3) A copy of a licence issued under this section shall be treated as if it were the licence.

Commencement

Brought into force by the Gambling Act 2005 (Commencement No 6 and Transitional Provisions) Order 2006, SI 2006/3272, art 2, Sch 1 as from 1 January 2007; for transitional provisions see art 6, Sch 4 thereto (as amended by SI 2007/1157, arts 7–12).

Sub-s (1): The Commission. Ie the Gambling Commission; see s 353(1). As to the establishment, etc of the Gambling Commission, see s 20, Sch 4, and the note 'Gambling Commission' to that section.

Sub-s (1): Operating licence. As to the nature, etc of operating licences, see s 65 and the note 'Operating licences' thereto.

Sub-s (2): Secretary of State. See the note to s 4.

Application

See the note to s 65.

Subordinate Legislation:

SI 2006/3284, 2007/269, 2007/1791.

As to regulations under this Act generally, see s 355.

Definitions

'the Commission': s 353(1)
'licensee' s 126(1)
'operating licence': s 353(1)

Explanatory Notes

323 [para **6.2008** below]

6.608 108 Production of licence

(1) A constable or enforcement officer may require the holder of an operating licence to produce it to the constable or enforcement officer within a specified period.

(2) A licensee commits an offence if he fails without reasonable excuse to comply with a requirement under subsection (1).

(3) A person guilty of an offence under subsection (2) shall be liable on summary conviction to a fine not exceeding level 2 on the standard scale.

Commencement

Brought into force by the Gambling Act 2005 (Commencement No 6 and Transitional Provisions) Order 2006, SI 2006/3272, art 2, Sch 1 as from 1 January 2007; for transitional provisions see art 6, Sch 4 thereto (as amended by SI 2007/1157, arts 7–12).

Sub-s (1): Constable. See the note to s 64.

Sub-s (1): Enforcement officer. As to enforcement officers, see, generally, s 303.

Sub-s (1): Operating licence. As to the nature, etc of operating licences, see s 65 and the note 'Operating licences' thereto.

Sub-s (2): Offence. For the power of the Gambling Commission and other specified persons to undertake activities for the purpose of assessing whether an offence is being committed under or by virtue of this Act, see s 27 and s 305; for the power of that Commission to investigate and prosecute offences, see s 28; as to offences committed by a body, see s 341; and for the time limit on prosecutions, see s 347. See also s 306 for powers of entry as respects a suspected offence, and s 345 as respects forfeiture of an article relating to an offence.

Sub-s (3): Summary conviction; standard scale. See the notes to s 33.

Application

See the note to s 65.

Definitions

'enforcement officer': s 353(1)
'holder': s 126(1)

'operating licence': s 353(1)

Explanatory Notes

323 [para **6.2008** below]

6.609 109 Conviction

(1) If the holder of an operating licence is convicted of an offence by or before a court in Great Britain he shall as soon as is reasonably practicable notify the Commission of—

(a) his conviction, and

(b) any sentence passed in respect of it.

(2) If the holder of an operating licence is convicted of a relevant offence by or before a court in Great Britain he shall immediately inform the court that he is the holder of an operating licence.

(3) If the holder of an operating licence is convicted of a relevant offence by or before a court outside Great Britain he shall as soon as is reasonably practicable notify the Commission of—

(a) his conviction, and

(b) any sentence passed in respect of it.

(4) A person commits an offence if he fails without reasonable excuse to comply with any of subsections (1) to (3).

(5) A person guilty of an offence under subsection (4) shall be liable on summary conviction to a fine not exceeding level 2 on the standard scale.

Commencement

Brought into force by the Gambling Act 2005 (Commencement No 6 and Transitional Provisions) Order 2006, SI 2006/3272, art 2, Sch 1 as from 1 January 2007; for transitional provisions see art 6, Sch 4 thereto (as amended by SI 2007/1157, arts 7–12).

Sub-s (1): Operating licence. As to the nature, etc of operating licences, see s 65 and the note 'Operating licences' thereto.

Sub-s (1): Great Britain. See the note to s 12.

Sub-s (1): Notify. See further, in connection with a requirement under this Act to give a notice, s 353(4).

Sub-s (1): The Commission. Ie the Gambling Commission; see s 353(1). As to the establishment, etc of the Gambling Commission, see s 20, Sch 4, and the note 'Gambling Commission' to that section.

Sub-s (4): Offence. For the power of the Gambling Commission and other specified persons to undertake activities for the purpose of assessing whether an offence is being committed under or by virtue of this Act, see s 27 and s 305; for the power of that Commission to investigate and prosecute offences, see s 28; as to offences committed by a body, see s 341; and for the time limit on prosecutions, see s 347. See also s 306 for powers of entry as respects a suspected offence, and s 345 as respects forfeiture of an article relating to an offence.

Sub-s (5): Summary conviction; standard scale. See the notes to s 33.

Application

See the note to s 65.

Definitions

'the Commission': s 353(1)
'conviction': s 126(1)
'holder': s 126(1)
'operating licence': s 353(1)
'relevant offence': ss 126(2), (3), 353(1), Sch 7

Explanatory Notes

324–327 [para **6.2008** below]

Duration

6.610 110 Indefinite duration

An operating licence shall continue to have effect unless and until it ceases to have effect in accordance with—

(a) a determination under section 111, or

(b) section 113, 114, 115, 118 or 119.

Commencement

Brought into force by the Gambling Act 2005 (Commencement No 6 and Transitional Provisions) Order 2006, SI 2006/3272, art 2, Sch 1 as from 1 January 2007; for transitional provisions see art 6, Sch 4 thereto (as amended by SI 2007/1157, arts 7–12).

Operating licence

As to the nature, etc of operating licences, see s 65 and the note 'Operating licences' thereto.

Application

See the note to s 65.

Definitions

'operating licence': s 353(1)

Explanatory Notes

328, 329 [para **6.2008** below]

6.611 111 Power to limit duration

(1) The Commission may determine that operating licences, or a specified class of operating licence, shall cease to have effect at the end of a specified period (unless terminated earlier in accordance with section 113, 114, 115 or 119).

(2) The period specified under subsection (1)—

(a) in the case of an operating licence issued after the determination, must begin with the date on which the licence is issued, and

(b) in the case of an operating licence issued before the determination, must begin with the date of the determination.

(3) The Commission—

(a) may determine different periods under subsection (1) for operating licences authorising different classes of activity (but may not otherwise determine different periods for different licences),

(b) may alter a determination under subsection (1) (but an alteration shall have effect only in relation to licences issued after the alteration), and

(c) may revoke a determination under subsection (1) (in which case the determination shall cease to have effect in relation to licences already issued).

(4) The Commission shall publish any determination under subsection (1) as part of a statement (or revised statement) under section 23.

Note

In 'Statement of Principles for Licensing and Regulation' (December 2006) at para 3.18 the Gambling Commission has stated that it does not currently intend to exercise this power (see para **6.2040** of *Paterson 2008* and *2009*).

Commencement

Brought into force by the Gambling Act 2005 (Commencement No 6 and Transitional Provisions) Order 2006, SI 2006/3272, art 2, Sch 1 as from 1 January 2007; for transitional provisions see art 6, Sch 4 thereto (as amended by SI 2007/1157, arts 7–12).

Sub-s (1): The Commission. Ie the Gambling Commission; see s 353(1). As to the establishment, etc of the Gambling Commission, see s 20, Sch 4, and the note 'Gambling Commission' to that section.

Sub-s (1): May determine. Where an operating licence is subject to a determination under this section, the licensee may apply to the Gambling Commission for renewal of the licence; see s 112.

Sub-s (1): Operating licences. As to the nature, etc of operating licences, see s 65 and the note 'Operating licences' thereto.

Application

See the note to s 65.

Definitions

'the Commission': s 353(1)
'operating licence': s 353(1)

Explanatory Notes

328, 329 [para **6.2008** below]

6.612 112 Renewal of licence

(1) Where an operating licence is subject to a determination under section 111, the licensee may apply to the Commission for renewal of the licence.

(2) The provisions of this Part shall apply in relation to an application for renewal as they apply in relation to an application for a licence—

(a) subject to the provisions of this section, and
(b) with any other necessary modifications.

(3) An application for renewal of an operating licence may be made only during the period which—

(a) begins three months before the date on which the licence would otherwise expire by virtue of section 111, and
(b) ends one month before the date on which the licence would otherwise expire by virtue of that section.

(4) Where an application for renewal of an operating licence is awaiting determination on the date when it would expire by virtue of section 111, the licence shall continue to have effect by virtue of this subsection until the application is determined (unless it ceases to have effect by virtue of section 113, 114, 115, 118 or 119).

(5) A direction or regulations under this Part which relate to an application for an operating licence may make—

(a) provision which applies only in the case of an application for renewal;
(b) provision which does not apply in the case of an application for renewal;
(c) different provision in relation to an application for renewal from that made in relation to an application for an operating licence.

(6) An application for renewal must (in addition to anything required by section 69) be accompanied by—

(a) the licence to be renewed, or
(b) a statement explaining why it is not reasonably practicable to submit the licence to be renewed.

(7) The Commission shall determine the period during which a renewed operating licence is to have effect (subject to sections 113, 114, 115, 118 and 119); and the Commission—

(a) may determine different periods for operating licences authorising different classes of activity (but may not otherwise determine different periods for different licences),
(b) may alter a determination (but an alteration shall have effect only in relation to licences issued after the alteration), and
(c) shall publish any determination under this subsection as part of a statement (or revised statement) under section 23.

(8) The Secretary of State may by order amend subsection (3) so as to substitute a different time for a time specified.

Commencement

Brought into force by the Gambling Act 2005 (Commencement No 6 and Transitional Provisions) Order 2006, SI 2006/3272, art 2, Sch 1 as from 1 January 2007; for transitional provisions see art 6, Sch 4 thereto (as amended by SI 2007/1157, arts 7–12).

Sub-s (1): Operating licence. As to the nature, etc of operating licences, see s 65 and the note 'Operating licences' thereto.

Sub-s (1): May apply, etc. The Gambling Commission may require the holder of an operating licence to submit it to the Commission for the purpose of amendment to reflect the grant of an application for renewal under this section; see s 105.

As to appeals to the Gambling Appeals Tribunal, see s 141.

Sub-s (1): The Commission. Ie the Gambling Commission; see s 353(1). As to the establishment, etc of the Gambling Commission, see s 20, Sch 4, and the note 'Gambling Commission' to that section.

Sub-s (2): This Part. Ie Pt 5 (ss 65–126 and Sch 7) of this Act.

Sub-s (8): Secretary of State. See the note to s 4.

Application

See the note to s 65.

Orders under this section

At the time of going to press no orders had been made under this section.

As to orders under this Act generally, see s 355.

Definitions

'the Commission': s 353(1)
'licensee': s 126(1)
'operating licence': s 353(1)

Explanatory Notes

330 [para **6.2008** below]

6.613 113 Surrender

An operating licence shall cease to have effect if the licensee—

(a) notifies the Commission of his intention to surrender the licence, and
(b) gives the Commission either—
  (i) the licence, or
  (ii) a written statement explaining why it is not reasonably practicable to produce the licence.

Commencement

Brought into force by the Gambling Act 2005 (Commencement No 6 and Transitional Provisions) Order 2006, SI 2006/3272, art 2, Sch 1 as from 1 January 2007; for transitional provisions see art 6, Sch 4 thereto (as amended by SI 2007/1157, arts 7–12).

Operating licence

As to the nature, etc of operating licences, see s 65 and the note 'Operating licences' thereto.

Notifies

See further, in connection with a requirement under this Act to give a notice, s 353(4).

The Commission

Ie the Gambling Commission; see s 353(1). As to the establishment, etc of the Gambling Commission, see s 20, Sch 4, and the note 'Gambling Commission' to that section.

Written

See the note 'Writing' to s 39.

Application

See the note to s 65.

Definitions

'the Commission': s 353(1)
'licensee': s 126(1)
'operating licence': s 353(1)

Explanatory Notes

331, 332 [para **6.2008** below]

6.614 114 Lapse

(1) In the case of an operating licence issued to an individual, the licence shall lapse if—

(a) the licensee dies,

(b) the licensee becomes, in the opinion of the Commission as notified to the licensee, incapable of carrying on the licensed activities by reason of mental or physical incapacity,

(c) the licensee becomes bankrupt (within the meaning of section 381 of the Insolvency Act 1986 (c 45)) [or a debt relief order is made in respect of the licensee (under Part 7A of the Insolvency Act 1986),], or

(d) sequestration of the licensee's estate is awarded under section 12(1) of the Bankruptcy (Scotland) Act 1985 (c 66).

(2) In any other case an operating licence shall lapse if the licensee—

(a) ceases to exist, or

(b) goes into liquidation (within the meaning of section 247(2) of the Insolvency Act 1986).

Commencement

Brought into force by the Gambling Act 2005 (Commencement No 6 and Transitional Provisions) Order 2006, SI 2006/3272, art 2, Sch 1 as from 1 January 2007; for transitional provisions see art 6, Sch 4 thereto (as amended by SI 2007/1157, arts 7–12).

Amendment

Sub-s (1): in para (c) words in square brackets inserted by SI 2012/2404, art 3(2), Sch 2, para 55.

Sub-s (1): Operating licence. As to the nature, etc of operating licences, see s 65 and the note 'Operating licences' thereto.

Sub-s (1): The Commission. Ie the Gambling Commission; see s 353(1). As to the establishment, etc of the Gambling Commission, see s 20, Sch 4, and the note 'Gambling Commission' to that section.

Sub-s (1): Notified. See further, in connection with a requirement under this Act to give a notice, s 353(4). As to appeals to the Gambling Appeals Tribunal, see s 141.

Application

See the note to s 65.

Definitions

'the Commission': s 353(1)
'the licensed activities': s 126(1)
'licensee': s 126(1)
'operating licence': s 353(1)

Explanatory Notes

331, 332 [para **6.2008** below]

6.615 115 Forfeiture

(1) Where the holder of an operating licence is convicted of a relevant offence by or before a court in Great Britain the court may order forfeiture of the licence.

(2) Forfeiture under this section shall be on such terms (which may include terms as to suspension) as may be specified by—

(a) the court which orders forfeiture,

(b) a court to which an appeal against the conviction, or against any order made on the conviction, has been or could be made, or

(c) the High Court, if hearing proceedings relating to the conviction.

(3) Subject to any express provision made under subsection (2), an operating licence shall cease to have effect on the making of a forfeiture order under subsection (1).

(4) The terms on which a forfeiture order is made under this section shall, in particular, include a requirement that the licensee deliver to the Commission, within such time as the order may specify—

(a) the licence, or

(b) a statement explaining why it is not reasonably practicable to produce the licence.

(5) As soon as is reasonably practicable after making an order for forfeiture under this section the court shall notify the Commission.

Commencement

Brought into force by the Gambling Act 2005 (Commencement No 6 and Transitional Provisions) Order 2006, SI 2006/3272, art 2, Sch 1 as from 1 January 2007; for transitional provisions see art 6, Sch 4 thereto (as amended by SI 2007/1157, arts 7–12).

Sub-s (1): Operating licence. As to the nature, etc of operating licences, see s 65 and the note 'Operating licences' thereto.

Sub-s (1): Great Britain. See the note to s 12.

Sub-s (4): The Commission. Ie the Gambling Commission; see s 353(1). As to the establishment, etc of the Gambling Commission, see s 20, Sch 4, and the note 'Gambling Commission' to that section.

Sub-s (5): Notify. See further, in connection with a requirement under this Act to give a notice, s 353(4).

Application

See the note to s 65.

Definitions

'the Commission': s 353(1)
'conviction': s 126(1)
'holder': s 126(1)
'licensee': s 126(1)
'operating licence': s 353(1)
'relevant offence': ss 126(2), (3), 353(1), Sch 7

Explanatory Notes

333 [para **6.2008** below]

Regulation

6.616 116 Review

(1) The Commission may in relation to operating licences of a particular description review—

(a) the manner in which licensees carry on licensed activities, and

(b) in particular, arrangements made by licensees to ensure compliance with conditions attached under section 75, 77 or 78.

(2) The Commission may review any matter connected with the provision of facilities for gambling as authorised by an operating licence if the Commission—

(a) has reason to suspect that activities may have been carried on in purported reliance on the licence but not in accordance with a condition of the licence,

(b) believes that the licensee, or a person who exercises a function in connection with or is interested in the licensed activities, has acquired a conviction of a kind mentioned in section 71(1), or

(c) for any reason—

(i) suspects that the licensee may be unsuitable to carry on the licensed activities[1], or

(ii) thinks that a review would be appropriate.

(3) For the purposes of subsection (2)(c) a reason—

(a) may, in particular, relate to the receipt of a complaint about the licensee's activities;

(b) need not relate to any suspicion or belief about the licensee's activities.

(4) Before commencing a review of an operating licence under subsection (2) the Commission shall—

(a) notify the licensee, and

(b) inform him of the procedure to be followed in the conduct of the review.

(5) In conducting a review of an operating licence under subsection (2) the Commission—

(a) shall give the licensee an opportunity to make representations, and

(b) may give other persons an opportunity to make representations.

Commencement

Subsections (1), (2)(a) brought into force as from 1 September 2007 by the Gambling Act 2005 (Commencement No 6 and Transitional Provisions) Order 2006, SI 2006/3272, art 2; for transitional provisions see art 6, Sch 4 thereto (as amended by SI 2007/1157, arts 7–12). Subsections (2)(b), (c), (3)–(5) brought into force by the Gambling Act 2005 (Commencement No 6 and Transitional Provisions) Order 2006, SI 2006/3272, art 2, Sch 1 as from 1 January 2007; for transitional provisions see art 6, Sch 4 thereto (as amended by SI 2007/1157, arts 7–12).

Sub-s (1): The Commission. Ie the Gambling Commission; see s 353(1). As to the establishment, etc of the Gambling Commission, see s 20, Sch 4, and the note 'Gambling Commission' to that section.

Sub-s (1): Operating licences. As to the nature, etc of operating licences, see s 65 and the note 'Operating licences' thereto.

Sub-s (1): Review. For the powers of the Gambling Commission following a review under sub-s (1) or (2) above, see ss 117–120.

Sub-s (4): Notify. See further, in connection with a requirement under this Act to give a notice, s 353(4).

Sub-s (5): Persons. See the note to s 23.

Application

See the note to s 65.

Subordinate Legislation:

ss 116–120 are modified in respect of non-payment of the Levy to the Levy Board by SI 2007/2159, Art 3.

Definitions

'the Commission': s 353(1)
'conviction': s 126(1)
'the licensed activities': s 126(1)
'licensee': s 126(1)
'operating licence': s 353(1)
'providing facilities for gambling': ss 5, 353(2)(i)

Explanatory Notes

334–338 [para **6.2008** below]

---

[1] An example of possible unsuitability in the case of gaming machine suppliers is to be found in the Gambling Commission's letter on the topic dated 21 August 2009 available on its website.

6.617 117 Regulatory powers

(1) Following a review under section 116(1) or (2) the Commission may—

(a) give the holder of an operating licence a warning;

(b) attach an additional condition to a licence under section 77;

(c) remove or amend a condition attached to a licence under section 77;

(d) . . .

(e) exercise the power under section 118 to suspend a licence;

(f) exercise the power under section 119 to revoke a licence;

(g) exercise the power under section 121 to impose a penalty.

(2) Where the Commission determines to take action under subsection (1) in respect of a licence it shall as soon as is reasonably practicable notify the licensee of—

(a) the action, and

(b) the Commission's reasons.

(3) In determining what action to take under subsection (1) following a review the Commission may have regard to a warning under that subsection given to the licensee following an earlier review (whether or not of that licence).

Commencement

Brought into force for certain purposes as from 1 January 2007, for remaining purposes as from 1 September 2007 by the Gambling Act 2005 (Commencement No 6 and Transitional Provisions) Order 2006, SI 2006/3272, art 2, Sch 1; for transitional provisions see art 6, Sch 4 thereto (as amended by SI 2007/1157, arts 7–12).

Sub-s (1): The Commission may, etc. Ie the Gambling Commission; see s 353(1). As to the establishment, etc of the Gambling Commission, see s 20, Sch 4, and the note 'Gambling Commission' to that section.

As to appeals to the Gambling Appeals Tribunal, see s 141.

Sub-s (1): Operating licence. As to the nature, etc of operating licences, see s 65 and the note 'Operating licences' thereto.

Sub-s (1): Attach an additional condition; amend a condition. The Gambling Commission may require the holder of an operating licence to submit it to the Commission for the purpose of amendment to reflect the attachment of an additional condition, or the amendment of a condition, under this section; see s 105.

Sub-s (1)(d): repealed by SI 2007/2321, reg 2(b).

Sub-s (2): Notify. See further, in connection with a requirement under this Act to give a notice, s 353(4).

Application

See the note to s 65.

Definitions

'the Commission': s 353(1)
'holder': s 126(1)
'licensee': s 126(1)
'operating licence': s 353(1)

Explanatory Notes
339–344 [para **6.2008** below]

6.618 118 Suspension

(1) The Commission may suspend an operating licence if following a review under section 116(1) or (2) the Commission thinks that any of the conditions specified in section 120(1) applies.

(2) The Commission may suspend an operating licence if at the time of deciding to conduct a review under section 116(1) or (2), or at any time during the course of a review, the Commission suspects that any of the conditions specified in section 120(1) may apply.

(3) The Commission may suspend an operating licence if it thinks that any of the conditions specified in section 120(2) applies.

(4) Where the Commission suspends an operating licence it—

(a) shall specify the time when the suspension takes effect,

(b) shall specify either—

(i) a period for which the suspension shall last (which is without prejudice to the re-exercise of the power under subsection (1) on or after the expiry of that period), or

(ii) that the suspension shall last until some specified event occurs (which may be the giving of a notice by the Commission), and

(c) may make saving or transitional provision (which may, in particular, provide for a licence to continue to have effect in relation to a gaming machine supplied, or another thing done, before the time when the suspension takes effect for other purposes).

(5) An operating licence shall have no effect in respect of anything done while it is suspended under this section.

Commencement

Brought into force for certain purposes as from 1 January 2007, for remaining purposes as from 1 September 2007 by the Gambling Act 2005 (Commencement No 6 and Transitional Provisions) Order 2006, SI 2006/3272, art 2, Sch 1; for transitional provisions see art 6, Sch 4 thereto (as amended by SI 2007/1157, arts 7–12).

Sub-s (1): The Commission. Ie the Gambling Commission; see s 353(1). As to the establishment, etc of the Gambling Commission, see s 20, Sch 4, and the note 'Gambling Commission' to that section.

Sub-s (1): May suspend. As to appeals to the Gambling Appeals Tribunal, see s 141.

Sub-s (1): Operating licence. As to the nature, etc of operating licences, see s 65 and the note 'Operating licences' thereto.

Sub-s (4): Notice. See further, in connection with a requirement under this Act to give a notice, s 353(4).

Application
See the note to s 65.

Definitions
'the Commission': s 353(1)
'gaming machine': ss 235, 353(1)
'operating licence': s 353(1)
'supply': s 353(1)

Explanatory Notes
339–344 [para **6.2008** below]

6.619 119 Revocation

(1) The Commission may revoke an operating licence if following a review under section 116(1) or (2) the Commission thinks that any of the conditions specified in section 120(1) applies.

(2) The Commission may revoke an operating licence if it thinks that any of the conditions specified in section 120(2) applies.

(3) The Commission shall revoke an operating licence if the licensee fails to pay the annual fee in accordance with section 100; but the Commission may disapply this subsection if it thinks that a failure to pay is attributable to administrative error.

(4) Where the Commission revokes an operating licence it—

(a) shall specify the time when the revocation takes effect, and

(b) may make saving or transitional provision (which may, in particular, provide for a licence to continue to have effect in relation to a gaming machine supplied, or another thing done, before the time when the revocation takes effect for other purposes).

Commencement

Brought into force for certain purposes as from 1 January 2007, for remaining purposes as from 1 September 2007 by the Gambling Act 2005 (Commencement No 6 and Transitional Provisions) Order 2006, SI 2006/3272, art 2, Sch 1; for transitional provisions see art 6, Sch 4 thereto (as amended by SI 2007/1157, arts 7–12).

Sub-s (1): The Commission. Ie the Gambling Commission; see s 353(1). As to the establishment, etc of the Gambling Commission, see s 20, Sch 4, and the note 'Gambling Commission' to that section.

Sub-s (1): Revoke. Revocation of an operating licence under s 102 is to be treated for all purposes (including the application of this section) as revocation under this section; see s 103(7).

As to appeals to the Gambling Appeals Tribunal, see s 141.

Sub-s (1): Operating licence. As to the nature, etc of operating licences, see s 65 and the note 'Operating licences' thereto.

Application

See the note to s 65.

Definitions

'the Commission': s 353(1)
'gaming machine': ss 235, 353(1)
'licensee': s 126(1)
'operating licence': s 353(1)
'supply': s 353(1)

Explanatory Notes

339–344 [para 6.2008 below]

6.620 120 Conditions for suspension or revocation

(1) The conditions referred to in sections 118(1) and (2) and 119(1) are—

(a) that a licensed activity is being or has been carried on in a manner which is inconsistent with the licensing objectives,

(b) that a condition of the licence has been breached,

(c) that the licensee has failed to cooperate with a review under section 116(1) or (2), or

(d) that the licensee is unsuitable to carry on the licensed activities.

(2) The conditions referred to in sections 118(3) and 119(2) are—

(a) that the licensee has failed to comply with a requirement of regulations under section 101, or

(b) that the licensee has failed to submit the licence to the Commission for amendment in accordance with section 105.

(3) In considering a licensee's suitability for the purpose of subsection (1)(d) the Commission may, in particular, have regard to—

(a) the integrity of the licensee or of any person who exercises a function in connection with or is interested in the licensed activities;

(b) the competence of the licensee, or of any person who exercises a function in connection with the licensed activities, to carry on the licensed activities in a manner consistent with pursuit of the licensing objectives;

(c) the financial and other circumstances of the licensee or of any person who exercises a function in connection with or is interested in the licensed activities (and, in particular, the resources available for the purpose of carrying on the licensed activities).

Commencement

Brought into force for certain purposes as from 1 January 2007, for remaining purposes as from 1 September 2007 by the Gambling Act 2005 (Commencement No 6 and Transitional Provisions) Order 2006, SI 2006/3272, art 2, Sch 1; for transitional provisions see art 6, Sch 4 thereto (as amended by SI 2007/1157, arts 7–12).

Sub-s (2): The Commission. Ie the Gambling Commission; see s 353(1). As to the establishment, etc of the Gambling Commission, see s 20, Sch 4, and the note 'Gambling Commission' to that section.

Application

See the note to s 65.

Definitions

'the Commission': s 353(1)
'the licensed activities': s 126(1)
'licensee': s 126(1)
'the licensing objectives': ss 1, 353(1)

Explanatory Notes

339–344 [para **6.2008** below]

6.621 121 Financial penalty

(1) The Commission may require the holder of an operating licence to pay a penalty if the Commission thinks that a condition of the licence has been breached.

(2) Before imposing a requirement on a licensee to pay a penalty under this section the Commission must notify him—

(a) that the Commission proposes to require him to pay a penalty,

(b) of the amount of the proposed penalty,

(c) of the Commission's reasons, and

(d) of a period within which he may make representations to the Commission.

(3) The Commission may not give a notice under subsection (2) in respect of the breach of a condition after the end of the period of two years beginning with—

(a) the day on which the breach occurred or began to occur, or

(b) if later, the day on which the breach came to the knowledge of the Commission.

(4) After the end of the period specified under subsection (2)(d) the Commission may give the licensee a notice requiring him to pay a penalty under this section.

(5) A penalty imposed by notice under subsection (4)—

(a) shall be payable by the licensee to the Commission,

(b) may be enforced as if it were a debt owed by the licensee to the Commission, and

(c) on receipt by the Commission shall be paid into the Consolidated Fund after deduction of a sum which represents the direct costs to the Commission of, and a reasonable share of expenditure by the Commission which is indirectly referable to—

(i) the investigation by the Commission of the matter in respect of which the penalty is imposed (whether by review under section 116 or otherwise), or

(ii) the imposition and enforcement of the penalty.

(6) The Commission shall—

(a) prepare a statement setting out the principles to be applied by the Commission in exercising the powers under this section,

(b) review the statement from time to time,

(c) revise the statement when the Commission thinks it necessary,

(d) as soon as is reasonably practicable—

(i) send the statement and any revision to the Secretary of State, and

(ii) publish the statement and any revision, and

(e) have regard to the statement when exercising a power under this section.

(7) The statement maintained under subsection (6) must, in particular, require the Commission in considering the imposition of a penalty under this section or the amount of a penalty to have regard, in particular, to—

(a) the seriousness of the breach of condition in respect of which the penalty is proposed,

(b) whether or not the licensee knew or ought to have known of the breach, and

(c) the nature of the licensee (including, in particular, his financial resources).

(8) Before preparing or revising a statement under subsection (6) the Commission shall consult—

(a) the Secretary of State,

(b) the Lord Chancellor, and

(c) such other persons as the Commission thinks appropriate.

Note

See the Gambling Commission's 'Statement of Principles for Determining Financial Penalties' September 2009 (see para **6.2076** below).

Commencement

Brought into force by the Gambling Act 2005 (Commencement No 6 and Transitional Provisions) Order 2006, SI 2006/3272, art 2 as from 1 September 2007; for transitional provisions see art 6, Sch 4 thereto (as amended by SI 2007/1157, arts 7–12).

Sub-s (1): The Commission. Ie the Gambling Commission; see s 353(1). As to the establishment, etc of the Gambling Commission, see s 20, Sch 4, and the note 'Gambling Commission' to that section.

Sub-s (1): Operating licence. As to the nature, etc of operating licences, see s 65 and the note 'Operating licences' thereto.

Sub-s (1): To pay a penalty. For the power of the Gambling Commission to exercise the power under this section to impose a penalty, following a review under s 116(1) or (2), see s 117.

Sub-s (2): Notify. See further, in connection with a requirement under this Act to give a notice, s 353(4).

Sub-s (4): Requiring him to pay a penalty. As to appeals to the Gambling Appeals Tribunal, see s 141.

Sub-s (6): Secretary of State. See the note to s 4.

Sub-s (8): Persons. See the note to s 23.

Application

See the note to s 65.

Definitions

'the Commission': s 353(1)
'holder': s 126(1)
'licensee': s 126(1)
'operating licence': s 353(1)

Explanatory Notes

339–344 [para **6.2008** below]

6.622 122 Information

(1) The holder of an operating licence shall comply with a request of the Commission to—

(a) produce a written or electronic record relating to the licensed activities;

(b) provide a copy of a written or electronic record relating to the licensed activities;

(c) provide information about the licensed activities.

(2) A request under subsection (1) may specify—

(a) the form and manner in which a record or information is to be produced or provided;

(b) the period within which a record or information is to be produced or provided.

(3) The Commission may retain anything provided under subsection (1).

(4) The Commission may exercise a power under this section only for the purpose of—

(a) determining whether activities have been carried on in purported reliance on the licence but not in accordance with a condition of the licence, or

(b) determining the suitability of the licensee to carry on the licensed activities.

(5) A person commits an offence if he fails without reasonable excuse to comply with subsection (1).

(6) A person guilty of an offence under subsection (5) shall be liable on summary conviction to a fine not exceeding level 2 on the standard scale.

Commencement

Brought into force by the Gambling Act 2005 (Commencement No 6 and Transitional Provisions) Order 2006, SI 2006/3272, art 2, Sch 1 as from 1 January 2007; for transitional provisions see art 6, Sch 4 thereto (as amended by SI 2007/1157, arts 7–12).

Sub-s (1): Operating licence. As to the nature, etc of operating licences, see s 65 and the note 'Operating licences' thereto.

Sub-s (1): The Commission. Ie the Gambling Commission; see s 353(1). As to the establishment, etc of the Gambling Commission, see s 20, Sch 4, and the note 'Gambling Commission' to that section.

Sub-s (1): Written. See the note 'Writing' to s 39.

Sub-s (5): Offence. For the power of the Gambling Commission and other specified persons to undertake activities for the purpose of assessing whether an offence is being committed under or by virtue of this Act, see s 27 and s 305; for the power of that Commission to investigate and prosecute offences, see s 28; as to offences committed by a body, see s 341; and for the time limit on prosecutions, see s 347. See also s 306 for powers of entry as respects a suspected offence, and s 345 as respects forfeiture of an article relating to an offence.

Sub-s (6): Summary conviction; standard scale. See the notes to s 33.

Application

See the note to s 65.

Definitions

'the Commission': s 353(1)
'holder': s 126(1)
'the licensed activities': s 126(1)
'licensee': s 126(1)
'operating licence': s 353(1)

Explanatory Notes
345 [para **6.2008** below]

General

6.623 123 Levy

(1) The Secretary of State may make regulations requiring holders of operating licences to pay an annual levy to the Commission.

(2) The regulations shall, in particular, make provision for—

(a) the amount of the levy;

(b) timing of payment of the levy.

(3) The regulations may, in particular, make provision—

(a) determining the amount of the levy by reference to a percentage of specified receipts of an operating licence holder,

(b) determining the amount of the levy by reference to a percentage of specified profits of an operating licence holder,

(c) determining the amount of the levy by reference to a percentage of the annual fee under section 100,

(d) providing for the determination of the amount of the levy according to a specified formula, or

(e) providing for the determination of the amount of the levy in some other way.

(4) Any sum due by way of levy by virtue of this section shall be treated for the purposes of this Act as if it were due by way of annual fee under section 100.

(5) The Commission shall, with the consent of the Treasury and of the Secretary of State, expend money received by way of levy for purposes related to, or by providing financial assistance for projects related to—

(a) addiction to gambling,

(b) other forms of harm or exploitation associated with gambling, or

(c) any of the licensing objectives.

(6) In subsection (5) the reference to financial assistance is a reference to grants, loans and any other form of financial assistance, which may be made or given on terms or conditions (which may include terms and conditions as to repayment with or without interest).

(7) The Secretary of State shall consult the Commission before making regulations under this section.

Commencement
Brought into force by the Gambling Act 2005 (Commencement No 6 and Transitional Provisions) Order 2006, SI 2006/3272, art 2 as from 1 September 2007; for transitional provisions see art 6, Sch 4 thereto (as amended by SI 2007/1157, arts 7–12).

Sub-s (1): Secretary of State. See the note to s 4.

Sub-s (1): Operating licences. As to the nature, etc of operating licences, see s 65 and the note 'Operating licences' thereto.

Sub-s (1): The Commission. Ie the Gambling Commission; see s 353(1). As to the establishment, etc of the Gambling Commission, see s 20, Sch 4, and the note 'Gambling Commission' to that section.

Application
See the note to s 65.

Regulations under this section
At the time of going to press no regulations had been made under this section.
As to regulations under this Act generally, see s 355.

Definitions

'the Commission': s 353(1)
'gambling': ss 3, 353(1)
'holder': s 126(1)
'the licensing objectives': ss 1, 353(1)
'operating licence': s 353(1)

Explanatory Notes

346–349 [para **6.2008** below]

6.624 124 Directions and requirements

Where the Commission has power under this Part to give a direction or impose a requirement it may give different directions or impose different requirements in relation to different cases or circumstances.

Commencement

Brought into force by the Gambling Act 2005 (Commencement No 6 and Transitional Provisions) Order 2006, SI 2006/3272, art 2, Sch 1 as from 1 January 2007; for transitional provisions see art 6, Sch 4 thereto (as amended by SI 2007/1157, arts 7–12).

The Commission

Ie the Gambling Commission; see s 353(1). As to the establishment, etc of the Gambling Commission, see s 20, Sch 4, and the note 'Gambling Commission' to that section.

This Part

Ie Pt 5 (ss 65–126 and Sch 7) of this Act.

Application

See the note to s 65.

Definitions

'the Commission': s 353(1)

Explanatory Notes

350 [para **6.2008** below]

6.625 125 Relevant offence: disapplication of rehabilitation

Section 4 of the Rehabilitation of Offenders Act 1974 (c 53) (effect of rehabilitation) shall not apply for the purposes of or in connection with—

(a) section 69(2)(d), or
(b) section 71(1).

Commencement

Brought into force by the Gambling Act 2005 (Commencement No 6 and Transitional Provisions) Order 2006, SI 2006/3272, art 2, Sch 1 as from 1 January 2007; for transitional provisions see art 6, Sch 4 thereto (as amended by SI 2007/1157, arts 7–12).

Application

See the note to s 65.

6.626 126 Interpretation

(1) In this Part—

'conviction'—

(a) has the meaning given by section 1(4) of the Rehabilitation of Offenders Act 1974, and
(b) includes, to the extent required by section 125, a spent conviction within the meaning of that Act,

'holder', in relation to an operating licence, means the person to whom the licence is issued, 'the licensed activities' in relation to an operating licence means the activities which it authorises, and

'licensee', in relation to an operating licence, means the person to whom the licence is issued.

(2) In this Act 'relevant offence' means—

(a) an offence listed in Schedule 7, and

(b) an offence under the law of a country or territory outside the United Kingdom (a 'foreign offence') which prohibits a kind of activity prohibited by an offence listed in that Schedule (a 'domestic offence').

(3) For the purpose of subsection (2)(b) it is immaterial—

(a) whether or not the foreign offence prohibits all the kinds of activity prohibited by the domestic offence, and

(b) whether or not the foreign offence prohibits kinds of activity not prohibited by the domestic offence.

Commencement

Brought into force by the Gambling Act 2005 (Commencement No 6 and Transitional Provisions) Order 2006, SI 2006/3272, art 2, Sch 1 as from 1 January 2007; for transitional provisions see art 6, Sch 4 thereto (as amended by SI 2007/1157, arts 7–12).

Sub-s (1): This Part. Ie Pt 5 (ss 65–126 and Sch 7) of this Act.

Sub-s (1): Operating licences. As to the nature, etc of operating licences, see s 65 and the note 'Operating licences' thereto.

Sub-s (1): Person. See the note 'Persons' to s 23.

Sub-s (2): United Kingdom. See the note to s 36.

Application

See the note to s 65.

Definitions

'operating licence': s 353(1)

Explanatory Notes

351 [para **6.2008** below]

PART 6
PERSONAL LICENCES

6.627 127 Nature of personal licence

(1) For the purposes of this Act a 'personal licence' is a licence which authorises an individual to perform the functions of a specified management office, or to perform a specified operational function, in connection with—

(a) the provision of facilities for gambling, or

(b) a person who provides facilities for gambling.

(2) In this section 'management office' and 'operational function' have the same meaning as in section 80.

Commencement

Brought into force by the Gambling Act 2005 (Commencement No 2 and Transitional Provisions) Order 2005, SI 2005/2455, art 2 and Schedule, as from 1 October 2005.

Sub-s (1): Personal licence. See further s 128 (application of provisions of Pt 5); s 129 (exemption for small-scale operators); s 130 (application); s 131 (duration); s 132 (fees); s 133 (multiple licences); s 134 (production of licence); s 135 (review); s 136 (disqualification); s 137 (notification of operating licensee); s 138 (conviction); and s 139 (breach of personal licence condition).

For offences in connection with the provision of facilities for gambling, see ss 33–36, for offences in connection with the use of premises, see ss 37–40, and for miscellaneous offences, see ss 41–44. Provisions for the protection of children and young persons are contained in Pt 4 of this Act.

The Gambling Commission may require the holder of an operating licence to submit it to the Commission for the purpose of amendment to reflect anything done in relation to a personal licence under this Part of this Act; see s 105.

Sub-s (1): Person. See the note 'Persons' to s 23.

Definitions

'providing facilities for gambling': ss 5, 353(2)(i)

Explanatory Notes

356–359 [para **6.2009** below]

6.628 128 Application of provisions of Part 5

(1) The provisions of Part 5 (other than section 65(2), (4) and (5)) shall apply to a personal licence as they apply to an operating licence, with—

(a) the modifications and exclusions specified in this Part,

(b) such modifications and exclusions as the Secretary of State may specify by regulations, and

(c) any other necessary modifications.

(2) Regulations under a provision of Part 5—

(a) may make different provision for purposes of this Part and for purposes of that Part, and

(b) in making provision for purposes of this Part, may make different provision in relation to personal licences authorising—

(i) the performance of different kinds of function, or

(ii) the performance of functions in different circumstances.

Commencement

Brought into force, in so far as it applies to s 75(1) and (2), s 76(1) to (3) and s 79, by the Gambling Act 2005 (Commencement No 2 and Transitional Provisions) Order 2005, SI 2005/2455, art 2 and Schedule, as from 1 October 2005. Brought into force for certain purposes as from 1 January 2007, for remaining purposes as from 1 September 2007 by the Gambling Act 2005 (Commencement No 6 and Transitional Provisions) Order 2006, SI 2006/3272, art 2, Sch 1; for transitional provisions see art 6, Sch 4 thereto (as amended by SI 2007/1157, arts 7–12).

Sub-s (1): Part 5. Ie Pt 5 (ss 65–126 and Sch 7) of this Act.

Sub-s (1): Personal licence. As to the nature, etc of personal licences, see s 127 and the note 'Personal licence' thereto.

Sub-s (1): Operating licence. As to the nature, etc of operating licences, see s 65 and the note 'Operating licences' thereto.

Sub-s (1): Secretary of State. See the note to s 4.

Sub-s (2): This Part. Ie Pt 6 (ss 127–139) of this Act.

As to regulations under this Act generally, see s 355.

Subordinate Legislation:

SI 2006/3267, 2006/3285.

Definitions

'operating licence': s 353(1)

'personal licence': ss 127, 353(1)

Explanatory Notes

360–362 [para **6.2009** below]

6.629 129 Exemption for small-scale operators

(1) A condition may not be attached to an operating licence under section 75, 77 or 78 requiring possession of a personal licence if the licensee is a small-scale operator.

(2) In this section 'small-scale operator' shall have such meaning as the Secretary of State may prescribe by regulations.

(3) Regulations under subsection (2) may, in particular, make provision by reference to—

(a) the size or value of business carried on, or expected to be carried on, in reliance on an operating licence;

(b) the number of persons employed, or expected to be employed, by the licensee.

(4) A constable or enforcement officer may under section 108(1) require a small-scale operator to produce his operating licence—

(a) within a specified period, or

(b) while the operator is carrying on a licensed activity, immediately.

Commencement

Brought into force by the Gambling Act 2005 (Commencement No 6 and Transitional Provisions) Order 2006, SI 2006/3272, art 2, Sch 1 as from 1 January 2007; for transitional provisions see art 6, Sch 4 thereto (as amended by SI 2007/1157, arts 7–12).

Sub-s (1): Operating licence. As to the nature, etc of operating licences, see s 65 and the note 'Operating licences' thereto.

Sub-s (1): Personal licence. As to the nature, etc of personal licences, see s 127 and the note 'Personal licence' thereto.

Sub-s (2): Secretary of State. See the note to s 4.

Sub-s (4): Constable. See the note to s 64.

Sub-s (4): Enforcement officer. As to enforcement officers, see, generally, s 303.

Sub-s (4): Licensed activity. Cf the definition of 'the licensed activities' in s 126(1).

As to regulations under this Act generally, see s 355.

Subordinate Legislation:

SI 2006/3266.

Definitions

'enforcement officer': s 353(1)
'operating licence': s 353(1)
'personal licence': ss 127, 353(1)

Explanatory Notes

363, 364 [para 6.2009 below]

6.630 130 Application

(1) A direction under section 69(2)(c) or (f) (as applied by section 128) may, in particular, require that an application—

(a) be signed by the applicant's employer;

(b) contain or be accompanied by information provided by the applicant's employer or relating to his employment.

(2) The Commission may under section 73(1)(a) (as applied by section 128) require an applicant to obtain information from his employer.

(3) For the purposes of this section a reference to an applicant's employer is a reference to any person for whom the applicant, in the course of a business (but whether or not under a contract of employment)—

(a) provides services,

(b) has provided services, or

(c) intends to provide services.

(4) Neither this section nor any other provision of this Act shall be treated as preventing a person who is not employed from applying for a personal licence.

Commencement

Brought into force for certain purposes as from 1 January 2007, for remaining purposes as from 1 September 2007 by the Gambling Act 2005 (Commencement No 6 and Transitional Provisions) Order 2006, SI 2006/3272, art 2, Sch 1; for transitional provisions see art 6, Sch 4 thereto (as amended by SI 2007/1157, arts 7–12).

Sub-s (2): The Commission. Ie the Gambling Commission; see s 353(1). As to the establishment, etc of the Gambling Commission, see s 20, Sch 4, and the note 'Gambling Commission' to that section.

Sub-s (3): Person. See the note 'Persons' to s 23.

Sub-s (4): Personal licence. As to the nature, etc of personal licences, see s 127 and the note 'Personal licence' thereto.

Definitions

'the Commission': s 353(1)
'personal licence': ss 127, 353(1)

Explanatory Notes

365 [para 6.2009 below]

6.631 131 Duration

A personal licence shall continue to have effect unless and until it ceases to have effect in accordance with section 113, 114, 115 or 119 (as applied by section 128).

Commencement

Brought into force by the Gambling Act 2005 (Commencement No 6 and Transitional Provisions) Order 2006, SI 2006/3272, art 2 as from 1 September 2007; for transitional provisions see art 6, Sch 4 thereto (as amended by SI 2007/1157, arts 7–12).

Personal licence

As to the nature, etc of personal licences, see s 127 and the note 'Personal licence' thereto.

Definitions

'personal licence': ss 127, 353(1)

Explanatory Notes

366, 367 [para 6.2009 below]

6.632 132 Fees

(1) Section 100 shall not have effect in relation to personal licences.

(2) The Secretary of State may make regulations requiring the holder of a personal licence to pay to the Commission specified fees in respect of specified periods during which the licence is held.

(3) Regulations under this section may, in particular, make different provision for—

(a) different kinds of licence, or
(b) different circumstances.

(4) In its application to this part by virtue of section 128, the reference in section 119(3) to failure to pay an annual fee shall be construed as a reference to failure to comply with regulations under this section.

Commencement

Brought into force by the Gambling Act 2005 (Commencement No 6 and Transitional Provisions) Order 2006, SI 2006/3272, art 2, Sch 1 as from 1 January 2007; for transitional provisions see art 6, Sch 4 thereto (as amended by SI 2007/1157, arts 7–12).

Sub-s (1): Personal licences. As to the nature, etc of personal licences, see s 127 and the note 'Personal licence' thereto.

Sub-s (2): Secretary of State. See the note to s 4.

Sub-s (2): The Commission. Ie the Gambling Commission; see s 353(1). As to the establishment, etc of the Gambling Commission, see s 20, Sch 4, and the note 'Gambling Commission' to that section.

As to regulations under this Act generally, see s 355.

Subordinate Legislation:

SI 2006/3285.

Definitions

'the Commission': s 353(1)

'personal licence': ss 127, 353(1)

Explanatory Notes

368 [para **6.2009** below]

6.633 133 Multiple licences

(1) The Commission may not issue a personal licence to an individual who already holds one.

(2) But a personal licence may authorise the performance of more than one function.

Commencement

Brought into force by the Gambling Act 2005 (Commencement No 6 and Transitional Provisions) Order 2006, SI 2006/3272, art 2, Sch 1 as from 1 January 2007; for transitional provisions see art 6, Sch 4 thereto (as amended by SI 2007/1157, arts 7–12).

Sub-s (1): The Commission. Ie the Gambling Commission; see s 353(1). As to the establishment, etc of the Gambling Commission, see s 20, Sch 4, and the note 'Gambling Commission' to that section.

Sub-s (1): Personal licence. As to the nature, etc of personal licences, see s 127 and the note 'Personal licence' thereto.

Definitions

'the Commission': s 353(1)

'personal licence': ss 127, 353(1)

Explanatory Notes

369 [para **6.2009** below]

6.634 134 Production of licence

(1) A constable or enforcement officer may under section 108 (as applied by section 128) require the individual who holds a personal licence to produce the licence—

- (a) within a specified period,
- (b) while the individual is carrying on a licensed activity, immediately, or
- (c) while the individual is on premises in respect of which a premises licence has effect, immediately.

(2) A licensee commits an offence if he fails without reasonable excuse to comply with a requirement under subsection (1).

(3) A person guilty of an offence under subsection (2) shall be liable on summary conviction to a fine not exceeding level 2 on the standard scale.

Commencement

Brought into force by the Gambling Act 2005 (Commencement No 6 and Transitional Provisions) Order 2006, SI 2006/3272, art 2 as from 1 September 2007; for transitional provisions see art 6, Sch 4 thereto (as amended by SI 2007/1157, arts 7–12).

Sub-s (1): Constable. See the note to s 64.

Sub-s (1): Enforcement officer. As to enforcement officers, see, generally, s 303.

Sub-s (1): Personal licence. As to the nature, etc of personal licences, see s 127 and the note 'Personal licence' thereto.

Sub-s (1): Licensed activity. Cf the definition of 'the licensed activities' in s 126(1).

Sub-s (1): Premises licence. As to the nature, etc of premises licences, see s 150 and the note 'Premises licence' thereto.

Sub-s (2): Offence. For the power of the Gambling Commission and other specified persons to undertake activities for the purpose of assessing whether an offence is being committed under or by virtue of this Act, see s 27 and s 305; for the power of that Commission to investigate and prosecute offences, see s 28; as to offences committed by a body, see s 341; and for the time limit on prosecutions, see s 347. See also s 306 for powers of entry as respects a suspected offence, and s 345 as respects forfeiture of an article relating to an offence.

Sub-s (3): Summary conviction; standard scale. See the notes to s 33.

Definitions

'enforcement officer': s 353(1)
'personal licence': ss 127, 353(1)
'premises': s 353(1), (2)(g)
'premises licence': s 353(1)

Explanatory Notes

370 [para 6.2009 below]

6.635 135 Review

Section 116(1) shall not apply in relation to personal licences.

Commencement

Brought into force by the Gambling Act 2005 (Commencement No 6 and Transitional Provisions) Order 2006, SI 2006/3272, art 2 as from 1 September 2007; for transitional provisions see art 6, Sch 4 thereto (as amended by SI 2007/1157, arts 7–12).

Personal licences

As to the nature, etc of personal licences, see s 127 and the note 'Personal licence' thereto.

Definitions

'personal licence': ss 127, 353(1)

6.636 136 Disqualification

(1) A court which may order the forfeiture of an individual's personal licence under section 115 (as applied by section 128) may, whether or not it makes an order for forfeiture, make an order disqualifying the individual from holding a personal licence for a specified period, not exceeding ten years, beginning with the date of the order.

(2) The Commission shall not issue a personal licence to a person while a disqualification order under this section has effect in respect of him.

(3) Subsections (2) to (5) of section 115 shall have effect in relation to an order under this section (and in relation to a licence held by the person disqualified) as they have effect in relation to an order under that section (and in relation to the licence forfeited).

Commencement

Brought into force by the Gambling Act 2005 (Commencement No 6 and Transitional Provisions) Order 2006, SI 2006/3272, art 2, Sch 1 as from 1 January 2007; for transitional provisions see art 6, Sch 4 thereto (as amended by SI 2007/1157, arts 7–12).

Sub-s (1): Personal licence. As to the nature, etc of personal licences, see s 127 and the note 'Personal licence' thereto.

Sub-s (2): The Commission. Ie the Gambling Commission; see s 353(1). As to the establishment, etc of the Gambling Commission, see s 20, Sch 4, and the note 'Gambling Commission' to that section.

Definitions

'the Commission': s 353(1)
'personal licence': ss 127, 353(1)

Explanatory Notes

371 [para 6.2009 below]

6.637 137 Notification of operating licensee

(1) This section applies where the Commission—

(a) suspends a personal licence under section 118 (as applied by section 128),
(b) revokes a personal licence under section 119 (as applied by section 128),
(c) is informed by a court of the making of a forfeiture order in respect of a personal licence under section 115 (as applied by section 128), or
(d) is informed by a court of the making of a disqualification order under section 136.

(2) If the Commission believes that the holder of the personal licence, or the subject of the disqualification order, is providing services to the holder of an operating licence in connection with the licensed activities, the Commission shall as soon as is reasonably practicable notify the holder of the operating licence of the matter specified in subsection (1).

Commencement

Brought into force by the Gambling Act 2005 (Commencement No 6 and Transitional Provisions) Order 2006, SI 2006/3272, art 2 as from 1 September 2007; for transitional provisions see art 6, Sch 4 thereto (as amended by SI 2007/1157, arts 7–12).

Sub-s (1): The Commission. Ie the Gambling Commission; see s 353(1). As to the establishment, etc of the Gambling Commission, see s 20, Sch 4, and the note 'Gambling Commission' to that section.

Sub-s (1): Personal licence. As to the nature, etc of personal licences, see s 127 and the note 'Personal licence' thereto.

Sub-s (2): Operating licence. As to the nature, etc of operating licences, see s 65 and the note 'Operating licences' thereto.

Sub-s (2): Licensed activities. Cf the definition of 'the licensed activities' in s 126(1).

Sub-s (2): Notify. See further, in connection with a requirement under this Act to give a notice, s 353(4).

Definitions

'the Commission': s 353(1)
'operating licence': s 353(1)
'personal licence': ss 127, 353(1)

Explanatory Notes

372 [para **6.2009** below]

6.638 138 Conviction

(1) This section applies if the holder of a personal licence is convicted of a relevant offence by or before a court (whether inside or outside Great Britain).

(2) The holder of any relevant operating licence shall notify the Commission of the conviction, and of any sentence passed in respect of it, as soon as is reasonably practicable after becoming aware of it.

(3) A person commits an offence if he fails without reasonable excuse to comply with subsection (2).

(4) A person guilty of an offence under subsection (3) shall be liable on summary conviction to a fine not exceeding level 2 on the standard scale.

(5) For the purposes of subsection (2) an operating licence is relevant if the holder of the personal licence acts in connection with activities authorised by the operating licence.

(6) The duty under subsection (2) is in addition to any duty of the holder of the personal licence under section 109 (as applied by section 128).

Commencement

Brought into force by the Gambling Act 2005 (Commencement No 6 and Transitional Provisions) Order 2006, SI 2006/3272, art 2 as from 1 September 2007; for transitional provisions see art 6, Sch 4 thereto (as amended by SI 2007/1157, arts 7–12).

Sub-s (1): Personal licence. As to the nature, etc of personal licences, see s 127 and the note 'Personal licence' thereto.

Sub-s (2): Operating licence. As to the nature, etc of operating licences, see s 65 and the note 'Operating licences' thereto.

Sub-s (2): Notify. See further, in connection with a requirement under this Act to give a notice, s 353(4).

Sub-s (2): The Commission. Ie the Gambling Commission; see s 353(1). As to the establishment, etc of the Gambling Commission, see s 20, Sch 4, and the note 'Gambling Commission' to that section.

Sub-s (3): Person. See the note 'Persons' to s 23.

Sub-s (3): Offence. For the power of the Gambling Commission and other specified persons to undertake activities for the purpose of assessing whether an offence is being committed under or by virtue of this Act, see s 27 and s 305; for the power of that Commission to investigate and prosecute offences, see s 28; as to offences committed by a body, see s 341; and for the time limit on prosecutions, see s 347. See also s 306 for powers of entry as respects a suspected offence, and s 345 as respects forfeiture of an article relating to an offence.

Sub-s (4): Summary conviction; standard scale. See the notes to s 33.

Definitions

'act which is authorised by a licence': s 353(5)
'the Commission': s 353(1)
'operating licence': s 353(1)
'personal licence': ss 127, 353(1)
'relevant offence': ss 126(2), (3), 353(1), Sch 7

Explanatory Notes

372 [para 6.2009 below]

6.639 139 Breach of personal licence condition

(1) This section applies where—

(a) a condition attached to an operating licence includes provision for a personal licence in accordance with section 80,

(b) an individual who holds a personal licence under this Part acts in the course of or in connection with any of the activities authorised by the operating licence, and

(c) the individual's action is not in accordance with the terms and conditions of the personal licence.

(2) The individual commits an offence.

(3) The individual may be proceeded against for the offence under subsection (2) whether or not the holder of the operating licence is proceeded against for an offence under section 33 (by reason of a breach of the condition under section 80).

(4) An individual guilty of an offence under this section shall be liable on summary conviction to—

(a) imprisonment for a term not exceeding 51 weeks,

(b) a fine not exceeding level 5 on the standard scale, or

(c) both.

(5) In the application of subsection (4) to Scotland the reference to 51 weeks shall have effect as a reference to six months.

Commencement

Brought into force by the Gambling Act 2005 (Commencement No 6 and Transitional Provisions) Order 2006, SI 2006/3272, art 2 as from 1 September 2007; for transitional provisions see art 6, Sch 4 thereto (as amended by SI 2007/1157, arts 7–12).

Sub-s (1): Operating licence. As to the nature, etc of operating licences, see s 65 and the note 'Operating licences' thereto.

Sub-s (1): Personal licence. As to the nature, etc of personal licences, see s 127 and the note 'Personal licence' thereto.

Sub-s (1): This Part. Ie Pt 6 (ss 127–139) of this Act.

Sub-s (2): Offence. For the power of the Gambling Commission and other specified persons to undertake activities for the purpose of assessing whether an offence is being committed under or

by virtue of this Act, see s 27 and s 305; for the power of that Commission to investigate and prosecute offences, see s 28; for the time limit on prosecutions, see s 347. See also s 306 for powers of entry as respects a suspected offence, and s 345 as respects forfeiture of an article relating to an offence.

Sub-s (4): Summary conviction; standard scale. See the notes to s 33.

Definitions

'act which is authorised by a licence': s 353(5)
'operating licence': s 353(1)
'personal licence': ss 127, 353(1)

Explanatory Notes

373 [para **6.2009** below]

PART 7
OPERATING AND PERSONAL LICENCES: APPEALS

6.640 [140 Definition of "the Tribunal"]

[In this Part "the Tribunal" means the First-tier Tribunal.][1]

Commencement

Brought into force by the Transfer of Tribunal Functions Order 2010 (SI 2010/22), art 1 as from 18 January 2010.

Sub-s (1): The Tribunal. See further s 141 (appeal to Tribunal), s 144 (powers of Tribunal), s 145 (stay pending appeal), s 146 (Tribunal Procedure Rules) and s 148 (legal assistance).

Sub-s (3): This Part. Ie Pt 7 (ss 140–149 and Sch 8) of this Act.

Explanatory Notes

375 [para **6.2010** below]

---

1 Substituted by SI 2010/22, art 5(1), Sch 2, paras 93, 94.

6.641 141 Appeal to Tribunal

(1) Where the Commission determines an application under section 69 or 112 (including either of those sections as applied by section 128) for the issue or renewal of an operating licence or a personal licence, the applicant may appeal to the Tribunal.

(2) Where the Commission attaches a condition to a licence under section 77 (including that section as applied by section 128) the licensee may appeal to the Tribunal.

(3) Where the Commission determines an application under section 102(2)(b) the applicant may appeal to the Tribunal.

(4) Where the Commission determines an application under section 104 (including that section as applied by section 128) the applicant may appeal to the Tribunal.

(5) Where the Commission gives a notice under section 114(1)(b) (including that section as applied by section 128) the licensee may appeal to the Tribunal.

(6) Where the Commission takes action, or determines to take action, under section 117 (including that section as applied by section 128) in respect of a licence, the licensee may appeal to the Tribunal.

(7) Where the Commission takes action, or determines to take action, under section 118 (including that section as applied by section 128) in respect of a licence, the licensee may appeal to the Tribunal.

(8) Where the Commission takes action, or determines to take action, under section 119 (including that section as applied by section 128) in respect of a licence, the licensee may appeal to the Tribunal.

(9) Where the Commission gives a notice imposing a penalty on a licensee under section 121(4) (including that section as applied by section 128) the licensee may appeal to the Tribunal.

6: Gambling Act 2005: Statutes

Commencement

Brought into force by the Gambling Act 2005 (Commencement No 6 and Transitional Provisions) Order 2006, SI 2006/3272, art 2, Sch 1 as from 1 January 2007; for transitional provisions see art 6, Sch 4 thereto (as amended by SI 2007/1157, arts 7–12).

Sub-s (1): The Commission. Ie the Gambling Commission; see s 353(1). As to the establishment, etc of the Gambling Commission, see s 20, Sch 4, and the note 'Gambling Commission' to that section.

Sub-s (1): Operating licence. As to the nature, etc of operating licences, see s 65 and the note 'Operating licences' thereto.

Sub-s (1): Personal licence. As to the nature, etc of personal licences, see s 127 and the note 'Personal licence' thereto.

Sub-s (1): The Tribunal. Ie the First-tier Tribunal; see s 140.

Definitions

'the Commission': s 353(1)
'operating licence': s 353(1)
'personal licence': ss 127, 353(1)
'the Tribunal': s 140

Explanatory Notes

376 [para **6.2010** below]

6.642 142 . . .

. . . [1]

[1] Repealed by SI 2010/22, art 5(1), Sch 2, paras 93, 95.

6.643 143 . . .

. . . [1]

[1] Repealed by SI 2010/22, art 5(1), Sch 2, paras 93, 96.

6.644 144 Powers of Tribunal

(1) On an appeal under section 141 against a decision or action taken by the Commission the Tribunal may—

(a) affirm the Commission's decision or action;
(b) quash the Commission's decision or action in whole or in part;
(c) substitute for all or part of the Commission's decision or action another decision or action of a kind that the Commission could have taken;
(d) add to the Commission's decision or action a decision or action of a kind that the Commission could have taken;
(e) remit a matter to the Commission (generally, or for determination in accordance with a finding made or direction given by the Tribunal);
(f) reinstate a lapsed or revoked licence.

(2) In determining an appeal instituted out of time under [Tribunal Procedure Rules][1] or following a direction under section 145(2) the Tribunal may, in addition to the matters specified in subsection (1) above, make any order that it thinks appropriate.

(3) In determining an appeal the Tribunal shall have regard to any relevant provision of a code of practice issued by the Commission under section 24.

(4) In determining an appeal the Tribunal may take account of evidence which was not available to the Commission.

(5) Section 141 applies to a decision or action of the Commission following remittal under subsection (1)(e) above.

Commencement

Brought into force by the Gambling Act 2005 (Commencement No 6 and Transitional Provisions) Order 2006, SI 2006/3272, art 2, Sch 1 as from 1 January 2007; for transitional provisions see art 6, Sch 4 thereto (as amended by SI 2007/1157, arts 7–12).

Sub-s (1): The Commission. Ie the Gambling Commission; see s 353(1). As to the establishment, etc of the Gambling Commission, see s 20, Sch 4, and the note 'Gambling Commission' to that section.

Sub-s (1): The Tribunal. Ie the First-tier Tribunal; see s 140.

Definitions

'the Commission': s 353(1)
'the Tribunal': s 140

Explanatory Notes

379–382 [para **6.2010** below]

1 Sub-s (2): words "Tribunal Procedure Rules" in square brackets substituted by SI 2010/22, art 5(1), Sch 2, paras 93, 97 with effect from 18 January 2010.

6.645 145 Stay pending appeal

(1) A decision or other action under Part 5 or 6 shall have no effect while an appeal under section 141—

(a) could be brought (ignoring the possibility of an appeal out of time under [Tribunal Procedure Rules][1]), or

(b) has been brought and has not yet been either finally determined or abandoned.

(2) But when making a decision or taking other action under Part 5 or 6 the Commission may direct that subsection (1) shall not apply.

Commencement

Brought into force by the Gambling Act 2005 (Commencement No 6 and Transitional Provisions) Order 2006, SI 2006/3272, art 2, Sch 1 as from 1 January 2007; for transitional provisions see art 6, Sch 4 thereto (as amended by SI 2007/1157, arts 7–12).

Sub-s (1): Part 5 or 6. Ie Pt 5 (ss 65–126 and Sch 7) or 6 (ss 127–139) of this Act.

Sub-s (2): The Commission. Ie the Gambling Commission; see s 353(1). As to the establishment, etc of the Gambling Commission, see s 20, Sch 4, and the note 'Gambling Commission' to that section.

Definitions

'the Commission': s 353(1)

Explanatory Notes

383, 384 [para **6.2010** below]

1 Sub-s (1): in para (a) words "Tribunal Procedure Rules" in square brackets substituted by SI 2010/22, art 5(1), Sch 2, paras 93, 98.

6.646 146 [Tribunal Procedure Rules][1]

[(1) Tribunal Procedure Rules may make provision—

(a) regulating the exercise of a right of appeal under this Act to the Tribunal;

(b) for the suspension by the Tribunal of decisions of the Commission (whether or not they have already taken effect).][2]

(2) . . .[3]

(3) [In the case of proceedings before the Tribunal under this Act, Tribunal Procedure Rules may][4] provide—

6: Gambling Act 2005: Statutes

(a) that a person commits an offence if without reasonable excuse he fails to comply with a requirement of a specified kind imposed by or in accordance with the rules, and

(b) that a person guilty of the offence shall be liable on summary conviction to a fine not exceeding level 3 on the standard scale.

Commencement

Brought into force by the Gambling Act 2005 (Commencement No 6 and Transitional Provisions) Order 2006, SI 2006/3272, art 2, Sch 1 as from 1 January 2007; for transitional provisions see art 6, Sch 4 thereto (as amended by SI 2007/1157, arts 7–12).

Sub-s (1): May make rules. See further in relation to such rules, Sch 8, paras 9(2), 13, 14.

Sub-s (1): The Tribunal. Ie the First-tier Tribunal; see s 140.

Sub-s (2): Person. See the note 'Persons' to s 23.

Sub-s (3): Summary conviction; standard scale. See the notes to s 33.

Subordinate Legislation

Gambling Appeals Tribunal Rules 2006, SI 2006/3293.

Gambling Appeals Tribunal (Amendment) Rules 2007, SI 2007/577.

The Tribunal Procedure (Amendment) Rules 2010, SI 2010/43.

As to rules under this Act generally, see s 355.

Definitions

'the Tribunal': s 140

Explanatory Notes

385 [para **6.2010** below]

[1] Section heading: substituted by SI 2010/22, art 5(1), Sch 2, paras 93, 99(a).

[2] Sub-s (1): substituted by SI 2010/22, art 5(1), Sch 2, paras 93, 99(b).

[3] Sub-s (2): repealed by SI 2010/22, art 5(1), Sch 2, paras 93, 99(c).

[4] Sub-s (3): words from "In the case" to "Tribunal Procedure Rules may" in square brackets substituted by SI 2010/22, art 5(1), Sch 2, paras 93, 99(d).

6.647 147 . . .

. . . [1]

[1] Repealed by SI 2010/22, art 5(1), Sch 2, paras 93, 100.

6.648 148 Legal assistance

(1) The Lord Chancellor may by regulations establish a scheme for the provision of legal assistance to appellants to the Tribunal.

(2) Regulations under subsection (1) may, in particular—

(a) specify the kinds of assistance that may be provided;

(b) specify the classes of person by whom assistance may be provided;

(c) . . . [1]

(d) . . . [1]

(e) enable the Tribunal to determine eligibility for assistance by reference to criteria specified in the regulations;

(f) make provision for an appeal against refusal of assistance;

(g) enable assistance to be granted subject to conditions or restrictions imposed by the Tribunal (which may, in particular, include conditions requiring—

(i) a person receiving assistance to contribute towards its cost;

(ii) a person who received assistance to defray all or part of its cost in specified circumstances);

(h) enable the Tribunal to vary or revoke a decision that assistance should be provided;
(i) include provision for enforcement of a duty of payment arising under the regulations (which may, in particular, confer jurisdiction on a court).

(3) Regulations under subsection (1) may, in particular, apply generally or only—
(a) in relation to specified kinds of appeal;
(b) in specified circumstances.

(4) The Lord Chancellor shall defray the costs of assistance provided under the scheme (subject to subsection (2)(g)).

(5) Regulations under this section shall have no effect in relation to proceedings heard or to be heard by the Tribunal sitting in Scotland.

Commencement

Brought into force by the Gambling Act 2005 (Commencement No 6 and Transitional Provisions) Order 2006, SI 2006/3272, art 2, Sch 1 as from 1 January 2007; for transitional provisions see art 6, Sch 4 thereto (as amended by SI 2007/1157, arts 7–12).

Sub-s (1): The Tribunal. Ie the First-tier Tribunal; see s 140.

Sub-s (2): Person. See the note 'Persons' to s 23.

Regulations under this section

At the time of going to press no regulations had been made under this section.

As to regulations under this Act generally, see s 355.

Definitions

'the Tribunal': s 140

Explanatory Notes

388 [para **6.2010** below]

---

[1] Sub-s (2): paras (c), (d) repealed by SI 2010/22, art 5(1), Sch 2, paras 93, 101.

6.649 149 . . .

. . . [1]

---

[1] Repealed by SI 2010/22, art 5(1), Sch 2, paras 93, 102.

PART 8
PREMISES LICENCES

The licence

6.650 150 Nature of licence

(1) A premises licence is a licence which states that it authorises premises to be used for—
(a) the operation of a casino (a 'casino premises licence'),
(b) the provision of facilities for the playing of bingo (a 'bingo premises licence'),
(c) making Category B gaming machines available for use (an 'adult gaming centre premises licence'),
(d) making Category C gaming machines available for use (a 'family entertainment centre premises licence'), or
(e) the provision of facilities for betting, whether by making or accepting bets, by acting as a betting intermediary or by providing other facilities for the making or accepting of bets (a 'betting premises licence').

(2) A casino premises licence is—
  (a) a 'regional casino premises licence' if it relates to a regional casino,
  (b) a 'large casino premises licence' if it relates to a large casino, and
  (c) a 'small casino premises licence' if it relates to a small casino

(3) Neither a premises licence nor any provision of this Part disapplies or provides a defence to the offence under section 33.

Commencement

Brought into force by the Gambling Act 2005 (Commencement No 6 and Transitional Provisions) Order 2006, SI 2006/3272, art 2, Sch 2 as from 30 April 2007; for transitional provisions see art 6, Sch 4 thereto (as amended by SI 2007/1157, arts 7–12).

Sub-s (1): Premises licence. See further s 60 (temporary use notices and occasional use notices); s 151 (form of licence); s 152 (combined licence, etc); ss 153–156 (licensing authorities' functions); ss 157, 158 (other relevant persons); ss 159–161 (application for licence); ss 162–166 (determination of application); ss 167–171 (conditions); ss 172–183 and Sch 9 (specific cases); ss 184–190 (maintenance); ss 191–196 (duration); ss 197–203 (review); ss 204, 205 (provisional statement); ss 206–209 (appeals); and ss 210–213 (general).

For offences in connection with the provision of facilities for gambling, see ss 33–36, for offences in connection with the use of premises, see ss 37–40, and for miscellaneous offences, see ss 41–44. Provisions for the protection of children and young persons are contained in Pt 4 of this Act.

An order under s 38(1) may make consequential amendment of this section, any other provision of this Part of this Act, and any provision of this Act, or of another enactment, that relates to this Part; see s 38(4).

For powers of entry in connection with premises licences, see ss 307, 313.

Sub-s (1): Casino premises licence. See the note 'Premises licence' above, and see, in particular, as respects casino premises licences, s 166 (resolution not to issue casino licences), s 172(3)–(6), (10), (11) (gaming machines), s 173 (virtual gaming), s 174 (casino premises licence), s 175 and Sch 9 (casino premises licence: overall limits), s 177 (credit), and s 181(2), (3) (betting machines). The unauthorised use of premises as a casino is an offence under s 37; for offences in connection with inviting a child or young person to enter premises if a casino licence has effect in respect of those premises, see s 47(1)–(3); and for offences in connection with the employment of a child or young person in a casino, see s 55.

Sub-s (1): Bingo premises licence. See the note 'Premises licence' above, and see, in particular, as respects bingo premises licences, s 172(7), (10), (11) (gaming machines), and s 177 (credit). The unauthorised use of premises for providing facilities for the playing of bingo is an offence under s 37, and for offences in connection with the employment of a child on bingo premises, see s 53.

Sub-s (1): Gaming machines. See the note 'Premises licence' above, and see, in particular, as respects gaming machines, s 172. The unauthorised use of premises for making a gaming machine available for use is an offence under s 37, and for offences in connection with the employment of a child or young person on premises with gaming machines, see s 54.

As to the categories of gaming machine, see s 236.

Sub-s (1): Adult gaming centre premises licence. See the note 'Premises licence' above, and see, in particular, as respects adult gaming centre premises licences, s 172(1), (10), (11) (gaming machines). For offences in connection with inviting a child or young person to enter premises if an adult gaming centre premises licence has effect in respect of those premises, see s 47(5).Only sub-categories B3 and B4 are included here: SI 2007/2158, reg 6(2).

Sub-s (1): Family entertainment centre premises licence. See the note 'Premises licence' above, and see, in particular, as respects family entertainment centre premises licences, s 172(2), (10), (11) (gaming machines). For offences in connection with inviting a child or young person to enter premises if the premises are a licensed family entertainment centre, see s 47(7).

Sub-s (1): Betting premises licence. See the note 'Premises licence' above, and see, in particular, as respects betting premises licences, s 172(8)–(11) (gaming machines), s 173 (virtual gaming), s 179 (pool betting on track), s 180 (pool betting on dog races), and s 181(1), (3) (betting machines). The unauthorised use of premises for providing facilities for betting is an offence under s 37. For offences in connection with inviting a child or young person to enter premises if a betting premises licence has effect in respect of those premises, see s 47(4).

Sub-s (3): This Part. See Pt 8 (ss 150–213 and Sch 9) of this Act.

Application

This Part of this Act is applied, with modifications, in relation to an application for the variation of a premises licence by s 187(3), (4), in relation to an application for transfer of a premises licence by s 188(2), in relation to an application for reinstatement by s 195(3), and in relation to an application for a provisional statement by s 204(2).

Regulations under s 185 may apply, or make provision similar to any provision of, this Part of this Act to renewal of a premises licence; see s 191(2).

Definitions

'accepting a bet': s 353(2)(a)
'acting as a betting intermediary': s 13(2)
'betting': ss 9–11, 353(1)
'betting intermediary': ss 13(1), 353(1)
'bingo': s 353(1)
'casino': ss 7, 353(1)
'Category B gaming machine': s 353(1)
'Category C gaming machine': s 353(1)
'premises': s 353(1), (2)(g) and see *Majorstake Ltd v Curtis* [2008] 1 A.C. 787, [2006] EWCA Civ 1171.
'premises licence': s 353(1)
'providing facilities for gambling': ss 5, 353(2)(i)

Explanatory Notes

409, 410 [para **6.2011** below]

6.651 151 Form of licence

(1) A premises licence must—

(a) specify the name of the person to whom it is issued,
(b) specify a home or business address of that person,
(c) specify the premises to which it relates,
(d) specify the activities for which it authorises the premises to be used,
(e) specify any condition attached by the licensing authority under section 169(1)(a),
(f) specify any exclusion of a default condition effected by the licensing authority under section 169(1)(b),
(g) include a plan of the premises, and
(h) if a period is prescribed under section 191 at the end of which the licence will expire (unless renewed or terminated earlier), specify the period.

(2) The Secretary of State may make regulations about—

(a) the form of a premises licence, and
(b) the content of a premises licence (which may, in particular, require the inclusion of information about mandatory conditions, default conditions or conditions attached to the licence by virtue of a provision of this Part).

(3) In relation to a premises licence issued in Scotland, subsection (2) shall have effect as if the reference to the Secretary of State were a reference to the Scottish Ministers.

Commencement

Brought into force by the Gambling Act 2005 (Commencement No 6 and Transitional Provisions) Order 2006, SI 2006/3272, art 2, Sch 2 as from 30 April 2007; for transitional provisions see art 6, Sch 4 thereto (as amended by SI 2007/1157, arts 7–12).

Sub-s (1): Premises licence. As to the nature, etc of premises licences, see s 150 and the note 'Premises licence' thereto.

Sub-s (1): Person. See the note 'Persons' to s 23.

Sub-s (1): Address. As to notification of a change of circumstances, see s 186.

Sub-s (1): Licensing authority. For the licensing authorities for the purposes of this Act, see s 2. As to the licensing authorities' functions, see ss 153–156.

Sub-s (2): Secretary of State. See the note to s 4.

Sub-s (2): This Part. Ie Pt 8 (ss 150–213 and Sch 9) of this Act.

Sub-s (3): Scottish Ministers. See the note to s 25.

Application

See the note to s 150.

Subordinate Legislation

Gambling Act 2005 (Premises Licences and Provisional Statements) Regulations 2007, SI 2007/459 (made under sub-s (2)).

As to regulations under this Act generally, see s 355.

Definitions

'a licensing authority': ss 2, 353(1)
'the licensing authority': s 213(f)
'premises': s 353(1), (2)(g)
'premises licence': s 353(1)

Explanatory Notes

411, 412 [para **6.2011** below]

6.652 152 Combined licence, &c

(1) A premises licence—

(a) may not authorise the use of premises for activities of more than one of the kinds specified in section 150(a) to (e) (subject to sections 172 to 174 and subsection (2) below), and

(b) may not be issued in respect of premises if a premises licence already has effect in relation to the premises (subject to subsection (3)).

(2) Subsection (1)(a) does not apply in the case of a track.

(3) More than one premises licence may have effect in relation to a track provided that—

(a) each licence relates to a specified area of the track, and

(b) not more than one premises licence has effect in relation to any area of the track.

(4) If a person applies for a premises licence in respect of an area of a track ('a subsidiary licence') and a premises licence already has effect in respect of the whole track or a part of the track that includes that area ('the main licence')—

(a) the application for the subsidiary licence must be accompanied by an application under section 187 to vary the main licence so that it does not have effect in relation to the area to which the subsidiary licence is to relate, and

(b) the application for the subsidiary licence may be granted only after, or together with, the grant of the application for variation.

Commencement

Brought into force by the Gambling Act 2005 (Commencement No 6 and Transitional Provisions) Order 2006, SI 2006/3272, art 2, Sch 2 as from 30 April 2007; for transitional provisions see art 6, Sch 4 thereto (as amended by SI 2007/1157, arts 7–12).

Sub-s (1): Premises licence. As to the nature, etc of premises licences, see s 150 and the note 'Premises licence' thereto.

Sub-s (4): Person. See the note 'Persons' to s 23.

Application

See the note to s 150.

Definitions

'premises': s 353(1), (2)(g)
'premises licence': s 353(1)
'track': s 353(1)

Explanatory Notes

413, 414 [para **6.2011** below]

Licensing authorities' functions

6.653 153 Principles to be applied

(1) In exercising their functions under this Part a licensing authority shall aim to permit the use of premises for gambling in so far as the authority think it—

(a) in accordance with any relevant code of practice under section 24,

(b) in accordance with any relevant guidance issued by the Commission under section 25,

(c) reasonably consistent with the licensing objectives (subject to paragraphs (a) and (b)), and

(d) in accordance with the statement published by the authority under section 349 (subject to paragraphs (a) to (c)).

(2) In determining whether to grant a premises licence a licensing authority may not have regard to the expected demand for the facilities which it is proposed to provide.

(3) This section is subject to section 166.

Commencement

Brought into force by the Gambling Act 2005 (Commencement No 6 and Transitional Provisions) Order 2006, SI 2006/3272, art 2, Sch 2 as from 30 April 2007; for transitional provisions see art 6, Sch 4 thereto (as amended by SI 2007/1157, arts 7–12).

Sub-s (1): This Part. Ie Pt 8 (ss 150–213 and Sch 9) of this Act.

Sub-s (1): Licensing authority. For the licensing authorities for the purposes of this Act, see s 2. As to the licensing authorities' functions, see also ss 154–156.

Sub-s (1): The Commission. Ie the Gambling Commission; see s 353(1). As to the establishment, etc of the Gambling Commission, see s 20, Sch 4, and the note 'Gambling Commission' to that section.

Application

See the note to s 150.

Sub-s (1) above is applied by s 224(7).

Definitions

'the Commission': s 353(1)
'gambling': ss 3, 353(1)
'a licensing authority': ss 2, 353(1)
'the licensing objectives': ss 1, 353(1)
'premises': s 353(1), (2)(g)

Explanatory Notes

415, 416 [para **6.2011** below]

6.654 154 Delegation of licensing authority functions: England and Wales

(1) The functions under this Part of a licensing authority in England and Wales are by virtue of this subsection delegated to the licensing committee of the authority established under section 6 of the Licensing Act 2003 (c 17).

(2) But—

(a) a licensing authority's functions under section 166 are not delegated by virtue of subsection (1) and may not be delegated by the authority,

(b) a licensing authority's functions under section 212 are not delegated by virtue of subsection (1) but may be delegated by the authority, and

(c) a licensing authority's function under section 349 is not delegated by virtue of subsection (1) and may not be delegated by the authority.

(3) The following provisions of the Licensing Act 2003 shall apply in relation to a function delegated to a licensing committee by virtue of subsection (1) or (2)(b) as they apply in relation to a function delegated under that Act—

(a) section 7(9) (referral back to licensing authority), and

(b) section 10 (sub-delegation).

(4) In the application of section 10(4) of that Act (matters not to be delegated to officer) by virtue of subsection (3) above, the following shall be substituted for the list of functions—

(a) determination of an application for a premises licence in respect of which representations have been made under section 161 (and not withdrawn),

(b) determination of an application for the variation of a premises licence in respect of which representations have been made under section 161 as applied by section 187 (and not withdrawn),

(c) determination of an application for transfer following representations by the Commission,

(d) determination of an application for a provisional statement under section 204 in respect of which representations have been made under section 161 as applied by section 204 (and not withdrawn), and

(e) a review of a premises licence under section 201.

(5) The provisions of section 9 of that Act and regulations under it apply to proceedings of licensing committees and their sub-committees in relation to the exercise of functions under this Part; and for that purpose regulations may, in particular, make provision which applies—

(a) only in relation to functions under that Act,

(b) only in relation to functions under this Part, or

(c) differently in relation to functions under that Act and functions under this Part.

Commencement

Subsections (1), (2)(b) brought into force for the purpose of enabling a licensing authority to delegate their functions under GA 2005, s 212 as from 13 November 2006 by the Gambling Act 2005 (Commencement No 4) Order 2006, SI 2006/2964, art 2(a); sub-ss (1), (2)(b) brought into force for remaining purposes by the Gambling Act 2005 (Commencement No 6 and Transitional Provisions) Order 2006, SI 2006/3272, art 2, Sch 2 as from 30 April 2007; for transitional provisions see art 6, Sch 4 thereto (as amended by SI 2007/1157, arts 7–12). Subsections (2)(a), (c), (3)–(5) brought into force by the Gambling Act 2005 (Commencement No 6 and Transitional Provisions) Order 2006, SI 2006/3272, art 2, Sch 2 as from 30 April 2007; for transitional provisions see art 6, Sch 4 thereto (as amended by SI 2007/1157, arts 7–12).

Sub-s (1): This Part. Ie Pt 8 (ss 150–213 and Sch 9) of this Act.

Sub-s (1): Licensing authority. For the licensing authorities for the purposes of this Act, see s 2. As to the licensing authorities' functions, see also s 153, ss 155, 156.

Sub-s (1):England; Wales.

See the note to s 2.

Sub-s (4): Premises licence. As to the nature, etc of premises licences, see s 150 and the note 'Premises licence' thereto.

Sub-s (4): The Commission. Ie the Gambling Commission; see s 353(1). As to the establishment, etc of the Gambling Commission, see s 20, Sch 4, and the note 'Gambling Commission' to that section.

Application

See the note to s 150.

This section is applied by Sch 10, para 6, Sch 12, para 28, Sch 13, para 3, Sch 14, para 7.

Subordinate Legislation

Gambling Act 2005 (Proceedings of Licensing Committees and Sub-committees) (Premises Licences and Provisional Statements) (England and Wales) Regulations 2007, SI 2007/173 (made under sub-s (5)).

Definitions
'the Commission': s 353(1)
'a licensing authority': ss 2, 353(1)
'premises licence': s 353(1)

Explanatory Notes
417, 418 [para **6.2011** below]

6.655 155 Delegation of functions under Part 8: Scotland

[(1) Subject to subsection (2), a licensing authority in Scotland may arrange for the discharge of any of its functions under this Part by—
(a) any member of the authority,
(b) any committee established by the authority,
(c) the clerk of the authority, or
(d) any member of staff provided under paragraph 8(1)(b) of schedule 1 to the Licensing (Scotland) Act 2005 (asp 16).][1]

(2) A licensing authority are not to make any arrangements under subsection (1)—
(a) in relation to their power under section 166 or their function under section 349, or
(b) for the discharge by the clerk of the authority or any [member of staff provided under paragraph 8(1)(b) of schedule 1 to the Licensing (Scotland) Act 2005][2] of any of the authority's functions mentioned in paragraphs (a) to (e) of section 154(4).

(3) The procedures applicable to the proceedings of licensing boards in the exercise or their functions under the Licensing (Scotland) Act [2005][3] apply to the proceedings of those boards in the exercise of their functions under this Part: and for that purpose regulations made by the Scottish Ministers may, in particular, make provision which applies—
(a) only in relation to functions under that Act,
(b) only in relation to functions under this Part, or
(c) differently in relation to functions under that Act and functions under this Part.

Commencement
Brought into force by the Gambling Act 2005 (Commencement No 6 and Transitional Provisions) Order 2006, SI 2006/3272, art 2, Sch 2 as from 30 April 2007; for transitional provisions see art 6, Sch 4 thereto (as amended by SI 2007/1157, arts 7–12).

Sub-s (1): Licensing authority. For the licensing authorities for the purposes of this Act, see s 2. As to the licensing authorities' functions, see also ss 153, 154, s 156.

Sub-s (1): This Part. Ie Pt 8 (ss 150–213 and Sch 9) of this Act.

Sub-s (3): Scottish Ministers. See the note to s 25.

Application
See the note to s 150.
This section is applied by Sch 10, para 6, Sch 12, para 28, Sch 13, para 3, Sch 14, para 7.

Regulations under this section
As to regulations under this Act generally, see s 355.

Definitions
'a licensing authority': ss 2, 353(1)

Explanatory Notes
419–422 [para **6.2011** below]

---

1 Sub-s (1): substituted by SSI 2009/248, art 2(1), Sch 1, Pt 1, para 12(1), (4)(a).

2 Sub-s (2): in sub-para (b) words from "member of staff" to "the Licensing (Scotland) Act

6: Gambling Act 2005: Statutes

2005" in square brackets substituted by SSI 2009/248, art 2(1), Sch 1, Pt 1, para 12(1), (4)(b).

3 Sub-s (3): reference to "2005" in square brackets substituted by SSI 2009/248, art 2(1), Sch 1, Pt 1, para 12(1), (4)(c).

6.656 156 Register

(1) A licensing authority shall—

(a) maintain a register of premises licences issued by the authority together with such other information as may be prescribed,

(b) make the register and information available for inspection by members of the public at all reasonable times, and

(c) make arrangements for the provision of a copy of an entry in the register, or of information, to a member of the public on request.

(2) A licensing authority may refuse to provide a copy of an entry or of information unless the person seeking it pays a reasonable fee specified by the authority.

(3) The Secretary of State may make regulations about—

(a) the form of the register;

(b) the manner in which it is maintained.

(4) The Secretary of State may make regulations—

(a) requiring licensing authorities to give to the Commission specified information about premises licences issued by them,

(b) requiring the Commission to maintain a register of the information provided to it under paragraph (a),

(c) requiring the Commission to grant access to the register to members of the public (without charge),

(d) requiring the Commission to make copies of entries available on request, and on payment of a reasonable fee, to members of the public, and

(e) excusing licensing authorities, wholly or partly, from compliance with subsection (1).

Commencement

Brought into force by the Gambling Act 2005 (Commencement No 6 and Transitional Provisions) Order 2006, SI 2006/3272, art 2, Sch 2 as from 30 April 2007; for transitional provisions see art 6, Sch 4 thereto (as amended by SI 2007/1157, arts 7–12).

Sub-s (1): Licensing authority. For the licensing authorities for the purposes of this Act, see s 2. As to the licensing authorities' functions, see also ss 153–155.

Sub-s (1): Premises licences. As to the nature, etc of premises licences, see s 150 and the note 'Premises licence' thereto.

Sub-s (3): Secretary of State. See the note to s 4.

Sub-s (4): The Commission. Ie the Gambling Commission; see s 353(1). As to the establishment, etc of the Gambling Commission, see s 20, Sch 4, and the note 'Gambling Commission' to that section.

Application

See the note to s 150.

Regulations under this section

At the time of going to press no regulations had been made under this section.

As to regulations under this Act generally, see s 355.

Definitions

'the Commission': s 353(1)
'a licensing authority': ss 2, 353(1)
'premises licence': s 353(1)
'prescribed': s 213(g)

Explanatory Notes
423, 424 [para **6.2011** below]

Other relevant persons

6.657 157 Responsible authorities

For the purposes of this Part the following are responsible authorities in relation to premises—

(a) a licensing authority in England and Wales in whose area the premises are wholly or partly situated,

(b) the Commission,

(c) either—

  (i) in England and Wales, the chief officer of police for a police area in which the premises are wholly or partly situated, or

  (ii) in Scotland, the chief constable of the police force maintained for a police area in which the premises are wholly or partly situated,

(d) the fire and rescue authority for an area in which the premises are wholly or partly situated,

(e) either—

  (i) in England and Wales, the local planning authority, in accordance with Part I of the Town and Country Planning Act 1990 (c 8), for an area in which the premises are wholly or partly situated, or

  (ii) in Scotland, the planning authority, in accordance with Part 1 of the Town and Country Planning (Scotland) Act 1997 (c 8), for an area in which the premises are wholly or partly situated,

(f) the [relevant authority as defined in section 6 of the Fire (Scotland) Act 2005 (asp 5)][1] for an area in which the premises are wholly or partly situated,

(g) an authority which has functions by virtue of an enactment in respect of minimising or preventing the risk of pollution of the environment or of harm to human health in an area in which the premises are wholly or partly situated,

(h) a body which is designated in writing for the purposes of this paragraph, by the licensing authority for an area in which the premises are wholly or partly situated, as competent to advise the authority about the protection of children from harm,

(i) Her Majesty's [Commissioners for Her Majesty's Revenue and Customs] 2, and

(j) any other person prescribed for the purposes of this section by regulations made by the Secretary of State.

Commencement
Brought into force by the Gambling Act 2005 (Commencement No 6 and Transitional Provisions) Order 2006, SI 2006/3272, art 2, Sch 2 as from 30 April 2007; for transitional provisions see art 6, Sch 4 thereto (as amended by SI 2007/1157, arts 7–12).

This Part
Ie Pt 8 (ss 150–213 and Sch 9) of this Act.

Licensing authority
For the licensing authorities for the purposes of this Act, see s 2. As to the licensing authorities' functions, see ss 153–156.

England; Wales
See the note to s 2.

The Commission

Ie the Gambling Commission; see s 353(1). As to the establishment, etc of the Gambling Commission, see s 20, Sch 4, and the note 'Gambling Commission' to that section.

Writing

See the note to s 39.

Commissioners for Her Majesty's Revenue and Customs

See the note to s 23.

Secretary of State

See the note to s 4.

Application

See the note to s 150.

Subordinate Legislation

SI 2006/636; SI 2007/459.

As to regulations under this Act generally, see s 355.

Definitions

'chief officer of police': s 213(b)
'chief officer's area': s 213(c)
'child': ss 45(1), 353(1)
'the Commission': s 353(1)
'a licensing authority': ss 2, 353(1)
'the licensing authority': s 213(f)
'premises': s 353(1), (2)(g)
'prescribed': s 213(g)

Explanatory Notes

425 [para 6.2011 below]

---

1 In para (f) words in square brackets substituted, in relation to Scotland, by SSI 2006/475, art 2(1), Sch 1, para 16(1), (2).

2 Words in square brackets substituted by virtue of the Commissioners for Revenue and Customs Act 2005, s 50(1), (7).

6.658 158 Interested party

For the purposes of this Part a person is an interested party in relation to a premises licence or in relation to an application for or in respect of a premises licence if, in the opinion of the licensing authority which issues the licence or to which the application is made, the person—

(a) lives sufficiently close to the premises to be likely to be affected by the authorised activities,

(b) has business interests that might be affected by the authorised activities, or

(c) represents persons who satisfy paragraph (a) or (b).

Commencement

Brought into force by the Gambling Act 2005 (Commencement No 6 and Transitional Provisions) Order 2006, SI 2006/3272, art 2, Sch 2 as from 30 April 2007; for transitional provisions see art 6, Sch 4 thereto (as amended by SI 2007/1157, arts 7–12).

This Part

Ie Pt 8 (ss 150–213 and Sch 9) of this Act.

Person

See the note 'Persons' to s 23.

Premises licence

As to the nature, etc of premises licences, see s 150 and the note 'Premises licence' thereto.

Licensing authority

For the licensing authorities for the purposes of this Act, see s 2. As to the licensing authorities' functions, see ss 153–156.

Subordinate Legislation

SI 2006/636.

Application

See the note to s 150.

Definitions

'authorised activity': s 213(a)
'the licensing authority': s 213(f)
'premises': s 353(1), (2)(g)
'premises licence': s 353(1)

Explanatory Notes

426 [para **6.2011** below]

Application for licence

6.659 159 Making of application

(1) A person may apply to a licensing authority for a premises licence to be issued to him authorising the use of premises to carry on an activity listed in section 37(1).

(2) An application must be made to a licensing authority in whose area the premises are wholly or partly situated.

(3) An application may be made only by a person who—

(a) holds an operating licence which authorises him to carry on the activity in respect of which the premises licence is sought, or

(b) has made an application, which has not yet been determined, for an operating licence which authorises him to carry on the activity in respect of which the premises licence is sought.

(4) But subsection (3) does not apply to an application for a premises licence which authorises a track to be used for accepting bets (and which does not also, otherwise than by virtue of section 172, authorise it to be used for another purpose).

(5) An application may be made only by a person who has a right to occupy the premises to which the application relates.

(6) An application must—

(a) be made in the prescribed form and manner,

(b) contain or be accompanied by the prescribed information or documents, and

(c) be accompanied by the prescribed fee.

(7) Regulations prescribing a matter for the purposes of this section may, in particular, make different provision for—

(a) applications in respect of different classes of activity, or

(b) different circumstances.

(8) In this section 'prescribed' means—

(a) in relation to applications to authorities in England and Wales, prescribed by regulations made by the Secretary of State, and

(b) in relation to applications to authorities in Scotland, prescribed by regulations made by the Scottish Ministers.

Commencement

Brought into force for certain purposes by the Gambling Act 2005 (Commencement No 6 and Transitional Provisions) Order 2006, SI 2006/3272, art 2, Schs 2, 3 as from 30 April and 1 June

2007; for transitional provisions see art 6, Sch 4 thereto (as amended by SI 2007/1157, arts 7–12). Brought into force for remaining purposes by the Gambling Act 2005 (Commencement No 6 and Transitional Provisions) Order 2006, SI 2006/3272, art 2 as from 1 September 2007; for transitional provisions see art 6, Sch 4 thereto (as amended by SI 2007/1157, arts 7–12). Appointment (for certain purposes): 20 May 2008: see SI 2008/1326, art 2, Schedule.

Sub-s (1): Person. See the note 'Persons' to s 23.

Sub-s (1): May apply. See further as respects applications for a premises licence, s 160 (notice of application), s 161 (representations), ss 162–166 (determination of applications), ss 167–171 (conditions), and ss 206–209 (appeals).

Sub-s (1): Licensing authority. For the licensing authorities for the purposes of this Act, see s 2. As to the licensing authorities' functions, see ss 153–156.

Sub-s (1): Premises licence. As to the nature, etc of premises licences, see s 150 and the note 'Premises licence' thereto.

Sub-s (3): Operating licence. As to the nature, etc of operating licences, see s 65 and the note 'Operating licences' thereto.

Sub-s (8): England; Wales.

See the note to s 2.

Sub-s (8): Secretary of State. See the note to s 4.

Sub-s (8): Scottish Ministers. See the note to s 25.

Application

See the note to s 150.

Subordinate Legislation

Gambling Act 2005 (Premises Licences and Provisional Statements) Regulations 2007, SI 2007/459 (made under sub-ss (6)–(8)).

Gambling (Premises Licence Fees) (England and Wales) Regulations 2007, SI 2007/479 (made under sub-ss (6), (7), (8)(a)).

Gambling Act 2005 (Premises Licences and Provisional Statements) (Amendment) (England and Wales) Regulations 2007, SI 2007/1775 (made under sub-ss (6)–(8)).

Gambling (Inviting Competing Applications for Large and Small Casino Premises Licences) Regulations 2008, SI 2008/469.As to regulations under this Act generally, see s 355.

Definitions

'accepting a bet': s 353(2)(a)
'a licensing authority': ss 2, 353(1)
'operating licence': s 353(1)
'premises': s 353(1), (2)(g)
'premises licence': s 353(1)
'track': s 353(1)

Explanatory Notes

427–432 [para **6.2011** below]

6.660 160 Notice of application

(1) The Secretary of State may make regulations requiring an applicant for a premises licence—

(a) to publish notice of his application;

(b) to give notice of his application to the responsible authorities in relation to the premises;

(c) to give notice of his application to other persons.

(2) Regulations under subsection (1) shall include provision—

(a) about the manner and form in which notice is to be published or given,

(b) about the period of time within which notice is to be published or given, and

(c) for the consequences of failure to comply with the regulations.

(3) In so far as this section has effect in relation to applications to authorities in Scotland, the reference to the Secretary of State shall have effect as a reference to the Scottish Ministers.

Commencement

Brought into force for certain purposes by the Gambling Act 2005 (Commencement No 6 and Transitional Provisions) Order 2006, SI 2006/3272, art 2, Schs 2, 3 as from 30 April and 1 June 2007; for transitional provisions see art 6, Sch 4 thereto (as amended by SI 2007/1157, arts 7–12). Brought into force for remaining purposes by the Gambling Act 2005 (Commencement No 6 and Transitional Provisions) Order 2006, SI 2006/3272, art 2 as from 1 September 2007; for transitional provisions see art 6, Sch 4 thereto (as amended by SI 2007/1157, arts 7–12). Appointment (for certain purposes): 20 May 2008: see SI 2008/1326, art 2, Schedule.

Sub-s (1): Secretary of State. See the note to s 4.

Sub-s (1): Applicant. As to the making of an application for a premises licence, see s 159.

Sub-s (1): Premises licence. As to the nature, etc of premises licences, see s 150 and the note 'Premises licence' thereto.

Sub-s (1): Give notice. See further, in connection with a requirement under this Act to give a notice, s 353(4).

Sub-s (1): Responsible authorities. See s 157.

Sub-s (1): Persons. See the note to s 23.

Sub-s (3): Scottish Ministers. See the note to s 25.

Application

See the note to s 150.

Subordinate Legislation

Gambling Act 2005 (Premises Licences and Provisional Statements) Regulations 2007, SI 2007/459 (made under sub-ss (1), (2)).

Gambling Act 2005 (Premises Licences and Provisional Statements) (Amendment) (England and Wales) Regulations 2007, SI 2007/1775 (made under sub-ss (1), (2)).

As to regulations under this Act generally, see s 355.

Definitions

'premises': s 353(1), (2)(g)
'premises licence': s 353(1)
'publication': s 353(2)(j)

Explanatory Notes

427–432 [para **6.2011** below]

6.661 161 Representations

(1) Where an application is made to a licensing authority for a premises licence, an interested party or responsible authority in relation to the premises may make representations in writing to the licensing authority.

(2) Representations under subsection (1) must be made within such period as the Secretary of State shall prescribe by regulations.

(3) In so far as this section has effect in relation to applications to authorities in Scotland, the reference to the Secretary of State shall have effect as a reference to the Scottish Ministers.

Commencement

Brought into force for certain purposes by the Gambling Act 2005 (Commencement No 6 and Transitional Provisions) Order 2006, SI 2006/3272, art 2, Schs 2, 3 as from 30 April and 1 June 2007; for transitional provisions see art 6, Sch 4 thereto (as amended by SI 2007/1157, arts 7–12). Brought into force for remaining purposes by the Gambling Act 2005 (Commencement No 6 and Transitional Provisions) Order 2006, SI 2006/3272, art 2 as from 1 September 2007; for transitional provisions see art 6, Sch 4 thereto (as amended by SI 2007/1157, arts 7–12). Appointment (for certain purposes): 20 May 2008: see SI 2008/1326, art 2, Schedule.

Sub-s (1): Application is made. As to the making of an application for a premises licence, see s 159.

Sub-s (1): Licensing authority. For the licensing authorities for the purposes of this Act, see s 2. As to the licensing authorities' functions, see ss 153–156.

Sub-s (1): Premises licence. As to the nature, etc of premises licences, see s 150 and the note 'Premises licence' thereto.

Sub-s (1): Interested party. See s 158.

Sub-s (1): Responsible authority. See s 157.

Sub-s (1): May make representations. As to the holding of hearings where representations have been made under this section, see s 162.

Sub-s (1): Writing. See the note to s 39.

Sub-s (2): Secretary of State. See the note to s 4.

Sub-s (3): Scottish Ministers. See the note to s 25.

Application

See the note to s 150.

Subordinate Legislation

Gambling Act 2005 (Premises Licences and Provisional Statements) Regulations 2007, SI 2007/459 (made under sub-s (2)).

Gambling Act 2005 (Premises Licences and Provisional Statements) (Amendment) (England and Wales) Regulations 2007, SI 2007/1775 (made under sub-s (2)).

As to regulations under this Act generally, see s 355.

Definitions

'a licensing authority': ss 2, 353(1)
'the licensing authority': s 213(f)
'premises': s 353(1), (2)(g)
'premises licence': s 353(1)

Explanatory Notes

427–432 [para **6.2011** below]

Determination of application

6.662 162 Requirement for hearing

(1) In determining an application for a premises licence a licensing authority must hold a hearing if—

(a) an interested party or responsible authority has made (and not withdrawn) representations about the application under section 161,
(b) the authority propose to attach a condition to the licence under section 169(1)(a), or
(c) the authority propose to exclude under section 169(1)(b) a condition that would otherwise be attached to the licence under section 168.

(2) But a licensing authority may determine an application for a premises licence without a hearing despite subsection (1) with the consent of—

(a) the applicant, and
(b) any interested party or responsible authority who has made (and not withdrawn) representations about the application under section 161.

(3) A licensing authority may also determine an application for a premises licence without a hearing despite subsection (1)(a) if the authority think that the representations made under section 161—

(a) are vexatious,
(b) are frivolous, or
(c) will certainly not influence the authority's determination of the application.

(4) If a licensing authority propose to determine an application in reliance on subsection (3) they shall as soon as is reasonably practicable notify any person who made representations under section 161.

Commencement

Brought into force for certain purposes by the Gambling Act 2005 (Commencement No 6 and Transitional Provisions) Order 2006, SI 2006/3272, art 2, Schs 2, 3 as from 30 April and 1 June 2007; for transitional provisions see art 6, Sch 4 thereto (as amended by SI 2007/1157, arts 7–12). Brought into force for remaining purposes by the Gambling Act 2005 (Commencement No 6 and Transitional Provisions) Order 2006, SI 2006/3272, art 2 as from 1 September 2007; for transitional provisions see art 6, Sch 4 thereto (as amended by SI 2007/1157, arts 7–12). Appointment (for certain purposes): 20 May 2008: see SI 2008/1326, art 2, Schedule.

Sub-s (1): Application. As to the making of an application for a premises licence, see s 159.

Sub-s (1): Premises licence. As to the nature, etc of premises licences, see s 150 and the note 'Premises licence' thereto.

Sub-s (1): Licensing authority. For the licensing authorities for the purposes of this Act, see s 2. As to the licensing authorities' functions, see ss 153–156.

Sub-s (1): Interested party. See s 158.

Sub-s (1): Responsible authority. See s 157.

Sub-s (4): Notify. See further, in connection with a requirement under this Act to give a notice, s 353(4).

Sub-s (4): Person. See the note 'Persons' to s 23.

Application

See the note to s 150.

Definitions

'a licensing authority': ss 2, 353(1)
'premises licence': s 353(1)

Explanatory Notes

433–437 [para **6.2011** below]

6.663 163 Determination of application

(1) On considering an application for a premises licence (whether at a hearing or not) a licensing authority shall—

(a) grant it, or

(b) reject it.

(2) A licensing authority shall not determine an application for a premises licence made in reliance on section 159(3)(b) until the relevant operating licence has been issued (in a form which authorises the applicant to carry on the activity in respect of which the premises licence is sought).

Commencement

Brought into force for certain purposes by the Gambling Act 2005 (Commencement No 6 and Transitional Provisions) Order 2006, SI 2006/3272, art 2, Schs 2, 3 as from 30 April and 1 June 2007; for transitional provisions see art 6, Sch 4 thereto (as amended by SI 2007/1157, arts 7–12). Brought into force for remaining purposes by the Gambling Act 2005 (Commencement No 6 and Transitional Provisions) Order 2006, SI 2006/3272, art 2 as from 1 September 2007; for transitional provisions see art 6, Sch 4 thereto (as amended by SI 2007/1157, arts 7–12). Appointment (for certain purposes): 20 May 2008: see SI 2008/1326, art 2, Schedule.

Sub-s (1): Application. As to the making of an application for a premises licence, see s 159.

Sub-s (1): Premises licence. As to the nature, etc of premises licences, see s 150 and the note 'Premises licence' thereto.

Sub-s (1): Licensing authority. For the licensing authorities for the purposes of this Act, see s 2. As to the licensing authorities' functions, see ss 153–156.

Sub-s (2): Operating licence. As to the nature, etc of operating licences, see s 65 and the note 'Operating licences' thereto. This sub-s is omitted in respect of the Tote: SI 2007/2102, Art 4.

Application

See the note to s 150.

Definitions

'a licensing authority': ss 2, 353(1)
'operating licence': s 353(1)
'premises licence': s 353(1)

Explanatory Notes

433–437 [para **6.2011** below]

6.664 164 Grant of application

(1) Where a licensing authority grant an application for a premises licence they shall as soon as is reasonably practicable—

(a) give notice of the grant to—

(i) the applicant,

(ii) the Commission,

(iii) any person who made representations about the application under section 161,

(iv) in England and Wales, the chief officer of police for any area in which the premises are wholly or partly situated,

(v) in Scotland, the chief constable of the police force maintained for a police area in which the premises are wholly or partly situated, and

(vi) Her Majesty's [Commissioners for Her Majesty's Revenue and Customs][1],

(b) issue a premises licence to the applicant, and

(c) give the applicant a summary of the terms and conditions of the licence in the prescribed form.

(2) A notice under subsection (1)(a)—

(a) must be in the prescribed form,

(b) if the licensing authority have attached a condition to the licence under section 169(1)(a) or excluded under section 169(1)(b) a condition that would otherwise have attached by virtue of section 168, must give the authority's reasons, and

(c) if representations were made about the application under section 161, must give the authority's response to the representations.

(3) In this section 'prescribed' means—

(a) in relation to authorities in England and Wales, prescribed by regulations made by the Secretary of State, and

(b) in relation to authorities in Scotland, prescribed by regulations made by the Scottish Ministers.

Commencement

Brought into force for certain purposes by the Gambling Act 2005 (Commencement No 6 and Transitional Provisions) Order 2006, SI 2006/3272, art 2, Schs 2, 3 as from 30 April and 1 June 2007; for transitional provisions see art 6, Sch 4 thereto (as amended by SI 2007/1157, arts 7–12). Brought into force for remaining purposes by the Gambling Act 2005 (Commencement No 6 and Transitional Provisions) Order 2006, SI 2006/3272, art 2 as from 1 September 2007; for transitional provisions see art 6, Sch 4 thereto (as amended by SI 2007/1157, arts 7–12). Appointment (for certain purposes): 20 May 2008: see SI 2008/1326, art 2, Schedule.

Sub-s (1): Licensing authority. For the licensing authorities for the purposes of this Act, see s 2. As to the licensing authorities' functions, see ss 153–156.

Sub-s (1): Application. As to the making of an application for a premises licence, see s 159.

Sub-s (1): Premises licence. As to the nature, etc of premises licences, see s 150 and the note 'Premises licence' thereto.

Sub-s (1): Notice. See further, in connection with a requirement under this Act to give a notice, s 353(4).

Sub-s (1): The Commission. Ie the Gambling Commission; see s 353(1). As to the establishment, etc of the Gambling Commission, see s 20, Sch 4, and the note 'Gambling Commission' to that section.

Sub-s (1): Person. See the note 'Persons' to s 23.

Sub-s (1): England; Wales. See the note to s 2.

Sub-s (1): Commissioners for Her Majesty's Revenue and Customs. See the note to s 23.

Sub-s (3): Secretary of State. See the note to s 4.

Sub-s (3): Scottish Ministers. See the note to s 25.

Application

See the note to s 150.

Subordinate Legislation

Gambling Act 2005 (Premises Licences and Provisional Statements) Regulations 2007, SI 2007/459.

As to regulations under this Act generally, see s 355.

Definitions

'chief officer of police': s 213(b)
'chief officer's area': s 213(c)
'the Commission': s 353(1)
'a licensing authority': ss 2, 353(1)
'premises': s 353(1), (2)(g)
'premises licence': s 353(1)

Explanatory Notes

433–437 [para **6.2011** below]

---

1 Words in square brackets substituted by virtue of the Commissioners for Revenue and Customs Act 2005, s 50(1), (7).

6.665 165 Rejection of application

(1) Where a licensing authority reject an application for a premises licence they shall as soon as is reasonably practicable give notice of the rejection to—

(a) the applicant,

(b) the Commission,

(c) any person who made representations about the application under section 161,

(d) either—

(i) in England and Wales, the chief officer of police for any area in which the premises are wholly or partly situated, or

(ii) in Scotland, the chief constable of the police force maintained for a police area in which the premises are wholly or partly situated, and

(e) Her Majesty's [Commissioners for Her Majesty's Revenue and Customs] [1].

(2) A notice under subsection (1)—

(a) must be in the prescribed form, and

(b) must give the authority's reasons for rejecting the application.

(3) In this section 'prescribed' means—

(a) in relation to authorities in England and Wales, prescribed by regulations made by the Secretary of State, and

(b) in relation to authorities in Scotland, prescribed by regulations made by the Scottish Ministers.

6: Gambling Act 2005: Statutes

Commencement

Brought into force for certain purposes by the Gambling Act 2005 (Commencement No 6 and Transitional Provisions) Order 2006, SI 2006/3272, art 2, Schs 2, 3 as from 30 April and 1 June 2007; for transitional provisions see art 6, Sch 4 thereto (as amended by SI 2007/1157, arts 7–12). Brought into force for remaining purposes by the Gambling Act 2005 (Commencement No 6 and Transitional Provisions) Order 2006, SI 2006/3272, art 2 as from 1 September 2007; for transitional provisions see art 6, Sch 4 thereto (as amended by SI 2007/1157, arts 7–12). Appointment (for certain purposes): 20 May 2008: see SI 2008/1326, art 2, Schedule.

Sub-s (1): Licensing authority. For the licensing authorities for the purposes of this Act, see s 2. As to the licensing authorities' functions, see ss 153–156.

Sub-s (1): Application. As to the making of an application for a premises licence, see s 159.

Sub-s (1): Premises licence. As to the nature, etc of premises licences, see s 150 and the note 'Premises licence' thereto.

Sub-s (1): Notice. See further, in connection with a requirement under this Act to give a notice, s 353(4).

Sub-s (1): The Commission. Ie the Gambling Commission; see s 353(1). As to the establishment, etc of the Gambling Commission, see s 20, Sch 4, and the note 'Gambling Commission' to that section.

Sub-s (1): Person. See the note 'Persons' to s 23.

Sub-s (1): England; Wales. See the note to s 2.

Sub-s (1): Commissioners for Her Majesty's Revenue and Customs. See the note to s 23.

Sub-s (3): Secretary of State. See the note to s 4.

Sub-s (3): Scottish Ministers. See the note to s 25.

Application

See the note to s 150.

Subordinate Legislation

Gambling Act 2005 (Premises Licences and Provisional Statements) Regulations 2007, SI 2007/459 (made under sub-ss (2), (3)).

As to regulations under this Act generally, see s 355.

Definitions

'chief officer of police': s 213(b)
'chief officer's area': s 213(c)
'the Commission': s 353(1)
'a licensing authority': ss 2, 353(1)
'premises': s 353(1), (2)(g)
'premises licence': s 353(1)

Explanatory Notes

433–437 [para **6.2011** below]

---

1 Words in square brackets substituted by virtue of the Commissioners for Revenue and Customs Act 2005, s 50(1), (7).

6.666 166 Resolution not to issue casino licences

(1) A licensing authority may resolve not to issue casino premises licences.

(2) In passing a resolution under subsection (1) a licensing authority may have regard to any principle or matter.

(3) A resolution under subsection (1)—

- (a) must apply to the issue of casino premises licences generally,
- (b) must specify the date on which it takes effect,
- (c) may be revoked by a further resolution, and
- (d) shall lapse at the end of the period of three years beginning with the date on which it takes effect (without prejudice to the ability to pass a new resolution).

(4) A resolution under subsection (1)—

(a) may be passed whether or not the licensing authority has already issued casino premises licences,

(b) shall have no effect in relation to a casino premises licence issued before the resolution takes effect,

(c) shall have no effect in relation to premises in respect of which a provisional statement relating to the operation of a casino is in force when the resolution takes effect,

(d) shall have no effect in relation to anything converted into a casino premises licence by virtue of Schedule 18,

(e) shall not affect the issuing of a casino premises licence in accordance with a requirement by virtue of Schedule 18, and

(f) may not be taken into account in conducting a review of a casino premises licence under section 201.

(5) A resolution under subsection (1) shall be published by being included in a statement or revision under section 349.

(6) Section 153 is subject to this section.

(7) The Secretary of State may by order require a licensing authority to consider whether or not to pass a resolution under subsection (1).

(8) An order under subsection (7) may—

(a) be directed to a particular licensing authority or to a class or description of licensing authority;

(b) require the licensing authority to consult such persons or classes of persons as they think are likely to be affected by the resolution (having regard to any guidance given by the Secretary of State);

(c) require the licensing authority to take other procedural steps;

(d) specify a period within which the consideration must take place;

(e) require consideration once or at specified intervals.

Commencement

Section brought into force by the Gambling Act 2005 (Commencement No 3) Order 2006, SI 2006/631, art 2 as from 31 March 2006.

Sub-s (1): Licensing authority. For the licensing authorities for the purposes of this Act, see s 2. As to the licensing authorities' functions, see ss 153–156.

Sub-s (1): Premises licence. As to the nature, etc of premises licences, see s 150 and the note 'Premises licence' thereto.

Sub-s (7): Secretary of State. See the note to s 4.

Sub-s (8): Persons. See the note to s 23.

Application

See the note to s 150.

Orders under this section

At the time of going to press no orders had been made under this section.

As to orders under this Act generally, see s 355.

Definitions

'a licensing authority': ss 2, 353(1)
'the licensing authority': s 213(f)
'premises': s 353(1), (2)(g)
'premises licence': s 353(1)

Explanatory Notes

438–441 [para **6.2011** below]

Conditions

6.667 167 Mandatory conditions

(1) The Secretary of State may by regulations provide for a specified condition to be attached to premises licences.

(2) Regulations under this section may, in particular—

(a) make provision which applies generally, only to premises licences in a specified class or only in specified circumstances;

(b) make different provision for different classes of licence or for different circumstances.

(3) In relation to premises licences issued in Scotland subsection (1) shall have effect as if the reference to the Secretary of State were a reference to the Scottish Ministers.

Commencement

Brought into force by the Gambling Act 2005 (Commencement No 6 and Transitional Provisions) Order 2006, SI 2006/3272, art 2, Sch 2 as from 30 April 2007; for transitional provisions see art 6, Sch 4 thereto (as amended by SI 2007/1157, arts 7–12).

Sub-s (1): Secretary of State. See the note to s 4.

Sub-s (1): Provide for a specified condition to be attached. See, however, ss 170, 171. See also, as respects the attachment of conditions under this section, s 174(6)–(8) (casino premises licences), s 178 (door supervision), s 181 (betting machines), and s 186(8) (change of circumstances).

For the power of a licensing authority to review arrangements made by licensees to ensure compliance with condition attached under this section, see s 200(1).

Sub-s (1): Premises licences. As to the nature, etc of premises licences, see s 150 and the note 'Premises licence' thereto.

Sub-s (3): Scottish Ministers. See the note to s 25.

Application

See the note to s 150.

Subordinate Legislation

SI 2007/1409.

As to regulations under this Act generally, see s 355.

Definitions

'premises licence': s 353(1)

Explanatory Notes

442–446 [para **6.2011** below]

6.668 168 Default conditions

(1) The Secretary of State may by regulations prescribe for a specified condition to be attached to any premises licence unless excluded by the authority who issue the licence.

(2) Regulations under this section may, in particular—

(a) make provision which applies generally, only to premises licences in a specified class or only in specified circumstances;

(b) make different provision for different classes of licence or for different circumstances.

(3) In relation to a premises licence issued by an authority in Scotland subsection (1) shall have effect as if the reference to the Secretary of State were a reference to the Scottish Ministers.

Commencement

Brought into force by the Gambling Act 2005 (Commencement No 6 and Transitional Provisions) Order 2006, SI 2006/3272, art 2, Sch 2 as from 30 April 2007; for transitional provisions see art 6, Sch 4 thereto (as amended by SI 2007/1157, arts 7–12).

Sub-s (1): Secretary of State. See the note to s 4.

Sub-s (1): Prescribe for a specified condition to be attached. See, however, ss 170, 171. See also, as respects the attachment of conditions under this section, s 174(7), (8) (casino premises licences), s 178 (door supervision), s 181 (betting machines), and s 186(8) (change of circumstances).

The holder of a premises licence may apply to the licensing authority to vary the licence by excluding a condition attached by virtue of this section; see s 187.

For the power of a licensing authority to review arrangements made by licensees to ensure compliance with condition attached under this section, see s 200(1), and for the power of the licensing authority to exclude a condition attached to a licence under this section or remove or amend an exclusion following a review under s 201, see s 202.

Sub-s (1): Premises licences. As to the nature, etc of premises licences, see s 150 and the note 'Premises licence' thereto.

Sub-s (1): Unless excluded. See s 169(1)(b).

Sub-s (3): Scottish Ministers. See the note to s 25.

Application

See the note to s 150.

Subordinate Legislation

SI 2007/1409.

As to regulations under this Act generally, see s 355.

Definitions

'premises licence': s 353(1)

Explanatory Notes

442–446 [para **6.2011** below]

6.669 169 Conditions imposed or excluded by licensing authority

(1) Where a licensing authority issue a premises licence they may—

(a) attach a condition to the licence;

(b) exclude a condition that would otherwise be attached to the licence by virtue of section 168.

(2) A condition attached to the licence under subsection (1)(a) may, in particular, address a matter addressed by a condition excluded under subsection (1)(b).

(3) A condition attached to the licence under subsection (1)(a) may apply in relation to the premises generally or only in relation to a specified part of the premises.

(4) A licensing authority may not attach a condition to a premises licence which prevents compliance with a condition of the operating licence which authorises the holder to carry out the activity in respect of which the premises licence is granted.

Commencement

Brought into force by the Gambling Act 2005 (Commencement No 6 and Transitional Provisions) Order 2006, SI 2006/3272, art 2, Sch 2 as from 30 April 2007; for transitional provisions see art 6, Sch 4 thereto (as amended by SI 2007/1157, arts 7–12).

Sub-s (1): Licensing authority. For the licensing authorities for the purposes of this Act, see s 2. As to the licensing authorities' functions, see ss 153–156.

Sub-s (1): Premises licence. As to the nature, etc of premises licences, see s 150 and the note 'Premises licence' thereto.

Sub-s (1): Attach . . . exclude a condition. See, however, ss 170, 171. See also, as respects the attachment of conditions under this section, s 174(8) (casino premises licences), s 178 (door supervision), s 181 (betting machines), s 186(8) (change of circumstances), and s 211(2) (vehicles and vessels). See also SI 2007/479, Art 9.

A premises licence must specify any condition attached under sub-s (1)(a) above and any exclusion of a default condition effected under sub-s (1)(b) above; see s 151(1)(e), (f).

As to the holding of hearings where the licensing authority propose to attach a condition under this section or propose to exclude a default condition under sub-s (1)(b) above, see s 162.

The holder of a premises licence may apply to the licensing authority to vary the licence by adding, amending or removing a condition attached under this section; see s 187.

For the power of a licensing authority to review arrangements made by licensees to ensure compliance with condition attached under this section, see s 200(1), and for the power of the licensing authority to add, remove or amend a condition under this section following a review under s 201, see s 202.

Sub-s (4): Operating licence. As to the nature, etc of operating licences, see s 65 and the note 'Operating licences' thereto.

Application

See the note to s 150.

Definitions

'holder': s 213(d)
'a licensing authority': ss 2, 353(1)
'operating licence': s 353(1)
'premises': s 353(1), (2)(g)
'premises licence': s 353(1)

Explanatory Notes

442–446 [para **6.2011** below]

6.670 170 Membership

A premises licence may not be subject to a condition (whether imposed by virtue of section 167, 168 or 169)—

(a) requiring all or part of the premises, or any activity taking place on the premises, to be operated or carried on as a club or other body with membership, or

(b) restricting use of any part of the premises wholly or partly by reference to membership of a club or other body.

Commencement

Brought into force by the Gambling Act 2005 (Commencement No 6 and Transitional Provisions) Order 2006, SI 2006/3272, art 2, Sch 2 as from 30 April 2007; for transitional provisions see art 6, Sch 4 thereto (as amended by SI 2007/1157, arts 7–12).

Premises licence

As to the nature, etc of premises licences, see s 150 and the note 'Premises licence' thereto.

Application

See the note to s 150.

Definitions

'premises': s 353(1), (2)(g)
'premises licence': s 353(1)

Explanatory Notes

442–446 [para **6.2011** below]

6.671 171 Stakes, &c

(1) A premises licence may not be subject to a condition (whether imposed by virtue of section 167, 168 or 169) imposing limits on—

(a) stakes,
(b) fees,
(c) winnings, or
(d) prizes.

(2) The prohibition in subsection (1)(b) shall not prevent the imposition by virtue of section 167 of a condition about fees for admission to a track.

Commencement

Brought into force by the Gambling Act 2005 (Commencement No 6 and Transitional Provisions) Order 2006, SI 2006/3272, art 2, Sch 2 as from 30 April 2007; for transitional provisions see art 6, Sch 4 thereto (as amended by SI 2007/1157, arts 7–12).

Sub-s (1): Premises licence. As to the nature, etc of premises licences, see s 150 and the note 'Premises licence' thereto.

Application

See the note to s 150.

Definitions

'premises licence': s 353(1)
'prize': ss 6(5), 239, 353(1)
'stake': s 353(1)
'track': s 353(1)
'winnings': s 353(1)

Explanatory Notes

442–446 [para **6.2011** below]

Specific cases

6.672 172 Gaming machines

(1) An adult gaming centre premises licence shall, by virtue of this section, authorise the holder—

[(a) to make available for use on the premises a number of Category B gaming machines not exceeding 20 per cent of the total number of gaming machines which are available for use on the premises,][1]

(b) to make any number of Category C gaming machines available for use on the premises, and

(c) to make any number of Category D gaming machines available for use on the premises.

(2) A family entertainment centre premises licence shall, by virtue of this section, authorise the holder—

(a) to make any number of Category C gaming machines available for use on the premises, and

(b) to make any number of Category D gaming machines available for use on the premises.

(3) A casino premises licence for a regional casino using at least 40 gaming tables shall by virtue of this section authorise the holder to make gaming machines available for use on the premises provided that—

(a) each gaming machine is of Category A, B, C or D, and

(b) the number of gaming machines—

(i) is not more than 25 times the number of gaming tables used in the casino, and

(ii) is not more than 1250.

(4) A casino premises licence for a large casino using at least one gaming table, or for a regional casino using fewer than 40 gaming tables, shall by virtue of this section authorise the holder to make gaming machines available for use on the premises provided that—

(a) each gaming machine is of Category B, C or D, and

(b) the number of gaming machines—

(i) is not more than 5 times the number of gaming tables used in the casino, and

(ii) is not more than 150.

(5) A casino premises licence for a small casino using at least one gaming table shall by virtue of this section authorise the holder to make gaming machines available for use on the premises provided that—

(a) each gaming machine is of Category B, C or D, and

(b) the number of gaming machines—

(i) is not more than twice the number of gaming tables used in the casino, and

(ii) is not more than 80.

(6) The Secretary of State may by regulations—

(a) define 'gaming table' for the purposes of subsections (3) to (5);

(b) provide that a gaming table is to be treated as being used in a casino for the purposes of those subsections only if used—

(i) for a specified purpose,

(ii) in specified circumstances, and

(iii) to a specified extent;

(c) provide for a number of tables are to be treated as if they were a single gaming table in specified circumstances.

(7) A bingo premises licence shall, by virtue of this section, authorise the holder—

[(a) to make available for use on the premises a number of Category B gaming machines not exceeding 20 per cent of the total number of gaming machines which are available for use on the premises,][2]

(b) to make any number of Category C gaming machines available for use on the premises, and

(c) to make any number of Category D gaming machines available for use on the premises.

(8) A betting premises licence shall, by virtue of this section, authorise the holder to make up to four gaming machines, each of which must be of Category B, C or D, available for use.

(9) But subsection (8) applies to a betting premises licence in respect of a track only if the holder also holds a pool betting operating licence.

(10) A premises licence may not (whether by way of condition or otherwise)—

(a) make provision about the number or categories of gaming machine that may be made available for use that contradicts a provision of this section,

(b) make provision that contradicts a provision of regulations under section 236, 240 or 241, or

(c) make provision of a kind prohibited by regulations under any of those sections.

(11) The Secretary of State may by order amend a provision of this section so as to vary—

(a) the number of machines authorised by a specified kind of premises licence;

(b) the category of machines authorised by a specified kind of premises licence.

Commencement

Brought into force by the Gambling Act 2005 (Commencement No 6 and Transitional Provisions) Order 2006, SI 2006/3272, art 2 as from 1 September 2007; for transitional provisions see art 6, Sch 4 thereto (as amended by SI 2007/1157, arts 7–12).

Sub-s (1): Premises licence. As to the nature, etc of premises licences, see s 150 and the note 'Premises licence' thereto.

Sub-s (1): Gaming machines. As to the categories of gaming machine, see s 236 and SI 2007/2158, reg 6(3).

Sub-s (3), (4), and (5): References to Category B excludes B3A: SI 2007/2158, reg 6(3).

Sub-s (6): Secretary of State. See the note to s 4. **Gaming table:** see SI 2009/1970.

Sub-s 7: Reference to Category B includes only B3 and B4: SI 2007/2158, reg 6(3).

Sub-s 8: Category B includes only B2, B3 and B4: SI 2007/2158, reg 6(3).

Sub-s (9): Operating licence. As to the nature, etc of operating licences, see s 65 and the note 'Operating licences' thereto.

Application

See the note to s 150.

Subordinate legislation

Gambling Act 2005 (Gaming Machines in Bingo Premises) Order 2009, SI 2009/324 (made under sub-s (11)(a)).

Definitions

'casino': ss 7, 353(1)
'Category A gaming machine': s 353(1)
'Category B gaming machine': s 353(1)
'Category C gaming machine': s 353(1)
'Category D gaming machine': s 353(1)
'gaming machine': ss 235, 353(1)
'holder': s 213(d)
'operating licence': s 353(1)
'premises': s 353(1), (2)(g)
'premises licence': s 353(1)
'track': s 353(1)

Explanatory Notes

447–451 [para **6.2011** below]

---

1 Sub-s (1): para (a) substituted by SI 2011/1710, art 2. Date in force: 13 July 2011: see SI 2011/1710, art 1; for transitional provisions see arts 4, 5 thereof.

2 Sub-s (7): para (a) substituted by SI 2011/1710, art 3. Date in force: 13 July 2011: see SI 2011/1710, art 1; for transitional provisions see arts 4, 5 thereof.

6.673 173 Virtual gaming

(1) The kinds of premises licence specified in subsection (2) shall by virtue of this section authorise the holder to make facilities available for betting on the outcome of a virtual game, race, competition or other event or process.

(2) Those kinds of licence are—

(a) a casino premises licence, and

(b) a betting premises licence.

Commencement

Brought into force by the Gambling Act 2005 (Commencement No 6 and Transitional Provisions) Order 2006, SI 2006/3272, art 2 as from 1 September 2007; for transitional provisions see art 6, Sch 4 thereto (as amended by SI 2007/1157, arts 7–12).

Sub-s (1): Premises licence. As to the nature, etc of premises licences, see s 150 and the note 'Premises licence' thereto.

Application

See the note to s 150.

Definitions

'betting': ss 9–11, 353(1)
'holder': s 213(d)
'premises licence': s 353(1)
'providing facilities for gambling': ss 5, 353(2)(i)
'virtual game, race or other event or process': s 353(3)

Explanatory Notes

452 [para **6.2011** below]

6.674 174 Casino premises licence

(1) A casino premises licence may be issued only in respect of—

(a) a regional casino,

(b) a large casino, or

(c) a small casino.

(2) A casino premises licence shall, by virtue of this section and subject to subsections (3) and (4), authorise the holder to use the premises to make available any number of games of chance other than casino games.

(3) A casino premises licence shall, by virtue of this subsection and subject to subsection (4), authorise the holder, and any person authorised by him in writing, to use the premises for the provision of facilities for—

(a) bingo,

(b) betting, or

(c) both.

(4) In respect of a small casino, subsection (3) shall not apply in so far as it authorises bingo.

(5) The Secretary of State may by order repeal subsection (4) (and this subsection).

(6) Regulations under section 167 shall, in particular, make provision in relation to casino premises licences imposing limits in respect of machines of a kind that would be gaming machines but for section 235(2)(i); and the limits may, in particular, operate by reference to—

(a) the number of machines, or

(b) the number of players that the machines are designed or adapted to accommodate.

(7) Regulations under section 167 or 168 may, in particular, make provision in relation to casino premises licences, or in relation to a class of casino premises licence, for a condition requiring the provision of recreational or other facilities of a specified kind.

(8) Subsection (7) is without prejudice to the generality of sections 167, 168 and 169.

Commencement

Subsection (1) brought into force by the Gambling Act 2005 (Commencement No 6 and Transitional Provisions) Order 2006, SI 2006/3272, art 2, Sch 2 as from 30 April 2007; for transitional provisions see art 6, Sch 4 thereto (as amended by SI 2007/1157, arts 7–12).

Subsections (2)–(8) brought into force by the Gambling Act 2005 (Commencement No 6 and Transitional Provisions) Order 2006, SI 2006/3272, art 2 as from 1 September 2007; for transitional provisions see art 6, Sch 4 thereto (as amended by SI 2007/1157, arts 7–12).

Sub-s (1): Premises licence. As to the nature, etc of premises licences, see s 150 and the note 'Premises licence' thereto.

Sub-s (3): Writing. See the note to s 39.

Sub-s (5): Secretary of State. See the note to s 4.

Production of authorisations on demand

See s 316.

Application

See the note to s 150.

Orders under this section

At the time of going to press no orders had been made under this section.

As to orders under this Act generally, see s 355.

Definitions

'betting': ss 9–11, 353(1)
'bingo': s 353(1)
'casino game': ss 7(2), (3), 353(1)
'game of chance': ss 6, 353(1)
'gaming machine': ss 235, 353(1)
'holder': s 213(d)
'machine': ss 235(3)(a), 353(1)
'premises': s 353(1), (2)(g)
'premises licence': s 353(1)
'providing facilities for gambling': ss 5, 353(2)(i)

Explanatory Notes

453–456 [para **6.2011** below]

6.675 175 Casino premises licence: overall limits

(1) No more than one casino premises licence may have effect at any time in respect of regional casinos.

(2) No more than eight casino premises licences may have effect at any time in respect of large casinos.

(3) No more than eight casino premises licences may have effect at any time in respect of small casinos.

(4) The Secretary of State shall, having consulted the Scottish Ministers and the National Assembly for Wales, by order make provision for determining the geographical distribution of casino premises licences within the limits specified in subsections (1) to (3); for which purpose the order shall—

(a) specify which licensing authorities may issue casino premises licences of a specified kind, and

(b) in respect of each specified authority, specify the number of casino premises licences of each kind issued by the authority that may have effect at any time.

(5) An application for a casino premises licence may not be made to a licensing authority if subsections (1) to (3) and the order under subsection (4) would prevent the authority from granting the application.

(6) An application for a provisional statement may not be made to a licensing authority if it relates to a casino and is made at a time when subsections (1) to (3) and the order under subsection (4) would prevent the authority from granting a casino premises licence in response to an application made in reliance on the provisional statement.

(7) Schedule 9 (which makes provision about the treatment of applications for casino premises licences and provisional statements) shall have effect.

(8) The Secretary of State may by order—

(a) amend any of subsections (1), (2) and (3) so as to substitute a new maximum number of casino premises licences;

(b) repeal any of subsections (1), (2) and (3).

Commencement

Brought into force by the Gambling Act 2005 (Commencement No 6 and Transitional Provisions) Order 2006, SI 2006/3272, art 2, Sch 3 as from 1 June 2007; for transitional provisions see art 6, Sch 4 thereto (as amended by SI 2007/1157, arts 7–12). Sub-ss (2)–(8): Appointment (for certain purposes): 20 May 2008: see SI 2008/1326, art 2, Schedule.

Sub-s (1): Premises licence. As to the nature, etc of premises licences, see s 150 and the note 'Premises licence' thereto.

Sub-s (4): Secretary of State. See the note to s 4.

Sub-s (4): Scottish Ministers. See the note to s 25.

Sub-s (4): Licensing authorities. For the licensing authorities for the purposes of this Act, see s 2. As to the licensing authorities' functions, see ss 153–156.

Sub-s (5): Application.

As to the making of an application for a premises licence, see s 159.

Application

See the note to s 150.

Subordinate legislation

Gambling (Geographical Distribution of Large and Small Casino Premises Licences) Order 2008, SI 2008/1327 (made under sub-s (4)).

As to orders under this Act generally, see s 355.

Definitions

'casino': ss 7, 353(1)
'a licensing authority': ss 2, 353(1)
'premises licence': s 353(1)

Explanatory Notes

457 [para **6.2011** below]

6.676 176 Casino premises licence: access by children

(1) The Commission shall issue one or more codes of practice under section 24 about access to casino premises for children and young persons.

(2) The code or codes issued in accordance with subsection (1) shall, in particular—

(a) require the holder of a casino premises licence to take specified steps to ensure that no child or young person enters premises or a part of premises which it would be an offence under section 47 to permit him to enter ('prohibited premises or areas'),

(b) for that purpose, require the holder of a casino premises licence to ensure—

(i) that each entrance to prohibited premises or to a prohibited area is supervised by one or more persons whose responsibilities include ensuring compliance with the code of practice ('the supervisor'), and

(ii) that arrangements are made to require evidence of age to be produced by any person seeking admission to prohibited premises or to a prohibited area unless the supervisor, reasonably, is certain that the person seeking admission is an adult, and

(c) make provision about the nature of evidence that may be used for the purpose of arrangements made in accordance with paragraph (b)(ii).

(3) A casino premises licence shall by virtue of this section be subject to the condition that the licensee ensures compliance with any relevant code of practice issued in accordance with subsection (1).

Note

See LCCP, Part II, December 2011 (see para **6.2060** below).

Commencement

Subsections (1), (2) brought into force by the Gambling Act 2005 (Commencement No 6 and Transitional Provisions) Order 2006, SI 2006/3272, art 2, Schs 2, 3 as from 30 April 2007; for transitional provisions see art 6, Sch 4 thereto (as amended by SI 2007/1157, arts 7–12).

Subsection (3) brought into force by the Gambling Act 2005 (Commencement No 6 and Transitional Provisions) Order 2006, SI 2006/3272, art 2 as from 1 September 2007; for transitional provisions see art 6, Sch 4 thereto (as amended by SI 2007/1157, arts 7–12).

Sub-s (1): The Commission. Ie the Gambling Commission; see s 353(1). As to the establishment, etc of the Gambling Commission, see s 20, Sch 4, and the note 'Gambling Commission' to that section.

Sub-s (2): Premises licence. As to the nature, etc of premises licences, see s 150 and the note 'Premises licence' thereto.

Application

See the note to s 150.

Definitions

'adult': s 353(1)
'casino': ss 7, 353(1)
'child': ss 45(1), 353(1)
'the Commission': s 353(1)
'holder': s 213(d)
'licensee': s 213(e)
'premises': s 353(1), (2)(g)
'premises licence': s 353(1)
'young person': ss 45(2), 353(1)

Explanatory Notes

461–463 [para **6.2011** below]

6.677 177 Credit

(1) This section applies to—

(a) casino premises licences, and
(b) bingo premises licences.

(2) A premises licence to which this section applies shall by virtue of this section be subject to the condition that the licensee does not—

(a) give credit in connection with gambling authorised by the licence, or
(b) participate in, arrange, permit or knowingly facilitate the giving of credit in connection with gambling authorised by the licence.

(3) But the condition in subsection (2) shall not prevent the licensee from permitting the installation and use on the premises of a machine enabling cash to be obtained on credit from a person (the 'credit provider') provided that—

(a) the licensee has no other commercial connection with the credit provider in relation to gambling,
(b) the licensee neither makes nor receives any payment or reward (whether by way of commission, rent or otherwise) in connection with the machine, and
(c) any conditions about the nature, location or use of the machine attached by virtue of section 167, 168 or 169 are complied with.

(4) In this section 'credit' has the same meaning as in section 81.

Commencement

Brought into force by the Gambling Act 2005 (Commencement No 6 and Transitional Provisions) Order 2006, SI 2006/3272, art 2 as from 1 September 2007; for transitional provisions see art 6, Sch 4 thereto (as amended by SI 2007/1157, arts 7–12).

Sub-s (1): Premises licence. As to the nature, etc of premises licences, see s 150 and the note 'Premises licence' thereto.

Sub-s (3): Person. See the note 'Persons' to s 23.

Application

See the note to s 150.

Definitions

'gambling': ss 3, 353(1)
'licensee': s 213(e)
'machine': ss 235(3)(a), 353(1)
'premises licence': s 353(1)

Explanatory Notes

464, 465 [para **6.2011** below]

6.678 178 Door supervision

(1) Where a condition for door supervision is attached to a premises licence (whether by virtue of section 167, 168 or 169) subsection (3) shall apply in relation to the licence.

(2) In subsection (1) 'condition for door supervision' means a condition requiring that one or more persons be responsible for guarding the premises against unauthorised access or occupation, against outbreaks of disorder or against damage.

(3) If the person carrying out the guarding mentioned in subsection (2) is required by the Private Security Industry Act 2001 (c 12) to hold a licence under that Act authorising the guarding, the requirement under that Act shall be treated for the purposes of this Act as if it were a condition of the premises licence attached by virtue of this section.

Commencement

Brought into force by the Gambling Act 2005 (Commencement No 6 and Transitional Provisions) Order 2006, SI 2006/3272, art 2 as from 1 September 2007; for transitional provisions see art 6, Sch 4 thereto (as amended by SI 2007/1157, arts 7–12).

Sub-s (1): Premises licence. As to the nature, etc of premises licences, see s 150 and the note 'Premises licence' thereto.

Application

See the note to s 150.

Definitions

'premises': s 353(1), (2)(g)

'premises licence': s 353(1)

Explanatory Notes

466, 467 [para **6.2011** below]

6.679 179 Pool betting on track

(1) A betting premises licence in respect of a track may not authorise the acceptance of bets by way of pool betting except in a case to which subsection (2) applies.

(2) This subsection applies to the acceptance of bets, by way of pool betting on horse-racing or dog-racing—

(a) by the holder of the betting premises licence, or

(b) in accordance with arrangements made by him.

(3) The Secretary of State may by order amend this section so as to—

(a) add an exception to subsection (1),

(b) amend an exception to subsection (1), or

(c) remove an exception to subsection (1).

Commencement

Brought into force by the Gambling Act 2005 (Commencement No 6 and Transitional Provisions) Order 2006, SI 2006/3272, art 2 as from 1 September 2007; for transitional provisions see art 6, Sch 4 thereto (as amended by SI 2007/1157, arts 7–12).

Sub-s (1): Premises licence. As to the nature, etc of premises licences, see s 150 and the note 'Premises licence' thereto.

Sub-s (3): Secretary of State. See the note to s 4.

Application

See the note to s 150.

Orders under this section

At the time of going to press no orders had been made under this section.

As to orders under this Act generally, see s 355.

Definitions

'accepting a bet': s 353(2)(a)
'holder': s 213(d)
'pool betting': ss 12, 353(1)
'premises licence': s 353(1)
'track': s 353(1)

Explanatory Notes

468–471 [para **6.2011** below]

6.680 180 Pool betting on dog races

(1) A betting premises licence in respect of premises other than a dog track shall by virtue of this section be subject to the condition that pool bets may not be accepted in reliance on the licence in respect of dog-racing other than in accordance with arrangements made with the occupier of the dog track on which the racing takes place.

(2) The Secretary of State may by order repeal this section.

(3) A repeal by order under subsection (2) shall cause the condition attached by subsection (1) to premises licences in force on the date of the repeal to lapse in respect of anything done on or after the date of the repeal.

(4) This section shall cease to have effect at the end of 31st December 2012 (and the condition attached by subsection (1) to premises licences in force on that date shall lapse in respect of anything done after that date).

Commencement

Brought into force by the Gambling Act 2005 (Commencement No 6 and Transitional Provisions) Order 2006, SI 2006/3272, art 2 as from 1 September 2007; for transitional provisions see art 6, Sch 4 thereto (as amended by SI 2007/1157, arts 7–12).

Sub-s (1): Premises licence. As to the nature, etc of premises licences, see s 150 and the note 'Premises licence' thereto.

Sub-s (2): Secretary of State. See the note to s 4.

Application

See the note to s 150.

Orders under this section

At the time of going to press no orders had been made under this section.

As to orders under this Act generally, see s 355.

Definitions

'dog track': s 353(1)
'premises': s 353(1), (2)(g)
'premises licence': s 353(1)

Explanatory Notes

472, 473 [para **6.2011** below]

6.681 181 Betting machines

(1) A condition of a betting premises licence may relate to—

(a) the number of machines used on the premises for the purpose of making or accepting bets;

(b) the nature of those machines;

(c) the circumstances in which those machines are made available for use.

(2) A condition of a casino premises licence may relate to—

(a) the number of machines used on the premises for the purpose of making or accepting bets;

(b) the nature of those machines;

(c) the circumstances in which those machines are made available for use.

(3) In this section 'condition' means a condition imposed by virtue of section 167, 168 or 169.

Commencement

Brought into force by the Gambling Act 2005 (Commencement No 6 and Transitional Provisions) Order 2006, SI 2006/3272, art 2, Sch 2 as from 30 April 2007; for transitional provisions see art 6, Sch 4 thereto (as amended by SI 2007/1157, arts 7–12).

Sub-s (1): Premises licence. As to the nature, etc of premises licences, see s 150 and the note 'Premises licence' thereto.

Application

See the note to s 150.

Definitions

'accepting a bet': s 353(2)(a)
'machine': ss 235(3)(a), 353(1)
'premises': s 353(1), (2)(g)
'premises licence': s 353(1)

Explanatory Notes

474, 475 [para **6.2011** below]

6.682 182 Exclusion of children from track areas

(1) A premises licence in respect of a track shall by virtue of this section be subject to the condition that the licensee shall ensure that children and young persons are excluded from—

(a) any area where facilities for betting are provided, and

(b) any area where a gaming machine, other than a Category D machine, is situated.

(2) But subsection (1)(a)—

(a) shall not apply to a dog track on a day on which dog-racing takes place, or is expected to take place, on the track, . . . [1]

(b) shall not apply to a horse-race course on a day on which horse-racing takes place, or is expected to take place, on the course[, and][1]

[(c) shall not apply to any other track on a day on which a race or other sporting event takes place, or is expected to take place, on the track][1].

(3) For the purposes of this section a reference to the area where facilities are provided or where a machine is situated is a reference to any place in which it is possible to take advantage of the facilities or use the machine.

(4) The Secretary of State may by order amend this section so as to—

(a) provide an additional exception to subsection (1)(a),

(b) remove an exception to subsection (1)(a), or

(c) amend an exception to subsection (1)(a).

Commencement

Brought into force by the Gambling Act 2005 (Commencement No 6 and Transitional Provisions) Order 2006, SI 2006/3272, art 2 as from 1 September 2007; for transitional provisions see art 6, Sch 4 thereto (as amended by SI 2007/1157, arts 7–12).

Sub-s (1): Premises licence. As to the nature, etc of premises licences, see s 150 and the note 'Premises licence' thereto.

Sub-s (1): Are excluded. A person commits an offence if he invites or permits a child or young person to enter an area from which children and young persons are required to be excluded by virtue of this section; see s 47(6).

Sub-s (1): Category D gaming machine. As to the categories of gaming machine, see s 236.

Sub-s (4): Secretary of State. See the note to s 4.

Application

See the note to s 150.

This section is applied in relation to a notice treated as a premises licence by virtue of s 60(1) by s 60(2).

Orders under this section

At the time of going to press no orders had been made under this section.

As to orders under this Act generally, see s 355.

Definitions

'betting': ss 9–11, 353(1)
'Category D gaming machine': s 353(1)
'child': ss 45(1), 353(1)
'dog track': s 353(1)
'gaming machine': ss 235, 353(1)
'horse-race course': s 353(1)
'licensee': s 213(e)
'premises licence': s 353(1)
'providing facilities for gambling': ss 5, 353(2)(i)
'track': s 353(1)
'young person': ss 45(2), 353(1)

Explanatory Notes

476, 477 [para **6.2011** below]

---

1 Word omitted repealed, word and para (c) inserted by SI 2007/1410, art 2.

6.683 183 Christmas Day

A premises licence shall, by virtue of this section, be subject to the condition that the premises shall not be used to provide facilities for gambling on Christmas Day.

Commencement

Brought into force by the Gambling Act 2005 (Commencement No 6 and Transitional Provisions) Order 2006, SI 2006/3272, art 2 as from 1 September 2007; for transitional provisions see art 6, Sch 4 thereto (as amended by SI 2007/1157, arts 7–12).

Premises licence

As to the nature, etc of premises licences, see s 150 and the note 'Premises licence' thereto.

Application

See the note to s 150.

Definitions

'gambling': ss 3, 353(1)
'premises': s 353(1), (2)(g)
'premises licence': s 353(1)
'providing facilities for gambling': ss 5, 353(2)(i)

Maintenance

6.684 184 Annual fee

(1) The holder of a premises licence—

(a) shall pay a first annual fee to the licensing authority within such period after the issue of the licence as may be prescribed, and

(b) shall pay an annual fee to the licensing authority before each anniversary of the issue of the licence.

(2) In this section 'annual fee' means a fee of such amount as may be prescribed; and 'prescribed' means prescribed by regulations made—

(a) in relation to premises licences issued by authorities in England and Wales, by the Secretary of State, and

(b) in relation to premises licences issued by authorities in Scotland, by the Scottish Ministers.

(3) Regulations prescribing the annual fee may, in particular, make different provision for—

(a) licences authorising different classes of activity, or

(b) different circumstances.

(4) The Secretary of State may by regulations—

(a) require a licensing authority to refund a prescribed part of an annual fee paid under this section where a premises licence ceases to have effect otherwise than on or immediately before an anniversary of its issue,

(b) require a licensing authority to refund a prescribed part of an annual fee paid under this section if a premises licence is altered under section 186, 187, 188 or 202 and the annual fee for the licence as altered is less than the annual fee for the licence before alteration, and

(c) require a licensee to pay an additional amount by way of annual fee if a premises licence is altered under section 186, 187, 188 or 202 and the annual fee for the licence as altered is more than the annual fee for the licence before alteration.

(5) In relation to premises licences issued by authorities in Scotland, subsection (4) shall have effect as if the reference to the Secretary of State were a reference to the Scottish Ministers.

(6) Subsection (1)(b) does not apply in relation to an anniversary of the issue of a licence on or immediately before which the licence expires in accordance with regulations under section 191(1).

Commencement

Brought into force by the Gambling Act 2005 (Commencement No 6 and Transitional Provisions) Order 2006, SI 2006/3272, art 2, Sch 2 as from 30 April 2007; for transitional provisions see art 6, Sch 4 thereto (as amended by SI 2007/1157, arts 7–12).

Sub-s (1): Premises licence. As to the nature, etc of premises licences, see s 150 and the note 'Premises licence' thereto.

Sub-s (1): Annual fee. For the power of the licensing authority to revoke an premises licence if the holder fails to pay the annual fee in accordance with regulations under this section, see s 193.

Sub-s (1): Licensing authority. For the licensing authorities for the purposes of this Act, see s 2. As to the licensing authorities' functions, see ss 153–156.

Sub-s (2): England; Wales.

See the note to s 2.

Sub-s (2): Secretary of State. See the note to s 4.

Sub-s (2): Scottish Ministers. See the note to s 25.

Application

See the note to s 150.

Subordinate Legislation

Gambling (Premises Licence Fees) (England and Wales) Regulations 2007, SI 2007/479 (made under sub-ss (1)–(4)).

As to regulations under this Act generally, see s 355.

Definitions

'holder': s 213(d)

'a licensing authority': ss 2, 353(1)

'the licensing authority': s 213(f)

'premises licence': s 353(1)

Explanatory Notes

479, 480 [para **6.2011** below]

6.685 185 Availability of licence

(1) The holder of a premises licence shall—

(a) keep the licence on the premises, and

(b) arrange for the licence to be made available on request to—

(i) a constable,

(ii) an enforcement officer, or

(iii) an authorised local authority officer.

(2) A person commits an offence if he fails without reasonable excuse to comply with subsection (1).

(3) A person guilty of an offence under subsection (2) shall be liable on summary conviction to a fine not exceeding level 2 on the standard scale.

Commencement

Brought into force by the Gambling Act 2005 (Commencement No 6 and Transitional Provisions) Order 2006, SI 2006/3272, art 2 as from 1 September 2007; for transitional provisions see art 6, Sch 4 thereto (as amended by SI 2007/1157, arts 7–12).

Sub-s (1): Premises licence. As to the nature, etc of premises licences, see s 150 and the note 'Premises licence' thereto.

Sub-s (1): Constable. See the note to s 64.

Sub-s (1): Enforcement officer. As to enforcement officers, see, generally, s 303.

Sub-s (2): Person. See the note 'Persons' to s 23.

Sub-s (2): Offence. For the power of the Gambling Commission and other specified persons to undertake activities for the purpose of assessing whether an offence is being committed under or by virtue of this Act, see s 27 and s 305; for the power of that Commission to investigate and prosecute offences, see s 28; as to offences committed by a body, see s 341; and for the time limit on prosecutions, see s 347. See also s 306 for powers of entry as respects a suspected offence, and s 345 as respects forfeiture of an article relating to an offence.

For the power of a licensing authority to institute criminal proceedings in respect of an offence under this section, see s 346.

Sub-s (3): Summary conviction; standard scale. See the notes to s 33.

Application

See the note to s 150.

Definitions

'authorised local authority officer': ss 304, 353(1)
'enforcement officer': s 353(1)
'holder': s 213(d)
'premises': s 353(1), (2)(g)
'premises licence': s 353(1)

Explanatory Notes

481 [para **6.2011** below]

6.686 186 Change of circumstance

(1) If the holder of a premises licence ceases to reside or attend at the address specified in the licence under section 151(1)(b) he shall as soon as is reasonably practicable—

(a) notify the licensing authority, and

(b) inform the licensing authority of a home or business address at which he resides or attends.

(2) The Secretary of State may make regulations requiring the holder of a premises licence—

(a) to notify the licensing authority of any change of circumstance of a prescribed kind in relation to him or to an authorised activity, and

(b) to give the licensing authority prescribed details of the change.

(3) If a change of circumstance notified under or by virtue of this section falsifies information contained in the premises licence in accordance with section 151, the notification must be accompanied by—

(a) the prescribed fee, and

(b) either—

(i) the licence, or

(ii) an application under section 190 for a copy of the licence.

(4) Where notification is accompanied by the licence, the licensing authority shall—

(a) make such alteration to the information contained in the licence as appears to them to be required by the change in circumstance, and

(b) return the licence to the licensee.

(5) Where the notification is accompanied by an application for a copy of the licence, the licensing authority shall, if they grant the application, issue the copy in a form which appears to them to reflect the change in circumstance.

(6) The holder of a premises licence commits an offence if he fails without reasonable excuse to comply with a provision of this section or of regulations made under this section.

(7) A person guilty of an offence under subsection (6) shall be liable on summary conviction to a fine not exceeding level 2 on the standard scale.

(8) This section does not prevent the imposition of a requirement to notify the licensing authority of a specified change of circumstance by way of the attachment of a condition to a premises licence.

(9) In subsection (3)(a) 'prescribed' means—

(a) in relation to notification given to authorities in England and Wales, prescribed by regulations made by the Secretary of State, and

(b) in relation to notifications given to authorities in Scotland, prescribed by regulations made by the Scottish Ministers.

Commencement

Brought into force by the Gambling Act 2005 (Commencement No 6 and Transitional Provisions) Order 2006, SI 2006/3272, art 2, Sch 2 as from 30 April 2007; for transitional provisions see art 6, Sch 4 thereto (as amended by SI 2007/1157, arts 7–12).

Sub-s (1): Premises licence. As to the nature, etc of premises licences, see s 150 and the note 'Premises licence' thereto.

Sub-s (1): Notify. See further, in connection with a requirement under this Act to give a notice, s 353(4).

Sub-s (1): Licensing authority. For the licensing authorities for the purposes of this Act, see s 2. As to the licensing authorities' functions, see ss 153–156.

Sub-s (2): Secretary of State. See the note to s 4.

Sub-s (6): Offence. For the power of the Gambling Commission and other specified persons to undertake activities for the purpose of assessing whether an offence is being committed under or by virtue of this Act, see s 27 and s 305; for the power of that Commission to investigate and prosecute offences, see s 28; as to offences committed by a body, see s 341; and for the time limit on prosecutions, see s 347. See also s 306 for powers of entry as respects a suspected offence, and s 345 as respects forfeiture of an article relating to an offence.

For the power of a licensing authority to institute criminal proceedings in respect of an offence under this section, see s 346.

Sub-s (7): Summary conviction; standard scale. See the notes to s 33.

Sub-s (9): England; Wales. See the note to s 2.

Sub-s (9): Scottish Ministers. See the note to s 25.

Application

See the note to s 150.

Subordinate Legislation

Gambling (Premises Licence Fees) (England and Wales) Regulations 2007, SI 2007/479 (made under sub-ss (3)(a), (9)(a)).

As to regulations under this Act generally, see s 355.

Definitions

'authorised activity': s 213(a)
'holder': s 213(d)
'licensee': s 213(e)
'the licensing authority': s 213(f)
'premises licence': s 353(1)
'prescribed': s 213(g)

Explanatory Notes

482 [para **6.2011** below]

6.687 187 Application to vary licence

(1) The holder of a premises licence may apply to the licensing authority to vary the licence by—

(a) adding, amending or removing an authorised activity,
(b) amending another detail of the licence,
(c) excluding a condition attached by virtue of section 168, or
(d) adding, amending or removing a condition attached to the licence under section 169.

(2) A licence may not be varied under this section so as to relate to premises to which it did not previously relate.

(3) The provisions of this Part shall apply in relation to an application for variation as they apply in relation to an application for a premises licence—

(a) subject to the provisions of this section, and
(b) with any other necessary modifications.

(4) Regulations under this Part which relate to an application for a premises licence may make—

(a) provision which applies only in the case of an application for variation;
(b) provision which does not apply in the case of an application for variation;
(c) different provision in relation to an application for variation from that made in relation to an application for a premises licence;
(d) different provision in relation to applications for variations of different kinds.

(5) An application for variation must (in addition to anything required by section 159) be accompanied by a statement of the variation sought.

(6) An application for variation must (in addition to anything required by section 159) also be accompanied by—

(a) the licence to be varied, or
(b) both—
    (i) a statement explaining why it is not reasonably practicable to produce the licence, and
    (ii) an application under section 190 for the issue of a copy of the licence.

(7) In granting an application for variation a licensing authority—

(a) shall specify a time when the variation shall begin to have effect, and
(b) may make transitional provision.

Commencement

Brought into force by the Gambling Act 2005 (Commencement No 6 and Transitional Provisions) Order 2006, SI 2006/3272, art 2, Sch 2 as from 30 April 2007; for transitional provisions see art 6, Sch 4 thereto (as amended by SI 2007/1157, arts 7–12).

Sub-s (1): Premises licence. As to the nature, etc of premises licences, see s 150 and the note 'Premises licence' thereto.

Sub-s (1): May apply. As to appeals, see ss 206–209.

Sub-s (1): Licensing authority. For the licensing authorities for the purposes of this Act, see s 2. As to the licensing authorities' functions, see ss 153–156.

Sub-s (3): This Part. Ie Pt 8 (ss 150–213 and Sch 9) of this Act.

Application

See the note to s 150.

Subordinate Legislation

Gambling Act 2005 (Premises Licences and Provisional Statements) Regulations 2007, SI 2007/459 (made under sub-ss (3), (4)).

Gambling (Premises Licence Fees) (England and Wales) Regulations 2007, SI 2007/479 (made under sub-ss (3), (4)).

Definitions

'authorised activity': s 213(a)
'holder': s 213(d)
'a licensing authority': ss 2, 353(1)
'the licensing authority': s 213(f)
'premises': s 353(1), (2)(g)
'premises licence': s 353(1)

Explanatory Notes

483–485 [para **6.2011** below]

6.688 188 Transfer

(1) A person may apply to a licensing authority for a premises licence to be transferred to him.

(2) The provisions of this Part shall apply in relation to an application for transfer as they apply in relation to an application for a premises licence—

(a) subject to the provisions of this section and section 189, and
(b) with any other necessary modifications.

(3) An application for transfer must (in addition to anything required by section 159)—

(a) specify the time when the transfer is to take effect, and
(b) be accompanied by a written statement by the licensee consenting to the transfer.

(4) A licensing authority shall grant an application for transfer unless they think it would be wrong to do so having regard to representations made under section 161 (as applied by subsection (2) above).

(5) On the grant of an application for the transfer of a premises licence the licensing authority—

(a) shall alter the licence so that the applicant for the transfer becomes the licensee,
(b) shall specify in the licence the time when the transfer takes effect (being either the time specified in the application under subsection (3) above or, if later, the time when the application is granted), and
(c) shall make such other alteration of the licence as appears to them to be required (which may, in particular, include an alteration to reflect a decision of the authority under section 169 as applied by subsection (2) above to make new or varied provision for the attachment or exclusion of conditions).

(6) A licence to which a condition is attached under section 169 for the purpose of giving effect to an agreement entered into under paragraph 5(3)(b) of Schedule 9 ('the original agreement') shall not be transferred unless—

(a) the transferee enters into an agreement ('the new agreement') which appears to the licensing authority to have substantially the same effect as the original agreement, and

(b) the condition is altered so as to give effect to the new agreement.

Commencement

Brought into force by the Gambling Act 2005 (Commencement No 6 and Transitional Provisions) Order 2006, SI 2006/3272, art 2, Sch 2 as from 30 April 2007; for transitional provisions see art 6, Sch 4 thereto (as amended by SI 2007/1157, arts 7–12).

Sub-s (1): Person. See the note 'Persons' to s 23.

Sub-s (1): May apply. As to appeals, see ss 206–209.

Sub-s (1): Licensing authority. For the licensing authorities for the purposes of this Act, see s 2. As to the licensing authorities' functions, see ss 153–156.

Sub-s (1): Premises licence. As to the nature, etc of premises licences, see s 150 and the note 'Premises licence' thereto.

Sub-s (2): This Part. Ie Pt 8 (ss 150–213 and Sch 9) of this Act.

Sub-s (3): Written. See the note 'Writing' to s 39.

Supplemental provisions

See s 189.

Application

See the note to s 150.

Subordinate Legislation

Gambling Act 2005 (Premises Licences and Provisional Statements) Regulations 2007, SI 2007/459 (made under sub-s (2)).

Gambling (Premises Licence Fees) (England and Wales) Regulations 2007, SI 2007/479 (made under sub-s (2)).

Definitions

'licensee': s 213(e)
'a licensing authority': ss 2, 353(1)
'the licensing authority': s 213(f)
'premises licence': s 353(1)

Explanatory Notes

486–493 [para **6.2011** below]

6.689 189 Transfer: supplemental

(1) If an application for transfer under section 188 states that the applicant has failed to contact the licensee having taken all reasonable steps to do so, the licensing authority shall—

(a) disapply section 188(3)(b) and take all reasonable steps to notify the licensee, or

(b) determine not to disapply section 188(3)(b) and notify the applicant of their determination and the reasons for it.

(2) An application for transfer must (in addition to anything required by section 159) be accompanied by—

(a) the licence, or

(b) both—

(i) a statement explaining why it is not reasonably practicable to produce the licence, and

(ii) an application by the licensee under section 190 for the issue of a copy of the licence.

(3) In relation to an application for transfer to which subsection (1) applies, for the purposes of any application under section 190 required in accordance with subsection (2)(b)(ii) above—

(a) the application under that section shall be made by the applicant for transfer, and

(b) a reference to the licence being lost, stolen or damaged shall be treated as a reference to the licence being unavailable to the applicant for transfer.

(4) Regulations under section 160, as they have effect in relation to applications for transfer by virtue of section 188(2), may require notice to be given to specified responsible authorities (and not to all responsible authorities).

(5) Section 161 shall have effect in relation to an application for transfer with the omission of the reference to interested parties.

(6) If an application for the transfer of a premises licence includes a request that this subsection apply, the licence shall have effect as if the applicant for transfer were the licensee during the period—

(a) beginning with the receipt of the application for transfer by the licensing authority, and

(b) ending with the determination of the application by the licensing authority.

Commencement

Brought into force by the Gambling Act 2005 (Commencement No 6 and Transitional Provisions) Order 2006, SI 2006/3272, art 2, Sch 2 as from 30 April 2007; for transitional provisions see art 6, Sch 4 thereto (as amended by SI 2007/1157, arts 7–12).

Sub-s (1): Licensing authority. For the licensing authorities for the purposes of this Act, see s 2. As to the licensing authorities' functions, see ss 153–156.

Sub-s (1): Notify. See further, in connection with a requirement under this Act to give a notice, s 353(4).

Sub-s (4): Responsible authorities. See s 157.

Sub-s (6): Premises licence. As to the nature, etc of premises licences, see s 150 and the note 'Premises licence' thereto.

Application

See the note to s 150.

Subordinate Legislation

Gambling Act 2005 (Premises Licences and Provisional Statements) Regulations 2007, SI 2007/459 (made under sub-s (4)).

Definitions

'licensee': s 213(e)
'the licensing authority': s 213(f)
'premises licence': s 353(1)

Explanatory Notes

486–493 [para **6.2011** below]

6.690 190 Copy of licence

(1) Where a premises licence issued, or a summary given, under section 164 is lost, stolen or damaged, the licensee may apply to the licensing authority for a copy.

(2) An application under subsection (1) must be accompanied by the prescribed fee.

(3) A licensing authority shall consider an application under this section as soon as is reasonably practicable and shall grant it if satisfied—

(a) that the licence or summary to which the application relates has been lost, stolen or damaged, and

(b) where the licence or summary has been lost or stolen, that the loss or theft has been reported to the police.

(4) As soon as is reasonably practicable after granting an application under this section a licensing authority shall issue a copy of the licence or summary to the applicant—

(a) certified by the authority as a true copy, and

(b) in, or in relation to, the form in which the licence had effect before the loss, theft or damage.

(5) A copy of a licence or summary issued under this section shall be treated as if it were the licence or summary.

(6) In subsection (2) 'prescribed' means—

(a) in relation to applications to authorities in England and Wales, prescribed by regulations made by the Secretary of State, and

(b) in relation to applications to authorities in Scotland, prescribed by regulations made by the Scottish Ministers.

Commencement

Brought into force by the Gambling Act 2005 (Commencement No 6 and Transitional Provisions) Order 2006, SI 2006/3272, art 2, Sch 2 as from 30 April 2007; for transitional provisions see art 6, Sch 4 thereto (as amended by SI 2007/1157, arts 7–12).

Sub-s (1): Premises licence. As to the nature, etc of premises licences, see s 150 and the note 'Premises licence' thereto.

Sub-s (1): May apply. As to appeals, see ss 206–209.

Sub-s (1): Licensing authority. For the licensing authorities for the purposes of this Act, see s 2. As to the licensing authorities' functions, see ss 153–156.

Sub-s (6): England; Wales. See the note to s 2.

Sub-s (6): Secretary of State. See the note to s 4.

Sub-s (6): Scottish Ministers. See the note to s 25.

Application

See the note to s 150.

Subordinate Legislation

Gambling (Premises Licence Fees) (England and Wales) Regulations 2007, SI 2007/479 (made under sub-ss (2), (6)(a)).

As to regulations under this Act generally, see s 355.

Definitions

'licensee': s 213(e)
'a licensing authority': ss 2, 353(1)
'the licensing authority': s 213(f)
'premises licence': s 353(1)

Explanatory Notes

494 [para **6.2011** below]

Duration

6.691 191 Initial duration

(1) The Secretary of State may by regulations prescribe a period at the end of which premises licences expire (unless they cease to have effect earlier in accordance with a provision of this Part).

(2) Regulations under this section may make provision about renewal (and may, in particular, apply or make provision similar to any provision of this Part about an application for a premises licence).

(3) Regulations under this section may make provision which applies to licences issued before the regulations are made.

(4) If the Secretary of State does not prescribe a period under this section in respect of a premises licence, it shall continue to have effect unless and until it ceases to have effect in accordance with a provision of this Part.

Commencement

Brought into force by the Gambling Act 2005 (Commencement No 6 and Transitional Provisions) Order 2006, SI 2006/3272, art 2 as from 1 September 2007; for transitional provisions see art 6, Sch 4 thereto (as amended by SI 2007/1157, arts 7–12).

Sub-s (1): Secretary of State. See the note to s 4.

Sub-s (1): Prescribe a period. A premises licence must, if a period is prescribed under this section at the end of which the licence will expire (unless renewed or terminated earlier), specify the period; see s 151(1)(h).

Sub-s (1): Premises licence. As to the nature, etc of premises licences, see s 150 and the note 'Premises licence' thereto.

Sub-s (1): This Part. Ie Pt 8 (ss 150–213 and Sch 9) of this Act.

Application

See the note to s 150.

Regulations under this section

At the time of going to press no regulations had been made under this section.

As to regulations under this Act generally, see s 355.

Definitions

'premises licence': s 353(1)

Explanatory Notes

495, 496 [para **6.2011** below]

6.692 192 Surrender

(1) A premises licence shall cease to have effect if the licensee—

(a) notifies the licensing authority of his intention to surrender the licence, and

(b) gives the licensing authority either—

(i) the licence, or

(ii) a written statement explaining why it is not reasonably practicable to produce the licence.

(2) As soon as is reasonably practicable after receipt of notification under subsection (1)(a) the licensing authority shall notify—

(a) the Commission,

(b) either—

(i) in England and Wales, the chief officer of police for any area in which the premises are wholly or partly situated, or

(ii) in Scotland, the chief constable of the police force maintained for a police area in which the premises are wholly or partly situated, and

(c) Her Majesty's [Commissioners for Her Majesty's Revenue and Customs] [1].

Commencement

Brought into force by the Gambling Act 2005 (Commencement No 6 and Transitional Provisions) Order 2006, SI 2006/3272, art 2, Sch 2 as from 30 April 2007; for transitional provisions see art 6, Sch 4 thereto (as amended by SI 2007/1157, arts 7–12).

Sub-s (1): Premises licence. As to the nature, etc of premises licences, see s 150 and the note 'Premises licence' thereto.

Sub-s (1): Licensing authority. For the licensing authorities for the purposes of this Act, see s 2. As to the licensing authorities' functions, see ss 153–156.

Sub-s (1): Written. See the note 'Writing' to s 39.

Sub-s (2): Notify. See further, in connection with a requirement under this Act to give a notice, s 353(4).

Sub-s (2): The Commission. Ie the Gambling Commission; see s 353(1). As to the establishment, etc of the Gambling Commission, see s 20, Sch 4, and the note 'Gambling Commission' to that section.

Sub-s (2): England; Wales. See the note to s 2.

Sub-s (2): Commissioners for Her Majesty's Revenue and Customs. See the note to s 23.

Application

See the note to s 150.

Definitions

'chief officer of police': s 213(b)
'chief officer's area': s 213(c)
'the Commission': s 353(1)
'licensee': s 213(e)
'the licensing authority': s 213(f)
'premises': s 353(1), (2)(g)
'premises licence': s 353(1)

Explanatory Notes

497 [para **6.2011** below]

---

[1] Words in square brackets substituted by virtue of the Commissioners for Revenue and Customs Act 2005, s 50(1), (7).

6.693 193 Revocation for failure to pay fee

(1) Where the holder of a premises licence fails to pay the annual fee in accordance with regulations under section 184 the licensing authority shall revoke the licence.

(2) But the licensing authority may disapply subsection (1) if they think that a failure to pay is attributable to administrative error.

Commencement

Brought into force by the Gambling Act 2005 (Commencement No 6 and Transitional Provisions) Order 2006, SI 2006/3272, art 2 as from 1 September 2007; for transitional provisions see art 6, Sch 4 thereto (as amended by SI 2007/1157, arts 7–12).

Sub-s (1): Premises licence. As to the nature, etc of premises licences, see s 150 and the note 'Premises licence' thereto.

Sub-s (1): Licensing authority. For the licensing authorities for the purposes of this Act, see s 2. As to the licensing authorities' functions, see ss 153–156.

Application

See the note to s 150.

Definitions

'holder': s 213(d)
'the licensing authority': s 213(f)
'premises licence': s 353(1)

Explanatory Notes

498 [para **6.2011** below]

6.694 194 Lapse

(1) In the case of a premises licence issued to an individual, the licence shall lapse if—

(a) the licensee dies,

(b) the licensee becomes, in the opinion of the licensing authority as notified to the licensee, incapable of carrying on the licensed activities by reason of mental or physical incapacity,

(c) the licensee becomes bankrupt (within the meaning of section 381 of the Insolvency Act 1986 (c 45)) [or a debt relief order is made in respect of the licensee (under Part 7A of the Insolvency Act 1986),], or

(d) sequestration of the licensee's estate is awarded under section 12(1) of the Bankruptcy (Scotland) Act 1985 (c 66).

(2) In any other case a premises licence shall lapse if the licensee—

(a) ceases to exist, or

(b) goes into liquidation (within the meaning of section 247(2) of the Insolvency Act 1986).

(3) If a licensing authority become aware that a premises licence issued by them has lapsed, they shall as soon as is reasonably practicable notify—

(a) the Commission,

(b) either—

(i) in England and Wales, the chief officer of police for any area in which the premises are wholly or partly situated, or

(ii) in Scotland, the chief constable of the police force maintained for a police area in which the premises are wholly or partly situated, and

(c) Her Majesty's [Commissioners for Her Majesty's Revenue and Customs].

Commencement

Brought into force by the Gambling Act 2005 (Commencement No 6 and Transitional Provisions) Order 2006, SI 2006/3272, art 2, Sch 2 as from 30 April 2007; for transitional provisions see art 6, Sch 4 thereto (as amended by SI 2007/1157, arts 7–12).

Amendment

Sub-s (1): in para (c) words in square brackets inserted by SI 2012/2404, art 3(2), Sch 2, para 55.

Sub-s (3): words in square brackets substituted by virtue of the Commissioners for Revenue and Customs Act 2005, s 50(1), (7).

Sub-s (1): Premises licence. As to the nature, etc of premises licences, see s 150 and the note 'Premises licence' thereto.

Sub-s (1): Shall lapse. As to reinstatement, see ss 195, 196.

Sub-s (1): Licensing authority. For the licensing authorities for the purposes of this Act, see s 2. As to the licensing authorities' functions, see ss 153–156.

Sub-s (3): Notify. See further, in connection with a requirement under this Act to give a notice, s 353(4).

Sub-s (3): The Commission. Ie the Gambling Commission; see s 353(1). As to the establishment, etc of the Gambling Commission, see s 20, Sch 4, and the note 'Gambling Commission' to that section.

Sub-s (3): England; Wales. See the note to s 2.

Sub-s (3): Commissioners for Her Majesty's Revenue and Customs. See the note to s 23.

Application

See the note to s 150.

Definitions

'chief officer of police': s 213(b)
'chief officer's area': s 213(c)
'the Commission': s 353(1)
'licensee': s 213(e)
'a licensing authority': ss 2, 353(1)
'the licensing authority': s 213(f)
'premises': s 353(1), (2)(g)
'premises licence': s 353(1)

Explanatory Notes

499, 500 [para **6.2011** below]

6.695 195 Reinstatement

(1) This section applies where a premises licence lapses under section 194.

(2) During the period of six months beginning with the date of the lapse of the premises licence a person may apply to the licensing authority for the licence to be reinstated with the applicant as the licensee.

(3) The provisions of this Part shall apply in relation to an application for reinstatement as they apply in relation to an application for a premises licence—

(a) subject to the provisions of this section and section 196, and

(b) with any other necessary modifications.

(4) An application for reinstatement must (in addition to anything required by section 159) request that the reinstatement take effect upon the application being granted.

(5) A licensing authority shall grant an application for reinstatement unless they think it would be wrong to do so having regard to representations made under section 161 (as applied by subsection (3) above).

(6) On the grant of an application for the reinstatement of a premises licence the licensing authority—

(a) shall alter the licence so that the applicant for reinstatement becomes the licensee,

(b) shall specify in the licence that the reinstatement takes effect at the time when the application is granted, and

(c) shall make such other alteration of the licence as appears to them to be required (which may, in particular, include an alteration to reflect a decision of the authority under section 169 as applied by subsection (3) above to make new or varied provision for the attachment or exclusion of conditions).

Commencement

Brought into force by the Gambling Act 2005 (Commencement No 6 and Transitional Provisions) Order 2006, SI 2006/3272, art 2, Sch 2 as from 30 April 2007; for transitional provisions see art 6, Sch 4 thereto (as amended by SI 2007/1157, arts 7–12).

Sub-s (1): Premises licence. As to the nature, etc of premises licences, see s 150 and the note 'Premises licence' thereto.

Sub-s (2): Person. See the note 'Persons' to s 23.

Sub-s (2): May apply. As to appeals, see ss 206–209.

Sub-s (2): Licensing authority. For the licensing authorities for the purposes of this Act, see s 2. As to the licensing authorities' functions, see ss 153–156.

Sub-s (3): This Part. Ie Pt 8 (ss 150–213 and Sch 9) of this Act.

Supplemental provisions

See s 196.

Application

See the note to s 150.

Subordinate Legislation

Gambling Act 2005 (Premises Licences and Provisional Statements) Regulations 2007, SI 2007/459 (made under sub-s (3)).

Gambling (Premises Licence Fees) (England and Wales) Regulations 2007, SI 2007/479 (made under sub-s (3)).

Definitions

'licensee': s 213(e)
'a licensing authority': ss 2, 353(1)
'the licensing authority': s 213(f)
'premises licence': s 353(1)

Explanatory Notes

501–505 [para **6.2011** below]

6.696 196 Reinstatement: supplemental

(1) An application under section 195 for the reinstatement of a premises licence must (in addition to anything required by section 159) be accompanied by—

(a) the licence, or

(b) both—

(i) a statement explaining why it is not reasonably practicable to produce the licence, and

(ii) an application under section 190 for the issue of a copy of the licence.

(2) In the case of an application under section 190 made in accordance with subsection (1)(b)(ii) above—

(a) the application shall be made by the applicant for reinstatement, and

(b) a reference to the licence being lost, stolen or damaged shall be treated as a reference to the licence being unavailable to the applicant for reinstatement.

(3) Regulations under section 160, as they have effect in relation to applications for reinstatement by virtue of section 195(3), may require notice to be given to specified responsible authorities (and not to all responsible authorities).

(4) Section 161 shall have effect in relation to an application for reinstatement with the omission of the reference to interested parties.

(5) Where an application is made under section 195 for the reinstatement of a premises licence, the licence shall have effect as if the applicant for reinstatement were the licensee during the period—

(a) beginning with the receipt of the application for reinstatement by the licensing authority, and

(b) ending with the determination of the application by the licensing authority.

Commencement

Brought into force by the Gambling Act 2005 (Commencement No 6 and Transitional Provisions) Order 2006, SI 2006/3272, art 2, Sch 2 as from 30 April 2007; for transitional provisions see art 6, Sch 4 thereto (as amended by SI 2007/1157, arts 7–12).

Sub-s (1): Premises licence. As to the nature, etc of premises licences, see s 150 and the note 'Premises licence' thereto.

Sub-s (3): Responsible authorities. See s 157.

Sub-s (5): Licensing authority. For the licensing authorities for the purposes of this Act, see s 2. As to the licensing authorities' functions, see ss 153–156.

Application

See the note to s 150.

Subordinate Legislation

Gambling Act 2005 (Premises Licences and Provisional Statements) Regulations 2007, SI 2007/459 (made under sub-s (3)).

Definitions

'licensee': s 213(e)
'the licensing authority': s 213(f)
'premises licence': s 353(1)

Explanatory Notes
501–505 [para **6.2011** below]

Review

6.697 197 Application for review

(1) A responsible authority or interested party may apply to the licensing authority for a review by the authority of a premises licence.

(2) An application must—

(a) be made in the prescribed form and manner,

(b) specify the grounds on which the review is sought, and

(c) contain or be accompanied by the prescribed information or documents.

(3) The Secretary of State may make regulations requiring an applicant—

(a) to give notice of his application to the licensee;

(b) to give notice of his application to the responsible authorities in relation to the premises.

(4) The Secretary of State may make regulations requiring the licensing authority to whom an application is made under this section to publish notice of the application.

(5) Regulations under subsection (2), (3) or (4) shall include provision—

(a) about the manner and form in which notice is to be published or given,

(b) about the period of time within which notice is to be published or given, and

(c) for the consequences of failure to comply with the regulations.

(6) Regulations by virtue of subsection (5)(a) shall, in particular, require a notice to specify a period of time during which representations about the application may be made to the licensing authority by—

(a) the licensee,

(b) a responsible authority, or

(c) an interested party.

(7) In relation to applications to authorities in Scotland, subsections (3) and (4) shall have effect as if the references to the Secretary of State were references to the Scottish Ministers.

Commencement

Brought into force by the Gambling Act 2005 (Commencement No 6 and Transitional Provisions) Order 2006, SI 2006/3272, art 2 as from 1 September 2007; for transitional provisions see art 6, Sch 4 thereto (as amended by SI 2007/1157, arts 7–12).

Sub-s (1): Responsible authority. See s 157.

Sub-s (1): Interested party. See s 158.

Sub-s (1): Licensing authority. For the licensing authorities for the purposes of this Act, see s 2. As to the licensing authorities' functions, see ss 153–156.

Sub-s (1): Review. See further as to reviews, s 198 (rejection of application); s 199 (grant of application); s 200 (initiation of review by licensing authority); s 201 (review); s 202 (action following review); and s 203 (determination).

Sub-s (1): Premises licence. As to the nature, etc of premises licences, see s 150 and the note 'Premises licence' thereto.

Sub-s (3): Secretary of State. See the note to s 4.

Sub-s (3): Notice. See further, in connection with a requirement under this Act to give a notice, s 353(4).

Sub-s (7): Scottish Ministers. See the note to s 25.

Application

See the note to s 150.

Subordinate Legislation:

SI 2007/2258.

As to regulations under this Act generally, see s 355.

Definitions

'licensee': s 213(e)
'the licensing authority': s 213(f)
'premises': s 353(1), (2)(g)
'premises licence': s 353(1)
'prescribed': s 213(g)
'publication': s 353(2)(j)

Explanatory Notes

506, 507 [para **6.2011** below]

6.698 198 Rejection of application

(1) A licensing authority may reject an application under section 197 for the review of a premises licence if they think that the grounds on which the review is sought—

(a) do not raise an issue relevant to the principles to be applied in accordance with section 153,

(b) are frivolous,

(c) are vexatious,

(d) will certainly not cause the authority to wish to take action of a kind specified in section 202(1),

(e) are substantially the same as the grounds specified in an earlier application under section 197 in respect of the premises licence, or

(f) are substantially the same as representations made under section 161 in relation to the application for the premises licence.

(2) In determining whether to exercise the power to reject an application under section 197 in accordance with subsection (1)(e) or (f), a licensing authority shall consider the length of time that has elapsed since the making of the earlier application or since the making of the representations under section 161.

(3) If a licensing authority consider that paragraphs (a) to (f) apply to some but not all of the grounds on which a review is sought, they may reject the application in so far as it relies on grounds to which those paragraphs apply.

(4) In this section a reference to section 161 includes a reference to that section as applied by section 187(3).

Commencement

Brought into force by the Gambling Act 2005 (Commencement No 6 and Transitional Provisions) Order 2006, SI 2006/3272, art 2 as from 1 September 2007; for transitional provisions see art 6, Sch 4 thereto (as amended by SI 2007/1157, arts 7–12).

Sub-s (1): Licensing authority. For the licensing authorities for the purposes of this Act, see s 2. As to the licensing authorities' functions, see ss 153–156.

Sub-s (1): May reject. As to appeals, see ss 206–209.

Sub-s (1): Premises licence. As to the nature, etc of premises licences, see s 150 and the note 'Premises licence' thereto.

Application

See the note to s 150.

Definitions

'a licensing authority': ss 2, 353(1)
'premises licence': s 353(1)

Explanatory Notes

508–510 [para **6.2011** below]

6.699 199 Grant of application

(1) This section applies where an application for review has been made to a licensing authority under section 197.

(2) If, or in so far as, the licensing authority do not reject the application under section 198 they shall grant it.

Commencement

Brought into force by the Gambling Act 2005 (Commencement No 6 and Transitional Provisions) Order 2006, SI 2006/3272, art 2 as from 1 September 2007; for transitional provisions see art 6, Sch 4 thereto (as amended by SI 2007/1157, arts 7–12).

Sub-s (1): Licensing authority. For the licensing authorities for the purposes of this Act, see s 2. As to the licensing authorities' functions, see ss 153–156.

Sub-s (2): Shall grant it. As to appeals, see ss 206–209.

Application

See the note to s 150.

Definitions

'a licensing authority': ss 2, 353(1)

Explanatory Notes

508–510 [para **6.2011** below]

6.700 200 Initiation of review by licensing authority

(1) A licensing authority may review in relation to premises licences of a particular class—

- (a) the use made of premises, and
- (b) in particular, arrangements made by licensees to ensure compliance with conditions attached under section 167, 168 or 169 or by a provision of this Part.

(2) A licensing authority may review any matter connected with the use of premises in reliance on a premises licence if the authority—

- (a) have reason to suspect that the premises may have been used in purported reliance on a licence but not in accordance with a condition of the licence, or
- (b) for any reason (which may relate to the receipt of a complaint about the use of the premises) think that a review would be appropriate.

(3) Before reviewing a premises licence under subsection (2) the licensing authority shall—

- (a) give notice of their intention to hold the review to the licensee, and
- (b) publish notice of their intention to hold the review.

(4) The Secretary of State may make regulations about—

- (a) the manner and form in which notice under subsection (3) is to be given or published, and
- (b) the period of time within which notice is to be given or published.

(5) Regulations by virtue of subsection (4)(a) shall, in particular, require a notice to specify a period of time during which representations about the review may be made to the licensing authority by—

- (a) the licensee,
- (b) a responsible authority, or
- (c) an interested party.

(6) In relation to notice given by a licensing authority in Scotland, subsection (4) shall have effect as if the reference to the Secretary of State were a reference to the Scottish Ministers.

Commencement

Brought into force by the Gambling Act 2005 (Commencement No 6 and Transitional Provisions) Order 2006, SI 2006/3272, art 2 as from 1 September 2007; for transitional provisions see art 6, Sch 4 thereto (as amended by SI 2007/1157, arts 7–12).

Sub-s (1): Licensing authority. For the licensing authorities for the purposes of this Act, see s 2. As to the licensing authorities' functions, see ss 153–156.

Sub-s (1): Review. See further as to reviews, s 201 (review); s 202 (action following review); and s 203 (determination).

Sub-s (1): Premises licence. As to the nature, etc of premises licences, see s 150 and the note 'Premises licence' thereto.

Sub-s (1): This Part. Ie Pt 8 (ss 150–213 and Sch 9) of this Act.

Sub-s (3): Notice. See further, in connection with a requirement under this Act to give a notice, s 353(4).

Sub-s (4): Secretary of State. See the note to s 4.

Sub-s (5): Responsible authority. See s 157.

Sub-s (5): Interested party. See s 158.

Sub-s (6): Scottish Ministers. See the note to s 25.

Application

See the note to s 150.

Subordinate Legislation:

SI 2007/2258.

As to regulations under this Act generally, see s 355.

Definitions

'licensee': s 213(e)
'a licensing authority': ss 2, 353(1)
'the licensing authority': s 213(f)
'premises': s 353(1), (2)(g)
'premises licence': s 353(1)

Explanatory Notes

511, 512 [para **6.2011** below]

6.701 201 Review

(1) This section applies where a licensing authority—

(a) have granted an application for a review of a premises licence under section 199, or

(b) have given notice under section 200 of their intention to hold a review of a premises licence.

(2) As soon as is reasonably practicable after the expiry of any period for representations prescribed under section 197(6) or 200(5), the licensing authority shall review the premises licence.

(3) The purpose of the review shall be to consider whether to take action of a kind specified in section 202(1) in relation to the licence.

(4) In conducting a review of a premises licence a licensing authority shall hold a hearing unless—

(a) the applicant for the review (if there is one), and each person who has made representations about the review under section 197(6) or 200(5), have consented to the conduct of the review without a hearing, or

(b) the licensing authority think that each representation made about the review in accordance with section 197(6) or 200(5)—

(i) is frivolous,

(ii) is vexatious, or

(iii) will certainly not influence the review.

(5) In considering whether to take action of a kind specified in section 202(1) the licensing authority shall have regard (in addition to the matters specified in section 153) to—

(a) any representations made in accordance with section 197(6) or 200(5),
(b) any representations made at the hearing of the review (if there is one), and
(c) in the case of a review held in response to an application under section 197, the grounds specified in the application for the review (apart from any in relation to which the application was rejected under section 198(3)).

Commencement

Brought into force by the Gambling Act 2005 (Commencement No 6 and Transitional Provisions) Order 2006, SI 2006/3272, art 2 as from 1 September 2007; for transitional provisions see art 6, Sch 4 thereto (as amended by SI 2007/1157, arts 7–12).

Sub-s (1): Licensing authority. For the licensing authorities for the purposes of this Act, see s 2. As to the licensing authorities' functions, see ss 153–156.

Sub-s (1): Premises licence. As to the nature, etc of premises licences, see s 150 and the note 'Premises licence' thereto.

Sub-s (2): Shall review. As to action following a review, see s 202, and as to decisions on a review, see s 203.

A resolution under s 166(1) may not be taken into account in conducting a review of a casino premises licence under this section; see s 166(4)(f).

For powers of entry in connection with a review, see s 313(2).

Application

See the note to s 150.

Definitions

'a licensing authority': ss 2, 353(1)
'the licensing authority': s 213(f)
'premises licence': s 353(1)

Explanatory Notes

513–518 [para **6.2011** below]

6.702 202 Action following review

(1) As a result of a review of a premises licence under section 201 a licensing authority may—
(a) revoke the licence;
(b) suspend the licence for a specified period not exceeding three months;
(c) exclude a condition attached to the licence under section 168 or remove or amend an exclusion;
(d) add, remove or amend a condition under section 169.

(2) If the licensing authority decide to take action of a kind specified in subsection (1) they shall specify the time at which the action shall take effect.

(3) A licensing authority may, in particular, take action under subsection (1) on the grounds that the licensee has not used the licence.

Commencement

Brought into force by the Gambling Act 2005 (Commencement No 6 and Transitional Provisions) Order 2006, SI 2006/3272, art 2 as from 1 September 2007; for transitional provisions see art 6, Sch 4 thereto (as amended by SI 2007/1157, arts 7–12).

Sub-s (1): Premises licence. As to the nature, etc of premises licences, see s 150 and the note 'Premises licence' thereto.

Sub-s (1): Licensing authority. For the licensing authorities for the purposes of this Act, see s 2. As to the licensing authorities' functions, see ss 153–156.

Sub-s (1): May revoke, etc. As to appeals, see ss 206–209.

Application

See the note to s 150.

Definitions

'licensee': s 213(e)
'a licensing authority': ss 2, 353(1)
'the licensing authority': s 213(f)
'premises licence': s 353(1)

Explanatory Notes

513–518 [para **6.2011** below]

6.703 203 Determination

(1) As soon as possible after completion of a review of a premises licence under section 201 a licensing authority shall give notice of their decision on the review to—

(a) the licensee,
(b) the applicant for the review (if any),
(c) the Commission,
(d) any person who made representations in accordance with section 197 or 200,
(e) either—
 (i) in England and Wales, the chief officer of police for any area in which the premises are wholly or partly situated, or
 (ii) in Scotland, the chief constable of the police force maintained for a police area in which the premises are wholly or partly situated, and
(f) Her Majesty's [Commissioners for Her Majesty's Revenue and Customs] 1.

(2) A notice under subsection (1)—

(a) must be in the prescribed form, and
(b) must give the authority's reasons for their decision.

Commencement

Brought into force by the Gambling Act 2005 (Commencement No 6 and Transitional Provisions) Order 2006, SI 2006/3272, art 2 as from 1 September 2007; for transitional provisions see art 6, Sch 4 thereto (as amended by SI 2007/1157, arts 7–12).

Sub-s (1): Premises licence. As to the nature, etc of premises licences, see s 150 and the note 'Premises licence' thereto.

Sub-s (1): Licensing authority. For the licensing authorities for the purposes of this Act, see s 2. As to the licensing authorities' functions, see ss 153–156.

Sub-s (1): Notice. See further, in connection with a requirement under this Act to give a notice, s 353(4).

Sub-s (1): The Commission. Ie the Gambling Commission; see s 353(1). As to the establishment, etc of the Gambling Commission, see s 20, Sch 4, and the note 'Gambling Commission' to that section.

Sub-s (1): Person. See the note 'Persons' to s 23.

Sub-s (1): England; Wales. See the note to s 2.Sub-s (1): Commissioners for Her Majesty's Revenue and Customs.

See the note to s 23.

Application

See the note to s 150.

Subordinate Legislation:

SI 2007/2258.

As to regulations under this Act generally, see s 355.

Definitions

'chief officer of police': s 213(b)
'chief officer's area': s 213(c)
'the Commission': s 353(1)

'licensee': s 213(e)
'a licensing authority': ss 2, 353(1)
'premises licence': s 353(1)
'prescribed': s 213(g)

Explanatory Notes

513–518 [para **6.2011** below]

---

1 Words in square brackets substituted by virtue of the Commissioners for Revenue and Customs Act 2005, s 50(1), (7).

Provisional statement

6.704 204 Application

(1) A person may make an application for a provisional statement in respect of premises—

(a) that he expects to be constructed,
(b) that he expects to be altered, or
(c) that he expects to acquire a right to occupy.

(2) The provisions of this Part shall apply in relation to an application for a provisional statement as they apply in relation to an application for a premises licence—

(a) subject to the provisions of this section and section 205, and
(b) with any other necessary modifications.

(3) An application for a provisional statement shall include such plans and other information in relation to the construction, alteration or acquisition as may be prescribed.

(4) Sections 152(1)(b) and 159(3) and (5) shall not apply in relation to an application for a provisional statement.

Commencement

Brought into force for certain purposes as from 30 April 2007 and for remaining purposes as from 1 June 2007 by the Gambling Act 2005 (Commencement No 6 and Transitional Provisions) Order 2006, SI 2006/3272, art 2, Schs 2, 3; for transitional provisions see art 6, Sch 4 thereto (as amended by SI 2007/1157, arts 7–12). Appointment (for certain purposes): 20 May 2008: see SI 2008/1326, art 2, Schedule.

Sub-s (1): Person. See the note 'Persons' to s 23.

Sub-s (1): Provisional statement. For the effect of such a statement, see s 205.

Sub-s (2): This Part. Ie Pt 8 (ss 150–213 and Sch 9) of this Act.

Sub-s (2): Premises licence. As to the nature, etc of premises licences, see s 150 and the note 'Premises licence' thereto.

Application

See the note to s 150.

Subordinate Legislation

Gambling Act 2005 (Premises Licences and Provisional Statements) Regulations 2007, SI 2007/459 (made under sub-ss (2), (3)).

Gambling (Premises Licence Fees) (England and Wales) Regulations 2007, SI 2007/479 (made under sub-s (2)).

Gambling Act 2005 (Premises Licences and Provisional Statements) (Amendment) (England and Wales) Regulations 2007, SI 2007/1775 (made under sub-s (2)).

As to regulations under this Act generally, see s 355.

Definitions

'premises': s 353(1), (2)(g)
'premises licence': s 353(1)

'prescribed': s 213(g)

Explanatory Notes

519–525 [para **6.2011** below]

6.705 205 Effect

(1) This section applies where—

(a) a licensing authority issue a provisional statement in respect of premises, and

(b) an application is made under section 159 for a premises licence in respect of the premises.

(2) The licensing authority shall disregard any representations made in relation to the application for the premises licence unless they think that the representations—

(a) address matters that could not have been addressed in representations in relation to the application for the provisional statement, or

(b) reflect a change in the applicant's circumstances.

(3) The licensing authority may refuse the application, or grant it on terms or conditions not included in the provisional statement, only by reference to matters which—

(a) the authority have considered in reliance on subsection (2)(a), or

(b) in the authority's opinion reflect a change in the applicant's circumstances.

(4) But subsections (2) and (3) do not apply in the case of a provisional statement issued in response to an application under section 204(1)(a) or (b) if the licensing authority think that the premises have been constructed or altered otherwise than in accordance with the plans and information included with the application for the provisional statement in accordance with section 204(3).

Commencement

Brought into force by the Gambling Act 2005 (Commencement No 6 and Transitional Provisions) Order 2006, SI 2006/3272, art 2, Sch 2 as from 30 April 2007; for transitional provisions see art 6, Sch 4 thereto (as amended by SI 2007/1157, arts 7–12).

Sub-s (1): Licensing authority. For the licensing authorities for the purposes of this Act, see s 2. As to the licensing authorities' functions, see ss 153–156.

Sub-s (1): Provisional statement. See s 204.

Sub-s (1): Premises licence. As to the nature, etc of premises licences, see s 150 and the note 'Premises licence' thereto.

Application

See the note to s 150.

Definitions

'a licensing authority': ss 2, 353(1)
'the licensing authority': s 213(f)
'premises': s 353(1), (2)(g)
'premises licence': s 353(1)

Explanatory Notes

519–525 [para **6.2011** below]

Appeals

6.706 206 Rights of appeal

(1) Where a licensing authority reject an application under this Part the applicant may appeal.

(2) Where a licensing authority grant an application under this Part either of the following may appeal—

(a) a person who made representations in relation to the application, and
(b) the applicant.

(3) Where a licensing authority take action under section 202 as a result of a review of a premises licence, or determine to take no action as a result of a review, any of the following may appeal—
(a) the licensee,
(b) a person who made representations in relation to the review,
(c) the person (if any) who applied for the review, and
(d) the Commission.

(4) Where a licensing authority take action or make a determination under section 188(4) or (5) either of the following may appeal—
(a) the licensee, and
(b) the applicant for transfer.

Commencement

Brought into force by the Gambling Act 2005 (Commencement No 6 and Transitional Provisions) Order 2006, SI 2006/3272, art 2, Sch 2 as from 30 April 2007; for transitional provisions see art 6, Sch 4 thereto (as amended by SI 2007/1157, arts 7–12).

Sub-s (1): Licensing authority. For the licensing authorities for the purposes of this Act, see s 2. As to the licensing authorities' functions, see ss 153–156.

Sub-s (1): This Part. Ie Pt 8 (ss 150–213 and Sch 9) of this Act.

Sub-s (1): May appeal. See further in relation to appeals, s 207 (process), s 208 (stay pending appeal), and s 209 (further appeal).

Sub-s (3): Premises licence. As to the nature, etc of premises licences, see s 150 and the note 'Premises licence' thereto.

Sub-s (3): The Commission. Ie the Gambling Commission; see s 353(1). As to the establishment, etc of the Gambling Commission, see s 20, Sch 4, and the note 'Gambling Commission' to that section.

Application

See the note to s 150.

Definitions

'the Commission': s 353(1)
'licensee': s 213(e)
'a licensing authority': ss 2, 353(1)
'premises licence': s 353(1)

Explanatory Notes

526–529 [para **6.2011** below]

6.707 207 Process

(1) An appeal under section 206 in relation to premises must be instituted—
(a) in the magistrates' court for a local justice area in which the premises are wholly or partly situated,
(b) by notice of appeal given to the designated officer, and
(c) within the period of 21 days beginning with the day on which the appellant receives notice of the decision against which the appeal is brought.[1]

(2) Where an appeal is brought under section 206 the licence holder (or the applicant in the case of an appeal against the grant of an application for a premises licence) shall be a respondent in addition to the licensing authority (unless he is the appellant).

(3) On an appeal under section 206 the magistrates' court may—
(a) dismiss the appeal;
(b) substitute for the decision appealed against any decision that the licensing authority could have made;

(c) remit the case to the licensing authority to decide in accordance with a direction of the court;

(d) make an order about costs.

(4) Section 206 applies to a decision of a licensing authority following remittal under subsection (3)(c) above.

(5) In relation to premises in Scotland—

(a) subsection (1)(a) shall have effect as if it referred to a sheriff within whose sheriffdom the premises are wholly or partly situated,

(b) subsection (1)(b) shall not have effect,

(c) the reference in subsection (3) to the magistrates' court shall have effect as a reference to the sheriff, and

(d) the reference in subsection (3) to costs shall have effect as a reference to expenses.

Commencement

Brought into force by the Gambling Act 2005 (Commencement No 6 and Transitional Provisions) Order 2006, SI 2006/3272, art 2, Sch 2 as from 30 April 2007; for transitional provisions see art 6, Sch 4 thereto (as amended by SI 2007/1157, arts 7–12).

Sub-s (1): Notice. See further, in connection with a requirement under this Act to give a notice, s 353(4).

Sub-s (2): Premises licence. As to the nature, etc of premises licences, see s 150 and the note 'Premises licence' thereto.

Sub-s (2): Licensing authority. For the licensing authorities for the purposes of this Act, see s 2. As to the licensing authorities' functions, see ss 153–156.

Application

See the note to s 150.

Definitions

'a licensing authority': ss 2, 353(1)
'the licensing authority': s 213(f)
'premises': s 353(1), (2)(g)
'premises licence': s 353(1)

Explanatory Notes

526–529 [para **6.2011** below]

---

[1] It would seem there is no power to extend the 21 day period: see *Stockton-on-Tees Borough Concil v Latif* [2009] EWHC 228 (Admin) and the radically different provisions of s 142(2).

6.708 208 Stay pending appeal

(1) A determination or other action under this Part shall have no effect while an appeal under section 206—

(a) could be brought, or

(b) has been brought and has not yet been either finally determined or abandoned.

(2) But a licensing authority making a determination or taking other action under this Part may direct that subsection (1) shall not apply (in which case the magistrates' court or sheriff determining an appeal may make any order that it or he thinks appropriate).

Commencement

Brought into force by the Gambling Act 2005 (Commencement No 6 and Transitional Provisions) Order 2006, SI 2006/3272, art 2, Sch 2 as from 30 April 2007; for transitional provisions see art 6, Sch 4 thereto (as amended by SI 2007/1157, arts 7–12).

Sub-s (1): This Part. Ie Pt 8 (ss 150–213 and Sch 9) of this Act.

Sub-s (2): Licensing authority. For the licensing authorities for the purposes of this Act, see s 2. As to the licensing authorities' functions, see ss 153–156.

Sub-s (2): Magistrates' court. See the note to s 207.

Application

See the note to s 150.

Definitions

'a licensing authority': ss 2, 353(1)

Explanatory Notes

526–529 [para **6.2011** below]

6.709 209 Further appeal

A party to an appeal under section 206 may appeal on a point of law—

(a) in relation to premises in England and Wales, to the High Court, or

(b) in relation to premises in Scotland, to the Court of Session.

Commencement

Brought into force by the Gambling Act 2005 (Commencement No 6 and Transitional Provisions) Order 2006, SI 2006/3272, art 2, Sch 2 as from 30 April 2007; for transitional provisions see art 6, Sch 4 thereto (as amended by SI 2007/1157, arts 7–12).

England; Wales

See the note to s 2.

Application

See the note to s 150.

Definitions

'premises': s 353(1), (2)(g)

Explanatory Notes

526–529 [para **6.2011** below]

General

6.710 210 Planning permission

(1) In making a decision in respect of an application under this Part a licensing authority shall not have regard to whether or not a proposal by the applicant is likely to be permitted in accordance with the law relating to planning or building.

(2) A decision by a licensing authority under this Part shall not constrain any later decision by the authority under the law relating to planning or building.

Commencement

Brought into force by the Gambling Act 2005 (Commencement No 6 and Transitional Provisions) Order 2006, SI 2006/3272, art 2, Sch 2 as from 30 April 2007; for transitional provisions see art 6, Sch 4 thereto (as amended by SI 2007/1157, arts 7–12).

Sub-s (1): This Part. Ie Pt 8 (ss 150–213 and Sch 9) of this Act.

Sub-s (1): Licensing authority. For the licensing authorities for the purposes of this Act, see s 2. As to the licensing authorities' functions, see ss 153–156.

Application

See the note to s 150.

Definitions

'a licensing authority': ss 2, 353(1)

Explanatory Notes

530 [para **6.2011** below]

6.711 211 Vehicles and vessels

(1) A premises licence—

(a) may not be issued in relation to a vehicle (or part of a vehicle),

(b) may be issued in relation to all or part of a passenger vessel,

(c) may be issued in relation to all or part of a vessel (within the meaning of section 353(1)) situated at a fixed place in or on water, and

(d) may not be issued in relation to all or part of a vessel to which neither of paragraphs (b) and (c) applies.

(2) A premises licence in relation to a vessel may include a condition imposed by virtue of section 169 about the location of the vessel.

(3) In relation to a vessel, a reference in this Part to a place in which premises are wholly or partly situated shall be construed—

(a) in the case of a vessel (within the meaning of section 353(1)) situated at a fixed place in or on water, as a reference to that place,

(b) in the case of a vessel which is permanently moored at a place, as a reference to that place,

(c) in the case of a vessel which is habitually moored at one place more frequently or for longer periods than at any other place, as a reference to that place, and

(d) in any other case, as a reference to any place at which a vessel is moored or is likely to be moored, or to the place in the United Kingdom nearest to any place at which a vessel is or is likely to be, while activities are carried on in the vessel in reliance on a premises licence.

(4) In relation to a vessel, the following are responsible authorities for the purposes of this Part (in addition to the persons listed in section 157)—

(a) a navigation authority, within the meaning of section 221(1) of the Water Resources Act 1991 (c 57), which has functions in relation to any place where the vessel is or is likely to be while activities are carried on in the vessel in reliance on a premises licence,

(b) the Environment Agency,

(c) the British Waterways Board, and

(d) the Secretary of State.

Commencement

Brought into force by the Gambling Act 2005 (Commencement No 6 and Transitional Provisions) Order 2006, SI 2006/3272, art 2, Sch 2 as from 30 April 2007; for transitional provisions see art 6, Sch 4 thereto (as amended by SI 2007/1157, arts 7–12).

Sub-s (1): Premises licence. As to the nature, etc of premises licences, see s 150 and the note 'Premises licence' thereto.

Sub-s (3): This Part. Ie Pt 8 (ss 150–213 and Sch 9) of this Act.

Sub-s (3): United Kingdom. See the note to s 36.

Sub-s (4): Secretary of State. See the note to s 4.

Application

See the note to s 150.

Definitions

'premises': s 353(1), (2)(g)
'premises licence': s 353(1)
'vehicle': s 353(1)
'vessel': s 353(1)

Explanatory Notes

531–534 [para **6.2011** below]

6.712 212 Fees

(1) Regulations under this Part prescribing a fee—

(a) may provide for the amount of the fee to be determined by a licensing authority, and

(b) may, if they make provision by virtue of paragraph (a), specify constraints on a licensing authority's power to determine the amount of the fee.

(2) Where provision is made under subsection (1) for the amount of a fee to be determined by a licensing authority, the authority—

(a) shall determine the amount of the fee,

(b) may determine different amounts for different classes of case specified in the regulations (but may not otherwise determine different amounts for different cases),

(c) shall publish the amount of the fee as determined from time to time, and

(d) shall aim to ensure that the income from fees of that kind as nearly as possible equates to the costs of providing the service to which the fee relates (including a reasonable share of expenditure which is referable only partly or only indirectly to the provision of that service).

(3) For the purposes of subsection (2)(d) a licensing authority shall compare income and costs in such manner, at such times and by reference to such periods as the authority, having regard to any guidance issued by the Secretary of State, think appropriate.

(4) Regulations by virtue of this section may (without prejudice to the generality of section 355)—

(a) make provision which applies generally or only to specified authorities or classes of authority,

(b) make different provision for different authorities or classes of authority, and

(c) make transitional provision in respect of a case where an authority enters or leaves a class.

(5) A class of authority for the purposes of subsection (4) may, in particular, be defined by reference to categories assigned under section 99 of the Local Government Act 2003 (c 26).

(6) This section does not apply to Scotland.

Commencement

Brought into force by the Gambling Act 2005 (Commencement No 6 and Transitional Provisions) Order 2006, SI 2006/3272, art 2, Sch 2 as from 30 April 2007; for transitional provisions see art 6, Sch 4 thereto (as amended by SI 2007/1157, arts 7–12).

Sub-s (1): This Part. Ie Pt 8 (ss 150–213 and Sch 9) of this Act.

Sub-s (1): Licensing authority. For the licensing authorities for the purposes of this Act, see s 2. As to the licensing authorities' functions, see ss 153–156.

Sub-s (3): Secretary of State. See the note to s 4.

Application

See the note to s 150.

This section is applied by ss 219(8), 227(6)(b).

Subordinate Legislation

Gambling (Premises Licence Fees) (England and Wales) Regulations 2007, SI 2007/479 (made under sub-ss (1), (4), (5)).

Gambling Act 2005 (Temporary Use Notices) Regulations 2007, SI 2007/3157.

Definitions

'a licensing authority': ss 2, 353(1)
'publication': s 353(2)(j)

Explanatory Notes

535–539 [para **6.2011** below]

6.713 213 Interpretation

In this Part—

(a) 'authorised activity', in relation to a premises licence, means an activity specified under section 151(1)(d),

(b) 'chief officer of police' has the meaning given by section 101(1) of the Police Act 1996 (c 16),

(c) a reference to a chief officer's area is a reference to the area in respect of which he has responsibility under that Act,

(d) 'holder', in relation to a premises licence, means the person to whom the licence is issued,

(e) 'licensee', in relation to a premises licence, also means the person to whom the licence is issued,

(f) 'the licensing authority', in relation to a premises licence, means the authority who issued the licence, and

(g) 'prescribed' means (except where the contrary is provided) prescribed by regulations made by the Secretary of State.

Commencement

Brought into force by the Gambling Act 2005 (Commencement No 6 and Transitional Provisions) Order 2006, SI 2006/3272, art 2, Sch 2 as from 30 April 2007; for transitional provisions see art 6, Sch 4 thereto (as amended by SI 2007/1157, arts 7–12).

This Part

Ie Pt 8 (ss 150–213 and Sch 9) of this Act.

Premises licence

As to the nature, etc of premises licences, see s 150 and the note 'Premises licence' thereto.

Person

See the note 'Persons' to s 23.

Secretary of State

See the note to s 4.

Application

See the note to s 150.

Definitions

'premises licence': s 353(1)

PART 9
TEMPORARY USE OF PREMISES

Temporary use notice

6.714 214 Exception to offence of using premises for gambling

(1) A person who uses premises to carry on an activity listed in section 37(1), or who causes or permits premises to be used to carry on an activity to which that section applies, does not commit an offence under that section if—

(a) a temporary use notice under this Part has effect in respect of the premises, and

(b) the activity is carried on in accordance with the terms of the notice.

Commencement

Brought into force by the Gambling Act 2005 (Commencement No 7) Order 2007, SI 2007/3155, art 2 as from 1 December 2007.

General Note

There is no sub-s (2) in the Queen's Printers' copy of this Act.

Person

See the note 'Persons' to s 23.

Temporary use notice

See further as to temporary use notices, s 215 (nature of notice); s 216 (form of notice); s 217 (effect of notice); s 218 (maximum permitted period); ss 219–228 (procedure); and ss 229–234 (miscellaneous).

For powers of entry in connection with a temporary use notice, see s 315.

This Part

Ie Pt 9 (ss 214–234) of this Act.

Definitions

'premises': s 353(1), (2)(g)
'temporary use notice': ss 215(1), 353(1)

Explanatory Notes

543–548 [para **6.2012** below]

6.715 215 Nature of notice

(1) A temporary use notice is a notice given in accordance with the provisions of this Part—

(a) by the holder of an operating licence, and
(b) stating his intention to carry on one or more specified prescribed activities.

(2) The Secretary of State may by regulations—

(a) prescribe activities which may be specified in a notice under subsection (1)(b);
(b) prescribe combinations of activity that may not be specified in a notice under subsection (1)(b);
(c) prescribe activities which may be specified under subsection (1)(b) only if no other prescribed activity is specified in the notice.

(3) A temporary use notice given by a person may specify an activity under subsection (1)(b) only if the person's operating licence authorises him to carry on the activity.

Commencement

Brought into force by the Gambling Act 2005 (Commencement No 7) Order 2007, SI 2007/3155, art 2 as from 1 December 2007.

Sub-s (1): Temporary use notice. See s 214 and the note 'Temporary use notice' thereto.

Sub-s (1): This Part. Ie Pt 9 (ss 214–234) of this Act.

Sub-s (1): Operating licence. As to the nature, etc of operating licences, see s 65 and the note 'Operating licences' thereto.

Sub-s (2): Secretary of State. See the note to s 4.

Sub-s (3): Person. See the note 'Persons' to s 23.

Subordinate legislation

Gambling Act 2005 (Temporary Use Notices) Regulations 2007, SI 2007/3157.

As to regulations under this Act generally, see s 355.

Definitions

'operating licence': s 353(1)

Explanatory Notes

543–548 [para **6.2012** below]

6.716 216 Form of notice

(1) A temporary use notice must—

(a) be in the prescribed form,

(b) specify the activity to be carried on in reliance on the notice,

(c) specify the premises on which the activity is to be carried on,

(d) specify the period of time during which the notice is to have effect,

(e) specify the times of day during that period at which the activity is to be carried on,

(f) specify any periods during the previous 12 months during which a temporary use notice has had effect in respect of the premises or any part of the premises,

(g) specify the date on which the notice is given, and

(h) contain any other prescribed information.

(2) In this section 'prescribed' means prescribed by regulations made by the Secretary of State.

(3) In subsection (1)(f) 'the previous 12 months' means the period of 12 months ending with the last day of the period specified under subsection (1)(d).

Commencement

Brought into force by the Gambling Act 2005 (Commencement No 7) Order 2007, SI 2007/3155, art 2 as from 1 December 2007.

Sub-s (1): Temporary use notice. See s 214 and the note 'Temporary use notice' thereto.

Sub-s (2): Secretary of State. See the note to s 4.

Subordinate legislation

Gambling Act 2005 (Temporary Use Notices) Regulations 2007, SI 2007/3157.

As to regulations under this Act generally, see s 355.

Definitions

'premises': s 353(1), (2)(g)

'temporary use notice': ss 215(1), 353(1)

Explanatory Notes

543–548 [para **6.2012** below]

6.717 217 Effect of notice

A temporary use notice shall, subject to the provisions of this Part and provided that the requirements of this Part are complied with, have effect during the period specified in the notice in accordance with section 216(1)(d).

Commencement

Brought into force by the Gambling Act 2005 (Commencement No 7) Order 2007, SI 2007/3155, art 2 as from 1 December 2007.

Temporary use notice

See s 214 and the note 'Temporary use notice' thereto.

This Part

Ie Pt 9 (ss 214–234) of this Act.

Definitions

'temporary use notice': ss 215(1), 353(1)

Explanatory Notes

543–548 [para 6.2012 below]

6.718 218 Maximum permitted period

(1) A set of premises may not be the subject of temporary use notification for more than 21 days in a period of 12 months.

(2) A set of premises may be the subject of more than one temporary use notice in a period of 12 months (provided that the aggregate of the periods for which the notices have effect does not exceed 21 days).

(3) If a temporary use notice is given to a licensing authority and subsection (1) would be contravened if the notice had effect for any part of the period specified in accordance with section 216(1)(d), the licensing authority shall give a counter-notice providing for the temporary use notice not to have effect.

(4) Subsections (5) and (6) apply where a temporary use notice is given to a licensing authority and—

(a) subsection (1) would be contravened if the notice had effect for the whole of the period specified in accordance with section 216(1)(d) ('the specified period'), but

(b) the notice could have effect for some part of the specified period without resulting in contravention of subsection (1).

(5) The licensing authority shall give a counter-notice providing that the temporary use notice—

(a) shall not have effect during such part of the specified period as the licensing authority may specify in the counter-notice ('the excluded period'), and

(b) shall be treated for the purposes of this Part as if it related only to the non-excluded period.

(6) Where there is a choice as to which part of the specified period to exclude under subsection (5), the licensing authority shall consult the person who gave the temporary use notice before giving a counter-notice by virtue of that subsection.

(7) A counter-notice under this section shall have effect; and subsections (4) and (6) of section 224 shall apply in relation to a counter-notice given under this section as they apply in relation to a counter-notice given under that section.

(8) For the purposes of this section a set of premises is the subject of temporary use notification (or of a notice) if any part of the premises is the subject of temporary use notification (or of a notice).

Commencement

Brought into force by the Gambling Act 2005 (Commencement No 7) Order 2007, SI 2007/3155, art 2 as from 1 December 2007.

Sub-s (1): Temporary use notification. See s 214 and the note 'Temporary use notice' thereto.

Sub-s (3): Licensing authority. For the licensing authorities for the purposes of this Act, see s 2. As to the licensing authorities' functions, see ss 232, 233.

Sub-s (5): This Part. Ie Pt 9 (ss 214–234) of this Act.

Sub-s (6): Person. See the note 'Persons' to s 23.

Definitions

'licensing authority': ss 2, 353(1)
'premises': s 353(1), (2)(g)
'temporary use notice': ss 215(1), 353(1)

Explanatory Notes

543–548 [para **6.2012** below]

Procedure

6.719 219 Giving notice

(1) A temporary use notice must be given to the licensing authority for the area in which the premises specified under section 216(1)(c) are situated.

(2) A temporary use notice must be given before the period of three months ending with the day before the period specified under section 216(1)(d).

(3) A temporary use notice given under subsection (1) must be accompanied by—

- (a) a copy of the notice, and
- (b) such fee as may be prescribed by regulations made—
  - (i) in relation to premises in England and Wales, by the Secretary of State, and
  - (ii) in relation to premises in Scotland, by the Scottish Ministers.

(4) A person who gives a temporary use notice must give a copy of it to—

- (a) the Commission,
- (b) either—
  - (i) in England and Wales, the chief officer of police for any area in which the premises specified in the notice are wholly or partly situated, or
  - (ii) in Scotland, the chief constable of the police force maintained for a police area in which the premises are wholly or partly situated, and
- (c) Her Majesty's [Commissioners for Her Majesty's Revenue and Customs] 1.

(5) A person who gives a temporary use notice must ensure that it, and any copy required by this section to be given, are received within the period of 7 days beginning with the date specified under section 216(1)(g).

(6) In the case of premises situated partly in the area of one licensing authority and partly in the area of another, the person giving the notice—

- (a) may give it to either authority, and
- (b) shall give a copy of the notice to the other authority.

(7) In this Part—

- (a) 'chief officer of police' has the meaning given by section 101(1) of the Police Act 1996 (c 16), and
- (b) a reference to a chief officer's area is a reference to the area in respect of which he has responsibility under that Act.

(8) Section 212 shall have effect in relation to fees under this section as it has effect in relation to fees under Part 8.

Commencement

Brought into force by the Gambling Act 2005 (Commencement No 7) Order 2007, SI 2007/3155, art 2 as from 1 December 2007.

Sub-s (1): Temporary use notice. See s 214 and the note 'Temporary use notice' thereto. As to acknowledgment of receipt, see s 214.

Sub-s (1): Licensing authority. For the licensing authorities for the purposes of this Act, see s 2. As to the licensing authorities' functions, see ss 232, 233.

Sub-s (3): England; Wales. See the note to s 2.

Sub-s (3): Secretary of State. See the note to s 4.

Sub-s (3): Scottish Ministers. See the note to s 25.

Sub-s (4): Person. See the note 'Persons' to s 23.

Sub-s (4): The Commission. Ie the Gambling Commission; see s 353(1). As to the establishment, etc of the Gambling Commission, see s 20, Sch 4, and the note 'Gambling Commission' to that section.

Sub-s (4): Commissioners for Her Majesty's Revenue and Customs. See the note to s 23.

Sub-s (7): This Part. Ie Pt 9 (ss 214–234) of this Act.

Sub-s (8): Part 8. Ie Pt 8 (ss 150–213 and Sch 9) of this Act.

Exclusion

Sub-ss (2), (3)(b) above are excluded by s 223(4).

Subordinate legislation

Gambling Act 2005 (Temporary Use Notices) Regulations 2007, SI 2007/3157.

As to regulations under this Act generally, see s 355.

Definitions

'the Commission': s 353(1)
'licensing authority': ss 2, 353(1)
'premises': s 353(1), (2)(g)
'temporary use notice': ss 215(1), 353(1)

Explanatory Notes

549–551 [para **6.2012** below]

---

[1] Words in square brackets substituted by virtue of the Commissioners for Revenue and Customs Act 2005, s 50(1), (7).

6.720 220 Acknowledgment of notice

Where a licensing authority receive a temporary use notice in accordance with section 219(1) they shall as soon as is reasonably practicable send a written acknowledgment of the notice to the person who gave it.

Commencement

Brought into force by the Gambling Act 2005 (Commencement No 7) Order 2007, SI 2007/3155, art 2 as from 1 December 2007.

Licensing authority

For the licensing authorities for the purposes of this Act, see s 2. As to the licensing authorities' functions, see ss 232, 233.

Temporary use notice

See s 214 and the note 'Temporary use notice' thereto.

Written

See the note 'Writing' to s 39.

Person

See the note 'Persons' to s 23.

Definitions

'licensing authority': ss 2, 353(1)
'temporary use notice': ss 215(1), 353(1)

Explanatory Notes

549–551 [para **6.2012** below]

6.721 221 Objections

(1) This section applies where a person receives a temporary use notice, or a copy of a temporary use notice, in accordance with section 219.

(2) If the person thinks that having regard to the licensing objectives the temporary premises notice should not have effect, or should have effect only with modification, he may give a notice of objection to the person who gave the temporary use notice.

(3) A person who gives a notice of objection under subsection (2) must give a copy of the notice to the licensing authority to which the temporary use notice was given (unless it is that licensing authority which give the notice of objection).

(4) A notice of objection and any copy required by subsection (3) must be given within the period of 14 days beginning with the date on which the temporary use notice is given as specified under section 216(1)(g).

(5) A notice of objection must state—

(a) that the person giving the notice objects to the temporary use notice, and

(b) the person's reasons.

(6) If the person who gives a notice of objection later withdraws it by notice in writing to the persons mentioned in subsections (2) and (3), the notice of objection shall be disregarded.

Commencement

Brought into force by the Gambling Act 2005 (Commencement No 7) Order 2007, SI 2007/3155, art 2 as from 1 December 2007.

Sub-s (1): Temporary use notice. See s 214 and the note 'Temporary use notice' thereto.

Sub-s (2): Notice of objection. See further, in connection with a requirement under this Act to give a notice, s 353(4). As to the hearing of objections, see s 222.

Sub-s (2): Person. See the note 'Persons' to s 23.

Sub-s (3): Licensing authority. For the licensing authorities for the purposes of this Act, see s 2. As to the licensing authorities' functions, see ss 232, 233.

Sub-s (6): Writing. See the note to s 39.

Definitions

'licensing authority': ss 2, 353(1)
'the licensing objectives': ss 1, 353(1)
'temporary use notice': ss 215(1), 353(1)

Explanatory Notes

552–554 [para **6.2012** below]

6.722 222 Hearing of objections

(1) This section applies where—

(a) a temporary use notice is given to a licensing authority in accordance with section 219, and

(b) a notice of objection is given in accordance with section 221.

(2) The licensing authority shall hold a hearing at which any of the following may make representations about the notice of objection—

(a) the person who gave the temporary use notice,

(b) the person who gave the notice of objection, and

(c) any other person who was entitled to receive a copy of the temporary use notice in accordance with section 219.

(3) But the licensing authority need not arrange a hearing if the authority and each person who would be entitled to make representations agree in writing that a hearing is unnecessary.

Commencement

Brought into force by the Gambling Act 2005 (Commencement No 7) Order 2007, SI 2007/3155, art 2 as from 1 December 2007.

Sub-s (1): Temporary use notice. See s 214 and the note 'Temporary use notice' thereto.

Sub-s (1): Licensing authority. For the licensing authorities for the purposes of this Act, see s 2. As to the licensing authorities' functions, see ss 232, 233.

Sub-s (2): Person. See the note 'Persons' to s 23.

Sub-s (3): Writing. See the note to s 39.

Definitions

'licensing authority': ss 2, 353(1)

'temporary use notice': ss 215(1), 353(1)

Explanatory Notes

552–554 [para **6.2012** below]

6.723 223 Modification by agreement

(1) This section applies where—

(a) a person has given a temporary use notice to a licensing authority in accordance with section 219,

(b) a notice of objection has been given by a person ('the objector') in accordance with section 221, and

(c) a hearing in accordance with section 222(2) has neither—

(i) taken place, nor

(ii) been dispensed with in accordance with section 222(3).

(2) The objector may by notice in writing to the person who gave the temporary use notice propose a modification of that notice.

(3) If the person who gave the temporary use notice accepts the modification—

(a) he shall give a new notice, incorporating the modification, in accordance with section 219, and

(b) the objection shall be treated as withdrawn (but without prejudice to the right of any person other than the objector to give a notice of objection in relation to the new notice).

(4) The following provisions of section 219 shall not apply to a temporary use notice given under subsection (3)(a) above—

(a) subsection (2), and

(b) subsection (3)(b).

Commencement

Brought into force by the Gambling Act 2005 (Commencement No 7) Order 2007, SI 2007/3155, art 2 as from 1 December 2007.

Sub-s (1): Person. See the note 'Persons' to s 23.

Sub-s (1): Temporary use notice. See s 214 and the note 'Temporary use notice' thereto.

Sub-s (1): Licensing authority. For the licensing authorities for the purposes of this Act, see s 2. As to the licensing authorities' functions, see ss 232, 233.

Sub-s (2): Notice. See further, in connection with a requirement under this Act to give a notice, s 353(4).

Sub-s (2): Writing. See the note to s 39.

Definitions

'licensing authority': ss 2, 353(1)

'temporary use notice': ss 215(1), 353(1)

Explanatory Notes

552–554 [para **6.2012** below]

6.724 224 Counter-notice

(1) This section applies where—

(a) a person has given a temporary use notice to a licensing authority in accordance with section 219,

(b) a notice of objection has been given in accordance with section 221, and

(c) a hearing—

(i) has taken place in accordance with section 222(2), or

(ii) has been dispensed with in accordance with section 222(3).

(2) If the licensing authority think that the temporary use notice should not have effect or should have effect only with modification, the authority may give a counter-notice under this subsection to the person who gave the temporary use notice.

(3) A counter-notice may provide for the temporary use notice—

(a) not to have effect;

(b) to have effect only in respect of a specified activity;

(c) to have effect only in respect of activity carried on during a specified period of time or at specified times of day;

(d) to have effect subject to compliance with a specified condition;

and provision made under this subsection shall have effect.

(4) A counter-notice must—

(a) be in the prescribed form,

(b) contain the prescribed information, and

(c) be given as soon as is reasonably practicable.

(5) A counter-notice must state the licensing authority's reasons for giving it.

(6) Where a licensing authority give a counter-notice they shall as soon as is reasonably practicable give a copy to any person who was entitled to receive a copy of the temporary use notice.

(7) Section 153(1) shall apply to the exercise of a licensing authority's functions under this section as it applies to the exercise of a licensing authority's functions under Part 8.

(8) In this section 'prescribed' means prescribed by regulations made by the Secretary of State.

Commencement

Brought into force by the Gambling Act 2005 (Commencement No 7) Order 2007, SI 2007/3155, art 2 as from 1 December 2007.

Sub-s (1): Person. See the note 'Persons' to s 23.

Sub-s (1): Temporary use notice. See s 214 and the note 'Temporary use notice' thereto.

Sub-s (1): Licensing authority. For the licensing authorities for the purposes of this Act, see s 2. As to the licensing authorities' functions, see ss 232, 233.

Sub-s (7): Part 8. Ie Pt 8 (ss 150–213 and Sch 9) of this Act.

Sub-s (8): Secretary of State. See the note to s 4.

Appeal

See s 226.

Application

Sub-ss (4), (6) above are applied by s 218(7).

Subordinate legislation.

Gambling Act 2005 (Temporary Use Notices) Regulations 2007, SI 2007/3157.

As to regulations under this Act generally, see s 355.

Definitions

'licensing authority': ss 2, 353(1)

'temporary use notice': ss 215(1), 353(1)

Explanatory Notes

555–562 [para **6.2012** below]

6.725 225 Dismissal of objection

(1) This section applies where—

(a) a person has given a temporary use notice to a licensing authority in accordance with section 219,

(b) a notice of objection has been given in accordance with section 221, and

(c) the licensing authority has determined not to give a counter-notice.

(2) The licensing authority shall as soon as is reasonably practicable give notice of their determination to—

(a) the person who gave the temporary use notice, and

(b) each person who received a copy of the temporary use notice in accordance with section 219.

Commencement

Brought into force by the Gambling Act 2005 (Commencement No 7) Order 2007, SI 2007/3155, art 2 as from 1 December 2007.

Sub-s (1): Person. See the note 'Persons' to s 23.

Sub-s (1): Temporary use notice. See s 214 and the note 'Temporary use notice' thereto.

Sub-s (1): Licensing authority. For the licensing authorities for the purposes of this Act, see s 2. As to the licensing authorities' functions, see ss 232, 233.

Sub-s (1): Counter notice. See s 224.

Sub-s (2): Notice. See further, in connection with a requirement under this Act to give a notice, s 353(4).

Appeal

See s 226.

Definitions

'licensing authority': ss 2, 353(1)
'temporary use notice': ss 215(1), 353(1)

Explanatory Notes

555–562 [para **6.2012** below]

6.726 226 Appeal

(1) This section applies where a licensing authority—

(a) give a counter-notice under section 224, or

(b) give a notice under section 225.

(2) Any of the following may appeal—

(a) the person who gave the temporary use notice, and

(b) a person who was entitled to receive a copy of the temporary use notice under section 219.

(3) An appeal under this section must be instituted—

(a) in the magistrates' court for a local justice area in which the premises to which the temporary use notice relates are wholly or partly situated,

(b) by notice of appeal given to the designated officer, and

(c) within the period of 14 days beginning with the day on which the appellant receives notice of the action against which the appeal is brought.

(4) A person who was entitled to receive a copy of the temporary use notice under section 219 must determine whether to appeal, and institute any appeal, as soon as is reasonably practicable.

(5) Where an appeal is brought against the giving of a notice under section 225 the person who gave the temporary use notice shall be a respondent in addition to the licensing authority.

(6) On an appeal under this section the magistrates' court may—

(a) dismiss the appeal;

(b) direct the licensing authority to take action of a specified kind;

(c) remit the case to the licensing authority to decide in accordance with a direction of the court;

(d) make an order about costs.

(7) Subsection (2) applies to a decision of a licensing authority following remittal under subsection (6)(c) above.

(8) A party to an appeal under this section may bring a further appeal to the High Court on a point of law.

(9) In relation to premises in Scotland—

(a) subsection (3)(a) shall have effect as if it referred to a sheriff within whose sheriffdom the premises are wholly or partly situated,

(b) subsection (3)(b) shall not have effect,

(c) the reference in subsection (6) to the magistrates' court shall have effect as a reference to the sheriff,

(d) the reference in subsection (6) to costs shall have effect as a reference to expenses, and

(e) the reference in subsection (8) to the High Court shall have effect as a reference to the Court of Session.

Commencement

Brought into force by the Gambling Act 2005 (Commencement No 7) Order 2007, SI 2007/3155, art 2 as from 1 December 2007.

Sub-s (1): Licensing authority. For the licensing authorities for the purposes of this Act, see s 2. As to the licensing authorities' functions, see ss 232, 233.

Sub-s (2): Person. See the note 'Persons' to s 23.

Sub-s (2): Temporary use notice. See s 214 and the note 'Temporary use notice' thereto.

Sub-s (3): Magistrates' court. See the note to s 207.

Definitions

'licensing authority': ss 2, 353(1)
'premises': s 353(1), (2)(g)
'temporary use notice': ss 215(1), 353(1)

Explanatory Notes

555–562 [para **6.2012** below]

6.727 227 Endorsement of notice

(1) This section applies where a temporary use notice has been given to a licensing authority under section 219.

(2) If no notice of objection is pending in relation to the temporary use notice when the 14 day period specified in section 221(4) expires, the licensing authority shall—

(a) endorse the copy submitted under section 219(3)(a) in such manner as may be prescribed by the Secretary of State by regulations, and

(b) return the endorsed copy, as soon as is reasonably practicable, to the person giving the notice.

(3) If a notice of objection is pending in relation to a temporary use notice when the 14 day period specified in section 221(4) expires, then as soon as is reasonably practicable after the completion of proceedings on the temporary use notice the licensing authority shall, unless they give a counter-notice under section 224(3)(a)—

(a) endorse the copy submitted under section 219(3)(a) in such manner as may be prescribed by the Secretary of State by regulations, and

(b) return the endorsed copy, as soon as is reasonably practicable, to the person giving the temporary use notice.

(4) For the purposes of this section a notice of objection is pending if it has been given in accordance with section 221 and—

(a) it has not been withdrawn, and

(b) it is not treated as withdrawn in accordance with section 223(3)(b).

(5) For the purposes of this section proceedings on a temporary use notice are completed—

(a) if any notice of objection given in relation to the temporary use notice has been withdrawn, or

(b) if the licensing authority has given a counter-notice under section 224 or a notice under section 225.

(6) A licensing authority shall make arrangements whereby if an endorsed copy of a temporary use notice is lost, stolen or damaged the person who gave the notice can obtain a new endorsed copy; and—

(a) the arrangements may include the charging of such fee as the Secretary of State may prescribe by regulations, and

(b) section 212 shall have effect in relation to fees under paragraph (a) above as it has effect in relation to fees under Part 8.

Commencement

Brought into force by the Gambling Act 2005 (Commencement No 7) Order 2007, SI 2007/3155, art 2 as from 1 December 2007.

Sub-s (1): Temporary use notice. See s 214 and the note 'Temporary use notice' thereto.

Sub-s (1): Licensing authority. For the licensing authorities for the purposes of this Act, see s 2. As to the licensing authorities' functions, see ss 232, 233.

Sub-s (2): Secretary of State. See the note to s 4.

Sub-s (2): Person. See the note 'Persons' to s 23.

Sub-s (6): Part 8. Ie Pt 8 (ss 150–213 and Sch 9) of this Act.

Subordinate legislation.

Gambling Act 2005 (Temporary Use Notices) Regulations 2007, SI 2007/3157.

As to regulations under this Act generally, see s 355.

Definitions

'licensing authority': ss 2, 353(1)

'temporary use notice': ss 215(1), 353(1)

Explanatory Notes

563–565 [para **6.2012** below]

6.728 228 Consideration by licensing authority: timing

(1) Where a licensing authority are given a temporary use notice in accordance with section 219 the authority shall complete proceedings on the notice before the end of the period of six weeks beginning with the date on which they receive the notice.

(2) In subsection (1) the reference to proceedings on a temporary use notice is a reference to—

(a) considering whether to give a notice of objection under section 221,

(b) holding a hearing in relation to any notice of objection given under section 221 (whether or not by the licensing authority) or agreeing to dispense with a hearing in accordance with section 222(3), and

(c) giving a counter-notice under section 224 or a notice under section 225.

Commencement

Brought into force by the Gambling Act 2005 (Commencement No 7) Order 2007, SI 2007/3155, art 2 as from 1 December 2007.

Sub-s (1): Licensing authority. For the licensing authorities for the purposes of this Act, see s 2. As to the licensing authorities' functions, see ss 232, 233.

Sub-s (1): Temporary use notice. See s 214 and the note 'Temporary use notice' thereto.

Definitions

'licensing authority': ss 2, 353(1)

'temporary use notice': ss 215(1), 353(1)

Explanatory Notes
566 [para **6.2012** below]

Miscellaneous

6.729 229 Availability of notice

(1) A person who gives a temporary use notice in respect of premises shall—

(a) arrange for a copy of the notice to be displayed prominently on the premises at any time when an activity is being carried on in reliance on the notice, and

(b) arrange for the notice endorsed by the licensing authority in accordance with section 227 to be produced on request to—

(i) a constable,

(ii) an officer of customs and excise,

(iii) an enforcement officer, or

(iv) an authorised local authority officer.

(2) A person commits an offence if he fails without reasonable excuse to comply with subsection (1).

(3) A person guilty of an offence under subsection (2) shall be liable on summary conviction to a fine not exceeding level 2 on the standard scale.

Commencement

Brought into force by the Gambling Act 2005 (Commencement No 7) Order 2007, SI 2007/3155, art 2 as from 1 December 2007.

Sub-s (1): Person. See the note 'Persons' to s 23.

Sub-s (1): Temporary use notice. See s 214 and the note 'Temporary use notice' thereto.

Sub-s (1): Licensing authority. For the licensing authorities for the purposes of this Act, see s 2. As to the licensing authorities' functions, see ss 232, 233.

Sub-s (1): Constable. See the note to s 64.

Sub-s (1): Enforcement officer. As to enforcement officers, see, generally, s 303.

Sub-s (2): Offence. For the power of the Gambling Commission and other specified persons to undertake activities for the purpose of assessing whether an offence is being committed under or by virtue of this Act, see s 27 and s 305; for the power of that Commission to investigate and prosecute offences, see s 28; as to offences committed by a body, see s 341; and for the time limit on prosecutions, see s 347. See also s 306 for powers of entry as respects a suspected offence, and s 345 as respects forfeiture of an article relating to an offence.

For the power of a licensing authority to institute criminal proceedings in respect of an offence under this section, see s 346.

Sub-s (3): Summary conviction; standard scale. See the notes to s 33.

Definitions
'authorised local authority officer': ss 304, 353(1)
'enforcement officer': s 353(1)
'licensing authority': ss 2, 353(1)
'premises': s 353(1), (2)(g)
'temporary use notice': ss 215(1), 353(1)

Explanatory Notes
567, 568 [para **6.2012** below]

6.730 230 Withdrawal of notice

If a person who gives a temporary use notice to a licensing authority in accordance with section 219 notifies the licensing authority that the notice is withdrawn—

(a) the notice shall have no effect (or, if it has started to have effect, shall cease to have effect), and

(b) no further proceedings shall take place in respect of the notice (except in respect of a matter arising during or in relation to a time at which the notice had effect).

Commencement

Brought into force by the Gambling Act 2005 (Commencement No 7) Order 2007, SI 2007/3155, art 2 as from 1 December 2007.

Person

See the note 'Persons' to s 23.

Temporary use notice. See s 214 and the note 'Temporary use notice' thereto.

Licensing authority

For the licensing authorities for the purposes of this Act, see s 2. As to the licensing authorities' functions, see ss 232, 233.

Notifies. See further, in connection with a requirement under this Act to give a notice, s 353(4).

Definitions

'licensing authority': ss 2, 353(1)
'temporary use notice': ss 215(1), 353(1)

Explanatory Notes

567, 568 [para **6.2012** below]

6.731 231 Vehicles and vessels

(1) A temporary use notice—

(a) may not be given in respect of a vehicle (or part of a vehicle),
(b) may be given in respect of all or part of a passenger vessel,
(c) may be given in respect of all or part of a vessel (within the meaning of section 353(1)) situated at a fixed place in or on water, and
(d) may not be given in respect of all or part of a vessel to which neither of paragraphs (b) and (c) applies.

(2) In relation to a vessel, a reference in this Part to a place in which premises are wholly or partly situated shall be construed—

(a) in the case of a vessel (within the meaning of section 353(1)) situated at a fixed place in or on water, as a reference to that place,
(b) in the case of a vessel which is permanently moored at a place, as a reference to that place,
(c) in the case of a vessel which is habitually moored at one place more frequently or for longer periods than at any other place, as a reference to that place, and
(d) in any other case, as a reference to any place at which a vessel is moored or is likely to be moored, or to the place in the United Kingdom nearest to any place at which a vessel is or is likely to be, while activities are carried on in the vessel in reliance on a temporary use notice.

(3) In relation to a vessel, the following are responsible authorities for the purposes of this Part (in addition to the persons listed in section 157)—

(a) a navigation authority, within the meaning of section 221(1) of the Water Resources Act 1991 (c 57), which has functions in relation to any place at which a vessel is moored or is likely to be moored, or to the place in the United Kingdom nearest to any place at which a vessel is or is likely to be, while activities are carried on in the vessel in reliance on a temporary use notice,
(b) the Environment Agency,
(c) the British Waterways Board, and
(d) the Secretary of State.

Commencement

Brought into force by the Gambling Act 2005 (Commencement No 7) Order 2007, SI 2007/3155, art 2 as from 1 December 2007.

Sub-s (1): Temporary use notice. See s 214 and the note 'Temporary use notice' thereto.

Sub-s (2): This Part. Ie Pt 9 (ss 214–234) of this Act.

Sub-s (2): United Kingdom. See the note to s 36.

Sub-s (3): Environment Agency; British Waterways Board. See the notes to s 211.

Sub-s (3): Secretary of State. See the note to s 4.

Definitions

'premises': s 353(1), (2)(g)
'temporary use notice': ss 215(1), 353(1)
'vehicle': s 353(1)
'vessel': s 353(1)

Explanatory Notes

569 [para **6.2012** below]

6.732 232 Delegation of licensing authority functions: England and Wales

(1) The functions under this Part of a licensing authority in England and Wales are by virtue of this subsection delegated to the licensing committee of the authority established under section 6 of the Licensing Act 2003 (c 17).

(2) The following provisions of the Licensing Act 2003 shall apply in relation to a function delegated to a licensing committee under this section as they apply in relation to a function delegated under that Act—

(a) section 7(9) (referral back to licensing authority), and
(b) section 10 (sub-delegation).

(3) In the application of section 10(4) of that Act (matters not to be delegated to officer) by virtue of subsection (2) above, for the list of functions there shall be substituted a reference to any function under section 224 of this Act.

(4) The provisions of section 9 of that Act and regulations under it apply to proceedings of licensing committees and their sub-committees in relation to the exercise of functions under this Part; and for that purpose regulations may, in particular, make provision which applies—

(a) only in relation to functions under that Act,
(b) only in relation to functions under this Part, or
(c) differently in relation to functions under that Act and functions under this Part.

Commencement

Brought into force by the Gambling Act 2005 (Commencement No 7) Order 2007, SI 2007/3155, art 2 as from 1 December 2007.

Sub-s (1): This Part. Ie Pt 9 (ss 214–234) of this Act.

Sub-s (1): Licensing authority. For the licensing authorities for the purposes of this Act, see s 2. As to the licensing authorities' functions, see also s 233.

Sub-s (1): England; Wales. See the note to s 2.

Definitions

'licensing authority': ss 2, 353(1)

Explanatory Notes

570 [para **6.2012** below]

6.733 233 Delegation of functions under Part 9: Scotland

[(1) Subject to subsection (2), a licensing authority in Scotland may arrange for the discharge of any of its functions under this Part by—

(a) any member of the authority,

(b) any committee established by the authority,
(c) the clerk of the authority, or
(d) any member of staff provided under paragraph 8(1)(b) of schedule 1 to the Licensing (Scotland) Act 2005 (asp 16)].[1]

(2) A licensing authority are not to make any arrangements under subsection (1) for the discharge by the clerk of the authority or any [member of staff provided under paragraph 8(1)(b) of schedule 1 to the Licensing (Scotland) Act 2005][2] of any of the authority's functions under section 224..

(3) The procedures applicable to the proceedings of licensing boards in the exercise of their functions under the Licensing (Scotland) Act [2005][3] apply to the proceedings of those boards in the exercise of their functions under this Part; and for that purpose regulations made by the Scottish Ministers may, in particular, make provision which applies—
(a) only in relation to functions under that Act,
(b) only in relation to functions under this Part,
(c) differently in relation to functions under that Act and functions under this Part.

Commencement

Brought into force by the Gambling Act 2005 (Commencement No 7) Order 2007, SI 2007/3155, art 2 as from 1 December 2007.

Sub-s (1): Licensing authority. For the licensing authorities for the purposes of this Act, see s 2. As to the licensing authorities' functions, see also s 232.

Sub-s (1): This Part. Ie Pt 9 (ss 214–234) of this Act.

Sub-s (3): Scottish Ministers. See the note to s 25.

Regulations under this section

As to regulations under this Act generally, see s 355.

Definitions

'licensing authority': ss 2, 353(1)

Explanatory Notes

571 [para **6.2012** below]

1 Sub-s (1): substituted by SSI 2009/248, art 2(1), Sch 1, Pt 1, para 12(1), (4)(a).

2 Sub-s (2): in sub-para (b) words from "member of staff" to "the Licensing (Scotland) Act 2005" in square brackets substituted by SSI 2009/248, art 2(1), Sch 1, Pt 1, para 12(1), (4)(b).

3 Sub-s (3): reference to "2005" in square brackets substituted by SSI 2009/248, art 2(1), Sch 1, Pt 1, para 12(1), (4)(c).

6.734 234 Register

(1) A licensing authority shall—
(a) maintain a register of temporary use notices given to them together with such other information as may be prescribed,
(b) make the register and information available for inspection by members of the public at all reasonable times, and
(c) make arrangements for the provision of a copy of an entry in the register, or of information, to a member of the public on request.

(2) A licensing authority may refuse to provide a copy of an entry or of information unless the person seeking it pays a reasonable fee specified by the authority.

(3) The Secretary of State may make regulations about—
(a) the form of the register;
(b) the manner in which it is maintained.

(4) The Secretary of State may make regulations—
- (a) requiring licensing authorities to give to the Commission specified information about temporary use notices given to them,
- (b) requiring the Commission to maintain a register of the information provided to it under paragraph (a),
- (c) requiring the Commission to grant access to the register to members of the public (without charge),
- (d) requiring the Commission to make copies of entries available on request, and on payment of a reasonable fee, to members of the public, and
- (e) excusing licensing authorities, wholly or partly, from compliance with subsection (1).

Commencement

Brought into force by the Gambling Act 2005 (Commencement No 7) Order 2007, SI 2007/3155, art 2 as from 1 December 2007.

Sub-s (1): Licensing authority. For the licensing authorities for the purposes of this Act, see s 2. As to the licensing authorities' functions, see ss 232, 233.

Sub-s (1): Temporary use notices. See s 214 and the note 'Temporary use notice' thereto.

Sub-s (3): Secretary of State. See the note to s 4.

Sub-s (4): The Commission. Ie the Gambling Commission; see s 353(1). As to the establishment, etc of the Gambling Commission, see s 20, Sch 4, and the note 'Gambling Commission' to that section.

Regulations under this section

At the time of going to press no regulations had been made under this section.

As to regulations under this Act generally, see s 355.

Definitions

'the Commission': s 353(1)
'licensing authority': ss 2, 353(1)
'temporary use notice': ss 215(1), 353(1)

Explanatory Notes

572, 573 [para **6.2012** below]

PART 10
GAMING MACHINES

6.735 235 Gaming machine

(1) In this Act 'gaming machine' means a machine which is designed or adapted[1] for use by individuals to gamble (whether or not it can also be used for other purposes).

(2) But—
- (a) a domestic or dual-use computer is not a gaming machine by reason only of the fact that it can be used to participate in remote gambling,
- (b) a telephone or other machine for facilitating communication (other than a computer) is not a gaming machine by reason only of the fact that it can be used to participate in remote gambling,
- (c) a machine is not a gaming machine by reason only of the fact that it is designed or adapted for use to bet on future real events,
- (d) a machine is not a gaming machine by reason only of the fact that it dispenses lottery tickets or otherwise enables a person to enter a lottery provided that the results of the lottery—
  - (i) are not determined by the machine, and
  - (ii) are not announced by being displayed or communicated by the machine without there being an interval, between each entry to the lottery and the announcement, of at least such duration as the Secretary of State shall prescribe by order,[2]

(e) a machine is not a gaming machine if—
(i) it is designed or adapted for the playing of bingo, and
(ii) it is used in accordance with a condition attached to a bingo operating licence under section 75 or 77 by virtue of section 85(2)(b),

(f) a machine is not a gaming machine if—
(i) it is designed or adapted for the playing of bingo by way of prize gaming, and
(ii) it is used in accordance with a condition attached to a gaming machine general operating licence under section 75 or 77 by virtue of section 85(2)(b),

(g) a machine is not a gaming machine if—
(i) it is designed or adapted for the playing of bingo by way of prize gaming,
(ii) it is made available for use in reliance on a family entertainment centre gaming machine permit or a prize gaming permit, and
(iii) any requirements prescribed for the purposes of this paragraph in a code of practice under section 24, as to the specification of the machine or the circumstances in which it is made available for use, are complied with,

(h) a machine is not a gaming machine by reason only of the fact that it is designed or adapted to be—
(i) controlled or operated by an individual employed or concerned in arranging for others to play a real game of chance, or
(ii) used in connection with a real game of chance the arrangements for which are controlled or operated by an individual, and

(i) a machine is not a gaming machine by reason only of the fact that it is designed or adapted to enable individuals to play a real game of chance, if—
(i) its design or adaptation is such that it does not require to be controlled or operated by a person employed or concerned in arranging for others to play the game,
(ii) it is not designed or adapted for use in connection with a game the arrangements for which are controlled or operated by an individual, and
(iii) it is used in accordance with a condition attached to a casino operating licence under section 75 or 77 by virtue of section 85(2)(b).

(3) In this Act—
(a) a reference to a machine is a reference to any apparatus which uses or applies mechanical power, electrical power or both,
(b) a reference to a machine being designed or adapted for a purpose includes—
(i) a reference to a computer being able to be used for that purpose (subject to subsection (2)), and
(ii) a reference to any other machine to which anything has been done as a result of which it can reasonably be expected to be used for that purpose (subject to subsection (2)),
(c) a reference to a part of a gaming machine—
(i) includes a reference to any computer software designed or adapted for use in a gaming machine, but
(ii) does not include a reference to a component of a gaming machine which does not influence the outcome of a game,

(d) a reference to installing a part of a gaming machine includes a reference to installing computer software for the purpose of altering the operation of a gaming machine,

(e) a reference to adapting a gaming machine includes a reference to adapting a machine so that it becomes a gaming machine, and

(f) 'domestic computer' and 'dual-use computer' shall have the meanings assigned by the Secretary of State by regulations.

(4) Regulations under subsection (3)(f) may, in particular, make provision by reference to—

(a) the location of a computer,

(b) the purposes for which a computer is used,

(c) the circumstances in which a computer is used,

(d) the software installed on a computer, or

(e) any other matter.

(5) The Secretary of State may make regulations providing for circumstances in which a single piece of apparatus is to be treated as more than one gaming machine for the purpose of provision made by or by virtue of this Act; and the regulations may, in particular, make provision by reference to the number of persons able to operate the apparatus at the same time.

Note

See the Gambling Commission publications at paras **6.2360**, **6.2520–6.2634.5**, **6.2657**, **6.2660–6.2671**, **6.2673–6.2674** and **6.2685–6.2686** below.

Commencement

(1), (2)(b)–(i), (3)(a)–(e), (5) brought into force by the Gambling Act 2005 (Commencement No 6 and Transitional Provisions) Order 2006, SI 2006/3272, art 2, Sch 1 as from 1 January 2007; for transitional provisions see art 6, Sch 4 thereto (as amended by SI 2007/1157, arts 7–12).

Subsections (2)(a), (3)(f), (4) brought into force by the Gambling Act 2005 (Commencement No 6 and Transitional Provisions) Order 2006, SI 2006/3272, art 2, Sch 2 as from 30 April 2007; for transitional provisions see art 6, Sch 4 thereto (as amended by SI 2007/1157, arts 7–12).

Sub-s (2): Operating licence. As to the nature, etc of operating licences, see s 65 and the note 'Operating licences' thereto.

Sub-s (2): Secretary of State. See the note to s 4.

Sub-s (2): Family entertainment centre gaming machine permit. See s 247.

Sub-s (2): Prize gaming permit. See s 289.

Territorial Application

For the territorial application of this Part of this Act, see s 251.

Subordinate Legislation:

SI 2007/2082, SI 2007/2289, SI 2007/2495

As to regulations under this Act generally, see s 355.

Definitions

'betting': ss 9–11, 353(1)
'bingo': s 353(1)
'family entertainment centre gaming machine permit': ss 247(2), 353(1)
'gambling': ss 3, 353(1)
'game of chance': ss 6, 353(1)
'installing computer software': s 353(2)(d)
'lottery': ss 14, 353(1)
'lottery ticket': ss 253(1), 353(1)
'operating licence': s 353(1)
'prize gaming': ss 288, 353(1)
'prize gaming permit: ss 289(2), 353(1)

'real': s 353(1)
'remote gambling': ss 4, 353(1)

Explanatory Notes

574–584 [para **6.2012** below]

---

[1] See *R (on the application of the Gambling Commission) v Bird* [2010] EWHC 995 (Admin) where it was decided that a machine which awarded credits from which prizes could be obtained was a gaming machine; the fact that it neither informed the player that he would be able to claim a prize nor had a mechanism to deliver a prize nor provided him with a document evidencing his right to claim was deemed irrelevant to the definition set out in s 235(1).

[2] See the Gambling Commission's publication of August 2012 'Comparing lottery ticket dispensers and category B3A gaming machines' available on the Commission's website.

6.736 236 Gaming machines: Categories A to D

(1) The Secretary of State shall make regulations defining four classes of gaming machine for the purposes of this Act (to be known as Categories A, B, C, and D).

(2) Regulations under subsection (1) shall—

(a) divide Category B into sub-categories, and

(b) make provision for determining to which sub-category (or sub-categories) of Category B a reference in this Act to Category B shall be treated as referring.

(3) Regulations under subsection (1) shall operate by reference to the nature of the facilities for gambling provided by the machine.

(4) Regulations under subsection (1) may, in particular, make provision by reference to—

(a) amounts paid in respect of the use of a machine;

(b) the value of prizes;

(c) the nature of prizes;

(d) the nature of the gambling for which the machine can be used;

(e) the premises where a machine is used.

(5) Regulations under subsection (1) may identify matters (whether or not addressed by other provisions of the regulations) as to which a condition may not be attached to an operating licence or to a premises licence.

(6) In accordance with regulations under subsection (1) a machine may change category as a result of a change of the mechanism, or the loading or removal of software, which alters the nature of the facilities for gambling provided by the machine.

Commencement

Brought into force by the Gambling Act 2005 (Commencement No 6 and Transitional Provisions) Order 2006, SI 2006/3272, art 2, Sch 2 as from 30 April 2007; for transitional provisions see art 6, Sch 4 thereto (as amended by SI 2007/1157, arts 7–12).

Sub-s (1): Secretary of State. See the note to s 4.

Sub-s (1): Regulations. An operating licence may not include a condition that contradicts a provision of regulations under this section or of a kind prohibited by regulations under this section (see s 86), and a premises licence may not make provision that contradicts a provision of regulations under this section or of a kind prohibited by regulations under this section (see s 172(10)).

Sub-s (5): Operating licence. As to the nature, etc of operating licences, see s 65 and the note 'Operating licences' thereto.

Sub-s (5): Premises licence. As to the nature, etc of premises licences, see s 150 and the note 'Premises licence' thereto.

Territorial Application

For the territorial application of this Part of this Act, see s 251.

Subordinate Legislation:

SI 2007/2158.

As to regulations under this Act generally, see s 355.

Definitions

'gaming machine': ss 235, 353(1)
'machine': ss 235(3)(a), 353(1)
'operating licence': s 353(1)
'premises': s 353(1), (2)(g)
'premises licence': s 353(1)
'prize': ss 239, 353(1)
'provide facilities for gambling': ss 5, 353(1)

Explanatory Notes

585–589 [para **6.2012** below]

6.737 237 Adult gaming centre

In this Act 'adult gaming centre' means premises in respect of which an adult gaming centre premises licence has effect.

Commencement

Brought into force by the Gambling Act 2005 (Commencement No 6 and Transitional Provisions) Order 2006, SI 2006/3272, art 2, Sch 1 as from 1 January 2007; for transitional provisions see art 6, Sch 4 thereto (as amended by SI 2007/1157, arts 7–12).

Premises licence

As to the nature, etc of premises licences, see s 150 and the note 'Premises licence' thereto.

Territorial application

For the territorial application of this Part of this Act, see s 251.

Definitions

'premises': s 353(1), (2)(g)
'premises licence': s 353(1)

6.738 238 Family entertainment centre

In this Act—

'family entertainment centre' means premises (other than an adult gaming centre) wholly or mainly used for making gaming machines available for use, and

'licensed family entertainment centre' means premises in respect of which a family entertainment centre premises licence has effect.

Commencement

Brought into force by the Gambling Act 2005 (Commencement No 6 and Transitional Provisions) Order 2006, SI 2006/3272, art 2, Sch 1 as from 1 January 2007; for transitional provisions see art 6, Sch 4 thereto (as amended by SI 2007/1157, arts 7–12).

Premises licence

As to the nature, etc of premises licences, see s 150 and the note 'Premises licence' thereto.

Territorial Application

For the territorial application of this Part of this Act, see s 251.

Definitions

'adult gaming centre': ss 237, 353(1)
'gaming machine': ss 235, 353(1)
'premises': s 353(1), (2)(g)
'premises licence': s 353(1)

6.739 239 Prize

In this Act 'prize' in relation to a gaming machine—

(a) includes any money, article, right or service won, whether or not described as a prize, but
(b) does not include an opportunity to play the machine again.

Commencement

Brought into force by the Gambling Act 2005 (Commencement No 6 and Transitional Provisions) Order 2006, SI 2006/3272, art 2, Sch 1 as from 1 January 2007; for transitional provisions see art 6, Sch 4 thereto (as amended by SI 2007/1157, arts 7–12).

Territorial application

For the territorial application of this Part of this Act, see s 251.

Definitions

'gaming machine': ss 235, 353(1)

Regulations

6.740 240 Use of machine

(1) The Secretary of State may make regulations controlling the circumstances in which a gaming machine is made available for use.

(2) Regulations under subsection (1) may, in particular, make provision by reference to—

(a) the method by which stakes may be deposited or payments made for the use of a machine;
(b) the nature of, or arrangements in respect of receiving or claiming, prizes;
(c) rollover of stakes or prizes;
(d) the proportion of amounts staked or paid that is returned by way of prizes;
(e) the display of information;
(f) any other matter relating to the manner in which a machine operates.

(3) Regulations under subsection (1) may identify matters (whether or not addressed by other provisions of the regulations) as to which a condition may not be attached to an operating licence or to a premises licence.

Note

In June 2007 the Gambling Commission issued a number of detailed documents concerned with machine standards see para **6.2520** ff below).

Commencement

Brought into force by the Gambling Act 2005 (Commencement No 6 and Transitional Provisions) Order 2006, SI 2006/3272, art 2, Sch 1 as from 1 January 2007; for transitional provisions see art 6, Sch 4 thereto (as amended by SI 2007/1157, arts 7–12).

Sub-s (1): Secretary of State. See the note to s 4.

Sub-s (1): Regulations. An operating licence may not include a condition that contradicts a provision of regulations under this section or of a kind prohibited by regulations under this section (see s 86), and a premises licence may not make provision that contradicts a provision of regulations under this section or of a kind prohibited by regulations under this section (see s 172(10)).

A person commits an offence if he makes a gaming machine available for use in contravention of regulations under this section; see s 242(2).

Sub-s (3): Operating licence. As to the nature, etc of operating licences, see s 65 and the note 'Operating licences' thereto.

Sub-s (3): Premises licence. As to the nature, etc of premises licences, see s 150 and the note 'Premises licence' thereto.

Territorial application

For the territorial application of this Part of this Act, see s 251.

Subordinate Legislation:
SI 2007/2319.

Definitions
'gaming machine': ss 235, 353(1)
'machine': ss 235(3)(a), 353(1)
'operating licence': s 353(1)
'premises licence': s 353(1)
'prize': ss 239, 353(1)
'stake': s 353(1)

Explanatory Notes
591–595 [para **6.2012** below]

6.741 241 Supply, &c

(1) The Secretary of State may make regulations about the supply, installation, adaptation, maintenance or repair of a gaming machine or part of a gaming machine.

(2) Regulations under subsection (1) may identify matters (whether or not addressed by other provisions of the regulations) as to which a condition may not be attached to an operating licence or to a premises licence.

Commencement

Brought into force by the Gambling Act 2005 (Commencement No 6 and Transitional Provisions) Order 2006, SI 2006/3272, art 2, Sch 1 as from 1 January 2007; for transitional provisions see art 6, Sch 4 thereto (as amended by SI 2007/1157, arts 7–12).

Sub-s (1): Secretary of State. See the note to s 4.

Sub-s (1): Regulations. An operating licence may not include a condition that contradicts a provision of regulations under this section or of a kind prohibited by regulations under this section (see s 86), and a premises licence may not make provision that contradicts a provision of regulations under this section or of a kind prohibited by regulations under this section (see s 172(10)).

A person commits an offence if he supplies, installs, adapts, maintains or repairs a gaming machine or part of a gaming machine and fails to comply with a provision of regulations under this section; see s 243(2).

Sub-s (2): Operating licence. As to the nature, etc of operating licences, see s 65 and the note 'Operating licences' thereto.

Sub-s (2): Premises licence. As to the nature, etc of premises licences, see s 150 and the note 'Premises licence' thereto.

Territorial application

For the territorial application of this Part of this Act, see s 251.

Subordinate Legislation:
SI 2007/2320.

Definitions
'adapting a gaming machine': s 235(3)(e)
'gaming machine': ss 235, 353(1)
'installing a part of a gaming machine': s 235(3)(d)
'operating licence': s 353(1)
'part of a gaming machine': s 235(3)(c)
'premises licence': s 353(1)
'supply': s 353(1)

Explanatory Notes

591–595 [para **6.2012** below]

Offences

6.742 242 Making machine available for use

(1) A person commits an offence if he makes a gaming machine available for use by another unless—

(a) he makes the machine available for use in accordance with an operating licence, or

(b) an exception in section 247, 248, 249, 271, 273, 282, 283 or 287 applies.

(2) A person commits an offence if he makes a gaming machine available for use in contravention of regulations under section 240.

Commencement

Brought into force by the Gambling Act 2005 (Commencement No 6 and Transitional Provisions) Order 2006, SI 2006/3272, art 2 as from 1 September 2007; for transitional provisions see art 6, Sch 4 thereto (as amended by SI 2007/1157, arts 7–12).

Sub-s (1): Person. See the note 'Persons' to s 23.

Sub-s (1): Offence. For the power of the Gambling Commission and other specified persons to undertake activities for the purpose of assessing whether an offence is being committed under or by virtue of this Act, see s 27 and s 305; for the power of that Commission to investigate and prosecute offences, see s 28; as to offences committed by a body, see s 341; and for the time limit on prosecutions, see s 347. See also s 306 for powers of entry as respects a suspected offence, and s 345 as respects forfeiture of an article relating to an offence. For territorial limitations on offences under this Part of this Act, see ss 359, 360.

For penalties, see s 246.

For the power of a licensing authority to institute criminal proceedings in respect of an offence under this section, see s 346.

Sub-s (1): Operating licence. As to the nature, etc of operating licences, see s 65 and the note 'Operating licences' thereto.

Territorial application

For the territorial application of this Part of this Act, see s 251.

Definitions

'gaming machine': ss 235, 353(1)
'operating licence': s 353(1)

Explanatory Notes

596–598 [para **6.2012** below]

6.743 243 Manufacture, supply, &c

(1) A person commits an offence if he manufactures, supplies, installs, adapts, maintains or repairs a gaming machine or part of a gaming machine unless—

(a) he acts in accordance with an operating licence, or

(b) an exception in or under section 248 or 250 applies.

(2) A person commits an offence if he—

(a) supplies, installs, adapts, maintains or repairs a gaming machine or part of a gaming machine, and

(b) fails to comply with a provision of regulations under section 241.

(3) Subsections (1) and (2) do not apply to the supply of a gaming machine, or part of a gaming machine—

(a) as scrap (without any element of salvage), or

(b) incidental to the sale or letting of property on which the machine has previously been used in reliance on a provision of this Act.

Commencement

Brought into force by the Gambling Act 2005 (Commencement No 6 and Transitional Provisions) Order 2006, SI 2006/3272, art 2 as from 1 September 2007; for transitional provisions see art 6, Sch 4 thereto (as amended by SI 2007/1157, arts 7–12).

Sub-s (1): Person. See the note 'Persons' to s 23.

Sub-s (1): Offence. For the power of the Gambling Commission and other specified persons to undertake activities for the purpose of assessing whether an offence is being committed under or by virtue of this Act, see s 27 and s 305; for the power of that Commission to investigate and prosecute offences, see s 28; as to offences committed by a body, see s 341; and for the time limit on prosecutions, see s 347. See also s 306 for powers of entry as respects a suspected offence, and s 345 as respects forfeiture of an article relating to an offence. For territorial limitations on offences under this Part of this Act, see ss 359, 360.

For penalties, see s 246, and for the power of the Secretary of Sate to make regulations creating exceptions from the offence under this section, see s 248(2).

Sub-s (1): Operating licence. As to the nature, etc of operating licences, see s 65 and the note 'Operating licences' thereto.

Territorial application

For the territorial application of this Part of this Act, see s 251.

Definitions

'adapting a gaming machine': s 235(3)(e)
'gaming machine': ss 235, 353(1)
'installing a part of a gaming machine': s 235(3)(d)
'operating licence': s 353(1)
'part of a gaming machine': s 235(3)(c)
'supply': s 353(1)

Explanatory Notes

599–601 [para **6.2012** below]

6.744 244 Linked machines

(1) A person commits an offence if—

(a) he makes a gaming machine ('the first gaming machine') available for use by another, and

(b) the amount or value of a prize available through use of the first gaming machine is or may be wholly or partly determined by reference to use made of another gaming machine ('the linked gaming machine').

(2) But subsection (1) does not apply where—

(a) the person who makes the first gaming machine available for use is the holder of a casino premises licence, and

(b) the first gaming machine and the linked gaming machine are situated on the same premises.

(3) The Secretary of State may by order amend, or modify the effect of, subsection (2) so that subsection (1) is disapplied to the linking of machines in casinos whether or not the machines are situated on the same premises—

(a) to such extent as the order may specify,

(b) in such circumstances as the order may specify, and

(c) subject to such conditions as the order may specify.

Note

In June 2007 the Gambling Commission published 'Machine Standards Linked Progressives' (see para **6.2560** below).

Commencement

Brought into force by the Gambling Act 2005 (Commencement No 6 and Transitional Provisions) Order 2006, SI 2006/3272, art 2 as from 1 September 2007; for transitional provisions see art 6, Sch 4 thereto (as amended by SI 2007/1157, arts 7–12).

Sub-s (1): Person. See the note 'Persons' to s 23.

Sub-s (1): Offence. For the power of the Gambling Commission and other specified persons to undertake activities for the purpose of assessing whether an offence is being committed under or by virtue of this Act, see s 27 and s 305; for the power of that Commission to investigate and prosecute offences, see s 28; as to offences committed by a body, see s 341; and for the time limit on prosecutions, see s 347. See also s 306 for powers of entry as respects a suspected offence, and s 345 as respects forfeiture of an article relating to an offence. For territorial limitations on offences under this Part of this Act, see ss 359, 360.

For penalties, see s 246.

Sub-s (2): Premises licence. As to the nature, etc of premises licences, see s 150 and the note 'Premises licence' thereto.

Sub-s (3): Secretary of State. See the note to s 4.

Territorial application

For the territorial application of this Part of this Act, see s 251.

Orders under this section

At the time of going to press no orders had been made under this section.

As to orders under this Act generally, see s 355.

Definitions

'casino': ss 7, 353(1)
'gaming machine': ss 235, 353(1)
'machine': ss 235(3)(a), 353(1)
'premises': s 353(1), (2)(g)
'premises licence': s 353(1)
'prize': ss 239, 353(1)

Explanatory Notes

602–604 [para **6.2012** below]

6.745

245 [*Repealed by SI 2007/2321, reg 2(c).*]

6.746 246 Penalty

(1) A person guilty of an offence under this Part shall be liable on summary conviction to—

(a) imprisonment for a term not exceeding 51 weeks,
(b) a fine not exceeding level 5 on the standard scale, or
(c) both.

(2) In the application of subsection (1) to Scotland the reference to 51 weeks shall have effect as a reference to six months.

Commencement

Brought into force by the Gambling Act 2005 (Commencement No 6 and Transitional Provisions) Order 2006, SI 2006/3272, art 2 as from 1 September 2007; for transitional provisions see art 6, Sch 4 thereto (as amended by SI 2007/1157, arts 7–12).

Sub-s (1): Person. See the note 'Persons' to s 23.

Sub-s (1): This Part. Ie Pt 10 (ss 235–251 and Sch 10) of this Act.

Sub-s (1): Summary conviction; standard scale. See the notes to s 33.

Territorial application

For the territorial application of this Part of this Act, see s 251.

Exceptions

6.747 247 Family entertainment centre gaming machine permit

(1) A person does not commit an offence under section 37 or 242 if he makes a Category D gaming machine available for use in accordance with a family entertainment centre gaming machine permit.

(2) A family entertainment centre gaming machine permit is a permit issued by a licensing authority authorising a person to make Category D gaming machines available for use in a specified family entertainment centre.

(3) Schedule 10 makes further provision about family entertainment centre gaming machine permits.

Commencement

Subsection (1) brought into force by the Gambling Act 2005 (Commencement No 6 and Transitional Provisions) Order 2006, SI 2006/3272, art 2 as from 1 September 2007; for transitional provisions see art 6, Sch 4 thereto (as amended by SI 2007/1157, arts 7–12).

Subsection (2) brought into force for certain purposes as from 13 November 2006 by the Gambling Act 2005 (Commencement No 4) Order 2006, SI 2006/2964, art 2(b).

Subsection (3) brought into force for certain purposes as from 13 November 2006 by the Gambling Act 2005 (Commencement No 4) Order 2006, SI 2006/2964, art 2(b) and for certain purposes as from 30 April 2007, for remaining purposes as from 1 September 2007 by the Gambling Act 2005 (Commencement No 6 and Transitional Provisions) Order 2006, SI 2006/3272, art 2, Sch 2; for transitional provisions see art 6, Sch 4 thereto (as amended by SI 2007/1157, arts 7–12).

Sub-s (1): Person. See the note 'Persons' to s 23.

Sub-s (1): Category D gaming machine. As to the categories of gaming machine, see s 236.

Sub-s (1): Family entertainment centre gaming machine permit. For powers of entry in connection with such a permit, see s 309.

Sub-s (2): Licensing authority. For the licensing authorities for the purposes of this Act, see s 2.

Sub-s (2): Person. See the note 'Persons' to s 23.

Territorial application

For the territorial application of this Part of this Act, see s 251.

Definitions

'Category D gaming machine': s 353(1)
'licensing authority: ss 2, 353(1)

Explanatory Notes

606, 607 [para **6.2012** below]

6.748 248 No prize

(1) A person does not commit an offence under section 37 or 242 if—

(a) he makes a gaming machine available for use by an individual, and

(b) the individual does not, by using the machine, acquire an opportunity to win a prize.

(2) The Secretary of State may make regulations creating exceptions from the offence under section 243 in connection with machines which, by virtue of their nature or any other specified matter, are not designed or expected to be used to provide an opportunity to win a prize.

Commencement

Subsection (1) brought into force by the Gambling Act 2005 (Commencement No 6 and Transitional Provisions) Order 2006, SI 2006/3272, art 2 as from 1 September 2007; for transitional provisions see art 6, Sch 4 thereto (as amended by SI 2007/1157, arts 7–12).

Subsection (2) brought into force by the Gambling Act 2005 (Commencement No 6 and Transitional Provisions) Order 2006, SI 2006/3272, art 2, Sch 1 as from 1 January 2007; for transitional provisions see art 6, Sch 4 thereto (as amended by SI 2007/1157, arts 7–12).

Sub-s (1): Person. See the note 'Persons' to s 23.

Sub-s (2): Secretary of State. See the note to s 4.

Territorial application

For the territorial application of this Part of this Act, see s 251.

Regulations under this section

At the time of going to press no regulations had been made under this section.

As to regulations under this Act generally, see s 355.

Definitions

'gaming machine': ss 235, 353(1)
'machine': ss 235(3)(a), 353(1)
'prize': ss 239, 353(1)

Explanatory Notes

613–615 [para **6.2013** below]

6.749 249 Limited prize

(1) A person does not commit an offence under section 37 or 242 if—

(a) he makes a gaming machine available for use by an individual, and

(b) the individual does not, by using the machine, acquire an opportunity to win a prize of a value in excess of the amount that he pays for or in connection with his use of the machine.

(2) For the purpose of subsection (1)(b)—

(a) the reference to paying includes a reference to—

(i) paying money by way of an entrance charge,

(ii) using a coin to activate a gaming machine where the coin will not or may not be returned,

(iii) transferring money's worth, and

(iv) paying for goods or services at a price or rate which reflects the opportunity to use a gaming machine, and

(b) it is immaterial—

(i) to whom payment is made, and

(ii) who receives benefit from the payment.

Commencement

Brought into force by the Gambling Act 2005 (Commencement No 6 and Transitional Provisions) Order 2006, SI 2006/3272, art 2 as from 1 September 2007; for transitional provisions see art 6, Sch 4 thereto (as amended by SI 2007/1157, arts 7–12).

Sub-s (1): Person. See the note 'Persons' to s 23.

Territorial application

For the territorial application of this Part of this Act, see s 251.

Definitions

'gaming machine': ss 235, 353(1)
'prize': ss 239, 353(1)

Explanatory Notes

613–615 [para **6.2013** below]

6.750 250 Single-machine supply and maintenance permits

(1) A person does not commit an offence under section 33 or 243(1) by reason only of the fact that he supplies, repairs, installs or maintains a gaming machine or part of a gaming machine in accordance with a permit under this section.

(2) A person may apply to the Commission for a permit authorising him to supply, repair, install or maintain a gaming machine or part of a gaming machine.

(3) An application under this section must—

(a) be made in writing,

(b) specify the gaming machine or part in relation to which the permit is sought,

(c) give such details of the activity in relation to which the permit is sought as the Commission may direct,

(d) be in such form, and contain such other information, as the Commission may direct, and
(e) be accompanied by the prescribed fee.

(4) On consideration of an application under this section the Commission may—
(a) grant the application and issue a permit to the applicant, or
(b) refuse the application.

(5) The Commission may grant an application under this section only if satisfied that the licensing objectives are irrelevant to the activity for which the permit is sought.

(6) A permit under this section must specify—
(a) a period, not exceeding one year, during which it has effect,
(b) the machine or part to which it relates, and
(c) the activities which it authorises.

(7) A permit under this section may be subject to a condition attached by the Commission.

(8) In subsection (3)(e) 'prescribed' means prescribed by regulations made by the Secretary of State.

Commencement

Brought into force by the Gambling Act 2005 (Commencement No 6 and Transitional Provisions) Order 2006, SI 2006/3272, art 2 as from 1 September 2007; for transitional provisions see art 6, Sch 4 thereto (as amended by SI 2007/1157, arts 7–12).

Sub-s (1): Person. See the note 'Persons' to s 23.

Sub-s (2): The Commission. Ie the Gambling Commission; see s 353(1). As to the establishment, etc of the Gambling Commission, see s 20, Sch 4, and the note 'Gambling Commission' to that section.

Sub-s (3): Writing. See the note to s 39.

Sub-s (8): Secretary of State. See the note to s 4.

Territorial application

For the territorial application of this Part of this Act, see s 251.

Subordinate Legislation

Gambling (Operating Licence and Single-Machine Permit Fees) Regulations 2006, SI 2006/3284 (made under sub-ss (3)(e), (8)).

As to regulations under this Act generally, see s 355.

Definitions

'the Commission': s 353(1)
'gaming machine': ss 235, 353(1)
'installing a part of a gaming machine': s 235(3)(d)
'the licensing objectives': ss 1, 353(1)
'part of a gaming machine': s 235(3)(c)
'supply': s 353(1)

Explanatory Notes

616–618 [para 6.2013 below]

General

6.751 251 Territorial application

This Part applies—
(a) to anything done in relation to a gaming machine which (or any part of which) is situated in Great Britain, and
(b) to anything done in Great Britain in relation to a gaming machine (irrespective of where it is situated).

Commencement

Brought into force by the Gambling Act 2005 (Commencement No 6 and Transitional Provisions) Order 2006, SI 2006/3272, art 2, Sch 1 as from 1 January 2007; for transitional provisions see art 6, Sch 4 thereto (as amended by SI 2007/1157, arts 7–12).

This Part

Ie Pt 10 (ss 235–251 and Sch 10) of this Act.

Great Britain

See the note to s 12.

Definitions

'gaming machine': ss 235, 353(1)
'part of a gaming machine': s 235(3)(c)

PART 11
LOTTERIES

Interpretation

6.752 252 Promoting a lottery

(1) For the purposes of this Act a person promotes a lottery if he makes or participates in making the arrangements for a lottery.

(2) In particular, a person promotes a lottery if he—

(a) makes arrangements for the printing of lottery tickets,
(b) makes arrangements for the printing of promotional material,
(c) arranges for the distribution or publication of promotional material,
(d) possesses promotional material with a view to its distribution or publication,
(e) makes other arrangements to advertise a lottery,
(f) invites a person to participate in a lottery,
(g) sells or supplies a lottery ticket,
(h) offers to sell or supply a lottery ticket,
(i) possesses a lottery ticket with a view to its sale or supply,
(j) does or offers to do anything by virtue of which a person becomes a member of a class among whom prizes in a lottery are to be allocated, or
(k) uses premises for the purpose of allocating prizes or for any other purpose connected with the administration of a lottery.

(3) In subsection (2) 'promotional material' means a document which—

(a) advertises a specified lottery,
(b) invites participation in a specified lottery,
(c) contains information about how to participate in a specified lottery, or
(d) lists winners in a specified lottery.

(4) Where arrangements for a lottery are made by an external lottery manager on behalf of a society or authority, for the purposes of this Act both the external lottery manager and the society or authority promote the lottery.

Commencement

Brought into force by the Gambling Act 2005 (Commencement No 6 and Transitional Provisions) Order 2006, SI 2006/3272, art 2, Sch 1 as from 1 January 2007; for transitional provisions see art 6, Sch 4 thereto (as amended by SI 2007/1157, arts 7–12).

Sub-s (1): Person. See the note 'Persons' to s 23.

Exclusion of the National Lottery and territorial application. See ss 264, 265.

Definitions

'advertising gambling': ss 327, 353(2)(b)
'external lottery manager': ss 257, 353(1)

'lottery': ss 14, 353(1)
'lottery ticket': ss 253(1), 353(1)
'participating in a lottery': ss 14, 353(2)(c)
'premises': s 353(1), (2)(g)
'prize': ss 14(4), 353(1)
'publication': s 353(2)(j)
'sale or supply of a lottery ticket': ss 253(2), 353(2)(k)
'society': s 353(1)
'supply': s 353(1)

Explanatory Notes

622, 623 [para **6.2014** below]

6.753 253 Lottery ticket

(1) For the purposes of this Act a document or article is a lottery ticket if it confers, or can be used to prove, membership of a class for the purpose of the allocation of prizes in a lottery.

(2) A reference in this Act to the sale or supply of a lottery ticket by a person includes a reference to a person doing anything as a result of which another person becomes a member of the class among whom prizes in a lottery are to be allocated.

(3) A reference in this Act to purchase of a lottery ticket includes a reference to any action by a person as a result of which he becomes a member of the class among whom prizes in a lottery are to be allocated.

Commencement

Brought into force by the Gambling Act 2005 (Commencement No 6 and Transitional Provisions) Order 2006, SI 2006/3272, art 2, Sch 1 as from 1 January 2007; for transitional provisions see art 6, Sch 4 thereto (as amended by SI 2007/1157, arts 7–12).

Sub-s (2): Person. See the note 'Persons' to s 23.

Exclusion of the National Lottery and territorial application. See ss 264, 265.

Definitions

'lottery': ss 14, 353(1)
'prize': ss 14(4), 353(1)
'supply': s 353(1)

Explanatory Notes

624 [para **6.2014** below]

6.754 254 Proceeds and profits

(1) In this Act a reference to the proceeds of a lottery is a reference to the aggregate of amounts paid in respect of the purchase of lottery tickets.

(2) In this Act a reference to the profits of a lottery is a reference to—

(a) the proceeds of the lottery, minus

(b) amounts deducted by the promoters of the lottery in respect of—

(i) the provision of prizes,

(ii) sums to be made available for allocation in another lottery in accordance with a rollover, or

(iii) other costs reasonably incurred in organising the lottery.

Commencement

Brought into force by the Gambling Act 2005 (Commencement No 6 and Transitional Provisions) Order 2006, SI 2006/3272, art 2, Sch 1 as from 1 January 2007; for transitional provisions see art 6, Sch 4 thereto (as amended by SI 2007/1157, arts 7–12).

Exclusion of the National Lottery and territorial application. See ss 264, 265.

Definitions

'lottery': ss 14, 353(1)
'lottery ticket': ss 253(1), 353(1)

'prize': ss 14(4), 353(1)
'promoting a lottery': ss 252, 353(2)(h)
'purchase of a lottery ticket': ss 253(3), 353(2)(k)
'rollover': ss 256, 353(1)

Explanatory Notes
625–628 [para **6.2014** below]

6.755 255 Draw

In this Act 'draw', in relation to a lottery, includes any process by which a prize in the lottery is allocated.

Commencement
Brought into force by the Gambling Act 2005 (Commencement No 6 and Transitional Provisions) Order 2006, SI 2006/3272, art 2, Sch 1 as from 1 January 2007; for transitional provisions see art 6, Sch 4 thereto (as amended by SI 2007/1157, arts 7–12).
Exclusion of the National Lottery and territorial application. See ss 264, 265.

Definitions
'lottery': ss 14, 353(1)
'prize': ss 14(4), 353(1)

Explanatory Notes
625–628 [para **6.2014** below]

6.756 256 Rollover

(1) In this Act 'rollover' in relation to a lottery means an arrangement whereby the fact that a prize is not allocated or claimed in one lottery increases the value of the prizes available for allocation in another lottery.

(2) For the purposes of this Act where prizes are allocated by means of more than one draw—

(a) the draws together constitute a single lottery if the class of persons among whom prizes are allocated is (and, by virtue of arrangements for the sale or supply of tickets, must be) the same in the case of each draw, and
(b) otherwise, the arrangements for each draw constitute a separate lottery.

Commencement
Brought into force by the Gambling Act 2005 (Commencement No 6 and Transitional Provisions) Order 2006, SI 2006/3272, art 2, Sch 1 as from 1 January 2007; for transitional provisions see art 6, Sch 4 thereto (as amended by SI 2007/1157, arts 7–12).
Exclusion of the National Lottery and territorial application. See ss 264, 265.

Definitions
'draw': ss 255, 353(1)
'lottery': ss 14, 353(1)
'prize': ss 14(4), 353(1)
'sale or supply of a lottery ticket': ss 253(2), 353(2)(k)
'supply': s 353(1)

Explanatory Notes
625–628 [para **6.2014** below]

6.757 257 External lottery manager

A person acts as an external lottery manager for the purposes of this Act if he makes arrangements for a lottery on behalf of a society or authority of which he is not—

(a) a member,
(b) an officer, or
(c) an employee under a contract of employment.

Commencement

Brought into force by the Gambling Act 2005 (Commencement No 6 and Transitional Provisions) Order 2006, SI 2006/3272, art 2, Sch 1 as from 1 January 2007; for transitional provisions see art 6, Sch 4 thereto (as amended by SI 2007/1157, arts 7–12).

Exclusion of the National Lottery and territorial application. See ss 264, 265.

Definitions

'lottery': ss 14, 353(1)
'society': s 353(1)

Explanatory Notes

629 [para **6.2014** below]

Offences

6.758 258 Promotion of lottery

(1) A person commits an offence if he promotes a lottery unless—

(a) the exception in subsection (2) or (3) applies, or

(b) the lottery is an exempt lottery.

(2) This section does not apply to activity by a person if—

(a) he holds an operating licence authorising the activity, and

(b) he acts in accordance with the terms and conditions of the licence.

(3) This section does not apply to activity by a person if—

(a) he acts, otherwise than as an external lottery manager, on behalf of a person who holds an operating licence authorising the activity, and

(b) the activity is carried on in accordance with the terms and conditions of the licence.

(4) It is a defence for a person charged with an offence under this section to show that he reasonably believed that—

(a) he was not committing the offence by reason of subsection (1)(b), (2) or (3),

(b) that the arrangement to which the charge relates was not a lottery, or

(c) that the arrangement to which the charge relates was a lottery forming part of the National Lottery.

(5) In this Act 'exempt lottery' means a lottery which is exempt by virtue of a provision of Schedule 11.

Commencement

Subsections (1)–(4) brought into force by the Gambling Act 2005 (Commencement No 6 and Transitional Provisions) Order 2006, SI 2006/3272, art 2 as from 1 September 2007; for transitional provisions see art 6, Sch 4 thereto (as amended by SI 2007/1157, arts 7–12).

Subsection (5) brought into force, in so far as it relates to the provisions of Schedule 11, paras 1–8, 10–12, 20, 30 and 31 (for the purposes of ss 17 and 18), by the Gambling Act 2005 (Commencement No 2 and Transitional Provisions) Order 2005, SI 2005/2455, art 2 and Schedule, as from 1 October 2005 and for remaining purposes by the Gambling Act 2005 (Commencement No 6 and Transitional Provisions) Order 2006, SI 2006/3272, art 2 as from 1 September 2007.

Sub-s (1): Person. See the note 'Persons' to s 23.

Sub-s (1): Offence. For the power of the Gambling Commission and other specified persons to undertake activities for the purpose of assessing whether an offence is being committed under or by virtue of this Act, see s 27 and s 305; for the power of that Commission to investigate and prosecute offences, see s 28; as to offences committed by a body, see s 341; and for the time limit on prosecutions, see s 347. See also s 306 for powers of entry as respects a suspected offence, and s 345 as respects forfeiture of an article relating to an offence. For territorial limitations on offences under this Part of this Act, see ss 359, 360.

For penalties, see s 263, and for a defence, see s 265(3).

For the power of a licensing authority to institute criminal proceedings in respect of an offence under this section, see s 346.

Sub-s (2): Operating licence. As to the nature, etc of operating licences, see s 65 and the note 'Operating licences' thereto.

Exclusion of the National Lottery and territorial application. See ss 264, 265.

Definitions

'acts as an external lottery manager': ss 257, 353(1)
'lottery': ss 14, 353(1)
'the National Lottery': s 353(1)
'operating licence': s 353(1)
'promoting a lottery': ss 252, 353(2)(h)

Explanatory Notes

630–633 [para **6.2014** below]

6.759 259 Facilitating a lottery

(1) A person commits an offence if he facilitates a lottery unless—

(a) the exception in subsection (3) applies, or
(b) the lottery is an exempt lottery.

(2) For the purposes of this section a person facilitates a lottery if (and only if) he—

(a) prints lottery tickets for a specified lottery,
(b) prints promotional material for a specified lottery, or
(c) advertises a specified lottery.

(3) This section does not apply to activity by a person if he acts in accordance with the terms and conditions of an operating licence.

(4) It is a defence for a person charged with an offence under this section to show that he reasonably believed—

(a) that he was not committing the offence by reason of subsection (1)(b) or (3), or
(b) that the arrangement to which the charge relates was not a lottery, or
(c) that the arrangement to which the charge relates was a lottery forming part of the National Lottery.

(5) In subsection (2)(b) 'promotional material' means a document which—

(a) advertises a specified lottery,
(b) invites participation in a specified lottery,
(c) contains information about how to participate in a specified lottery, or
(d) lists winners in a specified lottery.

Commencement

Brought into force by the Gambling Act 2005 (Commencement No 6 and Transitional Provisions) Order 2006, SI 2006/3272, art 2 as from 1 September 2007; for transitional provisions see art 6, Sch 4 thereto (as amended by SI 2007/1157, arts 7–12).

Sub-s (1): Person. See the note 'Persons' to s 23.

Sub-s (1): Offence. For the power of the Gambling Commission and other specified persons to undertake activities for the purpose of assessing whether an offence is being committed under or by virtue of this Act, see s 27 and s 305; for the power of that Commission to investigate and prosecute offences, see s 28; as to offences committed by a body, see s 341; and for the time limit on prosecutions, see s 347. See also s 306 for powers of entry as respects a suspected offence, and s 345 as respects forfeiture of an article relating to an offence. For territorial limitations on offences under this Part of this Act, see ss 359, 360.

For penalties, see s 263, and for a defence, see s 265(3).

For the power of a licensing authority to institute criminal proceedings in respect of an offence under this section, see s 346.

Sub-s (3): Operating licence. As to the nature, etc of operating licences, see s 65 and the note 'Operating licences' thereto.

Exclusion of the National Lottery and territorial application. See ss 264, 265.

Definitions

'advertising gambling': ss 327, 353(2)(b)
'exempt lottery': ss 258(5), 353(1)
'lottery': ss 14, 353(1)
'lottery ticket': ss 253(1), 353(1)
'the National Lottery': s 353(1)
'operating licence': s 353(1)
'participating in a lottery': ss 14, 353(2)(c)

Explanatory Notes

634–637 [para **6.2014** below]

6.760 260 Misusing profits of lottery

(1) This section applies to a lottery in respect of which the promoter has stated (in whatever terms) a fund-raising purpose for the promotion of the lottery.

(2) A person commits an offence if he uses any part of the profits of a lottery to which this section applies for a purpose other than that stated.

(3) The reference in subsection (2) to using profits includes a reference to permitting profits to be used.

(4) In subsection (1) the reference to a statement of a purpose for the promotion of a lottery is a reference to a statement appearing—

(a) on lottery tickets, or
(b) in an advertisement for the lottery.

(5) In subsection (4)(b) 'advertisement' in relation to a lottery includes any written notice announcing that a lottery will take place or inviting people to participate in a lottery (in either case whether or not it also gives other information).

Commencement

Brought into force by the Gambling Act 2005 (Commencement No 6 and Transitional Provisions) Order 2006, SI 2006/3272, art 2 as from 1 September 2007; for transitional provisions see art 6, Sch 4 thereto (as amended by SI 2007/1157, arts 7–12).

Sub-s (2): Person. See the note 'Persons' to s 23.

Sub-s (2): Offence. For the power of the Gambling Commission and other specified persons to undertake activities for the purpose of assessing whether an offence is being committed under or by virtue of this Act, see s 27 and s 305; for the power of that Commission to investigate and prosecute offences, see s 28; as to offences committed by a body, see s 341; and for the time limit on prosecutions, see s 347. See also s 306 for powers of entry as respects a suspected offence, and s 345 as respects forfeiture of an article relating to an offence. For territorial limitations on offences under this Part of this Act, see ss 359, 360.

For penalties, see s 263.

For the power of a licensing authority to institute criminal proceedings in respect of an offence under this section, see s 346.

Sub-s (5): Written. See the note 'Writing' to s 39.

Exclusion of the National Lottery and territorial application. See ss 264, 265.

Definitions

'advertising gambling': ss 327, 353(2)(b)
'lottery': ss 14, 353(1)
'lottery ticket': ss 253(1), 353(1)
'participating in a lottery': ss 14, 353(2)(c)
'profits of a lottery': ss 254(2), 353(1)
'promoting a lottery': ss 252, 353(2)(h)

Explanatory Notes

638 [para **6.2014** below]

6.761 261 Misusing profits of exempt lottery

(1) This section applies to the following kinds of lottery—

(a) an incidental non-commercial lottery (within the meaning of Part 1 of Schedule 11),

(b) a private society lottery (within the meaning of Part 2 of that Schedule), and

(c) a small society lottery (within the meaning of Part 4 of that Schedule).

(2) A person commits an offence if he uses any part of the profits of a lottery to which this section applies for a purpose other than one for which the lottery is permitted to be promoted in accordance with Schedule 11.

(3) Subsection (3) of section 260 shall have effect for the purpose of this section as it has effect for the purpose of that section.

Commencement

Brought into force by the Gambling Act 2005 (Commencement No 6 and Transitional Provisions) Order 2006, SI 2006/3272, art 2 as from 1 September 2007; for transitional provisions see art 6, Sch 4 thereto (as amended by SI 2007/1157, arts 7–12).

Sub-s (2): Person. See the note 'Persons' to s 23.

Sub-s (2): Offence. For the power of the Gambling Commission and other specified persons to undertake activities for the purpose of assessing whether an offence is being committed under or by virtue of this Act, see s 27 and s 305; for the power of that Commission to investigate and prosecute offences, see s 28; as to offences committed by a body, see s 341; and for the time limit on prosecutions, see s 347. See also s 306 for powers of entry as respects a suspected offence, and s 345 as respects forfeiture of an article relating to an offence. For territorial limitations on offences under this Part of this Act, see ss 359, 360.

For penalties, see s 263.

For the power of a licensing authority to institute criminal proceedings in respect of an offence under this section, see s 346.

Exclusion of the National Lottery and territorial application. See ss 264, 265.

Definitions

'lottery': ss 14, 353(1)
'profits of a lottery': ss 254(2), 353(1)
'using profits': s 260(3) (by virtue of sub-s (3) above)

Explanatory Notes

639 [para **6.2014** below]

6.762 262 Small society lottery: breach of condition

A non-commercial society commits an offence if—

(a) a lottery, purporting to be an exempt lottery under Part 4 of Schedule 11, is promoted on the society's behalf wholly or partly at a time when the society is not registered with a local authority in accordance with Part 5 of that Schedule,

(b) the society fails to comply with the requirements of paragraph 39 of that Schedule, or

(c) the society provides false or misleading information for the purposes of paragraph 39 of that Schedule.

Commencement

Brought into force by the Gambling Act 2005 (Commencement No 6 and Transitional Provisions) Order 2006, SI 2006/3272, art 2 as from 1 September 2007; for transitional provisions see art 6, Sch 4 thereto (as amended by SI 2007/1157, arts 7–12).

Sub-s (1): Offence. For the power of the Gambling Commission and other specified persons to undertake activities for the purpose of assessing whether an offence is being committed under or by virtue of this Act, see s 27 and s 305; for the power of that Commission to investigate and prosecute offences, see s 28; as to offences committed by a body, see s 341; and for the time limit on prosecutions, see s 347. See also s 306 for powers of entry as respects a suspected offence, and s 345 as respects forfeiture of an article relating to an offence. For territorial limitations on offences under this Part of this Act, see ss 359, 360.

For penalties, see s 263.

For the power of a licensing authority to institute criminal proceedings in respect of an offence under this section, see s 346.

Exclusion of the National Lottery and territorial application. See ss 264, 265.

Definitions

'exempt lottery': ss 258(5), 353(1)
'lottery': ss 14, 353(1)
'non-commercial society': ss 19, 353(1)
'promoting a lottery': ss 252, 353(2)(h)

Explanatory Notes

640 [para **6.2014** below]

6.763 263 Penalty

(1) A person guilty of an offence under this Part shall be liable on summary conviction to—

(a) imprisonment for a term not exceeding 51 weeks,
(b) a fine not exceeding level 5 on the standard scale, or
(c) both.

(2) In the application of subsection (1) to Scotland the reference to 51 weeks shall have effect as a reference to six months.

Commencement

Brought into force by the Gambling Act 2005 (Commencement No 6 and Transitional Provisions) Order 2006, SI 2006/3272, art 2 as from 1 September 2007; for transitional provisions see art 6, Sch 4 thereto (as amended by SI 2007/1157, arts 7–12).

Sub-s (1): Person. See the note 'Persons' to s 23.

Sub-s (1): This Part. Ie Pt 11 (ss 252–265 and Sch 11) of this Act.

Sub-s (1): Summary conviction; standard scale. See the notes to s 33.

Exclusion of the National Lottery and territorial application. See ss 264, 265.

Explanatory Notes

641 [para **6.2014** below]

Miscellaneous

6.764 264 Exclusion of the National Lottery

The preceding provisions of this Part do not apply to the National Lottery.

Commencement

Brought into force by the Gambling Act 2005 (Commencement No 6 and Transitional Provisions) Order 2006, SI 2006/3272, art 2 as from 1 September 2007; for transitional provisions see art 6, Sch 4 thereto (as amended by SI 2007/1157, arts 7–12).

This Part

Ie Pt 11 (ss 252–265 and Sch 11) of this Act.

Territorial application

See s 265.

Definitions

'the National Lottery': s 353(1)

Explanatory Notes
642 [para **6.2014** below]

General

6.765 265 Territorial application

(1) This Part applies to anything done in relation to a lottery—
(a) in Great Britain, or
(b) by the provision of, or by means of, remote gambling equipment situated in Great Britain.

(2) But this Part does not apply in relation to a lottery if—
(a) no person in Great Britain does anything by virtue of which he becomes a participant in the lottery, and
(b) no person in Great Britain possesses tickets for the lottery with a view to selling or supplying them to a person in Great Britain who thereby becomes a participant in the lottery.

(3) It is a defence for a person charged with an offence under section 258 or 259 to show that he reasonably believed that this Part did not and would not apply to the lottery, by reason of subsection (2) above.

Commencement
Brought into force by the Gambling Act 2005 (Commencement No 6 and Transitional Provisions) Order 2006, SI 2006/3272, art 2 as from 1 September 2007; for transitional provisions see art 6, Sch 4 thereto (as amended by SI 2007/1157, arts 7–12).
Sub-s (1): This Part. Ie Pt 11 (ss 252–265 and Sch 11) of this Act.
Sub-s (1): Great Britain. See the note to s 12.

Exclusion of the National Lottery
See s 264.

Definitions
'lottery': ss 14, 353(1)
'lottery ticket': ss 253(1), 353(1)
'participating in a lottery': ss 14, 353(2)(c)
'promoting a lottery': ss 252, 353(2)(h)
'remote gambling equipment': ss 36(4), (5), 353(1)
'sale or supply of a lottery ticket': ss 253(2), 353(2)(k)
'supply': s 353(1)

Explanatory Notes
643–646 [para **6.2014** below]

PART 12
CLUBS, PUBS, FAIRS, &C

Clubs

6.766 266 Members' club

(1) In this Act members' club means a club—
(a) which is established and conducted wholly or mainly for purposes other than the provision of facilities for gaming (subject to subsection (2)),
(b) which is established and conducted for the benefit of its members (and which is not otherwise established or conducted as a commercial enterprise),
(c) which is not established with the purpose of functioning only for a limited period of time, and

(d) which has at least 25 individual members.

(2) A club is a members' club for the purposes of this Act despite subsection (1)(a) if—

(a) it is established or conducted wholly or mainly for the purpose of the provision of facilities for gaming of a prescribed kind, and

(b) facilities are not provided for any other kind of gaming in the course of the club's activities.

Note

See the Gambling Commission publication of October 2010 on members' clubs and commercial clubs at para **6.2569** below.

Commencement

Brought into force by the Gambling Act 2005 (Commencement No 6 and Transitional Provisions) Order 2006, SI 2006/3272, art 2, Sch 3 as from 1 June 2007; for transitional provisions see art 6, Sch 4 thereto (as amended by SI 2007/1157, arts 7–12).

Subordinate Legislation:

SI 2007/1942.

As to regulations under this Act generally, see s 355.

Definitions

'gaming': ss 6, 353(1)
'prescribed': s 276
'providing facilities for gambling': ss 5, 353(2)(i)

Explanatory Notes

674–678 [para **6.2015** below]

6.767 267 Commercial club

(1) In this Act commercial club means a club—

(a) which is established and conducted wholly or mainly for purposes other than the provision of facilities for gaming (subject to subsection (2)),

(b) which is not established with the purpose of functioning only for a limited period of time, and

(c) which has at least 25 individual members.

(2) A club is a commercial club for the purposes of this Act despite subsection (1)(a) if—

(a) it is established or conducted wholly or mainly for the purpose of the provision of facilities for gaming of a prescribed kind, and

(b) facilities are not provided for any other kind of gaming in the course of the club's activities.

Note

See the Gambling Commission publication of October 2010 on members' clubs and commercial clubs at para **6.2569** below.

Commencement

Brought into force by the Gambling Act 2005 (Commencement No 6 and Transitional Provisions) Order 2006, SI 2006/3272, art 2, Sch 3 as from 1 June 2007; for transitional provisions see art 6, Sch 4 thereto (as amended by SI 2007/1157, arts 7–12).

Subordinate Legislation:

SI 2007/1942.

As to regulations under this Act generally, see s 355.

Definitions

'gaming': ss 6, 353(1)
'prescribed': s 276

'providing facilities for gambling': ss 5, 353(2)(i)

Explanatory Notes

674–678 [para **6.2015** below]

6.768 268 Miners' welfare institute

(1) In this Act miners' welfare institute means an association—

(a) which is established and conducted for social and recreational purposes, and

(b) which satisfies subsection (2) or (4).

(2) An association satisfies this subsection if its affairs are managed by a group of individuals of whom at least two thirds are miners' representatives.

(3) In subsection (2) 'miners' representative' means a person who—

(a) is nominated or appointed by a person who employs or has employed individuals in the course of a coal mining business,

(b) is nominated or appointed by the charitable trust known as the Coal Industry Social Welfare Organisation,

(c) is nominated or appointed by an organisation representing persons who are or were employed in connection with coal mining, or

(d) is or was employed in connection with coal mining;

and the group mentioned in subsection (2) must contain both one or more persons of a kind specified in paragraph (a) or (b) and one or more persons of a kind specified in paragraph (c) or (d).

(4) An association satisfies this subsection if—

(a) it operates on premises the use of which is regulated in accordance with a charitable trust, and

(b) the trust has received money from—

(i) the Miners' Welfare Fund established by section 20 of the Mining Industry Act 1920 (c 50),

(ii) the former body corporate which was known as the Coal Industry Social Welfare Organisation and incorporated under the Companies Act 1948 (c 38), or

(iii) the charitable trust known as the Coal Industry Social Welfare Organisation.

Commencement

Brought into force by the Gambling Act 2005 (Commencement No 6 and Transitional Provisions) Order 2006, SI 2006/3272, art 2, Sch 3 as from 1 June 2007; for transitional provisions see art 6, Sch 4 thereto (as amended by SI 2007/1157, arts 7–12).

Sub-s (3): Person. See the note 'Persons' to s 23.

Companies Act 1948. Repealed by the Companies Consolidation (Consequential Provisions) Act 1985, s 29, Sch 1.

Mining Industry Act 1920. Section 20 of that Act was repealed by the Miners' Welfare Act 1952, s 18(3), Sch 2.

Definitions

'premises': s 353(1), (2)(g)

Explanatory Notes

674–678 [para **6.2015** below]

6.769 269 Exempt gaming

(1) Sections 33 and 37 shall not apply to the provision of facilities for equal chance gaming which satisfies the conditions of this section by—

(a) a members' club,

(b) a commercial club,

(c) a club that would be a members' club but for section 266(1)(a),
(d) a club that would be a commercial club but for section 267(1)(a), or
(e) a miners' welfare institute.

(2) The first condition of gaming for the purposes of subsection (1) is that the arrangements for the gaming satisfy the prescribed requirements (if any) in relation to—
(a) amounts that may be staked, or
(b) the amount or value of a prize.

(3) The second condition of gaming for the purposes of subsection (1) is that no amount is deducted or levied from sums staked or won.

(4) The third condition of gaming for the purposes of subsection (1) is that any participation fee does not exceed such maximum as may be prescribed.

(5) The fourth condition of gaming for the purposes of subsection (1) is that a game played on one set of premises is not linked with a game played on another set of premises.

(6) The fifth condition of gaming for the purposes of subsection (1), which does not apply to a club of a kind mentioned in subsection (1)(b) or (d), is that each person who participates—
(a) is a member of the club or institute who applied for membership, was nominated for membership or became a member, at least 48 hours before he participates, or
(b) is a guest of a member of the club or institute who would be entitled to participate by virtue of paragraph (a).

Commencement

Brought into force by the Gambling Act 2005 (Commencement No 6 and Transitional Provisions) Order 2006, SI 2006/3272, art 2 as from 1 September 2007; for transitional provisions see art 6, Sch 4 thereto (as amended by SI 2007/1157, arts 7–12).

Supplementary provisions

See s 270.

Powers of entry

For powers of entry in connection with this section, see s 312.

Subordinate Legislation:

SI 2007/1944.

As to regulations under this Act generally, see s 355.

Definitions

'commercial club': ss 267, 353(1)
'deduction or levy': s 270(3)
'equal chance gaming': ss 8, 353(1)
'gaming': ss 6, 353(1)
'guest': s 270(6)
'linked': s 270(5)
'members' club': ss 266, 353(1)
'miners' welfare institute': ss 268, 353(1)
'participation fee': ss 344, 353(1)
'premises': s 353(1), (2)(g)
'prescribed': s 276
'prize': ss 6(5), 353(1)
'providing facilities for gambling': ss 5, 353(2)(i)
'provision of facilities by a club or institute': s 270(1)
'stake': s 353(1)

Explanatory Notes

679–681 [para **6.2015** below]

6.770 270 Section 269: supplementary

(1) In section 269(1) a reference to the provision of facilities by a club or institute includes a reference to any provision of facilities made—

(a) on behalf of or by arrangement with the club or institute, and

(b) in the course of its activities.

(2) Regulations prescribing requirements in relation to stakes or prizes for the purposes of section 269(2) may, in particular—

(a) make different provision for different classes of club or institute;

(b) make different provision for different classes or descriptions of game.

(3) In section 269(3) the reference to a deduction or levy in respect of gaming provided by, on behalf of or by arrangement with a club or institute is to a deduction or levy made by or on behalf of—

(a) the club or institute, or

(b) a person providing facilities for gaming on behalf of, or by arrangement with, the club or institute.

(4) Regulations prescribing a maximum charge for the purposes of section 269(4) may, in particular—

(a) make different provision for different classes of club or institute;

(b) make provision depending on whether a club or institute holds a club gaming permit;

(c) make different provision for different classes or descriptions of game;

(d) make different provision for different classes or descriptions of fee.

(5) For the purposes of section 269(5) two games are linked if—

(a) the result of one game is or may be wholly or partly determined by reference to the result of the other game, or

(b) the amount of winnings available in one game is or may be wholly or partly determined by reference to the amount of participation in the other game;

and if a single game is played partly on one set of premises and partly on another it shall be treated as two linked games.

(6) For the purposes of section 269(6) a person shall not be treated as the guest of a member if the member extends an invitation—

(a) having had no previous acquaintance with the person, and

(b) for the purpose only of enabling the person to take advantage of facilities for gaming provided by or for the club or institute.

Commencement

Brought into force by the Gambling Act 2005 (Commencement No 6 and Transitional Provisions) Order 2006, SI 2006/3272, art 2 as from 1 September 2007; for transitional provisions see art 6, Sch 4 thereto (as amended by SI 2007/1157, arts 7–12).

Sub-s (4): Club gaming permit. See, generally, s 271.

Subordinate Legislation:

SI 2007/1944.

Definitions

'club gaming permit': ss 271(2), 353(1)
'gaming': ss 6, 353(1)
'premises': s 353(1), (2)(g)
'prize': ss 6(5), 353(1)
'providing facilities for gambling': ss 5, 353(2)(i)
'regulations': s 276

'stake': s 353(1)
'winnings': s 353(1)

Explanatory Notes
679–681 [para **6.2015** below]

6.771 271 Club gaming permit

(1) Sections 33, 37 and 242 shall not apply to the provision of facilities for gaming in accordance with a club gaming permit.

(2) A club gaming permit is a permit issued by a licensing authority authorising the provision of facilities for gaming—

(a) on premises on which a members' club or a miners' welfare institute operates, and

(b) in the course of the activities of the club or institute.

(3) A club gaming permit shall, by virtue of this section, authorise—

(a) making up to three gaming machines available for use, each of which must be of Category B, C or D,

(b) the provision of facilities for gaming which satisfies the conditions in section 269 except for the first condition, and

(c) the provision of facilities for games of chance, of such class or description as may be prescribed, in accordance with the conditions specified in subsection (4).

(4) Those conditions are—

(a) that no participation fee is charged otherwise than in accordance with regulations (which may make provision about the circumstances in which a fee may be charged and about the amount of a fee),

(b) that no amount is deducted or levied from sums staked or won otherwise than in accordance with regulations (which may make provision about the circumstances in which an amount may be deducted or levied, about the amount of the deduction or levy and about the method by which the amount is determined),

(c) that the public is excluded from any area of the club's or institute's premises where gaming is taking place, and

(d) that children and young persons are excluded from any area of the club's or institute's premises where gaming is taking place.

(5) Regulations under subsection (4)(a) or (b) may—

(a) make different provision for different classes of club or institute;

(b) make different provision for different classes or descriptions of game;

(c) make different provision for different classes or descriptions of fee, deduction or levy.

(6) A club gaming permit shall, by virtue of this subsection, be subject to the condition that each person who participates in gaming in reliance on the permit—

(a) is a member of the club or institute who applied for membership, was nominated for membership or became a member, at least 48 hours before he participates, or

(b) is a guest of a member of the club or institute who would be entitled to participate by virtue of paragraph (a).

(7) A club gaming permit shall, by virtue of this subsection, be subject to the conditions—

(a) that no child or young person use a Category B or C gaming machine on the club's or institute's premises, and

(b) that the holder comply with any relevant provision of a code of practice under section 24 about the location and operation of a gaming machine.

Note

See the Gambling Commission's Code of Practice (June 2007) (see para **6.2660** below).

COMMENCEMENT

Subsections (1), (3)–(7) brought into force by the Gambling Act 2005 (Commencement No 6 and Transitional Provisions) Order 2006, SI 2006/3272, art 2 as from 1 September 2007; for transitional provisions see art 6, Sch 4 thereto (as amended by SI 2007/1157, arts 7–12).

Subsection (2) brought into force by the Gambling Act 2005 (Commencement No 6 and Transitional Provisions) Order 2006, SI 2006/3272, art 2, Sch 3 as from 1 June 2007; for transitional provisions see art 6, Sch 4 thereto (as amended by SI 2007/1157, arts 7–12).

Sub-s (2): Club gaming permit. A person commits an offence if he employs a child or young person to perform any function on premises where and at a time when facilities for gambling are provided in accordance with a club gaming permit; see s 53. For further provisions as respects club gaming permits, see s 274 and Sch 12.

For powers of entry in connection with such a permit, see s 312.

Sub-s (2): Licensing authority. For the licensing authorities for the purposes of this Act, see s 2.

Sub-s (3): Category B, C or D. As to the categories of gaming machine, see s 236 and SI 2007/2158.

Supplementary provisions

See s 272.

Subordinate Legislation:

SI 2007/1945.

As to regulations under this Act generally, see s 355.

Definitions

'area where gaming is taking place': s 272(3)
'Category B gaming machine': s 353(1)
'Category C gaming machine': s 353(1)
'Category D gaming machine': s 353(1)
'child': ss 45(1), 353(1)
'deduction or levy': s 272(1)
'game of chance': ss 6, 353(1)
'gaming': ss 6, 353(1)
'gaming machine': ss 235, 353(1)
'guest': s 272(4)
'licensing authority': ss 2, 353(1)
'members' club': ss 266, 353(1)
'miners' welfare institute': ss 268, 353(1)
'participation fee': ss 344, 353(1)
'premises': s 353(1), (2)(g)
'prescribed': s 276
'providing facilities for gambling': ss 5, 353(2)(i)
'the public': s 272(2)
'regulations': s 276
'young person': ss 45(2), 353(1)

Explanatory Notes

682–685 [para **6.2015** below]

6.772 272 Section 271: supplementary

(1) For the purposes of section 271(4)(b) the reference to a deduction or levy in respect of gaming provided by, on behalf of or by arrangement with a club or institute is to a deduction or levy made by or on behalf of—

(a) the club or institute, or

(b) a person providing facilities for gaming on behalf of, or by arrangement with, the club or institute.

(2) In section 271(4)(c) 'the public' means persons other than—

(a) members of the club or institute,

(b) guests of members of the club or institute,

(c) staff of the club or institute, and

(d) persons providing services to or for the club or institute.

(3) For the purposes of section 271(4)(c) and (d) a reference to an area where gaming is taking place is a reference to any place in which it is possible to participate in the gaming.

(4) For the purposes of section 271(6) and subsection (2) above a person shall not be treated as the guest of a member if the member extends an invitation—

(a) having had no previous acquaintance with the person, and

(b) for the purpose only of enabling the person to take advantage of facilities for gaming.

Commencement

Brought into force by the Gambling Act 2005 (Commencement No 6 and Transitional Provisions) Order 2006, SI 2006/3272, art 2 as from 1 September 2007; for transitional provisions see art 6, Sch 4 thereto (as amended by SI 2007/1157, arts 7–12).

Sub-s (1): Person. See the note 'Persons' to s 23.

Definitions

'gaming': ss 6, 353(1)

'providing facilities for gambling': ss 5, 353(2)(i)

Explanatory Notes

682–685 [para **6.2015** below]

6.773 273 Club machine permit

(1) Sections 37 and 242 shall not apply to making a gaming machine available for use in accordance with a club machine permit.

(2) A club machine permit is a permit issued by a licensing authority authorising up to three gaming machines, each of which must be of Category B, C or D, to be made available for use—

(a) on premises on which a members' club, a commercial club or a miners' welfare institute operates, and

(b) in the course of the activities of the club or institute.

(3) A club machine permit held by a members' club or a miners' welfare institute shall, by virtue of this subsection, be subject to the condition that each person to whom a machine is made available for use in reliance on the permit—

(a) is a member of the club or institute who applied for membership, was nominated for membership or became a member, at least 48 hours before he uses the machine, or

(b) is a guest of a member of the club or institute who would be entitled to use the machine by virtue of paragraph (a).

(4) A club machine permit shall, by virtue of this subsection, be subject to the conditions—

(a) that no child or young person use a Category B or C gaming machine on the club's or institute's premises, and

(b) that the holder comply with any relevant provision of a code of practice under section 24 about the location and operation of a gaming machine.

(5) For the purposes of subsection (3)(b) a person shall not be treated as the guest of a member if the member extends an invitation—

(a) having had no previous acquaintance with the person, and

(b) for the purpose only of enabling the person to take advantage of facilities for gaming.

Note

See the Gambling Commission's Code of Practice (June 2007) (see para **6.2660** below).

Commencement

Subsections (1), (3)–(5) brought into force by the Gambling Act 2005 (Commencement No 6 and Transitional Provisions) Order 2006, SI 2006/3272, art 2 as from 1 September 2007; for transitional provisions see art 6, Sch 4 thereto (as amended by SI 2007/1157, arts 7–12).

Subsection (2) brought into force by the Gambling Act 2005 (Commencement No 6 and Transitional Provisions) Order 2006, SI 2006/3272, art 2, Sch 3 as from 1 June 2007; for transitional provisions see art 6, Sch 4 thereto (as amended by SI 2007/1157, arts 7–12).

Sub-s (2): Club machine permit. A person commits an offence if he employs a child or young person to perform any function on premises where and at a time when facilities for gambling are provided in accordance with a club machine permit; see s 53. For further provisions as respects club machine permits, see s 274 and Sch 12.

For powers of entry in connection with such a permit, see s 312.

Sub-s (2): Licensing authority. For the licensing authorities for the purposes of this Act, see s 2.

Sub-s (2): Category B, C or D. As to the categories of gaming machine, see s 236 and SI 2007/2158.

Definitions

'Category B gaming machine': s 353(1)
'Category C gaming machine': s 353(1)
'Category D gaming machine': s 353(1)
'child': ss 45(1), 353(1)
'commercial club': ss 267, 353(1)
'gaming': ss 6, 353(1)
'gaming machine': ss 235, 353(1)
'licensing authority': ss 2, 353(1)
'members' club': ss 266, 353(1)
'miners' welfare institute': ss 268, 353(1)
'premises': s 353(1), (2)(g)
'young person': ss 45(2), 353(1)

Explanatory Notes

686, 687 [para **6.2015** below]

6.774 274 Procedure, &c

(1) Schedule 12 makes further provision about club gaming permits and club machine permits.

(2) Subsection (1) does not apply in relation to Scotland if the applicant for or holder of the permit in question is the holder of [. . .][1] a relevant Scottish licence or if he falls within such other description as may be specified in regulations under section 285(1).

Commencement

Brought into force for certain purposes by the Gambling Act 2005 (Commencement No 6 and Transitional Provisions) Order 2006, SI 2006/3272, art 2, Sch 3 as from 1 June 2007; for transitional provisions see art 6, Sch 4 thereto (as amended by SI 2007/1157, arts 7–12). Brought into force for remaining purposes by the Gambling Act 2005 (Commencement No 6 and Transitional Provisions) Order 2006, SI 2006/3272, art 2 as from 1 September 2007; for transitional provisions see art 6, Sch 4 thereto (as amended by SI 2007/1157, arts 7–12).

Sub-s (1): Club gaming permits; club machine permits. See, generally, ss 271, 273.

Definitions

'club gaming permit': ss 271(2), 353(1)
'club machine permit': ss 273(2), 353(1)

Explanatory Notes

688 [para **6.2015** below]

---

[1] Sub-s (2): words omitted repealed by SSI 2009/248, art 2(2), Sch 2.

6.775 275 Bingo

(1) The disapplication of section 33 by section 269 or 271 shall not apply to high turnover bingo played during a high turnover period.

(2) Bingo played in the course of the activities of a club or institute in any period of seven days is high turnover bingo if—

(a) the aggregate of stakes at bingo played during the period in the course of the activities of the club or institute exceeds £2,000, or

(b) the aggregate of prizes at bingo played during the period in the course of the activities of the club or institute exceeds £2,000.

(3) A high turnover period begins in relation to a club or institute at the end of a period of seven days during which—

(a) the aggregate of stakes at bingo played in the course of the activities of the club or institute exceeds £2,000, or

(b) the aggregate of prizes at bingo played in the course of the activities of the club or institute exceeds £2,000.

(4) A high turnover period expires at the end of the year beginning with the first day of the period of seven days which caused the high turnover period to begin.

(5) A period of seven days any of which is in a high turnover period does not cause a new high turnover period to begin.

(6) A club or institute in relation to which a high turnover period begins shall, unless the club or institute holds a bingo operating licence, inform the Commission as soon as is reasonably practicable.

(7) A club or institute commits an offence if it fails without reasonable excuse to comply with subsection (6).

(8) A club or institute guilty of an offence under subsection (7) shall be liable on summary conviction to a fine not exceeding level 3 on the standard scale.

(9) The Secretary of State may by order vary a monetary amount specified in this section.

Commencement

Brought into force by the Gambling Act 2005 (Commencement No 6 and Transitional Provisions) Order 2006, SI 2006/3272, art 2 as from 1 September 2007; for transitional provisions see art 6, Sch 4 thereto (as amended by SI 2007/1157, arts 7–12).

Sub-s (6): The Commission. Ie the Gambling Commission; see s 353(1). As to the establishment, etc of the Gambling Commission, see s 20, Sch 4, and the note 'Gambling Commission' to that section.

Sub-s (7): Offence. For the power of the Gambling Commission and other specified persons to undertake activities for the purpose of assessing whether an offence is being committed under or by virtue of this Act, see s 27 and s 305; for the power of that Commission to investigate and prosecute offences, see s 28; as to offences committed by a body, see s 341; and for the time limit on prosecutions, see s 347. See also s 306 for powers of entry as respects a suspected offence, and s 345 as respects forfeiture of an article relating to an offence.

Sub-s (8): Summary conviction; standard scale. See the notes to s 33.

Sub-s (9): Secretary of State. See the note to s 4.

Orders under this section

At the time of going to press no orders had been made under this section.

As to orders under this Act generally, see s 355.

Definitions
'bingo': s 353(1) and see fn to s 91.
'the Commission': s 353(1)
'stake': s 353(1)

Explanatory Notes
699–701 [para **6.2015** below]

6.776 276 Interpretation
In sections 266 to 275—
'prescribed' means prescribed by regulations, and
'regulations' means regulations made by the Secretary of State.

Commencement
Brought into force by the Gambling Act 2005 (Commencement No 6 and Transitional Provisions) Order 2006, SI 2006/3272, art 2, Sch 3 as from 1 June 2007; for transitional provisions see art 6, Sch 4 thereto (as amended by SI 2007/1157, arts 7–12).

Secretary of State
See the note to s 4.

Pubs, &c

6.777 277 Alcohol licence
In this Act—
(a) 'alcohol licence' means a premises licence under Part 3 of the Licensing Act 2003 (c 17),
(b) 'on-premises alcohol licence' means a premises licence under that Part which authorises the supply of alcohol for consumption on the licensed premises, and
[(c) "relevant Scottish licence" means a premises licence issued under the Licensing (Scotland) Act 2005, except where such a licence only applies to the sale of alcohol for consumption off the premises][1].

Commencement
Brought into force by the Gambling Act 2005 (Commencement No 6 and Transitional Provisions) Order 2006, SI 2006/3272, art 2, Sch 3 as from 1 June 2007; for transitional provisions see art 6, Sch 4 thereto (as amended by SI 2007/1157, arts 7–12).

Explanatory Notes
702–705 [para **6.2015** below]

[1] Para (c) substituted by SSI 2009/248, art 2(1), Sch 1, Pt 1, para 12(1), (6).

6.778 278 Application of sections 279 to 284
(1) Sections 279 to 284 apply to premises (other than a vehicle)—
(a) in respect of which an on-premises alcohol licence or relevant Scottish licence has effect,
(b) which contain a bar at which alcohol is served for consumption on the premises (without a requirement that alcohol is served only with food), and
(c) at a time when alcohol may be supplied in reliance on the alcohol licence or sold for consumption on the premises in reliance on the relevant Scottish licence.

(2) In those sections a reference to a licensing authority includes a reference to the Sub-Treasurer of the Inner Temple and the Under-Treasurer of the Middle Temple.

Commencement

Brought into force by the Gambling Act 2005 (Commencement No 6 and Transitional Provisions) Order 2006, SI 2006/3272, art 2, Sch 3 as from 1 June 2007; for transitional provisions see art 6, Sch 4 thereto (as amended by SI 2007/1157, arts 7–12).

Definitions

'alcohol licence': s 277(a)
'on-premises alcohol licence': s 277(b)
'premises': s 353(1), (2)(g)
'relevant Scottish licence': s 277(c)

Explanatory Notes

702–705 [para 6.2015 below]

6.779 279 Exempt gaming

(1) Sections 33 and 37 shall not apply to the provision of facilities for equal chance gaming which—

(a) takes place on premises to which this section applies, and
(b) satisfies the conditions of this section.

(2) The first condition of gaming for the purposes of subsection (1) is that the arrangements for the gaming satisfy the prescribed requirements in relation to—

(a) limiting amounts that may be staked, or
(b) limiting the amount or value of a prize.

(3) The second condition of gaming for the purposes of subsection (1) is that no amount is deducted or levied from sums staked or won.

(4) The third condition of gaming for the purposes of subsection (1) is that no participation fee is charged.

(5) The fourth condition of gaming for the purposes of subsection (1) is that a game played on one set of premises is not linked with a game played on another set of premises.

(6) The fifth condition of gaming for the purposes of subsection (1) is that children and young persons are excluded from participation.

Commencement

Brought into force by the Gambling Act 2005 (Commencement No 6 and Transitional Provisions) Order 2006, SI 2006/3272, art 2 as from 1 September 2007; for transitional provisions see art 6, Sch 4 thereto (as amended by SI 2007/1157, arts 7–12).

Sub-s (1): Sections 33 . . . shall not apply, etc. See, however, s 281.

Sub-s (1): Premises to which this section applies. See s 278.

Sub-s (1): Satisfies the conditions of this section. For powers of entry in connection with such conditions, see s 310(2).

Sub-s (4): Participation fee. For the purposes of this section, a membership subscription is a participation fee; see s 344(3).

Supplementary provisions

See s 280.

Removal of exemption

See s 284.

Subordinate Legislation:

SI 2007/1940.

As to regulations under this Act generally, see s 355.

Definitions

'child': ss 45(1), 353(1)
'equal chance gaming': ss 8, 353(1)
'gaming': ss 6, 353(1)
'linked': s 280(2)
'participation fee': ss 344, 353(1)
'premises': s 353(1), (2)(g)
'prescribed': s 280(1)
'prize': ss 6(5), 353(1)
'providing facilities for gambling': ss 5, 353(2)(i)
'young person': ss 45(2), 353(1)

Explanatory Notes

706–708 [para **6.2015** below]

6.780 280 Section 279: supplementary

(1) In section 279(2) 'prescribed' means prescribed by regulations made by the Secretary of State; and regulations may, in particular, make different provision for different classes or descriptions of game.

(2) For the purposes of section 279(5) two games are linked if—

(a) the result of one game is or may be wholly or partly determined by reference to the result of the other game, or

(b) the amount or value of a prize available in one game is or may be wholly or partly determined by reference to the extent of participation in the other game;

and if a single game is played partly on one set of premises and partly on another it shall be treated as two linked games.

Commencement

Brought into force by the Gambling Act 2005 (Commencement No 6 and Transitional Provisions) Order 2006, SI 2006/3272, art 2 as from 1 September 2007; for transitional provisions see art 6, Sch 4 thereto (as amended by SI 2007/1157, arts 7–12).

Sub-s (1): Secretary of State. See the note to s 4.

Sub-s (2): Premises. For the premises to which this section applies, see s 278.

Definitions

'premises': s 353(1), (2)(g)
'prize': ss 6(5), 353(1)

Explanatory Notes

706–708 [para **6.2015** below]

6.781 281 Bingo

(1) The disapplication of section 33 by section 279 shall not apply to high turnover bingo played during a high turnover period.

(2) Bingo played on premises in any period of seven days is high turnover bingo if—

(a) the aggregate of stakes at bingo played on the premises during the period exceeds £2,000, or

(b) the aggregate of prizes at bingo played on the premises during the period exceeds £2,000.

(3) A high turnover period begins in relation to premises at the end of a period of seven days during which—

(a) the aggregate of stakes at bingo played on the premises exceeds £2,000, or

(b) the aggregate of prizes at bingo played on the premises exceeds £2,000.

(4) A high turnover period expires at the end of the year beginning with the first day of the period of seven days which caused the high turnover period to begin.

(5) A period of seven days any of which is in a high turnover period does not cause a new high turnover period to begin.

(6) The holder of an on-premises alcohol licence or relevant Scottish licence for premises in relation to which a high turnover period begins shall, unless he holds a bingo operating licence, inform the Commission as soon as is reasonably practicable.

(7) A person commits an offence if he fails without reasonable excuse to comply with subsection (6).

(8) A person guilty of an offence under subsection (7) shall be liable on summary conviction to a fine not exceeding level 3 on the standard scale.

(9) The Secretary of State may by order vary a monetary amount specified in this section.

Commencement

Brought into force by the Gambling Act 2005 (Commencement No 6 and Transitional Provisions) Order 2006, SI 2006/3272, art 2 as from 1 September 2007; for transitional provisions see art 6, Sch 4 thereto (as amended by SI 2007/1157, arts 7–12).

Sub-s (2): Premises. For the premises to which this section applies, see s 278.

Sub-s (6): Operating licence. As to the nature, etc of operating licences, see s 65 and the note 'Operating licences' thereto.

Sub-s (6): The Commission. Ie the Gambling Commission; see s 353(1). As to the establishment, etc of the Gambling Commission, see s 20, Sch 4, and the note 'Gambling Commission' to that section.

Sub-s (7): Person. See the note 'Persons' to s 23.

Sub-s (7): Offence. For the power of the Gambling Commission and other specified persons to undertake activities for the purpose of assessing whether an offence is being committed under or by virtue of this Act, see s 27 and s 305; for the power of that Commission to investigate and prosecute offences, see s 28; as to offences committed by a body, see s 341; and for the time limit on prosecutions, see s 347. See also s 306 for powers of entry as respects a suspected offence, and s 345 as respects forfeiture of an article relating to an offence.

Sub-s (8): Summary conviction; standard scale. See the notes to s 33.

Sub-s (9): Secretary of State. See the note to s 4.

Powers of entry

For powers of entry in connection with this section, see s 310(2).

Subordinate Legislation:

SI 2007/1940.

As to orders under this Act generally, see s 355.

Definitions

'bingo': s 353(1)
'the Commission': s 353(1)
'on-premises alcohol licence': s 277(b)
'operating licence': s 353(1)
'premises': s 353(1), (2)(g)
'relevant Scottish licence': s 277(c)
'stake': s 353(1)

Explanatory Notes

699–701 [para **6.2015** below]

6.782 282 Gaming machines: automatic entitlement

(1) Sections 37 and 242 shall not apply to making one or two gaming machines, each of which is of Category C or D, available for use on premises to which this section applies, provided that the conditions in subsections (2) and (3) are satisfied.

(2) The first condition is that the person who holds the on-premises alcohol licence or the relevant Scottish licence sends the licensing authority—

(a) written notice of his intention to make gaming machines available for use in reliance on subsection (1), and

(b) the prescribed fee.

(3) The second condition is that any relevant provision of a code of practice under section 24 about the location and operation of a gaming machine is complied with.

(4) Subsection (1) does not disapply section 37 or 242 in respect of premises at a time when gaming machines are made available for use on those premises in reliance on a club gaming permit or a club machine permit.

(5) In this section 'prescribed' means—

(a) in the case of premises in respect of which an on-premises alcohol licence has effect, prescribed by regulations made by the Secretary of State, and

(b) in the case of premises in respect of which a relevant Scottish licence has effect, prescribed by regulations made by the Scottish Ministers.

Note

See the Gambling Commission's Code of Practice (June 2007) (see para **6.2660** below).

Commencement

Brought into force by the Gambling Act 2005 (Commencement No 6 and Transitional Provisions) Order 2006, SI 2006/3272, art 2 as from 1 September 2007; for transitional provisions see art 6, Sch 4 thereto (as amended by SI 2007/1157, arts 7–12).

Sub-s (1): Category C or D. As to the categories of gaming machine, see s 236.

Sub-s (1): Premises to which this section applies. See s 278.

Sub-s (2): Licensing authority. For the licensing authorities for the purposes of this Act, see s 2 (and see also s 278(2)).

Sub-s (2): Written. See the note 'Writing' to s 39.

Sub-s (2): Notice. See further, in connection with a requirement under this Act to give a notice, s 353(4).

Sub-s (4): Club gaming permit; club machine permit. See, generally, ss 271, 273.

Sub-s (5): Secretary of State. See the note to s 4.

Sub-s (5): Scottish Ministers. See the note to s 25.

Removal of exemption

See s 284.

Subordinate Legislation:

SI 2007/1832.

As to regulations under this Act generally, see s 355.

Definitions

'Category C gaming machine': s 353(1)
'Category D gaming machine': s 353(1)
'club gaming permit': ss 271(2), 353(1)
'club machine permit': ss 273(2), 353(1)
'gaming machine': ss 235, 353(1)
'licensing authority': ss 2, 278(2), 353(1)
'on-premises alcohol licence': s 277(b)
'premises': s 353(1), (2)(g)
'relevant Scottish licence': s 277(c)

Explanatory Notes

709, 710 [para **6.2016** below]

6.783 283 Licensed premises gaming machine permits

(1) A person does not commit an offence under section 37 or 242 if he makes a gaming machine of Category C or D available in accordance with a licensed premises gaming machine permit.

(2) A licensed premises gaming machine permit is a permit issued by a licensing authority authorising a person to make gaming machines of Category C or D (or both) available for use on premises to which this section applies.

(3) A licensed premises gaming machine permit shall, by virtue of this subsection, be subject to the condition that the holder comply with any relevant provision of a code of practice under section 24 about the location and operation of a gaming machine.

(4) Subsection (1) does not disapply section 37 or 242 in respect of premises at a time when gaming machines are made available for use on those premises in reliance on a club gaming permit or a club machine permit.

(5) Schedule 13, which makes further provision about licensed premises gaming machine permits, shall have effect except in relation to Scotland.

Note

See the Gambling Commission's Code of Practice (June 2007) (see para **6.2660** below).

Commencement

Subsections (1), (3), (4) brought into force by the Gambling Act 2005 (Commencement No 6 and Transitional Provisions) Order 2006, SI 2006/3272, art 2 as from 1 September 2007; for transitional provisions see art 6, Sch 4 thereto (as amended by SI 2007/1157, arts 7–12).

Subsection (2) brought into force by the Gambling Act 2005 (Commencement No 6 and Transitional Provisions) Order 2006, SI 2006/3272, art 2, Sch 3 as from 1 June 2007; for transitional provisions see art 6, Sch 4 thereto (as amended by SI 2007/1157, arts 7–12).

Subsection (5) brought into force for certain purposes as from 1 June 2007 and for remaining purposes as from 1 September 2007 by the Gambling Act 2005 (Commencement No 6 and Transitional Provisions) Order 2006, SI 2006/3272, art 2, Sch 3; for transitional provisions see art 6, Sch 4 thereto (as amended by SI 2007/1157, arts 7–12).

Sub-s (1): Person. See the note 'Persons' to s 23.

Sub-s (1): Category C or D. As to the categories of gaming machine, see s 236.

Sub-s (2): Licensing authority. For the licensing authorities for the purposes of this Act, see s 2 (and see also s 278(2)).

Sub-s (2): Premises to which this section applies. See s 278.

Sub-s (4): Club gaming permit; club machine permit. See, generally, ss 271, 273.

Definitions

'Category C gaming machine': s 353(1)
'Category D gaming machine': s 353(1)
'club gaming permit': ss 271(2), 353(1)
'club machine permit': ss 273(2), 353(1)
'gaming machine': ss 235, 353(1)
'licensing authority': ss 2, 278(2), 353(1)
'premises': s 353(1), (2)(g)

Explanatory Notes

711 [para **6.2016** below]

6.784 284 Removal of exemption

(1) A licensing authority may make an order disapplying section 279 or section 282(1) to specified premises.

(2) A licensing authority may make an order disapplying a section under subsection (1) only if they think that—

(a) the application of the section is not reasonably consistent with pursuit of the licensing objectives,

(b) gaming has taken place on the premises in purported reliance on the section but in breach of a condition of that section,

(c) the premises are mainly used or to be used for gaming, or

(d) an offence under this Act has been committed on the premises.

(3) Before making an order under subsection (1) a licensing authority shall—

(a) give the holder of the on-premises alcohol licence or of the relevant Scottish licence ('the licensee') at least 21 days' notice of the authority's intention to consider making an order,

(b) consider any representations made by the licensee,
(c) hold a hearing if the licensee requests one, and
(d) comply with any prescribed requirements for the procedure to be followed in considering whether to make an order.

(4) If a licensing authority make an order under subsection (1), they shall as soon as is reasonably practicable give the licensee—
(a) a copy of the order, and
(b) written reasons for the decision to make the order.

(5) A licensee may appeal against the making of an order under subsection (1).

(6) An appeal under subsection (5) must be instituted—
(a) in the magistrates' court for a local justice area in which the premises to which the appeal relates are wholly or partly situated,
(b) by notice of appeal given to the designated officer, and
(c) within the period of 21 days beginning with the day on which the appellant receives a copy of the order against which the appeal is brought.

(7) On an appeal the magistrates' court may—
(a) dismiss the appeal;
(b) allow the appeal and quash the order made by the licensing authority;
(c) make an order about costs.

(8) In relation to premises in Scotland—
(a) subsection (6)(a) shall have effect as if it referred to a sheriff within whose sheriffdom the premises are wholly or partly situated,
(b) subsection (6)(b) shall not have effect,
(c) the reference in subsection (7) to the magistrates' court shall have effect as a reference to the sheriff, and
(d) the reference in subsection (7)(c) to costs shall have effect as a reference to expenses.

(9) In this section, 'prescribed' means prescribed by regulations made by the Secretary of State.

Commencement

Brought into force by the Gambling Act 2005 (Commencement No 6 and Transitional Provisions) Order 2006, SI 2006/3272, art 2, Sch 3 as from 1 June 2007; for transitional provisions see art 6, Sch 4 thereto (as amended by SI 2007/1157, arts 7–12).

Sub-s (1): Licensing authority. For the licensing authorities for the purposes of this Act, see s 2 (and see also s 278(2)).

Sub-s (1): Premises. For the premises to which this section applies, see s 278.

Sub-s (3): Notice. See further, in connection with a requirement under this Act to give a notice, s 353(4).

Sub-s (4): Written. See the note 'Writing' to s 39.

Sub-s (6): Magistrates' court. See the note to s 207.

Sub-s (9): Secretary of State. See the note to s 4.

Regulations under this section

At the time of going to press no regulations had been made under this section.

As to regulations under this Act generally, see s 355.

Definitions

'gaming': ss 6, 353(1)
'licensing authority': ss 2, 278(2), 353(1)
'the licensing objectives': ss 1, 353(1)
'on-premises alcohol licence': s 277(b)
'premises': s 353(1), (2)(g)
'relevant Scottish licence': s 277(c)

Explanatory Notes

719–721 [para **6.2016** below]

Clubs, pubs &c: special provision for Scotland

6.785 285 Permits

(1) The Scottish Ministers may, with the consent of the Secretary of State, by regulations provide that such provisions as are set out in the regulations are to apply in relation to—

(a) a club gaming permit or club machine permit, in place of Schedule 12 if the applicant for or holder of the permit is the holder of . . . [1] a relevant Scottish licence [and the premises are premises to which section 125(1) of the Licensing (Scotland) Act 2005 applies][2], or

(b) a licensed premises gaming machine permit, in place of Schedule 13, if the applicant for or holder of the permit is the holder of a relevant Scottish licence [and the premises are premises to which section 125(1) of the Licensing (Scotland) Act 2005 does not apply][3],

or if the applicant for or holder of the permit falls within such other description as may be specified in the regulations.

(2) Regulations under subsection (1) may amend, revoke or otherwise modify any enactment in so far as it appears to the Scottish Ministers necessary or expedient to do so for the purposes of that subsection.

Commencement

Brought into force by the Gambling Act 2005 (Commencement No 6 and Transitional Provisions) Order 2006, SI 2006/3272, art 2, Sch 1 as from 1 January 2007; for transitional provisions see art 6, Sch 4 thereto (as amended by SI 2007/1157, arts 7–12).

Sub-s (1): Scottish Ministers. See the note to s 25.

Sub-s (1): Secretary of State. See the note to s 4.

Sub-s (1): Club gaming permit; club machine permit; licensed premises gaming machine permit. See, generally, ss 271, 273, 283.

Regulations under this section

As to regulations under this Act generally, see s 355.

Definitions

'club gaming permit': ss 271(2), 353(1)
'club machine permit': ss 273(2), 353(1)
'enactment': s 353(1)
'licensed premises gaming machine permit': ss 283(2), 353(1)
'relevant Scottish licence': s 277(c)

Explanatory Notes

722 [para **6.2016** below]

---

1 Sub-s (1): in para (a) words omitted repealed by SSI 2009/248, art 2(1), Sch 1, Pt 1, para 12(1), (7)(a)(i).

2 Sub-s (1): in para (a) words from "and the premises" to "the Licensing (Scotland) Act 2005 applies" in square brackets inserted by SSI 2009/248, art 2(1), Sch 1, Pt 1, para 12(1), (7)(a)(ii).

3 Sub-s (1): in para (b) words from "and the premises" to "does not apply" in square brackets inserted by SSI 2009/248, art 2(1), Sch 1, Pt 1, para 12(1), (7)(b).

Fairs

6.786 286 Interpretation: travelling fair

For the purposes of this Act—

(a) 'fair' means a fair consisting wholly or principally of the provision of amusements, and

(b) a fair held on a day in a calendar year is a 'travelling fair' if provided—

(i) wholly or principally by persons who travel from place to place for the purpose of providing fairs, and

(ii) at a place no part of which has been used for the provision of a fair on more than 27 days in that calendar year.

Commencement

Brought into force by the Gambling Act 2005 (Commencement No 6 and Transitional Provisions) Order 2006, SI 2006/3272, art 2 as from 1 September 2007; for transitional provisions see art 6, Sch 4 thereto (as amended by SI 2007/1157, arts 7–12).

Explanatory Notes

723, 724 [para **6.2016** below]

6.787 287 Gaming machines

A person does not commit an offence under section 37 or 242 if—

(a) he makes one or more Category D gaming machines available for use at a travelling fair, and

(b) facilities for gambling (whether by way of gaming machine or otherwise) amount together to no more than an ancillary amusement at the fair.

Commencement

Brought into force by the Gambling Act 2005 (Commencement No 6 and Transitional Provisions) Order 2006, SI 2006/3272, art 2 as from 1 September 2007; for transitional provisions see art 6, Sch 4 thereto (as amended by SI 2007/1157, arts 7–12).

Person

See the note 'Persons' to s 23.

Category D gaming machines. As to the categories of gaming machine, see s 236.

Definitions

'Category D gaming machine': s 353(1)
'fair': ss 286, 353(1)
'gaming machine': ss 235, 353(1)
'travelling fair': ss 286, 353(1)

Explanatory Notes

723, 724 [para **6.2016** below]

PART 13
PRIZE GAMING

6.788 288 Meaning of 'prize gaming'

Gaming is prize gaming for the purposes of this Act if neither the nature nor the size of a prize played for is determined by reference to—

(a) the number of persons playing, or

(b) the amount paid for or raised by the gaming.

Commencement

Brought into force by the Gambling Act 2005 (Commencement No 6 and Transitional Provisions) Order 2006, SI 2006/3272, art 2, Sch 1 as from 1 January 2007; for transitional provisions see art 6, Sch 4 thereto (as amended by SI 2007/1157, arts 7–12).

Definitions

'gaming': ss 6, 353(1)
'prize': ss 6(5), 353(1)

Explanatory Notes

730–732 [para **6.2017** below]

6.789 289 Prize gaming permits

(1) A person does not commit an offence under section 33 or 37 by providing facilities for prize gaming if—

(a) the gaming satisfies the conditions specified in section 293, and
(b) the facilities are provided in accordance with a prize gaming permit.

(2) A prize gaming permit is a permit issued by a licensing authority authorising a person to provide facilities for gaming with prizes on specified premises.

(3) Schedule 14 makes further provision about prize gaming permits.

Commencement

Subsection (1) brought into force by the Gambling Act 2005 (Commencement No 6 and Transitional Provisions) Order 2006, SI 2006/3272, art 2, Sch 1 as from 1 January 2007; for transitional provisions see art 6, Sch 4 thereto (as amended by SI 2007/1157, arts 7–12).

Subsection (2) brought into force by the Gambling Act 2005 (Commencement No 6 and Transitional Provisions) Order 2006, SI 2006/3272, art 2 as from 13 November 2006; for transitional provisions see art 6, Sch 4 thereto (as amended by SI 2007/1157, arts 7–12).

Subsection (3) brought into force for certain purposes as from 13 November 2006 and 30 April 2007, brought into force for remaining purposes as from 1 September 2007 by the Gambling Act 2005 (Commencement No 6 and Transitional Provisions) Order 2006, SI 2006/3272, art 2, Sch 2; for transitional provisions see art 6, Sch 4 thereto (as amended by SI 2007/1157, arts 7–12).

Sub-s (1): Person. See the note 'Persons' to s 23.

Sub-s (1): Does not commit an offence. See, however, s 294.

Sub-s (2): Prize gaming permit. For powers of entry in connection with such a permit, see s 311.

Sub-s (2): Licensing authority. For the licensing authorities for the purposes of this Act, see s 2.

Definitions

'licensing authority': ss 2, 353(1)
'premises': s 353(1), (2)(g)
'prize gaming': ss 288, 353(1)
'providing facilities for gambling': ss 5, 353(2)(i)

Explanatory Notes

733–739 [para **6.2017** below]

6.790 290 Gaming and entertainment centres

(1) A person does not commit an offence under section 33 or 37 by providing facilities for prize gaming if—

(a) the gaming satisfies the conditions specified in section 293, and
(b) the facilities are provided in—
  (i) an adult gaming centre, or
  (ii) a licensed family entertainment centre.

(2) A person does not commit an offence under section 33 or 37 by providing facilities for equal chance prize gaming if—

(a) the gaming satisfies the conditions specified in section 293, and
(b) the facilities are provided on premises in respect of which a family entertainment centre gaming machine permit has effect.

Commencement

Brought into force by the Gambling Act 2005 (Commencement No 6 and Transitional Provisions) Order 2006, SI 2006/3272, art 2 as from 1 September 2007; for transitional provisions see art 6, Sch 4 thereto (as amended by SI 2007/1157, arts 7–12).

Sub-s (1): Person. See the note 'Persons' to s 23.

Sub-s (1): Does not commit an offence. See, however, s 294.

Sub-s (2): Family entertainment centre gaming machine permit. See, generally, s 247, Sch 10.

Definitions

'adult gaming centre': ss 237, 353(1)
'equal chance gaming': ss 8, 353(1)
'family entertainment centre gaming machine permit': ss 247(2), 353(1)
'licensed family entertainment centre': ss 238, 353(1)
'premises': s 353(1), (2)(g)
'prize gaming': ss 288, 353(1)
'providing facilities for gambling': ss 5, 353(2)(i)

Explanatory Notes

740–742 [para **6.2017** below]

6.791 291 Bingo halls

(1) A person does not commit an offence under section 33 or 37 by providing facilities for prize gaming in premises in respect of which a bingo premises licence has effect.

(2) A condition may be attached under section 75 or 78 to an operating licence so as—

(a) to prevent facilities for a specified description of game from being provided in reliance on subsection (1), or

(b) to provide for subsection (1) to apply, whether generally or only in connection with a specified description of game, subject to specified conditions or only in specified circumstances.

(3) A condition attached under section 78 by virtue of subsection (2) above may, in particular, relate to a matter listed in section 91(1).

(4) Subsection (1) may not be disapplied or modified—

(a) by way of a condition attached to an operating licence under section 77, or

(b) by way of a condition attached to a premises licence under section 167, 168 or 169.

Commencement

Brought into force for certain purposes as from 1 January 2007, brought into force for remaining purposes as from 1 September 2007 by the Gambling Act 2005 (Commencement No 6 and Transitional Provisions) Order 2006, SI 2006/3272, art 2, Schs 1 and 2; for transitional provisions see art 6, Sch 4 thereto (as amended by SI 2007/1157, arts 7–12).

Sub-s (1): Person. See the note 'Persons' to s 23.

Sub-s (1): Premises licence. As to the nature, etc of premises licences, see s 150 and the note 'Premises licence' thereto.

Sub-s (2): Operating licence. As to the nature, etc of operating licences, see s 65 and the note 'Operating licences' thereto.

Subordinate Legislation:

SI 2007/2257.

Definitions

'operating licence': s 353(1)
'premises': s 353(1), (2)(g)
'premises licence': s 353(1)

'prize gaming': ss 288, 353(1)
'providing facilities for gambling': ss 5, 353(2)(i)

Explanatory Notes
743–745 [para **6.2017** below]

6.792 292 Fairs

A person does not commit an offence under section 33 or 37 by providing facilities for equal chance prize gaming if—

(a) the gaming satisfies the conditions specified in section 293,

(b) the facilities are provided at a travelling fair, and

(c) facilities for gambling (in whatever form) amount together to no more than an ancillary amusement at the fair.

Commencement
Brought into force by the Gambling Act 2005 (Commencement No 6 and Transitional Provisions) Order 2006, SI 2006/3272, art 2 as from 1 September 2007; for transitional provisions see art 6, Sch 4 thereto (as amended by SI 2007/1157, arts 7–12).

Person
See the note 'Persons' to s 23.
Does not commit an offence. See, however, s 294.

Definitions
'equal chance gaming': ss 8, 353(1)
'gambling': ss 3, 353(1)
'prize gaming': ss 288, 353(1)
'providing facilities for gambling': ss 5, 353(2)(i)
'travelling fair': ss 286, 353(1)

Explanatory Notes
740–742 [para **6.2017** below]

6.793 293 Conditions for prize gaming

(1) This section specifies the conditions mentioned in sections 289(1), 290(1) and (2) and 292 for prize gaming.

(2) The first condition is compliance with such limits as may be prescribed in respect of participation fees (and those limits may, in particular, relate to players, games or a combination; and different limits may be prescribed in respect of different classes or descriptions of fee).

(3) The second condition is that—

(a) all the chances to participate in a particular game must be acquired or allocated on one day and in the place where the game is played,

(b) the game must be played entirely on that day, and

(c) the result of the game must be made public—

(i) in the place where the game is played, and

(ii) as soon as is reasonably practicable after the game ends, and in any event on the day on which it is played.

(4) The third condition is that a prize for which a game is played, or the aggregate of the prizes for which a game is played—

(a) where all the prizes are money, must not exceed the prescribed amount, and

(b) in any other case, must not exceed the prescribed value.

(5) The fourth condition is that participation in the game by a person does not entitle him or another person to participate in any other gambling (whether or not he or the other person would also have to pay in order to participate in the other gambling).

(6) In this section 'prescribed' means prescribed by regulations made by the Secretary of State.

Commencement

Brought into force by the Gambling Act 2005 (Commencement No 6 and Transitional Provisions) Order 2006, SI 2006/3272, art 2 as from 1 September 2007; for transitional provisions see art 6, Sch 4 thereto (as amended by SI 2007/1157, arts 7–12).

Sub-s (6): Secretary of State. See the note to s 4.

Subordinate Legislation:

SI 2009/1272.

As to regulations under this Act generally, see s 355.

Definitions

'gambling': ss 3, 353(1)
'participation fee': ss 344, 353(1)
'prize': ss 6(5), 353(1)
'prize gaming': ss 288, 353(1)

Explanatory Notes

746 [para **6.2017** below]

6.794 294 Power to restrict exemptions

The Secretary of State may by order provide for sections 289, 290 and 292 not to have effect in relation to prize gaming of a specified description.

Commencement

Brought into force by the Gambling Act 2005 (Commencement No 6 and Transitional Provisions) Order 2006, SI 2006/3272, art 2 as from 1 September 2007; for transitional provisions see art 6, Sch 4 thereto (as amended by SI 2007/1157, arts 7–12).

Secretary of State

See the note to s 4.

Orders under this section

At the time of going to press no orders had been made under this section.

As to orders under this Act generally, see s 355.

Definitions

'prize gaming': ss 288, 353(1)

Explanatory Notes

747 [para **6.2017** below]

PART 14
PRIVATE AND NON-COMMERCIAL GAMING AND BETTING

Private gaming and betting

6.795 295 Interpretation

Schedule 15 (which defines private gaming and betting) shall have effect.

Commencement

Brought into force by the Gambling Act 2005 (Commencement No 6 and Transitional Provisions) Order 2006, SI 2006/3272, art 2 as from 1 September 2007; for transitional provisions see art 6, Sch 4 thereto (as amended by SI 2007/1157, arts 7–12).

6.796 296 Exceptions to offences

(1) A person does not commit an offence under section 33 by providing facilities for—

(a) private gaming, or
(b) private betting.

(2) Section 37 shall not apply to or in respect of the use of premises to carry on—

(a) private gaming, or
(b) private betting.

(3) A person does not commit an offence under section 33 or 37 by making or accepting a bet, or by offering to make or accept a bet, if he acts otherwise than in the course of a business.

Note

See the Gambling Commission advice note on non-commercial and private gaming and betting of January 2010 at para **6.2095** below.

Commencement

Brought into force by the Gambling Act 2005 (Commencement No 6 and Transitional Provisions) Order 2006, SI 2006/3272, art 2 as from 1 September 2007; for transitional provisions see art 6, Sch 4 thereto (as amended by SI 2007/1157, arts 7–12).

Sub-s (1): Person. See the note 'Persons' to s 23.

Definitions

'accepting a bet': s 353(2)(a)
'premises': s 353(1), (2)(g)
'private betting': ss 295, 353(1), Sch 15, Pt 2
'private gaming': ss 295, 353(1), Sch 15, Pt 1
'providing facilities for gambling': ss 5, 353(2)(i)

Explanatory Notes

750–753 [para **6.2018** below]

Non-commercial gaming and betting

6.797 297 Interpretation

(1) For the purposes of this Act gaming is non-commercial if it takes place at a non-commercial event (whether as an incidental activity or as the principal or only activity).

(2) An event is non-commercial if the arrangements for the event are such that no part of the proceeds is to be appropriated for the purpose of private gain.

(3) For the purposes of subsection (2) the proceeds of an event are—

(a) the sums raised by the organisers (whether by way of fees for entrance or for participation, by way of sponsorship, by way of commission from traders or otherwise), minus
(b) amounts deducted by the organisers in respect of costs reasonably incurred in organising the event.

Commencement

Brought into force by the Gambling Act 2005 (Commencement No 6 and Transitional Provisions) Order 2006, SI 2006/3272, art 2 as from 1 September 2007; for transitional provisions see art 6, Sch 4 thereto (as amended by SI 2007/1157, arts 7–12).

Definitions

'gaming': ss 6, 353(1)
'private gain': ss 19(3), 353(1)

Explanatory Notes

758–761 [para **6.2018** below]

6.798 298 Exceptions to offences

(1) A person does not commit an offence under section 33 by providing facilities for—

(a) non-commercial prize gaming which complies with the conditions in section 299, or

(b) non-commercial equal chance gaming which complies with the conditions in section 300.

(2) Section 37 shall not apply to or in respect of the use of premises to carry on—

(a) non-commercial prize gaming which complies with the conditions in section 299, or

(b) non-commercial equal chance gaming which complies with the conditions in section 300.

Commencement

Brought into force by the Gambling Act 2005 (Commencement No 6 and Transitional Provisions) Order 2006, SI 2006/3272, art 2 as from 1 September 2007; for transitional provisions see art 6, Sch 4 thereto (as amended by SI 2007/1157, arts 7–12).

Sub-s (1): Person. See the note 'Persons' to s 23.

Definitions

'equal chance gaming': ss 8, 353(1)
'non-commercial gaming': ss 297, 353(1)
'prize gaming': ss 288, 353(1)
'premises': s 353(1), (2)(g)
'providing facilities for gambling': ss 5, 353(2)(i)

Explanatory Notes

758–761 [para **6.2018** below]

6.799 299 Conditions for non-commercial prize gaming

(1) This section specifies the conditions for non-commercial prize gaming mentioned in section 298.

(2) The first condition is that players are informed that the purpose of the gaming is to raise money for a specified purpose other than that of private gain.

(3) The second condition is that the arrangements for the gaming are such that the profits will be applied for a purpose other than that of private gain.

(4) The third condition is that the non-commercial event of which the gaming is part does not take place—

(a) on premises, other than a track, in respect of which a premises licence has effect,

(b) on a track at a time when activities are being carried on in reliance on a premises licence, or

(c) on premises at a time when activities are being carried on in reliance on a temporary use notice.

(5) The fourth condition is that the gaming is not remote.

(6) In this section 'profits' in relation to gaming means—

(a) the aggregate of amounts—

(i) paid by way of stakes, or

(ii) otherwise accruing to the person organising the gaming directly in connection with it, minus

(b) amounts deducted by the person organising the gaming in respect of—

(i) the provision of prizes, or

(ii) other costs reasonably incurred in organising or providing facilities for the gaming.

Commencement

Brought into force by the Gambling Act 2005 (Commencement No 6 and Transitional Provisions) Order 2006, SI 2006/3272, art 2 as from 1 September 2007; for transitional provisions see art 6, Sch 4 thereto (as amended by SI 2007/1157, arts 7–12).

Sub-s (4): Premises licence. As to the nature, etc of premises licences, see s 150 and the note 'Premises licence' thereto.

Sub-s (4): Temporary use notice. See s 214 and the note 'Temporary use notice' thereto.

Definitions

'gaming': ss 6, 353(1)
'non-commercial event': s 297(2), (3)
'non-commercial gaming': ss 297, 353(1)
'premises': s 353(1), (2)(g)
'premises licence': s 353(1)
'private gain': ss 19(3), 353(1)
'prize': ss 6(5), 353(1)
'prize gaming': ss 288, 353(1)
'remote gambling': ss 4, 353(1)
'stake': s 353(1)
'temporary use notice': ss 215(1), 353(1)
'track': s 353(1)

Explanatory Notes

758–761 [para **6.2018** below]

6.800 300 Conditions for non-commercial equal-chance gaming

(1) This section specifies the conditions for non-commercial equal-chance gaming mentioned in section 298.

(2) The first condition is that persons participating in the gaming are informed that the purpose of the gaming is to raise money for a specified purpose other than that of private gain.

(3) The second condition is that the arrangements for the gaming are such that the profits will be applied for a purpose other than that of private gain.

(4) The third condition is that the arrangements for the gaming ensure compliance with regulations of the Secretary of State—

(a) limiting amounts staked;
(b) limiting participation fees;
(c) limiting other amounts paid by a person in connection with the gaming;
(d) limiting a combination of matters specified in paragraphs (a) to (c);
(e) limiting the amount or value of a prize;
(f) limiting the aggregate amount or value of prizes.

(5) Regulations under subsection (4) may, in particular—

(a) make provision by reference to whether or not a game is part of a series;
(b) make provision by reference to whether or not the non-commercial event of which the gaming is part is associated, as defined by the regulations, with another event;
(c) limit stakes in relation to a participant in more than one game;
(d) make different provision for different kinds of game or for games played in different circumstances.

(6) The fourth condition is that the non-commercial event of which the gaming is part does not take place—

(a) on premises, other than a track, in respect of which a premises licence has effect,
(b) on a track at a time when activities are being carried on in reliance on a premises licence, or
(c) on premises at a time when activities are being carried on in reliance on a temporary use notice.

(7) The fifth condition is that the gaming is non-remote.

(8) In this section 'profits' in relation to gaming means—

(a) the aggregate of amounts—

(i) paid by way of stakes, or

(ii) otherwise accruing to the person organising the gaming directly in connection with it, minus

(b) amounts deducted by the person organising the gaming in respect of—

(i) the provision of prizes, or

(ii) other costs reasonably incurred in organising or providing facilities for the gaming.

Commencement

Brought into force by the Gambling Act 2005 (Commencement No 6 and Transitional Provisions) Order 2006, SI 2006/3272, art 2 as from 1 September 2007; for transitional provisions see art 6, Sch 4 thereto (as amended by SI 2007/1157, arts 7–12).

Sub-s (4): Secretary of State. See the note to s 4.

Sub-s (6): Premises licence. As to the nature, etc of premises licences, see s 150 and the note 'Premises licence' thereto.

Sub-s (6): Temporary use notice. See s 214 and the note 'Temporary use notice' thereto.

Subordinate Legislation:

SI 2007/2041.

As to regulations under this Act generally, see s 355.

Definitions

'equal chance gaming': ss 8, 353(1)
'gaming': ss 6, 353(1)
'non-commercial event': s 297(2), (3)
'non-commercial gaming': ss 297, 353(1)
'participation fee': ss 344, 353(1)
'premises': s 353(1), (2)(g)
'premises licence': s 353(1)
'private gain': ss 19(3), 353(1)
'prize': ss 6(5), 353(1)
'remote gambling': ss 4, 353(1)
'stake': s 353(1)
'temporary use notice': ss 215(1), 353(1)
'track': s 353(1)

Explanatory Notes

758–761 [para **6.2018** below]

6.801 301 Misusing profits of non-commercial prize gaming

(1) This section applies to—

(a) non-commercial prize gaming in respect of which a fund-raising purpose has been specified as mentioned in section 299(2), and

(b) non-commercial equal-chance gaming in respect of which a fund-raising purpose has been specified as mentioned in section 300(2).

(2) A person commits an offence if he uses any part of the profits of gaming to which this section applies for a purpose other than that specified.

(3) The reference in subsection (2) to the use of profits includes a reference to permitting profits to be used.

(4) A person guilty of an offence under this section shall be liable on summary conviction to—

(a) imprisonment for a term not exceeding 51 weeks,

(b) a fine not exceeding level 5 on the standard scale, or

(c) both.

(5) In the application of subsection (4) to Scotland the reference to 51 weeks shall have effect as a reference to six months.

(6) In this section 'profits' has the same meaning as in sections 299 and 300.

Commencement

Brought into force by the Gambling Act 2005 (Commencement No 6 and Transitional Provisions) Order 2006, SI 2006/3272, art 2 as from 1 September 2007; for transitional provisions see art 6, Sch 4 thereto (as amended by SI 2007/1157, arts 7–12).

Sub-s (2): Person. See the note 'Persons' to s 23.

Sub-s (2): Offence. For the power of the Gambling Commission and other specified persons to undertake activities for the purpose of assessing whether an offence is being committed under or by virtue of this Act, see s 27 and s 305; for the power of that Commission to investigate and prosecute offences, see s 28; as to offences committed by a body, see s 341; and for the time limit on prosecutions, see s 347. See also s 306 for powers of entry as respects a suspected offence, and s 345 as respects forfeiture of an article relating to an offence.

Sub-s (4): Summary conviction; standard scale. See the notes to s 33.

Definitions

'equal chance gaming': ss 8, 353(1)
'non-commercial gaming': ss 297, 353(1)
'prize gaming': ss 288, 353(1)

Explanatory Notes

758–761 [para **6.2018** below]

6.802 302 Non-commercial betting

For the purposes of this Act a betting transaction is non-commercial betting if no party to the transaction—

(a) enters it in the course of a business, or
(b) holds himself out as being in business in relation to the acceptance of bets.

Commencement

Brought into force by the Gambling Act 2005 (Commencement No 6 and Transitional Provisions) Order 2006, SI 2006/3272, art 2 as from 1 September 2007; for transitional provisions see art 6, Sch 4 thereto (as amended by SI 2007/1157, arts 7–12).

Definitions

'accepting a bet': s 353(2)(a)

Explanatory Notes

762 [para **6.2018** below]

PART 15
INSPECTION

Inspectors

6.803 303 Enforcement officers

(1) The Commission—

(a) may designate employees of the Commission as enforcement officers for the purposes of this Act, and
(b) may appoint persons other than employees of the Commission as enforcement officers for the purposes of this Act.

(2) The Commission may pay to or in respect of an enforcement officer who is not an employee of the Commission sums by way of or in respect of—

(a) remuneration;
(b) allowances;
(c) expenses;

(d) pension;
(e) gratuity.

Note

See 'Compliance and Enforcement Policy Statement' published by the Gambling Commission in September 2009 (see para **6.2075** below).

Commencement

Brought into force by the Gambling Act 2005 (Commencement No 6 and Transitional Provisions) Order 2006, SI 2006/3272, art 2, Sch 2 as from 30 April 2007; for transitional provisions see art 6, Sch 4 thereto (as amended by SI 2007/1157, arts 7–12).

Sub-s (1): The Commission. Ie the Gambling Commission; see s 353(1). As to the establishment, etc of the Gambling Commission, see s 20, Sch 4, and the note 'Gambling Commission' to that section.

Definitions

'the Commission': s 353(1)

Explanatory Notes

764 [para **6.2019** below]

6.804 304 Authorised persons

(1) In this Act—

(a) 'authorised person' has the meaning given by this section, and
(b) a reference to an authorised local authority officer is a reference to a person who is an authorised person by virtue of subsection (2).

(2) An officer of a licensing authority is an authorised person for a purpose relating to premises if—

(a) the premises are wholly or partly situated in the authority's area, and
(b) the officer is designated by the authority as an authorised person for the purposes of this section.

(3) An officer of an authority other than a licensing authority is an authorised person for a purpose relating to premises if—

(a) the authority has statutory functions, for an area in which the premises are wholly or partly situated, in relation to minimising or preventing the risk of pollution of the environment or of harm to human health, and
(b) the officer is authorised by the authority for the purpose of exercising any of those statutory functions.

(4) The following are authorised persons for purposes relating to any premises—

(a) an inspector appointed under section 18 of the Fire Precautions Act 1971 (c 40) (enforcement),[1]
(b) an inspector appointed under section 19 of the Health and Safety at Work etc Act 1974 (c 37) (inspectors),
(c) an inspector or surveyor of ships appointed under section 256 of the Merchant Shipping Act 1995 (c 21) (enforcement),
(d) a person who is within a class prescribed by the Secretary of State by regulations.

Commencement

Brought into force by the Gambling Act 2005 (Commencement No 6 and Transitional Provisions) Order 2006, SI 2006/3272, art 2, Sch 2 as from 30 April 2007; for transitional provisions see art 6, Sch 4 thereto (as amended by SI 2007/1157, arts 7–12).

Sub-s (2): Licensing authority. For the licensing authorities for the purposes of this Act, see s 2.

Sub-s (4): Secretary of State. See the note to s 4.

Regulations under this section

At the time of going to press no regulations had been made under this section.

As to regulations under this Act generally, see s 355.

Definitions

'licensing authority': ss 2, 353(1)

'premises': s 353(1), (2)(g)

Explanatory Notes

765–766 [para **6.2019** below]

---

[1] Substituted in relation to Scotland by SSI 2006/475, art 2(1), Sch 1, para 16(1), (3).

Kinds of inspection

6.805 305 Compliance

A constable, enforcement officer or authorised person may undertake activities for the purpose of assessing—

(a) compliance with provision made by or by virtue of this Act;

(b) whether an offence is being committed under or by virtue of this Act.

Note

See 'Compliance and Enforcement Policy Statement' published by the Gambling Commission in September 2009 (see para **6.2075** below).

Commencement

Brought into force by the Gambling Act 2005 (Commencement No 6 and Transitional Provisions) Order 2006, SI 2006/3272, art 2 as from 1 September 2007; for transitional provisions see art 6, Sch 4 thereto (as amended by SI 2007/1157, arts 7–12).

Constable

See the note to s 64.

Enforcement officer. As to enforcement officers, see, generally, s 303.

Subordinate Legislation:

SI 2006/636.

Definitions

'authorised person': ss 304, 353(1)

Explanatory Notes

767 [para **6.2019** below]

6.806 306 Suspected offence

(1) A constable or enforcement officer may enter premises if he reasonably suspects that an offence under this Act may be—

(a) being committed on the premises, or

(b) about to be committed on the premises.

(2) A justice of the peace may on the application of a constable or enforcement officer issue a warrant authorising a constable or enforcement officer to enter premises if the justice of the peace is satisfied—

(a) that there are reasonable grounds for suspecting that an offence under this Act has been committed on the premises,

(b) that there are reasonable grounds for suspecting that evidence of the commission of the offence may be found on the premises, and

(c) that at least one of the conditions in subsection (3) is satisfied.

(3) Those conditions are—

(a) that admission to the premises has been refused,
(b) that admission to the premises is likely to be refused unless a warrant is produced,
(c) that the purpose of entry may be frustrated or seriously prejudiced unless a constable or enforcement officer arriving at the premises can secure immediate entry, and
(d) that there is likely to be nobody at the premises capable of granting admission.

(4) A warrant may be granted in reliance on subsection (3)(a) or (b) only if the justice of the peace is satisfied—
(a) that notice has been given to a person occupying the premises, or having responsibility for their management, of intent to apply for a warrant, or
(b) that the purpose of entry may be frustrated or seriously prejudiced by the giving of notice under paragraph (a).

(5) A warrant under subsection (2) shall cease to have effect at the end of the period of 28 days beginning with the day of issue.

(6) In the application of this section to Scotland, any reference to a justice of the peace is to be construed as a reference to the sheriff or a justice of the peace.

Commencement

Brought into force by the Gambling Act 2005 (Commencement No 6 and Transitional Provisions) Order 2006, SI 2006/3272, art 2 as from 1 September 2007; for transitional provisions see art 6, Sch 4 thereto (as amended by SI 2007/1157, arts 7–12).

Sub-s (1): Constable. See the note to s 64.

Sub-s (1): Enforcement officer. As to enforcement officers, see, generally, s 303.

Sub-s (4): Notice. See further, in connection with a requirement under this Act to give a notice, s 353(4).

Further provisions

See further in connection with the exercise of powers under this Part of this Act, s 317 (powers); s 318 (dwellings); s 319 (records); s 320 (timing); s 321 (evidence of authorisation); s 322 (information); s 323 (use of force); s 324 (person accompanying inspector, etc); s 325 (securing premises after entry); and s 326 (obstruction).

Definitions

'enforcement officer': s 353(1)
'premises': s 353(1), (2)(g)

Explanatory Notes

768–770 [para **6.2019** below]

6.807 307 Inspection of gambling

(1) A constable, enforcement officer or authorised person may enter premises to which this section applies for a purpose specified in subsection (3).

(2) This section applies to premises if a constable, enforcement officer or authorised person reasonably suspects that facilities for gambling other than private and non-commercial gaming or betting may be being provided, may be about to be provided or have been provided, on the premises.

(3) The purposes mentioned in subsection (1) are—
(a) to discover whether facilities for gambling other than private and non-commercial gaming or betting are being provided, are about to be provided or have been provided on the premises,
(b) to determine whether an operating licence or premises licence is held in respect of the provision of facilities for gambling on the premises, and
(c) to determine whether facilities are being, will be or have been provided in accordance with the terms and conditions of an operating licence or premises licence.

Commencement

Brought into force by the Gambling Act 2005 (Commencement No 6 and Transitional Provisions) Order 2006, SI 2006/3272, art 2 as from 1 September 2007; for transitional provisions see art 6, Sch 4 thereto (as amended by SI 2007/1157, arts 7–12).

Sub-s (1): Constable. See the note to s 64.

Sub-s (1): Enforcement officer. As to enforcement officers, see, generally, s 303.

Sub-s (3): Operating licence. As to the nature, etc of operating licences, see s 65 and the note 'Operating licences' thereto.

Sub-s (3): Premises licence. As to the nature, etc of premises licences, see s 150 and the note 'Premises licence' thereto.

Further provisions

See the note to s 306.

Definitions

'authorised person': ss 304, 353(1)
'enforcement officer': s 353(1)
'non-commercial betting': ss 302, 353(1)
'non-commercial gaming': ss 297, 353(1)
'operating licence': s 353(1)
'premises': s 353(1), (2)(g)
'premises licence': s 353(1)
'private betting': ss 295, 353(1), Sch 15, Pt 2
'private gaming': ss 295, 353(1), Sch 15, Pt 1
'providing facilities for gambling': ss 5, 353(2)(i)

Explanatory Notes

771, 772 [para **6.2019** below]

6.808 308 Operating licence holders

(1) A constable or enforcement officer may enter premises to which this section applies for the purpose specified in subsection (3).

(2) This section applies to premises which a constable or enforcement officer reasonably believes to be used by the holder of an operating licence wholly or partly for purposes connected with the licensed activities.

(3) The purpose mentioned in subsection (1) is to determine whether the licensed activities are being carried on in accordance with the terms and conditions of the operating licence.

Commencement

Brought into force by the Gambling Act 2005 (Commencement No 6 and Transitional Provisions) Order 2006, SI 2006/3272, art 2 as from 1 September 2007; for transitional provisions see art 6, Sch 4 thereto (as amended by SI 2007/1157, arts 7–12).

Sub-s (1): Constable. See the note to s 64.

Sub-s (1): Enforcement officer. As to enforcement officers, see, generally, s 303.

Sub-s (2): Operating licence. As to the nature, etc of operating licences, see s 65 and the note 'Operating licences' thereto.

Further provisions

See the note to s 306.

Definitions

'enforcement officer': s 353(1)
'operating licence': s 353(1)
'premises': s 353(1), (2)(g)

Explanatory Notes

773 [para **6.2019** below]

6.809 309 Family entertainment centres

(1) A constable, enforcement officer or authorised local authority officer may enter premises in respect of which an application has been made for a family entertainment centre gaming machine permit for a purpose connected with the consideration of the application.

(2) A constable, enforcement officer or authorised local authority officer may enter premises in respect of which a family entertainment centre gaming machine permit has effect for the purpose of determining whether the gaming machines used on the premises, and the arrangements for their use, comply with the requirements of this Act and regulations under it.

Commencement

Subsection (1) brought into force by the Gambling Act 2005 (Commencement No 6 and Transitional Provisions) Order 2006, SI 2006/3272, art 2, Sch 2 as from 30 April 2007; for transitional provisions see art 6, Sch 4 thereto (as amended by SI 2007/1157, arts 7–12).

Subsection (2) brought into force by the Gambling Act 2005 (Commencement No 6 and Transitional Provisions) Order 2006, SI 2006/3272, art 2 as from 1 September 2007; for transitional provisions see art 6, Sch 4 thereto (as amended by SI 2007/1157, arts 7–12).

Sub-s (1): Constable. See the note to s 64.

Sub-s (1): Enforcement officer. As to enforcement officers, see, generally, s 303.

Sub-s (1): Family entertainment centre gaming machine permit. See, generally, s 247, Sch 10.

Further provisions

See the note to s 306.

Definitions

'authorised local authority officer': ss 304, 353(1)
'enforcement officer': s 353(1)
'family entertainment centre gaming machine permit': ss 247(2), 353(1)
'gaming machine': ss 235, 353(1)
'premises': s 353(1), (2)(g)

Explanatory Notes

774 [para **6.2019** below]

6.810 310 Premises licensed for alcohol

(1) An enforcement officer or an authorised local authority officer may enter premises in respect of which an application has been made under Schedule 13 for a purpose connected with the consideration of the application.

(2) A constable, enforcement officer or authorised local authority officer may enter premises in respect of which an on-premises alcohol licence has effect for the purpose of—

(a) determining whether gaming carried on satisfies the conditions in section 279;

(b) in the case of bingo played on the premises, determining—

(i) whether the terms and conditions of any relevant operating licence are being complied with;

(ii) whether section 281 applies;

(c) ascertaining the number and category of gaming machines being made available for use on the premises.

Commencement

Subsection (1) brought into force by the Gambling Act 2005 (Commencement No 6 and Transitional Provisions) Order 2006, SI 2006/3272, art 2, Sch 3 as from 1 June 2007; for transitional provisions see art 6, Sch 4 thereto (as amended by SI 2007/1157, arts 7–12).

Subsection (2) brought into force by the Gambling Act 2005 (Commencement No 6 and Transitional Provisions) Order 2006, SI 2006/3272, art 2 as from 1 September 2007; for transitional provisions see art 6, Sch 4 thereto (as amended by SI 2007/1157, arts 7–12).

Sub-s (1): Enforcement officer. As to enforcement officers, see, generally, s 303.

Sub-s (2): Constable. See the note to s 64.

Sub-s (2): Category of gaming machines. As to the categories of gaming machine, see s 236.

Further provisions

See the note to s 306.

Definitions

'authorised local authority officer': ss 304, 353(1)
'bingo': s 353(1)
'enforcement officer': s 353(1)
'gaming': ss 6, 353(1)
'gaming machine': ss 235, 353(1)
'on-premise alcohol licence': ss 277(b), 353(1)
'premises': s 353(1), (2)(g)

Explanatory Notes

775, 776 [para **6.2019** below]

6.811 311 Prize gaming permit

(1) A constable, enforcement officer or authorised local authority officer may enter premises in respect of which an application has been made for a prize gaming permit for a purpose connected with the consideration of the application.

(2) A constable, enforcement officer or authorised local authority officer may enter premises in respect of which a prize gaming permit has effect for the purposes of determining whether prize gaming on the premises complies with the requirements of this Act and regulations under it.

Commencement

Subsection (1) brought into force by the Gambling Act 2005 (Commencement No 6 and Transitional Provisions) Order 2006, SI 2006/3272, art 2, Sch 2 as from 30 April 2007; for transitional provisions see art 6, Sch 4 thereto (as amended by SI 2007/1157, arts 7–12).

Subsection (2) brought into force by the Gambling Act 2005 (Commencement No 6 and Transitional Provisions) Order 2006, SI 2006/3272, art 2 as from 1 September 2007; for transitional provisions see art 6, Sch 4 thereto (as amended by SI 2007/1157, arts 7–12).

Sub-s (2): Constable. See the note to s 64.

Sub-s (1): Enforcement officer. As to enforcement officers, see, generally, s 303.

Sub-s (1): Prize gaming permit. See, generally, s 289.

Further provisions

See the note to s 306.

Definitions

'authorised local authority officer': ss 304, 353(1)
'enforcement officer': s 353(1)
'premises': s 353(1), (2)(g)
'prize gaming': ss 288, 353(1)
'prize gaming permit': ss 289(2), 353(1)

Explanatory Notes

777 [para **6.2019** below]

6.812 312 Clubs

(1) A constable or enforcement officer may enter premises to which this section applies for a purpose specified in subsection (3).

(2) This section applies to premises which a constable or enforcement officer reasonably believes to be used by a members' club, a commercial club or a miners' welfare institute.

(3) The purposes mentioned in subsection (1) are—

(a) to determine whether gaming is taking place on the premises or is about to take place on the premises,

(b) to determine whether any gaming that is taking place or is about to take place on the premises is in accordance with—

(i) section 269,

(ii) a club gaming permit, or

(iii) a club machine permit.

(4) An authorised local authority officer may enter premises in respect of which an application has been made for a club gaming permit or a club machine permit for a purpose connected with the consideration of the application.

Commencement

Subsections (1)–(3) brought into force by the Gambling Act 2005 (Commencement No 6 and Transitional Provisions) Order 2006, SI 2006/3272, art 2 as from 1 September 2007; for transitional provisions see art 6, Sch 4 thereto (as amended by SI 2007/1157, arts 7–12).

Subsection (4) brought into force by the Gambling Act 2005 (Commencement No 6 and Transitional Provisions) Order 2006, SI 2006/3272, art 2, Sch 3 as from 1 June 2007; for transitional provisions see art 6, Sch 4 thereto (as amended by SI 2007/1157, arts 7–12).

Sub-s (1): Constable. See the note to s 64.

Sub-s (1): Enforcement officer. As to enforcement officers, see, generally, s 303.

Sub-s (3): Club gaming permit; club machine permit. See, generally, ss 271, 273.

Further provisions

See the note to s 306.

Definitions

'authorised local authority officer': ss 304, 353(1)
'club gaming permit': ss 271(2), 353(1)
'club machine permit': ss 273(2), 353(1)
'commercial club': ss 267, 353(1)
'enforcement officer': s 353(1)
'gaming': ss 6, 353(1)
'members' club': ss 266, 353(1)
'miners' welfare institute': ss 268, 353(1)).
'premises': s 353(1), (2)(g)

Explanatory Notes

778–779 [para **6.2019** below]

6.813 313 Licensed premises

(1) A constable, enforcement officer or authorised person may enter premises in respect of which an application for a premises licence has been made to assess, having regard to the licensing objectives, the likely effects of activity carried on in reliance on the premises licence.

(2) A constable, enforcement officer or authorised person may enter premises in respect of which a premises licence has effect for a purpose connected with a review under section 201.

Commencement

Subsection (1) brought into force by the Gambling Act 2005 (Commencement No 6 and Transitional Provisions) Order 2006, SI 2006/3272, art 2, Sch 2 as from 30 April 2007; for transitional provisions see art 6, Sch 4 thereto (as amended by SI 2007/1157, arts 7–12).

Subsection (2) brought into force by the Gambling Act 2005 (Commencement No 6 and Transitional Provisions) Order 2006, SI 2006/3272, art 2 as from 1 September 2007; for transitional provisions see art 6, Sch 4 thereto (as amended by SI 2007/1157, arts 7–12).

Sub-s (1): Constable. See the note to s 64.

Sub-s (1): Enforcement officer. As to enforcement officers, see, generally, s 303.

Sub-s (1): Premises licence. As to the nature, etc of premises licences, see s 150 and the note 'Premises licence' thereto.

Further provisions

See the note to s 306.

Definitions

'authorised person': ss 304, 353(1)
'enforcement officer': s 353(1)
'the licensing objectives': ss 1, 353(1)
'premises': s 353(1), (2)(g)
'premises licence': s 353(1)

Explanatory Notes

780 [para **6.2019** below]

6.814 314 Lotteries: registered societies

Where a society is registered with a local authority in accordance with Part 5 of Schedule 11, an enforcement officer or an authorised local authority officer may enter premises owned or used by the society for the purpose of making inquiries in connection with a lottery promoted on behalf of the society.

Commencement

Brought into force by the Gambling Act 2005 (Commencement No 6 and Transitional Provisions) Order 2006, SI 2006/3272, art 2 as from 1 September 2007; for transitional provisions see art 6, Sch 4 thereto (as amended by SI 2007/1157, arts 7–12).

Enforcement officer. As to enforcement officers, see, generally, s 303.

Further provisions

See the note to s 306.

Definitions

'authorised local authority officer': ss 304, 353(1)
'enforcement officer': s 353(1)
'lottery': ss 14, 353(1)
'premises': s 353(1), (2)(g)
'promoting a lottery': ss 252, 353(2)(h)
'society': s 353(1)

Explanatory Notes

781 [para **6.2019** below]

6.815 315 Temporary use notice

(1) A constable, enforcement officer or authorised person may enter premises in respect of which a temporary use notice has been given to assess, having regard to the licensing objectives, the likely effects of activity carried on in reliance on the temporary use notice.

(2) A constable, enforcement officer or authorised person may enter premises in respect of which a temporary use notice has effect to determine whether an activity of a kind listed in section 37(1) is being carried on otherwise than in accordance with the temporary use notice.

Commencement

Brought into force by the Gambling Act 2005 (Commencement No 6 and Transitional Provisions) Order 2006, SI 2006/3272, art 2 as from 1 September 2007; for transitional provisions see art 6, Sch 4 thereto (as amended by SI 2007/1157, arts 7–12).

Sub-s (1): Constable. See the note to s 64.

Sub-s (1): Enforcement officer. As to enforcement officers, see, generally, s 303.

Sub-s (1): Temporary use notice. See s 214 and the note 'Temporary use notice' thereto.

Further provisions

See the note to s 306.

Definitions

'authorised person': ss 304, 353(1)
'enforcement officer': s 353(1)
'the licensing objectives': ss 1, 353(1)
'premises': s 353(1), (2)(g)
'temporary use notice': ss 215(1), 353(1)

Explanatory Notes

782 [para **6.2019** below]

6.816 316 Authorisations: production on demand

(1) A constable or enforcement officer may require the holder of an operating licence to produce to the constable or enforcement officer within a specified period a copy of any authorisation given by the holder of the licence under section 93(2) or (3) or 94(2).

(2) While a person is holding himself out as willing to accept bets on behalf of the holder of an operating licence in accordance with section 93(2) or (3) or 94(2), a constable or enforcement officer may require the person to produce a copy of his authorisation under that section—

(a) within a specified period, or
(b) immediately.

(3) A constable or enforcement officer may require the holder of a casino premises licence to produce to the constable or enforcement officer within a specified period a copy of any authorisation given by the holder of the licence under section 174(3).

(4) While a person is carrying on an activity in reliance on an authorisation under section 174(3), a constable or enforcement officer may require the person to produce a copy of his authorisation under that section—

(a) within a specified period, or
(b) immediately.

(5) A person commits an offence if he fails without reasonable excuse to comply with a requirement imposed under this section.

(6) A person guilty of an offence under subsection (5) shall be liable on summary conviction to a fine not exceeding level 2 on the standard scale.

Commencement

Brought into force by the Gambling Act 2005 (Commencement No 6 and Transitional Provisions) Order 2006, SI 2006/3272, art 2 as from 1 September 2007; for transitional provisions see art 6, Sch 4 thereto (as amended by SI 2007/1157, arts 7–12).

Sub-s (1): Constable. See the note to s 64.

Sub-s (1): Enforcement officer. As to enforcement officers, see, generally, s 303.

Sub-s (1): Operating licence. As to the nature, etc of operating licences, see s 65 and the note 'Operating licences' thereto.

Sub-s (3): Premises licence. As to the nature, etc of premises licences, see s 150 and the note 'Premises licence' thereto.

Sub-s (5): Person. See the note 'Persons' to s 23.

Sub-s (5): Offence. For the power of the Gambling Commission and other specified persons to undertake activities for the purpose of assessing whether an offence is being committed under or by virtue of this Act, see ss 27, 305; for the power of that Commission to investigate and prosecute offences, see s 28; as to offences committed by a body, see s 341; and for the time limit on prosecutions, see s 347. See also s 306 for powers of entry as respects a suspected offence, and s 345 as respects forfeiture of an article relating to an offence.

Sub-s (6): Summary conviction; standard scale. See the notes to s 33.

Further provisions
See the note to s 306.

Definitions
'accepting a bet': s 353(2)(a)
'enforcement officer': s 353(1)
'operating licence': s 353(1)
'premises licence': s 353(1)

Explanatory Notes
783, 784 [para **6.2019** below]

Powers and procedure

6.817 317 Powers

(1) A constable, enforcement officer or authorised person exercising a power under or by virtue of this Part to enter premises may—

(a) inspect any part of the premises and any machine or other thing on the premises;
(b) question any person on the premises;
(c) require access to any written or electronic record which is kept on the premises;
(d) require to be supplied with a copy, in such form as he directs, of an entry in a written or electronic record which is kept on the premises;
(e) remove and retain anything if he reasonably believes that it constitutes or contains evidence of—
  (i) the commission of an offence under this Act, or
  (ii) the breach of a term or condition of a licence issued under this Act;
(f) remove and retain anything if he reasonably believes that it is being used or has been used in the commission of an offence under this Act.

(2) The Secretary of State may by regulations make provision about the treatment of—

(a) copies supplied under subsection (1)(d), and
(b) things removed under subsection (1)(e) or (f).

(3) Regulations under subsection (2) may, in particular, make provision—

(a) about the retention, use, return, disposal or destruction of anything supplied or removed;
(b) conferring a right of appeal.

(4) The Secretary of State may by regulations make provision about the procedure to be followed in the exercise of a power under this section.

(5) Nothing in this Part authorises action to be taken in England and Wales in respect of anything of a kind specified in section 9(2) of the Police and Criminal Evidence Act 1984 (c 60) (legally privileged material, &c).

(6) A person exercising a power under or by virtue of this Part shall have regard to any relevant provision of a code of practice under that Act (and guidance under section 25 may refer to a provision of a code).

(7) Subsection (6) does not apply as respects the exercise of a power in relation to Scotland.

Commencement

Brought into force by the Gambling Act 2005 (Commencement No 6 and Transitional Provisions) Order 2006, SI 2006/3272, art 2, Sch 2 as from 30 April 2007; for transitional provisions see art 6, Sch 4 thereto (as amended by SI 2007/1157, arts 7–12).

Sub-s (1): Constable. See the note to s 64.

Sub-s (1): Enforcement officer. As to enforcement officers, see, generally, s 303.
Sub-s (1): This Part. Ie Pt 15 (ss 303–326) of this Act.
Sub-s (1): Written. See the note 'Writing' to s 39.
Sub-s (2): Secretary of State. See the note to s 4.

Further provisions

See the note to s 306.

Regulations under this section

At the time of going to press no regulations had been made under this section.
As to regulations under this Act generally, see s 355.

Definitions

'authorised person': ss 304, 353(1)
'enforcement officer': s 353(1)
'machine': ss 235(3)(a), 353(1)
'premises': s 353(1), (2)(g)

Explanatory Notes

785–789 [para **6.2019** below]

6.818 318 Dwellings

(1) A power under this Part to enter premises without a warrant does not apply in relation to a dwelling.

(2) A justice of the peace may on the application of a constable, enforcement officer or authorised person issue a warrant authorising a constable, enforcement officer or authorised person to enter premises if the justice of the peace is satisfied—

(a) that, but for subsection (1), a constable, enforcement officer or authorised person would be able to enter the premises without a warrant in reliance on a provision of this Part, and

(b) that at least one of the conditions in subsection (3) is satisfied.

(3) Those conditions are—

(a) that admission to the premises has been refused,

(b) that admission to the premises is likely to be refused unless a warrant is produced,

(c) that the purpose of entry may be frustrated or seriously prejudiced unless a constable, enforcement officer or authorised person arriving at the premises can secure immediate entry, and

(d) that there is likely to be nobody at the premises capable of granting admission.

(4) A warrant may be granted in reliance on subsection (3)(a) or (b) only if the justice of the peace is satisfied—

(a) that notice has been given to a person occupying the premises, or having responsibility for their management, of intent to apply for a warrant, or

(b) that the purpose of entry may be frustrated or seriously prejudiced by the giving of notice under paragraph (a).

(5) A warrant under subsection (2) shall cease to have effect at the end of the period of 28 days beginning with the day of issue.

(6) In the application of this section or section 319 to Scotland, any reference to a justice of the peace is to be construed as a reference to the sheriff or a justice of the peace.

Commencement

Brought into force by the Gambling Act 2005 (Commencement No 6 and Transitional Provisions) Order 2006, SI 2006/3272, art 2, Sch 2 as from 30 April 2007; for transitional provisions see art 6, Sch 4 thereto (as amended by SI 2007/1157, arts 7–12).

Sub-s (1): This Part. Ie Pt 15 (ss 303–326) of this Act.

Sub-s (2): Justice of the peace. See the note to s 306.
Sub-s (2): Constable. See the note to s 64.
Sub-s (2): Enforcement officer. As to enforcement officers, see, generally, s 303.
Sub-s (4): Notice. See further, in connection with a requirement under this Act to give a notice, s 353(4).

Further provisions
See the note to s 306.

Definitions
'authorised person': ss 304, 353(1)
'enforcement officer': s 353(1)
'premises': s 353(1), (2)(g)

Explanatory Notes
790–792 [para **6.2019** below]

6.819 319 Records

(1) A constable, enforcement officer or authorised person exercising a power of entry under or by virtue of this Part may exercise a power under section 317(1)(c) to (e) in relation to records (whether written or electronic) only if the records relate entirely to the matters to which the power of entry relates.

(2) A justice of the peace may on the application of a constable, enforcement officer or authorised person issue a warrant disapplying subsection (1) to a specified extent if the justice of the peace is satisfied that the disapplication is necessary.

(3) A warrant may be granted under subsection (2) only if the justice of the peace is satisfied—

(a) that notice has been given to a person in control of the records of intent to apply for a warrant, or

(b) that the purpose of exercising the power of entry may be frustrated or seriously prejudiced by the giving of notice under paragraph (a).

(4) A warrant under subsection (2) shall cease to have effect at the end of the period of 28 days beginning with the day of issue.

Commencement
Brought into force by the Gambling Act 2005 (Commencement No 6 and Transitional Provisions) Order 2006, SI 2006/3272, art 2, Sch 2 as from 30 April 2007; for transitional provisions see art 6, Sch 4 thereto (as amended by SI 2007/1157, arts 7–12).
Sub-s (1): Constable. See the note to s 64.
Sub-s (1): Enforcement officer. As to enforcement officers, see, generally, s 303.
Sub-s (1): This Part. Ie Pt 15 (ss 303–326) of this Act.
Sub-s (1): Written. See the note 'Writing' to s 39.
Sub-s (2): Justice of the peace. See the note to s 306.
Sub-s (3): Notice. See further, in connection with a requirement under this Act to give a notice, s 353(4).

Further provisions
See the note to s 306.

Definitions
'authorised person': ss 304, 353(1)
'enforcement officer': s 353(1)

Explanatory Notes
793 [para **6.2019** below]

6.820 320 Timing

A power under or by virtue of this Part may be exercised only at a reasonable time.

Commencement

Brought into force by the Gambling Act 2005 (Commencement No 6 and Transitional Provisions) Order 2006, SI 2006/3272, art 2, Sch 2 as from 30 April 2007; for transitional provisions see art 6, Sch 4 thereto (as amended by SI 2007/1157, arts 7–12).

This Part

Ie Pt 15 (ss 303–326) of this Act.

Further provisions

See the note to s 306.

Explanatory Notes

794 [para **6.2019** below]

6.821 321 Evidence of authorisation

An enforcement officer or authorised person seeking to exercise a power under or by virtue of this Part must produce evidence of his identity and authority to a person (if there is one) who appears to the enforcement officer or authorised person to be occupying the relevant premises or to have responsibility for their management.

Commencement

Brought into force by the Gambling Act 2005 (Commencement No 6 and Transitional Provisions) Order 2006, SI 2006/3272, art 2, Sch 2 as from 30 April 2007; for transitional provisions see art 6, Sch 4 thereto (as amended by SI 2007/1157, arts 7–12).

Enforcement officer.

As to enforcement officers, see, generally, s 303.

This Part

Ie Pt 15 (ss 303–326) of this Act.

Further provisions

See the note to s 306.

Definitions

'authorised person': ss 304, 353(1)
'enforcement officer': s 353(1)
'premises': s 353(1), (2)(g)

Explanatory Notes

795 [para **6.2019** below]

6.822 322 Information

(1) The Secretary of State shall make regulations requiring a person who exercises a power under or by virtue of this Part to provide information about the power and its exercise.

(2) Regulations under subsection (1) shall, in particular, make provision about—

- (a) the information to be provided (which may include ancillary information about a provision of this Act or another enactment or about a rule of law);
- (b) the form and manner in which the information is to be provided;
- (c) the person to whom, or the place at which, the information is to be provided (which may, in particular, include provision for the supply of a copy if requested by a person within a specified class);
- (d) timing.

(3) A constable, enforcement officer or authorised person exercising a power under or by virtue of this Part shall comply with any relevant provision of regulations under this section.

Commencement

Brought into force by the Gambling Act 2005 (Commencement No 6 and Transitional Provisions) Order 2006, SI 2006/3272, art 2, Sch 2 as from 30 April 2007; for transitional provisions see art 6, Sch 4 thereto (as amended by SI 2007/1157, arts 7–12).

Sub-s (1): Secretary of State. See the note to s 4.

Sub-s (1): This Part. Ie Pt 15 (ss 303–326) of this Act.

Sub-s (3): Constable. See the note to s 64.

Sub-s (3): Enforcement officer. As to enforcement officers, see, generally, s 303.

Further provisions

See the note to s 306.

Subordinate Legislation

Gambling Act 2005 (Inspection) (Provision of Information) Regulations 2007, SI 2007/319 (made under sub-ss (1), (2)).

As to regulations under this Act generally, see s 355.

Definitions

'authorised person': ss 304, 353(1)
'enforcement officer': s 353(1)

Explanatory Notes

796 [para **6.2019** below]

6.823 323 Use of force

(1) A constable may use reasonable force for the purpose of entering premises in pursuance of a power under or by virtue of this Part.

(2) An enforcement officer may use reasonable force for the purpose of entering premises in pursuance of a power under or by virtue of section 306 or 307.

(3) An authorised person may use reasonable force for the purpose of entering premises in pursuance of a power under section 307.

Commencement

Brought into force by the Gambling Act 2005 (Commencement No 6 and Transitional Provisions) Order 2006, SI 2006/3272, art 2, Sch 2 as from 30 April 2007; for transitional provisions see art 6, Sch 4 thereto (as amended by SI 2007/1157, arts 7–12).

Sub-s (1): Constable. See the note to s 64.

Sub-s (1): This Part. Ie Pt 15 (ss 303–326) of this Act.

Sub-s (2): Enforcement officer. As to enforcement officers, see, generally, s 303.

Further provisions

See the note to s 306.

Definitions

'authorised person': ss 304, 353(1)
'enforcement officer': s 353(1)
'premises': s 353(1), (2)(g)

Explanatory Notes

797 [para **6.2019** below]

6.824 324 Person accompanying inspector, &c

A constable, enforcement officer or authorised person exercising a power under or by virtue of this Part to enter premises may take one or more persons with him.

Commencement

Brought into force by the Gambling Act 2005 (Commencement No 6 and Transitional Provisions) Order 2006, SI 2006/3272, art 2, Sch 2 as from 30 April 2007; for transitional provisions see art 6, Sch 4 thereto (as amended by SI 2007/1157, arts 7–12).

Constable. See the note to s 64.

Enforcement officer. As to enforcement officers, see, generally, s 303.

This Part

Ie Pt 15 (ss 303–326) of this Act.

Further provisions

See the note to s 306.

Definitions

'authorised person': ss 304, 353(1)
'enforcement officer': s 353(1)
'premises': s 353(1), (2)(g)

Explanatory Notes

798 [para **6.2019** below]

6.825 325 Securing premises after entry

A person who enters premises in reliance on a power under or by virtue of this Part shall take reasonable steps to ensure that when he leaves the premises they are as secure as they were before he entered.

Commencement

Brought into force by the Gambling Act 2005 (Commencement No 6 and Transitional Provisions) Order 2006, SI 2006/3272, art 2, Sch 2 as from 30 April 2007; for transitional provisions see art 6, Sch 4 thereto (as amended by SI 2007/1157, arts 7–12).

This Part

Ie Pt 15 (ss 303–326) of this Act.

Further provisions

See the note to s 306.

Definitions

'premises': s 353(1), (2)(g)

Explanatory Notes

799 [para **6.2019** below]

6.826 326 Obstruction

(1) A person commits an offence if without reasonable excuse he obstructs, or fails to cooperate with, a constable, enforcement officer or authorised person who is exercising or seeking to exercise a power under or by virtue of this Part.

(2) A person guilty of an offence under this section shall be liable on summary conviction to a fine not exceeding level 3 on the standard scale.

Commencement

Brought into force by the Gambling Act 2005 (Commencement No 6 and Transitional Provisions) Order 2006, SI 2006/3272, art 2, Sch 2 as from 30 April 2007; for transitional provisions see art 6, Sch 4 thereto (as amended by SI 2007/1157, arts 7–12).

Sub-s (1): Person. See the note 'Persons' to s 23.

Sub-s (1): Offence. For the power of the Gambling Commission and other specified persons to undertake activities for the purpose of assessing whether an offence is being committed under or by virtue of this Act, see ss 27, 305; for the power of that Commission to investigate and prosecute offences, see s 28; as to offences committed by a body, see s 341; and for the time limit on prosecutions, see s 347. See also s 306 for powers of entry as respects a suspected offence, and s 345 as respects forfeiture of an article relating to an offence.

For the power of a licensing authority to institute criminal proceedings in respect of an offence under this section, see s 346.

Sub-s (1): Constable. See the note to s 64.

Sub-s (1): Enforcement officer. As to enforcement officers, see, generally, s 303.
Sub-s (1): This Part. Ie Pt 15 (ss 303–326) of this Act.
Sub-s (2): Summary conviction; standard scale. See the notes to s 33.

Further provisions
See the note to s 306.

Definitions
'authorised person': ss 304, 353(1)
'enforcement officer': s 353(1)

Explanatory Notes
800 [para **6.2019** below]

PART 16
ADVERTISING

6.827 327 Meaning of 'advertising'

(1) For the purposes of this Act a person advertises gambling if—

(a) he does anything to encourage one or more persons to take advantage (whether directly or through an agent) of facilities for gambling,

(b) with a view to increasing the use of facilities for gambling, he brings them or information about them to the attention of one or more persons, or

(c) he participates in or facilitates an activity knowing or believing that it is designed to—

(i) encourage one or more persons to take advantage (whether directly or through an agent) of facilities for gambling, or

(ii) increase the use of facilities for gambling by bringing them or information about them to the attention of one or more persons.

(2) For the purposes of subsection (1) a person shall be treated as bringing facilities for gambling to the attention of one or more persons with a view to increasing the use of the facilities if—

(a) he enters into arrangements (whether by way of sponsorship, brand-sharing or otherwise) under which a name is displayed in connection with an event or product, and

(b) either—

(i) the provision of facilities for gambling is the sole or main activity undertaken under that name, or

(ii) the manner or context in which the name is displayed is designed to draw attention to the fact that facilities for gambling are provided under that name.

Note
In September 2010 the Gambling Commission published a third edition of a Guide to Advertising Codes relevant to Gambling (see para **6.2086** below and see also paras **6.2087** and **6.2093** below).

Commencement
Brought into force by the Gambling Act 2005 (Commencement No 6 and Transitional Provisions) Order 2006, SI 2006/3272, art 2 as from 1 September 2007; for transitional provisions see art 6, Sch 4 thereto (as amended by SI 2007/1157, arts 7–12).
Sub-s (1): Person. See the note 'Persons' to s 23.

Definitions
'gambling': ss 3, 353(1)
'providing facilities for gambling': ss 5, 353(2)(i)

Explanatory Notes

802 [para **6.2020** below]

6.828 328 Regulations

(1) The Secretary of State may make regulations controlling the advertising of gambling.

(2) The regulations may, in particular, make provision about—

(a) the form of advertisements;

(b) the content of advertisements;

(c) timing;

(d) location.

(3) Regulations by virtue of subsection (2)(b) may, in particular, require specified words to be included in advertisements.

(4) In making regulations under this section the Secretary of State shall, in particular, have regard to the need to protect children and other vulnerable persons from being harmed or exploited by gambling.

(5) A person commits an offence if he contravenes a requirement of regulations under this section.

(6) Regulations under this section may provide defences (whether similar to those provided by section 330 or otherwise).

(7) A person guilty of an offence under subsection (5) shall be liable on summary conviction to—

(a) imprisonment for a term not exceeding 51 weeks,

(b) a fine not exceeding level 5 on the standard scale, or

(c) both.

(8) Where a person commits an offence under this section by causing an advertisement to be displayed or made accessible, he shall be treated as committing the offence on each day during any part of which the advertisement is displayed or made accessible.

(9) Regulations under this section may, in particular, make provision generally or by reference to—

(a) specified classes of gambling,

(b) specified classes of advertisement, or

(c) activity undertaken in or in connection with specified places.

(10) In the application of subsection (7) to Scotland the reference to 51 weeks shall have effect as a reference to six months.

Commencement

Brought into force by the Gambling Act 2005 (Commencement No 6 and Transitional Provisions) Order 2006, SI 2006/3272, art 2 as from 1 September 2007; for transitional provisions see art 6, Sch 4 thereto (as amended by SI 2007/1157, arts 7–12).

Sub-s (1): Secretary of State. See the note to s 4.

Sub-s (1): May make regulations. See further ss 329, 332(1), 333.

Sub-s (5): Person. See the note 'Persons' to s 23.

Sub-s (5): Offence. For the power of the Gambling Commission and other specified persons to undertake activities for the purpose of assessing whether an offence is being committed under or by virtue of this Act, see ss 27, 305; for the power of that Commission to investigate and prosecute offences, see s 28; as to offences committed by a body, see s 341; and for the time limit on prosecutions, see s 347. See also s 306 for powers of entry as respects a suspected offence, and s 345 as respects forfeiture of an article relating to an offence.

Sub-s (7): Summary conviction; standard scale. See the notes to s 33.

Regulations under this section

At the time of going to press no regulations had been made under this section.

As to regulations under this Act generally, see s 355.

Definitions

'advertising gambling': ss 327, 353(2)(b)
'child': ss 45(1), 353(1)
'gambling': ss 3, 353(1)

Explanatory Notes

803, 804 [para **6.2020** below]

6.829 329 Broadcasting

(1) Regulations under section 328 may not make provision about advertising by way of television or radio services to which section 319 of the Communications Act 2003 (c 21) applies.

(2) The Office of Communications shall under that section set, review and revise standards in respect of advertisements for gambling.

(3) In complying with subsection (2) the Office of Communications—

(a) shall consult the Gambling Commission, and
(b) shall ensure that the standards reflect the provisions of regulations under section 328.

(4) Regulations under section 328 may not make provision about advertising by way of a service which—

(a) is provided by the British Broadcasting Corporation, and
(b) would be licensable under Part 1 or 3 of the Broadcasting Act 1990 (c 42) or under Part 1 or 2 of the Broadcasting Act 1996 (c 55) were it provided by a person subject to licensing under that Part.

Commencement

Brought into force by the Gambling Act 2005 (Commencement No 6 and Transitional Provisions) Order 2006, SI 2006/3272, art 2 as from 1 September 2007; for transitional provisions see art 6, Sch 4 thereto (as amended by SI 2007/1157, arts 7–12).

Sub-s (3): Gambling Commission. As to the establishment, etc of the Gambling Commission, see s 20, Sch 4, and the note 'Gambling Commission' to that section.

Definitions

'advertising gambling': ss 327, 353(2)(b)
'gambling': ss 3, 353(1)

Explanatory Notes

805–807 [para **6.2020** below]

6.830 330 Unlawful gambling

(1) A person commits an offence if he advertises unlawful gambling.

(2) For the purposes of this section advertised gambling is unlawful if—

(a) in order for the gambling to take place as advertised without the commission of an offence under this Act it would or might be necessary to rely on a licence, notice, permit or registration under this Act or an exception to an offence under this Act, and
(b) at the time of advertising—
  (i) arrangements for a licence, notice, permit or registration, sufficient to prevent the commission of an offence under this Act if the gambling takes place as advertised, have not been completed, and
  (ii) the arrangements for the gambling as advertised are not such as to ensure that an exception to the offence will apply.

(3) Subsection (1) does not apply to anything done by way of promoting a lottery.

(4) It is a defence for a person charged with an offence under subsection (1) by reference to action of a kind described in section 327(1)(a) or (b) to show that he reasonably believed that the advertised gambling was lawful.

(5) Where a person acts in a way described in section 327(1)(c) he commits the offence under subsection (1) above only if he knows or should know that the advertised gambling is unlawful.

(6) A person does not commit an offence under subsection (1) by reason only of delivering, transmitting or broadcasting a communication or making data available if—

(a) he acts in the course of a business of delivering, transmitting or broadcasting communications (in whatever form or by whatever means) or making data available, and

(b) the nature of the business is such that persons undertaking it have no control over the nature or content of the communications or data.

(7) A person guilty of an offence under this section shall be liable on summary conviction to—

(a) imprisonment for a term not exceeding 51 weeks,

(b) a fine not exceeding level 5 on the standard scale, or

(c) both.

(8) Where a person commits an offence under this section by causing an advertisement to be displayed or made accessible, he shall be treated as committing the offence on each day during any part of which the advertisement is displayed or made accessible.

(9) In the application of subsection (7) to Scotland the reference to 51 weeks shall have effect as a reference to six months.

Note

See the Gambling Commission Advice Note, September 2009, on the sponsorship of British sporting clubs by foreign gambling operators at para **6.2093** below.

Commencement

Brought into force by the Gambling Act 2005 (Commencement No 6 and Transitional Provisions) Order 2006, SI 2006/3272, art 2 as from 1 September 2007; for transitional provisions see art 6, Sch 4 thereto (as amended by SI 2007/1157, arts 7–12).

Sub-s (1): Person. See the note 'Persons' to s 23.

Sub-s (1): Offence. For the power of the Gambling Commission and other specified persons to undertake activities for the purpose of assessing whether an offence is being committed under or by virtue of this Act, see ss 27, 305; for the power of that Commission to investigate and prosecute offences, see s 28; as to offences committed by a body, see s 341; and for the time limit on prosecutions, see s 347. See also s 306 for powers of entry as respects a suspected offence, and s 345 as respects forfeiture of an article relating to an offence.

For the territorial application of sub-s (1) above, see ss 332, 333.

Sub-s (7): Summary conviction; standard scale. See the notes to s 33.

Definitions

'advertising gambling': ss 327, 353(2)(b)
'gambling': ss 3, 353(1)
'lottery': ss 14, 353(1)
'promoting a lottery': ss 252, 353(2)(h)

Explanatory Notes

808–812 [para **6.2020** below]

6.831 331 Foreign gambling

(1) A person commits an offence if he advertises foreign gambling other than a lottery.

(2) In this section 'foreign gambling' means—

(a) non-remote gambling which is to take place in a non-EEA State, and

(b) remote gambling none of the arrangements for which are subject to the law about gambling of an EEA State (whether by being regulated, exempted, prohibited or otherwise).

(3) Subsection (2) shall apply to Gibraltar as it applies to EEA States.

(4) The Secretary of State may by regulations provide that a specified country or place is to be treated for the purposes of subsection (2) as if it were an EEA State.

(5) A person guilty of an offence under subsection (1) shall be liable on summary conviction to—

(a) imprisonment for a term not exceeding 51 weeks,

(b) a fine not exceeding level 5 on the standard scale, or

(c) both.

(6) In the application of subsection (5) to Scotland or Northern Ireland the reference to 51 weeks shall have effect as a reference to six months.

Commencement

Brought into force by the Gambling Act 2005 (Commencement No 6 and Transitional Provisions) Order 2006, SI 2006/3272, art 2 as from 1 September 2007; for transitional provisions see art 6, Sch 4 thereto (as amended by SI 2007/1157, arts 7–12).

Sub-s (1): Person. See the note 'Persons' to s 23.

Sub-s (1): Offence. For the power of the Gambling Commission and other specified persons to undertake activities for the purpose of assessing whether an offence is being committed under or by virtue of this Act, see ss 27, 305; for the power of that Commission to investigate and prosecute offences, see s 28; as to offences committed by a body, see s 341; and for the time limit on prosecutions, see s 347. See also s 306 for powers of entry as respects a suspected offence, and s 345 as respects forfeiture of an article relating to an offence.

For the territorial application of sub-s (1) above, see ss 332, 333.

Sub-s (4): Secretary of State. See the note to s 4.

Sub-s (5): Summary conviction; standard scale. See the notes to s 33.

Subordinate Legislation:

SI 2007/2329

As to regulations under this Act generally, see s 355.

Definitions

'advertising gambling': ss 327, 353(2)(b)
'EEA State': s 353(1)
'gambling': ss 3, 353(1)
'lottery': ss 14, 353(1)
'remote gambling': ss 4, 353(1)

Explanatory Notes

813–816 [para **6.2020** below]

6.832 332 Territorial application: non-remote advertising

(1) Regulations under section 328 shall apply to anything in the way of advertising which is done—

(a) wholly or partly in Great Britain, and

(b) otherwise than by way of remote communication.

(2) The prohibition in section 330(1) applies to anything in the way of advertising which is done—

(a) wholly or partly in Great Britain, and

(b) otherwise than by way of remote communication.

(3) The prohibition in section 331(1) applies to anything in the way of advertising which is done—

(a) wholly or partly in the United Kingdom, and

(b) otherwise than by way of remote communication.

(4) For the purposes of this section the following are immaterial—

(a) the nature of gambling to which advertising relates (whether remote or non-remote), and

(b) the location of the gambling to which advertising relates.

Commencement

Brought into force by the Gambling Act 2005 (Commencement No 6 and Transitional Provisions) Order 2006, SI 2006/3272, art 2 as from 1 September 2007; for transitional provisions see art 6, Sch 4 thereto (as amended by SI 2007/1157, arts 7–12).

Sub-s (1): Great Britain. See the note to s 12.

Sub-s (3): United Kingdom. See the note to s 36.

Definitions

'advertising gambling': ss 327, 353(2)(b)
'gambling': ss 3, 353(1)
'remote communication': ss 4(2), (3), 353(1)

Explanatory Notes

817, 818 [para **6.2020** below]

6.833 333 Territorial application: remote advertising

(1) Regulations under section 328 shall have effect in relation to advertising by way of remote communication only if—

(a) the advertising satisfies the test in subsection (4),
(b) the advertising satisfies the additional test in subsection (5) or (6), if relevant, and
(c) the gambling to which the advertising relates satisfies the test in subsection (9).

(2) The prohibition in section 330(1) applies to advertising by way of remote communication only if—

(a) the advertising satisfies the test in subsection (4),
(b) the advertising satisfies the additional test in subsection (5) or (6), if relevant, and
(c) the gambling to which the advertising relates satisfies the test in subsection (9).

(3) The prohibition in section 331(1) applies to advertising by way of remote communication only if the advertising satisfies the test in subsection (4); for which purpose a reference to Great Britain shall be taken as a reference to the United Kingdom.

(4) The test referred to in subsections (1)(a), (2)(a) and (3) is that the advertising involves—

(a) providing information, by whatever means (and whether or not using remote communication), intended to come to the attention of one or more persons in Great Britain,
(b) sending a communication intended to come to the attention of one or more persons in Great Britain,
(c) making data available with a view to its being accessed by one or more persons in Great Britain, or
(d) making data available in circumstances such that it is likely to be accessed by one or more persons in Great Britain.

(5) In the case of a broadcast by television, the additional test is that the broadcaster—

[(a) is under the jurisdiction of the United Kingdom for the purposes of Directive [2010/13/EU of the European Parliament and of the Council on the coordination of certain provisions laid down by law, regulation or administrative action in Member States concerning the provision of audiovisual media services][1], or
(b) is not under the jurisdiction of an EEA State for the purposes of that Directive.

(6) In the case of the dissemination of information by way of an information society service within the meaning of Directive 2000/31/EC on electronic commerce, the additional test is that the service provider—

(a) is established in the United Kingdom for the purposes of that Directive,

(b) is established in a non-EEA State for the purposes of that Directive, or

(c) has been notified that the conditions for derogation specified in Article 3(4) of that Directive are satisfied in relation to the application to the service provider of regulations under section 328 and of section 330.

(7) The reference to notification in subsection (6)(c) is a reference to written notice which—

(a) has been given by the Commission,

(b) has neither expired nor been withdrawn, and

(c) states whether the Commission's opinion as to satisfaction of the conditions for derogation relates—

(i) to the conditions specified in Article 3(4)(a) and (b), or

(ii) by virtue of Article 3(5), only to the conditions specified in Article 3(4)(a).

(8) In a case to which subsection (7)(c)(ii) applies, the Commission shall perform the duties of notification imposed on the United Kingdom by Article 3(5).

(9) The test referred to in subsections (1)(c) and (2)(c) is—

(a) in the case of non-remote gambling, that it is to take place in Great Britain, or

(b) in the case of remote gambling, that at least one piece of remote gambling equipment to be used in providing facilities for the gambling is or will be situated in Great Britain.

Commencement

Brought into force by the Gambling Act 2005 (Commencement No 6 and Transitional Provisions) Order 2006, SI 2006/3272, art 2 as from 1 September 2007; for transitional provisions see art 6, Sch 4 thereto (as amended by SI 2007/1157, arts 7–12).

Sub-s (3): United Kingdom. See the note to s 36.

Sub-s (4): Great Britain. See the note to s 12.

Sub-s (5): Directive 89/552/EEC. OJ L298 10.10.1989, p 23.

Sub-s (6): Directive 2000/31/EC. OJ L178 17.07.2000, p 1.

Sub-s (7): Written. See the note 'Writing' to s 39.

Sub-s (7): The Commission. Ie the Gambling Commission; see s 353(1). As to the establishment, etc of the Gambling Commission, see s 20, Sch 4, and the note 'Gambling Commission' to that section.

Definitions

'advertising gambling': ss 327, 353(2)(b)
'the Commission': s 353(1)
'EEA State': s 353(1)
'gambling': ss 3, 353(1)
'providing facilities for gambling': ss 5, 353(2)(i)
'remote communication': ss 4(2), (3), 353(1)
'remote gambling equipment': ss 36(4), (5), 353(1)

Explanatory Notes

819–826 [para **6.2020** below]

---

1 Sub-s (5): in para (a) words from "2010/13/EU of the" to "audiovisual media services" in square brackets substituted by SI 2010/1883, reg 6.

PART 17
LEGALITY AND ENFORCEABILITY OF GAMBLING CONTRACTS

6.834 334 Repeal of provisions preventing enforcement

(1) The following shall cease to have effect—

(a) section 1 of the Gaming Act 1710 (c 19) (voiding of security for winnings or for repayment of gaming loan, &c),

(b) remaining provisions of the Gaming Act 1835 (c 41) (security deemed given for illegal consideration),

(c) section 18 of the Gaming Act 1845 (c 109) (voiding of gaming contracts),

(d) section 1 of the Gaming Act 1892 (c 9) (voiding of promise to repay), and

(e) in section 412 of the Financial Services and Markets Act 2000 (c 8) (gaming contracts)—

(i) in subsection (1)(a), the words 'section 18 of the Gaming Act 1845, section 1 of the Gaming Act 1892 or', and

(ii) subsection (1)(b).

(2) The repeals in subsection (1) do not permit enforcement of a right which is created, or which emanates from an agreement made, before this section comes into force.

Commencement

Brought into force by the Gambling Act 2005 (Commencement No 6 and Transitional Provisions) Order 2006, SI 2006/3272, art 2 as from 1 September 2007; for transitional provisions see art 6, Sch 4 thereto (as amended by SI 2007/1157, arts 7–12).

Sub-s (2): Before this section comes into force. At the time of going to press no order had been made under s 358 post bringing this section into force.

Explanatory Notes

828 [para **6.2021** below]

6.835 335 Enforceability of gambling contracts

(1) The fact that a contract relates to gambling shall not prevent its enforcement.

(2) Subsection (1) is without prejudice to any rule of law preventing the enforcement of a contract on the grounds of unlawfulness (other than a rule relating specifically to gambling).

Commencement

Brought into force by the Gambling Act 2005 (Commencement No 6 and Transitional Provisions) Order 2006, SI 2006/3272, art 2 as from 1 September 2007; for transitional provisions see art 6, Sch 4 thereto (as amended by SI 2007/1157, arts 7–12).

Sub-s (1): The fact that, etc. Participating in a lottery which forms part of the National Lottery is gambling for the purposes of this section; see s 15(2).

Definitions

'gambling': ss 3, 353(1)

Explanatory Notes

829 [para **6.2021** below]

6.836 336 Power of Gambling Commission to void bet

(1) The Commission may make an order under this subsection in relation to a bet accepted by or through the holder of—

(a) a general betting operating licence,

(b) a pool betting operating licence, or

(c) a betting intermediary operating licence.

(2) Where the Commission makes an order under subsection (1) in relation to a bet—

6: Gambling Act 2005: Statutes

(a) any contract or other arrangement in relation to the bet is void, and
(b) any money paid in relation to the bet (whether by way of stake, winnings, commission or otherwise) shall be repaid to the person who paid it, and repayment may be enforced as a debt due to that person.

(3) The Commission may make an order under subsection (1) in relation to a bet only if satisfied that the bet was substantially unfair.

(4) In considering whether a bet was unfair the Commission shall, in particular, take account of any of the following that applies—

(a) the fact that either party to the bet supplied insufficient, false or misleading information in connection with it,
(b) the fact that either party to the bet believed or ought to have believed that a race, competition or other event or process to which the bet related was or would be conducted in contravention of industry rules,
(c) the fact that either party to the bet believed or ought to have believed that an offence under section 42 had been or was likely to be committed in respect of anything to which the bet related, and
(d) the fact that either party to the bet was convicted of an offence under section 42 in relation to the bet.

(5) An order under subsection (1) may be made in relation to a bet only during the period of six months beginning with the day on which the result of the bet is determined.

(6) But subsection (5) shall not apply to an order made taking account of the fact that a party to the bet was convicted of an offence under section 42 in relation to it.

Commencement

Brought into force by the Gambling Act 2005 (Commencement No 6 and Transitional Provisions) Order 2006, SI 2006/3272, art 2 as from 1 September 2007; for transitional provisions see art 6, Sch 4 thereto (as amended by SI 2007/1157, arts 7–12).

Sub-s (1): The Commission. Ie the Gambling Commission; see s 353(1). As to the establishment, etc of the Gambling Commission, see s 20, Sch 4, and the note 'Gambling Commission' to that section.

Sub-s (1): May make an order. A condition attached to an operating licence by virtue of s 88 may require a person to provide any information that he suspects may lead to the making of an order under this section; see s 88(2). See further as to orders under this section, s 337 (supplementary), and s 338 (interim moratorium).

Sub-s (1): Operating licence. As to the nature, etc of operating licences, see s 65 and the note 'Operating licences' thereto.

Subordinate Legislation:

SI 2007/2102, art 5.

Definitions

'the Commission': s 353(1)
'industry rules': s 337(7)
'operating licence': s 353(1)
'stake': s 353(1)
'winnings': s 353(1)

Explanatory Notes

830–834 [para **6.2021** below]

6.837 337 Section 336: supplementary

(1) Where the Commission makes an order under section 336(1) in relation to a bet a party to the bet or to any contract or other arrangement in relation to the bet may appeal to the [First-tier Tribunal][1]; and the following provisions of Part 7 shall have effect (with any necessary modifications) in relation to an appeal under this section as they have effect in relation to an appeal under that Part—

(a) . . . [2]
(b) . . . [2]
(c) section 144,
(d) section 145,
(e) section 146,
(f) . . . [2]
(g) . . . [2]

(2) The Commission may make an order under section 336(1) in relation to the whole, or any part or aspect of, a betting transaction.

(3) An order under section 336(1) may make incidental provision; in particular, an order may make provision about—

(a) the consequences of the order for bets connected with the bet which becomes void under the order;
(b) the consequences of the order for other parts or aspects of a betting transaction one part or aspect of which becomes void under the order.

(4) For the purposes of considering whether to make an order under section 336(1) in respect of a bet the Commission—

(a) may require a person by or through whom the bet is made or accepted to provide information or documents in relation to it, and
(b) may take into account information received from any other person.

(5) A person commits an offence if without reasonable excuse he fails to comply with a requirement under subsection (4).

(6) A person guilty of an offence under subsection (5) shall be liable on summary conviction to a fine not exceeding level 2 on the standard scale.

(7) In section 336(4)(b) 'industry rules' means rules established by an organisation having, by virtue of an agreement, instrument or enactment, responsibility for the conduct of races, competitions or other events or processes.

Commencement

Brought into force by the Gambling Act 2005 (Commencement No 6 and Transitional Provisions) Order 2006, SI 2006/3272, art 2 as from 1 September 2007; for transitional provisions see art 6, Sch 4 thereto (as amended by SI 2007/1157, arts 7–12).

Sub-s (1): The Commission. Ie the Gambling Commission; see s 353(1). As to the establishment, etc of the Gambling Commission, see s 20, Sch 4, and the note 'Gambling Commission' to that section.

Sub-s (4): Person. See the note 'Persons' to s 23.

Sub-s (5): Offence. For the power of the Gambling Commission and other specified persons to undertake activities for the purpose of assessing whether an offence is being committed under or by virtue of this Act, see ss 27, 305; for the power of that Commission to investigate and prosecute offences, see s 28; as to offences committed by a body, see s 341; and for the time limit on prosecutions, see s 347. See also s 306 for powers of entry as respects a suspected offence, and s 345 as respects forfeiture of an article relating to an offence.

Sub-s (6): Summary conviction; standard scale. See the notes to s 33.

Subordinate Legislation

SI 2007/2102.

Definitions

'betting': ss 9–11, 353(1)
'the Commission': s 353(1)

Explanatory Notes

835–837 [para **6.2021** below]

[1] Sub-s (1): words "First-tier Tribunal" in square brackets substituted by SI 2010/22, art 5(1), Sch 2, paras 93, 103(a).

[2] Sub-s (1): paras (a), (b), (f), (g) repealed by SI 2010/22, art 5(1), Sch 2, paras 93, 103(b).

6.838 338 Interim moratorium

(1) Where the Commission has reason to suspect that it may wish to make an order under section 336(1) in relation to a bet, the Commission may make an order under this subsection in relation to the bet.

(2) While an order under subsection (1) has effect in relation to a bet, an obligation to pay money in relation to the bet (whether by way of stake, winnings, commission or otherwise) shall have no effect.

(3) An order under subsection (1) shall have effect for the period of 14 days beginning with the day on which the order is made (subject to extension under subsection (4) and without prejudice to the making of a new order).

(4) The Commission may by order extend the period for which an order under subsection (1) has effect; and—

(a) an order under this subsection may extend that period by the addition of not more than 14 days, and

(b) more than one order may be made under this subsection in relation to a bet.

(5) The Commission may cancel an order under subsection (1) (without prejudice to the making of a new order).

(6) The Commission shall cancel an order under subsection (1) as soon as is reasonably practicable after it ceases to entertain the suspicion mentioned in that subsection.

(7) The Commission shall not be liable to make any payment on account only of the fact that it—

(a) has made an order under subsection (1), and

(b) not made a subsequent order under section 336(1).

(8) But subsection (7) is without prejudice to any power of a court in legal proceedings (whether for tort or otherwise).

Commencement

Brought into force by the Gambling Act 2005 (Commencement No 6 and Transitional Provisions) Order 2006, SI 2006/3272, art 2 as from 1 September 2007; for transitional provisions see art 6, Sch 4 thereto (as amended by SI 2007/1157, arts 7–12).

Sub-s (1): The Commission. Ie the Gambling Commission; see s 353(1). As to the establishment, etc of the Gambling Commission, see s 20, Sch 4, and the note 'Gambling Commission' to that section.

Subordinate Legislation:

SI 2007/2102, art 5.

Definitions

'the Commission': s 353(1)
'stake': s 353(1)
'winnings': s 353(1)

Explanatory Notes

838–842 [para **6.2021** below]

PART 18
MISCELLANEOUS AND GENERAL

Miscellaneous

6.839 339 Prize competitions

Participating in a competition or other arrangement under which a person may win a prize is not gambling for the purposes of this Act unless it is—

(a) gaming within the meaning of section 6,
(b) participating in a lottery within the meaning of section 14, or
(c) betting within the meaning of sections 9 to 11.

Commencement

Brought into force by the Gambling Act 2005 (Commencement No 6 and Transitional Provisions) Order 2006, SI 2006/3272, art 2 as from 1 September 2007; for transitional provisions see art 6, Sch 4 thereto (as amended by SI 2007/1157, arts 7–12).

Definitions

'gambling': ss 3, 353(1)

Explanatory Notes

844 [para **6.2022** below]

6.840 340 Foreign betting

Sections 9 to 9B of the Betting and Gaming Duties Act 1981 (c 63) (prohibitions, for protection of the revenue, in relation to foreign betting) shall cease to have effect.

Commencement

Brought into force by the Gambling Act 2005 (Commencement No 6 and Transitional Provisions) Order 2006, SI 2006/3272, art 2 as from 1 September 2007; for transitional provisions see art 6, Sch 4 thereto (as amended by SI 2007/1157, arts 7–12).

Explanatory Notes

845 [para **6.2022** below]

6.841 341 Offence committed by body

(1) Subsection (2) applies where an offence under this Act is committed by a body of persons corporate or unincorporate (other than a partnership) and it is proved that the offence was committed—

(a) with the consent or connivance of an officer of the body, or
(b) as a result of the negligence of an officer of the body.

(2) The officer, as well as the body, shall be guilty of the offence.

(3) In subsection (1) a reference to an officer of a body includes a reference to—

(a) a director, manager or secretary,
(b) a person purporting to act as a director, manager or secretary, and
(c) if the affairs of the body are arranged by its members, a member.

(4) Where an offence under this Act is committed by a partnership (other than a limited partnership) each partner shall be guilty of the offence.

(5) Where an offence under this Act is committed by a limited partnership, subsections (1) and (2) shall have effect, but as if a reference to an officer of the body were a reference to a partner.

(6) In relation to the prosecution of a body of persons unincorporate for an offence under this Act, the body shall be treated for all procedural purposes as if it were a body corporate.

(7) The Secretary of State may by regulations make provision for the modification of a provision of this section in its application to a body of persons formed under, or in so far as the body is recognised by, law having effect outside the United Kingdom.

Commencement

Brought into force as from 1 January 2007 for certain purposes and as from 1 September 2007 for remaining purposes by the Gambling Act 2005 (Commencement No 6 and Transitional Provisions) Order 2006, SI 2006/3272, art 2, Sch 1; for transitional provisions see art 6, Sch 4 thereto (as amended by SI 2007/1157, arts 7–12).

Sub-s (7): Secretary of State. See the note to s 4.

Sub-s (7): United Kingdom. See the note to s 36.

Regulations under this section

At the time of going to press no regulations had been made under this section.

As to regulations under this Act generally, see s 355.

Definitions

'director': s 353(1)

Explanatory Notes

846, 847 [para **6.2022** below]

6.842 342 False information

(1) A person commits an offence if without reasonable excuse he gives to the Commission or a licensing authority for a purpose connected with a provision of this Act (whether or not in relation to an application under this Act) information which is—

(a) false, or

(b) misleading.

(2) A person guilty of an offence under this section shall be liable on summary conviction to—

(a) imprisonment for a term not exceeding 51 weeks,

(b) a fine not exceeding level 5 on the standard scale, or

(c) both.

(3) In the application of subsection (2) to Scotland the reference to 51 weeks shall have effect as a reference to six months.

(4) Where it appears to the Commission or a licensing authority that a decision under this Act was taken by them in reliance upon false or misleading information, they may do anything that they think expedient for the purpose of cancelling, terminating or varying an effect of the decision (but action under this subsection shall not make unlawful anything done before the action is taken).

Commencement

Brought into force as from 1 January 2007 for certain purposes and as from 30 April 2007 for remaining purposes by the Gambling Act 2005 (Commencement No 6 and Transitional Provisions) Order 2006, SI 2006/3272, art 2, Schs 1 and 2; for transitional provisions see art 6, Sch 4 thereto (as amended by SI 2007/1157, arts 7–12).

Sub-s (1): Person. See the note 'Persons' to s 23.

Sub-s (1): Offence. For the power of the Gambling Commission and other specified persons to undertake activities for the purpose of assessing whether an offence is being committed under or by virtue of this Act, see ss 27, 305; for the power of that Commission to investigate and prosecute offences, see s 28; as to offences committed by a body, see s 341; and for the time limit on prosecutions, see s 347. See also s 306 for powers of entry as respects a suspected offence, and s 345 as respects forfeiture of an article relating to an offence.

For the power of a licensing authority to institute criminal proceedings in respect of an offence under this section, see s 346.

Sub-s (1): The Commission. Ie the Gambling Commission; see s 353(1). As to the establishment, etc of the Gambling Commission, see s 20, Sch 4, and the note 'Gambling Commission' to that section.

Sub-s (1): Licensing authority. For the licensing authorities for the purposes of this Act, see s 2.

Sub-s (2): Summary conviction; standard scale. See the notes to s 33.

Definitions

'the Commission': s 353(1)

'licensing authority': ss 2, 353(1)

Explanatory Notes

848 [para **6.2022** below]

6.843 343 Value of prize

(1) Regulations prescribing a maximum value of prizes for a purpose of this Act may include provision for determining the value of a prize.

(2) Regulations by virtue of subsection (1) may, in particular—

(a) apply (with or without modification) or make provision similar to a provision of section 20 of the Betting and Gaming Duties Act 1981 (c 63) (expenditure on bingo winnings);

(b) confer a discretion on the Secretary of State, on the Gambling Commission or on another person;

(c) provide for an appeal;

(d) confer jurisdiction on a court or tribunal.

(3) The imposition by or by virtue of this Act of a maximum on the value of a prize does not prevent an arrangement between a person who has won one or more prizes and a person who provides facilities for gambling whereby the prize or prizes are exchanged (whether for money or for one or more articles); provided that—

(a) the amount of money or the value of the articles for which the prize or prizes are exchanged does not exceed the maximum amount or value of the prize, or the aggregate maximum amount or value of the prizes, that the person could lawfully have won, and

(b) the nature of the substituted prize or prizes complies with any requirements of or by virtue of this Act as to the nature of the prize or prizes that the person could lawfully have won.

Commencement

Brought into force by the Gambling Act 2005 (Commencement No 6 and Transitional Provisions) Order 2006, SI 2006/3272, art 2, Sch 2 as from 30 April 2007; for transitional provisions see art 6, Sch 4 thereto (as amended by SI 2007/1157, arts 7–12).

Sub-s (2): Secretary of State. See the note to s 4.

Sub-s (2): Gambling Commission. As to the establishment, etc of the Gambling Commission, see s 20, Sch 4, and the note 'Gambling Commission' to that section.

Sub-s (2): Person. See the note 'Persons' to s 23.

Definitions

'prize': ss 6(5), 14(4), 239, 353(1)

'providing facilities for gambling': ss 5, 353(2)(i)

Explanatory Notes

849, 850 [para **6.2022** below]

6.844 344 Participation fees

(1) In this Act 'participation fee' means an amount paid in respect of entitlement to participate in gambling; and for that purpose—

(a) it is immaterial—

(i) how a fee is described,

(ii) whether a fee is payable in money or in money's worth,

(iii) when and how a fee is payable,

(iv) to whom a fee is payable,

(b) a charge for admission to premises where gambling takes place shall be treated as a participation fee,

(c) a membership subscription is not a participation fee (subject to subsections (2) and (3)), and

(d) a stake is not a participation fee.

(2) The Secretary of State may by regulations provide for a membership subscription to be treated as a participation fee in specified circumstances.

(3) For the purposes of section 279, a membership subscription is a participation fee.

(4) The Secretary of State may make regulations providing, in connection with the operation of a provision made by or by virtue of this Act in relation to a participation fee, for the apportionment of an amount which is payable partly in respect of entitlement to participate in gambling and partly in respect of another matter; and that provision may, in particular—

(a) provide for apportionment by a specified person;

(b) provide for apportionment in accordance with a specified formula or principle;

(c) refer to the concept of reasonableness.

Commencement

Brought into force by the Gambling Act 2005 (Commencement No 6 and Transitional Provisions) Order 2006, SI 2006/3272, art 2 as from 1 September 2007; for transitional provisions see art 6, Sch 4 thereto (as amended by SI 2007/1157, arts 7–12).

Sub-s (2): Secretary of State. See the note to s 4.

Regulations under this section

At the time of going to press no regulations had been made under this section.

As to regulations under this Act generally, see s 355.

Definitions

'gambling': ss 3, 353(1)
'premises': s 353(1), (2)(g)
'stake': s 353(1)

Explanatory Notes

851, 852 [para **6.2022** below]

6.845 345 Forfeiture

(1) A court by or before which a person is convicted of an offence under this Act may make an order for the forfeiture of an article that appears to the court to relate to the offence.

(2) A forfeiture order—

(a) may include such provision about the treatment of the article forfeited as the court thinks appropriate, and

(b) subject to any provision made under paragraph (a), shall be treated as requiring any person in possession of the article to surrender it to a constable as soon as is reasonably practicable.

(3) Where—

(a) a court proposes to make a forfeiture order in respect of an article, and

(b) a person notifies the court that he has an interest in the article,

the court may not make the order without first giving the person an opportunity to make representations.

(4) The court which made a forfeiture order may order that the forfeited article be given up to a person who claims to have an interest in it.

(5) A person commits an offence if he fails to—

(a) comply with a forfeiture order, or

(b) co-operate with a step taken for the purpose of giving effect to a forfeiture order.

(6) A person guilty of an offence under subsection (5) shall be liable on summary conviction to—

(a) imprisonment for a term not exceeding 51 weeks,

(b) a fine not exceeding level 5 on the standard scale, or

(c) both.

(7) In the application of subsection (6) to Scotland the reference to 51 weeks shall have effect as a reference to six months.

Commencement

Brought into force as from 1 January 2007 for certain purposes and as from 1 September 2007 for remaining purposes by the Gambling Act 2005 (Commencement No 6 and Transitional Provisions) Order 2006, SI 2006/3272, art 2, Sch 1; for transitional provisions see art 6, Sch 4 thereto (as amended by SI 2007/1157, arts 7–12).

Sub-s (1): Person. See the note 'Persons' to s 23.

Sub-s (2): Constable. See the note to s 64.

Sub-s (3): Notifies. See further, in connection with a requirement under this Act to give a notice, s 353(4).

Sub-s (5): Offence. For the power of the Gambling Commission and other specified persons to undertake activities for the purpose of assessing whether an offence is being committed under or by virtue of this Act, see ss 27, 305; for the power of that Commission to investigate and prosecute offences, see s 28; as to offences committed by a body, see s 341; and for the time limit on prosecutions, see s 347. See also s 306 for powers of entry as respects a suspected offence.

Sub-s (6): Summary conviction; standard scale. See the notes to s 33.

Explanatory Notes

853, 854 [para **6.2022** below]

6.846 346 Prosecution by licensing authority

(1) A licensing authority may institute criminal proceedings in respect of an offence under any of the following provisions of this Act—

(a) section 37,
(b) section 185,
(c) section 186,
(d) section 229,
(e) section 242,
(f) section 258,
(g) section 259,
(h) section 260,
(i) section 261,
(j) section 262,
(k) section 326,
(l) section 342,
(m) paragraph 20 of Schedule 10,
(n) paragraph 10 of Schedule 13, and
(o) paragraph 20 of Schedule 14.

(2) This section is without prejudice to section 222 of the Local Government Act 1972 (c 70) (power of local authorities to prosecute or defend legal proceedings).

(3) This section shall not apply to an authority in Scotland.

Commencement

Subsection (1) (a)–(k), (m)–(o) brought into force by the Gambling Act 2005 (Commencement No 6 and Transitional Provisions) Order 2006, SI 2006/3272, art 2 as from 1 September 2007; for transitional provisions see art 6, Sch 4 thereto (as amended by SI 2007/1157, arts 7–12).

Subsection (1)(l), (2), (3)brought into force by the Gambling Act 2005 (Commencement No 6 and Transitional Provisions) Order 2006, SI 2006/3272, art 2, Sch 2 as from 30 April 2007; for transitional provisions see art 6, Sch 4 thereto (as amended by SI 2007/1157, arts 7–12).

Sub-s (1): Licensing authority. For the licensing authorities for the purposes of this Act, see s 2.

Definitions

'licensing authority': ss 2, 353(1)

Explanatory Notes

855 [para **6.2022** below]

6.847 347 Prosecution: time limit

(1) A magistrates' court may try an information for an offence under this Act provided that the information was laid within the period of twelve months beginning with the date (or last date) on which the offence is alleged to have been committed.

(2) Section 127(1) of the Magistrates' Courts Act 1980 (c 43) shall not apply to an offence under this Act.

Commencement

Brought into force by the Gambling Act 2005 (Commencement No 6 and Transitional Provisions) Order 2006, SI 2006/3272, art 2 as from 1 September 2007; for transitional provisions see art 6, Sch 4 thereto (as amended by SI 2007/1157, arts 7–12).

Sub-s (1): Magistrates' court. See the note to s 207.

Explanatory Notes

856 [para **6.2022** below]

6.848 348 Excluded premises

(1) This Act shall have no effect in relation to anything done on, or in relation to any use of, premises of a kind specified for the purposes of this subsection by order of the Secretary of State.

(2) This Act shall have no effect in relation to anything done on, or in relation to any use of, premises certified for the purposes of this subsection, on grounds relating to national security, by the Secretary of State or the Attorney General.

Commencement

Brought into force by the Gambling Act 2005 (Commencement No 6 and Transitional Provisions) Order 2006, SI 2006/3272, art 2 as from 1 September 2007; for transitional provisions see art 6, Sch 4 thereto (as amended by SI 2007/1157, arts 7–12).

Sub-s (1): Secretary of State. See the note to s 4.

Orders under this section

At the time of going to press no orders had been made under this section.

As to orders under this Act generally, see s 355.

Definitions

'premises': s 353(1), (2)(g)

Explanatory Notes

857 [para **6.2022** below]

6.849 349 Three-year licensing policy

(1) A licensing authority shall before each successive period of three years—

(a) prepare a statement of the principles that they propose to apply in exercising their functions under this Act during that period, and

(b) publish the statement.

(2) A licensing authority shall—

(a) review their statement under this section from time to time,

(b) if they think it necessary in the light of a review, revise the statement, and

(c) publish any revision before giving it effect.

(3) In preparing a statement or revision under this section a licensing authority shall consult—

(a) either—

(i) in England and Wales, the chief officer of police for the authority's area, or

(ii) in Scotland, the chief constable of the police force maintained for the police area comprising that area,

(b) one or more persons who appear to the authority to represent the interests of persons carrying on gambling businesses in the authority's area, and

(c) one or more persons who appear to the authority to represent the interests of persons who are likely to be affected by the exercise of the authority's functions under this Act.

(4) The Secretary of State may make regulations about—

(a) the form of statements under this section;

(b) the procedure to be followed in relation to the preparation, review or revision of statements under this section;

(c) the publication of statements under this section.

(5) In relation to statements prepared under this section by licensing authorities in Scotland, subsection (4) shall have effect as if the reference to the Secretary of State were a reference to the Scottish Ministers.

(6) The Secretary of State shall by order appoint a day as the first day of the first period of three years for the purpose of this section[1].

(7) Where a licensing authority is specified in an order under section 175 they shall ensure that their statement under this section includes the principles that they propose to apply in making determinations under paragraph 5 of Schedule 9.[2]

Commencement

Section brought into force by the Gambling Act 2005 (Commencement No 3) Order 2006, SI 2006/631, art 2 as from 31 March 2006.

Sub-s (1): Licensing authority. For the licensing authorities for the purposes of this Act, see s 2.

Sub-s (1): Publish the statement. In exercising their functions under Pt 8 of this Act a licensing authority are to aim to permit the use of premises for gambling in so far as the authority think fit in accordance with the statement published under this section; see s 153(1)(d).

For restrictions on the delegation of the functions of a licensing authority under this section, see s 154(2)(c).

A resolution under s 166(1) must be published by being included in a statement or revision under this section; see s 166(5).

Sub-s (3): England; Wales

See the note to s 2.

Sub-s (3): Persons. See the note to s 23.

Sub-s (4): Secretary of State. See the note to s 4.

Sub-s (5): Scottish Ministers. See the note to s 25.

Subordinate Legislation

UK: Gambling Act 2005 (Licensing Authority Policy Statement) (England and Wales) Regulations 2006, SI 2006/636 (made under sub-s (4)).

Gambling Act 2005 (Licensing Authority Policy Statement) (First Appointed Day) Order 2006, SI 2006/637 (made under sub-s (6)).

Scotland: Gambling Act 2005 (Licensing Authority Policy Statement) (Scotland) Regulations 2006, SSI 2006/154 (made under sub-ss (4), (5)).

As to regulations and orders under this Act generally, see s 355.

Definitions

'gambling': ss 3, 353(1)
'licensing authority': ss 2, 353(1)
'publication': s 353(2)(j)

Explanatory Notes

858, 859 [para **6.2022** below]

[1] Appointed day (for the purposes of sub-s (6)): 31 January 2007: see 2006/637, art 2.

[2] This section was brought into force on 31 March 2006: see SI 2006/631, art 2(1)(a).

6.850 350 Exchange of information

(1) A person or body listed in Part 1 of Schedule 6 may provide information to any other person or body so listed for use in the exercise of a function under this Act.

(2) A person or body listed in Part 1 of Schedule 6 may provide information obtained in the course of the exercise of a function under this Act to Her Majesty's [Commissioners for Her Majesty's Revenue and Customs] for use in the exercise of any function.

(3) Provision of information in reliance on this section may be subject to conditions (whether as to use, storage, disposal or otherwise).

Commencement

Brought into force by the Gambling Act 2005 (Commencement No 6 and Transitional Provisions) Order 2006, SI 2006/3272, art 2, Sch 1 as from 1 January 2007; for transitional provisions see art 6, Sch 4 thereto (as amended by SI 2007/1157, arts 7–12).

Amendments. Sub-s (2): words in square brackets substituted by virtue of the Commissioners for Revenue and Customs Act 2005, s 50(1), (7).

Sub-s (2): Commissioners for Her Majesty's Revenue and Customs. See the note to s 23.

Explanatory Notes

860 [para **6.2022** below]

6.851 351 Power to amend Schedule 6

(1) The Secretary of State may by order amend Schedule 6 so as to—

(a) add an entry to a list (in Part 1, 2 or 3);

(b) remove an entry from a list (in Part 1, 2 or 3);

(c) move an entry from one list to another;

(d) add, remove or vary a Note.

(2) In particular, a Note relating to an entry for a person or body situated outside the United Kingdom may provide that the entry has effect only in relation to the law of a Part of the United Kingdom.

(3) An entry added to a list in Schedule 6 may specify a person or body or a class or description of persons or bodies.

(4) The power to add, remove or vary a Note may be exercised generally or in relation to a specified person or body or class or description of persons or bodies.

Commencement

Brought into force by the Gambling Act 2005 (Commencement No 6 and Transitional Provisions) Order 2006, SI 2006/3272, art 2, Sch 1 as from 1 January 2007; for transitional provisions see art 6, Sch 4 thereto (as amended by SI 2007/1157, arts 7–12).

Sub-s (1): Secretary of State. See the note to s 4.

Sub-s (2): United Kingdom. See the note to s 36.

Subordinate Legislation:

SI 2007/210.

As to orders under this Act generally, see s 355.

Explanatory Notes

861 [para **6.2022** below]

6.852 352 Data protection

Nothing in this Act authorises a disclosure which contravenes the Data Protection Act 1998 (c 29).

Commencement

Brought into force by the Gambling Act 2005 (Commencement No 2 and Transitional Provisions) Order 2005, SI 2005/2455, art 2 and Schedule, as from 1 October 2005.

Saving. See s 30(8).

Explanatory Notes

862 [para **6.2022** below]

6.852A [352A Wrongful disclosure

(1) Where the Commissioners for Her Majesty's Revenue and Customs provide information to a person under this Act, section 19 of the Commissioners for Revenue and Customs Act 2005 (c 11) (wrongful disclosure) shall apply to the disclosure of the information by the person as it applies to the disclosure of information in contravention of a provision of that Act.

(2) But section 19 shall not apply to disclosure—

(a) in accordance with this Act,

(b) in accordance with another enactment, or

(c) in circumstances specified in section 18(2)(c), (d), (e) or (h) of that Act.

(3) In subsection (1)—

(a) information provided to a person shall be treated as being provided both to him and to any person on whose behalf he acts or by whom he is employed, and

(b) the reference to disclosure by the person to whom information was provided includes a reference to disclosure by any person acting on behalf of, or employed by, the person to whom the information was provided (or a person to whom it is treated as being provided by virtue of paragraph (a)).

(4) In the application of section 18(2)(c) and (d) of that Act by virtue of subsection (2)(c) above a reference to functions of the Revenue and Customs shall be taken as a reference to functions of the person making the disclosure.

(5) In the application of section 19 of that Act by virtue of subsection (1) above "revenue and customs information" means information provided by the Commissioners (but subject to the express exclusion in section 19(2)).

(6) Section 19 of that Act shall, in so far as it applies by virtue of this section, be treated for the purposes of section 28 of this Act as an offence under this Act.]

Commencement

Inserted by the Finance Act 2006, s 177(1) as from 19 July 2006.

General

6.853 353 Interpretation

(1) In this Act, except where the context otherwise requires—

'adult' means an individual who is not a child or young person,

'adult gaming centre' has the meaning given by section 237,

'alcohol licence' has the meaning given by section 277,

'authorised local authority officer' has the meaning given by section 304,

'authorised person' has the meaning given by that section,
'betting' has the meaning given by sections 9 to 11, 37 and 150,
'betting intermediary' has the meaning given by section 13,
'bingo' means any version of that game, irrespective of by what name it is described,
'casino' has the meaning given by section 7,
'casino game' has the meaning given by that section,
'Category A gaming machine' (or B, C or D) means a gaming machine falling within Category A (or B, C or D) as prescribed under section 236,
'chief constables of police forces' has the same meaning in relation to England and Wales as in the Police Act 1996 (c 16),
'child' has the meaning given by section 45,
'club gaming permit' has the meaning given by section 271,
'club machine permit' has the meaning given by section 273,
'commercial club' has the meaning given by section 267,
'the Commission' means the Gambling Commission,
['director'—

(a) has the meaning given by section 250 of the Companies Act 2006, and
(b) includes a shadow director within the meaning of section 251 of that Act,][1]

'dog track' means premises which are designed, used or adapted for use for dog-racing,
'draw', in relation to a lottery, has the meaning given by section 255,
'EEA State' means a State which is a contracting party to the Agreement on the European Economic Area signed at Oporto on 2nd May 1992 (as it has effect from time to time),
'enactment' includes an enactment comprised in, or in an instrument made under, an Act of the Scottish Parliament,
'enforcement officer' means a person designated or appointed as an enforcement officer under section 303,
'equal chance gaming' has the meaning given by section 8,
'exempt lottery' has the meaning given by section 258,
'external lottery manager' has the meaning given by section 257,
'fair' has the meaning given by section 286,
'family entertainment centre' has the meaning given by section 238,
'family entertainment centre gaming machine permit' has the meaning given by section 247,
'football pools' means an arrangement whereby—

(a) people compete for prizes by forecasting the results of association football games, and
(b) each entry to the competition must forecast the results of at least four games,

'gambling' has the meaning given by section 3,
'gambling software' has the meaning given by section 41,
'game of chance' has the meaning given by section 6,
'gaming' has the meaning given by that section,
'gaming machine' has the meaning given by section 235,
'horse-race course' means premises which are designed, used or adapted for use for horse-racing,
'horse-race pool betting' has the meaning given by section 12,
'large casino' has the meaning given by regulations under section 7(5),
'licensed family entertainment centre' has the meaning given by section 238,

'licensed premises gaming machine permit' has the meaning given by section 283,
'the licensing objectives' has the meaning given by section 1,
'licensing authority' has the meaning given by section 2,
'lottery' has the meaning given by section 14 (and section 256),
'lottery manager's operating licence' has the meaning given by section 98,
'lottery ticket' has the meaning given by section 253,
'machine' has the meaning given by section 235(3)(a),
'members' club' has the meaning given by section 266,
'miners' welfare institute' has the meaning given by section 268,
'the National Lottery' has the meaning given by section 1 of the National Lottery etc Act 1993 (c 39)),
'non-commercial betting' has the meaning given by section 302,
'non-commercial gaming' has the meaning given by section 297,
'non-commercial society' has the meaning given by section 19,
'occasional use notice' means a notice given under section 39,
'operating licence' means a licence issued under Part 5,
'on-premises alcohol licence' has the meaning given by section 277,
'participant', in relation to a game of chance, includes a person who discharges an administrative or other function in relation to the game,
'participation fee' has the meaning given by section 344,
'passenger vessel' means a vessel which is carrying or expected to carry at least one passenger,
'personal licence' means a licence issued under Part 6,
'pool betting' has the meaning given by section 12,
'premises' includes any place and, in particular—

(a) a vessel, and
(b) a vehicle,

'premises licence' means a licence issued under Part 8,
'private betting' has the meaning given by section 295 and Part 2 of Schedule 15,
'private gaming' has the meaning given by section 295 and Part 1 of Schedule 15,
'private gain' is to be construed in accordance with section 19(3),
'prize' in relation to gaming (except in the context of a gaming machine) has the meaning given by section 6,
'prize' in relation to a gaming machine has the meaning given by section 239,
'prize' in relation to a lottery has the meaning given by section 14,
'prize gaming' has the meaning given by section 288,
'prize gaming permit' has the meaning given by section 289,
'proceeds', in relation to a lottery, has the meaning given by section 254,
'profits', in relation to a lottery, has the meaning given by that section,
'profits', in relation to non-commercial prize gaming, has the meaning given by section 299,
'racecourse' means premises on any part of which a race takes place or is intended to take place,
'real', in relation to a game, event or process means non-virtual,
'relevant offence' has the meaning given by section 126 and Schedule 7,
'remote communication' has the meaning given by section 4,
'remote gambling' has the meaning given by that section,
'remote gambling equipment' has the meaning given by section 36,
'remote operating licence' has the meaning given by section 67,
'rollover', in relation to a lottery, has the meaning given by section 256,
'small casino' has the meaning given by regulations under section 7(5),
'society' includes a branch or section of a society,

'stake' means an amount paid or risked in connection with gambling and which either—

(a) is used in calculating the amount of the winnings or the value of the prize that the person making the stake receives if successful, or

(b) is used in calculating the total amount of winnings or value of prizes in respect of the gambling in which the person making the stake participates,

'supply' includes—

(a) sale,

(b) lease, and

(c) placing on premises with permission or in accordance with a contract or other arrangement,

'temporary use notice' has the meaning given by section 215,

'track' means a horse-race course, dog track or other premises on any part of which a race or other sporting event takes place or is intended to take place,

'travelling fair' has the meaning given by section 286,

'vehicle' includes—

(a) a train,

(b) an aircraft,

(c) a seaplane, and

(d) an amphibious vehicle (other than a hovercraft within the meaning of the Hovercraft Act 1968 (c 59)),

'vessel' includes—

(a) anything, other than a seaplane or an amphibious vehicle, designed or adapted for navigation or other use in, on or over water,

(b) a hovercraft (within the meaning of the Hovercraft Act 1968), and,

(c) anything, or any part of any place, situated in or on water,

'virtual' has the meaning given by subsection (3) below,

'winnings', in relation to a bet, means anything won, whether in money or in money's worth, and

'young person' has the meaning given by section 45.

(2) In this Act, except where the context otherwise requires—

(a) a reference to accepting a bet includes a reference to negotiating a bet,

(b) a reference to advertising is to be construed in accordance with section 327,

(c) a reference to participating in a lottery is to be construed in accordance with section 14,

(d) a reference to installing computer software includes a reference to downloading computer software,

(e) a reference to paying winnings in relation to a bet includes a reference to providing a prize in money's worth,

(f) a reference to postal services does not include a reference to facsimile transmission,

(g) a reference to premises includes a reference to part of premises,

(h) a reference to promoting a lottery is to be construed in accordance with section 252,

(i) a reference to providing facilities for gambling is to be construed in accordance with section 5,

(j) a reference to publication includes a reference to display, and

(k) a reference to the sale, supply or purchase of a lottery ticket is to be construed in accordance with section 253.

(3) For the purposes of this Act a reference to a virtual game, race or other event or process is a reference to—

(a) images generated by computer so as to resemble all or part of a game, race or other event or process of a kind that is played by or involves actual people, animals or things,

(b) images generated by computer so as to represent an imaginary game, race or other event or process, or

(c) any game, race or other event or process the result of which is determined by computer.

(4) A requirement under this Act to give a notice (or to notify) is a requirement to give notice in writing; and for that purpose—

(a) a message sent by facsimile transmission or electronic mail shall be treated as a notice given in writing, and

(b) a notice sent to a licensee at the address specified for that purpose in the licence shall, unless the contrary is proved, be treated as reaching him within a period within which it could reasonably be expected to reach him in the ordinary course of events.

(5) A reference in this Act to an act which is authorised by a licence or other document does not include a reference to an act which would be authorised by the licence or document but for failure to comply with a term or condition.

Commencement

Brought into force by the Gambling Act 2005 (Commencement No 6 and Transitional Provisions) Order 2006, SI 2006/3272, art 2, Sch 1 as from 1 January 2007; for transitional provisions see art 6, Sch 4 thereto (as amended by SI 2007/1157, arts 7–12).

Sub-s (1): England; Wales

See the note to s 2.

Sub-s (1): Gambling Commission. As to the establishment, etc of the Gambling Commission, see s 20, Sch 4, and the note 'Gambling Commission' to that section.

Sub-s (1): Part 6. Ie Pt 6 (ss 127–139) of this Act.

Sub-s (1): Part 8. Ie Pt 8 (ss 150–213 and Sch 9) of this Act.

Sub-s (4): Writing. See the note to s 39.

Explanatory Notes

863, 864 [para **6.2022** below]

---

1 Sub-s (1): definition substituted by SI 2007/2194, art 10(1), (2), Sch 4, Pt 3, para 109.

6.854 354 Crown application

(1) This Act binds the Crown.

(2) But this Act shall have no effect in relation to anything done on, or in relation to any use of, premises occupied (temporarily or permanently) by *Her Majesty's naval forces, military forces or air forces (within the meaning given by section 225(1) of the Army Act 1955 (c 18))*[1].

(3) Section 40(3) of the Fire Precautions Act 1971 (c 40) (conversion of reference to fire and rescue authority into reference to Her Majesty's Fire Inspectorate in relation to Crown premises) shall apply to a provision of this Act as it applies to provisions of that Act (but with the substitution for the reference to section 40(1) of a reference to subsection (1) above).[2]

Commencement

Brought into force by the Gambling Act 2005 (Commencement No 2 and Transitional Provisions) Order 2005, SI 2005/2455, art 2 and Schedule, as from 1 October 2005.

Definitions

'premises': s 353(1), (2)(g)

Explanatory Notes

865, 866 [para **6.2022** below]

---

1 Words in italics repealed and words "any of Her Majesty's forces (within the meaning of the Armed Forces Act 2006)" substituted by the Armed Forces Act 2006, s 378(1), Sch 16, para 245 from a date to be appointed.

2 Substituted in relation to Scotland by SSI 2006/475, art 2(1), Sch 1, para 16(1), (4).

6.855 355 Regulations, orders and rules

(1) Regulations or rules under this Act, or an order of the Secretary of State under this Act—

(a) may make provision which applies generally or only for specified purposes or in specified cases or circumstances,

(b) may make different provision for different purposes, cases or circumstances, and

(c) may include incidental, consequential or transitional provision.

(2) A provision of this Act which permits regulations, rules or an order to make provision of a specified kind is without prejudice to the generality of subsection (1).

(3) Regulations or rules under this Act, or an order of the Secretary of State under this Act, shall be made by statutory instrument.

(4) Regulations under any of the following provisions shall not be made by the Secretary of State unless a draft has been laid before and approved by resolution of each House of Parliament—

(a) section 4,

(b) section 6,

(c) section 7,

(d) section 14,

(e) section 78,

(f) section 123,

(g) section 167,

(h) section 168,

(i) section 236, and

(j) section 328.

(5) Regulations or rules made by a Minister of the Crown under any other provision of this Act shall be subject to annulment in pursuance of a resolution of either House of Parliament.

(6) An order of the Secretary of State under this Act shall not be made unless a draft has been laid before and approved by resolution of each House of Parliament (subject to subsections (7) and (8)).

(7) Subsection (6) shall not apply to an order under section 349(6), to an order under section 351 other than an order adding an entry to the list in Part 2 or 3 of Schedule 6 or to an order under Part 2 of Schedule 7 or Part 2 of Schedule 18, which shall instead be subject to annulment in pursuance of a resolution of either House of Parliament.

(8) Subsection (6) shall not apply to an order under section 358; but—

(a) an order under section 358(1) which includes provision made by virtue of section 358(4) or by virtue of Part 1 of Schedule 18 shall be subject to annulment in pursuance of a resolution of either House of Parliament, and

(b) an order under section 358(5) or (6) shall not be made unless a draft has been laid before and approved by resolution of each House of Parliament.

(9) Regulations under a provision specified in subsection (4) or under section 285 shall not be made by the Scottish Ministers unless a draft has been laid before and approved by resolution of the Scottish Parliament.

(10) Regulations made by the Scottish Ministers under any other provision of this Act shall be subject to annulment in pursuance of a resolution of the Scottish Parliament.

Commencement

Brought into force by the Gambling Act 2005 (Commencement No 1) Order 2005, SI 2005/2425, art 2, as from 28 August 2005.

Sub-s (1): Secretary of State. See the note to s 4.

Sub-s (9): Scottish Ministers. See the note to s 25.

Explanatory Notes

867, 868 [para **6.2022** below]

6.856 356 Amendments and repeals

(1) Schedule 16 (minor and consequential amendments) shall have effect.

(2) An amendment in that Schedule shall have the same extent as the enactment amended (or as the relevant portion of the enactment amended).

(3) The following shall cease to have effect—

(a) the Gaming Act 1710 (c 19),

(b) the Gaming Act 1738 (c 28),

(c) the Gaming Act 1835 (c 41),

(d) the Gaming Act 1845 (c 109),

(e) the Gaming Act 1892 (c 9),

(f) the Betting, Gaming and Lotteries Act 1963 (c 2),

(g) the Gaming Act 1968 (c 65),

(h) the Lotteries Act 1975 (c 58), and

(i) the Lotteries and Amusements Act 1976 (c 32).

(4) The enactments listed in Schedule 17 are hereby repealed to the extent specified.

(5) A repeal in that Schedule shall have the same extent as the provision repealed (subject to the Note to that Schedule).

Commencement

Subsections (1) and (2), in so far as they relate to Sch 16, paras 3(1), (3)–(6), 5–7, 9, 13, 14, 16, 19 and 21, and subss (4) and (5), in so far as they relate to the entry in Sch 17 relating to the Gaming Act 1968, brought into force by the Gambling Act 2005 (Commencement No 2 and Transitional Provisions) Order 2005, SI 2005/2455, art 2 and Schedule, as from 1 October 2005. Subsections (1) and (2), in so far as they relate to Sch 16 para 3(2) brought into force by SI 2005/2455, art 2 as from 24 November 2005. Subsections (1) and (2), in so far as they relate to Sch 16, para 3(7) and (8) brought into force by SI 2005/2455, art 2 as from 25 November 2005.

Subsections (1), (2), (4), (5) brought into force for certain purposes as from 1 January 2007: see SI 2006/3272, art 2(1), Sch 1; for transitional provisions see art 6, Sch 4 thereto (as amended by SI 2007/1157, arts 7–12).

Sub-ss (1), (2): brought into force for remaining purposes as from 1 September 2007: see SI 2006/3272, art 2(4); for transitional provisions see art 6, Sch 4 thereto (as amended by SI 2007/1157, arts 7–12).

Subsection (3)(a)–(e), (h) brought into force as from 1 September 2007: see SI 2006/3272, art 2(4); for transitional provisions see art 6, Sch 4 thereto (as amended by SI 2007/1157, arts 7–12).

Subsection (3)(f), (g), (i) brought into force as from 1 September 2007: see SI 2006/3272, arts 3, 4, 5; for savings and transitional provisions see arts 3(2)–(8), 6, Sch 4 thereto.

Subsections (4), (5) brought into force as from 1 September 2007: see SI 2006/3272, arts 2–5; for savings and transitional provisions see arts 3(2)–(8), 4(2)–(5), 5(2)–(6), 6, Sch 4 thereto.

Explanatory Notes

869, 870 [para **6.2022** below]

6.857 357 Money

(1) Expenditure of a Minister of the Crown in connection with this Act shall be paid out of money provided by Parliament.

(2) A sum received by a Minister of the Crown in connection with this Act shall be paid into the Consolidated Fund.

Commencement

Brought into force by the Gambling Act 2005 (Commencement No 2 and Transitional Provisions) Order 2005, SI 2005/2455, art 2 and Schedule, as from 1 October 2005.

Sub-s (2): Consolidated Fund. See the note to s 121.

Explanatory Notes

871 [para **6.2022** below]

6.858 358 Commencement

(1) The preceding provisions of this Act shall come into force in accordance with provision made by the Secretary of State by order.

(2) An order under subsection (1) may (without prejudice to the generality of section 355(1))—

- (a) bring only specified provisions into force;
- (b) bring different provisions into force at different times;
- (c) bring a provision into force for a specified purpose only;
- (d) bring a provision into force at different times for different purposes;
- (e) in particular, bring Part 2 into force only for specified preliminary purposes relating to the establishment of the Commission (which may include the assumption of functions of the Gaming Board for Great Britain pending the commencement of repeals made by this Act);
- (f) in particular, bring a provision of this Act into force for the purpose of enabling an advance application for a licence or permit to be made, considered and determined;
- (g) in particular, bring an offence or other provision of this Act into force only in relation to gambling of a specified class or in specified circumstances;
- (h) include transitional provision modifying the application of a provision of this Act pending the commencement of, or pending the doing of anything under, a provision of another enactment.

(3) Schedule 18 (transitional) shall have effect.

(4) Without prejudice to the generality of section 355(1)(c) or of Schedule 18, an order under this section may—

- (a) make savings (with or without modification) or transitional provision in connection with Part 1 or 2 of the Horserace Betting and Olympic Lottery Act 2004 (c 25) (sale of the Horserace Totalisator Board ('the Tote') and abolition of the horserace betting levy system);
- (b) modify a provision of this Act in its application in relation to a matter addressed by Part 1 or 2 of that Act or so as to reflect a provision of Part 1 or 2 of that Act;
- (c) modify a provision of Part 1 or 2 of that Act (including a provision which amends another enactment) so as to reflect a provision of this Act.

(5) If the Secretary of State brings into force a repeal effected by this Act at a time when the appointed day for the purposes of Part 1 of that Act has not been appointed or has not arrived, he may by order—

- (a) save, with or without modification, a provision repealed by this Act in so far as it relates to the Tote;

(b) make provision in connection with the Tote of a kind similar to provision made by a provision repealed by this Act;
(c) modify a provision of this Act for a purpose connected with the Tote;
(d) modify a provision of Part 1 of that Act (including a provision which amends another enactment) so as to reflect a provision of this Act.

(6) If the Secretary of State wholly or partly brings into force the repeal by this Act of the Betting, Gaming and Lotteries Act 1963 (c 2) at a time when the provisions listed in section 15(1)(a) to (c) of the Horserace Betting and Olympic Lottery Act 2004 (horserace betting levy system) have not been entirely repealed by order under that section, he may by order—
(a) save any of those provisions, with or without modification;
(b) make provision of a kind similar to any of those provisions;
(c) modify a provision of this Act for a purpose connected with a matter addressed by any of those provisions or by Part 2 of that Act;
(d) modify a provision of Part 2 of that Act (including a provision which amends another enactment) so as to reflect a provision of this Act.

Commencement

7 April 2005 (the date of royal assent); see s 358(1).

Sub-s (1): Secretary of State. See the note to s 4.

Sub-s (2): Part 2. Ie Pt 2 (ss 20–32 and Schs 4–6) of this Act.

Sub-s (2): The Commission. Ie the Gambling Commission; see s 353(1). As to the establishment, etc of the Gambling Commission, see s 20, Sch 4, and the note 'Gambling Commission' to that section.

Subordinate legislation

Gambling Act 2005 (Commencement No 1) Order 2005, SI 2005/2425 (made under sub-ss (1), (2)).

Gambling Act 2005 (Commencement No 2 and Transitional Provisions) Order 2005, SI 2005/2455 (made under sub-ss (1), (2)).

Gambling Act 2005 (Commencement No 3) Order 2006, SI 2006/631 (made under sub-ss (1), (2)).

Gambling Act 2005 (Commencement No 4) Order 2006, SI 2006/2964 (made under sub-ss (1), (2)).

Gambling Act 2005 (Commencement No 5) Order 2006, SI 2006/3220 (made under sub-ss (1), (2)).

Gambling Act 2005 (Commencement No 6 and Transitional Provisions) Order 2006, SI 2006/3272 (made under sub-ss (1), (2)).

Gambling Act 2005 (Commencement No 6 and Transitional Provisions) (Amendment) Order 2006, SI 2006/3361 (made under sub-ss (1), (2)).

Gambling Act 2005 (Commencement and Transitional Provisions) (Amendment) Order 2007, SI 2007/1157 (made under sub-ss (1), (2)).

Gambling Act 2005 (Commencement No 6 and Transitional Provisions) (Amendment) Order 2007, SI 2007/1527 (made under sub-ss (1), (2)).

Gambling Act 2005 (Horserace Totalisator Board) Order 2007, SI 2007/2102 (made under sub-s (5)).

Gambling Act 2005 (Horserace Betting Levy) Order 2007, SI 2007/2159 (made under sub-s (6)).

Gambling Act 2005 (Commencement No 6 and Transitional Provisions) (Amendment) (No 2) Order 2007, 2007/2169 (made under sub-ss (1), (2), (4)).

Gambling Act 2005 (Commencement No 7) Order 2007, SI 2007/3155 (made under sub-ss (1), (2)).

Gambling Act 2005 (Commencement No 8) Order 2008, SI 2008/1326 (made under sub-ss (1), (2)).

As to orders under this Act generally, see s 355.

Definitions

'the Commission': s 353(1)

Explanatory Notes

872–877 [para **6.2022** below]

6.859 359 Vessels: territorial limitations

(1) A person does not commit an offence under Part 3, 4, 10 or 11 of this Act if—

(a) the conduct which would otherwise constitute the offence takes place on board a vessel (within the meaning of section 353(1)), and

(b) the vessel is on a journey which has taken it or is intended to take it into international waters.

(2) Subject to subsection (1) a provision of this Act which applies in relation to a thing done in Great Britain applies to that thing if done on or in the territorial sea adjacent to Great Britain.

(3) In this section—

'international waters' means waters outside the territorial sea adjacent to Great Britain, and

'the territorial sea' has the meaning given by section 1 of the Territorial Sea Act 1987 (c 49).

Commencement

7 April 2005 (the date of royal assent); see s 358(1).

Sub-s (1): Person. See the note 'Persons' to s 23.

Sub-s (1): Part 3 . . . of this Act. Ie ss 33–44.

Sub-s (1): Part 4 . . . of this Act. Ie ss 45–64.

Sub-s (1): Part 10 . . . of this Act. Ie ss 235–251 and Sch 10.

Sub-s (1): Part 11 of this Act. Ie ss 252–265 and Sch 11.

Sub-s (2): Great Britain. See the note to s 12.

Explanatory Notes

878 [para **6.2022** below]

6.860 360 Aircraft: territorial limitations

(1) A person does not commit an offence under Part 3, 4, 10 or 11 of this Act if the conduct which would otherwise constitute the offence takes place—

(a) on board an aircraft, and

(b) at a time when the aircraft is in international airspace.

(2) In this section 'international airspace' means airspace other than airspace above Great Britain or above the territorial sea adjacent to Great Britain (within the meaning given by section 1 of the Territorial Sea Act 1987).

Commencement

7 April 2005 (the date of royal assent); see s 358(1).

Sub-s (1): Person. See the note 'Persons' to s 23.

Sub-s (1): Part 3 . . . of this Act. Ie ss 33–44.

Sub-s (1): Part 4 . . . of this Act. Ie ss 45–64.

Sub-s (1): Part 10 . . . of this Act. Ie ss 235–251 and Sch 10.

Sub-s (1): Part 11 of this Act. Ie ss 252–265 and Sch 11.

Sub-s (2): Great Britain. See the note to s 12.

Explanatory Notes

878 [para **6.2022** below]

6.861 361 Extent

(1) The following provisions of this Act extend to England and Wales, Scotland and Northern Ireland—

(a) section 43,

(b) section 331, and
(c) section 340 (and the related entry in Schedule 17).

(2) The other provisions of this Act shall extend only to—
(a) England and Wales, and
(b) Scotland.

(3) This section is subject to section 356.

Commencement

7 April 2005 (the date of royal assent); see s 358(1).

Sub-s (1): England; Wales.

See the note to s 2.

Explanatory Notes

879 [para **6.2022** below]

6.862 362 Short title

This Act may be cited as the Gambling Act 2005.

Commencement

7 April 2005 (the date of royal assent); see s 358(1).

SCHEDULES

SCHEDULE 1
BETTING: PRIZE COMPETITIONS: DEFINITION OF PAYMENT TO ENTER
Section 11

Introduction

[6.863]

1. This Schedule makes provision about the circumstances in which a person is to be or not to be treated for the purposes of section 11(1)(b) as being required to pay to participate in an arrangement.

Meaning of payment

2. For the purposes of section 11 and this Schedule a reference to paying includes a reference to—
   (a) paying money,
   (b) transferring money's worth, and
   (c) paying for goods or services at a price or rate which reflects the opportunity to participate in an arrangement under which a participant may win a prize.

3. It is immaterial for the purposes of section 11 and this Schedule—
   (a) to whom a payment is made, and
   (b) who receives benefit from a payment.

4. It is also immaterial for the purposes of section 11 and this Schedule whether a person knows when he makes a payment that he thereby participates in an arrangement as a result of which he may win a prize.

Stamps, telephone calls, &c

5. (1) For the purposes of section 11 and this Schedule a reference to paying does not include a reference to incurring the expense, at a normal rate, of—
   (a) sending a letter by ordinary post,
   (b) making a telephone call, or
   (c) using any other method of communication.

(2) For the purpose of sub-paragraph (1)—
   (a) a 'normal rate' is a rate which does not reflect the opportunity to participate in an arrangement under which a person may win a prize, and
   (b) ordinary post means ordinary first-class or second-class post (without special arrangements for delivery).

Payment to discover whether prize won

6. For the purposes of section 11 and this Schedule a requirement to pay in order to discover whether a prize has been won under an arrangement shall be treated as a requirement to pay to participate in the arrangement.

Payment to claim prize

7. For the purposes of section 11 and this Schedule a requirement to pay in order to take possession of a prize which a person has or may have won under an arrangement shall be treated as a requirement to pay to participate in the arrangement.

Choice of free entry

8. (1) For the purposes of section 11 and this Schedule an arrangement shall not be treated as requiring a person to pay to participate if under the arrangement—

(a) each person who is eligible to participate has a choice whether to participate by paying or by sending a communication,

(b) the communication mentioned in paragraph (a) may be—

(i) a letter sent by ordinary post, or

(ii) another method of communication which is neither more expensive nor less convenient than participating by paying,

(c) the choice is publicised in such a way as to be likely to come to the attention of each person who proposes to participate, and

(d) the system for allocating prizes does not differentiate between those who participate by paying and those who participate by sending a communication.

(2) In this paragraph 'ordinary post' has the meaning given by paragraph 5(2)(b).

Power to make regulations

9. The Secretary of State may make regulations providing that an activity of a specified kind or performed in specified circumstances is to be or not to be treated for the purposes of section 11 as paying to participate in an arrangement.

Commencement

Brought into force by the Gambling Act 2005 (Commencement No 2 and Transitional Provisions) Order 2005, SI 2005/2455, art 2 and Schedule, as from 1 October 2005.

Para 9: Secretary of State. See the note to s 4.

Regulations under this Schedule. At the time of going to press no regulations had been made under this Schedule.

As to regulations under this Act generally, see s 355.

Definitions

'participant': s 353(1)

'prize': ss 6(5), 11(4), 353(1)

Explanatory Notes

83–87 [para **6.2004** below]

SCHEDULE 2
LOTTERIES: DEFINITION OF PAYMENT TO ENTER
Section 14

Introduction

[6.864]

1. This Schedule makes provision about the circumstances in which an arrangement is to be or not to be treated for the purposes of section 14 as requiring persons to pay in order to participate in an arrangement.

Meaning of payment

2. For the purposes of section 14 and this Schedule a reference to paying includes a reference to—

(a) paying money,

(b) transferring money's worth, and

(c) paying for goods or services at a price or rate which reflects the opportunity to participate in an arrangement.

3. It is immaterial for the purposes of section 14 and this Schedule—
(a) to whom a payment is made, and
(b) who receives benefit from a payment.

4. It is also immaterial for the purposes of section 14 and this Schedule whether a person knows when he makes a payment that he thereby participates in an arrangement.

Stamps, telephone calls, &c

5. (1) For the purposes of section 14 and this Schedule a reference to paying does not include a reference to incurring the expense, at a normal rate, of—
(a) sending a letter by ordinary post,
(b) making a telephone call, or
(c) using any other method of communication.

(2) For the purpose of sub-paragraph (1)—
(a) a 'normal rate' is a rate which does not reflect the opportunity to enter a lottery, and
(b) ordinary post means ordinary first-class or second-class post (without special arrangements for delivery).

Payment to discover whether prize won

6. For the purposes of section 14 and this Schedule a requirement to pay in order to discover whether a prize has been won under an arrangement shall be treated as a requirement to pay in order to participate in the arrangement.

Payment to claim prize

7. For the purposes of section 14 and this Schedule a requirement to pay in order to take possession of a prize which has or may have been allocated to a person under an arrangement shall be treated as a requirement to pay in order to participate in the arrangement.

Choice of free entry

8. (1) For the purposes of section 14 and this Schedule an arrangement shall not be treated as requiring persons to pay in order to participate if under the arrangement—
(a) each individual who is eligible to participate has a choice whether to participate by paying or by sending a communication,
(b) the communication mentioned in paragraph (a) may be—
(i) a letter sent by ordinary post, or
(ii) another method of communication which is neither more expensive nor less convenient than entering the lottery by paying,
(c) the choice is publicised in such a way as to be likely to come to the attention of each individual who proposes to participate, and
(d) the system for allocating prizes does not differentiate between those who participate by paying and those who participate by sending a communication.

(2) In this paragraph 'ordinary post' has the meaning given by paragraph 5(2)(b).

Power to make regulations

9. Regulations under section 14(7) may, in particular, provide that an activity of a specified kind or performed in specified circumstances is to be or not to be treated as paying to enter a lottery.

Commencement

Brought into force by the Gambling Act 2005 (Commencement No 2 and Transitional Provisions) Order 2005, SI 2005/2455, art 2 and Schedule, as from 1 October 2005.

Power to amend. For the power of the Secretary of State to amend this Schedule, see s 14(7).

Definitions

'lottery': ss 14, 353(1)
'prize' (in relation to a lottery): ss 14(4), 353(1)

Explanatory Notes

88, 89 [para **6.2004** below]

SCHEDULE 3
AMENDMENT OF NATIONAL LOTTERY ETC ACT 1993 (C 39)
Section 15

Annual levy

[6.865]

1. After section 10B of the National Lottery etc Act 1993 (financial penalties: appeal) insert—

'10C **Annual levy**

(1) The Secretary of State may make regulations requiring holders of licences under section 5 or 6 to pay an annual levy to the Gambling Commission.

(2) The regulations shall, in particular, make provision for—
- (a) timing of payment of the levy, and
- (b) the amount of the levy.

(3) The regulations may, in particular, make provision—
- (a) determining the amount of the levy by reference to a percentage of specified receipts of the holder of a licence under section 5 or 6,
- (b) determining the amount of the levy by reference to a percentage of specified profits of the holder of a licence under section 5 or 6,
- (c) providing for the determination of the amount of the levy according to a specified formula, or
- (d) providing for the determination of the amount of the levy in some other way.

(4) Any sum due by way of levy by virtue of this section shall be treated for the purposes of this Act as if its payment were a condition of the licence under section 5 or 6.

(5) The Gambling Commission shall, with the consent of the Treasury and of the Secretary of State, expend money received by way of levy for purposes related to, or by providing financial assistance for projects related to—
- (a) addiction to gambling,
- (b) other forms of harm or exploitation associated with gambling, or
- (c) any of the licensing objectives for the purposes of the Gambling Act 2005.

(6) In subsection (5) the reference to financial assistance is a reference to grants, loans and any other form of financial assistance, which may be made or given on terms or conditions (which may include terms and conditions as to repayment with or without interest).

(7) The Secretary of State may make regulations under this section only if—
- (a) he has made regulations under the Gambling Act 2005 requiring holders of operating licences to pay an annual levy to the Gambling Commission, and

(b) he has consulted the National Lottery Commission.

(8) The Gambling Commission shall consult the National Lottery Commission before incurring expenditure under subsection (5).'

Consultation with Gambling Commission

2. After section 4 of the National Lottery etc Act 1993 (c 39) (overriding duties) insert—

'4A Consultation with Gambling Commission

(1) If in the course of the exercise of its functions the National Lottery Commission becomes aware of a matter about which the Gambling Commission is likely to have an opinion, the National Lottery Commission shall consult the Gambling Commission.

(2) The National Lottery Commission shall comply with any direction of the Secretary of State (which may be general or specific) to consult the Gambling Commission.'

Definition of 'lottery'

3. In section 20 of the National Lottery etc Act 1993 (interpretation) after the definition of 'contravention' insert—

'"lottery" has the same meaning as in the Gambling Act 2005;'.

Commencement

Paras 1, 3 brought into force as from 1 September 2007 by the Gambling Act 2005 (Commencement No 6 and Transitional Provisions) Order 2006, SI 2006/3272, art 2; for transitional provisions see art 6, Sch 4 thereto (as amended by SI 2007/1157, arts 7–12).

Paragraph 2 brought into force by the Gambling Act 2005 (Commencement No 2 and Transitional Provisions) Order 2005, SI 2005/2455, art 2 and Schedule, as from 1 October 2005.

Para 1: Section 10C(1): Gambling Commission. As to the establishment, etc of the Gambling Commission, see Pt 2 of this Act.

Para 1: Section 10C(5): Licensing objectives, etc. See s 1 of this Act.

Regulations. At the time of going to press no regulations had been made under the National Lottery etc Act 1993, s 10C, as inserted by para 1 above.

Explanatory Notes

90 [para **6.2004** below]

SCHEDULE 4
THE GAMBLING COMMISSION
Section 20

Constitution

[6.866]

1. The Gambling Commission shall consist of a chairman and other commissioners appointed by the Secretary of State.

Tenure

2. (1) A commissioner shall hold and vacate office in accordance with the terms of his appointment (subject to this Schedule).

(2) A commissioner may resign by notice in writing to the Secretary of State.

(3) If the Secretary of State thinks that a commissioner is unable, unfit or unwilling to perform his functions, the Secretary of State may dismiss the commissioner.

3. The chairman—
- (a) shall hold and vacate office in accordance with the terms of his appointment (subject to this Schedule),
- (b) may resign by notice in writing to the Secretary of State, and
- (c) shall cease to be chairman if he ceases to be a commissioner.

4. The Secretary of State may not appoint a person as commissioner—
- (a) for a period of more than five years, or
- (b) for periods (whether or not consecutive) exceeding ten years in aggregate.

Staff

5. (1) The Commission may, with the Secretary of State's consent as to terms and conditions of employment, appoint a chief executive.

(2) A person—
- (a) may hold appointment both as the chief executive and as a commissioner, but
- (b) may not hold appointment both as the chief executive and as the chairman.

(3) Where a person holds appointment both as the chief executive and as a commissioner, if he ceases to be the chief executive he shall cease to be a commissioner.

6. The Commission may, with the Secretary of State's consent as to terms and conditions of employment, appoint other staff.

Proceedings

7. The Commission shall—
- (a) determine arrangements for the conduct of its proceedings (which may, in particular, include arrangements for a quorum), and
- (b) publish those arrangements.

8. (1) The Commission may delegate a function to—
- (a) a commissioner,
- (b) a committee consisting of commissioners, or
- (c) an employee of the Commission.

(2) Sub-paragraph (1) applies to any function of the Commission including, in particular—
- (a) a discretionary function;
- (b) the function of conducting a review;
- (c) the function of determining whether to revoke a licence or of determining whether to impose a requirement to pay a penalty.

Money

9. The Commission may, with the consent of the Secretary of State, pay to or in respect of a commissioner or employee sums by way of or in respect of—
- (a) remuneration;
- (b) allowances;
- (c) expenses;
- (d) pension;
- (e) gratuity.

10. The Secretary of State may make payments to the Commission for the purpose of enabling the Commission to meet such of its expenses as cannot be met out of fees paid to the Commission under this Act.

11. The Commission may, with the consent of the Secretary of State, borrow money.

12. The Commission may pay money into the Consolidated Fund.

13. The Commission shall keep accounting records in such form as the Secretary of State may direct.

14. (1) The Commission shall prepare a statement of accounts for each financial year in such form as the Secretary of State may direct.

(2) The Commission shall send a copy of a statement of accounts under sub-paragraph (1) to—

(a) the Secretary of State, and

(b) the Comptroller and Auditor General.

(3) The Commission must comply with sub-paragraph (2) within such period, beginning with the end of the financial year to which the accounts relate, as the Secretary of State may specify.

(4) The Comptroller and Auditor General shall—

(a) examine a statement sent to him under sub-paragraph (2),

(b) report on it, and

(c) lay a copy of his report before Parliament.

15. (1) The financial year of the Commission shall be the period of 12 months ending with 31st March.

(2) But the first financial year of the Commission shall be the period—

(a) beginning with the commencement of section 20, and

(b) ending with the following 31st March.

Annual report

16. (1) As soon as is reasonably practicable after the end of each financial year the Commission shall send to the Secretary of State a report about the activities of the Commission during the year.

(2) Where the Secretary of State receives a report under sub-paragraph (1)—

(a) he shall lay a copy before Parliament, and

(b) he may arrange for the report to be published.

Status

17. (1) The Commission shall not be regarded as the servant or agent of the Crown or as enjoying any status, immunity or privilege of the Crown.

(2) Property of the Commission shall not be regarded as property of or held on behalf of the Crown.

(3) Membership of or employment by the Commission is not employment in the civil service of the State.

Consent

18. Consent given by the Secretary of State for the purposes of this Schedule may be general or specific.

Commencement

Brought into force by the Gambling Act 2005 (Commencement No 2 and Transitional Provisions) Order 2005, SI 2005/2455, art 2 and Schedule, as from 1 October 2005.

Para 1: Chairman and other commissioners. As to the treatment of members of the Gaming Board for Great Britain and the chairman of that Board as commissioners of the Gambling Commission and the chairman of that Commission, see s 21(3), (4).

Para 1: Secretary of State. See the note to s 4.

Para 2: Writing. See the note to s 39.

Para 12: Consolidated Fund. See the note to s 121.

Para 14: Comptroller and Auditor General. See the note to s 30.

Explanatory Notes

120–126 [para **6.2005** below]

SCHEDULE 5
TRANSFER FROM GAMING BOARD TO GAMBLING COMMISSION: SUPPLEMENTARY PROVISION
Section 21

[6.867]

1. In this Schedule—

'the Board' means the Gaming Board for Great Britain,

'commencement' means the coming into force of section 21, and

'the Commission' means the Gambling Commission.

2. Anything done by or in relation to the Board which has effect immediately before commencement shall, so far as necessary for continuing its effect after commencement, have effect as if done by or in relation to the Commission.

3. Anything (including any legal proceedings) which immediately before commencement is in the process of being done by or in relation to the Board may be continued by or in relation to the Commission.

4. So far as necessary or appropriate in consequence of section 21, on and after commencement a reference to the Board in an enactment, instrument or other document shall be treated as a reference to the Commission.

5. (1) Section 21(2) shall operate in relation to rights and liabilities—

(a) whether or not they would otherwise be capable of being transferred by the Board, and

(b) without any instrument or other formality being required.

(2) In so far as section 21(2) transfers to the Commission liabilities under contracts of employment nothing in that section or this Schedule shall affect the operation of—

(a) the Transfer of Undertakings (Protection of Employment) Regulations 1981 (SI 1981/1794), or

(b) regulations under section 38 of the Employment Relations Act 1999 (c 26) (replication of the TUPE regulations).

Commencement

Brought into force by the Gambling Act 2005 (Commencement No 2 and Transitional Provisions) Order 2005, SI 2005/2455, art 2 and Schedule, as from 1 October 2005.

Para 1: Gaming Board for Great Britain. The Gaming Board for Great Britain was established in accordance with the Gaming Act 1968, s 10, Sch 1 (repealed by ss 21(1), 356(4), Sch 17), and its functions, rights and liabilities are transferred to the Gambling Commission in accordance with s 21(2).

Para 1: Coming into force of section 21. At the time of going to press no order had been made under s 358 bringing s 21 into force.

Para 1: Gambling Commission. As to the establishment, etc of the Gambling Commission, see s 20, Sch 4, and the note 'Gambling Commission' to that section.

Explanatory Notes

127, 128 [para **6.2005** below]

SCHEDULE 6
EXCHANGE OF INFORMATION: PERSONS AND BODIES
Sections 30 and 350

PART 1
PERSONS AND BODIES WITH FUNCTIONS UNDER THIS ACT

6.868–6.869 A constable or police force
An enforcement officer
A licensing authority
[Commissioners for Her Majesty's Revenue and Customs][1]
[The First-tier Tribunal][2]
The National Lottery Commission
The Secretary of State
The Scottish Ministers

Commencement

Brought into force by the Gambling Act 2005 (Commencement No 2 and Transitional Provisions) Order 2005, SI 2005/2455, art 2 and Schedule, as from 1 October 2005.

Constable. See the note to s 64.

Enforcement officer. As to enforcement officers, see, generally, s 303.

Licensing authority

For the licensing authorities for the purposes of this Act, see s 2.

Commissioners for Her Majesty's Revenue and Customs. See the note to s 23.

Gambling Appeal Tribunal. As to the establishment of the Gambling Appeals Tribunal, see s 140, Sch 8.

Secretary of State

See the note to s 4.

Scottish Ministers. See the note to s 25.

Further provisions. See Pt 4 of this Schedule. See also s 350 as respects the exchange of information by persons or bodies listed in this Part of this Schedule.

Power to amend. See s 351.

Definitions

'enforcement officer': s 353(1)
'licensing authority': ss 2, 353(1)

Explanatory Notes

129–131 [para **6.2005** below]

1 Words in square brackets substituted by virtue of the Commissioners for Revenue and Customs Act 2005, s 50(1), (7).

2 Entry "The First-tier Tribunal", substituted for entry "The Gambling Appeals Tribunal", as originally enacted, by SI 2010/22, art 5(1), Sch 2, paras 93, 104.

PART 2
ENFORCEMENT AND REGULATORY BODIES

6.870 . . .
The Charity Commission
The Financial Services Authority
[The Horserace Betting Levy Board]

. . .

. . .

The Office of Fair Trading
[The Pensions Regulator]
The Serious Fraud Office
[The Serious Organised Crime Agency]

Notes

Initial Commencement

To be appointed

To be appointed: see s 358(1).

Appointment

Appointment: 1 October 2005: see SI 2005/2455, art 2(1), Schedule.

Amendment

Entries 'The Director and staff of the Assets Recovery Agency', 'The Director General and staff of the National Crime Squad', 'The Director General and staff of the National Criminal Intelligence Service' (omitted) repealed by the Serious Crime Act 2007, ss 74(2)(g), 92, Sch 8, Pt 7, para 176(a), Sch 14.

Entry 'The Horserace Betting Levy Board' inserted by SI 2007/2101, art 2(a).

Entry omitted revoked by SI 2012/1633, art 2(a).

Entry 'The Pensions Regulator' inserted by SI 2012/1633, art 2(b).

Entry 'The Serious Organised Crime Agency' inserted by the Serious Crime Act 2007, s 74(2)(g), Sch 8, Pt 7, para 176(b).

PART 3
SPORT GOVERNING BODIES

6.871 [The Association of European Professional Football Leagues (established in Switzerland)
Bowls England]
[The British Boxing Board of Control Limited]
[The British Darts Organisation Limited
The British Horseracing Authority Limited
British Lions Limited (incorporated in Ireland)
Celtic Rugby Limited (incorporated in Ireland)
The Commonwealth Games federation
England Hockey
England Squash and Racketball Limited]
The England and Wales Cricket Board Limited
[The European Rugby Cup Limited (incorporated in Ireland)
Fédération Internationale de Football Association]
The Football Association Limited
The Football Association of Wales Limited
[The Greyhound Board of Great Britain Limited
The International Association of Athletics Federations
The International Cricket Council
The International Hockey Federation
The International Olympic Committee
The International Rugby Board
The International Tennis Federation (incorporated in the Bahamas as ITF Limited)]
The Lawn Tennis Association
The Irish Football Association Limited
The Jockey Club

[The London Marathon Limited
The Motor Sports Association Limited]
. . .
The Professional Golfers' Association Limited
[The Rugby Football League Limited]
The Rugby Football Union
[The Rugby League International Federation]
. . .
The Scottish Football Association Limited
[The Scottish Rugby Union PLC
Six Nations Rugby Limited]
UK Athletics Limited
[The Union of European Football Associations]
The Welsh Rugby Union Limited
[The World Darts Federation
The World Professional Billiards and Snooker Association Limited]

Commencement

Brought into force by the Gambling Act 2005 (Commencement No 2 and Transitional Provisions) Order 2005, SI 2005/2455, art 2 and Schedule, as from 1 October 2005.

Amendment

Entries 'The Association of European Professional Football Leagues (established in Switzerland)' and 'Bowls England' inserted by SI 2012/1633, art 3(a); entry 'The British Boxing Board of Control Limited' inserted by SI 2007/2101, art 2(b); entries 'The British Darts Organisation Limited' to 'England Squash and Racketball Limited' inserted by SI 2012/1633, art 3(b); entries 'The European Rugby Cup Limited (incorporated in Ireland)' and 'Fédération Internationale de Football Association' inserted by SI 2012/1633, art 3(c); entries from 'The Greyhound Board of Great Britain Limited' to 'The International Tennis Federation (incorporated in the Bahamas as ITF Limited)' substituted by SI 2012/1633, art 3(d); entries 'The London Marathon Limited' and 'The Motor Sports Association Limited' inserted by SI 2012/1633, art 3(e); entry omitted revoked by SI 2012/1633, art 6(f); entry 'The Rugby Football League Limited' substituted by SI 2012/1633, art 3(g); entry 'The Rugby League International Federation' inserted by SI 2012/1633, art 3(h); entry omitted revoked by SI 2012/1633, art 3(i); entries 'The Scottish Rugby Union PLC' and 'Six Nations Rugby Limited' inserted by SI 2012/1633, art 3(j); entry 'The Union of European Football Associations' inserted by SI 2012/1633, art 3(k); entries 'The World Darts Federation' and 'The World Professional Billiards and Snooker Association Limited' inserted by SI 2012/1633, art 3(l).

Further provisions. See Pt 4 of this Schedule.

Power to amend. See s 351.

Explanatory Notes

129–131 [para **6.2005** below]

PART 4
NOTES

[6.872]

1. Where a person or body listed in this Schedule is by virtue of an enactment restricted in the use that may be made of information provided to him or it by another person or body, nothing in section 30 or 350 overrides that restriction—

(a) in relation to information provided to the person or body by the Commission, or

(b) so as to permit the person or body to disclose to the Commission information provided to the person or body by another.

2. Where by virtue of an enactment the use that may be made of information supplied by a person or body listed in this Schedule is restricted, or where the information may be further disclosed only with the consent of the person or body which provided the information, the prohibition or restriction on further disclosure shall apply to—

(a) the supply of information by virtue of this Act, and

(b) the supply of information to the Gambling Commission (whether or not by virtue of this Act).

3. Information provided to a person or body by Her Majesty's [Commissioners for Her Majesty's Revenue and Customs][1] in reliance on a provision of this Act may not be provided by that person or body to any other person or body without the consent of the Commissioners.

Commencement

Brought into force by the Gambling Act 2005 (Commencement No 2 and Transitional Provisions) Order 2005, SI 2005/2455, art 2 and Schedule, as from 1 October 2005.

Para 1: Person. See the note 'Persons' to s 23.

Para 1: The Commission. Ie the Gambling Commission; see s 353(1). As to the establishment, etc of the Gambling Commission, see s 20, Sch 4, and the note 'Gambling Commission' to that section.

Para 3: Commissioners for Her Majesty's Revenue and Customs. See the note to s 23.

Power to amend. See s 351.

Definitions

'the Commission': s 353(1)

'enactment': s 353(1)

Explanatory Notes

129–131 [para **6.2005** below]

---

1 Para 3: words in square brackets substituted by virtue of the Commissioners for Revenue and Customs Act 2005, s 50(1), (7).

SCHEDULE 7
RELEVANT OFFENCES
Section 126

PART 1
THE OFFENCES

Gambling offences

[6.873]–[6.874]

1. An offence under—

(a) this Act,

(b) the Betting, Gaming and Lotteries Act 1963 (c 2),

(c) the Gaming Act 1968 (c 65),

(d) the Lotteries and Amusements Act 1976 (c 32),

(e) the National Lottery etc Act 1993 (c 39), or

(f) the National Lottery Act 1998 (c 22).

Theft, &c

2. An offence under any of the following provisions of the Theft Act 1968 (c 60)—

(a) section 1 (theft),

(b) section 8 (robbery),

(c) section 9 (burglary),
(d) section 10 (aggravated burglary),
(e) section 11 (theft from exhibition, &c),
(f) section 12A (aggravated vehicle-taking),
(g) section 13 (abstracting electricity),
(h) section 15 (obtaining property by deception),
(i) section 15A (obtaining money transfer by deception),
(j) section 16 (obtaining pecuniary advantage by deception),
(k) section 17 (false accounting),
(l) section 19 (false statement by director, &c),
(m) section 20 (suppression of document, &c),
(n) section 21 (blackmail),
(o) section 22 (handling stolen goods),
(p) section 24A (retaining wrong credit), and
(q) section 25 (going equipped for stealing, &c).

3. An offence under section 1 or 2 of the Theft Act 1978 (c 31) (obtaining services, or evading liability, by deception).

[**3A.** An offence under the Fraud Act 2006.][1]

4. An offence under section 170 or 170B of the Customs and Excise Management Act 1979 (c 2) (evasion of duty).

5. An offence under section 58(1) of the Civic Government (Scotland) Act 1982 (c 45) (convicted thief in possession).

6. Both in England and Wales and in Scotland, the offence at common law of conspiracy to defraud.

7. In Scotland the offences at common law of—

(a) theft,
(b) robbery,
(c) theft by housebreaking,
(d) fraud,
(e) extortion, and
(f) reset.

Miscellaneous

[**8.** An offence listed in Part 2 of Schedule 15 to the Criminal Justice Act 2003 (specified sexual offences).

8A. An offence under any of the following provisions of the Sexual Offences Act 1956—

(a) section 8 (intercourse with a defective);
(b) section 12 (buggery); and
(c) section 18 (fraudulent abduction of an heiress).

8B. An offence under section 3 of the Sexual Offences (Amendment) Act 2000 (abuse of trust).

9. An offence under the law of England and Wales which leads, or is intended to lead, to a person's death or to physical injury to a person.

9A. An offence of arson under section 1 of the Criminal Damage Act 1971 (destroying or damaging property)][2].

10. An offence under—

(a) the Firearms Act 1968 (c 27), or
(b) the Firearms (Amendment) Act 1988 (c 45).

11. An offence under any of the following provisions of the Misuse of Drugs Act 1971 (c 38)—

(a) section 4(2) (production),

(b) section 4(3) (supply),
(c) section 5(3) (possession with intent to supply), and
(d) section 8 (permitting activity on premises).

12. An offence under the Forgery and Counterfeiting Act 1981 (c 45), except for sections 18 and 19 (reproduction and imitation notes and coins).

13. An offence under section 3 of the Private Security Industry Act 2001 (c 12) (unlicensed activity).

14. An offence under section 70 of the Army Act 1955 (c 18) in so far as it relates to an offence listed elsewhere in this Schedule.

15. An offence under section 70 of the Air Force Act 1955 (c 19) in so far as it relates to an offence listed elsewhere in this Schedule.

16. An offence under section 42 of the Naval Discipline Act 1957 (c 53) in so far as it relates to an offence listed elsewhere in this Schedule.[2A]

17. An offence under section 52 or 52A of the Civic Government (Scotland) Act 1982 (offences relating to indecent photographs of children).

18. An offence under any of the following provisions of the Criminal Law (Consolidation) (Scotland) Act 1995 (c 39)—
(a) section 1 (incest),
(b) section 2 (intercourse with a stepchild),
(c) section 3 (intercourse with child under 16 by person in position of trust),
(d) section 5 (unlawful intercourse with a girl under 16),
(e) section 6 (indecent behaviour towards girl between 12 and 16),
(f) section 8 (detention of woman in brothel or other premises),
(g) section 10 (person having parental responsibilities causing or encouraging sexual activity in relation to a girl under 16), and
(h) section 13(5) (homosexual offences).

[**18A.** An offence under either of the following provisions of the Mental Health (Scotland) Act 1984—
(a) section 106 (protection of mentally handicapped females), and
(b) section 107 (protection of patients).

18B. An offence under either of the following provisions of the Mental Health (Care and Treatment) (Scotland) Act 2003—
(a) section 311 (non-consensual sexual acts), and
(b) section 313 (persons providing care services: sexual offences).

18C. An offence under any of the following provisions of the Protection of Children and Prevention of Sexual Offences (Scotland) Act 2005—
(a) section 1 (meeting a child following certain preliminary contact),
(b) section 9 (paying for sexual services of a child),
(c) section 10 (causing or inciting provision by child of sexual services or child pornography), and
(d) section 11 (controlling a child providing sexual services or involved in pornography).][3]

19. In Scotland, the offences at common law of—
(a) rape,
(b) clandestine injury to women,
(c) abduction of a woman or girl with intent to rape or ravish,
(d) assault with intent to rape or ravish,
(e) indecent assault,
(f) lewd, indecent or libidinous behaviour or practices,
(g) shameless indecency,
(h) sodomy,
(i) murder,

(j) culpable homicide, . . . [4]
(k) assault,
[(l) wilful fireraising,
(m) culpable and reckless fireraising, and
(n) bestiality][4].

20. In Scotland, the offence at common law of uttering and fraud.

21. An inchoate offence relating to an offence listed elsewhere in this Schedule.

22. A reference in this Part of this Schedule to an offence under an Act or a provision of an Act includes a reference to an offence under subordinate legislation made under that Act or provision.[5]

Commencement

Brought into force by the Gambling Act 2005 (Commencement No 6 and Transitional Provisions) Order 2006, SI 2006/3272, art 2, Sch 1 as from 1 January 2007; for transitional provisions see art 6, Sch 4 thereto (as amended by SI 2007/1157, arts 7–12).

Application

See the note to s 65.

Para 6: England; Wales. See the note to s 2.

Power to amend. See Pt 2 of this Schedule.

Explanatory Notes

352–355 [para 6.2008 below]

---

1 Para 3A: inserted by the Fraud Act 2006, s 14(1), Sch 1, para 38.

2 Paras 8, 8A, 8B, 9, 9A: substituted, for paras 8, 9 as originally enacted, by the Gambling Act 2005 (Relevant Offences) (Amendment) Order 2006, SI 2006/3391, art 2.

2A Paras 14-16: substituted by para 14A by the Armed Forces Act 2006, s 378(1), Sch 16, para 246(a) from a date to be appointed as follows:

"An offence under section 42 of the Armed Forces Act 2006 as respects which the corresponding offence under the law of England and Wales (within the meaning given by that section) is an offence listed elsewhere in this Schedule."

3 Paras 18A–18C: inserted by the Gambling Act 2005 (Relevant Offences) (Amendment) Order 2006, SI 2006/3391, art 3(1).

4 Para 19: in sub-para (j) word omitted repealed and sub-paras (l)–(n) inserted by the Gambling Act 2005 (Relevant Offences) (Amendment) Order 2006, SI 2006/3391, art 3(2).

5 Para 22A: inserted by the Armed Forces Act 2006, s 378(1), Sch 16, para 246(b) from a date to be appointed as follows:

"Section 48 of the Armed Forces Act 2006 (attempts, conspiracy, incitement and aiding and abetting outside England and Wales) applies for the purposes of this Act as if the reference in subsection (3)(b) to any of the following provisions of that Act were a reference to any provision of this Act."

PART 2
POWER TO AMEND PART 1

[6.875]

23. The Secretary of State may by order amend Part 1 of this Schedule so as to—
(a) add an entry,
(b) vary an entry, or
(c) remove an entry.

Commencement

Brought into force by the Gambling Act 2005 (Commencement No 5) Order 2006, SI 2006/3220, art 2 as from 5 December 2006.

Para 23: Secretary of State. See the note to s 4.

Application

See the note to s 65.

Subordinate Legislation under this Part of this Schedule. Gambling Act 2005 (Relevant Offences) (Amendment) Order 2006, SI 2006/3391 (made under para 23).

As to orders under this Act generally, see s 355.

Explanatory Notes

352–355 [para **6.2008** below]

SCHEDULE 8

. . . [1]

. . . [1]

[1] Repealed by SI 2010/22, art 5(1), Sch 2, paras 93, 105.

SCHEDULE 9
APPLICATIONS FOR CASINO PREMISES LICENCES
Section 175

Introduction

[6.877]

1. (1) This Schedule applies to an application for a casino premises licence of a kind in respect of which a limit under section 175 has effect.

(2) An application for the variation or transfer of a premises licence is not to be treated for the purposes of this Schedule as an application for a premises licence (despite sections 187(3) and 188(2)).

Competition for licences

2. (1) Before considering an application to which this Schedule applies a licensing authority shall comply with regulations of the Secretary of State about inviting competing applications.

(2) The regulations shall, in particular, make provision—

(a) about the publication of invitations (including provision as to the manner and timing of publication and the matters to be published), and

(b) about the timing of responses.

Two-stage consideration

3. Paragraph 4 applies where (whether or not as a result of the competition provided for by paragraph 2)—

(a) a number of applications for a casino premises licence are made to a licensing authority ('the competing applications'), and

(b) as a result of section 175 and the order under it the authority are able to grant one or more, but not all, of the competing applications.

4. (1) The licensing authority shall first consider in respect of each application whether they would grant it under section 163 if section 175 did not apply.

(2) For that purpose—

(a) the authority shall not have regard to whether any of the other competing applications is more deserving of being granted,

(b) subject to paragraph (a), each competing applicant is an interested party in relation to each of the other competing applications, and

(c) Part 8 shall apply, but with the substitution for a reference to the grant of an application in sections 163(1)(a) and 206(2) of a reference to a provisional decision to grant an application subject to the provisions of paragraph 5 below.

5. (1) This paragraph applies if a licensing authority determine under paragraph 4 that they would grant a number of competing applications greater than the number which they can grant as a result of section 175 and the order under it.

(2) The authority shall then determine which of those applications to grant under section 163(1)(a).

(3) For that purpose the authority—

(a) shall determine which of the competing applications would, in the authority's opinion, be likely if granted to result in the greatest benefit to the authority's area,

(b) may enter into a written agreement with an applicant, whether as to the provision of services in respect of the authority's area or otherwise,

(c) may determine to attach conditions under section 169 to any licence issued so as to give effect to an agreement entered into under paragraph (b), and

(d) may have regard to the effect of an agreement entered into under paragraph (b) in making the determination specified in paragraph (a).

(4) Having determined to grant one or more applications under sub-paragraph (2) the authority shall—

(a) grant that application or those applications under section 163(1)(a), and

(b) reject the other competing applications under section 163(1)(b).

(5) The list in section 164(1)(a) shall be treated as including any competing applicant whose application the authority decided provisionally to grant under paragraph 4.

6. (1) The Secretary of State may issue a code of practice about—

(a) the procedure to be followed in making the determinations required by paragraphs 4 and 5, and

(b) matters to which a licensing authority should have regard in making those determinations.

(2) A licensing authority shall comply with a code of practice under sub-paragraph (1).

7. (1) Where a licensing authority issue a casino premises licence following a determination to grant an application in accordance with paragraph 5, a condition attached to the licence under section 169 may, in particular, give effect to any agreement entered into under paragraph 5(3)(b) above.

(2) In that case—

(a) the condition shall refer to the agreement,

(b) a copy of the agreement shall be attached to the licence, and

(c) a variation of the agreement shall have effect only if accompanied by variation of the condition under section 187.

8. (1) An appeal may be brought under section 206(1) or (2) in respect of a decision under paragraph 4.

(2) While an appeal under section 206 could be brought by virtue of sub-paragraph (1), or has been brought by virtue of that sub-paragraph and has not yet been either finally determined or abandoned, the licensing authority shall take no action under paragraph 5(2).

(3) Sub-paragraph (2) has effect in place of section 208 in respect of an appeal by virtue of sub-paragraph (1).

(4) No appeal may be brought under section 206 in respect of a decision under paragraph 5.

Provisional statements

9. A reference in this Schedule to an application for a casino premises licence includes a reference to an application for a provisional statement where this Schedule would apply to an application for a premises licence made in reliance on the provisional statement.

10. (1) This paragraph applies where the process described in paragraphs 3 to 5 results in the issue of a provisional statement.

(2) Paragraphs 2 to 5 shall not apply by reason only of the fact that an application for a casino premises licence is made—

(a) in reliance on the provisional statement, and

(b) while it has effect.

(3) The licensing authority may provide in the provisional statement for it to cease to have effect at the end of a specified period.

(4) A licensing authority may extend a period specified under sub-paragraph (3) on the application of the person to whom the provisional statement is issued; and—

(a) the Secretary of State may by regulations provide for the procedure to be followed in relation to an application under this subsection, and

(b) sections 206 to 209 shall apply but—

(i) with the omission of section 206(2)(a),

(ii) as if section 208(1) referred not to a determination or other action under this Part but to a provision included in a provisional statement under sub-paragraph (3) above, and

(iii) with any other necessary modifications.

Commencement

Brought into force by the Gambling Act 2005 (Commencement No 6 and Transitional Provisions) Order 2006, SI 2006/3272, art 2, Sch 3 as from 1 June 2007; for transitional provisions see art 6, Sch 4 thereto (as amended by SI 2007/1157, arts 7–12). Appointment (for certain purposes): 20 May 2008: see SI 2008/1326, art 2, Schedule.

Para 1: Premises licence. As to the nature, etc of premises licences, see s 150 and the note 'Premises licence' thereto.

Para 2: Licensing authority. For the licensing authorities for the purposes of this Act, see s 2. As to the licensing authorities' functions, see ss 153–155.

Para 2: Secretary of State. See the note to s 4.

Para 5: Written. See the note 'Writing' to s 39.

Para 9: Provisional statement. See s 204, 205.

Para 10: Person. See the note 'Persons' to s 23.

Para 10: This Part. Ie Pt 8 (ss 150–213 and Sch 9) of this Act.

Application

See the note to s 150.

Subordinate Legislation

Gambling (Inviting Competing Applications for Large and Small Casino Premises Licences) Regulations 2008, SI 2008/469 (made under para 2).

As to regulations under this Act generally, see s 355.

Definitions

'a licensing authority': ss 2, 353(1)
'the licensing authority': s 213(f)
'premises licence': s 353(1)

'publication': s 353(2)(j)

Explanatory Notes

458–460 [para **6.2011** below]

SCHEDULE 10
FAMILY ENTERTAINMENT CENTRE GAMING MACHINE PERMITS
Section 247

Interpretation

[6.878]

1. In this Schedule—
'holder', in relation to a permit, means the person to whom the permit is issued,
'the licensing authority'—
(a) in relation to an application, means the licensing authority to whom the application is made, and
(b) in relation to a permit, means the licensing authority who issue it,
'permit' means a family entertainment centre gaming machine permit,
'the premises', in relation to an application or permit, means the premises in respect of which the permit is sought or issued, and
'prescribed' means prescribed by regulations made by the Secretary of State except that in paragraphs 5(d) and 21(2) it means, where the application is made to a licensing authority in Scotland, prescribed by regulations made by the Scottish Ministers.

Making of application

2. (1) An application for a permit may be made only by a person who—
(a) occupies or proposes to occupy the premises, and
(b) proposes to use the premises as an unlicensed family entertainment centre.

(2) If the applicant for a permit is an individual, he must be an adult.

3. An application for a permit may not be made if a premises licence has effect in respect of the premises.

4. An application for a permit must be made to a licensing authority in whose area the premises are wholly or partly situated.

5. An application for a permit must—
(a) be made in such form and manner as the licensing authority may direct,
(b) specify the premises in respect of which the permit is sought,
(c) contain or be accompanied by such other information or documents as the licensing authority may direct, and
(d) be accompanied by the prescribed fee[1].

Consideration of application

6. Sections 154 and 155 shall have effect in relation to the functions of a licensing authority under this Schedule as they have effect in relation to functions of a licensing authority under Part 8.

7. (1) A licensing authority may prepare a statement of principles that they propose to apply in exercising their functions under this Schedule.

(2) A statement under sub-paragraph (1) may, in particular, specify matters that the licensing authority proposes to consider in determining the suitability of an applicant for a permit.

(3) In exercising their functions under this Schedule a licensing authority—

(a) need not (but may) have regard to the licensing objectives, and
(b) shall have regard to any relevant guidance issued by the Commission under section 25.

Determination of application

8. (1) On considering an application for a permit a licensing authority may—
(a) grant it, or
(b) refuse it.

(2) A licensing authority may not attach conditions to a permit.

(3) As soon as is reasonably practicable after granting an application a licensing authority shall issue a permit to the applicant.

(4) As soon as is reasonably practicable after refusing an application a licensing authority shall notify the applicant of—
(a) the refusal, and
(b) the reasons for it.

9. A licensing authority may grant an application for a permit only if they—
(a) are satisfied that the applicant intends to use the premises as an unlicensed family entertainment centre, and
(b) have consulted the chief officer of police for a police area in which the premises are wholly or partly situated.

10. (1) A licensing authority may not refuse an application unless they have—
(a) notified the applicant of their intention to refuse the application and of their reasons, and
(b) given the applicant an opportunity to make representations.

(2) A licensing authority may satisfy sub-paragraph (1)(b) by giving the applicant an opportunity to make—
(a) oral representations,
(b) written representations, or
(c) both.

Form of permit

11. (1) A permit must be in the prescribed form[2] and must specify—
(a) the person to whom it is issued,
(b) the premises, and
(c) the date on which it takes effect.

(2) If the person to whom a permit is issued changes his name or wishes to be known by another name—
(a) he may send the permit to the licensing authority with—
(i) the prescribed fee[3], and
(ii) a request that a new name be substituted for the old name, and
(b) the licensing authority shall comply with the request and return the permit to the holder.

Duration

12. A permit shall cease to have effect at the end of the period of ten years beginning with the date specified under paragraph 11(1)(c) unless—
(a) it ceases to have effect before that time in accordance with a provision of this Schedule, or
(b) it is renewed in accordance with paragraph 18.

13. (1) A permit shall lapse if the holder ceases to occupy the premises specified under paragraph 11(1)(b).

6: Gambling Act 2005: Statutes

(2) A permit shall not take effect if on the date specified under paragraph 11(1)(c) the person to whom the permit is issued is not an occupier of the premises specified under paragraph 11(1)(b).

14. A permit shall lapse if the licensing authority notify the holder that the premises are not being used as a family entertainment centre.

15. (1) A permit held by an individual shall lapse if—

(a) he dies,

(b) he becomes, in the opinion of the licensing authority as notified to him, incapable of carrying on the activities authorised by the permit by reason of mental or physical incapacity,

(c) he becomes bankrupt (within the meaning of section 381 of the Insolvency Act 1986 (c 45)) [or a debt relief order is made in respect of him (under Part 7A of the Insolvency Act 1986)], or

(d) sequestration of his estate is awarded under section 12(1) of the Bankruptcy (Scotland) Act 1985 (c 66).

(2) In any other case a permit shall lapse if the holder—

(a) ceases to exist, or

(b) goes into liquidation (within the meaning of section 247(2) of the Insolvency Act 1986).

(3) During the period of six months beginning with the date on which a permit lapses under this paragraph the following may rely on it as if it had effect and were issued to them—

(a) the personal representatives of the holder (in the case of an individual holder who dies),

(b) the trustee of the bankrupt's estate (in the case of an individual holder who becomes bankrupt), and

(c) the liquidator of the company (in the case of a company holder that goes into liquidation).

16. A permit shall cease to have effect if the holder gives to the licensing authority—

(a) notice of surrender, and

(b) either—

(i) the permit, or

(ii) a statement explaining why it is not reasonably practicable to produce the permit.

17. (1) Where the holder of a permit is convicted of a relevant offence the court by or before which he is convicted may order forfeiture of the permit.

(2) Forfeiture under this paragraph shall be on such terms (which may include terms as to suspension) as may be specified by—

(a) the court which orders forfeiture,

(b) a court to which an appeal against the conviction, or against any order made on the conviction, has been or could be made, or

(c) the High Court, if hearing proceedings relating to the conviction.

(3) Subject to any express provision made under sub-paragraph (2), a permit shall cease to have effect on the making of a forfeiture order under this paragraph.

(4) The terms on which forfeiture is ordered under this paragraph shall, in particular, include a requirement that the holder of the permit deliver to the licensing authority within such time as the order may specify—

(a) the permit, or

(b) a statement explaining why it is not reasonably practicable to produce the permit.

(5) As soon as is reasonably practicable after making or suspending an order for forfeiture under this paragraph a court shall notify the licensing authority.

Renewal

18. (1) The holder of a permit may apply to the licensing authority for renewal[4] of the permit.

(2) An application for renewal may not be made—

(a) before the period of six months ending with the date on which the permit would otherwise expire in accordance with paragraph 12, or

(b) after the beginning of the period of two months ending with that date.

(3) The provisions of this Schedule shall have effect (with any necessary modifications) in relation to an application for renewal as they have effect in relation to an application for a permit.

(4) A licensing authority may refuse an application for renewal of a permit only on the grounds—

(a) that an authorised local authority officer has been refused access to the premises without reasonable excuse, or

(b) that renewal would not be reasonably consistent with pursuit of the licensing objectives.

(5) Paragraph 12 shall have effect in relation to a renewed permit as if the date of renewal were the date specified under paragraph 11(1)(c).

(6) A permit shall not cease to have effect by virtue only of paragraph 12 while—

(a) an application for renewal of the permit is pending, or

(b) an appeal against a decision on an application for renewal of the permit is pending.

Maintenance

19. The holder of a permit shall keep it on the premises.

20. (1) An occupier of premises in respect of which a permit has effect commits an offence if without reasonable excuse he fails to produce the permit on request for inspection by—

(a) a constable,

(b) an enforcement officer, or

(c) an authorised local authority officer.

(2) A person guilty of an offence under this paragraph shall be liable on summary conviction to a fine not exceeding level 2 on the standard scale.

21. (1) Where a permit is lost, stolen or damaged, the holder may apply to the licensing authority for a copy.

(2) An application under sub-paragraph (1) must be accompanied by the prescribed fee.[5]

(3) A licensing authority shall consider an application under this paragraph and shall grant it if satisfied—

(a) that the permit has been lost, stolen or damaged, and

(b) where the permit has been lost or stolen, that the loss or theft has been reported to the police.

(4) As soon as is reasonably practicable after granting an application under this paragraph a licensing authority shall issue a copy of the permit certified by the authority as a true copy.

(5) A copy of a permit issued under this paragraph shall be treated as if it were the permit.

Appeal

22. (1) The applicant for or holder of a permit may appeal if the licensing authority—

(a) reject an application for the issue or renewal of a permit,

6: Gambling Act 2005: Statutes

(b) give a notice under paragraph 14, or
(c) give a notice under paragraph 15(1)(b).

(2) An appeal under this paragraph must be instituted—
(a) in the magistrates' court for a local justice area in which the premises to which the appeal relates are wholly or partly situated,
(b) by notice of appeal given to the designated officer, and
(c) within the period of 21 days beginning with the day on which the appellant or holder receives notice of the decision against which the appeal is brought.

(3) On an appeal the magistrates' court may—
(a) dismiss the appeal;
(b) substitute for the decision appealed against any decision that the licensing authority could have made (with effect from such date and on such transitional or other terms as the court may specify);
(c) restore a permit (with effect from such date and on such transitional or other terms as the court may specify);
(d) remit the case to the licensing authority to decide in accordance with a direction of the court;
(e) make an order about costs.

(4) Sub-paragraph (1) applies to a decision of a licensing authority following remittal under sub-paragraph (3)(d).

(5) In relation to premises in Scotland—
(a) sub-paragraph (2)(a) shall have effect as if it referred to a sheriff within whose sheriffdom the premises are wholly or partly situated,
(b) sub-paragraph (2)(b) shall not have effect,
(c) the reference in sub-paragraph (3) to the magistrates' court shall have effect as a reference to the sheriff, and
(d) the reference in sub-paragraph (3) to costs shall have effect as a reference to expenses.

Register

23. (1) A licensing authority shall—
(a) maintain a register of permits issued by the authority together with such other information as may be prescribed,
(b) make the register and information available for inspection by members of the public at all reasonable times, and
(c) make arrangements for the provision of a copy of an entry in the register, or of information, to a member of the public on request.

(2) A licensing authority may refuse to provide a copy of an entry or of information unless the person seeking it pays a reasonable fee specified by the authority.

(3) The Secretary of State may make regulations about—
(a) the form of the register;
(b) the manner in which it is maintained.

(4) The Secretary of State may make regulations—
(a) requiring licensing authorities to give to the Commission specified information about permits issued by them;
(b) requiring the Commission to maintain a register of the information provided to it under paragraph (a);
(c) requiring the Commission to grant access to the register to members of the public (without charge);
(d) requiring the Commission to make copies of entries available on request, and on payment of a reasonable fee, to members of the public;

(e) excusing licensing authorities, wholly or partly, from compliance with sub-paragraph (1).

Vehicles and vessels

24. A permit may not be issued in respect of a vehicle or vessel (or part of a vehicle or vessel).

Commencement

Paras 1, 7(1), (2): brought into force as from 13 November 2006 by the Gambling Act 2005 (Commencement No 4) Order 2006, SI 2006/2964, art 2.

Paras 2–6, 8–11, 22 brought into force for certain purposes as from 30 April 2007 by the Gambling Act 2005 (Commencement No 6 and Transitional Provisions) Order 2006, SI 2006/3272, art 2, Sch 2; for transitional provisions see art 6, Sch 4 thereto (as amended by SI 2007/1157, arts 7–12).

Paras 2, 6, 8–11, 22 Appointment (for remaining purposes): 1 September 2007 by the Gambling Act 2005 (Commencement No 6 and Transitional Provisions) Order 2006, SI 2006/3272, art 2; for transitional provisions see art 6, Sch 4 thereto (as amended by SI 2007/1157, arts 7–12).

Para 7(3) brought into force for the purpose of enabling a licensing authority to carry out their functions under para 7(1), (2) as from 13 November 2006 by the Gambling Act 2005 (Commencement No 6 and Transitional Provisions) Order 2006, SI 2006/2964, art 2, for remaining purposes as from 30 April 2007 by the Gambling Act 2005 (Commencement No 6 and Transitional Provisions) Order 2006, SI 2006/3272, art 2, Sch 2; for transitional provisions see art 6, Sch 4 thereto (as amended by SI 2007/1157, arts 7–12).

Paras 12(a), 13, 15–17, 21, 23, 24: brought into force as from 30 April 2007 by the Gambling Act 2005 (Commencement No 6 and Transitional Provisions) Order 2006, SI 2006/3272, art 2, Sch 2; for transitional provisions see art 6, Sch 4 thereto (as amended by SI 2007/1157, arts 7–12).

Paras 12(b), 14, 18–20: Appointment: 1 September 2007 by the Gambling Act 2005 (Commencement No 6 and Transitional Provisions) Order 2006, 2006/3272, art 2; for transitional provisions see art 6, Sch 4 thereto (as amended by SI 2007/1157, arts 7–12).

Amendment

Para 15: in para (1)(c) words in square brackets inserted by SI 2012/2404, art 3(2), Sch 2, para 55.

Para 1: Person. See the note 'Persons' to s 23.

Para 1: Licensing authority. For the licensing authorities for the purposes of this Act, see s 2.

Para 1: Secretary of State. See the note to s 4.

Para 1: Scottish Ministers. See the note to s 25.

Para 3: Premises licence. As to the nature, etc of premises licences, see s 150 and the note 'Premises licence' thereto.

Para 6: Part 8. Ie Pt 8 (ss 150–213 and Sch 9) of this Act.

Para 7: The Commission. Ie the Gambling Commission; see s 353(1). As to the establishment, etc of the Gambling Commission, see s 20, Sch 4, and the note 'Gambling Commission' to that section.

Para 8: Notify. See further, in connection with a requirement under this Act to give a notice, s 353(4).

Para 9: Chief officer of police. See the note to s 349.

Para 9: Police area. See the note to s 157.

Para 10: Written. See the note 'Writing' to s 39.

Para 15: Months. See the note to s 76.

Para 17: High Court. See the note to s 115.

Para 20: Offence. For the power of the Gambling Commission and other specified persons to undertake activities for the purpose of assessing whether an offence is being committed under or by virtue of this Act, see ss 27, 305; for the power of that Commission to investigate and prosecute offences, see s 28; as to offences committed by a body, see s 341; and for the time limit on prosecutions, see s 347. See also s 306 for powers of entry as respects a suspected offence, and s 345 as respects forfeiture of an article relating to an offence. For territorial limitations on offences under this Part of this Act, see ss 359, 360.

For penalties, see s 246.

For the power of a licensing authority to institute criminal proceedings in respect of an offence under para 20 above, see s 346.

Para 20: Constable. See the note to s 64.

Para 20: Enforcement officer. As to enforcement officers, see, generally, s 303.

Para 20: Summary conviction; standard scale. See the notes to s 33.

Para 22: Magistrates' court. See the note to s 207.

Territorial application. For the territorial application of this Part of this Act, see s 251.

Subordinate Legislation

Gambling Act 2005 (Family Entertainment Centre Gaming Machine) (Permits) Regulations 2007, SI 2007/454 (made under paras 5(d), 11, 18(3), 21(2)).

As to regulations under this Act generally, see s 355.

Definitions

'adult': s 353(1)
'authorised local authority officer': ss 304, 353(1)
'the Commission': s 353(1)
'enforcement officer': s 353(1)
'family entertainment centre': ss 238, 353(1)
'family entertainment centre gaming machine permit': ss 247(2), 353(1)
'licensing authority: ss 2, 353(1)
'the licensing objectives': ss 1, 353(1)
'premises': s 353(1), (2)(g)
'premises licence': s 353(1)
'relevant offence': ss 126(2), (3), 353(1), Sch 7
'vehicle': s 353(1)
'vessel': s 353(1)

Explanatory Notes

608–612 [para **6.2013** below]

---

1 See SI 2007/454, reg 3.

2 SI 2007/454, reg 4 and Sch 1.

3 SI 2007/454, reg 5.

4 See SI 2007/454, reg 3(c).

5 See SI 2007/454, reg 6.

SCHEDULE 11
EXEMPT LOTTERIES
Section 258

6.879–6.880

Explanatory Notes

647, 648 [para **6.2014** below]

PART 1
INCIDENTAL NON-COMMERCIAL LOTTERIES

The exemption

1. (1) A lottery is exempt if—

(a) it is incidental to a non-commercial event within the meaning of paragraph 2 ('the connected event'), and

(b) the conditions specified in this Part are satisfied.

(2) A lottery to which sub-paragraph (1) applies is referred to in this Part as an incidental non-commercial lottery.

2. An event is non-commercial if no sum raised by the organisers of the event (whether by way of fees for entrance or for participation, by way of sponsorship, by way of commission from traders or otherwise) is appropriated for the purpose of private gain.

Deductions from proceeds[1]

3. The promoters of an incidental non-commercial lottery may not deduct from the proceeds of the lottery more than the prescribed sum in respect of the cost of the prizes (irrespective of their actual cost).

4. The promoters of an incidental non-commercial lottery may not deduct from the proceeds of the lottery more than the prescribed sum in respect of costs incurred in organising the lottery (irrespective of the amount of the costs incurred).

Purpose of lottery

5. An incidental non-commercial lottery must be promoted wholly for a purpose other than that of private gain.

No rollover

6. The arrangements for an incidental non-commercial lottery must not include a rollover.

Connection between lottery and event

7. (1) No lottery ticket for an incidental non-commercial lottery may be sold or supplied otherwise than—

(a) on the premises on which the connected event takes place, and

(b) while the connected event is taking place.

(2) The results of the lottery must be made public while the connected event is taking place.

Interpretation: 'prescribed'

8. In this Part 'prescribed' means prescribed by the Secretary of State by regulations.

Commencement

Paragraphs 1 to 8, 10 to 12, 20, 30 and 31 brought into force for the purposes of ss 17 and 18 by the Gambling Act 2005 (Commencement No 2 and Transitional Provisions) Order 2005, SI 2005/2455, art 2 and Schedule, as from 1 October 2005. Brought into force for remaining purposes as from 1 September 2007 by the Gambling Act 2005 (Commencement No 4) Order 2006, SI 2006/2964, art 2; for transitional provisions see art 6, Sch 4 thereto (as amended by SI 2007/1157, arts 7–12).

Para 5: Must be promoted wholly for a purpose, etc. Misuse of the profits of an incidental non-commercial lottery is an offence; see s 261.

The promotion of an incidental non-commercial lottery does not constitute a licensable activity by reason only of one or more of the prizes in the lottery consisting of or including alcohol, provided that the alcohol is in a sealed container; see the Licensing Act 2003, s 175, as substituted by s 356(1), Sch 16, para 20.

Para 8: Secretary of State. See the note to s 4.

Exclusion of the National Lottery and territorial application. See ss 264, 265.

Regulations under this Part of this Schedule. At the time of going to press no regulations had been made under this Part of this Schedule.

As to regulations under this Act generally, see s 355.

Definitions

'lottery': ss 14, 353(1)

'lottery ticket': ss 253(1), 353(1)

'premises': s 353(1), (2)(g)
'private gain': ss 19(3), 353(1)
'prize': ss 14(4), 353(1)
'proceeds of a lottery': ss 254(1), 353(1)
'promoting a lottery': ss 252, 353(2)(h)
'rollover': ss 256, 353(1)
'sale or supply of a lottery ticket': ss 253(2), 353(2)(k)
'supply': s 353(1)

Explanatory Notes

649, 650 [para **6.2014** below]

---

1 See SI 2007/2040.

PART 2
PRIVATE LOTTERIES

The exemption

[6.881]

9. (1) A lottery is exempt if—

(a) it is a private society lottery, a work lottery or a residents' lottery within the meaning of paragraphs 10 to 12, and
(b) the other conditions specified in this Part are satisfied.

(2) In this Part a reference to a private lottery is a reference to a private society lottery, a work lottery or a residents' lottery.

Private society lottery

10. (1) A lottery is a private society lottery if—

(a) it is promoted only by authorised members of a society, and
(b) each person to whom a ticket is sold is either a member of the society or on premises wholly or mainly used for the administration of the society or the conduct of its affairs ('society premises').

(2) In this Part 'society' means any group or society established and conducted for purposes not connected with gambling.

(3) In sub-paragraph (1)(a) 'authorised' means authorised in writing by the society or, if it has one, its governing body.

(4) In relation to a society which has branches or sections, the reference to a society in sub-paragraph (1)(a) is a reference to a single branch or section.

Work lottery

11. (1) A lottery is a work lottery if—

(a) the promoters work on a single set of premises ('the work premises'), and
(b) each person to whom a ticket is sold or supplied also works on the work premises.

(2) For the purposes of this paragraph a person works on premises if he—

(a) is employed under a contract of employment to work at or from the premises,
(b) undertakes to work at or from the premises (whether or not for remuneration), or
(c) conducts a business at or from the premises.

Residents' lottery

12. (1) A lottery is a residents' lottery if—

(a) the promoters live in a single set of premises ('the residential premises'), and

(b) each person to whom a ticket is sold or supplied also lives in the residential premises.

(2) For the purposes of this paragraph a person lives in premises if he habitually resides in any part of the premises (whether or not there are other premises in which he also habitually resides).

Purpose of lottery

13. (1) A private society lottery may be promoted for any of the purposes for which the society is conducted.

(2) A work lottery or residents' lottery must be organised in such a way as to ensure that no profits are made.

Advertising

14. (1) No advertisement for a private society lottery may be—

(a) displayed or distributed except on the society premises, or

(b) sent to any other premises.

(2) No advertisement for a work lottery may be—

(a) displayed or distributed except on the work premises, or

(b) sent to any other premises.

(3) No advertisement for a residents' lottery may be—

(a) displayed or distributed except on the residential premises, or

(b) sent to any other premises.

Lottery tickets

15. Each ticket in a private lottery must be a document (without prejudice to section 253).

16. (1) A ticket in a private lottery may be sold or supplied only by or on behalf of the promoters.

(2) The rights conferred by the sale or supply of a ticket in a private lottery shall not be transferable (and any purported transfer shall be treated by the promoters of the lottery as being ineffective).

17. Each ticket in a private lottery—

(a) must state the name and an address of each of the promoters of the lottery,

(b) must specify the class of persons to whom the promoters are willing to sell or supply tickets, and

(c) must explain the condition in paragraph 16(2).

Price

18. The price payable for each ticket in a private lottery—

(a) must be the same,

(b) must be shown on the ticket, and

(c) must be paid to the promoters of the lottery before any person is given the ticket or any right in respect of membership of the class among whom prizes are to be allocated.

No rollover

19. The arrangements for a private lottery must not include a rollover.

Commencement

Paras 9, 13–19 brought into force for remaining purposes as from 1 September 2007 by the Gambling Act 2005 (Commencement No 4) Order 2006, SI 2006/2964, art 2.

Paras 10–12 brought into force for certain purposes as from 1 October by the Gambling Act 2005 (Commencement No 2 and Transitional Provisions) Order 2005, for remaining purposes as from 1 September 2007 by the Gambling Act 2005 (Commencement No 6 and Transitional Provisions) Order 2006, SI 2006/3272, art 2; for transitional provisions see art 6, Sch 4 thereto (as amended by SI 2007/1157, arts 7–12).

Para 10: Writing. See the note to s 39.

Para 13: May be promoted for any of the purposes, etc. Misuse of the profits of a private society lottery is an offence; see s 261.

Exclusion of the National Lottery and territorial application. See ss 264, 265.

Exclusion in relation to vessels. See Pt 7, para 63 of this Schedule.

Definitions

'advertisement': Sch 11, Pt 7, para 61(a), (c)
'advertising gambling': ss 327, 353(2)(b)
'business': Sch 11, Pt 7, para 62
'displaying an advertisement' Sch 11, Pt 7, para 61(b)
'gambling': ss 3, 353(1)
'lottery': ss 14, 353(1)
'lottery ticket': ss 253(1), 353(1)
'premises': s 353(1), (2)(g)
'prize': ss 14(4), 353(1)
'profits of a lottery': ss 254(2), 353(1)
'promoting a lottery': ss 252, 353(2)(h)
'rollover': ss 256, 353(1)
'sale or supply of a lottery ticket': ss 253(2), 353(2)(k)
'society': s 353(1) (and para 10(2), (4) above)
'supply': s 353(1)

Explanatory Notes

651, 652 [para **6.2014** below]

PART 3
CUSTOMER LOTTERY

The exemption

[6.882]

20. (1) A lottery is exempt if—

(a) it is promoted by a person ('the promoter') who occupies premises in Great Britain in the course of a business ('the business premises'),

(b) no ticket in the lottery is sold or supplied to a person except at a time when he is on the business premises as a customer of the promoter, and

(c) the other conditions of a customer lottery specified in this Part are satisfied.

(2) A lottery to which sub-paragraph (1) applies is referred to in this Part as a customer lottery.

(3) For the purposes of sub-paragraph (1)(a)—

(a) it is immaterial whether persons other than the person who occupies the business premises also perform activities which amount to promotion of the lottery in accordance with section 252, but

(b) a reference in this Part to the promoter does not include a reference to any of those other persons.

No profits

21. A customer lottery must be organised in such a way as to ensure that no profits are made.

Advertising

22. No advertisement for a customer lottery may be—

(a) displayed or distributed except on the business premises, or
(b) sent to any other premises.

Lottery tickets

23. Each ticket in a customer lottery must be a document (without prejudice to section 253).

24. (1) A ticket in a customer lottery may be sold or supplied only by or on behalf of the promoter.

(2) The rights conferred by the sale or supply of a ticket in a customer lottery shall not be transferable (and any purported transfer shall be treated by the promoter of the lottery as being ineffective).

25. Each ticket in a customer lottery—

(a) must state the name and an address of the promoter of the lottery,
(b) must specify the class of persons to whom the promoter is willing to sell or supply tickets, and
(c) must explain the condition in paragraph 24(2).

Price

26. The price payable for each ticket in a customer lottery—

(a) must be the same,
(b) must be shown on the ticket, and
(c) must be paid to the promoter of the lottery before any person is given the ticket or any right in respect of membership of the class among whom prizes are to be allocated.

Maximum prize

27. It must not be possible for the purchaser of a ticket in a customer lottery to win by virtue of that ticket more than £50 (whether in money, money's worth, or partly the one and partly the other).

No rollover

28. The arrangements for a customer lottery must not include a rollover.

Frequency

29. A draw in a customer lottery must not take place during a period of seven days beginning with a previous draw in—

(a) that customer lottery, or
(b) another customer lottery promoted on the business premises.

Commencement

Para 20 brought into force for certain purposes as from 1 October 2005 by the Gambling Act 2005 (Commencement No 2 and Transitional Provisions) Order 2005, SI 2005/2455, art 2 and Schedule, for remaining purposes as from 1 September 2007 by the the Gambling Act 2005 (Commencement No 6 and Transitional Provisions) Order 2006, SI 2006/3272, art 2; for transitional provisions see art 6, Sch 4 thereto (as amended by SI 2007/1157, arts 7–12).

Paras 21–29 brought into force as from 1 September 2007 by the Gambling Act 2005 (Commencement No 6 and Transitional Provisions) Order 2006, SI 2006/3272, art 2; for transitional provisions see art 6, Sch 4 thereto (as amended by SI 2007/1157, arts 7–12).

Para 20: Person. See the note 'Persons' to s 23.

Para 20: Great Britain. See the note to s 12.

Para 27: £50. For the power of the Secretary of State to vary this sum, see Pt 6, para 60 of this Schedule.

Exclusion of the National Lottery and territorial application. See ss 264, 265.

Exclusion in relation to vessels. See Pt 7, para 63 of this Schedule.

Definitions

'advertisement': Sch 11, Pt 7, para 61(a), (c)
'advertising gambling': ss 327, 353(2)(b)
'business': Sch 11, Pt 7, para 62
'draw': ss 255, 353(1)
'lottery': ss 14, 353(1)
'lottery ticket': ss 253(1), 353(1)
'premises': s 353(1), (2)(g)
'prize': ss 14(4), 353(1)
'profits of a lottery': ss 254(2), 353(1)
'promoting a lottery': ss 252, 353(2)(h)
'rollover': ss 256, 353(1)
'sale or supply of a lottery ticket': ss 253(2), 353(2)(k)
'supply': s 353(1)

Explanatory Notes

653, 654 [para **6.2014** below]

PART 4
SMALL SOCIETY LOTTERIES

The exemption

[6.883]

30. (1) A lottery is exempt if—

(a) it is promoted wholly on behalf of a non-commercial society ('the promoting society'),

(b) it is a small lottery (within the meaning of paragraph 31), and

(c) the other conditions of a small society lottery specified in this Part are satisfied.

(2) A lottery promoted wholly on behalf of a non-commercial society is referred to in this Part as a small society lottery.

31. (1) For the purposes of this Part a society lottery is a small lottery unless it is a large lottery by virtue of any of sub-paragraphs (2) to (5).

(2) A society lottery is a large lottery if the arrangements for it are such that its proceeds may exceed £20,000.

(3) A society lottery is a large lottery if it is promoted wholly or partly at a time in a calendar year at which the aggregate of the promoting society's proceeds from society lotteries promoted wholly or partly during that year exceeds £250,000.

(4) A society lottery is a large lottery if the arrangements for it are such that (disregarding any other society lottery the sale of tickets for which is not concluded) it may during its promotion become a large lottery by virtue of sub-paragraph (3).

(5) If a society promotes a lottery that is a large society lottery by virtue of sub-paragraph (2), (3) or (4) ('the first lottery'), any other society lottery promoted by that society is a large lottery if it is wholly or partly promoted—

(a) after the beginning of the promotion of the first lottery and in a calendar year during which the first lottery is wholly or partly promoted, or

(b) in any of the three calendar years successively following the last calendar year during which the first lottery was wholly or partly promoted.

Purpose of lottery

32. A small society lottery may be promoted for any of the purposes for which the promoting society is conducted.

Minimum distribution for fund-raising purpose

33. The arrangements for a small society lottery must ensure that at least 20% of the proceeds of the lottery are applied to a purpose for which the society is conducted.

Maximum prize

34. It must not be possible for the purchaser of a ticket in a small society lottery to win by virtue of that ticket (whether in money, money's worth, or partly the one and partly the other) more than £25,000.

Rollover

35. (1) The arrangements for a small society lottery may include a rollover only if each other lottery which may be affected by the rollover is a small society lottery promoted by or on behalf of the same society.

(2) This paragraph is subject to paragraph 34.

Tickets

36. (1) Where a person purchases a lottery ticket in a small society lottery he must receive a document which—

(a) identifies the promoting society,

(b) states the price of the ticket,

(c) states the name and an address of—

(i) a member of the society who is designated, by persons acting on behalf of the society, as having responsibility within the society for the promotion of the lottery, or

(ii) if there is one, the external lottery manager, and

(d) either—

(i) states the date of the draw (or each draw) in the lottery, or

(ii) enables the date of the draw (or each draw) in the lottery to be determined.

(2) For the purpose of sub-paragraph (1) a reference to a person receiving a document includes, in particular, a reference to a message being sent or displayed to him electronically in a manner which enables him to—

(a) retain the message electronically, or

(b) print it.

Price

37. (1) The price payable for each ticket in a small society lottery—

(a) must be the same, and

(b) must be paid to the promoter of the lottery before any person is given the ticket or any right in respect of membership of the class among whom prizes are to be allocated.

(2) Membership of the class among whom prizes in a small society lottery are allocated may not be dependent on making any payment (apart from payment of the price of a ticket).

Registration

38. The promoting society of a small society lottery must, throughout the period during which the lottery is promoted, be registered with a local authority in accordance with Part 5 of this Schedule.

Filing of records

39. (1) The promoting society of a small society lottery must send to the local authority with which the society is registered under Part 5 of this Schedule a statement of the matters specified in sub-paragraph (2).

(2) Those matters are—

(a) the arrangements for the lottery (including the dates on which tickets were available for sale or supply, the dates of any draw and the arrangements for prizes (including any rollover),

(b) the proceeds of the lottery,

(c) the amounts deducted by the promoters of the lottery in respect of the provision of prizes (including the provision of prizes in accordance with any rollover),

(d) the amounts deducted by the promoters of the lottery in respect of other costs incurred in organising the lottery,

(e) any amount applied to a purpose for which the promoting society is conducted, and

(f) whether any expenses in connection with the lottery were defrayed otherwise than by deduction from proceeds, and, if they were—

(i) the amount of the expenses, and

(ii) the sources from which they were defrayed.

(3) The statement must be sent to the local authority during the period of three months beginning with the day on which the draw (or the last draw) in the lottery takes place.

(4) The statement must be—

(a) signed by two members of the society who are appointed for the purpose in writing by the society or, if it has one, its governing body, and

(b) accompanied by a copy of the appointment under paragraph (a).

(5) A member signing a statement in accordance with sub-paragraph (4) must be an adult.

40. (1) If after receiving a statement under paragraph 39 a local authority think that the lottery to which the statement relates was a large lottery, they shall notify the Commission in writing.

(2) A notice under sub-paragraph (1) shall be accompanied by a copy of—

(a) the statement relating to the lottery, and

(b) the statement relating to any other lottery as a result of which the lottery mentioned in paragraph (a) is a large lottery.

Commencement

Paras 30, 31 brought into force for certain purposes as from 1 October 2005 by the Gambling Act 2005 (Commencement No 2 and Transitional Provisions) Order 2005, SI 2005/2455, art 2 and Schedule, for remaining purposes as from 1 September 2007 the Gambling Act 2005 (Commencement No 6 and Transitional Provisions) Order 2006, SI 2006/3272, art 2; for transitional provisions see art 6, Sch 4 thereto (as amended by SI 2007/1157, arts 7–12).

Paras 32–40 brought into force as from 1 September 2007 by the Gambling Act 2005 (Commencement No 6 and Transitional Provisions) Order 2006, SI 2006/3272, art 2; for transitional provisions see art 6, Sch 4 thereto (as amended by SI 2007/1157, arts 7–12).

Para 31: £20,000; £250,000. For the power of the Secretary of State to vary these sums, see Pt 6, para 60 of this Schedule.

Para 32: May be promoted for any of the purposes, etc. Misuse of the profits of a small society lottery is an offence; see s 261.

Para 33: 20%. For the power of the Secretary of State to vary this percentage, see Pt 6, para 60 of this Schedule.

Para 34: £25,000. For the power of the Secretary of State to vary this sum, see Pt 6, para 60 of this Schedule.

Para 39: Must send to the local authority, etc. A non-commercial society commits an offence if the society fails to comply with the requirements of para 39 above or the society provides false or misleading information for the purposes of that paragraph; see s 262.

Para 39: Months. See the note to s 76.

Para 39: Writing. See the note to s 39.

Para 40: Notify. See further, in connection with a requirement under this Act to give a notice, s 353(4).

Para 40: The Commission. Ie the Gambling Commission; see s 353(1). As to the establishment, etc of the Gambling Commission, see s 20, Sch 4, and the note 'Gambling Commission' to that section.

Exclusion of the National Lottery and territorial application. See ss 264, 265.

Definitions

'adult': s 353(1)
'the Commission': s 353(1)
'draw': ss 255, 353(1)
'external lottery manager': ss 257, 353(1)
'lottery': ss 14, 353(1)
'lottery ticket': ss 253(1), 353(1)
'non-commercial society': ss 19, 353(1)
'proceeds of a lottery' ss 254(1), 353(1)
'promoting a lottery': ss 252, 353(2)(h)
'prize': ss 14(4), 353(1)
'purchase of a lottery ticket': ss 253(3), 353(2)(k)
'rollover': ss 256, 353(1)
'sale or supply of a lottery ticket': ss 253(2), 353(2)(k)
'supply': s 353(1)

Explanatory Notes

655–663 [para **6.2014** below]

PART 5
REGISTRATION WITH LOCAL AUTHORITY

Local authority

[6.884]

41. In this Part 'local authority' means—
(a) in relation to England—
(i) a district council,

(ii) a county council for a county in which there are no district councils,
(iii) a London borough council,
(iv) the Common Council of the City of London, and
(v) the Council of the Isles of Scilly,

(b) in relation to Wales,
(i) a county council, and
(ii) a county borough council, and

(c) in relation to Scotland, a licensing board [continued in existence by or established under section 5 of the Licensing (Scotland) Act 2005 (asp 16)] [4].

Application

42. (1) A society may apply to the relevant local authority for registration under this Part.

(2) An application under this paragraph—[1]

(a) must be in the prescribed form,
(b) must specify the purposes for which the society is conducted,
(c) must contain such other information, and be accompanied by such documents, as may be prescribed, and
(d) must be accompanied by the prescribed fee.

43. In relation to the registration of a society, the relevant local authority is the local authority for the area in which the principal premises of the society are situated.

Registration

44. As soon as is reasonably practicable after receipt of an application under paragraph 42 a local authority shall, subject to paragraphs 47 and 48—

(a) enter the applicant, together with such information as may be prescribed [2], in a register kept by the authority for the purposes of this Part,
(b) notify the applicant of his registration, and
(c) notify the Commission of the registration.

Gambling Commission

45. As soon as is reasonably practicable after receipt of notice of a registration under paragraph 44(c) the Commission shall record the registration.

46. (1) A notice under paragraph 44(c) must be accompanied by such part of the application fee as may be prescribed.

(2) In sub-paragraph (1) 'application fee' means the fee accompanying an application under paragraph 42.

Refusal of registration

47. A local authority shall refuse an application for registration if in the period of five years ending with the date of the application—

(a) an operating licence held by the applicant for registration has been revoked under section 119(1), or
(b) an application for an operating licence made by the applicant for registration has been refused.

48. A local authority may refuse an application for registration if they think that—

(a) the applicant is not a non-commercial society,
(b) a person who will or may be connected with the promotion of the lottery has been convicted of a relevant offence, or

(c) information provided in or with the application for registration is false or misleading.

49. A local authority may not refuse an application for registration unless they have given the applicant an opportunity to make representations.

Revocation

50. (1) A local authority may revoke a registration under this Part if they think that they would be obliged or permitted to refuse an application for the registration were it being made anew.

(2) Where a local authority revoke a registration under this Part they shall specify that the revocation takes effect—

(a) immediately, or

(b) at the end of such period, beginning with the day of the revocation and not exceeding two months, as they may specify.

(3) A local authority may not revoke a registration under this Part unless they have given the registered society an opportunity to make representations.

Appeal

51. (1) If a local authority refuse or revoke registration under this Part—

(a) the authority shall notify the applicant society or the formerly registered society as soon as is reasonably practicable, and

(b) the society may appeal to a magistrates' court.

(2) An appeal under this paragraph must be instituted—

(a) in a magistrates' court for a local justice area which is wholly or partly within the area of the local authority against whose decision the appeal is brought,

(b) by notice of appeal given to the designated officer, and

(c) in the period of 21 days beginning with the day on which the society is notified of the refusal or revocation of registration, and

(3) On an appeal under this paragraph a magistrates' court may—

(a) affirm the local authority's decision;

(b) reverse the local authority's decision;

(c) make any other order (which may include transitional provision).

(4) In relation to registration in Scotland—

(a) sub-paragraph (1)(b) shall have effect as if the reference to a magistrate's court were a reference to a sheriff whose sheriffdom is wholly or partly within the area of the local authority against whose decision the appeal is brought,

(b) sub-paragraph (2)(a) and (b) shall not have effect, and

(c) sub-paragraph (3) shall have effect as if the reference to a magistrate's court were a reference to the sheriff.

Cancellation

52. A registered society may apply in writing to the registering authority for the registration to be cancelled.

53. As soon as is reasonably practicable after receipt of an application under paragraph 52 a local authority shall—

(a) cancel the registration,

(b) notify the formerly registered society of the cancellation, and

(c) notify the Commission of the cancellation.

Annual fee[3]

54. (1) A registered society shall pay an annual fee to the registering local authority.

(2) An annual fee—

(a) shall be paid within such period before each anniversary of the registration as may be prescribed, and

(b) shall be of the prescribed amount.

(3) If a registered society fails to comply with this paragraph the registering authority may cancel the society's registration.

(4) If a local authority cancel a registration under sub-paragraph (3) the authority shall as soon as is reasonably practicable notify—

(a) the formerly registered society, and

(b) the Commission.

Retention of records

55. (1) Where a statement is sent to a local authority under paragraph 39 the authority shall—

(a) retain it for at least 18 months,

(b) make it available for inspection by members of the public at all reasonable times, and

(c) make arrangements for the provision of a copy of it or part of it to any member of the public on request.

(2) But a local authority may refuse to provide access or a copy unless the person seeking access or a copy pays a fee specified by the authority.

(3) A local authority may not specify a fee under sub-paragraph (2) which exceeds the reasonable cost of providing the service sought (but in calculating the cost of providing a service to a person the authority may include a reasonable share of expenditure which is referable only indirectly to the provision of that service).

Interpretation: 'prescribed'

56. In this Part 'prescribed' means prescribed by the Secretary of State by regulations except that, in the following provisions, it means prescribed by the Scottish Ministers by regulations—

(a) in paragraph 42(2)(d), where the application is made to a local authority in Scotland,

(b) in paragraph 46(1), where the local authority giving notice is in Scotland, and

(c) in paragraph 54(2)(b), where the registering local authority is in Scotland.

Commencement

Brought into force as from 1 September 2007 by the Gambling Act 2005 (Commencement No 6 and Transitional Provisions) Order 2006, SI 2006/3272, art 2; for transitional provisions see art 6, Sch 4 thereto (as amended by SI 2007/1157, arts 7–12).

Para 41: England; Wales; district council; county council; London borough council; Common Council of the City of London; Isles of Scilly; county borough council. See the notes to s 2.

Para 42: May apply . . . for registration, etc. A non-commercial society commits an offence if a lottery, purporting to be an exempt lottery under Pt 4 of this Schedule, is promoted on the society's behalf wholly or partly at a time when the society is not registered with a local authority under this Part of this Schedule; see s 262.

For powers of entry in connection with a lottery promoted by or on behalf of a society registered in accordance with this Part of this Schedule, see s 314.

Para 44: Notify. See further, in connection with a requirement under this Act to give a notice, s 353(4).

Para 44: The Commission. Ie the Gambling Commission; see s 353(1). As to the establishment, etc of the Gambling Commission, see s 20, Sch 4, and the note 'Gambling Commission' to that section.

Para 47: Operating licence. As to the nature, etc of operating licences, see s 65 and the note 'Operating licences' thereto.

Para 50: Months. See the note to s 76.

Para 51: Magistrates' court. See the note to s 207.

Para 52: Writing. See the note to s 39.

Para 56: Secretary of State. See the note to s 4.

Para 56: Scottish Ministers. See the note to s 25.

Exclusion of the National Lottery and territorial application. See ss 264, 265.

Regulations under this Part of this Schedule. At the time of going to press no regulations had been made under this Part of this Schedule.

As to regulations under this Act generally, see s 355.

Definitions

'the Commission': s 353(1)
'lottery': ss 14, 353(1)
'non-commercial society': ss 19, 353(1)
'operating licence': s 353(1)
'premises': s 353(1), (2)(g)
'promoting a lottery': ss 252, 353(2)(h)
'relevant offence': ss 126(2), (3), 353(1), Sch 7

Explanatory Notes

655–663 [para **6.2014** below]

---

1 See SI 2007/2328.

2 See SI 2007/2328.

3 See SI 2007/2328.

4 Para 41: in sub-para (c) words from "continued in existance" to "the Licensing (Scotland) Act 2005 (asp 16)" in square brackets substituted by SSI 2009/248, art 2(1), Sch 1, Pt 1, para 12(1), (8).

PART 6
POWERS TO IMPOSE ADDITIONAL RESTRICTIONS, &C.

Distributing lottery tickets by

[6.885]

57. (1) The Secretary of State may by regulations impose a condition in relation to exempt lotteries requiring that tickets purchased be delivered to the purchaser by hand at the time of purchase and not by post.

(2) Regulations under this paragraph may apply generally, only in relation to a specified class of lottery or only in specified circumstances.

Rollover

58. (1) The Secretary of State may by regulations impose in relation to exempt lotteries conditions or limitations in respect of the use of a rollover (in addition to any conditions or limitations set out in this Schedule).

(2) Regulations under this paragraph may apply generally, only in relation to a specified class of lottery or only in specified circumstances.

Other additional provision

59. (1) The Secretary of State may by order impose in relation to a class of lottery a condition (in addition to any specified in this Schedule) with which a lottery must comply if it is to be an exempt lottery within the meaning of this Schedule.

(2) A condition imposed under this paragraph may, in particular, relate to—

(a) the persons who may sell or supply lottery tickets;

(b) the persons who may buy lottery tickets;

(c) the circumstances in which lottery tickets are sold or supplied;

(d) the nature of lottery tickets and information appearing on them;

(e) arrangements for advertising the lottery;

(f) the deductions which promoters may make from the proceeds of a lottery.

(3) The Secretary of State may by order restrict the extent to which a person may carry on activities in reliance on an exemption under this Schedule.

(4) An order under sub-paragraph (3) may, in particular, make provision—

(a) restricting the number of lotteries that may be promoted on behalf of a person wholly or partly within a specified period;

(b) prescribing a minimum interval between activity in connection with one lottery promoted on behalf of a person and activity in connection with another lottery promoted on behalf of that person.

(5) Before making an order under this paragraph the Secretary of State must consult the Commission.

Variation of monetary limits and percentages

60. The Secretary of State may by order vary a monetary amount or a percentage in this Schedule.

Commencement

Brought into force as from 1 September 2007 by the Gambling Act 2005 (Commencement No 6 and Transitional Provisions) Order 2006, SI 2006/3272, art 2; for transitional provisions see art 6, Sch 4 thereto (as amended by SI 2007/1157, arts 7–12).

Para 57: Secretary of State. See the note to s 4.

Para 59: Person. See the note 'Persons' to s 23.

Para 59: The Commission. Ie the Gambling Commission; see s 353(1). As to the establishment, etc of the Gambling Commission, see s 20, Sch 4, and the note 'Gambling Commission' to that section.

Exclusion of the National Lottery and territorial application. See ss 264, 265.

Regulations under this Part of this Schedule. At the time of going to press no regulations had been made under this Part of this Schedule.

As to regulations under this Act generally, see s 355.

Orders under this Part of this Schedule. At the time of going to press no orders had been made under this Part of this Schedule.

As to orders under this Act generally, see s 355.

Definitions

'advertising gambling': ss 327, 353(2)(b)
'the Commission': s 353(1)
'exempt lottery': ss 258(5), 353(1)
'lottery': ss 14, 353(1)
'lottery ticket': ss 253(1), 353(1)
'proceeds of a lottery' ss 254(1), 353(1)
'promoting a lottery': ss 252, 353(2)(h)
'purchase of a lottery ticket': ss 253(3), 353(2)(k)
'rollover': ss 256, 353(1)
'sale or supply of a lottery ticket': ss 253(2), 353(2)(k)

'supply': s 353(1)

Explanatory Notes

664–647 [para **6.2014** below]

PART 7
GENERAL

Interpretation: advertisement

[6.886]

61. For the purposes of this Schedule—
- (a) 'advertisement', in relation to a lottery, includes any document, or electronic communication, announcing that a lottery will take place or inviting people to participate in a lottery (in either case whether or not it also gives other information),
- (b) a reference to displaying an advertisement includes a reference to publishing a notice, and
- (c) in the case of an advertisement in the form of an electronic communication, the communication is to be treated as being—
  - (i) distributed to any place at which a person can access it, and
  - (ii) sent to any premises at which a person can access it.

Interpretation: business

62. In this Schedule 'business' includes trade and profession.

Vessels

63. Nothing in Part 2 or 3 of this Schedule applies to anything done on a vessel.

Commencement

Brought into force as from 1 September 2007 by the Gambling Act 2005 (Commencement No 6 and Transitional Provisions) Order 2006, SI 2006/3272, art 2; for transitional provisions see art 6, Sch 4 thereto (as amended by SI 2007/1157, arts 7–12).

Exclusion of the National Lottery and territorial application. See ss 264, 265.

Definitions

'lottery': ss 14, 353(1)
'participating in a lottery': ss 14, 353(2)(c)
'premises': s 353(1), (2)(g)
'publication': s 353(2)(j)
'vessel': s 353(1)

Explanatory Notes

668 [para **6.2014** below]

SCHEDULE 12
CLUB GAMING PERMITS AND CLUB MACHINE PERMITS
Section 274

Application

[6.887]

1. (1) A members' club or miners' welfare institute may apply to a licensing authority for a club gaming permit.

(2) A members club, commercial club or miners' welfare institute may apply to a licensing authority for a club machine permit.

2. An application must—
   (a) be made to a licensing authority in whose area the premises are wholly or partly situated,
   (b) specify the premises in relation to which the permit is sought,
   (c) be made in the prescribed form and manner[1],
   (d) contain or be accompanied by the prescribed information and documents, and
   (e) be accompanied by the prescribed fee.[1]

3. (1) A club or institute making an application for a permit must within the prescribed time[1] send a copy of the application and of any accompanying documents to—
   (a) the Commission, and
   (b) the chief officer of police for any police area in which the premises are wholly or partly situated.

(2) If a club or institute fails to comply with sub-paragraph (1) the application, and any permit issued in response to it, shall have no effect.

Consideration of application

4. A person who receives a copy of an application for a permit in accordance with paragraph 3 may object to the application within the prescribed period of time and in the prescribed manner.[2]

5. The licensing authority to whom an application for a permit is made shall consider the application and—
   (a) grant it, or
   (b) refuse it.

6. (1) A licensing authority may refuse an application for a permit only on one or more of the following grounds (having regard to the matters mentioned in paragraph 27)—
   (a) that the applicant is not—
      (i) in the case of an application for a club gaming permit, a members' club or a miners' welfare institute, or
      (ii) in the case of an application for a club machine permit, a members' club, a commercial club or a miners' welfare institute,
   (b) that the premises on which the applicant conducts its activities are used wholly or mainly by children, by young persons or by both,
   (c) that an offence, or a breach of a condition of a permit, has been committed in the course of gaming activities carried on by the applicant,
   (d) that a permit held by the applicant has been cancelled during the period of ten years ending with the date of the application, or
   (e) that an objection to the application has been made under paragraph 4.

(2) If a licensing authority are satisfied in relation to an application for a permit of the matters specified in sub-paragraph (1)(a) or (b), they shall refuse the application.

7. (1) Before refusing an application for a permit a licensing authority must hold a hearing to consider the application and any objection made under paragraph 4.

(2) But a licensing authority may dispense with the requirement for a hearing with the consent of—
   (a) the applicant, and
   (b) any person who has made (and not withdrawn) an objection under paragraph 4.

8. (1) Where a licensing authority grant an application for a permit they shall as soon as is reasonably practicable—

(a) give notice of their decision and, where an objection was made under paragraph 4, of the reasons for it to—
(i) the applicant,
(ii) the Commission, and
(iii) the chief officer of police for any area in which the premises specified in the application are wholly or partly situated, and

(b) issue the permit to the applicant.

(2) A licensing authority may not attach conditions to a permit.

9. Where a licensing authority reject an application for a permit they shall as soon as is reasonably practicable give notice of their decision and the reasons for it to—
(a) the applicant,
(b) the Commission, and
(c) the chief officer of police for any area in which the premises specified in the application are wholly or partly situated.

Fast-track procedure for holder of club premises certificate

10. (1) This paragraph applies to an application if—
(a) the applicant for a permit is the holder of a club premises certificate under section 72 of the Licensing Act 2003 (c 17), and
(b) the application asserts that paragraph (a) is satisfied and is accompanied by the certificate.

(2) In the case of an application to which this paragraph applies—
(a) paragraphs 3 to 6 shall not apply, and
(b) paragraphs 7 and 8 shall apply with the omission of any reference to objections.

(3) The authority to whom an application to which this paragraph applies is made shall grant it unless they think—
(a) that the applicant is established or conducted wholly or mainly for the purposes of the provision of facilities for gaming, other than gaming of a prescribed kind,[3]
(b) that the applicant is established or conducted wholly or mainly for the purposes of the provision of facilities for gaming of a prescribed kind[4] and also provides facilities for gaming of another kind, or
(c) that a club gaming permit or club machine permit issued to the applicant has been cancelled during the period of ten years ending with the date of the application.

(4) Regulations[5] prescribing anything for the purposes of this Act may, in particular, make provision that differs in effect according to whether or not a permit is granted in pursuance of an application to which this paragraph applies.

(5) This paragraph does not apply to Scotland.

Form of permit

11. (1) A permit must be in the prescribed form[6] and must specify—
(a) the name of the club or institute in respect of which it is issued,
(b) the premises to which it relates,
(c) whether it is a club gaming permit or a club machine permit,
(d) the date on which it takes effect, and
(e) such other information as may be prescribed.

(2) If the application for the permit was made in accordance with paragraph 10, the permit must also identify the club premises certificate under section 72 of the Licensing Act 2003 (c 17).

Maintenance

12. The holder of a permit shall keep it on the premises to which it relates.

13. (1) An occupier of premises to which a permit relates commits an offence if without reasonable excuse he fails to produce the permit on request for inspection by—

(a) a constable, or

(b) an enforcement officer.

(2) A person guilty of an offence under sub-paragraph (1) shall be liable on summary conviction to a fine not exceeding level 2 on the standard scale.

14. (1) The holder of a permit—

(a) shall pay a first annual fee to the issuing licensing authority within such period after the issue of the permit as may be prescribed[7], and

(b) shall pay an annual fee[8] to the issuing licensing authority before each anniversary of the issue of the permit.

(2) In this paragraph 'annual fee' means a fee of such amount as may be prescribed.

(3) Sub-paragraph (1)(b) does not apply in relation to an anniversary of the issue of a permit immediately before which the permit expires in accordance with paragraph 17.

15. (1) If information contained in a permit ceases to be accurate the holder of the permit shall as soon as is reasonably practicable apply to the issuing licensing authority to have the permit varied.

(2) An application under sub-paragraph (1) must be accompanied by—

(a) the prescribed fee[9], and

(b) either—

(i) the permit, or

(ii) a statement explaining why it is not reasonably practicable to produce the permit.

(3) The licensing authority to whom an application is made under sub-paragraph (1) shall issue a copy of the permit varied in accordance with the application (and the copy shall be treated as if it were the original permit).

(4) But if the authority think that they would refuse an application for the permit were it made anew, they may—

(a) refuse the application for variation, and

(b) cancel the permit.

(5) Paragraphs 7, 9 and 25 apply in relation to a decision under sub-paragraph (4) as they apply in relation to a decision to refuse an application for a permit (and paragraph 21 shall not apply).

(6) The holder of a permit commits an offence if without reasonable excuse he fails to comply with sub-paragraph (1).

(7) A person guilty of an offence under sub-paragraph (6) shall be liable on summary conviction to a fine not exceeding level 2 on the standard scale.

16. (1) Where a permit is lost, stolen or damaged, the holder may apply to the issuing licensing authority for a copy.

(2) An application under sub-paragraph (1) must be accompanied by the prescribed fee[10].

(3) A licensing authority shall grant an application under sub-paragraph (1) if satisfied—

(a) that the permit has been lost, stolen or damaged, and

(b) where the permit has been lost or stolen, that the loss or theft has been reported to the police.

(4) As soon as is reasonably practicable after granting an application under sub-paragraph (1) a licensing authority shall issue a copy of the permit certified by the authority as a true copy (and the copy shall be treated as if it were the original permit).

Duration

17. (1) A permit shall cease to have effect at the end of the period of ten years beginning with the date on which it is issued unless—

(a) it ceases to have effect before that time in accordance with a provision of this Schedule, or

(b) it is renewed in accordance with paragraph 24.

(2) But a permit issued in pursuance of an application to which paragraph 10 applies—

(a) shall not cease to have effect by virtue of sub-paragraph (1),

(b) may cease to have effect in accordance with paragraph 19, 21, 22 or 23, and

(c) shall lapse if the club premises certificate on which the application relied ceases to have effect.

18. (1) If the holder of a permit ceases to be a members' club (whether or not it becomes a commercial club), a commercial club or a miners' welfare institute, the permit shall lapse.

(2) But this paragraph does not apply to a permit issued in pursuance of an application to which paragraph 10 applies.

19. (1) A permit shall cease to have effect upon being surrendered by notice given by the holder of the permit to the issuing licensing authority.

(2) A notice under sub-paragraph (1) must be accompanied by—

(a) the permit, or

(b) a statement explaining why it is not reasonably practicable to produce the permit.

20. (1) The licensing authority which issues a permit shall as soon as is reasonably practicable inform the persons specified in sub-paragraph (2) if the authority—

(a) believe that the permit has lapsed under paragraph 17(2)(c) or 18, or

(b) receive notice of surrender under paragraph 19.

(2) The persons mentioned in sub-paragraph (1) are—

(a) the Commission, and

(b) the chief officer of police for any area in which the premises to which the permit relates are wholly or partly situated.

Cancellation and forfeiture

21. (1) The licensing authority which issued a permit may cancel it if the authority think—

(a) that the premises on which the holder of the permit conducts its activities are used wholly or mainly by children, by young persons or by both, or

(b) that an offence, or a breach of a condition of a permit, has been committed in the course of gaming activities carried on by the holder of the permit.

(2) Before cancelling a permit under this paragraph a licensing authority shall—

(a) give the holder of the permit at least 21 days' notice of the authority's intention to consider cancelling the permit,

(b) consider any representations made by the holder,

(c) hold a hearing if the holder requests one, and

(d) comply with any prescribed requirements for the procedure to be followed in considering whether to cancel a permit.

(3) If a licensing authority cancel a permit they shall as soon as is reasonably practicable give notice of the cancellation and the reasons for it to—

(a) the holder,

(b) the Commission, and

(c) the chief officer of police for any area in which the premises to which the permit relates are wholly or partly situated.

(4) The cancellation of a permit shall not take effect until—

(a) the period specified in paragraph 25(5)(c) has expired without an appeal being brought, or

(b) any appeal brought has been determined.

22. (1) The licensing authority which issued a permit shall cancel it if the holder fails to pay the annual fee in accordance with paragraph 14.

(2) But a licensing authority may disapply sub-paragraph (1) if they think that a failure to pay is attributable to administrative error.

23. (1) Where the holder of a permit, or an officer of the holder of a permit, is convicted of an offence under this Act by or before a court in Great Britain, the court may order forfeiture of the permit.

(2) Forfeiture under this paragraph shall be on such terms (which may include terms as to suspension) as may be specified by—

(a) the court which orders forfeiture,

(b) a court to which an appeal against the conviction, or against any order made on the conviction, has been or could be made, or

(c) the High Court, if hearing proceedings relating to the conviction.

(3) Subject to any express provision made under sub-paragraph (2), a permit shall cease to have effect on the making of a forfeiture order under sub-paragraph (1).

(4) The terms on which a forfeiture order is made under this paragraph shall, in particular, include a requirement that the holder deliver to the licensing authority who issued the permit, within such time as the order may specify—

(a) the permit, or

(b) a statement explaining why it is not reasonably practicable to produce the permit.

(5) As soon as is reasonably practicable after making an order for forfeiture under this paragraph the court shall notify the licensing authority who issued the permit.

Renewal

24. (1) The holder of a permit may apply to the issuing authority for its renewal.

(2) An application for the renewal of a permit may not be made—

(a) before the period of three months ending with the date on which the permit would otherwise expire, or

(b) after the beginning of the period of six weeks ending with that date.

(3) The provisions of this Schedule shall have effect (with any necessary modifications)[11] in relation to an application for renewal as they have effect in relation to an application for a permit.

(4) Paragraph 17 shall have effect in relation to a renewed permit with the substitution of the date of renewal for the date of issue.

(5) A permit shall not cease to have effect by virtue only of paragraph 17 while—

(a) an application for renewal of the permit is pending, or

(b) an appeal against a decision on an application for renewal of the permit is pending.

Appeal

25. (1) Where a licensing authority reject an application for the issue or renewal of a permit the applicant may appeal.

(2) Where a licensing authority grant an application for the issue or renewal of a permit in relation to which an objection was made under paragraph 4, the person who made the objection may appeal.

(3) Where a licensing authority cancel a permit the holder may appeal.

(4) Where a licensing authority determine not to cancel a permit, any person who in accordance with regulations under paragraph 21(2)(d) made representations to the authority in connection with their consideration whether to cancel the permit may appeal.

(5) An appeal under this paragraph must be instituted—

(a) in the magistrates' court for a local justice area in which the premises to which the appeal relates are wholly or partly situated,

(b) by notice of appeal given to the designated officer, and

(c) within the period of 21 days beginning with the day on which the appellant receives notice of the decision against which the appeal is brought.

(6) On an appeal a magistrates' court may—

(a) dismiss the appeal;

(b) substitute for the decision appealed against any decision that the licensing authority could have made;

(c) restore a permit (with effect from such date and on such transitional or other terms as the court may specify);

(d) remit the case to the licensing authority to decide in accordance with a direction of the court;

(e) make an order about costs.

(7) In relation to premises in Scotland—

(a) sub-paragraph (5)(a) shall have effect as if it referred to a sheriff within whose sheriffdom the premises are wholly or partly situated,

(b) sub-paragraph (5)(b) shall not have effect,

(c) the reference in sub-paragraph (6) to the magistrates' court shall have effect as a reference to the sheriff, and

(d) the reference in sub-paragraph (6)(e) to costs shall have effect as a reference to expenses.

(8) Sub-paragraphs (1) to (4) apply to a decision of a licensing authority following remittal under sub-paragraph (6)(d) above.

Register

26. (1) A licensing authority shall—

(a) maintain a register of permits issued by the authority together with such other information as may be prescribed,

(b) make the register and information available for inspection by members of the public at all reasonable times, and

(c) make arrangements for the provision of a copy of an entry in the register, or of information, to a member of the public on request.

(2) A licensing authority may refuse to provide a copy of an entry or of information unless the person seeking it pays a reasonable fee specified by the authority.

(3) The Secretary of State may make regulations about—

(a) the form of the register;

(b) the manner in which it is maintained.

(4) The Secretary of State may make regulations—

(a) requiring licensing authorities to give to the Commission specified information about permits issued by them;

(b) requiring the Commission to maintain a register of the information provided to it under paragraph (a);

(c) requiring the Commission to grant access to the register to members of the public (without charge);

(d) requiring the Commission to make copies of entries available on request, and on payment of a reasonable fee, to members of the public;

(e) excusing licensing authorities, wholly or partly, from compliance with sub-paragraph (1).

Exercise of functions by licensing authority: general

27. In exercising a function under this Schedule a licensing authority shall have regard to—

(a) any relevant guidance under section 25, and

(b) subject to paragraph (a), the licensing objectives.

28. (1) Sections 154 and 155 shall have effect in relation to the functions of a licensing authority under this Schedule as they have effect in relation to functions of a licensing authority under Part 8.

(2) In the application of section 154 to this Schedule the following shall be substituted for the list of functions in subsection (4) (which itself substitutes a list of functions for that in section 10(4) of the Licensing Act 2003)—

(a) determination of an application for a permit in respect of which an objection has been made under this Schedule (and not withdrawn), and

(b) cancellation of a permit under paragraph 21.

Vehicles and vessels

29. A club gaming permit or club machine permit may not be issued in respect of a vehicle or vessel (or part of a vehicle or vessel).

Interpretation

30. In this Schedule 'prescribed' means prescribed by the Secretary of State by regulations except that in paragraphs 2(e), 15(2)(a) and 16(2) it means, where the application in question is made to a licensing authority in Scotland, prescribed by the Scottish Ministers by regulations.

31. This Schedule shall, in its application to Scotland, have effect as if references to a chief officer of police were references to a chief constable.

Commencement

Paras 1–11, 25 brought into force for certain purposes as from 1 June 2007 and for remaining purposes as from 1 September 2007 by the Gambling Act 2005 (Commencement No 6 and Transitional Provisions) Order 2006, SI 2006/3272, art 2, Sch 3; for transitional provisions see art 6, Sch 4 thereto (as amended by SI 2007/1157, arts 7–12).

Paras 12–14, 22, 24 brought into force as from 1 September 2007 by the Gambling Act 2005 (Commencement No 6 and Transitional Provisions) Order 2006, SI 2006/3272, art 2; for transitional provisions see art 6, Sch 4 thereto (as amended by SI 2007/1157, arts 7–12).

Paras 15–21, 23, 26–31 brought into force as from 1 June 2007 by the Gambling Act 2005 (Commencement No 6 and Transitional Provisions) Order 2006, SI 2006/3272, art 2, Sch 3; for transitional provisions see art 6, Sch 4 thereto (as amended by SI 2007/1157, arts 7–12).

Para 1: Licensing authority. For the licensing authorities for the purposes of this Act, see s 2.

Para 1: Club gaming permit; club machine permit. See, generally, ss 271, 273.

Para 3: The Commission. Ie the Gambling Commission; see s 353(1). As to the establishment, etc of the Gambling Commission, see s 20, Sch 4, and the note 'Gambling Commission' to that section.

Para 3: Chief officer of police. See the note to s 349.

Para 8: Notice. See further, in connection with a requirement under this Act to give a notice, s 353(4).

Para 13: Offence. For the power of the Gambling Commission and other specified persons to undertake activities for the purpose of assessing whether an offence is being committed under or by virtue of this Act, see ss 27, 305; for the power of that Commission to investigate and prosecute offences, see s 28; as to offences committed by a body, see s 341; and for the time limit on prosecutions, see s 347. See also s 306 for powers of entry as respects a suspected offence, and s 345 as respects forfeiture of an article relating to an offence.

Para 13: Constable. See the note to s 64.

Para 13: Enforcement officer. As to enforcement officers, see, generally, s 303.

Para 13: Summary conviction; standard scale. See the notes to s 33.

Para 23: Great Britain. See the note to s 12.

Para 23: High Court. See the note to s 115.

Para 24: Months. See the note to s 76.

Para 25: Magistrates' court. See the note to s 207.

Para 26: Secretary of State. See the note to s 4.

Para 28: Part 8. Ie Pt 8 (ss 150–213 and Sch 9) of this Act.

Para 30: Scottish Ministers. See the note to s 25.

As to regulations under this Act generally, see s 355.

Definitions

'child': ss 45(1), 353(1)
'club gaming permit': ss 271(2), 353(1)
'club machine permit': ss 273(2), 353(1)
'commercial club': ss 267, 353(1)
'the Commission': s 353(1)
'enforcement officer': s 353(1)
'gaming': ss 6, 353(1)
'licensing authority': ss 2, 353(1)
'the licensing objectives': ss 1, 353(1)
'members' club': ss 266, 353(1)
'miners' welfare institute': ss 268, 353(1)
'premises': s 353(1), (2)(g)
'providing facilities for gambling': ss 5, 353(2)(i)
'vehicle': s 353(1)
'vessel': s 353(1)
'young person': ss 45(1), 353(1)

Explanatory Notes

689–698 [para **6.2015** below]

---

1 See SI 2007/1834.
2 See SI 2007/1834.
3 See SI 2007/1942.
4 See SI 2007/1942.
5 See SI 2007/1834.
6 See SI 2007/1834.
7 See SI 2007/1834.
8 See SI 2007/1834.
9 See SI 2007/1834.
10 See SI 2007/1834.
11 See SI 2007/1834.

SCHEDULE 13
LICENSED PREMISES GAMING MACHINE PERMITS
Section 283

Making of application

[6.888]

1. (1) A person who applies to a licensing authority (in its capacity as a licensing authority under the Licensing Act 2003 (c 17)) for an on-premises alcohol licence or who holds an on-premises alcohol licence issued by a licensing authority (in that capacity) may apply to that licensing authority (in its capacity as a licensing authority under this Act) for a licensed premises gaming machine permit.

(2) An application may not be made under this Schedule if a licence under Part 8 has effect in relation to the premises.

2. An application for a permit must—

(a) be made in such form and manner as the licensing authority may direct,
(b) specify the premises in respect of which the permit is sought,
(c) specify the number and category of gaming machines in respect of which the permit is sought,
(d) contain or be accompanied by such other information or documents as the licensing authority may direct, and
(e) be accompanied by the prescribed fee[1].

3. Sections 154 and 155 shall have effect in relation to the functions of a licensing authority under this Schedule as they have effect in relation to functions of a licensing authority under Part 8.

4. (1) A licensing authority to whom an application is made under this Schedule shall consider it having regard to the licensing objectives, any relevant guidance issued by the Commission under section 25 and such other matters as they think relevant.

(2) On considering an application for a permit a licensing authority shall—

(a) grant the application,
(b) refuse the application, or
(c) grant it in respect of—
   (i) a smaller number of machines than that specified in the application,
   (ii) a different category of machines from that specified in the application, or
   (iii) both.

5. (1) A licensing authority may not attach conditions to a permit.

(2) As soon as is reasonably practicable after granting an application, a licensing authority shall issue a permit to the applicant.

(3) As soon as is reasonably practicable after refusing an application a licensing authority shall notify the applicant of—

(a) the refusal, and
(b) the reasons for it.

6. (1) A licensing authority may grant an application under this Schedule only if the applicant holds an on-premises alcohol licence.

(2) A licensing authority may not refuse an application, or grant an application in respect of a different category or smaller number of gaming machines than that specified in the application, unless they have—

(a) notified the applicant of their intention to refuse the application, or grant the application in respect of—
   (i) a smaller number of machines than that specified in the application,

(ii) a different category of machines from that specified in the application, or

(iii) both, and

(b) given the applicant an opportunity to make representations.

(3) A licensing authority may satisfy sub-paragraph (2)(b) by giving the applicant an opportunity to make—

(a) oral representations,

(b) written representations, or

(c) both.

(4) Sub-paragraph (2)(b) shall not apply in respect of a refusal if the refusal was by virtue of sub-paragraph (1).

Form of permit

7. (1) A permit must be in the prescribed form[2] and must specify—

(a) the person to whom it is issued,

(b) the premises,

(c) the number and category of gaming machines which it authorises, and

(d) the date on which it takes effect.

(2) If the person to whom a permit is issued changes his name or wishes to be known by another name—

(a) he may send the permit to the licensing authority with—

(i) the prescribed fee[3], and

(ii) a request that a new name be substituted for the old name, and

(b) the licensing authority shall comply with the request and return the permit to the holder.

Maintenance

8. The holder of a permit shall keep it on the premises to which it relates.

9. (1) The holder of a permit—

(a) shall pay a first annual fee[4] to the issuing licensing authority within such period[5] after the issue of the permit as may be prescribed, and

(b) shall pay an annual fee to the issuing licensing authority before each anniversary of the issue of the permit[6].

(2) In this paragraph 'annual fee' means a fee of such amount as may be prescribed.

10. (1) An occupier of premises in respect of which a permit has effect commits an offence if without reasonable excuse he fails to produce the permit on request for inspection by—

(a) a constable,

(b) an enforcement officer, or

(c) an authorised local authority officer.

(2) A person guilty of an offence under this paragraph shall be liable on summary conviction to a fine not exceeding level 2 on the standard scale.

11. (1) Where a permit is lost, stolen or damaged, the holder may apply to the licensing authority for a copy.

(2) An application under sub-paragraph (1) must be accompanied by the prescribed fee[7].

(3) A licensing authority shall consider an application under this paragraph and shall grant it if satisfied—

(a) that the permit has been lost, stolen or damaged, and

(b) where the permit has been lost or stolen, that the loss or theft has been reported to the police.

(4) As soon as is reasonably practicable after granting an application under this paragraph a licensing authority shall issue a copy of the permit certified by the authority as a true copy.

(5) A copy of a permit issued under this paragraph shall be treated as if it were the permit.

12. A permit shall continue to have effect unless and until it ceases to have effect in accordance with a provision of this Schedule.

13. A permit shall cease to have effect if—

(a) an on-premises alcohol licence ceases to have effect with respect to the premises to which it relates, or

(b) the permit holder ceases to be the holder of an on-premises alcohol licence.

14. A permit shall cease to have effect if the permit holder gives to the licensing authority—

(a) notice of surrender, and

(b) either—

(i) the permit, or

(ii) a statement explaining why it is not reasonably practicable to produce the permit.

Variation

15. (1) The holder of a permit may apply to the licensing authority to vary the number or category (or both) of gaming machines authorised by the permit.

(2) Paragraphs 1 to 7 and 21 shall have effect (with any necessary modifications) in relation to an application for variation under this paragraph as they have effect in relation to an application for the issue of a permit.

Cancellation and forfeiture

16. (1) The licensing authority which issued a permit may cancel it, or may vary the number or category (or both) of gaming machines authorised by it, if they think that—

(a) it would not be reasonably consistent with pursuit of the licensing objectives for the permit to continue to have effect,

(b) gaming has taken place on the premises in purported reliance on the permit but otherwise than in accordance with the permit or a condition of the permit,

(c) the premises are mainly used or to be used for making gaming machines available, or

(d) an offence under this Act has been committed on the premises.

(2) Before cancelling or varying a permit under this paragraph a licensing authority shall—

(a) give the permit holder at least 21 days' notice of the authority's intention to consider cancelling or varying the permit,

(b) consider any representations made by the holder,

(c) hold a hearing if the holder requests one, and

(d) comply with any prescribed requirements for the procedure to be followed in considering whether to cancel or vary a permit.

(3) If a licensing authority cancel or vary a permit under this paragraph they shall as soon as is reasonably practicable give notice of the cancellation or variation and the reasons for it to—

(a) the permit holder, and

(b) the Commission.

(4) The cancellation or variation of a permit shall not take effect until—

(a) the period specified in paragraph 21(2)(c) has expired without an appeal being brought, or

(b) any appeal brought has been determined.

17. (1) The licensing authority which issued a permit shall cancel it if the holder fails to pay the annual fee in accordance with paragraph 9.

(2) But a licensing authority may disapply sub-paragraph (1) if they think that a failure to pay is attributable to administrative error.

18. (1) Where a permit holder, or the officer of a permit holder, is convicted of a relevant offence the court by or before which he is convicted may order forfeiture of the permit.

(2) Forfeiture under this paragraph shall be on such terms (which may include terms as to suspension) as may be specified by—

(a) the court which orders forfeiture,

(b) a court to which an appeal against the conviction, or against any order made on the conviction, has been or could be made, or

(c) the High Court, if hearing proceedings relating to the conviction.

(3) Subject to any express provision made under sub-paragraph (2), a permit shall cease to have effect on the making of a forfeiture order under this paragraph.

(4) The terms on which forfeiture is ordered under this paragraph shall, in particular, include a requirement that the permit holder deliver to the licensing authority within such time as the order may specify—

(a) the permit, or

(b) a statement explaining why it is not reasonably practicable to produce the permit.

(5) As soon as is reasonably practicable after making or suspending an order for forfeiture under this paragraph a court shall notify the licensing authority.

Transfer of permit

19. (1) A person may apply for the transfer of a permit to him if—

(a) he is applying for the transfer of an on-premises alcohol licence to him in accordance with—

(i) section 42 of the Licensing Act 2003 (c 17) (application for transfer), or

(ii) section 50 of that Act (transfer following death of holder), and

(b) a permit has effect in respect of the same premises.

(2) The provisions of this Schedule shall have effect (with any necessary modifications) in relation to an application for the transfer of a permit as they have effect in relation to an application for the issue of a permit.

(3) A person applying for the transfer of a permit to him must supply with his application—

(a) the permit, or

(b) a statement explaining why it is not reasonably practicable to produce the permit.

(4) A licensing authority may not approve an application for the transfer of a permit under this paragraph unless the transfer of the on-premises alcohol licence is approved under section 45 of the Licensing Act 2003 (determination of application).

(5) Where a licensing authority refuse an application for the transfer of a permit under this paragraph by virtue of sub-paragraph (4), the provisions of paragraph 6(2)(b) shall not apply to the refusal.

20. (1) This paragraph applies where—

(a) the transfer of an on-premises alcohol licence is to be given immediate effect under section 43 of the Licensing Act 2003 (interim effect of transfer application), and

(b) the applicant has also made an application under paragraph 19.

(2) A permit in respect of those premises shall have effect during the application period as if the applicant for the transfer were the permit holder.

(3) In this paragraph 'application period' has the same meaning as in section 43 of the Licensing Act 2003.

Appeal

21. (1) The applicant for or holder of a permit may appeal if the licensing authority—

(a) reject an application for a permit,

(b) grant an application for a permit in respect of a smaller number of machines than that specified in the application or a different category of machines from that specified in the application (or both), or

(c) give a notice under paragraph 16.

(2) An appeal under this paragraph must be instituted—

(a) in the magistrates' court for a local justice area in which the premises to which the appeal relates are wholly or partly situated,

(b) by notice of appeal given to the designated officer, and

(c) within the period of 21 days beginning with the day on which the appellant or holder receives notice of the decision against which the appeal is brought.

(3) On an appeal the magistrates' court may—

(a) dismiss the appeal;

(b) substitute for the decision appealed against any decision that the licensing authority could have made (with effect from such date and on such transitional or other terms as the court may specify);

(c) restore a permit (with effect from such date and on such transitional or other terms as the court may specify);

(d) remit the case to the licensing authority to decide in accordance with a direction of the court;

(e) make an order about costs.

(4) Sub-paragraph (1) applies to a decision of a licensing authority following remittal under sub-paragraph (3)(d).

Register

22. (1) A licensing authority shall—

(a) maintain a register of permits issued by the authority together with such other information as may be prescribed,

(b) make the register and information available for inspection by members of the public at all reasonable times, and

(c) make arrangements for the provision of a copy of an entry in the register, or of information, to a member of the public on request.

(2) A licensing authority may refuse to provide a copy of an entry or of information unless the person seeking it pays a reasonable fee specified by the authority.

(3) The Secretary of State may make regulations about—

(a) the form of the register;

(b) the manner in which it is maintained.

(4) The Secretary of State may make regulations—

(a) requiring licensing authorities to give to the Commission specified information about permits issued by them;

(b) requiring the Commission to maintain a register of the information provided to it under paragraph (a);
(c) requiring the Commission to grant access to the register to members of the public (without charge);
(d) requiring the Commission to make copies of entries available on request, and on payment of a reasonable fee, to members of the public;
(e) excusing licensing authorities, wholly or partly, from compliance with sub-paragraph (1).

Interpretation

23. In this Schedule—
'permit' means a licensed premises gaming machine permit, and
'prescribed' means prescribed by regulations made by the Secretary of State.

Commencement

Paras 1–7, 22 brought into force for certain purposes as from 1 June 2007 and for remaining purposes as from 1 September 2007 by the Gambling Act 2005 (Commencement No 6 and Transitional Provisions) Order 2006, SI 2006/3272, art 2, Sch 3; for transitional provisions see art 6, Sch 4 thereto (as amended by SI 2007/1157, arts 7–12).

Paras 8–10 brought into force as from 1 September 2007 by the Gambling Act 2005 (Commencement No 6 and Transitional Provisions) Order 2006, SI 2006/3272, art 2; for transitional provisions see art 6, Sch 4 thereto (as amended by SI 2007/1157, arts 7–12).

Paras 11–20, 22, 23 brought into force as from 1 June 2007 by the Gambling Act 2005 (Commencement No 6 and Transitional Provisions) Order 2006, SI 2006/3272, art 2, Sch 3; for transitional provisions see art 6, Sch 4 thereto (as amended by SI 2007/1157, arts 7–12).

Para 1: Person. See the note 'Persons' to s 23.

Para 1: Licensing authority. For the licensing authorities for the purposes of this Act, see s 2.

Para 1: May apply, etc. For powers of entry where an application has been made under this Schedule, see s 310.

Para 1: Part 8. Ie Pt 8 (ss 150–213 and Sch 9) of this Act.

Para 4: The Commission. Ie the Gambling Commission; see s 353(1). As to the establishment, etc of the Gambling Commission, see s 20, Sch 4, and the note 'Gambling Commission' to that section.

Para 5: Notify. See further, in connection with a requirement under this Act to give a notice, s 353(4).

Para 6: Written. See the note 'Writing' to s 39.

Para 10: Offence. For the power of the Gambling Commission and other specified persons to undertake activities for the purpose of assessing whether an offence is being committed under or by virtue of this Act, see ss 27, 305; for the power of that Commission to investigate and prosecute offences, see s 28; as to offences committed by a body, see s 341; and for the time limit on prosecutions, see s 347. See also s 306 for powers of entry as respects a suspected offence, and s 345 as respects forfeiture of an article relating to an offence.

For the power of a licensing authority to institute criminal proceedings in respect of an offence under para 10 above, see s 346.

Para 10: Constable. See the note to s 64.

Para 10: Enforcement officer. As to enforcement officers, see, generally, s 303.

Para 10: Summary conviction; standard scale. See the notes to s 33.

Para 18: High Court. See the note to s 115.

Para 21: Magistrates' court. See the note to s 207.

Para 22: Secretary of State. See the note to s 4.

As to regulations under this Act generally, see s 355.

Definitions

'authorised local authority officer': ss 304, 353(1)
'the Commission': s 353(1)
'enforcement officer': s 353(1)
'gaming': ss 6, 353(1)

'gaming machine': ss 235, 353(1)
'licensed premises gaming machine permit': ss 283(2), 353(1)
'licensing authority': ss 2, 353(1)
'the licensing objectives': ss 1, 353(1)
'on-premises alcohol licence': s 277(b)
'premises': s 353(1), (2)(g)
'relevant offence': ss 126(2), (3), 353(1), Sch 7

Explanatory Notes

712–718 [para **6.2016** below]

---

1 See SI 2007/1833.

2 See SI 2007/1833.

3 See SI 2007/1833.

4 See SI 2007/1833.

5 See SI 2007/1833.

6 See SI 2007/1833.

7 See SI 2007/1833.

SCHEDULE 14
PRIZE GAMING PERMITS
Section 289

Interpretation

[6.889]

1. In this Schedule—
'holder', in relation to a permit, means the person to whom the permit is issued,
'the licensing authority'—
(a) in relation to an application, means the licensing authority to whom the application is made, and
(b) in relation to a permit, means the licensing authority who issue it,
'permit' means a prize gaming permit,
'the premises', in relation to an application or permit, means the premises in respect of which the permit is sought or issued, and
'prescribed' means prescribed by regulations made by the Secretary of State except that in paragraphs 6(e) and 21(2) it means, where the application in question is made to a licensing authority in Scotland, prescribed by regulations made by the Scottish Ministers.

2. This Schedule shall, in its application to Scotland, have effect as if references to a chief officer of police were references to a chief constable.

Making of application

3. (1) An application for a permit may be made only by a person who occupies or proposes to occupy the premises.
(2) If the applicant for a permit is an individual, he must be an adult.

4. An application for a permit may not be made if—
(a) a premises licence has effect in respect of the premises, or
(b) a club gaming permit has effect in respect of the premises.

5. An application for a permit must be made to a licensing authority in whose area the premises are wholly or partly situated.

6. An application for a permit must—

(a) be made in such form and manner as the licensing authority may direct,
(b) specify the premises,
(c) specify the nature of the gaming in respect of which the permit is sought,
(d) contain or be accompanied by such other information or documents as the licensing authority may direct, and
(e) be accompanied by the prescribed fee[1].

Consideration of application

7. Sections 154 and 155 shall have effect in relation to functions of a licensing authority under this Schedule as they have effect in relation to the functions of a licensing authority under Part 8.

8. (1) A licensing authority may prepare a statement of principles that they propose to apply in exercising their functions under this Schedule.

(2) A statement under sub-paragraph (1) may, in particular, specify matters that the licensing authority propose to consider in determining the suitability of an applicant for a permit.

(3) In exercising their functions under this Schedule a licensing authority—
(a) need not (but may) have regard to the licensing objectives, and
(b) shall have regard to any relevant guidance issued by the Commission under section 25.

Determination of application

9. (1) On considering an application for a permit a licensing authority may—
(a) grant it, or
(b) refuse it.

(2) A licensing authority may not attach conditions to a permit.

(3) As soon as is reasonably practicable after granting an application a licensing authority shall issue a permit to the applicant.

(4) As soon as is reasonably practicable after refusing an application a licensing authority shall notify the applicant of—
(a) the refusal, and
(b) the reasons for it.

10. A licensing authority may grant an application for a permit only if they have consulted the chief officer of police for a police area in which the premises are wholly or partly situated.

11. (1) A licensing authority may not refuse an application unless they have—
(a) notified the applicant of their intention to refuse the application and of their reasons, and
(b) given the applicant an opportunity to make representations.

(2) A licensing authority may satisfy sub-paragraph (1)(b) by giving the applicant an opportunity to make—
(a) oral representations,
(b) written representations, or
(c) both.

Form of permit

12. (1) A permit must be in the prescribed form[2] and must specify—
(a) the person to whom it is issued,
(b) the nature of the gaming in respect of which it has effect,
(c) the premises, and
(d) the date on which it takes effect.

(2) If the person to whom a permit is issued changes his name or wishes to be known by another name—

(a) he may send the permit to the licensing authority with—

(i) the prescribed fee, and

(ii) a request that a new name be substituted for the old name, and

(b) the licensing authority shall comply with the request and return the permit to the holder.

Duration

13. A permit shall cease to have effect at the end of the period of ten years beginning with the date specified under paragraph 12(1)(d) unless—

(a) it ceases to have effect before that time in accordance with a provision of this Schedule, or

(b) it is renewed in accordance with paragraph 18.

14. (1) A permit shall lapse if the holder ceases to occupy the premises specified under paragraph 12(1)(c).

(2) A permit shall not take effect if on the date specified under paragraph 12(1)(d) the person to whom the permit is issued is not an occupier of the premises specified under paragraph 12(1)(c).

15. (1) A permit held by an individual shall lapse if—

(a) he dies,

(b) he becomes, in the opinion of the licensing authority as notified to the individual, incapable of carrying on the activities authorised by the permit by reason of mental or physical incapacity,

(c) he becomes bankrupt (within the meaning of section 381 of the Insolvency Act 1986 (c 45)) [or a debt relief order is made in respect of him, (under Part 7A of the Insolvency Act 1986)], or

(d) sequestration of his estate is awarded under section 12(1) of the Bankruptcy (Scotland) Act 1985 (c 66).

(2) In any other case a permit shall lapse if the holder—

(a) ceases to exist, or

(b) goes into liquidation (within the meaning of section 247(2) of that Act).

(3) During the period of six months beginning with the date on which a permit lapses under this paragraph the following may rely on it as if it had effect and were issued to them—

(a) the personal representatives of the holder (in the case of an individual holder who dies),

(b) the trustee of the bankrupt's estate (in the case of an individual holder who becomes bankrupt),

(c) the holder's interim or permanent trustee (in the case of an individual holder whose estate is sequestrated), and

(d) the liquidator of the company (in the case of a company holder that goes into liquidation).

(4) In relation to premises in Scotland—

(a) sub-paragraph (2)(a) shall have effect as if it referred to a sheriff within whose sheriffdom the premises are wholly or partly situated,

(b) sub-paragraph (2)(b) shall not have effect,

(c) the reference in sub-paragraph (3) to a magistrate's court shall have effect as a reference to the sheriff, and

(d) the reference in sub-paragraph (3)(d) to costs shall have effect as a reference to expenses.

16. A permit shall cease to have effect if the holder gives to the licensing authority—

(a) notice of surrender, and

(b) either—
(i) the permit, or
(ii) a statement explaining why it is not reasonably practicable to produce the permit.

17. (1) Where the holder of a permit is convicted of a relevant offence the court by or before which he is convicted may order forfeiture of the permit.

(2) Forfeiture under this paragraph shall be on such terms (which may include terms as to suspension) as may be specified by—
(a) the court which orders forfeiture,
(b) a court to which an appeal against the conviction, or against any order made on the conviction, has been or could be made, or
(c) the High Court, if hearing proceedings relating to the conviction.

(3) Subject to any express provision made under sub-paragraph (2), a permit shall cease to have effect on the making of a forfeiture order under this paragraph.

(4) The terms on which forfeiture is ordered under this paragraph shall, in particular, include a requirement that the holder of the permit deliver to the licensing authority within such time as the order may specify—
(a) the permit, or
(b) a statement explaining why it is not reasonably practicable to produce the permit.

(5) As soon as is reasonably practicable after making or suspending an order for forfeiture under this paragraph a court shall notify the licensing authority.

Renewal

18. (1) The holder of a permit may apply to the licensing authority for renewal[3] of the permit.

(2) An application for renewal may not be made—
(a) before the period of six months ending with the date on which the permit would otherwise expire in accordance with paragraph 13, or
(b) after the beginning of the period of two months ending with that date.

(3) The provisions of this Schedule shall have effect (with any necessary modifications) in relation to an application for renewal as they have effect in relation to an application for a permit.

(4) Paragraph 13 shall have effect in relation to a renewed permit as if the date of renewal were the date specified under paragraph 12(1)(d).

(5) A permit shall not cease to have effect by virtue only of paragraph 13 while—
(a) an application for renewal of the permit is pending, or
(b) an appeal against a decision on an application for renewal of the permit is pending.

Maintenance

19. The holder of a permit shall keep it on the premises.

20. (1) An occupier of premises in respect of which a permit has effect commits an offence if without reasonable excuse he fails to produce the permit on request for inspection by—
(a) a constable, or
(b) an enforcement officer,
(c) an authorised local authority officer.

(2) A person guilty of an offence under this paragraph shall be liable on summary conviction to a fine not exceeding level 2 on the standard scale.

21. (1) Where a permit is lost, stolen or damaged, the holder may apply to the licensing authority for a copy.

6: Gambling Act 2005: Statutes

(2) An application under sub-paragraph (1) must be accompanied by the prescribed fee[4].

(3) A licensing authority shall consider an application under this paragraph and shall grant it if satisfied—

(a) that the permit has been lost, stolen or damaged, and

(b) where the permit has been lost or stolen, that the loss or theft has been reported to the police.

(4) As soon as is reasonably practicable after granting an application under this paragraph a licensing authority shall issue a copy of the permit certified by the authority as a true copy.

(5) A copy of a permit issued under this paragraph shall be treated as if it were the permit.

Appeal

22. (1) Where a licensing authority reject an application for the issue or renewal of a permit the applicant may appeal.

(2) An appeal under this paragraph must be instituted—

(a) in the magistrates' court for a local justice area in which the premises to which the appeal relates are wholly or partly situated,

(b) by notice of appeal given to the designated officer, and

(c) within the period of 21 days beginning with the day on which the appellant receives notice of the decision against which the appeal is brought.

(3) On an appeal a magistrates' court may—

(a) dismiss the appeal;

(b) substitute for the decision appealed against any decision that the licensing authority could have made;

(c) remit the case to the licensing authority to decide in accordance with a direction of the court;

(d) make an order about costs.

(4) Sub-paragraph (1) applies to a decision of a licensing authority following remittal under sub-paragraph (3)(c) above.

Register

23. (1) A licensing authority shall—

(a) maintain a register of permits issued by the authority together with such other information as may be prescribed,

(b) make the register and information available for inspection by members of the public at all reasonable times, and

(c) make arrangements for the provision of a copy of an entry in the register, or of information, to a member of the public on request.

(2) A licensing authority may refuse to provide a copy of an entry or of information unless the person seeking it pays a reasonable fee specified by the authority.

(3) The Secretary of State may make regulations about—

(a) the form of the register;

(b) the manner in which it is maintained.

(4) The Secretary of State may make regulations—

(a) requiring licensing authorities to give to the Commission specified information about permits issued by them;

(b) requiring the Commission to maintain a register of the information provided to it under paragraph (a);

(c) requiring the Commission to grant access to the register to members of the public (without charge);

(d) requiring the Commission to make copies of entries available on request, and on payment of a reasonable fee, to members of the public;

(e) excusing licensing authorities, wholly or partly, from compliance with sub-paragraph (1).

Vehicles and vessels

24. A permit may not be issued in respect of a vehicle or vessel (or part of a vehicle or vessel).

Commencement

Paras 1, 8(1), (2) brought into force as from 13 November 2006 by the Gambling Act 2005 (Commencement No 4) Order 2006, SI 2006/2964, art 2.

Paras 2, 13(a), 14–17, 21, 23, 24 brought into force as from 30 April 2007 by the Gambling Act 2005 (Commencement No 6 and Transitional Provisions) Order 2006, SI 2006/3272, art 2, Sch 2; for transitional provisions see art 6, Sch 4 thereto (as amended by SI 2007/1157, arts 7–12).

Paras 3–7, 9–12, 22 brought into force for certain purposes as from 30 April 2007 and for remaining purposes as from 1 September 2007 by the Gambling Act 2005 (Commencement No 6 and Transitional Provisions) Order 2006, SI 2006/3272, art 2, Schs 2 and 3; for transitional provisions see art 6, Sch 4 thereto (as amended by SI 2007/1157, arts 7–12).

Paras 8(3) brought into force for the purpose of enabling a licensing authority to carry out their functions under para 8(1), (2) as from 13 November 2006 by the Gambling Act 2005 (Commencement No 4) Order 2006, SI 2006/2964, art 2 and for remaining purposes as from 30 April 2007 by the Gambling Act 2005 (Commencement No 6 and Transitional Provisions) Order 2006, SI 2006/3272, art 2, Sch 2; for transitional provisions see art 6, Sch 4 thereto (as amended by SI 2007/1157, arts 7–12).

Paras 13(b), 18–20 brought into force as from 1 September 2007 by the Gambling Act 2005 (Commencement No 6 and Transitional Provisions) Order 2006, SI 2006/3272, art 2; for transitional provisions see art 6, Sch 4 thereto (as amended by SI 2007/1157, arts 7–12).

Amendment

Para 15: in para (1)(c) words in square brackets inserted by SI 2012/2404, art 3(2), Sch 2, para 55.

General note. It is thought that para 15(4) above should have been drafted as para 22(5) of this Schedule.

Para 1: Person. See the note 'Persons' to s 23.

Para 1: Licensing authority. For the licensing authorities for the purposes of this Act, see s 2.

Para 1: Secretary of State. See the note to s 4.

Para 1: Scottish Ministers. See the note to s 25.

Para 4: Premises licence. As to the nature, etc of premises licences, see s 150 and the note 'Premises licence' thereto.

Para 4: Club gaming permit. See, generally, s 271.

Para 7: Part 8. Ie Pt 8 (ss 150–213 and Sch 9) of this Act.

Para 8: The Commission. Ie the Gambling Commission; see s 353(1). As to the establishment, etc of the Gambling Commission, see s 20, Sch 4, and the note 'Gambling Commission' to that section.

Para 9: Notify. See further, in connection with a requirement under this Act to give a notice, s 353(4).

Para 10: Chief officer of police. See the note to s 349.

Para 10: Police area. See the note to s 157.

Para 11: Written. See the note 'Writing' to s 39.

Para 15: Months. See the note to s 76.

Para 17: High Court. See the note to s 115.

Para 20: Offence. For the power of the Gambling Commission and other specified persons to undertake activities for the purpose of assessing whether an offence is being committed under or by virtue of this Act, see ss 27, 305; for the power of that Commission to investigate and prosecute offences, see s 28; as to offences committed by a body, see s 341; and for the time limit on prosecutions, see s 347. See also s 306 for powers of entry as respects a suspected offence, and s 345 as respects forfeiture of an article relating to an offence.

For the power of a licensing authority to institute criminal proceedings in respect of an offence under para 20 above, see s 346.

Para 20: Constable. See the note to s 64.

Para 20: Enforcement officer. As to enforcement officers, see, generally, s 303.

Para 20: Summary conviction; standard scale. See the notes to s 33.

Para 22: Magistrates' court. See the note to s 207.

Subordinate Legislation

Gambling Act 2005 (Prize Gaming) (Permits) Regulations 2007, SI 2007/455 (made under paras 6(e), 12, 18(3), 21(2)).

As to regulations under this Act generally, see s 355.

Definitions

'adult': s 353(1)
'authorised local authority officer': ss 304, 353(1)
'club gaming permit': ss 273(2), 353(1)
'the Commission': s 353(1)
'enforcement officer': s 353(1)
'gaming': ss 6, 353(1)
'licensing authority': ss 2, 353(1)
'the licensing objectives': ss 1, 353(1)
'premises': s 353(1), (2)(g)
'premises licence': s 353(1)
'relevant offence': ss 126(2), (3), 353(1), Sch 7
'vehicle': s 353(1)
'vessel': s 353(1)

Explanatory Notes

733–739 [para **6.2017** below]

---

1 See SI 2007/455.

2 See SI 2007/455.

3 See SI 2007/455.

4 See SI 2007/455.

SCHEDULE 15
PRIVATE GAMING AND BETTING
Section 295

PART 1
GAMING

Introduction

[6.890]–[6.891]

1. Gaming is private if it satisfies the conditions specified in this Part of this Schedule.

2. (1) For the purposes of this Part of this Schedule gaming is domestic if it takes place—

(a) in a private dwelling, and
(b) on a domestic occasion.

(2) For the purposes of this Part of this Schedule gaming is residential if—

(a) it takes place in a hostel, hall of residence or similar establishment which is not administered in the course of a trade or business, and

(b) more than half of the participants are residents of the hostel, hall or establishment.

No charge for participation

3. (1) It is a condition of private gaming that no charge is made for participation.

(2) For the purposes of this paragraph—

(a) it is immaterial how a charge is described,

(b) it is immaterial whether a charge is in money or money's worth,

(c) an amount deducted or levied, by a person providing facilities for gaming, from sums staked or won in the course of gaming is a charge for participation in the gaming,

(d) a charge for admission to premises where gaming takes place shall be treated as a charge for participation in the gaming, and

(e) a stake is not a charge for participation.

Equal chance gaming

4. (1) It is a condition of private gaming that it is equal chance gaming.

(2) But this condition does not apply in relation to domestic or residential gaming.

Privacy

5. It is a condition of private gaming that it does not occur in a place to which the public have access (whether or not on payment).

Commencement

Brought into force as from 1 September 2007 by the Gambling Act 2005 (Commencement No 6 and Transitional Provisions) Order 2006, SI 2006/3272, art 2; for transitional provisions see art 6, Sch 4 thereto (as amended by SI 2007/1157, arts 7–12).

Definitions

'equal chance gaming': ss 8, 353(1)
'gaming': ss 6, 353(1)
'premises': s 353(1), (2)(g)
'providing facilities for gambling': ss 5, 353(2)(i)
'stake': s 353(1)

Explanatory Notes

745, 746 [para **6.2018** below]

PART 2
BETTING

Introduction

[6.892]

6. Betting is private betting if it is—

(a) domestic betting, or

(b) workers' betting.

Domestic betting

7. (1) A betting transaction is domestic betting if made on premises in which each party to the transaction lives.

(2) For the purposes of this paragraph a person lives in premises if he habitually resides in any part of the premises (whether or not there are other premises in which he also habitually resides).

Workers' betting

8. A betting transaction is workers' betting if made between persons each of whom is employed under a contract of employment with the same employer.

Commencement

Brought into force as from 1 September 2007 by the Gambling Act 2005 (Commencement No 6 and Transitional Provisions) Order 2006, SI 2006/3272, art 2; for transitional provisions see art 6, Sch 4 thereto (as amended by SI 2007/1157, arts 7–12).

Definitions

'betting': ss 9–11, 353(1)
'premises': s 353(1), (2)(g)

Explanatory Notes

757 [para **6.2018** below]

SCHEDULE 16
MINOR AND CONSEQUENTIAL AMENDMENTS
Section 356

PART 1
MINOR AMENDMENTS

Metropolitan Police Act 1839 (c 47)

[6.893]–[6.894]

1. In section 44 of the Metropolitan Police Act 1839 (refreshment houses)—
(a) omit ', or knowingly suffer any unlawful games or any gaming whatsoever therein,', and
(b) in the heading, omit ', or gaming'.

Libraries Offences Act 1898 (c 53)

2. Section 2(3) of the Libraries Offences Act 1898 (offence of annoying library users) shall cease to have effect.

Gaming Act 1968 (c 65)

3. (1) The Gaming Act 1968 shall be amended as follows.

(2) For section 6(2) (premises licensed for the sale of alcohol) substitute—

'(2) This section applies to any premises in England and Wales—
(a) in respect of which a premises licence under Part 3 of the Licensing Act 2003 (c 17) has effect,
(b) which contain a bar at which alcohol is served for consumption on the premises (without a requirement that alcohol is served only with food), and
(c) at a time when alcohol may be supplied in reliance on the premises licence under Part 3 of the Licensing Act 2003.'

(3) In section 12(3)—
(a) in paragraph (a) the words from 'and at that time' to the end of the paragraph shall cease to have effect,

(b) in paragraph (b) the words from 'and at that time' to the end of the paragraph shall cease to have effect, and

(c) in paragraph (c) the words from 'and at that time' to the end of the paragraph shall cease to have effect.

(4) For section 20(5) substitute—

'(5) Section 12(3) shall not apply in relation to any club to which this section applies.'

(5) In section 31—

(a) in subsection (2)(c) for 'ten' substitute 'twenty',

(b) for subsection (3E) substitute—

'(3E) The initial amount must not exceed the higher of—

(a) the highest coin value, or

(b) the charge for playing a game once by means of the machine.', and

(c) in subsection (3G) for 'the highest coin value' substitute

'the higher of—

(a) the highest coin value, or

(b) the charge for playing a game once by means of the machine.'

(6) In section 51(3) after 'regulations' insert 'or an order'.

(7) In paragraph 10A(1) of Schedule 9, leave out 'sub-paragraph (a) or'.

(8) After paragraph 10A of Schedule 9 insert—

'10AA.

A permit in respect of premises to which sub-paragraph (a) of paragraph 1 of this Schedule applies shall be subject to the conditions that a machine must—

(a) be located on premises which contain a bar at which alcohol is served for consumption on the premises (without a requirement that alcohol is served only with food), and

(b) be made available for use only at a time when alcohol may be supplied in reliance on the premises licence under Part 3 of the Licensing Act 2003.'

Chronically Sick and Disabled Persons Act 1970 (c 44)

4. Section 8B(2)(c) of the Chronically Sick and Disabled Persons Act 1970 (report by Secretary of State on access to betting offices) shall cease to have effect.

Commencement

Paras 1, 2, 4 brought into force as from 1 September 2007 by the Gambling Act 2005 (Commencement No 6 and Transitional Provisions) Order 2006, SI 2006/3272, art 2; for transitional provisions see art 6, Sch 4 thereto (as amended by SI 2007/1157, arts 7–12).

Paras 3(1), 3(3)–(6) brought into force by the Gambling Act 2005 (Commencement No 2 and Transitional Provisions) Order 2005, SI 2005/2455, art 2 and Schedule, as from 1 October 2005.

Paras 3(2) brought into force 24 November 2005 and paras 3(7), (8) brought into force 25 November 2005 by the Gambling Act 2005 (Commencement No 2 and Transitional Provisions) Order 2005, SI 2005/2455, art 2.

Para 3: England; Wales. See the note to s 2.

PART 2
CONSEQUENTIAL AMENDMENTS

Parliamentary Commissioner Act 1967 (c 13)

[6.895]

5. In Schedule 2 to the Parliamentary Commissioner Act 1967 (bodies subject to investigation) for 'Gaming Board for Great Britain.' substitute 'Gambling Commission.'

Superannuation Act 1972 (c 11)

6. In Schedule 1 to the Superannuation Act 1972 (employment to which superannuation schemes may extend) for 'Gaming Board for Great Britain.' substitute 'Gambling Commission.'

House of Commons Disqualification Act 1975 (c 24)

7. In Part II of Schedule 1 to the House of Commons Disqualification Act 1975 (c 24) (disqualifying offices) for 'The Gaming Board for Great Britain.' substitute 'The Gambling Commission.'

Local Government (Miscellaneous Provisions) Act 1976 (c 57)

8. In section 20(9) of the Local Government (Miscellaneous Provisions) Act 1976 (sanitation) for the definition of 'betting office' substitute—

> '"betting office' means premises, other than a track within the meaning of the Gambling Act 2005, in respect of which a betting premises licence under Part 8 of that Act has effect;'.

Race Relations Act 1976 (c 74)

9. . . . [2]

London Local Authorities Act 1995 (c x)

10. In section 14 of the London Local Authorities Act 1995 (interpretation of licensing provisions) for the provision excluding premises licensed under Part II of the Gaming Act 1968 substitute: 'does not include premises in respect of which a casino premises licence, bingo premises licence, adult gaming centre premises licence, family entertainment centre premises licence or betting premises licence under Part 8, or a family entertainment centre gaming permit under section 247, of the Gambling Act 2005 has effect;'.

Employment Rights Act 1996 (c 18)

11. For section 233 of the Employment Rights Act 1996 (betting workers) substitute—

> **'233 Betting workers**
>
> (1) In this Act "betting worker" means an employee who under his contract of employment is or may be required to do betting work.
>
> (2) In this Act "betting work" means—
>
> (a) work which consists of or includes dealing with betting transactions at a track in England or Wales and which is carried out for a person who holds a general betting operating licence, a pool betting operating licence or a horse-race pool betting operating licence, and
>
> (b) work on premises in respect of which a betting premises licence has effect at a time when the premises are used for betting transactions.
>
> (3) In subsection (2) "betting transactions" includes the collection or payment of winnings.
>
> (4) Expressions used in this section and in the Gambling Act 2005 have the same meaning in this section as in that Act.
>
> (5) In this Act—

"notice period", in relation to an opted-out betting worker, has the meaning given by section 41(3),

"opted-out", in relation to a betting worker, shall be construed in accordance with section 41(1) and (2),

"opting-in notice", in relation to a betting worker, has the meaning given by section 36(6),

"opting-out notice", in relation to a betting worker, has the meaning given by section 40(2), and

"protected", in relation to a betting worker, shall be construed in accordance with section 36(1) to (5).'

Police Act 1997 (c 50)

12. In section 115 of the Police Act 1997 (enhanced criminal record certificates) for subsection (5)(a) to (c) substitute—

'(a) a process under the Gambling Act 2005'.

Terrorism Act 2000 (c 11)

13. In paragraph 4 of Schedule 3A to the Terrorism Act 2000 (regulated sector and supervisory authorities) for 'Gaming Board for Great Britain' substitute 'Gambling Commission'.

Regulation of Investigatory Powers Act 2000 (c 23)

14. In paragraph 20A of Schedule 1 to the Regulation of Investigatory Powers Act 2000 (relevant public authorities) for 'Gaming Board for Great Britain' substitute 'Gambling Commission'.

Postal Services Act 2000 (c 26)

15. . . . [3]

Freedom of Information Act 2000 (c 36)

16. In Part 6 of Schedule 1 to the Freedom of Information Act 2000 (public authorities to which the Act applies) for 'Gaming Board of Great Britain' substitute 'Gambling Commission.

Private Security Industry Act 2001 (c 12)

17. . . . [4]

Criminal Justice and Police Act 2001 (c 16)

18. (1) In Schedule 1 of the Criminal Justice and Police Act 2001 (seizure powers to which extending provision of section 50 applies)—

(a) paragraphs 6, 11 and 20 cease to have effect,

(b) at the end of Part 1 (renumbering the entry for the Licensing Act 2003 as paragraph 73E) add—

'Gambling Act 2005

73F.

The powers conferred by section 317 of the Gambling Act 2005 (inspection powers).',

(c) paragraphs 89, 93 and 97 cease to have effect, and

(d) at the end of Part 3 (renumbering the entry for the Licensing Act 2003 as paragraph 111) add—

'*Gambling Act 2005*

112.

The powers conferred by section 317 of the Gambling Act 2005 (inspection powers).'

(2) For the purposes of the amendments made by this paragraph, the powers in section 317(1)(d), (e) and (f) are powers of seizure.

Proceeds of Crime Act 2002 (c 29)

19. In Part 2 of Schedule 9 to the Proceeds of Crime Act 2002 (supervisory authorities) in paragraph 4(g) for 'Gaming Board for Great Britain' substitute 'Gambling Commission'.

Licensing Act 2003 (c 17)

20. (1) The Licensing Act 2003 shall be amended as follows.

(2) For section 175 (exemption for raffle, tombola, &c.) substitute—

'175 Exemption for incidental non-commercial lottery

(1) The promotion of a lottery to which this section applies shall not constitute a licensable activity by reason only of one or more of the prizes in the lottery consisting of or including alcohol, provided that the alcohol is in a sealed container.

(2) This section applies to an incidental non-commercial lottery (within the meaning of Part 1 of Schedule 11 to the Gambling Act 2005).'

(3) In paragraph 10(3) of Schedule 1 (provision of regulated entertainment) for 'section 22 of the Lotteries and Amusements Act 1976 (c 32)' substitute 'section 19(3) of the Gambling Act 2005'.

(4) In Schedule 4 (relevant offences) after paragraph 20 insert—

'21.

An offence under section 46 of the Gambling Act 2005 if the child or young person was invited, caused or permitted to gamble on premises in respect of which a premises licence under this Act had effect.'

Note

21. The amendments made by this Schedule are without prejudice to the generality of paragraph 4 of Schedule 5.

Commencement

Paras 5 to 7, 9, 13, 14, 16, 19 and 21 brought into force by the Gambling Act 2005 (Commencement No 2 and Transitional Provisions) Order 2005, SI 2005/2455, art 2 and Schedule, as from 1 October 2005.

Paras 8, 10, 11, 15, 17, 18, 20 brought into force as from 1 September 2007 by the Gambling Act 2005 (Commencement No 6 and Transitional Provisions) Order 2006, SI 2006/3272, art 2; for transitional provisions see art 6, Sch 4 thereto (as amended by SI 2007/1157, arts 7–12).

Para 12 brought into force for certain purposes as from 1 January 2007 and for remaining purposes as from 1 September 2007 by the Gambling Act 2005 (Commencement No 6 and Transitional Provisions) Order 2006, SI 2006/3272, art 2, Sch 1; for transitional provisions see art 6, Sch 4 thereto (as amended by SI 2007/1157, arts 7–12).

Para 5: Gambling Commission. As to the establishment, etc of the Gambling Commission, see s 20, Sch 4, and the note 'Gambling Commission' to that section.

Para 11: Person. See the note 'Persons' to s 23.

---

1 Para 17: repealed by the Policing and Crime Act 2009, s 112(2), Sch 8, Pt 13.

2 Para 9: repealed by the Equality Act 2010, s 211(2), Sch 27, Pt 1A (as inserted by SI 2011/1060, art 3(1), (3)(a), Sch 3). Date in force: 4 April 2011: see SI 2011/1060, art 1(2).

3 Para 15: repealed by the Postal Services Act 2011, s 91(1), (2), Sch 12, Pt 3, para 172. Date in force: 1 October 2011: see SI 2011/2329, art 3(1).

4 Para 17: repealed by the Policing and Crime Act 2009, s 112(2), Sch 8, Pt 13. Date in force: 12 January 2010: see the Policing and Crime Act 2009, s 116(6)(b).

SCHEDULE 17
REPEALS
Section 356

6.896

Enactment	Repeal
Gaming Act 1710 (c 19)	The whole Act.
Gaming Act 1738 (c 28)	The whole Act.
Gaming Act 1835 (c 41)	The whole Act.
Metropolitan Police Act 1839 (c 47)	The words ', or knowingly suffer any unlawful games or any gaming whatsoever therein,'.
Gaming Act 1845 (c 109)	The whole Act.
Gaming Act 1892 (c 9)	The whole Act.
Libraries Offences Act 1898 (c 53)	Section 2(3).
Betting, Gaming and Lotteries Act 1963 (c 2)	The whole Act.[1]
Police Act 1964 (c 48)	In Schedule 9, the entry for the Betting, Gaming and Lotteries Act 1963.
Local Government Act 1966 (c 42)	In Schedule 3, paragraph 23.
Theft Act 1968 (c 60)	In Schedule 2, the entry for the Gaming Act 1845.
Gaming Act 1968 (c 65)	The whole Act.
Decimal Currency Act 1969 (c 19)	In Schedule 2, paragraph 17.
Family Law Reform Act 1969 (c 46)	In Schedule 1, the entry for the Betting, Gaming and Lotteries Act 1963.
Chronically Sick and Disabled Persons Act 1970 (c 44)	Section 8B(2)(c).
Courts Act 1971 (c 23)	In Schedule 6, paragraph 6.
	In Schedule 9
	(a) the entry for the Betting, Gaming and Lotteries Act 1963, and
	(b) the entry for the Gaming Act 1968.
Local Government Act 1972 (c 70)	In Schedule 29, paragraph 13.
Gaming (Amendment) Act 1973 (c 12)	The whole Act.
Lotteries Act 1975 (c 58)	The whole Act.
Lotteries and Amusements Act 1976 (c 32)	The whole Act.
Licensing (Scotland) Act 1976 (c 66)	Section 133.
Criminal Law Act 1977 (c 45)	In Schedule 1, paragraph 17.

Enactment	Repeal
	In Schedule 6, the entry for the Gaming Act 1968.
	In Schedule 12, the entry for the Gaming Act 1968.
Gaming (Amendment) Act 1980 (c 8)	The whole Act.
Local Government, Planning and Land Act 1980 (c 65)	In Schedule 8, the entry for the Lotteries and Amusements Act 1976.
Supreme Court Act 1981 (c 54)	In section 28(2)(b), the references to the Betting, Gaming and Lotteries Act 1963 and the Gaming Act 1968.
Betting and Gaming Duties Act 1981 (c 63)	Sections 9 to 9B.
Gaming (Amendment) Act 1982 (c 22)	The whole Act.
Criminal Justice Act 1982 (c 48)	In Schedule 3, the entry for the Betting, Gaming and Lotteries Act 1963.
Lotteries (Amendment) Act 1984 (c 9)	The whole Act.
Betting, Gaming and Lotteries (Amendment) Act 1984 (c 25)	The whole Act.
Police and Criminal Evidence Act 1984 (c 60)	In Schedule 6, paragraph 12.
Companies Consolidation (Consequential Provisions) Act 1985 (c 9)	In Schedule 2, the entry for the Betting, Gaming and Lotteries Act 1963.
Betting, Gaming and Lotteries (Amendment) Act 1985 (c 18)	The whole Act.
Gaming (Bingo) Act 1985 (c 35)	The whole Act.
Local Government Act 1985 (c 51)	In Schedule 8, paragraph 6.
Social Security Act 1985 (c 53)	Section 25.
Gaming (Amendment) Act 1986 (c 11)	The whole Act.
Gaming (Amendment) Act 1987 (c 11)	The whole Act.
Companies Act 1989 (c 40)	In Schedule 10, paragraph 25.
Gaming (Amendment) Act 1990 (c 26)	The whole Act.
Bingo Act 1992 (c 10)	The whole Act.
National Lottery etc Act 1993 (c 39)	Section 2.
	Section 18(1) to (4).
	Section 45.
	Section 46(3).
	Sections 47 to 59.
	In Schedule 1, paragraphs 1 and 2.
	Schedules 7 to 9.
Local Government (Wales) Act 1994 (c 19)	In Schedule 16, paragraph 50.
Coal Industry Act 1994 (c 21)	Section 68(2)(d)(iv).
	In Schedule 9, paragraph 12.
Deregulation and Contracting Out Act 1994 (c 40)	Section 20.
Civil Evidence Act 1995 (c 38)	In Schedule 1, paragraph 4.
Employment Rights Act 1996 (c 18)	In Schedule 1, paragraph 9.
Access to Justice Act 1999 (c 22)	In Schedule 13, paragraphs 32 to 35.

Enactment	Repeal
Financial Services and Markets Act 2000 (c 8)	In section 412(1)
	(a) in paragraph (a), the words 'section 18 of the Gaming Act 1845, section 1 of the Gaming Act 1892 or', and
	(b) paragraph (b).
Criminal Justice and Police Act 2001 (c 16)	Section 63(2)(d).
	In Schedule 1, paragraphs 6, 11, 20, 89, 93 and 97.
Licensing Act 2003 (c 17)	In Schedule 6, paragraphs 29 to 31, 48 to 52 and 62 to 66.
Courts Act 2003 (c 39)	In Schedule 8, paragraphs 113 to 115 and 132.
Criminal Justice Act 2003 (c 44)	In Schedule 25, paragraph 54.

1 In fact various provisions of this Act have been saved: see the introductory note to Pt 7, s 1 below.

Commencement

In so far as it relates to the repeal of section 10 of, and Sch 1 to, the Gaming Act 1968, Sch 17 brought into force by the Gambling Act 2005 (Commencement No 2 and Transitional Provisions) Order 2005, SI 2005/2455, art 2 and Schedule, as from 1 October 2005.Further brought into force in part as from 1 January and for all remaining pupposes as from 1 September by the Gambling Act 2005 (Commencement No 6 and Transitional Provisions) Order 2006, SI 2006/3272, arts 2–5, Sch 1; for transitional provisions see art 6, Sch 4 thereto (as amended by SI 2007/1157, arts 7–12).

Transitional provisions

See s 358(3), Sch 18.

Note

The repeal of section 2 of the National Lottery etc Act 1993 shall not extend to Northern Ireland.

SCHEDULE 18
TRANSITIONAL
Section 358

PART 1
TRANSITIONAL CONTINUATION OF OLD LICENCES, &C

Introduction

[6.897]–[6.898]

1. (1) In this Part a reference to a commencement order is a reference to an order under section 358(1).

(2) This Part is without prejudice to the generality of section 355(1)(c).

Transitional continuation of licences, &c

2. A commencement order may—

(a) provide for a licence or other document issued under an enactment repealed by this Act to have such effect as the order may specify after the commencement of the repeal until a time specified by or determined in accordance with the order;

(b) provide for the application of this Act, with any specified modifications, in relation to a licence or document to which paragraph (a) applies;

(c) disapply, or modify the application of, a provision of this Act in relation to specified things done in reliance on a licence or document to which paragraph (a) applies.

Transitional protection for casinos below minimum licensable size

3. A commencement order may—

(a) disapply section 174(1) in respect of premises that are in use, or could lawfully be used, for the operation of a casino (within the meaning of section 7(1) to (3)) when Part 8 of this Act comes into force;

(b) provide for the application of this Act, with any specified modifications, in relation to premises of that kind;

(c) disapply, or modify the application of, a provision of this Act in relation to specified things done on or in relation to premises of that kind.

References to procedures under this Act

4. A commencement order may include provision for a reference in this Act or in another enactment to anything done under or by virtue of this Act to be taken, for such transitional purposes as may be specified, as including a reference to a thing done under or by virtue of an enactment repealed by this Act.

Commencement

7 April 2005 (the date of royal assent); see s 358(1).

Para 2: Enactment repealed by this Act. See s 356(4), Sch 17.

Para 3: Part 8 of this Act. Ie ss 150–213 and Sch 9.

Definitions

'enactment': s 353(1)

'premises': s 353(1), (2)(g)

Explanatory Notes

872–877 [para **6.2022** below]

PART 2
ADVANCE AND INTERIM APPLICATIONS, AND CONVERSION

Advance applications

[6.899]

5. In this Schedule a reference to an advance application for a licence or permit is a reference to an application made in advance of the commencement of the offence or other provision of this Act in connection with which the licence or permit is required.

6. The Secretary of State may by order—

(a) make provision about the making, consideration or determination of an advance application for a licence or permit;

(b) make provision about the effect of a licence or permit issued in response to an advance application;

(c) require the person to whom an advance application for a licence or permit under this Act is made to determine the application within a specified period;

(d) make provision for an advance application for a licence or permit under this Act to be treated as granted (for such purposes, with such effect and for such period as the order may specify) if not determined in accordance with a requirement imposed under paragraph (c).

7. An order under paragraph 6—

(a) may make provision about advance applications generally or only if made before a specified date or during a specified period, and

(b) may make different provision in relation to different classes of advance application or different classes of activity.

Interim applications

8. The Secretary of State may by order make provision for or about the grant or renewal of a licence or other document, or a registration, under an enactment to be repealed by this Act during a specified period between the passing of this Act and the commencement of the repeal.

Conversion of existing licences, &c

9. The Secretary of State may by order—

(a) make provision for the conversion of a licence or other document under an enactment to be repealed by this Act into a licence or permit under this Act (which may, in particular, include provision requiring a person to whom an advance application is made to grant it in specified circumstances or to a specified extent);

(b) make provision for the conversion of registration under an enactment to be repealed by this Act into registration under this Act or into possession of a licence or permit under this Act (which may, in particular, include provision requiring a person to whom an advance application is made to grant it in specified circumstances or to a specified extent).

10. An order under paragraph 9 may provide for conversion of licences, other documents or registrations generally or by reference to—

(a) the use made of a licence, document or registration,

(b) the age or duration of a licence, document or registration, or

(c) any other matter.

Orders: general

11. An order under this Part—

(a) may include provision modifying the effect of a provision of this Act or the effect of a provision to be repealed by this Act, and

(b) may apply or replicate a provision of this Act with or without modification (including a provision conferring a discretion or providing for the payment of a fee).

Commencement

7 April 2005 (the date of royal assent); see s 358(1).

Para 6: Secretary of State. See the note to s 4.

Para 8: Enactment to be repealed by this Act. See s 356(4), Sch 17.

Subordinate Legislation under this Part of this Schedule. Gambling Act 2005 (Transitional Provisions) Order 2006, SI 2006/1038 (made under paras 8, 11).

Gambling Act 2005 (Transitional Provisions) (No 2) Order 2006, SI 2006/1758 (made under paras 8, 11).

Gambling Act 2005 (Commencement No 6 and Transitional Provisions) Order 2006, SI 2006/3272.

Gambling (Premises Licence Fees) (England and Wales) Regulations 2007, SI 2007/479 (made under paras 6, 7, 11).

As to orders under this Act generally, see s 355.

Definitions

'enactment': s 353(1)

'premises': s 353(1), (2)(g)

Explanatory Notes

872–877 [para **6.2022** below]

Section 3

Statutory Instruments

GAMBLING ACT 2005 (LICENSING AUTHORITY POLICY STATEMENT) (ENGLAND AND WALES) REGULATIONS 2006

(SI 2006/636)

Made . . . . *5th March 2006*
Laid before Parliament . . . . *9th March 2006*
Coming into force . . . . *31st March 2006*

The Secretary of State makes the following Regulations in exercise of the powers conferred by section 349(4) of the Gambling Act 2005.

6.1510 1 Citation, commencement and extent

(1) These Regulations may be cited as the Gambling Act 2005 (Licensing Authority Policy Statement) (England and Wales) Regulations 2006 and shall come into force on 31st March 2006.

(2) These Regulations shall extend to England and Wales.

6.1511 2 Interpretation

In these Regulations—

"the Act" means the Gambling Act 2005;

"authority" means a licensing authority within the meaning of section 2 of the Act;

"revision" means a revision of a statement under section 349(2) of the Act;

"statement" means the statement of principles that the authority is required to prepare under section 349(1) of the Act.

6.1512 3 Form of the statement or revision

Subject to regulations 4, 5 and 6, the form of the statement or any revision is to be for the authority to determine.

6.1513

4 (1) The statement shall include an introductory section at or near the beginning, summarising the matters dealt with in the statement.

(2) The introductory section shall also include—

(a) a description of the geographical area in respect of which the authority exercises functions under the Act, and

(b) a list of the persons whom the authority has consulted in preparing the statement.

(3) The authority may satisfy the requirement in paragraph (a) by including a plan of the area to which the statement applies.

6.1514

5 The following matters shall each be set out in a separate section within the statement—

(a) the principles to be applied by the authority in exercising the powers under section 157(h) of the Act to designate, in writing, a body which is competent to advise the authority about the protection of children from harm;

(b) the principles to be applied by the authority in exercising the powers under section 158 of the Act to determine whether a person is an interested party in relation to a premises licence, or an application for or in respect of a premises licence;

(c) the principles to be applied by the authority in exercising the functions under sections 29 and 30 of the Act with respect to the exchange of information between it and the Gambling Commission, and the functions under section 350 of the Act with respect to the exchange of information between it and the other persons listed in Schedule 6 to the Act;

(d) the principles to be applied by the authority in exercising the functions under Part 15 of the Act with respect to the inspection of premises; and the powers under section 346 of the Act to institute criminal proceedings in respect of the offences specified in that section.

6.1515

6 (1) Regulation 4(1) shall apply to a revision as it applies to a statement.

(2) The introductory section of a revision shall include a list of the persons whom the authority has consulted in preparing the revision.

(3) In so far as a revision deals with any of the matters referred to in regulation 5, the form of the revision shall be in accordance with those provisions.

6.1516 7 Procedure to be followed in preparing or publishing a statement or revision

(1) Before a statement or revision comes into effect, the authority that prepared it must—

(a) publish the statement or revision in accordance with paragraph (2); and

(b) advertise the publication of the statement or revision by publishing a notice in accordance with paragraphs (3) and (4).

(2) The statement or revision must be published by being made available for a period of at least 4 weeks before the date on which it will come into effect—

(a) on the authority's internet website; and

(b) for inspection by the public at reasonable times in one or both of the following places—

(i) one or more public libraries situated in the area covered by the statement or revision;

(ii) other premises situated in that area.

(3) The notice referred to in paragraph (1)(b) shall specify—

(a) the date on which the statement or revision will be published;

(b) the date on which the statement or revision will come into effect;

(c) the internet address where the statement or revision will be published in accordance with paragraph (2)(a); and

(d) the address of the library or other premises at which the statement or revision may be inspected in accordance with paragraph (2)(b).

(4) That notice shall be published no later than the first day on which the statement or revision is published in accordance with paragraph (2)—

(a) on the authority's internet website, and

(b) in or on one or more of the following places—

(i) a local newspaper circulating in the area covered by the statement;

(ii) a local newsletter, circular, or similar document circulating in the area covered by the statement;

(iii) a public notice board in or near the principal office of the authority;

(iv) a public notice board on the premises of public libraries in the area covered by the statement.

GAMBLING ACT 2005 (LICENSING AUTHORITY POLICY STATEMENT) (FIRST APPOINTED DAY) ORDER 2006

(SI 2006/637)

Made . . . . *5th March 2006*
Laid before Parliament . . . . *9th March 2006*
Coming into force . . . . *31st March 2006*

The Secretary of State makes the following Order in exercise of the powers conferred by section 349(6) of the Gambling Act 2005:

6.1520 1 Citation, commencement and interpretation

(1) This Order may be cited as the Gambling Act 2005 (Licensing Authority Policy Statement) (First Appointed Day) Order 2006 and shall come into force on 31st March 2006.

(2) In this Order, "the Act" means the Gambling Act 2005.

6.1521 2 First appointed day

For the purposes of section 349 of the Act (requirement on licensing authorities to publish a policy statement every three years), the first appointed day shall be 31st January 2007.

GAMBLING ACT 2005 (TRANSITIONAL PROVISIONS) ORDER 2006

(SI 2006/1038)

Made . . . . *3rd April 2006*
Laid before Parliament . . . . *4th April 2006*
Coming into force . . . . *29th April 2006*

The Secretary of State makes the following Order in exercise of the powers conferred by section 355(1) of, and paragraphs 8 and 11 of Schedule 18 to, the Gambling Act 2005:

6.1522 1 Citation, commencement and interpretation

(1) This Order may be cited as the Gambling Act 2005 (Transitional Provisions) Order 2006 and shall come into force on 29th April 2006.

(2) In this Order—

"the 1968 Act" means the Gaming Act 1968;

"casino licence" means a licence under the 1968 Act other than a bingo club licence (within the meaning of paragraph 2(2) of Schedule 2 to that Act);

"consent application in respect of a casino licence" means an application for a certificate of consent under paragraph 4 of Schedule 2 to the 1968 Act for the purposes of an application under that Act for the grant of a casino licence; and

"licensing board area" means the area of a licensing board constituted under section 1 of the Licensing (Scotland) Act 1976.

6.1523 2 Modification of the powers of the Gambling Commission to issue certificates of consent

(1) This article applies to the exercise by the Gambling Commission of its powers to issue a certificate of consent under paragraph 4 of Schedule 2 to the 1968 Act

during the period beginning on the date on which this Order comes into force and ending on the date on which the repeal of that paragraph by section 356(3)(g) and (4) of, and Schedule 17 to, the Gambling Act 2005 takes effect for all purposes.

(2) Where a consent application in respect of a casino licence is made on or after 29th April 2006, the Gambling Commission may only issue a certificate of consent on that application in the circumstances specified in paragraph (3).

(3) The circumstances are that—

(a) the person making the application holds one or more casino licences in respect of premises in the same licensing area; and

(b) the Gambling Commission is satisfied that the applicant intends to relinquish such a casino licence if the casino licence in respect of which the consent application is made is granted.

(4) In paragraph (3)(a) the reference to the same licensing area is—

(a) where the premises to which the consent application relates are in England or Wales, to the local justice area in which those premises are situated; and

(b) where the premises to which the consent application relates are in Scotland, to the licensing board area in which those premises are situated.

6.1524 3 Modification of the powers of the Gambling Commission to revoke certificates of consent

(1) Paragraph 35 of Schedule 2 to the 1968 Act (powers of the Gambling Commission to revoke a certificate of consent) is to be modified as follows in its application to a certificate of consent issued by the Gambling Commission on a consent application in respect of a casino licence made on or after 29th April 2006.

(2) Paragraph 35 is to have effect as if, in addition to the matters referred to in sub-paragraphs (2) and (3), it provided for the Gambling Commission to have power to revoke a certificate of consent where—

(a) the casino licence to which the certificate relates has been issued and premises are being used in reliance on that licence, but

(b) the holder of the licence has not relinquished a casino licence falling within the description in article 2(3)(a).

GAMBLING ACT 2005 (TRANSITIONAL PROVISIONS) (NO 2) ORDER 2006

(SI 2006/1758)

Made . . . . *4th July 2006*
Laid before Parliament . . . . *5th July 2006*
Coming into force . . . . *1st August 2006*

The Secretary of State makes the following Order in exercise of the powers conferred by section 355(1) of, and paragraphs 8 and 11 of Schedule 18 to, the Gambling Act 2005:

6.1525 1 Citation, commencement and interpretation

(1) This Order may be cited as the Gambling Act 2005 (Transitional Provisions) (No 2) Order 2006 and shall come into force on 1st August 2006.

(2) In this Order—

"the 1968 Act" means the Gaming Act 1968;

6.1525A 2 Betting, Gaming and Lotteries Act 1963: grant of new track betting licences

(1) This article applies to any track betting licence which is due to expire in accordance with paragraph 8 of Schedule 3 to the 1963 Act in the period beginning on 1st September 2006 and ending on 30th August 2007.

(2) Subject to paragraph (10), if a track betting licence to which this article applies (referred to below as "the previous track betting licence") is still in force immediately before it is due to expire, the licensing authority which granted the licence are to be treated as having granted a new track betting licence in respect of the track to which the previous track betting licence related.

(3) A licence granted in accordance with paragraph (2) is to be treated as having been granted when the previous track betting licence expires to the person who held that licence immediately before it expired.

(4) A licence granted in accordance with paragraph (2) is referred to in this article as a "new track betting licence".

(5) Paragraph 8 of Schedule 3 to the 1963 Act is to have effect in relation to a new track betting licence as if it provided for the licence to be in force until the end of 31st August 2007, unless cancelled under paragraph 10 or revoked under paragraph 13 of that Schedule.

(6) Where—

(a) the holder of a new track betting licence makes a request in writing to the relevant licensing authority for a copy of the licence, and

(b) that request is made in accordance with paragraph (7),

the authority must comply with the request as soon as reasonably practicable.

(7) When making a request under paragraph (6), the holder of a new track betting licence must include the previous track betting licence or, if for any reason that is not reasonably practicable, he must include a written statement—

(a) explaining why it is not reasonably practicable to provide that licence, and

(b) indicating—

(i) the premises to which the licence related,

(ii) the date on which it was granted, and

(iii) the date on which it expired.

(8) Paragraph (9) applies where before the previous track betting licence expires—

(a) the holder of that licence applies to the licensing authority which granted it for the grant of a further track betting licence in respect of the same track, or

(b) he gives notice under paragraph 5 of Schedule 3 to the 1963 Act to the licensing authority that he intends to make such an application.

(9) Where this paragraph applies—

(a) paragraph 12(1) of Schedule 3 to the 1963 Act (which provides for the payment of an application fee in respect of applications for track betting licences) is not to apply in relation to the application for the grant of a track betting licence;

(b) the licensing authority may not determine the application until the previous track betting licence has expired, and they may only do so after the licence expires if a new track betting licence is not granted in accordance with paragraph (2);

(c) where a new track betting licence is granted in accordance with paragraph (2), the notice or application referred to in paragraph (8) is to be treated on and after the date on which that licence is granted as if it were a request made under paragraph (6); and

(d) the requirement to comply with that request is to apply irrespective of whether the notice or application is accompanied by the previous track betting licence or includes the information specified in paragraph (7).

(10) Paragraphs (2) to (9) are not to apply where before the date on which this Order comes into force—

(a) the holder of the previous track betting licence applies under paragraph 3 of Schedule 3 to the 1963 Act for the grant of a track betting licence to have effect in respect of the same track, and

(b) the licensing authority determine that application.

(11) In this article "track" and "track betting licence" have the meanings given to them by sections 55(1) and 6(1) of the 1963 Act respectively, and "licensing authority" is to have the same the meaning as in Schedule 3 to that Act.

5.1526 3 Gaming Act 1968: renewal of licences

(1) This article applies to any licence under the 1968 Act which is due to expire in accordance with paragraph 52 of Schedule 2 to that Act in the period beginning on 1st September 2006 and ending on 30th August 2007.

(2) If the licence is still in force immediately before it is due to expire, the licensing authority is to be treated as having renewed the licence immediately before it expires.

(3) Section 48(3)(b) and (4)(b) of, and paragraph 63 of Schedule 2 to, the 1968 Act (which provide for the payment of a fee on renewal) are not to apply in relation to the renewal of a licence in accordance with paragraph (2).

(4) Where a licence is renewed under paragraph (2)—

(a) it is to be subject to the same restrictions as had effect in relation to the licence before it was renewed, and paragraphs 24 to 26 of Schedule 2 to the 1968 Act are to have effect in relation to the licence as if modified accordingly; and

(b) paragraph 52 of that Schedule is to have effect in relation to the licence as if it provided for it to be in force until the end of 31st August 2007 (unless cancelled before that date under any provision of that Schedule).

(5) Where—

(a) the holder of a licence renewed in accordance with paragraph (2) makes a request in writing to the relevant licensing authority for a copy of the licence as so renewed, and

(b) that request is made in accordance with paragraph (6),

the authority must comply with the request as soon as reasonably practicable.

(6) When making a request under paragraph (5), the holder of the licence must include the licence held by him or, if for any reason that is not reasonably practicable, he must include a written statement—

(a) explaining why it is not reasonably practicable to provide the licence, and

(b) indicating—

(i) the premises to which the licence relates,

(ii) the date on which it was granted or (as the case may be) last renewed before its renewal in accordance with paragraph (2), and

(iii) the date on which it was due to expire before being renewed in accordance with that paragraph.

6.1527 4 Gaming Act 1968: circumstances in which a licence is not to be treated as being automatically renewed

(1) Despite the provisions of article 3 (which provide for the automatic renewal of licences under the 1968 Act), the holder of a licence to which that article applies may make an application under paragraph 12 of Schedule 2 to that Act for its renewal; and, subject to the following provisions of this article, where such an application is made paragraphs (2) to (5) of article 3 are not to apply to the renewal of the licence.

(2) Where an application for renewal is made under paragraph 12 of Schedule 2 to the 1968 Act, paragraphs (2) to (5) of article 3 are still to apply to the renewal of the licence if either paragraph (3) or (4) applies.

(3) This paragraph applies where—

(a) the application for renewal is made later than is required by sub-paragraph (1) of paragraph 12 of that Schedule, and

(b) the licensing authority do not entertain the application in exercise of their powers under sub-paragraph (2) of that paragraph.

(4) This paragraph applies where the application for renewal is withdrawn at any time before any hearing is held by the licensing authority for the purposes of determining the application.

(5) Where a licence to which article 3 applies is renewed on an application made under paragraph 12 of Schedule 2 to the 1968 Act, paragraph 52 of that Schedule is to have effect in relation to the licence as if it provided for the licence to be in force until the end of 31st August 2007 (unless cancelled before that date under any provision of that Schedule).

6.1528 5 Gaming Act 1968: renewal of section 34 permits granted in respect of amusement machine premises

(1) This article applies to any permit under section 34 of the 1968 Act (which provides for the use of machines for amusement purposes), granted in respect of amusement machine premises, which is due to expire in accordance with paragraph 18 of Schedule 9 to that Act in the period beginning on 1st September 2006 and ending on 30th August 2007.

(2) Subject to paragraph (7), if the permit still has effect immediately before it is due to expire, the appropriate authority is to be treated as having renewed the permit immediately before it expires.

(3) Section 48(3)(h) and (i) and (4B) of, and paragraph 21 of Schedule 9 to, the 1968 Act (which provide for the payment of a fee on renewal) are not to apply in relation to the renewal of a permit in accordance with paragraph (2).

(4) Where—

(a) the holder of a permit renewed in accordance with paragraph (2) makes a request in writing to the appropriate authority for a copy of the permit as so renewed, and

(b) that request is made in accordance with paragraph (5),

the authority must comply with the request as soon as reasonably practicable.

(5) When making a request under paragraph (4), the holder of the permit must include the permit held by him or, if for any reason that is not reasonably practicable, he must include a written statement—

(a) explaining why it is not reasonably practicable to provide the permit, and

(b) indicating—

(i) the premises to which the permit relates,

(ii) the date on which it was granted or (as the case may be) last renewed before its renewal in accordance with paragraph (2), and

(iii) the date on which it was due to expire before being renewed in accordance with that paragraph.

(6) Where before its renewal in accordance with paragraph (2) the holder of the permit makes an application to the appropriate authority in accordance with paragraph 5(2) of Schedule 9 to the 1968 Act for the renewal of the permit—

(a) the appropriate authority may not determine the application before the permit is due to expire;

(b) where the permit is renewed in accordance with paragraph (2), the application is to be treated on and after the permit's renewal as if it were a request made under paragraph (4); and

(c) the requirement to comply with that request is to apply irrespective of whether the application is accompanied by the permit or includes the information specified in paragraph (5).

(7) Paragraphs (2) to (6) are not to apply where before the date on which this Order comes into force—

(a) the holder of the permit applies under paragraph 5(2) of Schedule 9 to the 1968 Act for the renewal of the permit, and

(b) the appropriate authority determine that application.

(8) Paragraph 18 of Schedule 9 to the 1968 Act is to have effect in relation to the renewal of a permit to which this article applies as if it provided for the permit to have effect until the end of 31st August 2007 unless cancelled before that date under section 39 of that Act.

(9) In this article "appropriate authority", in relation to a permit under section 34 of the 1968 Act, has the meaning given to it (as the case may be) by paragraph 1(b) or (d) of Schedule 9 to the 1968 Act.

6.1529 6 Gaming Act 1968: restrictions on the grant of section 34 permits

(1) This article applies to the grant or renewal of permits under section 34 of the 1968 Act by the authority mentioned in paragraph 1(b) or (d) of Schedule 9 to that Act during the period beginning on the date on which this Order comes into force and ending on the date on which the repeal of that section and that Schedule by section 356(3)(g) and (4) of, and Schedule 17 to, the Gambling Act 2005 takes effect for all purposes.

(2) Where the application is made on or after 1st August 2006, the authority may only grant or renew the permit if it relates to amusement machine premises.

(3) Paragraph (2) is without prejudice to article 5.

(4) Where a permit is granted or renewed during the period mentioned in paragraph (1) with respect to premises other than amusement machine premises, it is to cease to have effect on 31st July 2009 (unless it is cancelled before that date under section 39 of the 1968 Act); and paragraph 18 of Schedule 9 to that Act is to have effect in relation to such a permit as if modified accordingly.

6.1530 7 Lotteries and Amusements Act 1976: renewal of section 16 permits

(1) This article applies to any permit under section 16 of the 1976 Act (which relates to the provision of amusements with prizes at certain commercial entertainments) which is due to expire in accordance with paragraph 15 of Schedule 3 to that Act in the period beginning on 1st September 2006 and ending on 30th August 2007.

(2) Subject to paragraphs (7) and (8), if the permit still has effect immediately before it is due to expire, the appropriate authority is to be treated as having renewed the permit immediately before it expires.

(3) Paragraph 18 of Schedule 3 to the 1976 Act (which provides for the payment of a fee on grant or renewal of a permit) is not to apply in relation to the renewal of a permit in accordance with paragraph (2).

(4) Where—

(a) the holder of a permit renewed in accordance with paragraph (2) makes a request in writing to the appropriate authority for a copy of the permit as so renewed, and

(b) that request is made in accordance with paragraph (5),

the authority must comply with the request as soon as reasonably practicable.

(5) When making a request under paragraph (4), the holder of the permit must include the permit held by him or, if for any reason that is not reasonably practicable, he must include a written statement—

(a) explaining why it is not reasonably practicable to provide the permit, and

(b) indicating—

(i) the premises to which the permit relates,

(ii) the date on which it was granted or (as the case may be) last renewed before its renewal in accordance with paragraph (2), and

(iii) the date on which it was due to expire before being renewed in accordance with that paragraph.

(6) Where before its renewal in accordance with paragraph (2) the holder of the permit makes an application to the appropriate authority in accordance with paragraph 4(2) of Schedule 3 to the 1976 Act for the renewal of the permit—

(a) the appropriate authority may not determine the application before the permit is due to expire;

(b) where the permit is renewed in accordance with paragraph (2), the application is to be treated on and after the permit's renewal as if it were a request made under paragraph (4); and

(c) the requirement to comply with that request is to apply irrespective of whether the application is accompanied by the permit or includes the information specified in paragraph (5).

(7) Paragraphs (2) to (6) are not to apply where before the date on which this Order comes into force—

(a) the holder of the permit applies under paragraph 4(2) of Schedule 3 to the 1976 Act for the renewal of the permit, and

(b) the appropriate authority determine that application.

(8) Paragraphs (2) to (6) are also not to apply where—

(a) a resolution is passed by the appropriate authority under paragraph 2(b) of Schedule 3 to the 1976 Act with the effect that the authority will not renew permits under section 16 of that Act in respect of premises of a class which includes the premises to which the permit relates, and

(b) that resolution is in force—

(i) in relation to paragraph (6)(a), when the relevant application is made, or

(ii) in the case of any other provision, when the permit is due to expire.

(9) Paragraph 15 of Schedule 3 to the 1976 Act is to have effect in relation to the renewal of a permit to which this article applies as if it provided for the permit to have effect until the end of 31st August 2007, unless cancelled before that date under section 17(2) of that Act.

(10) In this article, "appropriate authority" is to have the meaning given to it by paragraph 1(1) of Schedule 3 to the 1976 Act.

GAMBLING ACT 2005 (DEFINITION OF SMALL-SCALE OPERATOR) REGULATIONS 2006

(SI 2006/3266)

Made ....*6th December 2006*
Laid before Parliament ....*7th December 2006*
Coming into force ....*1st January 2007*

The Secretary of State, in exercise of the powers conferred by section 129(2) of the Gambling Act 2005, makes the following Regulations:

6.1531 1 Citation, commencement and interpretation

(1) These Regulations may be cited as the Gambling Act 2005 (Definition of Small-scale Operator) Regulations 2006 and shall come into force on 1st January 2007.

(2) In these regulations "the Act" means the Gambling Act 2005.

6.1532 2 Definition of small-scale operator

(1) For the purposes of section 129 of the Gambling Act 2005, and subject to regulation 3, the holder of an operating licence (the licensee) is a small-scale operator if, in relation to the activity authorised by that operating licence (the licensed activity)—

(a) there are no more than 3 qualifying positions in or in respect of the licensee or in connection with the licensed activity, and

(b) each qualifying position is occupied by a qualified person.

(2) In this regulation "qualifying position" means a position which is held by a person who, by the terms of his appointment, has primary responsibility for—

(a) the management of the licensed activity;

(b) the management of the financial affairs of the licensee;

(c) ensuring the licensee complies with the requirements of the Act;

(d) the marketing of the licensed activity;

(e) the management of the information technology facilities used in the provision of the licensed activity;

(f) the management of the licensed activity for a particular locality or area in Great Britain in which there are situated 5 or more sets of premises in respect of each of which the licensee holds a premises licence; or

(g) the management of a single set of premises in respect of which a casino or bingo premises licence has effect.

(3) In this regulation "qualified person" means a person who is—

(a) named on the operating licence as a person who holds a qualifying position; or

(b) the subject of an application to vary the operating licence under section 104(1)(b) of the Act (application to vary licence) to add his name as a person holding a qualifying position, and—

(i) the application complies with sections 69(2)(g) (fee) and 104(5) (accompanying statement) of the Act; and

(ii) the application has not been withdrawn or finally determined.

(4) For the purposes of paragraph (3) an application to vary an operating licence, which has been rejected by the Gambling Commission, is to be treated as having been finally determined—

(a) where there is no appeal to the [First-tier Tribunal][1], on the expiry of the period for appealing

(b) where such an appeal is made, and the appeal is either withdrawn or allowed, (subject to sub-paragraph (e)) when the appeal is withdrawn, or, as the case may be, determined;

(c) where the appeal to the [First-tier Tribunal][2] is refused and no appeal is made [to the Upper Tribunal],[3] on the expiry of the period for appealing against the decision of the Gambling Appeals Tribunal;

(d) where an appeal is made [to the Upper Tribunal],[4] (subject to sub-paragraph (e)) on the date on which the appeal is determined or withdrawn;

(e) where the result of an appeal is that the matter is remitted to the body against whose decision the appeal is made, when any subsequent proceedings relating to the decision to reject the application are finally determined (as determined in accordance with sub-paragraphs (a) to (d)).

---

[1] Para (4): in sub-para (a) words "First-tier Tribunal" in square brackets substituted by SI 2010/22, art 5(2), Sch 3, para 138(a).

[2] Para (4): in sub-para (c) words "First-tier Tribunal" in square brackets substituted by SI 2010/22, art 5(2), Sch 3, para 138(a).

[3] Para (4): in sub-para (c) words "to the Upper Tribunal" in square brackets substituted by SI 2010/22, art 5(2), Sch 3, para 138(b).

[4] Para (4): in sub-para (d) words "to the Upper Tribunal" in square brackets substituted by SI 2010/22, art 5(2), Sch 3, para 138(b).

6.1533 3 Loss of Exemption

For the purposes of section 129 of the Act a person shall not cease to be a small-scale operator if he no longer complies with the conditions specified in regulation 2 unless he fails to comply with them—

(a) for a period of more than 28 days; or

(b) for two periods, each of more than 14 days, where one period occurs within 28 days of the other.

GAMBLING (PERSONAL LICENCES) (MODIFICATION OF PART 5 OF THE GAMBLING ACT 2005) REGULATIONS 2006

(SI 2006/3267)

Made ....*6th December 2006*
Laid before Parliament ....*7th December 2006*
Coming into force ....*1st January 2007*

The Secretary of State makes the following Regulations in exercise of the powers conferred by section 128(1)(b) the Gambling Act 2005:

6.1534 1 Citation and commencement

(1) These Regulations may be cited as the Gambling (Personal Licences) (Modification of Part 5 of the Gambling Act 2005) Regulations 2006 and shall come into force on 1st January 2007.

6.1535 2 Modification of Part 5 of the Gambling Act 2005

(1) The provisions of Part 5 of the Gambling Act 2005 listed in Table 1 in the Schedule are not to apply to personal licences.

(2) The provisions of that Part listed in column 1 of Table 2 in the Schedule shall apply to personal licences, subject to the modifications specified in the corresponding entry in column 2 of that table.

SCHEDULE

Regulation 2

6.1536

Table 1
Sections of the Gambling Act 2005 excluded from applying to personal licences

Section 72 (Consideration of application: demand)

Section 80 (Requirement for personal licence)

Section 81 (Credit and inducements)

Sections 85 to 87 (Equipment, gaming machines and membership)

Sections 89 to 99 (Rules for particular kinds of licence)

Sections 102 and 103 (Change of corporate control and supplemental)

Sections 110 to 112 (Duration)
Section 123 (Levy)

Table 2
Modifications to Part 5 of the Gambling Act 2005

Section 66(1) (Form of licence)	To have effect as if paragraph (b) was omitted.
Section 67 (Remote gambling)	To have effect as if— (a) the following was substituted for subsection (1)— "(1) A personal licence is a "remote personal licence" if it authorises an individual to perform functions which include the functions of a specified management office in connection with the provision of facilities for remote gambling."; (b) subsection (2) was omitted; and (c) the following was substituted for subsection (3)— "(3) A personal licence must state whether it is a remote personal licence or not.".
Section 69(2) and (3) (Application)	To have effect as if (a) the following was substituted for paragraph (a) of subsection (2)— "(a) Specify— (i) any management office the performance of whose functions are to be authorised by the licence, and (ii) any operational function to be authorised by the licence."; and (b) Paragraph (b) of subsection (3) was omitted.
Section 70 (Consideration of application: general principles)	To have effect as if— (a) in subsection (1), paragraphs (c) and (d) were omitted, (b) in subsection (2), the words "or of a person relevant to the application", wherever they appear, were omitted, (c) subsections (3), (6), (8) and (10) were omitted, (d) in subsection (7), the words "or other person" were omitted, and (e) in subsection (9), paragraph (b) was omitted.
Section 71 (Consideration of application: criminal record)	To have effect as if— (a) in subsection (1), the words "or a person relevant to the application" were omitted, and

	(b) subsection (3) was omitted.
Section 73 (Procedure)	To have effect as if paragraph (b) in each of subsections (2) and (3) was omitted.
Section 75(2) (General conditions imposed by Commission)	To have effect as if, in paragraph (c), the words from "or of another person" to the end of the paragraph were omitted.
Section 79 (Scope of powers to attach conditions)	To have effect as if— (a) in paragraph (c) of subsection (3), the words from "or of another person" to the end of the paragraph were omitted, (b) subsections (4), (6) and (7) were omitted, and (c) in subsection (5), the words from "or of another person" to the end of the subsection were omitted.
Section 82 (Compliance with code of practice)	To have effect as if (a) the following paragraph was substituted for paragraph (a) of subsection (2)— "(a) the reference to the licensee includes, where the licence authorises the performance of the functions of a management office, a reference to a person for whom the licensee is responsible,"; and (b) the following subsections were inserted after subsection (3)— "(4) For the purposes of subsection (2)(a), the licensee is responsible for a person if— (a) the licensee is required by the terms of his appointment, to take or share responsibility for the conduct of that person, and (b) that person performs an operational function in connection with an activity performed in reliance on a relevant operating licence. (5) In subsection (4), the reference to a relevant operating licence is to any operating licence in connection with which the licensee performs the functions authorised by his personal licence.".
Section 83 (Return of stakes to children)	To have effect as if— (a) the following subsections were substituted for subsection (1)— "(1) This section applies to a personal licence which authorises the licensee to perform a specified operational function in connection with the provision of facilities for gambling under an operating licence. (1A) The personal licence shall by virtue of this section be subject to the condition that, if the licensee becomes aware that a child or young person is using or has used facilities for gambling provided in reliance on the operating licence, the licensee—

(a) must return any money paid in respect of the use of those facilities (whether by way of fee, stake or otherwise) by the child or young person as soon as is reasonably practicable, and

(b) may not give a prize to the child or young person.

(1B) Subsection (1A) does not apply where the licensee does not have authority under the terms or conditions of his appointment to act in the way required by that subsection; but, in such a case, the licensee must take all reasonable steps to inform a person having the appropriate authority of the relevant matters relating to the child or young person referred to in that subsection.";

(b) in subsection (3) the words "The condition in subsection (1)" were omitted and replaced with "Subject to subsection (1B), the condition in subsection (1A)"; and

(c) subsection (4)(a) was omitted.

Section 84(1) (Premises)	To have effect with the omission of paragraph (b).
Section 88 (Information)	To have effect as if—

(a) the following was substituted for paragraph (a) of subsection (2)—

"(a) relate to information about the use made of facilities provided in accordance with a relevant operating licence;"; and

(b) the following subsection was inserted after subsection (2)—

"(2A)In subsection (2)(a), the reference to a relevant operating licence is to any operating licence in connection with which the licensee performs the functions authorised by his personal licence,".

Section 114 (Lapse)	To have effect with the omission of subsection (2).
Section 116 (Review)	To have effect as if the following were substituted for subsections (2) and (3)—

"(2) The Commission may review any matter connected with the performance of the functions authorised by the licence if the Commission—

(a) has reason to suspect that the functions have not been performed in accordance with a condition of the licence,

(b) believes that the licensee has acquired a conviction of a kind mentioned in section 71(1), or

(c) for any reason—

(i) suspects that the licensee may be unsuitable to carry on the licensed activities, or

(ii) thinks that a review would be appropriate.

(3) For the purposes of subsection (2)(c) a reason—

	(a) may, in particular, relate to the receipt of a complaint about the performance of the functions authorised by the licence; (b) need not relate to any suspicion or belief about the performance of those functions.”.
Section 117(1) (Regulatory powers)	To have effect with the omission of paragraph (d).
Section 119 (Revocation)	To have effect as if the following was substituted for subsection (3)— “(3) The Commission shall revoke a personal licence if the licensee fails to pay any fee payable in accordance with section 132; but the Commission may disapply this subsection if it thinks that a failure to pay is attributable to administrative error.”
Section 120(3) (Conditions for suspension or revocation)	To have effect as if— (a) in paragraphs (a) and (c), the words “or of any person who exercises a function in connection with or is interested in the licensed activities” were omitted, and (b) in paragraph (b), the words “, or of any person who exercises a function in connection with the licensed activities,” were omitted.
Section 126(1) (Interpretation)	To have effect as if the following was substituted for the definition of “licensed activities”— ““licensed activities” in relation to a personal licence means the functions whose performance is authorised by the licence, and”.

GAMBLING ACT 2005 (COMMENCEMENT NO 6 AND TRANSITIONAL PROVISIONS) ORDER 2006

(SI 2006/3272)

Made ....*6th December 2006*
Laid before Parliament ....*8th December 2006*
Coming into force ....*1st January 2007*

The Secretary of State makes the following Order in exercise of the powers conferred by sections 355(1) and 358(1) and (2) of, and paragraphs 2 to 11 of Schedule 18 to, the Gambling Act 2005:

6.1537 1 Citation, commencement and interpretation

(1) This Order may be cited as the Gambling Act 2005 (Commencement No 6 and Transitional Provisions) Order 2006 and shall come into force on 1st January 2007.

(2) In this Order—

“the 1963 Act” means the Betting, Gaming and Lotteries Act 1963;

“the 1968 Act” means the Gaming Act 1968;

“the 1976 Act” means the Lotteries and Amusements Act 1976;

[“the 2004 Act” means the Horserace Betting and Olympic Lottery Act 2004;][1]

"the 2005 Act" means the Gambling Act 2005;

"advance application", in relation to an application for a licence or permit under the 2005 Act, means an application made before 1st September 2007 (being the commencement date for the offences and other provisions of the 2005 Act in connection with which the licence or permit is required);

"amusement machine premises" means premises used wholly or mainly for the provision of amusements by means of machines to which Part 3 of the 1968 Act applies;

"non-conversion application for a casino premises licence" has the meaning given by paragraph 66(4) of Schedule 4 to this Order; . . . [2]

"point to point certificate" has the meaning given by paragraph 53(7) of Schedule 4 to this Order[; and][3]

["the successor company" means the company which is nominated for the purposes of section 2 of the 2004 Act by the Secretary of State in accordance with subsection (2)(a) of that section][4].

---

1 Definition "the 2004 Act" inserted by SI 2007/2169, art 2(a).

2 In definition "non-conversion application for a casino premises licence" word omitted revoked by SI 2007/2169, art 2(b).

3 In definition "point to point certificate" word "; and" in square brackets inserted by SI 2007/2169, art 2(c).

4 Definition "the successor company" inserted by SI 2007/2169, art 2(d).

6.1538 2 Commencement of provisions of the Gambling Act 2005

(1) The provisions of the 2005 Act specified in column 1 of Schedule 1 shall come into force on 1st January 2007, but where a particular purpose is specified in relation to any such provision in column 2 of that Schedule, the provision concerned shall come into force on that date for that purpose only.

[(1A) Section 182(4) of the 2005 Act shall come into force on 30th April 2007.][1]

(2) The provisions of the 2005 Act specified in column 1 of Schedule 2 shall come into force on [21st May][2] 2007, but where a particular purpose is specified in relation to any such provision in column 2 of that Schedule, the provision concerned shall come into force on that date for that purpose only.

(3) . . . [3]

[(3A) The provisions of the 2005 Act specified in column 1 of Schedule 3A shall come into force on 1st August 2007, but where a particular purpose is specified in relation to any such provision in column 2 of that Schedule, the provision shall come into force on that date for that purpose only.][4]

[(4) Save as provided by articles 3 to 5, the 2005 Act apart from the provisions listed in column 1 of Schedule 3B shall come into force on 1st September 2007.

(5) Where a particular purpose is specified in column 2 of Schedule 3B in relation to any provision listed in that Schedule, the reference to that provision in paragraph (4) is only to that provision for the purpose so specified.][5]

---

1 Inserted by SI 2007/1157, art 3(1), (2).

2 Words "21st May" in square brackets substituted by SI 2007/1157, art 3(1), (3).

3 Revoked by SI 2007/1527, art 2(1), (2)(a).

4 Inserted by SI 2007/1157, art 3(1), (4).

5 Paras (4), (5): substituted, for para (4) as originally enacted, by SI 2007/2169, art 3.

6.1539 3 Repeal of the Betting, Gaming and Lotteries Act 1963

(1) The repeal of the 1963 Act by section 356(3)(f), (4) and (5) of, and Schedule 17 to, the 2005 Act shall, to the extent that it is not already in force, come into force on 1st September 2007—

(a) for all purposes in relation to—

(i) any licence or other document issued under the 1963 Act, or

(ii) any registration under Schedule 2 to the 1963 Act (which relates to the registration of pool promoters),

which has effect immediately before that date; and

(b) for all other purposes except as provided in the following provisions of this article.

(2) The 1963 Act is to continue to have effect on and after 1st September 2007 in so far as is necessary to continue to give effect to [section 31][1] of that Act.

(3) The 1963 Act is to continue to have effect on and after 1st September 2007 for the purposes of enabling any of the following applications to be determined (including, where appropriate, by way of appeal), where the application is made but not determined before that date—

(a) an application for a certificate of approval under section 13 of the 1963 Act (other than an application for a point to point certificate);

(b) an application under Schedule 1 to that Act for the grant of a bookmaker's permit, betting agency permit or betting office licence;

(c) an application under paragraph 5 of Schedule 2 to that Act for the registration of a person as a registered pool promoter;

(d) an application for the grant or transfer of a track betting licence under Schedule 3 to that Act;

(e) an application for a licence authorising an inter-track betting scheme under paragraph 2 of Schedule 5ZA to that Act.

(4) The 1963 Act is to continue to have effect on and after 1st September 2007 for the purposes of enabling a certificate of approval under section 13 of that Act, a betting office licence or a track betting licence to be granted, where the application for its grant is one falling within paragraph (3)(a), (b) or (d).

(5) Paragraph 1(a) of Schedule 1 to the 1963 Act (which provides for the establishment of licensing committees) is to continue in force on and after 1st September 2007 for the purposes of providing for there to be a licensing committee for each local justice area.

(6) Paragraph (5) is to have effect whether or not there are any applications for the grant of a bookmaker's permit, betting agency permit or betting office licence which the licensing committee for a particular area are required to determine by virtue of paragraph (3)(b).

(7) For the purposes of this article, where an application is refused it is not to be treated as having been determined until any period for appealing against the refusal of the application has elapsed; or, if an appeal is made, until the appeal is determined or abandoned.

(8) In this article, "betting agency permit", "betting office licence", "bookmaker's permit" and "track betting licence" shall be construed in accordance with section 55(1) of the 1963 Act.

---

1 Words "section 31" in square brackets substituted by SI 2007/2169, art 4.

6.1540 4 Repeal of the Gaming Act 1968

(1) The repeal of the 1968 Act by section 356(3)(g), (4) and (5) of, and Schedule 17 to, the 2005 Act shall, to the extent that it is not already in force, come into force on 1st September 2007—

(a) for all purposes in relation to—

(i) any licence or other document issued under the 1968 Act, or
(ii) any registration under Part 2 or 3 of that Act,

which has effect immediately before that date; and

(b) for all other purposes except as provided in the following provisions of this article.

(2) The 1968 Act is to continue to have effect on and after 1st September 2007 for the purposes of enabling any of the following applications to be determined (including by way of appeal), where the application is made but not determined before that date—

(a) an application under paragraph 4 of Schedule 2 to that Act for the grant of a certificate of consent to apply for a licence under that Act;
(b) an application under paragraph 56 of that Schedule for a certificate of consent for the transfer of a licence under that Act;
(c) an application under paragraph 5 of that Schedule for the grant of a licence under that Act;
(d) an application under paragraph 12 of that Schedule for the renewal of a licence under that Act;
(e) an application under paragraph 58 of that Schedule for the transfer of a licence under that Act;
(f) an application under Schedule 3 or 4 to that Act for the registration of a members' club or miners' welfare institute under Part 2 of that Act;
(g) an application under Schedule 3 or 4 to that Act for the renewal of the registration of a members' club or miners' welfare institute under Part 2 of that Act;
(h) an application under paragraph 1 of Schedule 5 to that Act for a certificate under section 19 of that Act;
(i) an application under Schedule 6 to that Act for the grant or renewal of a certificate under section 27 of that Act;
(j) an application under Schedule 7 or 8 to that Act for the registration of a members' club, commercial club or miners' welfare institute under Part 3 of that Act;
(k) an application under Schedule 7 or 8 to that Act for the renewal of the registration of members' club, commercial club or miners' welfare institute under Part 3 of that Act;
(l) an application under paragraph 5 of Schedule 9 to that Act for the grant or renewal of a permit under section 34 of that Act in respect of amusement machine premises; and
(m) an application under that paragraph for the grant or renewal of a permit under section 34 of that Act in respect of any other premises.

(3) The 1968 Act is to continue to have effect on and after 1st September 2007 for the purposes of enabling a certificate, licence or permit to be granted or renewed, where the application for its grant or renewal is one falling within paragraph (2).

(4) The 1968 Act is to continue to have effect on and after 1st September 2007 for the purposes of enabling a club or miners' welfare institute to be registered under Part 2 or 3 of the 1968 Act, or for such a registration to be renewed, where the application for the registration or the renewal of the registration is one falling within paragraph (2)(f), (g), (j) or (k).

(5) For the purposes of this article—

(a) where an application is refused, it is not to be treated as having been determined until any period for appealing against the refusal of the application has elapsed; or, if an appeal is made, until the appeal is determined or abandoned;
(b) where a permit is granted on an application falling within sub-paragraph (m) of paragraph (2), but it is granted subject to a condition

limiting the number of machines to which Part 3 of the 1968 Act applies which may be made available for gaming on the relevant premises, the application is not to be treated as having been determined until any period for appealing against that decision has elapsed; or, if an appeal is made, until the appeal is determined or abandoned.

6.1541 5 Repeal of the Lotteries and Amusements Act 1976

(1) The repeal of the 1976 Act by section 356(3)(i), (4) and (5) of, and Schedule 17 to, the 2005 Act shall, to the extent that it is not already in force, come into force on 1st September 2007—

(a) for all purposes in relation to—

(i) any certificate or permit issued under the 1976 Act, or

(ii) any registration under that Act,

which has effect immediately before that date; and

(b) for all other purposes except as provided in the following provisions of this article.

(2) The 1976 Act is to continue to have effect on and after 1st September 2007 for the purposes of enabling any of the following applications to be determined (including by way of appeal), where the application is made but not determined before that date—

(a) an application for the registration of a society under Schedule 1 or 1A to that Act;

(b) an application for the registration of a scheme submitted by a local authority under Schedule 2 to that Act;

(c) an application for the grant of a lottery manager's certificate under paragraph 1 of Schedule 2A to that Act; and

(d) an application under paragraph 4 of Schedule 3 for the grant or renewal of a permit under section 16 of that Act.

(3) The 1976 Act is to continue to have effect on and after 1 September 2007 for the purposes of enabling a society to be registered under Schedule 1 or 1A to the 1976 Act, where the application for its registration is one falling within paragraph (2)(a).

(4) The 1976 Act is to continue to have effect on and after 1st September 2007 for the purposes of enabling a scheme submitted by a local authority under Schedule 2 to the 1976 Act to be registered, where the application for its registration is one falling within paragraph (2)(b).

(5) The 1976 Act is to continue to have effect on and after 1st September 2007 for the purposes of enabling a permit under section 16 of that Act to be granted or renewed, where the application for its grant or renewal is one falling within paragraph (2)(d).

(6) For the purposes of this article, where an application is refused, the application is not to be treated as having been determined until any period for appealing against the refusal of the application has elapsed; or, if an appeal is made, until the appeal is determined or abandoned.

6.1542 6 Transitional provisions

The transitional provisions in Schedule 4 shall have effect.

6.1543 [7 Modification of Part 1 of the Horserace Betting and Olympic Lottery Act 2004]

[(1) Section 8 of the 2004 Act (exclusive licence for the right to carry on horse-race pool betting) shall have effect subject to the following modifications.

(2) A term or condition of the exclusive licence under that section shall be of no effect to the extent that it is inconsistent with a term or condition of an operating licence issued to the successor company.

(3) A term or condition of an authorisation given to a person under subsection (5)(a) of that section shall be of no effect to the extent that it is inconsistent with a term or condition of any authorisation given by the successor company to that person under section 94 of the 2005 Act.

(4) Subsection (7)(b) of that section shall have effect as if it also provided for the Secretary of State to have power to direct the Gambling Commission to make an order revoking the exclusive licence under that section if any operating licence issued to the successor company ceases to have effect.][1]

---

1 Inserted by SI 2007/2169, art 5.

6.1544 [8 Modification of the Gambling Act 2005 to reflect provisions of Part 1 of the Horserace Betting and Olympic Lottery Act 2004]

[(1) In respect of any time when the exclusive licence issued to the successor company under section 8 of the 2004 Act has effect—

(a) section 33 of the 2005 Act (which makes it an offence to provide facilities for gambling without the appropriate authorisation under that Act) shall have effect subject to the modification in paragraph (2); and

(b) Part 8 of the 2005 Act shall have effect subject to the modification in paragraph (3).

(2) A person who acts in contravention of section 8(5)(b) of the 2004 Act shall be treated as having committed an offence under section 33 of the 2005 Act irrespective of whether or not he would otherwise have committed the offence.

(3) A premises licence issued under that Part shall not authorise the use of premises for doing anything prohibited by section 8(5)(b) of the 2004 Act.

(4) Part 5 of the 2005 Act (which makes provision with respect to operating licences under that Act) shall have effect in relation to the successor company subject to the modifications in the following provisions of this paragraph.

(5) If the Gambling Commission issues the exclusive licence to the successor company under section 8 of the 2004 Act, the Commission must (if it has not already done so) issue a remote and a non-remote pool betting operating licence to the successor company which will have the effect of authorising the activities which the exclusive licence grants the successor company the right to perform.

(6) An operating licence issued in accordance with paragraph (5) must provide for section 94 of the 2005 Act to apply to the licence.

(7) Paragraph (5) applies whether or not the successor company is applying under section 69 of the 2005 Act for a remote or a non-remote pool betting operating licence when the exclusive licence is issued.

(8) If the successor company holds a remote or a non-remote operating licence when the exclusive licence is issued, the Gambling Commission must (if necessary) vary the licence so that it will—

(a) have the effect of authorising the activities referred to in paragraph (5), and

(b) provide for section 94 of the 2005 Act to apply to the licence.

(9) Subsection (6) of section 104 of the 2005 Act applies to the variation of the operating licence under paragraph (8) as it applies to the variation of an operating licence on an application being made under that section.][1]

---

1 Inserted by SI 2007/2169, art 5.

6.1545

SCHEDULE 1
PROVISIONS COMING INTO FORCE ON 1ST JANUARY 2007
Article 2(1)

Column 1	Column 2
Section 28	In so far as it relates to an offence under section 342.
Section 65 (to the extent that section is not already in force) and sections 66 to 74	For the purpose of—
	(a) enabling advance applications for operating licences to be made, considered and determined; and
	(b) enabling such licences to be issued before 1st September 2007.
Sections 75, 76 and 79 (to the extent that those sections are not already in force)	
Sections 77 and 78	
[Section 80 (to the extent that that section is not already in force) and sections 81] and 84 to 88	
Section 89 (apart from subsections (2) and (3))	
Sections 90 to 99	
Sections 100 to 107	
Section 109	
Sections 113 to 115	
Subsections (2)(b) and (c) and (3) to (5) of section 116	
Sections 117 to 120	In so far as those sections relate to a review under paragraph (b) or (c) of section 116(2).
Section 122	
Sections 124 to 126	
Section 128 (to the extent that section is not already in force) and section 130	For the purpose of applying the provisions listed above in Column 1 to—
	(a) the making, consideration and determination of advance applications for personal licences; and
	(b) personal licences issued on the grant of such applications.
Sections 129, 132, 133 and 136	
Sections 140 to 149	
Section 235 (other than subsections (2)(a), (3)(f) and (4))	

Column 1	Column 2
Sections 237 to 241, 248(2) and 251	
Sections 252 to 257	
Sections 285 and 288	
Section 291	For the purpose of enabling conditions to be attached to an operating licence under section 75 or section 78 in connection with any of the matters referred to in subsections (2) and (3) of section 291.
Section 342	In so far as it relates to the provision of information to the Gambling Commission.
Sections 341 and 345	In so far as each of these provisions relate to an offence under section 342.
Sections 350 to 353	
Section 356(1) and (2)	In so far as it relates to paragraph 12 of Schedule 16.
Section 356(4) and (5)	In so far as it relates to the entry in Schedule 17 specified below (whose purpose is limited as specified below).
Schedule 7 (for all remaining purposes	
Schedule 8	
Paragraph 12 of Schedule 16	For the purposes of enabling a person to obtain an enhanced criminal records certificate under section 115 of the Police Act 1997 in respect of an advance application for an operating or a personal licence. This is to be without prejudice to paragraphs (a) to (c) of section 115(5) of that Act continuing to have effect without the amendment made by paragraph 2 of Schedule 16 for the purposes of the matters referred to in those paragraphs.
In Schedule 17, the entry relating to the 1963 Act	For the purposes of repealing paragraph 10 of Schedule 2 to that Act.
In Schedule 17, the entry relating to the Gaming (Bingo) Act 1985	For the purposes of repealing paragraph 5(b) of the Schedule to that Act.

1 In Column 1 words "Section 80 (to the extent that that section is not already in force) and sections 81" in square brackets substituted by SI 2006/3361, art 2(1), (2).

6.1546

SCHEDULE 2
PROVISIONS COMING INTO FORCE ON [21ST MAY] 2007

Schedule heading: words "21st May" in square brackets substituted by SI 2007/1157, art 4(1), (2).

Date in force: 29 April 2007: see SI 2007/1157, art 1(1).

Article 2(2)

Column 1	Column 2
. . . [1]	
Sections 150 to 153	

Column 1	Column 2
Section 154 (for all remaining purposes)	
Sections 155 to 158	
Sections 159 to 165	(1) Subject to paragraph (3) below, sections 159 to 165 are to have effect for the purpose of enabling advance applications for premises licences under Part 8 of the 2005 Act to be made, considered and determined; and for enabling such licences to be issued before 1st September 2007. [(2) Sections 159 to 165 are also to have effect for the purposes of applications under section 187 (applications to vary a premises licence), section 188 (applications to transfer a premises licence), section 195 (applications for the reinstatement of a premises licence) and section 204 (applications for a provisional statement).][2] (3) The reference in paragraph (1) to applications for premises licences is not to include non-conversion applications for casino premises licences.
Sections 167 to 171	
Sections 174(1), 176(1) and (2)	
Section 181	
Section 184 [(for all remaining purposes)][3]	
Sections 186 to 189	
Sections 190 and 192	
Sections 194 to 196	
Section 204	(1) Subject to paragraph (2) below, section 204 is to have effect for the purposes of enabling applications for a provisional statement to be made, considered and determined; and for enabling such statements to be issued. (2) The reference in paragraph (1) to applications for a provisional statement is not to include applications for a provisional statement in respect of a casino
Section 205	
Sections 206 to 209	
Sections 210 to 213	
. . . [4]	
. . . [5]	
Section 247(3)	In so far as it relates to the provisions of Schedule 10 specified below in this Schedule.
. . . [6]	
Section 289(3)	In so far as it relates to the provisions of Schedule 14 specified below in this Schedule.
Sections 303, 304, 309(1), 311(1), 313(1) and 317 to 326	

Column 1	Column 2
Section 342 (for all remaining purposes)	
Section 343	
Section 346(1)(l), (2) and (3)	
[Section 347][7]	
In Schedule 10, [paragraphs 2 to 5][8], 8 to 11 and 22	For the purposes of— (a) enabling advance applications for family entertainment centre gaming machine permits to be made, considered and determined; (b) enabling appeals in connection with such applications to be made, considered and determined; and (c) enabling such permits to be issued before 1st September 2007.
In Schedule 10, paragraph 7(3) (for all remaining purposes) and [paragraphs 6, 12(a)][9], 13, 15 to 17, 21, 23 and 24	
In Schedule 14, [paragraphs 3 to 6][10], 9 to 12 and 22	For the purposes of— (d) enabling advance applications for prize gaming permits to be made, considered and determined; (e) enabling appeals in connection with such applications to be made, considered and determined; and (f) enabling such permits to be issued before 1st September 2007.
In Schedule 14, [paragraphs 2, 7][11], 8(3) (for all remaining purposes), 13(a), 14 to 17, 21, 23 and 24	

1 In Column 1 entry "Section 7(5) to (7)" (omitted) revoked by SI 2007/1157, art 4(1), (3)(a)(i).

2 In Column 2 in entry relating to "Sections 159 to 165" para (2) substituted by SI 2007/1157, art 4(1), (4).

3 In Column 1 in entry relating to "Section 184" words "(for all remaining purposes)" in square brackets inserted by SI 2007/1157, art 4(1), (3)(b).

4 In Column 1 entry "Section 235 (for all remaining purposes)" (omitted) revoked by SI 2007/1157, art 4(1), (3)(a)(ii).

5 In Column 1 entry "Section 236" (omitted) revoked by SI 2007/1157, art 4(1), (3)(a)(iii).

6 In Column 1 entry "Section 285" (omitted) revoked by SI 2006/3361, art 2(1), (3).

7 In Column 1 entry "Section 347" inserted by SI 2007/1157, art 4(1), (3)(c).

8 In Column 1 in first entry relating to "Schedule 10" words "paragraphs 2 to 5" in square brackets substituted by SI 2007/1157, art 4(1), (3)(d).

9 In Column 1 in second entry relating to "Schedule 10" words "paragraphs 6, 12(a)" in square brackets substituted by SI 2007/1157, art 4(1), (3)(e).

10 In Column 1 in first entry relating to "Schedule 14" words "paragraphs 3 to 6" in square brackets substituted by SI 2007/1157, art 4(1), (3)(f).

11 In Column 1 in second entry relating to "Schedule 14" words "paragraphs 2, 7" in square brackets substituted by SI 2007/1157, art 4(1), (3)(g).

6.1547

SCHEDULE 3

. . .

[Article 2(3)]

. . .

[Revoked by SI 2007/1527, art 2(1), (3).]

6.1548

[SCHEDULE 3A
PROVISIONS COMING INTO FORCE ON 1ST AUGUST 2007]
[Article 2(3A)]

[Column 1	Column 2
Sections 266 to 268	
Sections 271(2) and 273(2)	
Section 274	In so far as it relates to the provisions of Schedule 12 specified below in this Schedule.
Section 276	
Sections 277 and 278	
Subsection (2) of section 282	For the purposes of enabling a person to comply with the condition in that subsection before 1st September 2007 (being the date on which section 282 comes into force).
Section 283(2)	
Section 283(5)	In so far as it relates to the provisions of Schedule 13 specified below in this Schedule.
Section 284	
Sections 310(1) and 312(4)	
In Schedule 12, paragraphs 1 to 11 and 25	For the purposes of— (a) enabling advance applications for club gaming permits and club machine permits to be made, considered and determined; (b) enabling appeals in connection with such applications to be made, considered and determined; and (c) enabling such permits to be issued before 1st September 2007.
In Schedule 12, paragraphs 14 to 21, 23 and 26 to 31	
In Schedule 13, paragraphs 1, 2, 4 to 7 and 21	For the purposes of— (a) enabling advance applications for licensed premises gaming machine permits to be made, considered and determined; (b) enabling appeals in connection with such applications to be made, considered and determined; and

[Column 1	Column 2
	(c) enabling such permits to be issued before 1st September 2007.][1]
In Schedule 13, paragraphs 3, 9, 11 to 20, 22 and 23	

1 Inserted by SI 2007/1157, art 6, Sch 2.

6.1549

[SCHEDULE 3B
PROVISIONS EXCLUDED FROM COMING INTO FORCE ON 1ST SEPTEMBER 2007]
[Article 2(4) and (5)]

[Column 1	Column 2
Section 7(5) to (7)	
Section 89(2) and (3)	
Sections 159 to 165	For the purposes of enabling a non-conversion application for a casino premises licence to be made, considered and determined; and for the purposes of enabling a regional, large or small casino premises licence to be issued on such an application.
Section 175	
Section 204	For the purposes of enabling applications for a provisional statement with respect to a casino to be made, considered and determined; and for the purposes of enabling such statements to be issued.
Sections 214 to 234	
Section 245	
Schedule 9	
Paragraph 17 of Schedule 16][1]	

1 Inserted by SI 2007/2169, art 6, Schedule.

6.1549A

SCHEDULE 4
TRANSITIONAL PROVISIONS
Article 6

PART 1
GENERAL

6.1550 1 Interpretation

(1) In this Schedule—

"amusement machine premises" has the meaning given by section 34(7A) of the 1968 Act;

"bingo club licence" means a licence under the 1968 Act granted in respect of any premises, where the licence, as it has effect immediately before 1st September 2007, is subject to restrictions under paragraph 25 of Schedule 2 to that Act under which gaming on those premises to which Part 2 of that Act applies is limited to the playing of bingo;

"casino licence" means a licence under the 1968 Act other than a bingo club licence.

(2) For the purposes of this Schedule (and unless the contrary intention appears) where—

(a) the licensing authority under the 2005 Act is to be determined by reference to which authority's area premises are situated in, and

(b) the premises are situated in the area of more than one authority,

the licensing authority is the authority in whose area the greater or greatest part of the premises is situated.

(3) The following provisions of this paragraph are to have effect for the purposes of determining, where an application for an operating or personal licence is rejected, when that application is to be treated as having been finally determined for the purposes of this Schedule.

(4) If there is no appeal to the Gambling Appeals Tribunal the application is to be treated as having been finally determined on the expiry of the period for appealing.

(5) Where such an appeal is made and—

(a) the appeal is withdrawn, or

(b) the appeal is allowed,

then (subject to sub-paragraph (8)) the application is to be treated as having been finally determined when the appeal is withdrawn or, as the case may be, determined.

(6) Where the appeal to the Gambling Appeals Tribunal is refused and no appeal is made under section 143 of the 2005 Act, the application is to be treated as having been finally determined on the expiry of the period for appealing against the decision of the Gambling Appeals Tribunal.

(7) Where an appeal is made under section 143 of the 2005 Act, then (subject to sub-paragraph (8)) the application is to be treated as having been finally determined on the date on which the appeal is determined or withdrawn.

(8) Where the result of an appeal is that the matter is remitted to the body against whose decision the appeal is made, the application is to be treated as having been finally determined when any subsequent proceedings relating to the decision to reject the application are finally determined (as determined in accordance with sub-paragraphs (4) to (7)).

PART 2
TRANSITIONAL PROVISIONS RELATING TO THE GRANT AND RENEWAL OF LICENCES AND OTHER DOCUMENTS, AND REGISTRATIONS, UNDER ENACTMENTS TO BE REPEALED BY THE GAMBLING ACT 2005

6.1550A 2 Betting, Gaming and Lotteries Act 1963: restrictions on applications

(1) This paragraph and paragraphs 3 and 4 apply with respect to the grant of licences and other documents, and registrations, under the 1963 Act during the period beginning on the date on which this Order comes into force and ending on the date on which the repeal of that Act for all purposes takes effect.

(2) [Subject to sub-paragraph (3),][1] any application under the 1963 Act of the following kinds may be granted only where the application is made before 28th April 2007 and, in a case to which paragraph 4 applies, the condition referred to in sub-paragraph (3) of that paragraph is met—

(a) an application under paragraph 5 of Schedule 1 for the grant of a bookmaker's permit, betting agency permit or betting office licence;

(b) an application under paragraph 5 of Schedule 2 for the registration of a person as a pool promoter;

(c) an application under paragraph 3 of Schedule 3 for the grant of a track betting licence;

(d) an application for a certificate of approval under section 13 for a ground to be used as a horse racecourse;

(e) an application for a licence authorising an inter-track betting scheme under paragraph 2 of Schedule 5ZA.

[(3) Sub-paragraph (2)(a) does not apply in relation to any application under Schedule 1 to the 1963 Act for the grant of a bookmaker's permit where the application is made by the company which is nominated by the Secretary of State for the purposes of section 2 of the Horserace Betting and Olympic Lottery Act 2004 in accordance with subsection (2)(a) of that section.][2]

3 Betting, Gaming and Lotteries Act 1963: period for which licences and other documents and registrations are to have effect

(1) Any licence or permit, granted under Schedule 1 or 3 to the 1963 Act on or after the date on which this Order comes into force but before 1st September 2007, is to cease to have effect at the end of 31st August 2007; and paragraph 29 of Schedule 1 to the 1963 Act and paragraph 8 of Schedule 3 to that Act are to have effect as if modified accordingly.

(2) Sub-paragraph (1) is without prejudice to any provisions of Schedule 1 or 3 to the 1963 Act under which such a licence or permit may be revoked or cancelled before the date on which it is due to expire.

(3) Where a person is registered as a pool promoter under Schedule 2 to the 1963 Act on or after the date on which this Order comes into force, the registration is to cease to have effect at the end of 31st August 2007 (unless revoked before that date under paragraph 5 of that Schedule).

(4) Where on or after the date on which this Order comes into force the Levy Board issue a certificate of approval under section 13 of the 1963 Act for a horse racecourse, the certificate is to cease to have effect at the end of 31st August 2007 (unless revoked before that date under that section).

(5) Where any licence authorising an inter-track betting scheme is granted under Schedule 5ZA to the 1963 Act on or after the date on which this Order comes into force, the licence is to cease to have effect at the end of 31st August 2007 (unless revoked before that date under paragraph 11 of that Schedule); and paragraph 7 of that Schedule is to have effect as if modified accordingly.

4 Betting, Gaming and Lotteries Act 1963: grant of licences etc on or after 1st September 2007

(1) This paragraph applies to an application for—

(a) a betting office licence under Schedule 1 to the 1963 Act,

(b) a track betting licence under Schedule 3 to that Act, or

(c) certificate of approval under section 13 of that Act (other than a point to point certificate),

which is not determined before 1st September 2007.

(2) Such a licence or certificate is referred to in this paragraph as a licence or certificate under the 1963 Act.

(3) A licence or certificate under the 1963 Act may only be granted on such an application if—

(a) the applicant is applying under Part 8 of the 2005 Act for a premises licence in respect of the same or substantially the same premises as those in respect of which the licence or certificate under the 1963 has effect, and

(b) he qualifies for the purposes of that application as the existing premises operator (within the meaning of paragraph 53 of this Schedule) in relation to the premises by virtue of the fact that he is applying for the licence or certificate under the 1963 Act.

(4) Where a licence or certificate under the 1963 Act is granted in accordance with sub-paragraph (3)—

(a) it is only to have effect for the purposes of Part 7 of this Schedule (which provides for the conversion of licences etc under enactments to be repealed by the 2005 Act into premises licences under that Act), and

(b) it is to cease to have effect when the application for a premises licence referred to in sub-paragraph (3) is determined or withdrawn.

5 Gaming Act 1968: restrictions on applications

(1) This paragraph and paragraphs 6 to 11 apply with respect to the grant or renewal of licences, registrations and permits under the 1968 Act during the period beginning on the date on which this Order comes into force and ending on the date on which the repeal of that Act for all purposes takes effect.

(2) Any application of the following kinds may be granted only where the application for the licence or permit is made before 28th April 2007 and, in a case to which paragraph 9 or 11 applies, the condition referred to in sub-paragraph (2) of that paragraph is met—

(a) a licence under the 1968 Act;

(b) a permit under section 34 of that Act (which makes provision about the use for gaming of machines to which Part 3 of that Act applies) in respect of amusement machine premises.

(3) The restriction in sub-paragraph (2) with respect to applications made on or after 28 April 2007 does not apply where—

(a) the application is for a casino licence;

(b) the applicant holds one or more other casino licences in respect of premises in the same licensing area; and

(c) the certificate of consent issued under paragraph 4 of Schedule 2 to the 1968 Act for the purposes of the application was issued by the Gambling Commission in pursuance of article 2(2) and (3) of the Gambling Act 2005 (Transitional Provisions) Order 2006 (which specifies the circumstances in which the Commission may issue a certificate of consent for a casino licence where the application is made on or after 29th April 2006).

(4) In sub-paragraph (3)(b) the reference to the same licensing area is—

(a) where the premises to which the application relates are in England or Wales, to the local justice area in which those premises are situated; and

(b) where the premises to which the application relates are in Scotland, to the area of the licensing board (being the licensing board constituted under section 1 of the Licensing (Scotland) Act 1976) in which those premises are situated.

(5) The Gambling Commission may grant an application for the renewal of a certificate under section 27 of the 1968 Act (which makes provision about the sale, supply and maintenance of machines to which Part 3 of that Act applies) only where the certificate is due to expire in accordance with paragraph 3 of Schedule 6 to that Act before 31st August 2007.

(6) The licensing authority (within the meaning of, as the case may be, Schedule 3, 4, 7 or 8 to the 1968 Act) may grant an application for the renewal of a registration under Part 2 or 3 of that Act only where the registration is due to expire before 31st August 2007.

(7) The appropriate authority (within the meaning of paragraph 1(a) or (c) of Schedule 9 to the 1968 Act) may grant an application for the renewal of a permit

under section 34 of that Act only where the permit is due to expire in accordance with paragraph 18 of that Schedule before 31st August 2007.

6 Gaming Act 1968: applications for the grant of a licence under that Act where a certificate of consent has been applied for but not obtained

(1) A person may apply for the grant or transfer of a licence under the 1968 Act provided that—

(a) the relevant consent application has been made to the Gambling Commission,

(b) and that application has not been withdrawn or refused.

(2) Sub-paragraph (1) is to apply whether or not the relevant consent application has been approved; and (as the case may be) paragraph 3 or 55 of Schedule 2 to the 1968 Act is to have effect as if modified accordingly.

(3) Where an application for the grant or transfer of a licence under the 1968 Act is made before a certificate of consent has been issued by the Gambling Commission with respect to the application, paragraph 5(2) or (as the case may be) paragraph 58(1) of Schedule 2 to that Act is to have effect as if it required the application to be accompanied by a copy of the relevant consent application.

(4) Paragraphs 6 and 7 of Schedule 2 to the 1968 Act are only to apply in a case falling within sub-paragraph (3) where a certificate of consent is issued on the grant of the relevant application; and in such a case those paragraphs are to have effect as provided in sub-paragraph (5).

(5) Where in a case falling within sub-paragraph (3) a certificate of consent is issued on the grant of the relevant consent application—

(a) sub-paragraph (1) of paragraph 6 of Schedule 2 to the 1968 Act is to have effect as if it required the person applying for the grant of the 1968 Act licence to do the things referred to in that sub-paragraph not later than 14 days after the date on which he receives the certificate of consent issued on the relevant consent application; and

(b) sub-paragraph (1) of paragraph 7 of that Schedule is to have effect as if it required the applicant to send the licensing authority a copy of the certificate of consent at the same time as it sends the things referred to in that sub-paragraph.

(6) The Gambling Commission must notify the licensing authority responsible for determining the application for the grant or transfer of the 1968 Act licence if the relevant consent application is refused.

(7) The licensing authority must refuse the application for the grant or transfer of a 1968 Act licence if the relevant consent application is refused.

(8) In this paragraph, references to the relevant consent application, in relation to an application for the grant or transfer of a casino licence, are to an application for a certificate of consent under (as the case may be) paragraph 4 or 56 of Schedule 2 to the 1968 Act, where the application—

(a) is in respect of the same premises as those to which the application for the grant or transfer of the casino licence relates, and

(b) where the application relates to the grant of a casino licence, is not made only for the purposes of an application for the grant of a bingo club licence.

(9) In this paragraph, references to the relevant consent application, in relation to an application for the grant or transfer of a bingo club licence, are to an application for a certificate of consent under (as the case may be) paragraph 4 or 56 of Schedule 2 to the 1968 Act where the application—

(a) is in respect of the same premises as those to which the application for the grant or transfer of the bingo club licence relates, and

(b) where the application relates to the grant of a bingo club licence, is made only for the purposes of an application for the grant of a bingo club licence.

7 Gaming Act 1968: restrictions on applications for a certificate of approval under section 19

(1) The Gambling Commission may issue a certificate under section 19 of the 1968 Act only where the application is made before 1st June 2007.

[(1A) Paragraph (1) does not apply where—

(a) the application is made by a person who, when the application is made, holds a certificate under section 19 of the 1968 Act ("the existing certificate");

(b) the effect of the certificate being applied for ("the new certificate") would be to authorise the performance of functions to which section 19(1) of the 1968 Act applies; and

(c) the new certificate would apply to different premises from those to which the existing certificate applies.][3]

(2) Where—

(a) a notice is issued under subsection (3) of section 19 of the 1968 Act before 1st June 2007, but

(b) no application for a certificate under subsection (4) of that section is made before that date,

the notice is to cease to have effect on that date.

(3) Where such a notice is issued on or after 1st June 2007, subsection (4) of section 19 of the 1968 Act is to have effect in relation to the notice as if—

(a) it required the person on whom it is served, before the end of such period (not being less than 21 days from the date of service of the notice) as may be specified in the notice, to obtain a personal licence under the 2005 Act whose effect would be to authorise the performance of the functions to which the notice relates; and

(b) it prohibited that person from performing those functions once that period has expired unless—

(i) such a personal licence has been granted to him by the Gambling Commission and has effect for the time being for the purposes of that subsection, or

(ii) he is applying for such a personal licence and that application has not been finally determined or withdrawn.

8 Gaming Act 1968: period for which licences, registrations, and permits are to have effect

(1) Subject to paragraph 62 below, where a licence under the 1968 Act is granted or renewed under Schedule 2 to that Act on or after the date on which this Order comes into force but before 1st September 2007, the licence is to cease to have effect at the end of 31st August 2007; and paragraph 52 of that Schedule is to have effect as if modified accordingly.

(2) Sub-paragraph (1) is without prejudice to any provisions of Schedule 2 to the 1968 Act under which a licence may be cancelled (whether in consequence of the revocation of the certificate of consent or by virtue of a disqualification order under that Schedule or otherwise).

(3) Where on or after the date on which this Order comes into force but before 1st September 2007—

(a) a club or miners' welfare institute is registered under Part 2 or Part 3 of the 1968 Act, or

(b) such a registration is renewed,

6: Gambling Act 2005: SIs

the registration is to cease to have effect at the end of 31st August 2007; and paragraph 19 of Schedule 3, paragraph 17 of Schedule 4 and paragraph 22 of Schedule 7 to that Act (including as that provision has effect in relation to Scotland by virtue of paragraph 3 of Schedule 8 to that Act) are to have effect as if modified accordingly.

(4) Sub-paragraph (3) is without prejudice to any provisions of the Schedules referred to in that sub-paragraph under which the registration of a club or miners' welfare institute may be cancelled.

(5) Where a permit under section 34 of the 1968 Act is granted in respect of amusement machine premises at any time on or after the date on which this Order comes into force, the permit is to cease to have effect at the end of 31st August 2007; and paragraph 18 of Schedule 9 to that Act is to have effect as if modified accordingly.

(6) Sub-paragraph (5) is without prejudice to the cancellation of any such permit under section 39 of the 1968 Act.

9 Gaming Act 1968: grant of licences under the 1968 Act on or after 1st September 2007

(1) This paragraph applies to an application for a licence under the 1968 Act which is not determined before 1st September 2007.

(2) A licence under the 1968 Act may only be granted on such an application if—

(a) the applicant is applying under Part 8 of the 2005 Act for a premises licence in respect of the same or substantially the same premises as those in respect of which the licence under the 1968 Act has effect, and

(b) he qualifies for the purposes of that application as the existing premises operator in relation to the premises because he is applying for the licence under the 1968 Act.

(3) Where a licence under the 1968 Act is granted in accordance with sub-paragraph (2)—

(a) it is only to have effect for the purposes of Part 7 of this Schedule (which provides for the conversion of licences etc under enactments to be repealed by the 2005 Act into premises licences under that Act), and

(b) it is to cease to have effect when the application for a premises licence referred to in that sub-paragraph is determined or withdrawn.

10 Gaming Act 1968: registrations under Part 2 or 3 after 1st September 2007

Where a members' club, commercial club or miners' welfare institute is registered under Part 2 or 3 of the 1968 Act on or after 1st September 2007—

(a) the registration is only to have effect for the purposes of Part 9 of this Schedule (which provides for the conversion of club registrations under the 1968 Act into club gaming and machine permits under the 2005 Act), and

(b) it is to cease to have effect on the date on which the information specified in, as the case may be, paragraph 79 or 87 of this Schedule is sent to the relevant licensing authority (within the meaning of that paragraph).

11 Gaming Act 1968: grant of permits under section 34 on or after 1st September 2007

(1) This paragraph applies to an application for a permit under section 34 of the 1968 Act in respect of amusement machine premises which is not determined before 1st September 2007.

(2) A permit under section 34 of the 1968 Act may only be granted on such an application if—

(a) the applicant is applying for a premises licence under Part 8 of the 2005 Act, or a family entertainment centre gaming machine permit, in respect of the same or substantially the same premises as those in respect of which the permit under section 34 of the 1968 Act has effect, and

(b) he qualifies for the purposes of that application as the existing premises operator, or (as the case may be) the existing family entertainment centre operator, in relation to the premises because he is applying for the permit under section 34 of the 1968 Act.

(3) Where a permit under section 34 of the 1968 Act is granted in accordance with sub-paragraph (2)—

(a) it is only to have effect for the purposes of, as the case may be—

(i) Part 7 of this Schedule (which provides for the conversion of licences and permits etc under enactments to be repealed by the 2005 Act into premises licences under that Act), or

(ii) Part 10 of this Schedule (which provides for the conversion of permits under section 34 of the 1968 Act into family entertainment centre gaming machine permits); and

(b) it is to cease to have effect when the application for a premises licence, or a family entertainment centre gaming machine permit, referred to in sub-paragraph (2) is determined or withdrawn.

12 Effect of references in the Gaming Act 1968 to the licensing authority on and after 1st September 2007

(1) In relation to any time on or after 1st September 2007 any reference in the 1968 Act to a licensing authority is—

(a) in respect of a local justice area in England and Wales, to the licensing committee for that area established and constituted under paragraph 1 of Schedule 1 to the 1963 Act; and

(b) in respect of any area in Scotland, to the licensing board for that area constituted under section 1 of the Licensing (Scotland) Act 1976.

(2) Sub-paragraph (1)(a) is to apply irrespective of whether or not the licensing committee for a particular local justice area continues to be responsible under that Schedule for the grant or renewal of bookmaker's permits, betting agency permits and betting office licences in that area.

13 Lotteries and Amusements Act 1976: restrictions on applications

(1) This paragraph and paragraphs 14 to 16 apply with respect to the grant of certificates, permits and registrations under the 1976 Act during the period beginning on the date on which this Order comes into force and ending on the date on which the repeal of that Act for all purposes takes effect.

(2) The Gambling Commission may grant an application under paragraph 1 of Schedule 2A to the 1976 Act for a person to be registered under that Schedule as a lottery manager only where the application is made before 28th April 2007.

(3) An application under paragraph 4 of Schedule 3 to the 1976 Act for the grant of a permit under section 16 of that Act may be granted only where the application is made before 28th April 2007 and, in a case to which paragraph 16 applies, the condition referred to in sub-paragraph (2) of that paragraph is met.

14 Lotteries and Amusements Act 1976: period for which registrations, certificates and permits are to have effect

(1) Where on or after the date on which this Order comes into force but before 1st September 2007—

(a) a society is registered under Schedule 1 to the 1976 Act;

(b) a society is registered under Schedule 1A to that Act; or

(c) a local authority scheme is registered under Schedule 2 to that Act,

the registration is to cease to have effect at the end of 31st August 2007.

(2) Sub-paragraph (1) is without prejudice to the revocation of any such registration under a provision of the relevant Schedule referred to in that sub-paragraph.

(3) Any lottery manager's certificate granted under Schedule 2A to the 1976 Act on or after the date on which this Order comes into force is to have effect until 31st August 2007 (unless revoked by the Gambling Commission before that date); and paragraph 5 of that Schedule is to have effect as if modified accordingly.

(4) Any permit under section 16 of the 1976 Act granted or renewed under Schedule 3 to that Act on or after the date on which this Order comes into force is to have effect until 31st August 2007 (unless cancelled before that date under section 17(2) of that Act); and paragraph 15 of that Schedule is to have effect as if modified accordingly.

15 Lotteries and Amusements Act 1976: society and local authority scheme registrations taking effect on or after 1st September 2007

(1) Where a society or local authority scheme is registered on or after 1st September 2007 under, as the case may be, Schedule 1, 1A or 2 to the 1976 Act—

(a) the registration is only to have effect for the purposes of Part 8 of this Schedule (which provides for the conversion of registrations under the 1976 Act into lottery operating licences and registrations under Part 5 of Schedule 11 to the 2005 Act); and

(b) it is to cease to have effect in accordance with the following provisions of this paragraph.

(2) Where a society or local authority scheme is registered under Schedule 1A or 2 to the 1976 Act, the registration is to cease to have effect on the date on which a converted lottery operating licence (within the meaning of Part 8 of this Schedule) is issued to, as the case may be, the society or the local authority.

(3) Where a society is registered under Schedule 1 to the 1976 Act, the registration is to cease to have effect on the date on which the society is registered under Part 5 of Schedule 11 to the 2005 Act in accordance with paragraph 74 of this Schedule.

16 Lotteries and Amusements Act 1976: grant of permits under section 16 on or after 1st September 2007

(1) This paragraph applies to an application for a permit under section 16 of the 1976 Act which is not determined before 1st September 2007.

(2) A permit under section 16 of the 1976 Act may only be granted on such an application if—

(a) the applicant is applying for a prize gaming permit in respect of the same or substantially the same premises as those in respect of which the permit under section 16 of the 1976 Act has effect, and

(b) he qualifies for the purposes of that application as an existing operator because he is applying for the permit under section 16 of the 1976 Act.

(3) Where a permit under section 16 of the 1976 Act is granted in accordance with sub-paragraph (2)—

(a) it is only to have effect for the purposes of Part 11 of this Schedule (which provides for the conversion of permits under section 16 of the 1976 Act into prize gaming permits), and the case may be—

(b) it is to have effect until the application for a premises licence referred to in that sub-paragraph is determined or withdrawn.

---

1 Words "Subject to sub-paragraph (3)," in square brackets inserted by SI 2007/1157, art 7(1), (2).

2 Sub-para (3) inserted by SI 2007/1157, art 7(1), (3).

3 Sub-para (1A) inserted by SI 2007/2169, art 7(1), (2).

PART 3
CONTINUATION OF CERTIFICATES AND PERMITS ISSUED UNDER THE GAMING ACT 1968

6.1551 17 Continuation of certificates and permits granted under section 27 of the Gaming Act 1968

(1) This paragraph applies to a certificate or permit under section 27 of the 1968 Act (which makes provision as to the sale, supply and maintenance of machines to which Part 3 of that Act applies) which—

(a) is in force immediately before 1st September 2007, or

(b) is granted or renewed on or after that date.

(2) A certificate or permit to which this paragraph applies is referred to in this paragraph and in paragraphs 18 to 22 as a section 27 certificate or, as the case may be, a section 27 permit.

(3) A section 27 certificate or permit is to have effect on and after 1st September 2007.

(4) Where a section 27 certificate has effect in accordance with sub-paragraph (3)—

(a) if it was issued for the purposes of subsection (1) of section 27 of the 1968 Act, its effect is to authorise the holder—

(i) to sell or supply a gaming machine or part of a gaming machine, or

(ii) to cause or permit another person to sell or supply a gaming machine or part of a gaming machine on his behalf;

(b) if it was issued for the purposes of subsection (5) of that section, its effect is to authorise the holder—

(i) to maintain or repair a gaming machine or part of a gaming machine, or

(ii) to cause or permit another person to maintain or repair a gaming machine or part of a gaming machine on his behalf;

(c) if it was issued for the purposes of both those subsections, its effect is to authorise the activities described in both paragraphs (a) and (b).

(5) On and after 1st September 2007 a section 27 certificate is to have effect subject to any relevant operating licence conditions.

(6) In sub-paragraph (5), the reference to relevant operating licence conditions is to—

[(a) any conditions in relation to gaming machine technical operating licences—

(i) for the time being specified by the Gambling Commission under section 75 of the 2005 Act, or

(ii) for the time being specified by the Secretary of State in regulations under section 78 of that Act,

and which apply to the activities authorised by the certificate;

(aa) the condition specified in section 82(1) of the 2005 Act; and][1]

(b) any conditions attached to the certificate under paragraph 21(3).

(7) Where a section 27 permit has effect on or after 1st September 2007—

(a) if it was issued for the purposes of subsection (1) of section 27 of the 1968 Act, its effect is to authorise the holder—

(i) to sell or supply the gaming machine specified in the permit or a part of that machine, or

(ii) to cause or permit another person to sell or supply that gaming machine on his behalf;

(b) if it was issued under subsection (5) of that section, its effect is to authorise the holder—

(i) to maintain or repair the gaming machine specified in the permit or a part of that machine, or

(ii) to cause or permit another person to maintain that machine or a part of that machine on his behalf.

18 Duration of section 27 certificates

(1) Subject to the following provisions of this paragraph, a section 27 certificate is to have effect—

(a) where the application for the certificate is granted on or after 1st September 2007, for a period of 5 years beginning on the date on which the certificate is issued; or

(b) in any other case, until the date on which, as the certificate had effect immediately before 1st September 2007, it was due to expire in accordance with paragraph 3 of Schedule 6 to the 1968 Act.

(2) Where the holder of a section 27 certificate applies for a gaming machine technical operating licence at least two months before the date on which the certificate is due to expire, the certificate is not to cease to have effect by virtue of sub-paragraph (1) before that application is finally determined or is withdrawn.

(3) A section 27 certificate is to cease to have effect before the date determined in accordance with sub-paragraph (1) if before that date the holder of the certificate is granted a gaming machine technical operating licence.

(4) Where sub-paragraph (3) applies, the certificate is to cease to have effect immediately before the gaming machine technical operating licence has effect.

(5) This paragraph is without prejudice to sections 113 to 115 and 119 of the 2005 Act (which provide respectively for the surrender, lapse, forfeiture and revocation of operating licences) as those sections have effect in relation to section 27 certificates by virtue of paragraphs 20 and 21.

19 Duration of section 27 permits

(1) Subject to sub-paragraph (2), a section 27 permit is to have effect until the date on which, as it had effect immediately before 1st September 2007, the permit was due to expire.

(2) A section 27 permit is to cease to have effect if before that date the holder of the permit is granted a single-machine supply and maintenance permit under section 250 of the 2005 Act in respect of the gaming machine to which the section 27 permit relates.

(3) Where sub-paragraph (2) applies, the permit is to cease to have effect immediately before the permit under section 250 of the 2005 Act has effect.

20 Application of the Gambling Act 2005 to section 27 certificates

(1) The 2005 Act is to apply to a section 27 certificate having effect on or after 1st September 2007 with the modifications specified in the following provisions of this paragraph and in paragraph 21.

(2) Section 33 (which makes it an offence to provide facilities for gambling without the appropriate authorisation) is to have effect as if it provided for subsection (1) of that section also not to apply to any activity by a person if—

(a) he holds a section 27 certificate, or is acting as the servant or agent of any person who holds such a certificate,

(b) the activity is authorised by the certificate, and

(c) in carrying out the activity he complies with any relevant operating licence conditions.

(3) Sections 113 to 115 are to apply to section 27 certificates and the holders of such certificates as they apply to gaming machine technical operating licences and the holders of such licences.

(4) Section 243 (which makes it an offence to manufacture, supply, install etc a gaming machine without the appropriate authorisation) is to have effect as if it provided for a person not to commit the offence under subsection (1) of that section if—

(a) he holds a section 27 certificate or is acting as the servant or agent of any person who holds such a certificate, and

(b) the activity is authorised by the certificate, and

(c) in carrying out the activity he complies with any relevant operating licence conditions.

(5) Section 308 (which provides for the inspection of premises used by an operating licence holder) is to apply to section 27 certificates and the holders of such certificates as it applies to gaming machine technical operating licences and the holders of such licences with the modifications specified in sub-paragraph (7).

(6) In section 308, in relation to a section 27 certificate—

(a) any reference to the licensed activities is to have effect as a reference to the activities authorised by the certificate, and

(b) in subsection (3), the reference to the terms and conditions of the operating licence is to have effect as a reference to any relevant operating licence conditions having effect in relation to the certificate.

(7) In this paragraph, "relevant operating licence conditions" has the meaning given by paragraph 17(6).

21 Application of review provisions to section 27 certificates

(1) Sections 116 to 122 of the 2005 Act (which make provision with respect to the review of operating licences) are to apply to section 27 certificates and the holders of such certificates as they apply to gaming machine technical operating licences and the holders of such licences, but with the modifications specified in the following provisions of this paragraph.

(2) In section 116 (scope of Gambling Commission's powers to carry out a review)—

(a) in subsection (1)—

(i) the reference to the licensed activities is to have effect as a reference to the activities authorised by the section 27 certificate; and

(ii) the reference to ensuring compliance with conditions attached under section 75, 77 or 78 is to have effect as a reference to ensuring compliance with any relevant operating licence conditions; and

(b) in subsection (2)—

(i) the reference to activities carried on otherwise than in accordance with a condition of the operating licence is to have effect as a reference to activities carried on otherwise than in accordance with any relevant operating licence conditions, and

(ii) references to the licensed activities are to have effect as references to the activities authorised by the section 27 certificate.

(3) Following a review under either subsection (1) or (2) of section 116, the Gambling Commission may—

(a) attach an additional condition to the certificate, or

(b) remove or amend a condition attached under this sub-paragraph as a result of a previous review under either subsection.

(4) Subsection (1) of section 117 (regulatory powers of the Gambling Commission on a review) is to have effect—

(a) as if paragraph (b) provided for the Gambling Commission to have power to attach an additional condition to the certificate under sub-paragraph (3) above,

(b) as if paragraph (c) provided for the Gambling Commission to have power to remove or amend a condition attached to the certificate under that sub-paragraph, and

(c) as if paragraph (d) were omitted.

(5) Section 118 (powers of Gambling Commission to suspend an operating licence following a review) is to have effect with the omission of subsection (3).

(6) Section 119 (powers of Gambling Commission to revoke an operating licence following a review) is to have effect with the omission of subsections (2) and (3).

(7) Section 120 (which specifies the conditions which are to apply if the Gambling Commission is to exercise its powers to suspend or revoke an operating licence) is to have effect with the omission of subsection (2) and in that section—

(a) in subsection (1)(b), the reference to a condition of the licence having been breached is to have effect as a reference to a relevant operating licence condition having been breached; and

(b) in subsections (1)(d) and (3), a reference to the licensed activities is to have effect as a reference to the activities authorised by the section 27 certificate.

(8) In section 121 (which enables the Gambling Commission to impose financial penalties on operating licence holders) any reference (however expressed) to a breach of a condition of an operating licence is to have effect as a reference to a breach of a relevant operating licence condition.

(9) In section 122 (which enables the Gambling Commission to require an operating licence holder to provide information)—

(a) In subsections (1)(c) and (4)(b), a reference to the licensed activities is to have effect as a reference to the activities authorised by the section 27 certificate; and

(b) In subsection (4)(a), the reference to activities carried on otherwise than in accordance with a condition of the operating licence is to have effect as a reference to activities carried on otherwise than in accordance with any relevant operating licence condition.

(10) Section 141 of the 2005 Act (which provides for appeals to the Gambling Appeals Tribunal) is to have effect in relation to a section 27 certificate as if—

(a) in subsections (6) to (8), references to the Gambling Commission taking action, or determining to take action, under section 117, 118 or 119 included references to the Gambling Commission taking action, or determining to take action, under any of those sections in relation to the certificate;

(b) in subsection (9), the reference to the Gambling Commission giving notice of a penalty under section 121(4) included giving such a notice in relation to the certificate; and

(c) references to a licensee in those subsections included a reference to the holder of the certificate.

(11) In this paragraph, "relevant operating licence conditions" has the meaning given by paragraph 17(6).

22 Application of the Gambling Act 2005 to section 27 permits

(1) The 2005 Act is to apply to a section 27 permit having effect on or after 1st September 2007 with the modifications specified in the following provisions of this paragraph.

(2) Subsection (1) of section 250 is to have effect as if the reference to a permit under that section included a reference to a section 27 permit.

(3) In section 243(1), the reference to section 250 is to have effect as a reference to that section as modified by sub-paragraph (2).

23 Continuation of permits granted under section 34 of the Gaming Act 1968 in respect of alcohol licensed premises

(1) This paragraph applies to a permit under section 34 of the 1968 Act (which makes provision with respect to the use for gaming of machines to which Part 3 of that Act applies) granted by the authority mentioned in sub-paragraph (a) or (c) of paragraph 1 of Schedule 9 to the 1968 Act which—

(a) is in force immediately before 1st September 2007, or

(b) (if not so in force) is granted or renewed on or after that date.

(2) A permit to which this paragraph applies is referred to in this paragraph and in paragraphs 24 to 26 as an alcohol licensed premises gaming machine permit.

(3) An alcohol licensed premises gaming machine permit is to have effect on and after 1st September 2007.

(4) Where an alcohol licensed premises gaming machine permit has effect in accordance with sub-paragraph (3), its effect is to authorise the holder to make available on the premises to which the permit relates a number of Category C or D gaming machines equal to the number of AWP machines which the permit would have authorised him to make available under the 1968 Act.

(5) An alcohol licensed premises gaming machine permit is to be subject to the conditions that any gaming machine must—

(a) be located on premises which contain a bar at which alcohol is served for consumption on the premises (without a requirement that alcohol is served only with food), and

(b) be made available for use only at a time when (as the case may be)—

(i) alcohol may be supplied in reliance on the premises licence under Part 3 of the Licensing Act 2003, or

(ii) alcohol may be sold for consumption on the premises in reliance on the relevant Scottish licence.

(6) In this paragraph and in paragraph 27, "AWP machine" means a machine—

(a) to which Part 3 of the 1968 Act applies,

(b) which is used for gaming (within the meaning of that Act), and

(c) which complies with the conditions specified in subsections (2), (3) and (5) of section 34 of that Act or those specified in subsections (5B) to (5C) of that section.

24 Duration of alcohol licensed premises gaming machine permits

(1) Subject to the following provisions of this paragraph, an alcohol licensed premises gaming machine permit is to have effect until—

(a) in a case falling within paragraph 23(1)(a), whichever is the earlier of—

(i) 31st August 2010, or

(ii) the date on which the permit, as it had effect immediately before 1st September 2007, was due to expire in accordance with paragraph 18 of Schedule 9 to the 1968 Act; or

(b) in a case falling within paragraph 23(1)(b), for a period of 3 years beginning on the date on which the permit is granted or renewed.

(2) Where in a case falling within paragraph 23(1)(a)—

(a) the permit has effect immediately before 1st September 2007 by virtue of paragraph 19 of Schedule 9 to the 1968 Act; and

(b) the application under Schedule 9 to that Act for the renewal of the permit is granted on or after that date,

the permit is to have effect until 31st August 2010.

(3) Where the holder of a permit under section 34 of the 1968 Act granted by the authority mentioned in sub-paragraph (a) or (c) of paragraph 1 of Schedule 9 to the 1968 Act applies for a licensed premises gaming machine permit . . . [2] before the date on which the permit under section 34 of the 1968 Act is due to expire, the permit

is not to cease to have effect by virtue of sub-paragraph (1) or (2) until the application for the licensed premises gaming machine permit is determined or is withdrawn.

(4) An alcohol licensed premises gaming machine permit is to cease to have effect before the date referred to in sub-paragraph (1) if before that date—

(a) the holder of the permit is granted a licensed premises gaming machine permit; or

(b) section 282 of the 2005 Act (which enables up to 2 Category C or D gaming machines to be made available in alcohol licensed premises) applies to the premises specified in the permit.

(5) Where sub-paragraph (4) applies, the permit is to cease to have effect immediately before the licensed premises gaming machine permit or section 282 of the 2005 Act has effect in relation to the premises specified in the permit.

(6) This paragraph is subject to paragraphs 25(8), 28(5) and 29(4) and (5).

25 Application of the Gambling Act 2005 to alcohol licensed premises gaming machine permits

(1) The 2005 Act is to apply to an alcohol licensed premises gaming machine permit having effect on or after 1st September 2007 with the modifications specified in the following provisions of this paragraph.

(2) Subsections (1), (3) and (4) of section 283 of the Act (which enables Category C and D gaming machines to be made available under the authority of a licensed premises gaming machine permit) are to have effect as if the reference to a licensed premises gaming machine permit included a reference to an alcohol licensed premises gaming machine permit.

(3) In sections 37(7)(e) and 242(1) (which make it an offence respectively to use premises for providing facilities for gambling and to make gaming machines available for use), the reference to section 283 is to have effect as a reference to that section as modified by sub-paragraph (2).

(4) The provisions of Schedule 13 to the 2005 Act (which relates to licensed premises gaming machine permits) specified in sub-paragraph (5) are to apply to an alcohol licensed premises gaming machine permit as they apply to a licensed premises gaming machine permit.

(5) The provisions of Schedule 13 referred to in sub-paragraph (4) are paragraphs 7(2), 8, 10 to 14, 16, 18 to 20 and 21 (as that last paragraph has effect for the purposes of appeals under sub-paragraph (1)(c) of that paragraph).

(6) In paragraphs 7(2), 11, 16, 18(4), 19(4) and (5), and 21(3) of Schedule 13, any reference to the licensing authority is to have effect as a reference to the licensing authority which in its capacity as a licensing authority under the Licensing Act 2003 granted the premises licence under Part 3 of the Licensing Act 2003 in respect of the premises to which the permit relates.

(7) Sub-paragraph (6) is subject to paragraph 26(4).

(8) Paragraph 12 of Schedule 13 is to have effect as if it provided for a permit to continue to have effect until the date determined in accordance with paragraph 24 above, unless and until it ceases to have effect before that time in accordance with any of the provisions of that Schedule specified in sub-paragraph (5).

26 Continuation of alcohol licensed premises gaming machine permits: application of the Gambling Act 2005 in relation to permits in Scotland

(1) Despite Schedule 13 to the 2005 Act not applying in relation to Scotland, the provisions of that Schedule specified in sub-paragraph (5) of paragraph 25 (other than paragraphs 19 and 20 of that Schedule) are to apply to alcohol licensed premises gaming machine permits issued in Scotland.

(2) The provisions of Schedule 13 to the 2005 Act referred to in sub-paragraph (1) are to apply to alcohol licensed premises gaming machine permits issued in Scotland with—

(a) the modification specified in sub-paragraph (8) of paragraph 25, and
(b) the modifications specified in sub-paragraphs (3) and (4) below.

(3) In relation to alcohol licensed premises gaming machine permits issued in Scotland—

(a) paragraph 13 of Schedule 13 is to have effect as if any reference to an on-premises alcohol licence was to a relevant Scottish licence;
(b) paragraph 18(2)(c) of that Schedule is to have effect as if the reference to the High Court was a reference to the Court of Session; and
(c) paragraph 21 of that Schedule is to have effect as if—
  (i) sub-paragraph (2)(a) referred to a sheriff within whose sheriffdom the premises to which the permit relates are wholly or partly situated;
  (ii) sub-paragraph (2)(b) was omitted;
  (iii) the reference in sub-paragraph (3) to the magistrates' court was to the sheriff; and
  (iv) the reference in sub-paragraph (3) to costs was to expenses.

(4) Any reference to the licensing authority in the provisions of Schedule 13 to the 2005 Act mentioned in paragraph 25(6) is to have effect as a reference to the licensing authority which in its capacity as a licensing board under the Licensing (Scotland) Act 1976 granted the relevant Scottish licence in respect of the premises to which the permit relates.

27 Conversion of permits under section 34 of the Gaming Act 1968 into licensed premises gaming machine permits

(1) This paragraph applies where—

[(a) the holder of a permit under section 34 of the 1968 Act—
  (i) granted by the authority mentioned in sub-paragraph (a) or (c) of paragraph 1 of Schedule 9 to the 1968 Act, or
  (ii) granted by the authority mentioned in sub-paragraph (d) of that paragraph in respect of premises in respect of which a relevant Scottish licence has effect,

applies for a licensed premises gaming machine permit;][3]

(b) that permit authorises the holder to make available a number of gaming machines, being a number which is greater than two;
(c) that permit is due to expire in accordance with paragraph 24(1) or (2)[, or (as the case may be) paragraph 31(5) or (5A),][4] on a date on or after 1st September 2007;
[(cc) the application for the licensed premises gaming machine permit relates to the same or substantially the same premises as those in respect of which the permit under section 34 of the 1968 Act has effect;][5]
(d) the application for the licensed premises gaming machine permit is made . . . [6] before the date on which the permit under section 34 of the 1968 Act is due to expire in accordance with paragraph 24(1) or (2) [or (as the case may be) paragraph 31(5) or (5A)][7]; and
(e) (where the applicant holds a premises licence under Licensing Act 2003 in respect of the premises to which the application relates) the application for the licensed premises gaming machine permit complies with sub-paragraphs (b), (c), and (e) of paragraph 2 of Schedule 13 to the 2005 Act.

(2) In sub-paragraph (1)(b) the reference to gaming machines is—

(a) in relation to any time before 1st September 2007, to AWP machines, and
(b) in relation to any time on or after that date, to Category C or D gaming machines.

(3) Sub-paragraph (1) applies whether the application is made before, on or after 1st September 2007.

(4) If the application is in respect of a number of gaming machines which does not exceed the number of AWP machines or Category C or D gaming machines authorised by the permit under section 34 of the 1968 Act (referred to in this paragraph as "the authorised number"), the licensing authority must grant the application.

(5) If the application is in respect of a number of gaming machines which is greater than the authorised number, the licensing authority must grant the application in respect of a number of gaming machines which is no smaller than the authorised number.

(6) In a case to which sub-paragraph (5) applies, where the number of Category C gaming machines specified in the application does not exceed the [relevant number][8], the licensing authority may not grant the application in respect of a smaller number of Category C gaming machines than that specified in the application.

[(6A) In sub-paragraph (6), the relevant number is the authorised number unless the authorised number is less than two, in which case the relevant number is two.][9]

(7) Where the application referred to in sub-paragraph (1) is made before 1st September 2007—

(a) the licensing authority must not grant the application for the licensed premises gaming machine permit until that date, and

(b) sub-paragraphs (4) to (6) are not to apply if the permit under section 34 of the 1968 Act ceases to have effect before 1st September 2007.

(8) Sub-paragraphs (4) to (6) also do not apply where, after the application for the licensed premises gaming machine permit has been made, the permit under section 34 of the 1968 Act is cancelled or forfeited under paragraph 16 or 18 of Schedule 13 to the 2005 Act (as those provisions have effect by virtue of paragraph 25(4) above).

(9) Where the premises to which the permit under section 34 of the 1968 Act relates are situated in England or Wales, sub-paragraphs (4) to (6) are to be subject to paragraph 6(1) of Schedule 13 to the 2005 Act (which prohibits the grant of a licensed premises gaming machine permit to a person who does not hold an on-premises alcohol licence).

28 Failure to make the application for a licensed premises gaming machine permit in the appropriate form or manner

(1) This paragraph applies to any application for a licensed premises gaming machine permit made to a licensing authority in England or Wales which meets the conditions in paragraphs (a) to (e) of paragraph 27(1) above, but does not comply with a requirement imposed under sub-paragraph (a) or (d) of paragraph 2 of Schedule 13 to the 2005 Act.

(2) Where the licensing authority give notice in writing to the applicant requesting him to do anything which is necessary for the purposes of complying with any such requirement, the licensing authority are to cease to be under a duty by virtue of paragraph 27(4) to (6) to grant the application, or to grant the application in respect of a specified number and type of gaming machines, until such time as the applicant complies with the request.

(3) The applicant must comply with any request made under sub-paragraph (2) within such period as may be specified in the notice (such period not being less than 14 days from the date on which the notice is received).

(4) Sub-paragraph (5) applies where the applicant fails to comply with the notice within the period referred to in sub-paragraph (3).

(5) Where an alcohol licensed premises gaming machine permit has effect in respect of the premises to which the application relates—

(a) paragraph 24(3) is not to apply to the permit, and

(b) if the permit has effect by virtue of that provision, the permit is to lapse on the expiry of the period referred to in sub-paragraph (3).

29 Applications for conversion of permits under section 34 of the Gaming Act 1968: provisions applying to Scotland

(1) This paragraph is only to have effect if on [1st August][10] 2007 regulations under section 285(1)(b) of the 2005 Act are not in force setting out provisions which are to have effect in place of Schedule 13 to that Act in relation to an application for a licensed premises gaming machine permit where the applicant is the holder of a relevant Scottish licence.

(2) Sub-paragraph (3) modifies the effect of paragraph 27 in relation to such an application where—

(a) the person making the application holds a permit under section 34 of the 1968 Act in respect of the premises to which the application relates, and

(b) that permit is due to expire in accordance with [paragraph 24(1) or 31(5)][11] on a date which is no more than [one month][12] after the date on which the provisions referred to in sub-paragraph (1) come into force.

[(3) Paragraph (d) of paragraph 27(1) is to have effect as if it required the application for the licensed premises gaming machine permit to be made on or before the date which is one month after the date on which the provisions referred to in paragraph (1) come into force.][13]

(4) Where—

(a) a permit under section 34 of the 1968 Act in respect of premises is held by a person who also holds a relevant Scottish licence in respect of the premises, and

(b) that permit is due to expire in accordance with [paragraph 24(1) or 31(5)] on a date which is before the date referred to in sub-[paragraph (3)][14],

then (subject to sub-paragraph (5)) [paragraph 24(1) or 31(5)][15] is to have effect as if it provided for the permit to continue in force until the date referred to in sub-[paragraph (3)][16].

(5) Where in a case falling within sub-paragraph (4)—

(a) the holder of the permit under section 34 of the 1968 Act applies for a licensed premises gaming machine permit, and

(b) that application meets the conditions in paragraphs (a) to (e) of paragraph 27(1) (as modified by sub-paragraph (3)),

the permit under section 34 of the 1968 Act is not to cease to have effect by virtue of sub-paragraph (4) until the application for the licensed premises gaming machine permit is determined or is withdrawn.

30 Special provision with respect to alcohol licensed premises within tracks in England and Wales

(1) This paragraph applies where—

(a) a person holds a permit under section 34 of the 1968 Act granted by the authority mentioned in sub-paragraph (a) or (c) of paragraph 1 of Schedule 9 to the 1968 Act, and

(b) the premises to which that permit relates form part of a track, and are situated in England or Wales.

(2) Where—

(a) the holder of the permit applies for a licensed premises gaming machine permit, and

(b) the application is one to which paragraph 27 applies,

Schedule 13 to the 2005 Act is to have effect in relation to that application as if paragraph 1(2) of that Schedule were omitted.

31 Continuation of other permits granted under section 34 of the Gaming Act 1968

(1) This paragraph applies to a permit under section 34 of the 1968 Act granted by the authority mentioned in paragraph 1(b) or (d) of Schedule 9 to that Act in respect of non-amusement premises which—

(a) is in force immediately before 1st September 2007, or

(b) (if not so in force) is granted or renewed on or after that date.

(2) A permit to which this paragraph applies is referred to in this paragraph and in paragraphs 32 and 33 as a Category D gaming machine permit.

(3) A Category D gaming machine permit is to continue to have effect on and after 1st September 2007.

(4) Where a Category D gaming machine permit has effect in accordance with sub-paragraph (3), it is to authorise the holder to make available on the premises to which the permit relates a number of Category D gaming machines equal to the number of lower value AWP machines which the permit would have authorised him to make available under the 1968 Act.

(5) A Category D gaming machine permit is to have effect until—

(a) in a case falling within paragraph (a) of sub-paragraph (1), whichever is the earlier of 31st July 2009 or the relevant expiry date; or

(b) in a case falling within paragraph (b) of that sub-paragraph, 31st July 2009.

[(5A) Where in a case falling within sub-paragraph (5)(a)—

(a) the permit has effect immediately before 1st September 2007 by virtue of paragraph 19 of Schedule 9 to the 1968 Act; and

(b) the application under that Schedule for the renewal of the permit is granted on or after that date,

the permit is to have effect until 31st July 2009.][16]

(6) [Sub-paragraphs (5) and (5A) are][17] subject to paragraph 33(8).

(7) In this paragraph—

(a) "lower value AWP machine" means a machine—

(i) to which Part 3 of the 1968 Act applies,

(ii) which is used for gaming (within the meaning of that Act), and

(iii) which complies with the conditions mentioned in subsection (1) of section 34 of that Act;

(b) "non-amusement premises" means any premises other than amusement machine premises; and

(c) "relevant expiry date", in relation to a Category D gaming machine permit, means the date on which, as it had effect immediately before 1st September 2007, the permit was due to expire.

32 Continuation of Category D gaming machine permits: provision of information where permit issued in Scotland

(1) This paragraph applies to a Category D gaming machine permit which was granted in Scotland by the appropriate authority mentioned in paragraph 1(d) of Schedule 9 to the 1968 Act (being a council constituted under section 2 of the Local Government etc (Scotland) Act 1994).

(2) The council which granted the permit must on the relevant date, or as soon as practicable after that date, provide the relevant licensing board with the information specified in sub-paragraph (3).

(3) The information to be provided is—

(a) the name and address of the permit holder,

(b) the premises to which the permit relates,

(c) the date on which the permit was granted or last renewed, and

(d) in a case falling within paragraph 31(1)(a), the date on which, as it had effect immediately before 1st September 2007, the permit was due to expire.

(4) In this paragraph—

(a) a reference to the relevant date is to—

(i) 1st September 2007, or

(ii) in a case falling within paragraph 31(1)(b), the date on which the permit is granted; and

(b) a reference to the relevant licensing board is to the licensing authority under the 2005 Act in whose area the premises to which the permit relates are situated.

33 Application of the Gambling Act 2005 to Category D gaming machine permits

(1) The 2005 Act is to apply to a Category D gaming machine permit on or after 1st September 2007 with the modifications specified in the following provisions of this paragraph.

(2) Subsection (1) of section 247 (which provides for Category D gaming machines to be made available under the authority of a family entertainment centre gaming machine permit) is to have effect as if the reference to a family entertainment centre gaming machine permit included a reference to a Category D gaming machine permit.

(3) In sections 37(7)(c) and 242(1) (which make it an offence respectively to use premises for providing facilities for gambling or to make gaming machines available for use), the reference to section 247 is to have effect as a reference to that section as modified by sub-paragraph (2).

(4) Section 309(2) (which provides for the inspection of premises in respect of which a family entertainment centre gaming machine permit has effect) is to have effect as if any reference to a family entertainment centre gaming machine permit included a reference to a Category D gaming machine permit.

(5) The provisions of Schedule 10 to the 2005 Act (which relates to family entertainment centre gaming machine permits) specified in sub-paragraph (6) are to apply to a Category D gaming machine permit as they apply to a family entertainment centre gaming machine permit.

(6) The provisions of Schedule 10 referred to in sub-paragraph (5) are paragraphs 11(2), 12(a), 13(1), 15 to 17, 19 to 21 and 22 (as that last paragraph has effect for the purposes of appeals under sub-paragraph (1)(c) of that paragraph).

(7) In paragraphs 11(2), 15(1), 16, 17(4) and 21 of Schedule 10 to the 2005 Act, any reference to the licensing authority is to have effect as a reference to the licensing authority in whose area the premises to which the permits relates are situated.

(8) Paragraph 12(a) of Schedule 10 to the 2005 Act is to have effect as if it provided for the permit to cease to have effect on the date determined in accordance with [paragraphs 31(5) and (5A)][18] above unless it ceases to have effect before that time in accordance with any of the provisions of that Schedule specified in sub-paragraph (6).

(9) Paragraph 13(1) of Schedule 10 to the 2005 Act is to have effect as if the reference to the premises specified under paragraph 11(1)(b) of that Schedule was a reference to the premises specified in the Category D gaming machine permit.

1 Para 17: sub-para (6)(a), (aa) substituted, for sub-para (6)(a) as originally enacted, by SI 2007/2169, art 8.

2 Para 24: in sub-para (3) words omitted revoked by SI 2007/1157, art 8(1), (2).

3 Para 27: sub-para (1)(a) substituted by SI 2007/1157, art 8(1), (3)(a)(i).

4 Para 27: in sub-para (1)(c) words ", or (as the case may be) paragraph 31(5) or (5A)," in square brackets inserted by SI 2007/1157, art 8(1), (3)(a)(ii).

5 Para 27: sub-para (1)(cc) inserted by SI 2007/1157, art 8(1), (3)(a)(iii).

[6] Para 27: in sub-para (1)(d) words omitted revoked by SI 2007/1157, art 8(1), (3)(a)(iv).

[7] Para 27: in sub-para (1)(d) words "or (as the case may be) paragraph 31(5) or (5A)" in square brackets inserted by SI 2007/1157, art 8(1), (3)(a)(iv).

[8] Para 27: in sub-para (6) words "relevant number" in square brackets substituted by SI 2007/1157, art 8(1), (3)(b).

[9] Para 27: sub-para (6A) inserted by SI 2007/1157, art 8(1), (3)(c).

[10] Para 29: in sub-para (1) words "1st August" in square brackets substituted by SI 2007/1157, art 8(1), (4)(a).

[11] Para 29: in sub-para (2)(b) words "paragraph 24(1) or 31(5)" in square brackets substituted by SI 2007/1157, art 8(1), (4)(b)(i).

[12] Para 29: in sub-para (2)(b) words "one month" in square brackets substituted by SI 2007/1157, art 8(1), (4)(b)(ii).

[13] Para 29: sub-para (3) substituted by SI 2007/1157, art 8(1), (4)(c).

[14] Para 29: in sub-para (4) words "paragraph 24(1) or 31(5)" in square brackets in both places they occur substituted by SI 2007/1157, art 8(1), (4)(d)(i).

[15] Para 29: in sub-para (4) words "paragraph (3)" in square brackets in both places they occur substituted by SI 2007/1157, art 8(1), (4)(d)(ii).

[16] Para 31: sub-para (5A) inserted by SI 2007/1157, art 8(1), (5)(a).

[17] Para 31: in sub-para (6) words "Sub-paragraphs (5) and (5A) are" in square brackets substituted by SI 2007/1157, art 8(1), (5)(b).

[18] Para 33: in sub-para (8) words "paragraphs 31(5) and (5A)" in square brackets substituted by SI 2007/1157, art 8(1), (6).

PART 4
LICENCES ETC GRANTED UNDER THE GAMBLING ACT 2005 BEFORE 1ST SEPTEMBER 2007

6.1552 34 Licences etc issued under the Gambling Act 2005 before 1st September 2007

(1) Where a licence or permit is issued under the 2005 Act before 1st September 2007 (including where it is issued by virtue of a provision of this Schedule), it is not to take effect until that date.

(2) Sub-paragraph (1) is subject to paragraph 52 (which relates to personal licences issued before 1st September 2007).

35 Operating licences issued before 1st September 2007

(1) Where an operating licence is issued before 1st September 2007, section 100(1) of the 2005 Act (which makes operating licences subject to an annual fee) is to have effect in relation to the licence as if it provided for the holder to pay—

(a) a first annual fee to the Gambling Commission within the relevant period after 1st September 2007, and

(b) an annual fee to the Commission before 1st September in each year following 2007.

(2) In sub-paragraph (1), the relevant period is a period equal in length to the period prescribed for the purposes of section 100(1)(a) of the 2005 Act (as that provision has effect in relation to operating licences issued on or after 1st September 2007).

36 Premises licences issued before 1st September 2007

(1) Where a premises licence is issued before 1st September 2007, section 184(1) of the 2005 Act (which makes premises licences subject to an annual fee) is to have effect in relation to the licence as if it provided for the holder to pay—

(a) a first annual fee to the licensing authority within the relevant period after 1st September 2007, and

(b) an annual fee to the licensing authority before 1st September in each year following 2007.

(2) In sub-paragraph (1), the relevant period is a period equal in length to the period prescribed for the purposes of section 184(1)(a) of the 2005 Act (as that provision has effect in relation to premises licences issued on or after 1st September 2007 [and which take effect on the date of issue][1]).

37 Club gaming and machine permits issued before 1st September 2007

(1) Where a club gaming or club machine permit is issued before 1st September 2007, paragraph 14(1) of Schedule 12 to the 2005 Act (which makes club gaming and machine permits subject to an annual fee) is to have effect in relation to the permit as if it provided for the holder to pay—

(a) a first annual fee to the issuing licensing authority within the relevant period after 1st September 2007, and

(b) an annual fee to the issuing licensing authority before 1st September in each year following 2007.

(2) In sub-paragraph (1), the relevant period is a period equal in length to the period prescribed for the purposes of paragraph 14(1)(a) of Schedule 12 to the 2005 Act (as that provision has effect in relation to permits issued on or after 1st September 2007 [and which take effect on the date of issue][2]).

(3) Where a club gaming or club machine permit is issued before 1st September 2007, paragraph 17(1) of Schedule 12 to the 2005 Act (which provides for the duration of club gaming and machine permits) is to have effect in relation to the permit as if it provided for the permit to cease to have effect at the end of the period of ten years beginning on that date unless—

(a) it ceases to have effect before that time in accordance with a provision of that Schedule, or

(b) it is renewed in accordance with paragraph 24 of that Schedule.

38 Licensed premises gaming machine permits issued before 1st September 2007

(1) Where a licensed premises gaming machine permit is issued before 1st September 2007, paragraph 9(1) of Schedule 13 to the 2005 Act (which makes licensed premises gaming machine permits subject to an annual fee) is to have effect in relation to the permit as if it provided for the holder to pay—

(a) a first annual fee to the issuing licensing authority within the relevant period after 1st September 2007, and

(b) an annual fee to the issuing licensing authority before 1st September in each year following 2007.

(2) In sub-paragraph (1), the relevant period is a period equal in length to the period prescribed for the purposes of paragraph 9(1)(a) of Schedule 13 to the 2005 Act (as that provision has effect in relation to permits issued on or after 1st September 2007 [and which take effect on the date of issue][3]).

---

1 Para 36: in sub-para (2) words "and which take effect on the date of issue" in square brackets inserted by SI 2007/1157, art 9.

2 Para 37: in sub-para (2) words "and which take effect on the date of issue" in square brackets inserted by SI 2007/2169, art 9.

3 Para 38: in sub-para (2) words "and which take effect on the date of issue" in square brackets inserted by SI 2007/2169, art 9.

PART 5
ADVANCE APPLICATIONS FOR OPERATING LICENCES BY EXISTING OPERATORS

6.1553 39 Meaning of existing operator

(1) This paragraph specifies the circumstances in which a person making an advance application for an operating licence is to be treated for the purposes of this Part as an existing operator.

(2) Where the advance application is for a remote or non-remote casino operating licence, a person is an existing operator if on the date on which the advance application is made—

(a) he holds a certificate of consent issued under paragraph 4 of Schedule 2 to the 1968 Act for the purposes of the grant of a casino licence; or

(b) he is applying for such a certificate and the application has not been withdrawn or refused.

(3) Where the advance application is for a remote or non-remote casino operating licence, a person (referred to in this sub-paragraph as "the first person") is also an existing operator if on the date on which the advance application is made—

(a) another person holds a certificate of consent issued under paragraph 56 of Schedule 2 to the 1968 Act, and the certificate relates to the transfer to the first person of a casino licence; or

(b) that other person is applying for such a certificate and the application has not been withdrawn or refused.

(4) Where the advance application is for a remote or non-remote bingo operating licence, a person is an existing operator if on the date on which the advance application is made—

(a) he holds a certificate of consent issued under paragraph 4 of Schedule 2 to the 1968 Act for the purposes of the grant of a bingo club licence; or

(b) he is applying for such a certificate and the application has not been withdrawn or refused.

(5) Where the advance application is for a remote or non-remote bingo operating licence, a person (referred to in this sub-paragraph as "the first person") is also an existing operator if on the date on which the advance application is made—

(a) another person holds a certificate of consent issued under paragraph 56 of Schedule 2 to the 1968 Act, and the certificate relates to the transfer to the first person of a bingo club licence; or

(b) that other person is applying for such a certificate and the application has not been withdrawn or refused.

(6) Where the advance application is for a remote bingo operating licence, a person is also an existing operator if on the date on which the advance application is made—

(a) he holds a multiple bingo certificate issued under the Schedule to the Gaming (Bingo) Act 1985, or

(b) he is applying to the Gambling Commission for such a certificate and the application has not been withdrawn or refused.

(7) [Subject to sub-paragraph (7A)][1] where the advance application is for a remote or non-remote general betting operating licence, a person is an existing operator if on the date on which the advance application is made—

(a) he holds a bookmaker's permit or a betting agency permit issued under Schedule 1 to the 1963 Act; or

(b) he is applying to the appropriate authority for such a permit, and the application (including any appeal) has not been withdrawn or finally determined.

[(7A) The Horserace Totalisator Board is an existing operator in relation to any advance application the Board makes for a remote or non-remote general betting operating licence.][2]

(8) Subject to sub-paragraph (9), where the advance application is for a remote or non-remote pool betting operating licence, a person is an existing operator if on the date on which the advance application is made—

(a) he is registered as a pool promoter under Schedule 2 to the 1963 Act; or

(b) he is applying to be so registered, and the application (including any appeal) has not been withdrawn or finally determined.

(9) Where the advance application is for a non-remote pool betting operating licence to authorise the provision of facilities for pool betting in connection with dog-racing, a person is an existing operator if on the date on which the advance application is made any of sub-paragraphs (10) to (12) applies.

(10) This sub-paragraph applies where the applicant for the non-remote pool betting operating licence—

(a) holds a track betting licence issued under that Schedule; or

(b) he is applying to the appropriate authority for such a licence, and the application (including any appeal) has not been withdrawn or finally determined.

(11) This sub-paragraph applies where—

(a) another person who holds a track betting licence is applying for the transfer of that licence to the applicant for the non-remote pool betting operating licence, and

(b) the application has not been finally determined.

(12) This sub-paragraph applies where the applicant for the non-remote pool betting operating licence operates a totalisator under the written authority of the occupier of a track given under section 16(1) of the 1963 Act.

(13) Where the advance application is for a remote pool betting operating licence to authorise the provision of facilities for pool betting in connection with dog-racing, a person is an existing operator if on the date on which the advance application is made—

(a) he holds a licence for an inter-track betting scheme granted under Schedule 5ZA to the 1963 Act; or

(b) he is applying for such a licence, and the application (including any appeal) has not been withdrawn or finally determined.

(14) Where the advance application is for a gaming machine general operating licence in respect of an adult gaming centre or a family entertainment centre, a person is an existing operator if on the date on which the advance application is made—

(a) he holds a permit under section 34 of the 1968 Act—

(i) granted by one of the authorities mentioned in paragraph 1(b) or (d) of Schedule 9 to that Act in respect of amusement machine premises; and

(ii) which is expressed to be granted for the purposes of subsection (5E) of that section; or

(b) he is applying to the appropriate authority for such a permit, and the application (including any appeal) has not been withdrawn or finally determined.

(15) Where the advance application is for a remote or non-remote lottery operating licence of the kind described in section 98(2)(c) of the 2005 Act (a lottery manager's operating licence), a person is an existing operator if on the date on which the advance application is made—

(a) he holds a lottery manager's certificate granted under Schedule 2A to the 1976 Act; or

(b) he is applying for such a certificate, and the application has not been withdrawn or finally determined.

40 Interim operating licences

(1) This paragraph applies where—

(a) an advance application for an operating licence is made by a person who is an existing operator in respect of one or more of the kinds of operating licence to which the application relates;

(b) the application is made before 28th April 2007; and

(c) the application complies with section 69(2)(g) and (3) of the 2005 Act.

(2) This paragraph also applies where—

(a) a person makes an advance application for an operating licence and the application is for, or includes an application for—

(i) a betting intermediary operating licence,

(ii) a gaming machine technical operating licence where the activity specified in the application is restricted to the manufacture of gaming machines or parts of gaming machines,

(iii) a gaming machine technical operating licence where the activities specified in the application are restricted to the installation, adaptation, maintenance or repair of gaming machines or parts of gaming machines otherwise than for valuable consideration, or

(iv) a gambling software operating licence;

(b) the application is made before 28th April 2007; and

(c) the application complies with section 69(2)(g) and (3) of the 2005 Act.

(3) The Gambling Commission must determine any such application within a period of four months beginning on the date on which the application is made.

(4) If the application is not finally determined within the period referred to in sub-paragraph (3), the applicant is to be treated, from the day immediately following that period until such time as the application is finally determined, as if he had been issued with an operating licence of the same description as that being applied for.

(5) Where—

(a) the application is for an operating licence of more than one of the kinds described in section 65(2) of the 2005 Act, and

(b) the applicant is an existing operator in respect of one or more, but not all, of the kinds of licence for which the application is made,

sub-paragraph (4) only has effect to provide for the grant of an operating licence of those kinds in respect of which the applicant is an existing operator.

(6) For the purposes of sub-paragraph (5), a person who makes an application to which sub-paragraph (2) applies is to be treated as an existing operator in relation to any part of the application falling within sub-paragraphs (i) to (iii) of paragraph (a) of that sub-paragraph.

(7) An operating licence granted by virtue of sub-paragraph (4) is referred to in this Schedule as an interim operating licence.

(8) Sub-paragraphs (3) and (4) are not to apply where a permit, registration or certificate, by virtue of which a person making an application for an operating licence qualifies as an existing operator, is revoked or cancelled before the end of the period referred to in sub-paragraph (3).

(9) Where such a permit, registration or certificate is revoked or cancelled after the end of that period but before the application for the operating licence is determined, any interim operating licence deemed to have been issued to the applicant by virtue of sub-paragraph (4) is to lapse.

(10) For the purposes of sub-paragraphs (8) and (9), a permit or registration is not to be treated as being revoked or cancelled until any period for appealing against that

decision has elapsed; and, if an appeal is made, it is not to be treated as being revoked or cancelled unless and until the appeal is dismissed or abandoned.

(11) Sub-paragraphs (8) and (9) are subject to sub-paragraphs (12) and (13).

(12) Where in a case to which sub-paragraph (8) or (9) applies—

(a) the application is for an operating licence of more than one of the kinds described in section 65(2) of the 2005 Act, and

(b) the applicant is an existing operator in respect of more than one of the kinds of operating licence to which the application relates,

sub-paragraphs (8) and (9) are not to apply to the application, or any interim operating licence issued on the application, to the extent that the application is for a kind of operating licence where the applicant qualifies as an existing operator otherwise than by virtue of the permit, registration or certificate referred to in sub-paragraph (8).

(13) Sub-paragraphs (8) and (9) are not to apply where, notwithstanding the revocation or cancellation of a permit or certificate, the person making the application for an operating licence qualifies as an existing operator by reason of holding the same kind of permit or certificate in respect of different premises.

41 Modifications where the applicant qualifies as an existing operator because he is applying for a permission under the existing legislation

(1) This paragraph applies where a person qualifies as an existing operator in relation to a particular kind of operating licence only by reason of the fact that—

(a) on the date on which the application for an operating licence is made—

(i) he is applying to the Gambling Commission for a certificate of consent for the grant of a casino or bingo club licence, or

(ii) another person is applying under paragraph 56 of Schedule 2 to the 1968 Act for a certificate of consent to the transfer of a casino or bingo club licence to him;

(b) on that date he is applying to the Gambling Commission for a lottery manager's certificate under Schedule 2A to the 1976 Act;

(c) on that date he is applying to the Gambling Commission for a multiple bingo certificate under the Schedule to the Gaming (Bingo) Act 1985;

(d) on that date he is applying for—

(i) a bookmaker's or betting agency permit under the 1963 Act,

(ii) registration as a pool promoter under the 1963 Act, or

(iii) a permit under section 34 of the 1968 Act; or

(e) on that date—

(i) he is applying under Schedule 3 to the 1963 Act for a track betting licence, or

(ii) another person is applying for the transfer of such a licence to him.

(2) Sub-paragraphs (3) and (4) of paragraph 40 are not to apply where the application referred to in sub-paragraph (1) ("the application under the existing legislation") is withdrawn or refused before the end of the period referred to in sub-paragraph (3) of that paragraph.

(3) Where, in any other case, the application under the existing legislation is withdrawn or refused before 1st September 2007, or is not determined by that date, any interim operating licence deemed to have been granted to the applicant by virtue of sub-paragraph (4) is to lapse.

(4) Sub-paragraphs (5) and (6) apply in relation to any application for an operating licence falling within paragraph (d) or (e) of sub-paragraph (1).

(5) The applicant must notify the Gambling Commission in writing if the application under the existing legislation is granted, and the notification must be given

before the end of the period of 14 days beginning on the day on which the application is granted.

(6) Where the applicant fails to notify the Gambling Commission within the period specified in sub-paragraph (5), paragraph 40(4) is to cease to apply in relation to the application for the operating licence after the end of that period.

42 Application of the Gambling Act 2005 to interim operating licences

(1) Section 74(2) of the 2005 Act (which requires the Gambling Commission to notify the applicant and issue the operating licence as soon as reasonably practicable after its grant) is not to have effect in relation to an interim operating licence.

(2) In exercising its powers under section 75 of the 2005 Act (powers of Gambling Commission to impose general conditions on operating licences), the Gambling Commission must specify any conditions which are to apply to an interim operating licence or an interim operating licence falling within a specified class.

(3) Where an interim operating licence has effect before the date on which the Commission publish in accordance with section 76(3) of the 2005 Act the specification of any condition which applies to the licence, the licence is to be subject to the condition on and after that date.

(4) Where an interim operating licence has effect on or after the date on which the Commission so publish the specification of any condition which applies to the licence, the licence is to be subject to the condition as soon as it has effect.

(5) Regulations under section 78 of the 2005 Act (which allows conditions to be imposed on operating licences by the Secretary of State) may specify conditions which are to apply to each interim operating licence or to interim operating licences falling within a specified description.

(6) In subsection (2) of section 78 of the 2005 Act, the reference to licences issued before regulations under that section are made is to include a reference to interim operating licences having effect before such regulations are made.

(7) The following provisions of the 2005 Act are not to apply to interim operating licences—

- (a) section 100 (which provides for the payment of an annual fee by the holder of an operating licence);
- (b) sections 104 to 107 (which make provision respectively for applications to vary operating licences, amendments to licences, registration of licences, copies of licences and production of licences); and
- (c) section 111 (which provides for the Gambling Commission to have power to limit the duration of operating licences) and section 112 (which makes provision about the renewal of operating licences).

(8) Section 110 (which provides for the duration of operating licences) is to have effect in relation to an interim operating licence as if it provided for the licence to cease to have effect when the advance application made by the existing operator is finally determined, unless and until it ceases to have effect before that date in accordance with section 113, 114, 115, 118 or 119 of the 2005 Act (which provide respectively for the surrender, lapse, forfeiture, suspension and revocation of operating licences).

43 Premises restriction applying to certain dog racing interim pool betting operating licences

(1) This paragraph applies where—

- (a) a person holds a non-remote interim pool betting operating licence which authorises the provision of facilities for pool betting in connection with dog-racing, and
- (b) he holds that licence by reason of the fact that, on the date on which he made the advance application for the relevant operating licence, he was authorised in writing under section 16 of the 1963 Act by the occupier of a track to operate a totalisator on the track.

(2) Subject to the following provisions of this paragraph, section 84 of the 2005 Act (which makes provision about the conditions attached to operating licences about the provision of the licensed activities on specified premises) is to have effect in relation to the interim operating licence as if it provided for the licence to have effect subject to a condition requiring the holder to carry on the activities authorised by the licence only at the track referred to in sub-paragraph (1)(b).

(3) Sub-paragraph (4) applies where, on the date on which the holder of the interim operating licence made the advance application for the relevant operating licence, he was authorised under section 16 of the 1963 Act to operate a totalisator at more than one track.

(4) Where this sub-paragraph applies, section 84 of the 2005 Act is to have effect in relation to the interim operating licence as if it provided for the licence to have effect subject to a condition requiring the holder to carrying on the activities authorised by the licence only at those tracks where he was authorised under section 16 of the 1963 Act to operate a totalisator on the date on which he made the advance application for the relevant operating licence.

---

1 Para 39: in sub-para (7) words "Subject to sub-paragraph (7A)" in square brackets inserted by SI 2007/1157, art 10(1), (2).

2 Para 39: sub-para (7A) inserted by SI 2007/1157, art 10(1), (3).

PART 6
TRANSITIONAL ARRANGEMENTS WITH RESPECT TO PERSONAL LICENCES

6.1554 44 Interpretation of Part 6

Any reference in this Part of this Schedule to a provision of Part 5 of the 2005 Act is to have effect as a reference to that provision as applied by section 128 of that Act.

45 Continuation of certificates under section 19 of the Gaming Act 1968 on and after 1st September 2007

(1) This paragraph applies to a certificate issued under section 19 of the 1968 Act (which provides for persons exercising specified functions on premises licensed under that Act to be approved by the Gambling Commission) which—

(a) is in force immediately before 1st September 2007, or

(b) is granted on or after that date.

(2) A certificate to which this paragraph applies is referred to in this Part as a section 19 certificate.

(3) A section 19 certificate is to have effect on and after 1st September 2007.

(4) Subject to [sub-paragraphs (5) to (6C)][1], where a section 19 certificate has effect in accordance with sub-paragraph (3), its effect is to authorise the person to whom it was issued, in connection with the provision of facilities for gambling in reliance on a non-remote casino or bingo operating licence—

(a) to perform the functions specified in the certificate on the premises so specified, or

(b) to perform any functions reasonably necessary for the purposes of acting in the capacity specified in the certificate in relation to the premises so specified.

(5) Sub-paragraph (6) applies to any certificate under section 19 of the 1968 Act where the holder of the certificate applies (whether before, on or after 1st September 2007) for a personal licence to authorise the performance of functions which include the functions authorised by the certificate.

(6) The section 19 certificate is to have effect on and after—

(a) 1st September 2007, or

(b) if the application referred to in paragraph (5) is [made][2] after that date, the date on which the application is [made][2],

as if it authorised the holder to perform the functions referred to in the certificate in or in relation to any premises in respect of which, as the case may be, a casino or bingo premises licence has effect (and not only in or in relation to the premises specified in the certificate).

[(6A) Sub-paragraph (6B) applies to any section 19 certificate ("the existing certificate") where—

(a) the holder of the certificate is applying for a new certificate under section 19 of the 1968 Act ("the new certificate"), and

(b) immediately before 1st September 2007 that application has not been determined or withdrawn.

(6B) In sub-paragraph (6A), the reference to an application for a new section 19 certificate is to an application for a certificate under section 19 of the 1968 Act—

(a) whose effect would be to authorise the performance of functions to which subsection (1) of that section applies, and

(b) which would apply to different premises from those to which the existing certificate applies.

(6C) The existing certificate is to have effect on and after 1st September 2007 as if it authorised the holder to perform functions in or in relation to the premises to which the new certificate would apply (as well as in or in relation to the premises specified in the existing certificate).

(6D) If the application for a personal licence referred to in sub-paragraph (5) or the application for a certificate under section 19 of the 1968 Act referred to in sub-paragraph (6A) is rejected, sub-paragraph (6) or (as the case may be) sub-paragraph (6C) shall cease to have effect in relation to the section 19 certificate.][3]

(7) On and after 1st September 2007 a section 19 certificate is to have effect subject to any relevant personal licence conditions.

(8) In sub-paragraph (7), references to relevant personal licence conditions in relation to a section 19 certificate are to—

(a) any conditions in relation to personal licences—

(i) for the time being specified by the Gambling Commission under section 75 of the 2005 Act, or

(ii) for the time being specified by the Secretary of State in regulations under section 78 of that Act,

and which apply to the performance of the functions authorised by the certificate; [4] . . .

[(aa) the conditions specified in sections 82(1) and 83(1) of the 2005 Act; and][5]

(b) any conditions attached to the certificate by virtue of paragraph 48(3).

46 Duration of section 19 certificates

(1) Subject to the following provisions of this paragraph, a section 19 certificate is to have effect until 31st December 2009.

(2) Where—

(a) the holder of a section 19 certificate applies for a personal licence to authorise the performance of functions which include the functions authorised by the certificate, and

(b) that application is made before 31st August 2009,

the certificate is not to cease to have effect by virtue of paragraph (1) before the application is finally determined or is withdrawn.

(3) A section 19 certificate is to cease to have effect before 31st December 2009 if it ceases to have effect in accordance with—

(a) section 113, 114, 115, 118 or 119 of the 2005 Act (which, as applied by section 128, provide respectively for the surrender, lapse, forfeiture, suspension and revocation of personal licences), or

(b) sub-paragraphs (4) and (5).

(4) A section 19 certificate is to cease to have effect if the person to whom it was issued is granted a personal licence authorising the performance of functions which include all the functions authorised by the certificate.

(5) Where sub-paragraph (4) applies, the certificate is to cease to have effect immediately before the personal licence has effect.

47 Application of the Gambling Act 2005 to section 19 certificates

(1) This paragraph applies where an operating licence is subject to a condition that a specified function is to be performed—

(a) by an individual who holds a personal licence authorising the performance of that function, and

(b) in accordance with the terms and conditions of the personal licence.

(2) The condition referred to in sub-paragraph (1) is to be treated as having been complied with if—

(a) the function is performed by an individual who holds a section 19 certificate authorising the performance of the function, and

(b) it is performed in accordance with any relevant personal licence conditions having effect in relation to the certificate.

(3) The following provisions of the 2005 Act are to have effect in relation to a section 19 certificate as if any reference in those provisions to a personal licence included a reference to the certificate—

(a) in Part 5, section 107 (which enables the Gambling Commission to issue copies of personal licences where lost, stolen or damaged), 113, 114 and 115, and

(b) in Part 6—

(i) section 134 (which requires a personal licence holder to produce the licence to a constable or enforcement officer),

(ii) section 138 (which specifies actions to be taken by an operating licence holder where the holder of a personal licence is convicted of a relevant offence), and

(iii) section 139 (which makes it an offence for the holder of a personal licence to act outside the terms and conditions of his licence in relation to activities authorised by an operating licence).

(4) In this paragraph, "relevant personal licence conditions" has the meaning given by paragraph 45(8).

48 Application of review provisions to section 19 certificates

(1) Sections 116 to 122 of the 2005 Act (which make provision with respect to the review of operating licences) are to apply to section 19 certificates and the persons to whom such certificates are issued as they apply to personal licences and the holders of such licences, but with the modifications specified in the following provisions of this paragraph.

(2) In section 116(2) (scope of Gambling Commission's powers to carry out a review) the reference to a condition of the personal licence is to have effect as a reference to any relevant personal licence conditions having effect in relation to the section 19 certificate.

(3) Following a review under subsection (2) of section 116, the Gambling Commission may—

(a) attach an additional condition to the certificate, or

(b) remove or amend a condition attached under this paragraph as a result of a previous review under that subsection

(4) Section 117(1) (regulatory powers of the Gambling Commission on a review) is to have effect—

(a) as if paragraph (b) provided for the Gambling Commission to have power to attach an additional condition to the certificate under sub-paragraph (3) above,

(b) as if paragraph (c) provided for the Gambling Commission to have power to remove or amend a condition attached to the certificate under that sub-paragraph, and

(c) as if paragraph (d) were omitted.

(5) Section 118 (powers of Gambling Commission to suspend a personal licence following a review) is to have effect with the omission of subsection (3).

(6) Section 119 (powers of Gambling Commission to revoke a personal licence following a review) is to have effect with the omission of subsections (2) and (3).

(7) Section 120 (which specifies the conditions which are to apply if the Gambling Commission is to exercise its powers to suspend or revoke a personal licence) is to have effect with the omission of subsection (2), and in that section—

(a) in subsection (1)(b), the reference to a condition of the licence having been breached is to have effect as a reference to a relevant personal licence condition having been breached; and

(b) in subsection (3), the reference to carrying on the licensed activities is to have effect as a reference to performing the functions to which the section 19 certificate relates.

(8) In section 121 (which enables the Gambling Commission to impose financial penalties on personal licence holders) any reference (however expressed) to a breach of a condition of a personal licence is to have effect as a reference to a breach of a relevant personal licence condition.

(9) In section 122 (which enables the Gambling Commission to require a personal licence holder to provide information)—

(a) in subsection (1)(c), the reference to the licensed activities is to have effect as a reference to the performance of the functions to which the section 19 certificate relates;

(b) in subsection (4)—

(i) in paragraph (a), the reference to a condition of the personal licence is to have effect as a reference to any relevant personal licence conditions; and

(ii) in paragraph (b), reference to carrying on the licensed activities is to have effect as a reference to performing the functions to which the section 19 certificate relates.

(10) Section 141 of the 2005 Act (which provides for appeals to the Gambling Appeals Tribunal) is to have effect in relation to a section 19 certificate as if—

(a) in subsections (6) to (8), references to the Gambling Commission taking action, or determining to take action, under section 117, 118 or 119, included references to the Gambling Commission taking action, or determining to take action, under any of those sections in relation to the certificate;

(b) in subsection (9), the reference to the Gambling Commission giving notice of a penalty under section 121(4) included giving such a notice in relation to the certificate; and

(c) references to a licensee in those subsections included a reference to the holder of the certificate.

(11) In this paragraph, "relevant personal licence conditions" has the meaning given by paragraph 45(8).

49 Interim personal licences

(1) This paragraph applies to—

(a) an advance application for a personal licence authorising the performance of the functions of a specified management office; or

(b) an advance application for a personal licence authorising the performance of a relevant operational function, where the application is made by a person who holds a section 19 certificate.

(2) Where the application—

(a) is made before 30th June 2007, and

(b) complies with the requirements of section 69(2)(g) and (3) of the 2005 Act,

the Gambling Commission must determine the application and inform the applicant of its decision before the end of the period of two months beginning on the day after the day on which the application is made.

(3) Where the application is not finally determined before the end of the period referred to in sub-paragraph (2), the Gambling Commission is to be treated as having issued to the applicant on the day immediately following the end of that period a personal licence of the same description as that being applied for.

(4) Where the application is for a multiple licence which authorises the performance of more than one function, sub-paragraph (2) is to have effect as if it provided for the Gambling Commission to be treated as having issued a personal licence which—

(a) in a case falling within sub-paragraph (1)(a), authorises the performance of the functions of any management office specified in the application;

(b) in a case falling within sub-paragraph (1)(b), authorises the performance of any relevant operational functions specified in the application, or

(c) in a case falling within both paragraphs (a) and (b) of sub-paragraph (1), authorises the performance of the functions of any management office and any relevant operational functions specified in the application.

(5) A personal licence deemed to have been granted by virtue of sub-paragraph (3) is referred to in this Part as an interim personal licence.

(6) In this paragraph—

(a) "management office" has the meaning given to it by section 80(5) of the 2005 Act,

(b) "operational function" has the meaning given to it by section 80(6) of that Act, and

(c) "relevant operational function" means an operational function—

(i) which is to be performed in premises in respect of which a casino or bingo premises licence has effect, and

(ii) which falls within any of the descriptions in subsection (2) of section 19 of the 1968 Act.

50 Application of Part 5 of the Gambling Act 2005 to interim personal licences

(1) Part 5 of the 2005 Act (as applied by section 128 of that Act to personal licences) is to have effect in relation to interim personal licences subject to the modifications specified in the following provisions of this paragraph.

(2) In exercising its powers under section 75 (powers of Gambling Commission to impose general conditions on personal licences), the Gambling Commission must specify any conditions which are to apply to an interim personal licence or an interim personal licence falling within a specified class.

(3) Where an interim personal licence has effect before the date on which the Commission publish in accordance with section 76(3) the specification of any condition which applies to the licence, the licence is to be subject to the condition on and after that date.

(4) Where an interim personal licence has effect on or after the date on which the Commission so publish the specification of any condition which applies to the licence, the licence is to be subject to the condition as soon as it has effect.

(5) Regulations under section 78 (which allows the Secretary of State to make regulations specifying conditions to be imposed on operating licences) may specify conditions which are to apply to each interim personal licence or to interim personal licences falling within a specified description.

(6) In subsection (2) of section 78, the reference to licences issued before regulations under that section are made is to include a reference to interim personal licences having effect before such regulations are made.

(7) Part 5 of the 2005 Act is to have effect as if sections 104 to 106 (which make provision respectively for applications to vary personal licences, amendments to licences, registration of licences and copies of licences) were omitted.

51 Application of Part 6 of the Gambling Act 2005 to interim personal licences

(1) Part 6 of the 2005 Act is to have effect in relation to interim personal licences subject to the modifications specified in the following provisions of this paragraph.

(2) Section 131 (which provides for the duration of personal licences) is to have effect as if it provided for an interim personal licence to cease to have effect when the application referred to in paragraph 49(1) is finally determined, unless and until it ceases to have effect before that date in accordance with section 113, 114, 115, or 119 of the 2005 Act (which provide respectively for the surrender, lapse, forfeiture and revocation of operating licences).

(3) Part 6 is to have effect as if sections 132 and 134 (which make provision as to fees and the production of personal licences) were omitted.

52 Personal licences issued before 1st September 2007

(1) Subject to the following provisions of this paragraph, where a personal licence (including an interim personal licence) is issued under the 2005 Act before 1st September 2007, it is not to take effect until that date.

(2) Where a personal licence authorises a person to carry out one or more of the functions described in subsection (2) of section 19 on premises in respect of which a casino or bingo premises licence has effect, that person is to be treated for the purposes of subsection (1) of that section as if he had been issued with a certificate certifying that he has been approved by the Gambling Commission to perform the functions concerned on any premises in respect of which a licence under the 1968 Act has effect.

(3) Where a person is served with a notice under subsection (3) of section 19 of the 1968 Act, the person on whom the notice is served is to be treated for the purposes of subsection (4) of that section as having been approved by the Commission to act in the capacity for which the notice requires him to obtain approval if—

(a) he has been granted a personal licence authorising the performance of the functions to which the notice relates, or

(b) he has applied for such a licence and the application has not been finally determined.

(4) Where before 1st September 2007 the Gambling Commission revoke a personal licence to which sub-paragraph (2) or (3) applies in exercise of their powers under section 119 of the 2005 Act, the person who held the licence is to cease to be treated for the purposes of section 19(1) or (4) of the 1968 Act as having been approved to perform the functions whose performance had been authorised by the licence.

---

1 Para 45: in sub-para (4) words "sub-paragraphs (5) to (6C)" in square brackets substituted by SI 2007/2169, art 10(1), (2).

2 Para 45: in sub-para (6)(b) word "made" in square brackets in both places it occurs substituted by SI 2007/2169, art 10(1), (3).

3 Para 45: sub-paras (6A)–(6D) inserted by SI 2007/2169, art 10(1), (4).

4 Para 45: in sub-para (8)(a) word omitted revoked by SI 2007/2169, art 10(1), (5)(a).

[5] Para 45: sub-para (8)(aa) inserted by SI 2007/2169, art 10(1), (5)(b).

PART 7
CONVERSION OF LICENCES ETC ISSUED UNDER ENACTMENTS TO BE REPEALED INTO PREMISES LICENCES UNDER THE GAMBLING ACT 2005

6.1555 53 Existing premises operators

(1) This paragraph specifies the circumstances in which a person is to be treated for the purposes of this Part as the existing premises operator in relation to premises which are the subject of an application for a premises licence.

(2) Where the application is for a casino premises licence, a person is the existing premises operator in relation to the premises to which the application relates if—

(a) on the date on which the application is made he holds a casino licence in respect of the same or substantially the same premises; or

(b) on that date—

(i) he is applying for the grant of such a licence, and

(ii) the application (including any appeal) has not been finally determined or withdrawn.

(3) . . . [1]

(4) Where the application is for a bingo premises licence, a person is the existing premises operator in relation to the premises to which the application relates if—

(a) on the date on which the application is made he holds a bingo club licence in respect of the same or substantially the same premises; or

(b) on that date—

(i) he is applying for the grant of such a licence, and

(ii) the application (including any appeal) has not been finally determined or withdrawn.

(5) . . . [2]

(6) Where the application is for a betting premises licence, a person is the existing premises operator in relation to the premises to which the application relates if—

(a) on the date on which the application is made he is—

(i) the holder of a betting office licence issued under Schedule 1 to the 1963 Act in respect of the same or substantially the same premises,

(ii) the holder of a track betting licence issued under Schedule 3 to the 1963 Act in respect of the same or substantially the same premises, or

(iii) the holder of a certificate of approval issued under section 13 of that Act (which provides for the approval of horse racecourses by the Levy Board), other than a point to point certificate, in respect of the same or substantially the same premises; or

(b) on that date—

(i) he is applying to the appropriate authority for the grant of such a licence or certificate, and

(ii) the application (including any appeal) has not been finally determined or withdrawn.

(7) In sub-paragraph (6)(a)(iii), the reference to a point to point certificate is to a certificate issued under section 13 of the 1963 Act which is subject to the restriction that the premises to which it relates may only be used for the purposes of a horse racecourse on a limited number of days during a specified period of no more than 12 months.

(8) . . . [3]

(9) Where the application is for an adult gaming centre premises licence or a family entertainment centre premises licence, a person is the existing premises operator in

relation to the premises to which the application relates if on the date on which the application is made the conditions in sub-paragraph (10) or (11) are met.

(10) The conditions are that—

(a) the person concerned holds a permit under section 34 of the 1968 Act (which makes provision with respect to the use of machines to which Part 3 of that Act applies for gaming) granted by one of the authorities mentioned in paragraph 1(b) or (d) of Schedule 9 to that Act;

(b) the permit relates to the same or substantially the same premises as those to which the application for the premises licence relates, and those premises are amusement machine premises; and

(c) the permit is expressed to be granted for the purposes of section 34(5E) of that Act.

(11) The conditions are that—

(a) the person concerned is applying to the relevant authority referred to in paragraph (a) of sub-paragraph (10) for a permit of the description mentioned in paragraphs (b) and (c) of that sub-paragraph, and

(b) the application (including any appeal) has not been finally determined or withdrawn.

54 Conversion of existing licences etc into premises licences

[(1) Subject to paragraph 66(4)(b), this paragraph applies to an advance application for a premises licence which—

(a) meets the conditions in sub-paragraphs (1A), (1B) and (1D), and

(b) in a case to which sub-paragraph (1B)(b) applies, also meets the condition in sub-paragraph (1E).

(1A) The first condition is that the application relates to premises in respect of which a person is an existing premises operator.

(1B) The second condition is that the application is made by—

(a) the existing premises operator in relation to those premises; or

(b) a person who is acting with the written consent of the existing premises operator.

(1C) Sub-paragraph (1B)(b) is only to apply where the person who is the existing premises operator in relation to the premises to which the application relates qualifies as such by reason of the fact that he holds—

(a) a licence under the 1968 Act,

(b) a betting office licence issued under Schedule 1 to the 1963 Act,

(c) a track betting licence issued under Schedule 3 to the 1963 Act,

(d) a certificate of approval issued under section 13 of the 1963 Act, or

(e) a permit under section 34 of the 1968 Act.

(1D) The third condition is that the application complies with any conditions or requirements of subsections (1) to (5) and (6)(c) of section 159 of the 2005 Act (which specifies the conditions and requirements to be met by a person applying for a premises licence).

(1E) The fourth condition, which only applies in a case falling within sub-paragraph (1B)(b), is that the application for the premises licence is accompanied by—

(a) the document containing the written consent of the existing premises operator, and

(b) a copy of the licence, certificate or permit referred to in sub-paragraph (1C) or, where it is not reasonably practicable to produce a copy of the licence, certificate or permit, a statement explaining why it is not reasonably practicable to do so.][4]

(2) An application to which this paragraph applies is referred to in this Part as a conversion application.

(3) Part 8 of the 2005 Act is to have effect in relation to the making and determination of a conversion application subject to the following provisions of this Part.

(4) Subject to [sub-paragraph (5A) and][5] paragraphs 55(2) and (3), 58(1) [and 59(4) and (5)][6], the licensing authority must grant the application.

(5) Section 163(2) of the 2005 Act (which prohibits a licensing authority from determining an application for a premises licence if the applicant does not hold a relevant operating licence) is not to have effect in relation to a conversion application; but any licence issued on such an application in accordance with sub-paragraph (4) is to lapse if the holder's application for a relevant operating licence is rejected when it is finally determined.

[(5A) Where—

(a) a person making a conversion application does not hold a relevant operating licence on the date on which he makes the application, and

(b) that person's application for a relevant operating licence is rejected before the conversion application is granted,

the licensing authority must reject the conversion application; and if the licensing authority grant the conversion application, any premises licence issued on such an application shall be of no effect.][7]

(6) In sub-paragraph (5) the reference to a relevant operating licence is to an operating licence which authorises the holder to carry on the activity to which the premises licence relates.

(7) Subject to sub-paragraph (8), section 206(2) of the 2005 Act (which provides for rights of appeal in connection with applications under Part 8 of that Act) is not to apply where an application is granted in pursuance of sub-paragraph (4).

(8) Sub-paragraph (7) is without prejudice to the right of—

(a) the applicant, or

(b) a person who made representations in relation to the application,

to appeal against any conditions attached by virtue of section 169(1) of the 2005 Act to a premises licence issued in pursuance of sub-paragraph (4).

[(9) In this paragraph "relevant operating licence" in relation to a conversion application means an operating licence (other than an interim operating licence) which authorises the person making the application to carry on the activity in respect of which the premises licence is sought.][8]

55 Failure to make the application for a premises licence in the appropriate form or manner

(1) This paragraph applies to any application for a premises licence which—

(a) is a conversion application, but

(b) either—

(i) does not comply with a requirement imposed under paragraph (a) or (b) of section 159(6) of the 2005 Act, or

(ii) includes a plan of the proposed licensed premises which is incompatible with any conditions which would be attached to the premises licence by virtue of regulations under section 167 of the 2005 Act.

(2) Where—

(a) the applicant has failed to comply with a requirement imposed under paragraph (a) or (b) of section 159(6) of the 2005 Act, and

(b) the licensing authority give notice in writing to the applicant requesting him to do anything which is necessary for the purposes of complying with the requirement,

the licensing authority are to cease to be under a duty by virtue of paragraph 54(4) to grant the application until such time as the applicant complies with the request.

(3) Where the application includes a plan of the proposed licensed premises which is incompatible with any conditions which would be attached to the premises licence by virtue of regulations under section 167 of the 2005 Act, the licensing authority—

(a) may not grant the application until such time as the applicant has submitted an amended plan which is compatible with the relevant conditions, and

(b) must give the applicant notice in writing—

(i) indicating that the plan is incompatible with specified conditions to be attached to the premises licence, and

(ii) requesting the applicant to submit an amended plan which is compatible with those conditions.

(4) In the case of an application made before [31st July][9], the applicant must comply with any request made under sub-paragraph (2) or (3) within such period as may be specified in the relevant notice (such period not being less than 14 days from the date on which the notice is received).

(5) If, in a case to which paragraph 62 applies, the applicant fails to comply with the request within the period specified in accordance with sub-paragraph (4)—

(a) that paragraph is to cease to apply after the end of that period; and

(b) where that period expires on or after 1st September 2007, the existing licence, permit or certificate (within the meaning of that paragraph) is to cease to have effect immediately following the expiry of that period.

56 Non-fast track applications: modification of provisions of the Gambling Act 2005

(1) This paragraph applies to a conversion application which is accompanied by a request made by the applicant for the licensing authority to exercise its powers under section 169(1) of the 2005 Act to exclude, or vary in a specified manner, a condition which would otherwise be attached to the licence by virtue of regulations under section 168 of that Act (which provides for default conditions to be prescribed by regulations).

(2) In this Part any reference to a non-fast track application is to an application to which this paragraph applies.

(3) Section 169 of the 2005 Act is to have effect in relation to a premises licence issued on a non-fast track application subject to the following modifications.

(4) Subject to sub-paragraph (5) [and paragraph 57A][10], in issuing the premises licence the licensing authority may only exercise its powers under section 169(1) for the purposes of complying with the request referred to in sub-paragraph (1).

(5) Where the licensing authority exercises its powers under subsection (1) of section 169 for the purposes of complying with the request referred to in sub-paragraph (1), it may also exercise its powers under that subsection to attach one or more other conditions to the licence.

57 Fast track applications: modification of provisions of the Gambling Act 2005

(1) This paragraph applies to a conversion application which is not a non-fast track application.

(2) In this Part any reference to a fast track application is to an application to which this paragraph applies.

(3) Part 8 of the 2005 Act is to have effect subject to the modifications specified below.

(4) Section 160(1) of the 2005 Act (which enables the Secretary of State by regulations to require applicants for premises licences to give notice of their applications) is to have effect as if the reference in that provision to an applicant for a premises licence did not include a person making a fast track application.

(5) Sections 161 and 162 of that Act (which respectively provide for representations to be made by persons with respect to premises licence applications,

and specify the circumstances in which a hearing is to take place) are not to apply to fast track applications.

(6) [Subject to paragraph 57A,][11] the powers of the licensing authority under section 169(1) of the 2005 Act—

(a) to attach conditions on issuing a premises licence, and

(b) to exclude a condition that would otherwise be attached to the licence by virtue of regulations under section 168 of that Act,

are not to apply to a licence issued on a fast track application.

(7) A person may make either a fast-track or a non-fast track application, but not both in respect of the same premises; and, where a person submits both a fast-track and a non-fast track application, the licensing authority must reject the non-fast track application.

[57A Attaching a condition restricting the use of premises to specified periods

(1) This paragraph applies to a conversion application which includes a request for the licensing authority to exercise its powers under section 169(1)(a) of the 2005 Act to attach a condition so that facilities for gambling may only be provided in reliance on the licence during one or more specified periods in a year.

(2) Despite paragraphs 56(4) and 57(6)(a), where the licensing authority issue a premises licence in pursuance of paragraph 54, they may exercise their powers under section 169(1)(a) of the 2005 Act to attach the condition referred to in sub-paragraph (1).][12]

58 Effect of revocation or cancellation of existing licence etc

(1) Where—

(a) a person makes a conversion application, and

(b) the licence, permit or certificate by virtue of which he qualifies as the existing premises operator in relation to the application ("the existing licence, permit or certificate") is revoked or cancelled,

the licensing authority must reject the application.

(2) Where despite sub-paragraph (1) the licensing authority purport to grant the premises licence in respect of which the application is made, the licence is to be of no effect.

(3) Where the existing licence, permit or certificate is revoked or cancelled after the licensing authority has issued a premises licence in pursuance of paragraph 54(4), the premises licence is to lapse on the date on which the existing licence is revoked or cancelled.

(4) Where the existing licence is a casino licence or a bingo club licence, any reference in this paragraph to the licence being revoked is to include a reference to the licence ceasing to have effect by virtue of paragraph 35(6) of Schedule 2 to the 1968 Act because the relevant certificate of consent issued under that Schedule has been revoked.

59 Conversion of existing licences etc into premises licences: supplementary provisions

(1) This paragraph applies to an advance application for a premises licence made by a person who qualifies as the existing premises operator in relation to the premises because on the date on which the application is made an application is also being made for—

(a) the grant of a betting office licence under the 1963 Act,

(b) the grant . . . [13] of a track betting licence under that Act,

(c) the grant of a certificate of approval under section 13 of that Act,

(d) the grant . . . [13] of a casino licence under the 1968 Act,

(e) the grant . . . [13] of a bingo club licence under that Act, or

6: Gambling Act 2005: SIs

(f) the grant of a permit under section 34 of that Act in respect of amusement machine premises.

(2) Any reference in this Part to the application under the existing legislation (including any reference to the application for transfer under the existing legislation) is to the relevant application referred to in sub-paragraph (1).

(3) . . . [14]

(4) Where the application is a conversion application, sub-paragraph (4) of paragraph 54 is to be modified so that—

(a) the licensing authority may not determine the application for the premises licence before being notified in writing by the applicant that the application under the existing legislation has been determined; and

(b) the licensing authority are to be under a duty to grant the application for a premises licence only where the application under the existing legislation is granted and the applicant has sent them a copy of the relevant licence, permit or certificate.

(5) Where the application under the existing legislation is refused, the licensing authority must reject the application for the premises licence.

(6) Where despite the refusal of the application under the existing legislation the licensing authority purport to grant the premises licence, the licence is to be of no effect.

(7) Where, in a case to which paragraph 54 applies, the application under the existing legislation is granted before 1st September 2007, paragraph 58 is to apply to a licence, permit or certificate granted on such an application as it applies to the existing licence, permit or certificate in a case to which that paragraph applies.

60 . . . [15]

61 Special provisions where the application for the premises licence and the application under the existing legislation are being made to the same authority

(1) Sub-paragraph (4) applies to a conversion application for an adult gaming centre premises licence or a family entertainment centre premises licence where—

(a) the person making the application qualifies as the existing premises operator by reason of the fact that on the date on which he makes the application he is also applying for a permit under section 34 of the 1968 Act in respect of amusement machine premises, and

(b) both the application for the premises licence and the application for the permit are being made to the same local authority in England or Wales.

(2) Sub-paragraph (4) also applies to any of the applications specified in sub-paragraph (3) where—

(a) the person making the application qualifies as the existing premises operator by reason of the fact that on the date on which he makes the application he is also making an application of one of the types referred to in paragraph (a), (d) or (e) of paragraph 59(1), and

(b) both the application for the premises licence and the application under the 1963 Act or the 1968 Act are being made to the same licensing board in Scotland.

(3) The applications referred to in sub-paragraph (2) are—

(a) a conversion application for a casino premises licence,

(b) a conversion application for a bingo premises licence, and

(c) a conversion application for a betting premises licence.

(4) Where this sub-paragraph applies, paragraph 59 is to have effect as if in sub-paragraph (4)(b), the words "and the applicant has sent them a copy of the relevant licence, permit or certificate" were omitted.

(5) . . . [16]

62 Continuation of existing licences, permits and certificates on and after 1st September 2007

(1) Subject to . . . [17] paragraph 55(5), this paragraph and paragraphs 63 and 64 apply where—

(a) a conversion application is made before 31st July 2007;

(b) [the person, who is the existing premises operator in relation to the premises to which the application relates,][18] is the holder immediately before 1st September 2007 of a licence, permit or certificate of one of the kinds described in paragraph 53 (referred to in this paragraph and in paragraphs 63 and 64 as "the existing licence, permit or certificate"); and—

(i) it is by virtue of that licence, certificate or permit that he qualifies as the existing premises operator for the purposes of the application, or

(ii) it is by virtue of an application for the grant . . . [19] of that licence, certificate of permit that he qualifies as the existing premises operator for the purposes of the application;

(c) the licensing authority are under a duty to grant the application by virtue of paragraph 54(4); and

(d) the licensing authority have not issued the premises licence to the applicant before 1st September 2007.

(2) The existing licence, permit or certificate is to continue in force on and after 1st September 2007.

[(2A) Where the person making the conversion application is not the existing premises operator, the existing licence, permit or certificate is to be treated for the purposes of this paragraph and paragraphs 63 and 64 as if it was issued to the person making the conversion application; and it is to have effect on and after 1st September 2007 accordingly.][20]

(3) Sub-paragraph (2) is to apply whether or not the existing licence, permit or certificate was due to expire at the end of 31st August 2007.

(4) Where the application for the premises licence is one to which paragraph 59 applies, sub-paragraph (2) is not to apply, or (as the case may be) is to cease to apply, to the existing licence, permit or certificate unless—

(a) the applicant notifies the licensing authority in writing of the grant of the existing licence, permit or certificate before the end of the period of 14 days beginning on the day on which it is granted, and

(b) provides the authority with a copy of the relevant licence, permit or certificate.

(5) Sub-paragraph (4) does not apply where the application for the premises licence is one to which paragraph 61(4) applies.

(6) On and after 1st September 2007—

(a) a casino licence is to have effect to authorise the licensed premises to be used for providing facilities for gambling as if it were a converted casino premises licence;

(b) a bingo club licence is to have effect to authorise the licensed premises to be used for providing facilities for gambling as if it were a bingo premises licence;

(c) a betting office licence under the 1963 Act, a track betting licence under that Act or a certificate of approval under section 13 of that Act is to have effect to authorise the premises to which the licence or certificate relates to be used for providing facilities for gambling as if it were a betting premises licence;

(d) a permit under section 34 of the 1968 Act is to have effect to authorise the premises to which the permit relates to be used for the purposes of providing facilities for gambling as if it were a relevant premises licence.

(7) In sub-paragraph (6)(d) the reference to a relevant premises licence is to—

(a) an adult gaming centre premises licence, if the conversion application is for a adult gaming centre premises licence;

(b) a family entertainment centre premises licence, if the conversion application is for a family entertainment centre premises licence.

(8) On and after 1st September 2007 the existing licence, permit or certificate is to have effect—

(a) subject to any relevant premises licence conditions, and

(b) until the premises licence which is being applied for has been issued or, [in a case to which sub-paragraph (5A) of paragraph 54 applies, until the date on which the application for the relevant operating licence referred to in that sub-paragraph is rejected][21].

(9) In sub-paragraph (8) and in paragraph 64, references to relevant premises licence conditions are to—

(a) any conditions which premises licences of the relevant kind are subject to by virtue of any provision of the 2005 Act (including any provision of that Act as modified by a provision of this Schedule),

(b) any conditions which premises licences of the relevant kind are subject to by virtue of regulations under section 167 of that Act,

(c) any default conditions, and

(d) any conditions attached to the existing licence, permit or certificate under paragraph 64(3).

(10) In sub-paragraph (9)(c) and paragraph 64, references to default conditions are to any conditions prescribed in regulations under section 168 in relation to premises licences of the relevant kind.

(11) Sub-paragraph (9)(c) is subject to paragraph 64(3)(a).

63 Application of the Gambling Act 2005 to the existing licence, permit or certificate

(1) The 2005 Act is to apply to the existing licence, permit or certificate on or after 1st September 2007 with the modifications specified in the following provisions of this paragraph and in paragraph 64.

(2) Section 37 (which makes it an offence to use premises for providing facilities for gambling) is to have effect as if it provided for subsection (1) of that section not to apply to the use of the premises to which the existing licence, permit or certificate relates by—

(a) the person to whom the existing licence, permit or certificate was issued, or

(b) a person acting in the course of a business carried on by the person referred to in paragraph (a),

if the use is authorised by the licence, permit or certificate.

(3) Where the premises concerned are a track, section 37 is to have effect as if it provided for subsection (1) of that section not to apply to the use of the track by a person for accepting bets if the use is authorised by the existing licence or certificate.

64 Application of review provisions to the existing licence, permit or certificate

(1) Sections 197 to 203 of the 2005 Act (which provide for the review of premises licences by licensing authorities) are to apply to the existing licence, permit or certificate and the holder of the existing licence, permit or certificate as they apply to premises licences and the holder of such licences, but with the modifications specified in sub-paragraphs (2) to (4).

(2) In subsection (2)(a) of section 200 (which specifies the circumstances in which a licensing authority may carry out a review), the reference to a condition of the licence

is to have effect as a reference to any relevant premises licence conditions having effect in relation to the existing licence, permit or certificate.

(3) Following a review under section 201 (which specifies the procedure on a review), the licensing authority may—

(a) exclude a default condition, or remove or amend an exclusion having effect by virtue of this sub-paragraph as a result of a previous review, or

(b) attach a condition, or remove or amend a condition attached under this sub-paragraph as a result of a previous review.

(4) Subsection (1) of section 202 (which makes provision as to the action which may be taken following a review) is to have effect—

(a) as if paragraph (c) provided for the licensing authority to have power to exclude a default condition, or remove or amend an exclusion having effect by virtue of sub-paragraph (3)(a) above, and

(b) as if paragraph (d) provided for the licensing authority to have power to attach a condition to the existing licence, permit or certificate under sub-paragraph (3)(b) above.

(5) Section 206(3) of the 2005 Act (which makes provision for appeals against actions taken by licensing authorities on a review) is to have effect in relation to the existing licence, permit or certificate as if—

(a) a reference to a licensing authority taking action under section 202 as a result of a review, or determining to take no action as a result of a review, included a reference to the licensing authority taking such action, or determining to take no such action, in relation to the existing licence, permit or certificate; and

(b) the reference to the licensee included a reference to the holder of the existing licence, permit or certificate.

(6) Section 313(2) of the 2005 Act (which provides for the inspection of premises in respect of which a premises licence has effect) is to apply to the premises in respect of which the existing licence, permit or certificate has effect as it applies to premises in respect of which a premises licence has effect.

65 Application of the Gambling Act 2005 to casino premises licences granted on a conversion application

(1) This paragraph applies to—

(a) a conversion application for a casino premises licence, and

(b) a casino premises licence issued on the grant of such an application in pursuance of paragraph 54(4).

(2) This paragraph is without prejudice to paragraphs 54 to 61.

(3) Part 8 of the 2005 Act is to have effect subject to the modifications specified in the following provisions of this paragraph.

(4) Section 150(2) (which describes the kinds of casino premises licences) is not to apply to a casino premises licence to which this paragraph applies and instead such a licence is to be referred to as a converted casino premises licence.

(5) A converted casino premises licence is a licence which states that it authorises premises to be used for the operation of a casino or for providing other facilities for gaming (apart from bingo); and section 150(1)(a) is to be modified accordingly.

(6) Section 172 (which makes provision as to the effect of a premises licence in authorising the making available of gaming machines) is to be modified so as to provide for a converted casino premises licence to authorise the holder of the licence either—

(a) to make 20 gaming machines available for use on the premises where at least one of the machines is of Category B and provided that each machine is of Category B, C or D; or

(b) to make available for use on the premises any number of Category C or D gaming machines.

(7) Section 174(1) (which makes provision as to the kinds of premises in respect of which a casino premises licence may be granted) is not to apply where the application is for a converted casino premises licence.

(8) Section 174(2) (which provides for casino premises licences to authorise the holder to make available any number of games of chance other than casino games)—

(a) is not to have effect to authorise the playing of bingo in premises in respect of which a converted casino premises licence has effect;

(b) is to have effect to authorise the holder of a converted casino premises licence to make available other games of chance which are not casino games, irrespective of whether or not casino games are also made available on the premises.

(9) Section 174(3) (which provides for casino premises licences to authorise the holder to use the premises for the provision of bingo, betting or both) is not to apply to a converted casino premises licence to which this paragraph applies.

(10) A converted casino premises licence is not to count for the purposes of any of the limits in section 175(1) to (3) (which limit the overall numbers of specified kinds of casino premises licences).

(11) Subsections (5) and (7) of section 175 and Schedule 9 (which make provision about applications for casino premises licences) are not to apply to an application for a converted casino premises licence.

(12) The licence holder may apply under section 187 to vary a converted casino premises licence so that it relates to premises which are different from those to which it previously related, and subsection (2) of that section (which prohibits a premises licence from being varied so as to relate to premises to which it did not previously relate) is accordingly not to have effect in relation to a converted casino premises licence.

(13) Where a converted casino premises licence is varied to relate to premises to which it did not previously relate, those premises must be wholly or partly situated in the area of the licensing authority which issued the licence.

66 Non-conversion applications for casino premises licences

(1) Where a converted casino premises licence has effect in respect of premises, nothing in Part 8 of the 2005 Act is to be taken as preventing the licence holder from making a non-conversion application for a casino premises licence which relates to or includes the same or substantially the same premises.

(2) Sub-paragraph (1) is to apply irrespective of whether or not the non-conversion application is made before, on or after 1st September 2007; or whether a previous non-conversion application has been made which relates to or includes the same or substantially the same premises.

(3) Where a non-conversion application for a casino premises licence is granted, the converted casino premises licence is to lapse when the licence issued on the grant of the non-conversion application takes effect.

(4) In this paragraph a "non-conversion application for a casino premises licence" means an application for a casino premises licence—

(a) to which paragraph 54 does not apply, or

(b) in a case in which that paragraph would otherwise apply, where the applicant includes a statement in the application indicating that that paragraph is not to apply to the application.

---

1 Para 53: sub-para (3) revoked by SI 2007/1157, art 11(1), (2).

2 Para 53: sub-para (5) revoked by SI 2007/1157, art 11(1), (2).

3 Para 53: sub-para (8) revoked by SI 2007/1157, art 11(1), (2).

4 Para 54: sub-paras (1), (1A)–(1E) substituted, for sub-para (1) as originally enacted, by SI 2007/1157, art 11(1), (3)(a).

5 Para 54: in sub-para (4) words "sub-paragraph (5A) and" in square brackets inserted by SI 2007/2169, art 11(1), (2)(a).

6 Para 54: in sub-para (4) words "and 59(4) and (5)" in square brackets substituted by SI 2007/1157, art 11(1), (3)(b).

7 Para 54: sub-para (5A) inserted by SI 2007/2169, art 11(1), (2)(b).

8 Para 54: sub-para (9) inserted by SI 2007/2169, art 11(1), (2)(c).

9 Para 55: in sub-para (4) words "31st July" in square brackets substituted by SI 2007/2169, art 11(1), (3).

10 Para 56: in sub-para (4) words "and paragraph 57A" in square brackets inserted by SI 2007/1157, art 11(1), (4).

11 Para 57: in sub-para (6) words "Subject to paragraph 57A," in square brackets inserted by SI 2007/1157, art 11(1), (5).

12 Para 57A: inserted by SI 2007/1157, art 11(1), (6).

13 Para 59: in sub-para (1) words omitted revoked by SI 2007/1157, art 11(1), (7).

14 Para 59: sub-para (3) revoked by SI 2007/1157, art 11(1), (8).

15 Para 60: revoked by SI 2007/1157, art 11(1), (8).

16 Para 61: sub-para (5) revoked by SI 2007/1157, art 11(1), (8).

17 Para 62: in sub-para (1) words omitted revoked by SI 2007/1157, art 11(1), (9)(a)(i).

18 Para 62: in sub-para (1)(b) words from "the person, who" to "the application relates," in square brackets substituted by SI 2007/1157, art 11(1), (9)(a)(ii)(aa).

19 Para 62: in sub-para (1)(b)(ii) words omitted revoked by SI 2007/1157, art 11(1), (9)(a)(ii)(bb).

20 Para 62: sub-para (2A) inserted by SI 2007/1157, art 11(1), (9)(b).

21 Para 62: in sub-para (8) words from "in a case" to "sub-paragraph is rejected" in square brackets substituted by SI 2007/2169, art 11(1), (5).

PART 8
CONVERSION OF LOTTERY REGISTRATIONS UNDER THE LOTTERIES AND AMUSEMENTS ACT 1976 INTO OPERATING LICENCES OR REGISTRATIONS UNDER THE GAMBLING ACT 2005

6.1556 67 Conversion of society registrations into lottery operating licences

(1) This paragraph applies where—

(a) a society is registered under Schedule 1A to the 1976 Act, and

(b) the registration has effect immediately before 1st September 2007.

(2) This paragraph also applies where a society is registered under Schedule 1A to the 1976 Act on or after 1st September 2007.

(3) The Gambling Commission must issue a lottery operating licence to the society on the relevant date or as soon as practicable after that date.

(4) Such a licence—

(a) is referred to in this paragraph and in paragraph 68 as a converted society lottery operating licence, and

(b) is included in any reference to a converted lottery operating licence in paragraphs 71 and 72.

(5) A converted society lottery operating licence is to have effect as both a remote and non-remote lottery operating licence; and section 67(2) and (3) of the 2005 Act (which prohibits an operating licence from being both a remote and non-remote licence) is not to apply to the licence.

(6) In exercising its powers under section 75 of the 2005 Act (powers of Gambling Commission to impose general conditions on operating licences), the Commission must specify any conditions which are to apply to—

(a) a converted society lottery operating licence, or

(b) a converted society lottery operating licence falling within a specified class.

(7) Regulations under section 78 of the 2005 Act (which allows the Secretary of State to make regulations specifying conditions to be imposed on operating licences) may specify conditions which are to apply to a converted society lottery operating licence or to converted society lottery operating licences falling within a specified description.

(8) In this paragraph a reference to the relevant date is to—

(a) 1st September 2007, or

(b) in a case falling within sub-paragraph (2), the date on which the society is registered under Schedule 1A to the 1976 Act.

68 Conversion of society registrations: transitional provisions

(1) A society falling within sub-paragraph (1) of paragraph 67 is to be treated as if it holds a converted society lottery operating licence during the period beginning on 1st September 2007 and ending immediately before the converted society lottery operating licence issued to the society takes effect.

(2) Where the society or a person acting on its behalf carries out activities in reliance on sub-paragraph (1) they are to comply with any relevant operating licence conditions.

(3) Section 258 of the 2005 Act (which makes it an offence to promote a lottery other than in specified circumstances) is not to apply to activity by a society acting in reliance on sub-paragraph (1) if the activity is carried on in accordance with any relevant operating licence conditions.

(4) Section 258 of the 2005 Act is not to apply to activity by a person acting on behalf of a society to which sub-paragraph (1) applies if—

(a) he acts otherwise than as an external lottery manager, and

(b) the activity is carried on in accordance with any relevant operating licence conditions.

(5) In this paragraph, any reference to relevant operating licence conditions is to—

(a) any conditions specified by the Gambling Commission under section 75 of the 2005 Act which would be attached in accordance with subsection (3) of that section to a converted society lottery operating licence; and

(b) any conditions specified by the Secretary of State in regulations under section 78 of that Act which would be attached to such a licence.

69 Conversion of local lottery scheme registrations into lottery operating licences

(1) This paragraph applies where—

(a) a scheme approved by a local authority in connection with the promotion of lotteries is registered under Schedule 2 to the 1976 Act, and

(b) the registration has effect immediately before 1st September 2007.

(2) This paragraph also applies where a scheme is registered under Schedule 2 to the 1976 Act on or after 1st September 2007.

(3) The Gambling Commission must issue a lottery operating licence to the local authority on the relevant date or as soon as practicable after that date.

(4) Such a licence—

(a) is referred to in this paragraph and in paragraph 70 as a converted local authority lottery operating licence, and

(b) is included in any reference to a converted lottery operating licence in paragraphs 71 and 72.

(5) A converted local authority lottery operating licence is to have effect as both a remote and non-remote lottery operating licence; and section 67(2) and (3) of the 2005 Act is not to apply to the licence.

(6) In exercising its powers under section 75 of the 2005 Act, the Commission must specify any conditions which are to be attached to—

(a) a converted local authority lottery operating licence, or

(b) a converted local authority lottery operating licence falling within a specified class.

(7) Regulations under section 78 of the 2005 Act may specify conditions which are to be attached to a converted local authority lottery operating licence or to converted local authority lottery operating licences falling within a specified description.

(8) In this paragraph a reference to the relevant date is to—

(a) 1st September 2007, or

(b) in a case falling within sub-paragraph (2), the date on which the scheme is registered.

70 Conversion of local lottery scheme registrations: transitional provisions

(1) A local authority to which sub-paragraph (1) of paragraph 69 applies is to be treated as if it holds a converted local authority lottery operating licence during the period beginning on 1st September 2007 and ending when the licence issued to the authority in accordance with that paragraph takes effect.

(2) Where the local authority or a person acting on its behalf carries out activities in reliance on sub-paragraph (1) they are to comply with any relevant operating licence conditions.

(3) Section 258 of the 2005 Act is not to apply to activity by a local authority acting in reliance on sub-paragraph (1) if the activity is carried on in accordance with any relevant operating licence conditions.

(4) Section 258 of the 2005 Act is not to apply to activity by a person acting on behalf of a local authority to which sub-paragraph (1) applies if—

(a) he acts otherwise than as an external lottery manager, and

(b) the activity is carried on in accordance with any relevant operating licence conditions.

(5) In this paragraph, any reference to relevant operating licence conditions is to—

(a) any conditions specified by the Gambling Commission under section 75 of the 2005 Act which would be attached in accordance with subsection (3) of that section to a converted local lottery operating licence, and

(b) any conditions specified by the Secretary of State in regulations under section 78 of that Act which would be attached to such a licence.

71 Duration of converted lottery operating licences

(1) Subject to the following provisions of this paragraph, a converted lottery operating licence is to cease to have effect on the last day of the period of three years beginning with the date on which the last 1976 Act fee was payable.

(2) Subject to sub-paragraph (3), where—

(a) the holder of a converted lottery operating licence applies for a lottery operating licence at least two months before the date on which the converted lottery operating licences is due to expire in accordance with sub-paragraph (1), and

(b) that application complies with section 69(2)(g) and (3) of the 2005 Act,

the converted lottery operating licence is not to cease to have effect by virtue of sub-paragraph (1) until the application is finally determined or is withdrawn.

(3) A converted lottery operating licence may cease to have effect before the date determined in accordance with sub-paragraphs (1) and (2) by virtue of section 113, 114, 115, 118 or 119 of the Act (which provide respectively for the surrender, lapse, forfeiture, suspension and revocation of operating licences).

(4) The reference in sub-paragraph (1) to the date on which the last 1976 Act fee was payable is to the last date before 1st September 2007 on which a fee was payable in respect of the registration by virtue of (as the case may be) paragraph 6(1)(a) of

Schedule 1A or paragraph 7(1)(b) of Schedule 2 to the 1976 Act( ) (each of which provides for the payment of periodic fees in respect of registrations under respectively Schedule 1A or 2 to the 1976 Act).

(5) Where no fee is payable before 1st September 2007 under the provisions of the 1976 Act referred to in sub-paragraph (4), the reference in sub-paragraph (1) to the date on which the last 1976 Act fee was payable is to be treated as a reference to the date on which the society or the local authority scheme was registered under that Act.

72 Application of Part 5 of the Gambling Act 2005 to converted lottery operating licences

(1) Part 5 of the 2005 Act is to be modified as follows in its application to a converted lottery operating licence.

(2) Section 99 (which specifies mandatory conditions of lottery operating licences) is to be modified so that, for the period beginning on the date on which the licence is issued and ending on 31st December 2007, the requirement specified in subsection (3)(b) is that the aggregate of the proceeds of lotteries promoted wholly or partly in reliance on the licence may not exceed—

$$£10,000,000 - (A + B)$$

where—

A is the total value of tickets or chances sold in the period beginning on 1st January 2007 and ending on 31st August 2007 in any lottery promoted wholly or partly in reliance on the 1976 Act registration, and

B is the aggregate amount of the proceeds of lotteries promoted wholly or partly under, as the case may be, paragraph 68 or 70.

(3) Sub-paragraph (2) only applies where the converted lottery operating licence is held by a society or local authority to which sub-paragraph (1) of (as the case may be) paragraph 67 or 69 applies.

(4) In sub-paragraph (2), "the 1976 Act registration" means—

(a) in relation to a converted lottery operating licence held by a society, the registration of the society under Schedule 1A to the 1976 Act which had effect immediately before 1st September 2007, and

(b) in relation to a converted lottery operating licence held by a local authority, the registration under Schedule 2 to the 1976 Act which had effect immediately before 1st September 2007.

(5) Sections 110 to 112 (which relate to duration of operating licences) are not to apply.

73 Application of the Gambling Act 2005 to lotteries begun before 1st September 2007

(1) A lottery operating licence is to authorise the holder to continue to promote a lottery which the holder began promoting before 1st September 2007 in reliance on the 1976 Act registration.

(2) Where before 1st September 2007 a person is able to participate in such a lottery by purchasing a chance (whether participation in the lottery in this way is offered in addition to or instead of participation by purchasing a ticket), persons may continue on and after that date to purchase a chance and not a ticket in the lottery if the condition in sub-paragraph (3) is met.

(3) The condition is that the arrangements for the lottery provide for each and every draw in the lottery to take place before 1st March 2009.

(4) Section 99 of the 2005 Act (which makes provision about the conditions to be attached to lottery operating licences) is to have effect subject to the following modifications in relation a lottery which falls within the description in sub-paragraph (2) and complies with the condition in sub-paragraph (3).

(5) Subject to sub-paragraph (6), subsections (4), (6) and (8) of that section are to have effect as if any reference to a person purchasing a ticket in the lottery (irrespective

of how it is described) included a reference to a person purchasing a chance in the lottery.

(6) Section 99 of the 2005 Act is to have effect as if the requirement in paragraph (b) of subsection (6) only applies where a person purchases a ticket in order to participate in the lottery.

(7) In sub-paragraph (1), "the 1976 Act registration" is to be construed in accordance with paragraph 72(4).

74 Conversion of society lottery registrations into registrations under the Gambling Act 2005

(1) This paragraph applies where—

(a) a society is registered under Schedule 1 to the 1976 Act, and

(b) the registration has effect immediately before 1st September 2007.

(2) This paragraph also applies where a society becomes registered under Schedule 1 to the 1976 Act on or after 1st September 2007.

(3) In England and Wales, the local authority which registered the society must on the relevant date, or as soon as practicable after that date, register the society under Part 5 of Schedule 11 to the 2005 Act.

(4) In Scotland, the council which registered the society must on the relevant date, or as soon as practicable after that date, provide the relevant licensing board with the information specified in sub-paragraph (5).

(5) The information to be provided is—

(a) the name and address of the society,

(b) the purposes for which the society is established,

(c) the date on which the society was registered under Schedule 1 to 1976 Act, and

(d) copies of any returns submitted in respect of the society in accordance with paragraph 11 of Schedule 1 to the 1976 Act.

(6) As soon as practicable after receiving the information specified in sub-paragraph (5), the relevant licensing board must register the society under Part 5 of Schedule 11 to the 2005 Act.

(7) In this paragraph—

(a) a reference to registering a society under Part 5 of Schedule 11 to the 2005 Act is to entering the society, together with such information as may be prescribed by regulations in accordance with paragraph 44(a) of that Schedule, in the register kept for the purposes of that Part;

(b) a reference to the relevant date is to—

(i) 1st September 2007, or

(ii) in a case falling within sub-paragraph (2), the date on which the society is registered under the 1976 Act; and

(c) a reference to the relevant licensing board is to the licensing board constituted under section 1 of the Licensing (Scotland) Act 1976 in whose area are situated the principal premises of the society.

75 Conversion of society lottery registrations: modification of Part 5 of Schedule 11 to the 2005 Act

(1) Paragraphs 44 and 46 of Schedule 11 to the 2005 Act are not to apply where a society is registered under Part 5 of that Schedule in pursuance of paragraph 74 above.

(2) Sub-paragraph (1) is subject to sub-paragraph (7)(a) of paragraph 74 above.

(3) Paragraph 54(2) of that Schedule is to have effect in relation to such a society as if for the reference to each anniversary of the registration of the society there were substituted a reference to 1st January in each year after 2007 on which the society is registered.

(4) In England and Wales, where a local authority registers a society under Part 5 of Schedule 11 to the 2005 Act in pursuance of paragraph 74 above, it must notify the society in writing of the registration before the beginning of the period referred to in sub-paragraph (2) of paragraph 54 of that Schedule (as that sub-paragraph has effect by virtue of sub-paragraph (3) above) when that period occurs for the first time during the registration.

(5) In Scotland, the council referred to in sub-paragraph (4) of paragraph 74 must at the same time as it provides the information referred to in that sub-paragraph give written notice to the society—

- (a) informing it that it is to be registered by the relevant licensing board under Part 5 of Schedule 11 to the 2005 Act, and
- (b) explaining the effect of sub-paragraphs (2) to (4) of paragraph 76.

(6) In sub-paragraph (5)(a), "the relevant licensing board" is to have the meaning given in paragraph 74(7)(c).

76 Conversion of society lottery registrations: transitional provisions

(1) Where—

- (a) a local authority in England or Wales or a licensing board in Scotland are required under paragraph 74 to register a society under Part 5 of Schedule 11 to the 2005 Act, but
- (b) the society is not so registered until after the relevant date (within the meaning of that paragraph),

during the period beginning on that date and ending immediately before the society is so registered ("the transitional period") Part 4 of that Schedule is to have effect in relation to the society as if modified in accordance with sub-paragraphs (2) to (4) below.

(2) Paragraph 38 of Schedule 11 to the 2005 Act is not to apply to the society during the transitional period.

(3) Paragraph 39 of that Schedule is to have effect during the transitional period as if the reference to the local authority with which the society is registered was a reference to the authority which is required to register the society under paragraph 74 above.

(4) Paragraph 55 of that Schedule is to have effect as if the reference to a statement sent to a local authority under paragraph 39 of that Schedule included a reference to a statement sent under that paragraph in pursuance of sub-paragraph (3) above.

(5) Sub-paragraph (6) applies where—

- (a) a lottery is promoted by a society which was registered under Schedule 1 to the 1976 Act immediately before 1st September 2007 (referred to in that sub-paragraph as "the 1976 Act registration"), and
- (b) it is promoted wholly or partly in the period beginning on that date and ending on 31st December 2007,

(6) Paragraph 31(3) of Schedule 11 to the 2005 Act is to have effect in relation to such a lottery as if it provided for the lottery to be a large lottery if it is promoted wholly or partly at a time at which the aggregate of the society's proceeds from society lotteries promoted wholly or partly during the period referred to in sub-paragraph (5) exceeds—

$$£250,000 - A,$$

where

A is the total value of tickets or chances sold in the period beginning on 1st January 2007 and ending on 31st August 2007 in any lottery promoted in reliance on the 1976 Act registration.

77 Application of Schedule 11 to the Gambling Act 2005 to lotteries begun before 1st September 2007

(1) Subject to the following provisions of this paragraph, Schedule 11 to the 2005 Act is to apply to a lottery whose promotion was begun (but not completed) before 1st September 2007 in the same way as it applies to a lottery which is wholly promoted on or after that date.

(2) Where before 1st September 2007 a person is able to participate in such a lottery by purchasing a chance (whether participation in the lottery in this way is offered in addition to or instead of participation by purchasing a ticket), persons may continue on and after that date to purchase a chance and not a ticket in the lottery if the condition in sub-paragraph (3) is met.

(3) The condition is that the arrangements for the lottery provide for each and every draw in the lottery to take place before 1st March 2009.

(4) Schedule 11 to the 2005 Act is to have effect subject to the following modifications in relation to a lottery which falls within the description in sub-paragraph (2) and complies with the condition in sub-paragraph (3).

(5) Subject to the following provisions of this paragraph any reference in that Schedule to a ticket is to include a reference to a chance.

(6) Where the lottery is a private lottery, paragraphs 15 and 18(b) of that Schedule are not to apply if a person purchases a chance (as opposed to a ticket) to participate in the lottery.

(7) Where the lottery is a small society lottery, paragraph 36 of that Schedule is only to apply where a person purchases a ticket to participate in the lottery.

PART 9
CONVERSION OF CLUB REGISTRATIONS UNDER THE GAMING ACT 1968 INTO CLUB GAMING AND MACHINE PERMITS UNDER THE GAMBLING ACT 2005

6.1557 78 Conversion of a club registration under Part 2 of the Gaming Act 1968 into a club gaming permit: scope of application of provisions

(1) Paragraphs 79 to 81, 83 and 84 apply to a members' club or miners' welfare institute where—

(a) the club or institute is registered under Part 2 of the 1968 Act, and

(b) the registration has effect immediately before 1st September 2007.

(2) Paragraphs 79 to 81, 83 and 84 also apply to a members' club or miners' welfare institute which is registered under Part 2 of the 1968 Act on or after 1st September 2007.

(3) In paragraphs 79, 80, 83 and 84, a reference to the relevant licensing authority is to the licensing authority (within the meaning of the 2005 Act) in whose area are situated the premises in respect of which the club or institute was registered under Part 2 of the 1968 Act.

79 Conversion of club registrations under Part 2 of the Gaming Act 1968: provision of information by the 1968 Act registration authority

(1) In England and Wales, the designated officer for the authority which registered the club or institute must on the relevant date, or as soon as practicable after that date, provide the relevant licensing authority with the information specified in sub-paragraph (3).

(2) In Scotland, the sheriff clerk to the sheriff who registered the club or institute must on the relevant date, or as soon as practicable after that date, provide the relevant licensing authority with the information specified in sub-paragraph (3).

(3) The information to be provided is—

(a) the name of the club or institute,

(b) a description of the purposes for which the club is established or, in the case of a miners' welfare institute, a statement that it is such;

(c) a description of the premises to which the registration relates,

(d) the address of those premises,

(e) the date of registration or, where the registration has been renewed, the date on which it was last renewed,

(f) in a case falling within paragraph 78(1) (other than one to which sub-paragraph (6) below applies), the date on which the registration, as it had effect immediately before 1st September 2007, was due to expire, and

(g) the name and address of the chairman or secretary of the club or institute as recorded in the register under Part 2 of the 1968 Act.

(4) This paragraph is subject to paragraph 81.

(5) Subject to sub-paragraph (6), a reference in this paragraph to the relevant date is to—

(a) 1st September 2007, or

(b) in a case falling within paragraph 78(2), the date on which the club or institute is registered.

(6) Where a club or institute's registration has effect immediately before 1st September 2007 by virtue of paragraph 22 of Schedule 3, or paragraph 20 of Schedule 4, to the 1968 Act (both of which provide for registrations under Part 2 of that Act to be extended where an application for renewal of the registration has not been determined), the relevant date is the date on which the application for renewal of the registration is granted.

80 Duty of licensing authority to convert a registration under Part 2 of the Gaming Act 1968 into a club gaming permit

(1) Subject to paragraphs 81 to 85, where—

(a) a members' club or miners' welfare institute applies to the relevant licensing authority for the grant of a club gaming permit in respect of the same or substantially the same premises as those to which the registration under Part 2 of the 1968 Act relates;

(b) the application complies with sub-paragraphs (b) and (e) of paragraph 2 and (where applicable) paragraph 3 of Schedule 12 to the 2005 Act; and

(c) the application is made . . . [1] before the relevant date,

the licensing authority must grant that application.

(2) Paragraphs 4, 5(b), 6, 7 and 10 of Schedule 12 to the 2005 Act are not to apply to an application falling within sub-paragraph (1), and paragraph 8 is to apply with the omission of any reference to objections.

(3) Subject to sub-paragraphs (4) and (5), in sub-paragraph (1)(c) "the relevant date" means the date on which the club or institute's registration, as it had effect immediately before 1st September 2007, was due to expire in accordance with (as the case may be) paragraph 19 of Schedule 3 or paragraph 17 of Schedule 4 to the 1968 Act (both of which provide for the duration of registrations under Part 2 of that Act).

(4) Where the club or institute's registration has effect immediately before 1st September 2007 by virtue of paragraph 22 of Schedule 3, or paragraph 20 of Schedule 4, to the 1968 Act, the relevant date is the last day of the period of 10 years beginning on the date on which the registration is renewed.

(5) Where the club or institute is registered on or after 1st September 2007, the relevant date is the last day of the period of one year beginning on the date on which it is registered.

81 Exclusion of cases where an application for the renewal of the registration under Part 2 is rejected on or after 1st September 2007

(1) This paragraph applies where—

(a) a club or institute's registration under Part 2 of the 1968 Act has effect immediately before 1st September 2007 by virtue of paragraph 22 of Schedule 3, or paragraph 20 of Schedule 4, to the 1968 Act; and

(b) the application for renewal of the registration is withdrawn or rejected on or after that date.

(2) Paragraphs 79 and 80(1) are not to apply in a case to which this paragraph applies.

(3) Paragraph 84(1) is to cease to apply to the club or institute on the date on which the application for renewal of the registration is withdrawn or rejected.

82 Conversion of club registrations under Part 2 of the Gaming Act 1968: applications made before 1st September 2007

(1) This paragraph applies where—

(a) a members' club or miners' welfare institute applies for the grant of a club gaming permit before 1st September 2007;

(b) when the application is made, the club or institute is registered under Part 2 of the 1968 Act in respect of the same, or substantially the same, premises as those to which the application relates;

(c) the registration under Part 2 of the 1968 Act is due to expire in accordance with (as the case may be) paragraph 19 of Schedule 3 or paragraph 17 of Schedule 4 to the 1968 Act on or after 1st September 2007;

(d) the application complies with paragraphs (b) and (e) of paragraph 2 and, where applicable, paragraph 3 of Schedule 12 to the 2005 Act; and

(e) the application is made . . . [2] before the relevant date (as that expression is defined in paragraph [80(3) and (4)][3]).

(2) The licensing authority may not determine the application before 1st September 2007.

83 Failure to make the application for a club gaming permit in the appropriate form or manner

(1) This paragraph applies to any application for a club gaming permit which meets the conditions in paragraphs (a) to (c) of paragraph 80(1), but does not comply with a requirement imposed under sub-paragraph (c) or (d) of paragraph 2 of Schedule 12 to the 2005 Act.

(2) Where the relevant licensing authority give notice in writing to the members' club or miners' welfare institute making the application requesting it to do anything which is necessary for the purposes of complying with any such requirement, the authority are to cease to be under a duty by virtue of paragraph 80(1) to grant the application until such time as the club or institute complies with the request.

(3) The applicant must comply with any request made under sub-paragraph (2) within such period as may be specified in the relevant notice (such period not being less than 14 days from the date on which the notice is received).

(4) Paragraph 84(1) is to cease to apply if the club or institute fails to comply with a request made under sub-paragraph (2) within the period specified in accordance with sub-paragraph (3).

84 Conversion of club registrations under Part 2 of the Gaming Act 1968: transitional provisions

(1) At any time on or after 1 September 2007 until the date on which the club gaming permit is granted in accordance with paragraph 80, a members' club or miners' welfare institute is to be treated for the purposes of the 2005 Act as if it had been granted such a permit in relation to the premises in respect of which the registration under Part 2 of the 1968 Act had effect.

(2) In a case falling within paragraph 78(2), sub-paragraph (1) is not to apply until the date on which the club or institute is registered under Part 2 of the 1968 Act.

(3) Where the club or institute fails to apply for a club gaming permit . . . [4] before the relevant date (within the meaning of paragraph 80(3) to (5)), sub-paragraph (1) is to have effect as if it provided for the club or institute to be treated as holding such a permit until the relevant date.

(4) Paragraph 80 and sub-paragraph (1) of this paragraph are to be subject to the following provisions of this paragraph.

(5) Paragraph 80 and sub-paragraph (1) of this paragraph are to cease to apply if the members' club or miners' welfare institute ceases to be such a club or institute within the meaning of sections 266 and 268 of the 2005 Act.

(6) Paragraph 80 and sub-paragraph (1) of this paragraph are to cease to apply to a members' club or miners' welfare institute if notice to that effect is given by the club or institute to the relevant licensing authority.

(7) The relevant licensing authority shall as soon as reasonably practicable inform the persons specified in sub-paragraph (8) if the authority—

(a) believe that sub-paragraph (5) applies, or

(b) receive notice given under sub-paragraph (6).

(8) The persons mentioned in sub-paragraph (7) are—

(a) the Gambling Commission, and

(b) the chief officer of police for any area in which the premises referred to in sub-paragraph (1) are situated.

(9) The relevant licensing authority may give notice in writing to a members' club or miners' welfare institute that paragraph 80 and sub-paragraph (1) of this paragraph are to be disapplied in relation to the club or institute.

(10) The relevant licensing authority may only give notice in accordance with sub-paragraph (9) if the authority think—

(a) that the premises on which the club or institute conducts its activities are used wholly or mainly by children, by young persons or by both, or

(b) that an offence, or a breach of a condition of section 271 of the 2005 Act (which makes provision with respect to club gaming permits), has been committed in the course of gaming activities carried on by the club or institute.

(11) Sub-paragraphs (2) to (4) of paragraph 21 and paragraph 25 of Schedule 12 to the 2005 Act (which provide respectively for cancellation of club gaming permits, and appeals) are to apply to the giving of a notice under sub-paragraph (9) of this paragraph as they apply to the cancellation of a club gaming permit under paragraph 21(1) of that Schedule.

(12) Paragraph 23 of Schedule 12 to the 2005 Act (which provides for forfeiture of club gaming permits on conviction of offences under the 2005 Act) is to apply as if—

(a) the reference in that paragraph to the holder of a club gaming permit, or the officer of the holder of such a permit holder, included a reference to a members' club or miners' welfare institute to which paragraph 80 and sub-paragraph (1) of this paragraph apply or the officer of such a club or institute; and

(b) the reference to the court having power to order forfeiture of the permit included a reference to the court having power to order that paragraph 80 and sub-paragraph (1) of this paragraph should be disapplied in relation to the club or miners' welfare institute concerned.

(13) Paragraph 28 of Schedule 12 to the 2005 Act (which makes provision about the delegation of licensing authority functions) is to apply to the exercise of functions by the relevant licensing authority under this paragraph and under paragraph 80 as it applies to the exercise of functions of a licensing authority under that Schedule.

(14) Despite section 274(2) of the 2005 Act (which disapplies Schedule 12 in relation to specified clubs etc in Scotland), the provisions of that Schedule referred to

in sub-paragraphs (11) to (13) are also to apply to a members' club or miners' welfare institute in Scotland in the same way as they apply to a club or institute in England and Wales.

85 Special provisions applying to clubs etc in Scotland

(1) This paragraph modifies paragraphs 80 and 82 to 84 in their application to members' clubs or miners' welfare institutes in respect of which a certificate of registration under section 105 of the Licensing (Scotland) Act 1976 has effect (referred to in this paragraph as a "certificate of registration").

(2) The following are not to apply where an application for a club gaming permit is made in relation to a members' club or miners' welfare institute in respect of which a certificate of registration has effect—

(a) the condition in paragraph (b) of paragraph 80(1),

(b) paragraph 80(2),

(c) the condition in paragraph (d) of paragraph 82, and

(d) paragraph 83.

(3) The following provisions of this paragraph are only to have effect if on [1st August][5] 2007 regulations under section 285(1)(a) of the 2005 Act are not in force setting out the provisions which are to have effect in place of Schedule 12 to that Act in relation to an application for a club gaming permit where the applicant is the holder of a certificate of registration.

(4) Paragraph (c) of paragraph 80(1) is to have effect as if it required such an application to be made on or before the date which is the later of—

(a) one month after the date on which the provisions referred to in sub-paragraph (3) come into force, or

(b) . . . [6] the relevant date (within the meaning of paragraph 80(3)).

(5) Paragraph 84(3) is not to apply in any case where the effect of paragraph 80(1) (as modified by sub-paragraph (4)) is to require the application to be made on or before the date which is one month after the date on which the provisions referred to in sub-paragraph (3) come into force.

(6) In such a case sub-paragraph (7) is to have effect in place of paragraph 84(3).

(7) Where the holder of the certificate of registration fails to apply for a club gaming permit on or before the date referred to in sub-paragraph (4)(a), paragraph 84(1) is to have effect as if it provided for the club or institute to be treated as holding such a permit until that date.

86 Conversion of a club registration under Part 3 of the Gaming Act 1968 into a club machine permit

(1) Paragraphs 87 to 89, 91 and 92 apply to a members' club, commercial club or miners' welfare institute where—

(a) the club or institute is registered under Part 3 of the [1968][7] Act, and

(b) the registration has effect immediately before 1st September 2007.

(2) Paragraphs 87 to 89, 91 and 92 also apply to a members' club, commercial club or miners' welfare institute which is registered under Part 3 of the 1968 Act on or after 1st September 2007.

(3) In paragraphs 87, 88, 91 and 92, any reference to the relevant licensing authority is to the licensing authority (within the meaning of the 2005 Act) in whose area are situated the premises in respect of which the club or institute was registered under Part 3 of the Act.

87 Conversion of club registrations under Part 3 of the Gaming Act 1968: provision of information by the 1968 Act licensing authority

(1) In England and Wales the designated officer for the authority which registered the club or institute must on the relevant date, or as soon as practicable after that date,

provide the relevant licensing authority with the information specified in sub-paragraph (3).

(2) In Scotland, the sheriff clerk to the sheriff who registered the club or institute must on the relevant date, or as soon as practicable after that date, provide the relevant licensing authority with the information specified in sub-paragraph (3).

(3) The information to be provided is—

(a) the name of the club or institute,

(b) a description of the purposes for which the club is established or, in the case of a miners' welfare institute, a statement that it is such;

(c) a description of the premises to which the registration relates,

(d) the address of those premises,

(e) the date of registration or, where the registration has been renewed, the date on which it was last renewed,

(f) in a case falling within paragraph 86(1) (other than one to which sub-paragraph (6) below applies), the date on which the registration, as it had immediately before 1st September 2007, was due to expire, and

(g) the name and address of the chairman or secretary of the club or institute as recorded in the register under Part 3 of the 1968 Act.

(4) This paragraph is subject to paragraph 89.

(5) Subject to sub-paragraph (6), a reference in this paragraph to the relevant date is to—

(a) 1st September 2007, or

(b) in a case falling within paragraph 86(2), the date on which the club or institute is registered.

(6) Where a club or institute's registration has effect immediately before 1st September 2007 by virtue of paragraph 23 of Schedule 7 to the 1968 Act (which provides for registrations under Part 3 of that Act to be extended where an application for renewal of the registration has not been determined), including as that paragraph has effect in relation to Scotland by virtue of paragraph 3 of Schedule 8 to that Act, the relevant date is the date on which the application for renewal of the registration is granted.

88 Duty of licensing authority to convert a registration under Part 3 of the Gaming Act 1968 into a club machine permit

(1) Subject to the following provisions of this Part, where—

(a) a members' club, commercial club or miners' welfare institute applies to the relevant licensing authority for the grant of a club machine permit in respect of the same or substantially the same premises as those to which the registration under Part 3 of the 1968 Act relates;

(b) the application complies with sub-paragraphs (b) and (e) of paragraph 2 and (where applicable) paragraph 3 of Schedule 12 to the 2005 Act; and

(c) the application is made . . . [8] before the relevant date

the relevant licensing authority must grant that application.

(2) Paragraphs 4, 5(b), 6, 7 and 10 of Schedule 12 to the 2005 Act are not to apply to an application falling within sub-paragraph (1), and paragraph 8 is to apply with the omission of any reference to objections.

(3) Subject to sub-paragraphs (4) and (5), in sub-paragraph (1)(c), "the relevant date" means the date on which the club or institute's registration, as it had immediately before 1st September 2007, was due to expire in accordance with paragraph 22 of Schedule 7 to the 1968 Act (which provides for the duration of registrations under Part 2 of that Act) including as that paragraph has effect in relation to Scotland by virtue of paragraph 3 of Schedule 8 to that Act.

(4) Where the club or institute's registration has effect immediately before 1st September 2007 by virtue of paragraph 23 of Schedule 7 to the 1968 Act (including as

that paragraph has effect in relation to Scotland by virtue of paragraph 3 of Schedule 8 to that Act), the relevant date is the last day of the period of 5 years beginning on the date on which the registration is renewed.

(5) Where the club or institute is registered on or after 1st September 2007, the relevant date is the last day of the period of 5 years beginning on the date on which it is registered.

89 Exclusion of cases where an application for the renewal of the registration under [Part 3][9] is rejected on or after 1st September 2007

(1) This paragraph applies where—

(a) a club or institute's registration under Part 3 of the 1968 Act has effect immediately before 1st September 2007 by virtue of paragraph 23 of Schedule 7 to the 1968 Act (including as that paragraph has effect in relation to Scotland by virtue of paragraph 3 of Schedule 8 to that Act); and

(b) the application for renewal of the registration is withdrawn or rejected on or after that date.

(2) Paragraphs 87 and 88(1) are not to apply in a case to which this paragraph applies.

(3) Paragraph 92(1) is to cease to apply to the club or institute on the date on which the application for renewal of the registration is withdrawn or rejected.

90 Conversion of club registrations under [Part 3][10] of the 1968 Act: applications made before 1st September 2007

(1) This paragraph applies where—

(a) a members' club, commercial club or miners' welfare institute applies for the grant of a club machine permit before 1st September 2007;

(b) when the application is made, the club or institute is registered under Part 3 of the 1968 Act in respect of the same, or substantially the same, premises as those to which the application relates;

(c) the registration under Part 3 of the 1968 Act is due to expire in accordance with paragraph 22 of Schedule 7 to the 1968 Act (including as that paragraph has effect in relation to Scotland by virtue of paragraph 3 of Schedule 8 to that Act) on a date on or after 1st September 2007;

(d) the application complies with sub-paragraphs (b) and (e) of paragraph 2 and, where applicable, paragraph 3 of Schedule 12 to the 2005 Act; and

(e) the application is made . . . [11] before the relevant date (as that expression is defined in paragraph [88(3) and (4)][12]).

(2) The licensing authority may not determine the application before 1st September 2007.

91 Failure to make the application for a club machine permit in the appropriate form or manner

(1) This paragraph applies to any application for a club machine permit which meets the conditions in paragraphs (a) to (c) of paragraph 88(1), but does not comply with a requirement imposed under sub-paragraph (c) or (d) of paragraph 2 of Schedule 12 to the 2005 Act.

(2) Where the relevant licensing authority give notice in writing to the club or miners' welfare institute making the application requesting it to do anything which is necessary for the purposes of complying with any such requirement, the authority are to cease to be under a duty by virtue of paragraph 88(1) to grant the application until such time as the club or institute complies with the request.

(3) The applicant must comply with any request made under sub-paragraph (2) within such period as may be specified in the relevant notice (such period not being less than 14 days from the date on which the notice is received).

(4) Paragraph 92(1) is to cease to apply if the club or institute fails to comply with a request made under sub-paragraph (2) within the period specified in accordance with sub-paragraph (3).

92 Conversion of club registrations under Part 3 of the 1968 Act: transitional provisions

(1) At any time on or after 1st September 2007 until the date on which the club machine permit is granted in accordance with paragraph 88, a club or miners' welfare institute is to be treated for the purposes of the Act as if it had been granted such a permit in relation to the premises in respect of which the registration under Part 3 of the 1968 Act had effect.

(2) In a case falling within paragraph 86(2), sub-paragraph (1) is not to apply until the date on which the club or institute is registered under Part 3 of the 1968 Act.

(3) Where the club or institute fails to apply for a club machine permit . . . [13] before the relevant date (within the meaning of paragraph 88(3) to (5)), sub-paragraph (1) is to have effect as if it provided for the club or institute to be treated as holding such a permit until the relevant date.

(4) Paragraph 88 and sub-paragraph (1) of this paragraph are to be subject to the following provisions of this paragraph.

(5) Paragraph 88 and sub-paragraph (1) of this paragraph are to cease to apply if the members' club, commercial club or miners' welfare institute ceases to be such a club or institute within the meaning of sections 266 to 268 of the 2005 Act.

(6) Paragraph 88 and sub-paragraph (1) of this paragraph are to cease to apply to a club or miners' welfare institute if notice to that effect is given by the club or institute to the relevant licensing authority.

(7) The relevant licensing authority shall as soon as reasonably practicable inform the persons specified in sub-paragraph (8) if the authority—

(a) believe that sub-paragraph (5) applies, or

(b) receive notice given under sub-paragraph (6).

(8) The persons mentioned in sub-paragraph (7) are—

(a) the Gambling Commission, and

(b) the chief officer of police for any area in which the premises referred to in sub-paragraph (1) are situated.

(9) The relevant licensing authority may give notice in writing to a club or miners' welfare institute that paragraph 88 and sub-paragraph (1) of this paragraph are to be disapplied in relation to the club or institute.

(10) The relevant licensing authority may only give notice in accordance with sub-paragraph (9) if the authority think—

(a) that the premises on which the club or institute conducts its activities are used wholly or mainly by children, by young persons or by both, or

(b) that an offence, or a breach of a condition of section 273 of the 2005 Act, has been committed in the course of gaming activities carried on by the club or institute.

(11) Sub-paragraphs (2) to (4) of paragraph 21, and paragraph 25, of Schedule 12 to the 2005 Act (which provide respectively for cancellation of club machine permits, and appeals) are to apply to the giving of a notice under sub-paragraph (9) of this paragraph as they apply to the cancellation of a club machine permit under paragraph 21(1) of that Schedule.

(12) Paragraph 23 of Schedule 12 to the 2005 Act (which provides for forfeiture of club machine permits on conviction of offences under the 2005 Act) is to apply as if—

(a) the reference in that paragraph to the holder of a club machine permit, or the officer of the holder of such a permit holder, included a reference to a club or miners' welfare institute to which paragraph 88 and sub-paragraph (1) of this paragraph apply, or the officer of such a club or institute; and

(b) the reference to the court having power to order forfeiture of the permit included a reference to the court having power to order that paragraph 88 and sub-paragraph (1) of this paragraph should be disapplied in relation to the club or miners' welfare institute concerned.

(13) Paragraph 28 of Schedule 12 to the 2005 Act (which makes provision about the delegation of licensing authority functions) is to apply to the exercise of functions by the relevant licensing authority under this paragraph and paragraph 88 as it applies to the exercise of functions of a licensing authority under that Schedule.

(14) Despite section 274(2) of the 2005 Act (which disapplies Schedule 12 in relation to specified clubs etc in Scotland), the provisions of that Schedule referred to in sub-paragraphs (10) to (12) are also to apply to any club or miners' welfare institute in Scotland in the same way as they apply to a club or institute in England and Wales.

93 Special provisions applying to clubs etc in Scotland

(1) This paragraph modifies paragraphs 88, 90, 91 and 92 in their application to members' clubs, commercial clubs or miners' welfare institutes in respect of which a certificate of registration under section 105 of the Licensing (Scotland) Act 1976 has effect (referred to in this paragraph as a "certificate of registration").

(2) The following are not to apply where an application for a club machine permit is made in relation to a club or miners' welfare institute in respect of which a certificate of registration has effect—

(a) the condition in paragraph (b) of paragraph 88(1),

(b) paragraph 80(2),

(c) the condition in paragraph (d) of paragraph 90, and

(d) paragraph 91.

(3) The following provisions of this paragraph are only to apply if on [1st August] [14] 2007 regulations under section 285(1)(a) of the 2005 Act are not in force setting out the provisions which are to have effect in place of Schedule 12 to that Act in relation to an application for a club machine permit where the applicant is the holder of a certificate of registration.

(4) Paragraph (c) of paragraph 88(1) is to have effect as if it required such an application to be made on or before the date which is the later of—

(a) one month after the date on which the provisions referred to in sub-paragraph (3) come into force, or

(b) . . . [15] the relevant date (within the meaning of paragraph 88(3)).

(5) Paragraph 92(3) is not to apply in any case where the effect of paragraph 88(1) (as modified by sub-paragraph (4)) is to require the application to be made or before the date which is one month after the date on which the provisions referred to in sub-paragraph (3) come into force.

(6) In such a case sub-paragraph (7) is to have effect in place of paragraph 92(3).

(7) Where the holder of the certificate of registration fails to apply for a club machine permit on or before the date referred to in sub-paragraph (4)(a), paragraph 92(1) is to have effect as if it provided for the club or institute to be treated as holding such a permit until that date.

---

1 Para 80: in sub-para (1)(c) words omitted revoked by SI 2007/1157, art 12(1), (2)(a).

2 Para 82: in sub-para (1)(e) words omitted revoked by SI 2007/1157, art 12(1), (3)(a).

3 Para 82: in sub-para (1)(e) words "80(3) to (4)" in square brackets substituted by SI 2007/1157, art 12(1), (3)(b).

4 Para 84: in sub-para (3) words omitted revoked by SI 2007/1157, art 12(1), (2)(b).

5 Para 85: in sub-para (3) words "1st August" in square brackets substituted by SI 2007/1157, art 12(1), (5)(a).

6 Para 85: in sub-para (4)(b) words omitted revoked by SI 2007/1157, art 12(1), (4)(a).

[7] Para 86: in sub-para (1)(a) reference to "1968" in square brackets substituted by SI 2007/1157, art 12(1), (6).

[8] Para 88: in sub-para (1)(c) words omitted revoked by SI 2007/1157, art 12(1), (2)(c).

[9] Para 89 heading: words "Part 3" in square brackets substituted by SI 2007/1157, art 12(1), (7).

[10] Para 90 heading: words "Part 3" in square brackets substituted by SI 2007/1157, art 12(1), (7).

[11] Para 90: in sub-para (1)(e) words omitted revoked by SI 2007/1157, art 12(1), (8)(a).

[12] Para 90: in sub-para (1)(e) words "88(3) and (4)" in square brackets substituted by SI 2007/1157, art 12(1), (8)(b).

[13] Para 92: in sub-para (3) words omitted revoked by SI 2007/1157, art 12(1), (9).

[14] Para 93: in sub-para (3) words "1st August" in square brackets substituted by SI 2007/1157, art 12(1), (5)(b).

[15] Para 93: in sub-para (4)(b) words omitted revoked by SI 2007/1157, art 12(1), (4)(b).

PART 10
CONVERSION OF PERMITS UNDER SECTION 34 OF THE GAMING ACT 1968 INTO FAMILY ENTERTAINMENT CENTRE GAMING MACHINE PERMITS

6.1558 94 Meaning of existing operator for the purposes of applications for family entertainment centre gaming machine permits

(1) This paragraph specifies the circumstances in which a person applying for a family entertainment centre gaming machine permit (referred to in this Part as a "FEC gaming machine permit") is to be treated for the purposes of this Part as an existing family entertainment centre operator.

(2) A person is an existing family entertainment centre operator if on the date on which he makes the application for the FEC gaming machine permit—

- (a) he holds a permit under section 34 of the 1968 Act (referred to in this Part as a "section 34 permit")—
  - (i) granted by one of the authorities mentioned in paragraph 1(b) or (d) of Schedule 9 to the 1968 Act in respect of amusement machine premises, and
  - (ii) which is expressed to be granted for the purposes of section 34(1) of the 1968 Act; or
- (b) he is applying for such a permit, and the application (including any appeal) has not been finally determined or withdrawn.

95 Conversion of section 34 permits into FEC gaming machine permits

(1) Subject to the following provisions of this Part, where—

- (a) an existing family entertainment centre operator makes an advance application for a FEC gaming machine permit under Schedule 10 to the 2005 Act,
- (b) the application relates to the same or substantially the same premises as those to which the section 34 permit relates, and
- (c) the application complies with any requirements imposed by or under paragraphs 2 to 4 and 5(b) and (d) of that Schedule,

the licensing authority must grant that application.

(2) Paragraphs 8(1)(b), 9 and 10 of Schedule 10 to the 2005 Act are not to apply to such an application.

96 Failure to make the application for a FEC gaming machine permit in the appropriate form or manner

(1) This paragraph applies to any application for a FEC gaming machine permit which meets the conditions in paragraphs (a) to (c) of paragraph 95(1), but does not comply with a requirement imposed under sub-paragraph (a) or (c) of paragraph 5 of Schedule 10 to the 2005 Act.

(2) Where the licensing authority give notice in writing to the applicant requesting him to do anything which is necessary for the purposes of complying with any such requirement, the licensing authority are to cease to be under a duty by virtue of paragraph 95(1) to grant the application until such time as the applicant complies with the request.

(3) In the case of an application made before 31st July 2007, the applicant must comply with any request made under sub-paragraph (2) within such period as may be specified in the relevant notice (such period not being less than 14 days from the date on which the notice is received).

(4) If, in a case to which paragraph 98 applies, the applicant fails to comply with the request within the period specified in accordance with sub-paragraph (3) above—

(a) sub-paragraph (3) of that paragraph is to cease to apply to the application after the end of that period; and

(b) where the relevant FEC gaming machine permit is treated as having been issued to the applicant by virtue of that sub-paragraph, the permit is to lapse.

97 Effect of cancellation of section 34 permit

(1) Where—

(a) a person makes an application for a FEC gaming machine permit which meets the conditions in paragraphs (a) to (c) of paragraph 95(1), and

(b) the section 34 permit by virtue of which he qualifies as an existing family entertainment centre operator is cancelled,

the licensing authority must reject the application.

(2) Where despite sub-paragraph (1) the licensing authority purport to grant the FEC gaming machine permit in respect of which the application is made, the permit is to be of no effect.

(3) Where the section 34 permit is cancelled after the licensing authority have issued the FEC gaming machine permit in pursuance of paragraph 95(1), the permit is to lapse on the date on which the section 34 permit is cancelled.

98 Provisions to ensure that existing family entertainment centre operators can continue to operate on and after 1st September 2007

(1) This paragraph applies to an application for a FEC gaming machine permit which meets the conditions in paragraphs (a) to (c) of sub-paragraph (1) of paragraph 95, but where in addition the application is made before 31st July 2007.

(2) The licensing authority must determine any such application within a period of one month beginning on the date on which the application is made.

(3) If the licensing authority do not determine the application within the period referred to in sub-paragraph (2)—

(a) the application is to be treated as having been granted, and

(b) the relevant FEC gaming machine permit as having been issued to the applicant,

on the day immediately following the end of that period.

(4) Where by virtue of sub-paragraph (3) above a FEC gaming machine permit is treated as having been issued to a person, paragraph 8(3) of Schedule 10 to the 2005 Act (which makes provision about the issuing of FEC gaming machine permits) is to have effect as if it required the licensing authority to provide the applicant with a copy of the permit as soon as practicable on or after the date of issue.

(5) For the purposes of paragraph 11(1)(c) of Schedule 10 to the 2005 Act (which requires the date on which a FEC gaming machine permit takes effect to be specified in the permit), the licensing authority are to specify 1st September 2007 as the date on which the FEC gaming machine permit takes effect.

99 Conversion of section 34 permits into FEC gaming machine permits: supplementary provisions

(1) This paragraph applies to an advance application for a FEC gaming machine permit where the person making the application qualifies as an existing family entertainment centre operator by virtue of paragraph 94(2)(b).

(2) Paragraph 95(1) is to have effect in relation to such an application as if the following paragraph was substituted for paragraph (b)—

"(b) the application relates to the same or substantially the same premises as those to which the application for the section 34 permit relates, and".

(3) Where the application meets the conditions in paragraphs (a) to (c) of sub-paragraph (1) of paragraph 95, that sub-paragraph is to be modified so that—

(a) the licensing authority may not determine the application for a FEC gaming machine permit before the application for the section 34 permit has been determined;

(b) the licensing authority are only to be under a duty to grant the application for a FEC gaming machine permit if the application for the section 34 permit is granted; and

(c) the licensing authority must reject the application for a FEC gaming machine permit if the application for the section 34 permit is refused.

(4) Sub-paragraph (3) is subject to paragraph 100(2).

(5) The following provisions of this paragraph apply where the application is one to which paragraph 98 applies.

(6) Sub-paragraph (2) of paragraph 98 is to be subject to paragraph (3) above.

(7) Where—

(a) the application for the section 34 permit is granted before 1st September 2007, but

(b) it is granted after the day referred to in sub-paragraph (3) of paragraph 98,

that sub-paragraph is to have effect as if it provided for the application to be treated as having been granted and the relevant FEC gaming machine permit issued on the date on which the application for the section 34 permit is granted.

(8) Sub-paragraphs (2) and (3) of paragraph 98 are not to apply where the application for the section 34 permit is refused or withdrawn, or is not granted before 1st September 2007.

(9) For the purposes of this paragraph, where an application for a section 34 permit is refused, it is not to be treated as having been determined or refused until the period for appealing against the decision to refuse the permit has elapsed; or, if an appeal is made, unless and until the appeal is dismissed or abandoned.

100 Conversion of section 34 permits into FEC gaming machine permits: supplementary provisions where premises are situated in Scotland

(1) This paragraph applies in any case falling within paragraph 99 where the premises to which the application for the section 34 permit relates are situated in Scotland.

(2) Paragraph 99 is to have effect as if for sub-paragraph (3) there were substituted—

"(3) Where the application meets the conditions in paragraphs (a) to (c) of sub-paragraph (1) of paragraph 95, that sub-paragraph is to be modified so that—

(a) the licensing authority may not determine the application for a FEC gaming machine permit until the applicant notifies it in writing of the determination of the application for the section 34 permit;

(b) the licensing authority are only to be under a duty to grant the application for a FEC gaming machine permit if—

(i) the application for the section 34 permit is granted, and

(ii) the applicant has given the authority written notice of that fact and provided it with a copy of the permit; and

(c) the licensing authority must reject the application for a FEC gaming machine permit if the application for the section 34 permit is refused."

(3) Subject to sub-paragraphs (4) and (5) below, where sub-paragraph (3) of paragraph 98 applies because the application for the section 34 permit is granted before 1st September 2007, sub-paragraph (4) of that paragraph is to have effect as if it required the licensing authority to provide the applicant with a copy of the FEC gaming machine permit as soon as practicable on or after the date on which they are notified of the grant of the application for the section 34 permit and provided with a copy of the permit.

(4) Where paragraph 98(3) applies because the application for the section 34 permit is granted before 1st September 2007, the applicant must notify the licensing authority of the fact that the application has been granted, and provide them with a copy of the section 34 permit, before the end of the period of 14 days beginning on the day on which the application is granted.

(5) Where the applicant fails to do the things referred to in sub-paragraph (4) within the period specified in that sub-paragraph, the licensing authority may revoke the permit issued in accordance with paragraph 98(3).

PART 11
CONVERSION OF PERMITS UNDER SECTION 16 OF THE LOTTERIES AND AMUSEMENTS ACT 1976 INTO PRIZE GAMING PERMITS

6.1558A 101 Meaning of existing operator for the purposes of an application for a prize gaming permit

(1) This paragraph specifies the circumstances in which a person applying for a prize gaming permit under Schedule 14 to the 2005 Act (referred to in this Part as a "prize gaming permit") is to be treated for the purposes of this Part as an existing operator.

(2) A person is an existing operator if on the date on which he makes the application for the prize gaming permit—

(a) he holds a permit issued under section 16 of the 1976 Act (which provides for permits authorising the provision of amusements with prizes at certain commercial entertainments) (referred to in this Part as a "section 16 permit"), or

(b) he is applying for such a permit, and the application (including any appeal) has not been finally determined or withdrawn.

102 Conversion of section 16 permits into prize gaming permits

(1) Where—

(a) an existing operator makes an advance application for a prize gaming permit,

(b) the application relates to the same or substantially the same premises as those to which the section 16 permit relates, and

(c) the application complies with the requirements of paragraphs 3 to 5 and 6(b), (c) and (e) of Schedule 14 to the Act,

the licensing authority must grant that application.

(2) Paragraphs 9(1)(b), 10 and 11 of Schedule 14 to the 2005 Act are not to apply to such an application.

103 Failure to make the application for a prize gaming permit in the appropriate form or manner

(1) This paragraph applies to any application for a prize gaming permit which meets the conditions in paragraphs (a) to (c) of paragraph 102(1), but does not comply with a requirement imposed under sub-paragraph (a) or (d) of paragraph 6 of Schedule 14 to the 2005 Act.

(2) Where the licensing authority give notice in writing to the applicant requesting him to do anything which is necessary for the purposes of complying with any such requirement, the licensing authority are to cease to be under a duty by virtue of paragraph 102(1) to grant the application until such time as the applicant complies with the request.

(3) In the case of an application made before 31st July 2007, the applicant must comply with any request made under sub-paragraph (2) within such period as may be specified in the relevant notice (such period not being less than 14 days from the date on which the notice is received).

(4) If, in a case to which paragraph 105 applies, the applicant fails to comply with the request within the period specified in accordance with sub-paragraph (3) above—

(a) sub-paragraph (3) of that paragraph is to cease to apply to the application after the end of that period; and

(b) where the relevant prize gaming permit is treated as having been issued to the applicant by virtue of that sub-paragraph, the permit is to lapse.

104 Effect of cancellation of section 16 permit

(1) Where—

(a) a person makes an application for a prize gaming permit which meets the conditions in paragraphs (a) to (c) of paragraph 102(1), and

(b) the section 16 permit by virtue of which he qualifies as an existing operator is cancelled,

the licensing authority must reject the application.

(2) Where despite sub-paragraph (1) the licensing authority purport to grant the prize gaming permit in respect of which the application is made, the permit is to be of no effect.

(3) Where the section 16 permit is cancelled after the licensing authority have issued the prize gaming permit in pursuance of paragraph 102(1), the permit is to lapse on the date on which the section 16 permit is cancelled.

105 Provisions to ensure that existing operators can continue to operate on and after 1st September 2007

(1) This paragraph applies to an application for a prize gaming permit which meets the conditions in paragraphs (a) to (c) of paragraph 102(1), but where in addition the application is made before 31st July 2007.

(2) The licensing authority must determine any such application within a period of one month beginning on the date on which the application is made.

(3) If the licensing authority do not determine the application within the period referred to in sub-paragraph (2)—

(a) the application is to be treated as having been granted, and

(b) the relevant prize gaming permit as having been issued to the applicant,

on the day immediately following the end of that period.

(4) Where by virtue of sub-paragraph (3) above a prize gaming permit is treated as having been issued to a person, paragraph 9(3) of Schedule 14 to the 2005 Act (which makes provision about the issuing of prize gaming permits) is to have effect as if it

required the licensing authority to provide the applicant with a copy of the permit as soon as practicable on or after the date of issue.

(5) For the purposes of paragraph 12(1)(d) of Schedule 14 to the 1968 Act (which requires the date on which a prize gaming permit takes effect to be specified in the permit), the licensing authority are to specify 1st September 2007 as the date on which the prize gaming permit takes effect.

106 Conversion of section 16 permits into prize gaming permits: supplementary provisions

(1) This paragraph applies to an application for a prize gaming permit where the person making the application qualifies as an existing operator by virtue of paragraph 101(2)(b).

(2) Paragraph 102(1) is to have effect in relation to such an application as if the following paragraph was substituted for paragraph (b)—

"(b) the application relates to the same or substantially the same premises as those to which the application for the section 16 permit relates, and".

(3) Where the application meets the conditions in paragraphs (a) to (c) of paragraph 102(1), that sub-paragraph is to be modified so that—

(a) the licensing authority may not determine the application for a prize gaming permit before the application for the section 16 permit has been determined;

(b) the licensing authority are only to be under a duty to grant the application for a prize gaming permit if the application for the section 16 permit is granted; and

(c) the licensing authority must reject the application for a prize gaming permit if the application for the section 16 permit is refused.

(4) Sub-paragraph (3)(b) is subject to paragraph 107(2).

(5) The following provisions of this paragraph apply where the application is one to which paragraph 105 applies.

(6) Sub-paragraph (2) of paragraph 105 is to be subject to paragraph (3) above.

(7) Where—

(a) the application for the section 16 permit is granted before 1st September 2007, but

(b) it is granted after the day referred to in sub-paragraph (3) of paragraph 105,

that sub-paragraph is to have effect as if it provided for the application to be treated as having been granted and the relevant prize gaming permit issued on the date on which the application for the section 16 permit is granted.

(8) Sub-paragraphs (2) and (3) of paragraph 105 are not to apply where the application for the section 16 permit is refused or withdrawn, or is not granted before 1st September 2007.

(9) For the purposes of this paragraph, where an application for a section 16 permit is refused, it is not to be treated as having been determined or refused until the period for appealing against the decision to refuse the permit has elapsed; or, if an appeal is made, unless and until the appeal is dismissed or abandoned.

107 Conversion of section 16 permits into prize gaming permits: supplementary provisions where premises are situated in Scotland

(1) This paragraph applies in any case falling within paragraph 106 where the premises to which the application for the section 16 permit relates are situated in Scotland.

(2) Paragraph 106 is to have effect as if for sub-paragraph (3) there were substituted—

"(3) Where the application meets the conditions in paragraphs (a) to (c) of paragraph 102(1), that sub-paragraph is to be modified so that—

(a) the licensing authority may not determine the application for a prize gaming permit until the applicant notifies it in writing of the determination of the application for the section 16 permit; and

(b) the licensing authority are only to be under a duty to grant the application for a prize gaming permit if—

(i) the application for the section 16 permit is granted, and

(ii) the applicant has given the authority written notice of that fact and provided it with a copy of the permit;

(c) the licensing authority must reject the application for a prize gaming permit if the application for the section 16 permit is refused."

(3) Subject to sub-paragraphs (4) and (5) below, where sub-paragraph (3) of paragraph 105 applies because the application for the section 16 permit is granted before 1st September 2007, sub-paragraph (4) of that paragraph is to have effect as if it required the licensing authority to provide the applicant with a copy of the prize gaming permit as soon as practicable on or after the date on which they are notified of the grant of the application for the section 16 permit and provided with a copy of the permit.

(4) Where paragraph 105(3) applies because the application for the section 16 permit is granted before 1st September 2007, the applicant must notify the licensing authority of the fact that the application has been granted, and provide them with a copy of the section 16 permit, before the end of the period of 14 days beginning on the day on which the application is granted.

(5) Where the applicant fails to do the things referred to in sub-paragraph (4) within the period specified in that sub-paragraph, the licensing authority may revoke the permit issued in accordance with paragraph 105(3).

GAMBLING (OPERATING LICENCE AND SINGLE-MACHINE PERMIT FEES) REGULATIONS 2006

(SI 2006/3284)

Made . . . . *10th December 2006*
Laid before Parliament . . . . *11th December 2006*

The Secretary of State makes the following Regulations in exercise of the powers conferred by sections 69(2)(g) and (5), 100(2) and (3), 103(2), 104(3) and (4), 107(2)(a), 250(3)(e) and (8) and 355(1) of the Gambling Act 2005:

PART 1
INTRODUCTORY

6.1558B 1 Citation and commencement

(1) These Regulations may be cited as the Gambling (Operating Licence and Single-Machine Permit Fees) Regulations 2006.

(2) Regulations 1 to 26 and Schedules 1 to 6 come into force on 1st January 2007.

(3) Regulation 27 comes into force on 1st September 2007.

6.1558C 2 General interpretation

(1) In these Regulations—

"the Act" means the Gambling Act 2005;

"ancillary remote operating licence" has the meaning given in regulation 14;

"annual fee" in relation to a licence means the fee prescribed under section 100(1)(b) for that licence;

"application fee" in relation to an application for a licence means the fee prescribed under section 69(2)(g) to accompany an application for that licence;

["betting intermediary (trading room only) operating licence" means a betting intermediary operating licence (as defined in section 65(2)(e) of the Act) which does not authorise the holder ("H") to act as a betting intermediary except where—

(a) any betting facilitated by a service provided by H pursuant to the licence is carried out only—

(i) by persons physically present on the premises from which H is providing the service;

(ii) by means of remote communication; and

(iii) through intermediaries other than H[, or with a person other than H who is either the holder of a remote general betting (standard) operating licence or provides facilities for remote betting the arrangements for which are subject to the law about gambling of an EEA state, Gibraltar or a country or place specified in regulations made under section 331(4) of the Act]; and

(b) H is not a party to any bet made or accepted by the persons referred to in sub-paragraph (a)(i) above];

"combined operating licence" has the meaning given in regulation 15;

'combined non-remote operating licence' has the meaning given in regulation [15(1)(a)];

'combined remote operating licence' has the meaning given in regulation [15(1)(b)];

"converted casino premises licence" means a casino premises licence issued pursuant to an order made under paragraph 9 of Schedule 18 to the Act;

["converted lottery operating licence" has the same meaning as in paragraph 71 of Schedule 4 to the Transitional Order;]

"existing casino operating licence" means a non-remote casino operating licence which authorises the licensee to operate a casino only in premises in respect of which a converted casino premises licence has effect;

"first annual fee" in relation to a licence means the fee prescribed under section 100(1)(a) in relation to that licence;

"gaming machine technical (full) operating licence" means a gaming machine technical operating licence which authorises the licensee to carry out all of the activities described in section 65(2)(h);

"gaming machine technical (software) operating licence" means a gaming machine technical operating licence which only authorises the licensee to manufacture, [supply, install or adapt] software for a gaming machine;

"gaming machine technical (supplier) operating licence" means a gaming machine technical operating licence which only authorises the licensee to supply, install, adapt, maintain or repair a gaming machine, or part of a gaming machine;

"general betting (limited) operating licence" means—

(a) a non-remote general betting operating licence which is subject to a condition that the licensee may not hold a betting premises licence, or

(b) a remote general betting operating licence that—

(i) is subject to a condition that the licensee may not hold a non-remote betting operating licence, and

(ii) only authorises the licensee to—

(aa) provide facilities for betting [in circumstances in which each bet made or accepted pursuant to the licence occurs—

(i) by means of a telephone or by email, and

(ii) otherwise than by wholly automated means], and

(bb) generate an annual gross gambling yield which does not exceed [£550,000];

[(c) in paragraph (b)(ii)(aa)(ii), a bet occurs otherwise than by wholly automated means if the arrangements for it are provided, operated or administered by an individual;]

"general betting (standard) operating licence" means—

(a) a non-remote general betting operating licence that is not a general betting (limited) operating licence, or

(b) a remote general betting operating licence that is not a general betting (limited) operating licence;

["general betting (standard) (real events) operating licence" means a licence which falls within paragraph (b) of the definition of a "general betting (standard) operating licence", but which is not a general betting (standard) (virtual events) operating licence";

['general betting (standard) (remote platform) operating licence' means a licence which—

(a) falls within paragraph (b) of the definition of a general betting (standard) operating licence, and

(b) authorises the licensee to provide facilities for gambling only by means of a service supplied by—

(i) the holder of a remote betting intermediary operating licence,

(ii) the holder of a remote general betting (standard) operating licence, or

(iii) any other person who provides facilities for remote betting the arrangements for which are subject to the law about gambling of an EEA state, Gibraltar or a country or place specified in regulations made under section 331(4) of the Act;]

"general betting (standard) (virtual events) operating licence" means a licence which falls within paragraph (b) of the definition of a "general betting (standard) operating licence" and which only authorises the holder to provide facilities for betting on the outcome of a virtual game, race or other event or process;]

['group company' means in respect of a company 'A' any other company which is a subsidiary or holding company of A (as those terms are defined in section 1159 of the Companies Act 2006) or any subsidiary of such holding company;]

"lottery operating (external lottery manager) licence" means a lottery operating licence issued to a person proposing to act as an external lottery manager on behalf of a non-commercial society or local authority;

"lottery operating (society) licence" means a lottery operating licence which is not a lottery operating (external lottery manager) licence;

"new casino operating licence" means a non-remote casino operating licence which does not authorise the licensee to operate a casino in premises in respect of which a converted casino premises licence has effect;

["new controller" has the same meaning as in section 102(2) of the Act];

"remote communication equipment" means electronic or other equipment that—

(a) is used to facilitate remote communication, but

(b) is not a gaming machine.

"single premises gaming" means gaming that—

(a) takes place on one set of premises, and

(b) is not linked with gaming that takes place on another set of premises;

. . .

[["supplementary gambling software operating licence" means a gambling software operating licence (as defined in section 65(2)(i) of the Act)] which does not authorise the holder of the licence ("H")—

(a) to manufacture, supply, install or adapt gambling software other than software for use in connection with gambling facilities provided by H; or

(b) to incur, for the purpose of carrying out activities authorised by the licence, costs of more than £50,000 during the period of one year commencing on the day after the day on which the licence is granted, or in any subsequent one year period;

"supplementary gaming machine technical operating licence" means a gaming machine technical operating licence (as defined in section 65(2)(h) of the Act) which does not—

(a) authorise the holder of the licence ("H") to–

(i) manufacture a gaming machine (or part of such a machine); or

(ii) supply, install, adapt, maintain or repair a gaming machine (or part of such a machine) except where H is the only person who makes the machine available for use; or

(b) authorise H to incur, for the purpose of carrying out activities authorised by the licence, costs of more than £50,000 during the period of one year commencing on the day after the day on which the licence is granted, or in any subsequent one year period;

"supplementary operating licence" means a supplementary gambling software operating licence or a supplementary gaming machine technical operating licence;"];

["supply" does not include install, adapt, maintain or repair;]

["the Transitional Order" means the Gambling Act 2005 (Commencement No 6 and Transitional Provisions) Order 2006].

(2) A reference in these Regulations to a section is, unless the contrary intention appears, a reference to a section of the Act.

Amendment

Para (1): definition 'betting intermediary' inserted by SI 2008/1803, regs 2, 3(a); in definition 'betting intermediary (trading room only) operating licence' in para (a)(iii) words from ', or with a ' to 'of the Act' in square brackets inserted by SI 2012/829, regs 2, 3(1); in definition 'combined non-remote operating licence' reference to '15(1)(a)' in square brackets substituted by SI 2012/829, regs 2, 3(2); in definition 'combined remote operating licence' reference to '15(1)(b)' in square brackets substituted by SI 2012/829, regs 2, 3(3); definition 'converted lottery operating licence' inserted by SI 2007/1791, reg 3(1), (2); in definition 'gaming machine technical (software) operating licence' words 'supply, install or adapt' in square brackets inserted by SI 2008/1803, regs 2, 3(d); in definition 'general betting (limited) operating licence' in para (b)(ii)(aa) words from 'in circumstances in' to 'wholly automated means' in square brackets substituted by SI 2012/829, regs 2, 3(4)(a); in definition 'general betting (limited) operating licence' in para (b)(ii)(bb) sum '£550,000' in square brackets substituted by SI 2012/829, regs 2, 3(4)(b); in definition 'general betting (limited) operating licence' para (c) inserted by SI 2012/829, regs 2, 3(4)(c); definitions 'general betting (standard) (real events) operating licence' and 'general betting (standard) (virtual events) operating licence' inserted by SI 2009/1837, regs 2, 3(a); definition 'general betting (standard) (remote platform) operating licence' inserted by SI 2012/829, regs 2, 3(5); definition 'group company' inserted by SI 2012/829, regs 2, 3(6); definition 'new controller' inserted by SI 2008/1803, regs 2, 3(b); original definition 'supply' (omitted) revoked by SI 2009/1837, regs 2, 3(b); definitions 'supplementary gambling software operating licence', 'supplementary gaming machine technical operating licence' and 'supplementary operating licence' inserted by SI 2008/1803, regs 2, 3(c); in definition 'supplementary gambling software operating licence' words from "supplementary gambling software' to 'of the Act)' in square brackets substituted by SI 2009/1837, regs 2, 3(c); new definition 'supply' inserted by SI 2009/1837, regs 2, 3(d); definition 'the Transitional Order' inserted by SI 2007/1791, reg 3(1), (4).

6.1558D 3 Units of division

(1) This regulation defines the units by reference to which licences are to be assigned to categories for the purpose of prescribing certain fees (see regulations 6 and 10).

(2) The units are—

(a) in relation to an operating licence—

(i) the annual gross gambling yield as calculated in accordance with the following formula—

$$A + B - C$$

where—

A is the total of any amounts that will be paid to the licensee by way of stakes in the relevant period in connection with the activities authorised by the licence,

B is the total of any amounts (exclusive of value added tax) that will otherwise accrue to the licensee in the relevant period directly in connection with the activities authorised by the licence, and

C is the total of any amounts that will be deducted by the licensee in respect of the provision of prizes or winnings in the relevant period in connection with the activities authorised by the licence; or

(ii) the value of annual gross sales, which is the total amount in money or money's worth that will accrue to the licensee from sales of goods and services authorised by the licence in the relevant period;

(b) in relation to a non-remote existing casino operating licence the annual gross gaming yield, which is [the aggregate of] the gross gaming yield within the meaning of section 11(8) of the Finance Act 1997 [and gaming machine revenue] to be generated in the relevant period from the premises on which gaming authorised by the licence takes place;

[(ba) in sub-paragraph (b) 'gaming machine revenue' means the total of amounts paid by persons in respect of the use of gaming machines less the value in money or money's worth of the prizes won in respect of such use;]

(c) in relation to a lottery operating licence the annual proceeds, which is the aggregate of the proceeds of lotteries authorised by the licence to be promoted wholly or partly in the relevant period;

[(d) in relation to a non-remote general betting (limited) operating licence (other than one falling within subparagraph (e)), the number of working days being the maximum number of days in the relevant period on which the licence will authorise the licensee to undertake activities authorised by it;

(e) in relation to a non-remote general betting (limited) operating licence under the authority of which the licensee provides, from a dog track, facilities for betting on the outcome of greyhound races taking place at that track ('relevant betting facilities'), the number of working days as calculated in accordance with the following formula—

A – B

where—

(i) A is the total number of working days in the relevant period on which the licence holder undertakes activities authorised by the licence, and

(ii) B is the total number of working days in the relevant period on which the licence holder provides relevant betting facilities in connection with relevant greyhound races but does not undertake any other activity authorised by the licence;

(f) in relation to a non-remote general betting (standard) operating licence the number of licensed premises, which is the maximum number of sets of premises on which the licence will authorise the licensee to carry on the activities authorised by the licence in the relevant period].

(3) In paragraph (2)—

(a) a reference to anything authorised by, or that will happen pursuant to a licence includes, for the purpose of determining an application fee for that licence, anything included in the application as something to be authorised by the licence; and

(b) 'relevant period' in relation to a licence means the period of 12 months beginning—

(i) where that paragraph is applied for the purpose of determining the amount of an application fee, on the day on which the licence would, if issued, take effect;

(ii) where that paragraph is applied for the purpose of determining the amount of a first annual fee, on the effective date;

(iii) where that paragraph is applied for the purpose of determining the amount of an annual fee, on the anniversary of the effective date that occurs on, or is the next to occur after, the date on which the fee becomes payable.

[(c) a reference to 'relevant greyhound races' means greyhound races that—

(i) take place between the hours of 8:00 am and 7:00 pm; and

(ii) are shown live on television at premises at which facilities for betting are provided by the holder of a general betting (standard) operating licence].

(4) In paragraph (3)(b) 'effective date', in relation to a licence in respect of which an annual fee or first annual fee is prescribed, means the day on which the licence took effect.

Amendment

Para (2): in sub-para (b) words 'the aggregate of' in square brackets inserted by SI 2012/829, regs 2, 4(1)(a); in sub-para (b) words 'and gaming machine revenue' in square brackets inserted by SI 2012/829, regs 2, 4(1)(b); sub-para (ba) inserted by SI 2012/829, regs 2, 4(2); sub-paras (d)–(f) substituted, for sub-paras (d), (e) as originally enacted, by SI 2009/1837, regs 2, 4(a).

Para (3): sub-para (c) inserted by SI 2009/1837, regs 2, 4(b).

6.1558E [3A Converted lottery operating licence]

[(1) For the purposes of these Regulations a converted lottery operating licence is to be treated as if it is a non-remote lottery operating (society) licence.

(2) But this regulation does not apply to regulation 8(5).]

Amendment

Inserted by SI 2007/1791, regs 2, 4.

PART 2
NON-REMOTE OPERATING LICENCES—APPLICATION FEES AND ANNUAL FEES

6.1558F 4 Application of this Part

(1) This Part applies in respect of non-remote operating licences.

(2) A non-remote operating licence is any of the following that is not a remote operating licence within the meaning of section 67 of the Act (remote gambling):

(a) an existing casino operating licence;
(b) a new casino operating licence;
(c) a bingo operating licence;
(d) a general betting (limited) operating licence;
(e) a general betting (standard) operating licence;
(f) a pool betting operating licence;
(g) a betting intermediary operating licence;
(h) a gaming machine general operating licence for an adult gaming centre;
(i) a gaming machine general operating licence for a family entertainment centre;
(j) a gaming machine technical (full) operating licence;
(k) a gaming machine technical (supplier) operating licence;
(l) a gaming machine technical (software) operating licence;
(m) a gambling software operating licence;
(n) a lottery operating (external lottery manager) licence; . . .
[(o) a lottery operating (society) licence, or
(p) a supplementary operating licence].

Amendment

Para (2): in sub-para (n) word omitted revoked by SI 2008/1803, regs 2, 4(a); sub-paras (o), (p) substituted, for sub-para (o) as originally enacted, by SI 2008/1803, regs 2, 4(b).

6.1558F.1 [4A Fees for non-remote supplementary operating licences

(1) The application fee for a supplementary operating licence to which this Part applies is £165.

(2) The annual fee for such a licence is £375.

(3) The first annual fee for such a licence is £281.25.]

Amendment

Inserted by SI 2008/1803, regs 2, 5.

6.1558G 5 Non-remote new casino operating licences: fee categories

A new casino operating licence to which this Part applies:

(a) is a category A licence if it does not authorise the holder to operate a casino other than a casino in respect of which a small casino premises licence has effect;
(b) is a category B licence if it does not authorise the holder to operate a casino other than a casino in respect of which a small casino premises licence or a large casino premises licence has effect;
(c) is a category C licence if it authorises the licensee to operate a casino in respect of which a small, large or regional casino premises licence has effect.

6.1558H 6 Other non-remote operating licences: fee categories

(1) A licence to which this Part applies (other than a new casino operating licence [or a supplementary operating licence]) is a licence of the category indicated in the table in Schedule 1.

(2) In that table:

(a) column (1) indicates the description of licence;

(b) column (2) indicates the unit of division (as defined in regulation 3) by reference to which licences within that description are assigned to categories; and

(c) columns [(3) to (14)] indicate the category to which a licence within that description is assigned, according to the range into which the number or amount of the unit of division authorised by the licence for the relevant period falls.

(3) In this regulation "relevant period" has the same meaning as in regulation 3.

Amendment

Para (1): words 'or a supplementary operating licence' in square brackets inserted by SI 2008/1803, regs 2, 6.

Para (2): in sub-para (c) words '(3) to (14)' in square brackets substituted by SI 2012/829, regs 2, 5.

6.1558I 7 Application fees for non-remote operating licences

(1) Subject to [regulations 8A, 16 and [18 to 20A]], the application fee—

(a) for a category A licence is the amount indicated in column (2) of the table in Schedule 2 adjacent to the description of the licence in column (1) of that table;

(b) for a category B licence is the amount indicated in column (3) of that table adjacent to the description of the licence in column (1);

(c) for a category C licence is the amount indicated in column (4) of that table adjacent to the description of the licence in column (1);

(d) for a category D licence is the amount indicated in column (5) of that table adjacent to the description of the licence in column (1);

(e) for a category E licence is the amount indicated in column (6) of that table adjacent to the description of the licence in column (1).

[(f) for a category E1 licence is the amount indicated in column (7) of that table adjacent to the description of the licence in column (1);

(g) for a category E2 licence is the amount indicated in column (8) of that table adjacent to the description of the licence in column (1);

(h) for a category E3 licence is the amount indicated in column (9) of that table adjacent to the description of the licence in column (1);

(i) for a category E4 licence is the amount indicated in column (10) of that table adjacent to the description of the licence in column (1);

(j) for a category E5 licence is the amount indicated in column (11) of that table adjacent to the description of the licence in column (1);

(k) for a category E6 licence is the amount indicated in column (12) of that table adjacent to the description of the licence in column (1);

(l) for a category E7 licence is the amount indicated in column (13) of that table adjacent to the description of the licence in column (1)].

(2) In applying regulations 5 and 6 for the purposes of calculating the amount of an application fee under this regulation any reference to—

(a) the activities authorised by the licence (regulation 5), or

(b) the number or amount of the unit of division authorised by the licence (regulation 6), is to be treated (as appropriate) as a reference to the activities, number or amount that the licence would authorise if granted in accordance with the application.

Amendment

Para (1): words in square brackets beginning with the words 'regulations 8A, 16 and' substituted by SI 2009/1837, regs 2, 5; words '18 to 20A' in square brackets substituted by SI 2012/829, regs 2, 6(1); sub-paras (f)–(l) inserted by SI 2012/829, regs 2, 6(2).

6.1558J 8 Annual fees and first annual fees for non-remote operating licences

(1) Subject to [regulations 8A, [17, 21 and 21A]], the annual fee—

(a) for a category A licence is the amount indicated in column (2) of the table in Schedule 3 adjacent to the description of the licence in column (1) of that table;

(b) for a category B licence is the amount indicated in column (3) of that table adjacent to the description of the licence in column (1);

(c) for a category C licence is the amount indicated in column (4) of that table adjacent to the description of the licence in column (1);

(d) for a category D licence is the amount indicated in column (5) of that table adjacent to the description of the licence in column (1);

(e) for a category E licence is the amount indicated in column (6) of that table adjacent to the description of the licence in column (1).

[(f) for a category E1 licence is the amount indicated in column (7) of that table adjacent to the description of the licence in column (1);

(g) for a category E2 licence is the amount indicated in column (8) of that table adjacent to the description of the licence in column (1);

(h) for a category E3 licence is the amount indicated in column (9) of that table adjacent to the description of the licence in column (1);

(i) for a category E4 licence is the amount indicated in column (10) of that table adjacent to the description of the licence in column (1);

(j) for a category E5 licence is the amount indicated in column (11) of that table adjacent to the description of the licence in column (1);

(k) for a category E6 licence is the amount indicated in column (12) of that table adjacent to the description of the licence in column (1);

(l) for a category E7 licence is the amount indicated in column (13) of that table adjacent to the description of the licence in column (1)].

(2) In applying this regulation the category to which a particular licence is assigned is to be determined as at the date by which the annual fee for the licence is payable.

(3) [Subject to paragraphs [(4) to (8)], the] first annual fee for a licence to which this Part applies is 75 per cent of the annual fee for that licence, as determined in accordance with paragraph (1).

[(4) Where the holder of a gaming machine technical (full) operating licence held a certificate under section 27 of the 1968 Act immediately before the issue of the licence, the first annual fee for the licence is the amount calculated in accordance with the following formula—

$$A - ((B / 60) \times C)$$

where—

A is the first annual fee that would, but for this paragraph, be payable for the licence under paragraph (3),

B is the amount of the last fee paid under section 48(3)(g) of 1968 Act for the certificate (whether it was in respect of the issue or renewal of the certificate), and

C is the number of whole calendar months between the date on which the licence was issued and—

(a) where the certificate was issued or renewed on or after 1st September 2007, the date which is 5 years after the date of its issue or renewal, whichever is the later, or

(b) in any other case, the date on which, as the certificate had effect immediately before 1st September 2007, it was due to expire in accordance with paragraph 3 of Schedule 6 to the 1968 Act.

(5) Where the holder of a lottery operating (society) licence ("the new licence") held a converted lottery operating licence ("the old licence") immediately before the issue of the new licence, the first annual fee for the new licence is the amount calculated in accordance with the following formula—

$$A - ((B/12) \times C)$$

where—

A is the first annual fee that would, but for this paragraph, be payable for the new licence under paragraph (3),

B is the amount of the last fee paid under section 100 of the Act for the old licence (whether it was a first annual fee or an annual fee), and

C is the number of whole calendar months between—

(a) the date on which the old licence ceased to have effect in accordance with paragraph 71 of Schedule 4 to the Transitional Order, and

(b) the next anniversary of the issue of the old licence.

(6) In paragraph (4) "the 1968 Act" means the Gaming Act 1968.]

[(7) The first annual fee for a new casino operating licence is 50 per cent of the annual fee for that licence as determined in accordance with paragraph (1).

(8) The annual fee for a new casino operating licence that is not operational is 50 per cent of the annual fee for that licence as determined in accordance with paragraph (1).

(9) For the purposes of paragraph (8), a new casino operating licence is operational if—

(a) in reliance on the licence a casino is trading from premises in respect of which a casino premises licence has effect, or

(b) (i) the holder of the licence has, in accordance with a condition of the licence, notified the Commission of a date upon which it is proposed that a casino will commence trading in reliance on the licence ('the opening date'), and

(i) the holder of the licence has, in accordance with a condition of the licence, notified the Commission of a date upon which it is proposed that a casino will commence trading in reliance on the licence ('the opening date'), and

(ii) the date by which the annual fee for the licence is payable is less than twelve months before the opening date.]

Amendment

Para (1): words in square brackets beginning with the words 'regulation 8A,' substituted by SI 2009/1837, regs 2, 6(1); words '17, 21 and 21A' in square brackets substituted by SI 2012/829, regs 2, 7(1)(a); sub-paras (f)–(l) inserted by SI 2012/829, regs 2, 7(1)(b).

Para (3): words in square brackets beginning with the words 'Subject to paragraphs' substituted by SI 2007/1791, reg 5(1), (2); words '(4) to (8)' in square brackets substituted by SI 2012/829, regs 7(2).

Paras (4)–(6): inserted by SI 2007/1791, reg 5(1), (3). Paras (7)–(9): inserted by SI 2012/829, regs 2, 7(3).

6.1558J.1 [8A Application, annual and first annual fees for non-remote general betting (standard) operating licences]

[(1) This regulation applies in respect of a non-remote general betting (standard) operating licence if—

(a) the licensee does not at any time during the relevant period make a gaming machine available for use at premises in respect of which the licensee holds a betting premises licence, and

(b) the licensee holds such a licence for the duration of that period in respect of—

(i) four or fewer premises,

(ii) five to fifteen premises, or

(iii) sixteen to fifty premises.

(2) Subject to regulations 16 and [18 to 20A], the application fee for a licence to which this regulation applies is to be determined in accordance with paragraph (3).

(3) The application fee is—

(a) for a licence to which paragraph (1)(b)(i) or (ii) applies, £977;

(b) for a licence to which paragraph (1)(b)(iii) applies, £3,417.

(4) Subject to regulations [17, 21 and 21A] the annual fee for a licence to which this regulation applies is to be determined in accordance with paragraph (5).

(5) The annual fee is—

(a) for a licence to which paragraph (1)(b)(i) applies, [£1,461];

(b) for a licence to which paragraph (1)(b)(ii) applies, [£6,582];

(c) for a licence to which paragraph (1)(b)(iii) applies, £16,860.

(6) The first annual fee for a licence to which this regulation applies is 75 per cent of the annual fee for that licence, as determined in accordance with paragraph (5).

(7) In this regulation—

(a) "relevant period" has the same meaning as in regulation 3;

(b) a reference to anything authorised by, or that will happen pursuant to a licence includes, for the purpose of determining an application fee for that licence, anything included in the application as something to be authorised by the licence.]

Amendment

Inserted by SI 2009/1837, regs 2, 6(2).

Para (2): words '18 to 20A' in square brackets substituted by SI 2012/829, regs 2, 8(a).

Para (4): words '17, 21 and 21A' in square brackets substituted by SI 2012/829, regs 2, 8(b).

Para (5): in sub-para (a) sum '£1,461' in square brackets substituted by SI 2012/829, regs 2, 8(c); in sub-para (b) sum '£6,582' in square brackets substituted by SI 2012/829, regs 2, 8(d).

PART 3
REMOTE OPERATING LICENCES—APPLICATION FEES AND ANNUAL FEES

6.1558K 9 Application of this Part

This Part applies in respect of any of the following that is a remote operating licence within the meaning of section 67 of the Act (remote gambling):

(a) a casino operating licence;

(b) a bingo operating licence;

(c) a general betting (limited) operating licence;

(d) [a general betting (standard) (real events) operating licence];

[(da) a general betting (standard) (remote platform) operating licence;

(db) a general betting (standard) (virtual events) operating licence;]

(e) a betting intermediary operating licence;
(f) a pool betting operating licence;
(g) a gaming machine technical (full) operating licence;
(h) a gaming machine technical (supplier) operating licence;
(i) a gaming machine technical (software) operating licence;
(j) a gambling software operating licence;
(k) a lottery operating (external lottery manager) licence; . . .
[(l) a lottery operating (society) licence;
(m) a supplementary operating licence; or
(n) a betting intermediary (trading room only) operating licence].

Amendment

In para (d) words 'a general betting (standard) (real events) operating licence' in square brackets substituted by SI 2012/829, regs 2, 9(1); paras (da), (db) inserted by SI 2012/829, regs 2, 9(2); para (k): word omitted revoked by SI 2008/1803, regs 2, 7(a); paras (l)–(n) substituted, for para (l) as originally enacted, by SI 2008/1803, regs 2, 7(b).

6.1558L 10 Remote operating licences: fee categories

(1) A licence to which this Part applies [(other than a remote general betting (limited) operating licence, [a general betting (standard) (remote platform) operating licence,] an ancillary remote operating licence or a remote supplementary operating licence)] is a licence of the category indicated in the table in Schedule 4.

(2) In that table:

(a) column (1) indicates the description of the licence;
(b) column (2) indicates the unit of division (as defined in regulation 3) by reference to which licences within that description are assigned to categories; and
(c) [columns (3) to (9)] indicate the category to which a licence within that description is assigned, according to the range into which the number or amount of the unit of division authorised by the licence for the relevant period falls.

(3) In this regulation "relevant period" has the same meaning as in regulation 3.

Amendment

Para (1): words from '(other than a' to 'supplementary operating licence)' in square brackets substituted by SI 2008/1803, regs 2, 8; words 'a general betting (standard) (remote platform) operating licence,' in square brackets inserted by SI 2012/829, regs 2, 10.

Para (2): in sub-para (c) words 'columns (3) to (9)' in square brackets substituted by SI 2009/1837, regs 2, 7.

6.1558M 11 Application fees for remote operating licences

(1) Subject to regulations 13(1), 14(6), 16 and [18 to 20A], the application fee—

(a) for a category F licence is the amount indicated in column (2) of the table in Schedule 5 adjacent to the description of the licence in column (1) of that table;
(b) for a category G licence is the amount indicated in column (3) of that table adjacent to the description of the licence in column (1);
(c) for a category H licence is the amount indicated in column (4) of that table adjacent to the description of the licence in column (1).
[(d) for a category I licence is the amount indicated in column (5) of that table adjacent to the description of the licence in column (1);
(e) for a category J licence is the amount indicated in column (6) of that table adjacent to the description of the licence in column (1);
(f) for a category K licence is the amount indicated in column (7) of that table adjacent to the description of the licence in column (1);

(g) for a category L licence is the amount indicated in column (8) of that table adjacent to the description of the licence in column (1)].

(2) In applying regulation 10 for the purposes of calculating the amount of an application fee under this regulation any reference to the number or amount of the unit of division authorised by the licence is to be treated as a reference to the number or amount that the licence would authorise if granted in accordance with the application.

Amendment

Para (1): words '18 to 20A' in square brackets substituted by SI 2012/829, regs 2, 11; sub-paras (d)–(g) inserted by SI 2009/1837, regs 2, 8.

6.1558N 12 Annual fees and first annual fees for remote operating licences

(1) Subject to regulations 13(2)(b), 14(7), [17(2), 21 and 21A], the annual fee—

(a) for a category F licence is the amount indicated in column (2) of the table in Schedule 6 adjacent to the description of the licence in column (1) of that table;

(b) for a category G licence is the amount indicated in column (3) of that table adjacent to the description of the licence in column (1);

(c) for a category H licence is the amount indicated in column (4) of that table adjacent to the description of the licence in column (1).

[(d) for a category I licence is the amount indicated in column (5) of that table adjacent to the description of the licence in column (1);

(e) for a category J licence is the amount indicated in column (6) of that table adjacent to the description of the licence in column (1);

(f) for a category K licence is the amount indicated in column (7) of that table adjacent to the description of the licence in column (1);

(g) for a category L licence is the amount indicated in column (8) of that table adjacent to the description of the licence in column (1)].

(2) In applying this regulation the category into which a particular licence falls is to be determined as at the date by which the annual fee for the licence is payable.

(3) Subject to regulations 13(2)(a), 14(8), 17(3) and 21, the first annual fee for a remote operating licence is the same amount as the annual fee.

Amendment

Para (1): words '17(2), 21 and 21A' in square brackets substituted by SI 2012/829, regs 2, 12; sub-paras (d)–(g) inserted by SI 2009/1837, regs 2, 9.

6.1558O 13 Fees for remote general betting (limited) operating licences

(1) Subject to regulations 16 and [18 to 20A], the application fee for a remote general betting (limited) operating licence is [£593].

(2) Subject to regulations 17 and 21—

(a) the first annual fee for a remote general betting (limited) operating licence is [£1,594]; and

(b) the annual fee for such a licence is [£1,594].

Amendment

Para (1): words '18 to 20A' in square brackets substituted by SI 2012/829, regs 2, 13(1)(a); sum '£593' in square brackets substituted by SI 2012/829, regs 2, 13(1)(b).

Para (2): in sub-para (a) sum '£1,594' in square brackets substituted by SI 2012/829, regs 2, 13(2); in sub-para (b) sum '£1,594' in square brackets substituted by SI 2012/829, regs 2, 13(3).

6.1558OA [13A Fees for general betting (standard) (remote platform) operating licences]

[(1) [Except as provided in paragraph (2) or (3)]—

(a) the application fee for a general betting (standard) (remote platform) operating licence is £198;
(b) the first annual fee for such a licence is £280;
(c) the annual fee for such a licence is £280.

[(2) Where a person applies for a general betting (standard) (remote platform) operating licence and holds or is also applying for—
(a) a remote general betting (limited) operating licence,
(b) a non-remote general betting (standard) operating licence, or
(c) a non-remote general betting (limited) operating licence,

there is no application fee for that general betting (standard) (remote platform) operating licence.]

[(3) At any time when a person who holds a general betting (standard) (remote platform) operating licence also holds—
(a) a remote general betting (limited) operating licence,
(b) a non-remote general betting (standard) operating licence, or
(c) a non-remote general betting (limited) operating licence,

there is no first annual fee and no annual fee for that general betting (standard) (remote platform) operating licence.]

Amendment

Inserted by SI 2012/829, regs 2, 14.

Para (1): words 'Except as provided in paragraph (2) or (3)' substituted by SI 2012/1851, reg 4(1)(a).

Para (2): substituted by SI 2012/1851, reg 4(1)(b).

Para (3): substituted by SI 2012/1851, reg 4(1)(c).

6.1558P 14 Fees for ancillary remote operating licences

(1) An ancillary remote operating licence is a licence to which any of paragraphs (2) to (5) applies.

(2) This paragraph applies to a remote operating licence which—
(a) is held by the holder of a non-remote casino operating licence, and
(b) only authorises the licensee to provide facilities for single premises gaming by means of remote communication equipment that is situated entirely on the set of premises on which the gaming takes place.

(3) This paragraph applies to a remote operating licence which—
(a) is held by the holder of a non-remote bingo operating licence, and
(b) does not authorise the licensee to provide facilities for the playing of bingo other than—
  (i) by means of remote communication equipment, and
  (ii) by people who are situated on licensed premises.

[(4) This paragraph applies to a remote operating licence which—
(a) is held by the holder of a non-remote general betting (limited) operating licence;
(b) authorises the licensee to provide facilities for betting only in circumstances in which each bet made or accepted pursuant to the licence occurs—
  (i) by means of a telephone or by email, and
  (ii) otherwise than by wholly automated means; and
(c) authorises the licensee only to generate an annual gross gambling yield which—
  (i) is less than the annual gross gambling yield generated by activities authorised by the non-remote operating licence, and
  (ii) does not in any event exceed £550,000;

(d) In sub-paragraph (b)(ii), a bet occurs otherwise than by wholly automated means if the arrangements for it are provided, operated or administered by an individual.]

[(4A) This paragraph applies to a remote operating licence which—

(a) is held by the holder of a non-remote general betting (standard) operating licence;

(b) authorises the licensee to provide facilities for betting only—

(i) by means of a machine, other than a gaming machine, used for the purpose of making or accepting bets on premises in respect of which a betting premises licence has effect, or

(ii) in circumstances in which each bet made or accepted pursuant to the licence occurs— (aa) by means of a telephone or by email, and (bb) otherwise than by wholly automated means; and

(aa) by means of a telephone or by email, and

(bb) otherwise than by wholly automated means; and

(c) in respect of facilities for betting to which sub-paragraph (b)(ii) applies, authorises the licensee only to generate an annual gross gambling yield which—

(i) is less than the annual gross gambling yield generated by activities authorised by the non-remote operating licence, and

(ii) does not in any event exceed £550,000;

(d) In sub-paragraph (b)(ii)(bb), a bet occurs otherwise than by wholly automated means if the arrangements for it are provided, operated or administered by an individual.

(4B) This paragraph applies to a remote operating licence which—

(a) is held by the holder of a non-remote pool betting operating licence; and

(b) authorises the licensee to accept bets only by means of a machine, other than a gaming machine, used for the purpose of making or accepting bets on premises in respect of which a betting premises licence has effect.

(4C) This paragraph applies to a remote operating licence which—

(a) is held by the holder of a non-remote lottery operating (society) licence; and

(b) authorises the licensee to accept payments for participation in a lottery only—

(i) by means of remote communication, and

(ii) up to an aggregate sum of £250,000 during each period of 12 months ending on an anniversary of the date of issue of the licence.]

(5) This paragraph applies to a remote operating licence which—

(a) is held by the holder of any of the following licences—

(i) a non-remote gaming machine technical (full) operating licence,

(ii) a non-remote gaming machine technical (supplier) operating licence,

(iii) a non-remote gaming machine technical (software) operating licence, or

(iv) a non-remote gambling software operating licence, and

(b) only authorises the licensee to supply software by email.

(6) The application fee for an ancillary remote operating licence is £100.

[(6A) There is no first annual fee and no annual fee for an ancillary remote operating licence to which any of paragraphs (2) to (4B) or (5) applies.

(6B) The first annual fee for an ancillary remote operating licence to which paragraph (4C) applies is £50.

(6C) The annual fee for such a licence is £50.]

(7) . . .

(8) . . .

(9) Nothing in this regulation limits the generality of the powers conferred by sections 75, 77 and 78 of the Act (conditions imposed by Commission (general and individual) and the Secretary of State) to attach conditions to ancillary remote operating licences.

Amendment

Para (4): substituted by SI 2012/829, regs 2, 15(1).

Paras (4A)–(4C): inserted by SI 2012/829, regs 2, 15(2).

Paras (6A)–(6C): inserted by SI 2012/829, regs 2, 15(3).

Paras (7), (8): revoked by SI 2012/829, regs 2, 15(4).

6.1558P.1 [14A Fees for . . . supplementary operating licences

(1) The application fee for a supplementary operating licence to which this Part applies is £165.

(2) The annual fee for such a licence is £375.

(3) The first annual fee for such a licence is £281.25].

Amendment

Inserted by SI 2008/1803, regs 2, 9.

Provision heading: word omitted revoked by SI 2012/829, regs 2, 16.

PART 4
COMBINED AND MULTIPLE OPERATING LICENCES—APPLICATION FEES AND ANNUAL FEES

6.1558Q 15 [Interpretation of Part 4]

For the purposes of this Part, a combined operating licence is an operating licence which either—

[(1)]

(a) combines more than one of the kinds of licence described in regulation 4 (a 'combined non-remote operating licence'), or

(b) combines more than one [of] the kinds of licence described in regulation 9 (a 'combined remote operating licence').

[(2) But in the application of this Part—

(a) a supplementary operating licence that is combined with one or more other kinds of licence; and

(b) an application for a supplementary operating licence

are to be disregarded].

[(3) This Part does not apply to a general betting (standard) (remote platform) operating licence [for which there is no application fee by virtue of paragraph (2) or, as the case may be, no first annual fee or no annual fee by virtue of paragraph (3) of regulation 13A].]

Amendment

Provision heading: substituted by SI 2008/1803, regs 2, 10(a).

Para (1): numbered as such by SI 2008/1803, regs 2, 10(b); in sub-para (b) word 'of' in square brackets inserted by SI 2008/1803, regs 2, 10(c).

Para (2): inserted by SI 2008/1803, regs 2, 10(d).

Para (3): inserted by SI 2012/829, regs 2, 17; words in square brackets substituted by SI 2012/1851, reg 5.

6.1558R 16 Application fee for combined operating licence

Subject to [regulations 16A and [18 to 20A]], the application fee for a combined operating licence is the sum of—

(a) the application fee which is the highest of those payable in respect of the different kinds of licence to which the combined licence relates; and

(b) 25 per cent of each of the other application fees payable in respect of the licences to which the combined licence relates.

Amendment

Words in square brackets beginning with the words 'regulations 16A and' substituted by SI 2009/1837, regs 2, 10; words '18 to 20A' in square brackets substituted by SI 2012/829, regs 2, 18.

6.1558R.1 [16A Application fee for certain combined remote licences]

[(1) [Subject to regulation 20A, this regulation] applies to a combined remote operating licence which combines two or three of the following kinds of licence (and no other kind of licence)—

(a) a remote casino operating licence;

(b) a remote bingo operating licence;

(c) a general betting (standard) (virtual events) operating licence.

(2) The application fee for a licence to which this regulation applies is the sum of the principal amount determined in accordance with paragraph (3) and the additional amount determined in accordance with paragraph (4).

(3) Where the annual gross gambling yield in respect of the licence—

(a) is less than £500,000, the principal amount is £2,933;

(b) is £500,000 or greater but less than £5 million, the principal amount is £7,169;

(c) is £5 million or greater but less than £25 million, the principal amount is £11,274;

(d) is £25 million or greater but less than £100 million, the principal amount is £16,551;

(e) is £100 million or greater but less than £250 million, the principal amount is £26,641;

(f) is £250 million or greater but less than £500 million, the principal amount is £37,591;

(g) is £500 million or greater, the principal amount is £63,671.

(4) Where the licence combines—

(a) two of the kinds of licence referred to in paragraph (1), the additional amount is £1,050,

(b) three of those kinds of licence, the additional amount is £2,100.

(5) The reference in paragraph (3) to the annual gross gambling yield is a reference to the annual gross gambling yield calculated in accordance with regulation 3(2)(a)(i).]

Amendment

Inserted by SI 2009/1837, regs 2, 11.

Para (1): words 'Subject to regulation 20A, this regulation' in square brackets substituted by SI 2012/829, regs 2, 19.

6.1558S 17 Annual fees and first annual fees for combined operating licences

(1) This regulation is subject to [regulations [17A, 21 and 21A]].

(2) The annual fee for a combined operating licence shall be the aggregate of—

(a) the annual fee which is the highest of those payable in respect of the different kinds of licence to which the combined licence relates[, but ignoring any new casino operating licence that is not operational]; and

(b) [95 per cent] of each of the other annual fees payable in respect of the licences to which the combined licence relates[, but ignoring any new casino operating licence that is not operational, and]

[(c) 50 per cent of the amount of the annual fee for a new casino operating licence that is not operational].

[(2A) Regulation 8(9) applies for the purposes of paragraph (2) as it applies for the purposes of regulation 8(8).]

(3) The first annual fee for—

(a) a combined non-remote operating licence[, which does not include a new casino operating licence,] is 75 per cent of the amount of the annual fee that would be payable for such a licence under paragraph (2) (were the annual fee to be payable when the first annual fee is payable);

[(aa) a combined non-remote operating licence that includes a new casino operating licence is the aggregate of—

(i) 75 per cent of the amount of the annual fee which is the highest of those payable in respect of the different kinds of licence to which the combined licence relates, but excluding the new casino operating licence;

(ii) 71.25 per cent of each of the other annual fees payable in respect of the licences to which the combined licence relates, but excluding the new casino operating licence; and

(iii) 50 per cent of the amount of the annual fee for a new casino operating licence;]

(b) a combined remote operating licence is the same amount as the annual fee so prescribed (were the annual fee to be payable when the first annual fee is payable).

Amendment

Para (1): words in square brackets beginning with the word 'regulations' substituted by SI 2009/1837, regs 2, 12(a); words '17A, 21 and 21A' in square brackets substituted by SI 2012/829, regs 2, 20(1).

Para (2): in sub-para (a) words ', but ignoring any new casino operating licence that is not operational' in square brackets inserted by SI 2012/829, regs 2, 20(2); in sub-para (b) words '95 per cent' in square brackets substituted by SI 2009/1837, regs 2, 12(b); in sub-para (b) words ', but ignoring any new casino operating licence that is not operational, and' in square brackets inserted by SI 2012/829, regs 2, 20(3); sub-para (c) inserted by SI 2012/829, regs 2, 20(4).

Para (2A): inserted by SI 2012/829, regs 2, 20(5).

Para (3): in sub-para (a) words ', which does not include a new casino operating licence,' in square brackets inserted by SI 2012/829, regs 2, 20(6)(a); sub-para (aa) inserted by SI 2012/829, regs 2, 20(6)(b).

6.1558S.1 [17A Annual fees and first annual fees for certain combined remote licences]

[(1) [Subject to regulation 21A, this regulation] applies to a combined remote operating licence which combines two or three of the following kinds of licence (and no other kind of licence)—

(a) a remote casino operating licence;

(b) a remote bingo operating licence;

(c) a general betting (standard) (virtual events) operating licence.

(2) The annual fee for a licence to which this regulation applies is the sum of the principal amount determined in accordance with paragraph (4) and the additional amount determined in accordance with paragraph (5).

(3) The first annual fee for a licence to which this regulation applies is the same amount as the annual fee determined in accordance with paragraph (2) (were the annual fee to be payable when the first annual fee is payable).

(4) Where the annual gross gambling yield in respect of the licence—

(a) is less than £500,000, the principal amount is £3,188;

(b) is £500,000 or greater but less than £5 million, the principal amount is £9,563;

(c) is £5 million or greater but less than £25 million, the principal amount is £13,529;

(d) is £25 million or greater but less than £100 million, the principal amount is £38,128;

(e) is £100 million or greater but less than £250 million, the principal amount is £74,012;

(f) is £250 million or greater but less than £500 million, the principal amount is £117,746;

(g) is £500 million or greater, the principal amount is £155,425.

(5) Where the licence combines—

(a) two of the kinds of licence referred to in paragraph (1), the additional amount is £2,500;

(b) three of those kinds of licence, the additional amount is £5,000.

(6) The reference in paragraph (4) to the annual gross gambling yield is a reference to the annual gross gambling yield calculated in accordance with regulation 3(2)(a)(i).]

Amendment

Inserted by SI 2009/1837, regs 2, 13.

Para (1): words 'Subject to regulation 21A, this regulation' in square brackets substituted by SI 2012/829, regs 2, 21.

6.1558T 18 Fee for simultaneous applications for two operating licences

(1) [Subject to regulation 20A, this regulation] applies where a person applies for—

(a) a non-remote operating licence, and

(b) a remote operating licence (other than an ancillary remote operating licence),

at the same time.

(2) The relevant licence is the licence referred to in paragraph (1) the application for which, apart from this regulation, would attract the lesser application fee.

(3) The application fee for the relevant licence is 25 per cent of the application fee that would, but for this regulation, be payable in respect of that licence.

Amendment

Para (1): words 'Subject to regulation 20A, this regulation' in square brackets substituted by SI 2012/829, regs 2, 22.

6.1558U 19 Fee payable on application for a licence when another application is pending

(1) [Subject to regulation 20A, this regulation] applies where a person who has applied for an operating licence ('the first application') applies for another operating licence ('the second application') before the first application has been determined in accordance with section 74.

(2) Where—

(a) the application fee that would, but for this regulation, be payable for the second application ("the usual fee") is less than the application fee payable for the first application, the application fee for the second application is 25 per cent of the usual fee;

(b) the usual fee is greater than the application fee payable for the first application, the application fee for the second application is the usual fee less 75 per cent of the fee paid in respect of the first application.

(3) In paragraph (1) "operating licence" does not include an ancillary remote operating licence.

Amendment

Para (1): words 'Subject to regulation 20A, this regulation' in square brackets substituted by SI 2012/829, regs 2, 23.

6.1558V 20 Fee payable when holder of existing licence applies for another licence

(1) Subject to regulation 20A, this regulation] applies where a person who holds an operating licence [other than a supplementary operating licence] ('the first licence') applies for another operating licence ('the second application').

(2) Where—

(a) the application fee that would, but for this regulation, be payable for the second application ('the usual fee') is less than the application fee paid for the first licence, the application fee for the second application is 25 per cent of the usual fee;

(b) the usual fee is greater than the application fee paid for the first licence, the application fee for the second application is the usual fee less 75 per cent of the fee paid in respect of the first licence.

(3) In paragraph (1) 'operating licence' does not include an ancillary remote operating licence.

Amendment

Para (1): words 'Subject to regulation 20A, this regulation' in square brackets substituted by SI 2012/829, regs 2, 24; words 'other than a supplementary operating licence' in square brackets inserted by SI 2008/1803, regs 2, 11.

6.1558VA [20A Reduced fee for applications for licences in certain circumstances]

(1) Where paragraph (2) or (3) applies, the application fee is 25 per cent of the application fee which, but for this regulation, would be payable.

(2) This paragraph applies to an application for a licence where—

(a) the applicant is the transferee of the whole of the business, including the property and liabilities, of another person ('the transferor');

(b) at the date of the application the transferor is the holder of a licence ('the existing licence')—

(i) of the same kind, or

(ii) if a combined licence, of one which includes the same kind, or

(iii) where the application is for a combined licence, of one which comprises at least the kind of licence to which the application relates;

(c) if the application is for a licence of a kind in respect of which these Regulations provide for separate fee categories, it is for a licence of the same category or a lower category (by reference to the fee payable) as the existing licence;

(d)

(i) the transferor is the kind of person listed in one of the lines in column A in Table 1;

(ii) the applicant is the kind of person listed in the corresponding line in column B; and

6: Gambling Act 2005: SIs

(iii) the condition set out in column C is satisfied; and

(e) the transferor has given notice to the Gambling Commission of the transferor's intention to surrender the existing licence conditional only upon the grant of the application.

Table

	Column A (Transferor)	*Column B (Applicant)*	*Column C (Condition)*
1	Individual	Company limited by shares	The transferor is the sole shareholder and sole director of the applicant.
2	Individual	Partnership	The transferor is a partner in the applicant, the applicant has only one other partner, and that other partner: (a) holds an operating or personal licence, or (b) is a qualified person within the meaning of regulation 2(3) of the Gambling Act 2005 (Definition of Small Scale Operator) Regulations 2006, or (c) was a person relevant to an application for an operating licence to whose integrity, competence and financial and other circumstances the Commission had regard in granting the licence.
3	Individual	Limited Liability Partnership	The transferor is a member of the applicant, the applicant has only one other member, and that other member: (a) holds an operating or personal licence, or (b) is a qualified person within the meaning of regulation 2(3) of the Gambling Act 2005 (definition of Small Scale Operators) Regulations 2006; or (c) was a person relevant to an application for an operating licence to whose integrity, competence and financial and other circumstances the Commission had regard in granting the licence.
4	Partnership	Individual	The applicant was one of only two partners in the transferor and paragraph (7) of this regulation does not apply.
5	Partnership	Company limited by shares	All persons who are shareholders or directors of the applicant were partners in the transferor.
6	Partnership	Limited Liability Partnership	All persons who are members of the applicant were partners in the transferor.
7	Company limited by shares	Individual	The applicant is the sole shareholder and sole director of the transferor.
8	Company limited by shares	Limited Liability Partnership	All persons who are members of the applicant were shareholders or directors in the transferor.
9	Company limited by shares	Partnership	All persons who are partners in the applicant were shareholders or directors in the transferor.

10	Limited Liability Partnership	Individual	The applicant was one of only two members of the transferor.
11	Limited Liability Partnership	Company limited by shares	All persons who are shareholders or directors of the applicant were members of the transferor.
12	Limited Liability Partnership	Partnership	All persons who are partners in the applicant were members of the transferor.

(3) This paragraph applies to an application for a licence where—

(a) the applicant is a person who, subject to being granted an operating licence, intends to carry on a business which was, at the date of the death of an individual ('the deceased'), being carried on by the deceased in reliance on an operating licence held by the deceased ('the former licence');

(b) the application is for a licence—

(i) of the same kind as the former licence,

(ii) where the former licence was a combined licence, of one of the kinds comprised in the former licence, or

(iii) where the application is for a combined licence, it is for one which comprises only kinds of licence which were comprised in the former licence;

(c) if the application is for a licence of a kind in respect of which these Regulations provide for separate fee categories, it is for a licence of the same category or a lower category (by reference to the fee payable) as the former licence;

(d) the application is made within six months of the date of death of the deceased; and

(e) the applicant is the kind of person listed in one of the lines in column A in Table 2 and the conditions set out in columns B and C are each satisfied.

	Column A (Applicant)	*Column B (Condition 1)*	*Column C (Condition 2)*
1	Individual	The applicant is the spouse, civil partner or child of the deceased	The person who, by the terms of their appointment, will have primary responsibility for the management of the licensed activity, either (a) holds an operating or personal licence, or (b) was a person relevant to an application for an operating licence to whose integrity, competence and financial and other circumstances the Commission had regard in granting the licence.

2	[Partnership]	Each partner in the applicant is the spouse, civil partner or child of the deceased	The person who, by the terms of their appointment, will have primary responsibility for the management of the licensed activity, either (a) holds an operating or personal licence, or (b) was a person relevant to an application for an operating licence to whose integrity, competence and financial and other circumstances the Commission had regard in granting the licence.
3	[Limited Liability Partnership]	Each member of the applicant is the spouse, civil partner or child of the deceased	The person who, by the terms of their appointment, will have primary responsibility for the management of the licensed activity, either (a) holds an operating or personal licence, or (b) was a person relevant to an application for an operating licence to whose integrity, competence and financial and other circumstances the Commission had regard in granting the licence.
4	[Company limited by shares]	Each shareholder and director of the applicant is the spouse, civil partner or child of the deceased	The person who, by the terms of their appointment, will have primary responsibility for the management of the licensed activity, either (a) holds an operating or personal licence, or (b) was a person relevant to an application for an operating licence to whose integrity, competence and financial and other circumstances the Commission had regard in granting the licence.

(4) Where paragraph (2) of this regulation would apply but for either or both of—

(a) the requirement contained in paragraph (2)(c), or

(b) the condition set out in column C of Table 1, the application fee is 75 per cent of the application fee which, but for this regulation, would be payable.

(5) Where paragraph (3) of this regulation would apply but for either or both of—

(a) the requirement contained in paragraph 3(c), or

(b) the condition set out in column C of Table 2,

the application fee is 75 per cent of the application fee which, but for this regulation, would be payable.

(6) Where paragraph (7) of this regulation applies the application fee is £100.

(7) This paragraph applies to an application for a licence where—

(a) the applicant is an individual who, subject to being granted an operating licence, intends to carry on a business ('the business') previously carried on by a partnership;

(b) the business was carried on pursuant to an operating licence ('the former licence') of the same kind and, if the application is for a licence of a kind in respect of which these Regulations provide for separate fee categories, the same category as that to which the application relates;

(c) the partnership comprised two partners only, of which the applicant was one, and

(d) the former licence— (i) has lapsed pursuant to section 114(1)(a) of the Act by virtue of the death of the other partner, or (ii) will lapse, pursuant to section 114(2)(a) of the Act by virtue of the retirement of the other partner.

(8) This regulation does not apply to an application for an ancillary remote operating licence or a supplementary operating licence.]

Amendment

Inserted by SI 2012/829, regs 2, 25.

Para (3): Table 2, in item 2 in column A word 'Partnership' in square brackets substituted by SI 2012/1851, reg 6(a); Table 2, in item 3 in column A words 'Limited Liability Partnership' in square brackets substituted by SI 2012/1851, reg 6(b); Table 2, in item 4 in column A words in square brackets substituted by SI 2012/1851, reg 6(c).

6.1558W 21 Annual fees for holders of two operating licences

(1) This regulation applies where a person holds both—

(a) a non-remote operating licence [that is not a supplementary operating licence], and

(b) a remote operating licence that is not an ancillary remote [or supplementary] operating licence,

('the licences').

(2) Where a first annual fee ('the relevant first annual fee') is paid—

(a) for both of the licences on the same day, the lower of the two fees is reduced by [5 per cent];

(b) for one of the licences and that fee is lower than the first annual fee previously paid for the other licence, the relevant first annual fee is reduced by [5 per cent];

(c) for one of the licences and that fee is greater than the first annual fee previously paid for the other licence, the relevant first annual fee is reduced by an amount equal to [5 per cent] of the fee already paid.

(3) Where an annual fee ('the relevant annual fee') is paid—

(a) for both of the licences on the same day, the lower of the two fees is reduced by [5 per cent];

(b) for one of the licences and that fee is lower than the annual fee paid for the other licence (on the last occasion on which it was paid), the relevant annual fee is reduced by [5 per cent];

(c) for one of the licences and that fee is greater than the annual fee paid for the other licence (on the last occasion on which it was paid), the relevant annual fee is reduced by an amount equal to [5 per cent] of the fee already paid.

(4) Paragraph (3) is not to apply where the annual fee which was previously paid in respect of the other licence was reduced in accordance with that paragraph.

Amendment

Para (1): in sub-para (a) words 'that is not a supplementary operating licence' in square brackets inserted by SI 2008/1803, regs 2, 12(a); in sub-para (b) words 'or supplementary' in square brackets inserted by SI 2008/1803, regs 2, 12(b).

Para (2): in sub-paras (a)–(c) words '5 per cent' in square brackets substituted by SI 2012/829, regs 2, 26.

Para (3): in sub-paras (a)–(c) words '5 per cent' in square brackets substituted by SI 2009/1837, regs 2, 14.

6.1558WA [21A Reduced first annual fee in certain circumstances]

[(1) This regulation applies in any case where any of paragraphs (2), (3), (4), (5) or (7) of regulation 20A applied to the application for the licence.

(2) In this regulation 'the old licence' means— (a) in a case to which paragraph (2) or (4) of regulation 20A applies, the existing licence; (b) in a case to which paragraph (3), (5) or (7) of regulation 20A applies, the former licence. (3)

(a) a non-remote operating licence [that is not a supplementary operating licence], and

(b) a remote operating licence that is not an ancillary remote [or supplementary] operating licence,

('the licences').

(2) Where a first annual fee ('the relevant first annual fee') is paid—

(a) for both of the licences on the same day, the lower of the two fees is reduced by [5 per cent];

(b) for one of the licences and that fee is lower than the first annual fee previously paid for the other licence, the relevant first annual fee is reduced by [5 per cent];

(c) for one of the licences and that fee is greater than the first annual fee previously paid for the other licence, the relevant first annual fee is reduced by an amount equal to [5 per cent] of the fee already paid.

(3) Subject to paragraph (4), where this regulation applies the first annual fee for the licence is the amount calculated in accordance with the following formula—

$$A - ((B \div 12) \times C]$$

where—

A is the first annual fee that would, but for this paragraph, be payable in respect of a licence of the kind and category being applied for;

B is the amount of the last fee paid under section 100 of the Act for the old licence (whether it was a first annual fee or an annual fee); and

C is the number of whole calendar months between—

(a) the date on which the old licence ceased to have effect, and

(b) the next anniversary of the issue of the old licence.

(4) Where application of the formula set out in paragraph (3) produces a negative figure there is no first annual fee for the licence.]

Amendment

Inserted by SI 2012/829, regs 2, 27.

6.1558X 22 Interpretation

In regulations 18 and 21—

"non-remote operating licence" includes a combined non-remote operating licence, and

"remote operating licence" includes a combined remote operating licence.

PART 5
OTHER PRESCRIBED FEES RELATING TO OPERATING LICENCES

6.1558Y.1 [23 Change in corporate control application fee]

[(1) Regulation 23A applies to an application under section 102(2)(b) ('a change application') [except where regulation 23B applies].

[(2) Regulation 23B applies to a change application where at the time the application is made the new controller—

(a) is the holder of an operating licence; or

(b) is a financial institution (as defined by article 4.5 of the Banking Consolidation Directive)—

(i) regulated by the Financial Services Authority, or

(ii) which has its registered office or, if it has no registered office, its head office, in an EEA state other than the United Kingdom and which is regulated by its home state regulator as defined in paragraph 9 of Schedule 3 to the Financial Services and Markets Act 2000.]

(3) Regulation 15(2) applies for the purposes of regulation 23A(1)(a) and (2) to (4) and [regulation 23B(2)(a) and (3) to (5)] in the same way as it applies in the application of Part 4.]

Amendment

Substituted, together with regs 23A, 23B, for reg 23 as originally enacted, by SI 2008/1803, regs 2, 13.

Para (1): words 'except where regulation 23B applies' in square brackets substituted by SI 2012/829, regs 2, 28.

Para (2): substituted by SI 2012/829, regs 2, 29.

Para (3): words 'regulation 23B(2)(a) and (3) to (5)' in square brackets substituted by SI 2009/1837, regs 2, 15.

6.1558Y.2

[**23A** (1) Where this regulation applies the fee to accompany a change application in relation to an operating licence is—

(a) if the licence is a combined operating licence, 75 per cent of the fee referred to in regulation 16(a);

(b) if paragraph (2) applies, the amount determined in accordance with paragraphs (3) and (4); . . .

[(ba) if paragraph (5) applies, the amount determined in accordance with paragraph (6), and]

(c) in any [other] case, 75 per cent of the application fee which would be payable in respect of an operating licence of the same kind at the time the change application is made (as determined by [regulations] 7, 11 and 12(1)).

(2) This paragraph applies to change applications made by a person simultaneously in relation to—

(a) a non-remote operating licence, and

(b) a remote operating licence (other than an ancillary remote operating licence), . . .

[held by that person].

(3) The fee to accompany each of the applications referred to in paragraph (2) is the amount calculated in accordance with the following formula—

$$[(0.75 \times A) + (0.75 \times B)] / 2$$

where A and B are the respective application fees payable for each of the licences referred to in that paragraph at the time the change applications are made (as determined in accordance with regulations 7, 11 and 13(1)).

(4) In paragraph (2)—

"non-remote operating licence" includes a combined non-remote operating licence, and

"remote operating licence" includes a combined remote operating licence].

[(5) This paragraph applies to change applications made by two or more holders of operating licences where—

(a) the applications are made on the same occasion and in respect of the same new controller, and

(b) each applicant is, in respect of each other applicant, a group company.

(6) Except where paragraph (c) applies, the fee payable in respect of the applications referred to in paragraph (5) is—

(a) in the case of the application for which the fee would be the highest if the fee for each application were calculated in accordance with paragraph (1) (but ignoring paragraph (1)(c)), the fee so calculated;

(b) in the case of each of the other applications, £100.

(c) In the case of two or more of the applications being of equally highest fee (if the fee for each application were calculated in accordance with paragraph (1)) (but ignoring paragraph (1)(c)), the fee payable—

(i) for each application of equally highest fee is to be determined in accordance with the following formula—

$$(X \div Y) + ((£100 \times (Y - 1)) / Y$$

where X is the highest fee payable and Y is the number of applications of equally highest fee; and

(ii) in the case of each of the other applications, is £100.]]

Amendment

Substituted, together with regs 23, 23B, for reg 23 as originally enacted, by SI 2008/1803, regs 2, 13.

Para (1): in sub-para (b) word omitted revoked by SI 2012/829, regs 2, 30(1); sub-para (ba) inserted by SI 2012/829, regs 2, 30(2); in sub-para (c) word 'other' in square brackets inserted by SI 2012/829, regs 2, 30(3); in sub-para (c) word 'regulations' in square brackets substituted by SI 2009/1837, regs 2, 16(a).

Para (2): in sub-para (b) words omitted revoked by SI 2009/1837, regs 2, 16(b)(i); words 'held by that person' in square brackets inserted by SI 2009/1837, regs 2, 16(b)(ii).

Paras (5), (6): inserted by SI 2012/829, regs 2, 30(4).

6.1558Y.3

[23B (1) Where this regulation applies the fee to accompany a change application is £100 if the new controller becomes a controller within the meaning of section 422 of the Financial Services and Markets Act 2000 ("the FSMA") solely by acquiring a holding of 10% or more of the shares in the company.

(2) But if the new controller becomes a controller within the meaning of section 422 of the FSMA in circumstances other than those falling within paragraph (1) the fee is—

(a) 25 per cent of the fee referred to in regulation 16(a) if the licence to which the application relates is a combined operating licence;

(b) the amount determined in accordance with paragraphs (4) and (5) if the application is one to which paragraph (3) applies; . . .

[(ba) the amount determined in accordance with paragraph (7) if the application is one to which paragraph (6) applies; or]

(c) in any other case, 25 per cent of the application fee which would be payable in respect of a licence of the same kind as that to which the change application relates at the time the change application is made (as determined by paragraphs 7, 11 and 13(1)).

(3) This paragraph applies to change applications made by a person simultaneously in relation to—

(a) a non remote operating licence, and

(b) a remote operating licence (other than an ancillary remote operating licence), . . .

[held by that person].

(4) The fee to accompany each of the applications to which paragraph [(3)] applies is the amount calculated in accordance with the following formula—

$$[(0.25 \times A) + (0.25 \times B)] / 2$$

where A and B are the respective application fees payable for each of the licences referred to in that paragraph at the time the change applications are made (as determined in accordance with regulations 7, 11 and 13(1)).

(5) In paragraph [(3)]—

"non remote operating licence" includes a combined non remote operating licence, and

"remote operating licence" includes a combined remote operating licence"].

[(6) This paragraph applies to change applications made by two or more holders of operating licences where—

(a) the applications are made on the same occasion and in respect of the same new controller, and

(b) each applicant is, in respect of each other applicant, a group company.

(7) Except where paragraph (c) applies, the fee payable in respect of the applications referred to in paragraph (6) is—

(a) in the case of the application for which the fee would be the highest if the fee for each application were calculated in accordance with paragraph (1) (but ignoring paragraph (1)(c)), the fee so calculated;

(b) in the case of each of the other applications, £100.

(c) In the case of two or more of the applications being of equally highest fee (if the fee for each application were calculated in accordance with paragraph (1)) (but ignoring paragraph (1)(c)), the fee payable—

(i) for each application of equally highest fee is to be determined in accordance with the following formula—

$$(X \div Y) + ((£100 \times (Y - 1)) / Y$$

where X is the highest fee payable and Y is the number of applications of equally highest fee; and

(ii) in the case of each of the other applications, is £100.]]

Amendment

Substituted, together with regs 23, 23A, for reg 23 as originally enacted, by SI 2008/1803, regs 2, 13.

Para (2): in sub-para (b) word omitted revoked by SI 2012/829, regs 2, 31(1); sub-para (ba) inserted by SI 2012/829, regs 2, 31(2).

Para (3): in sub-para (b) words omitted revoked by SI 2009/1837, regs 2, 17(a)(i); words 'held by that person' in square brackets inserted by SI 2009/1837, regs 2, 17(a)(ii).

Para (4): reference to '(3)' in square brackets substituted by SI 2009/1837, regs 2, 17(b).

Para (5): reference to '(3)' in square brackets substituted by SI 2009/1837, regs 2, 17(c).

Paras (6), (7): inserted by SI 2012/829, regs 2, 31(3).

6.1558Y.4 24 Fees for applications to vary operating licences

[(1) Subject to regulation 24A, the fee to accompany an application under section 104(1)(a) to vary a licence by adding a licensed activity is 25 per cent of the application fee for a licence that would authorise the licensee to engage only in the licensed activity to be added.]

(2) The fee to accompany an application under section 104(1)(a) to vary a licence by removing a licensed activity is £25.

(3) [[Except as provided in paragraph (3A), and subject] to paragraph (8), the] fee to accompany an application under section 104(1)(b) to vary a licence by amending another detail of the licence is £25.

[(3A) Where an application has been made under section 104(1)(b) to vary a non-remote general betting (standard) operating licence or a non-remote general betting (limited) operating licence, the fee specified in paragraph (3) is not payable in respect of any application under section 104(1)(b) to vary a general betting (standard) (remote platform) operating licence to the same extent.]

(4) [Subject to paragraph (8) [and regulation 24A], the] fee to accompany an application under section 104(1)(c) to vary a condition attached to a licence shall be determined in accordance with the following paragraphs.

[(5) Where the effect of the application (if granted) would be to bring the licence within a new category (pursuant to regulation 5, 6 or 10), the fee is—

(a) if the new category is higher than the category into which the licence falls at the time the application is made, [20 per cent] of the application fee for a licence that falls within the new category, and

(b) in all other cases £25].

(6) In any other case, the fee is 25 per cent of the application fee for a licence in the category to which the condition sought to be varied relates.

(7) But if the condition which it is sought to vary relates to more than one category, the fee shall be 25 percent of the highest of the application fees payable for licences in the categories to which the condition relates.

[(8) The fee to accompany an application under paragraph (3) or (4) is £100 where—

(a) the application is to vary a licence so as to change a reference to an individual, to an office or a post held by an individual, or to the responsibilities of an individual, an office or a post, and

(b) the change is of a kind in respect of which the Commission have published a notice (on their website and by any other means they consider appropriate) before the application is made to the effect that such a change requires them to examine the criminal record of any person before making the change.

(9) For the purposes of paragraph (5)(a) one category is higher than another if the letter used to denote it comes later in the alphabet].

Amendment

Para (1): substituted by SI 2012/829, regs 2, 32(1).

Para (3): words beginning 'Subject' in square brackets substituted by SI 2012/1851, reg 7(a); words 'to paragraph (8), the' in square brackets substituted by SI 2008/1803, regs 2, 14(a).

Para (3A): inserted by SI 2012/1851, reg 7(b).

Para (4): words in square brackets beginning with the words 'Subject to paragraph (8)' substituted by SI 2008/1803, regs 2, 14(a); words 'and regulation 24A' in square brackets inserted by SI 2012/829, regs 2, 32(2).

Para (5): substituted by SI 2008/1803, regs 2, 14(b); in sub-para (a) words '20 per cent' in square brackets substituted by SI 2012/829, regs 2, 32(3).

Paras (8), (9): inserted by SI 2008/1803, regs 2, 14(c).

6.1558Y.5 [24A Fees for applications to vary certain remote operating licences]

[(1) This paragraph applies to an application under section 104(1)(a) to vary a remote licence by adding a licensed activity in circumstances where, were the application to be granted, the resulting combined remote operating licence would be one to which regulation 16A applies.

(2) The fee to accompany an application to which paragraph (1) applies is—

(a) £1,050 if the application is to add a single additional licensed activity, and

(b) £2,100 if it is to add two additional licensed activities.

(3) This paragraph applies to an application to which paragraph (1) applies and which also comprises an application under section 104(1)(c) to vary a condition attached to the licence, the effect of which would be to bring the licence within a new category pursuant to regulation 10.

(4) The fee to accompany an application to which paragraph (3) applies is the aggregate of the fee prescribed under paragraph (2) plus—

(a) where the new category is higher than the category into which the licence falls at the time the application is made, 20 per cent of the application fee for a licence that falls within the new category, or

(b) where sub-paragraph (a) does not apply, £25.]

Amendment

Inserted by SI 2012/829, regs 2, 33.

6.1558ZA 25 Maximum fee for copy of operating licence

The fee for issuing a copy of an operating licence under section 107 shall not exceed £25.

PART 6
OPERATING LICENCES: GENERAL

6.1558ZB [26 Date for payment of first annual fee]

[(1) Except where paragraph (2) applies, the first annual fee for a licence shall be paid within 30 days of the date on which the licence was issued.

(2) This paragraph applies to a new casino operating licence.

(3) Where paragraph (2) applies the first annual fee for a licence shall be paid within six months of the date on which the licence was issued.]

Amendment

Substituted by SI 2012/829, regs 2, 34.

PART 7
SINGLE-MACHINE SUPPLY AND MAINTENANCE
PERMITS—APPLICATION FEE

6.1558ZC 27 Application fee for single-machine supply and maintenance permit

The fee to accompany an application for a permit under section 250(2) is £25.

6.1558ZD

[SCHEDULE 1
CATEGORIES OF NON-REMOTE OPERATING LICENCES]
Regulation 6

Description of licence	*Unit of division*	*Category A*	*Category B*	*Category C*	*Category D*	*Category E*	*Category E1*	*Category E2*	*Category E3*	*Category E4*	*Category E5*	*Category E6*	*Category E7*
Existing casino operating licence	Annual gross gaming yield	Less than £5.5 million	£5.5 million or greater, up to but excluding £27.5 million	£27.5 million or greater, up to but excluding £110 million	£110 million or greater, [up to] but excluding £275 million	£275 million or greater							
New casino operating licence	Nature of premises licence	Small	Large										
Bingo operating licence	Number of licensed premises	4 or fewer	5 to 15	16 to 50	51 to 99	100 or more							
General betting (standard) operating licence	Number of licensed premises	4 or fewer	5 to 15	16 to 50	51 to 99	Not applicable	100 to 199	200 to 349	350 to 499	500 to 999	1000 to 1499	1500 to 1999	2000 or more
General betting (limited) operating licence	Number of working days	75 or fewer	76 to 199	200 or more									

Description of licence	*Unit of division*	*Category A*	*Category B*	*Category C*	*Category D*	*Category E*	*Category E1*	*Category E2*	*Category E3*	*Category E4*	*Category E5*	*Category E6*	*Category E7*
Pool betting operating licence	Annual gross gambling yield	Less than £550,000	£550,000 [or greater] up to but excluding £2.5 million	£2.5 million or greater, up to but excluding £5.5 million	£5 million or greater, up to but excluding £10 million	£10 million or greater							
Betting intermediary operating licence	Annual gross gambling yield	Less than £5.5 million	£5.5 million or greater, up to but excluding £110 million	£110 million or greater									
Gaming machine general operating licence for an adult gaming centre	Number of licensed premises	4 or fewer	5 to 15	16 to 50	51 to 99	not applicable	100 to 199	200 to 299	300 to 399	400 or more			
Gaming machine general operating licence for a family entertainment centre	Number of licensed premises	4 or fewer	5 to 15	16 to 50	51 to 99	100 or more							

Description of licence	*Unit of division*	*Category A*	*Category B*	*Category C*	*Category D*	*Category E*	*Category E1*	*Category E2*	*Category E3*	*Category E4*	*Category E5*	*Category E6*	*Category E7*
Gaming machine technical (full) operating licence	Value of annual gross sales	Less than £550,000	£550,000 or greater, up to but excluding £6.6 million	£6.6 million or greater									
Gaming machine technical (supplier) operating licence	Value of annual gross sales	Less than £550,000	£550,000 or greater, up to but excluding £6.6 million	£6.6 million or greater									
Gaming machine technical (software) operating licence	Value of annual gross sales	Less than £550,000	£550,000 or greater, up to but excluding £6.6 million	£6.6 million or greater									
Gambling software operating licence	Value of annual gross sales	Less than £550,000	£550,000 or greater, up to but excluding £6.6 million	£6.6 million or greater									
Lottery operating (external lottery manager) licence	Annual proceeds	Less than [£550,000]	£550,000 [or greater] , up to but excluding £2.5 million	£2.5 million or greater, up to but excluding £10 million	£10 million or greater								

Description of licence	*Unit of division*	*Category A*	*Category B*	*Category C*	*Category D*	*Category E*	*Category E1*	*Category E2*	*Category E3*	*Category E4*	*Category E5*	*Category E6*	*Category E7*
Lottery operating (society) licence	Annual proceeds	Less than £100,000	£100,000 or greater, up to but excluding £500,000	[£500,000 or greater]									

Amendment

Substituted by SI 2012/829, regs 2, 35, Sch 1.

Set out as amended by SI 2012/1851, reg 8.

6.1558ZE

[SCHEDULE 2

APPLICATION FEES FOR NON-REMOTE OPERATING LICENCES]

Regulation 7

Description of licence	*Category A*	*Category B*	*Category C*	*Category D*	*Category E*	*Category E1*	*Category E2*	*Category E3*	*Category E4*	*Category E5*	*Category E6*	*Category E7*
Existing casino operating licence	£6,509	£9,763	£19,528	£19,528	£19,528							
New casino operating licence	£28,641	£37,591										
Bingo operating licence	£977	£1,627	£3,255	£17,087	£20,504							

Description of licence	*Category A*	*Category B*	*Category C*	*Category D*	*Category E*	*Category E1*	*Category E2*	*Category E3*	*Category E4*	*Category E5*	*Category E6*	*Category E7*
General betting (standard) operating licence	£977	£977	£3,417	£17,087	none applicable	£19,087	£22,087	£31,032	£40,032	£40,032	£40,032	£40,032
General betting (limited) operating licence	£178	£355	£979									
Pool betting operating licence	£651	£977	£1,274	£1,627	£4,882							
Betting intermediary operating licence	£198	£198	£198									
Gaming machine general operating licence for an adult gaming centre	£977	£977	£1,627	£4,882	none applicable	£16,274	£16,274	£16,274	£16,274			

Description of licence	*Category A*	*Category B*	*Category C*	*Category D*	*Category E*	*Category E1*	*Category E2*	*Category E3*	*Category E4*	*Category E5*	*Category E6*	*Category E7*
Gaming machine general operating licence for a family entertainment centre	£977	£977	£1,627	£4,882	£16,274							
Gaming machine technical (full) operating licence	£977	£1,627	£16,274									
Gaming machine technical (supplier) operating licence	£977	£1,627	£4,882									
Gaming machine technical (software) operating licence	£977	£4,882	£16,274									
Gambling software operating licence	£977	£4,882	£16,274									

Description of licence	*Category A*	*Category B*	*Category C*	*Category D*	*Category E*	*Category E1*	*Category E2*	*Category E3*	*Category E4*	*Category E5*	*Category E6*	*Category E7*
Lottery operating (external lottery manager) operating licence	£977	£1,627	£1,878	£2,278	£2,527							
Lottery operating (society) licence	£163	£244	£325]									

Amendment

Substituted by SI 2012/829, regs 2, 36, Sch 2.

6.1558ZF

[SCHEDULE 3

ANNUAL FEES FOR NON-REMOTE OPERATING LICENCES]

Regulation 8

Description of licence	*Category A*	*Category B*	*Category C*	*Category D*	*Category E*	*Category E1*	*Category E2*	*Category E3*	*Category E4*	*Category E5*	*Category E6*	*Category E7*
Existing casino operating licence	£17,378	£23,112	£74,112	£329,711	£443,526							

Description of licence	*Category A*	*Category B*	*Category C*	*Category D*	*Category E*	*Category E1*	*Category E2*	*Category E3*	*Category E4*	*Category E5*	*Category E6*	*Category E7*
New casino operating licence	£51,877	£108,132										
Bingo operating licence	£1,531	£6,894	£17,914	£43,921	£95,840							
General betting (standard) operating licence	£1,531	£6,894	£17,914	£45,426	none applicable	£51,555	£113,960	£169,960	£244,960	£264,960	£284,960	Where the number of licensed premises operated by the holder of the licence is 2,000 to 2,499, £304,960 Where the number of licensed premises operated by the holder of the licence is 2,500 or more, £304,960 plus £25,000 for each block of up to 500 premises over 2,499.
General betting (limited) operating licence	£200	£467	£1,346									

Description of licence	Category A	Category B	Category C	Category D	Category E	Category E1	Category E2	Category E3	Category E4	Category E5	Category E6	Category E7
Pool betting operating licence	£2,222	£2,879	£4,277	£6,477	£12,137							
Betting intermediary operating licence	£280	£4,277	£4,338									
Gaming machine general operating licence for an adult gaming centre	£1,523	£6,297	£13,736	£32,505	none applicable	£45,236	£50,236	£55,236	Where the number of licensed premises operated by the holder of the licence is 400 to 499, £60,236. Where the number of licensed premises operated by the holder of the license is 500 or more, £60,236 plus £5,000 for each block of up to 100 premises over 499.			

Description of licence	*Category A*	*Category B*	*Category C*	*Category D*	*Category E*	*Category E1*	*Category E2*	*Category E3*	*Category E4*	*Category E5*	*Category E6*	*Category E7*
Gaming machine general operating licence for a family entertainment centre	£1,020	£4,562	£9,950	£26,124	£43,921							
Gaming machine technical (full) operating licence	£3,102	£6,625	£15,813									
Gaming machine technical (supplier) operating licence	£1,258	£3,397	£4,338									
Gaming machine technical (software) operating licence	£1,608	£4,044	£6,575									
Gambling software operating licence	£1,608	£4,044	£6,575									

Description of licence	*Category A*	*Category B*	*Category C*	*Category D*	*Category E*	*Category E1*	*Category E2*	*Category E3*	*Category E4*	*Category E5*	*Category E6*	*Category E7*
Lottery operating (external lottery manager) licence	£2,075	£2,368	£4,044	£6,675	£15,813							
Lottery operating (society) licence	£348	£692	£1,458]									

Amendment

Substituted by SI 2012/829, regs 2, 37, Sch 3.

6.1558ZG

SCHEDULE 4
CATEGORIES OF REMOTE OPERATING LICENCES
Regulation 10

[Description of licence	*Unit of division*	*Category F*	*Category G*	*Category H*	*Category I*	*Category J*	*Category K*	*Category L*
Casino operating licence	Annual gross gambling yield	Less than £0.5 million	£0.5 million or greater, up to but excluding £5 million	£5 million or greater, up to but excluding £25 million	£25 million or greater, up to but excluding £100 million	£100 million or greater, up to but excluding £250 million	£250 million or greater, up to but excluding £500 million	£500 million or greater

[Description of licence	Unit of division	Category F	Category G	Category H	Category I	Category J	Category K	Category L
Bingo operating licence	Annual gross gambling yield	Less than £0.5 million	£0.5 million or greater, up to but excluding £5 million	£5 million or greater, up to but excluding £25 million	£25 million or greater, up to but excluding £100 million	£100 million or greater, up to but excluding £250 million	£250 million or greater, up to but excluding £500 million	£500 million or greater
General betting (standard) (virtual events) operating licence	Annual gross gambling yield	Less than £0.5 million	£0.5 million or greater, up to but excluding £5 million	£5 million or greater, up to but excluding £25 million	£25 million or greater, up to but excluding £100 million	£100 million or greater, up to but excluding £250 million	£250 million or greater, up to but excluding £500 million	£500 million or greater
General betting (standard) (real events) operating licence	Annual gross gambling yield	Less than £5.5 million	£5.5 million or greater, up to but excluding £55 million	£55 million or greater, up to but excluding £110 million	£110 million or greater, up to but excluding £220 million	£220 million or greater, up to but excluding £550 million	£550 million or greater	
General betting (limited) operating licence	Annual gross gambling yield	Less than £550,000						
Pool betting operating licence	Annual gross gambling yield	Less than £1.5 million	£1.5 million or greater, up to but excluding £5.5 million	£5.5 million or greater, up to but excluding £55 million	£55 million or greater, up to but excluding £110 million	£110 million or greater, up to but excluding £220 million	£220 million or greater, up to but excluding £550 million	£550 million or greater
Betting intermediary operating licence	Annual gross gambling yield	Less than £5.5 million	£5.5 million or greater, up to but excluding £55 million	£55 million or greater, up to but excluding £110 million	£110 million or greater, up to but excluding £220 million	£220 million or greater, up to but excluding £550 million	[£550 million] or greater	

[*Description of licence*	*Unit of division*	*Category F*	*Category G*	*Category H*	*Category I*	*Category J*	*Category K*	*Category L*
Betting intermediary (trading room only) operating licence	Annual gross gambling yield	Less than £550,000	£550,000 or greater, up to but excluding £6.6 million	£6.6 million or greater				
Gaming machine technical (full) operating licence	Value of annual gross sales	Less than £550,000	£550,000 or greater, up to but excluding £6.6 million	£6.6 million or greater				
Gaming machine technical (supplier) operating licence	Value of annual gross sales	Less than £550,000	£550,000 or greater, up to but excluding £6.6 million	£6.6 million or greater				
Gaming machine technical (software) operating licence	Value of annual gross sales	Less than £550,000	£550,000 or greater, up to but excluding £6.6 million	£6.6 million or greater				
Gambling software operating licence	Value of annual gross sales	Less than £550,000	£550,000 or greater, up to but excluding £6.6 million	£6.6 million or greater				
Lottery operating (external lottery manager) licence	Annual proceeds	Less than £550,000	£550,000 [or greater], up to but excluding £2.5 million	£2.5 million or greater, up to but excluding £5.5 million	£5.5 million or greater, up to but excluding £10 million	£10 million or greater		
Lottery operating (society) licence	Annual proceeds	Less than £100,000	£100,000 or greater, up to but excluding £500,000	[£500,000 or greater]]				

Amendment

Substituted by SI 2012/829, regs 2, 38, Sch 4.

Set out as amended by SI 2012/1851, reg 9.

6.1558ZH

[SCHEDULE 5
APPLICATION FEES FOR REMOTE OPERATING LICENCES
Regulation 11

[*Description of licence*	*Category F*	*Category G*	*Category H*	*Category I*	*Category J*	*Category K*	*Category L*
New casino operating licence	£2,933	£7,169	£11,274	£16,551	£26,641	£37,591	£63,671
Bingo operating licence	£2,933	£7,169	£11,274	£16,551	£26,641	£37,591	£63,671
General betting (limited) (virtual events) operating licence	£2,933	£7,169	£11,274	£16,551	£26,641	£37,591	£63,671
General betting (limited) (real events) operating licence	£3,259	£7,169	£16,274	£19,551	£28,641		
General betting (telephone only) operating licence	£593						
Pool betting operating licence	£651	£982	£1,627	£4,882	£4,882	£4,882	£4,882
Betting intermediary operating licence	£6,346	£13,018	£14,784	£16,274	£19,551	£28,641	
Betting intermediary (trading rooms) operating licence	£593	£977	£1,627				
Gaming machine technical (full) operating licence	£977	£1,627	£16,274				
Gaming machine technical (supplier) operating licence	£977	£1,627	£4,882				

6: Gambling Act 2005: SIs

[Description of licence	Category F	Category G	Category H	Category I	Category J	Category K	Category L
Gaming machine technical (software) operating licence	£977	£4,882	£16,274				
Gambling software operating licence	£6,346	£13,018	£16,274				
Lottery operating (external lottery manager) licence	£977	£1,627	£1,879	£2,278	£2,463		
Lottery operating (society) licence	£163	£244	£325]				

Amendment

Substituted by SI 2012/829, regs 2, 39, Sch 5.

6.1558ZI

[SCHEDULE 6
ANNUAL FEES FOR REMOTE OPERATING LICENCES
Regulation 12

[Description of licence	Category F	Category G	Category H	Category I	Category J	Category K	Category L
New casino operating licence	£3,188	£9,563	£13,529	£38,128	£74,012	£117,746	£155,425
Bingo operating licence	£3,188	£9,563	£13,529	£38,128	£74,012	£117,746	£155,425
General betting (standard) (virtual events) operating licence	£3,188	£9,563	£13,529	£38,128	£74,012	£117,746	£155,425
General betting (standard) (real events) operating licence	£13,529	£38,128	£48,893	£74,012	£117,746	£155,425	
General betting (telephone only) operating licence	£1,594						
Pool betting operating licence	£1,594	£13,529	£38,128	£48,893	£74,012	£117,746	£155,425
Betting intermediary operating licence	£13,529	£38,128	£48,893	£74,012	£117,746	£155,425	

[*Description of licence*	*Category F*	*Category G*	*Category H*	*Category I*	*Category J*	*Category K*	*Category L*
Betting intermediary (trading rooms) operating licence	£1,594	£6,765	£19,063				
Gaming machine technical (full) operating licence	£6,765	£19,063	£37,006				
Gaming machine technical (supplier) operating licence	£6,765	£19,063	£37,006				
Gaming machine technical (software) operating licence	£6,765	£19,063	£37,006				
Gambling software operating licence	£6,765	£19,063	£37,006				
Lottery operating (external lottery manager) licence	£6,765	£19,063	£24,372	£37,006	£48,893		
Lottery operating (society) licence	£348	£692	£1,458]				

Amendment

Substituted by SI 2012/829, regs 2, 40, Sch 6.

GAMBLING (PERSONAL LICENCE FEES) REGULATIONS 2006

(SI 2006/3285)

Made . . . . *10th December 2006*
Laid before Parliament . . . . *11th December 2006*
Coming into force . . . . *1st January 2007*

The Secretary of State makes the following Regulations in exercise of the powers conferred by sections 69(2)(g) and (5), 104(3) and (4), 107(2)(a), 128, 132(2) and (3) and 355(1) of the Gambling Act 2005:

6.1559 1 Citation and commencement

These Regulations may be cited as the Gambling (Personal Licence Fees) Regulations 2006 and shall come into force on 1st January 2007.

6.1560 2 Interpretation

(1) In these Regulations—

"the Act" means the Gambling Act 2005;

"maintenance fee" means a fee payable in accordance with section 132(2) of the Act (as specified in regulation 4);

"personal management licence" means a personal licence which authorises an individual to perform the functions of a management office within the meaning of section 80(5) (whether or not the licence also authorises the individual to perform a specified operational function within the meaning of section 80(6)); and

"personal functional licence" means a personal licence which does not authorise an individual to perform any function other than an operational function within the meaning of section 80(6).

(2) A reference in these Regulations to a section is a reference to a section of the Act.

(3) A reference in regulations 3, 5 and 6 to a section is a reference to that section as applied to personal licences by section 128(1).

6.1561 3 Application fees for personal licences

(1) The fee to accompany an application for a personal licence under section 69 is—

(a) [£370], if the application is for a personal management licence; or

(b) [£185], if the application is for a personal functional licence.

(2) But if an application for a personal licence is made by means of the Commission's website, the fee to accompany that application is 90 per cent of the fee that would, but for this paragraph, be payable under paragraph (1).

(3) For the purposes of paragraph (2), an application shall not be regarded as being made by means of the Commission's website unless it contains the information or documents required by section 69(2)(a), (b), (d), (e) and (f), to the extent that such information or documents can be transmitted electronically.

Amendment

Para (1): in sub-para (a) sum '£370' in square brackets substituted by SI 2009/1971, regs 2, 3(a); in sub-para (b) sum '£185' in square brackets substituted by SI 2009/1971, regs 2, 3(b).

6.1562 4 Maintenance fees for personal licences

(1) The holder of a personal licence shall pay a first maintenance fee to the Commission within 30 days of the fifth anniversary of the date on which the licence was issued.

(2) Thereafter the holder of a personal licence shall pay a further maintenance fee to the Commission every five years, within 30 days of the anniversary of the date on which the licence was issued.

(3) The maintenance fees payable pursuant to paragraphs (1) and (2) are—

(a) [£370], if the maintenance fee is in respect of a personal management licence; or

(b) [£145], if the maintenance fee is in respect of a personal functional licence.

Amendment

Para (3): in sub-para (a) sum '£370' in square brackets substituted by SI 2009/1971, regs 2, 4(a); in sub-para (b) sum '£145' in square brackets substituted by SI 2012/1851, reg 3.

6.1563 5 Fees for applications to vary personal licences

(1) The fee to accompany an application under section 104(1)(a) to vary a personal licence is—

(a) 25 per cent of the fee payable in respect of an application for a licence of the kind sought to be varied (determined in accordance with regulation 3(1)), if the application is to add or amend a licensed activity; or

(b) £25, if the application is to remove a licensed activity.

(2) The fee to accompany an application under section 104(1)(b) to vary a personal licence is £25.

(3) The fee to accompany an application under section 104(1)(c) to vary a personal licence is 25 per cent of the fee payable in respect of an application for a licence of the kind sought to be varied (determined in accordance with regulation 3(1)).

(4) In determining the fee to which a percentage reduction is made under this regulation, regulations 3(2) and (3) do not apply.

6.1564 6 Maximum fee for copy of personal licence

The fee for issuing a copy of a personal licence under section 107 shall not exceed £25.

GAMBLING APPEALS TRIBUNAL FEES REGULATIONS 2006

(SI 2006/3287)

6.1565–6.1571 . . . [1]

1 These Rules were revoked by SI 2010/22, art 5(3), Sch 4, Pt 1, as from 18 January 2010; for transitional provisions and savings see art 5(4), Sch 5 thereto.

GAMBLING APPEALS TRIBUNAL RULES 2006

(SI 2006/3293)

6.1572–6.1613 . . . [1]

[1] These Rules were revoked by SI 2010/22, art 5(3), Sch 4, Pt 1, as from 18 January 2010; for transitional provisions and savings see art 5(4), Sch 5 thereto.

GAMBLING ACT 2005 (PROCEEDINGS OF LICENSING COMMITTEES AND SUB-COMMITTEES) (PREMISES LICENCES AND PROVISIONAL STATEMENTS) (ENGLAND AND WALES) REGULATIONS 2007

(SI 2007/173)

Made . . . . *27th January 2007*
Laid before Parliament . . . . *29th January 2007*
Coming into force . . . . *30th April 2007*

The Secretary of State makes the following Regulations in exercise of the powers conferred by sections 9(2) and 197(2) of the Licensing Act 2003 and section 154(5) of the Gambling Act 2005.

6.1614 1 Citation, commencement and extent

(1) These Regulations may be cited as the Gambling Act 2005 (Proceedings of Licensing Committees and Sub-committees) (Premises Licences and Provisional Statements) (England and Wales) Regulations 2007 and shall come into force on 30th April 2007.

(2) These Regulations extend to England and Wales only.

6.1615 2 Interpretation

(1) In these Regulations—

"the Act" means the Gambling Act 2005;

"applicant" means a person who makes an application;

"application" means an application made under sections 159, 187, 188, 195, 197 or 204;

"relevant committee" means a licensing committee to which functions are delegated by virtue of section 154(1), or a licensing sub-committee empowered to discharge such functions by arrangement under section 10(1) of the Licensing Act 2003;

"notice of hearing" means a notice given to a party in accordance with regulation 5;

"party" means a person to whom a notice of hearing is given in accordance with regulation 5(1);

"representations" means representations made in accordance with regulations under section 161 in relation to an application, or section 197(6) or 200(5) in relation to a review;

"review" means a review under section 201; and

"working day" means a day which is not a Saturday or a Sunday, Christmas Day, Good Friday or a bank holiday in England and Wales under the Banking and Financial Dealings Act 1971.

(2) For the purposes of these Regulations, a reference to a review being determined is a reference to the [relevant committee][1] deciding what, if any, action it proposes to take under section 202 following a review.

(3) A reference in these regulations to a numbered section or subsection is a reference to that section or subsection of the Act so numbered, unless the contrary is indicated.

---

1 Words "relevant committee" in square brackets substituted by SI 2010/2440, reg 16.

6.1616 3 Scope

(1) These Regulations apply to the proceedings of a relevant committee in relation to the exercise of its functions under the following provisions of the Act—

- (a) subsections (1) and (2) of section 162 (which make provision about the circumstances in which a hearing is required to be held in relation to an application); or
- (b) section 201(4) (which makes provisions about the circumstances in which a hearing is required to be held in relation to a review).

(2) Subject to the provisions of these Regulations, it is for the relevant committee to determine the procedure to be followed in relation to the functions specified in paragraph (1).

(3) The Licensing Act 2003 (Hearings) Regulations 2005 do not apply to the proceedings of a relevant committee specified in paragraph (1).

6.1617 4 Period of time within which a hearing is to be held

(1) Where a hearing is required to be held under section 162(1) or section 201(4) in relation to a procedure listed in column 1 of the table in the Schedule, the relevant committee must arrange for the hearing to be commenced as soon as is reasonably practicable after the expiry of any period for representations prescribed under sections 161(2), 197(6) or 200(5).

(2) In any case where the hearing is to be held on more than one day, the relevant committee must arrange for the hearing to take place on consecutive working days.

6.1618 5 Notice of hearing

(1) A relevant committee must give notice of any hearing which is required to be held in relation to a procedure listed in column 1 of the table in the Schedule, to each of the relevant persons listed in column 2 of that table.

(2) A relevant committee must ensure that the notice referred to in paragraph (1)—

- (a) specifies the date on which, the place at which and the time when the hearing is to take place;
- (b) states that the relevant committee will make available the documents listed in the relevant entry in column 3 of the table in the Schedule to the following persons if those persons request them—
  - (i) any person who has made representations (unless the relevant committee considers that the representations are vexatious, frivolous or will certainly not influence the determination of the application), and
  - (ii) in the case of an application under section 188 for the transfer of a premises licence, the licensee; and
- (c) is sent so that, in the ordinary course of events, it is received no later than 10 working days before the first day on which the hearing is to be held (as specified in the notice).

6.1619 6 Information and documents to accompany the notice of hearing

(1) The notice of hearing must be accompanied by information in writing explaining the following—

(a) the consequences provided for under regulation 10(1) where a party informs the relevant committee that he does not wish to attend or be represented at the hearing, or fails to inform the relevant committee whether he wishes to attend or be represented at the hearing;

(b) the requirements imposed on the relevant committee in conducting a hearing as set out in regulations 8 and 9;

(c) the consequences provided for in regulation 10(2) where a party has indicated that he wishes to attend or be represented at the hearing, but fails to attend or be represented at the hearing;

(d) the procedure to be followed at the hearing;

(e) the time limit and method, if any, by which a party should inform the relevant committee that he wishes to attend or address the hearing;

(f) the time limit and method, if any, by which a party should inform the relevant committee that he wishes to be assisted or represented by another person;

(g) the time limit and method, if any, by which a party should inform the licensing authority that he will want to call a witness to give evidence at the hearing, and the matters in relation to which he wishes that witness to give evidence;

(h) the time limit and method, if any, by which a party should inform the relevant committee that he wishes to withdraw any representations;

(i) the time limit and method, if any, by which a party should inform the relevant committee that he is willing to consent to the application being determined without a hearing;

(j) the matters, if any, on which the relevant committee considers at the time that it will want clarification at the hearing from a party.

(2) Where a hearing is required to be held in relation to a procedure listed in column 1 of the table in the Schedule, a relevant committee must send the documents listed in the relevant entry in column 3 of the table in the Schedule—

(a) to the following persons—

(i) the applicant, and

(ii) in the case of a review, the licensee; and

(b) if requested by him, to—

(i) a person who has made representations in relation to the application or review (unless the relevant committee considers that the representations are vexatious, frivolous or will certainly not influence the determination of the application), and

(ii) in the case of an application under section 188 for a premises licence, the licensee.

6.1620 7 Power to postpone

(1) A relevant committee may at any time—

(a) postpone a hearing to a specified date, or

(b) arrange for a hearing to be held on a date specified by the committee.

(2) A relevant committee may take the actions specified in paragraph (1) if it considers it necessary—

(a) to enable it to consider any information or documents provided by any party in response to a notice under regulation 6, or at the hearing, or

(b) having regard to the ability of any party, person representing a party or witness to attend the hearing.

(3) Where a relevant committee has adjourned a hearing to a specified date it must, as soon as reasonably practicable, notify the parties of the new date, time and place for the hearing.

(4) Where a relevant committee has arranged for the hearing to be held on a specified additional date it must, as soon as reasonably practicable, notify the parties of the additional date, time and place for the hearing.

6.1621 8 Hearings to be public

(1) Subject to paragraph (2), the hearing must take place in public.

(2) A relevant committee may direct that all or part of a hearing must be in private if it is satisfied that it is necessary in all the circumstances of the case, having regard to—

- (a) any unfairness to a party that is likely to result from a hearing in public; and
- (b) the need to protect as far as possible, the commercial or other legitimate interests of a party.

6.1622 9 Proceedings of a relevant committee in conducting a hearing

(1) Subject to regulations 8 and 11, a relevant committee must permit a party to attend a hearing and be assisted or represented by any person whether or not that person is legally qualified.

(2) At the beginning of the hearing the relevant committee must explain the procedure that it proposes to follow in conducting the hearing.

(3) In conducting a hearing the relevant committee must ensure that each party is given the opportunity to—

- (a) address the relevant committee on any matter that is relevant to the application or review, or any representations made on the application or review;
- (b) call witnesses to give evidence on any matter that is relevant to the application or review, or any representations made on the application or review;
- (c) provide further information on, or explanation of, any matter on which the relevant committee has indicated that it will want further clarification under regulation 6(1)(j).

(4) In conducting a hearing the relevant committee must also—

- (a) permit any party to question any other party or person representing a party on any matter that is relevant to the application or review, or any representations made on the application or review, where the relevant committee considers that in all the circumstances it is appropriate to do so; and
- (b) take into consideration documentary or other information in support of the application or representations produced by a party—
  - (i) before the hearing; or
  - (ii) at the hearing, with the consent of all the other parties attending the hearing.

(5) Without prejudice to paragraphs (3) and (4), a hearing must be conducted so that it takes the form of a discussion led by the relevant committee, and the committee must not permit any cross-examination unless it considers that cross-examination is required for it properly to consider the application or representations made by any party.

6.1623 10 Failure of parties to attend the hearing

(1) A relevant committee may proceed with a hearing in the absence of a party or a party's representative if the party has—

6: Gambling Act 2005: SIs

(a) informed the committee that he does not intend to attend or be represented at the hearing (and has not subsequently advised the committee otherwise);
(b) failed to inform the committee whether he intends to attend or be represented at the hearing; or
(c) left the hearing in circumstances enabling the committee reasonably to conclude that he does not intend to participate further.

(2) If a party has indicated that he does intend to attend or be represented at the hearing, but fails to so attend or be so represented, the relevant committee may—
(a) adjourn the hearing to a specified date if it considers it to be in the public interest, or
(b) proceed with the hearing in the party's absence.

(3) Where the hearing proceeds in the absence of a party, the relevant committee must consider at the hearing the application or representations made by that party.

(4) Where, under this Regulation, the relevant committee adjourns the hearing to a specified date it must, as soon as reasonably practicable, notify the parties of the date, time and place to which the hearing has been adjourned.

6.1624 11 Exclusion of disruptive persons

(1) The relevant committee may require any person attending the hearing who in their opinion is behaving in a disruptive manner, or in breach of conditions specified under this paragraph, to leave the hearing and may—
(a) refuse to permit him to return, or
(b) permit him to return only on such conditions as the relevant committee may specify.

(2) The relevant committee may allow a person who is attending the hearing and in their opinion is behaving in a disruptive manner, or in breach of conditions specified under paragraph (1), to remain at the hearing only on such conditions as the committee may specify.

(3) Where a person is required to leave the hearing in accordance with paragraph (1), the relevant committee must—
(a) permit him to submit in writing, before the end of the hearing, any information which he would have been entitled to give orally had he not been required to leave; and
(b) take into account that information in reaching a determination of the application or review.

6.1625 12 Procedure where a hearing is not to take place

Where the parties have notified the relevant committee that they consent to the application or review being determined without a hearing under sections 162(2) or 201(4)(a), the relevant committee must, as soon as reasonably practicable—
(a) notify all the parties that the hearing has been dispensed with, and
(b) determine the application or review.

6.1626 13 Determination of an application or a review

Following a hearing under section 162(1) or 201(4), a relevant committee must determine the application or review before the end of the period of 5 working days starting with the day after the last day of the hearing.

6.1627 14 Power to extend time

(1) A relevant committee may extend the time limit provided for in regulation 13 for a specified period where it considers an extension to be in the public interest.

(2) Where the relevant committee has extended the time limit in accordance with paragraph (1), it must, as soon as reasonably practicable, give a notice of the extension to the parties stating the period of the extension and the reasons for it.

6.1628 15 Record of proceedings

(1) The relevant committee must ensure that a record of the hearing is taken in a permanent and intelligible form.

(2) The relevant committee must ensure that any such record is kept for a period of six years from the date that the application or review is finally determined (including, in either case, any appeal or judicial review).

6.1629 16 Irregularities

(1) Subject to paragraph (2), a relevant committee may disregard any irregularity resulting from a failure to comply with a provision of these Regulations, or with a procedure otherwise determined by the relevant committee in accordance with regulation 3(2), where that irregularity comes to its attention prior to it making a determination of the application or review.

(2) If the relevant committee considers that any person may have been prejudiced by any such irregularity, it must take such steps that it considers necessary to remedy the consequences of the irregularity, before reaching its determination.

6.1630 17 Clerical mistakes

A relevant committee may correct clerical mistakes in any document recording a determination of the committee, or errors arising in such a document from an accidental slip or omission.

6.1631 18 Notices etc

Except where otherwise provided, a requirement under these Regulations to give a notice (or to notify) is a requirement to give notice in writing; and for that purpose, a message sent by facsimile transmission or electronic mail must be treated as a notice given in writing.

6.1632

SCHEDULE 1

Regulations 4(1), 5(1), 6(2)

Column 1	Column 2	Column 3
Procedure in relation to which a hearing is required to be held	Persons to whom notice must be given	Copies of documents to accompany the notice of hearing
Application for a premises licence under section 159	(1) The applicant (2) Any person who has made (and not withdrawn) representations about the application	Representations made in relation to the application (unless the relevant committee considers that the representations are vexatious, frivolous or will certainly not influence the determination of the application)
Application to vary a premises licence under section 187	(1) The applicant (2) Any person who has made (and not withdrawn) representations about the application	Representations made in relation to the application (unless the relevant committee considers that the representations are vexatious, frivolous or will certainly not influence the determination of the application)

Column 1	Column 2	Column 3
Application for a premises licence to be transferred under sections 188 and 189	(1) The applicant (2) Any person who has made (and not withdrawn) representations about the application (3) The licensee	Representations made in relation to the application (unless the relevant committee considers that the representations are vexatious, frivolous or will certainly not influence the determination of the application)
Application for a licence to be reinstated under sections 195 and 196	(1) The applicant (2) Any person who has made (and not withdrawn) representations about the application	Representations made in relation to the application (unless the relevant committee considers that the representations are vexatious, frivolous or will certainly not influence the determination of the application)
Application for a provisional statement under section 204	(1) The applicant (2) Any person who has made (and not withdrawn) representations about the application	Representations in relation to the application (unless the relevant committee considers that the representations are vexatious, frivolous or will certainly not influence the determination of the application)
Review of a premises licence under section 201	(1) The applicant (2) Any person who has made (and not withdrawn) representations about the review (3) The licensee	Representations made in relation to the review (unless the relevant committee considers that the representations are vexatious, frivolous or will certainly not influence the determination of the review)

GAMBLING ACT 2005 (INSPECTION) (PROVISION OF INFORMATION) REGULATIONS 2007

(SI 2007/319)

Made . . . . *8th February 2007*
Laid before Parliament . . . . *8th February 2007*
Coming into force . . . . *21st May 2007*

The Secretary of State makes the following regulations in exercise of the powers conferred by sections 322(1) and (2) and of the Gambling Act 2005:

6.1636 1 Citation and commencement

These Regulations may be cited as the Gambling Act 2005 (Inspection) (Provision of Information) Regulations 2007 and shall come into force on 21st May 2007.

6.1637 2 Interpretation

(1) In these Regulations—

"the Act" means the Gambling Act 2005;

"appropriate recipient" means a person present at a premises at any time during an inspection, and who appears to the inspector to occupy the premises or to be responsible for their management;

"inspection" means the entry of an inspector into premises pursuant to a power conferred by Part 15, and the carrying out there of activities authorised under that Part;

"inspector" means a constable, enforcement officer or authorised person;

"interested person" in relation to an inspection means any of the following:

(a) the Gambling Commission;

(b) an appropriate recipient;

(c) the holder of a relevant authorisation in relation to the premises;

(d) where an inspection occurs pursuant to section 315 (which enables an inspector to enter premises in respect of which a temporary use notice has been given), the person who gave the temporary use notice;

(e) a society registered with a local authority in accordance with Part 5 of Schedule 11 of the Act, where the premises are owned or used by that society at the time of the inspection;

(f) a person who occupies the premises or is responsible for their management at the time of the inspection;

"relevant authorisation" in relation to the premises means a premises licence, a permit issued under the Act or an on-premises alcohol licence that has effect in relation to the premises at the time the inspection takes place;

(2) A reference in these Regulations to a numbered Part or section is a reference to that Part or section of the Act so numbered.

6.1638 3 Evidence of identity

Whilst an inspection is taking place, an inspector must ensure that a person who accompanies him pursuant to section 324 produces evidence of his identity to an appropriate recipient, or if there is no appropriate recipient, to a person who works at the premises and is there in his capacity as an employee.

6.1639 4 Statement on entry

(1) Where—

(a) an appropriate recipient is present at the premises at the start of an inspection, or

(b) such a recipient arrives at the premises during the inspection,

an inspector carrying out the inspection must communicate to the recipient the information set out in paragraph (2) (whether orally or in writing) as soon as reasonably practicable after the start of the inspection or the arrival of the recipient.

(2) The information is—

(a) that anyone who is an interested person in relation to the premises may, following the inspection, make a request in writing for the inspector to provide a written record of the inspection;

(b) the manner in which and the person to whom an interested person can make that request; and

(c) the persons, or categories of persons, who are interested persons in relation to those premises.

(3) Paragraph (1) does not apply where the information set out in paragraph (2) has already been communicated to an appropriate recipient during the inspection.

(4) If at no time during an inspection an appropriate recipient is present at the premises, an inspector must leave a written notice on the premises setting out—

(a) the fact that the premises have been inspected;

(b) the name of any inspector who carried out the inspection;

(c) the date of the inspection; and
(d) the information referred to in paragraph (2).

6.1640
5 If—
(a) an inspector questions a person on the premises under section 317(1)(b), and
(b) that person refuses to answer the question,

the inspector must orally inform the person that he is exercising a power to question under section 317(1)(b) and that it is an offence under section 326 if, without reasonable excuse, a person obstructs, or fails to cooperate with, an inspector who is exercising or seeking to exercise a power under or by virtue of Part 15.

6.1641 6 Written record of inspection

(1) If, following an inspection, an interested person makes a request in writing for a written record of the inspection, the inspector must, as soon as reasonably practicable after receipt of the request, supply the person with a written record including the information set out in paragraph (2).

(2) The information is, in relation to that inspection—
(a) the postal address of the premises;
(b) the name of the inspector who visited the premises and the name of any person accompanying him;
(c) the date and time when the inspector entered the premises;
(d) a description of the power that the inspector exercised to enter the premises, together with a reference to the relevant section of the Act;
(e) a record of any part of the premises, or any machine or other thing on the premises, that was inspected in exercise of the inspector's power under section 317(1)(a);
(f) a record of any written or electronic record to which the inspector required access under section 317(1)(c);
(g) a description of any copies of written or electronic records that were supplied to the inspector in compliance with his request under section 317(1)(d), specifying the form in which they were supplied;
(h) a record of anything that was removed from the premises and the reasons for its removal;
(i) a record of whether any force was used for the purpose of entering the premises, by whom it was used and the reason why it was used;
(j) if force was used for the purpose of entering the premises, a record of what steps were taken in accordance with section 325, to ensure that when the inspector left the premises they were as secure as they were before he entered;
(k) a record of any damage caused during the inspection, and of the circumstances in which it was caused.

GAMBLING ACT 2005 (FAMILY ENTERTAINMENT CENTRE GAMING MACHINE) (PERMITS) REGULATIONS 2007

(SI 2007/454)

Made . . . . *19th February 2007*
Laid before Parliament . . . . *20th February 2007*
Coming into force . . . . *21st May 2007*

The Secretary of State makes the following Regulations in exercise of the powers conferred by section 355(1) and paragraphs 5(d), 11, 18(3) and 21(2) of Schedule 10 to the Gambling Act 2005:

6.1642 1 Commencement, citation and application

(1) These Regulations may be cited as the Gambling Act 2005 (Family Entertainment Centre Gaming Machine) (Permits) Regulations 2007 and shall come into force on 21st May 2007.

(2) These Regulations apply to England and Wales and Scotland, except regulations 3 and 6 which apply only to England and Wales.

6.1643 2 Interpretation

(1) In these Regulations—

"the Act" means the Gambling Act 2005;

"existing operator" means a person who—

(a) makes an application for a permit before 1st September 2007;

(b) on the date on which he makes the application—

(i) holds a permit issued under section 34 of the Gaming Act 1968 (a "section 34 permit"), or

(ii) is applying to the appropriate authority (within the meaning of paragraph 1 of Schedule 9 to the Gaming Act 1968) for a section 34 permit, and the application (including any appeal) has not been finally determined; and

(c) the application relates to the same or substantially the same premises as those to which the section 34 permit, or the application for a section 34 permit, relates.

"permit" means a family entertainment centre gaming machine permit;

(2) A reference in these Regulations to a numbered paragraph is a reference to that paragraph of Schedule 10 to the Act so numbered.

6.1644 3 Application fee

For the purposes of paragraph 5(d)—

(a) (subject to sub-paragraphs (b) and (c)) the fee to accompany an application for a permit is £300;

(b) the fee to accompany an application for a permit made by an existing operator is £100;

(c) the fee to accompany an application for renewal of a permit under paragraph 18(1) is £300.

Extent

This regulation does not extend to Scotland: see reg 1(2).

6.1645 4 Form of Permit

A permit must be in the form prescribed in Schedule 1.

6.1646 5 Fee for change of name

For the purposes of paragraph 11(2)(a)(i), the fee to be sent with a request that a new name be substituted for the old name specified on a permit is £25.

6.1647 6 Fee for copy of permit

For the purposes of paragraph 21(2), the fee to accompany an application for a copy of a permit is £15.

6.1648
SCHEDULE 1
Regulation 4

This form is prescribed by regulation 4 of the Gambling Act 2005 (Family Entertainment Centre Gaming Machine) (Permits) Regulations 2007
Family Entertainment Centre Gaming Machine Permit
This family entertainment centre gaming machine permit authorises . . . . *(name of permit holder)* to make Category D gaming machines available for use on the following premises . . . . *(address of premises, including postcode)*
Date on which this permit takes effect or is renewed:
. . . .
Date on which this permit expires:
. . . .
This permit is issued by . . . . *(Name and address of licensing authority issuing permit)*

GAMBLING ACT 2005 (PRIZE GAMING) (PERMITS) REGULATIONS 2007

(SI 2007/455)

Made . . . . *19th February 2007*
Laid before Parliament . . . . *20th February 2007*
Coming into force . . . . *21st May 2007*

The Secretary of State makes the following Regulations in exercise of the powers conferred by section 355(1) and paragraphs 6(e), 12, 18(3) and 21(2) of Schedule 14 to the Gambling Act 2005:

6.1649 1 Commencement, citation and application

(1) These Regulations may be cited as the Gambling Act 2005 (Prize Gaming) (Permits) Regulations 2007 and shall come into force on 21st May 2007.

(2) These Regulations apply to England and Wales and Scotland, except regulations 3 and 6 which apply only to England and Wales.

6.1650 2 Interpretation

(1) In these Regulations—

"the Act" means the Gambling Act 2005;

"existing operator" means a person who—

(a) makes an application for a permit before 1st September 2007;

(b) on the date on which he makes the application—

(i) holds a permit issued under section 16 of the Lotteries and Amusements Act 1976 (a "section 16 permit"), or

(ii) is applying to the appropriate authority (within the meaning of paragraph 1(1) of Schedule 3 to the Lotteries and Amusements Act 1976) for a section 16 permit, and the application (including any appeal) has not been finally determined; and

(c) the application relates to the same or substantially the same premises as those to which the section 16 permit, or the application for a section 16 permit, relates.

"permit" means a prize gaming permit;

(2) A reference in these Regulations to a numbered paragraph is a reference to that paragraph of Schedule 14 to the Act so numbered.

6.1651 3 Application fee

For the purposes of paragraph 6(e)—

(a) (subject to sub-paragraphs (b) and (c)) the fee to accompany an application for a permit is £300;

(b) the fee to accompany an application for a permit made by an existing operator is £100;

(c) the fee to accompany an application for renewal of a permit under paragraph 18(1) is £300.

6.1652 4 Form of Permit

A permit must be in the form prescribed in Schedule 1.

6.1653 5 Fee for change of name

For the purposes of paragraph 12(2)(a)(i), the fee to be sent with a request that a new name be substituted for the old name specified on a permit is £25.

6.1654 6 Fee for copy of permit

For the purposes of paragraph 21(2), the fee to accompany an application for a copy of a permit is £15.

6.1655

SCHEDULE 1

Regulation 4

This form is prescribed by regulation 4 of the Gambling Act 2005 (Prize Gaming) (Permits) Regulations 2007

Prize Gaming Permit

This permit does not authorise the holder to make gaming machines available for use.

This prize gaming permit authorises . . . . (name of permit holder) to provide facilities for prize gaming (as described below) on the following premises . . . . (address of premises, including postcode) in respect of . . . . (nature of the gaming in respect of which permit has effect)

Date on which this permit takes effect or is renewed:

. . . .

Date on which this permit expires:

. . . .

This permit is issued by . . . . (Name and address of licensing authority issuing permit)

6: Gambling Act 2005: SIs

GAMBLING ACT 2005 (PREMISES LICENCES AND PROVISIONAL STATEMENTS) REGULATIONS 2007

(SI 2007/459)

Made .... *19th February 2007*
Laid before Parliament .... *20th February 2007*
Coming into force .... *21st May 2007*

The Secretary of State makes the following Regulations in exercise of the powers conferred by sections 151(2), 159(6) to (8), 160(1) and (2), 161(2), 164, 165(2) and (3), 187(3) and (4), 188(2), 189(4), 195(3), 196(3), 204(2) and (3) and 355(1) of the Gambling Act 2005.

PART 1
GENERAL

6.1656 1 Citation, commencement and application

(1) These Regulations may be cited as the Gambling Act 2005 (Premises Licences and Provisional Statements) Regulations 2007 and shall come into force on 21st May 2007.

(2) Subject to paragraph (3), these Regulations apply only—

(a) applications made to licensing authorities in England and Wales, and

(b) premises licences and provisional statements issued by licensing authorities in England and Wales.

(3) Paragraphs (2) to (4) of regulation 10, in so far as they relate to applications under section 204 for a provisional statement in respect of premises which the applicant expects to be constructed or altered, apply to applications made to licensing authorities in England and Wales and Scotland.

6.1657 2 Interpretation

(1) In these Regulations—

"the Act" means the Gambling Act 2005;

"application", unless the contrary appears, means any of the following—

(a) an application under section 159 for a premises licence;

(b) an application under section 187 to vary a premises licence;

(c) an application under section 188 to transfer a premises licence;

(d) an application under section 195 for the reinstatement of a premises licence;

(e) an application under section 204 for a provisional statement;

"the Commencement and Transitional Provisions Order" means the Gambling Act 2005 (Commencement No 6 and Transitional Provisions) Order 2006;

"converted premises licence" means a premises licence issued in pursuance of paragraph 54 of Schedule 4 to the Commencement and Transitional Provisions Order (which provides for the conversion of licences and other documents under enactments to be repealed by the Act into premises licences under that Act); and any reference to a "converted casino premises licence" is to be construed accordingly;

"the licensing authority" means—

(a) in relation to an application, the licensing authority to whom the application is made, and

(b) in relation to a premises licence or a provisional statement, the licensing authority who issued the licence or statement;

"operating licence number", in relation to an operating licence, means the reference number given by the Gambling Commission to the operating licence which is unique to that licence and which is specified in it;

"relevant operating licence" means—

(a) in relation to a person holding a premises licence, an operating licence which authorises the person to carry out the activities for which the premises licence authorises the premises to be used;

(b) in relation to a person to whom a provisional statement is issued, an operating licence which authorises the person to carry out the activities for which the premises to which the statement relates would be used.

"summary" means a summary of the terms and conditions of a premises licence issued under section 164(1)(c);

"working day" means a day which is not a Saturday or a Sunday, Christmas Day, Good Friday or a bank holiday in England and Wales under the Banking and Financial Dealings Act 1971.

(2) A reference in these Regulations to a numbered section is a reference to the section of the Act so numbered.

PART 2
FORM AND CONTENT OF APPLICATIONS

6.1658 3 Form and content of applications for a premises licence

(1) Subject to the following provisions of this paragraph, an application for a premises licence under section 159 shall be in the form, and contain the information, specified in Part 1 of Schedule 1.

(2) Subject to paragraph (3), an application for a premises licence in respect of premises which are a vessel shall be in the form, and contain the information, specified in Part 2 of Schedule 1.

(3) An application for a converted premises licence shall be in the form, and contain the information, specified in—

(a) Part 3 of Schedule 1, if it is in respect of premises which are not a vessel; or

(b) Part 4 of Schedule 1, if it is in respect of premises which are a vessel.

(4) This regulation is subject to regulation 11.

6.1659 4 Plan to accompany applications for a premises licence

(1) An application for a premises licence under section 159 shall be accompanied by a scale plan of the premises to which the application relates which complies with the following provisions of this regulation.

(2) The plan must show—

(a) the extent of the boundary or perimeter of the premises;

(b) where the premises include, or consist of, one or more buildings, the location of any external or internal walls of each such building;

(c) where the premises form part of a building, the location of any external or internal walls of the building which are included in the premises;

(d) where the premises are a vessel or a part of a vessel, the location of any part of the sides of the vessel, and of any internal walls of the vessel, which are included in the premises;

(e) the location of each point of entry to and exit from the premises, including in each case a description of the place from which entry is made or to which the exit leads; and

(f) any other matter required in accordance with the following provisions of this regulation.

(3) Where the application is for a casino premises licence [other than a converted casino premises licence][1], the plan must show—

(a) the principal entrance to the premises of those identified in accordance with paragraph (2)(e);

(b) the location and extent of any part of the premises which will be a table gaming area;

(c) the location and extent of any other part of the premises which will be used for providing facilities for gambling in reliance on the licence; and

(d) the location and extent of any part of the premises which will be a non-gambling area.

(4) Where the application is for a regional casino premises licence, the plan must show—

(a) the location and extent of any part of the premises to which children or young persons, or both, will have access;

(b) where any part of the premises referred to in sub-paragraph (a) is immediately adjacent to any part of the casino which will be used to provide facilities for gambling in reliance on the licence, the nature and location of any barrier or other thing separating the two parts of the casino

[(4A) Subject to paragraph (4B), where the application is for a converted casino premises licence, the plan must show—

(a) the principal entrance to the premises of those identified in accordance with paragraph (2)(e); and

(b) the location and extent of any part of the premises which will be used for providing facilities for gambling in reliance on the licence; and

(c) the location and extent of any part of the premises which will be a non-gambling area.

(4B) The requirement imposed by sub-paragraph (c) of paragraph (4A) only applies where the combined floor area of those parts of the casino identified in accordance with sub-paragraph (b) of that paragraph is 200 square metres or more.][2]

(5) Where the application is for a bingo premises licence in respect of premises to which children or young persons will be permitted to have access, the plan must show—

(a) the location and extent of any part of the premises which will be used to provide facilities for gaming in reliance on the licence (other than those parts which include Category B or C gaming machines);

(b) the location and extent of any part of the premises in which Category B or C gaming machines will be made available for use in reliance on the licence;

(c) the nature and location of any barrier or other thing separating any part of the premises in which Category B or C gaming machines will be made available for use from any other part of the premises.

(6) Where the application is for an adult gaming centre premises licence, the plan must show the location and extent of any part of the premises in which gaming machines will be made available for use in reliance on the licence.

(7) Where the application is for a family entertainment centre premises licence, the plan must show—

(a) the location and extent of any part of the premises in which Category C gaming machines will be made available for use in reliance on the licence;

(b) the location and extent of any part of the premises in which Category D gaming machines will be made available for use in reliance on the licence; and

(c) the nature and location of any barrier or other thing separating any part of the premises in which Category C gaming machines will be made available for use from any other part of the premises.

(8) Where the application is for a betting premises licence, other than in respect of a track, the plan must show the location and extent of any part of the premises which will be used to provide facilities for gambling in reliance on the licence.

(9) Where the application is for a betting premises licence in respect of a track, the plan must show—

(a) the location and extent of any part of the premises which is a five times rule betting area;

(b) the location and extent of any other parts of the premises which will be used for providing facilities for betting in reliance on the licence;

(c) the location and extent of any part of the premises in which Category B or C gaming machines will be made available for use in reliance on the licence;

(d) the nature and location of any barrier or other thing separating any part of the premises in which Category B or C gaming machines will be made available for use from any other part of the premises.

(10) In this regulation—

(a) "betting operator" means a person who accepts or negotiates bets in the course of the business of the holder of a general betting operating licence or a pool betting operating licence;

(b) "five times betting rule area", in relation to a track, means any part of the track in respect of which, in accordance with conditions attached under section 167, the charge for admission to that part of the track payable by betting operators may not exceed five times the cost of the highest charge paid by members of the public who are authorised to enter that part of the track;

(c) "non-gambling area" means any part of the proposed casino—

(i) which will be made available to customers but will not be used for providing facilities for gambling, and

(ii) which, unless it is a lobby area or toilet facilities, will contain recreational facilities for use by customers on the premises;

(d) "partially automated gaming table" means equipment that would fall within the definition of gaming machine in section 235 but for its exclusion from that definition by subsection (2)(h) of that section;

(e) "table gaming area" means any part of the proposed casino which is to be used for—

(i) casino games played on gaming tables (including wholly or partially automated gaming tables); or

(ii) real games of equal chance, other than bingo, played on a table; and

(f) "wholly automated gaming table" means equipment that would fall within the definition of a gaming machine in section 235 but for its exclusion from that definition by subsection (2)(i) of that section.

---

1 Words "other than a converted casino premises licence" in square brackets inserted by SI 2007/1775, reg 2(1), (2)(a).

2 Paras (4A), (4B): inserted by SI 2007/1775, reg 2(1), (2)(b).

6.1660 5 Documents to accompany applications for a converted premises licence

(1) An application under section 159 for a converted premises licence shall be accompanied by—

(a) a copy of the equivalent permission under the existing legislation; or

(b) where the applicant is applying for but has not been granted the equivalent permission under the existing legislation, copies of the documents submitted by the applicant in applying for the permission.

(2) Where an applicant is unable to comply with paragraph (1)(a) because it is not reasonably practicable for him to produce a copy of the relevant permission under the existing legislation, he must include with the application under section 159 a statement—

(a) explaining why it is not reasonably practicable to do so, and

(b) setting out the nature of the permission, the date on which it was granted and by whom.

(3) In this regulation and in regulation 6, "the equivalent permission under the existing legislation", in relation to an application for a converted premises licence, means the licence or permit under the Betting, Gaming and Lotteries Act 1963 or the Gaming Act 1968—

(a) held by the applicant in respect of the premises to which the application relates, and

(b) by virtue of which the applicant is entitled to be issued with a converted premises licence.

6.1661 6 Written statement to accompany applications for a casino premises licence

(1) Where a person who is applying for a casino premises licence—

(a) is entitled to apply for a converted casino premises licence in respect of the premises to which the application relates, but

(b) does not want the application to be treated as an application for a converted casino premises licence,

the application must be accompanied by a written statement confirming that the applicant does not want paragraph 54 of Schedule 4 to the Commencement and Transitional Provisions Order (which provides for the grant of applications for a premises licence made by a person holding the equivalent permission under the existing legislation) to apply.

6.1662 7 Form and content of applications to vary a premises licence

(1) Subject to regulation 11, an application under section 187 to vary a premises licence shall be in the form, and contain the information, specified in Schedule 2.

(2) Where the application includes an application to vary the plan which forms part of the premises licence under section 151(1)(g), the application must be accompanied by a scale plan which complies with paragraph (3).

(3) The plan must show the matters which it would be required to show under regulation 4 if the application were for the issue of a premises licence—

(a) of the same type as that to which the application relates; and

(b) which included the variations specified in the application.

6.1663 8 Form and content of applications to transfer a premises licence

Subject to regulation 11, an application under section 188 for the transfer of a premises licence shall be in the form, and contain the information, specified in Schedule 3.

6.1664 9 Form and content of applications for the reinstatement of a premises licence

Subject to regulation 11, an application under section 195 for the reinstatement of a premises licence shall be in the form, and contain the information, specified in Schedule 4.

6.1665 10 Form and content of applications for a provisional statement

(1) Subject to regulation 11, an application under section 204 for a provisional statement shall be in the form, and contain the information, specified in—

(a) Part 1 of Schedule 5, if it is in respect of premises or proposed premises which are not a vessel; or

(b) Part 2 of Schedule 5, if it is in respect of premises or proposed premises which are a vessel.

(2) An application under section 204 for a provisional statement must be accompanied by a scale plan which complies with the requirements of paragraphs (2) to (9) of regulation 4 (as modified in accordance with the following provisions of this regulation).

(3) Where the application relates to premises which the applicant expects to be constructed or altered, any reference in paragraphs (2) to (9) of regulation 4 to the premises to which the application relates is to have effect for the purposes of this regulation as a reference to those premises as they are expected to be when constructed or altered.

(4) Any reference in paragraphs (3) to (9) of regulation 4 to an application for a particular kind of premises licence is to have effect for the purposes of this regulation as a reference to an application for a provisional statement in respect of premises whose use would require the same kind of premises licence.

6.1666 11 Matters not required to be included in an application

(1) Where matters are included in square brackets in any form in Schedules 1 to 5, they are intended to indicate and explain the information to be specified in the application to which the form relates, and are not required to be included in the application.

(2) The first page of the form used for an application may include any symbol or logo which is commonly used by the licensing authority to identify documents produced by it.

PART 3
NOTICE OF APPLICATION AND PERIOD FOR REPRESENTATIONS

6.1667 12 Notice of application

(1) Subject to paragraph (2) a person making an application (other than a fast track application) must give notice of the application to each of the authorities which in accordance with section 157 are the responsible authorities in relation to the premises to which the application relates.

(2) Where the application is for the transfer or reinstatement of a premises licence, the applicant must give notice of his application only to the authorities mentioned in paragraphs (a), (b), (c), (h) and (i) of section 157.

(3) Subject to paragraphs (10) and (11), a notice under paragraph (1) must be in the form specified in—

(a) Part 1 of Schedule 6, where the application is for a premises licence;

(b) Part 3 of that Schedule, where the application is to vary a premises licence;

(c) Part 5 of that Schedule, where the application is to transfer a premises licence;

(d) Part 6 of that Schedule, where the application is for the reinstatement of a premises licence; and

(e) Part 7 of that Schedule, where the application is for a provisional statement.

(4) A notice under paragraph (1) must be given within a period of 7 days beginning on the date on which the application is made.

(5) Paragraph (6) applies where a person has made an application—

(a) under section 159 for a premises licence (other than where the application is a fast track application),
(b) under section 187 to vary a premises licence, or
(c) under section 204 for a provisional statement.

(6) Where this paragraph applies the applicant must publish notice of his application—
(a) in a local newspaper or, if there is none, a local newsletter, circular or similar document, circulating within the licensing authority's area on at least one occasion during the period of ten working days starting with the day after the day on which the application is made to the authority; and
(b) by displaying a notice on the premises to which the application relates—
(i) in a place at which it can conveniently be read by members of the public from the exterior of the premises;
(ii) for a period of no less than 28 consecutive days starting on the day on which the application is made to the licensing authority.

(7) Paragraph (8) applies in a case where—
(a) the application is for a provisional statement in respect of premises, and
(b) the premises have not been constructed, or the applicant does not have the right to occupy the premises, on the date on which the application is made.

(8) In any case to which this paragraph applies, paragraph (6)(b)(i) is to have effect as if it required the applicant to display the notice at a place—
(a) which is as near as reasonably practicable to the premises or proposed premises, and
(b) where it can conveniently be read by members of the public.

(9) Subject to paragraphs (10) and (11), a notice under sub-paragraph (a) or (b) of paragraph (6) is to be in the form specified in—
(a) Part 2 of Schedule 6, where the application is for a premises licence;
(b) Part 4 of that Schedule, where the application is to vary a premises licence; and
(c) Part 8 of that Schedule, where the application is for a provisional statement.

(10) Where matters are included in square brackets in any form in Schedule 6, they are intended to indicate and explain the information to be specified in the notice to which the form relates, and are not required to be included in the notice.

(11) The first page of a notice given or published under this regulation may include any symbol or logo which is commonly used by the licensing authority to identify documents produced by it.

(12) In this regulation, "fast track application" means an application for a premises licence to which paragraph 57 of Schedule 4 to the Commencement and Transitional Provisions Order (which modifies Part 8 of the Act in its application to certain applications for a converted premises licence) applies.

6.1668 13 Failure to give proper notice of application to a responsible authority

(1) This regulation applies where a person, who gives notice to a responsible authority under paragraph (1) of regulation 12, fails to give proper notice of his application within the period provided for under paragraph (4) of that regulation.

(2) For the purposes of paragraph (1), a person fails to give proper notice of his application if he fails to give a notice which complies with the requirements of these Regulations as to the form or manner in which it is to be given.

(3) The applicant must give notice to the responsible authority in a form and manner which complies with the requirements of these Regulations (other than as to the period within which the notice is to be given) as soon as practicable after the end of the period referred to in paragraph (1).

(4) In a case to which this regulation applies, the responsible authority concerned must make any representations under section 161 within the period of 28 days beginning on the day on which it receives the notice referred to in paragraph (3).

(5) The licensing authority may not grant the application until—

(a) notice has been given by the applicant in accordance with paragraph (3); and

(b) the period referred to in paragraph (4) has elapsed,

and if it purports to do so any licence issued by the authority shall be of no effect.

(6) Subject to paragraph (5), the licensing authority may disregard any irregularity in relation to the giving of notice under [regulation 12(1)][1].

---

[1] Words "regulation 12(1)" in square brackets substituted by SI 2007/1775, reg 2(1), (4).

6.1669 14 Failure properly to publish notice of an application

(1) This regulation applies where a person, who publishes notice of his application under sub-paragraph (a) or (b) of paragraph (6) of regulation 12, fails to publish a proper notice of his application within the period provided for under the relevant sub-paragraph.

(2) For the purposes of paragraph (1), a person fails to publish a proper notice of his application if the published notice does not comply with the requirements of these Regulations as to the form or manner in which it is to be published.

(3) The applicant must publish notice of the application in a form and manner which complies with the requirements of these Regulations (other than as to the timing of the publication) as soon as practicable after the end of the period referred to in paragraph (1).

(4) In a case to which this regulation applies an interested party must make any representations under section 161 within the period of 28 days beginning on the day on which the notice referred to in paragraph (3) is published.

(5) The licensing authority may not grant the application until—

(a) notice has been published by the applicant in accordance with paragraph (3); and

(b) the period referred to in paragraph (4) has elapsed,

and if it purports to do so any licence issued by the authority shall be of no effect.

(6) Subject to paragraph (5), the licensing authority may disregard any irregularity in relation to the publication of the notice under sub-paragraph (a) or (b) of paragraph (6) of regulation 12.

6.1670 15 Period within which representations are to be made by an interested party or responsible authority

(1) This regulation prescribes, for the purposes of section 161, the period within which a responsible authority or interested party may make representations in relation to an application.

(2) Subject to regulations 13(4) and 14(4), any representations must be made within a period of 28 days beginning on the date on which the application was made to the licensing authority.

PART 4
MANNER OF MAKING AND GIVING APPLICATIONS AND NOTICES

6.1671 16 Manner of making and giving applications and notices

(1) An application, or a notice under Part 3 of these Regulations, must be made or given in writing.

(2) For the purposes of paragraph (1), an application or notice which is sent by facsimile transmission or electronic mail shall be treated as being made or given in writing if it meets the conditions in paragraph (3).

(3) The conditions are that—

(a) the text of the application or notice—

(i) is capable of being accessed by the recipient,

(ii) is legible in all material respects, and

(iii) is capable of being read and reproduced in written form and used for subsequent reference by the recipient; and

(b) the person to whom the application or notice is to be made or given has agreed in advance that an application or notice may be made or given by the particular electronic means used.

(4) Subject to paragraph (5), where an application or notice is sent by facsimile transmission or electronic mail, it is to be treated as having been made or given at the time the conditions specified in paragraph (3)(a) are satisfied.

(5) An application is not to be treated as having been made until—

(a) the prescribed fee has been received by the licensing authority, or

(b) where any document required to accompany the application has not been sent by electronic means, or has been sent in a form that does not meet the conditions in paragraph (3), any such document has been received by the licensing authority in hard copy.

(6) In this regulation—

(a) "legible in all material respects" means, in relation to an application or notice sent by electronic means, that the information contained in the application or notice is available to the recipient to no lesser extent than it would be if given by means of a document in written form; and

(b) "the prescribed fee", in relation to an application, means the fee determined in accordance with regulations made under Part 8 of the Act which an applicant is required to pay in connection with the making of the application;

(c) any reference to a document in hard copy is to a written document or a document in the form of a plan.

PART 5
FORM OF NOTICE TO BE GIVEN ON GRANT OR REJECTION OF APPLICATIONS

6.1672 17 Form of notice to be given on grant of application

(1) This regulation prescribes the form of the notice which a licensing authority is required to give under section 164(1)(a) (notice of grant of application).

(2) Subject to the following provisions of this regulation and regulation 19, the notice shall be in the form specified in—

(a) Part 1 of Schedule 7, where it relates to the grant of an application for a premises licence;

(b) Part 2 of that Schedule, where it relates to the grant of an application to vary a premises licence;

(c) Part 3 of that Schedule, where it relates to the grant of an application to transfer a premises licence;

(d) Part 4 of that Schedule, where it relates to the grant of an application for the reinstatement of a premises licence; and

(e) Part 5 of that Schedule, where it relates to the grant of an application for a provisional statement.

(3) Where, on granting an application, the licensing authority exercise their powers to attach one or more conditions to the licence, the notice under section 164(1)(a) must include an annex in the form set out in Part 6 of Schedule 7—

(a) setting out the conditions, and

(b) in relation to each condition, giving the authority's reasons for attaching it to the licence.

(4) Where, on granting an application, the licensing authority exercise their powers to exclude one or more conditions that would otherwise be attached to the licence, the notice under section 164(1)(a) must include an annex in the form set out in Part 7 of Schedule 7—

(a) setting out the conditions to be excluded, and

(b) in relation to each condition, giving the authority's reasons for excluding it.

(5) Where representations are made under section 161 in relation to an application which is granted by a licensing authority, the notice under section 164(1)(a) must include an annex in the form set out in Part 8 of Schedule 7—

(a) setting out the representations, and

(b) giving the authority's response to the representations.

(6) In relation to an application for a provisional statement—

(a) any reference in paragraph (3) to conditions attached by the licensing authority is to have effect as a reference to those conditions which the authority would attach under section 169(1)(a) if a premises licence were granted in respect of the premises to which the provisional statement relates; and

(b) any reference in paragraph (4) to conditions excluded by the licensing authority is to have effect as a reference to those conditions which the authority would exclude under section 169(1)(a) if a premises licence were granted in respect of the premises to which the provisional statement relates.

6.1673 18 Form of notice to be given on rejection of application

(1) This regulation prescribes the form of the notice which a licensing authority is required to give under section 165(1) (notice of rejection of application).

(2) Subject to regulation 19, the notice shall be in the form specified in—

(a) Part 1 of Schedule 8, where it relates to the rejection of an application for a premises licence;

(b) Part 2 of that Schedule, where it relates to the rejection of an application to vary a premises licence;

(c) Part 3 of that Schedule, where it relates to the rejection of an application to transfer a premises licence;

(d) Part 4 of that Schedule, where it relates to the rejection of an application for the reinstatement of a premises licence; and

(e) Part 5 of that Schedule, where it relates to the rejection of an application for a provisional statement.

6.1674 19 Matters not required to be included in a notice

(1) Where matters are included in square brackets in any form in Schedule 7 or 8, they are intended to indicate and explain the information to be specified in the notice to which the form relates, and are not required to be included in the notice.

(2) The first page of a notice given by a licensing authority under section 164(1) or 165(1) may include any symbol or logo which is commonly used by that authority to identify documents produced by it.

PART 6
FORM OF PREMISES LICENCES, SUMMARIES AND
PROVISIONAL STATEMENTS

6.1675 20 Information to be included in a premises licence

(1) Subject to the following provisions of this regulation, a premises licence shall in addition to the matters set out in section 151(1) of the Act, contain the following information—

(a) the date on which the licence takes effect;

(b) the operating licence number of the relevant operating licence held by the holder of the premises licence;

(c) the name of the licensing authority which issued the licence and the address of its principal office;

(d) the number of the premises licence (being a number given by the licensing authority to the licence which is unique to that licence).

(2) Paragraph (1)(b) is not to apply in any case where paragraph (3) or (4) applies.

(3) This paragraph applies where the premises licence authorises a track to be used for accepting bets.

(4) This paragraph applies where—

(a) the premises licence is a converted premises licence, and

(b) the holder of the licence is applying for a relevant operating licence but the application has not been determined.

(5) Where a premises licence is varied, the licence shall specify the date on which the variations to the licence take effect.

6.1676 21 Matters to be included in the plan accompanying a premises licence

(1) The plan which is to be included in the premises licence by virtue of section 151(1)(g) must be a scale plan which complies with the requirements of paragraphs (2) to (9) of regulation 4 (as modified in accordance with the following provisions of this regulation).

(2) Any reference to the premises to which the application relates in paragraphs (2) to (9) of regulation 4 is to have effect for the purposes of this regulation as a reference to the premises to which the premises licence relates.

(3) Where a requirement of paragraphs (3) to (9) of regulation 4 is expressed only to apply to an application for a premises licence of a particular kind, for the purposes of this regulation that requirement is to apply only to a premises licence of the same kind.

6.1677 22 Form of a premises licence

(1) Subject to the following provisions of this regulation, a premises licence is to be in the form set out in Schedule 9.

(2) The matters in square brackets in the form in Schedule 9, and the guidance notes at the end of that Schedule, indicate and explain matters to be included in a premises licence and are not required to be included in the licence.

(3) The first page of a premises licence issued by a licensing authority may include any symbol or logo which is commonly used by that authority to identify documents produced by it.

6.1678 23 Form of summary

(1) Subject to the following provisions of this regulation, a summary shall be in the form set out in Schedule 10.

(2) Any matters in square brackets in the form in Schedule 10, and the guidance notes at the end of that Schedule, indicate and explain the matters to be included in a summary and are not required to be included in the summary.

(3) The first page of a summary issued by a licensing authority may include any symbol or logo which is commonly used by that authority to identify documents produced by it.

6.1679 24 Information to be included in a provisional statement

(1) A provisional statement shall in addition to the matters set out in section 151(1) (as applied by section 204(2)), contain the following information—

(a) the date on which the provisional statement is issued;

(b) the operating licence number of the relevant operating licence, if such a licence is held by the person to whom the provisional statement is issued;

(c) the number of the provisional statement (being a number given by the licensing authority to the provisional statement which is unique to that statement); and

(d) the name of the licensing authority which issued the provisional statement and the address of its principal office.

(2) Paragraph (1)(b) is not to apply where the provisional statement relates to a track to be used for accepting bets.

6.1680 25 Matters to be included in the plan accompanying a provisional statement

(1) The plan which is to be included in the provisional statement by virtue of section 151(1)(g) (as applied by section 204(2)) must be a scale plan which complies with the requirements of paragraphs (2) to (9) of regulation 4 (as modified in accordance with the following provisions of this regulation).

(2) Any reference in paragraphs (2) to (9) of regulation 4 to the premises to which the application relates is to have effect for the purposes of this regulation as a reference to the premises or proposed premises to which the provisional statement relates.

(3) Where a requirement of paragraphs (3) to (9) of regulation 4 is expressed only to apply to an application for a premises licence of a particular kind, for the purposes of this regulation that requirement is to apply only to a provisional statement which relates to premises or proposed premises of the same kind.

6.1681 26 Form of a provisional statement

(1) Subject to the following provisions of this regulation a provisional statement shall be in the form set out in Schedule 11.

(2) Any matters in square brackets in the form in Schedule 11, and the guidance notes at the end of that Schedule, indicate and explain the matters to be included in a provisional statement and are not required to be included in the statement.

(3) The first page of a provisional statement issued by a licensing authority may include any symbol or logo which is commonly used by that authority to identify documents produced by it.

6.1682

SCHEDULE 1

FORM AND CONTENT OF APPLICATIONS FOR A PREMISES LICENCE

Regulation 3

PART 1

FORM OF APPLICATION FOR A PREMISES LICENCE

Application for a premises licence under the Gambling Act 2005 (standard form)

PLEASE READ THE FOLLOWING INSTRUCTIONS FIRST

If you are completing this form by hand, please write legibly in block capitals using ink. Use additional sheets if necessary (marked with the number of the relevant question). You may wish to keep a copy of the completed form for your records.

Where the application is—

- **In respect of a vessel, or**
- **To convert an authorisation granted under the Betting, Gaming and Lotteries Act 1963 or the Gaming Act 1968,**

the application should be made on the relevant form for that type of premises or application.

Part 1 – Type of premises licence applied for

Regional casino ☐ **Large casino** ☐ **Small casino** ☐

Bingo ☐ **Adult gaming centre** ☐ **Family entertainment centre** ☐

Betting (Track) ☐ **Betting (Other)** ☐

Do you hold a provisional statement in respect of the premises? Yes ☐ **No** ☐

If the answer is "yes", please give the unique reference number for the provisional statement (as set out at the top of the first page of the statement):

....

Part 2 – Applicant details

If you are an individual, please fill in section A. If the application is being made on behalf of an organisation (such as a company or partnership), please fill in Section B.

Section A
Individual applicant

1. Title: Mr ☐ Mrs ☐ Miss ☐ Ms ☐ Dr ☐ Other (please specify)

....

2. Surname: .... Other name(s): ....
[*Use the names given in the applicant's operating licence or, if the applicant does not hold an operating licence, as given in any application for an operating licence*]

3. Applicant's address (home or business [*delete as appropriate*]):

....

....

.... Postcode:..

4(a) The number of the applicant's operating licence (as set out in the operating licence):

....

4(b) If the applicant does not hold an operating licence but is in the process of applying for one, give the date on which the application was made:

....

5. Tick the box if the application is being made by more than one person. ☐

[*Where there are further applicants, the information required in questions 1 to 4 should be included on additional sheets attached to this form, and those sheets should be clearly marked "Details of further applicants".*]

Section B
Application on behalf of an organisation

6. Name of applicant business or organisation:

....
[*Use the names given in the applicant's operating licence or, if the applicant does not hold an operating licence, as given in any application for an operating licence.*]

7. The applicant's registered or principal address:

....

....

....Postcode: ....

8(a) The number of the applicant's operating licence (as given in the operating licence):

....

8(b) If the applicant does not hold an operating licence but is in the process of applying for one, give the date on which the application was made:

....

9. Tick the box if the application is being made by more than one organisation. ☐

[*Where there are further applicants, the information required in questions 6 to 8 should be included on additional sheets attached to this form, and those sheets should be clearly marked "Details of further applicants"*.]

Part 3 – Premises Details

10. Proposed trading name to be used at the premises (if known):

....

11. Address of the premises (or, if none, give a description of the premises and their location):

....

....

....

....

....Postcode: ....

12. Telephone number at premises (if known):...

13. If the premises are in only a part of a building, please describe the nature of the building (for example, a shopping centre or office block). The description should include the number of floors within the building and the floor(s) on which the premises are located.

....

....

....

....

....

14(a) Are the premises situated in more than one licensing authority area? **Yes/No**
[*delete as appropriate*]

14(b) If the answer to question 14(a) is yes, please give the names of all the licensing authorities within whose area the premises are partly located, **other than the licensing authority to which this application is made**.

....

....

Part 4 – Times of operation

15(a) Do you want the licensing authority to exclude a default condition so that the premises may be used for longer periods than would otherwise be the case? **Yes/ No**
[*delete as appropriate*]
[*Where the relevant kind of premises licence is not subject to any default conditions, the answer to this question will be no.*]

15(b) If the answer to question 15(a) is yes, please complete the table below to indicate the times when you want the premises to be available for use under the premises licence

	Start	*Finish*	*Details of any seasonal variation*
Mon			
Tues			
Wed			
Thurs			
Fri			
Sat			
Sun			

16 If you wish to apply for a premises licence with a condition restricting gambling to specific periods in a year, please state the periods below using calendar dates:

....

Part 5 – Miscellaneous

17. Proposed commencement date for licence (leave blank if you want the licence to commence as soon as it is issued):

……../……../……………(dd/mm/yyyy)

18(a) Does the application relate to premises which are part of a track or other sporting venue which already has a premises licence?

Yes/ No
[*delete as appropriate*]

18(b) If the answer to question 18(a) is yes, please confirm by ticking the box that an application to vary the main track premises licence has been submitted with this application. ☐

19(a) Do you hold any other premises licences that have been issued by this licensing authority?

Yes/ No
[*delete as appropriate*]

19(b) If the answer question 19(a) is yes, please provide full details: ……………………

……………………………………………………………………………………

……………………………………………………………………………………

……………………………………………………………………………………

20. Please set out any other matters which you consider to be relevant to your application:

……………………………………………………………………………………

……………………………………………………………………………………

……………………………………………………………………………………

……………………………………………………………………………………

……………………………………………………………………………………

……………………………………………………………………………………

……………………………………………………………………………………

……………………………………………………………………………………

……………………………………………………………………………………

Part 6 – Declarations and Checklist (*Please tick*)

I/ We confirm that, to the best of my/ our knowledge, the information contained in this application is true. I/ We understand that it is an offence under section 342 of the Gambling Act 2005 to give information which is false or misleading in, or in relation to, this application. ☐

I/ We confirm that the applicant(s) have the right to occupy the premises. ☐

Checklist:

- **Payment of the appropriate fee has been made/is enclosed** ☐
- **A plan of the premises is enclosed** ☐
- **I/ we understand that if the above requirements are not complied with the application may be rejected** ☐
- **I/ we understand that it is now necessary to advertise the application and give the appropriate notice to the responsible authorities** ☐

Part 7 – Signatures

21. Signature of applicant or applicant's solicitor or other duly authorised agent If signing on behalf of the applicant, please state in what capacity:

Signature: ....

Print Name: ....

Date: .... Capacity:...

22. For joint applications, signature of 2nd applicant, or 2nd applicant's solicitor or other authorised agent. If signing on behalf of the applicant, please state in what capacity:

Signature: ....

Print Name: ....

Date: .... Capacity:...

[*Where there are more than two applicants, please use an additional sheet clearly marked "Signature(s) of further applicant(s)". The sheet should include all the information requested in paragraphs 21 and 22.*]

[*Where the application is to be submitted in an electronic form, the signature should be generated electronically and should be a copy of the person's written signature.*]

Part 8 – Contact Details

23(a) Please give the name of a person who can be contacted about the application:

....

23(b) Please give one or more telephone numbers at which the person identified in question 23(a) can be contacted:

....

24. Postal address for correspondence associated with this application:

....

....

.... Postcode:..

25. If you are happy for correspondence in relation to your application to be sent via e-mail, please give the e-mail address to which you would like correspondence to be sent:

....

PART 2
FORM OF APPLICATION FOR A PREMISES LICENCE IN RESPECT OF PREMISES WHICH ARE A VESSEL

[6.1683]

Application for a premises licence under the Gambling Act 2005 (vessel)

PLEASE READ THE FOLLOWING INSTRUCTIONS FIRST

If you are completing this form by hand, please write legibly in block capitals using ink. Use additional sheets if necessary (marked with the number of the relevant question). You may wish to keep a copy of the completed form for your records.

Applications in respect of premises which are not a vessel should be made on the relevant form for that type of premises.

Part 1 – Type of premises licence applied for

Regional Casino ☐ Large Casino ☐ Small Casino ☐
Bingo ☐ Adult Gaming Centre ☐ Family Entertainment Centre ☐
Betting ☐

Do you hold a provisional statement in respect of the premises? Yes ☐ No ☐

If the answer is "yes", please give the unique reference number for the provisional statement (as set out at the top of the first page of the provisional statement):

Part 2 – Applicant Details

If you are an individual, please fill in Section A. If the application is being made on behalf of an organisation (such as a company or partnership), please fill in Section B.

Section A
Individual applicant

1. Title: Mr ☐ Mrs ☐ Miss ☐ Ms ☐ Dr ☐ Other (please specify)

2. Surname: Other name(s):
[Use the names given in the applicant's operating licence or, if the applicant does not hold an operating licence, as given in any application for an operating licence]

3. Applicant's address (home or business – *[delete as appropriate]*):

Postcode:

4(a) The number of the applicant's operating licence (as set out in the operating licence):

4(b) If the applicant does not hold an operating licence but is in the process of applying for one, give the date on which the application was made:

5. Tick the box if the application is being made by more than one person. ☐

[Where there are further applicants, the information required in questions 1 to 4 should be included on additional sheets attached to this form, and those sheets should be clearly marked "Details of further applicants".]

Section B

Applicant on behalf of an organisation

6. Name of applicant business or organisation:

[Use the names given in the applicant's operating licence or, if the applicant does not hold an operating licence, as given in any application for an operating licence]

7. The applicant's registered or principal address:

Postcode:

8(a) The number of the applicant's operating licence (as given in the operating licence):

8(b) If the applicant does not hold an operating licence but is in the process of applying for one, give the date the application was made:

9. Tick the box if application is being made by more than one organisation. ☐

[Where there are further applicants, the information required in questions 6 to 8 should be included on additional sheets attached to this form, and those sheets should be clearly marked "Details of further applicants".]

Part 3 – Premises Details

10. Name of vessel to be licensed:

11. Country in which vessel is registered:

12(a) Give the place in the licensing authority's area at which the vessel is or will be situated or moored (Give an address with postcode if available):

12(b) Please confirm by ticking the appropriate box whether the place stated in question 12(a) is:

(i) a fixed place in or on water at which the vessel is situated; or ☐

(ii) a place at which the vessel is permanently moored; or ☐

(iii) a place at which the vessel is habitually moored; or ☐

(iv) in any other case, a place at which the vessel is moored or is likely to be moored or a place in the United Kingdom nearest to any place at which a vessel is, or is likely to be while activities are carried on in the vessel in reliance on the premises licence. ☐

13. If you have ticked box (iii) or (iv) in your answer to question 12(b), please indicate the number of days or months in a year when you expect the vessel to be moored at the place stated in question 12(a):

14. If you have ticked box (iii) or (iv) in your answer to question 12(b), please describe the other places where, and/or any other circumstances in which, the vessel will be used in reliance on the premises licence:

15. Please give a brief description of the vessel. Please describe the location of your premises within the vessel and indicate the uses of the other parts of the vessel:

Part 4 – Times of operation

16(a) Do you want the licensing authority to exclude a default condition so that the premises may be used for longer periods than would otherwise be the case? Yes/No *[delete as appropriate]*
[Where the relevant kind of premises licence is not subject to any default conditions, the answer to this question will be no.]

16(b) If the answer to question 16(a) is yes, please complete the table below to indicate the times when you want the premises to be available for use under the premises licence.

	Start	*Finish*	*Details of any seasonal variation*
Mon	*hh:mm*	*hh:mm*	
Tue			
Wed			
Thurs			
Fri			
Sat			
Sun			

17. If you wish to apply for a premises licence with a condition restricting gambling to specific periods in a year, please state the periods below using calendar dates:

Part 5 – Miscellaneous

18 Proposed commencement date for licence (leave blank if you want the licence to commence as soon as it is issued):

(dd/mm/yyyy)

19(a) Do you hold any other premises licences that have been issued by this licensing authority?
Yes/No *[delete as appropriate]*

19(b) If the answer question 19(a) is yes, please provide full details:

20 Please set out any other matters which you consider to be relevant to your application:

Part 6 – Declarations and Checklist (*Please tick*)

I/ We confirm that, to the best of my/ our knowledge, the information contained in this application is true. I/ We understand that it is an offence under section 342 of the Gambling Act 2005 to give information which is false or misleading in, or in relation to, this application. ☐

I/ We confirm that the applicant(s) have the right to occupy the premises. ☐

Checklist:

- Payment of the appropriate fee has been made/is enclosed ☐
- A plan of the premises is enclosed ☐
- I/ we understand that if the above requirements are not complied with the application may be rejected ☐
- I/ we understand that it is now necessary to advertise the application and give the appropriate notice to the responsible authorities ☐

Part 7 – Signatures

21. Signature of applicant or applicant's solicitor or other duly authorised agent. If signing on behalf of the applicant, please state in what capacity:

Signature:

Print Name:

Date: (dd/mm/yyyy) Capacity:

22. For joint applications, signature of 2nd applicant, or 2nd applicant's solicitor or other authorised agent. If signing on behalf of the applicant, please state in what capacity:

Signature:

Print Name:

Date: (dd/mm/yyyy) Capacity:

[Where there are more than two applicants, please use an additional sheet clearly marked "Signature(s) of further applicant(s)". The sheet should include all the information requested in paragraphs 21 and 22.]

[Where the application is to be submitted in an electronic form, the signature should be generated electronically and should be a copy of the person's written signature.]

Part 8 – Contact Details

23(a) Please give the name of a person who can be contacted about the application:

23(b) Please give one or more telephone numbers at which the person identified in question 23(a) can be contacted:

24. Postal address for correspondence associated with this application:

Postcode:

25. If you are happy for correspondence in relation to your application to be sent via e-mail, please give the e-mail address to which you would like correspondence to be sent:

PART 3
FORM OF APPLICATION FOR A CONVERTED PREMISES LICENCE

[6.1684]

Application for a premises licence under the Gambling Act 2005 (transitional conversion application)

PLEASE READ THE FOLLOWING INSTRUCTIONS FIRST

If you are completing this form by hand, please write legibly in block capitals using ink. Use additional sheets if necessary (marked with the number of the relevant question). You may wish to keep a copy of the completed form for your records.

Transitional conversion applications in respect of vessels should be made on the relevant form for that type of premises.

Part 1 – Type of premises licence applied for

Converted casino ☐ **Bingo** ☐ **Adult gaming centre** ☐

Family entertainment centre ☐ **Betting (Track)** ☐ **Betting (Other)** ☐

Tick this box if you want the application dealt with under the fast track procedure ☐

Part 2 – Applicant details

If you are an individual, please fill in section A. If the application is being made on behalf of an organisation (such as a company or partnership), please fill in Section B.

Section A
Individual applicant

1. Title: Mr ☐ Mrs ☐ Miss ☐ Ms ☐ Dr ☐ Other (please specify)

....

2. Surname: .... Other name(s): ....
[*Use the names given in the applicant's operating licence or, if the applicant does not hold an operating licence, as given in any application for an operating licence*]

3. Applicant's address (home or business – [*delete as appropriate*]):

....

....

....Postcode:..

6: Gambling Act 2005: SIs

4(a) The number of the applicant's operating licence (as set out in the operating licence):

....

4(b) If the applicant does not hold an operating licence but is in the process of applying for one, give the date on which the application was made:

....

5. Tick the box if the application is being made by more than one person. ☐

[*Where there are further applicants, the information required in questions 1 to 4 should be included on additional sheets attached to this form, and those sheets should be clearly marked "Details of further applicants".*]

Section B
Application on behalf of an organisation

6. Name of applicant business or organisation:

....

[*Use the names given in the applicant's operating licence or, if the applicant does not hold an operating licence, as given in any application for an operating licence*]

7. The applicant's registered or principal address:

....

....

....Postcode: ....

8(a) The number of the applicant's operating licence (as given in the operating licence):

....

8(b) If the applicant does not hold an operating licence but is in the process of applying for one, give the date on which the application was made:

....

9. Tick the box if the application is being made by more than one organisation. ☐

[*Where there are further applicants, the information required in questions 6 to 8 should be included on additional sheets attached to this form, and those sheets should be clearly marked "Details of further applicants".*]

Part 3 – Premises Details

10. Proposed trading name to be used at the premises (if known):

....

11. Address of the premises (or, if none, give a description of the premises and their location):

....

....

....

....Postcode: ....

12. Telephone number at premises (if known):...

13(a) Will the premises which are the subject of the application occupy the whole of the building in which they are located, or only part of it? If the premises are not a building or part of a building, please describe the nature of the premises.

....

....

....

....

....

13(b) If the premises will occupy only part of a building, please describe the nature of the building and the part of it in which the premises will be located. The information given should include a description of the building itself (whether it is primarily a shopping mall, residential, office space etc), whether it is multi-level or multi-units on one level; and in which units or on which floor the gambling premises will be located.

....

....

....

....

....

14(a) Are the premises situated in more than one licensing authority area? **Yes/No**
[*delete as appropriate*]

14(b) If the answer to question 14(a) is yes, please give the names of all the licensing authorities within whose area the premises are partly located, **other than the licensing authority to which this application is made.**

....

....

15(a) Give details of the existing gambling licence or permit held by the applicant(s) with respect to the premises:

....

....

....

15(b) Where no existing licence or permit is held, give details of the application which is being made for the grant or transfer of such a licence or permit to the applicant(s). Please specify the authority to which the application is being made:

....

....

....

Part 4 – Times of operation

16(a) Do you want the licensing authority to exclude a default condition so that the premises may be used for longer periods than would otherwise be the case? **Yes/ No**
[*delete as appropriate*]

[*Where the relevant kind of premises licence is not subject to any default conditions, the answer to this question will be no.* ***In all cases the answer to this question will be no, if you have indicated on the first page of the form that you want the application to be treated as a fast track application.***]

16(b) If the answer to question 16(a) is yes, please complete the table below to indicate the times when you want the premises to be available for use under the premises licence.

	Start	*Finish*	*Details of any seasonal variation*
Mon			
Tues			
Wed			
Thurs			
Fri			
Sat			
Sun			

17. If you wish to apply for a premises licence with a condition restricting gambling to specific periods in a year, please state the periods below using calendar dates

…………………………………………………………………………………………

Part 5 – Miscellaneous

18(a) Do you hold any other premises licences that have been issued by this licensing authority, or are you applying for any such licences?

Yes/ No
[*delete as appropriate*]

18(b) If the answer question 18(a) is yes, please provide full details: ……………………

…………………………………………………………………………………………

…………………………………………………………………………………………

…………………………………………………………………………………………

…………………………………………………………………………………………

19. Please set out any other matters which you consider to be relevant to your application:

…………………………………………………………………………………………

…………………………………………………………………………………………

…………………………………………………………………………………………

…………………………………………………………………………………………

…………………………………………………………………………………………

…………………………………………………………………………………………

…………………………………………………………………………………………

…………………………………………………………………………………………

Part 6 – Declarations and Checklist (*Please tick*)

I/ We confirm that, to the best of my/ our knowledge, the information contained in this application is true. I/ We understand that it is an offence under section 342 of the Gambling Act 2005 to give information which is false or misleading in, or in relation to, this application. ☐

I/ We confirm that the applicant(s) have the right to occupy the premises. ☐

Checklist:

- **Payment of the appropriate fee has been made/is enclosed** ☐
- **A plan of the premises is enclosed** ☐
- **A copy of the applicant's existing gambling licence or permit relating to the premises is enclosed; or where none exists, a copy of the application which is being made in respect of the premises is enclosed** ☐
- **I/ we understand that if the above requirements are not complied with the application may be rejected** ☐
- **I/ we understand that, if it is not a fast track application, it is now necessary to advertise the application and give the appropriate notice to the responsible authorities** ☐

Part 7 – Signatures

20. Signature of applicant or applicant's solicitor or other duly authorised agent If signing on behalf of the applicant, please state in what capacity:

Signature: ....

Print Name: ....

Date: .... Capacity:..

21. For joint applications, signature of 2nd applicant, or 2nd applicant's solicitor or other authorised agent. If signing on behalf of the applicant, please state in what capacity:

Signature: ....

Print Name: ....

Date: .... Capacity:..

[*Where there are more than two applicants, please use an additional sheet clearly marked "Signature(s) of further applicant(s)". The sheet should include all the information requested in paragraphs 20 and 21.*]

[*Where the application is to be submitted in an electronic form, the signature should be generated electronically and should be a copy of the person's written signature.*]

Part 8 – Contact Details

22(a) Please give the name of a person who can be contacted about the application:

....

22(b) Please give one or more telephone numbers at which the person identified in question 22(a) can be contacted:

....

23. Postal address for correspondence associated with this application:

....

....

.... Postcode:..

24. If you are happy for correspondence in relation to your application to be sent via e-mail, please give the e-mail address to which you would like correspondence to be sent:

....

PART 4
FORM OF APPLICATION FOR A CONVERTED PREMISES LICENCE IN RESPECT OF A VESSEL

[6.1685]

Application for a premises licence under the Gambling Act 2005 (transitional conversion application) (vessel)

PLEASE READ THE FOLLOWING INSTRUCTIONS FIRST

If you are completing this form by hand, please write legibly in block capitals using ink. Use additional sheets if necessary (marked with the number of the relevant question). You may wish to keep a copy of the completed form for your records.

Transitional conversion applications in respect of premises which are not a vessel should be made on the relevant form for that type of premises.

Part 1 – Type of premises licence applied for

Converted casino ☐ **Bingo** ☐ **Adult gaming centre** ☐

Family entertainment centre ☐ **Betting** ☐

Tick this box if you want the application dealt with under the fast track procedure ☐

Part 2 – Applicant details

If you are an individual, please fill in section A. If the application is being made on behalf of an organisation (such as a company or partnership), please fill in Section B.

Section A
Individual applicant

1. Title: Mr ☐ Mrs ☐ Miss ☐ Ms ☐ Dr ☐ Other (please specify)

....

2. Surname: .... Other name(s): ....
[*Use the names given in the applicant's operating licence or, if the applicant does not hold an operating licence, as given in any application for an operating licence*]

3. Applicant's address (home or business – [*delete as appropriate*]):

....

....

.... Postcode:...................................

4(a) The number of the applicant's operating licence (as set out in the operating licence):

....

4(b) If the applicant does not hold an operating licence but is in the process of applying for one, give the date on which the application was made:

....

5. Tick the box if the application is being made by more than one person. ☐

[*Where there are further applicants, the information required in questions 1 to 4 should be included on additional sheets attached to this form, and those sheets should be clearly marked "Details of further applicants".*]

Section B
Application on behalf of an organisation

6. Name of applicant business or organisation:

....

[*Use the names given in the applicant's operating licence or, if the applicant does not hold an operating licence, as given in any application for an operating licence*]

7. The applicant's registered or principal address:

....

....

....Postcode: ....

8(a) The number of the applicant's operating licence (as given in the operating licence):

....

8(b) If the applicant does not hold an operating licence but is in the process of applying for one, give the date on which the application was made:

....

9. Tick the box if the application is being made by more than one organisation. ☐

[*Where there are further applicants, the information required in questions 6 to 8 should be included on additional sheets attached to this form, and those sheets should be clearly marked "Details of further applicants".*]

Part 3 – Premises Details

10. Name of vessel to be licensed:..

11. Country in which vessel is registered:...

12(a) Give the place in the licensing authority's area at which the vessel is or will be situated or moored (Give an address with postcode if available):

....

....

....

12(b) Please confirm by ticking the appropriate box whether the place stated in question 12(a) is:

(i) a fixed place in or on water at which the vessel is situated; or ☐

(ii) a place at which the vessel is permanently moored; or ☐

(iii) a place at which the vessel is habitually moored; or ☐

(iv) in any other case, a place at which the vessel is moored or is likely to be moored, or a place in the United Kingdom nearest to any place at which a vessel is, or is likely to be while activities are carried on in the vessel in reliance on the premises licence. ☐

13. If you have ticked box (iii) or (iv) in your answer to question 12(b), please indicate the number of days or months in a year when you expect the vessel to be moored at the place stated in question 12(a):

....

14. If you have ticked box (iii) or (iv) in your answer to question 12(b), please describe the other places where, and/or any other circumstances in which, the vessel will be used in reliance on the premises licence:

....

....

....

15. Please give a brief description of the vessel. Please describe the location of your premises within the vessel and indicate the uses of the other parts of the vessel:

....

....

....

....

....

16(a) Give details of the existing gambling licence or permit held by the applicant(s) with respect to the premises:

....

....

....

....

16(b) Where no existing licence or permit is held, give details of the application which is being made for the grant or transfer of such a licence or permit to the applicant(s). Please specify the authority to which the application is being made:

....

....

....

....

....

Part 4 – Times of operation

17(a) Do you want the licensing authority to exclude a default condition so that the premises may be used for longer periods than would otherwise be the case? **Yes/ No**
[*delete as appropriate*]

[*Where the relevant kind of premises licence is not subject to any default conditions, the answer to this question will be no.* ***In all cases the answer to this question will be no, if you have indicated on the first page of the form that you want the application to be treated as a fast track application.***]

17(b) If the answer to question 17(a) is yes, please complete the table below to indicate the times when you want the premises to be available for use under the premises licence.

	Start	*Finish*	*Details of any seasonal variation*
Mon			
Tues			
Wed			
Thurs			
Fri			
Sat			
Sun			

18. If you wish to apply for a premises licence with a condition restricting gambling to specific periods in a year, please state the periods below using calendar dates:

....

Part 5 – Miscellaneous

19(a) Do you hold any other premises licences that have been issued by this licensing authority, or are you applying for any such licences?

Yes/ No
[*delete as appropriate*]

19(b) If the answer question 19(a) is yes, please provide full details: ....

....

....

....

....

20. Please set out any other matters which you consider to be relevant to your application:

....

....

....

....

....

....

....

....

Part 6 – Declarations and Checklist (*Please tick*)

I/ We confirm that, to the best of my/ our knowledge, the information contained in this application is true. I/ We understand that it is an offence under section 342 of the Gambling Act 2005 to give information which is false or misleading in, or in relation to, this application. ☐

I/ We confirm that the applicant(s) have the right to occupy the premises. ☐

Checklist:

- **Payment of the appropriate fee has been made/is enclosed** ☐
- **A plan of the premises is enclosed** ☐
- **A copy of the applicant's existing gambling licence or permit relating to the premises is enclosed; or where none exists, a copy of the application which is being made in respect of the premises is enclosed** ☐
- **I/ we understand that if the above requirements are not complied with the application may be rejected** ☐
- **I/ we understand that, if it is not a fast track application, it is now necessary to advertise the application and give the appropriate notice to the responsible authorities** ☐

Part 7 – Signatures

21. Signature of applicant or applicant's solicitor or other duly authorised agent If signing on behalf of the applicant, please state in what capacity:

Signature: ....

Print Name: ....

Date: .... Capacity:...

22. For joint applications, signature of 2nd applicant, or 2nd applicant's solicitor or other authorised agent. If signing on behalf of the applicant, please state in what capacity:

Signature: ....

Print Name: ....

Date: .... Capacity:...

[*Where there are more than two applicants, please use an additional sheet clearly marked "Signature(s) of further applicant(s)". The sheet should include all the information requested in paragraphs 21 and 22.*]

Where the application is to be submitted in an electronic form, the signature should be generated electronically and should be a copy of the person's written signature.

Part 8 – Contact Details

23(a) Please give the name of a person who can be contacted about the application:

....

23(b) Please give one or more telephone numbers at which the person identified in question 23(a) can be contacted:

....

24. Postal address for correspondence associated with this application:

....

....

.... Postcode:...

25. If you are happy for correspondence in relation to your application to be sent via e-mail, please give the e-mail address to which you would like correspondence to be sent:

....

6.1686

SCHEDULE 2
FORM AND CONTENT OF APPLICATION TO VARY A PREMISES LICENCE
Regulation 7

Application to vary a premises licence under the Gambling Act 2005

PLEASE READ THE FOLLOWING INSTRUCTIONS FIRST

If you are completing this form by hand, please write legibly in block capitals using ink. Use additional sheets if necessary (marked with the number of the relevant question). You may wish to keep a copy of the completed form for your records.

Part 1 – Applicant details

If you are an individual, please fill in section A. If the application is being made on behalf of an organisation (such as a company or partnership), please fill in Section B.

Section A
Individual applicant

1. Title: Mr ☐ Mrs ☐ Miss ☐ Ms ☐ Dr ☐ Other (please specify)

....

2. Surname: .... Other name(s): ....
[*Use the names given in the applicant's operating licence or, if the applicant does not hold an operating licence, as given in any application for an operating licence*]

3. Applicant's address (home or business – [*delete as appropriate*]):

....

....

.... Postcode:...

4(a) The number of the applicant's operating licence (as set out in the operating licence):

....

4(b) If the applicant does not hold an operating licence but is in the process of applying for one, give the date on which the application was made:

....

6: Gambling Act 2005: SIs

5. Tick the box if the application is being made by more than one person. ☐

[*Where there are further applicants, the information required in questions 1 to 4 should be included on additional sheets attached to this form, and those sheets should be clearly marked "Details of further applicants".*]

Section B
Application on behalf of an organisation

6. Name of applicant business or organisation:

....

[*Use the names given in the applicant's operating licence or, if the applicant does not hold an operating licence, as given in any application for an operating licence*]

7. The applicant's registered or principal address:

....

....

....Postcode: ....

8(a) The number of the applicant's operating licence (as given in the operating licence):

....

8(b) If the applicant does not hold an operating licence but is in the process of applying for one, give the date on which the application was made:

....

9. Tick the box if the application is being made by more than one organisation. ☐

[*Where there are further applicants, the information required in questions 6 to 8 should be included on additional sheets attached to this form, and those sheets should be clearly marked "Details of further applicants".*]

Part 2 – Premises Details

10. Trading name used at licensed premises:

....

11. Give the address of the premises or, if none, give a description of the premises and its location. Where the premises are a vessel, give the place indicated in the premises licence as the place in the licensing authority's area where the vessel is wholly or partly situated. Where possible this should include an address with postcode:

....

....

....Postcode: ....

12. Telephone number at premises (if known):..

13. Type of premises licence to be varied:

Regional Casino ☐ Large Casino ☐ Small Casino ☐

Converted Casino ☐ Bingo ☐ Adult Gaming Centre ☐

Betting (track) ☐ Betting (other) ☐ Family Entertainment Centre ☐

14. Premises licence number (if known):..

15. If you are making this application alongside an application for transfer or reinstatement of the premises licence into your name, please give name of the current licence holder as it appears on the premises licence (if known):

Surname: .... Other names: ....

Part 3 – Details of variations applied for

16(a) Please give details of any variation which is being applied for. Where the application includes an application to exclude or vary a condition of the premises licence, identify the relevant condition here (unless it relates to hours of operation which are dealt with in questions 16(b) and 16(c)):

....

....

....

....

....

....

....

....

....

16(b) Do you want the licensing authority to exclude or vary a condition of the licence so that the premises may be used for longer periods than would otherwise be the case?

Yes/ No

[*delete as appropriate*]

16(c) If the answer to question 16(b) is yes, please complete the table below to indicate the times when you want the premises to be available for use under the premises licence.

	Start	*Finish*	*Details of any seasonal variation*
Mon			
Tues			
Wed			
Thurs			
Fri			
Sat			
Sun			

17. Please indicate any particular date on which you want the variation to take effect if approved:

……../……../……………(dd/mm/yyyy)

18. Please set out any other matters which you consider to be relevant to your application:

……………………………………………………………………………………………

……………………………………………………………………………………………

……………………………………………………………………………………………

……………………………………………………………………………………………

……………………………………………………………………………………………

……………………………………………………………………………………………

……………………………………………………………………………………………

……………………………………………………………………………………………

Part 4 – Declarations and Checklist (*Please tick as appropriate*)

I/ We confirm that, to the best of my/ our knowledge, the information contained in this application is true. I/ We understand that it is an offence under section 342 of the Gambling Act 2005 to give information which is false or misleading in, or in relation to, this application. ☐

I/ We confirm that the applicant(s) have the right to occupy the premises. ☐

Checklist:

- **Payment of the appropriate fee has been made/is enclosed** ☐
- **A plan of the premises is enclosed** ☐
- **The existing premises licence is enclosed** ☐
- **The existing premises licence is not enclosed, but the application is accompanied by—**
  - **A statement explaining why it is not reasonably practicable to produce the licence and,** ☐
  - **An application under section 190 of the Gambling Act 2005 for the issue of a copy of the licence** ☐
- **I/ we understand that if the above requirements are not complied with the application may be rejected** ☐
- **I/ we understand that it is now necessary to advertise the application and give the appropriate notice to the responsible authorities** ☐

Part 5 – Signatures

19. Signature of applicant or applicant's solicitor or other duly authorised agent If signing on behalf of the applicant, please state in what capacity:

Signature: ....

Print Name: ....

Date: .... Capacity:..

20. For joint applications, signature of 2nd applicant, or 2nd applicant's solicitor or other authorised agent. If signing on behalf of the applicant, please state in what capacity:

Signature: ....

Print Name: ....

Date: .... Capacity:..

[*Where there are more than two applicants, please use an additional sheet clearly marked "Signature(s) of further applicant(s)". The sheet should include all the information requested in paragraphs 19 and 20.*]

[*Where the application is to be submitted in an electronic form, the signature should be generated electronically and should be a copy of the person's written signature.*]

Part 6 – Contact Details

21(a) Please give the name of a person who can be contacted about the application:

....

21(b) Please give one or more telephone numbers at which the person identified in question 21(a) can be contacted:

....

22. Postal address for correspondence associated with this application:

....

....

.... Postcode:...

23. If you are happy for correspondence in relation to your application to be sent via e-mail, please give the e-mail address to which you would like correspondence to be sent:

....

6.1687

SCHEDULE 3
FORM AND CONTENT OF APPLICATION TO TRANSFER A PREMISES LICENCE
Regulation 8

Application to transfer a premises licence under the Gambling Act 2005

PLEASE READ THE FOLLOWING INSTRUCTIONS FIRST

If you are completing this form by hand, please write legibly in block capitals using ink. Use additional sheets if necessary (marked with the number of the relevant question). You may wish to keep a copy of the completed form for your records.

Part 1 – Applicant details

If you are an individual, please fill in section A. If the application is being made on behalf of an organisation (such as a company or partnership), please fill in Section B.

Section A
Individual applicant

1. Title: Mr ☐ Mrs ☐ Miss ☐ Ms ☐ Dr ☐ Other (please specify)

....

2. Surname: .... Other name(s): ....
[*Use the names given in the applicant's operating licence or, if the applicant does not hold an operating licence, as given in any application for an operating licence*]

3. Applicant's address (home or business – [*delete as appropriate*])

....

....

.... Postcode:..

4(a) The number of the applicant's operating licence (as set out in the operating licence):

....

4(b) If the applicant does not hold an operating licence but is in the process of applying for one, give the date on which the application was made:

....

6: Gambling Act 2005: SIs

5. Tick the box if the application is being made by more than one person. ☐

[*Where there are further applicants, the information required in questions 1 to 4 should be included on additional sheets attached to this form, and those sheets should be clearly marked "Details of further applicants".*]

Section B
Application on behalf of an organisation

6. Name of applicant business or organisation:

....

[*Use the names given in the applicant's operating licence or, if the applicant does not hold an operating licence, as given in any application for an operating licence*]

7. The applicant's registered or principal address:

....

....

.... Postcode: ....

8(a) The number of the applicant's operating licence (as given in the operating licence):

....

8(b) If the applicant does not hold an operating licence but is in the process of applying for one, give the date on which the application was made:

....

9. Tick the box if the application is being made by more than one organisation. ☐

[*Where there are further applicants, the information required in questions 6 to 8 should be included on additional sheets attached to this form, and those sheets should be clearly marked "Details of further applicants".*]

Part 2 – Premises Details

10. Trading name used at licensed premises:

....

11. Give the address of the premises or, if none, give a description of the premises and its location. Where the premises are a vessel, give the place indicated in the premises licence as the place in the licensing authority's area where the vessel is wholly or partly situated. Where possible this should include an address with postcode:

....

....

....

.... Postcode: ....

12. Telephone number at premises (if known):...

13. Type of premises licence to be transferred:

Regional Casino ☐ Large Casino ☐ Small Casino ☐

Converted Casino ☐ Bingo ☐ Adult Gaming Centre ☐

Betting (track) ☐ Betting (other) ☐ Family Entertainment Centre ☐

14. Premises licence number (if known):...

15. Please give name of the current licence holder as it appears on the premises licence (if known):

Surname: .... Other names: ....

Part 3 – Details of application for transfer

16. Give the date on which you want the transfer to take effect if approved:

......../......../..............(dd/mm/yyyy)

17. If you want section 189(6) of the Gambling Act 2005 to apply, please tick the box ☐

[*Section 189(6) of the Gambling Act 2005 enables the applicant to be treated as the premises licence holder from the date on which this application is made until the date on which it is decided.*]

18(a) Have you contacted the holder of the premises licence? **Yes/ No**
[*delete as appropriate*]

18(b) If the answer to question 18(a) is no, please confirm by ticking the box that you have take all reasonable steps to contact the person or persons holding the premises licence. ☐

18(c) If you have answered question 18(b) by ticking the box, please give full details of the steps that you have taken to contact the holder of the premises licence:

....

....

....

....

....

....

6: Gambling Act 2005: SIs

19. Please set out any other matters which you consider to be relevant to your application:

....

....

....

....

....

....

....

....

....

Part 4 – Declarations and Checklist (*Please tick as appropriate*)

I/ We confirm that, to the best of my/ our knowledge, the information contained in this application is true. I/ We understand that it is an offence under section 342 of the Gambling Act 2005 to give information which is false or misleading in, or in relation to, this application. ☐

I/ We confirm that the applicant(s) have the right to occupy the premises. ☐

Checklist:

- **Payment of the appropriate fee has been made/is enclosed** ☐
- **A plan of the premises is enclosed** ☐
- **The existing premises licence is enclosed** ☐
- **The existing premises licence is not enclosed, but the application is accompanied by—**
  - **A statement explaining why it is not reasonably practicable to produce the licence and,** ☐
  - **An application under section 190 of the Gambling Act 2005 for the issue of a copy of the licence** ☐
- **I/ we understand that if the above requirements are not complied with the application may be rejected** ☐

Part 5 – Signatures

20. Signature of applicant or applicant's solicitor or other duly authorised agent If signing on behalf of the applicant, please state in what capacity:

Signature: ....

Print Name: ....

Date: .... Capacity:..

21. For joint applications, signature of 2nd applicant, or 2nd applicant's solicitor or other authorised agent. If signing on behalf of the applicant, please state in what capacity:

Signature: ....

Print Name: ....

Date: .... Capacity:..

[*Where there are more than two applicants, please use an additional sheet clearly marked "Signature(s) of further applicant(s)". The sheet should include all the information requested in paragraphs 20 and 21.*]

[*Where the application is to be submitted in an electronic form, the signature should be generated electronically and should be a copy of the person's written signature.*]

Part 6 – Contact Details

22(a) Please give the name of a person who can be contacted about the application:

....

22(b) Please give one or more telephone numbers at which the person identified in question 22(a) can be contacted:

....

23. Postal address for correspondence associated with this application:

....

....

.... Postcode:...

24. If you are happy for correspondence in relation to your application to be sent via e-mail, please give the e-mail address to which you would like correspondence to be sent:

....

6.1688

SCHEDULE 4
FORM AND CONTENT OF APPLICATION FOR REINSTATEMENT OF A PREMISES LICENCE
Regulation 9

Application for the reinstatement of a premises licence under the Gambling Act 2005

PLEASE READ THE FOLLOWING INSTRUCTIONS FIRST

If you are completing this form by hand, please write legibly in block capitals using ink. Use additional sheets if necessary (marked with the number of the relevant question). You may wish to keep a copy of the completed form for your records.

Part 1 – Applicant details

If you are an individual, please fill in section A. If the application is being made on behalf of an organisation (such as a company or partnership), please fill in Section B.

Section A
Individual applicant

1. Title: Mr ☐ Mrs ☐ Miss ☐ Ms ☐ Dr ☐ Other (please specify)

....

2. Surname: .... Other name(s): ....
[*Use the names given in the applicant's operating licence or, if the applicant does not hold an operating licence, as given in any application for an operating licence*]

3. Applicant's address (home or business – [*delete as appropriate*]):

....

....

.... Postcode:..

4(a) The number of the applicant's operating licence (as set out in the operating licence):

....

4(b) If the applicant does not hold an operating licence but is in the process of applying for one, give the date on which the application was made:

....

5. Tick the box if the application is being made by more than one person. ☐

[*Where there are further applicants, the information required in questions 1 to 4 should be included on additional sheets attached to this form, and those sheets should be clearly marked "Details of further applicants".*]

Section B
Application on behalf of an organisation

6. Name of applicant business or organisation:

....

[*Use the names given in the applicant's operating licence or, if the applicant does not hold an operating licence, as given in any application for an operating licence*]

7. The applicant's registered or principal address:

....

....

....Postcode: ....

8(a) The number of the applicant's operating licence (as given in the operating licence):

....

8(b) If the applicant does not hold an operating licence but is in the process of applying for one, give the date on which the application was made:

....

9. Tick the box if the application is being made by more than one organisation. ☐

[*Where there are further applicants, the information required in questions 6 to 8 should be included on additional sheets attached to this form, and those sheets should be clearly marked "Details of further applicants".*]

Part 2 – Premises Details

10. Trading name used at premises:

....

11. Give the address of the premises or, if none, give a description of the premises and its location. Where the premises are a vessel, give the place indicated in the premises licence as the place in the licensing authority's area where the vessel is wholly or partly situated. Where possible this should include an address with postcode:

....

....

.... Postcode: ....

12. Telephone number at premises (if known):...

13. Type of premises licence to be reinstated:

Regional Casino	☐	Large Casino	☐	Small Casino	☐
Converted Casino	☐	Bingo	☐	Adult Gaming Centre	☐
Betting (track)	☐	Betting (other)	☐	Family Entertainment Centre	☐

14. Premises licence number (if known):...

15. If known, please give the name of the person who held the premises licence immediately before it lapsed:

Surname: .... Other names: ....

16. Please indicate as accurately as you can the date on which the premises licence

lapsed:...

Part 3 – Details of application for reinstatement

17. Please confirm by ticking the box that you are applying for the reinstatement to take effect on the date on which the application is granted. ☐

18. Please set out any other matters which you consider to be relevant to your application:

....

....

....

....

....

....

....

....

Part 4 – Declarations and Checklist (*Please tick as appropriate*)

I/ We confirm that, to the best of my/ our knowledge, the information contained in this application is true. I/ We understand that it is an offence under section 342 of the Gambling Act 2005 to give information which is false or misleading in, or in relation to, this application. ☐

I/ We confirm that the applicant(s) have the right to occupy the premises. ☐

Checklist:

- **Payment of the appropriate fee has been made/is enclosed** ☐
- **A plan of the premises is enclosed** ☐
- **The existing premises licence is enclosed** ☐
- **The existing premises licence is not enclosed, but the application is accompanied by—**
  - **A statement explaining why it is not reasonably practicable to produce the licence and,** ☐
  - **An application under section 190 of the Gambling Act 2005 for the issue of a copy of the licence** ☐
- **I/ we understand that if the above requirements are not complied with the application may be rejected** ☐

Part 5 – Signatures

19. Signature of applicant or applicant's solicitor or other duly authorised agent If signing on behalf of the applicant, please state in what capacity:

Signature: ....

Print Name: ....

Date: .... Capacity:..

20. For joint applications, signature of 2nd applicant, or 2nd applicant's solicitor or other authorised agent. If signing on behalf of the applicant, please state in what capacity:

Signature: ....

Print Name: ....

Date: .... Capacity:..

[*Where there are more than two applicants, please use an additional sheet clearly marked "Signature(s) of further applicant(s)". The sheet should include all the information requested in paragraphs 19 and 20.*]

[*Where the application is to be submitted in an electronic form, the signature should be generated electronically and should be a copy of the person's written signature.*]

Part 6 – Contact Details

21(a) Please give the name of a person who can be contacted about the application:

....

21(b) Please give one or more telephone numbers at which the person identified in question 21(a) can be contacted:

....

22. Postal address for correspondence associated with this application:

....

....

.... Postcode:..................................

23. If you are happy for correspondence in relation to your application to be sent via e-mail, please give the e-mail address to which you would like correspondence to be sent:

....

6.1689

SCHEDULE 5
FORM AND CONTENT OF APPLICATION FOR A PROVISIONAL STATEMENT
Regulation 10(1)

PART 1
FORM OF APPLICATION FOR A PROVISIONAL STATEMENT

Application for a provisional statement under the Gambling Act 2005 (standard form)

PLEASE READ THE FOLLOWING INSTRUCTIONS FIRST

If you are completing this form by hand, please write legibly in block capitals using ink. Use additional sheets if necessary (marked with the number of the relevant question). You may wish to keep a copy of the completed form for your records.

Where the application is in respect of a vessel the application should be made on the relevant form for that type of premises

Part 1 – Type of premises to which the application relates

Regional casino ☐ **Large casino** ☐ **Small casino** ☐

Bingo ☐ **Adult gaming centre** ☐ **Family entertainment centre** ☐

Betting (Track) ☐ **Betting (Other)** ☐

Part 2 – Applicant details

If you are an individual, please fill in section A. If the application is being made on behalf of an organisation (such as a company or partnership), please fill in Section B.

Section A
Individual applicant

1. Title: Mr ☐ Mrs ☐ Miss ☐ Ms ☐ Dr ☐ Other (please specify)

....

2. Surname: .... Other name(s): ....
[Use the names given in the applicant's operating licence or, if the applicant does not hold an operating licence, as given in any application for an operating licence]

3. Applicant's address (home or business – [*delete as appropriate*])

....

....

.... Postcode:...

4(a) The number of the applicant's operating licence (as set out in the operating licence):

....

4(b) If the applicant does not hold an operating licence but is in the process of applying for one, give the date on which the application was made:

....

5. Tick the box if the application is being made by more than one person. ☐

[*Where there are further applicants, the information required in questions 1 to 4 should be included on additional sheets attached to this form, and those sheets should be clearly marked "Details of further applicants".*]

Section B
Application on behalf of an organisation

6. Name of applicant business or organisation:

....

[*Use the names given in the applicant's operating licence or, if the applicant does not hold an operating licence, as given in any application for an operating licence*]

7. The applicant's registered or principal address:

....

....

....Postcode: ....

8(a) The number of the applicant's operating licence (as given in the operating licence):

....

8(b) If the applicant does not hold an operating licence but is in the process of applying for one, give the date on which the application was made:

....

9. Tick the box if the application is being made by more than one organisation. ☐

[*Where there are further applicants, the information required in questions 6 to 8 should be included on additional sheets attached to this form, and those sheets should be clearly marked "Details of further applicants".*]

Part 3 – Premises Details

10. Proposed trading name to be used at the premises (if known):

....

11. Address of the premises (or, if none, give a description of the premises or proposed premises and their location):

....

....

....

....

....Postcode: ....

12. Telephone number at premises (if known):..

13. If the premises are in only a part of a building, please describe the nature of the building (for example, a shopping centre or office block). The description should include the number of floors within the building and the floor(s) on which the premises are located.

....

....

....

....

....

14(a) Are the premises or proposed premises situated in more than one licensing authority area? **Yes/No**

[*delete as appropriate*]

14(b) If the answer to question 14(a) is yes, please give the names of all the licensing authorities within whose area the premises or proposed premises are partly located, **other than the licensing authority to which this application is made**.

....

....

Part 4 – Times of operation

15(a) Do you want the licensing authority to exclude a default condition so that the premises may be used for longer periods than would otherwise be the case?

Yes/ No

[*delete as appropriate*]

[*Where the relevant kind of premises licence is not subject to any default conditions, the answer to this question will be no.*]

15(b) If the answer to question 15(a) is yes, please complete the table below to indicate the times when you want the premises to be available for use under the premises licence

	Start	*Finish*	*Details of any seasonal variation*
Mon			
Tues			
Wed			
Thurs			
Fri			
Sat			
Sun			

16. If you want the premises licence to have a condition restricting gambling to specific periods in a year, please state the periods below using calendar dates:

....

Part 5 – Miscellaneous

17(a) Does the application relate to premises or proposed premises which are part of a track or other sporting venue which already has a premises licence:

Yes/ No

[*delete as appropriate*]

17(b) If the answer to question 17(a) is yes, please confirm by ticking the box that an application to vary the main track premises licence has been submitted with this application. ☐

18(a) Do you hold any other premises licences that have been issued by this licensing authority?

Yes/ No
[*delete as appropriate*]

18(b) If the answer question 18(a) is yes, please provide full details: ....

....

....

....

19. Please set out any other matters which you consider to be relevant to your application:

....

....

....

....

....

....

....

....

Part 6 – Declarations and Checklist (*Please tick*)

I/ We confirm that, to the best of my/ our knowledge, the information contained in this application is true. I/ We understand that it is an offence under section 342 of the Gambling Act 2005 to give information which is false or misleading in, or in relation to, this application. ☐

Checklist:

- **Payment of the appropriate the fee has been made/is enclosed** ☐
- **A plan of the premises or proposed premises is enclosed** ☐
- **I/ we understand that if the above requirements are not complied with the application may be rejected** ☐
- **I/ we understand that it is now necessary to advertise the application and give the appropriate notice to the responsible authorities** ☐

Part 7 – Signatures

20. Signature of applicant or applicant's solicitor or other duly authorised agent If signing on behalf of the applicant, please state in what capacity:

Signature: ....

Print Name: ....

Date: .... Capacity:..

21. For joint applications, signature of 2nd applicant, or 2nd applicant's solicitor or other authorised agent. If signing on behalf of the applicant, please state in what capacity:

Signature: ....

Print Name: ....

Date: .... Capacity:..

[*Where there are more than two applicants, please use an additional sheet clearly marked "Signature(s) of further applicant(s)". The sheet should include all the information requested in paragraphs 20 and 21.*]

[*Where the application is to be submitted in an electronic form, the signature should be generated electronically and should be a copy of the person's written signature.*]

Part 8 – Contact Details

22(a) Please give the name of a person who can be contacted about the application:

....

22(b) Please give one or more telephone numbers at which the person identified in question 22(a) can be contacted:

....

23. Postal address for correspondence associated with this application:

....

....

.... Postcode:..

24. If you are happy for correspondence in relation to your application to be sent via e-mail, please give the e-mail address to which you would like correspondence to be sent:

....

PART 2
FORM OF APPLICATION FOR A PROVISIONAL STATEMENT (VESSEL)

[6.1690]

Application for a provisional statement under the Gambling Act 2005 (vessel)

PLEASE READ THE FOLLOWING INSTRUCTIONS FIRST

If you are completing this form by hand, please write legibly in block capitals using ink. Use additional sheets if necessary (marked with the number of the relevant question). You may wish to keep a copy of the completed form for your records.

Applications in respect of premises which are not a vessel should be made on the relevant form for those types of premises.

Part 1 – Type of premises to which the application relates

Regional casino ☐ **Large casino** ☐ **Small casino** ☐

Bingo ☐ **Adult gaming centre** ☐ **Family entertainment centre** ☐

Betting ☐

Part 2 – Applicant details

If you are an individual, please fill in section A. If the application is being made on behalf of an organisation (such as a company or partnership), please fill in Section B.

Section A
Individual applicant

1. Title: Mr ☐ Mrs ☐ Miss ☐ Ms ☐ Dr ☐ Other (please specify)

....

2. Surname: .... Other name(s): ....
[*Use the names given in the applicant's operating licence or, if the applicant does not hold an operating licence, as given in any application for an operating licence*]

3. Applicant's address (home or business – [*delete as appropriate*]):

....

....

.... Postcode:..

4(a) The number of the applicant's operating licence (as set out in the operating licence):

....

4(b) If the applicant does not hold an operating licence but is in the process of applying for one, give the date on which the application was made:

....

5. Tick the box if the application is being made by more than one person. ☐

[*Where there are further applicants, the information required in questions 1 to 4 should be included on additional sheets attached to this form, and those sheets should be clearly marked "Details of further applicants".*]

Section B
Application on behalf of an organisation

6. Name of applicant business or organisation:

....

[*Use the names given in the applicant's operating licence or, if the applicant does not hold an operating licence, as given in any application for an operating licence*]

7. The applicant's registered or principal address:

....

....

....Postcode: ....

8(a) The number of the applicant's operating licence (as given in the operating licence):

....

8(b) If the applicant does not hold an operating licence but is in the process of applying for one, give the date on which the application was made:

....

9. Tick the box if the application is being made by more than one organisation. ☐

[*Where there are further applicants, the information required in questions 6 to 8 should be included on additional sheets attached to this form, and those sheets should be clearly marked "Details of further applicants".*]

Part 3 – Premises Details

10. Name of vessel to which the application relates (if known):

....

11. Country in which vessel is registered (if known):

....

12(a) Give the place in the licensing authority's area at which the vessel is or will be situated or moored (Give an address with postcode if available):

....

....

....

12(b) Please confirm by ticking the appropriate box whether the place stated in question 12(a) is:

(i) a fixed place in or on water at which the vessel is situated; or ☐

(ii) a place at which the vessel is permanently moored; or ☐

(iii) a place at which the vessel is habitually moored; or ☐

(iv) in any other case, a place at which the vessel is moored or is likely to be moored or a place in the United Kingdom nearest to any place at which a vessel is, or is likely to be while activities are carried on in the vessel in reliance on the premises licence. ☐

13. If you have ticked box (iii) or (iv) in your answer to question 12(b), please indicate the number of days or months in a year when you expect the vessel to be moored at the place stated in question 12(a):

....

14. If you have ticked box (iii) or (iv) in your answer to question 12(b), please describe the other places where, and/or any other circumstances in which, the vessel will be used in reliance on the premises licence:

....

....

....

....

15. Please give a brief description of the vessel. Please describe the location of your premises within the vessel and indicate the uses of the other parts of the vessel:

....

....

....

....

....

....

Part 4 – Times of operation

16(a) Do you want the licensing authority to exclude a default condition so that the premises may be used for longer periods than would otherwise be the case? **Yes/ No**
[*delete as appropriate*]
[*Where the relevant kind of premises licence is not subject to any default conditions, the answer to this question will be no.*]

16(b) If the answer to question 16(a) is yes, please complete the table below to indicate the times when you want the premises to be available for use under the premises licence.

	Start	*Finish*	*Details of any seasonal variation*
Mon			
Tues			
Wed			
Thurs			
Fri			
Sat			
Sun			

17. If you want the premises licence to have a condition restricting gambling to specific periods in a year, please state the periods below using calendar dates:

....

Part 5 – Miscellaneous

18(a) Do you hold any other premises licences that have been issued by this licensing authority?

Yes/ No
[*delete as appropriate*]

18(b) If the answer question 18(a) is yes, please provide full details: ....

....

....

....

....

19. Please set out any other matters which you consider to be relevant to your application:

....

....

....

....

....

....

....

Part 6 – Declarations and Checklist (*Please tick*)

I/ We confirm that, to the best of my/ our knowledge, the information contained in this application is true. I/ We understand that it is an offence under section 342 of the Gambling Act 2005 to give information which is false or misleading in, or in relation to, this application. ☐

Checklist:

- **Payment of the appropriate fee has been made/is enclosed** ☐
- **A plan of the premises or proposed premises is enclosed** ☐
- **I/ we understand that if the above requirements are not complied with the application may be rejected** ☐
- **I/ we understand that it is now necessary to advertise the application and give the appropriate notice to the responsible authorities** ☐

Part 7 – Signatures

20. Signature of applicant or applicant's solicitor or other duly authorised agent. If signing on behalf of the applicant, please state in what capacity:

Signature: ....

Print Name: ....

Date: .... Capacity:...

21. For joint applications, signature of 2nd applicant, or 2nd applicant's solicitor or other authorised agent. If signing on behalf of the applicant, please state in what capacity:

Signature: ....

Print Name: ....

Date: .... Capacity:...

[*Where there are more than two applicants, please use an additional sheet clearly marked "Signature(s) of further applicant(s)". The sheet should include all the information requested in paragraphs 20 and 21.*]

[*Where the application is to be submitted in an electronic form, the signature should be generated electronically and should be a copy of the person's written signature.*]

Part 8 – Contact Details

22(a) Please give the name of a person who can be contacted about the application:

....

22(b) Please give one or more telephone numbers at which the person identified in question 22(a) can be contacted:

....

23. Postal address for correspondence associated with this application:

....

....

....Postcode:..............................

24. If you are happy for correspondence in relation to your application to be sent via e-mail, please give the e-mail address to which you would like correspondence to be sent:

....

6.1691

SCHEDULE 6
FORM OF NOTICE OF APPLICATION
Regulation 12

PART 1
APPLICATION FOR A PREMISES LICENCE: FORM OF NOTICE TO BE GIVEN TO THE RESPONSIBLE AUTHORITIES

Two forms are specified for the purposes of this Part. Form A is to be used where there is only one applicant. Form B is to be used where there are two or more applicants.

NOTICE OF APPLICATION FOR A PREMISES LICENCE

This notice is issued in accordance with regulations made under section 160 of the Gambling Act 2005

Notice is hereby given that:

....

[*Give the full name of the applicant as set out in Part 2 of the application for a premises licence*]

of the following address:..

....

....

....Postcode.................................

[*Give the full address of the applicant as set out in Part 2 of the application for a premises licence*]

the number of whose operating licence is ..../

who applied for an operating licence on..

[*Delete as appropriate. Insert the reference number of the applicant's operating licence (as set out in the operating licence). Where an application for an operating licence is in the process of being made, indicate the date on which the application was made.*]

has made an application for a .... premises licence.
[*Insert here the kind of premises licence being applied for*]

The application relates to the following premises:

....

....

....

....

....

....

[*Give the trading name to be used at the premises, and the address of the premises (or, if none, give a description of the premises and their location).*]

The application for a premises licence has been made to the following licensing authority:

....

....

....

....Postcode.......................................

Website:..

[*Insert name of the licensing authority and the address of its principal office, followed by the address of its website*]

Information about the application is available from the licensing authority, including the arrangements for viewing the details of the application.

The following person connected with the applicant is able to give further information about the application:

....

[*This entry is optional and is to be included if the applicant wishes to provide the name, telephone number and (if available) e-mail address of a person connected with the applicant who is able to answer questions and provide further information about the application.*]

Any representations under section 161 of the Gambling Act 2005 must be made no later than the following date:

....

[*Please insert last day on which representations may be made in relation to the application. The period for making representations is 28 days (inclusive) starting with the day on which the application for the premises licence was made to the licensing authority.*]

NOTICE OF APPLICATION FOR A PREMISES LICENCE

This notice is issued in accordance with regulations made under section 160 of the Gambling Act 2005

Notice is hereby given that the persons or organisations whose details are given in the Schedule to this notice have made an

application for a ....premises licence
[*Insert here the kind of premises licence being applied for*]

The application relates to the following premises:

....

....

....

....

....
[*Give the trading name to be used at the premises, and the address of the premises (or, if none, give a description of the premises and their location).*]

The application for a premises licence has been made to the following licensing authority:

....

....

....

....Postcode..........................

Website:...
[*Insert name of the licensing authority and the address of its principal office, followed by the address of its website*]

Information about the application is available from the licensing authority, including the arrangements for viewing the details of the application.

The following person connected with the applicant is able to give further information about the application:

....
[*This entry is optional and is to be included if the applicant wishes to provide the name, telephone number and (if available) e-mail address of a person connected with the applicant who is able to answer questions and provide further information about the application.*]

6: Gambling Act 2005: SIs

Any representations under section 161 of the Gambling Act 2005 must be made no later than the following date:

....

[*Please insert last day on which representations may be made in relation to the application. The period for making representations is 28 days (inclusive) starting with the day on which the application for the premises licence was made to the licensing authority.*]

SCHEDULE OF APPLICANTS

The persons or organisations making the application are as follows:

Name of 1st Applicant::

....

[*Give the full name of the applicant as set out in Part 2 of the application for a premises licence is more than one applicant*]

Address of 1st Applicant:...

....

....

....Postcode..................................

[*Give the full address of the applicant as set out in Part 2 of the application for a premises licence*]

The number of the operating licence held by 1st Applicant is:.../

The 1st Applicant applied for an operating licence on..

[*Delete as appropriate. Insert the reference number of the applicant's operating licence (as set out in the operating licence). Where an application for an operating licence is in the process of being made, indicate the date on which the application was made.*]

Name of 2nd Applicant:..

[*Give the full name of the applicant as set out in Part 2 of the application for a premises licence is more than one applicant*]

Address of 2nd Applicant:...

....

....

....Postcode..................................

[*Give the full address of the applicant as set out in Part 2 of the application for a premises licence*]

The number of the operating licence held by 2nd Applicant is:....................................../

The 2nd Applicant applied for an operating licence on..

[*Delete as appropriate. Insert the reference number of the applicant's operating licence (as set out in the operating licence). Where an application for an operating licence is in the process of being made, indicate the date on which the application was made.*]

[***Where there are more than two applicants, also give the same information for the other applicants.***]

PART 2
APPLICATION FOR A PREMISES LICENCE: FORM OF NOTICE TO BE PUBLISHED

[6.1692]

NOTICE OF APPLICATION FOR A PREMISES LICENCE UNDER THE GAMBLING ACT 2005

Notice is hereby given that:

....

[*Give the full name of the applicant(s)*]

of the following address:...

....

....

....

is/ are applying for a ....premises licence under section 159 of the Gambling Act 2005. [*Insert kind of premises licence being applied for*]

The application relates to the following premises:

....

....

....

....

[*Give the trading name to be used at the premises, and the address of the premises (or, if none, give a description of the premises and their location)*]

The application has been made to:...
[*Specify the name of the licensing authority to which the application has been made*]

Information about the application is available from the licensing authority, including the arrangements for viewing the details of the application.

Any of the following persons may make representations in writing to the licensing authority about the application:

- A person who lives sufficiently close to the premises to be likely to be affected by the authorised activities
- A person who has business interests that might be affected by the authorised activities
- A person who represents someone in any of the above two categories.

Any representations must be made by the following date:...

It is an offence under section 342 of the Gambling Act 2005 if a person, without reasonable excuse, gives to a licensing authority for a purpose connected with that Act information which is false or misleading.

PART 3
APPLICATION TO VARY A PREMISES LICENCE: FORM OF NOTICE TO BE GIVEN TO THE RESPONSIBLE AUTHORITIES

6.1693 Two forms are specified for the purposes of this Part. Form A is to be used where there is only one applicant. Form B is to be used where there are two or more applicants.

(Form A Individual Applicant)

NOTICE OF APPLICATION TO VARY A PREMISES LICENCE

This notice is issued in accordance with regulations made under section 160 of the Gambling Act 2005

Notice is hereby given that:

[*Give the full name of the applicant. The name should be the same as that given in Part 1 of the application to vary the premises licence.*]

of the following address:

Postcode

[*Give the full address of the applicant. The address should be the same as that set out in Part 1 of the application to vary the premises licence.*]

the number of whose operating licence is

who applied for an operating licence on

[*Delete as appropriate. Insert the reference number of the applicant's operating licence (as set out in the operating licence). Where an application for an operating licence is in the process of being made, indicate the date on which the application was made.*]

has applied for the vary to them of a premise licence of the following type:

[*Specify the type of premises licence to which the application relates*]

The application relates to the following licensed premises:

[*Give the trading name used at the premises, and the address of the premises (or, if none, give a description of the premises and their location)*]

Details of the variation sought:
The application has been made to the following licensing authority: Postcode: Website: [*Insert name of the licensing authority and the address of its principal office, followed by the address of its website*]
The current licence holder(s) is / are: [*Give the full name of the licence holder(s) as set out in the premises licence (if known). Where the applicant is the licence holder, it is sufficient to state "the applicant".*
(NB Reinstatement applications only delete as appropriate) The lapsed premises licence was held by: *[Give the full name of the licence holder(s) as set out in the premises licence (if known).]*
Information about the application is available from the licensing authority, including the arrangements for viewing the details of the application.
The following person connected with the applicant is able to give further information about the application: [*This entry is optional and is to be included if the applicant wishes to provide the name, telephone number and (if available) e-mail address of a person connected with the applicant who is able to answer questions and provide further information about the application.*]

Any representations under section 161 of the Gambling Act 2005 must be made no later than the following date:

[Please insert last day on which representations may be made in relation to the application. The period for making representations is 28 days (inclusive) starting with the day on which the application was made to the licensing authority.]

Form B

NOTICE OF APPLICATION TO VARY A PREMISES LICENCE

This notice is issued in accordance with regulations made under section 160 of the Gambling Act 2005

Notice is hereby given that the persons or organisations whose details are given in the Schedule to this notice have applied to vary a premises licence of the following type:

....

[*Specify the type of premises licence to which the application relates*]

The application relates to the following premises:

....

....

....

....

....

[*Give the trading name used at the premises, and the address of the premises (or, if none, give a description of the premises and their location).*]

Details of the variation sought:

....

....

....

....

....

....

The application has been made to the following licensing authority:

....

....

....

....Postcode....................................

Website:..

[*Insert name of the licensing authority and the address of its principal office, followed by the address of its website*]

The current licence holder(s) is/ are:

....

[*Give the full name of the licence holder(s) as set out in the premises licence (if known). Where the applicant is the licence holder, it is sufficient to state "the applicant".*]

Information about the application is available from the licensing authority, including the arrangements for viewing the details of the application.

The following person connected with the applicant is able to give further information about the application:

....

[*This entry is optional and is to be included if the applicant wishes to provide the name, telephone number and (if available) e-mail address of a person connected with the applicant who is able to answer questions and provide further information about the application.*]

Any representations under section 161 of the Gambling Act 2005 must be made no later than the following date:

....

[*Please insert last day on which representations may be made in relation to the application. The period for making representations is 28 days (inclusive) starting with the day after the day on which the application was made to the licensing authority.*]

SCHEDULE OF APPLICANTS

The persons or organisations making the application are as follows:

Name of 1st Applicant::

....

[*Give the full name of the applicant. The name should be the same as that given in Part 1 of the application to vary the premises licence.*]

Address of 1st Applicant:...

....

....

....Postcode...................................

[*Give the full address of the 1st Applicant. The address should be the same as that set out in Part 1 of the application to vary the premises licence.*]

The number of the operating licence held by 1st Applicant is:......................................./
The 1st Applicant applied for an operating licence on..

[*Delete as appropriate. Insert the reference number of the applicant's operating licence (as set out in the operating licence). Where an application for an operating licence is in the process of being made, indicate the date on which the application was made.*]

Name of 2nd Applicant:..

[*Give the full name of the applicant. The name should be the same as that given in Part 1 of the application to vary the premises licence.*]

Address of 2nd Applicant:...

....

....

....Postcode...................................

[*Give the full address of the applicant. The address should be the same as that set out in Part 1 of the application to vary the premises licence.*]

The number of the operating licence held by 2nd Applicant is:................................../

The 2nd Applicant applied for an operating licence on..

[*Delete as appropriate. Insert the reference number of the applicant's operating licence (as set out in the operating licence). Where an application for an operating licence is in the process of being made, indicate the date on which the application was made.*]

[***Where there are more than two applicants, also give the same information for the other applicants.***]

PART 4
APPLICATION TO VARY A PREMISES LICENCE: FORM OF NOTICE TO BE PUBLISHED

[6.1694]

NOTICE OF APPLICATION TO VARY A PREMISES LICENCE UNDER THE GAMBLING ACT 2005

Notice is hereby given that:

....

[Give the full name of the applicant(s)]

of the following address:..

....

....

is/ are applying under section 187 of the Gambling Act 2005 to vary a.............................. premises licence issued under that Act. [*Insert here the kind of premises licence to which the application relates*]

The application relates to the following premises:

....

....

....

[*Give the trading name used at the premises, and the address of the premises (or, if none, give a description of the premises and their location).*]

The application is to vary the licence as follows:

....

....

The application has been made to:...
[*Specify the name of the licensing authority to which the application has been made*]

Information about the application is available from the licensing authority, including the arrangements for viewing the details of the application.

Any of the following persons may make representations in writing to the licensing authority about the application:

- A person who lives sufficiently close to the premises to be likely to be affected by the authorised activities
- A person who has business interests that might be affected by the authorised activities
- A person who represents someone in any of the above two categories.

Any representations must be made by the following date:..

It is an offence under section 342 of the Gambling Act 2005 if a person, without reasonable excuse, gives to a licensing authority for a purpose connected with that Act information which is false or misleading.

6: Gambling Act 2005: SIs

PART 5
APPLICATION TO TRANSFER A PREMISES LICENCE: FORM OF NOTICE TO BE GIVEN TO THE RESPONSIBLE AUTHORITIES

6.1695 Two forms are specified for the purposes of this Part. Form A is to be used where there is only one applicant. Form B is to be used where there are two or more applicants.

(Form A Individual Applicant)

NOTICE OF APPLICATION TO TRANSFER A PREMISES LICENCE

This notice is issued in accordance with regulations made under section 160 of the Gambling Act 2005

Notice is hereby given that:

[*Give the full name of the applicant. The name should be the same as that given in Part 1 of the application to transfer the premises licence.*]

of the following address:

Postcode

[*Give the full address of the applicant. The address should be the same as that set out in Part 1 of the application to transfer the premises licence.*]

the number of whose operating licence is

who applied for an operating licence on

[*Delete as appropriate. Insert the reference number of the applicant's operating licence (as set out in the operating licence). Where an application for an operating licence is in the process of being made, indicate the date on which the application was made.*]

has applied for the transfer to them of a premise licence of the following type:

[*Specify the type of premises licence to which the application relates*]

The application relates to the following licensed premises:

[*Give the trading name used at the premises, and the address of the premises (or, if none, give a description of the premises and their location)*]

The application has been made to the following licensing authority:

Postcode

Website:

[*Insert name of the licensing authority and the address of its principal office, followed by the address of its website*]

The current licence holder(s) is / are:

[*Give the full name of the licence holder(s) as set out in the premises licence (if known). Where the applicant is the licence holder, it is sufficient to state "the applicant".*

(NB Reinstatement applications only delete as appropriate)

The lapsed premises licence was held by:

[Give the full name of the licence holder(s) as set out in the premises licence (if known).]

[NB variation, transfer, reinstatement applications only delete as appropriate

The number of the premises licence (if known):

[*Insert here the reference number of the premises licence as given in the licence itself.*]

Information about the application is available from the licensing authority, including the arrangements for viewing the details of the application.

The following person connected with the applicant is able to give further information about the application:

[*This entry is optional and is to be included if the applicant wishes to provide the name, telephone number and (if available) e-mail address of a person connected with the applicant who is able to answer questions and provide further information about the application.*]

Any representations under section 161 of the Gambling Act 2005 must be made no later than the following date:

[*Please insert last day on which representations may be made in relation to the application. The period for making representations is 28 days (inclusive) starting with the day on which the application was made to the licensing authority.*]

NOTICE OF APPLICATION TO TRANSFER A PREMISES LICENCE

This notice is issued in accordance with regulations made under section 160 of the Gambling Act 2005

Notice is hereby given that the persons or organisations whose details are given in the Schedule to this notice have applied for the transfer to them of a premises licence of the following type:

....

[*Specify the type of premises licence to which the application relates*]

The application relates to the following premises:

....

....

....

....

....

....

[*Give the trading name used at the premises, and the address of the premises (or, if none, give a description of the premises and their location).*]

The application has been made to the following licensing authority:

....

....

....

....Postcode..................................

Website:...

[*Insert name of the licensing authority and the address of its principal office, followed by the address of its website*]

The current licence holder(s) is/ are:

....

[*Give the full name of the licence holder(s) as set out in the premises licence (if known).*]

The number of the premises licence (if known):...

[*Insert here the reference number of the premises licence as given in the licence itself.*]

Information about the application is available from the licensing authority, including the arrangements for viewing the details of the application.

The following person connected with the applicant is able to give further information about the application:

....

[*This entry is optional and is to be included if the applicant wishes to provide the name, telephone number and (if available) e-mail address of a person connected with the applicant who is able to answer questions and provide further information about the application.*]

Any representations under section 161 of the Gambling Act 2005 must be made no later than the following date:

....

[*Please insert last day on which representations may be made in relation to the application. The period for making representations is 28 days (inclusive) starting with the day on which the application was made to the licensing authority.*]

SCHEDULE OF APPLICANTS

The persons or organisations making the application are as follows:

Name of 1st Applicant::

....

[*Give the full name of the applicant. The name should be the same as that given in Part 1 of the application to transfer the premises licence.*]

Address of 1st Applicant:...

....

....

....Postcode.................................

[*Give the full address of the 1st Applicant. The address should be the same as that set out in Part 1 of the application to transfer the premises licence.*]

The number of the operating licence held by 1st Applicant is:....................................../

The 1st Applicant applied for an operating licence on...

[*Delete as appropriate. Insert the reference number of the applicant's operating licence (as set out in the operating licence). Where an application for an operating licence is in the process of being made, indicate the date on which the application was made.*]

6: Gambling Act 2005: SIs

Name of 2nd Applicant:…………………………………………………………………………
[*Give the full name of the applicant. The name should be the same as that given in Part 1 of the application to transfer the premises licence.*]

Address of 2nd Applicant:……………………………………………………………………

……………………………………………………………………………………………………

……………………………………………………………………………………………………

……………………………………………………………Postcode……………………………
[*Give the full address of the applicant. The address should be the same as that set out in Part 1 of the application to transfer the premises licence.*]

The number of the operating licence held by 2nd Applicant is:……………………………/

The 2nd Applicant applied for an operating licence on……………………………………

[*Delete as appropriate. Insert the reference number of the applicant's operating licence (as set out in the operating licence). Where an application for an operating licence is in the process of being made, indicate the date on which the application was made.*]

[***Where there are more than two applicants, also give the same information for the other applicants.***]

PART 6
APPLICATION FOR THE REINSTATEMENT OF A PREMISES LICENCE: FORM OF NOTICE TO BE GIVEN TO THE RESPONSIBLE AUTHORITIES

6.1696

(Form A Individual Applicant)

NOTICE OF APPLICATION FOR THE REINSTATEMENT OF A PREMISES LICENCE

This notice is issued in accordance with regulations made under section 160 of the Gambling Act 2005

Notice is hereby given that:

[*Give the full name of the applicant. The name should be the same as that given in Part 1 of the application for reinstatement of the premises licence*]

of the following address:

Postcode

[*Give the full address of the applicant. The address should be the same as that set out in Part 1 of the application for reinstatement of the premises licence.*]

the number of whose operating licence is

who applied for an operating licence on

[*Delete as appropriate. Insert the reference number of the applicant's operating licence (as set out in the operating licence). Where an application for an operating licence is in the process of being made, indicate the date on which the application was made.*]

has made an application for the reinstatement of a premises licence of the following type:

[*Specify the type of premises licence to which the application relates*]

The application relates to the following licensed premises:

[*Give the trading name used at the premises, and the address of the premises (or, if none, give a description of the premises and their location)*

The application has been made to the following licensing authority: Postcode Website: [*Insert name of the licensing authority and the address of its principal office, followed by the address of its website*]
The lapsed premises licence was held by: [Give the full name of the licence holder(s) as set out in the premises licence (if known).]
(NB Reinstatement applications only delete as appropriate) The lapsed premises licence was held by: *[Give the full name of the licence holder(s) as set out in the premises licence (if known).]*
The number of the premises licence (if known): [*Insert here the reference number of the premises licence as given in the licence itself.*]
Information about the application is available from the licensing authority, including the arrangements for viewing the details of the application.
The following person connected with the applicant is able to give further information about the application: [*This entry is optional and is to be included if the applicant wishes to provide the name, telephone number and (if available) e-mail address of a person connected with the applicant who is able to answer questions and provide further information about the application.*]
Any representations under section 161 of the Gambling Act 2005 must be made no later than the following date: [*Please insert last day on which representations may be made in relation to the application. The period for making representations is 28 days (inclusive) starting with the day on which the application was made to the licensing authority.*]

NOTICE OF APPLICATION FOR THE REINSTATEMENT OF A PREMISES LICENCE

This notice is issued in accordance with regulations made under section 160 of the Gambling Act 2005

Notice is hereby given that the persons or organisations whose details are given in the Schedule to this notice have applied for the reinstatement of a premises licence of the following type:

....

[*Specify the type of premises licence to which the application relates*]

The application relates to the following premises:

....

....

....

....

....

....

[*Give the trading name used at the premises, and the address of the premises (or, if none, give a description of the premises and their location)*.]

The application has been made to the following licensing authority:

....

....

....

....Postcode..........................

Website:...

[*Insert name of the licensing authority and the address of its principal office, followed by the address of its website*]

The lapsed premises licence was held by:

....

....

[Give the full name of the licence holder(s) as given on the premises licence (if known).]

The number of the premises licence (if known):...

[*Insert here the reference number of the premises licence as given in the licence itself.*]

6: Gambling Act 2005: SIs

Information about the application is available from the licensing authority, including the arrangements for viewing the details of the application.

The following person connected with the applicant is able to give further information about the application:

....

[*This entry is optional and is to be included if the applicant wishes to provide the name, telephone number and (if available) e-mail address of a person connected with the applicant who is able to answer questions and provide further information about the application.*]

Any representations under section 161 of the Gambling Act 2005 must be made no later than the following date:

....

[*Please insert last day on which representations may be made in relation to the application. The period for making representations is 28 days (inclusive) starting with the day on which the application was made to the licensing authority.*]

SCHEDULE OF APPLICANTS

The persons or organisations making the application are as follows:

Name of 1st Applicant::

....

[*Give the full name of the applicant. The name should be the same as that given in Part 1 of the application for reinstatement of the premises licence.*]

Address of 1st Applicant:...

....

....

....Postcode...................................

[*Give the full address of the 1st Applicant. The address should be the same as that set out in Part 1 of the application for reinstatement of the premises licence.*]

The number of the operating licence held by 1st Applicant is:....................................../

The 1st Applicant applied for an operating licence on...

[*Delete as appropriate. Insert the reference number of the applicant's operating licence (as set out in the operating licence). Where an application for an operating licence is in the process of being made, indicate the date on which the application was made.*]

Name of 2nd Applicant:..
[*Give the full name of the applicant. The name should be the same as that given in Part 1 of the application for reinstatement of the premises licence.*]

Address of 2nd Applicant:..

....

....

....Postcode..
[*Give the full address of the applicant. The address should be the same as that set out in Part 1 of the application for reinstatement of the premises licence.*]

The number of the operating licence held by 2nd Applicant is:../

The 2nd Applicant applied for an operating licence on..

[*Delete as appropriate. Insert the reference number of the applicant's operating licence (as set out in the operating licence). Where an application for an operating licence is in the process of being made, indicate the date on which the application was made.*]

[***Where there are more than two applicants, also give the same information for the other applicants.***]

PART 7
APPLICATION FOR A PROVISIONAL STATEMENT: FORM OF NOTICE TO BE GIVEN TO THE RESPONSIBLE AUTHORITIES

6.1697 Two forms are specified for the purposes of this Part. Form A is to be used where there is only one applicant. Form B is to be used where there are two or more applicants.

NOTICE OF APPLICATION FOR A PROVISIONAL STATEMENT

This notice is issued in accordance with regulations made under section 160 of the Gambling Act 2005

Notice is hereby given that:

....

[*Give the full name of the applicant as set out in Part 2 of the application for a provisional statement*]

of the following address:...

....

....

....Postcode..................................

[*Give the full address of the applicant as set out in Part 2 of the application for a provisional statement*]

the number of whose operating licence is ..../

who applied for an operating licence on...

[*Delete as appropriate. Insert the reference number of the applicant's operating licence (as set out in the operating licence). Where an application for an operating licence is in the process of being made, indicate the date on which the application was made.*]

has made an application for a provisional statement in respect of the following type of premises;

....

[*Specify the type of premises to which the application relates*]

The application relates to the following premises or proposed premises:

....

....

....

....

....

[If known, give the trading name to be used at the premises and the address of the premises as given in Part 3 of the application. If the premises have no address, then describe the premises and the location in the same way as they are described in Part 3 of the application.]

The application has been made to the following licensing authority:

....

....

....

....Postcode..............................

Website:..

[Insert name of the licensing authority and the address of its principal office, followed by the address of its website]

Information about the application is available from the licensing authority, including the arrangements for viewing the details of the application.

The following person connected with the applicant is able to give further information about the application:

....

[This entry is optional and is to be included if the applicant wishes to provide the name, telephone number and (if available) e-mail address of a person connected with the applicant who is able to answer questions and provide further information about the application.]

Any representations under section 161 of the Gambling Act 2005 must be made no later than the following date:

....

[Please insert last day on which representations may be made in relation to the application. The period for making representations is 28 days (inclusive) starting with the day on which the application for a provisional statement was made to the licensing authority.]

NOTICE OF APPLICATION FOR A PROVISIONAL STATEMENT

This notice is issued in accordance with regulations made under section 160 of the Gambling Act 2005

Notice is hereby given that the persons or organisations whose details are given in the Schedule to this notice have made an application for a provisional statement in respect of the following type of premises:

....

[*Specify the type of premises to which the application relates*]

The application relates to the following premises:

....

....

....

....

....

[*If known, give the trading name to be used at the premises and the address of the premises as given in Part 3 of the application. If the premises have no address, then describe the premises and the location in the same way as they are described in Part 3 of the application.*]

The application has been made to the following licensing authority:

....

....

....

....Postcode...................................

Website:...

[*Insert name of the licensing authority and the address of its principal office, followed by the address of its website*]

Information about the application is available from the licensing authority, including the arrangements for viewing the details of the application.

The following person connected with the applicant is able to give further information about the application:

....

[*This entry is optional and is to be included if the applicant wishes to provide the name, telephone number and (if available) e-mail address of a person connected with the applicant who is able to answer questions and provide further information about the application.*]

Any representations under section 161 of the Gambling Act 2005 must be made no later than the following date:

....

[*Please insert last day on which representations may be made in relation to the application. The period for making representations is 28 days (inclusive) starting with the day after the day on which the application for a provisional statement was made to the licensing authority.*]

SCHEDULE OF APPLICANTS

The persons or organisations making the application are as follows:

Name of 1st Applicant::

....

[*Give the full name of the applicant as set out in Part 2 of the application for a provisional statement*]

Address of 1st Applicant:...

....

....

....Postcode....................................

[*Give the full address of the applicant as set out in Part 2 of the application for a provisional statement*]

The number of the operating licence held by 1st Applicant is:......................................./

The 1st Applicant applied for an operating licence on..

[*Delete as appropriate. Insert the reference number of the applicant's operating licence (as set out in the operating licence). Where an application for an operating licence is in the process of being made, indicate the date on which the application was made.*]

Name of 2nd Applicant:………………………………………………………………………

[*Give the full name of the applicant as set out in Part 2 of the application for a provisional statement*]

Address of 2nd Applicant:……………………………………………………………………

……………………………………………………………………………………………

……………………………………………………………………………………………

……………………………………………………………Postcode……………………………

[*Give the full address of the applicant as set out in Part 2 of the application for a provisional statement*]

The number of the operating licence held by 2nd Applicant is:……………………………/

The 2nd Applicant applied for an operating licence on………………………………………

[*Delete as appropriate. Insert the reference number of the applicant's operating licence (as set out in the operating licence). Where an application for an operating licence is in the process of being made, indicate the date on which the application was made.*]

[***Where there are more than two applicants, also give the same information for the other applicants.***]

PART 8
APPLICATION FOR A PROVISIONAL STATEMENT: FORM OF NOTICE TO BE PUBLISHED

[6.1698]

NOTICE OF APPLICATION FOR A PROVISIONAL STATEMENT UNDER THE GAMBLING ACT 2005

Notice is hereby given that:

....
[Give the full name of the applicant(s)]

of the following address:...

....

....

is/ are applying for a provisional statement under section 204 of the Gambling Act 2005. The application relates to the following type of premises:

....
[*Insert the type of premises to which the application relates*]

The application relates to the following premises:

....

....

....

....
[*Give the trading name to be used at the premises and the address of the premises. If no address is available, give a description of the premises and their location*]

The application has been made to:...
[*Specify the name of the licensing authority to which the application has been made*]

Information about the application is available from the licensing authority, including the arrangements for viewing the details of the application.

Any of the following persons may make representations in writing to the licensing authority about the application:

- A person who lives sufficiently close to the premises to be likely to be affected by the authorised activities
- A person who has business interests that might be affected by the authorised activities
- A person who represents someone in any of the above two categories.

Any representations must be made by the following date:..

It is an offence under section 342 of the Gambling Act 2005 if a person, without reasonable excuse, gives to a licensing authority for a purpose connected with that Act information which is false or misleading.

6.1699

SCHEDULE 7
FORM OF NOTICE OF GRANT OF AN APPLICATION
Regulation 17

PART 1
NOTICE OF THE GRANT OF AN APPLICATION FOR A PREMISES LICENCE

NOTICE OF GRANT OF AN APPLICATION FOR A PREMISES LICENCE

This notice is issued in accordance with regulations made under section 164(2) of the Gambling Act 2005

[*Insert here the name and address of the issuing licensing authority*]

An application for a premises licence of the following type:..
[*Insert type of premises licence to be granted*]

is granted to:

....
[*Insert name of person(s) to whom licence is issued*]

of the following address:...

....

....

....
[*Insert address(es) of the person(s) to whom the premises licence is issued as set out in Part 2 of the application for a premises licence*]

the number of whose operating licence is:

....
[*Insert the operating licence number given by the Gambling Commission to the applicant's operating licence. Leave out if no operating licence is held. Where there is more than one applicant who holds an operating licence, give all operating licence numbers.*]

The premises to which the application relates are:...

....

....

....

....

....

[*Give the address of the premises as set out in the premises licence. If the premises have no address, include the description of the premises and their location as set out in the premises licence.*]

The premises licence number is:...

The date on which the licence takes effect is: ....
[*This will generally be the date on which the licence is issued*]

The conditions set out in Annex A to this Notice have been attached to the premises licence under section 169(1)(a) of the Gambling Act 2005.
[*Set out the conditions and the reasons for imposing them in an annex in the appropriate form. Where no conditions are attached, omit this paragraph and the relevant annex.*]

The default conditions set out in Annex B to this Notice have been excluded under section 169(1)(b) of the Gambling Act 2005.
[*Set out the default conditions to be excluded, and the reasons for excluding them, in an annex in the appropriate form. Where no conditions are excluded, leave out this paragraph and the relevant annex.*]

The licensing authority did/did not [*delete as appropriate*] receive representations in relation to the application.

The representations received in relation to the application, together with the licensing authority's response, are set out in Annex C to this Notice.
[*Set out the representations by the licensing authority, together with the authority's response to them, in an annex in the appropriate form. Where no representations were received, leave out this paragraph and the relevant annex.*]

An appeal may be brought against the grant of the application, or the imposition or exclusion of the conditions referred to above by either the applicant, or any person who made representations in relation to the application. An appeal must be instituted:

- in the magistrates' court for a local justice area in which the premises are wholly or partly situated;
- by notice of appeal given to the designated officer;
- within 21 days beginning with the date of receipt of this notice of grant

PART 2
NOTICE OF THE GRANT OF AN APPLICATION TO VARY A PREMISES LICENCE

[6.1700]

NOTICE OF GRANT OF AN APPLICATION TO VARY A PREMISES LICENCE

This notice is issued in accordance with regulations made under section 164(2) of the Gambling Act 2005

[*Insert here the name and address of the issuing licensing authority*]

An application to vary a premises licence

is granted to:

....

[*Insert name of person(s) making the application*]

of the following address:..

....

....

....

[*Insert address(es) of the person(s) making the application as set out in Part 1 of the application*]

the number of whose operating licence is:

....

[*Insert the operating licence number given by the Gambling Commission to the applicant's operating licence. Leave out if no operating licence is held. Where there is more than one applicant who holds an operating licence, give all operating licence numbers.*]

The premises to which the application relates are:...

....

....

....

....

....

[*Give the address of the premises as set out in the premises licence. If the premises have no address, include the description of the premises and their location as set out in the premises licence*]

The premises licence number is:..

The premises licence is to be varied as follows:..

....

....

....

....

[*Describe the variations that are to be made to the premises licence on the grant of the application.*]

The variations take effect from: ....
[*Please insert the time and date from which the variations will take effect*]

In granting the application, the licensing authority have attached the conditions set out in Annex A to this Notice.
[*Set out the conditions and the reasons for imposing them in an annex in the appropriate form. Where no conditions are attached, omit this paragraph and the relevant annex.*]

In granting the application, the licensing authority have excluded the conditions set out in Annex B to this Notice.
[*Set out the conditions to be excluded, and the reasons for excluding them, in an annex in the appropriate form. Where no conditions are excluded, leave out this paragraph and the relevant annex.*]

The licensing authority did/did not [*delete as appropriate*] receive representations in relation to the application.

The representations received in relation to the application, together with the licensing authority's response, are set out in Annex C to this Notice.
[*Set out the representations by the licensing authority, together with the authority's response to them, in an annex in the appropriate form. Where no representations were received, leave out this paragraph and the relevant annex*.]

An appeal may be brought against the grant of the application, or the imposition or exclusion of the conditions referred to above by either the applicant, or any person who made representations in relation to the application. An appeal must be instituted:

- in the magistrates' court for a local justice area in which the premises are wholly or partly situated;
- by notice of appeal given to the designated officer;
- within 21 days beginning with the date of receipt of this notice of grant

PART 3
NOTICE OF THE GRANT OF AN APPLICATION FOR THE TRANSFER OF A PREMISES LICENCE

[6.1701]

NOTICE OF GRANT OF AN APPLICATION TO TRANSFER A PREMISES LICENCE

This notice is issued in accordance with regulations made under section 164(2) of the Gambling Act 2005

[*Insert here the name and address of the issuing licensing authority*]

An application to transfer a premises licence

is granted to:

....

[*Insert name of person(s) to whom licence is issued*]

of the following address:...

....

....

....

[*Insert address(es) of the person(s) to whom the premises licence is issued as set out in Part 1 of the application*]

the number of whose operating licence is:

....

[*Insert the operating licence number given by the Gambling Commission to the applicant's operating licence. Leave out if no operating licence is held. Where there is more than one applicant who holds an operating licence, give all operating licence numbers.*]

The premises to which the application relates are:...

....

....

....

....

....

[*Give the address of the premises as set out in the premises licence. If the premises have no address, include the description of the premises and their location as set out in the premises licence*]

The premises licence number is:..

The name of the person(s) from the whom the licence is transferred is/are:

....

The transfer takes effect from: ....
[*Give the date when the transfer will take effect*]

In granting the application, the licensing authority have attached the conditions set out in Annex A to this Notice.
[*Set out the conditions and the reasons for imposing them in an annex in the appropriate form. Where no conditions are attached, omit this paragraph and the relevant annex.*]

In granting the application, the licensing authority have excluded the conditions set out in Annex B to this Notice.
[*Set out the conditions to be excluded, and the reasons for excluding them, in an annex in the appropriate form. Where no conditions are excluded, leave out this paragraph and the relevant annex.*]

The licensing authority did/did not [*delete as appropriate*] receive representations in relation to the application.

The representations received in relation to the application, together with the licensing authority's response, are set out in Annex C to this Notice.
[*Set out the representations by the licensing authority, together with the authority's response to them, in an annex in the appropriate form. Where no representations were received, leave out this paragraph and the relevant annex.*]

An appeal may be brought against the grant of the application, or the imposition or exclusion of the conditions referred to above by either the applicant, or any person who made representations in relation to the application. An appeal must be instituted:

- in the magistrates' court for a local justice area in which the premises are wholly or partly situated;
- by notice of appeal given to the designated officer;
- within 21 days beginning with the date of receipt of this notice of grant

PART 4
NOTICE OF THE GRANT OF AN APPLICATION FOR THE REINSTATEMENT OF A PREMISES LICENCE

[6.1702]

NOTICE OF GRANT OF AN APPLICATION FOR THE REINSTATEMENT OF A PREMISES LICENCE

This notice is issued in accordance with regulations made under section 164(2) of the Gambling Act 2005

[*Insert here the name and address of the issuing licensing authority*]

An application for the reinstatement of a premises licence

is granted to:

....

[*Insert name of person(s) to whom licence is issued*]

of the following address:..

....

....

....

[*Insert address(es) of the person(s) to whom the premises licence is issued as set out in Part 1 of the application*]

the number of whose operating licence is:

....

[*Insert the operating licence number given by the Gambling Commission to the applicant's operating licence. Leave out if no operating licence is held. Where there is more than one applicant who holds an operating licence, give all operating licence numbers.*]

The premises to which the application relates are:..

....

....

....

....

....

[*Give the address of the premises as set out in the premises licence. If the premises have no address, include the description of the premises and their location as set out in the premises licence*]

The premises licence number is:...

The reinstatement takes effect from: ....
[*Insert the date on which the reinstatement will take effect. This will be the date on which the application was granted*]

In approving the application, the licensing authority have attached the conditons set out in Annex A to this Notice.
[*Set out the conditions and the reasons for imposing them in an annex in the appropriate form. Where no conditions are attached, omit this paragraph and the relevant annex.*]

In approving the application, the licensing authority have excluded the conditions set out in Annex B to this Notice.
[*Set out the conditions to be excluded, and the reasons for excluding them, in an annex in the appropriate form. Where no conditions are excluded, leave out this paragraph and the relevant annex.*]

The licensing authority did/did not [*delete as appropriate*] receive representations in relation to the application.

The representations received in relation to the application, together with the licensing authority's response, are set out in Annex C to this Notice.
[*Set out the representations by the licensing authority, together with the authority's response to them, in an annex in the appropriate form. Where no representations were received, leave out this paragraph and the relevant annex.*]

An appeal may be brought against the grant of the application, or the imposition or exclusion of the conditions referred to above by either the applicant, or any person who made representations in relation to the application. An appeal must be instituted:

- in the magistrates' court for a local justice area in which the premises are wholly or partly situated;
- by notice of appeal given to the designated officer;
- within 21 days beginning with the date of receipt of this notice of grant

PART 5
NOTICE OF THE GRANT OF AN APPLICATION FOR A PROVISIONAL STATEMENT

[6.1703]

NOTICE OF GRANT OF AN APPLICATION FOR A PROVISIONAL STATEMENT

This notice is issued in accordance with regulations made under section 164(2) of the Gambling Act 2005

[*Insert here the name and address of the issuing licensing authority*]

An application for a provisional statement in relation to the following type of premises:

....

[*Insert type of premises*]

is granted to:

....

[*Insert name of person(s) to whom the provisional statement is issued*]

of the following address:...

....

....

....

[*Insert address(es) of the person(s) to whom the provisional statement is issued as set out in Part 2 of the application*]

the number of whose operating licence is:

....

[*Insert the operating licence number given by the Gambling Commission to the applicant's operating licence. Leave out if no operating licence is held. Where there is more than one applicant who holds an operating licence, give all operating licence numbers.*]

The premises or proposed premises to which the application relates are:

....

....

....

....

....

[*Give the address of the premises as set out in the application. If the premises have no address, include the description of the premises and their location as set out in the application.*]

The provisional statement number is:...

If a premises licence for the type of premises specified in the provisional statement were to be issued, the licensing authority would attach the conditions set out in Annex A to this Notice, in exercise of their powers under section 169(1)(a) of the Gambling Act 2005.
[*Set out the conditions and the reasons for imposing them in an annex in the appropriate form. Where no conditions would be attached, omit this paragraph and the relevant annex.*]

If a premises licence for the type of premises specified in the provisional statement were to be issued, the licensing authority would exclude the default conditions set out in Annex B to this Notice, in exercise of their powers under section 169(1)(b) of the Gambling Act 2005.
[*Set out the default conditions to be excluded, and the reasons for excluding them, in an annex in the appropriate form. Where no conditions are excluded, leave out this paragraph and the relevant annex.*]

The licensing authority did/did not [*delete as appropriate*] receive representations in relation to the application.

The representations received in relation to the application, together with the licensing authority's response, are set out in Annex C to this Notice.
[*Set out the representations by the licensing authority, together with the authority's response to them, in an annex in the appropriate form. Where no representations were received, leave out this paragraph.*]

An appeal may be brought against the grant of the application, or the imposition or exclusion of the conditions referred to above by either the applicant, or any person who made representations in relation to the application. An appeal must be instituted:

- in the magistrates' court for a local justice area in which the premises are wholly or partly situated;
- by notice of appeal given to the designated officer;
- within 21 days beginning with the date of receipt of this notice of grant.

PART 6
ANNEX SETTING OUT CONDITIONS TO BE ATTACHED

[6.1704]

ANNEX A – CONDITIONS TO BE ATTACHED

Condition to be attached	*Reasons for attaching condition*

PART 7
ANNEX SETTING OUT CONDITIONS TO BE EXCLUDED

[6.1705]

ANNEX B – CONDITIONS TO BE EXCLUDED

Condition to be excluded	*Reasons for excluding condition*

PART 8
ANNEX SETTING OUT REPRESENTATIONS

[6.1706]

ANNEX C – REPRESENTATIONS

Representation	*Licensing authority's response*

6.1707

SCHEDULE 8
FORM OF NOTICE OF REJECTION OF APPLICATION
Regulation 18

PART 1
NOTICE OF THE REJECTION OF AN APPLICATION FOR A PREMISES LICENCE

NOTICE OF REJECTION OF AN APPLICATION FOR A PREMISES LICENCE

This notice is issued in accordance with regulations made under section 165(2) of the Gambling Act 2005

[*Insert here the name and address of the issuing licensing authority*]

An application for a premises licence of the following type:...
[*Insert type of premises licence*]

made by: ....

....
[*Insert name of person(s) by whom the application was made*]

of the following address:..

....

....

....
[*Insert address(es) of the person(s) making the application as set out in Part 2 of the application*]

the number of whose operating licence is:

....
[*Insert the operating licence number given by the Gambling Commission to the applicant's operating licence. Leave out if no operating licence is held. Where there is more than one applicant who holds an operating licence, give all operating licence numbers.*]

is rejected.

The premises to which this notice applies are:..

....

....

....

....

....

[*Give the trading name and address of the premises as set out in Part 3 of the application. If the premises have no address, include the description of the premises and their location as set out in the application.*]

The application has been rejected for the following reasons:

....

....

....

....

....

....

....

....

[*Give the reasons for the decision to reject. Continue as necessary*]

An appeal may be brought against the rejection of this application by the applicant. An appeal must be instituted:

- in the magistrates' court for a local justice area in which the premises are wholly or partly situated;
- by notice of appeal given to the designated officer;
- within 21 days beginning with the date of receipt of this notice of rejection.

PART 2
NOTICE OF THE REJECTION OF AN APPLICATION TO VARY A PREMISES LICENCE

[6.1708]

NOTICE OF REJECTION OF AN APPLICATION TO VARY A PREMISES LICENCE

This notice is issued in accordance with regulations made under section 165(2) of the Gambling Act 2005

[*Insert here the name and address of the issuing licensing authority*]

An application to vary a premises licence of the following type:....................................
[*Insert type of premises licence*]

made by:

....
[*Insert name of person(s) by whom the application was made*]

of the following address:..

....

....

....
[*Insert address(es) of the person(s) making the application as set out in Part 1 of the application*]

the number of whose operating licence is:

....
[*Insert the operating licence number given by the Gambling Commission to the applicant's operating licence. Leave out if no operating licence is held. Where there is more than one applicant who holds an operating licence, give all operating licence numbers.*]

is rejected.

6: Gambling Act 2005: SIs

The premises to which this notice applies are:..

....

....

....

....

....

[*Give the trading name and address of the premises as set out in the premises licence. If the premises have no address, include the description of the premises and their location as set out in the premises licence.*]

The application has been rejected for the following reasons:

....

....

....

....

....

....

....

....

[*Give the reasons for the decision to reject. Continue as necessary*]

An appeal may be brought against the rejection of this application by the applicant. An appeal must be instituted:

- in the magistrates' court for a local justice area in which the premises are wholly or partly situated;
- by notice of appeal given to the designated officer;
- within 21 days beginning with the date of receipt of this notice of rejection.

PART 3
NOTICE OF THE REJECTION OF AN APPLICATION TO TRANSFER A PREMISES LICENCE

[6.1709]

NOTICE OF REJECTION OF AN APPLICATION TO TRANSFER A PREMISES LICENCE

This notice is issued in accordance with regulations made under section 165(2) of the Gambling Act 2005

[*Insert here the name and address of the issuing licensing authority*]

An application to transfer a premises licence of the following type:

....

[*Insert type of premises licence*]

made by:

....

[*Insert name of person(s) by whom the application was made*]

of the following address:..

....

....

....

[*Insert address(es) of the person(s) making the application as set out in Part 1 of the application*]

the number of whose operating licence is:

....

[*Insert the operating licence number given by the Gambling Commission to the applicant's operating licence. Leave out if no operating licence is held. Where there is more than one applicant who holds an operating licence, give all operating licence numbers.*]

is rejected.

The premises to which this notice applies are:..

....

....

....

....

....

[*Give the trading name and address of the premises as set out in the premises licence. If the premises have no address, include the description of the premises and their location as set out in the premises licence.*]

The application has been rejected for the following reasons:

....

....

....

....

....

....

....

....

[*Give the reasons for the decision to reject. Continue as necessary*]

An appeal may be brought against the rejection of this application by the applicant. An appeal must be instituted:

- in the magistrates' court for a local justice area in which the premises are wholly or partly situated;
- by notice of appeal given to the designated officer;
- within 21 days beginning with the date of receipt of this notice of rejection.

PART 4
NOTICE OF THE REJECTION OF AN APPLICATION TO REINSTATE A PREMISES LICENCE

[6.1710]

NOTICE OF REJECTION OF AN APPLICATION FOR REINSTATEMENT OF A PREMISES LICENCE

This notice is issued in accordance with regulations made under section 165(2) of the Gambling Act 2005

[*Insert here the name and address of the issuing licensing authority*]

An application for the reinstatement of a premises licence of the following type:

....

[*Insert type of premises licence*]

made by:

....

[*Insert name of person(s) by whom the application was made*]

of the following address:...

....

....

....

[*Insert address(es) of the person(s) making the application as set out in Part 1 of the application*]

the number of whose operating licence is:

....

[*Insert the operating licence number given by the Gambling Commission to the applicant's operating licence. Leave out if no operating licence is held. Where there is more than one applicant who holds an operating licence, give all operating licence numbers.*]

is rejected.

6: Gambling Act 2005: SIs

The premises to which this notice applies are:...

....

....

....

....

....

[Give the trading name and address of the premises as set out in the premises licence. If the premises have no address, include the description of the premises and their location as set out in the premises licence.]

The application has been rejected for the following reasons:

....

....

....

....

....

....

....

....

[Give the reasons for the decision to reject. Continue as necessary]

An appeal may be brought against the rejection of this application by the applicant. An appeal must be instituted:

- in the magistrates' court for a local justice area in which the premises are wholly or partly situated;
- by notice of appeal given to the designated officer;
- within 21 days beginning with the date of receipt of this notice of rejection.

PART 5
NOTICE OF THE REJECTION OF AN APPLICATION FOR A PROVISIONAL STATEMENT

[6.1711]

NOTICE OF REJECTION OF AN APPLICATION FOR A PROVISIONAL STATEMENT

This notice is issued in accordance with regulations made under section 165(2) of the Gambling Act 2005

[*Insert here name and address of the issuing licensing authority*]

An application for a provisional statement in respect of the following type of premises:

....

[*Insert type of premises to which application relates*]

made by:

....

[*Insert name of person(s) by whom the application was made*]

of the following address:...

....

....

....

[*Insert address(es) of the person(s) making the application as set out in Part 2 of the application*]

the number of whose operating licence is:

....

[*Insert the operating licence number given by the Gambling Commission to the applicant's operating licence. Leave out if no operating licence is held. Where there is more than one applicant who holds an operating licence, give all operating licence numbers.*]

is rejected.

The premises to which this notice applies are:..

....

....

....

....

....

[*Give the trading name and address of the premises as set out in Part 3 of the application. If the premises have no address, include the description of the premises and their location as set out in the application.*]

The application has been rejected for the following reasons:

....

....

....

....

....

....

....

....

[*Give the reasons for the decision to reject. Continue as necessary*]

An appeal may be brought against the rejection of this application by the applicant. An appeal must be instituted:

- in the magistrates' court for a local justice area in which the premises are wholly or partly situated;
- by notice of appeal given to the designated officer;
- within 21 days beginning with the date of receipt of this notice of rejection.

SCHEDULE 9
FORM OF PREMISES LICENCE
Regulation 22

[6.1712]

No: [*Insert premises licence number*]

[*Insert type of licence. See Note 1*] **PREMISES LICENCE**

This licence is issued under section 164 of the Gambling Act 2005 by

[*Insert the name of the issuing licensing authority*]

Part 1 – Details of person to whom licence is issued

This premises licence is issued to:

....

[*Insert full name of person(s) or organisation(s) to whom the licence is issued. See Note 2*]

of the following address:

....

....

....

[*Insert address or addresses of person or organisations to whom the licence is issued. See Note 3*]

who holds an operating licence which has been given the following operating licence number by the Gambling Commission:

....

[*If appropriate, insert operating licence number. See Note 4.*]

Part 2 – Details of the premises in respect of which the licence is issued

Facilities for gambling may be provided in accordance with this licence on the following premises:

....

....

....

....

[*Give a description of the premises to which the licence relates. See Note 5.*]

The place in the area of the licensing authority in which the vessel is wholly or partly situated (within the meaning of section 211(3) of the Gambling Act 2005) is:

....

[*This entry is only to be included where the licensed premises are a vessel. See Note 6*]

Part 3 – Premises licence details

This licence came into effect on:

....

[*Set out the date on which the licence first took effect*]

This licence is of unlimited duration
[*See Note 7.*]

This licence has been re-issued following the grant of an application to vary the licence.

The variations to the licence take effect on:...
[*This entry is only to be included where the licence has been varied. Specify the date on which any variations took effect.*]

This licence has been re-issued following the grant of an application to transfer the licence.

The transfer of the licence takes effect on:...
[*This entry is only to be included where the licence has been transferred. Specify the date on which the transfer took effect.*]

This licence has been re-issued following the grant of an application for reinstatement of the licence. The reinstatement of the licence takes effect on the date on which the application was granted:

....

[*This entry is only to be included where the licence has been reinstated. State the date on which the application for reinstatement was granted. This will also be the date on which the reinstatement takes effect.*

The following conditions have been attached to the licence by the issuing authority under section 169(1)(a) of the Gambling Act 2005:

....

....

....

....

....

[*Insert any conditions attached to the licence under section 169(1)(a)*]

The following conditions, which would otherwise attach to the licence by virtue of regulations made under section 168 of the Gambling Act 2005, have been excluded by the issuing authority under section 169(1)(b) of that Act:

....

....

....

....

....

[*Insert any conditions that have been excluded under section 169(1)(b)*]

A scale plan is attached as an annex to this licence
[*Please ensure that the relevant plan of the premises is attached*]

Signed on behalf of the issuing licensing authority

....

[*Insert signature of person authorised to sign on behalf of the authority. Where the licence is issued electronically, the signature must be generated electronically and be a copy of the person's written signature*]

Guidance Notes

1. The type of premises licence should be inserted here. The following options are available:

— regional casino
— large casino
— small casino
— converted casino
— bingo
— adult gaming centre
— family entertainment centre
— betting

The type chosen should match the selection made by the applicant in Part 1 of the application form submitted to the licensing authority. If the premises licence is a betting premises licence, a suffix should also be added so that the title will read either "Betting Premises Licence (in respect of premises other than a track)" or "Betting Premises Licence (in respect of a track)"

2. Except where the licence is transferred or reinstated, the names or names given should reflect those given in Part 2 of the application for a premises licence.

3. Except where the licence is transferred or reinstated, the address or addresses given should reflect those given in Part 2 of the application for a premises licence.

4. Where the holder of the premises licence does not hold an operating licence then this entry is to be left out. A premises licence can be issued to a person who does not hold an operating licence:

— if the premises concerned are a track; or
— where the premises licence has been issued under transitional arrangements, and the holder of the premises licence is applying for an operating licence, but the application has not been granted by the date of issue.

5. Give the address of the premises as set out in Part 3 of the application for a premises licence. If the premises have no address, give a description of the premises and their location which as far as possible reflects that set out in the application for a premises licence. If the application is in respect of a vessel, the name and country of registration of the vessel should be entered here.

6. If the licence is in respect of a vessel, the place in the area of the licensing authority where the vessel is situated or moored for the purposes of the licence should be entered here. Unless varied, this place should be the same as that given in Part 3 of the application for a premises licence. If the application is not in respect of a vessel, this entry in the licence should be left out.

7. Licences run for an indefinite duration unless they are revoked, surrendered or lapse under Part 8 of the Gambling Act 2005.

6.1713

SCHEDULE 10
FORM OF SUMMARY
Regulation 23

SUMMARY OF THE TERMS AND CONDITIONS OF A PREMISES LICENCE

This summary is issued under section 164 of the Gambling Act 2005 by

[*Insert the name of the issuing licensing authority*]

This summary is issued to:

....

[*Insert full name of person(s) or organisation(s) to whom the summary is issued. See Note 1*]

of the following address:

....

....

....

[*Insert address of person(s) or organisation(s) to whom summary is issued. See Note 2*]

A premises licence of the following type:

....

[*Please specify type of premises licence*]

has been issued in respect of the following premises:

....

....

....

....

[*Give a description of the premises. See Note 3*]

The place in the area of the licensing authority in which the vessel is wholly or partly situated (within the meaning of section 211(3) of the Gambling Act 2005) is:

....

[*This entry is only to be included where the licensed premises are a vessel. See Note 4*]

Summary of the Terms and Conditions of the Premises Licence

1. The premises licence will run in perpetuity unless:
   — the Secretary of State prescribes a period after which the licence will expire under section 191 of the Gambling Act 2005;
   — the licence holder surrenders the licence under section 192 of the Gambling Act 2005
   — the licence lapses under section 194 of the Gambling Act 2005;
   — the licence is revoked under section 193 or 202(1) of the Gambling Act 2005.

2. The premises licence applies only in relation to the premises specified in Part 2 of the licence and may not be varied so that it applies to any other premises (except in the case of a converted casino premises licence).

3. The premises licence authorises the premises to be used for [*Insert a description of the activities for which the premises are authorised to be used*].

4. The premises licence is subject to:
   — any conditions specified on the face of the licence as being attached under section 169(1)(a) of the Gambling Act 2005;
   — any other conditions attached to the licence by virtue of regulations made under sections 167 and 168 of the Gambling Act 2005 (other than any conditions under section 168 which have been excluded by the licensing authority); and
   — any conditions attached to the licence by virtue of specific provisions of the Gambling Act 2005.

5. In particular, it is a condition of the premises licence under section 185 of the Gambling Act 2005 that the holder keeps the licence on the premises and arranges for it to be made available on request to a constable, enforcement officer or local authority officer. The holder of the licence commits an offence if he fails to comply with this condition.

Guidance Notes

1. The name or names should be those given in Part 1 of the premises licence.

2. The address of the person or organisation should be the address given in Part 1 of the premises licence.

3. The details entered here should be the details given in Part 2 of the premises licence. Note that these details will normally be the address of the premises, but they may be a description of the nature and location of the premises if no address is available. In the case of a vessel, the name and country of registration of the vessel should also be included.

4. If the licence is in respect of a vessel, the place where the vessel is situated or moored for the purposes of the premises licence should be entered here. This place will be the place given in Part 2 of the relevant premises licence. If the premises licence is not in respect of a vessel, this entry in the summary should be left out.

6.1714

SCHEDULE 11
FORM OF PROVISIONAL STATEMENT
Regulation 26

No: [*Insert provisional statement number*]

PROVISIONAL STATEMENT

This provisional statement is issued under section 164 of the Gambling Act 2005 (as applied by section 204(2) of that Act) by

[*Insert the name of the issuing licensing authority*]

Part 1 – Details of person to whom provisional statement is issued

This provisional statement is issued to:

....

[*Insert full name of person(s) or organisation(s) to whom the provisional statement is issued. See Note 1*]

of the following address:

....

....

....

[*Insert address or addresses of person(s) or organisation(s) to whom the provisional statement is issued. See Note 2*]

who holds an operating licence which has been given the following operating licence number by the Gambling Commission:

....

[*If an operating licence is held, insert operating licence number. See Note 3.*]

Part 2 – Details of the premises or proposed premises in respect of which the provisional statement is issued

This provisional statement has been issued in respect of the following premises or proposed premises:

....

....

....

....

....

[*Give a description of the premises to which the licence relates. See Note 4.*]

The place in the area of the licensing authority in which the vessel is wholly or partly situated (within the meaning of section 211(3) of the Gambling Act 2005) is:

....

[*This entry is only to be included where the premises are a vessel. See Note 5*]

Part 3 – Provisional statement details

This provisional statement confirms that the premises or proposed premises mentioned in Part 2 of this statement have in principle been deemed suitable to be licensed for use for the following type of activity:

....

[*Please indicate relevant activity. See note 6.*]

This provisional statement is issued on ....

[*Insert date on which the provisional statement is issued*]

If a premises licence for the type of premises referred to above in this Part were to be issued, the authority would attach the following conditions under section 169(1)(a) of the Gambling Act 2005:

....

....

....

....

and it would exclude the following default conditions in exercise of its powers under section 169(1)(b) of the Gambling Act 2005:

....

....

....

....

[*Insert any default conditions that the authority would be minded to exclude*]

A scale plan is attached as an annex to this statement

[*Please ensure that the relevant plan of the premises or proposed premises is attached*]

Signed on behalf of the issuing licensing authority

....

[*Insert signature of person authorised to sign on behalf of the authority. Where the statement is issued electronically, the signature must be generated electronically and be a copy of the person's written signature*]

Guidance Notes

1. The name of the person or organisation given here should be the same as that given in Part 2 of their application for a provisional statement.

2. The address of the person or organisation given here should be the same as that given in Part 2 of their application for a provisional statement.

3. Where the person or organisation to which the provisional statement is issued does not hold an operating licence then this entry is to be left out.

4. Give the proposed and address of the premises as set out in the application for a provisional statement. If the premises have no address, give a description of the premises and their location which as far as possible reflects that set out in the application for a provisional statement. If the application is in respect of a vessel, the name and country of registration of the vessel should if possible be given here.

5. If the provisional statement is in respect of a vessel, the place where the vessel is situated or moored for the purposes of the provisional statement should be entered here. This place should be the place entered in Part 3 of the provisional statement application. If the application is not in respect of a vessel, this entry in the provisional statement should be left out.

6. Specify here the activity which would be authorised by the premises licence if granted. The activities which can be authorised by a premises licence are:

— using premises for the operation of regional casino,
— using premises for the operation of a large casino,
— using premises for the operation of a small casino,
— using premises to provide facilities for the playing of bingo,
— using premises for the operation of an adult gaming centre
— using premises for the operation of a family entertainment centre, and
— using premises to provide facilities for betting.

GAMBLING (PREMISES LICENCE FEES) (ENGLAND AND WALES) REGULATIONS 2007

(SI 2007/479)

Made ....*21st February 2007*
Laid before Parliament ....*21st February 2007*
Coming into force ....*21st May 2007*

The Secretary of State makes the following Regulations in exercise of the powers conferred by sections 159(6), (7) and (8)(a), 184(1) to (4), 186(3)(a) and (9)(a), 187(3) and (4), 188(2), 190(2) and (6)(a), 195(3), 204(2), 212(1), (4) and (5), and 355(1) of, and paragraphs 6, 7 and 11 of Schedule 18 to, the Gambling Act 2005:

6.1715 1 Citation, commencement and extent

(1) These Regulations may be cited as the Gambling (Premises Licence Fees) (England and Wales) Regulations 2007 and shall come into force on 21st May 2007.

(2) These Regulations extend to England and Wales only.

6.1716 2 Interpretation

(1) In these Regulations—

"annual fee" in relation to a premises licence means the fee payable under section 184(1)(b) for the licence,

"application fee" means—

(a) in relation to an application for a premises licence under section 159(1) (whether it is a conversion or non-conversion application), the fee to accompany such an application payable under section 159(6)(c),

(b) in relation to an application to vary a premises licence under section 187(1), the fee to accompany such an application payable under section 159(6)(c) (as applied by section 187(3)),

(c) in relation to an application to transfer a premises licence under section 188(1), the fee to accompany such an application payable under section 159(6)(c) (as applied by section 188(2)),

(d) in relation to an application for a copy of a premises licence under section 190(1), the fee to accompany such an application payable under section 190(2),

(e) in relation to an application for reinstatement of a premises licence under section 195(2), the fee to accompany such an application payable under section 159(6)(c) (as applied by section 195(3)), and

(f) in relation to an application for a provisional statement under section 204(1), the fee to accompany such an application payable under section 159(6)(c) (as applied by section 204(2)),

"betting premises (other) licence" means a betting premises licence that is not a betting premises (track) licence,

"betting premises (track) licence" means a betting premises licence issued in respect of a track or any part of a track,

"conversion application" means an application to which paragraph 54 of Schedule 4 to the Transitional Order applies,

"converted casino premises licence" means a casino premises licence to which paragraph 65 of Schedule 4 to the Transitional Order applies, "fast track application" means an application to which paragraph 57 of Schedule 4 to the Transitional Order applies,

"first annual fee", in relation to a premises licence, means the fee payable under section 184(1)(a) for the licence,

"non-conversion application" means an application for a premises licence under section 159(1) that is not a conversion application,

"non-fast track application" means an application to which paragraph 56 of Schedule 4 to the Transitional Order applies,

"relevant licensing authority" means—

(a) in relation to an application for—

(i) a premises licence under section 159(1) (whether it is a conversion or non-conversion application), or

(ii) a provisional statement under section 204(1),

the licensing authority to whom the application is made, and

(b) in relation to—

(i) any other application,

(ii) a notification of a change of circumstance under section 186(1), or

(iii) the first annual fee or annual fee,

in respect of a premises licence, the licensing authority who issued the licence,

"the Table" means the table of maximum fees set out in the Schedule, and

"the Transitional Order" means the Gambling Act 2005 (Commencement No 6 and Transitional Provisions) Order 2006.

(2) A reference in these Regulations to a section of an Act is a reference to a section of the Gambling Act 2005.

6.1717 3 Classes of premises licence

(1) For the purposes of these Regulations, there are the following classes of premises licence—

(a) a regional casino premises licence,
(b) a large casino premises licence,
(c) a small casino premises licence,
(d) a converted casino premises licence,
(e) a bingo premises licence,
(f) an adult gaming centre premises licence,
(g) a betting premises (track) licence,
(h) a family entertainment centre premises licence, and
(i) a betting premises (other) licence.

(2) In applying regulations 4(2)(b), 5(2), 11(2), 12(2), 14(2) and 15(2)—

(a) the class of premises licence to which an application relates, or
(b) the relevant class of premises licence, in the case of an application for a provisional statement,

is to be determined as at the date that the application is made.

(3) In applying regulation 8(2), the class of premises licence to which an annual fee relates is to be determined as at the date by which the fee is payable.

6.1718 4 Application fee for conversion application

(1) The amount of the application fee for a conversion application shall be determined by the relevant licensing authority.

(2) But the amount of that fee shall not exceed—

(a) in the case of a fast track application, £300, and

(b) in the case of a non-fast track application, the amount specified in column (2) of the Table which is opposite the class of premises licence in column (1) to which the application relates.

6.1719 5 Application fee for non-conversion application

(1) The amount of the application fee for a non-conversion application shall be determined by the relevant licensing authority.

(2) But the amount of that fee shall not exceed—

(a) in the case of an application in respect of provisional statement premises, the amount specified in column (3) of the Table which is opposite the class of premises licence in column (1) to which the application relates, and

(b) in the case of an application in respect of any other premises, the amount specified in column (4) of the Table which is opposite the class of premises licence in column (1) to which the application relates.

(3) In paragraph (2) "provisional statement premises"—

(a) means premises in respect of which a licensing authority have issued a provisional statement under section 164 (as applied by section 204(2)), but

(b) does not include any such premises which have been constructed or altered otherwise than in accordance with the plans and information included with the application for the provisional statement in accordance with section 204(3).

6.1720 6 First annual fee for premises licence

(1) The amount of the first annual fee for a premises licence shall be determined by the relevant licensing authority.

(2) But the amount of that fee shall not exceed the amount of the annual fee for the licence as determined in accordance with regulation 8.

(3) In applying paragraph (2) the amount of the annual fee for the licence is to be determined—

(a) as at the date by which the first annual fee is payable, and

(b) as if the annual fee were payable by that date.

(4) This regulation is subject to regulation 9.

6.1721 7 Date by which first annual fee is payable

(1) Where a licence comes into effect on the issue date, the first annual fee for the licence shall be paid within 30 days after that date.

(2) Where a licence specifies that it is to come into effect on an effective date, the first annual fee for the licence shall be paid within—

(a) the relevant period, or

(b) 12 months,

after the issue date, whichever is sooner.

(3) Paragraph (2) does not apply to a premises licence issued before 1st September 2007.

(4) In this regulation—

"the effective date", in relation to a licence which specifies that it is to come into effect on a date after the issue date, means the date so specified,

"the issue date" means the date on which a licence is issued, and

"the relevant period", in relation to a licence, means the period which is equal to the sum of—

(a) the period between the issue date and the effective date, and

(b) 30 days.

6.1722 8 Annual fee for premises licence

(1) The amount of the annual fee for a premises licence shall be determined by the relevant licensing authority.

(2) But the amount of that fee shall not exceed the amount specified in column (5) of the Table which is opposite the class of premises licence in column (1) to which the fee relates.

(3) This regulation is subject to regulation 9.

6.1723 9 First annual and annual fees for premises licence that is subject to a seasonal condition

(1) Where a premises licence is subject to a seasonal condition, the relevant licensing authority may determine—

(a) a first annual fee, and

(b) an annual fee,

for the licence that are less than the first annual fee and annual fee respectively that would, but for this regulation, be payable in respect of the licence.

(2) In paragraph (1), "seasonal condition" means a condition attached to a licence by a licensing authority under section 169(1)(a) which provides that the premises to which the licence relates may be used for the activities specified in the licence for part of a year only.

6.1724 10 Change of circumstance fee

(1) The amount of the fee under section 186(3)(a) to accompany a notification of a change of circumstance under section 186(1) shall be determined by the relevant licensing authority.

(2) But the amount of that fee shall not exceed £50.

6.1725 11 Fee for application to vary licence

(1) The amount of the application fee for an application to vary a licence under section 187(1) shall be determined by the relevant licensing authority.

(2) But the amount of that fee shall not exceed the amount specified in column (6) of the Table which is opposite the class of premises licence in column (1) to which the application relates.

6.1726 12 Fee for application to transfer

(1) The amount of the application fee for an application to transfer a licence under section 188(1) shall be determined by the relevant licensing authority.

(2) But the amount of that fee shall not exceed the amount specified in column (7) of the Table which is opposite the class of premises licence in column (1) to which the application relates.

6.1727 13 Fee for application for copy of licence

(1) The amount of the application fee for an application for a copy of a licence under section 190(1) shall be determined by the relevant licensing authority.

(2) But the amount of that fee shall not exceed £25.

6.1728 14 Fee for application for reinstatement

(1) The amount of the application fee for an application for reinstatement of a licence under section 195(2) shall be determined by the relevant licensing authority.

(2) But the amount of that fee shall not exceed the amount specified in column (8) of the Table which is opposite the class of premises licence in column (1) to which the application relates.

6.1729 15 Fee for application for provisional statement

(1) The amount of the application fee for an application for a provisional statement under section 204(1) shall be determined by the relevant licensing authority.

(2) But the amount of that fee shall not exceed the amount specified in column (9) of the Table which is opposite the relevant class of premises licence in column (1).

(3) In paragraph (2), "the relevant class of premises licence", in relation to an application for a provisional statement in respect of premises, means the class of premises licence to which an application for a licence in respect of the premises would, if made, relate.

6.1730
SCHEDULE
TABLE OF MAXIMUM FEES

Column (1)	Column (2)	Column (3)	Column (4)	Column (5)	Column (6)	Column (7)	Column (8)	Column (9)
Classes of premises licence	Maximum conversion application fee for non-fast track application	Maximum non-conversion application fee in respect of provisional statement premises	Maximum non-conversion application fee in respect of other premises	Maximum annual fee	Maximum fee for application to vary licence	Maximum fee for application to transfer a licence	Maximum fee for application for reinstatement of a licence	Maximum fee for application for provisional statement
Regional casino premises licence		£8,000	£15,000	£15,000	£7,500	£6,500	£6,500	£15,000
Large casino premises licence		£5,000	£10,000	£10,000	£5,000	£2,150	£2,150	£10,000
Small casino premises licence		£3,000	£8,000	£5,000	£4,000	£1,800	£1,800	£8,000
Converted casino premises licence	£2,000			£3,000	£2,000	£1,350	£1,350	
Bingo premises licence	£1,750	£1,200	£3,500	£1,000	£1,750	£1,200	£1,200	£3,500
Adult gaming centre premises licence	£1,000	£1,200	£2,000	£1,000	£1,000	£1,200	£1,200	£2,000
Betting premises (track) licence	£1,250	£950	£2,500	£1,000	£1,250	£950	£950	£2,500

Column (1)	Column (2)	Column (3)	Column (4)	Column (5)	Column (6)	Column (7)	Column (8)	Column (9)
Classes of premises licence	Maximum conversion application fee for non-fast track application	Maximum non-conversion application fee in respect of provisional statement premises	Maximum non-conversion application fee in respect of other premises	Maximum annual fee	Maximum fee for application to vary licence	Maximum fee for application to transfer a licence	Maximum fee for application for reinstatement of a licence	Maximum fee for application for provisional statement
Family entertainment centre premises licence	£1,000	£950	£2,000	£750	£1,000	£950	£950	£2,000
Betting premises (other) licence	£1,500	£1,200	£3,000	£600	£1,500	£1,200	£1,200	£3,000

GAMBLING ACT 2005 (MANDATORY AND DEFAULT CONDITIONS) (ENGLAND AND WALES) REGULATIONS 2007

(SI 2007/1409)

Made ....*5th May 2007*
Coming into force ....*21st May 2007*

The Secretary of State makes the following Regulations in exercise of the powers conferred by sections 167, 168 and 355(1) of the Gambling Act 2005;

In accordance with section 355(4)(g) and (h) of that Act a draft of this instrument was laid before Parliament and approved by a resolution of each House of Parliament.

6.1731 1 Citation and commencement

(1) These Regulations may be cited as the Gambling Act 2005 (Mandatory and Default Conditions) (England and Wales) Regulations 2007 and shall come into force on whichever is the later of 21st May 2007 or the day after the Regulations are made.

(2) These Regulations shall extend to England and Wales.

3.1732 2 Interpretation

In these Regulations—

"the 1963 Act" means the Betting, Gaming and Lotteries Act 1963;

"the 2005 Act" means the Gambling Act 2005;

"alcohol" has the same meaning as in section 191 of the Licensing Act 2003;

"ATM" means a machine located on the premises which enables a person using it to obtain cash on credit;

"betting operator" means a person who in the course of the business of a general betting operating licence holder or pool betting operating licence holder accepts or negotiates bets; and "betting operator's assistant" means a person who carries out any other functions in the course of the business of a general betting operating licence holder or pool betting operating licence holder in connection with the licensed activities;

"betting machine" means a wholly automated machine designed or adapted only for use to bet on future real events, including—

(a) a machine that enables the customer to access an account on an internet website by means of which he is able to place a bet and receive winnings; and

(b) a machine which accepts bets made by the customer and issues a record of the betting transaction which enables the customer to claim his winnings from an individual on the betting premises, or from the machine;

"converted casino premises licence" means a premises licence issued in respect of a casino in accordance with transitional provisions made under paragraph 9 of Schedule 18 to the 2005 Act;

"gambling area", in relation to a casino premises licence, means those areas of the casino that are indicated on the plan as being the table gaming area, and any other area in which facilities for gambling may be provided;

"game card" means anything (including any electronic device) which provides an individual with the opportunity to win one or more prizes in respect of a game of bingo;

"non-gambling area" means those areas of the casino that are available to customers and are indicated on the plan as being areas other than gambling areas;

"ordinary gaming table" means a gaming table that is not a partially or wholly automated gaming table;

"partially automated gaming table" means equipment that would fall within the definition of gaming machine in section 235 of the 2005 Act but for its exclusion from that definition by subsection (2)(h) of that section;

"the plan", in relation to a premises licence, means the plan of the premises that forms part of the licence by virtue of section 151(1)(g) of the 2005 Act;

"street" includes any bridge, road, lane, footway, subway, square, court, alley or passage (including passages through enclosed premises such as shopping malls), whether a thoroughfare or not;

"table gaming" means—

(a) casino games played on ordinary, or partially or wholly automated gaming tables; and

(b) real games of equal chance, other than bingo, played on a table;

"table gaming area", in relation to a casino premises licence, means the area indicated on the plan as being for table gaming;

"track premises licence" means a betting premises licence in respect of a track;

"wholly automated gaming table" means equipment that would fall within the definition of a gaming machine in section 235 of the 2005 Act but for its exclusion from that definition by subsection (2)(i) of that section.

6.1733 3 Mandatory conditions attaching to every premises licence

(1) The conditions specified in paragraphs (2), (3) and (4) shall be attached to every premises licence.

(2) The summary of the terms and conditions of the premises licence issued under section 164(1)(c) of the 2005 Act shall be displayed in a prominent place within the premises.

(3) The layout of the premises shall be maintained in accordance with the plan.

(4) The premises shall not be used for—

(a) the sale of tickets in a private lottery or customer lottery, or

(b) the sale of tickets in any other lottery in respect of which the sale of tickets on the premises is otherwise prohibited.

(5) In this regulation—

(a) a "private lottery" means a private society lottery or a work lottery within the meaning of paragraphs 10 and 11 of Schedule 11 to the 2005 Act; and

(b) a "customer lottery" has the same meaning as in Part 3 of Schedule 11 to the 2005 Act.

6.1734 4 Mandatory conditions attaching to casino premises licences

The conditions specified in Part 1 of Schedule 1 shall be attached to all types of casino premises licences.

6.1735

5 The conditions specified in Part 2 of Schedule 1 shall, in addition to the conditions specified in Part 1 of that Schedule, be attached to regional casino premises licences.

6.1736

6 The conditions specified in Part 3 of Schedule 1 shall, in addition to the conditions specified in Part 1 of that Schedule, be attached to large casino premises licences.

6.1737

7 The conditions specified in Part 4 of Schedule 1 shall, in addition to the conditions specified in Part 1 of that Schedule, be attached to small casino premises licences.

6.1738
8 The conditions specified in Part 5 of Schedule 1 shall, in addition to the conditions specified in Part 1 of that Schedule, be attached to converted casino premises licences.

6.1739 9 Default conditions attaching to casino premises licences

The conditions specified in Part 6 of Schedule 1 shall be attached to casino premises licences unless excluded by the licensing authority who issue the licence, in exercise of their powers under section 169(1)(b) of the 2005 Act.

6.1740 10 Mandatory conditions attaching to bingo premises licences

The conditions specified in Part 1 of Schedule 2 shall be attached to bingo premises licences.

6.1741 11 Default conditions attaching to bingo premises licences

The conditions specified in Part 2 of Schedule 2 shall be attached to bingo premises licences unless excluded by the licensing authority who issue the licence, in exercise of their powers under section 169(1)(b) of the 2005 Act.

6.1742 12 Mandatory conditions attaching to adult gaming centre premises licences

The conditions specified in Schedule 3 shall be attached to adult gaming centre premises licences.

6.1743 13 Mandatory conditions attaching to family entertainment centre premises licences

The conditions specified in Schedule 4 shall be attached to family entertainment centre premises licences.

6.1744 14 Mandatory conditions attaching to betting premises licences other than track premises licences

The conditions specified in Part 1 of Schedule 5 shall be attached to betting premises licences other than track premises licences.

6.1745 15 Default conditions attaching to betting premises licences other than track premises licences

The conditions specified in Part 2 of Schedule 5 shall be attached to betting premises licences other than track premises licences unless excluded by the licensing authority who issue the licence, in exercise of their powers under section 169(1)(b) of the 2005 Act.

6.1746 16 Mandatory conditions attaching to track premises licences

(1) The conditions specified in Part 1 of Schedule 6 shall be attached to track premises licences.

(2) The conditions specified in Part 2 of Schedule 6 shall, in addition to the conditions specified in Part 1 of that Schedule, be attached to track premises licences in respect of premises that are horse-race courses.

(3) The conditions specified in Part 3 of Schedule 6 shall, in addition to the conditions specified in Part 1 of that Schedule, be attached to track premises licences in respect of premises that are dog tracks.

6.1747 17 Default conditions attaching to track premises licences

The conditions specified in Part 4 of Schedule 6 shall be attached to track premises licences unless excluded by the licensing authority who issue the licence, in exercise of their powers under section 169(1)(b) of the 2005 Act.

SCHEDULE 1
CONDITIONS ATTACHING TO CASINO PREMISES LICENCES
Regulations 4 to 9

PART 1
MANDATORY CONDITIONS ATTACHING TO CASINO PREMISES LICENCES

6.1748

1 (1) The principal entrance to the premises shall be from a street.

(2) No entrance to the premises shall be from premises that are used wholly or mainly by children, by young persons, or by both.

(3) No customer shall be able to enter the premises directly from any other premises in respect of which a licence issued under Part 8 of the Act, or a permit issued under Schedule 10, 12 or 13 to the Act, has effect.

2 A gap of at least 2 metres shall be maintained between any ordinary gaming table and any other equipment, apparatus or structure used by a person to gamble on the premises.

3 No more than 40 separate player positions may be made available for use in relation to wholly automated gaming tables at any time.

4 (1) The rules of each type of casino game that is available to be played on the premises shall be displayed in a prominent place within both the table gaming area and other gambling area of the premises to which customers wishing to use facilities for gambling have unrestricted access.

(2) The condition in sub-paragraph (1) may be satisfied by—

(a) displaying a clear and legible sign setting out the rules; or

(b) making available to customers leaflets or other written material containing the rules.

5 Any ATM made available for use on the premises shall be located in a place that requires any customer who wishes to use it to cease gambling at any gaming table, gaming machine or betting machine in order to do so.

PART 2
MANDATORY CONDITIONS ATTACHING TO REGIONAL CASINO PREMISES LICENCES

6.1749

1 A notice shall be displayed in a prominent place at every entrance to the gambling area of the premises stating that no person under the age of 18 years is permitted to enter that part of the premises.

2 The gambling area of the premises shall not be capable of being seen from any part of the premises to which children, young persons, or both, have access.

3 (1) The premises shall contain a table gaming area the floor area of which is no less than $1000m^2$.

(2) Subject to sub-paragraph (3), in determining the floor area of the table gaming area, any number of separate areas within the premises may be taken into account.

(3) Any separate area that comprises less than 12.5% of the minimum required table gaming area shall not be taken into account in determining the table gaming area.

(4) No gambling shall be permitted in the table gaming area of the premises other than gambling by way of table gaming.

4 (1) The premises shall contain a non-gambling area the floor area of which is no less than $1500m^2$.

(2) The non-gambling area may consist of one or more areas within the premises.

(3) Lobby areas and toilet facilities may be taken into account in calculating the non-gambling area; but the non-gambling area shall not consist exclusively of lobby areas and toilet facilities.

(4) Facilities for gambling shall not be provided in the non-gambling area.

(5) At any time during which facilities for gambling are provided on the premises, each separate area comprising the non-gambling area, other than the lobby areas and toilet facilities referred to in sub-paragraph (3), shall contain recreational facilities that are available for use by customers on the premises.

5 A notice shall be displayed in a prominent place in each part of the premises used for providing facilities for betting, setting out the terms on which persons are invited to bet on the premises.

6 (1) A notice setting out the information in sub-paragraph (2) shall be displayed in a prominent place at the main point on the premises where payment for the charge is to be made for a game card (or set of game cards) in respect of a game of bingo.

(2) The notice in sub-paragraph (1) shall include the following information—

- (a) the cost (in money) of each game card (or set of game cards) payable by an individual in respect of a game of bingo;
- (b) in respect of each game card (or set of game cards) referred to in paragraph (a), the maximum amount that will be charged by way of a participation fee for entitlement to participate in that game; and
- (c) a statement to the effect that all or part of the participation fee may be waived at the discretion of the person charging it.

(3) The notice may be displayed in electronic form.

(4) A reference in this paragraph to a charge in respect of gaming does not include an amount paid for an opportunity to win one or more prizes in gaming to which section 288 of the 2005 Act (meaning of "prize gaming") applies.

(5) The rules of each type of bingo game that is available to be played on the premises shall be made available to customers in each part of the premises used for providing facilities for bingo.

(6) The condition in sub-paragraph (5) may be satisfied by—

- (a) displaying a sign setting out the rules,
- (b) making available leaflets or other written material containing the rules, or
- (c) running an audio-visual guide to the rules prior to any bingo game being commenced.

7 No more than 40 separate betting positions may be made available for use in relation to betting machines at any time.

PART 3
MANDATORY CONDITIONS ATTACHING TO LARGE CASINO PREMISES LICENCES

6.1750

1 A notice stating that no person under the age of 18 years is permitted to enter the premises shall be displayed in a prominent place at every entrance to the premises.

2 (1) The premises shall contain a table gaming area, the floor area of which is no less than 1000m^2.

(2) Subject to sub-paragraph (3), in determining the floor area of the table gaming area, any number of separate areas within the premises may be taken into account.

(3) Any separate area that comprises less than 12.5% of the minimum required table gaming area shall not be taken into account in determining the table gaming area.

3 No gambling shall be permitted in the table gaming area of the premises other than gambling by way of table gaming.

4 (1) The premises shall contain a non-gambling area which comprises no less than 500m^2.

(2) The non-gambling area may consist of one or more areas within the premises.

(3) Lobby areas and toilet facilities may be taken into account in calculating the non-gambling area; but the non-gambling area shall not consist exclusively of lobby areas and toilet facilities.

(4) Facilities for gambling shall not be provided in the non-gambling area.

(5) At any time during which facilities for gambling are being provided on the premises, each separate area comprising of the non-gambling area, other than the lobby areas and toilet facilities referred to in sub-paragraph (3), shall contain recreational facilities that are available for use by customers on the premises.

5 A notice shall be displayed in a prominent place in each part of the premises used for providing facilities for betting, setting out the terms on which persons are invited to bet on the premises.

6 (1) A notice setting out the information in sub-paragraph (2) shall be displayed in a prominent place at the main point on the premises where payment for the charge is to be made for a game card (or set of game cards) in respect of a game of bingo.

(2) The notice in sub-paragraph (1) shall include the following information—

(a) the cost (in money) of each game card (or set of game cards) payable by an individual in respect of a game of bingo;

(b) in respect of each game card (or set of game cards) referred to in paragraph (a) the maximum amount that will be charged by way of a participation fee for entitlement to participate in that game; and

(c) a statement to the effect that all or part of the participation fee may be waived at the discretion of the person charging it.

(3) The notice may be displayed in electronic form.

(4) A reference in this paragraph to a charge in respect of gaming does not include an amount paid for an opportunity to win one or more prizes in gaming to which section 288 of the 2005 Act (meaning of "prize gaming") applies.

(5) The rules of each type of bingo game that is available to be played on the premises shall be made available to customers in each part of the premises used for providing facilities for bingo.

(6) The condition in sub-paragraph (5) may be satisfied by—

(a) displaying a sign setting out the rules,

(b) making available leaflets or other written material containing the rules, or

(c) running an audio-visual guide to the rules prior to any bingo game being commenced.

7 No more than 40 separate betting positions may be made available for use in relation to betting machines at any time.

PART 4
MANDATORY CONDITIONS ATTACHING TO SMALL CASINO PREMISES LICENCES

6.1751

1 A notice stating that no person under the age of 18 years is permitted to enter the premises shall be displayed in a prominent place at every entrance to the premises.

2 (1) The premises shall contain a table gaming area, the floor area of which is no less than $500m^2$.

(2) Subject to sub-paragraph (3), in determining the floor area of the table gaming area, any number of separate areas within the premises may be taken into account.

(3) Any separate area that comprises less than 12.5% of the minimum required table gaming area shall not be taken into account in determining the table gaming area.

3 No gambling shall be permitted in the table gaming area of the premises other than gambling by way of table gaming.

4 (1) The premises shall contain a non-gambling area which comprises no less than $250m^2$.

(2) The non-gambling area may consist of one or more areas within the premises.

(3) Lobby areas and toilet facilities may be taken into account in calculating the non-gambling area; but the non-gambling area shall not consist exclusively of lobby areas and toilet facilities.

(4) Facilities for gambling shall not be provided in the non-gambling area.

(5) At any time during which facilities for gambling are being provided on the premises, each separate area comprising the non-gambling area, other than the lobby areas and toilet facilities referred to in sub-paragraph (3), shall contain recreational facilities that are available for use by customers on the premises.

5 A notice shall be displayed in a prominent place in each part of the premises used for providing facilities for betting, setting out the terms on which persons are invited to bet on the premises.

6 No more than 40 separate betting positions may be made available for use in relation to betting machines at any time.

PART 5
MANDATORY CONDITIONS ATTACHING TO CONVERTED CASINO PREMISES LICENCES

6.1752

1 A notice shall be displayed in a prominent place at every entrance to the premises stating that no person under the age of 18 years is permitted to enter the premises.

2 (1) This paragraph shall apply to premises which have a gambling area the floor area of which is no less than $200m^2$.

(2) In determining the floor area of the gambling area, all areas in which facilities for gambling are provided on the premises shall be taken into account.

(3) The premises shall contain a non-gambling area, the floor area of which is no less than 10% of the floor area of the gambling area.

(4) The non-gambling area may consist of one or more areas within the premises.

(5) Lobby areas and toilet facilities may be taken into account in calculating the non-gambling area; but the non-gambling area shall not consist exclusively of lobby areas and toilet facilities.

(6) Facilities for gambling shall not be provided in the non-gambling area.

(7) At any time during which facilities for gambling are being provided on the premises, each separate area comprising the non-gambling area, other than the lobby areas and toilet facilities referred to in sub-paragraph (5), shall contain recreational facilities that are available for use by customers on the premises.

PART 6
DEFAULT CONDITIONS ATTACHING TO CASINO PREMISES LICENCES

6.1753 No facilities for gambling shall be provided on the premises between the hours of 6am and noon on any day.

SCHEDULE 2
CONDITIONS ATTACHING TO BINGO PREMISES LICENCES
Regulations 10 and 11

PART 1
MANDATORY CONDITIONS ATTACHING TO BINGO PREMISES LICENCES

6.1754

1 A notice stating that no person under the age of 18 years is permitted to play bingo on the premises shall be displayed in a prominent place at every entrance to the premises.

2 No customer shall be able to enter the premises directly from any other premises in respect of which one of the following permissions has effect—

(a) a casino premises licence;
(b) an adult gaming centre premises licence;
(c) a betting premises licence other than a track premises licence; and

3 (1) This paragraph shall apply where children or young persons or both are permitted by the licence holder to enter the premises, and Category B or C gaming machines are made available for use on the premises.

(2) Any area of the premises to which category B and C gaming machines are located—

(a) shall be separated from the rest of the premises by a physical barrier which is effective to prevent access other than by an entrance designed for the purpose;
(b) shall be supervised at all times to ensure children or young persons or both do not enter the area; and
(c) shall be arranged in such a way that ensures all parts of the area can be observed by the persons mentioned in sub-paragraph (3).

(3) The reference to supervision in this paragraph means supervision by—

(a) one or more persons whose responsibilities include ensuring children or young persons or both do not enter the area; or
(b) closed circuit television which is monitored by one or more persons whose responsibilities include ensuring that children or young persons or both do not enter the area.

(4) A notice stating that no person under the age of 18 years is permitted to enter the area shall be displayed in a prominent place at the entrance to any area of the premises in which Category B or C gaming machines are made available for use.

4 (1) In the case of a charge for admission to the premises, a notice of that charge shall be displayed in a prominent place at the principal entrance to the premises.

(2) In the case of any other charges in respect of gaming, a notice setting out the information in sub-paragraph (3) shall be displayed at the main point where payment for the charge is to be made.

(3) The notice in sub-paragraph (2) shall include the following information—

(a) the cost (in money) of each game card (or set of game cards) payable by an individual in respect of a game of bingo;
(b) in respect of each game card (or set of game cards) referred to in paragraph (a) the amount that will be charged by way of a participation fee for entitlement to participate in that game; and
(c) a statement to the effect that all or part of the participation fee may be waived at the discretion of the person charging it.

(4) The notice may be displayed in electronic form.

(5) A reference in this paragraph to a charge in respect of gaming does not include an amount paid for an opportunity to win one or more prizes in gaming to which section 288 of the 2005 Act (meaning of "prize gaming") applies.

5 (1) The rules of each type of game that is available to be played the premises other than games played on gaming machines shall be made available to customers within the premises.

(2) The condition in sub-paragraph (1) may be satisfied by—

(a) displaying a sign setting out the rules,
(b) making available leaflets or other written material containing the rules, or
(c) running an audio-visual guide to the rules prior to any bingo game being commenced.

6 Any ATM made available for use on the premises shall be located in a place that requires any customer who wishes to use it to cease gambling in order to do so.

PART 2
DEFAULT CONDITIONS ATTACHING TO BINGO PREMISES LICENCES

6.1755

1 Subject to paragraph 2, no facilities for gambling shall be provided on the premises between the hours of midnight and 9am.

2 The condition in paragraph 1 shall not apply to making gaming machines available for use.

SCHEDULE 3
MANDATORY CONDITIONS ATTACHING TO ADULT GAMING CENTRE PREMISES LICENCES
Regulation 12

6.1756

1 A notice stating that no person under the age of 18 years is permitted to enter the premises shall be displayed in a prominent place at every entrance to the premises.

2 No customer shall be able to access the premises directly from any other premises in respect of which a licence issued under Part 8 of the Act, or a permit issued under Schedule 10, 12 or 13 to the Act, has effect.

3 Any ATM made available for use on the premises shall be located in a place that requires any customer who wishes to use it to cease gambling at any gaming machine in order to do so.

4 (1) No alcohol shall be permitted to be consumed on the premises at any time during which facilities for gambling are being provided on the premises.

(2) A notice stating the condition in sub-paragraph (1) shall be displayed in a prominent place at every entrance to the premises.

SCHEDULE 4
MANDATORY CONDITIONS ATTACHING TO FAMILY ENTERTAINMENT CENTRE PREMISES LICENCES
Regulation 13

6.1757

1 No customer shall be able to access the premises directly from any other premises in respect of which one of the following premises licences has effect—

(a) a casino premises licence;

(b) an adult gaming centre premises licence;

(c) a betting premises licence other than a track premises licence.

2 Any ATM made available for use on the premises shall be located in a place that requires any customer who wishes to use it to cease gambling at any gaming machine in order to do so.

3 (1) Where Category C gaming machines are made available for use on the premises, any area of the premises in which those machines are located—

(a) shall be separated from the rest of the premises by a physical barrier which is effective to prevent access other than by an entrance designed for the purpose;

(b) shall be supervised at all times to ensure children or young persons or both do not enter the area; and

(c) shall be arranged in such a way so as to permit all parts of the area to be observed by the persons mentioned in sub-paragraph (2).

(2) The reference to supervision in this paragraph means supervision by—

(a) one or more persons whose responsibilities include ensuring children or young persons or both do not enter the area; or

(b) closed circuit television which is monitored by one or more persons whose responsibilities include ensuring that children or young persons or both do not enter the area.

(3) A notice stating that no person under the age of 18 years is permitted to enter the area shall be displayed in a prominent place at the entrance to any area of the premises in which Category C gaming machines are made available for use.

4 (1) No alcohol shall be permitted to be consumed on the premises at any time during which facilities for gambling are being provided on the premises.

(2) A notice stating the condition in sub-paragraph (1) shall be displayed in a prominent place at every entrance to the premises.

SCHEDULE 5
CONDITIONS ATTACHING TO BETTING PREMISES LICENCES
Regulations 14 and 15

PART 1
MANDATORY CONDITIONS ATTACHING TO BETTING PREMISES LICENCES (OTHER THAN TRACK PREMISES LICENCES)

6.1758

1 A notice stating that no person under the age of 18 years is permitted to enter the premises shall be displayed in a prominent place at every entrance to the premises.

2 (1) Access to the premises shall be from a street or from other premises with a betting premises licence.

(2) Without prejudice to sub-paragraph (1), there shall be no means of direct access between the premises and other premises used for the retail sale of merchandise or services.

3 Subject to anything permitted by virtue of the 2005 Act, or done in accordance with paragraphs 4, 5, 6 and 7 below, the premises shall not be used for any purpose other than for providing facilities for betting.

4 Any ATM made available for use on the premises shall be located in a place that requires any customer who wishes to use it to leave any gaming machine or betting machine in order to do so.

5 No apparatus for making information or other material available in the form of sounds or visual images may be used on the premises, except for apparatus used for the following purposes—

(a) communicating information about, or coverage of, sporting events, including—

(i) information relating to betting on such an event; and

(ii) any other matter or information, including an advertisement, which is incidental to such an event;

(b) communicating information relating to betting on any event (including the result of the event) in connection with which betting transactions may be or have been effected on the premises.

6 No publications, other than racing periodicals or specialist betting publications, may be sold or offered for sale on the premises.

7 No music, dancing or other entertainment shall be provided or permitted on the premises, save for entertainment provided in accordance with paragraph 5.

8 (1) No alcohol shall be permitted to be consumed on the premises at any time during which facilities for gambling are being provided on the premises.

(2) A notice stating the condition in sub-paragraph (1) shall be displayed in a prominent place at every entrance to the premises.

9 A notice setting out the terms on which customers are invited to bet on the premises shall be displayed in a prominent place on the premises to which customers have unrestricted access.

PART 2
DEFAULT CONDITIONS ATTACHING TO BETTING PREMISES LICENCES (OTHER THAN IN RESPECT OF TRACKS)

6.1759 No facilities for gambling shall be provided on the premises between the hours of 10pm on one day and 7am on the next day.

SCHEDULE 6
CONDITIONS ATTACHING TO TRACK PREMISES LICENCES
Regulations 16 and 17

PART 1
MANDATORY CONDITIONS ATTACHING TO ALL TRACK PREMISES LICENCES

6.1760

1 No customer shall be able to access the premises directly from any other premises in respect of which one of the following premises licences has effect—

(a) a casino premises licence;
(b) an adult gaming centre premises licence.

2 A notice stating that no person under the age of 18 is permitted to bet on the premises shall be displayed in a prominent place at every public entrance to the premises.

3 The terms on which a bet may be placed must be displayed in a prominent place within the premises to which customers wishing to use facilities for betting have unrestricted access.

4 The premises licence holder shall make arrangements to ensure that betting operators who are admitted to the premises for the purpose of accepting bets—

(a) will be operating under a valid operating licence; and
(b) are enabled to accept such bets in accordance with—
  (i) the conditions imposed under sections 92 (general betting operating licence) or 93 (pool betting operating licence) of the 2005 Act, or
  (ii) an authorisation under section 94 (horse-race pool betting operating licence) of that Act.

5 The premises licence holder shall make arrangements to ensure that reasonable steps are taken to remove from the premises any person who is found to be accepting bets on the premises otherwise than in accordance with the 2005 Act.

6 Any ATM made available for use on the premises shall be located in a place that requires any customer who wishes to use it to cease gambling in order to do so.

PART 2
MANDATORY CONDITIONS ATTACHING TO TRACK PREMISES LICENCES IN RESPECT OF PREMISES THAT ARE HORSE-RACE COURSES

6.1761

1 (1) This paragraph shall apply to converted track premises licences in respect of premises that are horse-race courses.

(2) The licence holder shall ensure that in respect of any part of the track, which immediately before 1st September 2007 was made available for the purposes of complying with a condition imposed under section 13(2) of the 1963 Act (which provides for conditions to be imposed on a certificate under section 13 relating to the places which are to be provided for enabling betting to take place on the track), that part shall continue to be made available for the purposes of enabling betting operators and betting operators' assistants to use it for carrying on business in connection with providing facilities for betting.

(3) Sub-paragraph (2) is without prejudice to any application under section 187 of the 2005 Act (application to vary a premises licence) to change the location of the part of the track to which that sub-paragraph applies.

(4) Where such an application is granted, sub-paragraph (2) is to have effect as if it required the licence holder to ensure that the part of the track identified in the application as the new location for the area referred to in that sub-paragraph is made available for the purposes of enabling betting operators and betting operators' assistants to carry on business in connection with providing facilities for betting.

(5) References in this paragraph to an "existing betting area" are to any part of the track which is required to be made available in accordance with the preceding provisions of this paragraph for the purposes of enabling betting operators and betting operators' assistants to carry on business in connection with providing facilities for betting.

(6) The charge for admission to an existing betting area for the purposes of carrying on business in connection with providing facilities for betting shall not exceed—

(a) where payable by a betting operator, five times the cost of the highest charge paid by members of the public who are authorised to enter that part of the track; and

(b) where payable by a betting operator's assistant, the cost of the highest charge paid by members of the public who are authorised to enter that part of the track.

(7) A betting operator or betting operator's assistant shall not be charged, for admission to an existing betting area, an amount which differs from that charged to any other betting operator or betting operator's assistant for admission to that part of the track.

(8) No charges may be made to betting operators and betting operators' assistants who are admitted to the existing betting areas of the track, other than—

(a) the charge for admission in accordance with sub-paragraphs (6) and (7), and

(b) charges levied to cover costs reasonably incurred in connection with enabling betting operators and betting operators' assistants to operate in the existing betting area.

(9) This paragraph shall not apply after 31st August 2012.

2 (1) This paragraph shall apply to all track premises licences in respect of premises that are horse-race courses.

(2) The licence holder shall provide a place on the premises where betting operators and betting operators' assistants, including small-scale operators, may carry on business in connection with providing facilities for betting and to which the public may resort for the purpose of betting.

(3) The reference in this paragraph to "small-scale operators" shall have the same meaning as prescribed in The Gambling Act 2005 (Definition of Small-scale Operator) Regulations 2006.

(4) This paragraph shall not apply to converted track premises licences before 1st September 2012.

3 In this Part "converted track premises licence" means a premises licence issued in respect of a track where—

(a) the holder of the licence held a certificate under section 13 of the 1963 Act, in respect of the same or substantially the same premises (referred to below as "the 1963 Act permission");

(b) the 1963 Act permission had effect immediately before 1st September 2007; and

(c) the holder of the licence was granted the premises licence, under transitional provisions made under paragraph 9 of Schedule 18 to the 2005 Act, by reason of his holding the 1963 Act permission.

PART 3
MANDATORY CONDITIONS ATTACHING TO TRACK PREMISES LICENCES IN RESPECT OF PREMISES THAT ARE DOG RACING TRACKS

6.1762

1 A totalisator on the premises shall only be operated—

(a) while the public are admitted to the premises for the purpose of attending dog races and no other sporting events are taking place on the premises; and

(b) for effecting with persons on the premises betting transactions on dog races taking place on the premises.

2 (1) At any time during which the totalisator is being lawfully used on the premises—

(a) no betting operator or betting operator's assistant shall be excluded from the premises by reason only of the fact that he proposes to accept or negotiate bets on the premises; and

(b) there shall be made available on the premises space for betting operators and betting operators' assistants where they can conveniently accept and negotiate bets in connection with dog races run on the premises on that day.

(2) This paragraph is without prejudice to section 180 (pool betting on dog races) of the 2005 Act.

3 For the purposes of this Part, "totalisator" means the apparatus for betting known as the totalisator or pari mutuel, or any other machine or instrument of betting of a like nature, whether mechanically operated or not.

PART 4
DEFAULT CONDITIONS ATTACHING TO ALL TRACK PREMISES LICENCES

6.1763

1 Subject to paragraph 2, no facilities for gambling shall be provided on the premises between the hours of 10pm on one day, and 7am on the next day.

2 The prohibition in paragraph 1 does not apply on days when a sporting event is taking place on the premises, in which case gambling transactions may take place at any time during that day.

GAMBLING ACT 2005 (EXCLUSION OF CHILDREN FROM TRACK AREAS) ORDER 2007

(SI 2007/1410)

Made ....*5th May 2007*
Coming into force ....*1st September 2007*

The Secretary of State makes the following Order in exercise of the powers conferred by section 182(4) of the Gambling Act 2005.

In accordance with section 355(6) of that Act, a draft of this instrument was laid before Parliament and approved by resolution of each House.

6.1764 1 Citation and commencement

This Order may be cited as the Gambling Act 2005 (Exclusion of Children from Track Areas) Order 2007 and shall come into force on 1st September 2007.

6.1765 2 Amendment to section 182(2) of the Gambling Act 2005

Section 182(2) of the Gambling Act 2005 shall be amended as follows—

(a) at the end of paragraph (a) delete the word "and";
(b) in paragraph (b) substitute "." with ", and"; and
(c) after paragraph (b) insert—
"(c) shall not apply to any other track on a day on which a race or other sporting event takes place, or is expected to take place, on the track.".

GAMING MACHINES IN ALCOHOL LICENSED PREMISES (NOTIFICATION FEE) (ENGLAND AND WALES) REGULATIONS 2007

(SI 2007/1832)

Made . . . . *26th June 2007*
Laid before Parliament . . . . *26th June 2007*
Coming into force . . . . *1st August 2007*

The Secretary of State makes the following Regulations in exercise of the powers conferred by section 282(2)(b) of the Gambling Act 2005.

6.1770 1 Commencement, citation and application

(1) These Regulations may be cited as the Gaming Machines in Alcohol Licensed Premises (Notification Fee) (England and Wales) Regulations 2007 and shall come into force on 1st August 2007.

(2) These Regulations apply to England and Wales.

6.1771 2 Interpretation

In these Regulations "the Act" means the Gambling Act 2005.

6.1772 3 Fee for automatic entitlement

For the purposes of section 282(2)(b) of the Act, the fee to be sent with written notice of intention to make gaming machines available for use in reliance on section 282(1) of the Act is £50.

GAMBLING ACT 2005 (LICENSED PREMISES GAMING MACHINE PERMITS) (ENGLAND AND WALES) REGULATIONS 2007

(SI 2007/1833)

Made . . . . *26th June 2007*
Laid before Parliament . . . . *26th June 2007*
Coming into force . . . . *1st August 2007*

The Secretary of State makes the following Regulations in exercise of the powers conferred by section 355(1) of, and paragraphs 2(e), 7(1)(a) and (2)(a)(i), 9, 11(2), 15(2) and 19(2) of Schedule 13 to, the Gambling Act 2005.

6.1773 1 Commencement, citation and application

(1) These Regulations may be cited as the Gambling Act 2005 (Licensed Premises Gaming Machine Permits) (England and Wales) Regulations 2007 and shall come into force on 1st August 2007.

(2) These Regulations apply to England and Wales.

6.1774 2 Interpretation

(1) In these Regulations—

"the 1968 Act" means the Gaming Act 1968;

"application" means an application for a licensed premises gaming machine permit under paragraph 1(1);

"existing operator" means a person who makes an application and—

(a) on the date on which he makes the application, holds a permit issued under section 34 of the 1968 Act by the authority mentioned in sub-paragraph (a) of paragraph 1 of Schedule 9 to the 1968 Act (a "section 34 permit");

(b) that section 34 permit—

(i) authorises him to make available a number of gaming machines, being a number which is greater than two, and

(ii) is due to expire in accordance with paragraph 24(1) or (2) of Schedule 4 to the Order on a date on or after 1st September 2007;

(c) the application for the permit is made before the date on which the section 34 permit is due to expire in accordance with paragraph 24(1) or (2) of Schedule 4 to the Order; and

(d) the application relates to the same or substantially the same premises as those to which the section 34 permit relates;

"the Order" means the Gambling Act 2005 (Commencement No 6 and Transitional Provisions) Order 2006; and

"permit" means a licensed premises gaming machine permit, unless the contrary is indicated.

(2) A reference in these Regulations to a numbered paragraph is a reference to that paragraph of Schedule 13 to the Gambling Act 2005 so numbered.

6.1775 3 Application fees

For the purposes of paragraph 2(e)—

(a) subject to sub-paragraphs (b) and (c), the fee to accompany an application for a permit under paragraph 1(1) is—

(i) £100, if it is made by an existing operator, and

(ii) £150 in all other cases;

(b) the fee to accompany an application to vary a permit under paragraph 15(1) is £100;

(c) the fee to accompany an application to transfer a permit under paragraph 19(1) is £25.

6.1776 4 Form of Permit

A permit must be in the form prescribed in the Schedule to these Regulations.

6.1777 5 Annual Fees

The first annual fee for a permit payable to the issuing licensing authority under paragraph 9(1)(a) is £50.

6.1778

6 The annual fee for a permit payable to the issuing licensing authority under paragraph 9(1)(b) is £50.

6.1779 7 Date by which first annual fee is payable

(1) Where a permit comes into effect on the issue date, the first annual fee for the permit shall be paid within 30 days after that date.

(2) Where a permit specifies that it is to come into effect on a date after the issue date, the first annual fee for the permit shall be paid within—

(a) the relevant period, or
(b) 12 months,

after the issue date, whichever is sooner.

(3) Paragraph (2) does not apply to a permit issued before 1st September 2007.

(4) In this regulation—

"the effective date", in relation to a permit which specifies that it is to come into effect on a date after the issue date, means the date so specified,

"the issue date" means the date on which a permit is issued, and

"the relevant period", in relation to a permit, means the period which is equal to the sum of—

(a) the period between the issue date and the effective date, and
(b) 30 days.

6.1780 8 Other fees

For the purposes of paragraph 7(2)(a)(i), the fee to be sent with a request that a new name be substituted for the old name specified on a permit is £25.

6.1781

9 For the purposes of paragraph 11(2), the fee to accompany an application for a copy of a permit is £15.

6.1782
SCHEDULE
Regulation 4

This form is prescribed by regulation 4 of the Gambling Act 2005 (Licensed Premises Gaming Machine Permits) (England and Wales) Regulations 2007

Licensed Premises Gaming Machine Permit

No:...*(insert licensed premises gaming machine permit number)*

This licensed premises gaming machine permit authorises...
....
....
....*(name of permit holder)*
to make gaming machines, of the category and number specified below, available for use on the following premises...
....
....
....
....
....
....
(address of premises, including postcode)

Number of Category C gaming machines authorised by this permit:...............................*(if no machines of this category are authorised, insert '0')*

Number of Category D gaming machines authorised by this permit:...............................*(if no machines of this category are authorised, insert '0')*

Date on which this permit takes effect:
....

This permit is issued by...
....
....
....
....
....
....
....................*(Name and address of licensing authority issuing permit)*

GAMBLING ACT 2005 (CLUB GAMING AND CLUB MACHINE PERMITS) REGULATIONS 2007

(SI 2007/1834)

Made .... *26th June 2007*
Laid before Parliament .... *26th June 2007*
Coming into force .... *1st August 2007*

The Secretary of State makes the following Regulations in exercise of the powers conferred by section 355(1) of, and paragraphs 2(c) to (e), 3(1), 4, 10(4), 11(1), 14(1)(a) and (2), 15(2)(a), 16(2) and 24(3) of Schedule 12 to, the Gambling Act 2005.

6.1783 1 Citation, commencement and application

These Regulations may be cited as the Gambling Act 2005 (Club Gaming and Club Machine Permits) Regulations 2007 and shall come into force on 1st August 2007.

6.1784

2 These regulations apply to England and Wales and Scotland, except regulations 8, 15 and 16, which apply only to England and Wales.

6.1785 3 Interpretation

(1) In these Regulations—

"the Act" means the Gambling Act 2005;

"the 1968 Act" means the Gaming Act 1968;

"applicant" means a members' club, commercial club or miners' welfare institute that is making an application under paragraph 1(1) or (as the case may be) paragraph 1(2) or 24(1);

"application" means, unless otherwise specified, an application—

(a) for a club gaming permit under paragraph 1(1),

(b) for a club machine permit under paragraph 1(2), or

(c) to renew a club gaming or club machine permit under paragraph 24(1),

as the case may require;

"existing Part 2 operator" means an applicant—

(a) who is registered—

(i) under Part 2 of the 1968 Act (a "Part 2 registration") and the registration has effect immediately before 1st September 2007, or

(ii) under Part 2 of the 1968 Act on or after 1st September 2007; and

(b) whose application—

(i) relates to the same or substantially the same premises as those to which the Part 2 registration relates,

(ii) complies with sub-paragraphs (b) and (e) of paragraph 2 and (where applicable) paragraph 3, and

(iii) is made before the relevant date;

"existing Part 3 operator" means an applicant—

(a) who is registered—

(i) under Part 3 of the 1968 Act (a "Part 3 registration") and the registration has effect immediately before 1st September 2007, or

(ii) under Part 3 of the 1968 Act on or after 1st September 2007; and

(b) whose application—

(i) relates to the same or substantially the same premises as those to which the Part 3 registration relates,

(ii) complies with sub-paragraphs (b) and (e) of paragraph 2 and (where applicable) paragraph 3, and

(iii) is made before the relevant date;

"permit" means—

(a) a club gaming permit; or

(b) a club machine permit;

"relevant date"—

(a) in relation to a Part 2 registration, has the meaning given in paragraphs 80(3) to (5) of Schedule 4 to the Gambling Act 2005 (Commencement No 6 and Transitional Provisions) Order 2006 ("the Order"); and

(b) in relation to a Part 3 registration, has the meaning given in paragraphs 88(3) to (5) of Schedule 4 to the Order.

(2) A reference in these Regulations to a numbered paragraph is a reference to that paragraph of Schedule 12 to the Act so numbered.

6.1786 4 Form and manner of application for a permit and application fee

An application must be made in the form prescribed in Schedule 1.

6.1787

5 Where an application is made by an existing Part 2 or Part 3 operator, the application shall be accompanied by a copy of—

(a) the applicant's registration certificate within the meaning of paragraph 18(1) of Schedule 3 or paragraph 16(1) of Schedule 4 to the 1968 Act, if the applicant is an existing Part 2 operator, or

(b) a copy of the certificate issued to the applicant under paragraph 21 of Schedule 7 to the 1968 Act, if the applicant is an existing Part 3 operator.

6.1788

6 An application under paragraph 24(1) to renew a permit shall be accompanied by a copy of that permit.

6.1789

7 For the purposes of paragraph 3(1), an applicant must send a copy of an application and any accompanying documents to—

(a) the Commission, and

(b) the chief officer of police (within the meaning given in paragraph 3(1)(b)), or in Scotland the chief constable,

within a period of 7 days beginning on the date on which the application is made.

6.1790

8 (1) The fee to accompany an application, other than an application to renew a permit under paragraph 24(1), is £200 except that where—

(a) the application is made in accordance with paragraph 10 (which applies where the applicant for a permit is the holder of a club premises certificate under section 72 of the Licensing Act 2003), or

(b) the application is made by an existing Part 2 operator or an existing Part 3 operator,

the fee is £100.

(2) The fee to accompany an application to renew a permit under paragraph 24(1) is—

(a) subject to sub-paragraph (b), £200, or
(b) where the application is made in accordance with paragraph 10, £100.

6.1791 9 Objections

An objection under paragraph 4 to an application must be made—

(a) within a period of 28 days beginning on the date on which the application was made to the licensing authority;
(b) by sending to the licensing authority to whom the application is made, two copies of a written statement setting out the reasons for the objection.

6.1792 10 Form of Permit

A club gaming permit must be in the form prescribed in Schedule 2.

6.1793

11 A club machine permit must in the form prescribed in Schedule 3.

6.1794 12 Annual Fees

The first annual fee for a permit payable to the issuing licensing authority under paragraph 14(1)(a) is £50.

6.1795

13 The annual fee for a permit payable to the issuing licensing authority under paragraph 14(1)(b) is £50.

6.1796 14 Date by which first annual fee is payable

(1) Where a permit comes into effect on the issue date, the first annual fee for the permit shall be paid within 30 days after that date.

(2) Where a permit specifies that it is to come into effect on a date after the issue date, the first annual fee for the permit shall be paid within—

(a) the relevant period, or
(b) 12 months,

after the issue date, whichever is sooner.

(3) Paragraph (2) does not apply to a permit issued before 1st September 2007.

(4) In this regulation—

"the effective date", in relation to a permit which specifies that it is to come into effect on a date after the issue date, means the date so specified,

"the issue date" means the date on which a permit is issued, and

"the relevant period", in relation to a permit, means the period which is equal to the sum of—

(a) the period between the issue date and the effective date, and
(b) 30 days.

6.1797 15 Other Fees

The fee to accompany an application under paragraph 15(1) to vary a permit is £100.

6.1798

16 The fee to accompany an application under paragraph 16(1) for a copy of a permit is £15.

6.1799 17 Matters not required to be included in an application or permit

(1) The first page of the form prescribed in Schedule 1 may include any symbol or logo which is commonly used by a licensing authority to identify documents produced by it.

(2) Where matters are included in square brackets in any form in Schedules 1 to 3, they are intended to indicate and explain the information to be specified in the

application to which the form relates, and are not required to be included in the application.

6.1800

SCHEDULE 1[1]
Regulation 4

SCHEDULE 1

Regulation 4

This form is prescribed by regulation 4 of the Gambling Act 2005 (Club Gaming and Club Machine Permits) Regulations 2007

APPLICATION FORM FOR CLUB GAMING PERMIT OR CLUB MACHINE PERMIT

(FOR USE BY APPLICANTS - MEMBERS' CLUBS, COMMERCIAL CLUBS AND MINERS' WELFARE INSTITUTES)

If you are completing this form by hand, please write legibly in block capitals using ink.

To:	**Official use only** - licensing authority logo or symbol
[insert name and address of relevant licensing authority – this is the authority in whose area the premises relating to this application are wholly or partly situated]	

SECTION A – Type of Application

1. Please indicate type of application by ticking one of the boxes below:

☐ **Application for a club gaming permit**

☐ **Application for a club machine permit**

☐ **Application to renew a club gaming permit**

☐ **Application to renew a club machine permit**

SECTION B – Existing registration under Gaming Act 1968

[To be completed if the applicant wishes to apply as an existing Part 2 or Part 3 operator. Do not complete if applying to renew a permit]

Part I

2. Is this application made before 1st September 2007? Yes ☐ No ☐

If the answer to question 2 is 'Yes', complete questions 3 to 5, 11 and 12.
If the answer to question 2 is 'No', complete questions 6 to 12.

Application made before 1st September 2007

3. Is the applicant registered under Part 2 or Part 3 of the Gaming Act 1968? Yes ☐ No ☐

If the answer to question 3 is 'Yes', please indicate which type of registration:
Part 2 Registration ☐ Part 3 Registration ☐

4. When the registration was granted (or last renewed), was it fixed to expire on a date on or after 1st September 2007? Yes ☐ No ☐

5. Please indicate the date on which the registration was fixed to expire...
....

Application made on or after 1st September 2007

6. Did the applicant have a Part 2 or Part 3 Registration under the Gaming Act 1968 that had effect on 31st August 2007? Yes ☐ No ☐

7. If the answer to question 6 is 'Yes', please indicate the date on which the registration was due to expire (ie the date it was fixed to expire when the registration was granted or last renewed)........
....

8. If the date given in answer to question 7 is a date before 31st August 2007, was the applicant's registration renewed on or after 1st September 2007? Yes ☐ No ☐

Please give date of renewal...

9. If the answer to question 6 is 'No', was the applicant first registered under Part 2 or Part 3 of the Gaming Act 1968 on or after 1st September 2007? Yes ☐ No ☐

Please give date of registration..

10. If the answer to either question 6 or 9 is 'Yes', please indicate which type of registration:

Part 2 Registration ☐ Part 3 Registration ☐

Part II

11. Does this application relate to the same (or substantially the same) premises as those to which the registration relates? Yes ☐ No ☐

12. Is this application made before the 'relevant date'? Yes ☐ No ☐

[The 'relevant date' is the date on which the registration is due to expire, except where the applicant is registered on or after 1st September 2007, in which case the 'relevant date' for a Part 2 registration is the last day of the period of one year beginning on the date on which it is registered, and for a Part 3 registration is the last day of the period of five years beginning on the date on which it is registered.]

The applicant may apply as an existing operator if:
(a) the answer to questions 3, 11 and 12 is 'Yes' and the answer to question 4 is 'No' OR
(b) the answer to questions 6, 8, 11 and 12 is 'Yes' OR
(c) the answer to questions 9, 11 and 12 is 'Yes'

If the applicant is applying as an existing operator:

- **Do NOT complete SECTION C**
- **Relevant documentation must be provided – see SECTION H**
- **A different application fee is payable for an existing operator.**

SECTION C – Fast-track Procedure
[This section does not apply to Scotland]

13. Please indicate if this application is made under the fast-track procedure *[tick as appropriate]*:
Yes ☐ No ☐ *[to apply under the fast-track procedure, the applicant must be the holder of a club premises certificate under section 72 of the Licensing Act 2003]*

14. If the answer to question 13 is 'Yes', please complete the declaration below:

'I hereby certify that the applicant for a permit is the holder of a club premises certificate under section 72 of the Licensing Act 2003'

....*[full name]*

....*[signature]*

Capacity..

If the answer to question 13 is 'Yes' relevant documentation must be provided – see SECTION H

SECTION D – Contact Details of the Applicant

15. Name of applicant...
....

16. Address (including postcode) of premises on which the applicant operates.............................
....
....
....
....
....

[any gaming or gaming machines authorised by a relevant permit must take place or be located on these premises]

SECTION E – Information about the Applicant

If the applicant is a miners' welfare institute, complete questions 17 to 20:

17. Is the applicant established and conducted for social and recreational purposes?
Yes ☐ No ☐

18. Are the applicant's affairs managed by a group of individuals of whom at least two thirds are miners' representatives? Yes ☐ No ☐

19. Does the applicant operate on premises the use of which is regulated in accordance with a charitable trust? Yes ☐ No ☐

20. If the answer to question 19 is 'Yes', has the charitable trust received money from any of the following:
(a) the Miners' Welfare Fund established by section 20 of the Mining Industry Act 1920,
(b) the former body corporate which was known as the Coal Industry Social Welfare Organisation and incorporated under the Companies Act 1948, or
(c) the charitable trust known as the Coal Industry Social Welfare Organisation?
Yes ☐ No ☐

If the applicant is a members' club or commercial club, complete questions 21 to 26

21. Is the applicant established with the purpose of functioning only for a limited period of time?
Yes ☐ No ☐

22. Does the applicant have at least 25 individual members? Yes ☐ No ☐

23. Is the applicant established and conducted for the benefit of its members? Yes ☐ No ☐

24. Is the applicant established or conducted as a commercial enterprise? Yes ☐ No ☐

25. Describe the purpose(s) for which the applicant is wholly or mainly established and conducted
....
....
....
....
....
....

26. If the applicant is established or conducted wholly or mainly for the purpose of the provision of facilities for gaming, please specify the kinds of gaming..
....
....
....
....

SECTION F – General information about person completing this application form on behalf of applicant

27. Name..

28. Capacity...

29. Address (including postcode)...
....
....
....
....

SECTION G – Contact details for correspondence associated with this application

30. Please tick one box as appropriate:

Address in section E ☐ Address in section F ☐ Address below ☐ :

Address (including postcode)...
....
....
....

Telephone number...

E-mail address (if the applicant is happy for correspondence in relation to this application to be sent via e-mail)...
....

6: Gambling Act 2005: SIs

SECTION H – Declaration

31. Please complete the following declarations and checklist:

I *[full name]*..

a. make this application on behalf of the applicant and have authority to act on behalf of the applicant.

b. confirm that I am aware of any relevant provision of a code of practice issued by the Gambling Commission under section 24 of the Gambling Act 2005 about the location and operation of a gaming machine.

c. confirm that I am aware that the permit to which this application relates will be subject to the relevant conditions specified in section 271 or 273 of the Gambling Act 2005.

d. confirm that I am aware that (unless this application is made under the fast-track procedure) the applicant must send a copy of this application and any accompanying documents to the Gambling Commission and the chief officer of police (or chief constable in Scotland) within a period of seven days beginning on the date this application is made.

e. Checklist *[tick as appropriate]*:

☐ Payment of the appropriate fee of £.......................... is enclosed.

☐ A copy of the existing club gaming permit or club machine permit is enclosed *[only applies to applications to renew a permit]*

☐ A copy of the registration certificate issued under Part 2 of the Gaming Act 1968 is enclosed *[only applies if the applicant wishes to apply as an existing Part 2 operator]*

☐ A copy of the registration certificate issued under Part 3 of the Gaming Act 1968 is enclosed *[only applies if the applicant wishes to apply as an existing Part 3 operator]*

☐ The applicant's club premises certificate issued under section 72 of the Licensing Act 2003 is enclosed *[only applies if the applicant has completed the declaration in section C]*

f. **confirm that, to the best of my knowledge, the information contained in this application is true. I understand that it is an offence under section 342 of the Gambling Act 2005 to give information which is false or misleading in, or in relation to, this application.**

Signature..

Date..

Capacity..

1 Substituted by SI 2007/2689, reg 2, Schedule.

6.1801

SCHEDULE 2
Regulation 10

SCHEDULE 2

Regulation 10

This form is prescribed by regulation 10 of the Gambling Act 2005 (Club Gaming and Club Machine Permits) Regulations 2007

Club Gaming Permit

No:..*[insert club gaming permit number]*

This club gaming permit authorises..
....
....*[name of permit holder]*
to provide facilities for gaming in accordance with section 271 of the Gambling Act 2005, and to make available for use up to three gaming machines, each of which must be of Category B3A, B4, C, or D, on the following premises...
....
....
....
....
....
....
....
[address of premises, including postcode]

Club Premises Certificate Number (if any)..
[complete if permit holder is the holder of a club premises certificate under section 72 of the Licensing Act 2003 (c. 17)].

Date on which this permit takes effect or is renewed:
....

Date on which this permit expires:
....

This permit is issued by...
....
....
....
....
....
....
.....................*[Name and address of licensing authority issuing permit]*

6.1802

SCHEDULE 3

SCHEDULE 3

Regulation 11

This form is prescribed by regulation 11 of the Gambling Act 2005 (Club Gaming and Club Machine Permits) Regulations 2007

Club Machine Permit

No:..*[insert club gaming permit number]*

This club machine permit authorises..
....
....
....*[name of permit holder]*
to make available for use up to three gaming machines, each of which must be of Category B3A (except that category B3A machines may not be made available for use in commercial clubs), B4, C or D, on the following premises..
....
....
....
....
....
....
....
....
....
[address of premises, including postcode]

Club Premises Certificate Number (if any)...
[complete if permit holder is the holder of a club premises certificate under section 72 of the Licensing Act 2003 (c. 17)].

Date on which this permit takes effect or is renewed:
....

Date on which this permit expires:
....

This permit is issued by..
....
....
....
....
....
....
....................*[Name and address of licensing authority issuing permit]*

GAMBLING ACT 2005 (EXEMPT GAMING IN ALCOHOL-LICENSED PREMISES) REGULATIONS 2007

(SI 2007/1940)

Made .... *7th July 2007*
Laid before Parliament .... *9th July 2007*
Coming into force .... *1st September 2007*

The Secretary of State makes the following Regulations in exercise of the powers conferred by sections 279(2), 280(1) and 355(1) of the Gambling Act 2005:

6.1803 1 Citation, commencement and interpretation

(1) These Regulations may be cited as the Gambling Act 2005 (Exempt Gaming in Alcohol-Licensed Premises) Regulations 2007 and shall come into force on 1st September 2007.

(2) In these Regulations—

"the Act" means the Gambling Act 2005, and

"poker" includes any version of that game, whatever name it is called.

(3) For the purposes of these Regulations, a reference to a day is a reference to a period of 24 hours beginning at midday.

6.1804 2 Requirements in relation to stakes

(1) This regulation applies to the provision of facilities for equal chance gaming in accordance with section 279 of the Act, and prescribes, for the purposes of subsection (2)(a) of that section, requirements in relation to limiting amounts that may be staked.

(2) Subject to paragraphs (3) and (4), the amount that may be staked by a person on any game of chance, except dominoes and cribbage, must not exceed £5.

(3) Subject to paragraph (4) the aggregate of the amounts that may be staked on games of poker in any one day must not exceed £100.

6.1805 3 Requirements in relation to poker prize

(1) For the purposes of section 279(2)(b) of the Act, the maximum amount or value of a prize that may be won in any game of poker is £100.

GAMBLING ACT 2005 (GAMING IN CLUBS) REGULATIONS 2007

(SI 2007/1942)

Made .... *7th July 2007*
Laid before Parliament .... *9th July 2007*
Coming into force .... *1st August 2007*

The Secretary of State makes the following Regulations in exercise of the powers conferred upon her by sections 266(2)(a), 267(2)(a) and paragraphs 10(3)(a) and (b) of Schedule 12 to the Gambling Act 2005.

6.1806 1 Citation, commencement and interpretation

(1) These Regulations may be cited as the Gambling Act 2005 (Gaming in Clubs) Regulations 2007 and shall come into force on 1st August 2007.

(2) In these Regulations "the Act" means the Gambling Act 2005.

(3) A reference in these Regulations to a numbered paragraph is a reference to that paragraph of Schedule 12 to the Act so numbered.

6.1807 2 Members' clubs and commercial clubs

Bridge and whist are prescribed for the purposes of sections 266(2)(a) and 267(2)(a) of the Act (which provide that a club is respectively a members' club or commercial club if it is established or conducted wholly or mainly to provide facilities for gaming of a prescribed kind, but for no other kind of gaming).

6.1808 3 Fast-track procedure

Bridge and whist are prescribed for the purposes of paragraphs 10(3)(a) and (b) (which enable licensing authorities to refuse applications to which paragraph 10 applies, if the applicant is established or conducted to provide either gaming other than gaming of the prescribed kinds, or gaming of the prescribed kinds and also gaming of another kind).

GAMBLING ACT 2005 (EXEMPT GAMING IN CLUBS) REGULATIONS 2007

(SI 2007/1944)

Made . . . . *7th July 2007*
Laid before Parliament . . . . *9th July 2007*
Coming into force . . . . *1st September 2007*

The Secretary of State makes the following Regulations in exercise of the powers conferred by sections 269(2) and (4), 270(2) and (4), and 355(1) of the Gambling Act 2005.

6.1809 1 Citation, commencement and interpretation

(1) These Regulations may be cited as the Gambling Act 2005 (Exempt Gaming in Clubs) Regulations 2007 and shall come into force on 1st September 2007.

(2) In these Regulations—

"the Act" means the Gambling Act 2005;

"poker" includes any version of that game, whatever name it is called; and

"relevant club" means—

(a) a members' club,
(b) a commercial club,
(c) a club that would be a members' club but for section 266(1)(a) of the Act,
(d) a club that would be a commercial club but for section 267(1)(b) of the Act, or
(e) a miners' welfare institute.

(3) For the purposes of these Regulations, a reference to a day is a reference to a period of 24 hours beginning at midday.

6.1810 2 Requirements in relation to poker stakes

(1) This regulation applies to the provision of facilities for games of poker under section 269 of the Act (exempt gaming) and prescribes, for the purposes of subsection (2)(a) of that section, requirements in relation to amounts that may be staked.

(2) Subject to paragraphs (3) and (4), the amount that may be staked by a person on any game of poker must not exceed £10.

(3) Subject to paragraph (4), the aggregate of the amounts that may be staked on games of poker in any one day must not exceed £250.

(4) The aggregate of the amounts that may be staked on games of poker in any period of seven days must not exceed £1,000.

6.1811 3 Requirements in relation to poker prize

For the purposes of section 269(2)(b) of the Act, the maximum amount or value of a prize that may be won in any game of poker is £250.

6.1812 4 Participation fees where no club gaming permit is held

(1) This regulation prescribes the maximum participation fee that may be charged for the purposes of section 269(4) of the Act, where a relevant club does not hold a club gaming permit.

(2) The maximum participation fee that a relevant club may charge a person in respect of entitlement to participate in a particular kind of game on any one day is—

(a) £18 in respect of bridge or whist, if the game is played on a day on which no facilities for any kinds of gaming (other than bridge or whist) are provided by the relevant club on that day; and

(b) in any other circumstances—

(i) subject to paragraph (ii), £1; or

(ii) in the case of a commercial club that holds a club machine permit, £3.

6.1813 5 Participation fees where a club gaming permit is held

Where a members' club or miners' welfare institute holds a club gaming permit, the maximum participation fee that it may charge a person in respect of entitlement to participate in a particular kind of game in any one day is—

(a) £20 (exclusive of value added tax) in respect of bridge or whist, if the game is played on a day on which no facilities for any kinds of gaming (other than bridge or whist) are provided by the relevant club on that day; and

(b) £3 (exclusive of value added tax) for equal chance gaming in any other circumstances.

GAMBLING ACT 2005 (CLUB GAMING PERMITS) (AUTHORISED GAMING) REGULATIONS 2007

(SI 2007/1945)

Made . . . . *7th July 2007*
Laid before Parliament . . . . *9th July 2007*
Coming into force . . . . *1st September 2007*

The Secretary of State makes the following Regulations in exercise of the powers conferred by sections 271(3)(c), (4)(a) and (5) and 355(1) of the Gambling Act 2005.

6.1814 1 Commencement, citation and interpretation

(1) These Regulations may be cited as the Gambling Act 2005 (Club Gaming Permits) (Authorised Gaming) Regulations 2007 and shall come into force on 1st September 2007.

(2) In these Regulations "the Act" means the Gambling Act 2005.

6.1815 2 Games of chance authorised under a club gaming permit

(1) For the purposes of section 271(3)(c) of the Act, the games of chance the provision of facilities for which is authorised by a club gaming permit are pontoon and chemin de fer.

(2) The reference in paragraph (1) to the game of pontoon does not include a reference to the game of blackjack, or any other form of pontoon whose rules do not provide for the right to hold the bank to pass amongst players in certain events arising in the course of play.

6.1816 3 Authorisation to charge participation fees

(1) For the purposes of section 271(4)(a) of the Act, a participation fee may be charged in respect of any of the games of chance prescribed by regulation 2(1).

(2) The maximum participation fee that a person may be charged in respect of entitlement to participate on any one day in any of the games prescribed by regulation 2(1) is £3 (exclusive of value added tax).

(3) In this regulation, a reference to a day is a reference to a period of 24 hours beginning at midday.

GAMBLING ACT 2005 (INCIDENTAL NON-COMMERCIAL LOTTERIES) REGULATIONS 2007

(SI 2007/2040)

Made ....*14th July 2007*
Laid before Parliament ....*17th July 2007*
Coming into force ....*1st September 2007*

The Secretary of State makes the following Regulations in exercise of the powers conferred by paragraphs 3 and 4 of Schedule 11 to the Gambling Act 2005.

6.1817 1 Citation, commencement and interpretation

(1) These Regulations may be cited as the Gambling Act 2005 (Incidental Non-Commercial Lotteries) Regulations 2007 and shall come into force on 1st September 2007.

(2) In these Regulations—

"the Act" means the Gambling Act 2005;

"incidental non-commercial lottery" has the same meaning as in Part 1 of Schedule 11 to the Act.

6.1818 2 Limits for incidental non-commercial lotteries

(1) This regulation prescribes for the purposes of paragraphs 3 and 4 of Schedule 11 to the Act the maximum sums that promoters of an incidental non-commercial lottery may deduct from the proceeds of the lottery.

(2) In respect of the cost of the prizes awarded in the lottery the promoters may deduct no more than £500.

(3) In respect of the costs incurred in organising the lottery the promoters may deduct no more than £100.

GAMBLING ACT 2005 (NON-COMMERCIAL EQUAL-CHANCE GAMING) REGULATIONS 2007

(SI 2007/2041)

Made ....*14th July 2007*
Laid before Parliament ....*17th July 2007*
Coming into force ....*1st September 2007*

The Secretary of State makes the following Regulations in exercise of the powers conferred by section 300(4) of the Gambling Act 2005.

6.1819 1 Citation, commencement and interpretation

These Regulations may be cited as the Gambling Act 2005 (Non-Commercial Equal-Chance Gaming) Regulations 2007 and shall come into force on 1st September 2007.

6.1820

2 (1) In these Regulations—

"the Act" means the Gambling Act 2005;

"event" means a non-commercial event within the meaning of section 297 of the Act.

(2) A reference to a game in regulation 3 means a game that constitutes non-commercial equal chance gaming within the meaning of Part 14 of the Act.

6.1821 3 Limits for non-commercial equal-chance gaming

(1) This regulation limits certain payments, amounts or values for the purposes of section 300(4) of the Act (conditions for non-commercial equal-chance gaming). (Accordingly, arrangements for gaming must ensure compliance with this regulation in order to satisfy the third condition as set out in that subsection).

(2) No person is to make, or to be required to make more than one payment (whether by way of a participation fee, stake or other charge) in order to participate in each and every game played at an event, and the payment shall not exceed £8.

(3) Subject to paragraph (5)(b), in respect of all games played at an event the aggregate amount or value of prizes and awards distributed in respect of those games shall not exceed £600.

(4) Where two or more events are promoted on the same premises by the same person on the same day, the limits in paragraphs (2) and (3) shall apply in relation to those events collectively as if they were a single event.

(5) Where a series of events is held, other than in circumstances where paragraph (4) applies—

(a) the limits in paragraphs (2) and (3) shall apply separately in relation to each event in the series, and

(b) in respect of all games played at a final event the amount or value of prizes and awards distributed in respect of those games shall not exceed £900.

(6) In this regulation an event is a final event if—

(a) no other event is promoted on the same premises by the same person on the same day as that on which the event takes place, and

(b) each person taking part in the event is qualified to do so by reason of having taken part in games played at another event of the series held on a previous day.

GAMBLING ACT 2005 (GAMING MACHINES) (DEFINITIONS) REGULATIONS 2007

(SI 2007/2082)

Made ....*18th July 2007*
Laid before Parliament ....*20th July 2007*
Coming into force ....*1st September 2007*

The Secretary of State makes the following regulations in exercise of the powers conferred by sections 235(3)(f), 235(4) and 355(1) of the Gambling Act 2005.

6.1822 1 Citation, commencement and interpretation

(1) These Regulations may be cited as the Gambling Act 2005 (Gaming Machines) (Definitions) Regulations 2007 and shall come into force on 1st September 2007.

(2) In these Regulations—

"the Act" means the Gambling Act 2005;

"commercial arrangement", in connection with the use of a computer—

(a) includes any arrangement under which an owner of the computer, or a person connected with such an owner—

(i) makes or receives (or intends to make or reasonably expects to receive) any payment or reward (whether by way of commission, rent or otherwise), in connection with making the computer available for use, or

(ii) otherwise receives (or reasonably expects to receive) any benefit in connection with making the computer available for use by virtue of it being adapted or presented in such a way as to facilitate or draw attention to the possibility of its use for gambling;

(b) does not include an arrangement between an employer and his employee in connection with that employment, other than where a computer is made available to the employee by his employer for use wholly or mainly for recreational purposes;

"company" has the meaning given in section 735(1)(a) of the Companies Act 1985;

"owner", in relation to a computer, means any person who owns the computer or has any right to control (directly or indirectly) by whom it is used;

"private use" in relation to a computer means use of the computer by—

(a) an owner of the computer, or

(b) persons using it with the permission of an owner of the computer, other than under any commercial arrangement in connection with its use;

"subsidiary" has the meaning given in section 736 of the Companies Act 1985.

(3) In these Regulations, a person is connected with an owner of a computer where—

(a) the person and the owner are both companies and—

(i) one is a subsidiary of the other, or

(ii) both are subsidiaries of the same company;

(b) the person and the owner are carrying on a business in common with a view to profit; or

(c) the person is the owner's spouse, civil partner, sibling, ancestor, or lineal or collateral descendant.

6.1823 2 Dual-use computers

(1) A computer is a dual-use computer within the meaning of section 235(2)(a) of the Act if—

(a) it is capable of being used for a purpose that is not related to gambling, and

(b) either—

(i) it is not knowingly adapted or presented by or on behalf of an owner of the computer or a person connected with such an owner, in such a way as to facilitate, or to draw attention to the possibility of, its use for gambling, or

(ii) it is so adapted or presented, but only in the circumstances specified in paragraph (2) or (3).

(2) The circumstances specified in this paragraph are that the computer is being made available for use (other than in circumstances where it is being adapted, maintained or repaired), but its use is restricted or intended to be restricted to private use.

(3) The circumstances specified in this paragraph are that the computer is being adapted, maintained or repaired (whether or not it is also being made available for use), but its use is restricted or intended to be restricted to persons using it in connection with its adaptation, maintenance or repair in circumstances where—

(a) but for its adaptation, maintenance or repair, its use would otherwise be restricted or intended to be restricted to private use, and

(b) enabling or facilitating the use of the computer for gambling is not the main purpose of the adaptation, maintenance or repair.

6.1824 3 Domestic computers

For the purposes of section 235(2) of the Act, a domestic computer is a computer that—

(a) is capable of being used for a purpose that is not related to gambling,

(b) is located in a private dwelling, and

(c) if used, is used on a domestic occasion.

GAMBLING ACT 2005 (HORSERACE TOTALISATOR BOARD) ORDER 2007

(SI 2007/2102)

Made . . . . 19th July 2007

Coming into force in accordance with article 1(1)

The Secretary of State makes the following Order in exercise of the powers conferred by section 358(5) of the Gambling Act 2005.

A draft of this Order has been laid before Parliament in accordance with section 355(8)(b) of that Act, and has been approved by a resolution of each House of Parliament.

6.1825 1 Citation, commencement and interpretation

(1) This Order may be cited as the Gambling Act 2005 (Horserace Totalisator Board) Order 2007 and shall come into force on whichever is the later of 1st September 2007 or the day after the day on which the Order is made.

(2) In this Order—

"the 1963 Act" means the Betting, Gaming and Lotteries Act 1963;

"the 2005 Act" means the Gambling Act 2005;

"approved horse-race course" means any horse-race course in respect of which a betting premises licence or an occasional use notice for the time being has effect;

"the dissolution date" means the day appointed for the purposes of section 1 of the Horserace Betting and Olympic Lottery Act 2004 as the day on which the Tote ceases to exist;

"pool betting business" has the meaning given in the table in the Schedule;

"sponsored pool betting" has the meaning given in the table in the Schedule;

"sponsored pool betting business" means business involving the receiving or negotiating of bets made by way of sponsored pool betting; and

"the Tote" means the Horserace Totalisator Board.

(3) Any reference in this Order to a person infringing the right conferred on the Tote by section 14 of the 1963 Act shall be construed in accordance with subsection (2) of that section.

6.1826 2 Savings

(1) Despite the repeal of the 1963 Act by the 2005 Act, sections 12, 14 and 15 of the 1963 Act shall continue in force until immediately before the dissolution date, subject to the following modification.

(2) Section 14 shall have effect as if the expressions listed in column 1 of the table in the Schedule had the meanings given in the associated entry in column 2 of that table.

6.1827 3 Modification of section 33 of the Gambling Act 2005

(1) Section 33 of the 2005 Act shall have effect until immediately before the dissolution date with the following modifications.

(2) Subsection (1) does not apply to any activity by—

(a) the Tote in pursuance of the right conferred by section 14 of the 1963 Act, or

(b) any other person acting in the course of a business carried on by the Tote in pursuance of that right.

(3) Subsection (1) does not apply to any activity which—

(a) takes place on an approved horse-race course on a day on which horse races but no other races take place, and

(b) is carried out by a person acting in the course of an authorised pool betting business.

(4) Subsection (1) does not apply to any activity by a person acting in the course of a sponsored pool betting business.

(5) Subsections (2) and (3) do not apply to any activity by a person which infringes the right conferred on the Tote by section 14 of the 1963 Act whether or not those subsections would otherwise apply to the activity.

(6) In paragraph (3) "authorised pool betting business" means a pool betting business carried on, with the authority of the Tote, by the persons having the management of the horse-race course referred to in sub-paragraph (a) of that paragraph.

6.1828 4 Modification of section 163 of the Gambling Act 2005

Section 163 of the 2005 Act shall have effect in relation to an application by the Tote for a betting premises licence with the omission of subsection (2).

6.1829 5 Modification of sections 336 to 338 of the Gambling Act 2005

Sections 336 to 338 of the Gambling Act 2005 shall apply to a bet accepted by or through—

(a) the Tote;

(b) a person carrying on a sponsored pool betting business; or

(c) the persons having the management of an approved horse-race course, where the act of accepting the bet is an activity to which article 3(3) applies,

as those sections apply to a bet accepted by or through the holder of a pool betting operating licence.

6.1830

SCHEDULE

DEFINITIONS OF EXPRESSIONS USED IN SECTION 14 OF THE BETTING, GAMING AND LOTTERIES ACT 1963

Articles 1 and 2

Column 1	**Column 2**
Expression	**Meaning**
Approved horse racecourse	Any horse-race course in respect of which a betting premises licence or an occasional use notice for the time being has effect.
Pool betting	Pool betting within the meaning of section 12 of the 2005 Act.
Pool betting business	Business involving the receiving or negotiating of bets made by way of pool betting.
Recognised horse race	A horse race run on an approved horse-race course.
Sponsored pool betting	Pool betting by means of facilities provided by the Tote, or provided on an approved horse-race course with the authority of the Tote by the persons having the management of the course.

BETTING AND GAMING DUTIES ACT 1981 (BINGO MONETARY AMOUNTS) ORDER 2007

(SI 2007/2152)

Made . . . . *24th July 2007*
Laid before the House of Commons . . . . *24th July 2007*
Coming into force . . . . *1st September 2007*

The Commissioners for Her Majesty's Revenue and Customs make the following Order in exercise of the powers conferred by Schedule 3 paragraph 7 to the Betting and Gaming Duties Act 1981:

6.1831

1 This Order may be cited as the Betting and Gaming Duties Act 1981 (Bingo Monetary Amounts) Order 2007 and comes into force on 1st September 2007.

6.1832

2 (1) Schedule 3 paragraph 5(2)(b) to the Betting and Gaming Duties Act 1981 (exemption from bingo duty for small-scale bingo provided commercially) shall have effect as if there were substituted for the sum there "£500".

(2) Paragraph 5(2)(c) of that Schedule shall have effect as if there were substituted for the sum there "£50".

6.1833

3 (1) Article 5(b) of the Betting and Gaming Duties Act 1981 (Monetary Amounts) Order 1995 is omitted.

(2) The Betting and Gaming Duties Act 1981 (Bingo Prize Limit) Order 2004 is revoked.

Two of the Commissioners for Her Majesty's Revenue and Customs.

CATEGORIES OF GAMING MACHINE REGULATIONS 2007

(SI 2007/2158)

Made . . . .*23rd July 2007*
Coming into force . . . .*1st September 2007*

The Secretary of State makes the following Regulations in exercise of the powers conferred in sections 236 and 355(1) of the Gambling Act 2005.

In accordance with section 355(4)(i) of that Act a draft of this instrument was laid before Parliament and approved by a resolution of each House of Parliament.

6.1834 1 Citation and commencement

These Regulations—

(a) may be cited as the Categories of Gaming Machine Regulations 2007;

(b) come into force on the day after the day on which they are made, or 1st September 2007, whichever is the later.

6.1835 2 Interpretation

(1) In these Regulations—

"Act" means the Gambling Act 2005;

"charge for use" means the amount a person pays for using a gaming machine once;

"machine" means a gaming machine within the meaning of section 235 of the Act;

"prize value" means the amount or value of any prize which can be won as a result of use of a gaming machine once.

(2) Subject to paragraph (3), a person is to be treated for the purposes of these Regulations as using a gaming machine once, even where he uses the machine to gamble more than once, if the payment for each gamble is made before he is able to know the result of any of them.

(3) Paragraph (2) does not apply in relation to a gaming machine in respect of which—

(a) the charge for use may only be paid by means of a single coin or token,

(b) the coin or token must be inserted into the machine to pay the charge for use, and

(c) whether or not a person using the machine wins a prize is determined (wholly or in part) by—

(i) the position in which the coin or token comes to rest after it has been inserted into the machine, together with the position of other coins or tokens which have previously been inserted into the machine to pay a charge for use, or

(ii) if the insertion of a single coin to pay the charge for use enables the person using the machine to release one or more tokens within the machine, the position in which such tokens come to rest after being released, together with the position of other tokens which have previously been so released.

(4) In paragraph (3) "token" means an object of money's worth.

6.1836 [3 **Definition of Category D gaming machine**

(1) Where a machine is a money-prize machine, it is a Category D machine if

(a) the maximum charge for use is no more than 10 pence; and

(b) the maximum prize value is no more than £5.

(2) Where a machine is a non-money prize machine (other than a crane grab machine), it is a Category D machine if

(a) the maximum charge for use is no more than 30 pence; and

(b) the maximum prize value is no more than £8.

(3) Where a machine is a crane grab machine, it is a Category D machine if

(a) the maximum charge for use is no more than £1; and

(b) the maximum prize value is no more than £50.

(4) Where a machine is a coin pusher or penny fall machine, it is a Category D machine if

(a) the maximum charge for use is no more than 10 pence; and

(b) the maximum prize value is no more than £15, of which no more than £8 may be a money prize.

(5) any other case, a machine is a Category D machine if

(a) the maximum charge for use is no more than 10 pence; and

(b) the maximum prize value is no more than £8, of which no more than £5 may be a money prize.

(6) In this regulation a reference to

(a) a money prize machine is a reference to a machine in respect of which every prize which can be won as a result of using the machine is a money prize;

(b) a non-money prize machine is a reference to a machine in respect of which every prize which can be won as a result of using the machine is a non-money prize;

(c) a crane grab machine is a reference to a non-money prize machine in respect of which

(i) every prize which can be won as a result of using the machine consists of an individual physical object (such as a stuffed toy), and

(ii) whether or not a person using the machine wins a prize is determined by the person's success or failure in manipulating a device forming part of the machine so as to separate, and keep separate, one or more physical objects from a group of such objects;

(d) a coin pusher or penny fall machine is a reference to a machine of the kind referred to in regulation 2(3) which is neither a money prize machine nor a non-money prize machine.

(7) Subject to paragraph (8), in this regulation "money prize" means a prize

(a) in the form of cash or a cheque (or partly in the form of cash and partly in the form of a cheque), or

(b) in the form of a document or object which—

(i) enables the person entitled to it to redeem its value, on the premises where the machine is made available for use, in the form of cash or a cheque (or partly in the form of cash and partly in the form of a cheque), and

(ii) may, but need not, also enable that person to use it to pay for goods or services (including facilities for gambling) available on the premises where the machine is made available for use;

and "non-money prize" is any prize which is not a money prize.

(8) A document or object is not a money prize if it is something which ordinarily is capable of being used for a purpose other than one referred to in paragraph (7)(b).".][1]

6.1837 4 Definition of Category C gaming machine

A machine is a Category C machine if—

(a) the maximum charge for use is no more than [£1][1];

(b) the maximum prize value is no more than [£70][1]; and

(c) it is not a Category D machine.

6.1838 5 Definition of Category B gaming machine

(1) There shall be five sub-categories of Category B to be known as sub-categories B1, B2, B3, B3A and B4.

(2) A machine is a sub-category B4 machine if—

(a) the maximum charge for use is no more than £1;

(b) the maximum prize value is no more than £250; and

(c) it is not a Category C or D machine.

(3) A machine is a sub-category B3A machine if—

(a) it enables a person to participate in a lottery but not in any other form of gambling;

(b) it is made available for use by a members' club or a miners' welfare institute;

(c) the maximum charge for use is no more than £1;

(d) the maximum prize value is no more than £500; and

(e) it is not a sub-category B4 machine or a Category C or D machine.

(4) A machine is a sub-category B3 machine if—

(a) the maximum charge for use is no more than [£2][1];

(b) the maximum prize value is no more than £500; and

(c) it is not a sub-category B3A or B4 machine or a Category C or D machine.

(5) A machine is a sub-category B2 machine if—

(a) the maximum charge for use is no more than £100;

(b) the maximum prize value is no more than £500; and

(c) it is not a sub-category B3, B3A or B4 machine or a Category C or D machine.

(6) A machine is a sub-category B1 machine if—

(a) the maximum charge for use is no more than £2;

(b) the maximum prize value is no more than £4,000; and

(c) it is not a sub-category B2, B3, B3A or B4 machine or a Category C or D machine.

---

1 Para (4): in sub-para (a) sum "£2" in sqaure brackets substituted by SI 2011/1711, reg 2. Date in force: 13 July 2011: see SI 2011/1711, reg 1.

6.1839 6 Allocation of sub-categories

(1) The reference to a Category B machine in section 54(1)(a) (employment on premises with gaming machines) is to be treated as referring to any sub-category of Category B.

(2) The reference to a Category B machine in section 150(1)(c) (adult gaming centre premises licence) is to be treated as referring to sub-categories B3 or B4.

(3) A reference to a Category B machine in section 172 of the Act is to have effect as follows—

(a) in subsection (1)(a) (licensed adult gaming centres) it is to be treated as referring to sub-categories B3 or B4;

(b) in subsections (3)(a), (4)(a) and (5)(a) (licensed regional, large and small casinos) it is to be treated as referring to any sub-category of Category B, except sub-category B3A;

(c) in subsection (7)(a) (licensed bingo premises) it is to be treated as referring to sub-categories B3 or B4;

(d) in subsection (8) (licensed betting premises) it is to be treated as referring to sub-categories B2, B3 or B4.

(4) A reference to a Category B machine in section 271 (club gaming permit) or section 273 (club machine permit) is to be treated as referring to sub-category B3A or B4.

6.1840 7 Definition of Category A gaming machine

A Category A machine is a machine which is not a Category B, C or D machine.

[1] Amended by SI 2009/1502.

GAMBLING ACT 2005 (HORSERACE BETTING LEVY) ORDER 2007

(SI 2007/2159)

Made ....19th July 2007

Coming into force in accordance with article 1(1)

The Secretary of State makes the following Order in exercise of the powers conferred by section 358(6) of the Gambling Act 2005.

A draft of this Order has been laid before Parliament in accordance with section 355(8)(b) of that Act, and has been approved by resolution of each House.

6.1841 1 Citation, commencement and interpretation

(1) This Order may be cited as the Gambling Act 2005 (Horserace Betting Levy) Order 2007 and shall come into force on whichever is the later of 1st September 2007 or the day after the day on which the Order is made.

(2) In this Order—

"the 1963 Act" means the Betting, Gaming and Lotteries Act 1963;

"the 2005 Act" means the Gambling Act 2005;

"bookmakers' levy" means the levy payable under section 27 of the 1963 Act; and

"the dissolution date" means the date specified in an order made under section 15(1) of the Horserace Betting and Olympic Lottery Act 2004 as the date on which the Horserace Betting Levy Board ceases to exist.

6.1842 2 Savings

(1) Despite the repeal of the 1963 Act by the 2005 Act, sections 24 to 30 of the 1963 Act shall continue to have effect until immediately before the dissolution date subject to the modification in paragraph (2).

(2) Section 28(10) of the 1963 Act does not apply to any information provided by a member, officer or servant of the Horserace Betting Levy Board to the Gambling Commission for use by the Commission in the exercise of its functions (including any information provided for the purposes of sections 116 to 120 of the 2005 Act as modified by article 3 of this Order).

(3) Expressions used in sections 24 to 30 of the 1963 Act shall have the meanings given to them by section 55(1) of the 1963 Act (as that provision had effect immediately before 1st September 2007).

6.1843–6.1849 3 Modification of the Gambling Act 2005

(1) Sections 116 to 120 of the 2005 Act (review of operating licences) shall have effect until immediately before the dissolution date subject to the following modifications.

(2) The Gambling Commission must carry out a review of an operating licence under section 116(2)(c) if it is notified in writing by the Horserace Betting Levy Board that—

(a) the holder of the operating licence is in default of the bookmakers' levy and has been so for at least three months; and

(b) on a previous occasion (not being before the period of five years ending with the date on which the Gambling Commission receives the notice from the Horserace Betting Levy Board) he was so in default and had been so for at least three months.

(3) The Gambling Commission must exercise its powers under section 119 to revoke the operating licence (on the grounds that the condition in section 120(1)(d) applies) if—

(a) the Commission is satisfied that the matters referred to in sub-paragraphs (a) and (b) of paragraph (2) are in fact the case; and

(b) having notified the Horserace Betting Levy Board and the operating licence holder in writing of this decision, the Commission has received written confirmation from the Horserace Betting Levy Board that they want the operating licence to be revoked.

(4) The Gambling Commission must provide the holder of the operating licence with an opportunity to make representations on the matters referred to in sub-paragraphs (a) and (b) of paragraph (2) before reaching a decision under paragraph (3)(a).

(5) For the purposes of this article, a person is in default in respect of the bookmakers' levy if—

(a) there has become due from him under section 28(7) of the 1963 Act an amount assessed as payable by him by way of levy, and

(b) the whole or any part of that amount remains unpaid.

GAMBLING ACT 2005 (OPERATING LICENCE CONDITIONS) REGULATIONS 2007

(SI 2007/2257)

Made . . . . *27th July 2007*
Coming into force in accordance with regulation 1(1)

The Secretary of State makes the following Regulations in exercise of the powers conferred by sections 78, 291(2) and (3) and 355(1) of the Gambling Act 2005.

In accordance with section 355(4) of that Act, a draft of this instrument was laid before Parliament and approved by resolution of each House.

6.1850 1 Citation, commencement and interpretation

(1) These Regulations may be cited as the Gambling Act 2005 (Operating Licence Conditions) Regulations 2007 and shall come into force on whichever is the later of 1st September 2007 or the day after the day on which these Regulations are made.

(2) In these Regulations—

"the 2005 Act" means the Gambling Act 2005; and

"licensed bingo premises" means premises in respect of which a bingo premises licence for the time being has effect.

6.1851 2 Condition to be attached to casino operating licences

(1) The condition specified in this regulation shall be attached to each casino operating licence.

(2) Where, in reliance on the operating licence, a game is played on a wholly automated gaming table, the game must be capable of being played by four persons at the same time using four separate player positions.

(3) In this regulation "wholly automated gaming table" means equipment that would fall within the definition of a gaming machine in section 235 of the 2005 Act but for its exclusion from that definition by subsection (2)(i) of that section.

6.1852–6.1856 3 Condition to be attached to bingo operating licences in respect of prize gaming

(1) The condition specified in this regulation shall be attached to each bingo operating licence.

(2) Section 291(1) of the 2005 Act (which authorises the provision of facilities for prize gaming in licensed bingo premises) applies only in respect of facilities for prize gaming provided by the holder of the operating licence in accordance with the following provisions of this regulation.

(3) The amount charged by way of participation fee in respect of any one chance to win a prize in a particular game does not exceed [£1].[1]

(4) Where in paying for a chance to win a prize in a game a person acquires the chance to win more than one prize, the limit in paragraph (3) shall apply despite the fact that the chance provides the opportunity to win more than one prize.

(5) The aggregate amount of the participation fees charged for participating in a particular game does not exceed £500.

(6) Where a prize for which a game is played is money, the amount of that prize does not exceed—

(a) [£100],[2] if no person under the age of 18 years is permitted to be on the premises at any time when the game is being played, and

(b) [£70],[3] in all other cases.

(7) For the purposes of paragraph (6)(a) no account shall be taken of any person under the age of 18 years who is permitted to be on the premises if—

(a) he is employed to perform any function on the premises, and

(b) he is on the premises in the course of his employment.

(8) In paragraphs (6)(a) and (7), any reference to the premises is to the licensed bingo premises in which the game referred to in paragraph (6)(a) is being played.

(9) The aggregate amount or value of the prizes for which a game is played does not exceed £500.

6: Gambling Act 2005: SIs

1 Para (3): sum "£1" in square brackets substituted by SI 2010/774, reg 2(1), (2).

2 Para (6): in sub-para (a) sum "£100" in square brackets substituted by SI 2010/774, reg 2(1), (3)(a).

3 Para (6): in sub-para (b) sum "£70" in square brackets substituted by SI 2010/774, reg 2(1), (3)(b).

GAMBLING ACT 2005 (PREMISES LICENCES) (REVIEW) REGULATIONS 2007

(SI 2007/2258)

Made ....*27th July 2007*
Laid before Parliament ....*31st July 2007*
Coming into force ....*1st September 2007*

The Secretary of State makes the following Regulations in exercise of the powers conferred by sections 197(2) to (6), 200(4) and (5), 203(2) and 355(1) of the Gambling Act 2005.

6.1857 1 Commencement, citation and application

(1) These Regulations may be cited as the Gambling Act 2005 (Premises Licences) (Review) Regulations 2007 and shall come into force on 1st September 2007.

(2) Subject to paragraphs (3) and (4), these Regulations apply to applications to, and reviews held or to be held by, licensing authorities in England and Wales and Scotland.

(3) The following provisions apply only in relation to applications made to licensing authorities in England and Wales—

(a) regulations 4 to 7,

(b) regulation 12, in so far as it has effect in relation to a notice given under regulation 4, and

(c) regulation 14, in so far as it has effect in relation to the form of a notice given under regulation 4 or published under regulation 5.

(4) The following provisions apply only in relation to notices given or published under section 200(3) of the Act (notice of intention to hold a review) by licensing authorities in England and Wales—

(a) regulations 8 to 11,

(b) regulation 12, in so far as it has effect in relation to a notice given under section 200(3) of the Act, and

(c) regulation 14, in so far as it has effect in relation to the form of a notice given or published under section 200(3) of the Act.

6.1858 2 Interpretation

In these Regulations—

"the Act" means the Gambling Act 2005;

"application" means an application under section 197 of the Act for a review;

"review" means a review of a premises licence under section 201 of the Act; and

"working day" means a day which is not a Saturday or a Sunday, Christmas Day, Good Friday or a day which is a bank holiday in England and Wales under the Banking and Financial Dealings Act 1971.

6.1859 3 Form and content of applications for a review

Subject to regulation 14, an application must be in the form, and contain the information, specified in Schedule 1.

6.1860 4 Giving of notice of an application

(1) A person making an application must give notice of the application to—

(a) the person who holds the premises licence to which the application relates, and

(b) each of the authorities which in accordance with section 157 of the Act are the responsible authorities in relation to the premises to which the application relates.

(2) Where the application is made by a responsible authority, the reference in paragraph (1)(b) to each of the responsible authorities in relation to the premises does not include a reference to the authority making the application.

(3) Subject to regulation 14, a notice under paragraph (1) must be in the form specified in Schedule 2, and must in particular specify the period of 28 days starting on the relevant date as the period during which representations about the application may be made to the licensing authority by—

(a) the person who holds the premises licence to which the application relates,

(b) a responsible authority in relation to the premises, or

(c) a person who is an interested party in relation to the premises.

(4) A notice under paragraph (1) must be given within the period of 7 days starting on the date on which the application is made.

(5) In this regulation and regulation 5, "the relevant date" in relation to an application means the day immediately following the last day of the period referred to in paragraph (4).

6.1861 5 Publication of notice of an application by the licensing authority

(1) Where an application is made to a licensing authority, that authority must publish notice of the application—

(a) either—

(i) in a local newspaper or, if there is none, a local newsletter, circular or similar document, circulating within the licensing authority's area; or

(ii) on the licensing authority's internet website; and

(b) by displaying the notice at a place—

(i) which is as near as reasonably practicable to the premises to which the application relates, and

(ii) where it can conveniently be read by members of the public.

(2) Where a licensing authority have more than one website, paragraph (1)(a)(ii) requires the licensing authority to publish notice of the application on the website which is wholly or mainly used by them to publicise matters relating to the licensing of gambling.

(3) The notice referred to in paragraph (1)(a)(i) must be published on at least one occasion during the period of ten working days starting on the first working day after the day on which the application is made to the authority.

(4) The notice referred to in paragraph (1)(a)(ii) or (b) must be displayed or, as the case may be, published for a period of no less than 28 consecutive days starting on a date which is no later than the relevant date.

(5) Subject to regulation 14, any notice under paragraph (1) must be in the form specified in Schedule 3, and must in particular specify the period of 28 days starting on the relevant date as the period during which representations about the application may be made to the licensing authority by—

(a) the person who holds the premises licence to which the application relates,

(b) a responsible authority in relation to the premises, or

(c) a person who is an interested party in relation to the premises.

6.1862 6 Failure to give proper notice of an application

(1) This regulation applies where a person who is making an application fails to give proper notice of the application within the period provided for under regulation 4(4).

(2) For the purposes of paragraph (1), a person fails to give proper notice of an application if, in the case of any one or more of the notices which that person is required to give under regulation 4, the person fails to give a notice which complies with the requirements of these Regulations as to the form and manner in which it is to be given.

(3) Subject to paragraph (5), where the applicant fails to give proper notice of his application, as the case may be, to the person holding the premises licence or a responsible authority, the applicant must give notice to that person or the authority in a form and manner which complies with the requirements of these Regulations (other than as to the period within which the notice is to be given) as soon as practicable after the end of the period referred to in regulation 4(4)).

(4) In a case to which this regulation applies, the person holding the premises licence or, as the case may be, the responsible authority concerned may make any representations about the application within the period of 28 days starting on the day on which the notice referred to in paragraph (3) is received.

(5) Regulation 4(3) is to have effect in relation to the notice to be given under paragraph (3) as if it required the notice to specify the period referred to in paragraph (4) as the period during which representations about the application may be made by the person to whom the notice is given.

(6) The licensing authority may not grant the application until—

(a) notice has been given by the applicant in accordance with paragraph (3); and

(b) the period referred to in paragraph (4) has elapsed.

(7) Subject to paragraph (6), the licensing authority may disregard any irregularity in relation to the giving of notice under regulation 4.

6.1863 7 Failure properly to publish notice of an application

(1) This regulation applies where a licensing authority to whom an application is made fail to publish a proper notice of the application during or for the period provided for under (as the case may be) paragraph (3) or (4) of regulation 5.

(2) For the purposes of paragraph (1), a licensing authority fail to publish a proper notice of an application if—

(a) they fail to publish a notice which they are required to publish under sub-paragraph (a) or (b) of regulation 5(1), or

(b) the published notice does not comply with the requirements of these Regulations as to the form and manner in which it is to be published.

(3) Subject to paragraph (6), the licensing authority must publish notice of the application in a form and manner which complies with the requirements of these Regulations (other than as to the beginning of the period when publication is to be made) as soon as practicable after the end of the period referred to in (as the case may be) paragraph (3) or (4) of regulation 5.

(4) In a case to which this regulation applies an interested party may make any representations about the application within the period of 28 days starting on the day on which the notice referred to in paragraph (3) is published.

(5) Where the notice is published in one of the ways referred to in regulation 5(1)(a)(ii) or 5(1)(b), the period referred to in paragraph (4) above is to start on the date on which the notice is first published.

(6) Regulation 5(5) is to have effect in relation to the notice referred to in paragraph (3) as if it required the notice to specify the period referred to in that paragraph as the period during which representations about the application may be made by an interested party.

(7) The licensing authority may not grant the application until—

(a) notice has been published in accordance with paragraph (3); and

(b) the period referred to in paragraph (4) has elapsed.

(8) Subject to paragraph (7), the licensing authority may disregard any irregularity in relation to the publication of a notice under sub-paragraph (a) or (b) of paragraph (1) of regulation 5.

6.1864 8 Giving and publication of notice of intention to conduct a review

(1) Subject to regulation 14, a notice given under section 200(3)(a) of the Act (notice of intention to hold a review) must be in the form specified in Schedule 4.

(2) A notice under section 200(3)(a) of the Act must in particular specify the period of 28 days starting on the day on which the notice is given to the holder of the premises licence as the period during which representations about the application may be made to the licensing authority by—

(a) the person who holds the premises licence to which the review relates,

(b) each of the authorities which in accordance with section 157 of the Act are the responsible authorities in relation to the premises, or

(c) a person who is an interested party in relation to the premises.

(3) . . . [1]

(4) The following provisions of this regulation apply to a notice published by a licensing authority under section 200(3)(b) of the Act indicating that they intend to hold a review.

(5) Subject to regulation 14, the notice must be in the form specified in Schedule 5.

(6) The notice must in particular specify the period of 28 days starting on the day on which the notice under section 200(3)(a) of the 2005 Act is given to the holder of the premises licence as the period during which representations about the application may be made to the licensing authority by—

(a) the person who holds the premises licence to which the notice relates,

(b) a responsible authority in relation to the premises, or

(c) a person who is an interested party in relation to the premises.

(7) The licensing authority must publish notice of their intention to hold a review—

(a) either—

(i) in a local newspaper or, if there is none, a local newsletter, circular or similar document, circulating within the licensing authority's area; or

(ii) on the licensing authority's internet website; and

(b) by displaying the notice at a place—

(i) which is as near as reasonably practicable to the premises to which the application relates, and

(ii) where it can conveniently be read by members of the public.

(8) Where a licensing authority have more than one website, paragraph (7)(a)(ii) requires the licensing authority to publish notice of their intention to hold a review on the website which is wholly or mainly used by them to publicise matters relating to the licensing of gambling.

(9) The notice referred to in paragraph (7)(a)(i) must be published on at least one occasion during the period of ten working days starting on the first working day after

the day on which the licensing authority give notice under section 200(3)(a) of the Act to the holder of the premises licence of their intention to hold a review.

(10) The notice referred to in paragraph (7)(a)(ii) or (7)(b) must be displayed or, as the case may be, published for a period of no less than 28 consecutive days starting on the day on which the licensing authority give notice under section 200(3)(a) of the Act to the holder of the premises licence of their intention to hold a review.

---

1 Para (3): revoked by SI 2007/3539, reg 2(1), (2)(a).

6.1865 9 Failure to give proper notice of intention to hold a review to the holder of the premises licence

(1) This regulation applies where a licensing authority give notice under section 200(3)(a) of the 2005 Act to the holder of the premises licence and the notice is not given in all respects in the form and manner required by these Regulations.

(2) The notice given by the licensing authority is of no effect and the licensing authority must give a further notice which complies with the requirements of these Regulations as to the form and manner in which a notice under section 200(3)(a) of the 2005 Act is to be given.

6.1866 10 . . .[1]

---

1 Revoked by SI 2007/3539, reg 2(1), (2)(b).

6.1867 11 Failure properly to publish notice of intention to hold a review

(1) This regulation applies where a licensing authority fail to publish a proper notice of their intention to hold a review during or for the period provided for under (as the case may be) paragraph (9) or (10) of regulation 8.

(2) For the purposes of paragraph (1), a licensing authority fail to publish a proper notice of their intention to hold a review if—

(a) they fail to publish a notice under section 200(3)(b) of the Act in the manner in which they are required to publish the notice under sub-paragraph (a) or (b) of regulation 8(7), or

(b) the published notice does not comply with the requirements of these Regulations as to the form and manner in which it is to be published.

(3) Subject to paragraph (6), the licensing authority must publish the notice in a form and manner which complies with the relevant requirements of these Regulations (other than as to the beginning of the period when publication is to be made) as soon as practicable after the end of the period referred to in (as the case may be) paragraph (9) or (10) of regulation 8.

(4) In a case to which this regulation applies an interested party may make any representations about the review within the period of 28 days starting on the day on which the notice referred to in paragraph (3) is published.

(5) Where the notice is published in one of the ways referred to in regulation 8(7)(a)(ii) or 8(7)(b), the period referred to in paragraph (4) above is to start on the date on which the notice is first published.

(6) Regulation 8(6) is to have effect in relation to the notice referred to in paragraph (3) as if it required the notice to specify the period referred to in that paragraph as the period during which representations about the application may be made by an interested party.

(7) The licensing authority may not hold the review until—

(a) notice has been published in accordance with paragraph (3); and

(b) the period referred to in paragraph (4) has elapsed.

(8) Subject to paragraph (7), the licensing authority may disregard any irregularity in relation to the publication of a notice under section 200(3)(b) of the 2005 Act.

6.1868 12 Manner of making and giving of applications and notices

(1) An application, a notice under regulation 4 or a notice under section 200(3)(a) of the Act must be made or given in writing.

(2) For the purposes of paragraph (1), an application or notice which is sent by facsimile transmission or electronic mail shall be treated as being made or given in writing if it meets the conditions in paragraph (3).

(3) The conditions are that—

(a) the text of the application or notice—

(i) is capable of being accessed by the recipient,

(ii) is legible in all material respects, and

(iii) is capable of being read and reproduced in written form and used for subsequent reference by the recipient; and

(b) the person to whom the application or notice is to be made or given has agreed in advance that an application or notice may be made or given by the particular electronic means used.

(4) Subject to paragraph (5), where an application or notice is sent by facsimile transmission or electronic mail, it is to be treated as having been made or given at the time the conditions specified in paragraph (3)(a) are satisfied.

(5) Where—

(a) a person making an application specifies a document in the application as being a document which accompanies the application, and

(b) the document has been sent in a form that does not meet the conditions in paragraph (3),

the application is not to be treated as having been made until any such document has been received by the licensing authority in hard copy.

(6) In paragraph (5), any reference to a document in hard copy is to a written document or a document in the form of a plan.

6.1869 13 Notice of the licensing authority's decision on a review

Subject to regulation 14, a notice under section 203(1) of the Act (notice of a licensing authority's decision on a review) must be in the form specified in Schedule 6.

6.1870 14 Matters not required to be included in an application or notice

(1) Where matters are included in square brackets in any form in Schedules 1 to 6, they are intended to indicate and explain the information to be specified in the application or notice to which the form relates, and are not required to be included in the application or notice.

(2) The first page of the form used for an application or notice may include any symbol or logo which is commonly used by the licensing authority to identify documents produced by it.

(3) In paragraph (2) "the licensing authority" means—

(a) in relation to an application or a notice of an application under regulation 4, the licensing authority to whom the application is made, and

(b) in relation to a notice given or published by a licensing authority, that authority.

6.1871

SCHEDULE 1
FORM AND CONTENT OF APPLICATIONS FOR A REVIEW OF A PREMISES LICENCE
Regulation 3

Application for a review of a premises licence under the Gambling Act 2005

PLEASE READ THE FOLLOWING INSTRUCTIONS FIRST

If you are completing this form by hand, please write legibly in block capitals using ink. Use additional sheets if necessary (marked with the number of the relevant question). You may wish to keep a copy of the completed form for your records.

Part 1 – Applicant Details

1. Name of Applicant:
[Where the applicant is an individual please give your first name(s) as well as your surname]

2. Applicant's address (home ☐ or business ☐ *[check or tick appropriate box]*)

Postcode:

3(a) Are you making the application as a responsible authority? Yes ☐ No ☐

3(b) If the answer to question 3(a) is yes, indicate the type of responsible authority:

4(a) If the answer to question 3(a) is no, please confirm by ticking or checking the box that you are applying as an interested party ☐

4(b) If you have ticked or checked the box in answer to question 4(a), please indicate on what basis you qualify as an interested party:

[Where there are further applicants, the information required by questions 1 to 4(b) should be included on additional sheets attached to this form, and those sheets should be clearly marked "Details of further applicants"]

Part 2 – Premises Details

5. Give the trading name used at the licensed premises to which the application for a review relates:

6. Give the address of the premises or, if not known, give a description of the premises and its location. Where the premises are a vessel, then (if known) give the place indicated in the premises licence as the place in the licensing authority's area where the vessel is wholly or partly situated. If possible, any address should include a postcode:

Postcode:

7. Type of premises:

Casino ☐ Bingo Hall ☐ Adult Gaming Centre ☐ *(arcade restricted to those who are 18 or over)*

Betting (track) ☐ Betting (other) ☐ Family entertainment centre ☐ *(arcade which admits both over and under 18s)*

8. Premises licence (if known):

9. Give the name of the person(s) or organisation(s) in whose name the licence is held.

[Where an individual is the licence holder please give their first name(s) as well as their surname.]

Part 3 – Details of grounds on which a review is being sought

10(a) Please give details of the grounds on which a review is being sought.

10(b) Indicate any specific actions you consider the licensing authority should take following the review, including the reasons why you consider those actions are appropriate:

Part 4 – Supporting Documents

11. List any supporting documents which you are submitting with the application:

Part 5 – Declarations and Checklist

I/ We confirm that, to the best of my/ our knowledge, the information contained in this application is true. I/ We understand that it is an offence under section 342 of the Gambling Act 2005 to give information which is false or misleading in, or in relation to, this application. ☐

I/We understand that it is now necessary to give notice to the licence holder and the responsible authorities in relation to the premises ☐

Part 6 – Signatures

12. Signature of applicant or applicant's solicitor or other duly authorised agent. If signing on behalf of the applicant, please state in what capacity:

Signature:

Print Name:

Date: *(dd/mm/yyyy)*

Capacity:

[Where there is more than one applicant, please use an additional sheet clearly marked "Signature(s) of further applicant(s)". The sheet should include, for each additional applicant, all the information requested in paragraph 12.]

[Where the application is to be submitted in an electronic form, the signature should be generated electronically and should be a copy of the person's written signature.]

Part 7 – Contact Details

13(a) Please give the name of a person who can be contacted about the application:

13(b) Please give one or more telephone numbers at which the person identified in question 13(a) can be contacted:

14. Postal address for correspondence associated with this application:

Postcode:

15. If you are happy for correspondence in relation to the application to be sent via e-mail, please give the e-mail address to which you would like correspondence to be sent:

6.1872

SCHEDULE 2
FORM OF THE NOTICE OF APPLICATION TO BE GIVEN TO THE HOLDER OF THE PREMISES LICENCE AND THE RESPONSIBLE AUTHORITIES
Regulation 4(3)

Form of the notice of application to be given to the holder of the premises licence and the responsible authorities

NOTICE OF APPLICATION FOR A REVIEW OF A PREMISES LICENCE

This notice is given in accordance with regulations made under section 197 of the Gambling Act 2005

Notice is hereby given that:

....

[*Give the full name of the applicant(s) as set out in Part 1 of the application for a review of the premises licence*]

has made an application under section 197 of the Gambling Act 2005 for a review of the premises licence which is in force at the following premises:

....

....

....

....

....

....

....

[*Give the trading name used at the premises, and the address of the premises (or, if not known, give a description of the premises and their location).*]

The applicant is:

a responsible authority ☐ an interested party ☐ [*check or tick the appropriate box*]

The following type of premises licence has effect in respect of the premises:

....

[*Indicate the type of premises licence which applies to the premises, eg bingo premises licence, adult gaming centre premises licence etc.*]

The application for a review of the premises licence has been made to the following licensing authority:

....

....

....

....Postcode...

Website:..

[*Insert name of the licensing authority and the address of its principal office, followed by the address of its website*]

Information about the application is available from the licensing authority, including the arrangements for viewing the details of the application.

The following person connected with the applicant is able to give further information about the application:

....

[*This entry is optional and is to be included if the applicant wishes to provide the name, telephone number and (if available) e-mail address of a person connected with the applicant who is able to answer questions and provide further information about the application.*]

The grounds on which a review is being sought are:

....

....

....

....

....

Representations about the application may be made in writing to the licensing authority by the licence holder, a responsible authority or an interested party during

the period of 28 consecutive days beginning on.. (which is 7 days after the date on which the application for a review was made to the licensing authority). The last day for making representations is:

....

Following a review under section 201 of the Gambling Act 2005 a licensing authority may decide to take any of the following kinds of action:

- **revoke the licence**
- **suspend the licence for a specified period not exceeding 3 months**
- **add, remove or amend a condition attached to the licence**

6.1873

SCHEDULE 3
FORM OF THE NOTICE OF APPLICATION TO BE PUBLISHED BY A LICENSING AUTHORITY
Regulation 5(5)

NOTICE OF APPLICATION FOR A REVIEW OF A PREMISES LICENCE UNDER THE GAMBLING ACT 2005

An application has been made under section 197 of the Gambling Act 2005 for a review of the premises licence which is in force in respect of the following premises:

....

....

....

[*Give the trading name used at the premises, and the address of the premises (or, if not known, give a description of the premises and their location).*]

The following type of premises licence applies to the premises:..............................

A review is being sought on the following grounds:

....

....

....

The application has been made on:..
[*Insert the date on which the application has been made*]

The licence holder or a responsible authority may make representations in writing about the application, as may any of the following persons:

- A person who lives sufficiently close to the premises to be likely to be affected by the authorised activities
- A person who has business interests that might be affected by the authorised activities
- A person who represents someone in any of the above two categories

Any representations are to be made to the following licensing authority:

....

[*Insert the name of licensing authority*]

and may be made during the period of 28 consecutive days beginning 7 days after the date on which the application was made. That period ends on :

....

[*Insert last day on which representations may be made in relation to the application.*]

Information about the application is available from the licensing authority, including the arrangements for viewing the details of the application.

It is an offence under section 342 of the Gambling Act 2005 if a person, without reasonable excuse, gives to a licensing authority for a purpose connected with that Act information which is false or misleading.

6.1874

SCHEDULE 4
FORM OF THE NOTICE OF INTENTION TO HOLD A REVIEW TO BE GIVEN TO HOLDER OF THE PREMISES LICENCE . . . [1]
Regulation 8(1)

NOTICE OF INTENTION TO HOLD A REVIEW OF A PREMISES LICENCE

This notice is given in accordance with regulations made under section 200 of the Gambling Act 2005

Notice is hereby given that the following licensing authority:

....

whose address is:

....

....

....

....Postcode.................................

Website:...
[*Insert the address of the authority's principal office, followed by the address of its website*]

intends to hold a review under section 201 of the Gambling Act 2005 of the premises licence which is in force at the following premises:

....

....

....

....

....

....
[*Give the trading name used at the premises, and the address of the premises (or, if not known, give a description of the premises and their location).*]

The following type of premises licence has effect in respect of the premises:

....
[*Indicate the type of premises licence which applies to the premises, eg bingo premises licence, adult gaming centre premises licence etc.*]

6: Gambling Act 2005: SIs

The licensing authority intends to hold the review for the following reasons:

....

....

....

....

....

....

....

The following person connected with the licensing authority is able to give further information about the review:

....

Representations about the proposed review may be made in writing to the licensing authority by the licence holder, a responsible authority or an interested party during the period of 28 consecutive days beginning on the date on which the notice of the authority's intention to hold the review was given to the licence holder. The last day of the period for making representations is:

....

Following a review under section 201 of the Gambling Act 2005 a licensing authority may decide to take any of the following kinds of action:

- **revoke the licence**
- **suspend the licence for a specified period not exceeding 3 months**
- **add, remove or amend a condition attached to the licence**

---

1 Schedule heading: words omitted revoked by SI 2007/3539, reg 2(1), (2)(c).

6.1875

SCHEDULE 5
FORM OF THE NOTICE OF INTENTION TO HOLD A REVIEW TO BE PUBLISHED BY A LICENSING AUTHORITY
Regulation 8(5)

NOTICE OF INTENTION TO HOLD A REVIEW OF A PREMISES LICENCE UNDER THE GAMBLING ACT 2005

Notice is hereby given that the following licensing authority:

....

[*Give the name of the licensing authority*]

intends to hold a review under section 201 of the Gambling Act 2005 of the premises licence which is in force at the following premises:

....

....

....

[*Give the trading name used at the premises, and the address of the premises (or, if not known, give a description of the premises and their location).*]

The following type of premises licence applies to the premises:

....

The licensing authority intends to hold the review for the following reasons:

....

....

....

The licence holder or a responsible authority may make representations in writing to the licensing authority about the review, as may any of the following persons:

- A person who lives sufficiently close to the premises to be likely to be affected by the authorised activities
- A person who has business interests that might be affected by the authorised activities
- A person who represents someone in any of the above two categories

Representations may be made during the period of 28 consecutive days beginning on the date on which notice of the intention to hold a review was given to the licence holder. That period ends on:

....

[*Insert last day on which representations may be made in relation to the application.*]

Further information about the review is available from the licensing authority.

It is an offence under section 342 of the Gambling Act 2005 if a person, without reasonable excuse, gives to a licensing authority for a purpose connected with that Act information which is false or misleading.

6: Gambling Act 2005: SIs

6.1876

SCHEDULE 6
FORM OF THE NOTICE OF THE LICENSING AUTHORITY'S DECISION ON A REVIEW
Regulation 13

NOTICE OF THE DECISION ON A REVIEW OF A PREMISES LICENCE

This notice is given in accordance with regulations under section 203(2) of the Gambling Act 2005

[*Insert here the name and address of the issuing licensing authority*]

The licensing authority has carried out a review of the premises licence which is in force in respect of the following premises:

....

....

....

....

....

[*Give the trading name used at the premises, and the address of the premises (or, if not known, give a description of the premises and their location).*]

The licensing authority has decided to take the following action as a result of the review:

....

....

....

[*Where the licensing authority proposes to take no action following the review, the authority should indicate that here.*]

The reasons for the licensing authority's decision are as follows:

....

....

....

....

....

....

....

Any of the following may appeal against a decision taken by the licensing authority as a result of a review:

- The licensee
- A person who made representations on the review
- The person (if any) who applied for the review, and
- The Gambling Commission

An appeal must be brought:

- In England and Wales, in the magistrates' court for the local justice area in which the premises are wholly or partly situated; or
- In Scotland, to the sheriff within whose sheriffdom the premises are wholly or partly situated.

An appeal must be brought within 21 days of the date on which the appellant received notice of the licensing authority's decision

GAMING MACHINE (SINGLE APPARATUS) REGULATIONS 2007

(SI 2007/2289)

Made . . . . *27th July 2007*
Laid before Parliament . . . . *2nd August 2007*
Coming into force . . . . *1st September 2007*

The Secretary of State, in exercise of the powers conferred by section 235(5) of the Gambling Act 2005, makes the following Regulations.

6.1877 1 Citation and commencement

These Regulations shall be cited as the Gaming Machine (Single Apparatus) Regulations 2007 and come into force on 1st September 2007.

6.1878 2 Single apparatus

For the purposes of the Gambling Act 2005, where a single piece of apparatus is—

(a) a gaming machine, and

(b) made available for use to more than one person at a time,

it is to be treated as the number of gaming machines equal to the number of people able to use it at that time.

GAMING MACHINE (CIRCUMSTANCES OF USE) REGULATIONS 2007

(SI 2007/2319)

Made . . . . *6th August 2007*
Laid before Parliament . . . . *7th August 2007*
Coming into force in accordance with regulation 1

The Secretary of State makes the following Regulations in exercise of the powers conferred by sections 240 and 355(1) of the Gambling Act 2005.

6.1879 1 Citation and commencement

(1) These Regulations may be cited as the Gaming Machine (Circumstances of Use) Regulations 2007.

(2) Subject to paragraphs (3) and (4) these Regulations come into force on 1st September 2007.

(3) Paragraphs (1)(a) and (5)(b) of regulation 3 come into force on 1st November 2007.

(4) Regulations 10 and 11 come into force on 1st March 2008.

6.1880 2 Interpretation

(1) In these Regulations—

"the Act" means the Gambling Act 2005;

"autoplay facility" has the meaning given by regulation 10(6);

"category", in relation to a gaming machine, means the category of machine as defined in regulations made under section 236 of the Act, and "Category A", or B, C or D means that Category (or in the case of Category B, sub-category) as defined in such regulations;

"charge for use" means the amount a person pays for using a gaming machine once;

"committed amount" has the meaning given by regulation 9(4);

"the deposited sum" has the meaning given by regulation 9(9); and

"prize value" means the amount or value of any prize which can be won as a result of use of a gaming machine once.

(2) For the purposes of these Regulations a person is to be treated as using a gaming machine once, even where he uses the machine to gamble more than once, if the payment for each gamble is made before he is able to know the result of any of them.

(3) Paragraph (2) does not apply in relation to a gaming machine in respect of which—

(a) the charge for use may only be paid by means of a single coin or token;

(b) the coin or token must be inserted into the machine to pay the charge for use; and

(c) whether or not a person using the machine wins a prize is determined (wholly or in part) by—

(i) the position in which the coin or token comes to rest after it has been inserted into the machine, together with the position of other coins or tokens which have previously been inserted into the machine to pay a charge for use, or

(ii) if the insertion of a single coin to pay the charge for use enables the person using the machine to release one or more tokens within the machine, the position in which such tokens come to rest after being released, together with the position of other tokens which have previously been so released.

(4) In paragraph (3) "token" means an object of money's worth.

(5) Subject to paragraph (6), in these Regulations "money prize" means a prize—

(a) in the form of cash or a cheque (or partly in the form of cash and partly in the form of a cheque); or

(b) in the form of a document or object which—

(i) enables the person entitled to it to redeem its value, on the premises where the machine is made available for use, in the form of cash or a cheque (or partly in the form of cash and partly in the form of a cheque), and

(ii) may, but need not, also enable that person to use it to pay for goods or services otherwise available on the premises where the machine is made available for use, including facilities for gambling;

and "non-money prize" is any prize which is not a money prize.

(6) A document or object is not a money prize if it is something which ordinarily is capable of being used for a purpose other than one referred to in paragraph (5)(b).

6.1881 3 Display of information

(1) A gaming machine shall display the following information—

(a) the category, or sub-category, of the machine;

(b) the name and telephone number of a person from whom assistance may be obtained by people who are or may be affected by problems related to gambling; and

(c) unless it is a Category D gaming machine, information constituting a warning that the machine is not to be used by a child or young person.

(2) Subject to paragraphs (3) and (4), a gaming machine shall display information—

(a) about the proportion of amounts paid to use the machine that is returned by way of prizes; or

(b) about the odds of winning prizes from use of the machine.

(3) A gaming machine is to be treated as having complied with the requirement in paragraph (2) if—

(a) a notice is displayed on the machine at all times when it is made available for use indicating where the information referred to in paragraph (2) can be found, and

(b) that information is held by or in relation to the machine in a way that makes it readily accessible by a person using the machine.

(4) Paragraph (2) does not apply to a Category D gaming machine in relation to which there is no mechanism for recording—

(a) the aggregate of amounts paid to use the machine, and

(b) the aggregate of amounts won as prizes,

in which case the machine shall display information stating that the machine provides facilities for gambling.

(5) Subject to paragraph (3), the information required by paragraphs (1), (2) and (4)—

(a) shall be displayed on the machine at all times when the machine is made available for use;

(b) in the case of paragraph (1)(a), shall be displayed on the machine in a manner which makes it readily visible to a person inspecting the machine while it is being made available for use; and

(c) in all other cases shall be displayed on the machine in a manner which makes it readily visible to a person using the machine.

(6) Information displayed in accordance with this regulation may take the form of any combination of letters, numbers or symbols.

6.1882 4 Methods of payment

(1) A gaming machine shall not be made available for use if it is designed or adapted to permit money to be paid by means of a credit card or debit card.

(2) A person making a gaming machine available for use shall not participate in, arrange, permit or knowingly facilitate payment of a charge for use by means of a credit card.

(3) In this regulation—

"credit card" means a credit-token within the meaning of section 14 of the Consumer Credit Act 1974; and "debit card" means a card enabling payment to be debited against a person's banking account, and which is not a credit card.

6.1883 5 Minimum payment amount

A gaming machine shall not be made available for use if a person can use the machine to gamble once by paying an amount which is not a whole number of pence.

3.1884 6 Nature of prizes

(1) A Category A, B or C gaming machine shall not provide an opportunity to win a non-money prize from use of the machine.

(2) A Category D gaming machine shall not provide an opportunity to win a proscribed non-money prize from use of the machine.

(3) In this regulation "proscribed non-money prize" means a good or service which it is illegal to supply or sell to a child or young person under the laws of the place where the gaming machine is made available for use.

6.1885 7 Payment limits

(1) Subject to regulation 9, where a gaming machine is made available for use, a person must not be able, by means of a single action, to make a payment in respect of the use of the machine which exceeds, in any case to which paragraphs (2) to (7) apply, the amount specified in the relevant paragraph.

(2) In relation to—

(a) a Category A machine where the payment is of money or money's worth, and

(b) a Category B or C machine, where the payment is of money,

the amount is £20.

(3) In relation to a Category B or C machine where—

(a) the payment is of money's worth, and

(b) either—

(i) the machine is manufactured on or after 1st September 2007, or

(ii) it is a non-compliant machine,

the amount is £20.

(4) In relation to a Category B1, B2 or B3 machine where—

(a) the payment is of money's worth,

(b) the payment satisfies—

(i) the supervision condition in paragraph (8),

(ii) the collection condition in paragraph (9), or

(iii) partly satisfies the supervision condition, with the payment of the remaining amount satisfying the collection condition,

(c) the machine is manufactured before 1st September 2007, and

(d) immediately before that date the machine is designed or adapted for payments of money's worth to be made in relation to its use,

the amount is £100.

(5) In relation to a Category B1, B2 or B3 machine which meets the conditions in sub-paragraphs (a) to (c) of paragraph (4), but in respect of which the condition in sub-paragraph (b) is not met, the amount is £20.

(6) In relation to a Category B3A, B4 or C machine where—

(a) the payment is of money's worth, and

(b) the machine is manufactured before 1st September 2007,

the amount is £20.

(7) In relation to a Category D machine, where the payment is of money or money's worth, the amount is £2.

(8) The supervision condition is that a payment of money's worth in respect of the use of a Category B1, B2 or B3 gaming machine must—

(a) be made by means of a document or object which is purchased or obtained from a person acting in the course of a business carried on by an authorised person; or

(b) be processed by a person acting in the course of such a business.

(9) The collection condition is that a payment of money's worth in respect of the use of a Category B1, B2 or B3 gaming machine must be made by means of—

(a) a document or object collected as a prize from use of a gaming machine, or

(b) a document or object delivered by a gaming machine as a means of returning an amount held to the credit of the person using the machine.

(10) In this regulation—

"authorised person" means a person who holds an operating licence which authorises making gaming machines available for use;

"non-compliant machine" means a Category B gaming machine manufactured before 1st September 2007 which does not comply with the condition in paragraph (4)(d); and

"payment of money's worth" includes circumstances where—

(a) a person pays money in relation to use of a gaming machine, and

(b) that payment is made otherwise than by inserting money into the machine.

(11) Where a person makes a payment in respect of a gaming machine, only those amounts of the payment which are—

(a) used to pay a charge for use, or

(b) held to the credit of a person using the machine,

are to be counted for the purposes of paragraphs (1) to (7).

(12) Nothing in this regulation shall prevent a person, by means of a series of actions, from making one or more payments which exceed the limits specified in paragraphs (2) to (7) provided that in each case the amount paid by means of a single action complies with the relevant limit.

6.1886 8 Payment limits: transitional provisions

(1) The limits imposed by regulation 7 on payments in respect of the use of—

(a) a Category B1, B2 or B3 gaming machine which meets the conditions in sub-paragraphs (a) to (d) of paragraph (4), and

(b) a Category B3A, B4 or C gaming machine which meets the conditions in sub-paragraphs (a) and (b) of paragraph (6),

do not apply until 1st September 2008.

(2) The limit imposed by regulation 7 on payments made in respect of the use of a Category B or C gaming machine in the circumstances specified in paragraphs (3)(a) and (b) of that regulation does not apply in the case of a gaming machine manufactured before 1st March 2008, until 1st September 2008.

6.1887 9 Committed payment limits

(1) This regulation is subject to regulation 11.

(2) Where a Category A, B or C gaming machine is made available for use, a person must not be able, by means of a single action, to make a committed payment in respect of the use of the machine which exceeds—

(a) in relation to a Category A, B1, B2, B3 or B3A machine, £10, or

(b) in relation to a Category B4 or C machine, £5.

(3) A committed payment is a payment of money or money's worth where—

(a) the whole amount is used to pay a charge for use in respect of a gaming machine,

(b) the whole amount is held by or in relation to a gaming machine as a committed amount, or

(c) part is used to pay a charge for use, with the remaining amount being held by or in relation to the machine as a committed amount.

(4) In these Regulations "committed amount", in relation to a gaming machine, means an amount of money or money's worth—

(a) held to the credit of a person using the machine for the purposes of paying one or more charges for use, and

(b) which, immediately after it is paid or (as the case may be) immediately after the action referred to in paragraph (7) is taken in relation to it, is not recoverable by a person using the machine.

(5) Where a part (but not the whole) of a payment is treated in one of the ways described in paragraph (3) the amount of that part of the payment must not exceed the limit specified in paragraph (2) in relation to the relevant category of machine.

(6) Paragraph (5) is without prejudice to any limit which may apply to the whole of the payment by virtue of regulation 7.

(7) Where a person using a gaming machine performs an action whose effect is to cause an amount held as part of the deposited sum to be—

(a) used to pay a charge for use in respect of the machine,

(b) held by or in relation to the machine as a committed amount, or

(c) partly used to pay a charge for use, with the remaining amount held by or in relation to the machine as a committed amount,

that action is to be treated for the purposes of this regulation as the making of a committed payment.

(8) Nothing in this regulation shall prevent a person, by means of a series of actions, from making one or more payments which exceed the limits specified in paragraph (2) provided that in each case the amount paid by means of a single action complies with the relevant limit.

(9) In these Regulations "the deposited sum", in relation to a gaming machine, means the amount of money or money's worth—

(a) which for the time being is held by or in relation to the machine to the credit of a person using the machine, and

(b) none of which is held as a committed amount.

(10) The limit in paragraph (2) does not apply, in the case of a Category A or B2 gaming machine which is designed or adapted to allow a person to pay a charge for use by using an amount of the deposited sum in relation to the machine, until 1st March 2008.

6.1888 10 Autoplay

(1) This regulation applies to a gaming machine, other than a casino jackpot gaming machine, which—

(a) is made available for use, and

(b) is designed or adapted to allow a charge for use to be paid by using an amount of the deposited sum in relation to the machine.

(2) Subject to the following provisions of this regulation, a charge for use in respect of such a gaming machine must not be payable by means of an autoplay facility.

(3) The prohibition in paragraph (2) does not apply to a gaming machine which is designed or adapted so that it meets the conditions in paragraphs (4) and (5).

(4) The first condition is that—

(a) a person using the machine is required to perform at least one action in relation to the machine to make an amount of the deposited sum capable of being used to pay a charge for use by means of an autoplay facility, and

(b) any such action is in addition to a separate action that the person is required to perform to cause the whole or part of that amount to be used to pay more than one charge for use by means of such a facility.

(5) The second condition is that each amount dealt with in accordance with paragraph (4)(a) does not exceed—

(a) in relation to a Category A, B1, B2, B3, or B3A machine, £10; and

(b) in relation to a Category B4 or C machine, £5.

(6) In these Regulations—

"autoplay facility" means any facility which enables a person using a gaming machine to pay more than one charge for use in respect of the machine without performing at least one separate action in respect of each charge for use; and

"casino jackpot gaming machine" means a gaming machine which—

(a) immediately before 1st September 2007 is—

(i) a machine to which Part 3 of the Gaming Act 1968 applies, and

(ii) designed or adapted to be used for gaming in accordance with section 31 of that Act on premises in respect of which a licence under that Act is in force, other than bingo club premises (as defined in section 20 of that Act); and

(b) on or after 1st September 2007 is not adapted, other than—

(i) to alter its maximum charge for use or prize value; or

(ii) to comply with the requirements of regulation 3.

(7) The prohibition in paragraph (2) does not apply, in the case of a gaming machine manufactured before 1st March 2008, until 1st September 2008.

6.1889 11 Special provision for Category A and B2 machines

(1) This regulation applies to a Category A or B2 gaming machine which is designed or adapted to allow a person to pay a charge for use by using an amount of the deposited sum in relation to the machine.

(2) The limit specified in regulation 9(2)(a) does not apply to the payment, in relation to such a machine, of a charge for use which exceeds £10; and, instead, any such payment is subject to the following provisions of this regulation.

(3) Subject to paragraph (5), where the machine is made available for use, the arrangements for the use of the machine must ensure that, for each permitted amount that a person wants to include in the amount he pays as a charge for use, he performs a separate action in relation to the machine to indicate that he wants to use that amount for that purpose.

(4) In this regulation, "permitted amount" is an amount not exceeding £10.

(5) Paragraph (3) does not apply where the conditions set out in paragraph (6), and either the condition set out in paragraph (7) or that in paragraph (8), are met.

(6) The conditions are that—

(a) a person has previously paid a charge for use of an amount which exceeds £10;

(b) the payment for that charge for use was made in accordance with paragraph (3) or paragraphs (5) to (8);

(c) a person has used the machine in relation to that charge for use; and

(d) before another person has paid to use the machine, the person referred to in sub-paragraph (a) pays a further charge for use in respect of the machine.

(7) Where the charge for use referred to in paragraph (6)(d) does not exceed the amount referred to in paragraph (6)(a), a person is required to take at least two separate actions in relation to the machine in order to pay the charge for use.

(8) Where the charge for use referred to in paragraph (6)(d) exceeds the amount referred to in paragraph (6)(a), a person is required to perform at least the required actions in relation to the machine in order to pay that charge for use.

(9) In paragraph (8), the required actions are—

(a) a separate action to indicate that he wants to include the original sum in the amount he pays for the charge for use,

(b) a further separate action for each permitted amount in addition to the original sum that he wants to include in that amount, and

(c) a further separate action to pay the total amount as the charge for use.

(10) In paragraph (9), "the original sum" means the amount referred to in paragraph (6)(a).

6.1890 12 Residues

(1) A gaming machine which is made available for use may not retain the deposited sum in relation to the machine (referred to below as retaining a "residue") unless the deposited sum—

(a) consists entirely of cash held by the machine,

(b) is an amount of less than £1, and

(c) cannot be recovered because—

(i) the machine cannot pay the correct denomination of coins equal to the amount to be recovered, and

(ii) the machine has no alternative means for paying the amount to the person seeking to recover it.

(2) Where a gaming machine, which is designed or adapted to retain a residue as permitted by paragraph (1), is made available for use—

(a) the machine shall display a warning of that fact, stating the maximum amount which the machine is designed or adapted to retain; and

(b) the amount of any such residue shall be made available for paying the whole or part of a further charge for use in relation to the machine and for no other purpose.

(3) Where a gaming machine is designed or adapted to hold an amount of money or money's worth as a committed amount, any such amount may only be used for paying the whole or part of a further charge for use in relation to the machine and for no other purpose.

6.1891 13 Delivery of prizes: general

(1) Where—

(a) a gaming machine is made available for use,

(b) a person wins a prize by using that machine ("the winner"), and

(c) the prize is not made available automatically for collection from the machine at the time of winning,

the arrangements with respect to prizes won using the machine must comply with the provisions of this regulation and regulation 14.

(2) If the prize won is a non-money prize—

(a) the machine must provide the winner with the means for collecting that prize;

(b) information about the type of prize won must be displayed on the machine or upon the premises where the machine is situated; and

(c) where the prize is not held by the machine, the prize must be available for collection by the winner, or a person claiming under him—

(i) at the premises where the machine is situated, and

(ii) at a time when gaming machines are available for use on those premises.

(3) If the prize won is a money prize—

(a) the machine must provide the winner with information about the amount of the prize he has won;
(b) the winner must have an opportunity to collect the whole amount of the prize; and
(c) where the prize is not held by the machine it must be available for collection by the winner, or a person claiming under him—
 (i) at the premises where the machine is situated, and
 (ii) at a time when gaming machines are available for use on those premises.

(4) If the prize won is a money prize, the machine must not operate in a way so that the prize, if it is not collected by the winner, is automatically—
(a) used to pay a charge for use in respect of the machine,
(b) held by or in relation to the machine as a committed amount, or
(c) partly used to pay a charge for use, with the remaining amount of the prize held by or in relation to the machine as a committed amount.

(5) Where a gaming machine is—
(a) manufactured before 1st September 2007, and
(b) not adapted on or after 1st September 2007, other than—
 (i) to alter its maximum charge for use or prize value; or
 (ii) to comply with the requirements of regulation 3,

paragraph (3)(b) is to be treated as having been complied with where the whole amount of the prize is added to the deposited sum in relation to the machine, even if the effect of doing so is that an amount of the prize will not be recoverable by virtue of regulation 12.

(6) The requirement imposed by paragraph (3)(b) does not apply in the case of—
(a) a gaming machine manufactured between 1st September 2007 and 29th February 2008, or
(b) a non-compliant machine,

until 1st September 2008.

(7) In—
(a) paragraph (1), a reference to a machine making a prize available for collection automatically is to a machine making available a prize for collection without the person who has won the prize being required to perform any action to make it available; and
(b) paragraph (6), a reference to a "non-compliant machine" means a gaming machine manufactured before 1st September 2007 which does not comply with the conditions in paragraph (5)(b).

6.1892 14 Delivery of money prizes

(1) Subject to paragraph (2) where—
(a) a money prize is won by using a gaming machine which is designed or adapted to enable a person to pay a charge for use by using an amount of the deposited sum, and
(b) the prize—
 (i) in relation to a Category A, B1, B2, B3 or B3A machine, exceeds £50,
 (ii) in relation to a Category B4 or C machine, exceeds £10, or
 (iii) in relation to a Category D machine, is a money prize of any amount,

the prize may not be added to the deposited sum in relation to the machine until the winner has first had an opportunity to collect the full amount of the prize.

(2) Where a money prize is won by using a gaming machine which is designed or adapted to allow a charge for use to be paid by means of an autoplay facility in accordance with regulation 10(3) to (5)—

(a) paragraph (1) does not apply; but
(b) the prize may not be made available to pay a charge for use in relation to that machine unless—
(i) the winner is required to perform at least one action in relation to the machine to make an amount of the prize capable of being used to pay a charge for use by means of an autoplay facility; and
(ii) any such action is in addition to a separate action that the person is required to perform to cause the whole or part of that prize to be used to pay more than one charge for use by means of such a facility.

(3) The requirement imposed by paragraph (1) does not apply in the case of a gaming machine manufactured before 1st March 2008, until 1st September 2008.

GAMING MACHINE (SUPPLY &C) REGULATIONS 2007

(SI 2007/2320)

Made ....*6th August 2007*
Laid before Parliament ....*7th August 2007*
Coming into force ....*1st September 2007*

The Secretary of State makes the following Regulations in exercise of the powers conferred by section 241 of the Gambling Act 2005.

6.1893 1 Citation and commencement

These Regulations may be cited as the Gaming Machine (Supply &c) Regulations 2007 and come into force on 1st September 2007.

6.1894 2 Methods of Payment

(1) A gaming machine shall not be supplied or installed if it is designed or adapted to permit money to be paid by means of a credit card or debit card.

(2) In paragraph (1)—
(a) "credit card" means a credit-token within the meaning of section 14 of the Consumer Credit Act 1974; and
(b) "debit card" means a card enabling payment to be debited against a person's banking account, and which is not a credit card.

SMALL SOCIETY LOTTERIES (REGISTRATION OF NON-COMMERCIAL SOCIETIES) REGULATIONS 2007

(SI 2007/2328)

Made ....*6th August 2007*
Laid before Parliament ....*8th August 2007*
Coming into force ....*1st September 2007*

The Secretary of State makes the following Regulations in exercise of the powers conferred by section 355(1) of, and paragraphs 42(2), 44(a), and 54(2) of Schedule 11 to, the Gambling Act 2005.

6.1895 1 Commencement, citation and application

(1) These Regulations may be cited as the Small Society Lotteries (Registration of Non-Commercial Societies) Regulations 2007 and shall come into force on 1st September 2007.

(2) Subject to paragraphs (2) and (3), these Regulations apply to England and Wales and Scotland.

(3) Regulation 3(1)(b) does not apply where the application is made to a local authority in Scotland.

(4) Regulation 5(a) does not apply where the local authority giving notice is in Scotland.

6.1896 2 Interpretation

(1) In these Regulations "the Act" means the Gambling Act 2005.

(2) A reference in these Regulations to a numbered paragraph is a reference to the paragraph of Schedule 11 to the Act so numbered, unless the contrary is indicated.

6.1897 3 Application for registration

(1) An application for registration under Part 5 of Schedule 11 to the Act must be—

(a) made in the form prescribed in the Schedule to these Regulations ("the Schedule"), and

(b) accompanied by a fee of £40.

(2) The first page of the form prescribed in the Schedule may include any symbol or logo which is commonly used by a local authority to identify documents produced by it.

(3) Where matters are included in square brackets and italics in the form prescribed in the Schedule, they are intended to indicate and explain the information to be specified in the application to which the form relates, and are not required to be included in the application.

6.1898 4 Registration by local authority

For the purposes of paragraph 44(a), when entering an applicant in the register under that paragraph, the local authority must include with the entry the date on which that entry is made.

6.1899 5 Annual fees

The annual fee payable to the registering local authority under paragraph 54(1)—

(a) is £20, and

(b) must be paid within the period of two months which ends immediately before each anniversary of the registration.

6.1900
SCHEDULE
Regulation 3(1)(a)

This form is prescribed by regulation 3(1)(a) of the Small Society Lotteries (Registration of Non-Commercial Societies) Regulations 2007

APPLICATION FORM FOR REGISTRATION OF NON-COMMERCIAL SOCIETY

If you are completing this form by hand, please write legibly in block capitals using ink.

To:	**This section is for official use only** - local authority logo or symbol
[insert name and address of relevant local authority – this is the local authority for the area in which the principal premises of the society are situated]	

SECTION A – Details of society applying for registration

1. Name of society..
....

2. Address (including postcode) of office or head office of society.......................................
....
....
....
....

3. Telephone number of society...

4. Please state the purpose(s) for which the society is established and conducted..................
....
....
....
....
....
....
....

5. If the society is a registered charity, please give the society's unique charity registration number...

6. Has the society held an operating licence under the Gambling Act 2005 in the period of five years ending with the date of this application? 'Yes' ☐ 'No' ☐

7. If the answer to question 6 is 'Yes', has the operating licence been revoked in the period of five years ending with the date of this application? 'Yes' ☐ 'No' ☐

8. If the answer to question 7 is 'Yes', please state the reasons for revocation and enclose a copy of the notice of revocation if one is available.

....

....

....

....

9. Has the society applied for and been refused an operating licence in the period of five years ending with the date of this application? 'Yes' ☐ 'No' ☐

SECTION B – General information about person applying on behalf of society

10. Name..

11. Capacity..

12. Address (including postcode)..

....

....

....

....

13. Daytime telephone number...

SECTION C – Contact details for correspondence associated with this application

14. Please tick one box as appropriate to indicate address for correspondence in relation to this application:

Address in section A ☐ Address in section B ☐ Address below ☐:

Address (including postcode)...

....

....

....

....

Telephone number..

Email address (if the applicant is happy for correspondence in relation to this application to be sent via e-mail)...

....

SECTION D – Declaration

15. Please complete the following declaration and checklist:

I *[full name]*..

a. make this application on behalf of the society referred to in Section A and have authority to act on behalf of that society.

6: Gambling Act 2005: SIs

b. enclose payment of the registration fee of £40.

c. **confirm that, to the best of my knowledge, the information contained in this application is true. I understand that it is an offence under section 342 of the Gambling Act 2005 to give information which is false or misleading in, or in relation to, this application.**

Signature..

Date...

Capacity...

Note to societies applying for registration:

The application will be refused if in the period of five years ending with the date of the application:
(a) an operating licence held by the society has been revoked under section 119(1) of the Gambling Act 2005, or
(b) an application for an operating licence made by the society has been refused.

The application may be refused if the local authority think that:
(a) the society is not a non-commercial society,
(b) a person who will or may be connected with the promotion of the lottery has been convicted of a relevant offence, or
(c) information provided in or with the application is false or misleading.

GAMBLING ACT 2005 (ADVERTISING OF FOREIGN GAMBLING) REGULATIONS 2007

(SI 2007/2329)

Made . . . . *3rd August 2007*
Laid before Parliament . . . . *9th August 2007*
Coming into force . . . . *1st September 2007*

The Secretary of State makes the following Regulations in exercise of the powers conferred by sections 331(4) and 355(1) of the Gambling Act 2005.

6.1901 1 Citation, commencement and interpretation

(1) These Regulations may be cited as the Gambling Act 2005 (Advertising of Foreign Gambling) Regulations 2007 and shall come into force on 1st September 2007.

(2) In these Regulations "the Act" means the Gambling Act 2005.

6.1902 2 Exemption from prohibition on the advertising of foreign gambling

[(1) This regulation specifies for the purposes of subsection (4) of section 331 of the Act (prohibition on the advertising of gambling taking place or originating from a non-EEA State the places which are to be treated for the purposes of subsection (2) of that section as if they were an EEA State, but only in so far as that subsection applies to remote gambling.

(2) The places referred to in paragraph (1) are—

(a) the Island of Alderney,

(b) Tasmania and

(c) Antigua and Barbuda.][1]

[1] Substituted by SI 2008/2829, reg 2. Date in force: 20 November 2008: see SI 2008/2829, reg 1(1)

6.1903

3 (1) This regulation specifies for the purposes of subsection (4) of section 331 of the Act a place which is to be treated for the purposes of subsection (2) of that section as if it were an EEA State, but only in so far as that subsection applies to—

(a) remote gambling, and

(b) non-remote gambling which takes place in a casino

(2) The place referred to in paragraph (1) is the Isle of Man.

GAMBLING (LOTTERY MACHINE INTERVAL) ORDER 2007

(SI 2007/2495)

Made . . . . *28th August 2007*
Coming into force in accordance with article 1(b)

The Secretary of State makes the following Order in exercise of the powers conferred by section 235(2)(d)(ii) of the Gambling Act 2005.

In accordance with section 355(6) of that Act a draft of this instrument was laid before

Parliament and approved by a resolution of each House of Parliament.

6.1904 1 Commencement and citation

This Order—

(a) may be cited as the Gambling (Lottery Machine Interval) Order 2007; and

(b) comes into force on the day after the day on which it is made, or 1st September 2007, whichever is the later.

6.1905 2 Lottery machine interval

For the purposes of section 235(2)(d)(ii) of the Gambling Act 2005, where a machine dispenses lottery tickets or otherwise enables a person to enter a lottery, there must be an interval of not less than one hour between each entry to a lottery and any announcement by the machine of the results of that lottery.

GAMBLING ACT 2005 (TEMPORARY USE NOTICES) REGULATIONS 2007

(SI 2007/3157)

Made ....*1st November 2007*
Laid before Parliament ....*7th November 2007*
Coming into force ....*1st December 2007*

The Secretary of State makes the following Regulations in exercise of the powers conferred by sections 212, 215(2), 216, 219(3)(b) and (8), 224(4), 227(2), (3) and (6) and 355(1) of the Gambling Act 2005.

6.1906 1 Citation, commencement, application and interpretation

(1) These Regulations may be cited as the Gambling Act 2005 (Temporary Use Notices) Regulations 2007 and shall come into force on 1st December 2007.

(2) Subject to paragraph (3), these Regulations apply to England and Wales and Scotland.

(3) Regulation 7(1) applies only to temporary use notices given in respect of premises in England and Wales.

(4) In these Regulations "the Act" means the Gambling Act 2005.

6.1907 2 Activities which may be specified in a temporary use notice

(1) This regulation specifies for the purposes of section 215(2)(a) of the Act the activities which may be specified in a temporary use notice under Part 9 of the Act.

(2) The activities are providing facilities for any form of equal chance gaming where those participating in the gaming are taking part in a competition which is intended to produce a single, overall winner.

(3) In paragraph (2) the reference to providing facilities for equal chance gaming does not include providing such facilities in circumstances where any person participating in the gaming does so by means of a gaming machine.

6.1908 3 Form and content of a temporary use notice

(1) Subject to paragraph (2), a temporary use notice under Part 9 of the Act must be in the form, and contain the information, specified in Part 1 of Schedule 1.

(2) A temporary use notice given in respect of a vessel must be in the form, and contain the information, specified in Part 2 of Schedule 1.

(3) This regulation is subject to regulation 5.

6.1909 4 Form and content of a counter-notice

Subject to regulation 5, a counter-notice under Part 9 of the Act must be in the form, and contain the information, specified in Schedule 2.

6.1910 5 Matters not required to be included in a notice

(1) Where matters are included in square brackets in any form in Schedules 1 and 2, they are intended to indicate and explain the information to be specified in the notice to which the form relates, and are not required to be included in the notice.

(2) The first page of the form used for a temporary use notice or a counter-notice under Part 9 of the Act may include any symbol or logo which is commonly used by the licensing authority to identify documents produced by them.

(3) In paragraph (2) "the licensing authority" means—

(a) in relation to a temporary use notice, the licensing authority to whom the notice is given, and

(b) in relation to a counter-notice, the licensing authority by whom the notice is given.

6.1911 6 Endorsement of temporary use notices

(1) This regulation prescribes for the purposes of each of subsections (2)(a) and (3)(a) of section 227 of the Act the manner in which the copy of a temporary use notice submitted under section 219(3)(a) of the Act is endorsed.

(2) The copy of the notice is endorsed by the licensing authority to whom it is given completing the section of the notice headed "Endorsement of notice by licensing authority".

6.1912 7 Fees in connection with temporary use notices

(1) The fee payable under section 219(3)(b) of the Act on giving a temporary use notice shall be of such amount not exceeding £500 as may be determined by the licensing authority to whom the notice is given.

(2) The fee payable under section 227(6)(a) of the Act for the replacement of an endorsed copy of a temporary use notice—

(a) where the licensing authority responsible for issuing the copy of the notice is in England or Wales, shall be of such amount not exceeding £25 as the licensing authority may determine; or

(b) where the licensing authority responsible for issuing the copy of the notice is in Scotland, shall be £25.

6.1913

SCHEDULE 1
FORM AND CONTENT OF A TEMPORARY USE NOTICE

SCHEDULE 1

Regulation 3

Form and content of a temporary use notice

PART 1

Form and content of temporary use notice applying to premises other than a vessel

[*SPACE FOR LICENSING AUTHORITY LOGO ETC.*]

Gambling Act 2005 - Temporary Use Notice
(for premises other than vessels)

Notice is hereby given under Part 9 of the Gambling Act 2005 that:
[*Insert the name and address of the person or organisation giving the notice*]

....

....

....

intends to use the following premises:
[*Identify the premises giving an address and postcode*]

....

....

....

....

for carrying on the following activities:
[*Indicate the type of gaming which will take place under the notice*]

....

....

....

....

during the following period:

Start date	End date

Additional information

1. Please describe the nature of the premises to which the notice relates:
[*Where the activities to be authorised by the notice are to take place only in a part of the premises, include a description of the nature of the part of the premises in which the activities are taking place and its location within the premises.*]

....

....

....

....

....

....

2. Please describe the nature of the event which is to take place (including the number of persons who are expected to participate in the event):

....

....

....

....

....

3. Please give for each day of the period of the notice the times when activities are to begin and end.

Date	Start time	Finish time

[Use additional sheets if necessary. These should be headed "Additional information about times when premises are to be used under the notice", and attached to the notice.]

4. Please give the operating licence number of the person or organisation giving the notice:

....

5(a) Please give the name of a person who is responsible for the conduct of the event to which the notice relates, and who will be available to be contacted during the course of the event:

....

5(b) Please specify that person's role or title in connection with the event:

....

5(c) Please give a telephone number at which that person can be contacted when the event is taking place:

....

6(a) Have any activities taken place, or will any activities take place, on the premises under any other temporary use notice during the period of 12 months ending on the last day of the period specified in this notice?

Yes ☐ No ☐

6(b) Where the answer to question 6(a) is "yes", give the dates on which such activities have taken or will take place:

Start date	End date	Number of days

[Use additional sheets if necessary. These should be headed "Additional information on previous notice periods", and attached to the notice.]

This notice is given on:
[*Specify the date on which the notice is given. This is the date on which it is sent or delivered to the licensing authority.*]

....

Declarations and Checklist ***(please tick or check)***

I confirm that, to the best of my knowledge, the information contained in this notice is true. I understand that it is an offence under section 342 of the Gambling Act 2005 without reasonable excuse to give information which is false or misleading in, or in relation to, this notice. ☐

Checklist:

- **The date on which this notice is given is more than 3 months before the date on which the activities to which this notice relates are due to start** ☐
- **Payment of the appropriate fee has been made/is enclosed** ☐
- **I understand that premises cannot be used under temporary use notices for more than 21 days in any 12 month period. I confirm that the notice will not lead to this limit being exceeded** ☐
- **I understand that each of the following persons and organisations must be given a copy of the notice and that they must receive it no later than 6 days after the date on which it is sent or delivered to the licensing authority:**
    - **The Gambling Commission,**
    - **The chief officer of police, or in Scotland the chief constable of the police, for any area in which the premises are wholly or partly situated, and**
    - **The Commissioners for Her Majesty's Revenue and Customs.** ☐

Signature

Signature of the person giving the temporary use notice, or signature of the solicitor or other duly authorised agent acting on behalf of the person or organisation giving the notice. If you are signing on behalf of the person or organisation giving the notice, please state in what capacity:

Signature: ....

Print Name: ....

Date: ....Capacity:..

[*Where the notice is given in an electronic form, the signature should be generated electronically and should be a copy of the person's written signature.*]

Contact Details

The following person can be contacted about this temporary use notice:

.... Tel:.....................................

The postal and/ or e-mail address for any correspondence associated with the notice is:

....

....

....

ENDORSEMENT OF NOTICE BY LICENSING AUTHORITY

(For Licensing Authority use only)

Endorsed by:
[*Specify the name of the licensing authority by whom the notice is endorsed in accordance with section 227 of the Gambling Act 2005.*]

....

Signed on behalf of the licensing authority:

Signature:..

Name:..

Date: .... Capacity:..

[6.1914]

PART 2

Form and content of temporary use notices applying to a vessel

[*SPACE FOR LICENSING AUTHORITY LOGO ETC.*]

Gambling Act 2005 - Temporary Use Notice (Vessel)

Notice is hereby given under Part 9 of the Gambling Act 2005 that:
[*Insert the name and address of the person or organisation giving the notice*]

....

....

....

....

intends to use the following vessel:
[*Give the name of the vessel*]

....

for carrying on the following activities:
[*Indicate the type of gaming which will take place under the notice*]

....

....

....

....

....

during the following period:

Start date	End date

Additional information

1. Please give the country in which the vessel is registered:

....

2(a) Please give the place in the licensing authority's area at which the vessel is situated or moored: [*Give an address with postcode if available*]

....

....

....

2(b) Please confirm by ticking or checking the appropriate box whether the place stated in question 2(a) is:

(i) a fixed place in or on water at which the vessel is situated; or ☐

(ii) a place at which the vessel is permanently moored; or ☐

(iii) a place at which the vessel is habitually moored; or ☐

(iv) in any other case, a place at which the vessel is moored or is likely to be moored, or a place in the United Kingdom nearest to any place at which a vessel is or is likely to be, while activities are carried on in the vessel in reliance on this notice. ☐

2(c) Where either sub-paragraph (iii) or (iv) of question 2(b) has been ticked or checked, please indicate all the places where the vessel will be during the whole of the period of time covered by the notice.

....

....

....

....

3. Please describe the nature of the event which is to take place (including the number of persons who are expected to participate in the event):

....

....

....

....

....

4. Please indicate whether the activities to be authorised by the notice are to take place only in a part of the vessel; and, if so, please include a description of the part in which the activities are taking place and its location within the vessel:

....

....

....

....

....

....

5. Please give for each day of the period of the notice the times when activities are to begin and end.

Date	Start time	Finish time

[*Use additional sheets if necessary. These should be headed "Additional information about times when premises are to be used under the notice", and attached to the notice.*]

6. Please give the operating licence number of the person or organisation giving the notice:

....

7(a) Please give the name of a person who is responsible for the conduct of the event to which the notice relates, and who will be available to be contacted during the course of the event:

....

7(b) Please specify that person's role or title in connection with the event:

....

7(c) Please give a telephone number at which that person can be contacted when the event is taking place:

....

6: Gambling Act 2005: SIs

6.1915

SCHEDULE 2
FORM AND CONTENT OF A COUNTER-NOTICE
Regulation 4

SCHEDULE 2

Regulation 4

Form and content of a counter-notice

[*SPACE FOR LICENSING AUTHORITY LOGO ETC.*]

COUNTER-NOTICE
(Given in response to a temporary use notice under Part 9 of the Gambling Act 2005)

This counter-notice is given under section 224 of the Gambling Act 2005 and relates to a

temporary use notice given on ....in respect of the following premises:
[*Identify the premises to which the temporary use notice applies, giving where applicable an address and postcode*]

....

....

....

The temporary use notice was given by the following person or organisation:
[*Give the name and address of the person or organisation who gave the temporary use notice*]

....

....

....

The temporary use notice provided for the premises to be used for the following activities:

....

....

....

during the following period:

Start date	End date

The licensing authority have decided that the temporary use notice referred to in this counter-notice: [*tick or check the box or boxes which apply, and give any additional information as appropriate*]

- Is not to have effect ☐
- Is to have effect only in respect of the following activities: ☐

....

- Is to have effect only during the following period: ☐

Start date	End date

- Is to authorise the activities to take place only at the following times of day: ☐

Date	Start time	Finish time

- Is to have effect subject to the activities being carried out in accordance with the following condition(s) attached in accordance with section 224(3)(d) of the Gambling Act 2005: ☐

....

....

....

....

....

This decision has been taken by the licensing authority for the following reasons:

....

....

....

....

Signed on behalf of the licensing authority:

Signature: ……………………………………………………………………………………………

Print Name: ……………………………………………………………………………………………

Date: …………………………… Capacity:……………………………………………………………

GAMBLING (INVITING COMPETING APPLICATIONS FOR LARGE AND SMALL CASINO PREMISES LICENCES) REGULATIONS 2008

(SI 2008/469)

Made ....*25th February 2008*
Laid before Parliament ....*26th February 2008*
Coming into force ....*18th March 2008*

The Secretary of State makes the following Regulations in exercise of the powers conferred by section 355 of and paragraph 2 of Schedule 9 to the Gambling Act 2005.

6.1916 1 Citation and commencement

These Regulations may be cited as the Gambling (Inviting Competing Applications for Large and Small Casino Premises Licences) Regulations 2008 and shall come into force on 18th March 2008.

6.1917 2 Interpretation

In these Regulations—

"application" means—

(a) an application under section 159 for a large or small casino premises licence, or

(b) an application under section 204 for a provisional statement in respect of a large or small casino,

and a reference to an "applicant" shall be construed accordingly,

"application pack" has the meaning given in regulation 3(1)(b),

"closing date" has the meaning given in regulation 5(1)(b),

"invitation" has the meaning given in regulation 3(1)(a), and

"the licensing authority", in relation to an invitation, application pack or application means the licensing authority—

(a) who publish the invitation,

(b) who make the application pack available to a member of the public on request, or

(c) to whom the application is made.

(2) A reference in these Regulations to a section or Schedule is a reference to a section of or Schedule to the Gambling Act 2005.

6.1918 3 Invitations for competing applications and application packs

(1) Before considering an application, a licensing authority must—

(a) publish an invitation calling for applications ("invitation"), and

(b) make arrangements for the provision, free of charge, of a copy of information about an invited application ("application pack") to a person on request, until the closing date stated in the invitation to which the application pack relates.

(2) An invitation must—

(a) be published in a manner that complies with regulation 4, and

(b) contain the information required by regulation 5.

(3) An application pack must contain the information required by regulation 6.

6.1919 4 Manner of publication of invitation

(1) An invitation must be published in a manner which the licensing authority consider is most likely to bring it to the attention of as many potential applicants in the United Kingdom and abroad as possible.

(2) Without prejudice to the generality of paragraph (1), an invitation must be published at least once in a trade newspaper, journal or similar publication which the licensing authority consider is likely to be read by persons in the United Kingdom and abroad who are potential applicants.

6.1920 5 Information to be included in invitation

(1) An invitation must state—

(a) whether the licensing authority propose to issue a casino premises licence for a large or small casino,

(b) the latest date by which an application must be made in order to be considered by the licensing authority ("closing date"),

(c) the place from which a person may obtain an application pack, and

(d) such other information as the licensing authority consider appropriate.

(2) The closing date may not be earlier than the date which is 3 months after the later of—

(a) the date on which the invitation is last published, and

(b) the date on which the application pack is first available to a person on request.

6.1921 6 Information to be included in application pack

(1) An application pack must include—

(a) a statement that—

(i) an application must be made in the form and manner prescribed by the application regulations, and

(ii) no information, other than information required by the application regulations, may be included in or submitted with an application,

(b) a statement of the procedure that the licensing authority propose to follow to determine whether to grant or reject an application,

(c) a statement that, in making any determination required by paragraph 4 of Schedule 9, the licensing authority will not take into account information which is relevant to a determination under paragraph 5 of that Schedule unless that information is also relevant to the determination under paragraph 4,

(d) a statement of the principles that the licensing authority propose to apply in making any determination required by paragraph 5 of Schedule 9,

(e) the dates by which the licensing authority expect to make—

(i) the determination under 163 (if the licensing authority only receives one application), or

(ii) the determination under paragraph 4 of Schedule 9 and any determination under paragraph 5 of that Schedule that may be required (if the licensing authority receives more than one application), and

(f) such other information as the licensing authority consider appropriate.

(2) The statement required by paragraph (1)(b) must, in particular, include information about the two-stage consideration procedure under paragraphs 4 and 5 of Schedule 9.

(3) In this regulation "the application regulations" means the regulations made under section 159(6)(a)—

(a) in relation to applications to licensing authorities in England and Wales, by the Secretary of State, and

(b) in relation to applications to licensing authorities in Scotland, by the Scottish Ministers.

6.1922 7 Timing

(1) A licensing authority may not consider an application before the closing date stated in the invitation to which the application relates ("the relevant closing date").

(2) A licensing authority are not required to consider an application that is made after the relevant closing date.

(3) For the purposes of the Act and any regulations made under it, an application that is made before the relevant closing date shall be treated as if it were made on the relevant closing date.

GAMBLING (GEOGRAPHICAL DISTRIBUTION OF LARGE AND SMALL CASINO PREMISES LICENCES) ORDER 2008

(SI 2008/1327)

Made ....19th May 2008
Coming into force in accordance with article 1

The Secretary of State makes the following Order in exercise of the powers conferred by sections 175(4) and 355 of the Gambling Act 2005.

In accordance with section 175(4) of that Act the Secretary of State has consulted the Scottish Ministers and the Welsh Ministers.

In accordance with section 355(6) of that Act a draft of this Order was laid before and approved by a resolution of each House of Parliament.

6.1930 1 Citation and commencement

This Order may be cited as the Gambling (Geographical Distribution of Large and Small Casino Premises Licences) Order 2008 and shall come into force on the day after the day on which it is made.

6.1931 2 Licensing authorities who may issue large casino premises licences

(1) The following licensing authorities may issue large casino premises licences—

(a) Great Yarmouth Borough Council,
(b) Kingston upon Hull City Council,
(c) Leeds City Council,
(d) Middlesbrough Borough Council,
(e) Milton Keynes Borough Council,
(f) Newham London Borough Council,
(g) Solihull Metropolitan Borough Council, and
(h) Southampton City Council.

(2) No more than one such licence issued by each licensing authority may have effect at any time.

6.1932 3 Licensing authorities who may issue small casino premises licences

(1) The following licensing authorities may issue small casino premises licences—

(a) Bath and North East Somerset District Council,
(b) East Lindsey District Council,
(c) Luton Borough Council,
(d) Scarborough Borough Council,
(e) Swansea City and County Council,
(f) Torbay Borough Council,
(g) Wigtown Divisional Licensing Board in the area of Dumfries and Galloway Council, and

(h) Wolverhampton City Council.

(2) No more than one such licence issued by each licensing authority may have effect at any time.

CATEGORIES OF CASINO REGULATIONS 2008

(SI 2008/1330)

Made . . . . 19th May 2008
Coming into force in accordance with regulation 1(1)

The Secretary of State makes these Regulations in exercise of the powers conferred by sections 7(5) to (7) and section 355(1) of the Gambling Act 2005.

A draft of these Regulations was laid before Parliament and approved by a resolution of each House of Parliament in accordance with section 355(4)(c) of that Act.

6.1940 1 Citation, commencement and interpretation

(1) These Regulations may be cited as the Categories of Casino Regulations 2008 and come into force on the day after the day on which they are made.

(2) In these Regulations "casino premises licence" has the same meaning as in Part 8 of the Gambling Act 2005.

6.1941 2 Classification of casinos

(1) This regulation specifies the matters by reference to which a casino is to be classified for the purposes of the Gambling Act 2005 as—

(a) a large casino,
(b) a small casino, or
(c) below the minimum size for a licensed casino.

(2) A casino is a large casino if the combined floor area of those parts of the casino which are used for providing facilities for gambling is equal to or exceeds 1,500 square metres, but is less than 3,500 square metres.

(3) A casino is a small casino if the combined floor area of those parts of the casino which are used for providing facilities for gambling is equal to or exceeds 500 square metres, but is less than 1,500 square metres.

(4) A casino is below the minimum size for a licensed casino if the combined floor area of those parts of the casino which are used for providing facilities for gambling is less than 500 square metres.

(5) In this regulation a reference to parts of a casino used for providing facilities for gambling is a reference to—

(a) where a casino premises licence has effect in respect of the casino, those parts of the premises shown on the plan included in the licence as the parts that will be used for providing facilities for gambling in reliance on the licence;

(b) where an application for a casino premises licence in respect of the casino has been made and not determined, those parts of the premises shown on the plan that accompanied the application as the parts which will be used for providing facilities for gambling in reliance on the licence; or

(c) in any other case, those parts of the premises that would be required to be shown on the plan accompanying an application for a casino premises licence (were such an application to be made in respect of the premises) as the parts which would be used for providing facilities for gambling in reliance on the licence.

TRIBUNAL PROCEDURE (UPPER TRIBUNAL) RULES 2008

(SI 2008/2698)

Made ....*9th October 2008*
Laid before Parliament ....*15th October 2008*
Coming into force ....*3rd November 2008*

After consulting in accordance with paragraph 28(1) of Schedule 5 to, the Tribunals, Courts and Enforcement Act 2007 the Tribunal Procedure Committee has made the following Rules in exercise of the power conferred by sections 10(3), 16(9), 22 and 29(3) and (4) of, and Schedule 5 to, that Act.
The Lord Chancellor has allowed the Rules in accordance with paragraph 28(3) of Schedule 5 to the Tribunals, Courts and Enforcement Act 2007.

PART 1
INTRODUCTION

6.1941.1 1 Citation, commencement, application and interpretation

(1) These Rules may be cited as the Tribunal Procedure (Upper Tribunal) Rules 2008 and come into force on 3rd November 2008.

(2) These Rules apply to proceedings before the Upper Tribunal [except proceedings in the Lands Chamber].

(3) In these Rules—

"the 2007 Act" means the Tribunals, Courts and Enforcement Act 2007;

["appellant" means—

(a) a person who makes an appeal, or applies for permission to appeal, to the Upper Tribunal;

(b) in proceedings transferred or referred to the Upper Tribunal from the First-tier Tribunal, a person who started the proceedings in the First-tier Tribunal; or

(c) a person substituted as an appellant under rule 9(1) (substitution and addition of parties);]

"applicant" means a person who applies for permission to bring, or does bring, judicial review proceedings before the Upper Tribunal and, in judicial review proceedings transferred to the Upper Tribunal from a court, includes a person who was a claimant or petitioner in the proceedings immediately before they were transferred;

["appropriate national authority" means, in relation to an appeal, the Secretary of State, the Scottish Ministers or the Welsh Ministers, as the case may be;]

["authorised person" means an examiner appointed by the Secretary of State under section 66A of the Road Traffic Act 1988, or a person acting under the direction of such an examiner, who has detained the vehicle to which an appeal relates;]

. . .

"dispose of proceedings" includes, unless indicated otherwise, disposing of a part of the proceedings;

"document" means anything in which information is recorded in any form, and an obligation under these Rules or any practice direction or direction to provide or allow access to a document or a copy of a document for any purpose means, unless the Upper Tribunal directs otherwise, an obligation to provide or allow access to such document or copy in a legible form or in a form which can be readily made into a legible form;

"hearing" means an oral hearing and includes a hearing conducted in whole or in part by video link, telephone or other means of instantaneous two-way electronic communication;

"interested party" means—

(a) a person who is directly affected by the outcome sought in judicial review proceedings, and has been named as an interested party under rule 28 or 29 (judicial review), or has been substituted or added as an interested party under rule 9 (substitution and addition of parties); and

(b) in judicial review proceedings transferred to the Upper Tribunal under section 25A(2) or (3) of the Judicature (Northern Ireland) Act 1978 or section 31A(2) or (3) of the [Senior Courts Act 1981], a person who was an interested party in the proceedings immediately before they were transferred to the Upper Tribunal;

"judicial review proceedings" means proceedings within the jurisdiction of the Upper Tribunal pursuant to section 15 or 21 of the 2007 Act, whether such proceedings are started in the Upper Tribunal or transferred to the Upper Tribunal;

. . .

"mental health case" means proceedings before the Upper Tribunal on appeal against a decision in proceedings under the Mental Health Act 1983 or paragraph 5(2) of the Schedule to the Repatriation of Prisoners Act 1984;

["national security certificate appeal" means an appeal under section 28 of the Data Protection Act 1998 or section 60 of the Freedom of Information Act 2000 (including that section as applied and modified by regulation 18 of the Environmental Information Regulations 2004);]

"party" means a person who is an appellant, an applicant, a respondent or an interested party in proceedings before the Upper Tribunal, a person who has referred a question to the Upper Tribunal or, if the proceedings have been concluded, a person who was an appellant, an applicant, a respondent or an interested party when the Tribunal finally disposed of all issues in the proceedings;

"permission" includes leave in cases arising under the law of Northern Ireland;

"practice direction" means a direction given under section 23 of the 2007 Act;

["relevant minister" means the Minister or designated person responsible for the signing of the certificate to which a national security certificate appeal relates;]

"respondent" means—

(a) in an appeal, or application for permission to appeal, against a decision of another tribunal, any person other than the appellant who—

(i) was a party before that other tribunal;

(ii) . . .

(iii) otherwise has a right of appeal against the decision of the other tribunal and has given notice to the Upper Tribunal that they wish to be a party to the appeal;

(b) in an appeal against any other decision [except a decision of a traffic commissioner], the person who made the decision;

(c) in judicial review proceedings——

(i) in proceedings started in the Upper Tribunal, the person named by the applicant as the respondent;

(ii) in proceedings transferred to the Upper Tribunal under section 25A(2) or (3) of the Judicature (Northern Ireland) Act 1978 or section 31A(2) or (3) of the [Senior Courts Act 1981], a person who was a defendant in the proceedings immediately before they were transferred;

(iii) in proceedings transferred to the Upper Tribunal under section 20(1) of the 2007 Act, a person to whom intimation of the petition was made before the proceedings were transferred, or to whom the Upper Tribunal has required intimation to be made;

[(ca) in proceedings transferred or referred to the Upper Tribunal from the First-tier Tribunal, a person who was a respondent in the proceedings in the First-tier Tribunal;]

(d) in a reference under the Forfeiture Act 1982, the person whose eligibility for a benefit or advantage is in issue; or

(e) a person substituted or added as a respondent under rule 9 (substitution and addition of parties);

. . .

["tribunal" does not include a traffic commissioner;]

"working day" means any day except a Saturday or Sunday, Christmas Day, Good Friday or a bank holiday under section 1 of the Banking and Financial Dealings Act 1971.

6.1941.2 2 Overriding objective and parties' obligation to co-operate with the Upper Tribunal

(1) The overriding objective of these Rules is to enable the Upper Tribunal to deal with cases fairly and justly.

(2) Dealing with a case fairly and justly includes——

(a) dealing with the case in ways which are proportionate to the importance of the case, the complexity of the issues, the anticipated costs and the resources of the parties;

(b) avoiding unnecessary formality and seeking flexibility in the proceedings;

(c) ensuring, so far as practicable, that the parties are able to participate fully in the proceedings;

(d) using any special expertise of the Upper Tribunal effectively; and

(e) avoiding delay, so far as compatible with proper consideration of the issues.

(3) The Upper Tribunal must seek to give effect to the overriding objective when it—

(a) exercises any power under these Rules; or

(b) interprets any rule or practice direction.

(4) Parties must—

(a) help the Upper Tribunal to further the overriding objective; and

(b) co-operate with the Upper Tribunal generally.

6.1941.3 3 Alternative dispute resolution and arbitration

(1) The Upper Tribunal should seek, where appropriate—

(a) to bring to the attention of the parties the availability of any appropriate alternative procedure for the resolution of the dispute; and

(b) if the parties wish and provided that it is compatible with the overriding objective, to facilitate the use of the procedure.

(2) Part 1 of the Arbitration Act 1996 does not apply to proceedings before the Upper Tribunal.

PART 2
GENERAL POWERS AND PROVISIONS

6.1941.4 4 Delegation to staff

(1) Staff appointed under section 40(1) of the 2007 Act (tribunal staff and services) may, with the approval of the Senior President of Tribunals, carry out functions of a judicial nature permitted or required to be done by the Upper Tribunal.

(2) The approval referred to at paragraph (1) may apply generally to the carrying out of specified functions by members of staff of a specified description in specified circumstances.

(3) Within 14 days after the date on which the Upper Tribunal sends notice of a decision made by a member of staff under paragraph (1) to a party, that party may apply in writing to the Upper Tribunal for that decision to be considered afresh by a judge.

6.1941.5 5 Case management powers

(1) Subject to the provisions of the 2007 Act and any other enactment, the Upper Tribunal may regulate its own procedure.

(2) The Upper Tribunal may give a direction in relation to the conduct or disposal of proceedings at any time, including a direction amending, suspending or setting aside an earlier direction.

(3) In particular, and without restricting the general powers in paragraphs (1) and (2), the Upper Tribunal may—

- (a) extend or shorten the time for complying with any rule, practice direction or direction;
- (b) consolidate or hear together two or more sets of proceedings or parts of proceedings raising common issues, or treat a case as a lead case;
- (c) permit or require a party to amend a document;
- (d) permit or require a party or another person to provide documents, information, evidence or submissions to the Upper Tribunal or a party;
- (e) deal with an issue in the proceedings as a preliminary issue;
- (f) hold a hearing to consider any matter, including a case management issue;
- (g) decide the form of any hearing;
- (h) adjourn or postpone a hearing;
- (i) require a party to produce a bundle for a hearing;
- (j) stay (or, in Scotland, sist) proceedings;
- (k) transfer proceedings to another court or tribunal if that other court or tribunal has jurisdiction in relation to the proceedings and—
  - (i) because of a change of circumstances since the proceedings were started, the Upper Tribunal no longer has jurisdiction in relation to the proceedings; or
  - (ii) the Upper Tribunal considers that the other court or tribunal is a more appropriate forum for the determination of the case;
- (l) suspend the effect of its own decision pending an appeal or review of that decision;
- (m) in an appeal, or an application for permission to appeal, against the decision of another tribunal, suspend the effect of that decision pending the determination of the application for permission to appeal, and any appeal;
- [(n) require any person, body or other tribunal whose decision is the subject of proceedings before the Upper Tribunal to provide reasons for the decision, or other information or documents in relation to the decision or any proceedings before that person, body or tribunal].

6.1941.6 6 Procedure for applying for and giving directions

(1) The Upper Tribunal may give a direction on the application of one or more of the parties or on its own initiative.

(2) An application for a direction may be made—

(a) by sending or delivering a written application to the Upper Tribunal; or

(b) orally during the course of a hearing.

(3) An application for a direction must include the reason for making that application.

(4) Unless the Upper Tribunal considers that there is good reason not to do so, the Upper Tribunal must send written notice of any direction to every party and to any other person affected by the direction.

(5) If a party or any other person sent notice of the direction under paragraph (4) wishes to challenge a direction which the Upper Tribunal has given, they may do so by applying for another direction which amends, suspends or sets aside the first direction.

6.1941.7 7 Failure to comply with rules etc

(1) An irregularity resulting from a failure to comply with any requirement in these Rules, a practice direction or a direction, does not of itself render void the proceedings or any step taken in the proceedings.

(2) If a party has failed to comply with a requirement in these Rules, a practice direction or a direction, the Upper Tribunal may take such action as it considers just, which may include—

(a) waiving the requirement;

(b) requiring the failure to be remedied;

(c) exercising its power under rule 8 (striking out a party's case); or

(d) except in mental health cases, restricting a party's participation in the proceedings.

(3) Paragraph (4) applies where the First-tier Tribunal has referred to the Upper Tribunal a failure by a person to comply with a requirement imposed by the First-tier Tribunal—

(a) to attend at any place for the purpose of giving evidence;

(b) otherwise to make themselves available to give evidence;

(c) to swear an oath in connection with the giving of evidence;

(d) to give evidence as a witness;

(e) to produce a document; or

(f) to facilitate the inspection of a document or any other thing (including any premises).

(4) The Upper Tribunal may exercise its power under section 25 of the 2007 Act (supplementary powers of the Upper Tribunal) in relation to such non-compliance as if the requirement had been imposed by the Upper Tribunal.

6.1941.8 8 Striking out a party's case

(1) The proceedings, or the appropriate part of them, will automatically be struck out if the appellant or applicant has failed to comply with a direction that stated that failure by the appellant or applicant to comply with the direction would lead to the striking out of the proceedings or that part of them.

(2) The Upper Tribunal must strike out the whole or a part of the proceedings if the Upper Tribunal—

(a) does not have jurisdiction in relation to the proceedings or that part of them; and

(b) does not exercise its power under rule 5(3)(k)(i) (transfer to another court or tribunal) in relation to the proceedings or that part of them.

(3) The Upper Tribunal may strike out the whole or a part of the proceedings if—

(a) the appellant or applicant has failed to comply with a direction which stated that failure by the appellant or applicant to comply with the direction could lead to the striking out of the proceedings or part of them;

(b) the appellant or applicant has failed to co-operate with the Upper Tribunal to such an extent that the Upper Tribunal cannot deal with the proceedings fairly and justly; or

(c) in proceedings which are not an appeal from the decision of another tribunal or judicial review proceedings, the Upper Tribunal considers there is no reasonable prospect of the appellant's or the applicant's case, or part of it, succeeding.

(4) The Upper Tribunal may not strike out the whole or a part of the proceedings under paragraph (2) or (3)(b) or (c) without first giving the appellant or applicant an opportunity to make representations in relation to the proposed striking out.

(5) If the proceedings have been struck out under paragraph (1) or (3)(a), the appellant or applicant may apply for the proceedings, or part of them, to be reinstated.

(6) An application under paragraph (5) must be made in writing and received by the Upper Tribunal within 1 month after the date on which the Upper Tribunal sent notification of the striking out to the appellant or applicant.

(7) This rule applies to a respondent [or an interested party] as it applies to an appellant or applicant except that—

(a) a reference to the striking out of the proceedings is to be read as a reference to the barring of the respondent [or interested party] from taking further part in the proceedings; and

(b) a reference to an application for the reinstatement of proceedings which have been struck out is to be read as a reference to an application for the lifting of the bar on the respondent [or interested party] . . . taking further part in the proceedings.

(8) If a respondent [or an interested party] has been barred from taking further part in proceedings under this rule and that bar has not been lifted, the Upper Tribunal need not consider any response or other submission made by that respondent [or interested party, and may summarily determine any or all issues against that respondent or interested party].

6.1941.9 [9 Addition, substitution and removal of parties]

[(1) The Upper Tribunal may give a direction adding, substituting or removing a party as an appellant, a respondent or an interested party.

(2) If the Upper Tribunal gives a direction under paragraph (1) it may give such consequential directions as it considers appropriate.

(3) A person who is not a party may apply to the Upper Tribunal to be added or substituted as a party.

(4) If a person who is entitled to be a party to proceedings by virtue of another enactment applies to be added as a party, and any conditions applicable to that entitlement have been satisfied, the Upper Tribunal must give a direction adding that person as a respondent or, if appropriate, as an appellant.]

6.1941.10 [10 Orders for costs]

[(1) The Upper Tribunal may not make an order in respect of costs (or, in Scotland, expenses) in proceedings [transferred or referred by, or on appeal from,] another tribunal except—

[(aa) in a national security certificate appeal, to the extent permitted by paragraph (1A);]

(a) in proceedings [transferred by, or on appeal from,] the Tax Chamber of the First-tier Tribunal; or

(b) to the extent and in the circumstances that the other tribunal had the power to make an order in respect of costs (or, in Scotland, expenses).

[(1A) In a national security certificate appeal—

(a) the Upper Tribunal may make an order in respect of costs or expenses in the circumstances described at paragraph (3)(c) and (d);

(b) if the appeal is against a certificate, the Upper Tribunal may make an order in respect of costs or expenses against the relevant Minister and in favour of the appellant if the Upper Tribunal allows the appeal and quashes the certificate to any extent or the Minister withdraws the certificate;

(c) if the appeal is against the application of a certificate, the Upper Tribunal may make an order in respect of costs or expenses—

(i) against the appellant and in favour of any other party if the Upper Tribunal dismisses the appeal to any extent; or

(ii) in favour of the appellant and against any other party if the Upper Tribunal allows the appeal to any extent.]

(2) The Upper Tribunal may not make an order in respect of costs or expenses under section 4 of the Forfeiture Act 1982.

(3) In other proceedings, the Upper Tribunal may not make an order in respect of costs or expenses except—

(a) in judicial review proceedings;

(b) . . .

(c) under section 29(4) of the 2007 Act (wasted costs); or

(d) if the Upper Tribunal considers that a party or its representative has acted unreasonably in bringing, defending or conducting the proceedings.

(4) The Upper Tribunal may make an order for costs (or, in Scotland, expenses) on an application or on its own initiative.

(5) A person making an application for an order for costs or expenses must—

(a) send or deliver a written application to the Upper Tribunal and to the person against whom it is proposed that the order be made; and

(b) send or deliver with the application a schedule of the costs or expenses claimed sufficient to allow summary assessment of such costs or expenses by the Upper Tribunal.

(6) An application for an order for costs or expenses may be made at any time during the proceedings but may not be made later than 1 month after the date on which the Upper Tribunal sends—

(a) a decision notice recording the decision which finally disposes of all issues in the proceedings; or

(b) notice of a withdrawal under rule 17 which ends the proceedings.

(7) The Upper Tribunal may not make an order for costs or expenses against a person (the "paying person") without first—

(a) giving that person an opportunity to make representations; and

(b) if the paying person is an individual and the order is to be made under paragraph (3)(a), (b) or (d), considering that person's financial means.

(8) The amount of costs or expenses to be paid under an order under this rule may be ascertained by—

(a) summary assessment by the Upper Tribunal;

(b) agreement of a specified sum by the paying person and the person entitled to receive the costs or expenses ("the receiving person"); or

(c) assessment of the whole or a specified part of the costs or expenses incurred by the receiving person, if not agreed.

(9) Following an order for assessment under paragraph (8)(c), the paying person or the receiving person may apply—

(a) in England and Wales, to the High Court or the Costs Office of the Supreme Court (as specified in the order) for a detailed assessment of the costs on the standard basis or, if specified in the order, on the indemnity basis; and the Civil Procedure Rules 1998 shall apply, with necessary modifications, to that application and assessment as if the proceedings in the tribunal had been proceedings in a court to which the Civil Procedure Rules 1998 apply;

(b) in Scotland, to the Auditor of the Court of Session for the taxation of the expenses according to the fees payable in that court; or

(c) in Northern Ireland, to the Taxing Office of the High Court of Northern Ireland for taxation on the standard basis or, if specified in the order, on the indemnity basis.]

6.1941.11 11 Representatives

(1) A party may appoint a representative (whether a legal representative or not) to represent that party in the proceedings.

(2) If a party appoints a representative, that party (or the representative if the representative is a legal representative) must send or deliver to the Upper Tribunal . . . written notice of the representative's name and address.

[(2A) If the Upper Tribunal receives notice that a party has appointed a representative under paragraph (2), it must send a copy of that notice to each other party.]

(3) Anything permitted or required to be done by a party under these Rules, a practice direction or a direction may be done by the representative of that party, except signing a witness statement.

(4) A person who receives due notice of the appointment of a representative—

(a) must provide to the representative any document which is required to be provided to the represented party, and need not provide that document to the represented party; and

(b) may assume that the representative is and remains authorised as such until they receive written notification that this is not so from the representative or the represented party.

(5) At a hearing a party may be accompanied by another person whose name and address has not been notified under paragraph (2) but who, subject to paragraph (8) and with the permission of the Upper Tribunal, may act as a representative or otherwise assist in presenting the party's case at the hearing.

(6) Paragraphs (2) to (4) do not apply to a person who accompanies a party under paragraph (5).

(7) In a mental health case if the patient has not appointed a representative the Upper Tribunal may appoint a legal representative for the patient where—

(a) the patient has stated that they do not wish to conduct their own case or that they wish to be represented; or

(b) the patient lacks the capacity to appoint a representative but the Upper Tribunal believes that it is in the patient's best interests for the patient to be represented.

(8) In a mental health case a party may not appoint as a representative, or be represented or assisted at a hearing by—

(a) a person liable to be detained or subject to guardianship or after-care under supervision, or who is a community patient, under the Mental Health Act 1983; or

(b) a person receiving treatment for mental disorder at the same hospital home as the patient.

[(9) In this rule "legal representative" means [a person who, for the purposes of the Legal Services Act 2007, is an authorised person in relation to an activity which constitutes the exercise of a right of audience or the conduct of litigation within the meaning of that Act], an advocate or solicitor in Scotland or a barrister or solicitor in Northern Ireland.]

6.1941.12 12 Calculating time

(1) An act required by these Rules, a practice direction or a direction to be done on or by a particular day must be done by 5pm on that day.

(2) If the time specified by these Rules, a practice direction or a direction for doing any act ends on a day other than a working day, the act is done in time if it is done on the next working day.

(3) In a special educational needs case or a disability discrimination in schools case, the following days must not be counted when calculating the time by which an act must be done—

(a) 25th December to 1st January inclusive; and

(b) any day in August.

(4) Paragraph (3) does not apply where the Upper Tribunal directs that an act must be done by or on a specified date.

[(5) In this rule—

"disability discrimination in schools case" means proceedings concerning disability discrimination in the education of a child or related matters; and

"special educational needs case" means proceedings concerning the education of a child who has or may have special educational needs.]

6.1941.13 13 Sending and delivery of documents

(1) Any document to be provided to the Upper Tribunal under these Rules, a practice direction or a direction must be—

(a) sent by pre-paid post or [by document exchange, or delivered by hand,] to the address specified for the proceedings;

(b) sent by fax to the number specified for the proceedings; or

(c) sent or delivered by such other method as the Upper Tribunal may permit or direct.

(2) Subject to paragraph (3), if a party provides a fax number, email address or other details for the electronic transmission of documents to them, that party must accept delivery of documents by that method.

(3) If a party informs the Upper Tribunal and all other parties that a particular form of communication, other than pre-paid post or delivery by hand, should not be used to provide documents to that party, that form of communication must not be so used.

(4) If the Upper Tribunal or a party sends a document to a party or the Upper Tribunal by email or any other electronic means of communication, the recipient may request that the sender provide a hard copy of the document to the recipient. The recipient must make such a request as soon as reasonably practicable after receiving the document electronically.

(5) The Upper Tribunal and each party may assume that the address provided by a party or its representative is and remains the address to which documents should be sent or delivered until receiving written notification to the contrary.

6.1941.14 14 Use of documents and information

(1) The Upper Tribunal may make an order prohibiting the disclosure or publication of—

(a) specified documents or information relating to the proceedings; or

(b) any matter likely to lead members of the public to identify any person whom the Upper Tribunal considers should not be identified.

(2) The Upper Tribunal may give a direction prohibiting the disclosure of a document or information to a person if—

(a) the Upper Tribunal is satisfied that such disclosure would be likely to cause that person or some other person serious harm; and

(b) the Upper Tribunal is satisfied, having regard to the interests of justice, that it is proportionate to give such a direction.

(3) If a party ("the first party") considers that the Upper Tribunal should give a direction under paragraph (2) prohibiting the disclosure of a document or information to another party ("the second party"), the first party must—

(a) exclude the relevant document or information from any documents that will be provided to the second party; and

(b) provide to the Upper Tribunal the excluded document or information, and the reason for its exclusion, so that the Upper Tribunal may decide whether the document or information should be disclosed to the second party or should be the subject of a direction under paragraph (2).

(4) . . .

(5) If the Upper Tribunal gives a direction under paragraph (2) which prevents disclosure to a party who has appointed a representative, the Upper Tribunal may give a direction that the documents or information be disclosed to that representative if the Upper Tribunal is satisfied that—

(a) disclosure to the representative would be in the interests of the party; and

(b) the representative will act in accordance with paragraph (6).

(6) Documents or information disclosed to a representative in accordance with a direction under paragraph (5) must not be disclosed either directly or indirectly to any other person without the Upper Tribunal's consent.

(7) Unless the Upper Tribunal gives a direction to the contrary, information about mental health cases and the names of any persons concerned in such cases must not be made public.

[(8) The Upper Tribunal may, on its own initiative or on the application of a party, give a direction that certain documents or information must or may be disclosed to the Upper Tribunal on the basis that the Upper Tribunal will not disclose such documents or information to other persons, or specified other persons.

(9) A party making an application for a direction under paragraph (8) may withhold the relevant documents or information from other parties until the Upper Tribunal has granted or refused the application.

(10) In a case involving matters relating to national security, the Upper Tribunal must ensure that information is not disclosed contrary to the interests of national security.

(11) The Upper Tribunal must conduct proceedings and record its decision and reasons appropriately so as not to undermine the effect of an order made under paragraph (1), a direction given under paragraph (2) or (8) or the duty imposed by paragraph (10).]

6.1941.15 15 Evidence and submissions

(1) Without restriction on the general powers in rule 5(1) and (2) (case management powers), the Upper Tribunal may give directions as to—

(a) issues on which it requires evidence or submissions;

(b) the nature of the evidence or submissions it requires;

(c) whether the parties are permitted or required to provide expert evidence, and if so whether the parties must jointly appoint a single expert to provide such evidence;

(d) any limit on the number of witnesses whose evidence a party may put forward, whether in relation to a particular issue or generally;

(e) the manner in which any evidence or submissions are to be provided, which may include a direction for them to be given—

(i) orally at a hearing; or

(ii) by written submissions or witness statement; and

(f) the time at which any evidence or submissions are to be provided.

(2) The Upper Tribunal may—

(a) admit evidence whether or not—

(i) the evidence would be admissible in a civil trial in the United Kingdom; or

(ii) the evidence was available to a previous decision maker; or

(b) exclude evidence that would otherwise be admissible where—

(i) the evidence was not provided within the time allowed by a direction or a practice direction;

(ii) the evidence was otherwise provided in a manner that did not comply with a direction or a practice direction; or

(iii) it would otherwise be unfair to admit the evidence.

(3) The Upper Tribunal may consent to a witness giving, or require any witness to give, evidence on oath, and may administer an oath for that purpose.

6.1941.16 16 Summoning or citation of witnesses and orders to answer questions or produce documents

(1) On the application of a party or on its own initiative, the Upper Tribunal may—

(a) by summons (or, in Scotland, citation) require any person to attend as a witness at a hearing at the time and place specified in the summons or citation; or

(b) order any person to answer any questions or produce any documents in that person's possession or control which relate to any issue in the proceedings.

(2) A summons or citation under paragraph (1)(a) must—

(a) give the person required to attend 14 days' notice of the hearing or such shorter period as the Upper Tribunal may direct; and

(b) where the person is not a party, make provision for the person's necessary expenses of attendance to be paid, and state who is to pay them.

(3) No person may be compelled to give any evidence or produce any document that the person could not be compelled to give or produce on a trial of an action in a court of law in the part of the United Kingdom where the proceedings are due to be determined.

[(4) A person who receives a summons, citation or order may apply to the Upper Tribunal for it to be varied or set aside if they did not have an opportunity to object to it before it was made or issued.

(5) A person making an application under paragraph (4) must do so as soon as reasonably practicable after receiving notice of the summons, citation or order.

(6) A summons, citation or order under this rule must—

(a) state that the person on whom the requirement is imposed may apply to the Upper Tribunal to vary or set aside the summons, citation or order, if they did not have an opportunity to object to it before it was made or issued; and

(b) state the consequences of failure to comply with the summons, citation or order.]

6.1941.17 17 Withdrawal

(1) Subject to paragraph (2), a party may give notice of the withdrawal of its case, or any part of it——

(a) at any time before a hearing to consider the disposal of the proceedings (or, if the Upper Tribunal disposes of the proceedings without a hearing, before that disposal), by sending or delivering to the Upper Tribunal a written notice of withdrawal; or

(b) orally at a hearing.

(2) Notice of withdrawal will not take effect unless the Upper Tribunal consents to the withdrawal except in relation to an application for permission to appeal.

(3) A party which has withdrawn its case may apply to the Upper Tribunal for the case to be reinstated.

(4) An application under paragraph (3) must be made in writing and be received by the Upper Tribunal within 1 month after—

(a) the date on which the Upper Tribunal received the notice under paragraph (1)(a); or

(b) the date of the hearing at which the case was withdrawn orally under paragraph (1)(b).

(5) The Upper Tribunal must notify each party in writing of a withdrawal under this rule.

6.1941.18 18 Notice of funding of legal services

If a party is granted funding of legal services at any time, that party must as soon as practicable—

(a)

(i) if funding is granted by the Legal Services Commission or the Northern Ireland Legal Services Commission, send a copy of the funding notice to the Upper Tribunal; or

(ii) if funding is granted by the Scottish Legal Aid Board, send a copy of the legal aid certificate to the Upper Tribunal; and

(b) notify every other party in writing that funding has been granted.

6.1941.19 20 Power to pay expenses and allowances

(1) In proceedings brought under section 4 of the Safeguarding Vulnerable Groups Act 2006 . . . , the Secretary of State may pay such allowances for the purpose of or in connection with the attendance of persons at hearings as the Secretary of State may, with the consent of the Treasury, determine.

(2) Paragraph (3) applies to proceedings on appeal from a decision of—

(a) the First-tier Tribunal in proceedings under the Child Support Act 1991, section 12 of the Social Security Act 1998 or paragraph 6 of Schedule 7 to the Child Support, Pensions and Social Security Act 2000;

(b) the First-tier Tribunal in a war pensions and armed forces case (as defined in the Tribunal Procedure (First-tier Tribunal) (War Pensions and Armed Forces Compensation Chamber) Rules 2008); or

(c) a Pensions Appeal Tribunal for Scotland or Northern Ireland.

(3) The Lord Chancellor (or, in Scotland, the Secretary of State) may pay to any person who attends any hearing such travelling and other allowances, including compensation for loss of remunerative time, as the Lord Chancellor (or, in Scotland, the Secretary of State) may determine.

6.1941.20 [20A Procedure for applying for a stay of a decision pending an appeal]

[(1) This rule applies where another enactment provides in any terms for the Upper Tribunal to stay or suspend, or to lift a stay or suspension of, a decision which is or may be the subject of an appeal to the Upper Tribunal ("the substantive decision") pending such appeal.

(2) A person who wishes the Upper Tribunal to decide whether the substantive decision should be stayed or suspended must make a written application to the Upper Tribunal which must include—

(a) the name and address of the person making the application;

(b) the name and address of any representative of that person;

(c) the address to which documents for that person should be sent or delivered;

(d) the name and address of any person who will be a respondent to the appeal;

(e) details of the substantive decision and any decision as to when that decision is to take effect, and copies of any written record of, or reasons for, those decisions; and

(f) the grounds on which the person making the application relies.

(3) In the case of an application under paragraph (2) for a stay of a decision of a traffic commissioner—

(a) the person making the application must notify the traffic commissioner when making the application;

(b) within 7 days of receiving notification of the application the traffic commissioner must send or deliver written reasons for refusing or withdrawing the stay—

(i) to the Upper Tribunal; and

(ii) to the person making the application, if the traffic commissioner has not already done so.

(4) If the Upper Tribunal grants a stay or suspension following an application under this rule—

(a) the Upper Tribunal may give directions as to the conduct of the appeal of the substantive decision; and

(b) the Upper Tribunal may, where appropriate, grant the stay or suspension subject to conditions.

(5) Unless the Upper Tribunal considers that there is good reason not to do so, the Upper Tribunal must send written notice of any decision made under this rule to each party.]

PART 3
[PROCEDURE FOR CASES IN] THE UPPER TRIBUNAL

6.1941.21 21 Application to the Upper Tribunal for permission to appeal

(1) . . .

(2) A person may apply to the Upper Tribunal for permission to appeal to the Upper Tribunal against a decision of another tribunal only if—

(a) they have made an application for permission to appeal to the tribunal which made the decision challenged; and

(b) that application has been refused or has not been admitted.

(3) An application for permission to appeal must be made in writing and received by the Upper Tribunal no later than—

(a) in the case of an application under section 4 of the Safeguarding Vulnerable Groups Act 2006, 3 months after the date on which written notice of the decision being challenged was sent to the appellant; or

(b) otherwise, a month after the date on which the tribunal that made the decision under challenge sent notice of its refusal of permission to appeal, or refusal to admit the application for permission to appeal, to the appellant.

(4) The application must state—

(a) the name and address of the appellant;

(b) the name and address of the representative (if any) of the appellant;

(c) an address where documents for the appellant may be sent or delivered;

(d) details (including the full reference) of the decision challenged;

(e) the grounds on which the appellant relies; and

(f) whether the appellant wants the application to be dealt with at a hearing.

(5) The appellant must provide with the application a copy of—

(a) any written record of the decision being challenged;

(b) any separate written statement of reasons for that decision; and

(c) if the application is for permission to appeal against a decision of another tribunal, the notice of refusal of permission to appeal, or notice of refusal to admit the application for permission to appeal, from that other tribunal.

(6) If the appellant provides the application to the Upper Tribunal later than the time required by paragraph (3) or by an extension of time allowed under rule 5(3)(a) (power to extend time)—

(a) the application must include a request for an extension of time and the reason why the application was not provided in time; and

(b) unless the Upper Tribunal extends time for the application under rule 5(3)(a) (power to extend time) the Upper Tribunal must not admit the application.

(7) If the appellant makes an application to the Upper Tribunal for permission to appeal against the decision of another tribunal, and that other tribunal refused to admit the appellant's application for permission to appeal because the application for permission or for a written statement of reasons was not made in time—

(a) the application to the Upper Tribunal for permission to appeal must include the reason why the application to the other tribunal for permission to appeal or for a written statement of reasons, as the case may be, was not made in time; and

(b) the Upper Tribunal must only admit the application if the Upper Tribunal considers that it is in the interests of justice for it to do so.

6.1941.22 22 Decision in relation to permission to appeal

(1) If the Upper Tribunal refuses permission to appeal, it must send written notice of the refusal and of the reasons for the refusal to the appellant.

(2) If the Upper Tribunal gives permission to appeal—

(a) the Upper Tribunal must send written notice of the permission, and of the reasons for any limitations or conditions on such permission, to each party;

(b) subject to any direction by the Upper Tribunal, the application for permission to appeal stands as the notice of appeal and the Upper Tribunal must send to each respondent a copy of the application for permission to appeal and any documents provided with it by the appellant; and

(c) the Upper Tribunal may, with the consent of the appellant and each respondent, determine the appeal without obtaining any further response.

[(3) Paragraph (4) applies where the Upper Tribunal, without a hearing, determines an application for permission to appeal—

(a) against a decision of—

(i) the Tax Chamber of the First-tier Tribunal;

(ii) the Health, Education and Social Care Chamber of the First-tier Tribunal;

[(iia) the General Regulatory Chamber of the First-tier Tribunal;]

(iii) the Mental Health Review Tribunal for Wales; or

(iv) the Special Educational Needs Tribunal for Wales; or

(b) under section 4 of the Safeguarding Vulnerable Groups Act 2006.]

(4) In the circumstances set out at paragraph (3) the appellant may apply for the decision to be reconsidered at a hearing if the Upper Tribunal—

(a) refuses permission to appeal; or

(b) gives permission to appeal on limited grounds or subject to conditions.

(5) An application under paragraph (4) must be made in writing and received by the Upper Tribunal within 14 days after the date on which the Upper Tribunal sent written notice of its decision regarding the application to the appellant.

6.1941.23 23 Notice of appeal

[(1) This rule applies—

(a) to proceedings on appeal to the Upper Tribunal for which permission to appeal is not required, except proceedings to which rule 26A applies;

(b) if another tribunal has given permission for a party to appeal to the Upper Tribunal; or

(c) subject to any other direction by the Upper Tribunal, if the Upper Tribunal has given permission to appeal and has given a direction that the application for permission to appeal does not stand as the notice of appeal.

(2) The appellant must provide a notice of appeal to the Upper Tribunal so that it is received within 1 month after—

(a) the date that the tribunal that gave permission to appeal sent notice of such permission to the appellant; or

(b) if permission to appeal is not required, the date on which notice of decision to which the appeal relates was sent to the appellant.]

(3) The notice of appeal must include the information listed in rule 21(4)(a) to (e) (content of the application for permission to appeal) and, where the Upper Tribunal has given permission to appeal, the Upper Tribunal's case reference.

(4) If another tribunal has granted permission to appeal, the appellant must provide with the notice of appeal a copy of—

(a) any written record of the decision being challenged;

(b) any separate written statement of reasons for that decision; and

(c) the notice of permission to appeal.

(5) If the appellant provides the notice of appeal to the Upper Tribunal later than the time required by paragraph (2) or by an extension of time allowed under rule 5(3)(a) (power to extend time)—

(a) the notice of appeal must include a request for an extension of time and the reason why the notice was not provided in time; and

(b) unless the Upper Tribunal extends time for the notice of appeal under rule 5(3)(a) (power to extend time) the Upper Tribunal must not admit the notice of appeal.

[(6) When the Upper Tribunal receives the notice of appeal it must send a copy of the notice and any accompanying documents—

(a) to each respondent; or

(b) in an appeal against the decision of a traffic commissioner, to—

(i) the traffic commissioner;

(ii) the appropriate national authority; and

(iii) in a case relating to the detention of a vehicle, the authorised person.]

6.1941.24 24 Response to the notice of appeal

[(1) This rule and rule 25 do not apply to an appeal against a decision of a traffic commissioner, in respect of which Schedule 1 makes alternative provision.

(1A) Subject to any direction given by the Upper Tribunal, a respondent may provide a response to a notice of appeal.]

(2) Any response provided under paragraph [(1A)] must be in writing and must be sent or delivered to the Upper Tribunal so that it is received—

(a) [if an application for permission to appeal] stands as the notice of appeal, no later than 1 month after the date on which the Upper Tribunal sent notice that it had granted permission to appeal to the respondent; or

(b) in any other case, no later than 1 month after the date on which the Upper Tribunal sent a copy of the notice of appeal to the respondent.

(3) The response must state—

(a) the name and address of the respondent;
(b) the name and address of the representative (if any) of the respondent;
(c) an address where documents for the respondent may be sent or delivered;
(d) whether the respondent opposes the appeal;
(e) the grounds on which the respondent relies, including [(in the case of an appeal against the decision of another tribunal)] any grounds on which the respondent was unsuccessful in the proceedings which are the subject of the appeal, but intends to rely in the appeal; and
(f) whether the respondent wants the case to be dealt with at a hearing.

(4) If the respondent provides the response to the Upper Tribunal later than the time required by paragraph (2) or by an extension of time allowed under rule 5(3)(a) (power to extend time), the response must include a request for an extension of time and the reason why the [response] was not provided in time.

(5) When the Upper Tribunal receives the response it must send a copy of the response and any accompanying documents to the appellant and each other party.

6.1941.25 25 Appellant's reply

(1) Subject to any direction given by the Upper Tribunal, the appellant may provide a reply to any response provided under rule 24 (response to the notice of appeal).

(2) Any reply provided under paragraph (1) must be in writing and must be sent or delivered to the Upper Tribunal so that it is received within one month after the date on which the Upper Tribunal sent a copy of the response to the appellant.

(3) When the Upper Tribunal receives the reply it must send a copy of the reply and any accompanying documents to each respondent.

PART 4
JUDICIAL REVIEW PROCEEDINGS IN THE UPPER TRIBUNAL

6.1941.26 27 Application of this Part to judicial review proceedings transferred to the Upper Tribunal

(1) When a court transfers judicial review proceedings to the Upper Tribunal, the Upper Tribunal—
(a) must notify each party in writing that the proceedings have been transferred to the Upper Tribunal; and
(b) must give directions as to the future conduct of the proceedings.

(2) The directions given under paragraph (1)(b) may modify or disapply for the purposes of the proceedings any of the provisions of the following rules in this Part.

(3) In proceedings transferred from the Court of Session under section 20(1) of the 2007 Act, the directions given under paragraph (1)(b) must—
(a) if the Court of Session did not make a first order specifying the required intimation, service and advertisement of the petition, state the Upper Tribunal's requirements in relation to those matters;
(b) state whether the Upper Tribunal will consider summary dismissal of the proceedings; and
(c) where necessary, modify or disapply provisions relating to permission in the following rules in this Part.

6.1941.27 28 Applications for permission to bring judicial review proceedings

(1) A person seeking permission to bring judicial review proceedings before the Upper Tribunal under section 16 of the 2007 Act must make a written application to the Upper Tribunal for such permission.

(2) Subject to paragraph (3), an application under paragraph (1) must be made promptly and, unless any other enactment specifies a shorter time limit, must be sent or delivered to the Upper Tribunal so that it is received no later than 3 months after the date of the decision[, action or omission] to which the application relates.

(3) An application for permission to bring judicial review proceedings challenging a decision of the First-tier Tribunal may be made later than the time required by paragraph (2) if it is made within 1 month after the date on which the First-tier Tribunal sent—

(a) written reasons for the decision; or

(b) notification that an application for the decision to be set aside has been unsuccessful, provided that that application was made in time.

(4) The application must state—

(a) the name and address of the applicant, the respondent and any other person whom the applicant considers to be an interested party;

(b) the name and address of the applicant's representative (if any);

(c) an address where documents for the applicant may be sent or delivered;

(d) details of the decision challenged (including the date, the full reference and the identity of the decision maker);

(e) that the application is for permission to bring judicial review proceedings;

(f) the outcome that the applicant is seeking; and

(g) the facts and grounds on which the applicant relies.

(5) If the application relates to proceedings in a court or tribunal, the application must name as an interested party each party to those proceedings who is not the applicant or a respondent.

(6) The applicant must send with the application—

(a) a copy of any written record of the decision in the applicant's possession or control; and

(b) copies of any other documents in the applicant's possession or control on which the applicant intends to rely.

(7) If the applicant provides the application to the Upper Tribunal later than the time required by paragraph (2) or (3) or by an extension of time allowed under rule 5(3)(a) (power to extend time)—

(a) the application must include a request for an extension of time and the reason why the application was not provided in time; and

(b) unless the Upper Tribunal extends time for the application under rule 5(3)(a) (power to extend time) the Upper Tribunal must not admit the application.

(8) When the Upper Tribunal receives the application it must send a copy of the application and any accompanying documents to each person named in the application as a respondent or interested party.

6.1941.28 29 Acknowledgment of service

(1) A person who is sent a copy of an application for permission under rule 28(8) (application for permission to bring judicial review proceedings) and wishes to take part in the proceedings must send or deliver to the Upper Tribunal an acknowledgment of service so that it is received no later than 21 days after the date on which the Upper Tribunal sent a copy of the application to that person.

(2) An acknowledgment of service under paragraph (1) must be in writing and state—

(a) whether the person intends to [support or] oppose the application for permission;

(b) their grounds for any [support or] opposition under sub-paragraph (a), or any other submission or information which they consider may assist the Upper Tribunal; and

(c) the name and address of any other person not named in the application as a respondent or interested party whom the person providing the acknowledgment considers to be an interested party.

(3) A person who is sent a copy of an application for permission under rule 28(8) but does not provide an acknowledgment of service may not take part in the application for permission, but may take part in the subsequent proceedings if the application is successful.

6.1941.29 30 Decision on permission or summary dismissal, and reconsideration of permission or summary dismissal at a hearing

(1) The Upper Tribunal must send to the applicant, each respondent and any other person who provided an acknowledgment of service to the Upper Tribunal, and may send to any other person who may have an interest in the proceedings, written notice of—

(a) its decision in relation to the application for permission; and

(b) the reasons for any refusal of the application, or any limitations or conditions on permission.

(2) In proceedings transferred from the Court of Session under section 20(1) of the 2007 Act, where the Upper Tribunal has considered whether summarily to dismiss of the proceedings, the Upper Tribunal must send to the applicant and each respondent, and may send to any other person who may have an interest in the proceedings, written notice of—

(a) its decision in relation to the summary dismissal of proceedings; and

(b) the reasons for any decision summarily to dismiss part or all of the proceedings, or any limitations or conditions on the continuation of such proceedings.

(3) Paragraph (4) applies where the Upper Tribunal, without a hearing—

(a) determines an application for permission to bring judicial review proceedings and either refuses permission, or gives permission on limited grounds or subject to conditions; or

(b) in proceedings transferred from the Court of Session, summarily dismisses part or all of the proceedings, or imposes any limitations or conditions on the continuation of such proceedings.

(4) In the circumstances specified in paragraph (3) the applicant may apply for the decision to be reconsidered at a hearing.

(5) An application under paragraph (4) must be made in writing and must be sent or delivered to the Upper Tribunal so that it is received within 14 days after the date on which the Upper Tribunal sent written notice of its decision regarding the application to the applicant.

6.1941.30 31 Responses

(1) Any person to whom the Upper Tribunal has sent notice of the grant of permission under rule 30(1) (notification of decision on permission), and who wishes to contest the application or support it on additional grounds, must provide detailed grounds for contesting or supporting the application to the Upper Tribunal.

(2) Any detailed grounds must be provided in writing and must be sent or delivered to the Upper Tribunal so that they are received not more than 35 days after the Upper Tribunal sent notice of the grant of permission under rule 30(1).

6.1941.31 32 Applicant seeking to rely on additional grounds

The applicant may not rely on any grounds, other than those grounds on which the applicant obtained permission for the judicial review proceedings, without the consent of the Upper Tribunal.

6.1941.32 33 Right to make representations

Each party and, with the permission of the Upper Tribunal, any other person, may—

(a) submit evidence, except at the hearing of an application for permission;

(b) make representations at any hearing which they are entitled to attend; and

(c) make written representations in relation to a decision to be made without a hearing.

PART 5
HEARINGS

6.1941.33 34 Decision with or without a hearing

(1) Subject to paragraph (2), the Upper Tribunal may make any decision without a hearing.

(2) The Upper Tribunal must have regard to any view expressed by a party when deciding whether to hold a hearing to consider any matter, and the form of any such hearing.

6.1941.34 35 Entitlement to attend a hearing

[(1)] Subject to rule 37(4) (exclusion of a person from a hearing), each party is entitled to attend a hearing.

[(2) In a national security certificate appeal the relevant Minister is entitled to attend any hearing.]

6.1941.35 36 Notice of hearings

(1) The Upper Tribunal must give each party entitled to attend a hearing reasonable notice of the time and place of the hearing (including any adjourned or postponed hearing) and any change to the time and place of the hearing.

(2) The period of notice under paragraph (1) must be at least 14 days except that—

(a) in applications for permission to bring judicial review proceedings, the period of notice must be at least 2 working days; and

(b) the Upper Tribunal may give shorter notice—

(i) with the parties' consent; or

(ii) in urgent or exceptional cases.

6.1941.36 37 Public and private hearings

(1) Subject to the following paragraphs, all hearings must be held in public.

(2) The Upper Tribunal may give a direction that a hearing, or part of it, is to be held in private.

[(2A) In a national security certificate appeal, the Upper Tribunal must have regard to its duty under rule 14(10) (no disclosure of information contrary to the interests of national security) when considering whether to give a direction that a hearing, or part of it, is to be held in private.]

(3) Where a hearing, or part of it, is to be held in private, the Upper Tribunal may determine who is entitled to attend the hearing or part of it.

(4) The Upper Tribunal may give a direction excluding from any hearing, or part of it—

(a) any person whose conduct the Upper Tribunal considers is disrupting or is likely to disrupt the hearing;

(b) any person whose presence the Upper Tribunal considers is likely to prevent another person from giving evidence or making submissions freely;

(c) any person who the Upper Tribunal considers should be excluded in order to give effect to [the requirement at rule 14(11) (prevention of disclosure or publication of documents and information)]; . . .

(d) any person where the purpose of the hearing would be defeated by the attendance of that person[; or

(e) a person under the age of eighteen years].

(5) The Upper Tribunal may give a direction excluding a witness from a hearing until that witness gives evidence.

6.1941.37 38 Hearings in a party's absence

If a party fails to attend a hearing, the Upper Tribunal may proceed with the hearing if the Upper Tribunal—

(a) is satisfied that the party has been notified of the hearing or that reasonable steps have been taken to notify the party of the hearing; and

(b) considers that it is in the interests of justice to proceed with the hearing.

PART 6
DECISIONS

6.1941.38 39 Consent orders

(1) The Upper Tribunal may, at the request of the parties but only if it considers it appropriate, make a consent order disposing of the proceedings and making such other appropriate provision as the parties have agreed.

(2) Notwithstanding any other provision of these Rules, the Tribunal need not hold a hearing before making an order under paragraph (1) . . .

6.1941.39 40 Decisions

(1) The Upper Tribunal may give a decision orally at a hearing.

(2) . . . the Upper Tribunal must provide to each party as soon as reasonably practicable after making a decision which finally disposes of all issues in the proceedings (except a decision under Part 7)—

(a) a decision notice stating the Tribunal's decision; and

(b) notification of any rights of review or appeal against the decision and the time and manner in which such rights of review or appeal may be exercised.

(3) [Subject to rule [14(11) (prevention of disclosure or publication of documents and information)],] the Upper Tribunal must provide written reasons for its decision with a decision notice provided under paragraph (2)(a) unless—

(a) the decision was made with the consent of the parties; or

(b) the parties have consented to the Upper Tribunal not giving written reasons.

(4) The [Upper] Tribunal may provide written reasons for any decision to which paragraph (2) does not apply.

[(5) In a national security certificate appeal, when the Upper Tribunal provides a notice or reasons to the parties under this rule, it must also provide the notice or reasons to the relevant Minister and the Information Commissioner, if they are not parties.]

PART 7
CORRECTING, SETTING ASIDE, REVIEWING AND APPEALING DECISIONS OF THE UPPER TRIBUNAL

6.1941.40 41 Interpretation

In this Part—

"appeal"[, except in rule 44(2) (application for permission to appeal),] means the exercise of a right of appeal under section 13 of the 2007 Act; and

"review" means the review of a decision by the Upper Tribunal under section 10 of the 2007 Act.

6.1941.41 42 Clerical mistakes and accidental slips or omissions

The Upper Tribunal may at any time correct any clerical mistake or other accidental slip or omission in a decision or record of a decision by—

(a) sending notification of the amended decision, or a copy of the amended record, to all parties; and

(b) making any necessary amendment to any information published in relation to the decision or record.

6.1941.42 43 Setting aside a decision which disposes of proceedings

(1) The Upper Tribunal may set aside a decision which disposes of proceedings, or part of such a decision, and re-make the decision or the relevant part of it, if—

(a) the Upper Tribunal considers that it is in the interests of justice to do so; and

(b) one or more of the conditions in paragraph (2) are satisfied.

(2) The conditions are—

(a) a document relating to the proceedings was not sent to, or was not received at an appropriate time by, a party or a party's representative;

(b) a document relating to the proceedings was not sent to the Upper Tribunal at an appropriate time;

(c) a party, or a party's representative, was not present at a hearing related to the proceedings; or

(d) there has been some other procedural irregularity in the proceedings.

(3) a party applying for a decision, or part of a decision, to be set aside under paragraph (1) must make a written application to the Upper Tribunal so that it is received no later than 1 month after the date on which the Tribunal sent notice of the decision to the party.

6.1941.43 44 Application for permission to appeal

(1) A person seeking permission to appeal must make a written application to the Upper Tribunal for permission to appeal.

(2) Paragraph (3) applies to an application under paragraph (1) in respect of a decision—

(a) on an appeal against a decision in a social security and child support case (as defined in the Tribunal Procedure (First-tier Tribunal) (Social Entitlement Chamber) Rules 2008);

(b) on an appeal against a decision in proceedings in the War Pensions and Armed Forces Compensation Chamber of the First-tier Tribunal; . . .

[(ba) on an appeal against a decision of a Pensions Appeal Tribunal for Scotland or Northern Ireland; or]

(c) in proceedings under the Forfeiture Act 1982.

(3) Where this paragraph applies, the application must be sent or delivered to the Upper Tribunal so that it is received within 3 months after the date on which the Upper Tribunal sent to the person making the application—

(a) written notice of the decision;

(b) notification of amended reasons for, or correction of, the decision following a review; or

(c) notification that an application for the decision to be set aside has been unsuccessful.

(4) Where paragraph (3) does not apply, an application under paragraph (1) must be sent or delivered to the Upper Tribunal so that it is received within 1 month after the latest of the dates on which the Upper Tribunal sent to the person making the application—

(a) written reasons for the decision;

(b) notification of amended reasons for, or correction of, the decision following a review; or

(c) notification that an application for the decision to be set aside has been unsuccessful.

(5) The date in paragraph (3)(c) or (4)(c) applies only if the application for the decision to be set aside was made within the time stipulated in rule 43 (setting aside a

decision which disposes of proceedings) or any extension of that time granted by the Upper Tribunal.

(6) If the person seeking permission to appeal provides the application to the Upper Tribunal later than the time required by paragraph (3) or (4), or by any extension of time under rule 5(3)(a) (power to extend time)—

(a) the application must include a request for an extension of time and the reason why the application notice was not provided in time; and

(b) unless the Upper Tribunal extends time for the application under rule 5(3)(a) (power to extend time) the Upper Tribunal must refuse the application.

(7) An application under paragraph (1) must—

(a) identify the decision of the Tribunal to which it relates;

(b) identify the alleged error or errors of law in the decision; and

(c) state the result the party making the application is seeking.

6.1941.44 45 Upper Tribunal's consideration of application for permission to appeal

(1) On receiving an application for permission to appeal the Upper Tribunal may review the decision in accordance with rule 46 (review of a decision), but may only do so if—

(a) when making the decision the Upper Tribunal overlooked a legislative provision or binding authority which could have had a material effect on the decision; or

(b) since the Upper Tribunal's decision, a court has made a decision which is binding on the Upper Tribunal and which, had it been made before the Upper Tribunal's decision, could have had a material effect on the decision.

(2) If the Upper Tribunal decides not to review the decision, or reviews the decision and decides to take no action in relation to the decision or part of it, the Upper Tribunal must consider whether to give permission to appeal in relation to the decision or that part of it.

(3) The Upper Tribunal must send a record of its decision to the parties as soon as practicable.

(4) If the Upper Tribunal refuses permission to appeal it must send with the record of its decision—

(a) a statement of its reasons for such refusal; and

(b) notification of the right to make an application to the relevant appellate court for permission to appeal and the time within which, and the method by which, such application must be made.

(5) The Upper Tribunal may give permission to appeal on limited grounds, but must comply with paragraph (4) in relation to any grounds on which it has refused permission.

6.1941.45 46 Review of a decision

(1) The Upper Tribunal may only undertake a review of a decision—

(a) pursuant to rule 45(1) (review on an application for permission to appeal); or

(b) pursuant to rule 47 (reviews of decisions in proceedings under the Forfeiture Act 1982).

(2) The Upper Tribunal must notify the parties in writing of the outcome of any review and of any rights of review or appeal in relation to the outcome.

(3) If the Upper Tribunal decides to take any action in relation to a decision following a review without first giving every party an opportunity to make representations, the notice under paragraph (2) must state that any party that did not have an opportunity to make representations may apply for such action to be set aside

and for the decision to be reviewed again.

GAMBLING ACT 2005 (LIMITS ON PRIZE GAMING) REGULATIONS 2009

(SI 2009/1272)

Made . . . .*19th May 2009*
Laid before Parliament . . . .*20th May 2009*
Coming into force . . . .*11th June 2009*

The Secretary of State makes the following Regulations in exercise of the power conferred by sections 293(2) and (4) and 355(1) of the Gambling Act 2005.

6.1942 1 Citation, commencement and interpretation

(1) These Regulations may be cited as the Gambling Act 2005 (Limits on Prize Gaming) Regulations 2009 and come into force on 11th June 2009.

(2) In these Regulations "the Act" means the Gambling Act 2005.

6.1943 2 Limits on participation fees

(1) For the purposes of section 293(2) of the Act the following limits are prescribed in respect of participation fees for prize gaming—

(a) the participation fee charged for any one chance to win a prize in a game must not exceed £1;

(b) the aggregate amount of the participation fees charged for any one chance to win a prize in a game must not exceed £500.

(2) The limit referred to in paragraph (1)(a) applies even if the chance provides the opportunity to win more than one prize.

6.1944 3 Limits on prizes

(1) For the purposes of section 293(4)(a) of the Act the prescribed amount in respect of—

(a) any one prize is £70; and

(b) the aggregate of the prizes is £500.

(2) For the purposes of section 293(4)(b) of the Act the prescribed value in respect of—

(a) any one prize which is money is £70; and

(b) the aggregate of the prizes is £500.

6.1945 4 Revocation

The Gambling Act 2005 (Limits on Prize Gaming) Regulations 2007 are revoked.

GAMBLING ACT 2005 (GAMING TABLES IN CASINOS) (DEFINITIONS) REGULATIONS 2009

(SI 2009/1970)

Made . . . .*16th July 2009*
Laid before Parliament . . . .*20th July 2009*
Coming into force . . . .*11th August 2009*

The Secretary of State makes the following Regulations in exercise of the powers conferred by sections 172(6) and 355(1) of the Gambling Act 2005 ("the Act").

6.1946 1 Citation, commencement and interpretation

(1) These Regulations may be cited as the Gambling Act 2005 (Gaming Tables in Casinos) (Definitions) Regulations 2009 and come into force on 11th August 2009.

(2) In these Regulations "wholly automated gaming table" means an apparatus that is designed or adapted to enable individuals to play a real game of chance where—

(a) the design or adaptation is such that the apparatus is not required to be controlled or operated by an individual employed or concerned in arranging for others to play the game; and

(b) the apparatus is not designed or adapted for use in connection with a game the arrangements for which are controlled or operated by an individual.

6.1947 2 Gaming table: definition

A wholly automated gaming table is not a "gaming table" for the purposes of section 172(3) to (5) of the Act.

6.1948 3 Requirements for gaming tables to be treated as being used in a casino

For the purposes of section 172(3) to (5) of the Act, a gaming table is to be treated as being used in a casino at a particular time only if it is—

(a) being used to play a casino game at that time; or

(b) available at that time to be used for that purpose.

TRIBUNAL PROCEDURE (FIRST-TIER TRIBUNAL) (GENERAL REGULATORY CHAMBER) RULES 2009

(SI 2009/1976)

Made ....*16th July 2009*
Laid before Parliament ....*21st July 2009*
Coming into force ....*1st September 2009*

---

[1] Reproduced as amended.

After consulting in accordance with paragraph 28(1) of Schedule 5 to the Tribunals, Courts and Enforcement Act 2007, the Tribunal Procedure Committee has made the following Rules in exercise of the power conferred by sections 9(3), 22 and 29(3) and (4) of, and Schedule 5 to, that Act.
The Lord Chancellor has allowed the Rules in accordance with paragraph 28(3) of Schedule 5 to the Tribunals, Courts and Enforcement Act 2007.

PART 1
INTRODUCTION

6.1949 1 Citation, commencement, application and interpretation

(1) These Rules may be cited as the Tribunal Procedure (First-tier Tribunal) (General Regulatory Chamber) Rules 2009 and come into force on 1st September 2009.

(2) These Rules apply to proceedings before the Tribunal which have been allocated to the General Regulatory Chamber by the First-tier Tribunal and Upper Tribunal (Chambers) Order 2008.

(3) In these Rules—

"the 2007 Act" means the Tribunals, Courts and Enforcement Act 2007;

"appellant" means a person who—

(a) commences Tribunal proceedings, whether by making an appeal, an application, a claim, a complaint, a reference or otherwise; or

(b) is added or substituted as an appellant under rule 9 (addition, substitution and removal of parties);

"charities case" means an appeal or application in respect of a decision, order or direction of the Charity Commission, or a reference under Schedule 1D of the Charities Act 1993;

"document" means anything in which information is recorded in any form, and an obligation under these Rules or any practice direction or direction to provide or allow access to a document or a copy of a document for any purpose means, unless the Tribunal directs otherwise, an obligation to provide or allow access to such document or copy in a legible form or in a form which can be readily made into a legible form;

"General Regulatory Chamber" means the General Regulatory Chamber of the First-tier Tribunal established by the First-tier Tribunal and Upper Tribunal (Chambers) Order 2008;

"hearing" means an oral hearing and includes a hearing conducted in whole or in part by video link, telephone or other means of instantaneous two-way electronic communication;

"notice of appeal" means a document which starts proceedings;

"party" means—

(a) a person who is an appellant or a respondent;

(b) if the proceedings have been concluded, a person who was an appellant or a respondent when the Tribunal finally disposed of all issues in the proceedings;

"practice direction" means a direction given under section 23 of the 2007 Act;

"respondent" means—

(a) in proceedings appealing against or challenging a decision, direction or order, the person who made the decision, direction or order appealed against or challenged;

(b) a person against whom an appellant otherwise brings proceedings; or

(c) a person added or substituted as a respondent under rule 9 (addition, substitution and removal of parties);

"transport case" means proceedings under the Road Traffic Act 1988, the Road Traffic Offenders Act 1988, the Greater London Authority Act 1999, the Postal Services Act 2000, the Vehicle Drivers (Certificates of Professional Competence) Regulations 2007 and the European Communities (Recognition of Professional Qualifications) Regulations 2007;

"Tribunal" means the First-tier Tribunal.

6.1950 2 Overriding objective and parties' obligation to co-operate with the tribunal

(1) The overriding objective of these Rules is to enable the Tribunal to deal with cases fairly and justly.

(2) Dealing with a case fairly and justly includes—

(a) dealing with the case in ways which are proportionate to the importance of the case, the complexity of the issues, the anticipated costs and the resources of the parties;
(b) avoiding unnecessary formality and seeking flexibility in the proceedings;
(c) ensuring, so far as practicable, that the parties are able to participate fully in the proceedings;
(d) using any special expertise of the Tribunal effectively; and
(e) avoiding delay, so far as compatible with proper consideration of the issues.

(3) The Tribunal must seek to give effect to the overriding objective when it—
(a) exercises any power under these Rules; or
(b) interprets any rule or practice direction.

(4) Parties must—
(a) help the Tribunal to further the overriding objective; and
(b) co-operate with the Tribunal generally.

6.1951 3 Alternative dispute resolution and arbitration

(1) The Tribunal should seek, where appropriate—
(a) to bring to the attention of the parties the availability of any appropriate alternative procedure for the resolution of the dispute; and
(b) if the parties wish, and provided that it is compatible with the overriding objective, to facilitate the use of the procedure.

(2) Part 1 of the Arbitration Act 1996 does not apply to proceedings before the Tribunal.

PART 2
GENERAL POWERS AND PROVISIONS

6.1952 4 Delegation to staff

(1) Staff appointed under section 40(1) of the 2007 Act (tribunal staff and services) may, with the approval of the Senior President of Tribunals, carry out functions of a judicial nature permitted or required to be done by the Tribunal.

(2) The approval referred to at paragraph (1) may apply generally to the carrying out of specified functions by members of staff of a specified description in specified circumstances.

(3) Within 14 days after the date that the Tribunal sends notice of a decision made by a member of staff pursuant to an approval under paragraph (1) to a party, that party may apply in writing to the Tribunal for that decision to be considered afresh by a judge.

6.1953 5 Case management powers

(1) Subject to the provisions of the 2007 Act and any other enactment, the Tribunal may regulate its own procedure.

(2) The Tribunal may give a direction in relation to the conduct or disposal of proceedings at any time, including a direction amending, suspending or setting aside an earlier direction.

(3) In particular, and without restricting the general powers in paragraphs (1) and (2), the Tribunal may—
(a) extend or shorten the time for complying with any rule, practice direction or direction, unless such extension or shortening would conflict with a provision of another enactment containing a time limit;
(b) consolidate or hear together two or more sets of proceedings or parts of proceedings raising common issues, or treat a case as a lead case (whether under rule 18 or otherwise);
(c) permit or require a party to amend a document;

(d) permit or require a party or another person to provide documents, information or submissions to the Tribunal or a party;
(e) deal with an issue in the proceedings as a preliminary issue;
(f) hold a hearing to consider any matter, including a case management issue;
(g) decide the form of any hearing;
(h) adjourn or postpone a hearing;
(i) require a party to produce a bundle for a hearing;
(j) stay (or, in Scotland, sist) proceedings;
(k) transfer proceedings to another court or tribunal if that other court or tribunal has jurisdiction in relation to the proceedings and—
    (i) because of a change of circumstances since the proceedings were started, the Tribunal no longer has jurisdiction in relation to the proceedings; or
    (ii) the Tribunal considers that the other court or tribunal is a more appropriate forum for the determination of the case;
(l) suspend the effect of its own decision pending the determination by the Tribunal or the Upper Tribunal of an application for permission to appeal against, and any appeal or review of, that decision.

6.1954 6 Procedure for applying for and giving directions

(1) The Tribunal may give a direction on the application of one or more of the parties or on its own initiative.

(2) An application for a direction may be made—
(a) by sending or delivering a written application to the Tribunal; or
(b) orally during the course of a hearing.

(3) An application for a direction must include the reason for making that application.

(4) Unless the Tribunal considers that there is good reason not to do so, the Tribunal must send written notice of any direction to every party and to any other person affected by the direction.

(5) If a party or any other person sent notice of the direction under paragraph (4) wishes to challenge a direction which the Tribunal has given, they may do so by applying for another direction which amends, suspends or sets aside the first direction.

6.1955 7 Failure to comply with rules, practice directions or tribunal directions

(1) An irregularity resulting from a failure to comply with any provision of these Rules, a practice direction or a direction does not of itself render void the proceedings or any step taken in the proceedings.

(2) If a party has failed to comply with a requirement in these Rules, a practice direction or a direction, the Tribunal may take such action as the Tribunal considers just, which may include—
(a) waiving the requirement;
(b) requiring the failure to be remedied;
(c) exercising its power under rule 8 (striking out a party's case);
(d) exercising its power under paragraph (3); or
(e) barring or restricting a party's participation in the proceedings.

(3) The Tribunal may refer to the Upper Tribunal, and ask the Upper Tribunal to exercise its power under section 25 of the 2007 Act in relation to, any failure by a person to comply with a requirement imposed by the Tribunal—
(a) to attend at any place for the purpose of giving evidence;
(b) otherwise to make themselves available to give evidence;
(c) to swear an oath in connection with the giving of evidence;
(d) to give evidence as a witness;
(e) to produce a document; or

(f) to facilitate the inspection of a document or any other thing (including any premises).

6.1956 8 Striking out a party's case

(1) The proceedings, or the appropriate part of them, will automatically be struck out if the appellant has failed to comply with a direction that stated that failure by the appellant to comply with the direction would lead to the striking out of the proceedings or that part of them.

(2) The Tribunal must strike out the whole or a part of the proceedings if the Tribunal—

(a) does not have jurisdiction in relation to the proceedings or that part of them; and

(b) does not exercise its power under rule 5(3)(k)(i) (transfer to another court or tribunal) in relation to the proceedings or that part of them.

(3) The Tribunal may strike out the whole or a part of the proceedings if—

(a) the appellant has failed to comply with a direction which stated that failure by the appellant to comply with the direction could lead to the striking out of the proceedings or part of them;

(b) the appellant has failed to co-operate with the Tribunal to such an extent that the Tribunal cannot deal with the proceedings fairly and justly; or

(c) the Tribunal considers there is no reasonable prospect of the appellant's case, or part of it, succeeding.

(4) The Tribunal may not strike out the whole or a part of the proceedings under paragraph (2) or (3)(b) or (c) without first giving the appellant an opportunity to make representations in relation to the proposed striking out.

(5) If the proceedings, or part of them, have been struck out under paragraph (1) or (3)(a), the appellant may apply for the proceedings, or part of them, to be reinstated.

(6) An application under paragraph (5) must be made in writing and received by the Tribunal within 28 days after the date on which the Tribunal sent notification of the striking out to that party.

(7) This rule applies to a respondent as it applies to an appellant except that—

(a) a reference to the striking out of the proceedings is to be read as a reference to the barring of the respondent from taking further part in the proceedings; and

(b) a reference to an application for the reinstatement of proceedings which have been struck out is to be read as a reference to an application for the lifting of the bar on the respondent from taking further part in the proceedings.

(8) If a respondent has been barred from taking further part in proceedings under this rule and that bar has not been lifted, the Tribunal need not consider any response or other submission made by that respondent, and may summarily determine any or all issues against that respondent.

6.1957 9 Addition, substitution and removal of parties

(1) The Tribunal may give a direction adding, substituting or removing a party as an appellant or a respondent.

(2) If the Tribunal gives a direction under paragraph (1) it may give such consequential directions as it considers appropriate.

(3) Any person who is not a party may apply to the Tribunal to be added or substituted as a party.

(4) If a person who is entitled to be a party to proceedings by virtue of another enactment applies to be added as a party, and any conditions applicable to that entitlement have been satisfied, the Tribunal must give a direction adding that person as a respondent or, if appropriate, as an appellant.

6.1958 10 Orders for costs

(1) The Tribunal may make an order in respect of costs (or, in Scotland, expenses) only—

(a) under section 29(4) of the 2007 Act (wasted costs);

(b) if the Tribunal considers that a party has acted unreasonably in bringing, defending or conducting the proceedings; or

(c) where the Charity Commission [or the Information Commissioner] is the respondent and a decision, direction or order of the Charity Commission [or the Information Commissioner] is the subject of the proceedings, if the Tribunal considers that the decision, direction or order was unreasonable.

(2) The Tribunal may make an order under paragraph (1) on an application or on its own initiative.

(3) A person making an application for an order under this rule must—

(a) send or deliver a written application to the Tribunal and to the person against whom it is proposed that the order be made; and

(b) send or deliver a schedule of the costs or expenses claimed with the application.

(4) An application for an order under paragraph (1) may be made at any time during the proceedings but may not be made later than 14 days after the date on which the Tribunal sends to the person making the application the decision notice recording the decision which finally disposes of all issues in the proceedings.

(5) The Tribunal may not make an order under paragraph (1) against a person ("the paying person") without first—

(a) giving that person an opportunity to make representations; and

(b) if the paying person is an individual, considering that person's financial means.

(6) The amount of costs or expenses to be paid under an order under paragraph (1) may be ascertained by—

(a) summary assessment by the Tribunal;

(b) agreement of a specified sum by the paying person and the person entitled to receive the costs or expenses ("the receiving person"); or

(c) assessment of the whole or a specified part of the costs or expenses incurred by the receiving person, if not agreed.

(7) Following an order under paragraph (6)(c) a party may apply—

(a) in England and Wales, to the county court for a detailed assessment of costs in accordance with the Civil Procedure Rules 1998 on the standard basis or, if specified in the order, on the indemnity basis;

(b) in Scotland, to the Auditor of the Court of Session for the taxation of the expenses according to the fees payable in the Court of Session; or

(c) in Northern Ireland, to the county court for the costs to be taxed.

6.1959 11 Representatives

(1) A party may appoint a representative (whether legally qualified or not) to represent that party in the proceedings.

(2) If a party appoints a representative, that party must send or deliver to the Tribunal and to each other party written notice of the representative's name and address.

(3) Anything permitted or required to be done by or provided to a party under these Rules, a practice direction or a direction may be done by or provided to the representative of that party except—

(a) signing a witness statement; or

(b) sending or delivering a notice under paragraph (2), if the representative is not [a person who, for the purposes of the Legal Services Act 2007, is an authorised person in relation to an activity which constitutes the exercise of a right of audience or the conduct of litigation within the meaning of that Act], an advocate or solicitor in Scotland or a barrister or solicitor in Northern Ireland.

(4) A person who receives due notice of the appointment of a representative—

(a) must provide to the representative any document which is required to be sent to the represented party, and need not provide that document to the represented party; and

(b) may assume that the representative is and remains authorised until receiving written notification to the contrary from the representative or the represented party.

(5) At a hearing a party may be accompanied by another person whose name and address has not been notified under paragraph (2) but who, with the permission of the Tribunal, may act as a representative or otherwise assist in presenting the party's case at the hearing.

(6) Paragraphs (2) to (4) do not apply to a person who accompanies a party under paragraph (5).

6.1960 12 Calculating time

(1) An act required by these Rules, a practice direction or a direction to be done on or by a particular day must be done before 5pm on that day.

(2) If the time specified by these Rules, a practice direction or a direction for doing any act ends on a day other than a working day, the act is done in time if it is done on the next working day.

(3) In this rule "working day" means any day except a Saturday or Sunday, Christmas Day, Good Friday or a bank holiday under section 1 of the Banking and Financial Dealings Act 1971.

6.1961 13 Sending and delivery of documents

(1) Any document to be provided to the Tribunal under these Rules, a practice direction or a direction must be—

(a) sent by prepaid post or by document exchange, or delivered by hand to the address specified for the proceedings;

(b) sent by fax to the number specified for the proceedings; or

(c) sent or delivered by such other method as the Tribunal may permit or direct.

(2) Subject to paragraph (3), if a party provides a fax number, email address or other details for the electronic transmission of documents to them, that party must accept delivery of documents by that method.

(3) If a party informs the Tribunal and all other parties that a particular form of communication, other than pre-paid post or delivery by hand, should not be used to provide documents to that party, that form of communication must not be so used.

(4) If the Tribunal or a party sends a document to a party or the Tribunal by email or any other electronic means of communication, the recipient may request that the sender provide a hard copy of the document to the recipient. The recipient must make such a request as soon as reasonably practicable after receiving the document electronically.

(5) The Tribunal and each party may assume that the address provided by a party or its representative is and remains the address to which documents should be sent or delivered until receiving written notification to the contrary.

6.1962 14 Prevention of disclosure or publication of documents and information

(1) The Tribunal may make an order prohibiting the disclosure or publication of—

(a) specified documents or information relating to the proceedings; or

(b) any matter likely to lead members of the public to identify any person whom the Tribunal considers should not be identified.

(2) The Tribunal may give a direction prohibiting the disclosure of a document or information to a person if—

(a) the Tribunal is satisfied that such disclosure would be likely to cause that person or some other person serious harm; and

(b) the Tribunal is satisfied, having regard to the interests of justice, that it is proportionate to give such a direction.

(3) If a party ("the first party") considers that the Tribunal should give a direction under paragraph (2) prohibiting the disclosure of a document or information to another party ("the second party"), the first party must—

(a) exclude the relevant document or information from any documents that will be provided to the second party; and

(b) provide to the Tribunal the excluded document or information, and the reason for its exclusion, so that the Tribunal may decide whether the document or information should be disclosed to the second party or should be the subject of a direction under paragraph (2).

(4) If the Tribunal gives a direction under paragraph (2) which prevents disclosure to a party who has appointed a representative, the Tribunal may give a direction that the documents or information be disclosed to that representative if the Tribunal is satisfied that—

(a) disclosure to the representative would be in the interests of the party; and

(b) the representative will act in accordance with paragraph (5).

(5) Documents or information disclosed to a representative in accordance with a direction under paragraph (4) must not be disclosed either directly or indirectly to any other person without the Tribunal's consent.

(6) The Tribunal may give a direction that certain documents or information must or may be disclosed to the Tribunal on the basis that the Tribunal will not disclose such documents or information to other persons, or specified other persons.

(7) A party making an application for a direction under paragraph (6) may withhold the relevant documents or information from other parties until the Tribunal has granted or refused the application.

(8) Unless the Tribunal considers that there is good reason not to do so, the Tribunal must send notice that a party has made an application for a direction under paragraph (6) to each other party.

(9) In a case involving matters relating to national security, the Tribunal must ensure that information is not disclosed contrary to the interests of national security.

(10) The Tribunal must conduct proceedings and record its decision and reasons appropriately so as not to undermine the effect of an order made under paragraph (1), a direction given under paragraph (2) or (6) or the duty imposed by paragraph (9).

6.1963 15 Disclosure, evidence and submissions

(1) Without restriction on the general powers in rule 5(1) and (2) (case management powers), the Tribunal may give directions as to—

(a) the exchange between parties of lists of documents which are relevant to the appeal, or relevant to particular issues, and the inspection of such documents;

(b) the provision by parties of statements of agreed matters;

(c) issues on which it requires evidence or submissions;

(d) the nature of the evidence or submissions it requires;

(e) whether the parties are permitted or required to provide expert evidence, and if so whether the parties must jointly appoint a single expert to provide such evidence;

(f) any limit on the number of witnesses whose evidence a party may put forward, whether in relation to a particular issue or generally;

(g) the manner in which any evidence or submissions are to be provided, which may include a direction for them to be given—

(i) orally at a hearing; or

(ii) by written submissions or witness statement; and

(h) the time at which any evidence or submissions are to be provided.

(2) The Tribunal may—

(a) admit evidence whether or not—

(i) the evidence would be admissible in a civil trial in [the United Kingdom]; or

(ii) the evidence was available to a previous decision maker; or

(b) exclude evidence that would otherwise be admissible where—

(i) the evidence was not provided within the time allowed by a direction or a practice direction;

(ii) the evidence was otherwise provided in a manner that did not comply with a direction or a practice direction; or

(iii) it would otherwise be unfair to admit the evidence.

(3) The Tribunal may consent to a witness giving, or require any witness to give, evidence on oath, and may administer an oath for that purpose.

6.1964 16 Summoning or citation of witnesses and orders to answer questions or produce documents

(1) On the application of a party or on its own initiative, the Tribunal may—

(a) by summons (or, in Scotland, citation) require any person to attend as a witness at a hearing at the time and place specified in the summons or citation; or

(b) order any person to answer any questions or produce any documents in that person's possession or control which relate to any issue in the proceedings.

(2) A summons or citation under paragraph (1)(a) must—

(a) give the person required to attend 14 days' notice of the hearing or such shorter period as the Tribunal may direct; and

(b) where the person is not a party, make provision for the person's necessary expenses of attendance to be paid, and state who is to pay them.

(3) No person may be compelled to give any evidence or produce any document that the person could not be compelled to give or produce on a trial of an action in a court of law in the part of the United Kingdom where the proceedings are due to be determined.

(4) A summons, citation or order under this rule must—

(a) state that the person on whom the requirement is imposed may apply to the Tribunal to vary or set aside the summons, citation or order, if they have not had an opportunity to object to it; and

(b) state the consequences of failure to comply with the summons, citation or order.

6.1965 17 Withdrawal

(1) Subject to paragraph (2)[, and, in the case of a withdrawal of a reference from an ethical standards officer, to the provisions of regulation 5 of the Case Tribunals (England) Regulations 2008], a party may give notice of the withdrawal of its case, or any part of it—

(a) at any time before a hearing to consider the disposal of the proceedings (or, if the Tribunal disposes of the proceedings without a hearing, before that disposal), by sending or delivering to the Tribunal a written notice of withdrawal; or

(b) orally at a hearing.

(2) Notice of withdrawal will not take effect unless the Tribunal consents to the withdrawal.

(3) A party who has withdrawn their case may apply to the Tribunal for the case to be reinstated.

(4) An application under paragraph (3) must be made in writing and be received by the Tribunal within 28 days after—

(a) the date on which the Tribunal received the notice under paragraph (1)(a); or

(b) the date of the hearing at which the case was withdrawn orally under paragraph (1)(b).

(5) The Tribunal must notify each party in writing of a withdrawal under this rule.

6.1966 18 Lead cases

(1) This rule applies if—

(a) two or more cases have been started before the Tribunal;

(b) in each such case the Tribunal has not made a decision disposing of the proceedings; and

(c) the cases give rise to common or related issues of fact or law.

(2) The Tribunal may give a direction—

(a) specifying one or more cases falling under paragraph (1) as a lead case or lead cases; and

(b) staying (or, in Scotland, sisting) the other cases falling under paragraph (1) ("the related cases").

(3) When the Tribunal makes a decision in respect of the common or related issues—

(a) the Tribunal must send a copy of that decision to each party in each of the related cases; and

(b) subject to paragraph (4), that decision shall be binding on each of those parties.

(4) Within 28 days after the date on which the Tribunal sent a copy of the decision to a party under paragraph (3)(a), that party may apply in writing for a direction that the decision does not apply to, and is not binding on the parties to, a particular related case.

(5) The Tribunal must give directions in respect of cases which are stayed [(or, in Scotland, sisted)] under paragraph (2)(b), providing for the disposal of or further directions in those cases.

(6) If the lead case or cases lapse or are withdrawn before the Tribunal makes a decision in respect of the common or related issues, the Tribunal must give directions as to—

(a) whether another case or other cases are to be specified as a lead case or lead cases; and

(b) whether any direction affecting the related cases should be set aside or amended.

6.1967 [18A Entry directions]

[(1) This rule applies to an appeal against a decision of, or notice issued by, the Information Commissioner.

(2) The Tribunal may give a direction ("an entry direction") requiring the occupier of any premises ("the occupier"), including a party, to permit entry to specified persons in order to allow such persons to—

(a) inspect, examine, operate or test relevant equipment;

(b) inspect, examine or test relevant materials.

(3) In paragraph (2)—

"relevant equipment" means equipment on the premises used or intended to be used in connection with the processing of personal data, or the storage, recording or deletion of other information; and

"relevant materials" means any documents and other materials on the premises connected with the processing of personal data, or the storage, recording or deletion of other information.

(4) A direction under paragraph (2) may not require a person to permit the inspection, examination or testing of any document or other materials which a person could not be compelled to produce in the trial of an action in a court of law in the part of the United Kingdom where the proceedings are due to be determined.

(5) A direction under paragraph (2) must specify the date and time at which the entry is to take place.

(6) The Tribunal must send a copy of the direction to the occupier so that it is received at least 7 days before the date specified for the entry.]

6.1967.1 [19A Power to stay or sist decision pending an appeal to, or decision by, the Tribunal]

[(1) The Tribunal may suspend the effect of a decision of the Gambling Commission (whether or not the decision has already taken effect) while an appeal against that decision—

(a) could be brought within the time required by these Rules; or

(b) has been brought and has not yet been finally determined or withdrawn

(2) In an appeal against a decision of the Immigration Services Commissioner, the Tribunal may direct that while the appeal is being dealt with the decision appealed against shall have—

(a) no effect; or

(b) only such limited effect as is specified in the direction.

(3) If the Tribunal makes a direction under paragraph (2), the Tribunal must consider any application by the Immigration Services Commissioner for the cancellation or variation of the direction.

(4) The Tribunal may vary or cancel a direction made under paragraph 9(3) of Schedule 5 to the Immigration and Asylum Act 1999 (interim directions pending the decision of the Tribunal).

6.1968 20 Procedure for applying for a stay of a decision pending an appeal

(1) This rule applies where [rule 19A or] another enactment provides in any terms for the Tribunal to stay [(or, in Scotland, sist)] or suspend, or to lift a stay [(or, in Scotland, sist)] or suspension of, a decision which is or may be the subject of an appeal to the Tribunal ("the substantive decision") pending such appeal, including an enactment which provides for—

(a) an appeal to the Tribunal against a decision not to stay [(or, in Scotland, sist)] the effect of the substantive decision pending an appeal; or

(b) an application to the Tribunal for an order that the substantive decision shall take effect immediately.

(2) A person who wishes the Tribunal to decide whether the substantive decision should be stayed [(or, in Scotland, sisted)] or suspended must make a written application to the Tribunal which must include—

(a) the name and address of the person making the application;

(b) the name and address of any representative of that person;

(c) the address to which documents for that person should be sent or delivered;

(d) the name and address of any person who will be a respondent to the appeal;

(e) details of the substantive decision and any decision as to when that decision is to take effect, and copies of any written record of, or reasons for, those decisions; and

(f) the grounds on which the person making the application relies.

(3) In the case of an appeal against a refusal by the registrar to stay [(or, in Scotland, sist)] a decision to refuse an application for registration as a driving instructor, an application under paragraph (2) must be sent or delivered to the Tribunal so that it is received within 10 days after the date on which the registrar sent notice of the refusal to the person making the application.

(4) If the Tribunal grants a stay [(or, in Scotland, sist)] or suspension following an application under this rule—

(a) the Tribunal may give directions as to the conduct of the appeal of the substantive decision; and

(b) the Tribunal may, where appropriate, grant the stay [(or, in Scotland, sist)] or suspension subject to conditions.

(5) Unless the Tribunal considers that there is good reason not to do so, the Tribunal must send written notice of any decision made under this rule to each party.

PART 3
PROCEEDINGS BEFORE THE TRIBUNAL

CHAPTER 1
BEFORE THE HEARING—CASES OTHER THAN CHARITIES CASES

6.1969 21 Application of this Chapter

This Chapter applies to cases other than charities cases.

6.1970 22 The notice of appeal

(1) An appellant must start proceedings before the Tribunal by sending or delivering to the Tribunal a notice of appeal so that it is received—

[(a) if a time for providing the notice of appeal is set out in paragraph (6), within that time];

(b) otherwise, within 28 days of the date on which notice of the act or decision to which the proceedings relate was sent to the appellant.

(2) The notice of appeal must include—

(a) the name and address of the appellant;

(b) the name and address of the appellant's representative (if any);

(c) an address where documents for the appellant may be sent or delivered;

(d) the name and address of any respondent;

(e) details of the decision or act, or failure to decide or act, to which the proceedings relate;

(f) the result the appellant is seeking;

(g) the grounds on which the appellant relies; and

(h) any further information or documents required by a practice direction.

(3) If the proceedings challenge a decision, the appellant must provide with the notice of appeal a copy of any written record of that decision, and any statement of reasons for that decision that the appellant has or can reasonably obtain.

(4) If the appellant provides the notice of appeal to the Tribunal later than the time required by paragraph (1) or by any extension of time under rule 5(3)(a) (power to extend time)—

(a) the notice of appeal must include a request for an extension of time and the reason why the notice of appeal was not provided in time; and

(b) unless the Tribunal extends time for the notice of appeal under rule 5(3)(a) (power to extend time) the Tribunal must not admit the notice of appeal.

(5) When the Tribunal receives the notice of appeal[, subject to rule 19(2) (national security appeals),] it must send a copy of the notice of appeal and any accompanying documents to each respondent.

[(6) The time for providing the notice of appeal referred to in paragraph (1)(a) is as follows—

(a) in an appeal against a refusal or revocation of a licence to give driving instruction, within 14 days of the date on which notice of the decision was sent to the appellant;

(b) in an appeal under section 28(4) of the Data Protection Act 1998 or section 60(1) of the Freedom of Information Act 2000 (including that subsection as applied and modified by regulation 18 of the Environmental Information Regulations 2004), at any time during the currency of the disputed certificate to which it relates;

(c) in an appeal under section 28(6) of the Data Protection Act 1998 or section 60(4) of the Freedom of Information Act 2000 (including that subsection as applied and modified by regulation 18 of the Environmental Information Regulations 2004), within 28 days of the date on which the claim was made that the certificate applies to the information or data in question;

(d) in the case of a reference from an ethical standards officer made in accordance with sections 63(3)(b) or section 65(4) of the Local Government Act 2000, within 28 days of the completion of the report made in accordance with sections 63(3)(a) and 65(1) of that Act; or

(e) in the case of a reference from a Standards Committee under the Local Government Act 2000 within 28 days of the meeting which decided to make such a reference.]

6.1971 23 The response

(1) Each respondent must send or deliver to the Tribunal a response to the notice of appeal so that it is received—

(a) in a transport case, within 14 days after the date on which the respondent received the notice of appeal;

(b) otherwise, within 28 days after the date on which the respondent received the notice of appeal.

(2) The response must include—

(a) the name and address of the respondent;

(b) the name and address of the respondent's representative (if any);

(c) an address where documents for the respondent may be sent or delivered;

(d) any further information or documents required by a practice direction or direction; and

(e) whether the respondent would be content for the case to be dealt with without a hearing if the Tribunal considers it appropriate.

(3) The response must include a statement as to whether the respondent opposes the appellant's case and, if so, any grounds for such opposition which are not contained in another document provided with the response.

(4) If the proceedings challenge a decision, the respondent must provide with the response a copy of any written record of that decision, and any statement of reasons for that decision, that the appellant did not provide with the notice of appeal and the respondent has or can reasonably obtain.

(5) If the respondent provides the response to the Tribunal later than the time required by paragraph (1) or by any extension of time under rule 5(3)(a) (power to extend time), the response must include a request for an extension of time and the reason why the response was not provided in time.

(6) In a transport case, the Tribunal must send a copy of the response and any accompanying documents to each other party.

(7) In any other case, the respondent must send or deliver a copy of the response and any accompanying documents to each other party at the same time as it provides the response to the Tribunal.

6.1972 24 Appellant's reply

(1) The appellant may make a written submission and provide further documents in reply to a response.

(2) Any reply and accompanying documents provided under paragraph (1) must be sent or delivered to the Tribunal within 14 days after the date on which the respondent or the Tribunal sent the response to the appellant.

(3) If the appellant provides the reply to the Tribunal later than the time required by paragraph (2) or by any extension of time under rule 5(3)(a) (power to extend time) the reply must include a request for an extension of time and the reason why the reply was not provided in time.

(4) In a transport case, the Tribunal must send a copy of any reply and any accompanying documents to each other party.

(5) In any other case, the appellant must send or deliver a copy of any reply and any accompanying documents to each other party at the same time as it provides the reply to the Tribunal.

CHAPTER 2
BEFORE THE HEARING—CHARITIES CASES

6.1973 32 Decision with or without a hearing

(1) Subject to paragraphs (2) and (3), the Tribunal must hold a hearing before making a decision which disposes of proceedings unless—

(a) each party has consented to the matter being determined without a hearing; and

(b) the Tribunal is satisfied that it can properly determine the issues without a hearing.

(2) This rule does not apply to a decision under Part 4 (correcting, setting aside, reviewing and appealing Tribunal decisions).

(3) The Tribunal may in any event dispose of proceedings without a hearing under rule 8 (striking out a party's case).

(4) Notwithstanding any other provision in these Rules, if the Tribunal holds a hearing to consider a preliminary issue, and following the disposal of that preliminary issue no further issue remains to be determined, the Tribunal may dispose of the proceedings without holding any further hearing.

6.1974 33 Entitlement to attend and take part in a hearing

(1) Subject to rule 35(4) (exclusion of a person from a hearing) each party is entitled to—

(a) attend any hearing that is held; and

(b) send written representations to the Tribunal and each other party prior to the hearing.

(2) The Tribunal may give a direction permitting or requesting any person to—

(a) attend and take part in a hearing to such extent as the Tribunal considers proper; or

(b) make written submissions in relation to a particular issue.

6.1975 34 Notice of hearings

(1) The Tribunal must give each person entitled, permitted or requested to attend a hearing (including any adjourned or postponed hearing) reasonable notice of the time and place of the hearing and any changes to the time and place of the hearing.

(2) The period of notice under paragraph (1) in relation to a hearing to consider disposal of the proceedings must be at least 14 days, except that the Tribunal may give shorter notice—

(a) with the parties' consent; or
(b) in urgent or exceptional circumstances.

6.1976 35 Public and private hearings

(1) Subject to the following paragraphs, all hearings must be held in public.

(2) The Tribunal may give a direction that a hearing, or part of it, is to be held in private.

(3) Where a hearing, or part of it, is to be held in private, the Tribunal may determine who is permitted to attend the hearing or part of it.

(4) The Tribunal may give a direction excluding from any hearing, or part of it—

(a) any person whose conduct the Tribunal considers is disrupting or is likely to disrupt the hearing;
(b) any person whose presence the Tribunal considers is likely to prevent another person from giving evidence or making submissions freely;
(c) any person who the Tribunal considers should be excluded in order to give effect to the requirement at rule 14(10) (prevention of disclosure or publication of documents and information); or
(d) any person where the purpose of the hearing would be defeated by the attendance of that person.

(5) The Tribunal may give a direction excluding a witness from a hearing until that witness gives evidence.

6.1977 36 Hearings in a party's absence

If a party fails to attend a hearing the Tribunal may proceed with the hearing if the Tribunal—

(a) is satisfied that the party has been notified of the hearing or that reasonable steps have been taken to notify the party of the hearing; and
(b) considers that it is in the interests of justice to proceed with the hearing.

CHAPTER 4
DECISIONS

6.1978 37 Consent orders

(1) The Tribunal may, at the request of the parties but only if it considers it appropriate, make a consent order disposing of the proceedings and making such other appropriate provision as the parties have agreed.

(2) Notwithstanding any other provision of these Rules, the Tribunal need not hold a hearing before making an order under paragraph (1), or provide reasons for the order.

6.1979 38 Decisions

(1) The Tribunal may give a decision orally at a hearing.

(2) Subject to rule 14(10) (prevention of disclosure or publication of documents and information), the Tribunal must provide to each party as soon as reasonably practicable after making a decision which finally disposes of all issues in the proceedings (except a decision under Part 4)—

(a) a decision notice stating the Tribunal's decision;
(b) written reasons for the decision; and
(c) notification of any right of appeal against the decision and the time within which, and manner in which, such right of appeal may be exercised.

(3) The Tribunal may provide written reasons for any decision to which paragraph (2) does not apply.

PART 4
CORRECTING, SETTING ASIDE, REVIEWING AND APPEALING TRIBUNAL DECISIONS

6.1980 39 Interpretation

In this Part—

"appeal" means the exercise of a right of appeal on a point of law under section 11 of the 2007 Act [or by any other enactment]; and

"review" means the review of a decision by the Tribunal under section 9 of the 2007 Act.

6.1981 40 Clerical mistakes and accidental slips or omissions

The Tribunal may at any time correct any clerical mistake or other accidental slip or omission in a decision, direction or any document produced by it, by—

(a) sending notification of the amended decision or direction, or a copy of the amended document, to each party; and

(b) making any necessary amendment to any information published in relation to the decision, direction or document.

6.1982 41 Setting aside a decision which disposes of proceedings

(1) The Tribunal may set aside a decision which disposes of proceedings, or part of such a decision, and re-make the decision or the relevant part of it, if—

(a) the Tribunal considers that it is in the interests of justice to do so; and

(b) one or more of the conditions in paragraph (2) are satisfied.

(2) The conditions are—

(a) a document relating to the proceedings was not sent to, or was not received at an appropriate time by, a party or a party's representative;

(b) a document relating to the proceedings was not sent to the Tribunal at an appropriate time;

(c) a party, or a party's representative, was not present at a hearing related to the proceedings; or

(d) there has been some other procedural irregularity in the proceedings.

(3) A party applying for a decision, or part of a decision, to be set aside under paragraph (1) must make a written application to the Tribunal so that it is received no later than 28 days after the date on which the Tribunal sent notice of the decision to the party.

6.1983 42 Application for permission to appeal

(1) A person seeking permission to appeal must make a written application to the Tribunal for permission to appeal.

(2) An application under paragraph (1) must be sent or delivered to the Tribunal so that it is received no later than 28 days after the latest of the dates that the Tribunal sends to the person making the application—

(a) written reasons for the decision;

(b) notification of amended reasons for, or correction of, the decision following a review; or

(c) notification that an application for the decision to be set aside has been unsuccessful.

(3) The date in paragraph (2)(c) applies only if the application for the decision to be set aside was made within the time stipulated in rule 41 (setting aside a decision which disposes of proceedings) or any extension of that time granted by the Tribunal.

(4) If the person seeking permission to appeal sends or delivers the application to the Tribunal later than the time required by paragraph (2) or by any extension of time under rule 5(3)(a) (power to extend time)—

(a) the application must include a request for an extension of time and the reason why the application was not provided in time; and

(b) unless the Tribunal extends time for the application under rule 5(3)(a) (power to extend time) the Tribunal must not admit the application.

(5) An application under paragraph (1) must—

(a) identify the decision of the Tribunal to which it relates;

(b) identify the alleged error or errors of law in the decision; and

(c) state the result the party making the application is seeking.

6.1984 43 Tribunal's consideration of application for permission to appeal

(1) On receiving an application for permission to appeal the Tribunal must first consider, taking into account the overriding objective in rule 2, whether to review the decision in accordance with rule 44 (review of a decision).

(2) If the Tribunal decides not to review the decision, or reviews the decision and decides to take no action in relation to the decision, or part of it, the Tribunal must consider whether to give permission to appeal in relation to the decision or that part of it.

(3) The Tribunal must send a record of its decision to the parties as soon as practicable.

(4) If the Tribunal refuses permission to appeal it must send with the record of its decision—

(a) a statement of its reasons for such refusal; and

(b) notification of the right to make an application to the Upper Tribunal for permission to appeal and the time within which, and the method by which, such application must be made.

(5) The Tribunal may give permission to appeal on limited grounds, but must comply with paragraph (4) in relation to any grounds on which it has refused permission.

6.1985 44 Review of a decision

(1) The Tribunal may only undertake a review of a decision—

(a) pursuant to rule 43(1) (review on an application for permission to appeal); and

(b) if it is satisfied that there was an error of law in the decision.

(2) The Tribunal must notify the parties in writing of the outcome of any review, and of any right of appeal in relation to the outcome.

(3) If the Tribunal takes any action in relation to a decision following a review without first giving every party an opportunity to make representations, the notice under paragraph (2) must state that any party that did not have an opportunity to make representations may apply for such action to be set aside and for the decision to be reviewed again.

6.1986 45 Power to treat an application as a different type of application

The Tribunal may treat an application for a decision to be corrected, set aside or reviewed, or for permission to appeal against a decision, as an application for any other one of those things.

TRANSFER OF TRIBUNAL FUNCTIONS ORDER 2010

(SI 2010/22)

Made ....6th January 2010
Coming into force in accordance with article 1

The Lord Chancellor makes the following Order in exercise of the powers conferred by sections 30(1) and (4), 31(1), (2) and (9) and 38 of, and paragraph 30 of Schedule 5 to, the Tribunals, Courts and Enforcement Act 2007.

The Welsh Ministers have consented to the making of this Order in so far as their consent is required by section 30(8) of that Act.

A draft of this Order was laid before Parliament and approved by a resolution of each House of Parliament in accordance with section 49(5) of that Act.

6.1987 1 Citation, commencement and extent

(1) This Order may be cited as the Transfer of Tribunal Functions Order 2010 and, subject to paragraph (2), comes into force on 18th January 2010.

(3) Subject as follows, this Order extends to England and Wales, Scotland and Northern Ireland.

(4) Except as provided by paragraph (5), an amendment, repeal or revocation of any enactment by any provision of Schedule 2, 3 or 4 extends to the part or parts of the United Kingdom to which the enactment extends.

6.1988 2 Transfer of functions of certain tribunals

(1) The functions of the following tribunals are transferred to the First-tier Tribunal—

(c) the Gambling Appeals Tribunal;

6.1989 3 Abolition of tribunals

The tribunals mentioned in article 2(1), (2) and (3)(a) are abolished.

6.1990 4 Persons becoming judges and other members of the First-tier Tribunal and the Upper Tribunal

A person who, immediately before this Order comes into force, holds an office listed in a part of Schedule 1, is to hold the office or offices set out in the corresponding entry in the table below.

Part of Schedule 1	*Office or offices*
Part 1	Transferred-in judge of the Upper Tribunal
Part 2	Transferred-in other member of the Upper Tribunal
Part 3	Deputy judge of the Upper Tribunal and transferred in judge of the First-tier Tribunal
Part 4	Transferred-in judge of the First-tier Tribunal
Part 5	Transferred-in other member of the First-tier Tribunal

6.1991 5 Consequential, transitional and saving provisions

(1) Schedule 2 contains amendments to primary legislation as a consequence of the transfers effected by this Order.

(2) Schedule 3 contains amendments to secondary legislation as a consequence of the transfers effected by this Order.

(3) Schedule 4 contains repeals and revocations as a consequence of the amendments in Schedules 2 and 3.

(4) Schedule 5 contains transitional and saving provisions.

6.1992

SCHEDULE 1
PERSONS BECOMING JUDGES AND MEMBERS OF THE FIRST-TIER TRIBUNAL AND UPPER TRIBUNAL
Article 4

PART 3
PERSONS BECOMING DEPUTY JUDGES OF THE UPPER TRIBUNAL AND TRANSFERRED-IN JUDGES OF THE FIRST-TIER TRIBUNAL
President of the Gambling Appeals Tribunal appointed under paragraph 1(1)(a) of Schedule 8 to the Gambling Act 2005 (c 19)

PART 4
PERSONS BECOMING TRANSFERRED-IN JUDGES OF THE FIRST-TIER TRIBUNAL
Other member of the Gambling Appeals Tribunal appointed under paragraph 1(1)(b) of Schedule 8 to the Gambling Act 2005

6.1993

SCHEDULE 2
CONSEQUENTIAL AMENDMENTS TO PRIMARY LEGISLATION
Article 5(1)

93 Gambling Act 2005

The Gambling Act 2005 is amended as follows.

94 For section 140 (the Gambling Appeals Tribunal) substitute—

"**140 Definition of "the Tribunal"**

In this Part "the Tribunal" means the First-tier Tribunal.".

95 Omit section 142 (timing).

96 Omit section 143 (appeal from tribunal).

97 In section 144(2) (powers of tribunal) for"" "section 142(2)" substitute"" "Tribunal Procedure Rules"".

98 In section 145(1)(a) (stay pending appeal) for "section 142(2)" substitute "Tribunal Procedure Rules".

99 In section 146 (rules)—

(a) for the heading substitute "Tribunal Procedure Rules";

(b) for subsection (1) substitute—

"(1) Tribunal Procedure Rules may make provision—

(a) regulating the exercise of a right of appeal under this Act to the Tribunal;

(b) for the suspension by the Tribunal of decisions of the Commission (whether or not they have already taken effect).";

(c) omit subsection (2); and

(d) in subsection (3) for "Rules under this section may, in particular," substitute "In the case of proceedings before the Tribunal under this Act, Tribunal Procedure Rules may".

100 Omit section 147 (fees).

101 In section 148 (legal assistance) omit subsection (2)(c) and (d).

102 Omit section 149 (enforcement of costs orders).

103 In section 337(1) (section 336: supplementary)—

(a) for "Gambling Appeals Tribunal" substitute "First-tier Tribunal"; and

(b) omit paragraphs (a), (b), (f) and (g).

104 In Part 1 of Schedule 6 (persons and bodies with functions under this Act) for "The Gambling Appeals Tribunal" substitute "The First-tier Tribunal".

105 Omit Schedule 8 (Gambling Appeals Tribunal).

6.1994

SCHEDULE 3
CONSEQUENTIAL AMENDMENTS TO SECONDARY LEGISLATION
Article 5(2)

138 Gambling Act 2005 (Definition of Small-scale Operator) Regulations 2006

In regulation 2(4) of the Gambling Act 2005 (Definition of Small-scale Operator) Regulations 2006 (definition of small-scale operator)—

(a) in sub-paragraphs (a) and (c) for "Gambling Appeals Tribunal" substitute "First-tier Tribunal"; and

(b) in sub-paragraph (c) and (d) for "under section 143 of the Act" substitute "to the Upper Tribunal".

6.1995

SCHEDULE 4
REPEALS AND REVOCATIONS
Article 5(3)

PART 1
COMING INTO FORCE ON 18TH JANUARY 2010

Enactment repealed/revoked	*Reference*	*Extent of repeal / revocation*
Gambling Appeals Tribunal Fees Regulations 2006	SI 2006/3287	The whole of the Regulations
Gambling Appeals Tribunal Rules 2006	SI 2006/3293	The whole of the Rules
Gambling Appeals Tribunal (Amendment) Rules 2007	SI 2007/577	The whole of the Rules

6.1996

SCHEDULE 5
TRANSITIONAL AND SAVING PROVISIONS
Article 5(4)

1 Interpretation of Schedule 5

In this Schedule—

"old tribunal" means a tribunal, the functions of which are transferred by article 2, but does not include the Pensions Regulator Tribunal in respect of its functions exercisable in Northern Ireland;

"new tribunal" means—

(a) the Upper Tribunal, in respect of—

(i) the functions of the Financial Services and Markets Tribunal and the Pensions Regulator Tribunal;

(ii) the functions of the Information Tribunal of deciding appeals under section 28 of the Data Protection Act 1998 or section 60 of the Freedom of Information Act 2000 (including that section as applied and modified by regulation 18 of the Environmental Information Regulations 2004) (appeals in relation to national security certificates);

(b) the First-tier Tribunal, in respect of—

(i) the tribunal functions mentioned in article 2(1);

(ii) the functions of the Information Tribunal other than those mentioned in paragraph (a)(ii);

"transfer date" means the date on which the functions of an old tribunal are transferred to a new tribunal by article 2.

2 Transitional and saving provisions

Any proceedings before an old tribunal which are pending immediately before the transfer date shall continue on and after the transfer date as proceedings before the new tribunal.

3 (1) The following sub-paragraphs apply where proceedings are continued in a new tribunal by virtue of paragraph 2.

(2) Where a hearing began before the transfer date but was not completed by that date, the new tribunal must be comprised for the continuation of that hearing of the person or persons who began it.

(3) The new tribunal may give any direction to ensure that proceedings are dealt with fairly and, in particular, may—

(a) apply any provision in procedural rules which applied to the proceedings before the transfer date; or

(b) disapply provisions of Tribunal Procedure Rules.

(4) In sub-paragraph (3) "procedural rules" means provision (whether called rules or not) regulating practice or procedure before a tribunal.

(5) Any direction or order given or made in proceedings which is in force immediately before the transfer date remains in force on and after that date as if it were a direction or order of the new tribunal.

(6) A time period which has started to run before the transfer date and which has not expired shall continue to apply.

(7) An order for costs may only be made if, and to the extent that, an order for costs could have been made by the old tribunal before the transfer date.

4 Paragraph 5 applies where—

(a) an appeal lies to a court from any decision made by an old tribunal before the transfer date;

(b) that right of appeal has not been exercised; and

(c) the time to exercise that right of appeal has not expired prior to the transfer date.

5 In the circumstances set out at paragraph 4, such of the following provisions as is appropriate shall apply as if the decision were a decision made on or after the transfer date by the new tribunal—

(a) section 11 of the Tribunals, Courts and Enforcement Act 2007 (right to appeal to Upper Tribunal);

(b) section 13 of the Tribunals, Courts and Enforcement Act 2007 (right to appeal to Court of Appeal);

(c) section 78(9A) to (9D) or section 78B(4) to (7) of the Local Government Act 2000 (as inserted or amended by Schedule 2 to this Order).

6 Any case to be remitted by a court on or after the transfer date and which, if it had been remitted before the transfer date, would have been remitted to an old tribunal, shall be remitted to the new tribunal.

7 Staff appointed to an old tribunal before the transfer date are to be treated on and after that date, for the purpose of any enactment, as if they had been appointed by the Lord Chancellor under section 40(1) of the Tribunals, Courts and Enforcement Act 2007 (tribunal staff and services).

8 A decision made by an old tribunal before the transfer date is to be treated on or after the transfer date as a decision of the new tribunal.

FIRST-TIER TRIBUNAL (GAMBLING) FEES ORDER 2010

(SI 2010/42)

Made . . . .*10th January 2010*
Laid before Parliament . . . .*12th January 2010*
Coming into force . . . .*18th January 2010*

The Lord Chancellor makes the following Order in exercise of the power conferred by section 42 of the Tribunals, Courts and Enforcement Act 2007.

In accordance with section 42(5) of that Act the Lord Chancellor has consulted the Senior President of Tribunals and the Administrative Justice and Tribunals Council.

6.1997 1 Citation and commencement

This Order may be cited as the First-tier Tribunal (Gambling) Fees Order 2010 and comes into force on 18 January 2010.

6.1998 2 Fee for bringing an appeal under the Gambling Act 2005

(1) Subject to paragraph (2) and articles 3 and 4, the fees set out in column 2 of the table in the Schedule are payable in relation to an appeal to the First-tier Tribunal under the Gambling Act 2005 listed in column 1 of that table.

(2) Where an appeal relates to a combination of any of the licences listed in fees 1.1 to 1.12 of column 1 of the table in the Schedule, only one fee is payable, and if those fees are different, only the highest fee is payable.

6.1999 3 Exemption from fees

(1) No fee is payable under this Order by a person bringing an appeal ("an appellant") who, at the time that the fee would otherwise become payable, is in receipt of any qualifying benefit.

(2) The following are qualifying benefits for the purpose of paragraph (1)—

- (a) income support under the Social Security Contributions and Benefits Act 1992;
- (b) working tax credit under the Tax Credits Act 2002, provided that—
  - (i) child tax credit is being paid to the appellant, or otherwise following a claim made jointly by the appellant and another person as a couple under section 3(3) of that Act; or
  - (ii) there is a disability element or severe disability element (or both) to the tax credit received by the appellant,

  and the gross annual income taken into account for the calculation of the working tax credit is £17,474 or less;
- (c) income-based jobseeker's allowance under the Jobseekers Act 1995;
- (d) guarantee credit under the State Pension Credit Act 2002;
- (e) income-related employment and support allowance payable under Part 1 of the Welfare Reform Act 2007.

6.1999.1 4 Reduction and remission of fees

Where the payment of any fee prescribed by this Order would, owing to the exceptional circumstances of the particular case, involve undue financial hardship to the appellant, the Lord Chancellor may reduce or remit the fee.

6.1999.2 5 Refunds

(1) Subject to paragraph (2), where a fee has been paid at a time—

(a) when, under article 3, it was not payable, the fee will be refunded;

(b) when the Lord Chancellor, if all the circumstances had been known, would have reduced the fee under article 4, the amount by which the fee would have been reduced will be refunded;

(c) when the Lord Chancellor, if all the circumstances had been known, would have remitted the fee under article 4, the fee will be refunded.

(2) No refund shall be made under paragraph (1) unless the appellant applies in writing within 6 months of paying the fee.

(3) The Lord Chancellor may extend the period of 6 months referred to in paragraph (2) if the Lord Chancellor considers that there is good reason for an application being made after the end of the period of 6 months.

6.1999.3
[SCHEDULE
FEES TO BE TAKEN]
[Article 2]

[Appeal	Column A	Column B
	New fee	Old fee
1 On filing an appeal under section 141 of the Gambling Act 2005 in relation to—		
1.1 a casino operating licence referred to in section 65(2)(a) of that Act	£14,000	£13,070
1.2 a bingo operating licence referred to in section 65(2)(b) of that Act	£3,100	£2,905
1.3 a general betting operating licence referred to in section 65(2)(c) of that Act	£10,000	£9,335
1.4 a pool betting operating licence referred to in section 65(2)(d) of that Act	£10,000	£9,335
1.5 a betting intermediary operating licence referred to in section 65(2)(e) of that Act	£10,000	£9,335
1.6 a gaming machine general operating licence for an adult gaming centre referred to in section 65(2)(f) of that Act	£1,600	£1,450

[Appeal	Column A	Column B
	New fee	Old fee
1.7 a gaming machine general operating licence for a family entertainment centre referred to in section 65(2)(g) of that Act	£1,600	£1,450
1.8 a gaming machine technical operating licence referred to in section 65(2)(h) of that Act	£1,600	£1,450
1.9 a gambling software operating licence referred to in with section 65(2)(i) of that Act	£1,600	£1,450
1.10 a lottery operating licence referred to in section 65(2)(j) of that Act	£9,400	£8,710
1.11 a personal management office licence referred to in section 127 of that Act	£1,600	£1,450
1.12 a personal operational function licence referred to in section 127 of that Act	£800	£755
2 On filing an appeal under section 337(1) of the Gambling Act 2005 against the Gambling Commission's order to void a bet under section 336(1) of that Act	£9,400	£8,710]

Section 4

Additional Material

Contents

GENERAL

BETTING

LOTTERIES

ADULT GAMING CENTRES

FAMILY ENTERTAINMENT CENTRES

REMOTE GAMBLING

We set out below the edited texts of those documents published by DCMS and the Gambling Commission which we consider are most likely to prove useful to practitioners. We do not, however, for reasons of certainty and space, reproduce the numerous consultation papers published by those bodies. Some of the documents such as Codes of Practice have formal status under s 24 of the 2005 Act; a failure to comply with them is likely to have regulatory implications and may provide a foundation for criminal or civil liability (see s 24(8) and (9)). Other documents set out conditions imposed by the Commission under s 75; a failure to comply with them is likely to give rise to criminal liability under s 33 (see s 33(2)(b)). Further documents despite not having any formal status under the Act will, in many cases, assist in resolving ambiguities in the Act and/or give indications of policy/legislative steer. There is a general section as some documents are not sector specific and a few have been consigned to the miscellaneous section.

GENERAL

GAMBLING ACT 2005 – EXPLANATORY NOTES

INTRODUCTION

6.2000 1. These explanatory[1] notes relate to the Gambling Act 2005 (c 19). They have been prepared by the Department for Culture, Media and Sport. They do not form part of the Act and have not been endorsed by Parliament.

2. These notes should be read in conjunction with the Act. They are not, and are not meant to be, a comprehensive description of the Act. Therefore, where a section or a part of a section does not seem to require any explanation or comment, none is given.

[1] For a brief discussion of the status of Explanatory Notes, see para **6.1** of the commentary on the Gambling Act 2005.

BACKGROUND

3. The Gambling Act 2005 ('the Act') gives effect to the Government's proposals for reform of the law on gambling. The Act contains a new regulatory system to govern the provision of all gambling in Great Britain, other than the National Lottery and spread betting. The Act received royal assent on 7th April 2005. A table of references to Hansard, reproducing the proceedings for the passage of the Gambling Act through Parliament, is set out at the end of these notes.
4. A draft Bill was published in November 2003 (Cm 6014), and further draft clauses were published in February and March 2004. The Bill followed on from the publication of a Government White Paper 'A Safe Bet for Success' (Cm 5397) published in March 2002. The White Paper was itself the Government's response to the report of the Gambling Review Body (Cm 5206) published in July 2001. The purpose of the publication of the draft Bill was to enable pre-legislative scrutiny to take place, by a Joint Committee of both Houses. The Joint Committee was convened on 16th September 2003, and produced two reports on 7th April 2004 (HL paper 63-1; HC 139-1) and 22nd July 2004 (HL Paper 146-1; HC 843-1). The Government's responses to these reports were published on 14th June 2004 (Cm 6253) and 22nd September 2004 (Cm 6330).

SUMMARY OF THE ACT

6.2001 5. The Act repeals the Betting, Gaming and Lotteries Act 1963 (c 2), the Gaming Act 1968 (c 65) and the Lotteries and Amusements Act 1976 (c 32).
6. Gambling will be unlawful in Great Britain, unless permitted by:
- the measures contained in this Act; or
- measures contained in the National Lottery etc Act 1993 (c 39), or pursuant to the Financial Services and Markets Act 2000 (c 8).

7. Two comprehensive offences are established: providing facilities for gambling or using premises for gambling, in either case without the appropriate permission. Such permission may come from a licence, permit, or registration granted pursuant to the Act or from an exemption given by the Act. Where authority to provide facilities for gambling is obtained under the Act, it will be subject to varying degrees of regulation, depending on the type of gambling, the means by which it is conducted, and the people by whom and to whom it is offered.
8. The Act introduces a unified regulator for gambling in Great Britain, the Gambling Commission ('the Commission'), and a new licensing regime for commercial gambling (to be conducted by the Commission or by licensing authorities, depending on the matter to be licensed). The Act removes from licensing justices all responsibility for granting gaming and betting permissions, which they exercised previously. Instead, the Commission and licensing authorities will share between them responsibility for all those matters previously regulated by licensing justices.
9. The Commission will not regulate spread betting, which is currently the preserve of the Financial Services Authority (at least for the time being), or the National Lottery, which is regulated by the National Lottery Commission. Those aside, the Commission will regulate all commercial gambling in Great Britain.
10. The Commission will take over from the Gaming Board for Great Britain. In addition to assuming responsibility for the Board's current remit of regulating gaming and certain lotteries, the Commission will take on responsibility for regulating betting. The Commission will be responsible for granting operating and personal licences for commercial gambling operators and personnel working in the industry. It will also regulate certain lottery managers and promoters. The Act sets out different types of operating licence that cover the full spectrum of commercial gambling activities conducted in Great Britain. It also makes provision for the Commission to have powers of entry and inspection to regulate gambling, with safeguards for those subject to the powers.
11. The Act establishes a Gambling Appeals Tribunal to hear appeals from decisions made by the Commission.

12. Licensing authorities will have new powers to license gambling premises within their area, as well as undertaking functions in relation to lower stake gaming machines and clubs and miners' welfare institutes. In England and Wales local authorities are given these responsibilities; in Scotland they are given to licensing boards. There will be a new system of temporary use notices. These will authorise premises that are not licensed generally for gambling purposes to be used for certain types of gambling, for limited periods.

13. The Act contains three licensing objectives which underpin the functions that the Commission and licensing authorities will perform. These objectives are central to the new regulatory regime created by the Act. They are:

- Protecting children and other vulnerable people from being harmed or exploited by gambling;
- Preventing gambling from being a source of crime or disorder, being associated with crime or disorder, or being used to support crime; and
- Ensuring that gambling is conducted in a fair and open way.

14. Regulation of gambling in Great Britain will be achieved through a variety of measures established under the Act. These include:

- Secondary Legislation;
- Conditions on Licences;
- Codes of Practice; and
- Guidance.

15. The Act recognises and accommodates the significant technological changes that have taken place in the last 40 years. The Act requires regulation of gambling where the player is not present on the operator's premises. For example, operators based in Great Britain must obtain an operating licence to authorise the provision of gambling via remote communication eg via interactive television or the internet. Moreover, the new licensing system has been designed to keep pace with technological developments, so that, subject to appropriate Parliamentary approval, gambling delivered by new, unforeseen, methods can be regulated in the future.

16. The Act revises the law of gambling. For example commercial bingo premises and casinos will no longer have to operate as clubs with a 24 hour membership rule (making them places to which the public will now have access); and a new class of betting intermediary operating licence has been introduced, to cater for the development of betting exchanges. The Act also repeals legislation that has prevented contracts relating to gambling from being enforceable through the courts.

17. The Act makes significant changes to the regime for casinos. It removes certain regulatory controls which existed under the Gaming Act 1968 (for example, 'permitted' areas and the demand test). Three categories of casino are introduced (regional, large and small). These are defined according to a casino's size. A casino's category affects what forms of gambling can be provided at the casino. For example, a casino's gaming machine entitlement depends upon which category it falls into. There will be a minimum size limit for new casinos established under the Act.

18. The Act imposes an initial limit of 1 regional casino, and 8 small and 8 large casinos, to be licensed under the Act. There are powers to amend these limits or remove them entirely, subject to appropriate Parliamentary approval. Casinos which are in operation, or which can lawfully be operated, immediately before the casino provisions of the Act come into force will be allowed to continue to operate. This will be provided for by means of transitional provisions. A power is provided for licensing authorities to pass resolutions not to licence any new casinos premises in their area.

19. The Act introduces a new regime for gaming machines. A new definition of gaming machine is provided, together with power to prescribe categories. The Act provides certain entitlements for commercial operators to use specified numbers and categories of machines in consequence of their licences. It also establishes permit procedures for authorising use of the lower stake gaming machines in specific locations.

20. The Act provides protection for children and vulnerable adults from the effects of harmful gambling. It does this through a number of specific offences that will prevent

children and young people from being given access to inappropriate or harmful gambling opportunities. In particular, it will be an offence to invite or permit a child or a young person to gamble contrary to the provisions of the Act. The Commission is required to promote socially responsible gambling through licence conditions and codes of practice directed at those providing facilities for gambling. The Act also provides powers for the Commission to void bets that are unfair, for example due to cheating.

21. A revised regime for the law of lotteries is contained in the Act, building upon that contained in the Lotteries and Amusements Act 1976, which the Act repeals. The Act regulates lotteries in two ways: either as exempt lotteries, or as licensable lotteries.

22. The Act makes provision for the advertising of gambling, creating new offences relating to the advertising of unlawful gambling and providing powers for the Secretary of State to make regulations controlling the content of gambling advertisements.

23. The Act establishes a series of authorisations for private and non-commercial gambling in Great Britain. This includes authorisations for domestic gaming and betting, and provisions for gaming and lotteries at non-commercial events.

STRUCTURE OF THE ACT

6.2002 24. The Act is set out as follows:

Part 1, and Schedules 1 and 2 introduce the fundamental concepts used in the Act, including definitions for 'gambling', 'betting', 'gaming', 'lottery' 'casino', 'remote gambling' and 'licensing authorities'. Part 1 also makes provision for situations where activities may fall into more than one category of gambling, and ensures that the forms of gambling regulated by the Act do not generally include entering a lottery forming part of the National Lottery. Schedule 3 makes amendments to the National Lottery etc Act 1993.

Part 2, and Schedules 4 and 5 establish the Gambling Commission, define its powers and give effect to the transfer from the Gaming Board of Great Britain. The core powers and duties of the Commission are set out, including its consultation obligations.

Part 3 sets out the general offences, including two key offences: the unlawful provision of facilities for gambling and the unlawful use of premises for gambling. Part 3 also makes provision for the prohibition of 'chain gifting schemes', a revised offence of cheating, and provisions on the manufacture of gambling software.

Part 4 establishes a number of specific offences that involve the participation of children and young people in gambling, their employment in relation to gambling and their entry to premises licensed to provide gambling.

Part 5 and Schedule 7 concern operating licences issued by the Commission. This Part establishes:

- The different types of licence and the rules relating to them;
- The conditions which may be attached to them;
- The required procedure for applying for them;
- The requirements as to their duration and validity; and
- A review procedure, including powers to revoke licenses and impose financial penalties.

Part 5 also provides powers for the raising of a levy on operating licence holders.

Part 6 concerns personal licences issued by the Commission. It defines the circumstances in which the Commission can impose requirements upon a person to hold a personal licence, and the procedures and rules relating to personal licences.

Part 7 and Schedule 8 create a tribunal to hear appeals from decisions taken by the Commission and provide the relevant powers and procedures for bringing an appeal. It includes powers to be exercised by the Lord Chancellor.

Part 8 concerns premises licences issued by licensing authorities. This Part describes the functions of licensing authorities, the various types of premises licence and the procedures for application. It sets out powers for licensing authorities and the Secretary of State or Scottish Ministers to attach conditions to licences. There are provisions on the duration, transfer and review of licences, and the mechanisms by which appeals can be made.

Part 8 also contains provisions for determining limits on the number of casino premises licences which may be granted under the Act. Schedule 9 makes provision for dealing with applications where such limits are in place.

Part 9 provides a procedure for authorising the temporary use of non-gambling premises for gambling. Licensing authorities are responsible for these authorisations, which are time limited.

Part 10 and Schedule 10 provide a new framework of regulation for gaming machines. There is power for the Secretary of State to prescribe categories of machine, by reference to the levels of charge and prize, the nature of the prize or the gambling, and the premises where the machine is to be located. Manufacture and supply of a gaming machine will require an operating licence from the Commission, and making a gaming machine available for use without the necessary permission is an offence.

Part 11 and Schedule 11 establish a new regime for lotteries, which is based upon, but revises the regime set out in the Lotteries and Amusements Act 1976. Part 5 also contains provisions for licensing lotteries. A new category of lawful lottery, the customer lottery, is created in Schedule 11. There are a number of new rules concerning the operation and promotion of lotteries.

Part 12 and Schedule 12 establish a new regime for gambling in clubs and miners' welfare institutes, developed from the regime in the Gaming Act 1968. It makes provision for the grant of permits by licensing authorities where gaming exceeds certain levels or where it involves the provision of gaming machines. There is also a requirement for bingo operating licences to be obtained, where the size of the bingo games played exceeds a specified threshold.

Part 12 and Schedule 13 make provision for gaming and gaming machines in premises holding an alcohol licence. Part 12 is also concerned with the use of gaming machines at travelling fairs.

Part 13 and Schedule 14 make provision for prize gaming which is to be permitted in certain locations, subject to specific rules.

Part 14 and Schedule 15 make provision for private and non-commercial gambling, which the Act authorises without any requirement for further permission.

Part 15 deals with the inspection rights and powers that are needed by the police, Commission enforcement officers, and local authority officers so that they can carry out their functions under the Act. Safeguards are afforded to those who may be the subject of inspection.

Part 16 provides a new regime for the advertising of gambling, replacing a number of provisions spread across different pieces of legislation, which the Act repeals. It creates new offences relating to the advertising of unlawful and foreign gambling, and provides powers for the Secretary of State to make regulations controlling the advertising of gambling.

Part 17 makes new provision for contracts relating to gambling. It repeals a number of statutes, dating from the eighteenth and nineteenth centuries, which prevented gambling contracts from being enforceable at law. It also makes provision for contracts relating to bets to be made void in circumstances where the Commission believes the bet was unfair, in particular as a result of misuse of information or cheating.

Part 18 provides an interpretation section and a number of general provisions applicable to the Act as a whole. Part 18 and Schedule 6 also provide powers for the Commission to exchange information with other bodies in the exercise of their functions.

Part 18 and Schedule 18 give the Secretary of State power to make regulations to provide for the transition from the old regime for gambling regulation to the new regime established by the Act.

Schedules 16 and 17 provide for consequential amendments to other legislation and for repeals as a result of the Act.

TERRITORIAL EXTENT

6.2003 25. The Act generally extends to England and Wales, and to Scotland with the exception of sections 148 (legal assistance scheme), 221 (fees) and 346 (prosecution by licensing authority). Sections 43 (chain gift schemes), 331 (foreign gambling) and 340 (foreign betting) apply to Northern Ireland.

TERRITORIAL APPLICATION: WALES

26. The Act's effect in Wales is the same as in England. The Act contains no provisions that relate exclusively to Wales, or affect the National Assembly for Wales.

TERRITORIAL APPLICATION: SCOTLAND

27. The Act's effect in Scotland is the same as in England, with the exception of the following sections:

- sections 148 (legal assistance scheme), 212 (fees) and 346 (prosecution by licensing authority) are not applicable in Scotland;
- sections 151 (form of licence), 159 (making of application), 160 (notice of application), 161 (representation), 164 and 165 (grant and rejection of application), 167 (mandatory conditions), 168 (default conditions), 184 (annual fee), 190 (copy of licence), 197 and 200 (review), 219 (giving notice), 349 (three-year licensing policy), and paragraphs (5)(d) of Schedule 10 (FEC permits) and 6 (e) and 21(2) of Schedule 14 (prize gaming permits) provide Scottish Ministers with the power to make their own regulations in respect of premises licence and permit matters in Scotland;
- section 285 (clubs, pubs etc: special provision for Scotland) enables Scottish Ministers, with the consent of the Secretary of State, to make provision by regulations in respect of club gaming and machine permits in place of that in Schedule 12; and in respect of licensed premises gaming machine permits in place of that in Schedule 13; and
- sections 33 (provision of facilities for gambling), 37 (use of premises), 41 (gambling software), 42 (cheating), 43 (chain gift schemes), 62 (penalty), 139 (breach of personal licence condition), 246 (penalty), 263 (penalty), 301 (misusing profits of non-commercial prize gaming), 328 (regulations), 330 (unlawful gambling), 331 (foreign gambling), 342 (false information) and 345 (forfeiture) make provision for a term of imprisonment on summary conviction not to exceed 51 weeks. The application of these sections to Scotland differs in that the maximum term of imprisonment is 6 months.
- Section 155 (delegation of functions under Part 8: Scotland) contains particular provisions regarding the delegation arrangements within licensing boards for functions conferred under the Act.

TERRITORIAL LIMITS – VESSELS AND AIRCRAFT

28. Sections 359 and 360 contain provisions for determining the territorial extent of the Act in relation to vessels and aircraft.

PART 1: INTERPRETATION OF KEY CONCEPTS

6.2004 29. Part 1 sets out definitions for the most important expressions and concepts that run through the Act. Part 18 also contains an interpretation section.

SECTION 1: THE LICENSING OBJECTIVES

30. The Act sets out licensing functions to be exercised by the Commission in relation to operating and personal licences, and by licensing authorities in relation to the

licensing of premises and the grant of certain permits. In exercising these functions, the Commission and licensing authorities must be guided by the licensing objectives, which underpin the new regulatory regime. The licensing objectives for the Act are:

- Preventing gambling from being a source of crime or disorder, being associated with crime or disorder or being used to support crime;
- Ensuring that gambling is conducted in a fair and open way; and
- Protecting children and other vulnerable people from being harmed or exploited by gambling.

SECTION 2: LICENSING AUTHORITIES

31. This section defines the term 'licensing authority' and therefore determines who is to discharge the licensing authority's functions under the Act. These functions include the licensing of gambling premises under Parts 8 and 9; the issue of permits authorising gaming and gaming machines in other premises under Parts 10, 12 and 13; and the registration of certain lotteries under Part 11. In England and Wales, local authorities are to act as the licensing authority for the purposes of the Act. In Scotland, licensing authorities are to be licensing boards constituted under section 1 of the Licensing (Scotland) Act 1976 (c 66).

32. The definition of 'licensing authority' mirrors that in the Licensing Act 2003 (c 17), omitting (except in relation to the provisions of Part 12 governing gaming and gaming machines in alcohol-licensed premises) certain bodies who should have functions only in relation to the subject matter of that Act. This will allow licensing authorities in England and Wales to coordinate their functions in relation to alcohol licensing and the licensing of gambling premises, as is already possible in Scotland. Part 8 makes further provision to achieve this.

33. Although there is no specific reference to a 'metropolitan council' or a 'unitary council' in the list of licensing authorities, these councils are types of district or county council and are therefore already covered in the list.

SECTION 3: GAMBLING

34. This section defines 'gambling' as meaning betting, gaming and participating in a lottery (within the meaning of those expressions as defined in subsequent provisions of Part 1). This is the first time that legislation has provided a generic concept of gambling, of which gaming, betting and lotteries are specific kinds. The Act adopts the approach recommended by the Gambling Review Body that there should be a single regulatory system for gambling, with different and distinctive provision for any of its specific forms, as appropriate. Accordingly, a definition of 'gambling' is provided which defines the forms of gambling which are to be brought within the system of regulation set out in the Act, and distinguishes them from activities which, although they combine expenditure and the influence of chance, should not be treated as gambling for the purposes of regulation.

SECTION 4: REMOTE GAMBLING

35. The Act contains specific provisions concerned with the regulation of the various technological means by which gambling activities can now be conducted. The Act adopts the concept of 'remote gambling' to cover gambling where the participants are not face to face on the same premises.

36. This section defines 'remote gambling' to mean gambling where people are participating by means of 'remote communication'. The types of remote communication by which people may participate in remote gambling are:

- the internet;
- telephone;
- television;

- radio; or
- any other kind of electronic or other technology for facilitating communication.

37. This list encompasses modern means of communication such as interactive television and mobile telephony, and is able, by virtue of subsection (2)(e), to ensure that the definition keeps pace with future developments in this field. However, in order to ensure clarity as well as flexibility for the regulation of gambling, the Secretary of State may specify in regulations that a specified system or method of communication is, or is not, to be treated as a form of remote communication for the purpose of the definition.

SECTION 5: FACILITIES FOR GAMBLING

38. The fundamental concept in the Act is the provision of facilities for gambling. It underpins the offences in Parts 3 and 4, and the requirements for licensing in Parts 5, 6 and 8. There are many ways in which individuals and organisations can provide gambling activities, or take part in them, whether through remote communication or in more traditional ways. This section defines the activities which are subject to regulation under the Act.
39. Subsection (1) sets out the circumstances in which a person is to be treated as providing facilities for gambling.
40. The list in paragraphs (a) to (c) of subsection (1) is aimed at different levels and aspects of the operation of gambling. Paragraph (a) is aimed at people and companies who are in the business of providing gambling. Any person who offers the opportunity for people to gamble, whether at a casino or licensed betting premises or through a website, will expressly or by implication be inviting people to gamble in accordance with arrangements made by them.
41. In paragraph (b), the reference to providing arrangements for gambling carries a general flavour of causing facilities to be available. The reference to operating arrangements for gambling is apt for mechanical arrangements such as a roulette wheel. Administering arrangements for gambling is a wide concept carrying a general flavour of control.
42. Paragraph (c) is concerned with those people who are directly involved in the gambling operation itself. People who participate in the operation of gambling by others will include those who actually play a part in the gambling transaction. An example might be a croupier at a gaming table. People who participate in the administration of gambling will include those who, whilst they do not actually operate the gambling, nevertheless provide direct administrative back-up to the gambling transaction. An example would be a person who hands out betting slips for the completion of a betting transaction.
43. Subsection (2) restricts the scope of subsection (1) by providing for certain exceptions. The exceptions cover:

- the supply of goods (other than a gaming machine) to a person who intends to use them to provide facilities for gambling (paragraph (a)), eg the supplier of gaming chips to a casino;
- the supply of goods to a person who may use them for gambling (but not where the supply is in the course of any of the activities referred to in subsection (1)(b) or (c)) (paragraph (b)), eg a retailer supplying a pack of playing cards to a person for domestic use; and
- electronic communications providers who do nothing more than act as a carrier of information for people providing facilities for gambling or consumers partaking in gambling (paragraph (c)), eg an internet service provider or mobile telephone operator.

44. Subsection (3) sets out the circumstances in which, despite the exception in subsection (2)(c), making available a means of remote communication will be providing facilities for gambling under the Act. This will be so where, because of the way in which the facilities have been adapted or presented, either they cannot reasonably be expected

to be used for purposes other than gambling, or they are intended to be used wholly or mainly for gambling. This might include, for example, where an internet connected personal computer is adapted so that it has a home page menu dedicated to providing links to gambling websites. It would also cover the situation where an internet connected personal computer was surrounded by signs indicating that it was available for use for gambling, and giving details of specific web pages where gambling was available.

45. Subsection (4) adds to the provision in subsection (3). It confers an order making power on the Secretary of State to clarify those cases where facilities for remote communication can or cannot reasonably be expected to be used for purposes other than gambling; or where facilities are to be taken as being intended, or not intended, to be used wholly or mainly for gambling.

SECTION 6: GAMING AND GAME OF CHANCE

46. This section defines 'gaming' for the purposes of the Act as playing a game of chance for a prize, and then further defines the meaning of a 'game of chance' and the concept of playing. The definitions are based on the relevant provisions in section 52 of the Gaming Act 1968, revised for the requirements of the Act. In particular, subsection (3) provides that a person can play a game of chance even if there are no other players, or the actions of a computer stand in for another player. This ensures that gaming on a machine or with virtual games is brought within the scope of the Act.

47. Subsection (6) provides the Secretary of State with the power to prescribe whether a particular activity (or an activity carried on in specified circumstances) does or does not amount to:

- a game;
- a game of chance; or
- a sport,

for the purpose of defining gaming under this section. The purpose of subsection (6) is to cater for circumstances, which might arise in the future, where either a new product or activity is introduced and there is doubt as to its treatment under this section, or where the interpretation being given to this section means it would be prudent to put beyond doubt the proper classification of a particular activity in relation to the definition of gaming.

SECTION 7: CASINO

48. This section provides a statutory definition of a 'casino' for the first time in British law.

49. The definition establishes that a casino is an arrangement (whether on premises or via remote communication such as the internet) where people can participate in casino games. Subsection (2) defines 'casino games' as games which are not equal chance games. This means that any games which involve playing or staking against a bank, or where the chances are not equally favourable to all the players, will be casino games.

50. Subsection (3) enables the Secretary of State to provide in regulations for a specified activity to be, or not to be, treated as a casino game for the purposes of the definition of casino. This power is not the same as specifying what kinds of casino games (eg roulette or blackjack) may be played in a licensed casino. Separate powers to specify such matters are provided in Part 5 on operating licences, specifically section 90.

51. The Act regulates casinos in different ways, depending on their size and the facilities they provide. Subsection (5) provides for four categories of casino, to be defined in regulations made by the Secretary of State; and subsection (6) specifically enables casinos to be classified by reference to a number of different matters. These include:

- the number of gaming tables at which casino games (or classes of casino games) are made available;

- the location and concentration of gaming tables; and
- the use and designation of floor areas for particular purposes.

52. In making such regulations, the Secretary of State can include provisions for determining what is and is not to be treated as a gaming table for the purposes of the casino definition, and for calculating when a floor area is to be treated as being used or designated for a particular purpose (see subsection (7)).

53. The three categories of casino to be licensed under the Act are: regional, large, and small. A regional casino will have the largest floor space requirements, followed by large casinos, and then small casinos. There is a fourth class of casino, which is a casino below the minimum size for a licensed casino (subsection (5)(d)). Casinos which have been licensed under the Gaming Act 1968, and which are too small to comply with the minimum requirements specified for regional, large or small casinos will fall into this fourth category. Transitional arrangements, under Part 18 of the Act, will be made to permit this fourth class of casino to continue in operation.

54. The Regulatory Impact Assessment published alongside the Act contains full details of the proposed specifications for regional, large and small casinos.

55. Sections 90, 166, 174, 175, 176 and Schedule 9, while not an exhaustive list, all contain particular provisions relevant to the regulation of casinos under the Act.

SECTION 8: EQUAL CHANCE GAMING

56. Under the Gaming Act 1968, the distinction is drawn between games of equal chance and games of unequal chance (including bankers' games). The Act maintains this distinction, and offers different degrees of regulation and control depending on which types of facilities for gaming are being offered. This section provides a definition of equal chance gaming.

57. At a number of places in the Act rights to conduct equal chance gaming are granted. See, for example, Part 12 on clubs, and the provisions of Part 14 on private and non-commercial gaming. By contrast, unequal chance gaming or bankers' games may only be made available, under the Act, in limited circumstances, the main example being that of a licensed casino.

SECTION 9: BETTING: GENERAL

58. This section defines 'betting' for the purposes of the Act. The present law contains no statutory definition of 'betting' as an activity. In broad terms it is taken to mean the staking of money or other value on the outcome of a doubtful issue. Betting can be at fixed odds, by means of a spread, or by way of pool betting.

59. By virtue of this section (which is subject to the qualification in Section 10) betting covers making, accepting or negotiating a bet in relation to:

- the outcome of any race, competition or event,
- the likelihood of anything occurring or not occurring, or
- whether something is true or not.

60. Subsections (2) and (3) extend the meaning of the term to include bets on races, competitions, or events that have occurred in the past.

SECTION 10: SPREAD BETS ETC

61. Spread bets or other bets, which are subject to regulation under section 22 of the Financial Services and Markets Act 2000, are excluded from the definition of betting in this Part. Section 22 of the 2000 Act provides for regulated activities under that Act to be specified in an order. The relevant order is the Financial Services and Markets Act 2000 (Regulated Activities) Order 2001 (SI 2001/544). Article 85 of that Order specifies as a regulated activity investments in rights under:

- a contract for differences, or

- any other contracts the purpose or pretended purpose of which is to secure a profit or avoid a loss by reference to fluctuations in the price or value of property, or fluctuations in an index or other factor specified in the contract,
- and spread bets are accepted as falling within this description.

62. If a class of bet ceases to be subject to such regulation as a result of an order under section 22 of that Act, it automatically becomes subject to regulation under the Act. Subsection (2) enables transitional provisions to be included in any such order under section 22 to ensure that the switch to regulation under the Act happens in an orderly way.

SECTION 11: BETTING: PRIZE COMPETITIONS

63. Schemes purporting to be prize competitions will fall within the definition of betting in this Part, even though they may not involve the deposit of a stake in the way normal to betting, if they satisfy specified conditions. One of the conditions is a requirement to pay to enter; and Schedule 1 defines what amounts to 'payment to enter'.

64. The effect of making such schemes subject to regulation as betting is to ensure that all the relevant protections provided by the Act in respect of betting apply. Therefore, schemes such as 'fantasy football' competitions or the Racing Post's 'Ten to Follow' competition will be regulated in the same way as bets placed on single events. However, the definition is intended to exclude prize competitions (such as prize crosswords) where the elements of prediction and wagering are not both present.

SECTION 12: POOL BETTING

65. This section defines 'pool betting'. It is based on the definition in section 10 of the Betting and Gaming Duties Act 1981 (c.63), and has been amended to remove those various elements which are no longer relevant to the definition for the purposes of the Act.

SECTION 13: BETTING INTERMEDIARY

66. A person who provides a service for others to make or accept bets is called a 'betting intermediary' in the Act. Such a person does not, himself, partake in the bet. The definition includes betting exchanges. There is a separate class of operating licence for betting intermediaries.

SECTION 14: LOTTERY

67. This section provides a definition of a lottery. It is intended to give statutory effect to the broad definition which the courts have evolved over recent years, while making specific additional provision in relation to arrangements whose status under the current law has proved problematic or uncertain.

68. The definition of lottery recognises that a lottery may involve more than one process for determining who the prize winners are. Where an arrangement involves more than one process then it fulfils the definition of a lottery if the first of those processes relies wholly on chance; and this is so even if subsequent processes require the lottery entrant to exercise skill or judgment. Conversely, where the first of these processes does not rely wholly on chance, the arrangement will not be a lottery, even if subsequent processes do not require any skill or judgment to be exercised whatsoever.

69. An arrangement will only be a lottery if the participants are required to pay to enter. Schedule 2 gives further detail on what amounts to 'payment to enter' for the purposes of this section.

70. The definition of lottery also contains provisions which replace section 14 of the Lotteries and Amusements Act 1976. Section 14 of that Act made provision about the

level of skill required for a legal prize competition. There is no direct equivalent of section 14 in this Act. Instead, competitions that do not require a minimum level of skill (according to the test in subsection (5)) are treated as relying wholly on chance, and therefore fall within the definition of a lottery (provided the other elements of the definition are satisfied).

71. Genuine prize competitions are not prohibited. So, under subsection (5), a process is not to be treated as relying wholly on chance if it contains a requirement to exercise skill and judgement, or knowledge that is reasonably likely to:

(a) prevent a significant proportion of people who wish to participate from doing so; or

(b) prevent a significant proportion of people who participate from receiving a prize.

72. If either one of these barriers to entry or success can be shown, the process will not be deemed to rely wholly on chance, and the arrangement will not be a lottery.

73. The test in subsection (5) is intended to be a practical one. So, for example, the level of skill or judgement required to win or go forward to the next round in a children's competition should be set at an appropriate level for the age of the children at which the competition is aimed. Equally, a competition in a specialist magazine needs to be suitably challenging for the specialists likely to read the magazine and enter the competition. The requirements of subsection (5) are not, therefore, necessarily satisfied by requiring a level of skill or judgment that could be expected to challenge the public at large.

74. Subsection (7) gives the Secretary of State power to provide in regulations whether a particular arrangement or a particular kind of arrangement is, or is not, to be treated as a lottery. The purpose of subsection (7) is to cater for circumstances which might arise in the future, such as where a new product or activity is introduced and there is doubt as to its treatment under this section. This enables the matter to be put beyond doubt.

SECTION 15: NATIONAL LOTTERY

75. This section ensures that participating in lotteries forming part of the National Lottery is not regulated as gambling under the Act. This is subject to two exceptions: section 42, which creates the offence of cheating; and section 335, which concerns the enforceability of gambling contracts.

SECTION 16: BETTING AND GAMING

76. Gambling transactions where there is an overlap between betting and gaming will be treated as gaming for the purposes of the Act, unless the betting in question constitutes pool betting. This ensures, amongst other things, that activities which are available in licensed gaming premises are not also available on licensed betting premises because, like roulette, they involve placing bets.

SECTION 17: LOTTERIES AND GAMING

77. Where gambling transactions satisfy the definitions of both games of chance and lotteries, then the arrangements fall under the controls on gaming unless they constitute a lawful lottery. The exception to this rule is transactions that require a person to participate, or be successful, in more than three processes. In that case, regardless of whether the transaction satisfies the definition of a lottery, it is always gaming. This broadly maintains the position in the current law (section 52 of the Gaming Act 1968).

SECTION 18: LOTTERIES AND BETTING

78. Transactions that satisfy both:

- the definition of pool betting or a betting prize competition, and

- the definition of entering a lottery,
- are to be treated as betting unless they form part of a lawful lottery. This section does not apply to lotteries forming part of the National Lottery which are excluded from being betting for the purposes of the Act by section 15(4).

SECTION 19: NON-COMMERCIAL SOCIETY

79. This section defines the circumstances in which a society is to be treated as non-commercial for the purposes of Part 11 and Schedule 11. It also contains the definition of 'private gain' for the purpose of Part 14.
80. Societies that are established for cultural or sporting purposes are deemed to be non-commercial societies under subsection (1). This is so, even if they provide benefits to individuals (subsection (3)).
81. Societies other than those with charitable or sporting purposes will only be non -commercial if their purposes are for something other than private gain. Therefore, these societies will be considered commercial, if their purpose is to provide benefit to a particular individual or individuals.
82. To illustrate, genuine societies that are set up to provide a child with medical care or sports sponsorship are likely to be non-commercial societies under this section. However, a society set up for political purposes would need to be set up to promote the party or group as a whole, rather than to have as its purpose the payment of sums to the benefit of particular individuals, for their own benefit.

SCHEDULE 1: BETTING: PRIZE COMPETITIONS: DEFINITION OF PAYMENT TO ENTER

83. Schedule 1 defines the circumstances in which someone is to be treated as having to pay to participate for the purposes of the 'betting: prize competitions' definition in section 11. The definition covers cases where a participant has to send money (or its equivalent), and also transferring money's worth and paying for goods and services at a price or rate which reflects the opportunity to participate in the prize competition.
84. Entry by standard rate telephone call, ordinary post (such as ordinary first class post) or by the use of another comparable service at its standard price to submit an entry, or to claim a prize, is not to be regarded as payment for entry.
85. Where an operator or any third party earns income from the prize competition because an entrant has to pay to discover whether a prize has been won or to take possession of the prize (for example, by means of a premium rate telephone line), then this is to be treated as payment to participate.
86. A prize competition is not to be regarded as requiring payment for entry, provided that a free entry route is offered for the competition (for example, a letter sent by ordinary post or another method of communication which is neither more expensive or less convenient than participating by paying). However, to qualify, the free entry route must be displayed with equal prominence as the other means of paid entry, and entries which are not paid for must be no less likely to win all or any of the prizes than entries which are paid for.
87. The Schedule confers a power on the Secretary of State to make regulations which determine whether or not a specified arrangement is to count as requiring payment to participate. New schemes and kinds of competition are always being devised; and this power will enable any uncertainty which might arise about payment to be resolved in the regulations.

SCHEDULE 2: LOTTERIES: DEFINITION OF PAYMENT TO ENTER

88. Part 1 contains the definition of a lottery for the purposes of the Act. The definition consists of three elements, one of which is that people are required to pay to

enter the lottery. Schedule 2 sets out what is meant by payment to enter for the purposes of a lottery. The provisions of this Schedule closely follow those in Schedule 1 for prize competitions.

89. It will not be possible for an operator to circumvent the provisions on payment to enter, explained above in relation to Schedule 1, by providing two methods of entry, both of which are communication at a premium rate, or one of which is a payment and the other is communication at a premium rate. This is because any method of communication that is charged at above the normal rate (ie at a rate that reflects the opportunity to enter the lottery) is deemed to be 'payment' under paragraph 2(c). So, where there is a choice between payment to enter, and entry through, say, a premium rate telephone line, there is no choice of free entry under paragraph 8, and both methods constitute payment. The arrangement will therefore be a lottery.

SCHEDULE 3: AMENDMENT OF THE NATIONAL LOTTERY ETC ACT 1993 (C 39)

90. Schedule 3 amends the National Lottery etc Act 1993. It inserts a new provision in the 1993 Act which will allow the Secretary of State to make regulations providing for the holders of licences under Part 1 of that Act to pay an annual levy to the Gambling Commission. The provision is based on that for operating licence holders under section 123 of the Act, and is subject to the condition that a levy will only be imposed where regulations have also been made under that section for a levy on operating licence holders. Schedule 3 also amends the 1993 Act to require the National Lottery Commission to consult the Gambling Commission where it becomes aware of any matter about which the Commission is likely to have an opinion, or where directed to do so by the Secretary of State.

PART 2: THE GAMBLING COMMISSION

6.2005 91. The Act creates a new, unified regulator for betting, gaming and lotteries in Great Britain called the Gambling Commission ('the Commission').

SECTION 20: ESTABLISHMENT OF THE COMMISSION

92. This section establishes the Commission, which will be the central regulatory body for gambling in Great Britain. Schedule 4, explained below, sets out the constitution of the Commission and its proceedings, the appointment of Commissioners and staff, as well as its financial and reporting arrangements.

SECTION 21: GAMING BOARD: TRANSFER TO COMMISSION

93. The Commission will take over from the Gaming Board of Great Britain, which was established under the Gaming Act 1968 and currently regulates gaming and certain types of lotteries. When commenced, this section, and Schedule 5, will transfer the Gaming Board's functions, rights and liabilities (including property) to the Commission. This section also provides for the chairman and members of the Gaming Board in post immediately before the establishment of the Commission to become chairman and commissioners in the new organisation.

SECTION 22: DUTY TO PROMOTE THE LICENSING OBJECTIVES

94. In carrying out its functions under the Act, the Commission must aim to pursue, and, wherever appropriate, have regard to the licensing objectives (as defined in section 1) and must aim to permit gambling in so far as it thinks such permission is reasonably consistent with pursuit of those objectives. Therefore, in carrying out its licensing functions under Parts 5 and 6 of the Act, or in issuing guidance and codes of

practice or advising the Secretary of State in accordance with Part 2, the Commission will have regard to the licensing objectives.

SECTION 23: POLICY FOR LICENSING AND REGULATION

95. Once established, the Commission will be responsible for licensing gambling operators and personnel working in the gambling industry under the provisions of Part 5 (operating licences) and Part 6 (personal licences) of the Act. This will be the primary licensing activity of the Commission, although the Act also provides it with other regulatory and advisory functions concerned with the proper conduct and control of gambling in Great Britain. The Commission will have investigation, enforcement and prosecution powers.
96. This section requires the Commission to prepare, publish, and keep under review, a statement that sets out the principles which will govern the exercise of its functions, and, in particular, explain how such principles will assist the Commission in its pursuit of the licensing objectives. This statement will underpin the work of the Commission.
97. Examples of specific matters for inclusion in the statement are: the principles, practice and procedure which the Commission will apply in considering applications for operating and personal licences under Parts 5 and 6.
98. Before issuing or revising a statement, subsection (5) provides that the Commission must consult the following:

- The Secretary of State;
- Representatives of local authorities (including, in Scotland, licensing boards);
- Representatives of Chief Constables of police forces;
- Representatives of gambling businesses;
- Commissioners of Customs and Excise;
- People with knowledge of social problems that may be associated with gambling; and
- The public, to such and extent, and in such a way as it thinks appropriate.

99. The statement and any revisions to the statement must be published.

SECTION 24: CODES OF PRACTICE

100. This section requires the Commission, as part of its regulatory functions, to publish codes of practice about the manner in which facilities for gambling are provided. These may be directed at the holders of operating or personal licences, or any other person involved in providing facilities for gambling. In particular, the Commission is required to publish a social responsibility code, which should describe the arrangements which a person providing facilities for gambling is to make for:

- ensuring that gambling is conducted in a fair and open way,
- protecting children and other vulnerable persons from harm or exploitation, and
- making help available to those who are, or may be, affected by problems related to gambling.

101. The Commission is required to publish its codes of practice, and all revisions, in a way that will ensure that those to whom they are addressed are made aware of them. A code, and any revision thereto, must state clearly when it is to come into effect. The Commission has the ability to revoke codes at any time.
102. Under Part 5, an operating licence is subject to the condition that the licensee complies with any relevant provision of a social responsibility code. Furthermore, it is open to the Commission to attach general or individual conditions to a licence requiring compliance with a provision of any other code (as further provided under Part 5). The same applies in relation to the Secretary of State's power to attach conditions to an operating licence.
103. A failure to comply with a code will not, of itself, render a person liable to prosecution or civil action. However, the codes can be used as evidence for criminal or civil proceedings; are to be taken into account by a court or tribunal in any case where

it appears relevant; and are to be taken into account by the Commission in exercising any of its functions. For example, where a licence holder has his operating licence reviewed by the Commission for potential breach of a licence condition, under the powers provided in Part 5, the Commission will refer to a code of practice, where it is relevant.

104. Before issuing a code of practice, subsection (10) requires the Commission to consult:

- The Secretary of State;
- People with knowledge of social problems that may be associated with gambling;
- Commissioners of Customs and Excise;
- People who appear to the Commission to represent gambling businesses, which are likely to be affected by the code or revision; and
- Where a provision in a code is about the advertising of facilities for gambling, people who appear to the Commission to have a relevant responsibility for regulating the advertising industry.

105. Subsection (11) requires the Commission to consult the following people as well, but only to the extent that it thinks it appropriate depending on the context and subject matter of the code:

- Representatives of local authorities (including, in Scotland, licensing boards);
- Representatives of Chief Constables of police forces;
- Representatives of gambling businesses other than mandatory consultees under subsection (10) (such as, those persons who are unlikely to be directly affected by the code); and
- The public (in such a manner as the Commission thinks fit).

106. The references to consultation of local authorities in sections 23 and 24 are to be read in the wider context, and includes parts of a local authority other than that responsible for licensing matters. This is to ensure that relevant parts of local government (in England, Scotland, and Wales) are consulted, where appropriate, in respect of the Commission's policy statement and codes of practice.

SECTION 25: GUIDANCE TO LOCAL AUTHORITIES

107. Under the Act, licensing authorities (local authorities in England and Wales, licensing boards in Scotland, and, where applicable, the Sub-Treasurer of the Inner Temple and the Under- Treasurer of the Middle Temple) are required to undertake various regulatory functions in relation to a number of gambling activities. They are responsible for:

- licensing of premises for gambling activities (Parts 8 and 9);
- regulating members' clubs and miners' welfare institutes which wish to undertake certain gaming activities (Part 12 and Schedule 12);
- regulating gaming and gaming machines in premises licensed to supply alcohol under the Licensing Act 2003. This includes granting licensed premises gaming machine permits (Part 12 and Schedule 13);
- granting permits to family entertainment centres for the use of certain lower stake gaming machines (Part 10 and Schedule 10);
- granting permits for prize gaming (Part 13 and Schedule 14); and
- registering societies' lotteries which fall below certain prescribed thresholds (Schedule 11, Part 5).

108. In order to assist licensing authorities to perform these various licensing and regulatory functions, this section requires the Commission to issue and publish guidance about how licensing authorities are to exercise their functions under the Act, including the principles to be applied in exercising those functions.

109. Licensing authorities are under a duty to have regard to such guidance.

110. Before issuing guidance to licensing authorities, subsection (4) requires the Commission to consult:

- The Secretary of State,
- The Scottish Ministers,
- Commissioners of Customs and Excise,
- Representatives of local authorities (as defined by this section),
- Representatives of gambling businesses, and
- People with knowledge of social problems that may be associated with gambling.

111. Depending on the nature of the code, or any revision, subsection (5) also requires the Commission to consult if, and to the extent it thinks it appropriate to do so:

- Representatives of Chief Constables of police forces; and
- Members of the public (in such a manner as the Commission thinks fit).

SECTION 26: DUTY TO ADVISE THE SECRETARY OF STATE

112. One of the functions of the Commission is to provide advice to the Secretary of State on matters relating to gambling as described in this section. This section permits the Commission to give advice about gambling to the Secretary of State either in response to a request or on its own initiative. Copies of any such advice will be sent to the Scottish Ministers also.

SECTION 27: COMPLIANCE

113. This section gives the Commission power to undertake activities for the purpose of assessing compliance with the provisions of the Act, or whether an offence has been committed under the Act. In particular, the Commission will be able to use children and young persons in test purchasing activities to assess whether the provisions for prevention of under-age gambling in Part 4 of the Act are being complied with. Section 64 exempts children, and people acting in the course of their duty, from committing an offence in these circumstances.

SECTION 28: INVESTIGATION AND PROSECUTION OF OFFENCES

114. The Commission has the power to investigate whether an offence has been committed under the Act, and to pursue criminal proceedings if this is the case. The Commission can do this on its own initiative or acting on other information. The power for the Commission itself to bring criminal proceedings does not apply in Scotland, due to the particular requirements of the criminal justice system in that jurisdiction.

SECTION 29: LICENSING AUTHORITY INFORMATION

115. Under the Act, Commission and licensing authorities must maintain registers containing appropriate details of licences that they have each issued. These registers will be open to the public. There will be circumstances where the Commission will need to obtain information directly from licensing authorities. For example, such information may be needed by the Commission to fulfil its duty under this Part to advise the Secretary of State. This section places an obligation on licensing authorities to comply with requests from the Commission for information contained in a register maintained by the authority, or for information in the authority's possession in consequence of their licensing and regulatory functions.

SECTION 30: OTHER EXCHANGE OF INFORMATION

116. This section permits the Commission to pass on information received in the course of its functions to those people or organisations listed in Parts 1 and 2 of Schedule 6, for use in the course of their, or the Commission's, business. This

section also provides a reciprocal power for the bodies listed in the Schedule to provide information to the Commission. Conditions may be imposed where information is provided under this section. The Commission may also provide information to the Comptroller and Auditor General for use in the exercise of his functions or to a person for use in a criminal investigation or criminal proceedings.

SECTION 31: CONSULTATION WITH THE NATIONAL LOTTERY COMMISSION

117. The National Lottery will continue to be regulated by the National Lottery Commission (NLC). This section requires the Commission to consult the NLC about matters in which the NLC is likely to have an interest or where the Secretary of State directs them to do so.

118. The sorts of issues which are likely to be of common concern between the NLC and the Commission are the way in which lotteries are conducted, and in particular those matters with respect to the conduct of lotteries that are liable to present risks to those taking part. There may be also a mutual interest in whether a particular activity is properly to be described as a lottery or a form of betting.

SECTION 32: CONSULTATION WITH COMMISSIONERS OF CUSTOMS AND EXCISE

119. This section requires the Gambling Commission to consult HM Commissioners of Customs and Excise on matters upon which HMCE are likely to have an opinion, or where it is directed to do so by the Secretary of State. This is in addition to the specific requirements for the Commission to consult HMCE concerning its policy statement, codes of practice, and guidance for local authorities.

SCHEDULE 4: THE GAMBLING COMMISSION

120. Schedule 4 provides for the constitution and membership of the Commission established under Part 2 of the Act.

121. The Commission will consist of a chairman and other commissioners. The Secretary of State will appoint all of these. The precise number of Commissioners will be a matter for the discretion of the Secretary of State. The Secretary of State may not appoint a commissioner for a single period of office in excess of five years, or for periods exceeding ten years in total.

122. The chief executive may also hold a position as a commissioner. However, the chief executive may not hold office as chairman. If a person ceases to be chief executive then that also brings to an end that person's appointment as a commissioner.

123. The Commission may also appoint other staff. The terms and conditions of employment of the chief executive and other staff are subject to the consent of the Secretary of State.

124. The Commission may determine its own proceedings, and must publish details of the arrangements it makes. In doing so, the Commission may delegate a function under the Act to: a commissioner, a commissioners' committee, or an employee of the Commission. Such delegation may include any discretionary function, a review function, or the exercise of a regulatory power.

125. Paragraph 9 authorises the Commission, with the consent of the Secretary of State, to make payments by way of remuneration, allowances, expenses, pensions and gratuities, to commissioners and Commission staff. Paragraph 10 provides that the Secretary of State may make payments to the Commission to meet such costs as cannot be met out of fees paid to the Commission under the Act. Paragraph 11 allows the Commission to borrow money, with the approval of the Secretary of State. Paragraphs 12 to 15 describe the accounting requirements for the Commission, which include a requirement for the Commission's annual statement of accounts to be examined and reported on to Parliament, by the Comptroller and Auditor General.

126. Paragraph 16 provides that after the end of each financial year the Commission must send a report of its activities to the Secretary of State. The Secretary of State must lay a copy before Parliament and may arrange for its publication.

SCHEDULE 5: TRANSFER FROM GAMING BOARD TO GAMBLING COMMISSION: SUPPLEMENTARY PROVISION

127. Paragraphs 1 to 5 of Schedule 5 make a number of technical provisions to achieve the legal transfer of the Gaming Board to the Commission pursuant to section 21. It allows the Commission to step into the shoes of the Board, without prejudicing any action, decision or pending proceedings of the Board. Upon commencement, references to the Board in any legislation or document will be construed as a reference to the Commission. To the extent that the Act has the effect of transferring staff contracts, it is not to affect the protections enjoyed by the staff of the Board under:

- the Transfer of Undertakings (Protection of Employment) Regulations 1981 (TUPE) (SI 1981/1794); or
- any regulations made under section 38 of the Employment Relations Act 1999 (c.26) (which have the effect of replicating TUPE in circumstances where they would not otherwise apply).

128. In accordance with the Cabinet Office Statement of Practice on Staff Transfers in the Public Sector (January 2000), the Government intend to ensure that those who are currently working for the Gaming Board and who wish to transfer to the Commission are able to do so. To the extent that TUPE does not apply to the transfer of all such staff, provision will be made by regulations under section 38 of the Employment Relations Act 1999 to ensure that in practice its provisions are applied in all cases.

SCHEDULE 6: EXCHANGE OF INFORMATION: PERSONS AND BODIES

129. Schedule 6 lists the bodies with which the Commission can exchange information. Under Part 18 of the Act, those bodies listed in Part 1 of Schedule 6 can also pass information to each other.
130. Paragraph 1 of Part 3 of Schedule 6 imposes restrictions on information exchanged between the Commission and a Schedule 6 body. In particular, where legislation restricts a Schedule 6 body in the way that it can use information provided to it, the exchange of information provisions in Parts 1 and 18 of the Act cannot override that restriction.
131. Paragraph 2 of Part 3 is concerned with information provided to a Schedule 6 body by HM Customs and Excise (HMCE) under this Act. It requires the consent of HMCE to be obtained before that information is passed on to any other body.

PART 3: GENERAL OFFENCES

6.2006 132. Part 3 contains general offences concerning the provision of facilities for gambling and the use of premises for that purpose. It also contains specific gambling related offences, such as the offences concerned with cheating at gambling and chain gift schemes. In addition to the offences in this Part, the Act contains specific offences concerning particular forms of gambling eg making gaming machines available for use (Part 10) or promoting or facilitating a lottery (Part 11) and specific offences relating to gambling involving children and young people (Part 4).
133. All offences under the Act are summary offences, with the exception of the offence of cheating in section 42.

SECTIONS 33 TO 35: PROVISION OF FACILITIES FOR GAMBLING

134. These sections establish the general principle that the provision of facilities for gambling (as defined in section 5) is unlawful unless it is either:

- authorised by an operating licence, or
- covered by a specific exception.

135. The specific exceptions relate to activities which do not require an operating licence under the Act, but which either depend on the issue of a permit or other authorisation, or fall within a category of gambling which may be carried on under the Act without the need for a specific authorisation or permission.

136. There are two further exceptions. The offence does not apply to the provision of facilities for a lottery; and the offence does not apply to making a gaming machine available for use. Specific offences concerning providing facilities in relation to these are contained at Parts 11 and 10 of the Act respectively.

137. Subsections (4) and (5) of section 33 provides for the offence to be a summary offence, with a maximum penalty on conviction of imprisonment for 51 weeks for England and Wales (or six months in Scotland), a level 5 fine on the standard scale, or both.

SECTION 36: TERRITORIAL APPLICATION

138. This section makes provision with respect to the territorial application of the offence of providing facilities for gambling. It provides that, where a person is providing facilities for gambling, it is immaterial whether the facilities are provided wholly or partly by means of remote communication, or inside, outside or partly inside and partly outside the UK. However, where what is involved is remote gambling (defined in section 4 to mean gambling in which those participating do so by means of remote communication), the offence will only apply if at least one piece of remote gambling equipment used in providing the facilities is located in Great Britain.

139. This means that, where gambling takes place remotely, the person providing the facilities for gambling will not fall within the scope of the offence if he does not have relevant equipment within Great Britain. This is so even if people within Great Britain can receive the gambling he is providing (eg over the internet). On the other hand, where at least one piece of remote gambling equipment is located in Great Britain, a person providing facilities for remote gambling will come within the scope of the offence. Therefore, a person commits the offence if any part of his remote equipment is located in Great Britain and he does not have the required authorisation or is not covered by one of the exceptions. This is so regardless of whether the gambling facilities are provided to people in Great Britain or outside.

140. Subsection (4) defines 'remote gambling equipment' for the purposes of the Act:

- Subsection (4)(a) captures equipment which stores information eg a computer database or server, about a person's participation in gambling. This includes the 'game history' of a player, including the player's identity and records of their wins and losses. Equipment used for storage of information for general promotional purposes would not be caught by the definition, unless the information relates to someone's participation in gambling;
- Subsection (4)(b) captures equipment used for generating and presenting virtual gambling;
- Subsection 4(c) captures equipment used by the person providing the gambling (or on his behalf) for determining the result or the effect of the result of the particular transaction. This covers random number generators used in virtual gaming, or the equipment for calculating whether someone has won or lost a bet on a real event;
- Subsection 4(d) captures equipment used to store information relating to a result. This is different to equipment under subsection 4(c) which covers the act of generation of a result, not its subsequent retention.

141. Subsection (5) excludes equipment used by a person who is participating in the remote gambling (ie the computer keyboard and screen), provided that the equipment has not been provided by the supplier of the remote gambling.

142. This section does not restrict the Commission from attaching licence conditions to remote operating licences about the collection and retention of information generally

by an operator (under its powers in Part 5). The purpose of this section is to establish whether a remote operator is within the jurisdiction for the purposes of the offence in section 33.

143. In the case of non-remote gambling (ie where remote communication is not used by those participating in the gambling), then the offence will apply if anything done in the course of the provision of the facilities for gambling is done in Great Britain.

SECTIONS 37 AND 38: USE OF PREMISES

144. This section makes it an offence to use premises, or cause or allow premises to be used, for the gambling activities set out in subsection (1) unless such use is:

- authorised by an appropriate licence or other permission obtained under the Act; or
- covered by an exception provided in the Act.

145. The principal authorisations which prevent a person committing an offence under this section are:

- a premises licence under Part 8;
- a temporary use notice under Part 9;
- an occasional use notice under this Part;
- premises used in connection with the provision of facilities for football pools in accordance with an authorisation under this Part;
- a family entertainment centre gaming machine permit under Part 10;
- a club gaming or gaming machine permit, or licensed premises gaming machine permit under Part 12; or
- a prize gaming permit under Part 13.

146. In addition, there are express exceptions which permit premises to be used for the provision of specified facilities for gambling without the need for a licence or permit, including the provision of gaming machines in premises with an alcohol licence and travelling fairs, and gaming at non- commercial events.

147. Subsection (4) provides an exception for people who are accepting bets on a track, where that track is covered by a premises licence issued under Part 8. In these circumstances the person accepting bets does not himself have to hold a premises licence. This subsection accommodates on-course betting operations, preventing each on-course operator from requiring a separate premises licence, provided the track itself is subject to the appropriate premises licence.

148. Subsection (5) ensures that casino operators can provide betting and (in the case of regional and large casinos) bingo under their casino premises licences without the need for a separate premises licence relating to those facilities.

149. Subsection (6) ensures that no offence is committed where premises are used to provide the facilities listed in subsection (1), provided that those facilities are used only by people who are not on the premises. An example of this is where premises house a server used for the purposes of remote gambling. Subsection (6) also exempts premises which are used only by people acting in the course of business. For example, a telephone call centre set up by a betting operator to accept telephone bets.

150. This is a summary offence with a maximum penalty on conviction of imprisonment for a term not exceeding 51 weeks for England and Wales (or 6 months in Scotland), a level 5 fine on the standard scale, or both.

151. Section 38 confers power on the Secretary of State to vary, by order, the gambling activities to which the section 37 offence applies. This includes the power to add or remove a gambling activity to the list provided, or to vary the entry for a gambling activity. The purpose of this provision is, in particular, to ensure that it is possible to bring within the scope of the offence any gambling activities which may be invented in the future, but which are not covered by the list in subsection (1). Where a new gambling activity is added, the Secretary of State may make consequential amendments to Part 8, to provide for an appropriate premises licence, and matters such as machine entitlements.

152. In particular, an order may have the effect of extending the offence to spread bets or other bets which are subject to regulation under the Financial Services and Markets Act 2000. Spread betting, which is regulated under the 2000 Act, is generally excluded from the scope of this Act (see section 10). The effect of section 38 is to allow the scope of this Act to be extended so that the use of premises to provide facilities for spread betting is also regulated under this Act. In these circumstances, amendments would also be required to Part 8 to enable premises licences to be granted under the Act, authorising premises to be used for the provision of facilities for spread betting.

SECTION 39: EXCEPTION: OCCASIONAL USE NOTICE

153. This section provides a means for tracks to be authorised for the provision of facilities for betting, where the use (for betting) will be for no more than 8 days a year: the occasional use notice. This notice, when in operation, excepts people on the track from committing the offence of using premises unlawfully for the provision of facilities for gambling. Tracks are defined in the interpretation section in section 353 as a racecourse, dog track or any other premises used or intended for races or other sporting events. The purpose of the section is to ensure that point-to-point racecourses which are used for only a few days a year, and tracks such as golf courses where betting facilities are provided for major competitions, but not otherwise, do not have to obtain a full premises licence in order to avoid the main offence in this Part.
154. Subsections (2) to (6) specify the procedure for serving an occasional use notice. An occasional use notice must be served by an occupier of the track, or a person who is responsible for the administration of races or sporting events on the track. It must be sent to the licensing authority with a copy sent to the police force for the area, and must specify the day on which it is to have effect. An occasional use notice cannot be given for a day in a calendar year if eight occasional use notices have already been given for days in that year. Therefore, a track that is used more frequently for betting will need a premises licence, or temporary use notice, under Parts 8 or 9.
155. Any person providing betting facilities pursuant to an occasional use notice will still require the appropriate authorisation to act as a betting operator: in general this will be a betting operating licence, or (in the case of pool betting) authorisation by the holder of a pool betting licence under Part 5.

SECTION 40: EXCEPTION: FOOTBALL POOLS

156. Holders of a pool betting operating licence, under section 93, can authorise people who are not their employees to dispense coupons, collect entries and stakes, and pay winnings, on football pools competitions. Collectors can operate, for example, door to door, or from ordinary retail premises such as newsagents.
157. This section provides an exception for such people from the premises offence in this Part. Collectors can therefore use premises to accept football pools entries, or pay out winnings without committing that offence. Subsection (2) gives the Secretary of State power to make regulations, to disapply this concession to particular types of premises.

SECTION 41: GAMBLING SOFTWARE

158. The Act places controls on people who wish to provide facilities for gambling by means of remote communication. This section concerns computer software for gambling that is used in connection with such facilities, but not software designed for use in a gaming machine.
159. It is an offence under subsection (1) to manufacture, supply, install or adapt, in the course of a business, computer software for remote gambling, unless an operating licence is held for such activity. The purpose of this offence is to ensure that people responsible for generating gambling software do so in a regulated environment, to

ensure, in particular, fairness for players. While an operating licence for remote gambling covers someone offering gambling, for example by means of the internet, it does not, itself, cover someone who is manufacturing the gambling software that will be used in providing such facilities (ie the software supplier to a remote gambling operator). This section covers this latter situation.

160. The maximum penalty for the offence is a maximum term or imprisonment of 51 weeks in England and Wales (or 6 months in Scotland), and/or a fine up to level 5 on the standard scale.

161. Computer software for gambling for use in a gaming machine is expressly excluded from this offence (in subsection (2)(b)) because the definition of gaming machine in Part 10 already includes such computer software. Someone manufacturing computer software for a gaming machine would therefore be subject to the provisions (and the offences) contained in Part 10.

162. Subsection (3) ensures that a communications service provider, who enables someone to download or send gambling software to another person, is not treated as himself supplying or installing that gambling software. This is an exception for 'mere carriers' of the software.

SECTION 42: CHEATING

163. This section creates a criminal offence for cheating at gambling, and repeals the old offence of cheating in section 17 of the Gaming Act 1845 (c.109). The word 'cheating' is not defined but has its normal, everyday meaning. The offence is committed by both cheating directly or by doing something for the purpose of assisting or enabling another person to cheat. A person who does something inadvertently which enables another person to cheat, will not, therefore, commit an offence.

164. Subsection (2) provides that a person will commit the offence irrespective of whether he actually wins anything as a result of the cheating, or whether the cheating has the effect of improving the cheat's chances of winning. This means that an inept cheat, or one who cheats for another person's benefit, will still commit an offence. Subsection (3) provides that, in particular, cheating may include actions that involve actual or attempted deception or interference with the processes involved in the conduct of gambling, or with any other game, race or other event or process to which gambling relates. Events can be either real or virtual. Subsection (3) does not provide an exhaustive definition of cheating. It is made expressly without prejudice to the general meaning of cheating established in subsection (1).

165. Subsections (4) and (5) provide for penalties that may be imposed upon conviction of the offence. Unlike other offences created under the Act, this offence is capable of being tried either summarily or on indictment. On summary conviction the penalty is a maximum term or imprisonment of 51 weeks (or 6 months in Scotland), and/or a fine up to level 5 on the standard scale. On conviction on indictment the maximum penalty is imprisonment for a term not exceeding two years, an unlimited fine, or both.

SECTION 43: CHAIN-GIFT SCHEMES

166. This section makes provision for the prohibition of chain-gift schemes. The offence extends to Northern Ireland, as well as England, Scotland and Wales.

167. A chain-gift scheme is an arrangement in which, in order to join, people must pay a joining fee to one or more of the other participants in the scheme. People who take part in the scheme are required or invited to encourage other people to join. A person who participates in the arrangement does so having been encouraged to believe that he will receive back more than his initial joining fee, from the fees paid by other participants. The joining fee must be a payment of money or money's worth, but it does not include goods or services.

168. Subsection (1) makes it an offence to invite another person to join such a scheme. It is also an offence to knowingly participate in the promotion of the scheme.

It will not, however, be an offence for a person merely to join the scheme. People who participate unwittingly in the promotion of a chain gift scheme, such as the host of an internet discussion forum upon which a posting promoting a chain- gift scheme has been made, will not commit an offence, provided they are unaware that the posting promotes a chain-gift scheme. People who knowingly participate in the administration or management of the scheme will also commit an offence.

169. Subsection (3)(b) provides that the offence is committed irrespective of whether the joining fees are paid directly between the participants in the scheme or through a person responsible for managing or administering the scheme. The penalty is a maximum term or imprisonment of 51 weeks in England and Wales (or 6 months in Scotland and Northern Ireland), and/or a fine up to level 5 on the standard scale.

SECTION 44: PROVISION OF UNLAWFUL FACILITIES ABROAD

170. This section gives the Secretary of State power to specify countries or places as prohibited territories, with the result that it will be an offence for a person to invite or enable a person in a prohibited territory to participate in remote gambling, where the person making the invitation or enabling the activity does anything in Great Britain or uses any remote gambling equipment in Great Britain so to do.

171. The Secretary of State's decision whether or not to exercise this power could depend on matters such as: the development of the global gambling market; the laws which other countries establish to permit, constrain or prohibit the use of remote gambling; the practical measures employed by those countries to secure compliance with such laws; and the extent to which it is possible to reach international agreements about the cross-border use of the internet for gambling.

172. In the event that the Secretary of State makes an order designating countries or places as prohibited territories the order must also prescribe the mode of trial and maximum penalty for the offence.

PART 4: PROTECTION OF CHILDREN AND YOUNG PERSONS

6.2007 173. Part 4 of the Act creates a number of offences that establish the extent to which children and young people may become involved in gambling, whether in terms of participation in the gambling, entry into gambling premises, or employment in relation to the provision of such facilities.

SECTION 45: MEANING OF CHILD AND YOUNG PERSON

174. Under the Act, any person aged less than sixteen years is defined as a child. Any person aged sixteen years or more, but who is not yet eighteen, is defined as a young person.

SECTIONS 46 AND 48: INVITING CHILDREN AND YOUNG PERSONS TO GAMBLE; PARTICIPATION BY YOUNG PERSONS IN GAMBLING

175. In broad terms, people aged under eighteen are not to be permitted to gamble. Therefore, it is an offence for a person to invite, cause or permit a person under eighteen to gamble. It is also to be an offence for the young person to gamble (those aged sixteen and seventeen). However, children (those not yet aged sixteen) do not commit an offence if they gamble.

176. There are some exceptions to the general prohibition on gambling by children and young people. Children and young persons may participate in all forms of private or non-commercial gaming and betting. Young persons may participate in lotteries and pool betting on association football. Children and young persons may use the category of gaming machine with the lowest stakes and prizes (Category D). They may also take part in equal chance prize gaming at certain premises, as provided under Part 13 of the Act.

177. The offence of inviting a child or young person to gamble is to include advertising and other actions that bring attention to the facilities available for gambling. A person may be liable to commit the offence where his or her name or contact details are included in the information provided to the child or young person, and that person is someone to whom payment may be made or from whom information about the gambling may be obtained. However, in such a case, the person has a defence if he can prove that the information was provided without his consent or authority. A further defence is also available in a case where information is brought to a child's attention (as opposed to being sent to the child). In those circumstances, the person whose contact details appear in the information will have a defence if he can demonstrate that it was brought to the child's attention incidentally to it being brought to the attention of adults.

SECTIONS 47 AND 49: INVITATION TO ENTER PREMISES; YOUNG PERSONS ENTERING PREMISES

178. Children and young persons may not enter a casino, a betting shop or an adult gaming centre at any time when facilities for gambling are being provided on the premises in reliance on the relevant premises licence. This is subject to the exception that children and young persons may enter the non -gambling area of a regional casino, but they may not enter the gambling area.

179. Under Part 8, a betting premises licence for a track is subject to the condition that children and young persons are excluded from any area where a Category C gaming machine is available for use or any area where facilities for betting are provided. However, the latter restriction does not apply in the case of a dog-race track or a horse-race course on any day on which racing takes place (see section 182).

180. Children are equally not permitted to enter areas of family entertainment centres where Category C gaming machines are available for use.

181. Any person who invites a child or young person to enter these premises, or the parts of the premises described above, commits an offence. Where a young person enters these areas, he too commits an offence.

182. As a consequence of these provisions, a person of any age may enter bingo premises, the betting areas of a horse racecourse or a greyhound track on days on which races are being run, or the non-gambling area of a regional casino. A person of any age may also enter any area of a family entertainment centre where no Category C gaming machines are provided at that place. This does not mean that they can necessarily partake in any gambling on the premises, see sections 46 and 48.

SECTION 50: PROVISION OF FACILITIES FOR GAMBLING

183. A young person commits an offence if he provides facilities for gambling, except in connection with private or non-commercial gaming and betting, lotteries, football pools and prize gaming at a travelling fair.

SECTIONS 51 TO 55: EMPLOYMENT OFFENCES

184. It is an offence to employ children and young persons to provide facilities for gambling, except in the case of private or non-commercial gaming and betting and in relation to prize gaming at a travelling fair. There is a further exception in the case of lotteries and football pool betting. In those cases, the offence only extends to the employment of children and not young persons. The National Lottery is excluded from this provision. Regulations made under the National Lottery etc Act 1993 already prohibit the sale of National Lottery tickets to those under 16.

185. Restrictions are imposed on the ways in which children and young people can be employed to work on premises where facilities for gambling are provided, even if they are not engaged to perform any gambling activities themselves. This is to ensure that children and young people are not afforded undesirable exposure to gambling.

186. It is an offence to employ children to work in premises at any time when facilities for the playing of bingo are being provided on the premises. It is also an offence to employ children at a club or institute at any time when facilities for gambling are being provided pursuant to a permit (section 53).

187. In relation to any premises where gaming machines of any category are situated, then any child or young person employed may not perform any function that involves the gaming machine. Therefore, for example, a child may be employed in a family entertainment centre to undertake non-gambling activities, although he may not operate or handle the machine or pay customers prizes in the event that the machine has insufficient money in it (and he may not enter the area where the Category C machines are located) (section 54).

188. Generally children and young persons are not allowed to be employed in any capacity in casinos, betting premises and adult gaming centres. This is subject to an exception in the case of regional casinos where children and young persons can be employed in non-gambling areas. It is possible, however, for children and young persons to be employed in adult only gambling premises (small and large casinos, the gambling area of regional casinos, betting offices and adult gaming centres) when no facilities for gambling are being provided. Therefore, for example, a sixteen-year-old apprentice joiner may undertake improvement works on the structure of a bar in a casino when it is closed (section 55).

189. There is also an effective prohibition on children and young persons being employed in the betting areas of certain tracks and the adult-only areas of family entertainment centres. This follows the provisions referred to above which generally prohibit children and young persons from being able to enter such areas (sections 47 and 49).

SECTION 56: INVITATION TO PARTICIPATE IN LOTTERY

190. This section makes it an offence to invite, cause or permit a child to take part in a lottery, for example, by selling him a ticket. However, this offence does not apply to two types of lottery allowed under the Act, that is, private lotteries and incidental non-commercial lotteries (see Schedule 11, Parts 1 and 2). This means that the section does not, for example, prevent the sale to children of tickets in events such as the tombola at a school or church fete. The National Lottery is also excluded from this provision.

191. The Act does not criminalise the purchase by a child of a ticket in any form of lottery.

SECTION 57: INVITATION TO PARTICIPATE IN FOOTBALL POOLS

192. Young people are to be permitted to participate in football pools, and it is, therefore, permissible for the operators of football pools to provide information to young persons, or to direct advertisements to young persons. However, children may not participate in football pools and this section makes it an offence to invite, cause or permit a child to do so.

SECTION 58: RETURN OF STAKE

193. Under Part 5, all operating licences for gambling are subject to a condition requiring licence holders to return any money paid to them by children or young persons, where the person concerned is not permitted to participate in the gambling activity (section 83). It also requires the licence holder to withhold any winnings that would otherwise be payable. This section makes it an offence for a licence holder to fail to do so.

SECTION 59: AGE LIMIT FOR CATEGORY D MACHINES

194. The Act does not set a minimum age limit for the use of Category D gaming machines. This section gives the Secretary of State power by order to establish one, by creating an offence of inviting, causing or permitting a child or young person below a specified age to use a Category D gaming machine.

195. Before making such an order, the Secretary of State is required to consult the Commission, people who appear to the Secretary of State to represent the interests of gambling businesses and people who have knowledge about problem gambling. An order need not apply to all types of Category D machine, which means that an age limit can be imposed on particular types of Category D machine. Therefore, if the evidence dictates that only certain types of machine require an age limit (as a result of harm), the section ensures that only those machines will be covered by the limit.

SECTION 60: TEMPORARY USE NOTICE

196. Temporary use notices issued under Part 9 may authorise gambling at premises that do not have a premises licence. The same applies in the case of premises subject to an occasional use notice. For the purposes of this Part, the relevant areas of such premises are to be regarded as being subject to the equivalent premises licence. Therefore, where a temporary use notice authorises gaming in one part of a hotel, a young person working in the hotel may not enter that area during the time that the notice has effect.

SECTION 61: MEANING OF EMPLOYMENT

197. For the purposes of this Part, employment is to be regarded as having a wide meaning. For example, as well as direct employees of the licence holder, people engaged temporarily through an employment agency are equally to be regarded as employees of the licence holder.

198. Any offence committed under this Part will be treated as a continuing offence which means that a new offence will be committed on each day that the employment continues. This increases the level of penalty that will be available in sentencing.

SECTION 62: PENALTY

199. Offences under this Part are to be punishable on conviction by a maximum term of imprisonment of up to 51 weeks in England and Wales (or 6 months in Scotland), or a fine not exceeding level 5 on the standard scale, or both. Where it is young person who is convicted, imprisonment is not to be available and any fine imposed may not exceed level 3 on the standard scale.

SECTION 63: REASONABLE BELIEF ABOUT A PERSON'S AGE

200. Where a person is charged with an offence under this Part of doing anything in relation to a child or young person it is to be a defence for the person to prove that he took all reasonable steps to determine the relevant person's age and he reasonably believed that the person was not a child or a young person.

SECTION 64: USE OF CHILDREN IN ENFORCEMENT OPERATIONS

201. This section will enable children and young persons to be used in test purchasing operations for the purpose of assessing whether the provisions in this Part, prohibiting under-age gambling, are being complied with. For example, a constable, enforcement officer or authorised person will not commit an offence under section 46 if, in the course of their duty, they invite a child or young person to gamble. Equally, a young person will not commit an offence under section 48 if he gambles at the request of a constable, enforcement officer or authorised officer who is acting in the course of his

functions.

PART 5: OPERATING LICENCES

6.2008 202. Operating licences are one of the principal forms of authorisation under the Act for the lawful provision of facilities for gambling. A person holding an operating licence, and providing facilities within the terms and conditions of that licence, will not commit the offence of unlawful provision of facilities for gambling under Part 3.

203. The sections in this Part describe the licensing regime to be administered by the Commission for granting operating licences. Matters covered include the principles to be applied by the Commission in considering applications for operating licences, powers for conditions to be attached to licences, and the review procedures once licences have been granted.

204. There are different kinds of operating licences for the various forms of gambling facilities eg to operate a casino, to provide facilities for betting, or to act as a betting intermediary. An operating licence for each kind of activity can authorise the provision of facilities on premises generally ('non-remote provision') or for the provision of those facilities by means of remote communication ('remote provision'). However, it is not possible to combine a licence for both remote and non-remote provision (but one person can be granted both a remote licence for betting and a non-remote licence for betting).

205. An operating licence for non-remote provision gives a general authorisation for the operator to provide gambling facilities on premises. However, before being able to use any particular premises, the holder of an operating licence will also need an authorisation under the Act to use such premises for gambling. The principal form of such permission is a premises licence granted under Part 8 of the Act, although there are other forms of permission eg an occasional use notice (section 39) or a temporary use notice (Part 9).

206. In addition to authorising the provision of facilities for gambling, operating licences can be obtained to authorise:

- the manufacture, supply, installation, adaptation, maintenance and repair of gaming machines; and
- the manufacture, supply, installation and adaptation of gambling computer software.

207. Part 1 of the Act defines 'betting', 'gaming' and 'lottery', and a number of related concepts. Part 18 of the Act contains further interpretation provisions relevant to Part 5.

SECTION 65: NATURE OF LICENCE

208. There are ten different kinds of operating licence:
(a) a casino operating licence;
(b) a bingo operating licence;
(c) a general betting operating licence;
(d) a pool betting operating licence;
(e) a betting intermediary operating licence;
(f) a gaming machine general operating licence for an adult gaming centre;
(g) a gaming machine general operating licence for a family entertainment centre;
(h) a gaming machine technical licence;
(i) a gambling software operating licence; and
(j) a lottery operating licence.

209. Subsection (1) empowers the Commission to issue these operating licences. Subsection (4) allows the Secretary of State, through secondary legislation, to amend this list so as to add, vary or delete a class of operating licence.

SECTION 66: FORM OF LICENCE

210. A licence must specify the person to whom it is issued; how long it has effect; and any condition attached to the licence by the Commission (subsection (1)). The Secretary of State may set out in regulations further details of what information a licence must contain, and the form in which it is to be issued (subsection (2)).

SECTION 67: REMOTE GAMBLING

211. Facilities for gambling can be provided remotely (ie by technology which means the player is not in the same place as the person offering the facilities), or non-remotely (ie face to face on premises). This section defines a 'remote operating licence' as an operating licence which authorises someone to provide remote gambling, and requires all licences to state whether they are a remote operating licence or a non-remote operating licence. An operating licence cannot be both.
212. The effect of this section is that for each of the ten kinds of operating licence listed in section 65, there are two basic types: a remote operating licence which authorises, for example, the provision of particular facilities by means of the internet; and a non-remote licence, which authorises the same facilities to be provided from premises. It will not be possible for one operating licence to combine authorisations for providing both remote and non-remote facilities for gambling. One person can hold both types of licence, but he will need to be granted each separately.
213. Further provisions on the conditions which can be attached to a remote licence allow the Commission to limit the particular forms of remote communication by which gambling is offered under a remote licence. Therefore, a remote licence does not automatically confer an entitlement to use all forms of remote communication eg television, radio and the internet. Instead, conditions can limit provision to one, or any combination of the different forms of remote communication defined in Part 1.

SECTION 68: COMBINED LICENCE

214. While there is a distinction between remote and non-remote operating licences, meaning that they cannot be combined in one licence, the Commission can issue operating licences which cover more than one of the ten kinds of licence, provided they are all either remote, or non-remote.
215. The starting point, in subsection (1), is that one operating licence can authorise a combination of the different kinds of activities that make up the ten kinds of operating licence. However, this is subject to certain rules and limitations.
216. Under subsection (3) a casino operating licence also authorises the provision of facilities for betting on the outcome of a virtual game, race, competition or other event or process (to the extent that this is not restricted or excluded by a condition imposed by the Commission), and the provision of equal chance gaming, other than bingo. This means that a casino operator does not need to obtain a betting operating licence if he wishes to offer this form of betting, and can automatically offer equal chance gaming, other than bingo. If he does wish to offer bingo, he will need to obtain a bingo operating licence as well. Under rules in Part 8 of the Act, a small non-remote casino cannot offer bingo from its premises.
217. Under subsection (4), a betting operating licence authorises the provision of facilities for betting on the outcome of a virtual game, race, competition or other event or process (other than a game of chance), but only to the extent that this is not restricted or excluded by a condition imposed by the Commission. This gives the Commission power to regulate virtual betting if the need arises.
218. Neither subsections (3) or (4) are authorisations for virtual gambling by machine. Machine gambling is regulated by Parts 8 and 10 of the Act. These subsections concern over-the- counter, person to person, betting on virtual events, or remote gambling where no gaming machine is involved.

219. There are two types of operating licence specifically designed for authorising the provision of gaming machines: the gaming machine general operating licence for adult gaming centres and the gaming machine general operating licence for family entertainment centres. These specifically authorise the licence holder to make gaming machines available for use. However, under subsection (5) certain other types of operating licence also bring with them a general entitlement to make gaming machines available for use:

- a non-remote casino operating licence;
- a non-remote bingo operating licence;
- a non-remote general betting operating licence; and
- a non-remote pool betting operating licence.

220. Apart from these four types of operating licence (and the two general gaming machine operating licences) no other operating licences may authorise the making available of gaming machines. Therefore, no remote operating licence confers a right to make gaming machines available for use.

221. Moreover, the fact that certain operating licences provide this authorisation, does not entitle the holder of the licence to use any number or category of gaming machines, on any particular premises. The purpose of subsection (5) is to provide a generic authority for the operator to make gaming machines available for use, in the same way as a casino operating licence gives authority to provide facilities to operate a casino (in the general sense). The provisions of Parts 8 (premises licences) and 10 (gaming machines) control the precise locations where gaming machines may be used, and an operator must comply with the requirements of these Parts to make a gaming machine available for use lawfully.

SECTION 69: APPLICATION

222. This section sets out who may apply for an operating licence and the type of information that must accompany an application. Applications are to be made to the Commission and such other people as the Secretary of State directs. The application, in particular, must contain details of the gambling activities that the operator wishes to provide (eg which of the ten types of licence he wishes to obtain, and whether remotely or non-remotely), and state whether the applicant has been convicted of a relevant offence (as defined in the interpretation section for this Part).

223. An application fee is payable, which may vary for different types of licence (ie different kinds of gambling activity) or different circumstances (subsections (2)(g) and (5)). Such fees will be prescribed by the Secretary of State in regulations. It is anticipated that fees will vary across sectors to reflect the Commission's differing costs of regulation.

SECTION 70: CONSIDERATION OF APPLICATIONS: GENERAL PRINCIPLES

224. This section sets out the general principles which the Commission will apply in determining applications, and particular matters which they may take into account. The detail of how the Commission will consider applications, and, for example, what evidence it will seek, will be set out in the statement of licensing policy that the Commission is required to produce under Part 2 of the Act.

225. The purpose of this section is to outline the principles which will govern the Commission's decision-making in relation to the consideration of applications. The two main matters are: to have regard to the licensing objectives, and to have regard to the applicant's suitability, including his integrity, competence, and financial circumstances. The assessment may also cover the suitability of equipment to be used in connection with the proposed activities.

226. The Commission's assessment may cover not just the applicant, but also people who are connected to the applicant because they are likely to exercise a function in connection with, or have an interest in, the gambling activities.

227. Subsection (3) makes specific provision for those cases where the application is for a non-remote casino operating licence. In such cases, the Commission must have

regard to the applicant's commitment to protecting vulnerable people from being harmed or exploited by gambling, and to making assistance available to people who may be affected by problem gambling. This requirement reflects the particular risks presented by casinos in relation to problem gambling.

228. There may be circumstances where the Commission will wish to assume that a class of applicant will automatically fulfil the requirement of integrity for the purpose of assessing suitability. In these circumstances the Commission's statement may make a determination to this effect. For example, the Commission could decide that local authorities, seeking a lottery operating licence, do not need to supply evidence of integrity as part of the application process.

229. The Commission can also deem particular equipment or gaming machines to be suitable, in accordance with standards or tests that it has established, or asked others to establish for it. This is designed to aid both the Commission and applicants in making the application process as efficient as possible.

SECTION 71: CONSIDERATION OF APPLICATION: CRIMINAL RECORD

230. One of the licensing objectives is to keep gambling crime free. This section provides that the Commission may refuse an application for an operating licence if the applicant has a conviction for a relevant offence. This is without prejudice to the suitability of the applicant generally, but permits the Commission to reject an application by reason of the conviction for the relevant offence, should it consider this appropriate. 'Relevant offence' is defined in the interpretation section for this Part.

SECTION 72: CONSIDERATION OF APPLICATION: DEMAND

231. Under the Betting, Gaming and Lotteries Act 1963 and the Gaming Act 1968, one of the considerations for the grant of a permit or licence was whether there was unmet demand for the specified gambling facilities in the particular area to which an application related. This section revokes this principle, as unmet demand is not a relevant criterion, under the Act, for determining whether or not to grant an operating licence. This section also abolishes the 'permitted areas' for casinos which were established under the Gaming Act 1968. Similar provisions are contained in Part 8, in relation to the consideration of premises licences. The necessary repeals for these various matters are set out in Schedule 17.

SECTION 73: PROCEDURE

232. This section sets out the powers of the Commission to require information from an applicant, and to have regard to information provided by other people when considering an application. In particular, the Commission may require the production of an enhanced criminal record certificate under the Police Act 1997 (c.50). This applies to the applicant or people relevant to the application.

233. The licensing policy statement produced by the Commission under Part 2 must specify the procedures to be operated by the Commission, including the Commission's practice with regard to delegating functions, holding hearings, and requiring evidence. Schedule 4 also makes provisions with regard to the general proceedings of the Commission.

SECTION 74: DETERMINATION OF APPLICATION

234. This section provides the range of determinations the Commission can make having considered an application and the actions consequent upon a determination, including a requirement to give reasons where an application is rejected.

SECTIONS 75 TO 78: LICENCE CONDITIONS

235. There are three types of licence condition that may be attached to operating licences under the Act: general conditions and individual conditions, both of which are attached by the Commission; and conditions imposed by the Secretary of State.
236. Sections 75 and 76 concern general conditions, which are conditions the Commission may specify for an operating licence or a class of operating licence, and which have general application. So, for example, the Commission could specify a general condition that applied to all general betting operating licences, that the rules of the bet must be on display to customers (whether on premises, or over the internet). This condition would apply to everyone holding a general betting operating licence.
237. Section 76 sets out the procedures which the Commission must follow in specifying general conditions. These include holding general consultations (with some mandatory consultees) on the terms of the condition, and publishing conditions. In addition, the Commission must notify licensees in advance of a proposed imposition, modification or revocation of a general condition, giving three months notice, unless the matter is urgent. This ensures that licensees have adequate notice of general conditions and changes that may be made to them over time.
238. Additionally, the Commission has power, under section 77 to impose specific conditions on individual operating licences. These conditions are not subject to any publication or general consultation requirements, in contrast with general conditions. Rather, these conditions will address particular matters concerning an individual operator and its activities, where the Commission considers it appropriate. So, for example, the Commission could attach an individual condition on a particular casino operating licence that not more than five casino premises can be operated under it, due to the financial strength of the operator. Every operating licence issued must specify any individual conditions attached to it under this section.
239. Alongside the powers of the Commission to attach conditions to operating licences, the Secretary of State may make regulations which provide for a specific condition to be attached to a class of operating licence, under section 78.

SECTION 79: SCOPE OF POWERS TO ATTACH CONDITIONS

240. This section gives specific examples of the matters to which general, individual or Secretary of State conditions may relate. The section does not limit the breadth of the matters with which these three types of condition can deal. Instead, this section helps provide some understanding of the matters which conditions may cover.
241. A condition may:

- limit or restrict the nature or extent of the gambling facilities provided, or control the circumstances in which they are carried on;
- make provision about the facilities that may be provided, the manner in which the facilities are provided or the number of people employed in providing facilities;
- make provision about the financial resources available to the licensee, including the maintenance of reserves in respect of potential liabilities;
- where it is a remote operating licence, may restrict the methods of remote communication that may be used;
- make provision about the advertising or description of facilities for gambling (which could include the name given to a gambling product);
- make provision about assistance to people who are or may be affected by problem gambling; and
- require the operator to identify or record the identity of users of his facilities.

SECTION 80: REQUIREMENT FOR PERSONAL LICENCE

242. Part 6 of the Act provides the licensing system for personal licences. This section sets out the relationship between an operating licence and the need for an operator to use people holding personal licences to provide certain functions and facilities for gambling.

243. When the Commission considers an application for an operating licence, it will consider what offices or functions in the organisation should be performed by a personal licence holder, and attach conditions to the licence specifying what the requirements for personal licences are to be. These conditions could be set by general or individual condition, or the Secretary of State may set generic conditions by regulations to apply to classes of operating licence.

244. There will be one mandatory condition on every operating licence, which is that every operating licence must specify at least one management office which is to be occupied by a person who holds a personal licence (subsection (1)). This will be set as a general or individual condition, not a Secretary of State condition. Beyond this one mandatory personal licence, the Commission may identify any additional number of posts in an operator's organisation which must be filled by a personal licence holder (subsections (2) to (4)). Such conditions will always relate to either a management office or an operational function.

245. Management office (subsection (5)) means:

- A director of a company;
- A partner;
- An officer in an unincorporated association; and
- Any position which (by reason of the terms of the appointment) carries responsibility for:
  - the conduct of a person who performs an operational function; or
  - facilitating or ensuring compliance with the terms of the operating licence.

246. Operational function (subsection (6)) means:

- any function that enables the person to influence the outcome of gambling;
- receiving or paying money in connection with the gambling; or
- specified activities in relation to the manufacture and supply of gaming machines.

247. The Secretary of State has the power to amend these definitions through secondary legislation (subsection (8)).

248. These broad definitions will enable the Commission to consider the particular circumstances of each operator (irrespective of the job titles the operator may use) and identify those functions and offices within an organisation that will require a person to hold a personal licence when carrying them out. This section is not intended to require everyone performing any management office or operational function (as described above) to hold a personal licence. The Commission will decide what the appropriate licensing requirements are to be, either on an individual basis, or, where it is able to do so, according to classes of operating licence.

249. If an operator does not use a person holding an appropriate personal licence to perform an office or function identified by the Commission, it will breach a condition of its operating licence.

250. While this section provides the mechanism for operating licences to contain conditions about matters to be undertaken by a personal licence holder, it does not cover the process for obtaining a personal licence. That is set out at Part 6 of the Act.

251. Subsection (9) contains an exemption from the requirements of this section for clubs or miners' welfare institutes holding a bingo operating licence. Part 12 requires clubs or miners' welfare institutes which provide facilities for bingo that exceed a specified threshold in terms of stakes or prizes in any week, to obtain a bingo operating licence. Games played below this threshold are authorised by other provisions in Part 12. Officers of these associations are not required to hold personal licences in relation to their additional bingo operating licence, and this subsection exempts them accordingly.

SECTION 81: CREDIT AND INDUCEMENTS

252. This section concerns restrictions on the offering of credit and inducements by operating licence holders. Subsection (1) provides that a condition may be attached by the Commission to an operating licence relating to:

- the giving of credit in relation to the licensed gambling activities;
- making offers or inducements designed to induce participation in the licensed gambling activities; or
- being party to arrangements for inducing, permitting or assisting person to gamble.

253. In addition to this general condition-making power, subsection (2) provides that holders of non-remote casino or bingo licences may not themselves give any form of credit to people using their facilities. Nor may they arrange, permit or knowingly facilitate credit in connection with their gambling facilities. This means that credit cards cannot be used to pay for gambling offered by casino or bingo operators. A similar restriction is placed upon the relevant premises licences in Part 8, and Part 10 prevents credit cards being used to pay for gaming machines.

254. Subsection (3) allows cash-withdrawal machines accepting credit cards to be used by casino or bingo operators, provided that:

- the nature and location of the machines complies with any relevant licence conditions; and
- the provider of the machine and the gambling operator are unconnected, and no payment is made or received in connection with the machine.

255. Subsection 4 defines 'credit' to include any form of financial accommodation and the acceptance of payment of a fee, charge, or stake in anything other than cash, cheque or debit card payment is considered credit.

SECTION 82: COMPLIANCE WITH CODE OF PRACTICE

256. This section makes it a condition of all operating licences that the holder must comply with any code of practice relating to social responsibility which is relevant to them. Codes of practice issued by the Commission under Part 2 are not of themselves automatically binding on operators, but are part of the overall scheme of regulation. However, this section provides that social responsibility provisions in any code are incorporated as conditions to an operating licence.

SECTION 83: RETURN OF STAKES TO CHILDREN

257. The Act contains a range of provisions designed to prevent children and young people from gambling. Under this section a condition is imposed on all operating licences which requires operators to take certain steps in the event that they become aware that a child or young person has used their facilities to gamble. A child is a person under 16, and a young person a person under 18.

258. If an operator becomes aware that a child or young person has used his gambling facilities, then the operator must return any money paid by the child or young person as soon as practicable, and must not pay out any winnings (although if winnings have been paid out before the operator is aware of the claimant's age, he may not demand repayment).

259. This section does not apply to the use of the lowest stake gaming machine (a Category D machine) or equal chance gaming at a licensed Family Entertainment Centre (which can be played pursuant to authorisations under Part 13). The section only applies to children (and not a young person) when the gambling activity concerned is football pools or a lottery. The condition imposed by this section cannot be overridden by any contract or other agreement.

SECTION 84: PREMISES

260. It is the role of licensing authorities to licence specific premises upon which facilities for gambling may be provided in Great Britain. These matters are regulated by Part 8 of the Act. Therefore, an operating licence cannot be subject to a condition which specifies particular premises upon which gambling activities must or must not be carried on. However, conditions may be attached to operating licences which deal with the number of sets of premises on which the licensed activities may be carried on (eg a maximum of 100 betting shops) or the number of people for whom facilities may be provided on any premises where the licensed activities are carried on.

261. An operating licence is not limited to authorising the provision of facilities in one place. The fact that an operating licence is a 'casino' operating licence or an operating licence for an 'adult gaming centre' does not mean this only authorises the provision of one such facility. An operating licence gives a generic entitlement, to be used alongside any number of premises licences, subject to any conditions imposed under subsection (1) of this section.

SECTION 85: EQUIPMENT

262. In issuing an operating licence, the Commission may attach a condition about the amount or specification of equipment to be used in the licensed gambling activities. Such equipment may include computers or devices for playing casino games, but does not include a gaming machine. This ties in with the powers of the Commission to consider the suitability of equipment when considering an application for a licence.

263. The section contains a specific provision for equipment used for playing bingo. Under subsection (2)(a) a condition cannot be attached to a licence about the number of pieces of equipment used for playing bingo. This means that equipment such as 'mechanised cash bingo equipment', used under the Gaming Act 1968 regime, cannot be subject to control about its numbers. It can be subject to licence conditions about its specification under subsection (2)(b), and such specification will enable this equipment to fall outside the definition of gaming machine in Part 10.

264. Similarly, the Commission can use subsection (2)(b) to specify equipment for playing bingo in adult gaming centres or licensed family entertainment centres, (bingo played pursuant to the prize gaming entitlements in Part 13). Where it does so, such equipment will not constitute a gaming machine.

SECTION 86: GAMING MACHINES

265. While certain operating licences confer general permissions to use gaming machines, under section 68, the permission to use gaming machines on particular premises is contained in Parts 8 and 10 of the Act. This means that the Commission should not attach conditions to operating licences concerning numbers or categories of gaming machines which an operator is entitled to use. Therefore, subsection (1) prevents operating licences having conditions attached to them about:

- the number or categories of gaming machine that may be made available for use in accordance with an operating licence; or
- anything that contradicts regulations concerning the use of gaming machines, made by the Secretary of State under Part 10.

266. This does not mean that the Commission cannot regulate the manufacture and supply of machines. Section 96 makes express provision for the Commission to set standards for the gaming machine technical operating licence.

267. Subsection (2) provides a mechanism for the Commission to require operators to stop using machines that have been illegally manufactured, supplied, or handled. The Commission may notify an operator that a machine is not covered by an appropriate gaming machine technical operating licence, or does not comply with Commission standards. After such notification, the Commission may place a

condition on the relevant operating licence requiring the operator to stop making the machine available for use. Failure to do so will amount to breach of the licence.

SECTION 87: MEMBERSHIP

268. Under the Gaming Act 1968 it is a requirement that gaming licences under Part II of that Act can only be held by casinos or bingo halls that operate as a members' club. That rule is abolished by this Act, and as a result, this section provides that neither the Commission nor the Secretary of State can impose a condition on an operating licence requiring facilities to be provided on the basis of a club or on any other membership basis. However, nothing in this section or the rest of the Act prevents organisations from operating as a members' club if they so wish.

SECTION 88: INFORMATION

269. This section permits the Commission or the Secretary of State to impose licence conditions requiring operators to pass information to the Commission or to such other people as may be specified. The purpose of this power is to promote information exchange between the Commission, operators and, for example, sporting regulators. The type of information which could be covered includes information concerning cheating or breach of sporting rules. Licence conditions could also be used to supplement the voiding of bets powers in Part 17. Voluntary codes are already in place in parts of the gambling industry to allow such information exchange. This section allows a uniform approach for different sectors to be established, as appropriate.

SECTION 89: REMOTE OPERATING LICENCE

270. This section sets out particular rules applying to a remote operating licence.

271. It is a presumption of a remote operating licence that remote gambling equipment used by the operator in providing facilities for gambling must be located in Great Britain. This is set out in subsection (1). Part 3 contains the definition of remote gambling equipment.

272. Subsection (2) empowers the Commission to depart from this general presumption, in certain circumstances. The Commission may allow an operator to site particular pieces of specified remote gambling equipment off-shore, provided the Commission is satisfied that to do so is consistent with the licensing objectives in section 1. For example, the power could be used in relation to equipment facilitating player to player games which can involve individuals in different jurisdictions being pooled by operators. The matter is one of discretion, for the Commission.

273. Without prejudice to its other condition-making powers, the Commission may establish, or authorise others to establish on its behalf, standards in respect of systems and processes used for remote gambling. These standards will be relevant to the consideration of applications for remote operating licences, made under section 69. The Commission can enforce these standards through licence conditions, including the testing of the operator's systems, on application and from time to time.

SECTION 90: CASINO OPERATING LICENCE

274. Part 1 provides a definition of casino, and gives the Secretary of State powers to define categories of casino. Under subsection (1) the Commission or the Secretary of State can impose conditions on any casino operating licence which restricts the type of casino game that can be made available. Under the Gaming Act 1968 these restrictions were imposed by secondary legislation. Under the Act the Commission has the power to achieve this by licence condition, or the Secretary of State may do so by regulations.

275. Subsection (2) provides that the Commission may specify rules for casino games or any equal chance game played in a casino. Again, this power replaces the position under the Gaming Act where these matters were prescribed in secondary legislation.

SECTION 91: BINGO OPERATING LICENCE

276. The Secretary of State may use her regulation making to attach conditions to bingo operating licences on the matters specified in subsection (1). This includes power to limit the amount of stakes or participation fees or value of prizes; or requiring a specified proportion of stakes to be paid out by way or prizes, or imposing requirements specific to bingo games that are played on more than one set of premises. Subsection (2) then lists matters about which conditions cannot be made in relation to bingo operating licences. This means that the Commission has no power to set conditions on these matters, and, to the extent that it is not expressly permitted by subsection (1), nor does the Secretary of State.

277. The introduction of remote operating licences, together with the Secretary of State's power to impose requirements that are specific to games played on more than one set of premises, at subsection (1)(e), replace the statutory provisions relating to 'multiple' and 'linked' bingo that are repealed by this Act. Remote operating licences will be required by those wishing to provide bingo by means of remote communication, even where the bingo is played partly on licensed bingo premises. The fees for these licences will be commensurate with the regulatory costs for the particular activities concerned.

278. Subsection (2)(f) prevents a condition being attached to a bingo operating licence which prohibits or limits the roll-over of prizes between bingo games. Neither the Secretary of State, nor the Commission can attach a condition relating to the roll-over of prizes.

279. In setting participation fees under subsection (1), different types of fee may be set, as amplified by section 344. For example, fees for admission to the premises can be distinguished from a fee to participate in a particular game. Fees can also be apportioned between gambling and non-gambling purposes.

SECTION 92: GENERAL BETTING OPERATING LICENCE

280. A general betting operating licence will be required by anyone wishing to accept or make bets by way of business (this includes negotiation of bets). If someone wishes to provide facilities merely for other people to accept and make bets, then the relevant operating licence will be a betting intermediary operating licence, not a general betting operating licence, as the latter is relevant only for people who are themselves making or accepting bets in the course of a business. See also sections 353(2)(a), 296(3) and 302.

281. This licence replaces the bookmaker's permit under section 2 of, and Schedule 1, to the Betting, Gaming and Lotteries Act 1963.

282. Subsection (1) sets out who is empowered to accept bets under the terms of a general betting operating licence: this will be the licence holder, an employee of the licence holder and any other holder of a general betting operating licence. No other person may accept or make bets under the authorisation of a general betting operating licence.

283. Subsection (2) makes it clear that a general betting operating licence contains an implied term permitting the making of bets via postal services. This prevents any question of the need for a remote licence arising in relation to bets made by post.

SECTION 93: POOL BETTING OPERATING LICENCE

284. Where an operator is making or accepting pool bets (as defined in section 12), then the appropriate operating licence will be a pool betting operating licence. This type of licence may cover any form of pool betting, but conditions may limit the particular pool betting activities an operator may provide. For example, a pool betting operating licence may specify that the operator may only operate pool betting in relation to football pools.

285. This licence replaces the system for registration of pools promoters under section 4 of, and Schedule 2 to, the Betting, Gaming and Lotteries Act 1963. It is also the form of authorisation that will be required by operators of pool betting on dog-tracks, previously authorised by section 4(1)(b) of the 1963 Act. Part 8 of this Act contains separate provisions governing the use of dog- track premises for pool betting. Horserace pool betting is dealt with in the next section.
286. As with the general betting operating licence, there are restrictions on who is permitted to accept pool bets under the licence. The restrictions are the same as those for the general betting operating licence, except that pool betting operators will also be allowed to authorise agents to accept bets on their behalf in certain circumstances. Those circumstances are:

- where the agent is on a track in reliance on an occasional use notice and is accepting bets in relation to a horse-race or a dog race on that track. In these circumstances the agent must be an adult and be authorised in writing to accept bets on behalf of the licensee (subsection (2)); or
- where the pool betting operating licence permits the operator to provide football pools and the operator has given written authority to an adult or young person to receive entries or payments on football pools on his behalf ('authorised collector') (subsections (3) to (6)). In these circumstances the authorised collector may provide coupons, receive entries and payments, and pay winnings, pursuant to the operating licence. Conditions may also be imposed on the operating licence specific to the authorised collectors.

287. Under subsection (9) the Secretary of State may change, by order, the types of event on a track (subject to an occasional use notice) for which an agent may be authorised to take pool bets under subsection (2), and may add sports to the matters for which agents can be authorised under subsection (3), in addition to football pools.
288. Subsection (7) makes it clear that a pool betting operating licence contains an implied term permitting the making of pool bets via postal services. This prevents any question of the need for a remote licence.

SECTION 94: HORSE-RACE POOL BETTING OPERATING LICENCE

289. Where a pool betting licence authorises the provision of horserace pool betting, then the operating licence may specify that this section has effect. The intention is that this section will be needed in circumstances where only one licence for horserace pool betting has effect in Great Britain.
290. Under subsection (2), the holder of a pool betting licence, who is licensed to conduct horserace pool betting, may authorise in writing any person to provide facilities for horserace pool betting, and this authorisation may include terms as to payment. This means that, for example, such an authority may be used by a person to accept pool bets on horse races on premises with a betting premises licence, or pursuant to an occasional use notice. This authorisation may also be made the subject of specific conditions on the operating licence (subsection (5)). Subsection (6) makes it clear that a pool betting operating licence contains an implied term permitting the making of pool bets via postal services.
291. The Secretary of State has the power to repeal this section if circumstances dictate that it is no longer needed ie if there are no longer exclusive arrangements for horserace pool betting in Great Britain. In such circumstances, the pool betting operating licence would become the only kind of licence relevant to pool betting in Great Britain, and would also cover horserace pool betting. Section 358(4) to (6) makes specific provision concerning commencement of this Act, and transitional powers relating to the Horserace Betting Olympic Lottery Act 2004 (c.25).

SECTION 95: BETTING ON THE NATIONAL LOTTERY

292. This section replaces provisions in the Betting, Gaming and Lotteries Act 1963 which caused a bookmaker to lose his licence if he took bets on the outcome of the

National Lottery (Schedule 1, paragraph 18A). Under this section, all types of operating licences permitting betting are subject to a mandatory condition that no betting takes place on the outcome of the National Lottery.

SECTION 96: GAMING MACHINE TECHNICAL OPERATING LICENCE

293. Without prejudice to other condition-making powers, the Commission may establish, or authorise others to establish on its behalf, standards in respect of systems and processes used for the manufacture, supply, installation, adaptation, maintenance or repair of a gaming machine, or software for use in a gaming machine (subsection (1)). These standards must be consistent with the rules concerning gaming machines contained in Part 10 (subsection (2)).

294. These standards may cover technical matters about the functioning of the machines. Under subsection (3) they may also cover matters such as the nature of the gambling involved, the way in which the results are presented or determined, and the nature of the information displayed on the machine. This is intended to be used, in particular, to provide standards which discourage repetitive play and protect children.

295. The Commission can enforce these standards through licence conditions, including the testing of the operator's systems on application, and from time to time.

SECTION 97: GAMBLING SOFTWARE: OPERATING LICENCE: STANDARDS

296. This section permits the Commission to set standards for gambling software supply and manufacture for use in remote gambling. Similar powers are set out in sections 89 and 96 for remote gambling and gaming machines respectively. The section describes the powers the Commission has, including authorising individuals to test software, or a random sample of software and requiring licensees to make software available for testing.

SECTION 98: LOTTERY OPERATING LICENCES

297. This section provides for the Commission to issue licences for the operation of lotteries. Lotteries which form part of the National Lottery (which are not covered by this Act), or that are classed as 'exempt' lotteries under Schedule 11, will not require a licence under these provisions.

298. A lottery operating licence may only be issued to the following:

- non-commercial societies;
- local authorities; and
- external lottery managers.

299. Section 18 of the Act contains a definition of 'non-commercial society'. A non-commercial society, which wishes to hold lotteries, will only require an operating licence under this section if the proceeds of the lotteries they promote exceed the thresholds set out in Part 4 of Schedule 11 to the Act. Below these thresholds, the lottery will be classified as a 'small society lottery', and will be exempt from the requirement to obtain a licence (although they will require registration with a local authority).

300. The types of local authority which may promote a lottery are broadly defined, and include parish councils in England, and community councils in Wales (subsection (7)).

301. Subsection (2) allows the Commission flexibility in terms of the scope of operating licences. A licence may authorise promotion generally, or specific promotion activities. It may authorise promotion of lotteries generally, or only in connection with lotteries of certain types or in certain circumstances.

302. A licence may authorise a person to act as an external lottery manager, to provide lottery management services on behalf of local authorities, and on behalf of non-commercial societies, whether licensed or exempt. The Commission has the power to include a condition on a lottery operating licence that all of the arrangements for the

lottery are to be made by an external lottery manager. If the Commission does so, it will not be required to form an opinion about the suitability of the local authority or non-commercial society in terms of integrity, competence or financial and other circumstances (under section 70 (2)), when considering their application for a licence. Their assessment will be of the lottery manager only. The Commission may similarly assume the integrity of particular classes of applicant, and, for example, could do so where a local authority is making the application (see section 70(7)).

303. Subsections (4) and (5) ensure that it will not be possible to prohibit the delivery of lottery tickets by post in relation to these lotteries, either by regulations made by the Secretary of State, or by conditions made by the Commission. Subsection (6) specifically empowers the Commission to attach conditions to the licence concerning rollovers, that is the carry over of prizes from one lottery to another, as defined in Part 11.

SECTION 99: MANDATORY CONDITIONS OF LOTTERY OPERATING LICENCE

304. This section provides that the Commission must attach certain conditions to lottery operating licences issued to non-commercial societies and local authorities, for the purpose of achieving the requirements set out in the section. The Commission is not restricted to these conditions, and may attach conditions which are similar, but more onerous, than those specified here.

305. Various conditions must be attached to licences which set money or percentage limits in relation to proceeds and prizes. At least 20% of the proceeds of any lottery promoted under the licence must go to good causes. In the case of a non-commercial society, this means that a minimum of 20% of the proceeds must be used for the purposes for which the society is conducted. In the case of a local authority, 20% of the proceeds must be put towards a purpose for which it has the power to incur expenditure. Under all lottery operating licences, the proceeds of any single lottery must be limited, and the proceeds of all lotteries in one year are restricted to an overall upper limit. There is also an upper limit on the size of a prize in a licensed lottery. These limits are set out in subsections (2) to (4).

306. Conditions must be attached to the licence prescribing certain requirements in relation to tickets. In particular, the information specified in subsections (5) and (6) must be included on the ticket. One ticket may provide entry to a number of lotteries, provided the information contained on it is sufficient that the dates of the draws in those lotteries are able to be determined. A ticket need not be a paper document, but if it is in electronic form, it must be capable of being printed out or electronically stored (subsection (7)). This will permit, for example, entry to a lottery over the internet. No additional payment apart from the ticket price may be required for entry into the lottery (subsection (8)).

307. The Secretary of State has power to vary, by order, the money amounts and percentages set out in this section (subsection (10)).

SECTION 100: ANNUAL FEE

308. The holder of an operating licence must pay a fee to the Commission for the licence to have effect ('the first annual fee'), and, thereafter must pay an annual fee before each anniversary of the issue of the licence. These annual fees acts as renewal fees in the sense that failure to pay them can lead to revocation of the licence. These fees are different to the application fee required when making an application for a licence. The Secretary of State will use regulations to set the fees and the period within which the first annual fee must be paid. Different fees may be set for different kinds of operating licences and different circumstances.

SECTION 101: CHANGE OF CIRCUMSTANCE

309. If an operator has a change of circumstance after an operating licence is issued he may be required, by regulations (under this section) or by conditions attached to his licence, to inform the Commission of the change of circumstance. There is a fee to be paid by for the operator. The Commission must then amend the licence as appropriate to reflect the change in circumstances.

310. This section sets out the regulation making power of the Secretary of State, and provides that a licence holder commits an offence if he fails, without reasonable excuse, to comply with a requirement to inform the Commission of a change of circumstance. The maximum penalty for the offence is a fine not exceeding level 2 on the standard scale. The Commission may also suspend or revoke an operating licence if the holder fails to comply with regulations under this section.

SECTIONS 102 AND 103: CHANGE OF CORPORATE CONTROL

311. If the holder of an operating licence is a company limited by shares, a mechanism is needed to allow the Commission to approve a change of control of that company (ie following sale, transfer, allotment or issue of shares). These sections provide that mechanism.

312. This mechanism applies to any kind of operating licence, but the Secretary of State may make regulations exempting specified kinds of operating licence from these requirements.

313. This section uses the definitions set out in the Financial Services and Markets Act 2000. It provides that if a person becomes a 'controller' of a company which holds an operating licence ('the company'), then the company must surrender the licence to the Commission, or apply to the Commission for approval for the licence to continue to have effect.

314. If the company wishes to apply for approval for the licence to continue to have effect (which will attract a fee to be set by the Secretary of State), then the Commission may require information about the change of control and the new controller. The Commission may give approval if it is satisfied that that it would have granted the operating licence at the time of the original application, had the new controller been the controller of the company at the time. If it is not so satisfied, then the Commission must revoke the operating licence. A company has five weeks from the date when the new controller takes over in which to surrender its licence, or apply for a continuation, otherwise the Commission will revoke the licence (unless the Commission chooses to extend this period, which it may do, even after the 5 weeks has expired, provide the licence has not already been revoked).

315. In requiring information in relation to a change of control, the Commission is required to have regard to normal commercial practices concerning confidentiality.

316. These sections apply to the merger or division of companies, but where this is the cause of a change of controller, the Secretary of State may set reduced fees for applications in these circumstances.

SECTION 104: APPLICATION TO VARY LICENCE

317. Holders of operating licences may, for their own commercial reasons, wish to vary the gambling facilities that they provide, whether that is to cease carrying out an activity, or to start a new activity. Equally, they may wish to vary an individual condition that has been attached to their licence. In such circumstances, the holder of an operating licence will need to apply to the Commission to vary the terms of the licence.

318. This section permits holders to apply for a variation of an operating licence, and applies the provisions of Part 5, modified as appropriate, to the variation process. Regulations by the Secretary of State will provide the relevant procedures.

319. An application for variation cannot be used to transfer an operating licence to another person. Operating licences are non-transferable.

SECTION 105: AMENDMENT

320. This section provides that the Commission may require the holder of an operating licence to submit the licence to the Commission for amendment in a number of circumstances where it requires changes to be made to it.
321. A licence holder has 14 days to comply with a requirement to send his licence to the Commission in response to a request, and commits an offence if he fails to do so without reasonable excuse. The maximum penalty is a fine not exceeding level 2 on the standard scale. The Commission also has power to suspend or revoke a licence if the holder fails to comply with the requirements set out here.

SECTION 106: REGISTER OF OPERATING LICENCES

322. To allow the public to find out whether a person providing gambling facilities holds the necessary permission, licence or permit, the Act contains a series of requirements for various registers to be maintained. This section requires the Commission to maintain a register of operating licences and to make it available to the public. A fee may be payable to gain access to the register, but the fee must not exceed the reasonable cost of providing the service.

SECTIONS 107 AND 108: COPY OF LICENCE AND PRODUCTION OF LICENCE

323. These sections allow the Commission:
- to issue to a licence holder a copy of the licence in the event that it has been lost, stolen or damaged; and
- (together with the police) to require the holder of an operating licence to produce it within a specified period. The licensee will be committing an offence if he fails without reasonable excuse to comply with this requirement. The maximum penalty is a fine not exceeding level 2 on the standard scale.

SECTION 109: CONVICTION

324. One of the licensing objectives in the Act is to prevent gambling from being a source of crime or disorder, being associated with crime or disorder or being used to support crime. This section requires holders of operating licences to take certain steps in the event that they are convicted of a criminal offence in Great Britain or abroad.
325. Where the holder of an operating licence is convicted of an offence in Great Britain, or of a relevant offence by a court outside Great Britain, he must inform the Commission as soon as reasonably practical. This ensures that the Commission has the necessary information it needs to regulate licence holders, and could, if it wished, commence a review of the licence.
326. If the holder of an operating licence is convicted of a relevant offence before a court in Great Britain he must inform the court immediately that he holds an operating licence. This is so that the court can consider whether it should exercise its powers to order forfeiture of the operating licence as part of the sentence it imposes for the offence.
327. A list of offences which are 'relevant offences' is set out at Schedule 7. These are offences under British law (the jurisdictions of England and Wales, and Scotland). An offence under the law of another country is a relevant offence if it is similar in nature to an offence listed in Schedule 7. This ensures that a person's suitability to hold a licence is considered in relation to any criminal conviction for a serious offence, not just those in Great Britain (see section 126 for the definition of 'relevant offence').

SECTIONS 110 AND 111: DURATION

328. As a general rule, operating licences will be of indefinite duration, subject to rules about lapse, forfeiture and the Commission's regulatory powers. However, the Commission has power to determine that operating licences, or a particular class of operating licence, should be given a particular duration. Such a determination will be made and promulgated as part of the Commission's licensing policy statement under Part 2.

329. Where the Commission determines a particular duration under section 111, this will apply to existing and future licences. However, for existing licences the duration will begin from the date of publication of the determination rather than the date the licence was granted.

SECTION 112: RENEWAL OF LICENCE

330. This section provides that where the Commission has decided that operating licences are to have a fixed duration under section 111, procedures for the renewal of licences can be put in place.

SECTIONS 113 AND 114: SURRENDER AND LAPSE

331. A licence ceases to have effect if it is surrendered to the Commission. This provides a voluntary procedure for a licence holder to give up his licence if he so wishes.

332. A licence will lapse, and is not transferable, if the licence holder:

- Dies;
- In the opinion of the Commission becomes incapable of carrying out the licensed activities (from which there is a right of appeal); or
- Becomes bankrupt or goes into liquidation.

SECTION 115: FORFEITURE

333. This section provides courts with the power to order forfeiture of an operating licence where it is sentencing the holder of a licence on conviction for a relevant offence, as defined in section 126. This allows the courts to take appropriate steps to bring a licence to an end, without the Commission needing to take separate regulatory action.

SECTION 116: REVIEW

334. Section 110 provides that operating licences are granted for an indefinite period. However, the Commission has power to introduce time limits for licences if it believes there is a regulatory need to do so. Therefore, the general position is that licences will not need to be renewed at any point. Section 116 gives the Commission the power to review, over time, the performance of licence holders and the operation of licence conditions.

335. First, under subsection (1) the Commission may review matters relating to a class of operating licence ie not an individual licence, but a type of licence. For example, the Commission could review the operation of all gaming machine general operating licences. The purpose will be to review the manner in which licensees, as a whole, carry on licensed activities, and particularly, how licensees comply with the conditions attached to the class of operating licence. The purpose of this type of review could be to consider whether any changes to general conditions on licences are needed.

336. Secondly, under subsection (2), the Commission has power to review any matter relating to an individual operating licence on any of three grounds:

- If the Commission suspects that conditions of an operating licence are being breached;
- If the Commission believes that the licence holder or any person connected with the gambling activities, has been convicted of a relevant offence in Great Britain or abroad; or

- If the Commission for any reason:
  - suspects that the licence holder may be unsuitable to perform the licensed activities; or
  - thinks that a review would be appropriate.

337. The section makes it clear that a review can be carried out even if there is no suspicion or belief about the licence holder's activities. This ensures that a licence could be reviewed solely on the grounds, for example, that it had been held for a long period of time, and that the Commission considered a review prudent.

338. In the event that the Commission decides to carry out a review of an individual licence there are procedural requirements to ensure that the licence holder can take part in the review (subsections (4) and (5)).

SECTIONS 117 TO 121: REGULATORY POWERS

339. The Commission has a range of powers available to it, exercisable after a review, or in circumstances where a licence holder has failed to comply with other requirements specified in Part 5 of the Act (eg to pay the annual fee). These sections outline these powers, and the procedural steps the Commission must take before exercising them.

340. The Commission can:

- give the licensee a warning;
- add, remove or vary a condition to the licence;
- make, amend or remove an exclusion;
- suspend or revoke the licence; or
- impose a financial penalty.

341. Suspension powers are available to the Commission at the outset of, and during, a review. Therefore, if the Commission considers a matter sufficiently serious, it can require the operator to suspend all or part of his activities pending the outcome of the review. The Commission also has powers to suspend a licence following a review.

342. Where the Commission concludes that a licence holder has breached the conditions of his licence, it may impose a financial penalty on the licence holder. The Commission must take a number of procedural steps before it can impose such a penalty, which include providing the licence holder with reasons for the proposed penalty, and time in which to make representations to the Commission. The Commission is subject to a time limit for imposing a penalty of two years following the date of the breach, or the date the Commission becomes aware of the breach, whichever is later.

343. To ensure that licence holders are aware of the way in which the Commission intends to use its power to impose financial penalties, the Commission must prepare and publish a statement of the principles it will apply in exercising these powers. In particular, the Commission must, in considering the imposition of a penalty, have regard for the seriousness of the breach of condition, whether the licensee knew or ought to have known of the breach and the nature of the licensee (including his financial resources). Before preparing or revising such a statement the Commission must consult the Secretary of State, the Lord Chancellor and other people as the Commission thinks appropriate.

344. All the regulatory powers available to the Commission under these sections are subject to full rights of appeal for those affected by them, under Part 7, to the Gambling Appeals Tribunal.

SECTION 122: INFORMATION

345. To assist the Commission to carry out its functions, this section sets out obligations on licence holders to comply with requests for information. These cannot be 'fishing exercises' by the Commission, but must concern questions of whether the licence holder has breached his licence conditions, or is unsuitable to carry on gambling activities. Non-compliance without reasonable excuse is an offence that will attract a fine not exceeding level 2 on the standard scale.

SECTION 123: LEVY

346. This section provides the Secretary of State with reserve powers to impose an annual financial levy on the holders of all operating licences. The power cannot be exercised in relation to particular classes of operating licence. If introduced, the levy will apply to all classes of operating licence. The levy would be paid to the Commission, and treated as if it were part of the annual fee. This means that a licence would be revocable if the levy was not paid.
347. The money raised by a levy would be used for alleviating problem gambling. Thus, the Commission could spend it on purposes or projects related to gambling addiction or other forms of harm or exploitation associated with gambling. The Treasury and the Secretary of State must consent to the Commission's expenditure of the levy. Such projects need not be undertaken by the Commission itself, but the Commission could fund others (including other public sector bodies) who are undertaking projects connected with problem gambling.
348. The section sets out the matters relating to the levy which must be set out in the regulations. A number of alternative methods for calculating the levy are listed, but none are mandatory. Depending on the method of calculation chosen, different levies could be charged to different operators. Before making these regulations imposing a levy, the Secretary of State must consult the Commission.
349. Provision is made, under Schedule 3 to the Act, for the National Lottery to be made subject to levy requirements also. A levy in these circumstances could not be imposed until the powers under this section had been exercised.

SECTION 125: RELEVANT OFFENCE: DISAPPLICATION OF REHABILITATION

350. This section identifies certain circumstances when section 4 of the Rehabilitation of Offenders Act 1974 (c.53) will not apply. This means that the Commission will be able to look at spent convictions in some cases. Where a person has a conviction for a relevant offence (defined in section 126) then the Commission will be able to consider a spent conviction for the offence when a person applies for an operating licence.

SECTION 126: INTERPRETATION

351. This section provides definitions for terms used throughout Part 5, including 'relevant offence'.

SCHEDULE 7: RELEVANT OFFENCES

352. This Schedule lists the British offences which are 'relevant offences' for the purposes of the Act (in England, Wales and Scotland). Under section 126 a relevant offence can also be a foreign offence which is equivalent to an offence listed in Schedule 7.
353. Under Part 5 of the Act, the Commission has power to take relevant offences into account when considering applications for operating and personal licences. Where an offence is a relevant offence, the Commission may consider such offences during the application process, even though they are spent within the terms of the Rehabilitation of Offenders Act 1974.
354. When sentencing a person convicted of a relevant offence, a court in Great Britain may order forfeiture of an operating or personal licence held by that person as part of the sentence. Where the licence held is a personal licence, the court may also disqualify the person from holding a personal licence for a period of up to 10 years, when it is sentencing for a relevant offence.
355. While the Commission may take account of a domestic, unspent conviction for any offence when considering an application for a licence under Part 5 of the Act, it is only those offences listed in this Schedule that attract the particular provisions

regarding spent convictions, foreign offences, forfeiture and disqualification.

PART 6: PERSONAL LICENCES

6.2009 356. This Part of the Act deals with personal licences, which certain individuals working in the gambling industry will be required to hold. The Commission will grant these licences, which are of indefinite duration. This regime is also relevant to operating licence holders, who will be required to use personnel who hold a personal licence. Unless the operator is a small-scale operator, the Commission is obliged to use its condition making powers to ensure that, for each operating licence, at least one person occupies a specified management office and holds a personal licence authorising them to perform the functions of the office.

357. Part 6 operates on the basis that many of the provisions contained in Part 5 on operating licences are also relevant to personal licences. So, in relation to many of the procedural requirements which the Commission will need to undertake for the personal licensing regime, the sections in Part 5 are deemed to apply to personal licences under Part 6. Powers are taken for the Secretary of State to make necessary modifications to the Part 5 procedures. This approach has been adopted to avoid repetition of large amounts of material in both Parts 5 and 6. Where particular matters need a self-standing provision for personal licences, Part 6 provides accordingly.

SECTION 127: NATURE OF PERSONAL LICENCE

358. A personal licence will authorise the holder to perform a specified management office or specified operational function, in connection with either the provision of facilities for gambling or a person who provides such facilities. The definitions of 'management office' and 'operational function' are set out in section 80.

359. By attaching conditions to operating licences under Part 5, the Commission will identify posts which must be held by a personal licence holder. These fall into the two groups of management offices and operational functions. Therefore, personal licences may need to be held by those directly providing the facilities for gambling, such as a croupier, or those who perform certain functions in a gambling operation but do not actually themselves provide the facilities, such as a compliance officer. Not everyone who works in the gambling industry will need a personal licence. It will be the task of the Commission, in granting operating licences, to determine which posts within any organisation need to be held by someone with a personal licence, and operators must employ people accordingly.

SECTION 128: APPLICATION OF PROVISIONS OF PART 5

360. The personal licensing system under Part 6 is not intended to be a free-standing regime in its own right, but instead sits alongside the regime for operating licences in Part 5. This section specifies that Part 6 is to be read as incorporating the features of the operating licence system, except where:

- it is modified by Part 6, or as necessary; or
- it is amended by regulations made by the Secretary of State.

361. As a result, the basic procedures for application for, determination of, and review of licences will be the same for both operating and personal licences, except where this Part (or the natural context) demands otherwise. Personal licences may be subject to general or specific conditions imposed by the Commission, or conditions imposed by the Secretary of State in regulations.

362. Personal licences are different to the ten types of operating licence specified in section 65(2).

SECTION 129: EXEMPTION FOR SMALL SCALE OPERATORS

363. Part 5 requires that anyone holding an operating licence must have at least one person in a management office holding a personal licence. However, this sec-

tion exempts small-scale operators from this requirement. This is because, in small operations, the operating licence will achieve the same purpose as a personal licence. For example, an independent on-course betting operator, employing only one or two people is likely to be the sort of operator who will be excused from holding a personal licence under this section.

364. The Secretary of State will define the meaning of 'small scale operator' in particular by reference to the size and value of the business, and the number of employees (subsection (2)). Subsection (4) requires an operator, who benefits from this exemption, to produce his operating licence, as if it were a personal licence. Section 134 sets out the requirements for producing a personal licence.

SECTION 130: APPLICATION

365. The application procedures set by the Commission for personal licences will mirror those set out in Part 5, with suitable modifications. In particular, the licensing objectives, and the applicant's suitability (including integrity and competence) will be taken into account by the Commission in deciding whether to grant a licence. This section makes it clear that the Commission can require the applicant's employer or intended employer to take part in the application process for a personal licence (subsections (1) and (2)). However, a person does not have to be employed in order to apply for a personal licence (subsection (4)). A person may acquire a licence prior to seeking employment in order, for example, to improve his chances of finding work.

SECTIONS 131 AND 135: DURATION AND REVIEW

366. Subject to surrender, lapse, forfeiture or revocation, all personal licences will be of unlimited duration. The Commission does not have the power to introduce limited durations for personal licences, as it can for operating licences under Part 5.

367. The review procedures for individual licences contained in section 116 will apply to personal licences, with any appropriate modification. However, the power to review classes of licence is not available for personal licences.

SECTION 132: FEES

368. Personal licences will be subject to an application fee. Under this section the Secretary of State also has power to specify periodic fees to be paid by a personal licence holder to the Commission to maintain his licence. Unlike operating licence maintenance fees, these will not necessarily be annual fees. Instead, the Secretary of State may set the amount and the period for which the fees must be paid. Non-payment can lead to revocation of a personal licence. The maintenance fees will be used by the Commission to cover the costs of regulation.

SECTION 133: MULTIPLE LICENCES

369. An individual will not be allowed to hold more than one personal licence, but a personal licence can cover a number of management or operational functions. This allows one individual to conduct a number of functions relying upon one licence.

SECTION 134: PRODUCTION OF LICENCE

370. This section gives police constables and Commission enforcement officers the power to require a personal licensee to produce his licence within a specified period. If the individual is carrying on a licensed activity, or is on licensed premises, then the licence must be produced immediately. This means that a personal licence holder will be required to keep the licence on his person when at work. This is in contrast to the operating licence holder, who, unless they are a 'small scale operator' can only be

required to produce the operating licence within a specified period. Failing to comply with these requirements will be an offence, attracting a fine not exceeding level 2 upon conviction.

SECTION 136: DISQUALIFICATION

371. In addition to being able to order forfeiture of a personal licence as part of the sentence for a relevant offence, this section allows a court to order that the person be disqualified from holding a personal licence for a period of up to ten years. This can be instead of, or in addition to, an order for forfeiture. Relevant offences are defined under section 126 of the Act.

SECTIONS 137 AND 138: NOTIFICATION REQUIREMENTS

372. Where the Commission suspends or revokes a personal licence, or a court orders forfeiture or disqualification, the operating licence holder is entitled to be notified by the Commission of what has happened to the personal licence. Equally, where an operating licence holder is aware that a personal licensee has been convicted of a relevant offence, he must inform the Commission of the fact.

SECTION 139: BREACH OF PERSONAL LICENCE CONDITION

373. This section makes it an offence for the holder of a personal licence to breach a condition of his licence, when acting in the course of (or in connection with) an activity authorised by an operating licence, which itself requires the personal licence to be held. The holder of the operating licence may also commit an offence, on the same set of facts, under Part 5, but this section provides that the individual personal licence holder can be proceeded against for the offence, irrespective of what steps are taken against the operator. The penalty for the personal licence holder is a maximum period of imprisonment in England or Wales of 51 weeks, and in Scotland of 6 months, and/or a fine not exceeding level 5.

PART 7: OPERATING AND PERSONAL LICENCES: APPEALS

6.2010 374. Part 7 provides for the formation and operation of an independent tribunal to deal with gambling matters. It will deal with appeals against decisions taken by the Commission in respect of operating and personal licences (Parts 5 and 6 of the Act), as well as appeals in relation to a decision by the Commission to void a bet under Part 17.

SECTION 140: THE GAMBLING APPEALS TRIBUNAL[1]

375. This section provides for the establishment of the Gambling Appeals Tribunal. The requirements for the foundation and operation of the tribunal are set out in Schedule 8 to the Act. The purpose of the Tribunal is to hear appeals against the decisions of the Commission. The mechanism for appeals against the decisions of licensing authorities are set out in those Parts and Schedules of the Act which deal with the functions of such authorities eg Part 8 on premises licences and Part 9 on temporary use notices.

[1] Note; as Part 7 has now been heavily amended and the GAT replaced, since January 2010 by the First-tier Tribunal (see SI 2010/22) not all Notes 375 – 399 are now relevant.

SECTION 141: APPEAL TO TRIBUNAL

376. Rights of appeal are available to people affected by the decisions of the Commission. This section sets out the particular circumstances under which holders of, and applicants for, operating and personal licences will have a right of appeal against decisions of the Commission:

- A person who has applied for grant of an operating or personal licence, (or, when relevant, an existing licence holder who has applied for renewal of their licence), will have the right of appeal against the Commission's decision.
- Where the Commission attach an individual condition to an operating or personal licence, the holder of the licence will have the right of appeal against the decision.
- An operating licence holder that is a company limited by shares, which has applied for the operating licence to continue to have effect when a new controller takes over, can appeal against the Commission's determination.
- The holder of an operating or personal licence who has applied to the Commission for variation of the licence by adding, amending or removing an authorised activity; amending another detail of the licence; or adding, amending or removing an individual condition attached to the licence, may appeal against the Commission's decision.
- The holder of an operating or personal licence can appeal against a decision by the Commission that they are incapable of carrying on their licensed activities by reason of mental or physical incapacity.
- The holder of an operating or personal licence can appeal against the Commission's use of its regulatory powers in connection with a review: that means that an appeal can be made against the issue of a warning to the licence holder; the variation or removal of a condition or exclusion, or attachment of a new condition or exclusion to the licence; suspension or revocation of the licence; or imposition of a financial penalty.

SECTION 142: TIMING

377. This section provides for a time limit within which an appeal must be commenced. An appeal must be made within one month of the date of decision or action that is to be appealed against. However, the Tribunal has discretion to permit an appeal to be started after this period.

SECTION 143: APPEAL FROM TRIBUNAL

378. This section provides that parties to an appeal before the Tribunal may appeal the Tribunal's decision to either the High Court, or, in Scotland, the Court of Session. The right only extends to appeals based on a point of law, and appeals may only be brought with the permission of the Tribunal or, if this is denied, the relevant appeal court. A higher court to which an appeal is brought under this section can affirm or quash the Tribunal's decision, or remit the matter back to the Tribunal for a re-determination. There is no power for the higher court to make a fresh determination based on the facts of the case.

SECTION 144: POWERS OF TRIBUNAL

379. This section provides for the Tribunal's powers following an appeal. It allows the Tribunal to either uphold or overturn all of, or part of, the Commission's decision. The Tribunal can also substitute a decision or action taken by the Commission for another. In so doing, it is limited to taking only decisions or actions of a kind which the Commission is empowered to take. For example; if the Commission recommended that a financial penalty be imposed, the Tribunal could rule that a more appropriate

decision would be to revoke the licence, or to issue a warning. But the Tribunal cannot order something which the Commission could not have ordered in the first place.

380. The Tribunal can also add to the Commission's decisions, ie it could uphold a decision to impose a financial penalty, and add that the licence should also be revoked. This section also allows for the Tribunal to refer a matter back to the Commission for further consideration, following which there will again be the right to appeal to the Tribunal under this Part from the new decision made by the Commission.

381. The Tribunal can also re-instate a lapsed or revoked licence following a successful appeal.

382. When determining an appeal, the Tribunal can take into account evidence that was not previously available to the Commission, and it must ensure that it considers any relevant code of practice issued by the Commission.

SECTION 145: STAY PENDING APPEAL

383. This section provides that a decision or action of the Commission, in relation to an operating or personal licence, will not have effect until either the period for bringing an appeal has expired, or if an appeal is in progress, until the appeal has been finally determined or abandoned. For example, if a financial penalty is imposed, and this is appealed against, the penalty cannot be enforced until the Tribunal decides, following that appeal, whether to uphold the decision to impose the penalty.

384. However, the Commission has the discretion to disapply this stay in a particular case if, for example, it considers that it is necessary that a particular licence is revoked or suspended with immediate effect. In such circumstances, the bringing of an appeal will not prevent the Commission's decision having effect, pending the outcome of the appeal. This power is provided so that the Commission can ensure fairness to players, protection of children and the vulnerable, and the prevention of crime (the licensing objectives).

SECTION 146: RULES

385. This section gives the Lord Chancellor the power to make secondary legislation in relation to the regulation of appeals to the Tribunal, and the procedure of proceedings before the Tribunal. In particular, these rules may specify who can be a party to proceedings, including, specifically, for the purposes of an appeal against a decision of the Tribunal. Paragraph 14 of Schedule 8 gives a non- exhaustive list of matters about which rules can be made. It includes:

- the manner and time in which appeals are instituted;
- determination of ongoing issues during the course of proceedings and other ancillary matters;
- issuing directions to parties;
- disclosure;
- joining the Commission to proceedings;
- suspension of Commission decisions;
- giving evidence and production of documents;
- administration of oaths to witnesses;
- public admission to proceedings;
- representation of parties;
- withdrawal of proceedings;
- recording and declaration of decisions;
- award of costs or expenses;
- variation or revocation of Tribunal decisions.

386. Rules made under this section may make it an offence not to comply with certain requirements.

SECTION 147: FEES

387. This section enables the Lord Chancellor, through regulations, to set the level of fees to be paid by a person when bringing an appeal to the Tribunal. Different fees for different types of case or circumstance may be charged, and the Tribunal may waive a fee where it deems it appropriate. The Lord Chancellor must consult the Secretary of State before exercising this power.

SECTION 148: LEGAL ASSISTANCE

388. This section enables the Lord Chancellor, through regulations, to establish a legal assistance scheme to provide financial assistance to appellants who might otherwise be unable to instigate an appeal to the Tribunal. Regulations may specify the kinds of assistance that may be provided and the classes of person by whom assistance may be provided. They may also include provision about applications to the Tribunal for assistance, including a requirement to provide information. The Lord Chancellor may state the criteria to be used by the Tribunal in determining eligibility for legal assistance, and may make provision for an applicant to appeal against a decision to refuse assistance. This section does not apply to Scotland, where different powers for affording legal assistance are available.

SECTION 149: ENFORCEMENT OF COSTS ORDERS

389. This section enables an award of costs made by the Tribunal to be enforced as though it was an order of the county court. The judgement creditor must apply to the county court for the district in which the debtor resides and payment may be enforced in accordance with Part V of the County Courts Act 1984. This includes the power to call in the bailiffs if necessary.

SCHEDULE 8: GAMBLING APPEALS TRIBUNAL

390. This schedule sets out the provisions for the establishment, constitution, and procedure of the Gambling Appeals Tribunal, and should be read in conjunction with this Part.

PARAGRAPHS 1 AND 2: PRESIDENT, DEPUTY AND MEMBERS

391. The Lord Chancellor will appoint a President and has the authority to appoint other members to the Tribunal. Only those with appropriate legal qualifications can be appointed. The Lord Chancellor can also appoint one or more members of the Tribunal to be its deputy President, who will act when the President is absent, and will undertake other duties delegated by the President.

PARAGRAPH 3: TENURE

392. The duration of post of the President or other members of the Tribunal is dependent upon the terms and conditions of appointment. Resignation must be in writing to the Lord Chancellor. The Lord Chancellor has the power to dismiss Tribunal members, including the President and deputy President, for misbehaviour, or if they are unable or unwilling to undertake their duties. The retirement provisions contained in the Pensions and Retirement Act 1993 will apply to all tribunal members.

PARAGRAPH 4: STAFF

393. The Lord Chancellor can appoint staff for the Tribunal.

PARAGRAPHS 5 TO 8: MONEY

394. The Lord Chancellor has the power to pay Tribunal members, including the President and deputy President, and staff. He also has the power to pay other expenses of the Tribunal. Money received by way of appeal fees is to be paid into the Consolidated Fund. The President of the Gambling Appeals Tribunal qualifies for a pension under the Judicial Pensions and Retirement Act 1993.

PARAGRAPH 9 TO 11: SITTINGS

395. The Tribunal President will direct when and where the Tribunal sits and will decide which members are to be present at each sitting. This is in line with general arrangements made by the Lord Chancellor. At each sitting of the Tribunal, the President or a Tribunal member must be present. It will also be possible for the President to sit with two Tribunal members, for example, in a case which is considered to be particularly complex. The arrangements may provide that in some cases, a three member Tribunal may be obliged to continue sitting with only one or two members. In such a case, if sitting with just one other member, the arrangements may include provision for the President to have a casting vote.
396. The President will determine the constitution of the Tribunal and the times and places at which it will sit, in accordance with the general arrangements made by the Lord Chancellor. The Lord Chancellor must consult the President before making general arrangements. Arrangements made by the Lord Chancellor will be published.

PARAGRAPHS 12 TO 14: PROCEDURE

397. Tribunal decisions are to be taken by a majority vote. The President is empowered to give directions about the practice and procedure of the Tribunal, as long as these do not conflict with the rules made by the Lord Chancellor.

PARAGRAPH 15: COUNCIL ON TRIBUNALS

398. The Gambling Appeals Tribunal will be subject to the scrutiny of the Council on Tribunals, which is responsible for the supervision, constitution and working of Tribunals and Inquiries in England, Scotland and Wales, under the Tribunals and Inquiries Act 1992 (c.53).

PARAGRAPH 16: DISQUALIFICATION

399. This paragraph disqualifies any member of the Tribunal from being a member of the House of Commons and prevents the President of the Tribunal from practising as a solicitor or barrister whilst in post.

PART 8: PREMISES LICENCES

6.2011 400. Part 8 of the Act describes the new regime for the licensing of premises where facilities for gambling may be provided. Premises licences are the third main category of licence (operating and personal licences being the other two) that will be issued under the Act. Premises licences will be granted by licensing authorities (as defined in section 2), not the Commission.
401. In England and Wales licensing authority functions are conferred on local authorities, and in Scotland upon licensing boards, as defined in Part 1 of the Act. Scottish Ministers will exercise a number of powers under this Part, prescribing procedures and fees for the premises licensing system in Scotland.
402. Premises licences can authorise the provision of facilities on:

- Casino premises;

- Bingo premises;
- Betting premises, including tracks and premises used by betting intermediaries;
- Adult Gaming Centres (for Category B,C and D machines); and
- Family Entertainment Centres (for Category C and D machines)

403. However, premises licences are not the only form of authorisation for the use of premises for providing gambling facilities. Under the Act, permission may also be obtained through:

- Occasional use notices or football pools authorisations under Part 3 of the Act;
- Temporary use notices under Part 9 of the Act;
- Permits for family entertainment centres (Category D machines only) under Part 10 of the Act;
- Authorisations for alcohol licensed premises; clubs and miners' welfare institutes and travelling fairs, all under Part 12 of the Act;
- Permissions for prize gaming under Part 13 of the Act; and
- Authorisations for private and non-commercial gaming and betting under Part 14 of the Act.

404. Applicants for premises licences are required to hold a relevant operating licence before being granted a premises licence under this Part, except in the case of tracks, where an operating licence need not be held in all cases. This is to enable trackside betting operators (also known as on-course bookmakers) with operating licences to benefit from the track premises licence held by the occupier of the track. Pool-betting on a track, by the track occupier, will require a pool betting operating licence to be held. The definition of a 'track' is contained in section 353.

405. Premises licences, unlike operating licences, are transferable between occupiers (who hold operating licences), on application to the licensing authority. Conditions on premises licences can be set by the licensing authority, and by the Secretary of State, or Scottish Ministers. Licensing authorities have powers to review licences, with associated regulatory powers. A provisional statement may be obtained from a licensing authority, in advance of a premises licence, where premises are to be constructed or altered, or where someone has yet to acquire the right to occupy premises.

406. Part 8 provides appeals mechanisms for people affected by the decisions of licensing authorities.

407. Part 18 contains provisions requiring all licensing authorities to set three- year licensing policies in respect of all of their functions under the Act, including premises licences. It also provides prosecution powers for licensing authorities in relation to their licensing functions.

408. Part 10 contains provisions concerning gaming machines, and the categorisation of machines by the Secretary of State. A reference to a Commission code of practice in this Part is a reference to a statutory code of practice issued under Part 2 of the Act.

SECTION 150: NATURE OF LICENCE

409. This section describes, in subsection (1), the premises licences that may be issued by a licensing authority. They are:

- A licence for the operation of a casino;
- A licence for the provision of facilities for playing bingo;
- A licence for making Category B gaming machines available for use (an adult gaming centre);
- A licence for making Category C gaming machines available for use (a family entertainment centre); and
- A licence for the provision of facilities for betting, including betting intermediary facilities

410. Under Part 1 of the Act, the Secretary of State will make regulations defining classes of casinos. As a result, casino premises licences are divided into three types:

- Regional casino premises licences;
- Large casino premises licence;

- Small casino premises licence
- Section 151: Form of licence

411. Premises licences must include the information described in this section. The Secretary of State may make further regulations about the form and content of the licence. These regulations may, in particular, specify how conditions, including mandatory conditions specified by the Secretary of State, are to appear on the licence.
412. In Scotland, the powers of the Secretary of State in relation to the form of the licence are to be carried out by the Scottish Ministers.

SECTION 152: COMBINED LICENCE

413. The general position for premises licensing is that premises may only be subject to one premises licence at a time. Subsection (1) provides for this. The effect of this requirement is to limit the principal activity on the premises to the provision of facilities for a particular type of gambling activity.
414. However, there are some exceptions to this approach. One exception is set out in this section. Subsections (2) and (3) provide that a betting track may be subject to more than one premises licence, but that no more than one premises licence can operate in relation to any area of the track. Subsection (4) provides that where a particular area of a track is already subject to a premises licence, and a person wishes to apply for a licence to offer another type of gambling activity in that area, an application must be made to vary the original licence under section 187. The new licence for the track can only be granted at the same time as, or after, the original licence has been varied. Other sections in this Part give permission for particular kinds of premises licence to authorise more than one type of activity.

SECTION 153: PRINCIPLES TO BE APPLIED

415. This section sets out the principles that licensing authorities should apply when exercising their premises licensing functions under this Part. They must to aim to permit the use of premises for gambling, in so far as the authority thinks that permission:
- accords with relevant Commission codes of practice and guidance under sections 24 and 25;
- is reasonably consistent with the licensing objectives; and
- is in accordance with the authority's three-year licensing policy (established by the authority under section 349 of the Act).

416. Under legislation repealed by this Act, it has been a requirement that the grant of certain gambling permissions should take account of whether there is unfulfilled demand for the facilities. This is the case, for example, for a casino licence under Part II of the Gaming Act 1968 or a bookmaker's permit under the Betting, Gaming and Lotteries Act 1963. Unmet demand is not to be a criterion that a licensing authority is permitted to take into account when considering an application for a premises licence, and subsection (2) provides for this.

SECTION 154: DELEGATION TO LICENSING COMMITTEE

417. With respect to England and Wales, this section provides that, with three exceptions, the functions of licensing authorities under Part 8 are delegated to the licensing committees established under section 6 of the Licensing Act 2003 (c.17). The three exceptions are:
- Functions relating to resolutions by the licensing authority not to issue casino licences under section 166;
- Formulation of the three year licensing policy under section 349; and
- Determination of premises licence fees under section 212.

The first two matters are not, and cannot be, delegated to a licensing committee, and must be taken by the authority as a whole. Decisions on fees are not automatically delegated, but can be.

418. Section 10(4) of the Licensing Act 2003 limits the matters that may be delegated to an officer of the authority. In relation to gambling functions, under subsection (4) the matters that may not be delegated to an officer are:

- Determination of an application for a premises licence or a provisional statement in respect of which representations have been made under section 161 and have not been withdrawn;
- Determination of an application for of a premises licence in respect of which representations have been made under section 161 by virtue of section 187 and not withdrawn; or of an application for transfer of a licence following representations by the Commission;
- Review of a premises licence.

SECTION 155: DELEGATION OF FUNCTIONS UNDER PART 8: SCOTLAND

419. This section provides that, in relation to Scotland, the functions of licensing authorities may be delegated to a committee of the authority, a member or members of the authority, the clerk of the authority, or any person appointed to assist the clerk.

420. The three exceptions to this are:

- Resolutions by the licensing authority not to issue casino licences under section 166;
- Formulation of the three year licensing policy under section 349; and
- The matters listed in subsection (4) of section 154.

421. The first two matters may not be delegated at all, but the third matter may be delegated to a committee of the authority, or to a member or members of the authority.

422. In Scotland, licensing authorities are licensing boards established under section 1 of the Licensing (Scotland) Act 1976. The procedures that apply to the proceedings of licensing boards in the exercise of their functions under that Act apply to the proceedings of those boards in relation to their functions under this Part. Regulations made by the Scottish Ministers dealing with the proceedings of licensing boards may make separate provision for the functions of the boards under the Licensing (Scotland) Act and under this Part.

SECTION 156: REGISTER

423. Under this section, licensing authorities must maintain a register of premises licences they have granted in their area, together with such other information as may be prescribed in regulations made by the Secretary of State. This register and information must be made available for inspection by the public. Licensing authorities must also provide a copy of an entry to the register, or of information, to a member of public on request, although they may charge for this service.

424. The section also provides that the Secretary of State may, by regulations, require licensing authorities to give the Commission specified information about premises licenses issued by them; and may require the Commission to maintain a register and grant public access to it. Regulations made under this section may also excuse licensing authorities from part or all of their duties to maintain a register and provide access to it.

SECTION 157: RESPONSIBLE AUTHORITIES

425. This section lists the people who are to be regarded as responsible authorities for the purposes of this Part. As responsible authorities they have particular rights to be involved and/or consulted in relation to applications for premises licences and other procedures under this Part. The Commission is a responsible authority, as are the police.

SECTION 158: INTERESTED PARTY

426. In addition to responsible authorities, a wider group of people may play a role in the premises licensing process under this Part. These people are called 'interested parties', and are defined in this section. Interested parties are:

- people who live sufficiently close to premises in respect of which a premises licence has been granted or applied for, that they are likely to be affected by activities authorised by the licence; and
- those with business interests who might be affected by the authorised activities; or
- representatives of either of these groups.

SECTIONS 159 TO 161: APPLICATIONS

427. These sections prescribe the procedure for making an application for a premises licence. Only people with a right to occupy premises are eligible to apply for a premises licence. The notes relating to prize gaming permits under Part 14 expand upon the meaning of 'occupy' for these purposes. Applicants must have an operating licence, or have made an application for one. A premises licence will not be issued until to an applicant until he holds an operating licence. The exception to this is an applicant for a premises licence that authorises a track to be used for accepting bets. These applicants do not need to hold, or have applied for, an operating licence.
428. Applications for premises licences must be made to the licensing authority in whose area the premises are wholly or partly situated; and must be in the prescribed form and manner, accompanied by the prescribed fee. Other sections in this Part describe the fee-setting powers relevant to premises licences.
429. The Secretary of State is given the power to make regulations which require an applicant for a premises licence to publish notice of his application, to give notice of it to responsible authorities and other people.
430. Responsible authorities and interested parties may make representations in writing to a licensing authority about a particular application. The period of time within which representations must be made will be prescribed in regulations.
431. Scottish Ministers exercise the powers of the Secretary of State under these sections in relation to Scotland.
432. Additional procedures apply in the case of applications for a casino licence. These are provided for in section 175 and Schedule 9.

SECTIONS 162 TO 165: DETERMINATION OF APPLICATION

433. These sections set out the procedure for determining an application. The procedures vary, depending on whether representations have been made, and what the licensing authority proposes to do with regard to licence conditions.
434. Where representations have been made by a responsible authority or an interested party (and not been withdrawn); or the licensing authority proposes to impose conditions on the licence, or exclude default conditions, a licensing authority is required to hold a hearing. The licensing authority may determine the application without a hearing, however, if either the applicant or any interested party has consented; or if the licensing authority considers that the representations made are vexatious, frivolous, or concern matters that will not influence their decision. Where the authority proposes to determine an application without a hearing, it must notify any person who made a representation as soon as reasonably practicable.
435. Following the grant or rejection of a premises licence, the authority must notify the applicant, the Commission, any person who made representations, the police, and HM Customs and Excise of their decision as soon as reasonably practicable.
436. Where the licensing authority determines to grant the licence, they must give reasons for the attachment or exclusion of any conditions. The premises licence issued

by the licensing authority must be accompanied by a summary of the terms and conditions attaching to it. Where the licence is refused, the licensing authority must give reasons for their decision.

437. Sections 206 to 209 set out the appeal rights in relation to a decision of a licensing authority to grant or reject an application for a premises licence. Where the licensing authority rejects an application for a licence, the applicant may appeal. Where the licensing authority grants an application, a person who made representations may appeal.

SECTION 166: RESOLUTION NOT TO ISSUE CASINO LICENCE

438. Part 8 requires licensing authorities to permit the use of premises for gambling, in so far as the authority thinks that permission accords with relevant Commission codes of practice and guidance, is reasonably consistent with the licensing objectives, and is in accordance with the authority's three-year licensing policy (established by the authority under Part 18 of the Act).

439. This section provides an exception to this requirement. Licensing authorities are given the power to decide not to issue further casino premises licences in their area. This decision is to be taken by the licensing authority as a whole, and may not be delegated to the licensing committee under sections 154 and 155. The licensing authority may take into account any principle or matter in making its decision, and may pass a resolution giving effect to their decision at any time. Such a resolution must be published as part of the authority's licensing policy statement made under Part 18, and lasts for 3 years from the date it takes effect.

440. There are a number of restrictions on the scope of a resolution, as follows:

- A resolution can only apply to the grant of future applications for casino premises licences;
- It cannot have any effect on casino licences that have already been granted, (including licences that have been converted into casino licences or issued under transitional provisions under Part 18);
- It cannot have effect in relation to a provisional statement that has already been granted for a casino;
- A resolution must apply to all types of casino premises licence (eg regional, large and small); and
- A resolution may not be taken into account when reviewing a casino licence.

441. Subsections 7 and 8 provide the Secretary of State with the power to order a particular licensing authority, or class of licensing authority to consider whether to issue a resolution under this section. Such an order may require, amongst other things, the authority to consult people likely to be affected by the resolution.

SECTIONS 167 TO 171: CONDITIONS

442. These sections provide the Secretary of State, Scottish Ministers and licensing authorities with powers to place conditions on premises licences.

443. The Secretary of State and the Scottish Ministers have power to issue mandatory conditions on premises licences, for England and Wales, and Scotland respectively. Such conditions will be specified in regulations, and must be included in all premises licences, or classes of premises licence, to which they apply. These powers can apply to all premises licences, or classes of licence or to licences in specified circumstances.

444. The Secretary of State and Scottish Ministers have further powers to impose default conditions by regulations, for England and Wales, and Scotland respectively. These conditions are ones which apply to a licence unless the licensing authority decides to exclude them (in which case the authority can impose alternative conditions relating to the same matter). These powers can apply to all premises licences, or classes of licence, or to licences in specified circumstances.

445. In addition, licensing authorities have power to set individual conditions for a premises licence when they grant it. In doing so, they may impose a condition on a

licence, or exclude default conditions (in which case they may impose alternative conditions relating to the same matter). Their power to impose conditions is subject to the matters listed below.

446. A premises licence not may be subject to a condition imposed by a licensing authority:

- that would prevent compliance with a condition on an operating licence which authorises the gambling activity (section 169(4));
- that requires the premises, or any part of it, to operate as a club or another body requiring membership (section 170);
- that imposes limits on stakes, fees, winnings or prizes (except in relation to fees for admission to a track) (section 171).

SECTION 172: GAMING MACHINES

447. Part 10 of the Act defines a gaming machine, and gives the Secretary of State power to make rules about their categorisation and use or manufacture and supply. This section contains the gaming machine entitlements which apply to the different types of premises licence issued under this Part. Licensing authorities may not vary these entitlements.

448. The entitlements are:

- Adult gaming centres: up to four Category B machines and any number of Category C and D machines;
- Licensed family entertainment centres: any number of machines of Category C or D;
- Casinos:
  - Small casinos: 2 machines per gaming table used in the casino, up to a maximum of 80 machines. Machines may be of Category B,C or D;
  - Large casinos: 5 machines per gaming table used in the casino, up to a maximum of 150 machines. Machines may be of Category B, C or D;
  - Regional casinos: 25 machines per gaming table used in the casino, provided there are at least 40 tables, and up to a maximum of 1250 machines. Machines may be of Category A, B, C or D. If a regional casino has fewer than 40 tables, its entitlement is that of a large casino.
- Bingo premises: up to 4 Category B gaming machines, and any number of machines of Category C and D;
- Betting premises: up to 4 gaming machines of Category B, C or D;
- Tracks: Where the track licensee is permitted to offer pool betting: up to 4 machines of Category B, C or D.

449. The Secretary of State may amend these entitlements in secondary legislation.

450. In relation to casino entitlements, the Secretary of State can make regulations defining 'gaming table', and, in particular may specify when a gaming table is to be treated as being used in a casino. These regulations could cover matters such as whether appropriate numbers of staff are trained to operate the tables, and the extent to which such staff (and therefore tables) are available for use.

451. These regulations can also specify when tables, which are linked together by electronic means for example, are to count as a single table for the purpose of machine entitlements under this section. This could be the case where one roulette wheel is operated by a croupier, but a number of associated banks of terminals allow players to take part in the game. The regulations will determine whether the banks of terminals count as a table in their own right. Part 10 of the Act contains provisions on when such equipment counts as a gaming machine.

SECTION 173: VIRTUAL GAMING

452. This section authorises the provision of facilities for 'virtual' betting in casinos and on betting premises. Section 353(3) contains a definition of 'virtual' for these purposes.

SECTION 174: CASINO PREMISES LICENCE

453. Casino premises licences will be available for 'small', 'large' and 'regional' casinos and will authorise the playing of casino games and equal chance games on the premises. Relevant definitions of these terms are set out in Part 1.

454. A casino premises licence will also authorise the provision of facilities for betting, where the licensee or a person authorised in writing by the licensee holds a relevant betting operating licence. Large and regional casino premises licences also authorise the provision of facilities for bingo, again, provided there is a valid bingo operating licence held by the person providing the activity. Provision of facilities for bingo may not be made in a small casino, but the Secretary of State has power to repeal this restriction by order.

455. Subsection (6) allows the Secretary of State to make regulations that impose mandatory conditions on casino premises licences in relation to equipment used for playing automated games of chance. Such equipment, which neither involves nor is linked to a game requiring human operation, is not a gaming machine provided it is used in accordance with Commission licence conditions set under this subsection (section 235(2)(i)). An example of this equipment is a roulette wheel which is completely mechanised, and works without the need for any croupier to rotate the wheel, spin the ball or accept stakes. Conditions may, in particular, limit the number of machines that may be provided in a casino and the number of player positions that may be provided for use of the machines.

456. Subsection (7) allows the Secretary of State to use her powers via regulation to control the non-gambling facilities provided in casinos by attaching licence conditions. This does not prevent the licensing authority imposing conditions on such matters under section 169, subject to any mandatory conditions which the Secretary of State may prescribe under section 167.

SECTION 175: CASINO PREMISES LICENCE: OVERALL LIMITS

457. This section sets an initial limit of 1 regional casino, and 8 small and 8 large casinos. The Secretary of State will, by order, determine the locations of the new casinos after consulting Scottish Ministers and the Welsh Assembly. The Secretary of State may by order vary the limits on the numbers of different categories of casino, or lift the limits altogether. Orders under this section are subject to the affirmative resolution procedure.

SCHEDULE 9: APPLICATIONS FOR CASINO PREMISES LICENCES

458. Schedule 9 sets out the process by which an operator may obtain a casino premises licence where there is a limit on the number of the particular category of casino.

459. As a first step a licensing authority must comply with regulations made by the Secretary of State about inviting competing applications. Where that leads to a number of applications, which is greater than the number of available premises licences, a two-stage process is to take place in accordance with paragraphs 4 and 5. Under paragraph 4, the first stage of the process is for the licensing authority to undertake a regulatory test on all the applications to ensure that they all satisfy the regulatory premises licensing requirements already contained in Part 8 of the Act. The second stage of the process, described in paragraph 5, only applies if more applicants pass this test than the number of available premises licences. In those circumstances, the licensing authority will run a competition to determine which of the competing applications, if successful, would offer the greatest benefits to the local area. Paragraph 6 requires licensing authorities, in running this competition, to comply with any code of practice issued by the Secretary of State. Paragraph 7 enables any commitments entered into by the successful applicant during the competition to be attached as conditions to the premises licence.

460. Paragraph 8 makes provision for appeals against decisions of licensing authorities under paragraph 4. By virtue of paragraph 8(4) no appeal may be brought against a decision of a licensing authority under paragraph 5. Paragraphs 9 and 10 make provision for the issuing of provisional statements, including allowing licensing authorities to set a time limit on the duration of a provisional statement.

SECTION 176: CASINO PREMISES LICENCE: ACCESS BY CHILDREN

461. Under section 47 it is an offence to invite or permit children and young people to enter small or large casinos or the gambling area of a regional casino. Under this section the Commission must issue one or more codes of practice with respect to the arrangements which the holders of casino premises licences are to take to ensure that children and young people do not enter any areas where access is prohibited by virtue of section 47.
462. The codes or codes must also require that each entrance to prohibited areas is supervised (by one or more persons required to ensure compliance with the code of practice); and, unless the person supervising the entrance is reasonably certain that a person wishing to enter is an adult, must require arrangements to be put in place which require the person seeking to enter to show evidence of their age. The type of evidence that is acceptable for proof of age is also to be set out in the code or codes of practice.
463. Subsection (3) makes it a condition of all casino premises licences that the licensee ensures compliance with a code of practice issued in accordance with subsection (1).

SECTION 177: CREDIT

464. Section 81 contains restrictions on the holders of bingo and casino operating licences giving, arranging, permitting or knowingly facilitating credit in connection with the facilities for gambling they provide. This section contains equivalent provisions for the holders of casino and bingo premises licences. This ban on credit extends to any gambling facilities offered on the premises, because the holder of the premises licence must not permit or knowingly facilitate the giving of credit to take place on those premises. This therefore covers, for example, the provision of facilities for betting in a casino, pursuant to a betting operating licence and section 174(3). It will be a breach of the premises licence for credit to be offered in contravention of this section.
465. Subsection (3) contains an exception for cash withdrawal machines operated by credit card, located on the premises, in similar terms to the exception set out in section 81(3) and described in the note for that section.

SECTION 178: DOOR SUPERVISION

466. Where the Secretary of State or a licensing authority places a condition for door supervision on a premises licence, this will require entry to the premises to be supervised in order to prevent unauthorised access or occupation, outbreaks of disorder, or damage. Where such a condition is imposed, it a requirement of this section that the person undertaking the door supervision is licensed under the Private Security Industry Act 2001 (c.12), where his conduct is licensable under that Act.
467. Schedule 16, at paragraph 17 makes minor amendments to the 2001 Act, which preserve the exemption from licensing afforded to bingo and casino operators under that Act.

SECTION 179: POOL BETTING ON TRACK

468. Under the Betting, Gaming and Lotteries Act 1963, occupiers of licensed dog-tracks and the Totalisator Board ('the Tote') at approved horse racecourses enjoy

certain exclusive rights to conduct pool betting on the races taking place there. These are the only tracks where pool betting is permitted. This section replaces those provisions in the 1963 Act.

469. Under subsection (1) the only tracks where pool betting is permitted, pursuant to a track betting premises licence, are dog tracks and horse racecourses. However, the Secretary of State may amend this by order, and add further types of track, or remove them (subsection (3)). So, for example, football stadium could be added to the list, by order.

470. On licensed dog tracks and horse racecourses, the holder of the track betting premises licence is given the exclusive right to offer pool betting on dog-racing or horse-racing respectively. He may authorise other people to conduct such pool-betting on his behalf. In all cases a relevant operating licence will be required. Track betting premises licences for dog tracks and horserace courses will be subject to mandatory licence conditions requiring access to be offered at the track-side to general betting operators. A licence condition will also be imposed for a transitional period, limiting the admission fee that can be charged to five times the public admission fee.

471. There is no longer any special procedure for the licensing of inter-track betting schemes for dog racing (section 16A of the 1963 Act). Pool betting operating licences (which may be held for remote operations) and the track premises licence will cover, between them, all the activities that could be carried on under an inter-track licence.

SECTION 180: POOL BETTING ON DOG RACES

472. This section contains a transitional measure for holders of dog-track betting premises licences. Holders of all betting premises licences (other than for a dog-track) may not permit pool betting on dog races to take place on their premises, unless it is in accordance with arrangements made with the occupier of the dog track on which the races take place. This means that a high street betting office cannot be used for pool betting on dog racing, unless it is covered by arrangements made between that office, and the relevant dog-track.

473. The Secretary of State can repeal this measure, and, in any event, the section lapses after 31st December 2012.

SECTION 181: BETTING MACHINES

474. Conditions attached to betting premises licences and casino premises licences may relate to the number of machines on the premises used for making or accepting bets; the nature of those machines and the circumstances of their use.

475. This provision is relevant to machines used for making or accepting bets on real events. Such machines are excluded from the definition of gaming machine in Part 10 of the Act. Another section in this Part imposes restrictions on the number of gaming machines that may be made available for use on licensed premises, and this section enables similar restrictions to be imposed on machines used for making or accepting bets on real events. Likewise, there is an express regulation making power for controlling the use of gaming machines in Part 10, and this section enables similar controls to be imposed on real betting machines.

SECTION 182: EXCLUSION OF CHILDREN FROM TRACK AREAS

476. It is a mandatory condition of premises licences in relation to a track that children and young people are to be excluded from any area where betting facilities are provided, or gaming machines, other than Category D machines, are made available for use. The exclusion from an area where betting facilities are provided does not apply to a dog-racing track or horse-racing track on a day on which racing takes place or is expected to take place. For the purposes of this section, an area where facilities are provided or a machine is situated is a place where it is possible to take advantage of the facilities or to use the machine.

477. The Secretary of State has the power to alter the places that children and young people are excluded from, and the circumstances in which they may be permitted access.

SECTION 183: CHRISTMAS DAY

478. This section imposes a condition on all premises licenses that the premises shall not be used to provide facilities for gambling on Christmas Day.

SECTION 184: ANNUAL FEE

479. A premises licence holder must pay a fee to the licensing authority upon the grant of the licence, and annually thereafter. The Secretary of State (and, in Scotland, the Scottish Ministers) will prescribe in regulations the amount of the fee, and the period within which the initial fee must be paid. Such regulations may make different provisions for different classes of licences and different circumstances. Further provision for the setting of premises licence fees in England and Wales is made later in this Part.

480. The section also makes provision for the Secretary of State, or in Scotland, the Scottish Ministers, to set fees for circumstances where a premises licence is altered (following, for example, a change of circumstances, a variation, transfer or review) and, as a consequence, a different annual fee (either more or less than the original) is applicable.

SECTION 185: AVAILABILITY OF LICENCE

481. Holders of premises licences must keep a copy of their licence on the premises and make it available to a police constable, a Commission enforcement officer or an authorised local authority officer. Failure to present the licence without reasonable excuse when requested by such people is an offence, for which the maximum penalty will be a fine of level 2 on the standard scale.

SECTION 186: CHANGE OF CIRCUMSTANCE

482. The licence holder commits an offence if he fails to inform the licensing authority if his home or business address (on the licence) changes, or where another change of a type specified in regulations by the Secretary of State takes place. If, because of the change, information on the licence is rendered incorrect then the licence holder must send, with his notification, his licence (or an application for a copy of it under section 190), and the prescribed fee. The licensing authority will then alter the licence and send it back, or issue a copy in a form that reflects the change in circumstance. If a person fails to comply with the requirements of this section, or the regulations made under it, he commits an offence. The penalty is a fine not exceeding level 2.

SECTION 187: APPLICATION TO VARY LICENCE

483. Licensees may apply to the licensing authority for a variation to their licence which will alter the authorised activities, change the conditions of the licence, or alter some other detail of the licence. A licence may not be varied so that it relates to premises to which it did not previously relate.

484. The procedures in this Part for licence applications will apply to procedures for variation; however, the Secretary of State may make regulations providing for different procedures, including different procedures for different types of variation. These powers may be used to provide that a different fee applies for applications for variation from that which applies in respect of applications for a licence.

485. An application for variation must be accompanied by the licence and a statement of the variation requested. If the licence cannot be provided, a statement explaining why the licence cannot be provided and an application for a copy must accompany the application.

SECTIONS 188 AND 189: TRANSFER

486. Unlike operating licences, premises licences can be transferred, provided the transfer is to another operating licence holder (except in the case of betting premises licences in respect of tracks, where the transfer can be to any person). The procedures under this Part for premises licence applications will apply to applications for transfer with any necessary modifications. A different fee may be prescribed in relation to applications for transfer to that which applies in relation to an application for a licence.
487. Where a licensing authority grants the application for transfer, it must alter the licence so that the applicant for transfer becomes the licensee; specify in the licence the time at which the transfer takes place; and make any alteration that appears to them to be required. This includes an alteration to attach or remove any condition.
488. Where a licence has a condition attached in order to give effect to an agreement made for the provision of services by the licensee in the context of a competition for a casino premises licence under Schedule 9, that licence cannot be transferred unless the transferee enters into an new agreement that appears to the licensing authority to have substantially the same effect as the original agreement. The condition of the licence to which the agreement relates must then be altered to reflect the new agreement.
489. Applications for transfer must state when the transfer is to take place and be accompanied by a written statement from the existing licence holder consenting to the transfer. It is possible for a transfer application to proceed without such a statement if the applicant has been unable to contact the existing licence holder, having taken all reasonable steps to do so. In such circumstances the licensing authority may disapply the requirement for consent from the licence holder and take all reasonable steps to notify the existing licence holder of their decision.
490. The licence or an application for a copy of the licence must accompany the application. Where the existing licensee is not contactable, the licence will be treated as being lost, stolen or damaged and the applicant must apply for a copy under section 190.
491. If the application for transfer so requests, the applicant will be treated as though he were the licensee from the point that the application is received by the licensing authority to the determination of the application by the licensing authority.
492. Regulations can be made to require an applicant for transfer to publish or give notice of his application to responsible authorities and other people specified. A responsible authority may make representations about the application to the licensing authority.
493. A licensing authority will grant an application for transfer, unless they think it would be wrong to do so having regard to any representations that have been made. Decisions made under this section will be subject to rights of appeal by the licensee or the applicant for transfer.

SECTION 190: COPY OF LICENCE

494. Where a premises licence, or summary of the terms and conditions, is lost, stolen or damaged, then the licence holder may apply to the licensing authority for a copy of the licence. The licensing authority must grant a copy if it is satisfied that the licence or summary has been lost, stolen or damaged and that the loss or theft has been reported to the police. A fee is payable, which will be set by the Secretary of State (and Scottish Ministers) in regulations. A copy of the licence or summary issued under this section shall be treated as though it were the original.

SECTION 191: INITIAL DURATION

495. Premises licences are of unlimited duration, unless:

- the Secretary of State exercises powers under this section to impose a time limit on premises licences, or a class of premises licences, by secondary legislation.; or
- the licence ceases to have effect in accordance with other provisions in this Part.

496. Regulations made by the Secretary of State under this section may have retrospective effect, and can make provision about renewals

SECTION 192: SURRENDER

497. Licensees may surrender their licences by writing to the licensing authority to give notice of their wish to do so, and enclosing the licence, or a written explanation of why it is not possible to provide the licence. The licensing authority must notify the surrender to the Commission, the police, and Her Majesty's Commissioners of Customs and Excise.

SECTION 193: REVOCATION FOR FAILURE TO PAY FEE

498. A premises licence will be revoked if the licence holder fails to pay the relevant annual fee (required under section 184), unless the failure to pay can be explained by an administrative error.

SECTION 194: LAPSE

499. Where the licensee dies, becomes (in the opinion of the licensing authority) incapable of carrying out the licensed activities due to physical or mental incapacity; or becomes bankrupt; insolvent; ceases to exist; or goes into liquidation, then the licence will lapse. A lapsed licence may be reinstated under sections 195 and 196.

500. When a licensing authority becomes aware of the lapse of a licence, it must, as soon as reasonably practicable, notify the Commission, the police, and Her Majesty's Commissioners of Customs and Excise.

SECTIONS 195 AND 196: REINSTATEMENT

501. For a period of 6 months beginning with the day on which the premises licence lapses, a person may apply for the licence to be reinstated in their name, instead of the person whose name is on the lapsed licence. The licence, or a statement of why the licence cannot be provided (along with an application for a copy of the licence), must accompany the application. The person seeking reinstatement must hold a relevant operating licence (except in the case of except in the case of betting premises licences in respect of tracks) in order for the licensing authority to be able to grant transfer. The requirements for licence applications are set out in section 159.

502. Regulations may be made requiring the applicant for reinstatement to publish or give notice of his application to certain specified (but not all) responsible authorities. A responsible authority may make representations about the application to the licensing authority.

503. The provisions in this Part relating to applications for premises licences apply to applications for reinstatement with any necessary modifications. The licensing authority will grant the application for reinstatement, unless they conclude that it would be wrong to do so, taking account of representations made by responsible authorities. On grant of the application, the licensing authority must alter the licence so that the applicant becomes the licensee; must specify that reinstatement take effect at the time when the application is granted; and must make any other alteration to the licence that they deem necessary.

504. An applicant shall be treated as being the licensee during the period between the application for reinstatement being received by the licensing authority and the determination of that application.

505. There is a right of appeal against the decision of the licensing authority to accept or reject an application for reinstatement under section 206.

SECTION 197: APPLICATION FOR REVIEW

506. Under this Part, a premises licence may be reviewed:

- in response to an application to the licensing authority by a responsible authority or interested party (section 197); or
- on the initiation of the licensing authority (section 200).

507. This section deals with applications by responsible authorities or interested parties. Applications must be in the form and manner prescribed by regulations made by the Secretary of State and Scottish Ministers. Regulations may also require an applicant to give notice of the application in a prescribed form and manner, to the licensee, and/or the responsible authorities in relation to the premises. In addition, the licensing authority may be required to publish notice of the application in the prescribed form and manner. Such notice must specify a period of time within which the licensee, a responsible authority or an interested party can make representations about the application.

SECTIONS 198 AND 199: CONSIDERATION OF APPLICATION

508. Section 198 specifies the grounds on which a licensing authority may reject an application for a review made by a responsible authority or an interested party. They include that the application is frivolous or vexatious, or that it does not raise any new grounds to those previously raised during the original consideration of the grant of relevant premises licence, or on a previous application for review of that licence. An application for review can also be rejected because it does not raise any issue which is relevant to the principles which the authority is required to consider in granting a premises licence application.

509. In determining whether to reject an application for a review, the licensing authority must consider the length of time that has elapsed since the last review and/or the grant of the relevant premises licence.

510. If the licensing authority thinks that some of the grounds on which an application for a review may be rejected apply, they may reject the relevant parts of the application for the review. To the extent that a licensing authority does not reject an application for review, they must, under section 199, accept it.

SECTION 200: INITIATION OF REVIEW BY LICENSING AUTHORITY

511. Where a review is initiated by a licensing authority, the authority may:

- review a particular class of premises licences, to assess the use of those premises or the arrangements made to ensure compliance with licence conditions (subsection (1)); or
- review a particular premises licence, where it suspects that the premises have not been used in accordance with a condition of a licence, or if it thinks that a review would be appropriate for any other reason. Before conducting such a review, the licensing authority must give notice of its intention to review the licence to the affected licensee, and also publish its intention.

512. The Secretary of State may specify the form and manner of the notice of intention to review, and also the period of time within which notice is to be given. Where such regulations are made, they must specify a period of time within which representations about the review may be made by the licensee, a responsible authority or an interested party.

SECTIONS 201 TO 203: REVIEW

513. Where a licensing authority has granted an application for a review, or has given notice of its intention to initiate a review, it must review the licence as soon as reasonably practicable (after the period for giving representations has expired) in order to determine what, if any, action should be taken under this Part.
514. In conducting the review, the licensing authority must hold a hearing unless the applicant for the review and any person who made representations has consented to the hearing being waived; or the licensing authority considers that all the representations made following notice of the review are frivolous, vexatious or will not influence their decision.
515. When determining what, if any, action under section 202(1) to take, the licensing authority must take into account representations made before or during the hearing, and the grounds specified in any application for a review made by a responsible authority or an interested party.
516. Following a review, a licensing authority may:
- suspend (for a period not exceeding 3 months) or revoke a licence; or
- amend, add or exclude the conditions attached to the licence. This includes reinstating a condition imposed under section 168 that they excluded under section 169.

517. After completing a review of a licence, the licensing authority must notify the licensee, the applicant for a review (if any), the Commission, any person who made representations, the police and Customs and Excise of their decision as soon as possible after it has been made. Notification must give reasons for the decision.
518. A right of appeal is provided against a determination by the licensing authority to take, or not to take, action under these sections. An appeal may be made by the licensee; any person who made representations in relation to a review; the person (if any) who applied for the review; and the Commission.

SECTIONS 204 AND 205: PROVISIONAL STATEMENT

519. Where a person expects premises to be constructed or altered, or expects to acquire a right to occupy premises, he may apply for a provisional statement from the licensing authority, in advance of a full premises licence.
520. Subject to any necessary modifications, the provisions relating to applications for premises licences under this Part apply to applications for provisional statements. A person does not require a right to occupy the premises, or an operating licence in order to be granted a provisional statement.
521. An application for a provisional statement must include plans, and information in relation to the construction, alteration or acquisition of property as may be prescribed by the Secretary of State in regulations.
522. Where granted, the provisional statement offers a degree of certainty to the applicant when he comes to apply for a premises licence because, unless the property has not been constructed or altered in accordance with the plans submitted to the licensing authority, when considering the application for the premises licence:
- the licensing authority must disregard any representations made, except where they relate to matters that could not have been addressed in relation to the application for a provisional statement; or where they reflect a change of circumstances relating to the applicant; and
- the licensing authority may only refuse the application for the premises licence or impose conditions not included in the provisional statement, by taking into account matters which are valid representations (as defined above) or where there has been a change in the circumstances of the applicant.

523. An example of a change in an applicant's circumstances that might be relevant may be where the applicant has been convicted of a relevant offence following his application for a provisional statement; such that the applicant is now unable to get an operating licence.

524. If the property in respect of which the application has been made has been altered or constructed in a way that is not in accordance with the plans that were submitted with the application for a provisional statement, the licensing authority are not limited in their consideration of the application for the premises licence in the ways outlined above.

525. Where a provisional statement is granted in respect of a casino premises, under Schedule 9, paragraphs 9 and 10, the licensing authority may specify a time period for which it is to have effect. In such a case, the period may be extended by the licensing authority on application by the holder.

SECTIONS 206 TO 209: RIGHTS OF APPEAL

526. These sections set out which licensing authority decisions under this Part are subject to appeal, and by whom. They include a decision to reject or grant an application (including rejection or grant of an application to reinstate a licence, and an application for a provisional statement); a decision whether to take action as a result of a review; and a decision whether to transfer a licence. In addition, Schedule 9 provides that an applicant may appeal against a decision to impose a time limit on the period for which a provisional casino premises licence applies.

527. Appeals under this Part must be made, in England and Wales, to the magistrates' court within 21 days of the relevant decision. Unless he is the appellant, the licence holder or applicant, as the case may be, must be joined as a respondent in addition to the licensing authority.

528. The magistrates may dismiss the appeal, substitute a new decision that could have been made by the licensing authority, remit the case back to the licensing authority, and also make an order about costs. Where the case is remitted, there is a further right of appeal on the same terms. In Scotland, appeals will be made to the sheriff on the same terms, except that there will be no right for the sheriff to substitute his own decision.

529. Any determination or action under this Part will be stayed during an appeal, or during the period within which an appeal could have been brought, unless the licensing authority, when making a determination or taking action, directs otherwise (in which case the magistrates' court or sheriff may make any appropriate order). There is a further right of appeal on a point of law to the High Court in England and Wales, or the Court of Session in Scotland.

SECTION 210: PLANNING PERMISSION

530. This section makes it clear that a licensing authority is not to have regard to planning or building law matters when considering an application under Part 8. It also provides that any decision on the application by a licensing authority is not to constrain a later decision by the authority under planning or building law.

SECTION 211: VESSELS AND VEHICLES

531. This section provides that premises licences may be granted to passenger vessels, but may not be granted to vehicles. The interpretation section in Part 18 contains provisions for defining vessels and vehicles, and this section contains rules for determining where vessels are located for the purpose of applying for a premises licence. Section 359 defines the territorial limitations on the Act in relation to vessels.

532. Where an application for a premises licence is made in respect of a vessel, the bodies listed in subsection (4) will be responsible bodies, with the same rights as responsible authorities generally under this Part.

533. The effect of this section (together with other provisions in the Act in relation to vehicles) is that gaming and betting on vehicles is unlawful under the Act, unless the

gambling constitutes private gaming or betting within the meaning of Part 14 and Schedule 15. Section 360 defines the territorial limitations on the Act in relation to aircraft.

534. Schedule 11 contains rules on the lawful promotion of exempt lotteries on vessels. Permits under Schedules 10, 12 and 14 may not be granted to vessels or vehicles. Authorisations under Schedule 13 will be available for vessels and vehicles to the same extent that they are available to them under the Licensing Act 2003.

SECTION 212: FEES

535. At a number of sections in this Part, provision is made for fees to be payable to licensing authorities, and for those fees to be set by the Secretary of State, or Scottish Ministers. Under this section, the Secretary of State may devolve to licensing authorities in England and Wales the freedom to set fees for premises licence applications relating to their area, subject to any constraints specified in the regulations.

536. Where licensing authorities are given power to determine a fee:

- they may set different fees for different classes of case specified in the regulations eg for different types of licence (but not otherwise); and
- they must aim to ensure that the income from the fees they set equals (as nearly as possible) the costs of providing the particular services to which the fee relates. In determining whether this cost recovery principle is being met, licensing authorities may make a comparison between costs and fees over whatever period it considers to be appropriate. The Secretary of State may issue guidance to licensing authorities on the appropriate periods for comparison. Where she does so, the licensing authority must take account of that guidance.

537. This permits the Secretary of State to set bands of minimum or maximum fees, within which a licensing authority can set its individual charges. Alternatively, the Secretary of State can give an authority complete discretion to set its own fees, subject always to the cost recovery principle.

538. Regulations under this section need not apply to all licensing authorities in England and Wales and may, in particular, apply only to categories of authority. In England, such categorisation could be achieved by reference to categories assigned under section 99 of the Local Government Act 2003 (c.26) (Comprehensive Performance Assessment).

539. This section does not apply to Scotland.

PART 9: TEMPORARY USE OF PREMISES

6.2012 540. Part 9 makes provision for the use of premises for gambling where there is no premises licence in respect of those premises, but an operating licence holder wishes to use the premises, temporarily, for providing facilities for gambling.

541. Temporary use notices, endorsed by licensing authorities, will authorise the provision of gambling activities temporarily on specific premises. The nature of the gambling activities that can be provided under such notices will be controlled by the Secretary of State in regulations. Examples of premises which could be subject to a temporary use notice are hotels, exhibition centres or entertainment venues.

542. Part 1 defines the licensing authorities which will consider temporary use notices, and Part 18 requires licensing authorities to make a licensing policy statement in relation to their functions under this Part.

SECTIONS 214 TO 218: TEMPORARY USE NOTICE

543. Where an operating licence holder wishes to provide facilities for gambling temporarily on premises, he may give notice in writing (a 'temporary use notice') that he intends to use the premises for the provision of facilities for gambling. Only a holder

of an operating licence may give a temporary use notice, and the activity that he wishes to provide must be the same activity that he is authorised to provide facilities for under the terms of his operating licence.

544. The temporary use notice must be in the form prescribed by the Secretary of State, and must specify the information listed in section 216(1).

545. A temporary use notice cannot authorise any gambling activities. It can only authorise such gambling activities as the Secretary of State may specify in regulations, and which are set out in the notice. These regulations may also specify combinations of activities that may not be provided together under a temporary use notice. For example, if facilities for poker, blackjack and pool betting were to be authorised by the Secretary of State, a temporary use notice could not permit the provision of such facilities at the same time, on the same premises.

546. Section 218 provides that a set of premises cannot be subject to a temporary use notices for more than 21 days in any 12 month period. This means that, while several different temporary use notices may have effect for a set of premises over a period of time, the aggregate period of these notices cannot exceed 21 days in a 12 month period. This is the case even if the gambling activities taking place under the notices are different activities. The maximum period of 21 days applies to all gambling carried on pursuant to notices, not merely one type of gambling.

547. These sections set out procedures for the licensing authority to ensure that these time periods are complied with. If any notice is served which is in breach of these requirements, the authority must serve a counter-notice which prevents the temporary use notice authorising gambling for anything over the permitted 21 days.

548. A valid (ie endorsed) temporary use notice, which complies with the requirements of this Part, will authorise gambling carried on pursuant to it, and no offences under Part 3 of the Act will be committed.

SECTIONS 219 AND 220: GIVING NOTICE: PROCEDURE

549. A temporary use notice must be served upon a licensing authority for the area in which the premises are situated. It must be given at least three months before it is proposed to have effect. It must arrive with both the licensing authority and any other person entitled to receive it within 7 days of the date on which it is stated to have been given.

550. A number of procedural requirements must be followed, including the payment of any fee that is prescribed by the Secretary of in regulations. In England and Wales this fee setting power may be devolved to licensing authorities in accordance with section 212. In addition, the person giving notice must also give a copy of it to the Commission, the police, and Her Majesty's Commissioners of Customs and Excise. This allows these people to object to the proposed notice, as outlined below.

551. The licensing authority receiving a notice must acknowledge its receipt as soon as practicable thereafter.

SECTIONS 221 TO 223: OBJECTIONS AND MODIFICATION BY AGREEMENT

552. The licensing authority or anyone else entitled to receive a copy of a notice may object to it. The grounds for objections are that, having regard to the licensing objectives set out in Part 1 of the Act, the notice should not have effect, or should only have effect with modifications. A notice of objection must be served upon the person seeking to make the facilities for gambling available (ie the server of the temporary use notice) within 14 days of the date of the temporary use notice, and must state the reasons for the objection. A copy must also be given to the licensing authority.

553. Where objection notices have been served, the licensing authority must hold a hearing at which representations may be made by the person who gave the temporary use notice, the people who objected, and any other people who were entitled to receive

a copy of the notice. This requirement may be waived if the licensing authority, and each person who would be entitled to make representations, agree in writing that a hearing is unnecessary.

554. Where an objection has been made to a temporary use notice, but a hearing has not taken place (either because it has not yet happened, or because it has been dispensed with), anyone who has raised objections under these sections may propose a modification to the notice. If the modifications are agreed, a new temporary use notice, incorporating the modifications, can be served and the original notice will be treated as withdrawn. In these circumstances, the three-month time limit and fee will not apply to the new temporary use notice. If all objections are dealt with by modifications then this will dispense with the further need to hold a hearing in relation to the notice. If not, then those with objections outstanding can continue to contest the notice.

SECTIONS 224 TO 226: COUNTER-NOTICES AND DISMISSAL OF OBJECTIONS

555. Where:

- an objection notice has been served;
- modification has not removed the objection; and
- either a hearing has taken place, or been dispensed with,
- the licensing authority may determine that the temporary use notice should not have effect, or should only have effect with modifications. The principles it must apply in reaching a view are the same as those it applies when determining premises licence applications. Therefore, it should aim to permit the temporary use of premises for gambling, in so far as it thinks that permission:
- accords with relevant Commission codes of practice and guidance;
- is reasonably consistent with the licensing objectives; and
- is in accordance with the authority's three-year licensing policy (established by the authority under section 349 of the Act).

556. If the authority concludes that the temporary use notice should not have effect, or should only have effect with modifications, it must serve a counter-notice upon the person who served the temporary use notice. This counter-notice may provide that the temporary use notice:

- will not have effect;
- will have effect only in respect of a certain activity;
- will only have effect in relation to an activity for a certain period of time or during certain hours of the day; or
- will be subject to a condition.

557. A counter notice must be in the prescribed form and state the licensing authority's reasons for giving it. A copy must be given to any person who was entitled to receive a copy of the temporary use notice under section 219.

558. If the authority concludes that it will not give any counter-notice, then it must inform all relevant parties of this fact. The effect is that any objection notices have been dismissed by the authority.

559. Rights of appeal are available following an authority's decision to issue a counter-notice or to dismiss objections under these sections. The person who gave the temporary use notice, and any person entitled to receive a copy of it, may appeal. An appeal lies to the magistrates' court, and must be made within 14 days of receiving notice of the licensing authority's decision. In Scotland, the appeal will be to the sheriff in whose area the premises are located. If the appeal is against the decision of the licensing authority not to issue a counter notice, then the person giving the temporary use notice will also be a respondent in the case.

560. Where the decision to appeal may be made by a person entitled to receive a copy of the notice under section 219, they must decide whether to appeal, and to institute any appeal as soon as is reasonably practicable.

561. The magistrates' court or sheriff may, on hearing an appeal, dismiss it; direct the licensing authority to take some specified action; remit it back to the licensing authority

to decide in accordance with a direction of the court; and make an order as to costs (or expenses). Where the decision is remitted to the licensing authority, the same rights of appeal will flow from their new decision as applied to their original one.

562. A further right of appeal exists to the High Court or Court of Session on a point of law.

SECTION 227: ENDORSEMENT OF NOTICE

563. If no objections are raised to a temporary use notice during the 14-day period after it is made, then the licensing authority will return the notice to the person who gave it, endorsing it as valid. The Secretary of State may prescribe the precise method of endorsement in regulations.

564. If a notice of objection was served, but did not result in a counter-notice being served (ie the objections were dismissed) then the temporary use notice must similarly be endorsed and returned, as soon as reasonably practicable, to the person who gave it.

565. An endorsed temporary use notice provides authorisation for the specified facilities for gambling to be provided at the relevant premises, in accordance with its terms.

SECTION 228: CONSIDERATION BY LICENSING AUTHORITY: TIMING

566. Licensing authorities will have six weeks from the date of the temporary use notice to complete proceedings on the notice. This includes proceedings to consider whether to give a notice of objection; holding a hearing or agreeing to dispense with one, and giving a counter notice or a notice dismissing any objections.

SECTIONS 229 AND 230: MISCELLANEOUS PROVISIONS

567. An endorsed temporary use notice must be displayed on the premises to which it relates at any time when it is being relied upon. It must also be made available on request to a police constable, a Commission enforcement officer, an authorised local authority officer, or an officer of Her Majesty's Customs and Excise. If a person fails to display or produce his notice as required, he will commit an offence for which he will be liable to a fine not exceeding level 2 on the standard scale.

568. A person who has given a temporary use notice to a licensing authority may withdraw it at any time. It will then cease to have effect and any proceedings relevant to it will cease, except in relation to a matter which arose during, or in relation to, any time during which it was in effect.

SECTION 231: VEHICLES AND VESSELS

569. A temporary use notice may be given in respect of a passenger vessel, but may not be given in relation to a vehicle. The interpretation section in Part 18 contains provisions for defining vessels and vehicles, and this section contains rules for determining where vessels are located for the purpose of a licensing authority's functions under this Part. See also the note on section 211.

SECTION 232: DELEGATION OF LICENSING AUTHORITY FUNCTIONS: ENGLAND AND WALES

570. This section provides that the provisions of Part 8 of the Act, in relation to the delegation of functions to a licensing committee established under the Licensing Act 2003, and further delegation to officers of the authority under sections 154 and 155, apply similarly to this Part. The only matter that may not be sub-delegated under this Part is the decision under section 224 to issue a counter notice. That decision must be made by the licensing committee.

SECTION 233: DELEGATION OF LICENSING AUTHORITY FUNCTIONS: SCOTLAND

571. This section provides that the provisions of Part 8 of the Act, in relation to the delegation of functions of Scottish licensing authorities, apply similarly to this Part. The decision to issue a counter-notice under this Part may not, however, be delegated to the clerk of the authority, or a person appointed to assist him.

SECTION 234: REGISTER

572. This section makes provision for licensing authorities to maintain a register of temporary use notices in a form and manner specified by the Secretary of State in regulations. The register must be available for inspection by members of the public at all reasonable times, and a copy must be provided to a member of the public on request. A charge may be made for copies.
573. The Secretary of State may also, in regulations, require licensing authorities to provide information about temporary use notices to the Commission in a specified fashion. The Commission may then be required to keep its own register of the information provided to it, and may relieve licensing authorities from the need to maintain a register under this section.

PART 10: GAMING MACHINES

6.2013 574. Part 10 contains the main provisions of the Act on gaming machines. It sets out a definition of 'gaming machine' together with the offences relevant to illegal use or manufacture of a gaming machine. Parts 5 and 8 of the Act deal with certain authorisations and entitlements to use gaming machines that arise from operating or premises licences respectively. This Part provides general provisions which apply to the use of any gaming machine, and includes regulation-making powers for the Secretary of State to set categories of machine and rules on use.
575. Manufacture, supply, maintenance, repair, installation and adaptation of a gaming machine are all regulated activities under this Part.
576. This Part applies to any gaming machine situated in Great Britain, or anything done in Great Britain in relation to a gaming machine, wherever that machine is situated (section 251). For example, a gaming machine manufactured in Great Britain, for export to another country, will be covered by the provisions in Part 10. Accordingly, a gaming machine technical operating licence under Part 5 of the Act will be available to manufacturers and suppliers who wish to cater for the overseas market. Such machines need not comply with the categorisation regulations under section 236 if the machines are for export. Machines supplied for use in Great Britain will need to comply with the requirements of Part 10, even if manufactured abroad.

SECTION 235: GAMING MACHINE

577. This section provides a definition of a gaming machine for the Act. It is significantly broader than the definition of gaming machine in section 26 of the Gaming Act 1968, which the Act repeals. The new definition accommodates developments in technology which have taken place since the 1968 Act. It also covers a wide range of gambling activities which can take place on a machine, and includes betting on virtual events.
578. Subsection (1) defines a gaming machine as a machine that is designed or adapted for use by people to gamble (whether or not it can be used for other purposes). This is a wide definition. Subsection (3)(b) contains further detail about how the words 'designed or adapted' are to be interpreted, particularly in relation to a computer.
579. Subsection (2) then sets out a number of exceptions to subsection (1) which ensure that the gaming machine definition does not capture certain specified types of machine.

580. The definition at subsection (1) does not depend on any concept of players depositing payments into the machine, or on the gambling activity being generated from within the machine itself (as opposed to being transmitted to the machine from other equipment). Nor is it restricted solely to gaming. To the extent that these were requirements under the 1968 Act, they are no longer part of the new definition.

581. The exclusions at subsection (2) provide that the following are not gaming machines:

- A domestic or dual-use computer which can be used for participating in remote gambling. The Secretary of State will prescribe the meaning of 'domestic computer' and 'dual-use computer' in regulations. The purpose of this exception is to exempt internet terminals and home computer equipment, which are not dedicated or specifically configured for gambling activities, from the definition of gaming machine. The mere fact that a home computer can be used to access gambling facilities should not render the computer a gaming machine. However, someone offering the public access to the internet, via terminals, and configuring them to encourage gambling, is making a gaming machine available for use (unless any other exception applies, such as betting on real events). The regulations to be made under this power will set out the relevant criteria for determining whether equipment is a domestic or dual use computer, and can refer to matters such as the location of the computer, the software installed on the computer, and the circumstances in which the computer is used (subsections (2)(a), (3)(f) and (4));
- A telephone or other communications device that can be used for remote gambling (other than a computer). The fact that, with modern technology, a telephone or interactive television can be used to participate in gambling will not render the equipment a gaming machine (subsection (2)(b)). This exception does not apply to computers;
- A machine which is designed or adapted for betting only on future real events. This exemption is designed to prevent equipment, such as automated betting terminals, through which people place bets on real, not virtual, events, from being counted as gaming machines. The event must be a future event at the time the machine is used, meaning that betting on pre-recorded activities, where the result is already known, is not exempt. The exempt equipment is not unregulated. Making it available as part of a business will be providing facilities for betting, and will require the relevant operating licences under the Act. However, in regulatory terms, these machines are not to be treated as gaming machines (subsection (2) (c)).
- A machine upon which someone enters a lottery. Provided that the machine does not determine the result of the lottery, or announces it only after a specified period, then such a machine is not a gaming machine. This means that if a machine only dispenses lottery tickets (for a draw that takes place completely independent of the machine), or vends lottery paper scratchcards, then the machine is outsides the definition of a gaming machine. If the machine announces the results of the lottery, as well as selling tickets to it, then the machine will not be a gaming machine provided a prescribed interval has elapsed between the sale of the ticket and the announcement of the result. The Secretary of State will determine the duration of the period by order. In no circumstances can the machine determine the result of the lottery (subsection (2)(d)).
- A machine for playing bingo which is used by the holder of a bingo operating licence, in accordance with conditions attached by the Commission. This is designed to exempt what is known as 'mechanised cash bingo equipment which is used for playing real bingo games, but whose degree of computerisation or mechanisation means that it would otherwise be caught by the definition of gaming machine. The need for it to comply with Commission conditions ensures that the exemption is construed narrowly and not extended to any machine on which a virtual bingo game could be played (subsection (2) (e));

- A machine for playing bingo prize gaming which is used by the holder of a gaming machine general operating licence (for an adult gaming centre or a family entertainment centre), in accordance with conditions attached to those licences by the Commission. This is designed to exempt equipment used for playing real prize bingo, in accordance with the terms of Part 13 of the Act. The need for it to comply with Commission conditions ensures that the exemption is construed narrowly and not extended to any machine on which a virtual bingo game could be played (subsection (2)(f));
- A machine for playing bingo prize gaming which is used by an unlicensed family entertainment centre or pursuant to a prize gaming permit, in accordance with any Commission code of practice. This exemption is similar to that at subsection (2)(g), but applies to different types of operator who have prize gaming rights under Part 13 (subsection (2)(g));
- A machine which is used for playing manual games of chance. This is a machine which:
  - is controlled or operated by someone employed to do so (eg a croupier spinning a roulette wheel); or
  - is used in connection with a real game of chance which is controlled or operated by an individual (eg a computer terminal for staking on the outcome of a roulette wheel that is spun by a croupier) (subsection (2)(h)).
- In both these instances the equipment could be construed as a gaming machine under the broad definition, but the fact that it is operated as part of a real game of chance means that it is not to be regulated under the gaming machine provisions. Such equipment and activities will be regulated under other parts of the Act.
- A machine which is used for playing automated games of chance in a casino. This is equipment used for playing a real game of chance, pursuant to a casino operating licence, but which has no human involvement from the organisers of the casino game, and which is not linked to a game which does have such human involvement. For example, apparatus such as a roulette wheel which is completely mechanised, and works without the need for any croupier to rotate the wheel, spin the ball or accept stakes. This equipment is not a gaming machine provided it is used in accordance with Commission licence conditions. Section 174(6) contains further provisions in relation to this equipment in casinos.

582. These various exemptions prevent the broad definition of gaming machine from capturing equipment unintentionally. The definition in subsection (1) is intended to cover a gaming machine that is used for taking part in virtual gaming, virtual betting or a virtual lottery (where the draw is part of the activity determined by the machine).

583. Subsection (3) provides clarification about the characteristics of a gaming machine. Reference to part of a gaming machine includes computer software to be used in a gaming machine, but does not include a component of a gaming machine which does not influence the outcome of the gambling (subsection (3)(c)). This means that where a gaming machine technical operating licence is required for the manufacture, installation etc of gaming machines, computer software intended for use in the machine is included within the licensing requirement. However, the plywood from which the machine is constructed is not. References to installing part of a gaming machine include installing computer software (subsection (3)(d)). This is required because machines can be configured or changed by the downloading of gambling software, without any need to physically interfere with the machine.

584. Subsection (5) allows the Secretary of State to make regulations concerning the sub-division of apparatus into individual gaming machines. It is no longer the case that a gaming machine will take the form of a stand-alone machine in the form of a traditional 'fruit-machine'. A single computer can be linked to a number of player positions and offer each player the experience of playing a gaming machine, although the apparatus forms one large whole. To tackle the possibility of evasion of the

Act's regulation for gaming machines, this power allows rules to be made for calculating when a single piece of apparatus counts as more than one machine, and, in particular, can focus on the number of player positions available. These regulations will supplement other parts of the Act, where numerical limits are placed on the entitlements to make gaming machines available for use.

SECTION 236: GAMING MACHINES: CATEGORIES A TO D

585. Gaming machines will be divided into categories, with different entitlements set out in the Act to use the various categories. This section requires the Secretary of State to define, in regulations, four classes of gaming machine, to be known as categories A, B, C and D. Category B may also be sub-divided into further sub-categories, and these regulations may identify to which sub-category of B machine an entitlement relates (subsections (1) and (2)).

586. The categorisation will refer to the particular facilities for gambling which are offered on the machine. In particular, under subsection (4), the regulations can specify:

- the maximum amounts that can be paid to use the machine;
- the value or nature of the prize delivered as a result of its use;
- the nature of the gambling for which the prize is used; or
- the types of premises on which it can be used.

587. These matters can be combined so that, for example, one category of machine could have different maximum use charges dependent on the nature of the prize offered by the machine.

588. Details of the proposed A to D categorisation of gaming machines is set out in the Regulatory Impact Assessment published alongside the Act. The intention is that Category D will have the lowest levels of charge and prizes, and that these will increase in value, up to Category A, which will be a machine with no limits as to charges and prizes.

589. Part 8 of the Act contains the principal commercial entitlements for different types of licensed gambling premises to use different categories of machines. Different permissions are also available under Part 12 of the Act, for clubs, miners' welfare institutes, alcohol licensed premises and travelling fairs, and, also, pursuant to this Part, for family entertainment centres.

SECTIONS 237 TO 239: OTHER DEFINITIONS

590. These sections set out definitions for an adult gaming centre, a family entertainment centre, (including a licensed family entertainment centre), and a 'prize' in relation to a gaming machine.

SECTIONS 240 AND 241: USE AND SUPPLY OF MACHINES

591. The Secretary of State can make regulations about the way in which gaming machines can operate. It will be an offence to make a gaming machine available for use if the machine does not comply with such regulations.

592. Under subsection (2), the regulations may provide, in particular, for rules about:

- The method by which payment may be made for use of machine (ie whether coins, banknotes, smartcards, tokens or other methods can be used). It is a separate offence, under this Part, to supply, install or make a machine available which can be paid for by a credit card;
- The nature of, and arrangements, for receiving or claiming prizes;
- The rollover of stakes or prizes (ie the carry over of amounts paid or won to a subsequent use of the machine);
- The proportion of stakes or sums paid for use which must be returned as prizes;
- The display of information on or around the machine (eg information on minimum age of use); or

- Any other matter relating to the way that the machine works (eg whether it must operate randomly or not).

593. The Secretary of State may also make regulations about the supply, installation, adaptation, maintenance or repair of a gaming machine.

594. The penalty for making a machine available for use, in breach of these regulations, is a maximum term of imprisonment of 51 weeks in England and Wales, or 6 months in Scotland, or a fine up to level 5, or both.

595. Regulatory steps taken by the Commission, and any licence conditions it sets, must not conflict with these regulations. The Secretary of State can also identify matters about which licence conditions cannot be made in relation to machines. The Commission is empowered in Part 5 to set standards for gaming machines under section 96, and regulation of gaming machines is therefore a dual function of both the Secretary of State, and the Commission.

SECTION 242: MAKING MACHINE AVAILABLE FOR USE

596. The principal offence of making a gaming machine available for use unlawfully is set out in this section. A person will commit an offence if he makes any gaming machine available for use unless:

- He holds an operating licence which permits such use;
- He holds a family entertainment centre permit;
- He holds a club gaming permit or a club machine permit under Part 12;
- He has appropriate permission for alcohol licensed premises under Part 12;
- He makes gaming machines available at a travelling fair as permitted by Part 12, or;
- The machine offers no, or a limited, prize (as defined in this Part).

597. Under Part 3 of the Act it is a separate offence for a person to use premises for making a gaming machine available for use without the necessary authorisation or exemption, such as a premises licence or a Category D gaming machine permit. It will also be an offence under this section to make a gaming machine available for use if the machine does not comply with regulations made by the Secretary of State under section 240.

598. The penalty for this offence is a maximum term of imprisonment of 51 weeks in England and Wales, or 6 months in Scotland, and/or a fine up to level 5.

SECTION 243: MANUFACTURE, SUPPLY ETC

599. As well as setting requirements about the use of machines, the Act stipulates that various activities concerning the manufacture or supply of a gaming machine must also be regulated by the Commission. Under Part 5 of the Act, gaming machine technical operating licences are available for those wishing to manufacture, supply, install, adapt, maintain or repair a gaming machine. Failure to hold such an operating licence, when undertaking any of these activities, is an offence under this section. The penalty is a maximum term of imprisonment of 51 weeks in England and Wales, or 6 months in Scotland, and/or a fine up to level 5.

600. Exceptions from this offence exist:

- for those holding a single machine supply and maintenance permit under this Part;
- for machines exempted by regulations under section 248(2) (no prize);
- where the activities relate to a gaming machine that is for scrap; or
- where the supply is incidental to the sale or letting of a property.

601. This means that no operating licence is required where a machine is being broken up and no further use is made of it for gaming machine purposes, and where the machines are ancillary to the sale of a business which uses gaming machines. Any use, after sale, will continue to be subject to the other requirements of the Act.

SECTION 244: LINKED MACHINES

602. It is an offence, under this section, for gaming machines to be linked so that they operate together, and the value of the prize available on one machine is determined to any extent by use of the other machine. There is one exception to this, which is that subsection (2) permits machines to be linked at licensed casino premises provided that all of the machines are situated on the same premises. Linkage of gaming machines in this way does not authorise casino licensees to offer maximum prizes in excess of those allowed for the category of machine being used.

603. No linking between licensed casino premises is permitted, but subsection (3) gives the Secretary of State power to lift this prohibition, subject to appropriate Parliamentary approval.

604. The penalty, upon conviction for this offence, is a maximum term of imprisonment of 51 weeks in England and Wales, or 6 months in Scotland, or a fine up to level 5, or both.

SECTION 245: CREDIT

605. It is an offence for a person to supply, install or make available a gaming machine which allows payment to be made by means of a credit card. The penalty, upon conviction for this offence, is a maximum term of imprisonment of 51 weeks in England and Wales, or 6 months in Scotland, or a fine up to level 5, or both.

SECTION 247: FAMILY ENTERTAINMENT CENTRE PERMITS

606. Family entertainment centre ('FEC') gaming machine permits allow certain gaming machines to be made available for use without an operating or premises licence. These permits are issued by licensing authorities using the procedure set out in Schedule 10. They relate to the lowest category of machine. If an FEC wished to use Category C and D machines, it would require an appropriate operating and premises licence, under Parts 5 and 8 of the Act. The permits provided for here only relate to Category D machines.

607. Only premises which are wholly or mainly used for making gaming machines available for use may hold an FEC gaming machine permit. This is a change from the position prior to the Act, when any premises could apply for a permit allowing them to use an 'amusements with prizes' gaming machine (the nearest equivalent to a Category D machine). The intention is that gaming machines in certain non-gambling premises, like those now sometimes located in fish and chip shops and taxi cab ranks, should be removed. Once these provisions are commenced, permits previously granted under Schedule 9 to the Gaming Act 1968 will no longer be available under the Act, except to the extent that they relate to premises wholly or mainly used for making gaming machines available for use. Transitional provisions, under Part 18, will give effect to this change, and allow existing permits to continue after the repeal of the relevant provisions of the 1968 Act, until the date on which they would otherwise have expired if those provisions had continued in force. The position of premises holding an alcohol licence is dealt with separately in Part 12.

SCHEDULE 10: FAMILY ENTERTAINMENT CENTRE GAMING MACHINE PERMITS

608. This schedule sets out the procedures for the application for and grant of an FEC gaming machine permit by licensing authorities. It also regulates the permit's form and maintenance. Provision is made for the licensing authority to maintain a register of permits issued. Permits cannot be issued to vessels or vehicles.

609. Under paragraphs 6 to 10, the authority may prepare a statement of its principles in respect of the issue of these permits, and this can include matters which

they propose to take into account in considering the suitability of an applicant. In exercising its functions under Schedule 10, including determining any application, the authority may have regard to the licensing objectives but must have regard to any guidance issued by the Commission. The authority must consult the local police prior to granting an application.

610. Paragraph 11 concerns the form and content of permits. Under paragraphs 12 to 21, permits will normally last 10 years, but will lapse if the holder ceases to occupy the premises, dies, becomes unfit to hold the licence or becomes bankrupt or insolvent. The notes relating to prize gaming permits under Part 14 expand upon the meaning of 'occupy' for these purposes. Lapsed permits may, however, remain in force for up to six months. This is to allow an orderly transfer of the affairs of the licence holder, and the maintenance of the business (with its machines) while a new permit is obtained. Permits cannot be transferred, but must be re-applied for if there is a new occupier of the premises to which the permit relates.

611. Holders may surrender their permits voluntarily, and a court may order forfeiture of a permit if the holder is convicted of any relevant offence (see section 126). Permits can be renewed, and a licensing authority may only refuse the application for renewal if access to the FEC by an authorised officer has been refused without reasonable excuse, or renewal would not be reasonably consistent with pursuit of the licensing objectives.

612. There is an appeal mechanism provided for those who wish to contest a decision of a licensing authority under this Schedule.

SECTIONS 248 AND 249: NO AND LIMITED PRIZES

613. Making a gaming machine available for use will be an offence under Part 10, unless the required authorisation, licence or permit is held for the machine. However, in a number of circumstances no offence will be committed where someone makes a gaming machine available for use. These are:

- Where a person using a machine has no opportunity to win a prize, whether or not he pays for use of the machine (section 248). If a prize (as defined in the Act) is available, a machine is a gaming machine, even if there is no payment required to use it;
- Where a person, whether they pay for the machine or not, has the opportunity to win only a limited prize as follows:
  - Solely another opportunity to play the machine (sections 248 and 239); or
  - A prize whose value does not exceed any payment made for use of the machine (section 249).

614. The sections define payment for use broadly, and this includes payments which entitle someone to use a machine eg entrance charges to premises where machines are located. Section 343 contains powers for the Secretary of State to make rules about how to determine the value of a prize.

615. Power is also provided for the Secretary of State to make regulations which exempt certain gaming machines from the licensing requirements for manufacture, supply, etc (section 248(2)). This will be where a machine is not designed or expected to be used to provide an opportunity to win a prize. An example of the type of machine which will be included in such regulations is a pin-ball machine, where a game of chance is offered by the machine, but with no prize, or no more than the possibility of another free go on the machine. In these circumstances there is no regulatory requirement for the machine to be manufactured or supplied under licence. This is a change to the regime under the Gaming Act 1968, where machines continued to require a certificate under section 27 of that Act, even if their subsequent use was not regulated as use of a gaming machine. Machines which offer a limited prize within the meaning of section 249 will require a gaming machine technical operating licence.

SECTION 250: SINGLE-MACHINE SUPPLY AND MAINTENANCE PERMITS

616. This section sets out an exception to the general rule that a person who supplies, etc, a gaming machine must hold a gaming machine technical operating licence. It allows the Commission to issue a permit in relation to a specific gaming machine that authorises its supply, repair, installation, or maintenance without an operating licence. A fee is payable for the permit.

617. The Commission can only grant a single-machine permit if it believes that the supply etc, of the machine will not have any impact on the licensing objectives. This permit procedure replaces the permits issued by the Gaming Board under section 27 of the Gaming Act 1968, to individuals outside the gambling business who have single machines which they wish to dispose of, or repair.

618. Regulations under section 248(2) could also be used to deal with circumstances where obtaining a permit was considered an onerous obligation for the particular activity concerned, and the gaming machine was not to be used in a manner which permitted it to deliver prizes.

PART 11: LOTTERIES

6.2014 619. This Part of the Act makes provision with respect to lotteries, and should be read in conjunction with Schedules 2 and 11. The provisions here are built upon the foundation of the Lotteries and Amusements Act 1976, which will be repealed by this Act on commencement.

620. The core definition of a lottery is set out in Part 1 of the Act (section 14), as are sections dealing with the overlap between betting, gaming and a lottery.

621. The promotion of a lottery is unlawful under the Act unless the lottery is of a type that is specifically permitted. There are two permitted types of lottery under the Act:

- lotteries that are run in accordance with an operating licence issued under Part 5; and
- exempt lotteries under Schedule 11. There are four types of exempt lottery set out in Schedule 11.

SECTION 252: PROMOTING A LOTTERY

622. This section clarifies what is meant by the promotion of a lottery. Subsection (2) sets out the activities which constitute promoting a lottery. A person promotes a lottery if (amongst other things) he arranges for the printing, distribution or publication of promotional material. Subsection (3) defines 'promotional material' as a document that advertises, invites participation in, contains information about how to participate in, or lists winners in, a particular lottery.

623. Where an external lottery manager is retained to carry out the arrangements for a lottery on behalf of a society or local authority, a lottery is regarded, for the purposes of the Act, as being promoted by both the lottery manager and the society or local authority itself.

SECTION 253: LOTTERY TICKET

624. This section describes the types of item that may constitute a lottery ticket. It includes any document or article which confers or proves membership of the class eligible for prizes. The definition is deliberately wide so as to include electronic tickets and other items that may not be in the traditional paper format. The terms 'sale', 'supply' and 'purchase' are defined here in relation to lottery tickets. Requirements as to the form and content of a lottery ticket are set out in section 99 (in respect of licensed lotteries) and Schedule 11 (in respect of exempt lotteries).

SECTIONS 254 TO 256: KEY TERMS

625. These sections define certain key terms in relation to lotteries. 'Proceeds' is the total amount paid for the tickets in the lottery, before any deductions. 'Profits' refers to that amount, less deductions for prizes, sums 'rolled over' to another lottery, and reasonable organisational expenses.
626. Section 255 explains what is meant by the term 'draw' in a lottery. The term is defined widely, to include any process by which a prize in a lottery is allocated.
627. A definition of 'rollover' in relation to a lottery is provided in section 256. A rollover occurs when a prize that has not been allocated in one lottery, is added to prizes available for allocation in a subsequent lottery. Where prizes from previous draws are made available in the next draw of the same lottery, this will not be a rollover.
628. This section also explains where the line is to be drawn between one lottery and another. A lottery may have more than one draw, but multiple draws will only be part of the same lottery where the lottery is arranged in such a way that the class of persons eligible for prizes remains the same. A new lottery will begin where the class of persons eligible for prizes changes, or may change.

SECTION 257: EXTERNAL LOTTERY MANAGER

629. The term 'external lottery manager' is defined here as a person independent of the society or local authority for whom the lottery is run, who makes the arrangements for the lottery on behalf of the society or local authority. The purpose of this section, when read together with sections 258(3) and 259(3) is to provide that those persons who work with, or on behalf of, societies and local authorities to set up and run the lottery are external lottery managers. Other individuals, who are involved in some ancillary way (for example by selling tickets), are not making arrangements for the lottery and are therefore not external lottery managers. Such individuals do not commit any offence under this Part if they act in accordance with an operating licence held by an external lottery manager or a society or local authority.

SECTION 258: PROMOTION OF LOTTERY

630. This section makes it an offence to promote a lottery, but no offence is committed under this section if the person concerned holds and complies with an appropriate operating licence; or the person acts (except as an external lottery manager) on behalf of someone who holds such a licence, and the activity in question is carried on in compliance with that licence. Operating licences can be issued to local authorities, larger non-commercial societies, or to an external lottery manager acting on their behalf (see Part 5 for details of these procedures).
631. In addition, no offence is committed if the lottery falls into one of the exempt categories set out in Schedule 11. These are:

- incidental non-commercial lotteries;
- private lotteries;
- customer lotteries; and
- small society lotteries (ie society lotteries which do not generate sufficient proceeds to require an operating licence from the Commission, and are instead required to be registered with the local authority).

632. It will be a defence for the person to show that he reasonably believed that he was not committing the offence because:

- the lottery was an exempt lottery under Schedule 11, or a lottery operating licence was held and complied with;
- the arrangement was part of the National Lottery; or
- the arrangement did not fall within the definition of 'lottery' under Part 1.

633. There is a further defence set out in section 265, where a person reasonably believed that the lottery was not one to which this Part applied because it was outside the territorial application of this Part.

SECTION 259: FACILITATING A LOTTERY

634. This section makes it an offence to facilitate a lottery, which means in this context, advertising a particular lottery, or printing tickets or promotional material for it. Since it is provided that these actions must be with respect to a 'particular lottery', this offence is not intended to capture those who, for example, print generic tickets that can be used in lotteries generally.

635. The offence will not apply if the lottery is exempt, or if a person acts in accordance with the terms and conditions of an operating licence. A person does not need to be a licence holder themselves to benefit from this exemption; they will be covered if they act for the licence holder (for example, if they are an employee, or someone who provides services, such as a printing company).

636. It will be a defence for the person to show that he reasonably believed that:

- the lottery was an exempt lottery under Schedule 11, or a lottery operating licence was held and complied with;
- the arrangement was part of the National Lottery; or
- the arrangement did not fall within the definition of 'lottery' under Part 1.

637. As with the offence of promoting a lottery, there is a further defence to the offence in this section set out in section 265, where a person reasonably believed that the lottery was not one to which this Part applied because it was outside the territorial application of this Part.

SECTION 260: MISUSING PROFITS OF LOTTERY

638. This section provides for a general offence of misusing the profits of a lottery. A person will commit the offence if the promoter has, in a statement appearing on the lottery tickets or in an advertisement for a lottery ticket, declared that the proceeds of the lottery are to be used for a particular purpose, and the person uses (or permits to be used) all or any of the proceeds for something other than the purpose stated. This offence is not restricted to any particular type of lottery, and can apply to any lottery where such a fund-raising purpose has been declared.

SECTION 261: MISUSING PROFITS OF AN EXEMPT LOTTERY

639. This section applies only to certain kinds of exempt lottery (incidental non-commercial lotteries, private society lotteries and small society lotteries), in respect of which there are restrictions on the purposes for which the lottery can be promoted. Under this provision, it will be an offence for a person to use (or permit to be used) any part of the profits of the lottery for a purpose other than a permitted one.

SECTION 262: SMALL SOCIETY LOTTERY: BREACH OF CONDITION

640. This section provides that a non-commercial society commits an offence if a small society lottery is promoted on its behalf without the necessary registration with the local authority. It is also an offence to fail to comply with the obligation to file a statement of the matters prescribed in paragraph 39 of Schedule 11 with the registering authority, or to submit false or misleading information in that statement.

SECTION 263: PENALTY

641. The maximum penalty upon conviction for any of the offences contained in this Part is a term of imprisonment of up to 51 weeks in England and Wales, or 6 months in Scotland, together with a fine not exceeding level 5 on the standard scale.

SECTION 264: EXCLUSION OF THE NATIONAL LOTTERY

642. This section excludes lotteries that form part of the National Lottery from the provisions of this Part. The National Lottery is regulated under the National Lottery etc Act 1993 (c.39), but see also Part 1 of this Act.

SECTION 265: TERRITORIAL APPLICATION

643. This section sets out the territorial area over which Part 11 is to apply. It provides that Part 11 applies to anything done in relation to a lottery in Great Britain, or by means of remote gambling equipment in Great Britain. So, if a lottery is provided electronically, and the servers are located in Great Britain, that may be a lottery that falls to be regulated under this Part.

644. However, the territorial application of Part 11 is limited by this section, so that Part 11 does not regulate any lottery where:

- the only people who become participants in it are outside Great Britain; and
- where there is no-one in Great Britain who possesses tickets with the intention of selling or supplying them to other individuals in Great Britain.

645. The effect of this is that as soon as a person in Britain becomes a participant in a lottery, or a person possesses tickets with a view to their sale in Great Britain, the lottery will be regulated by Part 11.

646. This section also provides a defence where a person reasonably believed that no person in Great Britain would become a participant in the lottery; or that there was no intention to sell tickets to people in Great Britain. Without this defence, innocent printers and distributors could be guilty of promoting or facilitating a lottery, even where they had honestly believed that the tickets they were printing or distributing would only be sold abroad.

SCHEDULE 11: EXEMPT LOTTERIES

6.2015 647. This Schedule sets out the requirements that must be complied with in order for a lottery to be classed as 'exempt'. Exempt lotteries are those that are permitted to be run without an operating licence. There are four types of exempt lottery: incidental non- commercial lotteries, private lotteries, customer lotteries, and small society lotteries.

648. Part 1 of this Schedule deals with incidental non-commercial lotteries; Part 2 with private lotteries; Part 3 with customer lotteries; and Parts 4 and 5 with small society lotteries and their registration with the local authority. Part 6 sets out certain additional powers of the Secretary of State, and Part 7 is interpretative.

PART 1: INCIDENTAL NON-COMMERCIAL LOTTERIES

649. This type of lottery replaces those permitted under section 3 (small lotteries incidental to exempt entertainments) and section 15 (provision of amusements with prizes at exempt entertainments) of the Lotteries and Amusements Act 1976 (c.32). An incidental non-commercial lottery is one that is incidental to a non-commercial event, and in respect of which, all the conditions set out in the rest of this Part are complied with. An event is a non-commercial event if the money raised from the event goes entirely to purposes that are not for private gain (paragraph 2).

650. The conditions that must be complied with are:

- The promoters of the lottery cannot deduct money from the proceeds of the lottery, for prizes or other costs, in excess of any sums prescribed by the Secretary of State in regulations;
- The lottery must itself be promoted for a purpose other than that of private gain;
- The lottery cannot involve a rollover; and
- Tickets must be sold at the event location during the event, and the result made public while the event is going on.

PART 2: PRIVATE LOTTERIES

651. There are three types of 'private lottery' which qualify as exempt lotteries:

- A private society lottery: this must be promoted for, and by, members of a society, although people on the society's premises (as defined in paragraph 10(1)(b)) may also purchase tickets. The lottery may be promoted for a purpose for which the society is conducted (paragraph 13), and the society can be any group or society, provided it is not established and conducted for purposes connected to gambling;
- A work lottery: this must not make any profit (ie all the proceeds must be used for prizes or reasonable costs – see paragraph 13), and must be promoted for and by people working on the same premises (as defined in paragraph 11(2)); and
- A residents' lottery: this must not make any profit (ie all the proceeds must be used for prizes or reasonable costs), and must be promoted for and by persons who live in a single set of premises (for instance, a hall of residence). The residency requirement can still be satisfied, where the premises are not the sole premises in which a person resides (paragraph 12(2)).

652. All three types of private lottery must comply with the conditions set out in Part 2. These conditions concern:

- Advertising (paragraph 14);
- Rollovers (paragraph 19); and
- Conditions relating to the price and format of lottery tickets (paragraphs 15 to 18).

PART 3: CUSTOMER LOTTERY

653. Under Part 3, a customer lottery is a lottery run by occupiers of business premises, who sell tickets only to customers present on their premises. All the conditions in this Part must be satisfied. These include that:

- the lottery must be arranged to ensure that no profits are made, ie the proceeds must be exhausted entirely in the reasonable expenses of the lottery and in the provision of prizes;
- the lottery may only be advertised on the premises on which it is held; and
- no ticket may result in the winner receiving a prize worth more than £50 (the Secretary of State can vary this amount by order, under Part 6 of this Schedule).

654. Other conditions prohibit rollover, set rules on the frequency with which customer lotteries can be conducted, and make rules relating to lottery tickets.

PARTS 4 AND 5: SMALL SOCIETY LOTTERIES

655. Under Part 4, a small society lottery is a lottery promoted on behalf of a non-commercial society (as defined in section 19 of the Act), the proceeds of which fall below the thresholds set out in paragraph 31 of this Part. Such a lottery will be exempt only if all relevant conditions set out in Parts 4 and 5 are complied with.

656. Small society lotteries are distinguished from large society lotteries by the amount of the proceeds that they generate. A large society lottery requires an operating licence from the Commission under Part 5 of the Act. A lottery is a large society lottery if its proceeds exceed the thresholds set out in paragraph 31.

657. Where the proceeds fall below these thresholds, the lottery qualifies as a small society lottery, and is regulated by these Parts of Schedule 11. The Secretary of State may change these thresholds in regulations.

658. A small society lottery may be promoted for any of the purposes of the society (paragraph 32). As with large society lotteries, at least 20% of the proceeds must go to a purpose for which the society is conducted (paragraph 33). No single prize may be worth more than the amount set out in paragraph 34. Small society lotteries may have

rollovers, although rollovers are only permitted where every lottery that may be affected by the rollover is also a small society lottery and the rollover will not permit any person to win more than the amount in paragraph 34 (paragraphs 34 and 35). This amount may be varied by the Secretary of State in regulations under Part 6.

659. Conditions are also set out in paragraphs 36 and 37 relating to the format and price of tickets. As is the case for large society lotteries, one document can be a ticket for the purpose of entering a number of lotteries, so long as the dates of the draw in those lotteries can be ascertained from the information on the ticket. Tickets for small society lotteries need not be paper documents – they may also be electronic. If a ticket is an electronic ticket, however, it must be capable of being printed, or stored electronically.

660. A society must be registered with a local authority (in England and Wales) or licensing board (in Scotland), in accordance with Part 5 of the Schedule while any small society lottery is being promoted.

661. The society must send to the local authority with which it is registered, a statement of the matters listed in paragraph 39(2). This includes information as to:

- The arrangements for the lottery (dates, prizes, proceeds etc);
- Amounts deducted by the promoters for prizes and costs;
- Whether any other costs were paid, other than from the proceeds of the lottery.

662. Two members of the society, or its governing body, must sign a statement sent to the local authority. If a local authority receives a statement, and they think that the lottery was, in fact, a large lottery, they must notify the Commission.

663. The provisions for registration, in Part 5, set out the mechanisms for application, registration, refusal, revocation, cancellation and appeal against decisions made in relation to the registration of a small society lottery. Appeal is to the Magistrates Court and, in Scotland, to the Sheriff. There is an annual registration fee of an amount to be prescribed by the Secretary of State and Scottish Ministers in regulations. Local authorities and licensing boards must keep a register of all societies registered under this Part, and must notify the Commission when they register any society.

PART 6: POWERS TO IMPOSE ADDITIONAL RESTRICTIONS

664. Part 6 sets out the powers for the Secretary of State to impose additional restrictions, by regulations, on the exempt lotteries described in this Part:

- requiring that tickets are distributed by hand rather than post; and
- relating to the use of rollover arrangements.

665. This Part also gives the Secretary of State the power to make orders relating to classes of lottery with the following effect:

- imposing further conditions on exempt lotteries (in particular in relation to those matters listed in paragraph 59(2));
- restricting the extent to which a person can rely on the exemptions set out in Schedule 11. Such an order may, in particular, further restrict the number of exempt lotteries that may be promoted in any period or the minimum interval between two exempt lotteries promoted on behalf of any person.

666. Before exercising these powers, the Secretary of State must consult the Commission.

667. The Secretary of State may also, by order, vary a monetary amount or a percentage set out in this Schedule.

PART 7: GENERAL

668. Part 7 explains terms and phrases used in Schedule 11. It also clarifies that, other than in respect of private lotteries or customer lotteries, the provisions of the Schedule

apply to activities on a vessel.

PART 12: CLUBS, PUBS, FAIRS, ETC

6.2016 669. This Part provides certain gaming allowances, and additional authorisation procedures for gaming and gaming machines for:

- Members' clubs;
- Commercial clubs;
- Miners' welfare institutes;
- Alcohol licensed premises; and
- Travelling fairs.

670. Under the Gaming Act 1968 these various associations, premises and entities are afforded particular gaming entitlements, either as of right, or with express permission. Once commenced, this Act repeals those provisions of the 1968 Act, and this Part provides a replacement regime. This Part does not provide any entitlements to conduct betting or lotteries, only gaming and the use of gaming machines.

671. Part 10 of the Act contains power for the categorisation of gaming machines, which is relevant to this Part. Part 18 of the Act contains sections which make provision for determining the value of a prize, and defining participation fee and stake.

672. Where a reference is made in this Part to a Commission code of practice, it means a statutory code of practice, issued under the Commission's powers in Part 2 of the Act.

673. This Part contains powers for Scottish Ministers to make regulations about the procedural requirements for club gaming permits and club gaming machine permits and licensed premises gaming machine permits in Scotland.

SECTIONS 266 TO 268: DEFINITIONS OF ELIGIBLE CLUBS

674. There are three categories of eligible club: members' clubs, commercial clubs and miners' welfare institutes. To take advantage of the various gaming rights in Part 12 a club has to bring itself within one of these categories (although not all gaming rights are equally available to all three categories of club).

675. Members' clubs must have at least 25 members and be established and conducted wholly or mainly for purposes other than gaming (unless the gaming is of a prescribed kind). They are to be established and conducted for the benefit of their members. They are also to be established with the intention of operating on an ongoing basis, and not temporarily. Examples of such clubs would include local political associations, working men's clubs or branches of the Royal British Legion.

676. Subsection (2) permits the Secretary of State to prescribe particular kinds of gaming. It is proposed that bridge and whist be so prescribed. This allows members' clubs established for the purposes of providing such gaming to take advantage of rights under Part 12, notwithstanding the restriction in subsection (1)(a). This maintains the position under the Gaming Act 1968. See also the provision for exempt gaming under section 269(1)(c).

677. Commercial clubs are subject to the same conditions as members' clubs, except that members' clubs must not operate as a commercial enterprise which benefits a class of people different to the members. Commercial clubs, on the other hand, can. These clubs can also be known as proprietary clubs. An example of a commercial club would be a snooker club. Like members' clubs, commercial clubs may also be gaming clubs, provided the gaming is of a type prescribed in regulations under subsection (2), although this proviso does not apply to exempt gaming under section 269.

678. The definition of miners' welfare institutes has been amended from that contained in the Gaming Act 1968. Under Part 12 miners' welfare institutes are associations established for social or recreational purposes, where the association is either managed by a group of miners' representatives or uses premises regulated under a charitable trust, where the trust has, at some time, received funds from one of a

number of mining related organisations. The definition of 'miners' representative' has been revised to take account of changes in mining communities and ex-mining communities. Furthermore, the alternative limb for qualification as a miners' welfare institute has been amended to allow for the broader social aims that institutes in ex-mining areas now promote. The definition in section 268 replaces that in the Gaming Act 1968.

SECTIONS 269 AND 270: EXEMPT GAMING

679. This section permits members' clubs, commercial clubs and miners' welfare institutes to provide certain facilities for gaming without the need for any express authorisation. In order to qualify for this exemption the gaming must meet a number of conditions:

- It must be equal chance gaming, as defined in Part 1 of the Act;
- Stakes and prizes must be in accordance with any rules or limits prescribed in regulations;
- The club must not deduct any amounts from sums staked or won in the gaming;
- Any charge for participation (which is broadly defined) must not exceed amounts prescribed in regulations (and see section 344);
- The games played may only take place on one set of premises meaning there may not be any linking of games between premises; and
- People may only participate in the gaming if they have been a member of the club (or applied or were nominated for membership) at least 48 hours before playing, or are the genuine guests of such a person (but this does not apply to commercial clubs).

680. These conditions are similar to those set out in section 40 of the 1968 Act, which the Act repeals, with the exception of the restriction on linking games and the addition of a power to prescribe maximum stakes and prizes, which are new. The gaming allowances under section 269 may be used by any members' or commercial club that is permanent and has at least 25 members, even if it is established for gaming. There is no requirement for the gaming to be of a prescribed kind (see section 269(1)(c) and (d)).

681. Under section 270, subsections (2) and (4), different requirements about the limits on stakes, prizes, and participation fees may be set for different types of club or institute, for different types of game, and for different types of fee.

SECTIONS 271 AND 272: CLUB GAMING PERMIT

682. Members' clubs (but not commercial clubs) and miners' welfare institutes may apply for a club gaming permit from a licensing authority to authorise the provision of games of chance and gaming machines on premises from which the club operates. This permit allows clubs and institutes to offer gaming facilities, in addition to those available under the exempt gaming allowances. Schedule 12 sets out the procedure and rules for this permit.

683. The club gaming permit will authorise the provision of up to 3 gaming machines in categories B, C or D (but no more than 3 machines in total). The permit is subject to the condition that no person under 18 shall use a Category B or C machine, and the holder of the permit must comply with a Commission code of practice about the location and operation of gaming machines.

684. The club gaming permit will also authorise additional gaming facilities to be provided. This gaming falls into two types:

- Equal chance gaming. This is equivalent to that authorised under the exempt gaming allowances in sections 269 and 270, but without any prescribed limits on maximum stakes or prizes. The other conditions set for exempt gaming apply equally to this entitlement; and
- Such games of chance as are prescribed in regulations. This provision allows the Secretary of State to authorise particular games involving a bank or unequal

chance games to be played under the permit. Under the Gaming Act 1968 pontoon and chemin de fer were permitted. This gaming is subject to a number of conditions set out in section 217(4), and also rules which the Secretary of State may prescribe.

685. The Secretary of State may make regulations which set different maximum participation fees for exempt gaming and gaming authorised by a club gaming permit. By this means a club which holds a club gaming permit can be permitted to make different charges for equal chance gaming, to a club which relies solely on the exempt gaming provisions in section 269.

SECTION 273: CLUB MACHINE PERMIT

686. Under this section a club machine permit is available to a members' club, miners' welfare institute or a commercial club. This type of permit authorises the holder to provide up to 3 gaming machines in Category B, C or D (but no more than 3 machines in total) on premises from which the club operates. It does not authorise the provision of any other type of facilities for gaming. Three conditions are automatically attached to a club machine permit. These relate to prior membership for use of the machines (but not for a commercial club), restrictions on giving children and young people access to Category C or B machines; and requiring compliance with Commission codes of practice about the location and operation of machines.

687. Schedule 12 sets out the procedure in relation to an application for a club machine permit, and the rules which apply to its maintenance and validity.

SECTION 274: PROCEDURE

688. Schedule 12 contains the detailed rules for the two types of club permit, in relation to England and Wales. In relation to Scotland, different procedures to those in Schedule 12 will apply if Scottish Ministers exercise their powers under section 285. These powers enable different procedural rules to be set for clubs or institutes holding a certificate of registration under the Licensing (Scotland) Act 1976, or for clubs or institutes of such other type as may be specified in the regulations.

SCHEDULE 12: CLUB GAMING PERMITS AND CLUB MACHINE PERMITS

689. Schedule 12 contains the procedures for obtaining club gaming and club machine permits, and the rules for their duration, maintenance, renewal and cancellation. Licensing authorities will issue both types of permit, and must keep registers of permits granted.

690. By virtue of paragraphs 27 and 28 a licensing authority must have regard to Commission guidance and the licensing objectives in undertaking its functions under this Schedule.

691. Paragraphs 1 to 9 include a requirement that applications for a permit are copied to the Commission and the police, who may object to the application, in which case a hearing will be required, unless all the parties agree otherwise.

692. Under paragraph 6 the licensing authority may only refuse an application on certain grounds. These grounds are that:

- The applicant does not fulfil the requirements for a members' or commercial club or miners' welfare institute and therefore is not entitled to receive the type of permit for which it has applied;
- The applicant's premises are used wholly or mainly by children or young people;
- An offence under the Act or a breach of a permit has been committed by the applicant while providing gaming facilities;
- A permit held by the applicant has been cancelled in the previous 10 years; or
- An objection has been lodged by the Commission or the police.

693. If the authority is satisfied that (a) or (b) are the case it must refuse the application. If (c), (d) or (e) is at issue the licensing authority may reject the licence if they think fit, taking account of any relevant guidance issued by the Commission and the licensing objectives.

694. A licensing authority has no discretion to attach conditions to a club machine permit or club gaming permit. Part 12 of the Act sets out particular conditions which are to apply universally to permits of either type.

695. Paragraph 10 provides a fast track procedure for clubs or institutes in England and Wales which hold a club premises certificate under section 72 of the Licensing Act 2003 (authorising the sale or supply of alcohol or provision of regulated entertainment). Under the fast-track procedure there is no opportunity for objections to be made by the Commission or the police, and the grounds upon which an authority can refuse a permit are reduced. This is because the club or institute will already have been through a licensing process in relation to its club premises certificate under the 2003 Act, and to impose the full requirements of Schedule 12 would produce unwarranted duplication and cost. This fast track procedure does not apply in Scotland. Instead, Scottish Ministers can make alternative provision using their powers under section 285.

696. Paragraph 11 deals with the form and content of permits, and paragraphs 12 to 16 with their maintenance, including variation of permits if the information in them becomes inaccurate. Paragraphs 17 to 20 provide that permits, with one exception, will last for ten years (in which case they can be renewed) unless they cease to have effect under another provision of the Schedule. These provisions are those for: lapse, surrender, cancellation and forfeiture.

697. The exception to the ten year duration is that where a permit has been granted under the fast track procedure under paragraph 10, such permits last indefinitely unless the club premises certificate under the Licensing Act 2003 ceases to have effect, or is surrendered, cancelled, or forfeited.

698. Paragraph 25 sets out full appeal rights from the decisions of licensing authorities under this Schedule.

SECTIONS 275 AND 281: BINGO IN CLUBS AND ALCOHOL LICENSED PREMISES

699. These sections contain particular provisions regulating bingo played pursuant to any of the authorisations in this Part by clubs or miners' welfare institutes, or on alcohol licensed premises. The purpose of sections 275 and 281 is to prevent facilities for bingo being offered on a large scale (high turnover bingo) under the various authorisations in this Part. Where a club, miners' welfare institute, or alcohol licensed premises wishes to offer high turnover bingo it will require a bingo operating licence from the Commission, under Part 5. In such cases, clubs and miners' welfare institutes are relieved from the general obligation under Part 5 to have at least one management office in the organisation held by a personal licence holder, under section 80(9).

700. The trigger for needing a bingo operating licence is that 'high turnover bingo' is played in a 'high turnover period', and sections 275 and 281 provide identical and comprehensive definitions for both terms. The key element is that the total stakes or prizes for bingo games played in any period for 7 days exceed £2000. Subject to appropriate Parliamentary approval, this figure can be amended by the Secretary of State by order.

701. If a club or institute plays high turnover bingo without the appropriate operating licence it will commit an offence under section 33. Sections 275 and 281 operate in a way which means that offences are only committed after a club or institute has had its first week of high turnover bingo. Once that has happened an offence takes place if high turnover bingo is played again in the following 12 month period, unless a bingo operating licence has been obtained. In addition, a club or institute must inform

the Commission whenever a high turnover period first begins (ie when it has had its first week of high turnover bingo), and failure to so is an offence, with a maximum penalty of a level 3 fine.

SECTIONS 277 AND 278: ALCOHOL LICENSED PREMISES

702. Sections 279 to 284 are concerned with the provision of gaming, and the making available of gaming machines, in certain premises which are licensed to supply alcohol for consumption on the premises under Part 3 of the Licensing Act 2003 or under section 9(1) of the Licensing (Scotland) Act 1976.

703. The relevant premises are those which contain a bar at which alcohol is served for consumption on the premises. This means that premises such as restaurants which do not have a bar for serving drinks to customers will fall outside the scope of the premises to which sections 279 to 284 apply. The sections also do not apply to vehicles.

704. The gaming and gaming machine exemptions conferred by sections 279 to 284 only apply at those times when alcohol is authorised to be sold at the premises.

705. A reference to 'alcohol licensed premises' in these notes means premises which are within the scope of sections 277 and 278.

SECTIONS 279 AND 280: EXEMPT GAMING

706. This section authorises the provision of gaming facilities on alcohol licensed premises, provided the gaming complies with certain conditions. No further authorisation is required to make the gaming lawful, provided the conditions are complied with.

707. The conditions are as follows:

- The facilities are limited to equal chance gaming;
- Stakes and prizes for the gaming must not exceed any limits as to value or amount prescribed by the Secretary of State;
- No amount may be deducted or levied from amounts staked or won;
- No participation fees may be charged (and this includes membership subscriptions, see section 344(3));
- The games played may only take place on one set of alcohol-licensed premises, ie there may not be any linking of games between premises; and
- Children and young people must be excluded from the gaming.

708. Under section 6 of the Gaming Act 1968 (general provisions as to gaming on premises licensed for retail sale of liquor) cribbage and dominoes may be played for winnings at premises licensed to sell alcohol for consumption on the premises. It is also possible, under section 6, for the holder of such a licence to apply for permission for other forms of gaming on the premises. In all cases conditions may be made to prevent high-stake gaming taking place, and to ensure the gaming does not become the main inducement to attend the premises. The Act repeals this section, and sections 279 and 280 contain the replacement provisions.

SECTION 282: GAMING MACHINES: AUTOMATIC ENTITLEMENT

6.2017 709. This section authorises up to 2 Category C or D gaming machines to be made available on alcohol licensed premises. It does this by exempting such premises from the premises offence in Part 3 (section 37) and the offence relating to making gaming machines available in Part 10 (section 242). This exemption only applies if the person who holds the relevant alcohol licence has notified the licensing authority of his intention to make gaming machines available, and has paid the required notification fee. The section is also subject to the condition that gaming machines are to be made available in compliance with any relevant provision of a code of practice issued by the Gambling Commission.

710. This section, together with the other provisions of this Part on gaming machines in alcohol licensed premises, replace the provisions of section 34 of, and Schedule 9 to, the Gaming Act 1968 for the grant of permits to alcohol licensed premises.

SECTION 283: LICENSED PREMISES GAMING MACHINE PERMITS

711. This section allows further Category C or D gaming machines to be made available in alcohol licensed premises (in addition to the two machines authorised under section 282) in accordance with a permit known as a licensed premises gaming machine permit. No limit is imposed on the number of gaming machines that can be made available under this section. The permit will provide in each case for the number of Category C or D gaming machines that it authorises.

SCHEDULE 13: LICENSED PREMISES GAMING MACHINE PERMITS

712. This Schedule makes further provision with respect to licensed premises gaming machine permits. This Schedule does not have effect in relation to Scotland. Section 285 enables Scottish Ministers to make provision by regulations in respect of licensed premises gaming machine permits which is to have effect in place of that in Schedule 13.
713. Paragraphs 1 to 6 set out the process for making applications for such a permit. By virtue of paragraph 5, a licensing authority may not attach conditions to a permit. Under paragraph 6, a licensing authority may not refuse an application or grant a permit for a different category or a smaller number of gaming machines unless they have notified the applicant and given him the opportunity to make representations.
714. There is no limit on the duration of a permit. Paragraph 12 provides for it to continue unless and until it ceases to have effect under a provision of the Schedule.
715. Paragraph 16 enables the licensing authority to cancel or vary the permit. The authority may only take such action in the circumstances specified in sub-paragraph (1), namely if—

- it would not be reasonably consistent with pursuit of the licensing objectives for the permit to continue to have effect;
- gaming has taken place on the premises in breach of the permit or a condition of the permit;
- the premises are mainly used for making gaming machines available; or
- an offence under the Act has been committed on the premises.

716. The licensing authority is required, before cancelling or varying a permit, to give the permit holder at least 21 days' notice and to consider any representations made by the permit holder. The authority is required to hold a hearing if the permit holder requests one.
717. Paragraphs 19 and 20 make provision for transfer of permits. Paragraph 21 sets out rights of appeal.
718. Paragraph 22 requires the licensing authority to maintain a register of permits. The Secretary of State may make regulations about how the licensing authority record and use this information.

SECTION 284: REMOVAL OF EXEMPTION

719. This section enables the licensing authority to make an order in respect of specific premises, removing the right to provide exempt gaming at those premises under section 279 or the right to make up to 2 gaming machines available for use in accordance with section 282.
720. The licensing authority may only make an order under this section if—

- it would not be reasonably consistent with pursuit of the licensing objectives for the exemption or entitlement conferred by the relevant section to continue to have effect;
- gaming has taken place on the premises in reliance on the exemption or entitlement conferred by the relevant section, but in breach of a condition of that

section. An example of such a breach would be where gaming machines were made available in breach of a relevant code of practice issued by the Gambling Commission;

- the premises are mainly used for gaming; or
- an offence under the Act has been committed on the premises.

721. Before making an order under this section, the licensing authority must give 21 days' notice to the holder of the alcohol licence, allow representations to be made, and hold a hearing if the licensee requests one. The licensee also has a right to appeal to a magistrates' court (or sheriff's court in Scotland) against any decision of the licensing authority under this section.

SECTION 285: PERMITS FOR CLUBS, PUBS ETC: SPECIAL PROVISION FOR SCOTLAND

722. This section enables Scottish Ministers, with the consent of the Secretary of State, to make provision by regulations in respect of club gaming and machine permits in place of that in Schedule 12, and in respect of licensed premises gaming machine permits in place of that in Schedule 13.

SECTIONS 286 AND 287: TRAVELLING FAIRS

723. These sections:

- define a 'travelling fair' for the purposes of the Act, and
- grant travelling fairs the right to provide unlimited numbers of Category D gaming machines, provided any facilities for gambling offered at the fair are no more than an ancillary amusement.

724. Fairs are also entitled to offer equal chance prize gaming, under Part 13 of the Act. This means that any prize gaming and any gaming machines made available must not be the principal activities at the fair. Instead, in order to offer these limited gambling facilities, the fair must be composed mainly of non-gambling amusements and activities.

PART 13: PRIZE GAMING

6.2018 725. Part 13 contains authorisations for prize gaming. This is a type of gaming where the organiser puts up the prizes in advance, as distinct from gaming where the stakes of the participants make up the winnings. Prize gaming is intended to permit low level gaming, for small participation fees, and modest prizes. Bingo played at seaside amusement arcades is a typical venue for such gaming.

726. The definition of 'gaming' in Part 1 covers any sort of gaming for prizes or winnings. Therefore, a provision in the Act which authorises gaming generally, also authorises prize gaming. For example, a bingo operating licence authorises the playing of games of bingo for prizes or winnings. However, in this Part the permissions relate exclusively to prize gaming.

727. The premises which can receive authorisations under this Part are: adult gaming centres, licensed or unlicensed family entertainment centres, and travelling fairs. There is also a permit for authorising other premises to provide prize gaming, under Schedule 14, and particular allowances for bingo operators.

728. This Part is derived from provisions in section 16 (provisions of amusements with prizes at certain commercial entertainments) of the Lotteries and Amusements Act 1976 (which is repealed by this Act) and section 21 (special provisions as to gaming for prizes) of the Gaming Act 1968 (which is repealed by this Act). This Part does not replicate every aspect of those sections. In particular, lotteries may not be promoted under this Part.

729. Where machines are used for playing prize games, these may or may not count as gaming machines. This will depend on whether the machine complies with the

exemptions in section 235(2)(e), (f) or (g). If it does, it will not be subject to the Part 10 gaming machine regime, but will be subject to regulation by this Part, together with relevant licence conditions and codes of practice. If it does not, it will be a gaming machine, and that regime will apply.

SECTION 288: MEANING OF 'PRIZE GAMING'

730. To be prize gaming, the prize for which the gaming is played must comply with the following requirements:

- the nature or size of the prize must not be determined by reference to the number of people playing the game; and
- the nature or size of the prize must not be determined by reference to the amount paid for or raised by the gaming.

731. This gaming is therefore different to gaming where the stakes paid by the players are used to calculate the winnings available. The effect of the definition is that in prize gaming the prizes available will be determined by the operator of the gaming before play commences, and the payments he receives from the players will not be put directly to any prize on offer. This does not stop operators from estimating what money will be raised from gaming, or predicting the numbers who will take part. Its purpose is to stop the actual amounts raised in a particular game being used to determine the prize in that particular game. Prize gaming can cover both money and non-money prizes.

732. Section 288 does not prevent prizes being won in a way that depends on the progress or outcome of the game. This means that if different prizes can be claimed dependent on how quickly a win takes place (for example, calling 'house' in a game of bingo within a certain number of calls), this is permitted.

SECTION 289: PRIZE GAMING PERMITS AND SCHEDULE 14

733. One way of authorising prize gaming is to obtain a prize gaming permit from a licensing authority. This section and Schedule 14 make provision for the grant and maintenance of prize gaming permits. Anyone who occupies, or proposes to occupy, premises may apply for a permit, but a permit is not available in respect of premises which are subject to a premises licence under Part 8, or a club gaming permit under Part 12. This is because those licences and permits already give such premises the relevant rights to offer prize gaming, where appropriate. A permit cannot be granted for a vessel or a vehicle.

734. The reference to 'occupy' in this context means a legal right to be in occupation of the premises. This can either be by having a freehold or leasehold interest in the property, or holding it on a tenancy agreement. A person who is seeking a prize gaming permit must have a right to occupy the premises where the prize gaming takes place. For example, if 'A' has a prize gaming permit and owns the freehold of the premises where the prize gaming is taking place, and leases the property to 'B', then (subject to the terms of the lease), A will no longer have the right to be in occupation of the premises. On this basis, the permit shall lapse in accordance with paragraph 14 of Schedule 14. If 'B' wishes to offer prize gaming at the premises then he will need to make an application for a new permit under paragraph 3. In these circumstances, 'B's' permit will not take effect until the lease has formally been executed in his favour (see paragraph 14(2)).

735. By virtue of the provisions of Part 4 of the Act, children and young people may only participate in equal chance prize gaming, and not any other form of prize gaming made available pursuant to a permit. There are a number of conditions applicable to prize gaming permits, which are common to all prize gaming authorised by this Part, contained in section 293.

736. Schedule 14 covers the process and procedure of the grant and maintenance of a prize gaming permit. The requirements are similar, but not identical, to those

applicable to family entertainment centre gaming machine permits under Part 10 of and Schedule 12 to the Act. The licensing authority must maintain a register of prize gaming permits.

737. Under paragraph 8 of Schedule 14 a licensing authority can prepare a statement of principles which they propose to use for determining applications for permits, and, in particular, the suitability of an applicant. In exercising their functions in relation to prize gaming permits, a licensing authority may have regard to the licensing objectives set out in Part 1 of the Act, but must have regard to any relevant guidance issued by the Commission (paragraph 8(3)). Subject to this, an authority has discretion whether to grant or refuse a permit. Paragraph 10 requires the authority to consult the police prior to issuing a permit.

738. Under paragraphs 13 to 17, a permit will expire after ten years (when it can be renewed) unless it lapses (in which case certain transitional provisions are made), is surrendered or is forfeited under the provisions of these paragraphs. Renewal applications are considered on the same grounds as an original application (this is different to the renewal of a family entertainment centre gaming machine permit under Schedule 12, where the grounds for refusing renewal are more narrowly defined). Forfeiture can be ordered by any court sentencing a permit holder for a relevant offence, as defined in section 126.

739. Paragraph 22 provides a full appeals procedure for anyone wishing to appeal against the decisions of a licensing authority under this Schedule.

SECTIONS 290 AND 292: PRIZE GAMING IN GAMING AND ENTERTAINMENT CENTRES AND FAIRS

740. As a separate authorisation to the prize gaming permit, these sections grant rights to conduct prize gaming to licensed adult gaming centres (AGCs), licensed and unlicensed family entertainment premises (FECs), and to travelling fairs. Licensed AGCs and FECs may offer any type of prize gaming, but an unlicensed FEC (ie one with a permit under Schedule 10 to the Act), and a travelling fair, may only offer equal chance prize gaming.

741. The prize gaming which can be offered under these sections is subject to conditions under section 293. In addition, under Part 4 of the Act, children and young people can only participate in equal chance gaming at a licensed or unlicensed FEC or travelling fair. Therefore, if a licensed FEC chooses to offer unequal chance prize gaming, children and young people may not participate in it (people under 18 are not allowed into AGCs at all).

742. In addition, for prize gaming to be offered lawfully at a fair, the prize gaming, together with any other facilities for gambling offered (eg gaming machines), must be ancillary to the other amusements and activities offered at the fair.

SECTION 291: BINGO HALLS

743. Under a bingo operating licence, any form of bingo may be offered. This means prize bingo and cash bingo, as developed under the Gaming Act 1968, are both permitted by the bingo operating licence. However, section 21 of the 1968 Act conferred certain entitlements to offer gaming for prizes upon premises licensed under Part II of that Act, which are not covered entirely by the terms of the bingo operating licence.

744. Section 291 permits holders of a bingo premises licence (and necessarily a bingo operating licence) to offer prize gaming, provided the gaming complies with any conditions attached to the relevant bingo operating licence. Such conditions may be added as general conditions by the Commission or imposed by the Secretary of State (see the notes on Part 5 for an explanation of these). In particular, the conditions may restrict the types of games offered under this authorisation. Conditions imposed by the

Secretary of State may also relate to any of the matters set out in section 91(1) eg impose limits on the size of payments made by players to participate in the gaming, or on the size of prizes.

745. Under the terms of Part 1 and Part 5 of the Act, casinos are granted permission to offer any form of gaming (subject to conditions which may be imposed on a casino operating licence), and no longer need any express permission similar to that offered by section 21 of the 1968 Act. Therefore, Part 13 does not cover casinos.

SECTION 293: CONDITIONS FOR PRIZE GAMING

746. There are four conditions that prize gaming permit holders, licensed AGCs, licensed FECs, FECs with permits and fairs must comply with in order for them to offer prize gaming lawfully under this Part:

- The amounts charged to players to take part in the prize gaming must not exceed any amounts prescribed by the Secretary of State, and these may differ according to different matters (and see section 344 for the definition of participation fee);
- The prizes offered in the prize gaming must not exceed any value set by the Secretary of State (and this may cover money and/or non-money prizes). The limits may be set by reference to each prize that is offered in a game or all the prizes that are offered in a game;
- The prize gaming must take place on the relevant premises, in the course of one day only, and the results must be announced on the premises, and as soon as possible after the game ends; and
- Participation in a game must not entitle the player to participate in any other gambling. In other words, the prize gaming must be free-standing and self-contained, and not linked with other gambling.

SECTION 294: POWER TO RESTRICT EXEMPTIONS

747. This section gives the Secretary of State the power to remove some, or all, of the prize gaming entitlements conferred in this Part. The purpose of this section is to provide flexibility in the event that, for example, an additional class of operating licence is added to Part 5 of the Act which covers matters dealt with under the prize gaming sections. If this were to happen, it would be necessary to remove the entitlements from Part 13, in order for new operating licence requirements to apply. This power is included to deal with such future contingencies.

PART 14: PRIVATE AND NON-COMMERCIAL GAMING AND BETTING

6.2019 748. This Part provides authorisations for gambling to take place in private, or on non-commercial terms. In particular, it permits various forms of domestic gambling, and also provides authorisations for gaming to take place at non-commercial events.

749. These sections replace various provisions of the Betting, Gaming and Lotteries Act 1963, the Gaming Act 1968, and the Lotteries and Amusements Act 1976. In particular, this Part replaces section 41 (gaming at entertainments not held for private gain) of the 1968 Act and section 15 (provision of amusements with prizes at exempt entertainments) of the 1976 Act. This Part does not provide any authority for the promotion of lotteries. Those elements of the 1976 Act which dealt with lotteries at exempt entertainments (specifically sections 3 and 15) are now dealt with under Part 11 and Schedule 11. The 'incidental non -commercial lottery' is the new type of exempt lottery, for what were lotteries at exempt entertainments.

SECTIONS 295 AND 296: PRIVATE BETTING AND GAMING

750. These sections enable people to participate in and offer facilities for betting and gaming, including on premises, without committing any offence under the Act,

provided their activity meets the various conditions for private gaming and betting. Schedule 15 sets out the various conditions.

751. In addition, these sections contain protection for people who bet, but who are not doing so in the course of a business. The definitions set out in Part 1 of the Act mean that both parties to a bet (sometimes known as the 'backer' and the 'layer') are capable of providing facilities for betting. This means that, ordinarily, anyone who offers a bet, or accepts a bet will be committing an offence under Part 3, unless he has authorisation under the Act.

752. Where a person is offering or negotiating bets in the course of a business, (commonly known as 'bookmaking'), he will require a betting operating licence under Part 5. Similarly, if someone is using betting as a way of earning a living, so that it renders it a business activity, that too may require a licence. However, there is no regulatory requirement for people who use the services of a betting operator on a non-commercial basis to obtain a licence. Nor should private bets, ie between friends, require any form of express authorisation. These sections make it clear that a person does not commit any offence under the Act if he makes or accepts a bet, or offers to do so, provided he is acting in a personal capacity, and not in the course of business.

753. These provisions apply equally to those using the services of a betting intermediary ie an internet betting exchange. The intermediary will require an operating licence under Part 5, but the users of the exchange will benefit from the exemption in these sections, provided their use is in a non-business capacity.

SCHEDULE 15: PRIVATE GAMING AND BETTING

Part 1: Gaming

754. Part 1 of the Schedule defines what private gaming constitutes for the purposes of the Act, and identifies two sub-sets of private gaming: domestic gaming and residential gaming.

755. Gaming is private gaming when:

- it is equal chance gaming;
- no charge is made for participation; and
- the gaming is conducted entirely in private (ie in a place to which the public do not have access).

756. However, where private gaming meets the conditions for domestic or residential gaming, then there is no need for this to be equal chance gaming, and therefore bankers' games and games of unequal chance may be played in these situations.

Part 2: Betting

757. There are two types of private betting: domestic betting and workplace betting.

SECTIONS 297 TO 301: NON-COMMERCIAL GAMING

758. These sections authorise certain types of gaming to be provided at non-commercial events. A non-commercial event is an event where the money raised from the event is not used for private gain eg it is for used for charitable or other generally beneficial purposes. Section 19, by virtue of section 353(1), provides a definition of private gain for these purposes.

759. These sections require that both money raised from the non-commercial event, and the profits made from the gaming itself, are not used for private gain. This means that if someone other than the organiser of the event provides the facilities for gaming, they too must ensure that the profits go to good causes.

760. The gaming permitted by these sections is prize gaming (as defined in section 288) and equal chance gaming which complies with a number of conditions:

All players must be told what purpose the money raised from the gaming is going to be used for (this must be something other than private gain), and the profits must be applied to that purpose;
The non-commercial event cannot take place on premises with a premises licence (under Part 8) or a temporary use notice (under Part 9). There is nothing to stop such premises running charitable or other gambling events to raise money for good causes, but they should do so using the gambling permissions granted to them by their premises licence or use notice. They cannot rely upon any of the allowances granted in Part 14. The one exception to this is that a non-commercial event can take place at a track licensed under Part 8, and rely upon the allowances in Part 14, provided no licensed activities are taking place at the time. This permits the use of tracks for non-commercial gambling on when races are not taking place.
The gaming (whether prize or equal chance) cannot be remote gaming. These permissions are only intended to be used at events, on premises, and for gaming in person.
If the gaming is equal chance gaming, then the gaming must comply with any regulations made by the Secretary of State setting limits on:

- The stakes, fees or charges for the gaming; and
- The amount or value of any prize available.

There are no limits on the fees, charges or value of prizes for prize gaming at a non-commercial event.

761. In all cases the money raised from the gaming must be used for the fund-raising purpose specified at the event, and if someone uses any profits from the gaming for something else, then they commit an offence under section 301. The maximum penalty, upon conviction for an offence, is a term of imprisonment not exceeding 51 weeks for England and Wales (six months in Scotland), and/or a level 5 fine.

SECTION 302: NON-COMMERCIAL BETTING

762. This section provides a definition for non-commercial betting. This is betting where neither party is acting in the course of business.

PART 15: INSPECTION

6.2020 763. Part 15 deals with the powers of entry to and inspection of premises. It sets out the different kinds of inspection and the people who may carry them out, the powers available to such people. both in relation to the circumstances of entry, and activity once on the premises, and the offences for non-compliance with the provisions of this Part. The provisions contain safeguards to ensure that any invasion of privacy is minimised and is proportionate to the purpose for which entry is made. For example, it will not be possible to enter a dwelling under this Part for any reason without a judicial warrant.

SECTION 303: ENFORCEMENT OFFICERS

764. The Commission will have power to appoint enforcement officers whose powers are set out in this Part. Enforcement officers may be, but need not be, employees of the Commission.

SECTION 304: AUTHORISED PERSONS

765. This section makes provision for persons to be 'authorised persons' for the purposes of the Act. Authorised persons are given various powers and functions under the Act in relation to inspection of premises in particular when someone is applying for a premises licence. Designated officers of licensing authorities and officers of other authorities who are authorised to exercise certain statutory functions in a particular

area are 'authorised persons' in relation to premises wholly or partly situated within that area. Subsection (4) provides for certain people to be 'authorised persons' in relation to any premises wherever situated.

766. An 'authorised local authority officer' is a person designated as such by a licensing authority for a purpose relating to premises within the area of the licensing authority.

SECTION 305: COMPLIANCE

767. This section confers express powers on constables, authorised persons and enforcement officers to undertake activities to assess whether a provision of the Act is being complied with or whether an offence is being committed. This provision is connected to section 64. That section provides for the actions of a constable, enforcement officer or authorised person (or those of a child or young person acting at his request) not to be unlawful under Part 4 if done in performance of his functions under the Act.

SECTION 306: SUSPECTED OFFENCE

768. Under this section a constable or enforcement officer may enter premises if it is reasonably suspected that an offence under this Act has been, is being or is about to be committed on the premises. Where it is suspected that the offence is being or is about to be committed entry can be made without a warrant (unless the premises is a dwelling). In cases regarding the past commission of an offence, a constable or enforcement officer may only enter the premises under the authority of a judicial warrant. An application must be made to a justice of the peace or the sheriff in Scotland to issue a warrant to enter the premises. A warrant can only be issued where the justice of the peace or sheriff is satisfied there are reasonable grounds for suspecting that an offence has been committed and that evidence of the offence may be found on the premises. The justice of the peace or sheriff must also be satisfied that one of the following conditions listed in subsection (3) is met:

- Admission to the premises has previously been refused;
- Admission is likely to be refused without a warrant;
- A search may be frustrated or endangered if immediate entry is not secured; and
- There is likely to be no-one present to grant admission to the premises.

769. If a warrant is to be granted for reasons in subsection (3)(a) or (b), the justice of the peace or sheriff must be satisfied that notice of the intention to apply for a warrant has been given to the appropriate person (ie the occupier of the premises or the person with responsibility for their management). Where no notice has been given, he must be satisfied that the giving of notice would seriously prejudice the purpose of the search.

770. Subsection (5) provides that a warrant under subsection (2) will have effect for 28 days from the date of issue.

SECTION 307: INSPECTION OF GAMBLING

771. A constable, enforcement officer or authorised person has the power to enter premises if it is reasonably suspected that facilities for gambling are being, are about to be or have been provided on the premises. This does not apply if the suspected gambling is private or non-commercial gaming or betting.

772. This power to enter will apply for the following purposes: to establish whether facilities for gambling are, were or are about to be provided; to ascertain whether there is an appropriate licence in force; or to determine whether the terms and conditions of the licence are, have been or will be complied with.

SECTION 308: OPERATING LICENCE HOLDERS

773. A constable or enforcement officer has the power to enter premises where it is reasonably believed to be in use by the holder of an operating licence partly or entirely for purposes connected with the licensed activities. This provision is intended to provide a power of entry to premises where the gambling itself may not necessarily take place, but which are being used in connection with licensed activities, such as the head office of a business running a casino. A constable or enforcement officer may only exercise powers of entry under this section to determine whether the terms and conditions of the operating licence are being met.

SECTION 309: FAMILY ENTERTAINMENT CENTRES

774. Where an application for a family entertainment centre gaming machine permit has been made, a constable, enforcement officer or authorised local authority officer may enter the premises for a purpose connected with the consideration of the application. Once the permit is in effect, the same may enter the premises to determine whether the gaming machines and the arrangements for their use comply with the requirements of the Act and any regulations made under it. Although constables, enforcement officers and authorised local authority officers have powers of entry under this section, it is anticipated that local authority officers will be primarily involved in the continuing inspection and enforcement of these types of premises. This is because it is the local authority which is responsible for issuing permits for these premises.

SECTION 310: PREMISES LICENSED FOR ALCOHOL

775. Part 12 and Schedule 13 make provision for Category C or D gaming machines to be made available on certain premises which are licensed to supply alcohol for consumption on the premises. This includes making gaming machines available under a licensed premises gaming machine permit. This section enables an enforcement officer or authorised local authority officer to enter premises in respect of which an application for such a permit has been made for a purpose connected with the consideration of the application.

776. Subsection (2) specifies other circumstances in which a constable, enforcement officer or authorised local authority officer may enter premises which are subject to a licence to supply alcohol for consumption on the premises. Entry may be made to determine whether the gaming taking place satisfies the conditions for exempt gaming under Part 12; whether the terms and conditions of any relevant operating licence are being complied with where bingo is played on the premises; or whether section 281 applies (which is concerned with high turnover bingo). Entry may also be made to ascertain the number and category of gaming machines being made available for use on the premises.

SECTION 311: PRIZE GAMING PERMIT

777. This section allows a constable, enforcement officer or authorised local authority officer to enter premises in respect of which an application for a prize gaming permit has been made. Once such a permit has effect, the same persons are given the power to enter the premises to determine whether the prize gaming complies with the requirements of the Act or regulations made under it.

SECTION 312: CLUBS

778. This section allows authorised local authority officers to enter premises, where an application for a club gaming or club machine permit has been made, for a purpose connected with the application.

779. The section also specifies the purposes for which a constable or enforcement officer may enter premises which are reasonably believed to be used by a members' club, a commercial club or a miners' welfare institute. These are to determine whether gaming is taking or is about to take place, or whether any gaming that is or is about to take place is in accordance with the provisions for exempt gaming under Part 12, a club gaming permit or a club machine permit.

SECTION 313: LICENSED PREMISES

780. This section gives the right of entry to a constable, enforcement officer or authorised person, to premises in respect of which an application for a premises licence has been made. This is to assess the likely impact of a licence being granted, in light of the licensing objectives. Once a licence is in force, there is also a power to enter the premises for a purpose connected with a review of the licence under Part 8.

SECTION 314: LOTTERIES: REGISTERED SOCIETIES

781. An enforcement officer or an authorised local authority officer may enter premises owned or used by a society registered with a local authority for the purpose of making inquiries about a lottery being promoted on behalf of the society. It is likely that authorised local authority officers will primarily exercise this power to enter. This is because the local authority is responsible for the registration of societies under the provisions for registered society lotteries.

SECTION 315: TEMPORARY USE NOTICE

782. This section allows a constable, enforcement officer or authorised person to enter premises for which a temporary use notice has effect to determine whether the activities being carried on are in accordance with the terms of the notice. The right of entry will also apply where a notice has been given, but before it has effect. This will enable an assessment to be made of the likely effects of the premises being used for this purpose, in the light of the licensing objectives.

SECTION 316: AUTHORISATIONS: PRODUCTION ON DEMAND

783. This section allows a constable or enforcement officer to require an operating licence holder who has given a written authorisation, or the person to whom the authorisation has been given, to produce a copy of the authorisation. Failure to comply, without reasonable excuse, is an offence. The maximum penalty for the offence is a fine not exceeding level 2 on the standard scale.

784. The types of authorisation which can be demanded under this section are:

- In relation to a pool betting operating licence, where the licence holder has authorised a person to accept bets on his behalf on a horserace course or dog track;
- In relation to a pool betting operating licence where the licence authorises the provision of facilities for football pools, where the licence holder has authorised a person to receive payments or entries on his behalf;
- In relation to a pool betting operating licence where the licence authorises horserace pool betting, where the licence holder has authorised a person to provide facilities for horserace pool betting; and
- In relation to a casino premises licence, where the licence holder has authorised a person or persons to use that premises for providing betting, bingo or both.

SECTION 317: POWERS

785. This section sets out the powers which a constable, enforcement officer or authorised person may exercise when entering premises under this Part.

6: Gambling Act 2005: Additional Material

786. Those exercising powers of entry may inspect any part of the premises and any machine or other thing on them. There is also power to question any person on the premises, to access any written or electronic record on the premises, and to request copies. Those entering will also have the right to seize and retain material, but only where the person entering believes that it contains or constitutes evidence of an offence under the Act or a breach of licence conditions. Through regulations the Secretary of State will have the power to set rules concerning the treatment of copies of written or electronic records supplied, and items removed as evidence of an offence (past or present) or breach of licence condition. Regulations may also include provision regarding the retention, use, return or destruction of items supplied or removed and the conferring of a right of appeal.

787. Restrictions are imposed on the extent to which a person entering premises can have access to and seize records without a warrant. It is only where a record (whether written or electronic) relates entirely to the matters to which the power of entry relates that it can be accessed or seized without a warrant. This is dealt with in further detail below in the note on section 319.

788. A constable, enforcement officer or authorised person when exercising powers under this Part is not entitled to take any action in relation to anything of a kind specified in section 9(2) of the Police and Criminal Evidence Act 1984 (for example, legally privileged material). This restriction only applies in England or Wales.

789. A constable, enforcement officer or authorised person must have regard to any relevant provision of a code of practice under the Police and Criminal Evidence Act 1984 in exercising any powers under this Part. This requirement does not apply in Scotland.

SECTION 318: DWELLINGS

790. A person exercising a power of entry under this Part may only enter a dwelling where authorised to do so by judicial warrant. A justice of the peace or the sheriff in Scotland may only issue a warrant if he is satisfied that, but for the requirement for a warrant, the person would be able to enter the premises in reliance on a provision of this Part. The justice of the peace or sheriff must also be satisfied that one of the following conditions listed in subsection (3) is met:

- Admission to the premises has previously been refused;
- Admission is likely to be refused without a warrant;
- A search may be frustrated or endangered if immediate entry is not secured; and
- There is likely to be no-one present to grant admission to the premises.

791. If a warrant is to be granted for reasons in subsection (3)(a) or (b), the justice of the peace or sheriff must be satisfied that notice of the intention to apply for a warrant has been given to the appropriate person (ie the occupier of the premises or the person with responsibility for their management). Where no notice has been given, he must be satisfied that the giving of notice would seriously prejudice the purpose of the search.

792. Subsection (5) provides that a warrant issued under this section is to have effect for 28 days from the date of issue.

SECTION 319: RECORDS

793. A person entering under this Part may only inspect or seize records (whether written or electronic) without a warrant where the records relate entirely to the matters to which the power of entry relates. Where records also contain information which is not relevant to those matters (ie where they are 'mixed' records), then they may only be inspected or seized under the powers in paragraphs (c) to (e) of section 317(1) under the authority of a judicial warrant. For example, 'mixed' records may contain information relating to personnel matters or may be commercially sensitive material irrelevant to the matters for which the powers of entry have been exercised. A justice of the peace may

only issue such a warrant if he is satisfied that it is necessary to allow inspection of mixed records. The justice of the peace must also be satisfied that one of the following conditions is met:

- Notice has been given to a person in control of the records of the intention to apply for a warrant, or
- The purpose of exercising the power may be frustrated or seriously prejudiced by the giving of such a notice.

SECTION 320: TIMING

794. A power under this Part can only be exercised at a reasonable time. Reasonable time may depend on the circumstances. If the reason for the entry requires it to be made at a time that would generally be perceived as an unreasonable time, then that time might nevertheless be reasonable in the circumstances of a particular case. For example, in a case where the person making the entry suspects that an offence is or is about to be committed and there is a strong likelihood that any evidence of the offence will be lost if entry is not made during night time hours.

SECTION 321: EVIDENCE OF AUTHORISATION

795. An enforcement officer or authorised person wishing to exercise a power under this Part is required to produce evidence of identity and authority to a person (if there is one) who appears to be occupying the premises or to have responsibility for their management.

SECTION 322: INFORMATION

796. This section requires the Secretary of State to make regulations about the information to be provided by those entering premises in reliance on a power under this Part. The regulations are to make provision about the nature of the information to be provided. They are also to prescribe the form and manner in which the information is to be provided, the person to whom it is to be provided and the timing of its provision. Subsection (3) imposes a duty on a constable, enforcement officer or authorised person exercising a power under this Part to comply with any relevant provision of regulations made under this section.

SECTION 323: USE OF FORCE

797. A constable has the authority to use reasonable force to enter premises when exercising powers under this Part. An enforcement officer has the authority to use reasonable force to enter premises where the entry is because he suspects that an offence under the Act has been, is being or is about to be committed on the premises. An authorised person or enforcement officer has the authority to use reasonable force to enter premises if he suspects that gambling (other than private or non-commercial gaming or betting) is taking place.

SECTION 324: PERSON ACCOMPANYING INSPECTOR, &C.

798. This section allows a constable, enforcement officer or authorised person to be accompanied by others when exercising a power to enter premises under this Part.

SECTION 325: SECURING PREMISES AFTER ENTRY

799. A constable, enforcement officer or authorised person who enters premises under this Part is required to take reasonable steps to ensure that premises remain as secure as they were when they entered.

SECTION 326: OBSTRUCTION

800. This section makes it an offence to obstruct or fail to cooperate with a constable, enforcement officer or authorised person exercising a power under this Part. For example, it will be an offence to block the doorway to premises where an enforcement officer has requested entry. The maximum penalty for the offence is a fine not exceeding level 3 on the standard scale.

PART 16: ADVERTISING

6.2021 801. Part 16 makes provision relating to the advertising and promotion of gambling.

SECTION 327: MEANING OF 'ADVERTISING'

802. This section sets out what it means to advertise gambling for the purposes of the Act. The definition is very broad and covers anything which is done to encourage people to take advantage of facilities for gambling (subsection (1)(a)). It also covers bringing information about gambling facilities to people's attention with a view to increasing the use of those facilities (subsection (1)(b)). As well as covering the activities of those who act with the specific intention of encouraging the use of facilities for gambling as described in subsection (1)(a) and (b), the definition also provides for the advertising of gambling to include those who participate in or facilitate such activities. Advertising includes entering into arrangements such as sponsorship or brand-sharing agreements.

SECTION 328: REGULATIONS

803. This section gives the Secretary of State power to make regulations controlling the form, content, timing and location of advertisements for gambling, including requirements for specified words to be included in advertisements. A specific duty is imposed on the Secretary of State to have regard to the need to protect children and other vulnerable persons from being harmed or exploited by gambling. This reflects the licensing objectives of the Act concerning the protection of children and vulnerable people. Regulations under this section will apply to advertising by both 'remote' means (such as email or television) and 'non-remote' means (such as a poster on a hoarding or a magazine page). Specific provision about this is made in subsequent sections in this Part.

804. It is an offence under this section to contravene a requirement of the regulations and any person guilty of an offence shall be liable on summary conviction to imprisonment for a term not exceeding 51 weeks (6 months for Scotland), a fine not exceeding level 5 on the standard scale, or both. An offence committed under this section shall be treated as a continuing offence which means that an offence shall be committed on each day during any period that the regulations are contravened.

SECTION 329: BROADCASTING

805. There are restrictions on the extent to which regulations controlling the form, content, timing and location of gambling advertisements, under this Part, may make provision about broadcast advertising. In particular, subsection (1) of this section prohibits the regulations under section 328 from making provision about advertising by means of television or radio services to which section 319 of the Communications Act 2003 (c.21) applies. This is broadly a reference to those broadcast television and radio services which are subject to regulation by the Office of Communications ('OFCOM') under Part 3 of that Act. Section 319 imposes a duty on OFCOM to set, and from time to time to review and revise, standards for the content of programmes to be included in television and radio services.

806. Subsection (2) requires OFCOM to set, review and revise standards for the advertising of gambling under section 319 of the Communications Act 2003. The standards must reflect the provisions of regulations controlling the form, content, timing and location of advertising of gambling made under this Part. OFCOM must also consult the Commission before setting or revising the standards.
807. Subsection (4) ensures that all broadcast television and radio services of the BBC do not fall within the scope of regulations controlling the form, content, timing and location of advertising of gambling made under this Part. This includes the BBC World Service which is not to any extent a service to which section 319 of the Communications Act 2003 applies.

SECTION 330: UNLAWFUL GAMBLING

808. This section makes it an offence to advertise unlawful gambling. For these purposes, advertised gambling is unlawful if it requires a licence, notice, permit, registration or exception under this Act ('a licence etc'), in order for the gambling to take place without an offence under the Act being committed, and arrangements for the licence etc have not been made at the time of advertising, or the exception does not apply to the arrangements. Take, for example, facilities for casino gaming which require operating, personal and premises licences to be obtained in order that the gaming can be provided without an offence being committed. Unless the necessary licences have been obtained at the time of advertising, any advertising of the gambling will constitute an offence under this section. The offence covers advertising of unlawful gambling whether the advertising takes place by remote or non-remote means, and sections 332 and 333 make specific provision about this.
809. The offence does not apply to lotteries. Part 11 of the Act contains separate provisions relating to the advertising of unlawful lotteries.
810. A person who commits the offence by doing anything to encourage people to gamble, or bringing facilities for gambling or information about them to the attention of others with a view to increasing their use, will have a defence if they can show that they reasonably believed the gambling to be lawful. People who commit the offence by participating in or facilitating such an activity will only commit the offence if they know or ought to have known the gambling to be unlawful.
811. There is also an exemption from this offence for peoples who advertise gambling because they merely deliver, transmit, broadcast or make data available in the course of business, without having any editorial control over the nature or content of the material.
812. A person guilty of an offence under this section shall be liable on summary conviction to imprisonment for a term not exceeding 51 weeks for England and Wales (6 months for Scotland), a fine not exceeding level 5 on the standard scale, or both. An offence committed under this section shall be treated as a continuing offence which means that an offence shall be committed on each day during any period that the advertisement is displayed or made accessible.

SECTION 331: FOREIGN GAMBLING

813. This section makes it an offence to advertise non-EEA (or 'foreign') gambling. Foreign gambling is gambling which either physically takes place in a non- EEA state (eg a casino in Australia), or gambling by remote means which is not regulated by the gambling law of any EEA state (the interpretation section in Part 18 defines 'EEA state'). For the purposes of this section, Gibraltar is treated as if it is an EEA state, which will allow gambling operators based in Gibraltar to advertise their services in the United Kingdom. The offence covers advertising of gambling whether the advertising takes place by remote or non-remote means, and sections 332 and 333 make specific provision about this. This section extends to Northern Ireland.
814. The offence does not apply to lotteries. Part 11 of the Act contains separate provisions relating to the advertising of foreign lotteries.

815. It will be open to the Secretary of State, however, to make regulations specifying countries or places which are to be treated as though they were EEA states for the purposes of this section. The effect of this will be to put any advertising of gambling taking place in that country or place outside the scope of the offence.

816. The maximum penalty upon conviction for an offence under this section is a term of imprisonment of 51 weeks in England and Wales (6 months in Scotland and Northern Ireland), together with a fine up to level 5 on the standard scale.

SECTION 332: TERRITORIAL APPLICATION: NON-REMOTE ADVERTISING

817. This section clarifies the application of Part 16 where the advertising is by non-remote means, for example a poster on a hoarding.

818. Where the advertising is by non-remote means:

- regulations controlling the form, content, timing and location of advertising under this Part; and
- the offence of advertising unlawful gambling under this Part;
- will only apply where the advertising takes place wholly or partly in Great Britain; and:
- the offence of advertising foreign gambling under this Part,
- will only apply where the advertising takes place wholly or partly in the United Kingdom.

SECTION 333: TERRITORIAL APPLICATION: REMOTE ADVERTISING

819. This section clarifies the application of these provisions where the advertising is by remote means, for example by email or television broadcast.

820. For remote advertising of gambling to fall within the scope of Part 16 it has to satisfy three tests. In the case of section 331 (the remote advertising of foreign gambling), it is only the first of the three tests which has to be satisfied. Furthermore, in the case of foreign gambling, the references to Great Britain in the first test should be read as references to the United Kingdom, because section 331 extends to Northern Ireland.

821. The first test is broadly that the advertising must be targeted at people in Great Britain. In particular the advertising must involve:

- providing information intended to come to the attention of a person in Great Britain;
- sending a communication intended to come to the attention of a person in Great Britain;
- or making data available with a view to its being accessed by a person in Great Britain or in circumstances where that is likely to happen.

822. The second test applies in the case of advertising that is either broadcast by television or constitutes an information society service within the meaning of Directive 98/34/EC (on electronic commerce). Information society service means 'any service normally provided for remuneration, at a distance, by means of electronic equipment for the processing and storage of data, and at the individual request of a recipient of a service'.

823. Where the advertising is broadcast by television the provisions of Part 16 will only apply if the broadcaster is either under the jurisdiction of the United Kingdom for the purposes of Directive 89/552/EEC (Television Without Frontiers) or is not under the jurisdiction of an EEA state for the purposes of that Directive. The purpose of this particular test is to ensure that the provisions do not apply to advertising where the broadcaster is properly regulated by another EEA State.

824. Where the advertising constitutes an information society service, the provisions of Part 16 only apply where the service provider:

- is established in the United Kingdom for the purposes of Directive 2000/31/EC,
- is established in a non-EEA state for those purposes, or

- has been notified that the conditions for derogation in Article 3(2) of that Directive have been satisfied in relation to the service provider.

825. Directive 2000/31/EC is concerned with contributing to the proper functioning of the Internal Market by ensuring the free movement of information society services between Member States. In broad terms the Directive establishes that a provider of information society services is to be regulated by the State in which it is established. Therefore, in general, where advertising constitutes an information society service, the provisions of Part 16 only apply where the provider is either established in the United Kingdom or outside the EEA. Article 3(4) of the Directive enables Member States to derogate from this general rule where the provider of an information society service not established in its country presents a serious and grave risk in respect of public policy matters such as the protection of consumers. The possibility to derogate under Article 3(4) of the Directive is also reflected in the section.

826. The third test is that the gambling itself takes place in Great Britain where it is non-remote gambling; or, where it is remote gambling, that at least one piece of remote gambling equipment is situated in Great Britain.

PART 17: LEGALITY AND ENFORCEMENT OF GAMBLING CONTRACTS

6.2022 827. This Part deals with the legality and enforcement of gambling contracts. As a result of the sections in this Part, contracts made for gambling purposes are to be treated similarly to other contracts. In particular, any debts that arise from gambling will be capable of enforcement in the same way as any other personal or business debts. All statutory provisions which prevented such contracts from being enforced are repealed by the Act. However, the Commission is given power to void betting contracts in certain circumstances. These powers (set out in this Part) are intended to promote the licensing objectives (under Part 1) and enable the Commission to take specific action if it is satisfied that a bet was substantially unfair.

SECTION 334: REPEAL OF PROVISIONS PREVENTING ENFORCEMENT

828. This section repeals all statutory provisions which provide that gambling contracts are unenforceable. The repeals will not apply retrospectively, so any gambling contract made, or right arising from an agreement made, before this section comes into force will not be enforceable.

SECTION 335: ENFORCEABILITY OF GAMBLING CONTRACTS

829. This section expressly provides that a contract will be capable of being enforced irrespective of the fact that it is a contract relating to gambling. This does not, however, override any other rule of law that prevents enforcement on the grounds of unlawfulness. Therefore gambling contracts may be void on the same basis as any other contract (for example, on the basis of lack of intention, mistake or illegality).

SECTION 336: POWER OF GAMBLING COMMISSION TO VOID BET

830. This section provides the Commission with the power to make an order that a bet accepted by, or through, the holder of a general betting operating licence, a pool betting operating licence, or a betting intermediary operating licence, is to be void.

831. Where the Commission exercises this power, any contract or other arrangement relating to the bet will be void, and any money paid in relation to the bet must be returned to the person who paid it. So, for example, a person who places a stake on a bet that the Commission orders should be made void, must have their stake returned to them. Equally, any winnings must be repaid to the person who accepted the bet. Such repayments will be enforceable as a debt.

832. The Commission may only make an order under this section where it is satisfied that the bet was substantially unfair. In considering whether a bet is substantially unfair, the Commission must, in particular, have regard to any of the factors listed in subsection (4) that apply. These are:

- that one or both of the parties to the bet (whether they made or accepted the bet) supplied information in connection with it that was insufficient, false or misleading;
- that one or both of the parties to the bet believed, or ought to have believed, that the race or event about which the bet was made was, or would be, conducted in contravention of the industry rules (as defined in section 337(7)) that apply to the event. This might apply where, for example, one party to a bet knew that players in a youth football match were in fact over the legal age for participation, but nonetheless offered a bet on the match;
- The fact that one or both of the parties to the bet believed, or ought to have believed, that the offence of cheating (as set out in section 42) had been, or was likely to be, committed in relation to the bet. This could apply where, for example, a person connected to a racehorse owner became aware that the horse had been deliberately injured prior to a race in which it was to run and, on the basis of that knowledge, made a bet on that horse through a betting intermediary;
- The fact that one or both parties to the bet have been convicted of the offence of cheating as set out in section 42 of the Act.

833. The effect of this section is that the Commission will not automatically void a bet where one of the factors listed in subsection (4) applies; it will only cancel a bet where it is satisfied that it was substantially unfair. This will allow for the situation where both parties to the bet knew about the cheating, for example, and so no unfairness arises.

834. The power to void a bet will be available to the Commission for a period of six months from the day on which the result of the bet is determined, except where there has been a conviction for cheating, in which case there is no time limit. Provision is made in section 337 for rights of appeal in relation to orders made by the Commission under this section.

SECTION 337: SUPPLEMENTARY

835. Subsection (1) of this section provides for a right of appeal to the Gambling Appeals Tribunal where the Commission makes an order to void a bet. Either party to the bet, and any other person who was a party to a contract or arrangement relating to the bet, will be able to appeal. This means that, for example, betting intermediaries who may lose money as a result of a bet being void, but who are not a party to the actual bet, are provided with a right of appeal. Further provision is made about the Gambling Appeals Tribunal in Part 7 of the Act.

836. Subsections (2) and (3) give the Commission power to void any part of a betting transaction, and to determine the consequences for any bets connected with a bet or betting transaction that is made void. Such a determination might, for example, require all the successive bets in an 'accumulator' bet to be made void.

837. When investigating whether to order that a bet should be made void, the Commission may require any person by or through whom the bet is made or accepted (such as a party to the bet or a betting intermediary), to provide information or documents in relation to the bet. A person who does not comply with this requirement commits an offence, unless they have a reasonable excuse. The penalty for the offence will be a maximum fine of level 2 on the standard scale. In conducting its investigation, the Commission may also take into account any other information that it receives.

SECTION 338: INTERIM MORATORIUM

838. The Commission will have the power to make an order freezing any obligation to pay money in relation to a bet, where it suspects that it may need to make an order that the bet is void under section 336. The effect of this interim moratorium is to protect any payments that would otherwise have been made in relation to a bet, but which might be difficult to recover if the Commission later decides that the bet should be made void. So, whilst the interim moratorium is in place, a betting operator need not pay a customer any winnings; and the customer will not be required to pay any stake or commission.

839. The Commission need not be certain that a voiding order will be made before imposing the interim moratorium.

840. An interim moratorium will last for a period of 14 days, beginning on the day that it is made. It will be possible for the Commission to extend an interim moratorium by a further period of up to 14 days. There is no limit to the number of interim moratoriums that the Commission may impose in relation to any bet, although the time limit of 6 months for making an order to void a bet will continue to apply during any period when an interim moratorium is in place.

841. The Commission may cancel an order for an interim moratorium before it expires; and must cancel one if it ceases to think that it might want to make an order to void the bet.

842. Where the Commission decides to impose an interim moratorium, but then decides not to void the bet, the Commission will not be liable to make any payment (such as interest on the payments that have been frozen) simply because it has taken such action.

PART 18: MISCELLANEOUS AND GENERAL

6.2023 843. Part 18 contains a number of miscellaneous provisions. It provides powers for transitional arrangements to be made for implementation of the various new licensing and permit regimes established by the Act. It covers matters such as application of the Act to the Crown, and the prosecution powers of licensing authorities. It sets out a comprehensive interpretation section, and it provides for repeals and consequential amendments and the general extent of the Act.

SECTION 339: PRIZE COMPETITIONS

844. Participating in competitions in which there is a prize is not to be regarded as gambling as long as the activities involved in the competition do not amount to betting, gaming or participating in a lottery as defined in the Act.

SECTION 340: FOREIGN BETTING

845. This section repeals sections 9 to 9B of the Betting and Gaming Duties Act 1981 (c.63), which imposes prohibitions on certain activities relating to overseas betting, for the protection of the revenue. The provisions of Part 16 will provide a complete regime for the regulation of advertising, and as a result, these sections of the 1981 Act are no longer required.

SECTION 341: OFFENCE COMMITTED BY BODY

846. If a body (such as a company) commits an offence under the Act, persons of authority in the body (known as officers) may be prosecuted if the offence resulted from their consent, connivance or their negligence. The body may be prosecuted also. Officers can include directors, managers, secretaries and members of a body. Where a body is a partnership then each partner is individually responsible for offences arising in these circumstances. Unincorporated bodies and their officers may also be prosecuted in the same way.

847. Subsection (7) allows the Secretary of State to make regulations dealing with the application of this section to bodies formed outside the United Kingdom.

SECTION 342: FALSE INFORMATION

848. Any person giving false or misleading information to the Commission or to a licensing authority, without a reasonable excuse, commits an offence. If convicted, the person may be imprisoned for up to 51 weeks in England and Wales, or 6 months in Scotland, and may also be fined an amount up to level 5 on the standard scale. If the Commission or a licensing authority have taken a decision on the basis of false information they may do whatever in their judgement is necessary to alter or remedy the effects of that decision.

SECTION 343: VALUE OF PRIZE

849. This section is concerned with determining how the value of a prize is to be calculated. A number of provisions in the Act give powers to the Secretary of State to prescribe the maximum value of a prize that may be won at gambling. This section allows such regulations to include provision for determining what is meant by the value of a prize, where they are non-monetary prizes.
850. Subsection (3) authorises a practice commonly known as 'trading- up'. This is where a person who has won two or more separate prizes from a gaming machine can swap the prizes won for another, different, prize. In the exchange, the value of the prize received must not be greater than the total value of the prizes that could have been won by the player from his winning turns on the machine. Thus, if a person wins two small toys from a Category D machine (and the maximum value of each prize is £8 under the Category D classification), then the two small toys can be swapped for one big toy provided the value of the big toy does not exceed £16 (2 x £8 prizes). The swap must also comply with any rules about the nature or type of prize that could have been delivered by the machine.

SECTION 344: PARTICIPATION FEES

851. This section provides a definition of 'participation fee' for the purposes of the Act. Under various Parts of the Act, powers are taken to prescribe maximum participation fees for gambling (eg under Parts 5 and 12), or participation fees are prohibited in relation to certain forms of gambling (eg private gaming under Part 14). This section describes the matters which may or may not count as a participation fee. It gives the Secretary of State power to provide that a membership subscription is to be treated as a participation fee, as an exception to the general rule set out in subsection (1).
852. Subsection (4) allows the Secretary of State to deal with the apportionment of participation fees where the fee covers both gambling and non-gambling activities. An example of when this could be used is where a participation fee limit is set for the admission charge to premises where gambling takes place (see subsection (1)(b)), but some of that sum is referable to non-gambling activities. In such circumstances the fee could be apportioned, and only the gambling element of it limited. This power applies to all participation fee powers under the Act.

SECTION 345: FORFEITURE

853. Courts may order the forfeiture of items, like gaming machines, which are involved in the commission of offences under the Act. Items will be surrendered to the police. Persons who have not been convicted may make representations about any items that are the subject of a forfeiture order, where they believe they have an interest in the article, and the court may order that the article be given to that person.

854. It will be an offence to fail to co-operate with a forfeiture order, the maximum penalty upon conviction being a maximum term of imprisonment of 51 weeks in England and Wales, or 6 months in Scotland, and/or a fine up to level 5.

SECTION 346: PROSECUTION BY LICENSING AUTHORITY

855. Local authorities have general powers to prosecute and defend legal proceedings, but this section provides power for them to institute proceedings with respect to specified offences under the Act. The section identifies those matters for which licensing authorities have express power to prosecute. This section does not apply to Scotland.

SECTION 347: PROSECUTION: TIME LIMIT

856. This Section disapplies section 127(1) of the Magistrates' Courts Act 1980 (c.43). That section limits the time for bringing a prosecution in the Magistrates' court to six months from the date upon which the offence was alleged to have been committed. Subsection (1) imposes a longer time limit, of 12 months from the date upon which the offence was alleged to have been committed.

SECTION 348: EXCLUDED PREMISES

857. The Act generally applies to gambling on any premises in Great Britain, including vessels and vehicles. However, this Section provides an exception to this general provision by excluding from the Act premises which are subject to a national security certificate, issued by the Secretary of State or the Attorney General, or premises which are otherwise of a kind specified by the Secretary of State by order.

SECTION 349: THREE-YEAR LICENSING POLICY

858. Licensing authorities perform a number of different functions under the Act. They issue premises licences under Part 8, temporary use notices under Part 9, and a range of permits, under Parts 10, 12 and 13 and Schedules 10, 12, 13 and 14. To assist them in this task, and to provide transparency for those wishing to apply to a licensing authority for a permission under the Act, all authorities are required to prepare a licensing policy, covering all their functions.

859. This section sets out the procedures authorities must follow in preparing such a policy. Following widespread consultation, licensing authorities will publish a licensing policy statement describing the principles they intend to apply in exercising their various functions. The policy will have effect for three years, but the authority may review and alter the policy during that period. Regulations may be made by the Secretary of State (or Scottish Ministers in relation to Scotland) about the form of statements, the procedure to be followed in relation to them and their publication. An order of the Secretary of State will fix the first day of the initial three year period.

SECTION 350: EXCHANGE OF INFORMATION

860. Part 2 of the Act contains provisions which enable the Commission to exchange information with the bodies listed in Schedule 6. This section allows the bodies listed in Part 1 of that Schedule to exchange information amongst themselves for use in the exercise of a function under the Act. It also allows those bodies to provide information obtained in the course of functions under the Act to Her Majesty's Customs and Excise. The provision of information under this section may be made subject to conditions.

SECTION 351: POWER TO AMEND SCHEDULE 6

861. This section confers power on the Secretary of State by order to amend the lists of bodies in Schedule 6. In particular, it allows entries to be added to or removed from a list, and for entries to be moved from one list to another.

SECTION 352: DATA PROTECTION

862. The Act contains various provisions enabling bodies, including the Commission, to provide information to other organisations. This section makes it clear that nothing in the Act is to be taken as authorising a disclosure of information which would contravene the Data Protection Act 1998 (c.29).

SECTION 353: INTERPRETATION

863. This section provides the general definitions and meanings of expressions for the Act. Particular definitions of substance, in subsection (1), are provided for:
- Director;
- EEA State;
- Football pools;
- Premises;
- Stake;
- Track (and dog tracks and horse-race courses);
- Vehicle; and
- Vessel.

864. Subsection (2) contains a number of interpretative provisions for references in the Act. Subsection (3) provides a definition of what is meant by 'virtual game, race or other event or process', and subsection (4) covers what is meant by giving notice under the Act.

SECTION 354: CROWN APPLICATION

865. The Act applies to the Crown, which includes government departments and crown servants. However, the Act has no effect in relation to anything done on premises occupied by the armed forces.
866. Subsection (3) ensures that a reference to 'fire and rescue authority' in the Act will be substituted with a reference to 'Her Majesty's Fire Inspectorate' in relation to premises for which Her Majesty's Fire Inspectorate is the proper fire authority. In particular, in respect of those properties for which they have responsibility, Her Majesty's Fire Inspectorate will be a responsible authority under Parts 8 and 9 and will be required to be notified of any application for a premises licence in relation to those premises.

SECTION 355: REGULATIONS, ORDERS AND RULES

867. This section contains provisions governing the form and procedure for regulations, rules and orders made by the Secretary of State (or the Lord Chancellor) under the Act. Similar provision is made for regulations made by Scottish Ministers.
868. Most regulations made under the Act are to be made by statutory instrument, pursuant to the negative resolution procedure. However, subsection (4) lists particular regulation-making powers which must be made pursuant to the affirmative resolution procedure (where made by the Secretary of State) or be approved by resolution of the Scottish Parliament (where made by the Scottish Ministers). Orders (with the exception of those listed in subsection (7)) are to be made by statutory instrument subject to the affirmative resolution procedure. By virtue of subsection (8) commencement orders under section 358 are not subject to any Parliamentary procedure except as provided in that subsection.

SECTION 356: AMENDMENTS AND REPEALS

869. As a result of the substantive provisions in the Act, there need to be consequential amendments made to provisions in other legislation and repeal of other Acts, in part or in their entirety. This section lists the major enactments repealed by the Act.

870. Schedule 16 contains the minor and consequential amendments arising from provisions of the Act. The minor amendments in Part 1 of Schedule 16 include amendments to the Gaming Act 1968. The amendments relate to the provisions of that Act concerned with gaming and gaming machines in premises licensed to supply alcohol. They also affect premises licensed under that Act, including in particular casinos. The amendments to the 1968 Act will apply until the repeal of that Act by this Act. Schedule 17 lists provisions repealed by the Act, and the extent of their repeal.

SECTION 357: MONEY

871. This section makes provision for expenditure and receipt of sums by a Minister of the Crown under the Act.

SECTION 358: COMMENCEMENT AND SCHEDULE 18

872. This section makes provision for the commencement of the Act. It provides for the preceding provisions of the Act to be brought into force by commencement order made by the Secretary of State. It is the Government's intention that the Act be brought into effect in stages. This section makes this possible by allowing different parts of the Act to be brought into force at different times and in relation to different classes of activity under the Act.

873. Subsection (2)(e) specifically allows a commencement order to be made for the purposes of establishing the Commission so that it can carry out preparatory work prior to the repeal of the existing licensing regimes. Subsection (2)(f) makes it possible for provisions to be brought into force so that people who wish to provide facilities for gambling may make advance applications for a licence or permit under the Act, and for those advance applications to be considered and determined.

874. Subsections (4) to (6) enable savings, modifications and transitional arrangements to be made in the context of the Horserace Betting and Olympic Lottery Act 2004. This will enable provisions to be made that ensure the new licensing regime under the Act is compatible with that legislation.

875. This section and, in particular, Schedule 18 provide powers to effect transition to the new regulatory regime and also allow effect to be given to what have become known as 'grandfather rights'. This means making provision whose effect is to require relevant authorities to grant new permissions to people making applications if they held equivalent permissions under the previous law.

876. Part 1 of Schedule 18 deals with the transitional continuation of old licences and permissions. In particular, paragraph 3 allows particular provision to be made for casinos which are below the minimum licensable size, as defined by regulations pursuant to section 7 of the Act. This will allow such casinos to continue to operate, with controls, but without requiring them to meet the minimum size requirements.

877. Part 2 of this Schedule deals with advance and interim applications, and the need for licences to be converted from old licences to new licences in certain circumstances. The Government intend that these conversion powers will be used primarily in relation to applications for premises licences under Part 8, family entertainment centre gaming machine permits under Schedule 10, lottery registrations under Schedule 11, prize gaming permits under Schedule 14, and in relation to the gaming activities of clubs and pubs under Part 12. There is to be no automatic conversion for operating and personal licences.

SECTIONS 359 AND 360: VESSELS AND AIRCRAFT: TERRITORIAL LIMITATION

878. The Act applies to vessels and vehicles. See, for example, sections 211 and 231. Sections 359 and 360 establish the territorial limitation to the Act's regulation of vessels and aircraft.

SECTION 361: EXTENT

879. The Act applies to Scotland, England and Wales, but not generally to Northern Ireland. There are three exceptions to this. The offence of chain gifting in Part 3 and that of advertising foreign gambling in Part 16 apply to Northern Ireland, as does the repeal of sections 9 to 9B of the Betting and Gaming Duties Act 1981 contained in this Part.

COMMENCEMENT

6.2024 880. The provisions of the Act (other than sections 358 to 362 which deal with commencement, territorial limitations, extent etc) will be brought into force on dates appointed by the Secretary of State by commencement order. It has been the Government's intention to commence Part 2, which will provide for the establishment of the Gambling Commission, by October 2005. Schedule 16 includes amendments to the Gaming Act 1968 which will have effect until replaced by the relevant provisions of the Act. The intention has been also to bring these amendments into force at that time. Other provisions of the Act will be brought into force in stages after that with the intention that the Act should be fully in force by September 2007.

STATEMENT OF PRINCIPLES FOR LICENSING AND REGULATION

September 2009

1 INTRODUCTION

THE PURPOSE OF THIS STATEMENT OF PRINCIPLES FOR LICENSING AND REGULATION

6.2040 1.1 This statement sets out the principles that the Gambling Commission (the Commission) will apply in exercising its functions under the Gambling Act 2005 (the Act) and explains how these principles are expected to assist the Commission in its pursuit of the licensing objectives in the Act.

THE LICENSING OBJECTIVES

1.2 The licensing objectives are set out in the Act[1] and are:

- preventing gambling from being a source of crime or disorder, being associated with crime or disorder or being used to support crime
- ensuring that gambling is conducted in a fair and open way
- protecting children and other vulnerable persons from being harmed or exploited by gambling.

THE DUTY TO PURSUE THE LICENSING OBJECTIVES AND PERMIT GAMBLING

1.3 In exercising its functions under the Act the Commission is under a duty to pursue, and wherever appropriate to have regard to, the licensing objectives, and permit gambling, in so far as the Commission thinks it reasonably consistent with pursuit of the licensing objectives[2].

STATUTORY REQUIREMENTS AND BETTER REGULATION PRINCIPLES

1.4 This statement has been prepared in accordance with the requirements of sections 23, 70, 73, 111, 112, 116 and 128 of the Act. The Commission has also had regard to the

- Regulators' Compliance Code[3]
- report of the Hampton Review[4]
- report of the Macrory Review[5]
- Enforcement Concordat[6]
- Cabinet Office Code of Practice on Consultation[7]
- Scottish Improving Regulation Report 2008[8]
- reports of the Regulatory Review Group in Scotland[9]
- Hampton Implementation Review Report into the Gambling Commission[10].

STATUTORY REQUIREMENTS AND BETTER REGULATION PRINCIPLES

1.5 This statement will be reviewed by the Commission from time to time and revised when appropriate. Before revising the statement, the Commission will consult on its proposed changes in accordance with section 23(5) of the Act.

THE COMMISSION'S JURISDICTION

1.6 The Commission's jurisdiction covers Great Britain – England, Scotland and Wales. The Commission will maintain appropriate working relationships with each administration and will take account of the differences between them.

2 THE COMMISSION'S STATUTORY FUNCTIONS

INTRODUCTION

2.1 The Commission's functions in relation to licensing and regulation can broadly be categorised as those of licensing, compliance and enforcement. In particular, the Commission has the power to:

- determine applications for operating and personal licences, specify the (general and individual) conditions to be contained in such licences, limit the duration of such licences[11], and determine applications to vary or renew operating and personal licences
- undertake activities for the purpose of assessing compliance with the Act and with any licence condition, code of practice or other provision made by or by virtue of the Act, and also for the purpose of assessing whether an offence is being committed under or by virtue of the Act (including the power to request information from operating and personal licence holders under section 122 of the Act, to commence reviews under section 116 of the Act, and to carry out inspections under Part 15 of the Act)
- take regulatory action against an operating or personal licence holder following a review under section 116 of the Act (including the power to issue a formal warning, to attach, remove or amend a licence condition, to suspend or revoke a licence, and to impose a financial penalty), to void a bet and require repayment of any money paid in relation to it, and to investigate and prosecute[12] offences committed under the Act.

THE FRAMEWORK OF POLICIES AND PROCEDURES

2.2 This Statement of principles for licensing and regulation underpins the work of the Commission. The Commission has also developed a number of policies which build on the principles in this document and govern how the Commission will carry out its work, including:

- Licensing, compliance and enforcement policy statement
- Statement of principles for determining financial penalties
- Licence Conditions and Codes of Practice
- Complaints procedure
- Corporate governance framework
- Regulatory panel procedures.

WHAT THE COMMISSION EXPECTS FROM APPLICANTS FOR LICENCES

2.3 The Commission expects applicants for licences to:

- be able to demonstrate that they can meet the Commission's suitability assessment
- ensure that the activities they plan to carry out will be conducted in a manner which minimises the risks to the licensing objectives
- work with the Commission in an open and co-operative way
- disclose to the Commission anything which the Commission would reasonably expect to know.

WHAT THE COMMISSION EXPECTS FROM LICENSEES

2.4 The Commission expects licensees to conduct their gambling operations in a way that does not put the licensing objectives at risk. The Licence Conditions and Codes of Practice are designed to ensure this.

2.5 The Commission also expects those holding licences, including, as appropriate, personal licences, to:

- conduct their business with integrity
- act with due care, skill and diligence
- take care to organise and control their affairs responsibly and effectively and have adequate systems and controls to minimise the risks to the licensing objectives
- maintain adequate financial resources
- have due regard to the interests of customers and treat them fairly
- have due regard to the information needs of customers and communicate with them in a way that is clear, not misleading, and allows them to make a properly informed judgment about whether to gamble
- manage conflicts of interest fairly
- work with the Commission in an open and co-operative way
- disclose to the Commission anything which the Commission would reasonably expect to know.

3 APPLICABLE PRINCIPLES

INTRODUCTION

3.1 The Commission will apply the following principles in exercising its functions under the Act. These principles have been formulated with a view to ensuring that the Commission regulates gambling in a transparent, accountable, proportionate, consistent and targeted manner.

REGULATING GAMBLING IN THE PUBLIC INTEREST

3.2 The Commission will regulate gambling in the public interest, having regard to, and in pursuit of, the licensing objectives in the Act. In doing so the Commission will work with licensees and other stakeholders and will ensure that it takes into account:

- the need to protect the public
- the need to maintain public confidence in the gambling industry and the Commission
- the importance of declaring and upholding proper standards of conduct and competence by licence holders.

PRECAUTIONARY APPROACH

3.3 The Commission will adopt a precautionary approach when interpreting evidence, where this is appropriate, having regard to its duty to promote the licensing objectives in the Act.

KEEPING THE COMMISSION'S REGULATORY APPROACH UNDER REVIEW

3.4 The Commission will keep its regulatory approach under review, and will make changes to that approach when appropriate (for example, to reflect experience or new developments).

CONSULTATION

3.5 The Commission will consult on changes to its regulatory approach where it is appropriate to do so, having regard to the Cabinet Office Code of Practice on Consultation[13] and will ensure that:

- consultation takes place when proposals are still at a formative stage
- sufficient information is provided to allow consultees to respond meaningfully
- adequate time is allowed for responses
- all responses are taken into account in reaching a final decision.

THE COMMISSION'S DECISION MAKING PROCESSES

3.6 The Commission will ensure that licensing and regulatory decisions are properly reasoned and evidence-based[14] and taken at the most appropriate level. The Commission will adopt a presumption in favour of decisions being made at the lowest appropriate level within the Commission[15], so that decisions of similar complexity and impact are generally made at similar levels within the Commission.

CONFIRMING LICENSING AND REGULATORY DECISIONS

3.7 The Commission will provide written notification of licensing and regulatory decisions, including:

- a clear explanation of the reasons on which the decision is based (in a level of detail proportionate to its impact)
- details of any appeal mechanism(s).

THE RELEVANCE OF CRIMINAL CONVICTIONS

3.8 The Commission will determine the weight it will attach to convictions for relevant offences and unspent convictions for other offences committed by licence applicants or persons relevant to applications for operating or personal licences[16] having regard to the nature and seriousness of the offence and the time which has elapsed since the offence was committed.

FAILURE TO DECLARE CONVICTIONS

3.9 The Commission will attach significant weight to failure by a licence applicant to declare a conviction for a relevant offence or unspent conviction for any other offence committed by it or a person relevant to the application, in the absence of a reasonable excuse for such failure.

THE OPPORTUNITY TO MAKE ORAL REPRESENTATIONS

3.10 The Commission will provide an opportunity for licence applicants to make oral representations to it in appropriate circumstances[17].

THE SUITABILITY OF LOCAL AUTHORITIES TO RUN LOTTERIES

3.11 The Commission will assume integrity when assessing the suitability of any local authority to run a lottery[18].

IMPOSING THE MINIMUM BURDEN NECESSARY TO PROMOTE THE LICENSING OBJECTIVES

3.12 The Commission will ensure that its regulatory approach imposes the minimum burden necessary to promote the licensing objectives in the Act – having regard to its impact on different types and sizes of licence applicant and licence holder – and does not unduly hinder economic progress.

REQUESTS FOR INFORMATION

3.13 The Commission will request only that information which it requires[19] and will avoid duplicating requests by seeking to obtain information from government bodies (for example, the Serious Fraud Office) and other regulators (for example, the National Lottery Commission, the Office of Fair Trading, the Office of Communications and the Financial Services Authority) where it is possible, and appropriate, to do so.

FOCUSING ON PREVENTATIVE ACTIVITY

3.14 The Commission will focus on preventative activity by keeping the gambling industry fully informed of the requirements of the regulatory regime and providing general information, advice and guidance, both on request and on its own initiative, with a view to aiding regulatory compliance.

COMPLAINTS

3.15 The Commission will treat all complaints seriously and will address them in accordance with its published complaints procedure.

ADOPTING A RISK-BASED APPROACH

3.16 The Commission will adopt a risk-based approach to regulation to ensure that its resources are concentrated where they are needed most and can be most effective.

PROPORTIONALITY

3.17 The Commission will generally use the least intrusive regulatory tool to achieve compliance and will ensure that any regulatory action is proportionate to the importance of the matters to which it relates, having regard to its risk assessment.

TAKING REGULATORY ACTION IN PREFERENCE TO CRIMINAL ACTION

3.18 The Commission will take regulatory action in preference to commencing criminal investigations unless it is appropriate to do otherwise.

LICENCE REVIEWS AND CRIMINAL CONVICTIONS

3.19 The Commission will commence a review under section 116 of the Act where a relevant offence is committed by an operating or personal licence holder or a person relevant to any such licence, except in exceptional circumstances.

PUBLICATION OF REGULATORY ACTION

3.20 The Commission will publish details of any regulatory action taken, except where it considers that this may have a disproportionately damaging effect on the licence holder.

ENFORCOMENT OF GAMBLING CONTRACTS

3.21 The Commission expects parties to gambling contracts to take private law action in respect of any breach. The Commission will not, except in exceptional circumstances, undertake reviews where debt enforcement proceedings could be brought by the parties to a gambling contract.

FOCUS ON INVESTIGATING OFFENCES IN WHICH GAMBLING IS AN INTRINSIC ELEMENT

3.22 The Commission will focus on investigating offences under the Act, such as crimes in which gambling is an intrinsic element (for example, illegal gambling) and crimes which affect the outcome of gambling (for example, cheating), together – in conjunction with government bodies and/or other regulators as necessary – with any other offences related to gambling (for example, money laundering offences under the Proceeds of Crime Act 2002 and illegal money lending).

CONSIDERING THE OUTCOME OF INVESTIGATIONS INTO OFFENCES NOT RELATED TO GAMBLING

3.23 The Commission will not itself investigate offences which are not related to gambling, but will have regard to the outcome of investigations carried out by other bodies (for example, burglary of premises licensed under the Act or theft by staff) where they raise issues regarding the continuing suitability of licence holders.

COORDINATING REGULATORY ACTION

3.24 The Commission will take coordinated regulatory action with government bodies and/or other regulators where it is appropriate to do so.

4 PROMOTING THE LICENSING OBJECTIVES

INTRODUCTION

4.1 The Commission expects the principles set out above to assist the pursuit of the statutory licensing objectives in the following ways.

PREVENTING GAMBLING FROM BEING A SOURCE OF CRIME OR DISORDER, BEING ASSOCIATED WITH CRIME OR DISORDER OR BEING USED TO SUPPORT CRIME

4.2 The Commission's licensing, compliance and enforcement processes are designed to prevent gambling from being a source of crime or disorder, being associated with crime or disorder or being used to support crime, and will ensure that:

- only suitable applicants will be granted operating licences or personal licences
- the suitability of licence holders will be assessed on an ongoing basis as part of the Commission's compliance activities
- compliance activity is targeted where the risks to the licensing objectives are greatest
- the suitability of licence holders will be reconsidered in the light of any subsequent criminal activity or connection with such activity.

4.3 The Commission will take a serious view of applicants and licensees who have convictions for relevant offences[20]. Each case will be considered on its merits, but there will be a presumption in favour of refusing an application or reviewing a licence in such cases.

4.4 The Commission will examine the corporate control structures and ownership of operators to enable the Commission to identify and satisfy itself of the integrity of controllers of companies[21] and others relevant to the operation of gambling.

4.5 The Commission will provide advice of a general nature about compliance to licensed operators and potential operators.

4.6 The Commission will provide guidance to local licensing authorities and to British Police Forces.

4.7 The Commission will make available general advice to the public on what activities are permissible without a licence.

4.8 The Commission will employ staff with the necessary skills and knowledge and will delegate to them the necessary powers they need to carry out compliance and enforcement functions.

4.9 In relation to the prevention, investigation and prosecution[22] of offences under the Act, and other offences related to gambling, the Commission will give priority, based on the level of risk posed to the licensing objectives, to:

- crimes in which gambling is an intrinsic element, for example illegal gambling
- financial crimes which operators should seek to prevent, such as money laundering and offences under the Proceeds of Crime Act, and

- crimes which affect the outcome of gambling for other participants.

4.10 Although the Commission will focus on crimes within the Act, rather than those unrelated to the Act such as burglary of gambling-licensed premises or theft by employees, the Commission may have an interest in the outcome of such investigations if they raise issues of relevance to the continuing suitability of persons licensed by the Commission. In appropriate cases the Commission may separately commence a review of the licence.

4.11 The Commission will seek to build and maintain good liaison and working relationships with local authorities, other regulators and law enforcement bodies The Commission will work closely with licensing authorities, other law enforcement agencies and other regulators to share relevant information and, where appropriate, investigate offences.

4.12 While the Commission recognises that licensing authorities will have the principal role in ensuring that premises based gambling is not a source of disorder, the Commission will also have a key role in this and will advise licensing authorities on the responsibilities that they have in relation to premises licensing. Where the Commission becomes aware that there are problems arising from disorder at gambling premises, the Commission may decide to commence a review of the licence.

ENSURING THAT GAMBLING IS CONDUCTED IN A FAIR AND OPEN WAY

4.13 The Commission expects that not only is gambling fair in the way it is played, but that the rules are transparent to players and they know what to expect.

4.14 The Commission will ensure that operating and personal licences are issued only to those who are suitable to offer gambling facilities or work in the industry.

4.15 The Commission will ensure that the rules are fair and that easily understandable information is made available by operators to players about, for example: the rules of the game, the probability of losing or winning, and the terms and conditions on which business is conducted.

4.16 The Commission will ensure that appropriate advertising codes continue to be in place to prevent consumers from being misled.

4.17 The Commission will require operators to make public the results of events and competitions on which commercial gambling takes place.

4.18 The Commission will ensure that the licences it issues, together with the licence conditions it imposes and the codes of practice it publishes, set appropriate standards of conduct for licence holders (for example, in respect of the terms on which gambling is offered and the transparency of such terms) and appropriate technical standards for gaming machines and other equipment used in connection with any licensed activity.

4.19 In the event of non-compliance, the Commission will ensure that sanctions are imposed which, among other things, deter future non-compliance on the part of the relevant licence holder and other licence holders more generally.

4.20 The Commission will ensure that the investigation and prosecution[23] of offences under the Act – including the offence of cheating under section 42 of the Act – is given priority based on the level of risk posed to the licensing objectives.

PROTECTING CHILDREN AND OTHER VULNERABLE PERSONS FROM BEING HARMED OR EXPLOITED BY GAMBLING

4.21 The Commission has issued and will from time to time revise its guidance to licensing authorities about how they can ensure that gambling premises are presented in such a way that access by children can be prevented.

4.22 The Commission has issued and will from time to time revise a code about access to casino premises in accordance with section 176, and will require persons operating casinos to take measures, such as supervision of entrances and training of staff, to prevent access by children and young persons.

4.23 The Commission will require persons operating remote gambling to ensure that there are adequate age verification measures in place to prevent children and young persons gambling on their sites.

4.24 The Commission will work with the Committees of Advertising Practice to develop advertising codes on gambling and will ensure that these are backed by effective enforcement action if those codes are breached.

4.25 With regard to 'vulnerable persons' the Commission considers that this group will include:

- people who gamble more than they want to
- people who gamble beyond their means; and/or
- people who may not be able to make informed or balanced decisions about gambling, for example because of mental health problems, learning disability, or substance misuse relating to alcohol or drugs.

4.26 Although the Commission's role does not, for example, extend to treatment or care of those who have gambling problems, the Commission does have an interest in keeping up to date with developments and trends in work of that kind.

4.27 The Commission will issue codes that include social responsibility requirements, setting out what practical measures operators must take in relation to social responsibility.

4.28 The Commission will ensure that marketing practices (including advertising and inducements) do not exaggerate the chances of winning or encourage players to gamble more than they can afford or want to.

4.29 The Commission will work with other bodies to build and maintain knowledge about problem gambling and the measures that may be taken to reduce the prevalence of problem gambling and will undertake regular prevalence surveys.

4.30 The Commission will normally rely on external research but may find it helpful to carry out, or commission, applied research on the effectiveness of particular measures – both before they are implemented and to monitor how effective they are in practice. In interpreting the available evidence, the Commission will take a precautionary approach. For example, caution may be justified where evidence is mixed or inconclusive, and the Commission would not want to restrict its discretion by requiring conclusive evidence that something was unsafe before taking measures to restrict it.

4.31 The Commission's focus will be on identifying best practice in protecting vulnerable people from being harmed or exploited by gambling, and, where appropriate, placing requirements on operators to put particular measures in place and to monitor their compliance.

Compliance will be kept regularly under review, with activity by the Commission targeted where the risks to the licensing objectives are greatest.

4.32 In the event of non-compliance, sanctions may be imposed which, among other things, are intended to deter future non-compliance on the part of the relevant licence holder and other licence holders more generally.

4.33 The Commission will also give priority to the investigation and prosecution[24] of offences under the Act – including those offences relating to children under sections 46, 47 and 51 to 57 of the Act – where appropriate, based on the level of risk posed to the licensing objectives.

---

1 Section 1 Gambling Act 2005.

2 Section 22 Gambling Act 2005.

3 Regulators' Compliance Code: Statutory Code of Practice for Regulators, Department for Business, Enterprise and Regulatory Reform, 17 December 2007.

4 Reducing Administrative Burdens: Effective Inspection and Enforcement, Philip Hampton, March 2005.

5 Regulatory Justice: Making Sanctions Effective, Professor Richard B. Macrory, November 2006.

6 Concordat on Good Enforcement, Cabinet Office, March 1998.

7 Code of Practice on Consultation, Cabinet Office, January 2004.

8 The Scottish Improving Regulation Report 2008, July 2008.

9 Interim Report from the Regulatory Review Group for the Scottish Group, February 2008; Regulatory Review Group Annual Report, July 2008.

10 Gambling Commission: A Hampton Implementation Review Report, April 2009.

11 The Commission has not made any determinations regarding the duration of an operating or personal licence, or a specified class of operating or personal licence, under section 111 of the Act. Nor, as a result, has it made any determinations regarding the duration of a renewed operating or personal licence, or a specified class of operating or personal licence, under section 112 of the Act. If any such determinations are made in due course, they will be published as part of a revised version of this statement in accordance with the requirements of sections 111(4) and 112(7) of the Act respectively.

12 The Commission has no power to prosecute offences in Scotland. That power rests solely with the Crown Office and Procurator Fiscal Service, to whom the Commission can refer the results of an investigation.

13 Code of Practice on Consultation, Cabinet Office, January 2004.

14 The kind of evidence to which the Commission will have regard when assessing the integrity, competence and financial or other circumstances of a licence applicant and in considering the suitability of a gaming machine or of other equipment is specified in the Licensing, Compliance and Enforcement Policy Statement. The relevant aspects of that document are incorporated into this statement by reference, in accordance with the requirements of sections 70(5) and 70(6) of the Act respectively.

15 The Commission's practice regarding the delegation of functions in relation to licence applications is specified in its Corporate Governance Policy (as amended from time to time). Those parts of Appendix 8 which deal with the grant or refusal of licence applications are incorporated into this statement by reference, in accordance with the requirements of section 73(4) of the Act.

16 Under section 70(9)(b) of the Act, a person is relevant to a licence application if, in particular, he is likely to exercise a function in connection with, or to have an interest in, the licensed activities.

17 The Commission's practice in relation to the holding of oral hearings of licence applications is specified in the Licensing, Compliance and Enforcement Policy Statement. The relevant aspects of that document are incorporated into this statement by reference, in accordance with the requirements of section 73(4) of the Act.

18 This assumption is specified in accordance with section 70(7) of the Act. The Commission has not identified a class of gaming machine or other equipment in relation to which it will or may assume suitability under section 70(8) of the Act, and therefore makes no specification in that regard.

19 The Commission's practice in relation to evidence required or accepted in connection with licence applications is specified in the Licensing, Compliance and Enforcement Policy Statement. The relevant aspects of that document are incorporated into this statement by reference, in accordance with the requirements of section 73(4) of the Act.

20 As defined in schedule 7, Gambling Act 2005.

21 Within the meaning of section 422 of the Financial Services and Markets Act 2000.

22 In Scotland the power to prosecute offences rests with the Crown Office and Procurator Fiscal Service, to whom the Commission can refer the results of an investigation.

23 In Scotland the power to prosecute rests solely with the Crown Office and Procurator Fiscal Service, to whom the Commission can refer the results of an investigation.

24 In Scotland the power to prosecute offences rests solely with the Crown Office and Procurator Fiscal Service, to whom the Commission can refer the results of an investigation.

Gambling Commission September 2009

GAMBLING ACT 2005 'WHITE-LISTING'

January 2007

1. INTRODUCTION

STATEMENT OF PURPOSE

6.2055 1.1 This guidance document describes the process, and sets out the criteria, which the Secretary of State will employ when considering whether to permit gambling operators based in a country, territory or jurisdiction outside the EEA to advertise their gambling activities in the United Kingdom, from September 2007. This process has also been referred to as 'white-listing' but that is an informal term which is not recognised in the relevant legislation and is not, therefore, used within this guidance document.

LEGISLATIVE BACKGROUND

1.2 The provisions of the Gambling Act 2005 (the 'Act') are expected to come fully into force, with effect from 1 September 2007. All of the Act's provisions apply to Great Britain (England, Wales and Scotland). Only the provisions in sections 43, 331 and 340 (including the related entry in Schedule 17) apply to the United Kingdom (Great Britain and Northern Ireland).

1.3 The provisions concerning advertising remote and non-remote gambling under the new licensing regime are contained in Part 16 of the Act. All guidance concerning the advertising in the UK of gambling activities should be read in conjunction with the relevant guidance published by the Committee of Advertising Practice (CAP), the Broadcast Committee of Advertising Practice (BCAP), OFCOM and the Gambling Commission.

1.4 As stated in paragraph 1.1 above, this document sets out the criteria which the Secretary of State will employ to specify which non-EEA countries, territories or jurisdictions should be treated as if they were an EEA State, and therefore exempt from the provisions in section 331 which forbid the advertising, in the UK, of gambling based in a non-EEA State. It also describes the process which the Secretary of State intends to employ in her deliberations.

1.5 Section 331 of the Act sets out restrictions on the advertisement of foreign gambling in the UK. From September 2007, countries, territories or jurisdictions that are situated outside the EEA and Gibraltar, will not be permitted to advertise foreign gambling, within the definition set out in section 331(2) of the Act, unless they can demonstrate that they have a satisfactory regulatory regime in place.

1.6 A country, territory or jurisdiction (from hereon referred to as a jurisdiction), which is situated outside the EEA and Gibraltar, which has the right to legislate for and regulate gambling activities based in, or offered from within, its geographical borders; and, is able to show that a satisfactory regulatory regime exists and operates within its jurisdiction, may make representations to the Secretary of State, and be considered for a special 'exemption' under section 331(4) of the Act. This 'exemption' will permit a gambling operator based in, and regulated by, the jurisdiction to advertise in the UK as if he were based in an EEA state or Gibraltar.

MAKING REPRESENTATIONS

1.7 The guidance in this document is intended to assist a jurisdiction when submitting representations to the Secretary of State for consideration under section 331(4). Such representations will be considered *only* if they are submitted by the Government which holds the relevant legislative and/or regulatory authority within a jurisdiction. Representations made by other persons or organisations will be considered only in the context of additional or supporting evidence and will not, otherwise, be considered.

1.8 The use of the word exemption in paragraph 1.7 above and elsewhere in this guidance document should not be inferred as meaning an exemption from stringent regulatory control. It is UK Government policy that any jurisdiction making representations will be required to demonstrate that its gambling licensees operate within a robust regulatory environment and that its regulator(s) is(are) required to operate continual licensing and regulatory enforcement of gambling operations within that jurisdiction. Furthermore, all gambling operators permitted to advertise their gambling activities in the UK will be subject to strict rules regarding the form and content of advertising in the UK, as well as to the robust gambling regulation in their home jurisdiction.

1.9 A jurisdiction may make representations to the Secretary of State in respect of the terrestrial (premises-based) gambling it regulates; the remote gambling it regulates; or both. In any event, the Secretary of State will require the jurisdiction to set out very clearly which gambling activities it licenses that it proposes should be permitted to advertise in the UK. A jurisdiction may make representations in respect of all the gambling activities which it licenses (except state, national or other lotteries – see paragraph 1.10), but will be required to provide full and detailed information about the regulatory nature and compliance and enforcement systems in place for each gambling activity. Information about enforcement systems should include details about the manner in which technical standards and requirements are effectively enforced, including details of testing procedures.

1.10 The advertising of state, national or other lotteries does not come within the scope of this part of the Act and section 331(4) does not, therefore, apply to the advertising of any lottery. If a jurisdiction makes representations in respect of a lottery the Secretary of State will not be permitted to consider those representations.

1.11 As a first step, when considering the robustness of its regulatory regime, a jurisdiction wishing to make representations to the Secretary of State should consider how its jurisdiction would meet the licensing objectives of the Act (set out in paragraph 2.1) and whether the regulatory obligations it places on its gambling operators meet the standards that will be required of the gambling operators to be licensed by the Gambling Commission under the Act.

1.12 Therefore, a jurisdiction will need to consider the application of our gambling licensing objectives (set out in paragraph 2.1) to the licensing regime(s) it applies to each and every category of commercial gambling for which it wishes to make representations, and compare how it would achieve those objectives for those gambling activities through the measures and protections within its regulatory and licensing regime(s).

1.13 In practice, in Britain, the Gambling Commission will attach conditions to operating and personal licences which will specify how British gambling operators can use their facilities for gambling. In addition, the Secretary of State may impose additional conditions on those licence holders. The Gambling Commission will also issue codes of practice about the conduct of gambling and its social impact to which gambling operators will also be subject and will provide guidance to local licensing authorities about their licensing obligations, including the licence conditions they may apply to gambling operators premises licences.

1.14 On 27 November 2006, the Gambling Commission published the licence conditions and codes of practice which will form the backbone of its licensing regime, that is, the regulatory obligations which will placed on all British gambling operators, terrestrial or remote, from September 2007. A supplement on financial requirements was published by the Commission at the end of December. Any breaches by a licensee may lead to heavy penalties, including stiff fines and, potentially, loss of licence or criminal prosecution.

1.15 We do not propose to prescribe the conditions which a jurisdiction must apply to its licensing regime in order to qualify for consideration under section 331(4). Neither do we propose to demand that a jurisdiction's regime must mirror the licensing regime which will be in operation in Britain from September 2007 in order to qualify. However, a jurisdiction wishing to make representations should refer to the relevant documentation on the Gambling Commission's website www.gamblingcommission.gov.uk and set out in writing how the issues which the Gambling Commission has addressed through its licensing regime are addressed with substantially similar intention and effect in the jurisdiction's regulatory regime and through the obligations placed on the operators it licenses.

1.16 Furthermore, it is vital that the Secretary of State may be assured that a jurisdiction has the capacity; technical and regulatory ability; and political impetus necessary, to enforce its regulation. The Secretary of State will be seeking evidence and firm commitment in this regard and a jurisdiction wishing to make representations should refer to the licensing, compliance and enforcement consultation documents on the Gambling Commission's website www.gamblingcommission.gov.uk for guidance about the sort of evidence we are expecting to receive.

1.17 In short, we expect that all those jurisdictions whose representations to the Secretary of State under section 331(4) are successful, to have embedded within their licensing regimes the values which underpin our licensing regime, that is to say, that they too regulate gambling in order to protect children and vulnerable people from being harmed or exploited; to keep crime out; and to ensure that gambling is conducted fairly, and that they have the facilities and resources in place to ensure compliance and enforcement with those values and the regulatory regime in operation.

1.18 There is no formal application form but a jurisdiction making representations to the Secretary of State is requested to state clearly which categories of gambling activities its representations concern and to formulate its representations around the three licensing objectives (set out in paragraph 2.1) for each of those categories; to consider the Gambling Commission's codes of practice and licence conditions and the issues they address for each of those categories (or individual activities) and set out how its regime addresses those issues for each of those categories (or individual activities); and to provide full details of how it enforces the licensing regime for each of those categories (or individual activities).

1.19 In addition, jurisdictions need to be aware that, in addition to UK law and regulations, there are a number of EU-wide regulations and policies with which British-based gambling operators must comply, such as on money-laundering. A jurisdiction making representations must confirm that its gambling regime and gambling operators are subject to rules on money-laundering, specifically, and financial probity, in general, which are no less stringent.

1.20 In developing its representations, a jurisdiction may also find it useful to consider the policy documents which Government used to formulate the new legislative framework and licensing arrangements (see paragraph 11).

1.21 Jurisdictions must also demonstrate that they adhere to fair tax principles, in particular, they will be judged on openness, equal availability and equal treatment.

1.22 All representations to the Secretary of State must be in English.

1.23 Ideally, we would like to receive all representations via email and for those representations, which must include an executive summary; information about the nature of the relevant regulatory regime(s) in the jurisdiction; contact details; and relevant supporting documentation, to not exceed a total of150 pages.

1.24 **As the UK Government is subject to 'Freedom of Information' legislation, it is vital that all commercially sensitive or otherwise sensitive information is included only in annexes and clearly labelled as such, with non-sensitive references to the sensitive information in the main text only (solely for the purpose of directing the reader to where the sensitive information can be found in the annexes).**

1.25 Please note that all information in responses, including personal information, may be subject to publication or disclosure under the Freedom of Information Act 2000. Confidentiality cannot be guaranteed, and will only be protected if considered appropriate under the legislation.

1.26 Lastly, jurisdictions should note that the Secretary of State reserves the right to remove a jurisdiction from any list of states or territories permitted to be treated as a

EEA state for the purposes of section 331(2) of the Act, under the provision of section 331(4) if, at any stage, there is concern that the jurisdiction no longer satisfies the criteria set out in this document.

1.27 In the paragraphs which follow this, we aim to explain, in greater detail, how the Act will apply to British premises-based gambling operators and British-based remote gambling operators from September 2007; and to explain the role of the Gambling Commission, which will regulate all British-based operators, except the National Lottery and spread betting. The purpose of this is to give a clearer indication about the issues which a jurisdiction must address in its representations but must be read in conjunction with the Gambling Commission's Licence Conditions and Codes of Practice document and its Licensing, Compliance and Enforcement consultation document and with the Act.

1.28 It may be helpful for a jurisdiction to set out its representations in much the same way as the Gambling Commission has set out the issues, and methods to address those issues, in these documents (see paragraph 1.27). However, we do not propose to prescribe this or any other layout.

MEETING THE UK GOVERNMENT'S REGULATORY REQUIREMENTS

2 KEY REGULATORY CONCEPTS

2.1 The licensing and regulatory objectives informing the jurisdiction's gambling regulatory regime, should, in practice, broadly, achieve the objectives under which the British gambling regulatory regime will operate, which are stated in section 1 of the Act, namely:

- To prevent gambling from being a source of crime or disorder, being associated with crime or disorder or being used to support crime;
- To ensure that gambling is conducted in a fair and open way; and
- To protect children and other vulnerable persons from being harmed or exploited by gambling.

3 KEEPING OUT CRIME

3.1 The UK Government has stated that 'one of the prime objectives of gambling regulation must be to combat criminality'. It has further commented that, 'this means having appropriate barriers to entry for those wanting to join the industry, and having effective mechanisms for policing new and existing gambling operators'.

3.2 Combating criminality is therefore a key component of the UK Government's policy towards the effective regulation of the gambling industry, protecting and regulating both operators and participants alike. To achieve this for our jurisdiction, we have established a thorough and robust licensing system, enforced by a tough regulatory body (the Gambling Commission), which will be expected to ensure that the gambling operators it licenses comply with high standards of probity and integrity.

3.3 The regulator has a wide range of enforcement and inspection powers, backed-up by 'statutory gateways', which are mechanisms which facilitate the transfer of information between the Gambling Commission and other organisations. These include law enforcement and financial regulatory bodies such as the police, National Crime Squad, National Criminal Intelligence Service, Serious Fraud Office and the Financial Services Authority.

3.4 In the UK, all gambling businesses are also required by law to comply with provisions, concerning the prevention and detection of money laundering, in the Proceeds of Crime Act 2002 and the Terrorism Act 2000. Casino operators (whether offering terrestrial (premises-based) gambling or remote gambling) are also subject to additional controls arising from the provisions of the Money Laundering Regulations 2003.

3.5 Other notable criminal prevention measures in the Act include the facility for the Gambling Commission to void bets (section 336); and an offence of cheating (section 42), designed to protect consumers, operators and the betting events or products from unscrupulous persons attempting to benefit from corrupting those events or products.

3.6 The UK Government believes that the Act provides the powers required to combat criminality, through the detection and prosecution of any person attempting to use gambling to conduct a criminal activity, such as money laundering, within its licensing jurisdiction.

3.7 A jurisdiction making representations will be required to demonstrate that it too has appropriate mechanisms in place to combat any criminality which may be linked to gambling, and that those mechanisms will also permit and facilitate 'policing' and prosecution of illegal gambling activities.

4 ENSURING THAT GAMBLING IS CONDUCTED IN A FAIR AND OPEN WAY

4.1 Consumers should be confident that a gambling service or product is operated in a fair and transparent manner. The UK Government believes that customers should be able to gamble, fully aware of the terms under which they participate, and confident in the financial reliability and probity of operators. Effective and transparent means of money transfer should be in operation, notably secure procedures for the acceptance of stakes and the prompt payment of winnings. The rules, or odds, for each type of gambling activity will, undoubtedly, vary depending upon the product, as it may between gambling operators. However, the terms under which gambling is offered should be readily available to customers and easy for them to access. It should also be written in simple, easy to understand, language.

4.2 The Act (section 335) makes gambling debts legally enforceable in Great Britain and the terms under which operators deal with customers will become contractual as soon as the relevant provisions of the Act have been implemented (currently planned for September 2007).

4.3 In Great Britain, licensed operators will be expected to make adequate provision for the handling of both complaints and dispute resolution. The dispute resolution process must include opportunity for recourse to an independent body or person. Licensed operators will be required, as part of their licence conditions, to maintain records of both complaints and disputes. The records must be available to the Gambling Commission.

4.4 A jurisdiction making representations will be required to demonstrate that it has in place sufficient regulatory controls to ensure that customers of those gambling products, for which it wishes to make representations, including those customers based outside the jurisdiction, will:

- Have ready access to the rules under which the gambling is offered and that those rules which will be available in the English language;
- May claim any prizes or winnings within a reasonable period; and
- Have ready access to dispute resolution and information about how to resolve any dispute with a gambling operator, including to the regulator, if necessary.

4.5 Jurisdictions should take note that the Gambling Commission may impose additional licence conditions on the gambling operators it licenses where it feels that there are sufficient concerns which would warrant the imposition of such conditions. The Secretary of State has similar powers. We would expect a jurisdiction making representations to provide evidence that it too has a regulatory regime which has sufficient mechanisms in place to respond to changing priorities and needs, as these arise.

5 PROTECTION OF CHILDREN AND THE VULNERABLE

5.1 The UK Government places great emphasis on licensed gambling operators conducting their business in a socially responsible way, in particular, with regard to children and vulnerable persons for which gambling presents particular risks that other forms of leisure may not.

5.2 Consequently, the new regulatory controls we have introduced for Great Britain are based around a set of statutory safeguards governing specific gambling activities, and – running alongside them – a commitment by all licensed gambling operators to conduct their business in a way which is socially responsible. The provisions of the Act also mean that licensed operators will be committing an offence if they invite or permit a child or young person to enter adult only premises or to participate in activities which are not permitted for that age group (Part 4 of the Act refers).

5.3 Additionally, the Act (section 83) imposes a condition that prevents operators from profiting from underage gambling. Operators who become aware that a child or young person is, or has used, their facilities for gambling:

- Must return any money paid in respect of the use of those facilities (whether by way of fee, stake or otherwise) by the child or young person as soon as is reasonably practicable; and
- May not give a prize to the child or young person.

5.4 An operator licensed by the Gambling Commission will be expected to put in place effective and robust protective measures to control entry to play, including seeking proof of age, where appropriate. Operators who breach their obligations could face criminal sanctions and wide-ranging licensing penalties, including the loss of licence and the right to operate.

5.5 British-based online gambling operators will be expected to put in place payment systems and other controls to prevent children using online gambling sites. Certain forms of payment may be deemed as potentially 'at risk', for example, due to their availability to children, and may, therefore, require greater age checks to be carried out on those customers before access to gambling facilities are permitted.

5.6 The Act aims to give adults the right to make informed choices about their gambling activities where socially responsible measures can be put in place to diminish any adverse effects. The licensing regime is sufficiently flexible to allow the Government and Gambling Commission to readily adapt and amend licence conditions and codes of practice to meet the challenges raised by changing technologies, new gambling products and developments in payment methods.

5.7 Nevertheless, even with these extensive safeguards, the Government recognises that access to any gambling facilities – legal or illegal; commercial or private - may produce instances of problem gambling. We are addressing this through a number of measures, such as a reserve power in the Act compelling British based operators to pay an annual levy, in addition to taxation, which the Secretary of State will introduce if we consider that the industry is not sufficiently fulfilling its obligations to demonstrate social responsibility.

5.8 It should, therefore, be very clear that positive socially responsible practices, notably regarding children and other vulnerable people, including those at risk of becoming problem gamblers, are a critical part of meeting the Government's regulatory aims.

5.9 A jurisdiction making representations will need to demonstrate that a similar importance and commitment is placed on social responsibility within its jurisdiction; backed up by a sufficiently tough regulatory regime. In effect, this means that jurisdictions will be expected to require licence holders to contribute to research, to education about the risks of gambling and to the treatment of problem gamblers. Furthermore, we will be looking for evidence that there is a facility within a jurisdiction's regulation to promptly, and effectively, put measures in place to address developments in technology or products linked to the gambling activities for which the jurisdiction wishes to make representations.

6 INDEPENDENT REGULATORY BODY WITH INSPECTION AND ENFORCEMENT POWERS

6.1 The Government has established a central body for the regulation of the British-based gambling industry, covering both remote and non-remote products and operations (the only exceptions being the National Lottery and spread betting, which have their own statutorily competent regulatory bodies, specifically the National Lottery Commission and the Financial Services Authority). This provides a single system of licensing for commercial gambling in Britain and ensures that entry and compliance controls can be applied consistently and proportionately across all sectors of the industry.

6.2 In addition to its licensing role, the Gambling Commission also has responsibility for investigating and taking action against illegal gambling which is taking place within Great Britain. The Act provides the Gambling Commission with wide ranging powers enabling it to ensure compliance and to investigate and prosecute offences, including powers to access licensed and unlicensed premises, and premises used in conjunction with gambling (such as a gambling operator's head office); and powers to access key gambling equipment. In exercising this function in an effective and proactive manner, the Gambling Commission will be able to work with and call upon other regulatory and investigative bodies, including local licensing authorities, the police and Her Majesty's Revenue and Customs.

6.3 The Act (section 30) makes statutory provision for the exchange of information between the Gambling Commission and other regulatory and investigative bodies. These 'statutory gateways' facilitate communication and cooperation between the Commission and these other bodies, most notably law enforcement agencies.

6.4 Licensed operators are also required to provide the Gambling Commission with information about the licensed activities (section 122). In addition, a licensed operator may be required to pass on information relating to a breach of a sporting rule (section 88).

6.5 The Gambling Commission has been provided with sufficient powers to fully and properly enforce its regulatory role and to fulfil the statutory requirement to pursue the Gambling Act's three key licensing objectives (as set out in paragraph 2.1).

6.6 A jurisdiction making representations will need to provide evidence that its regulator (or an appropriate investigative body) has sufficient power and mechanisms in place to ensure compliance with its regulatory regime and to investigate and, if appropriate, prosecute breaches in compliance, and that it is properly resourced to carry out those functions. We shall also be seeking evidence of information gathering and dissemination systems, including the capability and willingness to cooperate and work with international regulatory and investigative agencies, such as Interpol, and other national regulators, including the Gambling Commission.

6.7 A jurisdiction making representations must be prepared to demonstrate, also, that its regulator's internal systems and decision making processes are subject to public accountability and are not subject to competing non-regulatory Government

7 LICENSING (AND CODES OF PRACTICE) ARRANGEMENTS

7.1 In Great Britain, under the Act, the regulatory regime, which will be in operation from 1 September 2007, will take the form of operating licences issued by the Gambling Commission permitting the holders to offer specific gambling activities and setting conditions on the way in which they offer those specified gambling activities. The operating licences, and the obligations imposed on the gambling operators holding them, will be tailored in order to meet the specific regulatory challenges posed by each specified gambling activity. In addition, premises-based British gambling operations will be subject to premises licensing arrangements with additional conditions setting out how the gambling operators may use their premises for gambling. Lastly, all gambling operators may find that key personnel within their organisations are required to obtain personal licences from the Gambling Commission.

7.2 This licensing regime is explained in more detail below (paragraphs 7.6 – 7.30), but for more detailed information a jurisdiction should refer to the Gambling Commission's Licence Conditions and Codes of Practice document, which is available on the Gambling Commission's website, and the Act.

7.3 The Gambling Commission will issue operating and personal licences (under parts 5 and 6 of the Act). Premises licences (under part 8 of the Act) will be issued by the relevant licensing authorities, although the Gambling Commission will provide guidance to those licensing authorities, on the manner in which and the principles to be applied in exercising their functions under the Act, in order to ensure fairness and consistency throughout this jurisdiction.

7.4 The Act also permits the Government to impose specific conditions for operating licences (section 78) and for premises licences (section 167), in addition to those imposed on the gambling operator by the Gambling Commission and the licensing authority. The Act sets out the broad parameters for who requires and who may obtain a personal licence, and the Government has powers to amend those parameters

7.5 The UK Government is not expecting a jurisdiction making representations to have in place a licensing regime which is identical to this one. Details about the licensing system, which will operate in Great Britain under the Act, (set out in paragraphs 7.6 – 7.30), are provided for information and guidance. However, as stated throughout, the Secretary of State will wish to see how a jurisdiction has addressed each of the issues identified, for the gambling activities for which it wishes to make representations, within its regulatory regime.

Gambling Commission Licences

7.6 The Gambling Commission will operate controls on entry to the British gambling industry, issuing operating and personal licences on the basis of an assessment of honesty, competence and, in the case of operators, financial means.

7.7 This statement of approach has been statutorily underlined by the provisions of section 70 of the Act. The licensing process is a key stage in ensuring that those permitted to operate gambling facilities in this jurisdiction are of the utmost probity and integrity. They should also be able to demonstrate an appropriate level of competence and suitability to run such operations and that adequate financial resources are available.

7.8 This is complemented by the information sharing facilities between the Gambling Commission and other organisations, notably law enforcement agencies; and the Gambling Commission's information enforcement powers over licensed operators (see paragraph 6).

7.9 The licensing process should therefore be a tough and thorough procedure, acting as a significant deterrent to crime (see paragraph 3), ensuring that the gambling activity is conducted fairly (see paragraph 4), and that children and other vulnerable people are sufficiently protected (see paragraph 5). It must also ensure that those responsible for providing gambling have been subject to thorough background checks to ensure their personal and financial probity.

Operating Licences

7.10 The Act provides that the Gambling Commission shall have regard to the suitability of a gambling operator to operate and, in assessing suitability, may consider the gambling operator's integrity, competence, financial and other circumstances. In awarding licences, the Gambling Commission can (and in some cases must) attach conditions to those licences. The Gambling Commission's powers to attach conditions to licences are wide (sections 75 and 77 of the Act), essentially permitting the Gambling Commission to attach any condition that comes within the scope of the Gambling Commission's remit to control the way in which gambling may be offered. In addition, the Gambling Commission will issue codes of practice about the manner in which facilities for gambling are provided, again, with wide scope. This means that the Gambling Commission has very wide scope to influence or determine the way in which licensed operators conduct their affairs.

7.11 Operating licences, issued by the Gambling Commission, will be the main form of authorisation for providing facilities for commercial gambling in Great Britain. Where authority to provide facilities for gambling has been granted, it will be subject to varying degrees of regulation depending on: the type of gambling; the means by which the gambling is conducted; and the people by whom, and to whom, the gambling is offered.

7.12 To cater for the differing regulatory requirements that may be necessary for each form of gambling activity. There are ten different kinds of operating licence (listed in section 65 of the Act), each of which will have specific licence conditions:

(a) a casino operating licence;
(b) a bingo operating licence;
(c) a general betting operating licence;
(d) a pool betting operating licence;
(e) a betting intermediary operating licence;
(f) a gaming machine general operating licence for an adult gaming centre;
(g) a gaming machine general operating licence for a family entertainment centre;
(h) a gaming machine technical licence;
(i) a gambling software operating licence; and

7.13 Facilities for gambling can be provided remotely (ie by technology which means the player is not in the same place as the person offering the facilities), or non-remotely (ie face to face on premises). 'Remote gambling' means gambling in which persons participate by the use of remote communication (this includes (a) the internet, (b) the telephone, (c) television, (d) radio or (e) any other kind of electronic or other technology for facilitiating communication). For each of the ten kinds of operating licence, there are two basic types: a remote operating licence which authorises, for example, the provision of particular facilities by means of the internet; and a non-remote licence, which authorises the same facilities to be provided from premises. An operating licence must either be remote or non-remote but cannot be both.

7.14 In addition, the Act provides for premises to be licensed by licensing authorities (local authorities in England and Wales, and licensing boards in Scotland) for the provision of gambling facilities. It also provides for personal licences to be issued by the Gambling Commission for certain personnel within a gambling operator.

Personal Licences

7.15 The Act provides for two types of personal licences, for:

- management functions (section 80(5)); and
- operational functions (section 80(6)).

7.16 The Act requires all licensed operators (except those determined as small scale operators) to have at least one personal management licence holder for each specified management office and may also, in addition, impose personal licences for certain operational functions.

7.17 Personal licences do not remove the overall responsibility from the operator but reinforce the importance of an individual's responsibility, in enforcing the licensing objectives. This individual responsibility will include ensuring that any and all necessary training is undertaken, so that they are equipped with the skills to enable them to meet the regulatory requirements.

7.18 Those individuals who may be required to hold a personal management licence include staff at the following levels: managing director/chief executive; finance director; compliance director; and marketing director or equivalent positions. Regional, area, sector or site managers may also require a personal management licence.

7.19 Personal licences for operational functions may also be required in circumstances where an employee of an operator may have the potential to manipulate the outcome of a gambling product for their own (or others') advantage. Individuals who may be required to hold a licence of this nature include: bingo club managers; casino executives and managers; and casino gaming staff (dealers, cashiers, inspectors, security staff and supervisors).

7.20 As with the operating licence regime, the Gambling Commission will need to

Premises Licences

7.21 Part 8 of the Act describes the regime for the licensing of premises for gambling. This licensing role is the responsibility of licensing authorities (local authorities in England and Wales, and licensing boards in Scotland).

7.22 Premises licences may authorise the provision of gambling facilities on:

- casino premises;
- bingo premises;
- betting premises (including horseracing and greyhound racing tracks, and betting intermediaries);
- adult gaming centres; and
- family entertainment centres.

7.23 Applicants for premises licences will be required to hold an operating licence permitting the relevant gambling activity, (except in the case of operators of racing tracks or licensed sports stadia) and will, therefore, need to have satisfactorily demonstrated that they fulfil those stringent operating licensing requirements in addition to meeting premises licensing requirements.

7.24 Conditions on a premises licence may be set by the licensing authority and also by the Government. However, each licensing authority will be required to conduct its licensing functions with reference to guidance provided by the Gambling Commission (section 153 of the Act), in order to ensure fairness and consistency throughout the jurisdiction.

7.25 The Gambling Commission will issue guidance on how the inspection regime, in Great Britain, will work. The purpose of the inspection regime is to ensure that licensed activities are being conducted fairly; and for investigating and taking action against illegal gambling. Inspections will be conducted in proportion to the assessed risk attached to each type of gambling product. The Act has provided the Gambling Commission, and other regulatory organisations, with wide-ranging powers to inspect licensed and unlicensed premises, and equipment.

7.26 Wholly remote operators, such as those operators which offer only online gambling, will not require a premises licence, but must comply fully with the personal and operating licensing regimes.

Gaming Machine Permits (and other permissions)

7.27 The Act also includes a system of permits which will be granted by licensing authorities (local authorities in England and Wales, and licensing boards in Scotland). Permits are required when premises provide a gambling facility but either the stakes or prizes involved in the gambling activity are very low, or gambling is not the main function of the premises. The permits regulate gambling and the use of gaming machines (slot machines) in a specific premises and are subject to the same values which underpin the licensing regime: to protect children and vulnerable people from

Register of Licence Holders

7.28 The Gambling Commission will hold and maintain a register of all the holders of the operating and personal licences it has issued, which will be accessible to the public.

7.29 This register will contain information which is not commercially sensitive, such as: the company name; address; licence number; date of issue; any licensing restrictions; and any sanctions that have been imposed. (In the interests of privacy, the personal addresses of personal licensees will not be included in the register.)

7.30 Each local licensing authority will also be required to maintain a register of the premises licences it has issued and for that information to be publicly available.
7.31 To reiterate, the Secretary of State does not expect applicant jurisdictions to mirror our licensing regime but she does expect a jurisdiction making representations to demonstrate that its licensing regime(s) effectively addresses each of the issues to be covered in Britain by the operating, personal and premises licensing regimes.

8 ADDITIONAL REQUIREMENTS

Fair Tax Criteria

8.1 The UK Government recognises that national governments and parliaments must be free to set their own tax structures and rates, nevertheless we want to ensure that jurisdictions outside the EEA wishing to advertise their gambling services in the UK adhere to fair tax principles
8.2 These tax criteria only apply to the jurisdiction's gambling specific tax regimes.
8.3 The three criteria against a jurisdiction's gambling tax regime will be judged are:

Openness

8.4 The tax base and rates of any gambling taxes should be clear, should be properly enforced and be applied to all operators.

Equal availability

8.5 The tax regime should be available to all operators whether owned domestically or by overseas interests and should be available to all operators who wish to be based in that jurisdiction. In particular there should not be especial low or "designer" tax rates available only to selected foreign operators.

Equal Treatment

8.6 Tax rates should be applied equally to gambling services supplied for both domestic and overseas consumption, in particular there should not be discounted rates of duty for export services.

9. CONSIDERATION OF REPRESENTATIONS

9.1 Jurisdictions making representations should email those representations to the Secretary of State at mailto://whitelisting@culture.gsi.gov.uk no later than 17:00 GMT on 2 April 2007.
9.2 It is vital that any jurisdiction that wishes to be treated as an EEA-state under the advertising provisions of section 331 of the Act, from the time at which those provisions come into effect (1 September 2007), ensures that the Secretary of State is in receipt of their completed representations no later than the date set out in paragraph 9.1.
9.3 Any representations received after that date; or any applications that were received on time but are substantially incomplete, are unlikely to be assessed in time to be included on the list of jurisdictions that will be treated as EEA-states from 1 September 2007.
9.4 The Secretary of State may request any other information or evidence deemed necessary to consider a jurisdiction's representation(s). Failure to comply with such a request, and within a reasonable time, may lead the Secretary of State to view the representation(s) as insufficient to meet the criteria or to consider the representation(s) to be void on the grounds that the jurisdiction in question has failed to comply with the request.

9.5 Please note that all information in responses, including personal information, may be subject to publication or disclosure under the Freedom of Information Act 2000. Confidentiality cannot be guaranteed, and will only be protected if considered appropriate under the legislation.
9.6 When the Secretary of State has decided what country or place will be specified under s331(4), she will provide for this in Regulations that are intended to come into force on 1 September 2007.
9.9 In the event that a jurisdiction is permitted to be treated as an EEA-state for the purposes of section 331(2), the Secretary of State will require a list of all the gambling operators legally licensed within that jurisdiction, which offer the gambling activity or activities for which the provision applies, and will require to be informed about any changes to that list for the full period of time that the jurisdiction enjoys this status.
9.10 For further information, please contact Moira Redmond in the Department for Culture, Media and Sport at:

Email: moira.redmond@culture.gsi.gov.uk
Tel: +44 20 7211 6483

Postal address: Moira Redmond
Gambling and National Lottery Licensing Division
Department for Culture, Media and Sport
2-4 Cockspur Street
London SW1Y 5DH

United Kingdom

10 A NEGATIVE DECISION

10.1 There is no formal appeals procedure and the Secretary of State's decision whether or not to recommend to Parliament that a jurisdiction should be permitted to be treated as an EEA-state for the purposes of section 331(2), under the provision of section 331(4), and for which gambling activities those provisions apply, is final.
10.2 Jurisdictions wishing to respond to a negative decision may do so, and the Secretary of State will consider new information, if such is available. However, jurisdictions will need to note that the deadline constraints listed in the previous chapter will still apply.

11 INFORMATION LINKS

Organisations

Department for Culture, Media and Sport (DCMS)
www.culture.gov.uk
Gambling Commission
www.gamblingcommission.gov.uk
Responsibility in Gambling Trust (RIGT)
www.rigt.org.uk
Committee on Advertising Practice (CAP)
www.cap.org.uk/cap/
Broadcast Committee on Advertising Practice (BCAP)
www.cap.org.uk/cap/about/cap_broadcast/
Advertising Standards Authority (ASA)
www.asa.org.uk/asa/
Ofcom
www.ofcom.org.uk
HM Treasury
www.hm-treasury.gov.uk/

Documents

Gambling Review Report (published in July 2001)
www.culture.gov.uk/Reference_library/Publications/archive_2001/gamb_rev_report.htm
A Safe Bet for Success (published in March 2002)
www.culture.gov.uk/Reference_library/Publications/archive_2002/safe_bet_for_success.htm
Gambling Act 2005
www.opsi.gov.uk/ACTS/acts2005/20050019.htm
Gambling Commission's Licence Conditions and Codes of Practice
www.gamblingcommission.gov.uk/Client/detail.asp?ContentId=103
Gambling Commission's Licensing, Compliance and Enforcement
www.gamblingcommission.gov.uk/Client/detail.asp?ContentId=77
www.gamblingcommission.gov.uk/client/news/pressrelease_detail.asp?id=15
Committee on Advertising Practice and Broadcast Committee on Advertising Practice – Consultation on Proposed Rules on Broadcast and Non-Broadcast Gambling Advertising (consultation closed)
www.cap.org.uk/cap/Consultations/closed/gambling_consultation/gambling-consultation.htm
Gambling Commission Consultation on Gambling Advertisements and Impact on Responsible Gambling
www.gamblingcommission.gov.uk/UploadDocs/Contents/Documents/Advertising%20impact%20on%20responsible%20gambling.pdf
Gambling Commission January 2007

LICENCE CONDITIONS AND CODES OF PRACTICE (CONSOLIDATED VERSION)

December 2011

INTRODUCTION

6.2060 1. This document sets out the Gambling Commission's general licence conditions and associated codes of practice (LCCP) under the Gambling Act 2005 (the Act). The last general revision of the conditions and codes was published in October 2008 and came into force for gambling operating and personal licensees on 1 January 2009. After that a number of subsequent changes were made and published in the form of supplements to the LCCP. The last consolidation of supplements into the main LCCP document was published in March 2011 in a single document.

2. Since that date, three further changes have been made, which were included in the following separate publications:

- Supplement 8: Types and rules of casino and other games (amending licence condition 9), July 2011
- Supplement 9: Casino gaming reserve (revoking licence condition 3.2), September 2011
- Supplement 10: Technical changes in respect of 2005 Act casinos, November 2011

3. The LCCP document sets out:

- the suite of general conditions to be attached to operating licences
- the suite of general conditions to be attached to personal licences
- the principal codes of practice, distinguishing between 'social responsibility'
- provisions and 'ordinary' provisions (the social responsibility provisions are in shaded boxes within the text).

4. Copies of this and the other documents mentioned above can be obtained from the Commission's website: www.gamblingcommission.gov.uk or by writing to:

Gambling Commission
Victoria Square House
Victoria Square
Birmingham B2 4BP
T 0121 230 6666
F 0121 230 6720
E info@gamblingcommission.gov.uk

PART I: GENERAL CONDITIONS IMPOSED BY THE GAMBLING COMMISSION

SUITE OF GENERAL CONDITIONS TO BE ATTACHED TO OPERATING LICENCES UNDER SECTION 75 OF THE GAMBLING ACT 2005 ('THE ACT')

1 Qualified persons and personal licences

1.1 Qualified persons

All operating licences, except ancillary remote licences, issued to small-scale operators

In this condition the terms 'small-scale operator', 'qualifying position' and 'qualified person' have the meanings respectively ascribed to them by the Gambling Act 2005 (Definition of Small-scale Operator) Regulations 2006.

Schedule X[1] lists those individuals notified to the Commission as qualified persons.

If, whilst the licensee remains a small-scale operator, an individual begins or ceases to occupy a qualifying position in relation to the licensee, the licensee must within 28 days apply to the Commission under s104(1)(b) for amendment of the details of the licence set out in Schedule X[1].

An application for amendment under s104(1)(b) may be made in advance of an individual beginning or ceasing to occupy a qualifying position provided it specifies the date from which the change to which it relates is to be effective.

All non-remote general betting operating licences issued to small-scale operators

Schedule Y[1] to this licence lists those of the licensee's employees whose details have been provided to the Commission as authorised by the licensee to accept bets on the licensee's behalf on a track otherwise than under the supervision of a qualified person present on the same track.

Should the licensee wish to add an individual to the list or remove the name of an individual from the list the licensee must make application to the Commission under s104(1)(b) for amendment of that detail of the licence. Any employee the licensee wishes to add to the list may act unsupervised pending amendment of the licence provided a valid amendment application has been lodged with the Commission.

In this condition 'qualified person' has the same meaning as in the Gambling Act 2005 (Definition of Small-scale Operator) Regulations 2006.

[1] The schedules mentioned here will be attached to individual licences.

1.2 Personal licences

All casino, bingo, general and pool betting, betting intermediary, gaming machine general, gaming machine technical, gambling software and lottery managers licences except ancillary remote licences

(a) Subject to (e) and (f) below licensees must ensure:
   (i) that each individual who occupies one of the management offices specified in (b) below in or in respect of the licensee or in connection with

the licensed activities holds a personal licence authorising the performance of the functions of that office (hereafter 'a personal management licence')

(ii) that at least one person occupies at least one of those offices.

(b) The specified management offices are those offices (whether or not held by a director in the case of a licensee which is a company, a partner in the case of a licensee which is a partnership or an officer of the association in the case of a licensee which is an unincorporated association) the occupier of which is by virtue of the terms of their appointment responsible for:

- the overall management and direction of the licensee's business or affairs
- the licensee's finance function as head of that function
- the licensee's gambling regulatory compliance function as head of that function
- the licensee's marketing function as head of that function
- the licensee's information technology function as head of that function in so far as it relates to gambling-related information technology and software
- oversight of the day to day management of the licensed activities at an identified number of premises licensed under Part 8 of the Act or across an identified geographical area
- in the case of casino and bingo licences only, oversight of the day to day management of a single set of premises licensed under Part 8 of the Act.

(c) Licensees must take all reasonable steps to ensure that anything done in the performance of the functions of a specified management office is done in accordance with the terms and conditions of the holder's personal management licence.

(d) Where an individual is authorised by a personal licence and that licence comes under review under section 116(2) of the Act, the operating licensee must comply with any conditions subsequently imposed on that licence by the Commission about redeployment, supervision, or monitoring of the individual's work and any requirements of the Commission in respect of such matters applicable during the period of the review.

(e) Paragraphs (a) to (d) above shall not apply to a licensee for so long as the licensee is a 'small-scale operator' as defined in the Gambling Act 2005 (Definition of Small-scale Operator) Regulations 2006 ('the Regulations').

(f) During the period of 3 years commencing with the date on which a licensee ceases to be a small-scale operator paragraphs (a) to (e) above shall apply subject to the proviso that the phrase 'each individual' in paragraph (a)(i) shall not include any individual who was a 'qualified person' (as defined in the Regulations) in relation to the licensee 28 days immediately prior to the licensee ceasing to be a small-scale operator.

All casino operating licences, except ancillary remote licences

In addition to paragraphs (a) to (f) above, licensees must ensure that if any of the following operational functions:

- dealer in respect of casino games
- cashier
- inspector
- security staff employed to watch gaming
- supervisor of gaming activities

is performed in connection with the licensed activities, it is performed by an individual who holds a personal licence authorising performance of the function (hereafter 'a personal functional licence'). Licensees must take all reasonable steps to ensure that anything done in the performance of those functions is done in accordance with the terms and conditions of the personal functional licence.

All lottery operating licences issued to non-commercial societies and local authorities

(a) Subject to (e) below licensees must ensure that the individual who occupies the management office specified in (b) below in or in respect of the licensee or in connection with the licensed activities holds a personal licence authorising the performance of the functions of that office (hereafter 'a personal management licence').

(b) The specified management office is that director's post in the case of a licensee which is a company, that partner in the case of a licensee which is a partnership, or that office in a licensee which is an unincorporated association or local authority, the occupier of which has overall management responsibility for the promotion of the lottery.

(c) Licensees must take all reasonable steps to ensure that anything done in the performance of the functions of a specified management office is done in accordance with the terms and conditions of the holder's personal management licence.

(d) Where an individual is authorised by a personal licence and that licence comes under review under section 116(2) of the Act, the operating licensee must comply with any conditions subsequently imposed on that licence by the Commission about redeployment, supervision, or monitoring of the individual's work and any requirements of the Commission in respect of such matters applicable during the period of the review.

(e) Paragraphs (a) to (d) above shall not apply to a licensee for so long as the licensee is a 'small-scale operator' as defined in the Gambling Act 2005 (Definition of Small-scale Operator) Regulations 2006.

2 Technical standards and equipment specifications

All non-remote gaming machine technical and gambling software licences and remote operating licences, including remote gaming machine technical, remote gambling software and betting ancillary remote licences, but not remote betting intermediary (trading rooms only) licences

Licensees must comply with the Commission's technical standards and with requirements set by the Commission relating to the timing and procedures for testing.

Non-remote bingo operating licences and bingo ancillary remote licences

Licensees must comply with the Commission's specifications for bingo equipment.

Non-remote casino operating licences and casino ancillary remote licences

Licensees must comply with the Commission's specifications for casino equipment.

3 Financial robustness

3.1 NOTIFICATION OF SHAREHOLDERS

All operating licences, except ancillary remote licences, issued to companies

All company licensees must notify the Commission of the name and address of any person who becomes a shareholder in the company or its holding company holding 3% or more of the issued share capital of the company or its holding company; or any existing shareholder who acquires a holding of 3% or more of the issued share capital of the company or its holding company.

In this condition 'holding company' has the meaning ascribed to that term by section 1159 of the Companies Act 2006 or any statutory modification or re-enactment thereof.

4 Protection of customer funds

All operating licences except gaming machine technical, gambling software, ancillary remote bingo, ancillary remote casino and lottery licences issued to non commercial societies or local authorities

Licensees who hold customer funds for use in future gambling must set out clearly, in information made available to customers in writing, whether they protect customers' funds in the event of insolvency and the method by which this is achieved.

All lottery managers' operating licences

Licensees must credit all lottery proceeds to a bank account or accounts having trustee status and at all times maintain a separation between those funds and their own trading income, or have in place other arrangements which provide legal protection, in the event of the licensee's insolvency, for society and local authority lottery funds the licensee manages.

5 Cash handling

All operating licences (including remote betting intermediary (trading rooms only) licences), except gaming machine technical, gambling software and remote licences

Licensees, as part of their internal controls and financial accounting systems, must have and put into effect policies and procedures concerning the handling of cash, and cash equivalents (ie bankers drafts, cheques and debit cards), designed to minimise the risk of crimes such as money laundering, to avoid the giving of illicit credit and to provide assurance that gambling activities are being conducted fairly.

6 Provision of credit by licensees and the use of credit cards

All gaming machine general operating licences for adult gaming centres and family entertainment centres

Licensees must neither:

- provide credit themselves in connection with gambling; nor
- participate in, arrange, permit or knowingly facilitate the giving of credit in connection with gambling.

7 General 'fair and open' provisions

All operating licences except gaming machine technical and gambling software licences

Licensees must satisfy themselves that the terms on which gambling is offered are not unfair under the Unfair Terms in Consumer Contracts Regulations 1999 and, where applicable, meet the reasonableness test under the Unfair Contract Terms Act 1977. An accurate summary of the contractual terms on which gambling is offered must be made available to customers and set out in plain and intelligible language.
Customers must be notified of changes to terms before they come into effect.

8 Display of licensed status

All lottery operating licences

Lottery promoters must display 'licensed by the Gambling Commission' and details of the Gambling Commission website on lottery tickets.

All remote bingo, casino, general betting, betting intermediary and pool betting operating licences, except ancillary remote licences and remote betting intermediary (trading rooms only) licences

Licensees offering gambling on websites must:

(a) display the following information on a page which, by virtue of the construction of the website, customers access before gambling:

(i) a statement that they are licensed and regulated by the Gambling Commission
(ii) their licence number and
(iii) a link to the Gambling Commission's website
(b) display at least the information at (i) above on each page of the website which offers facilities for gambling in reliance on the licence
(c) where they offer on pages of the website, or by means of a link from the website, facilities for gambling which are not provided in reliance on their Gambling Commission licence, clearly distinguish those products which are regulated by the Commission from those which are not.

All gaming machine technical and gambling software licences
Licensees offering the supply of gaming machines or gambling software on websites must:
(a) display the following information on the first page of the website which offers gaming machines or gambling software in reliance on the licence:
(i) a statement that they are licensed and regulated by the Gambling Commission
(ii) their licence number and
(iii) a link to the Commission's website
(b) display at least the information at (i) above on each page of the website which offers gaming machines or gambling software in reliance on the licence
(c) where they offer on pages of, or by means of a link from, their website, the supply of gaming machines or gambling software which are not provided in reliance on their licence, clearly distinguish those products which are regulated by the Commission from those which are not.

9 Types and rules of casino and other games

All non-remote casino operating licences
Licensees must not offer or permit to be played casino games that appear on any list of games prohibited by the Commission.

All non-remote bingo operating licences
Licensees must not offer or permit to be played prize gaming games that appear on any list of games prohibited by the Commission.

10 Tipping of casino employees

All non-remote casino operating licences

Licensees must only permit tipping of staff holding personal licences where a tronc system is operated; that is to say, where all tips are pooled and distributed amongst the employees concerned. A separate tronc may be operated for each of a number of categories of licensed staff.

11 Lotteries

All lottery operating licences

Licensees must ensure that at least 20% of the proceeds of any lottery promoted in reliance on the licence are applied to a purpose for which the promoting non-commercial society is conducted or the promoting local authority has power to incur expenditure.
The proceeds of any lottery promoted in reliance on this licence must not exceed £4,000,000 and the aggregate of the proceeds of lotteries promoted wholly or partly in a calendar year in reliance on the licence must not exceed £10,000,000.
The rules of any lottery promoted in reliance on this licence must be such as to ensure:

(a) that it is not possible for the purchaser of a ticket in the lottery to win by virtue of that ticket (whether in money, money's worth, or partly the one and partly the other and including any winnings arising from a rollover) more than:
- £25,000
- if more, 10% of the proceeds of the lottery.

(b) that membership of the class among whom prizes are allocated does not depend on making any payment (apart from payment of the price of a ticket).

A lottery promoted in reliance on this licence must not be linked to any other lottery, free draw or prize competition.

For the purposes of this condition:

(a) two or more lotteries are linked if any of them is so structured that a person who wins a prize in that lottery will also win a prize in some or all of the others, unless the maximum amount which a person can win is no more than £400,000 in aggregate. In determining whether two or more lotteries are linked it is immaterial how many of them are promoted in reliance on this licence

(b) a lottery is linked to a free draw or prize competition if:
  (i) a person's participation in, or his being allocated a prize in, the lottery is a means of establishing his eligibility to enter the draw or competition and
  (ii) the arrangements for the lottery and/or the draw or competition are such that a person may win more than £400,000 in aggregate as a result of his participation in the lottery and the draw or competition.

If a lottery, whilst not a linked lottery, has the feature that by selecting the same numbers, or combination of numbers in the lottery and in one or more other lottery or lotteries the participant in those lotteries may win prizes which, in aggregate, exceed £400,000, no advertisement for, nor other marketing of, the lottery may make any reference to that feature.

In the case of lottery operating licences issued to non-commercial societies and lottery managers' operating licences, licensees must ensure that each person who purchases a ticket in a lottery promoted in reliance on this licence, or promoted on behalf of a society in reliance on this licence, receives a document which:
- identifies the promoting society
- states the name and address of a member of the society who is designated, by persons acting on behalf of the society, as having responsibility within the society for the promotion of the lottery
- either states the date of the draw (or each draw) in the lottery, or enables the date of the draw (or each draw) in the lottery to be determined.

Licensees must display 'licensed by the Gambling Commission' and details of the Gambling Commission website on lottery tickets.

The price payable for purchasing each ticket in a lottery promoted in reliance on this licence:
- must be the same
- must be shown on the ticket or in a document received by the purchaser; and
- must be paid to the promoter of the lottery before any person is given a ticket or any right in respect of membership of the class among whom prizes are to be allocated.

For the purposes of these conditions, reference to a person receiving a document includes a reference to a message being sent or displayed to him electronically in a manner which enables him, without incurring significant expense or delay, to:
- retain the message electronically
- print it.

Licensees must lodge with the Commission a description of, and a copy of the rules of, any lottery intended to be promoted in reliance on this licence, and any amendment to the rules of a lottery previously notified to the Commission, at least 28 days before any tickets in such lottery, or amended lottery, are put on sale.

Lottery tickets must not be sold to a person in any street. But tickets may be sold by a person present in a kiosk or shop premises having no space for the accommodation of customers or door to door. For the purposes of this condition 'street' includes any bridge, road, lane, footway, subway, square, court, alley or passage (including passages through enclosed premises such as shopping malls) whether a thoroughfare or not.

In respect of each lottery promoted in reliance on this licence, a lottery submission must be sent to the Commission within three months of the date of the determination of the lottery or, in the case of an 'instant lottery', within three months of the last date on which tickets in the lottery were on sale. It must show the total proceeds and how they have been distributed between prizes and expenses and the amount applied directly to the society's purposes or, in the case of licences issued to local authorities, the amount applied directly to purposes for which the authority has power to incur expenditure.

Every lottery submission must contain or be accompanied by a declaration that the information given in it is correct to the best of the signatory's knowledge and belief. The submission must be signed by:

(a) the holder of a personal licence issued under Part 6 of the Act or

(b) a 'qualified person' as defined in the Gambling Act 2005 (Definition of Smallscale Operator) Regulations 2006 or

(c) the designated person named on tickets in a lottery promoted by or on behalf of a noncommercial society as having responsibility within the society for the promotion of the lottery.

Accounting records and copies of lottery submissions must be retained for a minimum of three years from the date of any lottery to which they relate and be made available for inspection by the Commission on request. Accounting records must contain, in respect of each lottery, details of the total proceeds of the lottery, the expenses of the lottery and the sum allocated from the proceeds to cover those expenses, and the number of sold and unsold tickets.

For any calendar year in which the cumulative proceeds of lotteries promoted in reliance on this licence exceed £1,000,000 the licensee must provide the Commission with written confirmation from a qualifying auditor confirming that the proceeds of those lotteries have been fully accounted for in their annual audited accounts. Such confirmation must be provided within ten months of the date to which the accounts are made up.

A qualifying auditor means a person who is eligible for appointment as a company auditor under section 25 of the Companies Act 1989 but, in the case of a lottery promoted by or on behalf of a non-commercial society, is not:

(a) a member of the society

(b) a partner, officer or employee of such a member or

(c) a partnership of which a person falling within (a) or (b) is a partner.

Accurate records for each lottery must be kept by the operator to support the data in the lottery submissions and must be made available for inspection by the Commission when required. Such records must include:

- the total proceeds in each lottery
- the percentage of proceeds allocated to prizes in each lottery
- the amount of proceeds allocated to expenses and details of those expenses for each lottery
- the number of sold and unsold tickets in each lottery.

In the case of lottery managers' operating licences only, all licensees must have procedures in place designed to ensure that funds belonging to a society or local authority whose lotteries they manage in reliance on this licence are accounted for to them in a timely manner.

6: Gambling Act 2005: Additional Material

12 Betting intermediaries

All non-remote betting intermediary operating licences

Licensees must not lay bets on their own behalf when operating in their capacity as a public tic-tac on a track.

Tic-tacs must act only in relation to bets between holders of general betting operating licences (whether acting as principal or agent or through their authorised employees).

13 Pool betting

All pool betting operating licences except those restricted to football pools

Licensees must inform the Commission, within 14 days, in writing, of any person they authorise under section 93(2) of the Act to offer pool betting on a track in connection with a horserace or dog race in reliance on an occasional use notice. In doing so, they must include the terms and conditions under which this has been agreed, and provide contact details of the management and key staff of those that are authorised.

Licensees and any person they so authorise must produce and retain a record of the transactions relevant to each pool that they offer. The record must be capable of identifying individual bets into the pool and relating these to subsequent payment of winnings where applicable. Licensees must make this information available to the Commission on request.

All pool betting operating licences which authorise football pools

Licensees must inform the Commission, within 14 days, in writing, of any person they authorise under Section 93(3) of the Act in respect of football pool betting. In doing so, they must include the terms and conditions under which this has been agreed.

Licensees and any person they so authorise must produce and retain a record of the transactions relevant to each pool that they offer. The record must be capable of identifying individual bets into the pool and relating these to the subsequent payment of winnings where applicable. Licensees must make this information available to the Commission on request.

All pool betting operating licences

Licensees must produce annual accounts which should be certified by a qualified independent accountant. Licensees must make copies available to the Commission.

14 Access to premises

All operating licences

Licensees must have and put into effect policies and procedures (including staff training programmes) designed to ensure that their staff co-operate with the Commission's enforcement officers in the proper performance of their compliance functions and are made aware of those officers' rights of entry to premises contained in Part 15 of the Act.

15 Information requirements

15.1 Reporting suspicion of offences etc

All operating licences except betting, betting intermediary, ancillary remote betting and remote betting intermediary (trading rooms only) licences

Licensees must provide the Commission with any information that they know relates to or suspect may relate to the commission of an offence under the Act, including an offence resulting from a breach of a licence condition or a code provision having the effect of a licence condition.

All betting operating licences, including betting intermediary, ancillary remote betting and remote betting intermediary (trading rooms only) licences

Licensees must provide the Commission with any information that they:

- know relates to or suspect may relate to the commission of an offence under the Act, including an offence resulting from a breach of a licence condition or a code provision having the effect of a licence condition
- suspect may lead the Commission to consider making an order to void a bet.

Licensees who accept bets, or facilitate the making or acceptance of bets between others, on the outcome of horse races or other sporting events governed by one of the sport governing bodies for the time being included in Part 3 of Schedule 6 to the Act must also provide the relevant sport governing body with sufficient information to conduct an effective investigation if the licensee suspects that information in their possession may:

- lead the Commission to consider making an order to void a bet
- relate to a breach of a rule on betting applied by that sport governing body.

15.2 Reporting 'Key Events'

All operating licences, except ancillary remote licences

A key event is an event that could have a significant impact on the nature or structure of a licensee's business. Licensees must notify the Commission of the occurrence of any of the following key events as soon as reasonably practicable and in any event within five working days of the licensee becoming aware of the event's occurrence[2].

- in the case of licensees which are companies, a petition being presented for their winding up or the winding up of any group company of theirs, or they or any group company being placed in administration or receivership: in this condition a 'group company' is any subsidiary or holding company of the licensee – as those terms are defined in section 1159 of the Companies Act 2006 or any statutory modification or re-enactment thereof – and any subsidiary of such holding company
- in the case of a licensee who is an individual (or a partner in a partnership licensee) their being presented with a petition for their bankruptcy or sequestration or their entering into an individual voluntary agreement
- where the licensee is required to have their accounts independently audited, any unplanned change of auditor including a change prompted by a dispute or resulting from auditors being unable or unwilling to sign an unqualified audit report
- the departure from the licensee's business of any person occupying a 'qualifying position' as defined by Regulation 2(2) of the Gambling Act 2005 (Definition of Small-scale Operator) Regulations 2006
- any breach of a covenant given to a bank or other lender
- any default in making repayment of the whole or any part of a loan on its due date
- any court judgments remaining unpaid 14 days after the date of judgment
- the commencement of any material litigation against the licensee
- the imposition of a disciplinary sanction, including dismissal, against the holder of a personal licence or a person occupying a qualifying position for gross misconduct; or the resignation of a personal licence holder or person occupying a qualifying position following commencement of disciplinary proceedings in respect of gross misconduct against that person
- in the case of remote gambling, the commencement or cessation of trading on website domains (including WAP URLs) or broadcast media through which the licensee provides gambling facilities.

[2] Key events can be reported securely online at the Commission's website at www.gamblingcommission.gov.uk or by email to key.events@gamblingcommission.gov.uk or posted to Key

Events, Compliance Administration Team, Gambling Commission, Victoria Square House, Victoria Square, Birmingham B2 4BP

15.3 General and Regulatory Returns

All operating licences

On request, licensees must provide the Commission with such information as the Commission may require about the use made of facilities provided in accordance with this licence, and the manner in which gambling authorised by this licence and the licensee's business in relation to that gambling are carried on, including in particular information about:

- the numbers of people making use of the facilities and the frequency of such use
- the range of gambling activities provided by the licensee and the numbers of staff employed in connection with them
- the licensee's policies in relation to, and experiences of, problem gambling.

In particular within 28 days of the end of each quarterly period or, for those only submitting annual returns, within 42 days of the end of each annual period, licensees must submit a Regulatory Return to the Commission containing such information as the Commission may from time to time require[3].

[3] Regulatory returns can be submitted securely online at the Commission's website at www.gamblingcommission.gov.uk For operators unable to access this system, the forms and a guide to completing them can be requested from the Commission and returned by email to Regulatory.Returns@gamblingcommission.gov.uk or by post to Regulatory Returns, Compliance Administration Team, Gambling Commission, Victoria Square House, Victoria Square, Birmingham, B2 4BP

16 Primary gambling activity

Non-remote bingo operating licences, except where bingo is offered under a 2005 Act casino premises licence

Gaming machines may be made available for use in licensed bingo premises only on those days when sufficient facilities for playing bingo are also available for use.

In cases where bingo is exclusively offered by means of electronic bingo terminals or bingo machines, there must be more individual player positions made available for bingo than there are gaming machines made available for use.

Non-remote existing casino operating licences, except 2005 Act casino operating licences

Gaming machines may be made available for use in licensed casino premises only on those days when sufficient facilities for playing casino games and/or games of equal chance are also available for use.

When a casino exclusively offers fully automated casino games, there must be more individual player positions made available for these games than there are gaming machines made available for use.

Non-remote general betting licences, except where betting is offered under a 2005 Act casino premises licence

Gaming machines may be made available for use in licensed betting premises only at times when there are also sufficient facilities for betting available.

Such facilities for betting must include the provision of information that enables the customer to access details of the events on which bets can be made and to be able to place those bets, obtain details of the outcome of the events, calculate the outcome of their bets and be paid or credited with any winnings.

Where licensees provide facilities for betting only by means betting machines (machines which are designed or adapted for the purpose of making or accepting bets on future real events) the licensee must ensure that the number of betting machines is greater than the number of gaming machines which are made available for use in reliance on the premises licence.

SUITE OF GENERAL CONDITIONS TO BE ATTACHED TO PERSONAL LICENCES UNDER SECTION 75 OF THE GAMBLING ACT 2005

1 Personal licence holders must take all reasonable steps to ensure that the way in which they carry out their responsibilities in relation to licensed activities does not place the holder of the operating or any relevant premises licence in breach of their licence conditions.

2 Personal licence holders must keep themselves informed of developments in gambling legislation, codes of practice and any Commission guidance (whether issued on the Commission website or communicated direct to licence holders) relevant to their role. Holders of personal functional licences must keep their technical competence in respect of their licensed activities up to date.

3 Personal licence holders must notify the Commission of the occurrence of any of the following key events within five working days, or as soon as reasonably practicable after the licensee becomes aware of the event's occurrence[4]:

- the imposition of a disciplinary sanction against them, including dismissal, for gross misconduct
- their resignation from a position for which a personal licence is required following commencement of disciplinary proceedings in respect of gross misconduct
- their disqualification from acting as a company director
- the entry of any court judgment against them
- the presentation of a petition for their bankruptcy or sequestration or their entering into an individual voluntary agreement
- their conviction for any criminal offence or receipt of a formal police caution or any other out-of-court disposal
- the imposition of any sanction or penalty against them following an investigation by any professional, statutory, regulatory or government body
- a change in their name or address.

---

4 Key events can be reported securely online at the Commission's website at www.gamblingcommission.gov.uk or by email to key.events@gamblingcommission.gov.uk or posted to Key Events, Compliance Administration Team, Gambling Commission, Victoria Square House, Victoria Square, Birmingham, B2 4BP

PART II: CODES OF PRACTICE

INTRODUCTION

These are the Commission's principal codes of practice, issued under section 24 of the Gambling Act 2005. These codes will come into effect on 1 January 2009. There are two types of provisions in this document:

- social responsibility code provisions: compliance with these is a condition of licences; therefore any breach of them by an operator may lead the Commission to review the operator's licence with a view to suspension, revocation or the imposition of a financial penalty and would also expose the operator to the risk of prosecution; these provisions are in shaded boxes in this section
- ordinary code provisions: these do not have the status of licence conditions, but are admissible in evidence in criminal or civil proceedings and must be taken into account in any case in which the court or tribunal think them relevant and by the Commission in the exercise of its functions; any breach of ordinary code provisions by an operator may be taken into account by the Commission on a

licence review, but cannot lead to imposition of a financial penalty; these code provisions are in the unshaded parts of this section and generally set out good practice in these areas.

CODE PROVISIONS

1 Financial requirements

All remote and non-remote casino licences

Ordinary code provision

In order to help prevent activities related to money laundering and terrorist financing, licensees should act in accordance with the Commission's guidance on anti-money laundering, *The Prevention of Money Laundering and Combating the Financing of Terrorism - Guidance for remote and non-remote casinos.*

All remote and non-remote betting licences, except those restricted to football pools only and except remote betting intermediary (trading rooms only) licences

Ordinary code provision

As part of their procedures for compliance with the requirements in respect of the prevention and detection of money laundering in the Proceeds of Crime Act 2002 and the Terrorism Act 2000, licensees should:

- unless there is a specific reason not to do so, appoint one or more nominated officers whose duty it is to take overall responsibility for the anti-money laundering procedures within the operation, in particular with respect to Suspicious Activity Reporting; and ensure, through appropriate training and guidance, that all staff who handle money or accounts or accept bets are aware of their duties under anti-money laundering legislation to report all suspicious activity to the nominated officer in a timely manner or, where there is no such nominated officer, directly and promptly to the police. It is the nominated officer's duty to consider such reports and to forward them where appropriate to the Serious Organised Crime Agency
- adopt (or reflect in their procedures) the Association of British Bookmakers' guidelines.

All licences, except casino licences

Ordinary code provision

In order to help prevent activities related to money laundering licensees should take into account the Commission's advice on the Proceeds of Crime Act 2002, *Duties and responsibilities under the Proceeds of Crime Act 2002. Advice for operators (excluding casino operators).*

2 *Protection of children and other vulnerable persons*

2.1 Combating problem gambling

All licences

Social responsibility code provision

Licensees must have and put into effect policies and procedures intended to promote socially responsible gambling.

Licensees' policies and procedures for socially responsible gambling must include but need not be confined to:

- the specific policies and procedures required by the following provisions of section 2 of this code
- a commitment to and how they will contribute to research into the prevention and treatment of problem gambling
- a commitment to and how they will contribute to public education on the risks of gambling and how to gamble safely
- a commitment to and how they will contribute to the identification and treatment of problem gamblers.

2.2 Access to gambling by children and young persons

All non-remote casino licences

Social responsibility code provision

Licensees must have and put into effect policies and procedures designed to prevent underage gambling, and monitor the effectiveness of these.

Licensees must designate one or more supervisors for each casino entrance.

A supervisor's responsibilities include ensuring compliance with this section of the code.

A supervisor must implement the following procedures:

- checking the age of customers who appear to be, or are suspected of being, underage
- refusing entry to anyone unable to produce an acceptable form of identification, ie one which:
  - contains a photograph from which the individual can be identified
  - states the individual's date of birth
  - is valid
  - is legible and shows no signs of tampering or reproduction
- taking action when there are unlawful attempts to enter the premises, including removing anyone who appears to be underage who tries to access gambling facilities and cannot produce an acceptable form of identification.

Licensees must not deliberately provide facilities for gambling in such a way as to appeal particularly to children or young people, for example by reflecting or being associated with youth culture.

In premises restricted to adults, service must be refused in any circumstances where any adult is accompanied by a child or young person.
Licensees must take all reasonable steps to ensure that all staff understand their responsibilities for preventing underage gambling. This should include appropriate training which must cover the legal requirements on returning stakes and not paying prizes to underage customers.

All non-remote casino licences

Ordinary code provision

There should be a sufficient number of supervisors at casino entrances to enable a considered judgement to be made about the age of everyone attempting to enter the casino and to take the appropriate action (for example checking identification) whilst at the same time not allowing others to enter unsupervised. The nature of this task means that it cannot be properly accomplished only by using CCTV; it will require a physical presence. Heavily used entrances may require more than one designated supervisor.
Supervisors may be assisted by other door keepers provided the supervisor retains the responsibility for compliance with this section of the code and deals personally with any case where there is any doubt or dispute as to someone's eligibility to enter.
The Commission considers acceptable forms of identification to include: any identification carrying the PASS logo (for example Citizencard or Validate); a driving licence (including provisional licence) with photocard; or a passport.
Licensees should put into effect procedures that require their staff to check the age of any customer who appears to them to be under 21.
Licensees should consider permanent exclusion from premises of any adult accompanied by a child or young person on more than one occasion to premises restricted to adults, or if there is reason to believe the offence was committed knowingly or recklessly.
Procedures should be put into effect for dealing with cases where a child or young person repeatedly attempts to gamble on premises restricted to adults, including oral warnings, reporting the offence to the Gambling Commission and the police, and making available information on problem gambling.

All adult gaming centre licences

Social responsibility code provision

Licensees must have and put into effect policies and procedures designed to prevent underage gambling, and monitor the effectiveness of these.
This must include procedures for:

- checking the age of apparently underage customers
- removing anyone who appears to be under age who tries to access the gambling facilities and cannot produce an acceptable form of identification
- taking action when there are attempts by under-18s to enter the premises.

Licensees must not deliberately provide facilities for gambling in such a way as to appeal particularly to children or young people, for example by reflecting or being associated with youth culture.
In premises restricted to adults, service must be refused in any circumstances where any adult is accompanied by a child or young person.

Licensees must take all reasonable steps to ensure that all staff understand their responsibilities for preventing underage gambling. This must include appropriate training which must cover the legal requirements on returning stakes and not paying prizes to underage customers.

Licensees must only accept identification which:

- contains a photograph from which the individual can be identified
- states the individual's date of birth
- is valid
- is legible and has no visible signs of tampering or reproduction.

All adult gaming centre licences

Ordinary code provision

The Commission considers acceptable forms of identification to include any identification carrying the PASS logo (for example Citizencard or Validate); a driving licence (including a provisional licence) with photocard; or a passport.

Licensees should put into effect procedures that require their staff to check the age of any customer who appears to them to be under 21.

Licensees should consider permanent exclusion from premises for any adult accompanied by a child or young person on more than one occasion to premises restricted to adults, or if there is reason to believe the offence was committed knowingly or recklessly.

Procedures should be put into effect for dealing with cases where a child or young person repeatedly attempts to gamble on premises restricted to adults, including oral warnings, reporting the offence to the Gambling Commission and the police, and making available information on problem gambling.

All non-remote bingo and family entertainment centre licences

Social responsibility code provision

Licensees must have and put into effect policies and procedures designed to prevent underage gambling, and monitor the effectiveness of these.

This must include procedures for:

- checking the age of apparently underage customers
- refusing entry to any adult-only areas to anyone unable to produce an acceptable form of identification
- taking action when there are unlawful attempts to enter the adult-only areas.

Licensees must not permit children or young people to gamble in the adults-only areas of premises to which they have access. If there is a 'no under-18s' premises policy, licensees must pay particular attention to the procedures they use at the entrance to the premises to check customers' ages.

Licensees must take all reasonable steps to ensure that all staff understand their responsibilities for preventing underage gambling, returning stakes and not paying prizes to underage customers and particularly for challenging any adult who may be complicit in allowing a child or young person to gamble.

Licensees must only accept identification which:

- contains a photograph from which the individual can be identified
- states the individual's date of birth
- is valid

6: Gambling Act 2005: Additional Material

- is legible and has no visible signs of tampering or reproduction.

All non-remote bingo and family entertainment centre licences

Ordinary code provision

The Commission considers acceptable forms of identification to include: any identification carrying the PASS logo (for example Citizencard or Validate); a driving licence (including a provisional licence) with photocard; or a passport.

Licensees should require a person who appears to relevant staff to be under the age of 21 to be asked to produce proof of age, either at the point of entry to the gambling area or as soon as it comes to the attention of staff that they wish to access gambling facilities.

Licensees should have procedures for dealing with cases where an adult knowingly or recklessly allows a child or young person to gamble. These procedures might include refusing to allow the adult to continue to gamble, removing them from the premises, and reporting the incident to the police or local authorities, or taking action where forged identification is produced.

Procedures should be put into effect for dealing with cases where a child or young person repeatedly attempts to gamble on their premises, including oral warnings, reporting the offence to the Gambling Commission and the police, and making available information on problem gambling to the child or young person concerned.

Where it is likely that customers' young or otherwise vulnerable children will be left unattended on or adjacent to their premises, licensees should consider reminding customers of their parental responsibilities and assess whether there is a need to develop procedures for minimising the risk to such children.

All non-remote betting and remote betting intermediary (trading rooms only) licences

Social responsibility code provision

Licensees must have and put into effect policies and procedures designed to prevent underage gambling, and monitor the effectiveness of these.

This must include procedures for:

- checking the age of apparently underage customers
- removing from adult-only licensed premises anyone who appears to be underage who tries to access the gambling facilities and cannot produce an acceptable form of identification
- taking action when there are attempts by under-18s to enter adult-only premises
- refusing entry to any adult-only area of a track to anyone unable to produce an acceptable form of identification
- taking action when there are unlawful attempts to enter the adult-only areas.

Licensees must not deliberately provide facilities for gambling in such a way as to appeal particularly to children or, except in the case of football pools, young people, for example by reflecting or being associated with youth culture.

In premises restricted to adults, service must be refused in any circumstances where any adult is accompanied by a child or young person.

Licensees must take all reasonable steps to ensure that all staff understand their responsibilities for preventing underage gambling. This must include appropriate training which must cover the legal requirements on returning stakes and not paying prizes to underage customers.

Licensees must only accept identification which:

- contains a photograph from which the individual can be identified
- states the individual's date of birth
- is valid
- is legible and has no visible signs of tampering or reproduction.

In the case of non-remote pool betting licensees, where pool entries or payments are collected door to door by the licensee or the licensee's authorised agent the licensee's procedures must include procedures for:

- checking the age of apparently underage entrants to the pool; and
- taking action when there are unlawful attempts to enter the pool.

All non-remote betting and remote betting intermediary (trading rooms only) licences

Ordinary code provision

The Commission considers acceptable forms of identification to include any identification carrying the PASS logo (for example Citizencard or Validate); a driving licence (including a provisional licence) with photocard; or a passport.

Licensees should put into effect procedures that require their staff to check the age of any customer who appears to them to be under 21.

Licensees should consider permanent exclusion from premises for any adult accompanied by a child or young person on more than one occasion to premises restricted to adults, or if there is reason to believe the offence was committed knowingly or recklessly.

Procedures should be put into effect for dealing with cases where a child or young person repeatedly attempts to gamble on premises restricted to adults, including oral warnings, reporting the offence to the Gambling Commission and the police, and making available information on problem gambling.

All non-remote lottery licences

Social responsibility code provision

Licensees must have and put into effect policies and procedures designed to minimise the risk of lottery tickets being sold to children (that is, persons under 16). This must include procedures for:

- checking the age of apparently underage purchasers of lottery tickets
- taking action when there are unlawful attempts to purchase tickets.

Licensees must take all reasonable steps to ensure that all those engaged in the promotion of lotteries in reliance on the licence understand their responsibilities for preventing underage gambling, returning stakes and not paying prizes to underage customers.

All non-remote lottery licences

Ordinary code provision

Licensees should require a person who appears to be under the age of 16 to be asked to produce proof of identity and age before purchasing a lottery ticket.

All remote licences (including ancillary remote betting licences), except gaming machine technical, gambling software, ancillary remote casino, ancillary remote bingo and remote betting intermediary (trading rooms only) licences

Social responsibility code provision

Licensees must have and put into effect policies and procedures designed to prevent underage gambling, and monitor the effectiveness of these.

Such procedures must include:

(a) warning potential customers that underage gambling is an offence;

(b) requiring customers to affirm that they are of legal age;

(c) regularly reviewing their age verification systems and implementing all reasonable improvements that may be made as technology advances and as information improves;

(d) ensuring that relevant staff are properly trained in the use of their age verification procedures; in particular customer services staff must be appropriately trained in the use of secondary forms of identification when initial verification procedures fail to prove that an individual is of legal age;

(e) enabling their gambling websites to permit filtering software to be used by adults (such as parents or within schools) in order to restrict access to relevant pages of those sites;

(f) in the case of any UK resident customer who deposits money using any type of payment method other than a credit card, and unless the licensee has established that a third party has satisfactorily carried out age verification, the following age verification procedures:

  (i) verifying additional information about the customer, such as carrying out searches of credit reference and other databases that list names and addresses of individuals over the age of 18;

  (ii) carrying out secondary age verification checks in any circumstances which give the operator reason to suspect that the person may be underage;

  (iii) not permitting the customer to withdraw any winnings from their account until age verification has been satisfactorily completed; and

  (iv) in any event, a requirement that if age verification has not been satisfactorily completed within 72 hours of the customer applying to register to gamble and depositing money:

  - the account will be frozen
  - no further gambling will be permitted until age verification has been successfully completed
  - if on completion of age verification the customer is shown to be underage, the operator must return to the customer any money paid in respect of the use of the gambling facilities, but no winnings shall be paid.

(g) in the case of any non-UK resident customer who deposits money using any type of payment method other than a credit card, and unless the licensee has established that a third party has satisfactorily carried out age verification, the following age verification procedures:

  (i) taking all reasonable steps to make use of information available for age verification purposes from whichever country the potential customer is resident in; and

(ii) each of the following steps, unless they can not reasonably be implemented or, in the case of the fourth bullet point, a period of more than 72 hours was reasonably required:
- verifying additional information about the customer, such as carrying out searches of credit reference and other databases that list names and addresses of individuals over the age of 18
- carrying out secondary age verification checks in any circumstances which give the operator reason to suspect that the person may be underage
- not permitting the customer to withdraw any winnings from their account until age verification has been satisfactorily completed
- a requirement that if age verification has not been satisfactorily completed within 72 hours of the customer applying to register to gamble and depositing money:
  - the account will be frozen;
  - no further gambling will be permitted until age verification has been successfully completed; and
  - if on completion of age verification the customer is shown to be underage all deposits held by the operator are returned to the customer and no winnings paid.

(h) in the case of any customer who registers to gamble and deposits money using a credit card, conducting a programme of random checks of credit card users for compliance with age restrictions.

All remote licences (including ancillary remote betting licences), except gaming machine technical, gambling software, ancillary remote bingo, ancillary remote casino and remote betting intermediary (trading rooms only) licences

Ordinary code provision
Licensees should, and should request their contracted partners to, draw attention to parental responsibility as part of the purchasing process of facilities such as mobile phones and interactive television.

2.3 Information on how to gamble responsibly and help for problem gamblers

All licences except gaming machine technical, gambling software, ancillary remote bingo and ancillary remote casino licences

Social responsibility code provision

Licensees must make information readily available to their customers on how to gamble responsibly and how to access information about, and help in respect of, problem gambling.
The information must cover:
- any measures provided by the licensee to help individuals monitor or control their gambling, such as restricting the duration of a gambling session or the amount of money they can spend

6: Gambling Act 2005: Additional Material

- timers or other forms of reminders or 'reality checks' where available
- self-exclusion options
- information about the availability of further help or advice.

The information must be directed to all customers whether or not licensees also make available material which is directed specifically at customers who may be 'problem gamblers'.

For gambling premises, information must be available in all areas where gambling facilities are provided and adjacent to ATMs where these are not located in a gambling area. As a minimum, information must be displayed prominently on posters appropriate to the size and layout of the premises and contained in leaflets that may be taken away. Licensees must take all reasonable steps to ensure that this information is also readily accessible in locations which enable the customer to obtain it discreetly.

All licences except gaming machine technical, gambling software, ancillary remote bingo and ancillary remote casino licences

Ordinary code provision

Licensees who market their services in one or more foreign languages should make available in that, or those, foreign languages:

- the information on how to gamble responsibly and access to help referred to above
- the players' guides to any game, bet or lottery required to be made available to customers under provisions in this code
- the summary of the contractual terms on which gambling is offered, which is required to be provided to customers as a condition of the licensee's operating licence.

2.4 CUSTOMER INTERACTION

All licenses except gaming machine technical and gambling software licences

Social responsibility code provision

Licensees must put into effect policies and procedures for customer interaction where they have concerns that a customer's behaviour may indicate problem gambling. The policies must include:

- identification of the appropriate level of management who may initiate customer interaction and the procedures for doing so
- the types of behaviour that will be logged/reported to the appropriate level of staff and which may trigger customer interaction at an appropriate moment
- the circumstances in which consideration should be given to refusing service to customers and/or barring them from the operator's gambling premises
- training for all staff on their respective responsibilities, in particular so that they know who is designated to deal with problem gambling issues.

But such policies and procedures must be consistent with, and implemented with due regard to, licensees' duties in respect of the health and safety of their staff.

2.5 Self-exclusion

All non-remote licences and remote betting intermediary (trading rooms only) licences, but not gaming machine technical and gambling software licences

Social responsibility code provision

Licensees must have and put into effect procedures for self-exclusion and take all reasonable steps to refuse service or to otherwise prevent an individual who has entered a self-exclusion agreement from participating in gambling.

Licensees must, as soon as practicable, take all reasonable steps to prevent any marketing material being sent to a self-excluded customer.

Licensees must take steps to remove the name and details of a self-excluded individual from any marketing databases used by the company or group (or otherwise flag that person as an individual to whom marketing material must not be sent), within two days of receiving the completed self-exclusion notification. This covers any marketing material relating to gambling, or other activities that take place on the premises where gambling may take place. However, it would not extend to blanket marketing which is targeted at a particular geographical area and where the excluded individual would not knowingly be included.

Licensees must close any customer accounts of an individual who has entered a self exclusion agreement and return any funds held in the customer account. It is not sufficient merely to prevent an individual from withdrawing funds from their customer account whilst still accepting wagers from them. Where the giving of credit is permitted, the licensee may retain details of the amount owed to them by the individual, although the account must not be active.

Licensees must put into effect procedures designed to ensure that an individual who has self-excluded cannot gain access to gambling. These procedures must include:

- a register of those excluded with appropriate records (name, address, other details, and any membership or account details that may be held by the operator)
- photo identification (where available and in particular where enforcement of the system may depend on photographic ID), and a signature
- staff training to ensure that staff are able to enforce the systems
- the removal of those persons found in the gambling area or attempting to gamble from the premises.

All non-remote licences and remote betting intermediary (trading rooms only) licences, but not gaming machine technical and gambling software licences

Ordinary code provision

Self-exclusion procedures should require individuals to take positive action in order to self-exclude. This can be a signature on a self-exclusion form.

Wherever practicable, individuals should be able to self-exclude without having to enter gambling premises.

Before an individual self-excludes, licensees should provide or make available sufficient information about what the consequences of self-exclusion are.

Licensees should take all reasonable steps to extend the self-exclusion to premises of the same type owned by the operator in the customer's local area. In setting the bounds of that area licensees may take into account the customer's address (if known to them), anything else known to them about the distance the customer ordinarily travels to gamble and any specific request the customer may make.

Licensees should encourage the customer to consider extending their self exclusion to other licensees' gambling premises in the customer's local area.

Customers should be given the opportunity to discuss self-exclusion in private, where possible.

Licensees should take steps to ensure that:

- the self-exclusion period is a minimum of six months and give customers the option of extending this to a total of at least five years
- a customer who has decided to enter a self-exclusion agreement is given the opportunity to do so immediately without any cooling-off period. However, if the customer wishes to consider the self-exclusion further (for example to discuss with problem gambling groups) the customer may return at a later date to enter into self-exclusion
- at the end of the period chosen by the customer (and at least six months later), the self-exclusion remains in place, unless the customer takes positive action in order to gamble again. No marketing material should be sent to the individual unless the individual has taken positive action in order to gamble again, and has agreed to accept such material
- where a customer chooses not to renew the self-exclusion, and makes a positive request to begin gambling again, the customer is given one day to cool off before being allowed access to gambling facilities. The contact must be made via telephone or in person.

The licensee should retain the records relating to a self-exclusion agreement at least until the agreement has been formally ended.

(Please note that the Commission does not require the licensee to carry out any particular assessment or make any judgement as to whether the previously self-excluded individual should again be permitted access to gambling. The requirement to take positive action in person or over the phone is purely to a) check that the customer has considered the decision to access gambling again and allow them to consider the implications; and b) implement the one day cooling-off period and explain why this has been put in place.)

All remote licences (including ancillary remote betting licences), except gaming machine technical, gambling software, ancillary remote bingo, ancillary remote casino and remote betting intermediary (trading rooms only) licences

Social responsibility code provision

Licensees must have and put into effect procedures for self-exclusion and take all reasonable steps to refuse service or to otherwise prevent an individual who has entered a self-exclusion agreement from participating in gambling.

Licensees must, as soon as practicable, take all reasonable steps to prevent any marketing material being sent to a self-excluded customer.

Licensees must take steps to remove the name and details of a self-excluded individual from any marketing databases used by the company or group (or otherwise flag that person as an individual to whom marketing material must not be sent), within two days of receiving the completed self-exclusion notification. This covers any marketing material relating to gambling. However, it would not extend to blanket marketing which is targeted at a particular geographical area and where the excluded individual would not knowingly be included.

Licensees must close any customer accounts of an individual who has entered a self-exclusion agreement and return any funds held in the customer account. It is not sufficient merely to prevent an individual from withdrawing funds from their customer account whilst still accepting wagers from them. Where the giving of credit is permitted, the licensee may retain details of the amount owed to them by the individual, although the account must not be active.

Licensees must put into effect procedures designed to ensure that an individual who has self-excluded cannot gain access to gambling. These procedures must include:

- a register of those excluded with appropriate records (name, address, other details, and any membership or account details that may be held by the operator)
- a record of the card numbers to be excluded
- staff training to ensure that staff are able to enforce the systems
- the removal of access from those persons found to have gambled or who have attempted to gamble on the facilities.

All remote licences (including ancillary remote betting licences), except gaming machine technical, gambling software, ancillary remote bingo, ancillary remote casino and remote betting intermediary (trading rooms only) licences

Ordinary code provision

Self-exclusion procedures should require individuals to take positive action in order to self-exclude:

- over the **internet**; this can be a box that must be ticked in order to indicate that they understand the system
- by **telephone**; this can be a direct question asking whether they understand the system.

Before an individual self-excludes, licensees should provide or make available sufficient information about what the consequences of self-exclusion are.

Licensees should encourage the customer to consider extending their self exclusion to other remote gambling operators currently used by the customer.

Customers should be given the opportunity to self-exclude by contacting customer services and in addition, where technically possible, by entering an automated process using remote communication. In order to avoid inadvertent self-exclusion it is acceptable for an automated process to include an additional step that requires the customer to confirm that they wish to self-exclude. The licensee should ensure that all staff who are involved in direct customer service are aware of the self-exclusion system in place, and are able to direct that individual to an immediate point of contact with whom/which to complete that process.

Within the licensee's information about self-exclusion policies, the licensee should provide a statement to explain that software is available to prevent an individual computer from accessing gambling internet sites. The licensee should provide a link to a site where further information is available.

Licensees should take all reasonable steps to ensure that:

- the self-exclusion period is a minimum of six months and give customers the option of extending this to a total of at least five years
- a customer who has decided to enter a self-exclusion agreement is given the opportunity to do so immediately without any cooling-off period. However, if the customer wishes to consider the self-exclusion further (for example to discuss with problem gambling groups) the customer may return at a later date to enter into self-exclusion
- at the end of the period chosen by the customer (and at least six months later), the self-exclusion remains in place, unless the customer takes positive action in order to gamble again. No marketing material should be sent to the individual unless the individual has taken positive action in order to gamble again, and has agreed to accept such material
- where a customer chooses not to renew the self-exclusion, and makes a positive request to begin gambling again, the customer is given one day to cool off before being allowed access to the gambling facilities. The contact must be made via telephone or in person; re-registering online is not sufficient.

The licensee should retain the records relating to a self-exclusion agreement at least until the agreement has been formally ended.

(Please note that the Commission does not require the licensee to carry out any particular assessment or make any judgement as to whether the previously self excluded individual should again be permitted access to gambling. The requirement to take positive action in person or over the phone is purely to a) check that the customer has considered the decision to access gambling again and allow them to consider the implications; and b) implement the one day cooling-off period and explain why this has been put in place.)

2.6 Employment of children and young persons

All lottery licences and pool betting licences restricted to football pools

Ordinary code provision

Licensees who employ young persons (16 and 17 year olds) to sell tickets, collect payments or pay out winnings should have and put into effect policies and procedures designed to ensure that all staff, including staff who are young persons themselves, are made aware that the law prohibits underage gambling, and that tickets may only be sold to persons aged 16 or over.

All non-remote bingo licences

Ordinary code provision

Licensees who employ children (under-16-year-olds) and young persons (those aged 16 or 17) should be aware that it is an offence:

(a) to employ them to provide facilities for playing bingo;
(b) for their contracts of employment to require them, or for them to be permitted, to perform a function in connection with a gaming machine; and

(c) to employ a child to perform any function on premises where, and at a time when, facilities are being provided for playing bingo.

As to b) it should be noted that in the Commission's view the relevant provision of the Act applies to any function performed in connection with a gaming machine. This includes servicing or cleaning such a machine.

Accordingly, licensees should have and put into effect policies and procedures designed to ensure that:

- children and young persons are never asked to perform tasks within a) or b) above
- all staff, including those who are children and young persons themselves, are instructed about the laws relating to access to gambling by children and young persons.

and should consider adopting a policy that:

- children are not employed to work on bingo licensed premises at any time when the premises are open for business
- neither children nor young persons are in any event asked to work in areas where gaming machines are situated.

All non-remote casino licences

Ordinary code provision

Licensees who employ children (under-16-year-olds) and young persons (those aged 16 and 17) should be aware that it is an offence:

(a) to employ them to provide facilities for gambling;

(b) if gaming machines are sited on the premises, for their contracts of employment to require them, or for them to be permitted, to perform a function in connection with a gaming machine at any time; and

(c) to employ them to carry out any other function on casino licensed premises while any gambling activity is being carried on in reliance on the premises licence (except that they can be employed on a part of regional casino premises when that part of the premises is not being used for the provision of facilities for gambling).

As to b) it should be noted that in the Commission's view the relevant provision of the Act applies to any function performed in connection with a gaming machine. This includes servicing or cleaning such a machine.

Accordingly, licensees should have and put into effect policies and procedures designed to ensure that:

- children and young persons are never asked to perform tasks within a) or b) above
- all staff, including those who are children or young persons themselves, are instructed about the laws relating to access to gambling by children and young persons

and should consider adopting a policy that:

- children and young persons are not employed to work on casino licensed premises (other than in an area of a regional casino where gambling does not take place) at any time when the premises are open for business
- gaming machines are turned off if children and young persons are working on the premises outside the hours when the premises are open for business.

All non-remote general, pool betting and remote betting intermediary (trading rooms only) licences

Ordinary code provision

Licensees who employ children (under-16-year-olds) and young persons (those aged 16 and 17) should be aware that it is an offence:

(a) to employ children to provide facilities for gambling in connection with football pools;

(b) otherwise to employ children and young persons to provide facilities for gambling;

(c) if gaming machines are sited on the premises, for their contracts of employment to require them, or for them to be permitted, to perform a function in connection with a gaming machine at any time; and

(d) to employ them to carry out any other function on betting licensed premises while any gambling activity is being carried on in reliance on the premises licence.

As to c) it should be noted that in the Commission's view the relevant provision of the Act applies to any function performed in connection with a gaming machine. This includes servicing or cleaning such a machine.

Accordingly, licensees should have and put into effect policies and procedures designed to ensure that:

- children are never asked to perform tasks within (a) above
- children and young persons are never asked to perform tasks within b) above
- all staff, including those who are children or young persons themselves, are instructed about the laws relating to access to gambling by children and young persons

and should consider adopting a policy that:

- children and young persons are not employed to work on betting licensed premises at any time when the premises are open for business
- gaming machines are turned off if children and young persons are working on the premises outside the hours when the premises are open for business.

All adult gaming centre licences

Ordinary code provision

Licensees who employ children (under-16-year-olds) and young persons (those aged 16 and 17) should be aware that it is an offence:

(a) to employ them to provide facilities for gambling;

(b) if gaming machines are sited on the premises, for their contracts of employment to require them, or for them to be permitted, to perform a function in connection with a gaming machine at any time; and

(c) to employ them to carry out any other function on adult gaming centre licensed premises while any gambling activity is being carried on in reliance on the premises licence;

As to b) it should be noted that in the Commission's view the relevant provision of the Act applies to any function performed in connection with a gaming machine. This includes servicing or cleaning such a machine.

Accordingly, licensees should have and put into effect policies and procedures designed to ensure that:

- children and young persons are never asked to perform tasks within a) or b) above
- all staff, including those who are children or young persons themselves, are instructed about the laws relating to access to gambling by children and young persons

and should consider adopting a policy that:

- children and young persons are not employed to work on adult gaming centre licensed premises at any time when the premises are open for business
- gaming machines are turned off if children and young persons are working on the premises outside the hours when the premises are open for business.

All family entertainment centre licences

Ordinary code provision

Licensees who employ children (under-16-year-olds) and young persons (those aged 16 and 17) should be aware that it is an offence:

(a) to employ them to provide facilities for gambling; and

(b) if gaming machines are sited on the premises, for their contracts of employment to require them, or for them to be permitted, to perform a function in connection with a gaming machine at any time.

As to b) it should be noted that in the Commission's view the relevant provision of the Act applies to any function performed in connection with a gaming machine. This includes servicing or cleaning such a machine.

Accordingly, licensees should have and put into effect policies and procedures designed to ensure that:

- children and young persons are never asked to perform tasks within a) or b) above
- all staff, including those who are children or young persons themselves, are instructed about the laws relating to access to gambling by children and young persons

and should consider adopting a policy that:

- children and young persons are not employed to carry out any work in an adult-only area of family entertainment licensed premises at a time when any gambling is taking place
- gaming machines sited in adult-only areas are turned off if children and young persons are working on the premises outside the hours when the premises are open for business.

All remote licences except remote lottery, remote pool betting, remote gaming machine technical, remote gambling software, ancillary remote bingo, ancillary remote casino and remote betting intermediary (trading rooms only) licences

Ordinary code provision

Licensees who employ children (under-16-year-olds) and young persons (those aged 16 and 17) should be aware that it is an offence to employ them to provide facilities for gambling.

All remote pool betting licences

Ordinary code provision

Licensees who employ children (under-16-year-olds) and young persons (those aged 16 and 17) should be aware that it is an offence:

(a) to employ children to provide facilities for gambling in connection with football pools; and

(b) otherwise to employ children and young persons to provide facilities for gambling.

2.7 Provision of credit by licensees and the use of credit cards

All non-remote general betting licences, except where betting is offered under a 2005 Act casino premises licence, pool betting, betting intermediary and lottery licences and all remote licences, except gaming machine technical, gambling software, ancillary remote casino, ancillary remote bingo and remote betting intermediary (trading rooms only) licences

Social responsibility code provision

Licensees who choose to accept credit cards must:

- accept payment by credit card for gambling only where that payment is made to a customer account

- make available for gambling, funds deposited via credit card only after the card issuer has approved the transaction.

All non-remote general betting licences, except where betting is offered under a 2005 Act casino premises licence, pool betting licences and all remote licences (including ancillary remote betting licences), except gaming machine technical, gambling software, ancillary remote casino, ancillary remote bingo and remote betting intermediary (trading rooms only) licences

Ordinary code provision
Licensees who choose to offer credit to members of the public who are not themselves gambling operators should also:

- have procedures for checking and scoring applications for credit from such customers, for setting, and for the increase of, credit limits
- explain these procedures to customers
- set a maximum credit limit for each customer and not permit customers to exceed that limit without further application
- apply a 24-hour delay between receiving a request for an increase in a credit limit and granting it in those cases where the limit exceeds that which the operator previously set
- not require a minimum spend within a set time period
- take all reasonable steps to ensure that offers of credit are not sent to vulnerable persons, including those who have self-excluded from gambling
- ensure that information about an offer of credit includes a risk warning of what may happen in the event of default.

2.8 MONEY LENDING BETWEEN CUSTOMERS

All non-remote casino licences

Ordinary code provision

Licensees should take steps to prevent systematic or organised money lending between customers on their premises.
While the nature of those steps will depend to some extent on the layout and size of the premises, they should cover matters such as:

- systems for monitoring for such activity
- instructions to staff concerning what they should do if they spot what they believe to be significant money lending and to managers about the ways in which they should handle and act on any such lending
- excluding from the premises, either temporarily or permanently as appropriate, any person whom the evidence suggests has become involved in organised or systematic money lending.

There should be appropriate arrangements in place to cover any cases where it appears that the lending may be commercial in nature or may involve money laundering. In the latter case, the requirements in respect of reporting suspicious transactions must be followed. In all cases where the operator encounters systematic or organised money lending, a report should be made to the Commission.

All non-remote bingo, general betting, adult gaming centre, family entertainment centre and remote betting intermediary (trading rooms only) licences

Ordinary code provision
Licensees should seek to prevent systematic or organised money lending between customers on their premises. As a minimum, they should have arrangements in place to ensure staff are requested to report any instances of substantial money lending when they become aware of them.

2.9 Identification of individual customers

All remote licences (including ancillary remote betting licences) except gaming machine technical, gambling software, ancillary remote bingo, ancillary remote casino and remote betting intermediary (trading rooms only) licences

Social responsibility code provision

Licensees must have and put into effect policies and procedures designed to identify separate accounts which are held by the same individual.

Where licensees allow customers to hold more than one account with them, the licensee must link all of a customer's such accounts to that customer and ensure that:

- if a customer opts to self-exclude from one account they are excluded from all accounts they hold with the licensee
- all of a customer's accounts are monitored and decisions that trigger customer interaction are based on the observed behaviour and transactions across all the accounts
- where credit is offered or allowed the maximum credit limit is applied on an aggregate basis across all accounts
- individual financial limits can be implemented across all of a customer's accounts.

All remote licences (including ancillary remote betting licences) except gaming machine technical, gambling software, ancillary remote bingo, ancillary remote casino and remote betting intermediary (trading rooms only) licences

Ordinary code provision

Where a licensee:

(i) is a company, the licensee should take all reasonable steps to comply with the above social responsibility code provision as if it also applied to accounts held in respect of gambling carried on in reliance on a remote operating licence held by any Group Company;

(ii) also holds a licence in another jurisdiction permitting it to provide facilities for remote gambling (a 'foreign licence') or is a company one or more of whose Group Companies holds one or more foreign licences, the licensee should take all reasonable steps to comply with the above social responsibility code provision as if it applied also to accounts held in respect of gambling carried on in reliance on a foreign licence held by the licensee or any Group Company.

A company is a Group Company in relation to a licensee if it is the holding company of, subsidiary of, or shares a common holding company with, the licensee. For these purposes 'holding company' and 'subsidiary' respectively have the meanings ascribed to them by section 1159 of the Companies Act 2006 or any statutory modification or re-enactment thereof.

3 'Fair and open' provisions

All licences except gaming machine technical and gambling software licences

Social responsibility code provision

Licensees must be able to provide evidence to the Commission, if required, showing how they satisfied themselves that their terms are not unfair.

All non-remote casino licences

Social responsibility code provision

In complying with any condition on a casino premises licence requiring the display of rules about gaming, licensees must ensure that the following are included:

- the rules of each type of casino game available to be played
- a player's guide to the house edge
- a player's guide to the rules of any equal chance games which are made available.

All non-remote bingo licences

Social responsibility code provision

In complying with any condition on a bingo premises licence or a 2005 Act large casino premises licence requiring the display of rules about gaming, licensees must ensure that the following are included:

- rules about each variant of bingo made available
- rules about any prize gaming made available.

All remote licences (including ancillary remote betting licences), except gaming machine technical, gambling software, ancillary remote bingo, ancillary remote casino and remote betting intermediary (trading rooms only) licences

Social responsibility code provision

Licensees must make the following available to customers:

- a player's guide to each gambling opportunity (bet, game or lottery) made available by the operator
- such additional information relating to the available gambling as the Commission shall from time to time publish to licensees: the current requirements are set out in an Annex to

the Commission's Technical Standards.

All remote licences (including ancillary remote betting licences), except gaming machine technical, gambling software, ancillary remote bingo, ancillary remote casino and remote betting intermediary (trading rooms only) licences

Ordinary code provision

Where practicable, the player's guide and additional information referred to in the social responsibility code should be made available through the medium in which the remote gambling is to be conducted. Where that is not practicable, licensees should either:

- send a copy of the guide and required additional information by post, fax or email or
- make these available to the customer in another medium to which he has access.

All non-remote casino licences

Social responsibility code provision

Licensees must have and put into effect policies and procedures designed to ensure that proper supervision of gaming at tables is carried out by supervisors, pit bosses and croupiers in order to ensure the integrity of the gaming is not compromised. Such policies and procedures must take into account, but need not be limited by, any mandatory premises licence conditions relating to the layout of premises.

All general betting and betting intermediary licences, except remote betting intermediary (trading rooms only) licences

Social responsibility code provision

Licensees must set out within the full rules that they make available, the core elements for the acceptance and settlement of bets. These rules must cover:

- the circumstances under which the operator will void a bet
- treatment of errors, late bets and related contingencies
- availability of odds for any ante-post, early show or starting price betting, and treatment of place, forecast bets etc
- treatment of withdrawals, non-runners, and reformed markets
- maximum payout limiting liability for a specific betting product or generally
- any charges made to customers for the use of betting services or products, and how these are calculated (including deductions from winnings for commission, or in respect of withdrawn horses etc)
- means or medium by which the outcome of an event will be determined
- the rules for the event itself to be specified (eg horserace bets only to be accepted where the racing is subject to Horseracing Regulatory Authority rules)
- where bets are accepted on 'pari-mutuel' terms
- any special arrangements for settling bets on 'coupled' horses.

Where special rules have been agreed in relation to a particular bet these must not be overridden by any conflicting rules or subsequent rule changes.

Licensees must issue a betting slip or an electronic acknowledgement (other than in the case of telephone betting) for each transaction which includes information as to the operator's name and contact details, and words equivalent to 'Bets are accepted in accordance with the operator's rules'.

All non-remote general betting licences

Social responsibility code provision

In their terms on which bets may be placed (required to be displayed in accordance with mandatory conditions attaching to their premises licences) licensees must give prominence to their rules concerning voiding, late bets and maximum payouts.

When providing facilities for betting on-course, licensees must display on their 'joints' in an intelligible format:

- any rules that differ from Tattersalls' 'Rules on Betting' or the British Greyhound Racing Board's 'Regulations for the conduct of on-course bookmaking' as applicable[5]
- any types of unorthodox bets accepted (such as forecast betting, betting without the favourite, distance betting etc)
- whether win-only or each way bets are accepted
- any concessions or bonuses offered
- all of the runners and the odds available to the public
- the operator's trading name and contact address
- the minimum bet accepted
- the maximum guaranteed liability.

Licensees operating within the ring at horserace tracks must issue customers with a betting slip or ticket for each transaction accepted. Betting slips or tickets must include the following information:

- operator's name and contact details
- race day name or code, date and race number
- name and/or number of the selection
- the stake and potential return
- the odds, or whether the bet will be settled according to the Starting Price
- the type of bet.

Any special rules which have been agreed in relation to a particular bet must not be overridden by any conflicting rules or subsequent rule changes.

[5] The references to Tattersalls' 'Rules on Betting' and the British Greyhound Racing Board's Regulations for the conduct of on-course bookmaking' reflect the current position and may need to be amended in future.

included in these codes of practice as if they were explicitly covered. Licensees should also follow any relevant industry code of practice on advertising.

However, the particular restriction on allowing people aged under 25 to appear in adverts need not be applied to point of sale advertising material, provided that the images used depict the sporting activity that may be gambled on and not the activity of gambling itself and do not offend any other aspect of the advertising codes.

All remote licences except gaming machine technical, gambling software and ancillary remote licences

Ordinary code provision

Licensees should ensure that the terms on which they contract with their affiliates (that is those who are given a right to advertise, or provide a hyper-link to, a licensee's gambling website) enable them to terminate the affiliate's rights promptly if, in the licensee's opinion, the affiliate is in breach of the advertising codes.

5 Complaints and disputes

All licences (including ancillary remote licences), except gaming machine technical and gambling software licences

Social responsibility code provision

Licensees must put into effect a written procedure for handling customer complaints and disputes.

In this code a 'complaint' means a complaint about any aspect of the licensee's conduct of the licensed activities, and a 'dispute' is any complaint which:

(a) is not resolved at the first stage of the complaints procedure; and

(b) relates to the outcome of the complainant's gambling transaction.

Licensees must ensure that:

- customers are told the name and status of the person to contact about their complaint
- customers are given a copy of the complaints procedure on request or on making a complaint
- all complaints are handled in accordance with the procedure.

Licensees must also ensure that they have arrangements in place for disputes to be referred to an independent third party. Customers whose disputes are not resolved to their satisfaction by use of the operator's complaints procedure may refer those disputes to this independent third party. The arrangements under which such complaints are referred may, but need not, provide for the third party's decision to be binding on the licensee and the customer.

Licensees must keep a record of all complaints that are not resolved at the first stage of the complaints procedure.

Licensees must arrange for a copy of the decision on, or a note of the outcome of, each dispute referred to the independent party to be provided to the Commission quarterly, either by the independent party or by the licensee.

6 Gambling licensees' staff

All non-remote casino licences

Social responsibility code provision

Licensees must have and put into effect policies and procedures to manage relationships between staff and customers, based on the principle that in carrying out their duties staff must not engage in any conduct which is, or could be, likely to prejudice the licensing objectives.

All licences including betting ancillary remote licences, but not other ancillary remote licences

Social responsibility code provision

Licensees must take all reasonable steps to ensure that staff involved in the provision of facilities for gambling are made aware of advice on socially responsible gambling and of where to get confidential advice should their gambling become hard to control.

7 Pool betting

All pool betting licences

Social responsibility code provision

Licensees or any person they authorise to offer pool betting on their behalf under authority of section 93 of the Act must publish their rules relevant to the following:

- the deduction levels for overheads, taxes, profits etc, expressed as a percentage, from each available pool
- the rounding of winning dividends to a whole unit
- the procedure for when there is no winner of the pool, and the circumstances in which the pool is carried over
- the period of time in which a winning bet may be claimed from the pool operator.

All non-remote pool betting licences authorised to offer pool betting on dog races

Social responsibility code provision

Licensees or any person they authorise to offer pool betting on their behalf under authority of section 93 of the Act, must only accept bets through equipment capable of communicating bets to a central recording system.

The equipment must supply the person placing the bet with a betting slip or ticket containing the following information:

- the date on which the bet is made
- the amount of the stake
- the identity of the track, the number or time of the race and the pool in respect of which the bet is made
- the selection or selections or combination of selections as indicated
- means of identifying the equipment recording the bet.

The central recording system must collect all bets made to each of the operator's pools and all information required to calculate the winnings of each pool and be capable of storing this information for subsequent retrieval if required by the Commission.

Licensees and any person they authorise to offer pool betting on their behalf under authority of section 93 of the Act must:

- provide a public display system within sight of all of the operator's terminals capable of accepting pool bets situated on-course. The system must display the potential dividend returns in respect of win and place outcomes from each pool operated, and in at least one place the units staked on all types of combination bets offered. This information is to be updated whilst the pool market is open. Following conclusion of the event to which the pool relates, the total amount payable as winning dividends must be displayed as soon as practicable
- display prominently the minimum stake that will be accepted as a bet.

8 Information requirements

All licences, except ancillary remote licences

Ordinary code provision

The Commission expects licensees to work with the Commission in an open and cooperative way and to inform the Commission of any matters that the Commission would reasonably need to be aware of in exercising its regulatory functions. These are matters that will have a material impact on the licensee's business or on the licensee's ability to conduct its business. Such matters, which should be notified to the Commission as soon as reasonably practicable[6], include the following:

- the departure from the licensee's business of any person named in the licence application, or that person's successor, who holds a personal management licence, but who does not occupy a 'qualifying position'
- any reduction in the number of staff employed by the licensee where that has a material impact on the licensee's business
- the acquisition or disposal by the licensee of gambling premises or pitches where that has a material impact on the size or nature of the licensee's business

- in the case of corporate licensees, the disposal or acquisition of any group company where that has a material impact on the licensee's ability to conduct its business
- any disposal of the licensee's assets where that has a material impact on the licensee's business
- any investigation by a professional, statutory, regulatory or government body into the licensee's activities, or the activities in relation to the licensed entity of a personal licence holder or a person occupying a qualifying position employed by them, where such an investigation could result in the imposition of a sanction or penalty which, if imposed, could reasonably be expected to raise doubts about the licensee's continued suitability to hold a Gambling Commission licence
- any instance of criminal activity, including repeated instances of small-scale theft or fraud, where that has a material impact on the licensee's business
- any major breach in the licensee's information security where that adversely affects the confidentiality of customer data or prevents customers from accessing their accounts for a substantial period of time
- any other matters that have a material impact on the licensee's business or on the licensee's ability to conduct its business.

---

[6] These matters can be reported securely online at the Commission's website at www.gamblingcommission.gov.uk or by email to key.events@gamblingcommission.gov.uk or posted to Key Events, Compliance Administration Team, Gambling Commission, Victoria Square House, Victoria Square, Birmingham, B2 4BP

9 Primary gambling activity

Non-remote general betting, bingo and casino operating licences, except where facilities are offered under a 2005 Act casino premises licence

Ordinary code provision

In order to demonstrate that the primary gambling activity for which an operating licence has been issued is being offered in each licensed premises, licensees should have regard to the following general factors:

- the ratio of the space available to customers allocated to the primary gambling activity, to that allocated to other gambling activities
- the extent to which the primary gambling activity is promoted on the premises and by way of external advertising compared to other gambling activities
- the use, either expected or actual, to be made of the different gambling facilities.

Licensees should also have regard to the following additional sector specific factors:

Non-remote bingo licences, except where bingo is offered under a 2005 Act casino premises licence

Ordinary code provision

- the frequency and extent that bingo is, or is intended to be played on the premises, compared with the periods when the premises are open
- whether there is:
  - capacity on the premises for the generation of main stage bingo numbers
  - a facility to sell tickets or cards for bingo games on the premises
  - bingo available to be played whenever sessions are advertised
  - display of prize board information
  - a means of stopping a game to claim a win.

Not all the indicators would need to be present in a particular case, nor do they preclude others, but the combination of those factors that are present should be sufficient to indicate that the activity is the primary one in any given premises.

Non-remote casino operating licences, except 2005 Act casino premises licences

Ordinary code provision

- the proportion of the gaming day for which live tables are, or will, be made available on demand.

Not all the indicators would need to be present in a particular case, nor do they preclude others, but the combination of those factors that are present should be sufficient to indicate that the activity is the primary one in any given premises.

Non-remote general betting licences, except where betting is offered under a 2005 Act casino premises licence

Ordinary code provision

- the range and frequency of events on which bets can be made.

Not all the indicators would need to be present in a particular case, nor do they preclude others, but the combination of those factors that are present should be sufficient to indicate that the activity is the primary one in any given premises.
Gambling Commission December 2011

LICENSING, COMPLIANCE AND ENFORCEMENT POLICY STATEMENT

6.2075 September 2009

1 INTRODUCTION

THE ROLE OF THE COMMISSION

1.1 The Gambling Commission (the Commission) regulates commercial gambling in Great Britain. The principal ways in which the Commission does this are by:

- licensing operators and key personnel
- setting appropriate licence conditions and codes of practice
- carrying out compliance activities
- enforcement and prosecution work
- providing advice.

THE LICENSING OBJECTIVES

1.2 The Gambling Act 2005 (the Act) sets out the licensing objectives, which are:

- preventing gambling from being a source of crime or disorder, being associated with crime or disorder or being used to support crime
- ensuring that gambling is conducted in a fair and open way
- protecting children and other vulnerable people from being harmed or exploited by gambling.

1.3 In carrying out its functions, the Commission is under a statutory duty to pursue and have regard to the licensing objectives. The Commission must also permit gambling, in so far as it thinks it reasonably consistent with pursuit of the licensing objectives.

STATEMENT OF PRINCIPLES FOR LICENSING AND REGULATION

1.4 The Commission is required to prepare, publish, and keep under review, a statement that sets out the principles which will govern the exercise of its functions, and, in particular, explains how those principles will assist the Commission in its pursuit of the licensing objectives. The statement of principles for licensing and regulation underpins all of the work of the Commission and can be found on the Commission's website at www.gamblingcommission.gov.uk.

PURPOSE OF THIS DOCUMENT

1.5 This document should be read in conjunction with Statement of principles for licensing and regulation, which it builds on by setting out the Gambling Commission's regulatory policies in relation to:

- assessing risk
- licensing operators and key personnel
- carrying out compliance activities
- enforcement.

OTHER POLICY DOCUMENTS

1.6 The Commission has also developed a number of further documents which build on the statement of principles for licensing and regulation and govern how it carries out its functions:

- Statement of principles for determining financial penalties
- Corporate governance framework
- Regulatory panel procedures.

These documents are available online at www.gamblingcommission.gov.uk.

2 ASSESSING RISK

2.1 The Commission's approach to risk underpins its licensing, compliance and enforcement functions. This chapter sets out the key elements of the Commission's risk methodology, including the processes for addressing and reviewing risk.

2.2 The Commission's risk methodology is applied in order to establish a regulatory risk rating for licence holders. This informs the level and nature of regulatory engagement by the Commission with those operators.

2.3 The methodology is based upon assessing the likelihood of risk presented by operators and the potential impact that the risk if realised will have upon the licensing objectives. The assessment of likelihood will relate to key regulatory risk groups within the operators control, whilst the assessment of impact will be related to the size and market scope of an operator's activity.

REGULATORY RISK GROUPS

2.4 The Commission has identified key regulatory risk groups – those related to the suitability of the licence holder, those which relate to the gambling facilities themselves, and finally those which relate to the manner in which the gambling facilities are provided. Each risk group will contain information elements to which an assessment will address itself.

2.5 The risks related to suitability of the licence holder include:

- staff and management integrity and competence
- controller[1] integrity
- business integrity:
  - — financial circumstances
  - — governance, structure and resource.

2.6 The risks related to the type of gambling facility offered include:

- gambling product or facility
- market scope.

2.7 The risks presented through the provision of gambling facilities include:

- location and operating environment
- consistency with the licensing objectives.

IDENTIFYING RISK

2.8 With any aspect of regulatory engagement (licensing, compliance and so on), an initial identification of the risk(s) presented will be made. For example, with a licence application the consideration will necessarily involve a wide range of risks. A compliance visit may involve a similar broad assessment or may relate to specific potential risks identified as a result of information received or previous operator engagement. The assessment of risk may focus upon any combination of the regulatory risk groups and the elements there within.

2.9 An example of risk related to employees or management integrity would be the risk posed by a personal management licence holder being convicted of a relevant criminal offence indicating dishonesty. An example of risk related to the provision of gambling facilities would be the manner in which a licensed operator might seek to comply with the requirements of the Act and the Commission's Licence Conditions and Codes of Practice (LCCP).

ASSESSING RISK

2.10 Having identified relevant risks, the next consideration is the likelihood of a risk or risks occurring (provided it has not already occurred) and the likely impact.

2.11 The Commission's focus will determine the risk categories and elements against which information will be sought. The elements assessed in respect of likelihood may include how compliant an operator is, or is likely to be, with the requirements of the Act, the LCCP and also organisational considerations such as accountability and governance, competence and integrity of staff, and effectiveness of policies and procedures in minimising risk to the licensing objectives.
2.12 A significant part of this relates to the assessment of suitability. The assessment of suitability is a key element of the Commission's licensing process and continues, after a licence has been granted, in the Commission's compliance processes[2].
2.13 The Commission will assess the likely impact of a risk based primarily on the size and market scope of an operator (actual or potential). This may include size of customer base, number of premises, turnover or gaming yield and extent of licensed activity. This latter consideration covers not only those operators which offer gambling across more than one sector but also those where the nature of a single licensed activity extends across multiple sectors. Gambling software development and gaming machine manufacture are examples of this where the potential market impact is high if the end product presents risk to the licensing objectives once it is made available.

ADDRESSING THE RISK

2.14 The impact and likelihood of a given risk (or risks) is then taken into account as part of an overall risk assessment rating. This will determine the degree and type of regulatory engagement that may be required, although impact will be the primary consideration in this determination. The Commission considers that some operators will always be higher impact because of the size and scale, or nature of their operations. Those who have extensive operations (in terms of impact) or a significant market share will always receive a greater degree of regulatory oversight due to the market impact (actual or potential) should regulatory risk materialise or be identified. This is why additional information may be required at the licensing application stage and also why the Commission has adopted a relationship management approach (through the National Compliance Managers) for certain licensed operators.
2.15 Once an assessment has been completed, the Commission will, as appropriate, share with the operator its considerations as to the level of risk considered to exist. This will provide the basis of the Commission's further engagement and operators should use the information to inform their risk controls. The Commission will, as appropriate, provide information about its assessments to operators. Assessments will not be shared with other operators or parties.
2.16 The approach will allow a focused approach to managing risk to the licensing objectives, and the Commission would expect this to facilitate a productive engagement and assist operators in developing effective risk management strategies. By building up a picture over time, the Commission would expect to be able to identify risk movements within individual operators and identify major issues within sectors or impact groups.
2.17 Those operators which demonstrate good governance and a high level of compliance at all levels are less likely to present a risk to the licensing objectives and will receive less regulatory oversight as a result, although this reduced oversight will be proportionate to their potential impact.

REVIEWING THE RISK

2.18 Once any regulatory action is completed, the risk is re-assessed to determine whether the desired outcome has been met in addressing the risk(s) or further attention is needed.

3 LICENSING

3.1 This chapter sets out the Commission's approach to considering operating and personal licence applications, the kinds of evidence considered when assessing an application, and the process for assessing applications and notifying the outcome.

WHO NEEDS A LICENCE?

3.2 Most providers of commercial gambling based in Great Britain require an operating licence. Further guidance as to the types of operation or activity that might be exempt from requiring an operating licence can be found on the Commission's website at www.gamblingcommission.gov.uk.

3.3 Personal licences are required by those performing a specified management or operational function. The Commission consulted on the definitions of those who needed personal licences and of small scale operators[3] (where personal licence holders are not required) in 2006. The definitions subsequently adopted are outlined in the Licence Conditions and Codes of Practice (LCCP), a copy of which can be obtained from the Commission's website.

3.4 Those seeking a licence are required to submit an application form with the prescribed fee and supporting documentation.

INFORMATION AND EVIDENCE

3.5 All applicants are required to supply the Commission with sufficient and complete information to support their application and in particular information that will enable an assessment on their suitability to be made. However, the Commission takes a risk based and proportionate approach to the amount and detail of information an applicant is required to provide. Guidance on the type of information required is included in the guidance notes that accompany the application form[4].

3.6 The Commission may also seek evidence or opinions from other sources where that is appropriate or where its initial review has highlighted areas of concern. The sources the Commission may access include, but are not restricted to:

- Criminal Records Bureau (CRB) and Disclosure Scotland
- Court records
- Company Watch
- Companies House
- Dun & Bradstreet
- Equifax
- Financial Services Authority
- HMRC
- The Insolvency Service
- The Solicitors Regulation Authority
- The Law Society of Scotland
- Serious Organised Crime Agency
- sports governing bodies
- open source internet searches
- other regulators
- overseas gambling regulators
- police forces in UK and abroad
- references provided to the Commission

3.7 If an application is incomplete or information required to support the application is missing or not provided upon request then it may be determined on the basis of the information the Commission has available to it. This may affect the decision on whether a licence can be granted.

ASSESSMENT AND DETERMINATION OF THE APPLICATION

3.8 Each application is considered on merit and on the evidence available. In considering an application the Commission has regard to the licensing objectives and whether they are likely to be compromised, and the suitability of an applicant to carry out the licensed activities.

3.9 In considering operating licence applications the Commission will include assessment of the suitability of those persons considered relevant to the application. Those persons considered relevant may vary depending on the information provided in the operating licence application and on company structure but are likely to exercise a function in connection with, or to have an interest in, the licensed activities. General guidance on who may be considered relevant is available on the Commission's website and in regulations[5].

SUITABILITY

3.10 When considering the suitability of an applicant the Commission has regard to the following elements and seeks evidence to support and enable an assessment to be made against each one:

- **Identity and ownership** – the identity of the applicant and or person(s) relevant to the application and in the case of an application for an operating licence, who ultimately owns a corporate applicant.
- **Finances** – financial and other circumstances of the applicant past and present and or person(s) relevant to the application. For operating licences this will include the resources likely to be available to carry out the licensed activities.
- **Integrity** – the honesty and trustworthiness of the applicant and or persons relevant to the application.
- **Competence** – The experience, expertise, qualifications and history of the applicant and or persons relevant to the application.
- **Criminality** – criminal record of the applicant and or person(s) relevant to the application.

UPHOLDING THE LICENSING OBJECTIVES

3.11 Applicants for an operating licence are asked about their policies for ensuring that the licensing objectives will be adhered to. Guidance is provided on the Commission's website and in the guidance notes that accompany the application form.

3.12 In assessing policies the Commission is looking for understanding of the legislation overall and evidence that arrangements will address the social responsibility requirements.

CONSIDERING APPLICATIONS

3.13 On considering an application for a licence the Commission is required to either: grant it; reject it; or, grant it in respect of one or more of the specified activities and reject it in respect of the others. In some circumstances the Commission may attach specific conditions to the licence, which may, for example, have the effect of restricting the activities that may be carried out in reliance of the licence.

3.14 The Commission evaluates the information it receives on each element of the assessment on a four point scale. The categories are as follows:

Inadequate

This indicates that an applicant poses a substantial risk to the licensing objectives; or there are significant concerns about an applicant's suitability; or there is a risk of significant non-compliance with the requirements of the Act and the Commission's LCCP.

Just adequate

This indicates that there is less risk to the licensing objectives; the applicant meets the minimum expectations regarding suitability; the applicant just meets the requirements of the Act and the Commission's LCCP.

Adequate

This indicates that the applicant is unlikely to pose a risk to the licensing objectives; the applicant appears to be suitable to carry on the licensed activities in question; the applicant appears likely to be able to meet the requirements of the Act and the Commission's LCCP.

Good

This indicates that the applicant is unlikely to pose a risk to the licensing objectives; the applicant has a proven track record of being able to carry on the licensed activities in question; the applicant has a proven track record of being able to meet the requirements of the Act and the Commission's LCCP.

3.15 The Commission will keep applicants up to date with the progress of their application. Where the initial assessment gives rise to any concerns or doubts, the Commission will, if it is possible to do so, seek to address those concerns or doubts with the applicant by requesting additional information or clarification. The one possible exception to this would be the criminal record of the applicant where the Act [6] allows for the refusal of an application if the applicant or a person relevant to the application has a conviction for a relevant offence[7].

IDENTITY AND OWNERSHIP

3.16 The Commission requires individuals to provide identification information, as recommended by the CRB, which is checked in accordance with their advice. The Commission will seek to follow up and resolve any inconsistencies, such as an indication on the CRB record that states aliases have been used by an applicant. The Commission also asks for current photographs of personal licence applicants and will check that these are consistent with any photographs on identity documents.

3.17 The Commission will check records about companies and directors' records to ensure that we are clear that the correct entity is being licensed and to check whether there are any other related companies in a group, or historically related or common Directors across a number of companies. If this is the case we may investigate related companies to understand the relationship.

3.18 The Commission will also want to ensure that it can establish who benefits from the gambling provided and therefore require that any shareholders with a 3% holding are listed and that those with over 10% holding complete an Annex A form to enable further checks to be carried out on them. If the beneficiary of any business is a Trust then the Commission will want to know who the beneficiaries of that Trust are.

3.19 If the applicant is a company based overseas or part of the company structure is based overseas then we would want a full description of the company structure and would satisfy ourselves that the overseas elements were either listed companies or that we knew of nothing untoward about them. We might carry out checks with overseas regulators.

FINANCES

3.20 For operating licence applications, the Commission will ask for accounts from existing businesses or financial projections where the applicant is a new business. Our main focus is on assessing the resources likely to be available to enable a licensee to carry on the licensed activities.

3.21 The Commission's approach is slightly different depending on whether an applicant is a new start up or an existing business. With new businesses we consider the overall viability of the business and may wish to make further enquiries if it appears that the resources available are inadequate or not properly secured. With existing businesses the Commission will consider the resources devoted to the gambling operation and the degree to which they could deliver the necessary arrangements for the provision to be compliant with the Act.

INTEGRITY

3.22 The Commission will consider whether the information it collects raises any concerns about integrity. This involves an assessment of an applicant's criminal record (further details of which appear below) or past involvement in civil or regulatory investigations or proceedings.

3.23 The Commission will consider the evidence and findings of complaints about the applicant and investigations by other regulators. The Commission will look into the applicant and other relevant persons to see if there has been a history of problems or business failure and will use open source checks to assist with that.

COMPETENCE

3.24 The Commission will take up references and may review the CVs of the applicant or other relevant persons to assess their work experience and the training they have received which demonstrates their competence to carry out the role required of them.

3.25 For individuals who are likely to fulfil key senior roles, the Commission will look for evidence that the individual has some demonstrable experience, where appropriate, of working in a regulated industry and, if an individual has had no gambling experience, that suitable training or briefing in gambling regulation is planned.

CRIMINALITY

3.26 The fact that an applicant has been convicted of a relevant offence will result in the criminality element of the assessment being marked inadequate. This does not mean that the application will automatically be refused. Each case will be considered on its individual facts and merits and consideration will be given to the seriousness, relevance and date of the conviction. The Commission may consider relevant offences which would otherwise be considered 'spent' under the Rehabilitation of Offenders Act 1974 when considering an application for a licence.[8] More information on the treatment of criminal convictions is set out below.

3.27 Once the assessment has been completed for each element of the application then an overall view is taken and marked on the same basis. The fact that one or more elements are 'just adequate' or less does not always mean that the licence will be refused. The overall evaluation is judged on a case by case basis having regard to the importance of the matters to which it relates and risk to the licensing objectives.

3.28 When considering the relevance of an offence the Commission will start from the basis that it will accept the information it receives regarding convictions from the Criminal Records Bureau or Disclosure Scotland or the Police as likely to be accurate. If there is any doubt about the accuracy of the information then it is the responsibility of the applicant to rectify the error with the reporting body. In any event, the Commission's processes are not a forum for running arguments which could have been put in a criminal appeal.

3.29 The fact that a person has been convicted of an offence will be considered as a contra-indicator of that person's suitability as it raises a question about the character and behaviour of the individual in question.

3.30 In evaluating the seriousness and relevance of an offence, the Commission's assessment will focus on whether the conviction has a potential bearing on suitability to hold a licence and will have regard to the public interest, which includes taking account of:

- the protection of the public
- the maintenance of public confidence
- the importance of upholding proper standards of conduct and competence by licensees.

3.31 Broadly, the Commission considers that the impact of a conviction on an applicant's suitability to hold a licence is likely to be a function of:

- the nature and seriousness of the offence
- the relevance of the offence in the context of the licensed activities.

3.32 In order to assess the nature and seriousness of the offence the Commission will take account of all the evidence and information available about the offence. This will involve consideration of the facts and circumstances of the offence, including the individual's explanation and any further information about the offence, for example through any Amplified Police Report (APR) and sentencing remarks made by a Court.

3.33 Consideration of the nature and seriousness of an offence includes consideration of:

- the seriousness of the offence, its legal definition, the relevant criminal behaviour, including the degree of dishonesty, intent or recklessness involved
- the sentence imposed
- whether there is repeat offending or a pattern of offending, including the time period over which the offending occurred and the age and experience of the applicant at the time
- evidence of rehabilitation or the lack of a capacity for rehabilitation
- harm or loss suffered by any victim(s) of the crime and the nature of any victim(s).

3.34 The assessment of relevance will include consideration of whether, if at all:

- the offence is a 'relevant offence' listed in Schedule 7 of the Act
- the behaviour which led to the conviction was not only criminal but was also inconsistent with the licensing objectives
- the relevance of the offence to the activities which the applicant would be permitted to carry out if granted a licence.

3.35 The Rehabilitation of Offenders Act provides that, after a prescribed period of time, certain convictions become 'spent'. This means that a person who was convicted of an offence is after that time 'rehabilitated' and is to be treated for all purposes in law as if he had never been charged with, convicted of or sentenced for the offence.

3.36 However, as indicated above, by virtue of section 125 of the Gambling Act 2005, the Rehabilitation of Offenders Act does not apply to any offence specified in Schedule 7 of the Gambling Act 2005 as a 'relevant offence'. Therefore applicants must disclose relevant offences even if they would normally be spent and the Commission may refuse a licence on the grounds that the applicant (or a person relevant to the application) has a conviction for a 'relevant offence'.

3.37 When deciding what weight is to be attached to a conviction for a 'relevant offence', the Commission will take into account the passage of time since the offence was committed, the applicants' explanations of the circumstances of the offences and any information or reports which are available relating to the conviction.

3.38 When considering the applicant's suitability to carry on the licensed activities, as required by section 70 of the Act, the Commission will also have regard to the applicant's unspent convictions. Again, the Commission will take into account the passage of time since the offences were committed and the applicant's explanations of the circumstances of the offences.

3.39 The Commission will disregard spent convictions that do not relate to 'relevant offences'.

COMMUNICATING THE FINAL DECISION

3.40 All applicants will be informed in writing of the decision on their application. Where the Commission is minded to make a decision to refuse the application, grant in part or to attach specific conditions to the licence the applicant will be given the opportunity to make representations before that decision is finalised. Details of these arrangements and subsequent appeals processes including appeals to the Gambling Appeal Tribunal are contained on the Commission's website.

3.41 If the applicant is successful then a licence will be issued either by email or in hard copy. For operating and personal licences relevant details of the licence will be published in the public register[9] on the Commission's website.

WHAT HAPPENS AFTER THE LICENCE HAS BEEN ISSUED?

3.42 Once a licence has been granted and issued, it is important that licensees read though it to check that the details on the licence are correct and that they are familiar with the conditions attached to the licence and the changes and matters that licensees must keep the Commission informed of whilst they are the holder of a licence[10].

3.43 The Act requires the holders of operating licences to pay an annual fee for their licence, in advance. The first annual fee is due within 30 days of the licence being issued. Subsequent payments will be required before the anniversary date, that is the date of issue of the licence[11]. The Commission will remind licensees about the need to pay their annual fee approximately six weeks before each fee is due. Failure to pay annual fees by the due date may lead to the revocation of a licence.

3.44 Holders of personal licences will be required to pay a fee every five years to maintain their licence.[12] Full details of the fee to be paid and any additional information the Commission may require will be requested at least six weeks before the fee is due. Failure to pay the fee will ultimately lead to the revocation of a licence.

4 COMPLIANCE

4.1 Once an operator or individual holds a licence, the Commission seeks to ensure, through its compliance work, that the licensee remains suitable to hold licences and that they conduct themselves in a way which is consistent with the licensing objectives, the requirements of the Act and the conditions of their licences and related codes of practice. This chapter of the document outlines the manner in which the Commission will carry out its compliance activities.

ADVICE AND ASSESSMENT

4.2 The Commission will undertake compliance activity in a variety of ways. The Commission will provide advice to licensees to help them comply with the requirements of the legislation and the licence conditions and codes of practice which apply to them.

4.3 The Commission may also undertake desk based assessment, or may telephone licensees to assess compliance.

THE PURPOSE OF ASSESSMENTS AND VISITS

4.4 The purpose of an assessment and visit is to:

- ensure that the licensee remains suitable to hold a licence
- check that the licensee is conducting their activities in a manner which is consistent with the licensing objectives
- ensure that the licensee is complying with the requirements of the Act and relevant regulations
- ensure that the licensee is complying with the Commission's LCCP that apply to the licence held.

4.5 Assessments and visits will be used proportionately, as the Commission will seek to target those areas of greatest risk to the licensing objectives.
4.6 Assessments and visits also offer an opportunity for the Commission to promote good practice, as well as offering licensees an opportunity to seek advice and to provide feedback to the Commission, which can be used to continually improve its processes and procedures.

NOTIFICATION

4.7 The Commission may give advance notice of its intention to visit a licensee and provide details of the process and procedures to be followed. This will provide the licensee with clarity about what will be required and gives the licensee an opportunity to prepare and to minimise potential disruption to the licensed activities being undertaken. However, assessment visits may be made without prior notice.

THE FREQUENCY OF ASSESSMENTS AND VISITS

4.8 The frequency and focus of assessments and visits is based on the risk assessment of the licensee, which takes into account a variety of factors, including the likelihood and potential impact of non compliance by the licensee.

GENERAL CONDUCT

4.9 The Commission will:

- act reasonably in discharging its powers under the Act and conducting assessments and visits
- exercise its powers under the Act fairly, responsibly and with due respect for other parties involved
- explain what information is required, and why, to ensure requests are appropriate, proportionate, minimise disruption to the business, and enable the relevant person to comply fully with the request
- seek the co-operation of others wherever possible and only use its statutory powers when necessary.

REQUESTS FOR INFORMATION

4.10 A request for the production of any records or to provide an explanation of records will be made either orally or in writing, dependent upon the individual circumstances of each case. Wherever possible, licensees will be given a reasonable period of time to comply with the request. The Commission will seek to take into account the burden placed on the individual or business when removing records so that it causes minimal disruption.
4.11 The Commission will only ask a licensee to produce documents or records which it needs and will only remove them if it is necessary. Generally, the Commission will copy documents or records and leave the original records with the licensee. When any document or record is removed, the Commission will give an explanation of why this is necessary and provide a receipt. Any documents which have been removed will be returned as soon as possible after the need for their retention has passed. Where an information request is made orally on a visit a record will be made of the request, what has been requested and the time and place for its production.

THE DATA PROTECTION ACT

4.12 The Commission considers that licensees will not breach the requirements of the Data Protection Act if they supply information that the Commission has requested even if this relates to personal information that they hold. The Commission has the power to request this information under the Act.

PUBLICATION OF ASSESSMENT REPORTS

4.13 When an assessment has been carried out, the licensee will be notified of the result and any further action that is being taken, or should be taken, as soon as possible. The Commission will not normally give, either orally or in writing, any indication as to the result of the assessment at the time it is conducted.

DEALING WITH COMPLIANCE ISSUES

REQUIRED IMPROVEMENTS

4.14 During the course of an assessment visit, compliance issues may be identified which require improvements to be made. Wherever possible, the Commission will explain to the licensee why any changes need to be made, the basis for requiring the changes and a timeframe in which required improvements should be carried out.

COMPLAINTS ABOUT LICENSEES

4.15 Whilst the Commission does not have a specific statutory duty to investigate complaints about licensees, depending on the issues raised the Commission may decide to look into matters relating to the complaint. Further details of the Commission's approach to complaints can be found in the Commission's Complaints Policy which is on the Commission's website.

RISK ASSESSMENT AND PROPORTIONALITY

4.16 The decision about how best to deal with any issues will be informed by an assessment of risk. This will ensure that the Commission's resources are focussed primarily on those operators, individuals and activities which present the greatest risks to the licensing objectives.

EVALUATION

4.17 As part of its compliance activities, the Commission will:

- assess and evaluate compliance consistently and in accordance with the Commission's Risk Assessment methodology
- consider the ongoing suitability of the licensee by looking at the following factors, plus other matters, where appropriate (the list is not exhaustive):
  - — finances
  - — integrity
  - — competence
  - — criminality
- consider whether the licensed activities are being conducted in a manner which is consistent with the licensing objectives
- check that the licensee is complying with the requirements of the Act
- ensure compliance with the licence conditions and codes of practice that apply to the licence, amongst other things by reference to the controls which the licensee has put in place.

4.18 In carrying out this assessment, the Commission will use the following framework, which mirrors the framework for assessing licence applications:

Inadequate

This indicates that a substantial risk to the licensing objectives; or significant concerns about the licensee's suitability; or significant non-compliance with the requirements of the Act and the Commission's LCCP.

Just adequate

This indicates that there is less risk to the licensing objectives; the licensee meets the minimum expectations regarding suitability; the licensee just meets the requirements of the Act and the Commission's LCCP.

Adequate

This indicates that the licensee is unlikely to pose a risk to the licensing objectives; the licensee appears to be suitable to carry on the licensed activities in question; the licensee appears to be meeting the requirements of the Act and the Commission's LCCP.

Good

This indicates that the licensee is unlikely to pose a risk to the licensing objectives; the licensee is able to clearly demonstrate that the licensed activities in question are being conducted in accordance with the requirements of the Act and the Commission's LCCP.

PROVIDING ADVICE

4.19 Where the assessment of a licensee identifies an issue which needs to be addressed, where appropriate the Commission will seek to encourage the licensee to take action to address the issue. This may be done by officials, in addition to issuing standard documentation required under the inspection regulations, providing information to the licensee. Where such information is provided, the Commission will endeavour to distinguish between what are mandatory requirements and what is advice or guidance about what is desirable but not mandatory.

CONCERNS ABOUT SUITABILITY

4.20 Where the Commission's compliance activities give rise to concerns about the suitability of the licensee to carry out the licensed activities, or concerns about the circumstances under which the licensed activities are being carried on, the matter may be dealt with in accordance with the Commission's procedures for enforcement, which are set out below in Chapters 5 and 6.

5 REGULATORY ENFORCEMENT

5.1 In its widest sense, enforcement includes the regulatory or criminal investigation processes, which may result in the exercise of the Commission's regulatory powers under the Act, or the commencement of a prosecution and the laying of criminal charges. Enforcement forms an essential part of the Commission's work to keep gambling fair and safe for all.

5.2 This chapter sets out the Commission's policy in relation to its regulatory enforcement functions, namely:

- licence reviews
- the exercise of the Commission's regulatory powers after a licence review
- the exercise of the Commission's other regulatory powers.

LICENCE REVIEWS

WHAT ARE LICENCE REVIEWS?

5.3 Section 116 of the Act gives the Commission the power to review, over time, the performance of licence holders and the operation of licence conditions. The section provides for two different types of review.

5.4 Under section 116(1) of the Act the Commission may review matters relating to a class, or type, of licence. The purpose of such a review will be to review the manner in which a particular class of licensees carry on the licensed activities authorised by their licences, and, in particular, how the licensees in question comply with the conditions attached to the class of operating licence.

5.5 Section 116(2) of the Act gives the Commission the power to review any matter relating to an individual licence if the Commission:

- suspects that conditions of a licence have been or are being breached
- believes that the licence holder or any person connected with the gambling activities, has been convicted of a relevant offence in Great Britain or abroad; or
- for any reason:
  - — suspects that the licence holder may be unsuitable to perform the licensed activities
  - — thinks that a review would be appropriate.

5.6 A review can be carried out even if there is no suspicion or belief about the licence holder's activities. This means that a licence could be reviewed solely on the grounds that the Commission considers a review would be appropriate. There will, however, always be a reason for a review to be commenced and the Commission will ensure that the letters sent to licensees when a review is being initiated clearly explain the grounds for the review.

THE PROCESS FOR REVIEWING A CLASS OR TYPE OF LICENCE

5.7 The Commission may decide to review a class or type of licence. There are many reasons why the Commission may wish to do this. For example, the Commission may wish to assess the manner in which the licensed activities authorised by a class or type of licence are being carried out; the Commission may wish to review whether the conditions attached to the class of operating licence are being complied with; or, the Commission may decide to review a class of licences in order to ensure that the conditions that apply to those licences remain appropriate.

5.8 In practice, most reviews carried out under section 116 of the Act remain likely to take place in relation to individual licences.

THE PROCESS FOR REVIEWING AN INDIVIDUAL LICENCE

5.9 At any stage in the review process the Commission has the option to:

- decide that there should be no further action
- decide to issue advice to the licensee rather than continue the review
- agree to a licensee's proposals regarding voluntary settlement.

5.10 There may also be occasions when information gathered during the review leads the Commission to conclude that it should commence a criminal investigation, or should refer the matter to the police or another regulatory body for consideration by them.

COMMENCING A REVIEW OF AN INDIVIDUAL LICENCE

5.11 Before commencing a review of an individual operating or personal licence, the Commission must notify the licensee and inform him or her of the procedure to be followed in the conduct of the review. In most cases the Commission will fulfil this obligation by issuing a notice to the licensee, which sets out:

- the grounds for commencing a review
- the procedure to be followed
- confirmation of the licensee's right to make representations, the form of those representations (oral and written) and when those representations should be made.

5.12 The Commission will normally include an indication of whether it intends to give other persons an opportunity to make representations. The notice will confirm the fact that the Commission is undertaking a licence review, as opposed to a criminal investigation, and that the Commission will only take criminal action where, in response to a request for information, the licensee or any person appointed to act on behalf of the licensee provides false or misleading information to the Commission.

5.13 In the case of reviews of operating licences, the holder of an operating licence will also be reminded that it is an offence, under section 122 of the Act, to fail without reasonable excuse to comply with a request to produce written or electronic records or information about the licensed activities.

INITIAL MEETING

5.14 The Commission may, either when it is considering whether to commence a licence review, or after notifying a licensee that it proposes to commence a review but, before proceeding with the review or requesting specified information, hold an initial meeting with the licensee to clarify and narrow the issues and to establish exactly what information will be required by the Commission if it commences a review.

INTERVIEWS

5.15 In addition to requesting specified information, the Commission may wish to interview persons who it considers can supply relevant information in connection with the review. Such interviews may be recorded on tape and where necessary the person being interviewed will be reminded that the Commission may draw adverse inferences if they do not provide answers to the Commission's questions.

5.16 In Scotland, where the Commission determines to carry out an interview of an individual suspected of committing an offence that person will be issued with a caution but under Scottish law no adverse inference may be drawn from a failure to answer questions.

PRELIMINARY FINDING

5.17 At the conclusion of the review, the Commission will send a preliminary findings letter to the licensee. The letter and documents which accompany it will contain details of:

- the facts found during the review
- where relevant, how those facts relate to any apparent breach of a licence condition or a code of practice
- a preliminary assessment of the seriousness of the case in terms of possible outcomes
- any relevant policy considerations
- in appropriate cases, that the decision what (if any) regulatory action should follow the review will be taken by a Regulatory Panel.

5.19 The preliminary findings letter will also normally set out the details of the documents, and other evidence on which the Commission relies and details of any documents which might be said to undermine the Commission's or assist the licensee's case.

REPRESENTATIONS BY THE LICENSEE

5.19 The licensee will then be offered the opportunity to make written representations in response to the Commission's preliminary findings. Licensees will normally be given 28 days to make representations, but there may be occasions when a shorter period is appropriate.

5.20 Personal licensees who feel unable to prepare a written response will be offered the opportunity to make oral representations, which will be recorded in writing by the Commission.

THE COMMISSION'S REGULATORY POWERS

5.21 Following a review under section 116(1) or (2) of the Act, the Commission may:

- decide to take no further action
- decide to give the licensee advice as to conduct
- give the licensee a warning
- add, remove or vary a condition to the licence
- suspend a licence
- revoke a licence
- impose a financial penalty.

FINANCIAL PENALTIES

5.22 A financial penalty can be imposed either following a review, or without a review having taken place, but may only be imposed where the Commission thinks that a condition of a licence has been breached (which by virtue of section 82 of the Act includes a breach of a social responsibility provision of a code of practice).

5.23 Section 121(6) of the Gambling Act 2005 requires the Commission to prepare a statement setting out the principles to be applied by the Commission in exercising its powers to impose financial penalties and to have regard to the statement when exercising a power under this section. A copy of the Statement of Principles for Determining Financial Penalties can be found on the Commission's website.

SUSPENSION AT THE OUTSET OR DURING A REVIEW

5.24 The Commission has the power to suspend a licence at the outset of, or during, a review if the Commission suspects that:

- a licensed activity is being or has been carried on in a manner which is inconsistent with the licensing objectives
- a condition of the licence has been breached
- a licensee has failed to cooperate with a review
- the licensee is unsuitable to carry on the licensed activities.

5.25 Therefore, if the Commission considers a matter sufficiently serious, it can require an operator to suspend all or part of the activities authorised by the licence pending the outcome of the review.

5.26 If the Commission decides to suspend a licence in such circumstances, the licensee will be informed that they may have that decision reviewed by the Commission's Regulatory Panel. If such a review is requested, a meeting of the Regulatory Panel will be convened as soon as practical, normally within three days.

5.27 As an alternative to suspension the Commission may be prepared to agree conditions under which the licensee may continue to operate or work, for example subject to the Commission receiving satisfactory undertakings restricting, or accepting supervision arrangements in respect of, the activities which will be carried on whilst the review is in progress.

SUSPENSION OR REVOCATION OF A LICENCE FOLLOWING A REVIEW

5.28 The Commission may suspend or revoke a licence if, following a review, the Commission considers that:

- a licensed activity is being or has been carried on in a manner which is inconsistent with the licensing objectives
- a condition of the licence has been breached
- a licensee has failed to co-operate with a review
- the licensee is unsuitable to carry on the licensed activities.

ASSESSING SUITABILITY

5.29 In assessing the suitability of an applicant to carry on licensed activities, section 120 of the Act provides that the Commission may, in particular, have regard to:

- the integrity of the licensee or of any person who exercises a function in connection with or is interested in the licensed activities
- the competence of the licensee, or of any person who exercises a function in connection with the licensed activities, to carry on the licensed activities in a manner consistent with pursuit of the licensing objectives
- the financial and other circumstances of the licensee or of any person who exercises a function in connection with or is interested in the licensed activities (and, in particular, the resources available for the purpose of carrying on the licensed activities).

5.30 This means that the Commission will consider, amongst other things, a licensee's integrity (which includes an assessment of his or her honesty and openness), his or her competence and any other relevant financial or other circumstances including the resources available to carry on the licensed activities (for example, human resources, financial resources and the adequacy and effectiveness of the systems and controls which are in place).

5.31 The assessment of suitability in relation to the Commission's enforcement functions will assess many of the same matters which were assessed when the licence was originally granted. However, the Commission may also look at other matters as circumstances require. As such the factors described above are not intended to be an exhaustive list of the factors to be considered.

ASSESSING WHETHER THE LICENSED ACTIVITIES ARE BEING CARRIED OUT IN A MANNER WHICH IS INCONSISTENT WITH THE LICENSING OBJECTIVES

5.32 In deciding whether or not a person has carried on a licensed activity in a manner which is inconsistent with the licensing objectives, the Commission will have regard to its own codes of practice and any other statements it has made (for example, through guidance notes or advice as to conduct letters) about pursuing the objectives.

VOLUNTARY SETTLEMENT IN RELATION TO LICENCE REVIEWS

5.33 Carrying out licence reviews can be expensive and time-consuming. The Commission is therefore keen to encourage licensees to come forward and make full disclosure of all the relevant facts relating to a matter, at as early a stage as possible.

5.34 Where a licensee makes a full disclosure of all the relevant facts, the Commission will consider whether its investigations need to continue, or whether the Commission is prepared to agree the facts and the nature of the sanction (if any) which ought to be imposed, or in appropriate cases what action short of formal sanction should be taken.

5.35 The earlier disclosure is made in the investigation process, the more credit will be given to the licensee for making full disclosure of all the relevant facts. Licensees will also be given credit for disclosing a regulatory breach to the Commission before a licence review has commenced.

5.36 The Commission will not initiate the voluntary settlement process, but will remind licensees at the outset of the review process, that such an option exists.

VOLUNTARY SETTLEMENT IN RELATION TO CRIMINAL INVESTIGATIONS

5.37 The voluntary settlement process will not apply where the Commission decides to carry out a criminal investigation.

THE COMMISSION'S OTHER REGULATORY POWERS

WHAT OTHER REGULATORY POWERS DOES THE COMMISSION HAVE?

5.38 The Commission has regulatory powers which it can exercise without carrying out a licence review. The Act gives the Commission the power to:

- impose a financial penalty, where the Commission thinks that a condition of a licence has been breached
- void a bet
- decide that a licence has lapsed if a licensee becomes incapable of carrying on the licensed activities by reason of mental or physical incapacity,
- revoke a licence for non-payment of an annual fee.

FINANCIAL PENALTIES

5.39 The Commission has the power to impose a financial penalty, without a review having taken place, where the Commission considers that a condition of a licence has been breached (which by virtue of section 82 of the Act includes a breach of a social responsibility provision of a code of practice).

5.40 As indicated above, the Commission has prepared a Statement of Principles for Determining Financial Penalties which can be found on the Commission's website at www.gamblingcommission.gov.uk.

VOIDING BETS

5.41 The Commission has the power to make an order voiding an individual bet accepted by, or through, the holder of a general betting operating licence, a pool betting operating licence, or a betting intermediary operating licence. Where the Commission exercises this power, any contract or other arrangement relating to the bet will be void, and any money paid in relation to the bet must be returned to the person who paid it. Such repayments will be enforceable as a debt. The power to void a bet only applies to the parties to a specific bet; it does not apply to all bets placed on an event.

5.42 The Commission may only make an order to void a bet if it is satisfied that the bet was substantially unfair. In considering whether a bet is substantially unfair, the Commission must, in particular, have regard to any of the following factors:

- that one or both of the parties to the bet (whether they made or accepted the bet) supplied information in connection with it that was insufficient, false or misleading
- that one or both of the parties to the bet believed, or ought to have believed, that the race or event about which the bet was made was, or would be, conducted in contravention of the industry rules that apply to the event
- the fact that one or both of the parties to the bet believed, or ought to have believed, that the offence of cheating (as set out in section 42) had been, or was likely to be, committed in relation to the bet
- the fact that one or both parties to the bet have been convicted of the offence of cheating as set out in section 42 of the Act.

5.44 It follows that the Commission will not automatically void a bet where one of the factors listed above exists; it will only void a bet where it is satisfied that it was substantially unfair.

5.45 The power to void a bet will be available to the Commission for a period of six months from the day on which the result of the bet is determined, except where there has been a conviction for cheating, in which case there is no time limit.

5.46 The Commission also has the power, under section 338 of the Act, to make an order freezing any obligation to pay money in relation to a bet, where it suspects that it may need to make an order that the bet is void under section 336. The effect of this interim moratorium is to protect any payments that would otherwise have been made in relation to a bet. The Commission need not be certain that a voiding order will be made before imposing the interim moratorium.

5.47 An interim moratorium will last for a period of 14 days, beginning on the day that it is made. The Commission may extend an interim moratorium by a further period of up to 14 days and there is no limit to the number of interim moratoria that the Commission may impose in relation to any bet, although the time limit of six months for making an order to void a bet will continue to apply during any period when an interim moratorium is in place.

5.48 The Commission may cancel an order for an interim moratorium before it expires; and must cancel it if it ceases to think that it might want to make an order to void the bet.

SURRENDER OF A LICENCE

5.48 A licence ceases to have effect if it is surrendered to the Commission. This provides a voluntary procedure for a licence holder to give up their licence if they so wish.

5.49 However, if a licensee surrenders the licence whilst a licence review under section 116 of the Act is underway, the Commission may decide to continue its investigations in order to determine the facts of the case so that they can be referred to in the future, for example if the licensee subsequently applies for a new licence.

LAPSE

5.50 A licence will lapse, and is not transferable, if the licence holder dies or becomes bankrupt or goes into liquidation. A licence will also lapse if, in the Commission's view, the licensee becomes incapable of carrying out the licensed activities by reason of mental or physical incapacity. In such cases, the Commission will consider all of the circumstances of the case before making a decision, which may involve seeking medical advice about the licensee.

REVOCATION FOR NON-PAYMENT OF ANNUAL FEE

5.51 Failure to pay annual fees by the fee due date may lead to the revocation of an operator's licence.

6 INVESTIGATION AND PROSECUTION OF OFFENCES UNDER THE GAMBLING ACT 2005

6.1 This chapter sets out the Commission's policy in relation to the investigation and prosecution of offences under the Act, including the Commission's powers, and the relationship between criminal and regulatory investigations.

THE PREVENTION OF ILLEGAL GAMBLING

6.2 The general framework set by the Act is that providing facilities for gambling is illegal unless provided:

- in accordance with certain specific exemptions in the Act
- in certain cases (for example, machine gaming in pubs and clubs and small scale lotteries) under permits or other arrangements administered by local authorities
- by a person who holds a licence issued by the Commission.

6.3 The prevention of illegal gambling is a key priority for the Commission. The Commission's Strategic Assessment and Tactical Assessments will set the Commission's enforcement priorities. Those priorities will alter to meet changes in the assessment of risks and the Commission will allocate enforcement resources to the areas of greatest risk.

6.4 Combating illegal gambling also benefits licensed operators, as the provision of illegal unregulated gambling has both a reputational and economic impact on the gambling industry as a whole.

THE COMMISSION'S POWERS TO INVESTIGATE OFFENCES UNDER THE ACT

6.5 Under section 27 of the Act the Commission may undertake activities for the purpose of assessing compliance with provision made by or by virtue of the Act and whether an offence is being committed under the Act. By virtue of section 28 of the Act the Commission has the power to investigate whether an offence has been committed under the Act and may institute criminal proceedings in respect of offences under the Act in England and Wales. In Scotland, the power to institute criminal proceedings rests solely with the Crown Office and Procurator Fiscal Service (COPFS). At the conclusion of an investigation in Scotland, the Commission may prepare a report to COPFS recommending criminal proceedings.

THE RELATIONSHIP BETWEEN REGULATORY AND CRIMINAL INVESTIGATIONS

6.6 As a general rule the Commission will not normally pursue a criminal investigation into a licensed operator, as in most cases the matter under investigation is likely to be capable of being dealt with by the exercise of the Commission's regulatory powers. However, there might be circumstances where the commencement of a criminal investigation was merited, for example, if a licensee were suspected of cheating under section 42 of the Act (which carries the possibility of a longer period of imprisonment, if convicted), or if a licensee knowingly misled or provided false information to the Commission, contrary to section 342 of the Act.
6.7 There may be circumstances where the Commission's investigations uncover evidence that a serious criminal offence may have been committed, which falls outside the Commission's jurisdiction to investigate. In such cases the Commission may pass the information it possesses to the Police, or another body, for consideration by them.

DECIDING WHETHER TO INSTITUTE CRIMINAL PROCEEDINGS

6.8 The Commission recognises that there should be a separation of functions between the investigative process and the decision regarding whether or not a criminal prosecution should take place. At the conclusion of a criminal investigation, the case will be thoroughly reviewed before a decision is taken. In Scotland, this review will take place before a decision is taken on whether or not to report a case to COPFS.
6.9 The Commission will apply the Code for Crown Prosecutors when deciding whether criminal proceedings should be commenced, which involves a two-stage test:

- first, the evidence will be reviewed and an assessment made about whether there is a realistic prospect of conviction
- secondly, if there is sufficient evidence to mean that there is a realistic prospect of conviction, an assessment will be made about whether it is in the public interest for a prosecution to take place.

6.10 The Code for Crown Prosecutors lists a number of common public interest factors which either favour or are against prosecution. A copy of the code can be found on the Crown Prosecution Service's website[13] and in the event that the Code is revised the Commission may need to review its own processes accordingly.
6.11 In Scotland the Commission will follow the guidance to Specialist Reporting Agencies in the preparation of reports to COPFS.

TIME LIMITS

6.12 Section 347 of the Act establishes prosecution time limits for relevant offences and disapplies section 127(1) of the Magistrates Courts Act 1980. This means that any information in connection with an offence committed under the Act has to be laid before the Magistrates within the period of 12 months beginning with the date (or last date) on which the offence was alleged to have been committed. Where an offence is continuing in nature then the relevant date is the last date on which the offence was committed.

6.13 This time limit does not apply to the offence of cheating, under section 42 of the Act as cheating is triable either way. Conviction on indictment also carries the possibility of a longer sentence of imprisonment than other offences under the Act.

CAUTIONS

6.14 In appropriate cases, where the Commission has investigated a matter and both the evidential and public interest tests are met, the Commission may decide to issue a caution to the alleged offender, rather than pursue a prosecution. Where a caution is administered, details of the caution will be kept on file and may be taken into account in the future if further breaches occur.

PROSECUTIONS IN SCOTLAND

6.15 The Commission does not have the power to commence criminal proceedings in Scotland, but as a Specialist Reporting Agency can recommend criminal proceedings to the COPFS. Therefore the Commission has the power to carry out investigations in Scotland and where it does so it will investigate the matter in accordance with the requirements of the Scottish legal system and in accordance with the COPFS Guidance to Specialist Reporting Agencies. A case file/report will be prepared for submission to the COPFS, who will make the decision on whether or not to prosecute.

6.16 The Commission will work towards presenting the file/report to the Crown Office Procurator Fiscal Service within six months of the alleged offence(s).

6.17 The capacity to issue a formal caution for a criminal offence does not exist in Scotland. The COPFS has the power to issue warnings and impose financial penalties as a direct alternative to prosecution.

PROCEEDS OF CRIME

6.18 The Commission is committed to a multi-agency approach to ensuring that crime does not pay.

6.19 The Commission is an accredited agency and has powers under the Proceeds of Crime Act 2002 (POCA)[14]. Where the Commission has secured a criminal conviction in respect of an offence under the Act, it will use its powers under POCA and will work with other agencies to take appropriate action to ensure that the proceeds of gambling crime are confiscated. The Commission will also bear in mind the possibility that some regulatory cases could meet the Assets Recovery Agency (ARA) referral criteria.

6.20 The Commission is already the supervisory body for the casino industry for the purposes of the money laundering rules and uses its powers under the Act to exchange information on proceeds of crime issues with the Serious Organised Crime Agency and other law enforcement partners involved in taking action under the POCA.

---

1 Within the meaning of section 422 of the Financial Services and Markets Act 2000.

2 Further details of the Commission's current risk modelling and compliance visit programme can be found in the document The Compliance process; the Risk Modelling System (RMS) and Annual Visit Programme (AVP).

3 The Gambling Act 2005 (Definition of Small-scale Operator) Regulations 2006.

[4] Operating Licence Application Forms Guidance Notes and the Personal Licence Application Forms Guidance Notes (as amended from time to time).

[5] The Gambling Act 2005 (Definition of Small-scale Operator) Regulations 2006.

[6] Section 71 Gambling Act 2005.

[7] Schedule 7 Gambling Act 2005.

[8] Section 125 Gambling Act 2005.

[9] The Commission maintains a register of operating licences relating to each licence under the provisions of Section 106 of the Act.

[10] Licence Conditions and Codes of Practice (as amended from time to time).

[11] The Gambling (Operating Licence and Single-Machine Permit Fees) Regulations 2006 (as amended).

[12] The Gambling (Personal Licence Fees) Regulations 2006 (as amended).

[13] www.cps.gov.uk.

[14] The Commission's powers under POCA do not extend to Scotland.

Gambling Commission September 2009

STATEMENT OF PRINCIPLES FOR DETERMINING FINANCIAL PENALTIES

September 2009

1 INTRODUCTION

THE PURPOSE OF THIS STATEMENT OF PRINCIPLES FOR DETERMINING FINANCIAL PENALTIES

6.2076 1.1 This statement sets out the principles that the Gambling Commission (the Commission) will apply in exercising its powers to require the holder of an operating licence to pay a financial penalty.

THE FRAMEWORK OF POLICIES AND PROCEDURES

1.2 The Commission has developed a number of policies which govern how it carries out its statutory functions. As such this document needs to be read in conjunction with the following documents:

- Statement of principles for licensing and regulation
- Licensing, compliance and enforcement policy statement
- Licence Conditions and Codes of Practice
- Complaints procedure
- Corporate governance framework
- Regulatory panel procedures.

THE LEGAL FRAMEWORK

1.3 Section 121 of the Gambling Act 2005 (the Act) provides that the Commission may require the holder of an operating licence to pay a penalty if the Commission thinks that a condition of the licence has been breached. The Commission may impose a financial penalty following a review under section 116(1) or (2) of the Act. The Commission also has the power to impose a financial penalty without carrying out a licence review.

THE SCOPE OF THIS DOCUMENT

1.4 Section 121(6) of the Act requires the Commission to, among other things, prepare a statement setting out the principles to be applied by the Commission in exercising its powers to impose financial penalties and to have regard to the statement when exercising a power under this section. In particular the Commission will have regard to:

- the seriousness of the breach of condition in respect of which the penalty is proposed
- whether or not the licensee knew or ought to have known of the breach
- the nature of the licensee (including, in particular, the licensee's financial resources).

1.5 This document sets out the principles which the Commission will apply and will have regard to when exercising its powers under section 121 of the Act.

2 APPLICABLE PRINCIPLES

THE PURPOSE OF IMPOSING A FINANCIAL PENALTY

2.1 The primary purpose of the Commission's exercise of its regulatory powers is to protect the interests of the public, although they may have a punitive effect. The primary aims of financial penalties will be to:

- change the behaviour of the licensee

- eliminate any financial gain or benefit from non-compliance with licence conditions
- be proportionate to the nature of the breach of licence condition and the harm caused
- aim to deter future non-compliance.

CRITERIA FOR THE IMPOSITION OF A FINANCIAL PENALTY

2.2 By virtue of section 121(7), in considering the imposition of a penalty, the Commission must have regard to:

- the seriousness of the breach of the licence condition in respect of which the penalty is proposed
- whether the licensee knew or ought to have known of the breach
- the nature of the licensee (including, in particular, the licensee's financial resources).

2.3 In deciding whether it would be appropriate to impose a penalty, the Commission will take full account of the particular facts and circumstances of the breach under consideration. Factors which the Commission will take into consideration include (the list is not exhaustive):

- the extent to which the circumstances from which the contravention or failure arose were within the control of the licensee
- the presence or absence of internal controls or procedures which were intended to prevent the breach
- the steps that the licensee has taken since the breach was identified to avoid recurrence of the breach.

2.4 A financial penalty allows the Commission, amongst other things, to eliminate financial gain or benefit from non-compliance. A financial penalty may be appropriate in the following circumstances (the list is not exhaustive):

- where the breach of a licence condition was committed deliberately or recklessly
- the licensee was aware or should have been aware of the breach
- repeated breach of a licence condition
- systemic failure to comply with a condition of the licence
- where the breach gave rise to financial gain
- where the breach of a licence condition had an impact on customers
- where the licensee did not report the breach of a licence condition.

2.5 A financial penalty will not normally be used in the following circumstances (the list is not exhaustive):

- if the breach of a licence condition was minor in nature
- if the breach, or possibility of a breach of a licence condition, would not have been likely to be apparent to a diligent licensee
- if the Commission considers that other regulatory action is more appropriate.

CRITERIA FOR DETERMINING THE QUANTUM OF A FINANCIAL PENALTY

2.6 Although the Act does not set a limit for a financial penalty, a penalty will be set at a level which the Commission considers to be proportionate to the breach and will take into account the financial situation of the licensee, including the ability to pay. The Commission will also take into account all the other circumstances of the case, which may include (the list is not exhaustive):

- the impact on the licensing objectives
- whether there has been a repeated breach or failure
- whether the breach continued after the licensee became aware of it
- the scale of the breach of a licence condition across the licensed entity
- the involvement of senior management
- the level of any attempt to make financial gain from the breach
- the extent of any attempt to conceal the failure or breach

- the impact on customers
- the absence of internal controls or procedures intended to prevent the breach
- the duration of the breach
- the extent of steps taken to remedy the breach
- reporting the breach to the Commission
- co-operation with any investigation undertaken by the Commission.

PROCEDURAL MATTERS

2.7 Section 121 imposes a number of procedural steps which must be taken before the Commission can impose a financial penalty. Before imposing a requirement on a licensee to pay a penalty under this section the Commission must notify a licensee:

- that the Commission proposes to require him to pay a penalty
- of the amount of the proposed penalty
- of the Commission's reasons
- of a period within which the licensee may make representations to the Commission.

2.8 The Commission will normally give licensees 14 days to make representations.

TIME LIMITS

2.9 By virtue of section 121(3) the Commission may not give a notice in respect of the breach of a condition after the end of the period of two years beginning with the day on which the breach occurred or began to occur, or, if later, the day on which the breach came to the knowledge of the Commission.
Gambling Commission September 2009

THE COMPLIANCE PROCESS, THE RISK MODELLING SYSTEM (RMS) AND THE ANNUAL VISIT PROGRAMME (AVP)
Information paper, August 2007

INTRODUCTION

6.2080 This information document is divided into three parts.

PART 1 BACKGROUND AND CONTEXT

i. The first part sets out how the Gambling Commission should carry out the management of compliance due to the changes introduced by the Gambling Act 2005; the current regulatory environment in the Great Britain and the rationale for a risk based visit programme. Part 1 also describes how the visit appraisal process differs for lower-risk and higher-risk premises and operators. Part One also specifies how the concepts of lower-risk and higher-risk will affect the apportionment of compliance attention.

PART 2 HOW THE RMS OPERATES

ii. This details how the RMS and AVP are formulated and how the various parts of the model work together to determine a premises or operator's risk band. This part of the paper also sets out all the different steps and stages of the AVP. Part Two also describes how a premises or operator are assigned to a risk band.

PART 3 THE RISK ASSESSMENT PROCESS

iii. The last part describes the various Key Risk Areas and Risk Categories that combine to form a premises or operator's risk band. Part Three also details how the visit process will be carried out and how the work of Compliance Managers contributes to the final determination of the risk band of a operator which is moderated when combined with premises' risk evaluations.

> **"Comprehensive risk assessment should be the foundation of all regulators' enforcement programmes." (Hampton, 2005)**

1 BACKGROUND AND CONTEXT

COMPLIANCE

1.1 The Gambling Commission (the Commission) has powers under Part 15 of the Gambling Act 2005 (the Act) to carry out inspections 'to determine whether the licensed activities are being carried on in accordance with the terms and conditions of the operating licence' [s308(3)]. The terms and conditions are set out in the Licensing Conditions and Code of Practice (LCCP) document (June 2007). The LCCP lists the:

- general conditions for operating and personal licences;
- code of practice to be attached to casino premises licences for access by young persons and children; and
- code of practice detailing the ordinary provisions and the social responsibility provisions.

1.2 In order to carry out their functions and exercise powers under Part 15 of the Act (such as entering premises or requiring copies of documents) our Compliance Managers have to be designated as 'Enforcement Officers' and all designated 'officers' will carry identity and evidence of their authority. The Commission has made it clear that there is a clear distinction between compliance and enforcement with compliance being a collaborative process between an operator and the Commission. If we are taking formal regulatory enforcement action against an operator this will be preceded by the issue of a statutory notice so operators should not be alarmed by the prospect of being dealt with by an 'Enforcement Officer' on compliance and risk assessment visits (please see the policy document on compliance and enforcement for further details).

1.3 Compliance activity and the exercise of powers under Part 15 of the Act are governed by the Gambling Act 2005 (Inspection) (Provision of Information) Regulations 2007 ('the regulations'). The regulations are designed to ensure that we are transparent about the way we exercise our powers and we have designed our processes to ensure that we are compliant with and abide by the spirit of those regulations. We have also produced an information leaflet which sets out our powers, what operators can expect from our compliance staff (in terms of help and advice) and the information we have to provide to you.

1.4 If our Compliance Managers are exercising an entry power in order to carry out a compliance visit, then they must complete a written record of the inspection. They should also inform the occupier or a responsible person as soon as is reasonably practical about their rights to be supplied with a copy of that inspection record following a written request to the Commission. (A copy of our 'Record of Inspection' form is at Appendix 13)

1.5 We intend to comply with the regulations by issuing operators (or a responsible member of staff) at the start of the visit with a notice which sets out the right to make a written request for a copy of the inspection record. This will be a duplicated form a copy of which will be retained by the Commission for its records. (A copy of this form can be found at Appendix 12)

1.6 At the conclusion of the visit the operator or a responsible person will be given an Operator/Licensee Information form which summarises the salient points of the visit including any details of remedial action required. (A copy of this form is at Appendix 14)

1.7 Where the visit is made to an operator's retail premises (as opposed to the headquarters office) then a letter will be sent to the headquarters office making clear

that the operator can request a copy of the inspection record and enclosing a copy of the Operator/Licensee Information form that has also been left on the premises. This is to ensure that operators are fully aware of all visits that have been made to their premises and the issues arising.
1.8 As well as issuing standard documentation, we will also confirm any significant findings or requirements in writing.

RISK ASSESSMENT

1.9 The Commission has embraced the better regulation agenda and we have already made clear in our policy statement on compliance and enforcement that in developing our policy and processes, we have adopted the Hampton principles.[1] In particular our approach is risk-based and is intended to minimise the burden on the compliant while concentrating resources on the areas that most need them.
1.10 The Commission's primary responsibility is to issue operating licences having satisfied itself that an operator can meet the licensing objectives and is suitable to carry on licensed activities. Assessing suitability means making judgements about an operator's integrity, competence and financial and other resources. Once an operator is licensed, the Commission has an obligation to keep these factors under review and to assure itself that operators do not breach the law, continue to carry on licensed activities in a manner that is consistent with the three licensing objectives and with the licensing conditions and codes of practice.
1.11 Any risk assessment should therefore be based around an operator's ability to structure and manage itself properly to ensure that the risks posed to the three licensing objectives are minimised. For this reason the Commission proposes to make a provisional risk assessment based on organisational risk and the risks to the three licensing objectives, but also take into account the risks posed by any external factors which might impact on the ability of the business to remain compliant.
1.12 Although the principal focus should be on assessing operator risk, many operators have multi site retail premises and the challenge for operators is to ensure that regulatory policies and procedures developed at senior management level are effectively delivered by and through staff at the customer facing end of the business. So there must also be an assessment of how effective senior management are at implementing regulatory policies and procedures at all levels of the business and ensuring effective delivery. For this reason the risk assessment process is in two stages. Firstly an assessment at management level (with the approach being adapted to suit the size of the business) and then a validation of the effectiveness of implementation and monitoring procedures at premises level. The risk assessment at management or headquarters level will then be moderated by the outcome of premises risk assessments which will be used to validate the overall risk ratings. Only a sample of premises for multi site operators will be visited and for small operators with restricted numbers of premises, the approach will be simplified.
1.13 As well as regulating over 3000 operators, the Commission has direct or indirect responsibility for regulating approximately:

- 8,000 betting shops,
- 660 registered society lotteries,
- 679 certified bingo clubs,
- betting facilities and operations at 59 horse tracks,
- 170 section 27 certificated gaming machine operators,
- betting facilities and operations at 31 licensed greyhound tracks,
- over 4,000 adult gaming and family entertainment centres, and
- 165 licensed casinos, and a number of new casinos

(above estimated list correct as at 30 June 2007)
1.14 This number and range of operators and premises means that the Commission has had to develop an approach to organising the AVP and reviewing any premises or operator's level of compliance that takes a comprehensive risk-based approach and

aligns limited resources to areas of greatest risk. The RMS upon which the AVP is based will need continuous revision in the light of new information and the process is cyclical.

---

1 Reducing administrative burdens: effective inspection and enforcement, Philip Hampton, March 2005.

"Risk based regulation is a means of objectively demonstrating reasonable steps were taken to reduce and manage risks." (LSE Paper 33, 2005)

1.15 The proposed approach recognises that compliance with licence conditions is the common goal of the Commission and gambling operators. Good compliance performance by operators should be encouraged. Poor performance should be addressed. In this sense, it is essential that follow-up activity takes place in a consistent manner to reinforce the compliance activities undertaken. As with compliance reviews, follow-up effort should be focused on higher-risk operators or operators found to be borderline compliant or non-compliant with an aspect of their licence conditions or other regulatory requirements. To ensure that resources are focussed where they can be most effective a risk profile of each category and type of operator is required. Risk profiling provides the basis for determining where we need to focus attention to maximise compliance with the regulatory framework

1.16 Risk profiling will be completed for each category and type of operator as a part of the annual planning exercise. The main source of information and guidance will be the internal Gambling Commission Strategic Intelligence Assessments. Profiles for each establishment, industry and organisation will be used to determine the focus and scope of the compliance review to be performed. This allows flexible and targeted compliance reviews that consider the risks of particular operators or sectors to ensure that work is focused on those areas of greatest concern. For operators assessed as very low risk, compliance reviews will predominantly take place by way of an evaluation of specific information and documentation supplied by an operator to determine compliance. Site visits would not normally be undertaken, but the degree of examination could be increased or extended, including the potential for site visits, if it was determined necessary after reviewing the documentation or due to updated or further risk profiling.

1.17 For operators or particular premises assessed as a higher-risk, compliance reviews will predominantly take a targeted approach preceded by a substantial planning element. Compliance reviews will generally take a 'no surprises' approach, particularly when presenting the results of review findings. As far as possible, examinations of a premises or operator's compliance would be undertaken in-situ allowing more opportunity for interaction and discussion of actual or potential issues identified during the review, including with a premises or operator's principals. This approach will also provide greater visibility of compliance staff and more opportunity for interaction, relationship building and education. Greater emphasis will be placed on the education rather than compliance of a premises or operator, including the development of a strategic approach that takes account of both formal and informal education opportunities. More emphasis will also be directed towards ensuring that an operator assumes responsibility for putting in place policies and procedures that enable them to comply with licence conditions. Likewise, reviewing an operator's policies and procedures at headquarters and premises level will provide an indicator of its ability and willingness to comply with licence conditions (including at site level).

1.18 The in-built incentive for attaining a lower risk rating is earned autonomy. The more effort an operator makes and the more compliant they are then the less rigorous and frequent regulatory compliance attention they will experience. A 'sliding' level of inspection scheduling is the fairest and most equitable method by which a regulator can structure their compliance and inspection regime and it means that as an operator (or one of their respective premises) improves their risk level they gain the reward of being subject to lower levels of inspection and a general reduction in regulatory intervention.

1.19 In the future it is envisaged that for each industry type a customised self-assessment guide will become available to all types of premises, operators and stakeholders on the Commission's website. This will be done in an effort to encourage voluntary compliance and provide premises and operators with the ability to determine and gauge their own level of compliance with their particular licence conditions. Completion by premises or operators of self-assessment templates has benefits from both compliance and education perspectives and will be encouraged.

2 HOW THE RMS OPERATES

2.1 Each year an AVP will be developed and based on a detailed RMS that assesses individual premises or operators using the guiding principles contained within the three objectives of the Act. The Strategic Intelligence Assessment (SIA) will be the primary source utilised to inform and develop the AVP – the SIA is formulated by utilising multiple sources of information guided by the Act. The SIA surveys and details the current and long–term issues affecting the Commission. The SIA makes many recommendations covering the work of the Commission including the identification and evaluation of higher–risk priorities and emerging threats. The SIA is also the main source of guidance during the risk profiling stage but must be supplemented by other sources such as

- recent inspection trends,
- individual one-off inspection discoveries,
- thematic compliance activity
- input from the National Compliance Managers,
- input from Commission research and external research,
- input from the Commission's Policy section,
- input from Commission's Licensing section, and
- input from Commission's Investigations section.

2.2 Once the initial AVP has been developed the visit process will commence. After each visit an appraisal for each of the five Key Risk Areas will be produced by a Commission Compliance Manager. Each of these five appraisals are combined with an impact level to assign a premises or operator to a risk band. Our approach is in line with accepted risk management standards[2]. After the inspection process has been operating for sometime the number of premises and operators in each risk band will accrue and these placements and their movements (higher and lower – both individually and collectively) will inform future AVP planning.

2.3 An Impact rating for every premises and operator will be calculated. The overall risk band for any premises or operator is produced by the combination of Likelihood (Probability) and Consequence (Impact). Using the objectives of the Act as the overall guidance initially the Impact rating will be a combination of two factors:

- size/turnover; and
- customer base.

2.4 The National Compliance Managers classified each premises or operator within their jurisdiction into three ascending bands in terms of annual gambling turnover and customer base – this information will in future be primarily sourced from regulatory returns.

2.5 The two factors used to create the impact measure (size/turnover and customer base) have a range spreading from 'A' through to 'D'. The Impact measure for each premises and operator is calculated by combining the gambling turnover range (A, B, C or D), with the customer base range (A, B, C or D).

2.6 In the longer term the Commission will compile data at a finer resolution than Local Authority level as well as more varied gambling specific data to increase the sensitivity and utility of the impact measure.

---

2 ISO/IEC Guide 73:2002; ISO Guide 72:2001; British Standard BS-6079-3:2000; Australia/New Zealand Risk Management Standard 4360:2000; Canadian Risk Management

Guideline CAN/CSA-Q850-97

2.7 Some large operators, because of the size and scale of their operation will always be high impact which is the reason why the Commission has adopted a relationship management approach through the National Compliance Managers. For this reason these large operators will always receive some degree of regulatory attention due to their market coverage and market impact. This does not mean that such operators are automatically considered 'high risk'

2.8 The visit appraisal is based on an impartial, straightforward and moderated visit guide that covers the key categories of risks to gambling for each industry type. Visit guides were developed using key Commission documents such as the Act and the Licensing Conditions and Codes of Practice (2006). The guides were designed by the Commission's National Compliance Managers. Impact level and visit appraisals are used to assign a premises or operator to a risk band. In the longer term this will enable the development of a more informed and refined AVP. The RMS & AVP will be subject to a full review after an entire AVP has concluded. The review will be guided by an annual visit programme that has produced specific assessments for each premises or operators and over time collective premises ratings at the operator level and various geographic levels. A graphic summary and overview of how the AVP cycle will operate is at Appendix 2.

2.9 Once the AVP is set and all the visit plans are developed a number of methods are being considered and developed so that the AVP can be modified to cater for unforeseen developments. By way of example, one product that may be developed internally is an intelligence based product which alerts GC officers about the details of a recent issue and/or vulnerability that requires immediate escalation such as recent research findings, planned policy changes or an emerging visit trend.

2.10 The content and number of Evaluation Guides varies for each gambling sector depending on the market structure. However for all large corporate headquarters there is one Evaluation Guide. At Appendix 3 is the generic strategic Evaluation Guide for all gambling sectors and very large operators at the corporate level. For betting, arcades and lotteries there are two Evaluation guides: guide A for the management level and guide B for the premises. They can found at attachments 4-9. For the casinos (Attachment 10) and the bingo (Attachment 11) sector there is only one combined (A & B) Evaluation Guide which encompasses management and premises level specific risk items in the one document.

2.11 Evaluation Guides are being developed for machine manufacturers and suppliers. These guides will be finalised in the near future after all standards and other associated matters are finalised.

3 THE RISK ASSESSMENT PROCESS

3.1 The rationale behind a risk based visit process is to enable resources to be focussed on the areas of greatest risk, to identify emerging risk and to increase effectiveness. The success of the approach should be measured on an outcome basis ie overtime a reduction in the number of 'high risk' operators/premises and an increase in the number of low risk operators/premises.

3.2 When a Compliance Officer is conducting a visit they appraise various key identified risks within the various Risk Categories which make up the five Key Risk Areas. Each Compliance Officer will have a visit guide with key risks that they must assess to get an overall appraisal for each Risk Category. The five Key Risk Areas are:

(1) organisational;
(2) crime and disorder;
(3) fair and open;
(4) children and other vulnerable people; and
(5) external risk.

3.3 Each Compliance Officer will have an Evaluation Guide with the aspects that they must assess. They will apply the visit guide using their professional judgement and independent evidence taking account of the size, type and role of a premises. All five Key Risk Area appraisals are then combined with the impact level.

3.4 Based on the visit and appraisal process the premises and/or operator will be assigned a range of four risk descriptors. The table below depicts a typical guide a Compliance Manager may follow when assessing a premises or operator's performance against risks in the LCCP – the appraisal given by a Compliance Manager is used to assign risk descriptors to a premises or operator. By way of example this guide could be for any of the items in the Evaluation Guides contained within the Attachments to this document. A Compliance Officer uses the visit guide to appraise a premises or operator against the aforementioned example.

Risk Level	Guide criteria for a visit assessment
Low	Comprehensive clear evidence exists in relation to this LCCP standard that the premises or operator demonstrated that there are effective policies, systems & procedures in place and are being operated across all areas for this size and type of premises or operator when contrasted to comparable premises or operators. There is a continual good compliance record in all areas. Trends indicate good and improving performance. Staff are knowledgeable, well trained and highly skilled. Management are competent, confident and continually monitoring and responding professionally to change.
Medium low	Evidence exists that for more than half the requirements of this LCCP standard there has been a reasonable performance for this size and type of premises or operator when contrasted to comparable premises or operators. Management and staff are reasonably trained and skilled but there is room for improvement.
Medium high	Some evidence exists to show that systems are in place to manage and satisfactorily operate in terms this LCCP standard for this size and type of premises or operator when contrasted to comparable premises or operators. Overall the operation of this premises or operator for this aspect of the LCCP standard is at best unstructured and limited. There is a lack of regular business requirements such as training and management measuring of performance of the business. There is a slight lack of confidence in the management of this premises or operator in terms of this LCCP standard.
High	Very little to no evidence that appropriate systems are in place for this size and type of operator or premises when contrasted to comparable operators or premises in respect of this LCCP standard. Trends indicate poor historical performance in terms of complaints and/or inspections for this LCCP standard. There are instances of deliberate non-compliance. There are facets that need immediate significant attention.

3.5 The Commission considers that an operator's risk assessment is a matter between that operator and Commission staff and represents the Commission's perception of the risks (not the operators). Plainly the Commission will discuss the risk assessment outcomes with the Operator's senior management and take into account their views but the particular risk rating is ultimately a matter for the Commission's judgment. As risk assessments will be based on a knowledge of an operator's business and systems they are therefore considered to be commercially sensitive.

3.6 The Commission from time to time and for the purpose of measuring outcomes may publish generic risk assessment data, but will ensure that individual operator risk data is not published.

NEXT STEPS

3.7 As stated in the paper the basis for the RMS is to ensure that the Commission takes a comprehensive risk-based approach and aligns limited resources to the areas of greatest risk. The RMS proposed is based on the guidance in the Act and the current regulatory benchmark standards.

3.8 We will also be working further on continually enhancing and modifying the RMS and consequently the AVP to ensure it is always constantly improving. However, it is envisaged that the overall strategy and design will remain for the foreseeable future.

3.9 It is intended that the RMS and AVP will begin operating from 1 September although inevitably the first year's AVP has had to be based on limited data largely culled from applications. You are welcome to make the Commission aware of any comments you have on the RMS or AVP.

RESPONSES TO THIS DOCUMENT AND FURTHER INFORMATION

For more information on the Commission, including on licence conditions and codes of practice, please visit www.gamblingcommission.gov.uk

If you wish to comment about this information paper, please state whether you are responding as an individual or representing the views of an organisation. If responding on behalf of an organisation, please make clear who that organisation represents. If responding as an individual, please mention your own interest.

If you have any comments you can send your comments to info@gamblingcommission.gov.uk, or by post to:

Gambling Commission
Victoria Square House
Victoria Square
Birmingham B2 4BP

Gambling Commission August 2007

APPENDIX 1

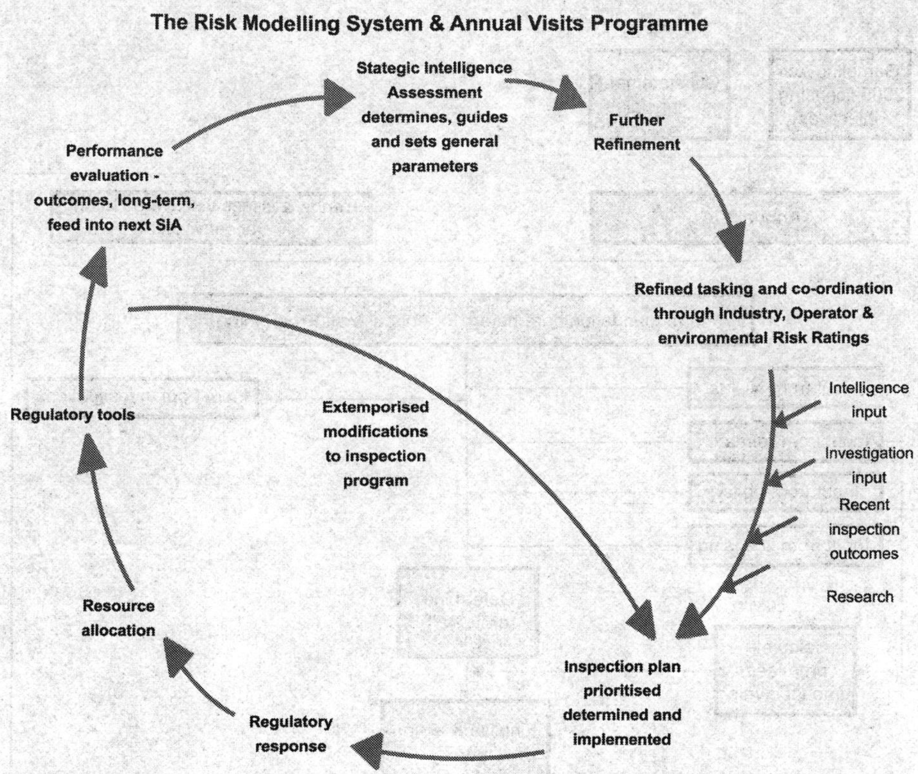

APPENDIX 2

ANNUAL VISIT PROGRAMME (AVP)

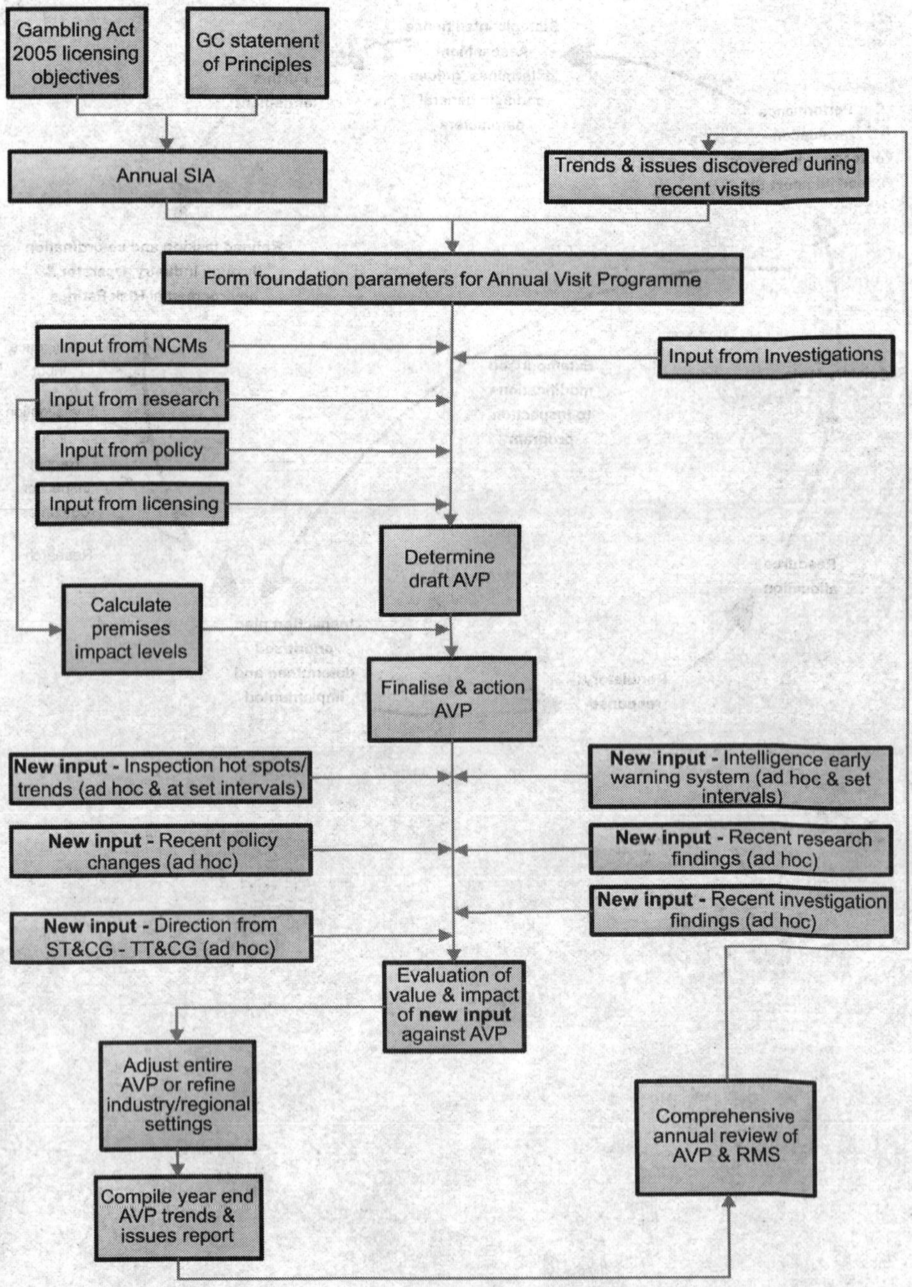

APPENDIX 3

GAMBLING COMMISSION

CORPORATE EVALUATION GUIDE

Operator Details	
Name of Operator	
Name of Holding Company (e.g. Rank)	
Address of Registered Office of Operator (if different from Head Office address below)	
Address of Head Office of Operator	
Type of Operating Licence	
Operating Licence Number	

Gambling Commission personnel, etc, details	
National Compliance Manager's name or other Enforcement Officer's name	
Name(s) of any other accompanying person(s)	
Date(s) of visit(s) & details of premises visited	
Date/premises visited	

OPERATIONAL RISK **Yes / Some / No**		
1	Is there a widely communicated internal statement of commitment to the Licensing objectives and/or the regulatory framework by either: (A) The Board, (B) Chairman (C) Chief Executive	☐ ☐ ☐ ☐ ☐ ☐
2	Is there any evidence of positive resistance or hostility to the new regulatory regime (this does not mean general complaints about the regime or any perceived regulatory burden)?	☐ ☐ ☐
3	Is there someone at Board level holding overall responsibility for regulatory compliance? (The Compliance Director does not have to be a Board member, but must be directly answerable to someone who has overall responsibility for regulatory compliance and is a Key PML) Yes/No	☐ ☐
4	Is corporate governance embedded in the organisation (i.e. does the business broadly follow the combined code)? Yes/No	☐ ☐
5	Is there a compliance or risk committee (a sub committee reporting to the Board of the licensed entity or the Group Board) that deals with regulatory compliance issues? Yes/No	☐ ☐
6	Is there apparent commitment to risk management within the organisation (corporate and divisional risk registers)? Yes/No	☐ ☐

7	Is there a recognition that there are risks associated with running a gambling business? (children and young persons, problem gambling, criminal spend, customer understanding etc)	☐ ☐ ☐
8	Has the operator carried out a documented risk assessment of the ability of the whole business to comply with LCCP (check lists, internal audit, risk register)? Yes/No	☐ ☐
9	Are there documented internal controls in place to manage regulatory risk (a widely available compliance or procedure manual, instructions to all layers of management and staff?	☐ ☐ ☐
10	Is there evidence that the business has effective and efficient performance measures in place to monitor regulatory compliance?	☐ ☐ ☐
11	Is there evidence that senior management monitor the performance measures in ITEM 10?	☐ ☐ ☐

OPERATIONAL RISK (CONTINUED) **Yes / Some / No**		
12	Is there evidence that senior management are proactive in checking that policies and procedures relating to regulatory compliance are fully implemented across the business (internal audit reports, management inspection, internal reporting etc)?	☐ ☐ ☐
13	Is there a documented regulatory training programme in place with regulatory compliance being part of an individual's training requirements? Yes/No	☐ ☐
14	Have management and staff at all levels been trained in their obligations under the new regulatory framework?	☐ ☐ ☐
15	(A) Overall, do all key PMLs have a good overall understanding of the regulatory framework and where applicable their specific obligations under the regulatory framework (this can be established by interview or other indirect evidence)? Specifically for the following persons do they have a thorough understanding and knowledge of ITEM 15(A)? (B) Chief Executive (or equivalent) (C) Finance Director (or equivalent) (D) Compliance Director (E) Marketing Director (F) IT Director (where applicable) (G) Regional/Area managers	☐ ☐ ☐ ☐
16	Are regulatory responsibilities clearly defined and allocated with clear management structures defined, responsibilities documented and Staff aware of their own specific responsibilities?	☐ ☐ ☐
17	Is there in-house or external resource available to advise on legal or technical issues relating to the regulatory framework?	☐ ☐ ☐
18	Do staff have ready access to sources of regulatory information?	☐ ☐ ☐
19	Do management have ready access to sources of regulatory information?	☐ ☐ ☐
20	Is there a business wide awareness of the powers of "enforcement officers" under Part 15 of the Act and the duty to cooperate with the	☐ ☐ ☐

	Commission and to provide information where requested?	
21	Are procedures in place to ensure that any information they suspect may relate to the commission of an offence under the Act or LCCP is reported to the Commission?	☐ ☐ ☐
22	Are procedures in place to ensure that 'Key Events' (LCCP 15.2) are reported to the Commission?	☐ ☐ ☐
23	Are procedures in place to assist personal licence holders in discharging their responsibilities under S75 of the Act in relation to their personal licences?	☐ ☐ ☐
CRIME & DISORDER RISK **Yes / Some / No**		
24	Is the reduction of crime and disorder a stated operational priority for senior management? Yes/No	☐ ☐
25	Is it clear which senior manager takes overall responsibility for this licensing objective? Yes/No	☐ ☐
26	Is there a commitment in this area in terms of dedicated specialist resource (Security, MLRO – where appropriate)?	☐ ☐ ☐
27	Does the operator participate in forums (trade associations etc) where best practice to reduce crime and disorder is discussed?	☐ ☐ ☐
28	Are there clear documented instructions for staff and a central reporting point for the reporting of suspicious activity?	☐ ☐ ☐
29	Is there evidence that management and staff have received training in their general and specific responsibilities under the POCA?	☐ ☐ ☐
CRIME & DISORDER RISK (CONTINUED) **Yes / Some / No**		
30	Are there documented internal controls to prevent internal fraud/theft (cash handling etc)	☐ ☐ ☐
31	Are there documented controls (security, opening closing procedures etc) to protect the business from theft/robbery/cheating etc	☐ ☐ ☐
32	Are there documented controls to minimise disorder (keep out alcohol, deal with violent customers, prevent staff being abused or intimidated etc)?	☐ ☐ ☐
33	Are there controls (security cameras, zero tolerance policy, door staff, supervision, central support for crime and disorder partnership engagement) to minimise non gambling crime from being committed on the premises (drug taking, stolen goods, customer intimidation etc)	☐ ☐ ☐
34	Are there clear documented procedures for recording incidents of gambling and non gambling crime and ensuring that such incidents are escalated to relevant senior managers	☐ ☐ ☐
35	Are there clear and documented procedures for recording breaches of LCCP and ensuring that such incidents are escalated to relevant senior managers?	☐ ☐ ☐
FAIR & OPEN RISK **Yes / Some / No**		
36	Is the compliance department (or the senior manager responsible for regulatory compliance) consulted before advertising and marketing content is sent for publication?	☐ ☐ ☐
37	Does the compliance department have authority to overrule other departments or senior management (including the Marketing director or equivalent) where it deems that advertising or marketing material is non compliant?	☐ ☐ ☐

38	If the answer to ITEM 37 is 'NO', is it clear who has final responsibility for signing off advertising and marketing content? Yes/No	☐ ☐
39	Are there clear documented procedures to ensure that advertising and marketing material is compliant (including local marketing initiatives)? Yes/No	☐ ☐
40	Are there documented policies and procedures on how staff deal with complaints or gambling disputes (including internal escalation)?	☐ ☐ ☐
41	Is there senior management awareness of the need to establish procedures to ensure that unresolved disputes are referred to an independent third party?	☐ ☐ ☐
42	Is there a documented commitment on the part of senior management to ensure that customers fully understand the nature of the gambling transaction they are entering into?	☐ ☐ ☐
43	Is there documentary evidence (not just assertions) that senior management are committed to the principles of customer transparency and treating their customers fairly?	☐ ☐ ☐
CHILDREN & OTHER VULNERABLE PEOPLE RISK **Yes / Some / No**		
44	Are there clear written procedures on the exclusion of children and young persons from premises (or restricted areas)?	☐ ☐ ☐
45	Does the operator have clearly documented social responsibility policy? Yes/No	☐ ☐
46	If the answer to ITEM 45 is 'YES' does the policy so contain the following key elements? (A) Combating problem gambling? (B) Access to gambling by children and young persons? (C) Information on how to gamble responsibly and help for problem gamblers? (D) Customer interaction? (E) Self exclusion?	 ☐ ☐ ☐ ☐ ☐ ☐ ☐ ☐ ☐ ☐ ☐ ☐ ☐ ☐ ☐
47	For everything listed in ITEM 46 are there clear documented procedures for staff and management that are well understood?	☐ ☐ ☐
48	Does the business have a self exclusion process including standardised forms and a centralised reporting process?	☐ ☐ ☐
49	Is there evidence that all management and staff are trained in all relevant aspects of social responsibility?	☐ ☐ ☐

CHILDREN & OTHER VULNERABLE PEOPLE RISK (CONTINUED) **Yes / Some / No**		
50	Are there documented policies and procedures for staff on how they should escalate concerns about problem gambling?	☐ ☐ ☐
51	Are there management checks and internal controls to ensure that all staff clearly understand their social responsibility obligations?	☐ ☐ ☐
EXTERNAL RISK **Yes / Some / No**		
52	Are there any external commercial, environmental or other pressures that will impact on the ability of the business to comply with the regulatory regime either by effecting financial and other resources or by limiting compliance capability? There will be some subjective judgment required, but there must be positive evidence to support conclusions i.e. statements by management staff or other stakeholders, observations, evidence such as imminent reduction in size of business or closure.	☐ ☐ ☐

APPENDIX 4

EVALUATION GUIDE A –
BETTING – MANAGEMENT

GAMBLING
COMMISSION

Location details			
Name of Business			
License Type & Category		Licence Number	
Address			
Gambling Commission personnel, etc, details			
Enforcement officer's name			
Name(s) of any other accompanying personnel			
Date, etc, details			
Date premises visited			

OPERATIONAL RISK **Yes / Some / No**		
1	Is there an awareness of the role of the Gambling Commission?	☐ ☐ ☐
2	Is there knowledge of the Act and the new regulatory framework?	☐ ☐ ☐
3	Is there awareness of the source of legal and regulatory information (The Act, LCCP, trade association membership, consultation documents etc)?	☐ ☐ ☐
4	Is there any evidence of efforts to access this information (documents on site, website knowledge etc etc)?	☐ ☐ ☐
5	Is there evidence of willingness or a statement of intent to comply with the new regulatory regime?	☐ ☐ ☐
6	Is there any evidence of positive resistance or hostility to the new regulatory regime (this does not mean general complaints about the regime) ?	☐ ☐ ☐
7	Is there knowledge of the three licensing objectives? 1. The crime and disorder objective 2. The fairness objective 3. Protecting children and vulnerable persons	 ☐ ☐ ☐ ☐ ☐ ☐ ☐ ☐ ☐
8	Is there a recognition that there are risks associated with running a gambling business (children & young persons, problem gambling criminal spend, customer understanding etc)?	☐ ☐ ☐
9	Has the operator carried out a risk assessment of the ability of the business to comply with the LCCP (checklists, audits, evidence of consideration etc)? Is there evidence of any shortfalls being addressed?	☐ ☐ ☐
10	Is there evidence of efforts to implement the requirements of LCCP?	☐ ☐ ☐

11	Are there controls in place to manage these risks (self exclusion, preventing underage entry etc) ?	☐ ☐ ☐
12	Is there any evidence of policies being developed in respect of the three licensing objectives?	☐ ☐ ☐
13	Are responsibilities within the business clearly defined and allocated (who does what, documented procedures or for very small micro businesses clear verbal instructions)?	☐ ☐ ☐
14	Has training been given to staff or is training planned in respect of the regulatory framework? Are there procedures in place to monitor the effectiveness of the training?	☐ ☐ ☐
15	Is there awareness of the powers of "enforcement officers" and the duty to cooperate with the Commission and to provide information?	☐ ☐ ☐
16	Is there an awareness of the need for the business to keep records of certain regulatory matters i.e. complaints/disputes, breaches of the Act or LCCP?	☐ ☐ ☐
CRIME & DISORDER RISK **Yes / Some / No**		
17	Is there knowledge of the POCA regime and the need to report suspicious activity where appropriate?	☐ ☐ ☐
18	Are there internal controls to prevent internal fraud/theft (cash handling etc)?	☐ ☐ ☐
19	Are there controls (security, opening closing procedures etc) to protect the business from theft/robbery/cheating etc?	☐ ☐ ☐
20	Is there evidence that crime and disorder is a problem for this business (incident logs, observation, staff/management experience)?	☐ ☐ ☐
21	Are there controls to minimise disorder (keep out alcohol, deal with violent customers, prevent staff being abused or intimidated etc)?	☐ ☐ ☐
22	Are there controls (security cameras, zero tolerance policy, door staff, supervision, local crime and disorder arrangements) to minimise non gambling crime from being committed on the premises (drug taking, stolen goods, customer intimidation etc)?	☐ ☐ ☐
23	Are there written policies and procedures (or for a micro business clear verbal instructions) in this area?	☐ ☐ ☐
FAIR & OPEN RISK **Yes / Some / No**		
24	Are the rules of the business (win limits, complaint procedures, circumstances for voiding bets etc) relating to gambling (games) clearly displayed for customers?	☐ ☐ ☐
25	Are there internal instructions on how staff deal with complaints or gambling disputes (including internal escalation)?	☐ ☐ ☐
26	If so is there an awareness of the Commission's complaints and disputes requirements including the need to refer disputes to a third party?	☐ ☐ ☐
27	Are such incidents recorded?	☐ ☐ ☐
CHILDREN & OTHER VULNERABLE PEOPLE RISK **Yes / Some / No**		
28	Where appropriate, does the business have to prevent children and young persons from entering its premises (or excluded areas) from time to time?	☐ ☐ ☐

29	Does the business have to prevent children and young persons from attempting to gamble (where they are prohibited) from time to time?	☐ ☐ ☐
30	Are there clear written instructions to staff on the exclusion of children and young persons from premises?	☐ ☐ ☐
31	In reference to ITEM 30 - Are these incidents recorded?	☐ ☐ ☐
32	Does the operator have a written social responsibility policy?	☐ ☐ ☐
34	In reference to ITEM 32 - Does it contain all the key elements relating to:	
	1. Combating problem gambling? yes/no	☐ ☐
	2. Access to gambling by children and young persons? yes/no	☐ ☐
	3. Information on how to gamble responsibly and help for problem gamblers? yes/no	☐ ☐
	4. Customer interaction? yes/no	☐ ☐
	5. Self exclusion? yes/no	☐ ☐

CHILDREN & OTHER VULNERABLE PEOPLE RISK (CONTINUED) Yes / Some / No		
35	NB in making this assessment, reference should be made to the internal social responsibility guidance note.	
	1. Are problem gambling literature and posters displayed?	☐ ☐ ☐
	2. Are there written instructions to staff about what to do following a request for self exclusion?	☐ ☐ ☐
	3. Does the business have self exclusion forms readily available?	☐ ☐ ☐
	4. Are staff and management trained or imminently planning training in social responsibility (mere expressions of intent do not constitute imminent planning)?	☐ ☐ ☐
	5. Are there clear instructions to staff on how they should escalate concerns about problem gambling?	☐ ☐ ☐
EXTERNAL RISK Yes / Some / No		
36	Are there any external commercial, environmental or other pressures that will impact on the ability of the business to comply with the regulatory regime either by effecting financial and other resources or by limiting compliance capability? NB there will be some subjective judgment required, but there must be positive evidence to support conclusions i.e. statements by management staff or other stakeholders, observations, evidence such as imminent reduction in size of business or closure.	☐ ☐ ☐

Please provide narrative on the visit record form

32	(A) Are there any external local factors that may have impacted the ability of the operator to achieve the licensing objectives e.g. 1. New competitor 2. Police activity and subsequent recommendations 3. Local neighbourhood group action 4. Any other relevant local factor (B) Have the staff taken sufficient action to minimise these risks?	☐ ☐ ☐ ☐ ☐ ☐ ☐ ☐ ☐ ☐ ☐ ☐

APPENDIX 6

EVALUATION GUIDE A – AGC AND LICENSED FEC

GAMBLING COMMISSION

Location details			
Name of Business			
License Type & Category		Licence Number	
Address			
Gambling Commission personnel, etc, details			
Enforcement officer's name			
Name(s) of any other accompanying personnel			
Date, etc, details			
Date premises visited			

OPERATIONAL RISK **Yes / Some / No**		
1	Is there an awareness of the role of the Gambling Commission?	☐ ☐ ☐
2	Is there knowledge of the Act and the new regulatory framework?	☐ ☐ ☐
3	Is there awareness of the source of legal and regulatory information (The Act, LCCP, trade association membership, consultation documents etc)?	☐ ☐ ☐
4	Is there any evidence of efforts to access information concerning ITEMS 2 & 3 (documents on site, website knowledge etc)?	☐ ☐ ☐
5	Is there evidence of willingness or a statement of intent to comply with the new regulatory regime?	☐ ☐ ☐
6	Is there any evidence of positive resistance or hostility to the new regulatory regime (this does not mean general complaints about the regime)?	☐ ☐ ☐
7	Is there knowledge of the three licensing objectives? (A) The crime and disorder objective (B) The fairness objective (C) Protecting children and vulnerable persons	☐ ☐ ☐ ☐ ☐ ☐ ☐ ☐ ☐ ☐ ☐ ☐
8	Is there recognition that there are risks associated with running a gambling business (children & young persons, problem gambling criminal spend, customer understanding etc)?	☐ ☐ ☐
9	Has the operator carried out a risk assessment of the ability of the business to comply with the LCCP (checklists, audits, evidence of consideration etc)?	☐ ☐ ☐
10	Is there evidence of efforts to implement the requirements of LCCP?	☐ ☐ ☐
11	Are there controls in place to manage risks? (self exclusion, preventing underage entry etc)	☐ ☐ ☐

APPENDIX 7

EVAULATION GUIDE B – AGC AND LICENSED FEC

GAMBLING COMMISSION

Location details			
Name of Business			
Licence Type & Category		Licence Number	
Address			
Gambling Commission personnel, etc, details			
Enforcement officer's name			
Name(s) of any other accompanying personnel			
Date, etc, details			
Date premises visited			

OPERATIONAL RISK Yes / Some / No		
1	Is there knowledge of the three licensing objectives? (A) The crime and disorder objective (B) The fairness objective (C) Protecting children and vulnerable persons	☐ ☐ ☐ ☐ ☐ ☐ ☐ ☐ ☐
2	Is there awareness of the three licensing objectives? (A) The crime and disorder objective (B) The fairness objective (C) Protecting children and vulnerable persons	☐ ☐ ☐ ☐ ☐ ☐ ☐ ☐ ☐
3	Is there staff knowledge of the Act and role of the Commission's compliance?	☐ ☐ ☐
4	Is there willingness to comply with the new regulatory regime?	☐ ☐ ☐
5	Is there any evidence of positive resistance or hostility to the new regulatory regime? (this does not mean general complaints about the regime)	☐ ☐ ☐
6	Is there recognition of the risks associated with running a gambling business?	☐ ☐ ☐
7	In regards to ITEM 6 is there recognition of the risks associated with running a gambling business especially children & young persons?	☐ ☐ ☐
8	In regards to ITEM 6 is there recognition of the risks associated with running a gambling business especially concerning problem gambling?	☐ ☐ ☐
9	Are there adequate and effective controls in place to manage the following two risks? (A) Preventing underage entry (B) Self exclusions	☐ ☐ ☐ ☐ ☐ ☐

10	Is there any evidence of knowledge and awareness in staff of policies being developed in respect of the three licensing objectives?	☐ ☐ ☐
11	Has training been given to staff or has been planned in respect of: (A) Children and young person attempting to gamble (B) Problem gambling and self exclusion (C) Complaints / disputes (recording of disputes)	☐ ☐ ☐ ☐ ☐ ☐ ☐ ☐ ☐
12	Is there staff awareness and knowledge as to their role, responsibilities and company procedures with respect to ITEM 11?	☐ ☐ ☐

CRIME & DISORDER RISK **Yes / Some / No**		
13	Are there written policies and procedures for dealing with suspicious transactions	☐ ☐ ☐
14	In reference to ITEM 13 are staff aware of their responsibilities?	☐ ☐ ☐
15	Are there controls to minimise disorder (keep out alcohol, deal with violent customers, prevent staff being abused or intimidated etc)?	☐ ☐ ☐
16	Are there adequate and effective controls (security cameras, zero tolerance policy, door staff, supervision, local crime and disorder arrangements) to minimise non-gambling crime from being committed on the premises (drug taking, stolen goods, customer intimidation etc)?	☐ ☐ ☐
FAIR & OPEN RISK **Yes / Some / No**		
17	Are the rules of the business (win limits, complaint procedures etc) relating to gambling clearly displayed for customers?	☐ ☐ ☐
18	Are there internal instructions as to how staff should deal with complaints or gambling disputes (including internal escalation)?	☐ ☐ ☐
19	In regards to ITEM 18 is there an awareness of the Commission's complaints and disputes requirements including the need to refer disputes to a third party?	☐ ☐ ☐
20	In regards to ITEM 18 are such incidents recorded and staff aware of their responsibilities?	☐ ☐ ☐
21	In regards to ITEM 18 are staff aware of their responsibilities?	☐ ☐ ☐
CHILDREN & OTHER VULNERABLE PEOPLE RISK **Yes / Some / No**		
22	Are there policies and procedures to prevent children or young persons from being employed to provide facilities for gambling or to perform any function in connection with a gaming machine (adult only areas)?	☐ ☐ ☐
23	Where appropriate, does the business have policies and procedures to prevent children and young persons from entering the premises (or excluded areas)?	☐ ☐ ☐
24	In reference to ITEM 23 is there clear door or area signage informing customers as to any age restrictions?	☐ ☐ ☐
25	In reference to ITEM 23 is there "No under age" signage on machines (where applicable)?	☐ ☐ ☐
26	In reference to ITEM 23 is there sufficient supervision (entry controls) of adult only area to prevent access by children or young persons?	☐ ☐ ☐
27	In reference to ITEM 23 is there clear written instructions to staff on the exclusion of children and young persons?	☐ ☐ ☐
28	Are there policies and procedures to verify a customers age?	☐ ☐ ☐

29	In reference to ITEM 28 are staff knowledgeable and aware of their responsibilities?	☐ ☐ ☐
30	Does the business have policies and procedures to prevent children and young persons from attempting to gamble (where they are prohibited)?	☐ ☐ ☐
31	In reference to ITEM 30 are staff knowledgeable and aware of their responsibilities?	☐ ☐ ☐
32	Where a child or young person has been gambling within an adult area are there policies and procedures to prevent the payment of prizes and the returning of stakes?	☐ ☐ ☐
33	In reference to ITEM 32 are staff knowledgeable and aware of their responsibilities?	☐ ☐ ☐
34	In reference to ITEM 30 are such incidents recorded?	☐ ☐ ☐

CHILDREN & OTHER VULNERABLE PEOPLE RISK (CONTINUED) **Yes / Some / No**		
35	Does the premises have a written social responsibility policy? If **YES** does it contain all the key elements? (A) Combating problem gambling? Yes/no (B) Access to gambling by children and young persons? yes/no (C) Information on how to gamble responsibly and help for problem gamblers? yes/no (D) Customer interaction? yes/no (E) Self exclusion? yes/no	☐ ☐ ☐ ☐ ☐ ☐ ☐ ☐ ☐ ☐ ☐
33	Is problem gambling literature displayed?	☐ ☐ ☐
34	Are problem gambling posters displayed?	☐ ☐ ☐
35	Are there written instructions to staff about what to do following a request for self exclusion?	☐ ☐ ☐
36	Does the business have self exclusion forms readily available?	☐ ☐ ☐
37	In reference to ITEMS 35 & 36 are staff knowledgeable and aware of their responsibilities?	☐ ☐ ☐
38	Are staff and management trained or imminently planning training in social responsibility? (mere expressions of intent do not constitute imminent planning)?	☐ ☐ ☐
39	Are there clear instructions to staff on how they should escalate concerns about problem gambling?	☐ ☐ ☐
40	In reference to ITEM 39 are staff knowledgeable and aware of their responsibilities?	☐ ☐ ☐
EXTERNAL RISK **Yes / Some / No**		
41	(A) Are there any external local factors that may have impacted the ability of the premises to achieve the licensing objectives e.g. ➢ New Competitor ➢ Police activity and subsequent recommendations	☐ ☐ ☐

	➢ Advice from trade bodies ➢ Local neighbourhood group action ➢ Any other relevant local factor (B) Have staff taken sufficient action to minimise these risks? Please provide narrative on the visit record form	☐ ☐ ☐

APPENDIX 8

EVALUATION GUIDE A – SOCIETY AND LOCAL AUTHORITY LOTTERIES AND EXTERNAL LOTTERY MANAGERS (ELM)

GAMBLING COMMISSION

Location details			
Name of Society, local authority or ELM			
Address			
Licence Type & Category		Licence Number	
Gambling Commission personnel, etc, details			
Enforcement officer's name			
Name(s) of any other accompanying personnel			
Date, etc, details			
Date premises visited			

OPERATIONAL RISK **Yes / Some / No**		
1	Is there an awareness of the role of the Gambling Commission?	☐ ☐ ☐
2	Is there knowledge of the Act and the new regulatory framework?	☐ ☐ ☐
3	Is there awareness of the source of legal and regulatory information (The Act, LCCP, trade association membership, consultation documents etc)?	☐ ☐ ☐
4	Is there any evidence of efforts to access this information (documents on site, website knowledge etc etc)?	☐ ☐ ☐
5	Is there evidence of willingness or a statement of intent to comply with the new regulatory regime?	☐ ☐ ☐
6	Is there any evidence of positive resistance or hostility to the new regulatory regime (this does not mean general complaints about the regime) ?	☐ ☐ ☐
7	Is there knowledge of the three licensing objectives? 1. The crime and disorder objective 2. The fairness objective 3. Protecting children and vulnerable persons	☐ ☐ ☐
8	Is there a recognition that there are risks associated with running a lottery (children, problem gambling criminal spend, customer understanding etc)?	☐ ☐ ☐
9	Has the operator carried out a risk assessment of the ability of the business to comply with the LCCP (checklists, audits, evidence of consideration etc)?	☐ ☐ ☐

10	Is there evidence of efforts to implement the requirements of LCCP?	☐ ☐ ☐
11	Are there controls in place to manage these risks (self exclusion, preventing underage gambling etc) ?	☐ ☐ ☐
12	Is there any evidence of policies being developed in respect of the three licensing objectives?	☐ ☐ ☐
13	Are responsibilities within the society, local authority or ELM clearly defined and allocated i.e. who does what?	☐ ☐ ☐
14	Has training been given to staff or is training planned in respect of the regulatory framework?	☐ ☐ ☐
15	Is there awareness of the powers of "enforcement officers" and the duty to cooperate with the Commission and to provide information?	☐ ☐ ☐
16	Is there an awareness of the need for the operator to keep records of certain regulatory matters i.e. complaints/disputes, breaches of the Act or LCCP?	☐ ☐ ☐

CRIME & DISORDER RISK **Yes / Some / No**		
17	Is there knowledge of the POCA regime and the need to report suspicious activity where appropriate?	☐ ☐ ☐
18	Are there internal controls to prevent internal fraud/theft (cash handling etc)?	☐ ☐ ☐
19	Are there controls to protect the lottery from theft/robbery/cheating etc?	☐ ☐ ☐
20	Is there evidence that crime and disorder is a problem for the lottery (incident logs, observation, staff/management experience)?	☐ ☐ ☐
FAIR & OPEN RISK **Yes / Some / No**		
21	Are the rules of the lottery including stake limits, complaint procedures etc easily accessible to customers?	☐ ☐ ☐
22	Are there instructions on how staff deal with complaints or gambling disputes (including internal escalation)?	☐ ☐ ☐
23	If so is there an awareness of the Commission's complaints and disputes requirements including the need to refer disputes to a third party?	☐ ☐ ☐
24	Are the incidents mentioned above recorded?	☐ ☐ ☐
CHILDREN & OTHER VULNERABLE PEOPLE RISK **Yes / Some / No**		
25	Are there clear written instructions to staff on the exclusion of children from the lottery?	☐ ☐ ☐
26	Does the society, local authority or ELM have to prevent children from entering its lottery from time to time?	☐ ☐ ☐
27	In reference to ITEM 26 - are these incidents recorded?	☐ ☐ ☐
28	Does the operator have a written social responsibility policy?	☐ ☐ ☐
29	In reference to ITEM 28 - Does it contain all the key elements relating to: 6. Combating problem gambling? Yes/no 7. Access to gambling by children and young persons? yes/no	 ☐ ☐ ☐ ☐

	8. Information on how to gamble responsibly and help for problem gamblers? yes/no	☐ ☐
	9. Customer interaction? yes/no	☐ ☐
	10. Self exclusion? yes/no	☐ ☐
30	NB in making this assessment, reference should be made to the internal social responsibility guidance note.	
	6. Is problem gambling literature available and posters displayed?	☐ ☐ ☐
	7. Are there written instructions to staff about what to do following a request for self exclusion?	☐ ☐ ☐
	8. Does the society, local authority and ELM have self exclusion forms readily available?	☐ ☐ ☐
	9. Are staff and management trained or imminently planning training in social responsibility (mere expressions of intent do not constitute imminent planning)?	☐ ☐ ☐
	10. Are there clear instructions to staff on how they should escalate concerns about problem gambling?	☐ ☐ ☐

EXTERNAL RISK **Yes / Some / No**		
31	Are there any external commercial, environmental or other pressures that will impact on the ability of the society or ELM to comply with the regulatory regime either by effecting financial and other resources or by limiting compliance capability? NB there will be some subjective judgment required, but there must be positive evidence to support conclusions i.e. statements by management staff or other stakeholders, observations, evidence such as imminent reduction in size of business or closure. Please provide narrative on the visit record form	☐ ☐ ☐

APPENDIX 9

EVALUATION GUIDE B – SOCIETY AND LOCAL AUTHORITY LOTTERIES AND EXTERNAL LOTTERY MANAGERS (ELM)

GAMBLING COMMISSION

Location details			
Name of Society, local authority or ELM			
Licence Type & Category		Licence Number	
Address			
Gambling Commission personnel, etc, details			
Enforcement officer's name			
Name(s) of any other accompanying personnel			
Date, etc, details			
Date society, local authority or ELM offices visited			

OPERATIONAL RISK		**Yes / No**
1	Is there at least one Personal Management Licence (PML) holder at the society or local authority or if a small scale operator at least one person in a qualifying position who has been vetted and approved by the Gambling Commission?	☐ ☐
2	Does the person in ITEM 1 above have day to day management responsibility for the running of the lottery?	☐ ☐
3	Does the person in ITEMS 1 & 2 above have a sound knowledge of the relevant sections of the Gambling Act and the Licence Conditions and Codes of Practice?	☐ ☐
4	For ELMs: if not a small scale operator does everyone in a qualifying position hold a PML?	☐ ☐
5	(A) If someone other than those persons specified at the ITEMS above has day to day management responsibility for the lottery are they in a qualifying position? (B) Does the person in ITEM 5A have a sound knowledge of the relevant sections of the Gambling Act and the Licence Conditions and Codes of Practice?	☐ ☐ ☐ ☐
6	Is the manager of the lottery at the society or local authority or the ELM aware of the specified "key events" and are there arrangements in place to notify the Commission within 5 working days?	☐ ☐
7	Is the manager of the lottery at the society, local authority or ELM aware of the statutory monetary limits including, maximum prizes, expenses and percentage to the beneficiary and the maximum number	☐ ☐

	tickets that can be sold in one year and in individual lotteries?	
8	(A) Have there been any breaches of the monetary limits during the past 12 months? (B) If yes – Have steps been taken to ensure against any future breaches?	☐ ☐ ☐ ☐
9	Are there arrangements in place to ensure that lottery returns showing the required information are submitted to the Commission within 3 months of the lottery draw?	☐ ☐

CRIME & DISORDER RISK **Yes / No**		
10	(A) Are lottery tickets sold in the street? (B) If yes, are they sold from a kiosk or shop premises?	☐ ☐ ☐ ☐
11	If retailers, door to door ticket agents or other external ticket sellers are used by the society, local authority or ELM to sell tickets are controls in place in respect of cash handling to prevent fraud and theft?	☐ ☐
12	(A) Are unsolicited lottery tickets sent to people who are not members of the society? (B) If yes – does the operator limit the value of lottery tickets sent to £20? (C) Does the operator keep records of where unreturned tickets were sent?	☐ ☐ ☐ ☐ ☐ ☐
13	**Societies and local authorities only –** (A) Do they employ someone else other an employee of the society or local authority to manage any part of their lottery? (B) If yes – is that person an ELM holding a lottery manager operating licence issued by the Gambling Commission?	 ☐ ☐ ☐ ☐
14	**ELM's only –** Do all the society lotteries managed either hold a current operating license issued by the Gambling Commission or a registration with a local authority?	 ☐ ☐
FAIR & OPEN RISK **Yes / No**		
15	Are players informed about the terms and conditions and the rules of the lottery and notified of changes?	☐ ☐
16	In reference to ITEM 15 – is this information notified to the player on the ticket, website or a separate leaflet?	☐ ☐

	If yes – is this leaflet or other communication sent or provided to every player?	☐ ☐
	Are the terms and conditions and rules clearly expressed and easily accessible by players?	☐ ☐
17	Required information that has to be clearly displayed on lottery tickets – must include –	
	(A) the name of the society	☐ ☐
	(B) the price of the ticket	☐ ☐
	(C) the date of the draw	☐ ☐
	(D) the name and address of the person responsible for the promotion of the lottery	☐ ☐
	(E) the fact that the lottery is licensed by the Gambling Commission and the Commission's website address.	☐ ☐
18	Are there arrangements in place to notify the Commission of any changes to the rules of the lottery 28 days before tickets are put on sale?	☐ ☐

CHILDREN & OTHER VULNERABLE PERSONS RISK **Yes / No**		
19	Does everyone at the society, local authority or ELM receive training in respect of	
	(A) minimum age requirements,	☐ ☐
	(B) age verification procedures	☐ ☐
	(C) the operator's policies and procedures in respect of preventing problem gambling	☐ ☐
	before they are allowed to sell a lottery ticket?	
20	In relation to the training in ITEM 19 above – What form of training is given?	
	(A) Written guidelines?	☐ ☐
	(B) Internal face to face training by a member or employee of the society, local authority or ELM ?	☐ ☐
	(C) External face to face training by specialist trainers?	☐ ☐
	(D) Are regular training updates given to everyone who sells lottery tickets?	☐ ☐
21	Where external agents, retailers, telephone call centres etc are used to	

	sell tickets does the operator ensure that they are aware of – (A) minimum age requirements, (B) age verification procedures (C) policies and procedure in respect of problem gambling ?	☐ ☐ ☐ ☐ ☐ ☐
22	In respect of the training and procedures mentioned in the previous ITEMS is the operator satisfied that these arrangements are sufficient?	☐ ☐
23	Does the operator carry out regular checks to ensure that external agents, retailers etc abide by their policies and procedures?	☐ ☐
24	Does the operator make clear and easily accessible information available to players on how to gamble responsibly?	☐ ☐
25	Does the operator have procedures in place to allow players to exclude themselves from the lottery or limit there spend?	☐ ☐
26	Does the operator employ young people (16 and 17 year olds) to sell lottery tickets?	☐ ☐
27	If yes to ITEM 26 above – Does the operator provide specific training to ensure that young people who sell lottery tickets are aware that the law prohibits their sale to anyone under 16 years of age ?	☐ ☐
EXTERNAL RISK **Yes / No**		
28	**New lotteries –** (A) Is the operator confident that the expenses and prizes of the lottery will stay within the 80% of proceeds limit? (B) Will the expenses of the lottery reduce once the lottery is established (6 -12 months) ?	☐ ☐ ☐ ☐

APPENDIX 10

EVALUATION GUIDE A & B – CASINO PREMISES

GAMBLING COMMISSION

Location details	
Name of Casino	
Address of Casino	
Name of Holding Company (e.g. Stanley, LCI etc.)	
Operating Licence No.	
Premises Licence No. & Issuing Authority	
Gambling Commission personnel, etc, details	
Compliance Manager's name	
Details of any other accompanying personnel	
Date, etc, details	
Date premises visited	

Priority should be given to the items in the 'white' numbered boxes below.		
OPERATIONAL RISK **Yes / Some / No**		
1	Do gaming staff have a sound knowledge of the Act and the new regulatory framework?	☐ ☐ ☐
2	Do gaming staff have an awareness of the source of legal and regulatory information? (The Act, LCCP, consultation documents etc)?	☐ ☐ ☐
3	Do gaming staff have knowledge of the three licensing objectives? (A) The crime and disorder objective (B) The fairness objective (C) Protecting Children & vulnerable persons	☐ ☐ ☐ ☐ ☐ ☐ ☐ ☐ ☐
4	Do staff recognise there are risks associated with (A) running a gambling business (B) children & young persons (C) problem gambling (D) criminal spend	☐ ☐ ☐ ☐ ☐ ☐ ☐ ☐ ☐

	(E) customer understanding	☐ ☐ ☐
5	Do the persons with oversight of the day to day management of the premises hold a relevant PML or C of A? (LCCP 1.2)	☐ ☐ ☐

OPERATIONAL RISK (CONTINUED) **Yes / Some / No**		
6	Do all staff carrying out the following operational functions hold a relevant PFL or C of A (LCCP 1.2) – (A) Dealers (B) Cashiers (C) Inspectors (D) Security staff employed to watch gaming (E) Supervisors of gaming activities?	☐ ☐ ☐ ☐ ☐ ☐ ☐ ☐ ☐ ☐ ☐ ☐ ☐ ☐ ☐
7	Do written policies and procedures exist concerning the handling of cash and cash equivalents? (LCCP 5)	☐ ☐ ☐
8	Are those policies effective in minimising the risk of: (A) Money laundering, i.e. compliance with the Commissions guidance. (B) The giving of illicit credit, i.e. compliance with S 81 of the Act. (LCCP 5)	 ☐ ☐ ☐ ☐ ☐ ☐
9	Do written policies and procedures exist which are designed to ensure that proper supervision of gaming tables is carried out to prevent overcrowding or jostling of players to a standard required by any mandatory premises licence conditions? (LCCP C of P 3)	☐ ☐ ☐
10	Are those policies and procedures effective in preventing overcrowding and jostling? (LCCP C of P 3)	☐ ☐ ☐
11	Do written policies and\or procedures exist in respect of the tipping of licensed staff? (LCCP 10)	☐ ☐ ☐
12	Is all permitted tipping of licensed staff operated via a tronc system where all tips are pooled and distributed amongst the employees concerned? (LCCP 10)	☐ ☐ ☐
13	Are written policies and procedures in place designed to ensure staff co-operate with the Commission's enforcement officers? (LCCP 14)	☐ ☐ ☐
14	Can the casino director\general manager provide an assurance that any information which they suspect may relate to the commission of an offence under the Act (as defined in 15.1) has been provided to the Commission's Compliance Manager within 5 working days of the matter coming to the Licensees attention? (e.g. offences by the licensee, certificated staff, cheats etc) (LCCP 15.1)	☐ ☐ ☐
15	Do Personal Licence (C of A) holders take all reasonable steps to ensure that the way in which they discharge their responsibilities in relation to licensed activities does not place the holder of the operating or premises licences in breach of their licence conditions? Rate the performance in respect of the following:	☐ ☐ ☐

	(A) The Compliance Manager's monitoring of breaches to detect adverse trends in respect of individual premises and or personal licence holders. (B) Select a random sample of licensed staff and question them as to how they discharge their responsibilities in relevant areas, e.g. acceptance of tips or following the rules of specific casino games etc. (C) Select a random sample of licensed staff and test their understanding, relevant to the position they hold within the company, of the requirements set out in LCCP 15.1, 15.2 & 15.3. (LCCP Conditions attached to personal licences 1)	☐ ☐ ☐ ☐ ☐ ☐ ☐ ☐ ☐
16	Do Personal Licence holders keep themselves informed of developments in gambling legislation, codes of practice and any Commission guidance (whether on the Commission website or communicated direct) relevant to their role; and (for personal functional licenses only) keep their technical competence up to date? (LCCP Conditions attached to personal licences 2)	☐ ☐ ☐

OPERATIONAL RISK (CONTINUED) **Yes / Some / No**		
17	Where licensees pay fees or other remuneration to representatives engaged to promote their business (whether in the UK or overseas), can the General Manager\Director provide assurances and relevant documentation to show the amounts of such payments are not directly related to the level of customers' prospective losses at gambling nor dependent upon, nor calculated by reference to, the length of time for which, or frequency with which, the customer gambles? (LCCP C of P 4)	☐ ☐ ☐
18	Do written policies and procedures exist to manage relationships between staff and customers? (LCCP C of P 6)	☐ ☐ ☐
19	Are staff aware of their responsibilities under the policies? (LCCP C of P 6)	☐ ☐ ☐
CRIME & DISORDER RISK **Yes / Some / No**		
20	Are there internal controls to prevent internal fraud/theft (cash handling etc)?	☐ ☐ ☐
21	Are there controls (security, opening closing procedures etc) to protect the business from theft/robbery/cheating etc?	☐ ☐ ☐
22	Is there evidence that crime and disorder is a problem for this business (incident logs, observation, staff/management experience)?	☐ ☐ ☐
23	Are there controls to minimise disorder (controlling alcohol, dealing with violent customers, prevent staff being abused or intimidated etc)?	☐ ☐ ☐
24	Are there controls (security cameras, zero tolerance policy, door staff, supervision, local crime and disorder arrangements) to minimise non-gambling crime from being committed on the premises (drug taking, stolen goods, customer intimidation etc)?	☐ ☐ ☐
25	Are procedures in place to ensure the gaming manager, or other nominated member of staff, can be kept informed of customers transactions across the complete range of gaming and cash desk (or 'cashless') facilities to prevent money laundering? (LCCP C of P 1) (Reference should be made to the Proceeds of Crime Act 2002, Money	☐ ☐ ☐

	Laundering Regulations 2003 and the Terrorism Act 2000)	
26	Are procedures in place to verify and record the identity of all customers who enter the gambling facilities? e.g. this may be via a membership system or other methods of recording identification details by the use of technology or otherwise, at the entry points. (LCCP C of P 1)	☐ ☐ ☐
27	Are procedures in place to record transactions above the GC's 'trigger limits'? e.g. this could be in a dedicated book\diary or by the use of technology. (LCCP C of P 1)	☐ ☐ ☐
28	Are staff trained to a standard which enables them to recognise and deal with transactions which may be related to money laundering? Such training should take place whenever the regulations or guidance changes and thereafter at least on an annual basis. (LCCP C of P 1)	☐ ☐ ☐
29	Are staff aware of the detailed requirements relevant to their role, e.g. cash desk transactions, suspicious play at the tables etc? (LCCP C of P 1)	☐ ☐ ☐
30	Are suspicious activity reports (SARS) are passed in a timely manner to the Money Laundering Reporting Officer (MLRO)? (LCCP C of P 1)	☐ ☐ ☐
31	After consideration by the MLRO, are relevant SAR's forwarded to the Serious Organised Crime Agency (SOCA)? (LCCP C of P 1)	☐ ☐ ☐
32	Are money laundering records (as above) retained for a minimum period of 5 years? (See 2003 Money Laundering Regulations for precise details). (LCCP C of P 1)	☐ ☐ ☐
FAIR & OPEN RISK **Yes / Some / No**		
33	Do all games offered appear on the Commission's list of approved games or form part of a trial approved by the Commission? (LCCP 9)	☐ ☐ ☐
34	Do the rules of approved games follow the rules as prescribed by the Commission? (LCCP - 9)	☐ ☐ ☐
35	Can Licensees provide evidence showing how they satisfied themselves that their terms are not unfair? (LCCP C of P 3)	☐ ☐ ☐
36	In order to comply with any condition on a casino premises licence requiring the display of rules about gaming, can the licensee demonstrate that the following are displayed and readily available to customers: (A) The rules of each type of casino game available to be played. (B) A player's guide to the house edge. (C) A player's guide to the rules of any equal chance games which are made available. (LCCP C of P 3)	☐ ☐ ☐ ☐ ☐ ☐ ☐ ☐ ☐
37	Where a licensee makes available to any customer or potential customer any incentive or reward scheme or other arrangement under which the customer may receive money, goods, services or any other advantage (including the discharge in whole or in part of any liability of his) ('the benefit') how well does the scheme comply with the following? (A) The circumstances in which, and conditions subject to which, the benefit is available are clearly set out and readily accessible to customers. (B) either the receipt nor the value or amount of the benefit is: (i) dependent on the customer gambling for a pre-determined length of time	☐ ☐ ☐ ☐ ☐ ☐ ☐ ☐ ☐ ☐ ☐ ☐

	or with a pre-determined frequency; or ii) dependent on the amount the customer spends on gambling within a predetermined length of time which is shorter than the whole of the period during which the particular benefit is made available. (C) If the value of the benefit increases with the amount the customer spends it does so at a rate no greater than that at which the amount spent increases; and further that: (D) If the benefit comprises free or subsidised travel or accommodation which facilitates the customer's attendance at particular licensed premises the terms on which it is offered are not directly related to the level of the customer's prospective gambling. (LCCP C of P 4)	☐ ☐ ☐
38	Where incentive or reward schemes are offered is the benefit available proportionate to the type and level of customers' gambling? (LCCP C of P 4)	☐ ☐ ☐
39	Has the licensee put in place written procedures for handling customer complaints and disputes? (LCCP C of P 5)	☐ ☐ ☐
40	Do the procedures in ITEM 39 include: (A) Customers being told the name and status of the person to contact about their complaint. (B) Giving customers a copy of the complaints procedure on request or on making a complaint. (C) All complaints being handled in accordance with the procedure. (D) Arrangements to ensure that customers whose disputes are not resolved to their satisfaction by use of the complaints procedure may refer them to an independent third party. NB 'independent third party' is not defined and Compliance Managers will need to exercise keen judgement across a range of procedures. e.g. the BCA are considering a panel of suitably experienced people, BACTA and the BA may act as the 'independent party' for each others disputes. (E) Keeping a record of all complaints that are not resolved at the first stage of the procedure. (F) For a copy of the decision on, or a note of the outcome of, each dispute referred to the independent party to be provided to the Commission on a quarterly basis? (LCCP C of P 5)	☐ ☐ ☐ ☐ ☐ ☐ ☐ ☐ ☐ ☐ ☐ ☐ ☐ ☐ ☐ ☐ ☐ ☐
41	Do Licensees comply with the advertising codes of practice which apply to the form and media in which they advertise their gambling facilities or services? (LCCP C of P 4)	☐ ☐ ☐
42	Where Licensees market their services in one or more foreign languages, do they make available in that, or those, foreign languages: (A) The information on how to gamble responsibly and access to help referred to Above. (B) The players' guides to any game, bet or lottery required to be made available to customers under provisions in this code.	☐ ☐ ☐ ☐ ☐ ☐ ☐ ☐ ☐

	(C) The summary of the contractual terms on which gambling is offered, which is required to be provided to customers as a condition of the operating licence. (LCCP CofP 2.4)	
43	Is an accurate summary of the contractual terms on which gambling is offered made available to customers and set out in plain and intelligible language? (LCCP 7)	☐ ☐ ☐
44	Are customers notified of changes to terms before they come into effect? (LCCP 7)	☐ ☐ ☐
45	Is the Licensee able to demonstrate how they have satisfied themselves that the terms on which gambling is offered are not unfair? (LCCP C of P 3)	☐ ☐ ☐

CHILDREN & OTHER VULNERABLE PEOPLE RISK **Yes / Some / No**		
46	Does the Licensee have policies and procedures in place intended to promote socially responsible gambling which include the following as a minimum: (A) A commitment to and how they will contribute to research into the prevention and treatment of problem gambling, e.g. a commitment and contribution to RIGT. (B) A commitment to and how they will contribute to public education on the risks of gambling and how to gamble safely, e.g. making literature available. (C) A commitment to and how they will contribute to the identification of and treatment of problem gamblers, e.g. by having an 'customer interaction' policy in place. (LCCP C of P 2.1)	☐ ☐ ☐ ☐ ☐ ☐ ☐ ☐ ☐
47	Does the Licensee have and put into practice policies and procedures designed to prevent underage gambling, and monitor their effectiveness, e.g. number of breaches and incidents? Do those procedures include: (A) Checking the age of apparently underage customers, e.g. checking the age of customers who appear to be under the age of 21. (B) Removing anyone who appears to be under age who cannot produce an acceptable form of identification, e.g. Citizencard etc. (see ITEM 48). (C) Taking action when there are attempts by under-18's to enter the premises, e.g. reporting the incidents to the Commission and making available information on problem gambling. (LCCP C of P 2.2)	☐ ☐ ☐ ☐ ☐ ☐ ☐ ☐ ☐ ☐ ☐ ☐
48	In relation to ITEM 47B do the policies and procedures specify that identification can only be accepted which: (A) Contains a photograph from which the individual can be identified. (B) States the individual's date of birth. (C) Is valid. (D) Is legible and has no visible signs of tampering or reproduction? (The Commission considers acceptable forms of identification to include any identification carrying the PASS logo (eg Citizencard, Validate and the Government's own Connexions card); a driving licence, including a	☐ ☐ ☐ ☐ ☐ ☐ ☐ ☐ ☐ ☐ ☐ ☐

	provisional licence, with photocard; and a passport). (LCCP C of P 2.2)	
49	Does the Licensee deliberately provide facilities for gambling in such a way as to appeal particularly to children or young people, e.g. reflecting or being associated with youth culture? (LCCP C of P 2.2)	☐ ☐ ☐
50	In premises restricted to adults and does the Licensee refuse service to adults where they are accompanied by a child or young person? (LCCP C of P 2.2)	☐ ☐ ☐
51	Have all staff have received training sufficient for them to understand their responsibilities for preventing underage gambling? This should specifically cover the legal requirements on returning stakes and not paying prizes to underage customers. (LCCP C of P 2.2)	☐ ☐ ☐
52	Are procedures in place for dealing with cases where a child or young person repeatedly attempts to gamble on premises restricted to adults, including oral warnings, reporting the offence to the Gambling Commission and the police, and making available information on problem gambling? (LCCP C of P 2.2)	☐ ☐ ☐
53	Does the Licensee designate sufficient 'supervisors' (as defined in s.176) for each casino entrance, whose responsibilities include ensuring compliance with this code? (Heavily used entrances may require more than one designated supervisor as there must be a sufficient number of designated supervisors to enable a considered judgment to be made about the age of everyone attempting to enter the casino and to take the appropriate action (for example checking identification) whilst at the same time not allowing others to enter unsupervised. The nature of this task means that it cannot be properly accomplished only by using CCTV; it will require a physical presence. Supervisors may be assisted by other door keepers provided the supervisor retains the responsibility for compliance with this code and deals personally with any case where there is any doubt or dispute as to someone's eligibility to enter). (It is a statutory condition of each casino premises licence that the licensee ensures compliance with this code: s176 (3) Gambling Act 2005). (LCCP C of P on access to casino premises for C & YP).	☐ ☐ ☐

CHILDREN & OTHER VULNERABLE PEOPLE RISK (CONTINUED) **Yes / Some / No**		
54	Is the supervisor (at ITEM 53) able to implement the following procedures: (A) Checking the age of apparently underage customers, in particular asking individuals for proof of age if there is any doubt as to whether the individual is 18 or over. (B) Refusing entry to anyone unable to produce an acceptable form of identification, ie one which: (i) contains a photograph from which the individual can be identified. (ii) states the individual's date of birth.	☐ ☐

	(iii) is valid. (iv) is legible and shows no signs of tampering or reproduction. (C) Taking action when there are unlawful attempts to enter the premises. (D) Dealing with cases where a child or young person repeatedly attempts to gamble on premises restricted to adults including oral warnings, reporting the offence to the police, and making available information on problem gambling. (It is a statutory condition of each casino premises licence that the licensee ensures compliance with this code: s176 (3) Gambling Act 2005). (LCCP C of P on access to casino premises for C & YP).	☐ ☐ ☐
55	Does the Licensee make information readily available to their customers on how to gamble responsibly and how to access information about and help in respect of problem gambling? e.g. by making leaflets available, by displaying posters or notices etc. (LCCP C of P 2.3)	☐ ☐ ☐
56	Does the Licensee take all reasonable steps to ensure that this information (at ITEM 55) is readily accessible including in locations which enable the customer to obtain it discreetly? For casinos this should include: (A) Information in the gambling area, near gaming machines and near to where ATMs are located. (B) Posters, or leaflets that may be collected discreetly and taken away, in other areas (e.g. toilets and near to exit doors). (The information must be prominent, and appropriate to the size and layout of the premises, e.g. where there is a large gaming floor, the information should be available in more than one location). (LCCP C of P 2.3)	☐ ☐ ☐ ☐ ☐ ☐ ☐ ☐ ☐
57	Is the information (at ITEMS 55/56) directed to all customers who wish to enjoy gambling as entertainment and not just targeted at those the operator perceives to be 'problem gamblers'? (LCCP C of P 2.3)	☐ ☐ ☐
58	Does the information cover? (A) The availability of measures that are accessible to help an individual monitor or control their gambling, such as to restrict the duration of a gambling session or the amount of money they can spend. (B) The availability of timers or any other forms of reminders or 'reality checks' that may be available; (C) Self-exclusion options. (D) Information about the availability of further help or advice? (LCCP C of P 2.3)	☐ ☐ ☐ ☐ ☐ ☐ ☐ ☐ ☐ ☐ ☐ ☐
59	Does the Licensee have and implement policies and procedures for customer interaction where they have concerns that a customer's behavior may indicate problem gambling? (LCCP C of P 2.4)	☐ ☐ ☐
60	Do the policies for ITEM 59 include: (A) Identification of the appropriate level of management who may initiate customer interaction and the procedures for doing so. (B) The types of behaviour that will be logged/reported to the appropriate level of staff and which may trigger customer interaction at an appropriate moment; (C) The circumstances in which consideration should be given to	☐ ☐ ☐ ☐ ☐ ☐ ☐ ☐ ☐ ☐ ☐ ☐

	refusing service to customers and/or barring them from the operator's gambling premises. (D) Training for all staff on their respective responsibilities, in particular so that they know who is designated to deal with problem gambling issues. (Such policies and procedures should be consistent with, and implemented with due regard to, licensees' duties in respect of the health and safety of their staff). (LCCP C of P 2.4)	
61	Does the Licensee have in place procedures for self-exclusion and take all reasonable steps to refuse service or to otherwise prevent an individual who has entered a self exclusion agreement from participating in gambling? (e.g. 'traffic cards' or other records pertaining to the individual are appropriately endorsed, and entry procedures are sufficiently robust to detect self-excluded persons). (LCCP C of P 2.5)	☐ ☐ ☐
62	Do the procedures designed to ensure that an individual who has self-excluded include: (A) A register of those excluded with appropriate records (name, address, other details, and any membership or account details that may be held by the operator). (B) Photo identification (where available and in particular where enforcement of the system may depend on photographic ID), and a signature. (C) Staff training to ensure that staff are able to enforce the systems. (D) The removal of those persons found in the gambling area or attempting to gamble from the premises? (LCCP C of P 2.5)	☐ ☐ ☐ ☐ ☐ ☐ ☐ ☐ ☐ ☐ ☐ ☐
63	Does the Licensee close any customer accounts of an individual who has entered a self exclusion agreement and return any funds held in the customer account? (It is not sufficient merely to prevent an individual from withdrawing funds from their customer account whilst still accepting wagers from them. Where the giving of credit is permitted, the licensee may retain details of the amount owed to them by the individual, although the account must not be active). (LCCP C of P 2.5)	☐ ☐ ☐
64	Do the Self-exclusion procedures require individuals to take positive action in order to self-exclude? This can be a signature on a self-exclusion form. (Wherever practicable, individuals should be able to self-exclude without having to enter gambling premises). (LCCP C of P 2.5)	☐ ☐ ☐
65	Before an individual self-excludes, does the Licensee provide or make available sufficient information about what the consequences of self-exclusion are? (Customers should be given the opportunity to discuss self-exclusion in private, where possible). (LCCP C of P 2.5)	☐ ☐ ☐
66	Does the Licensee take all reasonable steps to extend the self-exclusion to premises of the same type owned by the operator in the customer's local area? (In setting the bounds of that area licensees may take into account the customer's address (if known to them), anything else known to them about the distance the customer ordinarily travels to gamble and any specific request the customer may make). (LCCP C of P 2.5)	☐ ☐ ☐
67	Does the Licensee encourage the customer to consider extending their self exclusion to other licensees' gambling premises in the customer's local area? (LCCP C of P 2.5)	☐ ☐ ☐
68	Does the Licensee take all reasonable steps to ensure that: (A) The self-exclusion period is a minimum of six months and give	

	customers the option of extending this to a total of at least five years. (B) A customer who has decided to enter a self-exclusion agreement is given the opportunity to so do immediately without any cooling-off period. However, if the customer wishes to consider the self-exclusion further (for example to discuss with problem gambling groups) the customer may return at a later date to enter into self-exclusion. (C) At the end of the period chosen by the customer (and at least six months later), maintain the self-exclusion in place, unless the customer takes positive action in order to gamble again. No marketing material may be sent to the individual unless the individual has taken positive action in order to gamble again, and has agreed to accept such material. (D) Where a customer chooses not to renew, and makes a positive request to begin gambling again, give the customer one day to cool off before being allowed access to gambling facilities. The contact must be made via telephone or in person. (LCCP C of P 2.5)	☐ ☐ ☐ ☐ ☐ ☐ ☐ ☐ ☐ ☐ ☐ ☐
69	Does the Licensee, or any contractor\supplier employ children or young persons on the casino premises? (LCCP C of P 2.6)	☐ ☐ ☐
70	**This question only applies where the reply to ITEM 69 is 'yes'.** Where the Licensee employs children (under-16s) and young persons (those aged 16 and 17), are they aware that it is an offence: A) To employ them to provide facilities for gambling. B) If gaming machines are sited on the premises, for their contracts of employment to require them, or for them to be permitted, to perform a function in connection with a gaming machine at any time. C) To employ them to carry out any other function on casino licensed premises while any gambling activity is being carried on in reliance on the premises licence (except that they can be employed on a part of regional casino premises when that part of the premises is not being used for the provision of facilities for gambling). As to (B) it should be noted that in the Commission's view the relevant provision of the Act applies to any function performed in connection with a gaming machine. This includes servicing or cleaning such a machine. Accordingly, licensees should have policies and procedures designed to ensure that children and young persons are never asked to perform tasks within 70 (A) or 70 (B).	☐ ☐ ☐ ☐ ☐ ☐ ☐ ☐ ☐
71	**This question only applies where the reply to ITEM 69 is 'yes'.** (A) All staff, including those who are children or young persons themselves, are instructed about the laws relating to access to gambling by children and young persons. (B) The management are considering adopting a policy that: (i) children and young persons are not employed to work on casino licensed premises (other than in an area of a regional casino where gambling does not take place) at any time when the premises are open for business. (ii) gaming machines are turned off if children and young persons are working on the premises outside the hours when the premises are open for business. (LCCP C of P 2.6)	☐ ☐ ☐ ☐ ☐ ☐ ☐ ☐ ☐
72	Does the Licensee take all reasonable steps to ensure that staff involved in the provision of facilities for gambling are made aware of	☐ ☐ ☐

	advice on socially responsible gambling and of where to get confidential advice should their gambling become hard to control? (LCCP C of P 6)	
73	Where the Licensee offers customers free or discounted alcoholic drinks for consumption on the premises, do they do so on terms which do not in any way link the availability of such drinks to whether, or when, the customer begins, or continues, to gamble? (LCCP C of P 4)	☐ ☐ ☐
74	Does the Licensee make unsolicited offers of free alcoholic drinks for immediate consumption by customers at a time when they are participating in a casino game, playing a gaming machine? (LCCP C of P 4)	☐ ☐ ☐
75	Does the Licensee take steps to remove the name and details of a self-excluded individual from any marketing databases used by the company or group (or otherwise flag that person as an individual to whom marketing material must not be sent), within two days of receiving the completed self-exclusion notification. (LCCP C of P 2.5)	☐ ☐ ☐
76	Does the Licensee take all reasonable steps to prevent any marketing material being sent to a self-excluded customer as soon as practicable? This covers any marketing material relating to gambling, or other activities that take place on the premises where gambling may take place. However, it would not extend to blanket marketing which is targeted at a particular geographical area and where the excluded individual would not knowingly be included. The realistic timescale may depend upon lead in times for the despatch of such material and Compliance Managers will have to exercise keen judgement on these issues. (LCCP C of P 2.5)	☐ ☐ ☐
77	Where a premises is restricted to adults, does the Licensee consider the permanent exclusion of any adult who was accompanied by a child or young person on more than one occasion or where there is reason to believe the offence was committed knowingly or recklessly?	☐ ☐ ☐
78	Does the Licensee take steps to prevent systematic or organised money lending between customers on their premises? While the nature of those arrangements will depend to some extent on the layout and size of the premises, they should cover matters such as: ➢ Systems for monitoring for such activity; ➢ Instructions to staff concerning what they should do if they spot what they believe to be significant money lending and to managers about the ways in which they should handle and act on any such lending; and ➢ Excluding from the premises, either temporarily or permanently as appropriate, ➢ any person whom the evidence suggests has become involved in organised or ➢ systematic money lending. Particular care should be taken to ensure that there are appropriate arrangements in place to cover any cases where it appears that the lending may be commercial in nature or may involve money laundering. In the latter case, the requirements in respect of reporting suspicious transactions must be followed. In all cases where the operator encounters systematic or organised money lending, a report should be made to the Commission. (LCCP C of P 2.8)	☐ ☐ ☐

EXTERNAL RISK **Yes / Some / No**		
79	Are there any external commercial, environmental or other pressures that will impact on the ability of the business to comply with the regulatory regime either by effecting financial and other resources or by limiting compliance capability? NB there will be some subjective judgment required, but there must be positive evidence to support conclusions i.e. statements by management staff or other stakeholders, observations, evidence such as imminent reduction in size of business or closure. Please provide narrative on the visit record form.	☐ ☐ ☐

APPENDIX 11

GAMBLING COMMISSION

EVALUATION GUIDE A & B – BINGO

Location details	
Name of Bingo Club	
Address of Bingo Club	
Name of Holding Company (e.g. Rank)	
Operating Licence No.	
Premises Licence No. & Issuing Authority	
Gambling Commission personnel, etc, details	
Compliance Manager's name	
Details of any other accompanying person(s)	
Date, etc, details	
Date premises visited	

OPERATIONAL RISK		**Yes / Some / No**
1	Do all staff who are involved in the delivery of the bingo activity have a sound knowledge of the Act and the new regulatory framework?	☐ ☐ ☐
2	Do staff have an awareness of the source of legal and regulatory information? (The Act, LCCP, consultation documents etc)?	☐ ☐ ☐
3	Do gaming staff have knowledge of the three licensing objectives? (A) The crime and disorder objective (B) The fairness objective (C) Protecting Children & vulnerable persons	☐ ☐ ☐ ☐ ☐ ☐ ☐ ☐ ☐
4	Is there any evidence of policies being developed in respect of the three licensing objectives?	☐ ☐ ☐
5	Is there evidence of efforts to implement the requirements of LCCP?	☐ ☐ ☐
6	Are there controls in place to manage LCCP risks (self exclusion, preventing underage entry etc) ?	☐ ☐ ☐
7	Does the person(s) with oversight of the day to day management of the premises hold a relevant PML or Certificate of Approval?	☐ ☐ ☐
8	Has training been given to staff or is training planned in respect of the new act?	☐ ☐ ☐

	(mere expressions of intent do not constitute imminent planning)	
9	Does the bingo equipment comply with the bingo technical standards issued by the Commission?	☐ ☐ ☐
10	If any bingo equipment is offered where the player's money is held on deposit (smartcard, swipe-card or other back office banking arrangement) is there information available (in writing) as to what would happen to such funds in the event that the company became insolvent?	☐ ☐ ☐
11	Do written policies and procedures exist concerning the handling of cash and cash equivalents?	☐ ☐ ☐
12	Are there policies and procedures in place to ensure that licensees do not arrange, permit or knowingly facilitate the giving of credit in connection with gambling?	☐ ☐ ☐
13	Are the policies in ITEM 12 effective in minimising the risk of: (A) Crime. (B) Giving illicit credit. (i.e. compliance with S 81 of the Act)	 ☐ ☐ ☐ ☐ ☐ ☐
14	Are there written policies and procedures in place designed to ensure staff understand and co-operate with the Commission's enforcement officers?	☐ ☐ ☐
15	Can the bingo general manager provide evidence that any information which they suspect may relate to the commission of an offence under the Act (as defined in 15.1 of LCCP) has been provided to the Commission?	☐ ☐ ☐
16	Is the licence holder aware that he must notify the Commission of the occurrence of 'key events' as defined in LCCP, as soon as reasonably practicable and in any event within 5 working days of its occurrence?	☐ ☐ ☐
17	In respect of some of the ITEMS listed above in the ORGANISATIONAL RISK section do staff demonstrate knowledge as to their role, responsibilities and company procedures?	☐ ☐ ☐
CRIME AND DISORDER RISK **Yes / Some / No**		
18	Are there controls to prevent internal fraud/theft (e.g. cash handling etc)?	☐ ☐ ☐
19	Are there controls (e.g. security, CCTV, machine data management systems) to protect the business from theft/robbery/cheating etc?	☐ ☐ ☐
20	Are there controls to minimise disorder? (control of alcohol, dealing with abusive customers, prevent staff from being abused or intimidated etc)	☐ ☐ ☐
21	Are there controls (CCTV, zero tolerance policy, door staff, supervision, local crime and disorder arrangements) to minimise non-gambling crime from being committed on the premises (drug offences, stolen goods, customer intimidation?)	☐ ☐ ☐
22	Are there clear written policies setting out the strategy of how crime and disorder will be managed?	☐ ☐ ☐
FAIR AND OPEN RISK **Yes / Some / No**		
23	Are there policies and procedures in place to ensure that any terms	☐ ☐ ☐

	on which gambling is offered have met the reasonableness test under the Unfair Contract Terms Act 1977?	
24	In complying with any condition on a bingo premises licence requiring the display of rules about gaming, have licensees ensured that the following are included: (A) Rules about each variant of bingo made available. (B) Rules about any prize gaming made available.	☐ ☐ ☐ ☐ ☐ ☐
24	Can licensees provide evidence showing how satisfied they are that their terms are not unfair?	☐ ☐ ☐
25	Are there rules covering each game variant available on request to any person requiring same?	☐ ☐ ☐
27	Are there rules covering prize gaming available on request to any person requiring same?	☐ ☐ ☐
28	Are staff members conversant about policies issued by the licensee in terms of fair and open provisions?	☐ ☐ ☐
29	Does the licensee offer customers or potential customers any incentive or reward scheme or other arrangement under which the customer may receive money, goods, services or any other advantage?	☐ ☐ ☐
30	Are the conditions subject to which the benefits are available clearly set out and readily accessible to customers?	☐ ☐ ☐
31	Have licensees ensured neither the receipt nor the value or amount of a benefit is dependent on the customer gambling for a pre-determined length of time or with a pre-determined frequency?	☐ ☐ ☐
32	Do licensees offer free or discounted alcoholic drinks on the premises on the condition that a customer begins, continues to gamble or increases their gambling spend?	☐ ☐ ☐
33	Do licensees make unsolicited offers of free alcoholic drinks for immediate consumption when the customer is playing a bingo game or playing gaming machines on the condition that a customer continues to gamble, prolongs their gambling or increases their gambling spend?	☐ ☐ ☐
34	Has the licensee put in place written procedures for handling customer complaints and disputes?	☐ ☐ ☐
35	Do those procedures follow the guidance as laid down in Section 5 of the LCCP document	☐ ☐ ☐
36	Do licensees comply with the advertising codes of practice which apply to the form and media in which they advertise their gambling facilities or services?	☐ ☐ ☐
37	Do licensees market their services in one or more foreign languages and do they make available in that language(s) information on how to gamble responsibly?	☐ ☐ ☐
38	Are customers notified of changes to terms before they come into effect?	☐ ☐ ☐
39	In respect of some of the ITEMS listed above in the FAIR & OPEN RISK section do staff demonstrate knowledge as to their role, responsibilities and company procedures?	☐ ☐ ☐
CHILDREN & OTHER VULNERABLE PEOPLE RISK Yes / Some / No		
40	Has the licensee introduced policies and procedures that are intended to promote socially responsible gambling?	☐ ☐ ☐
41	Does the licensee have policies and procedures designed to prevent underage gambling?	☐ ☐ ☐

42	Do the policies include procedures for: (A) Checking the age of apparently underage customers. (B) Refusing entry to any adult-only areas to anyone unable to produce an acceptable form of identification. (C) Taking action when there are unlawful attempts to enter the adult-only areas.	☐ ☐ ☐ ☐ ☐ ☐ ☐ ☐ ☐
43	Does the licensee only accept identification which: (A) Contains a photograph from which the individual can be identified. (B) States the individual's date of birth. (C) Is valid. (D) Is legible and has no visible signs of tampering or reproduction?	☐ ☐ ☐ ☐ ☐ ☐ ☐ ☐ ☐ ☐ ☐ ☐
44	Does the licensee have a policy to prevent children and young persons from gambling in the adults-only areas of the premises to which they have access?	☐ ☐ ☐
45	If the licensee operates a 'no under 18s' premises policy, are procedures in place that ensure that age verification is checked at the entrance to the premises?	☐ ☐ ☐
46	Does the licensee have policies and procedures that reasonable steps are taken to ensure that staff understand their responsibility for preventing underage gambling, returning stakes and not paying prizes to underage customers, and for challenging any adult who may be complicit in allowing a child or young person to gamble?	☐ ☐ ☐
47	Does the licensee have information readily available to customers as how to gamble responsibly and how to access information about help in respect of problem gambling?	☐ ☐ ☐
48	Has the licensee taken all reasonable steps to ensure that this information is readily available including in locations which enable customers to obtain it discreetly (e.g. toilet areas, near to ATMs and exits)	☐ ☐ ☐
49	Does the information meet all the requirements as laid down in LCCP? (e.g. self exclusion options)	☐ ☐ ☐
50	Does the licensee have policies and procedures for customer interaction where they have concerns that a customer's behaviour may indicate problem gambling?	☐ ☐ ☐
51	Do the policies cover all the requirements as laid down in LCCP (e.g. appropriate level of management who may initiate customer interaction, types of behaviour to be logged etc)?	☐ ☐ ☐
52	Has the licensee put procedures in place for self exclusion and taken all reasonable steps to refuse service or to otherwise prevent an individual who has entered a self exclusion agreement from participating in gambling?	☐ ☐ ☐
53	Do licensees have policies and procedures designed to ensure that children and young persons employed by the licensee do not perform tasks connected to providing facilities for playing bingo or to perform functions in connection with a gaming machine?	☐ ☐ ☐
54	Does the licensee have policies and procedures for dealing with cases where an adult knowingly or recklessly allows a child or young person to gamble?	☐ ☐ ☐

55	Does the licensee have policies and procedures for dealing with cases where a child or young person repeatedly attempts to gamble on their premises, including oral warnings, reporting the offence to the Gambling Commission and the police and making available information on problem gambling to the young person concerned?	☐ ☐ ☐
56	In respect of some of the ITEMS listed above in the CHILDREN & OTHER VULNERABLE PEOPLE RISK section do staff demonstrate knowledge as to their role, responsibilities and company procedures?	☐ ☐ ☐
EXTERNAL RISK **Yes / Some / No**		
57	Are there any external commercial, environmental or other pressures that will impact on the ability of the business to comply with the regulatory regime either by effecting financial and other resources or by limiting compliance capability? NB there will be some subjective judgement required, but there must be positive evidence to support conclusions i.e. statements by management staff or other stakeholders, observations, evidence such as imminent reduction in size of business or closure. Please provide narrative on the visit record form	☐ ☐ ☐

APPENDIX 12

GAMBLING COMMISSION

GC ref

Operator's address

Dear Sir/Madam

Gambling Act 2005
Gambling Act 2005 (Inspection) (Provision of Information) Regulations 2007

This is to inform you that on the .... (*enter date*) an officer from the Gambling Commission visited the following premises:

....
....
....(*enter premises address*)

Please find enclosed a copy of:

- a form ('Inspection Record Request') detailing how you can obtain information about what statutory powers an officer used whilst carrying out the visit to the above premises. A copy of this 'Inspection Record Request' form was also left at the visited premises.

- the 'Operator/Licensee Information' form that was given to the occupier of the premises stated above. This particular form provides a brief summary of the results of the visit and if applicable explains what remedial action is required to be taken. When any remedial action is required in order to correct any non-compliance with the provisions of the Gambling Act 2005, a letter providing further detail will be supplied. If, at the time of the visit, no person was present a copy of this 'Operator/Licensee Information' form would have been left, with the 'Inspection Record Request' form, in a prominent place on the premises.

Should you have any queries about this letter please contact Compliance Administration at the address below.

Yours faithfully

W. Pearson
Head of Compliance

Victoria Square House
Victoria Square
Birmingham B2 4BP

T 0121 230 6500
F 0121 230 6720
www.gamblingcommission.gov.uk

complianceadmin@gamblingcommission.gov.uk

APPENDIX 13

TOP COPY – PREMISES
REF: 00000

GAMBLING COMMISSION

Inspection Record Request

<u>Gambling Act 2005 (Inspection) (Provision of Information) Regulations 2007</u>

This notice is to inform you that, under the provisions of the Gambling Act 2005, an inspection of the premises (stated below):

- is being undertaken*
- was undertaken in the absence of the occupier or a person responsible for their management*

and that if you are any of the following:

i) the occupier of the premises inspected,

ii) responsible for the management of such premises,

iii) the holder of a Gambling Act 2005 premises licence/permit that is in effect at the time of the premises inspection,

iv) the holder of an on-premises alcohol licence which is in effect at the time of the premises inspection,

v) a person who has provided a Gambling Act 2005 temporary use notice for the premises,

vi) a society registered with a local authority and these premises are owned by the society or being used by that society at the time of the inspection.

You may request a written record of the inspection. Please note that your request <u>must be in writing</u> and should be sent to the Gambling Commission at the address below.

[* delete as appropriate]

Name of premises	
Premises' address	

Name of Gambling Commission officer who carried out the inspection	
Date of inspection	

Victoria Square House
Victoria Square
Birmingham B2 4BP

T 0121 230 6500
F 0121 230 6720
www.gamblingcommission.gov.uk

APPENDIX 14

GAMBLING COMMISSION

RECORD OF INSPECTION

(Gambling Act 2005 (Inspection) (Provision of Information) Regulations 2007)

Location details	
Name of premises	
Address	

Gambling Commission personnel, etc, details	
Enforcement officer's name	
Name(s) of any other accompanying personnel	

Date, etc, details			
Date premises entered		Time of entry	

Gambling Act 2005: Entry to premises - powers available to Gambling Commission enforcement officers ("officers")		
Section	Statutory power description	Tick if power used
306	Premises (other than a dwelling) may be entered if an officer reasonably suspects an offence is being, or about to be, committed; any premises may be entered by virtue of a warrant issued by a Justice of the Peace on suspicion an offence has been committed and evidence may be found on the premises.	
307	Premises (other than a dwelling) may be entered if an officer reasonably suspects that facilities for gambling other than private or non-commercial gaming or betting may be being provided, may be about to be provided, or have been provided, for the purpose of establishing whether gambling facilities are being provided and , if so, in accordance with a licence.	
308	Premises (other than a dwelling) may be entered if an officer reasonably believes them to be used by a holder of an operating licence wholly or partly for purpose connected with the licensed activities, for the purpose of determining whether the activities are being carried on in accordance with the operating licence.	
309	Family entertainment centres may be entered by an officer for a purpose of checking compliance with the statutory provisions relating to gaming machines.	
310	Premises holding an on-premises alcohol licence may be entered by	

	an officer for a purpose connected to considering any application for a licensed premises gaming machine permit, or checking compliance with the statutory provisions relating to gaming machines or exempt gaming including bingo.	
311	Premises (other than a dwelling) may be entered by an officer for a purpose connected with the consideration of any application for a prize gaming permit, or checking compliance with the statutory provisions relating to such permits.	
312	Premises(other than a dwelling) reasonably believed by an officer to be used by a members'/commercial club or a miners' welfare institute can be entered to determine whether any gaming is taking, or about to take, place and if so whether in accordance with statutory provisions and/or relevant permits.	
313	Premises for which an application for a premises licence is pending may be entered to assess the likely effects of the proposed licensed activity; and licensed premises for purposes connected with a review of the licence.	
314	Registered society lottery premises may be entered by an officer for the purpose of making inquiries in connection with a lottery promoted by the society.	
315	Premises (other than a dwelling) in respect of which a temporary use notice has been given may be entered to assess the likely effects of the authorised activities, and when the notice is in effect to determine whether activities are being carried on in accordance with the notice.	
318	A dwelling may only be entered by an officer if a warrant has been issued by a Justice of the Peace.	
320	All powers of entry must be exercised at a reasonable time	
323	Reasonable force may be used by an officer to enter premises in reliance on section 306 or 307.	

RECORD OF INSPECTION

(Gambling Act 2005 (Inspection) (Provision of Information) Regulations 2007)

Record of any part of the premises, or any machine or other thing on the premises inspected under section 317(1)(a)	
Item no.	Details

Record of any written or electronic record to which access was required under section 317(1)(c)	
Item no.	Details

Description of any copies of written or electronic records that were supplied to the officer in compliance with a request under section 317(1)(d) and the form in which they were supplied		
Item no.	Details	Format

RECORD OF INSPECTION

(Gambling Act 2005 (Inspection) (Provision of Information) Regulations 2007)

Record of items removed from premises		
Description of item	Reason for removal	Location of item on premises

6: Gambling Act 2005: Additional Material

Details of any force used to enter premises	
Was any force used to enter the premises?	
Who used force to enter premises?	
Why was force used?	
Steps taken to secure premises	
Details of any damage caused and circumstances in which it was caused	

APPENDIX 15

TOP COPY – OPERATOR/LICENSEE

REF: 00000

GC REF No: ______________

GAMBLING COMMISSION

OPERATOR/LICENSEE INFORMATION

OPERATOR'S/LICENSEE'S NAME: ______________________________

PREMISES ADDRESS: ______________________________

....

....

....

....

....

....

....

....

....

GAMBLING COMMISSION OFFICER

SIGNED: .... NAME: ....

DATE: .... POSITION: ....

OPERATOR/LICENSEE

SIGNED: .... NAME: ....

DATE: .... POSITION: ....

Victoria Square House
Victoria Square
Birmingham B2 4BP

T 0121 230 6500
F 0121 230 6720
www.gamblingcommission.gov.uk

info@gamblingcommission.gov.uk

APPENDIX 16

GAMBLING COMMISSION

VISIT RECORD FORM

GC REF No:____________ OFFICER:__________________________ DATE:_____________

OPERATOR'S NAME: ____

PREMISES ADDRESS:

____

Type of visit – tick as appropriate					
Programmed ☐	Advisory ☐	Complaint ☐	Revisit ☐	Survey ☐	Other ☐
Time of entry onto premises			Time left premises		

Risks assessed	
LCCP etc risk	Details of assessment

Key Risk Areas – Risk Rating				
Organisational	Crime and disorder	Fair and open	Children and vulnerable people	External
☐	☐	☐	☐	☐

Gambling Commission August 2007

GAMBLING ACT 2005 – JOINT COMPLIANCE AND ENFORCEMENT STATEMENT BETWEEN THE GAMBLING COMMISSION, LOCAL AUTHORITIES COORDINATORS OF REGULATORY SERVICES (LACORS) AND THE ASSOCIATION OF CHIEF POLICE OFFICERS (ACPO)

6.2085 The Gambling Act 2005 (the Act) comprehensively updates existing gambling laws, providing new powers and protections for both new and old forms of gambling. The new regime is jointly administered by the Gambling Commission (the Commission) and local (licensing) authorities.

The Act has three licensing objectives:

- preventing gambling from being a source of crime and disorder;
- ensuring that gambling is fair and open; and
- protecting children and vulnerable people from being exploited or harmed by gambling.

Since January 2007 (operating & personal licences) and 21 May 2007 (premises licences), all operators requiring licensing under the new regime have had the opportunity to apply for their new licences. On 1 September 2007 the full provisions of the Act come into effect and from that day, all operators that require operating and premises licences (Adult Gaming Centres, Family Entertainment Centres, Bingo premises, Betting shops, Tracks, and Casinos) will need to be licensed under the new Act. Their existing licences will cease, regardless of the dates of expiry. Alcohol licensed premises and clubs will need to renew or convert their existing permits and registrations when they are due to expire.

Inevitably there will be a number of premises that will not have a new licence in place by the 1 September, or will not have renewed/converted their permit/ registration when they were required to do so. We therefore wish to set out our joint approach for dealing with unlicensed premises.

GENERAL PRINCIPLES

The Commission, LACORS and ACPO have agreed a framework in relation to dealing with unlicensed premises in the immediate post 1 September 2007 period. This is focused around pursuing the 3 licensing objectives. Central to this framework is partnership working between licensing authorities, the Commission and police forces. Any action taken will be decided on a case-by-case basis as we recognise that adopting a blanket approach will not be appropriate. Our ultimate aim is to have a properly regulated and licensed gambling industry.

COMPLIANCE AND ENFORCEMENT IN RELATION TO UNLICENSED PREMISES

With the underlying principle that all operators should have a licence/permit and should run their premises in accordance with the law, there will be a variety of reasons why licences/permits have not been obtained, not all of them wilful. Reasons could range from administrative issues, such as the licence/permit not yet having been issued, to operators not realising they had to apply. The steps an operator has taken to become licensed will be taken into account when determining the most appropriate course of action.

Local authorities are generally in the best position to proceed against individual unlicensed premises, although the Commission will be keen consider compliance activity

against operators who have a regional or national presence. The Commission and local authorities will also work together to identify and investigate organised or persistent illegal activity.

COMPLIANCE AND ENFORCEMENT IN RELATION TO LICENSED PREMISES

LACORS, the Commission and ACPO encourage a proportionate and risk individual assessed targeted approach towards compliance and enforcement.

- Licensing authorities will generally lead on matters relating to premises.
- The Gambling Commission will generally lead on matters relating to businesses with a national or regional presence.
- ACPO will support local authorities and the Commission in achieving the delivery of a properly regulated and licensed gambling industry.

The priorities for action will depend on the extent that the licensing objectives are threatened. Local flexibility is key when making decisions in respect of compliance and enforcement.

Derek Allen Executive
Director
LACORS
Jenny Williams
Chief Executive
Gambling Commission
ACC Ian Seabridge
Association of Chief
Police Officers

GUIDE TO GAMBLING ADVERTISING CODES
September 2010

1 BACKGROUND AND INTRODUCTION

6.2086 1.1 The Gambling Act 2005 (the Act) reforms virtually all of the previous restrictions on the advertising of gambling. The Gambling Commission (the Commission) has included an ordinary code provision within its Licence Conditions and Codes of Practice (*LCCP*) which requires licensees to comply with the advertising codes of practice that apply to the form and media in which they advertise their gambling facilities and services.

1.2 Advertising is subject to the CAP and BCAP advertising codes. The CAP and BCAP codes are administered by the Advertising Standards Authority (ASA). Operators should also follow the Gambling Industry Code for Socially Responsible Gambling. The Gambling Industry Code for Socially Responsible Gambling was published on 7 August 2007 and is monitored by the Review Group for Socially Responsible Advertising.

1.3 In September 2010, CAP and BCAP proposed new codes, following a systematic review and full 12-week consultation. The advertising codes apply to all gambling operators and advertisers permitted to advertise in Great Britain. This includes operators from the European Community jurisdictions and Gibraltar, and also the whitelisted[1] jurisdictions of Alderney, Antigua and Barbuda, Isle of Man, and Tasmania.

2 THE CODES

2.1 The CAP and BCAP codes cover the content and placement of advertising and ensure that gambling advertising is socially responsible. The rules ensure that gambling advertising is not aimed at children or young people and that it does not leave vulnerable people open to exploitation and harm.

2.2 The ASA investigates complaints about advertisements, which are alleged to be in breach of the CAP and BCAP codes. Where complaints are upheld the ASA requires advertisements to be amended or removed.

CAP CODE

2.3 Non-broadcast advertising is covered by the CAP code. A full copy of the code can be found at www.cap.org.uk

BCAP CODE

2.4 The first edition of the BCAP Code comes into force on 1 September 2010 and replaces the four previous separate BCAP Codes for broadcast advertising. The four previous codes have been merged into a single user-friendly code covering television and radio advertisements for the benefit of the public and broadcast advertising industry. A full copy of the code can be found at www.cap.org.uk
2.5 The revised CAP and BCAP codes now feature a new dedicated lotteries section; these can be found at section 18 of the BCAP Code and section 17 of the CAP code. These sections now include rules that have applied to society lotteries since the introduction of the Act in September 2007 and which, under the revised Codes, now also apply to the National Lottery. There is no change to the way in which society lotteries are treated under the revised Codes.

---

1 The 'whitelist' is a list of jurisdictions which are allowed to advertise gambling within the UK.

GAMBLING INDUSTRY CODE FOR SOCIALLY RESPONSIBLE GAMBLING

2.6 This code has been developed by the gambling industry to supplement the CAP and BCAP codes by setting minimum industry standards in a limited number of areas that are not covered by the CAP/BCAP rules. The areas covered by the industry code of practice are:

- social responsibility messages
- display of gambleaware website address
- broadcast media – messaging
- television advertising – watershed
- ban on children's merchandising as part of sporting sponsorships

3 OTHER USEFUL INFORMATION

CLEARANCE CENTRES

3.1 Pre-clearance for broadcast commercials is carried out by Clearcast. (CAP also undertake clearance services for non-broadcast).
3.2 Clearcast is a specialist body with responsibility for pre-transmission examination of television advertisements. All advertisements being transmitted as a national television campaign on UK terrestrial and satellite channels should be submitted to Clearcast for clearance.
3.3 All national, and certain special categories of local and regional, radio advertisements are vetted before transmission by the Radio Advertising Clearance Centre (RACC).

ADVERTISING STANDARDS AUTHORITY

3.4 The ASA's procedures for handling complaints under the CAP and BCAP codes can be found in full at www.asa.org.uk. Complaints about advertisements can be made via the ASA's website or by calling 020 7492 2222 (textphone 020 7242 8159).

WHERE TO ACCESS THE CODES

ASA	www.asa.org.uk	ASA procedures
CAP	www.cap.org.uk	CAP and BCAP codes
Clearcast	www.clearcast.co.uk/clearcast	Clearcast procedures
Gambling Commission	www.gamblingcommission.gov.uk	LCCP (October 2008) Copy of industry code
RACC	www.racc.co.uk	RACC procedures

4 THE LEGALITY OF ADVERTISING

4.1 Permission to advertise in Great Britain is restricted to operators licensed by the Commission, operators from EEA jurisdictions, Gibraltar, Alderney, Antigua and Barbuda, Isle of Man, and Tasmania. The Commission will take enforcement action against those not permitted to advertise if illegal advertising occurs, and may seek to prosecute.
Gambling Commission September 2010

ADVICE ON OFFERING FOREIGN GAMBLING AS PRIZES IN COMPETITIONS
December 2007

6.2087 It has come to the Commission's attention that a number of operators are offering places at overseas poker tournaments as prizes in UK based competitions. For example, a poker tournament played either at a UK Casino or online may offer the winner the chance to play in a cash prize tournament held outside the UK.
In the Commission's view, the offering of such a prize amounts to advertising of non-UK gambling, as defined by section 327 of the Gambling Act 2005. Unless the overseas tournament is based in the European Economic Area, Gibraltar, or in white-listed jurisdictions, the advert is likely to amount to the advertising of "foreign gambling", which constitutes an offence under section 331 of the Gambling Act 2005. Operators should take steps to ensure that any advertising which they are responsible for complies with the requirements of the Gambling Act 2005.
Gambling Commission December 2007

LICENSING DECISIONS: PROCEDURES AND GUIDANCE FOR THE REGULATORY PANEL
November 2010

1. INTRODUCTION

1.1 THE PURPOSE OF THIS GUIDANCE

6.2088 The purpose of this guidance is to assist the Regulatory Panel (the Panel) to carry out its functions in accordance with the Gambling Commission's (the Commission) policies and procedures and to comply with the law. A key aim of this guidance is to ensure that there are no grounds for suggesting that a decision maker has been biased, partial or that the decision is not well founded in any way. This guidance also seeks to ensure that the Commission meets the requirements of the Human Rights Act 1998 and the principles of natural justice.

This guidance needs to be read in conjunction with:
- the Statement of principles for licensing and regulation, issued pursuant to section 23 of the Gambling Act 2005 ('the Act')
- the Licensing, Compliance and Enforcement policy statement.

1.2 THE LICENSING OBJECTIVES

In carrying out its functions, the Commission must aim to pursue and have regard to the licensing objectives, which are:
- preventing gambling from being a source of crime or disorder, being associated with crime or disorder or being used to support crime
- ensuring that gambling is conducted in a fair and open way
- protecting children and other vulnerable people from being harmed or exploited by gambling.

The Commission must also aim to permit gambling, in so far as the Commission thinks it reasonably consistent with pursuit of the licensing objectives.

1.3 THE REGULATORY PANEL

Paragraph 8 of Schedule 4 of the Act provides that:

(1) The Commission may delegate a function to:
   (a) a Commissioner
   (b) a committee consisting of Commissioners
   (c) an employee of the Commission.

(2) Sub-paragraph (1) applies to any function of the Commission including in particular:
   (a) a discretionary function
   (b) the function of conducting a review
   (c) the function of determining whether to revoke a licence or of determining whether to impose a requirement to pay a penalty.

The Commission has delegated certain regulatory decisions to employees and other decisions to a Committee of Commissioners, known as the Regulatory Panel (the Panel).

1.4 REFERRAL OF CASE TO THE PANEL

There are three reasons why an application for a licence will be referred to the Panel:
- certain decisions will be reserved to the Panel for decision
- there may be cases where the particular circumstances of the case mean that it is appropriate for a case to be referred to the Panel for consideration
- where officials consider that an application should be refused, in whole or in part, a minded to refuse letter is sent to the applicant offering them a hearing before the Panel at which they will have an opportunity to appear or make further written representations before a final decision is made.

1.5 THE LEGAL FRAMEWORK FOR DECISION MAKING

The decisions to be taken by the Panel are all administrative decisions, which must be taken in accordance with the framework set out in the Act and the principles of fairness and natural justice.

The Commission exercises its functions in the public interest. Decisions must be made openly, impartially, with sound judgment and for justifiable reasons. This means that decision makers must:
- come to the decisions they make with an open mind and demonstrate they are open minded
- make a decision only after due consideration of all information reasonably required upon which to base such a decision

- seek further information if it is felt there is insufficient information to reach a decision.

It is important that decision makers have not already taken a firm view on a matter, nor give the appearance of having made up their mind before the formal consideration of an application. However, a decision maker will not have taken a firm view on a matter by just:

- listening to viewpoints from interested parties
- making comments or giving a provisional view, provided that it is clear that the issue has not been prejudged
- seeking information through appropriate channels
- asking questions at a hearing which reflect issues raised.

If a decision maker has any concerns about procedural fairness then they should seek advice from the Commission's legal advisers.

1.6 THE HUMAN RIGHTS ACT 1998

Article 6(1) of the European Convention on Human Rights (the Convention) provides, so far as relevant, as follows:

> "*In the determination of his civil rights and obligations . . . everyone is entitled to a fair and public hearing . . . by an independent and impartial tribunal . . .* "

The determination of a licence application is likely to amount to a determination of the applicant's civil rights or obligations within the meaning of Article 6(1) of the Convention. The Commission's procedures have therefore been designed to ensure, so far as possible, that the requirements of the Human Rights Act 1998 and the Convention are met. The right of appeal to the First-tier Tribunal (Gambling) is also an important element in ensuring that an individual's Convention rights are protected.

The purpose of the procedures which follow is to ensure a fair process, which accords with the requirements of natural justice and the Human Rights Act 1998. Inevitably there will be circumstances which have not been previously envisaged or anticipated and where it is necessary for the Chair of the Panel to exercise judgement and flexibility in the way that the procedures operate.

1.7 CONFLICTS OF INTEREST

Commissioners and senior employees are required to complete a declaration of their outside interests. The Commission also has a strict policy on the acceptance of gifts and hospitality. Even so, care must also be taken to ensure that in every case there is no conflict of interest or the risk that there may be a perception of a conflict of interest. Decision makers may have a conflict of interest in a matter if it affects them, their friends, relatives or employer. If a decision maker has a personal and potentially prejudicial interest in a matter then they:

- must not take a decision or sit as a member of a Panel, or otherwise take part in the decision making process
- must leave the room when that item is being discussed and must not participate in or give the appearance of trying to participate in the making of a decision
- must not lobby those who will be making the decision in question.

Decision makers must take care to avoid giving the impression that they are not independent or impartial or that their decision making process is biased, or there is a risk of apparent bias. The test for apparent bias was set out in Porter v Magill [2002] 2 AC 257: "The court must first ascertain all the circumstances which have a bearing on the suggestion that the judge was biased. It must then ask whether those circumstances would lead a fair-minded and informed observer to conclude that there was a real possibility . . . that the tribunal was biased." The test for apparent bias is an objective one, which requires an assessment to be made in the light of all of the facts of the case.

If a decision maker is in any doubt about whether there might be a possible conflict of interest then they should seek advice from the Commission's legal adviser.

2. PREPARING FOR THE HEARING

2.1 INTRODUCTION

The purpose of the hearing is to ensure that the Panel have all the information they require in order to determine the licence application before them. The Panel may therefore consider oral, documentary or other information which appears relevant to consideration of the case.

2.2 ADHERENCE TO TIME LIMITS

It is in everyone's interests for the time limits set out below to be adhered to. Adhering to the time limits supports proper case preparation, which in turn enhances the fairness and transparency of the process and avoids the possibility of postponement and delay. The Panel should therefore seek to ensure that time limits are met.

2.3 DOCUMENTARY AND OTHER EVIDENCE

The applicant and the Commission's representatives are expected to agree a bundle of relevant documents **at least 14 days prior to the hearing.** In the absence of an agreed bundle, the Commission's representatives will prepare a bundle of relevant documents. In some circumstances material which is not suitable for photocopying and distribution will be available for inspection by the Panel on the day, having previously been available for the applicant to inspect. In exceptional circumstances there may be material, which is relevant to the decision which the Panel must make, but which is not suitable for disclosure to the applicant or another person relevant to the application. Legal advice should be sought wherever this appears to be the case.

Save in exceptional circumstances, a copy of the bundle will normally be sent to the Panel and the legal adviser **no later than seven days prior to the hearing.**

2.4 CASE MANAGEMENT HEARINGS

In exceptional circumstances it may be necessary for there to be a case management hearing, at which the Panel may issue directions about the future conduct of the case. For example, the Panel may give directions about the service of documents or about who they expect to attend the substantive hearing on behalf of the applicant or the Commission.

If directions are issued, a formal record of the directions will be sent to the applicant **within seven days** of the case management hearing. Any such directions are binding on both the applicant and the Commission's representatives. In the event that directions are not complied with the Panel may draw such inference as it considers appropriate in relation to the admissibility of evidence or any other relevant matters.

These case management provisions are without prejudice to the ability of the Panel at the substantive hearing to give such directions for the management of the case as it sees fit.

3. THE HEARING

3.1 APPOINTMENT OF THE CHAIR

The Chairman of the Commission will, if present, preside at all meetings of the Panel. If the Chairman is not present, he may designate a Commissioner to chair the meeting. If there has been no such prior designation the Commissioners present at the meeting shall elect a Chair for the duration of the meeting.

3.2 VOTING

Decisions will normally be made by consensus. Where that cannot be achieved the Panel Members are required to vote, in which case the Chair of the Panel will have a casting vote in the event of a tie.

3.3 ATTENDANCE OF THE APPLICANT AND THEIR REPRESENTATIVES

The Panel would normally expect that the relevant persons identified by the Commission's officials will attend the hearing. Applicants may also be accompanied by a legal representative.
Where an applicant has indicated that they wish to appear or be represented before the Panel, but they or their representative then fail to attend at the hearing without good reason the Panel may continue in the applicant's or their representative's absence. No inference should be drawn from the applicant's absence.

3.4 ATTENDANCE OF REPRESENTATIVES FROM THE COMMISSION

The Chief Executive may designate such employees as she considers appropriate to attend meetings of the Panel to assist or advise the Panel, but those employees may not take part in the decision making process of the Panel. The Commission may also be legally represented at hearings before the Panel.

3.5 PROMOTING AN INVESTIGATIVE APPROACH AT HEARINGS

All those involved in hearings are expected to assist the Panel to determine the relevant facts and the Chair should direct those present to adopt an investigative rather than an adversarial approach. The purpose of this provision is twofold:

- to ensure that all relevant issues are explored fully
- to ensure that the process does not become unnecessarily adversarial in nature.

Should the Chair consider that the approach being taken by either the applicant, or their representative, is obstructive or unnecessarily adversarial, they should intervene to ask the applicant, or their representative, to refrain. If this does not resolve the matter, it may be necessary for the Panel to adjourn to consider the issue in private. The Chair may then decide to issue appropriate directions as to the future conduct of the hearing. The Chair and/or Commissioners should take an active role in the hearing through questioning the applicant, or the Commission's representatives who are present, and/or seeking clarification of points through the applicant's representative, if they have one. Where the Chair and Commissioners consider that all the relevant issues have not been raised or fully explored in the course of the evidence they will need to make sure that such issues or deficiencies are, as far as possible, covered through their questioning.

3.6 MEETINGS BY TELEPHONE OR VIDEO CONFERENCE

Meetings of the Panel may be conducted at a face to face hearing, or by telephone or video conference.

3.7 DEALING WITH APPLICATIONS ON THE PAPERS ALONE

If the applicant is content for matters to be dealt with on the papers alone, then the Panel may meet and carry out its work in the absence of the applicant. The Panel should still adopt the decision making process described below. No inference should be drawn from the applicant's absence.

3.8 DETERMINING WHETHER THE HEARING SHOULD BE IN PUBLIC OR PRIVATE

The Commission's policy is that hearings are held in private (ie in the absence of persons other than the directly interested parties). However, there may be occasions when the applicant whose case is being considered would like the hearing to be in public and as such careful consideration should be given to such a request. In deciding whether to grant such a request, the Panel will need to weigh up any potential prejudice to the rights of any third parties or prejudice to the overall fairness of the process against the applicant's reasons for requesting a public hearing. However, even if the Panel does decide to proceed in public, the Panel may decide to exclude the public and the press from all or part of the hearing where they consider that a public hearing may adversely affect the fairness of the process.

3.9 DELIBERATIONS IN PRIVATE

The Panel may determine, at any time, to deliberate in private (ie in the absence of any other person, including the directly interested parties). If legal advice is sought and given whilst the Panel is in private session the Chair should invite the legal adviser to repeat the advice in front of the applicant so that they have an opportunity to comment on the advice that has been given.

3.10 ROLE OF THE LEGAL ADVISER TO THE PANEL

A legal adviser will normally be present at all meetings of the Panel. The legal adviser's role is to provide the Panel with any advice they require to properly perform their functions, whether or not the Panel has requested that advice, on:

- questions of law and mixed fact and law
- matters of practice and procedure
- the range of outcomes available
- any relevant decisions of the superior courts or other guidelines
- other issues relevant to the matter before the Panel
- the appropriate decision-making structure to be applied in any given case.

The legal adviser may also:

- assist the Panel by reminding them of evidence
- ask questions in order to clarify the evidence and any issues in the case
- assist the Panel in formulating their reasons and recording the Panel's reasons.

Any legal advice given in private should be clearly stated to be provisional and the adviser should subsequently repeat the substance of the advice in open session and give the applicant an opportunity to make any representations relevant to the advice.

3.11 INTRODUCTIONS

The Chair should introduce the members of the Panel and confirm the identity of those appearing before the Panel. Appearing before a Panel may be a stressful experience for the individual involved. It is important that the Chair is sensitive to this and seeks to put them at their ease so that they can participate fully in the process.

3.12 REPRESENTATIONS AND EVIDENCE

The Panel may consider oral, documentary or other evidence which appears relevant to consideration of the case. The legal adviser can advise the Panel on any issue which arises as to the admissibility of, or the weight to be given to, any item of evidence.

At the start of the hearing, the Chair should confirm that the applicant and their representative are in possession of all relevant documentation and whether the bundle is agreed. The Chair should also check whether either the applicant or the Commission's representatives wish to rely on or to introduce any documents that are not already included in the case papers. If either party does wish to do so, then the Panel will need to consider the nature of any such document, the reasons for it being produced at a late stage and whether its admission would be likely to assist in the fair disposal of the hearing. It may be necessary to allow a brief adjournment for the applicant and/or the Commission's representatives to read the document in question. This is also the point at which any other issues relating to the documentation can be clarified.

3.13 DEALING WITH DISPUTED EVIDENCE CASES

Where some material facts of the case are disputed, the Commission's representative will be permitted to make an opening statement about the case. The applicant will then be given the opportunity to reply either in person or through their representative.
The Commission's representative and the applicant may present relevant written evidence relating to the facts in dispute and may, with the permission of the Panel, call witnesses.
As a general rule the Commission does not expect that it will be necessary for witnesses to attend hearings. In those exceptional cases where witnesses are to be called to give oral evidence, the Panel should seek confirmation at the outset of the hearing of which witnesses are to be called and how long their evidence might take.
In those cases where witnesses are to be called, any witness statements that have been prepared will normally be taken as the evidence-in-chief of that witness.
Normally whoever calls the witness will be allowed to ask some questions to clarify their statement before the witness is asked questions by the other party or the Panel.
The Chair should ensure that there is opportunity for the witness to be re-examined, if that is appropriate. However, such questioning should be confined to any 'new' areas arising from the questioning and should not repeat the original questions posed. Exceptionally, the Panel may allow further questioning by the other party on the new areas.
The Chair should ensure that this stage is limited to questioning of the witnesses and not to the making of statements.
Witnesses may be recalled at the discretion of the Panel, for example it may be appropriate if it is necessary to resolve any conflict in the evidence. If a witness is recalled it is for the Panel to determine the scope of any further questions but the applicant and the Commission's representative must have an opportunity to ask further questions.
After receiving evidence, the Chair may then ask whether the witnesses wish to remain in the hearing room or be released.

3.14 SUMMING UP

The Panel should normally permit both the applicant and the Commission's representatives to sum up. The Commission's representative should sum up first, followed by the applicant. Summing up must be confined to relevant matters which have been considered during the hearing. The Chair should ensure that under no circumstances is new evidence introduced during summing up.

3.15 REQUESTS FOR FURTHER INFORMATION

It is particularly important that the Panel is satisfied that they have enough information before them to make a decision. Where the Panel decides that they need further information before being able to make a final determination they may request the applicant or Commission's representatives to provide that information and may adjourn the hearing until the information is available. When adjourning for this purpose, the Panel should give directions about the time limits for the information to be provided.

3.16 ADJOURNMENTS

During the hearing it is important that the Chair allows sufficient breaks to avoid loss of concentration and fatigue on the part of participants. It may also be necessary to have adjournments during a hearing for the Panel to deliberate in private and/or to take advice on legal or procedural matters.

3.17 DECISION MAKING

In all cases the Panel will deliberate in private, in the presence of their legal adviser. The Secretary to the Regulatory Panel may also be present.

4. THE DECISION MAKING PROCESS FOR DETERMINING LICENCE APPLICATIONS

4.1 DETERMINING THE FACTS (TO BE CARRIED OUT IN EVERY CASE)

Stage one of the decision making process requires the Panel to determine the facts as relevant to the matter under consideration.
The Panel must be satisfied that the applicant is suitable to hold a licence and the Panel should assess and make findings of fact in relation to the following:

- Identity and ownership – the identity of the applicant and or person(s) relevant to the application and, in the case of an application for an operating licence, who ultimately owns a corporate applicant.
- Finances – the financial and other circumstances of the applicant, past and present, and or person(s) relevant to the application. For operating licences this will include the resources likely to be available to carry out the licensed activities.
- Integrity – the honesty and trustworthiness of the applicant and or persons relevant to the application.
- Competence – the experience, expertise, qualifications and history of the applicant and or persons relevant to the application.
- Criminality – the criminal record of the applicant and or person(s) relevant to the application.
- Upholding the licensing objectives – the applicant's policies for ensuring that the licensing objectives will be adhered to, the applicant's understanding of the legislation overall and evidence that arrangements will address the social responsibility requirements.

If there is a dispute about the facts of the case, the standard of proof required at all stages of the Panel's decision-making process is the civil standard, 'on the balance of probabilities'. The 'balance of probabilities' standard means that the Panel is satisfied an event occurred if the Panel considers that, on the evidence, the occurrence was more likely than not.

4.2 DECIDING WHETHER TO GRANT OR REFUSE THE APPLICATION (IN WHOLE OR IN PART)

When considering an application for a licence the Commission is required to either grant it (in whole or in part) or refuse it.
In deciding whether to grant a licence the Panel must:

- have regard to the licensing objectives
- form and have regard to an opinion of the applicant's suitability to carry on the licensed activities, for which purpose the Panel may, and would normally be expected to, have regard to his integrity, competence, and financial circumstances – including an assessment of people who are relevant to the application because they are likely to exercise a function in connection with, or have an interest in, the gambling activities.

4.3 DECIDING WHETHER TO IMPOSE AN INDIVIDUAL CONDITION

Where the Commission issues a licence it has the power, under section 77 of the Act, to attach a condition to the licence.

4.4 COMMUNICATING THE DECISION

The Panel's decision will be confirmed in writing within 14 days of the conclusion of a hearing. The written decision letter will normally comprise a statement of:

- the matter being considered by the Panel
- a summary of the evidence and representations
- the findings of fact
- the Panel's decision
- the reasons of the Panel.

Where appropriate, the decision letter will remind the recipient that they have the right to appeal to the First-Tier Tribunal (Gambling).
Gambling Commission November 2010

GUIDANCE ON REGULATORY DECISION MAKING AFTER A LICENCE REVIEW

November 2009

1 INTRODUCTION

6.2088.1 1.1 The decisions to be taken, whether by the Regulatory Panel or by employees acting under delegated powers are all administrative decisions, which must be taken in accordance with the framework set out in the Gambling Act 2005 ('the Act') and the principles of fairness and natural justice.

1.2 The Commission exercises its functions in the public interest. Decisions must be made openly, impartially, with sound judgment and for justifiable reasons. This means that decision makers must:

- come to the decisions they make with an open mind and demonstrate they are open minded
- make a decision only after due consideration of all information reasonably required upon which to base such a decision
- seek further information if it is felt there is insufficient information to reach a decision.

1.3 It is important that decision makers have not already taken a firm view on a matter, nor give the appearance of having made up their mind before the formal consideration of a matter. However, a decision maker will not have taken a firm view on a matter by:

- just listening to viewpoints from interested parties
- having prior knowledge of the issues, making comments or giving a provisional view, provided that it is clear that the issue has not been prejudged
- seeking information through appropriate channels; or
- asking questions at a hearing which reflect issues raised.

1.4 If a decision maker has any concerns about procedural fairness then they should seek advice from the Commission's legal advisers.

1.5 This guidance sets out a framework of matters which are relevant to decisions about whether the Commission should exercise its regulatory powers following a licence review under section 116 of the Act.

1.6 This guidance has been prepared in accordance with the requirements of the Act and the Commission has also had regard to the

- Statement of Principles for Licensing and Regulation

- Regulators' Compliance Code
- report of the Hampton Review
- report of the Macrory Review
- Enforcement Concordat
- Scottish Improving Regulation Report 2008
- reports of the Regulatory Review Group in Scotland
- Hampton Implementation Review Report into the Gambling Commission.

1.7 This guidance is a 'living document', which will be updated and revised as the need arises.

2 THE FRAMEWORK FOR CONSIDERING WHETHER TO EXERCISE THE COMMISSION'S REGULATORY POWERS AFTER A LICENCE REVIEW

2.1 In all cases due regard should be given to all the evidence gathered during a review, the facts that have been established and any evidence presented by way of mitigation by or on behalf of the licensee.

2.2 Following a review under section 116(1) or (2) of the Act, the Commission may:

- decide to take no further action
- decide to give the licensee advice as to conduct
- decide to exercise its powers under section 117[1] of the Act to:
    - give the licensee a warning
    - add, remove or vary a condition to the licence
    - suspend a licence
    - revoke a licence
    - impose a financial penalty.

2.3 The principal purpose of the Commission exercising its regulatory powers is to protect the public interest. In doing so, we will:

- seek to bring the licence holder back into compliance, where that can be achieved without undue risk to the licensing objectives or the public
- consider the necessity to deter the licence holder and others from future non-compliance
- consider, where appropriate and proportionate, the need to punish wrong doing

2.4 In deciding whether to exercise the Commission's regulatory powers the decision maker should have regard to risk to the licensing objectives[2] and apply the principle of proportionality, weighing the interests of the public (as above) against those of the licensee. The decision maker will also need to consider any mitigation in relation to the seriousness of the matters under consideration.

2.5 The Commission has developed policies which govern how it carries out its functions and this guidance needs to be read in conjunction with the following:

- Statement of Principles for Licensing and Regulation
- Licensing, Compliance and Enforcement Policy Statement
- Licence Conditions and Codes of Practice
- Corporate Governance Framework
- Regulatory Panel Procedures
- Statement of Principles for Determining Financial Penalties.

---

1 The powers under section 117 of the Gambling Act 2005 are not mutually exclusive and may, if appropriate, be exercised in combination.

2 Section 1 Gambling Act 2005

3 DECIDING WHAT TO DO AT THE CONCLUSION OF A LICENCE REVIEW

3.1 The paragraphs below outline each disposal option, stating the philosophy behind them and some broad criteria as to their use.

NO FURTHER ACTION AND ADVICE TO CONDUCT

3.2 The first step in the process is to decide whether the Commission's regulatory powers should be used at all. Deciding that there should be no further action is not in itself regulatory action, but it is a regulatory decision as it means that the Commission is bringing its investigations into regulatory concerns or issues to an end.

3.3 Deciding that there should be no further action will be appropriate if the decision maker considers that there is no case to answer or where further formal action would not be a proportionate response to the facts which have been established as there is no significant ongoing risk to the licensing objectives. In the latter case it may be appropriate to give the licensee some advice as to their future conduct.

3.4 The purpose of giving advice is to ensure future compliance with the Commission's requirements and to assist the licensee discharge their responsibilities in a compliant way in the future. If advice to conduct is given, consideration should also be given as to whether general advice should be published if it appears that the issue that gave rise to concerns may be prevalent in other parts of the industry.

3.5 An advice to conduct letter is not a formal warning. However, the Commission will keep a record of the fact that advice has been given and may refer to an advice to conduct letter in the future if circumstances require it.

3.6 It is difficult to be prescriptive about the circumstances in which an advice to conduct letter will be the most suitable means of disposal. The following examples are not intended to provide an exhaustive list, but are intended to provide some guidance on the type of situations which are likely to be suitable for advice to conduct:

- poor administrative and / or operational procedures, where the licensee demonstrates that they will take steps to improve them
- isolated minor breaches of licence conditions or social responsibility codes of practice, where the licensee demonstrates that they will take steps to improve compliance
- where disciplinary action has been taken by an employer against a personal licence holder, arising from circumstances of misconduct of a minor nature
- inappropriate behaviour by a personal licence holder on gambling licensed premises (on / off duty) which does not involve dishonesty
- cautions and convictions for offences involving minor instances of assault and / or disorderly behaviour (outside employed licensed duties).

WARNINGS

3.7 Where the decision maker decides that it is not sufficient to conclude a case without exercising the Commission's regulatory powers, then consideration should be given to whether a warning is appropriate. A warning may be appropriate where the concerns about a licensee are at the lower end of the spectrum in terms of seriousness of the event which occurred or existed and the risk to the licensing objectives, in order to mark the fact that the behaviour was unacceptable and must not happen again.

3.8 A warning allows the licence to continue. Warnings may also be taken into account in the future, if a licensee is the subject of another review.

3.9 **Warnings may be appropriate where most or all of the following factors are apparent[3]:**

- there is evidence that what happened did not seriously affect customers
- the licensee has demonstrated an understanding of the issues or concerns which gave rise to the licence review and / or there is not a significant risk of a repetition
- what happened was an isolated incident and was not deliberate
- the licensee has made a genuine expression of regret
- the licensee has previous good history
- there has been no repetition of behaviour since the incident
- the licensee has taken, or is taking, rehabilitative / corrective steps

- the licensee has produced relevant and appropriate references and testimonials.

AMENDING CONDITIONS OR IMPOSING ADDITIONAL CONDITIONS TO A LICENCE

3.10 Amending conditions or imposing additional conditions to a licence will allow a licence to continue. The conditions applied will set out the steps or controls which are considered necessary to minimise the risk to the licensing objectives in the future. Imposing licence conditions will also mean that it is possible to impose financial penalties on a licensee (as well as any other regulatory action deemed appropriate) if the conditions are not complied with.

3.11 Where conditions are imposed they should ensure that customers will not be seriously disadvantaged or affected either directly or indirectly as a result of the conditions imposed and that the conditions will protect customers and the public during the period they are in force. Conditions should also only be used where it is possible to formulate appropriate and practical conditions to impose on the licence.

3.12 **Imposing additional conditions may be appropriate when most or all of the following factors are apparent[4]:**

- what happened is not fundamentally incompatible with continuing to be licensed
- the licensee has demonstrated an understanding of the issues or concerns which gave rise to the review and / or there is no significant risk of repeating behaviour if the licence conditions are complied with
- there are identifiable areas of practice in need of retraining and the licensee has demonstrated their potential and willingness to respond positively to retraining.

FINANCIAL PENALTIES

3.13 Financial penalties can only be imposed when a licence condition has been breached. A financial penalty should aim to:

- change the behaviour of the licensee
- eliminate any financial gain or benefit from non-compliance with licence conditions
- be proportionate to the nature of the breach of licence condition and the harm caused
- deter future non-compliance by the relevant licence holder and other licence holders more generally.

[3] The examples are not intended to provide an exhaustive list, but are intended to provide some guidance on the type of situations which are likely to be suitable for warning.

[4] The examples are not intended to provide an exhaustive list, but are intended to provide some guidance on the type of situations which are likely to be suitable for imposing additional conditions.

3.14 More detailed guidance on financial penalties can be located in the Commission's 'Statement of Principles for Determining Financial Penalties'.

SUSPENSION

3.15 The Commission may only suspend a licence[5] if, following a review, the Commission considers that:

- a licensed activity is being or has been carried on in a manner which is inconsistent with the licensing objectives
- a condition of the licence has been breached
- a licensee has failed to cooperate with a review
- the licensee is unsuitable to carry on the licensed activities.

3.16 Suspension of a licence has a punitive effect, in that it prevents an individual or operator from carrying out regulated activities during the period of suspension.

3.17 Suspension is likely to be appropriate for misconduct or incompetence that is serious, but not so serious as to justify revocation of the licence. A period of suspension will allow a licensee to take steps to remedy the breach or concerns which gave rise the Commission's intervention, following which the licensee will be able to commence the licensed activities.

3.18 The length of the suspension is a matter for discretion, depending on the gravity of the particular case, but should be for as short a period as is appropriate to the circumstances of the case.

3.19 **Subject to the requirements for suspension outlined above being met, suspension may be appropriate when some or all of the following factors are apparent[6]:**

- suspension will prevent an ongoing breach or further breaches in the future and will be particularly appropriate for serious on-going breaches or concerns where continuation of the licensed activities is not in the public interest
- there has been a serious instance of unacceptable conduct and a lesser sanction is not sufficient
- what happened is not fundamentally incompatible with continuing to be licensed
- the licensee has demonstrated an understanding of the issues or concerns which gave rise to the review, with the result that there is no significant risk of repeating behaviour once the period of suspension has elapsed.

REVOCATION

3.20 The Commission may only revoke a licence if, following a review, the Commission considers that:

- a licensed activity is being or has been carried on in a manner which is inconsistent with the licensing objectives
- a condition of the licence has been breached
- a licensee has failed to cooperate with a review
- the licensee is unsuitable to carry on the licensed activities.

---

5 The Commission also has the power to suspend a licence when it commences a licence review, or during a licence review.

6 The examples are not intended to provide an exhaustive list, but are intended to provide some guidance on the type of situations which are likely to be suitable for suspension.

3.21 Revocation of an individual or an operator's licence is appropriate where this is the only means of protecting the public and maintaining public confidence. However, decision makers should not feel it necessary to revoke a licensee's licence in order to satisfy public demand for blame and punishment.

3.22 **Revocation is likely to be appropriate when what occurred is fundamentally incompatible with holding a licence and involves any of the following[7]:**

- there has been a serious departure from the Commission's Licensing Conditions or Social Responsibility Codes of Practice
- what happened seriously affected customers, either deliberately or through incompetence; particularly where there is a continuing risk that what happened will be repeated
- what happened involved abuse of position or trust
- dishonesty (especially where persistent and / or covered up)
- persistent lack of insight or understanding of the seriousness of what happened, the reasons that led up to a problem or the consequences.

[7] The examples are not intended to provide an exhaustive list, but are intended to provide some guidance on the type of situations which are likely to be suitable for revocation.

Gambling Commission November 2009

PRIZE COMPETITIONS AND FREE DRAWS: THE REQUIREMENTS OF THE GAMBLING ACT 2005

December 2009

1 INTRODUCTION

6.2089 1.1 Prize competitions and free draws are free of statutory regulatory control under the Gambling Act 2005 (the Act). Such competitions and draws can therefore be organised commercially for private benefit and profit. This contrasts with public lotteries, which are the preserve of good causes, and must, unless they qualify in one of the 'exempt' categories, operate under a licence issued by the Gambling Commission (the Commission). Lottery operating licences are only issued to non-commercial societies and external lottery managers who promote lotteries on their behalf.

1.2 The Act contains provisions designed to make clear the distinction between lotteries, prize competitions and free draws. Although the Commission has no regulatory responsibilities in respect of competitions and draws, we nonetheless monitor the boundary between them and lotteries. We also have powers in respect of pursuing and prosecuting illegal gambling and will act where schemes are organised and promoted that, in our view, amount to unlicensed and therefore illegal public lotteries.

1.3 Reflecting all this, the Commission is publishing this advice relating to prize competitions and draws, and in particular where the boundaries lie between them and lotteries. The purpose of this advice is to make those organising competitions and draws aware of what the Commission considers is needed to avoid breaches of the Act.

1.4 Organisers of competitions and free draws should also be aware that although they fall outside the ambit of the Gambling Act, there are other rules and regulations in place that they need to consider when developing and running their schemes. These include unfair trading and consumer protection laws and tax implications.

2 THE DISTINCTION BETWEEN LOTTERIES, PRIZE COMPETITIONS AND FREE DRAWS

2.1 The Act defines two types of lottery: a simple lottery and a complex lottery.

A simple lottery is where:
- persons are required to pay to participate
- one or more prizes are allocated to the participants in the scheme
- prizes are allocated wholly by chance.

A complex lottery is one where:
- persons are required to pay to participate
- one or more prizes are allocated to the participants in the scheme
- the prizes are allocated by a series of processes
- the first of these processes relies wholly on chance.

2.2 Any scheme that falls within either of these definitions needs to operate within the statutory provisions relating to lotteries in the Act if it is to be organised lawfully. These provisions are described in the Commission's publications Promoting society and local authority lotteries and Organising small lotteries (Gambling Act 2005).

2.3 In prize competitions, success depends, at least in part, on the exercise of skill, judgment or knowledge by the participants. This distinguishes them from lotteries, where either success depends wholly on chance or, in a complex lottery, the first stage relies wholly on chance. Section 14(5) of the Act addresses this distinction.

2.4 An arrangement is a lottery only if the participants are required to pay to enter. Therefore free draws are not lotteries and are exempt from statutory control. Schedule 2 to the Act gives details of what is to be treated as amounting to 'payment to enter' for the purposes of distinguishing free draws from lotteries.

3 PRIZE COMPETITIONS

3.1 As stated in paragraph 2.3 above, a prize competition is one where success depends on the exercise of skill, judgment or knowledge by the participants and does not, as it does in a lottery, rely wholly on chance. However, section 14(5) qualifies this distinction. It defines the circumstances in which arrangements requiring participants to exercise a degree of skill or judgment or to display knowledge are to be treated as relying wholly on chance. Such arrangements will therefore fall within the definition of a lottery provided the other elements of the definition (payment to participate and the allocation of prizes) are satisfied.

3.2 Section 14(5) says that 'a process which requires persons to exercise skill or judgment or to display knowledge shall be treated for the purposes of this section as relying wholly on chance if:

(a) the requirement cannot reasonably be expected to prevent a significant proportion of persons who participate in the arrangement of which the process forms part from receiving a prize; and

(b) the requirement cannot reasonably be expected to prevent a significant proportion of persons who wish to participate in that arrangement from doing so.'

3.3 It follows from this that a genuine prize competition is one that contains a requirement to exercise skill or judgment or to display knowledge and where it can reasonably be expected that the requirement will either:

(a) prevent a significant proportion of people who wish to participate from doing so (section 14(5)(b) of the 2005 Act); or

(b) prevent a significant proportion of people who participate from receiving a prize (section14(5)(a)).

If either one of these barriers to entry or success can be shown, the process will not be deemed to rely wholly upon chance, and the arrangement will not be a lottery.

3.4 Although the Commission can provide advice, only the courts can provide the definitive interpretation of the test in section 14(5) of the Act and decide whether or not an arrangement relies wholly on chance and consequently whether it is a prize competition or a lottery. With that proviso, the Commission offers the following advice as to the factors that will affect any decision we might take as to whether the statutory test has not, or may not have, been met.

3.5 First the intention of the law is clear: competitions that genuinely rely on skill, judgement or knowledge are to be permitted to operate free of any regulatory control under the Act. In many cases, it will be obvious that such competitions meet that test. A crossword puzzle, where entrants have to solve a large number of clues and where only fully completed entries are submitted, is an obvious example. Other types of word and number puzzles, such as those that feature in competition magazines, are further examples. The law makes it clear that these qualify as prize competitions even if those who successfully complete the puzzle are subsequently entered into a draw to pick the winner.

3.6 At the other extreme, there are some competitions that ask just one simple question, the answer to which is widely and commonly known or is blatantly obvious from the material accompanying the competition. The Commission considers that these do not meet the test in the Act. It is not easy to say where the dividing line between the two extremes lies. The more questions or clues that have to be solved, or the more obscure or specialist the subject, the more likely it is that application of the statutory test leads to the conclusion that the competition is not a lottery. But we do think that the requirement to exercise skill or knowledge in the test in the Act is not met where the answer can be found easily on the internet, is widely or commonly known by the general public, appears in the accompanying text or narrative, or is obvious within a programme.

3.7 In cases where it is not self-evident that the competition involves sufficient skill, judgment or knowledge, the test which must be applied is that in section 14(5) of the

Act. In other words the test is whether there is a reasonable expectation that the skill, judgment or knowledge requirement would either deter a significant proportion from entering or prevent a significant proportion from receiving a prize. In the Commission's view, in practical terms, there are two elements to this test. Did the skill, judgment or knowledge requirement in fact eliminate a significant proportion from participation or success and, if it did not, on what basis did the organisers conclude it was reasonable to expect that it would have done so?

3.8 On the first of these, the Act gives no indication of how the phrase, 'significant proportion' is to be interpreted. It should therefore take its ordinary, natural meaning. The Commission does not intend to set and promulgate any specific figure as, in any particular case, what is a significant proportion is likely to depend on the context and facts of the case.

3.9 Regardless of whatever level is regarded as 'significant', there is a related issue of how the proportion is to be calculated. In cases where organisers wish to defend their competitions by reference to subsection 14(5)(a) of the Act, it may be fairly easy to measure the actual proportions of those who participate who are eliminated by the skill, judgment or knowledge element. Organisers who seek to rely on subsection 14(5)(b), may have a more difficult evidential task. The test is whether a significant proportion of people who wish to participate can be expected to be deterred from doing so: in such competitions people may not enter unless they are confident they can pass the skill, judgment or knowledge hurdle. It may not be easy, as a result, to determine the numbers who wished to participate, against which the numbers who do so would need to be compared to establish that the former is a significant proportion of the whole.

3.10 In cases where the Commission forms a preliminary view that a particular competition appears to fall on the wrong side of the test in section 14(5) and therefore appears to be an illegal lottery, we will in the first instance approach the organisers to allow them to explain why they think their competition is compliant. In doing so, the Commission will take full account of the fact that the test in the Act is whether the skill, judgment or knowledge element could 'reasonably be expected' (the words in section 14(5)) to have eliminated a significant proportion. In other words, the Commission acknowledges that organisers may be able to demonstrate that they had reason to believe that the skill, judgment or knowledge element would eliminate a significant proportion even though in the event it does not.

3.11 Organisers are advised to consider how they will be able to demonstrate that their competition would meet the test in section 14(5). For example, they may choose to carry out research to test types of questions with viewer or reader panels to establish if a significant proportion would be deterred from entering, or would get the answer incorrect. The results of these tests could be recorded and passed to the Commission in the event that a competition gives rise to any regulatory concerns. Organisers may also use statistics showing results of similar previous competitions as a means of being reassured about future ones.

3.12 Organisers who decide to carry out research will need to consider how the outcome of that research relates to the context in which the competition is offered, as this may have an impact on the required element of skill, judgment or knowledge. For example, asking a panel a number of questions without any accompanying information is likely to produce very different results from asking questions following a television programme in which the correct answer has been given. In such cases, the Commission will consider both research carried out in advance of the competition and the context in which the competition is offered when making a judgment on whether the test at section 14(5) of the Act has been met.

3.13 The onus lies on the organisers of competitions to satisfy themselves that their competitions are compliant with the law. Consequently the Commission thinks it reasonable to ask those organisers how they have come to that view in cases where we have concerns about the legality of schemes. We acknowledge that it is open to them to refuse to respond, preferring instead to reserve their defence for any possible prosecution. But the Commission thinks that an approach on the lines we suggest will help avoid pursuing cases to prosecution and allow organisers the opportunity to withdraw or alter schemes where the Commission has concerns, without resort to costly litigation. Organisers should not however interpret any lack of action from the Commission as indicating specific approval of a scheme, nor as precluding subsequent action if the Commission later considers the event to be an illegal lottery. Under no circumstances will the Commission give clearance for schemes.

3.14 In cases where the organiser can produce figures which show that the skill, knowledge or judgment element eliminated a significant proportion of either actual or potential entrants, the Commission would not envisage taking the matter further. But where such figures are not available or where they show an insignificant proportion have been eliminated, the Commission will seek to establish the basis on which the organisers came to the view that the competition would in fact do so.

3.15 It is then for organisers to decide whether, or to what extent, they respond. But the Commission is likely to be satisfied where the organisers can produce material that demonstrates that they have taken steps to estimate the likely proportion of potential or actual participants, who are, or will be, eliminated by the skill, judgment or knowledge element. Where they seek to rely on the argument that significant proportions of potential entrants have been deterred, the Commission considers it will not be sufficient to compare numbers of entrants with, say, the audience figures for the TV programme or the readership figures for the newspaper carrying the competition. More is needed, for instance evidence of the propensity of the audience to enter such competitions. Similarly, for a competition made available on the internet, simple website traffic statistics that show large numbers went to the site but did not enter it are not, in the Commission's view, sufficient to suggest a significant proportion of persons who wished to participate were deterred. Again some more sophisticated analysis is needed which in some way is indicative of the fact that potential participants were deterred.

3.16 Where the Commission does have concerns about the legality of a scheme, we may be willing to accept that a misjudgement may be made on the first occasion that a particular type of competition is organised where steps have genuinely been taken by the organisers to establish the way the competition will operate in order to avoid being an illegal lottery. But further promotion of competitions of the same or similar types in the face of evidence to suggest that the particular skill etc element does not deter or eliminate a significant proportion of potential or actual participants must be much harder to defend. Where, by its nature, a competition can only involve one high value prize, as for example in the case of house sale competitions, the organisers will need to take particular care to justify their expectation that they are offering a genuine competition as there will be no opportunity to build up market data in successive competitions. We particularly recommend that organisers of these 'one-off' competitions learn from the experiences of previous examples of similar schemes, especially where these have been shown to give rise to concerns.

3.17 As it will not always be easy to establish empirically that the test in the Act has been met, the Commission has developed a number of indicators that we will consider when assessing whether the skill, knowledge or judgment element is sufficient. This is not a prescriptive list and following one or more of these indicators does not mean a competition will fully meet the requirements of the Act. It is your responsibility to ensure you meet the test in the Act. Some of the indicators we take into account are as follows:

- where a competition uses a multiple answer format, whether there are sufficient plausible alternative answers
- 'joke' answers are only used where there are sufficient plausible alternatives
- the correct answer is not obviously given close to the question
- the number of questions asked
- the types of formats used, for example, complex logic or mathematical puzzles which are demonstrably not simple to complete

- the cost of entry and/or the value of the prize; for instance the level of skill or knowledge needed to deter potential participants from entering a competition with a high value prize is likely to be greater than in the case where the value of the prize is low;

3.18 Schemes have been developed where some of the above elements are present, but where entrants are not required to pay until they give the correct answer. The Commission does not think these can be operated as prize competitions. The Commission considers that the test in the Act cannot be met as the element of skill, knowledge or judgment is not the determining factor in this type of scheme. The requirement for skill etc is negated by the fact that the participant does not have to pay until they are certain they have given the correct answer. In reality, the scheme splits into two parts, the first being the requirement to answer a question, and the second, which the participant only reaches if a correct answer has been given, a draw. Where entrants are in effect required to pay to enter that draw and then chance determines the winner of the prize, this second stage is a lottery. Even if the scheme cannot be split in this way, the Commission does not think the arrangement is likely to deter or eliminate a significant proportion of entrants as required by the test in the Act.

3.19 Ultimately however, the test remains that contained in the Act. If operators believe there is a risk of their competition being challenged as an illegal lottery, they will need to consider how they will be able to provide evidence of compliance, for instance by demonstrating from their records that a significant proportion of entrants either in that competition, or previous similar ones, had got the answers wrong. While it is a defence for a promoter that 'he reasonably believed that . . . the arrangement to which the charge relates was not a lottery' (sections 258(4)(b) and 259(4)(b)), promoters are expected to take steps to satisfy themselves that the requirements of the law are met. In our view that includes the need to consider our advice and whether specific legal advice is required.

3.20 Finally, competition organisers will need to consider whether their competition may involve betting as defined in section 9(1)(c), as applied by section 11 of the Act. These provisions are designed, amongst other things, to ensure that prediction competitions, such as 'fantasy football' games, are regulated as betting products and thus can only be offered under a relevant betting licence. However, a bet is defined by section 9 to include making a bet on 'whether anything is or is not true' and other competition organisers beyond those running 'fantasy football' type schemes will need to consider whether they are caught by this definition and thus whether their schemes involve betting.

4 FREE DRAWS

4.1 As stated in paragraph 2.4 above, an arrangement is a lottery only if the participants are required to pay to enter. Therefore, free draws always have been and remain exempt from statutory control. Schedule 2 to the Act gives details of what is to be treated as amounting to 'payment to enter' for the purposes of distinguishing free draws from lotteries.

4.2 The schedule envisages two circumstances. First, cases where there is only one entry route. Here, 'free' will include any method of communication (post, telephone or other) at a 'normal rate'. 'Normal rate' is defined as 'a rate which does not reflect the opportunity to enter a lottery' (paragraph 5(2)(a) of Schedule 2). It includes 'ordinary first-class or second- class post (without special arrangements for delivery)' (paragraph 5(2)(b)). There can be no additional payment over what it would normally cost to use the particular method of communication. Any competition that fails this test is deemed to require 'payment to enter' and will be a lottery if the other two elements (chance and prizes) are also present.

4.3 Secondly, cases where there is a choice of entry. Here, the arrangement will not be treated as requiring payment to participate in the arrangement and so will not be a lottery, if:

- each individual who is eligible to participate has a choice whether to do so by paying or by sending a communication
- that communication is either:
  - — a letter sent by ordinary post, again whether first or second class post
  - — or some other method which is neither more expensive nor less convenient than entering by the paid route. Again this method must be charged at the 'normal rate'; there can be no additional payment over what it would normally cost to use that method of communication
- the choice is publicised so that it is likely to come to the attention of all those intending to participate
- the system for allocating prizes does not distinguish between those using either route.

4.4 In both circumstances, the requirement to pay in order to participate also includes cases where there is 'a requirement to pay in order to discover whether a prize has been won under an arrangement' (paragraph 6 of Schedule 2 of the Act) and cases where there is 'a requirement to pay in order to take possession of a prize' (paragraph 7 of Schedule 2).

4.5 For the purpose of clarity:

- the implication of the second bullet point of paragraph 4.3 above is not that, if a competition organiser establishes two equally prominent and convenient methods of paying for entry and one costs less than the other, that is sufficient for the competition to meet the requirement. Both means of entry in such a case involve payment and the scheme will be a lottery. For the scheme to qualify as a free draw, the alternative route must itself meet the test in paragraph 5 of Schedule 2 (see paragraph 4.2 above)
- it is not sufficient to avoid classification as requiring 'payment to enter' that the alternative route costs the same as or less than ordinary first or second class post. To qualify as 'free', that route must still involve payment at no more than the 'normal rate' for that type of communication.

4.6 There have been advances in recent years in the numbers of different ways in which people communicate with each other. In addition to post and landline telephones, many people use mobile phones, text services, emails and other web based systems. The circumstances in which these do or do not involve 'payment to enter' a competition as defined in the Act will inevitably depend on the context and facts of each case. The following principles will however be relevant in reaching decisions in individual cases:

(i) It is irrelevant to whom the payment is made or who benefits from any payment (paragraph 3 of Schedule 2 of the Act). Hence, if a competition organiser makes no charge for entry but the telecommunications company does, over and above the 'normal rate' that still involves payment as defined in the Act.

(ii) The test to be applied where there is a choice of entry is that set out in paragraph 4.3. Hence, to qualify as a method which does not involve payment, it is not sufficient that the alternative route costs nothing for those who use it. It also has to be such that, for instance, individuals wishing to participate have a choice whether to use the alternative route and it is no less convenient than the paid route. As an example, many people do not have ready access to the internet at home. Although, for many of those that do, use of it costs nothing in the sense that they pay a single amount for access and nothing for subsequent use, others cannot access it, at least quickly. A competition which offers an alternative 'free' entry route via the web may not offer substantial proportions of those who wish to enter a genuine choice or at the very least that alternative may not be as convenient for them as the paid route. This is particularly the case where the need for immediate responses is emphasised to enable the participants to win the prizes on offer or the competitions are run only for relatively short periods. Reflecting all this, the Commission has developed the following principles, which we intend to use as a guide when considering whether web entry is a sufficient alternative route for those who seek to use it:

- potential participants who do not have home web access need sufficient time to gain web access elsewhere. The Commission considers three working days around the date of the particular draw as a reasonable length of time to obtain such access
- participation by web access should be available at all times while the scheme is being actively promoted and until the closing date/time for entries. Therefore, a quiz taking place during a television programme should permit web entries while the programme is being aired if entries by other means are permitted at that time as well
- the availability of free entry via the web should be made widely known, for example as the general policy for schemes organised by the operator concerned
- where any doubts exist as to whether the web entry arrangements in any particular case fully satisfy the Act's requirements, other routes, for example by post that has been specifically sanctioned by Parliament, should be offered in addition.

(iii) The test for whether a charge is at the 'normal rate' is whether or not it reflects the opportunity to enter the competition. This is a question of fact in each case. However, it is irrelevant to this test whether different methods of communication cost different amounts. For instance, different mobile phone operators have different tariffs. The fact that, as a result, some participants pay more than others for their call to enter a competition does not affect the question of whether or not that method involves 'payment to enter'. The test is rather whether the cost of the call includes an element which involves a payment to enter the competition. Therefore, if the cost of the call is what the user pays for any call to any other non-commercial user that is 'free' in the terms of the Act, regardless of who gets the payment and even if some part of that payment goes to the organiser of the draw. But if the call is charged at a tariff which includes an element of paying for a service (in this case, entering the competition), that involves, in the Commission's view, a payment, for the opportunity to enter, again regardless of who benefits from that element of the payment. Here there is some additional payment over that which relates to the provision of the telecommunications facilities.

(iv) As a general rule, the Commission does not think that the 'provision of data' by individuals amounts to 'payment' as intended by the Act. For instance, some organisations reward those who complete a survey form by entering them in a draw for one or more prizes. The Commission is of the opinion that such arrangements do not involve payment as that term is defined in paragraph 2 of Schedule 2 to the Act. In particular the Commission will not seek to argue that proportionate requests for data amount to payment because they involve 'transferring money's worth' (paragraph 2(b) of Schedule 2). The position might be different where large quantities of data are requested before entry to the draw takes place, particularly where data is obtained in circumstances where it is intended to be sold to third parties.

(v) As stated in paragraph 4.4, the definition of 'payment to enter' includes cases where there is a requirement to pay to collect the prize. In the Commission's view, that does not mean that prize winners cannot be required to pay normal delivery or other normal costs needed to obtain or use the prize. For instance, the Act's provisions do not, in the Commission's view, prevent the organiser of a competition in which a camera is a prize requiring the winner to pay normal delivery costs which might be charged if that same camera was bought from a retailer. Nor, clearly, does it prevent the winner of a car being required to pay road tax. But there can be no additional payment over what it would normally cost to pay for delivery or use.

4.7 As with prize competitions, in cases where the Commission forms a preliminary view that a particular scheme does not satisfy the requirements to qualify as a free draw, we would expect in the first instance to approach the operator to allow them the opportunity to explain why they think the arrangement is compliant. As has been said, in cases where there is a choice of entry route, any conclusion must focus on whether the arrangement satisfies the test set out in paragraph 4.3 above. But the Commission takes the view that it is not unreasonable to use, as a starting point, the proportion of entrants who have made use of each of the routes. Whilst such a test cannot be determinative one way or the other, in cases where operators are able and willing to provide such information, the Commission will see it as a relevant factor in reaching any conclusion as to whether or not the scheme is compliant with the law.

4.8 Finally, Schedule 2 to the Act also makes provision for product promotions. These are permitted where the price of the good or service does not include any element that reflects the opportunity to participate in the promotion (paragraph 2(c) of Schedule 2). Therefore draws tied to product promotions are not to be treated as requiring payment to enter and are not to be regarded as lotteries, so long as entry involves no cost beyond the cost of the product. Whether this is, or is not, so will be a question of fact in individual cases. As a general rule, a good linked to a promotion charged at a price that bears little relation either to its cost of production or to comparable products may mean the promotion will be challenged as an illegal lottery. On the other hand, an increase in price just before or coincident with the introduction of a promotion need not necessarily give rise to difficulty if it can be shown that the price rise is unrelated to the promotion itself, for instance because of higher costs of such things as raw materials or transport.

4.9 The Commission acknowledges that ultimately the costs of any product promotions must be recovered through the revenues obtained from sales. However, the test is whether an identifiable element within the price of the product during the promotion can be said to be a participation fee. Organisers do need to bear in mind that a promotional 'free draw' will involve payment, and as a result will be an illegal lottery, if a charge is made to discover whether a prize has been won or to take delivery of that prize (see paragraph 4.4 as qualified by paragraph 4.6 (v)).

4.10 An example of a typical product promotion is a scheme where persons buy a particular product at its usual price, such as a chocolate bar or magazine, and as a result they are given the chance to win a prize. Another example is where a retailer offers its customers the chance to win something, such as a discount, when they make a purchase.

5 DECIDING WHETHER TO INSTITUTE CRIMINAL PROCEEDINGS

5.1 If the Commission considers that what is in fact being offered is an illegal lottery, and/or we are unable to reach an appropriate outcome through discussions with the operator as set out above, we have the option to take forward criminal proceedings.

5.2 The following outlines our approach to deciding whether or not to institute such proceedings and is taken from our Licensing, Compliance and Enforcement Policy Statement, which provides more detail.

5.3 The Commission will apply the Code for Crown Prosecutors when deciding whether criminal proceedings should be commenced, which involves a two-stage test:

- first, the evidence will be reviewed and an assessment made as to whether there is a realistic prospect of conviction
- secondly, if there is sufficient such evidence, an assessment will be made as to whether it is in the public interest for a prosecution to take place.

5.4 The Code for Crown Prosecutors lists a number of common public interest factors which either favour or are against prosecution. A copy of the code can be found on the Crown Prosecution Service's website and in the event that the Code is revised the Commission may need to review its own processes accordingly.

Gambling Commission, December 2009

PRIZE COMPETITIONS AND FREE DRAWS: HOUSE COMPETITIONS — ADVICE NOTE
May 2009

6.2090 1.1 The Gambling Commission (the Commission) has received a number of enquiries from the public with regard to house competitions. A house competition refers to the attempted use of a prize competition by a homeowner to realise the value of their property.

1.2 The Commission regulates gambling and has no regulatory responsibility for prize competitions. It does however monitor the boundary between prize competitions, free draws and lotteries in order to ensure that those operating lotteries are properly licensed.

1.3 In October 2008 the Commission issued a press release entitled Homeowners urged to be aware of rules on house competitions which is available on our website. It set out the Commission's position with regard to house competitions and warned homeowners that attempts to sell homes using prize competition schemes could potentially fall foul of the Gambling Act 2005 (the Act).

1.4 Since that date a number of organisers have closed down or significantly amended their schemes following correspondence with the Commission. To avoid any misunderstandings, the Commission is now publishing this advice note. It draws on the Commission's experience to date in order to assist members of the public.

IN SUMMARY

- The Commission does not in any circumstances 'approve' prize competitions which remain free of statutory control under the Gambling Act 2005.
- Organisers considering running a house competition should read the Commission's guidance on prize competitions and free draws and take independent legal advice before proceeding.
- Organisers of house competitions are likely to attract regulatory intervention from the Commission.
- A decision over prosecution in a case where an operator persists in the face of the Commission's concern will be made with due regard to the public interest and in line with the Code for Crown Prosecutors.
- The circumstances in every case are different and a decision over prosecution in one case will not necessarily set a precedent for others.
- Organisers of house competitions may be liable for taxation and should contact HM Revenue and Customs before proceeding.

2 ARE HOUSE COMPETITIONS LAWFUL?

2.1 In principle an individual disposing of a property through a house competition can use a genuine prize competition to do so. Genuine prize competitions are free of statutory control under the Act provided they require sufficient skill, judgment or knowledge to either deter a significant proportion of potential entrants from participating or eliminate a significant proportion who do enter. House competitions that do not meet the test of skill, judgment or knowledge set out in section 14 of the Act are classed as lotteries.

2.2 Ultimately, it is the responsibility of organisers to ensure their house competition meets the requirements of a prize competition and that they are acting legally.

3 THE COMMISSION'S ROLE IN MONITORING THE BOUNDARY BETWEEN HOUSE COMPETITIONS AND LOTTERIES

3.1 The Commission monitors the boundary between prize competitions, free draws and lotteries in order to ensure that those operating lotteries are properly licensed. The Commission has no regulatory responsibility for prize competitions.

3.2 In some cases, we have become aware that the organisers of some house competitions claim to have received 'approval from the Gambling Commission'. This is not correct. The Commission does not, in any circumstances, approve house competitions.
3.3 In October last year a warning was published to all homeowners organising or considering such schemes that they risked prosecution if found to have promoted an illegal lottery. Anyone considering such a competition was advised to take account of the Commission's guidance Prize competitions free draws: the requirements of the Gambling Act 2005 which is available on our website and to take independent legal advice before proceeding.
3.4 Where we have concerns that a house competition may be an illegal lottery, the Commission will normally write to the organisers to alert them and to reiterate the tests that they will have to meet to ensure that their scheme meets the legal requirements in section 14 of the Act and is therefore not a lottery.
3.5 The letter requests information from the organisers in order to assess whether the scheme does amount to a genuine prize competition. We also advise the organisers to seek legal advice before commencing or continuing and where they cannot assure themselves of the legality of what they are doing; to cease activity and return monies already taken.
3.6 In practice, the Commission has written to over 50 organisers of house competitions and the majority appear to have had significant difficulty in satisfying themselves that their house competition is legal.

4 THE COMMISSION'S ROLE IN DEALING WITH POTENTIALLY UNLAWFUL HOUSE COMPETITION SCHEMES

4.1 Where the Commission considers that a scheme is an illegal lottery, a criminal investigation is likely to be commenced. This has already happened in one case.
4.2 At the conclusion of an investigation the Commission will decide whether to proceed with a prosecution and, in doing so, will have regard to the public interest and the Code for Crown Prosecutors. This means that a prosecution will not be pursued unless there is a realistic prospect of conviction and if it is considered to be in the public interest.
4.3 The circumstances in every case are different and a decision over prosecution in one case will not necessarily set a precedent for others.
Gambling Commission May 2009

THE GAMBLING ACT 2005, ADVICE FOR BRITISH POLICE SERVICES March 2009

Incorporating responses to the consultation

1 INTRODUCTION

6.2091 1.1 The Gambling Commission (the Commission) issued a consultation document in June 2008: *The Gambling Act 2005 – Advice for British police services*. We received four responses to the consultation and the comments have been noted and/or incorporated in this revised version. The aim is to provide a reference document for British police services with regard to their role and functions in the regulation of the gambling industry. The introduction in September 2007 of the new gambling legislation overhauled the licensing arrangements of the gambling industry and created a new regulatory regime. We have developed this document to highlight the extent of police involvement in supporting the various mechanisms of the regime.

1.2 The document is designed to act as a point of reference for police looking to identify specific information relating to the gambling industry, and includes suggestions as to how to achieve best practice.

1.3 This document sets out a number of topics which we consider to be important for the police, and offers advice on specific matters that they may encounter with regard to gambling premises operating in their individual areas.

1.4 Alongside the publication of this advice the Commission is working with the Association of Chief Police Officers for England, Wales and Northern Ireland (ACPO) and for Scotland (ACPOS) to complete a Memorandum of Understanding (MoU) which covers both information sharing and operational matters.

1.5 The Commission is in the early stages of developing an operational manual and accompanying training package for frontline officers in conjunction with ACPO and ACPOS.

2 AN OVERVIEW OF THE GAMBLING ACT 2005

2.1 The Gambling Act 2005 (the Act) received Royal Assent on 7 April 2005, and came fully into force on 1 September 2007. It repealed existing gambling legislation, namely the Betting, Gaming and Lotteries Act 1963, the Gaming Act 1968 and the Lotteries and Amusements Act 1976.

2.2 The Act makes it an offence to provide facilities for gambling or use premises for gambling without an appropriate permission. Such permission comes in the form of a licence, a permit, or a registration granted under the Act, or from an exemption stated within the Act.

2.3 The Act covers all gambling undertaken in England, Scotland and Wales, with the exception of:

- spread betting (which is regulated by the Financial Services Authority)
- the National Lottery (which is regulated by the National Lottery Commission).

2.4 It also created a new licensing regime for commercial gambling, and introduced the Commission as the industry regulator. Responsibility for issuing gaming and betting permissions that previously had rested with local magistrates has now been transferred to the Commission and licensing authorities.

THE LICENSING OBJECTIVES

2.5 The Act contains three licensing objectives, which are central to the regulatory regime and underpin functions carried out by the Commission and licensing authorities. These can be found at section 1 of the Act, and are:

- preventing gambling from being a source of crime or disorder, being associated with crime or disorder, or being used to support crime

- ensuring that gambling is conducted in a fair and open way
- protecting children and other vulnerable persons from being harmed or exploited by gambling.

GAMBLING COMMISSION

2.6 The Commission was established by the Act as the regulator for gambling in Great Britain (again with the exception of spread betting and the National Lottery). It replaced the Gaming Board for Great Britain.
2.7 The Commission is responsible for granting operating and personal licences to companies and individuals within the gambling industry. The Act also creates powers of entry and inspection for the Commission to regulate gambling, and sets out safeguards for those subject to the powers.

LICENCES, PERMITS AND NOTICES

2.8 Three types of licence and a number of types of permits and notices are issued under the Act. Collectively these permissions make up the regulatory framework for the gambling industry.

Operating licences

2.9 Individuals and companies providing facilities for certain types of gambling must obtain an operating licence from the Commission (section 65 of the Act). Operating licences authorise the holder to provide the facilities named on the licence, providing they do so in accordance with the conditions of their licence and any relevant codes of practice issued by the Commission.[1]
2.10 The Commission's *Licence Conditions and Codes of Practice* (LCCP) sets out the conditions and codes that apply to licences issued by the Commission to gambling operators and personal licence holders in Great Britain.
2.11 The conditions and codes set out the rules which operators must observe to meet the Commission's three licensing objectives of keeping crime out of gambling, ensuring that gambling is fair and open, and protecting children and other vulnerable people from being harmed or exploited by gambling.
2.12 The Commission has powers to prosecute operators who fail to maintain the standards it sets. A list of the licence conditions and codes relevant to each licence holder is issued as part of their Operating Licence.
2.13 Breach of an operating licence condition may give rise to a criminal offence. The Commission also has a range of regulatory penalties available to it which are separate from initiating criminal proceedings. These measures include issuing warnings, financial penalties and suspending or revoking a licence.
2.14 Operating licences may be issued to cover the provision of remote gambling facilities (using technology such as the internet) and non-remote facilities (ie premises-based, such as in a casino or a betting premises).

[1] Licence Conditions and Codes of Practice

Personal licences

2.15 The Commission is also responsible for issuing personal licences to key individuals within the gambling industry, in two categories:

- personal management licences – required by persons occupying specified management office positions for gambling operators, such as an Operations Director
- personal functional licences – required by persons performing a function that could enable them to influence the outcome of gambling or receive money in connection with gambling, such as a casino croupier.

Premises licences

2.16 Licensing authorities (as defined at section 2 of the Act) are responsible for issuing premises licences to enable gambling operators to provide different types of gambling facilities.

2.17 For the purposes of this Act the following are licensing authorities:

(a) in relation to England:

- (i) a district council
- (ii) a county council for a county in which there are no district councils
- (iii) a London borough council
- (iv) the Common Council of the City of London
- (v) the Council of the Isles of Scilly.

(b) in relation to Wales:

- (i) a county council
- (ii) a county borough council.

(c) in relation to Scotland:

- (i) a licensing board constituted under section 1 of the Licensing (Scotland) Act 1976 (c. 66).

2.18 The day to day work of the licensing authority is generally carried out by the licensing department.

2.19 The regime is similar in appearance to that created by the Licensing Act 2003 and the Licensing (Scotland) Act 2005, although the two regimes are entirely separate. The role played by police in premises licensing is discussed in section 7 of this document.

Permits and notices

2.20 In addition to issuing premises licences, licensing authorities issue permits and receive notices to authorise the provision of gambling facilities in a number of premises where gambling is not the primary activity (such as pubs and clubs). The role played by police towards permits and notices is discussed in section 6 of this document.

RESPONSIBLE AUTHORITIES AND INTERESTED PARTIES

2.21 The Act sets out two categories of organisations and individuals that are entitled to object to and comment on applications made to licensing authorities for gambling permissions such as premises licences. They are as follows:

- responsible authorities – these are bodies that are required by the Act to be notified of applications for certain gambling permissions made to licensing authorities. A full list of responsible authorities can be found at section 157 of the Act.
- interested parties – these are local groups that may be impacted by the gambling activities being proposed on an application, either by living sufficiently close to the premises where it is proposed the facilities will be offered that they may be affected, or if they have business interests that may be affected by the proposed gambling facilities.

2.22 Section 157 of the Act includes the chief officer of police of the area where a particular gambling premise is situated, as a responsible authority. **This is a key role for police, and the extent and manner in which they can make representations as a responsible authority is discussed in section 7 of this document.**

ACHIEVING COMPLIANCE WITH THE ACT

2.23 Facilities for gambling in Great Britain (besides the National Lottery and spread betting) must be compliant with the workings of the Act and the supporting legislation. The police play a key role in supporting the compliance and enforcement activity of the Commission and licensing authorities. This role is discussed in greater detail throughout this document.

3 POLICE POWERS CREATED BY THE GAMBLING ACT 2005

3.1 The Act creates a number of powers for police towards gambling premises and facilities. Most of these powers are shared with, for example, Commission enforcement officers and in some cases other authorised persons. Part 15 of the Act in particular creates a range of powers for entering premises. This section summarises those powers.
3.2 The Commission's compliance managers work closely with licensing authority colleagues and undertake a rolling risk-based programme of inspection activity. Police are advised in the first instance to contact the Commission's Enquiries desk (section 26 of this document) or, alternatively, the relevant licensing authority to discuss matters arising from the exercise of powers under Part 15 of the Act, or to identify the compliance manager covering their area.

GENERAL

3.3 Section 320 of the Act requires powers exercised under Part 15 of the Act to be exercised only at reasonable times.
3.4 Section 325 of the Act requires persons exercising powers under Part 15 of the Act to take reasonable steps to leave premises they have entered as secure as when they initially gained access.

POWERS RELATING TO INSPECTION ACTIVITY

Compliance activity – section 305

3.5 Police officers have powers to undertake activities for the purpose of assessing:
- compliance with provisions of the Act
- whether an offence under the Act is being committed.

Suspected offences – section 306

3.6 Police officers have powers to enter premises where they reasonably suspect an offence under the Act:
- is being committed on the premises
- is about to be committed on the premises.

3.7 Forces in England and Wales may apply to a justice of the peace for a 28-day entry warrant, (and in Scotland any application to a Sheriff for a warrant shall be made in accordance with current procedures through the Crown and Procurator Fiscal Service) to secure entry where:
- there are reasonable grounds for suspecting an offence under the Act has been committed on the premises
- there are reasonable grounds for suspecting that evidence of the commission of the offence may be found on the premises.

At least one of the following must also be satisfied:
- entry to the premises has already been refused
- entry is likely to be refused without a warrant
- the purpose of entry may be complicated or prejudiced unless police can ensure immediate entry
- there is likely to be nobody at the premises capable of granting entry.

Inspection of gambling facilities – section 307

3.8 Police officers may enter premises where they reasonably suspect facilities for gambling may be being provided or may be about to be provided, or were being provided, which they do not believe is consistent with 'exempt' forms of gambling, ie private and non-commercial gaming or betting (Part 14 of the Act). This type of inspection has to achieve one or more of the following:

- to discover whether any of the above suspicions are founded
- to determine whether an operating licence (issued by the Commission) and/or premises licence (issued by the local licensing authority) is held to cover the facilities being provided
- to determine whether the gambling facilities are being, will be, or have been provided in accordance with the terms and conditions of the operating licence or premises licence.

Inspection of gambling facilities provided under an operating licence – section 308

3.9 Where police officers reasonably believe premises are being used by an operating licence holder wholly or partly for purposes connected to the licensed activities, they may enter the premises using section 308 of the Act in order to determine whether the activities are being conducted in accordance with the terms and conditions of the licence.

Inspection of unlicensed family entertainment centre premises – section 309

3.10 Under section 309 of the Act police officers may:

- enter premises which are the subject of an application for a family entertainment centre permit for matters relating to the application
- enter premises which are the subject of a family entertainment centre permit in order to verify that the gaming machines are compliant with relevant provisions of the Act.

Inspection activity in alcohol-licensed premises – section 310

3.11 There are a number of powers of inspection available for police officers in England and Wales under section 310 of the Act. If a premises has an 'on-premises' alcohol licence issued under the Licensing Act 2003 a police officer may enter the premises in order to:

- determine whether any gaming taking place constitutes exempt gaming (section 279 of the Act)
- determine, where bingo is being played, if the terms and conditions of any relevant operating licence are being upheld and whether section 281 of the Act applies (which states that the bingo is high-turnover and requires an operating licence if the proceeds of the bingo are more than £2,000 per week)
- ascertain the number and types of gaming machines being used on the premises.

3.12 However, section 310 of the Act does not apply to police officers in Scotland, as it refers to schedule of the Act (13) which is disapplied for Scotland and premises that have an 'on-premises' alcohol licence issued under the Licensing Act 2003, but not the Licensing (Scotland) Act 2005. Therefore the powers of entry and inspection conferred by the Licensing (Scotland) Act 2005 are assumed to allow a police officer in Scotland to deal with any offence to which the Gambling Act applies, unless deemed to be a pre-planned operation, for which a warrant would be more appropriate.

Inspection activity in premises that are the subject of a prize gaming permit – section 311

3.13 Police officers may exercise their powers under section 311 of the Act as follows:

- entering a premises which is the subject of an application for a prize gaming permit for matters relating to the application
- entering a premises which is the subject of a prize gaming permit in order to verify that the gaming machines are compliant with relevant provisions of the Act.

Inspection activity in clubs – section 312

3.14 There are a number of powers of inspection available to police officers under section 312 of the Act. If a premises can reasonably be considered to be a members' club, a commercial club or a miner's welfare institute, a police officer may enter the premises in order to:

- determine whether any gaming is taking place or is about to take place
- determine where the gaming is taking place, that it is in accordance with section 269 of the Act (ie is permitted in clubs) or is in accordance with a club gaming permit or a club machine permit.

3.15 Police officers may also exercise this power in respect of premises that are the subject of an application for a club gaming permit or club machine permit in order to consider whether or not they will make representations.

Premises licences (gambling premises) – section 313

3.16 Section 313 of the Act entitles police officers to enter premises:

- that are the subject of an application for a premises licence under the Act to consider the effect of the proposed gambling premises upon the three licensing objectives
- that are already the subject of a premises licence issued under the Act, and the premises licence is the subject of a review, in order to determine whether they should make representations for inclusion in the review under section 201 of the Act.

Temporary use notices – section 315

3.17 Police officers may exercise their powers under section 315 of the Act to:

- enter premises for which a temporary use notice has been issued in order to assess (against the licensing objectives) the likely effects of the gaming due to take place
- enter premises where a temporary use notice is in effect in order to determine if the gaming is being carried out in accordance with the temporary use notice.

Production of authorisations – section 316

3.18 Police officers are entitled to view authorisations that betting operating licence holders may give to someone to carry out betting on their behalf (sections 93 and 94 of the Act), and can request that either the licence holder themselves or the person so authorised produces the authorisation within a specified period.

3.19 Similarly, a police officer may also require a casino premises licence holder to produce the authorisation given by them under section 174 of the Act permitting someone else to provide facilities for betting and/or bingo at the casino in question. The person so authorised can also be required to produce the authorisation within a specified period.

3.20 An offence is committed if the authorisation is not produced without a reasonable excuse.

POWERS UPON ENTRY

Powers upon entry – sections 317 and 322

3.21 Police officers exercising their powers under section 317 of the Act to enter premises may:

- inspect any part of the premises, any machine or any other thing on the premises
- question anyone on the premises
- request access to any written or electronic record kept on the premises

- require a copy of any entry made in a written or electronic record kept on the premises
- remove and retain anything that they believe is evidence (or is being used/has been used) for a breach of a term or condition under the Act, or commission of an offence under the Act.

3.22 Regulations have been laid setting out the information that police officers need to provide upon entry, and the written record of information that can be requested by the inspected person. These regulations are SI No 2007/319 The Gambling Act 2005 (Inspection) (Provision of information) regulations 2007.

Obtaining a warrant to enter a dwelling – section 318

3.23 Police officers may, under section 318 of the Act, apply to a justice of the peace or sheriff to obtain a 28 day warrant for use to enter a dwelling (as opposed to a licensed premises) within the provisions of the Act providing at least one of the conditions in section 318(3) of the Act are satisfied. Those conditions are as follows:

- that admission to the premises has been refused
- that admission to the premises is likely to be refused unless a warrant is produced
- that the purposes of entry may be frustrated or seriously prejudiced unless a police officer, enforcement officer or other authorised person arriving at the premises can secure immediate entry
- that there is likely to be nobody at the premises capable of granting admission.

Access to records – section 319

3.24 A police officer may apply to a justice of the peace or sheriff under section 319 of the Act to obtain a 28 day warrant if they believe they will require access to written or electronic records that may not be directly linked to the purposes of the inspection. The warrant will specify the extent to which it can be relied upon towards inspecting records.

Use of force – section 323

3.25 A police officer may use reasonable force under section 323 of the Act when entering premises in pursuance of a power under or by virtue of Part 15 of the Act. This section is disapplied in Scotland

Persons accompanying an inspector – section 324

3.26 A police officer, enforcement officer or authorised person exercising powers under Part 15 of the Act may take one or more persons with them. Examples include information technology technicians, contracted (civilian) investigation officers and police civilian licensing officers. This section is disapplied in Scotland.

EXERCISING POWERS OF INSPECTION AND ENTRY

3.27 The Commission's compliance managers work closely with licensing authorities throughout Great Britain on compliance and inspection activity relating to gambling, and as part of this work often engage with police.

3.28 It is an offence under section 326 of the Act to obstruct or fail to cooperate without reasonable excuse with a police officer, enforcement officer or authorised person carrying out inspection activity under Part 15 of the Act.

3.29 The Commission recommends that, where appropriate, police officers first contact the compliance manager covering their local area where they are seeking to exercise their powers of inspection for gambling premises. Information that police may require as a result of inspecting a gambling premises might already be in the possession of the local compliance manager, and there may be ongoing work being undertaken by the Commission and licensing authorities at the premises.

3.30 Contact details for the Commission's compliance managers can be found on the website www.gamblingcommission.gov.uk, or by calling 0121 230 6666. The details are also included in the *Police and Constabulary Almanac*.

4 INFORMATION EXCHANGE WITH POLICE SERVICES

OVERVIEW

4.1 The Commission is dependent on the exchange of information to uncover illegal activity associated with gambling, and to monitor the incidence of gambling in Great Britain.

4.2 Section 30 of the Act enables the Commission to exchange information with the police and other law enforcement agencies, including the bodies listed in Schedule 6 of the Act such as the National Crime Squad and the National Criminal Intelligence Service (now amalgamated into the Serious Organised Crime Agency), the Serious Fraud Office and the Scottish Crime and Drugs Enforcement Agency (SCDEA). The Commission also has separate signed memoranda of understanding with various other organisations. The exchange of information is for the purpose of:

- a criminal investigation (whether in the United Kingdom or elsewhere)
- criminal proceedings (whether in the United Kingdom or elsewhere).

4.3 Under sections 29 and 35 of the Data Protection Act 1998 personal data are exempt from the non-disclosure provisions where the disclosure is:

- for the prevention or detection of crime
- the apprehension or prosecution of offenders (section 29 of the Data Protection Act)
- required by law
- made in connection with legal proceedings
- for the purpose of obtaining legal advice (section 35 of the Data Protection Act). Requests for information should be made in writing to the intelligence unit at the Commission (see section 26 of this document). Annex G of this document provides a request proforma for use where appropriate.

The Commission's intelligence unit

4.4 The intelligence unit collects, collates, analyses and disseminates information about gambling to and from a wide range of sources, including the police and local authorities. Information of value to the unit includes, but is not restricted to:

- reports of police activity at gambling premises
- reports of suspected illegal gambling
- reports of underage gambling
- surveys undertaken by Crime and Disorder Reduction Partnerships highlighting gambling issues.

4.5 The intelligence unit periodically undertakes intelligence assessments, measuring compliance activity within the gambling industry and identifying information required to inform the Commission's intelligence regime.

NATIONAL INTELLIGENCE MODEL

4.6 The Commission's intelligence unit operates within the National Intelligence Model (NIM), in order to identify patterns of crime connected to gambling, to develop understanding of these patterns, and to share intelligence as appropriate with police, other law enforcement agencies and other relevant stakeholders.

5x5x5 reports

4.7 The Commission uses Intelligence Report Forms to receive and disseminate intelligence, more commonly known as 5x5x5 reports. This type of reporting is a NIM minimum standard, and ensures consistency of approach with other organisations that handle intelligence using NIM.

INTELLIGENCE COMING IN AND GOING OUT

Intelligence coming in

4.8 Police officers wishing to feed intelligence into the Commission should submit the information on a 5x5x5 report. The intelligence is then captured on the Commission's secure intelligence database. Reports should be sent via email to: intelligence-reports@gamblingcommission.gov.uk.

Intelligence going out

4.9 All intelligence is disseminated from the Commission on 5x5x5 reports. Extracts from intelligence assessments undertaken by the Commission may be made available from time to time on the website www.gamblingcommission.gov.uk.

What other information is the Commission able to provide police services?

4.10 Police officers may contact the intelligence unit when they require an intelligence check on individuals under investigation and there are suspected links to, for example, illegal gambling activity, gambling premises and so on. The details can be checked against the Commission's intelligence database to ascertain whether there is any relevant information available.

MONEY LAUNDERING

4.11 All gambling operators who hold an operating licence and offer premises-based gambling must put in place policies and procedures regarding the handling of cash in their premises, to minimise the risk of financial crimes such as money laundering.

4.12 In addition to this requirement, casinos operating in Great Britain (and therefore licensed by the Commission) are required to act in accordance with the provisions of the document *The prevention of money laundering and combating the financing of terrorism: Guidance for remote and non-remote casinos*. This document can be viewed on the Commission's website[2].

4.13 The guidance sets out how casino operators must comply with the Money Laundering Regulations (SI No 2007/2157) and the Proceeds of Crime Act 2002. It also includes reference to the role of police in issuing 'appropriate consent' to process suspicious transactions.

4.14 Police officers seeking specific information regarding money laundering within the gambling industry may contact the Commission using the details shown in section 26 of this document.

4.15 In addition the Commission will be publishing *Duties and responsibilities under the Proceeds of Crime Act 2002. Advice to Operators (excluding casino operators)*. This will be available via our web site later this year.

---

[2] The prevention of money laundering and combating the financing of terrorism: Guidance for remote and non-remote casino

5 OPERATIONAL ACTIVITY

5.1 The Commission and licensing authorities are responsible for undertaking compliance and enforcement activity towards the different types of gambling permissions issued under the Act (as set out in section 2 of this document).

5.2 Where the Commission and licensing authorities decide to take action under the provisions of the Act, whether in terms of operational breaches within the regulatory environment or the detection of illegal gambling, it will often be necessary for the police to be involved.

KEY DOCUMENTS

Memorandum of understanding between ACPO, the Commission and LACORS

5.3 Prior to the introduction of the Act on 1 September 2007, the Commission worked with the Local Authorities Coordinators of Regulatory Services (LACORS) and the ACPO to develop a joint statement towards compliance and enforcement in England and Wales.

5.4 The statement set out the initial approach for all three parties to apply towards any compliance and enforcement action required towards gambling premises in the months leading on from the Act's introduction. Broadly, this established that local authorities concentrate on premises related issues, the Commission's focus being wider or national operating issues, and the police provide support on criminal activity within these areas.

5.5 The statement also established a platform upon which to develop a longer-term collaborative approach towards compliance and enforcement. It can be viewed on the Commission's website[3].

5.6 As noted above (paragraph 1.4 of this document) the Commission, ACPO and ACPOS are currently completing a new Memorandum of Understanding.

---

[3] Joint compliance and enforcement statement

The Commission's compliance and enforcement policy statement

5.7 In June 2007 the Commission published the document *Compliance and enforcement policy statement* outlining its approach towards compliance and enforcement under the Act. This document is currently being updated and new version will be published in summer 2009.

5.8 The current version can be viewed on the Commission's website[4].

---

[4] Compliance and enforcement policy statement

Licensing authority policy statements

5.9 Each licensing authority is required under section 349 of the Act to produce a three-yearly statement of licensing policy setting out the broad principles they apply towards exercising their powers and responsibilities under the Act. Many of the statements include references to how local compliance activity is undertaken, and are generally available for viewing on each licensing authority's website.

REGIONAL ENFORCEMENT AGREEMENTS AND LICENSING WORKING GROUPS

5.10 The introduction of the Licensing Act 2003 prompted many local authorities in England and Wales to establish regional working groups, where licensing matters could be discussed at regular intervals and appropriate local policy and enforcement activity agreed on. These groups generally consist of licensing officers from neighbouring licensing authorities, but also include representatives from police and crime reduction partnerships, and other attendees such as representatives from the local fire service or environmental health departments.

5.11 The Commission is aware that many of these groups now also discuss relevant matters surrounding gambling premises, and licences and permits issued under the Act, and many have extended invitations to the Commission's local compliance managers to attend meetings. The introduction of the Licensing (Scotland) Act 2005 is likely to encourage the development of similar groups in Scotland. The involvement of local compliance managers is key in terms of reinforcing a joined-up approach towards local compliance and enforcement activity, developing regional best-practice towards licensing of gambling premises, and encouraging sharing of information. Local compliance managers can be identified by calling the Commission's enquiries desk on 0121 230 6666 or checking the website (www.gamblingcommission.gov.uk).

ILLEGAL GAMING MACHINES

In what circumstances is a gaming machine illegal?

5.12 The Act permits four categories of gaming machines (A, B, C and D) and a number of sub- categories, as shown in Annex B of this document. The Act also sets out the types of premises that are entitled to provide gaming machines and the type of authorisation needed in order to site the machines.

5.13 A gaming machine can be illegal for a number of reasons including any one of the following:

- it is located in a premises that are not permitted under the Act to provide gaming machines
- the stakes, prizes or circumstances of use for a machine is not consistent with those set down in regulations (SI No 2007/2158 Betting, Gaming and Lotteries The Categories of Gaming Machine Regulations 2007, No. 2007/2320 The Gaming Machine (Supply &c) Regulations 2007 and 2007/2319 Gaming Machine (Circumstances of Use) Regulations 2007)
- it is supplied by a non-licensed supplier (ie a supplier that is not an operating licence holder)
- the operator does not hold the appropriate operating licence.

5.14 The appropriate course of action, and who will take the lead, will depend on the circumstances which have led to a gaming machine being considered illegal, or illegally sited. In some cases licensing authorities and local law enforcement agencies such as the police and HM Revenue and Customs will be best placed to take the lead, and in others the Commission will take action. Often a co-ordinated, joined up approach consisting of all of these bodies is most appropriate.

5.15 Since the introduction of the Act on 1 September 2007, police have assisted the Commission and licensing authorities to undertake a number of operations regarding the seizure of illegal gaming machines. Such operations have generally been undertaken using a multi-agency approach.

5.16 If police believe that there are illegal gaming machines in operation in their area, they should, in the first instance, contact the licensing authority and the Commission's local compliance manager (paragraph 3.30 of this document) to agree the most suitable approach.

CHEATING IN GAMBLING

5.17 It is an offence under section 42 of the Act to cheat at gambling, or to assist another person to cheat at gambling. The offence is still committed irrespective of whether the cheater actually wins or improves their chances of winning.

5.18 Section 42 of the Act states that cheating may include actual or attempted deception or interference connected to the way in which gambling is conducted, and connected to a game, an event or a race that relates to gambling in some way.

5.19 If police receive complaints or intelligence relating to allegations of cheating in gambling, the Commission would like to be informed of the circumstances and nature of the complaint (section 26 of this document). If the information relates to gambling associated with sporting events it may also be important to inform the relevant sporting authority as it may contravene their rules on betting. A list of sports authorities is provided at Annex E.

5.20 Similarly, the Commission may wish to engage with the police and sporting authorities over cheating issues that may be better investigated by the police or other law enforcement agencies, for example where fraud appears to be involved.

6 LICENSING AUTHORITY FUNCTIONS AND THE ROLE OF THE POLICE

6.1 The Act gives licensing authorities a number of important regulatory functions in relation to gambling carried out in Great Britain. Each authority is expected to ensure they fulfil these functions in their respective area. The principal functions are to:

- licence premises to provide gambling facilities
- consider notices served on them for the temporary use of premises for equal-chance gaming
- grant permits for gaming and gaming machines in clubs and institutes
- regulate gaming and gaming machines in alcohol licensed premises
- grant permits to family entertainment centres for the use of category D gaming machines (eg machines such as crane grabbers or penny pushers)
- grant permits to authorise prize gaming
- receive 'occasional use' notices served on them to permit betting to be provided at a temporary track
- register local societies to run small lotteries.

6.2 The police play a key role in the application and determination process undertaken by licensing authorities towards managing local gambling authorisations. This section sets out in greater detail the functions outlined above, and in each case summarises the extent of the role of police in the process.

PREMISES LICENCES

- **Relevant part of the Act: Part 8**
- **Regulations: SI No 2007/459 (The Gambling Act 2005 (Premises Licences and Provisional Statements) Regulations 2007) and SI No 2007/196 (The Gambling Act 2005 (Premises Licences and Provisional Statements)(Scotland) Regulations 2007)**

What is a premises licence?

6.3 A premises licence granted under the Act authorises the licensee to provide specific gambling facilities at the premises in question. Each licence contains a number of conditions that licensees must adhere to, which are set out for each premises type in the regulations listed above. They are issued by local licensing authorities.

6.4 A premises licence must contain the following information:

- the name of the person to whom it is issued
- the home or business address of that person
- the premises to which it relates
- the activities for which it authorises the premises to be used
- any conditions attached by the licensing authority (under section 169(1)(a) of the Act)
- any exclusion of a default condition effected by the licensing authority under section 169(1)(b) of the Act
- a plan of the premises

- if the licence is time limited, the expiry date.

The Secretary of State (in England) and Scottish Ministers (in Scotland) may make regulations about the form and content of a premises licence.

6.5 The licensing authority holds a register of premises licences issued and must make the register available to members of the public (section 156 of the Act).

6.6 A premises licence may contain, as a condition, a requirement for door supervision, ie a condition requiring one or more persons be responsible for guarding the premises against unauthorised access or occupation. If the person guarding the premises is required by the Private Security Industry Act 2001 to hold a licence then that condition also applies to the premises licence.

6.7 Gambling premises licences are granted by licensing authorities in the following categories:

- casino premises
- bingo premises
- betting premises (generally high-street bookmaker's shops), including track premises (venues such as permanently-situated racecourses and sports arenas such as football grounds where betting is provided) and remote betting (trading room only)
- adult gaming centres (arcade-type premises that can only admit people aged18 and over)
- family entertainment centres (arcade-type premises that can admit under-18s).

6.8 All gambling premises falling within the above categories must be the subject of a premises licence issued under the Act.

Vessels and vehicles

6.9 The Act permits premises licences to be granted for passenger vessels. Separate application forms are prescribed for vessels under the Premises Licences and Provisional Statements Regulations. The equivalent legislation in Scotland is the Gambling Act 2005 Premises Licences and Provisional Statements (Scotland) Regulations 2007. The definition of a vessel (section 353(1) of the Act) is:

- anything (other than a seaplane or amphibious vehicle), designed or adapted
- for use on water
- a hovercraft
- anything, or part of any place, situated on or in water.

6.10 For further details of these regulations see Annex D.

What other gambling permissions are required by a premises licence holder?

6.11 The premises licences listed above can only be issued to holders of a Commission operating licence, with the exception of track premises licences which can be issued to certain track owners without the need to hold an operating licence if they do not themselves provide any betting facilities.

6.12 The type of premises licence must correlate with the type of operating licence held – for example, an adult gaming centre premises licence can only be held in conjunction with an adult gaming centre operating licence, not another type such as a bingo operating licence.

6.13 Gambling operators can hold multiple premises licences, but are only required to hold one operating licence in respect of the type of gambling they offer. For example, a betting operator may own 100 betting shops, each of which would require an individual betting premises licence, but the operator would require only one betting operating licence.

Information that the police receive regarding premises licence applications

6.14 The chief officer of police is sent a notice of application each time one of the following is lodged with a licensing authority falling within that policing area:

- a notice of application for a new premises licence
- a notice of application to vary a feature of an existing premises licence
- a notice of application to transfer an existing premises licence to someone else
- a notice of application to reinstate a premises licence that has lapsed for some reason.
- In each case the applicant is responsible for sending notice of their application to the police (as a responsible authority), once they have lodged their application with the relevant licensing authority.

Making representations

6.15 Police are entitled to make representations towards the premises licence applications, where they feel necessary (paragraph 6.23 of this document). However there is no requirement for representations to be made for each application.

6.16 Each notice of application is required to state the period available to the receiving police service to make representations about the application if they choose to (the period is required to be no less than 28 days, starting from the date on which the application was made to the licensing authority).

6.17 During the period allowed for representations, police may wish to contact colleagues in the licensing departments of local authorities to discuss matters relating to the application and the premises in question.

6.18 Police are also entitled under section 313(1) of the Act to enter premises in respect of which a premises licence application has been made in order to assess the likely effects of the proposed gambling activity.

6.19 Before deciding whether or not to make a representation, it should be noted that licensing authorities are required to filter all representations they receive under the Act to ensure they identify those that are relevant, and those that are irrelevant. This requirement is set down in section 162 of the Act, as licensing authorities may be required to hold a hearing for any relevant representations.

6.20 Representations that are likely to be deemed relevant by licensing authorities are those that relate to at least one of the licensing objectives (paragraph 2.5 of this document). They may also be found relevant if they raise issues of concern connected to the content of the licensing authority's own policy statement or any of the Commission's guidance or codes of practice. This is set out at section 153 of the Act.

6.21 Unlike the Licensing Act 2003 and the Licensing (Scotland) Act 2005, the Act does not include the prevention of public nuisance as a licensing objective, and therefore representations concerning nuisance issues at gambling premises may be deemed irrelevant by a licensing authority (unless the activity leading to the public nuisance could be held as fitting with the licensing objective of preventing crime and disorder associated with gambling).

6.22 If police have concerns relating to a premises licence application that cannot be justified as a relevant representation, they may prefer to raise these with the licensing authority in question and seek to address them under other relevant legislation. Some examples of representations that may or may not be considered relevant can be found in the table on the following page.

	Example of representation	Relevant issues under the Act
Representations that would not be likely to be deemed relevant (and as such would be best tackled under other legislation apart from the Gambling Act 2005)	'There are already too many other gambling premises in the area'	The level of demand for gambling premises is not relevant as a consideration, under the provision of the Act
	'The location of the premises is likely to increase traffic congestion in the area'	Local traffic matters cannot be handled under the Act and are better managed through other legislation
	'The premises will lead to groups of people congregating in the area, increasing general nuisance and excessive noise'	The prevention of public nuisance is better managed through other legislation (unless activity connected to the congregation of people was held to be a relevant consideration towards the Act's licensing objective of preventing gambling being associated with crime and disorder)
Representations that may be likely to be deemed relevant (and as such could be addressed at application stage via a hearing)	'Other gambling premises in the area are routinely used for illegal activities such as drug-dealing'	The licensing authority may decide this could lead to the premises in question damaging the licensing objective of preventing gambling from being associated with crime
	'The existence of other similar premises in the area has been found to have contributed towards local disorder'	This may be a relevant consideration as it may lead to the premises in question damaging the licensing objective of preventing gambling from being associated with disorder
	'Other premises owned by this operator in the area have been known to have major problems with underage gambling'	The licensing authority may decide this could lead to the premises in question damaging the licensing objective of protecting children from being harmed or exploited by gambling

6.23 Where police do choose to make representations, they must do so formally in writing to the licensing authority that is considering the application. The licensing authority will advise police of the outcome of all applications, and confirm whether or not a hearing will be held following the closure of the representations period.

6.24 For further information about making representations see the Commission's *Guidance to Licensing Authorities 2nd Edition* pages 54-5[5].

[5] Guidance to Licensing Authorities

Other information relating to premises licences which is sent to the police

6.25 Licensing authorities are also required to inform the local chief officer of police when:

- a premises licence application is determined (whether granted or rejected)
- a premises licence is surrendered by the licence holder (section 192 of the Act)
- a premises licence lapses (for reasons including the licence holder dying or becoming bankrupt, as set out in section 194 of the Act).

Criminal record checks for premises licence applicants

6.26 All premises licence holders (with the exception of track premises licences) are required to also hold an operating licence issued by the Commission. As part of the operating licence application process, the Commission undertakes disclosure checks to verify the suitability of the applicant to hold an operating licence.

Relationship with premises licences issued under alcohol licensing legislation

6.27 Premises licences issued under the Gambling Act 2005 are entirely distinct from premises licences issued under alcohol licensing legislation, and the two type of premises licence exist and are regulated under separate legislation.

6.28 Premises licences issued under gambling and alcohol licensing legislation can, in some cases, co-exist at the same premises. However, some gambling premises licences prohibit customers from consuming alcohol on the premises. This is discussed for each premises type in the following paragraphs of this document.

Provision of premises licence

6.29 The premises licence has to be kept on the premises, and police are entitled to request to see the licence (or a suitable copy if the original licence is held at a head office) under section 185 of the Act. It is an offence if the holder, without reasonable excuse, fails to comply. If the licence holder ceases to reside or attend at the address on the licence they must notify the licensing authority and inform them of the new address where they reside or attend under section 186 of the Act.

6.30 A premises licence holder may apply to vary a licence, for example to add or remove an authorised activity; however it cannot be varied so as to relate to a different premises to the original one. The exception to this is casinos licensed under the 1968 Act (converted casinos) who may vary their licence so that it relates to a different premises within the same licensing authority area. Details can be found in Commencement No. 6 and Transitional Provisions Order 2006 (SI No 2006/3272) paragraph 65 (12) in Schedule 4 to the SI.

Lapse of licence

6.31 In the case of a premises licence issued to an individual, the licence shall lapse if, under section 194 of the Act:

- the licensee dies
- the licensee becomes, in the opinion of the licensing authority, unfit by reason of physical or mental incapacity
- the licensee becomes bankrupt (section 381 Insolvency Act 1986)
- sequestration of the licensee's estate is awarded (section 12(1) Bankruptcy (Scotland) Act 1985).

  A person may apply to reinstate a licence (section 195 of the Act) within six months of it having lapsed.

Loss / theft of licence

6.32 If a premises licence or summary of licence is lost or stolen, the licence holder must apply for a replacement copy from the issuing licensing authority. Before the replacement can be issued however, the licensing authority is required to ensure that the licence holder has reported the loss or theft to the police.

PROVISIONAL STATEMENTS

- **Relevant part of the Act: section 204**
- **Regulations: SI No 2007/459 (The Gambling Act 2005 (Club Gaming Permits) (Authorised Gaming) Regulations 2007) and SI No 2007/196 (The Gambling Act 2005 (Premises Licences and Provisional Statements) (Scotland) Regulations 2007)**

What is a provisional statement?

6.33 Application may be made to a licensing authority for a provisional statement in respect of premises that the applicant expects to be constructed or altered, or where they expect to acquire a right to occupy.
Developers may wish to apply for provisional statements before they enter into a contract to buy or lease property or land to judge whether a development is worth taking forward in light of the need to obtain a premises licence. It is also possible for an application for a provisional statement to be made for premises that already have a premises licence (either for a different type of gambling or the same type).

What other gambling permissions are required?

6.34 Applicants for premises licences must fulfil certain criteria. They must hold or have applied for an operating licence from the Commission (except in the case of a track), and they must have a right to occupy the premises in respect of which their premises licence application is made. There is a separate form for provisional statement applications. These restrictions do not apply in relation to an application for a provisional statement. In circumstances in which an applicant has also applied to the Commission for an operating licence, the Commission will not be able to comment on whether the application is likely to be granted; and the licensing authority should not speculate on or otherwise take into account the likelihood of an operating licence being granted in its consideration of the application for a provisional statement.

Applications

6.35 The local chief officer of police is sent a notice of each application for a provisional statement. The applicant is responsible for sending this. The notice states the date by which the police may make representations about the application, if they choose to (the period is required to be no less than 28 days, starting from the date on which the application was made to the licensing authority).

6.36 When determining whether or not to make representations, the advice set out at paragraphs 6.15 – 6.24 of this document may also be useful for provisional statement applications.

6.37 As with premises licence applications, representations should be made formally and in writing to the relevant licensing authority.

6.38 For further information about provisional statements refer to the Commission's *Guidance to Licensing Authorities 2nd edition*, updated October 2008[6].

6 Guidance to Licensing Authorities

FAMILY ENTERTAINMENT CENTRE GAMING MACHINE PERMITS

- **Relevant parts of the Act: Schedule 10, section 309**
- **Regulations: SI No 2007/454 (The Gambling Act 2005 (Family Entertainment Centre Gaming Machine) (Permits) Regulations 2007)**

Family entertainment centre gaming machine permits

6.39 This type of permit (often also referred to as an 'unlicensed FEC' or a 'UFEC') enables the holder to site gaming machines in a particular area. They are often found as arcades on sea-fronts in coastal resorts, but can also be found within venues such as airports and motorway service stations.

6.40 The permit holder is only entitled to site category D gaming machines (Annex B), such as penny pushers that can be played by under-18s. The premises that are the subject of the permit must be wholly or mainly used for the provision of gaming machines.

What other gambling permissions are required?

6.41 None. Permit holders do **not** need to also hold an operating licence issued by the Commission. The permit holder is however required to be 18 or over.

Role of police in application process

6.42 The local chief officer of police is consulted by the licensing authority on each application for this type of permit. Police may raise any matters they deem necessary on **any aspect of the application**. As part of the application process, police officers are permitted to enter the premises where the FEC is to be located, if they require to do so, under the powers of inspection created by section 309(1) of the Act.
6.43 Licensing authorities may approach police during the application process with regard to carrying out criminal disclosure checks on the applicant.

Provision of permit

6.44 The permit has to be kept on the premises, and police officers are entitled to request that the permit is produced under Schedule 10(20) of the Act.

Consumption of alcohol in premises that are the subject of a family entertainment centre gaming machine permit

6.45 Alcohol consumption is permitted in family entertainment centres that exist under this type of permit. Police officers should note that this is not the case for family entertainment centres that are the subject of premises licences – and have higher category gaming machines – where the consumption of alcohol is prohibited by a condition of the premises licence. More information on this restriction can be found in section 10 of this document.

Loss or theft of permit

6.46 If a family entertainment centre gaming machine permit is lost or stolen, the permit holder may apply for a replacement copy from the issuing licensing authority. Before the replacement can be issued however, the licensing authority is required (under Schedule 10(21) of the Act) to ensure that the permit holder reported the loss or theft to police.

CLUB GAMING PERMITS AND CLUB MACHINE PERMITS

- **Relevant part of the Act: Schedule 12**
- **Regulations: SI No 2007/1834 (The Gambling Act 2005 (Club Gaming and Club Machine Permits) Regulations 2007) and SI No 2007/504 (The Club Gaming and Club Machine Permits (Scotland) Regulations 2007) SI No 2007/1942 (The Gambling Act 2005 (Gaming in Clubs) Regulations 2007) SI No 2007/1944 (The Gambling Act 2005 (Exempt Gaming in Clubs) Regulations 2007) SI No 2007/1945 (The Gambling Act 2005 (Club Gaming Permits (Authorised Gaming)) Regulations 2007)**

Clubs and club permits

6.47 Club gaming and club gaming machine permits authorise the provision of certain gambling facilities in members clubs, commercial clubs and miners' welfare institutes, providing the club in question meets the definitions set out in sections 266, 267 and 268 of the Act.
6.48 Club permits have replaced the registration scheme that clubs previously used to obtain gambling permissions under the Betting, Gaming and Lotteries Act 1963. These were commonly referred to as Part II and Part III registrations.
6.49 More information on considerations for police towards gambling in clubs can be found in section 18 of this document.

What other gambling permissions are required in order to hold this type of permit?

6.50 Permit holders do not need to also hold an operating licence issued by the Commission. However, some clubs operate high-turnover bingo games (exceeding a turnover of £2,000 a week) and as such are required to hold a relevant operating licence from the Commission.

Provision of club permit

6.51 The permit has to be kept on the premises, and police are entitled to request that the permit is produced (under Schedule 12 (13) of the Act).

Applications

6.52 Applicants for club permits are required to send the local chief officer of police a copy of their application at the time as they send the application to the relevant licensing authority. At this stage, police may decide to contact the licensing authority to raise any matters they deem necessary regarding the application.
6.53 Licensing authorities may approach police during the application process with regard to carrying out criminal disclosure checks on the applicant.
6.54 Licensing authorities will inform police regarding the outcome of each application for club permits, and the reason for that decision if any objections to the permit application were received.

Relationship with club premises certificate

6.55 Applicants for club gaming permits or club machine permits in England and Wales that already have a club premises certificate issued under the Licensing Act 2003 can use a 'fast-track' application route when applying for their permit. This process is set out in Schedule 12(10) of the Act, and removes the requirement on the applicant to send a copy of their application to the local chief officer of police.
6.56 There is currently no equivalent 'fast-track' route available in the Act for clubs applying for permits in Scotland.

Is any other information relating to club permits sent to the police?

6.57 Licensing authorities are also required to inform their local chief officer of police when:

- they believe a club permit has lapsed (under Schedule 12(20) of the Act)
- they have been informed that a club permit holder is surrendering their permit (under Schedule 12(20) of the Act)
- they cancel a club permit (under Schedule 12(21(3)) of the Act).

Loss or theft of permit

6.58 If a club gaming or machine permit is lost or stolen, the permit holder can apply for a replacement copy from the issuing licensing authority. Before the replacement can be issued however, the licensing authority is required (under Schedule 12(16) of the Act) to ensure that the permit holder reported the loss/theft to police.

ALCOHOL-LICENSED PREMISES AUTOMATIC ENTITLEMENT TO TWO GAMING MACHINES

- **Relevant parts of the Act: section 282 and Schedule 13**

What is the automatic entitlement?

6.59 Holders of premises licences issued under the Licensing Act 2003 and relevant Scottish alcohol legislation are automatically entitled to make available up to two gaming machines within categories C and D (Annex B). This is not a permit, as the entitlement exists automatically by virtue of the existence of an on-premises alcohol licence. Consequently there is no application process that police will be involved in for this type of permission.

What other gambling permissions are required?

6.60 None.

Applications

6.61 The holder of the on-premises alcohol licence must inform their local licensing authority that they intend to make use of the automatic entitlement. Police are not consulted at any stage of this process.

LICENSED PREMISES GAMING MACHINE PERMITS

- **Relevant part of the Act: Schedule 13**
- **Regulations: SI No 2007/1833 (The Gambling Act 2005 (Licensed Premises Gaming Machine Permits) (England and Wales) Regulations 2007) and SI No 2007/505 (The Licensed Premises Gaming Machine Permits (Scotland) Regulations 2007)**

What is a licensed premises gaming machine permit?

6.62 Holders of premises licences issued under alcohol licensing legislation are also entitled to apply to their local licensing authority for a 'licensed premises gaming machine permit'. This type of permit allows the holder to provide higher numbers of category C and D gaming machines at their premises (Annex B). Application for a permit must be made to the licensing authority. The permit specifies the number of machines that are authorised.

What other gambling permissions are required?

6.63 None. The permit holder is however required to hold a suitable alcohol licence issued under the Licensing Act 2003 (for England and Wales) or the Licensing (Scotland) Act 2005.

Provision of permit

6.64 The permit has to be kept on the premises, and police are entitled to request that the permit is produced (under Schedule 13(10) of the Act).

Applications

6.65 Applicants for licensed premises gaming machine permits are **not** required to send the local chief officer of police a copy of their application.

Loss or theft of permit

6.66 If a licensed premises gaming machine permit is lost or stolen, the permit holder can apply for a replacement copy from the issuing licensing authority. Before the replacement can be issued however, the licensing authority is required (under Schedule 13(11) of the Act) to ensure that the permit holder reported the loss or theft to police.

TEMPORARY USE NOTICES

- **Relevant part of the Act: Part 9**
- **Regulations: SI No 2007/3157 (The Gambling Act 2005 (Temporary Use Notices) Regulations 2007a)**

What is a temporary use notice?

6.67 A temporary use notice may be served on licensing authorities where the issuer wishes to provide facilities for equal chance gaming (generally poker) temporarily at a premises. The gaming provided must take the form of a competition intended to produce a single overall winner. The notice authorises the premises to be used for the provision of equal chance gaming during the period specified in the notice (up to 21 days for a set of premises in a 12 month period). An example of how a temporary use notice might be used is where a poker tournament is being held in a hotel.

A temporary use notice must include, amongst other things (see Section 216 of the Act):

- the activity to be carried out
- the premises to be used
- period of time and times of day the activity will take place
- any periods during the previous 12 months when a temporary use notice has applied to the premises in the application.

Licensing authorities are obliged (section 234 of the Act) to maintain and make accessible to the public, a register of temporary use notices given.

A temporary use notice must be prominently displayed at the premises where the activity is taking place, during the times when it is taking place. The notice must also be made available to a police officer on request. It is an offence to fail to comply with either of these requirements (section 229 of the Act).

What other gambling permissions are required?

6.68 Temporary use notices may only be served on licensing authorities by operating licence holders.

Provision of permit

6.69 A copy of the temporary use notice endorsed by the licensing authority has to be kept on the premises whilst the event is taking place, and police are entitled to request that the notice is produced.

Applications

6.70 Applicants for temporary use notices are required to send a copy of their notice (as served on the licensing authority) to the local chief officer of police of the area where the event is to be held. Notices must be served on the licensing authority and police no less than three months in advance of the event taking place.

6.71 Upon receipt of a temporary use notice, police should consider whether they wish to object to any aspect of the notice. Specifically they should consider whether the gambling set out on the notice should take place, or only with modifications. They may wish to contact the licensing team at the local authority in question to discuss the notice.

6.72 The principles involved in deciding whether to grant a temporary use notice are the same as those in determining a premises licence application (section 6 of this document and Part 14 of the Commission's *Guidance to Licensing Authorities* [7]).

6.73 Objections must be lodged within 14 days of the date that the temporary use notice was issued to the licensing authority. They should be sent as a formal notice of objection to both the licensing authority and the person or organisation that issued the temporary use notice.

6.74 Police officers are entitled by virtue of section 315(1) of the Act to enter premises in respect of which a temporary use notice is being given, in order to assess the effect of the proposed gambling activity upon the licensing objectives (paragraph 2.5 of this document).

6.75 Where objections are received the licensing authority must hold a hearing to listen to responses from the person or organisation issuing the temporary use notice. If police have lodged objections they may attend and offer modifications to the notice that will alleviate their concerns. If the modifications are accepted by the applicant, a new temporary notice must be prepared and the original notice withdrawn.

6.76 Following a hearing, licensing authorities may issue a counter-notice if they believe that the temporary use notice should not take effect. The counter-notice can:

- prevent the temporary use notice from taking effect
- limit the activities that are permitted
- limit the time period of the gambling
- allow the activities to take place subject to a specified condition.

Again police will be copied with the counter-notice.

6.77 If no objections are made within 14 days of the date the temporary use notice was issued, the authority must endorse the notice as valid and return it to the person who gave it.

---

[7] Guidance to Licensing Authorities

OCCASIONAL USE NOTICES

- **Relevant part of the Act: section 39**

What is an occasional use notice?

6.78 Occasional use notices can be served on licensing authorities where the issuer wishes to temporarily permit betting to be provided at a track venue where a sporting event is due to take place. The track does not need to be a permanent fixture, and can be an area of land that has other uses besides being a track. It could for example be a night club where a sporting event was taking place for the purposes of the notice. The notice authorises the track premises to be used for the provision of betting during the period specified in the notice (up to eight days per calendar year for all notices relating to each temporary track). One of the most common uses for an occasional use notice is to permit betting facilities to be provided at point-to-point race meetings.

What other gambling permissions are required?

6.79 Occasional use notices can be served on licensing authorities by anyone with authority to use the land as a track for a sporting event (such as the land owner where the event is to take place). However, the betting facilities at the event can only be provided by betting operators that hold operating licences issued by the Commission.

Applications

6.80 Applicants for occasional use notices are required to send a copy of their notice (as served on the licensing authority) to the local chief officer of police of the area where the event is to take place.

6.81 However, unlike temporary use notices, there is no facility for issuing counter-notices to prevent an occasional use notice from taking effect. The only circumstance under which an occasional use notice can be dismissed is where the maximum eight day limit (per calendar year) for the track had been used already. This is a responsibility of the licensing authority to check.

PRIZE GAMING PERMITS

- **Relevant parts of the Act: sections 288, 289, 311, and Schedule 14**
- **Regulations: SI No 2007/455 (The Gambling Act 2005 (Prize Gaming) (Permits) Regulations 2007) SI No 2007/1777 (The Gambling Act 2005 (Limits on Prize Gaming) Regulations 2007)**

What is a prize gaming permit?

6.82 Prize gaming is defined by section 288 of the Act as gaming where the nature and size of the prize on offer is fixed by the gaming operator before the start of play, and is not determined by how many people play or how much is raised in the course of the gaming. This type of permit enables the holder to run prize gaming at a particular premises.

What other gambling permissions are required?

6.83 None.

Applications

6.84 Licensing authorities may only grant an application for a prize gaming permit if they have consulted the chief officer of police of the area where the premises are located. Section 311(1) of the Act entitles a police officer to enter premises which are the subject of this type of application if they require to do so as part of the application process.
6.85 Licensing authorities may approach police during the application process with regards to carrying out criminal disclosure checks on the applicant.

Provision of permit

6.86 A copy of the prize gaming permit has to be kept on the premises, and police officers are entitled to request that the notice is produced (under Schedule 14(20) of the Act).

Other information

6.87 Several gambling premises are entitled to offer prize gaming without necessarily needing to be the subject of a prize gaming permit, including bingo operators and adult gaming centres.
6.88 Unlike many other forms of gambling, under-18s are entitled to participate in prize gaming, providing it is equal chance prize gaming, such as bingo.

7 PREMISES LICENCE REVIEWS AND THE APPEALS PROCESS

7.1 The local licensing framework, described in this section, includes mechanisms by which the circumstances of a particular gambling premises can be reviewed. There is also a route of appeal available to gambling operators against decisions made by licensing authorities.
7.2 Police have an important role to play towards premises licence reviews and appeals, both in terms of supporting licensing authorities and in their capacity as a responsible authority under the Act. This section of the document looks at the structure of premises licence reviews and appeals, and how police may be involved in this process.
7.3 The premises licence review and appeal process towards gambling premises is similar in appearance to the review and appeal process for alcohol premises licences existing under the Licensing Act 2003 and Licensing (Scotland) Act 2005. However, it should be noted that there are different considerations within gambling legislation and alcohol licensing legislation governing when a premises licence should be the subject of a review. The considerations towards gambling premises are discussed in the remainder of this section.

APPLYING FOR, AND PARTICIPATING IN, A PREMISES LICENCE REVIEW

- **Relevant part of the Act: Part 8**
- **Regulations: SI No 2007/2258 (The Gambling Act 2005 (Premises Licences) (Review) Regulations 2007) SI No 2007/394 (The Gambling Act 2005 (Review of Premises Licences) (Scotland) Regulations 2007)**

Premises licence reviews

7.4 A premises licence issued under the Act may be reviewed by the issuing licensing authority of its own volition, or following the receipt of an application for a review from either an interested party or a responsible authority. Any aspect of the premises or the licence itself may be scrutinised as part of a review.

7.5 During a review, the licensing authority will evaluate the grounds for the review and determine if any action can be taken in relation to the premises licence. If it concludes that action should be taken, it can look to make changes to certain premises licence conditions, add certain new conditions, suspend the licence for up to three months, or even revoke the licence altogether.

Police involvement in premises licence reviews

7.6 As a responsible authority under the Act, police may request a review of a premises licence, in accordance with section 197 of the Act. They may also contribute to premises licence reviews that are requested by other parties, or that are initiated by licensing authorities themselves.

Reasons to request a review of a premises licence

7.7 If police are concerned about a particular gambling premises in their local area, for example if they are aware of criminal activity taking place at a specific premises, they may apply to the issuing licensing authority for a review of the premises licence. Section 198 of the Act sets out a number of criteria to which licensing authorities should refer to when deciding whether to accept the application for a review, namely that a licensing authority may decide to reject an application for a review if the grounds:

- are not relevant to the Commission's guidance or codes of practice, the licensing authority's policy statement, or the three licensing objectives
- are found to be frivolous, vexatious, or not going to lead to the licensing authority revoking or suspending the licence, or changing licence conditions
- are substantially the same as grounds previously reviewed against the premises in question
- are substantially the same as representations made at the time the premises licence was first applied for.

7.8 Therefore, before deciding whether to apply to a licensing authority for a review of a premises licence, police may look instead, in the first instance, to contact the licensing authority in question to discuss the specific concerns connected to the gambling premises. This may help both parties to agree whether a premises licence review would be helpful in addressing the issues raised, or whether another course of action is more appropriate (such as using powers under other legislation, or meeting with the owner of the gambling premises to talk about the concerns).

7.9 It should be noted that, unlike the Licensing Act 2003 and Licensing (Scotland) Act 2005, the Act does not include the prevention of public nuisance as a specific licensing objective (unless the activity leading to the public nuisance could be held as fitting with the licensing objective of preventing crime and disorder associated with gambling). Nuisance associated with gambling premises therefore is unlikely to be grounds for a review of a premises licence, and should instead be tackled directly under other relevant legislation.

Police contributions to premises licence reviews

7.10 Police are a responsible authority for premises licence reviews, and as such are sent a 'notice of intention to carry out a review' when a gambling premises in their local area is having its premises licence reviewed. The notice is sent to them by the organisation or individual applying for the review, and a period of 28 days is made available in which representations can be made to the licensing authority. Notice of the application for a premises licence review must be given to the licence holder and all other responsible authorities under the Act.

7.11 The licensing authority is required to publish a notice of the intention to carry out a review in a local newspaper or on their website, and to fix a notice outside the premises itself.

7.12 When considering whether or not to make representations to be taken into account as part of a gambling premises licence review, police are entitled to enter the premises in question (under section 313(2) of the Act).

7.13 Again, before deciding whether or not to make representations relating to a premises licence review, police services may want to check against the criteria shown in paragraph 7.7 of this document, which are the criteria against which a licensing authority will assess representations.

APPEALS PROCESS AND THE ROLE OF THE POLICE

- **Relevant parts of the Act: sections 206-209**

7.14 Decisions made by licensing authorities relating to gambling permissions issued under the Act can be subject to appeal.

Appealing decisions made regarding applications for premises licences or provisional statements

7.15 For example, where individuals or organisations make representations towards a premises licence application or a provisional statement application, and the application is then granted by the licensing authority, a route of appeal opens against the decision. Consequently, where police make a representation towards a premises licence or provisional statement application, they will be entitled to appeal the outcome of the application, as they will be a party to the decision. Appeals of this nature should be lodged with the local magistrates' court or sheriff within 21 days of the outcome of the application being formally communicated to the police (via a notice of determination).

Appealing decisions made regarding applications for club permits and temporary use notices

7.16 Police also have a right of appeal for licensing authority decisions where they have made representations relating to:

- club gaming permits and club machine permit applications (under Schedule 12(25) of the Act)
- temporary use notices (under section 226 of the Act).

7.17 Police will be sent details of the outcome of the club permit application, or in the case of temporary use notices a copy of the notice endorsed by the licensing authority, and again will then have 21 days from receiving this document in which to appeal to the local magistrates' court or sheriff.

Appealing decisions made following a premises licence review

7.18 The process described above also applies to decisions made by licensing authorities following a review of a premises licence – police who make representations during the course of the review will be entitled to appeal the final decision taken by the licensing authority.

8 BETTING

8.1 Commercial betting can take place in betting premises, which are found throughout Great Britain on most high streets, and are often referred to as bookmakers, licensed betting offices, or betting shops. They can also be found in other premises such as racetracks (section 13 of this document).

8.2 Betting premises may only exist under an operating licence, issued by the Commission, and a betting premises licence, issued by the licensing authority covering the area where the premises is situated.

UNDER-18S AND ENTRY TO BETTING PREMISES

8.3 Under-18s are not allowed to enter betting premises, and each premises is required (as a condition of their premises licence) to display a notice at each entrance stating this.

ALCOHOL CONSUMPTION IN BETTING PREMISES

8.4 It is a condition of every betting premises licence that no alcohol can be consumed on the premises when gambling is taking place. It is the responsibility of the licence holder and their employees to ensure that this is upheld.

DOOR SUPERVISION AT BETTING PREMISES

8.5 Door supervisors are not commonly found at betting premises. Age verification (in terms of ensuring under-18s are not permitted to enter the premises) is often carried out by cashiers challenging, for example, anyone appearing to be under 21 attempting to place a bet.
8.6 Licensing authorities have discretion to attach their own conditions to premises licences issued under the Act, and may seek to require door supervision at premises via this method. In the event that a licensing authority sets such a condition at a betting premises, section 178 of the Act requires that the supervisor(s) holds a suitable licence issued by the Security Industry Authority (SIA).

GAMING MACHINES IN BETTING PREMISES

8.7 Betting premises are entitled to provide up to four gaming machines for their customers, and these can be within categories B2 (often referred to as 'fixed odds betting terminals', or FOBTs) to D. A summary of the machine categories and premises types can be found in Annex B of this document.

CAN POLICE USE POWERS IN THE ACT TO TACKLE CRIME AND DISORDER AT BETTING PREMISES?

8.8 Police may use the powers of the Act to take action where a gambling-related offence is committed under the Act in accordance with the summary of offences shown in section 25 of this document and the powers shown in section 3 of this document.
8.9 However, crime and disorder that is not linked to an offence under the Act or to the actual gambling facilities provided at a betting premises should be tackled under other relevant legislation or as common law offences. For example, if money was stolen from a cashier in a betting premises it is likely that the offence should be handled under the same legislation that would be used for theft offences anywhere, as there is no provision for this within the Act.
8.10 Police are a responsible authority under the Act and may request that a licensing authority reviews a particular premises licence.

NON-COMMERCIAL AND PRIVATE BETTING

8.11 Betting can take place on a commercial basis provided it is carried out by suitably licensed individuals and organisations, and takes place on premises that are covered by the appropriate permission under the Act. Commercial betting is illegal if it takes place outside of these requirements.

8.12 For example, commercial betting in pubs is illegal. The Commission has published a leaflet called *Betting in pubs and clubs* which provides further information on this subject. This is available on the Commission's website[8].
8.13 However if the betting is non-commercial (where no part of any proceeds from the betting are taken for private gain) it may be legally carried out under Part 14 of the Act. An example might be a charity race night, that is a fund-raising event involving betting where the proceeds from the betting activity are used for non-commercial purposes.
8.14 Similarly, betting may also be legally carried out where it is private and taking place between co-workers or people living in the same premises. Private betting is defined at Schedule 15 of the Act.

---

[8] Betting in pubs and clubs

9 CASINOS

9.1 Casinos offer casino games such as roulette and blackjack. They exist under an operating licence issued by the Commission and a casino premises licence issued by the local licensing authority.

CASINOS AND UNDER-18S

9.2 It is illegal for under-18s to enter a casino and notices to this effect are required to be displayed at entrances.
9.3 Under the Act new categories of casino (Large and Small casinos) are to be permitted offering a wider range of gambling facilities in selected local authority areas.

ALCOHOL CONSUMPTION IN CASINOS

9.4 There are no restrictions in the Act with regard to the consumption of alcohol in casinos. However under the *Licence Conditions and Codes of Practice* if licensees offer customers free or discounted drinks for consumption on the premises, the availability of the drinks must not in any way be related to whether the customer either begins or continues to gamble. In addition licensees must not make unsolicited offers of free alcoholic drinks for immediate consumption by customers when they are participating in a casino game or playing a gaming machine.

---

[9] Licence Conditions and Codes of Practice

DOOR SUPERVISION AT CASINOS

9.5 Section 178 of the Act requires that where a licensing authority attaches a condition to a premises licence requiring door supervision, that the persons employed as door supervisors at the gambling premises hold a suitable licence issued by the Security Industry Authority (SIA). This requirement is relaxed for some door supervisors directly employed by the casinos.
9.6 If someone is employed as a door supervisor at a casino, and is employed directly by the casino itself (as 'in-house' staff), they are not be required to be licensed by the SIA, due to an exemption created through Schedule 2 of the Private Security Industry Act 2001.
9.7 However, the exemption does **not** apply to people working under a contract of employment with another company as door supervisors at casinos (so if they work at the casino but are actually employed by a security company, for example). Contract staff working as door supervisors at casinos must be SIA licensed.

GAMING MACHINES IN CASINOS

9.8 Casinos that existed under permissions granted to them before the introduction of the new gambling legislation on 1 September 2007 are entitled to provide up to 20 gaming machines for their customers within categories B to D, or they can provide unlimited category C or D gaming machines instead. There are higher machine entitlements for the 'new' casinos that will exist as Small and Large casinos under the Act.

9.9 A summary of the machine categories and premises types can be found in Annex B of this document.

CAN THE ACT BE USED TO TACKLE CRIME AND DISORDER AT CASINOS?

9.10 Police may use the powers of the Act to take action where a gambling-related offence is committed under the Act in accordance with the summary of offences shown in section 25 of this document and the powers shown in section 3 of this document.

9.11 However, crime and disorder that is not linked to an offence under the Act or to the actual gambling facilities provided at a casino premises should be tackled under other relevant legislation or as common law offences. For example, if money was stolen from a cashier in a casino premises it is likely that the offence should be handled under the same legislation that would be used for theft offences anywhere, as there is no provision for this within the Act.

9.12 Police are a responsible authority under the Act and may request that a licensing authority reviews a particular premises licence.

10 AMUSEMENT ARCADES

WHAT DIFFERENT TYPES OF ARCADE ARE THERE?

10.1 There are a number of different types of premises that may exist under the Act to offer gaming machines to their customers, and are often referred to collectively as arcades, as follows:

- adult gaming centres (AGCs)
- family entertainment centres (FECs)
- unlicensed family entertainment centres (UFECs)
- alcohol-licensed premises gaming machine permits.

10.2 The different types are permitted to offer different categories of gaming machine, ranging from category B machines with potential jackpots up to £500 through to category D machines which may be played by under-18s. A summary of the machine categories and premises types can be found in Annex B of this document.

10.3 Arcades are often found on high streets but can also be found as a premises occupying part of a larger complex, including for example a bowling alley, at an airport, or inside a motorway services station. They are also commonly located in coastal resorts, situated on piers and in holiday parks.

10.4 Some types of amusement arcade may offer prize gaming such as bingo to their customers. This is discussed in section 11 of this document.

COMMON CHARACTERISTICS OF AGCS

10.5 An AGC is a gaming machine premises that exists under an operating licence issued by the Commission and a premises licence from the local licensing authority, and is permitted to offer gaming machines in categories B3 and B4 (up to four machines in total) and C and D (an unlimited number).

10.6 It is illegal for under-18s to enter an adult gaming centre, and notices to this effect are required to be displayed at entrances.

10.7 Alcohol may not be consumed in an AGC when gambling facilities are being provided (ie when open for business as an AGC), and a notice to this effect must be displayed at entrances.

10.8 An AGC premises licence places no restrictions on hours of business.

COMMON CHARACTERISTICS OF FECS

10.9 An FEC is a gaming machine premises that exists under an operating licence issued by the Commission and a premises licence from the local licensing authority, and is permitted to offer an unlimited number of gaming machines in categories C and D.

10.10 Under-18s are permitted to enter an FEC. They are not however permitted to enter areas within the FEC where category C gaming machines are situated. It is a condition of FEC premises licences that areas with category C gaming machines are supervised at all times, are separated from the rest of the premises by a physical barrier, and that a notice is displayed at the entrance to category C areas stating that under-18s are not permitted to enter.

10.11 Alcohol may not be consumed in an FEC when gambling facilities are being provided (ie when open for business as an FEC), and a notice to this effect must be displayed at FEC entrances.

10.12 An FEC premises licence places no restrictions on hours of business.

COMMON CHARACTERISTICS OF UFECS

10.13 A UFEC is a gaming machine premises that exists under a permit issued by the local licensing authority. A UFEC is permitted to offer an unlimited number of category D gaming machines.

10.14 Under-18s may enter a UFEC and are free to use all gaming machines without supervision.

10.15 There are no restrictions within the Act or supporting legislation regarding alcohol consumption in UFECs.

10.16 UFEC opening hours are agreed with the licensing authority at the time of application for the permit (or at the time of conversion of an old 'section 34' permit into a permit under the Act).

COMMON CHARACTERISTICS OF GAMING MACHINE PERMITS IN ALCOHOL LICENSED PREMISES

10.17 This type of permit authorises the holder to provide a specified number of gaming machines from categories C and D in premises that have an 'on-premises' alcohol licence issued under relevant alcohol licensing legislation. The issuing licensing authority specifies the maximum number of gaming machines that are allowed at the premises. Such premises must not be primarily established to offer gaming machines; if they are they should instead be the subject of an AGC or FEC permission. The machines must be a subsidiary activity to the existence of the alcohol licence, and if customers were visiting the premises purely to use gaming machines the issuing licensing authority could look to restrict the number of gaming machines available via the permit.

10.18 Under-18s may enter this type of premises. However they are not permitted to play category C gaming machines. As a result, category C machines must be supervised in accordance with the Commission's *Gaming Machine Permits Code of Practice*, available from the Commission's website[10].

[10] Gaming Machine Permits Code of Practice

CAN THE ACT BE USED TO TACKLE CRIME AND DISORDER AT ARCADE PREMISES?

10.19 Police may use the powers of the Act to take action where a gambling-related offence is committed under the Act in accordance with the summary of offences shown in section 25 of this document and the powers shown in section 3 of this document.

10.20 However, crime and disorder that is not linked to an offence under the Act or to the actual gambling facilities provided at arcade premises should be tackled under other relevant legislation. For example, if gaming machines were broken by a customer attempting to get money from the machine, the offence committed should be approached under appropriate legislation for handling that type of crime, as there is no provision for this within the Act.
10.21 Police are a responsible authority under the Act and may request that a licensing authority reviews a particular premises licence.

11 BINGO

11.1 Bingo may be played commercially in different types of premises, including:
- bingo premises (ie bingo halls)
- amusement arcades (played as prize gaming at an AGC, an FEC or a UFEC)
- travelling fairs (played as prize gaming)
- pubs, clubs and institutes (played as equal chance gaming or prize gaming).

BINGO AND UNDER-18S

11.2 Under-18s are entitled to play bingo in certain circumstances, depending on where and in what context the bingo is being played. If it is prize gaming, where the bingo is played for a prize that remains the same regardless of how many people play, under-18s can participate. For example, premises such as FECs, UFECs, funfairs and some clubs will run bingo games as prize gaming.
11.3 However if the bingo is played in a dedicated bingo premises (where it is the primary purpose of the venue) under-18s cannot participate. Some bingo premises allow under-18s to enter as part of a family group for example, but the under-18s cannot join in the gaming.

ALCOHOL CONSUMPTION IN BINGO PREMISES

11.4 There are no automatic restrictions on a bingo premises licence with regard to the consumption of alcohol.

GAMING MACHINES IN BINGO PREMISES

11.5 Commercial bingo premises, where bingo is the primary purpose of the venue, are entitled to provide up to eight gaming machines within categories B3 and B4, and can also provide an unlimited number of category C and D machines for their customers.
11.6 A summary of the machine categories and premises types can be found in Annex B of this document.

DOOR SUPERVISION AT BINGO PREMISES

11.7 Section 178 of the Act requires that where a licensing authority attaches a condition to a premises licence requiring door supervision, that the persons employed as door supervisors at the gambling premises hold a suitable licence issued by the SIA. This requirement is relaxed for some door supervisors at bingo premises.
11.8 If someone is employed as a door supervisor at a bingo premises and is employed directly by the bingo premises itself (as 'in-house' staff) they are not required to be licensed by the SIA, due to an exemption created through Schedule 2 of the Private Security Industry Act 2001.
11.9 However the exemption does **not** apply to people working as door supervisors at bingo premises that are under a contract of employment with another company (so if they work at the bingo premises but are actually employed by a security company, for example). Contract staff working as door supervisors at bingo premises must be SIA licensed.

CAN THE ACT BE USED TO TACKLE CRIME AND DISORDER AT BINGO PREMISES?

11.10 Police may use the powers of the Act to take action where a gambling-related offence is committed under the Act in accordance with the summary of offences shown in section 25 of this document and the powers shown in section 3 of this document.
11.11 However, crime and disorder that is not linked to an offence under the Act or to the actual gambling facilities provided at a bingo premises should be tackled under other relevant legislation or as common law offences. For example, if gaming machines were damaged by a customer attempting to get money from the machine, the offence committed should be approached under appropriate legislation for the act of causing the damage, as there is no provision for this within the Act.
11.12 Police are a responsible authority under the Act and may request that a licensing authority reviews a particular premises licence.

12 FAIRS

12.1 A travelling fair is defined by section 286 of the Act as 'consisting wholly or principally for the provision of amusements'. Where a fair provides facilities for gambling it may provide these for up to 27 days per calendar year at a single premises. For example, if a fair is based in a park for 26 days, it could only return to that same park for one more day in the calendar year. Licensing authorities are responsible for monitoring this limit.
12.2 The gambling facilities that the Act permits to be provided at funfairs meeting the above definition are prize gaming and gaming machines.
12.3 In addition to the 27 day limit set down in the Act, local authorities may adopt byelaws to control travelling fairs under a discretionary power set out in section 75 of the Public Health Act 1961 (as amended by section 22 of the Local Government (Miscellaneous Provisions) Act 1976).

PRIZE GAMING AT TRAVELLING FAIRS

12.4 Section 292 of the Act allows travelling fairs to legally provide prize gaming such as bingo, providing the following conditions (at section 293 of the Act) are upheld:

- the prize gaming is an ancillary amusement (ie not the main purpose) of the fair
- all chances to participate in each game must only be sold on the day of the game and at the fair itself
- each game must be played in full on the day the chances to participate are sold
- the result of each game must be made publicly available where the game is played after the game has finished
- the gaming does not entitle a player to participate in another form of gambling
- the limits set down in regulations on prize gaming are adhered to (SI No 2007/1777 The Gambling Act 2005 (Limits on Prize Gaming) Regulations 2007)
- the participation fee per player per game cannot exceed 50p (and the aggregate amount for all participation fees in a game cannot exceed £500)
- if a prize is a cash prize, it cannot exceed £35
- if a competition involves more than one prize the value of all prizes cannot exceed £500.

12.5 Under-18s are allowed to participate in prize gaming played at travelling fairs.

GAMING MACHINES AT TRAVELLING FAIRS

12.6 Travelling fairs may also provide an unlimited number of category D gaming machines (see Annex B for details) without requiring a permit or permission from a licensing authority. As with prize gaming, the machines must be an ancillary part of the fair rather than the main attraction.

12.7 Any gaming machine provided at a travelling fair operating in Great Britain must be capable of meeting the technical standards set out by the Commission (available through the Commission's website).

CAN THE ACT BE USED TO TACKLE CRIME AND DISORDER AT TRAVELLING FAIRS?

12.8 Police may use the powers of the Act to take action where a gambling-related offence is committed under the Act in accordance with the summary of offences shown in section 25 of this document and the powers shown in section 3 of this document.
12.9 However, crime and disorder that is not linked to an offence under the Act or to the actual gambling facilities provided at a travelling fair should be tackled under other relevant legislation or as common law offences. For example, if money was stolen from a cashier in a travelling fair it is likely that the offence should be handled under the same legislation that would be used for theft offences anywhere, as there is no provision for this within the Act.
12.10 Police are a responsible authority under the Act and may request that a licensing authority reviews a particular premises licence.

13 TRACKS (HORSERACING, GREYHOUND STADIUMS ETC)

PERMANENTLY-SITUATED TRACKS

13.1 Section 353 of the Act defines a track as a horse-race course, a dog track, or another premises on any part of which a race or other sporting event takes place or is intended to take place. The definition therefore covers venues such as football grounds, motor-racing circuits, and other sports stadia where betting occurs on site.
13.2 As a result of this wide definition, it is likely that most forces will have at least one permanently-situated premises in their area that is defined as a track under the Act. Where such tracks provide facilities for betting, they are required to hold a track premises licence issued by the local licensing authority.

TEMPORARY TRACKS

13.3 However, the definition also captures places that are only being used temporarily to provide races or sporting events, and that have other purposes most of the time. For example, other premises that could be considered as a track under the Act include a hotel staging a snooker tournament for two weeks (even though primarily it is a hotel), a field being used to provide a point-to-point horseracing event, or a section of riverbank being used to host an angling contest.
13.4 Some forces will therefore have places that are used temporarily as a track in their area. Betting facilities need to be the subject of an occasional use notice, as described in paragraphs 6.78 – 6.81 of this document. The local chief officer of police is sent a copy of every occasional use notice issued.

WHAT GAMBLING TAKES PLACE AT A TRACK?

13.5 The Act permits certain gambling facilities to be provided at tracks. Although the main gambling type is betting, many tracks also have gaming machines available.

BETTING AT TRACKS

13.6 Tracks such as racecourses and dog tracks allow betting operators to go onto the track on race days and accept bets. All betting operators working on tracks must hold a suitable operating licence issued by the Commission – for example each betting operator that takes bets from a stand must be licensed.

13.7 Larger tracks such as football stadia will often have a contract with a high-street betting operator to provide betting facilities at the stadium from kiosks or from an actual betting premises that is located on the track. The operator providing the betting is required to be suitably licensed by the Commission.
13.8 Some dog track owners are entitled under the Act to offer facilities for pool betting at their track. Such track owners offering pool betting must hold a suitable operating licence in order to do so.

GAMING MACHINES AT TRACKS

13.9 Many permanently-situated tracks have an 'on-premises' alcohol licence, and as such are entitled to make use of their automatic gaming machine entitlement to have up to two gaming machines (within categories C and D). If the track also offers betting facilities it is required to be the subject of a track premises licence, and the existence of this licence prevents the track from holding a permit authorising more gaming machines. However before the introduction of the new gambling legislation on 1 September 2007 tracks were entitled to apply for a permit authorising them to have more gaming machines, and these permits have been protected under the new regulatory regime. Therefore some tracks are legally able to offer higher numbers of gaming machines via a permit (on the assumption that the permit holder made the correct application in time, the right to make available the same number of machines as were permitted under the previous legislation, will be preserved indefinitely).
13.10 Where a track has a betting premises situated on it (ie effectively a high-street betting shop in a track environment), the shop will be the subject of a betting premises licence issued by a licensing authority. The betting operator running the premises will be entitled to provide up to four gaming machines within the walls of the betting premises, and these can be within categories B2 to D (in addition to any gaming machines existing elsewhere at the track).
13.11 Where a dog track owner provides pool betting facilities under an operating licence, the owner is entitled to site up to four gaming machines on their track within categories B2 to D (in addition to any gaming machines existing in reliance on an alcohol licence).

UNDER-18S ON TRACKS

13.12 There are no restrictions within the Act on under-18s visiting a track or moving into the different areas of a track, and it is common practice for families to attend tracks to watch sport and other events. However, it is illegal for under-18s to place bets and as such all permanently-situated tracks where betting is offered are required (through their track premises licence) to place prominent notices at public entrances stating that no person under 18 is permitted to bet on the premises.
13.13 Similarly on temporary tracks existing under an occasional use notice, the betting operators working on tracks are required (as a condition of their operating licence) to ensure that they and their staff check the age of any customer who appears to be under the age of 21.
13.14 Under-18s are entitled to play any category D gaming machines found at tracks. It is illegal however for them to use any higher category gaming machines, and as such the usage of these machines is required to be supervised appropriately.

CAN THE ACT BE USED TO TACKLE CRIME AND DISORDER AT TRACKS?

13.15 Police may use the powers of the Act to take action where a gambling-related offence is committed under the Act in accordance with the summary of offences shown in section 25 of this document and the powers shown in section 3 of this document.
13.16 However, crime and disorder that is not linked to an offence under the Act or to the actual gambling facilities provided at a track should be tackled under other

relevant legislation or as common law offences. For example, if money was stolen from a cashier at a track it is likely that the offence should be handled under the same legislation that would be used for theft offences anywhere, as there is no provision for this within the Act.

13.17 Police are a responsible authority under the Act and may request that a licensing authority reviews a particular premises licence.

14 TAKEAWAY RESTAURANTS, TAXI OFFICES, GUESTHOUSES AND SIMILAR PREMISES

14.1 Until 1 August 2006, businesses such as chip shops and taxi offices were entitled to apply to their local authority for a 'section 34' permit issued under the Gaming Act 1968 which allowed them to provide certain gaming machines for their customers to use. The Act has not replicated this permission, so all businesses of this type with gaming machines will not be able to provide the machines when their 'section 34' permit expires. This will be no later than 31 July 2009.

14.2 Gaming machines are only permitted to be sited in premises authorised to do so under the Act, namely:

- where a relevant premises licence has effect (casino, AGC, FEC, betting, bingo or track)
- where a relevant permit has effect (UFEC, alcohol-licensed premises machine permit, club gaming permit or club machine permit)
- where an automatic entitlement has effect (premises with an 'on sales' alcohol licence).

14.3 Gaming machines in any other premises are therefore illegally sited, unless they exist under a 'section 34' permit running until no later than 31 July 2009. The removal of illegal machines can involve a multi-agency approach which includes the police, local authorities, and customs and excise. The Commission is also involved in machine removal as there may be wider implications connected to suppliers of illegal gaming machines (paragraphs 5.12 – 5.16 of this document).

15 POKER AND GAMES OF EQUAL CHANCE

15.1 The Act allows games such as poker to be played in certain gambling premises such as casinos. The Act also allows poker and other games of equal chance to be played in other environments.

POKER IN RESIDENTIAL DWELLINGS

15.2 Individuals may play poker with friends etc in a residential dwelling providing other members of the public are not invited to participate, and no charge is made to participate in the gaming.

POKER AS A NON-COMMERCIAL GAME

15.3 Poker may be played as a form of non-commercial gaming, to raise funds for good causes. The conditions for non-commercial gaming are described further in paragraphs 8.13 – 8.14 and 20.1 – 20.9 of this document.

POKER IN PUBS AND CLUBS

15.4 Regulations have been made relating to poker and other equal chance games played in places such as pubs. *Code of practice for equal chance gaming in clubs and premises with an alcohol licence*, which summarises how the gaming should take place and the limits on stakes and prizes, can be viewed on the Commission's website[11].

15.5 The Commission has also published an advice document to answer general enquiries about poker, and other games of equal chance, played in pubs. *Advice on gaming in clubs and alcohol licensed premises: Gambling Act 2005* and can be viewed on the Commission's website[12].

[11] Code of practice for equal chance gaming in clubs and premises with an alcohol licence

[12] Advice on gaming in clubs and alcohol licensed premises: Gambling Act 2005

16 PUBS AND OTHER ALCOHOL-LICENSED PREMISES

16.1 The Act enables pubs and premises that are licensed for the consumption of alcohol to provide gaming machines. It also allows certain types of gaming to be played in pubs.

GAMING MACHINES IN ALCOHOL-LICENSED PREMISES

16.2 Pubs and other alcohol licensed-premises in Great Britain are automatically entitled to provide a maximum of two gaming machines on their premises. The gaming machines have to be either categories C or D (or one of each type).
16.3 The automatic entitlement is not a permit as such, as it exists automatically by virtue of the existence of an alcohol licence. However it can only be activated by the holder of the alcohol premises licence informing their local licensing authority of their intention to provide gaming machines.
16.4 Holders of premises licences issued under alcohol-licensing legislation are also entitled to apply to their local licensing authority for a 'licensed premises gaming machine permit'. This type of permit allows the holder to provide higher numbers of category C and D gaming machines at their premises.

OTHER MACHINES IN ALCOHOL-LICENSED PREMISES

16.5 Machines that require the player to demonstrate skill or knowledge, such as quiz machines or video games, are not classed as gaming machines under the Act. These types of machine, therefore, do not contribute towards a pub's automatic machine entitlement.

17 ENTERTAINMENT COMPLEXES AND OTHER VENUES

17.1 Gaming machines are often found in premises that form part of bigger entertainment complexes, and are often provided as a subsidiary element of venues that are primarily intended to provide other types of entertainment. Such venues include theme parks and bowling alleys.
17.2 Gaming machines may also commonly be found as an ancillary feature of venues that the public might visit primarily for non-gambling related purposes, including shopping malls, motorway service stations and airports.
17.3 However all gaming machines that exist as a component of a larger venue can only be provided if an appropriate premises licence, permit or entitlement under the Act is in place. For example, an arcade area comprised of category D gaming machines at a motorway services can exist only if the area is the subject of a family entertainment centre permit, issued by the local licensing authority.
17.4 Venues that have a premises licence issued under relevant alcohol licensing legislation may also provide gaming machines through a licensed premises gaming machine permit. So for example, a bowling centre licensed to serve alcohol may have an arcade area within the centre that is the subject of this type of permit.

OTHER MACHINES

17.5 Machines that require the player to demonstrate skill or knowledge, such as quiz machines or video games, are not classed as gaming machines under the Act. These types of machine, therefore, may be provided without being subject to gambling legislation.

18 CLUBS

18.1 Members clubs and commercial clubs in Britain are entitled under the Act to offer certain types of gambling. Paragraphs 6.47 – 6.49 of this document identify the permits that clubs need to hold in order to provide gambling facilities for their members.

GAMING IN CLUBS

18.2 The Commission has published a document called *Code of Practice for equal chance gaming in clubs and premises with an alcohol licence*, which summarises the types of gaming that may be offered by clubs for their members. This is available on the Commission's website[13].

---

[13] Code of practice for equal chance gaming in clubs and premises with an alcohol licence

GAMING MACHINES IN CLUBS

18.3 Clubs holding a relevant permit from their licensing authority are entitled to offer gaming machines for their members. Up to three gaming machines can be made available. The category types for clubs can be found in Annex B of this document.

18.4 Members clubs, including working men's institutes, are allowed to offer a category of gaming machine known as B3A, which provide lottery games, as part of their machine entitlement. This type of machine cannot be provided in any other type of premises.

OTHER MACHINES IN CLUBS

18.5 Machines that require the player to demonstrate skill or knowledge, such as quiz machines or video games, are not classed as gaming machines under the Act. These types of machine, therefore, may be provided in a club without being subject to gambling legislation.

19 LOTTERIES AND RAFFLES

19.1 The Act entitles various types of lottery (including raffles) to be carried out lawfully. Lotteries may only be run as a way of raising funds for a particular good cause, in the following categories:

- a society lottery – these are lotteries designed to raise funds for non-commercial purposes and fund raising initiatives, where under-16s cannot participate and can only be run where the society is licensed by the Commission or registered by a local authority (depending on the size of the lottery in question).

19.2 Lotteries that are permitted to be run without requiring any licence or registration are as follows:

- incidental non-commercial lotteries – these are lotteries held as part of non-commercial events, such as a raffle held at a school's fund raising night
- private lotteries – these are lotteries run by societies for their members, by someone at a place of work for their colleagues, or by a resident of premises for other residents

- customer lotteries – where an occupier of business premises runs a lottery for customers on the business premises.

19.3 Police with specific queries about lotteries should refer to the Commission's publication entitled *Lotteries and the Law*. This is available from the Commission's website[14]. Alternatively police may contact the local licensing authority or the Commission's Enquiries team (using the contact details in section 26 of this document).

---

[14] Lotteries and the Law

MACHINES THAT VEND LOTTERY TICKETS

19.4 Societies raising money for non-commercial purposes may sell their lottery tickets from vending-style terminals, for example where players can insert money and buy a scratch card. Such machines can be situated in a variety of locations such as a pub. However, as the Act prohibits under-16s from entering lotteries, such machines must be supervised to prevent children from buying tickets.

POSSIBLE LOTTERY SCAMS

19.5 Police may be contacted by members of the public who are concerned about lottery-style games or possible scams that may appear in many respects to be gambling products. For more information see section 21 of this document.

20 GAMING CARRIED OUT AS PART OF A LOCAL EVENT

20.1 Part 14 of the Act allows gaming to be carried out at a non-commercial event to raise funds for a specific purpose, other than for private gain. The gaming can be either prize gaming or equal chance gaming.
20.2 The principal distinction between prize gaming and equal chance gaming is how the prize is awarded and communicated to players – in **prize gaming** the prize is fixed before the start of the game and remains the same throughout regardless of how many people take part, whereas in **equal chance gaming** the prize is dependant on many people take part in the game as it is made up from stakes and participation fees.
20.3 Whichever type of gaming is used, the Act allows the gaming organiser to deduct reasonable costs from the proceeds of the gaming to cover prizes and costs associated with providing the facilities for the gaming. However, an offence is committed if the remainder of the proceeds are not used for the purposes that were advertised (see section 25 of this document for details of this offence).
20.4 Police with specific concerns over gaming held at non-commercial events are advised in the first instance to contact the licensing authority covering the area where the event is taking place.

FOR NON-COMMERCIAL PRIZE GAMING

20.5 An example of an acceptable type of non-commercial prize gaming would be a charity event in a village hall, where the evening's entertainment includes a game of bingo with players buying a gamecard and playing to win a food hamper. The proceeds of the bingo game go towards a good cause. It would not be acceptable gaming if the proceeds were, for example, kept for personal use by the event organiser.
20.6 Providing the following conditions (from Part 14 of the Act) are met, the gaming will be deemed to be compliant:

- all players to be informed of the purpose of the gaming (ie what will the funds raised be used for)

- the profits from the gaming must be applied to a purpose other than private gain
- the gaming does not take place on a gambling premises (holding a premises licence issued under the Act), on a track when betting is taking place or at a premises which is the subject of a temporary use notice
- the gaming is not remote (ie provided through means such as the internet).

FOR NON-COMMERCIAL EQUAL CHANCE GAMING

20.7 An example of an acceptable type of non-commercial equal chance gaming would be a fund-raising night at a sports or social club, where the evening's entertainment includes a number of hands of poker, with the prize for the overall winner being determined by the number of players. It would not be acceptable gaming if, for example, the event organiser provided a set prize fund that remained the same regardless of how many people participated.

20.8 The regulations set limits on stakes and prizes for non-commercial equal chance gaming (SI No 2007/2041as follows: The Gambling Act 2005 (Non-commercial equal-chance gaming) regulations 2007 – 2007 No 2041) [*sic*]:

- each player can only be required to make one payment of up to £8 per game at the event
- the aggregate amount or value of all prizes awarded as a result of games at the event must not exceed £600
- if the event is part of a series of events, the amount or value of prizes in respect of games at the final event cannot exceed £900.

20.9 Providing the following conditions (from Part 14 of the Act) are met, the gaming will be deemed to be compliant:

- all players to be informed of the purpose of the gaming (ie what will the funds raised be used for)
- the profits from the gaming must be applied to a purpose other than private gain
- the gaming does not exceed the limits set out in the regulations stated above
- the gaming does not take place on a gambling premises (holding a premises licence issued under the Act), on a track when betting is taking place, or at a premises which is the subject of a temporary use notice
- the gaming is not remote (ie provided through means such as the internet).

21 SCAMS AND BOGUS LOTTERIES

21.1 Police may be aware of products being sold in or adjacent to their policing area that appear in some respects to be gambling products, such as lottery-style scratch cards or selling schemes that involve a seemingly random return to participants. This section looks at some common types of arrangement that demonstrate partial elements of gambling, but are in fact not gambling products or are illegal under the Act.

CHAIN-GIFT SCHEMES

21.2 A chain-gift scheme typically involves pyramid-style arrangements where the person at the top of the chain aims to recruit other members to the scheme to earn commission or goods. Membership to the chain is often sold on the understanding that all members will make profits as they reach the top of the chain, if they get more people to join the scheme.

21.3 Many of these types of arrangement are classed as gambling by virtue of people being asked to pay to participate in what is effectively a random arrangement. The Act makes it an offence to promote or invite others to participate in a chain-gift scheme. The offence is derived from the Fair Trading Act 1973 (as amended by the Trading Schemes Act 1996).

BOGUS LOTTERIES AND COMPETITIONS

21.4 Schemes also exist that are similar in appearance to lotteries or prize competitions but are in fact bogus arrangements or have misleading terms and conditions. The Office of Fair Trading (OFT) is responsible for monitoring this type of arrangement in the interests of consumer protection, and runs the 'Scambusters' group (comprised of organisations including the Commission), aimed at targeting scams in the interests of protecting the public from harm.

21.5 If police are contacted by members of the public regarding schemes of this nature, they should in the first instance refer to the trading standards department at the local authority covering the area where the members of the public are based. Trading standards officers and the OFT are responsible for dealing with chain gift schemes, lottery-style scams and similar arrangements.

STREET COLLECTORS SELLING GAMECARDS

21.6 Police may also be aware of street sellers in their areas approaching the public to sell them gamecards, often saying that the cards are being sold to raise money for good causes. If such cards require an element of skill on the part of the player, such as completing a tie- break question, this may be sufficient to distinguish them from a lottery.

21.7 It will be unlikely that the product being sold is a legal lottery. This is because societies running large lotteries are not permitted (by virtue of a condition on their operating licence) to sell lottery tickets in the street, and those running small lotteries are recommended (by virtue of the Commission's *Guidance to Licensing Authorities* document) to have a similar restriction imposed upon them by the local authority that registers them.

21.8 Police with concerns over street sales of products such as gamecards and scratchcards are advised to contact the licensing section and trading standards at the local authority covering the area where sales are being made. They will be able to advise whether what is being sold amounts to a gambling product, and agree on the best course of action.

22 RACE NIGHTS AND CASINO NIGHTS

22.1 Venues such as pubs and restaurants often provide themed evenings such as race nights and casino nights. These are often provided by specialist companies and are held for the enjoyment of customers but also as a fund-raising initiative.

22.2 Part 14 of the Act permits non-commercial gaming of this type, and sets out the conditions under which the gaming must be provided. The gaming has to be part of a non-commercial event (the race night itself, for example) where the fund-raising purpose of the event is communicated to all participants. The proceeds of the event cannot be used for commercial gain, and must go entirely to the fund-raising purpose of the event, although reasonable expenses associated with organising the event can be deducted.

22.3 Police with concerns over any particular aspect of an event held under the provisions in Part 14 of the Act are advised to liaise with the organiser of the event itself or the local licensing authority covering the area where the event is being held.

23 GAMBLING VIA TECHNOLOGY SUCH AS THE INTERNET

23.1 Gambling facilities that can be accessed by communication technology including the internet, television and telephone are collectively known as remote gambling. The Commission issues operating licences to gambling operators that provide gambling via remote means, where their key equipment for providing the remote gambling facilities is located in Great Britain.

23.2 Under the Act, British residents may legally gamble using remote technology, including using gambling websites.

23.3 If police receive complaints relating to gambling using remote methods, in the first instance they are advised to contact the Commission regarding the circumstances of the complaint.

24 GAMBLING AND ADVERTISING

24.1 From 1 September 2007 the Gambling Act 2005 reformed the law on the advertising of gambling. The Commission has included an ordinary code provision within its *Licence Conditions and Codes of Practice* (LCCP June 2007 and October 2008) which requires licensees to comply with the advertising codes of practice which apply to the form and media in which they advertise their gambling facilities and services.

24.2 Permission to advertise in the United Kingdom is restricted to operators licensed by the Commission and operators from European Economic Area jurisdictions including Gibraltar. Operators based in 'white listed' jurisdictions are also permitted to advertise in Great Britain. These jurisdictions are (March 2009) Alderney, the Isle of Man, Tasmania, Antigua and Barbuda (which are a single jurisdiction). The Commission will take enforcement action against those not permitted to advertise if illegal advertising occurs, and may seek to prosecute.

24.3 The Commission has published a short guide summarising the advertising codes that apply to different circumstances.[15]

[15] Guide to gambling advertising codes

25 SUMMARY OF OFFENCES UNDER THE GAMBLING ACT 2005

25.1 This section summarises the key offences under the Act.

GENERAL OFFENCES REGARDING THE PROVISION OF GAMBLING FACILITIES

Providing gambling facilities in Great Britain without a relevant licence, permit, notice, or exemption included under the Act.	**Section 33**
Using premises to provide gambling facilities from, or causing them to be provided, without a relevant licence, permit, notice or exemption under the Act.	**Section 37**

OFFENCE REGARDING CHEATING AT GAMBLING

Cheating, attempting to cheat, or assisting another person to cheat at gambling.	**Section 42**

OFFENCES COMMITTED TOWARDS OR BY UNDER-18S

Inviting, causing or permitting a child (under 16) or young person (16 – 17) to gamble, with the exception of:		**Section 46**
•	private / non-commercial gaming and betting	
•	participating in lotteries	
•	participating in football pools	
•	using a category D gaming machine	

• participating in equal chance gaming at premises subject of a prize gaming permit or an FEC premises licence	
• participating in prize gaming at a fair or an unlicensed FEC.	
This offence includes intentional distribution of advertising to under-18s where the intent is to encourage gambling.	
It is also an offence on the part of a young person to gamble with the exception of situations listed above.	**Section 48**
Inviting or permitting a child or young person to enter:	**Section 47**
• a casino	
• a betting premises (except for betting areas of horse and greyhound tracks on race days)	
• an adult gaming centre	
• areas of a family entertainment centre where category C gaming machines are situated.	
This offence is committed at all times when the premises listed above are being used in reliance on the premises licence.	
It is also an offence on the part of a young person to enter the premises listed above.	**Section 49**
Young person providing facilities for gambling, with the exception of:	**Section 50**
• private / non-commercial gaming and betting	
• a lottery	
• football pools	
• prize gaming at a travelling fair.	
Employing a child or young person to provide gambling facilities, with the exception of providing the following facilities:	**Section 51**
• private / non-commercial gaming and betting	
• prize gaming at a travelling fair.	
Employing a child to provide facilities in connection with:	**Section 52**
• a lottery	
• football pools.	
Employing a child for any purposes when bingo is provided or gambling provided in accordance with a club gaming permit or club machine permit.	**Section 53**
Employing a child or young person to perform any function connected to a gaming machine.	**Section 54**
It is also an offence on the part of a young person if they are employed in such a role.	
Employing a child or young person in a casino, an adult gaming centre, or at a betting premises, unless it is at a time when no activity is being carried on in reliance on the premises licence.	**Section 55**
It is also an offence on the part of a young person if they are employed in such a role.	
Inviting, causing or permitting a child to take part in football pools or a lottery with the exception of:	**Sections 56 and 57**
• an incidental non-commercial lottery	
• a private lottery	

• part of the National Lottery.	
Failure to comply with an operating licence condition to return stake to a child or young person.	**Section 58**

OFFENCES CONNECTED TO OPERATING LICENCES

Failure to comply with an operating licence condition to return stake to a child or young person.	**Section 58**
Failing without reasonable excuse to notify the Commission of change in circumstances.	**Section 101**
Licensee failing without reasonable excuse to produce their operating licence when requested by a police officer or enforcement officer.	**Section 108**
Licensee failing to notify the Commission without reasonable excuse and as soon as reasonably practicable about conviction of an offence.	**Section 109**
Licensee failing to notify the court upon conviction of a relevant offence that they are an operating licence holder.	**Section 109**
Licensee failing without reasonable excuse to produce records for the Commission relating to operating licensed activities or information about licensed activities.	**Section 122**
Operating licence holder fails without reasonable excuse to produce the authorisation they have given to someone to accept bets on their behalf, when asked to do so by a police officer or enforcement officer.	**Section 316**
This offence can also apply to the person that has been authorised to accept bets.	

OFFENCES CONNECTED TO PERSONAL LICENCES

Failure without reasonable excuse to produce a personal licence to a police officer or enforcement officer.	**Section 134**
Licensee failing to notify the Commission as soon as reasonably practicable about a conviction of offence.	**Section 138**
Licensee failing to act within the terms and conditions of their licence.	**Section 139**

GENERAL OFFENCES CONNECTED TO ALL PREMISES LICENCES

Licensee failing without reasonable excuse to keep premises licence on premises and make available for inspection to a police officer, enforcement officer or authorised person.	**Section 185**
Licensee failing to notify without reasonable excuse the licensing authority about change of residential address or other details on the licence.	**Section 186**

OFFENCES CONNECTED TO TEMPORARY USE NOTICES

Failure of premises licence holder to without reasonable excuse prominently display or make available their temporary use notice to a police officer, customs and excise officer, enforcement officer or licensing authority officer.	**Section 229**

OFFENCES CONNECTED TO GAMING MACHINES

Making a gaming machine available for use without a relevant licence or permit, or in contravention of regulations made under section 240 of the Act (SI No 2007/2319).		**Section 242**
Manufacturing, supplying, installing, adapting, maintaining, or repairing a gaming machine without a suitable operating licence, unless:		**Section 243**
•	the gaming machine is scrap with no commercial value	
•	the gaming machine is incidental to the sale/letting of previously-licensed property.	
Supplying, installing, adapting, maintaining or repairing a gaming machine (or part of) without complying with regulations made under section 241 of the Act (SI No 2007/2320), unless:		**Section 243**
•	the gaming machine is scrap with no commercial value	
•	the gaming machine is incidental to the sale/letting of previously-licensed property.	
Supplying, installing or making available for use a gaming machine allowing payment by credit card.		**Section 245**

OFFENCES CONNECTED TO LOTTERIES

25.2 The offences listed here do not apply to lotteries or products forming part of the National Lottery, as the Act does not regulate the National Lottery. Police enquiries regarding offences connected to the National Lottery should be directed to the National Lottery Commission.

Promoting a non-exempt lottery without a suitable operating licence or on behalf of someone with a suitable operating licence.	**Section 258**
Facilitating a non-exempt lottery without holding a suitable operating licence (where facilitating includes functions such as advertising and printing tickets and promotional materials).	**Section 259**
Misusing profits from a lottery, ie using them or causing them to be used for purposes other than the advertised purpose of the lottery.	**Section 260**
Misusing profits from an incidental non-commercial lottery, a private society lottery, or a small society lottery.	**Section 261**
A non-commercial society promoting a lottery without being registered with a local authority, or failing to provide the local authority with returns (or providing false returns) following a small society lottery.	**Section 262**

OFFENCE CONNECTED TO BINGO PLAYED IN CLUBS AND INSTITUTES

Failing without reasonable excuse to inform the Commission of periods of high turnover bingo if the club or institute does not hold an operating licence (high turnover bingo being where the stakes or prizes of all games of bingo played in a seven day period exceed £2,000).	**Section 275**

OFFENCE CONNECTED TO USE OF PROCEEDS FROM GAMING AT NON-COMMERCIAL EVENTS

Using the profits (or permitting them to be used) from non-commercial prize gaming or equal chance gaming for a purpose other than that specified as the fund-raising purpose of the gaming.	**Section 301**

OFFENCE CONNECTED TO CASINO PREMISES LICENCES

Failure on the part of the casino premises licence holder to produce upon demand (by a police officer or enforcement officer) the authorisation they have given to someone to provide bingo or betting facilities at the casino in question. This offence can also be committed by the individual or organisation authorised by the casino premises licence holder if they fail to produce the authorisation.	**Section 316**

OFFENCE OF OBSTRUCTING OR FAILING TO CO-OPERATE DURING AN INSPECTION

Obstructing or failing to cooperate without reasonable excuse with a police officer, enforcement officer or authorised person carrying out inspection activity under Part 15 of the Act.	**Section 326**

OFFENCE OF PROVIDING FALSE OR MISLEADING INFORMATION

Providing false or misleading information to the Commission or a licensing authority regarding any provision of the Act.	**Section 342**

OFFENCES CONNECTED TO ADVERTISING OF GAMBLING FACILITIES

Contravention of any regulations relating to gambling advertising. (nb the Secretary of State for Culture, Media and Sport has chosen not to exercise their reserve powers to make such secondary legislation at this time).	**Section 328**
Knowingly advertising unlawful gambling without reasonable belief otherwise.	**Section 330**
Advertising foreign gambling facilities other than lotteries (in accordance with regulations SI No 2007/2329).	**Section 331**

OFFENCE OF FAILING TO COMPLY WITH A FORFEITURE ORDER

Failure to comply with a court's forfeiture order to surrender named materials to a police officer, or co-operate with steps to comply with the order.	**Section 345**

OFFENCE CONNECTED TO UNLICENSED FAMILY ENTERTAINMENT CENTRES

Occupier of premises failing without reasonable excuse to produce their family entertainment centre gaming machine permit for a police officer, enforcement officer or authorised officer.	**Schedule 10(20)**

OFFENCES CONNECTED TO CLUB GAMING AND CLUB MACHINE PERMITS

Failing without reasonable excuse to produce a club gaming permit or club machine permit for a police officer or enforcement officer.	**Schedule 12(13)**
Failure without reasonable excuse to have club gaming or club machine permits varied by the licensing authority as soon as practicable upon a change of circumstances.	**Schedule 12(15)**

OFFENCE CONNECTED TO ALCOHOL LICENSED PREMISES GAMING MACHINE PERMITS

Failure without reasonable excuse to produce a licensed premises gaming machine permit upon the request of a police officer, enforcement officer or authorised person.	**Schedule 13(10)**

OFFENCE CONNECTED TO PRIZE GAMING PERMITS

Failure without reasonable excuse to produce a prize gaming permit upon the request of a police officer, enforcement officer or authorised person.	**Schedule 14(20)**

OFFENCE CONNECTED TO GAMBLING SOFTWARE

Manufacturing, supplying, installing or adapting gambling software without holding a relevant operating licence.	**Section 41**

OFFENCE CONNECTED TO CHAIN-GIFT SCHEMES

Inviting another person to join chain-gift schemes or participating in the promotion of chain-gift schemes.	**Section 43**

26 CONTACT DETAILS

26.1 General enquiries to the Commission should be sent to:

Gambling Commission
Victoria Square House
Victoria Square
Birmingham B2 4BP
Tel: 0121 230 6666
Fax: 0121 230 6720
Email: info@gamblingcommission.gov.uk
Intelligence can be contacted via the number above or by emailing mailto://intelligence@gamblingcommission.gov.uk.

ANNEX A

SUMMARY OF RESPONSES TO THE CONSULTATION

1 Four responses were received to the consultation document. Both the British Casino Association and the Advertising Standards Association suggested minor clarifications and corrections which are now included in the current version of our *Advice for British police services* (Advice).

2 ACPOS offered various clarifications and elaborations, some of which were specific to the law as it applies in Scotland. All of these are included in the current document.

3 ACPO also suggested a number of additions to the Advice in order to clarify specific issues and ensure the document is as comprehensive as possible. Examples include a reference to the purpose of information sharing (paragraph 4.2 of this document) as cited in the Act; a list of the information required in a licence, a register and conditions for door supervision (paragraphs 8.5 – 8.6, 9.5 – 9.7, 11.7 – 11.9 of this document) and a list of persons who may reasonably be expected to accompany an officer when entering a premises (paragraph 3.26 of this document). These and the majority of others have been included in the current document.

4 ACPO noted the difficulties for licensing authorities regarding multiple Adult Gaming Centres (AGCs) and Family Entertainment Centres (FECs) operating in one building and suggested we reference current guidance from the Local Authorities Coordinators of Regulatory Services (LACoRS). The Commission has recently published a revised version of our *Guidance to Licensing Authorities* on this subject and we consider this addresses the concern.[16]

5 ACPO made two further specific suggestions which are included in the Advice as appendices: a glossary of terms and a copy of the 'request for/disclosure of intelligence form' drawn from the MoU (see above). The latter only applies to ACPO forces; it is anticipated that a similar form will be adopted by the Commission and ACPOS in due course.

6 ACPO suggested a confidential monthly 'Gambling Intelligence' bulletin for police only. The purpose of this would be to highlight criminal activity, networks, as well as enforcement actions and activity. They propose that the ACPO Regional Gambling Standard Working Group details could also be integrated within this bulletin in order to propagate intelligence networking and interagency operations.

7 The Commission supports this proposal and will work with ACPO and ACPOS to develop an appropriate vehicle for this to happen.

8 Another suggestion from ACPO was an electronic copy of the personal/operator licence application form, which provided details of the applicant's business or personal residence in any given Constabulary area. ACPO considers that this would allow for a more comprehensive awareness of the volume and location of licence holders (for strategic and tactical benefit), but also allow for the police to easily refer to

personal/operator licence details where the police consider it necessary to object to inappropriate premises licence and Temporary Use Notice applications.

9 The Commission does not consider it appropriate to supply an electronic version of individual applications. The reason being that a great deal of this information is commercially sensitive. We publish details of applicants on the public register which is available to any police force via the website. However, it is sometimes incomplete, as operators can request exclusion, but we are willing to explore the option of providing an unedited version similar to that supplied to Local Authorities via the Local Authorities Coordinators of Regulatory Services (LACoRS). If the police have any particular concerns about individuals identified from the register they could then seek further information from us. We prefer a 'single point of contact' (SPOC) system to process this information within police forces.

10 ACPO indicated that intelligence sharing between the Commission and the police may benefit from the use of a standard format premises and operator inspection form. Such a form would not only detail police powers under section 317 of the Act but also act as a useful aide memoire for police officers and become a 'notice of inspection' for licence holders.

11 The Commission, whilst fully supporting the importance of intelligence sharing, does not consider that this proposal would be beneficial. The primary reason being that the role of the Commission as a regulator requires a much more detailed system of inspection than that undertaken by police services. We regard the National Intelligence Report (NIR/5x5x5) (paragraph 4.7 of this document) as being the default system for the exchange of information.

12 The final proposal from ACPO is that the Commission assists in the development of a training package and operational manual for front line police officers to ensure that they are familiar with the Act and their powers under it. The development of the package is in its early stages. We aim to launch the programme in Spring 2009. We expect to develop a similar scheme for Scottish forces.

13 The Commission is grateful to all those who responded to the consultation. Updated versions of this Advice document will be issued as need arises.

16 Guidance to Licensing Authorities

ANNEX B

GAMING MACHINE CATEGORIES

Gaming Machine category	Maximum stake	Maximum prize
A	Unlimited	Unlimited
B1	£2	£4,000
B2	£100 (in multiples of £10)	£500
B3	£1	£500
B3A *	£1	£500
B4	£1	£250
C	50p	£35
D **	10p/30p	£5/£8

* Category B3A machines can only be situated in members clubs and some institutes with a suitable permit.

** Category D machines with a 10p stake are entitled to offer prizes of up to £5 in cash, or up to £5 in cash and £3 in non-monetary prizes. Category D machines with a 30p stake can offer

£8 in non-monetary prizes only.

GAMING MACHINE ENTITLEMENTS FOR GAMBLING PREMISES

Premises type	Machine entitlement
Regional casino	Maximum of 1,250 machines in categories A-D except for B3A machines
Large casino	Maximum of 150 machines in categories B-D except B3A machines
Small casino	Maximum of 80 machines in categories B-D except B3A machines
Pre-2005 Act casino	Maximum of 20 machines in categories B-D except B3A machines, or C and D machines instead
Betting premises and tracks with pool betting	Maximum of 4 machines in categories B2-D
Bingo premises	Maximum of 8 machines in categories B3-B4 except B3A machines, and unlimited number of C and D machines
Adult gaming centre	Maximum of 4 machines in categories B3-B4 except B3A machines, and unlimited number of C and D machines
Family entertainment centre (with premises licence)	No limit on category C and D machines
Family entertainment centre (with permit)	No limit on category D machines
Members clubs and miners welfare institutes (with permit)	Maximum of 3 machines in categories B3A-D
Commercial clubs (with permit)	Maximum of 3 machines in categories B4-D
Alcohol licensed premises (automatic entitlement)	Maximum of 2 machines in categories C-D
Alcohol licensed premises with machine permit	Number of category C-D machines is stated on permit
Travelling fair	No limit on category D machines

ANNEX C

SUMMARY OF WEBSITE LINKS FOR COMMISSION DOCUMENTS REFERRED TO

Guidance to Licensing Authorities
www.gamblingcommission.gov.uk/Client/mediadetail.asp?mediaid=138
Licence Conditions and Codes of Practice
www.gamblingcommission.gov.uk/UploadDocs/publications/Document/LCCP08%20final%20pdf.pdf
The prevention of money laundering and combating the financing of terrorism
http://www.gamblingcommission.gov.uk/Client/mediadetail.asp?mediaid=326&id=10
Joint compliance and enforcement statement between the Commission, LACORS and ACPO http://www.gamblingcommission.gov.uk/Client/mediadetail.asp?mediaid=221&id=5
Compliance and enforcement policy statement
http://www.gamblingcommission.gov.uk/Client/mediadetail.asp?mediaid=127
Gaming machine permits code of practice

http://www.gamblingcommission.gov.uk/Client/mediadetail.asp?mediaid=124
Technical standards for gaming machines
http://www.gamblingcommission.gov.uk/Client/mediadetail.asp?mediaid=131
Code of practice for equal chance gaming in clubs and premises with an alcohol licence
http://www.gamblingcommission.gov.uk/client/mediadetail.asp?mediaid=184
Advice on gaming in clubs and alcohol licensed premises: Gambling Act 2005
http://www.gamblingcommission.gov.uk/Client/mediadetail.asp?mediaid=319&id=9
Lotteries and the Law
http://www.gamblingcommission.gov.uk/Client/mediadetail.asp?mediaid=62&id=10
Gambling and advertising
http://www.gamblingcommission.gov.uk/Client/mediadetail.asp?mediaid=264

ANNEX D

VESSELS AND VEHICLES (CONTINUED FROM PARAGRAPH 6.9 OF THIS DOCUMENT)

Structures which are an extension of the land are not vessels, even if they arch over water. Thus, neither a pier nor a bridge are to be considered a vessel. Instead, they remain premises under the Act. This is important because not all forms of permit are available to vessels.
The Act will, for example, allow pleasure boats to apply for a premises licence. As with multi-purpose buildings, the part of the vessel where gambling takes place will be licensed and the usual restrictions on access for children will apply. The Act applies in relation to a vessel that is not permanently moored or berthed as if it were premises situated in a place where it is usually moored or berthed. The relevant licensing authority for considering an application for a premises licence in respect of a vessel is therefore the licensing authority for the area in which it is usually moored or berthed.
Vehicles (trains, road vehicles, aircraft, sea planes and amphibious vehicles other than a hovercraft) may not be the subject of a premises licence and therefore all forms of commercial betting and gaming will be unlawful in a vehicle in Great Britain. Certain allowances are made for private and non-commercial gaming or betting to take place in a vehicle, but these are subject to a number of stringent requirements. These ensure that at no point can the gambling become a commercial activity.
Where a premises licence is sought in connection with a vessel which will be navigated whilst licensable activities takes place, the licensing authority should be concerned with the promotion of the licensing objectives on board the vessel.
It should not focus on matters relating to safe navigation or operation of the vessel, the general safety of passengers or emergency provision, all of which are subject to regulations which must be met before the vessel is issued with its Passenger Certificate and Safety Management Certificate.
Gambling is not a licensable activity if it takes place aboard a vessel engaged on an international journey. Such gambling is exempted from the offences under the Act if the vessel is on a journey which has taken it, or is intended to take it, into international waters (ie beyond the 12 mile territorial limit, so this includes cross-channel ferries). In the case of aircraft, no offence takes place if the gambling takes place in international airspace.
Licensing authorities have jurisdiction over gambling conducted on vessels on all inland waterways, at permanent moorings, and on all aircraft on the ground or in domestic airspace. If an ocean-going vessel is involved, authorities will need to establish where the vessel has been, or is intending to go.

ANNEX E

SPORT GOVERNING BODIES

- The England and Wales Cricket Board Limited
- The Football Association Limited

- The Football Association of Wales Limited
- The Horseracing Regulatory Authority
- The Lawn Tennis Association
- The Irish Football Association Limited
- The Jockey Club
- The National Greyhound Racing Club Limited
- The Professional Golfers' Association Limited
- The Rugby Football League
- The Rugby Football Union
- The Scottish Rugby Union
- The Scottish Football Association Limited
- UK Athletics Limited
- The Welsh Rugby Union Limited

ANNEX F

GLOSSARY OF TERMS RELATED TO GAMBLING

ABB	Association of British Bookmakers
Adult gaming centre (AGC)	Arcades offering gaming machines. Entry is prohibited to anyone under the age of 18
AMLD	Amusement machine licence duty
AR	American roulette
ARA	Asset recovery agency
ARB	Association of Racecourse Bookmakers
ASA	Advertising Standards Authority
AWP	Amusement with prizes (machine)
BACTA	British Amusement catering Trades Association (gaming machine manufacturers, suppliers and users)
BALPPA	The British Association of Leisure Parks, Piers and Attractions Ltd
BA	Bingo Association
BBPA	British Beer and Pub Association
BCA	British Casino Association
BETA	Betting Exchange Trade Association
Betting	Betting means making or accepting a bet on: • the outcome of a race, competition or other event or process • the likelihood of anything occurring or not occurring • whether anything is or is not true
BGRB	British Greyhound Racing Board
BHA	British Horseracing Authority
BII	British Institute of Innkeepers
BHHPA	British Holiday and Home Parks Association
Bingo	**All winners:** games played weekly/daily with the winners going on to a grand final **Link game:** game that is played live and simultaneously between two or more bingo clubs for the same prize

	National game: a game of multiple bingo operated by the national Bingo Game Association where all licensed bingo clubs are permitted to play
BISL	Business in Sport and Leisure
BJ	Blackjack
Casino	A casino is defined as an arrangement whereby people are given the chance to participate in casino games (games of chance which are not equal chance gaming). It is immaterial whether the gaming takes place on one set of premises or is provided wholly or partly by means of remote communication. Equipment includes roulette wheels, card shufflers, automated terminals and touch bet machines.
Child	An individual who is less than 16 years old
CHIS	Covert human intelligence source
CLG	Community liaison group
COA	Casino Operators Association
CoC	Certificate of Consent
CMMG	Casino Machine Manufacturers Group
Competition	A game of skill that cannot be based on the outcome of a future event. There is no legal definition of skill. Legal advice is required.
COPFS	Crown Office and Procurator Fiscal Service
COSLA	Convention of Scottish Local Authorities
CCJ and in Scotland a Decree	Incurred when a County Court rules against an individual for defaulting on a debt, it will make an order that they must repay a creditor the debt
CSP	Casino stud poker
CTPN	Charges to play notice
Data Protection Act 1998 (DPA)	The law which applies to the gathering, storage and use of personal data, and which is overseen by the independent Information Commissioner
DCMS	Department for Culture, Media and Sport
Decree (in Scotland)	See CCJ
Director	Has the meaning given by Section 741 of the Companies Act 1985
EBT	Electronic bingo terminal
EDRM	Electronic Document Record Management
ELM	External Lottery Manager
Fair and open	Where the customer is given full information about the way in which the game is played (ie the rules of the game) or bet taken; about the odds of winning or losing in different scenarios; that any changes to the rules or odds are fully flagged up so that gamblers are not caught out.
Family entertainment centres (FECs)	Often known as amusement arcades offer machines for playing by children (Category D) and in some cases machines (category C) and prize bingo for over 18s
FIN-NET	Financial Crime Information Network

Fixed Odds Betting Terminal (FOBTs)	Software-driven terminals, about same size and shape as a floor-standing cash dispenser. They are used to bet on a variety of 'virtual' events whose outcome is driven by a random number generator operated by an independent third party and located remotely. The types of events on which users can bet includes horseracing, greyhound racing, football, penalty shootouts, numbers games and roulette.
FRB	Federation of Racecourse Bookmakers
FSA	Financial Services Authority
GA	Gamblers Anonymous
Gambling	In the Gambling Act this means gaming, betting or participating in a lottery
GAT	Gambling Appeals Tribunal – an independent body set up by the Department for Constitutional Affairs, dealing solely with gambling matters with the power to review decisions taken by the Gambling Commission relating to: • Operating licences • Personal licences • Decisions taken by the Commission to void bets
Gaming	Playing a game of chance for a prize
Gaming machines	The term covers all machines on which people can gamble. Exemptions to this include a home PC. See Section 235 of the Act for a full list
GC	Gambling Commission
GRA	Greyhound Racing Association
GREF	Gaming Regulators European Forum
GSG	Gaming Stakeholder Group
HBLB	Horserace Betting Levy Board
HRA	Horseracing Regulatory Authority (now BHA)
IBAS	Independent Betting Arbitration Service
ILG	Industry Liaison Group
IoL	Institute of Licensing
JMLSG	Joint Money Laundering Steering Group
Judgement	An official court order deciding the rights or claims of the parties in a legal proceeding
Keno	A game similar to Lotto in which numbered balls are drawn at random and players cover the corresponding numbers on their cards
LACoRS	Local Authorities Coordinators of Regulatory Services
LALG	Local Authorities Liaison Group
LBO	Licensed betting office
LC	Lotteries Council
LCE	Licensing, compliance and enforcement
Licence Conditions and Codes of Practice (LCCP)	The rules which operators must observe to meet the Commission's three licensing objectives: • Keeping crime out of gambling • Ensuring that gambling is fair and open • Protecting children and other vulnerable people from being harmed or exploited by gambling

6: Gambling Act 2005: Additional Material

LGA	Local Government Association
Licensing Authorities	**In England** • District Councils (including Metropolitan Councils) • County Councils (including Unitary Councils) or counties in which there are no District Councils • London Borough Councils • The Common Council of the City of London • The Council of the Isles of Scilly **In Wales** • County Councils or County Borough Councils **In Scotland** • Licensing Boards (the same bodies that currently grant casino and bingo licences in Scotland)
Licensing Justices	Magistrates who are specifically designated to issue licences
Licensing objectives	See LCCP above
Lotteries and Amusements Act 1976	Repealed by the Gambling Act 2005
Lotteries Act 1963	Repealed by the Gambling Act 2005
Lotteries	A lottery is a certain type of 'arrangement' that may be either 'simple' or 'complex' **Simple lottery** • Persons are required to pay to enter into the arrangement • In the course of the arrangement one or more prizes are allocated to one or more participants in the lottery • The prizes are allocated by a process that relies wholly on chance **Complex lottery** • Persons are required to pay to enter into the arrangement • In the course of the arrangement one or more prizes are allocated to one or more participants in the lottery • The prizes are allocated by a series of processes • The first process relies wholly on chance **Chance:** a process which requires persons to exercise skill or judgement or display knowledge is nevertheless to be treated as relying wholly on chance if: • The requirement cannot reasonably be expected to prevent a significant proportion of participants from receiving a prize • The requirement cannot reasonably be expected to prevent a significant proportion of those who wish to participate from doing so. An arrangement is not a lottery if there is a free entry route

	Skill: a merely 'cosmetic' skill element will not prevent an arrangement from being a lottery. Within the target audience, only a level of skill or knowledge which would weed out or deter a significant proportion of that target audience will prevent a scheme from being a lottery
MCB	Mechanised cash bingo
MLAC	Money Laundering Advisory Committee
MLR	Money Laundering Regulations
MLRO	Money Laundering Reporting Officer
MTR	Minded to revoke
NAB	National Association of Bookmakers
NAO	National Audit Office
NBGA	National Bingo Game Association
NLC	National Lottery Commission
OFCOM	Office of Communications
Off-course	The place where the bet is lodged if it is not physically made at the event
OFT	Office of Fair Trading
On-course	The place where the event takes place. Betting commonly takes place at horse and dog racecourses, as well as football, cricket and other sporting events
PASS	Proof of age standards scheme
PB	Punto Banco (also known as North American Baccarat)
Personal Licences	There are two categories of personal licence:
	Personal management licence (PML)
	This licence authorises an individual to perform the functions of a specified management office. The operator must ensure that for at least one of the following management officers holds a PML authorising the performance of the functions of that office: managing director/chief executive, finance director/head of finance, compliance director/head of compliance, marketing director/head of marketing
	Personal functional licence (PFL)
	PFLs are required by casino gaming staff below manager level eg dealers, cashiers, inspectors, security staff employed to watch gaming, supervisors of gaming activity.
PET	Personal electronic terminals
POCA	Proceeds of Crime Act
Private and non-commercial gaming	Certain types of gaming can be provided at non-commercial events, eg where the money and profits are used for charitable or other generally beneficial purposes rather than providing benefit to individuals
Problem gambling	Any gambling that goes beyond 'normal' bounds of gambling for fun, recreation or entertainment. The inability, over an extended period of time, to resist impulses to gamble. Often demonstrated by serious negative consequences for the individual.

Provides facilities for gambling	A person provides facilities for gambling if he/she: • invites others to gamble in accordance with arrangements made by him • provides operates or administers arrangements for gambling by others • participates in the operation or administration of gambling by others.
PSP	Progressive stud poker
Random Number Generator (RNG)	A computational or physical device designed to generate a sequence of numbers that does not have any easily discernable pattern and is used for, example, in gaming machines or to pick numbers for a game of bingo
RBA	Rails Bookmakers association
RCA	Racecourse Association
RCPA	Racecourse Promoters Association
Remote gambling	Facilities for gambling using a form of remote communications medium such as the internet, a mobile phone or interactive TV • Location of remote gambling equipment; equipment includes a computer database or server and it must be located within Great Britain • A remote operating licence is required for any form of remote gambling.
Revoke	To cancel or annul, for example, a licence
RIPA	Regulation of Investigatory Powers Act
RGA	Remote Gambling Association
S19	Section 19 certificate issued under the Gaming Act 1968 for gaming staff
S27	Section 27 certificate issued under the Gaming Act 1968 for gaming machine suppliers
SAR	Suspicious activities report
SB	Sic Bo (gambling game of Chinese origin also known as Tai Sai or Dai Siu meaning Big Small)
Self exclusion	A procedure which enables individuals to bar themselves voluntarily from gambling at particular venues or websites
SIA	Security Industry Association
Single machine Permit	A permit issued by the Commission for individuals who are not normally in the trade but who wish to make a one off sale or supply transaction, or to install, maintain or repair a gaming machine
SIBA	Scottish Independent Bookmakers Association
SIS	Satellite Information Services
Small scale operator	An operator is small scale if there are no more than 3 qualifying positions in the commercial gambling business which in each case are occupied by a qualified person

Social responsibility	Gambling operators must act with concern and sensitivity, and be aware of the impact of their actions on others, particularly the vulnerable. All holders of operating licences are required to comply with any relevant social responsibility provision of a code of practice issued by the Commission
SP	Starting price
SPRC	Starting Price Regulatory Commission
SRA	Solicitors Regulation Authority
SRF	Social Responsibility Forum
Technical standards	Established by the Commission in respect of remote gambling systems, gambling software and gaming machines to provide for a testing regime and their enforcement
TCP	Three card poker
TED	The electronic dauber (electronic hand held bingo machine)
UAT	User acceptance testing
Unfair Contract Terms	The law which relates to contracts. Under the Gambling
Act 1977	Act, gambling contracts are capable of being enforced but may be void on the same basis as any other contract eg on the basis of lack of intention, mistake or illegality
Vulnerable people	Assumed to include the following: • people who gamble more than they want to • people who gamble beyond their means • people who may not be able to make informed or balanced decisions about gambling due to a mental impairment, alcohol or drugs.
Young person	An individual who is not a child but who is less than 18 years old

ANNEX G

Gambling Commission / Police Information Request

The organisation requesting information should complete sections A, B & C. The receiving organisation should complete section D. All fields marked* should be completed.

This form should be transmitted via a method agreed between the Gambling Commission and Police Force

If you need any help completing this form, please contact the Commission Intelligence Team on 0121 230 6705

Section A – Request Details

A1 Request To:

Name*

Organisation*

A2 Request From:

Name*

Organisation*

Tel.* Fax.

Email

Section B – Enquiry Details

B1 Enquiry Date* Date Required*

B2 Individual / Organisation about whom information is sought:

Name

Address

Date of Birth

Other Relevant Information
(e.g. Description, Reference Numbers)

B3 Nature of Enquiry (Details of Investigation/Proceedings and purpose of enquiry)*:

B4 Information Sought*:

RESTRICTED when complete

Gambling Commission / Police Information Request

The organisation requesting information should complete sections A, B & C. The receiving organisation should complete section D. All fields marked* should be completed.

This form should be transmitted via a method agreed between the Gambling Commission and Police Force

If you need any help completing this form, please contact the Commission Intelligence Team on 0121 230 6705

Section A – Request Details

A1 Request To:

Name*

Organisation*

A2 Request From:

Name*

Organisation*

Tel.* Fax.

Email

Section B – Enquiry Details

B1 Enquiry Date* Date Required*

B2 Individual / Organisation about whom information is sought:

Name

Address

Date of Birth

Other Relevant Information
(e.g. Description, Reference Numbers)

B3 Nature of Enquiry (Details of Investigation/Proceedings and purpose of enquiry)*:

B4 Information Sought*:

RESTRICTED when complete

Gambling Commission March 2009

DUTIES AND RESPONSIBILITIES UNDER THE PROCEEDS OF CRIME ACT 2002
ADVICE TO OPERATORS (EXCLUDING CASINO OPERATORS)

September 2009

OVERVIEW

6.2092
(i) All gambling operators have a legal obligation to be alert to attempts by customers to gamble money acquired unlawfully, either to obtain 'clean' money in return or simply as a leisure activity. They must report any suspicion or knowledge they or their employees have of such attempts to the Serious Organised Crime Agency (SOCA) and, if circumstances permit, wait for clearance to deal with the customer or until a set period has elapsed.
(ii) This advice explains how operators can make sure they and their employees comply with their legal obligations under the Proceeds of Crime Act 2002 (POCA). The advice is inevitably detailed and aimed primarily at operators with a number of employees. Operators with few or no employees may find the quick guide published separately on the Commission's website helpful although it remains the operator's responsibility to understand and comply with the requirements of POCA.

PART 1: INTRODUCTION

WHO IS THIS INTENDED FOR?
(iii) This advice is directed at all gambling operating licence holders (see Annex A for a complete list), excluding holders of casino licences, who can find guidance on our website.

THE PURPOSE OF THIS ADVICE
(iv) This advice document sets out duties and obligations under POCA.
(v) The document covers a number of topics operators need to be aware of. It should help operators to comply with their responsibilities under POCA.
(vi) Operators should devise their own policies and procedures in order to meet their duties and responsibilities under POCA.

THE ROLE OF THE COMMISSION
(vii) The Gambling Commission (the Commission) licenses operators and one of the Commission's licensing objectives is to keep crime out of gambling. This advice document is an important tool in meeting that objective. Whilst potential breaches of POCA will normally be reported to SOCA and fall to the Police to investigate, the Commission has a duty to help operators meet their duties and responsibilities under POCA.
(viii) Should operators regularly and consistently ignore their duties and responsibilities under POCA, the Commission will consider reviewing the suitability of the operator to carry on the licensed activities. This could result in the suspension or revocation of the operator's licence under sections 118 and 119 of the Gambling Act 2005.
(ix) The Commission has the powers of accredited financial investigators under POCA in England and Wales.[1] This means, amongst other things, that the Commission can apply for orders and warrants in relation to money laundering, for the purpose of:
- requiring a specified person to produce certain material
- permitting the search of and seizure of material from specified premises
- requiring a financial institution to provide customer information relating to a specified person.

1 See Statutory Instrument No. 2009/975.

PART 2: THE ADVICE

1 WHAT IS MEANT BY THE PROCEEDS OF CRIME?

1.1 Broadly, the term 'proceeds of crime' refers to property from which a person benefits directly or indirectly, by being party to criminal activity, for example stolen money, money from drug dealing or property stolen in a burglary or robbery (this is commonly referred to as criminal property). It also includes property that a person gains by spending the proceeds of criminal activity, for example, if a person uses money earned from drug dealing to buy a car or a house, or spends money gained in a bank robbery to gamble.

2 THE PROCEEDS OF CRIME ACT 2002

2.1 In section 340 of POCA, criminal property is defined as property which:

- constitutes a person's benefit from criminal conduct or represents such a benefit, in whole or in part, and whether directly or indirectly
- and the alleged offender knows or suspects constitutes or represents such a benefit.

It is immaterial who carried out the criminal conduct, who benefited from it and whether the conduct occurred before or after the passing of POCA.[2]

2.2 Criminal conduct, in turn, is defined as conduct which:

- constitutes an offence in any part of the United Kingdom
- or would constitute an offence in any part of the United Kingdom if it occurred there.[3]

This means that offences from which the proceeds of crime are generated are relevant for these purposes even if the principal offence was committed abroad, so long as the principal offence would also be a crime if it was committed in the United Kingdom.

2.3 A person benefits from criminal conduct if he or she obtains property as a result of or in connection with the conduct. If a person benefits from criminal conduct, his or her benefit is the property obtained as a result of, or in connection with, the conduct. Property includes money, all forms of property, real (for example, land and buildings) or personal (for example, cars, furniture and clothing), inherited or moveable (for example, machinery and livestock), and intangible property (for example, trademarks, copyrights and patents). Property is gained by a person if he or she obtains an interest in it. This would mean that he or she has obtained benefit from the property.[4] Property is 'criminal property' if it is a benefit from criminal conduct, either directly or indirectly, as long as the alleged offender knows or suspects that it is such.

2.4 If a person gains a pecuniary advantage as a result of, or in connection, with criminal conduct, he or she is to be taken to have obtained a sum of money equal to the value of the pecuniary advantage.[5]

2.5 The three principal money laundering offences specified within POCA criminalise a person's dealings with criminal property, subject to certain exceptions. The principal offences and the exceptions are discussed next.

2 Section 340(3) and (4) of the Proceeds of Crime Act 2002.

3 Section 340(2) of the Proceeds of Crime Act 2002.

4 Section 340(5) to (9) of the Proceeds of Crime Act 2002.

5 Section 340(6) of the Proceeds of Crime Act 2002.

3 OFFENCES UNDER THE PROCEEDS OF CRIME ACT 2002

3.1 Criminal offences of money laundering were first introduced in the United Kingdom in the Criminal Justice Act 1988 and the Drug Trafficking Offences Act 1986. POCA consolidated, updated and reformed the criminal law relating to money laundering to cover all criminal offences including any dealing in criminal property.

3.2 POCA applies to everyone, although certain offences relating to the failure to report (except in relation to a nominated officer) and 'tipping off' only apply to those operating in the regulated sector. The businesses that fall within the regulated sector are specified in Schedule 9 to POCA, and include credit institutions, financial institutions, auditors, insolvency practitioners, external accountants, tax advisers, independent legal professionals, trust or company service providers, estate agents, high value dealers and casino operators.

3.3 POCA creates three principal offences that apply to everyone and criminalise any involvement in the proceeds of any crime if the person knows or suspects that the property is the proceeds of crime.[6] These offences relate to the concealing, arrangement and acquisition of criminal property. In respect of the gambling industry, this generally could involve the taking of cash, cheque, debit or credit card payments from persons in the form of a bet or wager, or holding money on account for a customer for the purposes of gambling.

3.4 Section 327 of POCA provides that a person commits an offence if he or she:

- conceals criminal property (for example, by depositing funds obtained through criminal activity in a gambling account)
- disguises criminal property (for example, by placing funds obtained through criminal activity in a gambling account and then withdrawing them at a later date)
- converts criminal property (for example, by placing bets in a gambling establishment and then cashing in the winnings)
- transfers criminal property (for example, by transferring property to another person or company)
- removes criminal property from the United Kingdom (for example, by taking his or her winnings overseas).

Concealing or disguising property includes concealing or disguising its nature, source, location, disposition, movement or ownership, or any rights with respect to it. Whilst 'converting' criminal property is not defined in POCA, it is suggested that this be given its conventional legal meaning, that is that the 'converter' has dealt with the property in a manner inconsistent with the rights of the true owner of the property. For example, a criminal steals cash in a bank robbery and then uses that cash to open a gambling account and place bets.

3.5 Section 328 of POCA provides that a person commits an offence if he or she enters into or becomes concerned in an arrangement which he or she knows or suspects facilitates, by whatever means, the acquisition, retention, use or control of criminal property by or on behalf of another person. An example of this in the gambling industry would be for an operator knowingly to accept stakes that are the proceeds of criminal activity.

3.6 Section 329 of POCA provides that a person commits an offence if he or she:

- acquires criminal property
- or uses criminal property
- or has possession of criminal property (for example, via stakes).

However, a person does not commit an offence if he or she acquired or used or had possession of the property for adequate consideration. What this means is that, if a person buys or exchanges something which is clearly below market value (inadequate consideration), then they will be committing an offence if the money or property is criminal property. If the person buys or exchanges something at its current market value (adequate consideration), then they will not be committing an offence if the money or property is criminal property. This defence protects operators who may be paid for a bet in the normal way with funds that appear to be suspicious, provided they report this suspicion (explained in paragraphs 5.17 to 5.20 below).

3.7 These are wide offences that can be committed by anyone, including employees of an operator, who have actual knowledge or suspicion that a customer is using the proceeds of crime. This means that the person must know or suspect that the property is the proceeds of crime in order to have committed the offence in section 329 of POCA.

3.8 The offence of money laundering, and the duty to report under POCA, apply in relation to the proceeds of any criminal activity, wherever conducted, including abroad, that would constitute an offence if it took place in the United Kingdom. However, a person does not commit an offence where it is known or believed, on reasonable grounds, that the conduct occurred outside the United Kingdom and the conduct was not criminal in the country where it took place.

3.9 While POCA places responsibilities on operators, the legislation also gives them protection if they report suspicious activity. It is a defence to the offences listed above for a person to show that he or she made an authorised disclosure under section 338 of POCA. Disclosure of suspicious activity will be discussed later in this document.

3.10 The penalty for conviction of an offence under sections 327, 328 or 329 of POCA is imprisonment for a term of a maximum of 14 years, a fine not exceeding the statutory maximum, or both. In addition, POCA contains provisions for the recovery of the proceeds of crime, regardless of whether a conviction for any offence has been obtained or is intended to be obtained. Criminal property can be recoverable even if it is disposed of to another person.

---

[6] Sections 327, 328 and 329 of the Proceeds of Crime Act 2002.

4 RISK-BASED APPROACH

Introduction

4.1 A risk-based approach involves a number of discrete steps to assess the most proportionate way to manage and mitigate the risks faced by the operator. These steps should include:

- identifying the money laundering risks that are relevant to the operator
- designing and implementing policies and procedures to manage and mitigate the assessed risks
- monitoring and improving the effective operation of these controls
- recording what has been done, and why.

4.2 The possibility of gambling being used by criminals to assist in spending the proceeds of their criminal activity poses many risks for operators. These include criminal and regulatory sanctions for operators, civil action against the operator and damage to the reputation of the operator, leading to a loss of business.

4.3 Operators need to identify, assess and prevent these risks, just like any other business risk. Operators should assess the level of money laundering risk applicable to their business and implement reasonable and considered controls to minimise the risks posed to their business by money launderers. This risk-based approach means that operators focus their resources on the areas which represent the greatest risk. The benefits of this approach include a more efficient and effective use of resources, minimising compliance costs and the flexibility to respond to new risks as money laundering methods change.

4.4 Most operators already manage their affairs with regard to the risks inherent in their business, and measure the effectiveness of the policies and procedures they have put in place to manage these risks. A similar approach is appropriate to manage the risks of the operator's business being used for money laundering purposes, including the spending of the proceeds of crime by customers. Existing risk management systems should address money laundering risks. The detail and complexity of these systems will depend on the operator's size and the complexity of their business.

4.5 Even though operators outside the regulated sector (clarified in paragraph 3.2 above) are not obliged to have systems and procedures in place, POCA, nonetheless, imposes requirements on all operators that must be satisfied, as a breach can constitute a criminal offence[7]. Systems and procedures can assist operators in complying with their obligations, particularly in relation to reporting suspicious transactions.

4.6 In order to detect customer activity that may be suspicious, it is necessary to monitor transactions or activity. The monitoring of customer activity should be carried out using a risk-based approach. Higher risk customers should be subjected to a frequency and depth of scrutiny greater than may be appropriate for lower risk customers.

4.7 Where a customer is assessed as presenting a higher risk it would be advisable to seek additional information in respect of that customer. This will help the operator to judge whether the higher risk that the customer is perceived to present is likely to materialise. Such additional information may include an understanding of where the customer's funds and wealth have come from. The need to 'know your customer' is particularly relevant here. While the Commission recognises that some relationships with customers will be transient or temporary in nature, operators still need to give consideration to this issue.

4.8 Deciding that a customer presents a higher risk of money laundering does not automatically mean that he or she is a criminal or is laundering money. Similarly, identifying a customer as having a low risk of money laundering does not mean that the customer is definitely not laundering money or spending the proceeds of crime. Operators, therefore, need to remain vigilant and use their experience and common sense in applying their risk-based criteria and rules.

4.9 No system of checks will detect and prevent all money laundering activity. A risk-based approach will, however, serve to balance the burden placed on operators and their customers with a realistic assessment of the threat of the operator being involved, albeit unintentionally, in money laundering. It focuses the effort where it is most needed and will have the most impact. It is not a blanket, one size fits all approach, and therefore operators have a degree of flexibility in their methods of compliance.

4.10 A risk-based approach requires the full commitment and support of senior management, and the active co-operation of all employees. The risk-based approach should be reflected in an operator's policies and procedures. There needs to be clear communication of the policies and procedures to all employees, along with robust mechanisms to ensure that they are carried out effectively, weaknesses are identified and improvements are made, wherever necessary.

---

[7] Sections 327 to 332 of the Proceeds of Crime Act 2002.

Identifying and assessing the risks faced by the operator

4.11 The operator should assess its risks in the context of how it is most likely to be involved in money laundering and the spending of the proceeds of crime. Assessment of risk is based on a number of questions, including:

- What risk is posed by the business profile and the profile of customers using the gambling facilities?
- Is the business high volume, consisting of many low spending customers?
- Is the business low volume, with high spending customers?
- Is the business a mixed portfolio, that is, customers are a mix of high spenders and lower spenders and/or a mix of regular and occasional customers?
- Are procedures in place to monitor customer transactions and mitigate any money laundering potential?
- Is the business local with regular and generally well known customers?

- Are there a large proportion of overseas customers using foreign currency or overseas based bank cheques or debit cards?
- Are customers likely to be engaged in a business which involves significant amounts of cash?
- Are there likely to be situations where the source of funds cannot be easily established or explained by the customer?
- Is the majority of business conducted through customer accounts or some other contractual arrangement?

4.12 An example of the risk to operators from exposure to criminal spend is a case where a known criminal, with a previous conviction for money laundering, was released from prison, claimed state benefits, but then spent millions of pounds in gambling establishments. Another case is that of a grandmother with no known gambling history, on a state pension, who began to make weekly bets of about £100. Investigations later revealed that the grandmother was placing the bets on behalf of her grandson, a known criminal, and that the money spent was the proceeds of his criminal activity.

4.13 Many customers carry a lower risk of money laundering. These might include customers who are regularly employed or who have a regular source of income from a known source which supports the activity being undertaken (this applies equally to pensioners, benefit recipients or to those whose income originates from their partner's employment or income).

4.14 Money laundering risk assessment is not a one-off exercise. Operators should ensure that their policies and procedures for managing money laundering risks, including the detection of the spending of the proceeds of crime, are kept under regular review.

5 DUTIES UNDER THE PROCEEDS OF CRIME ACT 2002

5.1 POCA imposes duties on all operators to:

- disclose instances where operators know or suspect that another person is engaged in money laundering
- and make disclosures in the prescribed form and manner
- and obtain appropriate consent to do a prohibited act, where appropriate.

Disclosure

5.2 If a person carries out any action falling under the principal offences discussed in paragraphs 3.3 to 3.6 above, then failure to make a disclosure to SOCA prior to carrying out the action can result in a criminal offence which can be committed by any employee of the operator. The employee does not commit any of these offences if a proper disclosure is made and, where applicable, appropriate consent is obtained from SOCA.[8]

5.3 SOCA was established by the Serious Organised Crime and Police Act 2005 and came into being on 1 April 2006. The functions of the UK Financial Intelligence Unit (UKFIU) are now placed within the Proceeds of Crime Department of SOCA. In addition, the Serious Crime Act 2007 provided for the merging of the Asset Recovery Agency and SOCA. This means that, with effect from 1 April 2008, SOCA also undertakes civil recovery and tax investigations in England, Wales and Northern Ireland. SOCA is an intelligence-led agency with law enforcement powers and harm-reduction responsibilities, where harm, in this context, is the damage caused to people and communities by serious organised crime.

5.4 The disclosure regime for money laundering is run by the UKFIU within SOCA. It receives and analyses suspicious activity reports (SARs) concerning instances of suspected spending of the proceeds of crime in order to counter money laundering, and makes those SARs available to law enforcement and taxation agencies so they can take the appropriate action.

5.5 In all instances where customers' funds are known or suspected of having criminal origins, a disclosure must be made to SOCA at the earliest opportunity using the methods set out on the SOCA website: www.soca.gov.uk.

5.6 Operators should have a system clearly setting out the requirements for making a disclosure. This system could include:

- the circumstances in which a disclosure is likely to be required
- how and when information is to be provided to the person responsible for making reports to SOCA
- resources which can be used to resolve difficult issues regarding a disclosure
- how and when a disclosure is to be made to SOCA
- how employees can manage a customer when a disclosure has been made and consent is awaited
- the need to be alert to circumstances which could lead to charges of prejudicing an investigation.

---

8 Sections 327(2), 328(2) and 329(2) of the Proceeds of Crime Act.

Appointment of nominated officer

5.7 Whilst it is only incumbent upon those companies in the regulated sector (which, in the gambling sector, only includes non-remote and remote casinos) to appoint nominated officers, operators in the non-regulated sector should also consider appointing a nominated officer, as this can help them meet their obligations under POCA more effectively. This can particularly assist in the reporting of suspicious activity to SOCA, as it is the nominated officer who will have this duty. The nominated officer can also give 'appropriate consent' to a transaction going ahead (this is discussed in paragraphs 5.38 and 5.40 below). Employees will also have protection from prosecution because, so long as they report any known or suspected money laundering activity to the nominated officer (this is called 'internal disclosure'), they cannot be prosecuted for the principal offences under POCA, as the decision whether to report or not to report to SOCA and request appropriate consent is the sole responsibility of the nominated officer.

5.8 The nominated officer should be of sufficient seniority to make decisions on reporting, which will have an impact on the operator's business relationship with its customers and its exposure to criminal, civil, regulatory and disciplinary sanctions. The nominated officer should also have sufficient responsibility to be allowed access to customer information and the operator's business information to enable informed decisions on suspicious activity to be made.

5.9 The nominated officer should receive all disclosures from employees and review them with a view to making a decision on whether to make a disclosure. Where necessary, the nominated officer must make the required disclosure to SOCA as soon as practicable after the information has come to him or her.

5.10 It is important to note, however, that the position of a nominated officer brings with it responsibilities and associated offences, if he or she fails to take the required action, even though the operator may be outside the regulated sector. The responsibilities of the nominated officer and the associated offences are discussed below. Further details can be found in Part 7 of POCA[9].

5.11 Operators with chains of outlets may have an employee who holds a Personal Management Licence issued by the Commission, who would be suitable to appoint as the nominated officer for that chain. In the case of small or solo operators, a person of reasonable standing in the business can act as the nominated officer.

5.12 Where the operator does not formally appoint a nominated officer, it is still advisable for a manager to take particular responsibility for complying with the operator's obligations under POCA.

[9] www.opsi.gov.uk/acts/acts2002/ukpga_20020029_en_22#pt7.

Role of the nominated officer

5.13 Where a nominated officer is appointed, he or she will normally be responsible for ensuring that, when appropriate, information or any other matter leading to knowledge or suspicion of money laundering is properly disclosed to SOCA. The decision to report or not to report suspicious activity is the personal responsibility of the nominated officer. The nominated officer must also liaise with SOCA or law enforcement agencies on the issue of whether to proceed with a transaction or what information may be disclosed to customers or third parties.

5.14 Where an operator has appointed a nominated officer, he or she will:

- receive internal disclosures under Part 7 of POCA
- decide whether these disclosures should be reported to SOCA
- if appropriate, make such external reports to SOCA
- ensure that appropriate consent is applied for as necessary.

5.15 The nominated officer should be able to monitor the day-to-day operation of the operator's anti-money laundering (AML) policies in general, including policies to deal with the spending of the proceeds of crime by customers, and respond promptly to any reasonable request for information made by the Commission or law enforcement bodies.

5.16 Where AML tasks are delegated by an operator's nominated officer to another employee, the nominated officer is still expected to take ultimate managerial responsibility for AML issues and he or she is likely to remain liable for the commission of any criminal offences relating to POCA. The Commission strongly recommends that in such circumstances:

- the fact, date and time of any delegation be entered immediately in a written record
- the delegate should counter-sign by way of acceptance of responsibility
- all employees who need to be aware of the delegation should be notified immediately.

Suspicious activities and reporting

5.17 Operators in the non-regulated sector are required to make a report in respect of information that comes to them within the course of their business:

- where they know
- or where they suspect

that a person is engaged in money laundering, including the spending of the proceeds of crime.

5.18 Operators will only need to consider making a disclosure if they have actual knowledge or subjective suspicion.

5.19 In order to provide a framework within which SARs may be raised and considered:

- each operator should ensure that employees make reports to the operato's nominated officer (where one has been appointed), or an employee in a managerial capacity, where they know or suspect that a person or customer is engaged in money laundering
- the nominated officer, or the manager, should consider each report, and determine whether it warrants the submission of a SAR
- operators should ensure that employees are appropriately trained in their obligations, and the requirements for making reports to their nominated officer or manager.

5.20 If the nominated officer or manager determines that a report warrants the submission of a SAR, he or she must report the matter to SOCA. Under POCA, the nominated officer or manager is required to make a report to SOCA as soon as is practicable if he or she has grounds for suspicion that another person, whether or not that person is a customer, is engaged in money laundering.

What is meant by knowledge and suspicion?

5.21 In the context of POCA, knowledge means actual knowledge. Having knowledge means actually knowing something to be true. In a criminal court, it must be proved that the individual in fact knew that a person was engaged in money laundering. Knowledge can be inferred from the surrounding circumstances, so, for example, a failure to ask obvious questions may be relied upon by a jury to infer knowledge. The knowledge must, however, have come to the operator (or to an employee) in the course of business or (in the case of a nominated officer) as a consequence of a disclosure by another employee. Information that comes to the operator or employee in other circumstances does not come within the scope of the obligation to make a report. This does not preclude a report being made should the operator choose to do so, or be obliged to do so by other parts of POCA. Further information can be found in Part 7 of POCA.[10]

5.22 Suspicion is more subjective and falls short of proof based on firm evidence. Suspicion has been defined by the courts as being beyond mere speculation and based on some foundation. As a judge put it: "It seems to us that the essential element in the word 'suspect' and its affiliates, in this context, is that the defendant must think that there is a possibility, which is more than fanciful, that the relevant facts exist. A vague feeling of unease would not suffice". There is no requirement for the suspicion to be clear or firmly based on specific facts, but there must be a degree of satisfaction, not necessarily amounting to belief, but at least extending beyond speculation.[11]

5.23 The test to decide whether you hold a suspicion is a subjective one. If you think a transaction is suspicious, you are not expected to know the exact nature of the criminal offence or that the funds were definitely those arising from the crime. You may notice something unusual or unexpected and, after making enquiries, the facts do not seem normal or do not make commercial or financial sense. You do not have to have evidence that the customer is using the proceeds of crime to have suspicion. Whether you have a suspicion is a matter for your own judgement. If you have not yet formed a suspicion but simply have cause for concern, you may choose to ask the customer or others more questions. This choice will depend on what you already know and how easy it is to make enquiries.

5.24 Unusual patterns of gambling, including gambling involving particularly large amounts of money, should receive attention, but unusual patterns of behaviour should not necessarily lead to knowledge or suspicion of money laundering, or the submission of a report to SOCA. Nominated officers or managers assigned AML duties should assess all of the circumstances. In cases where it is feasible, it may be helpful to ask customers discretely for more information, such as why they have a large cash amount to spend.

5.25 In order for a disclosure to be made, it is not necessary to know or to establish the exact nature of any underlying criminal offence, or that the particular funds or property were definitely those arising from a crime.

10 www.opsi.gov.uk/acts/acts2002/ukpga_20020029_en_22#pt7.

11 Longmore LJ, R v Da Silva [1996] EWCA Crim 1654.

What constitutes suspicious activity?

5.26 There are numerous things that can make someone either know or suspect that they are dealing with the proceeds of crime. Some common examples of how suspicions may be raised are listed below, although this is not an exhaustive list and there may well be other circumstances which raise suspicion.

EXAMPLES:

- A man convicted of dealing in drugs is released from prison and immediately starts gambling large amounts of money. He is known to be out of work and other customers inform employees that he is supplying drugs again. This will give rise to the suspicion that he is spending the proceeds of his criminal activity.
- Stakes wagered by a customer become unusually high or out of the ordinary and the customer is believed to be spending beyond his or her known means. This requires some knowledge of the customer but, nevertheless, there may be circumstances that appear very unusual and raise the suspicion that he or she is using money obtained unlawfully. It may be that the customer lives in low cost accommodation with no known source of income but nonetheless is spending money well above his or her apparent means. There is no set amount which dictates when a disclosure should be made and much will depend on what is known or suspected about the customer.
- A customer exhibits unusual gambling patterns with an almost guaranteed return or very little financial risk. It is accepted that some customers prefer to gamble in this way but, in some instances, the actions may raise suspicion because they are different from the customer's normal gambling practices.
- Money is deposited by a customer or held over a period and withdrawn by the customer without being used for gambling. For instance, suspicions should be raised by any large amounts deposited in gaming machines or gambling accounts that are then cashed or withdrawn after very little game play or gambling.
- A customer regularly gambles large amounts of money and appears to find an unusual level of losses acceptable. In this instance, the customer may be spending the proceeds of crime and sees the losses as an acceptable consequence of the process of laundering the proceeds of crime.
- Operators are advised that instances of high spend by customers that lead to commercial risk for the operator may also indicate suspicious activity.

Suspicious activity reports (SARs)

5.27 Disclosures under POCA of known or suspected money laundering activity must be made in the prescribed manner and form.[12] In this regard, the operator or operator's nominated officer (where one has been appointed) must disclose to SOCA any transaction or activity that, after his or her evaluation, he or she knows or suspects may be linked to money laundering. The prescribed form for the making of a disclosure to SOCA is a SAR. Such reports must be made as soon as is reasonably practicable after the information comes to the operator or nominated officer.

5.28 SOCA's preferred method for operators to submit their SARs is the 'SOCA Suspicious Activity Report Form'[13], which can be found on the SOCA website at www.soca.gov.uk/financialIntel/suspectActivity.html#forms. Guidance on completing the form can be found at www.soca.gov.uk/financialIntel/formsGuide.html. SOCA prefers these forms to be submitted electronically using SAR Online, SOCA's web based reporting mechanism. SAR Online can be used by anyone with access to the internet and can be found at www.ukciu.gov.uk/saronline.aspx.

5.29 Any reporter choosing not to use one of the electronic reporting methods is advised to obtain a copy of the SOCA preferred form. This form can be downloaded from the SOCA website and be completed by the person making the report on their own computer. However, in cases where it is not possible to complete the form on a computer, hard copy versions of the forms can be completed by hand. After completion, all forms should be posted to: UKFIU, PO Box 8000, London SE11 5EN. They can also be faxed to 0207 238 8286.

5.30 Operators should include in each SAR as much relevant information about the customer, transaction or activity that it has in its records. SOCA's website contains guidance on completing SARs in a way that gives most assistance to law enforcement (www.soca.gov.uk/financialIntel/formsGuide.html). In particular, SOCA has published a glossary of terms which they prefer operators to use when completing SARs (www.soca.gov.uk/financialIntel/SARglossary.html). This will also speed up consideration of the report by SOCA.

5.31 The bulk submission of SARs or those made through the SAR Online system will receive an acknowledgment of receipt, which will include an automatically generated ELMER (the SOCA database of SARs) reference number.

5.32 SOCA will not acknowledge receipt of any SARs sent by post or fax.

5.33 SARs will generally be the normal method of reporting, but reports may also take the form of a limited intelligence value report (LIVR), which may be appropriate in cases where operators know that a law enforcement agency already has an interest in the matter. SOCA provides detailed information on when LIVRs should be used (www.soca.gov.uk/financialIntel/suspectActivity.html), but it is suggested that, where operators are in doubt, they complete a SAR form.

5.34 In order that an informed overview of the situation may be maintained, all contact between operators, SOCA and other law enforcement agencies should be controlled through, or reported back to, the nominated officer (or a deputy acting in the absence of the nominated officer). Where a nominated officer has not been appointed, it is suggested that contact should be through a senior manager in the operator's organisation.

5.35 Should operators require assistance, the UK FIU postal address is: PO Box 8000, London, SE11 5EN. The Unit can also be contacted during office hours on: 020 7238 8282.

---

[12] Section 339(1) of the Proceeds of Crime Act 2002.

[13] Operators that already use 'Encrypted Bulk File' submission can continue to submit reports electronically by those means.

FIGURE 1: KNOWLEDGE OR SUSPICION OF SPENDING OF PROCEEDS OF CRIME (SUBJECTIVE TEST)

Figure 1: Knowledge or suspicion of spending of proceeds of crime (subjective test)

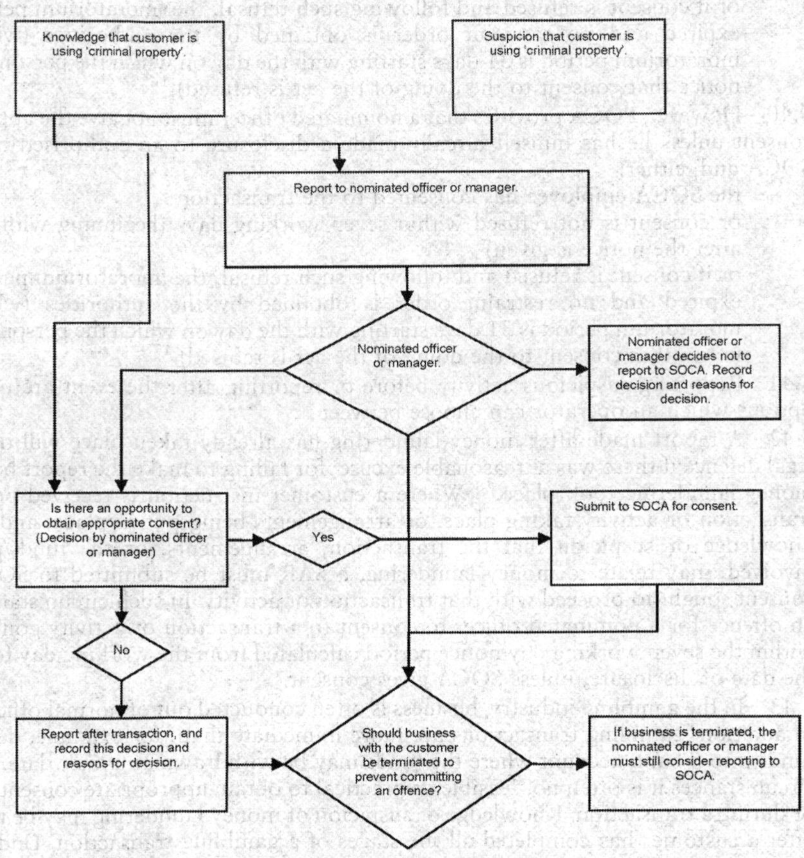

Appropriate consent

5.36 If operators handle any proceeds of crime, they may commit a principal money laundering offence. However, if the operator submits a SAR to SOCA, this can amount to a defence. The 'reporting defence' includes the statutory mechanism which allows SOCA either to agree to the transaction going ahead (this is called 'appropriate consent'), or to prevent the suspected money laundering going ahead.[14]

5.37 Operators need to consider how they will approach their reporting obligations and consider:

- the timing of the report(s) – particularly second or subsequent reports
- whether the operator wishes to continue to do business with the customer while it awaits appropriate consent.

5.38 A nominated officer (where one has been appointed by the operator), police constable, SOCA employee or customs officer can give a person (which may include employees of the operator) actual 'appropriate consent' to a suspect transaction proceeding.[15]

5.39 Alternatively, such a person will be treated as having the appropriate consent if notice is given to a police constable or customs officer (but, note, not the nominated officer) and either:

- consent is not refused within seven working days (beginning with the day after the notice is given)
- or if consent is refused and following such refusal, the 'moratorium period' has expired and no restraint order is obtained by the authorities (where the moratorium period is 31 days starting with the day on which the person receives notice that consent to the doing of the act is refused).[16]

5.40 However, POCA provides that a nominated officer must not give the appropriate consent unless he has himself already made a disclosure to an authorised officer of SOCA and, either:

- the SOCA employee has consented to the transaction
- or consent is not refused within seven working days (beginning with the day after the notice is given)
- or if consent is refused and following such refusal, the 'moratorium period' has expired and no restraint order is obtained by the authorities (where the moratorium period is 31 days starting with the day on which the person receives notice that consent to the doing of the act is refused).[17]

5.41 Reporting suspicious activity before or reporting after the event are not equal options which an operator can choose between.

5.42 A report made after money laundering has already taken place will only be a legal defence if there was a 'reasonable excuse' for failing to make the report before the money laundering took place.[18] Where a customer instruction is received prior to a transaction or activity taking place, or arrangements being put in place, and there is knowledge or suspicion that the transaction, arrangements, or the funds/property involved, may relate to money laundering, a SAR must be submitted to SOCA and consent sought to proceed with that transaction or activity. In such circumstances, it is an offence for a nominated officer to consent to a transaction or activity going ahead within the seven working day notice period calculated from the working day following the date of disclosure, unless SOCA gives consent.[19]

5.43 In the gambling industry, business is often conducted out of normal office hours. In addition, gambling transactions are more immediate than, for example, depositing funds into a bank account where the funds may be withdrawn at a later date. In these circumstances it is often not feasible or practical to obtain appropriate consent prior to or during a transaction. Knowledge or suspicion of money laundering may be triggered after a customer has completed all the stages of a gambling transaction. Under those circumstances it may be reasonable to report after the transaction. However, it should be noted that the defence of 'reasonable excuse' when reporting after the transaction is currently untested by case law and should be considered on a case-by-case basis.[20]

5.44 Where there is knowledge or suspicion of money laundering, particularly if this occurs out of normal office hours, there must be a mechanism for involvement of the senior manager on duty and contact with the nominated officer (where one has been appointed) as soon as is practicable. In circumstances where this is not possible, it will be advisable to report the matter to SOCA directly, where feasible.

5.45 Operators or nominated officers will need to think very carefully about whether or not they wish to continue to do business with the suspected customer. Relevant considerations should be the potential for criminal offences under POCA, as well as potential damage to business reputation and other commercial factors.

5.46 Operators should also note that the reporting defence is not intended to be used repeatedly in relation to the same customer. If patterns of gambling lead to a steadily increasing level of suspicion of money laundering or even to actual knowledge of money laundering, operators will need to seriously consider whether they wish to allow the customer to continue using their gambling facilities. Operators are, of course, free to terminate their business relationships if they wish and, provided this is handled sensitively, there should be no risk of prejudicing an investigation. However, given that operators will have previously reported the customer to SOCA, they should normally liaise with the agency about the best approach to turning the customer away.

5.47 How suspected customers will be dealt with is an important area of risk management for all operators. Operators should deal with the issue in their policies and procedures and, as all gambling operators are at risk of committing the principal offences, it is advisable for operators to consider these issues carefully before they occur in practice.

5.48 For example, the operator may consider one transaction to be suspicious and reports it to SOCA as such, but the operator may be less concerned that all of an individual's future transactions are suspicious. In these circumstances each transaction should be considered on a case-by-case basis and reports made accordingly. Where subsequent reports are also made after prohibited acts appear to have taken place, operators are encouraged to keep records about why reporting was delayed, and about why appropriate consent was not requested before the suspected money laundering took place.

---

14 Section 335 of the Proceeds of Crime Act 2002.

15 Section 335(1) of the Proceeds of Crime Act 2002.

16 Section 335(2) of the Proceeds of Crime Act 2002.

17 Section 336 of the Proceeds of Crime Act 2002.

18 Section 327(2)(b) of the Proceeds of Crime Act 2002.

19 Section 336(3) and (4) of the Proceeds of Crime Act 2002.

20 Section 327(2)(b) of the Proceeds of Crime Act 2002.

Applying for appropriate consent

5.49 Operators should apply for appropriate consent using the SAR Online facility (www.ukciu.gov.uk/saronline.aspx) where they have no existing arrangements to use other electronic media (bulk submission). Operators should complete the standard SAR form and ensure that they tick the "consent required" option and tick the option to indicate that they are disclosing under POCA. The SAR Online process provides an automatic acknowledgement of the report and an ELMER reference number.

5.50 In circumstances where operators are unable to use SAR Online (www.ukciu.gov.uk/saronline.aspx), they should fax their disclosure requesting consent to 0207 238 8286. They should use SOCA's standard SAR form which can be downloaded from the SOCA website (www.soca.gov.uk). Persons submitting the reports should ensure that they tick the "consent required" option and tick the option to indicate that they are disclosing under POCA.

5.51 Operators are strongly discouraged from using the postal system to submit SARs requiring consent as this may delay the decision on consent being relayed back to the operator.

5.52 Where operators have submitted a consent disclosure electronically or via fax, they are not required to post a duplicate report.

5.53 All requests for appropriate consent are treated as a priority within SOCA. The aim is to provide the quickest possible response to the person who has made the report. As soon as a decision has been made in relation to a request for consent it will be relayed to the person who has made the report without delay, but some consent decisions will take longer than others.

5.54 A consent decision will usually be communicated by telephone to the person who made the report in order to provide the quickest possible response. SOCA will also send a letter by post recording the decision, but there is no requirement to wait for this letter in order to proceed with the prohibited act if consent has already been granted verbally.

5.55 SOCA has indicated that it is mindful of the sensitivity of SARs, even within the same organisation, and endeavours to communicate only with persons whose details are verifiable by SOCA. The person who made the report may, therefore, wish to appoint a specified deputy to deal with decisions relating to the consent request in his or her absence, in order to avoid delays. Details of nominated officers, Money Laundering Reporting Officers or other persons responsible for making reports, and their deputies, including their direct contact telephone numbers, should be registered with SOCA. Registration is available through SAR Online (www.ukciu.gov.uk/saronline.aspx) or through forms available on the SOCA website (www.soca.gov.uk).

5.56 When consent is granted by SOCA or no response is received within seven working days, the operator is free to undertake the reported prohibited act(s) without committing a money laundering offence in relation to POCA. Operators should note that consent does not extend to any acts or criminal property not detailed in the initial disclosure or agreed with SOCA.

5.57 The seven day notice period commences on the day after a disclosure is made and excludes weekends and bank holidays. The purpose of the seven day notice period is to allow SOCA and its law enforcement partners sufficient time to assess the risk, and analyse, research and undertake further enquiries relating to the disclosed information, in order to determine the best response to the request for consent.

5.58 Where SOCA gives notice that consent to an act is refused, a further 31 day period (the 'moratorium') commences on the day that notice of refusal is given. The 31 days include weekends and bank holidays.[21] It is an offence to undertake the act during this period as the participant would not have the appropriate consent. The moratorium period enables SOCA to further their investigation into the reported matter using the powers within POCA in relation to the criminal property (for example, by applying to the courts for a restraint order). If the moratorium period expires and no such action has been taken, the operator is free to proceed with the act(s) detailed in the initial disclosure.

5.59 On 5 December 2008, the Home Office published a circular on the so-called'consent regime' in POCA.[22] This circular contains guidance on the operation of the regime and was drawn up in consultation with SOCA, the Association of Chief Police Officers, the Association of Chief Police Officers (Scotland), the Crown Prosecution Service, HM Revenue and Customs, the Revenue and Prosecution Office and others. It was issued to ensure consistency of practice by law enforcement agencies in considering requests for consent. The circular sets out the principles by which the law enforcement agencies should make decisions on consent and how those principles should be applied. Law enforcement agencies are encouraged to recognise the potential, significant impact that each SAR and consent decision can have. This includes, for example, whether or not the proceeds of crime are recovered, crime is prevented, honest individuals and operators are exposed to financial loss or litigation, and the smooth running of commercial business is disrupted.

---

21 Section 335 of the Proceeds of Crime Act 2002.

22 www.homeoffice.gov.uk/about-us/publications/home-office-circulars/circulars-2008/.

FIGURE 2: APPROPRIATE CONSENT

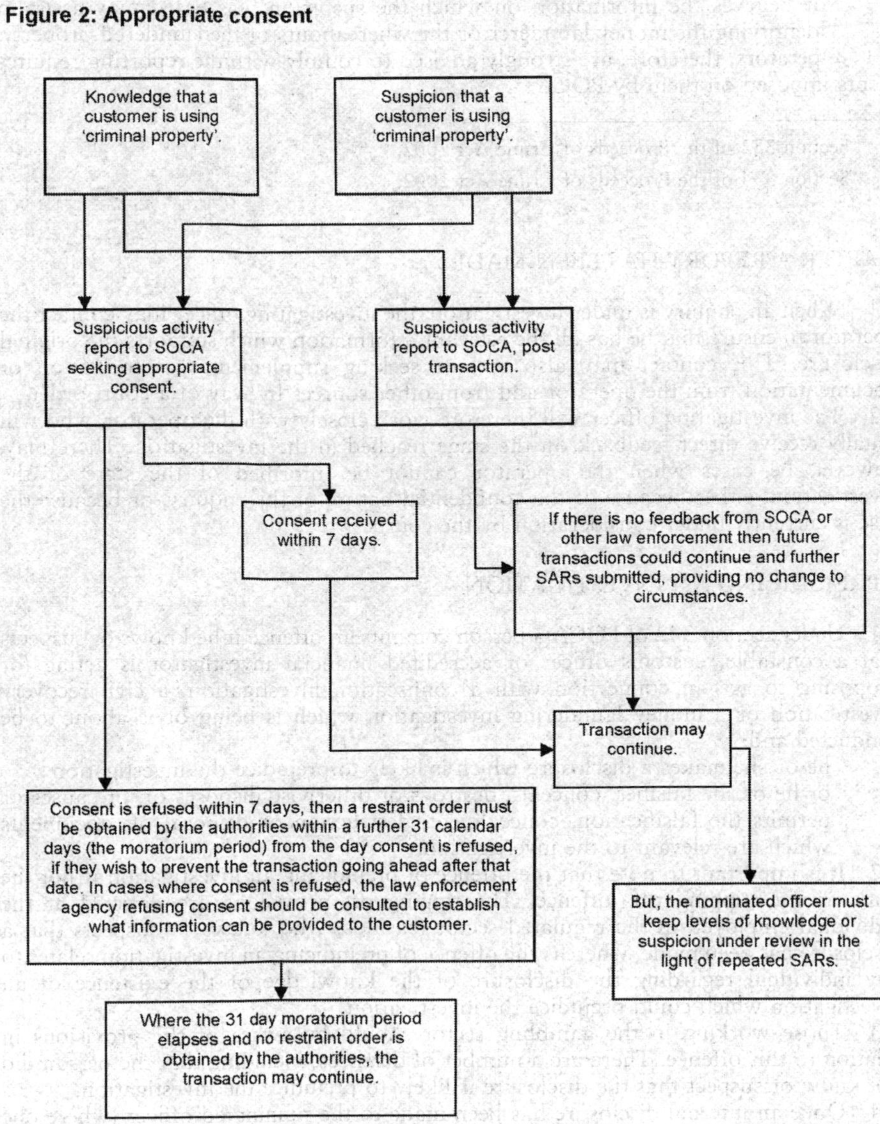

6 FAILING TO REPORT

6.1 POCA creates an offence of failing to report suspicious activity. Where a person nominated by the operator to receive disclosures (the nominated officer) fails to comply with the obligation to make a report to SOCA as soon as practicable after the information is received, they are open to criminal prosecution.[23] The criminal sanction under POCA is a prison term of up to five years and/or a fine.[24]

6.2 For all failure to disclose offences it will be necessary to prove that the person nominated to receive disclosures either:

- knows the identity of the money launderer or the whereabouts of the laundered property
- or believes the information on which the suspicion was based may assist in identifying the money launderer or the whereabouts of the laundered property.

6.3 Operators, therefore, are strongly advised to comply with the reporting requirements imposed on them by POCA.

---

23 Section 332 of the Proceeds of Crime Act 2002.

24 Section 334 of the Proceeds of Crime Act 2002.

7 AFTER A REPORT HAS BEEN MADE

7.1 When an enquiry is under investigation, the investigating officer may contact the operator to ensure that he has all the relevant information which supports the original disclosure. This contact may also include seeking supplementary information or documentation from the operator and from other sources by way of a court order.
7.2 The investigating officer will therefore work closely with the operator, who will usually receive direct feedback on the stage reached in the investigation. There may, however, be cases when the operator cannot be informed of the state of the investigation, either because of the confidential nature of the enquiry, or because the case is currently under consideration by the courts.

8 PREJUDICING AN INVESTIGATION

8.1 Under section 342 of POCA a person commits an offence if he knows or suspects that a constable, customs officer or accredited financial investigator is acting (or proposing to act) in connection with a confiscation investigation, a civil recovery investigation or a money laundering investigation which is being or is about to be conducted and:

- he or she makes a disclosure which is likely to prejudice the investigation
- or he or she falsifies, conceals, destroys or otherwise disposes of, or causes or permits the falsification, concealment, destruction or disposal of, documents which are relevant to the investigation.[25]

8.2 It is important to note that the offence of prejudicing an investigation is not the same as the 'tipping off' offence. The tipping off provisions are directed at the individual employed in the regulated sector (casinos) who knows or suspects that a disclosure has been made, whereas the offence of prejudicing an investigation relates to any individual regarding the disclosure of the knowledge of the existence of an investigation which could prejudice the investigation.
8.3 Those working in the gambling sector should be aware of the provisions in relation to this offence. There are a number of defences, including that the person did not know or suspect that the disclosure is likely to prejudice the investigation.
8.4 Once an internal disclosure has been made to the nominated officer (where one has been appointed) or an external SAR has been made to SOCA, it is a criminal offence for anyone to release information that is likely to prejudice an investigation.[26] Reasonable enquiries of a customer, conducted in a tactful manner, regarding the background to a transaction or activity that is inconsistent with the normal pattern of activity is prudent practice and should not result in the offence of prejudicing an investigation.
8.5 Where a confiscation investigation, a civil recovery investigation or a money laundering investigation is being, or is about to be, conducted, it is a criminal offence for anyone to release information which is likely to prejudice the investigation. It is also a criminal offence to falsify, conceal, destroy or otherwise dispose of documents which are relevant to the investigation (or to cause or permit these offences).[27] It is, however, a defence if the person does not know or suspect that disclosure of the information is

likely to prejudice the investigation, or if the disclosure is made in compliance with other provisions of POCA, or similar enactments.[28]

8.6 The offence of prejudicing an investigation can be committed before or after a disclosure has been made.

---

[25] Section 342(2) of the Proceeds of Crime Act 2002.

[26] Section 342(2)(a) of the Proceeds of Crime Act 2002.

[27] Section 342(1) of the Proceeds of Crime Act 2002.

[28] Section 342(3) of the Proceeds of Crime Act 2002.

9 TRAINING

9.1 All operators should consider awareness training for all relevant employees so that they have an understanding of what obligations are placed upon them and what action they must take to ensure that details are forwarded to and considered immediately by the nominated officer, manager or other employee responsible for making reports to SOCA. In the case of solo operators or operators without specific AML employees, advice is always available directly from SOCA.

9.2 One of the most important controls over the detection of the spending of the proceeds of crime and the prevention of money laundering is for an operator to have employees who are alert to the risks and who are well-trained in the identification of unusual activities or transactions which may prove to be suspicious. The effective application of even the best-designed control systems can be quickly compromised if the employees applying those systems are not adequately trained. The effectiveness of the training will therefore be important to the overall success of the operator's AML strategy.

9.3 Operators should devise and implement a clear and well articulated policy and procedure for ensuring that relevant employees are aware of their legal obligations in respect of POCA. They should also provide employees with regular training in the identification and reporting of anything that gives grounds for suspecting the spending of the proceeds of crime and money laundering activity.

9.4 Under POCA, individual employees face criminal penalties if they are involved in money laundering activity. If they do not make a report when required they may also face criminal sanctions. It is important, therefore, that employees are made aware of their legal obligations and are given training in how to correctly discharge them.

9.5 The content of any training, the frequency of training and the assessment of competence following training are matters for each operator to assess and decide in the light of the money laundering risks they identify. The Commission advises that such issues are covered in each operator's policies and procedures.

9.6 Operators should also take reasonable steps to ensure that relevant employees are aware of:

- their responsibilities under the operator's policies and procedures for the detection and prevention of money laundering
- the money laundering risks faced by an operator
- the operator's procedures for managing those risks
- the identity and responsibilities of the nominated officer (where one has been appointed) or the person responsible for making reports to SOCA
- the potential effect of a breach of POCA on the operator and its employees.

9.7 Where a nominated officer has been appointed, he or she should be actively involved in devising and managing the delivery of the training, taking particular care to ensure that systems are in place to cover all part-time or casual employees.

9.8 SOCA publishes a range of material at www.soca.gov.uk, such as threat assessments and risk profiles, of which operators may wish to make their employees aware. The information on the SOCA website could usefully be incorporated into operators' training materials. In addition, the Association of British Bookmakers (www.abb.uk-.com) has published useful guidelines on POCA and these can be obtained from them directly.

ANNEX A – APPLICABLE LICENCE TYPES

Licence type	Licence category											
	A	B	C	D	E	F	G	H	I	J	K	L
non-remote bingo licence	√	√	√	√	√							
general betting – standard licence	√	√	√	√	√							
non-remote general betting – limited licence	√	√	√									
non-remote pool betting licence	√	√	√									
non-remote betting intermediary licence	√	√	√									
gaming machine general AGC licence	√	√	√	√	√							
gaming machine general FEC licence	√	√	√	√	√							
non-remote external lottery manager licence	√	√	√									
non-remote society lottery licence	√	√	√									
remote bingo operating licence holder						√	√	√	√	√	√	√
general betting – standard virtual events licence						√	√	√	√	√	√	√
general betting – standard real events licence						√	√	√	√	√	√	√
remote general betting – limited licence						√						
remote pool betting licence						√	√	√	√	√		
remote betting intermediary licence						√	√	√	√	√		
remote betting intermediary (trading rooms) licence						√	√	√				
remote external lottery manager licence						√	√	√				
remote society lottery licence						√	√	√				

ANNEX B – GLOSSARY OF TERMS

AML	Anti-money laundering
Money laundering	The process by which criminal or 'dirty' money is legitimised or made 'clean', including any action taken to conceal, arrange, use or possess the proceeds of any criminal conduct.
POCA	The Proceeds of Crime Act 2002, which is intended to reduce money laundering and the profitability of organised crime through the use of tools such as asset recovery.
Proceeds of crime	Property from which a person benefits directly or indirectly, by being party to criminal activity, for example stolen money, money from drug dealing or property stolen in a burglary or robbery
SAR	A suspicious activity report – the means by which suspicious activity relating to possible money laundering or the financing of terrorism is reported to SOCA under POCA
SOCA	The Serious Organised Crime Agency, which was established by the Serious Organised Crime and Police Act 2005 and came into being on 1 April 2006. SOCA is an intelligence-led agency with law enforcement powers and the responsibility to reduce the harm caused to people and communities by serious organised crime). SOCA is the organisation to which suspicious activity is reported
UKFIU	The United Kingdom Financial Intelligence Unit, which is the unit within SOCA that operates the disclosure regime for money laundering

Gambling Commission September 2009

ADVICE NOTE, SPONSORSHIP OF BRITISH SPORTING CLUBS BY FOREIGN GAMBLING OPERATORS

September 2009

6.2093 A growing number of British sports clubs are obtaining sponsorship deals with gambling providers based outside Great Britain. Sports sponsorship falls within the definition of advertising in Section 327(2)(a) of the Gambling Act 2005 (the Act). Such sponsorship deals raise two principal issues, the first is whether foreign gambling providers may advertise within Great Britain; the second is the need to comply with the gambling industry code for socially responsible advertising.

Under section 331 of the Act, it is an offence to advertise foreign gambling. Any gambling operator who wishes to advertise within Great Britain must be licensed and regulated in either an EEA state (for the purposes of the Act, Gibraltar is considered an EEA state), or one of the states that have been approved by the Department for Culture,

Media and Sport (DCMS) on the Government's white list (currently Antigua & Barbuda, Alderney, the Isle of Man and Tasmania).

If a gambling sponsor does not meet one of these licensing criteria they are not permitted to advertise in Great Britain and clubs may not carry their branding. Section 331 can be read online here and clubs or operators in breach of Section 331 put themselves at risk of prosecution.

This should also be borne in mind when hosting international competitions. Care should be exercised to ensure that visiting teams' sponsors are permitted to advertise within Great Britain. As above, the advertising of a gambling sponsor on a visiting club's branded shirts will constitute an offence under section 331 if that sponsor does not meet the licensing criteria.

The second issue is with the branding of childrens' replica kits. The gambling industry code for socially responsible advertising (the industry code) covers this issue and states at paragraph 33 that:

> The advertising of adult-only gambling products or product suppliers should never be targeted at children. This applies equally to sponsorship and this code requires that gambling operators will not allow their logos or other promotional material to appear on any commercial merchandising which is designed for use by children. A clear example of this would be the use of logos on childrens' sports shirts which in future would not be permitted under the terms of this code. Children's shirts and other merchandise will be defined as those that do not attract VAT.

It should be noted that the industry code applies from 1 September 2007 and does not apply to sponsorship deals signed before this date. You can read the industry code online here.

Gambling Commission September 2009

RUNNING PRIZE COMPETITIONS AND FREE DRAWS

December 2009

6.2094 Prize competitions and free draws are free from control under the Gambling Act 2005 (the Act). They can be run for commercial or private gain and can be used as a fun way of offering prizes or promoting a product.

However, it is easy to cross the boundary and in fact be offering an illegal lottery.

This leaflet provides a brief introduction to running prize competitions and free draws and you should also read the detailed advice on our website.

The Gambling Commission (the Commission) strongly recommends that you seek legal advice if you are unsure about the legality of a competition or free draw.

WHAT IS A PRIZE COMPETITION?

A genuine prize competition is one where the outcome is determined by the application of skill, judgement or knowledge. Under the Act a genuine prize competition is one run in such a way that the organisers believe that the requirement for skill, knowledge or judgement will either:

- deter a significant proportion of those who wish to enter from doing so, or
- prevent a significant proportion of those who do enter from winning a prize.

WHAT IS A FREE DRAW?

Under the Act there are two types of free draw. The first is where all entries are free, and the second is where there is both a paid and free entry route. The Act defines 'free' as any method of communication charged at the normal rate, and specifically mentions the use of first or second class post. 'Normal rate' means that there can be no additional payment over what it normally costs to use a particular method of communication. For example, special delivery is not classed as free.

If you choose to run a free draw with a paid entry route, you must ensure that:

- people can genuinely choose to take part without paying
- the free entry route is no more expensive or no less convenient than the paid route and charged at its normal rate
- the choice is publicised so that it is likely to come to the attention of anyone intending to participate
- the system for allocating prizes does not distinguish between either route.

DO I NEED PERMISSION TO RUN A PRIZE COMPETITION OR FREE DRAW?

You do not need permission or a licence from the Commission or a licensing authority to run genuine prize competitions or free draws, as long as they are organised in a way that means they meet the requirements of the Act.

HOW DO I KNOW IF MY PRIZE COMPETITION OR FREE DRAW IS LEGAL?

The Commission does not approve prize competitions or free draws or help develop them, although we may raise any immediately obvious concerns with you. We strongly recommend that you seek legal advice if you are in any doubt as you must satisfy yourself that you are not running an illegal lottery.

WHAT HAPPENS IF MY PRIZE COMPETITION OR FREE DRAW DOESN'T MEET THE REQUIREMENTS?

If you do not meet the requirements it is likely that you are running an illegal lottery. Lotteries are regulated under the Act and are the preserve of good causes. They cannot be run for commercial or private gain, and, unless they are in one of a limited category of exempt lotteries, must be either licensed by the Commission or registered with a licensing authority. It is illegal if you run such a lottery without a licence or registration. More information about lotteries is available in *Promoting society and local authority lotteries* and *Organising small lotteries* on the Commission website.

WHY IS THE COMMISSION INTERESTED?

We monitor the boundary between prize competitions and free draws on the one hand and lotteries on the other. We also have a duty to pursue and prevent illegal gambling and may act where prize competitions and free draws are organised and promoted that, in our view, are illegal lotteries. If appropriate, we will prosecute.

FURTHER INFORMATION

For detailed advice on prize competitions and free draws you should read: *Prize competitions and free draws: the requirements of the Gambling Act 2005*, which can be found on the Gambling Commission website.
Gambling Commission December 2009

ADVICE ON NON-COMMERCIAL AND PRIVATE GAMING AND BETTING

January 2010

1 INTRODUCTION

6.2095 1.1 This advice is designed to provide help to people planning to offer gambling at non-commercial or private events

1.2 he rules governing non-commercial and private gaming and betting are complex and this advice is for guidance only. It is not a binding interpretation of the law and cannot cover every circumstance. Anyone intending to run events under these provisions should therefore refer to the Gambling Act 2005 (the Act) itself and, if necessary, seek independent legal advice to ensure that their plans conform to the law before proceeding.

2 DEFINING NON-COMMERCIAL AND PRIVATE GAMING AND BETTING

2.1 The Act permits gambling without any specific permission under limited circumstances. In summary these are:

- non-commercial gaming
- private gaming and betting
- incidental non-commercial lotteries
- private society lotteries
- work lotteries
- residents' lotteries
- customer lotteries.

2.2 The Act allows non-commercial gaming, that is to say gaming which takes place at a non-commercial event, either as an incidental or principal activity at the event. Events are non-commercial if no part of the proceeds is for private profit or gain. The proceeds of such events may benefit one or more individuals if the activity is organised:

- by, or on behalf of, a charity or for charitable purposes, or
- to enable participation in, or support of, sporting, athletic or cultural activities.

2.3 For example, it would be possible to raise funds for an individual as long as the proceeds were for a wheelchair or to support a sporting endeavour. Additionally, popular events such as race nights or casino nights may be permitted if they comply with the regulations and profits go to a 'good cause'. More details about these can be found later in this document.

2.4 Section 297(3) of the Act defines 'proceeds' as:

- the sums raised by the organisers (whether by way of fees for entrance or for participation, by way of sponsorship, by way of commission from traders, or otherwise)

  minus:
- amounts deducted by the organisers in respect of costs reasonably incurred in organising the event.

2.5 However, sums raised by other persons will not form part of the proceeds of the event and may be appropriated for private gain. An example would be refreshments provided at the event by an independent third party.

2.6 The Act identifies two types of permissible non-commercial gaming:

- prize gaming (which must comply with the conditions set out in section 299 of the Act)
- equal chance gaming (which must comply with the conditions set out in section 300 of the Act and the conditions prescribed in Regulations).

2.7 Gaming is private gaming provided it is equal chance gaming, there is no charge for participation and it takes place somewhere to which the public do not have access. That would include a workplace, for example. Domestic and residential gaming are subsets of private gaming where non-equal chance gaming is also allowed:

- Domestic gaming is allowed without the need for permissions if:

— it takes place in a private dwelling, and
— it is on a domestic occasion

- Residential gaming is allowed when:
  — it takes place in a hall of residence or hostel not administered in the course of a trade or business, and
  — more than 50% of the participants are residents.

2.8 Betting is private if it is domestic betting or workers' betting. Domestic betting is a betting transaction made on premises in which each party to the transaction habitually resides. Workers' betting is where a betting transaction is made between persons who are employed by the same employer.

2.9 With regard to exempt lotteries, this advice addresses incidental non-commercial lotteries only. If you would like further information about exempt lotteries in general, you are directed to the Gambling Commission's publication Organising small lotteries: *Advice on lotteries that do not require a licence or registration (November 2009).*

2.10 An incidental non-commercial lottery is a lottery which is incidental to a non-commercial event, that is, the lottery is not the main purpose of the event. Examples may include a lottery held at a school fete or at a social event such as a dinner dance.

3 NON-COMMERCIAL PRIZE GAMING

3.1 Section 288 defines gaming as prize gaming if neither the nature nor size of a prize is determined by the number of people playing or the amount paid for or raised by the gaming. The prizes will be determined by the operator before play commences. This is distinct from normal commercial gaming where the stakes and participation fees paid by the players go to make up the available winnings.

3.2 There are no statutory limits on stakes, prizes, participation fees or other charges for non-commercial prize gaming. In addition, no licence, permit or other form of permission is required to operate this kind of gaming, provided that the statutory conditions are complied with.

3.3 The conditions for non-commercial prize gaming, set out in section 299 of the Act, are as follows:

- All players must be told for what purpose the money raised from the gaming is going to be used (this must be something other than private gain), and the profits must be applied for that purpose
- The non-commercial event cannot take place on premises (other than a track) which hold a premises licence, nor on a track at a time when activities are being carried on in reliance on a premises licence, nor on premises at a time when activities are being carried on in reliance on a temporary use notice. There is nothing to stop such premises running charitable or other gambling events to raise money for good causes, but they should do so using the gambling permissions granted to them by their premises licence or temporary use notice. The one exception to this is that a non-commercial event can take place at a track or premises subject to a temporary use notice, provided no gambling activities are taking place in reliance on the licence or notice at the same time. This enables a track to be used for non-commercial gambling when races are not taking place
- The gaming must be non-remote gaming. In other words, the authorisation can only apply to gaming which takes place at events, on premises, and for gaming in person.

3.4 'Profits' in paragraph 3.3 above means:

- total amounts:
  — paid by way of stakes, or
  — accruing to the person organising the gaming directly in connection with it minus:
- amounts deducted by the person organising the gaming in respect of:
  — the provision of prizes, or

6: Gambling Act 2005: Additional Material

— other reasonable costs incurred in organising the gaming or providing facilities for the gaming.

3.5 A person commits an offence under section 301 of the Act if he or she uses any part of the profits from the gaming for purposes other than the specified non-commercial purpose. This includes permitting the profits to be used for other than the specified non-commercial purpose.

4 NON-COMMERCIAL EQUAL CHANCE GAMING

4.1 Equal chance gaming is gaming where the chances are equally favourable to all participants and players are not competing against a bank (section 8 of the Act). This includes games such as poker or bingo. In non-commercial equal chance gaming, the charitable funds are usually raised through an entrance fee, participation fee, or through other payments related to the gaming.

4.2 The conditions for non-commercial equal chance gaming, set out in section 300 of the Act, are as follows:

- All players must be told for what purpose the money raised from the gaming is going to be used (this must be something other than private gain), and the profits must be applied for that purpose
- The gaming must also comply with regulations[1] made, limiting:
  - — the maximum payment each player can be required to make to participate in all games at an event to £8
  - — the aggregate amount or value of prizes in all games played at an event to £600, although where an event is the final one of a series in which all of the players have previously taken part, a higher prize fund of up to £900 is permitted
- The non-commercial event cannot take place on premises (other than a track) which hold a premises licence, nor on a track at a time when activities are being carried on in reliance on a premises licence, nor on premises at a time when activities are being carried on in reliance on a temporary use notice. There is nothing to stop such premises running charitable or other gambling events to raise money for good causes, but they should do so using the gambling permissions granted to them by their premises licence or temporary use notice. The one exception to this is that a non-commercial event can take place at a track or premises subject to a temporary use notice, provided no gambling activities are taking place in reliance on the licence or notice at the same time. This enables a track to be used for non-commercial gambling when races are not taking place
- The gaming must be non-remote gaming. In other words, the authorisation can only apply to gaming which takes place at events, on premises, and for gaming in person.

4.3 'Profits' in paragraph 4.2 above means:

- total amounts:
  - — paid by way of stakes, or
  - — accruing to the person organising the gaming directly in connection with it

minus:

- amounts deducted by the person organising the gaming in respect of:
  - — the provision of prizes, or
  - — other reasonable costs incurred in organising the gaming or providing facilities for the gaming.

4.4 A person commits an offence under section 301 of the Act if he or she uses any part of the profits from the gaming for purposes other than the specified non-commercial purpose. This includes permitting the profits to be used for other than the specified non-commercial purpose.

[1] SI 2007 No. 2041: The Gambling Act 2005 (Non-Commercial Equal Chance Gaming) Regulations 2007.

5 PRIVATE GAMING

Gaming is only private gaming if it occurs in a place to which the public does not have access (normally a private dwelling, hostel, hall of residence or similar establishment). No charge may be made for participation in private gaming (and this includes an entrance fee or other charge for admission), nor may any amounts be deducted from stakes or prizes. No profits can be made from private gaming, irrespective of how the organiser intends to use those profits.

Private gaming is restricted to equal chance gaming (poker or bingo, for example), except where it is domestic or residential gaming.

Private gaming can potentially take place on commercial premises in circumstances where a members' club hires a room in, for example, a pub or hotel for a private function where equal chance gaming only is played. However, organisers would need to scrutinise very carefully the arrangements put in place to make sure that the particular area of the pub, hotel or other venue in which the gaming takes place is not, on the occasion of the private function, a place to which the public have access and that those participating are not selected by a process which means that, in fact, they are members of the public rather than members of the club. The law in this area is complex and organisers are strongly advised to seek their own legal advice before organising events of this nature.

6 NON-COMMERCIAL AND PRIVATE BETTING

6.1 The Act also says that betting is private if it is domestic betting or workers' betting. Domestic betting is a betting transaction made on premises in which each party to the transaction habitually resides. Workers' betting is where a betting transaction is made between persons who are employed by the same employer. A person does not commit an offence under section 33 or 37 of the Act if he or she provides facilities for private betting.

OCCASIONAL USE NOTICES

6.2 Section 39 of the Act provides that where there is betting on a track on eight days or fewer in a calendar year, betting may be permitted by an occasional use notice (OUN), without the need for a full premises licence.

6.3 While tracks are normally thought of as permanent racecourses, the meaning of 'track' in the Act covers not just horse racecourses or dog tracks, but also any other premises on any part of which a race or other sporting event takes place, or is intended to take place (see section 353(1) of the Act). This could include football grounds, cricket grounds, golf courses and the like.

6.4 This also means that land which has a number of uses, one of which fulfils the definition of a track, can qualify for the OUN provisions (for example, agricultural land on which a point-to-point meeting takes place). Land used temporarily as a track can qualify, provided races or sporting events take place or will take place there. The track need not be a permanent fixture.

6.5 The intention of OUNs is to permit licensed betting operators to use tracks for short periods for conducting betting, where the event upon which the betting is to take place is of a temporary, infrequent nature. OUNs dispense with the need for a betting premises licence for the track in these circumstances. OUNs can also potentially be used to facilitate betting at non-commercial or charity events.

6.6 It should be noted that betting operators cannot provide gaming machines at tracks by virtue of an OUN.

6.7 Non-commercial, fund raising race nights can be run as betting events at sporting venues under the authority of an OUN, whether or not the sporting event on which the bets are taken is held at that venue. The sporting event on which the bets are or will be taken also need not be taking place at the same time as the betting under the OUN.
6.8 An OUN must be sent in writing to the relevant local authority in advance of the event and be copied to the chief officer of police for the area in which the venue is located (or, in Scotland, the chief constable of the police force for the area) and specify a day on which it is to have effect. OUNs must be given for each day on which they are to have effect and must be given by the person responsible for the administration of events on the track or the occupier of the track.
6.9 No more that eight OUNs may be issued in a calendar year (that is, for a total of eight days per calendar year), in respect of any one venue. OUNs may be given for consecutive days, so long as the overall limit of eight days is not exceeded in the calendar year.

7 INCIDENTAL NON-COMMERCIAL LOTTERY

7.1 In simple terms, a lottery is a form of gambling that has three essential elements:
- payment is required to participate
- one or more prizes are awarded
- those prizes are awarded by chance.

This is set out more formally in the Act (section 14), which defines two types of lottery – a simple lottery and a complex lottery.
7.2 The conditions for an incidental non-commercial lottery are as follows:
- the promoters must not deduct from the proceeds of the lottery more than the prescribed[2] amount in respect of the cost of the prizes (currently £500), irrespective of their actual cost
- the promoters must not deduct from the proceeds of the lottery more than the prescribed[2] amount in respect of the costs incurred in organising the lottery (currently £100), irrespective of the amount of the costs incurred
- the lottery must be promoted for a purpose other than that of private gain
- the arrangements for the lottery must not include a rollover
- tickets in the lottery can only be sold during the event and on the premises where the event takes place.

7.3 If the gaming at a non-commercial event is not the only or main purpose of the event and meets the definition of a lottery, it is possible to operate it as an incidental non-commercial lottery.
7.4 If you would like further information about other exempt lotteries, you are directed to the Gambling Commission's publication Organising small lotteries: Advice on lotteries that do not require a licence or registration (November 2009).

---

2 SI 2007 No 2040: The Gambling Act 2005 (Incidental Non-Commercial Lotteries) Regulations 2007.

8 NON-COMMERCIAL 'CASINO NIGHT'

8.1 A non-commercial casino night is an event where participants stake money on casino-style games, such as poker or roulette, at a non-commercial event, where none of the money the organisers raise from the event is used for private gain.
8.2 Apart from reasonable costs, proceeds (including any entrance fees, sponsorship, the difference between stakes placed and payout made):
- must not be used for private gain
- must all be given to a good cause.

Reasonable costs would include costs incurred by providing the prizes. If third parties are selling goods or services at the event, for example if someone is selling refreshments, this does not count as money raised for the charity or good cause and can be retained by that third party.

8.3 A non-commercial casino night can be run without a licence, or any other form of permission, providing the operation of the gaming falls into one of the three categories discussed below.

8.4 Organisers should note that, under the Act, it is illegal to organise a commercial casino night outside of a licensed casino. As the law stands, only the holder of a valid non-remote casino operating licence can apply to a licensing authority for a temporary use notice (TUN) in respect of other premises to offer gaming on a commercial basis, and then only in respect of equal chance gaming organised on a tournament basis with a single overall winner.[3]

NON-COMMERCIAL PRIZE GAMING

8.5 Casino nights can be held as non-commercial prize gaming. The players must be told what good cause will benefit from the profits of the gaming before placing a bet. The prizes must be advertised in advance and must not depend on the number of people playing or the stakes raised. In non-commercial prize gaming, the casino gaming determines the individual winner or winners, for example by counting who has the most casino chips at a set time. The winners are then awarded the prizes that have been advertised in advance.

NON-COMMERCIAL EQUAL CHANCE GAMING

8.6 Casino nights can also be run as non-commercial equal chance gaming. Equal chance gaming is gaming where the chances are equally favourable to all participants and players are not competing against a bank. In non-commercial equal chance gaming, the charitable funds are usually raised through an entrance fee, participation fee, or through other payments related to the gaming. The maximum amount that a player may be charged is £8 per day (this includes entrance or participation fees, stakes and any other payments in relation to the gaming). Organisers must ensure that the total amount paid out in prizes remains below £600 in total across all players. However, where an event is the final one of a series in which all of the players have previously taken part, a higher prize fund of up to £900 is allowed.

PRIVATE GAMING

8.7 A casino night may also be run under the private gaming provisions in the Act. Private gaming may only occur in a place to which the public does not have access (normally a private dwelling, hostel, hall of residence or similar establishment). No charge may be made for participation in private gaming (and that includes an entrance fee or other charge for admission), nor may any amounts be deducted from stakes or prizes. No profits can be made from private gaming, irrespective of how the organiser intended to use those profits and, thus, even if intended for charitable purposes.

8.8 Private gaming is restricted to equal chance gaming (poker, for example), except where it is domestic or residential gaming.

8.9 Private gaming can potentially take place on commercial premises in circumstances where a members' club hires a room in, for example, a pub or hotel for a private function where equal chance gaming only is played. However, organisers would need to scrutinise very carefully the arrangements put in place to make sure that the particular area of the pub, hotel or other venue in which the gaming takes place is not, on the occasion of the private function, a place to which the public have access and that those participating are not selected by a process which means that, in fact, they are members of the public rather than members of the club. The law in this area is complex and organisers are advised to seek their own legal advice before organising events of this nature.

[3] SI 2007 No 3157: The Gambling Act 2005 (Temporary Use Notices) Regulations 2007.

9 NON-COMMERCIAL 'RACE NIGHT'

9.1 'Race nights' are permitted for charitable purposes. However, in some circumstances, they can only be undertaken by a licensed betting operator and after the premises owner has notified the local authority.

9.2 A non-commercial race night is an event where participants stake money on the outcome of live, recorded or virtual races. The money the organisers raise from the event is called the proceeds.

9.3 Apart from reasonable costs, proceeds (including any entrance fees, sponsorship, the difference between stakes placed and payout made):

- must not be used for private gain
- must all be given to a good cause.

Reasonable costs would include costs reasonably incurred, for example by providing any prizes and for betting slips. If third parties are selling goods or services at your event, for example if someone is selling refreshments, this does not count as money raised for the charity or good cause and can be retained by that third party.

9.4 Broadly there are three types of race nights which can be organised for charitable purposes.

NON-COMMERCIAL GAMING

9.5 The first type of race night occurs where the selection of a 'horse' by a participant is totally dependent on chance, and where no 'odds' or 'form' are available to assist the gambler's selection. An example would be the use of archive films of horseracing without revealing the details of each race.

9.6 Such nights can be run without a licence, or any other form of permission, providing the operation of the gaming falls into one of the three categories discussed below.

INCIDENTAL NON-COMMERCIAL LOTTERY

9.7 Where the race night is not the only or main purpose of a non-commercial event, it is possible to operate it as an incidental lottery. In this case there are no limits on the amount that players may be charged to participate, but no more than £500 may be deducted from the proceeds of the lottery for the cost of prizes (which may be in cash or in kind), and no more than £100 for other expenses. The organisers can only sell tickets at the event and they have to announce the results at the event. As an example, a 'horse' might be picked at random for each paying customer who is awarded a prize if the horse 'wins'.

NON-COMMERCIAL PRIZE GAMING

9.8 Race nights can be held as non-commercial prize gaming. The players must be told what good cause will benefit from the profits of the gaming. The prizes must be advertised in advance and must not depend on the number of people playing or the stakes raised. In non-commercial prize gaming, the 'race' determines the individual winner or winners, for example, those who have paid are allocated or select a named horse in the race. The winners are then awarded the prizes that had been advertised in advance.

NON-COMMERCIAL EQUAL CHANCE GAMING

9.9 Race nights can also be run as non-commercial equal chance gaming. Equal chance gaming, which also includes games such as poker or bingo, is gaming where the chances are equally favourable to all participants and players are not competing against a bank.

9.10 The maximum amount that a player may be charged is £8 per day (this includes entrance or participation fees, betting stakes and any other payments in relation to the gaming). Organisers must ensure that the total amount paid out in prizes remains below £600 in total across all players. However, where an event is the final one of a series in which all of the players have previously taken part, a higher prize fund of up to £900 is allowed. This could take place, for example, where each participant pays a fee for a randomly selected 'horse' in each 'race' and the participant with the winning horse or chooser of the winning horse receives a prize commensurate with the stakes placed.

OCCASIONAL USE NOTICES

9.11 The second type of race night relies on bets being taken by a licensed betting operator on events, including cases where odds and form are available to gamblers.
9.12 This type of race night can only be organised at sporting venues under the authority of an Occasional Use Notice (OUN). It does not matter, however, whether or not the sporting event on which the bets are taken is held at that venue. The sporting event on which the bets are or will be taken also need not be taking place at the same time as the betting under the OUN.
9.13 An OUN must be sent in writing to the relevant local authority in advance of the event and be copied to the chief officer of police for the area in which the venue is located (or, in Scotland, the chief constable of the police force for the area) and specify a day on which it is to have effect. OUNs must be given for each day on which they are to have effect and must be issued by the person responsible for the administration of events on the track or the occupier of the track.
9.14 No more than eight OUNs may be issued in a calendar year (that is, for a total of eight days per calendar year), in respect of any one venue. OUNs may be given for consecutive days, so long as the overall limit of eight days is not exceeded in the calendar year.
9.15 The person administering the betting under an OUN must have a Gambling Commission general betting operating licence (that is, he or she must be a licensed bookmaker).

PRIVATE GAMING

9.16 A non-commercial race night may also be run under the private gaming provisions in the Act. Private gaming may only occur in a place to which the public does not have access (a private dwelling, hostel, hall of residence or similar establishment). No charge may be made for participation in private gaming (and that includes an entrance fee or other charge for admission), nor may any amounts be deducted from stakes or prizes. Thus, no profits can be made from private gaming, irrespective of how the organiser intended to use those profits, and not even for charitable purposes.
Gambling Commission January 2010

CONCORDAT
GAMBLING ACT 2005 – CO-REGULATORS CONCORDAT BETWEEN THE GAMBLING COMMISSION AND LOCAL GOVERNMENT REGULATION (LG REGULATION)

September 2010

1 INTRODUCTION

6.2096 1.1 This Concordat is an agreement between the Gambling Commission (the Commission) and licensing authorities (LAs) in England and Wales, via Local

Government Regulation (LG Regulation – formerly LACORS). It is based on a set of principles which set out in general terms our shared understanding of how the Commission and LAs will carry out our respective duties under the Gambling Act 2005 (the Act).

1.2 The practical application of these principles is detailed in an accompanying set of protocols. The protocols reflect how the Commission and LAs will ensure compliance with the Act, the licensing objectives and the associated rules and regulations. The Concordat and protocols will, when need arises, be amended and new ones added to respond to changing circumstances. Such review will be a joint process between both parties.

2 PRINCIPLES

2.1 The Commission and LAs act jointly as co-regulators of the gambling industry under the Act. We regulate most commercial, and some non-commercial, gambling in Great Britain.

2.2 Section 1 of the Act sets out three licensing objectives that underpin our respective work as regulators. These are:

- preventing gambling from being a source of crime and disorder
- ensuring that gambling is fair and open
- protecting children and vulnerable people from being exploited or harmed by gambling.

2.3 The Commission must aim to permit gambling so far as it thinks it reasonably consistent with pursuit of the licensing objectives. The Act also requires the Commission to give advice to the Secretary of State about the incidence, manner, effects and regulation of gambling.

2.4 The Act requires the Commission to issue guidance from time to time on the manner in which licensing authorities are to exercise their functions under the Act and in particular, the principles that they should apply. LAs must have regard to such guidance, which will be reviewed and revised as required. The Commission will consult on any proposed changes and will aim to make the guidance easily understood and applied.

2.5 LAs must aim to permit the use of premises for gambling, in so far as they think that this:

- accords with the licence conditions, codes of practice and guidance issued by the Commission
- is reasonably consistent with the licensing objectives; and
- is in accordance with the LAs' three-year licensing policy.

2.6 LAs and the Commission aim to ensure that the gambling industry is correctly licensed and well regulated and that it operates in a compliant manner. We recognise that co-regulation requires a shared understanding of the responsibilities of each party and the ability both at local and national levels to work effectively together and resolve problems in a consistent and timely manner.

2.7 We are aware that a minority of operators will be non-compliant or operate illegally. We will take the appropriate and proportionate regulatory and enforcement action in such circumstances. We will both uphold the Act and protect the compliant industry from the threats that such activity poses. Where there is evidence of systematic illegality, LAs and the Commission will work together, and with other agencies as appropriate, to identify offenders and to ensure that they face action as required.

2.8 We aim to achieve regulatory outcomes in a way that minimises burdens imposed on business. Key to this is that we are risk based and proportionate in our decision making and transparent and accountable for our actions. Both LG Regulation and the Commission recognise that, in keeping with the Hampton principles of better regulation, we must minimise the risk of duplication or over-regulation and make the most efficient use of our resources.

2.9 The Commission recognises that LAs will each have different priorities and that this will have a bearing on their approach to the licensing of premises and to compliance. It is a matter for the local democratic process to make such decisions and to reflect local concerns. The Commission and LAs both operate a risk based methodology. The Commission's resources are prioritised on risks that are identified which are high in impact and of regional or national significance. LAs are concerned with risks within their geographical boundaries and which would have a high impact at a local level.

2.10 We recognise that our understanding of the Act is continuing to evolve and that as new circumstances emerge, and as operators develop new products and new methods of making gambling available; this will continue to be the case. The Commission will endeavour to ensure that, when elaborations of its understanding of the Act are required, LG Regulation and LAs are engaged at the earliest opportunity.

NOTE:

Various protocols relevant to the above Concordat concerning communication structures, exchange of information and compliance enforcement were published in November 2010. These are available on the websites of the Gambling Commission and Local Government Regulation.

Gambling Commission September 2010

APPROACH TO TEST PURCHASING – ENGLAND AND WALES ONLY

May 2011

1 INTRODUCTION

6.2097 1.1 Test purchasing is one method by which the Gambling Commission (the Commission) may measure the compliance of licensed operators, or groups of licensed operators, with aspects of the Gambling Act 2005 (the Act).

1.2 The purpose of this advice note is to set out the Commission's approach to test purchasing in England and Wales, providing clarity to operators, co-regulators and others about how they might reasonably expect the Commission to act.

2 TEST PURCHASING – THE COMMISSION'S APPROACH

TEST PURCHASING AS A REGULATORY TOOL

2.1 It is the responsibility of operators to manage the risks to the licensing objectives that their activities may present. The Commission expects this to be managed in the same way as any other core risk to their business. It is a matter for each operator to determine how they best manage risk. The Commission's focus of attention is with the outcome of the operator's actions.

2.2 Test purchasing is one means by which the Commission can measure the effectiveness of licensees' efforts to control risks to the licensing objectives. It is a targeted activity focused upon what the Commission considers to be important aspects of managing risk. Examples include the effectiveness of self exclusion procedures, controls on underage gambling and anti-money laundering policies and procedures.

2.3 The Commission will generally not prioritise test purchasing in sectors and on themes where it is satisfied that operators have in place their own arrangements for monitoring compliance, that those arrangements are effective and the results are made available to the Commission.

2.4 The Commission is most likely to use test purchasing for the following purposes:

- to assess thematic compliance of operators (with selected characteristics, eg from a sector) with aspects of the legislation and/or licence conditions and codes so as to be able to assess risk to the licensing objectives. This enables us to advise on the way in which gambling regulation is working and to take any necessary regulatory action whether in the form of advice or sharing of best practice or further refinement of licence conditions and codes

- in an enforcement context, to gather evidence in relation to breaches committed by individual operators.

2.5 It is anticipated that the majority of circumstances where the Commission carries out test purchasing will be under the first of the modes set out above, although it will act in the second mode where necessary.

2.6 Whatever the mode of operation, the Commission will conduct test purchasing in a way that is fair and objective. When assessing thematic compliance focused upon sectors, our aim is to build an understanding of specific risk within a sector and the degree of compliance with regulatory requirements, it is not to 'catch out' individual operators. Test purchasing activity will be designed so as to provide sufficient opportunity for operators to demonstrate compliance.

2.7 Normally when conducting thematic compliance test purchasing the Commission will give the sector potentially affected notice of its intentions in general terms before the exercise starts.

2.8 It is the responsibility of operators to manage the outcome of such testing in relation to their staff and the means by which future compliance is secured.

2.9 Dependent on the results of a test purchasing exercise operators may be requested to supply details of an improvement programme, if they are not already doing so, and to demonstrate, at a later date, the effectiveness of such a programme.

TEST PURCHASING BY THE COMMISSION AND BY LICENSING AUTHORITIES (LAS)

2.10 The Act created a framework for licensing, compliance and enforcement in which the Commission and LAs have overlapping but distinctive responsibilities. The most obvious distinction is between LAs who are the primary agency responsible for issues related to premises and the Commission who are responsible for the licensing of operators (and individuals), and this is reflected in the sources of income each agency receives to finance their duties under the Act. However, the matter is more nuanced than this.

2.11 The Act also makes LAs the agency responsible for either being notified of or granting permissions and permits for gambling activity that is predominantly 'local' in nature. Examples include occasional use notices, temporary use notices, club gaming permits and machine permits and small society lottery registrations.

2.12 This distinction between what is essentially localised and what has wider significance and the potential to have impact at a regional or national level is reflected in the Co-Regulators Concordat (March 2010) which states:

> 'The Commission's resources are prioritised on risks that are identified which are high in impact and of regional or national significance. LAs are concerned with risks within their geographical boundaries and which would have a high impact at a local level.'

2.13 This approach is expanded in the Compliance and Enforcement Protocol (which accompanies the Concordat) as follows:

> 'LAs are best placed to monitor and ensure compliance with the Act at a local level. For example, they are generally in the best position to proceed against individual licensed premises, where the impact is high in that local situation, although the Commission will consider compliance activity against operators who have a large regional or national presence and where the failing is more widespread.'

2.14 It therefore follows that in relation to compliance and regulatory effort generally, and test purchasing in particular, the Commission's focus is on operators whose scale of activity is such that non-compliance would have either a regional or national impact.

2.15 Both regulatory bodies work to the principles contained in the Hampton Report 1, something also explicitly acknowledged in the Concordat:

'We aim to achieve regulatory outcomes in a way that minimises burdens imposed on business. Key to this is that we are risk based and proportionate in our decision making and transparent and accountable for our actions. Both LG Regulation[2] and the Commission recognise that, in keeping with the Hampton principles of better regulation, we must minimise the risk of duplication or over-regulation and make the most efficient use of our resources.'

2.16 It is to mitigate this risk that the Protocol on Communication states the following:

'. . . . it is important that information is shared at an early stage where there is any risk to the duplication of effort of regulatory activity. One party will inform the other where there are either matters of non-compliance or illegality for which the other party is primarily responsible and/or where the other partner has the most appropriate powers to deal with it. Details of any ongoing action and the outcome of action taken on the basis of such reports will be shared subsequently.'

and the Protocol on Compliance and Enforcement states:

'Information which arises from compliance and enforcement activity, including test purchasing operations, will be shared between the Commission and the LAs where possible. This may include action plans produced by operators to address any shortcomings that were identified by the exercise.'

2.17 In summary therefore, in the normal course of business, the Commission would inform relevant LAs (those who have premises within their geographical boundaries which are planned to be included in a test purchasing operation) of the detail of the operation in advance. A similar expectation applies to such operations when the lead agency is a LA.

2.18 Forward planning of this kind ensures that, for example, the following do not occur:

- an operator or an individual premises is unnecessarily tested twice in a short period of time
- an operator who has been tested by one regulator, and has recently implemented an improvement plan, is then retested whilst implementing the plan
- an operator who is managing their business risk in a responsible manner by employing an independent third party to conduct test purchasing, and who is sharing those results and improvement plans with a regulator is tested without consideration first being given to the operator's actions to date (and taken into account in terms of risk assessment)
- a test purchasing exercise conflicts with other compliance or enforcement work that may be in process in relation to an individual operator, premises or personal licence holder.

2.19 The Commission has engaged with the Local Better Regulation Office (LBRO) and the Better Regulation Executive (BRE) on the subject of Primary Authority[3] schemes for some time. Whilst the question as to whether aspects of gambling regulation may be suitable for inclusion within the scheme are subject to further consultation it may be helpful to consider the Commission as acting akin to the Primary Authority. This applies particularly to aspects of compliance that are most likely to be of interest to LAs in relation to test purchasing – for example age verification. The operators concerned are the larger ones who have either a significant regional presence or a national footprint. As noted above (2.16), the Commission and LAs are committed to the sharing of information in advance of test purchasing exercises and that is the occasion when such issues can be discussed.

---

1 Reducing administrative burdens: effective inspection and enforcement (March 2005)

2 Formerly LACORS

[3] www.lbro.org.uk

2.20 A further two factors are also relevant. Firstly, whilst a gambling operator with multiple premises may be actively promoting compliance with policies and procedures, for example age verification training, and improving their results nationally, an individual premises that is a part of their estate may still be considered a significant risk by a LA. As noted above (2.12) the Concordat states that:

> 'LAs are concerned with risks within their geographical boundaries and which would have a high impact at a local level.'

2.21 Secondly, it should be recognised that LAs work within a wider local authority structure and set of policy priorities which will influence the approach they take to gambling in general and test purchasing in particular. As the Concordat notes:

> 'The Commission recognises that LAs will each have different priorities and that this will have a bearing on their approach to the licensing of premises and to compliance. It is a matter for the local democratic process to make such decisions and to reflect local concerns.'

2.22 For premises based operators tests may be conducted in conjunction with LAs and other local authority departments.

SAMPLE SIZE AND METHODOLOGY

2.23 Sample size will vary and will, at least in part, be dependent on the purpose of the exercise. In general terms the Commission seeks to minimise regulatory effort (and any consequent burden on operators) whilst maximising the impact of that effort in improving regulatory outcomes.

2.24 The Commission's test purchasing methodology is designed:

- to ensure that the work is conducted in a standardised way irrespective of the personnel employed. It is in part informed by the existing LG Regulation Guide to Test Purchasing (July 2009). The methodology is designed to ensure that tests are conducted fairly, for example an age verification exercise would not use a young person who appears to be older than they are and also avoids the risk of entrapment
- to ensure that the Commission complies with all relevant legal requirements, including but not limited to the Human Rights Act, Data Protection Act and Regulation of Investigatory Powers Act
- in such a way as to achieve an answer to the question being set – for example how effectively a policy and procedure is being implemented. Were a different question to be asked, a different methodology might apply.

INFORMATION SHARING AND DISCLOSURE

2.25 The Commission is committed to operating in an open and transparent manner. The inclination is to disclose information rather than retain it. Set against this there are a number of issues that require consideration. They include the following:

- legal requirements
- commercial confidentiality
- information which it is not in the public interest to disclose
- information which, if disclosed, may impede the desired regulatory outcomes.

2.26 The Commission will aim to inform the operator at the earliest opportunity once the testing of all of their premises (those that we plan to test) is complete to enable them to conduct any investigation that they consider necessary and to enable them to inspect records such as CCTV footage before it is deleted.

2.27 The expectation is that it is the responsibility of the operator to inform their staff of any test results as they see fit.

2.28 While the Commission will normally publish the results of thematic test purchase exercises at the earliest appropriate time, the Commission will not normally comment on specific enforcement activity until and unless formal regulatory action is taken (for example a formal warning or imposition of another sanction).

2.29 For test purchase exercises the Commission would expect to disclose, in aggregate terms, an operator's result but will not publicly disclose details relating to specific premises.

2.30 Both as a matter of courtesy and to allow for the correction of any factual errors operators may be offered advance sight of a press release.

2.31 When an exercise has involved joint working with LAs the relevant authorities could expect to be supplied with a copy of the Commission's press release in advance of publication. Should the LA decide to issue their own press release the expectation is that similarly, it will be shared with the Commission in advance of publication.

Gambling Commission May 2011

BETTING

CONDITIONS AND CODES OF PRACTICE APPLICABLE TO:
NON-REMOTE GENERAL BETTING LICENCES
NON-REMOTE POOL BETTING LICENCES
NON-REMOTE BETTING INTERMEDIARY LICENCES
October 2010

6.2100–6.2120 Your licence is subject to certain conditions and codes of practice, these are detailed in the following pages

STATUTORY CONDITIONS ATTACHED BY VIRTUE OF THE ACT

SOCIAL RESPONSIBILITY

This licence is subject to a condition that the licensee ensures compliance with any relevant social responsibility provision of a code of practice issued by the Commission. The social responsibility provisions that are relevant to the activities authorised by this licence are set out in the section entitled Codes of Practice.
(Sections 24 and 82(1) Gambling Act 2005)

RETURN OF STAKES TO CHILDREN

The following condition applies to all operating licences except pool betting operating licences restricted to football only

This licence is subject to a condition that if the licensee (or anyone employed by the licensee to perform an operational function within the meaning of Section 80 of the Act) becomes aware that a child or young person is using or has used facilities for gambling provided in reliance on the licence, the licensee:

(a) must return any money paid in respect of the use of those facilities (whether by way of fee, stake or otherwise) by the child or young person as soon as is reasonably practicable; and

(b) may not give a prize to the child or young person.

This condition does not apply to use of a Category D gaming machine.
(Section 83(1))

The following condition applies to pool betting operating licences restricted to football only

This licence is subject to a condition that if the licensee (or anyone employed by the licensee to perform an operational function within the meaning of Section 80 of the Act) becomes aware that a child is using or has used facilities for gambling provided in reliance on the licence, the licensee;

(a) must return any money paid in respect of the use of those facilities (whether by way of fee, stake or otherwise) by the child as soon as is reasonably practicable, and

(b) may not give a prize to the child.

This condition does not apply to use of a Category D gaming machine.
(Section 83(1))

OTHER STATUTORY CONDITIONS

This licence is subject to a condition that nothing may be done in reliance on the licence in relation to a bet on the outcome of a lottery which forms part of the National Lottery.

(Section 95(2))

The following condition applies to all general betting operating licences only

This licence is subject to a condition that bets may be accepted on behalf of the licensee only by:
(a) the licensee;
(b) a person employed by the licensee under a written contract of employment; or
(c) the holder of another general betting operating licence.
(Section 92(1))

The following condition applies to all pool betting operating licences only

This licence is subject to a condition that bets may be accepted on behalf of the licensee only:
(a) by the licensee,
(b) by a person employed by the licensee under a written contract of employment,
(c) by the holder of another pool betting operating licence, or
(d) by an agent, provided the agent is authorised by the licensee in writing to accept bets on behalf of the licensee, the agent is an adult, at the time of accepting the bet the agent is on a track, the bet is accepted in reliance on an occasional use notice and the bet is in connection with a horse race or dog race
(e) where this pool betting operating licence authorises (whether expressly or impliedly) the provision of facilities for football pools, by an adult or young person authorised by the licensee in writing to make documents or other facilities available in connection with the licensed activities, to receive entries on behalf of the licensee, to receive payments on behalf of the licensee, or to make payments of winnings on behalf of the licensee.
(Section 93(1),(2) &(3))

COMMISSION GENERAL CONDITIONS

The Commission's complete suite of Licence Conditions to be attached to operating licences pursuant to section 75 of the Act includes some conditions which may not apply to your licence. Where that is the case the irrelevant conditions have not been reproduced below. The full list of Licence Conditions and Codes of Practice are contained within the Commission's Publication "Licence Conditions and Codes of Practice"

QUALIFIED PERSONS AND PERSONAL LICENCES

Qualified persons

THE FOLLOWING CONDITION APPLIES TO ALL OPERATING LICENCES ISSUED TO SMALL-SCALE OPERATORS

In this condition the terms 'small-scale operator', 'qualifying position' and 'qualified person' have the meanings respectively ascribed to them by the Gambling Act 2005 (Definition of Small-scale Operator) Regulations 2006.
Schedule X[1] lists those individuals notified to the Commission as qualified persons.
If, whilst the licensee remains a small-scale operator, an individual begins or ceases to occupy a qualifying position in relation to the licensee, the licensee must within 28 days apply to the Commission under s104(1)(b) for amendment of the details of the licence set out in Schedule X[1].
An application for amendment under s104(1)(b) may be made in advance of an individual beginning or ceasing to occupy a qualifying position provided it specifies the date from which the change to which it relates is to be effective.

[1] The schedules mentioned here will be attached to individual licences.

THE FOLLOWING CONDITION APPLIES TO ALL GENERAL BETTING LICENCES ISSUED TO SMALL-SCALE OPERATORS

Schedule Y to this licence lists those of the licensee's employees whose details have been provided to the Commission as authorised by the licensee to accept bets on the licensee's behalf on a track otherwise than under the supervision of a qualified person present on the same track.

Should the licensee wish to add an individual to the list or remove the name of an individual from the list the licensee must make application to the Commission under s104(1)(b) for amendment of that detail of the licence. Any employee the licensee wishes to add to the list may act unsupervised pending amendment of the licence provided a valid amendment application has been lodged with the Commission.

In this condition 'qualified person' has the same meaning as in the Gambling Act 2005 (Definition of Small-scale Operator) Regulations 2006.

PERSONAL LICENCES

(a) Subject to (e) and (f) below licensees must ensure:
  (i) that each individual who occupies one of the management offices specified in (b) below in or in respect of the licensee or in connection with the licensed activities holds a personal licence authorising the performance of the functions of that office (hereafter 'a personal management licence')
  (ii) that at least one person occupies at least one of those offices.

(b) The specified management offices are those offices (whether or not held by a director in the case of a licensee which is a company, a partner in the case of a licensee which is a partnership or an officer of the association in the case of a licensee which is an unincorporated association) the occupier of which is by virtue of the terms of their appointment responsible for:
  - the overall management and direction of the licensee's business or affairs
  - the licensee's finance function as head of that function
  - the licensee's gambling regulatory compliance function as head of that function
  - the licensee's marketing function as head of that function
  - the licensee's information technology function as head of that function in so far as it relates to gambling-related information technology and software
  - oversight of the day to day management of the licensed activities at an identified number of premises licensed under Part 8 of the Act or across an identified geographical area
  - in the case of casino and bingo licences only, oversight of the day to day management of a single set of premises licensed under Part 8 of the Act.

(c) Licensees must take all reasonable steps to ensure that anything done in the performance of the functions of a specified management office is done in accordance with the terms and conditions of the holder's personal management licence.

(d) Where an individual is authorised by a personal licence and that licence comes under review under section 116(2) of the Act, the operating licensee must comply with any conditions subsequently imposed on that licence by the Commission about redeployment, supervision, or monitoring of the individual's work and any requirements of the Commission in respect of such matters applicable during the period of the review.

(e) Paragraphs (a) to (d) above shall not apply to a licensee for so long as the licensee is a 'small-scale operator' as defined in the Gambling Act 2005 (Definition of Small-scale Operator) Regulations 2006 ('the Regulations').

(f) During the period of 3 years commencing with the date on which a licensee ceases to be a small-scale operator paragraphs (a) to (e) above shall apply subject to the proviso that the phrase 'each individual' in paragraph (a)(i) shall not include any individual who was a 'qualified person' (as defined in the Regulations) in relation to the licensee 28 days immediately prior to the licensee ceasing to be a small-scale operator.

FINANCIAL ROBUSTNESS

Notification of shareholders

All company licensees must notify the Commission of the name and address of any person who becomes a shareholder in the company or its holding company holding 3% or more of the issued share capital of the company or its holding company; or any existing shareholder who acquires a holding of 3% or more of the issued share capital of the company or its holding company.

In this condition 'holding company' has the meaning ascribed to that term by section 1159 of the Companies Act 2006 or any statutory modification or re-enactment thereof.

PROTECTION OF CUSTOMER FUNDS

Licensees who hold customer funds for use in future gambling must set out clearly, in information made available to customers in writing, whether they protect customers' funds in the event of insolvency and the method by which this is achieved.

CASH HANDLING

Licensees, as part of their internal controls and financial accounting systems, must have and put into effect policies and procedures concerning the handling of cash, and cash equivalents (ie bankers drafts, cheques and debit cards), designed to minimise the risk of crimes such as money laundering, to avoid the giving of illicit credit and to provide assurance that gambling activities are being conducted fairly.

GENERAL 'FAIR AND OPEN' PROVISIONS

Licensees must satisfy themselves that the terms on which gambling is offered are not unfair under the Unfair Terms in Consumer Contracts Regulations 1999 and, where applicable, meet the reasonableness test under the Unfair Contract Terms Act 1977. An accurate summary of the contractual terms on which gambling is offered must be made available to customers and set out in plain and intelligible language.

Customers must be notified of changes to terms before they come into effect.

BETTING INTERMEDIARIES

The following condition applies to betting intermediary operating licences only

Licensees must not lay bets on their own behalf when operating in their capacity as a public tic-tac on a track.

Tic-tacs must act only in relation to bets between holders of general betting operating licences (whether acting as principal or agent or through their authorised employees).

POOL BETTING

The following condition applies to all pool betting operating licences except those restricted to football only

Licensees must inform the Commission, within 14 days, in writing, of any person they authorise under section 93(2) of the Act to offer pool betting on a track in connection with a horserace or dog race in reliance on an occasional use notice. In doing so, they must include the terms and conditions under which this has been agreed, and provide contact details of the management and key staff of those that are authorised.
Licensees and any person they so authorise must produce and retain a record of the transactions relevant to each pool that they offer. The record must be capable of identifying individual bets into the pool and relating these to subsequent payment of winnings where applicable. Licensees must make this information available to the Commission on request.

The following condition only applies to all pool betting operating licences which authorise football pools

Licensees must inform the Commission, within 14 days, in writing, of any person they authorise under Section 93(3) of the Act in respect of football pool betting. In doing so, they must include the terms and conditions under which this has been agreed.
Licensees and any person they so authorise must produce and retain a record of the transactions relevant to each pool that they offer. The record must be capable of identifying individual bets into the pool and relating these to the subsequent payment of winnings where applicable. Licensees must make this information available to the Commission on request.

The following condition applies to all pool betting operating licences only

Licensees must produce annual accounts which should be certified by a qualified independent accountant. Licensees must make copies available to the Commission.

ACCESS TO PREMISES

Licensees must have and put into effect policies and procedures (including staff training programmes) designed to ensure that their staff co-operate with the Commission's enforcement officers in the proper performance of their compliance functions and are made aware of those officers' rights of entry to premises contained in Part 15 of the Act.

INFORMATION REQUIREMENTS

Reporting suspicion of offences etc

Licensees must provide the Commission with any information that they:

- know relates to or suspect may relate to the commission of an offence under the Act, including an offence resulting from a breach of a licence condition or a code provision having the effect of a licence condition
- suspect may lead the Commission to consider making an order to void a bet.

Licensees who accept bets, or facilitate the making or acceptance of bets between others, on the outcome of horse races or other sporting events governed by one of the sport governing bodies for the time being included in Part 3 of Schedule 6 to the Act must also provide the relevant sport governing body with sufficient information to conduct an effective investigation if the licensee suspects that information in their possession may:

- lead the Commission to consider making an order to void a bet
- relate to a breach of a rule on betting applied by that sport governing body.

REPORTING 'KEY EVENTS'

A key event is an event that could have a significant impact on the nature or structure of a licensee's business. Licensees must notify the Commission of the occurrence of any of the following key events as soon as reasonably practicable and in any event within five working days of the licensee becoming aware of the event's occurrence[2].

- in the case of licensees which are companies, a petition being presented for their winding up or the winding up of any group company of theirs, or they or any group company being placed in administration or receivership: in this condition a 'group company' is any subsidiary or holding company of the licensee – as those terms are defined in section 1159 of the Companies Act 2006 or any statutory modification or re-enactment thereof – and any subsidiary of such holding company
- in the case of a licensee who is an individual (or a partner in a partnership licensee) their being presented with a petition for their bankruptcy or sequestration or their entering into an individual voluntary agreement
- where the licensee is required to have their accounts independently audited, any unplanned change of auditor including a change prompted by a dispute or resulting from auditors being unable or unwilling to sign an unqualified audit report
- the departure from the licensee's business of any person occupying a 'qualifying position' as defined by Regulation 2(2) of the Gambling Act 2005 (Definition of Small-scale Operator) Regulations 2006
- any breach of a covenant given to a bank or other lender
- any default in making repayment of the whole or any part of a loan on its due date
- any court judgments remaining unpaid 14 days after the date of judgment
- the commencement of any material litigation against the licensee
- the imposition of a disciplinary sanction, including dismissal, against the holder of a personal licence or a person occupying a qualifying position for gross misconduct; or the resignation of a personal licence holder or person occupying a qualifying position following commencement of disciplinary proceedings in respect of gross misconduct against that person
- in the case of remote gambling, the commencement or cessation of trading on website domains (including WAP URLs) or broadcast media through which the licensee provides gambling facilities.

---

2 Key events can be reported securely online at the Commission's website at www.gamblingcommission.gov.uk or by email to key.events@gamblingcommission.gov.uk or posted to Key Events, Compliance Administration Team, Gambling Commission, Victoria Square House, Victoria Square, Birmingham B2 4BP

GENERAL AND REGULATORY RETURNS

On request, licensees must provide the Commission with such information as the Commission may require about the use made of facilities provided in accordance with this licence, and the manner in which gambling authorised by this licence and the licensee's business in relation to that gambling are carried on, including in particular information about:

- the numbers of people making use of the facilities and the frequency of such use
- the range of gambling activities provided by the licensee and the numbers of staff employed in connection with them
- the licensee's policies in relation to, and experiences of, problem gambling.

In particular within 28 days of the end of each quarterly period or, for those only submitting annual returns, within 42 days of the end of each annual period, licensees must submit a Regulatory Return to the Commission containing such information as the Commission may from time to time require.[3]

[3] Regulatory returns can be submitted securely online at the Commission's website at www.gamblingcommission.gov.uk For operators unable to access this system, the forms and a guide to completing them can be requested from the Commission and returned by email to Regulatory.Returns@gamblingcommission.gov.uk or by post to Regulatory Returns, Compliance Administration Team, Gambling Commission, Victoria Square House, Victoria Square, Birmingham, B2 4BP.

PRIMARY GAMBLING ACTIVITY

Gaming machines maybe made available for use in licensed betting premises only at times when there are also sufficient facilities for betting available.
Such facilities for betting must include the provision of information that enables the customer to access details of the events on which bets can be made and to be able to place those bets, obtain details of the outcome of the events, calculate the outcome of their bets and be paid or credited with any winnings.
Where licensees provide facilities for betting only by means of betting machines (machines which are designed or adapted for the purpose of making of accepting bets on future real events) the licensee must ensure that the number of betting machines is greater than the number of gaming machines which are made available for use in reliance on the premises licence.

SECRETARY OF STATE GENERAL CONDITIONS

None at present

CODES OF PRACTICE

INTRODUCTION

This is the Commission's principal code of practice, issued under section 24 of the Gambling Act 2005, as revised with effect from 1 January 2009. There are two types of provision in the code:

- social responsibility provisions: compliance with these is a condition of licences; therefore any breach of them by an operator may lead the Commission to review the operator's licence with a view to suspension, revocation or the imposition of a financial penalty and would also expose the operator to the risk of prosecution; and
- ordinary code provisions: these do not have the status of licence conditions, but are admissible in evidence in criminal or civil proceedings and must be taken into account in any case in which the court or tribunal think them relevant and by the Commission in the exercise of its functions. Any breach of ordinary code provisions by an operator may be taken into account by the Commission on a licence review, but cannot lead to imposition of a financial penalty. These code provisions generally set out good practice in these areas.

FINANCIAL REQUIREMENTS

The following code applies to all general betting operating licences, all betting intermediary operating licences and all pool betting operating licences, except those restricted to football pools only

Ordinary code provision

As part of their procedures for compliance with the requirements in respect of the prevention and detection of money laundering in the Proceeds of Crime Act 2002 and the Terrorism Act 2000, licensees should:

- unless there is a specific reason not to do so, appoint one or more nominated officers whose duty it is to take overall responsibility for the anti-money laundering procedures within the operation, in particular with respect to Suspicious Activity Reporting; and ensure, through appropriate training and guidance, that all staff who handle money or accounts or accept bets are aware of their duties under anti-money laundering legislation to report all suspicious activity to the nominated officer in a timely manner or, where there is no such nominated officer, directly and promptly to the police. It is the nominated officer's duty to consider such reports and to forward them where appropriate to the Serious Organised Crime Agency
- adopt (or reflect in their procedures) the Association of British Bookmakers' guidelines.

Ordinary code provision

In order to help prevent activities related to money laundering licensees should take into account the Commission's advice on the Proceeds of Crime Act 2002, *Duties and responsibilities under the Proceeds of Crime Act 2002. Advice for operators (excluding casino operators).*

PROTECTION OF CHILDREN AND OTHER VULNERABLE PERSONS

Combating problem gambling

Social responsibility code provision

Licensees must have and put into effect policies and procedures intended to promote socially responsible gambling.

Licensees' policies and procedures for socially responsible gambling must include but need not be confined to:

- the specific policies and procedures required by the following provisions of section 2 of this code
- a commitment to and how they will contribute to research into the prevention and treatment of problem gambling
- a commitment to and how they will contribute to public education on the risks of gambling and how to gamble safely
- a commitment to and how they will contribute to the identification and treatment of problem gamblers.

ACCESS TO GAMBLING BY CHILDREN AND YOUNG PERSONS

Social responsibility code provision

Licensees must have and put into effect policies and procedures designed to prevent underage gambling, and monitor the effectiveness of these.

This must include procedures for:

- checking the age of apparently underage customers

- removing from adult-only licensed premises anyone who appears to be underage who tries to access the gambling facilities and cannot produce an acceptable form of identification
- taking action when there are attempts by under-18s to enter adult-only premises
- refusing entry to any adult-only area of a track to anyone unable to produce an acceptable form of identification
- taking action when there are unlawful attempts to enter the adult-only areas.

Licensees must not deliberately provide facilities for gambling in such a way as to appeal particularly to children or, except in the case of football pools, young people, for example by reflecting or being associated with youth culture.

In premises restricted to adults, service must be refused in any circumstances where any adult is accompanied by a child or young person.

Licensees must take all reasonable steps to ensure that all staff understand their responsibilities for preventing underage gambling. This must include appropriate training which must cover the legal requirements on returning stakes and not paying prizes to underage customers.

Licensees must only accept identification which:

- contains a photograph from which the individual can be identified
- states the individual's date of birth
- is valid
- is legible and has no visible signs of tampering or reproduction.

In the case of non-remote pool betting licensees, where pool entries or payments are collected door to door by the licensee or the licensee's authorised agent the licensee's procedures must include procedures for:

- checking the age of apparently underage entrants to the pool; and
- taking action when there are unlawful attempts to enter the pool.

Ordinary code provision

The Commission considers acceptable forms of identification to include any identification carrying the PASS logo (for example Citizencard or Validate); a driving licence (including a provisional licence) with photocard; or a passport.

Licensees should put into effect procedures that require their staff to check the age of any customer who appears to them to be under 21.

Licensees should consider permanent exclusion from premises for any adult accompanied by a child or young person on more than one occasion to premises restricted to adults, or if there is reason to believe the offence was committed knowingly or recklessly.

Procedures should be put into effect for dealing with cases where a child or young person repeatedly attempts to gamble on premises restricted to adults, including oral warnings, reporting the offence to the Gambling Commission and the police, and making available information on problem gambling.

INFORMATION ON HOW TO GAMBLE RESPONSIBLY AND HELP FOR PROBLEM GAMBLERS

Social responsibility code provision

Licensees must make information readily available to their customers on how to gamble responsibly and how to access information about, and help in respect of, problem gambling.

The information must cover:

- any measures provided by the licensee to help individuals monitor or control their gambling, such as restricting the duration of a gambling session or the amount of money they can spend
- timers or other forms of reminders or 'reality checks' where available
- self-exclusion options
- information about the availability of further help or advice.

The information must be directed to all customers whether or not licensees also make available material which is directed specifically at customers who may be 'problem gamblers'.

For gambling premises, information must be available in all areas where gambling facilities are provided and adjacent to ATMs where these are not located in a gambling area. As a minimum, information must be displayed prominently on posters appropriate to the size and layout of the premises and contained in leaflets that may be taken away. Licensees must take all reasonable steps to ensure that this information is also readily accessible in locations which enable the customer to obtain it discreetly.

Ordinary code provision

Licensees who market their services in one or more foreign languages should make available in that, or those, foreign languages:

- the information on how to gamble responsibly and access to help referred to above
- the players' guides to any game, bet or lottery required to be made available to customers under provisions in this code
- the summary of the contractual terms on which gambling is offered, which is required to be provided to customers as a condition of the licensee's operating licence.

CUSTOMER INTERACTION

Social responsibility code provision

Licensees must put into effect policies and procedures for customer interaction where they have concerns that a customer's behaviour may indicate problem gambling. The policies must include:

- identification of the appropriate level of management who may initiate customer interaction and the procedures for doing so
- the types of behaviour that will be logged/reported to the appropriate level of staff and which may trigger customer interaction at an appropriate moment
- the circumstances in which consideration should be given to refusing service to customers and/or barring them from the operator's gambling premises
- training for all staff on their respective responsibilities, in particular so that they know who is designated to deal with problem gambling issues.

But such policies and procedures must be consistent with, and implemented with due regard to, licensees' duties in respect of the health and safety of their staff.

SELF-EXCLUSION

Social responsibility code provision

Licensees must have and put into effect procedures for self-exclusion and take all reasonable steps to refuse service or to otherwise prevent an individual who has entered a self-exclusion agreement from participating in gambling.

Licensees must, as soon as practicable, take all reasonable steps to prevent any marketing material being sent to a self-excluded customer.

Licensees must take steps to remove the name and details of a self-excluded individual from any marketing databases used by the company or group (or otherwise flag that person as an individual to whom marketing material must not be sent), within two days of receiving the completed self-exclusion notification.

This covers any marketing material relating to gambling, or other activities that take place on the premises where gambling may take place. However, it would not extend to blanket marketing which is targeted at a particular geographical area and where the excluded individual would not knowingly be included.

Licensees must close any customer accounts of an individual who has entered a self exclusion agreement and return any funds held in the customer account. It is not

sufficient merely to prevent an individual from withdrawing funds from their customer account whilst still accepting wagers from them. Where the giving of credit is permitted, the licensee may retain details of the amount owed to them by the individual, although the account must not be active.
Licensees must put into effect procedures designed to ensure that an individual who has self-excluded cannot gain access to gambling. These procedures must include:

- a register of those excluded with appropriate records (name, address, other details, and any membership or account details that may be held by the operator)
- photo identification (where available and in particular where enforcement of the system may depend on photographic ID), and a signature
- staff training to ensure that staff are able to enforce the systems
- the removal of those persons found in the gambling area or attempting to gamble from the premises.

Ordinary code provision

Self-exclusion procedures should require individuals to take positive action in order to self-exclude. This can be a signature on a self-exclusion form.
Wherever practicable, individuals should be able to self-exclude without having to enter gambling premises.
Before an individual self-excludes, licensees should provide or make available sufficient information about what the consequences of self-exclusion are.
Licensees should take all reasonable steps to extend the self-exclusion to premises of the same type owned by the operator in the customer's local area. In setting the bounds of that area licensees may take into account the customer's address (if known to them), anything else known to them about the distance the customer ordinarily travels to gamble and any specific request the customer may make.
Licensees should encourage the customer to consider extending their self exclusion to other licensees' gambling premises in the customer's local area.
Customers should be given the opportunity to discuss self-exclusion in private, where possible.
Licensees should take steps to ensure that:

- the self-exclusion period is a minimum of six months and give customers the option of extending this to a total of at least five years
- a customer who has decided to enter a self-exclusion agreement is given the opportunity to do so immediately without any cooling-off period. However, if the customer wishes to consider the self-exclusion further (for example to discuss with problem gambling groups) the customer may return at a later date to enter into self-exclusion
- at the end of the period chosen by the customer (and at least six months later), the self-exclusion remains in place, unless the customer takes positive action in order to gamble again. No marketing material should be sent to the individual unless the individual has taken positive action in order to gamble again, and has agreed to accept such material
- where a customer chooses not to renew the self-exclusion, and makes a positive request to begin gambling again, the customer is given one day to cool off before being allowed access to gambling facilities. The contact must be made via telephone or in person.

The licensee should retain the records relating to a self-exclusion agreement at least until the agreement has been formally ended.
(Please note that the Commission does not require the licensee to carry out any particular assessment or make any judgement as to whether the previously self-excluded individual should again be permitted access to gambling. The requirement to take positive action in person or over the phone is purely to a) check that the customer has considered the decision to access gambling again and allow them to consider the implications; and b) implement the one day cooling-off period and explain why this has been put in place.)

EMPLOYMENT OF CHILDREN AND YOUNG PERSONS

The following code applies to all pool betting operating licences restricted to football only

Ordinary code provision

Licensees who employ young persons (16 and 17 year olds) to sell tickets, collect payments or pay out winnings should have and put into effect policies and procedures designed to ensure that all staff, including staff who are young persons themselves, are made aware that the law prohibits underage gambling, and that tickets may only be sold to persons aged 16 or over.

The following code applies to all general betting and all pool betting operating licences only

Ordinary code provision

Licensees who employ children (under-16-year-olds) and young persons (those aged 16 and 17) should be aware that it is an offence:

(a) to employ children to provide facilities for gambling in connection with football pools;
(b) otherwise to employ children and young persons to provide facilities for gambling;
(c) if gaming machines are sited on the premises, for their contracts of employment to require them, or for them to be permitted, to perform a function in connection with a gaming machine at any time; and
(d) to employ them to carry out any other function on betting licensed premises while any gambling activity is being carried on in reliance on the premises licence.

As to c) it should be noted that in the Commission's view the relevant provision of the Act applies to any function performed in connection with a gaming machine. This includes servicing or cleaning such a machine.

Accordingly, licensees should have and put into effect policies and procedures designed to ensure that:

- children are never asked to perform tasks within (a) above
- children and young persons are never asked to perform tasks within b) above
- all staff, including those who are children or young persons themselves, are instructed about the laws relating to access to gambling by children and young persons

and should consider adopting a policy that:

- children and young persons are not employed to work on betting licensed premises at any time when the premises are open for business
- gaming machines are turned off if children and young persons are working on the premises outside the hours when the premises are open for business.

PROVISION OF CREDIT BY LICENSEES AND THE USE OF CREDIT CARDS

Social responsibility code provision

Licensees who choose to accept credit cards must:

- accept payment by credit card for gambling only where that payment is made to a customer account
- make available for gambling, funds deposited via credit card only after the card issuer has approved the transaction.

The following code applies to all general betting and all pool betting operating licences only

Ordinary code provision

Licensees who choose to offer credit to members of the public who are not themselves gambling operators should also:

- have procedures for checking and scoring applications for credit from such customers, for setting, and for the increase of, credit limits
- explain these procedures to customers
- set a maximum credit limit for each customer and not permit customers to exceed that limit without further application
- apply a 24-hour delay between receiving a request for an increase in a credit limit and granting it in those cases where the limit exceeds that which the operator had previously set
- not require a minimum spend within a set time period
- take all reasonable steps to ensure that offers of credit are not sent to vulnerable persons, including those who have self-excluded from gambling
- ensure that information about an offer of credit includes a risk warning of what may happen in the event of default.

MONEY LENDING BETWEEN CUSTOMERS

The following code applies to all general betting operating licences only

Ordinary code provision

Licensees should seek to prevent systematic or organised money lending between customers on their premises. As a minimum, they should have arrangements in place to ensure staff are requested to report any instances of substantial money lending when they become aware of them.

'FAIR AND OPEN' PROVISIONS

Social responsibility code provision

Licensees must be able to provide evidence to the Commission, if required, showing how they satisfied themselves that their terms are not unfair.

The following code applies to all general betting and all betting intermediary operating licences only

Social responsibility code provision

Licensees must set out within the full rules that they make available, the core elements for the acceptance and settlement of bets. These rules must cover:

- the circumstances under which the operator will void a bet
- treatment of errors, late bets and related contingencies
- availability of odds for any ante-post, early show or starting price betting, and treatment of place, forecast bets etc
- treatment of withdrawals, non-runners, and reformed markets
- maximum payout limiting liability for a specific betting product or generally
- any charges made to customers for the use of betting services or products, and how these are calculated (including deductions from winnings for commission, or in respect of withdrawn horses etc)
- means or medium by which the outcome of an event will be determined
- the rules for the event itself to be specified (eg horserace bets only to be accepted where the racing is subject to Horseracing Regulatory Authority rules)
- where bets are accepted on 'pari-mutuel' terms

- any special arrangements for settling bets on 'coupled' horses.

Where special rules have been agreed in relation to a particular bet these must not be overridden by any conflicting rules or subsequent rule changes.

Licensees must issue a betting slip or an electronic acknowledgement (other than in the case of telephone betting) for each transaction which includes information as to the operator's name and contact details, and words equivalent to 'Bets are accepted in accordance with the operator's rules'.

The following code applies to all general betting operating licences only

Social responsibility code provision

In their terms on which bets may be placed (required to be displayed in accordance with mandatory conditions attaching to their premises licences) licensees must give prominence to their rules concerning voiding, late bets and maximum payouts.

When providing facilities for betting on-course, licensees must display on their 'joints' in an intelligible format:

- any rules that differ from Tattersalls' 'Rules on Betting' or the British Greyhound Racing Board's 'Regulations for the conduct of on-course bookmaking' as applicable[4]
- any types of unorthodox bets accepted (such as forecast betting, betting without the favourite, distance betting etc)
- whether win-only or each way bets are accepted
- any concessions or bonuses offered
- all of the runners and the odds available to the public
- the operator's trading name and contact address
- the minimum bet accepted
- the maximum guaranteed liability.

Licensees operating within the ring at horserace tracks must issue customers with a betting slip or ticket for each transaction accepted. Betting slips or tickets must include the following information:

- operator's name and contact details
- race day name or code, date and race number
- name and/or number of the selection
- the stake and potential return
- the odds, or whether the bet will be settled according to the Starting Price
- the type of bet.

Any special rules which have been agreed in relation to a particular bet must not be overridden by any conflicting rules or subsequent rule changes.

4 The references to Tattersalls' 'Rules on Betting' and the British Greyhound Racing Board's Regulations for the conduct of on-course bookmaking' reflect the current position and may need to be amended in future.

Ordinary code provision

Where licensees offer to accept bets, or facilitate the making or acceptance of bets between others, on the outcome of a sport regulated by a sport governing body for the time being included in Part 3 of Schedule 6 of the Act they should take all reasonable steps to familiarise themselves with the rules applied by that body on betting, in particular betting by registered participants.

MARKETING

Social responsibility code provision

If a licensee makes available to any customer or potential customer any incentive or reward scheme or other arrangement under which the customer may receive money, goods, services or any other advantage (including the discharge in whole or in part of any liability of his) ('the benefit') the scheme must be designed to operate, and be operated, in such a way that:

(a) the circumstances in which, and conditions subject to which, the benefit is available are clearly set out and readily accessible to the customers to whom it is offered;

(b) neither the receipt nor the value or amount of the benefit is:

   (i) dependent on the customer gambling for a pre-determined length of time or with a predetermined frequency; or

   (ii) altered or increased if the qualifying activity or spend is reached within a shorter time than the whole period over which the benefit is offered;

(c) if the value of the benefit increases with the amount the customer spends it does so at a rate no greater than that at which the amount spent increases;

and further that:

(d) if the benefit comprises free or subsidised travel or accommodation which facilitates the customer's attendance at particular licensed premises the terms on which it is offered are not directly related to the level of the customer's prospective gambling.

Ordinary code provision

Licensees should only offer incentive or reward schemes in which the benefit available is proportionate to the type and level of customers' gambling.

Ordinary code provision

All advertising of gambling products and services should be undertaken in a socially responsible manner. In particular, licensees should comply with the advertising codes of practice which apply to the form and media in which they advertise their gambling facilities or services, and for media not explicitly covered should apply the principles included in these codes of practice as if they were explicitly covered. Licensees should also follow any relevant industry code of practice on advertising.

However, the particular restriction on allowing people aged under 25 to appear in adverts need not be applied to point of sale advertising material, provided that the images used depict the sporting activity that may be gambled on and not the activity of gambling itself and do not offend any other aspect of the advertising codes.

COMPLAINTS AND DISPUTES

Social responsibility code provision

Licensees must put into effect a written procedure for handling customer complaints and disputes.

In this code a 'complaint' means a complaint about any aspect of the licensee's conduct of the licensed activities, and a 'dispute' is any complaint which:

(a) is not resolved at the first stage of the complaints procedure; and

(b) relates to the outcome of the complainant's gambling transaction.

Licensees must ensure that:

- customers are told the name and status of the person to contact about their complaint
- customers are given a copy of the complaints procedure on request or on making a complaint
- all complaints are handled in accordance with the procedure.

Licensees must also ensure that they have arrangements in place for disputes to be referred to an independent third party. Customers whose disputes are not resolved to their satisfaction by use of the operator's complaints procedure may refer those disputes to this independent third party.

The arrangements under which such complaints are referred may, but need not, provide for the third party's decision to be binding on the licensee and the customer.

Licensees must keep a record of all complaints that are not resolved at the first stage of the complaints procedure.
Licensees must arrange for a copy of the decision on, or a note of the outcome of, each dispute referred to the independent party to be provided to the Commission quarterly, either by the independent party or by the licensee.

GAMBLING LICENSEES' STAFF

Social responsibility code provision

Licensees must take all reasonable steps to ensure that staff involved in the provision of facilities for gambling are made aware of advice on socially responsible gambling and of where to get confidential advice should their gambling become hard to control.

POOL BETTING

The following code applies to all pool betting operating licences only

Social responsibility code provision

Licensees or any person they authorise to offer pool betting on their behalf under authority of section 93 of the Act must publish their rules relevant to the following:

- the deduction levels for overheads, taxes, profits etc, expressed as a percentage, from each available pool
- the rounding of winning dividends to a whole unit
- the procedure for when there is no winner of the pool, and the circumstances in which the pool is carried over
- the period of time in which a winning bet may be claimed from the pool operator.

The following code applies to all pool betting operating licences authorised to offer pool betting on dog races

Social responsibility code provision

Licensees or any person they authorise to offer pool betting on their behalf under authority of section 93 of the Act, must only accept bets through equipment capable of communicating bets to a central recording system.
The equipment must supply the person placing the bet with a betting slip or ticket containing the following information:

- the date on which the bet is made
- the amount of the stake
- the identity of the track, the number or time of the race and the pool in respect of which the bet is made
- the selection or selections or combination of selections as indicated
- means of identifying the equipment recording the bet.

The central recording system must collect all bets made to each of the operator's pools and all information required to calculate the winnings of each pool and be capable of storing this information for subsequent retrieval if required by the Commission.
Licensees and any person they authorise to offer pool betting on their behalf under authority of section 93 of the Act must:

- provide a public display system within sight of all of the operator's terminals capable of accepting pool bets situated on-course. The system must display the potential dividend returns in respect of win and place outcomes from each pool operated, and in at least one place the units staked on all types of combination bets offered. This information is to be updated whilst the pool market is open. Following conclusion of the event to which the pool relates, the total amount payable as winning dividends must be displayed as soon as practicable

- display prominently the minimum stake that will be accepted as a bet.

INFORMATION REQUIREMENTS

Ordinary code provision

The Commission expects licensees to work with the Commission in an open and cooperative way and to inform the Commission of any matters that the Commission would reasonably need to be aware of in exercising its regulatory functions. These are matters that will have a material impact on the licensee's business or on the licensee's ability to conduct its business. Such matters, which should be notified to the Commission as soon as reasonably practicable[5], include the following:

- the departure from the licensee's business of any person named in the licence application, or that person's successor, who holds a personal management licence, but who does not occupy a 'qualifying position'
- any reduction in the number of staff employed by the licensee where that has a material impact on the licensee's business
- the acquisition or disposal by the licensee of gambling premises or pitches where that has a material impact on the size or nature of the licensee's business
- in the case of corporate licensees, the disposal or acquisition of any group company where that has a material impact on the licensee's ability to conduct its business
- any disposal of the licensee's assets where that has a material impact on the licensee's business
- any investigation by a professional, statutory, regulatory or government body into the licensee's activities, or the activities in relation to the licensed entity of a personal licence holder or a person occupying a qualifying position employed by them, where such an investigation could result in the imposition of a sanction or penalty which, if imposed, could reasonably be expected to raise doubts about the licensee's continued suitability to hold a Gambling Commission licence
- any instance of criminal activity, including repeated instances of small-scale theft or fraud, where that has a material impact on the licensee's business
- any major breach in the licensee's information security where that adversely affects the confidentiality of customer data or prevents customers from accessing their accounts for a substantial period of time
- any other matters that have a material impact on the licensee's business or on the licensee's ability to conduct its business.

---

[5] These matters can be reported securely online at the Commission's website at www.gamblingcommission.gov.uk or by email to key.events@gamblingcommission.gov.uk or posted to Key Events, Compliance Administration Team, Gambling Commission, Victoria Square House, Victoria Square, Birmingham, B2 4BP

PRIMARY GAMBLING ACTIVITY

Ordinary code provision

In order to demonstrate that the primary gambling activity for which an operating licence has been issued is being offered in each licensed premises, licensees should have regard to the following general factors:

- the ratio of the space available to customers allocated to the primary gambling activity, to that allocated to other gambling activities
- the extent to which the primary gambling activity is promoted on the premises and by way of external advertising compared to other gambling activities
- the use, either expected or actual, to be made of the different gambling facilities

Licensees should also have regard to the following additional sector specific factors:

Ordinary code provision

- the range and frequency of events on which bets can be made.

Not all the indicators would need to be present in a particular case, nor do they preclude others, but the combination of those factors that are present should be sufficient to indicate that the activity is the primary one in any given premises.

Gambling Commission October 2010

CONDITIONS AND CODES OF PRACTICE APPLICABLE TO: REMOTE GENERAL BETTING LICENCES REMOTE POOL BETTING LICENCES REMOTE BETTING INTERMEDIARY LICENCES REMOTE GENERAL BETTING ANCILLARY LICENCES

October 2010

6.2125–6.2150 Your licence is subject to certain conditions and codes of practice, these are detailed in the following pages

STATUTORY CONDITIONS ATTACHED BY VIRTUE OF THE ACT

SOCIAL RESPONSIBILITY

This licence is subject to a condition that the licensee ensures compliance with any relevant social responsibility provision of a code of practice issued by the Commission. The social responsibility provisions that are relevant to the activities authorised by this licence are set out in the section entitled Codes of Practice.

(Sections 24 and 82(1) Gambling Act 2005)

RETURN OF STAKES TO CHILDREN

The following condition applies to all remote operating licences except remote pool betting operating licences restricted to football only

This licence is subject to a condition that if the licensee (or anyone employed by the licensee to perform an operational function within the meaning of Section 80 of the Act) becomes aware that a child or young person is using or has used facilities for gambling provided in reliance on the licence, the licensee:

(a) must return any money paid in respect of the use of those facilities (whether by way of fee, stake or otherwise) by the child or young person as soon as is reasonably practicable; and

(b) may not give a prize to the child or young person.

This condition does not apply to use of a Category D gaming machine.

(Section 83(1))

The following condition applies to remote pool betting operating licences restricted to football only

This licence is subject to a condition that if the licensee (or anyone employed by the licensee to perform an operational function within the meaning of Section 80 of the Act) becomes aware that a child is using or has used facilities for gambling provided in reliance on the licence, the licensee;

(a) must return any money paid in respect of the use of those facilities (whether by way of fee, stake or otherwise) by the child as soon as is reasonably practicable, and

(b) may not give a prize to the child.

This condition does not apply to use of a Category D gaming machine.
(Section 83(1))

OTHER STATUTORY CONDITIONS

This licence is subject to a condition that nothing may be done in reliance on the licence in relation to a bet on the outcome of a lottery which forms part of the National Lottery.
(Section 95(2))

The following condition applies to all remote general betting operating licences only

This licence is subject to a condition that bets may be accepted on behalf of the licensee only by:
(a) the licensee;
(b) a person employed by the licensee under a written contract of employment; or
(c) the holder of another general betting operating licence.
(Section 92(1))

The following condition applies to all remote pool betting operating licences only

This licence is subject to a condition that bets may be accepted on behalf of the licensee only:
(a) by the licensee,
(b) by a person employed by the licensee under a written contract of employment,
(c) by the holder of another pool betting operating licence, or
(d) by an agent, provided the agent is authorised by the licensee in writing to accept bets on behalf of the licensee, the agent is an adult, at the time of accepting the bet the agent is on a track, the bet is accepted in reliance on an occasional use notice and the bet is in connection with a horse race or dog race
(e) where this pool betting operating licence authorises (whether expressly or impliedly) the provision of facilities for football pools, by an adult or young person authorised by the licensee in writing to make documents or other facilities available in connection with the licensed activities, to receive entries on behalf of the licensee, to receive payments on behalf of the licensee, or to make payments of winnings on behalf of the licensee.
(Section 93(1),(2) &(3))

COMMISSION GENERAL CONDITIONS

The Commission's complete suite of Licence Conditions to be attached to operating licences pursuant to section 75 of the Act includes some conditions which may not apply to your licence. Where that is the case the irrelevant conditions have not been reproduced below. The full list of Licence Conditions and Codes of Practice are contained within the Commission's Publication "Licence Conditions and Codes of Practice"

QUALIFIED PERSONS AND PERSONAL LICENCES

Qualified persons

THE FOLLOWING CONDITION APPLIES TO ALL REMOTE OPERATING LICENCES, EXCEPT ANCILLARY REMOTE LICENCES, ISSUED TO SMALL-SCALE OPERATORS

In this condition the terms 'small-scale operator', 'qualifying position' and 'qualified person' have the meanings respectively ascribed to them by the Gambling Act 2005 (Definition of Small-scale Operator) Regulations 2006.

Schedule X[1] lists those individuals notified to the Commission as qualified persons.

If, whilst the licensee remains a small-scale operator, an individual begins or ceases to occupy a qualifying position in relation to the licensee, the licensee must within 28 days apply to the Commission under s104(1)(b) for amendment of the details of the licence set out in Schedule X[1].

An application for amendment under s104(1)(b) may be made in advance of an individual beginning or ceasing to occupy a qualifying position provided it specifies the date from which the change to which it relates is to be effective.

1 The schedules mentioned here will be attached to individual licences.

Personal licences

THE FOLLOWING CONDITION APPLIES TO ALL REMOTE OPERATING LICENCES EXCEPT ANCILLARY REMOTE LICENCES

(a) Subject to (e) and (f) below licensees must ensure:
  (i) that each individual who occupies one of the management offices specified in (b) below in or in respect of the licensee or in connection with the licensed activities holds a personal licence authorising the performance of the functions of that office (hereafter 'a personal management licence')
  (ii) that at least one person occupies at least one of those offices.

(b) The specified management offices are those offices (whether or not held by a director in the case of a licensee which is a company, a partner in the case of a licensee which is a partnership or an officer of the association in the case of a licensee which is an unincorporated association) the occupier of which is by virtue of the terms of their appointment responsible for:
- the overall management and direction of the licensee's business or affairs
- the licensee's finance function as head of that function
- the licensee's gambling regulatory compliance function as head of that function
- the licensee's marketing function as head of that function
- the licensee's information technology function as head of that function in so far as it relates to gambling-related information technology and software
- oversight of the day to day management of the licensed activities at an identified number of premises licensed under Part 8 of the Act or across an identified geographical area
- in the case of casino and bingo licences only, oversight of the day to day management of a single set of premises licensed under Part 8 of the Act.

(c) Licensees must take all reasonable steps to ensure that anything done in the performance of the functions of a specified management office is done in accordance with the terms and conditions of the holder's personal management licence.

(d) Where an individual is authorised by a personal licence and that licence comes under review under section 116(2) of the Act, the operating licensee must comply with any conditions subsequently imposed on that licence by the Commission about redeployment, supervision, or monitoring of the individual's work and any requirements of the Commission in respect of such matters applicable during the period of the review.

(e) Paragraphs (a) to (d) above shall not apply to a licensee for so long as the licensee is a 'small-scale operator' as defined in the Gambling Act 2005 (Definition of Small-scale Operator) Regulations 2006 ('the Regulations').

(f) During the period of 3 years commencing with the date on which a licensee ceases to be a small-scale operator paragraphs (a) to (e) above shall apply subject to the proviso that the phrase 'each individual' in paragraph (a)(i) shall not include any individual who was a 'qualified person' (as defined in the Regulations) in relation to the licensee 28 days immediately prior to the licensee ceasing to be a small-scale operator.

TECHNICAL STANDARDS AND EQUIPMENT SPECIFICATIONS

The following condition applies to all remote operating licences except remote betting intermediary (trading rooms only) licences

Licensees must comply with the Commission's technical standards and with requirements set by the Commission relating to the timing and procedures for testing.

FINANCIAL ROBUSTNESS

Notification of shareholders

THE FOLLOWING CONDITION APPLIES TO ALL REMOTE OPERATING LICENCES EXCEPT ANCILLARY REMOTE LICENCES

All company licensees must notify the Commission of the name and address of any person who becomes a shareholder in the company or its holding company holding 3% or more of the issued share capital of the company or its holding company; or any existing shareholder who acquires a holding of 3% or more of the issued share capital of the company or its holding company.

In this condition 'holding company' has the meaning ascribed to that term by section 1159 of the Companies Act 2006 or any statutory modification or re-enactment thereof.

PROTECTION OF CUSTOMER FUNDS

Licensees who hold customer funds for use in future gambling must set out clearly, in information made available to customers in writing, whether they protect customers' funds in the event of insolvency and the method by which this is achieved.

CASH HANDLING

The following condition only applies to remote betting intermediary (trading rooms only) operating licences

Licensees, as part of their internal controls and financial accounting systems, must have and put into effect policies and procedures concerning the handling of cash, and cash equivalents (ie bankers drafts, cheques and debit cards), designed to minimise the risk of crimes such as money laundering, to avoid the giving of illicit credit and to provide assurance that gambling activities are being conducted fairly.

GENERAL 'FAIR AND OPEN' PROVISIONS

Licensees must satisfy themselves that the terms on which gambling is offered are not unfair under the Unfair Terms in Consumer Contracts Regulations 1999 and, where applicable, meet the reasonableness test under the Unfair Contract Terms Act 1977. An accurate summary of the contractual terms on which gambling is offered must be made available to customers and set out in plain and intelligible language.

Customers must be notified of changes to terms before they come into effect.

DISPLAY OF LICENSED STATUS

The following condition applies to all remote operating licences except remote betting intermediary (trading rooms only) licences and ancillary remote licences

Licensees offering gambling on websites must:

(a) display the following information on a page which, by virtue of the construction of the website, customers access before gambling:
 (i) a statement that they are licensed and regulated by the Gambling Commission;
 (ii) their licence number; and
 (iii) a link to the Gambling Commission's website;

(b) display at least the information at (i) above on each page of the website which offers facilities for gambling in reliance on the licence;

(c) where they offer on pages of the website, or by means of a link from the website, facilities for gambling which are not provided in reliance on their Gambling Commission licence, clearly distinguish those products which are regulated by the Commission from those which are not.

POOL BETTING

The following condition applies to all remote pool betting operating licences except those restricted to football only

Licensees must inform the Commission, within 14 days, in writing, of any person they authorise under section 93(2) of the Act to offer pool betting on a track in connection with a horserace or dog race in reliance on an occasional use notice. In doing so, they must include the terms and conditions under which this has been agreed, and provide contact details of the management and key staff of those that are authorised.

Licensees and any person they so authorise must produce and retain a record of the transactions relevant to each pool that they offer. The record must be capable of identifying individual bets into the pool and relating these to subsequent payment of winnings where applicable. Licensees must make this information available to the Commission on request.

The following condition only applies to all remote pool betting operating licences which authorise football pools

Licensees must inform the Commission, within 14 days, in writing, of any person they authorise under Section 93(3) of the Act in respect of football pool betting. In doing so, they must include the terms and conditions under which this has been agreed.

Licensees and any person they so authorise must produce and retain a record of the transactions relevant to each pool that they offer. The record must be capable of identifying individual bets into the pool and relating these to the subsequent payment of winnings where applicable. Licensees must make this information available to the Commission on request.

The following condition applies to all remote pool betting operating licences only

Licensees must produce annual accounts which should be certified by a qualified independent accountant. Licensees must make copies available to the Commission.

ACCESS TO PREMISES

Licensees must have and put into effect policies and procedures (including staff training programmes) designed to ensure that their staff co-operate with the Commission's enforcement officers in the proper performance of their compliance functions and are made aware of those officers' rights of entry to premises contained in Part 15 of the Act.

INFORMATION REQUIREMENTS

Reporting suspicion of offences etc

Licensees must provide the Commission with any information that they:

- know relates to or suspect may relate to the commission of an offence under the Act, including an offence resulting from a breach of a licence condition or a code provision having the effect of a licence condition
- suspect may lead the Commission to consider making an order to void a bet.

Licensees who accept bets, or facilitate the making or acceptance of bets between others, on the outcome of horse races or other sporting events governed by one of the sport governing bodies for the time being included in Part 3 of Schedule 6 to the Act must also provide the relevant sport governing body with sufficient information to conduct an effective investigation if the licensee suspects that information in their possession may:

- lead the Commission to consider making an order to void a bet
- relate to a breach of a rule on betting applied by that sport governing body.

Reporting 'Key Events'

THE FOLLOWING CONDITION APPLIES TO ALL REMOTE OPERATING LICENCES EXCEPT ANCILLARY REMOTE LICENCES

A key event is an event that could have a significant impact on the nature or structure of a licensee's business. Licensees must notify the Commission of the occurrence of any of the following key events as soon as reasonably practicable and in any event within five working days of the licensee becoming aware of the event's occurrence[2].

- in the case of licensees which are companies, a petition being presented for their winding up or the winding up of any group company of theirs, or they or any group company being placed in administration or receivership: in this condition a 'group company' is any subsidiary or holding company of the licensee – as those terms are defined in section 1159 of the Companies Act 2006 or any statutory modification or re-enactment thereof – and any subsidiary of such holding company
- in the case of a licensee who is an individual (or a partner in a partnership licensee) their being presented with a petition for their bankruptcy or sequestration or their entering into an individual voluntary agreement
- where the licensee is required to have their accounts independently audited, any unplanned change of auditor including a change prompted by a dispute or resulting from auditors being unable or unwilling to sign an unqualified audit report
- the departure from the licensee's business of any person occupying a 'qualifying position' as defined by Regulation 2(2) of the Gambling Act 2005 (Definition of Small-scale Operator) Regulations 2006
- any breach of a covenant given to a bank or other lender
- any default in making repayment of the whole or any part of a loan on its due date
- any court judgments remaining unpaid 14 days after the date of judgment
- the commencement of any material litigation against the licensee
- the imposition of a disciplinary sanction, including dismissal, against the holder of a personal licence or a person occupying a qualifying position for gross misconduct; or the resignation of a personal licence holder or person occupying a qualifying position following commencement of disciplinary proceedings in respect of gross misconduct against that person
- in the case of remote gambling, the commencement or cessation of trading on website domains (including WAP URLs) or broadcast media through which the licensee provides gambling facilities.

[2] Key events can be reported securely online at the Commission's website at www.gamblingcommission.gov.uk or by email to key.events@gamblingcommission.gov.uk or posted to Key Events, Compliance Administration Team, Gambling Commission, Victoria Square House, Victoria Square, Birmingham B2 4BP

General and Regulatory Returns

On request, licensees must provide the Commission with such information as the Commission may require about the use made of facilities provided in accordance with this licence, and the manner in which gambling authorised by this licence and the licensee's business in relation to that gambling are carried on, including in particular information about:

- the numbers of people making use of the facilities and the frequency of such use
- the range of gambling activities provided by the licensee and the numbers of staff employed in connection with them
- the licensee's policies in relation to, and experiences of, problem gambling.

In particular, within 28 days of the end of each quarterly or annual period as the case may be, licensees must submit a Regulatory Return to the Commission containing such information as the Commission may from time to time require[3].

[3] Regulatory returns can be submitted securely online at the Commission's website at www.gamblingcommission.gov.uk For operators unable to access this system, the forms and a guide to completing them can be requested from the Commission and returned by email to Regulatory.Returns@gamblingcommission.gov.uk or by post to Regulatory Returns, Compliance Administration Team, Gambling Commission, Victoria Square House, Victoria Square, Birmingham, B2 4BP

SECRETARY OF STATE GENERAL CONDITIONS

None at present

CODES OF PRACTICE

Introduction

This is the Commission's principal code of practice, issued under section 24 of the Gambling Act 2005, as revised with effect from 1 January 2009. There are two types of provision in the code:

- social responsibility provisions: compliance with these is a condition of licences; therefore any breach of them by an operator may lead the Commission to review the operator's licence with a view to suspension, revocation or the imposition of a financial penalty and would also expose the operator to the risk of prosecution; and
- ordinary code provisions: these do not have the status of licence conditions, but are admissible in evidence in criminal or civil proceedings and must be taken into account in any case in which the court or tribunal think them relevant and by the Commission in the exercise of its functions. Any breach of ordinary code provisions by an operator may be taken into account by the Commission on a licence review, but cannot lead to imposition of a financial penalty. These code provisions are in italics in this section and generally set out good practice in these areas.

FINANCIAL REQUIREMENTS

The following code applies to all remote operating licences except remote pool betting operating licences restricted to football and remote betting intermediary (trading rooms only) licences

Ordinary code provision

As part of their procedures for compliance with the requirements in respect of the prevention and detection of money laundering in the Proceeds of Crime Act 2002 and the Terrorism Act 2000, licensees should:

- unless there is a specific reason not to do so, appoint one or more nominated officers whose duty it is to take overall responsibility for the anti-money laundering procedures within the operation, in particular with respect to Suspicious Activity Reporting; and ensure, through appropriate training and guidance, that all staff who handle money or accounts or accept bets are aware of their duties under anti-money laundering legislation to report all suspicious activity to the nominated officer in a timely manner or, where there is no such nominated officer, directly and promptly to the police. It is the nominated officer's duty to consider such reports and to forward them where appropriate to the Serious Organised Crime Agency
- adopt (or reflect in their procedures) the Association of British Bookmakers' guidelines.

PROTECTION OF CHILDREN AND OTHER VULNERABLE PERSONS

Combating problem gambling

Social responsibility code provision

Licensees must have and put into effect policies and procedures intended to promote socially responsible gambling.

Licensees' policies and procedures for socially responsible gambling must include but need not be confined to:

- the specific policies and procedures required by the following provisions of section 2 of this code
- a commitment to and how they will contribute to research into the prevention and treatment of problem gambling
- a commitment to and how they will contribute to public education on the risks of gambling and how to gamble safely
- a commitment to and how they will contribute to the identification and treatment of problem gamblers.

Access to gambling by children and young persons

THE FOLLOWING CODE ONLY APPLIES TO REMOTE BETTING INTERMEDIARY (TRADING ROOMS ONLY) OPERATING LICENCES

Social responsibility code provision

Licensees must have and put into effect policies and procedures designed to prevent underage gambling, and monitor the effectiveness of these.

This must include procedures for:

- checking the age of apparently underage customers
- removing from adult-only licensed premises anyone who appears to be underage who tries to access the gambling facilities and cannot produce an acceptable form of identification
- taking action when there are attempts by under-18s to enter adult-only premises

- refusing entry to any adult-only area of a track to anyone unable to produce an acceptable form of identification
- taking action when there are unlawful attempts to enter the adult-only areas.

Licensees must not deliberately provide facilities for gambling in such a way as to appeal particularly to children or, except in the case of football pools, young people, for example by reflecting or being associated with youth culture.

In premises restricted to adults, service must be refused in any circumstances where any adult is accompanied by a child or young person.

Licensees must take all reasonable steps to ensure that all staff understand their responsibilities for preventing underage gambling. This must include appropriate training which must cover the legal requirements on returning stakes and not paying prizes to underage customers.

Licensees must only accept identification which:

- contains a photograph from which the individual can be identified
- states the individual's date of birth
- is valid
- is legible and has no visible signs of tampering or reproduction.

In the case of non-remote pool betting licensees, where pool entries or payments are collected door to door by the licensee or the licensee's authorised agent the licensee's procedures must include procedures for:

- checking the age of apparently underage entrants to the pool; and
- taking action when there are unlawful attempts to enter the pool.

THE FOLLOWING CODE ONLY APPLIES TO REMOTE BETTING INTERMEDIARY (TRADING ROOMS ONLY) OPERATING LICENCES

Ordinary code provision

The Commission considers acceptable forms of identification to include any identification carrying the PASS logo (for example Citizencard or Validate); a driving licence (including a provisional licence) with photocard; or a passport.

Licensees should put into effect procedures that require their staff to check the age of any customer who appears to them to be under 21.

Licensees should consider permanent exclusion from premises for any adult accompanied by a child or young person on more than one occasion to premises restricted to adults, or if there is reason to believe the offence was committed knowingly or recklessly.

Procedures should be put into effect for dealing with cases where a child or young person repeatedly attempts to gamble on premises restricted to adults, including oral warnings, reporting the offence to the Gambling Commission and the police, and making available information on problem gambling.

THE FOLLOWING CODE APPLIES TO ALL REMOTE OPERATING LICENCES EXCEPT REMOTE BETTING INTERMEDIARY (TRADING ROOMS ONLY) LICENCES

Social responsibility code provision

Licensees must have and put into effect policies and procedures designed to prevent underage gambling, and monitor the effectiveness of these.

Such procedures must include:

(a) warning potential customers that underage gambling is an offence;
(b) requiring customers to affirm that they are of legal age;
(c) regularly reviewing their age verification systems and implementing all reasonable improvements that may be made as technology advances and as information improves;
(d) ensuring that relevant staff are properly trained in the use of their age verification procedures; in particular customer services staff must be appropri-

ately trained in the use of secondary forms of identification when initial verification procedures fail to prove that an individual is of legal age;

(e) enabling their gambling websites to permit filtering software to be used by adults (such as parents or within schools) in order to restrict access to relevant pages of those sites;

(f) in the case of any UK resident customer who deposits money using any type of payment method other than a credit card, and unless the licensee has established that a third party has satisfactorily carried out age verification, the following age verification procedures:

 (i) verifying additional information about the customer, such as carrying out searches of credit reference and other databases that list names and addresses of individuals over the age of 18;

 (ii) carrying out secondary age verification checks in any circumstances which give the operator reason to suspect that the person may be underage;

 (iii) not permitting the customer to withdraw any winnings from their account until age verification has been satisfactorily completed; and

 (iv) in any event, a requirement that if age verification has not been satisfactorily completed within 72 hours of the customer applying to register to gamble and depositing money:
 - the account will be frozen
 - no further gambling will be permitted until age verification has been successfully completed
 - if on completion of age verification the customer is shown to be underage, the operator must return to the customer any money paid in respect of the use of the gambling facilities, but no winnings shall be paid.

(g) in the case of any non-UK resident customer who deposits money using any type of payment method other than a credit card, and unless the licensee has established that a third party has satisfactorily carried out age verification, the following age verification procedures:

 (i) taking all reasonable steps to make use of information available for age verification purposes from whichever country the potential customer is resident in; and

 (ii) each of the following steps, unless they can not reasonably be implemented or, in the case of the fourth bullet point, a period of more than 72 hours was reasonably required:
 - verifying additional information about the customer, such as carrying out searches of credit reference and other databases that list names and addresses of individuals over the age of 18
 - carrying out secondary age verification checks in any circumstances which give the operator reason to suspect that the person may be underage
 - not permitting the customer to withdraw any winnings from their account until age verification has been satisfactorily completed
 - a requirement that if age verification has not been satisfactorily completed within 72 hours of the customer applying to register to gamble and depositing money:
   - the account will be frozen;
   - no further gambling will be permitted until age verification has been successfully completed; and
   - if on completion of age verification the customer is shown to be underage all deposits held by the operator are returned to the customer and no winnings paid.

(h) in the case of any customer who registers to gamble and deposits money using a credit card, conducting a programme of random checks of credit card users for compliance with age restrictions.

THE FOLLOWING CODE APPLIES TO ALL REMOTE OPERATING LICENCES EXCEPT REMOTE BETTING INTERMEDIARY (TRADING ROOMS ONLY) LICENCES

Ordinary code provision

Licensees should, and should request their contracted partners to, draw attention to parental responsibility as part of the purchasing process of facilities such as mobile phones and interactive television.

INFORMATION ON HOW TO GAMBLE RESPONSIBLY AND HELP FOR PROBLEM GAMBLERS

Social responsibility code provision

Licensees must make information readily available to their customers on how to gamble responsibly and how to access information about, and help in respect of, problem gambling.

The information must cover:

- any measures provided by the licensee to help individuals monitor or control their gambling, such as restricting the duration of a gambling session or the amount of money they can spend
- timers or other forms of reminders or 'reality checks' where available
- self-exclusion options
- information about the availability of further help or advice.

The information must be directed to all customers whether or not licensees also make available material which is directed specifically at customers who may be 'problem gamblers'.

For gambling premises, information must be available in all areas where gambling facilities are provided and adjacent to ATMs where these are not located in a gambling area. As a minimum, information must be displayed prominently on posters appropriate to the size and layout of the premises and contained in leaflets that may be taken away. Licensees must take all reasonable steps to ensure that this information is also readily accessible in locations which enable the customer to obtain it discreetly.

Ordinary code provision

Licensees who market their services in one or more foreign languages should make available in that, or those, foreign languages:

- the information on how to gamble responsibly and access to help referred to above
- the players' guides to any game, bet or lottery required to be made available to customers under provisions in this code
- the summary of the contractual terms on which gambling is offered, which is required to be provided to customers as a condition of the licensee's operating licence.

Customer interaction

Social responsibility code provision

Licensees must put into effect policies and procedures for customer interaction where they have concerns that a customer's behaviour may indicate problem gambling. The policies must include:

- identification of the appropriate level of management who may initiate customer interaction and the procedures for doing so
- the types of behaviour that will be logged/reported to the appropriate level of staff and which may trigger customer interaction at an appropriate moment

- the circumstances in which consideration should be given to refusing service to customers and/or barring them from the operator's gambling premises
- training for all staff on their respective responsibilities, in particular so that they know who is designated to deal with problem gambling issues.

But such policies and procedures must be consistent with, and implemented with due regard to, licensees' duties in respect of the health and safety of their staff.

Self-exclusion

THE FOLLOWING CODE ONLY APPLIES TO REMOTE BETTING INTERMEDIARY (TRADING ROOMS ONLY) OPERATING LICENCES

Social responsibility code provision

Licensees must have and put into effect procedures for self-exclusion and take all reasonable steps to refuse service or to otherwise prevent an individual who has entered a self-exclusion agreement from participating in gambling.

Licensees must, as soon as practicable, take all reasonable steps to prevent any marketing material being sent to a self-excluded customer.

Licensees must take steps to remove the name and details of a self-excluded individual from any marketing databases used by the company or group (or otherwise flag that person as an individual to whom marketing material must not be sent), within two days of receiving the completed self-exclusion notification.

This covers any marketing material relating to gambling, or other activities that take place on the premises where gambling may take place. However, it would not extend to blanket marketing which is targeted at a particular geographical area and where the excluded individual would not knowingly be included.

Licensees must close any customer accounts of an individual who has entered a self exclusion agreement and return any funds held in the customer account. It is not sufficient merely to prevent an individual from withdrawing funds from their customer account whilst still accepting wagers from them. Where the giving of credit is permitted, the licensee may retain details of the amount owed to them by the individual, although the account must not be active.

Licensees must put into effect procedures designed to ensure that an individual who has self-excluded cannot gain access to gambling. These procedures must include:

- a register of those excluded with appropriate records (name, address, other details, and any membership or account details that may be held by the operator)
- photo identification (where available and in particular where enforcement of the system may depend on photographic ID), and a signature
- staff training to ensure that staff are able to enforce the systems
- the removal of those persons found in the gambling area or attempting to gamble from the premises.

THE FOLLOWING CODE ONLY APPLIES TO REMOTE BETTING INTERMEDIARY (TRADING ROOMS ONLY) OPERATING LICENCES

Ordinary code provision

Self-exclusion procedures should require individuals to take positive action in order to self-exclude. This can be a signature on a self-exclusion form.

Wherever practicable, individuals should be able to self-exclude without having to enter gambling premises.

Before an individual self-excludes, licensees should provide or make available sufficient information about what the consequences of self-exclusion are.

Licensees should take all reasonable steps to extend the self-exclusion to premises of the same type owned by the operator in the customer's local area. In setting the bounds of that area licensees may take into account the customer's address (if known to them), anything else known to them about the distance the customer ordinarily travels to gamble and any specific request the customer may make.

Licensees should encourage the customer to consider extending their self exclusion to other licensees' gambling premises in the customer's local area.

Customers should be given the opportunity to discuss self-exclusion in private, where possible.

Licensees should take steps to ensure that:

- the self-exclusion period is a minimum of six months and give customers the option of extending this to a total of at least five years
- a customer who has decided to enter a self-exclusion agreement is given the opportunity to do so immediately without any cooling-off period. However, if the customer wishes to consider the self-exclusion further (for example to discuss with problem gambling groups) the customer may return at a later date to enter into self-exclusion
- at the end of the period chosen by the customer (and at least six months later), the self-exclusion remains in place, unless the customer takes positive action in order to gamble again. No marketing material should be sent to the individual unless the individual has taken positive action in order to gamble again, and has agreed to accept such material
- where a customer chooses not to renew the self-exclusion, and makes a positive request to begin gambling again, the customer is given one day to cool off before being allowed access to gambling facilities. The contact must be made via telephone or in person.

The licensee should retain the records relating to a self-exclusion agreement at least until the agreement has been formally ended.

(Please note that the Commission does not require the licensee to carry out any particular assessment or make any judgement as to whether the previously self-excluded individual should again be permitted access to gambling. The requirement to take positive action in person or over the phone is purely to a) check that the customer has considered the decision to access gambling again and allow them to consider the implications; and b) implement the one day cooling-off period and explain why this has been put in place.)

THE FOLLOWING CODE APPLIES TO ALL REMOTE OPERATING LICENCES EXCEPT REMOTE BETTING INTERMEDIARY (TRADING ROOMS ONLY) LICENCES

Social responsibility code provision

Licensees must have and put into effect procedures for self-exclusion and take all reasonable steps to refuse service or to otherwise prevent an individual who has entered a self-exclusion agreement from participating in gambling.

Licensees must, as soon as practicable, take all reasonable steps to prevent any marketing material being sent to a self-excluded customer.

Licensees must take steps to remove the name and details of a self-excluded individual from any marketing databases used by the company or group (or otherwise flag that person as an individual to whom marketing material must not be sent), within two days of receiving the completed self-exclusion notification.

This covers any marketing material relating to gambling. However, it would not extend to blanket marketing which is targeted at a particular geographical area and where the excluded individual would not knowingly be included.

Licensees must close any customer accounts of an individual who has entered a self-exclusion agreement and return any funds held in the customer account. It is not sufficient merely to prevent an individual from withdrawing funds from their customer account whilst still accepting wagers from them. Where the giving of credit is permitted, the licensee may retain details of the amount owed to them by the individual, although the account must not be active.

Licensees must put into effect procedures designed to ensure that an individual who has self-excluded cannot gain access to gambling. These procedures must include:

- a register of those excluded with appropriate records (name, address, other details, and any membership or account details that may be held by the operator)
- a record of the card numbers to be excluded
- staff training to ensure that staff are able to enforce the systems
- the removal of access from those persons found to have gambled or who have attempted to gamble on the facilities.

THE FOLLOWING CODE APPLIES TO ALL REMOTE OPERATING LICENCES EXCEPT REMOTE BETTING INTERMEDIARY (TRADING ROOMS ONLY) LICENCES

Ordinary code provision

Self-exclusion procedures should require individuals to take positive action in order to self-exclude:

- over the **internet**; this can be a box that must be ticked in order to indicate that they understand the system
- by **telephone**; this can be a direct question asking whether they understand the system.

Before an individual self-excludes, licensees should provide or make available sufficient information about what the consequences of self-exclusion are.

Licensees should encourage the customer to consider extending their self exclusion to other remote gambling operators currently used by the customer.

Customers should be given the opportunity to self-exclude by contacting customer services and in addition, where technically possible, by entering an automated process using remote communication. In order to avoid inadvertent self-exclusion it is acceptable for an automated process to include an additional step that requires the customer to confirm that they wish to self-exclude. The licensee should ensure that all staff who are involved in direct customer service are aware of the self-exclusion system in place, and are able to direct that individual to an immediate point of contact with whom/which to complete that process.

Within the licensee's information about self-exclusion policies, the licensee should provide a statement to explain that software is available to prevent an individual computer from accessing gambling internet sites. The licensee should provide a link to a site where further information is available.

Licensees should take all reasonable steps to ensure that:

- the self-exclusion period is a minimum of six months and give customers the option of extending this to a total of at least five years
- a customer who has decided to enter a self-exclusion agreement is given the opportunity to do so immediately without any cooling-off period. However, if the customer wishes to consider the self-exclusion further (for example to discuss with problem gambling groups) the customer may return at a later date to enter into self-exclusion
- at the end of the period chosen by the customer (and at least six months later), the self-exclusion remains in place, unless the customer takes positive action in order to gamble again. No marketing material should be sent to the individual unless the individual has taken positive action in order to gamble again, and has agreed to accept such material
- where a customer chooses not to renew the self-exclusion, and makes a positive request to begin gambling again, the customer is given one day to cool off before being allowed access to the gambling facilities. The contact must be made via telephone or in person; re-registering online is not sufficient.

The licensee should retain the records relating to a self-exclusion agreement at least until the agreement has been formally ended.

(Please note that the Commission does not require the licensee to carry out any particular assessment or make any judgement as to whether the previously self excluded individual should again be permitted access to gambling. The requirement to take positive action in person or over the phone is purely to a) check that the customer has considered the decision to access gambling again and allow them to consider the implications; and b) implement the one day cooling-off period and explain why this has been put in place.)

Employment of children and young persons

THE FOLLOWING CODE APPLIES TO ALL REMOTE POOL BETTING OPERATING LICENCES RESTRICTED TO FOOTBALL ONLY

Ordinary code provision

Licensees who employ young persons (16 and 17 year olds) to sell tickets, collect payments or pay out winnings should have and put into effect policies and procedures designed to ensure that all staff, including staff who are young persons themselves, are made aware that the law prohibits underage gambling, and that tickets may only be sold to persons aged 16 or over.

THE FOLLOWING CODE APPLIES TO ALL REMOTE OPERATING LICENCES EXCEPT REMOTE POOL BETTING OPERATING LICENCES AND REMOTE BETTING INTERMEDIARY (TRADING ROOMS ONLY) LICENCES

Ordinary code provision

Licensees who employ children (under-16-year-olds) and young persons (those aged 16 and 17) should be aware that it is an offence to employ them to provide facilities for gambling.

THE FOLLOWING CODE APPLIES TO ALL REMOTE POOL BETTING OPERATING LICENCES ONLY

Ordinary code provision

Licensees who employ children (under-16-year-olds) and young persons (those aged 16 and 17) should be aware that it is an offence:

(a) to employ children to provide facilities for gambling in connection with football pools; and

(b) otherwise to employ children and young persons to provide facilities for gambling.

Provision of credit by licensees and the use of credit cards

THE FOLLOWING CODE APPLIES TO ALL REMOTE OPERATING LICENCES EXCEPT REMOTE BETTING INTERMEDIARY (TRADING ROOMS ONLY) LICENCES

Social responsibility code provision

Licensees who choose to accept credit cards must:

- accept payment by credit card for gambling only where that payment is made to a customer account
- make available for gambling, funds deposited via credit card only after the card issuer has approved the transaction.

6: Gambling Act 2005: Additional Material

THE FOLLOWING CODE APPLIES TO ALL REMOTE OPERATING LICENCES EXCEPT REMOTE BETTING INTERMEDIARY (TRADING ROOMS ONLY) LICENCES

Ordinary code provision

Licensees who choose to offer credit to members of the public who are not themselves gambling operators should also:

- have procedures for checking and scoring applications for credit from such customers, for setting, and for the increase of, credit limits
- explain these procedures to customers
- set a maximum credit limit for each customer and not permit customers to exceed that limit without further application
- apply a 24-hour delay between receiving a request for an increase in a credit limit and granting it in those cases where the limit exceeds that which the operator had previously set
- not require a minimum spend within a set time period
- take all reasonable steps to ensure that offers of credit are not sent to vulnerable persons, including those who have self-excluded from gambling
- ensure that information about an offer of credit includes a risk warning of what may happen in the event of default.

Money lending between customers

THE FOLLOWING CODE ONLY APPLIES TO REMOTE BETTING INTERMEDIARY (TRADING ROOMS ONLY) OPERATING LICENCES

Ordinary code provision

Licensees should seek to prevent systematic or organised money lending between customers on their premises. As a minimum, they should have arrangements in place to ensure staff are requested to report any instances of substantial money lending when they become aware of them.

Identification of individual customers

THE FOLLOWING CODE APPLIES TO ALL REMOTE OPERATING LICENCES EXCEPT REMOTE BETTING INTERMEDIARY (TRADING ROOMS ONLY) LICENCES

Social responsibility code provision

Licensees must have and put into effect policies and procedures designed to identify separate accounts which are held by the same individual.

Where licensees allow customers to hold more than one account with them, the licensee must link all of a customer's such accounts to that customer and ensure that:

- if a customer opts to self-exclude from one account they are excluded from all accounts they hold with the licensee
- all of a customer's accounts are monitored and decisions that trigger customer interaction are based on the observed behaviour and transactions across all the accounts
- where credit is offered or allowed the maximum credit limit is applied on an aggregate basis across all accounts
- individual financial limits can be implemented across all of a customer's accounts.

THE FOLLOWING CODE APPLIES TO ALL REMOTE OPERATING LICENCES EXCEPT REMOTE BETTING INTERMEDIARY (TRADING ROOMS ONLY) LICENCES

Ordinary code provision

Where a licensee:

(i) is a company, the licensee should take all reasonable steps to comply with the above social responsibility code provision as if it also applied to accounts held in respect of gambling carried on in reliance on a remote operating licence held by any Group Company;

(ii) also holds a licence in another jurisdiction permitting it to provide facilities for remote gambling (a 'foreign licence') or is a company one or more of whose Group Companies holds one or more foreign licences, the licensee should take all reasonable steps to comply with the above social responsibility code provision as if it applied also to accounts held in respect of gambling carried on in reliance on a foreign licence held by the licensee or any Group Company.

A company is a Group Company in relation to a licensee if it is the holding company of, subsidiary of, or shares a common holding company with, the licensee. For these purposes 'holding company' and 'subsidiary' respectively have the meanings ascribed to them by section 1159 of the Companies Act 2006 or any statutory modification or re-enactment thereof.

'Fair and open' provisions

Social responsibility code provision

Licensees must be able to provide evidence to the Commission, if required, showing how they satisfied themselves that their terms are not unfair.

THE FOLLOWING CODE APPLIES TO ALL REMOTE OPERATING LICENCES EXCEPT REMOTE BETTING INTERMEDIARY (TRADING ROOMS ONLY) LICENCES

Social responsibility code provision

Licensees must make the following available to customers:

- a player's guide to each gambling opportunity (bet, game or lottery) made available by the operator
- such additional information relating to the available gambling as the Commission shall from time to time publish to licensees: the current requirements are set out in an Annex to the Commission's Technical Standards.

THE FOLLOWING CODE APPLIES TO ALL REMOTE OPERATING LICENCES EXCEPT REMOTE BETTING INTERMEDIARY (TRADING ROOMS ONLY) LICENCES

Ordinary code provision

Where practicable, the player's guide and additional information referred to in the social responsibility code should be made available through the medium in which the remote gambling is to be conducted. Where that is not practicable, licensees should either:

- send a copy of the guide and required additional information by post, fax or email; or
- make these available to the customer in another medium to which he has access.

THE FOLLOWING CODE APPLIES TO ALL REMOTE OPERATING LICENCES EXCEPT REMOTE POOL BETTING OPERATING LICENCES AND REMOTE BETTING INTERMEDIARY (TRADING ROOMS ONLY) LICENCES

Social responsibility code provision

Licensees must set out within the full rules that they make available, the core elements for the acceptance and settlement of bets. These rules must cover:

- the circumstances under which the operator will void a bet
- treatment of errors, late bets and related contingencies
- availability of odds for any ante-post, early show or starting price betting, and treatment of place, forecast bets etc
- treatment of withdrawals, non-runners, and reformed markets
- maximum payout limiting liability for a specific betting product or generally
- any charges made to customers for the use of betting services or products, and how these are calculated (including deductions from winnings for commission, or in respect of withdrawn horses etc)
- means or medium by which the outcome of an event will be determined
- the rules for the event itself to be specified (eg horserace bets only to be accepted where the racing is subject to Horseracing Regulatory Authority rules)
- where bets are accepted on 'pari-mutuel' terms
- any special arrangements for settling bets on 'coupled' horses.

Where special rules have been agreed in relation to a particular bet these must not be overridden by any conflicting rules or subsequent rule changes.

Licensees must issue a betting slip or an electronic acknowledgement (other than in the case of telephone betting) for each transaction which includes information as to the operator's name and contact details, and words equivalent to 'Bets are accepted in accordance with the operator's rules'.

THE FOLLOWING CODE APPLIES TO ALL REMOTE OPERATING LICENCES EXCEPT ANCILLARY REMOTE LICENCES

Ordinary code provision

Licensees should ensure that the terms on which they contract with third parties who provide user interfaces enabling customers to access their remote gambling facilities:

- include a term that any such user interface comply with the Commission's technical standards for remote gambling systems
- enable them to terminate the third party's contract promptly if, in the licensee's opinion, the third party is in breach of that term.

Ordinary code provision

Where licensees offer to accept bets, or facilitate the making or acceptance of bets between others, on the outcome of a sport regulated by a sport governing body for the time being included in Part 3 of Schedule 6 of the Act they should take all reasonable steps to familiarise themselves with the rules applied by that body on betting, in particular betting by registered participants.

Marketing

Social responsibility code provision

If a licensee makes available to any customer or potential customer any incentive or reward scheme or other arrangement under which the customer may receive money, goods, services or any other advantage (including the discharge in whole or in part of any liability of his) ('the benefit') the scheme must be designed to operate, and be operated, in such a way that:

(a) the circumstances in which, and conditions subject to which, the benefit is available are clearly set out and readily accessible to the customers to whom it is offered;

(b) neither the receipt nor the value or amount of the benefit is:
 (i) dependent on the customer gambling for a pre-determined length of time or with a predetermined frequency; or
 (ii) altered or increased if the qualifying activity or spend is reached within a shorter time than the whole period over which the benefit is offered;
(c) if the value of the benefit increases with the amount the customer spends it does so at a rate no greater than that at which the amount spent increases;

and further that:

(d) if the benefit comprises free or subsidised travel or accommodation which facilitates the customer's attendance at particular licensed premises the terms on which it is offered are not directly related to the level of the customer's prospective gambling.

Ordinary code provision

Licensees should only offer incentive or reward schemes in which the benefit available is proportionate to the type and level of customers' gambling.

Ordinary code provision

All advertising of gambling products and services should be undertaken in a socially responsible manner. In particular, licensees should comply with the advertising codes of practice which apply to the form and media in which they advertise their gambling facilities or services, and for media not explicitly covered should apply the principles included in these codes of practice as if they were explicitly covered. Licensees should also follow any relevant industry code of practice on advertising.

However, the particular restriction on allowing people aged under 25 to appear in adverts need not be applied to point of sale advertising material, provided that the images used depict the sporting activity that may be gambled on and not the activity of gambling itself and do not offend any other aspect of the advertising codes.

THE FOLLOWING CODE APPLIES TO ALL REMOTE OPERATING LICENCES EXCEPT ANCILLARY REMOTE LICENCES

Ordinary code provision

Licensees should ensure that the terms on which they contract with their affiliates (that is those who are given a right to advertise, or provide a hyper-link to, a licensee's gambling website) enable them to terminate the affiliate's rights promptly if, in the licensee's opinion, the affiliate is in breach of the advertising codes.

Complaints and disputes

Social responsibility code provision

Licensees must put into effect a written procedure for handling customer complaints and disputes.

In this code a 'complaint' means a complaint about any aspect of the licensee's conduct of the licensed activities, and a 'dispute' is any complaint which:

(a) is not resolved at the first stage of the complaints procedure; and
(b) relates to the outcome of the complainant's gambling transaction.

Licensees must ensure that:

- customers are told the name and status of the person to contact about their complaint
- customers are given a copy of the complaints procedure on request or on making a complaint
- all complaints are handled in accordance with the procedure.

Licensees must also ensure that they have arrangements in place for disputes to be referred to an independent third party. Customers whose disputes are not resolved to their satisfaction by use of the operator's complaints procedure may refer those disputes to this independent third party. The arrangements under which such complaints are referred may, but need not, provide for the third party's decision to be binding on the licensee and the customer.

Licensees must keep a record of all complaints that are not resolved at the first stage of the complaints procedure.

Licensees must arrange for a copy of the decision on, or a note of the outcome of, each dispute referred to the independent party to be provided to the Commission quarterly, either by the independent party or by the licensee.

Gambling licensees' staff

Social responsibility code provision

Licensees must take all reasonable steps to ensure that staff involved in the provision of facilities for gambling are made aware of advice on socially responsible gambling and of where to get confidential advice should their gambling become hard to control.

Pool betting

THE FOLLOWING CODE APPLIES TO ALL REMOTE POOL BETTING OPERATING LICENCES ONLY

Social responsibility code provision

Licensees or any person they authorise to offer pool betting on their behalf under authority of section 93 of the Act must publish their rules relevant to the following:

- the deduction levels for overheads, taxes, profits etc, expressed as a percentage, from each available pool
- the rounding of winning dividends to a whole unit
- the procedure for when there is no winner of the pool, and the circumstances in which the pool is carried over
- the period of time in which a winning bet may be claimed from the pool operator.

Information requirements

THE FOLLOWING CODE APPLIES TO ALL REMOTE OPERATING LICENCES EXCEPT ANCILLARY REMOTE LICENCES

Ordinary code provision

The Commission expects licensees to work with the Commission in an open and cooperative way and to inform the Commission of any matters that the Commission would reasonably need to be aware of in exercising its regulatory functions. These are matters that will have a material impact on the licensee's business or on the licensee's ability to conduct its business. Such matters, which should be notified to the Commission as soon as reasonably practicable[4], include the following:

- the departure from the licensee's business of any person named in the licence application, or that person's successor, who holds a personal management licence, but who does not occupy a 'qualifying position'
- any reduction in the number of staff employed by the licensee where that has a material impact on the licensee's business
- the acquisition or disposal by the licensee of gambling premises or pitches where that has a material impact on the size or nature of the licensee's business
- in the case of corporate licensees, the disposal or acquisition of any group company where that has a material impact on the licensee's ability to conduct its business

- any disposal of the licensee's assets where that has a material impact on the licensee's business
- any investigation by a professional, statutory, regulatory or government body into the licensee's activities, or the activities in relation to the licensed entity of a personal licence holder or a person occupying a qualifying position employed by them, where such an investigation could result in the imposition of a sanction or penalty which, if imposed, could reasonably be expected to raise doubts about the licensee's continued suitability to hold a Gambling Commission licence
- any instance of criminal activity, including repeated instances of small-scale theft or fraud, where that has a material impact on the licensee's business
- any major breach in the licensee's information security where that adversely affects the confidentiality of customer data or prevents customers from accessing their accounts for a substantial period of time
- any other matters that have a material impact on the licensee's business or on the licensee's ability to conduct its business.

[4] These matters can be reported securely online at the Commission's website at www.gambling-commission.gov.uk or by email to key.events@gamblingcommission.gov.uk or posted to Key Events, Compliance Administration Team, Gambling Commission, Victoria Square House, Victoria Square, Birmingham, B2 4BP

Gambling Commission October 2010

CHANGES TO LICENCE CATEGORIES FROM 1 AUGUST 2008

6.2167 Changes to certain operating licences and fee categories come into effect on 1 August 2008. Whilst the Gambling Commission (the Commission) has sought to contact all operators who may be affected it is quite possible that other operators may wish to take advantage of the new licences. In addition your business may have changed since applying for an operating licence.
Below are descriptions of the different types of licences and the activities related to them. Please read and check that you hold all the correct licences in order to continue to operate legally.
Holding one type of gambling licence does not always give you authority to carry out or provide facilities covered by another licence type.

WHAT ARE THE NEW LICENCES?

The Commission has introduced a number of new licence types. Four of the new licence types are linked activity licences, allowing operators to carry out activities which are linked to their main licence type eg gaming machine repair.
The Commission has also introduced a new remote betting intermediary (trading rooms only) licence for dedicated trading rooms.

WHAT IS THE DIFFERENCE BETWEEN A REMOTE BETTING INTERMEDIARY (TRADING ROOM ONLY) LICENCE AND A REMOTE BETTING INTERMEDIARY LICENCE?

Operators providing a service designed to facilitate the making or acceptance of bets between others by means of remote communication equipment require a remote betting intermediary operating licence.
The new licence allows an operator to act as a betting intermediary as described above, but is restricted to providing these facilities from licensed premises by providing a link by means of remote communication to a betting exchange.

For example by providing internet access to a licensed betting exchange in a dedicated room.

WHAT IS A LINKED ACTIVITY LICENCE?

The Commission has found that some operators provide in-house services such as maintaining or repairing their own gaming machines that would require a full operating licence if provided commercially. A linked activity licence allows the operator to carry out these activities on their own behalf but does not authorise them to be offered to third parties. Anyone thinking of applying for a linked licence should consider whether a full operating licence is necessary (see overleaf). Four types of linked activity licence are available:

A LINKED REMOTE GAMING MACHINE TECHNICAL (SUPPLIER) LICENCE

A remote gaming machine technical operating licence which does not authorise the licensee to manufacture gaming machines (or parts of, or software for, gaming machines) but does permit supply, installation, adaptation, maintenance or repair of a gaming machine, or part of a gaming machine (including software), provided (1) the licensee is the only operator making that machine available for use and (2) the licensee does not incur costs of more than £50,000 per annum in respect of those activities. It does not allow you to supply, install, adapt, maintain or repair machines that are not offered by you in reliance on your licence.

This licence would be of interest, for example, to an AGC operator which wished to install or adapt the software in machines in its arcades by means of remote communication.

A LINKED NON-REMOTE GAMBLING SOFTWARE LICENCE

A non-remote gambling software operating licence which only authorises you, the operator, to manufacture, supply, install or adapt gambling software for use in connection with gambling facilities provided by you, provided the costs incurred in carrying out activities authorised by the licence do not exceed £50,000 per year.

This licence would be of interest, for example, to a casino which wished to install or adapt software used in its automated roulette equipment.

DO I NEED ANOTHER OPERATING LICENCE RATHER THAN A LINKED LICENCE?

When considering your requirement for these additional linked licences please consider all of the costs that are involved with the supply, adaptation, maintenance or repair of gaming machines, including for example, any salary costs and the average annual cost of any parts or systems used.

If the costs total more than £50,000 per year then you must apply for one of the licences below:

- a gaming machine technical (supplier) licence (remote or non-remote)
- a gambling software licence (remote or non-remote)

If you require an additional licence or are unsure which licences you require contact us by email on enquiries@gamblingcommission.gov.uk or by phone on 0121 230 6666. For details of fees see www.gamblingcommission.gov.uk

BETTING INTEGRITY

Policy position paper, March 2009

1 INTRODUCTION AND DEFINITION

6.2168 1.1 In October 2007, the Gambling Commission (the Commission) published a paper on its approach to integrity in sports betting[1]. This followed public consultation on integrity in sports betting[2].

1.2 Since then the Commission has worked with sports governing bodies, the betting industry and others concerned with integrity in betting, such as the police, to develop our approach. We also consulted on an issues paper on in-running betting which invited views on the risks that posed for betting integrity.

1.3 This policy position paper summarises our work to date and the Commission's policy on betting integrity, which is primarily concerned with sports betting, but also covers betting on non-sporting events, for example the winners of film awards. Accordingly this paper is titled *Betting Integrity*, rather than *Integrity in Sports Betting* as previous documents on this topic have been.

1.4 Betting integrity is important to the Commission because of the risks any failure would pose to the licensing objectives of keeping gambling fair and open and keeping crime out of gambling. While any lack of integrity in the way in which an event is managed, or the results reported, will detract from the fairness and openness of any betting on that event, the Commission's focus is on integrity directly related to betting, specifically where the outcome of an event has been influenced with the intention of benefiting through betting on it, or where inside information is used improperly or unfairly in placing a bet. For example, if an individual pays (directly or indirectly) another to deliberately lose a game with the intention of profiting through betting on that outcome (directly or indirectly), that is a matter of concern to the Commission. The Commission does not consider it to be part of its core role to promote event integrity more widely, but would expect sports governing bodies to do this. For example, if a team does not put out its best available players for one match simply in order to be better prepared for another match, this would not normally be a matter for the Commission even if bets had been placed on the outcome (unless inside information is used improperly or unfairly in placing a bet). Generally speaking, those betting are aware of such wider risks to sporting or event integrity.

1.5 The Commission works on the principle of risk-based regulation and must act in a proportionate manner. However, while limited evidence has so far emerged to support it, the Commission recognises the widespread concern about the risks to betting integrity, particularly in relation to sporting events, and has been developing its policies and procedures to reduce such risks.

1.6 In summary, the Commission's approach is to work with the sporting bodies, licensed betting operators and others to strengthen the deterrents to corruption in betting by making it more likely that those involved can be identified and appropriate sanctions imposed. That process itself will help clarify the extent of any lack of integrity in betting and the need, if any, for further regulatory action. Such regulatory action could be in relation to more disclosure about, or restrictions on, types of bets, or on rules relating to use of 'inside' information or on who may bet on what. The Commission has dedicated a cross-functional betting integrity team to this work, with expertise that covers the whole of the regulatory process, from licensing through to enforcement and prosecution.

---

1 *Integrity in Sports Betting: Policy position paper* (October 2007)

2 *Issues Paper — Integrity in Sports Betting* (May 2007)

2 POLICY DEVELOPMENT

2.1 Since October 2007 the Commission's work in relation to betting integrity has focused on six main areas:

- work with sports governing bodies and operators
- sports governing bodies' rules
- information sharing
- specific bets and terms and conditions
- investigation and prosecution
- in-running betting
- This section describes our recent work and explains how we are building on, and expanding it.

WORK WITH SPORTS GOVERNING BODIES AND OPERATORS

2.2 The Commission has been working with sports governing bodies and the betting industry to help them better understand, and co-operate with, each other. To this end, we encouraged the Association of British Bookmakers to hold a seminar for sports bodies to meet and further their understanding of the betting industry. We are also working with CCPR[3] (Central Council of Physical Recreation) and supporting CCPR's survey of its members, which will assess how well equipped sports governing bodies are to manage any threat to integrity in their sport. The results of this survey will inform the Commission's work, particularly in helping to establish and promote best practice in relation to rules on betting and the use of 'inside' information (discussed in more detail below).

2.3 The Commission is also working directly with a number of sports governing bodies. We have developed, or are developing, memoranda of understanding (MOU) with some of these bodies setting out how we will work together, in particular in relation to the reporting of suspicious betting patterns. However, we also have good working relationships with a number of sports governing bodies without any formal MOU. We have also developed a memorandum of understanding with the European Sports Security Association (ESSA), an association of sports betting operators in Europe that looks to monitor any irregular betting patterns, or possible use of inside information.

[3] The CCPR are an alliance of governing and representative bodies of sports and recreations

SPORTS GOVERNING BODIES' RULES

2.4 We have taken a particular interest in the rules put in place by sports governing bodies. Clear, well publicised, rules on who can bet on what and effective sanctions for those found breaking those rules, alongside effective information sharing, can assist sports governing bodies to maintain integrity in their sports. Such rules will also help betting operators to decide if an individual is breaching their sports governing body's rules. Both sports governing bodies and the Commission have been identifying good practice and the Commission has been encouraging bodies to share that good practice with one another.

We have also been making sports governing bodies aware of our investigative techniques, procedures and evidential requirements to help them to build up their capacity to uphold their own rules and conduct investigations relating to their own sports. At the same time we have been learning more about the issues and approaches that are unique to each sport. We will continue to encourage, and help, sports governing bodies to develop effective rules and build capacity to maintain integrity in their sports. We will explore with the governing bodies and others concerned the scope for agreeing on what is best practice and for encouraging and promoting best practice and enforcing compliance with it.

INFORMATION SHARING

2.5 A key component of the Commission's work on betting integrity is the imposition of a licence condition (15.1) which requires betting operators to share information on suspicious transactions with the Commission and sports governing bodies. The condition, set out at appendix 1, was revised in *Licence Conditions and Codes of Practice* (October 2008) to clarify the degree of suspicion that would trigger a notification to the Commission by an operator. We have also addressed the concerns of some betting operators that the provision of such information might breach data protection requirements. We have confirmed with the Information Commissioner's Office that, provided that the operator can demonstrate the reasons behind, and justifications for, the disclosure, they will comply with their Data Protection Act obligations. Since the reason will be the obligation to report 'reasonable suspicion', and the rationale will be the operator's suspicions, it would follow that there would be sufficient reason and justification for the provision of information to the Commission and/ or the relevant sports governing body.

2.6 We will also be looking at the practices adopted by betting operators in making decisions about what to report under licence condition 15.1 and what not to report. Although the Commission receives reports under licence condition 15.1 we presently do not have a clear understanding of any underlying systemic problems indicated by the number of reports received. We are working with the relevant trade bodies to promote better understanding, and more effective use, of the information sharing provisions and will be discussing with them further advice to be provided to operators in the coming months. We also encourage sports governing bodies and operators to have direct agreements on how they will work together, such as the agreements Betfair has, and is developing, with sports governing bodies.

2.7 Since September 2007 the Commission has received reports relating to around 50 instances of suspicious betting activity. The majority of these were notified to the Commission by licence holders as required by licence condition 15.1, but some have come through other sources, for example sports governing bodies, the media or the public. All of these have been, or are being, examined by the relevant sport governing body or the Commission. In nearly half of these cases the grounds for suspicion have not been substantiated following an initial consideration. The remaining cases are under consideration, in some cases by sports governing bodies, and include a small number of active investigations in which the Commission is further involved.

2.8 While the number of live cases under active investigation remains small, the level of public concern remains high. A number of high profile admissions by sports participants and referees here and overseas have fuelled that concern. The sporting bodies' rules governing betting and the use of inside information vary enormously as do the effectiveness of their own integrity enforcement and sanctioning arrangements. Equally while certain betting exchanges' arrangements are well established and resourced, and larger betting operators are following suit, generally speaking smaller licensed betting operators' arrangements for supplying information on suspicious transactions are relatively new and need development. The Commission will make the effective working of licence condition 15.1 one of its compliance priorities over the coming months.

SPECIFIC BETS AND TERMS AND CONDITIONS

2.9 The Commission understands the importance of upholding betting integrity to sporting bodies, the betting industry and, of course, to the public, and is familiar with methods used in other countries to promote betting integrity, such as restricting the type of bets offered or approving sporting bodies' rules before allowing betting on those sports. The Commission has the power to impose such restrictions on its licensees but does not consider, based on the available evidence, that such intrusive or resource intensive methods are warranted or would be effective in Great Britain, although we will continue to monitor developments in this area. The Commission is, however, interested in working with the betting industry, sports governing bodies and others who are affected by non-sports betting to see if the deterrents to cheating or getting others to cheat (whether by improper use of inside information or by rigging the outcome of an event) can be strengthened.

2.10 In addition to the tightening up of sports bodies' rules and the provision of information mentioned above, the Commission plans to explore the scope for promoting integrity and deterring corruption by using information and publicity on which sporting events or types of bets are relatively low or high risk. Additionally, we will consider the scope for using employment terms and betting contract terms and conditions to make it easier to establish whether an offence has been committed and securing deterrent sanctions. For example, one possibility might be for the terms and conditions of betting to include a provision that the person placing/accepting the bet confirms both that they are not legally or contractually prohibited by any professional or employment requirements from betting on the event and that they do not already know the outcome of the event on which they are betting (using the earlier example, betting on a film awards when you already know the results); an individual misrepresenting their position would not only render the contract unenforceable, it would also engage the Commission's and sports governing bodies' enforcement and sanctioning powers, including, in the Commission's case, the power to void a bet.

INVESTIGATION AND PROSECUTION

2.11 In the meantime, the Commission has further developed its internal procedures, adopting a streamlined process of escalation and decision making which will enable us to take a prosecution or refer a case to the police in a more timely and cost effective way. The Commission has powers to take action in relation to cheating (under section 42 of the Act), void bets (section 336) and to obtain information (section 88). Ultimately, it will usually be for the police to take forward investigations as they have greater investigative powers (for example they can investigate bank accounts of those betting, which the Commission cannot) and are better equipped to undertake more complex investigations or those that may be linked to other criminal offences. However, it is still the case that the loss of career prospects relating to the particular sport or event is likely to be used more often as a sanction by the sports governing body and is likely to be faster than criminal proceedings. Additionally, it is worth noting that the Commission's powers to void a bet only apply to the corrupter's or corrupters' bets, not to whole markets.

2.12 The Commission is aware that regulatory bodies in other jurisdictions and sports governing bodies have set up, or have considered setting up mechanisms that look at betting data in real time. However, experience demonstrates that this requires considerable resource and expertise. The Commission is not persuaded that it would be proportionate or cost effective for the Commission to undertake such work, and considers that it might duplicate the work of others such as the BHA, or operators themselves. The Commission receives information from operators under licence condition 15.1 and works closely with other partners. At present the Commission considers this to be an appropriate way to manage this issue. However, experience from working together may lead to further proposals, for example, to pool expertise or to develop industry wide integrity units.

2.13 The Commission has been collating information since September 2007 when the Gambling Act 2005 fully came into force. We have been sharing that information when appropriate with partners here and abroad. The Commission is developing a memorandum of understanding with both the Association of Chief Police Officers (ACPO) and the Association of Chief Police Officers in Scotland (ACPOS) that will set out how we exchange information and work together. The Commission's powers do not extend beyond Great Britain and operators licensed with the Commission. As such, we rely on international police co-operation and relationships with other relevant bodies where the suspected source of corruption is based abroad. To that end we will continue to build relationships with other regulators and sports governing bodies overseas.

IN-RUNNING BETTING

2.14 The results of the Commission's specific consultation on issues raised by in–running betting[4] (published concurrently[5]) noted that while in-running betting theoretically gave more scope for event rigging or use of inside information, the evidence had not been provided to indicate that in practice there has been any significant increase. As the main ways of deterring or combating lack of integrity are the same for in–running and ante post betting, the Commission proposes to deal with in–running betting risks to integrity as part of its wider integrity programme.

---

4 In-running betting (or in-play or live betting as it is also known) is betting while the event to which the bet relates is actually taking place, for example, placing a bet on a horserace while the race is being run.

5 *In-running (In-play) betting: Position paper* (March 2009)

3 CONCLUSION

3.1 While there is limited evidence to support it, the Commission recognises the widespread concern about the risks to betting integrity particularly in relation to sporting events, and has been developing its policies and procedures to combat such risks. The workstream on betting integrity, taking forward the activities described in section two above, is one of the Commission's 2009/10 business plan priorities. The Commission's dedicated cross-functional betting integrity team will undertake this work.

3.2 While we are not persuaded that there is a sufficient case for restricting types of bets or dictating sporting bodies' rules in relation to betting at this time, we plan to monitor closely the effectiveness of the various actions being taken by the Commission, the industry and sporting bodies and will consider further regulatory measures if they appear warranted.

3.3 We will review this work programme in a year's time and publish a stock take of the progress made in relation to promoting integrity in betting.

APPENDIX 1

15.1 REPORTING SUSPICION OF OFFENCES ETC

All operating licences except betting, betting intermediary, ancillary remote betting and remote betting intermediary (trading rooms only) licences

Licensees must provide the Commission with any information that they know relates to or suspect may relate to the commission of an offence under the Act, including an offence resulting from a breach of a licence condition or a code provision having the effect of a licence condition.

All betting operating licences, including betting intermediary, ancillary remote betting and remote betting intermediary (trading rooms only) licences

Licensees must provide the Commission with any information that they:

- know relates to or suspect may relate to the commission of an offence under the Act, including an offence resulting from a breach of a licence condition or a code provision having the effect of a licence condition
- suspect may lead the Commission to consider making an order to void a bet.

Licensees who accept bets, or facilitate the making or acceptance of bets between others, on the outcome of horse races or other sporting events governed by one of the sport governing bodies for the time being included in Part 3 of Schedule 6 to the Act must also provide the relevant sport governing body with sufficient information to conduct an effective investigation if the licensee suspects that information in their possession may:

- lead the Commission to consider making an order to void a bet
- relate to a breach of a rule on betting applied by that sport governing body.

Gambling Commission March 2009

IN-RUNNING (IN-PLAY) BETTING: POSITION PAPER

March 2009

1 INTRODUCTION AND DEFINITION

6.2169 1.1 This paper sets out the Commission's position in relation to in-running betting. It is an updated version of the issues paper published in May 2008 for consultation and takes account of the responses we received (see the responses document published concurrently for a summary), the workshop held and our experience to date.

1.2 In-running betting (or in-play or live betting as it is also known) is betting while the event to which the bet relates is actually taking place, for example, placing a bet on a horserace while the race is being run. This form of betting takes place mainly, but not exclusively, on sporting events.

1.3 In-running betting is predominantly an online activity with bets being made via the internet using either a betting exchange or a traditional bookmaker's website, but it also takes place in betting shops or over the phone. In-running betting has become increasingly popular and a significant volume of betting takes place in-running.

2 SUMMARY OF THE COMMISSION'S POSITION

2.1 In-running betting is a popular and legitimate form of gambling. The operation of in-running betting, particularly through online facilities, raises a number of issues that have the potential to impact on the licensing objectives. These issues can be distilled into two groups: issues that concern the integrity of the betting and the subject of the betting; and, issues that relate to the fairness and openness of the betting.

2.2 In-running betting offers some increased potential for individuals to exploit this form of gambling illicitly for their own benefit. However, other forms of betting and gambling also have the potential for such exploitation. On the information currently available the Commission does not consider that in–running betting requires special regulatory treatment but it will be addressed as part of the Commission's wider efforts to maintain integrity in sports betting.

2.3 Similarly, with regard to the issues potentially affecting fairness and openness, such as speed of feeds or use of 'bots' (explained later in this document), in-running betting does not appear to generate specific additional risks to the licensing objectives as long as betting customers are sufficiently aware of their position and the respective positions of other players and the betting operators. This includes ensuring that any information deficit is clearly understood, as are any built-in time delays to the system. We do not consider it necessary to intervene to prevent some players using technology to gain an advantage in terms of speed of information, provided it is clear to all players that this can be done.

2.4 The Commission will continue to monitor the fairness and openness of in-running betting as part of its overall betting compliance programme and take its particular characteristics into account in its wider work on integrity in sports (and other) betting. The responses to its consultation document, the workshop and other enquiries over the past months, for example into potentially suspect betting patterns, do not suggest the need for any additional regulation at this stage.

3 ISSUES CONSIDERED

IN-RUNNING BETTING

3.1 In-running (or in-play) betting generally takes place on sporting events such as horseracing, football, tennis, golf and cricket. As in ante-post betting (betting taking place before the start of an event) the prices on the markets change according to the information available and where the money goes. The increased popularity of in-running betting has been brought about by technological developments that have enabled traditional bookmakers and betting exchanges to offer markets over the internet with up-to-date prices on events as they are taking place. As the in-running betting market is predominantly an internet activity this has allowed betting exchanges and traditional bookmakers to price up markets and amend them continuously, as well as allowing customers to take prices during the event that reflect the progress of that event.

3.2 It is not only betting exchanges but also traditional bookmakers that are involved in the in- running betting market. A number of bookmakers offer in-running betting through their website, over the phone or at their shops. The difference between traditional bookmakers and exchanges is that the bookmakers' markets do not change with anywhere near such speed or frequency as they are offering fixed-odds betting with themselves as the counterparty across a whole market, whereas a betting exchange matches bets at prices specified by the betting customers. Therefore the markets on betting exchanges are more fluid and vary in liquidity compared to the markets offered by a traditional bookmaker where the customers cannot choose the price.

3.3 In-running betting is often associated with short events, such as a horserace, where the action is immediate and fast-paced. However it is important to remember that in-running betting is also popular on much longer events such as a cricket test match or a golf tournament. This generates markets for the traditional bookmaker that can take bets in- running on these longer events, where fixed odds can be offered over the counter, that reflect the progress of the event. It also demonstrates the variety of events that have in- running betting markets and the varying lengths of time that the events take from start to finish; however some issues will be more relevant to the more fast-paced events than the longer-duration events.

3.4 Betting customers have traditionally sought better information when making their bets. These information advantages have traditionally been either access to inside information (potentially contrary to the rules of the sport) or else the studying of form and relevant statistics. Such information is used before the event takes place as well as in-running. But in-running betting customers are turning to other tools besides information in order to bet profitably. These advantages, in the context of in-running betting, are generally technological.

3.5 There are a number of areas where the technology may give some customers additional advantages over others. It has been suggested that there are a number of experienced and knowledgeable in-running betting customers who use advantages they have developed to win at the expense of less-experienced or less-knowledgeable betting customers. Although betting with varying levels of knowledge and skill is not unfair in itself, there may be a problem where betting customers perceive their chances to be better than they actually are due to a lack of knowledge of the in-running betting in terms of the subject- matter itself or the actual market and how it operates. For example, less well-informed betting customers could take part in in-running betting not realising that they may actually have an informational disadvantage due to the variable speed of information feeds. The concern is whether there is any possible unfairness or just insufficient awareness of the potential disparity in knowledge about how the market works, how the odds are generated and whether the betting customer is aware of what is going on at the event.

3.6 Despite some assertions to the contrary, what limited evidence we have seen to date indicates that the market for in-running betting is likely to be made up predominantly of knowledgeable and skilled betting customers. This is backed up by analysis which shows a success rate percentage for in-running betting with one company being slightly higher than successful bets made ante-post (that is prior to the event to which the bet relates starting). Additionally, no evidence has emerged from complaints or compliance work that would suggest there are specific concerns relating to differential knowledge levels. The feedback we received from the 2008 consultation suggests that further warnings are not necessary as customers are aware of the risks involved in betting in-running and the nature of such markets. However we do not rule out taking further action to ensure a level playing field in the future should any further evidence emerge suggesting this is required.

TECHNOLOGICAL ADVANTAGES

3.7 There is inequality between in-running betting customers when it comes to the availability of information and technology. This is manifested in three related areas: sources of information and time delays; availability of high-speed broadband; and computer software packages that are specifically designed to assist in-running betting customers (known as 'bots').

3.8 There are a number of feeds that inform people on live sports through television or radio with variable time delays between different feeds showing the same sporting event. For example, an analogue signal on television or radio will be slightly ahead of the equivalent digitally-sourced feed as it does not need to go through the compression and encoding/decoding process. Likewise a cable signal and a satellite feed, as different modes of transmission, will vary in how long the picture takes to be transmitted. Ultimately, the least delay is experienced by being at the event and watching it live.

3.9 Pictures of live sporting events that are shown in betting shops from broadcasters may be several seconds behind the actual event. This is due to the distance the signal has to travel to the studio via satellite and then out to the customers via another satellite (known as 'satellite latency'). The pictures also have to go through the encoding/decoding process twice in order to be beamed via satellite onto the television screen. This has created a gap in information between those who are at the live event and those who are watching the event through a feed.

3.10 There is also the gap between the speeds of the various feeds due to the technological process of producing the feed. A lot of betting customers will use the internet to source feeds showing the live sporting event. These delays vary tremendously and can be up to several minutes behind the action depending on the provider.

3.11 These variations in how a feed is sourced mean that, for example, two betting customers using the same betting exchange could be making bets on the same event and at the same time but based on different information. This gap in the speed of the source of information can be exploited by some betting customers. Those people who have a faster source of information can use it to take advantage of prices that do not reflect the actual progress of the event.

3.12 The variable time delays are of particular relevance to events where the action at the event can suddenly change over a short period of time and have an effect on the market. This is the case in most sports: from a faller at a horserace to a wicket being taken in a cricket match. When such occurrences happen that will change the odds available in a market, those who have access to the information fastest can potentially take advantage to make a profit.

3.13 It has been suggested to us that the ability to obtain information ahead of the rest of the market would constitute an unfair advantage. This could apply to betting customers with shorter time delays on their feed showing the event, or equally to the betting customer who is betting while actually at the live event. The counter-proposition is that provided that customers are fully informed of the risks that they run, they should be free to decide whether or not to bet.

3.14 The Commission's Remote Gambling and Software Technical Standards (RTS) already reflect this issue. Information Provision Annex 3 currently refers to in-running betting and sets out a provision to ensure customers are informed on this issue:

INFORMATION PROVISION ANNEX (IPA) 3 – IN-RUNNING BETTING

BETTING AND PEER-TO-PEER BETTING

IPA aim 3

To make the customer aware that they may not have the latest information available when betting on live events, and that they may be at a disadvantage to operators or other customers who have more up-to-date information.

IPA requirement 3A

Information must be made available that explains that 'live' TV or other broadcasts are delayed and that others may have more up-to-date information. Main in-running betting pages must be designed to include this information where practicable.

IPA implementation guidance 3A

(a) Brief information should be included on main in-running pages or screens, such as the in-running home page or screen. More detail should be provided in 'help' or 'how to' or other product pages or screens.

(b) For telephone betting the information should be included in the general betting or product information that is made available to and/or sent out to customers.

(c) Where a brief notice cannot be practicably included on the main pages or screens, the information should be provided on easily accessible 'help', 'how to' or other product pages or screens.

3.15 This provision in our RTS requires online operators offering in-running betting to put up a warning that feeds showing sporting events may have a time delay on them. It is designed to inform in-running betting customers that other people may have faster feeds and therefore better information for making their bets. It is a condition of a remote operator's licence that they comply with this standard.

3.16 The advent of broadband internet has brought about an increased popularity in using web- based companies for a number of different activities including betting. The variability in speed between dial-up and broadband, and between different broadband services, generates the ability for some betting customers to make their bets faster than others.

3.17 Again this is of particular relevance to a betting exchange, in that there will be betting customers who are at the front of the market and are able to respond more quickly to events as they happen in-running because of their high-speed internet connection.

3.18 Another technological advantage available to betting customers on exchanges is 'bots'. 'Bots' are complex software packages that are generally available to the public as downloads from the internet (usually at a cost). They have a number of different functions, depending on the package used, but include the ability to make bets much more rapidly which can allow the in-running betting customer to react much more quickly to events in a fast-paced market. This ability to be ahead of the market gives an inherent advantage in seeking to obtain the best possible price.

3.19 'Bots' also allow users to take part on a number of different betting markets at the same time and assist in calculating where a market is not efficient and taking full advantage of it. Among the other functions they can offer is the ability to allow a betting customer to automatically 'green up' on a market (ie backing and laying on the same outcome at different odds in a fluid market to ensure that they have a profit locked in whatever the outcome).

3.20 Betting customers using 'bots' obtain a number of advantages over other customers who either choose not to use a 'bot' or do not even know about them. The use of 'bots' automates the process of betting and turns it into a process more akin to trading on the stock exchange. Interest in, or knowledge of, the sporting event is unnecessary as the 'bot' enables the user to make decisions and place bets in order to make a profit by trading on their betting position using market fluctuations.
3.21 While there remains some concern on the part of commentators about the breadth of awareness among in-running betting customers about differential feed speeds, the risk of betting on different information and the possible use of 'bots', the level of awareness of variable time delays appears high and the availability and use of 'bots' is publicised. As with the fast feeds and variable time delays, it is the case that such equipment is publicly available, at a cost, and used for benefit in these particular markets. The limited evidence we have received indicates that the level of awareness of variable time delays and other technological advantages is high among in-running betting customers and there is no need for further information requirements relating to these issues at present.
3.22 The Commission would not take action against technological advances per se unless the risk to the licensing objectives were proven or probable. On the basis of our information to date there is an insufficient case in relation to any threat to the licensing objectives for regulatory action over the use of technological advantages such as differential feeds or use of bots.

TRADING ROOMS

3.23 Trading rooms are a recent innovation and represent a particular case of technological advantage. They are a similar concept to internet cafes but are dedicated to providing a service specifically for online betting customers, particularly those using exchanges. From the evidence we have, which includes consultation and workshop responses, as well as informal evidence gathering from such sources as the internet betting forums, we consider that there is a general awareness of the existence and purpose of trading rooms among in- running betting customers.
3.24 These trading rooms rent seats at a high-performance PC with high-speed broadband internet and dedicated sports feeds with some of the shortest time delays in order to put their customers in the best possible position for their betting. These trading rooms aim to maximise the potential technological advantages available on behalf of their customers in return for a fee for use of the PCs. Some also have commercial arrangements with a betting operator where they receive a percentage fee from their customers' winnings with that operator.
3.25 This concept is targeted particularly at customers who 'trade' on a betting exchange (ie rather than just having a few simple bets they will back and lay on a market to achieve a profitable outcome, akin to trading on the stock market) and who are betting mainly in- running in order to guarantee themselves profits by trading betting positions at optimal prices. These customers will pay the necessary charge to use the trading room in order to gain the technological advantages over other betting customers. As noted above, some argue that the technological advantages constitute an unfair advantage.
3.26 However it has also been suggested that the main profits from in-running betting come by being able to read and understand what is happening at the sporting event and this is the key driver for making a profit at in-running betting but that the increasing popularity of trading rooms is being driven by all the technological advantages available to assist betting customers in utilising their skill. Others point to non-monetary reasons why people use trading rooms, such as the opportunity to interact with others and view a wider range of sports feeds.
3.27 Trading rooms now have a specific licence fee category as a type of remote betting intermediary and are regulated by the Commission. The licence fees for trading rooms were set following a consultation exercise on the Gambling Commission fees

from 1 August 2008. The Commission has brought trading rooms within the licensing regime and considers this to be a suitable and proportionate response to the growth and development of trading rooms. We do not consider that any further action on trading rooms is required apart from continuing to police them in accordance with the existing licensing regime and to monitor the level of awareness among customers generally of the range of technological advantages.

TIME DELAYS IN BET PROCESSING

3.28 At present, operators set a time delay so that when a customer places an order for a bet in- running they will have to wait a number of seconds between pressing the 'place bet' button and receiving confirmation that the bet has been made. This is done in order to ensure that the odds on offer reflect the progress of the event and that bets made are a true reflection of what is happening with an up-to-date market. It should be noted that there is a difference in reasoning between traditional bookmakers and betting exchanges – exchanges put in place a standard delay to protect customers, traditional bookmakers put in a delay to ensure their own prices are correct. This delay usually covers the time delay in the speed of feed that is being used to adjust the market and a small margin to enable the operator to react to a significant event.

3.29 We are aware that there have been attempts to circumvent the time delay in the processing of bets. When this occurs, people are able to achieve far better odds than would be the case if the market followed the course of the event. For example, in a football match when a goal is scored the market needs to be corrected to reflect the progress of the game following the scoring of the goal.

3.30 These time delays may increase openness and fairness by allowing betting operators to suspend their in-running markets (ie preventing bets being taken) when a key event occurs that will affect the markets, and for traditional betting operators to correct them (this correction happens naturally on betting exchanges). It also allows betting exchanges to level the playing field for all customers by suspending markets before some people can take advantage of the market situation in the period between a significant event occurring and the market being corrected.

3.31 However there is the converse problem that the offer of a bet by the betting customer to the operator can be delayed during the action when a significant event occurs. In this scenario there is a lag between the offer of the bet and the accepting of the bet by someone with more up-to-date knowledge. This raises the related question of whether there should be more warning about time delays in processing and accepting bets so that betting customers understand when the contract is made and what their position is between when they think they have made the bet and when it is confirmed.

3.32 Some operators will use different time delays for different sports and the approach taken to the suspension of markets varies between sports and events. It is more feasible to suspend markets when a key event occurs for slower paced sports where the key events occur less frequently and are clearly defined (eg football and a goal being scored) than for faster paced events where what could be considered a key event happens very frequently (eg horseracing and a horse falling).

3.33 There are three prime factors affecting time delays when a betting customer goes to place a bet online. There is the delay, mentioned above, which the operator physically puts in to cover the risk of a customer being ahead of the other's knowledge as shown by the system. The second delay is the physical process of accepting the bet by the operator and the time taken to send a bet through the system. The quality of operators' technology to deal with online in-running betting may vary and we have heard of complaints from customers that the technological capacity of some operators' systems is insufficient, leaving them uncertain of whether their bet has been processed and the price they have received. There is, therefore, a tension between operators implementing a time delay to ensure market correction and having a fast-paced in-running opportunity but with the risk of old prices being available. The final delay is rarer and that is when a bet, frequently over the phone, is referred to a trader for approval. This referral necessarily causes a time delay while a decision is made; however we do not consider any action here to be required at the present time.

3.34 This leads to concerns that these delays put together could mean that customers betting on a fast-paced event in-running, or on a market where a significant event is likely to occur that will change the market, are put at unacceptable risk, in the sense that they are uncertain of the status of their bets and therefore their financial position, due to the amount of time it takes from making the bet to the bet actually being confirmed.

3.35 The Commission is clear that the existence of the time delays that are built into systems when bets are being processed should always be clearly communicated to customers, but is not convinced that it is necessary or practical at this stage to set out standards for time delays, bet acceptance and standard times for accepting or rejecting a bet. The Commission is aware that certain operators already provide clear information on delays in processing bets. We will monitor whether this is more widely adopted through our compliance activity and, if it is not, will consider whether any further steps can be taken to ensure awareness of these time delays.

CHEATING AND INTEGRITY IN SPORTS BETTING

3.36 A number of commentators and participants have raised the issue of whether in-running betting is more prone to potential cheating offences than regular ante-post betting. One well-publicised case, involving a tennis match, brought about a whole market being voided by an operator due to suspicious in-running betting patterns. Cheating, including collusion with sports players, could take place on an event where the betting customer obtains an advantage both ante-post and in-running but it is widely argued that there are specific inherent or greater risks involved with in-running betting that are not present or so great for ante-post betting.

3.37 There is a particular concern that the availability of in-running betting can have an effect on player performance. For example, in a sport between two individuals, one player can underperform deliberately to begin with so that his odds will drift out. The player can then perform at full potential and go on to win. This example was raised in research conducted by the University of Salford for the Central Council for Physical Recreation (CCPR)[1] which discusses theoretical risks that in-running betting could potentially pose to betting integrity.

---

[1] Available on CCPR's website.

3.38 The Salford research also discusses risk assessment of certain types of bets and highlights a number of types of bets that are available in-running that could potentially pose an increased risk to integrity in sports betting. It highlights underperformance of players as a potential risk for integrity in in-running sports betting. The research considers eight sports and sets out the range of bets that are typically available in-running. The types of in-running bets that are listed could be characterised as potentially producing additional risk due to their very nature, for example in-running bets where one sportsperson can affect the outcome of the bet, such as next man out in cricket. Others have raised concerns in relation to market suspensions and bets staked on photo finishes and stewards' enquiries.

3.39 While the Salford work identifies areas of theoretical risk to betting integrity, there have been relatively few incidents reported of concern over betting patterns and even fewer that still appear suspect after initial examination. Some find this reassuring; others doubt the effectiveness of the reporting requirements or investigations. To address the former concerns last October the Commission introduced a revised version of Licence Condition 15.1 in our updated Licence Conditions and Codes of Practice. This condition puts specific obligations on licensees to share any information with the Commission and the sport governing bodies in particular circumstances. This strengthened provision should help ensure that potential threats to betting integrity are highlighted and properly investigated. The Commission is also working with both betting operators and sport governing bodies to develop a common understanding and working practices for sharing information on suspicious betting patterns and tackling risks to betting integrity. This should also provide a better evidence base for considering if any further action is needed.

3.40 The updated position paper on betting integrity published concurrently[2] addresses the potential risk to integrity from in-running betting as part of the Commission's wider efforts to maintain betting integrity.

2 Betting Integrity: Policy position paper (March 2009).

PROBLEM GAMBLING

3.41 The Commission must also consider whether certain activities can lead to increases in problem gambling. People who bet in-running will frequently make a large volume of bets over the course of a betting session. This could be the normal activity of a skilful or committed customer who concentrates on betting in-running, or it could be symptomatic of problem gambling. It has been suggested that the potential for rapid, repetitive betting in in- running betting markets may increase the risk of problem gambling.

3.42 So far there has not been evidence to suggest that in-running betting poses a specific, identifiable risk to problem gambling as opposed to other forms of betting or online gambling.

SPREAD BETTING

3.43 In-running betting could be seen as similar to trading on the financial markets. In this context there is a parallel with spread betting, although spread betting is a different form of betting in the sense that instead of offering odds on an event happening, the market offers a price for a spread of points on a likely outcome where you can buy or sell points depending on your view of how the event will finish. The other key difference is that, in principle, losses in spread betting are not limited to the amount staked as they are in fixed odds betting.

3.44 There is a particular concern that the availability of in-running betting can have an effect on player performance. For example, in a sport between two individuals, one player can underperform deliberately to begin with so that his odds will drift out. The player can then perform at full potential and go on to win. This example was raised in research conducted by the University of Salford for the Central Council for Physical Recreation (CCPR)1 which discusses theoretical risks that in-running betting could potentially pose to betting integrity.

3.45 The FSA has its Conduct of Business rules which regulate how spread betting companies are to treat their clients. The overarching principles bear a significant similarity to how we approach regulation of betting operators although there are some differences in the detailed arrangements, with more constraints on inexperienced users of the spread betting markets but no provision for information exchange with sporting bodies. While there have been calls for spread betting operators to play a more active part in combating risks to sports betting integrity, there has been little call or evidence of the need for the sort of constraints on new players that exist in spread betting.

3.46 We will continue to liaise with the FSA to ensure we share best practice and keep under review the need for more constraints on new players.

4 CONCLUSION

4.1 Although in the last 18 months we have received few specific complaints about particular aspects of in-running betting we have heard from those who have general

concerns about in-running betting in the context of the three licensing objectives. However those concerned did not provide much by way of specific evidence or corroboration of those concerns. From the evidence we have received and considered to date, we have come to the conclusion that the current regulatory regime we have in place for in-running betting is sufficient and does not need further controls at this time. However we will continue to monitor in-running betting as part of the Commission's compliance programme. Particularly we will focus on developing information sharing under licence condition 15.1. We will address in-running betting's potential for facilitating cheating as part of the Commission's wider efforts to maintain integrity in betting.
Gambling Commission March 2009

THE GAMBLING COMMISSION'S BETTING INTEGRITY DECISION MAKING FRAMEWORK
December 2010

1 INTRODUCTION

6.2170 1.1 Under the Gambling Act 2005 (the Act) the Gambling Commission (the Commission) has powers to prosecute offences of cheating and to void bets. Our powers to prosecute cheating offences apply where a person cheats at gambling or where they do anything for the purposes of enabling or assisting another (person) to cheat at gambling.

1.2 We also have powers to make an order voiding an individual bet accepted by, or through, the holder of a betting specific licence. Where the Commission exercises this power, any contract or other arrangement relating to the bet will be void, and any money paid in relation to the bet must be returned to the person who paid it. The power to void a bet only applies to the parties to a specific bet; it does not apply to all bets placed on an event.

1.3 In addition a key component of the Commission's work on betting integrity is a licence condition (15.1)[1] which requires betting operators to share information on suspicious transactions with the Commission and sports governing bodies (SGBs).

1.4 In March 2009, the Commission published a policy position paper on betting integrity[2] that summarised the work we had done to date with sports governing bodies, the betting industry and others and outlined our commitment to strengthen the deterrents against corruption with a view to profit from betting.

1.5 Following on from the policy paper, in mid 2009, the then Minister for Sport, brought together a panel of experts, including key people from the principal organisations involved – from the betting industry, the police, players, fans, SGBs, the legal profession and the Commission, to look at a wide range of issues relating to sports betting integrity. They were asked to make recommendations on how the various bodies concerned could work together more effectively. The main focus was the design and implementation of an integrated strategy to uphold integrity in sports and associated betting.

1.6 One of the recommendations of the Panel was that:

> " . . . the Gambling Commission should work with the police and the Sports Betting Group to publish its decision making framework in the area of betting related corruption. This would provide greater clarity of expectation over when a particular incident might be treated as a criminal investigation or a sports disciplinary matter; and the circumstances under which police cooperation or, indeed, a police lead would be appropriate."

1.7 There are various published documents that help set out the Commission's decision making processes, most notably the Commission's document *Licensing, Compli-*

ance and Enforcement policy statement (September 2009)[3], or provide relevant information, such as the Sports Betting Intelligence Unit Terms of Reference (June 2010)[4]. This document sets out the Commission's processes and decision making framework, in the context of betting integrity and, in parts, in greater detail, from when it first receives a piece of information through to when a case is closed. The Commission's framework has been refined following the development of the Sport Betting Intelligence Unit (SBIU), another recommendation of the Panel. This document is aimed at those bodies the Commission might work with in respect of betting integrity.

1.8 This document may be revised from time to time to reflect any developments in the Commission's approach.

2 SUMMARY

2.1 The overall aim of the Commission, and its partners, is to reduce the likelihood of corruption and where it is discovered to cause it to end. This is best achieved by working together on a combination of prevention, disruption, deterrence and sanction opportunities.

2.2 Pursuing a criminal sanction will not always be possible, and often will not be the most effective or efficient approach to take. It is usually not possible to prove that the result of an event has been manipulated simply by watching the event; instead, a criminal case will very often rely on establishing relationships between those involved and following flows of money. As a result it can be both very time consuming and costly. The Commission noted in its policy position paper of March 2009 that investigation and sanction by the SGB may be a more appropriate approach to achieve our aim, be quicker than criminal investigation and therefore may be the more frequently taken approach.

2.3 A SGB sanction can act as a timely deterrent. In short this is because the standards of proof required for a civil sanction are lesser than those required for a criminal sanction and an SGB's rules, when effectively applied can be an effective control to achieve our joint aims. Our decision making framework reflects this aim and these issues. However, each case will be considered on its merits and appropriate action taken dependent on the circumstances. Furthermore, SGB action doesn't rule out the possibility of a criminal charge brought in an appropriate case.

2.4 Once a piece of information is received there are broadly four key partners who can be involved in a case – the Commission, SGBs, betting operators and the police (and/or other law enforcement agencies). The flow chart overleaf, in general terms, sets out how a case progresses and the decision making processes. However, it should be noted that this model does not purport to capture all circumstances and the approach may vary according to the occasion. The flow chart will be useful to understand the structure, and different sections, of this document.

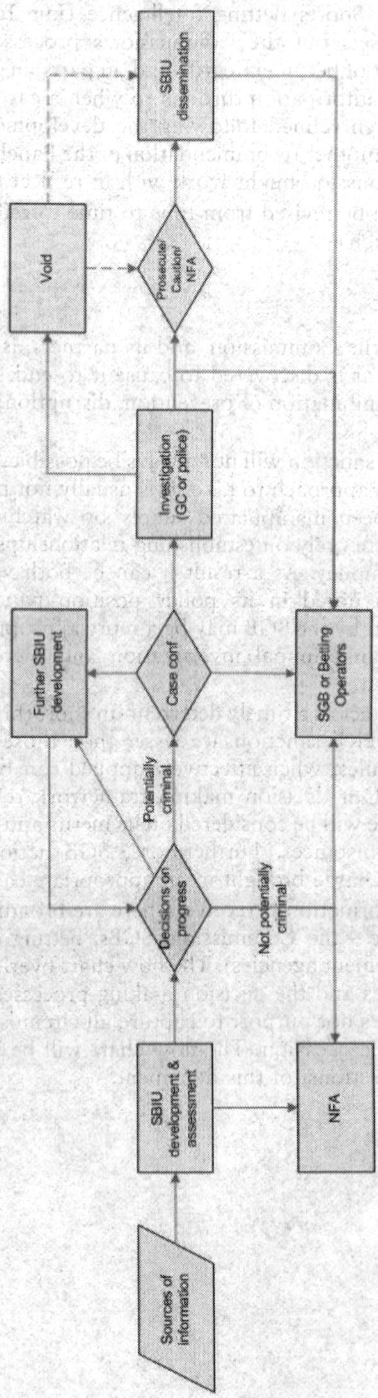
Sources of information
SBIU development & assessment
NFA
Decisions on progress
Not potentially criminal
Potentially criminal
Further SBIU development
Case conf
SGB or Betting Operators
Investigation (GC or police)
Void
Prosecute/ Caution/ NFA
SBIU dissemination

3 THE COMMISSION'S APPROACH AND DECISION MAKING FRAMEWORK

SOURCES OF INFORMATION

3.1 The Commission receives information from a variety of sources, including:

- betting operators
- sports governing bodies
- law enforcement
- other Commission work or other regulators
- Commission's confidential hotline
- media.

The majority of information comes from betting operators. They are required to provide us with information about suspicious betting as one of their licence conditions (15.1). Not doing so would threaten their licence. Betting operators are also obliged by this condition to pass information to SGBs where appropriate. However, betting operators can also pass other information that they consider might be of relevance to the SBIU, whether or not it reaches their criteria of "suspicious". The SBIU has been working closely with operators to embed this approach. The Commission is currently considering whether there is a need to amend licence condition 15.1 and related matters (a further recommendation of the Panel)[5]. The Commission can also request specific information under licence condition 15.3.

3.2 SGBs pass information to the Commission which can be information gained through their own means or that originally passed by a betting operator to which they have been able to add further detail.

3.3 Law enforcement and the media are other potential source of information, as are other regulators (for example gambling regulators overseas). The Commission might also develop information in the course of other work that is relevant to betting integrity (other betting integrity cases or regulatory work with operators) including that from our confidential hotline.

SBIU DEVELOPMENT AND ASSESSMENT

3.4 Having received the information, the SBIU will look to establish whether there is any potential criminal activity by ascertaining:

- whether there is an identifiable event (or events)
- whether there is an identifiable participant (or participants)
- whether there is an identifiable betting party (or parties)
- the scope and scale of activity
- any links to other intelligence or cases (Commission or otherwise).

The SBIU will also consider whether the activity falls within its terms of reference, in particular whether the activity:

- relates to a sporting event that occurred in Great Britain, and/ or
- involves parties based within Great Britain, and/ or
- occurred with a Gambling Commission licensed operator.

3.5 The quality and detail of information provided may vary substantially. Whilst the SBIU will assess all information provided it must prioritise its use of resources. Accordingly, it may be that not enough information is provided to warrant further work on an issue at that stage. For example, if a single individual or organisation considers a particular event as suspicious, but the SBIU is unable to verify important elements then it may not be considered appropriate for the SBIU to investigate it further at that stage. However, the information will be logged and if further relevant information came to light the issue could be looked at again.

3.6 The relevant SGB is often contacted at this stage. Where there is sufficient information to warrant further work the SBIU will attempt to ascertain the information set out at section 3.4.

3.7 It is important that those providing information to the Commission provide as much relevant detail as possible and provide it as early as possible (most notably the event/s, participant/s, betting party or parties and scope and scale of activity as set out in section 3.4). The more comprehensive the information that can be gained, and the quicker it is provided, the more efficiently and effectively the Commission can determine an appropriate course of action. Speed is important in processing information as the longer the period between the incident and investigation the greater the likelihood that certain evidence may no longer exist.

DECISIONS ON HOW TO PROGRESS THE INTELLIGENCE GATHERED

3.8 It may be quickly established that a referral is not suitable for investigation focused upon a criminal prosecution – for example, a player betting on themself to win might be against the sport's rules, but it is unlikely to be a criminal offence. The SBIU would be unlikely to look into this further, unless there were other issues of relevance. Our investigatory powers, such as those under Regulation of Investigatory Powers Act 2000 (RIPA) and Proceeds of Crime Act 2002 (POCA), can only be utilised when investigating (which covers intelligence work as well as enforcement work) a potential crime. As such we could not use our powers once we consider an issue unsuitable for investigation.

3.9 Once it has been established to the satisfaction of the SBIU that there is potential criminal activity (by reference to the information in section 3.4) a decision (by the Commission's intelligence and enforcement teams in collaboration is taken as to how to progress the issue. Broadly speaking this establishes whether the Commission could progress a case, whereas the case conference stage establishes whether it should.

3.10 There may be situations where the necessary information to establish whether there is any potentially criminal activity cannot be secured or cannot be secured in a reasonable time or without disproportionate effort. These situations would also be considered at this formal decision making stage as it is important to consider whether there may be sufficient information to make a decision on how to progress anyway.

3.11 The decision of how to progress an issue is based on an assessment of whether there is a potential criminal activity by considering whether there are/is:

- identifiable events
- identifiable participants
- identifiable betting patterns and activity
- identifiable links between them.

3.12 If there is no potential criminal activity the options are to go to the SGB, betting operator or take no further action. If there is potentially criminal activity the options are to progress this to a case conference, engage in further SBIU development or take no further action at this time

3.13 There are five decisions that could be made at this point:

- no further action – for example, this could be because there was an appropriate explanation for a suspicious pattern or insufficient information is available to proceed (in which case the information would be logged on our intelligence database)
- refer to SGB – this could be where there is potentially a breach of a sport's rule. The SGB would then decide how to proceed with it. Details of the Commission's approach to sharing information with partners can be found at section 3.35-3.39
- refer to betting operator/s – this could be where there is potentially a breach of a betting operator's terms and conditions or contracts of employment. The betting operator would then decide how to proceed with it. Details of the Commission's approach to sharing information with partners can be found at section 3.35-3.39

- progress to a case conference – this is where there is sufficient intelligence and evidence to progress the matter. There may be times where the significance of an issue might mean it is escalated to the case conference stage before all of the elements at 3.11 have been identified
- further SBIU development – to secure additional intelligence and evidence.

CASE CONFERENCE

3.14 The Statement of Principles for Licensing and Regulation (September 2009) sets out the principles which underpin the Commission's approach to investigations and prosecutions. The Commission's approach to betting integrity sits within this broad framework. As noted in paragraph 2.1 a SGB applying a sanction is likely to be a quicker and less costly deterrent than the Commission or police pursuing a criminal sanction. As such there is a presumption that only more serious cases would potentially be appropriate for a criminal sanction. Decisions on how to proceed from a case conference are based on what would be the most proportionate way to address an issue and will take into account:

- what would be the most effective and timely deterrent and sanction
- scope and scale of criminality
- harm to/ impact on victims, including the sport or betting customers
- scale of potential winnings
- evidential prospects
- available resources
- the need to collaborate with other law enforcement agencies or partners
- wider factors that may override these in certain circumstances.

3.15 To give an indication of how the criteria might be used:

- if the scope and scale of criminality is high (for example, a number of participants and betting parties are involved) and/ or there is a need for collaborations the Commission is likely to try to engage the police, most likely as the lead body. If the scope and criminality is high it is feasible that offences other than "cheat" might be relevant
- if a swift and significant sanction could be applied by the SGB (which offers an effective deterrent to others) then that might be the most appropriate route
- if the scale of criminality is low or the scale of the potential winnings and harm/ impact on victims is low it is more likely that the Commission will pass this to SGBs or operators to take disruptive action rather than prosecute. One example might be where the outcome of the event has not been influenced; another might be where those betting fairly have not been disadvantaged
- a theoretical example of an overriding factor might be where it is considered appropriate to take a case to prosecution in a particular sport (or against a particular type of participant) where a theme has developed to provide a deterrent effect – it is possible that a case might be taken where it would normally not be, based on the other factors alone
- a further example of an overriding factor might be where a precedent could be set and needs to be legally tested. The Commission is more likely to take such a case.

3.16 All of the factors above are taken into account when making a decision. There are no set limits for each or a sequential way in which they are considered. It is important to retain flexibility in what is progressed.

3.17 The potential outcomes from a case conference are:

- investigation (Commission or police led)
- disruptive (including disciplinary) action by SGBs or betting operators
- further development by the SBIU
- no further action.

3.18 The decision on how to progress a case is taken by the Commission's enforcement team, escalated appropriately dependent on the scale of resources that may need to be committed to conclude a case.

3.19 'Disruptive action' is a wide term that covers action taken to disrupt those seeking to corrupt sports betting integrity and can occur before the event has taken place, before winnings are collected or later, such that a repeat occurrence is made less likely. Even when an issue is potentially criminal, disruptive action might often be the most effective way of addressing it. Disruptive action would normally (but not exclusively) be carried out by the relevant SGB or betting operator on the basis of information provided by the Commission. Most frequently this would take the form of a disciplinary sanction which would have an impact on the participant and provide a wider deterrent within the sport. It might also take the form of pre-game warnings if the SGB is aware of an issue before the game or of the betting operator withholding payment on a bet.

3.20 Further SBIU development to gather additional information necessary might be required to take a decision as to how to proceed. This particularly might be the case if an issue had been escalated in the absence of all the necessary information (for example because it was taking longer to gather or the issue warranted early escalation), perhaps just to gather the full range of information (as noted at 3.10 and 3.13).

3.21 'No further action' might be an appropriate outcome where a SGB or betting operator has considered the issue and decided it is not appropriate or feasible for them to take disruptive action.

EFFECTIVE USE OF RESOURCES

3.22 An underlying aim of this approach is to ensure that criminality activity ceases and that the partners involved use their resources in the most effective and efficient way possible to achieve an effective combination of prevention, deterrence, disruption and sanction.

3.23 The issue of available resources applies to all parties. For example, it is feasible that something that might most appropriately be led by the police cannot be because the relevant force does not have the available resources at that time. Similarly, the Commission's resources are finite; it regulates the whole of the gambling industry and has a budget of £13m (which is reducing in the current economic climate) which is based on the workloads created by the operators we regulate.

INVESTIGATION (COMMISSION OR POLICE)

3.24 The Commission's broad policy framework in relation to the investigation and prosecution of offences under the Act, including the Commission's powers is set out in the Commission's document *Licensing, Compliance and Enforcement policy statement (September 2009)*[3]. Investigations in respect of betting integrity can be taken singularly by the police or Commission or the lead can be taken by one and supported by the other. This arrangement can change during the course of a case depending on developments.

3.25 The investigation process will seek to convert that intelligence into evidence and develop further lines of enquiry as required. The Commission will use the investigative resources available to it to establish whether the activity in question is consistent with cheating, for example our powers under RIPA or POCA. The Commission will generally work with relevant SGBs and betting operators during the investigation process.

3.26 The Commission may at times use expert witnesses to inform our understanding of a situation (or during a prosecution). The Commission will generally discuss with the relevant SGB (or potentially betting operator, depending on circumstances) who an appropriate expert witness might be. The Commission will not necessarily seek a definitive statement that an individual has cheated or not performed to the best of their abilities, but just a view on whether the performance is consistent with the allegation made.

INFORMATION TO SGBS AND OPERATORS DURING INVESTIGATIONS

3.27 The Commission may, where appropriate, share information with SGBs and betting operators during investigations (more information on information sharing is available from paragraph 3.35). It may be feasible for a SGB to prepare or progress disciplinary cases under sports rules at the same time as a criminal investigation (as noted in *The British Horseracing Authority and Integrity in Horseracing Review* by Dame Elizabeth Neville[6]) and it may be appropriate for betting operators to take appropriate action in their own right. These should be the subject of joint discussions to ensure neither the criminal nor the disciplinary action could negatively impact on the other.

VOIDING

3.28 The Commission has powers to void individual bets either as a disruptive end in itself or as a stage on the way to a prosecution. More detail about this power is set out in section 5.41 to 5.47 of *Licensing, Compliance and Enforcement policy statement (September 2009)*[3].

3.29 The Commission would normally only contemplate suspending or voiding bets where our investigations have established a pattern of apparently corrupt behaviour. This is because, although the evidential test for the Commission to be "satisfied that the bet was substantially unfair" is lower than the test for securing a criminal conviction for cheating, the evidential strands to substantiate a conclusion of that a bet is "substantially unfair" are broadly the same. In such circumstances the Commission, and/ or others, may monitor those suspected so that it is able to move to impose interim moratoria or void bets more swiftly in the future on the basis of the accumulated evidence and a pattern of suspicious activity or repeated suspicious circumstances.

PROSECUTION

3.30 Following an investigation the Commission may proceed to prosecution, issue a caution or decide to take no further action. Information concerning the framework for deciding how to proceed following a criminal investigation is set out in section 6.8 to 6.111 of *Licensing, Compliance and Enforcement policy statement (September 2009)* 3.

3.31 The Commission will apply the Code for Crown Prosecutors when deciding whether criminal proceedings should be commenced, which involves a two-stage test:

- first, the evidence will be reviewed and an assessment made about whether there is a realistic prospect of conviction
- secondly, if there is sufficient evidence to mean that there is a realistic prospect of conviction, an assessment will be made about whether it is in the public interest for a prosecution to take place.

If either of those tests is not met no further action relating to a criminal prosecution would be taken although referral to the relevant SGB may be considered appropriate.

3.32 Whilst the Commission can take prosecutions itself, often such court cases will be led by the Crown Prosecution Service (CPS), particularly where a police force has been involved, so whether or not to prosecute will often be a decision for them in the first instance. If the CPS does not think it appropriate to prosecute, the Commission is unlikely to proceed independently unless there are exceptional circumstances (for example, the need to set a legal precedent).

3.33 Section 6.14 of *Licensing, Compliance and Enforcement policy statement (September 2009)*[3] notes that in appropriate cases, where the Commission has investigated a matter and both the evidential and public interest tests are met, the Commission may decide to issue a caution to the alleged offender, rather than pursue a prosecution. Where a caution is administered, details of the caution will be kept on file and may be taken into account in the future if further offences occur.

SBIU DISSEMINATION

3.34 Following the outcome of a case, including where there is no further action, the SBIU may disseminate information to other parties. The information that can be shared will be dependent on the case and any legal restrictions which may apply. More information on this is set out in the section below. The SBIU would also welcome any relevant information from partners on the completion of any action taken by them regarding lessons learnt or emerging themes.

SHARING INFORMATION WITH PARTNERS

3.35 The Commission will generally look to share information with partners where it is considered appropriate to do so and having made the decision will do so as soon as possible. Generally, and particularly for non-law enforcement partners, this will be in a summarised format. The Commission is usually more able to share data with law enforcement agencies for the purpose of criminal investigations. However, there are constraints as to the circumstances in which the Commission can share data.

3.36 Section 30[7] and schedule 6[8] (which names a number of SGBs) of the Act provide a limited list of third parties with whom the Commission may provide information received by it in the course of its duties. However the Commission may choose to provide information to parties not listed where this is considered appropriate in furtherance of the licensing objectives and is not prohibited by any statutory provision or legal principle. Where necessary information provided by the Commission to third parties may be subject to conditions, including the requirement to apply good information handling procedures. The Commission would not be able to pass data to those that do not have appropriate information handling procedures.

3.37 All disclosures of personal data made by the Commission will be subject to the requirements of the Human Rights Act 1998 and the Data Protection Act 1998. This includes the principles of data protection as well as the data protection non-disclosure provisions which provide for the disclosure of personal data to third parties in particular circumstances. We will only share data which the recipient is clearly lawfully entitled to access to in pursuance of their duties.

3.38 We will also be mindful of the source of our information, the powers under which we secured it and, in light of that, whether it is proportionate to disclose. For example, if we secure information under RIPA in the course of investigating a potentially criminal action that identifies a relatively minor sports rule infraction it may not be appropriate to share that information. It would not be good practice to routinely pass information secured under criminal powers to other bodies to take a civil sanction; this could call into question the use of our powers.

However, it also should be noted that we do receive a significant amount of useful information from other sources, such as licence condition 15.1 or through our hotline which, subject to the restrictions noted in paragraph 3.37, we are able to pass to partners with less constraints.

3.39 Principle 8 of data protection states that personal data shall not be provided outside of the European Economic Area (EEA) unless an adequate level of protection is applied. The Commission will be particularly vigilant when sharing personal data in these circumstances.

---

1 Licence Conditions and Code of Practice- October 2008

2 Betting Integrity: Policy position paper — March 2009

3 Licensing, Compliance and Enforcement policy statement- September 2009

4 Sports Betting Intelligence Unit terms of reference- June 2010

5 Whilst nothing in such a review would undermine the principles here this section may be expanded in due course if necessary to reflect any changes made.

6 The British Horseracing Authority and Integrity in Horseracing Review, May 2008

[7] Section 30, Gambling Act 2005

[8] Schedule 6, Gambling Act 2005

Gambling Commission December 2010

IS A TRADING ROOM LICENCE REQUIRED? March 2011

1 INTRODUCTION

6.2171 1.1 The Gambling Commission (the Commission) is frequently asked whether a particular business arrangement requires a Betting Intermediary (trading room only) operating licence. The answer to that question depends upon whether the business configuration is offering facilities for gambling as defined in section 5 of the Gambling Act 2005 (the Act).

1.2 This advice note sets out the framework which the Commission applies when deciding whether it considers that a particular business model requires a licence.

1.3 The interpretation of the Act is, of course, ultimately a matter for the courts. Nevertheless, the Commission hopes that it will be helpful to stakeholders and licensing authorities for it to set out how it approaches the question of whether a trading room style offer of facilities at a premises amounts to a licensable gambling activity.

1.4 The Commission may update this advice note from time to time to reflect developments in the market.

2. BACKGROUND

2.1 Trading rooms have developed as a by-product of the emergence of betting exchanges and the popularity of 'in-running' betting. Typically, a trading room is characterised as premises which provide access to live sporting pictures and remote communication such as an internet-enabled computer intended to be used for betting via a betting exchange. Consumers wishing to bet in-running, most commonly through betting exchanges, pay the trading room operators for use of these facilities. The operator's involvement is limited to administering the arrangements for gambling by others.

2.2 Trading rooms are not defined in the Act. A definition is contained within The Gambling (Operating licence and Single-Machine Permit Fees) (Amendment) Regulations 2008. The explanatory memorandum to the Regulations explains that the definition is intended to include only those who operate trading rooms, that is those who provide facilities for individuals to place or accept bets through other intermediaries via remote communication, where the person providing the facilities does not place or accept any bet with those individuals.

2.4 The Commission has issued a number of trading room licences, which are typically sited at commercially based high street premises, offering remote communications (PCs and internet access) and providing access to live sporting pictures. Where it is considered the activity conducted at a premises requires an intermediary (trading room only) operating licence the operator should also obtain a betting premises licence from the local licensing authority.

2.5 The circumstances in each case will be a matter of fact and degree but in order to help businesses understand the Commission's approach to making a judgement in a particular case we have produced a list of characteristics of trading rooms. The characteristics set out below are not intended to be exhaustive, nor is any one of them by itself necessarily determinative. They do however set out some of the key indicative features to be considered to establish the principal business intention of the

premises.

3 ARE FACILITIES FOR GAMBLING BEING OFFERED?

3.1 In distinguishing whether the activity conducted at a premises requires a licence the Commission will have regard to the following indicative features amongst others.

3.2 **Business model**

Does the business model depend on the provision of facilities for gambling?

This might help, for example, to draw a distinction between a trading room and, say, an internet café. The business model of a trading room would depend on the provision of facilities for gambling; without that provision it would be hard for the business to remain viable. To take another example, if it were unlikely that corporate hospitality facilities at a racecourse would ever be expected to be used for purposes other than providing accommodation for in-running bettors, it may well indicate that those facilities should be treated as a trading room. A mixed use facility, not wholly dependent on gambling facilities, may still in some circumstances require an operating and premises licence to operate legally.

3.3 **Facilities**

Are the facilities provided, or the investment in facilities, consistent with the purported business model (with reference to the local context)?

The degree of investment in particular facilities will often provide an indication of the main purpose of the business. For example, the provision of a live feed to racing pictures will represent an expensive overhead for many businesses; it seems unlikely that an internet café would make such an investment; in contrast, it would usually be critical to the viability of a trading room business. However, consideration of this point needs to take place with reference to the local context. For example, a racecourse may provide live feeds throughout the complex, including to conference or hospitality facilities, and so the presence of such facilities may have less significance in the context of a track than it would, say, at purported conference facilities away from a track. Similarly, the provision of facilities at a hotel adjoining a racecourse should be viewed with reference to the local context and likely target clientele.

3.4 **Promotion**

How is the premises advertised and marketed, and is this in keeping with the purported business model?

How the business is marketed may provide an indication of its purpose. When considering this factor, the Commission is likely to look at both the positive presence of marketing relating to gambling and the absence of marketing relating to the purported purpose of the facilities. For example, not only would we expect a genuine corporate hospitality box **not** to be marketed on the basis of facilities provided for gambling in direct connection with that box, but we would also expect that it would be marketed positively in ways connected with its provision as corporate hospitality. As with the other factors, the Commission will consider the context within which the facilities are offered.

3.5 For further information and frequently asked questions please consult the Commission's website (www.gamblingcommission.gov.uk) or call (0121 230 6666).

Gambling Commission March 2011

INDICATORS OF BETTING AS PRIMARY GAMBLING ACTIVITY, COMPLIANCE FRAMEWORK

November 2011

1 INTRODUCTION

6.2172 1.1 The Gambling Commission's interpretation of the framework of the Gambling Act 2005 (the Act) is that holders of general betting standard non-remote operating licences must provide betting as the primary gambling activity on licensed betting premises. We reinforced this understanding of the Act in May 2009 with the introduction of licence condition 16 to the Commission's Licence Conditions and Codes of Practice (LCCP) to all holders of this particular operating licence.

1.2 The Commission continues to receive a number of regulatory returns from general betting standard non-remote operating licence holders, where betting activity accounts for a minimal proportion of gross gambling yield. It is likely that in these cases further regulatory activity will be necessary to assess whether the requirements of LCCP with regard to primary gambling activity are being met.

1.3 The six indicators below are used by the Commission when assessing compliance with LCCP at premises where betting is the primary gambling activity offered. The indicators are based on the requirements of LCCP and what is accepted as typical of commercial betting shop provision in the British market.

1.4 Each case will be judged on its merits but the indicators discussed below are relevant to the vast majority of betting premises - operators with specialist or niche betting operations will need to explain why these indicators are not applicable to them.

INDICATORS OF BETTING AS PRIMARY GAMBLING ACTIVITY

(1) The offer of established core products (including live event pictures and bet range)
(2) The provision of information on products and events
(3) The promotion of gambling opportunities and products
(4) The actual use made of betting facilities
(5) The size of premises
(6) The delivery of betting facilities

2. BACKGROUND

LCCP AND BETTING PRIMARY GAMBLING ACTIVITY

2.1 In respect of primary gambling activity for non-remote general betting standard licence holders, LCCP includes a specific licence condition and an ordinary code of practice.

Licence condition 16

'Gaming machines may be made available for use in licensed betting premises only at times when there are also sufficient facilities for betting available'.

2.2 Such facilities for betting must include:

- the provision of information that enables the customer to access details of the events on which bets can be made
- facilities to enable to place bets
- facilities to establish the outcome of the events
- facilities to calculate the outcome of their bets
- facilities to be paid or credited with any winnings.

2.3 Where licensees provide facilities for betting only by means of betting machines the licensee must ensure that the number of betting machines is greater than the number of gaming machines which are made available for use in reliance on the premises licence.

ORDINARY CODE PROVISION

2.4 The factors listed in the ordinary code provisions with regard to betting as the primary gambling activity are the principal factors to consider in determining whether sufficient facilities are being provided to satisfy the requirement for primary gambling activity.

2.5 The four indicators are as follows:
- the range and frequency of events on which bets can be made
- the ratio of the space available to customers allocated to the primary gambling activity, to that allocated to other gambling activities
- the extent to which the primary gambling activity is promoted on the premises and by way of external advertising compared to other gambling activities
- the use, either expected or actual, to be made of the different gambling facilities

3 COMPLIANCE INDICATORS

3.1 This section sets out the indicators used by the Commission in assessing whether betting is being offered as the primary gambling activity on a betting premises.
3.2 Each of the six indicators which make up the compliance framework are listed with a brief description of what the Commission considers that a typical betting shop offering betting as the primary gambling activity offers.

1 THE OFFER OF ESTABLISHED CORE PRODUCTS (INCLUDING LIVE EVENT PICTURES AND BET RANGE)

Overall range and frequency of events
3.3 High street bookmakers offering betting as a primary gambling activity typically look to increase customer spend and time spent per visit by offering regular betting opportunities during opening hours.
3.4 Shop opening times can vary slightly based on local business features between the hours of 8am-10pm. The Commission considers that a typical betting shop offering betting as the primary gambling activity would, within half an hour of shop opening to within half an hour of closing, broadcast live betting opportunities from the five core products listed below throughout the day. Based on the *Gambling Industry Statistics 2009/10 – Update July 2011* the off-course betting operator's average percentage of betting turnover on each product is:
- horseracing (59%)
- greyhound racing (15%)
- football (11%)
- numbers (9%)
- other (sports) (6%).

Range and frequency of events involving core products
3.5 The Commission considers that a typical betting shop offering betting as the primary gambling activity would offer the following range and frequency of betting events involving core products.
3.6 This list does not make it a requirement for operators to accept bets from all customers at all times on such events. Operators may well restrict access, partially or wholly, to markets for sound commercial reasons which can be evidenced.

Horse racing
- regular daily service offering horse racing betting from Great Britain and Ireland in line with the respective fixture lists
- foreign morning meetings, for example South African
- typical day will include two or more staggered British horse meetings with up to eight races per card.

Greyhound racing
- regular daily service offering greyhound betting from six venues equally divided into morning, afternoon and evening slots.

Football
- UK domestic league football
- domestic and European cup competitions
- international matches.

Numbers (including virtual betting products)

- numbers betting products (such as 49s and Irish Lottery)
- virtual racing events available throughout each day.

Other sports betting

- PGA and US PGA golf each week
- tennis
- international and domestic cricket.

Broadcasting of live event pictures for core products

3.7 The best source of promoting a betting event on a premises is live pictures. In relation to UK horse and dog racing these are commercially provided by Turf TV and SIS.

3.8 Events such as football, golf and tennis are often shown on terrestrial television or via commercial agreement with satellite providers such as Sky. Domestic coverage of the free- to-air listed sport events such as the Grand National is also made available.

3.9 Clearly the ability to watch an event has a positive promotional effect on turnover levels hence the cost involved in accessing the picture provider's content. Along with live pictures the broadcast media's audio support informs customers of upcoming events and details.

3.10 Premises offering betting as a primary gambling activity usually offer an audio service to remind operators of the live events that are imminent and available to bet on.

Range of bets available on core products

3.11 The Commission considers that a typical betting shop offering betting as the primary gambling activity offers a range of bets that includes the following:

- single bets on all of the five core products
- multiple bets across all of the above five categories. This should normally include some, or all, of the following: doubles, trebles, patents, Lucky 15s 31, 63's and Yankee and Super Yankee
- ante-post betting on high profile competitions in all core products

Specific bet type range by core product

3.12 In addition, the Commission considers that a typical betting shop offering betting as the primary gambling activity would offer the following specific bets for each of the core products:

Horse and greyhound racing

3.13 Forecast and tricast betting would normally be available when betting on horse or dog races.

3.14 A customer placing bets on horse or dog racing can choose between the current 'live show' price or the starting price.

Football

3.15 A betting premises offering betting as the primary gambling activity would typically offer first goalscorer, correct score and scorecast betting.

3.16 Dedicated football coupons tend to be available in midweek and weekend formats to facilitate the placing of multiple bets.

2 PROVISION OF INFORMATION ON PRODUCTS AND EVENTS

Customer information screens

3.17 A betting shop typically has a bank of screens providing customers with details of upcoming events and betting opportunities and also results of previous events. In particular they would show the following information on the next betting opportunity:

- event type
- participants
- odds of participants
- time and location of event
- each-way place terms.

Horse and dog events may also include details of going, jockey changes, non runners and rule four details.

Event details including form/results

3.18 Betting shops display details of the day's horse and dog meetings which include runners, form guides and tips most commonly provided by the Racing Post.

3.19 Publicising results in the customer area helps to promote the range of betting events available and reminds customers of the availability and the scope of individual betting products.

3 PROMOTION OF GAMBLING OPPORTUNITIES AND PRODUCTS

External promotion

3.20 The Commission considers that a typical betting shop offering betting as the primary gambling activity uses promotional posters to advertise products and betting events in their windows, in particular to generate interest/revenue in the build up to a significant sporting event, for example the Grand National or a live Premier League football match.

3.21 Where other advertising is used, the Commission considers that a typical betting shop offering betting as the primary gambling activity would reference betting products as part of their advertising.

3.22 Trading names used and other external fascia may also provide an indicator of the primary gambling activity of the business.

4 ACTUAL USE MADE OF BETTING FACILITIES

Betting vs gaming

3.23 The Commission considers that a typical betting shop offering betting as the primary gambling activity would attract a mixture of customers each day, some of whom would be placing bets.

3.24 There is an industry trend towards gaming machines and away from over the counter betting. Based on the latest industry statistics the average breakdown between gaming machines and betting gross gambling yield for the off-course betting industry are:

- betting – 54%
- gaming – 46%

3.25 The level of betting turnover cannot simply be compared to gaming machine turnover due to the churn effect of a gaming machine session of play. The Commission will therefore also consider the profit, slippage and staking of betting activity against industry averages when considering whether the actual use of made of betting facilities is indicative of a betting shop offering betting as the primary gambling activity.

3.26 The Commission considers that a typical betting shop offering betting as the primary gambling activity would have a clearly defined business plan setting out the expected use of betting versus gaming including interim targets (and supporting promotional activity).

5 SIZE OF PREMISES SUFFICIENT TO PROVIDE FACILITIES

3.27 In order to provide sufficient facilities for betting as outlined above the Commission will have regard to the actual size of the premises and whether the premises are adequate to provide betting facilities as the primary gambling activity rather than as ancillary to a gaming machines area.

6 DELIVERY OF BETTING FACILITIES

3.28 If an operator chooses to rely on betting terminals without a counter service to offer betting as the primary gambling activity, then they must site more betting terminals/machines than gaming machines.

3.29 A betting shop premises where the number of betting machines is equal to or less than the number of gaming machines, is required to have a counter service available with at least one member of staff present at all times to facilitate the placing of bets. An intermittent counter service in such circumstances would, at times, lead to the delivery of betting facilities relying solely on machines, meaning the operator would be in breach of Licence Condition 16.

Gambling Commission November 2011

PRIMARY GAMBLING ACTIVITY: COMMON MISUNDERSTANDINGS

August 2012

6.2173 As readers will know from previous articles, the Gambling Act 2005 has the effect of restricting B2 machines (FOBTs) to betting shops (and casinos). The question of what constitutes a genuine betting shop continues to be a subject of some debate and confusion, with a view gaining traction – erroneously says the Gambling Commission – that if gaming machine turnover exceeds betting turnover in a particular shop, it must fail the test of primary gambling activity.

'In reality, readers will not be surprised to learn that it is not as simple as that,' says Matthew Hill, the Commission's Director of Regulatory Risk and Analysis. 'There is a fundamental misconception at large – the 50/50 myth – that there must be more profit or turnover from betting than machines to satisfy primary gambling activity'.

> 'In making judgements about whether individual premises are being run as genuine betting businesses, we and others (for example local authorities) need to take into account both expected and actual use of the betting facilities being provided. What matters is whether there is, or is intended to be, sufficient betting to constitute a genuine betting business. In assessing this we take account of the actual use of premises in terms of, for example, gross gambling yield (GGY) or the number of bets taken as one of a wide range of factors in our consideration.
>
> Other relevant factors include the facilities that are actually in place – like the provision of information that enables the customer to access details of the events on which bets can be made and to be able to place those bets. Customers should be able to obtain details of the outcome of the events, calculate the outcome of their bets and be paid or credited with any winnings. The range and frequency of events on which bets can be made, the relative space allocated to each product and the extent to which betting is promoted are also considered.
>
> Although there is plenty of room for development of niche or novel betting businesses, we do expect all business models to be based on a core genuine betting business. Where actual GGY from betting is low, we are likely to wish to look at the facilities in place and the business projections and marketing plans of the operator. Some of the cases we have been dealing with in recent months involve extremely low numbers of bets, and the operators concerned have had difficulty making a convincing case that what they are running is a genuine betting business.
>
> It is of course also misleading to compare the turnover of over-the-counter betting with that from machines which, on average, pay out around 97% of the amount staked but which rely on players repeatedly re-staking their winnings. A successful (and genuine) betting business may well have a machine turnover greatly in excess of its over-the-counter business. What matters is whether there is, or is likely to be, sufficient betting business, and not whether the return from machines is larger.
>
> We appreciate that the situation can be complex but the simple message is that only genuine betting businesses are entitled to make B2 gaming machines available for use, so the focus is primarily on the facilities for betting and the use made of them.

Over the coming months we will continue to work with stakeholders to help improve understanding and to explain the position, as well as refining our published advice to improve accessibility and clarity.'

Gambling Commission August 2012

LICENSING AUTHORITY BULLETIN SPECIAL EDITION: PRIMARY GAMBLING ACTIVITY

August 2012

6.2174 This special edition of the Gambling Commission's licensing authority bulletin provides clarification on issues around primary gambling activity.

PRIMARY GAMBLING ACTIVITY: COMMON MISUNDERSTANDINGS AROUND BETTING SHOPS

Licensing authorities will be aware that the Gambling Act 2005 has the effect of restricting B2 gaming machines to betting shops (and casinos). In November 2011 the Commission issued details of the indicators the Commission uses when assessing premises where betting is the primary gambling activity offered. However the question of what constitutes a genuine betting shop continues to be a subject of some debate, with the growing misconception that if gaming machine turnover exceeds betting turnover in a particular shop, it must fail the test of primary gambling activity.

In making judgements about whether individual premises are being run as genuine betting businesses, the Commission needs to take into account both expected and actual use of the betting facilities being provided. What matters is whether there is, or is intended to be, sufficient betting to constitute a genuine betting business. In assessing this the Commission takes account of the actual use of premises in terms of, for example, gross gambling yield (GGY) or the number of bets taken as one of a wide range of factors for consideration.

Other relevant factors include the facilities that are actually in place – like the provision of information that enables the customer to access details of the events on which bets can be made and to be able to place those bets. Customers should be able to obtain details of the outcome of the events, calculate the outcome of their bets and be paid or credited with any winnings. The range and frequency of events on which bets can be made, the relative space allocated to each product and the extent to which betting is promoted are also considered.

Although there is plenty of room for development of niche or novel betting businesses, there is an expectation for all business models to be based on a core genuine betting business. Where actual GGY from betting is low, the Commission is likely to wish to look at the facilities in place and the business projections and marketing plans of the operator. It is also misleading to compare the turnover of over-the-counter betting with that from machines which, on average, pay out around 97% of the amount staked but which rely on players repeatedly re-staking their winnings. A successful (and genuine) betting business may well have a machine turnover greatly in excess of its over-the-counter business. What matters is whether there is, or is likely to be, sufficient betting business, and not whether the return from machines is larger.

Licensing authorities will want to have regard to the primary gambling indicators but must be careful not to just assume there that there must be more profit or turnover from betting than machines to satisfy primary gambling activity.

The simple message is that only genuine betting businesses are entitled to make B2 gaming machines available for use, so the focus is primarily on the facilities for betting and the use made of them. Over the coming months the Commission will

continue to work with our partners in licensing authorities and stakeholders from the industry to help improve understanding, to explain the position and refine its published advice to improve accessibility and clarity.
Gambling Commission August 2012

Note

Regulatory return forms (October 2011) and guides as to how to complete them (June 2011) are available from the Gambling Commission's website at www.gamblingcommission.gov.uk

TRACKS

ADVICE TO TRACK PREMISES LICENCE HOLDERS June 2007

1 INTRODUCTION

6.2175 1.1 In April 2007, the Department for Culture, Media and Sport (DCMS) and the Scottish Executive laid the regulations in relation to Premises Licences: Mandatory and Default Conditions[1].

---

[1] For England and Wales – SI 2007/1409 — The Gambling Act 2005 (Mandatory and Default Conditions) (England and Wales) Regulations 2007

For Scotland – SSI 2007/266 – The Gambling Act 2005 (Mandatory and Default Conditions) (Scotland) Regulations 2007.

1.2 In order to assist track premises licence holders (as opposed to other premises such as casinos, bingo halls, adult gaming centres, family entertainment centres and betting shops), the Gambling Commission (the Commission) has undertaken to provide tracks with advice that is supplementary to the mandatory and default conditions.

1.3 Therefore, in March 2007 we published the consultation document '*Advice to track premises licence holders*'. The purpose of this consultation document was to offer advice on other aspects of track management that may impact upon the licensing objectives, which are:

- preventing gambling from being a source of crime or disorder, being associated with crime or disorder, or being used to support crime;
- ensuring that gambling is conducted in a fair and open way;
- protecting children and other vulnerable persons from being harmed or exploited by gambling.

1.4 A list of the mandatory and default premises licence conditions that will affect track premises licence holders exclusively is provided in section 3 of this document. The full DCMS and Scottish Executive regulations contain some conditions that are designed specifically not to apply to tracks, although these are not covered in this advice.

1.5 The Commission is producing separate guidance to licensing authorities on what they need to do in order to licence tracks appropriately. Prospective track premises licence holders should consider the guidance to licensing authorities in tandem with this advice from the Commission.

1.6 The Commission has conducted a full and open consultation on this advice. A stakeholder meeting took place during the consultation period. A total of nine responses were received during the six-week consultation, and the consultation paper was downloaded 651 times from the Commission's website during the same period. We have given careful consideration to the consultation responses before finalising our policy position.

2 BACKGROUND AND SCOPE

DEFINITION OF A TRACK

2.1 Within the Gambling Act 2005 (the Act) a track is defined as a horse racecourse, dog track or other premises on any part of which a race or other sporting event takes place or is intended to take place[2].

---

[2] Section 353 Gambling Act 2005.

2.2 If betting takes place at a track then a premises licence, awarded by the local licensing authority[3], will be required[4].

[3] In England and Wales the appropriate local authority, in Scotland, a licensing board constituted under section 1 of the Licensing (Scotland) Act 1976.

[4] With the exception of occasional and temporary use notices under sections 39 and 214–234 of the Act; see sections 2.12 to 2.17 of this document for further details.

2.3 Betting facilities are offered on a wide variety of tracks – most notably the 59 principal horse racecourses approved by the Horserace Betting Levy Board (referred to in this consultation as 'racecourses') and greyhound tracks (both those approved by the National Greyhound Racing Club and independent tracks). The Act does not give a list of premises which are officially recognised as 'tracks' but there are a number of venues other than those mentioned above where sporting events do or could take place, and accordingly could accommodate the provision of betting facilities. Examples of tracks include:

- a point-to-point horserace meeting;
- football, cricket and rugby grounds;
- an athletics stadium;
- a golf course;
- venues hosting darts, bowls, or snooker tournaments;
- a premises staging boxing matches;
- a section of river hosting a fishing competition; and
- a motor racing event.

While many of these venues are not commonly understood to be 'tracks,' they fall within the definition of 'track' as defined by the Act.

2.4 In theory, betting could take place at any venue where a sporting or competitive event occurs. The Act provides for tracks which do not offer betting facilities currently but may elect to do so in the future.

2.5 There is a distinct difference between track premises licences and most other premises licences. Generally, a track owner admits third-party operators to provide betting facilities at the track whereas other premises licence holders provide the betting facilities themselves. Consequently, they are subject to the conditions of the operating licence as well as the premises licence.

2.6 However, there are a limited number of track premises licence holders who will have an operating licence because they operate a betting pool. An example of these would be the 29 greyhound tracks which are approved by the National Greyhound Racing Club[5]. In addition to admitting independent fixed-odds betting operators, these tracks may run their own pool betting as permitted by sections 179 and 180 of the Act, and will be subject to licence conditions applicable to their status as both betting operators and track premises licence holders.

[5] A small number of point-to-point track owners also offer pool betting. These tracks will be subject normally to occasional use notices, see sections 2.12 to 2.14 of this document for further details.

2.7 The track premises licence authorises anyone upon the premises with an operating licence to offer betting facilities, and the conduct of betting on track will be regulated primarily through these operating licences, since track betting operators will be subject to the provisions of their licence conditions while they are on track.

2.8 Most activities that the track premises licence holders will need to undertake to meet the licensing objectives are included in the mandatory and default conditions set by the Secretary of State. However, the Commission considers that there are other areas of activity that fall outside of the mandatory and default conditions: these are covered in section 4 of this advice.

2.9 The Commission will be a responsible authority[6] in relation to premises licences and will be able to request a review of a premises licence if it suspects the breach of a licence condition. The Commission will liaise with licensing authorities in reviewing the standards of compliance displayed by track premises licence holders and it is possible that the licensing authorities may attach conditions to premises licences where local problems have been identified.

---

[6] Section 157 of Gambling Act 2005.

DIFFERENT TYPES OF PERMISSION

2.10 There are three different types of permission which enable tracks to offer legitimate betting facilities. These are described in more detail in the '*Guidance to Licensing Authorities on tracks*' document that was published alongside this advice (available from the Commission's website).

Premises licences

2.11 Usually, for tracks that operate frequently, a premises licence will be required as described in part 8 of the Act. These licences would be appropriate for racecourses, greyhound tracks and most football stadia. However, for some tracks, a premises licence may not be required. Such tracks may offer betting facilities under an occasional or temporary use notice.

Occasional use notices

2.12 Section 39 of the Act enables a track occupier or administrator to issue an occasional use notice. An occasional use notice gives entitlement of up to eight[7] occasional uses of a track for betting purposes in any calendar year, so this permission would be suitable for, say, point-to-point racecourses, motor racing venues and some cricket grounds.

---

[7] The Secretary of State may by order amend this number.

2.13 We are taking guidance from DCMS on whether a 'day' refers to a calendar day or a period of 24 hours – for instance, noon until noon.

2.14 Tracks that operate under this notice are not required to comply with any of the mandatory and default conditions. However, only licensed betting operators may offer betting facilities at such tracks, otherwise an offence would be committed under section 33 of the Act.

2.15 Consequently, the Commission strongly advises track occupiers or administrators operating under an occasional use notice to satisfy themselves that only licensed betting operators are offering betting facilities at their tracks. One way of achieving this may be by following the advice in sections 3.10 to 3.12 of this advice. If evidence emerges that unlicensed betting operators have been allowed to offer betting facilities on tracks operating under an occasional use notice, the Commission will consider taking action against the illegal betting operators.

Temporary use notices

2.16 A temporary use notice is similar in some ways to an occasional use notice. Sections 214 to 234 of the Act explain the relevant provisions. Temporary use notices may be used for up to 21 days in a calendar year and may be used at premises such as hotels, exhibition centres or entertainment venues.

2.17 Temporary use notices are given by a holder of an operating licence rather than the owner or manager of the venue.

2.18 Temporary use notices are subject to regulations by the Secretary of State prescribing the activities which may be covered by the notice (see section 215(2) of the Act) and are subject to objections from the Commission, police and HM Revenue and Customs if they think that the notice may affect the licensing objectives (see section 221 of the Act). The Commission considers that these regulations will be sufficient to uphold the licensing objectives.

2.19 DCMS is consulting currently on temporary use notices prior to finalising the regulations[8]. DCMS proposes that the notices should be used to provide otherwise unlicensed premises with the opportunity to host equal chance gaming tournaments. Should this be confirmed in the regulations, tracks will only be eligible to host out-of-hours non-raceday betting by virtue of an occasional use notice.

[8] /NR/rdonlyres/D3CD77AA-11D7-4676-92F8-12407C989311/0/TemporaryUseNoticescon.pdf — reference correct at 1 June 2007

2.20 We will follow the progress of the DCMS consultation and revise our advice if necessary following the laying of regulations.

3 THE COMMISSION'S ADVICE ON THE REGULATIONS FOR TRACK PREMISES LICENCE HOLDERS

3.1 For ease of reference, the conditions as they apply to track premises licence holders have been extracted from the regulations and reproduced below, schedule by schedule. The supplementary advice given by the Commission follows each schedule of the mandatory or default conditions.

ADVICE ON REGULATIONS, SCHEDULE 6, PART 1

SCHEDULE 6
CONDITIONS ATTACHING TO TRACK PREMISES LICENCES
Regulations 16 and 17

PART 1
MANDATORY CONDITIONS ATTACHING TO ALL TRACK PREMISES LICENCES

1. No customer shall be able to access the premises directly from any other premises in respect of which one of the following premises licences has effect:
(a) a casino premises licence; (b) an adult gaming centre premises licence.

2. A notice stating that no person under the age of 18 is permitted to bet on the premises shall be displayed in a prominent place at every public entrance to the premises.

3. The terms on which a bet may be placed must be displayed in a prominent place within the premises to which customers wishing to use facilities for betting have unrestricted access.

4. The premises licence holder shall make arrangements to ensure that betting operators who are admitted to the premises for the purpose of accepting bets:
(a) will be operating under a valid operating licence; and (b) are enabled to accept such bets in accordance with:
(i) the conditions imposed under sections 92 (general betting operating licence) or 93 (pool betting operating licence) of the 2005 Act, or (ii) an authorisation under section 94 (horse-race pool betting operating licence) of that Act.

5. The premises licence holder shall make arrangements to ensure that reasonable steps are taken to remove from the premises any person who is found to be accepting bets on the premises otherwise than in accordance with the 2005 Act. 6. Any ATM made available for use on the premises shall be located in a place that requires any customer who wishes to use it to cease gambling in order to do so.

3.2 Subsection 1 is self-explanatory. It means that any adult gaming centre or casino located on a track (such as a 'racino,' the term used to refer to a casino located on a racecourse) must not be accessible by persons attempting entrance directly from within the track: it would be necessary for track patrons to leave the confines of the track and gain access from the street. 8

3.3 Subsection 2 is self-explanatory. In addition to placing underage gambling notices at each public entrance, we consider that it would be best practice for tracks to place a notice on underage gambling in the race card or programme and, at racecourses, adjacent to the prominently-displayed Tattersalls' Rules.

3.4 Subsection 3 places the onus on track premises licence holders to display in a prominent place the terms on which a bet may be placed ie the rules. We expect that betting operators will want to display the rules for their customers and will leave it to the tracks to decide how best this should be policed. However, the track is responsible for any non-compliance.

3.5 In relation to starting price facilities and the Tote, we consider that racecourses should oblige betting operators to display rules either in or adjacent to the main betting outlet only.

3.6 On racecourses, the generic rules – known as Tattersalls' Rules – that govern gambling in betting rings should be displayed in a prominent place by the racecourse. Any deviations from these rules must be displayed by the betting operators in accordance with their licence conditions.

3.7 We consider that track premises licence holders are best-placed to make arrangements to ensure that customers have 'unrestricted access' to the rules. We are aware that many tracks have different enclosures or stands where unhindered customer access to all areas is sometimes prohibited. Where appropriate arrangements to facilitate free access to the rules cannot be organised, we consider it would be best practice for the rules to be displayed in each distinct enclosure or area.

3.8 Where there is only a single central location for the displayed rules, and two or more different enclosures or stands, we consider that it would be best practice to refer to that location in the race card or programme.

3.9 We do not consider that it is necessary to introduce a code of practice relating to the display of rules on tracks.

3.10 Subsection 4 of the regulations provides that it is the responsibility of track premises licence holders to ensure that only Commission licensed betting operators and their properly contracted employees are allowed to provide betting facilities on their premises. This is a mandatory condition attached to the premises licence.

3.11 Track premises licence holders may introduce their own administrative arrangements for the positive identification of betting operators. Again, we do not need to be prescriptive on how this outcome is achieved as we expect track premises licence holders to set up appropriate procedures to meet their obligations. However, failure to do so may place track premises licence holders in breach of their licence conditions.

3.12 The Commission is considering what evidence needs to be in place in order for track premises licence holders to be satisfied that an operator's staff member (who is acting in the capacity of bookmaker or provider of betting facilities) is employed under contract. This advice will be updated once our approach is finalised.

3.13 On racecourses, the Commission does not consider that bookmakers' assistants, such as computer operators and floormen, need to be registered as workers in the future, as they are currently with the National Joint Pitch Council (NJPC). Neither would the Commission expect racecourses to require registration of other functional staff, such as Tote employees or workers at the racecourse betting shop. Similarly, the Commission does not consider that 'shop floor' staff at other tracks need to be identified, such as cashiers at football grounds. We would expect betting operators to exercise sufficient control over their businesses to ensure that only properly authorised people are allowed to conduct betting on their behalf. However, the Commission intends to monitor this situation in case evidence emerges that suggests that this is at odds with the licensing objectives.

3.14 Subsection 5 requires track premises licence holders to ensure that ATMs are situated away from gambling facilities and that any new gambling facilities take into account the location of pre-existing ATMs. Any ATM made available for use on the premises must be located in a place that requires any customer who wishes to use it to cease gambling at any booth, counter, stand, betting machine or any other betting facility.

3.15 Track premises licence holders are required by the mandatory condition in subsection 6 to take reasonable steps to remove from the track anybody found to be providing facilities for gambling without authorisation, ie illegal bookmakers. Failure to do so could result in action against the premises licence.

3.16 The Commission is not inclined to define 'reasonable steps' as that is a matter of construction by a court.

3.17 The Commission considers that it would be best practice for all instances of illegal betting to be recorded in writing by the track premises licence holder and reported to the Commission within 14 days.

3.18 The details included in the report should include the location of the offence, date, name and address of the illegal betting operator (if possible), a description of the circumstances and the action that the premises licence holder intends to take in order to prevent further similar instances of illegal gambling.

ADVICE ON REGULATIONS, SCHEDULE 6, PART 2

The regulations are reproduced below.

PART 2
MANDATORY CONDITIONS ATTACHING TO TRACK PREMISES LICENCES IN RESPECT OF PREMISES THAT ARE HORSE-RACE COURSES

1 (1) This paragraph shall apply to converted track premises licences in respect of premises that are horse-race courses.

(2) The licence holder shall ensure that in respect of any part of the track, which immediately before 1st September 2007 was made available for the purposes of complying with a condition imposed under section 13(2) of the 1963 Act (which provides for conditions to be imposed on a certificate under section 13 relating to the places which are to be provided for enabling betting to take place on the track), that part shall continue to be made available for the purposes of enabling betting operators and betting operators' assistants to use it for carrying on business in connection with providing facilities for betting.

(3) Sub-paragraph (2) is without prejudice to any application under section 187 of the 2005 Act (application to vary a premises licence) to change the location of the part of the track to which that sub-paragraph applies.

(4) Where such an application is granted, sub-paragraph (2) is to have effect as if it required the licence holder to ensure that the part of the track identified in the application as the new location for the area referred to in that sub-paragraph is made available for the purposes of enabling betting operators and betting operators' assistants to carry on business in connection with providing facilities for betting.

(5) References in this paragraph to an 'existing betting area' are to any part of the track which is required to be made available in accordance with the preceding provisions of this paragraph for the purposes of enabling betting operators and betting operators' assistants to carry on business in connection with providing facilities for betting.

(6) The charge for admission to an existing betting area for the purposes of carrying on business in connection with providing facilities for betting shall not exceed:

(a) where payable by a betting operator, five times the cost of the highest charge paid by members of the public who are authorised to enter that part of the track; and

(b) where payable by a betting operator's assistant, the cost of the highest charge paid by members of the public who are authorised to enter that part of the track.

(7) A betting operator or betting operator's assistant shall not be charged, for admission to an existing betting area, an amount which differs from that charged to any other betting operator or betting operator's assistant for admission to that part of the track.

(8) No charges may be made to betting operators and betting operators' assistants who are admitted to the existing betting areas of the track, other than:

(a) the charge for admission in accordance with sub-paragraphs (6) and (7), and

(b) charges levied to cover costs reasonably incurred in connection with enabling betting operators and betting operators' assistants to operate in the existing betting area.

(9) This paragraph shall not apply after 31 August 2012.

2 (1) This paragraph shall apply to all track premises licences in respect of premises that are horse-race courses.

(2) The licence holder shall provide a place on the premises where betting operators and betting operators' assistants, including small-scale operators, may carry on business in connection with providing facilities for betting and to which the public may resort for the purpose of betting.

(3) The reference in this paragraph to 'small-scale operators' shall have the same meaning as prescribed in The Gambling Act 2005 (Definition of Small-scale Operator) Regulations 2006.

(4) This paragraph shall not apply to converted track premises licences before 1 September 2012. 3. In this Part 'converted track premises licence' means a premises licence issued in respect of a track where:

(a) the holder of the licence held a certificate under section 13 of the 1963 Act, in respect of the same or substantially the same premises (referred to below as 'the 1963 Act permission');

(b) the 1963 Act permission had effect immediately before 1 September 2007; and

(c) the holder of the licence was granted the premises licence, under transitional provisions made under paragraph 9 of Schedule 18 to the 2005 Act, by reason of his holding the 1963 Act permission.

3.19 Subsections 1 and 2 provide that all existing betting areas (as defined in subsection 5) that are approved by the Horserace Betting Levy Board (HBLB) on 31 August 2007 (including those areas that are considered or named as 'temporary') will continue to allow access to betting operators for five years (as confirmed in subsection 9). These conditions do not apply to other tracks, including point-to-point racecourses. Racecourses should make clear in their applications to licensing authorities for premises licences precisely where their existing approved betting areas are located: this process is described in greater detail in the guidance to licensing authorities on tracks. 11

3.20 If track premises licence holders wish to vary the location of betting areas that are subject to the five times rule on 31 August 2007, then they may apply to the local licensing authority to vary the premises licence.

3.21 From 1 September 2007, racecourses will be permitted to establish new betting areas, which will not be subject to a mandatory condition replicating the 'five times rule'. The cost of establishing a pitch in these new areas will be left to regulation by the market.

3.22 Subsection 4 provides that any relocated betting area (that had previously been a HBLB approved betting area immediately prior to 1 September 2007) would be subject to the same obligations as if it were the original area.

3.23 Subsection 6 provides for the maximum charges that may be applied to betting operators and their assistants when working in existing betting areas. This appears to be self-explanatory, as does subsection 7 which provides that all betting operators and assistants within existing betting areas must be charged the same admission prices.

3.24 Subsection 8 provides that no additional charges may be applied to betting operators and their assistants over and above the admission charges and reasonable charges to reflect costs incurred in the administration of the betting ring. If deemed appropriate, these charges may be levied by a third-party administrative body appointed by the racecourses and/or the betting operators.
3.25 Subsection 2(2) provides that an area must be provided by racecourses for betting operators to conduct betting business after 31 August 2012.
3.26 Subsection 3 defines a converted track premises licence. 'Grandfather rights' give track operators with existing permissions to offer gambling under current legislation the right to be granted the equivalent type of permission in relation to their premises under the new legislation. For example, track operators under the existing legislation would be entitled to a betting premises licence under the new legislation, assuming that they had accepted the default licence conditions.

ADVICE ON REGULATIONS, SCHEDULE 6, PART 3

The regulations are reproduced below.

PART 3
MANDATORY CONDITIONS ATTACHING TO TRACK PREMISES LICENCES IN RESPECT OF PREMISES THAT ARE DOG RACING TRACKS
1 A totalisator on the premises shall only be operated:
(a) while the public are admitted to the premises for the purpose of attending dog races and no other sporting events are taking place on the premises; and (b) for effecting with persons on the premises betting transactions on dog races taking place on the premises.
2 (1) At any time during which the totalisator is being lawfully used on the premises:
(a) no betting operator or betting operator's assistant shall be excluded from the premises by reason only of the fact that he proposes to accept or negotiate bets on the premises; and
(b) there shall be made available on the premises space for betting operators and betting operators' assistants where they can conveniently accept and negotiate bets in connection with dog races run on the premises on that day. 12
(2) This paragraph is without prejudice to section 180 (pool betting on dog races) of the 2005 Act. 3. For the purposes of this Part, 'totalisator' means the apparatus for betting known as the totalisator or pari mutuel, or any other machine or instrument of betting of a like nature, whether mechanically operated or not.
3.27 These regulations above give clear guidance to greyhound track premises licence holders on the operation of totalisators, which facilitate pool betting, and access rights for general betting operators when the totalisator is being used.
3.28 Section 180 of the Act provides that pool betting on greyhound racing may be offered only in accordance with arrangements made with the occupier of the greyhound venue where the racing is taking place. This means that the greyhound track operator controls whether or not pool betting on the racing that takes place at his track is available at other licensed betting premises. If he does wish this to happen, he can make appropriate arrangements with other betting operating licence holders. This is a transitional measure that will lapse on 31 December 2012 unless it is repealed before then.
3.29 Subsection 2 grants mandatory access to greyhound tracks for general betting operators when the totalisator is in use ie during race meetings held at that track. The greyhound track premises licence holder must provide an area where the general betting operators can offer betting facilities when events are being held at the track. However, this does not mean that the totalisator may not be operated if general betting operators elect not to attend or are prevented from attending by circumstances outside the control of the track premises licence holders or themselves.

ADVICE ON REGULATIONS, SCHEDULE 6, PART 4

The regulations are reproduced below.

PART 4
DEFAULT CONDITIONS ATTACHING TO ALL TRACK PREMISES LICENCES

1 Subject to paragraph 2, no facilities for gambling shall be provided on the premises between the hours of 10pm on one day, and 7am on the next day.

2 The prohibition in paragraph 1 does not apply on days when a sporting event is taking place on the premises, in which case gambling transactions may take place at any time during that day.

3.30 The above is self-explanatory. The restrictions on the time during which gambling may take place on any track do not apply when the track is staging a sporting event. For instance, greyhound tracks often race beyond 10pm in the evening and it is permissible to offer betting facilities for races taking place after that time.

3.31 However, offering betting facilities after 10pm is not permissible if there is no sporting event being staged at the track. Such facilities may only be offered if the track premises licence holder applies to the local licensing authority for a variation to the default hours or an operator takes advantage of an occasional use notice. 13

4 ADDITIONAL ADVICE FOR TRACK PREMISES LICENCE HOLDERS

SOCIAL RESPONSIBILITY

4.1 While betting operators have primary responsibility for creating and implementing social responsibility policies and procedures, the Commission considers that track premises licence holders should accept some responsibility for supporting and promoting socially responsible gambling on their premises.

4.2 Track premises licence holders who are also pool betting operators, such as greyhound tracks, will have their own social responsibility policies as a result of their operating licences. However, as the hosts of betting facilities additionally provided by third-party betting operators, they should put in place proportionate measures to deal with customers who have social responsibility queries relating to those operators.

4.3 The Commission does not expect track premises licence holders to have lengthy and detailed policies relating to social responsibility. The policies should be commensurate with the volume and intensity of gambling that occurs on their premises. We are aware, however, that many customers will direct queries and comments to the track owner rather than the betting operator. As a minimum, therefore, we consider it to be best practice for track premises licence holders to have a brief knowledge of the typical social responsibility policies and procedures of the betting operators who are offering betting facilities on their premises, so that track staff are able to deal with queries and advise customers accordingly (although not in a counselling capacity). At the very least, we would expect track staff to be aware that all betting operators have a social responsibility policy and that customer queries should be directed back to the operators.

4.4 Track premises licence holders may wish also to consider more proactive measures, such as notices in programmes that promote responsible gambling or an appropriate location where they could display posters, leaflets and information relating to problem gambling.

BET RECEIPT TERMINALS

4.5 The supervision of bet receipt terminals is the responsibility of betting operators rather than premises licence holders. The premises licence holders, therefore, have no responsibility to ensure that bet receipt terminals are supervised appropriately. However, should the premises licence holder become aware that the betting operator has failed persistently to supervise the bet receipt terminals correctly, the track management should inform the Commission. The Commission may be contacted via email on info@gamblingcommission.gov.uk or by telephone on 0121 230 6666.

ADMINISTRATIVE ARRANGEMENTS

4.6 There are varying degrees of administrative and quasi-regulatory arrangements that have been in place on tracks up to now. Racecourses, for instance, have been subject to the administrative arrangements and rules/guidelines of the HBLB and the NJPC. In contrast, betting facilities at most events other than horse and greyhound racing (for example, football grounds) are provided by individual operators, generally from the major high street betting chains, who hold direct contracts with the track owner without the administration and supervision of a third party.

4.7 Consequently, there has been a significant difference in the level of supervision between different tracks: for example, racecourses have been subject to the administrative arrangements of the NJPC, which provides betting ring managers (BRMs) to monitor compliance with the National Pitch Rules (NPRs) at each race meeting, while most other track owners (including greyhound tracks) have required the track bookmakers to oversee themselves. 14

4.8 The Act repeals the Betting, Gaming and Lotteries Act 1963 and removes the authority of the provisions attached to Certificates of Approval issued by the HBLB and, also, removes the authority of the NPRs and of the NJPC to administer those rules.

4.9 The remit of the Commission is limited to the licensing objectives and so it is not for us to be prescriptive about which of the various current administrative systems should be maintained. The Commission is keen, however, that the levels of compliance and generally high standards of administrative order on all tracks are not lost as a result of the implementation of the Act.

4.10 Under the Act, track premises licence holders may undertake the administration of betting facilities themselves or they can make arrangements with another body to take on this work. It is for them, individually or collectively, to make that decision. Whichever way, the track premises licence holders retain the responsibility to meet all premises licence conditions, including those imposed by the licensing authorities.

4.11 Track premises licence holders will have a responsibility to report regulatory matters concerning the premises and issues relating to betting to the Commission. The licensing authority and/or Commission's compliance officers will visit tracks for the purpose of checking compliance with the Act, regulations and licence conditions and codes of practice.

4.12 With specific regard to racecourses, it is unclear what administrative arrangements will exist from September 2007. A working group has been set up to deal with these issues and the Commission will be guided by the recommendations of that body.

4.13 All tracks should seek independent legal advice if they are concerned that any arrangements which are in place to limit the number of betting operators at any given race meeting may be in breach of competition law. Similarly, any terms imposed on betting operators by track premises licence holders for access to betting areas must comply with the law, including competition law.

GAMING MACHINES

4.14 A betting premises licence in respect of a track does not of itself give any entitlement to use gaming machines. That is because this type of premises licence can be held without any corresponding operating licence. However, by virtue of section 172(9) of the Act, any track owner who holds both a betting premises licence and a pool betting operating licence (which means he will have judged by the Commission as suitable to provide gambling facilities), may site up to 4 gaming machines (in categories B2 to D) on the track.

4.15 Such machines will be subject to the licence conditions and codes of practice imposed upon the operator. These conditions and codes have been made available on the Commission's website. Further information relating to gaming machines can be found in the '*Guidance to Licensing Authorities on tracks*' document.

COMBINED LICENCES

4.16 The general position for premises licensing is that premises may only be subject to one premises licence at a time[9]. The effect of this requirement is to limit the principal activity on the premises to the provision of facilities for one type of gambling activity.

[9] Section 152(1) of Gambling Act 2005.

4.17 However, tracks are exempted from this approach. Subsections 2 and 3 of section 152 of the Act provide that a track may be subject to more than one premises licence, but that no more than one premises licence can operate in relation to any area of the track. Subsection 4 provides that where a particular area of a track is already subject to a premises licence, and a person wishes to apply for a licence to offer another type of gambling activity in that area, an application must be made to vary the original licence under section 187. The new licence for the track can only be granted at the same time as, or after, the original licence has been varied.

4.18 An example of where this may be relevant to tracks is the granting of separate premises licences for track betting shops. The Act gives discretion for such shops to be a part of the umbrella track premises licence or to be subject to a separate premises licence, which will contain its own licence conditions. The Commission expects that track premises licence holders will wish to liaise with betting operators to discuss what will be most appropriate for their particular circumstances.

STARTING PRICES

4.19 The Commission is aware that the betting market on racecourses and greyhound tracks is the source of the Starting Price (SP), via which approximately 80% of relevant off-course bets are settled. For this reason, these track betting markets have significance beyond the confines of the track.

4.20 SP's are returned usually by employees of the Press Association, who act according to pre-defined guidelines designed to protect the strength and integrity of the SP. At racecourses, specific measures to prevent the potential distortion of the SP are currently in place through NPR 18.1.

4.21 The procedures relating to the return of the racecourse SP are agreed by the Starting Price Regulatory Commission (SPRC). The agreement to transfer data (ie prices) to the off-course industry from the on-course industry is subject to a commercial agreement between Satellite Information Services and the Federation of Racecourse Bookmakers, which is the umbrella organisation for on-course bookmakers. The Commission is aware that the SPRC has completed a recent review of the SP returning procedures, some of which require the NJPC to ensure compliance by on-course bookmakers with some elements of the NPRs mentioned above.

4.22 The Commission considers that it would be inappropriate for it to become involved in any issues relating to the SP, or to place requirements on track premises licence holders that served to protect the strength and integrity of the SP. If evidence did emerge that the integrity of the SP was being compromised, the Commission may need to become involved given its duty to promote the licensing objective that gambling should be conducted in a fair and open way. It is more likely, however, that such action would be directed towards betting operators rather than track premises licence holders.

Gambling Commission June 2007

LETTER TO RACECOURSE MANAGERS: CORPORATE HOSPITALITY BOXES AT RACECOURSES
December 2009

6.2176 As you will be aware there has been considerable industry interest in the subject of corporate hospitality boxes at racecourses. The Commission is therefore writing to all racecourses to make clear our understanding of this matter.

As regards such boxes, whether racecourses are in breach of the Act seems to us to be a matter of fact and degree. Racecourses by their very nature provide facilities for viewing racing usually with screens to view live action and of course are permitted to allow bookmakers to offer betting without the need for any additional premises licence. Individuals at tracks, whether or not in a box, can use mobile phones or laptops to access remote betting sites licensed here or overseas.

It follows, in our view, that racecourses can provide telephones, pc and wi fi facilities, as can any internet café, for general use. Racecourses should be careful not to set up arrangements that amount to the track, or people who hire a box at the track, providing facilities for gambling. This would require an operating licence in addition to any premises licence which they may already hold.

We would have a concern should either a racecourse, or those hiring a box, advertise such a facility in a way which may be seen to be offering facilities for gambling.

I should also mention for the purposes of clarity that we see this as distinct from the question of whether there are unlicensed layers using betting exchanges to act in the course of business.

Yours sincerely

Mike Williams

Head of Enforcement and Regional Compliance

Gambling Commission December 2009

LETTER TO RACECOURSE MANAGERS: CORPORATE HOSPITALITY BOXES AT RACECOURSES
November 2010

6.2177 In December 2009 the Commission wrote to racecourses regarding the use of racecourse hospitality boxes for the provision of facilities for gambling. It is apparent from recent compliance activity that there remains some confusion regarding the issue and what is permissible under the Gambling Act 2005.

The Commission remain of the view that the question of whether a racecourse is providing facilities for gambling and requiring an operating licence is a matter of fact and degree. Racecourses by their very nature provide facilities for viewing racing usually with screens to view live action and are permitted to allow bookmakers to offer betting without the need for any additional premises licence. Individuals at tracks, whether or not in a box, can use mobile phones or laptops to access remote betting sites licensed here or overseas.

Therefore as long as no facilities additional to those available as standard hospitality are provided, and the service is not advertised or promoted as a betting facility, the use of corporate hospitality facilities for in-running betting by individuals is likely to be permissible under the Act.

Where configurations are in place which may constitute the offering of facilities for gambling the Commission will in the first instance assist our co regulatory partners in determining whether such arrangements represent a breach of the existing track premises licence.

Trading Room Licence

All racecourses have a track premises licence from their local authority which, subject to commercial arrangements with a licensed operator, allows betting to take place anywhere within the area covered by the licence. This does not cover trading rooms. Trading rooms are where you set up equipment that lets people bet with a third party such as a betting exchange, through the internet or other remote means.

In cases where additional facilities are made available by racecourses for in-running betting then it is likely that the racecourse is offering facilities for gambling and will require a separate operating licence and premises licence:

- A betting premises licence – Covering trading rooms is available from the local authority with fees set by each authority.
- A Betting Intermediary (Trading Room only) Operating Licence, available from the Gambling Commission. At present there is an application fee of £593, and an annual renewal fee of £1,594 (discounted in the first year).

If the proposed trading room were sited within the area covered by the existing track premises licence the relevant area must be de-licensed from the track premises licence and relicensed under its own premises licence. This area will then be considered a trading room 365 days per year, and restrictions regarding access by under 18s and the consumption of alcohol will apply at all times. Therefore, this area could not be used for either race day or non race day events where children would be present or alcohol served.

We have sent a copy of this letter to your local authority.

Yours sincerely

Mike Williams

Head of Enforcement and Regional Compliance

Gambling Commission

GAMING: CASINOS

CONDITIONS AND CODES OF PRACTICE APPLICABLE TO: REMOTE CASINO LICENCES REMOTE CASINO ANCILLARY LICENCES October 2010

6.2180–6.2200 Your licence is subject to certain conditions and codes of practice, these are detailed in the following pages

STATUTORY CONDITIONS ATTACHED BY VIRTUE OF THE ACT

SOCIAL RESPONSIBILITY

This licence is subject to a condition that the licensee ensures compliance with any relevant social responsibility provision of a code of practice issued by the Commission. The social responsibility provisions that are relevant to the activities authorised by this licence are set out in the section entitled Codes of Practice
(Sections 24 and 82(1) Gambling Act 2005)

RETURN OF STAKES TO CHILDREN

This licence is subject to a condition that if the licensee (or anyone employed by the licensee to perform an operational function within the meaning of section 80 of the Act) becomes aware that a child or young person is using or has used facilities for gambling provided in reliance on the licence, the licensee:

(a) must return any money paid in respect of the use of those facilities (whether by way of fee, stake or otherwise) by the child or young person as soon as is reasonably practicable; and

(b) may not give a prize to the child or young person.

This condition does not apply to use of a Category D gaming machine. **Section 83(1)**

COMMISSION GENERAL CONDITIONS

The Commission's complete suite of Licence Conditions to be attached to operating licences pursuant to section 75 of the Act includes some conditions which may not apply to your licence. Where that is the case the irrelevant conditions have not been reproduced below. The full list of Licence Conditions and Codes of Practice are contained within the Commission's Publication "Licence Conditions and Codes of Practice"

QUALIFIED PERSONS AND PERSONAL LICENCES

Personal licences

THE FOLLOWING CONDITION APPLIES TO ALL REMOTE CASINO OPERATING LICENCES EXCEPT ANCILLARY REMOTE LICENCES

(a) Subject to (e) and (f) below licensees must ensure:

  (i) that each individual who occupies one of the management offices specified in (b) below in or in respect of the licensee or in connection with the licensed activities holds a personal licence authorising the performance of the functions of that office (hereafter 'a personal management licence')

  (ii) that at least one person occupies at least one of those offices.

(b) The specified management offices are those offices (whether or not held by a director in the case of a licensee which is a company, a partner in the case of a

6: Gambling Act 2005: Additional Material

licensee which is a partnership or an officer of the association in the case of a licensee which is an unincorporated association) the occupier of which is by virtue of the terms of their appointment responsible for:

- the overall management and direction of the licensee's business or affairs
- the licensee's finance function as head of that function
- the licensee's gambling regulatory compliance function as head of that function
- the licensee's marketing function as head of that function
- the licensee's information technology function as head of that function in so far as it relates to gambling-related information technology and software
- oversight of the day to day management of the licensed activities at an identified number of premises licensed under Part 8 of the Act or across an identified geographical area
- in the case of casino and bingo licences only, oversight of the day to day management of a single set of premises licensed under Part 8 of the Act.

(c) Licensees must take all reasonable steps to ensure that anything done in the performance of the functions of a specified management office is done in accordance with the terms and conditions of the holder's personal management licence.

(d) Where an individual is authorised by a personal licence and that licence comes under review under section 116(2) of the Act, the operating licensee must comply with any conditions subsequently imposed on that licence by the Commission about redeployment, supervision, or monitoring of the individual's work and any requirements of the Commission in respect of such matters applicable during the period of the review.

(e) Paragraphs (a) to (d) above shall not apply to a licensee for so long as the licensee is a 'small-scale operator' as defined in the Gambling Act 2005 (Definition of Small-scale Operator) Regulations 2006 ('the Regulations').

(f) During the period of 3 years commencing with the date on which a licensee ceases to be a small-scale operator paragraphs (a) to (e) above shall apply subject to the proviso that the phrase 'each individual' in paragraph (a)(i) shall not include any individual who was a 'qualified person' (as defined in the Regulations) in relation to the licensee 28 days immediately prior to the licensee ceasing to be a small-scale operator.

THE FOLLOWING CONDITION APPLIES TO ALL REMOTE CASINO OPERATING LICENCES EXCEPT ANCILLARY REMOTE LICENCES

In addition to paragraphs (a) to (f) above, licensees must ensure that if any of the following operational functions:

- dealer in respect of casino games
- cashier
- inspector
- security staff employed to watch gaming
- supervisor of gaming activities

is performed in connection with the licensed activities, it is performed by an individual who holds a personal licence authorising performance of the function (hereafter 'a personal functional licence'). Licensees must take all reasonable steps to ensure that anything done in the performance of those functions is done in accordance with the terms and conditions of the personal functional licence.

TECHNICAL STANDARDS AND EQUIPMENT SPECIFICATIONS

The following condition applies to all remote casino operating licences except ancillary remote licences

Licensees must comply with the Commission's technical standards and with requirements set by the Commission relating to the timing and procedures for testing.

The following condition applies to ancillary remote casino operating licences only

Licensees must comply with the Commission's specifications for casino equipment.

FINANCIAL ROBUSTNESS

Notification of shareholders

THE FOLLOWING CONDITION APPLIES TO ALL REMOTE CASINO OPERATING LICENCES EXCEPT ANCILLARY REMOTE LICENCES

All company licensees must notify the Commission of the name and address of any person who becomes a shareholder in the company or its holding company holding 3% or more of the issued share capital of the company or its holding company; or any existing shareholder who acquires a holding of 3% or more of the issued share capital of the company or its holding company.

In this condition 'holding company' has the meaning ascribed to that term by section 1159 of the Companies Act 2006 or any statutory modification or re-enactment thereof.

PROTECTION OF CUSTOMER FUNDS

The following condition applies to all remote casino operating licences except ancillary remote licences

Licensees who hold customer funds for use in future gambling must set out clearly, in information made available to customers in writing, whether they protect customers' funds in the event of insolvency and the method by which this is achieved.

GENERAL 'FAIR AND OPEN' PROVISIONS

Licensees must satisfy themselves that the terms on which gambling is offered are not unfair under the Unfair Terms in Consumer Contracts Regulations 1999 and, where applicable, meet the reasonableness test under the Unfair Contract Terms Act 1977. An accurate summary of the contractual terms on which gambling is offered must be made available to customers and set out in plain and intelligible language.

Customers must be notified of changes to terms before they come into effect.

DISPLAY OF LICENSED STATUS

The following condition applies to all remote casino operating licences except ancillary remote licences

Licensees offering gambling on websites must:

(a) display the following information on a page which, by virtue of the construction of the website, customers access before gambling:

(i) a statement that they are licensed and regulated by the Gambling Commission;

(ii) their licence number; and
(iii) a link to the Gambling Commission's website;
(b) display at least the information at (i) above on each page of the website which offers facilities for gambling in reliance on the licence;
(c) where they offer on pages of the website, or by means of a link from the website, facilities for gambling which are not provided in reliance on their Gambling Commission licence, clearly distinguish those products which are regulated by the Commission from those which are not.

ACCESS TO PREMISES

Licensees must have and put into effect policies and procedures (including staff training programmes) designed to ensure that their staff co-operate with the Commission's enforcement officers in the proper performance of their compliance functions and are made aware of those officers' rights of entry to premises contained in Part 15 of the Act.

INFORMATION REQUIREMENTS

Reporting suspicion of offences etc

THE FOLLOWING CONDITION APPLIES TO ALL REMOTE CASINO OPERATING LICENCES EXCEPT ANCILLARY REMOTE LICENCES

Licensees must provide the Commission with any information that they know relates to or suspect may relate to the commission of an offence under the Act, including an offence resulting from a breach of a licence condition or a code provision having the effect of a licence condition.

Reporting 'Key Events'

THE FOLLOWING CONDITION APPLIES TO ALL REMOTE CASINO OPERATING LICENCES EXCEPT ANCILLARY REMOTE LICENCES

A key event is an event that could have a significant impact on the nature or structure of a licensee's business. Licensees must notify the Commission of the occurrence of any of the following key events as soon as reasonably practicable and in any event within five working days of the licensee becoming aware of the event's occurrence[1].

- in the case of licensees which are companies, a petition being presented for their winding up or the winding up of any group company of theirs, or they or any group company being placed in administration or receivership: in this condition a 'group company' is any subsidiary or holding company of the licensee – as those terms are defined in section 1159 of the Companies Act 2006 or any statutory modification or re-enactment thereof – and any subsidiary of such holding company
- in the case of a licensee who is an individual (or a partner in a partnership licensee) their being presented with a petition for their bankruptcy or sequestration or their entering into an individual voluntary agreement
- where the licensee is required to have their accounts independently audited, any unplanned change of auditor including a change prompted by a dispute or resulting from auditors being unable or unwilling to sign an unqualified audit report
- the departure from the licensee's business of any person occupying a 'qualifying position' as defined by Regulation 2(2) of the Gambling Act 2005 (Definition of Small-scale Operator) Regulations 2006
- any breach of a covenant given to a bank or other lender
- any default in making repayment of the whole or any part of a loan on its due date

- any court judgments remaining unpaid 14 days after the date of judgment
- the commencement of any material litigation against the licensee
- the imposition of a disciplinary sanction, including dismissal, against the holder of a personal licence or a person occupying a qualifying position for gross misconduct; or the resignation of a personal licence holder or person occupying a qualifying position following commencement of disciplinary proceedings in respect of gross misconduct against that person
- in the case of remote gambling, the commencement or cessation of trading on website domains (including WAP URLs) or broadcast media through which the licensee provides gambling facilities.

---

1 Key events can be reported securely online at the Commission's website at www.gamblingcommission.gov.uk or by email to key.events@gamblingcommission.gov.uk or posted to Key Events, Compliance Administration Team, Gambling Commission, Victoria Square House, Victoria Square, Birmingham B2 4BP

General and Regulatory Returns

On request, licensees must provide the Commission with such information as the Commission may require about the use made of facilities provided in accordance with this licence, and the manner in which gambling authorised by this licence and the licensee's business in relation to that gambling are carried on, including in particular information about:

- the numbers of people making use of the facilities and the frequency of such use
- the range of gambling activities provided by the licensee and the numbers of staff employed in connection with them
- the licensee's policies in relation to, and experiences of, problem gambling.

In particular within 28 days of the end of each quarterly period or, for those only submitting annual returns, within 42 days of the end of each annual period, licensees must submit a Regulatory Return to the Commission containing such information as the Commission may from time to time require[2].

---

2 Regulatory returns can be submitted securely online at the Commission's website at www.gamblingcommission.gov.uk. For operators unable to access this system, the forms and a guide to completing them can be requested from the Commission and returned by email to Regulatory.Returns@gamblingcommission.gov.uk or by post to Regulatory Returns, Compliance Administration Team, Gambling Commission, Victoria Square House, Victoria Square, Birmingham, B2 4BP

SECRETARY OF STATE GENERAL CONDITIONS

None at present

CODES OF PRACTICE

Introduction

This is the Commission's principal code of practice, issued under section 24 of the Gambling Act 2005, as revised with effect from 1 January 2009. There are two types of provision in the code:

- social responsibility provisions: compliance with these is a condition of licences; therefore any breach of them by an operator may lead the Commission to review the operator's licence with a view to suspension, revocation or the imposition of a financial penalty and would also expose the operator to the risk of prosecution; and

- ordinary code provisions: these do not have the status of licence conditions, but are admissible in evidence in criminal or civil proceedings and must be taken into account in any case in which the court or tribunal think them relevant and by the Commission in the exercise of its functions. Any breach of ordinary code provisions by an operator may be taken into account by the Commission on a licence review, but cannot lead to imposition of a financial penalty. These code provisions are in italics in this section and generally set out good practice in these areas.

Financial requirements

Ordinary code provision

In order to help prevent activities related to money laundering and terrorist financing, licensees should act in accordance with the Commission's guidance on anti-money laundering, *The Prevention of Money Laundering and Combating the Financing of Terrorism — Guidance for remote and non-remote casinos.*

Protection of children and other vulnerable persons

Combating problem gambling

Social responsibility code provision

Licensees must have and put into effect policies and procedures intended to promote socially responsible gambling.

Licensees' policies and procedures for socially responsible gambling must include but need not be confined to:

- the specific policies and procedures required by the following provisions of section 2 of this code
- a commitment to and how they will contribute to research into the prevention and treatment of problem gambling
- a commitment to and how they will contribute to public education on the risks of gambling and how to gamble safely
- a commitment to and how they will contribute to the identification and treatment of problem gamblers.

Access to gambling by children and young persons

The following code applies to all remote casino operating licences, except ancillary remote licences

Social responsibility code provision

Licensees must have and put into effect policies and procedures designed to prevent underage gambling, and monitor the effectiveness of these.

Such procedures must include:

(a) warning potential customers that underage gambling is an offence;
(b) requiring customers to affirm that they are of legal age;
(c) regularly reviewing their age verification systems and implementing all reasonable improvements that may be made as technology advances and as information improves;
(d) ensuring that relevant staff are properly trained in the use of their age verification procedures; in particular customer services staff must be appropriately trained in the use of secondary forms of identification when initial verification procedures fail to prove that an individual is of legal age;

(e) enabling their gambling websites to permit filtering software to be used by adults (such as parents or within schools) in order to restrict access to relevant pages of those sites;

(f) in the case of any UK resident customer who deposits money using any type of payment method other than a credit card, and unless the licensee has established that a third party has satisfactorily carried out age verification, the following age verification procedures:
  (i) verifying additional information about the customer, such as carrying out searches of credit reference and other databases that list names and addresses of individuals over the age of 18;
  (ii) carrying out secondary age verification checks in any circumstances which give the operator reason to suspect that the person may be underage;
  (iii) not permitting the customer to withdraw any winnings from their account until age verification has been satisfactorily completed; and
  (iv) in any event, a requirement that if age verification has not been satisfactorily completed within 72 hours of the customer applying to register to gamble and depositing money:
    - the account will be frozen
    - no further gambling will be permitted until age verification has been successfully completed
    - if on completion of age verification the customer is shown to be underage, the operator must return to the customer any money paid in respect of the use of the gambling facilities, but no winnings shall be paid.

(g) in the case of any non-UK resident customer who deposits money using any type of payment method other than a credit card, and unless the licensee has established that a third party has satisfactorily carried out age verification, the following age verification procedures:
  (i) taking all reasonable steps to make use of information available for age verification purposes from whichever country the potential customer is resident in; and
  (ii) each of the following steps, unless they can not reasonably be implemented or, in the case of the fourth bullet point, a period of more than 72 hours was reasonably required:
    - verifying additional information about the customer, such as carrying out searches of credit reference and other databases that list names and addresses of individuals over the age of 18
    - carrying out secondary age verification checks in any circumstances which give the operator reason to suspect that the person may be underage
    - not permitting the customer to withdraw any winnings from their account until age verification has been satisfactorily completed
    - a requirement that if age verification has not been satisfactorily completed within 72 hours of the customer applying to register to gamble and depositing money:
      – the account will be frozen;
      – no further gambling will be permitted until age verification has been successfully completed; and
      – if on completion of age verification the customer is shown to be underage all deposits held by the operator are returned to the customer and no winnings paid.

(h) in the case of any customer who registers to gamble and deposits money using a credit card, conducting a programme of random checks of credit card users for compliance with age restrictions.

THE FOLLOWING CODE APPLIES TO ALL REMOTE CASINO OPERATING LICENCES, EXCEPT ANCILLARY REMOTE LICENCES

ORDINARY CODE PROVISION

Licensees should, and should request their contracted partners to, draw attention to parental responsibility as part of the purchasing process of facilities such as mobile phones and interactive television.

Information on how to gamble responsibly and help for problem gamblers

THE FOLLOWING CODE APPLIES TO ALL REMOTE CASINO OPERATING LICENCES, EXCEPT ANCILLARY REMOTE LICENCES

SOCIAL RESPONSIBILITY CODE PROVISION

Licensees must make information readily available to their customers on how to gamble responsibly and how to access information about, and help in respect of, problem gambling.

The information must cover:

- any measures provided by the licensee to help individuals monitor or control their gambling, such as restricting the duration of a gambling session or the amount of money they can spend
- timers or other forms of reminders or 'reality checks' where available
- self-exclusion options
- information about the availability of further help or advice.

The information must be directed to all customers whether or not licensees also make available material which is directed specifically at customers who may be 'problem gamblers'.

For gambling premises, information must be available in all areas where gambling facilities are provided and adjacent to ATMs where these are not located in a gambling area. As a minimum, information must be displayed prominently on posters appropriate to the size and layout of the premises and contained in leaflets that may be taken away. Licensees must take all reasonable steps to ensure that this information is also readily accessible in locations which enable the customer to obtain it discreetly.

THE FOLLOWING CODE APPLIES TO ALL REMOTE CASINO OPERATING LICENCES, EXCEPT ANCILLARY REMOTE LICENCES

ORDINARY CODE PROVISION

Licensees who market their services in one or more foreign languages should make available in that, or those, foreign languages:

- the information on how to gamble responsibly and access to help referred to above
- the players' guides to any game, bet or lottery required to be made available to customers under provisions in this code
- the summary of the contractual terms on which gambling is offered, which is required to be provided to customers as a condition of the licensee's operating licence.

Customer interaction

SOCIAL RESPONSIBILITY CODE PROVISION

Licensees must put into effect policies and procedures for customer interaction where they have concerns that a customer's behaviour may indicate problem gambling. The policies must include:

- identification of the appropriate level of management who may initiate customer interaction and the procedures for doing so
- the types of behaviour that will be logged/reported to the appropriate level of staff and which may trigger customer interaction at an appropriate moment
- the circumstances in which consideration should be given to refusing service to customers and/or barring them from the operator's gambling premises
- training for all staff on their respective responsibilities, in particular so that they know who is designated to deal with problem gambling issues.

But such policies and procedures must be consistent with, and implemented with due regard to, licensees' duties in respect of the health and safety of their staff.

Self-exclusion

THE FOLLOWING CODE APPLIES TO ALL REMOTE CASINO OPERATING LICENCES, EXCEPT ANCILLARY REMOTE LICENCES

SOCIAL RESPONSIBILITY CODE PROVISION

Licensees must have and put into effect procedures for self-exclusion and take all reasonable steps to refuse service or to otherwise prevent an individual who has entered a self-exclusion agreement from participating in gambling.

Licensees must, as soon as practicable, take all reasonable steps to prevent any marketing material being sent to a self-excluded customer.

Licensees must take steps to remove the name and details of a self-excluded individual from any marketing databases used by the company or group (or otherwise flag that person as an individual to whom marketing material must not be sent), within two days of receiving the completed self-exclusion notification.

This covers any marketing material relating to gambling. However, it would not extend to blanket marketing which is targeted at a particular geographical area and where the excluded individual would not knowingly be included.

Licensees must close any customer accounts of an individual who has entered a self-exclusion agreement and return any funds held in the customer account. It is not sufficient merely to prevent an individual from withdrawing funds from their customer account whilst still accepting wagers from them. Where the giving of credit is permitted, the licensee may retain details of the amount owed to them by the individual, although the account must not be active.

Licensees must put into effect procedures designed to ensure that an individual who has self-excluded cannot gain access to gambling. These procedures must include:

- a register of those excluded with appropriate records (name, address, other details, and any membership or account details that may be held by the operator)
- a record of the card numbers to be excluded
- staff training to ensure that staff are able to enforce the systems
- the removal of access from those persons found to have gambled or who have attempted to gamble on the facilities.

THE FOLLOWING CODE APPLIES TO ALL REMOTE CASINO OPERATING LICENCES, EXCEPT ANCILLARY REMOTE LICENCES

ORDINARY CODE PROVISION

Self-exclusion procedures should require individuals to take positive action in order to self-exclude:

- over the **internet**; this can be a box that must be ticked in order to indicate that they understand the system
- by **telephone**; this can be a direct question asking whether they understand the system.

Before an individual self-excludes, licensees should provide or make available sufficient information about what the consequences of self-exclusion are.

Licensees should encourage the customer to consider extending their self exclusion to other remote gambling operators currently used by the customer.

Customers should be given the opportunity to self-exclude by contacting customer services and in addition, where technically possible, by entering an automated process using remote communication. In order to avoid inadvertent self-exclusion it is acceptable for an automated process to include an additional step that requires the customer to confirm that they wish to self-exclude. The licensee should ensure that all staff who are involved in direct customer service are aware of the self-exclusion system in place, and are able to direct that individual to an immediate point of contact with whom/which to complete that process.

Within the licensee's information about self-exclusion policies, the licensee should provide a statement to explain that software is available to prevent an individual computer from accessing gambling internet sites. The licensee should provide a link to a site where further information is available.

Licensees should take all reasonable steps to ensure that:

- the self-exclusion period is a minimum of six months and give customers the option of extending this to a total of at least five years
- a customer who has decided to enter a self-exclusion agreement is given the opportunity to do so immediately without any cooling-off period. However, if the customer wishes to consider the self-exclusion further (for example to discuss with problem gambling groups) the customer may return at a later date to enter into self-exclusion
- at the end of the period chosen by the customer (and at least six months later), the self-exclusion remains in place, unless the customer takes positive action in order to gamble again. No marketing material should be sent to the individual unless the individual has taken positive action in order to gamble again, and has agreed to accept such material
- where a customer chooses not to renew the self-exclusion, and makes a positive request to begin gambling again, the customer is given one day to cool off before being allowed access to the gambling facilities. The contact must be made via telephone or in person; re-registering online is not sufficient.

The licensee should retain the records relating to a self-exclusion agreement at least until the agreement has been formally ended.

(Please note that the Commission does not require the licensee to carry out any particular assessment or make any judgement as to whether the previously self excluded individual should again be permitted access to gambling. The requirement to take positive action in person or over the phone is purely to a) check that the customer has considered the decision to access gambling again and allow them to consider the implications; and b) implement the one day cooling-off period and explain why this has been put in place.)

Employment of children and young persons

THE FOLLOWING CODE APPLIES TO ALL REMOTE CASINO OPERATING LICENCES, EXCEPT ANCILLARY REMOTE LICENCES

ORDINARY CODE PROVISION

Licensees who employ children (under-16-year-olds) and young persons (those aged 16 and 17) should be aware that it is an offence to employ them to provide facilities for gambling.

Provision of credit by licensees and the use of credit cards

THE FOLLOWING CODE APPLIES TO ALL REMOTE CASINO OPERATING LICENCES, EXCEPT ANCILLARY REMOTE LICENCES

SOCIAL RESPONSIBILITY CODE PROVISION

Licensees who choose to accept credit cards must:

- accept payment by credit card for gambling only where that payment is made to a customer account
- make available for gambling, funds deposited via credit card only after the card issuer has approved the transaction.

THE FOLLOWING CODE APPLIES TO ALL REMOTE CASINO OPERATING LICENCES, EXCEPT ANCILLARY REMOTE LICENCES

ORDINARY CODE PROVISION

Licensees who choose to offer credit to members of the public who are not themselves gambling operators should also:

- have procedures for checking and scoring applications for credit from such customers, for setting, and for the increase of, credit limits
- explain these procedures to customers
- set a maximum credit limit for each customer and not permit customers to exceed that limit without further application
- apply a 24-hour delay between receiving a request for an increase in a credit limit and granting it in those cases where the limit exceeds that which the operator had previously set
- not require a minimum spend within a set time period
- take all reasonable steps to ensure that offers of credit are not sent to vulnerable persons, including those who have self-excluded from gambling
- ensure that information about an offer of credit includes a risk warning of what may happen in the event of default.

Identification of individual customers

THE FOLLOWING CODE APPLIES TO ALL REMOTE CASINO OPERATING LICENCES, EXCEPT ANCILLARY REMOTE LICENCES

SOCIAL RESPONSIBILITY CODE PROVISION

Licensees must have and put into effect policies and procedures designed to identify separate accounts which are held by the same individual.

Where licensees allow customers to hold more than one account with them, the licensee must link all of a customer's such accounts to that customer and ensure that:

- if a customer opts to self-exclude from one account they are excluded from all accounts they hold with the licensee
- all of a customer's accounts are monitored and decisions that trigger customer interaction are based on the observed behaviour and transactions across all the accounts
- where credit is offered or allowed the maximum credit limit is applied on an aggregate basis across all accounts
- individual financial limits can be implemented across all of a customer's accounts.

THE FOLLOWING CODE APPLIES TO ALL REMOTE CASINO OPERATING LICENCES, EXCEPT ANCILLARY REMOTE LICENCES

ORDINARY CODE PROVISION

Where a licensee:

(i) is a company, the licensee should take all reasonable steps to comply with the above social responsibility code provision as if it also applied to accounts held in respect of gambling carried on in reliance on a remote operating licence held by any Group Company;

(ii) also holds a licence in another jurisdiction permitting it to provide facilities for remote gambling (a 'foreign licence') or is a company one or more of whose Group Companies holds one or more foreign licences, the licensee should take all reasonable steps to comply with the above social responsibility code provision as if it applied also to accounts held in respect of gambling carried on in reliance on a foreign licence held by the licensee or any Group Company.

A company is a Group Company in relation to a licensee if it is the holding company of, subsidiary of, or shares a common holding company with, the licensee. For these purposes 'holding company' and 'subsidiary' respectively have the meanings ascribed to them by section 1159 of the Companies Act 2006 or any statutory modification or re-enactment thereof.

'Fair and open' provisions

SOCIAL RESPONSIBILITY CODE PROVISION

Licensees must be able to provide evidence to the Commission, if required, showing how they satisfied themselves that their terms are not unfair.

THE FOLLOWING CODE APPLIES TO ALL REMOTE CASINO OPERATING LICENCES, EXCEPT ANCILLARY REMOTE LICENCES

SOCIAL RESPONSIBILITY CODE PROVISION

Licensees must make the following available to customers:

- a player's guide to each gambling opportunity (bet, game or lottery) made available by the operator
- such additional information relating to the available gambling as the Commission shall from time to time publish to licensees: the current requirements are set out in an Annex to the Commission's Technical Standards.

THE FOLLOWING CODE APPLIES TO ALL REMOTE CASINO OPERATING LICENCES, EXCEPT ANCILLARY REMOTE LICENCES

ORDINARY CODE PROVISION

Where practicable, the player's guide and additional information referred to in the social responsibility code should be made available through the medium in which the remote gambling is to be conducted. Where that is not practicable, licensees should either:

- send a copy of the guide and required additional information by post, fax or email; or
- make these available to the customer in another medium to which he has access.

The following code applies to all remote casino operating licences, except ancillary remote licences

Ordinary code provision

Licensees should ensure that the terms on which they contract with third parties who provide user interfaces enabling customers to access their remote gambling facilities:

- include a term that any such user interface comply with the Commission's technical standards for remote gambling systems
- enable them to terminate the third party's contract promptly if, in the licensee's opinion, the third party is in breach of that term.

Marketing

Social responsibility code provision

If a licensee makes available to any customer or potential customer any incentive or reward scheme or other arrangement under which the customer may receive money, goods, services or any other advantage (including the discharge in whole or in part of any liability of his) ('the benefit') the scheme must be designed to operate, and be operated, in such a way that:

(a) the circumstances in which, and conditions subject to which, the benefit is available are clearly set out and readily accessible to the customers to whom it is offered;

(b) neither the receipt nor the value or amount of the benefit is:

  (i) dependent on the customer gambling for a pre-determined length of time or with a predetermined frequency; or

  (ii) altered or increased if the qualifying activity or spend is reached within a shorter time than the whole period over which the benefit is offered;

(c) if the value of the benefit increases with the amount the customer spends it does so at a rate no greater than that at which the amount spent increases;

and further that:

(d) if the benefit comprises free or subsidised travel or accommodation which facilitates the customer's attendance at particular licensed premises the terms on which it is offered are not directly related to the level of the customer's prospective gambling.

Ordinary code provision

Licensees should only offer incentive or reward schemes in which the benefit available is proportionate to the type and level of customers' gambling.

Ordinary code provision

All advertising of gambling products and services should be undertaken in a socially responsible manner. In particular, licensees should comply with the advertising codes of practice which apply to the form and media in which they advertise their gambling facilities or services, and for media not explicitly covered should apply the principles included in these codes of practice as if they were explicitly covered. Licensees should also follow any relevant industry code of practice on advertising.

However, the particular restriction on allowing people aged under 25 to appear in adverts need not be applied to point of sale advertising material, provided that the images used depict the sporting activity that may be gambled on and not the activity of gambling itself and do not offend any other aspect of the advertising codes.

THE FOLLOWING CODE APPLIES TO ALL REMOTE CASINO OPERATING LICENCES, EXCEPT ANCILLARY REMOTE LICENCES

ORDINARY CODE PROVISION

Licensees should ensure that the terms on which they contract with their affiliates (that is those who are given a right to advertise, or provide a hyper-link to, a licensee's gambling website) enable them to terminate the affiliate's rights promptly if, in the licensee's opinion, the affiliate is in breach of the advertising codes.

Complaints and disputes

SOCIAL RESPONSIBILITY CODE PROVISION

Licensees must put into effect a written procedure for handling customer complaints and disputes.

In this code a 'complaint' means a complaint about any aspect of the licensee's conduct of the licensed activities, and a 'dispute' is any complaint which:

(a) is not resolved at the first stage of the complaints procedure; and
(b) relates to the outcome of the complainant's gambling transaction.

Licensees must ensure that:

- customers are told the name and status of the person to contact about their complaint
- customers are given a copy of the complaints procedure on request or on making a complaint
- all complaints are handled in accordance with the procedure.

Licensees must also ensure that they have arrangements in place for disputes to be referred to an independent third party. Customers whose disputes are not resolved to their satisfaction by use of the operator's complaints procedure may refer those disputes to this independent third party. The arrangements under which such complaints are referred may, but need not, provide for the third party's decision to be binding on the licensee and the customer.

Licensees must keep a record of all complaints that are not resolved at the first stage of the complaints procedure.

Licensees must arrange for a copy of the decision on, or a note of the outcome of, each dispute referred to the independent party to be provided to the Commission quarterly, either by the independent party or by the licensee.

Gambling licensees' staff

THE FOLLOWING CODE APPLIES TO ALL REMOTE CASINO OPERATING LICENCES, EXCEPT ANCILLARY REMOTE LICENCES

SOCIAL RESPONSIBILITY CODE PROVISION

Licensees must take all reasonable steps to ensure that staff involved in the provision of facilities for gambling are made aware of advice on socially responsible gambling and of where to get confidential advice should their gambling become hard to control.

Information requirements

THE FOLLOWING CODE APPLIES TO ALL CASINO OPERATING LICENCES EXCEPT ANCILLARY REMOTE LICENCES

ORDINARY CODE PROVISION

The Commission expects licensees to work with the Commission in an open and cooperative way and to inform the Commission of any matters that the Commission would reasonably need to be aware of in exercising its regulatory functions. These are matters that will have a material impact on the licensee's business or on the licensee's ability to conduct its business. Such matters, which should be notified to the Commission as soon as reasonably practicable[3], include the following:

- the departure from the licensee's business of any person named in the licence application, or that person's successor, who holds a personal management licence, but who does not occupy a 'qualifying position'
- any reduction in the number of staff employed by the licensee where that has a material impact on the licensee's business
- the acquisition or disposal by the licensee of gambling premises or pitches where that has a material impact on the size or nature of the licensee's business
- in the case of corporate licensees, the disposal or acquisition of any group company where that has a material impact on the licensee's ability to conduct its business
- any disposal of the licensee's assets where that has a material impact on the licensee's business
- any investigation by a professional, statutory, regulatory or government body into the licensee's activities, or the activities in relation to the licensed entity of a personal licence holder or a person occupying a qualifying position employed by them, where such an investigation could result in the imposition of a sanction or penalty which, if imposed, could reasonably be expected to raise doubts about the licensee's continued suitability to hold a Gambling Commission licence
- any instance of criminal activity, including repeated instances of small-scale theft or fraud, where that has a material impact on the licensee's business
- any major breach in the licensee's information security where that adversely affects the confidentiality of customer data or prevents customers from accessing their accounts for a substantial period of time
- any other matters that have a material impact on the licensee's business or on the licensee's ability to conduct its business.

---

3 These matters can be reported securely online at the Commission's website at www.gambling-commission.gov.uk or by email to key.events@gamblingcommission.gov.uk or posted to Key Events, Compliance Administration Team, Gambling Commission, Victoria Square House, Victoria Square, Birmingham, B2 4BP

Gambling Commission October 2010

CONDITIONS AND CODES OF PRACTICE APPLICABLE TO: NON-REMOTE CASINO LICENCES

December 2011

6.2205–6.2215 **Your licence is subject to certain conditions and codes of practice,**

these are detailed in the following pages

STATUTORY CONDITIONS ATTACHED BY VIRTUE OF THE ACT

SOCIAL RESPONSIBILITY

This licence is subject to a condition that the licensee ensures compliance with any relevant social responsibility provision of a code of practice issued by the Commission. The social responsibility provisions that are relevant to the activities authorised by this licence are set out in the section entitled Codes of Practice.
(Sections 24 and 82(1) Gambling Act 2005)

RETURN OF STAKES TO CHILDREN

This licence is subject to a condition that if the licensee (or anyone employed by the licensee to perform an operational function within the meaning of section 80 of the Act) becomes aware that a child or young person is using or has used facilities for gambling provided in reliance on the licence, the licensee:

(a) must return any money paid in respect of the use of those facilities (whether by way of fee, stake or otherwise) by the child or young person as soon as is reasonably practicable; and

(b) may not give a prize to the child or young person.

This condition does not apply to use of a Category D gaming machine.
(Section 83(1))

OTHER STATUTORY CONDITIONS

This licence is subject to a condition that the licensee may not:

- give credit in connection with gambling; or
- participate in, arrange, permit or knowingly facilitate the giving of credit in connection with gambling.

But this condition shall not prevent the licensee from permitting the installation and use on their licensed premises of a machine enabling cash to be obtained on credit from a person (the "credit provider") provided that:

- the licensee has no other commercial connection with the credit provider in relation to gambling;
- the licensee neither makes nor receives any payment or reward (whether by way of commission, rent or otherwise) in connection with the machine; and
- any conditions about the nature, location or use of the machine which may be attached to this licence by the Commission or by virtue of regulations by the Secretary of State are complied with.

(Section 81(2))

COMMISSION GENERAL CONDITIONS

The Commission's complete suite of Licence Conditions to be attached to operating licences pursuant to section 75 of the Act includes some conditions which may not apply to your licence. Where that is the case the irrelevant conditions have not been reproduced below. The full list of Licence Conditions and Codes of Practice are contained within the Commissions Publication "Licence Conditions and Codes of Practice"

QUALIFIED PERSONS AND PERSONAL LICENCES

PERSONAL LICENCES

(a) Subject to (e) and (f) below licensees must ensure:

(i) that each individual who occupies one of the management offices specified in (b) below in or in respect of the licensee or in connection with the licensed activities holds a personal licence authorising the performance of the functions of that office (hereafter 'a personal management licence')

(ii) that at least one person occupies at least one of those offices.

(b) The specified management offices are those offices (whether or not held by a director in the case of a licensee which is a company, a partner in the case of a licensee which is a partnership or an officer of the association in the case of a licensee which is an unincorporated association) the occupier of which is by virtue of the terms of their appointment responsible for:

- the overall management and direction of the licensee's business or affairs
- the licensee's finance function as head of that function
- the licensee's gambling regulatory compliance function as head of that function
- the licensee's marketing function as head of that function
- the licensee's information technology function as head of that function in so far as it relates to gambling-related information technology and software
- oversight of the day to day management of the licensed activities at an identified number of premises licensed under Part 8 of the Act or across an identified geographical area
- in the case of casino and bingo licences only, oversight of the day to day management of a single set of premises licensed under Part 8 of the Act.

(c) Licensees must take all reasonable steps to ensure that anything done in the performance of the functions of a specified management office is done in accordance with the terms and conditions of the holder's personal management licence.

(d) Where an individual is authorised by a personal licence and that licence comes under review under section 116(2) of the Act, the operating licensee must comply with any conditions subsequently imposed on that licence by the Commission about redeployment, supervision, or monitoring of the individual's work and any requirements of the Commission in respect of such matters applicable during the period of the review.

(e) Paragraphs (a) to (d) above shall not apply to a licensee for so long as the licensee is a 'small-scale operator' as defined in the Gambling Act 2005 (Definition of Small-scale Operator) Regulations 2006 ('the Regulations').

(f) During the period of 3 years commencing with the date on which a licensee ceases to be a small-scale operator paragraphs (a) to (e) above shall apply subject to the proviso that the phrase 'each individual' in paragraph (a)(i) shall not include any individual who was a 'qualified person' (as defined in the Regulations) in relation to the licensee 28 days immediately prior to the licensee ceasing to be a small-scale operator.

In addition to paragraphs (a) to (f) above, licensees must ensure that if any of the following operational functions:

- dealer in respect of casino games
- cashier
- inspector
- security staff employed to watch gaming
- supervisor of gaming activities

is performed in connection with the licensed activities, it is performed by an individual who holds a personal licence authorising performance of the function (hereafter 'a personal functional licence'). Licensees must take all reasonable steps to ensure that anything done in the performance of those functions is done in accordance with the terms and conditions of the personal functional licence.

TECHNICAL STANDARDS AND EQUIPMENT SPECIFICATIONS

Licensees must comply with the Commission's specifications for casino equipment.

FINANCIAL ROBUSTNESS

Notification of shareholders

All company licensees must notify the Commission of the name and address of any person who becomes a shareholder in the company or its holding company holding 3% or more of the issued share capital of the company or its holding company; or any existing shareholder who acquires a holding of 3% or more of the issued share capital of the company or its holding company.

In this condition 'holding company' has the meaning ascribed to that term by section 1159 of the Companies Act 2006 or any statutory modification or re-enactment thereof.

PROTECTION OF CUSTOMER FUNDS

Licensees who hold customer funds for use in future gambling must set out clearly, in information made available to customers in writing, whether they protect customers' funds in the event of insolvency and the method by which this is achieved.

CASH HANDLING

Licensees, as part of their internal controls and financial accounting systems, must have and put into effect policies and procedures concerning the handling of cash, and cash equivalents (ie bankers drafts, cheques and debit cards), designed to minimise the risk of crimes such as money laundering, to avoid the giving of illicit credit and to provide assurance that gambling activities are being conducted fairly.

GENERAL 'FAIR AND OPEN' PROVISIONS

Licensees must satisfy themselves that the terms on which gambling is offered are not unfair under the Unfair Terms in Consumer Contracts Regulations 1999 and, where applicable, meet the reasonableness test under the Unfair Contract Terms Act 1977. An accurate summary of the contractual terms on which gambling is offered must be made available to customers and set out in plain and intelligible language.

Customers must be notified of changes to terms before they come into effect.

TYPES AND RULES OF CASINO AND OTHER GAMES

Licensees must not offer or permit to be plated casino games that appear on any list of games prohibited by the Commission.

TIPPING OF CASINO EMPLOYEES

Licensees must only permit tipping of staff holding personal licences where a tronc system is operated; that is to say, where all tips are pooled and distributed amongst the employees concerned. A separate tronc may be operated for each of a number of categories of licensed staff.

ACCESS TO PREMISES

Licensees must have and put into effect policies and procedures (including staff training programmes) designed to ensure that their staff co-operate with the Commission's enforcement officers in the proper performance of their compliance functions and are made aware of those officers' rights of entry to premises contained in Part 15 of the Act.

INFORMATION REQUIREMENTS

Reporting suspicion of offences etc

Licensees must provide the Commission with any information that they know relates to or suspect may relate to the commission of an offence under the Act, including an offence resulting from a breach of a licence condition or a code provision having the effect of a licence condition.

Reporting 'Key Events'

A key event is an event that could have a significant impact on the nature or structure of a licensee's business. Licensees must notify the Commission of the occurrence of any of the following key events as soon as reasonably practicable and in any event within five working days of the licensee becoming aware of the event's occurrence[1].

- in the case of licensees which are companies, a petition being presented for their winding up or the winding up of any group company of theirs, or they or any group company being placed in administration or receivership: in this condition a 'group company' is any subsidiary or holding company of the licensee – as those terms are defined in section 1159 of the Companies Act 2006 or any statutory modification or re-enactment thereof – and any subsidiary of such holding company
- in the case of a licensee who is an individual (or a partner in a partnership licensee) their being presented with a petition for their bankruptcy or sequestration or their entering into an individual voluntary agreement
- where the licensee is required to have their accounts independently audited, any unplanned change of auditor including a change prompted by a dispute or resulting from auditors being unable or unwilling to sign an unqualified audit report
- the departure from the licensee's business of any person occupying a 'qualifying position' as defined by Regulation 2(2) of the Gambling Act 2005 (Definition of Small-scale Operator) Regulations 2006
- any breach of a covenant given to a bank or other lender
- any default in making repayment of the whole or any part of a loan on its due date
- any court judgments remaining unpaid 14 days after the date of judgment
- the commencement of any material litigation against the licensee
- the imposition of a disciplinary sanction, including dismissal, against the holder of a personal licence or a person occupying a qualifying position for gross misconduct; or the resignation of a personal licence holder or person occupying a qualifying position following commencement of disciplinary proceedings in respect of gross misconduct against that person
- in the case of remote gambling, the commencement or cessation of trading on website domains (including WAP URLs) or broadcast media through which the licensee provides gambling facilities.

[1] Key events can be reported securely online at the Commission's website at www.gamblingcommission.gov.uk or by email to key.events@gamblingcommission.gov.uk or posted to Key Events, Compliance Administration Team, Gambling Commission, Victoria Square House, Victoria Square, Birmingham B2 4BP

6: Gambling Act 2005: Additional Material

General and Regulatory Returns

On request, licensees must provide the Commission with such information as the Commission may require about the use made of facilities provided in accordance with this licence, and the manner in which gambling authorised by this licence and the licensee's business in relation to that gambling are carried on, including in particular information about:

- the numbers of people making use of the facilities and the frequency of such use
- the range of gambling activities provided by the licensee and the numbers of staff employed in connection with them
- the licensee's policies in relation to, and experiences of, problem gambling.

In particular within 28 days of the end of each quarterly period or, for those only submitting annual returns, within 42 days of the end of each annual period, licensees must submit a Regulatory Return to the Commission containing such information as the Commission may from time to time require[2]

[2] Regulatory returns can be submitted securely online at the Commission's website at www.gamblingcommission.gov.uk For operators unable to access this system, the forms and a guide to completing them can be requested from the Commission and returned by email to Regulatory.Returns@gamblingcommission.gov.uk or by post to Regulatory Returns, Compliance Administration Team, Gambling Commission, Victoria Square House, Victoria Square, Birmingham, B2 4BP.

Primary gambling activity

The following condition applies to non-remote casino operating licences except 2005 Act casino operating licences

Gaming machines may be made available for use in licensed casino premises only on those days when sufficient facilities for playing casino games and/or games of equal chance are also available for use.

When a casino exclusively offers fully automated casino games, there must be more individual player positions made available for these games than there are gaming machines made available for use.

SECRETARY OF STATE GENERAL CONDITIONS

This licence is subject to a condition that where, in reliance on the operating licence, a game is played on a wholly automated gaming table, the game must be capable of being played by four persons at the same time using four separate player positions.

"Wholly automated gaming table" means equipment that would fall within the definition of a gaming machine in section 235 of the Gambling Act 2005 but for its exclusion from that definition by subsection (2)(i) of that section.

Regulation 2, Gambling Act 2005 (Operating Licence Conditions) Regulations 2007

CODES OF PRACTICE

INTRODUCTION

This is the Commission's principal code of practice, issued under section 24 of the Gambling Act 2005, as revised with effect from 1 January 2009. There are two types of provision in the code:

- social responsibility provisions: compliance with these is a condition of licences; therefore any breach of them by an operator may lead the Commission to review the operator's licence with a view to suspension, revocation or the imposition of a financial penalty and would also expose the operator to the risk of prosecution; and
- ordinary code provisions: these do not have the status of licence conditions, but are admissible in evidence in criminal or civil proceedings and must be taken into

account in any case in which the court or tribunal think them relevant and by the Commission in the exercise of its functions. Any breach of ordinary code provisions by an operator may be taken into account by the Commission on a licence review, but cannot lead to imposition of a financial penalty. These code provisions are in italics in this section and generally set out good practice in these areas.

FINANCIAL REQUIREMENTS

Ordinary code provision

In order to help prevent activities related to money laundering and terrorist financing, licensees should act in accordance with the Commission's guidance on anti-money laundering, *The Prevention of Money Laundering and Combating the Financing of Terrorism — Guidance for remote and non-remote casinos.*

PROTECTION OF CHILDREN AND OTHER VULNERABLE PERSONS

Combating problem gambling

Social responsibility code provision

Licensees must have and put into effect policies and procedures intended to promote socially responsible gambling.
Licensees' policies and procedures for socially responsible gambling must include but need not be confined to:

- the specific policies and procedures required by the following provisions of section 2 of this code
- a commitment to and how they will contribute to research into the prevention and treatment of problem gambling
- a commitment to and how they will contribute to public education on the risks of gambling and how to gamble safely
- a commitment to and how they will contribute to the identification and treatment of problem gamblers.

Access to gambling by children and young persons

Social responsibility code provision

Licensees must have and put into effect policies and procedures designed to prevent underage gambling, and monitor the effectiveness of these.
Licensees must designate one or more supervisors for each casino entrance.
A supervisor's responsibilities include ensuring compliance with this section of the code.
A supervisor must implement the following procedures:

- checking the age of customers who appear to be, or are suspected of being, underage
- refusing entry to anyone unable to produce an acceptable form of identification, ie one which:
  - contains a photograph from which the individual can be identified
  - states the individual's date of birth
  - is valid
  - is legible and shows no signs of tampering or reproduction
- taking action when there are unlawful attempts to enter the premises, including removing anyone who appears to be underage who tries to access gambling facilities and cannot produce an acceptable form of identification.

Licensees must not deliberately provide facilities for gambling in such a way as to appeal particularly to children or young people, for example by reflecting or being associated with youth culture.

In premises restricted to adults, service must be refused in any circumstances where any adult is accompanied by a child or young person.

Licensees must take all reasonable steps to ensure that all staff understand their responsibilities for preventing underage gambling. This should include appropriate training which must cover the legal requirements on returning stakes and not paying prizes to underage customers.

Ordinary code provision

There should be a sufficient number of supervisors at casino entrances to enable a considered judgement to be made about the age of everyone attempting to enter the casino and to take the appropriate action (for example checking identification) whilst at the same time not allowing others to enter unsupervised. The nature of this task means that it cannot be properly accomplished only by using CCTV; it will require a physical presence. Heavily used entrances may require more than one designated supervisor.

Supervisors may be assisted by other door keepers provided the supervisor retains the responsibility for compliance with this section of the code and deals personally with any case where there is any doubt or dispute as to someone's eligibility to enter.

The Commission considers acceptable forms of identification to include: any identification carrying the PASS logo (for example Citizencard or Validate); a driving licence (including provisional licence) with photocard; or a passport.

Licensees should put into effect procedures that require their staff to check the age of any customer who appears to them to be under 21.

Licensees should consider permanent exclusion from premises of any adult accompanied by a child or young person on more than one occasion to premises restricted to adults, or if there is reason to believe the offence was committed knowingly or recklessly.

Procedures should be put into effect for dealing with cases where a child or young person repeatedly attempts to gamble on premises restricted to adults, including oral warnings, reporting the offence to the Gambling Commission and the police, and making available information on problem gambling.

Information on how to gamble responsibly and help for problem gamblers

Social responsibility code provision

Licensees must make information readily available to their customers on how to gamble responsibly and how to access information about, and help in respect of, problem gambling.

The information must cover:

- any measures provided by the licensee to help individuals monitor or control their gambling, such as restricting the duration of a gambling session or the amount of money they can spend
- timers or other forms of reminders or 'reality checks' where available
- self-exclusion options
- information about the availability of further help or advice.

The information must be directed to all customers whether or not licensees also make available material which is directed specifically at customers who may be 'problem gamblers'.

For gambling premises, information must be available in all areas where gambling facilities are provided and adjacent to ATMs where these are not located in a gambling area. As a minimum, information must be displayed prominently on posters appropriate to the size and layout of the premises and contained in leaflets that may be taken away. Licensees must take all reasonable steps to ensure that this information is also readily accessible in locations which enable the customer to obtain it discreetly.

ORDINARY CODE PROVISION

Licensees who market their services in one or more foreign languages should make available in that, or those, foreign languages:

- the information on how to gamble responsibly and access to help referred to above
- the players' guides to any game, bet or lottery required to be made available to customers under provisions in this code
- the summary of the contractual terms on which gambling is offered, which is required to be provided to customers as a condition of the licensee's operating licence.

Customer interaction

SOCIAL RESPONSIBILITY CODE PROVISION

Licensees must put into effect policies and procedures for customer interaction where they have concerns that a customer's behaviour may indicate problem gambling. The policies must include:

- identification of the appropriate level of management who may initiate customer interaction and the procedures for doing so
- the types of behaviour that will be logged/reported to the appropriate level of staff and which may trigger customer interaction at an appropriate moment
- the circumstances in which consideration should be given to refusing service to customers and/or barring them from the operator's gambling premises
- training for all staff on their respective responsibilities, in particular so that they know who is designated to deal with problem gambling issues.

But such policies and procedures must be consistent with, and implemented with due regard to, licensees' duties in respect of the health and safety of their staff.

Self-exclusion

SOCIAL RESPONSIBILITY CODE PROVISION

Licensees must have and put into effect procedures for self-exclusion and take all reasonable steps to refuse service or to otherwise prevent an individual who has entered a self-exclusion agreement from participating in gambling.

Licensees must, as soon as practicable, take all reasonable steps to prevent any marketing material being sent to a self-excluded customer.

Licensees must take steps to remove the name and details of a self-excluded individual from any marketing databases used by the company or group (or otherwise flag that person as an individual to whom marketing material must not be sent), within two days of receiving the completed self-exclusion notification.

This covers any marketing material relating to gambling, or other activities that take place on the premises where gambling may take place. However, it would not extend to blanket marketing which is targeted at a particular geographical area and where the excluded individual would not knowingly be included.

Licensees must close any customer accounts of an individual who has entered a self exclusion agreement and return any funds held in the customer account. It is not sufficient merely to prevent an individual from withdrawing funds from their customer account whilst still accepting wagers from them. Where the giving of credit is permitted, the licensee may retain details of the amount owed to them by the individual, although the account must not be active.

Licensees must put into effect procedures designed to ensure that an individual who has self-excluded cannot gain access to gambling. These procedures must include:

- a register of those excluded with appropriate records (name, address, other details, and any membership or account details that may be held by the operator)
- photo identification (where available and in particular where enforcement of the system may depend on photographic ID), and a signature
- staff training to ensure that staff are able to enforce the systems
- the removal of those persons found in the gambling area or attempting to gamble from the premises.

ORDINARY CODE PROVISION

Self-exclusion procedures should require individuals to take positive action in order to self-exclude. This can be a signature on a self-exclusion form.

Wherever practicable, individuals should be able to self-exclude without having to enter gambling premises.

Before an individual self-excludes, licensees should provide or make available sufficient information about what the consequences of self-exclusion are.

Licensees should take all reasonable steps to extend the self-exclusion to premises of the same type owned by the operator in the customer's local area. In setting the bounds of that area licensees may take into account the customer's address (if known to them), anything else known to them about the distance the customer ordinarily travels to gamble and any specific request the customer may make.

Licensees should encourage the customer to consider extending their self exclusion to other licensees' gambling premises in the customer's local area.

Customers should be given the opportunity to discuss self-exclusion in private, where possible.

Licensees should take steps to ensure that:

- the self-exclusion period is a minimum of six months and give customers the option of extending this to a total of at least five years
- a customer who has decided to enter a self-exclusion agreement is given the opportunity to do so immediately without any cooling-off period. However, if the customer wishes to consider the self-exclusion further (for example to discuss with problem gambling groups) the customer may return at a later date to enter into self-exclusion
- at the end of the period chosen by the customer (and at least six months later), the self-exclusion remains in place, unless the customer takes positive action in order to gamble again. No marketing material should be sent to the individual unless the individual has taken positive action in order to gamble again, and has agreed to accept such material
- where a customer chooses not to renew the self-exclusion, and makes a positive request to begin gambling again, the customer is given one day to cool off before being allowed access to gambling facilities. The contact must be made via telephone or in person.

The licensee should retain the records relating to a self-exclusion agreement at least until the agreement has been formally ended.

(Please note that the Commission does not require the licensee to carry out any particular assessment or make any judgement as to whether the previously self-excluded individual should again be permitted access to gambling. The requirement to take positive action in person or over the phone is purely to a) check that the customer has considered the decision to access gambling again and allow them to consider the implications; and b) implement the one day cooling-off period and explain why this has been put in place.)

Employment of children and young persons

ORDINARY CODE PROVISION

Licensees who employ children (under-16-year-olds) and young persons (those aged 16 and 17) should be aware that it is an offence:

(a) to employ them to provide facilities for gambling;

(b) if gaming machines are sited on the premises, for their contracts of employment to require them, or for them to be permitted, to perform a function in connection with a gaming machine at any time; and

(c) to employ them to carry out any other function on casino licensed premises while any gambling activity is being carried on in reliance on the premises licence (except that they can be employed on a part of regional casino premises when that part of the premises is not being used for the provision of facilities for gambling).

As to b) it should be noted that in the Commission's view the relevant provision of the Act applies to any function performed in connection with a gaming machine. This includes servicing or cleaning such a machine.

Accordingly, licensees should have and put into effect policies and procedures designed to ensure that:

- children and young persons are never asked to perform tasks within a) or b) above
- all staff, including those who are children or young persons themselves, are instructed about the laws relating to access to gambling by children and young persons

and should consider adopting a policy that:

- children and young persons are not employed to work on casino licensed premises (other than in an area of a regional casino where gambling does not take place) at any time when the premises are open for business
- gaming machines are turned off if children and young persons are working on the premises outside the hours when the premises are open for business.

Money lending between customers

ORDINARY CODE PROVISION

Licensees should take steps to prevent systematic or organised money lending between customers on their premises.

While the nature of those steps will depend to some extent on the layout and size of the premises, they should cover matters such as:

- systems for monitoring for such activity
- instructions to staff concerning what they should do if they spot what they believe to be significant money lending and to managers about the ways in which they should handle and act on any such lending
- excluding from the premises, either temporarily or permanently as appropriate, any person whom the evidence suggests has become involved in organised or systematic money lending.

There should be appropriate arrangements in place to cover any cases where it appears that the lending may be commercial in nature or may involve money laundering. In the latter case, the requirements in respect of reporting suspicious transactions must be followed. In all cases where the operator encounters systematic or organised money lending, a report should be made to the Commission.

'Fair and open' provisions

SOCIAL RESPONSIBILITY CODE PROVISION

Licensees must be able to provide evidence to the Commission, if required, showing how they satisfied themselves that their terms are not unfair.

SOCIAL RESPONSIBILITY CODE PROVISION

In complying with any condition on a casino premises licence requiring the display of rules about gaming, licensees must ensure that the following are included:

- the rules of each type of casino game available to be played
- a player's guide to the house edge
- a player's guide to the rules of any equal chance games which are made available.

SOCIAL RESPONSIBILITY CODE PROVISION

Licensees must have and put into effect policies and procedures designed to ensure that proper supervision of gaming at tables is carried out by supervisors, pit bosses and croupiers in order to ensure the integrity of the gaming is not compromised. Such policies and procedures must take into account, but need not be limited by, any mandatory premises licence conditions relating to the layout of premises.

Marketing

SOCIAL RESPONSIBILITY CODE PROVISION

If a licensee makes available to any customer or potential customer any incentive or reward scheme or other arrangement under which the customer may receive money, goods, services or any other advantage (including the discharge in whole or in part of any liability of his) ('the benefit') the scheme must be designed to operate, and be operated, in such a way that:

(a) the circumstances in which, and conditions subject to which, the benefit is available are clearly set out and readily accessible to the customers to whom it is offered;

(b) neither the receipt nor the value or amount of the benefit is:

 (i) dependent on the customer gambling for a pre-determined length of time or with a predetermined frequency; or

 (ii) altered or increased if the qualifying activity or spend is reached within a shorter time than the whole period over which the benefit is offered;

(c) if the value of the benefit increases with the amount the customer spends it does so at a rate no greater than that at which the amount spent increases;

and further that:

(d) if the benefit comprises free or subsidised travel or accommodation which facilitates the customer's attendance at particular licensed premises the terms on which it is offered are not directly related to the level of the customer's prospective gambling.

ORDINARY CODE PROVISION

Licensees should only offer incentive or reward schemes in which the benefit available is proportionate to the type and level of customers' gambling.

SOCIAL RESPONSIBILITY CODE PROVISION

If licensees offer customers free or discounted alcoholic drinks for consumption on the premises they must do so on terms which do not in any way link the availability of such drinks to whether, or when, the customer begins, or continues, to gamble.

Licensees must not make unsolicited offers of free alcoholic drinks for immediate consumption by customers at a time when they are participating in a casino game, bingo game or playing a gaming machine.

SOCIAL RESPONSIBILITY CODE PROVISION

Where a licensee employs agents to promote its business (wherever that business is conducted), it must ensure that its agreement with any agent makes clear that the agent must not encourage players to play longer or wager more than the player might otherwise do.

In particular, payments should not be directly dependent upon, nor directly calculated by reference to, the length of time for which, or frequency with which, the customer gambles. If the payment to the agent increases with the amount the customer spends it must do so at a rate no greater than that at which the amount spent increases.

ORDINARY CODE PROVISION

All advertising of gambling products and services should be undertaken in a socially responsible manner. In particular, licensees should comply with the advertising codes of practice which apply to the form and media in which they advertise their gambling facilities or services, and for media not explicitly covered should apply the principles included in these codes of practice as if they were explicitly covered. Licensees should also follow any relevant industry code of practice on advertising.

However, the particular restriction on allowing people aged under 25 to appear in adverts need not be applied to point of sale advertising material, provided that the images used depict the sporting activity that may be gambled on and not the activity of gambling itself and do not offend any other aspect of the advertising codes.

Complaints and disputes

SOCIAL RESPONSIBILITY CODE PROVISION

Licensees must put into effect a written procedure for handling customer complaints and disputes.

In this code a 'complaint' means a complaint about any aspect of the licensee's conduct of the licensed activities, and a 'dispute' is any complaint which:

(a) is not resolved at the first stage of the complaints procedure; and
(b) relates to the outcome of the complainant's gambling transaction.

Licensees must ensure that:

- customers are told the name and status of the person to contact about their complaint
- customers are given a copy of the complaints procedure on request or on making a complaint
- all complaints are handled in accordance with the procedure.

Licensees must also ensure that they have arrangements in place for disputes to be referred to an independent third party. Customers whose disputes are not resolved to their satisfaction by use of the operator's complaints procedure may refer those disputes to this independent third party. The arrangements under which such complaints are referred may, but need not, provide for the third party's decision to be binding on the licensee and the customer.

Licensees must keep a record of all complaints that are not resolved at the first stage of the complaints procedure.

Licensees must arrange for a copy of the decision on, or a note of the outcome of, each dispute referred to the independent party to be provided to the Commission quarterly, either by the independent party or by the licensee.

Gambling licensees' staff

SOCIAL RESPONSIBILITY CODE PROVISION

Licensees must have and put into effect policies and procedures to manage relationships between staff and customers, based on the principle that in carrying out their duties staff must not engage in any conduct which is, or could be, likely to prejudice the licensing objectives.

SOCIAL RESPONSIBILITY CODE PROVISION

Licensees must take all reasonable steps to ensure that staff involved in the provision of facilities for gambling are made aware of advice on socially responsible gambling and of where to get confidential advice should their gambling become hard to control.

Information requirements

ORDINARY CODE PROVISION

The Commission expects licensees to work with the Commission in an open and cooperative way and to inform the Commission of any matters that the Commission would reasonably need to be aware of in exercising its regulatory functions. These are matters that will have a material impact on the licensee's business or on the licensee's ability to conduct its business. Such matters, which should be notified to the Commission as soon as reasonably practicable[3], include the following:

- the departure from the licensee's business of any person named in the licence application, or that person's successor, who holds a personal management licence, but who does not occupy a 'qualifying position'
- any reduction in the number of staff employed by the licensee where that has a material impact on the licensee's business
- the acquisition or disposal by the licensee of gambling premises or pitches where that has a material impact on the size or nature of the licensee's business
- in the case of corporate licensees, the disposal or acquisition of any group company where that has a material impact on the licensee's ability to conduct its business
- any disposal of the licensee's assets where that has a material impact on the licensee's business
- any investigation by a professional, statutory, regulatory or government body into the licensee's activities, or the activities in relation to the licensed entity of a personal licence holder or a person occupying a qualifying position employed by them, where such an investigation could result in the imposition of a sanction or penalty which, if imposed, could reasonably be expected to raise doubts about the licensee's continued suitability to hold a Gambling Commission licence
- any instance of criminal activity, including repeated instances of small-scale theft or fraud, where that has a material impact on the licensee's business
- any major breach in the licensee's information security where that adversely affects the confidentiality of customer data or prevents customers from accessing their accounts for a substantial period of time
- any other matters that have a material impact on the licensee's business or on the licensee's ability to conduct its business.

---

[3] These matters can be reported securely online at the Commission's website at www.gamblingcommission.gov.uk or by email to key.events@gamblingcommission.gov.uk or posted to Key Events, Compliance Administration Team, Gambling Commission, Victoria Square House, Victoria Square, Birmingham, B2 4BP

Primary gambling activity

The following condition applies to non-remote casino operating licences except 2005 Act casino operating licences

ORDINARY CODE PROVISION

In order to demonstrate that the primary gambling activity for which an operating licence has been issued is being offered in each licensed premises, licensees should have regard to the following general factors:

- the ratio of the space available to customers allocated to the primary gambling activity, to that allocated to other gambling activities
- the extent to which the primary gambling activity is promoted on the premises and by way of external advertising compared to other gambling activities
- the use, either expected or actual, to be made of the different gambling facilities.

Licensees should also have regard to the following additional sector specific factors:

- the proportion of the gaming day for which live tables are, or will, be made available on demand.

Not all the indicators would need to be present in a particular case, nor do they preclude others, but the combination of those factors that are present should be sufficient to indicate that the activity is the primary one in any given premises.
Gambling Commission December 2011

THE PREVENTION OF MONEY LAUNDERING AND COMBATING THE FINANCING OF TERRORISM
Guidance for remote and non-remote casinos (2nd edn)

6.2241 December 2011

PART 1 – SUMMARY OF THE GUIDANCE

PRINCIPLES TO BE FOLLOWED

i All casinos (both premises based and remote) must have appropriate systems and processes to forestall and prevent money laundering and terrorist financing. To achieve this they should:

- develop systems and controls that are appropriate for their businesses;
- adopt a risk-based approach that is flexible, effective, proportionate and cost-effective;
- have full commitment from, and responsibility resting with, senior management;
- regularly assess the adequacy of their systems and controls;
- maintain, where necessary, records of customers and transactions that meet the needs of law enforcement investigations tackling money laundering and terrorist financing;
- provide initial and ongoing training for all relevant employees;
- support their nominated officers with resources and authority to operate objectively and independently;
- engage with law enforcement bodies and the Gambling Commission (the Commission) by reporting suspicious activity; and
- participate in feedback and best practice forums.

RISK-BASED APPROACH

ii The Regulations require operators to have a policy and procedure in relation to risk assessment and management. The risk-based approach involves a number of discrete steps in assessing the most proportionate way to manage and mitigate the money laundering and terrorist financing risks faced by the operator. These steps require the operator to:

- identify the money laundering and terrorist financing risks that are relevant to the operator;
- design and implement policies and procedures to manage and mitigate these assessed risks;
- monitor and improve the effective operation of these controls; and
- record what has been done, and why.

iii A risk-based approach focuses the effort where it is most needed and will have most impact. It requires the full commitment and support of senior management, and the active co-operation of all employees.

iv The risk-based approach is discussed in section 2 of this guidance.

SENIOR MANAGEMENT RESPONSIBILITY

v Senior management must be fully engaged in the processes around an operator's assessment of risks for money laundering and terrorist financing, and must be involved at every level of the decision making to develop the operator's policies and processes to comply with the Money Laundering Regulations 2007 (the Regulations). Disregard for the legal requirements, for example, turning a blind eye to customers spending criminal proceeds, may result in criminal or regulatory action.

vi A member of senior management who consents to, or connives in, the commission of offences under the regulations, or where the commission of any such offence is attributable to any neglect on his part, will be individually liable for the offence.

vii Operators must establish and maintain appropriate written risk-sensitive policies and procedures relating to:

- customer due diligence (CDD) measures and ongoing monitoring;
- reporting;
- record keeping;
- internal control;
- risk assessment and management;
- training; and
- the monitoring and management of compliance with, and the internal communication of, such policies and procedures.

viii Senior management responsibility is discussed in section 3 of this guidance.

NOMINATED OFFICER

ix Nominated officers have responsibility for:

- making reports to senior management on anti-money laundering (AML) and countering terrorist financing (CTF) activity;
- receiving internal disclosures under Part 7 of the Proceeds of Crime Act 2002 (POCA) and Part 3 of the Terrorism Act 2000 (the Terrorism Act);
- deciding whether these should be reported to the Serious Organised Crime Agency (SOCA); and
- if appropriate, making such external reports.

x They must have the authority to act independently in carrying out their responsibilities, and have access to sufficient resources to carry out their duties.

xi Casinos must have contingency arrangements in place for circumstances where no nominated officer is in post, for example if on annual leave, long-term sick leave or if the nominated officer leaves the employ of the casino.

xii The responsibilities of the nominated officer are discussed in section 4 of this guidance.

CASINO EMPLOYEES

xiii Employees must report to their nominated officer any knowledge or suspicion of money laundering whether by customers, guests or other employees.

xiv Employees must follow casino policies and procedures for:

- CDD, including enhanced requirements for high risk customers, which includes politically exposed persons (PEPs);
- reporting suspicious activity to the nominated officer;
- where necessary, seeking appropriate consent to allow participation in gaming and to conduct gaming and other business transactions; and
- record keeping for those who exceed the threshold or who have a business relationship.

xv The duties of casino employees are discussed throughout sections 4, 5, 6 and 7 of this guidance.

CUSTOMER DUE DILIGENCE

xvi A key requirement in the regulations is the requirement to make checks on customers — CDD. Casino operators can use one of two approaches; identifying and verifying the identity of all customers on entry to the casino's licensed premises (the on entry approach) or undertaking identification and verification when a customer approaches the threshold set out in the Regulations (the threshold approach).

xvii Operators must conduct their CDD on the basis of risk assessment, including simplified due diligence and enhanced due diligence (which includes PEPs). Operators are also required to identify the beneficial owner of a customer and they will also need to have evidence of identity in place for all customers.

xviii Operators should note that CDD is ongoing and may need updating for changes in the customer's circumstances and personal details.

xix Customer de diligence is discussed in section 5 of this guidance.

RECORD KEEPING

xx The purpose of the record keeping requirement is to ensure that there is an audit trail that could assist in any financial investigation by a law enforcement body.

xxi The operator's record keeping policy and procedure should cover records in the following areas:

- details of how compliance has been monitored by the nominated officer;
- delegation of AML/CTF tasks by the nominated officer;
- nominated officer reports to senior management;
- information not acted upon by the nominated officer, with reasoning why no further action was taken;
- customer identification and verification information;
- supporting records in respect of business relationships or occasional transactions;
- employee training records;
- internal and external suspicious activity reports (SARs); and
- contact between the nominated officer and law enforcement or SOCA, including records connected to appropriate consent.

xxii Record keeping is discussed in section 6 of this guidance.

SUSPICIOUS ACTIVITY REPORTS

xxiii Employees in casinos are required to make a report in respect of information that comes to them within the course of business:

- where they know; or
- where they suspect; or

6: Gambling Act 2005: Additional Material

- where they have reasonable grounds for knowing or suspecting,

that a person is engaged in money laundering or terrorist financing.

xxiv Operators must ensure that any employee reports to the nominated officer where they have grounds for knowledge or suspicion that a person or customer is engaged in money laundering or terrorist financing. The operator's nominated officer must consider each report, and determine whether it gives grounds for knowledge or suspicion.

xxv If the nominated officer determines that a report does give rise to grounds for knowledge or suspicion, he must report the matter to SOCA. Under POCA, the nominated officer is required to make a report to SOCA as soon as is practicable if he has grounds for suspicion that another person, whether or not a customer, is enagaged in money laundering. Under the Terrorism Act, similar conditions apply in relation to disclosure where there are grounds for suspicion of terrorist financing.

xxvi Suspicious activities and reporting requirements are discussed in section 7 of this guidance.

OFFENCES

xxvii POCA and the Terrorism Act create offences of failing to report suspicious activity. Where a person fails to comply with the obligations to make disclosures to a nominated officer, or the nominated officer to SOCA, as soon as practicable after the information giving rise to the knowledge or suspicion comes to the employee, they are open to criminal prosecution.

xxviii In certain circumstances, a person also commits an offence under POCA if he discloses information that a SAR has been submitted that is likely to prejudice any investigation, or discloses information that an investigation into allegations that an offence under the Regulations has been committed, that is likely to prejudice the investigation.

xxix A person in the regulated sector also commits an offence if he knows or suspects that an appropriate officer or, in Scotland, a proper person is acting (or proposing to act) in connection with a confiscation investigation, a civil recovery investigation, a detained cash investigation or a money laundering investigation which is being or is about to be conducted, and falsifies, conceals, destroys or disposes of, or causes or permits the falsification, concealment, destruction or disposal of, documents which are relevant to the investigation.

xxx The offences are discussed in section 7 of this guidance.

PART 2 – THE GUIDANCE

1 INTRODUCTION

1.1 The law concerning money laundering is based on the general and wide ranging prevention and detection of the use of any proceeds of crime, the prevention and detection of terrorist financing, and for some businesses (including casinos) the more specific requirements of the business and its employees to have policies and procedures in place covering the risks it faces from money laundering.

1.2 Money laundering is a term that is often misunderstood. It is defined in section 340 of POCA and covers wide ranging circumstances involving any activity concerning the proceeds of any crime. This includes:

- trying to turn money raised through criminal activity into 'clean' money (that is, classic money laundering);
- possessing or transferring the benefit of acquisitive crimes such as theft and fraud, and funds generated from crimes like tax evasion;
- possessing or transferring stolen goods;
- being directly involved with any criminal or terrorist property, or entering into arrangements to facilitate the laundering of criminal or terrorist property; and
- criminals investing the proceeds of their crimes in the whole range of financial products.

1.3 Using money in casinos, regardless of the amount, that is the proceeds of any crime can amount to money laundering if the person using or taking the money knows or suspects that it is the proceeds of crime. Money laundering offences can be committed by both the customer and the casino employees, depending on respective levels of knowledge or suspicion.

1.4 The Regulations came into effect on 15 December 2007 and replaced the Money Laundering Regulations 2003 (the 2003 Regulations). Both remote and non-remote casinos licensed by the Commission are covered by the Regulations.

1.5 The Regulations are generated from the Third European Union Directive (2005) that was adopted in October 2005. This directive represents Europe's ongoing commitment to tackle the international problem of money laundering and terrorist financing by implementing the global standards produced by the Financial Action Task Force (FATF) in 2003.

1.6 The FATF recommendations that set the global standards single out the business sectors where there are believed to be the highest risks of money laundering and terrorist financing. This includes remote and non-remote casinos.

1.7 Criminal offences of money laundering were first introduced in the United Kingdom (UK) in the Criminal Justice Act 1988 and the Drug Trafficking Offences Act 1986. POCA consolidated, updated, and reformed, the criminal law relating to money laundering to include any dealing in 'criminal property', which is defined widely as the proceeds of any type of crime, however small the amount. POCA created three principal offences that between them criminalise any involvement in the proceeds of any crime if the person knows or suspects that the property is the proceeds of crime.[1]

1.8 These are wide offences that can be committed by any person, including a casino employee, who has actual knowledge or suspicion that a customer is using the proceeds of crime, or has possession of the proceeds of criminal activity.

1.9 Specific obligations to report suspected terrorist financing were included in the Terrorism Act, as amended by the Anti Terrorism Crime and Security Act 2001. This legislation creates criminal offences, most of which can be committed by anyone in the UK. Some of the offences are specific to people working in firms covered by the Regulations, and who are therefore in the regulated sector, which includes casinos.

1.10 The Regulations cover a range of businesses and professions, including remote and non-remote casinos licensed by the Commission. This guidance sets out how casino operators can and must comply with the law, which at times is complex and demanding. The law places responsibilities on the Commission as the supervisory authority for casinos. The Commission should produce guidance that helps casino operators to meet the requirements of the law, is workable in the remote and non-remote casino environments and is approved by HM Treasury. This guidance covers the full requirements of the UK law as it affects casinos.

1.11 The purpose of this guidance is to:

- outline the full legal framework for AML and CTF requirements and systems across the remote and non-remote casino sector;
- summarise the requirements of the relevant law and regulations, and how they may be implemented in practice;
- indicate good industry practice in AML/CTF procedures through a proportionate risk-based approach;
- assist operators to design and implement the policies and procedures necessary to mitigate the risks of being used in connection with money laundering and the financing of terrorism.

1.12 This guidance sets out what will be expected of casino operators and their employees in relation to the prevention of money laundering and terrorist financing, but allows them some discretion as to how they apply the requirements of the AML/CTF regime in the particular circumstances of their business.

1.13 This guidance will be of direct relevance to senior management and nominated officers in remote and non-remote casinos.

[1] Sections 327, 328 and 329 of POCA.

How should the guidance be used?

1.14 The purpose is to give guidance to those who set operators' risk management policies and procedures for preventing money laundering and terrorist financing. This guidance aims to assist operators with detail about how to comply with the Regulations and the wider legal requirements, and is intended to allow operators flexibility as to how they comply. Operators will need to establish their own, more detailed and more specific internal arrangements directed by senior management and nominated officers to reflect the risk profile of their business.

1.15 When provisions of the statutory requirements or the Commission's regulatory requirements are directly described in the text of the guidance and are obligatory, the guidance uses the term 'must', indicating that these provisions are mandatory. Where the guidance is merely advisory, the term 'should' is adopted. References to 'must' and 'should' in the text should therefore be construed accordingly.

1.16 This guidance is not intended to be a substitute for legal advice and operators' individual risk management plans. Operators should refer to the Regulations and associated legislation in making decisions in relation to the Regulations.

Content of the guidance

1.17 This guidance emphasises the responsibility of senior management to manage the operator's money laundering and terrorist financing risks, and how this should be carried out on a risk-based approach. It sets out a standard approach to the identification of customers and verification of their identities, separating out basic identity from other measures relating to customer due diligence, including the obligation to monitor customer activity.

1.18 It is accepted that a proportionate risk-based approach has to meet a variety of scenarios and, as such, has to be based on an understanding of how the business is designed to operate. There is, therefore, a need for ongoing and repeated assessments of risk to meet changing circumstances.

1.19 The guidance contains the following sections:

- the importance of adopting a risk-based approach;
- the importance of senior management taking responsibility for effectively managing the money laundering and terrorist financing risks faced by the operator's businesses;
- the role and responsibilities of the nominated officer;
- the proper carrying out of the CDD obligations, including monitoring customer transactions and activity;
- record keeping; and
- the identification and reporting of suspicious activity.

Status of the guidance

1.20 POCA requires a court to take account of industry guidance, such as this, that has been approved by a Treasury minister when considering whether a person within the regulated sector has committed the offence of failing to report. Similarly the Terrorism Act requires a court to take account of such approved industry guidance when considering whether a person has failed to report under that Act. The Regulations state that a court must consider whether someone has followed this guidance if they are prosecuted for failing to comply with the Regulations.[2] The first edition of this guidance was approved by HM Treasury on 27 July 2010.

1.21 Operators must be able to demonstrate that they have taken all reasonable steps to comply with all the AML requirements. If they can demonstrate to a court and/or the Commission that they have followed this guidance then the court or the Commission is obliged to take that into account.

1.22 The Commission is not a 'designated authority' under the Regulations and therefore has no powers to take action against operators that breach the Regulations.[3] However, an ordinary code provision within the Licence Conditions and Codes of Practice requires casino operators to act in accordance with this guidance. Should operators not follow the code provision, the Commission may consider reviewing the suitability of the operator to carry on the licensed activities. This could result in the suspension or revocation of the operator's licence under sections 118 and 119 of the Gambling Act 2005 (the Act).

1.23 The Commission also has employees who have the powers of accredited financial investigators under POCA in England and Wales.[4] This means that the Commission can apply for orders and warrants in relation to money laundering, for the purpose of:

- requiring a specified person to produce certain material
- permitting the search of and seizure of material from specified premises
- requiring a financial institution to provide customer information relating to a specified person.

1.24 The guidance provides a sound basis for operators to meet their legislative and regulatory obligations when tailored by operators to their particular business risk profile. Departures from this guidance, and the grounds for so doing, should be documented and may have to be justified, for example, to the Commission.

---

2 Sections 330 and 331 of POCA and Regulation 45.

3 Regulation 42.

4 See Statutory Instrument No 2009/975.

2 RISK-BASED APPROACH

Introduction

2.1 The Regulations impose compulsory compliance requirements and a breach can constitute a criminal offence.[5] However, within this legal framework of requirements, casinos have flexibility to devise policies and procedures which best suit their assessment of the money laundering and terrorist financing risks faced by their business. The Regulations require a policy and procedure in relation to risk assessment and management.[6]

2.2 Operators are already expected to manage their operations with regard to the risks posed to the licensing objectives in the Act, and measure the effectiveness of the policies and procedures they have put in place to manage those risks. The approach to managing the risks of the operator being used for money laundering or terrorist financing is consistent with the existing regulatory requirements.

2.3 The risk-based approach involves a number of discrete steps in assessing the most proportionate way to manage and mitigate the money laundering and terrorist financing risks faced by the operator. These steps require the operator to:

- identify the money laundering and terrorist financing risks that are relevant to the operator;
- design and implement policies and procedures to manage and mitigate these assessed risks;
- monitor and improve the effective operation of these controls; and
- record what has been done, and why.

2.4 A risk-based approach will serve to balance the burden placed on operators and their customers with a realistic assessment of the threat of the operator being misused in connection with money laundering or terrorist financing. It focuses the effort where it is most needed and will have most impact. It is not a blanket one size fits all approach, and therefore operators have a degree of flexibility in their methods of compliance.

2.5 A risk-based approach requires the full commitment and support of senior management, and the active co-operation of all employees. Senior management should ensure that the risk-based approach is part of the operator's philosophy and reflected in its policies and procedures. There needs to be a clear communication of the policies and procedures across the operator, along with robust mechanisms to ensure that they are carried out effectively, weaknesses are identified, and improvements are made wherever necessary.

---

5 Regulation 45.

6 Regulation 20(1)(e).

Identifying and assessing the risks faced by the operator

2.6 The operator should assess its risks in the context of how it is most likely be involved in money laundering or terrorist financing. Assessment of risk is based on a number of questions including:

- What risk is posed by the business profile and customers using the casino?
- Is the business high volume consisting of many low spending customers?
- Is the business low volume with high spending customers, perhaps who use and operate within their cheque cashing facilities?
- Is the business a mixed portfolio, ie customers are a mix of high spenders and lower spenders and/or a mix or regular and occasional customers?
- Are procedures in place to monitor customer transactions and mitigate any money laundering potential?
- Is the business local with regular and generally well known customers?
- Are there a large proportion of overseas customers using foreign currency or overseas based bank cheque or debit cards?
- Are customers likely to be individuals who hold public positions in countries which carry a higher exposure to the possibility of corruption, that is, a PEP?
- Are customers likely to be engaged in a business which involves significant amounts of cash?
- Are there likely to be situations where the source of funds cannot be easily established or explained by the customer?
- Are there likely to be situations where the customer's purchase or exchange of chips is irrational or not linked with gaming?
- Is the majority of business conducted in the context of business relationships?

2.7 Deciding that a customer is presenting a higher risk of money laundering or terrorist financing does not automatically mean that he is a money launderer or a financier of terrorism. Similarly, identifying a customer as presenting a low risk of money laundering or terrorist financing does not mean that the customer is definitely not money laundering. Employees therefore need to remain vigilant and use their experience and common sense in applying the operator's risk-based criteria and rules, seeking guidance from their nominated officer as appropriate.

2.8 Many customers carry a lower money laundering or terrorist financing risk. These might include customers who are regularly employed or who have a regular source of income from a known source which supports the activity being undertaken (this applies equally to pensioners, benefit recipients, or to those whose income originates from their partner's employment or income).

2.9 Where a customer is assessed as presenting higher risk it will be necessary to seek additional information in respect of the customer. This will help the operator judge whether the higher risk that the customer is perceived to present is likely to materialise. Such additional information may include an understanding of where the customer's funds and wealth have come from.

2.10 If casinos adopt the threshold approach to CDD, part of the risk-based approach will involve making decisions about whether or when verification should take place electronically. Operators must determine the extent of their CDD measures, over and above the minimum requirements, on a risk-sensitive basis depending on the risk posed by the customer and their level of gambling.

2.11 In order to be able to detect customer activity that may be suspicious, it is necessary to monitor transactions or activity.[7] Monitoring customer activity should be carried out using the risk-based approach, with higher risk customers being subjected to an appropriate frequency and depth of scrutiny, which is likely to be greater than may be appropriate for lower risk customers.

---

7 Regulation 8.

Risk management is dynamic

2.12 A money laundering/terrorist financing risk assessment is not a one-off exercise. Operators must therefore ensure that their policies and procedures for managing money laundering and terrorist financing risks are kept under regular review.

Remote casinos – enhanced due diligence

2.13 The Regulations view situations where a customer is not physically present for identification purposes as higher risk for money laundering and require an operator to take specific and adequate measures to compensate for the higher risk (referred to as enhanced customer due diligence and ongoing measures in the Regulations), for example by applying one or more of the following measures:[8]

(a) ensuring that the customer's identity is established by additional documents, data or information;

(b) supplementary measures to verify or certify the documents supplied, or confirmatory certification by a credit or financial institution which is subject to the money laundering directive; or

(c) ensuring that the first payment is carried out through an account opened in the customer's name with a credit institution.

2.14 Option (c) above will fit with remote casinos business methods where it is necessary for a customer to have a bank or credit card account, which must be in his name.

2.15 Remote operators also have the benefit of being able to withhold payment of winnings or remaining deposits until satisfied that CDD is satisfactorily done.

2.16 Remote operators should include in their policies how they will manage, on a risk-sensitive basis, the higher risks presented by customers not being physically present for identification purposes.

---

8 Regulation 14.

Figure 1: Risk-based approach

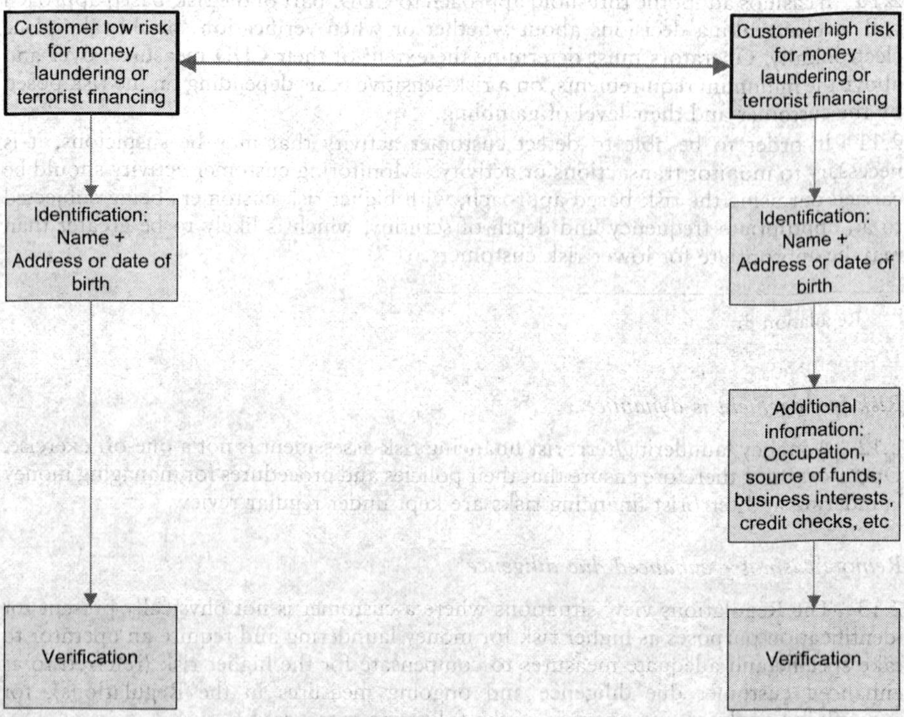

<u>Note</u>:
Casino operators should undertake risk assessments of each premises and each remote site and:
(a) look at the average drop/win per customer, and
(b) risk assess each customer.
See paragraphs 2.1 to 2.16 of this guidance for more detail on assessing risk.

3 SENIOR MANAGEMENT RESPONSIBILITY

Introduction

3.1 Senior management must be fully engaged in the processes around an operator's assessment of risks for money laundering and terrorist financing, and must be involved at every level of the decision making to develop the operator's policies and processes to comply with the Regulations. Disregard for the legal requirements, for example, turning a blind eye to customers spending criminal proceeds, may result in criminal or regulatory action.

3.2 It is considered best practice, and is explicit in parts of the Regulations, that a risk-based approach should be taken to tackling money laundering and terrorist financing.

3.3 Operators, using a risk-based approach, should start from the premise that most customers are not money launderers or terrorist financiers. However, operators should have policies and procedures in place to highlight those customers who, according to criteria established by the operator, may present a higher risk. The policies and procedures should be proportionate to the risks involved.

Obligations on all operators

3.4 An officer of a licensed operator which is subject to the Regulations (that is, a director, manager, secretary, chief executive, member of the management committee, or a person purporting to act in such a capacity) who consents to, or connives in, the commission of offences under the Regulations, or where the commission of any such offence is attributable to any neglect on his part, will be individually liable for the offence.[9]

3.5 The nominated officer should compile an annual report covering the operation and effectiveness of the operator's policies and procedures to combat money laundering. In practice, senior management should determine the depth and frequency of information they feel is necessary to discharge their responsibilities. The nominated officer may also wish to report to senior management more frequently than annually, as circumstances dictate. The nominated officer may not need to provide the names of suspected persons in any report.

---

[9] Regulation 47.

Policies and procedures

3.6 Operators must establish and maintain appropriate written risk-sensitive policies and procedures relating to:

- CDD measures and ongoing monitoring;
- reporting;
- record keeping;
- internal control;
- risk assessment and management;
- training; and
- the monitoring and management of compliance with, and the internal communication of, such policies and procedures.[10]

3.7 The operator's policies and procedures should cover:

- the arrangements for nominated officer reports to senior management;
- the systems for customer identification and verification, including enhanced arrangements for high risk customers, which included PEPs;
- the circumstances in which additional information in respect of customers will be sought in the light of their activity;
- the procedures for handling SARs, covering both reporting by employees and transmission to SOCA;
- the mechanisms for contact between the nominated officer and law enforcement or SOCA, including the circumstances in which appropriate consent should be sought
- the arrangements for recording information not acted upon by the nominated officer, with reasoning why no further action was taken;
- the monitoring and management of compliance with internal policies and procedures;
- the communication of such policies and procedures, including details of how compliance is monitored by the nominated officer, and the arrangements for communicating the policies and procedures to all relevant employees;
- employee training records; and
- supporting records in respect of business relationships, and the retention period for the records.

10 Regulation 20.

Training

3.8 The Regulations require that all relevant employees of casinos must be trained on the prescribed AML and CTF topics. Operators must ensure that their employees understand the Regulations and apply the operator's policies and procedures, including the requirements for CDD, record keeping and SARs.

3.9 One of the most important controls over the prevention and detection of money laundering is to have employees who are alert to the risks of money laundering and terrorist financing, and who are well trained in the identification of unusual activities or transactions which appear to be suspicious. The effective application of even the best designed control systems can be quickly compromised if the employees applying the systems are not adequately trained. The effectiveness of the training will therefore be important to the success of the operator's AML/CTF strategy.

3.10 Operators should devise and implement a clear and well articulated policy and procedure for ensuring that relevant employees are aware of their legal obligations in respect of the prevention of money laundering and terrorist financing, and for providing them with regular training in the identification and reporting of anything that gives grounds for suspicion of money laundering or terrorist financing.

3.11 Under POCA and the Terrorism Act, individual members of staff face criminal penalties if they are involved in money laundering or terrorist financing. If they do not make an internal report to their nominated officer when necessary they may also face criminal sanctions. It is important, therefore, that staff are made aware of their legal obligations, and are given training in how to discharge them.

3.12 The Regulations require operators to take appropriate measures so that all relevant employees are:

- made aware of the law relating to money laundering and terrorist financing; and
- regularly given training in how to recognise and deal with transactions and other activities which may be related to money laundering or terrorist financing.[11]

3.13 'Relevant employees' includes the holders of personal management licences and personal functional licences issued by the Commission as well as employees responsible for completing CDD measures. It does not include any ancillary employees such as catering and bar staff.

3.14 The content of any training, the regularity of training and the assessment of competence following training are matters for each operator to assess and decide in light of the money laundering risks they identify. The Commission will expect such issues to be covered in each operator's policies and procedures. This should make provision for the attainment of an appropriate competence level by the relevant employees identified in paragraph 3.13, prior to them undertaking the duties for which they will be responsible. This may, for example, be achieved by the attainment of an appropriate pass rate in a competency test following training.

3.15 Operators should also ensure that relevant employees are aware of and understand:

- their responsibilities under the operator's policies and procedures for the prevention of money laundering and terrorist financing;
- the money laundering and terrorist financing risks faced by an operator and each of its casino premises;
- the operator's procedures for managing those risks;
- the identity, role and responsibilities of the nominated officer, and what should be done in his absence;
- the potential effect of a breach upon the operator and upon its employees;
- how the casino will undertake CDD;
- how the casino will track customers when CDD is not undertaken on entry to the casino; and

- how PEPs will be identified.

3.16 There is no single solution when determining how to deliver training and a mix of training methods may, therefore, be appropriate. On-line training systems can provide a solution for many employees, but this approach may not be suitable for all employees. Classroom training can be more effective in these circumstances.

3.17 Procedure manuals, whether paper or electronic, are useful in raising employee awareness and can supplement more dedicated forms of training, but their main purpose is generally to provide ongoing reference rather than being written as training material.

3.18 Ongoing training should be given to all relevant employees at appropriate intervals. Records should be maintained to monitor who has been trained, when they received the training, the nature of the training and the effectiveness of the training.

3.19 The nominated officer should be heavily involved in devising and managing the delivery of such training, taking particular care to ensure that systems are in place to cover all part-time or casual employees.

3.20 SOCA publishes a range of material at www.soca.gov.uk, such as threat assessments and risk profiles, of which operators may wish to make their employees aware. The information on this website could usefully be incorporated into operators' training materials.

---

11 Regulation 21.

4 NOMINATED OFFICER

4.1 [12] Licensed casino operators must appoint a nominated officer, who is responsible for:

- receiving internal disclosures under Part 7 of POCA and Part 3 of the Terrorism Act;
- deciding whether these should be reported to SOCA;
- if appropriate, making such external reports; and
- ensuring that appropriate consent is applied as necessary.

4.2 A nominated officer should be able to monitor the effectiveness of the day-to-day operation of the operator's AML/CTF policies, and respond promptly to any reasonable request for information made by the Commission or law enforcement bodies.

4.3 The term 'nominated officer' is used and defined in the Regulations.

---

12 Regulation 20(2)(d)

Standing of the nominated officer

4.4 The nominated officer is responsible for the oversight of all aspects of the operator's AML/CTF activities at all premises. They are the focal point for all activity within the operator relating to AML. The individual appointed as nominated officer must have a sufficient level of seniority. The nominated officer must hold a personal management licence (PML) issued by the Commission. The job description of the nominated officer should clearly set out the extent of the responsibilities given to him and his objectives. The nominated officer will need to be involved in establishing the basis on which a risk-based approach to the prevention of money laundering and terrorist financing is put into practice.

4.5 The nominated officer must:

- have the authority to act independently in carrying out his responsibilities
- be free to have direct access to the Commission and appropriate law enforcement agencies, including SOCA, in order that any suspicious activity may be reported to the right quarter as soon as is practicable. He must

- be free to liaise with SOCA on any question of whether to proceed with a transaction in the circumstances, that is, in relation to appropriate consent

4.6 Senior management of the operator must ensure that the nominated officer has sufficient resources available to him, including appropriate employees and technology. This should include arrangements that apply in his temporary absence.

4.7 Where a nominated officer is temporarily unavailable another PML holder may deputise. Operators should consider the appointment of a permanent deputy nominated officer.

4.8 Where AML/CTF tasks are delegated by an operator's nominated officer, the Commission will expect the nominated officer to take ultimate managerial responsibility and they are likely to remain liable for the commission of any criminal offences relating to POCA, the Terrorism Act or the Regulations. The Commission strongly recommends that in such circumstances:

- the fact, date and time of such delegation be entered contemporaneously in a written record;
- the delegate counter-signs by way of acceptance of responsibility; and
- all employees who need to be aware of such delegation, are notified immediately.

Internal and external reports

4.9 An operator must require that anyone working for the operator, to whom information or other matter comes in the course of business, as a result of which they know or suspect, or have reasonable grounds for knowing or suspecting, that a person is engaged in money laundering or terrorist financing, must make an internal report to their nominated officer. Whilst disclosure to another of the fact that a person may be engaged in money laundering is generally an offence, such disclosures to a 'nominated officer' are specifically protected, where they are made as soon as is practicable and in the course of the discloser's employment.[13] It is recommended that employees be made aware that they have a legal defence to prosecution if they make an internal report to the nominated officer as soon as is reasonably practicable after the information or other matter comes to their attention.

4.10 Any internal report should be considered by the nominated officer, in the light of all other relevant information, to determine whether or not the information contained in the report leads them to form knowledge or suspicion, or reasonable grounds for knowledge or suspicion, of money laundering or terrorist financing.

4.11 The nominated officer should consider any information held about the customer's personal circumstances that might be available to the operator; and review other transaction patterns and volumes through the account or accounts in the same name, the length of the business relationship and identification records held.

4.12 The nominated officer must be fully conversant with his legal obligations to make external reports to SOCA.

4.13 Many of the records required by the Regulations relate to work done, or decisions made, by the nominated officer, including records of why reports have not been made to SOCA.

---

13 Section 337 of POCA.

5 CUSTOMER DUE DILIGENCE

Introduction

5.1 A key requirement in the Regulations is the requirement to make checks on customers, known as customer due diligence or CDD[14]. Casino operators may take one of two approaches; identifying and verifying the identity of all customers on entry to the casino's licensed premises or undertaking identification and verification when a customer approaches the threshold set out in the Regulations.

5.2 This requirement applies to customers of both remote and non-remote casinos. Aside from these checks being a statutory requirement in the Regulations, they also make sense in terms of helping operators avoid the commission of criminal offences under POCA.

5.3 The Regulations define casino as 'the holder of a casino operating licence'[15]. CDD therefore may be conducted just once by the holder of an operating licence and does not need to be repeated each time a customer visits another casino operated by that licensee. CDD records held by a casino operator will need to be available across the operator's different casino premises and the policies and procedures must include details of how the operator will manage this. Operators should note that CDD is ongoing and may need updating for changes in the customer's circumstances and personal details.

---

14 Regulation 10.

15 Regulation 3(13).

Threshold approach

5.4 The Regulations set out thresholds which, if customer transactions approach this level, require the casino operator to verify the identity of the customer. These limits are:

- in non-remote casinos the 'threshold approach for chips' – identification and verification is required when a customer purchases from or exchanges with the casino chips with a total value of €2,000 or more during any period of 24 hours;
- in non-remote casinos the 'threshold approach for gaming machines' – identification and verification is required when a customer pays €2,000 or more into the gaming machines during any period of 24 hours. This threshold amount does not include any winnings; or
- in remote casinos the 'threshold approach for remote gaming' – identification and verification is required when a customer pays to, or stakes with, the casino €2,000 during any period of 24 hours.

5.5 The gaming machine limits only apply in premises based casinos. By separating the purchase or exchange of chips from the payment to use gaming machines there is the potential for customers to spend up to €2,000 in the machines in addition to the purchase or exchange of chips up to €2,000. It should be noted that for the purpose of this guidance 'gaming machine' and 'stake' have the same meaning as that in the Act.

5.6 In premises based casinos automated and semi-automated table games such as touch-bet roulette are not defined as gaming machines and therefore the take in these games should be counted towards the threshold approach for chips.

Figure 2: Customer due diligence

Threshold model

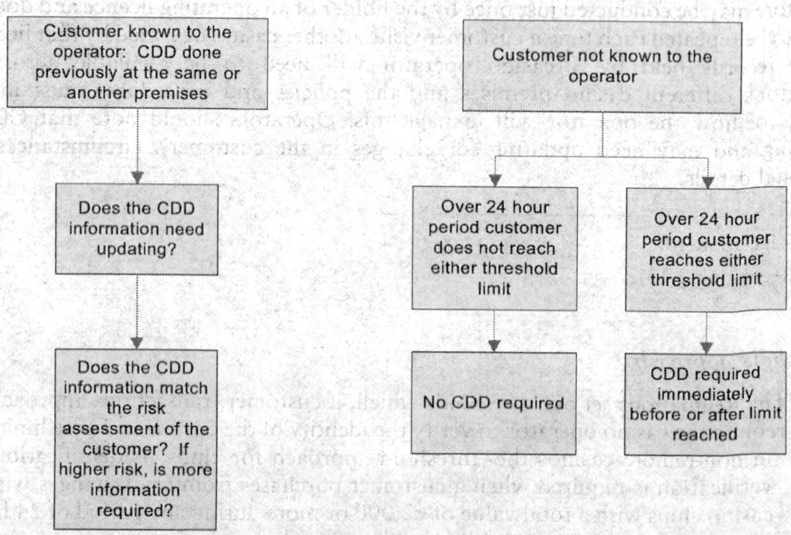

On entry model

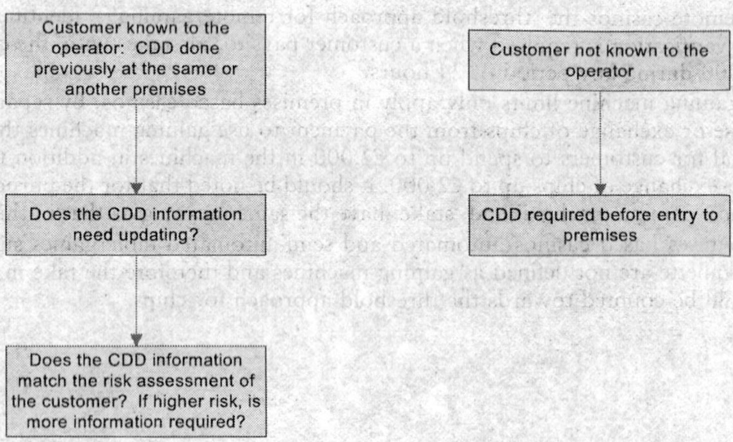

<u>Notes</u>:

1. Operator to be reasonably satisfied that the customer is who they claim to be.
2. The requirement applies to an operator, not to each premises.
3. Identification: Name, plus residential address or date of birth.
4. Verification: Documents or electronically.
5. Records of CDD to be kept for five years from the end of the business relationship or last visit to the premises run by the operator.

5.7 If casinos wish to adopt the threshold approach, the following two conditions must be satisfied:

- it must verify the identity of each customer before, or immediately after, the customer purchases, exchanges, pays or stakes €2,000 or more; and
- the Commission must be satisfied that the casino operator has appropriate procedures in place to monitor and record the total value of chips purchased from or exchanged with the casino, the total money paid for the use of gaming machines, or the total money paid or staked in connection with facilities for remote gaming by each customer.

5.8 Casino operators will have to satisfy the Commission that they have the mechanisms in place that are appropriate for the spend profile in each premises. For example, a casino with a customer drop/win average considerably below the threshold will need mechanisms in place to monitor customer transactions to be sure that any customer reaching either of the threshold levels is picked up in good time to allow CDD to be completed. Where the operator has a number of premises, the Commission will consider the use of the threshold approaches for each casino premises rather than for an operator.

5.9 Casinos adopting the threshold approach should think carefully about whether they wish to defer both identification and verification until the threshold is reached, or whether identification will be conducted on entry but verification deferred until the threshold is reached. For example, a premises based casino may operate a membership scheme where customers are identified on admission but verification only occurs once the threshold is approached. Similarly, remote casinos may require customers to identify themselves (and undertake age verification) on registering with the casino but only require verification of identity if the threshold is approached.

5.10 There may be significant advantages in asking customers for their identification on entry, even if verification of this information is deferred until the threshold is reached, for example, identifying customers on entry means it will not be necessary to interrupt the customer's gambling once the threshold is reached, and verification becomes necessary.

5.11 Casinos have to monitor both purchase and exchange of chips. If either hits the threshold CDD will be necessary.

5.12 A key challenge for casinos wishing to adopt the threshold approach is keeping track of the level of all an individual customer's purchases and exchanges of chips, and spends on the gaming machines. However, it is appropriate to do so in light of the known spend patterns in each premises.

5.13 Should casino operators choose to adopt the threshold approach, they must satisfy the Commission, on a premises-by-premises basis, that they have the appropriate procedures in place to manage the threshold in light of the assessed money laundering risk and spending profile at each premises.

Figure 3: Determining when the threshold is reached (non-remote casinos) – chips and gaming machines

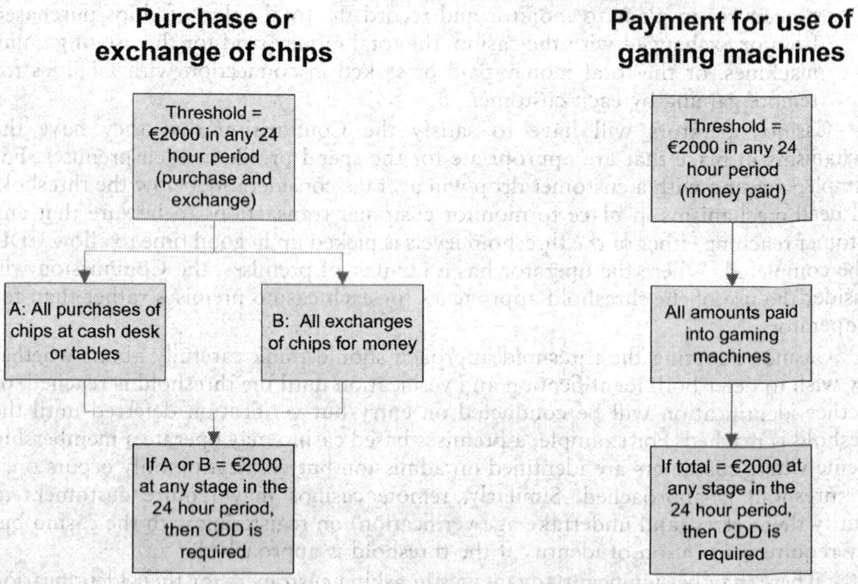

Notes:

1. The casino can set its own 24 hour period, for example the same hours as the business day, as appropriate to its business model.
2. A customer could spend €1800 on chips and a further €1800 in a gaming machine and not reach the threshold (see paragraph 5.5 of this guidance).
3. Risk-based approach – operator analysis of spending behaviours at each premises and an objective assessment made of the likelihood of customers reaching either threshold. Measures then put in place need to capture all customers likely to hit either threshold.

Figure 4: Determining when the threshold is reached (non-remote casinos) – casino account

Depositing or withdrawing casino account funds

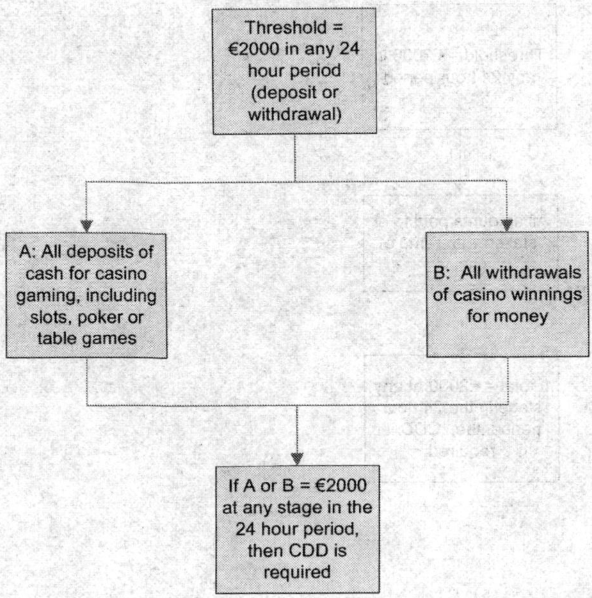

<u>Notes</u>:

1. The casino can set its own 24 hour period, for example the same hours as the business day, as appropriate to its business model.
2. Risk-based approach – operator analysis of spending behaviours at each premises and an objective assessment made of the likelihood of customers reaching the threshold. Measures then put in place need to capture all customers likely to hit the threshold.

Figure 5: Determining when the threshold is reached (remote casinos)

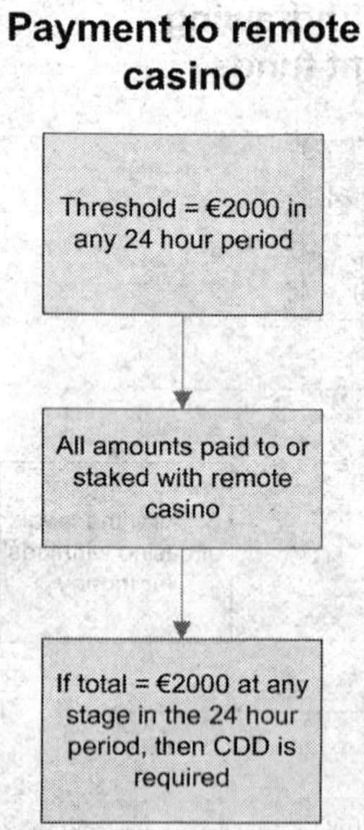

<u>Notes</u>:
1. The casino can set its own 24 hour period, for example the same hours as the business day, as appropriate to its business model.
2. "Stake" has the meaning in the Gambling Act 2005.
3. Risk-based approach – operator analysis of spending behaviours and an objective assessment made of the likelihood of customers reaching the threshold. Measures then put in place need to capture all customers likely to hit the threshold.

5.14 Some remote casinos operate a 'wallet' system which allows customers to use the money in their wallet in different parts of the operator's site. An operator's site may include some casino games as well as other games. It is only when a customer first enters the casino part of an operator's website and stakes money or chips that the CDD requirements apply. The Regulations do not apply to people 'window shopping' in a remote casino's website, it applies only when money is staked. Where an operator is unsure of what the funds in the wallet will be used for (for example, casino or sports betting) they should consider applying these controls to all customers.

5.15 Casinos using the 'threshold approach' must be sure that they are able to end transactions with a customer who reaches the threshold if they are unable to comply with the CDD requirements.

5.16 The Commission has not determined the start of a 24 hour period for the purposes of the Regulations. Casino operators are free to choose the start time of their 24 hour period (previously referred to as the 'business day') to meet the demands of their business.

Identification and verification on entry

5.17 The 'on entry' approach requires casinos to identify and verify the identity of the customer before entry to any premises where gaming facilities are provided, or before access is given to remote gaming. Once the customer's identity is verified he may commence gaming.

5.18 If a casino using the 'on entry' approach to CDD is unable to complete the appropriate CDD they must not allow the customer access to the premises or to the remote gaming. This puts a stop, in non-remote casinos, to the current practice of allowing guests of known customers a single entry without undertaking CDD. However, operators should consider using variations of the threshold CDD approach for guests of casino members.

Identification and verification

5.19 Applying CDD measures involves several steps. The operator is required to identify customers and then verify their identities, either upon entry or when reaching the threshold. Identification of a customer is being told or coming to know of the customer's identifying details, such as their name and address. Verification is obtaining some evidence which supports this claim of identity. The operator *identifies* the customer by obtaining a range of information about him. The *verification* of the identity consists of the operator verifying some of this information against documents, data or information obtained from a reliable and independent source.

5.20 Identification of customers consists of a number of aspects, including the customer's name, current and past addresses, date of birth, physical appearance, employment and financial history, and family circumstances.

5.21 Casino operators may identify their customers simply by asking them for personal information, including name, home address and date of birth. Other sources of identity can include:

- identity documents such as passports and photocard driving licences presented by customers;
- other forms of confirmation, including assurances from persons within the regulated sector (for example, banks) or employees within the same casino or casino group who have dealt with the customer for some time.

Some or all of this information will need to be verified. It may also be helpful to obtain information on customers' source of funds and level of legitimate income, for example occupation. This information may assist casinos with their assessments about whether a customer's level of gambling is in profile for their approximate income, or whether it is suspicious.

5.22 Information about customer identity must then be verified through documents, data and information which come from a reliable and independent source. There are a number of ways that a person's identity can be verified, including:

- obtaining or viewing original documents
- conducting electronic verification
- obtaining information from another person in the regulated sector (for example, banks).

No method of verification, either documentary or electronic, can conclusively prove that the customer definitely is who they claim to be. However, the Commission expects casinos to be reasonably satisfied following appropriate inquiry that customers are who they claim to be.

5.23 It is generally considered good practice to require either:

- one government document which verifies either name and address, or name and date of birth
- a government document which verifies the customer's full name and another supporting document which verifies their name and either their address or date of birth.

5.24 Some casinos have adopted the practice of allowing celebrities who are household names to by-pass the identification procedures agreed under the 2003 Regulations. Identification under these circumstances is not an issue. Verification may not be an issue owing to the easy availability of open source data and public knowledge that can be relied on as 'information from an independent and reliable source'. If such circumstances apply then the casino must keep records of the celebrity's presence at the casino, how their identity has been verified and where necessary the supporting records of their gaming. CDD using a customer's celebrity status is a subjective decision and must be supported by adequate records.

Electronic verification

5.25 Increasingly casinos use reliable electronic systems to help with verification. Some of these systems have the advantage of assisting in the identification of PEPs. The amount of information available about individuals will vary, depending on the extent of their electronic 'footprint'.

5.26 Electronic data sources can provide a wide range of confirmatory material without necessarily requiring the customer to produce documents. Electronic sources can be a convenient method of verification. They can be used either as the sole method of verification, or in combination with traditional document checks, on a risk basis. For an electronic check to provide satisfactory evidence of identity on its own it must use data from multiple sources, and across time, or incorporate qualitative checks that assess the strength of the information supplied. An electronic check that accesses data from a single source (eg a single check against the electoral roll) is not enough on its own to verify identity.

5.27 Where such sources are used for a credit check, the customer's permission is required under the Data Protection Act 1998 (the Data Protection Act). Credit checks can provide inexpensive information on which to assess a customer's access to funds and to obtain a credit profile to match against spending patterns. For example, a criminal spending large amounts of criminal property would most likely not match his or her credit profile. A search for identity verification for AML/CTF purposes, however, leaves a different 'footprint' on the customer's electronic file, and the customer's permission is not required, but they must be informed that this check is to take place. There are systems available that give typical financial and lifestyle profiles of people in a given postcode, such systems do not amount to credit check and do not require the use of personal information but can provide helpful indicators of someone's expected financial profile.

5.28 Some external electronic databases are accessible directly by casinos but it more likely they will be purchased from an independent third party organisation. The size of the electronic 'footprint' in relation to the depth, breadth and quality of data, and the degree of corroboration of the data supplied by the customer may provide a useful basis for an assessment of the degree of confidence in the product.

5.29 A number of commercial agencies which access many data sources are accessible online by operators, and may provide operators with a composite and comprehensive level of electronic verification through a single interface. Such agencies use databases of both positive and negative information, and many also access high-risk alerts that utilise specific data sources to identify high-risk conditions, for example, known identity frauds or inclusion on a sanctions list.

5.30 Positive information (relating to full name, current address, date of birth) can prove that an individual exists, but some can offer a higher degree of confidence than others. Such information should include data from more robust sources – where an individual has to prove their identity, or address, in some way in order to be included, as opposed to others, where no such proof is required.

5.31 Negative information includes consideration of lists of individuals known to have committed fraud, including identity fraud, and registers of deceased persons. Checking against such information may be appropriate where other factors suggest an increased risk of impersonation fraud.

Criteria for use of an electronic data provider

5.32 Before using a commercial agency for electronic verification, operators should be satisfied that information supplied by the data provider is considered to be sufficiently extensive, reliable and accurate. This judgement may be assisted by considering whether the provider meets all the following criteria:

- it is recognised, through registration with the Information Commissioner's Office, to store personal data;
- it uses a range of positive information sources that can be called upon to link an applicant to both current and previous circumstances;
- it accesses negative information sources, such as databases relating to identity fraud and deceased persons;
- it accesses a wide range of alert data sources; and
- it has transparent processes that enable the operator to know what checks were carried out, what the results of these checks were, and what they mean in terms of how much certainty they give as to the identity of the subject.

5.33 In addition, a commercial agency should have processes that allow the enquirer to capture and store the information they used to verify identity.

5.34 It is important that the process of electronic verification meets a standard level of confirmation before it can be relied on. The standard level of confirmation, in circumstances that do not give rise to concern or uncertainty, is:

- one match on an individual's full name and current address, and
- a second match on an individual's full name and either his current address or his date of birth.

5.35 Commercial agencies that provide electronic verification use various methods of displaying results – for example, by the number of documents checked, or through scoring mechanisms. Operators should ensure that they understand the basis of the system they use, in order to be satisfied that the sources of the underlying data meets the required standard.

Documentary evidence

5.36 If verification is undertaken using documents, casino operators should usually rely upon documents issued by government departments.

5.37 Original documents should be examined so that, as far as reasonably practicable, forgeries are not accepted. Casino operators should recognise that some documents are more easily forged than others. If suspicions are raised in relation to any document offered, operators should take whatever practical and proportionate steps are available to establish whether the document offered is a forgery or has been reported as lost or stolen. While the presentation of false documents does not, in itself, amount to money laundering, it may constitute an offence under the Fraud Act 2006 or Identity Cards Act 2006 and should, in appropriate circumstances, be reported to the police or SOCA. Casino operators should also be aware that even if documents appear to be legitimate and issued by a government department they may be false, for example the European driving permit that is freely available through the internet. Commercial software is available that checks the algorithms used to generate passport numbers. This can be used to check the validity of passports of any country that issues machine-readable passports.

5.38 If documents are in a foreign language appropriate steps should be taken to be reasonably satisfied that the documents in fact provide evidence of the customer's identity, for example a translation of the relevant sections.

5.39 Documentation purporting to offer evidence of identity may emanate from a number of sources. These documents differ in their integrity, reliability and independence. Some are issued after CDD on the holder of the document is carried out by the issuing authority. There is a broad hierarchy of documents.

5.40 Documents issued by government departments and agencies that contain a photograph may be considered reliable. In practical terms, for face-to-face verification conducted by non-remote casinos, production of a valid passport or photocard driving licence should enable most individuals to meet the identification requirement for AML/CTF purposes. These documents will also confirm either residential address or date of birth.

5.41 Alternatively government issued documents without a photograph may be used which incorporates the customer's full name, supported by a second document, which is ideally also government issued, or issued by a public sector body or authority. This second document must also include the customer's full name and either his residential address or his date of birth.

5.42 The following sources may, therefore, be useful for verification of UK-based customers:

- current signed passport
- birth certificate
- current photocard driving licence
- current EEA member state identity card
- current identity card issued by the Electoral Office for Northern Ireland
- residency permit issued by the Home Office
- firearms certificate or shotgun licence
- benefit book or original notification letter from the Department of Works and Pensions confirming the right to benefits
- council tax bill
- utility bill or statement (but not ones printed off the internet), or a certificate from a utilities supplier confirming an arrangement to pay services on pre-payment terms
- bank, building society or credit union statement or passbook containing current address (but not statements printed off the internet) — bank or credit cards alone will not be sufficient as these do not provide either residential address or date of birth
- confirmation from an electoral register that a person of that name lives at that address
- recent original mortgage statement from a recognised lender
- solicitor's letter confirming recent house purchase or land registry confirmation of address
- local council or housing association rent card or tenancy agreement
- HM Revenue and Customs (HMRC) self-assessment statement or tax demand
- house or motor insurance certificate.

5.43 Customers who are not resident in the UK should be asked to produce their passport, national identity card or photocard driving licence. If the casino has concerns that the identity document presented by a customer is not genuine, they should contact the relevant embassy or consulate. Confirmation of the customer's address can be obtained from:

- an official overseas government source
- a reputable directory of addresses
- a person regulated for money laundering purposes in the country where the customer is resident (for example, a casino or bank) who confirms that the customer is known to them and lives or works at the overseas address supplied.

5.44 Non-remote casinos have adopted the practice of photographing new customers on their first visit as part of the CDD records. Doing so assists with casino security issues and with customer tracking. It is a matter for each casino operator but the Commission views the use of customer photographs as good practice in the casino environment that contributes to the prevention and detection of money laundering and terrorist financing.

Politically exposed persons

Definition

5.45 A PEP is a person who is or has, at any time in the preceding year, been entrusted with prominent public functions outside the UK, a Community institution (for example, the European Parliament) or an international body (for example, the United Nations), including the following persons:

- heads of state, heads of government, ministers and deputy or assistant ministers
- members of parliament
- members of supreme courts, constitutional courts or other high-level judicial bodies whose decisions are not generally subject to further appeal, except in exceptional circumstances
- members of courts of auditors or of the boards of central banks
- ambassadors, charge d'affairs and high ranking officers in armed forces
- members of the administrative, management or supervisory bodies of state-owned enterprises.[16]

The following persons are also regarded as PEPs by virtue of their relationship or association with the persons listed above:

- family members of the persons listed above, including spouse, partner, children and their spouses or partners, and parents
- known close associates of the persons listed above, including persons with whom joint beneficial ownership of a legal entity or legal arrangement is held, with whom there are close business relationships, or who is a sole beneficial owner of a legal entity or arrangement set up by the PEP with whom they are associated.

PEP status itself does not incriminate individuals or entities. It may, however, put a customer into a higher risk category.

---

[16] Regulation 14(5) and Schedule 2.

Risk-based approach to PEPs

5.46 The nature and scope of a particular casino's business will help to determine the likelihood of PEPs in their customer base, and whether the operator needs to consider screening all customers for this purpose.

5.47 Establishing whether individuals are PEPs is not always straightforward and can present difficulties. Where operators need to carry out specific checks, they may be able to rely on an internet search engine, or consult relevant reports and databases on corruption risk published by specialised national, international, non-governmental and commercial organisations. Resources such as the Transparency International Corruption Perceptions Index, which ranks approximately 150 countries according to their perceived level of corruption, may be helpful in terms of assessing the risk. This may be found at www.transparency.org/policy_research/surveys_indices/cpi. If there is a need to conduct more thorough checks, or if there is a high likelihood of an operator having PEPs for customers, subscription to a specialist PEP database may be the only adequate risk mitigation tool.

5.48 New and existing customers may not initially meet the definition of a PEP, but that position may change over time. Equally, individuals who are initially identified as PEPs may cease to be PEPs, for example if they change their job or retire. The operator should, as far as practicable, be alert to public information relating to possible changes in the status of its customers with regard to political exposure. Casino operators should be alert to situations which suggest that the customer is a PEP. These situations include:

- receiving funds from a government account
- correspondence on an official letterhead from the customer or a related person
- general conversation with the customer or related person linking the person to a PEP
- news reports suggesting that your client is a PEP or is linked to one.

5.49 Although under the definition of a PEP an individual ceases to be so regarded after he has left office for one year, operators are encouraged to apply a risk-based approach in determining whether or when they should cease carrying out appropriately enhanced monitoring of transactions. In many cases, a longer period might be appropriate, in order to ensure that the higher risks associated with the individual's previous position have adequately abated.

5.50 Each operator's policies and procedures should cover when and how customers will be checked for PEP status.

PEPs requirements

5.51 An operator who proposes to allow a PEP to be a customer must:

- have approval from its senior management for establishing a business relationship with that person;
- take adequate measures to establish the source of wealth and source of funds which are involved in the proposed business relationship; and
- where a business relation is entered into, conduct enhanced ongoing monitoring of the relationship.

5.52 Each operator's policies and procedures should cover how and when senior management approval will be sought and provided, and deal with how the customer will be dealt with if there is any delay to approval being provided.

Failure to complete checks

5.53 Where a casino operator is unable to comply with the required CDD measures in relation to a customer, the operator:

- must not carry out a transaction with or for the customer through a bank account;
- must not establish a business relationship or carry out an occasional transaction with the customer;
- must terminate any existing business relationship with the customer; and
- must consider making a report to SOCA.[17]

5.54 Casinos must therefore have clear policies in place on how they will manage situations where they are unable to comply with the CDD measures.

---

[17] Regulation 11.

Requirements for remote casinos

5.55 In the light of the requirements imposed by regulation 11, where remote casinos use the threshold approach to CDD, they should adopt the following procedure:

- at the point that verification is triggered, operators should put all monies owed to the customer into an account (or equivalent) from which no withdrawals can be made
- further deposits can be made to that account as long as they too are 'locked' into it until CDD is completed
- bets can be made from the account, again providing any winnings are 'locked' until CDD is completed
- once CDD is completed, the account can be 'unlocked' and business continue as normal
- if it cannot be completed, then the operator must proceed in line with regulation 11(1) and terminate the business relationship with the customer
- if monies are to be repaid, then the amount repaid should consist of all monies owed to the customer at the point that the verification procedure was triggered plus all deposits made at that point and thereafter
- money should be refunded back to the originating account
- there should be risk mitigation, including the submission of any possible SARs or the seeking of appropriate consent
- if the refund if to be completed back to another account (whether partially or completely), risk assessment must be done that should take into account information such as:
  - multiple destinations – is the customer requesting that the money be sent to several bank accounts?
  - high risk destination – is the customer requesting that the money be returned to a country where there is a significant money laundering concern?
  - above €2000 – is the amount above the threshold for CDD?
- there should be ongoing monitoring of the account and, if necessary, reporting of findings via services such as CIFAS (the UK's Fraud Prevention Service).

5.56 The customer should be made fully aware of the procedures adopted by the operator when they first register so that there is no misunderstanding at a later stage.

Existing customers

5.57 Where the identity of an existing customer has already been established to the standards agreed following the 2003 Regulations then there is no need to undertake CDD to the new standards until the customer enters a casino again, or reaches a CDD threshold, depending on the CDD model in use by the operator.

List of persons subject to financial sanctions

5.58 The UK operates financial sanctions on persons and entities following their designation at the United Nations and/or European Union. The UK also operates a domestic counter-terrorism regime, where the Government decides to impose financial restrictions on certain persons and entities. There are specific financial restrictions targeted at the Al-Qaida network and terrorism.

5.59 Financial restrictions in the UK are governed by various pieces of legislation. The purpose of imposing financial restrictions is to restrict the access to finance by designated persons and to prevent the diversion of funds to terrorism and terrorist purposes. In all circumstances, where an asset freeze is imposed, it is unlawful to make payments to or allow payments to be made to designated persons.

5.60 A list of all financial restrictions currently in force in the UK is maintained by the Treasury's Asset Freezing Unit. The Consolidated List of persons designated as being subject to financial restrictions can be found on the HM Treasury web site at: www.hm-treasury.gov.uk/financialsanctions. Further information on financial restrictions can also be found via this website. The purpose of the HM Treasury list is to draw together, in one place, all the names of designated persons for the various financial regimes effective in the UK.

5.61 Under the relevant legislation, it is a criminal offence for any natural or legal person to:

- deal with the funds of designated persons;
- make funds and economic resources, and in the case of terrorism financial services, available directly or indirectly to or for the benefit of designated persons;
- knowingly and intentionally participate in activities that would directly or indirectly circumvent the financial restrictions or enable or facilitate the commission of an offence relating to the above.

5.62 In this context, 'deal with' means:

- in respect of funds, to use, alter, move, allow access to or transfer;
- in respect of funds, deal with in any other way that would result in any change in volume, amount, location, ownership, possession, character or destination; or
- in respect of funds, make any other change that would enable use, including portfolio management; and
- in respect of economic resources, to use to obtain funds, goods or services in any way, including (but not limited to) by selling, hiring or mortgaging the resources.

5.63 HM Treasury has the power to grant licences exempting certain transactions from the financial restrictions. Requests to disapply the financial restrictions in relation to a designated person are considered by the Treasury on a case-by-case basis to ensure that there is no risk of funds being diverted to otherwise restricted purposes. To apply for a licence, the Asset Freezing Unit at HM Treasury can be contacted using the contact details provided below.

5.64 Operators need to have the necessary policies and procedures in place to monitor financial transactions so that payments are not made to designated persons, thereby preventing breaches of the financial restrictions legislation. For manual checking, operators can register with the HM Treasury Asset Freezing Unit update service (directly or via a third party). If checking is automated, operators will need to ensure that the relevant software includes checks against the latest Consolidated List.

5.65 The Asset Freezing Unit may also be contacted to provide guidance and to assist with any concerns regarding financial restrictions at:

Asset Freezing Unit
Tel: 020 7270 5664/5454
Fax: 020 7451 7677
Email: assetfreezingunit@hmtreasury.gsi.gov.uk

5.66 In the event that a customer or payee is identified as a designated person, payments must not proceed unless a licence is granted by the Treasury, as this would be a breach of the financial restrictions. The Treasury should be informed immediately and the transaction suspended pending their advice. No funds should be returned to the designated person. The firm may also need to consider whether there is an obligation also to report to SOCA under POCA or the Terrorism Act.

5.67 Written reports can be made to the Asset Freezing Unit via email.

6 RECORD KEEPING

General legal and regulatory requirements

6.1 This chapter provides guidance on appropriate record keeping procedures required by the Regulations. The purpose of the record keeping requirement is to ensure that there is an audit trail that could assist in any financial investigation by a law enforcement body.

6.2 The operator's record keeping policy and procedure should cover records in the following areas:

- details of how compliance has been monitored by the nominated officer;
- delegation of AML/CTF tasks by nominated officer;
- nominated officer reports to senior management;
- information not acted upon by the nominated officer, with reasoning why no further action was taken;
- customer identification and verification information;
- supporting records in respect of business relationships or occasional transactions;
- employee training records;
- internal and external SARs; and
- contact between the nominated officer and law enforcement or SOCA, including records connected to appropriate consent.

6.3 The record keeping requirements for supporting records, that is, the records of ongoing transactions with a customer, are based on the nature of the relationship with that customer. There is either:

- no relationship;
- a 'business relationship', depending on the circumstances; or
- an 'occasional transaction'.

Business relationship

6.4 Casino operators form business relationships with their customers if, at the point that contact is established, the casino expects their relationship to have an element of duration. Casino operators are encouraged to interpret this definition widely.

6.5 Casinos are likely to form a business relationship when:

- the casino starts tracking a customer's drop/win figures;
- a customer opens an account with the operator or joins a membership scheme; or
- a customer obtains a cheque cashing facility.

6.6 'Ongoing monitoring of business relationships' is a requirement for casino operators and includes scrutiny of transactions undertaken throughout the course of the relationship (including, where necessary, the source of funds) to ensure that the transactions are consistent with the relevant person's knowledge of the customer, his business and risk profile.[18]

6.7 Casinos are expected to approach this requirement on a risk basis. Dependent on how frequently a casino forms 'business relationships' it may be good practice to apply ongoing monitoring more widely. Regular players should be the subject of closer scrutiny and their level of play should be assessed with reference to the information already known about them, and where necessary, additional information must be collected and retained about the source of their funds.

[18] Regulation 8(1)

Occasional transaction

6.8 A casino may undertake an occasional transaction with a customer when there is no business relationship but the customer purchases or exchanges chips over €15,000 in value. For example, a customer on a single visit to a casino while on holiday or a business trip who purchases or exchanges chips over the €15,000 limit constitutes an 'occasional transaction'. CDD will need to be done under these circumstances and the casino will have to retain the supporting records, that is the drop/win data, for five years after the date of the visit.

Other casino customers

6.9 Some casino customers may not fall into the business relationship or occasional transaction definitions. For example, customers spending low amounts at gaming during single, infrequent and irregular visits to a casino and who are not subject to tracking. There may be no expectation at any stage that there will be any duration to the relationship with the customer. Strictly speaking such business falls outside of the record-keeping requirements.

Customer information

6.10 In relation to the evidence of a customer's identity, operators must keep a copy of, or the references to, the verification evidence of the customer's identity obtained during the application of CDD measures.[19]

6.11 An operator may often hold additional information beyond identity in respect of a customer for the purposes of wider customer due diligence. As a matter of best practice this information and any relevant documents should also be retained.

6.12 There is a separate requirement in the Regulations to ensure that documents, data or information held by casinos are kept up to date.[20] A trigger event for refreshing and extending CDD may be if a customer returns to a casino after a period of non-attendance. Refreshing information about existing customers will ensure that matters such as change of address, or a customer being appointed into a role which attracts PEP status, will be picked up. Keeping information up to date is also a requirement under the Data Protection Act. How these issues which will be dealt with in practice should be covered a casino's policies and procedures.

19 Regulation 19(2).

20 Regulation 8(2)(b).

Figure 6: Record keeping

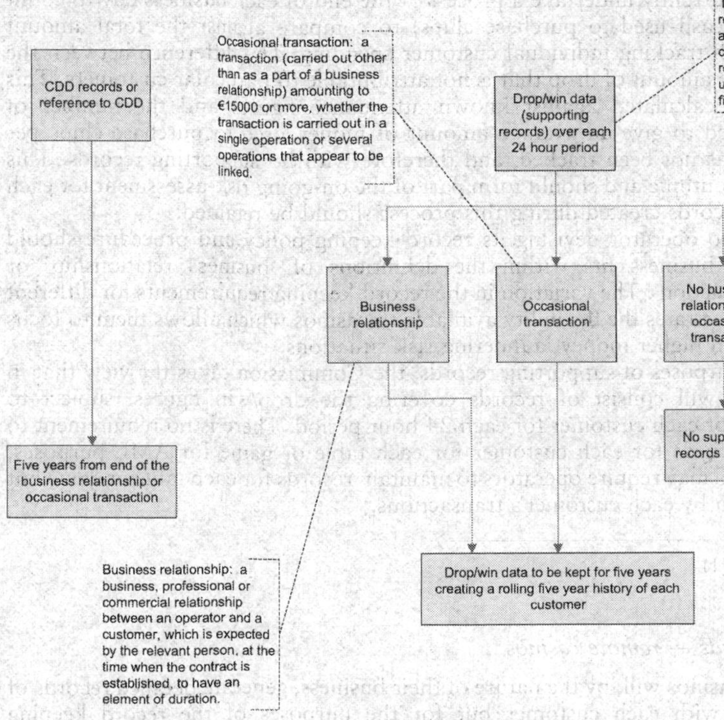

Note:
Operators should devise and implement a clear and articulated policy and procedure for ensuring all relevant employees are aware of their legal obligations in respect of the prevention of money laundering and terrorist financing.

6.13 Where documents verifying the identity of a customer are held in one casino premises they do not also need to be held in duplicate form in another premises in the same group. For the purposes of compliance with the Regulations the whole group forms part of the same 'relevant person'. The records need to be accessible to all premises that have contact with the customer, the nominated officer, and law enforcement. The Regulations accept that operators may have more than one casino premises or more than one remote casino site. It is sufficient for the operator to undertake identification and verification providing that the information is available to each premises or site.

Supporting records – non-remote casinos

6.14 The requirement to keep supporting records is linked to 'business relationships' and 'occasional transactions' which are defined in the Regulations[21] and the extent and nature of records created. In many casinos customers, regardless of whether or not they have formed a business relationship, or are part of an occasional transaction, purchase chips with cash at the gaming tables where, in low risk situations, no records are created and therefore not available to be kept.

6.15 The Commission expects casino operators to use reasonable endeavours to create and keep supporting records and to make it clear in their policies and procedures what records will be created in light of the known spending patterns and the assessed money laundering and terrorist financing risks at each premises.

6.16 Casinos currently undertake a process at the end of each business day to count the total drop (cash used to purchase chips) to compare against the total amount recorded through tracking individual customer spending. The difference between the two figures is the amount of drop that is not attributable to particular customers. This in turn can be calculated against known attendance figures and the number of customers tracked to give an average amount of money used to purchase chips per customer that has not been tracked, and therefore with no supporting records. This process should continue and should form part of the on-going risk-assessment for each premises. The records created during this process should be retained.

6.17 Any casino operator devising its record keeping policy and procedure should decide how its business fits within the definitions of 'business relationship' or 'occasional transaction'. The variation in the record-keeping requirements for different circumstances illustrates the flexibility available to casinos which allows them to focus their resources on higher money laundering risk situations.

6.18 For the purposes of supporting records, the Commission takes the view that in most cases this will consist of records covering the drop/win figures, subject to paragraph 6.9, for each customer for each 24 hour period. There is no requirement to keep detailed records for each customer for each table or game for AML purposes. However, HMRC may require operators to maintain records for each table or game but not broken down by each customer's transactions.

---

[21] Regulation 2(1).

Supporting records — remote casinos

6.19 Remote casinos will, by the nature of their business, generate detailed records of all transactions with each customer but for the purposes of the record keeping requirements it is sufficient to retain the drop/win figures for each named customer for each 24 hour period.

Supporting records — gaming machines

6.20 Cash-in with cash-out gaming machines do not produce any supporting records that can be attributed to a customer. They do generate overall cash-in and cash-out data that must be retained by the casino. However, 'ticket in, ticket out' (TITO) and 'smart card' technology may mean that, in the future, machines produce supporting records that can be attributed to a customer who falls within the record keeping requirements, in which case such records must be retained in accordance with the Regulations.

6.21 The essentials of any system of monitoring are that:

- it flags up transactions and/or activities for further examination;
- these reports are reviewed promptly by the nominated officer; and
- appropriate action is taken on the findings of any further examination.

6.22 Monitoring can be either:

- in real time, in that transactions and/or activities can be reviewed as they take place or are about to take place; or
- after the event, through the nominated officer's review of the transactions and/or activities that a customer has undertaken.

In either case, unusual transactions or activities will be flagged for further examination.

6.23 In designing monitoring arrangements, it is important that appropriate account be taken of the frequency, volume and size of transactions with customers, in the context of the assessed customer risk.

6.24 Monitoring is not a mechanical process and does not necessarily require sophisticated electronic systems. The scope and complexity of the process will be influenced by the operator's business activities, and whether the operator is large or small. The key elements of any system are having up-to-date customer information, on the basis of which it will be possible to spot the unusual, and asking pertinent questions to elicit the reasons for unusual transactions or activities in order to judge whether they may represent something suspicious.

Retention period

6.25 Records of identification and verification of customers must be kept for a period of at least five years after the relationship with the customer has ended.[22] The date the relationship with the customer ends is the last date on which they visit or use a casino.

6.26 Supporting records must be retained for a period of five years beginning on the date any transaction is completed where the records relate to a particular transaction. This creates a rolling five year history of drop/win data. Records of internal and external reports on suspicious activity should be retained for five years from when the report was made.[23]

---

22 Regulation 19(3).

23 Regulation 19(3).

Form in which records have to be kept

6.27 Most operators have record keeping procedures which they keep under review, and will seek to reduce the volume and density of records which have to be stored, whilst still complying with statutory requirements. Retention may therefore be:

- by way of original documents;
- by way of photocopies of original documents;
- on microfiche;
- in scanned form; or
- in computerised or electronic form.

6.28 Records relating to ongoing investigations should, where possible, be retained until the relevant law enforcement agency has confirmed that the case has been concluded.

6.29 Where the record keeping obligations under the Regulations are not observed, an operator or person is open to prosecution and sanctions, including imprisonment for up to two years and/or a fine, or regulatory censure.

7 SUSPICIOUS ACTIVITIES AND REPORTING

Introduction

7.1 Employees in casinos are required to make a report in respect of information that comes to them within the course of their business:

- where they know; or
- where they suspect; or
- where they have reasonable grounds for knowing or suspecting,

that a person is engaged in money laundering or terrorist financing. Within this guidance, the above obligations are collectively referred to as 'grounds for knowledge or suspicion'.

7.2 In order to provide a framework within which suspicion reports may be raised and considered:

- each operator must ensure that any employee reports to the operator's nominated officer where they have grounds for knowledge or suspicion that a person or customer is engaged in money laundering or terrorist financing;
- the operator's nominated officer must consider each such report, and determine whether it gives grounds for knowledge or suspicion;

- operators should ensure that employees are appropriately trained in their obligations, and in the requirements for making reports to their nominated officer.

7.3 If the nominated officer determines that a report does give rise to grounds for knowledge or suspicion, he must report the matter to SOCA. Under POCA, the nominated officer is required to make a report to SOCA as soon as is practicable if he has grounds for suspicion that another person, whether or not a customer, is engaged in money laundering. Under the Terrorism Act, similar conditions apply in relation to disclosure where there are grounds for suspicion of terrorist financing.

What Is meant by knowledge and suspicion?

7.4 Having knowledge means actually knowing something to be true. In a criminal court, it must be proved that the individual in fact knew that a person was engaged in money laundering. That said, knowledge can be inferred from the surrounding circumstances, so, for example, a failure to ask obvious questions may be relied upon by a jury to infer knowledge. The knowledge must, however, have come to the operator (or to the member of staff) in the course of casino business or (in the case of a nominated officer) as a consequence of a disclosure under section 330 of POCA. Information that comes to the operator or staff member in other circumstances does not come within the scope of the regulated sector obligation to make a report. This does not preclude a report being made should employees choose to do so. Employees may also be obliged to make a report by other parts of the Act.

Figure 7: Reasonable grounds to suspect (objective test)

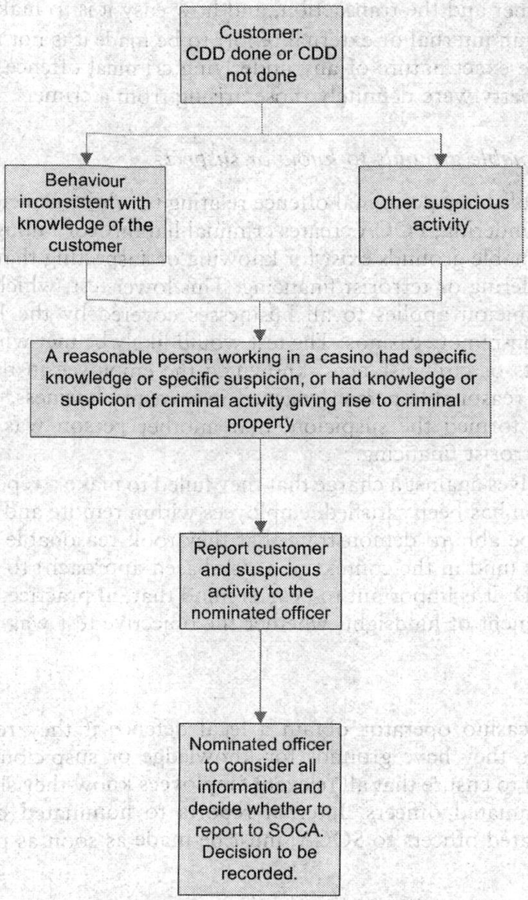

7.5 In the case of *Da Silva* [2006] EWCA Crim 1654, the Court of Appeal stated the following in relation to suspicion:

> 'It seems to us that the essential element in the word "suspect" and its affiliates, in this context, is that the defendant must think that there is a possibility, which is more than fanciful, that the relevant facts exist. A vague feeling of unease would not suffice.'

There is thus no requirement for the suspicion to be clear or firmly grounded on specific facts, but there must be a degree of satisfaction, not necessarily amounting to belief but at least extending beyond mere speculation, that an event has occurred or not.

7.6 Whether you hold suspicion or not is a subjective test. If you think a transaction is suspicious you are not expected to know the exact nature of the criminal offence or that particular funds are definitely those arising from the crime. You may have noticed something unusual or unexpected and, after making enquiries, the facts do not seem normal or make commercial sense. You do not need to have evidence that money laundering is taking place to have suspicion.

7.7 Unusual patterns of gambling, including the spending of particularly large amounts of money in relation to the casino or customer's profile, should receive attention, but unusual behaviour should not necessarily lead to grounds for knowledge or suspicion of money laundering, or the making of a report to SOCA. The nominated officer is required to assess all of the circumstances and, in some cases, it may be helpful to ask customer or others more questions. The choice depends on what is already known about the customer and the transaction, and how easy it is to make enquiries.

7.8 In order for either an internal or external report to be made it is not necessary to know or to establish the exact nature of any underlying criminal offence, or that the particular funds or property were definitely those arising from a crime.

What is meant by reasonable grounds to know or suspect?

7.9 In addition to establishing a criminal offence relating to when suspicion or actual knowledge of money laundering, POCA creates criminal liability for failing to disclose information when reasonable grounds exist for knowing or suspecting that a person is engaged in money laundering or terrorist financing. This lower test, which introduces an *objective* test of suspicion applies to all businesses covered by the Regulations, including remote and non-remote casinos. The test would likely be met when there are demonstrated to be facts or circumstances, known to the employee in the course of business, from which a reasonable person engaged in a casino business, would have inferred knowledge, or formed the suspicion, that another person was engaged in money laundering or terrorist financing.

7.10 To defend themselves against a charge that they failed to make a report when the objective test of suspicion has been satisfied, employees within remote and non-remote casinos would need to be able to demonstrate that they took reasonable steps in the particular circumstances (and in the context of a risk-based approach) to conduct the appropriate level of CDD. It is important to bear in mind that, in practice, a court will be deciding, with the benefit of hindsight, whether the objective test was met.

Internal reporting

7.11 Employees of a casino operator obtain a legal defence if they report to the nominated officer where they have grounds for knowledge or suspicion. All casino operators therefore need to ensure that all relevant employees know they should report suspicions to their nominated officers. Internal reports to nominated officers, and reports made by nominated officers to SOCA, must be made as soon as possible.

Figure 8: Knowledge or suspicion of money laundering or terrorist financing (subjective test)

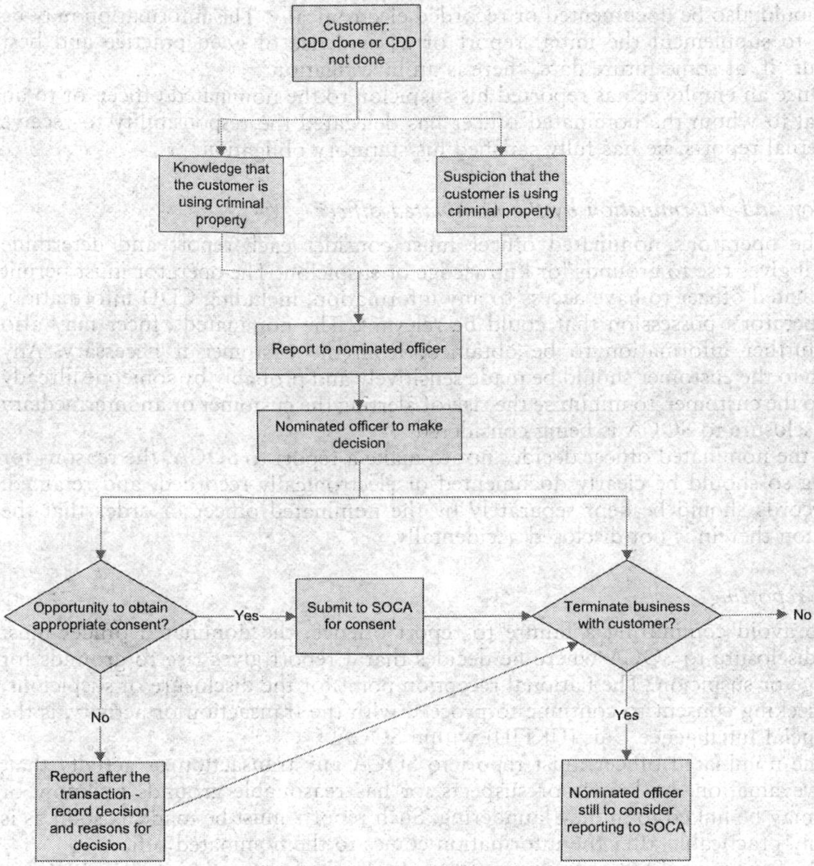

7.12 All suspicions reported to the nominated officer should be documented or electronically recorded. The report should include full details of the customer who is the subject of concern and as full a statement as possible of the information giving rise to the grounds for knowledge or suspicion. All internal enquiries made in relation to the report should also be documented or recorded electronically. This information may be required to supplement the initial report or as evidence of good practice and best endeavours if, at some future date, there is an investigation.

7.13 Once an employee has reported his suspicion to the nominated officer, or to an individual to whom the nominated officer has delegated the responsibility to receive such internal reports, he has fully satisfied his statutory obligation.

Evaluation and determination by the nominated officer

7.14 The operator's nominated officer must consider each report and determine whether it gives rise to grounds for knowledge or suspicion. The operator must permit the nominated officer to have access to any information, including CDD information, in the operator's possession that could be relevant. The nominated officer may also require further information to be obtained, from the customer if necessary. Any approach to the customer should be made sensitively and probably by someone already known to the customer, to minimise the risk of alerting the customer or an intermediary that a disclosure to SOCA is being considered.

7.15 If the nominated officer decides not to make a report to SOCA, the reasons for not doing so should be clearly documented or electronically recorded, and retained. These records should be kept separately by the nominated officer in order that the information therein is not disclosed accidentally.

External reporting

7.16 To avoid committing a failure to report offence, the nominated officer must make a disclosure to SOCA where he decides that a report gives rise to grounds for knowledge or suspicion. The national reception point for the disclosure of suspicions, and for seeking consent to continue to proceed with the transaction or activity, is the UK Financial Intelligence Unit (UKFIU) within SOCA.

7.17 The nominated officer must report to SOCA any transaction or activity that, after his evaluation, he knows or suspects, or has reasonable grounds to know or suspect, may be linked to money laundering. Such reports must be made as soon as is reasonably practicable after the information comes to the nominated officer.

7.18 The Secretary of State may by order prescribe the form and manner in which a disclosure under section 330, section 331, section 332, or section 338, may be made. A consultation paper on the form and manner or reporting was issued by the Home Office in the summer of 2007, however, the Home Office decided not to proceed with the introduction of a prescribed form and manner of reporting.

Submission of suspicious activity reports

7.19 SOCA accept the submission of SARs in three main ways:

- **Paper based reporting** using the standard SOCA Suspicious Activity Report From. SOCA prefers submissions to be typed to enable it to be scanned and prevent errors in data entry. The form is available from the SOCA website at www.soca.gov.uk/financialintel/suspectactivity.html#forms. Guidance on using the form can be found at www.soca.gov.uk/financialIntel/formsGuide.html. Completed forms should be posted to UKFIU, PO Box 8000, London SE11 5EN. If using the form to request appropriate consent, it should be faxed immediately to 0207 238 8286, but it is not necessary to post and fax a consent request.

  The paper based reporting system will not elicit an acknowledgment of receipt or an ELMER reference number for your records, and the SAR will take some time to reach investigators.

- **SAR Online** is a secure web based reporting system for small or medium sized reporting entities with access to the interney, which allows SARs to be submitted electronically through www.ukfiu.gov.uk/saronline.aspx. Reporters must register themselves as a source (reporting entity) on the system once, and then submit SARs by completing linked electronic screens that reflect the fields included in the paper based reports.
  Consent requests can be submitted using SAR Online, and as long as the box for consent is checked at the start of the process; the system alerts the Consent Team automatically, ensuring swift identification and management of appropriate consent. It is not necessary to send a consent fax as well as a submission on line.
  SAR Online is SOCA's preferred method for small and medium sized reporters to submit SARs. The benefit to the reporter is 24/7 reporting, an automatic acknowledgment of receipt with the ELMER reference number, an initial feedback report on the quality of the SARs submitted after 6 months, and investigators are able to access the information more repidly.
- **Encrypted bulk data exchange** is used by high volume reporters, that is reporters with more than 10,000 reports a month. If an operator believes this would be the most appropriate method of reporting for their group, contact the UKFIU on 0207 238 8282 to discuss the issue.

7.20 Operators should include in each SAR as much relevant information about the customer, transaction or activity that it has in its records. SOCA has published a glossary of terms which they prefer operators to use when completing SARs (www.soca.gov.uk/financialintel/SARglossary.html). This will assist in consideration of the report by SOCA.

7.21 In order that an informed overview of the situation may be maintained, all contact between operators and law enforcement agencies should be controlled through, or reported back to, the nominated officer or a deputy acting in the absence of the nominated officer.

Appropriate consent

7.22 If operators handle any proceeds of crime they may commit one of the POCA principal money laundering offences. However if the nominated officers makes a report to SOCA this can amount to a defence. The 'reporting defence' includes the statutory mechanism which allows SOCA either to agree to the transaction going ahead, or to prevent the suspected money laundering going ahead. This statutory mechanism is called 'appropriate consent.'

7.23 The nominated officer needs to consider how he will approach his reporting obligations and consider:

- the timing of the report(s) – particularly second or subsequent reports; and
- whether the operator wishes to continue to do business with the customer.

7.24 A nominated officer, police constable, SOCA employee or customs officer can give a person (which may include, for example, a casino employee) *actual* 'appropriate consent' to a suspect transaction proceeding. However, it should be noted that SOCA is the only body able to issue formal notification of consent by means of an official SOCA letter, which the nominated officer can then retain for his records.

Figure 9: Appropriate consent

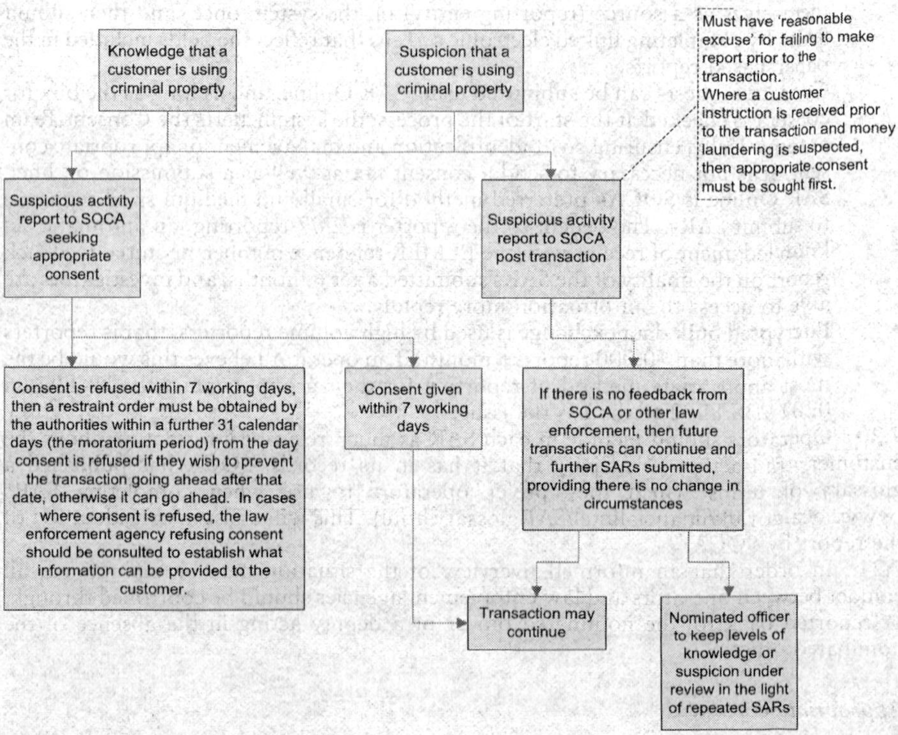

7.25 Alternatively, such a person will be *treated* as having the appropriate consent if notice is given to a police constable or customs officer (but not the nominated officer) and either:

- consent is not refused within seven working days (beginning with the day after the notice is given); or
- following such refusal, the 'moratorium period' (31 calendar days starting with the day on which the person receives notice that consent to the doing of the act is refused) has expired.

7.26 However, the Act provides that a nominated officer *must not* give the appropriate consent unless he has himself already made a disclosure to an authorised officer of SOCA and, either:

- the SOCA employee has consented to the transaction; or
- consent is not refused within seven working days (beginning with the day after the notice is given); or
- following such refusal, the 'moratorium period' (31 calendar days starting with the day on which the person receives notice that consent to the doing of the act is refused) has expired.

7.27 Reporting suspicious activity before or reporting after the event are not equal options which an operator can choose between. A report made after money laundering has already taken place will only be a legal defence if there was a 'reasonable excuse' for failing to make the report before the money laundering took place. Where a customer instruction is received prior to a transaction or activity taking place, or arrangements being put in place, and there are grounds for knowledge or suspicion that the transaction, arrangements, or the funds/property involved, may relate to money laundering, a report must be made to SOCA and consent sought to proceed with that transaction or activity. In such circumstances, it is an offence for a nominated officer to consent to a transaction or activity going ahead within the seven working day notice period from the working day following the date of disclosure, unless SOCA gives consent.

7.28 In the casino environment business is often conducted out of normal office hours and in circumstances where it is not feasible to obtain appropriate consent prior to or during a transaction. Grounds for knowledge or suspicion may be triggered after a customer has completed the three stages of a gambling transaction; that is they have bought in, they have played and they have cashed out. Under these circumstances it would be reasonable to report after the transaction. However, the defence of 'reasonable excuse' when reporting after the transaction is untested by case law, and would need to be considered on a case-by-case basis.

7.29 Casinos should include in their policies and procedures details on how they will manage circumstances where there is grounds for knowledge or suspicion of money laundering or terrorist financing. If knowledge or suspicion is present then there must be a mechanism for involvement of the senior manager on duty and contact with the nominated officer as soon as is practicable. If the circumstances amount to reasonable grounds to suspect, then reporting the matter to the nominated officer should be sufficient, and for the nominated officer to receive the matter at the earliest practicable opportunity.

7.30 The nominated officer will need to think very carefully about whether or not he wishes to continue to do business with the suspected customer. Relevant considerations should be the potential commission of criminal offences under POCA or the Terrorism Act, as well as potential damage to reputation and other commercial factors.

7.31 Operators should also note that in the Commission's view the reporting defence is not intended to be used repeatedly in relation to the same customer. If patterns of gambling lead to a steadily increasing level of suspicion of money laundering, or even to actual knowledge of money laundering, operators will no doubt seriously consider whether they wish to allow the customer to continue using their gaming facilities. Operators are of course free to terminate their business relationships if they wish, and provided this is handled sensitively there will be no risk of 'tipping off'. However, given that nominated officers will have previously reported the customer to SOCA they should liaise with the agency about the best approach to turning the customer away.

7.32 How customers suspected of money laundering will be dealt with is an important area of risk management for all operators. Casinos should deal with the issue in their policies and procedures under the Regulations and, as all gambling operators are at risk of committing the principal offences, it is advisable for all operators to consider these issues carefully before they arise in practice.

7.33 Although one transaction may be suspicious and be reported as such, there may be less concern that all of an individual's future transactions will be suspicious. In these circumstances, each transaction should be considered on a case-by-case basis and reports made accordingly. Where subsequent reports are also made after actual or suspected money laundering has taken place or appears to have taken place, the nominated officer is encouraged to keep records about why reporting was delayed, and about why appropriate consent was not requested before the suspected money laundering took place.

Applying for appropriate consent

7.34 When consent is needed reports should be faxed to the SOCA UKFIU Consent Desk (see SOCA website www.soca.gov.uk) or, where SAR Online is used, by checking the box requesting consent. The Consent Desk will apply the Association of Chief Police Officers (ACPO) agreed consent criteria to each request for consent, carry out the necessary internal enquiries, and will contact the appropriate law enforcement agency, where necessary, for a consent recommendation. Once SOCA's decision has been reached, the disclosing operator will be informed of the decision by telephone, and be given a consent number, which should be recorded. A formal consent letter from SOCA will follow.

7.35 As indicated, in the event that SOCA does not refuse consent within seven working days (the notice period) following the working day after the report is made, the operator may continue to do business with the customer. However, if consent is refused within that period, SOCA can interrupt business for a further 31 calendar days (the moratorium period) from the day consent is refused.

7.36 All consents are dealt with by SOCA on a case-by-case basis and while it may take the maximum of seven working days to deal with a consent request, in practice turnaround for most SARs is about three days.[24] Nominated officers should take this into account when deciding whether it is practical and reasonable to request consent prior to the transaction rather than making a report after the transaction or activity.

[24] SOCA Annual Report 2009/10.

Failing to report

7.37 POCA and the Terrorism Act create offences of failing to report suspicious activity. Where a person fails to comply with the obligations to make disclosures to a nominated officer and/or SOCA as soon as practicable after the information giving rise to the knowledge or suspicion comes to the employee they are open to criminal prosecution. The criminal sanction, under POCA or the Terrorism Act, is a prison term of up to five years, and/or a fine.

After a report has been made

7.38 Depending on the circumstances, an operator being served with a court order in relation to a customer may have cause for suspicion, or reasonable grounds for suspicion, in relation to that customer. In such an event, operators should review the information it holds about that customer, in order to determine whether or not such grounds exist, and if necessary make a report to SOCA.

7.39 When an enquiry is under investigation, the investigating officer may contact the nominated officer to ensure that he has all the relevant information which supports the original disclosure. This contact may also include seeking supplementary information or documentation from the reporting operator and from other sources by way of a court order. The investigating officer will therefore work closely with the nominated officer who will usually receive direct feedback on the stage reached in the investigation. There may, however, be cases when the nominated officer cannot be informed of the state of the investigation, either because of the confidential nature of the enquiry, or because the case is being considered by a court.

Tipping off, or prejudicing an investigation

7.40 Under section 333A of POCA a person commits an offence if:

(a) the person discloses that he or another person has made a disclosure under Part 7 of the Regulations to a constable, an officer of Revenue or Customers, a nominated officer or a member of staff of SOCA of information that came to that person in the course of a business in the regulated sector;

(b) the disclosure is likely to prejudice any investigation that might be conducted following the disclosure referred to in (a); and

(c) the information on which the disclosure is based came to the person in the course of a business in the regulated sector.

A person also commits an offence under section 333A if:

(a) the person discloses that an investigation into allegations that an offence under Part 7 of the Regulations has been committed, is being contemplated or is being carried out;

(b) the disclosure is likely to prejudice the investigation; and

(c) the information on which the disclosure is based came to the person in the course of a business in the regulated sector.

7.41 Under section 342 of POCA a person in the regulated sector also commits an offence if he:

- knows or suspects that an appropriate officer or, in Scotland, a proper person is acting (or proposing to act) in connection with a confiscation investigation, a civil recovery investigation, a detained cash investigation or a money laundering investigation which is being or is about to be conducted, and
- falsifies, conceals, destroys or otherwise disposes of, or causes or permits the falsification, concealment, destruction or disposal of, documents which are relevant to the investigation.

7.42 A person does not falsify, conceal, destroy or otherwise dispose of, or cause or permit the falsification, concealment, destruction or disposal of, documents which are relevant to the investigation if he

- does not know or suspect that the documents are relevant to the investigation
- does not intend to conceal any facts disclosed by the documents from any appropriate officer or (in Scotland) proper person carrying out the investigation.[25]

7.43 POCA therefore, in this regard, contains separate offences of tipping off and prejudicing an investigation. These offences are similar and overlapping, but there are also significant differences between them. It is important for those working in the regulated sector to be aware of the conditions for each offence. Each offence relates to situations where the information on which the disclosure was based came to the person making the disclosure in the course of a business in the regulated sector. The Terrorism Act contains similar offences. There are a number of disclosures which are permitted and that do not give rise to these offences (permitted disclosures) – see paragraphs 7.46 to 7.48.

7.44 Once an internal or external report of suspicious behaviour has been made, it is a criminal offence for anyone to release information that is likely to prejudice an investigation that might be conducted following that disclosure. An offence is not committed if the person dies not know or suspect that the disclosure is likely to prejudice an investigation, or if the disclosure is permitted under POCA or the Terrorism Act.[26] Reasonable enquiries of a customer, conducted in a tactful manner, regarding the background to a transaction or activity that is inconsistent with the normal pattern of activity is prudent practice, forms an integral part of CDD measures and should not give rise to tipping off.

7.45 Where a confiscation investigation, a civil recovery investigation, a detained cash investigation or a money laundering investigation is being, or is about to be, conducted, it is a criminal offence for anyone to disclose this fact if that disclosure is likely to prejudice the investigation. It is also a criminal offence to falsify, conceal, destroy or otherwise dispose of documents which are relevant to the investigation (or to cause or permit these offences). It is, however, a defence if the person does not know or suspect that disclosure is likely to prejudice the investigation, or if the disclosure is permitted under POCA or the Terrorism Act (see paragraphs 7.46 to 7.48).

7.46 An offence is not committed if the disclosure is made to the relevant supervisory authority (the Commission) for the purposes of:

- the detection, investigation or prosecution of a criminal offence in the UK or elsewhere
- an investigation under POCA
- the enforcement of any order of a court under POCA.[27]

7.47 An employee, officer or partner of a casino operator does not commit an offence under POCA or the Terrorism Act if the disclosure is to an employee, officer or partner of the casino operator.[28]

7.48 A person does not commit an offence under POCA if the person does not know or suspect that the disclosure is likely to prejudice

- any investigation that might be conducted following a disclosure; or
- an investigation into allegations that an offence under Part 7 of POCA has been committed, is being contemplated or is being carried out.[29]

7.49 The fact that a transaction is notified to SOCA before the event, and SOCA does not refuse consent within seven working days following the day after disclosure is made, or a restraint order is not obtained within the moratorium period, does not alter the position so far as 'tipping off' is concerned.

7.50 This means that an operator:

- cannot, at the time, tell a customer that a transaction is being delayed because a report is awaiting consent from SOCA;
- cannot, later, tell a customer that a transaction or activity was delayed because a report had been made under POCA or the Terrorism Act, unless law enforcement or SOCA agrees, or a court order is obtained permitting disclosure; and
- cannot tell the customer that law enforcement is conducting an investigation.

7.51 The case of *K v Natwest* [2006] EWCA Civ 1039 confirmed the application of these provisions. The judgement in this case also dealt with the issue of suspicion stating that the 'The existence of suspicion is a subjective fact. There is no legal requirement that there should be reasonable grounds for the suspicion. The relevant bank employee either suspects or he does not. If he does suspect, he must (either himself or through the Bank's nominated officer) inform the authorities.' It was further observed that the 'truth is that Parliament has struck a precise and workable balance of conflicting interests in the 2002 Act'. The Court appears to have approved of the seven and 31 day scheme and said that in relation to the limited interference with private rights that this scheme entails 'many people would think that a reasonable balance has been struck'. A copy of the judgement is available at www.jmlsg.org.uk/about-soca/library/cat_view/84-csar.

7.52 The existence of a SAR cannot be revealed to any customer of the casino at any time, whether or not consent has been requested. However, there is nothing in POCA which prevents operators from making normal enquiries about customer transactions in order to help remove any concerns about the transaction and enable the operator to decide whether to proceed with the transaction. These enquiries will only constitute tipping off if the operator discloses that a SAR has been made to SOCA or a nominated officer, or that a money laundering investigation is being carried out or is being contemplated.

7.53 The combined effect of these two offences is that one or other of them can be committed before or after a disclosure has been made.

7.54 The offence of money laundering, and the duty to report under POCA, apply in relation to the proceeds of any criminal activity, wherever conducted, including abroad, that would constitute an offence if it took place in the UK. A person does not commit an offence where it is known or believed on reasonable grounds that the conduct occurred outside the UK; and the conduct was not criminal in the country where it took place. However, if the criminal activity would constitute an offence in the UK if committed here and would be punishable by imprisonment for a maximum term in excess of twelve months then the defence does not apply except if the offence is an offence under section 23 or 25 of the Financial Services and Markets Act 2000.

7.55 There is also a specific offence of failure to disclose terrorist financing which was added to the Terrorism Act through the Anti Terrorism Crime and Security Act 2001. This offence is limited to the regulated sector, which includes casinos. The offence can be committed if a person forms knowledge or suspicion of terrorist financing or reasonable grounds for suspecting terrorist financing, during the course of working for a casino, but does not make a report. Guidance issued by the Commission and approved by Treasury must be taken into consideration by any court considering whether this offence has been committed.

---

[25] Section 342(6) of POCA.

[26] Section 342(3) of POCA.

[27] Section 333D of POCA.

[28] Section 333B of POCA.

[29] Section 333D of POCA.

ANNEX A – GLOSSARY OF TERMS

AML: Anti-money laundering

Business relationship: Abusiness, professional or commercial relationship between a casino operator and a customer, which is expected to have an element of duration.

CTF: Countering terrorist financing

Customer tracking: The process of capturing drop and win data for a customer.

Drop/win figures: Data recorded by casinos that covers the total value of chips purchased as well as the total loss or win for a customer over a 24 hour period.

ML: Money laundering.

Money laundering: The process by which criminal or 'dirty' money is legitimised or made 'clean', including any action taken to conceal, arrange, use or possess the proceeds of any criminal conduct. Defined in section 340 of POCA.

Non-remote casinos: Casinos licensed to operate commercial casino premises.

Operators: Firms holding an operator's licence issued by the Commission.

PFL: Personal functional licence.

POCA: The Proceeds of Crime Act 2002, which is intended to reduce money laundering and the profitability of organised crime through the use of tools such as asset recovery.

PML: Personal management licence.

Proceeds of crime: Property from which a person benefits directly or indirectly, by being party to criminal activity, for example stolen money, money from drug dealing or property stolen in a burglary or robbery.

Remote casinos: Casinos licensed to offer casino games by means of remote communication.

SAR: A suspicious activity report – the means by which suspicious activity relating to possible money laundering or the financing of terrorism is reported to SOCA under POCA.
SOCA: The Serious Organised Crime Agency, which was established by the Serious Organised Crime and Police Act 2005 and came into being on 1 April 2006. SOCA is an intelligence-led agency with law enforcement powers and the responsibility to reduce the harm caused to people and communities by serious organised crime. SOCA is the organisation to which suspicious activity is reported.
Supervisory authorities: Supervisory authorities, which are listed in regulation 23 of the Regulations. The Commission is the supervisory authority for casinos
The Commission: The Gambling Commission.
The Regulations: The Money Laundering Regulations 2007.
The Terrorism Act: The Terrorism Act 2000.
UKFIU: The United Kingdom Financial Intelligence Unit, which is the unit within SOCA that operates the disclosure regime for money laundering.
Gambling Commission December 2011

AML – ANTI MONEY LAUNDERING.

CODE OF PRACTICE

Determinations under Paragraphs 4 and 5 of Schedule 9 to the Gambling Act 2005 relating to Large and Small Casinos

6.2242 Issued by the Secretary of State for Culture, Media and Sport on 26th February 2008
Our aim is to improve the quality of life for all through cultural and sporting activities, support the pursuit of excellence, and champion the tourism, creative and leisure industries.

SECTION 1: INTRODUCTION

1.1 This Code of Practice is issued by the Secretary of State for Culture, Media and Sport under paragraph 6 of Schedule 9 to the Gambling Act 2005. It should be read alongside Part 8 of and Schedule 9 to that Act.
1.2 This Code of Practice is about:
1.2.1. the procedure to be followed by a licensing authority in making any determinations required by paragraphs 4 and 5 of Schedule 9 to the Gambling Act 2005; and
1.2.2. matters to which a licensing authority should have regard in making those determinations.
1.3 Under paragraph 6(2) of Schedule 9 to the Gambling Act 2005, a licensing authority must comply with this Code of Practice.

SECTION 2: DEFINITIONS

2.1 In this Code of Practice:
the Act means the Gambling Act 2005,
application, unless the contrary intention appears, means:
(a) an application under section 159 of the Act for a large or small casino premises licence, or
(b) an application under section 204 of the Act for a provisional statement in respect of a large or small casino,
and a reference to an **applicant** shall be construed accordingly,

the invitation regulations means the Gambling (Inviting Competing Applications for Large and Small Casino Premises Licences) Regulations 2008[1] and a reference to an **application pack** or **invitation** means an application pack made available or invitation published under those regulations,
second stage applicants has the meaning given in paragraph 5.4.1 below,
the Schedule means Schedule 9 to the Act, and
the second stage means the second stage of the two-stage consideration procedure under the Schedule, by which a licensing authority makes the determination required by paragraph 5 of the Schedule.

[1] S.I. 2008/469

SECTION 3: GENERAL PRINCIPLES TO GOVERN PROCEDURE

3.1 A licensing authority must ensure that the procedure they follow in making any determinations required by paragraphs 4 and 5 of the Schedule is fair, having regard to the provisions of the Act.
3.2 Subject to the provisions of the Act, the procedure must allow any person to make an application. It must also ensure that each application is determined by the licensing authority according to criteria which are:
3.2.1. the same for all applications;
3.2.2. made known to all applicants; and
3.2.3. not pre-selected to favour a particular applicant or application.
3.3 A licensing authority must ensure that any pre-existing contract, arrangement or other relationship they have with any person does not affect the procedure so as to make it unfair (or appear unfair) to any applicant. In particular, a licensing authority must:
3.3.1. in determining the principles that they propose to apply in making the determination under paragraph 5 of the Schedule, disregard any such contract, arrangement or other relationship;
3.3.2. before publishing an invitation, put in place arrangements to ensure that any such contract, arrangement or other relationship does not, actually or apparently, prejudice their ability to conduct the procedure fairly; and
3.3.3. after the closing date (as defined in the invitation regulations) but before considering an application, prepare a register of interests disclosing their interest in any contract, arrangement or other relationship with an applicant or a person connected or associated with an applicant.
3.4 A copy of the information in the register of interests referred to in paragraph 3.3.3 above must be provided by the licensing authority free of charge to each applicant and to any other person who requests it.
3.5 For the purposes of paragraph 3.3.3 above:
3.5.1. a person is "connected with" an applicant if, were the applicant a director of a company, the person would be connected with the applicant within the meaning of section 252 of the Companies Act 2006; and
3.5.2. a person is "associated with" an applicant if the applicant is a body corporate and the person is an associated body corporate under section 256 of the Companies Act 2006.
3.6 Paragraph 3.3 above does not apply to an agreement between a licensing authority and an applicant entered into during the second stage under paragraph 5(3)(b) of the Schedule.
3.7 Licensing authorities should bear in mind section 210 of the Act, which provides that:
3.7.1. in making a decision in respect of an application, a licensing authority shall not have regard to whether a not a proposal by the applicant is likely to be permitted in accordance with the law relating to planning or building; and

3.7.2. a decision in respect of an application shall not constrain any later decision by the authority under the law relating to planning or building.

SECTION 4: THE FIRST STAGE OF THE CONSIDERATION PROCEDURE

4.1 In making any determination required by paragraph 4 of the Schedule, a licensing authority must apply the procedure for assessing applications for premises licences which they ordinarily apply to such applications, subject to the modifications of that procedure noted in paragraph 4.2 below. That procedure is governed by Part 8 of the Act, including statutory instruments made under that Part.[2] Section 153 of the Act sets out the principles to be applied by a licensing authority in exercising their functions under Part 8.

4.2 For the purposes of making any determination under paragraph 4 of the Schedule, Part 8 of the Act is modified by paragraph 4(2)(b) and (c) of the Schedule. Paragraph 4(2)(b) provides that each competing applicant is an interested party in relation to each of the other competing applications.

4.3 In making any determination required by paragraph 4 of the Schedule, a licensing authority must not take into account any matters which they would not ordinarily take into account in determining an application for a premises licence. In particular, a licensing authority must comply with paragraph 4(2)(a) of the Schedule, which provides that an authority must not have regard to whether any of the competing applications is more deserving of being granted.

4.4 Regulation 6(1)(a) of the invitation regulations requires that an application pack include a statement that no information, other than information required by the regulations that govern the making of applications,3 be included in or submitted with an application. Where any such information (including information which is relevant to a determination under paragraph 5 of the Schedule but is not also relevant to the determination under paragraph 4) is nevertheless included in or submitted with an application, the licensing authority must:

4.4.1. disregard it in making the determination required by paragraph 4 of the Schedule; and

4.4.2. if possible, return it to the applicant.

4.2 Regulation 6(1)(b) and (2) of the invitation regulations requires that an application pack include a statement of the procedure the licensing authority propose to follow in making any determination required by paragraph 4 of the Schedule (together with the procedure the authority propose to follow in making any determination required by paragraph 5). As noted in paragraph 4.1 above, the procedure to be followed under paragraph 4 of the Schedule is the procedure for assessing applications for premises licences which a licensing authority ordinarily apply to such applications, subject to the modifications of that procedure noted in paragraph 4.2 above.

---

2 In particular, in relation to applications in England and Wales, the Gambling Act 2005 (Premises Licences and Provisional Statements) (England and Wales) Regulations 2007 (S.I. 2007/459); and in relation to applications in Scotland, the Gambling Act 2005 (Premises Licences and Provisional Statements) (Scotland) Regulations 2007 (S.S.I. 2007/196)

SECTION 5: THE SECOND STAGE OF THE CONSIDERATION PROCEDURE

5.1 Before publishing an invitation, a licensing authority must determine:

5.1.1. the procedure they propose to follow, and

5.1.2. the principles they propose to apply,

in making any determination required by paragraph 5 of the Schedule.

5.2 Regulation 6(1)(b), (d) and (2) of the invitation regulations requires that statements of:

5.2.1. that procedure (together with the procedure the authority propose to follow in making the determination required by paragraph 4 of the Schedule), and

5.2.2. those principles,
be included in an application pack.

5.3 In addition, section 349(7) of the Act requires that those principles be included in the licensing policy statement published by a licensing authority under that section.

5.4 The procedure a licensing authority propose to follow in making any determination required by paragraph 5 of the Schedule must provide for the following:

5.4.1. Where a licensing authority determine under paragraph 4 of the Schedule that they would, if they were able, grant more than one application, the applicants who made those applications ("the second stage applicants") must be invited to participate in the second stage.

5.4.2. During the second stage, each of the second stage applicants must be given an equal opportunity to demonstrate to the licensing authority how their application would, if granted, result in the greatest benefit to the authority's area.

5.4.3. At the outset of the second stage, each of the second stage applicants must be invited to submit information to the authority about how their application would, if granted, benefit the authority's area.

5.4.4. A licensing authority may engage in discussions or negotiations during the second stage with each second stage applicant with a view to the particulars of an application being refined, supplemented or otherwise altered so as to maximise the benefits to the authority's area that would result from it (were it granted).

5.4.5. A licensing authority may not, during the second stage, discuss the details of a person's application with the other competing applicants without the person's permission.

5.4.6. A licensing authority must put in place a protocol governing the storage of confidential information submitted to them during the second stage, so as to maintain the confidentiality of that information.

5.5 In determining the procedure, licensing authorities should bear in mind that, under paragraph 5(3)(b) of the Schedule, they may enter into a written agreement with an applicant during the second stage. Under paragraph 5(3)(d), a licensing authority may take any such agreement into account in determining, under paragraph 5(3)(a), which application would be likely if granted to result in the greatest benefit to the authority's area.

5.6 The power under paragraph 5(3)(b) of the Schedule is a broad one: an agreement may be "as to the provision of services in respect of an authority's area or otherwise". An agreement may, for example, record the outcome of the discussions or negotiations referred to in paragraph 5.4.4 above and may be conditional on a licensing authority granting a casino licence to the applicant that is party to the agreement. Licensing authorities should consider the effect (if any) of other legislation (for example the Public Contracts Regulations 2006) on an agreement proposed or entered into under paragraph 5(3)(b) of the Schedule.

5.7 In determining the principles they propose to apply in making any determination required by paragraph 5 of the Schedule a licensing authority:

5.7.1. must consider what aspects of an application will be relevant to determining which of the applications would if granted be likely to result in the greatest benefit to the authority's area;

5.7.2. should consider local issues and priorities;

5.7.3. must consult a person or people who appear to represent the interests of local people and businesses, although if they have already consulted about a related matter (for example, in relation to their licensing policy statement published under section 349 of the Act) they need not engage in further consultation, as long as the views expressed in the earlier consultation are taken into account; and

5.7.4. may wish to pay particular regard to the following:

(a) the provision that is made in an application for protecting children and other vulnerable people from harm or exploitation arising from gambling, whether in the proposed casino or the wider community,

(b) the provision that is made in an application for preventing gambling from being a source of crime or disorder, being associated with crime or disorder or being used to support crime,

(c) the provision that is made in an application for ensuring that gambling is conducted in a fair and open way,

(d) the likely effects of an application on employment and regeneration within the authority's area,

(e) the design and location of the development proposed in the application,

(f) the range and nature of non-gambling facilities to be offered as part of the development proposed in the application, and

(g) the financial and other contributions a second stage applicant proposes to make to the authority's area, whether pursuant to an agreement under paragraph 5(3)(b) of the Schedule or otherwise.

2-4 Cockspur Street
London SW1Y 5DH
www.culture.gov.uk

RULES OF CASINO GAMES IN GREAT BRITAIN
ARCHIVE VERSION
Effective only until June 2011

1 INTRODUCTION

6.2243 1.1 In March 2011 the Gambling Commission (the Commission) consulted on licence condition 9 of its Licence Conditions and Codes of Practice (LCCP): Types and rules of casino and other games. In an attempt to bring casinos more into line with the other gambling sectors, the Commission consulted on a number of proposals, which are reproduced below:

- The Rules of Casino Games in Great Britain document would be discontinued.
- In its place would be an amendment to the LCCP licence condition 9 (types and rules of casino and other games) to be confined only to the following condition for casinos[1]:

9 Types and rules of casino and other games

All non-remote casino operating licences

~~Licensees must:~~

- ~~with the exception of games made available for a specified period in accordance with a Commission approved trial of a proposed new game only offer or permit to be played casino games that appear on the Gambling Commission's list of approved games~~
- ~~follow any rules for the playing of approved casino games, or other games of chance, as may be set by the Commission.~~

Licensees must not offer or permit to be played casino games that appear on any list of games prohibited by the Commission.

All non-remote bingo operating licences

Licensees must not offer or permit to be played prize gaming games that appear on any list of ~~proscribed prize gaming~~ games ~~issued~~ prohibited by the Commission.

- The wording of the condition applying to all non-remote bingo operating licences would also be changed, as detailed above, so that the phrasing mirrors that of the revised casino condition. In this way the meaning of the condition would remain the same and would not constitute any sort of change, but the articulation of the idea would be standardised across the bingo and casino conditions.

- The provisions of code of practice 3 would then cover the requirements to provide and display the rules and house edge information, as now.
- In this way, the Commission would retain the ability to list any games that it did not consider should be played (as with the bingo condition) in the unlikely event that this should be required. However, if a game is not on a prohibited list, and otherwise conforms to the criteria for being a casino game under section 7 of the Gambling Act 2005, it would automatically be permitted.
- The Commission expects operators to explain their games clearly and transparently to customers. This deregulatory measure is in line with the Commission's general approach and places the onus on the individual operator to ensure that the licensing objectives are upheld.

[1] Existing text to be replaced is represented in strike-through; new text is underlined.

1.2 The new licence condition took effect from 16 June 2011. Alongside the revised licence condition the Commission committed to publishing two additional documents – a core rules document[2] covering the standard game rules for the five most popular games in GB casinos: blackjack, roulette, three card poker, punto banco and dice as well as one final edition of the *Rules of Casino Games in Great Britain*. This document therefore aims to incorporate all the games that operators have trialled successfully and asked to retain since the last edition was published in July 2008. It is hoped that this document will accurately represent the casino games market in Great Britain at the time the new licence condition takes effect. **Please note that this document serves only to represent the casino games market in Great Britain at the time the new licence condition came into effect. It does not prescribe rules or games that apply after that date, which are at the discretion of the individual licence holders.**

SCOPE OF THE DOCUMENT

1.3 This document sets out the rules, including layouts, odds and any side bets, for each game on the list of approved games.
1.4 The document has been created to ensure a consistent approach in providing casino games in Great Britain and accordingly is aimed at casino operators.
1.5 Any matters relating to game rules not specifically covered in this document may be interpreted at the discretion of the operator. The Commission's licence conditions and codes of practice require that all operators of these games have training, security, procedures and systems in place to ensure that all the games are played in an open and fair manner.

[2] This document can be found on the Commission's website.

2. GENERAL RULES

2.1 The following are standard non-remote casino house rules. The listed games may only be played for commercial gain on casino premises, licensed under the Act.

THE BANK

2.2 The following rules apply to **ALL** games listed in this document and cannot be varied:
(a) no person other than the holder of a licence under the Gambling Act 2005 for the premises where the game is played shall have any share or interest in the bank;
(b) the bank shall be held by the licence holder or a person acting in pursuance of a service agreement on their behalf; and

(c) all wagers will be made with the bank.

FULLY AND PARTLY AUTOMATED CASINO GAMES

2.3 **ALL** equipment used in fully and partly automated casino games must comply with technical standards set by the Commission in the current *Bingo and Casino Equipment Technical Requirements.*

PROGRESSIVE SIDE WAGERS

2.4 At the licence holder's discretion, a casino may introduce an additional feature into any game listed within this document, namely a 'Progressive Jackpot' wager, subject to specific rules and odds being detailed for that wager in the section relating to the game concerned. In such cases, the following standard rules will apply wherever a progressive jackpot wager is applied:

(a) operators will have systems and procedures in place to account for malfunctions and technical faults during the operation of the game;
(b) at least 70% of the total value of the progressive jackpot wagers placed at all tables, within the premises and at any tables on other premises, which are linked for the purposes of the progressive jackpot, shall be added to a cumulative prize fund (referred to in these rules as the 'Progressive Jackpot Meter');
(c) a licence holder may apply additional sums to the progressive jackpot meter (the Jackpot 'seed') from its own funds;
(d) equipment used to play the progressive wager must conform to the current *Bingo and Casino Equipment Technical Requirements* published by the Commission;
(e) operators must have procedures in place to account for the possibility of multiple wins occurring at the same time, either on the same table, same premises or premises located elsewhere that are linked into the same progressive jackpot meter;
(f) operators must have procedures and security systems in place to ensure the integrity of the funds held on the progressive jackpot meter, and to ensure that any wins can be substantiated to the satisfaction of the Commission; and
(g) a sign or notice must be displayed at each participating table showing the current progressive jackpot meter total.

MINIMUM ODDS AND PAY TABLES

2.5 Odds detailed in this document refer to the minimum odds that must be offered to players within a game. As detailed in rule 2.4e, more favourable odds may be offered to the player, on a permanent or temporary basis, provided the details are clearly displayed at the table.

2.6 However, whilst the minimum odds permissible for each individual wager are detailed in this document, operators may wish to change the whole pay table, rather than simply adjust one or more individual odds. This is in order to balance the house edge across the whole range of odds being applied. It is acceptable to replace complete pay tables in this way provided:

(a) the individual odds used within a pay table are not less than the individual minimum odds given within this document;
(b) house edge details relating to every pay table used in a particular premises are made clearly available to players;
(c) for the benefit of players, a sign or notice is displayed at each relevant gaming tables indicating which pay table is being used, so that players may compare the given odds against details of the house edge otherwise made available within the premises; and
(d) where a pay table is used that increases the minimum odds, but is otherwise not one of the pre-determined tables prescribed in both this document and the

House Edge leaflet, the sign or notice also shows the revised house edge for the game resulting from the revised pay table.

2.7 In some cases, the minimum odds given in this document serve only to show the lowest permitted odds, drawn from all of the pay tables listed for that game. As a result, the minimum odds are not always in themselves a well-balanced pay table. In such cases, this fact is indicated in the description of the minimum odds within this document, with a recommendation that one of the given pay tables is used.

3. ROULETTE

THE TABLE LAYOUTS

3.1 Figures 1 and 2 show examples of the style of game layouts that may be offered to the players. They also illustrate the full range of bets available, and the position that such bets must be placed on the layout, in accordance with the list given in paragraph 3.2.

Figure 1: American roulette

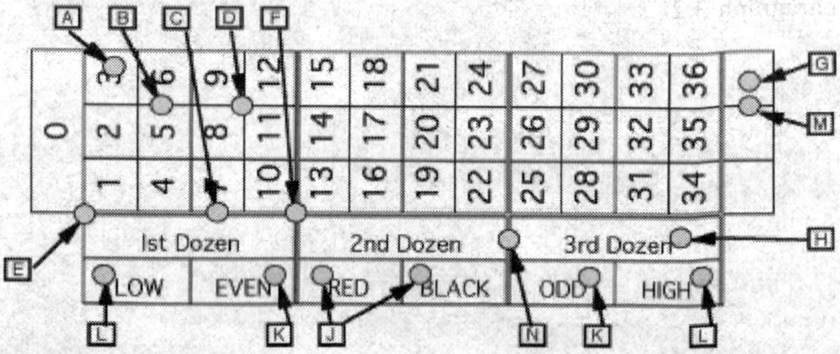

Figure 2: French roulette

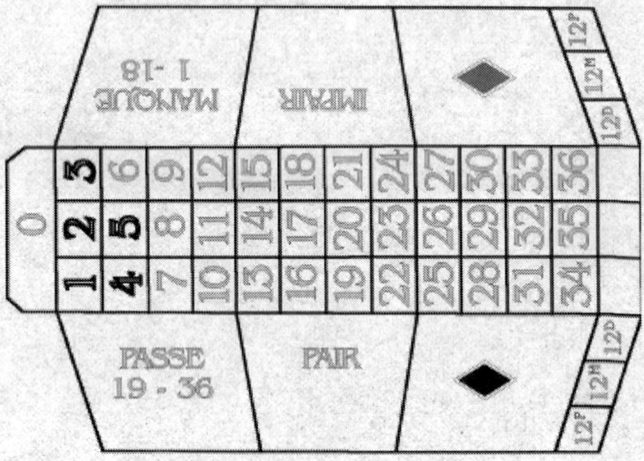

3.2 Any wager in relation to this game shall be payable, if won, at a minimum and with the odds indicated below:

American term	**French term**	**Minimum odds**
A. **Straight Up** – one specific number	En Plein	**35 to 1**
B. **Split** – one of two specific numbers	A Cheval	**17 to 1**
C. **Street** – one of three specific numbers	En Transversale	**11 to 1**
D. **Corner** – one of four specific numbers	En Carré	**8 to 1**
E. **First Four** – one of numbers 0 (or 00),1,2,3	Quatre Premiers	**8 to 1**
F. **Six Line** – one of six specific numbers	Sixain	**5 to 1**
G. **Column** – one of 12 specific numbers in a row	Sur une Colonne	**2 to 1**
H. **Dozen** – one of 12 specific numbers in a block	Sur une Douzaine	**2 to 1**
I. **Red or Black** – one of 18 specific numbers	Rouge ou Noir	**1 to 1**
J. **Odd or Even** – one of 18 specific numbers	Impair ou Pair	**1 to 1**
K. **Low or High** – one of 18 specific numbers	Manque ou Passe	**1 to 1**
L. **Split Columns** – one of 24 specific numbers in a row	A Cheval sur Deux Colonnes	**1 to 2**
M. **Split Dozens** – one of 24 specific numbers in a block	A Cheval sur Deux Douzaines	**1 to 2**

3.3 When the winning number is zero (or double zero, where available):

(a) wagers placed on zero, double zero or combination of either with one, two and/or three, shall win at odds in accordance with rule 3.2;

(b) either:

(i) half of each wager on any even money chance shall be lost and the remaining half returned to the player; or

(ii) all wagers on any even money chance shall be lost.[3]

(c) the whole of all other wagers shall be lost.

3.4 It is not a requirement that all wagers are made available on any particular table. However, no variation may be considered in addition to the wagers and minimum odds given in rule 3.2, other than in accordance with the rules detailed in section 2.3 and 2.4.

THE WHEEL

3.5 Other than any permitted variations detailed in rule 3.11 onwards, or otherwise in accordance with the rules detailed in section 2.3 and 2.4, the wheel used to play roulette shall have either:

(a) 37 equal compartments with one marked zero and the others marked 1 to 36, coloured alternately red and black, and in the same sequence as shown in Figure 3, below, or

(b) 38 equal compartments with one marked zero, one marked double zero and the others marked 1 to 36, coloured alternately red and black, and in the same sequence as shown, below:

0, 28, 9, 26, 30, 11, 7, 20, 32, 17, 5, 22, 34, 15, 3, 24, 36, 13, 1, 00, 27, 10, 25, 29, 12, 8, 19, 31, 18, 6, 21, 33, 16, 4, 23, 35, 14, 2

The house edge for whichever wheel options used must be detailed in the house edge leaflet or otherwise on the table(s) concerned. Where option b) is used, this fact must

6: Gambling Act 2005: Additional Material

be clearly highlighted on a notice at the table(s) concerned to ensure that players wishing to use neighbour bets are aware of the number order currently in play.

---

[3] Where option b) ii) is used, this fact must be clearly highlighted on a notice displayed at the table(s) and the house edge detailed in the appropriate leaflet or otherwise displayed at the table. Whichever option is used, the appropriate rule must be covered in any "How to Play" leaflets or material provided at the casino concerned.

Figure 3: The wheel

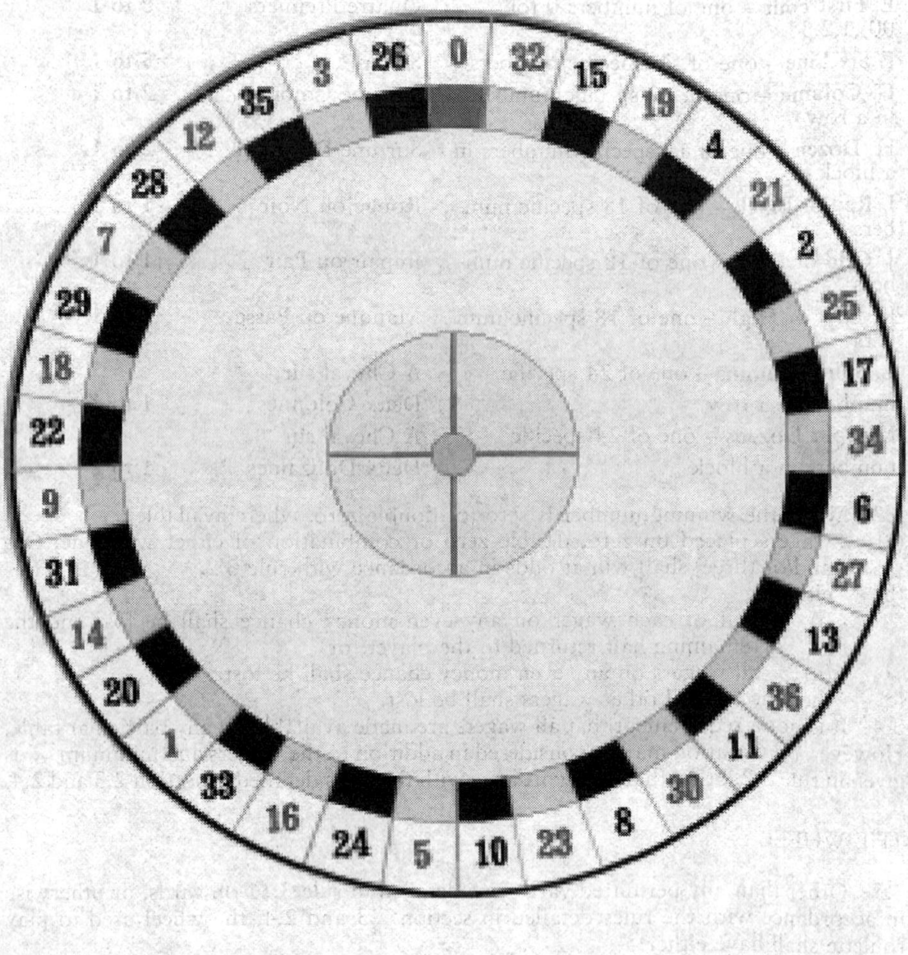

3.6 The ball shall be spun in the opposite direction to the wheel.
3.7 Operators must have procedures in place to ensure the security and integrity of the wheel. The wheel must comply with the standards set in the document, *Bingo and Casino Equipment Technical Requirements*, published by the Commission.

GENERAL RULES

3.8 Wagers orally declared shall be accepted only if accompanied by the placing of sufficient chips, wheel checks or cash on the table to cover the wager and verbally confirmed by the dealer.
3.9 Each player shall be responsible for the positioning of their own wager or wagers on the table, whether or not they are assisted by the dealer. The player must ensure that any instructions given are correctly carried out. Wagers shall be settled strictly in accordance with the position of chips (or as orally declared and confirmed) when the ball falls to rest in a compartment of the wheel.
3.10 The maximum and minimum wagers permitted shall be shown on a notice prominently displayed at the table. Display of the maximum wager is recommended but is otherwise at the discretion of the licence holder. Partnerships with a view to exceeding the maximum stake shall not be permitted.

PERMITTED VARIATIONS TO ROULETTE

3.11 Symbols other than the numbers 0-36 or 00 – 36 may be permitted on the wheel and layout within a game of roulette provided the order in which they appear on the wheel, and overall impact on the game, are the same as if they were numbers used within the standard rules of the game, as detailed in this section. Similarly, when using electronic versions of Roulette, instead of a wheel and ball it is permitted to use four, six sided dice, each containing symbols. When the dice are tumbled, the combination of these symbols may be used to generate a grid co-ordinate on the layout to determine the winning number and colour. This is only permitted where the possible combinations of symbols will only generate winning numbers between 0-36 or 00 to 36, exactly as if spun by a wheel, so that the overall impact on the game is the same.

Roulette Rage side wager

3.12 It is at the discretion of the licence holder whether or not to offer an additional feature called 'Roulette Rage' as an additional wager within a standard game of roulette. The proprietor of the side wager is TCSJohnHuxley Ltd and no variations may be put forward without their prior agreement.
3.13 The feature shall only be made available at a table or tables marked for the provision of the wager.
3.14 The Roulette Rage side wager is an optional wager that at least five consecutive numbers will be spun of the same colour. Higher odds are paid depending on the number of consecutively coloured numbers that are spun.
3.15 Wagers on the Roulette Rage side wager may only be placed after a different coloured number is spun to that spun immediately before it. For example, when a black number is spun after one or more red numbers.
3.16 Further wagers may not then be placed until a sequence of consecutive colours is broken by a number of a different colour being spun, or by zero, whichever is spun first.
3.17 The Roulette Rage side wager is not activated if zero is spun, which will be deemed to bring a previous consecutive sequence to an end. New wagers may only then be placed after a further number has been spun following the zero, or multiple zeros.
3.18 When a different coloured number is spun (as per rule 3.15), the dealer will invite all players at the table to place optional wagers on the Roulette Rage side wager, within the specified table limits. The first spin that determines the colour for the

Roulette Rage side wager will hereafter be known as the 'establishing spin'. This spin **will not** count towards the sequence of consecutive colours (ie the first number will register only if the establishing colour is repeated on the next spin).

3.19 Players need not have placed any other wager within the game in order to place a Roulette Rage side wager.

3.20 All Roulette Rage side wagers will be placed in the betting area marked for the purpose by the dealer after the establishing spin. No further side wagers may be accepted until the next establishing spin.

3.21 The roulette game will then continue as normal.

3.22 If a first number spun after the establishing spin is of the same colour, all Roulette Rage wagers will be moved into the circle marked '1', other than where rule 3.23 applies.

3.23 Operators may choose to have the current number of consecutive spins transmitted automatically from the wheel to an electronic number display. Provided players are able to clearly see the current number on the display, it is not then necessary to physically move the wagers from the betting area. This applies to all subsequent spins up to 15.

3.24 If the next number spun is not of the same colour as the establishing spin, then all Roulette Rage wagers will be lost and surrendered to the house. A new round of wagers may then be accepted, in accordance with rules 3.18 and 3.19.

3.25 If a second number of the same colour is spun after the establishing spin, all Roulette Rage wagers will be moved into the circle marked '2'. The same process continues on the next two spins, whereby all roulette rage wagers will be moved into the circle marked '3' or '4' respectively.

3.26 Rule 3.24 will apply if a different coloured number, or zero, is spun on either the first, second or third spin after the establishing spin. However, if the fourth spin after the establishing spin is the same colour, then all Roulette Rage wagers will win and qualify for a pay out as and when a different colour or zero is subsequently spun. The pay out will then relate to however many spins of the same colour had occurred before the sequence was broken. For example, if five red numbers are spun after the establishing spin, followed by a black number, the winning wagers will be paid the odds for five consecutive colours given in rule 3.28.

3.27 Wagers will only be paid out if the odds applicable for the highest number of consecutive spins are achieved, up to a maximum of 15, including the establishing spin. Any consecutive spins thereafter will not be counted. Rule 3.18 will then apply as soon as a different colour is spun, at which time winning wagers will be paid odds for 15 consecutive spins.

3.28 Winning Roulette Rage wagers will be paid the following minimum odds for achieving at least four consecutive spins of the same colour, after the establishing spin:

Number of consecutive spins of the same colour (*after* establishing spin)	Minimum odds
4	5 to 1
5	8 to 1
6	15 to 1
7	20 to 1
8	40 to 1
9	60 to 1
10	100 to 1
11	200 to 1
12	400 to 1
13	1000 to 1
14	2000 to 1

The above table shows the minimum permitted odds that may be paid for each consecutive spin, drawn from the pay tables given in this section.

3.30 However, the full list of minimum odds is not, in itself, a well-balanced pay table and in fact carries a house edge of 17.0%. It is therefore recommended that the minimum odds are only used as a guide and not as a pay table in themselves.

3.31 In addition to offering the minimum odds given in rule 3.28, odds for winning Roulette Rage wagers may be presented as complete pay tables, in accordance with rule 2.9 given in section 2. Permitted pay tables are as follows:

Pay table 1

Number of consecutive spins of the same colour	Minimum odds
4	6 to 1
5	10 to 1
6	20 to 1
7	30 to 1
8	40 to 1
9	60 to 1
10	100 to 1
11	200 to 1
12	400 to 1
13	1000 to 1
14	2000 to 1

Pay table 2

Number of consecutive spins of the same colour	Minimum odds
4	5 to 1
5	9 to 1
6	20 to 1
7	30 to 1
8	40 to 1
9	60 to 1
10	100 to 1
11	200 to 1
12	400 to 1
13	1000 to 1
14	2000 to 1

'Colours' Side Wager

3.32 It is at the discretion of the licence holder whether or not to offer an additional feature called 'Colours', as an additional wager within a standard game of roulette. The proprietor of the side wager is Casino Gaming LLC and no variations may be put forward without their prior agreement.

3.33 The feature shall only be made available at a table or tables marked for the provision of the wager.

3.34 The Colours side wager is an optional wager that three consecutive numbers will be spun of the same colour.

3.35 Wagers on Colours side wager cannot be removed until that wager is either won or lost.

3.36 If the player has placed a 'Colours' wager and three consecutive numbers are spun of the same colour. Then the wager placed on the related colour designated betting position will be paid at odds at a minimum of **7 to 1.**
3.37 All winning wagers are returned to the player, as the wager will then have been deemed spent.
3.38 If three consecutive numbers of the same colour are not spun, then any colours wagers placed on the related colour designated betting area shall be lost and surrendered to the house.
3.39 If zero is spun, then any colours wagers placed on any colour designated betting areas shall be lost and surrendered to the bank.
3.40 Players are not required to place any other wager within the game in order to place a colour side wager.

New AR side bet

3.41 It is at the discretion of the licence holder whether or not to offer an additional feature called 'NewAR' as an additional wager within a standard game of roulette. The proprietor of the side wager is NewAR and no variations may be put forward without their prior agreement.
3.42 The feature shall only be made available at a table or tables marked for the provision of the wager. An example game layout is shown below:

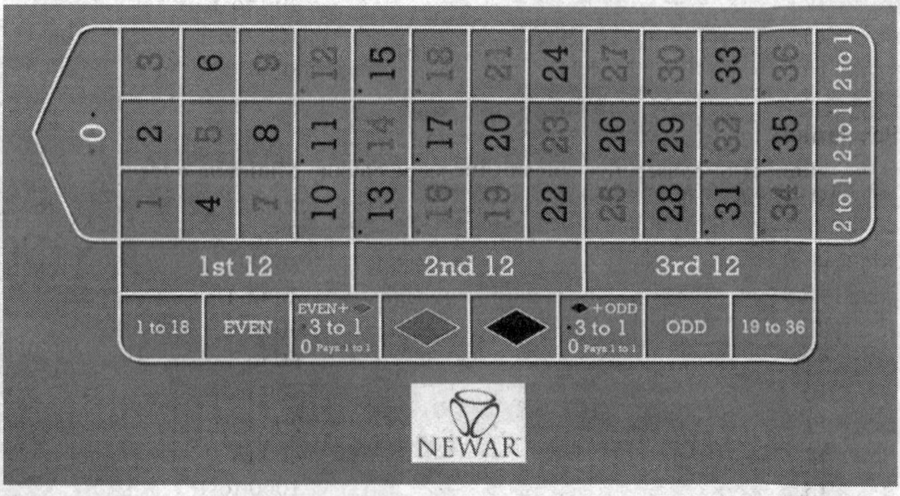

3.43 The bet groups together all Red, Even numbers in a defined betting area offering house chosen odds, and also include a 'bonus' number in this betting area where the house offers a different set of odds. Likewise, the NewAR side bets group together all Black, Odd numbers as a single spin betting option – again with a bonus number, and again with house selected odds.
3.44 Minimum permitted odds and House Edge are shown in the below table.

Black + Odd / Red + Even pays;	**Zero (or other selected bonus number) pays;**	**House Edge**
3-1	1-1	8.1%
3-1	3-2	6.75%
3-1	2-1	5.4%
3-1	5-2	4.05%
2-1	9-1	8.1%

Black + Odd / Red + Even pays;	Zero (or other selected bonus number) pays;	House Edge
2-1	9.5-1	6.75%
2-1	10-1	5.4%
2-1	10.5-1	4.05%

Crown Double Zero Roulette

3.45 It is at the discretion of the licence holder whether or not to offer the roulette variant Crown Double Zero Roulette. The proprietor of this roulette variant is Aspers Group Ltd and no variations may be put forward without their prior agreement.
3.46 The game is played with a wheel containing 38 compartments numbered from 1-36 and two zeros. The numbers from 1-36 are divided up equally and coloured either red or black. A single ball is spun and will land in one of the numbered compartments.
3.47 The object of the game is to predict which numbered compartment the ball will fall into by placing a wager on the appropriate number on the layout. Wagers may also be placed to predict a sequence of numbers. The best odds are given for predicting the number outright (straight up) and the odds diminish depending on the range of numbers in the sequence, line or block. Players are not normally limited in the number or range of bets they may place on the same 'spin' unless otherwise specified locally.
3.48 It is also possible to wager on whether the number will be red or black, odd or even, low or high (often called the 'outside / even chance bets'). Each of these consists of eighteen numbers and normally pays even money unless zero is spun whereby all of the even chance bets will be lost.
3.49 The usual odds paid are reproduced below:

Straight up (one specific number) aka *En Plein*	35 to 1
Split (one of two numbers) aka *Á Cheval*	17 to 1
Street (one of three specific numbers) aka *En Transversale*	11 to 1
Corner (one of four specific number) aka *En Carré*	8 to 1
First Four (one of numbers 0,1,2,3) aka *Quatre Premiers*	8 to 1
Six Line (one of six specific numbers) aka *Sixtain*	5 to 1
Column (one of 12 specific numbers in a row) *Sur une Colonne*	2 to 1
Dozen (one of 12 specific numbers) *Sur une Douzaine*	2 to 1
Red or Black (one of 18 specific numbers) *Rouge ou Noir*	1 to 1

3.50 The house edge on Crown Double Zero Roulette is 5.26%.

Double Action Roulette

3.51 It is at the discretion of the licence holder whether or not to offer the roulette variant Double Action Roulette. The proprietor of this roulette variant is TCS John Huxley and no variations may be put forward without their prior agreement.
3.52 Double Action Roulette is introduced by TCSJOHNHUXLEY and is played on their Mark VII Roulette Wheel. The game offers a unique variation to the traditional game of Roulette, delivering two winning numbers from a single spin. This is achieved using two sets of numbers (inner and outer rings) situated in opposing order on a single wheel, one spin marks two numbers.
3.53 The Double Action table layout consists of two identical betting areas. Each area accommodates bets for one of the two sets of numbers on the wheel. In addition, new areas including the Double Action Track are available for placing bets on double numbers occurring - paying up to 1200 to 1. The game demands no complicated rules.

THE WHEEL

3.54 The wheel is divided into two opposite spinning sets of numbers. Each wheel is evenly divided into 37 equal segments, numbered 1 to 36. Numbers are divided into red and black with the exception of 0, which is green.

3.55 The object of the game is to predict which numbered compartment the ball will fall into by placing a wager on the appropriate number on the layout or layouts. Wagers may also be placed

3.56 The usual odds paid are reproduced below:

1200 – 1	Ball lands within the same number on each wheel.
25 – 1	Dual Star bet. Both winning numbers are within 0 – 6 on each layout.
3 – 1 1 – 18/19 – 36	Both winning numbers to be within a certain criteria (ie bet black – both winning numbers must be black)
8 – 1	Dozens Columns – Both winning numbers to be in the same chosen column or dozen.
4 – 1	7 Star bet. Any number between 0 – 6 on the corresponding wheel/layout (ie outer wheel = outer layout)
2 – 1	Any twelve numbers (ie 7 – 18)
5 – 1	Any six numbers (ie 13 – 18)
8 – 1	Corner.Any four numbers (ie 1,2,7,8)
17 – 1	Split Any two numbers (5 + 11).
35 – 1	Any one number.
11 – 1	Any three numbers (ie 0,5,6)

3.57 House edge details are as follows:

Double Action™ (identical numbers)	12.27%
Dual star bet House Edge	6.94%
Outside chances House Edge	5.33%

Single outcomes:

Straight ups	2.7%
Single star bet House Edge	5.41%

4. BLACKJACK

THE TABLE LAYOUTS

4.1 Figures 4 and 5 show examples of the style of game layout that may be offered to players.

Figure 4

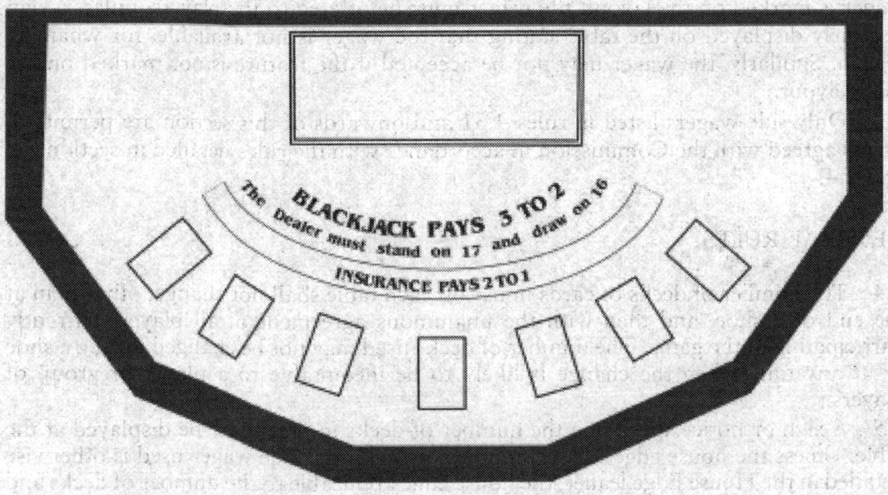

Figure 5

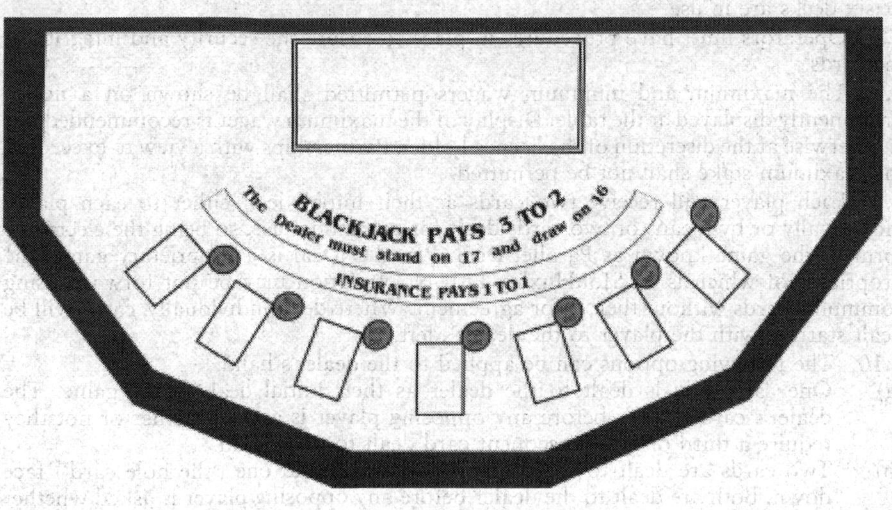

4.2 The layout must show any additional side wagers permitted by these rules, in cases where those wagers are made available on the table concerned. If an optional side wager is marked on the layout, the wager must be offered to the players, unless a sign is clearly displayed on the table stating that the wager is not available, for whatever reason. Similarly, the wager may not be accepted if the feature is not marked on the table layout.
4.3 Only side wagers listed in rules 4.31 and onwards of this section are permitted, unless agreed with the Commission in accordance with the rules detailed in section 2.3 and 2.4.

GENERAL RULES

4.4 The number of decks of cards in use on each table shall not change, other than at the end of a shoe, and then with the unanimous agreement of all players currently participating in the game. The number of decks used may not be changed during a shoe or at any time when the change is likely to be inequitable to a player or group of players.
4.5 A sign or notice specifying the number of decks in play must be displayed at the table. Unless the house edge for the number of decks and side wager used is otherwise detailed in the House Edge leaflet, the house edge applicable to the number of decks and side wager in play must be displayed on the sign or notice.
4.6 Certain side bets detailed in rules 4.31 onwards may **only** be offered where four or six decks are in use.
4.7 Operators must have procedures in place to ensure the security and integrity of the cards.
4.8 The maximum and minimum wagers permitted shall be shown on a notice prominently displayed at the table. Display of the maximum wager is recommended but is otherwise at the discretion of the licence holder. Partnerships with a view to exceeding the maximum stake shall not be permitted.
4.9 Each player will receive two cards as their initial deal, either to each player individually or by means of two cards dealt for communal use, so being the electronic form of the game known as Parallel Deal. Parrallel Deal is a proprietary game, the proprietor of which is TCSJohHuxley Ltd. No variation may be put forward using communal cards without their prior agreement. Where dealt individually, cards will be dealt starting with the player to the dealer's left.
4.10 The following options can be applied to the dealer's hand:
(a) One card only is dealt to the dealer as their initial deal in any game. The dealer's card is dealt before any opposing player is asked whether or not they require a third or any subsequent card dealt to their hand.
(b) Two cards are dealt to the dealer, one face up and one ('the hole card') face down. Both are dealt to the dealer before any opposing player is asked whether or not they require a third or subsequent card dealt to their hand.

Whichever option is used in a casino must be explained in the 'how to play' literature made readily available to all players.
4.11 The values of the cards dealt to any hand are as follows:
(a) the first Ace dealt to any one player in any game has the value of 11 unless that would give the player a score of more than 21 at the end of the game and, subject to that, any Ace has the value of 1;
(b) any card from 2 to 10 has its face value;
(c) any Jack, Queen or King has a value of ten; and
(d) any Ace together with a 10, Jack, Queen or King shall constitute a blackjack (ie a total card count of 21 with just two cards) but a blackjack cannot be obtained in any hand that is derived from splitting a pair, or pairs.

4.12 An opposing player is not required to take a third or any subsequent card if they do not wish to do so.

4.13 An opposing player who achieves a score of 21, either with a hand of two cards only (blackjack), or with a combination of additional cards, is not permitted to take any further cards.
4.14 Subject to rule 4.15, the dealer is required to draw further cards on their own hand when they have a score of 16 or less and is not permitted to take a further card once they have a score of 17 or more.
4.15 Where option b) is used in Rule 4.10, and the dealer's exposed card is an Ace or has a value of 10, customers dealt a score of 21 with their first two cards (a Blackjack) will be offered the insurance options detailed in Section 4.19 and 4.20.
4.17 Having done so, it is permitted for a secure device to be used that will allow the dealer to check the value of their hole card without it being exposed. If this shows that the hole card would make the dealer's hand a Blackjack, the dealer may reveal their full hand and immediately conclude the game before any further cards are dealt or decisions made. This is because all hands (other than player Blackjacks) will inevitably lose against the dealer's Blackjack.
4.18 Management may decide which of the following two options will apply to the dealer's hand:
(a) The first Ace dealt to the dealer in a game shall have a value of 11. If this gives a total of between 17 and 21 inclusive, the dealer must stand. For example, an Ace and 6 equals a score of 17. Alternatively, if this would give a score of more than 21 at the end of the game, and subject to that, an Ace shall have a value of 1;
(b) 'Soft 17' – an Ace dealt to a dealer's hand will count as 11, unless this gives a score of more than 21, or a total of 17, in which case it will count as one. Therefore, an Ace and 6 will equal 7, and not 17. If it gives a total of between 18 and 21 inclusive, the dealer must stand.

Where option b) is used, a notice must be displayed on the table clearly stating this fact.

WAGERS AND SETTLEMENT

4.19 Wagers on a participating player's hand shall be wagers that the hand will achieve a score not exceeding 21, and will win if either:
(a) the dealer's score exceeds 21; or
(b) the player achieves a higher score than the dealer using either the two cards initially dealt or those cards combined with any further cards subsequently drawn to the hand; or
(c) the player and the dealer both achieve a score of 21, but the player does so with a hand of two cards only, and the dealer does not.
4.20 The hand and wager shall be treated as void if the player and the dealer:
(a) both achieve the same score that is less than 21;
(b) both achieve a score of 21 with a hand of two cards only; or
(c) both achieve a score of 21 with more than two cards.
4.21 Subject to rules 2.3 and 2.4, a winning hand in accordance with rule 4.16 shall be paid minimum odds as follows:
(a) where the player achieves a winning score of 21 with a hand of two cards only (blackjack), the hand will be paid at **3 to 2**. However, where a single deck of cards is used, odds of 6 to 5 may be paid provided this is clearly displayed on the table concerned via a sign or notice.
(b) in any other case, the hand will be paid at **1 to 1**.

INSURANCE

4.22 When the dealer's first card is an Ace, any player with their first two cards may wager an amount equivalent to no more than half the amount staked on his initial wager that the dealer's second card will have a value of 10. Any wager which wins under this rule shall be payable at odds of **2 to 1**. All insurance wagers shall be made before a third card is dealt to any box (the subsequent deal).

4.23 Alternatively, when the dealer's first card is an Ace, any player who has a score of 21 with their first two cards (blackjack) may be offered the option of being paid at odds of 1 to 1 immediately. This has the same net effect as a winning wager of half the original stake winning at odds of 2 to 1, under rule 4.19.
4.24 During the subsequent deal, where the dealer's second card is not a 10, any insurance wagers under rule 4.19 which remain unsettled shall be lost, and should be collected by the dealer immediately after the drawing of that card.

'PLAYING BEHIND'

4.25 Decisions on the hand dealt to any particular playing position shall be made by the person seated at that position (the 'controlling player'), provided they have placed an initial wager on that position. Further players may place wagers on the same playing position ('playing behind'), but may not make decisions on the hand and must abide by the decisions made by the controlling player.
4.26 Wagers placed by people playing behind will win or lose in accordance with the outcome of the hand dealt to the controlling player in accordance with rules 4.16, 4.17 and 4.18.

DOUBLING DOWN

4.27 The player may double the amount of their initial stake, on the condition that they receive a third card and no more. Where the controlling player decides to double down in this way, players who are 'playing behind' on that hand may similarly double their wager, but the hand will receive only one more card, irrespective of whether they decide to do so. Management may decide which of the following options will apply:
(a) the double down option will only be offered where the player has a score of 9, 10 or 11; or
(b) the double down option will be offered when the player has any score.
Whichever option is used, the appropriate rule must be covered in any "How to Play" leaflets or material provided at the casino concerned.

SPLITTING PAIRS

4.28 Where the first two cards dealt to an opposing player's hand are cards of equal value (ie a pair), that player may elect to split the two cards into two separate hands. They must then make a further initial wager, equal to that already staked, on the second hand so formed. Management may decide which of the following options will apply:
(a) the option to split a pair will not apply when the player has a pair of 4s, 5s or 10s); or
(b) the option to split will apply to any pair.
Whichever option is used, the appropriate rule must be covered in any "How to Play" leaflets or material provided at the casino concerned.
4.29 The dealer will then deal a second card to each of the split cards which will be treated as separate hands. However, if the two cards being split are both Aces, the two cards being formed will only receive one further card each. Where electronic versions of the game are played, the first separate new hand may be completed before any further cards are dealt to the second separate hand (ie leaving the hand with only one card in the meantime). In such cases, the order in which cards are dealt to each of the split hands must be made clear to players via a notice or in the 'How to Play' literature.
4.30 A two-card total of 21 formed by a split hand in conformity with these rules will not constitute a blackjack, but will count as a score of 21 and be paid at odds of 1 to 1 if the hand wins.
4.31 The player will complete the first split hand before electing to draw cards to the second hand. If the cards dealt to a split hand result in a further pair of cards of equal value, the resulting pair may be split again and continue to be split if the resulting

hand(s) contain cards of the same value. Where electronic versions of the game are used, it is permitted to impose a restriction on the number of times a hand may be split due to the limitations of space on a video screen. In such cases, this restriction must be made clear to players via a notice or in the 'How to Play' literature.
4.32 Any person who is playing behind on the playing position, on which the controlling player has elected to split a pair, will also have the option of making a wager of an equal amount on the second hand. If they chose not to do so, they must identify on which of the two hands they wish their wager to be applied, either remaining on the original hand, or being transferred onto the second split hand if they prefer.
4.33 On a hand formed as a result of a split pair, players on that hand have the option of doubling their wager in accordance with rule 4.24.

PERMITTED VARIATIONS TO BLACKJACK

'21+3'

4.34 It is at the discretion of the licence holder whether or not to offer an additional feature called '21+3' as an additional wager within the standard game of blackjack. The proprietor of the side wager is Prime Table Games and no variations may be put forward without their prior agreement.
4.35 The feature shall only be available at a table or tables marked for the provision of the wager.
4.36 '21+3' is an optional wager that the first two cards dealt to the hand to which the wager relates will, when combined with the **first** card dealt to the dealer's hand, make a three card poker hand against the following list of winning hand:
Flush All three cards of the same suit (eg three Hearts, three Clubs etc).
Straight All three cards in sequence, but not of the same suit (eg 4 of Hearts, 5 of Diamonds and 6 of Clubs. Please note, this includes both Ace, 2, 3 and Queen, King and Ace).
Three of a Kind All three cards of the same rank (eg three 2s, three Queens etc).
Straight Flush All three cards in sequence **and** of the same suit (eg 4, 5 and 6 of Hearts. Please note, this includes both a sequence of Ace, 2 and 3 or of Queen, King and Ace).
Note: A Flush may include Three of a Kind within it, but this will count as only one winning hand.
4.37 If **any** of the hands given in section 4.33 is so formed, then any '21+3' winning wagers placed on the related hand will be paid odds at a minimum of **9 to 1**.
4.38 If none of the hands given in section 4.33 is so formed, then any '21+3' wagers placed on the related hand will lose.
4.39 The playing of a '21+3' wager shall not otherwise affect the manner in which a player may choose to play his hand in accordance with the practices and rules for blackjack given in this section.
4.40 A '21+3' wager may only be placed if the player has also placed a standard initial blackjack wager on the hand concerned.
4.41 All '21+3' wagers will be settled immediately after the initial deal, before any decisions are made, or further cards are dealt to the main blackjack game.

'Royal Match'

4.42 It is at the discretion of the licence holder whether or not to offer an additional feature called 'Royal Match' as an additional wager within a standard game of blackjack. The proprietor of the side wager is Shufflemaster Inc. and no variations may be put forward without their prior agreement.
4.43 The feature shall only be available at a table or tables marked for the provision of the wager. **The wager may only be offered where four or six decks are in use.**
4.44 'Royal Match' is a wager that the first two cards dealt to a hand to which the wager relates will both be of the same suit.

4.45 If both cards in a hand to which the wager relates are of the same suit, they will win and be paid, as a minimum, the range of odds shown below, depending on the value of the cards concerned:

Hand	**Minimum odds**
Royal Match – King and Queen of the same suit	30–1
Suited Pair – eg two 9s, 7s of the same suit	8–1
Straight Flush – two consecutive cards of the same suit	4–1
Two suited cards – any two cards of the same suit	3–2

Please note that the above table shows the minimum permitted odds that may be paid, drawn from the pay tables given in section 4.43. However, the full list of minimum odds is not, in itself, a well-balanced pay table and in fact carries a house edge of between 10.2% and 11.5% depending on the number of decks used. It is therefore recommended that they are only used as a guide and not as a pay table in themselves.

4.46 In addition to offering, as a minimum, the odds given in rule 4.42 above, odds may be presented as complete pay tables, in accordance with rule 2.9. Permitted pay tables are as follows:

Pay table 1

Royal Match	30–1
Suited Pair	9–1
Straight Flush	5–1
Two suited cards	3–2

Pay table 2

Royal Match	40–1
Suited Pair	8–1
Straight Flush	4–1
Two suited cards	3–2

4.47 If the first two cards dealt to a related hand are not of the same suit, then any related wagers placed on the Royal Match side wager for that hand will lose.

4.48 The playing of a Royal Match wager shall not otherwise affect the manner in which a player may choose to play his hand in accordance with the practices and rules for blackjack given in this section.

4.49 A Royal Match wager may only be placed if the player has also placed a standard initial blackjack wager on the hand concerned.

4.50 All Royal Match wagers will be settled immediately after the initial deal, before any decisions are made or further cards are dealt to the main blackjack game.

'Perfect Pairs'

4.51 It is at the discretion of the licence holder whether or not to offer an additional feature called 'Perfect Pairs' as an additional wager within a standard game of blackjack. The proprietor of the side wager is TCS John Huxley Ltd and no variations may be put forward without their prior agreement.

4.52 The feature shall only be available at a table or tables marked for the provision of the wager.

4.53 Perfect Pairs is a wager that the first two cards dealt to a hand to which the wager relates will be a pair of the same value.

4.54 If both cards dealt to a hand to which the wager relates are a pair of the same value (eg two 3s, two Queens etc) they will win and be paid, as a minimum, the range of odds shown below, depending on the suits and colours of the cards concerned:

Hand	**Minimum odds**
Mixed Pair – one red, one black	5–1
Coloured Pair – both red or black, but different suits	10–1
Perfect Pair – both of the same suit	25–1

Please note that the above table shows the minimum permitted odds that may be paid, drawn from the pay tables given in section 4.52. However, the full list of minimum odds is not, in itself, a well-balanced pay table and in fact carries a house edge of between 11.5% and 13.8%, depending on the number of decks used. It is therefore recommended that they are only used as a guide and not as a pay table in themselves.

4.55 In addition to offering, as a minimum, the odds given in rule 4.51 above, odds may be presented as complete pay tables, in accordance with rule 2.9. Permitted pay tables are as follows:

Pay table 1 (recommended by proprietor for four deck game)

Mixed Pair	5–1
Coloured Pair	12–1
Perfect Pair	30–1

Pay table 2 (recommended by proprietor for a six deck game)

Mixed Pair	5–1
Coloured Pair	10–1
Perfect Pair	30–1

Pay table 3 (recommended by proprietor for an eight deck game)

Mixed Pair	5 –1
Coloured Pair	12 –1
Perfect Pair	25 –1

4.56 If the first two cards dealt to a related hand are not a pair, then any related wagers placed on the Perfect Pairs side wager for that hand will lose.

4.57 The playing of a Perfect Pairs wager shall not otherwise affect the manner in which a player may choose to play his hand in accordance with the practices and rules for blackjack given in this section.

4.58 A Perfect Pairs wager may only be placed if the player has also placed a standard initial blackjack wager on the hand concerned.

4.59 All Perfect Pairs wagers will be dealt with immediately after the initial deal, before any decisions are made or further cards are dealt to the main blackjack game.

Blackjack Switch

4.60 It is at the discretion of the licence holder whether or not to offer a variation called 'Blackjack Switch' as an additional wager within the standard game of blackjack. The proprietor of the side wager is Customized Casino Games Ltd and no variations may be put forward without their prior agreement.

4.61 The feature shall only be made available at a table or tables marked for the provision of the wager. The wager may only be offered where six or eight decks are in use.

4.62 'Blackjack Switch' is an optional wager based on the player then receiving two initial hands rather than one, Having done so, the player is permitted to change over ('switch') the second card dealt on each hand in order to form two better hands.
4.63 The optional wager must be equal to the amount already staked.
4.64 All normal blackjack rules apply other than those stated in Section 4.62 and 4.63.
4.65 For any **winning** player hand on which a "Blackjack Switch" wager is in play, any player Blackjack obtained from the first two cards dealt to either hand is paid at odds of 1 to 1. However, if the player has switched their cards then the hand is instead deemed to have a score of 21 and not Blackjack.
4.66 A dealer total of 22 will be standoff against any player total of 21 or less. A player blackjack (a hand of two cards only which have not been switched) will still beat a dealer hand of 22.
Please note it is recommended that this version of Blackjack is dealt in conjunction with the 'Soft 17' option detailed in Rule 4.15 b).

Super Match side bet

4.67 It is at the discretion of the licence holder whether or not to offer an additional sidebet called 'Super Match' as an additional wager to Blackjack Switch. The proprietor of the side wager is Customized Casino Games Ltd
4.68 The feature shall only be available at a table or tables marked for the provision of both Blackjack Switch and the Super Match side wager. The wager may only be offered where six or eight decks are in use.
4.69 The 'Super Match' side wager is that the player's first four cards dealt to their two Switch hands contain of at least a pair, three cards matching, two pairs or all four cards matching. If the initial four cards dealt to the players two Switch hands forms one of these hands, the Super Match wager will win and be paid, as a minimum, the range of odds shown below.

Hand	Minimum odds
A single Pair (two cards of same denomination and suit)	1 - 1
Three of a kind (three cards of same denomination and suit)	3 – 1
Two Pairs (two single pairs)	5 – 1
Four of a kind (four cards of same denomination and suit)	25 – 1

Please note that the above table shows the minimum permitted odds that may be paid, drawn from the pay tables given in section 4.62. However, the full list of minimum odds is not, itself, a well-balanced pay table and in fact carries a house edge of 11.56% for six decks and 10.74% for eight decks. It is therefore recommended that it is only used as a guide and not as a pay table in themselves.
4.70 In addition to offering, as a minimum, the odds given in rule 4.61 above, odds may be presented as complete pay tables, in accordance with rule 2.9. Permitted pay tables are as follows:

Pay table 1 (recommended by proprietor for six decks)

A single Pair	1 - 1
Three of a Kind	5 – 1
Two Pairs	8 – 1
Four of a kind	40 – 1

Pay table 2 (recommended by proprietor for eight decks)

A single Pair	1 - 1
Three of a Kind	5 – 1
Two Pairs	7 – 1
Four of a kind	50 – 1

4.71 If the initial four cards dealt to the related do not contain one of the hands given in rule 4.67, then any Super Match side wager relating to those cards will lose and be surrendered to the house.
4.72 A 'Super Match' wager may only be placed if the player has also placed their 'Blackjack Switch' wagers on the hand concerned.
4.73 All 'Super Match' wagers will be settled immediately after the initial deal, before any decisions are made, or further cards are dealt to the main blackjack game.

NeverBust Blackjack

4.74 It is at the discretion of the licence holder whether or not to offer a variation of the game called NeverBust Blackjack. The proprietor of this version of the game is Customized Games Ltd and no variations to it may be put forward without their prior agreement.
4.75 The game is generally played in the same way as the standard game of Blackjack outlined in this section, with the following exceptions:
(i) Players may not split (see 3.23 to 3.28) or double down (see 3.22).
(ii) Each player's hand must be dealt to the same rules as the Dealer's hand (see 3.12), in that further a card must be drawn if the total is 16 or less and the hand must stand on a total of 17 or higher.
4.76 When either a player or the Dealer draws a card to their hand that will cause the total to exceed 21, the card concerned will be discarded and the hand will stand on whatever total was held before the card was dealt. For example, if the total was 14 and a 10 was drawn, the 10 will be discarded and the hand will stand on 14.
4.77 If the player's final total is higher than the Dealer's it will win and be paid even money.
4.78 If the Dealer's final total is higher than the Player's, the player's hand will lose and be collected by the house.
4.79 If the player's hand is a Blackjack, it will win and be paid odds of 3 to 2 unless the Dealer also has a Blackjack, in which case the hand will push and be declared a standoff.
4.80 If, after a card causing the Dealer's hand to exceed 21 has been discarded, the Dealer's final total is 15, then all player hands will be 'push' and be declared a stand off, regardless of whether they are higher or lower than the Dealer's total. The only exception is if the Player's hand is a Blackjack, in which case it will be paid 3 to 2 as normal.
4.81 Insurance wagers may be applied as in the normal game when the Dealer is showing an Ace, in accordance with rules 4.22 to 4.24.

5. THREE CARD POKER

THE TABLE LAYOUTS

5.1 Three Card Poker is a proprietary game licensed in the UK by the registered proprietor, Prime Table Games. Figure 6 shows a layout design approved by the registered owner, which must be offered to players in all formats of the game offered in the UK, unless otherwise agreed with the proprietor.

Figure 6

5.2 Only side bets listed in rules 5.24 and onwards in this section are permitted, unless agreed by both the Commission, in accordance with the rules detailed in section 2.3 and 2.4, and with the agreement of the proprietor.

GENERAL RULES

5.3 The game shall be played with a single deck of cards.
5.4 Operators must have procedures in place to ensure the security and integrity of the cards.
5.5 The maximum and minimum wagers permitted shall be shown on a notice prominently displayed at the table. Display of the maximum wager is recommended but is otherwise at the discretion of the licence holder. Partnerships with a view to exceeding the maximum stake shall not be permitted.
5.6 The payout odds for the Ante Bonus and Pair Plus shall be printed on the layout in accordance with a design approved by the registered owner or, where approved by the registered owner, shown on a sign or notice displayed at the table.
5.7 The relative value of each of the cards is as follows (in descending order): Ace, King, Queen, Jack, 10, 9, 8, 7, 6, 5, 4, 3, 2, except that the Ace may be used as a value of one in order to complete a Straight Flush or a Straight, as defined in rule 5.8 below (being 3, 2, Ace).
5.8 The terms used to describe the hands held by a participant in the game, and the ranking of hands from highest to lowest, are as follows:
(i) **Straight Flush** – three cards of consecutive values of the same suit;
(ii) **Three of a Kind** – three cards of the same value;
(iii) **Straight** – three cards of consecutive values not being a straight flush;
(iv) **Flush** – three cards of the same suit not being a straight flush;
(v) **Pair** – two cards of the same value; and
(vi) **High card** – the highest value single card.

INITIAL WAGER

5.9 Only one wager may be accepted on each playing position and no individual player may place a wager on more than one playing position.

5.10 An initial wager (comprising either, or both, of the wagers referred to in rule 5.11 i) and ii), below, as respectively an Ante wager and/or a Pair Plus wager) shall be made by each opposing player in the appropriate playing position, before any cards are dealt in the game.

5.11 Each opposing player may place either one, two or all three of the following wagers:

(i) A Pair Plus wager, being a wager that the player's hand will achieve a particular hand ranking, irrespective of the hand dealt to the dealer.

(ii) An Ante wager, being a wager that the player's hand will have a higher ranking than the dealer's hand.

(iii) A 'Prime' wager, being a wager that all three cards in the player's hand will be of the same colour, and may also be of the same colour as the three cards dealt to the dealer's hand.

5.12 Each player and the dealer will be dealt three cards face down starting with the player to the dealer's left.

SUBSEQUENT DEAL

5.13 An opposing player, who has made an Ante wager and who wishes to continue with that wager after the cards are dealt, shall make a further wager (referred to in these rules as a 'Play' wager) which must be of an equal amount to his Ante wager. They will place their cards in the 'Play' area with the wager on top.

5.14 An opposing player who has made an Ante wager but who does not make a subsequent 'Play' wager shall surrender the amount staked on the Ante wager to the bank.

5.15 A player who has **only** placed a Pair Plus wager (without also placing an Ante bet) will place their cards in the 'Play' area (this time without a wager on top) if their hand contains at least a pair.

5.16 The dealer's hand must have a value of 'Queen high' or better to qualify to play against the player's hands.

(a) If the dealer **does not** have a qualifying hand:
- (i) all 'play' bets are declared void and returned to the players;
- (ii) Ante bonuses are paid on all Straights or better;
- (iii) all Ante bets are won by the players and paid at the rate of **1 to 1**; and
- (iv) all Pair Plus wagers are paid or taken.

(b) If the dealer **does** have a qualifying hand:
- (i) the 'play' wagers are paid or taken;
- (ii) Ante bonuses are paid on all Straights or better;
- (iii) Ante bets are paid or taken; and
- (iv) Pair Plus wagers are paid or taken.

5.17 If after ranking the cards, the first two cards in the dealer's hand tie with a player's hand, the third card will determine the winner. A tied hand is a stand-off on the 'Play' and on the 'Ante'. However, the Ante Bonus and the Pair Plus wagers are always paid, where applicable.

5.18 If a player's hand beats the dealer's qualifying hand, the player wins on their Ante and Play wagers, both of which are paid at **1 to 1**.

5.19 If the dealer's hand has a higher poker ranking than the player's hand, in accordance with rule 5.8, the player loses both their Ante and Play wagers.

5.20 An opposing player who has made an Ante wager and a Play wager shall be paid an Ante Bonus, payable in respect of his Ante wager only and at the minimum odds set out in this rule, if, upon his hand being revealed, his hand consists of one of the following hands, as defined in rule 5.8:

(a) **Straight** – player will be paid at minimum odds of **1 to 1**

(b) **Three of a Kind** – player will be paid at minimum odds of **4 to1**

(c) **Straight Flush** – player will be paid at minimum odds of **5 to 1**

5.21 If both an opposing player's hand and the dealer's hand are of exactly equal ranking, the Ante and Play wagers on that hand shall be void.

5.22 The wager of an opposing player who has made a Pair Plus wager shall win and be paid at the following minimum odds if, upon his hand being revealed, it consists of one of the following rankings:
(a) **Pair** – player will be paid odds of **1 to 1**
(b) **Flush** – player will be paid odds of **4 to 1**
(c) **Straight** – player will be paid odds of **6 to 1**
(d) **Three of a Kind** – player will be paid odds of **33 to 1**
(e) **Straight Flush** – player will be paid at odds of **35 to 1**
5.23 The wager of an opposing player who has made a Pair Plus wager shall lose and the amount staked be surrendered to the bank if, upon his hand being revealed, his hand does not contain at least a Pair.

PERMITTED VARIATIONS TO THREE CARD POKER

Prime

5.24 It is at the discretion of the licence whether or not to offer an additional feature called 'Prime' as an additional wager within the standard game of Blackjack. The proprietor of the side wager is that of Three Card Poker itself, Prime Table Games.
5.25 The feature shall only be available at a table or tables marked for the provision of the wager.
5.26 'Prime' is an optional wager that either the three cards dealt to the hand to which the wager relates will be all of the same colour or, in addition, that all three cards in the Dealer's hand are also of the same colour to those in the Player's hand.
5.27 If the player's three cards are all of the same colour (ie all black or all red), but the Dealer's three cards are of a different, or mixed, colours, then any 'Prime' wager placed on the related hand will be paid minimum odds of 3 to 1.
5.28 If the player's three cards are all of the same colour (ie all black or all red) and all three of the Dealer's three cards are also of that same colour, then any 'Prime' wager placed on the related hand will be paid minimum odds of 4 to 1
5.29 If the player's three cards are of mixed colours (ie one is of a different colour to the other two), then any 'Prime' wager placed on the related hand will lose and be surrendered to the house.
5.30 If the Dealer's three cards are of the same colour as each other, but the Player's cards are of mixed colours, then any 'Prime' wager placed on the related hand will lose and be surrendered to the house.

6. PUNTO BANCO

THE TABLE LAYOUTS

6.1 Figures 7 and 8 show examples of the style of game layouts that may be offered to players. They also illustrate the full range of wagers available, and the position at which such wagers must be placed using the example playing positions.

Figure 7: Full Size Punto

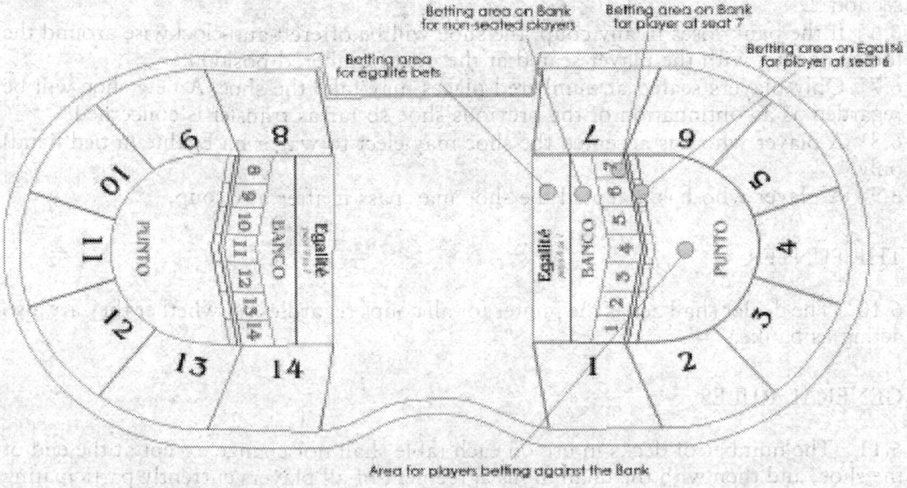

Figure 8: Mini Punto with Dragon Bonus side wager

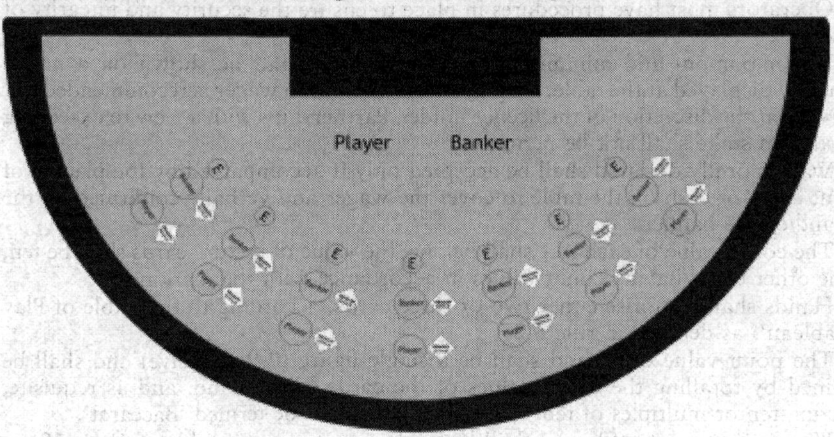

Only side wagers or variations listed in rules 6.28 and onwards in this section are permitted.

THE BANKER

6.2 There are two different methods of determining who is to fulfil the role of 'banker' within the context of the game, as follows:
(a) The dealer will at all times draw the cards and act as banker; or
(b) The shoe will be offered in turn to each player seated at the table, who will accept or refuse to take on the role of banker.

6.3 If the dealer is to act as banker, they will at all times retain the shoe and deal the cards into predetermined positions on the table in front of them.

6.4 If the players are to act in turn as banker, the shoe will be offered anti-clockwise around the table to the seated players, starting at the commencement of play with the player in seat 1.

6.5 A player accepting the shoe shall act as banker **ONLY** for the purposes of dealing the cards, and will not hold or control the bank itself, in accordance with rule 2.5 of section 2.
6.6 If the bank loses in any coup, the shoe will be offered anti-clockwise around the table, starting with the player seated at the next numbered position.
6.7 Only players seated at numbered places may take the shoe. A new shoe will be regarded as a continuation of the previous shoe so far as transfer is concerned.
6.8 A player who has accepted the shoe may elect to wager on Egalité (a tied hand) only.
6.9 A player who has accepted the shoe may pass it after any coup.

THE PUNTER

6.10 The dealer shall act as the punter for all coups regardless of whether they are also acting as banker.

GENERAL RULES

6.11 The number of decks in use on each table shall not change except at the end of the shoe, and then with the unanimous agreement of all players currently participating in the game. The number of decks used may not be changed during a shoe or at any time when the change is likely to be inequitable to a player or group of players.
6.12 Operators must have procedures in place to ensure the security and integrity of the cards.
6.13 The maximum and minimum wagers permitted shall be shown on a notice prominently displayed at the table. Display of the maximum wager is recommended but is otherwise at the discretion of the licence holder. Partnerships with a view to exceeding the maximum stake shall not be permitted.
6.14 Wagers orally declared shall be accepted only if accompanied by the placing of sufficient chips or cash on the table to cover the wager and verbally confirmed by the dealer and/or the banker.
6.15 The count value of each Ace shall be one, the value of picture cards shall be ten, with the other cards having count values in accordance with the markings.
6.16 Hands shall comprise either two or three cards, according to the Table of Play (the 'Tableau') as detailed in rule 6.27.
6.17 The point value of a hand shall be a single figure (0-9 inclusive) and shall be determined by totalling the count values of the cards in the hand, and as requisite, subtracting ten or multiples of ten. A point of zero shall be termed 'Baccarat'.
6.18 Winning wagers on 'Banco' shall be paid, as a minimum, odds of **19 to 20.**
6.19 Winning wagers on 'Punto' shall be paid, as a minimum, odds of **1 to 1.**
6.20 Winning wagers on Egalité shall be paid, as a minimum, odds of **8 to 1.**

THE INITIAL DEAL

6.21 For each coup the banker shall initially deal four cards in the sequence punter, banker, punter, banker.

THE PLAY

6.22 After the initial deal, the value of the punter's hand will be determined and, depending on the point value, the punter will proceed as follows:

Point value	**Action**
'Baccarat', 1, 2, 3, 4 or 5	Punter takes an additional card face upwards

Point value	**Action**
6 or 7	Punter stands
8 or 9	Punter stands

6.23 If either the punter or banker has a point of 8 or 9, the banker will deal no more cards for that coup.

6.24 If neither the punter nor the banker has a point of 8 or 9 on the Initial Deal, the banker shall, in accordance with the Table of Play in rule 6.27, either draw a card for his hand, or stand, as required.

6.25 The order of merit of hands at the conclusion shall be:

(1) A two card point of nine
(2) A two card point of eight
(3) A three card point of nine
(4) A three card point of eight
(5) A two card or three card point of seven
(6) A two card or three card point of six
(7) A two card or three card point of five
(8) A two card or three card point of four
(9) A two card or three card point of three
(10) A two card or three card point of two
(11) A two card or three card point of one
(12) 'Baccarat' (zero)

6.26 If the two hands are of equal merit, the wagers on punter and banker shall be void and the wagers on 'Egalité' shall win and be paid, at a minimum, odds of **8 to 1**.

6.27 Cards will be drawn strictly in accordance the Table of Play shown below.

		Punter given										
		0	1	2	3	4	5	6	7	8	9	No card
Banker's point	3	D	D	D	D	D	D	D	D	S	D	D
	4	S	S	D	D	D	D	D	D	S	S	D
	5	S	S	S	S	D	D	D	D	S	S	D
	6	S	S	S	S	S	S	D	D	S	S	S

D = Draw S = Stand

Banker:	Punter:
0, 1 or 2 – draws	0, 1, 2, 3, 4 or 5 – draws
3, 4, 5 or 6 – (see above)	6 or 7 – stands
7 – stands	8 or 9 – no further draw
8 or 9 – no further draw	

PERMITTED VARIATIONS TO PUNTO BANCO

Punto Banco 2000

6.28 The variation to the game known as Punto 2000 is played exactly as the standard game of Punto Banco, as detailed in this section, except that the minimum payment odds for any winning wagers on the banker (as given in rule 6.18) will not apply.

6.29 Instead, winning wagers on the banker shall be paid at a minimum, odds of **1 to 1**, other than circumstances where the banker wins with a card total of 6. In that case, the winning wager shall be paid at a minimum, odds of **1 to 2**.

6.30 Wagers may not be accepted for Punto 2000 during a game for which wagers on the standard game of Punto Banco, referred to in this document, are also accepted.

'Dragon Bonus' side wager

6.31 It is at the discretion of the licence holder whether or not to offer the 'Dragon Bonus' side wager as an additional, optional wager in the standard game of Punto Banco or Punto Banco 2000. The proprietor of the side wager is Shufflemaster Inc and no variations may be put forward without their prior agreement.
6.32 The feature shall only be available at a table or tables marked for the provision of the wager, hereafter called the 'Dragon Bonus' side wager.
6.33 Players do not need to place a standard wager on either the player, the banker or Egalité, in order to place a Dragon Bonus side wager.
6.34 Players may wager any amount within the table limits as their Dragon Bonus side wager, which must be wagered before any cards are dealt.
6.35 The player may place a Dragon Bonus side wager on either the player's hand or the dealer's hand, hereafter referred to as the 'selected hand', but not on both. To do so, they will place the wager in one of the dedicated betting positions in front of them, either alongside the player wager or the banker wager respectively.
6.36 After all standard wagers and Dragon Bonus wagers have been placed, a standard game of Punto Banco or Punto 2000 will take place, in accordance with the procedures in this section.
6.37 The dealer will reconcile the player's standard wager, where applicable, before dealing with any Dragon Bonus side wager on that playing position.
6.38 Players have two ways to win the Dragon Bonus side wager depending on whether the selected hand is a 'natural' winner (being a score of eight or nine with the first two cards dealt to that hand) or a 'non-natural' winner (being any winning score after a third card has been dealt to that hand) in accordance with the Table of Play given in rule 6.27.
6.39 If their selected hand is a natural winner, the Dragon Bonus side wager will win and be paid, as a minimum, odds of **1 to 1 (even money)**.
6.40 If the selected hand is a natural winner, but ties, then the Dragon Bonus side wager will be a stand off and the wager will be returned to the player.
6.41 If the selected hand for the Dragon Bonus wager is a 'non-natural' winning score, and wins by four clear points, the Dragon Bonus side wager will win and be paid, as a minimum, at the following odds:

Winning margin of non-natural winner	Minimum odds payable
Win by 9 points	20–1
Win by 8 points	8–1
Win by 7 points	4–1
Win by 6 points	4–1
Win by 5 points	2–1
Win by 4 points	1–1

Please note that the above table shows the minimum permitted odds that may be paid, drawn from the pay tables given in section 6.42. However, the full list of minimum odds is not, in itself, a well-balanced pay table and in fact carries a house edge of between 11.2% and 16.7%, depending on whether six or eight decks are used. It is therefore recommended that they are only used as a guide and not as a pay table in themselves.
6.42 In addition to offering, as a minimum, the odds given in rule 6.41 above, odds for non-natural winners may be presented as complete pay tables, in accordance with rule 2.9 given in section 2. Permitted pay tables are as follows:

Pay table 1

Win by 9 points	30–1
Win by 8 points	10–1
Win by 7 points	6–1
Win by 6 points	4–1
Win by 5 points	2–1
Win by 4 points	1–1

Pay table 2

Win by 9 points	20–1
Win by 8 points	8–1
Win by 7 points	7–1
Win by 6 points	4–1
Win by 5 points	3–1
Win by 4 points	1–1

Pay table 3

Win by 9 points	30–1
Win by 8 points	10–1
Win by 6-7 points	4–1
Win by 4-5 points	2–1

6.43 If the selected hand is a non-natural winner, with any score, but does not win by a clear four points, the Dragon Bonus side wager will lose and be surrendered to the house.
6.44 If the selected hand does not win, the Dragon Bonus side wager will lose and will be surrendered to the house.

'UR Way Egalité' Side Wager

6.45 It is at the discretion of the licence holder whether or not to offer the 'UR Way Egalité' side wager within the game Punto Banco. The proprietor of the side wager is TCS John Huxley Ltd and no variations may be put forward without their prior agreement or that of a subsequent proprietor.
6.46 The feature shall only be available at a table or tables marked for the provision of the wager, hereafter called the UR Way Egalité side wager.
6.47 It is at the discretion of the licence holder whether players need to also place a standard wager on the player or the banker, in order to place a 'UR Way Egalité' side wager. Whichever option is used at a particular club must be clearly displayed to players on either a sign or notice at the table or detailed within "how to play" leaflets or literature.
6.48 Players may wager any amount within the table limits as their UR Way Egalité' side wager, which must be wagered before any cards are dealt.
6.49 After all standard wagers and UR Way Egalité wagers have been placed a standard game of Punto Banco, Punto 2000 or EZ baccarat will take place, in accordance with the procedures in this section.
6.50 Players can select to place one or more wagers on the individual tied hands (Egalité) offered.
If the individual Egalité is drawn, the UR Way Egalité wager for that score will win and be paid, as a minimum, at the following minimum odds:

Winning Individual Egalité	Minimum odds payable
0	140 - 1
1	200 - 1
2	200 - 1
3	180 - 1
4	110 - 1
5	100 - 1
6	40 - 1
7	40 - 1
8	70 - 1
9	70 – 1

NB the above table shows the minimum permitted odds that may be paid for each Egalité, drawn from the Pay Tables given in Section 5.11. However, the full list of minimum odds is not, in itself, a well balance Pay Table and in fact carries a House Edge of 19.9%. It is therefore recommended that the minimum odds only be used as a guide and not as a Pay Table in themselves.

6.51 In addition to offering, as a minimum, the odds given in rule 5.10 above, odds for individual Egalités may be presented as complete pay tables, in accordance with rule 2.9 given in section 2. Permitted pay tables are as follows:

Pay table 1

0	150 - 1
1	215 - 1
2	225 - 1
3	200 - 1
4	120 - 1
5	110 - 1
6	45 - 1
7	45 - 1
8	80 - 1
9	80 – 1

This gives an overall House Edge of 11.7%

Pay table 2

0	150 - 1
1	200 - 1
2	210 - 1
3	190 - 1
4	120 - 1
5	110 - 1
6	45 - 1
7	45 - 1
8	80 - 1
9	80 – 1

This gives an overall House Edge of 14.4%

Pay table 3

0	140 - 1

1	200 - 1
2	210 - 1
3	190 - 1
4	110 - 1
5	100 - 1
6	40 - 1
7	40 - 1
8	75 - 1
9	75 - 1

This gives an overall House Edge of 17.9%

6.52 If the selected individual Egalité hand does not win, the UR Way Egalité side wager will lose and be surrendered to the house.

'Three Giving Eight (3g8)' side wager

6.53 It is at the discretion of the licence holder whether or not to offer the 'Three Giving Eight' side wager with the game Punto Banco. The proprietor of the side wager is CPE 18 Table Games Ltd and no variations may be put forward without their prior agreement.

6.54 The feature shall only be available at a table or tables marked for the provision of the wager, hereafter called the side wager.

6.55 It is at the discretion of the licence holder whether players do or do not need to place a standard wager on the player or the banker, in order to place a 'cpe18 table games Ltd' side wager.

6.56 3g8 is an optional wager that if the Banker's hand has 3 points with only two cards and the player's hand is entitled to receive another card that card being the third card to the players hand will win if it is an 8 (eight).

6.57 If the player has placed a 3g8 wager and in accordance with rule 6.63, then the wager placed on the designated betting position will be paid at minimum odds of **180 to 1.**

6.58 In addition, the 3g8 can also be offered as optional wager that if the Banker's hand has 3 points with only two cards and the player's hand is entitled to receive another card that card being the third card to the players hand will win.

6.59 If the player has placed a 3g8 wager and in accordance with rule 6.65, then the wager placed on the designated betting position shall win and be paid at minimum odds if:

Banker having 3 points and the player drawing an 8	100 to 1
Banker having 3 points and the player drawing any Card except an 8	6 to 1

6.60 After all standard wagers and 3g8 wagers have been placed; a standard game of Punto Banco, Punto 2000 or EZ baccarat will take place, in accordance with the rules in this section.

6.61 It is at the discretion of the Licence holder whether or not to offer one or both of the side wagers provided.

6.62 Players can select to place one or more wagers on the 3g8 wagers if offered.

6.63 If the selected hand does not win, the 3g8 side wager(s) will lose and be surrendered to the house.

Super Pay Egalité side wager

6.64 It is at the discretion of the licence holder whether or not to offer the Super Pay Egalité side wager as an additional, optional wager in the standard game of Punto Banco or Punto Banco 2000. The proprietor of the side wager is Grosvenor Casinos and no variations may be put forward without their prior agreement.

6.65 The feature shall only be available at a table, or tables, marked for the provision of the wager, hereafter called the Super Pay Egalité side wager.

6.66 Players do not need to place a standard wager on either the Player, the Banker or Egalité, in order to place a Super Pay Egalité side wager. They may place wagers on more than one Super Pay Egalité betting position if they wish to do so.

6.67 Players may wager any amount within the table limits as their Super Play Egalité Side wager, which must be wagered before any cards are dealt.

6.68 The wager is that the two hands will be of an equal score, (ie an Egalité) but will be in a range of specific scores. The wager will win if any of the specific scores in the selected range is the outcome of the tied hand, and will then be paid at the following minimum odds:

Tied hand score	*Minimum odds paid*
Zero	160-1
Either, 1, 2 or 3	70-1
Either 4 or 5	60-1
Either 6 or 7	22-1
Either 8 or 9	40-1

6.69 After all standard wagers, Egalité and Super Pay Egalité wagers have been placed, a standard game of Punto Banco or Punto 2000 will take place, in accordance with the procedures in this Section.

6.70 If the score is not an Egalité, all wagers on Super Pay Egalité will lose and be surrendered to the bank

6.71 If the score is an Egalité, all Super Pay Egalité on the specific range of numbers that includes the winning score will win, and be paid odds in accordance with section 1.05, above. All Super Pay Egalité wagers on a range of numbers that does not include the winning score will lose and be surrendered to the bank.

House Edge

6.72 The house edge information relating to the various Super Pay Egalité wagers are as follows:

Tied hand score	*Minimum odds paid*	*House Edge*
Zero	160-1	6.65%
Either, 1, 2 or 3	70-1	10.86%
Either 4 or 5	60-1	7.28%
Either 6 or 7	22-1	8.94%
Either 8 or 9	40-1	9.75%

BACCARAT PAIRS SIDE WAGER

TABLE LAYOUT

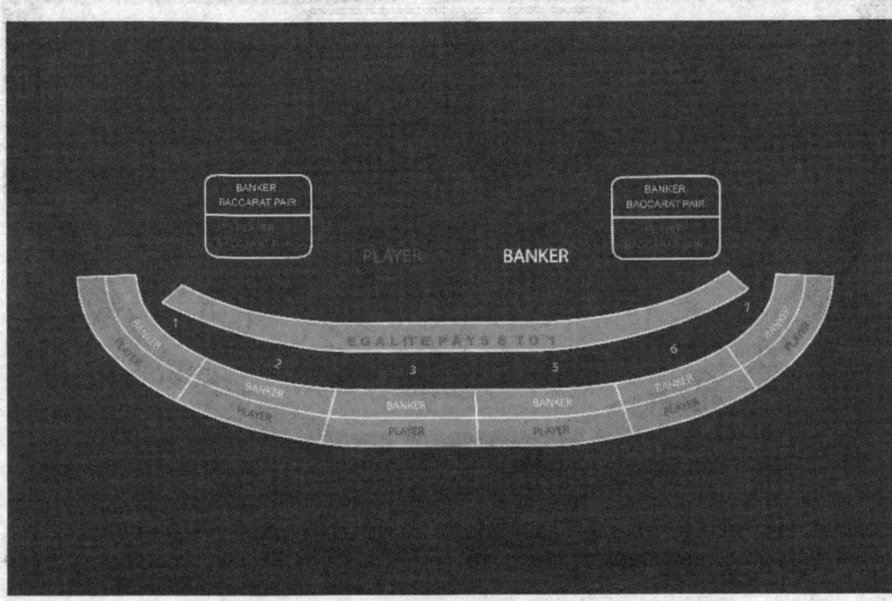

6.72 It is at the discretion of the licence holder whether or not to offer the 'Baccarat Pairs' side wager as an additional, optional wager in the standard game of Punto Banco or Punto Banco 2000.

6.73 The feature shall only be available at a table or tables marked for the provision of the wager, hereafter called the 'Baccarat Pairs' side wager.

6.74 Players do not need to place a standard wager on either the player, the banker or Egalité, in order to place a Baccarat Pairs side wager.

6.75 Players may wager any amount within the table limits as their Baccarat Pairs side wager, which must be wagered before any cards are dealt.

6.76 The player may place a Baccarat Pairs side wager on either the player's hand or the dealer's hand or on both. To do so, they will place the wager in one of the dedicated Baccarat Pairs betting positions so marked on the table, either alongside the player wager or the banker wager respectively.

6.77 After all standard wagers and Baccarat Pairs wagers have been placed, a standard game of Punto Banco or Punto 2000 will take place, in accordance with the procedures in this section.

6.78 Players win if the first two cards dealt to the Player or the Banker (as nominated by the player) constitute a pair (for example 10, 10 or K, K) and lose on all other outcomes in accordance with the Table of Play given in rule 6.27.

6.79 All winning Baccarat Pairs wagers will be paid, as a minimum, odds of **11 to 1**.

7. CASINO STUD POKER

THE TABLE LAYOUT

7.1 Figure 9 shows an example of the style of game layouts that may be offered to players. It also illustrates the full range of wagers available, including the optional Progressive and Bonus Insurance wagers, and the position at which such wagers must be placed on the layout.

Figure 9

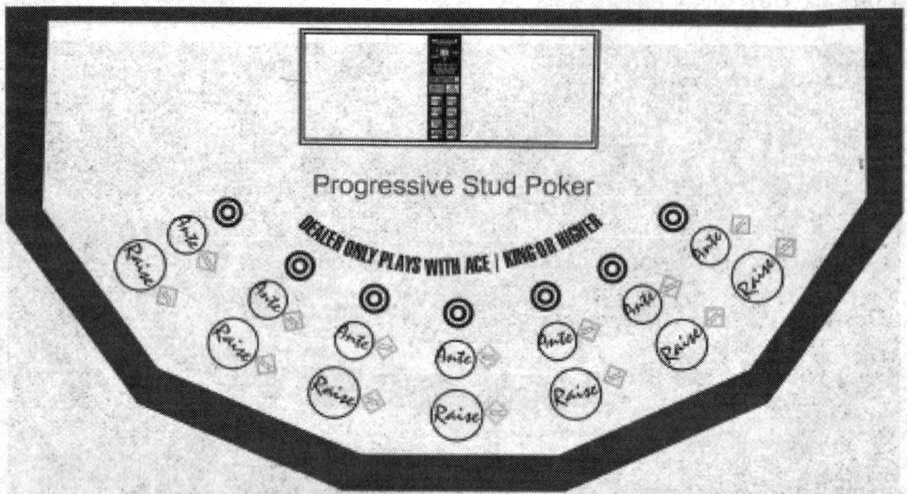

7.2 Other than the Progressive wager detailed in rules 7.16 to 7.21, only side wagers or variations listed in rules 7.22 and onwards of this section are permitted, unless agreed with the Commission in accordance with the rules detailed in section 2.3 and 2.4.

GENERAL RULES

7.3 Casino Stud Poker shall be played with a single pack of 52 cards.
7.4 Operators must have procedures in place to ensure the security and integrity of the cards.
7.5 The maximum and minimum wagers permitted shall be shown on a notice prominently displayed at the table. Display of the maximum wager is recommended but is otherwise at the discretion of the licence holder. Partnerships with a view to exceeding the maximum stake shall not be permitted.
7.6 The relative value of each of the cards is as follows (in descending order): Ace, King, Queen, Jack, 10, 9, 8, 7, 6, 5, 4, 3, and 2, except that the Ace may be used as a value of one in order to complete a Straight Flush or a Straight, as defined in rule 6.7 below (being 3, 2, Ace).
7.7 The terms used to describe the five cards held by a participant in the game of Casino Stud Poker shall be in accordance with the following meanings and hand rankings:
(a) **Royal Flush** – Ace, King, Queen, Jack and 10 of the same suit
(b) **Straight Flush** – five cards of consecutive values of the same suit
(c) **Four of a Kind** – four cards of the same value
(d) **Full House** – three cards of the same value together with two cards of the same value being different to the first value
(e) **Flush** – five cards of the same suit
(f) **Straight** – five cards of consecutive values not being a Royal Flush or a Straight Flush
(g) **Three of a Kind** – three cards of the same value
(h) **Two pairs** – two cards of the same value together with two cards of the same value being different to the first value
(i) **One pair** – two cards of the same value
(j) **No pair** – the highest value cards of the hand

INITIAL WAGER

7.8 Only one wager may be accepted on each playing position, and no individual player may place a wager on more than one playing position.
7.9 Any initial wager will be made by an opposing player against the dealer. The initial wager, hereafter referred to as the Ante, shall be made before any cards are dealt in the game, and shall be placed in the designated betting area.
7.10 Each opposing player and the dealer shall be dealt five cards, starting from the player to the dealer's left. All cards will be dealt face down with the exception of the dealer's fifth card, which shall be dealt face up.
7.11 It is the player's own responsibility to establish the value of their hand.
7.12 After looking at their cards, players who wish to continue in the game shall then make a second wager called the 'Raise' which must be exactly twice the original Ante wager. Those players not making the additional wager will surrender the amount staked on the Ante to the bank.
7.13 The remaining wagers will win if, on revealing the dealer's hand:
(a) The dealer does not have a hand containing Ace/King or better, in which case the hand will be complete and the Ante wager will only win, at a minimum, odds of **1 to 1**; and
(b) The dealer does have a hand containing Ace/King or better and the player has a hand which outranks it. The player's Ante wager will win, at a minimum, odds of **1 to 1**, and the Raise wager will win and be paid in accordance with the following minimum odds:
(i) Straight Flush – minimum odds payable 50 to 1
(ii) Four of a Kind – minimum odds payable 20 to 1
(iii) Full House – minimum odds payable 8 to 1
(iv) Flush – minimum odds payable 6 to 1
(v) Straight – minimum odds payable 4 to 1
(vi) Three of a Kind – minimum odds payable 3 to 1
(vii) Two pairs – minimum odds payable 2 to 1
(viii) One pair or less – minimum odds payable 1 to 1

A sign or notice will be displayed at the table showing the bonus odds payable for the above hands.
7.14 A player's hand that is outranked by the dealer's hand will lose both their Ante and Raise wagers.
7.15 Wagers will be void if the player's hand is of exactly equal ranking to the dealer's hand.

PROGRESSIVE WAGER

7.16 At the licence holder's discretion, a casino may introduce an additional feature into the game, namely a Progressive Jackpot wager. The general rules detailed in 2.7 of section 2 will apply.
7.17 A Progressive Jackpot wager shall be an optional wager that an opposing player may place at the same time as he places an Ante wager.
7.18 A Progressive Jackpot wager may not be placed unless an Ante wager has also been placed at the same time.
7.19 A Progressive Jackpot wager shall be placed in a designated slot, spot or dedicated area, set into or otherwise made available at each playing position.
7.20 A Progressive wager is a wager that the player will receive one of a specific set of hands, as per rule 7.21. If such a hand is dealt, the player will win regardless of whether the hand also beat the dealer, or whether the dealer receives Ace/King or better.
7.21 If upon the hand being revealed, an opposing player who has placed a Progressive Jackpot wager has a hand containing one of the following rankings, the player's Progressive Jackpot wager shall win, and be paid from the Progressive Jackpot Meter, the following minimum amounts:

(a) Royal Flush (**100% of the Progressive Jackpot Meter**)
(b) Straight Flush (**10% of the Progressive Jackpot Meter**)
(c) Four of a Kind (**100 times the value of the wager**)
(d) Full House (**75 times the value of the wager**)
(e) Flush (**50 times the value of the wager**)

PERMITTED VARIATIONS TO CASINO STUD POKER

Casino stud bonus insurance

7.22 It is at the discretion of the licence holder whether or not to offer Casino Stud Bonus Insurance (CSBI) as an additional, optional feature in the standard game of Casino Stud Poker. The proprietor of the CSBI side feature is Prime Table Games and no variations may be put forward without their prior agreement.
7.23 The feature shall only be available at a table or tables marked for the provision of the CSBI wagers, hereafter called the Insurance wager and Double wager.
7.24 A player may not place an Insurance wager unless they have also placed a standard initial Ante wager.
7.25 Players may wager any amount within the table limits as their Insurance wager, which must be wagered before any cards are dealt.
7.26 The dealer will conduct the initial deal and reveal the final card dealt to their own five-card hand, face up, in accordance with rule 7.10. This card is hereafter referred to as the 'dealer's up card'.
7.27 If the dealer's up card has a value of **two, three, four or five,** any player with an Insurance wager is then offered the opportunity to 'double'. They may then place a Double wager of an equal amount to their Insurance wager. If they do not wish to place a Double wager, the player may decline the opportunity and elect to stay with the original Insurance wager.
7.28 If the dealer's up card has a value **other than** two, three, four or five, all Insurance wagers will remain in place without the option to double.
7.29 Once all players have made their decisions to raise or fold and, where applicable, place a Double wager (in accordance with rules 7.27 and 7.28) the dealer will address the Ante wagers from each player who has elected to fold.
7.30 If a player who has elected to fold **does not** have any CSBI wagers (Insurance or Double), their Ante wager will lose and be surrendered to the bank. Their cards will then be collected by the dealer.
7.31 If a player who has elected to fold **does** have any CSBI wagers, their Ante wager will lose and be surrendered to the bank, **but their CSBI wager(s) and folded hand will remain in action.** The dealer must cover the player's Ante betting position with their cards face down to indicate that their CSBI wager(s) remain in action.

Dealer's qualifying hand

7.32 If the dealer has a qualifying hand of Ace/King or better at the end of the game, standard Ante and Raise wagers will be settled in accordance with rule 7.13(b), but all CSBI wagers will lose and be surrendered to the bank.

Dealer's non-qualifying hand

7.33 If the dealer **does not** have a qualifying hand of Ace/King or better at the end of the game, standard Ante and Raise wagers will be settled in accordance with rule 7.13(a). However, the player's Insurance wager and, where applicable, Double wager, will be paid according to the following minimum odds:
Royal Flush 100–1
Straight Flush 50–1
Four of a Kind 20–1
Full House 8–1

Flush 6–1

7.34 If a player has a hand with a ranking of a **Flush or higher**, in accordance with the card rankings given in rule 7.7, the minimum odds paid out to the Insurance wager and Double wager, where applicable, will be based on the value of the **player's own hand** ranking.

7.35 If the player has a hand ranking of **less than a Flush**, the minimum odds paid out to the Insurance wager and Double wager will be based on the value of the **dealer's** hand ranking in accordance with the following minimum odds:

Dealer hand	**Player with less than a Flush paid:**
7 High	5–1
8 High	4–1
9 or 10 High	2–1
Less than an Ace/King	1–1 (even money)

The player will only be paid one set of odds. For example, if the player has Four of a Kind and the dealer has 9-High, the player will be paid 20–1. However, they will not be paid both.

Mississippi Stud (Texas Hold Em Poker Variation)

TABLE LAYOUT

7.36 The diagram below shows an example of the style of game layout that may be offered to players. The proprietor of the game is Shufflemaster Inc and no variation to the game may be put forward without their prior agreement.

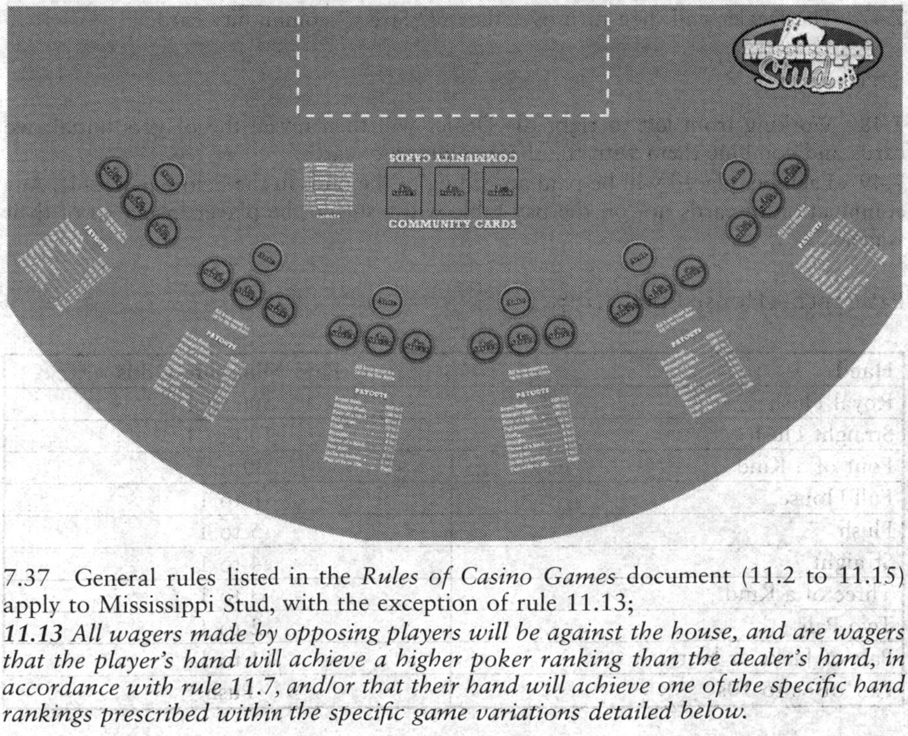

7.37 General rules listed in the *Rules of Casino Games* document (11.2 to 11.15) apply to Mississippi Stud, with the exception of rule 11.13;

***11.13** All wagers made by opposing players will be against the house, and are wagers that the player's hand will achieve a higher poker ranking than the dealer's hand, in accordance with rule 11.7, and/or that their hand will achieve one of the specific hand rankings prescribed within the specific game variations detailed below.*

6: Gambling Act 2005: Additional Material

7.38 In Mississippi Stud players compete against a pay table, not against the dealer or other players.

Initial Wager

7.39 Only one wager may be accepted on each playing position, and no individual player may place a wager on more than one playing position.
7.40 The initial wager for each participating player, hereafter referred to as the Ante wager, shall be made before any cards are dealt in the game. The Ante wager shall be placed in the designated betting area marked 'Ante'.

The Deal

7.41 After the initial wager has been placed, two cards will be dealt face down to each player and a further three cards placed face down in the 'community cards' area.
7.42 At this stage the player may view their cards and has two possible decisions:
- They may fold their hand and lose their initial wager (ante bet), or;
- Place a further wager of 1, 2 or 3 x their Ante on the "3rd Street" area.

7.43 The Dealer will then turn over the "3rd Street" community card.
7.44 At this stage the player has two possible decisions:
- They may fold their hand and lose their initial wager (ante bet) and their "3rd Street" bet, or;
- Place a further wager of 1, 2 or 3 x their Ante on the "4th Street" area.

7.45 The Dealer will then turn over the "4th Street" community card.
7.46 At this stage the player again has two possible decisions:
- They may fold their hand and lose their initial wager (ante bet), 3rd and 4th Streets bets, or;
- Place a further wager of 1, 2 or 3 x their Ante on the "5th Street" area.

7.47 The Dealer will then turn over the "5th Street" community card.

Settlement

7.48 Working from left to right the Dealer will then reveal the players initial two cards and combine them with the three community cards.
7.49 Each bet placed will be paid according to the odds in the below pay table. Any combination of cards not on the pay table will result in the player losing all of their wagers.

Pay table – House Edge 3.27%

Hand	Pays Minimum Odds
Royal Flush	500 to 1
Straight Flush	100 to 1
Four of a Kind	30 to 1
Full House	6 to 1
Flush	5 to 1
Straight	4 to 1
Three of a Kind	3 to 1
Two Pair	2 to 1
Pair of Jacks or better	1 to 1
Pair of 6s to 10s	Push

8. DICE/CRAPS

THE TABLE LAYOUT

8.1 Figure 10 shows an example of the style of game layout that may be offered to players. It also illustrates the full range of bets available.

Figure 10

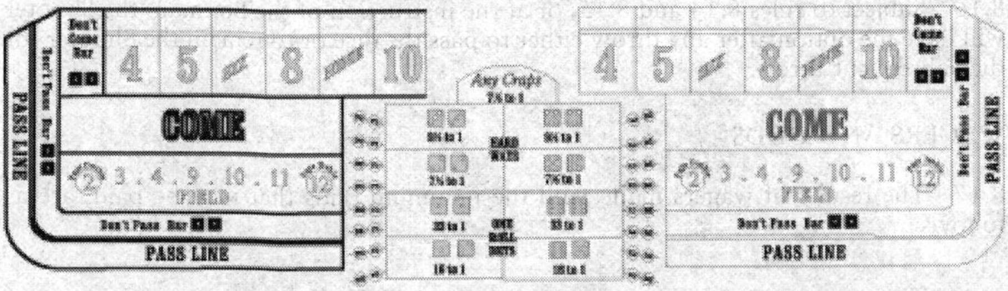

8.2 Only variations listed in rules 8.20 and onwards in this section are permitted, unless agreed by the Commission, in accordance with the rules detailed in section 2.3 and 2.4.

GENERAL RULES

8.3 Two dice shall be thrown at every throw made in the course of the game. The side of each of the dice shall be marked with values from 1 to 6, so arranged that the sum of the values of any pair of opposite sides total seven.
8.4 Operators must have procedures in place to ensure the security and integrity of the dice.
8.5 In these rules, the term 'Stickman' and/or 'Boxman' refer to people operating and controlling the game on behalf of the licence holder.
8.6 The maximum and minimum wagers permitted shall be shown on a notice prominently displayed at the table. Display of the maximum wager is recommended but is otherwise at the discretion of the licence holder. Partnerships with a view to exceeding the maximum stake shall not be permitted.
8.7 Wagers orally declared shall be accepted only if accompanied by the placing of sufficient chips or cash on the table to cover the wager and verbally confirmed by the Boxman or Stickman.
8.8 The dice shall be thrown by one of the players termed the 'Shooter'. To determine who shall be the Shooter at the commencement of play, the Stickman will offer the dice to the player immediately to the left of the Boxman. If that player does not accept, or otherwise on miniature versions of the game, the dice will be offered to each player in turn, clockwise around the table.
8.9 When a Shooter relinquishes the dice in the course of play, the dice will pass to the player immediately to the left of the previous Shooter and, if he does not accept, again to each of the players in turn clockwise around the table.
8.10 The Shooter must maintain a wager on the 'Win Line' or the 'Don't Win Line' (see rule 8.17).
8.11 The Shooter shall throw the two dice so that they leave his hand simultaneously, with a view to striking the end of the table furthest from him.
8.12 Any wager in relation to the game shall be of a kind specified in rule 8.17 and shall be payable if won and at the appropriate odds there specified.
8.13 The following terms shall have the following meanings in these rules:
(a) **'Point'** The sum of the two numbers shown on the uppermost faces of the two dice.

(b) **'Come Out Point'** A point of 4, 5, 6, 8, 9, or 10 thrown by the Shooter on his Come Out Roll and which, if thrown by him again before a total of 7 on his subsequent throw or throws, shall constitute a win for wagers on the Win Line (see rule 8.17).

(c) **'Loser 7'** A point of 7 thrown by the Shooter subsequent to his establishment of a Come Out Point.

8.14 The Shooter shall relinquish the dice if he throws a Loser 7 (see rule 8.13(c)).

8.15 If the Shooter throws a Come Out Point, he shall subject to rule 8.14, remain as the Shooter until he repeats that point on a subsequent throw.

8.16 Subject to rules 8.14 and 8.15, or at the instruction of the Boxman, the Shooter will have the option after any throw either to pass the dice or to remain the Shooter for the subsequent throw.

WAGERS AND ODDS

8.17 The results of wagers made, and the minimum odds that may be paid, are as follows:

Wagers on:	**Shall:**
a. Win (or Pass) Line	**Win** if 7 or 11 is thrown
- placed on the Shooter's first throw (the Come Out Roll)	**Lose** if 2, 3 or 12 is thrown
- at minimum odds of **1 to 1** other than these five is thrown, in which case that number, termed the Come Out Point is established and these wagers subsequently:	**Remain Unchanged** if any number
Win if the Come Out Point is thrown before a 7	
Lose if a 7 is thrown before the Come Out Point	
*See note at the end	
b. **Don't Win Line**	
(Don't Pass Line)	
- placed on the Shooter's first throw (the Come Out Roll)	**Win** if the 3 or 12 is thrown
	Lose if 7 or 11 is thrown
- at minimum odds of **1 to 1**	
	Be Void if a 2 is thrown
	Remained Unchanged if a Come Out Point is established in which case these wagers subsequently:
	Win if a 7 is thrown before the Come Out Point
	Lose if the Come Out Point is thrown again before a 7
c. **Come**	
- placed at any time after the	**Win, Lose or Remain Unchanged** in Shooter's Come Out Roll accordance with rule 8.17(a) above
- at minimum odds of **1 to 1** *See note at the end	
d. **Don't Come**	

- placed at any time after the Shooter's Come Out Roll 8.17(b) above	**Win, Lose, Be Void or Remain Unchanged** in accordance with rule
- at minimum odds of **1 to 1**	
e. **Behind the Win Line**	
- placed, after the establishment of a Come Out Point, by a player again before a 7 who already has a wager on the	**Win** if the Come Out point is thrown
Win Line	**Lose** if a 7 is thrown before the
Come Out Point	
- at odds depending on the point as follows:	**Remain Unchanged** if any other point is thrown and become subject
to the result of the subsequent throw	
4 or 10 at minimum odds of	
2 to 1	
5 or 9 at minimum odds of **3 to 2**	
6 or 8 at minimum odds of **6 to 5**	
f. **Behind the Don't Win Line**	
(Don't Win Lay Bets)	**Win** if a 7 is thrown before the Come Out point is thrown again
- placed by a player, after the establishment of a Come Out Point to win not more than the amount already being wagered against as follows:-	**Lose** if the Come Out Point is thrown before a 7
Remain Unchanged if any other point	
4 or 10 at minimum odds of **1 to 2**	is thrown and become subject to the result of the subsequent throw
5 or 9 at minimum odds of **2 to 3**	
6 or 8 at minimum odds of 5 to 6	
g. **Behind the Come**	
- placed by a player who has a wager of the same amount or larger on the Come on any Come Out Roll	**Win, Lose, Remain Unchanged** in accordance with rule 8.17(e) above except that these wagers are not valid unless
- at odds as in 8.20(e)	previously called 'On' (ie orally
declared to be in play by the player)	
h. **Behind the Don't Come**	
(Don't Come Lay Bets)	**Win, Lose, Remain Unchanged** in accordance with rule 8.17(f)
- placed by a player to win not more than the amount already being wagered by him on Don't Come on any Come Out Roll unless	These wagers shall remain in action
- at odds as in rule 8.20(f)	previously called 'Off' by the player
i. **Hardways**	
- placed by a player to wager that both dice will show the same number (a double) in one of the following combinations:	**Win** if the exact combination nominated is thrown before any other combination producing the same point or 7

Two 2s at minimum odds of 7½ **to 1** Two 3s at minimum odds of 9½ **to 1** Two 4s at minimum odds of 9½ **to 1** Two 5s at minimum odds of 7½ **to 1**	**Lose** if any other combination producing the same point or 7 is thrown before the exact combination
nominated	
Remain Unchanged if any other point is thrown, and becomes subject to the result of the next throw	
j. **Place Bets (Box Numbers) to Win**	
- at minimum odds depending on the point as follows: before a 7	**Win** if the Box Number is thrown
6 or 8 at minimum odds of **7 to 6**	
5 or 9 at minimum odds of **7 to 5** 4 or 10 at minimum odds of **9½ to 5**	**Lose** if 7 is thrown before the Box Number
Remain Unchanged if any other point is thrown and becomes subject to the result of the subsequent throw	
Except that these wagers shall not be valid on any Come Out Roll unless previously called 'On' (ie orally declared to be in play by the player)	
k. **Place Bets (Box Numbers) to Lose** (**Don't Lay Bets**)	**Win** if 7 is thrown before the Box Number
- at minimum odds depending on the point wagered against as follows:	**Lose** if the Box Number is thrown before a 7
6 or 8 at minimum odds of **4 to 5**	
5 or 9 at minimum odds of **5 to 8**	
4 or 10 at minimum odds of **5 to 11**	**Remain Unchanged** if any other point
is thrown and becomes subject to the result of the subsequent throw	
These wagers shall remain in action on any Come Out Roll unless previously called 'Off' by the player	
l. **Any Craps**	
- at minimum odds of **7½ to 1**	**Win** if 2, 3, or 12 is thrown
Lose if any other point is thrown	
m. **Craps 2**	
- at minimum odds of 33 to 1	**Win** if two 1s are thrown
Lose if any other point is thrown	
n. **Craps 3**	
- at minimum odds of 16 to 1	**Win** if 3 is thrown
Lose if any other point is thrown	
o. **Craps 12**	
- at minimum odds of 33 to 1	**Win** if 12 is thrown
Lose if any other point is thrown	
p. **Eleven**	
- at minimum odds of 16 to 1	**Win** if 11 is thrown
Lose if any other point is thrown	
q. **Any Seven**	

- at minimum odds of 4 to 1 — **Win** if 7 is thrown

Lose if any other point is thrown

r. **A Specific Pair Combination**

- at minimum odds of **33 to 1** — **Win** if specific pair is thrown (1,1)(2,2)

etc

Lose if any other combination is thrown

s. **A Specific Non-Pair Combination**

- at odds of 16 to 1 — **Win** if specific non-pair is thrown (1,3)

(2,4), etc

Lose if any other combination is thrown

t. **Field**

- at minimum odds depending on the point as follows: — **Win** if 2, 3, 4, 9, 10, 11 or 12 is thrown

3, 4, 9, 10 or 11 at **1 to 1**

2 at **2 to 1** — **Lose** if 5, 6, 7 or 8 is thrown

12 at **3 to 1**

* No stake wagered under 8.17(a) or 8.17(c) above shall be removed or reduced after the establishment of the respective Come Out or Come Point until that wager is either won or lost.

8.18 It is not a requirement that all bets are made available on any particular table. However, no variation may be considered in addition to the bets and minimum odds given in rule 8.17 above, other than in accordance with the rules detailed in section 2.3 and 2.4, or listed in rule 8.20.

8.19 Where any odds offered are higher than the minimum odds, the details of any change should be made clearly available to players on the table(s) concerned.

PERMITTED VARIATIONS TO DICE/CRAPS

'Rocket 7'

8.20 It is at the discretion of the licence holder whether or not to offer 'Rocket 7' as a variation to the standard game of Dice. The proprietor of the variation is International Casino Systems Europe, and no variations may be put forward without their prior agreement or that of a subsequent proprietor.

8.21 Rocket 7 is a simplified, one roll version of dice using a layout similar to the example given in the diagram below:

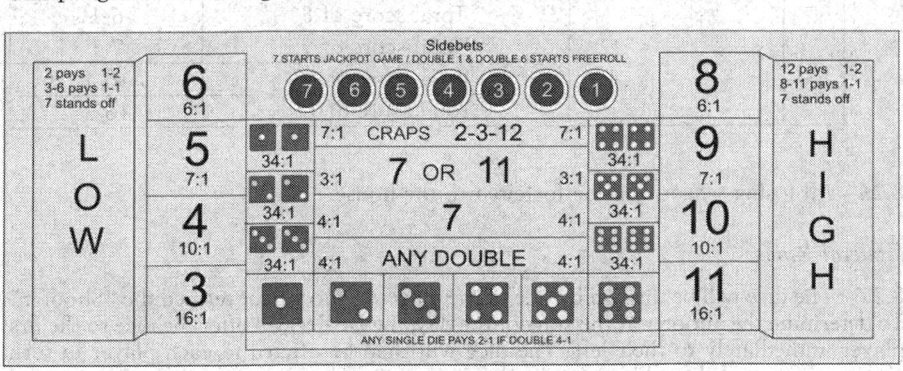

6: Gambling Act 2005: Additional Material

Example of Rocket 7 Layout

8.22 Two dice will be thrown at every throw made in the course of the game. The dice must comply with the marking requirements of rule 8.3 and the requirements of rule 8.4 regarding the security and integrity of the dice.

8.23 The Maximum and minimum wagers permitted shall be shown on a notice prominently displayed at the table. Partnerships with a view to exceeding the maximum shall not be permitted.

8.24 Wagers orally declared shall be accepted only if accompanied by the placing of sufficient chips or cash on the table to over the wager and verbally confirmed by the Dealer.

Wagers and Odds

8.25 Players may place wagers on any of the betting areas shown on the layout (see Figure 10a above). The type of wagers permitted for the standard game of Rocket 7, and the minimum odds that may be paid in each case, are as follows:

	Bet	Description	Minimum Odds
a.	**Low**	Total of 3,4,5 or 6	1-1
		Total of 2	1-2
		If score of seven	Standoff
b.	**High**	Total of 8,9,10 or 11	1-1
		Total of 12	1-2
		If score of 7	Stand off
c.	**Single die bet**	Score of 1,2,3,4,5 or 6 on one die	2-1
		If score appears on both die	4-1
d.	**Specific double**	A specific identical score on both dice (2 x 3s, 2 x 4s etc)	34-1
e.	**Any double**	Any identical score on both dice	4-1
f.	**7**	Total score of 7	4-1
g.	**7 or 11**	Total score of 7 or 11	3-1
h.	**Craps**	Total score of 2, 3 or 12	7-1
i.	**Specific score**	Total score of 3	16-1
		Total score of 4	10-1
		Total score of 5	7-1
		Total score of 6	6-1
		Total score of 8	6-1
		Total score of 9	7-1
		Total score of 10	10-1
		Total score of 11	16-1

8.26 All losing wagers will be forfeited to the house.

General Rules

8.27 The dice will be thrown by one of the players, who will be termed the "Shooter". To determine the Shooter at the start of the day, the Dealer will offer the dice to the first player immediately to their left. The dice will then be offered to each player in turn, clockwise around the table.

8.28 A Player must place a wager in accordance with rule 8.25 in order to become the Shooter. Otherwise the dice will pass to the next consecutive player who has placed a wager.
8.29 A player will normally act as Shooter for one throw before the dice pass to the next consecutive player. However, if the result of their throw is a score of seven, the same shooter will retain the dice for the next, and any number of subsequent throws, until they fail to score seven again. As soon as the Shooter throws a score other than a seven on a subsequent throw, the dice will pass to the next player.
8.30 The Dealer will have control of the dice at all times and will pass them to the Shooter only once all bets have been placed and a throw is required in the game.
8.31 Once handed the dice, the Shooter must immediately throw them both (within 3 seconds of receipt) so that they leave their hand simultaneously, with a view to striking the end of the table furthest from the Shooter.
8.32 The throw is invalid if both dice do not hit the wall, do not turn at least three times in the course of the throw, or if one die lands on top of the other.
8.33 The Dealer will announce the result, first by total and then by the score on each dice, from low to high. For example, if one dice lands on six and the other lands on one, the Dealer will announce a total score of seven with dice 1 and 6.

Progressive Jackpot and Bonus side bet Wagers

8.34 At the licence holder's discretion, a casino may introduce one or both of the two additional side bet features to Rocket 7, being the Rocket 7 Jackpot and/or the Free Roll Jackpot Game. The general rules for Progressive wagers given in Section 2.7 will apply.
8.35 Players wishing to place a side bets must have also placed a standard wager in order to do so.
8.36 Side wagers must be placed in the appropriately numbered, illuminated betting circle relating to the player's position on the table, starting from the Dealer's left. A maximum of one side bet per betting circle, is permitted.
8.37 The Rocket 7 Jackpot and Free Roll Jackpot Game are optional wagers that an opposing player may place at the same time as their standard Rocket 7 wager.
8.38 A player who places a single side bet wager will qualify for both the Rocket 7 Jackpot and the Free Roll Jackpot Game, where both are offered. It is recommended by the proprietor that the maximum permitted wager for the sidebet is set at the same value as the minimum permitted bet for the table.
8.39 The progressive jackpot fund is shared between the Rocket 7 Jackpot and the Free Roll Jackpot Game.
8.40 The Rocket 7 Jackpot is paid depending on a sequence of consecutive scores of seven being thrown. Winning wagers will be paid according to the following minimum pay table:

Sequence	Minimum Payout	Example for a £2 wager
Two consecutive throws with a total score of 7	2.5 x wager	£5
Three consecutive throws with a total score of 7	10 x wager	£20
Four consecutive throws with a total score of 7	75 x wager	£150
Five consecutive throws with a total score of 7	375 x wager	£750

6: Gambling Act 2005: Additional Material

Sequence	Minimum Payout	Example for a £2 wager
Six consecutive throws with a total score of 7	Jackpot	Jackpot

8.41 All players who have placed a sidebet will be paid after each occasion that a seven is thrown on two or more occasions. For example, they will all be paid £5 each after the second consecutive seven, then paid a further £20 each after the third, £150 after the fourth and so on.
8.42 Where the Jackpot is won for the Rocket 7 Jackpot sidebet, ie where six consecutive sevens are thrown, the jackpot pool will similarly be shared by all player who have placed a sidebet.
8.43 The Free Roll Jackpot Game is dependant on the outcome of a throw being either a double one or a double six. A player who throws a double one or a double six will therefore qualify for the Free roll.
8.44 The Free Roll means that the Shooter must now throw the dice three additional times in a row. During these throws, the standard Rocket 7 game is placed on hold and no further standard wagers may be accepted. The three additional throws relate only to the Free Roll Jackpot Game.
8.45 The Shooter will throw the dice three times, and the total of the three scores will be added together to make a total Free Roll score.
8.46 After the three throws have been completed, all Players will a side bet wager will be paid according to the following pay table for whichever total Free roll score is achieved:

	Total Low Free Roll score	*Total High Free Roll score*	*Minimum Pay-out*	*Example for a £2 bet*
Jackpot	6,7,8 or 9	33,34,35 or 36	Jackpot	Jackpot
Bonus 1	10,11,12 or 13	29,30,31 or 32	12.5 x wager	£25
Bonus 2	14, 15, 16,17 or 18	24,25,26,27 or 28	5 x wager	£10
Bonus 3	19,20,21,22, or 23		2.5 x wager	£5

For example, if the first throw is 1 & 3, the second throw 3 & 3 and the third throw 1 & 2, the total Free Roll score will be 13. All players with a £2 side bet will therefore be paid £25 each (Bonus 1). The Dealer should announce a running total of the individual and cumulative scores after each of the three Free Roll throws.
Where the Jackpot is won for the Free Roll Jackpot Game, it will be shared by all players who have placed a side bet wager.
8.47 After the third Free Roll throw, the dice will pass to the next consecutive player and the standard Rocket 7 game is resumed.
8.48 If neither a score of seven, double one or double six are thrown by the Shooter on their first throw, then all side bet wagers lose and are forfeited to the house.

Dice Magic

THE TABLE LAYOUT

8.49 The proprietor of Dice Magic is Gala Casinos and no variation to the game may be put forward without their prior agreement. The following diagram shows an example of the style of game layout that may be offered to the Players. It also illustrates the full range of bets available.

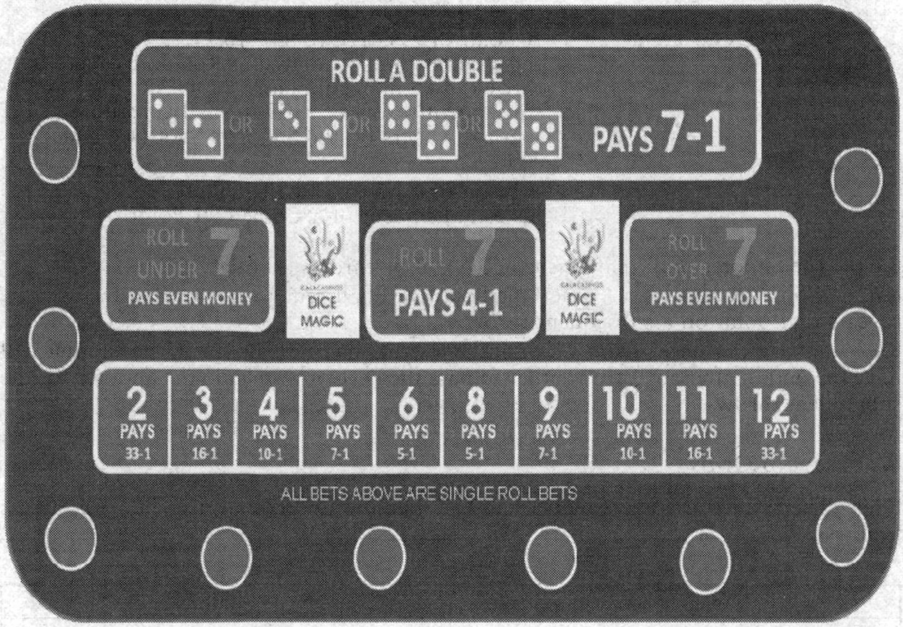

GENERAL RULES

8.50 Two Dice shall be thrown at every throw made in the course of the game. The side of each of the dice shall be marked with values from 1 to 6, so arranged that the sum of the values of any pair of opposite sides total seven.

8.51 Operators must have procedures in place to ensure the security and integrity of the Dice.

8.52 In these Rules, the term Stickman/ Boxman or Dice Hosts refer to persons operating and controlling the game on behalf of the Licence Holder.

8.53 The maximum and minimum wagers permitted shall be shown on a notice prominently displayed at the table. Partnerships with a view to exceeding the maximum stakes shall not be permitted.

8.54 Wagers orally declared shall be accepted only if accompanied by the placing of sufficient chips or cash on the table to cover the wager and verbally confirmed by the Boxman/Stickman or Dice Host.

8.55 The Dice shall be thrown by one of the players, termed the Shooter. To determine who shall be the Shooter at the commencement of play, the Stickman will offer the Dice to the Player immediately to the left of the Boxman. If that Player does not accept, (or otherwise on miniature versions of the game), the Dice will otherwise be offered to each player in turn, clockwise around the table.

8.56 When a Shooter relinquishes the Dice in the course of play, the Dice will pass to the player immediately to the left of the previous Shooter and, if he does not accept, again to each of the players in turn clockwise around the table.

8.57 The Shooter must and maintain a wager on the 'Shooters Spot'.
8.58 The Shooter shall throw the two Dice so that they leave his hand simultaneously, with a view to striking the end of the table furthest from him.
8.59 Any wager in relation to the game shall be of a kind specified in Rule 17 and shall be payable if won, at the appropriate odds there specified.
8.60 The following terms shall have the following meanings in these Rules:

a. Point	The sum of the two numbers shown on the uppermost faces of the two Dice.
b. Come Out Point	A point of 2,3,4, 5, 6, 8, 9,10,11,12 thrown by the shooter on his Come Out Roll and which, if thrown by him again before a total of 7 on his subsequent throw or throws, shall constitute a win for wagers on the Shooters Spot (see Rule 17).
c. Loser 7	A point of 7 thrown by the Shooter subsequent to his establishment of a Come Out Point.

8.61 The Shooter shall relinquish the Dice if he throws a Loser 7.
8.62 If Shooter throws a Come Out Point, he shall remain as the Shooter until he repeats that point on a subsequent throw.
8.63 Subject to Rules 14 and 15, or at the instruction of the Boxman, the Shooter will have the option after any throw either to pass the Dice or to remain the Shooter for the subsequent throw.

Wagers and Odds

8.64 The results of wagers made, and the minimum odds that may be paid, are as follows:

Wagers on:	Shall:
a. Shooters Spot - placed on the Shooter's first throw (the Come Out Roll) - at minimum odds of 1:1	Lose if a 7 is thrown Remain Unchanged if any number is thrown, in which case that number, termed the Come Out Point is established and these wagers subsequently:-Win if the Point is thrown before a 7.

Place Bets (Box Numbers) to Win on a single throw of the Dice - at minimum odds as follows:- 2 or 12 at minimum odds of 33/1 3 or 11 at minimum odds of 16/1 4 or 10 at minimum odds of 10/1 5 or 9 at minimum odds of 7/1 6 or 8 at minimum odds of 5/1	Lose if any other number is thrown.

Any Seven	Win if a 7 is thrown

- at minimum odds of 4 to 1	Lose if any other number is thrown
Under 7 - at minimum odds of 1 to 1	Win if 2,3,4,5 & 6 is thrown Lose if any other number is thrown
Over 7 - at minimum odds of 1 to 1	Win if 8,9,10,11 & 12 is thrown Lose if any other number is thrown

Roll a Double – At minimum odds of 7 to 1	Win if 4,6,8,10 are thrown with the combination of the 2 dice being either 2x2, 3x3, 4x4, 5x5. Lose if any other number is thrown or not thrown in the above combinations.

8.65 Where any odds offered are higher than the minimum odds, the details of any change should be made clearly available to Players on the table(s) concerned.

9. SIC BO

THE TABLE LAYOUT

9.1 Figures 11 and 12 show examples of the style of game layout that may be offered to players. They also illustrate the full range of bets available.

Figure 11: Example of 50 position layout

Figure 12: Example of 106 position layout

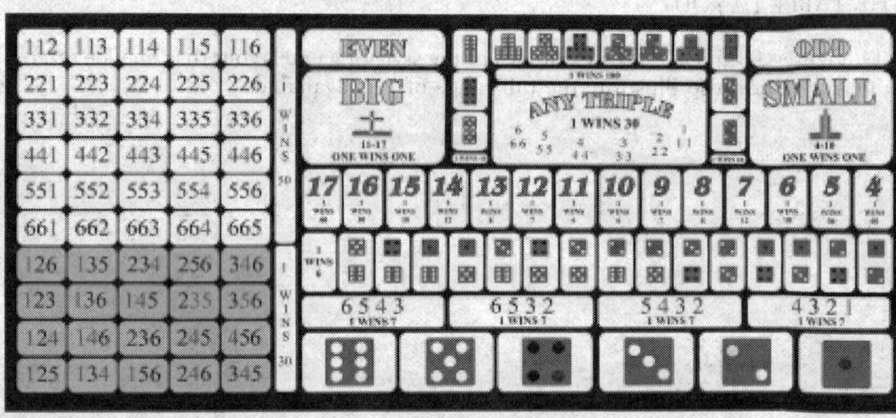

9.2 Only variations listed in rules 9.13 and onwards in this section are permitted.

GENERAL RULES

9.3 Three dice shall be thrown at every throw made in the course of the game. The side of each of the dice shall be marked with values from 1 to 6, so arranged that the sum of the values of any pair of opposite sides total seven.

9.4 Operators must have procedures in place to ensure the security and integrity of the dice.

9.5 The maximum and minimum wagers permitted shall be shown on a notice prominently displayed at the table. Display of the maximum wager is recommended but is otherwise at the discretion of the licence holder. Partnerships with a view to exceeding the maximum stake shall not be permitted.

9.6 Wagers orally declared shall be accepted only if accompanied by the placing of sufficient chips or cash on the table to cover the wager and verbally confirmed by the dealer.

9.7 A dice shaker/tumbler device, either manually or electrically operated, shall be used to tumble the dice.

9.8 The table shall be fitted with electrical equipment to illuminate the winning areas of the layout. The entry of a declared result of the game, by activation of the relevant numbered buttons on the control panel, shall cause all the winning areas of the layout to be illuminated.

9.9 Electrical devices and equipment used to operate the game of Sic Bo must conform to the technical standards as outlined in the Commission's publication entitled *Bingo and Casino Equipment Technical Requirements*.

9.10 Any wager in relation to the game shall be of a kind specified in rule 9.12 below, and shall be payable, if won, at the appropriate minimum odds there specified.

9.11 Each player shall be responsible for the positioning of his wager or wagers on the table, whether or not he is assisted by the dealer. The player must ensure that any instructions that he gives are correctly carried out. Wagers shall be settled strictly in accordance with the position of the chips on the layout at the time that the dice shaker is uncovered.

WAGERS AND ODDS

9.12 The available bets, and minimum odds payable are shown below. In this schedule, a 'Double' means two dice showing the same score and a 'Triple' means three dice showing the same score. Where any odds offered are higher than the minimum odds shown in this schedule, the details of any change should be made clearly available to players on the table or tables concerned:

(a) **Small:** a wager that the total score on the next throw of the dice will be 4, 5, 6, 7, 8, 9 or 10 in any combination with the exception of a triple. The minimum odds payable if the wager is won shall be **1 to 1.**

(b) **Big:** a wager that the total score on the next throw of the dice will be 11, 12, 13, 14, 15, 16 or 17 in any combination with the exception of a triple. The minimum odds payable if the wager is won shall be **1 to 1.**

(c) **Odd:** a wager that the total score on the next throw of the dice will be 5, 7, 9, 11, 13, 15 or 17 in any combination with the exception of a triple. The minimum odds payable if the wager is won shall be **1 to 1.**

(d) **Even:** a wager that the total score on the next throw of the dice will be 4, 6, 8, 10, 12, 14 or 16 in any combination with the exception of a triple. The minimum odds payable if the wager is won shall be **1 to 1.**

(e) **Specific Triples:** a wager that on the next throw of the dice a specific triple will appear. The minimum odds payable if the wager is won shall be **180 to 1.**

(f) **Specific Doubles:** a wager that on the next throw of the dice a specific double will appear. The minimum odds payable if the wager is won shall be **10 to 1.**

(g) **Any Triple:** a wager that on the next throw of the dice any of the triples will appear. The minimum odds payable if the wager is won shall be **30 to 1.**

(h) **Three Dice Total:** a wager that on the next throw of the dice a specific total score of 4, 5, 6, 7, 8, 9, 10, 11, 12, 13, 14, 15, 16 or 17 will appear. The minimum odds payable if the wager is won shall be, where the score wagered on is:
   - (i) 4 or 17, minimum odds payable **60 to 1**
   - (ii) 5 or 16, minimum odds payable **30 to 1**
   - (iii) 6 or 15, minimum odds payable **18 to 1**
   - (iv) 7 or 14, minimum odds payable **12 to 1**
   - (v) 8 or 13, minimum odds payable **8 to 1**
   - (vi) 9 or 12, minimum odds payable **7 to 1**
   - (vii) 10 or 11, minimum odds payable **6 to 1**

(i) **Dice Combinations:** a wager that on the next throw of the dice two of the three dice will show one of the following specific combinations, that is to say:
   - (i) the number 1 together with the specific number 2, 3, 4, 5 or 6
   - (ii) the number 2 together with the specific number 3, 4, 5 or 6
   - (iii) the number 3 together with the specific number 4, 5 or 6
   - (iv) the number 4 together with the specific number 5 or 6
   - (v) the number 5 together with the number 6

   The minimum odds payable if the wager is won shall be **6 to 1.**

(j) **Single Dice Bet:** a wager that on the next throw of the dice the specific number 1, 2, 3, 4, 5 or 6 will appear. The minimum odds payable if the wager is won shall be, if the number wagered on appears:
  (i) on one of the dice, **1 to 1**
  (ii) on two of the dice, **2 to 1**
  (iii) on three of the dice, **3 to 1**

(k) **Four Number Combination:** a wager that on the next throw of the dice any three of the four numbers in one of the following specific combinations will appear:
  (i) the numbers 6, 5, 4, 3
  (ii) the numbers 6, 5, 3, 2
  (iii) the numbers 5, 4, 3, 2
  (iv) the numbers 4, 3, 2, 1

  The minimum odds payable if the wager is won shall be **7 to 1**.

(l) **Three Single Number Combination:** a wager that on the next throw of the dice one of the following specific combinations will appear:
  (i) the numbers 1, 2, 6
  (ii) the numbers 1, 3, 5
  (iii) the numbers 2, 3, 4
  (iv) the numbers 2, 5, 6
  (v) the numbers 3, 4, 6
  (vi) the numbers 1, 2, 3
  (vii) the numbers 1, 3, 6
  (viii) the numbers 1, 4, 5
  (ix) the numbers 2, 3, 5
  (x) the numbers 3, 5, 6
  (xi) the numbers 1, 2, 4
  (xii) the numbers 1, 4, 6
  (xiii) the numbers 2, 3, 6
  (xiv) the numbers 2, 4, 5
  (xv) the numbers 4, 5, 6
  (xvi) the numbers 1, 2, 5
  (xvii) the numbers 1, 3, 4
  (xviii) the numbers 1, 5, 6
  (xix) the numbers 2, 4, 6
  (xx) the numbers 3, 4, 5

  The minimum odds payable if the wager is won shall be **30 to 1**.

(m) **Specific Double and Single Number Combination:** a wager that on the next throw of the dice two of the three dice will show a specific double and the third dice will show a specific single number other than that on the other two dice. The minimum odds payable if the wager is won shall be **50 to 1**.

PERMITTED VARIATIONS TO SIC BO

9.13 Any permitted variations to the existing game will be listed here. There are none at present.

10. BIG SIX (WHEEL OF FORTUNE)

THE WHEEL AND TABLE LAYOUT

10.1 Figure 13 shows an example of the wheel, and the order in which the symbols specified in rule 10.2 must be arranged around it. It also shows the style of game layout that may be offered to players and the minimum odds payable.

Figure 13: Order of symbols on the wheel and example of layout design

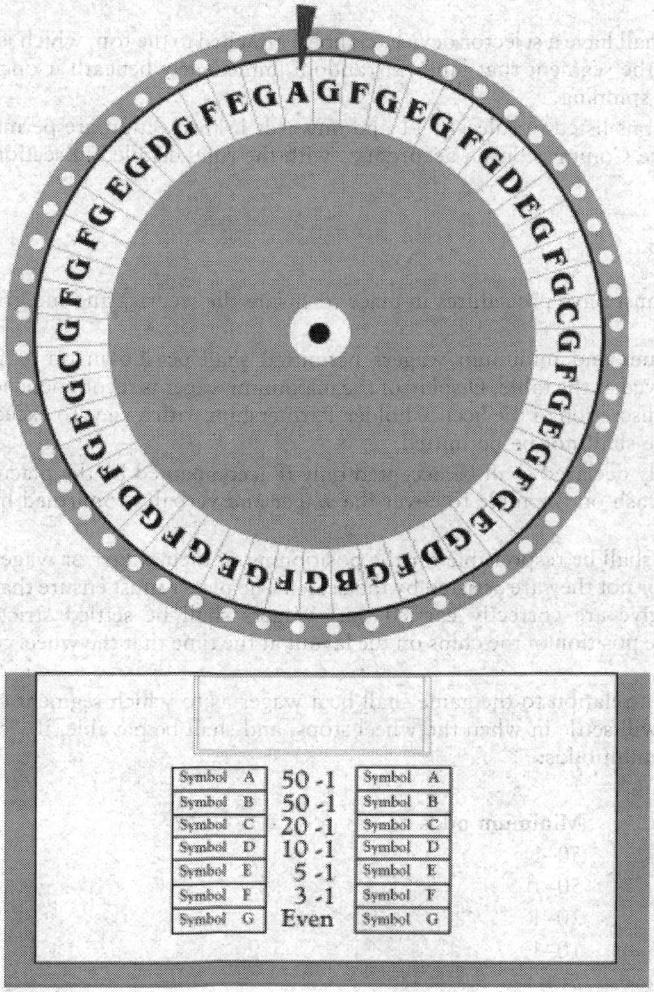

10.2 'Big Six' (or any other name used to portray the same game, such as Wheel of Fortune, Big Wheel etc) will be played with a circular wheel which shall have 52 equal compartments marked with seven different symbols. The numbers or designs used as symbols may be of any theme chosen by the operator. However, symbols or designs must be allocated to the 52 compartments (segments) in the order shown in Figure 13. The number of compartments allocated to each symbol will be as follows:

Symbol	Number of compartments
Type A	1
Type B	1
Type C	2
Type D	4
Type E	8
Type F	12

Symbol	Number of compartments
Type G	24

10.3 The wheel shall have a selector device (clapper) attached to the top, which is able to come to rest in the segment that lands at random immediately beneath it once the wheel has stopped spinning.
10.4 Only variations listed in rules 10.11 and onwards in this section are permitted, unless agreed by the Commission, in accordance with the rules detailed in section 2.3 and 2.4.

GENERAL RULES

10.5 Operators must have procedures in place to ensure the security and integrity of the wheel.
10.6 The maximum and minimum wagers permitted shall be shown on a notice prominently displayed at the table. Display of the maximum wager is recommended but is otherwise at the discretion of the licence holder. Partnerships with a view to exceeding the maximum stake shall not be permitted.
10.7 Wagers orally declared shall be accepted only if accompanied by the placing of sufficient chips or cash on the table to cover the wager and verbally confirmed by the dealer.
10.8 Each player shall be responsible for the positioning of their wager or wagers on the table, whether or not they are assisted by the dealer. The player must ensure that any instructions they give are correctly carried out. Wagers shall be settled strictly in accordance with the position of the chips on the layout at the time that the wheel comes to rest.
10.9 Any wager in relation to the game shall be a wager as to which segment of the wheel the clapper will settle in when the wheel stops, and shall be payable, if won, at the following minimum odds:

Symbol type	Minimum odds
Type A	50–1
Type B	50–1
Type C	20–1
Type D	10–1
Type E	5–1
Type F	3–1
Type G	1–1

10.10 If the clapper comes to rest between two segments, the casino licence holder has the option to do one of the following:
(a) declare the winning number to be the number previously passed; or
(b) declare the spin void and re-spin the wheel.
Whichever option a licence holder chooses from a) and b) above, a sign or notice shall be clearly displayed so that players are aware of this.

PERMITTED VARIATIONS TO BIG SIX

10.11 Any permitted variations to the existing game will be listed here. There are none at present.

11. TEXAS HOLD ’EM POKER

THE TABLE LAYOUTS

11.1 There are four casino variations of Texas Hold ’Em Poker approved by these rules. Each is a proprietary game licensed in the UK by the registered owner. Figures 18 to 21 show example layout designs for each variation.

Figure 18: WSOP Texas Hold ’Em Bonus Poker Copyright PGI

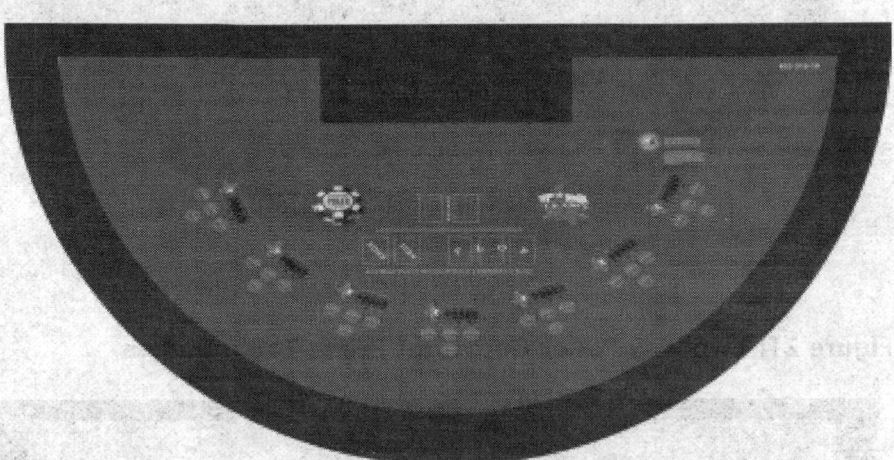

Figure 19: Ultimate Texas Hold ’Em Poker Copyright Shufflemaster

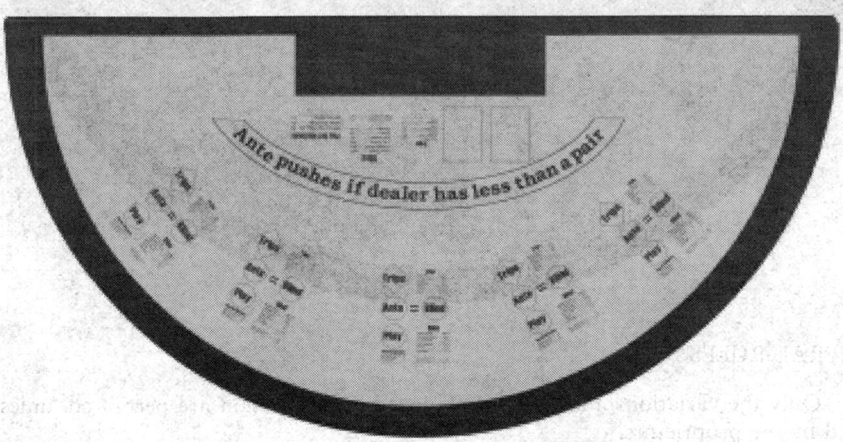

Figure 20: Casino Hold 'Em Poker Copyright TCSJohnHuxley

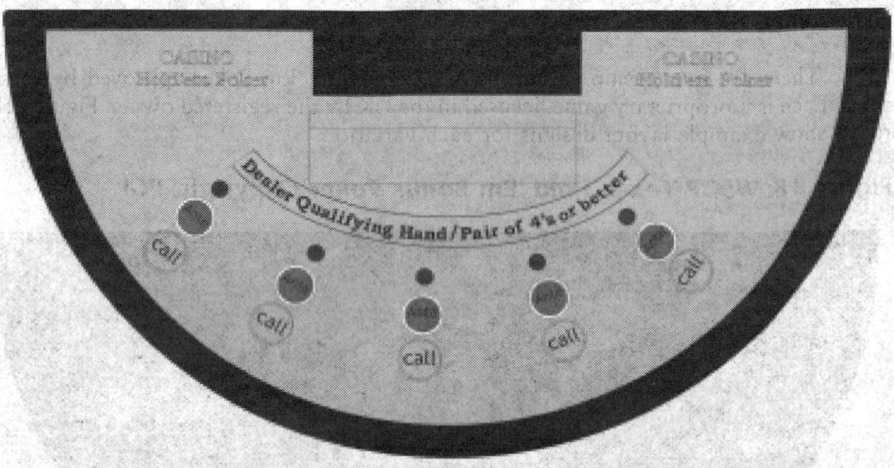

Figure 21: Two Way Poker Copyright Prime Table Games

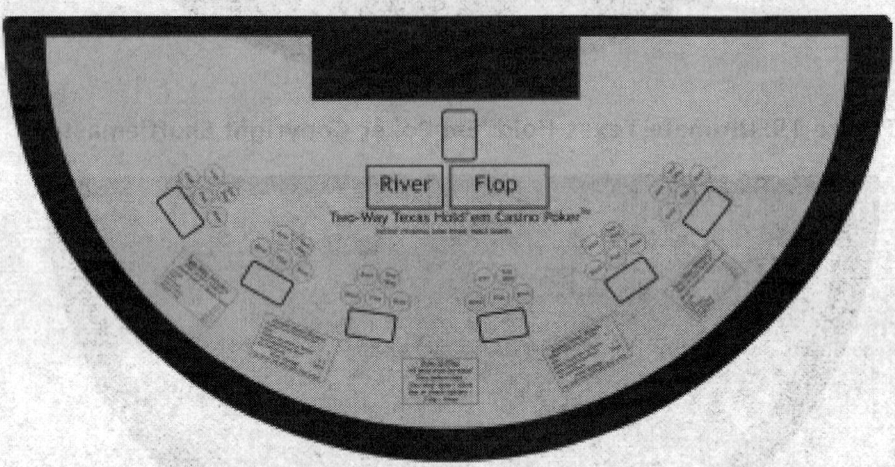

GENERAL RULES

11.2 Only the variations and side wagers listed in this section are permitted, unless agreed by the proprietors.

11.3 All versions of Texas Hold 'Em shall be played with a single pack of 52 cards.

11.4 Operators must have procedures in place to ensure the security and integrity of the cards.

11.5 The maximum and minimum wagers permitted shall be shown on a notice prominently displayed at the table. Display of the maximum wager is recommended but is otherwise at the discretion of the licence holder. Partnerships with a view to exceeding the maximum stake shall not be permitted.

11.6 The relative value of each of the cards is as follows (in descending order): Ace, King, Queen, Jack, 10, 9, 8, 7, 6, 5, 4, 3, and 2, except that the Ace may be used as a value of one in order to complete a Straight Flush or a Straight, as defined in rule 11.7 below (being 5, 4, 3, 2, and Ace).

11.7 The terms used to describe the five-card hands, and descending order of hand rankings, in all approved versions of Texas Hold 'Em Poker shall be in accordance with the following:

(a) **Royal Flush** – Ace, King, Queen, Jack and 10 of the same suit;
(b) **Straight Flush** – five cards of consecutive values of the same suit;
(c) **Four of a Kind** – four cards of the same value;
(d) **Full House** – three cards of the same value together with two cards of the same value being different to the first value;
(e) **Flush** – five cards of the same suit;
(f) **Straight** – five cards of consecutive values not being a Royal Flush or a Straight Flush;
(g) **Three of a Kind** – three cards of the same value;
(h) **Two pairs** – two cards of the same value together with two cards of the same value being different to the first value;
(i) **One pair** – two cards of the same value;
(j) **High Card/No pair** – the highest value cards of the hand.

11.8 The terminology used to describe the cards dealt within all versions of Texas Hold 'Em Poker is as follows:

(a) **'Hole Cards'** The two cards dealt to the player and dealer;
(b) **'The Flop'** The first three communal cards dealt;
(c) **'The Turn'** The fourth communal card dealt;
(d) **'The River'** The fifth and final communal card dealt.
(e) **'Playing the Board'** Where the best poker hand for one or more players and/or the dealer is actually to use all five communal cards, and neither of the player/dealer's two hole cards.
(f) **'Fold'** A player electing to throw in their hand and surrender their wagers to the house.

11.9 In all versions of the game detailed in this section, only one player may wager on each playing position, and no individual player may place a wager on more than one playing position.

11.10 In all versions of Texas Hold 'Em approved within this section, each participating player and the dealer will be dealt an initial hand of two cards (the hole cards), face downwards. Cards are always dealt starting from the player on the dealer's left. In all versions of the game detailed in this section, this is referred to as the 'Initial Deal'.

11.11 The five communal cards detailed in rule 11.8 will be dealt at appropriate stages of the game, as prescribed within the specific game variations detailed in this section.

11.12 The player and dealer's final hand is always their best five-card hand created by using one, both or neither of their two hole cards, together with some or all of the five communal cards. Any number of players and/or the dealer may 'Play the Board' if this creates their individual best hand.

11.13 All wagers made by opposing players will be against the house, and are wagers that the player's hand will achieve a higher poker ranking than the dealer's hand, in accordance with rule 11.7, and/or that their hand will achieve one of the specific hand rankings prescribed within the specific game variations detailed below.

11.14 Players will always be invited by the dealer to make any decisions required by the specific game variation, such as whether to 'bet or check', starting in order from the player to the dealer's left.

11.15 Wagers are always settled for each player in turn, starting with the player on the dealer's right.

TEXAS HOLD 'EM BONUS POKER

11.16 The following procedures describe the proprietary variation of Texas Hold 'Em called 'Texas Hold 'Em Bonus Poker'. The current proprietor of the game is Shufflemaster Gaming Inc. and no variations to the game may be put forward without either their prior agreement, or that of a subsequent proprietor.

11.17 The initial wager for each participating player, hereafter referred to as the Ante wager, shall be made before any cards are dealt in the game. The Ante wager shall be placed in the designated betting area marked 'Ante'.

11.18 At the same time, an optional additional side wager called Bonus Jackpot may also be wagered in the designated betting area marked 'Bonus', provided the participating player has also placed an Ante wager. The Bonus Jackpot is a wager that a player's two hole cards will achieve one of the specific hand rankings given in rule 11.33, irrespective of the hand dealt to the dealer (other than the optional top pay-out, which is dependent on the dealer hand being Ace-Ace).

11.19 If after the Initial Deal, an opposing player who has made an Ante wager wishes to continue with that wager, the player must make a further wager, referred to in these rules as the Flop wager. This shall be an amount of **twice the value** of the Ante wager and will be placed in the designated betting area marked 'Flop'.

11.20 An opposing player who has made an Ante wager but who does not wish to make a subsequent Flop wager after the Initial Deal shall surrender the amount staked on the Ante wager to the bank (Fold).

11.21 Once all participating players have made their decisions to either place a Flop wager or Fold, the dealer will draw three communal cards and place them face up in the designated area marked for the Flop.

11.22 The dealer will then ask each participating player with a Flop wager whether they wish to 'check or bet' before the fourth card (the Turn) is revealed.

11.23 If a player elects to bet, they must place a wager equal to the amount of their Ante wager in the designated betting area marked 'Turn'.

11.24 If the player elects to check they will remain in the game without placing a Turn wager.

11.25 Once all participating players have made their decision to check or bet, the dealer will then deal the next communal card face up and place it in the designated area marked for the Turn card.

11.26 The dealer will then invite each participating player with a Flop wager whether they wish to check or bet before the fifth card (the 'River') is revealed.

11.27 If a player elects to bet, they must place a wager equal to the amount of the Ante wager in the designated betting area marked 'River'.

11.28 If the player elects to check, they will remain in the game without placing a River wager.

11.29 Once all participating players have made their decision to check or bet, the dealer will then deal the final communal card face up and place it in the designated area marked for the River card.

11.30 Once all five communal cards have been dealt, the dealer will expose their own two hole cards face up and announce their best five card poker hand, in accordance with rule 11.7.

11.31 Dealing with each player in turn, the dealer will then expose the player's two hole cards and evaluate their best possible five card poker hand in accordance with rule 11.7.

11.32 The dealer will announce the player's hand ranking. If the player has a Bonus Jackpot wager, the dealer will also announce whether the player's two hole cards form a winning hand against the pay table given in rule 11.33.

11.33 A player with a Bonus Jackpot wager will win if their **two hole cards** alone form one of the following hands, and will be paid minimum odds as follows:

Player's two-card hand	**Minimum odds payable**
Ace–Ace at same time as dealer Ace–Ace	1000–1**
Ace–Ace	30–1
Ace–King (suited)	25–1
Ace–Queen or Ace–Jack (suited)	20–1
Ace–King (unsuited)	15–1
Pair of Jacks, Queens or Kings	10–1
Ace–Queen or Ace–Jack (unsuited)	5–1
Pair of 2s, 3s, 4s, 5s, 6s, 7s, 8s, 9s or 10s	3–1

** Available at the discretion of the operator

11.34 If the two hole cards held by a participating player with a Bonus Jackpot wager do not form one of the hands listed in rule 11.33, the wager will lose and will be surrendered to the bank.

***It is permissible to apply a maximum ceiling to the sterling amount that will be paid at a table to an individual who wins the Bonus Jackpot with Ace-Ace when the dealer has Ace-Ace, on a table where that outcome is offered. This is provided:-**

(a) **It applies only to odds of 1000-1 or above;**

(b) **There must be very clear signage at the table highlighting the maximum amount that will be paid regardless of the value of the wager;**

(c) **That all players who place wagers that would be impacted by the maximum payout are informed of this fact, so that they are in absolutely no doubt of the fact and have the opportunity to remove or adjust their wager before the game takes place if they wish.**

11.35 If the dealer's hand has a **higher** poker ranking than the player's five-card hand, the player's Ante, Flop and, where wagered, Turn and/or River wagers will lose and be surrendered to the bank.

11.36 If the player's hand is of exactly **equal** ranking to the dealer's hand, the hand is a stand off and the player's Ante, Flop and, where wagered, Turn and/or River wagers will all be returned to the player.

11.37 If the player's hand is of a higher poker ranking than the dealer's hand, the player's Flop and, where wagered, Turn and/or River wagers will win and each will be paid, as a minimum, odds of **even money (1–1)**.

11.38 If the player's winning hand against the dealer is a Straight or better their Ante wager will win and also be paid, as a minimum, odds of **even money (1–1)**. However, if the winning hand is a **less than a Straight** the Ante wager will be deemed a stand off and will instead be returned to the player.

PROGRESSIVE TEXAS HOLD 'EM BONUS WAGER

11.39 At the licence holder's discretion, a casino may introduce an additional feature into the game, namely a Progressive Jackpot wager, either in addition to, or instead of, the Bonus Jackpot wager.

11.40 A Progressive Jackpot wager shall be an optional wager that an opposing player may place at the same time as he places an Ante wager.

11.41 A Progressive Jackpot wager may not be placed unless an Ante wager has also been placed at the same time.

11.42 A Progressive Jackpot wager shall be placed in a designated slot, spot or dedicated area, set into, or otherwise made available at, each playing position.

11.43 A Progressive wager is a wager that the player will receive one of the specific five-card hands given in rule 11.44, using any combination of their two hole cards and the five community cards. If such a hand is dealt, the player will win regardless of whether the hand also beat the dealer. Where such a hand comprises all five community cards, all players with a Progressive wager are entitled to Play the Board, ie use the five community cards as their hand.

11.44 If upon the hand being revealed, an opposing player who has placed a Progressive Jackpot wager has a hand containing one of the following rankings, the player's Progressive Jackpot wager shall win, and be paid from the Progressive Jackpot Meter, the following **minimum** amounts:
(a) Royal Flush (**100% of the Progressive Jackpot Meter**)
(b) Straight Flush (**10% of the Progressive Jackpot Meter**)
(c) Four of a Kind (**500 times the value of the wager**)
(d) Full House (**100 times the value of the wager**)
(e) Flush (**50 times the value of the wager**)

11.45 Where one of winning hands given in rule 11.44 comprises all five community cards, all players with a Progressive wager are entitled to Play the Board.
(a) Where the winning hand is a Royal Flush, all winning players will share the jackpot meter equally.
(b) Where the winning hand is a Straight Flush made up of all five community cards, all winning players will receive an equal share equivalent to 10% of the jackpot total.
(c) Where the winning hand is a Four of a Kind or below, each player will receive the appropriate fixed payment detailed in points c), d) and e) in rule 11.44.

11.46 If one or more participating players is dealt a Royal Flush or Straight Flush using either or both of their hole cards together with a combination of community cards, payment will be made in seating order, starting from the dealer's right.

11.47 Progressive wagers will be settled after all five community cards have been dealt. If a player with a Progressive wager therefore elects to Fold, their cards will remain on the table until the Turn and River cards have been dealt and the outcome of the Progressive wager can be determined.

ULTIMATE TEXAS HOLD 'EM POKER

11.48 The following procedures describe the proprietary variation of Texas Hold 'Em called 'Ultimate Texas Hold 'Em Poker'. The proprietor of the game is Shufflemaster Gaming Inc. and no variations to the game may be put forward without their prior agreement.

11.49 An opposing player will make **two** initial wagers of equal amount. These wagers are hereafter referred to as the Ante wager and the Blind wager and shall be made before any cards are dealt in the game. The wagers will be placed in the designated betting areas marked 'Ante' and 'Blind'. These are initial wagers that the player's hand will have a higher ranking than the dealer's hand.

11.50 An optional additional side wager is called Trips Bonus. This side wager may be of any amount within the table limits, and is wagered in the designated betting area marked 'Trips' at the start of the game before any cards are dealt, provided the player has also placed an Ante and Blind wager. The Trips is a wager that the player's best five-card hand will achieve one of the particular hand ranking given in rule 11.72, irrespective of the hand dealt to the dealer.

11.51 Immediately after the Initial Deal, the dealer may deal the five communal cards face down in the area allocated on the table. This is permitted to allow a shuffle machine to deliver five cards followed by a succession of two for each player, regardless of the number of participants. Alternatively, the communal cards can be dealt as and when they are required in the course of the game. When all players have been dealt their hand, the dealer will ask each participating player with an Ante and Blind wager whether they wish to 'check or bet' before the Flop is revealed.

11.52 If the player elects to place an additional wager, hereafter called the Play wager, **before** the three communal Flop cards are dealt, they have the option of wagering either **three or four times** the amount of their Ante wager as their Play wager.

11.53 Having taken the option to place their Play wager before the Flop, a player may not then wager again during the remainder of the game, and cannot change their wager once the Flop has been dealt.

11.54 If the player elects instead to check, they will remain in the game without placing a Play wager before the Flop is dealt.
11.55 Once all opposing players have made their decision to check or bet, the dealer will then deal/reveal the three communal Flop cards.
11.56 The dealer will then invite each of the opposing players in turn who has not yet placed a Play wager, whether they wish to check or bet before the fourth and fifth cards (the Turn and River) are revealed.
11.57 If a player elects to bet, they must place a Play wager of **twice the amount of the Ante** wager in the designated betting area. They may not then wager again during the remainder of the game.
11.58 If the player again elects to check they will remain in the game without placing a Play wager before the Turn and River cards are dealt or revealed.
11.59 Once all relevant players have made their decision to check or bet, the dealer will then deal or reveal both the two remaining communal cards (the Turn and River).
11.60 Starting from the player on their left, the dealer will then invite all remaining opposing players in turn who have not yet placed a Play wager, whether they wish to bet or fold.
11.61 If a player elects to bet, they must place a Play wager of **an equal amount of the Ante** wager in the designated betting area.
11.62 If the player still does not wish to place a Play wager, they must fold. Their Ante, Blind and, where applicable, Trips Bonus wagers will then lose and the amount staked will be surrendered to the bank. However, if the folded hand contains three of a kind or better and thus qualifies for Trips Bonus wager pay out in accordance with rule 11.72, the Trips Bonus will be paid, irrespective of the hand being folded.
11.63 Once all remaining players have made their decision to check or fold, the dealer will expose their two hole cards face up and announce their best five card poker hand in accordance with rule 11.7.

Pay out if dealer has a Qualifying Hand in Ultimate Texas Hold 'Em Poker

11.64 The dealer's best hand must contain at least a pair to qualify, hereafter called a Qualifying Hand.
11.65 If the dealer **does** have a Qualifying Hand then they will compare it against each player's best five-card hand in turn.
11.66 If the dealer's Qualifying Hand is of identical value to the player's hand, the Ante, Play and Blind wagers will be returned to the player.
11.67 If the dealer's Qualifying Hand is of a higher ranking than the player's hand, the player's Ante, Play and Blind wagers are lost and surrendered to the house.
11.68 If the player's hand is of a higher ranking to the dealer's Qualifying Hand, their Ante and Play wager will be paid, at a minimum, odds of **even money (1–1)**.
11.69 If the player's hand is of a higher ranking than the dealer's hand, but **does not** contain a Straight or better, the Blind wager will be returned to the player.
11.70 If the player's hand is of a higher ranking than the dealer's hand, and **does** contain a Straight or better, their **Blind** wager will win and be paid odds at a minimum to the following pay table:

6: Gambling Act 2005: Additional Material

Player's five-card hand	Minimum odds payable
Royal Flush	500–1*
Straight Flush	50–1
Four of a Kind	10–1
Full House	3–1
Flush	3–2
Straight	1–1

*It is permissible to apply a maximum ceiling to the sterling amount that will be paid at a table to an individual who wins with a Royal Flush, provided:

(a) It applies only to odds of 500-1 or above;

(b) There must be very clear signage at the table highlighting the maximum amount that will be paid regardless of the value of the wager;

(c) That all players who place wagers that would be impacted by the maximum payout are informed of this fact, so that they are in absolutely no doubt of the fact and have the opportunity to remove or adjust their wager before the game takes place if they wish.

11.71 If the player's hand is of a lower ranking than the dealer's hand, their Play and Blind wagers will lose and be surrendered to the bank.

11.72 If a player who has placed the optional **Trips Bonus** has a hand containing Three of a Kind or better, the wager will win and be paid, as a minimum, the following odds:

Player's five-card hand	Minimum odds payable
Royal Flush	50–1
Straight Flush	40–1
Four of a Kind	20–1
Full House	7–1
Flush	6–1
Straight	4–1
Three of a Kind	3–1

Please note that the above table shows the minimum permitted odds that may be paid, drawn from the pay tables given in Section 11.73. However, the full list of minimum odds is not, in itself, a well-balanced pay table and in fact carries a house edge of 9.12%. It is therefore recommended that they are only used as a guide and not as a pay table in themselves.

11.73 In addition to offering, as a minimum, the odds given in rule 11.72 above, odds for the Trips Bonus may be presented as complete pay tables, in accordance with rule 2.9 given in section 2. Permitted pay tables are as follows:

Pay table 1

Royal Flush	50–1
Straight Flush	40–1
Four of a Kind	30–1
Full House	9–1
Flush	7–1
Straight	4–1
Three of a Kind	3–1

Pay table 2

Royal Flush	50–1
Straight Flush	40–1
Four of a Kind	30–1
Full House	8–1
Flush	6–1
Straight	5–1
Three of a Kind	3–1

Pay table 3

Pay table 4

Royal Flush	50–1	Royal Flush	50–1
Straight Flush	40–1	Straight Flush	40–1
Four of a Kind	30–1	Four of a Kind	20–1
Full House	8–1	Full House	7–1
Flush	7–1	Flush	6–1
Straight	4–1	Straight	5–1
Three of a Kind	3–1	Three of a Kind	3–1

11.74 If a player who has placed the optional Trips Bonus wager does not have a hand containing Three of a Kind or better, the Trips Bonus wager will lose and be surrendered to the House.

Pay out if dealer does not have a Qualifying Hand in Ultimate Texas Hold 'Em Poker

11.75 If the dealer **does not** have a Qualifying Hand in accordance with rule 11.64, then the Ante wager of each player who has not folded will be returned to them.
11.76 The dealer will then deal with the Play, Blind and optional Trips Bonus wagers for each player in turn in exactly the same way as for a Qualifying Hand, in accordance with rules 11.64 to 11.72.

CASINO HOLD 'EM POKER

11.77 The following procedures describe the proprietary variation of Texas Hold 'Em called 'Casino Hold 'Em Poker'. The proprietor of the game is TCS John Huxley Ltd, and no variations to the game may be put forward without their prior agreement.
11.78 Each opposing player places an initial wager, hereafter called the Ante wager, in the designated area marked 'Ante'.
11.79 An optional side wager called 'AA Bonus' may also be placed in the designated area marked 'AA', provided the player has also placed an Ante wager at the same time.
11.80 Immediately after the Initial Deal, the dealer will draw the first three communal cards and place them face up in the designated Flop area.
11.81 Any opposing player who has made an Ante wager and wishes to remain in the game shall then make a further wager of **twice the value** of their Ante wager (hereafter called the Call wager). This will place it in the designated area marked 'Call'.
11.82 If an opposing player does not wish to place a Call wager to remain in the game, they must Fold. Their Ante and optional AA Bonus wagers will then lose and be surrendered to the bank.
11.83 When all players have decided whether to Call or Fold, the dealer will then determine whether any player has a winning AA bonus hand, using their two hole cards and the three card flop.
Any player who has a Pair of Aces or better will win and be paid minimum odds in accordance with the following pay table:

Hand	**Minimum odds**
Flush or Higher	25–1
Pair of Aces to Straight	7–1

11.84 If a player with an AA Bonus wager does not have a Pair of Aces or better, the wager will lose and be surrendered to the bank.
11.85 Once all AA Bonus wagers have been settled or surrendered, the dealer will then draw the fourth and fifth communal cards together, and will place them face up in the area designated for the Turn and River cards.
11.86 The dealer will then reveal their own two hole cards and will declare their best five-card hand in accordance with rule 11.7.

11.87 The dealer must have at least a pair of fours to qualify (hereafter called a Qualifying Hand).

11.88 If the dealer **does not** have a Qualifying Hand then the Call wager for each remaining player will be returned. The dealer will determine the best five-card hand of each player in turn and the Ante wager for each player will be paid in accordance with the following minimum odds:

Hand	Minimum odds
Royal Flush	100–1
Straight Flush	20–1
Four of a Kind	10–1
Full House	3–1
Flush	2–1
Straight or less Even	(1–1)

11.89 If the dealer **does** have a Qualifying Hand, in accordance with rule 11.87, then the dealer will determine the best five-card hand for each player in turn.

11.90 If the dealer's Qualifying Hand is of a higher poker ranking than the player's hand, the player's Ante and Call wagers will lose and will be surrendered to the bank.

11.91 If the player's Qualifying Hand is of a higher poker ranking than the dealer's, the player's Call wager will be paid at minimum odds of **even money (1–1)**. Their Ante wager will be paid in accordance with the minimum odds given in rule 11.88.

PROGRESSIVE WAGER

11.92 At the licence holder's discretion, a casino may introduce an additional feature into the game, namely a Progressive Jackpot wager called 'Progressive 5/7', either in addition to, or instead of, the 'AA Bonus' wager. The general rules detailed in section 2.7 will apply.

11.93 The Progressive Jackpot wager shall be an optional wager that an opposing player may place at the same time as he places an Ante wager.

11.94 The Progressive Jackpot wager may not be placed unless an Ante wager has also been placed at the same time.

11.95 The Progressive Jackpot wager shall be placed in a designated slot, spot or dedicated area, set into or otherwise made available at each playing position.

11.96 The Progressive wager is a wager that the player will receive one of the specific five-card hands given in rule 11.97 using any combination of their two hole cards and the five community cards. If such a hand is dealt, the player will win regardless of whether the hand also beat the dealer.

11.97 If upon the hand being revealed, an opposing player who has placed a Progressive Jackpot wager has a hand containing one of the following rankings, the player's Progressive Jackpot wager shall win, and be paid from the Progressive Jackpot Meter, the following minimum amounts:

(a) Royal Flush **(100% of the Progressive Jackpot Meter)**
(b) Straight Flush **(10% of the Progressive Jackpot Meter)**
(c) Four of a Kind **(100 times the value of the wager)**
(d) Full House **(10 times the value of the wager)**

11.98 Where one of winning hands given in rule 11.97 comprises all five community cards, all players with a Progressive wager are entitled to Play the Board, ie use the five community cards as their hand:

(a) Where the winning hand is a Royal Flush, all winning players will share the jackpot meter equally.

(b) Where the winning hand is a Straight Flush made up of all five community cards, all winning players will receive an equal share equivalent to 10% of the jackpot total.
(c) Where the winning hand is a Four of a Kind or Full House, each player will receive the appropriate fixed payment detailed in points c) and d) in rule 11.97.

11.99 If one or more participating players is dealt a Royal Flush or Straight Flush, using either or both of their hole cards together with a combination of community cards, payment will be made in seating order starting from the dealer's right.

11.100 Progressive wagers will be settled after all five community cards have been dealt. If a player with a Progressive wager therefore elects to Fold, their cards will remain on the table until the Turn and River cards have been dealt and the outcome of the Progressive wager can be determined.

TWO WAY TEXAS HOLD 'EM CASINO POKER

11.101 The following procedures describe the proprietary variation of Texas Hold 'Em called 'Two Way Texas Hold 'Em Casino Poker'. The proprietor of the game is Prime Table Games, and no variations to the game may be put forward without their prior agreement.

11.102 The player shall place **three** initial wagers of equal amounts, hereafter called the Ante wager, the Blind wager and the Two Way wager before the Initial Deal. All subsequent optional wagers are placed **after** the cards are drawn.

11.103 The dealer will make the Initial Deal, and will then immediately draw the first three communal cards, which they will place face up in the area designated for the Flop.

11.104 All opposing players then have the opportunity to place an **optional** additional wager of equal amount to their Ante wager (hereafter called the Flop wager), which they will place in the designated betting area.

11.105 When all opposing players have made their decision whether or not to place a Flop wager, the dealer will draw the last two communal cards, and will place them face up in the area designated for the Turn and River cards.

11.106 All opposing players then have the opportunity to place an **optional** additional wager (hereafter called the River wager) which they will place in the designated betting area.

11.107 When all opposing players have made their decision whether or not to place a River wager, the dealer will reveal their own two hole cards, and will determine their best five-card hand.

11.108 The dealer must have at least a pair for their hand to qualify (hereafter called a Qualifying Hand).

11.109 If the dealer's hand does **not** qualify, the Blind wager and any optional Flop or River wagers for each opposing player will be returned. However, the **Ante wager remains 'in action'** and will be contested against the dealer's hand. The dealer will determine the best five-card hand of each player in turn.

11.110 If the dealer's hand does not qualify, and is of a **lower** ranking than the player's hand, the Ante wager will win and be paid minimum odds of **even money (1–1)**.

11.111 If the dealer's hand does not qualify, but is of a **higher** ranking than the player's hand, the Ante wager will lose and be surrendered to the bank.

11.112 If the dealer **does** qualify, they will determine the best five-card hand of each player in turn.

11.113 If the dealer's hand qualifies and has a **lower** ranking than the player's hand, the player's Ante, Blind and any Flop or River wagers will all be paid minimum odds of **even money (1–1)**.

11.114 If the dealer's hand qualifies and has a **higher** ranking than the player's hand, the player's Ante, Blind and any Flop or River wagers will all lose and be surrendered to the house.

11.115 The Two Way wager is unaffected by whether or not the dealer has a hand in Action. If neither the dealer's nor the player's hand contains a **Straight or better**, the player's Two Way wager will lose and be surrendered to the House.

11.116 If either the player and/or the dealer has a Straight or better, the player's Two Way wager will be paid the minimum odds given in rule 11.117 for **whichever** of the player or dealer hands has the higher ranking. For example, if the player has a Four of a Kind and the dealer only has a Full House, the player will be paid odds for Four of a Kind, as they have the higher ranking hand. However, if the player only has a Full House and the dealer has a higher ranking Four or a Kind, the player will be paid the higher odds for the dealer's Four of a Kind in settlement of their Two Way wager.
11.117 The table of minimum odds for settlement of Two Way wagers is as follows:

Hand	**Minimum odds**
Straight Flush	50–1
Four of a Kind	25–1
Full House	4–1
Flush	3–1
Straight	2–1

12. LET IT RIDE

THE TABLE LAYOUTS

12.1 Figure 23 shows an example of the style of game layout that may be offered to players. The proprietor of the game is Shufflemaster Inc and no variations to the game may be put forward without their prior agreement.

Figure 23

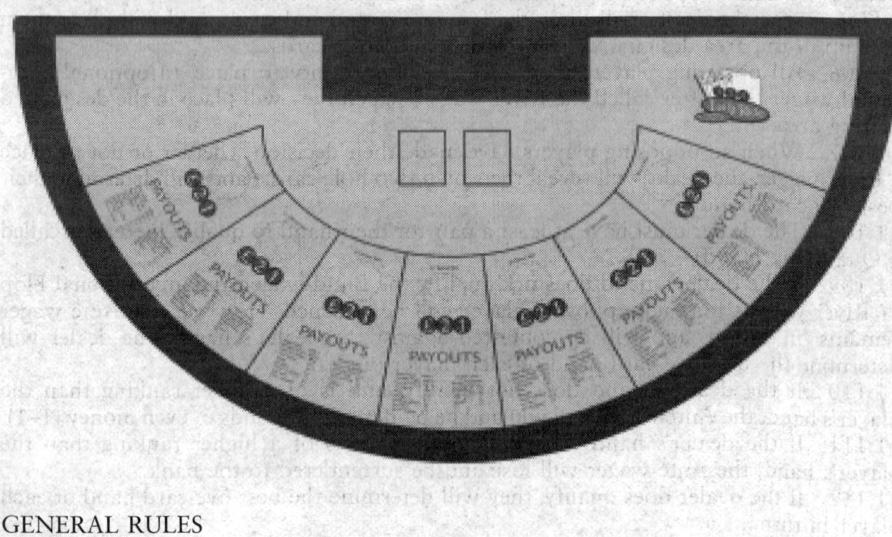

GENERAL RULES

12.2 Only the variations and side wagers listed in this section are permitted, unless agreed by the Proprietors and then approved by the Commission in accordance with the rules detailed in section 2.3 and 2.4.
12.3 The game shall be played with a single pack of 52 cards.
12.4 Operators must have procedures in place to ensure the security and integrity of the cards.
12.5 The maximum and minimum wagers permitted shall be shown on a notice prominently displayed at the table. Display of the maximum wager is recommended but

is otherwise at the discretion of the licence holder. Partnerships with a view to exceeding the maximum stake shall not be permitted.

12.6 The relative value of each of the cards is as follows (in descending order): Ace, King, Queen, Jack, 10, 9, 8, 7, 6, 5, 4, 3, and 2, except that the Ace may be used as a value of one, as detailed in 12.7 below, (being 3, 2, Ace).

12.7 The terms used to describe the five-card hands, and descending order of hand rankings, shall be in accordance with the following:

(a) **Royal Flush** – Ace, King, Queen, Jack and 10 of the same suit;
(b) **Straight Flush** – five cards of consecutive values of the same suit;
(c) **Four of a Kind** – four cards of the same value;
(d) **Full House** – three cards of the same value together with two cards of the same value being different to the first value;
(e) **Flush** – five cards of the same suit;
(f) **Straight** – five cards of consecutive values not being a Royal Flush or a Straight Flush;
(g) **Three of a Kind** – three cards of the same value;
(h) **Two pairs** – two cards of the same value together with two cards of the same value being different to the first value;
(i) **One pair** – two cards of the same value;
(j) **High Card/No pair** – the highest value cards of the hand.

The minimum winning hand in the game of Let it Ride is a pair of tens or better.

12.8 Only one wager may be accepted on each playing position and no individual player may place a wager on more than one playing position.

12.9 All wagers made by opposing players will be against the house. Players will wager that their hand achieves a particular hand ranking prescribed within the pay tables given in rule 12.27, when the three cards dealt to their hand are combined with the two community cards dealt to the dealer.

12.10 An additional optional side wager may be placed by participating players, which will be a wager that the three cards dealt to a player's hand will achieve a particular three-card hand ranking within the pay tables given in rule 12.30 and 12.31.

12.11 Cards will be dealt starting from the player to the dealer's left.

12.12 All settlement of bets and decisions as to whether a player wishes to Let it Ride will be made by each player in turn, starting from the player to the dealer's right.

INITIAL WAGER

12.13 Prior to any cards being dealt, all participating players must make three equal wagers (hereafter called the Mandatory Wagers) and place them in the betting positions marked '1', '2' and '£' on the playing position in front of them. The '£' wager is the minimum amount that the player must risk, whilst the first and second wagers ('1' and '2') may be pulled back during the course of the game, in accordance with the rules of this section.

12.14 Participating players who have placed the three Mandatory Wagers may also place an optional side wager (hereafter called the Three Card Bonus) of an amount no more or less than the minimum and maximum wager applicable to that table. The Three Card Bonus wager does not have to be of equal value to the Mandatory Wagers.

12.15 After all Mandatory Wagers and optional Three Card Bonus wagers have been placed, the dealer will deal three cards face down to each player, starting from the player to their left, and three cards to themselves. The dealer's cards are **not** considered as a separate hand.

12.16 The dealer's top **two** cards (hereafter called the 'community cards') will be placed face down in the area designated for the community cards. If a shuffle machine is used and dispatches three cards to the dealer, their third card (top or bottom) will be burned and placed in the discard.

12.17 Each player will decide whether their three card hand has the potential to achieve a minimum ranking of a pair of tens or better, when combined with the two (as yet unknown) community cards.

12.18 Each player will be invited to decide whether they wish to withdraw their first ('1') Mandatory Wager or Let it Ride, that is, remain in play.
12.19 If a player elects to withdraw their first wager, the dealer will return the wager to the player.
12.20 If the player elects to 'Let it Ride', it will be left in position '1' and will remain in play.
12.21 When all players have made their decision to either withdraw their first wager or Let it Ride, the dealer will reveal their first community card in front of them, being the card to their left.
12.22 Each player will then be invited to decide in turn whether to withdraw their second ('2') wager or Let it Ride.
12.23 If a player elects to withdraw their second wager, the dealer will return the wager to the player.
12.24 If the player elects to Let it Ride, it will be left in position '2' and will remain in play.
12.25 When all players have made their decision to either withdraw their second wager or Let it Ride, the dealer will reveal their second community card in front of them, being the card to their right.
12.26 Starting from the player to their right, the dealer will then determine whether each player has a winning five-card hand in accordance with rule 12.7, using all three of the player's cards combined with both the two community cards.
12.27 The Player will win if they have one of the hand rankings below:

Hand	Paid Minimum Odds
Royal Flush	100 – 1
Straight Flush	50 –1
Four of a Kind	25 –1
Full House	11 –1
Flush	8 – 1
Straight	5 – 1
Three of a Kind	3 – 1
Two Pairs	2 – 1
Pair of Tens, Jacks, Queens, Kings or Aces	Evens

NB the above table shows the minimum permitted odds that may be paid, drawn from the Pay Tables given below. However, the full list of minimum odds is not, in itself, a well balance Pay Table and in fact carries a House Edge of 5.25%. It is therefore recommended that they only be used as a guide and not as a Pay Table in themselves.
In addition to offering, as a minimum, the odds given above, above, odds for the standard wagers on Let it Ride may be presented as complete pay tables, in accordance with Rule 2.9 given in section 2of this document. Permitted pay tables are as follows:

Pay table 1

Hand	Paid Minimum Odds
Royal Flush	100 – 1
Straight Flush	50 –1
Four of a Kind	30 –1
Full House	15 –1
Flush	9 – 1
Straight	6 – 1
Three of a Kind	3 – 1

Hand	Paid Minimum Odds
Two Pairs	2 – 1
Pair of Tens, Jacks, Queens, Kings or Aces	Evens

Pay table 2

Hand	Paid Minimum Odds
Royal Flush	200 – 1
Straight Flush	100 –1
Four of a Kind	40 –1
Full House	15 –1
Flush	9 – 1
Straight	6 – 1
Three of a Kind	3 – 1
Two Pairs	2 – 1
Pair of Tens, Jacks, Queens, Kings or Aces	Evens

Pay table 3

Hand	Paid Minimum Odds
Royal Flush	500 – 1
Straight Flush	100 –1
Four of a Kind	25 –1
Full House	15 –1
Flush	10 – 1
Straight	5 – 1
Three of a Kind	3 – 1
Two Pairs	2 – 1
Pair of Tens, Jacks, Queens, Kings or Aces	Evens

Pay table 4

Hand	Paid Minimum Odds
Royal Flush	1000 – 1*
Straight Flush	200 –1
Four of a Kind	50 –1
Full House	11 –1
Flush	8 – 1
Straight	5 – 1
Three of a Kind	3 – 1
Two Pairs	2 – 1
Pair of Tens, Jacks, Queens, Kings or Aces	Evens

***It is permissible to apply a maximum ceiling to the total sterling amount that will be paid at a table to an individual who wins with a Royal Flush, provided:**

(a) **It applies only to the 1000-1 Royal Flush payout;**

(b) There is very clear signage at the table highlighting the maximum total amount that will be paid to that player for the standard wagers, regardless of the value of the bets placed or how many of the three standard wagers remain in play at the end of the game;

(c) That all players who have placed wagers that would be impacted by the maximum payout are informed of this fact before the game commences, so that they are in absolutely no doubt of the fact and have the opportunity to remove or adjust their wager before the game takes place if they wish.

12.28 If the player does not have a hand containing, as a minimum, a Pair of Tens or better, their hand will lose and however many of their three Mandatory Wagers are still in play will be surrendered to the bank.

12.29 If the player does have a hand containing, as a minimum, a Pair of Tens or better, then however many of their three Mandatory Wagers are left in play will each be paid the relevant minimum odds given in rule 12.27.

12.30 For Players who placed the optional Three Card Bonus wager at the beginning of the game, the Dealer will also determine whether the Player's own three card hand has achieved one of the following hand rankings:

Hand	**Paid Minimum Odds**
Mini Royal Flush (Suited Q,K,A)	50–1
Straight Flush	40–1
Three of a Kind	8–1
Straight	4–1
Flush	3–1
Pair	1–1

NB the above table shows the minimum permitted odds that may be paid, drawn from the Pay Tables given in Section 12.31. However, the full list of minimum odds is not, in itself, a well balance Pay Table and in fact carries a House Edge of 18.7%. It is therefore recommended that they only be used as a guide and not as a Pay Table in themselves.

12.31 In addition to offering, as a minimum, the odds given in rule 12.30, above, odds may be presented as complete pay tables, in accordance with rule 2.9 given in section 2. Permitted pay tables are as follows:

Pay table 1

Hand	**Paid minimum odds**
Mini Royal Flush (Suited Queen, King, Ace)	50–1
Straight Flush	40–1
Three of a Kind	30–1
Straight	6–1
Flush	4–1
Pair	1–1

Pay table 2

Hand	**Paid minimum odds**
Mini Royal Flush (Suited Queen, King, Ace)	50–1
Straight Flush	40–1
Three of a Kind	30–1
Straight	5–1

Hand	Paid minimum odds
Flush	4–1
Pair	1–1

Pay table 3

Hand	Paid minimum odds
Mini Royal Flush (Suited Queen, King, Ace)	50–1
Straight Flush	40–1
Three of a Kind	30–1
Straight	6–1
Flush	3–1
Pair	1–1

12.32 If the three cards dealt to the hand of a player with a Three Card Bonus wager do not contain at least a pair, their Three Card Bonus will lose and be surrendered to the house.
12.33 If the three cards dealt to the hand of a player with a Three Card Bonus wager do contain at least a pair, their Three Card Bonus wager will win and be paid the minimum odds given in rule 12.30.

13. PAI GOW POKER

THE TABLE LAYOUT

Figure 24 shows an example of the style of games layout that may be offered to players. It illustrates the range of wages available.

Figure 24:

GENERAL RULES

13.1 Only the variations and side wagers listed in this section are permitted, unless agreed by the proprietors and then approved by the Commission in accordance with the rules detailed in section 2.3 and 2.4.
13.2 The game shall be played with a single pack of 53 cards **including the joker**.

13.3 Operators must have procedures in place to ensure the security and integrity of the cards.
13.4 The maximum and minimum wagers permitted shall be shown on a notice prominently displayed at the table. Display of the maximum wager is recommended but is otherwise at the discretion of the licence holder. Partnerships with a view to exceeding the maximum stake shall not be permitted.
13.5 The relative value of each of the cards is as follows (in descending order): Ace, King, Queen, Jack, 10, 9, 8, 7, 6, 5, 4, 3, and 2, except that the Ace may be used as a value of one, as detailed in 12.7 below (being 3, 2, Ace). The Joker is valued in accordance with rule 13.9.
13.6 The player must set their best five-card hand **and** two-card hand from the seven cards they are dealt, in accordance with rule 13.19.
13.7 The terms used to describe the **five-card hands**, and descending order of hand rankings, shall be in accordance with the following:
(a) **Five Aces** – Four Aces and the Joker;
(b) **Royal Flush** – Ace, King, Queen, Jack and ten of the same suit;
(c) **Straight Flush** – five cards of consecutive values of the same suit. Please note, the second highest straight flush (to 10, Jack, Queen, King, Ace as the highest) is Ace, 2, 3, 4, 5 in Pai Gow Poker;
(d) **Four of a Kind** – four cards of the same value; 80
(e) **Full House** – three cards of the same value together with two cards of the same value being different to the first value;
(f) **Flush** – five cards of the same suit;
(g) **Straight** – five cards of consecutive values not being a Royal Flush or a Straight Flush. Please note, the second highest straight (to 10, Jack, Queen, King, Ace as the highest) is Ace, 2, 3, 4, 5 in Pai Gow Poker.
(h) **Three of a Kind** – three cards of the same value;
(i) **Two pairs** – two cards of the same value together with two cards of the same value being different to the first value;
(j) **One pair** – two cards of the same value;
(k) **High Card/No pair** – the highest value cards of the hand.
13.8 The **two-card hand** will be either a pair or two individual cards. The highest two card hand is a pair of Aces, and the lowest is 2-3. A Straight or a Flush do not apply within the ranking of the two-card hand.
13.9 **The Joker** can be used to complete a Straight, a Flush or a Straight Flush but is otherwise **treated as an Ace.**
13.10 Only one wager may be accepted on each playing position and no individual player may place a wager on more than one playing position.
13.11 All wagers made by opposing players will be against the house. Players will wager that **both** their five-card hand **and** their two-card hand achieve higher rankings than the equivalent hands dealt and arranged by the dealer.
13.12 Optional side wagers may be made available in the game, as described in rules 13.28 onwards. Only one form of optional side wager may be offered on any particular table.
13.13 Cards will be dealt starting from the player to the dealer's left.
13.14 All settlement of wagers will be made to each player in turn, starting from the player to the dealer's right.

INITIAL WAGER

13.15 Prior to any cards being dealt, all participating players must place a wager (Standard Wager).
13.16 At the same time, players may place an optional side wager as described in rule 13.28 onwards, provided they have also placed a Standard Wager.
13.17 Each participating player and the dealer will be dealt seven cards in turn, face down.

13.18 Each player will then set a five-card hand ('High') and a two-card hand ('Low') from the seven cards they are dealt. The five-card High Hand will be placed in the playing position marked 'H', which is also known as the 'Back'. The two-card Low hand will be placed in the playing position marked 'L', which is also known as the 'Front'.

13.19 When setting their hands, the player must make their best five-card hand as the High hand. **The player's two-card hand may not be higher than their five-card hand.** For example, if the player is dealt King, King, 2, 4, 6, 8, 10 of mixed suits and can therefore only make one pair from all the seven cards dealt, that pair must be set within the five-card hand. The pair cannot be set as the two-card hand, as it would then be better than the hand of five unrelated cards. If the player sets their hands with the two-card hand higher than the five-card hand, then a 'foul' is declared. At the licence holder's discretion the following two options may apply:

(a) Both player hands will automatically lose, regardless of their ranking against the dealer's hand; or

(b) The dealer may re-set the player's hands using the House Way detailed in rule 13.21 and allow them to then remain in play.

Whichever option is being applied, a sign or notice must be displayed at the table to inform players.

13.20 Other than abiding by rule 13.19, the player may set their two and five-card hands in whichever way they wish. However, the dealer must always set both their hands in accordance with the House rules ('the House Way') as detailed in rule 13.21.

13.21 When all opposing players have set their hands and placed them in the appropriate playing position, the dealer will reveal their own seven cards and set out their best five-card High hand, and their two-card Low hand, face up in the designated area. The dealer must set their hands in accordance with the House Way, as detailed below:

Seven Cards containing:	**Place in five-card hand ('Back')**	**Place in two-card hand ('Front')**
High Card/No Pair	**Highest Card**	**2nd and 3rd highest cards**
One Pair	Pair	Next two highest singleton cards
Two Pairs criteria given below using following groups: **2s – 6s = Low Pair** **7s – 10s = Medium Pair** **Js – Ks = High Pair**	(See below)	
Low Pair + Low Pair **or** **Low Pair + Medium Pair**	Split unless holding a King or better, in which case both pairs at the back and next highest two cards at the front	
Low Pair + High Pair **or** **Medium Pair + Medium Pair**	Split unless holding an Ace in which case both pairs at the back and next highest two cards at the front	
Medium Pair + High Pair **or** **High Pair + High Pair** **or** **Pair of Aces + Any other pair**	Always Split	

6: Gambling Act 2005: Additional Material

Seven Cards containing:	Place in five-card hand ('Back')	Place in two-card hand ('Front')
High Card/No Pair	Highest Card	2nd and 3rd highest cards
Three Pairs	2nd and 3rd highest pairs	Highest pair
Three of a Kind (other than Aces)	Three of a Kind	Next two highest cards
Three of a Kind Aces	Pair of Aces	Ace + one other card
Three of a Kind twice	Lowest three of a kind	Highest pair
Straights, Flushes, Straight Flushes and Royal Flushes	(See below)	(See below)
- with no pair	When choosing whether to play a Straight. Flush or Straight Flush, play the category that will allow the highest two cards in front	
- with 6th or 7th card included	Play the lower Straight or Flush in the back to place highest cards in front	
- with one pair	Play pair in the front only if a Straight, Flush or Straight Flush can be played in the back	
- with two pair	Use the two pair rules detailed above	
- with three pairs	Use the three pair rules detailed above	
One Pair	Pair	Next two highest singleton cards
Two Pairs criteria given below using following groups: 2s – 6s = Low Pair 7s – 10s = Medium Pair Js – Ks = High Pair	(See below)	
Low Pair + Low Pair or Low Pair + Medium Pair	Split unless holding a King or better, in which case both pairs at the back and next highest two cards at the front	
Low Pair + High Pair or Medium Pair + Medium Pair	Split unless holding an Ace in which case both pairs at the back and next highest two cards at the front	
Medium Pair + High Pair or High Pair + High Pair or Pair of Aces + Any other pair	Always Split	
Three Pairs	2nd and 3rd highest pairs	Highest pair
Three of a Kind (other than Aces)	Three of a Kind	Next two highest cards
Three of a Kind Aces	Pair of Aces	Ace + one other card
Three of a Kind twice	Lowest three of a kind	Highest pair

Seven Cards containing:	Place in five-card hand ('Back')	Place in two-card hand ('Front')
High Card/No Pair	Highest Card	2nd and 3rd highest cards
Straights, Flushes, Straight Flushes and Royal Flushes	(See below)	(See below)
- with no pair	When choosing whether to play a Straight, Flush or Straight Flush, play the category that will allow the highest two cards in front	
- with 6th or 7th card included	Play the lower Straight or Flush in the back to place highest cards in front	
- with one pair	Play pair in the front only if a Straight, Flush or Straight Flush can be played in the back	
- with two pair	Use the two pair rules detailed above	
- with three pairs	Use the three pair rules detailed above	
- with Three of a Kind	Play Pair in front	
- with Full House	Use Full House rules detailed below	
Full House	Always split unless includes a pair of two's and there is an Ace and a King to play in front	
- with three of a kind and two pairs or with three of a kind twice	Play highest pair in front	
- when 2s, 3s, 4s, 5s or 6s	Keep together and play Four of a Kind in back	
- when 7s, 8s, 9s or 10s	Split unless a King or better can be played in front	
- when Js, Qs or Ks	Split unless an Ace can be played in front	
- when four Aces	Always split	
- Four of a Kind with a pair	Play Pair in front	
Five Aces	Aces and play three Aces in back and two Aces in front, unless hand includes a pair of Kings, when all five Aces played in back and pair of Kings in front	

13.22 The dealer will then compare their own two hands against each opposing player's hands in turn. The player's five-card High hand will be compared against the dealer's **High** Hand first, followed by the two-card (Low) Hand, which is compared to the dealer's **Low** Hand. The dealer will assess the ranking of hands in accordance with rule 13.7. **Both** player hands must beat the dealer for the player's Standard Wager to win.

13.23 If the player's High Hand beats the dealer's equivalent High hand, but their Low hand does not beat the dealer's Low hand, (ie one wins and one loses) the player's Standard wager is a stand off and is returned to the player.

13.24 If both the player's High Hand **and** their Low Hand lose to the dealer, their Standard wager is lost and will be surrendered to the bank.

13.25 If there is an **exact** match between the player's High Hand and the dealer's High Hand, the dealer will win the High Hand. Similarly, if there is an **exact** match between the player's Low Hand and the dealer's Low Hand, the dealer will win the Low Hand.

13.26 If the player's High Hand beats the dealer's High Hand, and their Low Hand beats the dealer's Low hand (ie both hands win) the player's standard wager will win and be paid minimum odds of **even money less a 5% commission**.

13.27 The dealer will then settle the player's optional side wager, in accordance with rules 13.28 and onwards.

PERMITTED VARIATIONS TO PAI GOW POKER

'Fortune Pai Gow Poker' side wager

13.28 It is at the discretion of the licence holder whether or not to offer the 'Fortune Pai Gow' side wager as an additional, optional wager in the standard game of Pai Gow Poker. The proprietor of the side wager is Shufflemaster Inc and no variations may be put forward without their prior agreement.

13.29 The feature shall only be available at a table or tables marked for the provision of the wager, hereafter called the 'Fortune side wager'.

13.30 The Fortune side wager is an optional bonus wager that considers the player's best possible hand from all seven cards dealt to them, and is reconciled against an approved pay table (see rule 13.36).

13.31 Players may wager any amount within the table limits as their Fortune side wager, which must be wagered at the same time as the Standard wager, but need not be of equal value to it.

13.32 Players who place a Fortune side wager that is equal to, or exceeds, the amount prescribed under the house rules, will qualify for a potential 'Envy Bonus' as detailed in rule 13.38 onwards. Such a hand is hereafter referred to as an 'Envy Qualifying Hand'. The qualifying amount for an Envy Bonus must be clearly displayed at the table.

13.33 The dealer will place an Envy Bonus marker alongside all Fortune side wagers that relate to Envy Qualifying Hands.

13.34 Any Fortune side wagers will be settled at the same time as the Standard Pai Gow wager for each player.

13.35 If the player's hand **does not** achieve one of the hand rankings given in rule 13.36, it will not qualify for a Fortune Pai Gow pay out. Their Fortune side wager will lose and be surrendered to the house.

13.36 If the player's hand **does** achieve one of the following hand rankings, it will qualify for a Fortune Pai Gow pay out. The Fortune side wager will be settled and paid, as a minimum, the odds listed below:

Hand	**Minimum odds payable**
7 Card Straight Flush	2500–1*
Royal Flush + King/Queen of a same suit	1000–1*
7 Card Straight Flush with Joker	500–1
5 Aces (All four plus Joker)	250–1
5 card Royal Flush	100–1
5 card Straight Flush	50–1
Four of a Kind	20–1
Full House	5–1
5 card Flush	4–1
Three of a Kind	3–1
Five card Straight	2–1
Three Pair	Push/standoff**
**Available at discretion of operator	

Please note that the above table shows the minimum permitted odds that may be paid, drawn from the pay tables given in Section 13.37. However, the full list of minimum odds is not, in itself, a well-balanced Pay Table. It is therefore recommended that they are only used as a guide and not as a pay table in themselves.

13.37 In addition to offering, as a minimum, the odds given in rule 13.36 above, odds may be presented as complete pay tables, in accordance with rule 2.9 given in section 2 of this document. Permitted pay tables are as follows:

Pay table 1

7 Card Straight Flush	5000–1*
Royal Flush + King/Queen of a same suit	1000–1*
7 Card Straight Flush with Joker	750–1
5 Aces (All four plus Joker)	250–1
5 card Royal Flush	100–1
5 card Straight Flush	50–1
Four of a Kind	20–1
Full House	5–1
5 card Flush	4–1
Three of a Kind	3–1
Five card Straight 2–1	3–1
Three Pair	Push/standoff

Pay table 2

7 Card Straight Flush	8000–1*
Royal Flush + King/Queen of a same suit	2000–1*
7 Card Straight Flush with Joker	1000–1*
5 Aces (All four plus Joker)	400–1
5 card Royal Flush	150–1
5 card Straight Flush	50–1
Four of a Kind	25–1
Full House	5–1
5 card Flush	4–1
Three of a Kind	3–1
Five card Straight	2–1

*It is permissible to apply a maximum ceiling to the sterling amount that will be paid at a table to an individual who wins with a seven card straight flush or a Royal Flush+ king/ queen of a same suit, provided:

(a) It applies only to odds of 1000-1 or above;

(b) There must be very clear signage at the table highlighting the maximum amount that will be paid regardless of the value of the wager;

(c) That all players who place wagers that would be impacted by the maximum payout are informed of this fact, so that they are in absolutely no doubt of the fact and have the opportunity to remove or adjust their wager before the game takes place if they wish.

ENVY BONUS

13.38 If any player on the table has an Envy Bonus marker alongside their wager, in accordance with rule 13.33, all cards will be left in place until the dealer has settled the wagers for all opposing players. They will then assess whether one or more Envy Bonuses are payable to Envy Qualifying Hands.

13.39 If the player's hand qualifies for a Fortune Pai Gow pay out, and has a marker or other indicator to show that it qualifies for a potential Envy Bonus, in accordance with rule 13.33, the marker will be left in place after the dealer has settled all wagers for that player and remain there whilst they settle wagers for all remaining players.

13.40 After all hands and Standard wagers and Fortune side wagers for opposing players have been settled, the dealer will determine whether any player at the table has a seven-card hand that contains Four of a Kind or better.

13.41 A player cannot earn an Envy Bonus on his own hand, or for the dealer's hand.

13.42 If no player has a seven-card hand containing Four of a Kind or better, then no Envy Bonus is payable. The dealer will therefore collect the cards and Envy Bonus markers and the game will be over.

13.43 If one player has a seven-card hand containing Four of a Kind or better, then an Envy Bonus is payable to each player who has an Envy Qualifying Hand.

13.44 If more than one player has a seven-card hand containing Four of a Kind or better, then a separate Envy Bonus is payable for **each** of those winning hands to all Envy Qualifying hands.

13.45 Winning Envy bonuses on qualifying hands will be paid, as a minimum, the following amounts:

Seven card hand	Minimum amounts paid for Envy Bonus
7 Card Straight Flush	£500
Royal Flush + Royal Match	£125
7 card Straight Flush with Joker	£50
5 Aces (all four plus Joker)	£25
5 Card Royal Flush	£10
Straight Flush	£5
Four of a Kind	£2

In addition to offering, as a minimum, the odds given above, amounts may be presented for Envy Bonuses as complete pay tables, in accordance with rule 2.9 given in section 2 of this document. Examples permitted include:

Pay table 1
Minimum odds given above

Pay table 2

Seven card hand	Minimum amounts paid for Envy Bonus
7 Card Straight Flush	£2500
Royal Flush + Royal Match	£500
7 card Straight Flush with Joker	£250
5 Aces (all four plus Joker)	£100
5 Card Royal Flush	£25
Straight Flush	£10
Four of a Kind	£2

Jokolor side wager

13.46 It is at the discretion of the licence holder whether or not to offer the 'Jokolor' side wager as an additional, optional wager in the standard game of Pai Gow Poker. The proprietor of the side wager is Prime Table Games and no variations may be put forward without their prior agreement.

13.47 The feature shall only be available at a table or tables marked for the provision of the wager, hereafter called the Jokolor side wager.
13.48 The Jokolor side wager is an optional bonus wager payable if the player's seven card hand includes the Joker, if all seven cards are of the same colour, or where the hand consists of six cards of the same colour plus the Joker.
13.49 Players may wager any amount within the table limits as their Jokolor side wager, which must be placed at the same time as the Standard wager, but need not be of equal value.
13.50 Any Jokolor side wagers will be settled at the same time as the dealer reconciles the standard Pai Gow wager for each player.
13.51 If the player with a Jokolor side wager has one of the hands listed below, it will win and be paid, as a minimum, the following odds:

Seven-card hand	**Minimum odds payable for Jokolor**
Includes Joker	5–1
All seven cards of same colour	10–1
Six cards of same colour plus Joker	30–1

13.52 If the player's hand **does not** contain one of the hands listed in rule 13.51, their Jokolor side wager will lose and be surrendered to the house.

14. PAI GOW TILES

THE TABLE LAYOUTS

The diagrams below show examples of the style of game layout that may be offered to players.

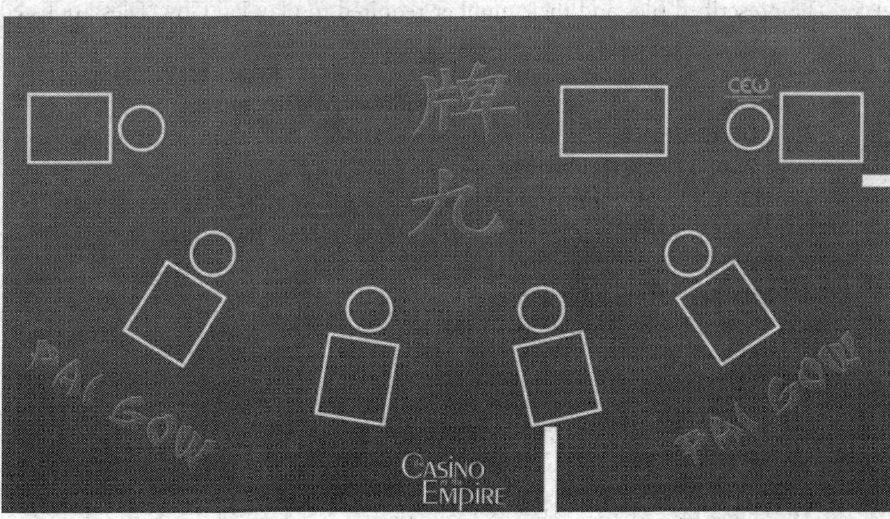

GENERAL RULES

14.1 Only the variations and side wagers listed in this section are permitted.
14.2 The game shall be played with 32 prescribed tiles (dominoes), three dice and a shaker. The tiles will be marked as follows:

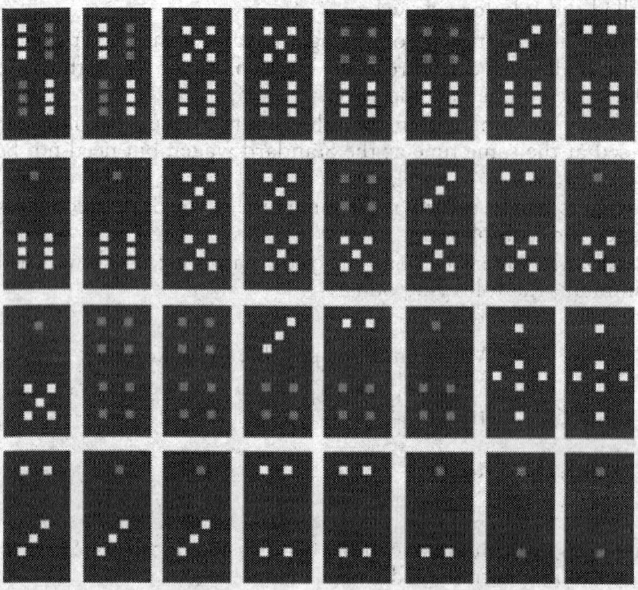

14.3 Operators must have procedures in place to ensure the security and integrity of the tiles and dice.

14.4 The minimum wagers permitted shall be shown on a notice prominently displayed at the table. Display of the maximum wager is recommended but is otherwise at the discretion of the licence holder. Partnerships with a view to exceeding the maximum stake shall not be permitted.

14.5 The prescribed tiles and their number required to play Pai Gow Tiles are listed below:

Tile	Number of Tiles in set
Twelve [6 – 6] (Double six)	2
Two [1 – 1] (Double one)	2
Eight [4 – 4] (Double four)	2
Four [1 – 3]	2
Ten [5 – 5] (Double five)	2
Six [3 – 3] (Double three)	2
Four [2 – 2] (Double two)	2
Eleven [5 – 6]	2
Ten [4 – 6]	2
Seven [1 – 6]	2
Six [1 – 5]	2
Nine [3 – 6]	1
Nine [4 – 5]	1
Eight [2 – 6]	1
Eight [3 – 5]	1
Seven [2 – 5]	1
Seven [3 – 4]	1
Six [2 – 4]	1

Tile	Number of Tiles in set
Five [1 – 4]	1
Five [2 – 3]	1
Three [1 – 2]	1

14.6 All the hands describe below have had the overall ranking and common tile hand name (where appropriate) attached to them. Some numbers are shown on the domino coloured red, but this does not affect the score or the ranking of the domino or pair.

14.7 The highest possible pair is the 'Supreme Pair', which is made up of two tiles:

14.8 The above tiles are the two 'wild tiles' and can be used as either a 3 or a 6 (ie they can substitute for each other) when making pairs only.

14.9 The next tier of hands are called Pairs (these can be referred to as Bo), their order of ranking from high to low are as follows:

	Pair	Common Pair name
2nd	[6 – 6] and [6 – 6]	Heaven
3rd	[1 – 1] and [1 – 1]	Earth
4th	[4 – 4] and [4 – 4]	Man
5th	[3 – 1] and [3 – 1]	Goose
6th	[5 – 5] and [5 – 5]	Plum Flower or Flower
7th	[3 – 3] and [3 – 3]	Long or Double Three
8th	[2 – 2] and [2 – 2]	Board
9th	[6 – 5] and [6 – 5]	Hatchet
10th	[6 – 4] and [6 – 4]	Red Ten
11th	[6 – 1] and [6 – 1]	Long Leg Seven
12th	[5 – 1] and [5 – 1]	Big head Six
13th	[6 – 3] and [5 – 4]	Mixed Nine
14th	[6 – 2] and [5 – 3]	Mixed Eight
15th	[5 – 2] and [4 – 3]	Mixed Seven
16th	[4 – 1] and [3 – 2]	Mixed Five

14.10 The next tier of hands are called Wongs (they are a nine combined with a double six or double one) which are combinations of tiles and in order of rank from high to low are as follows:

17th	[6 – 6] and [6 – 3]	King of Heaven
17th	[6 – 6] and [5 – 4]	King of Heaven
18th	[1 – 1] and [6 – 3]	King of Earth
18th	[1 – 1] and [5 – 4]	King of Earth

14.11 The next tier of hands are called Gongs (they are a eight combined with a double six or double one) which are combinations of tiles and in order of ranking from high to low they are as follows:

19th	[6 – 6] and [6 – 2]	Treasure of Heaven
19th	[6 – 6] and [5 – 3]	Treasure of Heaven
19th	[6 – 6] and [4 – 4]	Treasure of Heaven
20th	[1 – 1] and [6 – 2]	Treasure of Earth
20th	[1 – 1] and [5 – 3]	Treasure of Earth
20th	[1 – 1] and [4 – 4]	Treasure of Earth

14.12 If the player or dealer cannot obtain any of the above combination of tiles, then the number of points on the two tiles (dominoes) that form the hand will be added to form a total. This value shall be a single figure (0 – 9) inclusive should that sum exceed 9 (as nine is the highest possible value) then ten is subtracted from this figure to form the hand value. For example, 6 and 5 = 11, subtract 10 = 1.

14.13 In the event of a tie, the outcome of the hand is determined by the individual tile values and in order of rank from high to low they are as follows:

Tile	**Common Tile name**
[6 – 6]	Heaven
[1 – 1]	Earth
[4 – 4]	Man
[1 – 3]	Goose
[5 – 5]	Flower
[3 – 3]	Long
[2 – 2]	Board
[5 – 6]	Hatchet
[4 – 6]	Red Ten
[1 – 6]	Long leg
[1 – 5]	Big head
[3 – 6] or [4 – 5]	Mixed 9
[2 – 6] or [3 – 5]	Mixed 8
[2 – 5] or [3 – 4]	Mixed 7
[1 – 4] or [2 – 3]	Mixed 5
[2 – 4]	Mixed 6 (part of Supreme Pair)
1 – 2]	Mixed 6 (part of Supreme Pair)

Note that, whilst the two wild tiles (1-2 and 2 -4) combined together are the highest ranking hand (the supreme pair), the individual tiles individually are the lowest ranking.

14.14 The player must ensure that their High hand outranks their Low Hand.

14.15 A dice shaker/tumbler device, either manually or electrically operated, shall be used to tumble the dice.

14.16 Players may play more than one betting position. The number of positions a player may play will be determined by the House.

14.17 All wagers made by the opposing player will be against the House. Players will wager that both their High and Low hands achieve higher rankings than then the equivalent hands dealt and arranged by the dealer.

14.18 Optional side wagers may be made available in the game, as described in the rules 14.38 onwards. More than one form of optional side wager may be offered on any particular table.
14.19 Tiles can either be dealt starting from the player to the dealer's left or to their right. This will be determined by the House.
14.20 All settlement of wagers will be made to each player in turn, starting from the player to the dealer's right.
14.21 The Licence Holder may at its discretion allow the player(s) to hold the bank. The casino is permitted to charge a levy on the players' winnings of 5% of any excess of losing wagers over winning wagers.
14.22 Should the Casino operator wish to introduce rule 14.21, it must do so to ensure the rules are equally favourable to all the player's who hold the bank.
14.23 The rules for the player to hold the bank must be easily accessible to the players.

Initial Wager

14.24 Prior to any tiles being dealt, all participating players must place an initial wager (Standard Wager).
14.25 At the same time, players may place an optional side wager as described in rule 14.38 onwards, provided they also placed a Standard Wager.
14.26 Whilst doing so, the dealer will mix up the tiles, face down, and will place them into eight stacks of four each. The Dealer will tumble the dice, which will determined which player will receive the first stack of tiles. The Dealer (House) is always numbered 1, 9 or 17.
14.27 Each participating player, non-wagered betting position and dealer will be dealt a stack of four tiles in turn, face down.
14.28 Each player will then set a two-domino ('High') hand and a two-domino ('Low') hand from the stack they are dealt. The High hand must be placed in the designated position so marked for that hand. The Low hand must be placed in the designated position so marked for that hand.
14.29 When setting their hands, the players must ensure their two-domino High hand outranks and or is greater that the players two-domino Low hand.
If the player sets their tiles with the Low hand greater than the High hand, then a 'Foul' is declared. At the licence holder's discretion the following two options may then apply:
(a)
(b) both player hands will automatically lose, regardless of their ranking against the dealer's hand; or
(c) The dealer may re-set the player's tiles using the House Way detailed in rule 14. 25 and allow them to then remain in play.
The players must be made aware of this fact, by whatever means the casino feels is appropriate. (A notice, rules of the games leaflets etc).
14.30 Other than abiding by rule 14.29, the player may set their High and Low domino hands in whichever way they wish. However, the dealer must always set both their hands in accordance with the House rules (the House Way) as detailed in rule 14.31.
14.31 When all opposing players have set their hands and placed them in the appropriate playing position, the dealer will reveal their own four tiles and set out their High and Low hands, face up in the designated area. The dealer must set their tiles in accordance with the House Way, as detailed below:

PAIR	WHEN TO SPLIT BANKER
Supreme Pair (3/6) (1-2 & 4-2 Tiles)	Any 6 with 4, 5, 6 i.e make a 9 – 7 or better

PAIR	WHEN TO SPLIT **BANKER**
Heaven and Earth (2 or 12) (Double six or Double one tiles)	Gong with 7, 8, 9 4 with 6, 7, 8, 9 (6 or 7) with 5, 6, 7, 8, 9 8 with 5, 8 Mixed 8 with 9 9 with 5, 11 **OR** Split to make 6 – 8 or better With 9 and 11
Man (8) (Double four tiles)	If (2, 10,12) With 10 or 11 2 with 12 9 with 11
Goose (4) Pair of 3-1 tiles	NEVER SPLIT
Flower (10) Double five tiles	NEVER SPLIT
Long (6) Double three tiles	(2, 12) with (2, 11, 12) **OR** NEVER SPLIT
Board (4) Double Two Tiles	NEVER SPLIT
Hatchet (11) (6 – 5) Tiles	NEVER SPLIT
Red Ten (10) (6 – 4) Tiles	NEVER SPLIT
Long Leg Seven (6 – 1) Tiles	2 and 12 (2, 12) with (10, 11) 10 and 11 **OR** (2, 12) WITH 2, 10, 11 12
Big Head Six (5 – 1) Tiles	2 and 12 (2, 12) with (FLOWER 10, 11) **OR** NEVER SPLIT
Mixed Nine	2 and 12 10 with 2, 12 Unpaired 10s
Mixed Eight	2 and 12 (2, 10, 12) with 10, 11 9 and 11
Mixed Seven	2 and 12 (2, 10, 12) with 10, 11
Mixed Five	2 and 12 **OR**

PAIR	WHEN TO SPLIT BANKER NEVER SPLIT

However; additional local House Way Rules may be added and applied to the above House Way, such as 'Strengthen' and 'Balancing Hands' rules.

If these are applicable then **THEY MUST** be displayed.

14.32 The dealer will then compare their two hands against each opposing player's hands in turn. The player's High (two domino) hand will be compared against the dealer's **High** hand first, followed by the Low (two domino) hand, which is compared to the dealer's **Low** hand. The dealer will assess the ranking of the hands in accordance with rule 14.7. **Both** player hands must beat the dealer for the player's Standard Wager to win.

14.33 If the player's High hand beats the dealer's equivalent High hand, but their Low hand does not beat the dealer's Low hand, (ie one wins and one loses) the player's Standard wager is a stand off (Tie/push) and is returned to the bank.

14.34 If both the player's High Hand **and** their Low Hand lose to the dealer, their Standard wager is lost and will be surrendered to the bank.

14.35 If there is an **exact** match between the player's High Hand and the dealer's High Hand, the hand will then be determined by the higher ranking domino in each hand, if then there is still an **exact** match the dealer will win the High Hand. Similarly, if there is an exact match between the player's Low Hand and the dealer's Low Hand, the hand will then be determined by the higher ranking domino in each hand, if then there is still an exact match the dealer will win the Low Hand.

14.36 If the player's High Hand beats the dealer's High hand and their Low Hands beats the dealer's Low Hand (ie both hands win) the player's Standard wager will win and be paid minimum odds of **even money less a 5% commission**.

14.37 The dealer will then settle the player's optional side wager, in accordance with rules 14.38 and onwards.

Permitted Variations to Pai Gow Tiles

'Bonanza Pai Gow Tiles' side wager

14.38 It is at the discretion of the licence holder whether or not to offer the 'Bonanza Pai Gow' side wagers as an additional, optional wager in the standard game of Pai Gow Tiles. The proprietor of the side wager is Gambology Inc and no variations may be put forward without their prior agreement or that of a subsequent proprietor.

14.39 The feature shall only be available at a table or table(s) marked for the provision of the wagers, hereafter called the Bonanza side wagers.

14.40 The Bonanza side wagers comprise of two optional wagers. These are the Bonus and Tie wagers. The player has the option to wager on either one of the wagers or both.

14.41 Any Bonanza side wager(s) will be settled at the same time as the Standard Pai Gow wager for each player.

14.42 The Bonanza Bonus side wager is an optional wager that considers the player's possible four tiles (dominoes) hand dealt to them, and is reconciled against an approved pay table in rule 14.44.

14.43 If the player's hand does not achieve one of the hand rankings given in rule 14.45, it will not qualify for a Bonanza Bonus pay out. Their Bonanza Bonus side wager will lose and be surrender to the house.

14.44 If the player's four tiles hand **does** achieve one of the following hand rankings, it will qualify for a Bonanza Pai Gow Bonus pay out. The Bonanza Bonus side wager will be settled and paid, as a minimum, the odds listed below:

Hand	Minimum odds payable
Player 2 Pair Vs Dealer 2 Pair	150 – 1
Supreme Pair + Heaven Pair	60 – 1
Supreme Pair + Earth Pair	30 – 1
Lucky Duck (A High 6, A Low 6, Any 7 And Any 4)	10 – 1
Two Pair	6 – 1
Supreme, Heaven or Earth Pair	3 – 1
Wong or One Pair	2 – 1

Please note that the above table shows the minimum permitted odds that may be paid. However, the full list of minimum odds is not, in itself, a well-balanced Pay Table and in fact carries a House Edge of 13.2%. It is therefore recommended that they are only used as a guide and not as a pay table in themselves.

14.45 In addition to offering, as a minimum, the odds given in rule 14.44 above, odds may be presented as complete pay tables, in accordance with rule 2.9 given in section 2 of this document. Permitted pay tables are as follows:

Pay table 1

Player 2 Pair Vs Dealer 2 Pair	250 – 1
Supreme Pair + Heaven Pair	100 – 1
Supreme Pair + Earth Pair	50 – 1
Lucky Duck (A High 6, A Low 6, Any 7 And Any 4)	20 – 1
Two Pair	10 – 1
Supreme, Heaven or Earth Pair	4 – 1
Wong or One Pair	2 – 1

Pay table 2

Player 2 Pair Vs Dealer 2 Pair	200 – 1
Supreme Pair + Heaven Pair	80 – 1
Supreme Pair + Earth Pair	40 – 1
Lucky Duck (A High 6, A Low 6, Any 7 And Any 4)	20 – 1
Two Pair	10 – 1
Supreme, Heaven or Earth Pair	4 – 1
Wong or One Pair	2 – 1

Pay table 3

Player 2 Pair Vs Dealer 2 Pair	250 – 1
Supreme Pair + Heaven Pair	80 – 1
Supreme Pair + Earth Pair	50 – 1
Lucky Duck (A High 6, A Low 6, Any 7 And Any 4)	5 – 1
Two Pair	8 – 1
Supreme, Heaven or Earth Pair	4 – 1
Wong or One Pair	2 – 1

Pay table 4

Player 2 Pair Vs Dealer 2 Pair	500 – 1
Supreme Pair + Heaven Pair	100 – 1
Supreme Pair + Earth Pair	50 – 1
Lucky Duck (A High 6, A Low 6, Any 7 And Any 4)	15 – 1
Two Pair	8 – 1
Supreme, Heaven or Earth Pair	3 – 1
Wong or One Pair	2 – 1

14.46 The Bonanza Tie side wager is an optional wager that the player will win one hand and loses the other hand against the dealer in regard to the Standard Pai Gow Tile wager, and is reconciled against an approved pay table in rule 14.49.

14.47 If the player's Standard Pai Gow wager is not a standoff (tie/push) nor has a hand reconciled against an approved pay table in accordance with rule 14.49, it will not qualify for a Bonanza Tie pay out. Their Bonanza Tie side wager will lose and be surrender to the house.

14.48 A player may decide after viewing their Pai Gow tiles to surrender their Bonanza Pai Gow Tie side wager, in doing so; the player will **lose half** their Bonanza Pai Gow Tie side wager staked.

14.49 If the player's two hand **does** achieve one of the following hand rankings, it will qualify for a Bonanza Pai Gow Tie pay out. The Bonanza side wager will be settled and paid, as a minimum, the odds listed below:

Hand	**Minimum odds payable**
Tie	1 – 1
Automatic Winners	
Two Pair	1 – 1
Lucky Duck	1 – 1

14.50 In addition to offering, as a minimum, the odds given in rule 14.49 above, odds may be presented as complete pay tables. Permitted pay table are as follows:

Pay table 1

Tie	1 – 1
Automatic Winners	
Two Pair	2 – 1
Lucky Duck	2 – 1

Pay table 2

Tie	1 – 1
Automatic Winners	
Two Pair	3 – 1
Lucky Duck	3 – 1

15. CRAZY FOR POKER

THE TABLE LAYOUT

15.1 The diagram below shows an example of the style of game layout that may be offered to players. The proprietor of the game in Shufflemaster Inc and no variation to the game may be put forward without their prior agreement.

GENERAL RULES

15.2 Only the variations and side wagers listed in this section are permitted, unless first agreed by the Proprietors.
15.3 The game shall be played with a single pack of 52 cards.
15.4 Operators must have procedures in place to ensure the security and integrity of the cards.
15.5 The maximum and minimum wagers permitted shall be shown on a notice prominently displayed at the table. Partnerships with a view to exceeding the maximum stake shall not be permitted.
15.6 The relevant value of each of the cards (in descending order) is as follows:- Ace, King, Queen, Jack, 10,9,8,7,6,5,4,3 and 2, except that Ace may have a value of one when used in a sequence of 4,3,2-Ace, within a Straight or Straight Flush, (as defined in rule 15.7 below).
15.7 The terms used to describe the four best card hands, and descending order of hand rankings, shall be in accordance with the following:
(a) **Four of a Kind** – four cards of the same value;
(b) **Straight Flush** – Four cards of consecutive value of the same suit;
(c) **Three of a Kind** – Three cards of the same value;
(d) **Flush** – Four cards of the same suit;
(e) **Straight** – Four cards of consecutive value not of the same suit;
(f) Two Pairs – Two cards of the same value together with two further cards; of the same value but different to the first pair;
(g) **Pair** – two cards of the same value;
(h) **High Card** – The highest value card in the hand;

INITIAL WAGER

15.8 Only one wager may be accepted on each playing position, and no individual player may place a wager on more than one playing position.

15.9 All wagers made by opposing players will be against the house. An initial wager is required from each opposing player, as referred to in rule 15.10, below.

15.10 The following initial wagers apply:

(i) A mandatory Ante wager being a wager that the player's hand, using the best four cards, will have a higher ranking than the dealer's hand.

(ii) A mandatory Super Bonus wager, being a wager that the player's hand will contain at least a straight or better.

(iii) An **optional** Queens Up wager, being a wager that the player's hand will contain at least a pair of queens or better.

A player who places an Ante wager must also place a Super Bonus wager, but need not place the optional Queens Up side bet wager. They may not place a Queens Up wager on its own without also having placed an Ante and Super Bonus side bet wager.

15.11 Wagers on the Ante and Super Bonus must be of an equal amount. Wagers on the Queens Up side bet may be for any amount within the table limits.

15.12 All opposing players and the dealer will receive five cards each, face down, starting with the player to the dealer's left.

SUBSEQUENT WAGER

15.13 Once all cards have been dealt, each player will examine their hand and establish the best four card hand available, in accordance with the hand rankings detailed in rule15.7.

15.14 All players who have placed an Ante and Super Bonus wager, and who wish to remain in the game, shall then make a further wager known as a Play wager. This must be for an equal amount to the Ante wager, other than for players eligible for a triple down wager, as defined in rule 15.15.

15.15 Where a player has a hand containing a pair of Aces or better, they have the option to triple down and place a Play wager of up to three times the Ante value.

15.16 A player with an Ante and Super Bonus wager who does not wish to make a subsequent Play wager shall fold and surrender the amount staked on both the Ante and Super Bonus wagers to the house.

15.17 The player who wishes to make a subsequent "Play" wager will place their cards face down under the wager in the "Play" betting position. Although only four cards are used to make the player's hand, the unwanted fifth card will remain with the other cards.

SETTLEMENT

15.18 Once all players have made their decisions, the Dealer will reveal their own five cards and determine their best four card hand. The Dealer's hand must have a value of "King high" or better to qualify against the player's hand.

15.19 If the Dealer **does not** have a qualifying hand, all Play wagers will be paid at odds of 1 to 1 and all Ante wagers will be returned to the Players ("push")

15.20 If the Dealer **does** gave a qualifying hand, they will compare it against each individual player's hand in turn, starting from the player to their right. If the Dealer's hand is higher, the player will lose, and will surrender both their Ante and Play wagers to the house. If the Player's hand is higher, their Ante and Play wagers shall win and be paid odds of 1 to 1.

15.21 If the Dealer's hand qualifies but is of exactly the same value as the Player's hand, it will be declared a tie and both the Ante and Play wagers will be returned to the Player ("push").

15.22 The Super Bonus wager shall win if the player's hand contains a straight or better, regardless of the value of the Dealer's hand and whether or not it qualifies. The player will be paid odds for any winning hand (as defined in rule 15.7) in accordance with the following pay table:

Hand:	**Paysminimum odds of:**
Four Aces	**200-1**
Four of a Kind	**30-1**
Straight Flush	**15-1**
Three of a Kind	**2-1**
Flush	**3-2**
Straight	**1 to 1**

The Super Bonus does not necessarily lose if the player does not have a hand containing a Straight or better, as detailed in rule 15.24.

15.23 If the player does not place a Play wager, and therefore folds in accordance with rule 15.16, their Super Bonus wager will also be surrendered to the house. However, any Queens Up wager may remain in play if the player believes it to contain a winning hand but still wishes to fold on their Ante and Super Bonus. In such circumstances, the player will place their cards face down in front of the Queens Up wager. It is the player's responsibility to notify the dealer if they do not wish to fold on their Queens Up wager when otherwise folding on their Ante and Super Bonus.

15.24 If the player's hand contains less than a straight, the following circumstances will apply regardless of whether the Dealer's hand qualifies:

(a) If the Player's hand is found to be higher or ties with the Dealer's had, then the Super Bonus wager will be returned (Push)

(b) If Player's hand is lower than the dealer's, then the Super Bonus will lose and be surrendered to the house.

QUEENS UP SIDEBET

15.25 The optional Queens Up side bet may be wagered at the same time as the Initial Wager, as described in rules 15.10 and 15.11.

15.26 An opposing player who has made a Queen Up wager shall win and be paid at the following minimum odds if, upon their hand being revealed, it consists of a pair of Queens or better. The following minimum odds will then be paid for the relevant hand rankings, regardless of whether the Dealer's hand qualifies:

Hand	**Pays Minimum Odds**
Four of a Kind	50 to 1
Straight Flush	30 to 1
Three of a Kind	7 to 1
Flush	4 to 1
Straight	3 to 1
Two pairs	2 to 1
Pair of Queens or better	1 to 1

NB the above table shows the minimum permitted odds that may be paid, drawn from the pay tables given below. However, the full list of minimum odds is not, in itself, a well balanced pay table and in fact carries a much higher house edge. It is therefore recommended that they only be used as a guide and not as a pay table in themselves.

Odds for the Queens Up side bet wagers on Crazy 4 Poker may also be presented as complete pay tables, in accordance with rule 2.9 in Section Two of this document. Permitted pay tables are as follows:

Pay table 1

Hand	Pays Minimum Odds
Four of a Kind	50 to 1
Straight Flush	30 to 1
Three of a Kind	9 to 1
Flush	4 to 1
Straight	3 to 1
Two pairs	2 to 1
Pair of Queens or better	1 to 1
House edge of 3.06%	

Pay table 2

Hand	Pays Minimum Odds
Four of a Kind	50 to 1
Straight Flush	40 to 1
Three of a Kind	8 to 1
Flush	4 to 1
Straight	3 to 1
Two pairs	2 to 1
Pair of Queens or better	1 to 1
House edge of 4.52%	

Pay table 3

Hand	Pays Minimum Odds
Four of a Kind	50 to 1
Straight Flush	30 to 1
Three of a Kind	8 to 1
Flush	4 to 1
Straight	3 to 1
Two pairs	2 to 1
Pair of Queens or better	1 to 1
House edge of 5.32%	

Pay table 4

Hand	Pays Minimum Odds
Four of a Kind	50 to 1
Straight Flush	40 to 1
Three of a Kind	7 to 1

Hand	Pays Minimum Odds
Flush	4 to 1
Straight	3 to 1
Two pairs	2 to 1
Pair of Queens or better	1 to 1
House edge of 6.78%	

15.27 A player who has placed a Queens Up side wager, but whose hand does not contain a pair of Queens or better, will lose and the wager will be surrendered to the house.

16. LIVE DRAW POKER

THE TABLE LAYOUT

The diagram below shows an example of the style of game layout that may be offered to players.

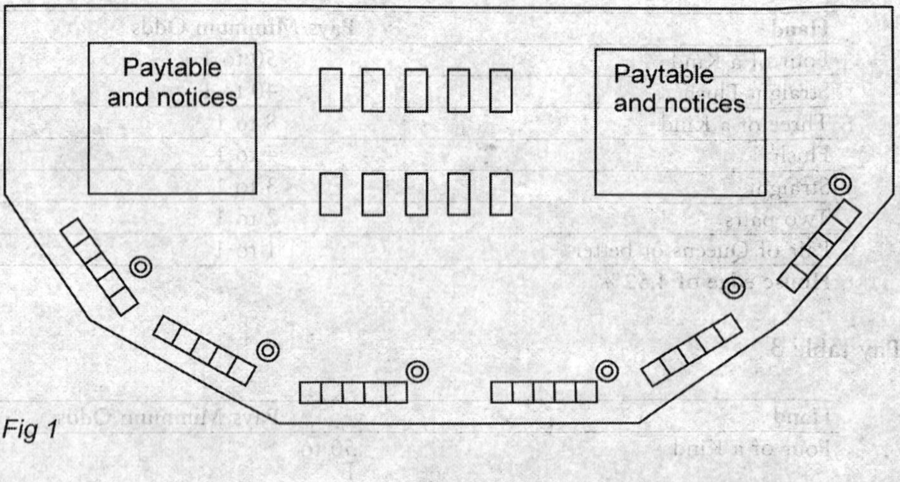

Fig 1

GENERAL RULES

16.1 The game shall be played with a single deck of 52 or 53 cards including the Joker.
16.2 A sign or notice specifying the number of cards in the deck shall be displayed at the table.
16.3 The house edge shall be detailed in the House Edge leaflet.
16.4 The pay table being used shall be displayed on a sign or notice at the table.
16.5 The deck shall be shuffled for each round of play. A manual shuffle or mechanical shuffler may be used.
16.6 Operators shall have procedures in place to ensure the security and integrity of the cards.
16.7 The cards shall at no stage be handled by the players.
16.8 The deck shall be dealt from a card shoe.
16.9 The maximum and minimum wagers permitted shall be shown on a notice prominently displayed at the table.

16.10 The relative value of each of the cards is as follows (in descending order): Ace, King, Queen, Jack, 10.9, 8, 7, 6, 5, 4, 3, 2, except that the Ace may be used as a value of one in order to complete a Straight Flush or a Straight, as defined in the rule 1.12 below.

16.11 The terms used to describe the hands held by a participant in the game, and the ranking from highest to lowest are as follows:

- Royal Flush – 10, Jack, Queen, King and Ace of the same suit. The order of cards being dealt is not a relevant factor
- Straight Flush – five cards of consecutive values of the same suit. The order of cards being dealt is not a relevant factor
- Five-of-a-Kind – four cards of the same value plus a Wild card
- Four-of-a-Kind – four cards of the same value
- Full House – five cards configured as a Three-of-a-Kind and a Pair
- Flush – five cards of the same suit not being a Royal Flush or a Straight Flush
- Straight – five cards of consecutive value not of the same suit
- Three-of-a-Kind – three cards of the same value
- Pair – two cards of the same value
- Jacks or Better – a pair of cards ranking Jacks or higher

16.12 Wild Card/s may be assigned. A wild card is one which may be assigned any value and suit in order to make a poker hand.

16.13 A Joker which acts as a Wild Card may be added to the deck.

METHOD OF DEALING

16.13 The dealer shall draw five cards in succession from the shuffled deck in the card shoe and place them face-up on the layout so as to allow each player the opportunity to see the values of all of the cards.

16.14 The players shall indicate to the dealer which cards they wish to keep in their poker hand in order that the hand may be improved by the replacement of other cards in the subsequent draw.

16.15 When either all of the players have made their decisions as to which cards, if any, are to be held or alternatively a reasonable period of time has been allowed for the players to have made such decision, the dealer draws sufficient cards so as to replace the cards in the poker hands of all players, which have not been held.

16.17 Where a player does not indicate any cards to be held, then all of the cards in the initial deal are replaced by the cards in the subsequent draw for that player's hand.

16.18 Where a player requires less cards than the cards actually dealt in the second round of cards, the players final hand will constitute his held cards and the first cards dealt to make up a five card hand. If for example he has held two cards then the first three cards dealt to the second round will make up his final 5 cards. When the draw is completed each player then has a fivecard poker hand according to the decision made or not made by the player with regard to holding cards.

16.19 The value of all the poker hands is evaluated and paid, or not paid, according to the odds.

WAGERS AND SETTLEMENT

16.20 Wagers on a participating player's hand shall be wagers that the hand will achieve a qualifying poker hand as per the displayed odds.

16.21 One or more wagers may be made on one or more playing positions.

16.22 Wagers are placed before any cards are dealt to the player.

16.23 Only the highest ranking hand is paid to the player. For example a Four-of-a-Kind hand is paid at odds of 25 for 1 only. There are no additional payments to the player for the Three-of-a- Kind, Two Pairs, or any other poker hand which may be a subset of the highest ranking hand.

16.24 Odds are expressed as "*x* for 1" which shall have the meaning that the bet placed is taken in by the bank and is included in the total amount paid back as winnings to the player.

VARIATIONS

16.25 It is at the discretion of the license holder to configure the odds offered for the poker hands in Rule 1.12.
16.26 It is at the discretion of the license holder to introduce a feature which improves the odds for a nominated poker hand or hands offered over time until such accumulated prize is won.
16.27 It is at the discretion of the license holder whether or not to introduce a Joker card or assign any other card as a Wild card.

PROGRESSIVE WAGER

16.28 At the license holder's discretion, a casino may introduce an optional progressive jackpot feature. The progressive jackpot may pay out to a Royal Flush.
16.29 All wagers placed will contain a specified percentage which will go into a jackpot fund.
16.30 The progressive jackpot fund may be shared equally by all players holding a Royal Flush.

EXPECTED RETURNS TO PLAYER

16.31 Three pay tables are shown below as examples of what may be offered to players and the estimated Return to Player expectations. Player's strategy will tend to vary according to the prizes offered and these choices are reflected in the differences in hand combination calculations below. Returns to Player in these examples are 96.06%, 95.78% and 94.63% respectively. The Odds which change in the pay tables are highlighted (expressed as the units paid including the return of 1 unit bet).

HAND	ODDS	COMBINATIONS	PROBABILITY	FREQUENCY	RETURN
Royal Flush	250	396,015,612	0.0000200	50,334.46	0.497%
Straight Flush	50	2,086,500,204	0.0001050	9,553.43	0.523%
Four of a Kind	25	47,152,135,212	0.0023660	422.74	5.914%
Full House	8	229,634,948,268	0.0115200	86.80	9.216%
Flush	5	226,047,920,664	0.0113400	88.18	5.670%
Straight	4	226,137,685,320	0.0113450	88.15	4.538%
Three of a Kind	3	1,484,761,801,884	0.0744870	13.43	22.346%
Two Pair	2	2,575,330,507,260	0.1291980	7.74	5.840%
Jacks or Better	1	4,289,619,749,004	0.2151990	4.65	21.520%
Nothing	0	10,852,063,253,772	0.5444210	1.84	0.000%
TOTALS		19,933,230,517,200	1.0000000	2.20	96.064%

HAND	ODDS	COMBINATIONS	PROBABILITY	FREQUENCY	RETURN
Royal Flush	100	348,521,940	0.0000170	57,193.62	0.175%

HAND	ODDS	COMBINATIONS	PROBABILITY	FREQUENCY	RETURN
Straight Flush	50	2,069,584,176	0.0001040	9,631.51	0.519%
Four of a Kind	25	47,178,839,244	0.0023670	422.50	5.917%
Full House	8	229,730,113,116	0.0115250	86.77	9.220%
Flush	5	226,398,400,764	0.0113580	88.04	5.679%
Straight	4	227,026,031,436	0.0113890	87.80	4.556%
Three of a Kind	3	1,485,715,778,040	0.0745350	13.42	22.360%
Two Pair	2	2,576,429,969,616	0.1292530	7.74	25.851%
Jacks or Better	1	4,286,468,469,924	0.2150410	4.65	21.504%
Nothing	0	10,851,864,808,944	0.5444110	1.84	0.000%
TOTALS		19,933,230,517,200	1.0000000	2.19	95.781%

HAND	ODDS	COMBINATIONS	PROBABILITY	FREQUENCY	RETURN
Royal Flush	100	348,606,048	0.000017	57179.82	0.17%
Straight Flush	50	2,070,602,760	0.000104	9626.777	0.52%
Four of a Kind	25	47,162,626,008	0.002366	422.6489	5.92%
Full House	7	229,670,200,872	0.011522	86.79067	8.07%
Flush	5	226,431,439,212	0.011359	88.03208	5.68%
Straight	4	228,005,927,304	0.011438	87.42418	4.58%
Three of a Kind	3	1,485,045,903,228	0.074501	13.42264	22.35%
Two Pair	2	2,575,490,418,756	0.129206	7.739586	25.84%
Jacks or Better	1	4,287,068,895,780	0.215071	4.649617	21.51%
Nothing	0	10,851,935,897,232	0.544414	1.836836	0.00%
TOTALS		19,933,230,517,200	1	2.194977	**94.63%**

17. CASINO WAR

TABLE LAYOUT

17.1 The proprietor of Casino War is Shufflemaster Inc and no variation to the game may be put forward without their prior agreement.

GENERAL RULES

17.2 The game is normally played with six standard decks of cards. Players purchase tokens from the table. Bets may only be placed in the betting position (box) before the first card is dealt. An additional bet may be made on Tie at the Player's discretion. No bets may be added to, reduced or retracted after the first card has been dealt.
17.3 A maximum of three players may play on one box. The maximum bet displayed on the table is for the box. Each box with a bet on it will receive one card face up.
17.4 The Dealer will deal to themself one card face up. If a Player has a card with a higher value than the Dealer then they will win Even Money. If the Dealer has a higher card value than the Player then the Player will lose their stake.
17.5 If the Dealer and the Player have cards of the same value then one of the following options must happen:

The Player must 'Go to War' and place an additional bet equal to their original wager.

The Player must 'Surrender' and lose half the value of their original wager.

If the Player 'Goes to War' they will be dealt a second card face up, then the Dealer will deal themselves a second card face up.

If the Players second card is of a higher or equal value to the Dealers second card they will win even money on the Go to War wager only. If it is of a lower value they will lose both the Go to War wager and the original wager.

Players may not at any point touch the cards on a Casino War table.

USUAL ODDS PAID

17.6 Original Wager – Player's First card of a higher value than the Dealer's First card 1 to 1.
17.7 'Go to War' Wager – Player elects to 'Go to War' and their Second card is of the same value as the Dealer's Second card 1 to 1.
17.8 Player elects to 'Go to War' and their Second card is of a higher value than the Dealer's Second card 1 to 1.
17.9 Tie Wager – The Player's First card if of the same value as the Dealer's First card 10 to 1.

HOUSE EDGE DETAILS

17.10 Details of the house edge are as follows:
Main game 2.88%
Tie Bet 18.65%

18. POCKET PAIRS

GENERAL RULES

18.1 Pocket Pairs is a banker's game played as part of an equal chance card room Poker game.
18.2 It can be played only on tables displaying the 'Pocket Pair' layout. 'Pocket Pairs' may be offered on any card room poker game of equal chance where the Players are dealt two cards in the initial deal.
18.3 The object of the game is to receive a 'same' colour or 'mixed' colour pair of cards from the initial two cards dealt to the Player. For this particular wager the Player is playing against the pay table and not against the Dealer or another Player. However all cards must still remain concealed until the conclusion of the hand.
18.4 Prior to any cards being dealt, the Player has the opportunity to place an optional side bet of the 'Pocket Pairs' wager. The 'Pocket Pair' wager is of an amount within the table minimums/maximums. Once the 'Ante' and/or 'Big and Little Blind' bets have been placed, the Dealer will ask the table if there are any Pocket Pair bets. Bets shall be collected from the players and placed in the corresponding Pocket Pair position in front of the Dealer to ensure the Dealer remains aware of which player has placed a 'Pocket Pair' bet.
18.5 Once all bets have been made the deal will commence as per normal for the desired Poker game. After this point no Pocket Pair wager may be altered or touched by a Player or any new Pocket Pair wagers accepted by the Dealer.
18.6 If a Player has made a bet on the 'Pocket Pairs' and consequently folds their hand, the cards remain in front of the Dealer in the designated area corresponding to the Player's seating position, face down, until the conclusion of the hand. Should the Player wish to fold their hand and forfeit their 'Pocket Pairs' wager then the Dealer will place their cards in the 'muck' and the 'Pocket Pair' wager will be taken into the float.
18.7 After the final round of betting, all Players who remain in the game reveal their hands (the showdown). The Dealer will then determine who holds the winning hand and the pot will be distributed accordingly.
18.8 Following the settlement of the pot, working from left (seating position 1) to right the Dealer begins to settle the Players Pocket Pairs wagers. Each wager is dealt within strict rotation. All hands are exposed and should a Player indicate that they do not want their cards exposed then the Dealer will 'clearly and verbally' advise them that their cards are Pocket Pairs bet is forfeited.

USUAL ODDS PAID

18.9 The odds are usually paid as follows:

Same Colour Pair	Mixed Colour Pair
Pays	Pays
25/1	11/1
24/1	11/1
23/1	11/1
23/1	12/1
22/1	12/1
21/1	12/1
21/1	13/1
20/1	13/1
19/1	13/1
19/1	14/1
18/1	14/1
17/1	14/1

House edge details

18.10 Details of the house edge are as follows:

Same Colour Pair	Mixed Colour Pair	House Edge
Pays	Pays	
25/1	11/1	1.96%
24/1	11/1	3.92%
23/1	11/1	5.88%
23/1	12/1	1.96%
22/1	12/1	3.92%
21/1	12/1	5.88%
21/1	13/1	1.96%
20/1	13/1	3.92%
19/1	13/1	5.88%
19/1	14/1	1.96%
18/1	14/1	3.92%
17/1	14/1	5.88%

Gambling Commission June 2011

RULES OF CORE CASINO GAMES IN GREAT BRITAIN

June 2011

1 INTRODUCTION

6.2244 1.1 This document sets out the standard house rules for the core non-remote casino games commonly played in Great Britain.

1.2 Any matters relating to game rules not specifically covered in this document may be interpreted at the discretion of the operator. The Commission's licence conditions and codes of practice require that all operators of these games have training, security procedures and systems in place to ensure that all games are played in an open and fair manner.

1.3 This document was created as a result of the consultation entitled *Review of the casino games trial approval process and amendment to licence condition 9 – September 2010*. This document is designed to set out the standard games rules for the five most popular games in GB casinos: blackjack, roulette, three card poker, punto banco and dice. This document does not set out the rules for side bets or variations to these games.

2 AMERICAN ROULETTE

BASIC OUTLINE RULES/HOW TO PLAY

2.1 The game is played with a wheel containing 37 or 38 compartments numbered from 1-36 and either one or two zeros. The numbers from 1-36 are divided up equally and coloured either red or black. A single ball is spun and will land in one of the numbered compartments.

2.2 The object of the game is to predict which numbered compartment the ball will fall into by placing a wager on the appropriate number on the layout. Wagers may also be placed to predict a sequence of numbers. The best odds are given for predicting the number outright ("straight up") and the odds diminish depending on the range of numbers in the sequence, line or block. Players are not normally limited in the number or range of bets they may place on the same "spin" unless otherwise specified locally.

2.3 It is also possible to wager on whether the number will be red or black, odd or even, low or high (often called the "outside / even chance bets"). Each of these consists of eighteen numbers and normally pays even money, unless zero is spun whereby either half or all of the even chance bets will be lost, depending on the rules of the club.

American term odds	**French term**	**Minimum**
A. **Straight Up** – one specific number	En Plein	**35 to 1**
B. **Split** – one of two specific numbers	A Cheval	**17 to 1**
C. **Street** – one of three specific numbers	En Transversale	**11 to 1**
D. **Corner** – one of four specific numbers	En Carré	**8 to 1**
E. **First Four** – one of numbers 0 (or 00), 1,2,3	Quatre Premiers	**8 to 1**
F. **Six Line** – one of six specific numbers	Sixain	**5 to 1**
G. **Column** – one of 12 specific numbers in a row	Sur une Colonne	**2 to 1**
H. **Dozen** – one of 12 specific numbers in a block	Sur une Douzaine	**2 to 1**
I. **Red or Black** – one of 18 specific numbers	Rouge ou Noir	**1 to 1**
J. **Odd or Even** – one of 18 specific numbers	Impair ou Pair	**1 to 1**
K. **Low or High** – one of 18 specific numbers	Manque ou Passe	**1 to 1**
L. **Split Columns** – one of 24 specific	A Cheval sur	
numbers in a row	Deux Colonnes	**1 to 2**
M. **Split Dozens** – one of 24 specific	A Cheval sur	
numbers in a block	Deux Douzaines	**1 to 2**

HOUSE EDGE DETAILS

Even chance bets	1.35% (if only half wager lost when zero spun)
Bets on the layout	2.70 % (5.26% on a double zero wheel)

3 BLACKJACK

BASIC OUTLINE RULES/HOW TO PLAY

3.1 The game is normally played with four or six decks of cards, unless otherwise specified in the club. Single Deck Blackjack is also possible.
3.2 Similar to Pontoon or 21, the aim is to achieve a score closer to 21 than the dealer, without going over. Each player is dealt two cards face down. The dealer is dealt one card face up. Depending on the rules of the club, the dealer may also be dealt their second card face down at the outset, or must otherwise wait until all hands are dealt with before receiving it.
3.3 Each player will be asked in turn to make their decisions as to whether or not to receive further cards (draw) to improve their score, or otherwise stand on their existing total. There is no limit to the number of further cards that can be drawn, provided the score does not exceed 21.
3.4 An Ace counts as either one or eleven, depending on whether it would cause the hand to exceed 21 ("bust"). All picture cards count as a score of 10. Suits are not relevant to the normal game.
3.5 An initial two card total of 21 is called a Blackjack and consists of a ten card and an Ace.
3.6 If the dealer receives the same score as the Player, the hand will be tied and the player's bet returned. A score of 21 achieved by three cards or splitting a pair would be beaten by a two card Blackjack. However, a dealer and player will tie if both have a Blackjack.
3.7 It is normally permitted for more than one player to play the same hand ("playing behind") but the seated player will make any decisions on whether to draw etc.
3.8 The dealer is not permitted to draw further cards to their hand on a score of 17, but must do so on anything up to a score of 16.

DOUBLING

3.9 A player may double their bet and receive just one further card only (total of three cards) if they wish to do so.

SPLITTING PAIRS

3.10 If a player's first two cards are a pair of the same denomination, they may elect to split them into two hands. Each hand must have a wager equivalent to the original bet and each hand will then be dealt with in turn. There is no limit to the number of times a hand may split, if further cards of the same denomination are dealt to either hand. A pair of Aces that is split will only receive one further card each, and the total will not count as a Blackjack if a ten is then dealt.

INSURANCE

3.11 If the player is dealt a Blackjack, but the Dealer's first card is an Ace, they may place an insurance wager of half their original stake. If the Dealer is then dealt a Blackjack, the insurance wager will be paid at 2 to 1 whilst the original hand will tie.

The same net affect is achieved by paying the hand even money (instead of the normal 3 to 2 for a Blackjack) if the player elects to accept it. They may otherwise take their chances against the dealer's hand.

SOFT 17

3.12 An Ace dealt to the dealer's hand will normally count as one or 11. However, where the soft 17 rule is applied, an Ace dealt to the dealer's hand that would give a score of 17 if counted as 11, will instead be counted as one. For example, a six and an Ace will equal seven, not seventeen.

USUAL ODDS PAYABLE

3.13 For a Blackjack, odds of 3 to 2 are usually paid. Insurance wagers are paid at 2 - 1.

HOUSE EDGE DETAILS

4 decks (best technique) -	0.51%
Where the dealer may draw on soft 17	0.85%
6 decks (best technique) -	0.55%
Where the dealer may draw on soft 17	0.89%

4 PUNTO BANCO

BASIC OUTLINE RULES/HOW TO PLAY

4.1 The game is normally played with six or eight decks of cards, unless otherwise specified in the club. Punto Banco is a derivation of the traditional game of Baccarat.
4.2 The game is normally played in one of two formats. One is the mini/midi format, where the dealer draws all cards and acts as the banker, whilst the other is the full size game, where the shoe is offered in turn to seated players to assume the role of banker (in such cases, the player only assumes the role for the purposes of dealing the cards and taking ownership of the banker hand. At no time does the player hold or control the bank itself).
4.3 Players wager on whether they believe the winning hand after all cards are dealt will be that of the player (Punto), the banker (Banco) or a tie (Egalité).
4.4 Normally, six or eight decks are used. Two hands are dealt consisting of two card each, one to the Player (Punto) and one to the Banker (Banco). The winning hand will be that with a score nearest to nine. Cards have a point value of 0-9 inclusive, whereby Ace counts as one, whilst tens, jacks, queens and kings count as zero. For example, 10+5=5, 10+1+5=6.
4.4 Hands will consist of two or three cards, according to a compulsory drawing table of play (the Tableau). This is as follows:

PLAYER'S HAND

Player having a two card total of:	**Third Card Determination**
0,1,2,3,4,5	Player dealt a third card unless Bank has 8 or 9 (natural)
6 – 7	Player Stands
8 – 9	Stands – no third card dealt to either hand

6: Gambling Act 2005: Additional Material

BANK'S HAND

Player having a two card total of:	Third Card Determination
0,1,2	Bank dealt a third card unless Punto has 8 or 9 (natural)
3	Bank dealt a third card unless Punto third card is an 8
4	Bank dealt a third card unless Punto third card is 0,1,8 or 9
5	Bank dealt a third card unless Punto third card is 0,1,2,3,8 or 9
6	Bank stands unless Punto third card is a 6 or 7
7	Bank Stands
8 or 9	Bank stands – no third card dealt to either hand

USUAL ODDS PAYABLE

4.5 Winning wagers on the Banco hand are normally paid 19 to 20
4.6 Winning wagers on the Punto hand are normally paid 1 to 1
4.7 Winning wagers on a tied hand (Egalité) are normally paid 8 to 1

HOUSE EDGE DETAILS

If Banco wins	1.06%
If Punto wins	1.24%

5 THREE CARD POKER

BASIC OUTLINE RULES/HOW TO PLAY

5.1 The game is played with one deck of cards. Ace is high, but may be used as a value of one within a Straight or Straight Flush (see below), being Ace, 2, 3.
5.2 Players may make an initial wager, comprising either or both of the following:
(i) An Ante wager – being that the player's hand will have a higher poker ranking than the dealer's.
(ii) A Pair Plus wager – being that the player's hand will achieve a particular hand ranking, irrespective of whether it beats the dealer.
5.3 Each player and the dealer is dealt three cards face down. Players may touch their cards to assess their hand.
5.4 A Player who has made an Ante wager who wishes to continue in the game must make a further wager, called the Play wager, of an equal amount to their Ante bet. Otherwise, their Ante bet will lose.
5.5 Players who only placed a Pair Plus wager, without an Ante bet, will remain in the game provided their hand contains at least a pair (see below).
5.6 Hands are ranked in descending order as follows:

STRAIGHT FLUSH – three cards of consecutive values of the same suit (eg 4H,5H,6H);

THREE OF A KIND – three cards of the same value (eg 3 x 7's, 3 x kings etc)

STRAIGHT – three cards of consecutive values but not the same suit (eg 4H,5C,6D);

FLUSH – three cards of the same suit but not consecutive values (eg 4H, 7H, 9H)

PAIR – two cards of the same value (eg 2 x 6's, 2 x 4's)

HIGH CARD – the highest single card in a hand that has none of the above rankings.

5.7 The Dealer must have a hand with at least "Queen High" to qualify against the Player's hand.

5.8 If the Dealer DOES NOT qualify:

(i) All Play bets are void ("stand off") and are returned to the players;

(ii) Ante Bonuses (see below) are paid on hands with a Straight or better;

(iii) All Ante bets win and are paid odds of 1 to 1

(iv) All Pair Plus wagers are paid or lose, according to whether they contain at least a Pair in the above table of rankings (see odds below)

5.9 If the Dealer DOES qualify:

(i) The Play wagers are paid or lose, depending on whether they have a higher ranking that the Dealer's hand in the above table.

(ii) Ante Bonuses are paid on all Straights or better (see odds below);

(iii) Ante bets are paid or taken (see odds below);

(iv) All Pair Plus wagers are paid or lose according to whether they contain at least a Pair in the above table of rankings (see odds below).

5.10 A tied hand is a stand off on the Play and Ante. However, the Ante Bonus and Pair Plus are always paid where the hand meets the required ranking.

5.11 If the Dealer qualifies and has a higher hand ranking than the player, the "Ante" and Play wagers will both lose.

5.12 If the Player has placed a Pair Plus wager but their hand does not contain at least a pair, the wager will lose.

USUAL ODDS PAYABLE

5.13 If the Player's hand beats the Dealer's qualifying hand, their Ante and Play wagers will win and normally be paid at odds of 1 to 1.

ANTE BONUS ODDS

5.14 A Player who has made both an Ante and a Play wager will win an Ante Bonus for the Ante wager if their hand contains one of the following:

- **Straight** – normally paid 1 to 1
- **Three of a Kind** – normally paid 4 to 1
- **Straight Flush** – normally paid 5 to 1

PAIR PLUS ODDS

- **Pair** – normally paid 1 to 1
- **Flush** – normally paid 4 to 1
- **Straight** – normally paid 6 to 1
- **Three of a kind** – normally paid 33 to 1
- **Straight Flush** – normally paid 35 to 1

HOUSE EDGE DETAILS

On Pair Plus wagers	2.7%
Overall game	2.0%

6 DICE/CRAPS

BASIC OUTLINE RULES/HOW TO PLAY

6.1 There are two parts to a dice game. The first part is called the 'Come Out Roll', this is indicated by the large round puck on the table layout placed in the 'Off' position.
6.2 When the puck is in the off position the 'shooter' rolls the dice. If they roll a 7, 11 or a 2, 3, 12 then the Pass/Win Line and Don't Pass/Win Line are paid accordingly.
6.3 Any other number rolled (4, 5, 6, 8, 9 or 10) becomes your 'Point'; this is indicated by the dealer moving the puck to the number rolled which is then flipped over to the 'On' position.
6.4 The object of the game is then to repeat the number first rolled (the Point) before rolling a 7. If a 7 is rolled before the point is achieved then it is called a '7 out'.
6.5 This signifies the end of a shooters roll, the dice are then passed to the next shooter. In both cases the puck is returned to the off position and a new game is started on the 'Come Out Roll'.
6.6 Note that 2, 3 and 12 are collectively known as the 'Craps' – the American name for the game.

USUAL ODDS PAID

6.7 **Pass/Win Line:** On the come out roll: Wins on a 7 or 11, loses on a 2, 3 or 12. When a point has been achieved: Wins when the point is rolled and loses on a 7. The Pass/Win Line pays even money.
6.8 **Don't Pass/Win Line:** On the come out roll: Wins on a 3 or 12, stands on 2, loses on 7 and 11. When a point is achieved: Wins when a 7 is rolled and loses if the point is rolled.
6.9 **Taking Odds:** Odds are placed behind a Pass/Win Line Bet when a point has been achieved and are paid accordingly:
6.10 Point of 4 or 10 – Pays 2 to 1. Point of 5 or 9 – Pays 3 to 2. Point of 6 or 8 – Pays 6 to 5. Odds are placed next to a Don't Pass/Win Line Bet and when a 7 is rolled are paid accordingly: Point of 4 or 10 – Pays 1 to 2. Point of 5 or 9 – Pays 2 to 3. Point of 6 or 8 – Pays 6 to 5.
6.11 **Field and Place bets:** 4 and 10 – Pays 91/2 to 5. 5 and 9 – Pays 7 to 5. 6 and 8 – Pays 7 to 6. All place bets lose on a 7 out.
6.12 **Hard Ways:** Hard 6 and 8 – Pays 91/2 to 1. Hard 4 and 10 – Pays 71/2 to 1. Centre Bets: 2 or 12 – Pays 33 to 1 3 or 11 – Pays 16 to 1 All Centre Bets are one roll bets.
6.13 **Any Crap:** An Any Crap Bet wins on 2, 3 or 12 and pays 71/2 to 1. All Any Crap Bets are one roll bets.
6.14 **Hopping Bets:** A Hopping Bet wins when the exact combination of the two dice is predicted on one roll of the dice. Hard way Hopping Bet – Pays 33 to 1 Regular Hopping Bets – Pays 16 to 1.

HOUSE EDGE DETAILS

6.15 **Varying from:**
For Front Line bets 1.4%to
For Hopping Bets 5.6%
'Any Seven' one roll bets 16.6%.
Gambling Commission June 2011

BINGO AND CASINO EQUIPMENT TECHNICAL REQUIREMENTS July 2008

1 INTRODUCTION

6.2244.1 The Gambling Act 2005 ('the Act') gives the Gambling Commission ('the Commission'), as part of its statutory role, the power to attach conditions to operating licences about equipment used in connection with gambling activities (section 85). In addition, the Commission has the power to set technical standards for remote gambling systems (including software) (section 89). Appropriate conditions have been attached to non-remote and ancillary remote bingo and casino operating licences.

These technical requirements will regulate bingo and casino equipment in two different situations: (a) equipment that is used on premises in Great Britain to provide casino games and bingo games to the public and (b) equipment used to provide such games in gambling premises by means of a remote communication system, where the provider is regulated by the Act. These Requirements cover a variety of equipment including a 'live' roulette wheel and bingo tickets. They do not cover gaming machines.

With the following exceptions, these technical requirements will come into force on 31 August 2008 and will replace the technical requirements published on 1 June 2007. The requirements of paragraphs 3.5d and 3.5e of the casino technical requirements and paragraphs 3.5d and 3.5e of the bingo technical requirements will come into force on a date or dates later than 31 August 2008, and the Commission will give at least three months notice of their implementation.

PART I: CASINO TECHNICAL REQUIREMENTS

Implementation

These requirements apply to gambling related equipment (excluding gaming machines) sited in licenced casinos after 31 August 2008.

1 GAME REQUIREMENTS

Speed of Play

1.1 An electronic terminal that gives a player the opportunity to bet on the outcome of a fully automated 'real' game must ensure that the game cannot be played at a speed significantly faster than the manually operated equivalent and that the player is given adequate time to place their initial and any subsequent bet(s) within the game.

For fully automated 'real' games played using electronic terminals the following game frequency must not be exceeded:

a.	games of roulette:	50 games per hour
b.	games played using dice:	50 games per hour
c.	games played using cards:	50 games per hour

Where electronic terminals provide a player with the opportunity to play multiple 'real' games on the same terminal, then the terminal must limit the play to a single game at a time. That is, the player must not be given the opportunity to stake on a second game until the first game is completed.

Display of Information on Players' Game Devices

1.2 Game devices must be capable of clearly displaying (either on screen or via labelling attached to the device), the following information:

6: Gambling Act 2005: Additional Material

(a) cost of bet(s) or stake(s) to play the game
(b) prize amounts available within the game, or the information necessary to calculate the prize amounts, for example, the odds for each type of bet in a game of roulette
(c) players' credit held on the system
(d) information describing how the game is played on the device – this is optional if the method of playing the game on the device is identical to the method of playing the actual table game
(e) information on how to gamble responsibly and help for problem gamblers; and alarm or fault information when needed

The game itself should be displayed in a recognisable form such that the player is able to follow the play and interact appropriately.

2 RANDOM NUMBER GENERATION

Random Number Generation

2.1 Random number generation (and game results) must be 'acceptably random'. Acceptably random here means that it is possible to demonstrate to a high degree of confidence that the output of the random number generators (RNG) is random, through, for example, statistical analysis using generally accepted tests and methods of analysis.

Random number generators should be capable of demonstrating the following qualities:

(a) the output from the RNG is uniformly distributed over the entire output range
(b) the output is unpredictable, ie it is computationally infeasible to predict what the next number will be, given complete knowledge of the algorithm or hardware generating the sequence, and all previously generated numbers
(c) random number generation does not reproduce the same output stream (cycle), and that two instances of a random number generator do not produce the same stream as each other (synchronise)
(d) any forms of seeding (the process of initialising the random number generation process) and re-seeding used do not introduce predictability
(e) any scaling applied to the random output complies with a) to d) above

Mechanically Based Rng Games

2.2 Mechanically based RNG games are games that use the laws of physics to generate the outcome of the game and must conform to the following rules:

(a) they must meet the requirements of Section 2.1
(b) the mechanical pieces must be constructed of materials that prevent decomposition of any component over its lifetime (for example, a ball must not disintegrate)
(c) the properties of physical items used to generate the random outcome must not be altered

Scaling Algorithms

2.3 If a random number with a range shorter than that provided by the RNG is required for some purpose within the gaming device, the method of re-scaling, (ie converting the number to the lower range), must be designed in such a way that all numbers within the lower range are equally probable.

Randomisation with Varying Class Size

2.4 Where a game is played using a finite set of randomised outcomes, eg a shuffled deck of cards, each outcome within the set must initially be equally probable as per

Section 2.1 to 2.3 above. However, it is accepted that as the finite set reduces in number, the outcome may become more predictable as the game progresses.

3 ELECTRONIC DEVICE AND SERVER BASED SYSTEM REQUIREMENTS

General Requirements

3.1 The following must apply:

(a) any server used in the gaming process must be housed securely

(b) an audit trail for all financial transactions, errors and significant events must be maintained either on the electronic device, on the server, or by some other secure means, such that it can be accessed for compliance audit purposes

(c) data must be regularly backed-up and the back-up stored in a secure location

Errors and significant events and the methods of dealing with them are listed in section 4 below.

Service Interruption and Resumption

3.2 Operators must take all reasonable steps to ensure that their policies for dealing with service interruptions are fair and do not systematically disadvantage customers. The system must not be adversely affected by the simultaneous or sequential activation of any inputs and outputs, such as 'play buttons', which might, whether intentionally or not, cause malfunctions or invalid results.

Where a peripheral device such as a note acceptor (accepting a note) or printer (printing a ticket/credit note) is in operation during a power failure it must, where practicable, on resumption of the power either complete or restart the task successfully or display an error message indicating that such a fault has occurred. The error message must remain until the fault has been resolved by either the automatic operation of the device or by the operator. In all circumstances the metering or audit controls must be able to identify any accounting anomalies for dispute resolution purposes.

Previous Game Recall on Electronic Gaming Devices

3.3 Information about the current game and previous games played must always be available to view for dispute and/or complaint resolution purposes on the operation of a suitable external key-switch, or other secure method that is not available to the player. Last play information must provide all information required to fully reconstruct the game play. All values must be displayed, including the initial credits, credits bet, credits won, and credits paid. The information must include the final game outcome, including all player choices and game features.

Historic game data must be stored such that it can be called upon for evidential purposes in the event of a dispute and/or complaint. If the data is required to resolve a continuing dispute or complaint and the system is incapable of continuing to operate without overwriting or losing that historic data, then the pertinent data must be stored 'offline' until the dispute and/or complaint is satisfactorily resolved.

System Clocks

3.4 The following must apply:

(a) gambling devices / systems used in a casino which incorporate an internal clock must use the time to provide an accurate time stamp of all financial transactions, errors and significant events

(b) all clocks or clock systems related to gambling within a casino that can be adjusted shall be set to the correct time

Cashless Play

3.5 Where a gaming device has the facility to accept a stake or participation fee from, and make payment of a prize to, the same medium of cashless payment, for example a smartcard ('the medium'), then the requirements of this section must be complied with. For the avoidance of doubt, neither ticket in and out (TITO) systems nor tokens are required to comply with this section. For the purposes of this section a 'token' is an object with a fixed monetary value (whether or not exchangeable for cash) that may be used for the purpose of paying a stake or participation fee or crediting a gaming device. The following will also apply:

(a) a secure player account database must be held within the system

(b) the system must allow the player to retrieve their funds at any reasonable time when the venue is open

(c) a facility must be available on the premises which will show the player their current monetary balance held on the medium without the requirement to transfer funds or a game having to be played. Such a facility must not offer any inducements to the player to commit money for play or further play

(d) a gaming device must have the facility to enable it to be rendered incapable of accepting funds from the medium at any time when the account holder has entered a self-exclusion agreement in respect of the premises where the device is sited. Activation and de-activation of such facility must require action by the site operator

(e) the players must have the facility to track and/or limit the amount of money they are able to deposit into the medium over a given period of time. The limit that the individual chooses to impose may only be set or modified once in any 24 hour period

Printers

3.6 If a gaming device is equipped with a printer that is used to make payments, it must be located in a locked or otherwise secure area of the gaming device (for example, require opening of the main door to access).

The printed ticket/voucher/hand pay receipt ('the ticket') must display sufficient information to allow the following to be determined:

(a) details of where and when the ticket originated

(b) details of the transaction type (for example, cash out ticket, hand pay receipt)

(c) value of the ticket

(d) unique ticket identifier (for example barcode and validation number)

This data must be stored such that it is available for audit or dispute resolution purposes.

Ticket Validation

3.7 Payment by ticket printer as a method of credit redemption is only permissible when there is an independent means to validate the printed ticket/voucher/hand pay receipt prior to any credit or other type of redemption. The validation system must be able to identify duplicate tickets to prevent fraud by reprinting and redeeming a ticket that was previously issued.

This data must be stored such that it is available for audit or dispute resolution purposes.

4 SPECIFIC ERROR CONDITIONS AND ALERT REQUIREMENTS

4.1 Devices must detect, display and alert the operator to the types of error conditions and significant events listed below. If the error or event affects the game-play in any way then the device should 'lock up' and allow no further game-play until the error or event is cleared either automatically or by operator intervention.

(a) events/errors related to payment to play, eg coins, notes
(b) events/errors related to operation of the device, eg battery failure, programme error
(c) events/errors related to security, eg door open
(d) events/errors related to payouts, eg printer jam, hopper empty

5 WIRELESS NETWORK SYSTEMS

Network Coverage

5.1 If a gaming device is designed to allow players to participate using a wireless network the following must be complied with:

(a) unless denoted by clear signage, there must be no areas where players may participate in any gambling using such a device where the communication signal is:
  (i) not available
  (ii) of poor quality such that interruptions in play would be likely
(b) there must be adequate wireless coverage so that the failure of a single transmitter does not significantly reduce the players' ability to participate in the game. This does not prohibit the use of a single transmitter

Network Failure

5.2 Where a network failure occurs:

(a) all devices must alert the player of the failure as soon as it is possible to do so. It is permissible for a device to continue with any game if the network connection is restored provided that the player is not disadvantaged in any way
(b) a manual alternative method of play (for example, keying in game outcome or other element as opposed to an automatic download via wireless network) is permissible where there is no disadvantage to the player and where there is adequate time to do so. Catch up facilities (for example, button pressed to bring device up to current position within game) may be used where the game that was in play when the network failure occurred has not been completed

Communication Requirements

5.3 All protocols must use communication techniques that have proper error detection and/or recovery mechanisms which are designed to prevent unauthorised access or tampering, employing Data Encryption Standards (DES) or equivalent encryption with secure seeds or algorithms.

Power Level Display Requirements

5.4 Portable devices must give warnings when the battery life of the device reaches a low level.

Audit Requirements

5.5 An audit log of sufficient time stamping of significant events must be maintained so as to be able to resolve any player disputes arising as a result of timing issues. It must be possible to display the audit log on the site operator's premises.

The Commission does not intend to set out exact requirements for time stamping of significant events as it is considered better that the manufacturer do so on the basis of the overall system design.

PART II: BINGO TECHNICAL REQUIREMENTS

Implementation

These requirements apply to gambling related equipment (excluding gaming machines) sited in licenced bingo premises after 31 August 2008.
However, in the circumstances referred to below, equipment used for the playing of interval bingo games (as defined at 1.1) need not adhere to the following requirements:

- section 1.3
- section 3.1b
- section 3.2
- section 3.4a

The circumstances referred to above are where the player plays the interval bingo game using bingo tickets (or representations thereof) which are not presented to the player in an electronic (virtual) form. If such games are presented to the player partly using electronic (virtual) tickets and partly using non electronic forms of tickets then the portion of the game played using the electronic (virtual) tickets must comply with these technical requirements in full.

1 GAME REQUIREMENTS

Definitions

Main Stage Bingo Game:	This is the primary game (or games) played in any bingo session, involving physical (paper) and/or virtual (electronic) tickets which are typically purchased before the bingo session starts.
Interval Bingo Game:	This is any game played outside of sessions of 'main stage bingo'. Entry into interval games is typically purchased prior to each game starting. An example of an interval game would be 'mechanised cash bingo'.

Prize Information Board

1.2 The prize information board together with any associated boards (if needed) must display the information listed below at all times during the game session (scrolling displays are permitted); and the vast majority of players must have a clear and unobstructed view of the board(s) during play, unless they can clearly view the same information, in real time, by other means.
Information to be displayed for main stage games:

(a) opening and closing numbers of tickets. Physical (paper) and virtual (electronic) tickets must be displayed separately. There must be provision to display both sets of numbers from any split series permutations
(b) total number of tickets in the game (whether tickets are paper, virtual or otherwise)
(c) total number of tickets not in the game, eg spoiled or unsold
(d) total prize fund (this may be subdivided into its constituent parts if required)
(e) details of allocation of prizes, eg one line, full house, value etc
(f) information to allow players to identify the ticket in play, eg book colour, page
(g) all previously called numbers within the game
(h) last number called

Additionally, during claim checking, a representation of the ticket being checked, including its relevant serial or permutation numbers must be shown, together with its status (valid, not valid, already checked).

If equipment manufactured before 31 August 2008 does not have the capability to display the information required at (f) above, the player must be provided with that information by some other means (eg orally).

Information to be displayed for interval bingo games:

(a) game number
(b) game type (eg prize, cash)
(c) cost per game (unless this is indicated orally to players)
(d) number of boards in play for linked games and number of boards or players in play for standards games
(e) prize (cash prizes only; non-cash prizes can be announced by other means)
(f) last number called

Additionally, during claim checking, a representation of the ticket being checked, including the card number, must be shown, together with its status (valid, not valid, already checked).

If equipment manufactured before 31 August 2008 does not have the capability to display the information required at (b) above, the player must be provided with that information by some other means (eg orally).

Display of Information on Players' Game Devices

1.3 Game devices must be capable of clearly displaying (either on screen or via labelling attached to the device), the following information:

(a) the information to be displayed for main stage games listed at 'a' to 'h', and information to be displayed for interval bingo games listed at 'a' to 'f', in Section 1.2, unless and to the extent the player can clearly see the prize information board(s) (or the same information in real time) during play
(b) the operator's policy on the charging of participation fees and the proportion of stakes to be paid out by way of prizes. This is optional if the player can clearly see this information from their playing position, eg on the prize information board(s), or clearly at the point of ticket purchase
(c) players' credit held on the system
(d) price of play information
(e) information describing how the game is played on the device – this is optional if the method of playing the game on the device is identical to the manual method of playing the game
(f) information on how to gamble responsibly and help for problem gamblers
(g) alarm or fault information when needed

The game itself should be displayed in a recognisable form such that the player is able to follow the play and interact appropriately.

2 RANDOM NUMBER GENERATION

Random Number Generation

2.1 Random number generation (and game results) must be 'acceptably random'.

'Acceptably random' means that it is possible to demonstrate to a high degree of confidence that the output of the random number generators (RNG) is random, through, for example, statistical analysis using generally accepted tests and methods of analysis. Random number generators should be capable of demonstrating the following qualities:

(a) the output from the RNG is uniformly distributed over the entire output range
(b) the output is unpredictable, ie it is computationally infeasible to predict what the next number will be, given complete knowledge of the algorithm or hardware generating the sequence, and all previously generated numbers
(c) random number generation does not reproduce the same output stream (cycle), and that two instances of a random number generator do not produce the same stream as each other (synchronise)

(d) any forms of seeding (the process of initialising the random number generation process) and re-seeding used do not introduce predictability
(e) any scaling applied to the random output complies with a) to d) above

Mechanically Based Rng Games

2.2 Mechanically based RNG games of bingo are games that use the laws of physics to generate the outcome of the game and must conform to the following rules:
(a) they must meet the requirements of Section 2.1
(b) the mechanical pieces must be constructed of materials that prevent decomposition of any component over its lifetime (for example, a ball must not disintegrate)
(c) the properties of physical items used to generate the random outcome must not be altered

Mechanical Ball Mixing Method

2.3 A mechanical device that uses air flow for mixing and randomly withdrawing balls to determine the letters, numbers or symbols to be used in a game of bingo must operate in the following manner:
(a) it must follow the rules for mechanically based RNG games
(b) it must allow participants full view of the mixing action of the balls
(c) it must not be possible to change the random placement of the balls at the exit receptacle of the device, except when the device is shut off

Scaling Algorithms

2.4 If a random number with a range shorter than that provided by the RNG is required for some purpose within the gaming device, the method of re-scaling, (ie converting the number to the lower range), is to be designed in such a way that all numbers within the lower range are equally probable.

Randomisation with Varying Class Size

2.5 Where a game is played using a finite set of randomised outcomes, eg a set of bingo balls; each outcome within the set must initially be equally probable as per Section 2.1 to 2.4 above. However, it is accepted that as the finite set reduces in number, the outcome may become more predictable as the game progresses.

3 ELECTRONIC DEVICE AND SERVER BASED SYSTEM REQUIREMENTS

General Requirements

3.1 The following must apply:
(a) any server used in the gaming process must be housed securely
(b) an audit trail for all financial transactions, errors and significant events must be maintained either on the electronic device, on the server, or by some other secure means such that it can be accessed for compliance audit purposes
(c) data must be regularly backed-up and the back-up stored in a secure location

Errors and significant events and the methods of dealing with them are listed in section 4 below.

Service Interruption and Resumption

3.2 Operators must take all reasonable steps to ensure that their policies for dealing with service interruptions are fair and do not systematically disadvantage customers. The system must not be adversely affected by the simultaneous or sequential activation of any inputs and outputs, such as ‘play buttons’, which might, whether intentionally or not, cause malfunctions or invalid results.

Where a peripheral device such as a note acceptor (accepting a note) or printer (printing a ticket/credit note) is in operation during a power failure it must, where practicable, on resumption of the power either complete or restart the task successfully or display an error message indicating that such a fault has occurred. The error message must remain until the fault has been resolved by either the automatic operation of the device or by the operator. In all circumstances the metering or audit controls must be able to identify any accounting anomalies for dispute resolution purposes.

Determination of Winners

3.3 Any determinant used in the game of bingo and distributed by any form of network must be transmitted simultaneously to all player devices designed to receive such information within that game. The receiving devices must be able to present the appropriate information such that no player is disadvantaged by the introduction of any delay.

This requirement does not apply to different venues involved in 'non simultaneous linked bingo games', providing that all players within a single venue receive their determinants simultaneously.

System Clocks

3.4 The following must apply:

(a) gambling devices / systems used in a bingo club which incorporate an internal clock must use the time to provide an accurate time stamp of all financial transactions, errors and significant events

(b) all clocks or clock systems related to gambling within a bingo club that can be adjusted shall be set to the correct time

Cashless Play

3.5 Where a gaming device has the facility to accept a stake or participation fee from, and make payment of a prize to, the same medium of cashless payment, for example a smartcard ('the medium'), then the requirements of this section must be complied with. For the avoidance of doubt, neither ticket in and out (TITO) systems nor tokens are required to comply with this section. For the purposes of this section a 'token' is an object with a fixed monetary value (whether or not exchangeable for cash) that may be used for the purpose of paying a stake or participation fee or crediting a gaming device. The following will also apply:

(a) a secure player account database must be held within the system

(b) the system must allow the player to retrieve their funds at any reasonable time when the venue is open

(c) a facility must be available on the premises which will show the player their current monetary balance held on the medium without the requirement to transfer funds or a game having to be played. Such a facility must not offer any inducements to the player to commit money for play or further play

(d) a gaming device must have the facility to enable it to be rendered incapable of accepting funds from the medium at any time when the account holder has entered a self-exclusion agreement in respect of the premises where the device is sited. Activation and de-activation of such facility must require action by the site operator

(e) the players must have the facility to track and/or limit the amount of money they are able to deposit onto the medium over a given period of time. The limit that the individual chooses to impose may only be set or modified once in any 24 hour period

Printers

3.6 If a gaming device is equipped with a printer that is used to make payments, it must be located in a locked or otherwise secure area of the gaming device (for example, require opening of the main door to access).
The printed ticket/voucher/hand pay receipt ('the ticket') must display sufficient information to allow the following to be determined:
(a) details of where and when the ticket originated
(b) details of the transaction type (for example, cash out ticket, hand pay receipt)
(c) value of the ticket
(d) unique ticket identifier (for example, barcode and validation number)
This data must be stored such that it is available for audit or dispute resolution purposes.

Ticket Validation

3.7 Payment by ticket printer as a method of credit redemption is only permissible when there is an independent means to validate the printed ticket/voucher/hand pay receipt prior to any credit or other type of redemption. The validation system must be able to identify duplicate tickets to prevent fraud by reprinting and redeeming a ticket that was previously issued.
This data must be stored such that it is available for audit or dispute resolution purposes.

4 SPECIFIC ERROR CONDITIONS AND ALERT REQUIREMENTS

4.1 Devices must detect, display and alert the operator to the types of error conditions and significant events listed below. If the error or event affects the game-play in any way, then the device should 'lock up' and allow no further game-play until the error or event is cleared either automatically or by operator intervention:
(a) events/errors related to payment to play, eg coins, notes
(b) events/errors related to operation of the device, eg battery failure, programme error
(c) events/errors related to security, eg door open
(d) events/errors related to payouts, eg printer jam, hopper empty
Equipment used for the playing of interval bingo games but which by reason of its design cannot meet the above requirement must indicate to the player whether they are entered into the game.

5 WIRELESS NETWORK SYSTEMS

Network Coverage

5.1 If a gaming device is designed to allow players to participate using a wireless network the following must be complied with:
(a) unless denoted by clear signage, there must be no areas where players may participate in any gambling using such a device where the communication signal is
  (i) not available
  (ii) of poor quality such that interruptions in play would be likely
(b) there must be adequate wireless coverage so that the failure of a single transmitter does not significantly reduce the players' ability to participate in the game. This does not prohibit the use of a single transmitter

Network Failure

5.2 Where a network failure occurs:

(a) all devices must alert the player of the failure as soon as it is possible to do so. It is permissible for the device to continue with any game if the network connection is restored provided that the player is not disadvantaged in any way
(b) a manual alternative method of play (for example, keying in game outcome or other element as opposed to an automatic download via wireless network) is permissible where there is no disadvantage to the player and where there is adequate time to do so. Catch up facilities (for example, button pressed to bring device up to current position within game) may be used where the game that was in play when the network failure occurred has not been completed

Communication Requirements

5.3 All protocols must use communication techniques that have proper error detection and/or recovery mechanisms which are designed to prevent unauthorized access or tampering, employing Data Encryption Standards (DES) or equivalent encryption with secure seeds or algorithms.

Power Level Display Requirements

5.4 Portable devices must give warnings when the battery life of the device reaches a low level.

Audit Requirements

5.5 An audit log of sufficient time stamping of significant events must be maintained so as to be able to resolve any player disputes arising as a result of timing issues. It must be possible to display the audit log on the site operator's premises.
The Commission does not intend to set out exact requirements for time stamping of significant events as it is considered better that the manufacturer do so on the basis of the overall system design.

6 BINGO TICKETS

Bingo Tickets

6.1 The requirements for bingo tickets are as follows:
(a) every ticket used in a game of bingo must consist of a unique set of letters, numbers or symbols. This applies whether the tickets in play are physical (paper), virtual (electronic), a mix of the two, or any other representations of bingo tickets and applies whether the game takes place in one or at multiple venues
(b) each ticket in play (whether paper, electronic or other) must have a unique reference number or code associated with it, which can be used for ticket verification purposes

Automatic Game Determinant Marking

6.2 In all circumstances, player participation is required to record the numbers or other game determinant called and to claim a win. The Commission does not intend to set rules as to what action the player must take in order to initiate the system to record the determinant(s) called, but this must involve a physical player interaction of some description.
This requirement does not prevent the use of catch up facilities within a game (for example, a button pressed to bring a device up to the current position within a game), providing the game is still in play.
Gambling Commission July 2008

Note

Regulatory return forms (October 2011) and guides as to how to complete them (June 2011) are available from the Gambling Commission's website at www.gamblingcommission.gov.uk

GAMING: BINGO

BINGO UNDER THE GAMBLING ACT 2005

CASH BINGO

6.2265 Cash bingo is primarily a commercial activity, and is licensed and regulated by the Gambling Commission. If you wish to provide cash bingo on a commercial basis you should consult the Commission: www.gamblingcommission.gov.uk.

PRIZE BINGO

Prize bingo is the kind normally played in funfairs and amusement arcades, for small participation fees and modest prizes.
It is typical of the prize gaming defined in section 288 of the Act, in which neither the nature nor the size of the prize are determined by the number of people playing or the amount paid for or raised by the gaming. Instead, the prize is put up in advance by the organiser of the game.
Under their existing permissions, bingo halls, adult gaming centres, travelling fairs, licensed family entertainment centres and holders of family entertainment centre gaming machine permits are automatically entitled to offer prize bingo. It may also be provided, for example in holiday camps and theme parks, under a prize gaming permit issued by a local licensing authority.
The maximum participation fee that may be charged for any one chance to win a prize in a game of prize bingo, wherever it is played, is 50 pence. The aggregate amount of participation fees, and the amount or value of prizes for which a game may be played, may not exceed £500.
Where prize bingo is played for money prizes, the following limits apply to the amount of a prize:

Adult Gaming Centres:	£50
Licensed bingo premises (where under 18s are excluded):	£50
Licensed bingo premises (where under 18s are permitted):	£35
All other cases:	£35

CLUB BINGO

Clubs and miners' welfare institutes that wish to provide facilities for bingo may do so under the "exempt gaming" provisions in Part 12 of the Act (section 269). Clubs need to meet a number of statutory criteria before they can offer gaming – please refer to the separate fact sheet on gaming in clubs.
The following rules apply to bingo played in clubs and institutes:

- no amounts may be deducted from sums staked or won;
- the maximum participation fee is £1 per person, per day (or £3 where a club gaming permit is held);
- there should be no linking of games between premises; and
- in the case of members' clubs and institutes, people may only participate in the gaming if they have been a member (or applied or were nominated for membership) at least 48 hours before playing, or are genuine guests of such a person.

There are no limits on stakes and prizes for individual games of club bingo.
However, clubs or institutes that wish to offer high turnover bingo (ie where stakes or prizes exceed £2000 per week) will require a bingo operating licence from the Gambling Commission. See the Commission's website (details above) for further

6: Gambling Act 2005: Additional Material

information.

PUB BINGO

Pubs that wish to provide facilities for bingo may do so under section 279 of the Act. The following rules apply:

- the maximum amount that may be staked by a player in a game of bingo is £5;
- no amounts may be deducted from sums staked or won;
- players may not be charged a fee for taking part;
- there should be no linking of games between premises; and,
- nobody under 18 may participate.

As with clubs, pubs that wish to offer high turnover bingo (ie where stakes or prizes exceed £2000 per week) will require a bingo operating licence from the Gambling Commission. See the Commission's website (details above) for further information.

BINGO FOR "GOOD CAUSES"

Organisations that wish to provide bingo (or other types of gaming) for charitable or other non-commercial purposes (eg to raise funds for a society) may do so under Part 14 of the Act. Non-commercial gaming may only take place at events where none of the proceeds from the event itself are used for private gain. There are two types of non-commercial gaming.

Prize gaming : where the prizes are put up in advance, and are not dependent on the number of players taking part or the amount of money staked. There are no statutory limits on stakes, prizes, participation fees or other charges for this type of gaming.

Equal chance gaming: where the amount or value of the prizes varies according to the number of players who participate and/or the amount of money they stake. Here a single payment of £8 per day may be charged to cover admission, stakes and any other charges for playing. The total value of prizes must not exceed £600 in one day. Where an event is the final one of series in which all of the players have previously taken part, a higher prize fund of no more than £900 is permitted.

In all cases, the players participating in non-commercial bingo must be told what "good cause" is to benefit from the profits from the gaming.

NB. This fact sheet is intended to provide a general explanation of the circumstances in which "bingo" can be played under the Gambling Act 2005. It does not deal with every detail of the legislative provisions, or with the individual circumstances of a particular case. This fact sheet does not constitute legal advice and is not a substitute for the relevant legal provisions. If you are in any doubt about the legality of any gambling activities that you intend to promote or for which you intend to provide facilities, you are strongly advised to seek independent legal advice.

Department for Culture Media and Sport

August 2007

CONDITIONS AND CODES OF PRACTICE APPLICABLE TO:
NON-REMOTE BINGO LICENCES

October 2010

6.2270–6.2275 **Your licence is subject to certain conditions and codes of practice,**

these are detailed in the following pages

STATUTORY CONDITIONS ATTACHED BY VIRTUE OF THE ACT

SOCIAL RESPONSIBILITY

This licence is subject to a condition that the licensee ensures compliance with any relevant social responsibility provision of a code of practice issued by the Commission. The social responsibility provisions that are relevant to the activities authorised by this licence are set out in the section entitled Codes of Practice.

(Sections 24 and 82(1) Gambling Act 2005)

RETURN OF STAKES TO CHILDREN

This licence is subject to a condition that if the licensee (or anyone employed by the licensee to perform an operational function within the meaning of section 80 of the Act) becomes aware that a child or young person is using or has used facilities for gambling provided in reliance on the licence, the licensee:

(a) must return any money paid in respect of the use of those facilities (whether by way of fee, stake or otherwise) by the child or young person as soon as is reasonably practicable; and

(b) may not give a prize to the child or young person.

This condition does not apply to use of a Category D gaming machine.

(Section 83(1))

OTHER STATUTORY CONDITIONS

This licence is subject to a condition that the licensee may not:

- give credit in connection with gambling; or
- participate in, arrange, permit or knowingly facilitate the giving of credit in connection with gambling.

But this condition shall not prevent the licensee from permitting the installation and use on their licensed premises of a machine enabling cash to be obtained on credit from a person (the "credit provider") provided that:

- the licensee has no other commercial connection with the credit provider in relation to gambling;
- the licensee neither makes nor receives any payment or reward (whether by way of commission, rent or otherwise) in connection with the machine; and
- any conditions about the nature, location or use of the machine which may be attached to this licence by the Commission or by virtue of regulations by the Secretary of State are complied with.

(Section 81(2))

COMMISSION GENERAL CONDITIONS

The Commission's complete suite of Licence Conditions to be attached to operating licences pursuant to section 75 of the Act includes some conditions which may not apply to your licence. Where that is the case the irrelevant conditions have not been reproduced below. The full list of Licence Conditions and Codes of Practice are contained within the Commissions Publication "Licence Conditions and Codes of Practice"

QUALIFIED PERSONS AND PERSONAL LICENCES

Qualified persons

THE FOLLOWING CONDITION APPLIES TO ALL OPERATING LICENCES ISSUED TO SMALL-SCALE OPERATORS

In this condition the terms 'small-scale operator', 'qualifying position' and 'qualified person' have the meanings respectively ascribed to them by the Gambling Act 2005 (Definition of Small-scale Operator) Regulations 2006.

Schedule X[1] lists those individuals notified to the Commission as qualified persons.

If, whilst the licensee remains a small-scale operator, an individual begins or ceases to occupy a qualifying position in relation to the licensee, the licensee must within 28 days apply to the Commission under s104(1)(b) for amendment of the details of the licence set out in Schedule X.

An application for amendment under s104(1)(b) may be made in advance of an individual beginning or ceasing to occupy a qualifying position provided it specifies the date from which the change to which it relates is to be effective.

---

1 The schedules mentioned here will be attached to individual licences.

PERSONAL LICENCES

(a) Subject to (e) and (f) below licensees must ensure:
   (i) that each individual who occupies one of the management offices specified in (b) below in or in respect of the licensee or in connection with the licensed activities holds a personal licence authorising the performance of the functions of that office (hereafter 'a personal management licence')
   (ii) that at least one person occupies at least one of those offices.

(b) The specified management offices are those offices (whether or not held by a director in the case of a licensee which is a company, a partner in the case of a licensee which is a partnership or an officer of the association in the case of a licensee which is an unincorporated association) the occupier of which is by virtue of the terms of their appointment responsible for:
   - the overall management and direction of the licensee's business or affairs
   - the licensee's finance function as head of that function
   - the licensee's gambling regulatory compliance function as head of that function
   - the licensee's marketing function as head of that function
   - the licensee's information technology function as head of that function in so far as it relates to gambling-related information technology and software
   - oversight of the day to day management of the licensed activities at an identified number of premises licensed under Part 8 of the Act or across an identified geographical area
   - in the case of casino and bingo licences only, oversight of the day to day management of a single set of premises licensed under Part 8 of the Act.

(c) Licensees must take all reasonable steps to ensure that anything done in the performance of the functions of a specified management office is done in accordance with the terms and conditions of the holder's personal management licence.

(d) Where an individual is authorised by a personal licence and that licence comes under review under section 116(2) of the Act, the operating licensee must comply with any conditions subsequently imposed on that licence by the Commission about redeployment, supervision, or monitoring of the individual's work and any requirements of the Commission in respect of such matters applicable during the period of the review.

(e) Paragraphs (a) to (d) above shall not apply to a licensee for so long as the licensee is a 'small-scale operator' as defined in the Gambling Act 2005 (Definition of Small-scale Operator) Regulations 2006 ('the Regulations').

(f) During the period of 3 years commencing with the date on which a licensee ceases to be a small-scale operator paragraphs (a) to (e) above shall apply subject to the proviso that the phrase 'each individual' in paragraph (a)(i) shall not include any individual who was a 'qualified person' (as defined in the Regulations) in relation to the licensee 28 days immediately prior to the licensee ceasing to be a small-scale operator.

TECHNICAL STANDARDS AND EQUIPMENT SPECIFICATIONS

Licensees must comply with the Commission's specifications for bingo equipment.

FINANCIAL ROBUSTNESS

Notification of shareholders

All company licensees must notify the Commission of the name and address of any person who becomes a shareholder in the company or its holding company holding 3% or more of the issued share capital of the company or its holding company; or any existing shareholder who acquires a holding of 3% or more of the issued share capital of the company or its holding company.
In this condition 'holding company' has the meaning ascribed to that term by section 1159 of the Companies Act 2006 or any statutory modification or re-enactment thereof.

PROTECTION OF CUSTOMER FUNDS

Licensees who hold customer funds for use in future gambling must set out clearly, in information made available to customers in writing, whether they protect customers' funds in the event of insolvency and the method by which this is achieved.

CASH HANDLING

Licensees, as part of their internal controls and financial accounting systems, must have and put into effect policies and procedures concerning the handling of cash, and cash equivalents (ie bankers drafts, cheques and debit cards), designed to minimise the risk of crimes such as money laundering, to avoid the giving of illicit credit and to provide assurance that gambling activities are being conducted fairly.

GENERAL 'FAIR AND OPEN' PROVISIONS

Licensees must satisfy themselves that the terms on which gambling is offered are not unfair under the Unfair Terms in Consumer Contracts Regulations 1999 and, where applicable, meet the reasonableness test under the Unfair Contract Terms Act 1977. An accurate summary of the contractual terms on which gambling is offered must be made available to customers and set out in plain and intelligible language.
Customers must be notified of changes to terms before they come into effect.

TYPES AND RULES OF CASINO AND OTHER GAMES

Licensees must not offer or permit to be played games that appear on any list of proscribed prize gaming games issued by the Commission.

ACCESS TO PREMISES

Licensees must have and put into effect policies and procedures (including staff training programmes) designed to ensure that their staff co-operate with the Commission's enforcement officers in the proper performance of their compliance functions and are made aware of those officers' rights of entry to premises contained in Part 15 of the Act.

INFORMATION REQUIREMENTS

Reporting suspicion of offences etc

Licensees must provide the Commission with any information that they know relates to or suspect may relate to the commission of an offence under the Act, including an offence resulting from a breach of a licence condition or a code provision having the effect of a licence condition.

Reporting 'Key Events'

A key event is an event that could have a significant impact on the nature or structure of a licensee's business. Licensees must notify the Commission of the occurrence of any of the following key events as soon as reasonably practicable and in any event within five working days of the licensee becoming aware of the event's occurrence[2].

- in the case of licensees which are companies, a petition being presented for their winding up or the winding up of any group company of theirs, or they or any group company being placed in administration or receivership: in this condition a 'group company' is any subsidiary or holding company of the licensee – as those terms are defined in section 1159 of the Companies Act 2006 or any statutory modification or re-enactment thereof – and any subsidiary of such holding company
- in the case of a licensee who is an individual (or a partner in a partnership licensee) their being presented with a petition for their bankruptcy or sequestration or their entering into an individual voluntary agreement
- where the licensee is required to have their accounts independently audited, any unplanned change of auditor including a change prompted by a dispute or resulting from auditors being unable or unwilling to sign an unqualified audit report
- the departure from the licensee's business of any person occupying a 'qualifying position' as defined by Regulation 2(2) of the Gambling Act 2005 (Definition of Small-scale Operator) Regulations 2006
- any breach of a covenant given to a bank or other lender
- any default in making repayment of the whole or any part of a loan on its due date
- any court judgments remaining unpaid 14 days after the date of judgment
- the commencement of any material litigation against the licensee
- the imposition of a disciplinary sanction, including dismissal, against the holder of a personal licence or a person occupying a qualifying position for gross misconduct; or the resignation of a personal licence holder or person occupying a qualifying position following commencement of disciplinary proceedings in respect of gross misconduct against that person
- in the case of remote gambling, the commencement or cessation of trading on website domains (including WAP URLs) or broadcast media through which the licensee provides gambling facilities.

---

2 Key events can be reported securely online at the Commission's website at www.gamblingcommission.gov.uk or by email to key.events@gamblingcommission.gov.uk or posted to Key Events, Compliance Administration Team, Gambling Commission, Victoria Square House, Victoria Square, Birmingham B2 4BP

GENERAL AND REGULATORY RETURNS

On request, licensees must provide the Commission with such information as the Commission may require about the use made of facilities provided in accordance with this licence, and the manner in which gambling authorised by this licence and the licensee's business in relation to that gambling are carried on, including in particular information about:

- the numbers of people making use of the facilities and the frequency of such use
- the range of gambling activities provided by the licensee and the numbers of staff employed in connection with them
- the licensee's policies in relation to, and experiences of, problem gambling.

In particular within 28 days of the end of each quarterly period or, for those only submitting annual returns, within 42 days of the end of each annual period, licensees must submit a Regulatory Return to the Commission containing such information as the Commission may from time to time require.[3]

[3] Regulatory returns can be submitted securely online at the Commission's website at www.gamblingcommission.gov.uk For operators unable to access this system, the forms and a guide to completing them can be requested from the Commission and returned by email to Regulatory.Returns@gamblingcommission.gov.uk or by post to Regulatory Returns, Compliance Administration Team, Gambling Commission, Victoria Square House, Victoria Square, Birmingham, B2 4BP.

PRIMARY GAMBLING ACTIVITY

Gaming machines may be made available for use in licensed bingo premises only on those days when sufficient facilities for playing bingo are also available for use.
In cases where bingo is exclusively offered by means of electronic bingo terminals or bingo machines, there must be more individual player positions made available for bingo than there are gaming machines made available for use.

SECRETARY OF STATE GENERAL CONDITIONS

CONDITION TO BE ATTACHED TO BINGO OPERATING LICENCES IN RESPECT OF PRIZE GAMING

(1) The amount charged by way of participation fee in respect of any one chance to win a prize in a particular game does not exceed £1.

(2) Where in paying for a chance to win a prize in a game a person acquires the chance to win more than one prize, the limit in paragraph (1) shall apply despite the fact that the chance provides the opportunity to win more than one prize.

(3) The aggregate amount of the participation fees charged for participating in a particular game does not exceed £500.

(4) Where a prize for which a game is played is money, the amount of that prize does not exceed:
   - (a) £100, if no person under the age of 18 years is permitted to be on the premises at any time when the game is being played, and
   - (b) £70, in all other cases.

(5) For the purposes of paragraph (4)(a) above, no account shall be taken of any person under the age of 18 years who is permitted to be on the premises if:
   - (a) they are employed to perform any function on the premises, and
   - (b) they are on the premises in the course of their employment.

Any reference to the premises is to the licensed bingo premises in which the game referred to in paragraph (4) is being played.

(6) The aggregate amount or value of the prizes for which a game is played does not exceed £500.

(Regulation 3 of the Gambling Act 2005 (Operating Licence Conditions) Regulations 2007)

CODES OF PRACTICE

INTRODUCTION

This is the Commission's principal code of practice, issued under section 24 of the Gambling Act 2005, as revised with effect from 1 January 2009. There are two types of provision in the code:

- social responsibility provisions: compliance with these is a condition of licences; therefore any breach of them by an operator may lead the Commission to review the operator's licence with a view to suspension, revocation or the imposition of a financial penalty and would also expose the operator to the risk of prosecution; and
- ordinary code provisions: these do not have the status of licence conditions, but are admissible in evidence in criminal or civil proceedings and must be taken into account in any case in which the court or tribunal think them relevant and by the Commission in the exercise of its functions. Any breach of ordinary code provisions by an operator may be taken into account by the Commission on a licence review, but cannot lead to imposition of a financial penalty. These code provisions are in italics in this section and generally set out good practice in these areas.

FINANCIAL REQUIREMENTS

Ordinary code provision

In order to help prevent activities related to money laundering licensees should take into account the Commission's advice on the Proceeds of Crime Act 2002, *Duties and responsibilities under the Proceeds of Crime Act 2002. Advice for operators (excluding casino operators).*

PROTECTION OF CHILDREN AND OTHER VULNERABLE PERSONS

Combating problem gambling

SOCIAL RESPONSIBILITY CODE PROVISION

Licensees must have and put into effect policies and procedures intended to promote socially responsible gambling.

Licensees' policies and procedures for socially responsible gambling must include but need not be confined to:

- the specific policies and procedures required by the following provisions of section 2 of this code
- a commitment to and how they will contribute to research into the prevention and treatment of problem gambling
- a commitment to and how they will contribute to public education on the risks of gambling and how to gamble safely
- a commitment to and how they will contribute to the identification and treatment of problem gamblers.

Access to gambling by children and young persons

Social responsibility code provision

Licensees must have and put into effect policies and procedures designed to prevent underage gambling, and monitor the effectiveness of these.

This must include procedures for:

- checking the age of apparently underage customers
- refusing entry to any adult-only areas to anyone unable to produce an acceptable form of identification
- taking action when there are unlawful attempts to enter the adult-only areas.

Licensees must not permit children or young people to gamble in the adults-only areas of premises to which they have access. If there is a 'no under-18s' premises policy, licensees must pay particular attention to the procedures they use at the entrance to the premises to check customers' ages.

Licensees must take all reasonable steps to ensure that all staff understand their responsibilities for preventing underage gambling, returning stakes and not paying prizes to underage customers and particularly for challenging any adult who may be complicit in allowing a child or young person to gamble.

Licensees must only accept identification which:

- contains a photograph from which the individual can be identified
- states the individual's date of birth
- is valid
- is legible and has no visible signs of tampering or reproduction.

Ordinary code provision

The Commission considers acceptable forms of identification to include: any identification carrying the PASS logo (for example Citizencard or Validate); a driving licence (including a provisional licence) with photocard; or a passport.

Licensees should require a person who appears to relevant staff to be under the age of 21 to be asked to produce proof of age, either at the point of entry to the gambling area or as soon as it comes to the attention of staff that they wish to access gambling facilities.

Licensees should have procedures for dealing with cases where an adult knowingly or recklessly allows a child or young person to gamble. These procedures might include refusing to allow the adult to continue to gamble, removing them from the premises, and reporting the incident to the police or local authorities, or taking action where forged identification is produced.

Procedures should be put into effect for dealing with cases where a child or young person repeatedly attempts to gamble on their premises, including oral warnings, reporting the offence to the Gambling Commission and the police, and making available information on problem gambling to the child or young person concerned.

Where it is likely that customers' young or otherwise vulnerable children will be left unattended on or adjacent to their premises, licensees should consider reminding customers of their parental responsibilities and assess whether there is a need to develop procedures for minimising the risk to such children.

Information on how to gamble responsibly and help for problem gamblers

Social responsibility code provision

Licensees must make information readily available to their customers on how to gamble responsibly and how to access information about, and help in respect of, problem gambling.

The information must cover:

- any measures provided by the licensee to help individuals monitor or control their gambling, such as restricting the duration of a gambling session or the amount of money they can spend
- timers or other forms of reminders or 'reality checks' where available
- self-exclusion options
- information about the availability of further help or advice.

The information must be directed to all customers whether or not licensees also make available material which is directed specifically at customers who may be 'problem gamblers'.

For gambling premises, information must be available in all areas where gambling facilities are provided and adjacent to ATMs where these are not located in a gambling area. As a minimum, information must be displayed prominently on posters appropriate to the size and layout of the premises and contained in leaflets that may be taken away. Licensees must take all reasonable steps to ensure that this information is also readily accessible in locations which enable the customer to obtain it discreetly.

Ordinary code provision

Licensees who market their services in one or more foreign languages should make available in that, or those, foreign languages:

- the information on how to gamble responsibly and access to help referred to above
- the players' guides to any game, bet or lottery required to be made available to customers under provisions in this code
- the summary of the contractual terms on which gambling is offered, which is required to be provided to customers as a condition of the licensee's operating licence.

Customer interaction

Social responsibility code provision

Licensees must put into effect policies and procedures for customer interaction where they have concerns that a customer's behaviour may indicate problem gambling. The policies must include:

- identification of the appropriate level of management who may initiate customer interaction and the procedures for doing so
- the types of behaviour that will be logged/reported to the appropriate level of staff and which may trigger customer interaction at an appropriate moment
- the circumstances in which consideration should be given to refusing service to customers and/or barring them from the operator's gambling premises
- training for all staff on their respective responsibilities, in particular so that they know who is designated to deal with problem gambling issues.

But such policies and procedures must be consistent with, and implemented with due regard to, licensees' duties in respect of the health and safety of their staff.

Self-exclusion

Social responsibility code provision

Licensees must have and put into effect procedures for self-exclusion and take all reasonable steps to refuse service or to otherwise prevent an individual who has entered a self-exclusion agreement from participating in gambling.

Licensees must, as soon as practicable, take all reasonable steps to prevent any marketing material being sent to a self-excluded customer.

Licensees must take steps to remove the name and details of a self-excluded individual from any marketing databases used by the company or group (or otherwise flag that person as an individual to whom marketing material must not be sent), within two days of receiving the completed self-exclusion notification.

This covers any marketing material relating to gambling, or other activities that take place on the premises where gambling may take place. However, it would not extend to blanket marketing which is targeted at a particular geographical area and where the excluded individual would not knowingly be included.

Licensees must close any customer accounts of an individual who has entered a self exclusion agreement and return any funds held in the customer account. It is not sufficient merely to prevent an individual from withdrawing funds from their customer account whilst still accepting wagers from them. Where the giving of credit is permitted, the licensee may retain details of the amount owed to them by the individual, although the account must not be active.

Licensees must put into effect procedures designed to ensure that an individual who has self-excluded cannot gain access to gambling. These procedures must include:

- a register of those excluded with appropriate records (name, address, other details, and any membership or account details that may be held by the operator)
- photo identification (where available and in particular where enforcement of the system may depend on photographic ID), and a signature
- staff training to ensure that staff are able to enforce the systems
- the removal of those persons found in the gambling area or attempting to gamble from the premises.

Ordinary code provision

Self-exclusion procedures should require individuals to take positive action in order to self-exclude. This can be a signature on a self-exclusion form.

Wherever practicable, individuals should be able to self-exclude without having to enter gambling premises.

Before an individual self-excludes, licensees should provide or make available sufficient information about what the consequences of self-exclusion are.

Licensees should take all reasonable steps to extend the self-exclusion to premises of the same type owned by the operator in the customer's local area. In setting the bounds of that area licensees may take into account the customer's address (if known to them), anything else known to them about the distance the customer ordinarily travels to gamble and any specific request the customer may make.

Licensees should encourage the customer to consider extending their self exclusion to other licensees' gambling premises in the customer's local area.

Customers should be given the opportunity to discuss self-exclusion in private, where possible.

Licensees should take steps to ensure that:

- the self-exclusion period is a minimum of six months and give customers the option of extending this to a total of at least five years
- a customer who has decided to enter a self-exclusion agreement is given the opportunity to do so immediately without any cooling-off period. However, if the customer wishes to consider the self-exclusion further (for example to discuss with problem gambling groups) the customer may return at a later date to enter into self-exclusion
- at the end of the period chosen by the customer (and at least six months later), the self-exclusion remains in place, unless the customer takes positive action in order to gamble again. No marketing material should be sent to the individual unless the individual has taken positive action in order to gamble again, and has agreed to accept such material
- where a customer chooses not to renew the self-exclusion, and makes a positive request to begin gambling again, the customer is given one day to cool off before being allowed access to gambling facilities. The contact must be made via telephone or in person.

The licensee should retain the records relating to a self-exclusion agreement at least until the agreement has been formally ended.
(Please note that the Commission does not require the licensee to carry out any particular assessment or make any judgement as to whether the previously self-excluded individual should again be permitted access to gambling. The requirement to take positive action in person or over the phone is purely to a) check that the customer has considered the decision to access gambling again and allow them to consider the implications; and b) implement the one day cooling-off period and explain why this has been put in place.)

Employment of children and young persons

ORDINARY CODE PROVISION

Licensees who employ children (under-16-year-olds) and young persons (those aged 16 or 17) should be aware that it is an offence:

(a) to employ them to provide facilities for playing bingo;
(b) for their contracts of employment to require them, or for them to be permitted, to perform a function in connection with a gaming machine; and
(c) to employ a child to perform any function on premises where, and at a time when, facilities are being provided for playing bingo.

As to b) it should be noted that in the Commission's view the relevant provision of the Act applies to any function performed in connection with a gaming machine. This includes servicing or cleaning such a machine.
Accordingly, licensees should have and put into effect policies and procedures designed to ensure that:

- children and young persons are never asked to perform tasks within a) or b) above
- all staff, including those who are children and young persons themselves, are instructed about the laws relating to access to gambling by children and young persons

and should consider adopting a policy that:

- children are not employed to work on bingo licensed premises at any time when the premises are open for business
- neither children nor young persons are in any event asked to work in areas where gaming machines are situated.

Money lending between customers

ORDINARY CODE PROVISION

Licensees should seek to prevent systematic or organised money lending between customers on their premises. As a minimum, they should have arrangements in place to ensure staff are requested to report any instances of substantial money lending when they become aware of them.

'FAIR AND OPEN' PROVISIONS

Social responsibility code provision

Licensees must be able to provide evidence to the Commission, if required, showing how they satisfied themselves that their terms are not unfair.

Social responsibility code provision

In complying with any condition on a bingo premises licence requiring the display of rules about gaming, licensees must ensure that the following are included:

- rules about each variant of bingo made available
- rules about any prize gaming made available.

MARKETING

Social responsibility code provision

If a licensee makes available to any customer or potential customer any incentive or reward scheme or other arrangement under which the customer may receive money, goods, services or any other advantage (including the discharge in whole or in part of any liability of his) ('the benefit') the scheme must be designed to operate, and be operated, in such a way that:

(a) the circumstances in which, and conditions subject to which, the benefit is available are clearly set out and readily accessible to the customers to whom it is offered;

(b) neither the receipt nor the value or amount of the benefit is:

 (i) dependent on the customer gambling for a pre-determined length of time or with a predetermined frequency; or

 (ii) altered or increased if the qualifying activity or spend is reached within a shorter time than the whole period over which the benefit is offered;

(c) if the value of the benefit increases with the amount the customer spends it does so at a rate no greater than that at which the amount spent increases;

and further that:

(d) if the benefit comprises free or subsidised travel or accommodation which facilitates the customer's attendance at particular licensed premises the terms on which it is offered are not directly related to the level of the customer's prospective gambling.

Ordinary code provision

Licensees should only offer incentive or reward schemes in which the benefit available is proportionate to the type and level of customers' gambling.

Social responsibility code provision

If licensees offer customers free or discounted alcoholic drinks for consumption on the premises they must do so on terms which do not in any way link the availability of such drinks to whether, or when, the customer begins, or continues, to gamble.

Licensees must not make unsolicited offers of free alcoholic drinks for immediate consumption by customers at a time when they are participating in a casino game, bingo game or playing a gaming machine.

Ordinary code provision

All advertising of gambling products and services should be undertaken in a socially responsible manner. In particular, licensees should comply with the advertising codes of practice which apply to the form and media in which they advertise their gambling facilities or services, and for media not explicitly covered should apply the principles included in these codes of practice as if they were explicitly covered. Licensees should also follow any relevant industry code of practice on advertising.

However, the particular restriction on allowing people aged under 25 to appear in adverts need not be applied to point of sale advertising material, provided that the images used depict the sporting activity that may be gambled on and not the activity of gambling itself and do not offend any other aspect of the advertising codes.

Complaints and disputes

SOCIAL RESPONSIBILITY CODE PROVISION

Licensees must put into effect a written procedure for handling customer complaints and disputes.

In this code a 'complaint' means a complaint about any aspect of the licensee's conduct of the licensed activities, and a 'dispute' is any complaint which:

(a) is not resolved at the first stage of the complaints procedure; and

(b) relates to the outcome of the complainant's gambling transaction.

Licensees must ensure that:

- customers are told the name and status of the person to contact about their complaint
- customers are given a copy of the complaints procedure on request or on making a complaint
- all complaints are handled in accordance with the procedure.

Licensees must also ensure that they have arrangements in place for disputes to be referred to an independent third party. Customers whose disputes are not resolved to their satisfaction by use of the operator's complaints procedure may refer those disputes to this independent third party. The arrangements under which such complaints are referred may, but need not, provide for the third party's decision to be binding on the licensee and the customer.

Licensees must keep a record of all complaints that are not resolved at the first stage of the complaints procedure.

Licensees must arrange for a copy of the decision on, or a note of the outcome of, each dispute referred to the independent party to be provided to the Commission quarterly, either by the independent party or by the licensee.

Gambling licensees' staff

SOCIAL RESPONSIBILITY CODE PROVISION

Licensees must take all reasonable steps to ensure that staff involved in the provision of facilities for gambling are made aware of advice on socially responsible gambling and of where to get confidential advice should their gambling become hard to control.

Information requirements

ORDINARY CODE PROVISION

The Commission expects licensees to work with the Commission in an open and cooperative way and to inform the Commission of any matters that the Commission would reasonably need to be aware of in exercising its regulatory functions. These are matters that will have a material impact on the licensee's business or on the licensee's ability to conduct its business. Such matters, which should be notified to the Commission as soon as reasonably practicable[4], include the following:

- the departure from the licensee's business of any person named in the licence application, or that person's successor, who holds a personal management licence, but who does not occupy a 'qualifying position'
- any reduction in the number of staff employed by the licensee where that has a material impact on the licensee's business
- the acquisition or disposal by the licensee of gambling premises or pitches where that has a material impact on the size or nature of the licensee's business
- in the case of corporate licensees, the disposal or acquisition of any group company where that has a material impact on the licensee's ability to conduct its business

- any disposal of the licensee's assets where that has a material impact on the licensee's business
- any investigation by a professional, statutory, regulatory or government body into the licensee's activities, or the activities in relation to the licensed entity of a personal licence holder or a person occupying a qualifying position employed by them, where such an investigation could result in the imposition of a sanction or penalty which, if imposed, could reasonably be expected to raise doubts about the licensee's continued suitability to hold a Gambling Commission licence
- any instance of criminal activity, including repeated instances of small-scale theft or fraud, where that has a material impact on the licensee's business
- any major breach in the licensee's information security where that adversely affects the confidentiality of customer data or prevents customers from accessing their accounts for a substantial period of time
- any other matters that have a material impact on the licensee's business or on the licensee's ability to conduct its business.

---

[4] These matters can be reported securely online at the Commission's website at www.gambling-commission.gov.uk or by email to key.events@gamblingcommission.gov.uk or posted to Key Events, Compliance Administration Team, Gambling Commission, Victoria Square House, Victoria Square, Birmingham, B2 4BP.

Primary gambling activity

ORDINARY CODE PROVISION

In order to demonstrate that the primary gambling activity for which an operating licence has been issued is being offered in each licensed premises, licensees should have regard to the following general factors:

- the ratio of space available to customers allocated to the primary gambling activity, to that allocated to other gambling activities
- the extent to which the primary gambling activity is promoted on the premises and by way of external advertising compared to other gambling activities
- the use, either expected or actual, to be made of the different gambling facilities

Licensees should also have regard to the following additional sector specific factors:

ORDINARY CODE PROVISION

The frequency and extent that bingo is, or is intended to be played on the premises, compared with the periods when the premises are open whether there is:

- capacity on the premises for the generation of main stage bingo numbers
- a facility to sell tickets or cards for bingo games on the premises
- bingo available to be played whenever sessions are advertised
- display of prize board information
- a means of stopping a game to claim a win.

Not all the indicators would need to be present in a particular case, nor do they preclude others, but the combination of those factors that are present should be sufficient to indicate that the activity is the primary one in any given premises.

Gambling Commission October 2010

CONDITIONS AND CODES OF PRACTICE APPLICABLE TO: REMOTE BINGO LICENCES REMOTE BINGO ANCILLARY LICENCES

October 2010

6.2280 Your licence is subject to certain conditions and codes of practice, these are detailed in the following pages

STATUTORY CONDITIONS ATTACHED BY VIRTUE OF THE ACT

SOCIAL RESPONSIBILITY

This licence is subject to a condition that the licensee ensures compliance with any relevant social responsibility provision of a code of practice issued by the Commission. The social responsibility provisions that are relevant to the activities authorised by this licence are set out in the section entitled Codes of Practice.
(Sections 24 and 82(1) Gambling Act 2005)

RETURN OF STAKES TO CHILDREN

This licence is subject to a condition that if the licensee (or anyone employed by the licensee to perform an operational function within the meaning of section 80 of the Act) becomes aware that a child or young person is using or has used facilities for gambling provided in reliance on the licence, the licensee:

(a) must return any money paid in respect of the use of those facilities (whether by way of fee, stake or otherwise) by the child or young person as soon as is reasonably practicable; and

(b) may not give a prize to the child or young person.

This condition does not apply to use of a Category D gaming machine.
(Section 83(1))

COMMISSION GENERAL CONDITIONS

The Commission's complete suite of Licence Conditions to be attached to operating licences pursuant to section 75 of the Act includes some conditions which may not apply to your licence. Where that is the case the irrelevant conditions have not been reproduced below. The full list of Licence Conditions and Codes of Practice are contained within the Commission's Publication "Licence Conditions and Codes of Practice"

QUALIFIED PERSONS AND PERSONAL LICENCES

Qualified persons

THE FOLLOWING CONDITION APPLIES TO ALL REMOTE BINGO OPERATING LICENCES, EXCEPT ANCILLARY REMOTE LICENCES, ISSUED TO SMALL-SCALE OPERATORS

In this condition the terms 'small-scale operator', 'qualifying position' and 'qualified person' have the meanings respectively ascribed to them by the Gambling Act 2005 (Definition of Small-scale Operator) Regulations 2006.

Schedule X[1] lists those individuals notified to the Commission as qualified persons.

If, whilst the licensee remains a small-scale operator, an individual begins or ceases to occupy a qualifying position in relation to the licensee, the licensee must within 28 days apply to the Commission under s104(1)(b) for amendment of the details of the licence set out in Schedule X[1].

An application for amendment under s104(1)(b) may be made in advance of an individual beginning or ceasing to occupy a qualifying position provided it specifies the date from which the change to which it relates is to be effective.

[1] The schedules mentioned here will be attached to individual licences.

Personal licences

THE FOLLOWING CONDITION APPLIES TO ALL REMOTE BINGO OPERATING LICENCES EXCEPT ANCILLARY REMOTE LICENCES

(a) Subject to (e) and (f) below licensees must ensure:
   (i) that each individual who occupies one of the management offices specified in (b) below in or in respect of the licensee or in connection with the licensed activities holds a personal licence authorising the performance of the functions of that office (hereafter 'a personal management licence')
   (ii) that at least one person occupies at least one of those offices.

(b) The specified management offices are those offices (whether or not held by a director in the case of a licensee which is a company, a partner in the case of a licensee which is a partnership or an officer of the association in the case of a licensee which is an unincorporated association) the occupier of which is by virtue of the terms of their appointment responsible for:
   - the overall management and direction of the licensee's business or affairs
   - the licensee's finance function as head of that function
   - the licensee's gambling regulatory compliance function as head of that function
   - the licensee's marketing function as head of that function
   - the licensee's information technology function as head of that function in so far as it relates to gambling-related information technology and software
   - oversight of the day to day management of the licensed activities at an identified number of premises licensed under Part 8 of the Act or across an identified geographical area
   - in the case of casino and bingo licences only, oversight of the day to day management of a single set of premises licensed under Part 8 of the Act.

(c) Licensees must take all reasonable steps to ensure that anything done in the performance of the functions of a specified management office is done in accordance with the terms and conditions of the holder's personal management licence.

(d) Where an individual is authorised by a personal licence and that licence comes under review under section 116(2) of the Act, the operating licensee must comply with any conditions subsequently imposed on that licence by the Commission about redeployment, supervision, or monitoring of the individual's work and any requirements of the Commission in respect of such matters applicable during the period of the review.

(e) Paragraphs (a) to (d) above shall not apply to a licensee for so long as the licensee is a 'small-scale operator' as defined in the Gambling Act 2005 (Definition of Small-scale Operator) Regulations 2006 ('the Regulations').

(f) During the period of 3 years commencing with the date on which a licensee ceases to be a small-scale operator paragraphs (a) to (e) above shall apply subject to the proviso that the phrase 'each individual' in paragraph (a)(i) shall not include any individual who was a 'qualified person' (as defined in the Regulations) in relation to the licensee 28 days immediately prior to the licensee ceasing to be a small-scale operator.

Technical standards and equipment specifications

THE FOLLOWING CONDITION APPLIES TO ALL REMOTE BINGO OPERATING LICENCES EXCEPT ANCILLARY REMOTE LICENCES

Licensees must comply with the Commission's technical standards and with requirements set by the Commission relating to the timing and procedures for testing.

THE FOLLOWING CONDITION APPLIES TO ANCILLARY REMOTE BINGO OPERATING LICENCES ONLY

Licensees must comply with the Commission's specifications for bingo equipment.

FINANCIAL ROBUSTNESS

Notification of shareholders

THE FOLLOWING CONDITION APPLIES TO ALL REMOTE BINGO OPERATING LICENCES, EXCEPT ANCILLARY REMOTE LICENCES

All company licensees must notify the Commission of the name and address of any person who becomes a shareholder in the company or its holding company holding 3% or more of the issued share capital of the company or its holding company; or any existing shareholder who acquires a holding of 3% or more of the issued share capital of the company or its holding company.
In this condition 'holding company' has the meaning ascribed to that term by section 1159 of the Companies Act 2006 or any statutory modification or re-enactment thereof.

Protection of customer funds

THE FOLLOWING CONDITION APPLIES TO ALL REMOTE BINGO OPERATING LICENCES, EXCEPT ANCILLARY REMOTE LICENCES

Licensees who hold customer funds for use in future gambling must set out clearly, in information made available to customers in writing, whether they protect customers' funds in the event of insolvency and the method by which this is achieved.

General 'fair and open' provisions

Licensees must satisfy themselves that the terms on which gambling is offered are not unfair under the Unfair Terms in Consumer Contracts Regulations 1999 and, where applicable, meet the reasonableness test under the Unfair Contract Terms Act 1977. An accurate summary of the contractual terms on which gambling is offered must be made available to customers and set out in plain and intelligible language.
Customers must be notified of changes to terms before they come into effect.

Display of licensed status

THE FOLLOWING CONDITION APPLIES TO ALL REMOTE BINGO OPERATING LICENCES, EXCEPT ANCILLARY REMOTE LICENCES

Licensees offering gambling on websites must:

(a) display the following information on a page which, by virtue of the construction of the website, customers access before gambling:
  (i) a statement that they are licensed and regulated by the Gambling Commission;

(ii) their licence number; and
(iii) a link to the Gambling Commission's website;

(b) display at least the information at (i) above on each page of the website which offers facilities for gambling in reliance on the licence;

(c) where they offer on pages of the website, or by means of a link from the website, facilities for gambling which are not provided in reliance on their Gambling Commission licence, clearly distinguish those products which are regulated by the Commission from those which are not.

ACCESS TO PREMISES

Licensees must have and put into effect policies and procedures (including staff training programmes) designed to ensure that their staff co-operate with the Commission's enforcement officers in the proper performance of their compliance functions and are made aware of those officers' rights of entry to premises contained in Part 15 of the Act.

INFORMATION REQUIREMENTS

Reporting suspicion of offences etc

Licensees must provide the Commission with any information that they know relates to or suspect may relate to the commission of an offence under the Act, including an offence resulting from a breach of a licence condition or a code provision having the effect of a licence condition.

Reporting 'Key Events'

THE FOLLOWING CONDITION APPLIES TO ALL REMOTE BINGO OPERATING LICENCES, EXCEPT ANCILLARY REMOTE LICENCES

A key event is an event that could have a significant impact on the nature or structure of a licensee's business. Licensees must notify the Commission of the occurrence of any of the following key events as soon as reasonably practicable and in any event within five working days of the licensee becoming aware of the event's occurrence[2].

- in the case of licensees which are companies, a petition being presented for their winding up or the winding up of any group company of theirs, or they or any group company being placed in administration or receivership: in this condition a 'group company' is any subsidiary or holding company of the licensee – as those terms are defined in section 1159 of the Companies Act 2006 or any statutory modification or re-enactment thereof – and any subsidiary of such holding company
- in the case of a licensee who is an individual (or a partner in a partnership licensee) their being presented with a petition for their bankruptcy or sequestration or their entering into an individual voluntary agreement
- where the licensee is required to have their accounts independently audited, any unplanned change of auditor including a change prompted by a dispute or resulting from auditors being unable or unwilling to sign an unqualified audit report
- the departure from the licensee's business of any person occupying a 'qualifying position' as defined by Regulation 2(2) of the Gambling Act 2005 (Definition of Small-scale Operator) Regulations 2006
- any breach of a covenant given to a bank or other lender
- any default in making repayment of the whole or any part of a loan on its due date
- any court judgments remaining unpaid 14 days after the date of judgment
- the commencement of any material litigation against the licensee

- the imposition of a disciplinary sanction, including dismissal, against the holder of a personal licence or a person occupying a qualifying position for gross misconduct; or the resignation of a personal licence holder or person occupying a qualifying position following commencement of disciplinary proceedings in respect of gross misconduct against that person
- in the case of remote gambling, the commencement or cessation of trading on website domains (including WAP URLs) or broadcast media through which the licensee provides gambling facilities.

[2] Key events can be reported securely online at the Commission's website at www.gamblingcommission.gov.uk or by email to key.events@gamblingcommission.gov.uk or posted to Key Events, Compliance Administration Team, Gambling Commission, Victoria Square House, Victoria Square, Birmingham B2 4BP

General and Regulatory Returns

On request, licensees must provide the Commission with such information as the Commission may require about the use made of facilities provided in accordance with this licence, and the manner in which gambling authorised by this licence and the licensee's business in relation to that gambling are carried on, including in particular information about:

- the numbers of people making use of the facilities and the frequency of such use
- the range of gambling activities provided by the licensee and the numbers of staff employed in connection with them
- the licensee's policies in relation to, and experiences of, problem gambling.

In particular within 28 days of the end of each quarterly period or, for those only submitting annual returns, within 42 days of the end of each annual period, licensees must submit a Regulatory Return to the Commission containing such information as the Commission may from time to time require.[3]

[3] Regulatory returns can be submitted securely online at the Commission's website at www.gamblingcommission.gov.uk For operators unable to access this system, the forms and a guide to completing them can be requested from the Commission and returned by email to Regulatory.Returns@gamblingcommission.gov.uk or by post to Regulatory Returns, Compliance Administration Team, Gambling Commission, Victoria Square House, Victoria Square, Birmingham, B2 4BP.

SECRETARY OF STATE GENERAL CONDITIONS

None at present

CODES OF PRACTICE

Introduction

This is the Commission's principal code of practice, issued under section 24 of the Gambling Act 2005, as revised with effect from 1 January 2009. There are two types of provision in the code:

- social responsibility provisions: compliance with these is a condition of licences; therefore any breach of them by an operator may lead the Commission to review the operator's licence with a view to suspension, revocation or the imposition of a financial penalty and would also expose the operator to the risk of prosecution; and
- ordinary code provisions: these do not have the status of licence conditions, but are admissible in evidence in criminal or civil proceedings and must be taken into

account in any case in which the court or tribunal think them relevant and by the Commission in the exercise of its functions. Any breach of ordinary code provisions by an operator may be taken into account by the Commission on a licence review, but cannot lead to imposition of a financial penalty. These code provisions are in italics in this section and generally set out good practice in these areas.

Financial requirements

Ordinary code provision

In order to help prevent activities related to money laundering licensees should take into account the Commission's advice on the Proceeds of Crime Act 2002, *Duties and responsibilities under the Proceeds of Crime Act 2002. Advice for operators (excluding casino operators).*

PROTECTION OF CHILDREN AND OTHER VULNERABLE PERSONS

Combating problem gambling

Social responsibility code provision

Licensees must have and put into effect policies and procedures intended to promote socially responsible gambling.

Licensees' policies and procedures for socially responsible gambling must include but need not be confined to:

- the specific policies and procedures required by the following provisions of section 2 of this code
- a commitment to and how they will contribute to research into the prevention and treatment of problem gambling
- a commitment to and how they will contribute to public education on the risks of gambling and how to gamble safely
- a commitment to and how they will contribute to the identification and treatment of problem gamblers.

Access to gambling by children and young persons

The following code applies to all remote bingo operating licences, except ancillary remote licences

Social responsibility code provision

Licensees must have and put into effect policies and procedures designed to prevent underage gambling, and monitor the effectiveness of these.

Such procedures must include:

(a) warning potential customers that underage gambling is an offence;
(b) requiring customers to affirm that they are of legal age;
(c) regularly reviewing their age verification systems and implementing all reasonable improvements that may be made as technology advances and as information improves;
(d) ensuring that relevant staff are properly trained in the use of their age verification procedures; in particular customer services staff must be appropriately trained in the use of secondary forms of identification when initial verification procedures fail to prove that an individual is of legal age;

(e) enabling their gambling websites to permit filtering software to be used by adults (such as parents or within schools) in order to restrict access to relevant pages of those sites;

(f) in the case of any UK resident customer who deposits money using any type of payment method other than a credit card, and unless the licensee has established that a third party has satisfactorily carried out age verification, the following age verification procedures:
- (i) verifying additional information about the customer, such as carrying out searches of credit reference and other databases that list names and addresses of individuals over the age of 18;
- (ii) carrying out secondary age verification checks in any circumstances which give the operator reason to suspect that the person may be underage;
- (iii) not permitting the customer to withdraw any winnings from their account until age verification has been satisfactorily completed; and
- (iv) in any event, a requirement that if age verification has not been satisfactorily completed within 72 hours of the customer applying to register to gamble and depositing money:
  - the account will be frozen
  - no further gambling will be permitted until age verification has been successfully completed
  - if on completion of age verification the customer is shown to be underage, the operator must return to the customer any money paid in respect of the use of the gambling facilities, but no winnings shall be paid.

(g) in the case of any non-UK resident customer who deposits money using any type of payment method other than a credit card, and unless the licensee has established that a third party has satisfactorily carried out age verification, the following age verification procedures:
- (i) taking all reasonable steps to make use of information available for age verification purposes from whichever country the potential customer is resident in; and
- (ii) each of the following steps, unless they can not reasonably be implemented or, in the case of the fourth bullet point, a period of more than 72 hours was reasonably required:
  - verifying additional information about the customer, such as carrying out searches of credit reference and other databases that list names and addresses of individuals over the age of 18
  - carrying out secondary age verification checks in any circumstances which give the operator reason to suspect that the person may be underage
  - not permitting the customer to withdraw any winnings from their account until age verification has been satisfactorily completed
  - a requirement that if age verification has not been satisfactorily completed within 72 hours of the customer applying to register to gamble and depositing money:
    - — the account will be frozen;
    - — no further gambling will be permitted until age verification has been successfully completed; and
    - — if on completion of age verification the customer is shown to be underage all deposits held by the operator are returned to the customer and no winnings paid.

(h) in the case of any customer who registers to gamble and deposits money using a credit card, conducting a programme of random checks of credit card users for compliance with age restrictions.

The following code applies to all remote bingo operating licences, except ancillary remote licences

Ordinary code provision

Licensees should, and should request their contracted partners to, draw attention to parental responsibility as part of the purchasing process of facilities such as mobile phones and interactive television.

Information on how to gamble responsibly and help for problem gamblers

The following code applies to all remote bingo operating licences, except ancillary remote licences

Social responsibility code provision

Licensees must make information readily available to their customers on how to gamble responsibly and how to access information about, and help in respect of, problem gambling.

The information must cover:

- any measures provided by the licensee to help individuals monitor or control their gambling, such as restricting the duration of a gambling session or the amount of money they can spend
- timers or other forms of reminders or 'reality checks' where available
- self-exclusion options
- information about the availability of further help or advice.

The information must be directed to all customers whether or not licensees also make available material which is directed specifically at customers who may be 'problem gamblers'.

For gambling premises, information must be available in all areas where gambling facilities are provided and adjacent to ATMs where these are not located in a gambling area. As a minimum, information must be displayed prominently on posters appropriate to the size and layout of the premises and contained in leaflets that may be taken away. Licensees must take all reasonable steps to ensure that this information is also readily accessible in locations which enable the customer to obtain it discreetly.

The following code applies to all remote bingo operating licences, except ancillary remote licences

Ordinary code provision

Licensees who market their services in one or more foreign languages should make available in that, or those, foreign languages:

- the information on how to gamble responsibly and access to help referred to above
- the players' guides to any game, bet or lottery required to be made available to customers under provisions in this code
- the summary of the contractual terms on which gambling is offered, which is required to be provided to customers as a condition of the licensee's operating licence.

Customer interaction

Social responsibility code provision

Licensees must put into effect policies and procedures for customer interaction where they have concerns that a customer's behaviour may indicate problem gambling. The policies must include:

- identification of the appropriate level of management who may initiate customer interaction and the procedures for doing so
- the types of behaviour that will be logged/reported to the appropriate level of staff and which may trigger customer interaction at an appropriate moment
- the circumstances in which consideration should be given to refusing service to customers and/or barring them from the operator's gambling premises
- training for all staff on their respective responsibilities, in particular so that they know who is designated to deal with problem gambling issues.

But such policies and procedures must be consistent with, and implemented with due regard to, licensees' duties in respect of the health and safety of their staff.

Self-exclusion

The following code applies to all remote bingo operating licences, except ancillary remote licences

Social responsibility code provision

Licensees must have and put into effect procedures for self-exclusion and take all reasonable steps to refuse service or to otherwise prevent an individual who has entered a self-exclusion agreement from participating in gambling.

Licensees must, as soon as practicable, take all reasonable steps to prevent any marketing material being sent to a self-excluded customer.

Licensees must take steps to remove the name and details of a self-excluded individual from any marketing databases used by the company or group (or otherwise flag that person as an individual to whom marketing material must not be sent), within two days of receiving the completed self-exclusion notification.

This covers any marketing material relating to gambling. However, it would not extend to blanket marketing which is targeted at a particular geographical area and where the excluded individual would not knowingly be included.

Licensees must close any customer accounts of an individual who has entered a self-exclusion agreement and return any funds held in the customer account. It is not sufficient merely to prevent an individual from withdrawing funds from their customer account whilst still accepting wagers from them. Where the giving of credit is permitted, the licensee may retain details of the amount owed to them by the individual, although the account must not be active.

Licensees must put into effect procedures designed to ensure that an individual who has self-excluded cannot gain access to gambling. These procedures must include:

- a register of those excluded with appropriate records (name, address, other details, and any membership or account details that may be held by the operator)
- a record of the card numbers to be excluded
- staff training to ensure that staff are able to enforce the systems
- the removal of access from those persons found to have gambled or who have attempted to gamble on the facilities.

The following code applies to all remote bingo operating licences, except ancillary remote licences

Ordinary code provision

Self-exclusion procedures should require individuals to take positive action in order to self-exclude:

- over the **internet**; this can be a box that must be ticked in order to indicate that they understand the system
- by **telephone**; this can be a direct question asking whether they understand the system.

Before an individual self-excludes, licensees should provide or make available sufficient information about what the consequences of self-exclusion are.

Licensees should encourage the customer to consider extending their self exclusion to other remote gambling operators currently used by the customer.

Customers should be given the opportunity to self-exclude by contacting customer services and in addition, where technically possible, by entering an automated process using remote communication. In order to avoid inadvertent self-exclusion it is acceptable for an automated process to include an additional step that requires the customer to confirm that they wish to self-exclude. The licensee should ensure that all staff who are involved in direct customer service are aware of the self-exclusion system in place, and are able to direct that individual to an immediate point of contact with whom/which to complete that process.

Within the licensee's information about self-exclusion policies, the licensee should provide a statement to explain that software is available to prevent an individual computer from accessing gambling internet sites. The licensee should provide a link to a site where further information is available.

Licensees should take all reasonable steps to ensure that:

- the self-exclusion period is a minimum of six months and give customers the option of extending this to a total of at least five years
- a customer who has decided to enter a self-exclusion agreement is given the opportunity to do so immediately without any cooling-off period. However, if the customer wishes to consider the self-exclusion further (for example to discuss with problem gambling groups) the customer may return at a later date to enter into self-exclusion
- at the end of the period chosen by the customer (and at least six months later), the self-exclusion remains in place, unless the customer takes positive action in order to gamble again. No marketing material should be sent to the individual unless the individual has taken positive action in order to gamble again, and has agreed to accept such material
- where a customer chooses not to renew the self-exclusion, and makes a positive request to begin gambling again, the customer is given one day to cool off before being allowed access to the gambling facilities. The contact must be made via telephone or in person; re-registering online is not sufficient.

The licensee should retain the records relating to a self-exclusion agreement at least until the agreement has been formally ended.

(Please note that the Commission does not require the licensee to carry out any particular assessment or make any judgement as to whether the previously self excluded individual should again be permitted access to gambling. The requirement to take positive action in person or over the phone is purely to a) check that the customer has considered the decision to access gambling again and allow them to consider the implications; and b) implement the one day cooling-off period and explain why this has been put in place.)

Employment of children and young persons

THE FOLLOWING CODE APPLIES TO ALL REMOTE BINGO OPERATING LICENCES, EXCEPT ANCILLARY REMOTE LICENCES

ORDINARY CODE PROVISION

Licensees who employ children (under-16-year-olds) and young persons (those aged 16 and 17) should be aware that it is an offence to employ them to provide facilities for gambling.

Provision of credit by licensees and the use of credit cards

THE FOLLOWING CODE APPLIES TO ALL REMOTE BINGO OPERATING LICENCES, EXCEPT ANCILLARY REMOTE LICENCES

SOCIAL RESPONSIBILITY CODE PROVISION

Licensees who choose to accept credit cards must:

- accept payment by credit card for gambling only where that payment is made to a customer account
- make available for gambling, funds deposited via credit card only after the card issuer has approved the transaction.

THE FOLLOWING CODE APPLIES TO ALL REMOTE BINGO OPERATING LICENCES, EXCEPT ANCILLARY REMOTE LICENCES

ORDINARY CODE PROVISION

Licensees who choose to offer credit to members of the public who are not themselves gambling operators should also:

- have procedures for checking and scoring applications for credit from such customers, for setting, and for the increase of, credit limits
- explain these procedures to customers
- set a maximum credit limit for each customer and not permit customers to exceed that limit without further application
- apply a 24-hour delay between receiving a request for an increase in a credit limit and granting it in those cases where the limit exceeds that which the operator had previously set
- not require a minimum spend within a set time period
- take all reasonable steps to ensure that offers of credit are not sent to vulnerable persons, including those who have self-excluded from gambling
- ensure that information about an offer of credit includes a risk warning of what may happen in the event of default.

Identification of individual customers

THE FOLLOWING CODE APPLIES TO ALL REMOTE BINGO OPERATING LICENCES, EXCEPT ANCILLARY REMOTE LICENCES

SOCIAL RESPONSIBILITY CODE PROVISION

Licensees must have and put into effect policies and procedures designed to identify separate accounts which are held by the same individual.

Where licensees allow customers to hold more than one account with them, the licensee must link all of a customer's such accounts to that customer and ensure that:

- if a customer opts to self-exclude from one account they are excluded from all accounts they hold with the licensee
- all of a customer's accounts are monitored and decisions that trigger customer interaction are based on the observed behaviour and transactions across all the accounts
- where credit is offered or allowed the maximum credit limit is applied on an aggregate basis across all accounts
- individual financial limits can be implemented across all of a customer's accounts.

THE FOLLOWING CODE APPLIES TO ALL REMOTE BINGO OPERATING LICENCES, EXCEPT ANCILLARY REMOTE LICENCES

ORDINARY CODE PROVISION

Where a licensee:

(i) is a company, the licensee should take all reasonable steps to comply with the above social responsibility code provision as if it also applied to accounts held in respect of gambling carried on in reliance on a remote operating licence held by any Group Company;

(ii) also holds a licence in another jurisdiction permitting it to provide facilities for remote gambling (a 'foreign licence') or is a company one or more of whose Group Companies holds one or more foreign licences, the licensee should take all reasonable steps to comply with the above social responsibility code provision as if it applied also to accounts held in respect of gambling carried on in reliance on a foreign licence held by the licensee or any Group Company.

A company is a Group Company in relation to a licensee if it is the holding company of, subsidiary of, or shares a common holding company with, the licensee. For these purposes 'holding company' and 'subsidiary' respectively have the meanings ascribed to them by section 1159 of the Companies Act 2006 or any statutory modification or re-enactment thereof.

'FAIR AND OPEN' PROVISIONS

SOCIAL RESPONSIBILITY CODE PROVISION

Licensees must be able to provide evidence to the Commission, if required, showing how they satisfied themselves that their terms are not unfair.

THE FOLLOWING CODE APPLIES TO ALL REMOTE BINGO OPERATING LICENCES, EXCEPT ANCILLARY REMOTE LICENCES

SOCIAL RESPONSIBILITY CODE PROVISION

Licensees must make the following available to customers:

- a player's guide to each gambling opportunity (bet, game or lottery) made available by the operator
- such additional information relating to the available gambling as the Commission shall from time to time publish to licensees: the current requirements are set out in an Annex to the Commission's Technical Standards.

THE FOLLOWING CODE APPLIES TO ALL REMOTE BINGO OPERATING LICENCES, EXCEPT ANCILLARY REMOTE LICENCES

ORDINARY CODE PROVISION

Where practicable, the player's guide and additional information referred to in the social responsibility code should be made available through the medium in which the remote gambling is to be conducted. Where that is not practicable, licensees should either:

- send a copy of the guide and required additional information by post, fax or email; or
- make these available to the customer in another medium to which he has access.

THE FOLLOWING CODE APPLIES TO ALL REMOTE BINGO OPERATING LICENCES, EXCEPT ANCILLARY REMOTE LICENCES

ORDINARY CODE PROVISION

Licensees should ensure that the terms on which they contract with third parties who provide user interfaces enabling customers to access their remote gambling facilities:

- include a term that any such user interface comply with the Commission's technical standards for remote gambling systems
- enable them to terminate the third party's contract promptly if, in the licensee's opinion, the third party is in breach of that term.

MARKETING

SOCIAL RESPONSIBILITY CODE PROVISION

If a licensee makes available to any customer or potential customer any incentive or reward scheme or other arrangement under which the customer may receive money, goods, services or any other advantage (including the discharge in whole or in part of any liability of his) ('the benefit') the scheme must be designed to operate, and be operated, in such a way that:

(a) the circumstances in which, and conditions subject to which, the benefit is available are clearly set out and readily accessible to the customers to whom it is offered;

(b) neither the receipt nor the value or amount of the benefit is:

 (i) dependent on the customer gambling for a pre-determined length of time or with a predetermined frequency; or

 (ii) altered or increased if the qualifying activity or spend is reached within a shorter time than the whole period over which the benefit is offered;

(c) if the value of the benefit increases with the amount the customer spends it does so at a rate no greater than that at which the amount spent increases;

and further that:

(d) if the benefit comprises free or subsidised travel or accommodation which facilitates the customer's attendance at particular licensed premises the terms on which it is offered are not directly related to the level of the customer's prospective gambling.

ORDINARY CODE PROVISION

Licensees should only offer incentive or reward schemes in which the benefit available is proportionate to the type and level of customers' gambling.

ORDINARY CODE PROVISION

All advertising of gambling products and services should be undertaken in a socially responsible manner. In particular, licensees should comply with the advertising codes of practice which apply to the form and media in which they advertise their gambling facilities or services, and for media not explicitly covered should apply the principles included in these codes of practice as if they were explicitly covered. Licensees should also follow any relevant industry code of practice on advertising.

However, the particular restriction on allowing people aged under 25 to appear in adverts need not be applied to point of sale advertising material, provided that the images used depict the sporting activity that may be gambled on and not the activity of gambling itself and do not offend any other aspect of the advertising codes.

The following code applies to all remote bingo operating licences, except ancillary remote licences

Ordinary code provision

Licensees should ensure that the terms on which they contract with their affiliates (that is those who are given a right to advertise, or provide a hyper-link to, a licensee's gambling website) enable them to terminate the affiliate's rights promptly if, in the licensee's opinion, the affiliate is in breach of the advertising codes.

Complaints and disputes

Social responsibility code provision

Licensees must put into effect a written procedure for handling customer complaints and disputes.

In this code a 'complaint' means a complaint about any aspect of the licensee's conduct of the licensed activities, and a 'dispute' is any complaint which:

(a) is not resolved at the first stage of the complaints procedure; and

(b) relates to the outcome of the complainant's gambling transaction.

Licensees must ensure that:

- customers are told the name and status of the person to contact about their complaint
- customers are given a copy of the complaints procedure on request or on making a complaint
- all complaints are handled in accordance with the procedure.

Licensees must also ensure that they have arrangements in place for disputes to be referred to an independent third party. Customers whose disputes are not resolved to their satisfaction by use of the operator's complaints procedure may refer those disputes to this independent third party. The arrangements under which such complaints are referred may, but need not, provide for the third party's decision to be binding on the licensee and the customer.

Licensees must keep a record of all complaints that are not resolved at the first stage of the complaints procedure.

Licensees must arrange for a copy of the decision on, or a note of the outcome of, each dispute referred to the independent party to be provided to the Commission quarterly, either by the independent party or by the licensee.

Gambling licensees' staff

The following code applies to all remote bingo operating licences, except ancillary remote licences

Social responsibility code provision

Licensees must take all reasonable steps to ensure that staff involved in the provision of facilities for gambling are made aware of advice on socially responsible gambling and of where to get confidential advice should their gambling become hard to control.

Information requirements

THE FOLLOWING CODE APPLIES TO ALL REMOTE BINGO OPERATING LICENCES, EXCEPT ANCILLARY REMOTE LICENCES

ORDINARY CODE PROVISION

The Commission expects licensees to work with the Commission in an open and cooperative way and to inform the Commission of any matters that the Commission would reasonably need to be aware of in exercising its regulatory functions. These are matters that will have a material impact on the licensee's business or on the licensee's ability to conduct its business. Such matters, which should be notified to the Commission as soon as reasonably practicable[4], include the following:

- the departure from the licensee's business of any person named in the licence application, or that person's successor, who holds a personal management licence, but who does not occupy a 'qualifying position'
- any reduction in the number of staff employed by the licensee where that has a material impact on the licensee's business
- the acquisition or disposal by the licensee of gambling premises or pitches where that has a material impact on the size or nature of the licensee's business
- in the case of corporate licensees, the disposal or acquisition of any group company where that has a material impact on the licensee's ability to conduct its business
- any disposal of the licensee's assets where that has a material impact on the licensee's business
- any investigation by a professional, statutory, regulatory or government body into the licensee's activities, or the activities in relation to the licensed entity of a personal licence holder or a person occupying a qualifying position employed by them, where such an investigation could result in the imposition of a sanction or penalty which, if imposed, could reasonably be expected to raise doubts about the licensee's continued suitability to hold a Gambling Commission licence
- any instance of criminal activity, including repeated instances of small-scale theft or fraud, where that has a material impact on the licensee's business
- any major breach in the licensee's information security where that adversely affects the confidentiality of customer data or prevents customers from accessing their accounts for a substantial period of time
- any other matters that have a material impact on the licensee's business or on the licensee's ability to conduct its business.

---

[4] These matters can be reported securely online at the Commission's website at www.gamblingcommission.gov.uk or by email to key.events@gamblingcommission.gov.uk or posted to Key Events, Compliance Administration Team, Gambling Commission, Victoria Square House, Victoria Square, Birmingham, B2 4BP

Gambling Commission October 2010

BINGO – WHAT DO WE MEAN BY 'BINGO'?

6.2295 Commercially run clubs, halls and other organisations that provide bingo games in a club or location open to the public, as well as those that offer bingo remotely (for example over the internet or by using a machine), must be licensed by the Gambling Commission.

Non-remote licences allow bingo to be offered in premises and remote licences allow for bingo to be played over the internet or through other communications device, or by using a machine.
Non-remote licensees who wish to offer their customers facilities for playing bingo by using remote communication equipment (all of which must be located on the premises), can apply for an ancillary remote operating licence.
Bingo halls are also permitted to have certain gaming machines on the premises.
Bingo licensees must not employ children (under 16s) or young people (16 and 17 year olds) to carry out tasks that relate to the provision of facilities for gambling – this includes tasks such as selling bingo books or tickets, handing out TED* machines, identifying winning players or paying out winnings/prizes, or any task in connection with a gaming machine.

1 TED - an electronic hand held system that allows people to play multiple packs at the same time

HOW IS BINGO REGULATED?

Most organisations and individuals that provide facilities for playing bingo require a licence to operate, whether the facilities are provided remotely (for example through the internet or telephone), or in premises. The Commission has developed licence conditions and codes of practice that govern licence holders and it can prosecute or impose fines on operators who breach their licence conditions.
There are three types of licence for those providing bingo:

- Operating licences are required by those that provide facilities for bingo in Britain.
- Personal licences are required by individuals in certain management positions except for those organisations categorised as small-scale operators.
- Premises licences are required where gambling services are provided to the public from fixed premises rather than remotely. These are issued by the local licensing authority.

BINGO FACTS AND FIGURES

- People mainly play bingo in dedicated bingo halls, holiday parks and resorts, although it is also popular in working men's and British Legion clubs and miners' institutes.
- There are over 650 dedicated bingo clubs operating at 31 March 2007, and over 1,000 other clubs and smaller institutions where bingo is played.
- £1,820 million was staked at bingo halls in 2006/07.
- The average spend is around £16.90 a night.
- Bingo is the only gambling activity more popular with women than men.

Gambling Commission August 2007

BINGO PREMISES LICENCE APPLICATIONS UNDER GAMBLING ACT 2005 17 April 2008 ADV 08/06

6.2296 The following information is to assist local authorities with determining bingo premises licence applications, to ensure the mandatory premises licence conditions[1] for bingo premises can be complied with at each individual premises.

1 As set down in statutory instruments 2007/1409 for England and Wales, and 2007/266 for Scotland.

FACILITIES FOR PLAYING BINGO MUST BE PROVIDED IN EACH BINGO PREMISES

The Commission has recently published its view that bingo must be offered (albeit not necessarily at all times) in each separate bingo premises, and that operators of such premises may not simply make gaming machines available. This was communicated to bingo trade associations in an open letter, which is available from this link: 1st letter on principal activity

We have also recently published a second letter which confirms our view that there needs to be an acceptable balance between the provision of the primary gambling activity and the provision of gaming machines: 2nd letter on principal activity

Local authorities will need to satisfy themselves that bingo can be played in any bingo premises for which they issue a premises licence. This may also be a relevant consideration where an existing bingo premises applies to vary their licence to exclude an area of the existing premises from its ambit and then applies for a new premises licence, or multiple licences, for that or those excluded areas.

The Commission recommends that local authorities contact their local compliance manager at the Commission (the contact details are available here) and that they may also want to contact the applicant to discuss how they intend to ensure bingo can be played in the new bingo premises being applied for.

THE SEPARATION OF PREMISES ADJOINING A BINGO PREMISES

The mandatory premises licence conditions for bingo premises restrict direct access from a bingo premises into a premises that is the subject of a casino, adult gaming centre, or betting premises licence. The licence conditions do not, however, require there to be no direct access from a bingo premises into another bingo premises.

Where a local authority receives applications that involve adjoining premises, each seeking a separate bingo premises licence they must be satisfied that each area is a separate set of premises capable of being identified as such, notwithstanding the fact that direct access between separate bingo premises is not prevented by licence conditions. The Commission has given guidance in this area in paragraphs 7.11 to 7.20 of its Guidance to Licensing Authorities (June 2007).

Where a local authority receives applications for other types of gambling premises adjoining bingo premises, the authority will need to ensure that direct access between the premises is prevented if the premises licence conditions require it. For example, an adult gaming centre premises adjoining a bingo premises would need to be properly separated in such a way that direct access is prevented. The Commission has already published guidance on direct access in such cases – for example in paragraph 21.6 of the its Guidance to Licensing Authorities (June 2007) referred to above.

GROUPING OF GAMING MACHINES

Every bingo premises is entitled to provide a maximum of four gaming machines in categories B3 or B4, and an unlimited number of category C and D gaming machines. These gaming machines must remain within the licensed area covered by each premises licence. Where an existing bingo premises covered by one premises licence applies to vary the licence and acquire additional bingo premises licences so that the area that was the subject of the original licence will become divided between a number of separate licensed premises, it is not permissible for all of the gaming machines to which each of the licences brings an entitlement to be grouped together within one of the licensed premises. So for example, where three bingo premises exist adjacent to each other, it is not permissible to locate 12 category B3 gaming machines in one of the premises (with none in the other two), as the gaming machine entitlement for that premises would be exceeded.

THE COMMISSION'S ROLE AS A RESPONSIBLE AUTHORITY

As a responsible authority under the Act, we receive notice of every premises licence application, and for each individual application we evaluate whether there are grounds for us to make representations. In some circumstances we will contact licensing authorities and the applicant themselves during the representation period regarding concerns over a particular premises licence application.

We receive as much information as any other responsible authority on which to consider if we will make representations. The Commission does not receive copies of plans of premises as there is no statutory requirement for plans to be sent to us or any other responsible authority. The premises licence application consideration process is the responsibility of licensing authorities and reflects the importance of local decision making, on a premises-by-premises basis.

Gambling Commission April 2008

BINGO AND CASINO EQUIPMENT TECHNICAL REQUIREMENTS

To avoid duplication this document has not been reproduced here but can be found at para **6.2244.1** above.

KEY CHARACTERISTICS OF BINGO
June 2009

6.2297 Following discussions with the Bingo Association and BACTA, the Gambling Commission has published a list of characteristics which it consider must be present in games, whether or not played by machine, to be classed as bingo.

The characteristics are particularly relevant to bingo machines. Machines that play bingo are exempt from limits on numbers, and stakes and prizes. If these characteristics are not present it is likely that the Commission will view the machines as gaming machines and regulate accordingly.

In the list below any reference to 'game' or 'games' means a bingo game/s

KEY CHARACTERISTICS OF BINGO

- Players' payments must be divided between stakes and participation fees, although they may consist entirely of stake or entirely of participation fee. The way that division is made must be transparent to the player and in particular there must be a notice displayed showing participation fees in a way that makes it readily accessible to players. Stakes must be returned to players either in the particular game or in a subsequent one.
- Each game must be played to a single set of numbers; drawing a second set of numbers starts a new game.
- Any bingo games must clearly be presented as offering the player the opportunity to participate in a game of bingo. This includes numbers (or symbols) being marked off and the game having the appearance of a game of bingo (rather than a gaming machine).
- All bingo games (including electronic) must require players to monitor games and claim prizes.
- Any added prize money, once offered, with the exception of time limited offers, must remain available until won in that or subsequent games; the operator cannot claim them back. Prizes clearly advertised as being offered only for a limited period can be claimed back if they are not won. All prizes offered in each game must be transparent to the player.

- Games may operate with a single player, provided there is a meaningful opportunity for other players to participate in the same game.
- The game must comply with the requirements of the Gambling Act 2005 and must be capable of audit, where appropriate, to demonstrate legal compliance. Such audit data will demonstrate for example how players' payments are split between stakes and participation fees and that all stakes are returned to the players, either in that game or subsequent games.

CHARACTERISTICS SPECIFIC TO BINGO MACHINES

- The speed of game including the time taken to join should be similar to that of an interval game. Games will not have an auto play function.
- The machines must provide the facility for the player to extend the playing time by a minimum of 100%.
- The amount that can be staked in a set period should be no greater than on a Category C machine.

REGULATIONS SPECIFIC TO BINGO MACHINES IN AGCS/FECS

- The nature or size of the prize offered may not be determined by the number of persons playing; or the amount paid for or raised by the game
- Bingo machines in FECs will not be made available in areas where children and young people (those under the age of 18) are permitted.

Manufacturers and operators will need to address these characteristics when developing bingo machines for bingo clubs, AGCs and FECs. We also have concerns about potential access to these machines by children and young people (those under the age of 18). Our intention is to restrict to adults the use of these machines in licensed FECs by attaching licence conditions under section 75 or 77 and in unlicensed FECs by a code of practice under section 24.

For the longer term, we need to decide to what extent we will incorporate the characteristics in our Technical Standards and Licence Conditions and Codes of Practice. In the meantime, we are content to provide the industry with an opportunity to secure the arrangements set out above on a voluntary basis. If that does not prove possible, we will pursue a more formal regulatory route. So far, both the Bingo Association and BACTA have issued these characteristics to their members as a Code of Practice.

Gambling Commission June 2009

Note

Regulatory return forms (October 2011) and guides as to how to complete them (June 2011) are available from the Gambling Commission's website at www.gamblingcommission.gov.uk

LOTTERIES

LOTTERIES AND THE LAW (2005 GAMBLING ACT)
Advice for society and local authority lotteries, May 2007

1 INTRODUCTION

6.2300 1.1 This advice provides a general guide to the main principles and requirements of lotteries law as contained in the Gambling Act 2005 which repeals the Lotteries and Amusements Act 1976. It is primarily intended as advice for large society and local authority lotteries promoted under licence from the Gambling Commission ("the Commission").

1.2 The advice is not comprehensive or a binding interpretation of the law and anyone intending to run a lottery should refer to the Gambling Act 2005 ("the Act") and if necessary seek independent legal advice to ensure that they conform to the law before proceeding. Separate advice has been issued to local authorities in respect of small society lotteries under their jurisdiction.

1.3 The Act introduces a new regulator for all gambling (except the National Lottery and spread betting) in Great Britain, the Gambling Commission. It also introduces a new licensing regime for society and local authority lotteries and a registration system for small society lotteries.

1.4 The Act creates two broad classes of lottery; first large society lotteries and lotteries run for the benefit of local authorities which will be licensed by the Gambling Commission, and secondly exempt lotteries, including small society lotteries which will be registered with licensing authorities (local authorities).

1.5 The Commission does not regulate the National Lottery, which continues to be regulated by the National Lottery Commission under separate legislation.

1.6 The Act has three licensing objectives which underpin the functions that the Commission and licensing authorities will perform. These objectives are central to the new regulatory regime created by the Act. They are:

- preventing gambling from being a source of crime or disorder, being associated with crime or disorder, or being used to support crime;
- ensuring that gambling is conducted in a fair and open way; and
- protecting children and other vulnerable people from being harmed or exploited by gambling.

1.7 The Gambling Act 2005 allows for a general relaxation of lottery law, in particular it:

- relaxes the limits on the percentage of proceeds that may be applied to expenses or prizes;
- allows rollovers of the prize fund from one lottery to another;
- allows for the sale of tickets by an automated process; and
- removes the maximum price for a lottery ticket.

2 DEFINITION OF A LOTTERY

2.1 An arrangement is a simple lottery if:

- persons are required to pay to participate in the arrangement;
- in the course of the arrangement one or more prizes are allocated to one or more members of a class; and
- the prizes are allocated by a process which relies wholly on chance.

2.2 An arrangement is a complex lottery if:

- persons are required to pay to participate in the arrangement;
- in the course of the arrangement one or more prizes are allocated to one or more members of a class;
- the prizes are allocated by a series of processes; and

- the first of those processes relies wholly on chance.

2.3 By virtue of section 14(5) of the Act, for the purpose of these definitions a process which requires persons to exercise skill or judgment or display knowledge is to be treated as relying wholly on chance if:

- the requirement cannot reasonably be expected to prevent a significant proportion of persons who participate in the arrangement from receiving a prize; and
- it cannot reasonably be expected to prevent a significant proportion of persons who wish to participate in the arrangement from doing so.

3 TYPES OF LOTTERIES

SOCIETY LOTTERIES

3.1 Society lotteries are lotteries promoted for the benefit of a non-commercial society. A society is non-commercial if it is established and conducted:

- or charitable purposes;
- for the purpose of enabling participation in, or of supporting, sport, athletics or a cultural activity, or
- for any other non-commercial purpose other than that of private gain.

LOCAL AUTHORITY LOTTERIES

3.2 A local authority may use the net proceeds of its lottery for any purpose for which it has power to incur expenditure.

EXEMPT LOTTERIES

3.3 Exempt lotteries do not require a licence from the Gambling Commission, although small society lotteries, are required to register with their local authority. In addition to small society lotteries, exempt lotteries include:

- incidental non-commercial lotteries – commonly held at charity fund raising events;
- private society lotteries – only members of the society and those on society premises can participate in the lottery;
- work lotteries – only people who work together on the same premises may participate;
- residents' lotteries – only people who live at the same premises may participate; and
- customer lotteries – only customers at the business premises may participate.

Detailed guidance on exempt lotteries is given at pages 13 to 15.

THE NATIONAL LOTTERY

3.4 The National Lottery, currently operated by Camelot, will continue to be regulated by the National Lottery Commission. Lotteries that are regulated by the National Lottery Commission will not require a Gambling Commission licence or registration with the licensing authority.

4 LARGE SOCIETY AND LOCAL AUTHORITY LOTTERY LICENSING REQUIREMENTS

4.1 If the arrangements for a society lottery are such that total proceeds (ticket sales) from it may in a single society lottery exceed £20,000 or proceeds of previous lotteries in the same calendar year have already reached or may, taking into account that lottery in question, reach £250,000 in one calendar year then the lottery is a large lottery and may only be run under a lottery operating licence issued by the Commission.

4.2 If a society promotes a lottery which, applying the above rules, is a large lottery ("the first lottery") then every subsequent lottery it promotes in that year and in the following three years will also be a large lottery and will require the society to hold a lottery operating licence issued by the Commission.

4.3 Society and local authority lotteries who allow players to participate in their lottery by means of remote communication will be required to hold a remote lottery operating licence, whether or not their activities also require them to hold a non remote lottery operating licence.

4.4 All local authority lotteries must be run under an operating licence issued by the Commission.

4.5 General information about the Gambling Commission's licensing requirements is given in this document. Specific guidance is available on the Commission's website under the heading "Applying for a licence".

5 SMALL SOCIETY LOTTERIES

5.1 Societies who run small society lotteries, that is to say lotteries which are not large lotteries (essentially those in which £20,000 (or less) worth of tickets are put on sale and where the society's aggregate proceeds from lotteries do not exceed £250,000 a year) may operate without a Gambling Commission licence provided they register with their local authority.

5.2 The promoting society of a small society lottery must, throughout the period during which the lottery is promoted, be registered with a local authority in England and Wales or licensing board in Scotland.

5.3 The societies will be required to be registered with their local authority in the area where their principal office is located. If the local authority believes that the society's principal office is situated in another area it should inform the society as soon as possible and if possible inform that other authority.

5.4 Details of registration requirements and procedures will be available from the licensing department of the relevant local authority.

5.6 Societies who run small society lotteries under registration with a local authority and who sell tickets by means of remote communication (Internet, telephone etc) will not be required to hold a remote gambling licence issued by the Commission.

6 PERSONAL MANAGEMENT LICENCES

6.1 A society or local authority licensed by the Gambling Commission is required to have at least one Personal Management Licence (PML) holder if they have more than three people in "qualifying positions".

6.2 A "qualifying position" is one where a person by the terms of their appointment has primary responsibility for:

- the management of the licensed activity (ie the lottery);
- the financial affairs of the society;
- ensuring the society complies with the requirements of the Gambling Act;
- the marketing of the lottery; or
- management of the IT used in connection with the lottery.

6.3 In deciding who should hold the PML a society or local authority should identify the relevant senior individual who can take overall management responsibility for the promotion and proper management of the lottery and for compliance with the regulatory regime as a whole. The PML holder must be a trustee or officer of an unincorporated society, a director of a corporate society or a partner where the society is a partnership. In the case of a local authority lottery the PML holder must be someone in a senior management post who holds the relevant delegated authority from the licensing authority.

6.4 If a society has three or fewer people in "qualifying positions" they will qualify as a small scale operator and will be exempt from the need to hold a PML. In those circumstances one person from the society who is identified as the senior person responsible for the overall conduct of the lottery (usually the chief executive, a trustee, director or member of the senior management board) must complete the personal declaration (Annex A) of the Operating Licence application form and submit it to the Commission along with a Criminal Records Bureau form.

6.5 Any change to the PML holder or the person notified as having responsibility for the lottery under the small scale operator exemption should be notified to the Gambling Commission as soon as practicable. Indeed, a change in the identity of those occupying "qualifying positions" requires a small-scale operator to apply to amend the details of its operating licence and a change of office holder requiring a PML in the case of other lottery licensees requires the new office holder to apply for a personal licence.

6.6 Detailed guidance on PMLs and the small scale operator exemption are available on the Commission's website.

7 EXTERNAL LOTTERY MANAGERS

7.1 A licensed or registered society or local authority may employ an external lottery manager (ELM) to run all or part of its lottery. An ELM is defined in section 257 of the Act as someone that is a person or a company who makes arrangements for a lottery on behalf of a society or local authority but is not a member, officer or employee of the society or authority.

7.2 All ELMs must hold a lottery manager's operating licence issued by the Commission before they can manage a licensed society or local authority lottery or a society lottery registered with a local authority. It is the responsibility of the society or local authority lottery to ensure that before employing anyone to manage all or part of their lottery they hold a valid lottery manager operating licence issued by the Commission. A list of licensed ELMs is available on the Commission's website.

7.3 The fact that a society or local authority may employ a licensed ELM to manage all or part of its lottery does not absolve the society or local authority from its responsibility for ensuring that the lottery is conducted in such a way as to ensure that it is lawful and fully complies with all licence conditions and the codes of practice.

7.4 ELMs are also required to hold Personal Management Licences for a range of directors and senior managers, including the managing director, chief executive, finance director, compliance, marketing and IT director.

7.5 ELMs are also required to hold a remote gambling licence if they intend to sell tickets by means of remote communication.

8 EXTERNAL LOTTERY MANAGERS AND SERVICE PROVIDERS

8.1 The Act specifies that a person promotes a lottery if he makes or participates in making the arrangements for a lottery. The Act states that promotion of a lottery includes:

- making arrangements for the printing of tickets;
- making arrangements for the printing, publication and distribution of promotional material;
- making arrangements to advertise a lottery;
- inviting a person to participate in a lottery;
- selling or supplying tickets; and
- offering to sell or supply tickets.

Full details are set out at section 252 of the Act.

8.2 A person commits an offence under the Act if they promote a lottery, unless;

- they are an officer, employee or a member of a licensed or registered society or local authority; or
- they are a licensed ELM directed by a society or local authority to run all or part of its lottery.

8.3 A person or company may provide services in connection with a lottery to a society or local authority (for example printing tickets or advertising a lottery) without being held to have promoted a lottery.

8.4 Section 252 of the Act provides a comprehensive definition of what amounts to promoting a lottery and section 257 provides a definition of an ELM. If there is doubt whether a person or company is acting in the role of an ELM or that of a service provider the Commission will have regard to the overall management and degree of control of the lottery undertaken by the society and the other party in question. Key indicators will include:

- who decides how the lottery scheme will operate and when changes to the scheme should be made;
- who controls the promotion, marketing and advertising of the lottery;
- who sells the tickets;
- who pays the prizes;
- who appoints and manages sub contractors;
- banking arrangements and the process for handling the proceeds of the lottery; and
- the contractual agreements between the society and the other party.

8.5 Where the person or company who makes any of the arrangements for a society or local authority lottery, for example has control of how the lottery is promoted and managed they will be acting as a ELM and they will need to hold the relevant operating licence issued by the Commission if they are to avoid committing an offence under the Act.

9 REMOTE LOTTERIES

9.1 Section 4 of the Gambling Act specifies that remote gambling means gambling in which people participate by the use of remote communication including the Internet, telephone, television, radio or any other electronic or technological method of communication. Note that normal letter post is not a form of remote communication for the purposes of the Act.

9.2 Society and local authority lotteries who allow players to participate in their lottery by means of remote communication will be required to hold a remote lottery operating licence.

9.3 Holders of a remote lottery operating licence will be required to comply with the technical standards and the other specific licence conditions and codes of practice issued by the Commission that relate to remote gambling. Details are available on the Commission's website.

9.4 Society lotteries registered with local authorities who allow persons to participate in their lottery by way of remote communication are not required to hold a remote lottery operating licence.

10 GAMBLING COMMISSION LICENCE CONDITIONS AND CODES OF PRACTICE

10.1 All lotteries licensed by the Commission will be required to comply with the specific licence conditions and codes of practice relevant to them. The specific licence conditions will be set out at the time a licence is issued.

10.2 Some of the licence conditions and requirements of the codes of practice are referred to in this document under the relevant headings. Specific details are contained in the Commission's 'Licence conditions and codes of practice' which is available on the Commission's website.

11 SOCIETY AND LOCAL AUTHORITY LOTTERIES – PROCEEDS AND OTHER MONETARY LIMITS

11.1 A society or local authority lottery must apply a minimum of 20% of the gross proceeds of each lottery directly to the purposes of the society or in the case of a local authority a purpose for which the authority has power to incur expenditure.

11.2 Up to a maximum of 80% of the gross proceeds of each lottery may be divided between prizes and the expenses of the lottery.

The maximum value of tickets that can be sold in a single large lottery is £2 million.

11.4 The maximum aggregate value of lottery tickets that can be sold in any calendar year is £10 million.
11.5 The maximum prize in a single lottery is £25,000 in the case of a small society lottery and £25,000 or 10% of the proceeds (gross ticket sales), whichever is greater, in the case of a large society or local authority lottery. Therefore, a society that sells the maximum number of tickets in a single large lottery (£2 million) could award a maximum top prize of £200,000.
11.6 Rollovers are permitted provided the maximum single prize limit is not breached.
11.7 Every ticket in the lottery must be the same price and the cost of purchased tickets must be paid to the society before entry into the draw is allowed.
11.8 There is no maximum price of a lottery ticket.
11.9 No lottery may operate in such a way that a player can win a prize greater than the statutory prize limit of £200,000.
11.10 No lottery may be linked to any other lottery in such a way that a person who wins a prize in one also wins a prize in another, unless the aggregate of those prizes is less than or equal to the statutory prize limit of £200,000.
11.11 Where separate lotteries have a feature that allows a player to win a larger prize than the statutory maximum of £200,000 by selecting the same numbers in different lotteries and these lotteries are decided by the same draw, no advertisement or other marketing of the lotteries may refer to this feature.

12 TICKET INFORMATION

12.1 All tickets in a society lottery licensed by the Commission or registered with a local authority must state:

- he name of the society on whose behalf the lottery is being promoted;
- the price of the ticket;
- the name and address of the member of the society responsible for the promotion of the lottery (in the case of a small society lottery run under local authority registration the name and address of the ELM if there is one may be given as an alternative).
- the date of the draw, or the means by which the date may be determined; and
- the fact, where that is the case, that the society is licensed by the Commission.

12.2 Tickets which are issued through a form of remote communication or any other electronic manner must specify this information to the purchaser of the ticket and ensure that the message can be either retained or printed.

13 SALE OF TICKETS

13.1 Tickets in society and local authority lotteries promoted under licence from the Commission must not be sold to any person in a street. Tickets may be sold by a person in a kiosk or shop premises (having no space for the accommodation of customers), or from door to door. The Act defines a street as any bridge, road, lane, footway, subway, square, court, alley or passage (including passages through enclosed premises such as shopping malls) whether a thoroughfare or not.
13.2 To minimise the risk of fraud societies licensed by the Commission should adopt one or more of the following measures when sending unsolicited mailings of lottery tickets:

- prohibit the unsolicited mailing of lottery tickets to non members of the promoting society;
- limit the value of tickets sent to any one address which is not that of a member of the promoting society to £20; or
- maintain records of tickets distributed and not returned; (the Commission recommends that these records should include details of the address to which the tickets have been sent, their total value and their serial number. Information on unsold tickets not returned by the date of the lottery draw should be retained for

at least six months.)

14 FINANCIAL REQUIREMENTS

14.1 For society and local authority lotteries promoted under licence from the Commission, accounting records must be retained for a minimum of three years from the date of any lottery to which they relate and they must be made available for inspection by the Commission on request. These records must contain, in respect of each lottery, details of the total proceeds of each lottery, the expenses of the lottery, and the number of sold and unsold tickets.

14.2 Where the cumulative proceeds of lotteries promoted by a society or local authority exceed £1,000,000 in a calendar year, the Commission must be sent a written confirmation from a qualifying auditor that the proceeds of those lotteries have been fully accounted for in annual audited accounts. Such confirmation must be provided within ten months of the end of the period to which the accounts relate.

14.3 A qualifying auditor is a person who is eligible for appointment as a company auditor under section 25 of the Companies Act 1989 but is not, in the case of a society:

- a member of the society;
- a partner, officer or employee of such a member; or
- a partnership of which a person falling within (a) or (b) is a partner.

15 LOTTERY RETURNS

15.1 Every society and local authority licensed by the Commission must submit a return for each lottery which shows the total proceeds and how they have been distributed between prizes and expenses and the amount applied directly to the society's purposes, or purpose for which the local authority has power to incur expenditure, as the case may be.

15.2 Every society registered with a local authority to run small society lotteries must submit a statement providing the following information:

- the date on which tickets were available for sale or supply and the date of the draw;
- the total proceeds of the lottery;
- the amounts deducted by promoters of the lottery in providing prizes, including rollovers;
- the amounts deducted by the promoters of the lottery in respect of costs incurred in organising the lottery;
- the amount applied directly to the purpose for which the promoting society is conducted or for which the local authority has power to incur expenditure (at least 20% of the gross proceeds); and
- whether any expenses incurred in connection with the lottery were not paid for by deduction from the proceeds, and, if so, the amount of expenses and the sources from which they were paid.

15.3 A licensed society or local authority's return must be sent to the Gambling Commission **no later than three months** after the date of the lottery draw or in the case of an 'instant' (scratchcard) lottery within three months of the last date on which tickets in the lottery were on sale. At the time it is submitted each return must be verified by a Personal Management Licence holder, a "qualified person" in the case of a small scale operator or the person named (in the case of societies) named on the lottery tickets as being responsible for the promotion of the lottery.

15.4 Returns can be submitted to the Commission on-line using the relevant form or it can be downloaded and submitted through the post.

15.5 A registered society's statement must be sent to the local authority within the three months beginning on the day on which the draw (or last draw) in the lottery took place. It must be signed by two members of the society appointed in writing for that purpose by the society's governing body and accompanied by a copy of that appointment.

16 SOCIAL RESPONSIBILITY

16.1 Lotteries are a form of gambling and as such societies and local authorities are required to ensure that children and other vulnerable people are not exploited by their lottery.

16.2 The minimum age for participation in a lottery is 16 years of age. A person commits an offence if they invite or allow a child to enter a lottery other than certain classes of exempt lottery (ie: incidental non-commercial lotteries, private lotteries, work lotteries and residents' lotteries). Societies and local authorities running lotteries must have written policies and procedures in place to help prevent and deal with cases of under-age play.

16.3 Licence holders must take all reasonable steps to ensure that information about how to gamble responsibly and how to access information and help in respect of problem gambling is readily available.

16.4 Further information about social responsibility requirements is contained in the Commission's Licence Conditions and Codes of Practice document.

17 EXEMPT LOTTERIES

17.1 Exempt lotteries are all those specified in the Gambling Act 2005 as permitted to be run without a licence from the Gambling Commission. These include small society lotteries which can be run under a registration with a local authority.

17.2 This section is intended to provide information on whether proposals for a lottery give rise to the need for either a Commission licence or registration with the local authority.

17.3 Apart from small society lotteries there are three types of exempt lottery: incidental noncommercial lotteries, private lotteries and customer lotteries.

INCIDENTAL NON-COMMERCIAL LOTTERIES

17.4 An incidental non-commercial lottery is one that is incidental to a non-commercial event. Examples may include a lottery held at a school fete or at a social event such as a dinner dance. An event is non-commercial if all the money raised at the event including entrance fees goes entirely to purposes that are not for private gain: therefore a fundraising social event with an entrance fee would be non-commercial if the profits went to a society but would not be non-commercial if the profits were retained by the organiser for private gain.

17.5 The Gambling Act 2005 specifies that:

- the promoters of the lottery may not deduct more than the amount prescribed by the Secretary of State (or Scottish Minister) from the proceeds in respect of the expenses, such as the cost of printing tickets, hire of equipment etc. This is currently £250; (this may increase to £500 following DCMS Consultation);
- not more than £250 can be spent on prizes; (this may increase to £500 following DCMS consultation);
- the lottery cannot involve a rollover of prizes from one lottery to another; and
- all tickets must be sold at the location during the event, and the result made public while the event takes place.

PRIVATE LOTTERIES

17.6 There are three types of private lotteries that qualify as exempt lotteries:

- Private lottery – these can only be promoted by one of its members and tickets can only be sold to other members of that same society and persons on premises used for the administration of the society. The lottery may only be promoted for a purpose for which the society is conducted, and the society can be any group or society, provided it is not established and conducted for purposes connected to gambling eg private members clubs.

- Work lottery – the promoter of the lottery must work on the premises and tickets can only be sold to other people who work on the same premises. The lottery must not be run for profit and all the proceeds must be used for prizes or reasonable expenses incurred in organising the lottery eg a Grand National sweepstake.
- Residents' lottery – these must not be run for profit and all the proceeds must be used for prizes or reasonable expenses. The promoter of the lottery must reside on the premises and tickets can only be sold to other residents of the same premises. The residency requirement can still be satisfied where the premises are not the sole premises in which a person resides eg a student halls of residence.

17.7 Private lotteries must comply with conditions relating to advertising which state that no advertisement for a private society, work or residents' lottery may be displayed or distributed except at the society or work premises, or the relevant residence, or sent to any other premises.

17.8 Private lotteries must comply with conditions set out in schedule 11 of the Act relating to tickets. In summary these are:

- A ticket in a private lottery may be sold or supplied only by or on behalf of the promoters
- Tickets (and the rights they represent) are non-transferable.
- Each ticket must state the name and address of the promoter of the lottery, the persons to whom the promoter can sell or supply tickets and the fact that they are not transferable.

17.9 Private lotteries cannot be conducted on vessels. The Act's definition of a vessel (section 353-1) is:

- anything (other than a seaplane or amphibious vehicle), designed or adapted for navigation or other use in, on or over water;
- a hovercraft; or
- anything, or any part of any place, situated on or in water.

17.10 The price paid for each ticket in a private lottery must be the same, must be shown on the ticket and must be paid to the promoters of the lottery before any person is given a ticket.

CUSTOMER LOTTERIES

17.11 A customer lottery is a lottery run by the occupiers of business premises, who sell tickets only to customers present on their premises.

17.12 The Act requires that in customer lotteries:

- the lottery must be arranged to ensure that no profit is made;
- tickets may be sold or supplied only by or on behalf of the promoter;
- no advertisement may be displayed or distributed except on the business premises nor sent to any other premises;
- another customer lottery cannot take place within seven days on the same business premises;
- tickets (and the rights they represent) are non transferable;
- no ticket may result in the winner receiving a prize worth more than £50;
- no rollovers of prizes are permitted.

Each ticket in a customer lottery must state;

- the name and address of the promoter of the lottery;
- the persons to whom the promoters can sell or supply tickets;
- that the rights conferred by the sale or supply of a ticket in a customer lottery

are not transferable.

18 PRIZE COMPETITIONS AND FREE PRIZE DRAWS

18.1 Prize competitions which are not otherwise betting, gaming or lotteries and free draws are exempt from regulatory control under the Gambling Act.

18.2 The Commission has no regulatory responsibilities in respect of competitions and draws, but it will monitor the boundary between them and lotteries. Where the Commission believes that a competition or draw is in fact an illegal unlicensed lottery it will have the power to investigate and if necessary prosecute.

PRIZE "SKILL" COMPETITIONS

18.3 Genuine prize competitions based on skill, judgement or knowledge are exempt from statutory control. The effect of section 14(5) of the Act is that a process is not to be treated as relying wholly on chance if it contains a requirement to exercise skill and judgement or knowledge that is reasonably likely to:

- prevent a significant proportion of people who wish to participate from doing so; or
- prevent a significant proportion of people who do participate from receiving a prize.

18.4 A competition that requires a payment to enter and does not meet the test set out above is likely to be an illegal lottery and the operators of such competitions be liable to prosecution.

FREE DRAWS

18.5 In order for an arrangement to be a lottery persons must be required to pay to participate. Accordingly a "free" draw is not a lottery and is exempt from statutory control. Schedule 2 of the Act lays down the rules as to what is to be treated as payment for the purposes of distinguishing free draws from lotteries.

18.6 The schedule envisages two circumstances.

First, cases where there is only one entry route. Here, 'free' will include any method of communication (post, telephone or other) at a 'normal rate'. 'Normal rate' is defined as "a rate which does not reflect the opportunity to enter a lottery" (paragraph 5 of Schedule 2). There can be no premium over what it would normally cost to use that method of communication.

Secondly, cases where there is a choice of entry route. Here, the arrangement will not be treated as requiring payment if:

(a) each individual has a choice whether to participate by paying or by sending a communication;

(b) that communication is either a letter sent by ordinary post or some other method which is neither more expensive nor less convenient than entering by the paid route (there can be no premium over what it would normally cost to use that method of communication);

(c) the choice must be publicised so that it is likely to come to the attention all potential participants; and

(d) the system for allocating prizes does not distinguish between using the paid or the free route.

18.7 Schedule 2 also makes provision for product promotions. These are permitted where the price of the good or service does not include any element which reflects the opportunity to participate in the promotion (paragraph 2(c) of Schedule 2).

18.8 A document setting out further details of the Commission's position on the issue of prize competitions and free draws is available on its website.

19 CHAIN GIFT SCHEMES

19.1 Section 43 of the Act makes it an offence to invite others to join a chain-gift scheme or to participate knowingly in the promotion or administration of such a scheme. A person found guilty of the offence could be liable to a fine or imprisonment.
19.2 These schemes have most of the relevant features of pyramid selling schemes, but escape the ban on them because they do not involve the sale of any product. An arrangement is a chain gift scheme if:

- person must pay a "joining fee" to participate; and
- he is encouraged to believe that he will receive the joining fees, or part of the joining fee, of other participants, to an amount in excess of the joining fee he paid.

19.3 The Commission is aware that the Office of Fair Trading and local authority trading standards officers have considerable relevant experience of dealing with chain gift schemes and are well placed to deal with schemes that arise from time to time. The Commission will keep its role in tackling chain gift schemes under review and will monitor developments so that if more concerted action is required centrally it can liaise with other bodies to determine what action should be taken.
19.4 The main element of consumer protection against these schemes is publicity to prevent people becoming involved in them. Local authorities may wish to use their websites and other publicity tools to educate consumers against participation in such schemes.]

20 LOTTERY SCAMS

20.1 Most lottery scams are advanced fee frauds where a person is invited to send a payment to claim a prize in a lottery or raffle that they were not aware they had entered. In most cases there is no lottery.
20.2 The advice to anyone who receives such a communication through the post, via e-mail or in any other way is:

- do not respond;
- never send any payment;
- do not release your bank account or credit card details;
- if you are asked to confirm your identity do not release any personal details or you may be at risk from identity fraud; and
- if you have been a victim of this type of fraud you should contact the police.

20.3 The Office of Fair Trading (OFT) is the lead co-ordination body in this field. The OFT has set up a multi-agency scams group as a forum for bringing together experience in dealing with scams of all kinds. The "Scams Enforcement Group" has been formed as part of the OFT's commitment to co-ordinate action against scams including bogus lotteries and deceptive premium rate prize promotions as a priority over the next three years. The Gambling Commission is a member of the Scams Enforcement Group and works closely with other agencies represented on the group to share information, co-operate in investigations and prosecutions and raise public awareness for example through use of its website. Further details of the work of the OFT can be found on its website www.oft.gov.uk.

21 CONTACTS

Gambling Commission — www.gamblingcommission.gov.uk
Department for Culture Media and Sport – www.culture.gov.uk
The Lotteries Council – www.lotteriescouncil.org.uk
Hospice Lotteries Association – www.hospicelotteries.org.uk
Gamcare – www.gamcare.org.uk
Responsibility in Gambling Trust – www.rigt.org.uk

Charity Commission for England & Wales – www.charity-commission.gov.uk
Office of the Scottish Charities Regulator – www.oscr.gov.uk
Office of Fair Trading (scams) – www.oft.gov.uk/consumer/scams
Trading Standards – www.tradingstandards.gov.uk
Local Authority Coordinators of Regulatory Services – www.lacors.gov.uk
Institute of Fundraising – www.institute-of-fundraising.org.uk
Charity Law Association – www.charitylawassociation.org.uk
Committee of Advertising Practice – www.cap.org.uk
Independent Committee for the Supervision of Standards of the Telephone Information Services(Premium rate services regulator) – www.icstis.org.uk
OFCOM – www.ofcom.org.uk
Gambling Commission May 2007

CONDITIONS AND CODES OF PRACTICE APPLICABLE TO:
REMOTE EXTERNAL LOTTERY MANAGER LICENCES
REMOTE NON-COMMERCIAL SOCIETY LOTTERY LICENCES
REMOTE LOCAL AUTHORITY LOTTERY LICENCES

October 2010

6.2305–6.2315 **Your licence is subject to certain conditions and codes of practice, these are detailed in the following pages**

STATUTORY CONDITIONS ATTACHED BY VIRTUE OF THE ACT

SOCIAL RESPONSIBILITY

This licence is subject to a condition that the licensee ensures compliance with any relevant social responsibility provision of a code of practice issued by the Commission. The social responsibility provisions that are relevant to the activities authorised by this licence are set out in the section entitled Codes of Practice.
(Sections 24 and 82(1) Gambling Act 2005)

RETURN OF STAKES TO CHILDREN

This licence is subject to a condition that if the licensee (or anyone employed by the licensee to perform an operational function within the meaning of Section 80 of the Act) becomes aware that a child is using or has used facilities for gambling provided in reliance on the licence, the licensee;
(a) must return any money paid in respect of the use of those facilities (whether by way of fee, stake or otherwise) by the child as soon as is reasonably practicable, and
(b) may not give a prize to the child.
This condition does not apply to use of a Category D gaming machine.
(Section 83(1))

OTHER STATUTORY CONDITIONS

The following condition applies to remote lottery manager operating licences only

To the extent this licence is relied on to authorise action as an external lottery manager in respect of lotteries promoted by societies or local authorities whose lottery operating licences require them to ensure that all the arrangements for the lottery are made by the holder of a lottery manager's licence, this licence is subject to any conditions attached to those licences by virtue of section 99(1).

COMMISSION GENERAL CONDITIONS

The Commission's complete suite of Licence Conditions to be attached to operating licences pursuant to section 75 of the Act includes some conditions which may not apply to your licence. Where that is the case the irrelevant conditions have not been reproduced below. The full list of Licence Conditions and Codes of Practice are contained within the Commission's Publication "Licence Conditions and Codes of Practice"

QUALIFIED PERSONS AND PERSONAL LICENCES

Qualified persons

THE FOLLOWING CONDITION APPLIES TO ALL REMOTE OPERATING LICENCES ISSUED TO SMALL-SCALE OPERATORS

In this condition the terms 'small-scale operator', 'qualifying position' and 'qualified person' have the meanings respectively ascribed to them by the Gambling Act 2005 (Definition of Small-scale Operator) Regulations 2006.

Schedule X[1] lists those individuals notified to the Commission as qualified persons.

If, whilst the licensee remains a small-scale operator, an individual begins or ceases to occupy a qualifying position in relation to the licensee, the licensee must within 28 days apply to the Commission under s 104(1)(b) for amendment of the details of the licence set out in Schedule X[1].

An application for amendment under s 104(1)(b) may be made in advance of an individual beginning or ceasing to occupy a qualifying position provided it specifies the date from which the change to which it relates is to be effective.

---

[1] The schedules mentioned here will be attached to individual licences.

Personal licences

THE FOLLOWING CONDITION APPLIES TO REMOTE LOTTERY MANAGER OPERATING LICENCES ONLY

(a) Subject to (e) and (f) below licensees must ensure:
   (i) that each individual who occupies one of the management offices specified in (b) below in or in respect of the licensee or in connection with the licensed activities holds a personal licence authorising the performance of the functions of that office (hereafter 'a personal management licence')
   (ii) that at least one person occupies at least one of those offices.
(b) The specified management offices are those offices (whether or not held by a director in the case of a licensee which is a company, a partner in the case of a licensee which is a partnership or an officer of the association in the case of a licensee which is an unincorporated association) the occupier of which is by virtue of the terms of their appointment responsible for:
   - the overall management and direction of the licensee's business or affairs
   - the licensee's finance function as head of that function
   - the licensee's gambling regulatory compliance function as head of that function
   - the licensee's marketing function as head of that function

- the licensee's information technology function as head of that function in so far as it relates to gambling-related information technology and software
- oversight of the day to day management of the licensed activities at an identified number of premises licensed under Part 8 of the Act or across an identified geographical area
- in the case of casino and bingo licences only, oversight of the day to day management of a single set of premises licensed under Part 8 of the Act.

(c) Licensees must take all reasonable steps to ensure that anything done in the performance of the functions of a specified management office is done in accordance with the terms and conditions of the holder's personal management licence.

(d) Where an individual is authorised by a personal licence and that licence comes under review under section 116(2) of the Act, the operating licensee must comply with any conditions subsequently imposed on that licence by the Commission about redeployment, supervision, or monitoring of the individual's work and any requirements of the Commission in respect of such matters applicable during the period of the review.

(e) Paragraphs (a) to (d) above shall not apply to a licensee for so long as the licensee is a 'small-scale operator' as defined in the Gambling Act 2005 (Definition of Small-scale Operator) Regulations 2006 ('the Regulations').

(f) During the period of 3 years commencing with the date on which a licensee ceases to be a small-scale operator paragraphs (a) to (e) above shall apply subject to the proviso that the phrase 'each individual' in paragraph (a)(i) shall not include any individual who was a 'qualified person' (as defined in the Regulations) in relation to the licensee 28 days immediately prior to the licensee ceasing to be a small-scale operator.

THE FOLLOWING CONDITION APPLIES TO ALL REMOTE LOTTERY OPERATING LICENCES ISSUED TO NON-COMMERCIAL SOCIETIES AND LOCAL AUTHORITIES

(a) Subject to (e) below licensees must ensure that the individual who occupies the management office specified in (b) below in or in respect of the licensee or in connection with the licensed activities holds a personal licence authorising the performance of the functions of that office (hereafter 'a personal management licence').

(b) The specified management office is that director's post in the case of a licensee which is a company, that partner in the case of a licensee which is a partnership, or that office in a licensee which is an unincorporated association or local authority, the occupier of which has overall management responsibility for the promotion of the lottery.

(c) Licensees must take all reasonable steps to ensure that anything done in the performance of the functions of a specified management office is done in accordance with the terms and conditions of the holder's personal management licence.

(d) Where an individual is authorised by a personal licence and that licence comes under review under section 116(2) of the Act, the operating licensee must comply with any conditions subsequently imposed on that licence by the Commission about redeployment, supervision, or monitoring of the individual's work and any requirements of the Commission in respect of such matters applicable during the period of the review.

(e) Paragraphs (a) to (d) above shall not apply to a licensee for so long as the licensee is a 'small-scale operator' as defined in the Gambling Act 2005 (Definition of Small-scale Operator) Regulations 2006.

TECHNICAL STANDARDS AND EQUIPMENT SPECIFICATIONS

Licensees must comply with the Commission's technical standards and with requirements set by the Commission relating to the timing and procedures for testing.

FINANCIAL ROBUSTNESS

Notification of shareholders

All company licensees must notify the Commission of the name and address of any person who becomes a shareholder in the company or its holding company holding 3% or more of the issued share capital of the company or its holding company; or any existing shareholder who acquires a holding of 3% or more of the issued share capital of the company or its holding company.

In this condition 'holding company' has the meaning ascribed to that term by section 1159 of the Companies Act 2006 or any statutory modification or re-enactment thereof.

PROTECTION OF CUSTOMER FUNDS

The following condition applies to remote lottery manager operating licences only

Licensees who hold customer funds for use in future gambling must set out clearly, in information made available to customers in writing, whether they protect customers' funds in the event of insolvency and the method by which this is achieved.

The following condition applies to remote lottery manager operating licences only

Licensees must credit all lottery proceeds to a bank account or accounts having trustee status and at all times maintain a separation between those funds and their own trading income, or have in place other arrangements which provide legal protection, in the event of the licensee's insolvency, for society and local authority lottery funds the licensee manages.

GENERAL 'FAIR AND OPEN' PROVISIONS

Licensees must satisfy themselves that the terms on which gambling is offered are not unfair under the Unfair Terms in Consumer Contracts Regulations 1999 and, where applicable, meet the reasonableness test under the Unfair Contract Terms Act 1977. An accurate summary of the contractual terms on which gambling is offered must be made available to customers and set out in plain and intelligible language.

Customers must be notified of changes to terms before they come into effect.

DISPLAY OF LICENSED STATUS

Lottery promoters must display 'licensed by the Gambling Commission' and details of the Gambling Commission website on lottery tickets.

LOTTERIES

Licensees must ensure that at least 20% of the proceeds of any lottery promoted in reliance on the licence are applied to a purpose for which the promoting non-commercial society is conducted or the promoting local authority has power to incur expenditure.

The proceeds of any lottery promoted in reliance on this licence must not exceed £4,000,000 and the aggregate of the proceeds of lotteries promoted wholly or partly in a calendar year in reliance on the licence must not exceed £10,000,000.

The rules of any lottery promoted in reliance on this licence must be such as to ensure:

(a) that it is not possible for the purchaser of a ticket in the lottery to win by virtue of that ticket (whether in money, money's worth, or partly the one and partly the other and including any winnings arising from a rollover) more than:
   - £25,000
   - if more, 10% of the proceeds of the lottery

(b) that membership of the class among whom prizes are allocated does not depend on making any payment (apart from payment of the price of a ticket).

A lottery promoted in reliance on this licence must not be linked to any other lottery, free draw or prize competition.

For the purposes of this condition:

(a) two or more lotteries are linked if any of them is so structured that a person who wins a prize in that lottery will also win a prize in some or all of the others, unless the maximum amount which a person can win is no more than £400,000 in aggregate. In determining whether two or more lotteries are linked it is immaterial how many of them are promoted in reliance on this licence.

(b) a lottery is linked to a free draw or prize competition if:
   (i) a person's participation in, or his being allocated a prize in, the lottery is a means of establishing his eligibility to enter the draw or competition; and
   (ii) the arrangements for the lottery and/or the draw or competition are such that a person may win more than £400,000 in aggregate as a result of his participation in the lottery and the draw or competition.

If a lottery, whilst not a linked lottery, has the feature that by selecting the same numbers, or combination of numbers in the lottery and in one or more other lottery or lotteries the participant in those lotteries may win prizes which, in aggregate, exceed £400,000, no advertisement for, nor other marketing of, the lottery may make any reference to that feature.

In the case of lottery operating licences issued to non-commercial societies and lottery managers' operating licences, licensees must ensure that each person who purchases a ticket in a lottery promoted in reliance on this licence, or promoted on behalf of a society in reliance on this licence, receives a document which:

- identifies the promoting society
- states the name and address of a member of the society who is designated, by persons acting on behalf of the society, as having responsibility within the society for the promotion of the lottery
- either states the date of the draw (or each draw) in the lottery, or enables the date of the draw (or each draw) in the lottery to be determined.

Licensees must display 'licensed by the Gambling Commission' and details of the Gambling Commission website on lottery tickets.

The price payable for purchasing each ticket in a lottery promoted in reliance on this licence:

- must be the same
- must be shown on the ticket or in a document received by the purchaser; and
- must be paid to the promoter of the lottery before any person is given a ticket or any right in respect of membership of the class among whom prizes are to be allocated.

For the purposes of these conditions, reference to a person receiving a document includes a reference to a message being sent or displayed to him electronically in a manner which enables him, without incurring significant expense or delay, to:

- retain the message electronically
- print it.

Licensees must lodge with the Commission a description of, and a copy of the rules of, any lottery intended to be promoted in reliance on this licence, and any amendment to the rules of a lottery previously notified to the Commission, at least 28 days before any tickets in such lottery, or amended lottery, are put on sale.

Lottery tickets must not be sold to a person in any street. But tickets may be sold by a person present in a kiosk or shop premises having no space for the accommodation of customers or door to door. For the purposes of this condition 'street' includes any bridge, road, lane, footway, subway, square, court, alley or passage (including passages through enclosed premises such as shopping malls) whether a thoroughfare or not.

In respect of each lottery promoted in reliance on this licence, a lottery submission must be sent to the Commission within three months of the date of the determination of the lottery or, in the case of an 'instant lottery', within three months of the last date on which tickets in the lottery were on sale. It must show the total proceeds and how they have been distributed between prizes and expenses and the amount applied directly to the society's purposes or, in the case of licences issued to local authorities, the amount applied directly to purposes for which the authority has power to incur expenditure.

Every lottery submission must contain or be accompanied by a declaration that the information given in it is correct to the best of the signatory's knowledge and belief. The submission must be signed by:

(a) the holder of a personal licence issued under Part 6 of the Act; or
(b) a 'qualified person' as defined in the Gambling Act 2005 (Definition of Small scale Operator) Regulations 2006; or
(c) the designated person named on tickets in a lottery promoted by or on behalf of a non commercial society as having responsibility within the society for the promotion of the lottery.

Accounting records and copies of lottery submissions must be retained for a minimum of three years from the date of any lottery to which they relate and be made available for inspection by the Commission on request. Accounting records must contain, in respect of each lottery, details of the total proceeds of the lottery, the expenses of the lottery and the sum allocated from the proceeds to cover those expenses, and the number of sold and unsold tickets.

For any calendar year in which the cumulative proceeds of lotteries promoted in reliance on this licence exceed £1,000,000 the licensee must provide the Commission with written confirmation from a qualifying auditor confirming that the proceeds of those lotteries have been fully accounted for in their annual audited accounts. Such confirmation must be provided within ten months of the date to which the accounts are made up.

A qualifying auditor means a person who is eligible for appointment as a company auditor under section 25 of the Companies Act 1989 but, in the case of a lottery promoted by or on behalf of a non-commercial society, is not:

(a) a member of the society;
(b) a partner, officer or employee of such a member; or
(c) a partnership of which a person falling within (a) or (b) is a partner.

Accurate records for each lottery must be kept by the operator to support the data in the lottery submissions and must be made available for inspection by the Commission when required. Such records must include:

- the total proceeds in each lottery
- the percentage of proceeds allocated to prizes in each lottery
- the amount of proceeds allocated to expenses and details of those expenses for each lottery
- the number of sold and unsold tickets in each lottery.

In the case of lottery managers' operating licences only, all licensees must have procedures in place designed to ensure that funds belonging to a society or local authority whose lotteries they manage in reliance on this licence are accounted for to them in a timely manner.

ACCESS TO PREMISES

Licensees must have and put into effect policies and procedures (including staff training programmes) designed to ensure that their staff co-operate with the Commission's enforcement officers in the proper performance of their compliance functions and are made aware of those officers' rights of entry to premises contained in Part 15 of the Act.

INFORMATION REQUIREMENTS

Reporting suspicion of offences etc

Licensees must provide the Commission with any information that they know relates to or suspect may relate to the commission of an offence under the Act, including an offence resulting from a breach of a licence condition or a code provision having the effect of a licence condition.

Reporting 'Key Events'

A key event is an event that could have a significant impact on the nature or structure of a licensee's business. Licensees must notify the Commission of the occurrence of any of the following key events as soon as reasonably practicable and in any event within five working days of the licensee becoming aware of the event's occurrence[2].

- in the case of licensees which are companies, a petition being presented for their winding up or the winding up of any group company of theirs, or they or any group company being placed in administration or receivership: in this condition a 'group company' is any subsidiary or holding company of the licensee – as those terms are defined in section 1159 of the Companies Act 2006 or any statutory modification or re-enactment thereof – and any subsidiary of such holding company
- in the case of a licensee who is an individual (or a partner in a partnership licensee) their being presented with a petition for their bankruptcy or sequestration or their entering into an individual voluntary agreement
- where the licensee is required to have their accounts independently audited, any unplanned change of auditor including a change prompted by a dispute or resulting from auditors being unable or unwilling to sign an unqualified audit report
- the departure from the licensee's business of any person occupying a 'qualifying position' as defined by Regulation 2(2) of the Gambling Act 2005 (Definition of Small-scale Operator) Regulations 2006
- any breach of a covenant given to a bank or other lender
- any default in making repayment of the whole or any part of a loan on its due date
- any court judgments remaining unpaid 14 days after the date of judgment
- the commencement of any material litigation against the licensee
- the imposition of a disciplinary sanction, including dismissal, against the holder of a personal licence or a person occupying a qualifying position for gross misconduct; or the resignation of a personal licence holder or person occupying a qualifying position following commencement of disciplinary proceedings in respect of gross misconduct against that person
- in the case of remote gambling, the commencement or cessation of trading on website domains (including WAP URLs) or broadcast media through which the licensee provides gambling facilities.

---

2 Key events can be reported securely online at the Commission's website at www.gamblingcommission.gov.uk or by email to key.events@gamblingcommission.gov.uk or posted to Key Events, Compliance Administration Team, Gambling Commission, Victoria Square House, Victoria Square, Birmingham B2 4BP

General and Regulatory Returns

On request, licensees must provide the Commission with such information as the Commission may require about the use made of facilities provided in accordance with this licence, and the manner in which gambling authorised by this licence and the licensee's business in relation to that gambling are carried on, including in particular information about:

- the numbers of people making use of the facilities and the frequency of such use
- the range of gambling activities provided by the licensee and the numbers of staff employed in connection with them
- the licensee's policies in relation to, and experiences of, problem gambling.

In particular within 28 days of the end of each quarterly period or, for those only submitting annual returns, within 42 days of the end of each annual period, licensees must submit a Regulatory Return to the Commission containing such information as the Commission may from time to time require[3].

---

[3] Regulatory returns can be submitted securely online at the Commission's website at www.gamblingcommission.gov.uk For operators unable to access this system, the forms and a guide to completing them can be requested from the Commission and returned by email to Regulatory.Returns@gamblingcommission.gov.uk or by post to Regulatory Returns, Compliance Administration Team, Gambling Commission, Victoria Square House, Victoria Square, Birmingham, B2 4BP.

SECRETARY OF STATE GENERAL CONDITIONS

None at present

CODES OF PRACTICE

INTRODUCTION

This is the Commission's principal code of practice, issued under section 24 of the Gambling Act 2005, as revised with effect from 1 January 2009. There are two types of provision in the code:

- social responsibility provisions: compliance with these is a condition of licences; therefore any breach of them by an operator may lead the Commission to review the operator's licence with a view to suspension, revocation or the imposition of a financial penalty and would also expose the operator to the risk of prosecution; and
- ordinary code provisions: these do not have the status of licence conditions, but are admissible in evidence in criminal or civil proceedings and must be taken into account in any case in which the court or tribunal think them relevant and by the Commission in the exercise of its functions. Any breach of ordinary code provisions by an operator may be taken into account by the Commission on a licence review, but cannot lead to imposition of a financial penalty. These code provisions are in italics in this section and generally set out good practice in these areas.

FINANCIAL REQUIREMENTS

Ordinary code provision

In order to help prevent activities related to money laundering licensees should take into account the Commission's advice on the Proceeds of Crime Act 2002, *Duties and responsibilities under the Proceeds of Crime Act 2002. Advice for operators (excluding casino operators).*

PROTECTION OF CHILDREN AND OTHER VULNERABLE PERSONS

Combating problem gambling

Social responsibility code provision

Licensees must have and put into effect policies and procedures intended to promote socially responsible gambling.
Licensees' policies and procedures for socially responsible gambling must include but need not be confined to:
- the specific policies and procedures required by the following provisions of section 2 of this code
- a commitment to and how they will contribute to research into the prevention and treatment of problem gambling
- a commitment to and how they will contribute to public education on the risks of gambling and how to gamble safely
- a commitment to and how they will contribute to the identification and treatment of problem gamblers.

Access to gambling by children and young persons

Social responsibility code provision

Licensees must have and put into effect policies and procedures designed to prevent underage gambling, and monitor the effectiveness of these.
Such procedures must include:
(a) warning potential customers that underage gambling is an offence;
(b) requiring customers to affirm that they are of legal age;
(c) regularly reviewing their age verification systems and implementing all reasonable improvements that may be made as technology advances and as information improves;
(d) ensuring that relevant staff are properly trained in the use of their age verification procedures; in particular customer services staff must be appropriately trained in the use of secondary forms of identification when initial verification procedures fail to prove that an individual is of legal age;
(e) enabling their gambling websites to permit filtering software to be used by adults (such as parents or within schools) in order to restrict access to relevant pages of those sites;
(f) in the case of any UK resident customer who deposits money using any type of payment method other than a credit card, and unless the licensee has established that a third party has satisfactorily carried out age verification, the following age verification procedures:
    (i) verifying additional information about the customer, such as carrying out searches of credit reference and other databases that list names and addresses of individuals over the age of 18;
    (ii) carrying out secondary age verification checks in any circumstances which give the operator reason to suspect that the person may be underage;
    (iii) not permitting the customer to withdraw any winnings from their account until age verification has been satisfactorily completed; and
    (iv) in any event, a requirement that if age verification has not been satisfactorily completed within 72 hours of the customer applying to register to gamble and depositing money:
    - the account will be frozen
    - no further gambling will be permitted until age verification has been successfully completed

- if on completion of age verification the customer is shown to be underage, the operator must return to the customer any money paid in respect of the use of the gambling facilities, but no winnings shall be paid.

(g) in the case of any non-UK resident customer who deposits money using any type of payment method other than a credit card, and unless the licensee has established that a third party has satisfactorily carried out age verification, the following age verification procedures:

(i) taking all reasonable steps to make use of information available for age verification purposes from whichever country the potential customer is resident in; and

(ii) each of the following steps, unless they can not reasonably be implemented or, in the case of the fourth bullet point, a period of more than 72 hours was reasonably required:

- verifying additional information about the customer, such as carrying out searches of credit reference and other databases that list names and addresses of individuals over the age of 18
- carrying out secondary age verification checks in any circumstances which give the operator reason to suspect that the person may be underage
- not permitting the customer to withdraw any winnings from their account until age verification has been satisfactorily completed
- a requirement that if age verification has not been satisfactorily completed within 72 hours of the customer applying to register to gamble and depositing money:
  – the account will be frozen;
  – no further gambling will be permitted until age verification has been successfully completed; and
  – if on completion of age verification the customer is shown to be underage all deposits held by the operator are returned to the customer and no winnings paid.

(h) in the case of any customer who registers to gamble and deposits money using a credit card, conducting a programme of random checks of credit card users for compliance with age restrictions.

Ordinary code provision

Licensees should, and should request their contracted partners to, draw attention to parental responsibility as part of the purchasing process of facilities such as mobile phones and interactive television.

Information on how to gamble responsibly and help for problem gamblers

Social responsibility code provision

Licensees must make information readily available to their customers on how to gamble responsibly and how to access information about, and help in respect of, problem gambling.

The information must cover:

- any measures provided by the licensee to help individuals monitor or control their gambling, such as restricting the duration of a gambling session or the amount of money they can spend
- timers or other forms of reminders or 'reality checks' where available
- self-exclusion options
- information about the availability of further help or advice.

The information must be directed to all customers whether or not licensees also make available material which is directed specifically at customers who may be 'problem gamblers'.
For gambling premises, information must be available in all areas where gambling facilities are provided and adjacent to ATMs where these are not located in a gambling area. As a minimum, information must be displayed prominently on posters appropriate to the size and layout of the premises and contained in leaflets that may be taken away. Licensees must take all reasonable steps to ensure that this information is also readily accessible in locations which enable the customer to obtain it discreetly.

ORDINARY CODE PROVISION

Licensees who market their services in one or more foreign languages should make available in that, or those, foreign languages:

- the information on how to gamble responsibly and access to help referred to above
- the players' guides to any game, bet or lottery required to be made available to customers under provisions in this code
- the summary of the contractual terms on which gambling is offered, which is required to be provided to customers as a condition of the licensee's operating licence.

Customer interaction

SOCIAL RESPONSIBILITY CODE PROVISION

Licensees must put into effect policies and procedures for customer interaction where they have concerns that a customer's behaviour may indicate problem gambling. The policies must include:

- identification of the appropriate level of management who may initiate customer interaction and the procedures for doing so
- the types of behaviour that will be logged/reported to the appropriate level of staff and which may trigger customer interaction at an appropriate moment
- the circumstances in which consideration should be given to refusing service to customers and/or barring them from the operator's gambling premises
- training for all staff on their respective responsibilities, in particular so that they know who is designated to deal with problem gambling issues.

But such policies and procedures must be consistent with, and implemented with due regard to, licensees' duties in respect of the health and safety of their staff.

Self-exclusion

SOCIAL RESPONSIBILITY CODE PROVISION

Licensees must have and put into effect procedures for self-exclusion and take all reasonable steps to refuse service or to otherwise prevent an individual who has entered a self-exclusion agreement from participating in gambling.
Licensees must, as soon as practicable, take all reasonable steps to prevent any marketing material being sent to a self-excluded customer.
Licensees must take steps to remove the name and details of a self-excluded individual from any marketing databases used by the company or group (or otherwise flag that person as an individual to whom marketing material must not be sent), within two days of receiving the completed self-exclusion notification.
This covers any marketing material relating to gambling. However, it would not extend to blanket marketing which is targeted at a particular geographical area and where the excluded individual would not knowingly be included.

Licensees must close any customer accounts of an individual who has entered a self-exclusion agreement and return any funds held in the customer account. It is not sufficient merely to prevent an individual from withdrawing funds from their customer account whilst still accepting wagers from them. Where the giving of credit is permitted, the licensee may retain details of the amount owed to them by the individual, although the account must not be active.

Licensees must put into effect procedures designed to ensure that an individual who has self-excluded cannot gain access to gambling. These procedures must include:

- a register of those excluded with appropriate records (name, address, other details, and any membership or account details that may be held by the operator)
- a record of the card numbers to be excluded
- staff training to ensure that staff are able to enforce the systems
- the removal of access from those persons found to have gambled or who have attempted to gamble on the facilities.

Ordinary code provision

Self-exclusion procedures should require individuals to take positive action in order to self-exclude:

- over the **internet**; this can be a box that must be ticked in order to indicate that they understand the system
- by **telephone**; this can be a direct question asking whether they understand the system.

Before an individual self-excludes, licensees should provide or make available sufficient information about what the consequences of self-exclusion are.

Licensees should encourage the customer to consider extending their self exclusion to other remote gambling operators currently used by the customer.

Customers should be given the opportunity to self-exclude by contacting customer services and in addition, where technically possible, by entering an automated process using remote communication. In order to avoid inadvertent self-exclusion it is acceptable for an automated process to include an additional step that requires the customer to confirm that they wish to self-exclude. The licensee should ensure that all staff who are involved in direct customer service are aware of the self-exclusion system in place, and are able to direct that individual to an immediate point of contact with whom/which to complete that process.

Within the licensee's information about self-exclusion policies, the licensee should provide a statement to explain that software is available to prevent an individual computer from accessing gambling internet sites. The licensee should provide a link to a site where further information is available.

Licensees should take all reasonable steps to ensure that:

- the self-exclusion period is a minimum of six months and give customers the option of extending this to a total of at least five years
- a customer who has decided to enter a self-exclusion agreement is given the opportunity to do so immediately without any cooling-off period. However, if the customer wishes to consider the self-exclusion further (for example to discuss with problem gambling groups) the customer may return at a later date to enter into self-exclusion
- at the end of the period chosen by the customer (and at least six months later), the self-exclusion remains in place, unless the customer takes positive action in order to gamble again. No marketing material should be sent to the individual unless the individual has taken positive action in order to gamble again, and has agreed to accept such material
- where a customer chooses not to renew the self-exclusion, and makes a positive request to begin gambling again, the customer is given one day to cool off before being allowed access to the gambling facilities. The contact must be made via telephone or in person; re-registering online is not sufficient.

The licensee should retain the records relating to a self-exclusion agreement at least until the agreement has been formally ended.
(Please note that the Commission does not require the licensee to carry out any particular assessment or make any judgement as to whether the previously self excluded individual should again be permitted access to gambling. The requirement to take positive action in person or over the phone is purely to a) check that the customer has considered the decision to access gambling again and allow them to consider the implications; and b) implement the one day cooling-off period and explain why this has been put in place.)

Employment of children and young persons

ORDINARY CODE PROVISION

Licensees who employ young persons (16 and 17 year olds) to sell tickets, collect payments or pay out winnings should have and put into effect policies and procedures designed to ensure that all staff, including staff who are young persons themselves, are made aware that the law prohibits underage gambling, and that tickets may only be sold to persons aged 16 or over.

Provision of credit by licensees and the use of credit cards

SOCIAL RESPONSIBILITY CODE PROVISION

Licensees who choose to accept credit cards must:

- accept payment by credit card for gambling only where that payment is made to a customer account
- make available for gambling, funds deposited via credit card only after the card issuer has approved the transaction.

ORDINARY CODE PROVISION

Licensees who choose to offer credit to members of the public who are not themselves gambling operators should also:

- have procedures for checking and scoring applications for credit from such customers, for setting, and for the increase of, credit limits
- explain these procedures to customers
- set a maximum credit limit for each customer and not permit customers to exceed that limit without further application
- apply a 24-hour delay between receiving a request for an increase in a credit limit and granting it in those cases where the limit exceeds that which the operator had previously set
- not require a minimum spend within a set time period
- take all reasonable steps to ensure that offers of credit are not sent to vulnerable persons, including those who have self-excluded from gambling
- ensure that information about an offer of credit includes a risk warning of what may happen in the event of default.

Identification of individual customers

SOCIAL RESPONSIBILITY CODE PROVISION

Licensees must have and put into effect policies and procedures designed to identify separate accounts which are held by the same individual.
Where licensees allow customers to hold more than one account with them, the licensee must link all of a customer's such accounts to that customer and ensure that:

- if a customer opts to self-exclude from one account they are excluded from all accounts they hold with the licensee
- all of a customer's accounts are monitored and decisions that trigger customer interaction are based on the observed behaviour and transactions across all the accounts
- where credit is offered or allowed the maximum credit limit is applied on an aggregate basis across all accounts
- individual financial limits can be implemented across all of a customer's accounts.

ORDINARY CODE PROVISION

Where a licensee:

(i) is a company, the licensee should take all reasonable steps to comply with the above social responsibility code provision as if it also applied to accounts held in respect of gambling carried on in reliance on a remote operating licence held by any Group Company;

(ii) also holds a licence in another jurisdiction permitting it to provide facilities for remote gambling (a 'foreign licence') or is a company one or more of whose Group Companies holds one or more foreign licences, the licensee should take all reasonable steps to comply with the above social responsibility code provision as if it applied also to accounts held in respect of gambling carried on in reliance on a foreign licence held by the licensee or any Group Company.

A company is a Group Company in relation to a licensee if it is the holding company of, subsidiary of, or shares a common holding company with, the licensee. For these purposes 'holding company' and 'subsidiary' respectively have the meanings ascribed to them by section 1159 of the Companies Act 2006 or any statutory modification or re-enactment thereof.

'FAIR AND OPEN' PROVISIONS

Social responsibility code provision

Licensees must be able to provide evidence to the Commission, if required, showing how they satisfied themselves that their terms are not unfair.

Social responsibility code provision

Licensees must make the following available to customers:

- a player's guide to each gambling opportunity (bet, game or lottery) made available by the operator
- such additional information relating to the available gambling as the Commission shall from time to time publish to licensees: the current requirements are set out in an Annex to the Commission's Technical Standards.

Ordinary code provision

Where practicable, the player's guide and additional information referred to in the social responsibility code should be made available through the medium in which the remote gambling is to be conducted. Where that is not practicable, licensees should either:

- send a copy of the guide and required additional information by post, fax or email; or
- make these available to the customer in another medium to which he has access.

Ordinary code provision

Licensees should ensure that the terms on which they contract with third parties who provide user interfaces enabling customers to access their remote gambling facilities:

- include a term that any such user interface comply with the Commission's technical standards for remote gambling systems
- enable them to terminate the third party's contract promptly if, in the licensee's opinion, the third party is in breach of that term.

MARKETING

Social responsibility code provision

If a licensee makes available to any customer or potential customer any incentive or reward scheme or other arrangement under which the customer may receive money, goods, services or any other advantage (including the discharge in whole or in part of any liability of his) ('the benefit') the scheme must be designed to operate, and be operated, in such a way that:

(a) the circumstances in which, and conditions subject to which, the benefit is available are clearly set out and readily accessible to the customers to whom it is offered;

(b) neither the receipt nor the value or amount of the benefit is:

(i) dependent on the customer gambling for a pre-determined length of time or with a predetermined frequency; or

(ii) altered or increased if the qualifying activity or spend is reached within a shorter time than the whole period over which the benefit is offered;

(c) if the value of the benefit increases with the amount the customer spends it does so at a rate no greater than that at which the amount spent increases;

and further that:

(d) if the benefit comprises free or subsidised travel or accommodation which facilitates the customer's attendance at particular licensed premises the terms on which it is offered are not directly related to the level of the customer's prospective gambling.

Ordinary code provision

Licensees should only offer incentive or reward schemes in which the benefit available is proportionate to the type and level of customers' gambling.

Ordinary code provision

With a view to minimising the risk of fraud, licensees who are non-commercial societies or external lottery managers should adopt one or more of the following measures:

- prohibit the unsolicited mailing of tickets to non-members of the promoting society
- limit the value of tickets sent to any one address which is not that of a member of the promoting society to £20
- maintain records of tickets distributed and not returned.

Ordinary code provision

All advertising of gambling products and services should be undertaken in a socially responsible manner. In particular, licensees should comply with the advertising codes of practice which apply to the form and media in which they advertise their gambling facilities or services, and for media not explicitly covered should apply the principles included in these codes of practice as if they were explicitly covered. Licensees should also follow any relevant industry code of practice on advertising.

However, the particular restriction on allowing people aged under 25 to appear in adverts need not be applied to point of sale advertising material, provided that the images used depict the sporting activity that may be gambled on and not the activity of gambling itself and do not offend any other aspect of the advertising codes.

Ordinary code provision

Licensees should ensure that the terms on which they contract with their affiliates (that is those who are given a right to advertise, or provide a hyper-link to, a licensee's gambling website) enable them to terminate the affiliate's rights promptly if, in the licensee's opinion, the affiliate is in breach of the advertising codes.

COMPLAINTS AND DISPUTES

Social responsibility code provision

Licensees must put into effect a written procedure for handling customer complaints and disputes.
In this code a 'complaint' means a complaint about any aspect of the licensee's conduct of the licensed activities, and a 'dispute' is any complaint which:
(a) is not resolved at the first stage of the complaints procedure; and
(b) relates to the outcome of the complainant's gambling transaction.
Licensees must ensure that:

- customers are told the name and status of the person to contact about their complaint
- customers are given a copy of the complaints procedure on request or on making a complaint
- all complaints are handled in accordance with the procedure.

Licensees must also ensure that they have arrangements in place for disputes to be referred to an independent third party. Customers whose disputes are not resolved to their satisfaction by use of the operator's complaints procedure may refer those disputes to this independent third party. The arrangements under which such complaints are referred may, but need not, provide for the third party's decision to be binding on the licensee and the customer.
Licensees must keep a record of all complaints that are not resolved at the first stage of the complaints procedure.
Licensees must arrange for a copy of the decision on, or a note of the outcome of, each dispute referred to the independent party to be provided to the Commission quarterly, either by the independent party or by the licensee.

GAMBLING LICENSEES' STAFF

Social responsibility code provision

Licensees must take all reasonable steps to ensure that staff involved in the provision of facilities for gambling are made aware of advice on socially responsible gambling and of where to get confidential advice should their gambling become hard to control.

INFORMATION REQUIREMENTS

Ordinary code provision

The Commission expects licensees to work with the Commission in an open and cooperative way and to inform the Commission of any matters that the Commission would reasonably need to be aware of in exercising its regulatory functions. These are matters that will have a material impact on the licensee's business or on the licensee's ability to conduct its business. Such matters, which should be notified to the Commission as soon as reasonably practicable[4], include the following:

- the departure from the licensee's business of any person named in the licence application, or that person's successor, who holds a personal management licence, but who does not occupy a 'qualifying position'
- any reduction in the number of staff employed by the licensee where that has a material impact on the licensee's business
- the acquisition or disposal by the licensee of gambling premises or pitches where that has a material impact on the size or nature of the licensee's business
- in the case of corporate licensees, the disposal or acquisition of any group company where that has a material impact on the licensee's ability to conduct its business
- any disposal of the licensee's assets where that has a material impact on the licensee's business
- any investigation by a professional, statutory, regulatory or government body into the licensee's activities, or the activities in relation to the licensed entity of a personal licence holder or a person occupying a qualifying position employed by them, where such an investigation could result in the imposition of a sanction or penalty which, if imposed, could reasonably be expected to raise doubts about the licensee's continued suitability to hold a Gambling Commission licence
- any instance of criminal activity, including repeated instances of small-scale theft or fraud, where that has a material impact on the licensee's business
- any major breach in the licensee's information security where that adversely affects the confidentiality of customer data or prevents customers from accessing their accounts for a substantial period of time
- any other matters that have a material impact on the licensee's business or on the licensee's ability to conduct its business.

[4] These matters can be reported securely online at the Commission's website at www.gamblingcommission.gov.uk or by email to key.events@gamblingcommission.gov.uk or posted to Key Events, Compliance Administration Team, Gambling Commission, Victoria Square House, Victoria Square, Birmingham, B2 4BP

Gambling Commission October 2010

CONDITIONS AND CODES OF PRACTICE APPLICABLE TO: NON-REMOTE EXTERNAL LOTTERY MANAGER LICENCES NON-REMOTE NON-COMMERCIAL SOCIETY LOTTERY LICENCES NON-REMOTE LOCAL AUTHORITY LOTTERY LICENCES

October 2010

6.2325–6.2335 Your licence is subject to certain conditions and codes of practice, these are detailed in the following pages

STATUTORY CONDITIONS ATTACHED BY VIRTUE OF THE ACT

SOCIAL RESPONSIBILITY

This licence is subject to a condition that the licensee ensures compliance with any relevant social responsibility provision of a code of practice issued by the Commission. The social responsibility provisions that are relevant to the activities authorised by this licence are set out in the section entitled Codes of Practice.
(Sections 24 and 82(1) Gambling Act 2005)

RETURN OF STAKES TO CHILDREN

This licence is subject to a condition that if the licensee (or anyone employed by the licensee to perform an operational function within the meaning of Section 80 of the Act) becomes aware that a child is using or has used facilities for gambling provided in reliance on the licence, the licensee;

(a) must return any money paid in respect of the use of those facilities (whether by way of fee, stake or otherwise) by the child as soon as is reasonably practicable, and

(b) may not give a prize to the child.

This condition does not apply to use of a Category D gaming machine.
(Section 83(1))

Other statutory conditions

THE FOLLOWING CONDITION APPLIES TO LOTTERY MANAGER OPERATING LICENCES ONLY

To the extent this licence is relied on to authorise action as an external lottery manager in respect of lotteries promoted by societies or local authorities whose lottery operating licences require them to ensure that all the arrangements for the lottery are made by the holder of a lottery manager's licence, this licence is subject to any conditions attached to those licences by virtue of section 99(1).

COMMISSION GENERAL CONDITIONS

The Commission's complete suite of Licence Conditions to be attached to operating licences pursuant to section 75 of the Act includes some conditions which may not apply to your licence. Where that is the case the irrelevant conditions have not been reproduced below. The full list of Licence Conditions and Codes of Practice are contained within the Commission's Publication "Licence Conditions and Codes of Practice"

QUALIFIED PERSONS AND PERSONAL LICENCES

Qualified persons

THE FOLLOWING CONDITION APPLIES TO ALL OPERATING LICENCES ISSUED TO SMALL-SCALE OPERATORS

In this condition the terms 'small-scale operator', 'qualifying position' and 'qualified person' have the meanings respectively ascribed to them by the Gambling Act 2005 (Definition of Small-scale Operator) Regulations 2006.

Schedule X[1] lists those individuals notified to the Commission as qualified persons.

If, whilst the licensee remains a small-scale operator, an individual begins or ceases to occupy a qualifying position in relation to the licensee, the licensee must within 28 days apply to the Commission under s104(1)(b) for amendment of the details of the licence set out in Schedule X[FN6.2325_1].

An application for amendment under s104(1)(b) may be made in advance of an individual beginning or ceasing to occupy a qualifying position provided it specifies the date from which the change to which it relates is to be effective.

Personal licences

THE FOLLOWING CONDITION APPLIES TO LOTTERY MANAGER OPERATING LICENCES ONLY

(a) Subject to (e) and (f) below licensees must ensure:

(i) that each individual who occupies one of the management offices specified in (b) below in or in respect of the licensee or in connection with the licensed activities holds a personal licence authorising the performance of the functions of that office (hereafter 'a personal management licence')

(ii) that at least one person occupies at least one of those offices.

(b) The specified management offices are those offices (whether or not held by a director in the case of a licensee which is a company, a partner in the case of a licensee which is a partnership or an officer of the association in the case of a licensee which is an unincorporated association) the occupier of which is by virtue of the terms of their appointment responsible for:

- the overall management and direction of the licensee's business or affairs
- the licensee's finance function as head of that function
- the licensee's gambling regulatory compliance function as head of that function
- the licensee's marketing function as head of that function
- the licensee's information technology function as head of that function in so far as it relates to gambling-related information technology and software
- oversight of the day to day management of the licensed activities at an identified number of premises licensed under Part 8 of the Act or across an identified geographical area
- in the case of casino and bingo licences only, oversight of the day to day management of a single set of premises licensed under Part 8 of the Act.

(c) Licensees must take all reasonable steps to ensure that anything done in the performance of the functions of a specified management office is done in accordance with the terms and conditions of the holder's personal management licence.

(d) Where an individual is authorised by a personal licence and that licence comes under review under section 116(2) of the Act, the operating licensee must comply with any conditions subsequently imposed on that licence by the Commission about redeployment, supervision, or monitoring of the individual's work and any requirements of the Commission in respect of such matters applicable during the period of the review.

(e) Paragraphs (a) to (d) above shall not apply to a licensee for so long as the licensee is a 'small-scale operator' as defined in the Gambling Act 2005 (Definition of Small-scale Operator) Regulations 2006 ('the Regulations').

(f) During the period of 3 years commencing with the date on which a licensee ceases to be a small-scale operator paragraphs (a) to (e) above shall apply subject to the proviso that the phrase 'each individual' in paragraph (a)(i) shall not include any individual who was a 'qualified person' (as defined in the Regulations) in relation to the licensee 28 days immediately prior to the licensee ceasing to be a small-scale operator.

---

1 The schedules mentioned here will be attached to individual licences.

THE FOLLOWING CONDITION APPLIES TO ALL LOTTERY OPERATING LICENCES ISSUED TO NONCOMMERCIAL SOCIETIES AND LOCAL AUTHORITIES

(a) Subject to (e) below licensees must ensure that the individual who occupies the management office specified in (b) below in or in respect of the licensee or in connection with the licensed activities holds a personal licence authorising the performance of the functions of that office (hereafter 'a personal management licence').

(b) The specified management office is that director's post in the case of a licensee which is a company, that partner in the case of a licensee which is a partnership, or that office in a licensee which is an unincorporated association or local authority, the occupier of which has overall management responsibility for the promotion of the lottery.

(c) Licensees must take all reasonable steps to ensure that anything done in the performance of the functions of a specified management office is done in accordance with the terms and conditions of the holder's personal management licence.

(d) Where an individual is authorised by a personal licence and that licence comes under review under section 116(2) of the Act, the operating licensee must comply with any conditions subsequently imposed on that licence by the Commission about redeployment, supervision, or monitoring of the individual's work and any requirements of the Commission in respect of such matters applicable during the period of the review.

(e) Paragraphs (a) to (d) above shall not apply to a licensee for so long as the licensee is a 'small-scale operator' as defined in the Gambling Act 2005 (Definition of Small-scale Operator) Regulations 2006.

FINANCIAL ROBUSTNESS

Notification of shareholders

All company licensees must notify the Commission of the name and address of any person who becomes a shareholder in the company or its holding company holding 3% or more of the issued share capital of the company or its holding company; or any existing shareholder who acquires a holding of 3% or more of the issued share capital of the company or its holding company.

In this condition 'holding company' has the meaning ascribed to that term by section 1159 of the Companies Act 2006 or any statutory modification or re-enactment thereof.

PROTECTION OF CUSTOMER FUNDS

The following condition applies to lottery manager operating licences only

Licensees who hold customer funds for use in future gambling must set out clearly, in information made available to customers in writing, whether they protect customers' funds in the event of insolvency and the method by which this is achieved.

The following condition applies to lottery manager operating licences only

Licensees must credit all lottery proceeds to a bank account or accounts having trustee status and at all times maintain a separation between those funds and their own trading income, or have in place other arrangements which provide legal protection, in the event of the licensee's insolvency, for society and local authority lottery funds the licensee manages.

CASH HANDLING

Licensees, as part of their internal controls and financial accounting systems, must have and put into effect policies and procedures concerning the handling of cash, and cash equivalents (ie bankers drafts, cheques and debit cards), designed to minimise the risk of crimes such as money laundering, to avoid the giving of illicit credit and to provide assurance that gambling activities are being conducted fairly.

GENERAL 'FAIR AND OPEN' PROVISIONS

Licensees must satisfy themselves that the terms on which gambling is offered are not unfair under the Unfair Terms in Consumer Contracts Regulations 1999 and, where

applicable, meet the reasonableness test under the Unfair Contract Terms Act 1977. An accurate summary of the contractual terms on which gambling is offered must be made available to customers and set out in plain and intelligible language.
Customers must be notified of changes to terms before they come into effect.

DISPLAY OF LICENSED STATUS

Lottery promoters must display 'licensed by the Gambling Commission' and details of the Gambling Commission website on lottery tickets.

LOTTERIES

Licensees must ensure that at least 20% of the proceeds of any lottery promoted in reliance on the licence are applied to a purpose for which the promoting non-commercial society is conducted or the promoting local authority has power to incur expenditure.
The proceeds of any lottery promoted in reliance on this licence must not exceed £4,000,000 and the aggregate of the proceeds of lotteries promoted wholly or partly in a calendar year in reliance on the licence must not exceed £10,000,000.
The rules of any lottery promoted in reliance on this licence must be such as to ensure:

(a) that it is not possible for the purchaser of a ticket in the lottery to win by virtue of that ticket (whether in money, money's worth, or partly the one and partly the other and including any winnings arising from a rollover) more than:
  - £25,000
  - if more, 10% of the proceeds of the lottery

(b) that membership of the class among whom prizes are allocated does not depend on making any payment (apart from payment of the price of a ticket).

A lottery promoted in reliance on this licence must not be linked to any other lottery, free draw or prize competition.
For the purposes of this condition:

(a) two or more lotteries are linked if any of them is so structured that a person who wins a prize in that lottery will also win a prize in some or all of the others, unless the maximum amount which a person can win is no more than £400,000 in aggregate. In determining whether two or more lotteries are linked it is immaterial how many of them are promoted in reliance on this licence.

(b) a lottery is linked to a free draw or prize competition if:
  - (i) a person's participation in, or his being allocated a prize in, the lottery is a means of establishing his eligibility to enter the draw or competition; and
  - (ii) the arrangements for the lottery and/or the draw or competition are such that a person may win more than £400,000 in aggregate as a result of his participation in the lottery and the draw or competition.

If a lottery, whilst not a linked lottery, has the feature that by selecting the same numbers, or combination of numbers in the lottery and in one or more other lottery or lotteries the participant in those lotteries may win prizes which, in aggregate, exceed £400,000, no advertisement for, nor other marketing of, the lottery may make any reference to that feature.
In the case of lottery operating licences issued to non-commercial societies and lottery managers' operating licences, licensees must ensure that each person who purchases a ticket in a lottery promoted in reliance on this licence, or promoted on behalf of a society in reliance on this licence, receives a document which:

- identifies the promoting society
- states the name and address of a member of the society who is designated, by persons acting on behalf of the society, as having responsibility within the society for the promotion of the lottery
- either states the date of the draw (or each draw) in the lottery, or enables the date of the draw (or each draw) in the lottery to be determined.

Licensees must display 'licensed by the Gambling Commission' and details of the Gambling Commission website on lottery tickets.
The price payable for purchasing each ticket in a lottery promoted in reliance on this licence:
- must be the same
- must be shown on the ticket or in a document received by the purchaser; and
- must be paid to the promoter of the lottery before any person is given a ticket or any right in respect of membership of the class among whom prizes are to be allocated.

For the purposes of these conditions, reference to a person receiving a document includes a reference to a message being sent or displayed to him electronically in a manner which enables him, without incurring significant expense or delay, to:
- retain the message electronically
- print it.

Licensees must lodge with the Commission a description of, and a copy of the rules of, any lottery intended to be promoted in reliance on this licence, and any amendment to the rules of a lottery previously notified to the Commission, at least 28 days before any tickets in such lottery, or amended lottery, are put on sale.
Lottery tickets must not be sold to a person in any street. But tickets may be sold by a person present in a kiosk or shop premises having no space for the accommodation of customers or door to door.
For the purposes of this condition 'street' includes any bridge, road, lane, footway, subway, square, court, alley or passage (including passages through enclosed premises such as shopping malls) whether a thoroughfare or not.
In respect of each lottery promoted in reliance on this licence, a lottery submission must be sent to the Commission within three months of the date of the determination of the lottery or, in the case of an 'instant lottery', within three months of the last date on which tickets in the lottery were on sale. It must show the total proceeds and how they have been distributed between prizes and expenses and the amount applied directly to the society's purposes or, in the case of licences issued to local authorities, the amount applied directly to purposes for which the authority has power to incur expenditure.
Every lottery submission must contain or be accompanied by a declaration that the information given in it is correct to the best of the signatory's knowledge and belief. The submission must be signed by:
(a) the holder of a personal licence issued under Part 6 of the Act; or
(b) a 'qualified person' as defined in the Gambling Act 2005 (Definition of Small scale Operator) Regulations 2006; or
(c) the designated person named on tickets in a lottery promoted by or on behalf of a non-commercial society as having responsibility within the society for the promotion of the lottery.

Accounting records and copies of lottery submissions must be retained for a minimum of three years from the date of any lottery to which they relate and be made available for inspection by the Commission on request. Accounting records must contain, in respect of each lottery, details of the total proceeds of the lottery, the expenses of the lottery and the sum allocated from the proceeds to cover those expenses, and the number of sold and unsold tickets.
For any calendar year in which the cumulative proceeds of lotteries promoted in reliance on this licence exceed £1,000,000 the licensee must provide the Commission with written confirmation from a qualifying auditor confirming that the proceeds of those lotteries have been fully accounted for in their annual audited accounts. Such confirmation must be provided within ten months of the date to which the accounts are made up.
A qualifying auditor means a person who is eligible for appointment as a company auditor under section 25 of the Companies Act 1989 but, in the case of a lottery promoted by or on behalf of a non-commercial society, is not:
(a) a member of the society;

(b) a partner, officer or employee of such a member; or
(c) a partnership of which a person falling within (a) or (b) is a partner.

Accurate records for each lottery must be kept by the operator to support the data in the lottery submissions and must be made available for inspection by the Commission when required. Such records must include:

- the total proceeds in each lottery
- the percentage of proceeds allocated to prizes in each lottery
- the amount of proceeds allocated to expenses and details of those expenses for each lottery
- the number of sold and unsold tickets in each lottery.

In the case of lottery managers' operating licences only, all licensees must have procedures in place designed to ensure that funds belonging to a society or local authority whose lotteries they manage in reliance on this licence are accounted for to them in a timely manner.

ACCESS TO PREMISES

Licensees must have and put into effect policies and procedures (including staff training programmes) designed to ensure that their staff co-operate with the Commission's enforcement officers in the proper performance of their compliance functions and are made aware of those officers' rights of entry to premises contained in Part 15 of the Act.

INFORMATION REQUIREMENTS

Reporting suspicion of offences etc

Licensees must provide the Commission with any information that they know relates to or suspect may relate to the commission of an offence under the Act, including an offence resulting from a breach of a licence condition or a code provision having the effect of a licence condition.

Reporting 'Key Events'

A key event is an event that could have a significant impact on the nature or structure of a licensee's business. Licensees must notify the Commission of the occurrence of any of the following key events as soon as reasonably practicable and in any event within five working days of the licensee becoming aware of the event's occurrence[2].

- in the case of licensees which are companies, a petition being presented for their winding up or the winding up of any group company of theirs, or they or any group company being placed in administration or receivership: in this condition a 'group company' is any subsidiary or holding company of the licensee – as those terms are defined in section 1159 of the Companies Act 2006 or any statutory modification or re-enactment thereof – and any subsidiary of such holding company
- in the case of a licensee who is an individual (or a partner in a partnership licensee) their being presented with a petition for their bankruptcy or sequestration or their entering into an individual voluntary agreement
- where the licensee is required to have their accounts independently audited, any unplanned change of auditor including a change prompted by a dispute or resulting from auditors being unable or unwilling to sign an unqualified audit report
- the departure from the licensee's business of any person occupying a 'qualifying position' as defined by Regulation 2(2) of the Gambling Act 2005 (Definition of Small-scale Operator) Regulations 2006
- any breach of a covenant given to a bank or other lender
- any default in making repayment of the whole or any part of a loan on its due date

- any court judgments remaining unpaid 14 days after the date of judgment
- the commencement of any material litigation against the licensee
- the imposition of a disciplinary sanction, including dismissal, against the holder of a personal licence or a person occupying a qualifying position for gross misconduct; or the resignation of a personal licence holder or person occupying a qualifying position following commencement of disciplinary proceedings in respect of gross misconduct against that person
- in the case of remote gambling, the commencement or cessation of trading on website domains (including WAP URLs) or broadcast media through which the licensee provides gambling facilities.

---

2 Key events can be reported securely online at the Commission's website at www.gamblingcommission.gov.uk or by email to key.events@gamblingcommission.gov.uk or posted to Key Events, Compliance Administration Team, Gambling Commission, Victoria Square House, Victoria Square, Birmingham B2 4BP

General and Regulatory Returns

On request, licensees must provide the Commission with such information as the Commission may require about the use made of facilities provided in accordance with this licence, and the manner in which gambling authorised by this licence and the licensee's business in relation to that gambling are carried on, including in particular information about:

- the numbers of people making use of the facilities and the frequency of such use
- the range of gambling activities provided by the licensee and the numbers of staff employed in connection with them
- the licensee's policies in relation to, and experiences of, problem gambling.

In particular within 28 days of the end of each quarterly period or, for those only submitting annual returns, within 42 days of the end of each annual period, licensees must submit a Regulatory Return to the Commission containing such information as the Commission may from time to time require[3].

---

3 Regulatory returns can be submitted securely online at the Commission's website at www.gamblingcommission.gov.uk For operators unable to access this system, the forms and a guide to completing them can be requested from the Commission and returned by email to Regulatory.Returns@gamblingcommission.gov.uk or by post to Regulatory Returns, Compliance Administration Team, Gambling Commission, Victoria Square House, Victoria Square, Birmingham, B2 4BP.

SECRETARY OF STATE GENERAL CONDITIONS

None at present

CODES OF PRACTICE

Introduction

This is the Commission's principal code of practice, issued under section 24 of the Gambling Act 2005, as revised with effect from 1 January 2009. There are two types of provision in the code:

- social responsibility provisions: compliance with these is a condition of licences; therefore any breach of them by an operator may lead the Commission to review the operator's licence with a view to suspension, revocation or the imposition of a financial penalty and would also expose the operator to the risk of prosecution; and

- ordinary code provisions: these do not have the status of licence conditions, but are admissible in evidence in criminal or civil proceedings and must be taken into account in any case in which the court or tribunal think them relevant and by the Commission in the exercise of its functions. Any breach of ordinary code provisions by an operator may be taken into account by the Commission on a licence review, but cannot lead to imposition of a financial penalty. These code provisions are in italics in this section and generally set out good practice in these areas.

Financial requirements

ORDINARY CODE PROVISION

In order to help prevent activities related to money laundering licensees should take into account the Commission's advice on the Proceeds of Crime Act 2002, *Duties and responsibilities under the Proceeds of Crime Act 2002. Advice for operators (excluding casino operators).*

Protection of children and other vulnerable persons

COMBATING PROBLEM GAMBLING

SOCIAL RESPONSIBILITY CODE PROVISION

Licensees must have and put into effect policies and procedures intended to promote socially responsible gambling.
Licensees' policies and procedures for socially responsible gambling must include but need not be confined to:

- the specific policies and procedures required by the following provisions of section 2 of this code
- a commitment to and how they will contribute to research into the prevention and treatment of problem gambling
- a commitment to and how they will contribute to public education on the risks of gambling and how to gamble safely
- a commitment to and how they will contribute to the identification and treatment of problem gamblers.

Access to gambling by children and young persons

SOCIAL RESPONSIBILITY CODE PROVISION

Licensees must have and put into effect policies and procedures designed to minimise the risk of lottery tickets being sold to children (that is, persons under 16). This must include procedures for:

- checking the age of apparently underage purchasers of lottery tickets
- taking action when there are unlawful attempts to purchase tickets.

Licensees must take all reasonable steps to ensure that all those engaged in the promotion of lotteries in reliance on the licence understand their responsibilities for preventing underage gambling, returning stakes and not paying prizes to underage customers.

ORDINARY CODE PROVISION

Licensees should require a person who appears to be under the age of 16 to be asked to produce proof of identity and age before purchasing a lottery ticket.

Information on how to gamble responsibly and help for problem gamblers

SOCIAL RESPONSIBILITY CODE PROVISION

Licensees must make information readily available to their customers on how to gamble responsibly and how to access information about, and help in respect of, problem gambling.

The information must cover:

- any measures provided by the licensee to help individuals monitor or control their gambling, such as restricting the duration of a gambling session or the amount of money they can spend
- timers or other forms of reminders or 'reality checks' where available
- self-exclusion options
- information about the availability of further help or advice.

The information must be directed to all customers whether or not licensees also make available material which is directed specifically at customers who may be 'problem gamblers'.

For gambling premises, information must be available in all areas where gambling facilities are provided and adjacent to ATMs where these are not located in a gambling area. As a minimum, information must be displayed prominently on posters appropriate to the size and layout of the premises and contained in leaflets that may be taken away. Licensees must take all reasonable steps to ensure that this information is also readily accessible in locations which enable the customer to obtain it discreetly.

ORDINARY CODE PROVISION

Licensees who market their services in one or more foreign languages should make available in that, or those, foreign languages:

- the information on how to gamble responsibly and access to help referred to above
- the players' guides to any game, bet or lottery required to be made available to customers under provisions in this code
- the summary of the contractual terms on which gambling is offered, which is required to be provided to customers as a condition of the licensee's operating licence.

Customer interaction

SOCIAL RESPONSIBILITY CODE PROVISION

Licensees must put into effect policies and procedures for customer interaction where they have concerns that a customer's behaviour may indicate problem gambling. The policies must include:

- identification of the appropriate level of management who may initiate customer interaction and the procedures for doing so
- the types of behaviour that will be logged/reported to the appropriate level of staff and which may trigger customer interaction at an appropriate moment
- the circumstances in which consideration should be given to refusing service to customers and/or barring them from the operator's gambling premises
- training for all staff on their respective responsibilities, in particular so that they know who is designated to deal with problem gambling issues.

But such policies and procedures must be consistent with, and implemented with due regard to, licensees' duties in respect of the health and safety of their staff.

Self-exclusion

SOCIAL RESPONSIBILITY CODE PROVISION

Licensees must have and put into effect procedures for self-exclusion and take all reasonable steps to refuse service or to otherwise prevent an individual who has entered a self-exclusion agreement from participating in gambling.

Licensees must, as soon as practicable, take all reasonable steps to prevent any marketing material being sent to a self-excluded customer.

Licensees must take steps to remove the name and details of a self-excluded individual from any marketing databases used by the company or group (or otherwise flag that person as an individual to whom marketing material must not be sent), within two days of receiving the completed self-exclusion notification.

This covers any marketing material relating to gambling, or other activities that take place on the premises where gambling may take place. However, it would not extend to blanket marketing which is targeted at a particular geographical area and where the excluded individual would not knowingly be included.

Licensees must close any customer accounts of an individual who has entered a self exclusion agreement and return any funds held in the customer account. It is not sufficient merely to prevent an individual from withdrawing funds from their customer account whilst still accepting wagers from them. Where the giving of credit is permitted, the licensee may retain details of the amount owed to them by the individual, although the account must not be active.

Licensees must put into effect procedures designed to ensure that an individual who has self-excluded cannot gain access to gambling. These procedures must include:

- a register of those excluded with appropriate records (name, address, other details, and any membership or account details that may be held by the operator)
- photo identification (where available and in particular where enforcement of the system may depend on photographic ID), and a signature
- staff training to ensure that staff are able to enforce the systems
- the removal of those persons found in the gambling area or attempting to gamble from the premises.

ORDINARY CODE PROVISION

Self-exclusion procedures should require individuals to take positive action in order to self-exclude. This can be a signature on a self-exclusion form.

Wherever practicable, individuals should be able to self-exclude without having to enter gambling premises.

Before an individual self-excludes, licensees should provide or make available sufficient information about what the consequences of self-exclusion are.

Licensees should take all reasonable steps to extend the self-exclusion to premises of the same type owned by the operator in the customer's local area. In setting the bounds of that area licensees may take into account the customer's address (if known to them), anything else known to them about the distance the customer ordinarily travels to gamble and any specific request the customer may make.

Licensees should encourage the customer to consider extending their self exclusion to other licensees' gambling premises in the customer's local area.

Customers should be given the opportunity to discuss self-exclusion in private, where possible.

Licensees should take steps to ensure that:

- the self-exclusion period is a minimum of six months and give customers the option of extending this to a total of at least five years
- a customer who has decided to enter a self-exclusion agreement is given the opportunity to do so immediately without any cooling-off period. However, if

the customer wishes to consider the self-exclusion further (for example to discuss with problem gambling groups) the customer may return at a later date to enter into self-exclusion

- at the end of the period chosen by the customer (and at least six months later), the self-exclusion remains in place, unless the customer takes positive action in order to gamble again. No marketing material should be sent to the individual unless the individual has taken positive action in order to gamble again, and has agreed to accept such material
- where a customer chooses not to renew the self-exclusion, and makes a positive request to begin gambling again, the customer is given one day to cool off before being allowed access to gambling facilities. The contact must be made via telephone or in person.

The licensee should retain the records relating to a self-exclusion agreement at least until the agreement has been formally ended.

(Please note that the Commission does not require the licensee to carry out any particular assessment or make any judgement as to whether the previously self-excluded individual should again be permitted access to gambling. The requirement to take positive action in person or over the phone is purely to a) check that the customer has considered the decision to access gambling again and allow them to consider the implications; and b) implement the one day cooling-off period and explain why this has been put in place.)

Employment of children and young persons

ORDINARY CODE PROVISION

Licensees who employ young persons (16 and 17 year olds) to sell tickets, collect payments or pay out winnings should have and put into effect policies and procedures designed to ensure that all staff, including staff who are young persons themselves, are made aware that the law prohibits underage gambling, and that tickets may only be sold to persons aged 16 or over.

Provision of credit by licensees and the use of credit cards

SOCIAL RESPONSIBILITY CODE PROVISION

Licensees who choose to accept credit cards must:

- accept payment by credit card for gambling only where that payment is made to a customer account
- make available for gambling, funds deposited via credit card only after the card issuer has approved the transaction.

'Fair and open' provisions

SOCIAL RESPONSIBILITY CODE PROVISION

Licensees must be able to provide evidence to the Commission, if required, showing how they satisfied themselves that their terms are not unfair.

Marketing

SOCIAL RESPONSIBILITY CODE PROVISION

If a licensee makes available to any customer or potential customer any incentive or reward scheme or other arrangement under which the customer may receive money, goods, services or any other advantage (including the discharge in whole or in part of any liability of his) ('the benefit') the scheme must be designed to operate, and be operated, in such a way that:

(a) the circumstances in which, and conditions subject to which, the benefit is available are clearly set out and readily accessible to the customers to whom it is offered;
(b) neither the receipt nor the value or amount of the benefit is:
  (i) dependent on the customer gambling for a pre-determined length of time or with a predetermined frequency; or
  (ii) altered or increased if the qualifying activity or spend is reached within a shorter time than the whole period over which the benefit is offered;
(c) if the value of the benefit increases with the amount the customer spends it does so at a rate no greater than that at which the amount spent increases;

and further that:

(d) if the benefit comprises free or subsidised travel or accommodation which facilitates the customer's attendance at particular licensed premises the terms on which it is offered are not directly related to the level of the customer's prospective gambling.

ORDINARY CODE PROVISION

Licensees should only offer incentive or reward schemes in which the benefit available is proportionate to the type and level of customers' gambling.

ORDINARY CODE PROVISION

With a view to minimising the risk of fraud, licensees who are non-commercial societies or external lottery managers should adopt one or more of the following measures:

- prohibit the unsolicited mailing of tickets to non-members of the promoting society
- limit the value of tickets sent to any one address which is not that of a member of the promoting society to £20
- maintain records of tickets distributed and not returned.

ORDINARY CODE PROVISION

All advertising of gambling products and services should be undertaken in a socially responsible manner. In particular, licensees should comply with the advertising codes of practice which apply to the form and media in which they advertise their gambling facilities or services, and for media not explicitly covered should apply the principles included in these codes of practice as if they were explicitly covered. Licensees should also follow any relevant industry code of practice on advertising.

However, the particular restriction on allowing people aged under 25 to appear in adverts need not be applied to point of sale advertising material, provided that the images used depict the sporting activity that may be gambled on and not the activity of gambling itself and do not offend any other aspect of the advertising codes.

Complaints and disputes

SOCIAL RESPONSIBILITY CODE PROVISION

Licensees must put into effect a written procedure for handling customer complaints and disputes.

In this code a 'complaint' means a complaint about any aspect of the licensee's conduct of the licensed activities, and a 'dispute' is any complaint which:

(a) is not resolved at the first stage of the complaints procedure; and
(b) relates to the outcome of the complainant's gambling transaction.

Licensees must ensure that:

- customers are told the name and status of the person to contact about their complaint
- customers are given a copy of the complaints procedure on request or on making a complaint
- all complaints are handled in accordance with the procedure.

Licensees must also ensure that they have arrangements in place for disputes to be referred to an independent third party. Customers whose disputes are not resolved to their satisfaction by use of the operator's complaints procedure may refer those disputes to this independent third party. The arrangements under which such complaints are referred may, but need not, provide for the third party's decision to be binding on the licensee and the customer.

Licensees must keep a record of all complaints that are not resolved at the first stage of the complaints procedure.

Licensees must arrange for a copy of the decision on, or a note of the outcome of, each dispute referred to the independent party to be provided to the Commission quarterly, either by the independent party or by the licensee.

Gambling licensees' staff

SOCIAL RESPONSIBILITY CODE PROVISION

Licensees must take all reasonable steps to ensure that staff involved in the provision of facilities for gambling are made aware of advice on socially responsible gambling and of where to get confidential advice should their gambling become hard to control.

Information requirements

ORDINARY CODE PROVISION

The Commission expects licensees to work with the Commission in an open and cooperative way and to inform the Commission of any matters that the Commission would reasonably need to be aware of in exercising its regulatory functions. These are matters that will have a material impact on the licensee's business or on the licensee's ability to conduct its business. Such matters, which should be notified to the Commission as soon as reasonably practicable[4], include the following:

- the departure from the licensee's business of any person named in the licence application, or that person's successor, who holds a personal management licence, but who does not occupy a 'qualifying position'
- any reduction in the number of staff employed by the licensee where that has a material impact on the licensee's business
- the acquisition or disposal by the licensee of gambling premises or pitches where that has a material impact on the size or nature of the licensee's business
- in the case of corporate licensees, the disposal or acquisition of any group company where that has a material impact on the licensee's ability to conduct its business
- any disposal of the licensee's assets where that has a material impact on the licensee's business
- any investigation by a professional, statutory, regulatory or government body into the licensee's activities, or the activities in relation to the licensed entity of a personal licence holder or a person occupying a qualifying position employed by them, where such an investigation could result in the imposition of a sanction or penalty which, if imposed, could reasonably be expected to raise doubts about the licensee's continued suitability to hold a Gambling Commission licence
- any instance of criminal activity, including repeated instances of small-scale theft or fraud, where that has a material impact on the licensee's business

- any major breach in the licensee's information security where that adversely affects the confidentiality of customer data or prevents customers from accessing their accounts for a substantial period of time
- any other matters that have a material impact on the licensee's business or on the licensee's ability to conduct its business.

---

4 These matters can be reported securely online at the Commission's website at www.gamblingcommission.gov.uk or by email to key.events@gamblingcommission.gov.uk or posted to Key Events, Compliance Administration Team, Gambling Commission, Victoria Square House, Victoria Square, Birmingham, B2 4BP

Gambling Commission October 2010

LOTTERIES – WHAT DO WE MEAN BY 'LOTTERIES'?

6.2350 Regulated lotteries are run in support of good causes; they cannot be run for private or commercial gain. Under the Gambling Act 2005, the Gambling Commission continues to regulate larger society lotteries with proceeds of over £20,000 in a single lottery or total proceeds of over £250,000 in a calendar year, and local authority lotteries.

Societies and local authorities promoting these lotteries and external lottery managers will need to be licensed by the Commission. Smaller society lotteries will be regulated, as now, by local authorities. The National Lottery is regulated under different legislation, by the National Lottery Commission. There are three classes of exempt lotteries (ie lotteries where the sales are restricted to a single site) which do not need to be registered with any regulator.

The key financial requirements for society lotteries include: a maximum of £2 million proceeds (ticket sales) in any one lottery; a maximum of £10 million aggregate annual proceeds (ticket sales) in successive lotteries; a maximum prize of £25,000 or 10 % of the proceeds if greater, up to a maximum prize of £200,000; and a requirement that at least 20 % of the proceeds go directly to the purposes of the society promoting the lottery.

Lottery providers and promoters must be licensed by the Commission and pursue the Act's licensing objectives. For example, lotteries are required to put in place procedures aimed at preventing tickets from being sold to children.

HOW ARE LOTTERIES REGULATED?

Most organisations and individuals that provide facilities for participating in a lottery require a licence to operate. The Commission has developed licence conditions and codes of practice that govern licence holders and has powers to prosecute or impose fines on operators who breach their licence conditions.

There are two types of licence required by those running a lottery:

- Operating licences are required by those that provide lotteries in Britain.
- Personal licences are required by individuals in certain management positions except for those organisations categorised as small-scale operators.

LOTTERY FACTS AND FIGURES

- Proceeds raised by societies' lotteries fell from £141.1 million in 2004/05 to £138.7 million in 2005/06, a decrease of £2.4 million or nearly 2%.
- Of the society ticket sales in 2005/06, around £29 million (21%) went on prizes, around £35 million (25%) went on expenses and the remaining £73 million (53%) went to the good cause.
- Gross gambling yield (ie the amount retained by operators after the payment of winnings but before the deduction of the costs of the operation) was estimated at £2,450 million in 2006.

Gambling Commission August 2007

PRIZE COMPETITIONS AND FREE DRAWS: THE REQUIREMENTS OF THE GAMBLING ACT 2005

To avoid duplication this document has not been reproduced here but can be found at para 6.2089 above.

LOTTERY GUIDANCE FOR CHARITY TRADING COMPANIES AND SPORTING CLUBS: GAMBLING ACT 2005

December 2007

CHARITY TRADING COMPANIES

6.2351–6.2352 A number of charities who run lotteries as one of their fundraising activities have traditionally done so through a trading company, and often it has been that company, rather than the charity itself, which registers with the Gambling Commission (and its predecessor, the Gaming Board for Great Britain) under Schedule 1A of the Lotteries & Amusements Act 1976.

Concern has been expressed in some quarters as to whether this practice may properly continue under the new licensing arrangements in the Gambling Act 2005 ("the Act"). Under the Act, a lottery operating licence may only be issued by the Commission to a non-commercial society, a local authority, or a person proposing to act as an external lottery manager on behalf of such societies or local authorities.

Section 19 of the Act defines a "non-commercial society" as follows:

NON-COMMERCIAL SOCIETY

(1) For the purposes of this Act a society is non-commercial if it is established and conducted –
   (a) for charitable purposes,
   (b) for the purpose of enabling participation in, or of supporting, sport, athletics or a cultural activity; or
   (c) for any other non-commercial purpose other than that of private gain.

(2) In subsection (1) "charitable purposes" means –
   (a) in relation to England and Wales, purposes which are exclusively charitable according to the law of England and Wales, and
   (b) in relation to Scotland, purposes which are charitable purposes only (that expression having the same meaning as in the Income Tax Acts).

(3) The provision of a benefit to one or more individuals is not a provision for the purpose of private gain for the purposes of this Act if made in the course of the activities of a society that is a non-commercial society by virtue of subsection (1)(a) or (b).

A question has arisen whether a charity's trading company can be regarded as established and conducted for a "non-commercial" purpose, particularly when the company may, typically, be involved not only in running a lottery to support its parent charity, but also in selling merchandise (perhaps from a charity shop) to generate profits which can be donated to that charity, or where the charity is a membership organisation, providing services to members with a view to a modest profit for charity funds.

Whilst the Courts are the only body that can provide a definitive ruling on the meaning of legislation, the Commission sets out here the circumstances in which it considers charity trading companies may satisfy the Act's "non-commercial" test.

Under paragraph 67 in Schedule 4 to The Gambling Act 2005 (Commencement No.6 and Transitional Provisions) Order 2006 (SI 2006 No 3272) the Commission has a duty to grant a lottery operating licence to every society which, as at 1 September 2007, has a registration with it according to Schedule 1A of the 1976 Act. That obligation will be honoured.

Looking to the future, the Commission appreciates that a charity's trading subsidiary has a "commercial" purpose in the sense that it intends its activities to generate profit; but the intention is to do so in order to pass that profit to its parent charity.

Accordingly, whilst the Commission takes the view that it would be entirely appropriate for any charity wishing to promote a lottery to raise funds, to obtain a lottery operating licence (whether it runs the lotteries in-house or engages the services of an external lottery manager), nevertheless the Commission will consider charities' trading subsidiaries as eligible to hold licences under section 19(1)(a) of the Act for so long as they are either:

- companies limited by guarantee whose member is the charity or whose members are the trustees of the charity;
- companies limited by shares and all of the shares are held by the charity, or its Trustees;
- in either case:
  - the company's purposes includes expressed or implied support of the charity;
  - the company's powers extend to the promotion of lotteries; and
  - the company's net profits in any trading period are subject only to a reasonable retention, (generally thought to be not more than 10%) for working capital purposes) donated to the charity under a Deed of Covenant or Gift Aid.

SPORTING CLUBS

In the issue of sporting clubs holding lottery licences, it is our view that these organisations fall within section 19(1)(b) and are therefore deemed non-commercial.

QUALIFYING AS NON-COMMERCIAL

If a charity is concerned whether its trading subsidiary would qualify as a non-commercial society, or a sporting club is concerned as to whether it can hold a lottery licence, please contact the Gambling Commission.

Gambling Commission December 2007

LICENCE CONDITION 2 – RANDOM NUMBER GENERATOR TESTING AND SECURITY AUDITS

14 April 2008

6.2353 Dear Colleague

This letter is relevant to holders of the following Gambling Commission licences:

- remote society lottery operating licences
- converted lottery operating licences (but only those licensees that run remote lotteries[1] themselves or via a lottery manager)
- remote lottery managers' operating licences (also known as external lottery managers)

Condition 2 of your licence states that "Licensees must comply with the Commission's technical standards and with requirements set out by the Commission relating to the timing and procedures for testing". The Commission's Remote Testing Strategy[2] provides for the Commission to change the testing requirements applicable to such licence holders based on the perceived risk they pose to the licensing objectives.

It is the Commission's view that lotteries in general pose a relatively low risk to the licensing objectives and that this should be reflected by the Commission in taking a proportionate approach to the requirements that:

- a Commission approved test house is used to conduct a test of random number generators (RNGs)
- a third party security audit firm is used to conduct an annual audit of information security

The Commission has set out below the criteria it will apply to remote lottery licensees (including external lottery managers) when determining the specific testing and audit arrangements it requires. Licensees will need to meet these criteria no later than 1 September 2008.

---

1 A remote lottery is where people participate in the lottery by using the internet, telephone, television, radio or any other kind of electronic or other technology for facilitating communication.

2 'Testing Strategy for Compliance with the Remote Gambling and Software Technical Standards – June 2007'.

TESTING OF THE RANDOM NUMBER GENERATOR

Holders of remote society lottery operating licences, converted lottery operating licences or remote lottery managers' licences that accept no more than £250,000 worth of entries per year by means of remote communication will not be required to submit their RNG for testing by a Commission approved test house.

Instead such licensees will be required to demonstrate that:

(1) their RNG has been tested or verified as being fair and random by an independent and suitably qualified third party. This fact should be supported by documentary evidence.

(2) they have policies and procedures in place which set out how they ensure the lottery draw is fair and open and can produce evidence of these procedures being followed.

Holders of such licences that accept more than £250,000 worth of entries per year by means of remote communication will be required to ensure their RNG is tested by a Commission approved test house as set out in the Commission's Remote Testing Strategy.

SECURITY AUDIT

The Remote Testing Strategy states that subscription lotteries[3] do not require a third party annual security audit but the Commission will audit the subscription lotteries against the requirements.

In addition holders of remote society lottery operating licences, converted lottery operating licences and remote lottery manager's licences that accept no more than £250,000 worth of entries per year by remote communication are not required to submit to a third party annual security audit.

Instead such licensees must have in place, and will be required to demonstrate to Commission Compliance managers during routine compliance visits that they comply with the security requirements set out in Annex C to the *Remote Gambling and Software Technical Standards*.

Holders of such licences that accept more than £250,000 worth of entries per year by means of remote communication will be required to submit to a third party annual security audit to show they comply with the security requirements set out in Annex C to the *Remote Gambling and Software Technical Standards*.

These criteria will be reflected in the next edition of the Commission's Remote Testing Strategy.

Yours sincerely

Cliff Young National Compliance Manager – Lotteries

[3] A subscription lottery is a series of lotteries (other than instant lotteries) promoted on behalf of the same noncommercial society or local authority in respect of which participants pay for participation in one or more future lotteries by regular subscription over a fixed or indefinite period of time.

Gambling Commission April 2008

ADVICE NOTE

Running a lottery including raffles, tombolas, sweepstakes and more

November 2009

6.2354 People have a variety of reasons for wanting to run a lottery. They may want to collect money for a good cause such as a charity or help their local sports club buy some equipment or simply to have some fun by running an office sweepstake.

Whatever the reason – fundraising or just fun – lotteries are a form of gambling and so there is a need for safeguards and other regulations.

These regulations are all set out in the Gambling Act 2005 and are the responsibility of the Gambling Commission, which has issued this leaflet.

We will try to answer some initial questions and help you to decide which type of lottery to go for.

The Gambling Commission does not regulate the National Lottery. The National Lottery Commission regulates all National Lottery products.

WHAT EXACTLY IS A LOTTERY?

A lottery is a kind of gambling which has three essential ingredients:

- You have to pay to enter the game
- There is always at least one prize
- Prizes are awarded purely on chance

Atypical small-scale lottery is a raffle where players buy a ticket with a number on it. The tickets are randomly drawn and those holding the same numbered ticket win a prize.

Another version is a sweepstake, for example, where the participants pay to randomly draw the names of a horse in a race. The person who draws the winning horse wins the entry money

There are other versions too, such as a tombola – often found at a funday or summer fete; or a 100 club which is often a weekly event organised, for members only, by a PTA.

As well as the three elements of a lottery outlined above, they all have something else in common: while there is no maximum price for a ticket, in each lottery all tickets must cost the same. That way, everyone has the same chance of winning for the same outlay.

TYPES OF LOTTERY UNDER THE GAMBLING ACT 2005

Types of lottery under the Gambling Act 2005For legal reasons, the Gambling Act has created eight categories of lottery, each of which has its own dos and don'ts. Here is a short description of them, together with a table on the back page to answer some initial queries.

These types of lottery require permission, find out more about them in *Promoting society and local authority lotteries* a publication on the Commission website.

Small society lotteries The society in question must be set up for non-commercial purposes eg sports, cultural or charitable. There is a top limit of £20,000 in ticket sales.

Large society lotteries Similar to the small society lottery, but there is a minimum of £20,000 in ticket sales.

Local authority lotteries Run by the local authority, to help with any expenditure it normally incurs.

These types of lottery do not require permission, find out more about them in *Organising small lotteries* a publication on the Commission website.

Private society lotteries Any group or society except those set up for gambling. The proceeds of the lottery must go to the purposes of the society.

Work lotteries These can only be run and played by colleagues at a particular place of work. This type of lottery cannot make a profit, and so is unsuitable for fundraising.

Residents' lotteries These can only be run and played by people living at a particular address. This type of lottery cannot make a profit, and so is unsuitable for fundraising.

Customer lotteries These can only be run by a business, at its own premises and for its own customers. No prize can be more than £50 in value. This type of lottery cannot make a profit, and so is unsuitable for fundraising.

Incidental non-commercial lotteries These are held at non-commercial events, such as school fetes etc. All the sales and the draw must take place during the main event, which may last more than a single day. Prizes cannot total more than £500.

WHAT ABOUT THE PRIZES?

Apart from the individual limit in customer lotteries and the overall limit in non-commercial lotteries, there are no restrictions. Prizes in all categories can be monetary or non-monetary; they can be cash, goods or services. Under the licensing laws alcohol must not be awarded to anyone under 18. The police or local authority can give advice on this.

The following refers to the table on the back page

SYSTEM A

Tickets must show the name of the society and/or the purpose of the lottery, the ticket price, the name and address of the organiser and the date of the draw.

SYSTEM B

Tickets must show the name and address of the organiser, the ticket price, any restrictions as to who may or may not buy a ticket, and state that the rights created by the ticket are non-transferable.

SYSTEM C

There are no specific requirements for tickets.

Type of lottery	Fund raising?	Who can play?	Who can run one?	Limits on time	Limits on place	Can I claim my costs?	Ticket system (see over)
Types of lottery that require permission							
Small society	Yes, at least 20% of the proceeds	Over 16s	Society members or nominated fundraisers	None	Check with licensing authority	Yes, for prizes and expense. Up to 80% of sales	A
Large society	Yes, at least 20% of the proceeds	Over 16s	Society members or nominated fundraisers	None	Not in public street	Yes, for prizes and expense. Up to 80% of sales	A
Local authority	Yes, at least 20% of the proceeds	Over 16s	Authority nominees	None	Not in public street	Yes, for prizes and expense. Up to 80% of sales	C
Types of lottery that do not require permission							
Private society	Yes	Members or guests on the premises	Society members	One-off. No rollovers	Members or guests must be on premises	Yes, for prizes and reasonable lottery running costs	B
work	No profit can be made	Employees at a single premises only	Any employees	One-off. No rollovers	No sales or ads off premises. Single premises only	Yes, for prizes and reasonable lottery running costs	B
Residents'	No profit can be made	Residents at a single premises only	Any residents	One-off. No rollovers	No ads off premises	Yes, for prizes and reasonable lottery running costs	B
Customer	No profit can be made	Your customers	Occupier of business premises	7 days between. No rollovers	No sales or ads off premises	Yes, for prizes and reasonable lottery running costs	B

Type of lottery	Fund raising?	Who can play?	Who can run one?	Limits on time	Limits on place	Can I claim my costs?	Ticket system (see over)
Types of lottery that require permission							
Incidental non-commercial	Yes	Anyone at the event	Anyone	One-off. Sales only at event.	Only at event	£100 max	C

Gambling Commission November 2009

REVERSE AUCTIONS
Frequently Asked Questions, June 2008

1 WHAT IS A REVERSE AUCTION?

6.2355 1.1 Reverse auctions are schemes where to win a prize participants must make the lowest unique bid (generally in pence). Depending on the format (online, TV, radio, SMS or print) the prize is shown or described (including the retail value) and participants are asked to submit a bid. Operators charge participants for each bid they make. Bids are generally made via text message (at a premium rate) or through registering with the operators website and paying by debit/credit card or pre-purchased credits.

1.2 The prize is won by the person who makes the lowest unique bid. As well as the cost of making each bid the winning participant is usually required to pay the amount of their winning bid to receive the prize.

1.3 Reverse auctions tend to fall into two categories:

- those where operators only provide participants with information on whether they were successful or not; or
- those where the operator provides additional information, usually following the submission of a first bid. For example:
  full bid history;
  placement of received bid; and/or
  current lowest unique bid.

2 WHAT IS THE GAMBLING COMMISSION'S INTEREST IN REVERSE AUCTIONS?

2.1 The Gambling Act 2005 (the Act) contains provisions designed to make clear the distinction between lotteries and prize competitions and free draws. Although the Gambling Commission (the Commission) has no regulatory responsibilities in respect of competitions and draws it does monitor the boundary between them and lotteries. The Commission has duties in respect of pursuing and prosecuting illegal gambling and will act where schemes are organised and promoted, that in our view, amount to unlicensed and therefore illegal lotteries.

2.2 Depending on how a reverse auction is operated it could be considered to be a lottery.

3 CAN REVERSE AUCTIONS BE OPERATED AS PRIZE COMPETITIONS UNDER THE GAMBLING ACT 2005?

3.1 A prize competition is one where success depends on the exercise of skill, judgement or knowledge by the participants and does not, as it does in a lottery rely wholly on chance.

3.2 Reverse auctions can be operated as prize competitions under the Gambling Act 2005, provided they comply with the test set out in the Act at section 14(5). This says that a genuine prize competition is one that contains a requirement to exercise skill or judgement or to display knowledge and where it can reasonably be expected that that requirement will either:

- prevent a significant proportion of people who wish to participate from doing so (section 14(5)(b) of the Act); or
- prevent a significant proportion of people who participate from receiving a prize (section 14(5)(a)).

4 WHAT CAN I DO TO ENSURE THE REVERSE AUCTIONS I OPERATE ARE COMPLIANT WITH THE GAMBLING ACT 2005?

4.1 To ensure that reverse auctions are compliant with the requirements in respect of prize competitions in the Gambling Act 2005 success must be dependent on the skill, judgement and knowledge of participants rather than chance.

4.2 Examples of factors that may enable operators of reverse auctions to ensure they are compliant include time limits for the submission of bids, the provision of information to participants about previous winning bids (for similar items) and updates on the status of their current bid(s). Operating reverse auctions of this type may make it possible for participants to apply a strategy to their bidding (demonstrating a requirement for a level of skill or application of knowledge).

5 WHAT WILL HAPPEN IF MY REVERSE AUCTION IS NOT COMPLIANT AND IS JUDGED TO BE AN UNLICENSED LOTTERY?

5.1 If a reverse auction does not meet the test for prize competitions set out in section 14 of the Act, and all the elements of a lottery are present — that is payment, chance and allocation of prizes — then it may be an unlicensed and therefore unlawful lottery.

5.2 The Commission has duties in respect of pursuing and prosecuting illegal gambling and will act where schemes are organised and promoted which, in our view, amount to unlicensed and therefore illegal public lotteries.

5.3 Operators of reverse auctions that do not meet the test in the Act have three options available to them:

- cease to operate;
- adapt their reverse auction schemes to ensure they are compliant with section 14 of the Act; or
- apply to the Commission for a Lottery Operating Licence, and be subject to the regulations and Licence Conditions and Codes of Practice associated with this type of licence.

5.4 The onus lies on the operators of reverse auctions to satisfy themselves that their schemes are compliant with the law. If they are in doubt, they should seek legal advice.

For further information or to register your interest in the Commission please visit our website at: www.gamblingcommission.gov.uk

Gambling Commission June 2008

PROMOTING SOCIETY AND LOCAL AUTHORITY LOTTERIES

Advice for society and local authority lotteries which require a licence or registration

November 2009

1 INTRODUCTION

6.2356–6.2357 1.1 Lotteries are illegal unless they fall into one of the categories specifically permitted by law. Apart from the National Lottery (which has its own dedicated legislation), the relevant law is contained in the Gambling Act 2005 (the Act). The Act creates eight categories of permitted lottery. Three of these categories (small and large society lotteries and local authority lotteries) require either a licence from the Gambling Commission (the Commission) if they are a large society or local authority lottery, or registration with a licensing authority if they are a small society lottery. This advice relates to these lotteries. Advice on the remaining five categories can be found in a separate document called Organising small lotteries (Gambling Act 2005).

1.2 This advice is not comprehensive or a binding interpretation of the law and anyone intending to run a lottery should refer to the Act and if necessary seek independent legal advice to ensure that they conform to the law before proceeding. Separate advice has been issued to local authorities in respect of small society lotteries under their jurisdiction.

1.3 The Act has three licensing objectives that are central to the regulatory regime and underpin the functions that the Commission and licensing authorities perform in respect of all types of gambling, including lotteries. These are:

- preventing gambling from being a source of crime or disorder, being associated with crime or disorder, or being used to support crime
- ensuring that gambling is conducted in a fair and open way
- protecting children and other vulnerable people from being harmed or exploited by gambling.

2 DEFINITION OF A LOTTERY

2.1 In simple terms a lottery is a kind of gambling that has three essential elements:

- payment is required to participate
- one or more prizes are awarded
- those prizes are awarded by chance.

This is set out more formally in the Act which defines two types of lottery, a simple lottery and a complex lottery.

2.2 An arrangement is a simple lottery if:

- people are required to pay to participate in the arrangement
- in the course of the arrangement one or more prizes are allocated to one or more people in a class
- the prizes are allocated by a process which relies wholly on chance.

2.3 An arrangement is a complex lottery if:

- people are required to pay to participate in the arrangement
- in the course of the arrangement one or more prizes are allocated to one or more people in a class
- the prizes are allocated by a series of processes
- the first of those processes relies wholly on chance.

2.4 In addition, section 14(5) of the Act stipulates that, for the purpose of these definitions, a process that requires people to exercise skill or judgment or display knowledge is to be treated as relying wholly on chance if:

- the requirement cannot reasonably be expected to prevent a significant proportion of people who participate in the arrangement from receiving a prize
- it cannot reasonably be expected to prevent a significant proportion of people who wish to participate in the arrangement from doing so.

3 MEANING OF SOCIETY AND LOCAL AUTHORITY LOTTERIES

SOCIETY LOTTERIES

3.1 Society lotteries are lotteries promoted for the benefit of a non-commercial society. Such societies are organisations that have distinct aims and objectives and meet the definition of a non-commercial society set out in the Act.

3.2 A society is non-commercial if it is established and conducted:

- for charitable purposes
- for the purpose of enabling participation in, or of supporting, sport, athletics or a cultural activity
- for any other non-commercial purpose other than that of private gain.

LOCAL AUTHORITY LOTTERIES

3.3 Local authority lotteries are lotteries promoted by local authorities themselves. These differ from society lotteries registered with a licensing authority. Authorities may use the net proceeds of such lotteries for any purpose for which they have power to incur expenditure.

4 LARGE SOCIETY AND LOCAL AUTHORITY LOTTERY LICENSING REQUIREMENTS

4.1 A society lottery is a large lottery and may only be run under an operating licence issued by the Commission if the arrangements for that lottery are such that total proceeds (ticket sales) from it:

- may in a single society lottery exceed £20,000,
- or the proceeds of previous lotteries in the same calendar year have already reached or may, taking into account the lottery in question reach £250,000 in one calendar year.

4.2 If a society promotes a lottery which, applying the above rules, is a large lottery (the first lottery) then every subsequent lottery it promotes in that year and in the following three years will also be a large lottery and will require the society to hold a lottery operating licence issued by the Commission.

4.3 All local authority lotteries must be run under an operating licence issued by the Commission.

4.4 Societies and local authorities that allow players to participate in their lotteries by means of remote communication (internet, telephone etc) will be required to hold a remote lottery operating licence, whether or not their activities also require them to hold a non remote lottery operating licence.

4.5 General information about the Commission's licensing requirements is given in this document. Specific guidance is available on the Commission's website.

5 SMALL SOCIETY LOTTERIES

5.1 Societies that run small society lotteries, that is to say lotteries in which no more than £20,000 worth of tickets are put on sale and where the society's aggregate proceeds from lotteries do not exceed £250,000 a year may operate without a Commission licence provided they register with their licensing authority. Where it becomes apparent that a small society lottery will exceed either of the monetary limits, it is the responsibility of the society to ensure they apply to the Commission for a licence, before the limit is exceeded.

5.2 The promoting society of a small society lottery must, throughout the period during which the lottery is promoted, be registered with a licensing authority in England and Wales or a licensing board in Scotland.

5.3 The societies are required to be registered with their licensing authority in the area where their principal office is located. If the local authority believes that the society's principal office is situated in another area it should inform the society as soon as possible and if possible inform that other authority.

5.4 Details of registration requirements and procedures can be obtained from the licensing department of the relevant local authority.

5.5 Societies that run small society lotteries under registration with a licensing authority and that sell tickets by means of remote communication (internet, telephone etc) are not required to hold a remote gambling licence issued by the Commission.

6 PERSONAL MANAGEMENT LICENCES

6.1 A society or local authority licensed by the Gambling Commission is required to have at least one Personal Management Licence (PML) holder if they have more than three people in qualifying positions.

6.2 A qualifying position is one where an individual by the terms of their appointment has primary responsibility for:

- the management of the licensed activity (ie the lottery)
- the financial affairs of the society
- ensuring the society complies with the requirements of the Gambling Act

- the marketing of the lottery
- management of the IT used in connection with the lottery.

6.3 In deciding who should hold the PML a society or local authority should identify the relevant senior individual who takes overall management responsibility for the promotion and proper management of the lottery and for compliance with the regulatory regime as a whole. The PML holder must be a trustee or officer of an unincorporated society, a director of a corporate society or a partner where the society is a partnership. In the case of a local authority lottery the PML holder must be someone in a senior management post who holds the relevant delegated authority from the licensing authority.

6.4 If a society has three or fewer people in qualifying positions they will qualify as a small scale operator and will be exempt from the need to have a PML holder. In those circumstances one individual from the society who is identified as the senior person responsible for the overall conduct of the lottery (usually the chief executive, a trustee, director or member of the senior management board) must complete the personal declaration (Annex A) of the Operating Licence application form and submit it to the Commission along with a Criminal Records Bureau form.

6.5 A society must not operate any lottery unless it has at least one PML holder or at least one Individual who has submitted an Annex A and is named on the operating licence. If the people holding PMLs or the people who have previously submitted Annex A Personal Declarations under the small scale operator exemption change, the society must notify the Commission as soon as possible. If departures leave the society without a PML holder or anyone who has submitted an Annex A, then a new individual needs to make an application for a PML, or in the case of those operators subject to the small scale operator exemption, submit an Annex A. The latter will also require an amendment to the operating licence. Both instances will require a Criminal Records Bureau check as well as appropriate payment.

6.6 Detailed guidance on PMLs and the small scale operator exemption are available on the Commission's website.

7 EXTERNAL LOTTERY MANAGERS

7.1 A licensed or registered society or local authority may employ an external lottery manager (ELM) to manage all or part of its lottery. An ELM is defined in section 257 of the Act as someone that is a person or a body who makes arrangements for a lottery on behalf of a society or local authority but is not a member, officer or employee of the society or authority.

7.2 All ELMs must hold a lottery manager's operating licence issued by the Commission before they can manage a licensed society or local authority lottery or a society lottery registered with a local authority. It is the responsibility of the society or local authority to ensure that before employing anyone to manage all or part of their lottery that person or body holds a valid lottery manager's operating licence issued by the Commission. A list of licensed ELMs is available on the Commission's website.

7.3 The fact that a society or local authority may employ a licensed ELM to manage all or part of its lottery does not absolve the society or local authority from its responsibility for ensuring that the lottery is conducted in such a way as to ensure that it is lawful and fully complies with all licence conditions and the codes of practice. Both the society or local authority and the ELM require an operating licence from the Commission.

7.4 ELMs are also required to hold Personal Management Licences for a range of directors and senior managers, including the managing director, chief executive, finance director, compliance manager, marketing manager and IT manager.

7.5 ELMs also need to hold a remote gambling licence if they intend to sell tickets by means of remote communication (internet, telephone etc).

8 EXTERNAL LOTTERY MANAGERS AND SERVICE PROVIDERS

8.1 Uncertainty can arise as to whether services provided to societies or local authorities amount to the promotion or facilitation of a lottery, in which case the provider needs an ELM licence if they are to avoid committing an offence, or instead amount to the provision of services which do not amount to promotion or facilitation, in which case no licence is needed. The following paragraphs give some guidance on the distinction. But anyone who is uncertain whether the services provided require the provider to hold an ELM licence should contact the Commission for advice.

8.2 Under section 252 of the Act, a person promotes a lottery if they make or participate in making the arrangements for a lottery. It says further that a person promotes a lottery in particular if they:

- make arrangements for the printing of tickets
- make arrangements for the printing, publication and distribution of promotional material
- make arrangements to advertise a lottery
- invite an individual to participate in a lottery
- sell or supply tickets
- offer to sell or supply tickets
- use premises for the purpose of allocating prizes or for any other purpose connected with the administration of a lottery.

Promotional material is defined as a document that advertises, invites participation, contains information about how to participate, or lists winners, in a particular lottery.

8.3 A person commits an offence under the Act if they carry out any of these activities on behalf of a society or local authority unless:

- they are an officer, employee or a member of a licensed or registered society or local authority
- or they are a licensed ELM directed by a society or local authority to run all or part of its lottery.

8.4 Under section 259, a person facilitates a lottery if they:

- print lottery tickets for a specified lottery
- print promotional material for a specified lottery
- advertise a specified lottery.

A person commits an offence of facilitating a society or local authority lottery unless they act in accordance with an operating licence.

8.5 Whether or not a person or body carrying out activities on behalf of a society or local authority requires licensing as an ELM will depend on the activities they conduct and whether they amount to either promoting or facilitating a lottery and, if so, the circumstances in which they carry out those activities. For instance companies which print tickets for or which advertise lotteries under direction from licensed or registered societies or licensed ELMs do not themselves require a licence because, although they are facilitating a lottery, they are acting in accordance with a licence held by someone else.

8.6 To take another example, direct mailing companies employed by society lotteries may be classed as either a service provider or ELM, depending on the functions they carry out. If their only role is to post tickets to people to participate in the lottery from a list provided by the society or ELM, the Commission does not think they are doing any of the things that fall into the definition above of promoting a lottery. However, where a person or body is responsible for and manages part or all of the lottery and decides issues such as where to target promotional material, sources people to enter the lottery and deals with ticket transactions, they are carrying out functions that are caught by the definition of promoting a lottery and require a licence.

8.7 The Commission considers that the Act provides a comprehensive definition of what amounts to promoting or facilitating a lottery for the purpose of determining whether an ELM licence is needed for people or bodies providing services to societies or local authorities. In cases where there is doubt whether or not a person or body is acting in the role of an ELM, the Commission will have regard to the overall management and degree of control of the lottery undertaken by the society and the other party in question. Where the person or body making any of the arrangements for a society or local authority lottery, for example, has control of how the lottery is promoted and managed, the Commission's view is that they will be acting as an ELM and will need to hold the relevant operating licence issued by the Commission if they are to avoid committing an offence under the Act. Key indicators the Commission uses in reaching a conclusion include:

- who decides how the lottery scheme will operate and when changes to the scheme should be made
- who controls the promotion, marketing and advertising of the lottery
- who sells the tickets
- who pays the prizes
- who appoints and manages sub contractors
- banking arrangements and the process for handling the proceeds of the lottery
- the contractual agreements between the society and the other party.

9 REMOTE LOTTERIES

9.1 Section 4 of the Gambling Act specifies that remote gambling means gambling in which people participate by the use of remote communication including the internet, telephone, television, radio or any other electronic or technological method of communication. Normal letter post is not a form of remote communication for the purposes of the Act.

9.2 Societies and local authorities requiring licensing by the Commission and which allow players to participate in their lotteries by means of remote communication will be required to hold a remote lottery operating licence. For example, those accepting payments by telephone, or over the internet, will require a remote operating licence.

9.3 Holders of a remote lottery operating licence will be required to comply with the technical standards and the other specific licence conditions and codes of practice issued by the Commission that relate to remote gambling. Only remote lottery operating licence holders that accept more than £250,000 worth of entries by remote means per year will be required to meet the full testing and third party security audit requirements. Further details are available on the Commission's website.

9.4 Societies registered with licensing authorities that allow people to participate in their lottery by way of remote communication are not required to hold a remote lottery operating licence.

10 GAMBLING COMMISSION LICENCE CONDITIONS AND CODES OF PRACTICE

10.1 All societies and local authorities licensed by the Commission to run lotteries are required to comply with the specific licence conditions and codes of practice relevant to them. The specific licence conditions are set out at the time a licence is issued.

10.2 Some of the licence conditions and requirements of the codes of practice are referred to below. Specific details are contained in the Commission's Licence Conditions and Codes of Practice, which is available on the Commission's website.

11 SOCIETY AND LOCAL AUTHORITY LOTTERIES – PROCEEDS AND OTHER MONETARY LIMITS

11.1 A society or local authority lottery must apply a minimum of 20% of the gross proceeds of each lottery directly to the purposes of the society or in the case of a local authority a purpose for which the authority has power to incur expenditure.

11.2 Up to a maximum of 80% of the gross proceeds of each lottery may be divided between prizes and the expenses of the lottery.

11.3 In a single large society or local authority lottery the maximum value of tickets that can be sold is £4 million. The maximum aggregate value of lottery tickets that can be sold in any calendar year is £10 million.
11.4 The maximum prize in a single lottery is £25,000 in the case of a small society lottery and £25,000 or 10% of the proceeds (gross ticket sales), whichever is greater, in the case of a large society or local authority lottery. Therefore, a society that sells the maximum number of tickets in a single large lottery (£4 million) could award a maximum top prize of £400,000.
11.5 Rollovers are permitted provided the maximum single prize limit is not breached.
11.6 Every ticket in the lottery must be the same price and the cost of purchased tickets must be paid to the society before entry into the draw is allowed.
11.7 There is no maximum price of a lottery ticket.
11.8 No lottery organised by a large society or local authority may operate in such a way that a player can win a prize greater than the statutory prize limit of £400,000.
11.9 No lottery organised by a large society or local authority may be linked to any other lottery in such a way that a person who wins a prize in one also wins a prize in another, unless the aggregate of those prizes is less than or equal to the statutory prize limit of £400,000.
11.10 Where separate lotteries have a feature that allows a player to win a larger prize than the statutory maximum of £400,000 by selecting the same numbers in different lotteries and these lotteries are decided by the same draw, no advertisement or other marketing of the lotteries may refer to this feature. A lottery cannot be linked to a prize competition or free draw if the maximum amount which a person can win is more that £400,000 in aggregate.

12 TICKET INFORMATION

12.1 All tickets in a society lottery licensed by the Commission or registered with a local authority must state:

- the name of the society on whose behalf the lottery is being promoted
- the price of the ticket
- the name and address of the member of the society responsible for the promotion of the lottery. In the case of a small society lottery run under local authority registration the name and address of the ELM if there is one may be given as an alternative
- the date of the draw, or the means by which the date may be determined
- the fact, where that is the case, that the society is licensed by the Commission
- the website address of the Commission, if licensed by the Commission.

12.2 Tickets that are issued through a form of remote communication or any other electronic manner must specify the information above to the purchaser of the ticket and ensure that the message can be either retained (saved) or printed.

13 SALE OF TICKETS

13.1 Tickets in society and local authority lotteries promoted under licence from the Commission must not be sold to anyone in a street. Tickets may be sold by a person in a kiosk or from a shop premises in a street, or from door to door. For this purpose a street includes any bridge, road, lane, footway, subway, square, court, alley or passage (including passages through enclosed premises such as shopping malls) whether a thoroughfare or not. The Commission has recommended to licensing authorities that they also apply this restriction to small society lotteries. Small societies should check the licensing authority they are registered with.
13.2 Lottery tickets must not be sold to, or by, those under the age of 16.
13.3 Society lottery tickets may be sold from vending machines. These machines may be sited anywhere that a society lottery ticket can be sold (see 13.1). They are not subject to restrictions on the number that can be sited and no licence is required to site

or supply them. However, licensed operators (societies and/or ELMs) must ensure that they fulfil their social responsibility duties under the licence conditions and codes of practice in respect of preventing underage play and problem gambling. In the case of lottery ticket vending machines the operator may wish to ensure that the machine is located in a supervised area or that some other arrangements are put in place to prevent underage and problem gambling.

13.4 To minimise the risk of fraud, societies licensed by the Commission should adopt one or more of the following measures when sending unsolicited mailings of lottery tickets:

- prohibit the unsolicited mailing of lottery tickets to non members of the promoting society
- limit the value of tickets sent to any one address which is not that of a member of the promoting society to £20
- maintain records of tickets distributed and not returned. The Commission recommends that these records should include details of the address to which the tickets have been sent, their total value and their serial number. Information on unsold tickets not returned by the date of the lottery draw should be retained for at least six months.

13.5 Society lottery operator licences (remote and non remote) from the Commission allow societies to sell lottery tickets within Great Britain (England, Scotland, and Wales). If you wish to sell lottery tickets outside of Great Britain you will need to check the laws that apply in that jurisdiction.

14 FINANCIAL REQUIREMENTS

14.1 For society and local authority lotteries promoted under licence from the Commission, accounting records must be retained for a minimum of three years from the date of any lottery to which they relate and they must be made available for inspection by the Commission on request. These records must contain, in respect of each lottery, details of the total proceeds of each lottery, the expenses of the lottery, and the number of sold and unsold tickets.

14.2 Where the cumulative proceeds of lotteries promoted by a society or local authority exceed £1,000,000 in a calendar year, the Commission must be sent a written confirmation from a statutory auditor that the proceeds of those lotteries have been fully accounted for in annual audited accounts. Such confirmation must be provided within ten months of the end of the period to which the accounts relate.

14.3 A statutory auditor is someone who is eligible for appointment as a company auditor under section 1210 of the Companies Act 2006 but is not, in the case of a society:

(a) a member of the society
(b) a partner, officer or employee of such a member
(c) a partnership of which a person falling within (a) or (b) is a partner.

15 LOTTERY SUBMISSIONS

15.1 Every society and local authority licensed by the Commission must provide a submission for each lottery. This must show the total proceeds and how they have been distributed between prizes and expenses and the amount applied directly to the society's purposes, or purpose for which the local authority has power to incur expenditure.

15.2 A licensed society's or local authority's submission must be sent to the Gambling Commission no later than three months after the date of the lottery draw or in the case of an instant (scratchcard) lottery within three months of the last date on which tickets in the lottery were on sale. At the time it is submitted each submission must be verified by a Personal Management Licence holder, a qualified person in the case of a small scale operator or the person (in the case of societies) named on the lottery tickets as being responsible for the promotion of the lottery.

15.3 Submissions can be sent to the Commission on-line using the relevant form or the form can be downloaded and sent through the post.

15.4 Every society registered with a local authority to run small society lotteries must submit a statement providing the following information:

- the date on which tickets were available for sale or supply and the date of the draw
- the total proceeds of the lottery (remote and non remote)
- the amounts deducted by promoters of the lottery in providing prizes, including rollovers
- the amounts deducted by the promoters of the lottery in respect of costs incurred in organising the lottery
- the amount applied directly to the purpose for which the promoting society is conducted or for which the local authority has power to incur expenditure (at least 20% of the gross proceeds)
- whether any expenses incurred in connection with the lottery were not paid for by deduction from the proceeds, and, if so, the amount of expenses and the sources from which they were paid.

15.5 A registered society's statement must be sent to the local authority within three months beginning on the day the draw (or last draw) in the lottery took place. It must be signed by two members of the society appointed in writing for that purpose by the society's governing body and accompanied by a copy of that appointment.

16 SOCIAL RESPONSIBILITY

16.1 Lotteries are a form of gambling and as such societies and local authorities are required to ensure that children and other vulnerable people are not exploited by their lottery.

16.2 The minimum age for participation in a society or local authority lottery is 16 years of age. A person commits an offence if they invite or allow a child to enter such a lottery. Licensed societies and local authorities running lotteries must have written policies and procedures in place to help prevent and deal with cases of under-age play.

16.3 Licence holders must take all reasonable steps to ensure that information about how to gamble responsibly and how to access information and help in respect of problem gambling is readily available.

16.4 Further information about social responsibility requirements is contained in the Commission's Licence Conditions and Codes of Practice document.

17 B3A LOTTERY MACHINES

17.1 Section 235(2)(d) of the Act and Regulations under that section define a B3A machine as one where the results of the lottery are determined by the machine and/or the machine displays the results of the lottery without an interval of at least one hour between the sale of the ticket and the announcement of the result. These machines can only be sited in a members' club or miners' welfare institute holding a club gaming or club machine permit issued by the licensing authority. Clubs and institutes are entitled to site one category B3A machine on the premises.

18 PROCEEDS AND PROFITS

18.1 Section 254 of the Act clarifies what is meant by 'proceeds' and 'profits' of alottery.

18.2 'Proceeds' are the total amount paid for tickets before any deductions.

18.3 'Profits' are the amount of proceeds less any deductions for prizes, rollovers, and reasonable expenses incurred in connection with running the lottery.

19 MISUSING PROFITS OF LOTTERIES

19.1 Under section 260 of the Act it is an offence to use or permit profits from a large society or local authority lottery to be used for any purposes other than for the purpose for which the lottery was permitted or promoted. Section 261 applies the same offence to small society lotteries.

20 CONTACTS

Gambling Commission
www.gamblingcommission.gov.uk
Department for Culture Media and Sport
www.culture.gov.uk
The Lotteries Council
www.lotteriescouncil.org.uk
Hospice Lotteries Association
www.hospicelotteries.org.uk
Gamcare
www.gamcare.org.uk
The GREaT Foundation
www.thegreatfoundation.org.uk
Charity Commission for England & Wales
www.charity-commission.gov.uk
Office of the Scottish Charities Regulator
www.oscr.gov.uk
Trading Standards
www.tradingstandards.gov.uk
Local Authority Coordinators of Regulatory Services
www.lacors.gov.uk
Institute of Fundraising
www.institute-of-fundraising.org.uk
Charity Law Association
www.charitylawassociation.org.uk
Committee of Advertising Practice
www.cap.org.uk
National Lottery Commission
www.natlotcomm.gov.uk
Gambling Commission November 2009

ORGANISING SMALL LOTTERIES

Advice on lotteries that do not require a licence or registration

November 2009

1 INTRODUCTION

6.2358 1.1 Lotteries are illegal unless they fall into one of the categories specifically permitted by law. Apart from the National Lottery (which has its own dedicated legislation), the relevant law is contained in the Gambling Act 2005 (the Act). The Act creates eight categories of permitted lottery. Three of these categories (small and large society lotteries and local authority lotteries) require either a licence from the Gambling Commission (the Commission) or registration with a licensing authority. Advice on these can be found in a separate document called Promoting society and local authority lotteries.

1.2 This document provides a general guide to the main provisions and requirements of the law relating to the only other types of permitted lotteries. Such lotteries are intended to be small-scale and as such they do not require either a licence or registration. These are customer lotteries; non-commercial lotteries that are incidental to some other event; and three types of permitted private lottery (private society lotteries; work lotteries; and residents' lotteries). Each of these is described separately below.

1.3 This advice is not comprehensive or a binding interpretation of the law and anyone intending to run such a lottery should refer to the Act and if necessary seek independent legal advice to ensure that they conform to the law before proceeding.

2 DEFINITION OF A LOTTERY

2.1 In simple terms a lottery is a kind of gambling that has three essential elements:

- payment is required to participate
- one or more prizes are awarded
- those prizes are awarded by chance.

This is set out more formally in the Act which defines two types of lottery, a simple lottery and a complex lottery.

2.2 An arrangement is a simple lottery if:

- people are required to pay to participate in the arrangement
- in the course of the arrangement one or more prizes are allocated to one or more people in a class
- the prizes are allocated by a process which relies wholly on chance.

2.3 An arrangement is a complex lottery if:

- people are required to pay to participate in the arrangement
- in the course of the arrangement one or more prizes are allocated to one or more people in a class
- the prizes are allocated by a series of processes
- the first of those processes relies wholly on chance.

3 TYPES OF LOTTERIES THAT DO NOT REQUIRE A LICENCE OR REGISTRATION

3.1 These are:

(a) incidental non-commercial lotteries – commonly held at charity fund raising events

(b) private lotteries
  - private society lotteries – only members of the society and those on society premises can participate in the lottery
  - work lotteries – only people who work together on the same premises may participate
  - residents' lotteries – only people who live at the same premises may participate

(c) customer lotteries – only customers at the business premises may participate

4 INCIDENTAL NON-COMMERCIAL LOTTERIES

4.1 An incidental non-commercial lottery is one that is incidental to a non-commercial event. Examples may include a lottery held at a school fete or at a social event such as a dinner dance. An event is non-commercial if all the money raised (proceeds) at the event including entrance fees, sales of food and drink and so on, goes entirely to purposes that are not for private gain: therefore a fundraising social event with an entrance fee would be non-commercial if the monies raised went to a society but would not be non-commercial if the monies were retained by the organiser for private gain. However, money raised by third parties will not form part of the proceeds of the event and so may be appropriated for private gain. An example of this would be refreshments or entertainment provided at the event by an independent third party.

4.2 The Gambling Act 2005 and a related Statutory Instrument1 specify that:

- the promoters of the lottery may not deduct more than £100 from the proceeds in respect of the expenses incurred in organising the lottery, such as the cost of printing tickets, hire of equipment and so on
- not more than £500 can be spent on prizes (but other prizes may be donated to the lottery)
- the lottery cannot involve a rollover of prizes from one lottery to another
- all tickets must be sold at the location during the event, and the result made public while the event takes place.

5 PRIVATE LOTTERIES

5.1 There are three types of private lotteries permitted by the Act:

- private society lottery
- work lottery
- residents' lottery.

5.2 Private lotteries must comply with conditions relating to advertising which state that no advertisement for a private society, work or residents' lottery may be displayed or distributed except at the society or work premises, or the relevant residence, nor may it be sent to any other premises.

5.3 Private lotteries must comply with conditions set out in Schedule 11 of the Act relating to tickets. In summary these are:

- a ticket in a private lottery may be sold or supplied only by or on behalf of the promoters
- tickets (and the rights they represent) are non-transferable
- each ticket must state the name and address of the promoter of the lottery, the people to whom the promoter can sell or supply tickets and the fact that they are not transferable.

5.4 Private lotteries cannot be conducted on vessels. The Act's definition of a vessel (section 353(1)) is:

- anything (other than a seaplane or amphibious vehicle), designed or adapted for navigation or other use in, on or over water
- a hovercraft
- anything, or any part of any place, situated on or in water.

5.5 The price paid for each ticket in a private lottery must be the same, must be shown on the ticket and must be paid to the promoters of the lottery before anyone is given a ticket.

5.6 The arrangements for private lotteries must not include a rollover of prizes from one lottery to another.

PRIVATE SOCIETY LOTTERIES

5.7 Private society lotteries can only be promoted by an authorised member of a society. The society can be any group or society, provided it is not established and conducted for purposes connected to gambling; for example private members clubs can organise such lotteries. Tickets can only be sold to other members of that society and to people on the premises used for the administration of the society. The lottery may only be promoted and raise proceeds for the purposes for which the society is conducted.

WORK LOTTERIES

5.8 Work lotteries can only be promoted by someone who works on the premises (see paragraph 5.10) and tickets can only be sold to other people who work on the same single set of premises. The lottery must not be run for profit (see paragraph 8 below) and all the proceeds (gross ticket sales) must be used for prizes or reasonable expenses incurred in organising the lottery. An arrangement such as a Grand National sweepstake held in an office is an example of a work lottery.

RESIDENTS' LOTTERIES

5.9 Residents' lotteries must not be run for profit (see section 8 below) and all the proceeds must be used for prizes or reasonable expenses. The promoter of the lottery must reside in the premises and tickets can only be sold to other residents of the same single set of premises. The residency requirement can still be satisfied where the premises are not the sole premises in which a person resides, for example student halls of residence.

DEFINITION OF 'SINGLE SET OF PREMISES'

5.10 The Commission is of the view that the wording 'single set of premises' was designed to include the situation where there might be multiple buildings on a single site, such as a hospital site or the many buildings which may exist within larger corporations. The term does not include multiple sites; for example a company with premises in more than one area would not be able to sell tickets for a single private lottery covering all of the sites.

6 CUSTOMER LOTTERIES

6.1 A customer lottery is a lottery promoted by the occupiers of business premises, who sell tickets only to customers present on their premises.

6.2 The Act requires that in customer lotteries:

- the lottery must be arranged to ensure that no profit is made (see section 8 below)
- tickets may be sold or supplied only by or on behalf of the promoter
- tickets must not be sold to children under 16 years of age
- no advertisement may be displayed or distributed except on the business premises nor may it be sent to any other premises
- another customer lottery cannot take place within seven days on the same business premises
- tickets (and the rights they represent) are non transferable
- no ticket may result in the winner receiving a prize worth more than £50
- no rollovers of prizes from one lottery to another are permitted.

Each ticket in a customer lottery must state:

- the name and address of the promoter of the lottery
- the people to whom the promoters can sell or supply tickets
- that the rights conferred by the sale or supply of a ticket in a customer lottery are not transferable.

6.3 Customer lotteries cannot be conducted on a vessel (see paragraph 5.4 for the definition of a vessel under the Act.)

7 PREMISES LICENCES AND LOTTERIES

7.1 Under section 167 of the Act, the Secretary of State and Scottish Ministers have made regulations setting mandatory and default conditions that are attached to gambling premises licences2. These include a mandatory condition that specifies premises licensed for gambling may not be used for the sale of tickets in a private society lottery, work lottery or a customer lottery. For example, a casino operator holding a premises licence will not be permitted to hold a work lottery for its staff on those premises. It also specifies that National Lottery products may not be sold on such

premises.

8 PROCEEDS AND PROFITS

8.1 Section 254 of the Act clarifies what is meant by 'proceeds' and 'profits' of a lottery.
8.2 'Proceeds' are the total amount paid for tickets before any deductions.
8.3 'Profits' are the amount of proceeds less any deductions for prizes, rollovers, and reasonable expenses incurred in connection with running the lottery.

9 MISUSING PROFITS OF LOTTERIES

9.1 Incidental non-commercial lotteries and private society lotteries can all be used to raise funds (profit) for a non-commercial society (whether that society is a charity or a club). Under section 261 of the Act it is an offence to use or permit profits from these types of lottery to be used for any purpose other than the purposes for which the lottery was permitted or promoted.
Gambling Commission November 2009

SOCIETY LOTTERIES, EXTERNAL LOTTERY MANAGERS AND SERVICE PROVIDERS

A quick guide for local authorities

6.2359 It is common practice in the lottery sector for organisers of lotteries to employ third parties to provide materials and services to assist in the promotion of lotteries. Those third parties are generally commercial companies and include ticket printers, advertising agencies, response handling, telemarketing and direct mail companies etc. In many cases those third parties will simply be acting as 'service providers' rather than being involved in the promotion or facilitation of the lottery and they will not require a licence or any other specific permission under the Gambling Act 2005 (the Act).

WHAT IS AN EXTERNAL LOTTERY MANAGER (ELM)?

Under the Act a third party will require an operating licence from the the Commission if the services the third party provides amounts to the promotion or facilitation of a lottery under section 252 or 259. Under the Act a society or local authority lottery may employ a third party (an ELM) to promote all or part of its lottery.
Section 257 of the Act defines an ELM as a person or body that makes arrangements for a lottery on behalf of a society or authority of which they are not a member, officer or employee. Further advice on the distinction between ELMs and service providers is given is in sections 7 and 8 of the Commission's advice document: ***Promoting society and local authority lotteries (November 2009)***, available on our website.

WHAT LICENCES DOES AN ELM NEED?

ELMs must hold a lottery manager's operating licence issued by the Commission before they can manage a licensed society, local authority lottery or a society lottery registered with a local authority.
It is the responsibility of the society or local authority to ensure that before employing anyone to manage all or part of their lottery that that person or body holds a valid lottery manager's operating licence issued by the Commission.
A list of licensed ELMs is available on the Commission's website.
Some ELMs are also required to hold Personal Management Licences and they must ensure that certain directors and senior managers, including the managing director, chief executive, finance director, compliance manager, marketing manager and IT manager hold licences.

ELMs will also need to hold a remote gambling licence if they are involved in the promotion of a society lottery where tickets are sold by means of remote communication (internet, telephone etc).

The fact that a society or local authority lottery employs a licensed ELM to manage all or part of its lottery does not absolve the society, or local authority, from its responsibility for ensuring that the lottery is conducted in such a way that it is lawful and fully complies with all licence or registration requirements. In cases where a licensed ELM is employed, the society or local authority lottery will still need to hold a licence(s) or a registration.

WHAT RESPONSIBILITIES DO LOCAL AUTHORITIES HAVE?

The Commission has responsibility for the licensing and regulation of ELMs. However, many ELMs and service providers supply materials and services to small society lotteries registered with local authorities where the Commission has no involvement or any direct regulatory responsibility.

It is recommended that, at the time a society applies to a local authority for a society lottery registration or makes their annual renewal payment for their registration, the local authority should ask the society to confirm whether or not they employ a person or body to promote all or part of their lottery, and if so, whether that person or body is licensed by the Commission as an ELM.

If that third party person or body is promoting a society lottery without a licence from the Commission they may be committing an offence under section 258 of the Act.

Where a local authority becomes aware of a person or body operating as an unlicensed ELM they should inform the Commission and provide details of that person or body.

The local authority should also inform the society that they may also be committing an offence under the Act by employing an unlicensed entity to promote all or part of its lottery.

In most cases where the Commission becomes aware of an unlicensed ELM it will investigate the circumstances. One option open to the Commission is to give the person or body in question the option of either applying for a lottery manager's operating licence or ceasing its business of promoting lotteries.

Where there is doubt about whether a third party is acting as an ELM or a service provider our advice in ***Promoting society and local authority lotteries (November 2009)***, available on our website, may help. The Commission's Contact Centre may also be able to give advice on **0121 230 6666.**

Gambling Commission January 2011

Note

Regulatory return forms (October 2011) and guides as to how to complete them (June 2011) are available from the Gambling Commission's website at www.gamblingcommission.gov.uk

PROMOTING MULTIPLE SOCIETY LOTTERIES

Advice for society lotteries and external lottery managers promoting individual lotteries under one brand (August 2011)

1 INTRODUCTION

6.2359A 1.1 The purpose of this note is to provide advice to society lottery promoters (society lottery operators and External Lottery Managers (ELMs)) and others about some of the factors the Gambling Commission (the Commission) is likely to take into account when making decisions about whether the requirements of the Gambling Act 2005 (the Act) are satisfied in a particular lottery scheme.

1.2 The interpretation of the Act is ultimately a matter for the courts but it is hoped that this note will be helpful to societies and ELMs in setting out some of the indicators to which the Commission has regard in determining whether a particular scheme is being properly promoted as a series of separate lotteries or is in reality a single lottery. These indicators may also be relevant, in appropriate cases, to the Commission's decision whether to grant an operating licence.

1.3 This note contains advice supplementary to the requirements of the Act, relevant regulations and the Licence Conditions and Codes of Practice. Operators must also ensure they meet those requirements. For further information see the Commission's document 'Promoting society and local authority lotteries, November 2009'.

1.4 To assist operators in ensuring that their lottery is being promoted lawfully and in line with the licensing objectives as set out in the Act, the Commission has prepared a series of indicators that may be taken into account when deciding whether or not a particular scheme is lawful. The indicators are neither exhaustive not exclusive and no single factor is likely to be determinant by itself.

1.5 The Commission may update this advice from time to time to reflect developments in the sector.

2 PROMOTING MULTIPLE SOCIETY LOTTERIES LAWFULLY

2.1 The Act permits licensed or registered non-commercial societies to promote lotteries. The intention of the relevant provisions is to make it possible for a non-commercial society to use a lottery as a means of retaining funds from the public for the cause promoted by the society. The provisions are relatively limited in scope.

2.2 The Act also allows those societies to appoint a person who is not a member, officer or employee of the society – an External Lottery Manager (ELM) – to make the arrangements for the lottery on their behalf. Where arrangements for the lottery are made by an ELM on behalf of a society both the ELM and society promote the lottery. The intention of these provisions is also relatively limited in scope: they are designed to do nothing more than allow a society to 'outsource' the running of its lottery to a third party.

2.3 It is the view of the Commission that where and EML, a society lottery operator or a collective of society lottery operators, promote multiple society lotteries under a single brand, each lottery must be organised and promoted in such a way as to ensure that the lotteries are not combined to form one single lottery, which could be a breach of the requirements of the Act and regulations.

2.4 The proceeds from one society's lottery may not be used to fund any of the prizes or expenses in a different society's lottery promoted under the same brand. For example proceeds from lottery A promoted by society A may not be rolled over to fund prizes in lottery B promoted by society B (a different society) or be used to pay or subsidise any prizes in society lottery B.

2.5 The relevant monetary limits set out in the Act apply to each of the individual society lotteries separately.

2.6 Under the Act the proceeds of each lottery draw are the responsibility of the individual lottery operators. It is each society operator's responsibility to ensure that the proceeds, including expenses and prizes, of its lottery are apportioned and distributed lawfully and that a minimum of 20% of the proceeds of each of its society lottery draws are applied to a purpose for which the promoting society is established.

2.7 Each society must meet the requirements of a non-commercial society set out in section 19 of the Act and any publicly available criteria relied upon by the Commission in assessing compliance with those requirements. The Commission will always look at the reality of each situation in determining whether the test for a non-commercial society is met, and when deciding the imposition of licence conditions

Control and accountability

2.8 There is no prohibition in the Act on society lottery operators coming together under a single brand and the results in those lotteries being determined by a single draw. However, the individual lotteries must remain separate, distinct entities. Indicators that may help make judgements in these circumstances include

- In cases where a number of societies come together to promote their lotteries under one brand, whether an ELM is involved or not, the extent to which each individual society is able to demonstrate that they retain overall management control of their lottery will be important. This will include the society demonstrating that they retain overall control of management and strategic decision-making relating to the promotion of the lottery, including control over social responsibility policies and the marketing of the lottery.
- The extent to which the proceeds of individual society lotteries are separated, for example through ring-fencing individual bank accounts from other societies, from the ELM and from any other related company or body.
- In cases where a number of societies come together to promote their lotteries under one brand, whether an ELM is involved or not, the extent to which each society has control of the proceeds of the lottery including how those proceeds are apportioned and distributed will be an important factor. Where multiple society lotteries are promoted under one brand, the proceeds cannot be pooled and distributed among all societies promoting their lottery under that brand.

Marketing

2.9 The Act requires each individual society lottery that forms part of a single branded scheme must be promoted separately, and it must be clear to a participant in the lottery which society lottery they are being asked to participate in. Where a number of society lotteries are promoted under one brand whether with an ELM or not the following indicators may assist decision making in this area:

- The extent to which the general advertising and marketing material relating to the promotion of the umbrella lottery brand makes it clear each draw will be on behalf of separate identified societies.
- Prior to each lottery draw the relative prominence of the name of the umbrella lottery brand in the advertising and marketing material compared to that of the name of the society or societies involved in the promotion of that particular draw.
- The extent to which the document (ticket) given to participants at the time they pay to enter the lottery clearly and prominently specified and displays the name of the individual society or societies involved in promoting each lottery draw.

Gambling Commission August 2011

OFFERING LOTTERY, GAMING AND BETTING PRODUCTS UNDER COMMON BRANDING

Advice for society lotteries and external lottery managers (June 2012)

1 INTRODUCTION

6.2359B 1.1 The Gambling Commission (the Commission) has a duty to pursue the three licensing objectives set out in the Gambling Act 2005 ('the Act'). The Commission's role is to permit gambling, in so far as the Commission thinks it is reasonably consistent with the pursuit of those objectives and where it is satisfied that the requirements of the Act will be met by operating licence holders.

1.2 The purpose of this note is to provide advice to lottery promoters (society lottery operators and External Lottery Managers (ELMs)) and others about the principles the Commission is likely to apply when making decisions regarding applications from operators who wish to combine the promotion of lotteries with provision of facilities for other types of gambling.

1.3 The interpretation of the Act and the Commission's powers is ultimately a matter for the courts but it is hoped that this note will be helpful to societies and ELMs in setting out the principles to which the Commission will have regard in determining whether a particular combination of lottery and other gambling products adequately meets the licensing objectives set out in Section 1 of the Act. These principles may also be relevant, in appropriate cases, to the Commission's decision whether to grant an operating licence, or whether to add specific conditions to the licence to ensure the operator offers gambling in a fair and open manner and protects children and other vulnerable persons from being harmed or exploited by gambling.

1.4 This note contains advice supplementary to the requirements of the Act, relevant regulations and the Licence Conditions and Codes of Practice. Operators must also ensure they meet those requirements. For further information see the Commissions document Promoting society and local authority lotteries, November 2009.

1.5 The Commission may update this advice note from time to time to reflect developments in the sector.

2 BACKGROUND

2.1 Over the past few years the Commission has seen a move away from traditional paper based weekly subscription lotteries to more diverse and innovative ways of selling lottery tickets including, for example, instant win scratchcards and online electronic lottery scratchcards.

2.2 We have also seen an increase in licence applications from ELMs who are arguably more commercially-focused and business-orientated, with emphasis on promoting the individual society lotteries that they manage under a common brand. Increasingly we are finding that ELMs are applying for licences to run lotteries under a brand name and looking at ways of maximising revenue through innovative marketing and through brand awareness. The promotion of lotteries online has also increased and with that some societies and ELMs are looking at what other online gambling products might also be offered on their websites.

2.3 In some cases the products being offered may satisfy both the statutory definition of a lottery and that of gaming or betting. Sections 17 and 18 of the Act were introduced to deal with these cross-category activities and apply the following criteria:

- If the arrangements satisfy the definition of both a lottery and gaming then, subject to the next sentence and unless the lottery is promoted under a lottery operating licence or satisfies the definition of an exempt lottery, the default position is that cross-category gambling is to be treated as gaming rather than a lottery. However, if the arrangement involves more than three processes in order to win a prize then the arrangement is always treated as gaming.
- Where the arrangements satisfy both the definition of a lottery and that of pool betting or a betting prize competition, the default position is that the arrangements are to be treated as betting rather than a lottery, unless they are promoted in reliance on a lottery operating licence or satisfy the definition of an exempt lottery.

Branding

2.4 It is generally accepted that, when framing the Act, Parliament considered lotteries to be a 'softer' form of gambling and that betting and gaming are 'harder' forms of gambling. Should an ELM or society offer both a lottery and gaming or betting under the same brand, especially on-line, there are concerns that players attracted, for example to a website, to play a lottery may also be offered gaming or betting products.

2.5 By offering gaming or betting under the same branding as lotteries, there is potential for players to become confused and believe that they are participating in a lottery rather than gaming or betting. Lotteries are promoted to support 'good causes' and many players are supporting their chosen 'good cause' as well as participating in gambling when they enter a lottery. There is a risk that those attracted to a lottery branded website would assume that all activities they were participating in under the single banner on that site would be in support of good causes rather than for private gain, and would be unaware that they were participating in a 'harder' form of gambling.

Marketing

2.6 The advertising/marketing of a lottery brand and use of the same brand for gaming or betting products may also draw into gambling young adults (16-17 year olds) who are permitted to participate in lotteries but not gaming or betting. This concern extends to the increasingly popular 'try for free' games widely available on the internet.

3 PRINCIPLES

3.1 In considering a scenario where an ELM (or society) wishes also to offer gaming or betting activities the Commission considers that there is a risk to the licensing objectives, in particular ensuring that gambling is conducted in a fair and open way and protecting children and vulnerable adults from being harmed or exploited by gambling if players are not clear about the characteristics of the gambling being promoted. The Commission does, however, believe that those risks could be mitigated or removed if the following principles were applied when considering an application.

3.2 Licensees wishing to offer betting or casino products alongside lotteries should be advised that the following principles will be applied, which may be attached as conditions to their licence, if an application were to be granted.

The Licensee should only use the word "lottery" in relation to products that fall within the legal definition of a lottery and are being promoted in reliance on a lottery operating licence.

Subject to that, the Licensee may offer lottery games and other forms of gambling via a single website, on associated web pages and under a single umbrella brand name, provided:

- Lottery games and other forms of gambling are offered on separate pages of the website.
- Each web page makes it clear to players which type of gambling is being offered on that page.
- It is made clear on the home page that the licensed activities authorised by any casino or betting operating licence are only available to and accessible by players aged 18 and over.
- Players must only be permitted to participate in gaming or betting (including "try" or "play for fun" activities) where they are registered to do so, and only after age verification has taken place.

The Licensee must ensure that any marketing material which expresses, or implies, an association with a lottery or lottery brand relates to lottery products only and not to any other type of facilities for gambling.

3.3 The principles above describe the Commission's current position on lottery promoters who intend to offer lottery products alongside betting or gaming remote activities. The Commission's intention is that these principles will be consulted on in the future with a view to incorporating them as a general condition on all relevant combined licences.

3.4 This advice is not comprehensive or a binding interpretation of the law and anyone intending to offer cross-gambling activities should refer to the Act and if necessary seek independent legal advice to ensure that they conform to the law before proceeding.

Gambling Commission June 2012

ADULT GAMING CENTRES

CONDITIONS AND CODES OF PRACTICE APPLICABLE TO: GAMING MACHINE GENERAL: ADULT GAMING CENTRE LICENCES GAMING MACHINE GENERAL: FAMILY ENTERTAINMENT CENTRE LICENCES

October 2010

6.2360 Your licence is subject to certain conditions and codes of practice, these are detailed in the following pages

STATUTORY CONDITIONS ATTACHED BY VIRTUE OF THE ACT

SOCIAL RESPONSIBILITY

This licence is subject to a condition that the licensee ensures compliance with any relevant social responsibility provision of a code of practice issued by the Commission. The social responsibility provisions that are relevant to the activities authorised by this licence are set out in the section entitled Codes of Practice.
(Sections 24 and 82(1) Gambling Act 2005)

RETURN OF STAKES TO CHILDREN

The following condition applies to gaming machine general: adult gaming centre operating licences only

This licence is subject to a condition that if the licensee (or anyone employed by the licensee to perform an operational function within the meaning of section 80 of the Act) becomes aware that a child or young person is using or has used facilities for gambling provided in reliance on the licence, the licensee:

(a) must return any money paid in respect of the use of those facilities (whether by way of fee, stake or otherwise) by the child or young person as soon as is reasonably practicable; and

(b) may not give a prize to the child or young person.

This condition does not apply to use of a Category D gaming machine.
(Section 83(1))

The following condition applies to gaming machine general: family entertainment centre operating licences only

This licence is subject to a condition that if the licensee (or anyone employed by the licensee to perform an operational function within the meaning of section 80 of the Act) becomes aware that a child or young person is using or has used facilities for gambling provided in reliance on the licence, the licensee;

(a) must return any money paid in respect of the use of those facilities (whether by way of fee, stake or otherwise) by the child or young person as soon as is reasonably practicable; and

(b) may not give a prize to the child or young person.

This condition does not apply to use of a Category D gaming machine, or equal chance gaming.
(Section 83(1))

COMMISSION GENERAL CONDITIONS

The Commission's complete suite of Licence Conditions to be attached to operating licences pursuant to section 75 of the Act includes some conditions which may not apply to your licence. Where that is the case the irrelevant conditions have not been reproduced below. The full list of Licence Conditions and Codes of Practice are contained within the Commission's Publication "Licence Conditions and Codes of Practice"

QUALIFIED PERSONS AND PERSONAL LICENCES

Qualified persons

THE FOLLOWING CONDITION APPLIES TO ALL OPERATING LICENCES ISSUED TO SMALL-SCALE OPERATORS

In this condition the terms 'small-scale operator', 'qualifying position' and 'qualified person' have the meanings respectively ascribed to them by the Gambling Act 2005 (Definition of Small-scale Operator) Regulations 2006.
Schedule X[1] lists those individuals notified to the Commission as qualified persons.
If, whilst the licensee remains a small-scale operator, an individual begins or ceases to occupy a qualifying position in relation to the licensee, the licensee must within 28 days apply to the Commission under s 104(1)(b) for amendment of the details of the licence set out in Schedule X[1].
An application for amendment under s 104(1)(b) may be made in advance of an individual beginning or ceasing to occupy a qualifying position provided it specifies the date from which the change to which it relates is to be effective.

---

[1] The schedules mentioned here will be attached to individual licences.

Personal licences

(a) Subject to (e) and (f) below licensees must ensure:
   (i) that each individual who occupies one of the management offices specified in (b) below in or in respect of the licensee or in connection with the licensed activities holds a personal licence authorising the performance of the functions of that office (hereafter 'a personal management licence')
   (ii) that at least one person occupies at least one of those offices.

(b) The specified management offices are those offices (whether or not held by a director in the case of a licensee which is a company, a partner in the case of a licensee which is a partnership or an officer of the association in the case of a licensee which is an unincorporated association) the occupier of which is by virtue of the terms of their appointment responsible for:
   - the overall management and direction of the licensee's business or affairs
   - the licensee's finance function as head of that function
   - the licensee's gambling regulatory compliance function as head of that function
   - the licensee's marketing function as head of that function
   - the licensee's information technology function as head of that function in so far as it relates to gambling-related information technology and software
   - oversight of the day to day management of the licensed activities at an identified number of premises licensed under Part 8 of the Act or across an identified geographical area
   - in the case of casino and bingo licences only, oversight of the day to day management of a single set of premises licensed under Part 8 of the Act.

(c) Licensees must take all reasonable steps to ensure that anything done in the performance of the functions of a specified management office is done in accordance with the terms and conditions of the holder's personal management licence.

(d) Where an individual is authorised by a personal licence and that licence comes under review under section 116(2) of the Act, the operating licensee must comply with any conditions subsequently imposed on that licence by the Commission about redeployment, supervision, or monitoring of the individual's work and any requirements of the Commission in respect of such matters applicable during the period of the review.

(e) Paragraphs (a) to (d) above shall not apply to a licensee for so long as the licensee is a 'small-scale operator' as defined in the Gambling Act 2005 (Definition of Small-scale Operator) Regulations 2006 ('the Regulations').

(f) During the period of 3 years commencing with the date on which a licensee ceases to be a small-scale operator paragraphs (a) to (e) above shall apply subject to the proviso that the phrase 'each individual' in paragraph (a)(i) shall not include any individual who was a 'qualified person' (as defined in the Regulations) in relation to the licensee 28 days immediately prior to the licensee ceasing to be a small-scale operator.

FINANCIAL ROBUSTNESS

Notification of shareholders

All company licensees must notify the Commission of the name and address of any person who becomes a shareholder in the company or its holding company holding 3% or more of the issued share capital of the company or its holding company; or any existing shareholder who acquires a holding of 3% or more of the issued share capital of the company or its holding company.

In this condition 'holding company' has the meaning ascribed to that term by section 1159 of the Companies Act 2006 or any statutory modification or re-enactment thereof.

PROTECTION OF CUSTOMER FUNDS

Licensees who hold customer funds for use in future gambling must set out clearly, in information made available to customers in writing, whether they protect customers' funds in the event of insolvency and the method by which this is achieved.

CASH HANDLING

Licensees, as part of their internal controls and financial accounting systems, must have and put into effect policies and procedures concerning the handling of cash, and cash equivalents (ie bankers drafts, cheques and debit cards), designed to minimise the risk of crimes such as money laundering, to avoid the giving of illicit credit and to provide assurance that gambling activities are being conducted fairly.

PROVISION OF CREDIT BY LICENSEES AND THE USE OF CREDIT CARDS

Licensees must neither:

- provide credit themselves in connection with gambling; nor
- participate in, arrange, permit or knowingly facilitate the giving of credit in connection with gambling.

GENERAL 'FAIR AND OPEN' PROVISIONS

Licensees must satisfy themselves that the terms on which gambling is offered are not unfair under the Unfair Terms in Consumer Contracts Regulations 1999 and, where applicable, meet the reasonableness test under the Unfair Contract Terms Act 1977. An accurate summary of the contractual terms on which gambling is offered must be made available to customers and set out in plain and intelligible language.

Customers must be notified of changes to terms before they come into effect.

ACCESS TO PREMISES

Licensees must have and put into effect policies and procedures (including staff training programmes) designed to ensure that their staff co-operate with the Commission's enforcement officers in the proper performance of their compliance functions and are made aware of those officers' rights of entry to premises contained in Part 15 of the Act.

INFORMATION REQUIREMENTS

Reporting suspicion of offences etc

Licensees must provide the Commission with any information that they know relates to or suspect may relate to the commission of an offence under the Act, including an offence resulting from a breach of a licence condition or a code provision having the effect of a licence condition.

Reporting 'Key Events'

A key event is an event that could have a significant impact on the nature or structure of a licensee's business. Licensees must notify the Commission of the occurrence of any of the following key events as soon as reasonably practicable and in any event within five working days of the licensee becoming aware of the event's occurrence[2].

- in the case of licensees which are companies, a petition being presented for their winding up or the winding up of any group company of theirs, or they or any group company being placed in administration or receivership: in this condition a 'group company' is any subsidiary or holding company of the licensee – as those terms are defined in section 1159 of the Companies Act 2006 or any statutory modification or re-enactment thereof – and any subsidiary of such holding company
- in the case of a licensee who is an individual (or a partner in a partnership licensee) their being presented with a petition for their bankruptcy or sequestration or their entering into an individual voluntary agreement
- where the licensee is required to have their accounts independently audited, any unplanned change of auditor including a change prompted by a dispute or resulting from auditors being unable or unwilling to sign an unqualified audit report
- the departure from the licensee's business of any person occupying a 'qualifying position' as defined by Regulation 2(2) of the Gambling Act 2005 (Definition of Small-scale Operator) Regulations 2006
- any breach of a covenant given to a bank or other lender
- any default in making repayment of the whole or any part of a loan on its due date
- any court judgments remaining unpaid 14 days after the date of judgment
- the commencement of any material litigation against the licensee
- the imposition of a disciplinary sanction, including dismissal, against the holder of a personal licence or a person occupying a qualifying position for gross misconduct; or the resignation of a personal licence holder or person occupying a qualifying position following commencement of disciplinary proceedings in respect of gross misconduct against that person
- in the case of remote gambling, the commencement or cessation of trading on website domains (including WAP URLs) or broadcast media through which the licensee provides gambling facilities.

---

2 Key events can be reported securely online at the Commission's website at www.gamblingcommission.gov.uk or by email to key.events@gamblingcommission.gov.uk or posted to Key

Events, Compliance Administration Team, Gambling Commission, Victoria Square House, Victoria Square, Birmingham B2 4BP

General and Regulatory Returns

On request, licensees must provide the Commission with such information as the Commission may require about the use made of facilities provided in accordance with this licence, and the manner in which gambling authorised by this licence and the licensee's business in relation to that gambling are carried on, including in particular information about:

- the numbers of people making use of the facilities and the frequency of such use
- the range of gambling activities provided by the licensee and the numbers of staff employed in connection with them
- the licensee's policies in relation to, and experiences of, problem gambling.

In particular within 28 days of the end of each quarterly period or, for those only submitting annual returns, within 42 days of the end of each annual period, licensees must submit a Regulatory Return to the Commission containing such information as the Commission may from time to time require[3].

---

[3] Regulatory returns can be submitted securely online at the Commission's website at www.gamblingcommission.gov.uk For operators unable to access this system, the forms and a guide to completing them can be requested from the Commission and returned by email to Regulatory.Returns@gamblingcommission.gov.uk or by post to Regulatory Returns, Compliance Administration Team, Gambling Commission, Victoria Square House, Victoria Square, Birmingham, B2 4BP.

SECRETARY OF STATE GENERAL CONDITIONS

None at present

CODES OF PRACTICE

INTRODUCTION

This is the Commission's principal code of practice, issued under section 24 of the Gambling Act 2005, as revised with effect from 1 January 2009. There are two types of provision in the code:

- social responsibility provisions: compliance with these is a condition of licences; therefore any breach of them by an operator may lead the Commission to review the operator's licence with a view to suspension, revocation or the imposition of a financial penalty and would also expose the operator to the risk of prosecution; and
- ordinary code provisions: these do not have the status of licence conditions, but are admissible in evidence in criminal or civil proceedings and must be taken into account in any case in which the court or tribunal think them relevant and by the Commission in the exercise of its functions. Any breach of ordinary code provisions by an operator may be taken into account by the Commission on a licence review, but cannot lead to imposition of a financial penalty. These code provisions are in italics in this section and generally set out good practice in these areas.

FINANCIAL REQUIREMENTS

Ordinary code provision

In order to help prevent activities related to money laundering licensees should take into account the Commission's advice on the Proceeds of Crime Act 2002, *Duties and responsibilities under the Proceeds of Crime Act 2002. Advice for operators (excluding casino operators).*

PROTECTION OF CHILDREN AND OTHER VULNERABLE PERSONS

Combating problem gambling

SOCIAL RESPONSIBILITY CODE PROVISION

Licensees must have and put into effect policies and procedures intended to promote socially responsible gambling.

Licensees' policies and procedures for socially responsible gambling must include but need not be confined to:

- the specific policies and procedures required by the following provisions of section 2 of this code
- a commitment to and how they will contribute to research into the prevention and treatment of problem gambling
- a commitment to and how they will contribute to public education on the risks of gambling and how to gamble safely
- a commitment to and how they will contribute to the identification and treatment of problem gamblers.

Access to gambling by children and young persons

THE FOLLOWING CODE APPLIES TO GAMING MACHINE GENERAL: ADULT GAMING CENTRE OPERATING LICENCES ONLY

SOCIAL RESPONSIBILITY CODE PROVISION

Licensees must have and put into effect policies and procedures designed to prevent underage gambling, and monitor the effectiveness of these.

This must include procedures for:

- checking the age of apparently underage customers
- removing anyone who appears to be under age who tries to access the gambling facilities and cannot produce an acceptable form of identification
- taking action when there are attempts by under-18s to enter the premises.

Licensees must not deliberately provide facilities for gambling in such a way as to appeal particularly to children or young people, for example by reflecting or being associated with youth culture.

In premises restricted to adults, service must be refused in any circumstances where any adult is accompanied by a child or young person.

Licensees must take all reasonable steps to ensure that all staff understand their responsibilities for preventing underage gambling. This must include appropriate training which must cover the legal requirements on returning stakes and not paying prizes to underage customers.

Licensees must only accept identification which:

- contains a photograph from which the individual can be identified
- states the individual's date of birth
- is valid
- is legible and has no visible signs of tampering or reproduction.

THE FOLLOWING CODE APPLIES TO GAMING MACHINE GENERAL: ADULT GAMING CENTRE OPERATING LICENCES ONLY

ORDINARY CODE PROVISION

The Commission considers acceptable forms of identification to include any identification carrying the PASS logo (for example Citizencard or Validate); a driving licence (including a provisional licence) with photocard; or a passport.

Licensees should put into effect procedures that require their staff to check the age of any customer who appears to them to be under 21.

Licensees should consider permanent exclusion from premises for any adult accompanied by a child or young person on more than one occasion to premises restricted to adults, or if there is reason to believe the offence was committed knowingly or recklessly.

Procedures should be put into effect for dealing with cases where a child or young person repeatedly attempts to gamble on premises restricted to adults, including oral warnings, reporting the offence to the Gambling Commission and the police, and making available information on problem gambling.

THE FOLLOWING CODE APPLIES TO GAMING MACHINE GENERAL: FAMILY ENTERTAINMENT CENTRE OPERATING LICENCES ONLY

SOCIAL RESPONSIBILITY CODE PROVISION

Licensees must have and put into effect policies and procedures designed to prevent underage gambling, and monitor the effectiveness of these.

This must include procedures for:

- checking the age of apparently underage customers
- refusing entry to any adult-only areas to anyone unable to produce an acceptable form of identification
- taking action when there are unlawful attempts to enter the adult-only areas.

Licensees must not permit children or young people to gamble in the adults-only areas of premises to which they have access. If there is a 'no under-18s' premises policy, licensees must pay particular attention to the procedures they use at the entrance to the premises to check customers' ages.

Licensees must take all reasonable steps to ensure that all staff understand their responsibilities for preventing underage gambling, returning stakes and not paying prizes to underage customers and particularly for challenging any adult who may be complicit in allowing a child or young person to gamble.

Licensees must only accept identification which:

- contains a photograph from which the individual can be identified
- states the individual's date of birth
- is valid
- is legible and has no visible signs of tampering or reproduction.

THE FOLLOWING CODE APPLIES TO GAMING MACHINE GENERAL: FAMILY ENTERTAINMENT CENTRE OPERATING LICENCES ONLY

ORDINARY CODE PROVISION

The Commission considers acceptable forms of identification to include: any identification carrying the PASS logo (for example Citizencard or Validate); a driving licence (including a provisional licence) with photocard; or a passport.

Licensees should require a person who appears to relevant staff to be under the age of 21 to be asked to produce proof of age, either at the point of entry to the gambling area or as soon as it comes to the attention of staff that they wish to access gambling facilities.

Licensees should have procedures for dealing with cases where an adult knowingly or recklessly allows a child or young person to gamble. These procedures might include refusing to allow the adult to continue to gamble, removing them from the premises, and reporting the incident to the police or local authorities, or taking action where forged identification is produced.
Procedures should be put into effect for dealing with cases where a child or young person repeatedly attempts to gamble on their premises, including oral warnings, reporting the offence to the Gambling Commission and the police, and making available information on problem gambling to the child or young person concerned.
Where it is likely that customers' young or otherwise vulnerable children will be left unattended on or adjacent to their premises, licensees should consider reminding customers of their parental responsibilities and assess whether there is a need to develop procedures for minimising the risk to such children.

Information on how to gamble responsibly and help for problem gamblers

Social responsibility code provision

Licensees must make information readily available to their customers on how to gamble responsibly and how to access information about, and help in respect of, problem gambling.
The information must cover:

- any measures provided by the licensee to help individuals monitor or control their gambling, such as restricting the duration of a gambling session or the amount of money they can spend
- timers or other forms of reminders or 'reality checks' where available
- self-exclusion options
- information about the availability of further help or advice.

The information must be directed to all customers whether or not licensees also make available material which is directed specifically at customers who may be 'problem gamblers'.
For gambling premises, information must be available in all areas where gambling facilities are provided and adjacent to ATMs where these are not located in a gambling area. As a minimum, information must be displayed prominently on posters appropriate to the size and layout of the premises and contained in leaflets that may be taken away. Licensees must take all reasonable steps to ensure that this information is also readily accessible in locations which enable the customer to obtain it discreetly.

Ordinary code provision

Licensees who market their services in one or more foreign languages should make available in that, or those, foreign languages:

- the information on how to gamble responsibly and access to help referred to above
- the players' guides to any game, bet or lottery required to be made available to customers under provisions in this code
- the summary of the contractual terms on which gambling is offered, which is required to be provided to customers as a condition of the licensee's operating licence.

Customer interaction

Social responsibility code provision

Licensees must put into effect policies and procedures for customer interaction where they have concerns that a customer's behaviour may indicate problem gambling. The policies must include:

- identification of the appropriate level of management who may initiate customer interaction and the procedures for doing so
- the types of behaviour that will be logged/reported to the appropriate level of staff and which may trigger customer interaction at an appropriate moment
- the circumstances in which consideration should be given to refusing service to customers and/or barring them from the operator's gambling premises
- training for all staff on their respective responsibilities, in particular so that they know who is designated to deal with problem gambling issues.

But such policies and procedures must be consistent with, and implemented with due regard to, licensees' duties in respect of the health and safety of their staff.

Self-exclusion

Social responsibility code provision

Licensees must have and put into effect procedures for self-exclusion and take all reasonable steps to refuse service or to otherwise prevent an individual who has entered a self-exclusion agreement from participating in gambling.

Licensees must, as soon as practicable, take all reasonable steps to prevent any marketing material being sent to a self-excluded customer.

Licensees must take steps to remove the name and details of a self-excluded individual from any marketing databases used by the company or group (or otherwise flag that person as an individual to whom marketing material must not be sent), within two days of receiving the completed self-exclusion notification.

This covers any marketing material relating to gambling, or other activities that take place on the premises where gambling may take place. However, it would not extend to blanket marketing which is targeted at a particular geographical area and where the excluded individual would not knowingly be included.

Licensees must close any customer accounts of an individual who has entered a self exclusion agreement and return any funds held in the customer account. It is not sufficient merely to prevent an individual from withdrawing funds from their customer account whilst still accepting wagers from them. Where the giving of credit is permitted, the licensee may retain details of the amount owed to them by the individual, although the account must not be active.

Licensees must put into effect procedures designed to ensure that an individual who has self-excluded cannot gain access to gambling. These procedures must include:

- a register of those excluded with appropriate records (name, address, other details, and any membership or account details that may be held by the operator)
- photo identification (where available and in particular where enforcement of the system may depend on photographic ID), and a signature
- staff training to ensure that staff are able to enforce the systems
- the removal of those persons found in the gambling area or attempting to gamble from the premises.

Ordinary code provision

Self-exclusion procedures should require individuals to take positive action in order to self-exclude. This can be a signature on a self-exclusion form.

Wherever practicable, individuals should be able to self-exclude without having to enter gambling premises.

Before an individual self-excludes, licensees should provide or make available sufficient information about what the consequences of self-exclusion are.

Licensees should take all reasonable steps to extend the self-exclusion to premises of the same type owned by the operator in the customer's local area. In setting the bounds of that area licensees may take into account the customer's address (if known to them), anything else known to them about the distance the customer ordinarily travels to gamble and any specific request the customer may make.

Licensees should encourage the customer to consider extending their self exclusion to other licensees' gambling premises in the customer's local area.

Customers should be given the opportunity to discuss self-exclusion in private, where possible.

Licensees should take steps to ensure that:

- the self-exclusion period is a minimum of six months and give customers the option of extending this to a total of at least five years
- a customer who has decided to enter a self-exclusion agreement is given the opportunity to do so immediately without any cooling-off period. However, if the customer wishes to consider the self-exclusion further (for example to discuss with problem gambling groups) the customer may return at a later date to enter into self-exclusion
- at the end of the period chosen by the customer (and at least six months later), the self-exclusion remains in place, unless the customer takes positive action in order to gamble again. No marketing material should be sent to the individual unless the individual has taken positive action in order to gamble again, and has agreed to accept such material
- where a customer chooses not to renew the self-exclusion, and makes a positive request to begin gambling again, the customer is given one day to cool off before being allowed access to gambling facilities. The contact must be made via telephone or in person.

The licensee should retain the records relating to a self-exclusion agreement at least until the agreement has been formally ended.

(Please note that the Commission does not require the licensee to carry out any particular assessment or make any judgement as to whether the previously self-excluded individual should again be permitted access to gambling.

The requirement to take positive action in person or over the phone is purely to a) check that the customer has considered the decision to access gambling again and allow them to consider the implications; and b) implement the one day cooling-off period and explain why this has been put in place.)

Employment of children and young persons

THE FOLLOWING CODE APPLIES TO GAMING MACHINE GENERAL: ADULT GAMING CENTRE OPERATING LICENCES ONLY

ORDINARY CODE PROVISION

Licensees who employ children (under-16-year-olds) and young persons (those aged 16 and 17) should be aware that it is an offence:

(a) to employ them to provide facilities for gambling;

(b) if gaming machines are sited on the premises, for their contracts of employment to require them, or for them to be permitted, to perform a function in connection with a gaming machine at any time; and

(c) to employ them to carry out any other function on adult gaming centre licensed premises while any gambling activity is being carried on in reliance on the premises licence;

As to b) it should be noted that in the Commission's view the relevant provision of the Act applies to any function performed in connection with a gaming machine. This includes servicing or cleaning such a machine.

Accordingly, licensees should have and put into effect policies and procedures designed to ensure that:

- children and young persons are never asked to perform tasks within a) or b) above

- all staff, including those who are children or young persons themselves, are instructed about the laws relating to access to gambling by children and young persons

and should consider adopting a policy that:

- children and young persons are not employed to work on adult gaming centre licensed premises at any time when the premises are open for business
- gaming machines are turned off if children and young persons are working on the premises outside the hours when the premises are open for business.

THE FOLLOWING CODE APPLIES TO GAMING MACHINE GENERAL: FAMILY ENTERTAINMENT CENTRE OPERATING LICENCES ONLY

ORDINARY CODE PROVISION

Licensees who employ children (under-16-year-olds) and young persons (those aged 16 and 17) should be aware that it is an offence:

(a) to employ them to provide facilities for gambling; and

(b) if gaming machines are sited on the premises, for their contracts of employment to require them, or for them to be permitted, to perform a function in connection with a gaming machine at any time.

As to b) it should be noted that in the Commission's view the relevant provision of the Act applies to any function performed in connection with a gaming machine. This includes servicing or cleaning such a machine.

Accordingly, licensees should have and put into effect policies and procedures designed to ensure that:

- children and young persons are never asked to perform tasks within a) or b) above
- all staff, including those who are children or young persons themselves, are instructed about the laws relating to access to gambling by children and young persons

and should consider adopting a policy that:

- children and young persons are not employed to carry out any work in an adult-only area of family entertainment licensed premises at a time when any gambling is taking place
- gaming machines sited in adult-only areas are turned off if children and young persons are working on the premises outside the hours when the premises are open for business.

MONEY LENDING BETWEEN CUSTOMERS

ORDINARY CODE PROVISION

Licensees should seek to prevent systematic or organised money lending between customers on their premises. As a minimum, they should have arrangements in place to ensure staff are requested to report any instances of substantial money lending when they become aware of them.

'Fair and open' provisions

SOCIAL RESPONSIBILITY CODE PROVISION

Licensees must be able to provide evidence to the Commission, if required, showing how they satisfied themselves that their terms are not unfair.

6: Gambling Act 2005: Additional Material

Marketing

SOCIAL RESPONSIBILITY CODE PROVISION

If a licensee makes available to any customer or potential customer any incentive or reward scheme or other arrangement under which the customer may receive money, goods, services or any other advantage (including the discharge in whole or in part of any liability of his) ('the benefit') the scheme must be designed to operate, and be operated, in such a way that:

(a) the circumstances in which, and conditions subject to which, the benefit is available are clearly set out and readily accessible to the customers to whom it is offered;

(b) neither the receipt nor the value or amount of the benefit is:

  (i) dependent on the customer gambling for a pre-determined length of time or with a predetermined frequency; or

  (ii) altered or increased if the qualifying activity or spend is reached within a shorter time than the whole period over which the benefit is offered;

(c) if the value of the benefit increases with the amount the customer spends it does so at a rate no greater than that at which the amount spent increases;

and further that:

(d) if the benefit comprises free or subsidised travel or accommodation which facilitates the customer's attendance at particular licensed premises the terms on which it is offered are not directly related to the level of the customer's prospective gambling.

ORDINARY CODE PROVISION

Licensees should only offer incentive or reward schemes in which the benefit available is proportionate to the type and level of customers' gambling.

ORDINARY CODE PROVISION

All advertising of gambling products and services should be undertaken in a socially responsible manner. In particular, licensees should comply with the advertising codes of practice which apply to the form and media in which they advertise their gambling facilities or services, and for media not explicitly covered should apply the principles included in these codes of practice as if they were explicitly covered. Licensees should also follow any relevant industry code of practice on advertising.

However, the particular restriction on allowing people aged under 25 to appear in adverts need not be applied to point of sale advertising material, provided that the images used depict the sporting activity that may be gambled on and not the activity of gambling itself and do not offend any other aspect of the advertising codes.

COMPLAINTS AND DISPUTES

Social responsibility code provision

Licensees must put into effect a written procedure for handling customer complaints and disputes.

In this code a 'complaint' means a complaint about any aspect of the licensee's conduct of the licensed activities, and a 'dispute' is any complaint which:

(a) is not resolved at the first stage of the complaints procedure; and

(b) relates to the outcome of the complainant's gambling transaction.

Licensees must ensure that:

- customers are told the name and status of the person to contact about their complaint
- customers are given a copy of the complaints procedure on request or on making a complaint

- all complaints are handled in accordance with the procedure.

Licensees must also ensure that they have arrangements in place for disputes to be referred to an independent third party. Customers whose disputes are not resolved to their satisfaction by use of the operator's complaints procedure may refer those disputes to this independent third party. The arrangements under which such complaints are referred may, but need not, provide for the third party's decision to be binding on the licensee and the customer.

Licensees must keep a record of all complaints that are not resolved at the first stage of the complaints procedure.

Licensees must arrange for a copy of the decision on, or a note of the outcome of, each dispute referred to the independent party to be provided to the Commission quarterly, either by the independent party or by the licensee.

GAMBLING LICENSEES' STAFF

Social responsibility code provision

Licensees must take all reasonable steps to ensure that staff involved in the provision of facilities for gambling are made aware of advice on socially responsible gambling and of where to get confidential advice should their gambling become hard to control.

INFORMATION REQUIREMENTS

Ordinary code provision

The Commission expects licensees to work with the Commission in an open and cooperative way and to inform the Commission of any matters that the Commission would reasonably need to be aware of in exercising its regulatory functions. These are matters that will have a material impact on the licensee's business or on the licensee's ability to conduct its business. Such matters, which should be notified to the Commission as soon as reasonably practicable[4], include the following:

- the departure from the licensee's business of any person named in the licence application, or that person's successor, who holds a personal management licence, but who does not occupy a 'qualifying position'
- any reduction in the number of staff employed by the licensee where that has a material impact on the licensee's business
- the acquisition or disposal by the licensee of gambling premises or pitches where that has a material impact on the size or nature of the licensee's business
- in the case of corporate licensees, the disposal or acquisition of any group company where that has a material impact on the licensee's ability to conduct its business
- any disposal of the licensee's assets where that has a material impact on the licensee's business
- any investigation by a professional, statutory, regulatory or government body into the licensee's activities, or the activities in relation to the licensed entity of a personal licence holder or a person occupying a qualifying position employed by them, where such an investigation could result in the imposition of a sanction or penalty which, if imposed, could reasonably be expected to raise doubts about the licensee's continued suitability to hold a Gambling Commission licence
- any instance of criminal activity, including repeated instances of small-scale theft or fraud, where that has a material impact on the licensee's business
- any major breach in the licensee's information security where that adversely affects the confidentiality of customer data or prevents customers from accessing their accounts for a substantial period of time
- any other matters that have a material impact on the licensee's business or on the licensee's ability to conduct its business.

---

4 These matters can be reported securely online at the Commission's website at www.gambling-commission.gov.uk or by email to key.events@gamblingcommission.gov.uk or posted to Key Events, Compliance Administration Team, Gambling Commission, Victoria Square House, Victoria Square, Birmingham, B2 4BP

Gambling Commission October 2010

Note

Regulatory return forms (October 2011) and guides as to how to complete them (June 2011) are available from the Gambling Commission's website at www.gamblingcommission.gov.uk

FAMILY ENTERTAINMENT CENTRES

CONDITIONS AND CODES OF PRACTICE APPLICABLE TO: GAMING MACHINE GENERAL: ADULT GAMING CENTRE LICENCES; GAMING MACHINE GENERAL: FAMILY ENTERTAINMENT CENTRE LICENCES

To avoid duplication this document has not been reproduced here but can be found at para 6.2360 above.

Note

Regulatory return forms (October 2011) and guides as to how to complete them (June 2011) are available from the Gambling Commission's website at www.gamblingcommission.gov.uk

REMOTE GAMBLING

INTERNATIONAL SUMMIT ON REMOTE GAMBLING
Communiqué

ASCOT RACECOURSE, BERKSHIRE, UNITED KINGDOM – 31 OCTOBER 2006

6.2395–6.2405 We agree:

That in enacting legislation or regulations in relation to remote gambling our principal and over-riding priorities are:

- That remote gambling should be conducted responsibly and with safeguards necessary to protect children and vulnerable people;
- That remote gambling should be regulated in accordance with generally accepted international standards to prevent fraud, money laundering and other crime, and should not be permitted to be a source of crime;
- That, where offered, remote gambling should be verifiably fair to the consumer.

We accept that each jurisdiction may choose to address these priorities differently and, within the scope of international law and trade agreements, may choose to control gambling within its borders in a way that is appropriate to its national regulatory approach and particular circumstances.

We also agree to actively explore the scope for greater international cooperation in the regulation of remote gambling.

Areas of cooperation include:

- Effective measures to protect children and vulnerable people;
- Sharing research and expertise on remote gambling and methods of preventing problem gambling;
- Promoting public awareness of how to gamble responsibly;
- Developing effective licensing regimes;
- Working with the financial sector to secure these priorities.

REMOTE GAMBLING AND SOFTWARE TECHNICAL STANDARDS
August 2009

1 INTRODUCTION

6.2410 1.1 This document sets out remote and gambling software technical standards issued by the Gambling Commission (the Commission) under section 89 and section 97 of the Gambling Act 2005 (the Act).

1.2 This document replaces the Remote gambling and software technical standards (RTS) – June 2007.

REVIEW OF RTS

1.3 The Commission has monitored RTS since they came into force on 1 September 2007. The Commission also carried out an initial review of RTS between October and December 2008 to determine whether there were any possible issues or changes that warranted a full consultation.

1.4 Feedback from stakeholders indicated that the RTS remain fit for purpose and there are no issues that required full consultation. The Commission published an information note on this in December 2008.

CHANGES TO RTS

1.5 This updated RTS document therefore does not include any changes to policy. However, the Commission has decided to publish an updated version to bring together other RTS requirements that were originally published separately.

1.6 This version now includes:

- a summary of the RTS security requirements that licence holders must meet (in chapter 5)
- signposting to the relevant testing and audit requirements that licence holders must meet (below).

TESTING AND AUDIT REQUIREMENTS

1.7 The Commission's 'Testing strategy for compliance with the remote gambling and software technical standards' (August 2009) sets out the Commission's current requirements for the timing and procedures for testing. Compliance with the RTS and testing strategy is a licence condition[1].

[1] Condition 2 in Licence Conditions and Codes of Practice (LCCP), October 2008.

1.8 Importantly it sets out the circumstances in which independent third party testing is required. The relevant standards are given in chapters 3 and 4 of this document.

1.9 The Testing strategy for compliance with the remote gambling and software technical standards also sets out the independent audit requirements that licence holders should fulfil. This is based on relevant sections of Annex A to ISO/IEC 27001: 2005 which are summarised in chapter 5 of this document.

APPLICATION TO REMOTE BINGO LICENCES

1.10 The following standards do not apply to holders of remote bingo licences when making facilities available by means of remote communication in respect of games of bingo played on more than one set of premises:

- RTS 1
- RTS 2
- RTS 6
- RTS 8
- RTS 9
- RTS 11
- RTS 12
- RTS 13
- RTS 14
- IPA 1-5
- IPA 7

GAMBLING SOFTWARE

1.11 In the case of gambling software, these technical standards only apply to manufacture, supply, installation or adaptation of software for use in connection with remote gambling which takes place in reliance on an operating licence issued by the Commission.

2 DEFINITION OF TERMS

2.1 In this document the following terms have the following meanings:

Compensated games or events	Games or virtual events that adjust the likelihood of winning outcomes occurring based on previous payouts or intake. Sometimes referred to as adaptive behaviour or percentage compensation.
Game	A game of chance as defined in section 6(2) of the Act
Instant lottery	A lottery in which the draw takes place before any of the tickets in the lottery are offered for sale.
Mapping	Is the process of selecting an outcome using the result from a Random Number Generator (RNG). For example, the result from a RNG is mapped to a reel strip symbol.
Lottery	As described by section 14 of the Act.
Lottery ticket	As described by section 253 of the Act and a reference in this document to a lottery ticket includes:
	• a lottery ticket which is sent by post following entry by means of remote communication
	• a message sent or displayed to a person electronically in a manner which enables him to
	(a) retain the message electronically, or (b) print it.
Non-commercial society	As described by section 19 of the Act.
Peer-to-peer gambling	A type of gambling where customers gamble against each other rather than against the house. For example, equal chance gaming such as poker or peer-to-peer betting through betting exchanges.
Progressive or progressive jackpot	An incremental prize that increases as a result of contributions from the monies staked within a game from pre-set base value.
Random Number Generator (RNG)	Refers to any item of hardware or software which is used to generate random numbers with the intended property of statistical randomness.
Restricted display device	A device such as a mobile phone or personal digital assistant which has limited space on which to display information, when used to access gambling facilities that the operator intends a customer to use by means of such a device.
Scaling	Scaling is the process used to convert the output from a RNG into the format required to produce a result for a particular gambling product. To illustrate, an RNG may produce a result of between 1 and 100,000 but these possible outcomes need to be scaled to the potential game outcomes of, for example, between 1 – 52 (ie to correspond to a standard pack of cards).
Seeding	Refers to the process used to determine the initial state of the RNG.
Subscription lottery	A series of lotteries (other than instant lotteries) promoted on behalf of the same non-commercial society or local authority in respect of which participants pay for participation in one or more future lotteries by regular subscription over a fixed or indefinite period.

Telephone gambling	Gambling which takes place via a telephone, without the use of visual displays, by interaction with a customer service agent or an automated system, such as intelligent voice recognition systems or touch tone.
Virtual	As described by s353(3) of the Act. Virtual event and virtual game are to be construed accordingly.

3 REMOTE GAMBLING AND SOFTWARE TECHNICAL STANDARDS (RTS)

RTS 1 – CUSTOMER ACCOUNT INFORMATION

All gambling – except subscription lotteries

RTS AIM 1

To provide customers with easily accessible information about their current balances.

RTS REQUIREMENT 1A

Where customers hold a credit or debit balance, the pages or screens used to move money into and out of accounts or products must be designed to display the customer's current account or product balance, either in the currency of their account or the currency of the gambling product (eg dollars, euros or pounds sterling), whenever that customer is logged in.

For telephone betting this information is to be delivered at the customer's request by the customer service agent or automated response system.

RTS IMPLEMENTATION GUIDANCE 1A

(a) Where funds are moved between products (for example, from a betting product to a gaming product) the balance does not necessarily have to represent all of the balances that a customer may hold with an operator in respect of those products.

RTS REQUIREMENT 1B

Where customers hold a credit or debit balance, the pages or screens used for gambling must be designed to display the customer's current account or product balance, or where this is not practical to display a link to a page or screen that shows the balance, whenever that customer is logged in. Balances are to be presented either in the currency of the customer's account or the currency of the gambling product (eg dollars, euros or pounds sterling).

For telephone betting this information is to be delivered at the customer's request by the customer service agent or automated response system.

RTS IMPLEMENTATION GUIDANCE 1B

(a) Where funds are moved between products, the balance does not necessarily have to represent all of the balances that a customer may hold with an operator in respect of other products.

(b) Gambling pages and screens include virtual game pages, sports betting coupons, and poker and other virtual gaming 'tables'.

RTS 2 – DISPLAYING TRANSACTIONS

All gambling

RTS AIM 2

To enable the customer to understand the value and content of their transactions.

RTS REQUIREMENT 2A

The remote gambling system must be designed to make available clear information about the amount of money being gambled by the customer, including any conversions from one form of currency to another, or from currency to credits, chips or other tokens etc, at the point of conversion.

For telephone gambling, this information is to be delivered by the customer service agent or automated response system.

RTS IMPLEMENTATION GUIDANCE 2A

(a) It is preferable for the amount being gambled to be displayed either in the currency of the customer's account or in the currency of the product. The use of credits, chips or other tokens with no face value should be avoided wherever possible.

(b) Any conversion from one currency to another should be clearly presented to the customer and any conversion rules are also to be presented. Where currency is converted into tokens, chips or credits, etc, the conversion should be clearly displayed.

(c) Information about the value of the gamble should be displayed including, as appropriate:
   (i) unit stake and total stake, whether currency, credit, tokens, chips, or any other form of payment;
   (ii) entry fees, for example, payment for entry to poker tournaments;
   (iii) the price of lottery tickets and the number of draws entered.

(d) For subscription lotteries, sending a confirmation by email or post and/or displaying the stake and the number of draws entered when the customer subscribes is sufficient.

RTS REQUIREMENT 2B

The gambling system must be designed to display sufficient relevant information about the customer's gamble so that the content of the gamble is clear. This information must be made available before the customer commits to the gamble including, for example, in the artwork and textual information displayed during gaming, or on an electronic equivalent of a betting slip or lottery ticket.

For telephone betting, this information is to be delivered by the customer service agent or automated response system.

RTS IMPLEMENTATION GUIDANCE 2B

(a) The following items provide guidelines about the type of information that may be relevant:
   (i) selections – the items the customer has chosen to gamble on;
   (ii) the bet type
   (iii) the accepted odds, for example current odds, starting price, first show, etc.

   These items, where relevant, are required on applications designed for use on restricted display devices.

(b) For telephone gambling the content of the customer's bet should be read back to them before the bet is confirmed.

(c) Where the customer is able to choose, through the use of a third party user-interface, to override the display of this information, this must not be the default option. That is, the customer must make an active choice not to have the information available or to install a user-interface that does not contain the information. The remote gambling system should continue to make available or send the information to the customer; it should not assume that the information is not required.

(d) For subscription lotteries, sending a confirmation by email or post and/or displaying the first draw and the number of draws for which the customer will be entered is sufficient.

RTS 3 – RULES, GAME DESCRIPTIONS AND THE LIKELIHOOD OF WINNING

Gaming (including bingo), lotteries and betting on virtual events

RTS AIM 3

To enable customers to make informed decisions about whether to gamble based on their chances of winning, the way the game, lottery or event works, the prizes or payouts on offer and the current state of multi-state games or events.

RTS REQUIREMENT 3A
An explanation of the applicable rules must be easily available to the customer before they commit to gamble. The content including artwork and text must be accurate, and sufficient to explain all of the applicable rules and how to participate. All reasonable steps must be taken to ensure that the content is understandable.

RTS IMPLEMENTATION GUIDANCE 3A
(a) Explanatory content includes information in artwork and text displayed within the virtual event, in 'help' or 'how to play' pages, or other supporting material.
(b) Links to the information should be prominently placed, for example on home pages for gaming sections, game selection pages or menus, or within individual games, so that customers can easily locate them.
(c) As a minimum, restricted display devices should provide explanatory content via a menu item or other link.
(d) The following items provide guidelines on the type of explanatory content that may be relevant and should be considered for inclusion:
  (i) the name of the game, lottery or virtual event
  (ii) the applicable rules, including clear descriptions of what constitutes a winning outcome iii. restrictions on play or betting, such as any play duration limits, maximum wins, etc
  (iii) the number of decks or frequency of shuffles in virtual card games
  (iv) whether there are contributions to jackpots (progressives) and the way in which the jackpot operates, for example, whether the jackpot is won by achieving a particular outcome
  (v) instructions on how to interact with the game
  (vi) rules pertaining to metamorphosis of games, for example, the number and type of tokens that need to be collected in order to qualify for a feature or bonus round and the rules and behaviour of the bonus round
  (vii) the rules for entering a single lottery draw or a series of lottery draws and the frequency of the draws.

RTS REQUIREMENT 3B
Where relevant, as the game or event progresses, information that may reasonably be expected to enable the customer to understand the current state must be displayed.

RTS IMPLEMENTATION GUIDANCE 3B

The following items provide guidelines on the type of information that may be relevant.

(a) Where a game builds up a collection of tokens (symbols etc), the current number collected.

(b) An indication of which rules are currently relevant, such as displaying 'bonus round' or other feature labels.

(c) This requirement does not apply to lotteries.

RTS REQUIREMENT 3C

For each virtual event, game (including bingo), or lottery, information that may reasonably be expected to enable the customer to make an informed decision about his or her chances of winning must be easily available before the customer commits to gamble. Information must include:

(i) a description of the way the game works and the way in which winners are determined and prizes allocated

(ii) house edge (or margin)

(iii) the return to player (RTP) percentage

(iv) the probability (likelihood) of winning events occurring.

RTS IMPLEMENTATION GUIDANCE 3C

(a) The following items provide further guidance on acceptable types of information about the likelihood of winning:

   (i) for types of peer-to-peer games where the likelihood of winning may depend on skill and/or the actions of other participants, a description of the way the game works and how winners are determined will be sufficient;

   (ii) for bingo, and some types of lottery or other games where it is not possible to determine the likelihood of winning because it depends on the eventual number of participants, a description of the way in which prizes are allocated will be sufficient.

   (iii) the average theoretical return to player percentage. Where an event (other than peer- to-peer) involves an element of skill, return to player percentage should be calculated using either the auto-play strategy or a standard/published strategy;

   (iv) the house edge, margin or over-round, for example for a virtual race;

   (v) the probability of each winning event occurring, or such information as may reasonably be expected to allow the customer to calculate the probability that the event will occur. The nature of some games may mean that the game itself provides sufficient information, for example, the likelihood of rolling a six on a six-sided die would not require further explanation.

(b) Information may be included in artwork and text displayed within the virtual game or event, in 'help' or 'how to play' pages, or other supporting material.

(c) Information should be easily accessible, for example by placing links on home pages for gaming or virtual event sections, game selection pages or menus, or within individual games.

RTS REQUIREMENT 3D

For each virtual event, game (including bingo), or lottery, content describing the potential prizes and payouts or the means by which these are calculated or determined must be easily available before the customer commits to gamble.

RTS IMPLEMENTATION GUIDANCE 3D

(a) Information should be made available about the amounts that customers may potentially win, for example in the form of pay-tables, or by showing the odds paid for particular outcomes.

(b) For peer-to-peer games where the prize is determined based on the actions of the participants, a description of the way the game works and the rake or commission taken will be sufficient.
(c) For lotteries and other types of events where the potential amount or prize paid out may not be known before the customer commits to gamble, describing the way in which the prize amount is determined will be sufficient.
(d) Information may be included in artwork and text displayed within the virtual event, in 'help' or 'how to play' pages, or other supporting material.
(e) Information should be easily accessible, for example by placing links on home pages for gaming sections, game selection pages or menus, or within individual games.
(f) Displays of jackpot amounts that change over time ('progressives') should be updated as frequently as practicable, particularly after the amount has been reset following a win.

RTS 4 – TIME-CRITICAL EVENTS

Gaming (including bingo), and betting on virtual events

RTS AIM 4
To reduce the risk that customers are unfairly disadvantaged by technical factors that may affect speed of response, where response time has a significant impact on the likelihood of winning.

RTS REQUIREMENT 4A
Where speed of interaction has a significant effect on the customer's chance of winning, operators must assess the level of risk and demonstrate to the Commission that they are taking reasonable steps to reduce the risk to customers.

RTS IMPLEMENTATION GUIDANCE 4A
Examples of possible approaches include:
(a) estimating the degree of network latency (delay) a customer is experiencing and displaying regularly updated information to the customer about any disadvantage that they may be operating under (eg high, medium, low)
(b) applying a handicapping system based on estimated performance and/or system latency
(c) treating winning responses that arrive within a period of time as simultaneous and implementing a policy on how simultaneous wins are to be dealt with.

RTS 5 – RESULT DETERMINATION

All gambling

RTS AIM 5
To ensure that the gambling system implements the operator's rules, game rules and betting rules as they are described to the customer.

RTS REQUIREMENT 5A
All reasonable steps should be taken to ensure that gambles are accepted, processed and settled in accordance with the operator's published terms and rules, and the rules of the specific game, event, or bet.
Where unexpected system flaws, faults, or errors that affect the customer occur, steps are to be taken as soon as practicable to remedy the problem and ensure that the customer is treated fairly according to the circumstances.

RTS IMPLEMENTATION GUIDANCE 5A

(a) Under normal operation, in the absence of technical faults, the system should act in accordance with the rules.

(b) Reasonable steps include testing of systems and new products against the published rules.

(c) Customers should be notified when errors that affect them, for example, incorrectly settled bets, have occurred as soon as practicable after the event occurs. Steps should be taken to rectify the error, for example, by manually adjusting the customer's account.

RTS 6 – RESULT DETERMINATION FOR PLAY-FOR-FUN GAMES

Gaming (including bingo), lotteries, and betting on virtual events

RTS AIM 6

To minimise the risk that customers are misled about the likelihood of winning due to the behaviour of play-for-fun games.

RTS REQUIREMENT 6A

Play-for-fun games must implement the same game rules as the corresponding play-for-money games. Operators must take all reasonable steps to ensure that play-for-fun games accurately represent the likelihood of winning and prize distribution in the play-for-money game. For the purpose of this requirement playing a game includes participating in a lottery and/or betting on a virtual event.

RTS IMPLEMENTATION GUIDANCE 6A

(a) The play-for-free game should use the same RNG as the corresponding play-for-money games, another RNG that fulfils the requirements set out in RTS requirement 7A, or a publicly available RNG, (such as those available as standard within operating systems) that may reasonably be expected to produce no systematic bias.

(b) Where 6a is not reasonably possible, it should be demonstrated that the method of producing outcomes does not introduce a systematic bias, for example:
  (i) if tables of random numbers are used, they should be sufficiently long to support a large number of games without repeating;
  (ii) the method should represent game probabilities accurately, ie it should not produce a higher than expected proportion of winning outcomes.

(c) The prize distribution should accurately represent the play-for-money game. For example, where play-for-fun games use virtual cash, the virtual cash payouts should be the same as the corresponding play-for-money game, and where tokens are used, the allocation of tokens as prizes should be proportionate to the stakes and prizes in the play-for-money game.

RTS 7 – GENERATION OF RANDOM OUTCOMES

Gaming (including bingo), lotteries, and betting on virtual events

RTS AIM 7

To ensure that games and other virtual events operate fairly.

RTS REQUIREMENT 7A

Random number generation and game results must be 'acceptably random'. Acceptably random here means that it is possible to demonstrate to a high degree of confidence that the output of the RNG, game, lottery and virtual event outcomes are random, through, for example, statistical analysis using generally accepted tests and methods of analysis. Adaptive behaviour (ie a compensated game) is not permitted.

Where lotteries use the outcome of other events external to the lottery, to determine the result of the lottery (for example, using numbers from the National Lottery) the outcome must be unpredictable and externally verifiable.

RTS IMPLEMENTATION GUIDANCE 7A

(a) RNG's should be capable of demonstrating the following qualities:
   (i) the output from the RNG is uniformly distributed over the entire output range and game, lottery, or virtual event outcomes are distributed in accordance with the expected/theoretical probabilities
   (ii) the output of the RNG, game, lottery, and virtual event outcomes should be unpredictable, for example, for a software RNG it should be computationally infeasible to predict what the next number will be without complete knowledge of the algorithm and seed value
   (iii) random number generation does not reproduce the same output stream (cycle), and that two instances of a RNG do not produce the same stream as each other (synchronise)
   (iv) any forms of seeding and re-seeding used do not introduce predictability
   (v) any scaling applied to the output of the random number generator maintains the qualities above.
(b) For lotteries using external events — where it is not practical to demonstrate 7a. — the events outcomes should be:
   (i) unpredictable, that is, events should be selected only where they may reasonably be assumed to be random events
   (ii) unable to be influenced by the lottery operator (or external lottery manager)
   (iii) publicly available and externally verifiable, for example, events that are published in local or national press would be acceptable.
(c) For games or virtual events that use the laws of physics to generate the outcome of the game (mechanical RNGs), the mechanical RNG used should be capable of meeting the requirements in a. where applicable and in addition:
   (i) the mechanical pieces should be constructed of materials to prevent decomposition of any component over time (eg a ball shall not disintegrate)
   (ii) the properties of physical items used to choose the selection should not be altered
   (iii) players should not have the ability to interact with, come into physical contact with, or manipulate the mechanics of the game.
(d) Restricting adaptive behaviour prohibits automatic or manual interventions that change the probabilities of game outcomes occurring during play. Restricting adaptive behaviour is not intended to prevent games from offering bonus or special features that implement a different set of rules, if they are based on the occurrence of random events.

RTS REQUIREMENT 7B

As far as is reasonably possible, games and events must be implemented fairly and in accordance with the rules and prevailing payouts, where applicable, as they are described to the customer.

RTS IMPLEMENTATION GUIDANCE 7B

(a) Games should implement the rules as described in the rules available to the customer before play commenced.
(b) The mapping of the random inputs to game outcomes should be in accordance with prevailing probabilities, pay tables, etc.

(c) When random numbers, scaled or otherwise, are received, eg following a game requesting a sequence of random numbers, they are to be used in the order in which they are received. For example, they may not be discarded due to adaptive behaviour.

(d) Numbers or sequences of numbers are not to be discarded, unless they fall outside the expected range of numbers required by the virtual event – such an occurrence should result in an error being logged and investigated.

RTS REQUIREMENT 7C

Game designs or features that may reasonably be expected to mislead the customer about the likelihood of particular results occurring are not permitted, including substituting losing events with near-miss losing events and simulations of real devices that do not simulate the real probabilities of the device.

RTS IMPLEMENTATION GUIDANCE 7C

(a) Where a virtual event simulates a physical device, the theoretical game probabilities should match the probabilities of the real device (for example, the probability of a coin landing heads must be 0.5 every time the coin is tossed).

(b) Where multiple physical devices are simulated the probabilities of each outcome should be independent of the other simulated devices.

(c) Games may not falsely display near-miss results, that is, the event may not substitute one losing outcome with a different losing outcome.

(d) Where the event requires a pre-determined layout (for example, hidden prizes on a map), the locations of the winning spots should not change during play, except as provided for in the rules of the game.

(e) Where games involve an element of skill, every outcome described in the virtual event rules or artwork should be possible, that is, the customer should have some chance of achieving an advertised outcome regardless of skill.

(f) Where a customer contributes to a jackpot pool, that customer should be eligible to win the jackpot whilst they are playing that game, in accordance with the game and jackpot rules.

RTS REQUIREMENT 7D

The rules, payouts and outcome probabilities of a virtual event or game may not be changed while it is available for gambling, except as provided for in the rules of the game, lottery or virtual event. Such changes must be brought to customer's attention.

RTS IMPLEMENTATION GUIDANCE 7D

(a) Changes to game or event rules, paytables or other parameters that change the way in which a game, lottery, or event works, the winnings paid, or likelihood of winning (except as described in 7Dc.), should be conducted with the game or event taken offline or suspended.

(b) Altered games, lotteries, and events should display a notice that informs customers that the game or event has been changed, for example, 'rules changed', 'new odds', or 'different payouts'. The notice should be displayed on game selection screens and on the events themselves if it is possible for the customer to go straight to the event without using a selection screen.

(c) This requirement is not intended to prevent games and virtual events where specified changes occur legitimately, in accordance with the game or event rules, for example:

   (i) virtual events, such as virtual racing products where the odds differ from event to event depending on the virtual runners

   (ii) virtual games, such as bingo where the odds of winning are dependent on the number of entrants

   (iii) games with progressive jackpots, where the amount that can be won changes over time

(iv) games with bonus rounds where different rules apply, so long as these rounds are properly described to the customer

(v) unspecified changes to rules, paytables or other parameters that change the way in which a game, lottery or event works are not permitted, for example, rules that state 'game rules may be changed at any time' would not be acceptable.

RTS REQUIREMENT 7E

Except in the case of subscription lotteries, the system must be designed to clearly and accurately display the result of the game or event and the customer's gamble. The result must be displayed for a length of time that may reasonably be expected to be sufficient for the customer to understand the result of the game or event in the context of their gamble.

RTS IMPLEMENTATION GUIDANCE 7E

The game artwork and text should be sufficient to provide the customer with all of the information required to determine whether they have lost or won, and the value of any winnings.

RTS 8 – AUTO-PLAY FUNCTIONALITY

Gaming

RTS AIM 8

To ensure that the customer is still in control of the gambling where auto-play functionality is provided.

RTS REQUIREMENT 8A

Auto-play must be implemented in such a way that the customer is able to control the amount gambled through selecting the stake and the number of auto-play gambles. The number of auto- play gambles may not exceed 25 in one batch.

RTS IMPLEMENTATION GUIDANCE 8A

(a) The customer should choose the stake and either the number of auto-play gambles or the total amount to be gambled.

(b) During auto-play the customer should be able to stop the auto-play regardless of how many auto-play gambles they initially chose or how many remain.

(c) Auto-play should not override any of the display requirements (for example, the result of each gamble must be displayed for a reasonable length of time before the next gamble commences, as set out in RTS 7E).

RTS 9 – SKILL AND CHANCE GAMES WITH AUTO-PLAY

Gaming

RTS AIM 9

To minimise the risk that auto-play functionality disadvantages a customer or that autoplay or other strategy advice is misleading.

RTS REQUIREMENT 9A

Strategy advice and auto-play functionality must be fair, not misleading and must not represent a poor choice.

RTS IMPLEMENTATION GUIDANCE 9A

(a) In implementing this control, the following should be considered, where appropriate:
   (i) if there is a standard strategy, for example, for well known games like blackjack, the standard strategy should be used
   (ii) strategies or auto-play should (theoretically) produce at least the average Return to Player (RTP) for the game over time.

RTS 10 – INTERRUPTED GAMBLING

Peer-to-peer betting and gaming (including bingo)

RTS AIM 10

To ensure that customers are treated fairly in the event of interrupted play or betting and that they are aware of how they will be treated if interruptions occur.

RTS REQUIREMENT 10A

Operators must take all reasonable steps to ensure that their policies for instigating or dealing with service interruptions are fair and do not systematically disadvantage customers.

RTS IMPLEMENTATION GUIDANCE 10A

(a) For gaming the following policies should be applied:
   (i) where an interruption occurs after the operator receives notification of the customer's gamble and where the customer can have no further influence on the outcome of the event or gamble the results of the gamble should stand;
   (ii) where an interruption to a single-participant single stage event occurs before an outcome has been generated the customer should have any deducted stake returned to their balance;
   (iii) for stateful games (games where there are multiple stages or decision points), all reasonable steps should be taken to restore the game to its last known state to enable the customer to complete the game;
   (iv) games with multiple participants (equal chance or otherwise) should be dealt with fairly on a case-by-case basis;
   (v) progressive jackpot values should be restored to their pre-failure state.
(b) For peer-to-peer betting the following policies should be applied:
   (i) where a service interruption is caused by failures in the gambling system, operators should suspend betting on all betting markets that have been affected by a significant event before service is restored;
   (ii) other failures should be dealt with fairly on a case-by-case basis.

RTS REQUIREMENT 10B

Systems must be capable of recovering from failures that cause interruptions to gambling, including where appropriate, the capability to void gambles (with or without manual intervention), the capability to suspend betting markets, and taking all reasonable steps to retain sufficient information to be able to restore events to their pre-failure state.

RTS IMPLEMENTATION GUIDANCE 10B

(a) For gaming the system should:
   (i) be capable of voiding gambles and restoring the amount gambled to the customer automatically, or in conjunction with manual operational controls; and

(ii) implement all reasonable measures to maintain sufficient information to be capable of automatically restoring an event to its pre-failure state so that it may be completed by the customer. The following information should be restored, as appropriate:
- the state of a deck of cards, and any hands that have been dealt
- number of tokens collected
- any other predetermined information, such as maps or prize layouts
- the value of any progressive jackpots
- the state of any gambles, eg who has staked what on what outcome
- bets placed or offered.

(b) For peer-to-peer betting, it should be possible to suspend betting markets manually or automatically.

RTS 11 – LIMITING COLLUSION/CHEATING

Peer-to-peer gaming

RTS AIM 11

To reduce the risk that cheating or collusion by players unfairly disadvantages another player.

RTS REQUIREMENT 11A
Measures intended to deter, prevent, and detect collusion and cheating must be implemented. Gambling systems must retain a record of relevant activities to facilitate investigation and be capable of suspending or disabling player accounts or player sessions.

RTS IMPLEMENTATION GUIDANCE 11A
(a) The Information Provision Annex standard 7 provides guidance on the minimum information that should be made available to deter cheating.
(b) Relevant activities to be recorded will vary by game but may include:
 (i) which players played at which tables
 (ii) the amounts won from and lost to accounts
 (iii) game activities to an individual bet/action level.
(c) Where appropriate, prevention measures may include:
 (i) taking steps to prevent a player from occupying more than one seat at any individual table.
(d) Detection measures may include, detecting and investigating the following, where appropriate:
 (i) players who frequently share the same tables;
 (ii) players from same address who share the same table;
 (iii) suspicious patterns of play (such as chip dumping).
(e) Customer complaints about cheating should be investigated.

RTS 12 – FINANCIAL LIMITS

All gambling

RTS AIM 12

To provide customers with facilities that may assist them in sticking to their personal budgets for gambling with the operator.

6: Gambling Act 2005: Additional Material

RTS REQUIREMENT 12A

The gambling system must provide easily accessible facilities that make it possible for customers to impose their own financial limits. Customers must be given the opportunity to set a limit as part of the registration process (or at the point at which the customer makes the first deposit or payment).

For lotteries, where the customer's spend is controlled through subscriptions, additional facilities do not have to be provided.

RTS IMPLEMENTATION GUIDANCE 12A

(a) For telephone gambling (except lotteries), customers should be asked if they would like to set a deposit or spend limit when they register. Customers should be able to request a limit at any point after registration. The limit should be implemented as soon as practicable after the customer's request. The customer should be informed when the limit will come into force.

(b) For other access media (including internet, interactive TV and mobile), customers should be offered the opportunity to select a deposit/spend limit from a list which may contain a 'no limit' option or to enter a limit of their choice as part of the registration or first deposit process. The 'no limit' option should not be the default option.

(c) Limits could be in the form of:
  (i) deposit limits: where the amount a customer deposits into their account is limited over a particular duration;
  (ii) spend limits: where the amount a customer spends on gambling (or specific gambling products) is restricted for a given period – this type of limit may be appropriate where the customer does not hold a deposit account with the operator;
  (iii) loss limits: where the amount lost (ie winnings subtracted from the amount spent) is restricted (for instance when a customer makes a £10 bet and wins £8, the loss is £2).

(d) The period/duration of the limit should be no less than one day (or 24 hours).
e. In addition:
  (i) limits may be implemented per customer, per account, or other means;
  (ii) limits could also be implemented across all products or channels or for individual products or channels;
  (iii) financial limit facilities should be provided via a link on the home page;
  (iv) facilities should be available on deposit pages/screens or via a link on these pages/screens.

RTS REQUIREMENT 12B

All reasonable steps must be taken to ensure that customer-led limits are only increased at the customer's request, and only after a cooling-off period of 24 hours has elapsed.

RTS IMPLEMENTATION GUIDANCE 12B

(a) Increases should not be implemented until a cooling-off period of at least 24 hours from the point at which the request to increase the limit was received. Where it is practicable to do so, the customer should be required to confirm that they still wish to increase the limit at the end of the cooling-off period.

(b) Where possible (for instance, unless systems/technical failures prevent it) limit reductions are to be implemented within 24 hours of the request being received.

RTS 13 – TIME REQUIREMENTS

All gambling except telephone gambling

RTS AIM 13

To provide customers with facilities to assist them to keep track of the time they spend gambling.

RTS REQUIREMENT 13A
Where the gambling system uses full screen client applications that obscure the clock on the customer's device the client application itself must display the time of day or the elapsed time since the application was started, wherever practicable.

RTS IMPLEMENTATION GUIDANCE 13A
(a) Time of day should either be taken from the customer's own device or 'server time' and should be displayed in hours and minutes.
(b) Operators will not be expected to detect whether or not customers have hidden their clocks. c. Elapsed time should be displayed in minutes and hours.
(c) For restricted display devices, time of day or elapsed time should be displayed where the device supports it.
(d) In addition, customers may be offered the ability to set a session or game-play duration reminder.

RTS 14 – RESPONSIBLE PRODUCT DESIGN

All gambling

RTS AIM 14

To ensure that products are designed responsibly and to minimise the likelihood that they exploit or encourage problem gambling behaviour.

RTS REQUIREMENT 14A
Gambling products must not actively encourage customers to chase their losses, increase their stake or increase the amount they have decided to gamble, or continue to gamble after they have indicated that they wish to stop.

RTS IMPLEMENTATION GUIDANCE 14A
(a) By actively encourage, we mean the inclusion of specific features, functions or information that could reasonably be expected to encourage a greater likelihood of the behaviours described occurring. For example:
  (i) the amount of funds taken into a product should not be topped up without the customer choosing to do so on each occasion, eg when a customer buys-in at a poker table they should have to choose to purchase more chips to play at the table – automatic re- buys should not be provided
  (ii) written or graphical information should not encourage customers to try to win back their losses
  (iii) customers who have chosen to exit a game should not be encouraged to continue playing by, for example, being offered a free game.
(b) This requirement is not intended to prevent operators from offering special features or well-known games such as blackjack that allow customers to

increase their stake on the occurrence of specific events (eg split).

4 INFORMATION PROVISION ANNEX (IPA) STANDARDS

IPA 1 – CUSTOMER ACCOUNT INFORMATION

All gambling except subscription lotteries

IPA AIM 1

To provide customers with facilities that enable them to review previous gambling and account transactions.

IPA REQUIREMENT 1A
Customers must have easy access to their account and gambling history. Where customers access operators' products or register via websites, it is acceptable to provide access to statements via these websites. For customers who do not access or register via websites, information is to be provided via the medium of access, or a copy must be sent via email, fax, or post.

IPA IMPLEMENTATION GUIDANCE 1A
(a) Account history should include credit and debit information such as deposits, withdrawals, movement of funds between products, payments off credit accounts, entry fee deductions, and bonus information, as appropriate.
(b) For betting, gambling history should include bets placed, and the results of bets, including winnings paid. For gaming (including bingo) full or summarised gaming information should be available, for example, £10 taken into game, £100 turned over, £3 taken away from game.
(c) Where customers are able to move funds between gambling products, account information and statements should clearly display movement of funds into and out of products.
(d) For telephone betting, where customers demonstrate that they also have access to websites – by registering online or using other online products – it is acceptable to provide access to statements via these websites, otherwise customers should be sent a regular copy of their statement via email, fax or post unless they elect not to receive this information. Customers should be sent a statement on request, even if they have opted out of receiving regular statements.
(e) For gaming, where detailed historic game information may not necessarily be directly available to customers, as a minimum, customers should have easy access to details of the last game played and summarised information for previous activities.
(f) For restricted display devices, where customers demonstrate that they also have access to websites – for example, by registering online or using other online products – it is acceptable to provide access to statements via these websites. Otherwise, if the information cannot practicably be provided on the device, customers should be sent a copy of the statement via email, fax or post.

IPA 2 – DISPLAYING TRANSACTIONS – THIRD PARTY USER-INTERFACES

IPA aim 2

To inform customers who choose to use third party user-interfaces that they may not receive full information about their gambles.

IPA REQUIREMENT 2A

Customers must be informed that third party interface applications may not display full information about the customer's gambles.

IPA IMPLEMENTATION GUIDANCE 2A

(a) Information should be included in terms and conditions, rules or other general information about the gambling product that is made available to and/or sent out to customers.

IPA 3 – IN-RUNNING BETTING

Betting and peer-to-peer betting

IPA AIM 3

To make the customer aware that they may not have the latest information available when betting on live events, and that they may be at a disadvantage to operators or other customers who have more up-to-date information.

IPA REQUIREMENT 3A

Information must be made available that explains that 'live' TV or other broadcasts are delayed and that others may have more up-to-date information. Main in-running betting pages must be designed to include this information where practicable.

IPA IMPLEMENTATION GUIDANCE 3A

(a) Brief information should be included on main in-running pages or screens, such as the in- running home page or screen. More detail should be provided in 'help' or 'how to' or other product pages or screens.

(b) For telephone betting the information should be included in the general betting or product information that is made available to and/or sent out to customers.

(c) Where a brief notice cannot be practicably included on the main pages or screens, the information should be provided on easily accessible 'help', 'how to' or other product pages or screens.

IPA 4 – USE OF AUTOMATED GAMBLING SOFTWARE

Peer-to-peer gambling

IPA AIM 4

To make customers in peer-to-peer(s) gambling aware that they may be gambling against a software program (designed to automatically participate in gambling within certain parameters), rather than another (human) participant. This software is sometimes referred to as a robot or bot.

IPA REQUIREMENT 4A

Where operators use programs to participate in gambling on their behalf in peer-to-peer gambling, easily accessible information must be displayed, which clearly informs customers that the operator uses this kind of software.

IPA IMPLEMENTATION GUIDANCE 4A

(a) Peer-to-peer(s) gambling operators that use software to gamble on their behalf (for example, poker robots) should display a notice to customers on the home pages or screens and in the game description, 'help' or 'how to play/bet' pages or screens.

(b) As a minimum, restricted display devices should provide a link to further information on gambling pages/screens or in 'help', 'about' or 'how to bet/play' pages or screens.

IPA REQUIREMENT 4B
Where peer-to-peer(s) customers may be gambling against programs deployed by other customers to play on their behalf, information should be made available that describes that this is possible, and if it is against the operator's terms and conditions to use robots, how to report suspected robot use.

IPA IMPLEMENTATION GUIDANCE 4B
(a) The warning and information about how to complain should be included in game descriptions, rules, terms and conditions, 'help', 'how to play' or other general product information pages.
(b) The warning should also inform customers that if they use a program to gamble on their behalf, other customers may be able to exploit it.

IPA 5 – TIME-CRITICAL EVENTS

Gaming (including bingo), betting on virtual events, and peer-to-peer betting

IPA AIM 5

To make the customer aware that they may be at a disadvantage due to technical characteristics, such as slower network connections or lower end user device performance, if they are participating in a time-critical form of gambling (where the customer's speed of interaction influences their chance of winning).

IPA REQUIREMENT 5A
For time-critical events, the customer should be informed that they might be at a disadvantage because of technical issues such as slower network speeds, or slower end user device performance.

IPA IMPLEMENTATION GUIDANCE 5A
(a) Information should be included in game descriptions, rules, 'help' or 'how to play' pages.

IPA 6 – INTERRUPTED GAMBLING

Gaming (including bingo), betting on virtual events, and peer-to-peer betting

IPA AIM 6

To inform customers about the operator's policies with regard to service interruptions and how they are likely to be treated if interruption occurs so that they may make an informed decision about whether to gamble and in what way.

IPA REQUIREMENT 6A
Operators must make available information about their policies regarding service interruptions in various different circumstances.

IPA IMPLEMENTATION GUIDANCE 6A
(a) Operators should make information available to customers about how they will be treated in various common scenarios. However, this does not mean that

operators have to detail all possible scenarios or responses to service interruptions.

IPA 7 – LIMITING COLLUSION/CHEATING

Peer-to-peer gaming

IPA AIM 7

To inform customers about the risks posed by collusion/cheating and to deter individuals from attempting to cheat.

IPA REQUIREMENT 7A

Information must be made available about the operator's policies and procedures with regard to cheating, and about how to complain if a customer suspects other participants are cheating.

IPA IMPLEMENTATION GUIDANCE 7A

(a) As a minimum deterrent, customers should be informed that accounts will be closed if the customer is found to have cheated.
(b) Relevant information should be included in terms and conditions or rules.

5 REMOTE GAMBLING AND SOFTWARE TECHNICAL STANDARDS – SECURITY REQUIREMENTS

5.1 This section sets out a summary of the RTS security requirements that licence holders must meet. The Commission has based the security requirements on the relevant sections of Annex A to the ISO/EIC 27001: 2005 standard. The full sections of the relevant security requirements can be obtained in paper format from the Commission. Alternatively a full copy of the British Standards can be obtained from BSI Customer Services, 389 Chiswick High Road, London, W4 4AL. Tel: ++ 44 (0)20 8996 9001. Email: mailto://cservices@bsigroup.com.

5.2 The Commission's aim in setting out the security standards is to ensure customers are not exposed to unnecessary security risks by choosing to participate in remote gambling. The Commission has highlighted those systems that are most critical to achieving the Commission's aims and the security standards apply to these critical systems:

- electronic systems that record, store, process, share, transmit or retrieve sensitive customer information, eg credit/debit card details, authentication information, customer account balances
- electronic systems that generate, transmit, or process random numbers used to determine the outcome of games or virtual events
- electronic systems that store results or the current state of a customer's gamble;
- points of entry to and exit from the above systems (other systems that are able to communicate directly with core critical systems)
- communication networks that transmit sensitive customer information.

SECURITY REQUIREMENTS SUMMARY

Standard – A.5 Security Policy

Requirement A.5.1.1 Information security policy document
Requirement A.5.1.2 Review of the information security policy

Standard – A.6 Organization of information policy

Requirement A.6.1 Internal organization
Requirement A.6.1.8 Independent review of information security

Standard – A.8 Human resources security

Requirement A.8.2 During employment
Requirement A.8.2.2 Information security awareness, education and training
Requirement A.8.3.3 Removal of access rights

Standard – A.9 Physical and environmental security

Requirement A.9.2.1 Equipment siting and protection Requirement A.9.2.6 Secure disposal or re-use of equipment

Standard – A.10 Communications and operations management

Requirement A.10.1.4 Separation of development, test and operational facilities
Requirement A.10.2 Third party service delivery management
Requirement A.10.2.1 Service delivery
Requirement A.10.2.2 Monitoring and review of third party services
Requirement A.10.2.3 Managing changes to third party services
Requirement A.10.4.1 Controls against malicious code
Requirement A.10.4.2 Controls against mobile code
Requirement A.10.5.1 Information back-up
Requirement A.10.6.1 Network controls
Requirement A.10.6.2 Security of network services
Requirement A.10.7.1 Management of removable data
Requirement A.10.7.2 Disposal of media
Requirement A.10.7.3 Information handling procedures
Requirement A.10.7.4 Security of system documentation
Requirement A.10.9.1 Electronic commerce
Requirement A.10.9.2 On-line transactions
Requirement A.10.10.1 Audit logging
Requirement A.10.10.2 Monitoring systems use
Requirement 10.10.3 Protection of log information
Requirement 10.10.4 Administrator and operator logs
Requirement 10.10.5 Fault logging
Requirement A.10.10.6 Clock synchronization

Standard – A.11 Business requirement for access control

Requirement A.11.1.1 Access control policy
Requirement A.11.2.1 User registration
Requirement A.11.2.2 Privilege management
Requirement A.11.2.3 User password management
Requirement A.11.2.4 Review of user access rights
Requirement A.11.3.1 Password use
Requirement A.11.3.2 Unattended user equipment
Requirement A.11.4.1 Policy on use of network services
Requirement A.11.4.2 User authentication for external connection
Requirement A.11.4.3 Equipment identification in networks
Requirement A.11.4.4 Remote diagnostic and configuration port protection
Requirement A.11.4.5 Segregation in networks
Requirement A.11.4.6 Network connection control
Requirement A.11.4.7 Network routing control
Requirement A.11.5.1 Secure log-on procedures

Requirement A.11.5.2 User identification and authentication
Requirement A.11.5.3 Password management system
Requirement A.11.5.4 Use of system utilities
Requirement A.11.5.5 Session time-out
Requirement A.11.5.6 Limitation of connection time
Requirement A.11.6.1 Information access restriction
Requirement A.11.6.2 Sensitive system isolation
Requirement A.11.7.1 Mobile computing and communications
Requirement A.11.7.2 Teleworking

Standard – A.12 Correct processing in applications

Requirement A.12.2.1 Input data validation
Requirement A.12.2.2 Control of internal processing
Requirement A.12.2.3 Message integrity
Requirement A.12.2.4 Output data validation
Requirement A.12.3.1 Policy on the use of cryptographic controls
Requirement A.12.3.2 Key management

These requirements were notified in draft to the European Commission in accordance with Directive 98/34/EC, as amended by Directive 98/48/EC.

Gambling Commission August 2009

TESTING STRATEGY FOR COMPLIANCE WITH REMOTE GAMBLING AND SOFTWARE TECHNICAL STANDARDS

August 2009

1 INTRODUCTION

6.2410.1 1.1 Sections 89 and 97 of the Gambling Act 2005 enable the Commission to set technical standards for remote gambling systems and gambling software respectively, to make arrangements for the administration of tests of compliance with standards and to provide for the enforcement of standards and submission to tests by attaching conditions to operating licences. Condition 2 of the Commission's Licence Conditions and Codes of Practice (LCCP) requires gambling software and remote operating licensees (including ancillary remote betting licensees) to comply with the Commission's technical standards and with requirements set by the Commission relating to the timing and procedures for testing.

1.2 This document sets out the Commission's current requirements for the timing and procedures for testing referred to in that Condition. It discusses the testing strategy for assessing compliance with the Remote Gambling and Software Technical Standards which were published in June 2007. Its publication follows discussions with operators and test houses on the Commission's proposed approach.

1.3 The Commission's approach to setting technical standards is outcome based to allow licensees flexibility as to the means of achieving the desired outcome. In a similar manner, the Commission takes a risk based approach to producing the testing strategy to ensure that its approach is reasonable, taking into account:

- the likelihood of non-compliance occurring
- the impact (on customers) of non-compliance
- the means available to assess compliance, and the likely burden imposed by the approach.

1.4 This document sets out:

- what the Commission would normally consider to be the types of testing required in order for it to be satisfied that the technical standards are being met
- who the Commission considers appropriate to carry out that testing

- the procedures for testing.

1.5 This is based on the potential impact of non-compliance on the customer and how obvious or easy it would be to determine whether a licensee and/or their systems are compliant.
1.6 There is scope for moderation or enhancement of the level of assurance required on these matters dependent on the Commission's view of the likelihood that any particular risk will crystallise for an individual licensee. The Commission will also have regard to a licensee's compliance record when determining if the current level of assurance is adequate.

2 APPROACH

2.1 In deciding what, and the level of, testing licensees are required to submit to we have categorised the 'visibility' (vis) of compliance. That is, how easy it is to see whether a system or licensee is compliant. For example, it is easy to see whether an operator has mitigated the risk that a customer will not understand the rules of the game by providing easily accessible information, whereas the underlying fairness of the game is more difficult to observe.

TABLE 1: HOW VISIBLE IS COMPLIANCE?

Visibility	**Description**
Low	Compliance is difficult to determine by external observation – functionality is within a technical solution rather than obvious procedural solution. eg do games operate fairly? Does the game correctly implement the rules?
Moderate	Moderately easy to spot non-compliance — eg does the operator have an internal policy and procedure that they follow or not?
High	Easy to spot non-compliance – it is obvious whether something is compliant or not. eg are terms and conditions accessible on a website?

2.2 We have also categorised the potential impact (imp) on the customer of non-compliance into three levels I, II, or III set out below.

TABLE 2: DEGREE OF POTENTIAL CUSTOMER IMPACT

Impact	**Description**
III	Unfair financial impact on customer(s). Potentially significant negative impact on responsible gambling. Loss of personal data.
II	Easily rectifiable financial impact (eg incorrectly settled bets). Game rules misleading to the player.
I	Inconvenience to customer(s). (Eg disabled website hyperlink. Temporary loss of access?)

2.3 Using these criteria we have categorised the risks and associated mitigating requirements and controls into three categories (cat).

TABLE 3: COMPLIANCE ASSURANCE CATEGORIES

Category	**Assurance category description**

3	Strongest degree of assurance required – normally requiring submission to a testing regime involving approved third parties.
2	Moderate amount of assurance required — normally requiring operator to present evidence that appropriate procedures are in place to assure compliance.
1	Lightest touch, compliance to be assessed by Commission, by for example, checking that operators have published the required information.

2.4 The individual technical requirements have been categorised into groups of requirements which can be treated in a similar way in terms of the category of assurance that is required and the timing of any testing or other assessment. For each group of requirements we set out the proposed type of assessment and timing of assessment.

TABLE 4: MAPPING OF RISK & VISIBILITY TO ASSURANCE CATEGORIES

Impact

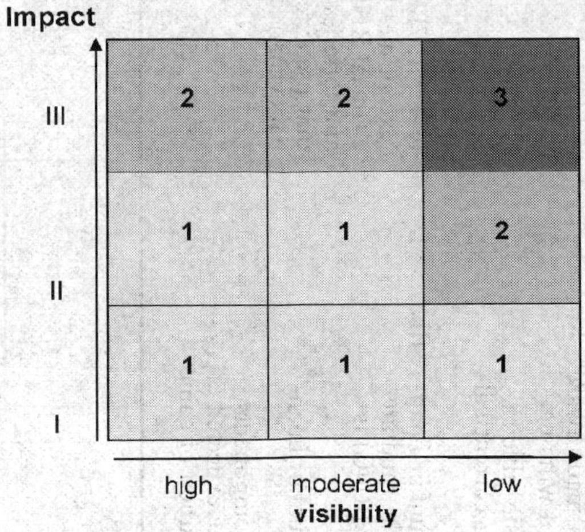

2.5 The following table sets out the Commissions current requirements. These will be kept under review.

TABLE 5: GENERAL RISK AND COMPLIANCE ASSURANCE ACTIVITIES

General risk description	Detailed risk examples (not exhaustive)	Imp	Vis	Relevant standard	Cat	Testing required/Assurance activities
Customers are not provided with sufficient information about their gambling activity, pertinent information about the site/operator's policies, and/or the rules of the gambling.	Customers do not understand what they are betting on Customers are not aware of their previous betting activity Customers are not made aware of pertinent information about the site (for example, the use of automated gambling software) Customers are not made aware of the likelihood of winning Customers not easily able to keep track of their current balance.	II	H	RTS 1A, 1B, 2A, 2B, 3A, 3B, 3C, 3D, 9A IPA 1-7	1	Commission checks for presence of required material accompanying live gambling products, for example, on websites, mobile phones, or in printed material.
Customers suffer financial loss because the results of virtual games or other virtual events are not generated fairly	Customers suffer unfair financial loss because the random number generator (RNG) is not 'random' Customers suffer unfair financial loss because scaling/mapping components do not produce the expected ('random') distribution of game outcomes.	III	L	RTS 7A, 7B (except mechanical RNGs and lotteries that use external events)	3	Approved third party test house performs statistical analysis of RNG and game outputs, prior to release.

Customers suffer financial loss because games or virtual events contain incorrect/malicious code components that do not operate in accordance with the published rules of the game.	Customers suffer unfair financial loss because RNG contains incorrect/malicious code causing non-random output Customers suffer unfair financial loss because scaling and/or mapping components contain incorrect/malicious code that causes the game to operate outside the published rules.	III	L	RTS 7A, 7B, 7C	3	Approved third party test house examines RNG, scaling and mapping components (to include source code review where considered appropriate by Commission/third party) to assess whether they operate in accordance with the rules of the virtual game or event, prior to release.
Customers suffer financial loss because the results of the mechanical RNG is not fair and external events used to determine the result can be influenced.	Customers suffer unfair financial loss because the RNG is not random Customers suffer unfair financial loss because the external event used to determine the result can be influenced.	III	M	RTS 7A (only mechanical RNG and lotteries that use external events)	2	Licensee must satisfy themselves and provide evidence that the mechanical RNG meets the guidelines set out in the standards and retain evidence to be reviewed by Commission during compliance visits. Lotteries will need to retain evidence that the event is external and cannot be influenced. To be reviewed by the Commission during compliance visits.

Customers are unfairly disadvantaged or misled by game design or functionality.	Customers are not aware of the result of the game Customers do not know what rules apply because rules are changed during play Customers are misled about the likelihood of winning because games that appear to simulate real devices do not accurately reflect the probabilities of the real device Customers unfairly disadvantaged by games that are affected by network or end-user systems performance.	III	M	RTS 4A, 7C, 7D, 7E	2	Where relevant (eg result display duration), product testing must be conducted prior to release by licensee . Commission will require evidence of testing to be made available. Internal control procedures, for example, game configuration change control, reviewed by Commission during compliance visits. Live* gambling products reviewed by Commission.
Customers are able to exploit methods of cheating and collusion to disadvantage other customers.	Customers experience unfair financial losses because other customers cheat or collude.	III	M	RTS 11A	2	Where technical solutions are implemented, testing must be conducted prior to release by licensee **. Commission will require evidence of testing to be made available. Commission review and approve procedures and technical solutions intended to deter, prevent and detect cheating and collusion prior to release.

Customer's gambles are not settled in accordance with the operator's rules, game rules and/or bet rules.	Customer suffers financial loss because bets are settled incorrectly (and not identified) or Customer is temporarily inconvenienced where bets are settled incorrectly and have to be adjusted at a later time.	III	M	RTS 5A	2	Product testing must be conducted prior to release by licensee **. Commission will require evidence of testing to be made available
Customers are misled about the likelihood of winning due to behaviour of play-for-fun games.	Play-for-fun games do not implement the same rules as the corresponding play-for-money games.	III	M	RTS 6A	2	Product testing must be conducted prior to release by licensee** or the Commission will require evidence that the play-for-fun game is the same base game as the play- for-money game.
Customers are placed at a higher risk from irresponsible gambling because responsible gambling facilities do not work correctly or are not provided.	Customers who want to use some form of personal spending limit to control the amount that they gamble are unable to do so because they are not provided Customers using spending limits spend more than they intended because the limit is not properly enforced.	III	H	RTS 12A, 12B, 13A	2	Product testing must be conducted prior to release by licensee **. Commission will require evidence of testing to be made available. Commission checks for presence of required facilities accompanying live * gambling products, for example, on websites, mobile phones, or printed material.

Customers suffer financial loss because systems are unable to adequately recover from or deal with the effects of service interruptions.	Customers suffer unfair financial loss because they are unable to remove a bet offer when a betting market changes Customers suffer unfair financial loss because they are unable to complete a multi-state game due to insufficient data being appropriately stored.	III	M	RTS 10A	2	Product testing must be conducted prior to release by licensee **. Commission will require evidence of testing to be made available. Commission review technical approach and operational control procedures invoked during/after service interruptions for live* gambling products.
Customers are treated unfairly in the event of a service interruption.	Customers are unable to make an informed choice about whether to gamble on multi-state games or events, because the operator's policies are not published Operator policy is systematically unfair in the event of a service interruption, that is, always operates in the operators favour.	II	H	RTS 10B	1	Commission checks that policies are easily available and accompany live* gambling products. Commission reviews service interruption policies.

Customers placed at greater degree of risk from irresponsible gambling because products are designed to exploit or encourage problem gambling behaviour.	Irresponsible product design encourages customers to gamble more than they intended or to continue gambling after they have indicated that they wish to stop Customers spend more than they intended because auto-play restrictions not in place to limit the number of transactions that can take place without customer interaction.	III	H	RTS 8A, 14A	2	Where appropriate (eg auto-play implementation), product testing must be conducted prior to release by licensee**. Commission will require evidence of testing to be made available. Commission review live* gambling products and may review product development policies and procedures during compliance visits.
Game integrity compromised because operators do not implement adequate security.	Customers suffer unfair financial loss because weaknesses in game security are exploited.	III	L	Security	3	Annual security audit carried out by qualified and independent third party ***
Customer data or information is disclosed to unauthorised entities because system security is inadequate.	Confidential customer information is disclosed to unauthorised entities leading to criminal or inappropriate use of customer information.	III	L	Security	3	Annual security audit carried out by qualified and independent third party ***
Customer information is lost due to inadequate security, backup or recovery provisions.	Customers suffer unfair financial loss where the content and/or value of customer transactions (gambles) is irrecoverably lost due to inadequate system security, backup and/or recovery provisions	III	L	Security	3	Annual security audit carried out by qualified and independent third party ***.

	Customers suffer unfair financial loss where customer account information is irrecoverably lost, for example, the current value of their deposits with the operator, due to inadequate system security, backup and/or recovery provisions.	

* Remote gambling products that are available to customers.

** Section 3 of this document sets out the circumstances in which operators will be permitted to carry out their own testing of gambling products.

*** Section 3 of this document explains security auditor requirements.

3 PROCEDURE FOR TESTING

THIRD PARTY TEST HOUSES

3.1 The Commission has published a list of approved test houses that can perform third party testing. This will be updated as new test houses are approved and can be found on our website at www.gamblingcommission.gov.uk. Licensees and their chosen test house will need to agree the scope of testing and this must be sufficient to ensure that testing will adequately assess compliance with the Commission's standards.

3.2 Licensees must send the results of testing (ie a test house's summary report) to the Commission on completion of satisfactory testing (but prior to release). As a minimum the report should include:

- licensee name
- date of testing
- game details – including game name, return to player (RTP), software number and game signature
- scope and approach to testing – for example, testing completed against the Gambling Commission's technical standards, in particular RTS 7A – 7D result of testing
- details of games/versions of games that the game supersedes

3.3 Once this has been provided, the successfully tested product can be released into the live environment.

3.4 Licensees also need to make the full test results available to the Commission on request.

3.5 If a licensee intends to run an off-the-shelf product (for example, a game developed by a third party software developer) they must ensure that the product is tested to confirm it meets the Commission's requirements.

3.6 If a third party software developer has already obtained satisfactory testing for its product by a Commission approved test house the licensee can only rely on this testing if it is able to demonstrate that the testing conducted is sufficient for the environment the product or game will operate in. If the testing obtained by the software developer is sufficient for the environment the product will operate in, the licensee must send the test house summary report to the Commission prior to release and make available full results to the Commission on request.

3.7 In circumstances where the operating environment differs from the testing environment the licensee will be required to obtain further testing by a test house. The Commission must receive all relevant testing reports to show the testing is sufficient to cover product or game in the operational environment prior to release. The Licensee will also need to make the full test results available to the Commission on request.

3.8 The licensees overall compliance with the technical standards and testing requirements (including those aspects requiring test house testing as well as internal testing) is the responsibility of the licensee.

TESTING CONDUCTED BY LICENSEE/OPERATOR

3.9 To be permitted to carry out their own testing of gambling products licensees will be required to provide a declaration to the Commission that they follow good practice in development, testing and release control of gambling products and/or systems. More details on what the Commission considers to be good practice can be found in section 4.

3.10 The Commission, on request or as part of a compliance visit, may require evidence from the licensee that it complies with its good practice guidelines.

3.11 All results from licensee testing should be retained and be made available to the Commission during compliance visits or on request.

THIRD PARTY ANNUAL SECURITY AUDIT

3.12 Table 5 sets out that an annual security audit must be carried out to assess compliance against the security requirements of the remote technical standards. The security requirements are based on relevant sections of Annex A to ISO/IEC 27001:2005 and these are listed in chapter 5 of the Remote Gambling and Software Technical Standards. The Commission does not intend to approve security audit firms to perform the security audit as many licensees already have arrangements with appropriate security auditors.

3.13 However, licensees must satisfy themselves that the third party security auditor is reputable, is suitably qualified to test compliance with BS ISO/IEC 27001:2005 and that the auditor is independent from the licensee.

3.14 Licensees must provide to the Commission copies of the audit summary and full report produced by the security auditor on completion of their audit.

3.15 The Commission is aware that many operators are also subject to PCI DSS[1] and are audited for those purposes. The Commission considers its security standards to be sufficiently broad that audits conducted against other standards may meet some of the Commission's requirements. Operators will need to ensure that their audits cover the scope of the security requirements as set out in chapter 5 of the Remote Gambling and Software Technical Standards.

3.16 The Commission has highlighted those systems that are most critical to achieving the Commission's aims and the security standards will apply to these critical systems:

- electronic systems that record, store, process, share, transmit or retrieve sensitive customer information, eg credit/debit card details, authentication information, customer account balances
- electronic systems that generate, transmit, or process random numbers used to determine the outcome of games or virtual events
- electronic systems that store results or the current state of a customer's gamble;
- points of entry to and exit from the above systems (other systems that are able to communicate directly with core critical systems)
- communication networks that transmit sensitive customer information.

TESTING AND AUDIT REQUIREMENTS FOR REMOTE LOTTERY LICENSEES [2]

3.17 It is the Commission's view that lotteries in general pose a relatively low risk to the licensing objectives. This section sets out the criteria that applies to remote lottery licensees[2] (including external lottery managers) when determining specific testing and audit requirements.

3.18 Holders of remote lottery licences2 that accept no more than £250,000 worth of entries per year by means of remote communication will not be required to submit their RNG for testing by a Commission approved test house or submit to a third party annual security audit.

3.19 Instead, and in terms of RNG testing, such licensees will need to demonstrate that:

- their RNG has been tested or verified as being fair and random by an independent and suitably qualified third party. This should be supported by documentary evidence
- they have policies and procedures in place which set out how they ensure the lottery draw is fair and open and can produce evidence that these procedures are followed.

3.20 In terms of the third party security audit requirement, such lottery licensees will instead be required to demonstrate to Commission compliance managers during compliance visits that they comply with the RTS security requirements as set out in chapter 5 of the Remote Gambling and Software Technical Standards.

3.21 Holders of such licences that accept more than £250,000 worth of entries by remote means per year will be required to meet the full RNG testing and third party security audit requirements as set out in table 5 above.

---

1 (PCI DSS) Payment Card Industry Data Security Standard.

2 By lottery licensees we mean, remote lottery operating licensees, converted lottery operating licensees (but only those licensees that run remote lotteries themselves or via a lottery manager) or remote lottery managers' operating licensees (also know as external lottery managers).

4 IN-HOUSE DEVELOPMENT, TESTING AND RELEASE – GOOD PRACTICE

4.1 Good practice gambling software development should possess the elements below. These specific controls would already exist in an organisation compliant with ISO17799.

4.2 Development process:

- source code should be held in a secure environment
- an audit log of all accesses to program source should be maintained
- old versions of source code and the dates they were retired should be retained
- access to source code by developers should be well controlled and based on a minimum access required for the job approach
- access to platform source code should not be granted to those working only on game specific development
- changes to critical modules need to be peer reviewed by appropriately skilled but independent developers to ensure all changes made are appropriate and in line with the change documentation. Any suspicious or unauthorised changes must be explained.

4.3 Testing Process:

- logically separate development and testing environments
- separate staff to those that developed should perform the testing
- an independent assessment of changes made by the developers should be performed to verify all changes are documented in the change documentation. This may involve the use of file comparison programs to quickly identify all changes.

4.4 Policies and processes should be in place for control of changes to operational environments including version control for software upgrades. To minimise threats to the operational environment operators should consider but not limit activities to ensuring:

- adequate testing and change control mechanisms and authorisations are in place for the migration of new or modified software into the operational environment; and
- appropriate testing, planning and migration control measures should be carried out when upgrading patches or new software versions to ensure the overall security of the agency operational environment is not adversely impacted.

Gambling Commission August 2009

REVIEW OF REMOTE TECHNICAL STANDARDS
Information note, December 2008

1 INTRODUCTION

6.2410.2 1.1 The Gambling Commission (the Commission) published its Remote Gambling and Software Technical Standards on 1 June 2007, which came into force on

1 September 2007. This included the remote technical standards (RTS) and the Information Provision Annex (IPA).

1.2 In August 2007 the Commission published a supplementary paper to RTS[1] which set out the relevant security requirements contained in ISO/EIC 27001:2005 that remote operating licence holders must meet. These were published in paper form only as required by the Commission's copyright agreement with the British Standards Institute (BSI). This followed an earlier summary document[2], published on our website in July 2007, which sign posted licensees to the relevant sections of ISO/EIC 27001:2005 ahead of publication of the full paper supplement.

1.3 As a result, the 1 June 2007 version of the RTS did not refer to the security requirements that also form part of the RTS. We understand that this may have caused some licensed operators to be unaware of the need to comply with these requirements and so the Commission has decided to address this issue in the updated version of the RTS.

1.4 The Commission has informally monitored the RTS since it came into force on 1 September 2007 and has received positive comments from various stakeholders that it remains fit for purpose.

---

1 Remote Gambling and Software Technical Standards Supplementary Paper – Security requirements (Annex C), August 2007

2 Remote Gambling and Software Technical Standards: Annex C – Security requirements, July 2007

2 THE REVIEW

2.1 In support of the Commission's ongoing dialogue with the industry, the Commission instigated an initial review of the RTS in October 2008.

2.2 The purpose of the initial review was to establish if there were any issues or possible changes that warranted a full consultation in 2009. The purpose of the review was not to review policy decisions taken during the original consultation. The Commission sought comments from stakeholders, via its e-bulletin and dialogue with trade associations, seeking comments identifying the following:

(a) areas where individual requirements were unclear and further clarification was needed

(b) errors in the original version

(c) important issues that should be covered in the RTS.

2.3 The feedback indicated that the RTS remains fit for purpose and there are no issues that require a full consultation.

3 UPDATED RTS

3.1 The Commission considers that the minor and cosmetic redrafting of the RTS document that clearly signposts the security requirements will assist operators, as the content of the document was sufficient and no changes to policy are required.

3.2 In the interests of Better Regulation and of minimising the regulatory burden, the Commission has concluded that it would be inappropriate and unnecessary to conduct a consultation on these cosmetic changes.

3.3 The Commission therefore intends to publish an updated version of the RTS in the new year, ensuring all relevant documents and security requirements are cross referenced. We intend to do this by incorporating the summary version of the security requirements[3] within the updated RTS document. The Commission will continue to provide copies of the full security supplement[4] available in accordance with its own licensing agreement with BSI.

3.4 It is worth acknowledging that the Commission is currently developing its policy on in-running betting and if there is any policy development it may be necessary to consider whether the RTS needs to be updated. If changes are required the Commission will also need to consider whether to consult at that time.

---

[3] Remote Gambling and Software Technical Standards: Annex C – Security requirements, July 2007

[4] Remote Gambling and Software Technical Standards Supplementary Paper – Security requirements (Annex C), August 2007

Gambling Commission December 2008

CONDITIONS AND CODES OF PRACTICE APPLICABLE TO: REMOTE GENERAL BETTING LICENCES; REMOTE POOL BETTING LICENCES; REMOTE BETTING INTERMEDIARY LICENCES; REMOTE GENERAL BETTING ANCILLARY LICENCES

To avoid duplication this document has not been reproduced here but can be found at para 6.2125 – 6.2150 above.

CONDITIONS AND CODES OF PRACTICE APPLICABLE TO: NON-REMOTE BINGO LICENCES

To avoid duplication this document has not been reproduced here but can be found at para 6.2270 – 6.2275 above.

CONDITIONS AND CODES OF PRACTICE APPLICABLE TO: REMOTE CASINO LICENCES; REMOTE CASINO ANCILLARY LICENCES

To avoid duplication this document has not been reproduced here but can be found at para 6.2180 – 6.2200 above.

CONDITIONS AND CODES OF PRACTICE APPLICABLE TO: NON-REMOTE GAMING MACHINE TECHNICAL: FULL LICENCES; NON-REMOTE GAMING MACHINE TECHNICAL: SUPPLIER LICENCES; NON-REMOTE GAMING MACHINE TECHNICAL: SOFTWARE LICENCES; NON-REMOTE GAMBLING SOFTWARE LICENCES

To avoid duplication this document has not been reproduced here but can be found at para 6.2590 – 6.2595 below.

CONDITIONS AND CODES OF PRACTICE APPLICABLE TO: REMOTE EXTERNAL LOTTERY MANAGER LICENCES REMOTE NON-COMMERCIAL SOCIETY LOTTERY LICENCES REMOTE LOCAL AUTHORITY LOTTERY LICENCES

To avoid duplication this document has not been reproduced here but can be found at para 6.2305 – 6.2315 above.

REMOTE GAMBLING – WHAT DO WE MEAN BY 'REMOTE GAMBLING'?

6.2510 Under the Gambling Act 2005, operators of remote gambling (via such means as the internet, digital TV and mobile phones) offering casino, bingo and machine-style gaming can lawfully establish their operations in Britain for the first time.
This means that the public will have the choice of gambling on sites that meet the high standards required by the Gambling Commission. Consumers will be able to tell who these operators are by a statement on their website which includes their Commission operating licence number and a link to the Commission's website.
It is a criminal offence to allow children or young people to game or bet remotely and licensed operators must have robust procedures in place to prevent underage gambling.

These include checks to verify age and making available filtering software to allow adults to block access by children. Operators must use the best publicly available information for age verification and must regularly review their age verification systems to ensure that they are keeping pace with technological advances.

Licensees are required to comply with the Commission's remote gambling and software technical standards and to have their products tested in line with the Commissions requirements for testing

HOW IS REMOTE GAMBLING REGULATED?

Organisations and individuals that provide facilities for betting or gaming remotely require a licence to operate. The Commission has developed licence conditions and codes of practice that govern licence holders and it has powers to prosecute or impose fines on operators who breach their licence conditions.

There are two types of licence required by remote operators:

- Operating licences are required by those that provide facilities for gambling in Britain.
- Personal licences are required by individuals in certain management positions except for those organisations categorised as small-scale operators.

REMOTE GAMBLING FACTS AND FIGURES

- Those participating in remote gambling are more likely to be male than female, and aged 18 — 34.
- 8.6% of the 8,000 adults surveyed over the four quarters to June 2007 (ie an average of figures for September 2006, December 2006, March 2007 and June 2007), said they had participated in at least one form of remote gambling (through a computer, mobile phone or interactive/digital TV) in the previous month. (This compares to the 2006 calendar year figure of 7.4%).
- Excluding those who only played the National Lottery remotely, 5.9% of respondents had participated in remote gambling.
- Remote gambling via a computer, laptop or handheld device was most popular (6.7% of all adult respondents), followed by gambling via mobile phone (2.9%) and interactive/digital TV (under 2%).

Gambling Commission August 2007

REMOTE GAMBLING EQUIPMENT
Advice note, March 2008

1 INTRODUCTION

6.2511 1.1 This document sets out our interpretation of which elements of a gambling system will meet the definition of remote gambling equipment ('key equipment') set out in the Act. It provides additional advice for those completing the Gambling Commission's application forms. Please see our website for the application forms and the standard Guidance Notes for those forms.

1.2 The information contained in this document is intended to provide advice to operators on identifying key equipment; it is not intended in any way to replace the definition set out in the Act.

2 BACKGROUND

2.1 If an operator providing facilities for remote gambling locates any 'remote gambling equipment' (sometimes referred to as 'key equipment') in Great Britain that operator will have to a hold a form of remote gambling licence whether or not those facilities are provided for use wholly or partly in the United Kingdom. The Act defines remote gambling equipment in Section 36(4) and sets out some specific exclusions in 36(5):

(4) In this Act 'remote gambling equipment' means, subject to subsection (5), electronic or other equipment used by or on behalf of a person providing facilities for remote gambling:
  (a) to store information relating to a person's participation in the gambling
  (b) to present, to persons who are participating or may participate in the gambling, a virtual game, virtual race or other virtual event or process by reference to which the gambling is conducted
  (c) to determine all or part of a result or of the effect of a result: or
  (d) to store information relating to a result

(5) In this Act 'remote gambling equipment' does not include equipment which:
  (a) is used by a person to take advantage of remote gambling facilities provided by another person; and
  (b) is not provided by that other person

3 READING THIS DOCUMENT

3.1 In this document we use the term 'component' to refer to software that is run by (executed) or data that is stored on a piece of equipment. A component fulfils a specific purpose (for example, an RNG is a component that generates random numbers); a piece of equipment may host one or more components.

3.2 Under the heading 'Facilities for gambling and remote gambling equipment' we provide advice on and specific examples of the Commission's interpretation of whether equipment is used in the provision of facilities for gambling.

3.3 Under the heading 'Remote gambling equipment' we list those components that we believe meet the definition set out in the Act.

3.4 In order to set the components into context this document also contains a gambling system overview, a component glossary and a number of high-level diagrams. The diagrams are not intended to describe any particular gambling system nor do they define the way a gambling system should be implemented.

4 FACILITIES FOR GAMBLING AND REMOTE GAMBLING EQUIPMENT

4.1 Based on our interpretation of the Act a piece of equipment is remote gambling equipment if it is "used in the provision of facilities for gambling" and the components deployed on it perform one or more of the functions set out in 36(4)(a) to (d).

4.2 In order to assist operators to identify their key equipment this section provides advice on our interpretation of "used in the provision of facilities for gambling" in the context of remote gambling equipment. Under the heading 'Remote gambling equipment' we list those components that we believe meet the definition set out in the Act.

4.3 We read "used in the provision of facilities for gambling" as relatively narrow and as not extending to all equipment used by a remote gambling operator generally in connection with, or incidentally to, the provision of the gambling. Thus, for example — and based on our present understanding of such systems in use in the remote gambling industry — we do not consider equipment used for integrity testing, money laundering compliance and monitoring, complaints handling and responsible gambling analysis to be "used in" the provision of the gambling activity because they are not used by the customer or operator as part of that gambling. Below are further specific examples.

5 MARKETING, BONUSES AND INCENTIVES

5.1 Operators typically keep some data about customers and their previous gambling activities for the purpose of marketing, including offering bonuses and other incentives related to the amount that a customer has gambled with the operator. This data may be stored separately from similar data stored in other parts of the operator's infrastructure.

5.2 In the case of equipment which stores information relating to customers' participation in the gambling and which is used for bonus and reward calculations, we consider only the core system whose principal function is to offer, operate and settle the gamble to be "used in" the provision of facilities for gambling. Therefore, whilst we would consider systems used to calculate bonuses or other rewards or incentives which are *awarded or determined during the course of a single gambling transaction or session of "play"* (whether the activity is betting, gaming or participating in a lottery) to be remote gambling equipment, we would not necessarily take the same view of systems that only operate to calculate rewards and incentives based on a customer's historic play. The latter we would normally regard as an aspect of marketing and not as tantamount to a prize related to specific gambling.

5.3 Table 1 on the following page provides examples of types of bonuses and incentives. In the examples set out below, numbers 1 to 5 are linked to the current gamble or session and equipment which stores or processes the relevant data would therefore be remote gambling (key) equipment. Examples 6 – 13 are not linked to the current gamble or session and only operate to calculate rewards and incentives based on a customer's historic play.

TABLE 1

	"type"	Linkage to gamble	Qualification for bonus	Reward example
linked to current gamble or current session (gaming)				
1	Game feature (random)	Current game (random)	Triggered by random event	Get 3 cherries on any TootyFruity game and win a free spin
2	Game feature (random)	Current game (random)	Triggered by random event	Pineapple feature doubles the win on your TootyFruity winning line
3	Winnings multiplier	Current bet	Placing a specific bet	Place a £10 bet on this match and we'll double your winnings
4	Free game (spend based)	Current session/game (accumulated spend)	Cumulative consecutive spend on single game	Stake £10 over any number of consecutive TootyFruity games and you'll earn a free £1 spin
5	Session spend	Current session (accumulated spend)	Spend in a single session	Stake £50 in this gaming session and we'll put £10 in your account (or give you £10 worth of free credits to spend in the game)
Not linked to current gamble or current session				
6	Loyalty scheme (points)	Current bet / accumulated spend	Accumulated amount spent/staked converted to loyalty points	For every whole £1 staked we'll give you 1 loyalty point — 100 pts may be redeemed for £10 (or a £10 free bet)

7	Loyalty scheme (cash / free bet)	Accumulated spend	Amount staked	Once you reach a total staked of £50 we'll put £10 into your account (or give you a free £10 bet)
8	Loyalty scheme (commission)	Accumulated activity over time-period	Amount regularly spent (peer to peer)	Varied commission bands depending on customer spend
9	Monthly loyalty bonus	Accumulated activity over time-period	Amount spent in specific time-frame	For every whole £20 staked in August, we'll give you a £10 free bet (or put £10 in your account)
10	Playing time	Accumulated duration of play	Amount of time spent playing	We'll put £5 into your account for every hour you play at poker
11	Deposit matching	Unrelated / accumulated spend	Registration, deposit amount and total amount staked	Register and deposit £30 and we'll put £30 into your account *after* your total stakes have exceeded £50
12	Deposit matching	Unrelated	Registration, deposit amount	Register and deposit £10 and we'll add another £10 to your account
13	Good will campaigns	Unrelated to gambling activity	Non-gambling customer attribute	Happy birthday . . . we've put £10 in your account (or have a free £10 bet on the tennis)

6 CLIENT APPLICATION DOWNLOAD SERVERS

6.1 Games may be deployed using a "client application", that is, a piece of software that is downloaded by and installed on the end-user's device to present a rich graphical and auditory interface that represents the game. Client applications are designed for a range of end-user devices including PCs, mobile phones or set-top boxes (interactive digital TV).

6.2 Operators may deploy specific equipment to make client applications available for download. To improve the speed with which the customer is able to download the application, such equipment may be placed in a number of geographical locations. Typically the equipment is also used to download patches and upgrades to the application and to verify the integrity of the installed application, that is, to check that the client software has not been tampered with before permitting access to gaming.

6.3 In the context of download servers, the Commission would not normally consider equipment that is used as described above as being used in the provision of facilities for gambling, as long as that equipment is only being used as a means of distributing, updating and checking applications to be installed on the end-user's device and is not involved once the gambling commences. To meet this distinction the same equipment must not be used to determine the results of virtual events, pass on the contents of gambles from the client application to the server, nor pass results from the server to the client.

6.4 For example, an offshore operator may choose to place a server in Great Britain that is used for downloading game applications but once the client application has been installed and the gaming has commenced the equipment is no longer involved. In that case the operator would not require a licence.

6.5 If however, an operator located a download server in Great Britain that was also used during gaming to exchange information about the content of the customer's gamble and the results of the virtual event, this equipment would, under our interpretation, be used in the provision of facilities for gambling. We would consider such equipment as being used "to present, to persons who are participating or may participate in the gambling, a virtual game, virtual race or other virtual event or process by reference to which the gambling is conducted" (s36(4)(b)). Therefore, in this example the operator would have to hold a remote casino licence.

7 BUSINESS CONTINUITY ARRANGEMENTS

7.1 Organisations will have in place systems and technologies that are intended to reduce the likelihood of operational downtime, prevent data loss, and to provide business continuity in the event of equipment failure, scheduled maintenance or loss of an operational data centre.

7.2 The equipment used for these purposes is likely to contain components and data set out in Table 2. In considering whether such systems are remote gambling equipment, the Commission draws a distinction between equipment used to store a backup of operational data for a gambling system and equipment that is used as a standby or disaster recovery system.

7.3 The Commission defines standby and disaster recovery equipment as equipment that the operator intends to use in, or as a replacement for, the 'live' system in the event that the equipment normally used is unavailable. Standby and disaster recovery equipment is, therefore, intended to be used in the provision of facilities for gambling and any such equipment used to deploy the components identified in table 2 would be remote gambling equipment, which if sited in Great Britain would require the operator to hold a form of remote gambling licence.

7.4 For example, if an operator's primary gaming system is located outside of Great Britain, but they choose to have a disaster recovery facility in Great Britain, which would become their live gaming system in the event that their primary data centre became unavailable, the operator would require a remote casino licence.

7.5 The Commission has also considered whether equipment that stores back-up data for gambling systems is remote gambling equipment. We define equipment used to store back-up data as equipment that holds a copy of operational data but which will not itself be used as part of the 'live' gambling system. The data will instead be restored onto 'live', standby or disaster recovery equipment. We would not normally consider such equipment to be "used in the provision of facilities for gambling".

7.6 For example, if an operator has a betting system located outside Great Britain but uses equipment in Great Britain to keep a mirror copy of their operational data, this operator will not require a remote betting licence as long as that equipment is only used to enable the data to be restored onto the offshore system and never itself used to provide facilities for gambling.

8 REMOTE GAMBLING EQUIPMENT

8.1 Whether or not any piece of equipment that is used in the provision of facilities for gambling will be classified as 'remote gambling equipment' is determined by the components that reside on it. If any of the components perform the functions listed in section 36(4) of the Act, then that piece of equipment is remote gambling equipment[1], regardless of what other components may be deployed on the equipment. Based on our present understanding of remote gambling systems, Table 2 summarises the components that meet our interpretation of the definition set out in the Act where they are used in the provision of facilities for gambling. A more detailed description of the components can be found in the Component Glossary.

8.2 Table 2 below identifies components that meet our interpretation of the definition set out in the Act.

[1] By virtue of Section 36(5), the Act excludes client devices, such as home PCs or mobile phones unless these devices are provided by an operator to enable a person to take advantage of facilities for gambling provided by that operator.

TABLE 2

Component	Act ref	Brief Description
Presentation Components		
Virtual Event and game 'Pages'	Section 36 (4)b	Equipment that serves 'pages' or other media that present virtual events on which people may gamble, including: ■ internet web pages (web server) ■ digital television (dTV server) 'pages' mobile 'pages' (WAP / mobile server) Equipment from which 'client applications' that present virtual events for gambling are downloaded, only where this equipment is used in the provision of facilities for gambling (see section 6 on Client application download servers)
Application Components		
Virtual Event Controller	Section 36 (4)c	Determining the result of a virtual event based on RNG output
Settling	Section 36 (4)c	Marking up (as winner or loser) and settling (determining the amount to be paid) of gambles
Random Number Generator	Section 36 (4)c	Generation of random data to be used by games / events
Data Components		
Gambling Transaction Record	Section 36 (4)a and d	Stored information about: An individual's gambling transactions (eg £10 single on Trap 3 in the 4.37 at Monmore, 01/12/06), bet logs, game logs. The results of an individual's gamble, eg win/loss amounts, including summarised information about an individuals wins or losses, where this is used in the provision of facilities for gambling (see section 4 on Facilities for gambling and remote gambling equipment)
Virtual Event State	Section 36 (4)a and d	Information stored in order to keep track of the last known state of a virtual event or virtual game that an individual participated in

9 GAMBLING SYSTEMS OVERVIEW

9.1 For the purpose of this document, gambling systems have been logically separated into five layers:

End-User Devices: the device used by the customer to access the gambling facilities. Some devices may be used in different ways, for example a mobile phone could access via specialised Java applications ('client application') provided by the operator or via the phone's built-in browser.

Presentation & Formatting: components concerned with the presentation and formatting of information that will be displayed on the end-user device and components that provide specialised interfaces for client applications (eg Betting Exchange Client, Casino Client).

Applications: the software components that process incoming or outgoing information, each providing a particular function, such as settling, or account management.

Data Storage: where data is physically stored after it has been processed by applications.

External Interfaces: components that handle communication with external systems, for example, between a sportsbook and a card processing service or Poker Room.

9.2 Traditional betting (eg sportsbook) and virtual event gambling (such as casino gaming, arcade, poker, virtual horse racing) systems have been considered separately for several reasons. Virtual event and betting systems use different terminology and have distinct technical impacts on the systems required to support them.

9.3 Virtual event systems require random inputs in order to determine the outcome of games, which are normally provided by internal or external Random Number Generators. Virtual event systems may also support multi-player games where multiple players 'sit' at the same table (whether they play against each other or against the house) and require systems to support multi-player tables.

9.4 Betting systems rely on external sources of information to determine the outcome of bets (eg sporting results), which are provided automatically through electronic 'data feeds' (eg from Satellite Information Services (SIS) or the Press Association (PA)) or are entered manually.

9.5 Some operators offer both betting ('sportsbooks') and virtual event gambling (such as online 'casinos', 'arcades', poker). For technical, commercial, and jurisdictional reasons these systems may be deployed separately. For example, British sportsbook operators may offer casino gambling from off-shore locations. The casinos may be hosted by third party providers and these providers may host 'virtual' casinos for several different operators on the same equipment. The operator allows the customer to purchase chips or tokens to take to the casino. The offshore host provides a 'shadow' account and transactional systems that keep track of the customer's chip/token balance and gambling activity ('bet record' or 'game log'). The betting system, in this instance, does not keep a record of the casino gaming activities, just a record of funds taken to and from the casino.

9.6 Poker (and similar) gambling represents a somewhat special case. Many operators offer their 'poker rooms' through a third party provider. Shared poker rooms are managed by a provider on behalf of a number of their licensees. As with integrated casinos, players normally purchase tokens/chips, which are transferred to the poker room and held in a shadow account.

9.7 The following pages present some simplified diagrams intended to represent the sort of components found in various types of gambling system. Items highlighted with bold text and cross-hatching fulfil our interpretation of remote gambling equipment.

9.8 Software can be deployed within remote gambling infrastructures in any number of ways. Although some operators will have dedicated presentation, application, data and interface servers, many operators will not. These logical diagrams do not, therefore, necessarily map directly onto any particular server infrastructure.

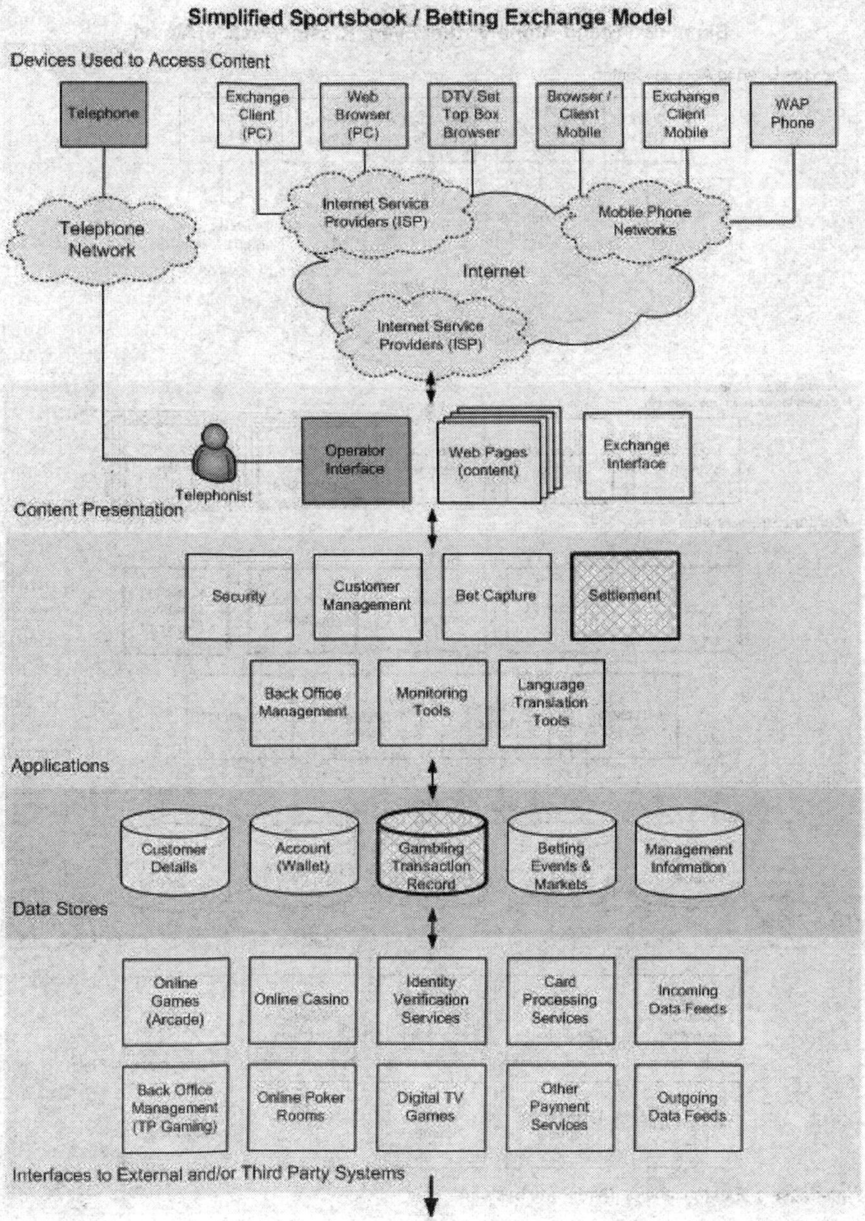
Simplified Sportsbook / Betting Exchange Model
Devices Used to Access Content
Telephone
Exchange Client (PC)
Web Browser (PC)
DTV Set Top Box Browser
Browser / Client Mobile
Exchange Client Mobile
WAP Phone
Telephone Network
Internet Service Providers (ISP)
Mobile Phone Networks
Internet
Internet Service Providers (ISP)
Operator Interface
Web Pages (content)
Exchange Interface
Telephonist
Content Presentation
Security
Customer Management
Bet Capture
Settlement
Back Office Management
Monitoring Tools
Language Translation Tools
Applications
Customer Details
Account (Wallet)
Gambling Transaction Record
Betting Events & Markets
Management Information
Data Stores
Online Games (Arcade)
Online Casino
Identity Verification Services
Card Processing Services
Incoming Data Feeds
Back Office Management (TP Gaming)
Online Poker Rooms
Digital TV Games
Other Payment Services
Outgoing Data Feeds
Interfaces to External and/or Third Party Systems

Simplified Stand-Alone Virtual Event (Casino/Arcade) Model

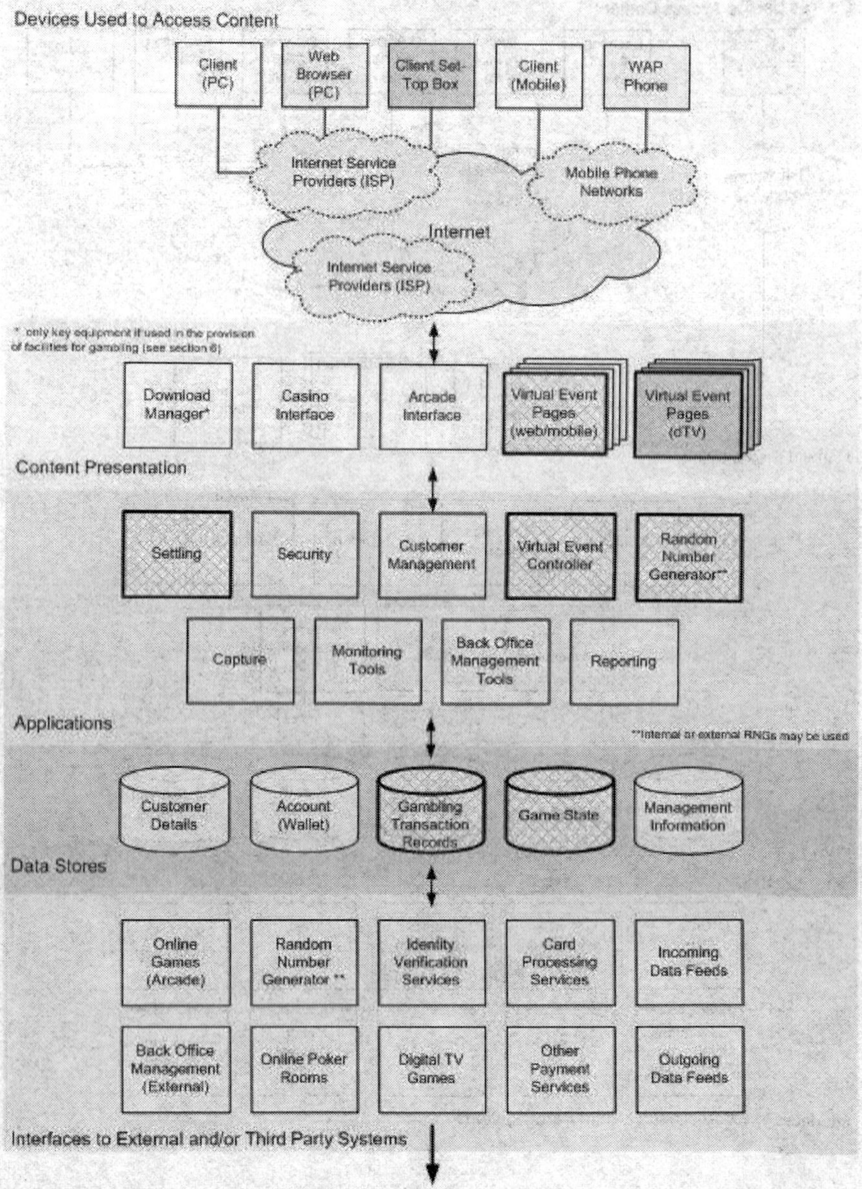

Simplified Integrated Virtual Event & Sportsbook Model

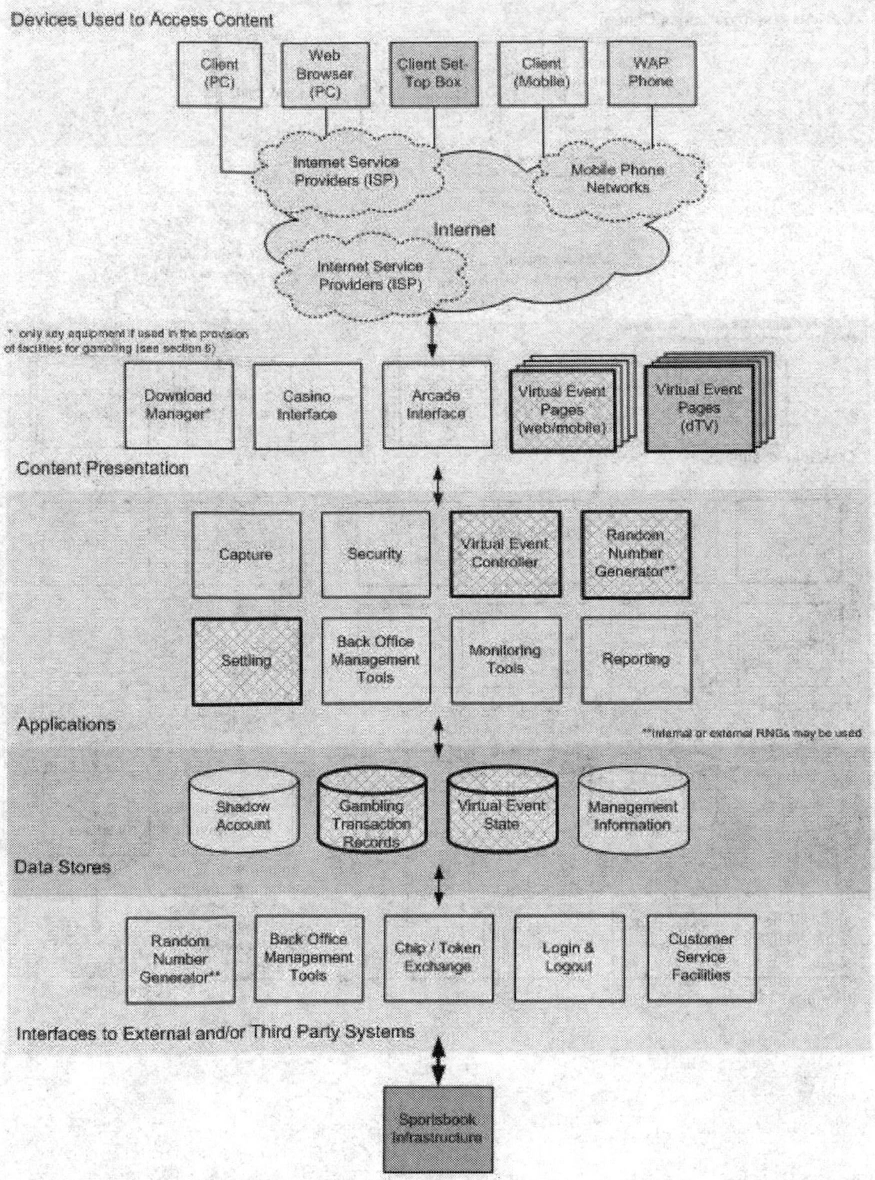

Simplified Shared Poker Room Model

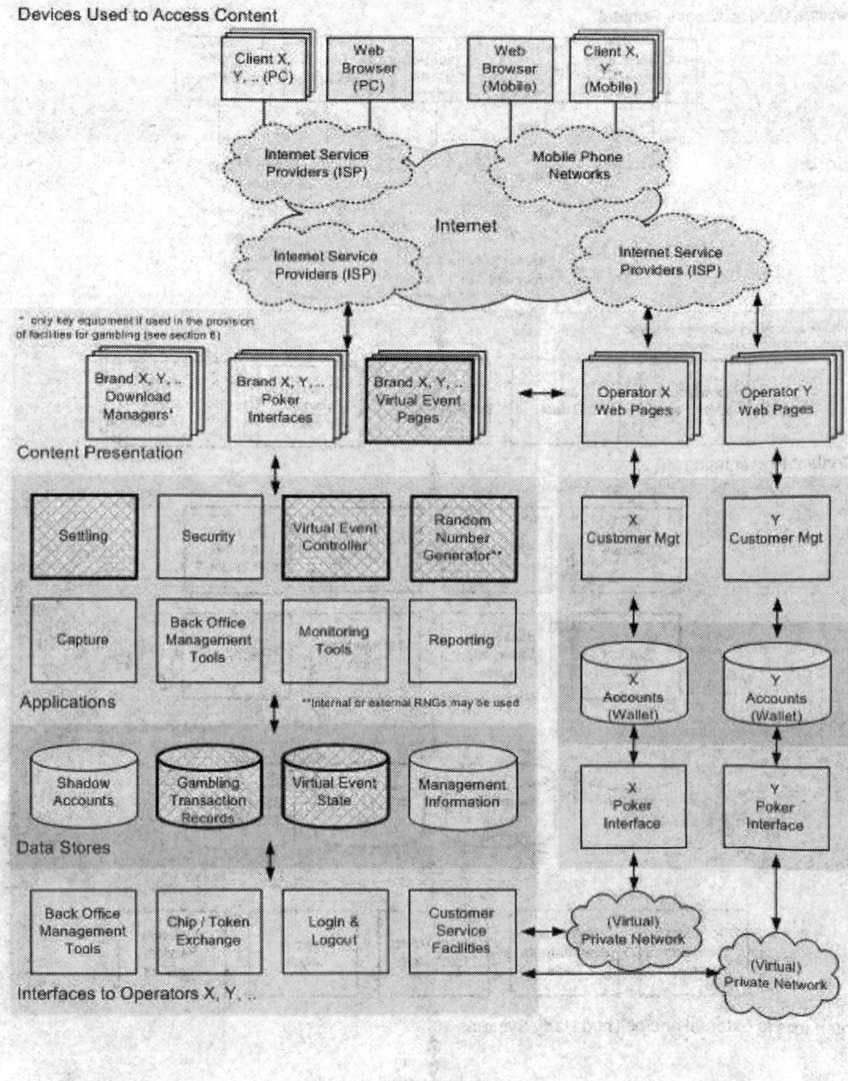

COMPONENT GLOSSARY

DEVICES

Many client devices can be used to interact with the gambling systems. The devices themselves may utilise different methods to interact with the gambling system. The software tool or application the customer actually interacts with is known as the 'user interface'; the three most common types of which are outlined below. Customer's devices are explicitly excluded from being classified as gambling equipment by the Gambling Act[2].

Browsers are non-specific applications that can be used to view any web page and may be on any supported device, such as a PC, mobile phone or other portable device.

Client applications have been developed specifically by operators or software developers to communicate with the core gambling system. Client applications typically provide a 'richer' visual and functional environment than can be achieved using a web browser. Importantly (for security) client applications do not contain any software that determines the result of a bet.

Telephones may be used to interact directly with the gambling system using touch-tone, Intelligent Voice Recognition (IVR) systems or via a telephonist.

[2] By virtue of Section 36(5), the Act excludes client devices, such as home PC's or mobile phones unless these devices are provided by an operator to enable a person to take advantage of facilities for gambling provided by that operator.

PRESENTATION/FORMATTING

It is common practice to deploy those software components concerned with the presentation or formatting of content (eg Web pages) and direct connection to end-user devices (eg Interfaces) on separate dedicated servers. These servers communicate with the rest of the infrastructure over communications networks which may be local or remote.

Web pages (content)

Web pages present text or graphical information to customers. The web page allows the customer to interact with a gambling system and brings together various sources of information allowing them to view their account history, gambling history, movement of funds between systems (eg sportsbook to casino) and to amend (permissible) details. For a betting operator these pages would normally be referred to as their 'sportsbook'. Web pages are also commonly used to display marketing, help or contact information. Web pages that contain animated or video content for virtual events are considered separately (see 'virtual event web pages').

Virtual event web pages

Virtual event web pages contain graphics, animation, text and sometimes sound that represents a game or other virtual event and displays results via the customer's browser. Several technologies are used including flash, java, shockwave, and mpeg-4.

Exchange/casino/arcade/sportsbook/digital TV application interfaces

Application Interfaces provide a way for remote client applications to interact with the core gambling system. The interface typically handles formatting and exchange of messages. Betting Exchanges typically use a dedicated client application in order to support the relatively rich content that the customer needs in order to be able to interact with the betting exchange. Similarly casino, arcades, sportsbook and digital TV interfaces are used to manage communication with specific client applications.

Download manager

Download managers store client applications and make them available for customers to download to their device (mobile phone, PC, etc). They may also keep track of versions and intelligently download newer versions or patches to existing client applications.

Telephonist user interface

The operator user interface provides a means for the telephonist to capture customer details, bets, financial transactions and queries.

APPLICATIONS

Applications may be deployed on a one-to-one basis (one application per server) however it is more common for multiple applications reside on the same physical piece of equipment for reasons of economy and performance.

System monitoring tools

Monitoring tools are frequently used to monitor the technical aspects of the gambling system including performance, resource utilisation, or the performance or interaction with external systems.

Reporting

Reporting applications gather and summarise information from the system, providing reports on most aspects of the system including ongoing liability, virtual event statistics, account activity (for example, large bets, large wins, summarised information) and profit/loss reports. Reports may be scheduled to run at particular times of day, run manually or triggered by unusual activities ('alerts').

Bet capture/bet matching

The capture component processes the information about the customer's gamble, validating the selections against the rules of the particular bet type, game or event/market before it is stored in the gambling transaction record. For a betting exchange this component would be the 'bet matching' component.

Customer management

Customer management applications provide facilities for customers to register their details, deposit funds, update account details and view their account history. Customer Support personnel use the same or similar components to manage aspects of customers accounts.

Settling

Settling is sometimes referred to in two parts, 'marking-up' (ie identifying individual gambles as winners or losers) and 'settling'. The term settling is used here to represent both parts. Settling determines whether or not a customer has won based on the outcome of some real or virtual event. If the customer has won, the settling component calculates the value of the return to the customer and corresponding adjustments are made to the customers account balance.

Random number generator (RNG)

Random number generators use specialised hardware and software to generate sequences of numbers that are unpredictable, that is, numbers that do not have a detectable pattern. Virtual events always require one or more numbers within a specific range (for example a Roulette game may request a number between 0 and 36). The output of the RNG must be 'scaled' to fit into this range. The scaling component may be part of the RNG, a separate component or part of the game depending on the deployment.

Virtual event control

Each virtual event has its own rules and behaviour. Virtual event control is used here as a generic term for components that handle:

- placing a request for random numbers and/or receiving random numbers
- the determination of the virtual event result using the random number input
- issuing instructions to the client application to display the result of the event and the result of the customer's gamble

Some virtual event gambling may also require components that coordinate activities in multi-player scenarios.

Back-office tools

Back-office tools provide a variety of functions that aid the smooth running of the system or allow operational personnel to perform tasks such as pricing and setting limits on betting opportunities, adjusting customer balances (for example, in the case of settlement errors), and changing event configurations.

Security

Security, for example authorisation and authentication (user-name, password, access rights, etc), and audit trails may be deployed within other components or applications, but may also be deployed as a separate component.

DATA

Data storage is frequently separated from applications and from presentation onto specialised 'database' (DBMS) servers, however, some applications may be operated or processing may occur on database servers and some operators deploy data and applications on the same equipment. The deployment of databases is further complicated because server hardware and the disks that physically store the data may be separate devices. Dedicated (and expensive) data storage equipment is often used by larger operators for performance and management purposes.

Operators normally have some form of back-up or archiving that keeps a copy of data that will be used in the event of loss of the main source of data, either directly or following restoration to the production system.

Customer details

Customer details include information about the customer, such as name, address, credit and debit cards and other payment-type information and account number(s). Customers may register their details whether they intend to gamble or not.

Customer account (wallet)

The customer account keeps track of the customer's balance and the transactions into and out of the account. The balance is amended by other components following deposits/payments, withdrawals, gambling transactions, etc. The information stored may also include monies taken to and from other wallets and/or shadow wallets. The account will be linked in some form to customer's gambling transaction records (see below) and may also be linked to external shadow wallets via a reference number or other identifier.

Shadow account (shadow wallet)

The shadow account or token/chip wallet is only relevant for integrated gambling systems where monies are moved from one product to another. Essentially the shadow account contains the customer's chip/token balance and a reference ID from the originating system.

Gambling transaction record (game/bet history)

This data store may be referred to as a virtual event log, game log, game history, bet log, bet record, or bet history. The gambling transaction record contains the details of the customer's gambling transactions such as selection, stake, odds, and bet type. The gambling transaction record also stores the result (win/loss) of the individual gambling transactions. Gambling transactions are linked to customer accounts, normally via the customer's account number so that account balances may be updated following settling processes.

Summarised information about amounts staked, amounts credited as winnings and amounts taken as losses would also be classed as gambling transaction records.

Events & markets

Information about sporting or other 'real' events, such as location, time and date, competitors, etc. (for example, Arsenal (home) vs Man Utd (away), on the 5th June, at 3pm), are stored along with associated betting markets, (if they exist, eg win/lose/draw) and the current and previous odds (where they exist). This information is commonly received from external sources, such as SIS or the PA in Britain, and is stored by other non-gambling organisations.

Virtual event state

Gambling systems may need to maintain a record of the event state in order to be able to recover interrupted gambling where, for example, a customer loses connectivity to the server part way through a multi-stage game.

Management & marketing information

Management information is non-production data, that is, data that is not intended to be used in 'live' systems in the provision of facilities for gambling. Management information is normally stored separately to be examined at a later point in time. Management information is used to explore trends, betting patterns, popularity of games or types of betting, successful promotions, etc. This may include data for marketing purposes or for the calculation of bonuses or incentives based on customer's accumulated gambling activity.

External interfaces

Interfaces to external systems (often referred to as Application Programming Interfaces or APIs) could be deployed anywhere within the infrastructure, though larger operators will often have dedicated equipment. Interfaces support the exchange of information with other organisations or other systems. Gambling systems have a variable number of external interfaces depending on the size and scope of the operation. As noted earlier, many operators offer sportsbook and virtual events including 'casinos' and 'poker rooms' often hosted/managed on their behalf by third parties. To gamble using these systems the customer purchases chips/token and the Interfaces are used to exchange information about the value of these and minimal information about the customer's identity (often just a reference ID).

DISASTER RECOVERY & BACKUP DATA

Disaster recovery

Most of the larger operators and many of the smaller ones have some kind of disaster recovery (DR) facility. DR facilities require data to be copied from the production infrastructure over to DR infrastructures, which may be identical to or be a trimmed down versions of the production infrastructure. DR facilities are normally only invoked after a significant failure event occurring in the production infrastructure. However, operators may also 'test' their disaster recovery processes and infrastructures by transferring live operations to them for short periods.

Backup data

Backup data is distinct from DR data since it is not intended to be used *directly* as a live source of data. Instead this data is used to restore information to a production facility (or a DR mirror).
Gambling Commission March 2008

CHANGES TO LICENCE CATEGORIES FROM 1 AUGUST 2008

To avoid duplication this document has not been reproduced here but can be found at para 6.2167 above.

IS A PRODUCT REMOTE BETTING OR REMOTE GAMING?

October 2009

1 INTRODUCTION

6.2513 1.1 The Gambling Commission (the Commission) has received a number of enquiries from the gambling industry about which products can be offered online under a remote general betting operating licence and which require a remote casino operating licence.
1.2 The purpose of this advice note is to provide a clearer distinction between betting and gaming by setting out for the gambling industry the test that the Commission will apply when considering whether a product is:

- a betting product which requires a remote general betting licence, whether for real events or virtual events or
- a gaming product which requires a remote casino licence.

1.3 As of 1 August 2009 the remote general betting operating licence has been split so that there are now separate operating licences for the provision of facilities for betting on real events and for betting on virtual events:

- A remote general betting (real events) operating licence authorises the provision of facilities for betting on the outcome of real races, competitions or other events or processes other than a game of chance.
- A remote general betting (virtual events) operating licence authorises the provision of facilities for betting on the outcome of virtual races, competitions or other events or processes other than a game of chance. Neither licence authorises the provision of facilities for gaming.
- The remote casino operating licence continues to exist.

1.4 The remote sector is innovative and there have been signs that some remote betting licensees are offering products that appear to be (or have the characteristics of) gaming products.

1.5 Remote betting products will generally involve placing a bet on the outcome of a race, competition or other event or process. This will often involve a future real sporting event (whereas gaming excludes sports) and no participation beyond the placing of a bet, unlike gaming which involves the playing of a game and thus, to varying degrees, participation in the game by players. Other products will involve virtual (computer generated) events. It is with these that this advice note is concerned.

1.6 The Commission considers it important that operators are appropriately licensed for the products they offer and is mindful that there are additional regulatory requirements on those holding a casino operating licence compared to those holding a general betting operating licence (whether for real or virtual events). For example, the Money Laundering Regulations 2007 apply to casino operators but not to betting operators. However all gambling operators are required to comply with the requirement of the Proceeds of Crime Act 2002 (POCA) and the Commission has published advice on its website to assist gambling operators to comply with their responsibilities under POCA.

1.7 This advice note is not concerned with whether a product may fall outside of betting or gaming ie products that are lotteries.

2 IS A PRODUCT BETTING OR GAMING?

2.1 The Commission has considered what factors are relevant, in the context of computer generated events, in order to distinguish between betting and gaming, or to determine whether what is being bet on is the outcome of a game of chance as opposed to some other event or process. But of course only the courts can provide a definitive view on the legal position. The Secretary of State also has power, by regulations under section 6(6) of the Gambling Act 2005 (the Act) to provide that a specific activity, or an activity carried on in specified circumstances, is or is not to be treated as a game, a game of chance or a sport. To date the Secretary of State has not exercised these powers.

2.2 In determining whether a remote gambling product involves gaming, or whether the outcome on which bets are placed is the outcome of a game of chance the Commission intends to adopt the following two stage test:

Test 1:

Is the product a virtual version of a known casino game, a derivative of one or designed to resemble one?

If the answer is yes then the Commission considers that the product is gaming and a remote casino operating licence is required.

If the answer to Test 1 is no then Test 2 becomes relevant.

Test 2:

Does the product meet the following criteria?

- Is it a virtual game which is not a sport?
- Do the customers participate in or bet on the outcome of the game?
- Is there an element of chance involved? Is the outcome determined by anything other than skill? The Act provides that a game which involves both an element of chance and an element of skill is a game of chance.
- Is there a prize? A prize can be in the form of money or money's worth.

If the answer to all of these four questions is yes then the Commission considers that the product is gaming or betting on a game of chance and a remote casino operating licence is required.

2.3 It is possible for a particular transaction to satisfy both the definition of betting in section 9 of the Act and the definition of gaming in section 6 of the Act. An obvious example is staking on a number at roulette in a casino. The Act provides (in section 16) for how such a transaction is to be regulated. If the transaction is pool betting within the meaning of section 12 of the Act then it falls to be regulated as betting; otherwise it falls to be regulated as gaming.

2.4 Consistent with the approach taken in section 16 of the Act, where a remote gambling product appears to have characteristics of gaming or betting on a game of chance the Commission's starting position will be that the activity requires a remote casino licence.

2.5 An operator may require more than one category of operating licence depending on the products they offer. For example some operators offer betting on real and virtual events as well as casino games and will require a remote casino licence; remote general betting (real events) licence; and remote general betting (virtual events) licence.

2.6 The Commission will continue to monitor licensees as part of compliance to ensure they are appropriately licensed. Where operators require an additional or different licence the Commission will expect operators to take steps to regularise their position and either (1) apply for the appropriate licence or (2) remove products that are not authorised by their existing licence.

2.7 Operators can obtain information about how to apply for a licence from our website at www.gamblingcommission.gov.uk.

Copies of this document are available in alternative formats on request.

Gambling Commission October 2009

Note

Regulatory return forms (October 2011) and guides as to how to complete them (June 2011) are available from the Gambling Commission's website at www.gamblingcommission.gov.uk

MACHINES

MACHINE STANDARDS DEFINITIONS
June 2007

6.2520

Address Space	A range of discrete addresses, each of which may correspond to a physical or virtual memory register, a network host, peripheral device, disk sector or other logical or physical entity.
Change	Money paid out which was inserted by the player that has neither been played nor committed to play.
Critical Game Files	All files that may affect the outcome of a game, including executables, data, and operating system files.
Critical Memory	Has the meaning ascribed to it in paragraph 3.1.
Critical Memory Clear	The process to reset the critical memory of a gaming machine, which configures the gaming machine into the 'as new' state.
Device	Any component of a gaming machine and, where the context requires, includes computer software used in a gaming machine.
Double-Up	Feature whereby the player is offered a gamble in which some or all of the winnings may be wagered at a 100% player return.
Enriched Periods	Where the machine deliberately forces winning outcomes over a series of games by use of any compensation or other controller mechanism.
Error Condition	A detectable event outside of the gaming machine's normal operating parameters.
Firmware	The embedded program memory of the gaming machine.
Gamble	A single act of staking on an outcome within a game.
Game	Any gambling opportunity offered to the user of a gaming machine whether it amounts to gaming, betting or participating in a lottery as those terms are defined in the Act.
Game Cycle	Has the meaning ascribed to it in paragraph 5.6.
Game Update	Any change to game configuration, pay table or any other software that may affect the gambling.
Gaming Machine	Has the meaning ascribed to it by section 235 of the Act.
Hashing Algorithm	Reproducible method of turning some kind of data into a (relatively) small number that may serve as a digital 'fingerprint' of the data.
Idle state	Where there are insufficient credits on a machine to enable a game to be played.
Live Jackpot Feature	A feature played on a single gaming machine which has a prize that may be increased from a pre-set or seeded value from game to game as contributions are made to it from monies staked.
Machine Malfunction	Any hardware and/or software fault that temporarily results in an unforeseen game outcome, or corruption and/or renders the machine unserviceable. Deliberate player actions to trigger a machine fault are not considered be a machine malfunction.
MD5 or SHA	Message-Digest Algorithm 5 and Secure Hash Algorithm respectively.

Multi-Station Game	A gaming machine which incorporates a number of player terminals which share a common device required for the game such as a random number generator.
Non-volatile Computer Memory	Memory that can retain the stored information even when not powered. eg. read-only memory, flash, hard disk, floppy disk, magnetic tape and optical disc drives.
Normal Mode	Where a gaming machine is in a configuration designed for play (not in test or other non-play mode) and in a serviceable condition with no errors detected.
'Off chip' Battery Source	Battery source independent of a data storage chip used for data refresh purposes (recharges state of data bytes when mains power is disconnected).
Passive Display Equipment	Devices only associated with viewing game outcome and not with player interaction such as touch screen displays.
Patch Wires and Track Cuts	Modifications to a circuit board, post manufacture, including soldering additional wires to bridge the electrical conductor paths or the addition of a component (patch wires) or to change the circuit path by cutting the copper conductor (track cut).
Program Storage Devices ('PSD')	Means any device used to store software code in read only or read write format as required by the gaming machine in its normal operation.
Raking Periods	Where a machine deliberately forces a series of losing games by use of any compensation or other controller mechanism.
ROM	Read only memory.
Seeding	Means an integer used to set the starting point for generating a series of random numbers.
Theoretical Target Percentage Return to Player	In the case of games in which the chances of winning are distributed randomly, the calculated probable percentage return to player at a 95% confidence level. In other cases, the target percentage return to player as determined by any controlling mechanism.
TITO	Ticket in, ticket out system.
Updates	Any software modification that may affect the outcome of the game.
Value of Total Play (VTP)	The aggregate of all charges for use paid in respect of the machine.

These requirements were notified in draft to the European Commission in accordance with Directive 98/34/EC, as amended by Directive 98/48/EC

Gambling Commission June 2007

MACHINE STANDARDS CATEGORY A & B1
June 2012

INTRODUCTION

6.2525 This standard is applicable to all category A & B1 gaming machines as defined under section 235 of the Gambling Act 2005 (the Act). This standard came into force for all category A & B1 gaming machines supplied or sited within Great Britain from 1 September 2007.
The purpose of the standard is to set out in detail Gambling Commission's (the Commission) requirements with respect to game features,

display notices and general machine operation including metering. These have been developed to help ensure the Commission's three licensing objectives are met. Those objectives are to:

- prevent gambling from being a source of crime or disorder, being associated with crime or disorder or being used to support crime;
- ensure that gambling is conducted in a fair and open way; and
- protect children and other vulnerable persons from being harmed or exploited by gambling.

Operators or end users should not rely upon these standards as a measure of reliability, quality or minimal security requirements.
These standards permit equivalence between different types of technology and do not specify proprietary products or technologies. Testing regimes for these standards will permit equivalent international standards (ISO). It is not intended to limit game content and the use of new technological developments provided that the objectives of the standard are met.

OTHER RELEVANT GAMING MACHINE TECHNICAL STANDARDS

- Technical Standards for Category B2, B3, B3A, B4, C and D Machines
- Technical Standards for Non-Complex Category D Machines
- Technical Standards for Legacy Machines[1] (Categories B3, B4, C and D Machines)
- Technical Standard for Server Networked & Downloadable Gaming Machines (All categories of machine)
- Technical Standard for Wireless Network Systems (All categories of machine)
- Technical Standard for Cashless Systems (All categories of machine)
- Technical Standard for Linked Progressives (All categories of machine)

---

1 Essentially 'legacy machines' are Category B3, B4, C or D machines which were lawfully in use on premises in Great Britain on 31 August 2007 which comply with the regulations made under s 240 of the Act and certain details of which have been notified to the Commission.

1.0 HARDWARE REQUIREMENTS

1.1 PHYSICAL SECURITY

All reasonable efforts should be made to ensure that a gaming machine is robust enough to withstand forced entry which would not leave behind evidence of the attempted entry. Where any form of attempted or forced entry causes an error condition, the machine must only commence play once the error condition has been cleared. Provided that any security device or sensor (eg door open sensor) which has detected an attempted entry no longer indicates there to be a problem the machine may automatically clear the error condition and commence play. Otherwise, operator action shall be required to clear the error condition.

1.2 MACHINE IDENTIFICATION

A gaming machine must have an identification plate of metallic construction or of an equally resilient material permanently affixed to the exterior of the cabinet by the manufacturer. This must not be easily removable, without leaving evidence of tampering. The following information shall be displayed on the identification plate:

(a) the manufacturer (machine manufacturer or brand name under which it is to be sold);
(b) a unique serial number;
(c) the gaming machine model number (which may refer to the cabinet type and not the game); and

(d) the date of manufacture.

The identification plate shall be mounted on the front or side of the cabinet where it is clearly visible.

1.3 GAMING MACHINE ALARM/ALERT REQUIREMENTS

Gaming machines must be designed to automatically prevent further play and alert the site management in the following situations:

(a) a player winning an amount or redeeming credits that the machine cannot automatically pay;

(b) an error condition occurring; or

(c) a machine fault occurring.

Such a system must be transparent to the player when activated and sufficiently able to attract the attention of the site management.

1.4 LOGIC AREA

Any electronic logic components that could significantly influence the operation of the gaming machine shall be housed in an area that can be separately locked (with its own locked door) and should only be able to be accessed with the appropriate key. There may be more than one such logic area in a gaming machine.

Electronic component items that are required to be housed in one or more logic areas are:

(a) central processing units and other electronic components involved in the operation and calculation of game play (eg game controller electronics and components housing the game or system firmware program storage media);

(b) electronics involved in the operation and calculation of game result determination;

(c) electronics involved in the calculation of game display, and components housing display program storage medium (other than passive display equipment);

(d) communication controller electronics, and components housing the communication program storage media may reside outside the gaming machine; and

(e) alterable storage media that hold control programs.

1.5 CONFIGURATION SETTINGS

It must not be possible to change a configuration setting in any manner that may obstruct the proper operation of an electronic accounting meter without a critical memory clear. A change to the accounting denomination must be done by a secure means, which includes access to the locked logic area.

All switches and/or jumpers must be fully documented and any hardware system within the machine which may alter the configuration settings such as pay tables, accounting denomination, or payout percentages in the operation of the gaming machine must be housed within a separately locked secure logic area. This includes top award changes (including progressives), selectable Blackjack settings, or any other option that would affect the payout percentage.

1.6 VIDEO MONITORS/TOUCH SCREENS

All video based games shall meet the following requirements:

(a) touch screens shall be accurate and, once calibrated, shall maintain that accuracy for at least the manufacturer's recommended maintenance period;

(b) a touch screen should be able to be re-calibrated without access to the machine cabinet other than opening the main door;

(c) there shall be no hidden or undocumented buttons/touch points anywhere on the screen that affect game play, except as provided for by the game rules; and

(d) section (1.6 c) does not apply to audit functions and controls which must be documented.

1.7 MECHANICAL DEVICES USED FOR DISPLAYING OF GAME OUTCOMES

If the game has mechanical or electro-mechanical devices, which are used for displaying game outcomes, the following rules shall be observed:
(a) electro-mechanically controlled display devices (eg reels or wheels) shall have a sufficiently closed loop of control so as to enable the software to detect a malfunction, or an attempt to interfere with the correct operation of that device. This requirement is designed to ensure that if a reel or wheel is not in the position it is supposed to be in, an error condition will be generated;
(b) mechanical assemblies (eg reels or wheels) shall have some mechanism that ensures the correct mounting of reels' artwork;
(c) displays shall be constructed in such a way that winning symbol combinations match up with pay lines or other indicators; and
(d) a mechanical assembly shall be so designed that it is not obstructed by any other components.

1.8 MULTI-STATION GAMES

In any multi-station game each player terminal and any other shared device must comply with the relevant sections of this standard, including its requirements for machine identification and metering.
All game rules shall be transparent to the player at each terminal and any shared device that is used to display information pertaining to the game shall be clearly visible to all players participating.

1.9 PATCH WIRES

All patch wires and track cuts shall be documented, in an appropriate manner, in the relevant service manual and/or service bulletin. This does not prohibit required repairs in the field.

2.0 SOFTWARE REQUIREMENTS

2.1 CONTROL PROGRAM AUTHENTICATION REQUIREMENTS

The control program must utilise an integrity check, suitable for the media, providing at least the level of integrity of CRC 16 (for non alterable storage media) or a secured hashing method such as MD5 or SHA (for alterable storage media) to authenticate that the program and/or support files have not been corrupted or altered prior to use/loading.
Any alterable media must be write protected. For non-alterable storage media it is acceptable to have a test methodology which detects at least 99.99% of all possible failures.
The program residing in the gaming machine or device must be contained in a storage medium, which cannot be altered through use of the circuitry or programming of the machine or device itself. If the program is contained in any other medium, then the following requirements must be met or an alternative method used providing at least this level of integrity:
(a) authentication is required for all critical game files. This authentication shall employ a hashing algorithm which produces a 'Message Digest' (the mathematical results/signature of the hashing algorithm) output of at least 128 bits[2];
(b) the Message Digest(s) for all files must reside on a memory device (ROM based or other medium) within the gaming machine or device. Message Digests which

reside on any other medium shall be encrypted or digitally signed, using a public/private key algorithm with a minimum of a 512 bit key or an equivalent encryption algorithm with similar security[3];

(c) the gaming machine or device shall authenticate all critical game files against the stored Message Digest(s);

(d) in the event of a failed authentication, after the game has been powered up, the gaming machine or relevant device should immediately enter an error condition and the operator be notified by the device accordingly. The machine should also record the details, including time and date of the error in a log. Clearing of such error condition must require operator intervention. The game must display specific error information and not clear until either the file authenticates properly, following the operator intervention, or the medium is replaced or corrected, and the device's memory cleared, the game restarted, and all files authenticated correctly; and

(e) the device must be capable of displaying the 'Message Digest' of any and all files on demand through the audit mode.

---

2 This requirement will be reviewed periodically as technology advances and new security methods become available

3 This requirement will be reviewed periodically as technology advances and new security methods become available

2.2 ALTERABLE STORAGE MEDIA DEVICES

Any gaming machine and any procedural requirements must include sufficient security to ensure that any software that can influence the game outcome, including configurable settings that reside on any alterable media, is a true replication of that version of the game, control or other software.

2.3 PROGRAM STORAGE MEDIUM IDENTIFICATION

Any program medium (ROMs, EPROMs, Alterable storage media, DVD and CD-ROM) placed in the field shall be uniquely identified, displaying:

(a) program ID number;

(b) manufacturer or game provider;

(c) version number;

(d) type and size of medium (unless located on the medium as purchased unused from the supplier); and

(e) location of installation in gaming machine or device, if potentially confusing.

The information a) to e) above must be available for inspection on the site operator's premises either on the label of the storage media or via video or display monitor. For EPROM based games, the identification label shall be placed over the UV window to avoid erasing or alteration of the program.

2.4 PROGRAM INTERRUPTION AND RESUMPTION

After a program interruption (eg power down or power failure), software must be able to recover to the state it was in immediately prior to the interruption occurring. If a gaming machine or device is powered down while in an error condition, and power is later restored, the gaming machine or device must either:

(a) detect that the error has been corrected, in which case play may continue; or

(b) if the error remains, continue to display the error message and cause the gaming device to remain locked-up.

The program must not be adversely affected by the simultaneous or sequential activation of the various inputs and outputs, such as 'play buttons', which might, whether intentionally or not, cause malfunctions or invalid results.

On program resumption, the following procedures must be performed as a minimum requirement:

(a) any communications to an external device must not begin until the program resumption routine, including self-tests, is completed successfully;

(b) gaming device control programs shall test themselves for possible corruption due to failure of the program storage media. The authentication may use the checksum; however, it is preferred that the Cyclic Redundancy Check (CRC) calculations are used as a minimum (at least 16 bit). Other test methodologies must be approved by the Commission, its agent or approved test house; and

(c) the integrity of all critical memory must be checked.

Where a peripheral device such as a note acceptor (accepting a note) or printer (printing a coupon/credit note) is in operation during a power failure it must, where practicable, on resumption of the power either complete or restart the task successfully or display an error message indicating that a fault has occurred. The error message must remain until the fault has been resolved by either the actions of the device or the operator. In all circumstances the metering or audit controls must be able to identify any accounting anomalies and a record be maintained for dispute resolution purposes.

Microprocessor controlled reels (eg stepper motor reels) must re-spin automatically to the last valid play-mode result when the play mode is re-entered, and the reel positions have been altered (eg when the main door is closed, power is restored, audit mode is exited, or an error condition cleared).

2.5 LAST GAME RECALL

Information on at least the last five games must be always retrievable on the operation of a suitable external key-switch, or another secure method not available to the player. Last play information must provide all information required to reconstruct fully the last five (5) plays. All values must be displayed, including the initial credits, credits bet, credits won, and credits paid. If a progressive prize was awarded (see Progressive Standard), it is sufficient to indicate that fact: the value need not be displayed. This information should include the final game outcome, including all player choices and bonus features. In addition, the results of any 'Double-up' or 'Gamble'.

The last five game re-call shall reflect bonus rounds in their entirety. If a bonus round lasts 'x number of events', each with separate outcomes, each of the 'x events' shall be displayed with its corresponding outcome, if the outcome results in an award. The recall shall also reflect position dependent events if the outcome results in an award. For games that may award unlimited free plays, there shall be a minimum of fifty plays recallable.

2.6 TEST/DIAGNOSTIC MODE

When a gaming machine or device is in a test mode, any test that involves credits entering or leaving the gaming machine or device (eg a hopper test) must be completed prior to resumption of normal operation. In addition, there must not be any test mode that increments any of the electronic meters. Any credits on the gaming machine or device accrued during the test mode must be cleared before the test mode is exited. Test meters are permissible provided the meter indicates that they are such.

The main cabinet door of a gaming machine may automatically place the machine in a service or test mode. Test/diagnostics mode may also be entered, via an appropriate instruction, by an attendant during an audit mode access.

When exiting from test mode, any game in play must return to the original state it was in when the test mode was entered. If the gaming machine or a device is in a game test mode, the machine must clearly indicate that it is in a test mode, not normal play.

2.7 SOFTWARE VERIFICATION

All gaming machines must be capable of permitting an independent integrity software check utilising an external device. This can be accomplished by the medium being able to be removed and authenticated by a third-party, or having an interface port for third-party equipment to authenticate the media. The purpose of such an integrity check is to provide a means for field testing the software to identify and validate the program.

3.0 CRITICAL MEMORY REQUIREMENTS

3.1 CONTENTS OF CRITICAL MEMORY

Critical memory means computer memory used to store all data that is vital to the continued operation of the gaming machine or device. This includes, but is not limited to, memory which records:

(a) the current value of:
- credit and bank (deposited, committed funds and winnings) values; and
- last bank note data.

(b) power up and door open occurrences;
(c) gaming device/game configuration data;
(d) information pertaining to the last five (5) plays with the RNG outcome (including the current game, if incomplete); and
(e) software state (ie the last normal state the gaming machine or device software was in before interruption).

3.2 MAINTENANCE OF CRITICAL MEMORY

Critical memory storage must be maintained by a methodology that enables errors to be identified and corrected in most circumstances. This methodology may involve signatures, checksums, partial checksums, multiple copies, timestamps and/or effective use of validity codes.

Comprehensive checks of critical memory must be made during each gaming machine or device restart (eg power up cycle).

Gaming machine or device control programs (software that operates the machine or device's functions) shall test for possible corruption caused by failure of the program storage medium and all critical game files. Test methodology must endeavour to detect 100 percent of all possible failures.

The control program (software that operates the gaming machine or device's functions) must allow for the machine or device to ensure the integrity of all control program components during execution of said components.

All program storage devices ('PSD') in the executable address space of a main processor shall be validated during the following conditions:

(a) any power up;
(b) the first time the files are loaded for use (even if only partially loaded).

Memory and PSD space that are not critical to machine security (eg video or sound ROM) are not required to be validated.

3.3 PROGRAM MEMORY, CRITICAL MEMORY AND NON-VOLATILE DEVICES USED TO STORE PROGRAM MEMORY

The following are requirements for critical memory:

(a) a battery back-up (where required), or an equivalent, must be installed on the gaming machine or device for the electronic meters and must be capable of maintaining the accuracy of all information required for thirty days after power is discontinued from the machine. The back-up device must be kept within the locked logic area;

6: Gambling Act 2005: Additional Material

(b) if the rechargeable battery back-up is used as an 'off chip' battery source it shall re-charge itself to its full potential in a maximum of twenty-four hours and have a shelf life of at least five years; and

(c) critical memory that uses an off-chip back-up power source to retain its contents when the mains power is switched off must have a detection system which will provide a method for software to interpret and act upon a low battery condition.

3.4 UNRECOVERABLE CRITICAL MEMORY

An un-correctable corruption of critical memory must result in an error condition. Critical memory should not be cleared automatically, but must only be cleared by an authorised person.

3.5 FUNCTION OF CRITICAL MEMORY RESET

Clearing critical memory must only be capable of being undertaken by accessing the logic area in which it is housed. Following the initiation of a critical memory reset procedure, the game program must execute a routine which initialises each and every bit in memory to the default state.

For machines that allow for partial critical memory clears, the methodology for doing so must be accurate and the machine must validate the un-cleared portions of memory. The default reel position or game display after a critical memory reset must not be the top award on any selectable line. The default game display, upon entering game play mode, must also not be the top award. This applies to the base game only and not to any secondary bonus devices.

4.0 MACHINE CREDIT AND PAYMENT REQUIREMENTS

4.1 COIN OR TOKEN AND NOTE ACCEPTORS AND OTHER METHODS OF INSERTING MONEY OR MONEY'S WORTH INTO THE MACHINE

All coin/token acceptors must meet the following requirements:

(a) the coin/token acceptor must be designed to prevent the use of cheating methods such as slugging (counterfeit coins/tokens), stringing (coin pullback), the insertion of foreign objects and other manipulation. The device must be capable of handling rapidly-fed coins/tokens so that the possibility of cheating is minimised. The devices must have suitable detectors for determining the direction and the speed of coin/token travel in the receiver. If a coin/token travelling at too slow a speed or in an invalid direction is detected, the gaming device shall enter an error condition and display an error condition for at least thirty seconds or be cleared by an attendant;

(b) other than for diagnostic purposes coins/tokens judged invalid by the acceptor must be rejected to the coin tray and shall not be counted as credits. Acceptance of coins/tokens for crediting to the credit meter must only be possible when the gaming machine is enabled for play. Other states, such as error conditions, including 'door open' and 'audit mode' must disable the coin/token acceptor system. Each coin/token inserted must register the actual monetary value or a number of credits on the player's credit meter for the current game or bet meter. If coins or tokens inserted in a machine are registered directly as credits, the conversion rate must be clearly stated, or be easily ascertainable from a help menu or similar;

(c) all acceptance devices must be able to detect the entry of valid notes, coupons, paper tokens, or other approved voucher, and provide a method to enable the gaming device software to interpret and act appropriately upon a valid or invalid input. Acceptance devices must be electronically-based and configured to ensure that they only accept valid banknotes, vouchers or paper tokens, and reject all other notes. The note input system must be constructed in a manner that protects against vandalism, abuse, or fraudulent activity. In addition, note acceptance devices must meet the following requirements:

(d) where a stacker is installed credits must only be registered when:
  (i) the note or other valid token has passed the point where it is accepted and stacked; and
  (ii) the acceptor has sent an 'irrevocably stacked' message to the machine.

(e) if note acceptors are designed to be factory set only, it must not be possible to access or conduct maintenance or adjustments to those note acceptors in the field, other than:
  (i) the selection of notes, coupons, or paper tokens and their limits;
  (ii) changing of EPROMs or downloading of software;
  (iii) adjustment of the tolerance level for accepting notes or tokens of varying quality should only be allowed with adequate levels of security in place. This can be accomplished through lock and key, physical switch settings, or other accepted methods approved on a case-by-case basis;
  (iv) maintenance, adjustment, and repair per factory approved procedures; or
  (v) options that set the direction or orientation of acceptance.

4.2 TOKENISATION

For games that may be played using tokens, the gaming machine or relevant device must receive from the acceptor and post to the player's 'bank' the entire amount inserted. If the currency amount is not an even multiple of the token for a game or the credit amount has a fractional component, the system must retain the value for the benefit of the next player.

4.3 PRINTERS

If a gaming machine is equipped with a printer that is used to make payments, the printer must be located in a locked area of the machine (eg require opening of the main door to access), but not in the logic area.

Any printed ticket/voucher/hand pay receipt must display the following information:

(a) operator's name or reference;
(b) gaming machine number;
(c) date and time (24-hour format) of issuance;
(d) alpha numeric currency amount;
(e) sequence number;
(f) validation number and/or unique identifier (eg bar code);
(g) transaction type (cash out ticket, hand pay receipt.); and
(h) duplicate ticket indicator (eg duplicate number 3).

4.4 TICKET VALIDATION

Payment by ticket printer as a method of credit redemption is only permissible when:

(a) there is an independent means to validate the printed ticket/voucher/hand pay receipt prior to any credit or other type of redemption; and
(b) such validation system is capable of identifying duplicate tickets to prevent fraud by reprinting and redeeming a ticket previously issued.

To meet this standard, an audit trail of at least one month's data relating to all ticket transactions must be maintained for dispute resolution purposes.

5.0 SPECIFIC GAME REQUIREMENTS

5.1 GENERAL REQUIREMENT

Where the outcome results in a player winning a prize, it must be determined randomly and in particular no compensator or regulator may be used to determine any stage of the game.

The machine must clearly display to the player either at all times when it is in operation, or at the point a game is selected for play, the following statement:

THIS MACHINE IS RANDOM

5.2 RANDOM NUMBER GENERATOR (RNG) REQUIREMENTS

Each possible permutation or combination of game elements that produces winning or losing game outcomes shall be available for random selection at the initiation of each play, unless otherwise clearly stated.

A gaming machine or device must use appropriate communication protocols to protect the RNG and random selection process from influence by associated equipment which may be communicating with the machine or device. The RNG must be protected from external influences, such as electromagnetic and electrostatic interference and radio waves. (Compliance with the Electromagnetic Regulations would satisfy these requirements.)

A machine or device must not present a losing game result which indicates a 'Near Miss', eg where the odds of the top award symbol landing on the pay line are limited it must not frequently appear above or below the pay line.

The selection process must:

(a) be distributed over the entire output range and pass appropriate statistical tests as defined in the test and approval requirements;

(b) ensure the output is unpredictable; and

(c) not reproduce the same output stream, nor must two instances of an RNG produce the same stream as each other. Where seeding is required to achieve this seeding should not introduce predictability.

If a gaming machine offers a game which is recognisable (eg Poker, Blackjack, Roulette) and is described as such by title or visual presentation and the chances of winning differ from an equivalent real game then this must be made plain to the player either via the artwork or help menus. In any event the rules of the simulated game must be evident and transparent to the player. In the case of other games (such as spinning reel games or video spinning reel games); the mathematical probability of each possible stage of the game outcome shall be constant.

5.3 MECHANICAL BASED RNG GAMES

Mechanical based RNG games are games that use the laws of physics to generate the outcome of the game. All mechanical based RNG games must meet the requirements of this standard with the exception of requirements in s 5.2 that are clearly applicable only to electronic RNGs. In addition, mechanical based RNG games must meet the following requirements:

(a) the mechanical pieces must be constructed of materials to prevent decomposition of any component over time (eg a ball shall not disintegrate);

(b) the properties of physical items used to choose the selection shall not be altered; and

(c) the player must not be able to interact with, come into physical contact with, or manipulate the mechanics of the game.

The above is not intended to prohibit mechanically based skill and chance features used for entertainment purposes which may form a part of an otherwise electronic game.

5.4 SCALING ALGORITHMS

If a random number with a range shorter than that provided by the RNG is required for some purpose within a game, the method of re-scaling, (ie converting the number to the lower range), is to be designed in such a way that all numbers within the lower range are equally probable.

5.5 SINGLE GAME REQUIREMENTS

The stakes for every gambling opportunity within a game selected by the player must be deducted from the credit or play meter prior to the outcome of any gambling opportunity being displayed to the player.
Before credit(s) for play in a game can be taken, the previous game must first have been completed in full and the result shown to the player.
This section does not preclude the use of multi lines, multi stake and multi reel games provided that the total stake and prize do not exceed the statutory maximum for the single game.

5.6 INITIATING THE NEXT GAME (AUTO START/PLAY)

Except where an 'auto play' or 'auto start' feature is permissible[4] it must always be necessary to release and then depress the machine's real or virtual 'start button' to start a game cycle.

---

[4] See Regulation 2, Gaming Machine (Circumstances of Use) Regulations 2007

5.7 GAME SPEED OF PLAY

Each game cycle must last at least 2.5 seconds.
A game cycle starts when a player using a gaming machine once[5] has paid for each gamble selected and depresses the 'start button' or takes equivalent action to initiate the game and ends when all money or money's worth staked or won during the game has been either lost or delivered to, or made available for collection by the player and the start button or equivalent becomes available to initiate the next game.
Where auto play or auto start is permitted then a game cycle is measured from the point at which the game is initiated by the system (equivalent to the player depressing the start button) to the point at which it is able to automatically start the next game.

---

[5] Within the meaning of the Category of Gaming Machine Regulations 2007

5.8 NOT APPLICABLE TO THESE CATEGORIES OF MACHINE.

5.9 LIVE JACKPOTS

Except for a live jackpot, no gaming machine shall offer prizes which increase or appear to increase from one game to the next. A live jackpot shall not be linked to any other gaming machine and must comply with the following rules:

(a) for an electronically displayed live jackpot the true value (the prize value which may be won within the game) must be displayed to the player at all times and must be available in every game. It may only be won as a result of either:
   - (i) a random outcome within the game; or
   - (ii) the proportion of total money contributed to the jackpot reaching a randomly pre-determined trigger limit;

(b) it is permissible to use physical coins in place of an electronically displayed equivalent provided that the value of prize which may be won by the player is transparent (the player must be able to reasonably assess the total prize value on offer);

(c) the live jackpot must be incremented in proportion to the money staked and by no more than the statutory maximum stake in any single game. For category A machines it shall not be increased by more than the value of the stake used to play the game in which it is incremented. It is not a requirement for the live jackpot and reserve (where used) to be incremented in unison or at the same rate;

(d) the prize awarded may be comprised of a fixed value (which must be transparent to the player at all times) together with the live jackpot provided that the total (including any other prize won in the game) does not exceed the statutory maximum;

(e) if an alternative prize option is selected, the live jackpot prize must remain unaffected. Once, however, the live jackpot option is selected, the live jackpot prize must be delivered and the live jackpot reduced to zero or its seeded value, regardless of whether the live jackpot is delivered directly or is subject to some intervening gamble or skill feature; and

(f) the value of the live jackpot or its reserve shall not influence the chance of achieving a win within the game or be used to imply that a win is more likely.

In this section, a 'reserve meter' is a second meter or display which is used to hold any value which may be raised at the same time as the live jackpot, or which holds any overspill once the live jackpot has reached the maximum level for that category of machine.

5.10 DOUBLE-UP

Any Double-up or Gamble options must have a theoretical return to the player of that displayed or suggested by the game graphic.

5.11 BONUS GAMES

If a game cycle contains a 'bonus feature' including a game within a game, the following rules must be met:

(a) it must be transparent to the player which game rules apply to the current game state;

(b) if the bonus game does not occur randomly, the machine must display to the player sufficient information to indicate the current status towards the triggering of the next bonus game (eg if the game requires the player to obtain several events/symbols to enter a bonus game, the number of events/symbols needed to enter the bonus game shall be indicated along with the number of events/symbols collected at that point);

(c) the game must not adjust the likelihood of a bonus occurring, based on the history of prizes obtained in previous games;

(d) if a game's bonus is triggered after accruing a certain number of events/symbols or combination of events/symbols of a different kind, the probability of obtaining like events/symbols must not deteriorate as the game progresses (eg for identical events/symbols it is not permissible that the last few events/symbols needed should be more difficult to obtain than the previous events/symbols of that kind); and

(e) it must be transparent to the player that the game is in a bonus mode.

5.12 ADDITIONAL CREDIT(S) STAKED DURING THE GAME

A machine must not permit players to stake any additional credit(s) during a game cycle unless the game complies with the following requirements:

(a) that the outcome of the game is not decided prior to any additional credit(s) being staked;

(b) that the outcome of the game following any additional credit(s) being staked is random and that all possible combinations associated with an equivalent real game under the same circumstances are available to the player;

(c) that the game does not modify the chance of achieving a win or the combinations available to the player associated with an equivalent real game as a result of their decision not to stake, or to stake additional credits within that game; and

(d) the player must not be deliberately misled or given a false impression that they have an enhanced chance of winning as a result of staking additional credits within the game.

Category A only

(e) That the total stake wagered within the game does not exceed 3 times (3x) the original stake wagered to start the game.

Category B1 only

(f) That the total stake wagered within the game does not exceed the relevant statutory maximum.

This section does not preclude the use of multi stake, multi line and multi reel game configurations provided that the player sets their total stake prior to the start of the game cycle.

5.13 PRE-GAMBLE

Where the player is given the opportunity at the start of the game to enter into a 'pre-gamble', and the prizes available or the odds of achieving those prizes in the game are linked to the odds of a successful outcome of the pre-gamble, the following rules shall be complied with:

(a) the player must always be given the option at the start of the game whether or not to use the pre-gamble feature;

(b) there must not be a difference of more than10% between the lowest percentage return to player (%RTP) offered to the player opting to use the pre-gamble feature and a player who does not opt to do so;

(c) the prize awards related to each pre-gamble option must be transparent to the player in that they must be fully aware of what they are playing for (or pre-gambling for);

(d) pre-gambles must be transparent in that they must be at natural odds, the player must get what he sees, and there must be no form of compensation or payment or retention of winnings in the event that a short or long series of game outcomes falls outside that which might be normally expected; and

(e) following a 20 second period in which there is no game played, and there is insufficient credit to play a game, any set gamble level is to be reset to 'no gamble'.

5.14 GAME LINKS

A 'game link' is where an element, feature or outcome from one game is either held over or made reference to (recreated) in the next game (eg reel band holds). Game links, with the exception of the live jackpot, are not permissible unless they comply with the following rules:

(a) any reference or link made to any previous game must occur randomly;

(b) linkages to a game are only permissible from the immediately preceding completed game;

(c) the chance of being awarded a link to the next game must be no better than even;

(d) the player must not be aware of whether a link will be given or have the opportunity to use it before he commits himself to the game; and

(e) no subsequent game link is permissible to the current game where a prize has been awarded, and delivered to the player. It is not permissible to force or create a series of wins (enriched periods) using any link feature(s).

5.15 MULTIPLE GAMES ON A GAMING MACHINE

(a) The methodology used to select and discard a particular game for play on a multi-game machine shall be transparent to the player.

(b) All applicable rules and/or the pay tables should be transparent and available to view for each game prior to any commitment to play.

(c) It must at all times be made transparent to the player which game has been selected for play or is being played.

(d) Committing to play a game must involve the player in at least two actions. Having selected a game, the player must be able to return to the main menu without playing.

(e) It should not be possible to start a new game before the current play is completed and all relevant meters have been updated (including features, gamble and other options of the game).

(f) The set of games offered to the player for selection, or the pay table, must be capable of being changed only by a secure method. This includes turning on and off games available for play through a suitable interface. The rules at section 1.5 of these standards shall govern the critical memory clear control requirements for these types of selections. However, for games that keep the previous pay tables (the pay table just turned off) data in memory, a critical memory clear is not required. Alternatively to a critical memory clear, a gaming system may record the data that is stored in critical memory on separately allocated memory exclusive to the game provided there are adequate safeguards to ensure critical memory integrity.

(g) No changes to the set of games offered to the player for selection (or to the pay table) are permitted while there are credits on the player's credit or bank meter or while a game is in progress unless there is evidence of game manipulation or fraud as a result of a security weakness.

(h) Where changes to the sets of games offered to the player for selection (or to the pay table) are performed outside of the site operator's opening hours it is permissible to do so while credits remain on the player's credit meter provided that there are adequate measures to ensure the machine is not accessible to players and that any credits are retained for the benefit of the next player following such a procedure.

6.0 SPECIFIC ERROR CONDITIONS AND ALERT REQUIREMENTS

6.1 GENERAL ALERT CONDITIONS

Gaming machines and devices must be capable of detecting, displaying and alerting the operator to the error conditions listed below. These must be cleared either by an attendant or upon initiation of a new play sequence and where any on-line monitoring and control system is networked to the machine details of the error should be communicated to it:

(a) coin-in jam (where the coin acceptor disables itself under such circumstances it is not a requirement that it display an error message);

(b) coin-out jam;

(c) hopper empty or timed out;

(d) hopper runaway or extra coin paid out;

(e) critical memory error (including an indication of battery failure or low battery power source);

(f) note acceptor-in jam;

(g) program error or authentication mismatch;

(h) door open (including note acceptor);

(i) reverse coin-in (coin travelling the wrong way through acceptor);

(j) reel spin errors, including a miss-index condition for rotating reels, that affect the outcome of the game:

  (i) the specific reel number must be identified in the error code;

  (ii) in the final positioning of the reel, if the position error exceeds one-half of the width of the smallest symbol excluding blanks on the reel strip; and

  (iii) microprocessor controlled reels must be monitored to detect malfunctions such as a reel which is jammed, or is not spinning freely, or any attempt to manipulate their final resting position.

(k) power reset; and
(l) logic cage open (where applicable).

NOTE: This rule also applies to 'Note Acceptor Error Conditions' as to which see 6.3 below.

For machines or devices or individual games that use error codes, a description of such codes and their meanings shall be affixed inside the machine or device. This does not apply to video-based games; however, video based games shall display meaningful text to describe the relevant error condition.

6.2 PRINTER ERROR CONDITIONS

A printer shall have mechanisms to allow software to interpret and act upon the following conditions:
(a) out of paper or paper low;
(b) presentation error (TITO only);
(c) printer jam/failure; and
(d) printer disconnected which may only be detected when the software tries to print.

These conditions shall trigger an error condition to indicate the error has occurred.

6.3 NOTE ACCEPTOR ERROR CONDITIONS

Each gaming machine or device (including note acceptors) must have the capability of detecting and displaying (for note acceptors, it is acceptable to disable or flash a light or lights) the following error conditions:
(a) Stacker Full (where installed) – a note acceptor should disable itself to accept no more notes. The game should not generate an error message when the stacker is full;
(b) Note Jams – it is acceptable for the note acceptor to indicate there is a note jam by disabling itself to accept no more notes or by some other method;
(c) Note Acceptor Door Open – where a note acceptor door is the glass door, a door open signal is sufficient; and
(d) Stacker Door Open (where installed) or Stacker Removed.

A note acceptor must perform a self-test at each power up. In the event of a self-test failure, the note acceptor must automatically disable itself (ie enter note reject state) until the error state has been cleared.

7.0 METER REQUIREMENTS

7.1 CREDIT/PLAY METER

Credits used to initiate a new game (see section 5.6) must come from a single meter which may be described as a credit or play meter. The player shall have the option to view any funds held in such a meter as a monetary value.

7.2 ACCOUNTING AND OCCURRENCE METERS

The machine must have at least one primary metering system which is independent of the main control system. All reasonable efforts should be made to ensure that data held by the primary metering system is true and accurate and impervious to tampering or unauthorised modification.

Accounting meters shall be at least eight (8) digits in length. If the meter is being used in Pounds (£) and Pence, at least seven (7) digits must be used for the Pound (£) amount. The meter must roll over to zero upon the next occurrence, any time the meter is eight (8) digits or higher and after 99,999,999 has been reached or any other value that is logical. Occurrence meters shall be at least three (3) digits in length and roll over to zero upon the next occurrence, any time the meter is higher that the maximum number of digits for that meter. The primary metering system as a minimum requirement shall be capable of recording the following data (accounting meters are designated with an asterisk '*'):

(a) the coins-in* (OR cash in) meter shall cumulatively count the total amounts staked during game play, except credits that are won during a game that are subsequently risked in a double up mode;

(b) the coins-out* (OR credit out) meter must cumulatively count all amounts won by the player at the end of the game, that were not paid out by an attendant, including amounts paid by a ticket printer. This meter must not increment for notes inserted and cashed out (ie when the device is used as a change machine);

(c) the drop* meter must maintain a cumulative count of the number of coins that have been diverted into a drop bucket and credit value of all notes and tickets/coupons inserted into the note acceptor for play. It is acceptable to have separate 'drop' meters for coins, notes, tickets and coupons;

(d) the hand pays* meter shall reflect the cumulative amounts paid by an attendant for progressive and non-progressive hand pays;

(e) the games-played meter must display the cumulative number of games played since the last critical memory clear.

(f) a cabinet door meter must display the number of times the front cabinet door was opened since the last critical memory clear;

(g) the drop door meter must display the number of times the drop door or the note acceptor door was opened since the last critical memory clear; and

(h) the progressive occurrence meter must count the number of times each progressive meter is activated. Note: there is a separate standard applicable to progressives.

In all cases the data held on the metering system must be such that the percentage return to player can be accurately calculated and available for inspection. In instances where a gaming machine or device is able to offer multiple games such information must be available for each game and game variant.

7.3 METERING OF NOTE ACCEPTOR EVENTS

A gaming machine or device's primary metering system must also maintain and be able to report the following:

(a) total monetary value of all items accepted;

(b) total number of all items accepted; and

(c) a break down of the notes accepted:

- (i) for banknotes, the device must report the number accepted for each denomination;
- (ii) for all other notes (non legal tender), the device must have a separate meter that reports the number accepted; and
- (iii) denomination of the last five banknotes inserted.

7.4 MULTI-GAME, GAME SPECIFIC METERS

In addition to the Accounting Meters required above, each individual game available for play shall have at least a separate 'Credits Bet' and 'Credits Won' meter designated in either credits or pounds (£).

Even if a 'Double up or Gamble' game is lost, the initial win amount/credits bet amount shall be recorded in the game specific meters. Alternatively, there may be separate meters that account for the Double-up or Gamble information. In either event the method of metering must be transparent.

7.5 DOOR OPEN/CLOSE METERING

The gambling machine or device shall be able to detect and meter access to the following doors or secure areas:

(a) all external doors;
(b) drop box door; and
(c) bill acceptor door.

8.0 ARTWORK AND GAME DISPLAY REQUIREMENTS

8.1 INFORMATION TO BE DISPLAYED

A gaming machine or relevant device shall display, on the machine itself or on screen, information to enable players to keep track of their gambling. As a minimum, the following information must be available to the player at all times the machine is available for play:

(a) the player's current bank balance (where relevant);
(b) number of plays available or current credit balance (monetary value);
(c) the current stake;
(d) all possible winning outcomes, or a link to where this information may be viewed for, eg on a help menu;
(e) win amounts or odds given for each possible winning outcome, or a link to where this information may be viewed, eg on a help menu. The win amount may be displayed as a multiple of the bet or may be shown indirectly by describing the method by which wins are awarded;
(f) the amount won for the last completed game; and
(g) the player options selected (eg total stake, lines played) for the last completed game (until the next game starts or a new selection is made).

Mystery wins are permissible provided it is transparent to the player as to how such a prize may be achieved.

It is not permissible to state or imply that a prize greater than the statutory maximum for a single game may be won by means of the machine nor to indicate that the machine is in a state which could be beneficial to the player (such as by way of a Cash Full Lamp).

8.2 MULTI-LINE GAMES

(a) Each individual line to be played shall be clearly indicated by the gaming machine or device so that the player is in no doubt as to which lines are being staked upon.
(b) The winning play line(s) shall be clearly discernable to the player (eg on a video game it may be accomplished by drawing a line over the symbols on the play line(s) and/or the flashing of winning symbols and line selection box. Where there are wins on multiple lines, each winning play line may be indicated in turn. This would not apply to reel based games).

8.3 DISPLAY NOTICE REQUIREMENTS

(a) If any display in respect of a game offered by a gaming machine (including reels) is capable of being taken to indicate odds which do not reflect the true odds in the game the following statement must be included on the face of the machine or at the time the game is selected where more than one game is offered to the player, clearly visible to the player:

THE OUTCOME OF ANY GAME OR FEATURE IS NOT NECESSARILY THAT SHOWN BY THE ODDS DISPLAYED

(b) The following statement must be displayed on the face of the machine or at the time the game is selected where more than one game is offered to the player, clearly visible to the player:

NO PRIZE GREATER IN VALUE THAN [JACKPOT] POUNDS CAN BE WON FROM THIS MACHINE IN ANY ONE GAME

(c) The theoretical target percentage return to player (for betting products this equates to 1 less the calculated hold) must be clearly displayed to the player on the machine in the appropriate alternative format below:

(i) in cases in which the percentage return to player does not depend upon the strategy used by the player

THIS MACHINE HAS AN AVERAGE PERCENTAGE PAYOUT OF AT LEAST (VALUE) %

Where there is a range (a lower and upper percentage return to player available within the same game) it must be the lower value that is displayed.

(ii) in cases in which the percentage return to player can vary depending upon the strategy used by the player

THE RETURN TO PLAYER BASED ON BEST STRATEGY IS (VALUE) %

In either case the percentage return to player should be calculated in the following manner:

Percentage return to player equals the value of total play divided by total win shown as a percentage

(d) Either of the following statements must be displayed on the machine, clearly visible to the player:

(i) MACHINE MALFUNCTION VOIDS GAME

Or

(ii) MALFUNCTION VOIDS PAYS AND PLAYS

For the purposes of this standard both statements mean that that a machine malfunction voids the game within which the malfunction occurs and does not affect the position of the player prior to that specific game including win and credit meters.

(e) Where the machine is designed such that the deposited sum cannot be delivered by the machine for any reason then the following statement must be clearly displayed on the machine:

THIS MACHINE PAYS (£ minimum value payable) ONLY ANY LESSER AMOUNTS WILL BE RETAINED FOR FUTURE USE

9.0 DEFINITIONS

Address Space	A range of discrete addresses, each of which may correspond to a physical or virtual memory register, a network host, peripheral device, disk sector or other logical or physical entity.
Change	Money paid out which was inserted by the player that has neither been played nor committed to play.
Critical Game Files	All files that may affect the outcome of a game, including executables, data, and operating system files.
Critical Memory	Has the meaning ascribed to it in paragraph 3.1.
Critical Memory Clear	The process to reset the critical memory of a gaming machine, which configures the gaming machine into the 'as new' state.
Device	Any component of a gaming machine and, where the context requires, includes computer software used in a gaming machine.

Double-Up	Feature whereby the player is offered a gamble in which some or all of the winnings may be wagered at a 100% player return.
Enriched Periods	Where the machine deliberately forces winning outcomes over a series of games by use of any compensation or other controller mechanism.
Error Condition	A detectable event outside of the gaming machine's normal operating parameters.
Firmware	The embedded program memory of the gaming machine.
Gamble	A single act of staking on an outcome within a game.
Game	Any gambling opportunity offered to the user of a gaming machine whether it amounts to gaming, betting or participating in a lottery as those terms are defined in the Act.
Game Cycle	Has the meaning ascribed to it in paragraph 5.7.
Game Update	Any change to game configuration, pay table or any other software that may affect the gambling.
Gaming Machine	Has the meaning ascribed to it by section 235 of the Act.
Hashing Algorithm	Reproducible method of turning some kind of data into a (relatively) small number that may serve as a digital 'fingerprint' of the data.
Idle state	Where there are insufficient credits on a machine to enable a game to be played.
Live Jackpot Feature	A feature played on a single gaming machine which has a prize that may be increased from a pre-set or seeded value from game to game as contributions are made to it from monies staked.
Machine Malfunction	Any hardware and/or software fault that temporarily results in an unforeseen game outcome, or corruption and/or renders the machine unserviceable. Deliberate player actions to trigger a machine fault are not considered be a machine malfunction.
MD5 or SHA	Message-Digest Algorithm 5 and Secure Hash Algorithm respectively.
Multi-Station Game	A gaming machine which incorporates a number of player terminals which share a common device required for the game such as a random number generator.
Non-volatile computer memory	Memory that can retain the stored information even when not powered. eg. read-only memory, flash, hard disk, floppy disk, magnetic tape and optical disc drives.
Normal Mode	Where a gaming machine is in a configuration designed for play (not in test or other non-play mode) and in a serviceable condition with no errors detected.
'Off chip' Battery Source	Battery source independent of a data storage chip used for data refresh purposes (recharges state of data bytes when mains power is disconnected).
Passive Display Equipment	Devices only associated with viewing game outcome and not with player interaction such as touch screen displays.
Patch Wires and Track Cuts	Modifications to a circuit board, post manufacture, including soldering additional wires to bridge the electrical conductor paths or the addition of a component (patch wires) or to change the circuit path by cutting the copper conductor (track cut).
Program Storage Devices ('PSD')	Means any device used to store software code in read only or read write format as required by the gaming machine in its normal operation.

Raking Periods	Where a machine deliberately forces a series of losing games by use of any compensation or other controller mechanism.
ROM	Read only memory.
Seeding	Means an integer used to set the starting point for generating a series of random numbers.
Theoretical Target Percentage Return to Player	In the case of games in which the chances of winning are distributed randomly, the calculated probable percentage return to player at a 95% confidence level. In other cases, the target percentage return to player as determined by any controlling mechanism.
TITO	Ticket in, ticket out system.
Updates	Any software modification that may affect the outcome of the game.
Value of Total Play (VTP)	The aggregate of all charges for use paid in respect of the machine.

These requirements were notified in draft to the European Commission in accordance with Directive 98/34/EC, as amended by Directive 98/48/EC
Gambling Commission June 2012

MACHINE STANDARDS CATEGORY B2
June 2012

INTRODUCTION

6.2530 This standard is applicable to all category B2 gaming machines as defined under section 235 of the Gambling Act 2005 (the Act). This standard came into force for all category B2 gaming machines supplied or sited within Great Britain from 1 September 2007.

The purpose of the standard is to set out in detail the Gambling Commission's (the Commission) requirements with respect to game features, display notices and general machine operation including metering. These have been developed to help ensure the Commission's three licensing objectives are met. Those objectives are to:

- prevent gambling from being a source of crime or disorder, being associated with crime or disorder or being used to support crime;
- ensure that gambling is conducted in a fair and open way; and
- protect children and other vulnerable persons from being harmed or exploited by gambling.

Operators or end users should not rely upon these standards as a measure of reliability, quality or minimal security standards.

These standards permit equivalence between different types of technology and do not specify proprietary products or technologies. Testing regimes for these standards will permit equivalent international standards (ISO). It is not intended to limit game content and the use of new technological developments provided that the objectives of the standard are met.

OTHER RELEVANT GAMING MACHINE TECHNICAL STANDARDS

- Technical Standards for Category A & B1, B3, B3A, B4, C and D Machines
- Technical Standards for Non-Complex Category D Machines
- Technical Standards for Legacy Machines[1] (Categories B3, B4, C and D Machines)

- Technical Standard for Server Networked & Downloadable Gaming Machines (All categories of machine)
- Technical Standard for Wireless Network Systems (All categories of machine)
- Technical Standard for Cashless Systems (All categories of machine)
- Technical Standard for Linked Progressives (All categories of machine)

[1] Essentially 'legacy machines' are Category B3, B4, C or D machines which were lawfully in use on premises in Great Britain on 31 August 2007 which comply with the regulations made under s 240 of the Act and certain details of which have been notified to the Commission.

1.0 HARDWARE REQUIREMENTS

1.1 PHYSICAL SECURITY

All reasonable efforts should be made to ensure that a gaming machine is robust enough to withstand forced entry which would not leave behind evidence of the attempted entry. Where any form of attempted or forced entry causes an error condition, the machine must only commence play once the error condition has been cleared. Provided that any security device or sensor (eg door open sensor) which has detected an attempted entry no longer indicates there to be a problem the machine may automatically clear the error condition and commence play. Otherwise, operator action shall be required to clear the error condition.

1.2 MACHINE IDENTIFICATION

A gaming machine must have an identification plate of metallic construction or of an equally resilient material permanently affixed to the exterior of the cabinet by the manufacturer. This must not be easily removable, without leaving evidence of tampering. The following information shall be displayed on the identification plate:

(a) the manufacturer (machine manufacturer or brand name under which it is to be sold);
(b) a unique serial number;
(c) the gaming machine model number (which may refer to the cabinet type and not the game); and
(d) the date of manufacture.

The identification plate shall be mounted on the front or side of the cabinet where it is clearly visible.

1.3 GAMING MACHINE ALARM/ALERT REQUIREMENTS

Gaming machines must be designed to automatically prevent further play, and alert the site management in the following situations:

(a) a player winning an amount or redeeming credits that the machine cannot automatically pay;
(b) an error condition occurring; or
(c) a machine fault occurring.

Such a system must be transparent to the player when activated and sufficiently able to attract the attention of the site management.

1.4 LOGIC AREA

Manufacturers must, so far as is reasonably practicable, incorporate in gaming machines design features aimed at preventing tampering with any electronic logic component that has the potential significantly to influence the operation of the machine.

1.5 CONFIGURATION SETTINGS

All switches and/or jumpers must be fully documented and any hardware system within the machine which may alter the configuration settings such as pay tables, accounting denomination, or payout percentages in the operation of the gaming machine must either be housed within a separately locked secure logic area or comply with the following two paragraphs. This includes top award changes (including progressives) or any other option that would affect the payout percentage.
As an alternative to a separate secure logic area, any change in configuration defined above must be logged and date stamped within the secure non-volatile memory of the machine. This log must cover a minimum period of not less than 1 month and be made available for display on demand with the test and diagnostic routine of the machine.
The data for the log file may be captured and held on a device independent of any player terminal (eg a back office or off site server) provided it complies with the following:
(a) the server or device holding the log file is robust enough to withstand forced entry or alternatively housed within a secure environment (eg locked within a room, enclosure or within dedicated IT environment);
(b) the log file covers a minimum period of not less than 1 month;
(c) the log file is available for inspection;
(d) all reasonable efforts are made to ensure that the log file cannot be tampered with or modified;
(e) the log file is backed up on regular basis and that those back ups are available for inspection; and
(f) the data written to and stored on the log file is true and accurate.

1.6 VIDEO MONITORS/TOUCH SCREENS

All video based games shall meet the following requirements:
(a) touch screens shall be accurate and once calibrated, shall maintain that accuracy for at least the manufacturer's recommended maintenance period;
(b) a touch screen should be able to be re-calibrated without access to the machine cabinet other than opening the main door;
(c) there shall be no hidden or undocumented buttons/touch points anywhere on the screen that affect game play, except as provided for by the game rules; and
(d) section (1.6 c) does not apply to audit functions and controls which must be documented.

1.7 MECHANICAL DEVICES USED FOR DISPLAYING OF GAME OUTCOMES

If the game has mechanical or electro-mechanical devices, which are used for displaying game outcomes, the following rules shall be observed:
(a) mechanical assemblies (eg reels or wheels) shall have some mechanism that ensures the correct mounting of reels' artwork;
(b) displays shall be constructed in such a way that winning symbol combinations match up with pay lines or other indicators; and
(c) a mechanical assembly shall be so designed that it is not obstructed by any other components.

1.8 MULTI-STATION GAMES

In any multi-station game each player terminal and any other shared device must comply with the relevant sections of this standard, including its requirements for machine identification and metering.
All game rules shall be transparent to the player at each terminal and any shared device that is used to display information pertaining to the game shall be clearly visible to all players participating.

1.9 PATCH WIRES

All patch wires and track cuts shall be documented, in an appropriate manner, in the relevant service manual and/or service bulletin. This does not prohibit required repairs in the field.

2.0 SOFTWARE REQUIREMENTS

2.1 CONTROL PROGRAM AUTHENTICATION REQUIREMENTS

The control program must utilise an integrity check, suitable for the media, providing at least the level of integrity of CRC 16 (for non-alterable storage media) or a secured hashing method such as MD5 or SHA (for alterable storage media) to authenticate that the program and/or support files have not been corrupted or altered prior to use/loading. Any error detected must result in the machine displaying the appropriate error message and being unavailable for play.
The integrity check must be carried out during each start up or at least once every 24 hours where the machine is specifically designed for permanent serviceable operation.

2.2 ALTERABLE STORAGE MEDIA DEVICES

Any gaming machine and any procedural requirements must include sufficient security to ensure that any software that can influence the game outcome, including configurable settings that reside on any alterable media is a true replication of that version of the game, control or other software.

2.3 PROGRAM STORAGE MEDIUM IDENTIFICATION

Any program medium (ROMs, EPROMs, Alterable storage media, DVD and CD-ROM) placed in the field shall be uniquely identified, displaying:
(a) program ID number;
(b) manufacturer or game provider;
(c) version number;
(d) type and size of medium (unless located on the medium as purchased unused from the supplier); and
(e) location of installation in gaming machine or device, if potentially confusing.
The information a) to e) above must be available for inspection on the site operator's premises either on the label of the storage media or via video or display monitor. For EPROM based games, the identification label shall be placed over the UV window to avoid erasing or alteration of the program.

2.4 NOT APPLICABLE TO THESE CATEGORIES OF MACHINE.
2.5 LAST GAME RECALL

Information on at least the last five games must be always retrievable on the operation of a suitable external key-switch, or another secure method not available to the player. Last play information must provide all information required to reconstruct fully the last five plays. If a progressive prize was awarded (see Progressive Standard) it is sufficient to indicate that fact: the value need not be displayed. All values must be displayed, including the initial credits, credits bet, credits won, and credits paid. This information should include the final game outcome, including all player choices and bonus features. In addition, the results of any 'Double-up' or 'Gamble'.
The last five game recalls shall reflect bonus rounds in their entirety. If a bonus round lasts 'x number of events', each with separate outcomes, each of the 'x events' shall be displayed with its corresponding outcome, if the outcome results in an award. The recall shall also reflect position dependent events if the outcome results in an award. For games that may award unlimited free plays, there shall be a minimum of fifty plays recallable.

2.6 TEST/DIAGNOSTIC MODE

When a gaming machine or device is in a test mode, any test that involves credits entering or leaving the gaming machine or device (eg a hopper test) must be completed prior to resumption of normal operation.
The main cabinet door of a gaming machine may automatically place the machine in a service or test mode. Test/diagnostics mode may also be entered, via an appropriate instruction, by an attendant during an audit mode access.
When exiting from test mode, any game in play must return to the original state it was in when the test mode was entered. If the gaming machine or a device is in a game test mode, the machine shall clearly indicate that it is in a test mode, not normal play.

2.7 SOFTWARE VERIFICATION

At a minimum, the machine must have the ability to allow visual inspection of the following using either an available matrix or video display. (It is permissible for the machine not to display such information during each start up but it must be accessible when required. This may involve the machine being restarted or an appropriate security key being used.)
(a) identity of the game provider;
(b) game identity code;
(c) version number of game software; and
(d) check sum of game software
And if the operating system is not proprietary to the manufacturer, game provider, supplier or operator then:
(e) identity of operating system; and
(f) version number of operating system.
On machines or terminals which offer the player a choice of games the above information concerning the game software must be made available for each game.

3.0 CRITICAL MEMORY REQUIREMENTS

3.1 CONTENTS OF CRITICAL MEMORY

Critical memory (that is non-volatile computer memory) must be used to store the following data:
(a) credit and bank values (deposited, committed and winning funds);
(b) electronic meters; and
(c) data for the 'last five games recall'.
The clearing or resetting of such data must require deliberate action by appropriately authorised personnel.

3.2 MAINTENANCE OF CRITICAL MEMORY

Critical memory storage must be maintained by a methodology that enables errors to be identified and corrected in most circumstances. This methodology may involve signatures, checksums, partial checksums, multiple copies, timestamps and/or effective use of validity codes.
Comprehensive checks of critical memory must be made during each gaming machine or device restart (eg power up cycle). Gaming machine or device control programs (software that operates the machine or device's functions) shall test for possible corruption caused by failure of the program storage medium and all critical game files. Test methodology must endeavour to detect 100 percent of all possible failures.
The control program (software that operates the gaming machine or device's functions) must allow for the machine or device to ensure the integrity of all control program components during execution of said components.

All program storage devices ('PSD') in the executable address space of a main processor shall be validated during the following conditions:
(a) any power up; and
(b) the first time the files are loaded for use (even if only partially loaded).
Memory and PSD space that are not critical to machine security (eg video or sound ROM) are not required to be validated.

3.3 PROGRAM MEMORY, CRITICAL MEMORY AND NON-VOLATILE DEVICES USED TO STORE PROGRAM MEMORY

The following are requirements for critical memory:
(a) a battery back-up (where required), or an equivalent, must be installed on the gaming machine or device for the electronic meters and must be capable of maintaining the accuracy of all information required for thirty days after power is discontinued from the machine The battery backup device must be kept within the locked logic area or if not available a secure location behind the locked main door;
(b) if the rechargeable battery back-up is used as an 'off chip' battery source, it shall re-charge itself to its full potential in a maximum of twenty-four hours and a specified shelf life of at least five years; and
(c) critical memory that uses an off-chip back-up power source to retain its contents when the main's power is switched off must have a detection system which will provide a method for software to interpret and act upon a low battery condition, or alternatively, use a suitable software check to ensure integrity of storage is maintained.

3.4 UNRECOVERABLE CRITICAL MEMORY

An un-correctable corruption of critical memory must result in an error condition. Critical memory should not be cleared automatically, but must only be cleared by an authorised person.

3.5 FUNCTION OF CRITICAL MEMORY RESET

Clearing critical memory must only be capable of being undertaken by accessing the logic area or secure location in which it is housed. Following the initiation of a critical memory reset procedure, the game program must execute a routine, which initialises each and every bit in memory to the default state. For machines that allow for partial critical memory clears, the methodology for doing so must be accurate and the machine must validate the un-cleared portions of memory.
The default reel position or game display after a critical memory reset must not be the top award on any selectable line. The default game display, upon entering game play mode, must also not be the top award. This applies to the base game only and not to any secondary bonus devices.

4.0 MACHINE CREDIT AND PAYMENT REQUIREMENTS

4.1 COIN OR TOKEN AND NOTE ACCEPTORS AND OTHER METHODS OF INSERTING MONEY OR MONEY'S WORTH INTO THE MACHINE

All coin/token acceptors must meet the following requirements:
(a) the coin/token acceptor must be designed to prevent the use of cheating methods such as slugging (counterfeit coins/tokens), stringing (coin pullback), the insertion of foreign objects and other manipulation; and
(b) other than for diagnostic purposes coins/tokens judged invalid by the acceptor must be rejected to the coin tray and shall not be counted as credits. Acceptance of coins/tokens for crediting to the credit meter must only be possible when the

gaming machine is enabled for play. Other states, such as error conditions, including 'door open' and 'audit mode' must disable the coin/token acceptor system. Each coin/token inserted must register the actual monetary value or a number of credits on the player's credit meter for the current game or bet meter. If coins or tokens inserted in a machine are registered directly as credits, the conversion rate must be clearly stated, or be easily ascertainable from a help menu or similar.

All acceptance devices must be able to detect the entry of valid notes, coupons, paper tokens, or other approved voucher and provide a method to enable the gaming device software to interpret and act appropriately upon a valid or invalid input. Acceptance devices must be electronically-based and be configured to ensure that they only accept valid banknotes, vouchers or paper tokens and reject all other notes. The note input system must be constructed in a manner that protects against vandalism, abuse, or fraudulent activity.

4.2 TOKENISATION

For games that may be played using tokens, the gaming machine or relevant device must receive from the acceptor and post to the player's 'bank' the entire amount inserted. If the currency amount is not an even multiple of the token for a game or the credit amount has a fractional component, the system must retain the value for the benefit of the next player.

4.3 PRINTERS

If a gaming machine is equipped with a printer that is used to make payments, the printer must be located in a locked area of the machine (eg require opening of the main door to access), but not in the logic area unless the alternative requirements in the second and third paragraphs of section 1.5 (configuration settings) are complied with.

Any printed ticket/voucher/hand pay receipt must display the following information:

(a) operator's name or reference;
(b) gaming machine number;
(c) date and time (24-hour format) of issuance;
(d) alpha numeric currency amount;
(e) sequence number;
(f) validation number and/or unique identifier (eg bar code);
(g) transaction type (cash out ticket, hand pay receipt); and
(h) duplicate ticket indicator (eg duplicate number 3).

4.4 TICKET VALIDATION

Payment by ticket printer as a method of credit redemption is only permissible when:

(a) there is an independent means to validate the printed ticket/voucher/hand pay receipt prior to any credit or other type of redemption; and
(b) such validation system is capable of identifying duplicate tickets to prevent fraud by reprinting and redeeming a ticket previously issued.

To meet this standard, an audit trail of at least one month's data relating to all ticket transactions must be maintained for dispute resolution purposes.

5.0 SPECIFIC GAME REQUIREMENTS

5.1 GENERAL REQUIREMENT

Where the outcome results in a player winning a prize, it must be determined randomly and in particular no compensator or regulator may be used to determine any stage of the game.

The machine must clearly display to the player either at all times when it is in operation or at the point a game is selected for play, the following statement:

THIS MACHINE IS RANDOM

5.2 RANDOM NUMBER GENERATOR (RNG) REQUIREMENTS

Each possible permutation or combination of game elements that produces winning or losing game outcomes shall be available for random selection at the initiation of each play, unless otherwise clearly stated.

A gaming machine or device must use appropriate communication protocols to protect the RNG and random selection process from influence by associated equipment, which may be communicating with the machine or device. The RNG must be protected from external influences, such as from electromagnetic and electrostatic interference and radio waves (Compliance with the Electromagnetic Compatibility Regulations would satisfy these requirements).

A machine or device must not present a losing game result which indicates a 'Near Miss'; eg where the odds of the top award symbol landing on the pay line are limited it must not frequently appear above or below the pay line.

The selection process must:

(a) be distributed over the entire output range and pass appropriate statistical tests as defined in the test and approval requirements (reference to document to be included);
(b) ensure the output is unpredictable; and
(c) not reproduce the same output stream, nor must two instances of an RNG produce the same stream as each other. Where seeding is required to achieve this it should not introduce predictability.

If a gaming machine offers a game which is recognisable (eg Poker, Blackjack, Roulette) and is described as such by title or visual presentation and the chances of winning differ from an equivalent real game then this must be made plain to the player either via the artwork or help menus. In any event the rules of the simulated game must be clear and transparent to the player. In the case of other games (such as spinning reel games or video spinning reel games) the mathematical probability of each possible stage of the game outcome shall be constant.

5.3 MECHANICAL BASED RNG GAMES

Mechanical based RNG games are games that use the laws of physics to generate the outcome of the game. All mechanical based RNG games must meet the requirements of this standard with the exception of requirements in s 5.2 that are clearly applicable only to electronic RNGs. In addition, mechanical based RNG games must meet the following requirements:

(a) the mechanical pieces must be constructed of materials to prevent decomposition of any component over time (eg a ball shall not disintegrate);
(b) the properties of physical items used to choose the selection shall not be altered; and
(c) the player must not be able to interact with, come into physical contact with or manipulate the mechanics of the game.

The above is not intended to prohibit mechanically based skill and chance features used for entertainment purposes which may form a part of an otherwise electronic game.

5.4 SCALING ALGORITHMS

If a random number with a range shorter than that provided by the RNG is required for some purpose within a game, the method of re-scaling, (ie converting the number to the lower range), is to be designed in such a way that all numbers within the lower range are equally probable.

5.5 SINGLE GAME REQUIREMENTS

The stakes for every gambling opportunity within a game selected by the player must be deducted from the credit or play meter prior to the outcome of any gambling opportunity being displayed to the player.
Before credit(s) for play in a game can be taken, the previous game must first have been completed in full and the result shown to the player.
This section does not preclude the use of multi lines, multi stake and multi reel games provided that the total stake and prize do not exceed the statutory maximum for the single game.

5.6 INITIATING THE NEXT GAME (AUTO START/PLAY)

Except where an 'auto play' or 'auto start' feature is permissible[2] it must always be necessary to release and then depress the machine's real or virtual 'start button' to start a game cycle.

[2] See Regulation 2, Gaming Machine (Circumstances of Use) Regulations 2007

5.7 GAME SPEED OF PLAY

Each game cycle must last at least 20 seconds to complete.
A game cycle starts when a player using a gaming machine once[3] has paid for each gamble selected and depresses the 'start button' or takes equivalent action to initiate the game and ends when all money or money's worth staked or won during the game has either been lost or delivered to, or made available for collection by the player and the start button or equivalent becomes available to initiate the next game.
Where auto play or auto start is permitted then a game cycle is measured from the point at which the game is initiated by the system (equivalent to the player depressing the start button) to the point at which it is able to automatically start the next game.

[3] Within the meaning of the Category of Gaming Machine Regulations 2007

5.8 NOT APPLICABLE TO THIS CATEGORY OF MACHINE

5.9 LIVE JACKPOTS

Except for a single live jackpot feature, no gaming machine shall offer prizes which increase or appear to increase from one game to the next. A live jackpot shall not be linked to any other gaming machine and must comply with the following rules:

(a) for an electronically displayed live jackpot the true value (the prize value which may be won within the game) must be displayed to the player at all times and must be available in every game. It may only be won as a result of either:
- a random outcome within the game; or
- the proportion of total money contributed to the jackpot reaching a randomly pre-determined trigger limit;

(b) it is permissible to use physical coins in place of an electronically displayed equivalent provided that the value of prize which may be won by the player is transparent (the player must be able to reasonably assess the total prize value on offer);

(c) the live jackpot must be incremented in proportion to the money staked and by no more than the value of the stake used to play the game once (as defined in the section 236 regulations) in which it is incremented. It is not a requirement for the live jackpot and reserve (where used) to be incremented in unison or at the same rate;

(d) the prize awarded may be comprised of a fixed value (which must be transparent to the player at all times) together with the live jackpot provided that the total (including any other prize won in the single game) does not exceed the statutory maximum;
(e) if an alternative prize option is selected, the live jackpot prize must remain unaffected. Once, however, the live jackpot option is selected, the live jackpot prize must be delivered and the live jackpot reduced to zero, regardless of whether the live jackpot is delivered directly or is subject to some intervening gamble or skill feature; and
(f) the value of the live jackpot or its reserve shall not influence the chance of achieving a win within the game or be used to imply that a win is more likely.

In this section, a 'reserve meter' is a second meter or display which is used to hold any value which may be raised at the same time as the live jackpot, or which holds any overspill once the live jackpot has reached the maximum level for that category of machine.

5.10 DOUBLE-UP

Any Double-up or Gamble options must have a theoretical return to the player of that displayed or suggested by the game graphic.

5.11 NOT APPLICABLE TO THIS CATEGORY OF MACHINE.

5.12 ADDITIONAL CREDIT(S) STAKED DURING THE GAME

A machine must not permit players to stake any additional credit(s) during a game cycle unless the game complies with the following requirements:
(a) that the outcome of the game is not decided prior to any additional credit(s) being staked;
(b) that the outcome of the game following any additional credit(s) being staked is random and that all possible combinations associated with an equivalent real game under the same circumstances are available to the player;
(c) that the game does not modify the chance of achieving a win or the combinations available to the player associated with an equivalent live game as a result of their decision not to stake, or to stake additional credits within that game;
(d) that player must not be deliberately misled or given a false impression that they have an enhanced chance of winning as a result of staking additional credits within the game; and
(e) that the total stake wagered within the game does not exceed the relevant statutory maximum.

This section does not preclude the use of multi stake, multi line and multi reel game configurations provided that the player sets their total stake prior to the start of the game cycle.

5.13 PRE-GAMBLE

Where the player is given the opportunity at the start of the game to enter into a pre-gamble and the prizes available or the odds of achieving those prizes in the game are linked to the odds of a successful outcome of the pre-gamble, the following rules shall be complied with:
(a) the player must always be given the option at the start of the game whether or not to use the pre-gamble;
(b) there must not be a difference of more than 10% between the lowest percentage return to player (%RTP) offered to the player when not opting to use the pre-gamble as against opting to do so;
(c) the prize awards related to each pre-gamble option must be transparent to the player in that they must be fully aware of what they are playing for (or pre-gambling for);

(d) pre-gambles must be transparent in that they must be at natural odds, the player must get what he sees, and there must be no form of compensation or payment or retention of winnings in the event that a short or long series of game outcomes falls outside that which might be normally expected; and

(e) following a 20 second period in which there is no game played, and there is insufficient credit to play a game, any set gamble level is to be reset to 'no gamble'.

5.14 GAME LINKS

A 'game link' is where an element, feature or outcome from one game is either held over or made reference to (recreated) in the next game (eg reel band holds). Game links, with the exception of the live jackpot, are not permissible unless they comply with the following rules:

(a) any reference or link made to any previous game must occur randomly;

(b) linkages to a game are only permissible from the immediately preceding completed game.

(c) the chance of being awarded a link to the next game must be no better than even;

(d) the player must not be aware of whether a link will be given or have the opportunity to use it before he commits himself to the game; and

(e) no subsequent game link is permissible to the current game where a prize has been awarded, and delivered to the player. It is not permissible to force or create a series of wins (enriched periods) using any link feature(s).

5.15 MULTIPLE GAMES ON A GAMING MACHINE

(a) the methodology used to select and discard a particular game for play on a multi-game machine shall be transparent to the player;

(b) all applicable rules and/or the pay tables should be transparent and available to view for each game prior to any commitment to play;

(c) it must at all times be made transparent to the player which game has been selected for play or is being played;

(d) committing to play a game must involve the player in at least two actions. Having selected a game, the player must be able to return to the main menu without playing;

(e) it should not be possible to start a new game before the current play is completed and all relevant meters have been updated (including features, gamble and other options of the game);

(f) the set of games offered to the player for selection, or the pay table, must be capable of being changed only by a secure method. This includes turning on and off games available for play through a suitable interface. The rules at section 1.5 of these standards shall govern the critical memory clear control requirements for these types of selections. However, for games that keep the previous pay tables (the pay table just turned off) data in memory, a critical memory clear is not required. Alternatively to a critical memory clear, a gaming system may record the data that is stored in critical memory on separately allocated memory exclusive to the game provided there are adequate safeguards to ensure critical memory integrity;

(g) no changes to the set of games offered to the player for selection (or to the pay table) are permitted while there are credits on the player's credit or bank meter or while a game is in progress unless there is evidence of game manipulation or fraud as a result of a security weakness; and

(h) where changes to the sets of games offered to the player for selection (or to the pay table) are performed outside of the site operator's opening hours it is permissible to do so while credits remain on the player's credit meter provided that there are adequate measures to ensure the machine is not accessible to players and that any credits are retained for the benefit of the next player following such a procedure.

6.0 SPECIFIC ERROR CONDITIONS AND ALERT REQUIREMENTS

6.1 GENERAL ALERT CONDITIONS

Gaming machines and devices must be capable of detecting, displaying and alerting the operator to the error conditions listed below. These must be cleared either by an attendant or upon initiation of a new play sequence and where any on-line monitoring and control system is networked to the machine details of the error should be communicated to it:

(a) coin-in jam (where the coin acceptor disables itself under such circumstances it is not a requirement that it display an error message);
(b) coin-out jam;
(c) hopper empty or timed out;
(d) hopper runaway or extra coin paid out;
(e) critical memory error (including an indication of battery failure or low battery power source);
(f) note acceptor-in jam;
(g) program error or authentication mismatch;
(h) main Door open;
(i) reverse coin-in (coin travelling the wrong way through acceptor);
(j) reel spin errors, including a miss-index condition for rotating reels, that affect the outcome of the game:
    (i) the specific reel number must be identified in the error code;
    (ii) in the final positioning of the reel, if the position error exceeds one-half of the width of the smallest symbol excluding blanks on the reel strip; and
    (iii) microprocessor controlled reels must be monitored to detect malfunctions such as a reel which is jammed, or is not spinning freely, or any attempt to manipulate their final resting position;
(k) power reset; and
(l) logic cage open (where applicable).

NOTE: This rule also applies to 'Note Acceptor Error Conditions' as to which see 6.3 below.

For machines or devices or individual games that use error codes, a description of such codes and their meanings shall be affixed inside the machine or device. This does not apply to video-based games; however, video based games shall display meaningful text to describe the relevant error condition.

6.2 PRINTER ERROR CONDITIONS

A printer shall have mechanisms to allow software to interpret and act upon the following conditions:

(a) out of paper or paper low;
(b) presentation error (TITO only);
(c) printer jam/failure (TITO only); and
(d) printer disconnected which may only be detected when the software tries to print (TITO only).

These conditions shall trigger an error condition to indicate the error has occurred.

6.3 NOTE ACCEPTOR ERROR CONDITIONS

Each gaming machine or device (including note acceptors) must have the capability of detecting and displaying (for note acceptors, it is acceptable to disable or flash a light or lights) the following error conditions:

(a) Note Jams – it is acceptable for the note acceptor to indicate there is a note jam by disabling itself from accepting any more notes or by some other method; and

(b) Stacker or Main Door Open (where stacker installed) or Stacker Removed.
A note acceptor must perform a self-test at each power up. In the event of a self-test failure, the note acceptor must automatically disable itself (ie enter note reject state) until the error state has been cleared.

7.0 METER REQUIREMENTS

7.1 CREDIT/PLAY METER

Credits used to initiate a new game (see section 5.6) must come from a single meter which may be described as a credit or play meter. The player shall have the option to view any funds held in such a meter as a monetary value.

7.2 ACCOUNTING AND OCCURRENCE METERS

The machine must have at least one primary metering system which is independent of the main control system. All reasonable efforts should be made to ensure that data held by the primary metering system is true and accurate and impervious to tampering or unauthorised modification.
The primary metering system must, as a minimum requirement, be capable of accurately recording the following data:
(a) cash in;
(b) cash out;
(c) change; and
(d) value of total play.
In addition, for machines or devices which offer the player a choice of more than one game the following minimum data must be accurately recorded for each game choice:
(e) value of total play; and
(f) winnings.
In all cases the data held on the metering system must be such that the percentage return to player can be accurately calculated and available for inspection. In instances where a gaming machine or device is able to offer multiple games such information must be available for each game and game variant.
Any meter used to record the above information must have a minimum capacity of seven digits.
It must not be possible for values on meters to increase or decrease while the machine cabinet doors are open.

7.3 METERING OF NOTE ACCEPTOR EVENTS (CATEGORIES A, B1, B2)

A gaming machine or device's primary metering system must also maintain and be able to report the following:
(a) total monetary value of all items accepted;
(b) total number of all items accepted; and
(c) denomination of the last five (5) banknotes inserted.

7.4 NOT APPLICABLE TO THIS CATEGORY OF MACHINE
7.5 NOT APPLICABLE TO THIS CATEGORY OF MACHINE

8.0 ARTWORK AND GAME DISPLAY REQUIREMENTS

8.1 INFORMATION TO BE DISPLAYED

A gaming machine or relevant device shall display, on the machine itself or on screen, information to enable players to keep track of their gambling. As a minimum, the following information must be available to the player at all times the machine is available for play:

(a) the player's current bank balance (where relevant);
(b) number of plays available or current credit balance (monetary value);
(c) the current stake;
(d) all possible winning outcomes, or a link to where this information may be viewed eg on a help menu;
(e) win amounts or odds given for each possible winning outcome, or a link to where this information may be viewed for example on a help menu. The win amount may be displayed as a multiple of the bet or may be shown indirectly by describing the method by which wins are awarded;
(f) the amount won for the last completed game; and
(g) the player options selected (eg total stake, lines played) for the last completed game (until the next game starts or a new selection is made).

Mystery wins are permissible provided it is transparent to the play as to how such a prize may be achieved.
It is not permissible to state or imply that a prize greater than the statutory maximum for a single game may be won by means of the machine nor to indicate that the machine is in a state which could be beneficial to the player (such as by way of a Cash Full Lamp).

8.2 MULTI-LINE GAMES
(a) Each individual line to be played shall be clearly indicated by the gaming machine or device so that the player is in no doubt as to which lines are being staked upon.
(b) The winning play line(s) shall be clearly discernable to the player. (eg, on a video game it may be accomplished by drawing a line over the symbols on the play line(s) and/or the flashing of winning symbols and line selection box. Where there are wins on multiple lines, each winning play line may be indicated in turn. This would not apply to reel based games).

8.3 DISPLAY NOTICE REQUIREMENTS
(a) If any display in respect of a game offered by a gaming machine (including reels) is capable of being taken to indicate odds which do not reflect the true odds in the game the following statement must be included on the face of the machine or at the time the game is selected where more than one game is offered to the player, clearly visible to the player:

THE OUTCOME OF ANY GAME OR FEATURE IS NOT NECESSARILY THAT SHOWN BY THE ODDS DISPLAYED

(b) The following statement must be displayed on the face of the machine or at the time the game is selected where more than one game is offered to the player, clearly visible to the player:

NO PRIZE GREATER IN VALUE THAN [JACKPOT] POUNDS CAN BE WON FROM THIS MACHINE IN ANY ONE GAME

(c) The theoretical target percentage return to player (for betting products this equates to 1 less the calculated hold) must be clearly displayed to the player on the machine in the appropriate alternative format below:
(d)
(i) in cases in which the percentage return to player does not depend upon the strategy used by the player

THIS MACHINE HAS AN AVERAGE PERCENTAGE PAYOUT OF AT LEAST (VALUE) %

Where there is a range (a lower and upper percentage return to player available within the same game) it must be the lower value that is displayed.

(ii) in cases in which the percentage return to player can vary depending upon the strategy used by the player

THE RETURN TO PLAYER BASED ON BEST STRATEGY IS (VALUE) %

In either case the percentage return to player should be calculated in the following manner:

Percentage return to player equals the value of total play divided by total win shown as a percentage

(e) Either of the following statements must be displayed on the machine, clearly visible to the player:
(i) MACHINE MALFUNCTION VOIDS GAME
Or
(ii) MALFUNCTION VOIDS PAYS AND PLAYS
For the purposes of this standard both statements mean that that a machine malfunction voids the game within which the malfunction occurs and does not affect the position of the player prior to that specific game including win and credit meters.

(f) Where the machine is designed such that the deposited sum cannot be delivered by the machine for any reason then the following statement must be clearly displayed on the machine:

THIS MACHINE PAYS (£ minimum value payable) ONLY ANY LESSER AMOUNTS WILL BE RETAINED FOR FUTURE USE

9.0 DEFINITIONS

Address Space	A range of discrete addresses, each of which may correspond to a physical or virtual memory register, a network host, peripheral device, disk sector or other logical or physical entity.
Change	Money paid out which was inserted by the player that has neither been played nor committed to play.
Critical Game Files	All files that may affect the outcome of a game, including executables, data, and operating system files.
Critical Memory	Has the meaning ascribed to it in paragraph 3.1.
Critical Memory Clear	The process to reset the critical memory of a gaming machine, which configures the gaming machine into the 'as new' state.
Device	Any component of a gaming machine and, where the context requires, includes computer software used in a gaming machine.
Double-Up	Feature whereby the player is offered a gamble in which some or all of the winnings may be wagered at a 100% player return.
Enriched Periods	Where the machine deliberately forces winning outcomes over a series of games by use of any compensation or other controller mechanism.
Error Condition	A detectable event outside of the gaming machine's normal operating parameters.
Firmware	The embedded program memory of the gaming machine.
Gamble	A single act of staking on an outcome within a game.

Game	Any gambling opportunity offered to the user of a gaming machine whether it amounts to gaming, betting or participating in a lottery as those terms are defined in the Act.
Game Cycle	Has the meaning ascribed to it in paragraph 5.7.
Game Update	Any change to game configuration, pay table or any other software that may affect the gambling.
Gaming Machine	Has the meaning ascribed to it by section 235 of the Act.
Hashing Algorithm	Reproducible method of turning some kind of data into a (relatively) small number that may serve as a digital 'fingerprint' of the data.
Idle state	Where there are insufficient credits on a machine to enable a game to be played.
Live Jackpot Feature	A feature played on a single gaming machine which has a prize that may be increased from a pre-set or seeded value from game to game as contributions are made to it from monies staked.
Machine Malfunction	Any hardware and/or software fault that temporarily results in an unforeseen game outcome, or corruption and/or renders the machine unserviceable. Deliberate player actions to trigger a machine fault are not considered be a machine malfunction.
MD5 or SHA	Message-Digest Algorithm 5 and Secure Hash Algorithm respectively.
Multi-Station Game	A gaming machine which incorporates a number of player terminals which share a common device required for the game such as a random number generator.
Non-volatile Computer Memory	Memory that can retain the stored information even when not powered. eg. read-only memory, flash, hard disk, floppy disk, magnetic tape and optical disc drives.
Normal Mode	Where a gaming machine is in a configuration designed for play (not in test or other non-play mode) and in a serviceable condition with no errors detected.
'Off chip' Battery Source	Battery source independent of a data storage chip used for data refresh purposes (recharges state of data bytes when mains power is disconnected).
Passive Display Equipment	Devices only associated with viewing game outcome and not with player interaction such as touch screen displays.
Patch Wires and Track Cuts	Modifications to a circuit board, post manufacture, including soldering additional wires to bridge the electrical conductor paths or the addition of a component (patch wires) or to change the circuit path by cutting the copper conductor (track cut).
Program Storage Devices ('PSD')	Means any device used to store software code in read only or read write format as required by the gaming machine in its normal operation.
Raking Periods	Where a machine deliberately forces a series of losing games by use of any compensation or other controller mechanism.
ROM	Read only memory.
Seeding	Means an integer used to set the starting point for generating a series of random numbers.
Theoretical Target Percentage Return to Player	In the case of games in which the chances of winning are distributed randomly, the calculated probable percentage return to player at a 95% confidence level. In other cases, the target percentage return to player as determined by any controlling mechanism.

TITO	Ticket in, ticket out system.
Updates	Any software modification that may affect the outcome of the game.
Value of Total Play (VTP)	The aggregate of all charges for use paid in respect of the machine.

These requirements were notified in draft to the European Commission in accordance with Directive 98/34/EC, as amended by Directive 98/48/EC

Gambling Commission June 2012

MACHINE STANDARDS CATEGORY B3 & B4
June 2012

INTRODUCTION

6.2535 This standard is applicable to all category B3 & B4 gaming machines as defined under section 235 of the Gambling Act 2005 (the Act). This standard came into force for all category B3 & B4 gaming machines supplied or sited within Great Britain from 1 September 2007.

The purpose of the standard is to set out in detail the Gambling Commission's (the Commission) requirements with respect to game features, display notices and general machine operation including metering. These have been developed to help ensure the Commission's three licensing objectives are met. Those objectives are to:

- prevent gambling from being a source of crime or disorder, being associated with crime or disorder or being used to support crime;
- ensure that gambling is conducted in a fair and open way; and
- protect children and other vulnerable persons from being harmed or exploited by gambling.

Operators or end users should not rely upon these standards as a measure of reliability, quality or minimal security standards.

These standards permit equivalence between different types of technology and do not specify proprietary products or technologies. Testing regimes for these standards will permit equivalent international standards (ISO). It is not intended to limit game content and the use of new technological developments provided that the objectives of the standard are met.

OTHER RELEVANT GAMING MACHINE TECHNICAL STANDARDS

- Technical Standards for Category A, B1, B2, B3A, C and D Machines
- Technical Standards for Non-Complex Category D Machines
- Technical Standards for Legacy Machines[1] (Categories B3, B4, C and D Machines)
- Technical Standard for Server Networked & Downloadable Gaming Machines (All categories of machine)
- Technical Standard for Wireless Network Systems (All categories of machine)
- Technical Standard for Cashless Systems (All categories of machine)
- Technical Standard for Linked Progressives (All categories of machine)

---

1 Essentially 'legacy machines' are Category B3, B4, C or D machines which were lawfully in use on premises in Great Britain on 31 August 2007 which comply with the regulations made under s 240 of the Act and certain details of which have been notified to the Commission.

1.0 HARDWARE REQUIREMENTS

1.1 PHYSICAL SECURITY

All reasonable efforts should be made to ensure that a gaming machine is robust enough to withstand forced entry which would not leave behind evidence of the attempted entry. Where any form of attempted or forced entry causes an error condition, the machine must only commence play once the error condition has been cleared. Provided that any security device or sensor (eg door open sensor) which has detected an attempted entry no longer indicates there to be a problem the machine may automatically clear the error condition and commence play. Otherwise, operator action shall be required to clear the error condition.

1.2 MACHINE IDENTIFICATION

A gaming machine must have an identification plate of metallic construction or of an equally resilient material permanently affixed to the exterior of the cabinet by the manufacturer. This must not be easily removable, without leaving evidence of tampering. The following information shall be displayed on the identification plate:

(a) the manufacturer (machine manufacturer or brand name under which it is to be sold);

(b) a unique serial number;

(c) the gaming machine model number (which may refer to the cabinet type and not the game); and

(d) the date of manufacture.

The identification plate shall be mounted on the front or side of the cabinet where it is clearly visible.

1.3 GAMING MACHINE ALARM/ALERT REQUIREMENTS

Gaming machines must be designed to automatically prevent further play of the game and alert the site management in the following situations:

(a) a player winning an amount or redeeming credits that the machine cannot automatically pay;

(b) an error condition occurring; or

(c) a machine fault occurring.

Such a system must be transparent to the player when activated and sufficiently able to attract the attention of the site management.

1.4 LOGIC AREA

Manufacturers must so far as is reasonably practicable, incorporate gaming machine design features aimed at preventing tampering with any electronic logic components that has the potential significantly to influence the operation of the gaming device.

1.5 CONFIGURATION SETTINGS

All switches and/or jumpers must be fully documented and any hardware system within the machine which may alter the configuration settings such as pay tables, accounting denomination, or payout percentages in the operation of the gaming machine must either be housed within a separately locked secure logic area or comply with the following paragraph. This includes top award changes (including progressives where applicable) or any other option that would affect the payout percentage.

As an alternative to a separate secure logic area, any change in configuration defined above must be logged and date stamped within the secure non-volatile memory of the machine. This log must cover a minimum period of not less than 1 month and be made available for display on demand with the test and diagnostic routine of the machine.

1.6 VIDEO MONITORS/TOUCH SCREENS

All video based games shall meet the following requirements:

(a) touch screens shall be accurate and, once calibrated, shall maintain that accuracy for at least the manufacturer's recommended maintenance period;

(b) a touch screen should be able to be re-calibrated without access to the machine cabinet other than opening the main door;

(c) there shall be no hidden or undocumented buttons/touch points anywhere on the screen that affect game play, except as provided for by the game rules.

(d) section (1.6 c) does not apply to audit functions and controls which must be documented.

1.7 MECHANICAL DEVICES USED FOR DISPLAYING OF GAME OUTCOMES

If the game has mechanical or electro-mechanical devices, which are used for displaying game outcomes, the following rules shall be observed:

(a) mechanical assemblies (eg reels or wheels) shall have some mechanism that ensures the correct mounting of reels' artwork;

(b) displays shall be constructed in such a way that winning symbol combinations match up with pay lines or other indicators; and

(c) a mechanical assembly shall be so designed that it is not obstructed by any other components.

1.8 MULTI-STATION GAMES

In any multi station game each player terminal and any other shared device must comply with the relevant sections of this standard, including its requirements for machine identification and metering.

All game rules shall be transparent to the player at each terminal and any shared device that is used to display information pertaining to the game shall be clearly visible to all players participating.

1.9 PATCH WIRES

All patch wires and track cuts shall be documented, in an appropriate manner, in the relevant service manual and/or service bulletin. This does not prohibit required repairs in the field.

2.0 SOFTWARE REQUIREMENTS

2.1 CONTROL PROGRAM AUTHENTICATION REQUIREMENTS

The control program must utilise an integrity check, suitable for the media, providing at least the level of integrity of CRC16 (for non-alterable storage media) or a secured hashing method such as MD5 or SHA (for alterable storage media) to authenticate that the program and/or support files have not been corrupted or altered prior to use/loading. Any error detected will result in the machine displaying the appropriate error message and being unavailable for play.

The integrity check must be carried out during each start up or at least once every 24 hours where the machine is specifically designed for permanent serviceable operation.

2.2 ALTERABLE STORAGE MEDIA DEVICES

Any gaming machine and any procedural requirements must include sufficient security to ensure that any software that can influence the game outcome, including configurable settings that reside on any alterable media is a true replication of that version of the game, control or other software.

2.3 PROGRAM STORAGE MEDIUM IDENTIFICATION

Any program medium (ROMs, EPROMs, Alterable storage media, DVD and CD-ROM) placed in the field shall be uniquely identified, displaying:

(a) program ID number;
(b) manufacturer or game provider;
(c) version number;
(d) type and size of medium (unless located on the medium as purchased unused from the supplier); and
(e) location of installation in gaming machine or device, if potentially confusing.

The information a) to e) above must be available for inspection on the site operator's premises either on the label of the storage media or via video or display monitor. For EPROM based games, the identification label shall be placed over the UV window to avoid erasing or alteration of the program.

2.4 NOT APPLICABLE TO THESE CATEGORIES OF MACHINE.

2.5 LAST GAME RECALL

Information on at least the last five games must be always retrievable on the operation of a suitable external key-switch, or another secure method not available to the player. This will be a minimum of any collected winnings and bank status for each of the five individual games.

2.6 TEST/DIAGNOSTIC MODE

When a gaming machine or device is in a test mode, any test that involves credits entering or leaving the gaming machine or device (eg a hopper test) must be completed prior to resumption of normal operation.
The main cabinet door of a gaming machine may automatically place the machine in a service or test mode. Test/diagnostics mode may also be entered, via an appropriate instruction, by an attendant during an audit mode access.
When exiting from test mode, any game in play must return to the original state it was in when the test mode was entered. If the gaming machine or a device is in a game test mode, the machine must clearly indicate that it is in a test mode, not normal play.

2.7 SOFTWARE VERIFICATION

At a minimum, the machine must have the ability to allow a visual inspection of the following using either an available matrix or video display. (It is permissible for the machine not to display such information during each start up but it must be accessible when required. This may involve the machine being restarted or an appropriate security key being used.)

(a) identity of the game provider;
(b) game identity code;
(c) version number of game software;
(d) check sum of game software;

And if the operating system is not proprietary to the manufacturer, game provider, supplier or operator then:

(e) identity of operating system; and
(f) version number of operating system

On machines or terminals which offer the player a choice of games the above information concerning the game software must be made available for each game.

3.0 CRITICAL MEMORY REQUIREMENTS

3.1 CONTENTS OF CRITICAL MEMORY

Critical memory (that is non-volatile computer memory) must be used to store a minimum of the following data:

(a) credit and bank values;
(b) electronic meters (if so fitted);
(c) data used in any control of the game (if the game is non-random); and
(d) data for the 'last five games recall'

The clearing or resetting of such data must require deliberate action by appropriately authorised personnel.

3.2 MAINTENANCE OF CRITICAL MEMORY

Critical memory storage must be maintained by a methodology that enables errors to be identified and corrected in most circumstances. This methodology may involve signatures, checksums, partial checksums, multiple copies, timestamps and/or effective use of validity codes.

Comprehensive checks of critical memory must be made during each gaming machine or device restart (eg power up cycle). Gaming machine or device control programs (software that operates the machine or device's functions) shall test for possible corruption caused by failure of the program storage medium and all critical game files. Test methodology must endeavour to detect 100 percent of all possible failures.

The control program (software that operates the gaming machine or device's functions) shall allow for the machine or device to ensure the integrity of all control program components during execution of said components.

All program storage devices (PSD), in the executable address space of a main processor, shall be validated during the following conditions:

(a) any power up;
(b) the first time the files are loaded for use (even if only partially loaded).

Memory and PSD space that are not critical to machine security (eg video or sound ROM) are not required to be validated.

3.3 PROGRAM MEMORY, CRITICAL MEMORY AND NON-VOLATILE DEVICES USED TO STORE PROGRAM MEMORY

The following are requirements for critical memory:

(a) a battery back-up (where required), or an equivalent, must be installed on the gaming machine or device for the electronic meters and must be capable of maintaining the accuracy of all information required for thirty days after power is discontinued from the machine The battery backup device must be kept within the locked logic area or if not available a secure location behind the locked main door
(b) if the rechargeable battery back-up is used as an 'off chip' battery source, it shall re-charge itself to its full potential in a maximum of twenty-four hours and have a shelf life of at least five years;
(c) critical memory that uses an off-chip back-up power source to retain its contents when the mains power is switched off must have a detection system which will provide a method for software to interpret and act upon a low battery condition, or alternatively, use a suitable software check to ensure integrity of the storage is maintained.

3.4 UNRECOVERABLE CRITICAL MEMORY

An uncorrectable corruption of critical memory must result in an error condition. Critical memory should not be cleared automatically, but must only be cleared by an authorised person.

3.5 FUNCTION OF CRITICAL MEMORY RESET

Clearing critical memory must only be capable of being undertaken by accessing the logic area or secure location in which it is housed. Following the initiation of a critical

memory reset procedure, the game program must execute a routine which initialises each and every bit in memory to the default state. For games that allow for partial critical memory clears, the methodology for doing so must be accurate and the game must validate the un-cleared portions of memory.
The default reel position or game display after a critical reset must not be the top award on any selectable line. The default game display, upon entering game play mode, must also not be the top award. This applies to the base game only and not to any secondary bonus devices.

4.0 MACHINE CREDIT AND PAYMENT REQUIREMENTS

4.1 COIN OR TOKEN AND NOTE ACCEPTORS AND OTHER METHODS OF INSERTING MONEY OR MONEY'S WORTH INTO THE MACHINE

All coin/token acceptors must meet the following requirements:
(a) the coin/token acceptor must be designed to prevent the use of cheating methods such as slugging (counterfeit coins/tokens), stringing (coin pullback), the insertion of foreign objects and other manipulation; and
(b) other than for diagnostic purposes coins/tokens judged invalid by the acceptor must be rejected to the coin tray and shall not be counted as credits. Acceptance of coins/tokens for crediting to the credit meter must only be possible when the gaming machine is enabled for play. Other states, such as error conditions, including 'door open' and 'audit mode' must disable the coin/token acceptor system. Each coin/token inserted must register the actual monetary value or a number of credits on the player's credit meter for the current game or bet meter. If coins or tokens inserted in a machine are registered directly as credits, the conversion must be clearly stated, or be easily ascertainable from a help menu or similar.

All acceptance devices must be able to detect the entry of valid notes, coupons, paper tokens, or other approved vouchers, and provide a method to enable the gaming device software to interpret and act appropriately upon a valid or invalid input. Acceptance devices must be electronically-based and be configured to ensure that they only accept valid banknotes, vouchers or paper tokens and reject all other notes. The note input system must be constructed in a manner that protects against vandalism, abuse, or fraudulent activity.

4.2 TOKENISATION

For games that may be played using tokens, the gaming machine or relevant device must receive from the acceptor and post to the player's 'bank' the entire amount inserted. If the current local currency amount is not an even multiple of the token for a game or the credit amount has a fractional component, the system must retain the value for the benefit of the next player.

4.3 PRINTERS

If a gaming machine is equipped with a printer that is used to make payments, the printer must be located in a locked area of the machine (eg require opening of the main door to access), but not in the logic area unless the alternative requirements in the second paragraph of section 1.5 (configuration settings) are complied with.
Any printed ticket/voucher/hand pay receipt must display the following information:
(a) operator's name or reference;
(b) gaming machine number;
(c) date and time (24-hour format) of issuance;
(d) alpha numeric currency amount;
(e) sequence number;
(f) validation number and/or unique identifier (eg bar code);

(g) transaction type (cash out ticket, hand pay receipt); and
(h) duplicate ticket indicator (eg duplicate number 3).

4.4 TICKET VALIDATION

Payment by ticket printer as a method of credit redemption is only permissible when:
(a) there is an independent means to validate the printed ticket/voucher/hand pay receipt prior to any credit or other type of redemption; and
(b) such validation system is capable of identifying duplicate tickets to prevent fraud by reprinting and redeeming a ticket previously issued.
To meet this standard, an audit trail of at least one month's data relating to all ticket transactions must be maintained for dispute resolution purposes.

5.0 SPECIFIC GAME REQUIREMENTS

5.1 GENERAL REQUIREMENT (RANDOM GAMES)

Where the outcome results in a player winning a prize, it must be determined randomly and in particular no compensator or regulator may be used to determine any stage of the game.
The machine must clearly display to the player either at all times when it is in operation or at the point a game is selected for play the following statement:

THIS MACHINE IS RANDOM

5.2 RANDOM NUMBER GENERATOR (RNG) REQUIREMENTS

Each possible permutation or combination of game elements that produces winning or losing game outcomes shall be available for random selection at the initiation of each play, unless otherwise clearly stated.
A gaming machine or device must use appropriate communication protocols to protect the RNG and random selection process from influence by associated equipment, which may be communicating with the machine or device. The RNG must be protected from external influences, such as from electromagnetic and electrostatic interference and radio waves. (Compliance with the Electromagnetic Compatibility Regulations would satisfy these requirements).
A machine or device must not present a losing game result which indicates a 'Near Miss', eg where the odds of the top award symbol landing on the pay line are limited it must not frequently appear above or below the pay line.
The selection process must:
(a) be distributed over the entire output range and pass appropriate statistical tests as defined in the test and approval requirements (reference to be included)
(b) ensure the output is unpredictable.
(c) not reproduce the same output stream, nor must two instances of an RNG produce the same stream as each other. Where seeding is required to achieve this it should not introduce predictability.
If a gaming machine offers a game which is recognisable (eg Poker, Blackjack, Roulette) and is described as such by title or visual presentation, and the chances of winning differ from an equivalent real game, then this must be made plain to the player either via the artwork or help menus. In any event the rules of the simulated game must be transparent to the player.

5.3 MECHANICAL BASED RNG GAMES

Mechanical based RNG games are games that use the laws of physics to generate the outcome of the game. All mechanical based RNG games must meet the requirements of this standard with the exception of requirements in s5.2 that are clearly applicable only to electronic RNGs. In addition, mechanical based RNG games must meet the following requirements:

(a) the mechanical pieces must be constructed of materials to prevent decomposition of any component over time (eg a ball shall not disintegrate);
(b) the properties of physical items used to choose the selection shall not be altered; and
(c) the player must not be able to interact with, come into physical contact with or manipulate the mechanics of the game.

The above is not intended to prohibit mechanically based skill and chance features, used for entertainment purposes, which may form a part of an otherwise electronic game.

5.4 SCALING ALGORITHMS

If a random number with a range shorter than that provided by the RNG is required for some purpose within a game, the method of re-scaling, (ie, converting the number to the lower range), is to be designed in such a way that all numbers within the lower range are equally probable.

5.5 SINGLE GAME REQUIREMENTS

The stakes for every gambling opportunity within a game selected by the player must be deducted from the credit or play meter prior to the outcome of any gambling opportunity being displayed to the player.
Before credit(s) for play in a game can be taken, the previous game must first have been completed in full and the result shown to the player.
This section does not preclude the use of multi lines, multi stake and multi reel games provided that the total stake and prize do not exceed the statutory maximum for the single game.

5.6 INITIATING THE NEXT GAME (AUTO START/PLAY)

Except where an 'auto play' or 'auto start' feature is permissible[2] it must always be necessary to release and then depress the machine's real or virtual 'start button' to start a game cycle.

[2] See Regulation 2, Gaming Machine (Circumstances of Use) Regulations 2007

5.7 GAME SPEED OF PLAY

Each game cycle must last at least 2.5 seconds.
A game cycle starts when a player using a gaming machine once[3] has paid for each gamble selected and depresses the 'start button' or takes equivalent action to initiate the game and ends when all money or money's worth staked or won during the game has been either lost or delivered to, or made available for collection by the player and the start button or equivalent becomes available to initiate the next game.
Where auto play or auto start is permitted then a game cycle is measured from the point at which the game is initiated by the system (equivalent to the player depressing the start button) to the point at which it is able to automatically start the next game.

[3] Within the meaning of the Category of Gaming Machine Regulations 2007

5.8 USE OF COMPENSATORS AND/OR REGULATORS

The use of compensators or regulators to determine any stage of the game outcome is permitted, except in the case of 'pre-gambles', provided that the following rules are complied with;

(a) each possible permutation or combination of game elements that produces winning or losing game outcomes must be available for selection at the initiation of each play.

(b) the outcome of any gamble must not be predictable to the player;

(c) cyclic periods of play must not be deliberately introduced and due care must be exercised to prevent their inadvertent occurrence;

(d) the chance of winning a prize must not be so altered as to deliberately create a series of losing (raking periods) or winning games (enriched periods);

(e) any sequence of wins must not exceed that to be expected from a random machine of a similar payout profile and running at the same payout percentage.

A gaming machine or device must not present a losing game result which indicates a 'Near Miss', eg where the odds of the top award symbol landing on the pay line are limited it must not frequently appear above or below the pay line.

A compensated game must clearly display to the player on the face of the machine at all times (when in operation) or at the point the game is selected for play (where operated on a multi-game terminal) the following statement:

> THIS GAME IS COMPENSATED AND MAY BE INFLUENCED BY PREVIOUS PLAY

Where a machine operates in such a way that a particular feature (such as Hi/Low or gamble) may invite a player to make a choice in circumstances in which they have no chance of success (defined by the probability of a win being reduced to less than 20% of that required to achieve the target percentage payout) then the following statement must be substituted for the above:

> THIS GAME IS COMPENSATED AND MAY BE INFLUENCED BY PREVIOUS PLAY AND OFFER THE PLAYER A CHOICE WHERE THERE IS LITTLE CHANCE OF SUCCESS

5.9 LIVE JACKPOTS

Except for a single live jackpot, no gaming machine shall offer prizes which increase or appear to increase from one game to the next. A live jackpot shall not be linked to any other gaming machine and must comply with the following rules:

(a) for an electronically displayed live jackpot the true value (the prize value which may be won within the game) must be displayed to the player at all times and must be available in every game. It may only be won as a result of either:
- a random outcome within the game; or
- the proportion of total money contributed to the jackpot reaching a randomly pre-determined trigger limit.

(b) it is permissible to use physical coins in place of an electronically displayed equivalent provided that the value of prize which may be won by the player is transparent (the player must be able to reasonably assess the total prize value on offer).

(c) the live jackpot must be incremented in proportion to the money staked and by no more than the statutory maximum stake in any single game. It is not a requirement for the live jackpot and reserve (where used) to be incremented in unison or at the same rate.

(d) the prize awarded may be comprised of a fixed value (which must be transparent to the player at all times) together with the live jackpot provided that the total (including any other prize won in the game) does exceed the statutory maximum.

(e) if an alternative prize option is selected, the live jackpot prize must remain unaffected. Once, however, the live jackpot option is selected, the live jackpot prize must be delivered and the live jackpot reduced to zero or its seeded value, regardless of whether the live jackpot is delivered directly or is subject to some intervening gamble or skill feature.

(f) the value of the live jackpot or its reserve shall not influence the chance of achieving a win within the game or be used to imply that a win is more likely.

In this section, a 'reserve meter' is a second meter or display which is used to hold any value which may be raised at the same time as the live jackpot, or which holds any overspill once the live jackpot has reached the maximum level for that category of machine.

5.10 DOUBLE-UP (RANDOM GAMES ONLY)

Any Double-up or Gamble options must have a theoretical return to the player of that displayed or suggested by the game graphic.

5.11 NOT APPLICABLE TO THIS CATEGORY OF MACHINE

5.12 ADDITIONAL CREDIT(S) STAKED DURING THE GAME

Machines must not permit players to stake any additional credit(s) during a game cycle, unless the game complies with the following requirements:

(a) that the outcome of the game is not decided prior to any additional credit(s) being staked;

(b) that the outcome of the game following any additional credit(s) being staked is random and that all possible combinations associated with an equivalent real game under the same circumstances are available to the player;

(c) that the game does not modify the chance of achieving a win or the combinations available to the player associated with an equivalent live game as a result of their decision not to stake, or to stake additional credits within that game;

(d) that player must not be deliberately misled or given a false impression that they have an enhanced chance of winning as a result of staking additional credits within the game; and

(e) that the total stake wagered within the game does not exceed the relevant statutory maximum.

This section does not preclude the use of multi stake, multi line and multi reel game configurations provided that the player sets their total stake prior to the start of the game cycle.

5.13 PRE-GAMBLE

Where the player is given the opportunity at the start of the game to enter into a gamble (pre-gamble), and the prizes available or the odds of achieving those prizes in the game are linked to the odds of a successful outcome of the pre-gamble, the following rules shall be complied with:

(a) the player must always be given the option at the start of the game whether or not to use the pre-gamble;

(b) there must not be a difference of more than 10% between the lowest percentage return to player (%RTP) offered to the player when not opting to use the pre-gamble as against opting to do so;

(c) the prize awards related to each pre-gamble option must be transparent to the player in that they must be fully aware of what they are playing for (or pre-gambling for);

(d) pre-gambles must be transparent in that they must be at natural odds, the player must get what he sees, and there must be no form of compensation or payment or retention of winnings in the event that a short or long series of game outcomes falls outside that which might be normally expected; and

(e) following a 20 second period in which there is no game played, and there is insufficient credit to play a game, any set gamble level is to be reset to 'no gamble'.

5.14 GAME LINKS

A 'game link' is where an element, feature or outcome from one game is either held over or made reference to (recreated) in the next game (eg reel band holds). Game links, with the exception of the live jackpot, are not permissible unless they comply with the following rules:

(a) any reference or link made to any previous game must occur randomly;
(b) linkages to a game are only permissible from the immediately preceding completed game.
(c) the percentage chance of being awarded a link to the next game must be no better than even;
(d) the player must not be aware of whether a link will be given or have the opportunity to use it before he commits himself to the game; and
(e) no subsequent game link is permissible to the current game where a prize has been awarded, and delivered to the player. It is not permissible to force or create a series of wins (enriched periods) using any link feature(s).

5.15 MULTIPLE GAMES ON THE GAMING DEVICE

(a) The methodology used to select and discard a particular game for play on a multi-game machine shall be transparent to the player.
(b) All applicable rules and/or the pay tables should be transparent and available to view for each game prior to any commitment to play.
(c) It must at all times be made transparent to the player which game has been selected for play or is being played.
(d) Committing to play a game must involve the player in at least two actions. Having selected a game, the player must be able to return to the main menu without playing
(e) It should not be possible to start a new game before the current play is completed and all relevant meters have been updated (including features, gamble and other options of the game).
(f) The set of games offered to the player for selection, or the pay table, must be capable of being changed only by a secure method. This includes turning on and off games available for play through a suitable interface. The rules at section 1.5 of these standards shall govern the critical memory clear control requirements for these types of selections. However, for games that keep the previous pay tables (the pay table just turned off) data in memory, a critical memory clear is not required. Alternatively to a critical memory clear, a gaming system may record the data that is stored in critical memory on separately allocated memory exclusive to the game provided there are adequate safeguards to ensure critical memory integrity.
(g) No changes to the set of games offered to the player for selection (or to the pay table) are permitted while there are credits on the player's credit or bank meter or while a game is in progress unless there is evidence of game manipulation or fraud as a result of a security weakness.
(h) Where changes to the sets of games offered to the player for selection (or to the pay table) are performed outside of the site operator's opening hours it is permissible to do so while credits remain on the player's credit meter provided that there are adequate measures to ensure the machine is not accessible to players and that any credits are retained for the benefit of the next player

following such a procedure.

6.0 SPECIFIC ERROR CONDITIONS AND ALERT REQUIREMENTS

6.1 GENERAL ALERT CONDITIONS

Gaming machines and devices must be capable of detecting, displaying and alerting the operator to the error conditions listed below. These must be cleared either by an attendant or upon initiation of a new play sequence and where any on-line monitoring and control system is networked to the machine details of the error should be communicated to it:

(a) coin-in jam (where the coin acceptor disables itself under such circumstances it is not a requirement that it display an error message);
(b) coin-out jam;
(c) hopper empty or timed out;
(d) hopper runaway or extra coin paid out;
(e) critical memory error (including an indication of battery failure or low battery power source);
(f) note acceptor-in jam;
(g) program error or authentication mismatch;
(h) main door open;
(i) reverse coin-in (coin travelling the wrong way through acceptor);
(j) reel spin errors, including a miss-index condition for rotating reels, that affect the outcome of the game:
  (i) the specific reel number must be identified in the error code;
  (ii) in the final positioning of the reel, if the position error exceeds one-half of the width of the smallest symbol excluding blanks on the reel strip; and
  (iii) microprocessor controlled reels must be monitored to detect malfunctions such as a reel which is jammed, or is not spinning freely, or any attempt to manipulate their final resting position;
(k) power reset; and
(l) logic cage open (where applicable).

NOTE: This rule also applies to the 'Note Acceptor Error Conditions' as to which see 6.3 below.

For machines or devices or individual games that use error codes, a description of such codes and their meanings shall be affixed inside the machine or device. This does not apply to video-based games; however, video based games shall display meaningful text to describe the relevant error condition.

6.2 PRINTER ERROR CONDITIONS

A printer shall have mechanisms to allow software to interpret and act upon the following conditions:

(a) out of paper or paper low;
(b) presentation error (TITO only);
(c) printer jam/failure; and
(d) printer disconnected which may only be detected when the software tries to print.

These conditions shall trigger an error condition to indicate the error has occurred.

6.3 NOTE ACCEPTOR ERROR CONDITIONS

Each gaming machine or device (including note acceptors) must have the capability of detecting and displaying (for note acceptors, it is acceptable to disable or flash a light or lights) the following error conditions:

(a) Note Jams – it is acceptable for the note acceptor to indicate there is a note jam by disabling itself from accepting any more notes or by some other method.

(b) Stacker or Main Door Open (where stacker installed) or Stacker Removed.

A note acceptor must perform a self-test at each power up. In the event of a self-test failure, the note acceptor must automatically disable itself (ie enter note reject state) until the error state has been cleared.

7.0 METER REQUIREMENTS

7.1 CREDIT/PLAY METER

Credits used to initiate a new game (see section 5.6) must come from a single meter which may be described as a credit or play meter. The player shall have the option to view any funds held in such a meter as a monetary value.

7.2 ACCOUNTING AND OCCURRENCE METERS

The machine must have at least one primary metering system which is independent of the main control system. All reasonable efforts should be made to ensure that data held by the primary metering system is true and accurate and impervious to tampering or any unauthorised modification.

The primary metering system must, as a minimum requirement, be capable of accurately recording the following data:

(a) cash in;
(b) cash out;
(c) change;
(d) value of total play;

In addition, for machines or devices which offer the player a choice of more than one game the following minimum data must be accurately recorded for each game choice:

(e) value of total play;
(f) winnings.

In all cases the data held on the metering system must be such that the percentage return to player can be accurately calculated and available for inspection. In instances where a terminal is able to offer multiple games such information shall be available for each title and variant where applicable.

Any meter used to record the above information must have a minimum capacity of seven digits.

It must not be possible for values on meters to increase or decrease in value while any of the machine cabinet doors are open.

7.3 NOT APPLICABLE TO THESE CATEGORIES OF MACHINE.
7.4 NOT APPLICABLE TO THESE CATEGORIES OF MACHINE.
7.5 NOT APPLICABLE TO THESE CATEGORIES OF MACHINE.

8.0 ARTWORK AND GAME DISPLAY REQUIREMENTS

8.1 INFORMATION TO BE DISPLAYED

A gaming machine or relevant device must display, on the machine itself or on screen, information to enable players to keep track of their gambling. As a minimum, the following information must be available to the player at all times the machine is available for player input:

(a) the player's current bank balance (where relevant);
(b) number of plays available or current credit balance (monetary value);
(c) the current stake;
(d) all possible winning outcomes, or a link to where this information may be viewed, eg on a help menu;
(e) win amounts or odds given for each possible winning outcome, or a link to where this information may be viewed, eg on a help menu. The win amount may

be displayed as a multiple of the bet or may be shown indirectly by describing the method by which wins are awarded;

(f) the amount won for the last completed game; and

(g) the player options selected (eg total stake, lines played) for the last completed game (until the next game starts or a new selection is made).

Mystery wins are permissible provided it is transparent to the player as to how such a prize may be achieved.

It is not permissible to state or imply that a prize greater than the statutory maximum for a single game may be won by means of the machine nor to indicate that the machine is in a state which could be beneficial to the player (such as by way of Cash Full Lamp).

8.2 MULTI-LINE GAMES

(a) Each individual line to be played shall be clearly indicated by the gaming machine or device so that the player is in no doubt as to which lines are being staked upon.

(b) The winning play line(s) shall be clearly discernable to the player (eg on a video game it may be accomplished by drawing a line over the symbols on the play line(s) and/or the flashing of winning symbols and line selection box. Where there are wins on multiple lines, each winning play line may be indicated in turn. This would not apply to reel based games).

8.3 DISPLAY NOTICE REQUIREMENTS

(a) If any display in respect of a game offered by a gaming machine (including reels) is capable of being taken to indicate odds which do not reflect the true odds in the game the following statement must be included on the face of the machine or at the time the game is selected where more than one game is offered to the player, clearly visible to the player:

THE OUTCOME OF ANY GAME OR FEATURE IS NOT NECESSARILY THAT SHOWN BY THE ODDS DISPLAYED

(b) The following statement must be displayed on the face of the machine or at the time the game is selected where more than one game is offered to the player, clearly visible to the player:

NO PRIZE GREATER IN VALUE THAN [JACKPOT] POUNDS CAN BE WON FROM THIS MACHINE IN ANY ONE GAME

(c) The theoretical target percentage return to player (for betting products this equates to 1 less the calculated hold) must be clearly displayed to the player on the machine in the appropriate alternative format below:

(i) in cases in which the percentage return to player does not depend upon the strategy used by the player

THIS MACHINE HAS AN AVERAGE PERCENTAGE PAYOUT OF AT LEAST (VALUE) %

Where there is a range (a lower and upper percentage return to player available within the same game) it must be the lower value that is displayed.

(ii) in cases in which the percentage return to player can vary depending upon the strategy used by the player

A. THE RETURN TO PLAYER BASED ON BEST STRATEGY IS (VALUE) %

In either case the percentage return to player should be calculated in the following manner:

Percentage return to player equals the value of total play divided by total win shown as a percentage

(d) Either of the following statements must be displayed on the machine, clearly visible to the player:
(i) MACHINE MALFUNCTION VOIDS GAME
Or
(ii) MALFUNCTION VOIDS PAYS AND PLAYS
For the purposes of this standard both statements mean that that a machine malfunction voids the game within which the malfunction occurs and does not affect the position of the player prior to that specific game including win and credit meters.

(e) Where the machine is designed such that the deposited sum cannot be delivered by the machine for any reason then the following statement must be clearly displayed on the face of the machine:

THIS MACHINE PAYS (£ minimum value payable) ONLY ANY LESSER AMOUNTS WILL BE RETAINED FOR FUTURE USE

(f) Where certain winning combinations may be excluded as a result of the way in which reel spin-distances are determined at the start of each game, the following statement must be displayed clearly to the player on the machine: DUE TO THE SEQUENCING OF THE REELS CERTAIN WINNING COMBINATIONS ARE NOT AVAILABLE IN EVERY GAME

9.0 DEFINITIONS

Address Space	A range of discrete addresses, each of which may correspond to a physical or virtual memory register, a network host, peripheral device, disk sector or other logical or physical entity.
Change	Money paid out which was inserted by the player that has neither been played nor committed to play.
Critical Game Files	All files that may affect the outcome of a game, including executables, data, and operating system files.
Critical Memory	Has the meaning ascribed to it in paragraph 3.1.
Critical Memory Clear	The process to reset the critical memory of a gaming machine, which configures the gaming machine into the 'as new' state.
Device	Any component of a gaming machine and, where the context requires, includes computer software used in a gaming machine.
Double-Up	Feature whereby the player is offered a gamble in which some or all of the winnings may be wagered at a 100% player return.
Enriched Periods	Where the machine deliberately forces winning outcomes over a series of games by use of any compensation or other controller mechanism.
Error Condition	A detectable event outside of the gaming machine's normal operating parameters.
Firmware	The embedded program memory of the gaming machine.
Gamble	A single act of staking on an outcome within a game.
Game	Any gambling opportunity offered to the user of a gaming machine whether it amounts to gaming, betting or participating in a lottery as those terms are defined in the Act.
Game Cycle	Has the meaning ascribed to it in paragraph 5.7.

Game Update	Any change to game configuration, pay table or any other software that may affect the gambling.
Gaming Machine	Has the meaning ascribed to it by section 235 of the Act.
Hashing Algorithm	Reproducible method of turning some kind of data into a (relatively) small number that may serve as a digital 'fingerprint' of the data
Idle state	Where there are insufficient credits on a machine to enable a game to be played.
Live Jackpot Feature	A feature played on a single gaming machine which has a prize that may be increased from a pre-set or seeded value from game to game as contributions are made to it from monies staked.
Machine Malfunction	Any hardware and/or software fault that temporarily results in an unforeseen game outcome, or corruption and/or renders the machine unserviceable. Deliberate player actions to trigger a machine fault are not considered be a machine malfunction.
MD5 or SHA	Message-Digest Algorithm 5 and Secure Hash Algorithm respectively.
Multi-Station Game	A gaming machine which incorporates a number of player terminals which share a common device required for the game such as a random number generator.
Normal Mode	Where a gaming machine is in a configuration designed for play (not in test or other non-play mode) and in a serviceable condition with no errors detected.
Non-volatile Computer Memory	Memory that can retain the stored information even when not powered. eg. read-only memory, flash, hard disk, floppy disk, magnetic tape and optical disc drives.
'Off chip' Battery Source	Battery source independent of a data storage chip used for data refresh purposes (recharges state of data bytes when mains power is disconnected).
Passive Display Equipment	Devices only associated with viewing game outcome and not with player interaction such as touch screen displays.
Patch Wires and Track Cuts	Modifications to a circuit board, post manufacture, including soldering additional wires to bridge the electrical conductor paths or the addition of a component (patch wires) or to change the circuit path by cutting the copper conductor (track cut).
Program Storage Devices ('PSD')	Means any device used to store software code in read only or read write format as required by the gaming machine in its normal operation.
Raking Periods	Where a machine deliberately forces a series of losing games by use of any compensation or other controller mechanism.
ROM	Read only memory.
Seeding	Means an integer used to set the starting point for generating a series of random numbers.
Theoretical Target Percentage Return to Player	In the case of games in which the chances of winning are distributed randomly, the calculated probable percentage return to player at a 95% confidence level. In other cases, the target percentage return to player as determined by any controlling mechanism.
TITO	Ticket in, ticket out system.
Updates	Any software modification that may affect the outcome of the game.

Value of Total Play (VTP)	The aggregate of all charges for use paid in respect of the machine.

These requirements were notified in draft to the European Commission in accordance with Directive 98/34/EC, as amended by Directive 98/48/EC

Gambling Commission June 2012

MACHINE STANDARDS CATEGORY C
June 2012

INTRODUCTION

6.2540 This standard is applicable to all category C gaming machines as defined under section 235 of the Gambling Act 2005 (the Act). This standard came into force for all category C gaming machines supplied or sited within Great Britain from 1 September 2007.

The purpose of the standard is to set out in detail the Gambling Commission's (the Commission) requirements with respect to game features, display notices and general machine operation including metering. These have been developed to help ensure the Commission's three licensing objectives are met. Those objectives are to:

- prevent gambling from being a source of crime or disorder, being associated with crime or disorder or being used to support crime;
- ensure that gambling is conducted in a fair and open way; and
- protect children and other vulnerable persons from being harmed or exploited by gambling.

Operators or end users should not rely upon these standards as a measure of reliability, quality or minimal security requirements.

These standards permit equivalence between different types of technology and do not specify proprietary products or technologies. Testing regimes for these standards will permit equivalent international standards (ISO). It is not intended to limit game content and the use of new technological developments provided that the objectives of the standard are met.

REVISIONS

A list of the revisions to this document are included in section 10.

OTHER RELEVANT GAMING MACHINE TECHNICAL STANDARDS

- Technical Standards for Category A, B1, B2, B3, B3A, B4 and D Machines
- Technical Standards for Non-Complex Category D Machines
- Technical Standards for Legacy Machines[1] (Categories B3, B4, C and D Machines)
- Technical Standard for Server Networked & Downloadable Gaming Machines (All categories of machine)
- Technical Standard for Wireless Network Systems (All categories of machine)
- Technical Standard for Cashless Systems (All categories of machine)
- Technical Standard for Linked Progressives (All categories of machine)

[1] Essentially 'legacy machines' are Category B3, B4, C or D machines which were lawfully in use on premises in Great Britain on 31 August 2007 which comply with the regulations made under s240 of the Act and certain details of which have been notified to the Commission.

1.0 HARDWARE REQUIREMENTS

1.1 PHYSICAL SECURITY

All reasonable efforts should be made to ensure that a gaming machine is robust enough to withstand forced entry which would not leave behind evidence of the attempted entry. Where any form of attempted or forced entry causes an error condition, the machine must only commence play once the error code has been cleared. Provided that any security device or sensor (eg door open sensor) which has detected an attempted entry no longer indicates there to be a problem the machine may automatically clear the error condition and commence play. Otherwise, operator action shall be required to clear the error condition.

1.2 MACHINE IDENTIFICATION

A gaming machine must have an identification plate of metallic construction or of an equally resilient material permanently affixed to the exterior of the cabinet by the manufacturer. This must not be easily removable, without leaving evidence of tampering. The following information shall be displayed on the identification plate:

(a) the manufacturer (machine manufacturer or brand name under which it is to be sold);
(b) a unique serial number;
(c) the gaming machine model number (which may refer to the cabinet type and not the game); and
(d) the date of manufacture.

The identification plate shall be mounted on the front or side of the cabinet where it is clearly visible.

1.3 GAMING MACHINE ALARM/ALERT REQUIREMENTS

Gaming machines must be designed to automatically prevent further play and alert the site management in the following situations:

(a) a player winning an amount or redeeming credits that the machine cannot automatically pay;
(b) an error condition occurring; or
(c) a machine fault occurring.

Such a system must be transparent to the player when activated and sufficiently able to attract the attention of the site management.

1.4 LOGIC AREA

Manufacturers must, so far as is reasonably practicable, incorporate in gaming machines design features aimed at preventing tampering with any electronic logic component that has the potential significantly to influence the operation of the machine.

1.5 CONFIGURATION SETTINGS

All switches and/or jumpers must be fully documented and any hardware system within the machine which may alter the configuration settings such as pay tables, accounting denomination, or payout percentages in the operation of the gaming machine must either be housed within a separately locked secure logic area or comply with the following paragraph. This includes top award changes (including progressives) or any other option that would affect the payout percentage.

As an alternative to a separate secure logic area, any change in configuration defined above must be logged and date stamped within the secure non-volatile memory of the machine. This log must cover a minimum period of not less than one month and made available for display on demand with the test and diagnostic routine of the machine or as appropriate.

1.6 VIDEO MONITORS/TOUCH SCREENS

All video based games shall meet the following requirements:
(a) touch screens shall be accurate and, once calibrated, shall maintain that accuracy for at least the manufacturer's recommended maintenance period;
(b) a touch screen should be able to be re-calibrated without access to the machine cabinet other than opening the main door;
(c) there shall be no hidden or undocumented buttons/touch points anywhere on the screen, that affect game play, except as provided for by the game rules; and
(d) section (1.6 c) does not apply to audit functions and controls which must be documented.

1.7 MECHANICAL DEVICES USED FOR DISPLAYING OF GAME OUTCOMES

If the game has mechanical or electro-mechanical devices, which are used for displaying game outcomes, the following rules shall be observed:
(a) mechanical assemblies (eg reels or wheels) shall have some mechanism that ensures the correct mounting of reels' artwork;
(b) displays shall be constructed in such a way that winning symbol combinations match up with pay lines or other indicators; and
(c) a mechanical assembly shall be so designed that it is not obstructed by any other components.

1.8 MULTI-STATION GAMES

In any multi-station game, each player terminal and any other shared device must comply with the relevant sections of this standard, including its requirements for machine identification and metering.
All game rules shall be transparent to the player at each terminal and any shared device that is used to display information pertaining to the game shall be clearly visible to all players participating.

1.9 PATCH WIRES

All patch wires and track cuts shall be documented, in an appropriate manner, in the relevant service manual and/or service bulletin. This does not prohibit required repairs in the field.

2.0 SOFTWARE REQUIREMENTS

2.1 CONTROL PROGRAM AUTHENTICATION REQUIREMENTS

The control program must utilise an integrity check, suitable for the media, providing at least the level of integrity of CRC 16 (for non-alterable storage media) or a secured hashing method such as MD5 or SHA (for alterable storage media) to authenticate that the program and/or support files have not been corrupted or altered prior to use/loading. Any error detected must result in the machine displaying the appropriate error message and being unavailable for play.
The integrity check must be carried out during each start up or at least once every 24 hours where the machine is specifically designed for permanent serviceable operation.

winning differ from an equivalent real game this must be made plain to the player either via the artwork or help menus. In any event the rules of the simulated game must be clear and transparent to the player.

5.3 MECHANICAL BASED RNG GAMES

Mechanical based RNG games are games that use the laws of physics to generate the outcome of the game. All mechanical based RNG games must meet the requirements of this standard with the exception of requirements in section 5.2 that are clearly applicable only to electronic random number generators. In addition, mechanical based RNG games must meet the following requirements:

(a) the mechanical pieces must be constructed of materials to prevent decomposition of any component over time (eg a ball shall not disintegrate);

(b) the properties of physical items used to choose the selection shall not be altered; and

(c) the player shall not have the ability to interact with or come into physical contact with or manipulate the mechanics of the game.

The above is not intended to prohibit mechanically based skill and chance features used for entertainment purposes which may form a part of an otherwise electronic game.

5.4 SCALING ALGORITHMS

If a random number with a range shorter than that provided by the RNG is required for some purpose within a game, the method of re-scaling, (ie converting the number to the lower range), is to be designed in such a way that all numbers within the lower range are equally probable.

5.5 SINGLE GAME REQUIREMENTS

The stakes for every gambling opportunity within a game selected by the player must be deducted from the credit or play meter prior to the outcome of any gambling opportunity being displayed to the player.
Before credit(s) for play in a game can be taken, the previous game must first have been completed in full and the result shown to the player.
This section does not preclude the use of multi lines, multi stake and multi reel games provided that the total stake and prize do not exceed the statutory maximum for the single game.

5.6 INITIATING THE NEXT GAME (AUTO START/PLAY)

Except where an 'auto play' or 'auto start' feature is permissible[2] it must always be necessary to release and then depress the machine's real or virtual 'start button' to start a game cycle.

[2] See Regulation 2, Gaming Machine (Circumstances of Use) Regulations 2007.

5.7 GAME SPEED OF PLAY

When played at the statutory maximum stake, each game cycle must take no less than 1.5 seconds to complete and the average duration of games, taken over one hour, should not be less than 2.5 seconds.
For this purpose, a game played at less than the statutory maximum stake should be considered as a proportion of one played at the maximum permissible stake (eg 2 x 50p games would be considered to be equivalent to 1 x £1 game) with regard to both average and minimum duration.

Regardless of stake, the minimum duration of any game should not be less than 1.0 second and the average duration of games, taken over one hour, should not be less than 1.25 seconds.

A game cycle starts when a player using a gaming machine once[3] has paid for each gamble selected and depresses the 'start button' or takes equivalent action to initiate the game and ends when all money or money's worth staked or won during the game has either been lost or delivered to, or made available for collection by the player and the start button or equivalent becomes available to initiate the next game.

Where auto play or auto start is permitted then a game cycle is measured from the point at which the game is initiated by the system (equivalent to the player depressing the start button) to the point at which it is able to automatically start the next game.

---

[3] Within the meaning of the Category of Gaming Machine Regulations 2007.

5.8 USE OF COMPENSATORS AND/OR REGULATORS

The use of compensators or regulators to determine any stage of the game outcome is permitted, except in the case of 'pre-gambles', provided that the following rules are complied with:

(a) each possible permutation or combination of game elements that produces winning or losing game outcomes must be available for selection at the initiation of each play;

(b) the outcome of any gamble must not be predictable to the player;

(c) cyclic periods of play must not deliberately be introduced and due care must be exercised to prevent their inadvertent occurrence;

(d) the chance of winning a prize must not be so altered as deliberately to create a series of losing (raking periods) or winning games (enriched periods); and

(e) any sequence of wins must not exceed that to be expected from a random machine of a similar payout profile and running at the same payout percentage.

A gaming machine or device must not present a losing game result which indicates a 'Near Miss'; for example where the odds of the top award symbol landing on the pay line are limited it must not frequently appear above or below the pay line.

A compensated game must clearly display to the player on the face of the machine at all times (when in operation) or at the point the game is selected for play (where operated on a multi-game terminal) the following statement:

> THIS GAME IS COMPENSATED AND MAY BE INFLUENCED BY PREVIOUS PLAY

Where a machine operates in such a way that a particular feature (such as Hi/Low or gamble) may invite a player to make a choice in circumstances in which they have no chance of success (defined by the probability of a win being reduced to less than 20% of that required to achieve the target percentage payout) then the following statement must be substituted for the above:

> THIS GAME IS COMPENSATED AND MAY BE INFLUENCED BY PREVIOUS PLAY AND OFFER THE PLAYER A CHOICE WHERE THERE IS LITTLE CHANCE OF SUCCESS

5.9 LIVE JACKPOTS

Except for a live jackpot, no gaming machine must offer prizes which increase or appear to increase from one game to the next. A live jackpot must not be linked to any other gaming machine and must comply with the following rules:

(a) for an electronically displayed live jackpot the true value (the prize value which may be won within the game) must be displayed to the player at all times and must be available in every game. It may only be won as a result of either:

(i) a random outcome within the game; or
(ii) the proportion of total money contributed to the jackpot reaching a randomly pre-determined trigger limit;
(iii) the trigger value of the live jackpot must not be predictable to the player.

(b) it is permissible to use physical coins in place of an electronically displayed equivalent provided that the value of prize which may be won by the player is transparent (the player must be able to reasonably assess the total prize value on offer);

(c) the live jackpot must not be incremented by more than the money staked since the previous increment. It is not a requirement for the live jackpot and reserve (where used) to be incremented in unison or at the same rate. The chance of randomly winning the pot must not be changed in relation to its value;

(d) the prize awarded may be comprised of a fixed value (which must be transparent to the player at all times) together with the live jackpot provided that the total (including any other prize won in the game) does not exceed the statutory maximum;

(e) if an alternative prize option is selected, the live jackpot prize must remain unaffected. Once, however, the live jackpot option is selected, the live jackpot prize must be delivered and the live jackpot reduced to zero or its seeded value, regardless of whether the live jackpot is delivered directly or is subject to some intervening gamble or skill feature; and

(f) the value of the live jackpot or its reserve shall not influence the chance of achieving a win within the game or be used to imply that a win is more likely.

In this section, a 'reserve meter' is a second meter or display which is used to hold any value which may be raised at the same time as the live jackpot, or which holds any overspill once the live jackpot has reached the maximum level for that category of machine.

5.10 DOUBLE-UP (RANDOM GAMES ONLY)

Any Double-up or Gamble options must have a theoretical return to the player of that displayed or suggested by the game graphic.

5.11 NOT APPLICABLE TO THIS CATEGORY OF MACHINE.

5.12 ADDITIONAL CREDIT(S) STAKED DURING THE GAME

Machines must not permit players to stake any additional credits during a game cycle unless the game complies with the following requirements:

(a) that the outcome of the game is not decided prior to any additional credit(s) being staked;

(b) that the outcome of the game following any additional credit(s) being staked is random and that all possible combinations associated with an equivalent real game under the same circumstances are available to the player;

(c) that the game does not modify the chance of achieving a win or the combinations available to the player associated with an equivalent live game as a result of their decision not to stake, or to stake additional credits within that game;

(d) that player must not be deliberately misled or given a false impression that they have an enhanced chance of winning as a result of staking additional credits within the game; and

(e) that the total stake wagered within the game does not exceed the relevant statutory maximum.

This section does not preclude the use of multi stake, multi line and multi reel game configurations provided that the player sets their total stake prior to the start of the game cycle.

5.13 PRE-GAMBLE

Where the player is given the opportunity at the start of the game to enter into a pre-gamble, and the prizes available or the odds of achieving those prizes in the game are linked to the odds of a successful outcome of the pre-gamble, the following rules shall be complied with:

(a) the player must always be given the option at the start of the game whether or not to use the pre-gamble;

(b) there must not be a difference of more than 10% between the lowest percentage return to player (%RTP) offered to the player when not opting to use the pre-gamble as against opting to do so;

(c) the prize awards related to each pre-gamble option must be transparent to the player in that they must be fully aware of what they are playing for (or pre-gambling for);

(d) pre-gambles must be transparent in that they must be at natural odds, the player must get what he sees, and there must be no form of compensation or payment or retention of winnings in the event that a short or long series of game outcomes falls outside that which might be normally expected; and

(e) following a 20 second period in which there is no game played, and there is insufficient credit to play a game, any set gamble level is to be reset to 'no gamble'.

5.14 GAME LINKS

5.14(A) GAME LINKS FOLLOWING A LOSING GAME

A 'game link' is where an element, feature or outcome from one game is either held over or made reference to (recreated) in the next game (eg reel band holds). Game links, with the exception of the live jackpot are not permissible unless they comply with the following rules:

(a) linkages to a game are only permissible from the immediately preceding completed game;

(b) it is not permissible to create a situation whereby the machine's control deliberately restores a link to any previous game by any means other than the immediately preceding completed game;

(c) it is not permissible deliberately to force or create a series of wins (enriched periods) using a link feature(s);

(d) it is not permissible to carry over a win unless section 5.14(b) is complied with;

(e) it is not permissible to link to the previous game if a prize had been awarded in that game unless section 5.14(b) is complied with.

5.14(B) GAME LINKS FOLLOWING A GAME WHICH AWARDS A PRIZE

A 'game link' is where an element, feature or outcome from one game is either held over or made reference to (recreated) in the next game (eg reel band holds). Game links, with the exception of the live jackpot are not permissible unless they comply with the following rules:

(a) subject to (g) any reference or link made to any previous game must occur randomly;

(b) linkages to a game are only permissible from the immediately preceding completed game;

(c) the chance of being awarded a link to the next game must be no better than even;

(d) it is not permissible to create a situation whereby the machine's control deliberately restores a link to any previous game by any means where it is broken as a result of an unfavourable outcome in a subsequent game;

(e) the player must not be aware as to whether a link will be given or have the opportunity to use it before there is sufficient credit available on the credit or play meter to play the same at least once by means of the machine[4];

(f) it is not permissible deliberately to force or create a series of wins (enriched periods) using a link feature(s);

(g) the table below sets out the permissible number of consecutive winning games that may be linked together by reference to the maximum prize awarded and delivered to a player in any single game of this linked series of winning games. For example where no prize in any single game of a linked series exceeds £15 then it is permissible to offer the player a maximum of six successful consecutive links.

Maximum prize value awarded in any single game of a linked series	**Maximum number of successful consecutive links permissible**
£10 or less	Unrestricted
£15 or less, greater than £10	6
£20 or less, greater than £15	5
£25 or less, greater than £20	4
£50 or less, greater than £25	3
£70 or less, greater than £50	2
£100 or less, greater than £70	1
In excess of £100	0

All games in a linked series will be otherwise separate and required to be purchased by an appropriate stake.

[1] In the Category C and complex D technical standards responses document (November 2011), Section 5.14b(e) was incorrectly shown with the original wording of the Standard and not the wording as modified by Gaming Machine Standards Supplement 1, paragraph 7.2, (July 2008).

5.15 MULTIPLE GAMES ON A GAMING MACHINE

(a) The methodology used to select and discard a particular game for play on a multi-game machine must be transparent to the player.

(b) All applicable rules and/or the pay tables must be transparent and available to view for each game prior to any commitment to play.

(c) It must at all times be made transparent to the player which game has been selected for play or is being played.

(d) Committing to play a game must involve the player in at least two actions. Having selected a game, the player must be able to return to the main menu without playing.

(e) It must not be possible to start a new game before the current play is completed and all relevant meters have been updated (including features, gamble and other options of the game).

(f) The set of games offered to the player for selection, or the pay table, must be capable of being changed only by a secure method. This includes turning on and off games available for play through a suitable interface. The rules at section 1.5 of these standards shall govern the critical memory clear control requirements for these types of selections. However, for games that keep the previous pay tables (the pay table just turned off) data in memory, a critical memory clear is not required. Alternatively to a critical memory clear, a gaming system may record the data that is stored in critical memory on separately allocated memory exclusive to the game provided there are adequate safeguards to ensure critical memory integrity.

(g) No changes to the set of games offered to the player for selection (or to the pay table) are permitted while there are credits on the player's credit or bank meter or while a game is in progress unless there is evidence of game manipulation or fraud as a result of a security weakness.

(h) Where changes to the sets of games offered to the player for selection (or to the pay table) are performed outside of the site operator's opening hours it is permissible to do so while credits remain on the player's credit meter provided that there are adequate measures to ensure the machine is not accessible to players and that any credits are retained for the benefit of the next player following such a procedure.

6.0 SPECIFIC ERROR CONDITIONS AND ALERT REQUIREMENTS

6.1 GENERAL ALERT CONDITIONS

Gaming machines and devices must be capable of detecting, displaying and alerting the operator to the error conditions listed below. These must be cleared either by an attendant or upon initiation of a new play sequence and where any on-line monitoring and control system is networked to the machine details of the error should be communicated to it:

(a) coin-in jam (where the coin acceptor disables itself under such circumstances it is not a requirement that it display an error message);
(b) coin-out jam;
(c) hopper empty or timed out;
(d) hopper runaway or extra coin paid out;
(e) critical memory error (including an indication of battery failure or low battery power source);
(f) note acceptor-in jam;
(g) program error or authentication mismatch;
(h) door open (including note acceptor);
(i) reverse coin-in (coin travelling the wrong way through acceptor);
(j) reel spin errors, including a miss-index condition for rotating reels, that affect the outcome of the game:
    (i) the specific reel number must be identified in the error code;
    (ii) in the final positioning of the reel, if the position error exceeds one-half of the width of the smallest symbol excluding blanks on the reel strip; and
    (iii) microprocessor controlled reels must be monitored to detect malfunctions such as a reel which is jammed, or is not spinning freely, or any attempt to manipulate their final resting position.
(k) power reset;
(l) logic cage open (where applicable).

NOTE: This rule also applies to 'Note Acceptor Error Conditions' as to which see 6.3 below.

For machines or devices or individual games that use error codes, a description of such codes and their meanings shall be affixed inside the machine or device. This does not apply to video-based games; however, video based games shall display meaningful text to describe the relevant error condition.

6.2 PRINTER ERROR CONDITIONS

A printer shall have mechanisms to allow software to interpret and act upon the following conditions:

(a) out of paper or paper low;
(b) presentation error (TITO only);
(c) printer jam/failure; and
(d) printer disconnected which may only be detected when the software tries to print.

These conditions shall trigger an error condition to indicate the error has occurred.

6.3 NOTE ACCEPTOR ERROR CONDITIONS

Each gaming machine or device (including note acceptors) must have the capability of detecting and displaying (for note acceptors, it is acceptable to disable or flash a light or lights) the following error conditions:

(a) Note Jams – it is acceptable for the note acceptor to indicate there is a note jam by disabling itself from accepting any more notes or by some other method;

(b) Stacker or Main Door Open (where stacker installed) or Stacker Removed.

A note acceptor must perform a self-test at each power up. In the event of a self-test failure, the note acceptor must automatically disable itself (ie enter note reject state) until the error state has been cleared.

7.0 METER REQUIREMENTS

7.1 CREDIT/PLAY METER

Credits used to initiate a new game (see section 5.6) must come from a single meter which may be described as a credit or play meter. The player shall have the option to view any funds held in such a meter as a monetary value.

7.2 ACCOUNTING AND OCCURRENCE METERS

The machine must have at least one primary metering system which is independent of the main control system (repairing the machine by replacing the electronic controls must leave the integrity of the primary metering system intact). All reasonable efforts should be made to ensure that data held by the primary metering system is true and accurate and impervious to tampering or unauthorised modification.

The primary metering system must, as a minimum requirement, be capable of accurately recording the following data:

(a) cash in;

(b) cash out;

(c) change; and

(d) value of total play.

In addition, for machines or devices which offer the player a choice of more than one game the following minimum data must be accurately recorded for each game choice:

(e) value of total play; and

(f) winnings.

In all cases the data held on the metering system must be such that the percentage return to player can be accurately calculated and available for inspection. In instances where a gaming machine or device is able to offer multiple games such information must be available for each game and game variant.

Any meter used to record the above information must have a minimum capacity of seven digits.

It must not be possible for values on meters to increase or decrease while any of the machine cabinet doors are open.

7.3 NOT APPLICABLE TO THIS CATEGORY OF MACHINE
7.4 NOT APPLICABLE TO THIS CATEGORY OF MACHINE
7.5 NOT APPLICABLE TO THIS CATEGORY OF MACHINE

8.0 ARTWORK AND GAME DISPLAY REQUIREMENTS

8.1 INFORMATION TO BE DISPLAYED

A gaming machine or relevant device must display on the machine itself or on screen, information to enable players to keep track of their gambling. As a minimum, the following information must be available to the player at all times the machine is available for play:

(a) the player's current bank balance (where relevant);
(b) number of plays available or current credit balance (monetary value);
(c) the current stake;
(d) all possible winning outcomes, or a link to where this information may be viewed, for example on a help menu;
(e) win amounts or odds given for each possible winning outcome, or a link to where this information may be viewed, for example on a help menu. The win amount may be displayed as a multiple of the bet or may be shown indirectly by describing the method by which wins are awarded;
(f) the amount won for the last completed game; and
(g) the player options selected (eg total stake, lines played) for the last completed game (until the next game starts or a new selection is made).

Mystery wins are permissible provided it is transparent to the player as to how such a prize may be achieved.
It is not permissible to state or imply that a prize greater than the statutory maximum for a single game may be won by means of the machine nor to indicate that the machine is in a state which could be beneficial to the player (such as by way of a Cash Full Lamp).

8.2 MULTI-LINE GAMES
(a) Each individual line to be played shall be clearly indicated by the gaming machine or device so that the player is in no doubt as to which lines are being staked upon.
(b) The winning play line(s) shall be clearly discernable to the player. (eg on a video game it may be accomplished by drawing a line over the symbols on the play line(s) and/or the flashing of winning symbols and line selection box. Where there are wins on multiple lines, each winning play line may be indicated in turn. This would not apply to reel based games).

8.3 DISPLAY NOTICE REQUIREMENTS
(a) If any display in respect of a game offered by a gaming machine (including reels) is capable of being taken to indicate odds which do not reflect the true odds in the game, the following statement must be included on the face of the machine or at the time the game is selected where more than one game is offered to the player, clearly visible to the player:

THE OUTCOME OF ANY GAME OR FEATURE IS NOT NECESSARILY THAT SHOWN BY THE ODDS DISPLAYED

(b) The following statement must be displayed on the face of the machine or at the time the game is selected where more than one game is offered to the player, clearly visible to the player:

NO PRIZE GREATER IN VALUE THAN [JACKPOT] POUNDS CAN BE WON FROM THIS MACHINE IN ANY ONE GAME

(c) The theoretical target percentage return to player (for betting products this equates to 1 less the calculated hold) must be clearly displayed to the player on the machine in the appropriate alternative format below:
(i) in cases in which the percentage return to player does not depend upon the strategy used by the player:

THIS MACHINE HAS AN AVERAGE PERCENTAGE PAYOUT OF AT LEAST (VALUE) %

Where there is a range (a lower and upper percentage return to player available within the same game) it must be the lower value that is displayed.

(ii) in cases in which the percentage return to player can vary depending upon the strategy used by the player:

THE RETURN TO PLAYER BASED ON BEST STRATEGY IS (VALUE) %

In either case the percentage return to player should be calculated in the following manner:

Percentage return to player equals the value of total play divided by total win shown as a percentage

(d) Either of the following statements must be displayed on the machine, clearly visible to the player:
(i) MACHINE MALFUNCTION VOIDS GAME
or
(ii) MALFUNCTION VOIDS PAYS AND PLAYS
For the purposes of this standard both statements mean that a machine malfunction voids the game within which the malfunction occurs and does not affect the position of the player prior to that specific game including win and credit meters.

(e) Where the machine is designed such that the deposited sum cannot be delivered by the machine for any reason then the following statement must be clearly displayed on the machine:

THIS MACHINE PAYS (£ minimum value payable) ONLY ANY LESSER AMOUNTS WILL BE RETAINED FOR FUTURE USE

(f) Where certain winning combinations may be excluded as a result of the way in which reel spin-distances are determined at the start of each game, the following statement must be displayed clearly to the player on the face of the machine:

DUE TO THE SEQUENCING OF THE REELS CERTAIN WINNING COMBINATIONS ARE NOT AVAILABLE IN EVERY GAME

9.0 DEFINITIONS

Address Space	A range of discrete addresses, each of which may correspond to a physical or virtual memory register, a network host, peripheral device, disk sector or other logical or physical entity.
Change	Money paid out which was inserted by the player that has neither been played nor committed to play.
Critical Game Files	All files that may affect the outcome of a game, including executables, data, and operating system files.
Critical Memory	Has the meaning ascribed to it in paragraph 3.1.
Critical Memory Clear	The process to reset the critical memory of a gaming machine, which configures the gaming machine into the 'as new' state.
Device	Any component of a gaming machine and, where the context requires, includes computer software used in a gaming machine.
Double-Up	Feature whereby the player is offered a gamble in which some or all of the winnings may be wagered at a 100% player return.
Enriched Periods	Where the machine deliberately forces winning outcomes over a series of games by use of any compensation or other controller mechanism.

6: Gambling Act 2005: Additional Material

Theoretical Target Percentage Return to Player	In the case of games in which the chances of winning are distributed randomly, the calculated probable percentage return to player at a 95% confidence level. In other cases, the target percentage return to player as determined by any controlling mechanism.
TITO	Ticket in, ticket out system.
Updates	Any software modification that may affect the outcome of the game.
Value of Total Play (VTP)	The aggregate of all charges for use paid in respect of the machine.

These requirements were notified in draft to the European Commission in accordance with Directive 98/34/EC, as amended by Directive 98/48/EC

Gambling Commission June 2012

MACHINE STANDARDS COMPLEX CATEGORY D
June 2012

INTRODUCTION

6.2540A This standard is applicable to all Complex Category D gaming machines as defined under section 235 of the Gambling Act 2005 (the Act). This standard came into force for all Complex Category D gaming machines supplied or sited within Great Britain from 1 September 2007.

The purpose of the standard is to set out in detail the Gambling Commission's (the Commission) requirements with respect to game features, display notices and general machine operation including metering. These have been developed to help ensure the Commission's three licensing objectives are met. Those objectives are to:

- prevent gambling from being a source of crime or disorder, being associated with crime or disorder or being used to support crime;
- ensure that gambling is conducted in a fair and open way; and
- protect children and other vulnerable persons from being harmed or exploited by gambling.

Operators or end users should not rely upon these standards as a measure of reliability, quality or minimal security requirements.

These standards permit equivalence between different types of technology and do not specify proprietary products or technologies. Testing regimes for these standards will permit equivalent international standards (ISO). It is not intended to limit game content and the use of new technological developments provided that the objectives of the standard are met.

OTHER RELEVANT GAMING MACHINE TECHNICAL STANDARDS

- Technical Standards for Category A, B1, B2, B3, B3A, B4 and C Machines
- Technical Standards for Non-Complex Category D Machines
- Technical Standards for Legacy Machines[1] (Categories B3, B4, C and D Machines)
- Technical Standard for Server Networked & Downloadable Gaming Machines (All categories of machine)
- Technical Standard for Wireless Network Systems (All categories of machine)
- Technical Standard for Cashless Systems (All categories of machine)
- Technical Standard for Linked Progressives (All categories of machine)

[1] Essentially 'legacy machines' are Category B3, B4, C or D machines which were lawfully in use on premises in Great Britain on 31 August 2007 which comply with the regulations made under s240 of the Act and certain details of which have been notified to the Commission.

1.0 HARDWARE REQUIREMENTS

1.1 PHYSICAL SECURITY

All reasonable efforts should be made to ensure that a gaming machine is robust enough to withstand forced entry which would not leave behind evidence of the attempted entry. Where any form of attempted or forced entry causes an error condition, the machine must only commence play once the error code has been cleared. Provided that any security device or sensor (eg door open sensor) which has detected an attempted entry no longer indicates there to be a problem the machine may automatically clear the error condition and commence play. Otherwise, operator action shall be required to clear the error condition.

1.2 MACHINE IDENTIFICATION

A gaming machine must have an identification plate of metallic construction or of an equally resilient material permanently affixed to the exterior of the cabinet by the manufacturer. This must not be easily removable, without leaving evidence of tampering. The following information shall be displayed on the identification plate:

(a) the manufacturer (machine manufacturer or brand name under which it is to be sold);
(b) a unique serial number;
(c) the gaming machine model number (which may refer to the cabinet type and not the game); and
(d) the date of manufacture.

The identification plate shall be mounted on the front or side of the cabinet where it is clearly visible.

1.3 GAMING MACHINE ALARM/ALERT REQUIREMENTS

Gaming machines must be designed to automatically prevent further play and alert the site management in the following situations:

(a) a player winning an amount or redeeming credits that the machine cannot automatically pay;
(b) an error condition occurring; or
(c) a machine fault occurring.

Such a system must be transparent to the player when activated and sufficiently able to attract the attention of the site management.

1.4 LOGIC AREA

Manufacturers must, so far as is reasonably practicable, incorporate in gaming machines design features aimed at preventing tampering with any electronic logic component that has the potential significantly to influence the operation of the machine.

1.5 CONFIGURATION SETTINGS

All switches and/or jumpers must be fully documented and any hardware system within the machine which may alter the configuration settings such as pay tables, accounting denomination, or payout percentages in the operation of the gaming machine must either be housed within a separately locked secure logic area or comply with the following paragraph. This includes top award changes (including progressives) or any other option that would affect the payout percentage.

As an alternative to a separate secure logic area, any change in configuration defined above must be logged and date stamped within the secure non-volatile memory of the machine. This log must cover a minimum period of not less than one month and made available for display on demand with the test and diagnostic routine of the machine or as appropriate.

1.6 VIDEO MONITORS/TOUCH SCREENS

All video based games shall meet the following requirements:

(a) touch screens shall be accurate and, once calibrated, shall maintain that accuracy for at least the manufacturer's recommended maintenance period;

(b) a touch screen should be able to be re-calibrated without access to the machine cabinet other than opening the main door;

(c) there shall be no hidden or undocumented buttons/touch points anywhere on the screen, that affect game play, except as provided for by the game rules; and

(d) section (1.6 c) does not apply to audit functions and controls which must be documented.

1.7 MECHANICAL DEVICES USED FOR DISPLAYING OF GAME OUTCOMES

If the game has mechanical or electro-mechanical devices, which are used for displaying game outcomes, the following rules shall be observed:

(a) mechanical assemblies (eg reels or wheels) shall have some mechanism that ensures the correct mounting of reels' artwork;

(b) displays shall be constructed in such a way that winning symbol combinations match up with pay lines or other indicators; and

(c) a mechanical assembly shall be so designed that it is not obstructed by any other components.

1.8 MULTI-STATION GAMES

In any multi-station game, each player terminal and any other shared device must comply with the relevant sections of this standard, including its requirements for machine identification and metering.

All game rules shall be transparent to the player at each terminal and any shared device that is used to display information pertaining to the game shall be clearly visible to all players participating.

1.9 PATCH WIRES

All patch wires and track cuts shall be documented, in an appropriate manner, in the relevant service manual and/or service bulletin. This does not prohibit required repairs in the field.

2.0 SOFTWARE REQUIREMENTS

2.1 CONTROL PROGRAM AUTHENTICATION REQUIREMENTS

The control program must utilise an integrity check, suitable for the media, providing at least the level of integrity of CRC 16 (for non-alterable storage media) or a secured hashing method such as MD5 or SHA (for alterable storage media) to authenticate that the program and/or support files have not been corrupted or altered prior to

use/loading. Any error detected must result in the machine displaying the appropriate error message and being unavailable for play.
The integrity check must be carried out during each start up or at least once every 24 hours where the machine is specifically designed for permanent serviceable operation.

2.2 ALTERABLE STORAGE MEDIA DEVICES

Any gaming machine and any procedural requirements must include sufficient security to ensure that any software that can influence the game outcome, including configurable settings that reside on any alterable media is a true replication of that version of the game, control or other software.

2.3 PROGRAM STORAGE MEDIUM IDENTIFICATION

Any program medium (ROMs, EPROMs, Alterable storage media, DVD and CD-ROM) placed in the field shall be uniquely identified, displaying:
(a) program ID number;
(b) manufacturer or game provider;
(c) version number;
(d) type and size of medium (unless located on the medium as purchased unused from the supplier); and
(e) location of installation in gaming machine or device, if potentially confusing.
The information a) to e) above must be available for inspection on the site operator's premises either on the label of the storage media or via video or display monitor. For EPROM based games, the identification label shall be placed over the UV window to avoid erasing or alteration of the program.

2.4 NOT APPLICABLE TO THIS CATEGORY OF MACHINE.
2.5 LAST GAME RECALL

Information on at least the last five games must always be retrievable on the operation of a suitable external key-switch, or another secure method not available to the player. This must be a minimum of any collected winnings and bank status for each of the five individual games.

2.6 TEST/DIAGNOSTIC MODE

When a gaming machine or device is in a test mode, any test that involves credits entering or leaving the gaming machine or device (eg a hopper test) must be completed prior to resumption of normal operation.
The main cabinet door of a gaming machine may automatically place the machine in a service or test mode. Test/diagnostics mode may also be entered, via an appropriate instruction, by an attendant during an audit mode access.
When exiting from test mode, any game in play must return to the original state it was in when the test mode was entered. If the gaming machine or a device is in a game test mode, the machine must clearly indicate that it is in a test mode, not normal play.

2.7 SOFTWARE VERIFICATION

At a minimum, the machine must have the ability to allow a visual inspection of the following using either an available matrix or video display. (It is permissible for the machine not to display such information during each start up but it must be accessible when required which may involve the machine being restarted or an appropriate security key being used.
(a) identity of the game provider;

(b) game identity code;
(c) version number of game software; and
(d) check sum of game software;

And if the operating system is not proprietary to the manufacturer, game provider, supplier or operator then:

(e) identity of operating system; and
(f) version number of operating system.

On machines or terminals which offer the player a choice of games the above information concerning the game software must be made available for each game.

3.0 CRITICAL MEMORY REQUIREMENTS
3.1 CONTENTS OF CRITICAL MEMORY

Critical memory (that is non-volatile memory) must be used to store a minimum of the following data:

(a) credit and bank values;
(b) electronic meters;
(c) data used in any control of the game (if the game is non-random); and
(d) data for the 'last five games recall'.

The clearing or resetting of such data must require deliberate action by appropriately authorised personnel.

3.2 MAINTENANCE OF CRITICAL MEMORY

Critical memory storage must be maintained by a methodology that enables errors to be identified and corrected in most circumstances. This methodology may involve signatures, checksums, partial checksums, multiple copies, timestamps and/or effective use of validity codes.

Comprehensive checks of critical memory must be made during each gaming machine or device restart (eg power up cycle). Gaming machine or device control programs (software that operates the machine or device's functions) shall test for possible corruption caused by failure of the program storage medium and all critical game files. Test methodology must endeavour to detect 100 percent of all possible failures.

The control program (software that operates the gaming machine or device's functions) must allow for the machine or device to ensure the integrity of all control program components during execution of said components.

All program storage devices ('PSD') in the executable address space of a main processor shall be validated during the following conditions:

(a) any power up; and
(b) the first time the files are loaded for use (even if only partially loaded).

Memory and PSD space that are not critical to machine security (eg video or sound ROM) are not required to be validated.

3.3 PROGRAM MEMORY, CRITICAL MEMORY AND NON-VOLATILE DEVICES USED TO STORE PROGRAM MEMORY

The following are requirements for critical memory:

(a) a battery back-up (where required), or an equivalent, must be installed on the gaming machine or device for the electronic meters and must be capable of maintaining the accuracy of all information required for thirty days after power is discontinued from the machine The backup device must be kept within the locked logic area or if not available a secure location behind the locked main door;
(b) if the rechargeable battery back-up is used as an 'off chip' battery source, it shall re-charge itself to its full potential in a maximum of twenty-four hours and a specified shelf life of at least five years; and

(c) critical memory that uses an off-chip back-up power source to retain its contents when the mains power is switched off must have a detection system which will provide a method for software to interpret and act upon a low battery condition or alternatively, use a suitable software check to ensure integrity of the storage is maintained.

3.4 UNRECOVERABLE CRITICAL MEMORY

An un-correctable corruption of critical memory must result in an error condition. Critical memory should not be cleared automatically, but must only be cleared by an authorised person.

3.5 FUNCTION OF CRITICAL MEMORY RESET

Clearing critical memory must only be capable of being undertaken by accessing the logic area or secure location in which it is housed. Following the initiation of a critical memory reset procedure, the game program shall execute a routine which initialises each and every bit in memory to the default state. For machines that allow for partial critical memory clears, the methodology for doing so must be accurate and the machine must validate the un-cleared portions of memory.
The default reel position or game display after a critical memory reset must not be the top award on any selectable line. The default game display, upon entering game play mode, must also not be the top award. This applies to the base game only and not to any secondary bonus devices.

4.0 MACHINE CREDIT AND PAYMENT REQUIREMENTS

4.1 COIN OR TOKEN AND NOTE ACCEPTORS AND OTHER METHODS OF INSERTING MONEY OR MONEY'S WORTH INTO THE MACHINE

All coin/token acceptor must meet the following requirements:
(a) the coin/token acceptor must be designed to prevent the use of cheating methods such as slugging (counterfeit coins/tokens), stringing (coin pullback), the insertion of foreign objects and other manipulation; and
(b) other than for diagnostic purposes coins/tokens judged invalid by the acceptor must be rejected to the coin tray and shall not be counted as credits. Acceptance of coins/tokens for crediting to the credit meter must only be possible when the gaming machine is enabled for play. Other states, such as error conditions, including 'door open' and 'audit mode' must disable the coin/token acceptor system. Each coin/token inserted must register the actual monetary value or a number of credits on the player's credit meter for the current game or bet meter. If coins or tokens inserted in a machine are registered directly as credits, the conversion rate must be clearly stated, or be easily ascertainable from a help menu or similar.

All acceptance devices must be able to detect the entry of valid notes, coupons, paper tokens, or other approved vouchers and provide a method to enable the gaming device software to interpret and act appropriately upon a valid or invalid input. Acceptance devices must be electronically-based and be configured to ensure that they only accept valid banknotes, vouchers or paper tokens and reject all other notes. The note input system must be constructed in a manner that protects against vandalism, abuse, or fraudulent activity.

4.2 TOKENISATION

For games that may be played using tokens, the gaming machine or relevant device must receive from the acceptor and post to the player's 'bank' the entire amount inserted. If the currency amount is not an even multiple of the token for a game or the credit amount has a fractional component, the system must retain the value for the benefit of the next player.

4.3 NOT APPLICABLE TO THIS CATEGORY OF MACHINE

4.4 NOT APPLICABLE TO THIS CATEGORY OF MACHINE

5.0 SPECIFIC GAME REQUIREMENTS

5.1 GENERAL REQUIREMENT (RANDOM GAMES)

Where the outcome results in a player winning a prize, it must be determined randomly and in particular no compensator or regulator may be used to determine any stage of the game.
The machine must clearly display to the player either at all times when it is in operation or at the point a game is selected for play, the following statement:

THIS MACHINE IS RANDOM

5.2 RANDOM NUMBER GENERATOR (RNG) REQUIREMENTS

Each possible permutation or combination of game elements that produces winning or losing game outcomes shall be available for random selection at the initiation of each play, unless otherwise clearly stated.
A gaming machine or device must use appropriate communication protocols to protect the random number generator and random selection process from influence by associated equipment which may be communicating with the machine or device. The RNG shall be protected from external influences, such as electromagnetic and electrostatic interference and radio waves. (Compliance with the Electromagnetic Compatibility Regulations is considered to satisfy these requirements)
A machine or device must not present a losing game result which indicates a 'Near Miss'; for example where the odds of the top award symbol landing on the pay line are limited it must not frequently appear above or below the pay line.
The selection process must:

(a) be distributed over the entire output range and pass appropriate statistical tests as defined in the test and approval requirements (reference to be included);
(b) ensure the output is unpredictable; and
(c) not reproduce the same output stream, nor must two instances of an RNG produce the same stream as each other. Where seeding is required to achieve this it should not introduce predictability.

If a gaming machine offers a game that is recognisable (for example Poker, Blackjack and Roulette) and is described as such by title or visual presentation and the chances of winning differ from an equivalent real game this must be made plain to the player either via the artwork or help menus. In any event the rules of the simulated game must be clear and transparent to the player.

5.3 MECHANICAL BASED RNG GAMES

Mechanical based RNG games are games that use the laws of physics to generate the outcome of the game. All mechanical based RNG games must meet the requirements of this standard with the exception of requirements in section 5.2 that are clearly applicable only to electronic random number generators. In addition, mechanical based RNG games must meet the following requirements:

(a) the mechanical pieces must be constructed of materials to prevent decomposition of any component over time (eg a ball shall not disintegrate);
(b) the properties of physical items used to choose the selection shall not be altered; and
(c) the player shall not have the ability to interact with or come into physical contact with or manipulate the mechanics of the game.

The above is not intended to prohibit mechanically based skill and chance features used for entertainment purposes which may form a part of an otherwise electronic game.

5.4 SCALING ALGORITHMS

If a random number with a range shorter than that provided by the RNG is required for some purpose within a game, the method of re-scaling, (ie converting the number to the lower range), is to be designed in such a way that all numbers within the lower range are equally probable.

5.5 SINGLE GAME REQUIREMENTS

The stakes for every gambling opportunity within a game selected by the player must be deducted from the credit or play meter prior to the outcome of any gambling opportunity being displayed to the player.
Before credit(s) for play in a game can be taken, the previous game must first have been completed in full and the result shown to the player.
This section does not preclude the use of multi lines, multi stake and multi reel games provided that the total stake and prize do not exceed the statutory maximum for the single game.

5.6 INITIATING THE NEXT GAME (AUTO START/PLAY)

Except where an 'auto play' or 'auto start' feature is permissible[2] it must always be necessary to release and then depress the machine's real or virtual 'start button' to start a game cycle.

[2] See Regulation 2, Gaming Machine (Circumstances of Use) Regulations 2007.

5.7 GAME SPEED OF PLAY

Where the stake is 60p or less, each game cycle must take no less than 1.5 seconds to complete and the average duration of games, taken over one hour, should not be less than 2.5 seconds.
Where the stake is greater than 60p, each game cycle must either:

- Take no less than 1.5 seconds to complete and the average duration of a game taken over one hour should not be less than 3 seconds; or
- Take no less than 2.5 second to complete.

A game cycle starts when a player using a gaming machine once[3] has paid for each gamble selected and depresses the 'start button' or takes equivalent action to initiate the game and ends when all money or money's worth staked or won during the game has either been lost or delivered to, or made available for collection by the player and the start button or equivalent becomes available to initiate the next game.
Where auto play or auto start is permitted then a game cycle is measured from the point at which the game is initiated by the system (equivalent to the player depressing the start button) to the point at which it is able to automatically start the next game.

[3] Within the meaning of the Category of Gaming Machine Regulations 2007.

5.8 USE OF COMPENSATORS AND/OR REGULATORS

The use of compensators or regulators to determine any stage of the game outcome is permitted, except in the case of 'pre-gambles', provided that the following rules are complied with:

(a) each possible permutation or combination of game elements that produces winning or losing game outcomes must be available for selection at the initiation of each play;

(b) the outcome of any gamble must not be predictable to the player;
(c) cyclic periods of play must not deliberately be introduced and due care must be exercised to prevent their inadvertent occurrence;
(d) the chance of winning a prize must not be so altered as deliberately to create a series of losing (raking periods) or winning games (enriched periods); and
(e) any sequence of wins must not exceed that to be expected from a random machine of a similar payout profile and running at the same payout percentage.

A gaming machine or device must not present a losing game result which indicates a 'Near Miss'; for example where the odds of the top award symbol landing on the pay line are limited it must not frequently appear above or below the pay line.
A compensated game must clearly display to the player on the face of the machine at all times (when in operation) or at the point the game is selected for play (where operated on a multi-game terminal) the following statement:

> THIS GAME IS COMPENSATED AND MAY BE INFLUENCED BY PREVIOUS PLAY

Where a machine operates in such a way that a particular feature (such as Hi/Low or gamble) may invite a player to make a choice in circumstances in which they have no chance of success (defined by the probability of a win being reduced to less than 20% of that required to achieve the target percentage payout) then the following statement must be substituted for the above:

> THIS GAME IS COMPENSATED AND MAY BE INFLUENCED BY PREVIOUS PLAY AND OFFER THE PLAYER A CHOICE WHERE THERE IS LITTLE CHANCE OF SUCCESS

5.9 LIVE JACKPOTS

Except for a live jackpot, no gaming machine must offer prizes which increase or appear to increase from one game to the next. A live jackpot must not be linked to any other gaming machine and must comply with the following rules:

(a) for an electronically displayed live jackpot the true value (the prize value which may be won within the game) must be displayed to the player at all times and must be available in every game. It may only be won as a result of either:
    (i) a random outcome within the game; or
    (ii) the proportion of total money contributed to the jackpot reaching a randomly pre-determined trigger limit;
    (iii) the trigger value of the live jackpot must not be predictable to the player.
(b) it is permissible to use physical coins in place of an electronically displayed equivalent provided that the value of prize which may be won by the player is transparent (the player must be able to reasonably assess the total prize value on offer);
(c) the live jackpot must not be incremented by more than the money staked since the previous increment. It is not a requirement for the live jackpot and reserve (where used) to be incremented in unison or at the same rate. The chance of randomly winning the pot must not be changed in relation to its value;
(d) the prize awarded may be comprised of a fixed value (which must be transparent to the player at all times) together with the live jackpot provided that the total (including any other prize won in the game) does not exceed the statutory maximum;
(e) if an alternative prize option is selected, the live jackpot prize must remain unaffected. Once, however, the live jackpot option is selected, the live jackpot prize must be delivered and the live jackpot reduced to zero or its seeded value, regardless of whether the live jackpot is delivered directly or is subject to some intervening gamble or skill feature; and
(f) the value of the live jackpot or its reserve shall not influence the chance of achieving a win within the game or be used to imply that a win is more likely.

In this section, a 'reserve meter' is a second meter or display which is used to hold any value which may be raised at the same time as the live jackpot, or which holds any overspill once the live jackpot has reached the maximum level for that category of machine.

5.10 DOUBLE-UP (RANDOM GAMES ONLY)

Any Double-up or Gamble options must have a theoretical return to the player of that displayed or suggested by the game graphic.

5.11 NOT APPLICABLE TO THIS CATEGORY OF MACHINE

5.12 ADDITIONAL CREDIT(S) STAKED DURING THE GAME

Machines must not permit players to stake any additional credits during a game cycle unless the game complies with the following requirements:

(a) that the outcome of the game is not decided prior to any additional credit(s) being staked;

(b) that the outcome of the game following any additional credit(s) being staked is random and that all possible combinations associated with an equivalent real game under the same circumstances are available to the player;

(c) that the game does not modify the chance of achieving a win or the combinations available to the player associated with an equivalent live game as a result of their decision not to stake, or to stake additional credits within that game;

(d) that player must not be deliberately misled or given a false impression that they have an enhanced chance of winning as a result of staking additional credits within the game; and

(e) that the total stake wagered within the game does not exceed the relevant statutory maximum.

This section does not preclude the use of multi stake, multi line and multi reel game configurations provided that the player sets their total stake prior to the start of the game cycle.

5.13 PRE-GAMBLE

Where the player is given the opportunity at the start of the game to enter into a pre-gamble, and the prizes available or the odds of achieving those prizes in the game are linked to the odds of a successful outcome of the pre-gamble, the following rules shall be complied with:

(a) the player must always be given the option at the start of the game whether or not to use the pre-gamble;

(b) there must not be a difference of more than 10% between the lowest percentage return to player (%RTP) offered to the player when not opting to use the pre-gamble as against opting to do so;

(c) the prize awards related to each pre-gamble option must be transparent to the player in that they must be fully aware of what they are playing for (or pre-gambling for);

(d) pre-gambles must be transparent in that they must be at natural odds, the player must get what he sees, and there must be no form of compensation or payment or retention of winnings in the event that a short or long series of game outcomes falls outside that which might be normally expected; and

(e) following a 20 second period in which there is no game played, and there is insufficient credit to play a game, any set gamble level is to be reset to 'no gamble'.

5.14 GAME LINKS

A 'game link' is where an element, feature or outcome from one game is either held over or made reference to (recreated) in the next game (eg reel band holds). Game links, with the exception of the live jackpot are not permissible unless they comply with the following rules:

(a) subject to (g) any reference or link made to any previous game must occur randomly;
(b) linkages to a game are only permissible from the immediately preceding completed game;
(c) the chance of being awarded a link to the next game must be no better than even;
(d) it is not permissible to create a situation whereby the machine's control deliberately restores a link to any previous game by any means where it is broken as a result of an unfavourable outcome in a subsequent game;
(e) the player must not be aware as to whether a link will be given or have the opportunity to use it before there is sufficient credit available on the credit or play meter to play the same at least once by means of the machine;
(f) it is not permissible deliberately to force or create a series of wins (enriched periods) using a link feature(s);
(g) the table below sets out the permissible number of consecutive winning games that may be linked together by reference to the maximum prize awarded and delivered to a player in any single game of this linked series of winning games. For example where no prize in any single game of a linked series exceeds £2 then it is permissible to offer the player a maximum of six successful consecutive links.

Maximum prize value awarded in any single game of a linked series	**Maximum number of successful consecutive links permissible**
£1 or less	Unrestricted
£2 or less, greater than £1	6
£3 or less, greater than £2	5
£4 or less, greater than £3	4
£5 or less, greater than £4	3
£70 or less, greater than £50	2
£100 or less, greater than £70	1
In excess of £100	0

All games in a linked series will be otherwise separate and required to be purchased by an appropriate stake.

5.15 MULTIPLE GAMES ON A GAMING MACHINE

(a) The methodology used to select and discard a particular game for play on a multi-game machine must be transparent to the player.
(b) All applicable rules and/or the pay tables must be transparent and available to view for each game prior to any commitment to play.
(c) It must at all times be made transparent to the player which game has been selected for play or is being played.
(d) Committing to play a game must involve the player in at least two actions. Having selected a game, the player must be able to return to the main menu without playing.
(e) It must not be possible to start a new game before the current play is completed and all relevant meters have been updated (including features, gamble and other options of the game).
(f) The set of games offered to the player for selection, or the pay table, must be capable of being changed only by a secure method. This includes turning on and

off games available for play through a suitable interface. The rules at section 1.5 of these standards shall govern the critical memory clear control requirements for these types of selections. However, for games that keep the previous pay tables (the pay table just turned off) data in memory, a critical memory clear is not required. Alternatively to a critical memory clear, a gaming system may record the data that is stored in critical memory on separately allocated memory exclusive to the game provided there are adequate safeguards to ensure critical memory integrity.

(g) No changes to the set of games offered to the player for selection (or to the pay table) are permitted while there are credits on the player's credit or bank meter or while a game is in progress unless there is evidence of game manipulation or fraud as a result of a security weakness.

(h) Where changes to the sets of games offered to the player for selection (or to the pay table) are performed outside of the site operator's opening hours it is permissible to do so while credits remain on the player's credit meter provided that there are adequate measures to ensure the machine is not accessible to players and that any credits are retained for the benefit of the next player following such a procedure.

6.0 SPECIFIC ERROR CONDITIONS AND ALERT REQUIREMENTS

6.1 GENERAL ALERT CONDITIONS

Gaming machines and devices must be capable of detecting, displaying and alerting the operator to the error conditions listed below. These must be cleared either by an attendant or upon initiation of a new play sequence and where any on-line monitoring and control system is networked to the machine details of the error should be communicated to it:

(a) coin-in jam (where the coin acceptor disables itself under such circumstances it is not a requirement that it display an error message);

(b) coin-out jam;

(c) hopper empty or timed out;

(d) hopper runaway or extra coin paid out;

(e) critical memory error (including an indication of battery failure or low battery power source);

(f) note acceptor-in jam;

(g) program error or authentication mismatch;

(h) door open (including note acceptor);

(i) reverse coin-in (coin travelling the wrong way through acceptor);

(j) reel spin errors, including a miss-index condition for rotating reels, that affect the outcome of the game:

   (i) the specific reel number must be identified in the error code;

   (ii) in the final positioning of the reel, if the position error exceeds one-half of the width of the smallest symbol excluding blanks on the reel strip; and

   (iii) microprocessor controlled reels must be monitored to detect malfunctions such as a reel which is jammed, or is not spinning freely, or any attempt to manipulate their final resting position.

(k) power reset;

(l) logic cage open (where applicable).

NOTE: This rule also applies to 'Note Acceptor Error Conditions' as to which see 6.3 below.

For machines or devices or individual games that use error codes, a description of such codes and their meanings shall be affixed inside the machine or device. This does not apply to video-based games; however, video based games shall display meaningful text to describe the relevant error condition.

6.2 NOT APPLICABLE TO THIS CATEGORY OF MACHINE

6.3 NOT APPLICABLE TO THIS CATEGORY OF MACHINE

7.0 METER REQUIREMENTS

7.1 CREDIT/PLAY METER

Credits used to initiate a new game (see section 5.6) must come from a single meter which may be described as a credit or play meter. The player shall have the option to view any funds held in such a meter as a monetary value.

7.2 ACCOUNTING AND OCCURRENCE METERS

The machine must have at least one primary metering system which is independent of the main control system (repairing the machine by replacing the electronic controls must leave the integrity of the primary metering system intact). All reasonable efforts should be made to ensure that data held by the primary metering system is true and accurate and impervious to tampering or unauthorised modification.
The primary metering system must, as a minimum requirement, be capable of accurately recording the following data:
(a) cash in;
(b) cash out;
(c) change; and
(d) value of total play.
In addition, for machines or devices which offer the player a choice of more than one game the following minimum data must be accurately recorded for each game choice:
(e) value of total play; and
(f) winnings.
In all cases the data held on the metering system must be such that the percentage return to player can be accurately calculated and available for inspection. In instances where a gaming machine or device is able to offer multiple games such information must be available for each game and game variant.
Any meter used to record the above information must have a minimum capacity of seven digits.
It must not be possible for values on meters to increase or decrease while any of the machine cabinet doors are open.

7.3 NOT APPLICABLE TO THIS CATEGORY OF MACHINE
7.4 NOT APPLICABLE TO THIS CATEGORY OF MACHINE
7.5 NOT APPLICABLE TO THIS CATEGORY OF MACHINE

8.0 ARTWORK AND GAME DISPLAY REQUIREMENTS

8.1 INFORMATION TO BE DISPLAYED

A gaming machine or relevant device must display on the machine itself or on screen, information to enable players to keep track of their gambling. As a minimum, the following information must be available to the player at all times the machine is available for play:
(a) the player's current bank balance (where relevant);
(b) number of plays available or current credit balance (monetary value);
(c) the current stake;
(d) all possible winning outcomes, or a link to where this information may be viewed, for example on a help menu;
(e) win amounts or odds given for each possible winning outcome, or a link to where this information may be viewed, for example on a help menu. The win

amount may be displayed as a multiple of the bet or may be shown indirectly by describing the method by which wins are awarded;
(f) the amount won for the last completed game; and
(g) the player options selected (eg total stake, lines played) for the last completed game (until the next game starts or a new selection is made).

Mystery wins are permissible provided it is transparent to the player as to how such a prize may be achieved.
It is not permissible to state or imply that a prize greater than the statutory maximum for a single game may be won by means of the machine nor to indicate that the machine is in a state which could be beneficial to the player (such as by way of a Cash Full Lamp).

8.2 MULTI-LINE GAMES
(a) Each individual line to be played shall be clearly indicated by the gaming machine or device so that the player is in no doubt as to which lines are being staked upon.
(b) The winning play line(s) shall be clearly discernable to the player. (eg, on a video game it may be accomplished by drawing a line over the symbols on the play line(s) and/or the flashing of winning symbols and line selection box. Where there are wins on multiple lines, each winning play line may be indicated in turn. This would not apply to reel based games).

8.3 DISPLAY NOTICE REQUIREMENTS
(a) If any display in respect of a game offered by a gaming machine (including reels) is capable of being taken to indicate odds which do not reflect the true odds in the game, the following statement must be included on the face of the machine or at the time the game is selected where more than one game is offered to the player, clearly visible to the player:

THE OUTCOME OF ANY GAME OR FEATURE IS NOT NECESSARILY THAT SHOWN BY THE ODDS DISPLAYED

(b) The following statement must be displayed on the face of the machine or at the time the game is selected where more than one game is offered to the player, clearly visible to the player:

NO PRIZE GREATER IN VALUE THAN [JACKPOT] POUNDS CAN BE WON FROM THIS MACHINE IN ANY ONE GAME

(c) The theoretical target percentage return to player (for betting products this equates to 1 less the calculated hold) must be clearly displayed to the player on the machine in the appropriate alternative format below:
(i) in cases in which the percentage return to player does not depend upon the strategy used by the player:

THIS MACHINE HAS AN AVERAGE PERCENTAGE PAYOUT OF AT LEAST (VALUE) %

Where there is a range (a lower and upper percentage return to player available within the same game) it must be the lower value that is displayed.
(ii) in cases in which the percentage return to player can vary depending upon the strategy used by the player:

THE RETURN TO PLAYER BASED ON BEST STRATEGY IS (VALUE) %

In either case the percentage return to player should be calculated in the following manner:

Percentage return to player equals the value of total play divided by total win shown as a percentage

(d) Either of the following statements must be displayed on the machine, clearly visible to the player:
(i) MACHINE MALFUNCTION VOIDS GAME
or
(ii) MALFUNCTION VOIDS PAYS AND PLAYS
For the purposes of this standard both statements mean that a machine malfunction voids the game within which the malfunction occurs and does not affect the position of the player prior to that specific game including win and credit meters.

(e) Where the machine is designed such that the deposited sum cannot be delivered by the machine for any reason then the following statement must be clearly displayed on the machine:

THIS MACHINE PAYS (£ minimum value payable) ONLY ANY LESSER AMOUNTS WILL BE RETAINED FOR FUTURE USE

(f) Where certain winning combinations may be excluded as a result of the way in which reel spin-distances are determined at the start of each game, the following statement must be displayed clearly to the player on the face of the machine:

DUE TO THE SEQUENCING OF THE REELS CERTAIN WINNING COMBINATIONS ARE NOT AVAILABLE IN EVERY GAME

9.0 DEFINITIONS

Address Space	A range of discrete addresses, each of which may correspond to a physical or virtual memory register, a network host, peripheral device, disk sector or other logical or physical entity.
Change	Money paid out which was inserted by the player that has neither been played nor committed to play.
Critical Game Files	All files that may affect the outcome of a game, including executables, data, and operating system files.
Critical Memory	Has the meaning ascribed to it in paragraph 3.1.
Critical Memory Clear	The process to reset the critical memory of a gaming machine, which configures the gaming machine into the 'as new' state.
Device	Any component of a gaming machine and, where the context requires, includes computer software used in a gaming machine.
Double-Up	Feature whereby the player is offered a gamble in which some or all of the winnings may be wagered at a 100% player return.
Enriched Periods	Where the machine deliberately forces winning outcomes over a series of games by use of any compensation or other controller mechanism.
Error Condition	A detectable event outside of the gaming machine's normal operating parameters.
Firmware	The embedded program memory of the gaming machine.
Gamble	A single act of staking on an outcome within a game.
Game	Any gambling opportunity offered to the user of a gaming machine whether it amounts to gaming, betting or participating in a lottery as those terms are defined in the Act.
Game Cycle	Has the meaning ascribed to it in paragraph 5.7.

Game Update	Any change to game configuration, pay table or any other software that may affect the gambling.
Gaming Machine	Has the meaning ascribed to it by section 235 of the Act.
Hashing Algorithm	Reproducible method of turning some kind of data into a (relatively) small number that may serve as a digital 'fingerprint' of the data.
Idle state	Where there are insufficient credits on a machine to enable a game to be played.
Live Jackpot Feature	A feature played on a single gaming machine which has a prize that may be increased from a pre-set or seeded value from game to game as contributions are made to it from monies staked.
Machine Malfunction	Any hardware and/or software fault that temporarily results in an unforeseen game outcome, or corruption and/or renders the machine unserviceable. Deliberate player actions to trigger a machine fault are not considered be a machine malfunction.
MD5 or SHA	Message-Digest Algorithm 5 and Secure Hash Algorithm respectively.
Multi-Station Game	A gaming machine which incorporates a number of player terminals which share a common device required for the game such as a random number generator.
Non-volatile Computer Memory	Memory that can retain the stored information even when not powered. eg. read-only memory, flash, hard disk, floppy disk, magnetic tape and optical disc drives.
Normal Mode	Where a gaming machine is in a configuration designed for play (not in test or other non-play mode) and in a serviceable condition with no errors detected.
'Off chip' Battery Source	Battery source independent of a data storage chip used for data refresh purposes (recharges state of data bytes when mains power is disconnected).
Passive Display Equipment	Devices only associated with viewing game outcome and not with player interaction such as touch screen displays.
Patch Wires and Track Cuts	Modifications to a circuit board, post manufacture, including soldering additional wires to bridge the electrical conductor paths or the addition of a component (patch wires) or to change the circuit path by cutting the copper conductor (track cut).
Program Storage Devices ('PSD')	Means any device used to store software code in read only or read write format as required by the gaming machine in its normal operation.
Raking Periods	Where a machine deliberately forces a series of losing games by use of any compensation or other controller mechanism.
ROM	Read only memory.
Seeding	Means an integer used to set the starting point for generating a series of random numbers.
Theoretical Target Percentage Return to Player	In the case of games in which the chances of winning are distributed randomly, the calculated probable percentage return to player at a 95% confidence level. In other cases, the target percentage return to player as determined by any controlling mechanism.
TITO	Ticket in, ticket out system.
Updates	Any software modification that may affect the outcome of the game.

Value of Total Play (VTP)	The aggregate of all charges for use paid in respect of the machine.

These requirements were notified in draft to the European Commission in accordance with Directive 98/34/EC, as amended by Directive 98/48/EC

Gambling Commission June 2012

MACHINE STANDARDS 'NON-COMPLEX' CATEGORY D
June 2007

INTRODUCTION

6.2545 This standard is applicable to 'non-complex' versions of category D gaming machines as defined under section 235 of the Gambling Act 2005 (the Act). It is a requirement that such gaming machines sited within Great Britain on or after 1 September 2007 comply with this standard in full.

The purpose of the standard is to set out in detail the Commission's requirements with respect to game features, display notices and general machine operation including metering. These have been developed to help ensure the Commission's three licensing objectives are met. Those objectives are to:

- prevent gambling from being a source of crime or disorder, being associated with crime or disorder or being used to support crime;
- ensure that gambling is conducted in a fair and open way; and
- protect children and other vulnerable persons from being harmed or exploited by gambling.

Operators or end users should not rely upon these standards as a measure of reliability, quality or minimal security requirements.

These standards permit equivalence between different types of technology and do not specify proprietary products or technologies. Testing regimes for these standards will permit equivalent international standards (ISO). It is not intended to limit game content and the use of new technological developments provided that the objectives of the standard are met.

OTHER RELEVANT GAMING MACHINE TECHNICAL STANDARDS

- Technical Standards for Category A, B1, B2, B3 & B4, C & Complex Category D Machines
- Technical standards for Legacy machines[1] (Category B3, B4, C and D machines)
- Technical Standards for Wireless Networks (All categories of machine)
- Technical Standard for Downloadable Gaming Machines (All categories of machine)
- Technical Standard for Cashless Systems (All categories of machine)
- Technical Standard for Linked Progressives (All categories of machine)

[1] Essentially 'legacy machines' are Category B3, B4, C or D machines which were lawfully in use on premises in Great Britain on 31 August 2007 which comply with the regulations made under s240 of the Act and certain details of which have been notified to the Commission.

1.0 THE GAMBLING COMMISSION'S APPROACH

The Commission will not require category D gaming machines which meet its definition of a 'non complex' machine to comply with the full technical standard for that category.

However, the Commission will keep matters under review and reserves the right to require that any specified type of gaming machine comply with the applicable technical standard where it considers that the licensing objectives might otherwise be compromised.

1.1 DEFINITION OF 'NON-COMPLEX' GAMING MACHINES

The Commission uses the term 'non-complex' to refer to machines where the game outcome is achieved by mechanical means such as a coin drop & moving decks, or electro-mechanical or electronic selected game outcomes which are not automated or capable of alteration through electronic or other circuitry, other than, in the case of Cranes only, a feedback control via a microprocessor (or equivalent) to maintain a winner percentage output.

These contrast to complex gaming machines where the outcome of a game is determined by a random number generator (or equivalent) and/or where there is invariably some form of closed loop feedback control (a measurement of game outcome used to determine or alter the chance of winning) to control the percentage return to the player.

The exemption from compliance with the Commission's full standard for category D machines applies to machines of the description at sections 1.2, 1.3 and 1.4 below provided they meet the requirements in section 1.5.

1.2 GENERIC NAME – CRANE

A Crane is a gaming machine in using which, a player attempts to retrieve an item by means of a mechanical grab arm, the positioning of which, he controls by the use of a joystick or direction indicator buttons. On reaching its intended position the grab closes. The player wins where a prize is picked up and it remains held by the grab mechanism until it is delivered to a payout position.

Whether the player wins is not dependant entirely on skill but is determined, in whole or in part, by timing or other compensating devices which determine whether the grab successfully closes on and/or lifts an item and/or the length of time for which it remains closed.

1.3 GENERIC NAME – PUSHER

A Pusher is a gaming machine in using which a player inserts coins which, together with coins previously inserted into the machine, come to rest on a fixed deck and are then pushed forward by the action of a second moving deck. The coins drop off the edge of the fixed deck to the win position if the player is successful, or to a lose position if the player is unsuccessful.

A Pusher may be fitted with further refinements including:

- a pin board where coins are scrambled before landing on the deck;
- replacement of the moving deck by individual paddle arms or eccentric cams;
- a feature which routes the coin through a specific path which in turn activates a bonus, the outcome of which results in further coins being dropped onto the deck; and
- the placing of small toys or gifts on the top of the coins on the fixed deck which are then conveyed by the action of the coins to the edge of the deck where they are delivered as an additional prize with the coins which are dropped.

1.4 GENERIC NAME – MULTI-SLOT

A Multi-slot is a gaming machine, whether designed for a single player or to accommodate use by a number of players at the same time, which features a player panel with a multiple choice of coin entry slots allowing stakes to be placed on each of a number of game elements.

For example, the machine might present a five horse race and have five slots each designated for betting on one of the horses. If a player selected the winning horse then a prize (in cash or tokens) would be delivered by the machine. The game 'outcome' is determined by an extremely simple pseudo-random selector (either electro-mechanical, or electronic).

This format can be used for a number of types of machine, always with some form of physical display, where each slot corresponds to a given horse, vehicle, item or, in the case of a colour wheel, a colour segment.

In the case of some Multi-slots the charge to play the game must be a single coin; in other formats the charge may be paid by way of a number of coins.

1.5 REQUIREMENTS – NON-COMPLEX MACHINE TYPES

A. MACHINE IDENTIFICATION

Each gaming machine must have an identification sticker or marking of a resilient material permanently affixed to the exterior of the cabinet by the manufacturer which must not be easily removable, without leaving evidence of tampering. The following information must be displayed:

(i) the manufacturer (machine manufacturer or brand name under which it is to be sold);

(ii) a unique serial number;

(iii) the gaming machine model number (which may refer to the cabinet type and not the game); and

(iv) the date of manufacture.

B. ADDITIONAL CREDIT(S) STAKED DURING GAME

In the case of Cranes and Multi-slots it must not be possible to place additional credits to the machine once a game has been initiated and until that game has concluded

C. DISPLAY NOTICES

The machine must display on its face in a clear manner the following display notice:

THIS MACHINE PROVIDES FACILITIES FOR GAMBLING

These requirements were notified in draft to the European Commission in accordance with Directive 98/34/EC, as amended by Directive 98/48/EC

* Paragraphs 5.7 and 5.14g updated by Gaming Machine Standards Supplement 2: Revisions to the speed of play and game links sections of the Machine Standards Category C and Complex Category D, June 2009.

Gambling Commission June 2007

MACHINE STANDARDS CASHLESS PAYMENT
June 2007

INTRODUCTION

6.2550 This standard is applicable to all categories of gaming machine as defined under section 235 of the Gambling Act 2005 (the Act). It is a requirement that where any gaming machine accepts or pays prizes in non-cash form and is sited within Great Britain on or after 1 September 2007 then it must comply with this standard in addition to the relevant category specific standard.

The purpose of the standard is to set out in detail the Commission's requirements with respect to game features, display notices and general machine operation including metering. These have been developed to help ensure the Commission's three licensing objectives are met. Those objectives are to:

- prevent gambling from being a source of crime or disorder, being associated with crime or disorder or being used to support crime;
- ensure that gambling is conducted in a fair and open way; and
- protect children and other vulnerable persons from being harmed or exploited by gambling.

Operators or end users should not rely upon these standards as a measure of reliability, quality or minimal security requirements.

These standards permit equivalence between different types of technology and do not specify proprietary products or technologies. Testing regimes for these standards will permit equivalent international standards (ISO). It is not intended to limit game content and the use of new technological developments provided that the objectives of the standard are met.

OTHER RELEVANT GAMING MACHINE TECHNICAL STANDARDS

- Technical Standards for Category A, B1, B2, B3 & B4, C & Complex Category D Machines
- Technical Standards for Non-Complex Category D machines
- Technical Standards for Legacy machines[1] (Categories B3, B4, C and D machine)
- Technical Standard for Wireless Systems (All categories of machine)
- Technical Standard for Downloadable Gaming Machines (All categories of machine)
- Technical Standard for Linked Progressives (All categories of machine)

[1] Essentially 'legacy machines' are Category B3, B4, C or D machines which were lawfully in use on premises in Great Britain on 31 August 2007 which comply with the regulations made under s240 of the Act and certain details of which have been notified to the Commission.

1.0 GENERAL STATEMENT

Where a gaming machine has the facility to accept a credit or charge for use from, and make payment of a prize to, the same medium of cashless payment, for example a smartcard ('the medium') then the requirements of this section must be complied with. For the avoidance of doubt, neither ticket in and out (TITO) systems nor tokens are required to comply with this section. For the purposes of this section a 'token' is an object with a fixed monetary value (whether or not exchangeable for cash) that may be used for the purpose of paying a charge for use or crediting a gaming machine.

1.1 CASHING OUT

A machine may allow players to pay only a portion of the funds held to their credit on a machine to the medium if they so choose, but they must always be given the option to pay the whole of their credit to the medium.

1.2 VIEWING FUNDS HELD

A facility must be available on the premises which will show the player their current monetary balance held on the medium without the requirement to transfer funds or use a gaming machine to play a game. Such a facility must not offer any inducements to the player to commit money for play or further play.

1.3 SELF EXCLUSION

A gaming machine must have the facility to enable it to be rendered incapable of accepting funds from the medium at any time when the account holder has entered a self-exclusion agreement in respect of the premises where the machine is sited. Activation and de-activation of such facility must require action by the site operator.

1.4 DEPOSIT LIMITS

Where there is the facility on the machine, players must be able to track and/or limit the amount of money they are able to deposit onto the medium over a given period of time, excluding monies won during play. The limit that the individual chooses to impose may only be set or raised once in any 24 hour period.
These requirements were notified in draft to the European Commission in accordance with Directive 98/34/EC, as amended by Directive 98/48/EC
Gambling Commission June 2007

MACHINE STANDARDS WIRELESS NETWORK
June 2007

INTRODUCTION

6.2555 This standard is applicable to all categories of gaming machine as defined under section 235 of the Gambling Act 2005 (the Act). It is a requirement that where any gaming machine (including a portable machine) sited within Great Britain on or after 1 September 2007, employs a wireless connection to communicate with any other device used in the provision of facilities for gambling it must comply with this standard in full.
The purpose of the standard is to set out in detail the Commission's requirements with respect to game features, display notices and general machine operation including metering. These have been developed to help ensure the Commission's three licensing objectives are met. Those objectives are to:

- prevent gambling from being a source of crime or disorder, being associated with crime or disorder or being used to support crime;
- ensure that gambling is conducted in a fair and open way; and
- protect children and other vulnerable persons from being harmed or exploited by gambling.

Operators or end users should not rely upon these standards as a measure of reliability, quality or minimal security requirements.
These standards permit equivalence between different types of technology and do not specify proprietary products or technologies. Testing regimes for these standards will permit equivalent international standards (ISO). It is not intended to limit game content and the use of new technological developments provided that the objectives of the standard are met.

OTHER RELEVANT GAMING MACHINE TECHNICAL STANDARDS

- Technical Standards for Category A, B1, B2, B3 & B4, C & Complex Category D Machines
- Technical standards for Non-Complex Category D machines
- Technical standards for Legacy machines[1] (Category B3, B4, C and D machines)
- Technical Standard for Downloadable Gaming Machines (All categories of machine)

- Technical Standard for Cashless Systems (All categories of machine)
- Technical Standard for Linked Progressives (All categories of machine)

---

[1] Essentially 'legacy machines' are Category B3, B4, C or D machines which were lawfully in use on premises in Great Britain on 31 August 2007 which comply with the regulations made under s240 of the Act and certain details of which have been notified to the Commission.

1.0 NETWORK COVERAGE

If a gaming machine is designed to allow players to participate in gambling using a wireless network the following must be complied with:

(a) unless denoted by clear signage there must be no areas where players may participate in any gambling using such a device where the communication signal is:
   (i) not available;
   (ii) of poor quality such that interruptions in play would be likely; and

(b) there must be adequate wireless coverage so that the failure of a single transmitter does not significantly reduce the players' ability to participate in gambling.

The term wireless network as used in this standard does not include any wireless communication link with an external device located off the licensed premises where the player is using a gaming machine.

1.1 NETWORK FAILURE

Where a network failure occurs:

(a) the device must alert the player within 10 seconds of it occurring. It is permissible for the device to continue with any gambling if the network connection is restored provided that the player is not disadvantaged in any way; and

(b) a manual alternative method of play (eg keying in game outcome or other element as opposed to an automatic download via wireless network) is permissible where there is no disadvantage to the player and that there is adequate time to do so. Catch up facilities (eg button pressed to bring device up to current position within game) may only be used where the game in which the credit was taken has not been completed.

The Commission does not intend to set any rules pertaining to voided games as a result of communication loss or other device malfunctions as it is expected that the operator will do so in their terms and conditions. Any such conditions must, however, be clearly expressed and made available to players prior to their use of a relevant gaming machine.

1.2 COMMUNICATION REQUIREMENTS

All protocols must use communication techniques that have proper error detection and/or recovery mechanisms which are designed to prevent unauthorized access or tampering, employing at a minimum Data Encryption Standards (DES) or equivalent encryption with secure seeds or algorithms.

1.3 POWER LEVEL DISPLAY REQUIREMENTS

Portable devices must ensure that players have adequate information as to the likely battery life (preferably in hours/minutes) and give additional warnings when this reaches a low level (eg 10 minutes charge remaining).

1.4 AUDIT REQUIREMENTS

An audit log of sufficient time stamping of significant events so as to be able to resolve any player disputes arising as a result of timing issues must be retained for a minimum of one month. It must be possible to display the audit log on the site operator's premises.

The Commission does not intend to set out exact requirements for time stamping of significant events as it is considered better that the manufacturers do so on the basis of the overall system design.

These requirements were notified in draft to the European Commission in accordance with Directive 98/34/EC, as amended by Directive 98/48/EC

Gambling Commission June 2007

MACHINE STANDARDS LINKED PROGRESSIVES
June 2007

INTRODUCTION

6.2560 This standard is applicable to any gaming machine designed or adapted to be capable of being made available for use as a linked gaming machine as defined in section 244 of the Gambling Act 2005 (the Act). It is a requirement that all linked gaming machines supplied or sited within Great Britain on or after 1 September 2007 comply with this standard in full.

The purpose of the standard is to set out in detail the Commission's requirements with respect to game features, display notices and general device operation including metering. These have been developed to help ensure the Commission's three licensing objectives are met. Those objectives are to:

- prevent gambling from being a source of crime or disorder, being associated with crime or disorder or being used to support crime;
- ensure that gambling is conducted in a fair and open way; and
- protect children and other vulnerable persons from being harmed or exploited by gambling.

Operators or end users should not rely upon these standards as a measure of reliability, quality or minimal security requirements.

These standards permit equivalence between different types of technology and do not specify proprietary products or technologies. Testing regimes for these standards will permit equivalent international standards (ISO). It is not intended to limit game content and the use of new technological developments provided that the objectives of the standard are met.

OTHER RELEVANT GAMING MACHINE TECHNICAL STANDARDS

- Technical Standards for Category A &B1, B2, B3 & B4, C & Complex category D Machines
- Technical Standards for Legacy Machines[1] (Categories B3, B4, C and D machine)
- Technical Standard for Downloadable Gaming Machines (All categories of machine)
- Technical Standard for Wireless Systems (All categories of machine)
- Technical Standard for Cashless Systems (All categories of machine)

---

[1] Essentially 'legacy machines' are Category B3, B4, C or D machines which were lawfully in use on premises in Great Britain on 31 August 2007 which comply with the regulations made

under s240 of the Act and certain details of which have been notified to the Commission.

1.0 GENERAL STATEMENT

A 'linked progressive' is any configuration whereby the same jackpot prize ('a progressive jackpot'), which may be of a fixed amount or increased in proportion to credits staked, is offered on more than one gaming machine

1.1 SOFTWARE REQUIREMENT

PROGRAM STORAGE MEDIUM IDENTIFICATION

Any program medium (ROMs, EPROMs, FLASH ROMs, DVD and CD-ROM) used in a gaming machine incorporating a linked progressive (referred to in this standard as a progressive device) must be uniquely identified by reference to:

(a) program ID number;
(b) manufacturer (machine manufacturer or brand name under which it is to be sold);
(c) version number;
(d) type and size of medium (unless located on the medium as purchased unused from the supplier); and
(e) a unique signature. For medium other than EPROM, a hashing algorithm shall be used.

The information a) to e) above must be available for inspection on the site operator's premises either on the label of the storage media, or via video or matrix display.

1.2 PROGRESSIVE DISPLAYS

A linked progressive display meter ('the progressive meter') must be visible to all players who are playing a gaming machine which may, deliver a progressive jackpot, if the appropriate combination or trigger event is achieved. It must be clear to the player that he is playing a progressive device.

Progressive meters must display the current total of the progressive jackpot in monetary value. It is appreciated that the polling cycle may cause some delay so that a meter does not reflect precisely the actual monies in the progressive pool at each instance, but meters should be designed to maximise the frequency at which they can be updated.

Where multiple items of information are displayed on a progressive meter, it is sufficient to have the information displayed in an alternating fashion provided that the monetary value that is available to win is clear to the player.

Where any gaming machine has a feature that performs a multiplication of a win (doubles, triples etc.) it must be made clear to the player if that does not apply to the progressive jackpot won during the feature.

1.3 TYPES OF UPDATING DISPLAYS

The use of odometer and other 'paced' updating displays is allowed. The progressive meter must display the winning value within 30 seconds of the jackpot being recognised by the central system. In the case of the use of paced updating displays, the system jackpot meter must display the winning value after the jackpot broadcast is received from the central system.

1.4 PROGRESSIVE DISPLAY DIGITAL LIMITATIONS

Once a progressive meter has reached its maximum display amount, the meter must freeze and remain at the maximum value until awarded to a player. Where a progressive jackpot is awarded by a trigger amount then this must always be less than the maximum displayable value.

1.5 PROGRESSIVE CONTROLLER DEFINITION

A progressive controller is all of the hardware and software that:

- controls all communications between progressive jackpots;
- that calculates the value of the progressive prizes;
- that displays the value of those prizes appropriately;
- together with associated progressive meters.

1.6 SETTING THE JACKPOT AMOUNT

The method by which system jackpot parameter values are modified or entered must be secure. The progressive system must be capable of displaying the following information for each progressive jackpot offered:

(a) current value: current prize amount;
(b) overflow: amount exceeding limit;
(c) hits: number of times this prize was won;
(d) wins: total value of wins for this prize or a history of the last hits;
(e) base: starting value;
(f) limit: progressive jackpot limit value (if the jackpot is capped at a maximum limit, it is not necessary to add the overflow amounts to the next starting value);
(g) increment: percentage increment rate;
(h) secondary increment: percentage increment rate after limit is reached;
(i) hidden increment: percentage increment rate for the reserve pool (the next base amount must be computed or posted to advise the player of this contribution);
(j) reset value: the amount the progressive jackpot meter resets to after the progressive jackpot is won; and
(k) the participating gaming machines.

1.7 PROGRESSIVE CONTROLLER PROGRAM INTERRUPTION

After a program interruption (eg power down), the software must be able to recover to the state it was in immediately prior to the interruption occurring.

1.8 PROGRESSIVE RESUMPTION

On program resumption, the following procedures must be performed as a minimum requirement:

(a) any communications to an external device must not begin until the program resumption routine, including self-tests, is completed successfully;
(b) progressive system control programs must test themselves for possible corruption due to failure of the program storage media. The authentication may use the checksum; however, it is preferred that the Cyclic Redundancy Check (CRC) calculations are used as a minimum (at least 16 bit). Other test methodologies are acceptable if they deliver a comparable level of integrity; and
(c) the integrity of all critical memory must be checked.

1.9 COMMUNICATION REQUIREMENTS FOR SIGNALLING OF A JACKPOT

There must be a secure, two-way communication protocol between the progressive controller and any gaming machine that is able to participate in the link. This must be used for signalling a jackpot hit between the machine and controller and for transferring a progressive win from the controller to the gaming machine.

1.10 MONITORING OF CREDITS STAKED

During 'Normal Mode' the progressive controller must continuously monitor each machine on the link for credits staked and multiply the same by the rate of progression and denomination in order to determine the correct amounts to apply to the progressive jackpot.

1.11 ACCESS TO THE PROGRESSIVE CONTROLLER

Every progressive controller must be housed in a secure environment allowing only authorised accessibility.

D.1.12 Progressive controller required meters

Every progressive controller or other progressive system component must keep the following information in non-volatile memory, which must be capable of being displayed:
(a) the number of progressive jackpots won on each progressive level if the progressive display has more than one winning amount;
(b) the cumulative amounts paid on each progressive level if the progressive display has more than one winning amount;
(c) the maximum amount of the progressive payout for each level displayed;
(d) the minimum amount of the progressive payout for each level displayed; and
(e) the rate of progression for each level displayed.

1.13 CONTROLLER AND DISPLAY FUNCTIONS DURING PROGRESSIVE JACKPOT WIN

When a progressive jackpot win is recorded on a gaming machine which is linked to the progressive controller, the progressive controller must allow for the following to occur on the progressive display and/or each gaming machine in the link:
(a) display of the winning amount;
(b) display of the electronic gaming machine identification that caused the progressive meter to activate;
(c) the progressive controller may automatically reset to the reset amount and continue normal play; and
(d) display the new progressive values.

1.14 PROGRESSIVE CONTROLLER ERROR CONDITIONS

When a progressive controller error occurs the system must display an appropriate error message that is visible to all players. The site system must also alert the casino to the error condition. All game(s) in progress must be disabled, and an error message clearly displayed to all players who might participate in a game linked to the progressive prize, whenever any of the following event(s) occur:
(a) during a communication failure;
(b) when there have been multiple communication errors;
(c) a controller checksum or signature has failed;
(d) a controller's RAM or PSD (program storage device) mismatch or failure;
(e) the current amount is larger than the limit, (see also 'Jackpot Limits');
(f) the jackpot configuration is lost or is not set;
(g) an unfeasible number or value of credits appears to have been staked (as defined by the parameters of the progressive set-up based on the ratio of number of machines to the amount staked ratio); or
(h) a gaming machine's and the progressive controller's meters do not reconcile.

1.15 TRANSFERRING OF PROGRESSIVE JACKPOT

The progressive controller must have a secure means of transferring a progressive jackpot win to the appropriate gaming machine and the process must be clear to the player.

1.16 JACKPOT LIMITS

Where there are any upper or lower limits imposed on the progressive jackpot via configuration settings this must be made clear to the players prior to play.

1.17 TIME LIMITS

A progressive controller may have the ability to limit the time during which a progressive jackpot is available. Where this is the case the rules applying to such time limits must be made clear to the players prior to play.

1.18 SWAPPING PROGRESSIVE LEVELS

When a winning combination may be evaluated as more than one of the available pay table combinations, the players must be paid the highest possible progressive value.

1.19 GAMING DEVICE REQUIREMENTS WHEN ANY PROGRESSIVE IS AWARDED

When a progressive jackpot prize has been awarded, a linked gaming machine must perform the following:

(a) an appropriate message must be displayed;
(b) the prize must be transferred to the gaming machine and the game shall lock up until the award has been paid; and
(c) all linked progressive related meters must be updated.

These requirements were notified in draft to the European Commission in accordance with Directive 98/34/EC, as amended by Directive 98/48/EC

Gambling Commission June 2007

MACHINE STANDARDS SERVER NETWORKED AND DOWNLOADABLE June 2007

INTRODUCTION

6.2565 This standard is applicable to all categories of gaming machine as defined under section 235 of the Gambling Act 2005 (the Act). This standard will come into force for any gaming machine terminal, sited within Great Britain on or after 1 September 2007, that is dependant upon some external device for the purpose of gambling (including software downloads, server based systems or external random number generators), subject to the Implementation Annex to this standard (published separately). That Annex identifies those requirements of the standard which will come into force on various dates in the period 1 September 2007 to 1 September 2008.

The purpose of the standard is to set out in detail the Gambling Commission's (the Commission) requirements with respect to game features, display notices and general machine operation including metering. These have been developed to help ensure the Commission's three licensing objectives are met. Those objectives are to:

- prevent gambling from being a source of crime or disorder, being associated with crime or disorder or being used to support crime;
- ensure that gambling is conducted in a fair and open way; and
- protect children and other vulnerable persons from being harmed or exploited by gambling.

Operators or end users should not rely upon these standards as a measure of reliability, quality or minimal security requirements.

These standards permit equivalence between different types of technology and do not specify proprietary products or technologies. Testing regimes for these standards will permit equivalent international standards (ISO). It is not intended to limit game content and the use of new technological developments provided that the objectives of the standard are met.

E. OTHER RELEVANT GAMING MACHINE TECHNICAL STANDARDS
- Technical Standards for Category A, B1, B2, B3 & B4, C & Complex Category D Machines
- Technical Standards for Non-Complex Category D machines
- Technical Standards for Legacy machines[1] (Category B3, B4, C& D machines)
- Technical Standard for Wireless Systems (All categories of machine)
- Technical Standard for Cashless Systems (All categories of machine)
- Technical Standard for Linked Progressives (All categories of machine)

---

[1] Essentially 'legacy machines' are Category B3, B4, C or D machines which were lawfully in use on premises in Great Britain on 31 August 2007 which comply with the regulations made under s240 of the Act and certain details of which have been notified to the Commission.

1.0 SERVER NETWORKED AND DOWNLOADABLE GAME REQUIREMENTS

This standard is applicable in any of the following circumstances:

(a) where a gaming machine is designed or adapted such that games are operated partly on a player terminal and partly on another device (eg server based systems);

(b) where the control software can be modified, removed or added to the player terminal via a network;

(c) where the control software can be modified, removed or added to the player terminal using a portable device without physical access to the gaming machine (eg a laptop temporarily networked to the gaming machine to update flash RAM); or

(d) where the RNG (Random number generator) is external to the player's terminal.

Examples of such systems are where the terminal control program, randomly generated game determinants or other game content is generated by a central server and downloaded to the player terminal for the operation of the game. This section does not apply to system triggered jackpots or game features which may be external to the player's terminal.

1.1 COMMUNICATION REQUIREMENTS

All communication protocols must have error detection and/or recovery mechanisms which are designed to prevent unauthorised access or tampering.

1.2 SOFTWARE VERIFICATION

Where any control software is modified or downloaded onto the player's terminal the following requirements must be met:

(a) the system responsible for the software upload must be capable of verifying that all control programs installed are true and exact replications of those communicated to the device in order to ensure game integrity. Where any error is detected an appropriate action must be taken to either remedy the fault or disable the game; and

(b) there are sufficient security measures to ensure that any control software residing on the player's terminal remains true and is an exact replication of that communicated to the device.

1.3 REMOTE ACCESS AND AUDIT REQUIREMENTS

Where a player terminal has the facility for remote access for the purpose of control software modification, deletions, additions or product support, the following must be met:

- there must be sufficient security measures to prohibit non-authorised access; and
- an audit log of the following must be retained for a minimum of twelve months:

(a) time and date of the access and/or event;
(b) log in name;
(c) download data files added, modified or deleted;
(d) the player terminal(s) which the file or program was downloaded to and, if applicable, the file or program it replaced; and
(e) modifications to the player terminal configuration settings and what the changes were.

It is preferred that such data as log on duration, the file size and easily identified program ID's are included in the log.

The audit log(s) and any applicable records must be available for inspection.

1.4 PAY TABLE/DENOMINATION CONFIGURATION CHANGES

Player terminal control programs that offer multiple pay tables and/or denominations that can be configured via an external communication must comply with the following:
(a) information relating to the player's likely return (%RTP) must be transparent to the player for the pay table in operation and in particular where any changes occur at times when the system is available for play;
(b) the game is in an idle state when any update occurs; and
(c) any change to the pay table will not cause inaccurate crediting or payment.

1.5 EXTERNAL RANDOM NUMBER GENERATOR

Where a random value or other element used to determine the game outcome is uploaded to the player terminal from a device external to its cabinet by means of electronic communication then the arrangement must comply with the following:
(a) the method of transmission must be secure, with error detection and/or recovery mechanisms;
(b) there must be a means of authentication which would alert the operator to any external tampering, modification or interception and replacement of the transmitted random variable that may be used to determine a game outcome;
(c) where an error occurs the terminal must display an error message with the appropriate audio and visual indicator, and record the details, including time and date of the error in a log. Correcting such an error must require operator intervention unless there is a secure automated process to do so; and
(d) an audit log of sufficient time stamping of significant events so as to be able to resolve any player disputes arising as a result of timing issues must be retained for a minimum of one month. The Commission does not intend to set out exact requirements for time stamping of significant events as it is considered better that the manufacturer do so on the basis of the overall game and system design.

The system must be capable of displaying the audit log on the site operator's premises.

These requirements were notified in draft to the European Commission in accordance with Directive 98/34/EC, as amended by Directive 98/48/EC

Gambling Commission June 2007

LEGACY MACHINES
Policy statement 30 April 2007

6.2570 Legacy machines are Category B3, B4, C and D machines which have already been manufactured, supplied into the market **and sited** prior to 1 September 2007. The Commission will put into place separate requirements for such machines so that they will not need significant adaptation. The rules ensure that operators do not have to make unreasonable technical adaptations to machines already in the market whilst also ensuring that only those machines genuinely in the market at the end of August and compliant with current requirements will be permitted to continue to operate.

The limitations that we intend are:

- operators and suppliers making available gaming machines will be required to supply the Commission (possibly facilitated by the trade associations) with a register of the machines in the market at 31 August 2007, with name and unique identification number, so that the machines can be identified and tracked;
- the machines will not be required to comply with the new standards but would be expected to continue to operate in the same way as they do under current legislation and current accepted practices. (Machines which meet the current agreed Commission-BACTA guidelines would meet these requirements);
- the machines will be able to move premises and be sold between operators so long as there is an ability to identify and track the machines;
- machines will be able to be downgraded through the categories, for example being changed from a category C in a pub, to a category D in a family entertainment centre (where only the stakes and prizes will be different and no software adaptation is required); and
- the machines will remain as legacy machines unless and until they are modified in order to take advantage of the new freedoms (eg higher stakes and prize rules, ability to accept a mix of cash and non-cash payments). If they are substantially altered so that they effectively become new machines they will cease to be legacy machines and thus will automatically be required meet the relevant new technical standards in full.[1]

---

1 [*Author's note*: see next document herein.]

Gambling Commission April 2007

MACHINE STANDARDS CATEGORY B3, B4, C & D (LEGACY MACHINES) June 2007

INTRODUCTION

6.2575 This standard is applicable to all 'Legacy Machines'.

A gaming machine, as defined by section 235 of the Gambling Act 2005 (the 2005 Act), is a legacy machine, if:

- it is of category B3, B4, C or D;
- it was available for lawful use on premises within Great Britain on 31 August 2007 (whether as a 'Jackpot' machine under the provisions of section 31 Gaming Act 1968 or as an 'amusement with prizes' machine under the provisions of section 34 of that Act);
- it is so configured as to comply with any regulations made under section 240 of the 2005 Act which apply to it; and
- prescribed details of it have been registered with the Gambling Commission by 31 August 2007.

The purpose of the Commission's standards is to set out in detail the Commission's requirements with respect to game features, display notices and general device operation including metering for machines. These have been developed to help ensure the Commission's three licensing objectives are met. Those objectives are to:

- prevent gambling from being a source of crime or disorder, being associated with crime or disorder or being used to support crime,
- ensure that gambling is conducted in a fair and open way, and
- protect children and other vulnerable persons from being harmed or exploited by gambling.

A legacy machine will not be required to comply with the Commission's full technical standards which would apply to a newly manufactured machine of the appropriate

category. Rather the purpose of this standard is to set out those minimum requirements legacy machines must continue to meet if they are to continue to be sited after 1 September 2007. These draw upon large parts of the existing industry and trade association voluntary guidelines on gaming machines.
In general, any legacy machine which is adapted after 1 September 2007 will thereafter be required to comply in full with the Commission's technical standard and test and approval processes for the relevant category of machine. However, downgrading a machine from one category to a lower category, or adapting it to take advantage of its relevant pre-existing stake or prize limits, will not disqualify a machine from its legacy status provided no other aspect of the machine's operation is affected.

OTHER APPLICABLE DOCUMENTS
(i) Section 240 regulations – (*Applicable S.I. Number*)
(ii) Section 236 regulations – (*Applicable S.I. Number*)

1. KEY POINTS

1.1 In this Standard the following terms have the same meaning as in the Gaming Machine (Circumstances of Use) Regulations 2007 (the Regulations):

- charge for use;
- committed amount;
- committed payment;
- deposited sum; and
- using a gaming machine once.

1.2 In this Standard:

- 'Bank' refers to a meter used to record uncollected winnings for Category C & D and in the case of categories B3 and B4 deposited sums and uncollected winnings;
- 'Credit' refers to a meter used to record the committed amount;
- 'Residue' refers to a meter used to record deposited sums only in each case irrespective of how the meter is described on any particular gaming machine.

1.3 Except for a live jackpot which complies with 2 below and reasonable percentage control parameters, no game must be linked to the previous game other than the last game played. The odds of such a link occurring must be no greater than 50%, and must be randomly determined.
1.4 No display other than those indicating the current value of a Bank, Credit or Residue must display values greater than the maximum prize value allowed for the category of legacy machine.
1.5 Statements for the player's benefit, such as information about any payout restrictions, must be truthful and clearly visible to the player.

2. LIVE JACKPOTS

2.1 Except for a single live jackpot feature, no machine must offer prizes which increase or appear to increase from one game to the next other than on a random basis and at odds of no more than evens.
2.2 The true value of the live jackpot, and any reserve if used, must be displayed to the player at all times.
2.3 The live jackpot and its reserve must start off from zero (except after a win when the live jackpot has been immediately replenished by the value in the reserve), and be increased only at random in proportion to the number of games played, and in no other way whatsoever, whether the live jackpot contains coins of a single denomination or a range of different denominations.
This restricts live jackpot prizes to a specific and pre-determined value, independent of the outcome of some other part of the game.
Note that this places no restriction on the rate of increase of the live jackpot and its reserve.

2.4 The reserve must contain the same range of coin values as the live jackpot and its rate of increase must also be the same.
2.5 The live jackpot must be available in every game and its contents, in whatever form, may not be used to enhance the chances of winning.
2.6 The live jackpot, when won, must be paid in full, without the addition of any further value other than as may be necessary to round up the value so as to be payable by the machine, and must be delivered in the game in which it is won.
2.7 Category B3 & B4 legacy machines may offer awards which comprise a fixed value together with the live jackpot, as long as the sum of these two components cannot exceed the statutory prize limit for the particular category of machine and that no reserve is used.
If an alternative prize option is selected, the live jackpot prize must remain unaffected. Once, however, the live jackpot option is selected, the live jackpot prize must be delivered and the live jackpot reduced to zero, regardless of whether the live jackpot is delivered directly or is subject to some intervening gamble or skill features.
2.8 If a repeat chance is offered when a live jackpot has been won, it must be available for every value of a live jackpot. The value of the repeat award must be the same as the original award.

3. DISPLAYS

3.1 No single display, other than any Bank, Credit, or Residue display, may show, or be presented in such a way that it could be taken to show, a value which exceeds the statutory prize limit for the machine. A plurality of such display elements is acceptable.
3.2 If any display (including reels) does not reflect the actual odds of the game presented the following statement must be included on the face of the machine, clearly visible to the player:

> THE OUTCOME OF ANY GAME OR FEATURE IS NOT NECESSARILY THAT SHOWN BY THE ODDS DISPLAYED.

3.3 Machines must display, clearly visible to the player, a sign in the form:

> NO PRIZE GREATER IN VALUE THAN [X] POUNDS CAN BE WON FROM THIS MACHINE IN ANY ONE GAME.

Where [X] is the maximum win achievable on the machine (which must be no greater than the statutory prize limit for the category of machine).
3.4 Where a Bank uses a pictorial representation for display it is acceptable to use a single symbol or facsimile representing £10 or more up to £20 even where this exceeds the maximum permitted prize for a machine of the relevant category.
Where a symbol (eg note) with a value equal to £20 is used, then no symbols in the Bank display must exceed the physical size of a current note of that value.

PERCENTAGE PAYOUT LABEL

3.5 Where regulation 3(2) of the Regulations applies any percentage payout labels displayed on the face of machines must be clearly visible to the player, and in the following form:

> THIS MACHINE HAS AN AVERAGE PAYOUT OF 70% OR GREATER.

LEVEL OF PRIZES

3.6 Each category B3 & B4 legacy machine must bear a statement of the monetary value of each prize, how it may or may not be won and of any special circumstances under which a prize may not be paid or may be modified. It is not necessary for these statements to be continuously displayed if the player can access the statements at any time, and the means to do so is clearly visible at all times when the machine is available for play.

Where there are insufficient coins to pay any prize in full then an illuminated warning sign on the machine clearly visible to the player must appear bearing the words -

WARNING — INSUFFICIENT COINS TO PAY MAJOR PRIZES.

CASH FULL LAMP

3.7 Any indicator which implies that the machine is in a state which could be beneficial to the player is unacceptable.

CATEGORY B3 & B4 LEGACY MACHINES – MYSTERY PRIZES

3.8 The circumstances in which any prize is not available on a category B3 or B4 legacy machine must be clearly displayed on the face of the machine before a player commits himself to play.

CATEGORY B3 & B4 LEGACY MACHINES – REEL SEQUENCING

3.9 Where certain winning combinations may be excluded as a result of the way in which reel spin-distances are determined at the start of each game, the following statement must be placed on the face of the machine, clearly visible to the player:-

DUE TO THE SEQUENCING OF THE REELS CERTAIN WINNING COMBINATIONS ARE NOT AVAILABLE IN EVERY GAME.

CATEGORY B3 & B4 LEGACY MACHINES — ROUNDING UP PRIZES

3.10 On machines in which whole pound devices only are provided the following notice must be incorporated on the face of the machine, clearly visible to the player:

THIS MACHINE PAYS OUT £1 COINS ONLY.

ALL PRIZES WILL BE ROUNDED UP TO THE NEAREST POUND.

4. BANK

4.1 A single Bank may be used to accumulate all winnings from machines over any number of games.

4.2 A single Bank display must show the contents of the Bank in monetary values, although a secondary display on a feature display shared with other machines may replicate the machine's Bank display whilst the machine is actively using this feature (otherwise this secondary display must read zero).

4.3 Accumulated winnings in a category C or D legacy machine's Bank may not be used to pay a charge for use of the machine (other than by payout of the Bank and re-insertion into the machine).

4.4 A display that incorporates a Bank can be used for other purposes providing that:

(a) the only time that the display shows an amount greater than the statutory maximum prize is when it is used in the Bank mode;

(b) it must be clearly stated on the machine when the display is in the Bank mode; and

(c) all uses of the display must fully comply with this standard.

4.5 The value of the Bank displayed on a category C or D legacy machine must not exceed five times the maximum permitted prize for machines of these categories. In the event that a win plus the current value of the Moneybank should exceed that limit, then:

(a) the machine must increment the Moneybank to momentarily display the true accumulated total; and
(b) the machine must immediately automatically pay out the Moneybank down to a value of four times the maximum permitted prize.

4.6 There must be no statement made on the machine which suggests that for any reason a payment to the Bank can exceed the permitted maximum prize for a machine of the relevant category.

4.7 Pictorial Bank displays must not be used to register the accumulated winnings awarded by a feature which repeats over successive games when such wins may total a sum greater than the permitted maximum for using the machine once.

5. LINKAGES

RANDOM HOLD

5.1 A random hold complies with this standard provided that:
(a) the operation of the hold device is completely random;
(b) the combined availability of reel hold and all other feature holds is no greater than 50%;
(c) the player is not offered the opportunity to hold before he commits himself to the game; and
(d) the descriptive flash on the machine fascia does not imply that a succession of holds will enable a player to win a sum greater than the maximum permitted prize. For example:
    (i) in a gamble feature consisting of a reel containing numbers to determine the outcome of a Hi-Lo selection made by the player and in which, when the reel is spun, a higher or lower number appears on the win line, it is unacceptable for that reel to remain in position over games more than 50% of the time; and
    (ii) A Spin to Last Win feature would generally be unacceptable because the probability of the immediately preceding win value remaining unchanged will invariably be greater than 50%.

5.2 Other than the Live Jackpot, machines must not be designed to create a real or perceived chance of a link between games which is greater than 50%. Any favourable combination remaining at the end of a game must be the result of the random action of the machine or a selection by the player (or a combination of the two) and must not derive from a characteristic inherent in the design of the machine.
For example, it is unacceptable for the last game in the series to drive the reels (or other feature) into a favourable combination as that may encourage the player to pay a further charge for use or make a further committed payment in a hope that the favourable situation can be improved to a winning combination in a subsequent game.

5.3 Captions which, when illuminated, suggest that the next game in a series may result in a maximum win are not acceptable.

LINKED OR PROGRESSIVE FEATURES

5.4 Any feature which builds up an enhanced payout as the result of the out-turn of a preceding game is unacceptable unless the probability of this occurring is no greater than 50%. For example, the following are unacceptable:
(a) machines which contain such features which operate on (say) every fifth game regardless of wins or losses in those games;
(b) machines which award a prize at the end of a losing sequence of a certain number of games; and
(c) a feature which enables a player to modify the combination standing over from a previous game.

5.5 A repeat win, when achieved, must be displayed on the same set of symbols as the original win.

'BUYING' A BENEFIT OR ADVANTAGE

5.6 A machine must not offer a 'token trade' or 'trade exchange' feature in which a part or all of a cash or token prize may be exchanged for a benefit or advantage (for example a nudge) carried forward into the next game.
However, it is permissible for a feature in a game to be used in that game or left unused with the possibility of its being held over into the next game at odds of no greater than 50% (for example, nudges which become available during the normal course of a game may be used during that game or 'banked' with the possibility that they may be carried forward into the next game).

RANDOM DEVICES

5.7 A benefit bestowed by a random device may consist of the opportunity to use a hold-and-draw feature, to use a 'nudger', to play an enriched game, or to play a separate game. All these are acceptable, provided they are only available to a player whilst using the machine once.

RANDOM EVENT

5.8 Where a number of events occur at random, the probability of any one of those events occurring must be the same as the probability of any other event occurring.
For example, where a machine is designed to offer a random chance of a repeat win, the probability of the repeat occurring must be the same whatever the value of the win. In particular, the probability must not be increased to a higher value after a major win and reduced to a lower percentage for other wins.

DUAL STAKE CATEGORY C AND D LEGACY MACHINES

5.9 Where category C and D legacy machines offer dual stakes:
(a) no reel or feature hold may be offered in any game in which the stake has been increased;
(b) on insertion of more than one charge for use ('credits') the player must either:
  (i) be 'locked in' to games at whatever fixed stake was initially selected until all credits are exhausted and, once all credits have been used, no reel or feature hold may be offered for the next game if an increase in stake is selected; or
  (ii) be allowed to change stake from game to game but without repeat reel or feature hold being offered in any game in which the stake has been increased;
(c) the fact that no reel or feature hold is available in a game in which the stake has been increased must be made clear to the player at all times;
(d) in any game in which the stake is reduced, only one random 50/50 decision is permitted (for example, if a reel or feature hold is available at one stake it should also be available if a lower stake game is selected); and
(e) reel or feature hold availability must not be shown to the player until after the desired stake has been selected.

6. GENERAL

6.1 Controls for Legacy Machines of the 'Fruit Machine' Type:
(a) any sequence of wins must not exceed that to be expected from a random machine of a similar payout profile and running at the same payout percentage;
(b) prior to the commencement of any game the outcome of that game must not be shown to or predictable by the player;
(c) any features that can be used to modify the outcome of a game by reference to the immediately preceding game must not be available at a greater than 50% probability (except for a live jackpot);

(d) if a feature is described as 'skill', it must be true skill; and
(e) the stated target percentage payout must be achieved within any 10,000 games in the case of category C & D legacy machines or 100,000 games in the case of category B3 and B4 legacy machines.

6.2 There must be no feature which offers, or appears to offer, a series of enriched games. For example:
(a) some live jackpots appear in the form of a multi-lamp display where the number of lamps illuminated increases as games are played, but where the number of lamps illuminated is not directly related to the true value of the live jackpot cash award that it represents. This type of display can make it appear that the live jackpot value increases only slowly at first, but at a faster rate as more games are played, thus giving the impression of a period of enriched play during the latter stages of a series of games. This is not permissible;
(b) some machines include win captions which, when illuminated, suggest that the next game or subsequent games may result in an improved win. If such captions are not permanently lit but illuminate at some stage during play, the effect is to imply that during the illuminated period the player will enjoy a series of enriched games. This arrangement is not permissible; and
(c) the value of a prize, other than a live jackpot prize, may be increased in any one game by the random operation of a bonus feature. However, a bonus may not be offered over a series of games, since this would create a period of enriched games. Equally, a pseudo-bonus feature which adds nothing to the value of the prize but which gives the impression of a series of enriched games is impermissible.

6.3 Machines may incorporate a change giving facility.

PERCENTAGE PAYOUT

6.4 All category B3, B4, C & D legacy machines must have a payout of at least 70%.

6.5 Category C & D Legacy Machines which accept smart cards:
(a) a facility must be available on the premises where such machines are sited which will show the player what credits his card holds without requiring credits to be spent or a game to be played;
(b) the machine must allow the player to pay a single charge for use and the smart card must be partly ejected for re-insertion for every £2 value of stake committed;
(c) smart card must be partly ejected by the machine and re-inserted by the player before any replayable token wins can be used to pay a charge for use or make a committed payment;
(d) cash winnings recorded as credits on the card must not be used to play further games — they must be exchanged for cash only; and
(e) the 'stake' purse must have a maximum value determined by the machine operator which reflects both the need for adequate security and the modes of operation required.

PRE-GAME GAMBLE

6.6 Where a pre-game gamble is offered to the players:
(a) if a pre-game gamble is offered in all games, the player must be given an option at the start of the game to use the pre-gamble or not;
(b) use of the pre-gamble must not cause the machine's percentage return to player to be enhanced by more than 10 percentage points;
(c) if no pre-gamble is used in any game, the machine percentage return to player must not be less than that stated on the glass artwork;
(d) the pre-gamble must be transparent: that is to say at natural odds, the player gets what he sees, and no compensation;

(e) the pay tables relating to each pre-gamble must be transparent to the player: they must know what they are playing for (or pre-gambling for);
(f) such gambles are to be optional, transparent and not used as part of the machine's payout controls; and
(g) after a 10 seconds period in which no game is played, and there is insufficient credit to play a game, any set gamble level must be reset to 'no gamble'.

7. PAYMENT METHODS AND METERS

GENERAL

7.1 The following general requirements will apply:
(a) for Category D machines the charge for playing a game once shall be by one or more coins or tokens inserted into the machine;
(b) notwithstanding the provisions in s6.5 above, category C legacy machines may be played only with coins or banknotes, and must pay out using coins or banknotes;
(c) category B3 & B4 legacy machines may be played with coins, banknotes, smartcard credits and tokens, and may pay out using coins, banknotes, smartcard credits, tokens, cheques and credit notes. In addition, payments to be made to and pay outs from such machines may be accepted or delivered by site staff (hand- pay) rather than by the machine itself; and
(d) category B3 & B4 legacy machines may use winnings to pay a charge for use or make a committed payment without these having first to be paid out.

NOTES ON MAXIMUM VALUE TRANSFERABLE TO CREDIT

7.2 The maximum value of a committed payment capable of being transferred to a credit meter to be held as a committed amount in any one tranche must not exceed £2.

BANK, CREDIT AND RESIDUE METERS

7.3 Credit includes all committed amounts derived from: coins and tokens inserted into category D legacy machines; coins and banknotes inserted into category C legacy machines; or coins, banknotes, smartcards and tokens inserted into category B3 & B4 legacy machines.
Residue includes all sums inserted into the machine, using banknotes or smartcards, which are not committed to Credit.
Bank includes all winnings and, for those category B3 & B4 legacy machines which display Bank and Credit only, it also includes the value of the Residue.
Category C, B3 & B4 legacy machines must record any deposited sums not committed to Credit as Residue, otherwise up to a maximum of £2 may be committed directly to the Credit either from a smartcard in the case of Category B3 & B4 legacy machines, or from a banknote in which case the uncommitted portion of the banknote value must be paid out to the player immediately.
The Bank and Residue values must be available for collection by the player, but the Credit balance need not except in the case of a category B3 & B4 legacy machine played using a smartcard when the value of any unplayable committed amount originating from the smartcard must be available for transfer back to the smartcard (subject to capacity).
Any Residue and Bank displays may contain monetary values which may exceed the statutory maximum prize for the category of machine.
A Credit display does not need to be shown as a monetary value and may exceed the statutory maximum prize for the category of machine.

MINIMUM COMMITMENT FOR PLAY

7.4 There is no requirement for category B3, B4 or C legacy machines to be capable of accepting money in any form which would allow the player to be able to pay a single charge for use only. But the maximum sum for any committed payment must be £2.

SMARTCARDS IN CATEGORY B3 & B4 LEGACY MACHINES

7.5 Those portions of a Bank or Residue, and any portion of the Credit which is too small to pay a charge for use, that either originated from a smartcard or (in the case of a Bank or Residue) represent winnings that resulted form staking credits which originated from a smartcard, must be paid back to the smartcard if capacity allows. No other portions of these meters may be paid to the smartcard.

A facility must be provided by the machine to show players what credits their smartcards hold without requiring credits to be used to pay a charge for use. The contents of the smartcard must be shown on a display until either the player transfers money from the smartcard or withdraws the smartcard. This display may show values greater than the statutory maximum prize allowed for the category of machine when operating in this mode. When being used to display the contents of the smartcard only, the machine must not offer any inducement for the player to make a committed payment.

A smartcard must have a maximum monetary capacity determined by the machine operator which reflects both the need for adequate security and the modes of operation required.

Upon completion of any game in respect of which the charge for use was paid for by use of a smartcard, the machine must display the value remaining on the smartcard on a suitable display. The player must then be able to:

(i) withdraw the card without transferring any money from the card;

(ii) transfer the appropriate portion of the Bank and/or Residue to the smartcard (subject to capacity), if this option is offered, without transferring any money from the smartcard;

(iii) press either the Transfer or Start button to transfer up to a maximum of £20 from the smartcard to the Bank or Residue of which up to £2 may be a committed payment automatically transferred to the Credit. Alternatively, up to a maximum of £2 may be transferred directly from the smartcard to the Credit without transferring any value to the Bank or Residue from the smartcard.

The player may at any time make a committed payment of up to £2 to Credit by pressing a transfer button provided for that purpose.

he maximum sum which may be transferred from a smartcard before it is withdrawn from the machine and re-inserted is £20. But unless the Bank, Residue or Credit limit would otherwise be reached, there is no restriction on the number of times a smartcard may be withdrawn and re-inserted.

BANKNOTES INSERTED INTO CATEGORY B3 B4 & C LEGACY MACHINES

7.6 The largest banknote which may be inserted is a £20 note.

The value of banknotes inserted may either be credited wholly to the Residue (or Bank in the case of a category B3 or B4 legacy machine) from which up to £2 may be automatically transferred as a committed payment to Credit; or be credited up to £2 to the Credit with immediate payout of the remainder.

A player may at any time make a committed payment of up to £2 to the Credit by pressing a Transfer button provided for that purpose.

Provided the Bank, Residue or Credit meter limits are not reached, there is no restriction on the number of banknotes which may be inserted at any one time.

TRANSFERRING FROM THE BANK TO CREDIT IN CATEGORY B3 AND B4 LEGACY MACHINES

7.7 Players may choose to commit up to £2 from the Bank to the Credit for further play by pressing a Transfer button provided for that purpose at any time.
Provided the Credit limit is not reached, there is no restriction on the number of times the Transfer button may be pressed at any time.

TRANSFER BUTTON

7.8 Where the Transfer button is also used to start a game, but there are insufficient credits to do so, then the change of the function of the button must be made clear to the player.

COLLECTING THE BANK, RESIDUE AND CREDIT

7.9 The player may collect whole pound values of either all or part of the Bank and the Residue at any reasonable time by pressing a button provided for this purpose.
In the case of category B3 & B4 legacy machines, if a smartcard is present with sufficient capacity, or hand-pay has been used then the entire value of the appropriate portion of the Bank and Residue together with any committed amount which is too small to pay a charge for use originating from the smartcard must be available for transfer back to the smartcard or payment to the player as the case may be.
A category C legacy machine may pay out in coins and banknotes.
For amounts other than those derived from using a smartcard, which must be paid to the smartcard, a category B3 or B4 legacy machine may payout in any suitable combination of coins, banknotes, tokens, cheques, and credit notes. In addition, machine payments may be made by site staff (hand-pay) on behalf of the machine provided the machine records that this process has been completed.
In the case of a category B3 or B4 legacy machine, if the smartcard does not have sufficient capacity to accept the whole of the amount to be paid, then either all or part of the payment must be made using coins, banknotes or a cheque. This may be limited to whole pound portions unless hand-pay is used.
In the event of the Bank or Residue containing cash which cannot be delivered by the machine for any reason, then the un-payable amount (which must be less than £1) may be retained by the machine for further play or for the benefit of the next player, and the machine must incorporate on its face, clearly visible to the player, a statement in the following form:

THIS MACHINE PAYS £1 COINS ONLY

ANY UNPAYABLE AMOUNTS WILL BE RETAINED FOR FUTURE USE

These requirements were notified in draft to the European Commission in accordance with Directive 98/34/EC, as amended by Directive 98/48/EC
Gambling Commission June 2007

IMPLEMENTATION ANNEXES TO GAMING MACHINE STANDARDS FOR CATEGORIES A & B1, B2, B3 & B4, C & D AND SERVER NETWORKED AND DOWNLOADABLE GAMES
July 2007

1 INTRODUCTION

6.2580 1.1 The machine standards for categories A and B1, B2, B3 and B4, C and D and Server Networked and Downloadable games published on 1 June 2007 by the

Gambling Commission stated that the standards would come into force for the gaming machines in the respective categories supplied or sited within Great Britain from 1 September 2007, subject to the Implementation Annex for each of the standards. This document includes the implementation annex for each set of standards. Each implementation annex identifies those requirements of the standard which will come into force on various dates in the period 1 September 2007 to 1 September 2008.

1.2 The Commission considers that some parts of the industry will not be able to comply with the new standards in full by 1 September 2007. The implementation annexes reflect this. A different approach is taken for category A, B1 and B2 compared to B3, B4, C and D, but the arrangements will give all parts of the industry between six months and one year to prepare for the full implementation of these standards.

1.3 The Commission will publish separately a document outlining the testing strategy for compliance with the standards.

1.4 The Commission has sought views from industry representative bodies before publishing this document.

2 MACHINE STANDARDS CATEGORIES A & B1: IMPLEMENTATION ANNEX

2.1 Category A and B1 gaming machines manufactured before 1 March 2008 will need to comply with all parts of the relevant standard by 1 September 2008. Category A and B1 gaming machines manufactured from 1 March 2008 will need to comply with the all parts of the relevant standard before they are supplied into the market.

3 MACHINE STANDARDS CATEGORY B2: IMPLEMENTATION ANNEX

3.1 Category B2 gaming machines manufactured before 1 March 2008 will need to comply with all parts of the relevant standard by 1 September 2008. Category B2 gaming machines manufactured from 1 March 2008 will need to comply with the all parts of the relevant standard before they are supplied into the market.

4 MACHINE STANDARDS CATEGORIES B3 & B4: IMPLEMENTATION ANNEX

4.1 Category B3 and B4 machines will need to comply with most sections of the standards on 1 September 2007. The table below sets out which sections will not come into force at 1 September 2007 and at what date each of those sections will come into force.

Section	Requirement	Coming into force date
Section 2	**Software requirements**	
2.1	Control program authentication requirements	31 August 2008
2.5	Last game recall	31 August 2008
2.6	Test/diagnostic mode	31 August 2008
2.7	Software verification	31 August 2008
Section 3	**Critical memory requirements**	
3.1	Contents of critical memory	31 August 2008
3.2	Maintenance of critical memory	31 August 2008
3.3	Program memory, critical memory and non-volatile devices used to store program memory	31 August 2008

Section	Requirement	Coming into force date
3.4	Unrecoverable critical memory	31 August 2008
3.5	Function of critical memory reset	31 August 2008
Section 6	**Specific error conditions and alert requirements**	
6.1	General alert conditions	31 August 2008
Section 7	**Meter requirements**	
Part of 7.1	The second sentence of this requirement (which states that 'The player shall have the option to view any funds held in such a [credit or play] meter as a monetary value.') (For the avoidance of doubt the first sentence of the requirement will come into force on 1 September 2007.)	31 August 2008

5 MACHINE STANDARDS CATEGORIES C & D: IMPLEMENTATION ANNEX

5.1 Category C and D machines will need to comply with most sections of the standards on 1 September 2007. The table below sets out which sections will not come into force at 1 September 2007 and at what date each of those sections will come into force.

Section	Requirement	Coming into force date
Section 2	**Software requirements**	
2.1	Control program authentication requirements	31 August 2008
2.5	Last game recall	31 August 2008
2.6	Test/diagnostic mode	31 August 2008
2.7	Software verification	31 August 2008
Section 3	**Critical memory requirements**	
3.1	Contents of critical memory	31 August 2008
3.2	Maintenance of critical memory	31 August 2008
3.3	Program memory, critical memory and non-volatile devices used to store program memory	31 August 2008
3.4	Unrecoverable critical memory	31 August 2008
3.5	Function of critical memory reset	31 August 2008
Section 6	**Specific error conditions and alert requirements**	
6.1	General alert conditions	31 August 2008

Section 7	Meter requirements	
Part of 7.1	The second sentence of this requirement (which states that 'The player shall have the option to view any funds held in such a [credit or play] meter as a monetary value.') (For the avoidance of doubt the first sentence of the requirement will come into force on 1 September 2007.)	31 August 2008

6 MACHINE STANDARDS CATEGORY SERVER NETWORKED AND DOWNLOADABLE: IMPLEMENTATION ANNEX

6.1 Server Networked and Downloadable category gaming machines manufactured before 1 March 2008 will need to comply with all parts of the relevant standard by 1 September 2008. Server Networked and Downloadable category gaming machines manufactured from 1 March 2008 will need to comply with the all parts of the relevant standard before they are supplied into the market.

Gambling Commission July 2007

GAMING AND GAMING MACHINES IN PUBS AND OTHER ALCOHOL-LICENSED PREMISES UNDER THE GAMBLING ACT 2005 – WHICH PREMISES ARE ELIGIBLE TO PROVIDE GAMING?

6.2581 Any premises that have an alcohol licence, and which have a bar at which alcohol is served for consumption on the premises without a requirement that alcohol is served only with food.

WHAT ABOUT CLUBS?

There are separate provisions covering gaming in clubs and miners' welfare institutes – please see the separate DCMS fact sheet.

What kind of gaming can pubs and other eligible premises provide?

Section 279 of the Gambling Act allows pubs and other eligible premises to provide what the Act calls "exempt gaming". There are a number of conditions:

it must be **equal chance gaming** (examples would be bingo, bridge and certain poker games);

stakes and prizes must comply with the limits prescribed in regulations;

no amount may be deducted or levied from amounts staked or won;

no participation fees may be charged;

the games played may only take place on one set of premises, ie there may not be any linking of games between premises; and

children and young people must be excluded from participation.

WHAT LIMITS ARE THERE ON STAKES AND PRIZES?

Different limits apply to different types of gaming.

For dominoes and cribbage there are no limits on either stakes or prizes.

For all other types of equal chance gaming there is a limit on stakes of £5 per person, per game.

For **poker**, a stakes limit of £5 per player **per game** (n.b. not per hand) applies, and the aggregate stakes limit for pub poker is £100 per day for each premises. So, for example, a pub could run a daily poker game involving 20 players staking £5 each. The maximum prize for a game of poker played in a pub is also £100.

WHAT ABOUT PUB BINGO?

Pubs that wish to provide facilities for bingo may do so under the Act's exempt gaming provisions. The following rules apply:

- the maximum amount that may be staked by a player in a game of bingo is £5;
- no amounts may be deducted from sums staked or won;
- players may not be charged a fee for taking part;
- there should be no linking of games between premises; and,
- nobody under 18 may participate.

As with clubs, pubs that wish to offer high turnover bingo (ie where stakes or prizes exceed £2000 per week) will require a bingo operating licence from the Gambling Commission. See the Commission's website (details above) for further information.

CAN PUBS CHARGE CUSTOMERS FOR TAKING PART IN GAMING, OR MAKE DEDUCTIONS FROM STAKES OR PRIZES?

No charges or deductions may be made.

CAN A PUB CHARGE A MEMBERSHIP FEE FOR GAMBLING?

No – under section 344(3) of the Act any membership fee charged in these circumstances would be regarded as a participation fee.

DO PUBS NEED A GAMBLING PERMIT OR LICENCE?

No licence or permit is required for pubs or other eligible premises providing gaming under the exempt gaming provisions (see above).

WHAT IF A PUB ONLY WANTS TO PROVIDE GAMING MACHINES?

Under section 282 of the Act alcohol-licensed premises are entitled to a maximum of two gaming machines (each of which may be category C or D) without the need for a permit or licence. To exercise this entitlement the person who holds the relevant alcohol licence should notify their local licensing authority of their intention to make gaming machines available, and pay the required notification fee. If a licensee wishes to make more than two gaming machines available he will need to obtain a **licensed premises gaming machine permit**, once again from the local licensing authority. There are a number of statutory conditions relating to the way in which gaming machines are used, and licensees will also need to ensure compliance with the Gambling Commission's code of practice on the location and operation of gaming machines. See the Commission's website – www.gamblingcommission.gov.uk — for further details.

WHAT IS THE MAXIMUM NUMBER OF GAMING MACHINES THAT A PUB MAY HAVE?

There is no statutory limit on the number of gaming machines that individual premises may apply for, but the licensing authority has the discretion to restrict the number of machines on individual premises (or change the category of the machines), having regard to the licensing objectives of the Gambling Act.

WHAT HAPPENS IF A PUB BREAKS THE RULES?

Licensees will be expected to monitor any gaming that takes place on their premises, and take all reasonable steps to ensure that it complies with the statutory requirements, including the limits on stakes and prizes. Under section 310(2) of the Act, a constable, Gambling Commission enforcement officer or authorised local authority officer may enter premises that hold an on-premises alcohol licence in order to determine whether gaming carried on there satisfies the statutory conditions. Any breach of those conditions in respect of particular premises would leave them liable to the loss of their entitlement to offer gaming and/or gaming machines, and criminal prosecution. Where a breach of the Gambling Act has implications for alcohol licensing objectives it may, as with breaches of other laws, be taken into account by licensing authorities and others in the exercise of their functions under the relevant legislation.

IS PRACTICAL ADVICE AVAILABLE ABOUT HOW TO OPERATE GAMING IN PUBS AND OTHER ELIGIBLE PREMISES?

The Gambling Commission has issued a statutory code of practice on gaming in clubs and alcohol-licensed premises, which is available from its website (see above).

NB. This fact sheet is intended to provide a general explanation of the regulatory regime under the Gambling Act 2005 and its subordinate legislation, and does not deal with every detail of the legislative provisions, or with the individual circumstances of a particular case. This fact sheet does not constitute legal advice and is not a substitute for the relevant legislative provisions. If you are in any doubt about the legality of any gambling activities that you intend to promote or for which you intend to provide facilities, you are strongly advised to seek independent legal advice.

DCMS
August 2007

REGISTRATION OF LEGACY GAMING MACHINES
August 2007

1 INTRODUCTION

6.2585 1.1 The Gambling Commission (the Commission) requires a register of legacy machines in order to:

- prevent further legacy machines being produced after 1 September 2007; and
- differentiate legacy machines from new machines which will be compliant with the technical standards that apply post 1 September.

1.2 The legacy standards require prescribed details of legacy machines to be registered with the Commission.

2 DEFINITION OF LEGACY MACHINES AND WHAT IT MEANS FOR OPERATORS

2.1 The definition of a legacy machine, which is set out in the legacy machine standards, is as follows:

A gaming machine, as defined by section 235 of the Gambling Act 2005 (the 2005 Act), is a legacy machine, if:

- *it is of category B3, B4, C or D;*
- *it was available for lawful use on premises within Great Britain on 31 August 2007 (whether as a 'Jackpot' machine under the provisions of section 31 Gaming Act 1968 or as an 'amusement with prizes' machine under the provisions of section 34 of that Act);*

- *it is so configured as to comply with any regulations made under section 240 of the 2005 Act which apply to it; and*
- *prescribed details of it have been registered with the Gambling Commission by 31 August 2007.*

This deadline has now changed, please see section 3 – Timing of Information for details.

2.2 This means that a B3, B4, C, or D (other than non-complex category D) gaming machine sited or in stock at a manufacturer or operator at 31 August 2007 is a legacy machine if it meets the other legacy requirements set out above. Non-complex category D machines (eg pushers and cranes) have specific standards that apply and do not need to be registered with the Commission as legacy machines.

2.3 The machines can be moved to other premises and be sold between operators. This will enable machines to be downgraded through the categories, for example being changed from a category C in a pub, to a category D in a family entertainment centre (where only the stakes and prizes will be different).

2.4 The machines can remain as legacy machines unless they are modified in order to take advantage of the new freedoms (eg ability to accept cash and non-cash payments or single metering); or unless they are substantially altered so that they effectively become new machines. If they are modified in this way, they will cease to be legacy machines and thus will automatically be required to meet the relevant new technical standards in full. They can be adapted to comply with any regulatory or other legislative requirements without losing their legacy status.

2.5 The Commission believes that this position will allow machines to move out of the market over time rather than having to be removed by 1 September 2007, whilst also ensuring that only those genuinely in the market at the end of August and compliant with the legacy standards will be permitted to continue to operate.

3 TIMING OF INFORMATION

3.1 The Commission requires the situation as at 31 August to be recorded on the register. This means that all machines for which legacy status is claimed that were supplied or owned by an individual or business at that date, even if they are subsequently sold, should be recorded. The information must be provided to the Commission (and any new identifier required displayed on the machine) by 1 December 2007. This is a change from the legacy machine technical standards which stated that prescribed details of each legacy machine should be registered with the Commission by 31 August 2007.

3.2 The Commission considers that it should be possible for the vast majority of legacy machines to be labelled and registered by 1 December 2007. There may be a minority of smaller suppliers where this may be more difficult. The Commission is willing to consider requests for extensions to this deadline, but cannot guarantee they will be granted.

4 THE RETURN

4.1 The owner of the machine will need to provide the return. This will often be the supplier, except where individuals or businesses own their machines outright. The Commission would prefer electronic returns, submitted in the attached spreadsheet. Electronic returns should be sent to: mailto://legacymachines@gamblingcommission.gov.uk

4.2 Written returns are also acceptable. They should be provided on a printed version of the spreadsheet or in a similar format including the same information. Written returns should be sent to:

Legacy Machines,
Compliance Administration Team
Gambling Commission
Victoria Square House
Victoria Square
Birmingham B2 4BP

LICENSEE INFORMATION

4.3 In the spreadsheet version of the return, the drop down menu asks the operator completing the return to state the type of licence the operator holds, giving options for AGC or FEC, Bingo, Casino, Manufacturer or Supplier, Non-commercial club and Other. In a further drop down menu it also asks who issued the operator's licence, giving options of the Commission, the Gaming Board or the local authority. We would prefer the Commission issued operating licence number where the person or company providing the return has one. Those providing a written return should also provide this information.

GAMING MACHINE DATA: UNIQUE IDENTIFIER

4.4 There are three options for what the unique identifier for each machine can be: the serial number of the machine, the asset number of the machine or, where those are appropriate, a new identifier based on the owner's postcode, address number and a five digit number unique to that machine.
4.5 The Commission's preference is for the full machine serial number to be used as the unique identifier. However, we understand that some suppliers do not use the full serial number on their computer systems and that this information is not easily provided. Where it is easier to provide, the Commission is content for the asset number of the machine to be used instead, provided that number is unique to that machine (compared to other machines administered by that supplier). In both cases this number would have to be displayed on the outside of the machine. For further details, please see the section titled 'identifier on the machine'.
4.5 Where a machine does not have a serial or asset number, the supplier or owner should generate their own identifier to put on the machine and include in the register. The identifier should consist of the post code of the supplier/ owner, their business address number or name and a 5 digit number unique to each machine logged by that supplier or owner. The identifier should be entered on the return in the format B2-4BP-1-00001.

GAMING MACHINE DATA: MANUFACTURER AND GAME TITLE

4.6 We also require the name of the company that manufactured the machine and the title of the game available on the machine.

5 INFORMATION ON THE MACHINE

IDENTIFIER ON THE MACHINE

5.1 The unique identifier will need to be displayed on the outside of the machine. Most serial or asset numbers are displayed on the back of the machine and that is acceptable. It is the supplier's or owner's responsibility to ensure that the identifier on the machine matches what is on the register. Unless the identifier on the machine matches the one on the register a machine will not have legacy status.
5.2 Where a new identifier has been generated it should be displayed on a sticker in a visible position on the machine. The identifier should ideally be printed, although clear handwritten stickers are acceptable.

CATEGORY STICKER

5.3 In addition to the identifier, DCMS regulations will require each machine to display what category it is. This will need to identify if it is a legacy machine. A new identifier could be on the same sticker as this category information.
Gambling Commission August 2007

TYPICAL LICENCE CONDITIONS AND CODES OF PRACTICE FOR: OPERATORS OF CONVERTED S27 GAMING MACHINE NOTICES August 2007

INTRODUCTION

6.2586 The Gambling Act 2005 (the Act) creates new arrangements that govern the way organisations and individuals involved in gambling can operate. From September 2007, most operators who wish to run a gambling business in Britain, and certain key individuals, need to be licensed by the Commission. There are some exemptions. The Commission has developed general licence conditions and codes of practice that govern how gambling facilities are provided and managed and gambling conducted.
This document sets out an example of the relevant conditions and code provisions for holders of a *Converted s27 (gaming machine) Notice* operating licence. It does not include statutory conditions, any licence conditions imposed by the Secretary of State or any conditions the Commission might attach solely to an individual licence.
This document is intended to be a general example only and does not replace the conditions and codes which will be attached to the operating and personal licences when these are issued. It should not be considered a definitive guide. However, this licensee-specific example will, we hope, aid operators' and stakeholders' understanding about the requirements on licensees.
Individual licence holders will receive copies of the conditions and codes which apply to their particular licence when their licence is issued to them. In some cases, the licence will set out individual conditions that are specific to that operator, based on the assessment of their licence application.
The Commission has powers to prosecute operators and can impose fines on operators who breach their licence conditions or social responsibility code of practice provisions, and can take breaches of the ordinary codes of practice into account as part of a prosecution. Licence conditions and social responsibility codes of practice detail the legal obligations attached to holding an operating licence. Ordinary codes of practice detail the manner in which facilities for gambling should be provided.
Part I of this documents sets out the Licence Conditions.
Part II of this document sets out the relevant provisions of the code of practice. The text in shaded boxes comprises the 'social responsibility provisions' and covers issues including the promotion of responsible gambling and marketing. The text that is not shaded which is titled 'ordinary code provisions' covers issues including the employment of children and young people and age verification.
Where a Condition or Code provision appears in the full Licence Conditions and Codes of Practice but does not apply for this type of licence, it has not been reproduced here. Where this is the case, there may gaps in the sequential numbering of the individual conditions.
You can obtain copies of this document and the other documents mentioned above from the Commission's website, www.gamblingcommission.gov.uk or by writing to:

Gambling Commission
Victoria Square House
Victoria Square
Birmingham B2 4BP

T 0121 230 6666
F 0121 230 6720
E info@gamblingcommission.gov.uk

PART I: GAMBLING COMMISSION GENERAL LICENCE CONDITIONS

LICENCE CONDITIONS APPLICABLE TO MANUFACTURING, SUPPLYING, INSTALLING, ADAPTING, MAINTAINING OR REPAIRING A GAMING MACHINE OR A PART OF A GAMING MACHINE

1 Personal licences and qualified persons

1.1 Qualified persons

Operating licences issued to small-scale operators

In this condition the terms 'small-scale operator', 'qualifying position' and 'qualified person' have the meanings respectively ascribed to them by the Gambling Act 2005 (Definition of Small-scale Operator) Regulations 2006.

Schedule X[1] lists those individuals notified to the Commission as qualified persons.

If, whilst the licensee remains a small-scale operator, an individual begins or ceases to occupy a qualifying position in relation to the licensee, the licensee must within 28 days apply to the Commission under s104(1)(b) for amendment of the details of the licence set out in Schedule X[1].

An application for amendment under s104(1)(b) may be made in advance of an individual beginning or ceasing to occupy a qualifying position provided it specifies the date from which the change to which it relates is to be effective.

---

1 The schedules mentioned here will be attached to individual licences.

1.2 Personal licences

(a) Subject to (e) and (f) below licensees must ensure:
  (i) that each individual who occupies one of the management offices specified in (b) below in or in respect of the licensee or in connection with the licensed activities holds a personal licence authorising the performance of the functions of that office (hereafter 'a personal management licence'); and
  (ii) that at least one person occupies at least one of those offices.

(b) The specified management offices are those offices (whether or not held by a director in the case of a licensee which is a company, a partner in the case of a licensee which is a partnership or an officer of the association in the case of a licensee which is an unincorporated association) the occupier of which is by virtue of the terms of their appointment responsible for:
  - the overall management and direction of the licensee's business or affairs;
  - the licensee's finance function as head of that function;
  - the licensee's gambling regulatory compliance function as head of that function;
  - the licensee's marketing function as head of that function;
  - the licensee's information technology function as head of that function in so far as it relates to gambling-related information technology and software; or
  - oversight of the day to day management of the licensed activities at an identified number of premises licensed under Part 8 of the Act or across an identified geographical area.

(c) Licensees must take all reasonable steps to ensure that anything done in the performance of the functions of a specified management office is done in accordance with the terms and conditions of the holder's personal management licence.

(d) Where an individual is authorised by a personal licence and that licence comes under review under section 116(2) of the Act, the operating licensee must comply with any conditions subsequently imposed on that licence by the Commission about redeployment, supervision, or monitoring of the individual's work and any requirements of the Commission in respect of such matters applicable during the period of the review.

(e) Paragraphs (a) to (d) above shall not apply to a licensee for so long as the licensee is a 'small-scale operator' as defined in the Gambling Act 2005 (Definition of Small-scale Operator) Regulations 2006 ('the Regulations').

(f) During the period of 3 years commencing with the date on which a licensee ceases to be a small-scale operator paragraphs (a) to (e) above shall apply subject to the proviso that the phrase 'each individual' in paragraph (a)(i) shall not include any individual who was a 'qualified person' (as defined in the Regulations) in relation to the licensee 28 days immediately prior to the licensee ceasing to be a small-scale operator.

2 Technical standards and equipment specifications

Licensees must comply with the Commission's and with requirements set by the Commission relating to the timing and procedures for testing.

3 Financial robustness

All company licensees must notify the Commission of the name and address of any person who becomes a shareholder in the company or its holding company holding 3% or more of the issued share capital of the company or its holding company; or any existing shareholder who acquires a holding of 3% or more of the issued share capital of the company or its holding company.

In this condition 'holding company' has the meaning ascribed to that term by section 736 of the Companies Act 1985 (as amended).

14 Access to premises

Licensees must have in place and implement written policies and procedures (including staff training programmes) designed to ensure that their staff co-operate with the Commission's enforcement officers in the proper performance of their compliance functions and are made aware of those officers' rights of entry to premises contained in Part 15 of the Act.

15 Information requirements

15.1 REPORTING SUSPICION OF OFFENCES ETC

Licensees must provide the Commission with any information that they suspect may relate to the commission of an offence under the Act, including an offence resulting from a breach of a licence condition or a code provision having the effect of a licence condition.

15.2 REPORTING 'KEY EVENTS'

Licensees must notify the Commission of the occurrence of any of the following key events as soon as reasonably practicable and in any event within 5 working days of its occurrence:

- in the case of licensees which are companies, their (or any group company of theirs) being placed in liquidation, administration or receivership: in this condition a 'group company' is any subsidiary or holding company of the licensee – as those terms are defined in s736 Companies Act 1985 or any statutory modification or re-enactment thereof – and any subsidiary of such holding company;
- in the case of a licensee who is an individual (or a partner in a partnership licensee) their becoming bankrupt within the meaning of section 381 of the Insolvency Act 1986 or sequestration of their estate under section 12(1) of the Bankruptcy (Scotland) Act 1985;
- where the licensee is required to have its accounts independently audited, any unplanned change of auditor including a change prompted by a dispute or resulting from auditors being unable or unwilling to sign an audit certificate;
- the departure from the licensee's business of any holder of a personal management licence, other than those with oversight of the day to day management of licensed premises of a licensee operating more than 4 licensed premises;
- any reduction in the licensee's employed staff by more than 10% provided that represents at least 3 individuals;
- the acquisition or disposal of gambling premises or pitches;
- in the case of corporate licensees, the disposal or acquisition of any group company;
- the disposal of assets to the value of 10% or more of the licensee's total net assets;
- any breach of a covenant given to a bank or other lender;
- any default in making repayment of the whole or any part of a loan on its due date;
- any court judgments remaining unpaid 14 days after the date of judgment;
- the commencement of any material litigation against the licensee;
- any instance of internal or external fraud or theft involving a sum in excess of £10,000; and
- the commencement of disciplinary action against the holder of a personal licence where the licence holder is suspended or serious misconduct is alleged.

15.3 General and Regulatory Returns

On request, licensees must provide the Commission with such information as the Commission may require about the use made of facilities provided in accordance with this licence, and the manner in which gambling authorised by this licence and the licensee's business in relation to that gambling are carried on, including in particular information about:

- the numbers of people making use of the facilities and the frequency of such use;
- the range of gambling activities provided by the licensee and the numbers of staff employed in connection with them; and
- the licensee's policies in relation to, and experiences of, problem gambling.

In particular within 28 days of the end of each quarterly period or, for those only submitting annual returns, within 42 days of the end of each annual period, licensees must submit a Regulatory Return to the Commission containing such information as the Commission may from time to time require[2, 3].

---

[2] The current forms of the sector specific returns and guidance notes for their completion are available on the Commission's website www.gamblingcommission.gov.uk and can also be obtained by writing to the Commission at Victoria Square House, Victoria Square, Birmingham B2 4BP.

[3] Paragraph replaced by LCCP, supplement 7.

PART II: GAMBLING COMMISSION CODES OF PRACTICE

CODES OF PRACTICE APPLICABLE TO MANUFACTURING, SUPPLYING, INSTALLING, ADAPTING, MAINTAINING OR REPAIRING A GAMING MACHINE OR A PART OF A GAMING MACHINE

2 Protection of children and other vulnerable persons

2.1 COMBATING PROBLEM GAMBLING

SOCIAL RESPONSIBILITY CODE PROVISION

Licensees must have and put into effect policies and procedures intended to promote socially responsible gambling.

Licensees' policies and procedures for socially responsible gambling must include but need not be confined to:

- the specific policies and procedures required by the following provisions of section 2 of this code;
- a commitment to and how they will contribute to research into the prevention and treatment of problem gambling;
- a commitment to and how they will contribute to public education on the risks of gambling and how to gamble safely; and
- a commitment to and how they will contribute to the identification of and treatment of problem gamblers.

4 Marketing

ORDINARY CODE PROVISION

Licensees should comply with the advertising codes of practice which apply to the form and media in which they advertise their gambling facilities or services.

6 Gambling licensees' staff

SOCIAL RESPONSIBILITY CODE PROVISION

Licensees must take all reasonable steps to ensure that staff involved in the provision of facilities for gambling are made aware of advice on socially responsible gambling and of where to get confidential advice should their gambling become hard to control.

Gambling Commission August 2007

CONDITIONS AND CODES OF PRACTICE APPLICABLE TO: NON-REMOTE GAMING MACHINE TECHNICAL: FULL LICENCES NON-REMOTE GAMING MACHINE TECHNICAL: SUPPLIER LICENCES NON-REMOTE GAMING MACHINE TECHNICAL: SOFTWARE LICENCES NON-REMOTE GAMBLING SOFTWARE LICENCES

October 2010

6.2590–6.2595 Your licence is subject to certain conditions and codes of practice,

these are detailed in the following pages

STATUTORY CONDITIONS ATTACHED BY VIRTUE OF THE ACT

SOCIAL RESPONSIBILITY

This licence is subject to a condition that the licensee ensures compliance with any relevant social responsibility provision of a code of practice issued by the Commission. The social responsibility provisions that are relevant to the activities authorised by this licence are set out in the section entitled Codes of Practice.
(Sections 24 and 82(1) Gambling Act 2005)

COMMISSION GENERAL CONDITIONS

The Commission's complete suite of Licence Conditions to be attached to operating licences pursuant to section 75 of the Act includes some conditions which may not apply to your licence. Where that is the case the irrelevant conditions have not been reproduced below. The full list of Licence Conditions and Codes of Practice are contained within the Commission's Publication "Licence Conditions and Codes of Practice"

QUALIFIED PERSONS AND PERSONAL LICENCES

Qualified persons

THE FOLLOWING CONDITION APPLIES TO ALL OPERATING LICENCES ISSUED TO SMALL-SCALE OPERATORS

In this condition the terms 'small-scale operator', 'qualifying position' and 'qualified person' have the meanings respectively ascribed to them by the Gambling Act 2005 (Definition of Small-scale Operator) Regulations 2006.
Schedule X[1] lists those individuals notified to the Commission as qualified persons.
If, whilst the licensee remains a small-scale operator, an individual begins or ceases to occupy a qualifying position in relation to the licensee, the licensee must within 28 days apply to the Commission under s 104(1)(b) for amendment of the details of the licence set out in Schedule X[1].
An application for amendment under s 104(1)(b) may be made in advance of an individual beginning or ceasing to occupy a qualifying position provided it specifies the date from which the change to which it relates is to be effective.

[1] The schedules mentioned here will be attached to individual licences.

Personal licences

(a) Subject to (e) and (f) below licensees must ensure:
  (i) that each individual who occupies one of the management offices specified in (b) below in or in respect of the licensee or in connection with the licensed activities holds a personal licence authorising the performance of the functions of that office (hereafter 'a personal management licence')
  (ii) that at least one person occupies at least one of those offices.
(b) The specified management offices are those offices (whether or not held by a director in the case of a licensee which is a company, a partner in the case of a licensee which is a partnership or an officer of the association in the case of a licensee which is an unincorporated association) the occupier of which is by virtue of the terms of their appointment responsible for:
  - the overall management and direction of the licensee's business or affairs

- the licensee's finance function as head of that function
- the licensee's gambling regulatory compliance function as head of that function
- the licensee's marketing function as head of that function
- the licensee's information technology function as head of that function in so far as it relates to gambling-related information technology and software
- oversight of the day to day management of the licensed activities at an identified number of premises licensed under Part 8 of the Act or across an identified geographical area
- in the case of casino and bingo licences only, oversight of the day to day management of a single set of premises licensed under Part 8 of the Act.

(c) Licensees must take all reasonable steps to ensure that anything done in the performance of the functions of a specified management office is done in accordance with the terms and conditions of the holder's personal management licence.

(d) Where an individual is authorised by a personal licence and that licence comes under review under section 116(2) of the Act, the operating licensee must comply with any conditions subsequently imposed on that licence by the Commission about redeployment, supervision, or monitoring of the individual's work and any requirements of the Commission in respect of such matters applicable during the period of the review.

(e) Paragraphs (a) to (d) above shall not apply to a licensee for so long as the licensee is a 'small-scale operator' as defined in the Gambling Act 2005 (Definition of Small-scale Operator) Regulations 2006 ('the Regulations').

(f) During the period of 3 years commencing with the date on which a licensee ceases to be a small-scale operator paragraphs (a) to (e) above shall apply subject to the proviso that the phrase 'each individual' in paragraph (a)(i) shall not include any individual who was a 'qualified person' (as defined in the Regulations) in relation to the licensee 28 days immediately prior to the licensee ceasing to be a small-scale operator.

TECHNICAL STANDARDS AND EQUIPMENT SPECIFICATIONS

Licensees must comply with the Commission's technical standards and with requirements set by the Commission relating to the timing and procedures for testing.

FINANCIAL ROBUSTNESS

Notification of shareholders

All company licensees must notify the Commission of the name and address of any person who becomes a shareholder in the company or its holding company holding 3% or more of the issued share capital of the company or its holding company; or any existing shareholder who acquires a holding of 3% or more of the issued share capital of the company or its holding company.

In this condition 'holding company' has the meaning ascribed to that term by section 1159 of the Companies Act 2006 or any statutory modification or re-enactment thereof.

DISPLAY OF LICENSED STATUS

Licensees offering the supply of gaming machines or gambling software on websites must:

(a) display the following information on the first page of the website which offers gaming machines or gambling software in reliance on the licence:

   (i) a statement that they are licensed and regulated by the Gambling Commission;
   (ii) their licence number; and
   (iii) a link to the Commission's website;

(b) display at least the information at (i) above on each page of the website which offers gaming machines or gambling software in reliance on the licence.

(c) where they offer on pages of, or by means of a link from, their website, the supply of gaming machines or gambling software which are not provided in reliance on their licence, clearly distinguish those products which are regulated by the Commission from those which are not.

ACCESS TO PREMISES

Licensees must have and put into effect policies and procedures (including staff training programmes) designed to ensure that their staff co-operate with the Commission's enforcement officers in the proper performance of their compliance functions and are made aware of those officers' rights of entry to premises contained in Part 15 of the Act.

INFORMATION REQUIREMENTS

Reporting suspicion of offences etc

Licensees must provide the Commission with any information that they know relates to or suspect may relate to the commission of an offence under the Act, including an offence resulting from a breach of a licence condition or a code provision having the effect of a licence condition.

Reporting 'Key Events'

A key event is an event that could have a significant impact on the nature or structure of a licensee's business. Licensees must notify the Commission of the occurrence of any of the following key events as soon as reasonably practicable and in any event within five working days of the licensee becoming aware of the event's occurrence[2].

- in the case of licensees which are companies, a petition being presented for their winding up or the winding up of any group company of theirs, or they or any group company being placed in administration or receivership: in this condition a 'group company' is any subsidiary or holding company of the licensee – as those terms are defined in section 1159 of the Companies Act 2006 or any statutory modification or re-enactment thereof – and any subsidiary of such holding company
- in the case of a licensee who is an individual (or a partner in a partnership licensee) their being presented with a petition for their bankruptcy or sequestration or their entering into an individual voluntary agreement
- where the licensee is required to have their accounts independently audited, any unplanned change of auditor including a change prompted by a dispute or resulting from auditors being unable or unwilling to sign an unqualified audit report
- the departure from the licensee's business of any person occupying a 'qualifying position' as defined by Regulation 2(2) of the Gambling Act 2005 (Definition of Small-scale Operator) Regulations 2006
- any breach of a covenant given to a bank or other lender
- any default in making repayment of the whole or any part of a loan on its due date
- any court judgments remaining unpaid 14 days after the date of judgment
- the commencement of any material litigation against the licensee
- the imposition of a disciplinary sanction, including dismissal, against the holder of a personal licence or a person occupying a qualifying position for gross

misconduct; or the resignation of a personal licence holder or person occupying a qualifying position following commencement of disciplinary proceedings in respect of gross misconduct against that person
- in the case of remote gambling, the commencement or cessation of trading on website domains (including WAP URLs) or broadcast media through which the licensee provides gambling facilities.

---

[2] Key events can be reported securely online at the Commission's website at www.gamblingcommission.gov.uk or by email to key.events@gamblingcommission.gov.uk or posted to Key Events, Compliance Administration Team, Gambling Commission, Victoria Square House, Victoria Square, Birmingham B2 4BP

General and Regulatory Returns

On request, licensees must provide the Commission with such information as the Commission may require about the use made of facilities provided in accordance with this licence, and the manner in which gambling authorised by this licence and the licensee's business in relation to that gambling are carried on, including in particular information about:
- the numbers of people making use of the facilities and the frequency of such use
- the range of gambling activities provided by the licensee and the numbers of staff employed in connection with them
- the licensee's policies in relation to, and experiences of, problem gambling.

In particular within 28 days of the end of each quarterly period or, for those only submitting annual returns, within 42 days of the end of each annual period, licensees must submit a Regulatory Return to the Commission containing such information as the Commission may from time to time require[3].

---

[3] Regulatory returns can be submitted securely online at the Commission's website at www.gamblingcommission.gov.uk For operators unable to access this system, the forms and a guide to completing them can be requested from the Commission and returned by email to Regulatory.Returns@gamblingcommission.gov.uk or by post to Regulatory Returns, Compliance Administration Team, Gambling Commission, Victoria Square House, Victoria Square, Birmingham, B2 4BP

SECRETARY OF STATE GENERAL CONDITIONS

None at present

CODES OF PRACTICE

Introduction

This is the Commission's principal code of practice, issued under section 24 of the Gambling Act 2005, as revised with effect from 1 January 2009. There are two types of provision in the code:
- social responsibility provisions: compliance with these is a condition of licences; therefore any breach of them by an operator may lead the Commission to review the operator's licence with a view to suspension, revocation or the imposition of a financial penalty and would also expose the operator to the risk of prosecution; and
- ordinary code provisions: these do not have the status of licence conditions, but are admissible in evidence in criminal or civil proceedings and must be taken into account in any case in which the court or tribunal think them relevant and by the Commission in the exercise of its functions. Any breach of ordinary code provisions by an operator may be taken into account by the Commission on a

licence review, but cannot lead to imposition of a financial penalty. These code provisions are in italics in this section and generally set out good practice in these areas.

Financial requirements

ORDINARY CODE PROVISION

In order to help prevent activities related to money laundering licensees should take into account the Commission's advice on the Proceeds of Crime Act 2002, *Duties and responsibilities under the Proceeds of Crime Act 2002. Advice for operators (excluding casino operators).*

Protection of children and other vulnerable persons

COMBATING PROBLEM GAMBLING

SOCIAL RESPONSIBILITY CODE PROVISION

Licensees must have and put into effect policies and procedures intended to promote socially responsible gambling.

Licensees' policies and procedures for socially responsible gambling must include but need not be confined to:

- the specific policies and procedures required by the following provisions of section 2 of this code
- a commitment to and how they will contribute to research into the prevention and treatment of problem gambling
- a commitment to and how they will contribute to public education on the risks of gambling and how to gamble safely
- a commitment to and how they will contribute to the identification and treatment of problem gamblers.

Marketing

ORDINARY CODE PROVISION

All advertising of gambling products and services should be undertaken in a socially responsible manner. In particular, licensees should comply with the advertising codes of practice which apply to the form and media in which they advertise their gambling facilities or services, and for media not explicitly covered should apply the principles included in these codes of practice as if they were explicitly covered. Licensees should also follow any relevant industry code of practice on advertising.

However, the particular restriction on allowing people aged under 25 to appear in adverts need not be applied to point of sale advertising material, provided that the images used depict the sporting activity that may be gambled on and not the activity of gambling itself and do not offend any other aspect of the advertising codes.

Gambling licensees' staff

SOCIAL RESPONSIBILITY CODE PROVISION

Licensees must take all reasonable steps to ensure that staff involved in the provision of facilities for gambling are made aware of advice on socially responsible gambling and of where to get confidential advice should their gambling become hard to control.

Information requirements

Ordinary code provision

The Commission expects licensees to work with the Commission in an open and cooperative way and to inform the Commission of any matters that the Commission would reasonably need to be aware of in exercising its regulatory functions. These are matters that will have a material impact on the licensee's business or on the licensee's ability to conduct its business. Such matters, which should be notified to the Commission as soon as reasonably practicable[4], include the following:

- the departure from the licensee's business of any person named in the licence application, or that person's successor, who holds a personal management licence, but who does not occupy a 'qualifying position'
- any reduction in the number of staff employed by the licensee where that has a material impact on the licensee's business
- the acquisition or disposal by the licensee of gambling premises or pitches where that has a material impact on the size or nature of the licensee's business
- in the case of corporate licensees, the disposal or acquisition of any group company where that has a material impact on the licensee's ability to conduct its business
- any disposal of the licensee's assets where that has a material impact on the licensee's business
- any investigation by a professional, statutory, regulatory or government body into the licensee's activities, or the activities in relation to the licensed entity of a personal licence holder or a person occupying a qualifying position employed by them, where such an investigation could result in the imposition of a sanction or penalty which, if imposed, could reasonably be expected to raise doubts about the licensee's continued suitability to hold a Gambling Commission licence
- any instance of criminal activity, including repeated instances of small-scale theft or fraud, where that has a material impact on the licensee's business
- any major breach in the licensee's information security where that adversely affects the confidentiality of customer data or prevents customers from accessing their accounts for a substantial period of time
- any other matters that have a material impact on the licensee's business or on the licensee's ability to conduct its business.

---

[4] These matters can be reported securely online at the Commission's website at www.gambling-commission.gov.uk or by email to key.events@gamblingcommission.gov.uk or posted to Key Events, Compliance Administration Team, Gambling Commission, Victoria Square House, Victoria Square, Birmingham, B2 4BP

Gambling Commission October 2010

CONDITIONS AND CODES OF PRACTICE APPLICABLE TO: REMOTE GAMING MACHINE TECHNICAL: FULL LICENCES REMOTE GAMING MACHINE TECHNICAL: SUPPLIER LICENCES REMOTE GAMING MACHINE TECHNICAL: SOFTWARE LICENCES REMOTE GAMBLING SOFTWARE LICENCES REMOTE GAMING MACHINE TECHNICAL: FULL ANCILLARY LICENCES REMOTE GAMING MACHINE TECHNICAL: SUPPLIER ANCILLARY LICENCES REMOTE GAMING MACHINE TECHNICAL: SOFTWARE ANCILLARY LICENCES REMOTE GAMBLING SOFTWARE ANCILLARY LICENCES

October 2010

6.2600 Your licence is subject to certain conditions and codes of practice, these are detailed in the following pages

STATUTORY CONDITIONS ATTACHED BY VIRTUE OF THE ACT

SOCIAL RESPONSIBILITY

This licence is subject to a condition that the licensee ensures compliance with any relevant social responsibility provision of a code of practice issued by the Commission. The social responsibility provisions that are relevant to the activities authorised by this licence are set out in the section entitled Codes of Practice.

(Sections 24 and 82(1) Gambling Act 2005)

COMMISSION GENERAL CONDITIONS

The Commission's complete suite of Licence Conditions to be attached to operating licences pursuant to section 75 of the Act includes some conditions which may not apply to your licence. Where that is the case the irrelevant conditions have not been reproduced below. The full list of Licence Conditions and Codes of Practice are contained within the Commission's Publication "Licence Conditions and Codes of Practice"

QUALIFIED PERSONS AND PERSONAL LICENCES

Qualified persons

THE FOLLOWING CONDITION APPLIES TO ALL REMOTE OPERATING LICENCES, EXCEPT ANCILLARY REMOTE LICENCES, ISSUED TO SMALL-SCALE OPERATORS

In this condition the terms 'small-scale operator', 'qualifying position' and 'qualified person' have the meanings respectively ascribed to them by the Gambling Act 2005 (Definition of Small-scale Operator) Regulations 2006.

Schedule X[1] lists those individuals notified to the Commission as qualified persons.

If, whilst the licensee remains a small-scale operator, an individual begins or ceases to occupy a qualifying position in relation to the licensee, the licensee must within 28 days apply to the Commission under s 104(1)(b) for amendment of the details of the licence set out in Schedule X[1].

An application for amendment under s 104(1)(b) may be made in advance of an individual beginning or ceasing to occupy a qualifying position provided it specifies the date from which the change to which it relates is to be effective.

---

1 The schedules mentioned here will be attached to individual licences.

Personal licences

THE FOLLOWING CONDITION APPLIES TO ALL REMOTE OPERATING LICENCES EXCEPT ANCILLARY REMOTE LICENCES

(a) Subject to (e) and (f) below licensees must ensure:
   (i) that each individual who occupies one of the management offices specified in (b) below in or in respect of the licensee or in connection with the licensed activities holds a personal licence authorising the performance of the functions of that office (hereafter 'a personal management licence')
   (ii) that at least one person occupies at least one of those offices.

(b) The specified management offices are those offices (whether or not held by a director in the case of a licensee which is a company, a partner in the case of a licensee which is a partnership or an officer of the association in the case of a licensee which is an unincorporated association) the occupier of which is by virtue of the terms of their appointment responsible for:
   - the overall management and direction of the licensee's business or affairs
   - the licensee's finance function as head of that function
   - the licensee's gambling regulatory compliance function as head of that function
   - the licensee's marketing function as head of that function
   - the licensee's information technology function as head of that function in so far as it relates to gambling-related information technology and software
   - oversight of the day to day management of the licensed activities at an identified number of premises licensed under Part 8 of the Act or across an identified geographical area
   - in the case of casino and bingo licences only, oversight of the day to day management of a single set of premises licensed under Part 8 of the Act.

(c) Licensees must take all reasonable steps to ensure that anything done in the performance of the functions of a specified management office is done in accordance with the terms and conditions of the holder's personal management licence.

(d) Where an individual is authorised by a personal licence and that licence comes under review under section 116(2) of the Act, the operating licensee must comply with any conditions subsequently imposed on that licence by the Commission about redeployment, supervision, or monitoring of the individual's work and any requirements of the Commission in respect of such matters applicable during the period of the review.

(e) Paragraphs (a) to (d) above shall not apply to a licensee for so long as the licensee is a 'small-scale operator' as defined in the Gambling Act 2005 (Definition of Small-scale Operator) Regulations 2006 ('the Regulations').

(f) During the period of 3 years commencing with the date on which a licensee ceases to be a small-scale operator paragraphs (a) to (e) above shall apply subject to the proviso that the phrase 'each individual' in paragraph (a)(i) shall not include any individual who was a 'qualified person' (as defined in the Regulations) in relation to the licensee 28 days immediately prior to the licensee ceasing to be a small-scale operator.

TECHNICAL STANDARDS AND EQUIPMENT SPECIFICATIONS

Licensees must comply with the Commission's technical standards and with requirements set by the Commission relating to the timing and procedures for testing.

FINANCIAL ROBUSTNESS

Notification of shareholders

THE FOLLOWING CONDITION APPLIES TO ALL REMOTE OPERATING LICENCES EXCEPT ANCILLARY REMOTE LICENCES

All company licensees must notify the Commission of the name and address of any person who becomes a shareholder in the company or its holding company holding 3% or more of the issued share capital of the company or its holding company; or any existing shareholder who acquires a holding of 3% or more of the issued share capital of the company or its holding company.

In this condition 'holding company' has the meaning ascribed to that term by section 1159 of the Companies Act 2006 or any statutory modification or re-enactment thereof.

DISPLAY OF LICENSED STATUS

Licensees offering the supply of gaming machines or gambling software on websites must:

(a) display the following information on the first page of the website which offers gaming machines or gambling software in reliance on the licence:
  (i) a statement that they are licensed and regulated by the Gambling Commission;
  (ii) their licence number; and
  (iii) a link to the Commission's website;

(b) display at least the information at (i) above on each page of the website which offers gaming machines or gambling software in reliance on the licence.

(c) where they offer on pages of, or by means of a link from, their website, the supply of gaming machines or gambling software which are not provided in reliance on their licence, clearly distinguish those products which are regulated by the Commission from those which are not.

ACCESS TO PREMISES

Licensees must have and put into effect policies and procedures (including staff training programmes) designed to ensure that their staff co-operate with the Commission's enforcement officers in the proper performance of their compliance functions and are made aware of those officers' rights of entry to premises contained in Part 15 of the Act.

INFORMATION REQUIREMENTS

Reporting suspicion of offences etc

Licensees must provide the Commission with any information that they know relates to or suspect may relate to the commission of an offence under the Act, including an offence resulting from a breach of a licence condition or a code provision having the effect of a licence condition.

Reporting 'Key Events'

THE FOLLOWING CONDITION APPLIES TO ALL REMOTE OPERATING LICENCES EXCEPT ANCILLARY REMOTE LICENCES

A key event is an event that could have a significant impact on the nature or structure of a licensee's business. Licensees must notify the Commission of the occurrence of any of the following key events as soon as reasonably practicable and in any event within five working days of the licensee becoming aware of the event's occurrence[2].

- in the case of licensees which are companies, a petition being presented for their winding up or the winding up of any group company of theirs, or they or any group company being placed in administration or receivership: in this condition a 'group company' is any subsidiary or holding company of the licensee – as those terms are defined in section 1159 of the Companies Act 2006 or any statutory modification or re-enactment thereof – and any subsidiary of such holding company
- in the case of a licensee who is an individual (or a partner in a partnership licensee) their being presented with a petition for their bankruptcy or sequestration or their entering into an individual voluntary agreement
- where the licensee is required to have their accounts independently audited, any unplanned change of auditor including a change prompted by a dispute or resulting from auditors being unable or unwilling to sign an unqualified audit report
- the departure from the licensee's business of any person occupying a 'qualifying position' as defined by Regulation 2(2) of the Gambling Act 2005 (Definition of Small-scale Operator) Regulations 2006
- any breach of a covenant given to a bank or other lender
- any default in making repayment of the whole or any part of a loan on its due date
- any court judgments remaining unpaid 14 days after the date of judgment
- the commencement of any material litigation against the licensee
- the imposition of a disciplinary sanction, including dismissal, against the holder of a personal licence or a person occupying a qualifying position for gross misconduct; or the resignation of a personal licence holder or person occupying a qualifying position following commencement of disciplinary proceedings in respect of gross misconduct against that person
- in the case of remote gambling, the commencement or cessation of trading on website domains (including WAP URLs) or broadcast media through which the licensee provides gambling facilities.

---

2 Key events can be reported securely online at the Commission's website at www.gamblingcommission.gov.uk or by email to key.events@gamblingcommission.gov.uk or posted to Key Events, Compliance Administration Team, Gambling Commission, Victoria Square House, Victoria Square, Birmingham B2 4BP

GENERAL AND REGULATORY RETURNS

On request, licensees must provide the Commission with such information as the Commission may require about the use made of facilities provided in accordance with this licence, and the manner in which gambling authorised by this licence and the licensee's business in relation to that gambling are carried on, including in particular information about:

- the numbers of people making use of the facilities and the frequency of such use
- the range of gambling activities provided by the licensee and the numbers of staff employed in connection with them
- the licensee's policies in relation to, and experiences of, problem gambling.

In particular within 28 days of the end of each quarterly period or, for those only submitting annual returns, within 42 days of the end of each annual period, licensees must submit a Regulatory Return to the Commission containing such information as the Commission may from time to time require[3].

---

3 Regulatory returns can be submitted securely online at the Commission's website at www.gamblingcommission.gov.uk For operators unable to access this system, the forms and a guide to

completing them can be requested from the Commission and returned by email to Regulatory.Returns@gamblingcommission.gov.uk or by post to Regulatory Returns, Compliance Administration Team, Gambling Commission, Victoria Square House, Victoria Square, Birmingham, B2 4BP

SECRETARY OF STATE GENERAL CONDITIONS

None at present

CODES OF PRACTICE

INTRODUCTION

This is the Commission's principal code of practice, issued under section 24 of the Gambling Act 2005, as revised with effect from 1 January 2009. There are two types of provision in the code:

- social responsibility provisions: compliance with these is a condition of licences; therefore any breach of them by an operator may lead the Commission to review the operator's licence with a view to suspension, revocation or the imposition of a financial penalty and would also expose the operator to the risk of prosecution; and
- ordinary code provisions: these do not have the status of licence conditions, but are admissible in evidence in criminal or civil proceedings and must be taken into account in any case in which the court or tribunal think them relevant and by the Commission in the exercise of its functions. Any breach of ordinary code provisions by an operator may be taken into account by the Commission on a licence review, but cannot lead to imposition of a financial penalty. These code provisions are in italics in this section and generally set out good practice in these areas.

FINANCIAL REQUIREMENTS

Ordinary code provision

In order to help prevent activities related to money laundering licensees should take into account the Commission's advice on the Proceeds of Crime Act 2002, Duties and responsibilities under the Proceeds of Crime Act 2002. Advice for operators (excluding casino operators).

PROTECTION OF CHILDREN AND OTHER VULNERABLE PERSONS

Combating problem gambling

SOCIAL RESPONSIBILITY CODE PROVISION

Licensees must have and put into effect policies and procedures intended to promote socially responsible gambling.

Licensees' policies and procedures for socially responsible gambling must include but need not be confined to:

- the specific policies and procedures required by the following provisions of section 2 of this code
- a commitment to and how they will contribute to research into the prevention and treatment of problem gambling
- a commitment to and how they will contribute to public education on the risks of gambling and how to gamble safely
- a commitment to and how they will contribute to the identification and treatment of problem gamblers.

MARKETING

Ordinary code provision

All advertising of gambling products and services should be undertaken in a socially responsible manner. In particular, licensees should comply with the advertising codes of practice which apply to the form and media in which they advertise their gambling facilities or services, and for media not explicitly covered should apply the principles included in these codes of practice as if they were explicitly covered. Licensees should also follow any relevant industry code of practice on advertising.

However, the particular restriction on allowing people aged under 25 to appear in adverts need not be applied to point of sale advertising material, provided that the images used depict the sporting activity that may be gambled on and not the activity of gambling itself and do not offend any other aspect of the advertising codes.

GAMBLING LICENSEES' STAFF

The following code applies to all remote operating licences except ancillary remote licences

Social responsibility code provision

Licensees must take all reasonable steps to ensure that staff involved in the provision of facilities for gambling are made aware of advice on socially responsible gambling and of where to get confidential advice should their gambling become hard to control.

INFORMATION REQUIREMENTS

The following code applies to all remote operating licences except ancillary remote licences

Ordinary code provision

The Commission expects licensees to work with the Commission in an open and cooperative way and to inform the Commission of any matters that the Commission would reasonably need to be aware of in exercising its regulatory functions.

These are matters that will have a material impact on the licensee's business or on the licensee's ability to conduct its business. Such matters, which should be notified to the Commission as soon as reasonably practicable[4], include the following:

- the departure from the licensee's business of any person named in the licence application, or that person's successor, who holds a personal management licence, but who does not occupy a 'qualifying position'
- any reduction in the number of staff employed by the licensee where that has a material impact on the licensee's business
- the acquisition or disposal by the licensee of gambling premises or pitches where that has a material impact on the size or nature of the licensee's business
- in the case of corporate licensees, the disposal or acquisition of any group company where that has a material impact on the licensee's ability to conduct its business
- any disposal of the licensee's assets where that has a material impact on the licensee's business
- any investigation by a professional, statutory, regulatory or government body into the licensee's activities, or the activities in relation to the licensed entity of a personal licence holder or a person occupying a qualifying position employed by them, where such an investigation could result in the imposition of a sanction

or penalty which, if imposed, could reasonably be expected to raise doubts about the licensee's continued suitability to hold a Gambling Commission licence

- any instance of criminal activity, including repeated instances of small-scale theft or fraud, where that has a material impact on the licensee's business
- any major breach in the licensee's information security where that adversely affects the confidentiality of customer data or prevents customers from accessing their accounts for a substantial period of time
- any other matters that have a material impact on the licensee's business or on the licensee's ability to conduct its business.

4 These matters can be reported securely online at the Commission's website at www.gamblingcommission.gov.uk or by email to key.events@gamblingcommission.gov.uk or posted to Key Events, Compliance Administration Team, Gambling Commission, Victoria Square House, Victoria Square, Birmingham, B2 4BP

Gambling Commission October 2010

INFORMATION NOTE – GAMBLING COMMISSION'S TESTING STRATEGY 24/8/2007

6.2605 A recent press release by eCOGRA on 21 August 2007 includes some misunderstandings about the testing required for remote gambling operators licensed by the Gambling Commission. This information note clarifies the position in relation to the Commission's remote testing strategy which was published on 27 July 2007.
The Commission has taken a risk based approach when producing the testing strategy to ensure the approach is proportionate yet still meets our licensing objectives.
Importantly the testing strategy provides for various methods of testing. In many cases, output based testing alone will not provide the required degree of confidence that the product fully meets the technical standards.
For certain high risk areas like the systems that produce the results of a game, third party testing of games will need to be conducted by an approved test house before they are released. The Commission has provisionally approved eight test houses to test compliance against the Commission's technical standards.
Licensed operators will need to contract with test houses and agree on the scope of testing. This scope must be sufficient to ensure that testing adequately covers the Commission's technical standards.
eCOGRA is not a Commission approved test house. For an up to date list of test houses currently approved, click here [www.gamblingcommission.gov.uk/Client/mediadetail.asp?mediaid=18]

GAMING MACHINE TESTING STRATEGY FOR CATEGORIES A & B1, B2, B3 & B4, C & D, SERVER NETWORKED AND DOWNLOADABLE, CASHLESS PAYMENT, LINKED PROGRESSIVES AND WIRELESS NETWORKS August 2007

1 INTRODUCTION

6.2620 1.1 Sections 96 and 97 of the Gambling Act 2005 (the Act) enable the Gambling Commission (the Commission) to set technical standards for gaming machines and gambling software respectively, to make arrangements for the administration of tests of compliance with standards and to provide for the enforcement of standards and submission to tests by attaching conditions to operating licences. Condition 2 of the Commission's *Licence Conditions and Codes of Practice (LCCP June 2007)* requires gambling software and gaming machine technical licensees to comply with the Commission's technical standards and with requirements set by the Commission relating to the timing and procedures for testing.

1.2 This document sets out the testing requirements for each set of standards. This includes who can test against the standards, what will need to be tested and the deadlines for testing. It discusses the testing strategy for assessing compliance with the machine standards for categories A & B1, B2, B3, B4, C & D, Server Networked and Downloadable games, Cashless Payment machine systems, Linked Progressives and Wireless Networks published on 1 June 2007. It also covers the B3A standard (which is yet to be published), system integration testing and commercial site testing. Its publication follows discussions with industry representative bodies, operators and test houses on the Commission's proposed approach.

1.3 The Commission is aware that testing cannot be completed prior to release for new gaming machines coming on to the market in the first few months without causing substantial delays. This has been taken into account in this strategy.

1.4 The Commission has published separately the implementation annexes for each category of gaming machine, setting out the timetable for compliance. This document should be read alongside the corresponding implementation annexes.

2 MACHINE STANDARDS CATEGORIES A & B1 AND B2

2.1 Category A & B1 and B2 game titles manufactured from 1 September 2007 will be required to be tested against all sections of the applicable standard, and relevant regulatory requirements in force at the time of testing, by a Commission approved third party test house.

Such tests may be carried out retrospectively for game titles manufactured prior to 1 September 2008 (after the machine has been supplied into the market) provided that the required testing has been completed by 31 August 2008. Manufacturers should ensure that machines supplied into the market prior to testing comply with the standards as far as possible, although the Commission recognises that there may be elements of some machines that are not fully compliant until the machine has been retrospectively modified.

2.2 Manufacturers may opt to have their game titles tested against the regulations that will be in force at 1 September 2008 if they choose to do so. Where any regulation has not come into force at the time the machine is tested the Commission would not require it be retrospectively re-tested, subject to section 12 (Change controls), unless any non-compliance issue(s) are identified (where the modification is required to comply with regulations).

2.3 Game titles manufactured from 1 September 2008 will be required to be tested by a Commission approved third party test house prior to being commercially exploited subject to section 11 (site testing for commercial purposes).

2.4 The Commission does not intend to test retrospectively any category A & B1 and B2 game titles manufactured, or machines converted, before 1 September 2007, including those subsequently modified to comply with the applicable technical standard and/or regulations unless any non-compliance issue(s) are identified, in which case the Commission, on a risk assessment basis, may require that the machine be tested by a Commission approved third party test house.

3 MACHINE STANDARDS CATEGORY B3

3.1 Category B3 game titles manufactured from 1 September 2007 will be required to be tested against the sections of the applicable standard and relevant regulatory requirements in force at the time of testing by a Commission approved third party test house. Such tests may be carried out retrospectively for machines manufactured prior to 1 September 2008 (after the game titles has been supplied into the market) provided that all reasonable steps have been taken to ensure that the game title complies with the applicable standard and relevant regulations and the required testing has been completed by 31 August 2008.

3.2 Manufacturers may opt to have their game titles tested against the standards and regulations that will be in force at 1 September 2008 if they choose to do so. Where any sections of the standards or regulations have not come into force at the time the game title is tested the Commission would not require it be retrospectively re-tested, subject to section 12 (Change controls), unless any non-compliance issue(s) are identified (where the modification is required to comply with regulations). Game titles that comply with the Commission's standards in force at the time of manufacture (for those manufactured after between 1 September 2007 and 31 August 2008) do not have to be modified to comply with those standards that come into force on 1 September 2008.

3.3 Game titles manufactured from 1 September 2008 will be required to be tested by a Commission approved third party test house prior to being commercially exploited subject to section 11 (site testing for commercial purposes).

3.4 The Commission does not intend to test retrospectively any category B3 game titles manufactured or machines converted before 1 September 2007 that comply with the new or legacy standards. This includes game titles or machines subsequently modified to comply with the applicable technical standard and regulations that come into force later (between 1 September 2007 and 31 August 2008) unless any non-compliance issue(s) are identified, in which case the Commission, on a risk assessment basis, may require that the machine be tested by a Commission approved third party test house.

3.5 "Legacy machines" may continue to be operated indefinitely provided that where adapted to comply with any regulatory or other legislative requirements they continue to comply with the Commission's legacy standard. The Commission does not intend to test retrospectively such machines. Where a legacy machine is modified after 1 September 2007 such that it no longer complies with the legacy standards it will be treated as being manufactured after 31 August 2007 and will be subject to the applicable technical and test requirements.

4 MACHINE STANDARDS CATEGORY B3A

4.1 Category B3A game titles manufactured and supplied from the incept date of the B3A technical standard will be required to be tested against all sections of that standard and relevant regulatory requirements in force at the time of testing by a Commission approved third party test house. Such tests may be carried out retrospectively for game titles manufactured up to one year after the game title has been supplied into the market provided that the required testing has been completed within 12 months following the incept date of the technical standard.

4.2 Game titles manufactured 12 months after the incept of the technical standard will be required to be third party tested by a Commission approved third party test house prior to being commercial exploited, subject to section 11 (site testing for commercial purposes).

4.3 Manufacturers may opt to have their game titles tested against the regulations that will be in force at 1 September 2008 if they choose to do so. Where any regulation has not come into force at the time the game title is tested the Commission would not require it be retrospectively re-tested, subject to section 12 (change controls), unless any non-compliance issue(s) are identified (where the modification is required to comply with regulations).

4.4 The Commission does not intend to test retrospectively category B3A game titles manufactured and supplied before the incept date of the B3A technical standard, including those subsequently modified to comply with the applicable standard and/or regulations unless any non-compliance issue(s) are identified whereby the Commission, on a risk assessment basis, may request that the game title be tested by a Commission approved third party test house.

5 MACHINE STANDARDS CATEGORY B4

5.1 The Commission considers that category B4 machines should be tested in the same way as category B3 machines. However, the Commission has received a last minute request to re-consider this view and treat B4 machines in the same way as C and D machines. The Commission expects to be sent the detail to support this request shortly and will set out the testing arrangements for category B4 machines in due course.

6 MACHINE STANDARDS CATEGORY C & D

6.1 Category C & D game titles manufactured from 1 September 2007 can be tested against the sections of the applicable standard and relevant regulatory requirements in force at the time of testing by a Commission approved third party test house (in the same fashion as for category A and B game titles) or by the manufacturer where they able to provide assurance of independence between the testing function and commercial operation and comply with sections 9.4 – 9.6 (testing conducted by licensee/ operator). Such tests may be carried out retrospectively for machines manufactured prior to 1 September 2008 (after the game titles has been supplied into the market) provided that all reasonable steps have been taken to ensure that the game title complies with the applicable standard and relevant regulations and that the required testing has been completed by 31 August 2008.

6.2 Manufacturers may opt to have their game titles tested against the standards and regulations that will be in force at 1 September 2008 if they choose to do so. Where any section of the standards or regulations have not come into force at the time the game title is tested the Commission would not require it be retrospectively re-tested, subject to section 12 (change controls), unless any non-compliance issue(s) are identified (where the modification is required to comply with regulations). Game titles that comply with the Commission's standards in force at the time of manufacture (for those manufactured after between 1 September 2007 and 31 August 2008) do not have to be modified to comply with those standards that come into force on 1 September 2008.

6.3 Where the manufacturer opts to test and approve game titles in-house they will be required to have one game title (of a machine type) tested by a Commission approved third party test house within a 12 to 24 months period at the Commission's discretion. The Commission will decide on the frequency of test for each operator based on our compliance risk assessment programme. The term "machine type" refers to the machine's architecture and configuration and where significantly different to other products manufactured it would be considered a machine type in its own right. Where any non-compliance issues arise the Commission may require that further game titles be tested by a Commission approved third party test house on a risk assessment basis.

6.4 In instances where a game title had already been tested by a Commission approved third party test house the Commission would not require that it be re-tested unless any non-compliance issues are identified.

6.5 The Commission does not intend to test retrospectively any category C and D game titles manufactured or machines converted before 1 September 2007 that comply with the new or legacy standards. This includes game titles or machines subsequently modified to comply with the applicable technical standard and regulations that come into force later (between 1 September 2007 and 31 August 2008) unless any non-compliance issue(s) are identified, in which case the Commission, on a risk assessment basis, may request that the machine be tested by a Commission approved third party test house.

6.6 "Legacy machines" may continue to be operated indefinitely provided that where adapted to comply with any regulatory or other legislative requirements they continue to comply with the Commission's legacy standard. The Commission does not intend to test retrospectively such machines. Where a legacy machine is modified after 1 September 2007 such that it no longer complies with the legacy standards it will be treated as being manufactured after 31 August 2007 and will be subject to the applicable technical and test requirements.

7 MACHINE STANDARDS CATEGORY SERVER NETWORKED AND DOWNLOADABLE, CASHLESS PAYMENT MACHINE SYSTEMS, LINKED PROGRESSIVES AND WIRELESS NETWORKS

7.1 Equipment of the above categories manufactured from 1 September 2007 will be required to be tested against the sections of the applicable standard by a Commission approved third party test house. Such tests may be carried out retrospectively for equipment manufactured prior to 1 September 2008 (after the equipment has been supplied into the market) provided that all reasonable steps have been taken to ensure that the game title complies with the applicable standard and relevant regulations and that the required testing has been completed by 31 August 2008. Provided that the system (which has been tested) is not modified then it will not be a requirement for such tests to be repeated when used for different applications. The Commission is still considering testing arrangements for downloadable gaming systems where components manufactured by different entities are subsequently integrated (see system integration testing section below).

8 SYSTEM INTEGRATION TESTING

8.1 The Commission is still considering the appropriate testing arrangements where components such as the player terminal, RNG or game system are purchased separately and integrated by the end user or supplier. Examples of this arrangement are existing fixed odds betting terminals where the random number generator is separate to the terminal and terminals where games from different suppliers are loaded by the end user, supplier or operator.

9 PROCEDURE FOR TESTING

THIRD PARTY TEST HOUSES

9.1 In June 2007 the Commission published a list of test houses that are approved to test gaming machines against its technical standards. The list, which can be found on the Commission's website at www.gamblingcommission.gov.uk, will be updated as new test houses are approved.

9.2 Licensees must send to the Commission on completion of satisfactory testing (but prior to release) the results of testing (ie a test house's summary report). Where practicable the Commission is content to receive this directly from the test house. Once this has been provided, the successfully tested product can be commercially exploited, subject to section 11 (site testing for commercial purposes).

9.3 Licensees on request will need to make available to the Commission the full test results supplied by the approved third party test house. Where practicable the Commission is content to receive this directly from the test house.

TESTING CONDUCTED BY LICENSEE/OPERATOR

9.4 To be permitted to carry out their own testing of gambling products the licensee should follow good practice in the development and testing cycle for gaming machines. Examples of what the Commission considers to be good practice can be found in section 10 below. Manufacturers can depart from the good practice set out in section 10, but must be able to demonstrate as to how their alternative procedures mitigate the risks associated with software development, implementation and testing procedures.

9.5 The Commission, on request or as part of a compliance visit, may require evidence from the licensee that it follows good practice and may inspect any documentation relating to the development and testing of any game title manufactured after 31 August 2007.

9.6 All results from licensee testing should be retained for 10 years after the final production of a game title and be made available to the Commission during compliance visits or on request. A summary of each game title approved in-house should be submitted to the Commission. The summary should include the game title, version number and confirmation that good practice procedures for development and testing are in place and that the standards and relevant DCMS regulations have been complied with. This must be signed as being the case by a Personal Management Licence (PML) holder or an appropriate company director in the case of a small scale operator (where there is no PML holder).

10 IN-HOUSE DEVELOPMENT, TESTING AND RELEASE – EXAMPLES OF GOOD PRACTICE

10.1 Examples of good practice gaming machine and gambling software development are set out as follows.

10.2 Development process.

- Master source code should be held securely (such that the source cannot be tampered with by unauthorised persons).
- An audit log of all accesses to master source code should be maintained.
- Old versions of source code and the dates they were retired should be retained for 10 years.
- Access to source code by developers should be well controlled and based on a minimum access required for the job approach.
- Access to platform source code should not be granted to those working only on game specific development.
- Changes to critical modules must be logged and should be peer reviewed by an appropriately skilled independent person (who can be from the same company) to ensure all changes made are appropriate and in line with the change documentation. Any suspicious or unauthorised changes must be explained.

10.3 Testing Process.

- Logically separate development and testing environments should be adapted.
- Separate staff to those that developed should perform the testing.
- An independent assessment of changes made by the developers should be performed (this can be performed by someone from the same company) to verify all changes are documented in the change documentation. This may involve the use of file comparison programs to quickly identify all changes.

11 SITE TESTING FOR COMMERCIAL PURPOSES

11.1 Commercial site testing of game titles prior to them being formally tested is permitted providing the following is adhered to:

- the manufacturer must follow good practice (examples are given above in section 10) in the development and approval of games for commercial site testing and take all reasonable steps to ensure that any test machine complies with applicable technical standards and regulations in force at the time it is manufactured;
- a maximum of 50 machines may be site tested;
- the testing must last no longer than sixteen weeks (taken from the date the first machine of that title is sited);
- the machines must be clearly identified as being on a commercial site test; and
- the entity responsible for the test machine must also keep adequate records of the above, the site locations for inspection purposes and any modification made as a result of non-compliance with standards or regulations.

11.2 The Commission will keep commercial site testing under review and will amend these arrangements if necessary.

12 CHANGE CONTROLS

12.1 Where a gaming machine's hardware or software is modified such that it could potentially affects the fairness of the game (eg pay-tables or game personality) or randomness (where applicable) then it must be resubmitted for testing to ensure compliance. Otherwise the machine need not be re-tested but any modification to hardware or software must be documented and signed as being compliant with the Commission's requirements by a PML holder or a company director in the case of a small scale operator.
12.2 Where the manufacturer tests the machine internally they must ensure that all reasonable steps are taken to ensure continued compliance with the technical standards and/or regulations.
12.3 Updated game version numbers must be submitted to the Commission and referenced against an existing game title prior to its release. Documentation relating to sections 12.1 and 12.2 above must be retained for a minimum of 10 years.
Gambling Commission August 2007

GAMING MACHINE TESTING STRATEGY SUPPLEMENT 1: SYSTEM INTEGRATION

December 2008

1 INTRODUCTION

6.2621 1.1 This document sets out a revision to section 8 of the *Gaming Machine Testing Strategy for Categories A & B1, B2, B3 & B4, C & D, Server Networked and Downloadable, Cashless Payment, Linked Progressives and Wireless Networks*
1.2 The Commission is concerned that game fairness may be adversely affected where a gaming system is comprised of modular components (cabinet, RNG, game content) from various manufacturers which are not sufficiently tested in combination, albeit that each may have been tested in isolation.
1.3 In the gaming machine testing strategy published in August 2007 the Commission indicated that it was still considering what arrangements would be appropriate for such system integration. The Commission has been discussing this issue with the industry during the course of the year, including at the test house and manufacturers forum in late May. As a result of these discussions the Commission is content for system integration to be tested in any of three ways, as set out below. These methodologies will give the industry flexibility in how they test system integration, utilising methods already in use, whilst at the same time giving the Commission assurance that adequate system integration testing has taken place.

2 CHANGE TO TEXT

2.1 The text at section 8 of *Gaming Machine Testing Strategy for Categories A & B1, B2, B3 & B4, C & D, Server Networked and Downloadable, Cashless Payment, Linked Progressives and Wireless Networks* should be changed to:

8 SYSTEM INTEGRATION TESTING

8.1 System integration describes the situation where primary elements of a gaming machine such as the cabinet, random number generator, operating system or game content are used in different combinations, by manufacturers, suppliers or operators.

Examples of this arrangement are video terminals (category B2 gaming machines) such as those operated in licensed betting premises (formerly referred to as fixed odds betting terminals) whereby multiple game content supplied by various vendors is offered.

8.2 The Commission intends to take a flexible approach to integration testing and therefore the following approaches are permitted.

Internal testing

8.3 Internal testing is where the platform provider supplies sufficient software interface details to the game vendor with respect to system integration and the software vendor ensures compliance of their game software via the Commission's testing requirements as normal. It should be clear in the appropriate contractual arrangements between the game vendor, terminal provider and any other interested party who is responsible for system integration testing.

8.4 To be permitted to carry out their own testing of gambling products the licensee(s) must follow good practice in the development and testing cycle for gaming machines (as set out at section 10 of the testing strategy). Any internal testing carried out must be documented for the purpose of any later audit by the Commission.

External testing

8.5 This option requires each cabinet and game combination to be tested via an external test house. This allows both fairness and integration testing to be carried out simultaneously.

Partial system integration testing carried out by an external testing house

8.6 Under this option each cabinet type undergoes system integration testing against a manufacturer's game software using an external testing laboratory (in particular the interface between the hardware and the game software). Provided that there are no modifications to the interface between the hardware and the game software then there would be no further system integration testing required for any subsequent new title. Game software is still required to undergo fairness testing as set out in the Commission's testing strategy.

8.7 To be permitted to carry out their own testing of gambling products the licensee must follow good practice in the development and testing cycle for gaming machines (as set out at section 10 of the testing strategy). Any internal testing carried out must be documented for the purpose of any later audit by the Commission.

Gambling Commission December 2008

GAMING MACHINES AND SOFTWARE – WHAT DO WE MEAN BY 'GAMING MACHINES & SOFTWARE'?

6.2625–6.2630 There are 4 main categories of gaming machines regulated by the Gambling Commission, ranging from category A to category D. The maximum stakes and prizes for these machines are set out in regulations under the Gambling Act 2005. Gaming machines may be located in a wide variety of locations including betting shops, bingo halls and alcohol-licensed premises. They are being phased out of premises such as taxi offices and chip shops to restrict their availability to children.

Software that is used to facilitate machine or remote gambling is also regulated by the Commission. Those that manufacture, supply, install or adapt gaming machines or gambling software must be licensed by the Commission and must adhere to strict technical requirements.

HOW ARE MACHINES AND SOFTWARE REGULATED?

Most organisations and individuals that offer machines or software for gambling require a licence to operate, whether the facilities are provided remotely (for example through the internet or telephone), or in premises. The Commission has developed licence conditions and codes of practice that govern all licence holders and it can prosecute or impose fines on operators who breach their licence conditions.
There are two types of licence for gaming machines and software providers:

- Operating licences are required by those that provide gambling machines and software in Britain.
- Personal licences are required by individuals in certain management positions except for those organisations categorised as small-scale operators.

MACHINES AND SOFTWARE FACTS AND FIGURES

- There are an estimated 260,000 gaming machines in the UK.
- 14% of the population play gaming machines.
- Gaming machines are most popular amongst younger age groups with 32% of those aged 16-24 playing them.
- Men are more likely than women to play gaming machines.
- Gaming machines in 2006/07 (including FOBTs) were estimated to be located as follows: family entertainment centres 31%, adult gaming centres 13%, pubs 28%, casinos 1%, clubs 6%, motorway services 1%, bingo halls 9%, licensed betting offices 2%, licensed betting offices (inc FOBTs) 9%, other locations 1%.

Category of machine (typical location)	Maximum stakes and prizes	
	Stake	Prize
A (jackpot machines in a regional casino)	unlimited	unlimited
B1 (jackpot machines in casinos)	£2	£4000
B2 (fixed odds betting terminals in betting shops)	£100	£500
B3 (jackpot machines in bingo halls and adult gaming centres)	£1	£500
B3A (lottery style machines in members' clubs and miners' welfare institutes)	£1	£500
B4 (jackpot machines in registered clubs)	£1	£250
C (amusement with prizes machines in alcohol licences premises and arcades)	50p	£35
D (amusement with prizes machines in arcades)	10p	£5
	30p	£8 (non-monetary)

Gambling Commission August 2007

ADVICE ON PART-EXCHANGING GAMING MACHINES
December 2007

6.2631 The Commission has been asked to consider whether a supplier's licence to provide a gaming machine in part exchange. The Commission has also been asked whether section 16 or section 21 machines can be part-exchanged.

An operator who provides a gaming machine in part exchange for another gaming machine, which is provided by a licensed supplier of such machines, will not require a supplier's licence or permit. Non-compliant section 16 or section 21 machines can also be part-exchanged.
Gambling Commission December 2007

ADVICE REGARDING WHEN A MACHINE IS 'AVAILABLE FOR USE'

December 2007

6.2632 1.1 The Commission is aware that there has been some confusion about when a gaming machine is considered 'available for use' given that the Gambling Act 2005 says that only a limited number of certain categories of machines may be made 'available for use' on a premises.

1.2 The Commission considers that a gaming machine is available for use if a person can play it. It follows that more than the permitted number of machines may be physically located on a premises, provided the operator has a robust system in place that ensures no more than the permitted number are 'available for use' at any one time. The operator must control this system. We remind operators that if two people can play a gaming machine simultaneously, then the machine counts as two machines.

1.3 An example of an appropriate system may be a situation where the power supply for machines of a certain category is controlled by the operator (and is not accessible to the player) so that one machine must be unplugged before another machine can be played. An example of an inappropriate system would be where an additional machine was located on premises and there was a spare plug which a player could plug the machine into at will, allowing play on more than the permitted number of machines.

1.4 If an operator does want to put more than the permitted number of machines in a public area the onus will be on the operator to demonstrate that no more than the permitted number of machines are 'available for use' at any one time. The Commission will not hesitate to take action if it finds that more than the permitted number of machines is 'available for use'.

1.5 A machine that can operate at more than one category, which is operating at a lower category, does not contribute to the number of machines 'available for use' at a higher category until it switches to that category. However, the operator must also have a system in place for these machines which ensures no more than the permitted number are 'available for use' at any one time.

1.6 The Commission permits systems in which a number of machines network so that the player can select which game and category they play at, but which adhere to any restrictions on the number of machines at a certain category.

1.7 This note clarifies the position for regulatory purposes. Operators will also need to consider any amusement machine licence duty implications associated with the siting of broken down or spare machines.
Gambling Commission December 2007

MACHINE STANDARDS CATEGORY B3A
June 2008

INTRODUCTION

6.2633 This standard is applicable to category B3A gaming machines as defined in Article 5 of The Categories of Gaming Machine Regulations 2007. Category B3A gaming machines manufactured before 27 December 2008 will need to comply with all parts of the relevant standard by 27 June 2009. Category B3A gaming machines manufactured from 27 December 2008 will need to comply with all parts of the relevant standard before they are supplied into the market.

The purpose of the standard is to set out in detail the Gambling Commission's (the Commission's) requirements with respect to game features, display notices and general machine operation including metering. These have been developed to help ensure the Commission's three licensing objectives are met. Those objectives are to:

- prevent gambling from being a source of crime or disorder, being associated with crime or disorder or being used to support crime
- ensure that gambling is conducted in a fair and open way
- protect children and other vulnerable persons from being harmed or exploited by gambling.

Operators or end users should not rely upon these standards as a measure of reliability, quality or minimal security standards.

These standards permit equivalence between different types of technology and do not specify proprietary products or technologies. Testing regimes for these standards will permit equivalent international standards (ISO). Whilst what is provided on a B3A machine must be a lottery, it is not intended further to limit game content and the use of new technological developments provided that the objectives of the standards are met.

OTHER RELEVANT GAMING MACHINE TECHNICAL STANDARDS AND RELATED DOCUMENTS

- Technical Standard for Server Networked & Downloadable Gaming Machines (All categories of machine)
- Technical Standard for Wireless Network Systems (All categories of machine)
- Technical Standard for Cashless Systems (All categories of machine)
- Gaming machines testing strategy

1.0 HARDWARE REQUIREMENTS

1.1 PHYSICAL SECURITY

All reasonable efforts should be made to ensure that a gaming machine is robust enough to withstand forced entry which would not leave behind evidence of the attempted entry. Where any form of attempted or forced entry causes an error condition, the machine must only commence play once the error condition has been cleared. Provided that any security device or sensor (eg door open sensor) which has detected an attempted entry no longer indicates there to be a problem the machine may automatically clear the error condition and commence play. Otherwise, operator action shall be required to clear the error condition.

1.2 MACHINE IDENTIFICATION

A gaming machine must have an identification plate of metallic construction or of an equally resilient material permanently affixed to the exterior of the cabinet by the manufacturer. This must not be easily removable, without leaving evidence of tampering. The following information shall be displayed on the identification plate:

(a) the manufacturer (machine manufacturer or brand name under which it is to be sold)
(b) a unique serial number
(c) the gaming machine model number (which may refer to the cabinet type and not the lottery)
(d) the date of manufacture.

The identification plate shall be mounted on the front or side of the cabinet where it is clearly visible.

1.3 GAMING MACHINE ALARM/ALERT REQUIREMENTS

Gaming machines must be designed to automatically prevent further play within the lottery and alert the site management in the following situations:

(a) a player winning an amount or redeeming credits that the machine cannot automatically pay

(b) an error condition occurring

(c) a machine fault occurring.

Such a system must be transparent to the player when activated and sufficiently able to attract the attention of the site management.

1.4 LOGIC AREA

Manufacturers must so far as is reasonably practicable, incorporate gaming machine design features aimed at preventing tampering with any electronic logic components that has the potential to significantly influence the operation of the gaming device.

1.5 CONFIGURATION SETTINGS

All switches and/or jumpers must be fully documented and any hardware system within the machine which may alter the configuration settings such as accounting denomination must either be housed within a separately locked secure logic area or comply with the following paragraph.

As an alternative to a separate secure logic area, any change in configuration defined above must be logged and date stamped within the secure non-volatile memory of the machine. This log must cover a minimum period of not less than one month and be made available for display on demand with the test and diagnostic routine of the machine.

1.6 VIDEO MONITORS/TOUCH SCREENS

All video based lotteries shall meet the following requirements:

(a) touch screens shall be accurate and, once calibrated, shall maintain that accuracy for at least the manufacturer's recommended maintenance period

(b) a touch screen should be able to be re-calibrated without access to the machine cabinet other than opening the main door

(c) there shall be no hidden or undocumented buttons/touch points anywhere on the screen that affect play within the lottery, except as provided for by the lottery rules

(d) section (1.6 c) does not apply to audit functions and controls which must be documented.

1.7 MECHANICAL DEVICES USED FOR DISPLAYING OF LOTTERY OUTCOMES

If the machine has mechanical or electro-mechanical devices, which are used for displaying lottery outcomes, the following rules shall be observed:

(a) mechanical assemblies (eg reels or wheels) shall have some mechanism that ensures the correct mounting of reels' artwork

(b) displays shall be constructed in such a way that winning symbol combinations match up with pay lines or other indicators

(c) a mechanical assembly shall be so designed that it is not obstructed by any other components.

1.8 NOT APPLICABLE TO THIS CATEGORY OF MACHINE

1.9 PATCH WIRES

All patch wires and track cuts shall be documented, in an appropriate manner, in the relevant service manual and/or service bulletin. This does not prohibit required repairs in the field.

2.0 SOFTWARE REQUIREMENTS

2.1 CONTROL PROGRAM AUTHENTICATION REQUIREMENTS

The control program must utilise an integrity check, suitable for the media, providing at least the level of integrity of CRC16 (for non-alterable storage media) or a secured hashing method such as MD5 or SHA (for alterable storage media) to authenticate that the program and/or support files have not been corrupted or altered prior to use/loading. Any error detected will result in the machine displaying the appropriate error message and being unavailable for play. The integrity check must be carried out during each start up or at least once every 24 hours where the machine is specifically designed for permanent serviceable operation.

2.2 ALTERABLE STORAGE MEDIA DEVICES

Any gaming machine and any procedural requirements must include sufficient security to ensure that any software that can influence the lottery outcome, including configurable settings and classes that reside on any alterable media is a true replication of that version of the lottery, control or other software.

2.3 PROGRAM STORAGE MEDIUM IDENTIFICATION

Any program medium (ROMs, EPROMs, Alterable storage media, DVD and CD-ROM) placed in the field shall be uniquely identified, displaying:

(a) program ID number
(b) manufacturer or lottery system provider
(c) version number
(d) type and size of medium (unless located on the medium as purchased unused from the supplier)
(e) location of installation in gaming machine or device, if potentially confusing.

The information in points a to e above must be available for inspection on the site operator's premises either on the label of the storage media or via video or display monitor. For EPROM based lotteries, the identification label shall be placed over the UV window to avoid erasing or alteration of the program.

2.4 NOT APPLICABLE TO THIS CATEGORY OF MACHINE.

2.5 LAST LOTTERY CHANCE RECALL

Information on at least the last fifty lottery tickets purchased on the machine must always be retrievable on the operation of a suitable external key-switch, or another secure method not available to the player. This information must include a minimum of which lottery has been entered (but only if several exist on the machine), timestamp of ticket purchase, unique ticket identifier (if system uses one), bank/credit meter details and outcome (losing chance or win amount).

2.6 TEST/DIAGNOSTIC MODE

When a gaming machine is in a test mode, any test that involves credits entering or leaving the gaming machine must be completed prior to resumption of normal operation. The main cabinet door of a gaming machine may automatically place the machine in a service or test mode. Test/diagnostics mode may also be entered, via an appropriate instruction, by an attendant during an audit mode access.

When exiting from test mode, any lottery in play must return to the original state it was in when the test mode was entered. If the gaming machine is in a test mode, the machine must clearly indicate that it is in a test mode, not normal play.

2.7 SOFTWARE VERIFICATION

At a minimum, the machine must have the ability to allow a visual inspection of the following using either an available matrix or video display. (It is permissible for the machine not to display such information during each start up but it must be accessible when required. This may involve the machine being restarted or an appropriate security key being used.)

(a) identity of the lottery system provider
(b) lottery system identity code
(c) version number of lottery system software
(d) check sum of lottery system software

And if the operating system is not proprietary to the manufacturer, lottery system provider, supplier or operator then:

(e) identity of operating system
(f) version number of operating system

On machines or terminals, which offer the player a choice of lotteries, the above information concerning the lottery software must be made available for each lottery.

3.0 CRITICAL MEMORY REQUIREMENTS

3.1 CONTENTS OF CRITICAL MEMORY

Critical memory (that is non-volatile computer memory) must be used to store a minimum of the following data:

(a) credit and bank values
(b) electronic meters (if so fitted)
(c) previous lottery ticket data, as required by section 2.5

The clearing or resetting of such data must require deliberate action by appropriately authorised personnel.

3.2 MAINTENANCE OF CRITICAL MEMORY

Critical memory storage must be maintained by a methodology that enables errors to be identified and corrected in most circumstances. This methodology may involve signatures, checksums, partial checksums, multiple copies, timestamps and/or effective use of validity codes.

Comprehensive checks of critical memory must be made during each gaming machine or device restart (eg power up cycle). Gaming machine or device control programs (software that operates the machine or device's functions) shall test for possible corruption caused by failure of the program storage medium and all critical lottery files. Test methodology must endeavour to detect 100 percent of all possible failures.

The control program (software that operates the gaming machine or device's functions) shall allow for the machine or device to ensure the integrity of all control program components during execution of said components.

All program storage devices (PSD), in the executable address space of a main processor, shall be validated (including an integrity check of all lottery chance classes) during the following conditions:

(a) any power up
(b) the first time the files are loaded for use (even if only partially loaded).

Memory and PSD space that are not critical to machine security (eg video or sound ROM) are not required to be validated.

3.3 PROGRAM MEMORY, CRITICAL MEMORY AND NON-VOLATILE DEVICES USED TO STORE PROGRAM MEMORY

The following are requirements for critical memory:

(a) a battery back-up (where required), or an equivalent, must be installed on the gaming machine or device for the electronic meters and must be capable of maintaining the accuracy of all information required for thirty days after power is discontinued from the machine The battery backup device must be kept within the locked logic area or if not available in a secure location behind the locked main door

(b) if the rechargeable battery back-up is used as an 'off chip' battery source, it shall re-charge itself to its full potential in a maximum of twenty-four hours and have a shelf life of at least five years

(c) critical memory that uses an off-chip back-up power source to retain its contents when the mains power is switched off must have a detection system which will provide a method for software to interpret and act upon a low battery condition, or alternatively, use a suitable software check to ensure integrity of the storage is maintained.

3.4 UNRECOVERABLE CRITICAL MEMORY

An uncorrectable corruption of critical memory must result in an error condition. Critical memory should not be cleared automatically, but must only be cleared by an authorised person.

3.5 FUNCTION OF CRITICAL MEMORY RESET

Clearing critical memory must only be capable of being undertaken by accessing the logic area or secure location in which it is housed. Following the initiation of a critical memory reset procedure, the lottery program must execute a routine which initialises each and every bit in memory to the default state. For machines that allow for partial critical memory clears, the methodology for doing so must be accurate and the machine must validate the un-cleared portions of memory.

If a pseudo 'game' is used to display the result of the ticket, the default reel position or lottery 'game' display after a critical reset must not be the top award on any selectable line. The default lottery 'game' display, upon entering lottery 'game' play mode, must also not be the top award. This applies to the base lottery 'game' only and not to any secondary bonus devices.

4.0 MACHINE CREDIT AND PAYMENT REQUIREMENTS

4.1 COIN OR TOKEN AND NOTE ACCEPTORS AND OTHER METHODS OF INSERTING MONEY OR MONEY'S WORTH INTO THE MACHINE

All coin/token acceptors must meet the following requirements:

(a) the coin/token acceptor must be designed to prevent the use of cheating methods such as slugging (counterfeit coins/tokens), stringing (coin pullback), the insertion of foreign objects and other manipulation

(b) other than for diagnostic purposes coins/tokens judged invalid by the acceptor must be rejected to the coin tray and shall not be counted as credits. Acceptance of coins/tokens for crediting to the credit meter must only be possible when the gaming machine is enabled for play. Other states, such as error conditions, including 'door open' and 'audit mode' must disable the coin/token acceptor system. Each coin/token inserted must register the actual monetary value or a number of credits on the player's credit meter for the current lottery. If coins or tokens inserted in a machine are registered directly as credits, the conversion must be clearly stated, or be easily ascertainable from a help menu or similar.

All acceptance devices must be able to detect the entry of valid notes, coupons, paper tokens, or other approved vouchers, and provide a method to enable the gaming device software to interpret and act appropriately upon a valid or invalid input. Acceptance devices must be electronically-based and be configured to ensure that they only accept valid banknotes, vouchers or paper tokens and reject all other notes. The note input system must be constructed in a manner that protects against vandalism, abuse, or fraudulent activity.

4.2 TOKENISATION

For lotteries that may be played using tokens, the gaming machine or relevant device must receive from the acceptor and post to the player's 'bank' the entire amount inserted. If the current local currency amount is not an even multiple of the token for a lottery or the credit amount has a fractional component, the system must retain the value for the benefit of the next player.

4.3 PRINTERS

If a gaming machine is equipped with a printer that is used to make payments, the printer must be located in a locked area of the machine (eg require opening of the main door to access), but not in the logic area unless the alternative requirements in the second paragraph of section 1.5 (configuration settings) are complied with.

Any printed ticket/voucher/hand pay receipt must display the following information in addition to that required by the provisions of the Gambling Act 2005 (the Act) which apply to the particular type of lottery concerned (eg: a private society lottery or small society lottery):

(a) date and time (24-hour format) of issuance
(b) alpha numeric currency amount
(c) validation number and/or unique identifier (eg bar code)
(d) duplicate ticket indicator (eg duplicate number 3).

4.4 TICKET VALIDATION

Payment by ticket printer as a method of credit redemption is only permissible when:

(a) there is a means to validate the printed ticket/voucher/hand pay receipt prior to any credit or other type of redemption
(b) such validation system is capable of identifying duplicate tickets to prevent fraud by reprinting and redeeming a ticket previously issued.

To meet this standard, an audit trail of at least one month's data relating to all ticket transactions must be maintained for dispute resolution purposes.

5.0 SPECIFIC LOTTERY REQUIREMENTS

5.1 GENERAL REQUIREMENT

The outcome of the lottery must not be determined or influenced by means of the machine. To stop a class before it has completed there must be a valid reason such as evidence of fraud or manipulation. A class may only be suspended, stopped or replaced by a new class by a secure operator action.

However, it is permissible for a machine to randomly select a new class of lottery tickets (when the current class is completed) from a previously randomised selection of classes, which have been pre-loaded into the machine, but the new class selected must be different from the class just completed. This requirement that the new class selected

must be different from the class just completed only applies to machines that are manufactured from [six months after publication].
The machine must clearly display to the player either at all times when it is in operation or at the point a lottery is selected for play the following statement:

THIS IS A LOTTERY MACHINE

5.2 NOT APPLICABLE TO THIS CATEGORY OF MACHINE
5.2A CLASS SIZE AND CHANCE DISTRIBUTION WITHIN A CLASS

Class sizes within any lottery must contain a minimum number of chances, with chances awarding wins (ie winning tickets) randomly distributed among the chances not awarding wins (ie losing tickets).
The minimum number of chances depends on how the next class is selected:

(a) if the next class is selected from a limited number of re-usable classes then the minimum class size is 10,000. The number of classes from which a re-useable class is selected from must be sufficient to provide a reasonable assurance that there is no possibility that a payer or observer is able to predict the order in which chances have been randomised within a class.
(b) if the next class is not selected from a limited number of re-usable classes (eg a new class is downloaded from a server each time) then the minimum class size is 1,000 chances.

The randomisation process must:

(c) ensure chances which award prizes and the value of those prizes are randomly distributed over the entire range and pass appropriate statistical tests
(d) ensure prize awards are randomly distributed over the entire range
(e) ensure the output is unpredictable
(f) not reproduce the same output stream, nor must two instances of an RNG produce the same stream as each other. Where seeding is required to achieve this it should not introduce predictability.

A machine or device must not present a losing lottery ticket result which indicates a 'Near Miss', eg where the odds of the top award symbol landing on the pay line are limited it must not frequently appear above or below the pay line.
If a gaming machine uses a pseudo 'game' to display the result of a lottery ticket which is recognisably a known game (eg poker, reels, bingo) and is described as such by title or visual presentation, it must be made clear to the player that the chances of winning in the lottery differ from an equivalent real game and that the outcome of the 'game' is totally dependant upon the result obtained from the next chance drawn from the class.

5.3 NOT APPLICABLE TO THIS CATEGORY OF MACHINE
5.4 NOT APPLICABLE TO THIS CATEGORY OF MACHINE
5.5 SINGLE LOTTERY CHANCE REQUIREMENTS

The price for any lottery ticket purchased by the player must be deducted from the credit or play meter prior to the outcome of the chance in the class represented by that ticket being displayed to the player.
This section does not preclude the use of multi-line and multi-reel pseudo 'games' to display the result of the lottery ticket(s) provided that the aggregate ticket price and total prize do not exceed the statutory maxima.

5.6 INITIATING THE NEXT LOTTERY CHANCE CYCLE (AUTO START/ PLAY)

Except where an 'auto play' or 'auto start' feature is permissible[1] it must always be necessary to release and then depress the machine's real or virtual 'start button' to start a lottery chance cycle.

5.7 SPEED OF PLAY

Each lottery chance cycle must last at least 2.5 seconds.
A lottery chance cycle starts when a player using a gaming machine once[2] has paid for a lottery ticket and depresses the 'start button' or takes equivalent action to determine if his ticket is a winning ticket and ends when the result of the lottery chance represented by that ticket has been displayed to the player and any prize has been paid to, or made available for collection by the player and the start button or equivalent becomes available to determine the fate of the next lottery chance.
Where auto play or auto start is permitted then a lottery chance cycle is measured from the point at which the lottery chance purchase is initiated by the system (equivalent to the player depressing the start button) to the point at which it is able to automatically start the next lottery chance.

5.8 NOT APPLICABLE TO THIS CATEGORY OF MACHINE
5.9 NOT APPLICABLE TO THIS CATEGORY OF MACHINE
5.10 NOT APPLICABLE TO THIS CATEGORY OF MACHINE
5.11 NOT APPLICABLE TO THIS CATEGORY OF MACHINE
5.12 NOT APPLICABLE TO THIS CATEGORY OF MACHINE
5.13 NOT APPLICABLE TO THIS CATEGORY OF MACHINE
5.14 NOT APPLICABLE TO THIS CATEGORY OF MACHINE
5.15 MULTIPLE LOTTERIES ON THE GAMING DEVICE

(a) The methodology used to select and discard a particular lottery for play on a multi-lottery machine shall be transparent to the player.

(b) All applicable rules and/or the pay tables should be transparent and available to view for each lottery prior to any commitment to play.

(c) It must at all times be made transparent to the player which lottery has been selected for play or is being played.

(d) Committing to play a lottery must involve the player in at least two actions. Having selected a lottery, the player must be able to return to the main menu without playing.

(e) It should not be possible to start a new lottery before the current play is completed and all relevant meters have been updated (including features and other options of a pseudo 'game').

(f) The set of lotteries offered to the player for selection must be capable of being changed only by a secure method. This includes turning on and off lotteries available for play through a suitable interface. The rules at section 1.5 of these standards shall govern the critical memory clear control requirements for these types of selections. A lottery gaming system may record the data that is stored in critical memory on separately allocated memory exclusive to the lottery provided there are adequate safeguards to ensure critical memory integrity.

(g) No changes to the set of lotteries offered to the player for selection are permitted while there are credits on the player's credit or bank meter or while a lottery is in progress unless there is evidence of lottery manipulation or fraud as a result of a security weakness. This requirement does not prohibit the loading of a new class of lottery chances should an existing lottery class be completed.

(h) Where changes to the set of lotteries offered to the player for selection are performed outside of the site operator's opening hours it is permissible to do so while credits remain on the player's credit meter provided that there are adequate measures to ensure the machine is not accessible to players and that any credits are retained for the benefit of the next player following such a procedure.

(i) Where allowed by this section, the set of lotteries offered to the player may be modified as long as any changes made do not in any way affect any lottery class (or classes) provided on the machine until all tickets within that class (or classes) have been purchased. This is to ensure that any changes made, affect the whole class and not simply a part of a class. This requirement does not apply if changes to the set of lottery games are being made because there is evidence of lottery manipulation or fraud as a result of a security weakness.

[1] See Regulation 2 and 10, Gaming Machine (Circumstances of Use) Regulations 2007

[2] Within the meaning of the Categories of Gaming Machine Regulations 2007

6.0 SPECIFIC ERROR CONDITIONS AND ALERT REQUIREMENTS

6.1 GENERAL ALERT CONDITIONS

Gaming machines and devices must be capable of detecting, displaying and alerting the operator to the error conditions listed below. These must be cleared either by an attendant or upon initiation of a new play sequence and where any on-line monitoring and control system is networked to the machine details of the error should be communicated to it:

(a) coin-in jam (where the coin acceptor disables itself under such circumstances it is not a requirement that it display an error message)
(b) coin-out jam
(c) hopper empty or timed out
(d) hopper runaway or extra coin paid out
(e) critical memory error (including an indication of battery failure or low battery power source);
(f) note acceptor-in jam
(g) program error or authentication mismatch
(h) main door open
(i) reverse coin-in (coin travelling the wrong way through acceptor)
(j) reel spin errors, including a miss-index condition for rotating reels, that affect the outcome of a pseudo 'game' used to display the result of a lottery chance:
    (i) the specific reel number must be identified in the error code
    (ii) in the final positioning of the reel, if the position error exceeds one-half of the width of the smallest symbol excluding blanks on the reel strip
    (iii) microprocessor controlled reels must be monitored to detect malfunctions such as a reel which is jammed, or is not spinning freely, or any attempt to manipulate their final resting position
(k) power reset
(l) logic cage open (where applicable).

NOTE: This rule also applies to the 'Note Acceptor Error Conditions' as to which see 6.3 below.

For machines or devices or individual lottery systems that use error codes, a description of such codes and their meanings shall be affixed inside the machine or device. This does not apply to video-based lotteries; however, video based lotteries shall display meaningful text to describe the relevant error condition.

6.2 PRINTER ERROR CONDITIONS

A printer shall have mechanisms to allow software to interpret and act upon the following conditions:

(a) out of paper or paper low
(b) presentation error (TITO only)
(c) printer jam/failure
(d) printer disconnected which may only be detected when the software tries to print.

These conditions shall trigger an error condition to indicate the error has occurred.

6.3 NOTE ACCEPTOR ERROR CONDITIONS

Each gaming machine or device (including note acceptors) must have the capability of detecting and displaying (for note acceptors, it is acceptable to disable or flash a light or lights) the following error conditions:

(a) Note Jams – it is acceptable for the note acceptor to indicate there is a note jam by disabling itself from accepting any more notes or by some other method.

(b) Stacker or Main Door Open (where stacker installed) or Stacker Removed.

A note acceptor must perform a self-test at each power up. In the event of a self-test failure, the note acceptor must automatically disable itself (ie enter note reject state) until the error state has been cleared.

7.0 METER REQUIREMENTS

7.1 CREDIT/PLAY METER

Credits used to purchase a new lottery ticket (see section 5.7) must come from a single meter which may be described as a credit or play meter. The player shall have the option to view any funds held in such a meter as a monetary value.

7.2 ACCOUNTING AND OCCURRENCE METERS

The machine must have at least one primary metering system which is independent of the main control system. All reasonable efforts should be made to ensure that data held by the primary metering system is true and accurate and impervious to tampering or any unauthorised modification.

The primary metering system must, as a minimum requirement, be capable of accurately recording the following data:

(a) cash in

(b) cash and/or ticket value out

(c) change (if available)

(d) winnings

For machines or devices which offer the player a choice of more than one lottery the above data must be accurately recorded for each lottery offered.

In all cases the data held on the metering system must be such that the percentage return to player can be accurately calculated and available for inspection for each class of lottery in use. In instances where a terminal is able to offer multiple lotteries such information shall be available for each lottery.

Any meter used to record the above information must have a minimum capacity of seven digits.

It must not be possible for values on meters to increase or decrease in value while any of the machine cabinet doors are open.

7.3 NOT APPLICABLE TO THIS CATEGORY OF MACHINE.
7.4 NOT APPLICABLE TO THIS CATEGORY OF MACHINE.
7.5 NOT APPLICABLE TO THIS CATEGORY OF MACHINE.

8.0 ARTWORK AND LOTTERY DISPLAY REQUIREMENTS

8.1 INFORMATION TO BE DISPLAYED

A gaming machine or relevant device must display, on the machine itself or on screen, information to enable players to keep track of their gambling. As a minimum, the following information must be available to the player at all times the machine is available for player input:

(a) the player's current bank balance (where relevant)

(b) number of plays available or current credit balance (monetary value)

(c) the cost to enter the lottery or each lottery if more than one is provided
(d) all possible winning outcomes, or a link to where this information may be viewed, eg on a help menu
(e) win amounts for each possible winning outcome, or a link to where this information may be viewed, eg on a help menu
(f) the player options selected (eg which lottery is in play) for the last purchased lottery ticket (until the next ticket is purchased or a new selection is made).

It is not permissible to state or imply that a prize greater than the statutory maximum for a single lottery may be won by means of the machine nor to indicate that the machine is in a state which could be beneficial to the player (such as number of 'tickets' left in the class or prizes yet to be won).

8.2 MULTI-LINE PSEUDO 'GAMES'

(a) Each individual line to be played shall be clearly indicated by the gaming machine or device so that the player is in no doubt as to which lines are involved in the pseudo 'game'.
(b) The winning play line(s) shall be clearly discernable to the player (eg on a video display it may be accomplished by drawing a line over the symbols on the play line(s) and/or the flashing of winning symbols and line selection box. Where there are wins on multiple lines, each winning play line may be indicated in turn. This would not apply to reel based pseudo 'games').

8.3 DISPLAY NOTICE REQUIREMENTS

(a) The following statement must be displayed on the face of the machine or at the time the lottery is selected where more than one lottery is offered to the player, clearly visible to the player:

    NO PRIZE GREATER IN VALUE THAN [JACKPOT] POUNDS CAN BE WON FROM THIS MACHINE AS A RESULT OF PLAYING THE MACHINE ONCE

(b) The actual percentage return to player for each lottery class must be clearly displayed to the player on the machine in the format below.:

    ON COMPLETION THE LOTTERY SELECTED HAS A PERCENTAGE PAYOUT OF (VALUE)%

    Percentage return to player equals the total value of all wins within an entire lottery class divided by the total cost of all 'tickets' in an entire lottery class, shown as a percentage.
    This figure must be calculated prior to the sale of any 'tickets' within the class and must not be updated as 'tickets' are sold.

(c) The following statement must be displayed on the machine, clearly visible to the player:

    MALFUNCTION VOIDS PAYS AND PLAYS

    For the purposes of this standard this statement means that a machine malfunction voids the chance in the lottery within which the malfunction occurs and does not affect the position of the player prior to that specific lottery chance, including win and credit meters.

(d) Where the machine is designed such that the deposited sum cannot be delivered by the machine for any reason then the following statement must be clearly displayed on the face of the machine:

    THIS MACHINE PAYS (£ minimum value payable) ONLY ANY LESSER AMOUNTS WILL BE RETAINED FOR FUTURE USE

9.0 DEFINITIONS

Address Space	A range of discrete addresses, each of which may correspond to a physical or virtual memory register, a network host, peripheral device, disk sector or other logical or physical entity.
Chance (within a class)	single result (win or lose) from the full set of possible results available within a lottery class. One chance is represented by one ticket.
Chance Cycle	as the meaning ascribed to it in paragraph 5.7.
Change	Money paid out which was inserted by the player that has neither been played nor committed to play.
Class	A finite set of lottery results made up from winning and losing chances.
Critical Lottery Files	All files that may affect the outcome of a lottery, including executables, data, and operating system files.
Critical Memory	Has the meaning ascribed to it in paragraph 3.1.
Critical Memory Clear	The process to reset the critical memory of a gaming machine, which configures the gaming machine into the 'as new' state.
Device	Any component of a gaming machine and, where the context requires, includes computer software used in a gaming machine.
Error Condition	A detectable event outside of the gaming machine's normal operating parameters.
Gaming Machine	Has the meaning ascribed to it by section 235 of the Act.
Hashing Algorithm	Reproducible method of turning some kind of data into a (relatively) small number that may serve as a digital 'fingerprint' of the data
Lottery	Has the meaning ascribed to it by section 14 of the Act.
Machine Malfunction	Any hardware and/or software fault that temporarily results in an unforeseen lottery outcome, or corruption and/or renders the machine unserviceable. Deliberate player actions to trigger a machine fault are not considered to be a machine malfunction.
MD5 or SHA	Message-Digest Algorithm 5 and Secure Hash Algorithm respectively.
Normal Mode	Where a gaming machine is in a configuration designed for play (not in test or other non-play mode) and in a serviceable condition with no errors detected.
Non-volatile Computer Memory	Memory that can retain the stored information even when not powered. Eg read-only memory, flash, hard disk, floppy disk, magnetic tape and optical disc drives.
'Off chip' Battery Source	Battery source independent of a data storage chip used for data refresh purposes (recharges state of data bytes when mains power is disconnected).
Patch Wires and Track Cuts	Modifications to a circuit board, post manufacture, including soldering additional wires to bridge the electrical conductor paths or the addition of a component (patch wires) or to change the circuit path by cutting the copper conductor (track cut).
Pseudo 'Game'	A portrayal of a game which is used to display the outcome of a lottery chance. This is a display method only and nothing done within the game may affect the outcome of the lottery chance.

Program Storage Devices ('PSD')	Means any device used to store software code in read only or read write format as required by the gaming machine in its normal operation.
ROM	Read only memory.
Seeding	Means an integer used to set the starting point for generating a series of random numbers.
Percentage Return to Player	Percentage return to player equals the total value of all wins within a lottery class divided by total cost of all 'tickets' in a lottery class, shown as a percentage
Ticket	A 'ticket' includes a document or article which can be used to prove membership of a class for the purpose of the allocation of prizes in a lottery, but references to purchase of a ticket include doing any thing to acquire one chance in the lottery.
TITO	Ticket in, ticket out system.
Updates	Any software modification that may affect the outcome of the lottery.

Gambling Commission June 2008

SKILL WITH PRIZES MACHINES

13 July 2009

Leslie Macleod-Miller
BACTA
Alders House
133 Aldersgate Street
London EC1A 4JA

Dear Leslie

6.2634 As you are aware, the Gambling Commission (the Commission) has been reviewing recent developments with respect to skill with prizes machines (SWPs) in order to ascertain whether or not some games described as SWPs are in fact gaming machines as defined in the Gambling Act 2005 (the Act). This is in line with our commitment in my letter to you of 17 November 2007 to keep the issue under consideration in the light of developments.

I am writing now to let you know that the Commission is of the view that 'skill games' which are designed to look like recognised games of chance (such as roulette or bingo) are being presented as involving an element of chance and are therefore games of chance according to section 6 (2)(a)(iii) of the Act.

Such machines are subject to all the regulations and controls which apply to gaming machines, for example in relation to supply, location, numbers, stakes and prizes and technical standards. In this respect, we believe at least some machines are being illegally sited and operated. We are contacting the manufacturers of such machines.

In addition, and in the light of what BACTA has told us, the Commission has also developed grounds for concern regarding the compensation or control mechanism used in some types of machines. In particular whether in reality the compensation or control mechanism operates in such a way that it introduces an element of chance into the way the game is played, at least on some occasions. If so, the machines are gaming machines as defined by section 6(2)(a)(i) of the Act.

More widely, we would like to work with the industry (including BACTA), HMRC and others to develop a list of characteristics exhibited by genuine SWP machines to provide the industry, regulators and the public with greater clarity about the status of individual machines. We will be in touch in due course with our initial thoughts on such a list.

Yours sincerely

James Holdaway
Policy Programme Manager
Gambling Commission July 2009

JOINT STATEMENT BETWEEN HMRC AND THE GAMBLING COMMISSION IN RELATION TO AMUSEMENT MACHINES WHICH OFFER GAMES DESIGNED TO LOOK LIKE RECOGNISED GAMES OF CHANCE

14 December 2009

6.2634.1 This joint statement outlines HMRC's policy and the Gambling Commission's views in relation to amusement machines which offer games which are designed to look like recognised games of chance.

BACKGROUND

HMRC and the Gambling Commission are aware that manufacturers have produced amusement machines marketed as skill with prize but which offer games which are designed to look like recognised games of chance (such as roulette, bingo or poker). In our view, such games are being presented as involving an element of chance and are therefore games of chance by dint of section 6 (2)(a)(iii) of the Gambling Act 2005. Further the machines on which the games are played are gaming machines under s25 of the Betting and Gaming Duties Act 1981 and s235 of the Gambling Act 2005.

GUIDANCE

Machines which offer such games that are presented as involving an element of chance are liable to Amusement Machine Licence Duty (AMLD) unless they fall within one of the exemptions for machines with small stakes and prizes. Further, such games must only be sited where the correct permissions for a gaming machine are in force under the Gambling Act 2005. Anybody wishing to manufacture, supply or maintain such a machine must also obtain the applicable operating licence from the Gambling Commission.

A GAME OF CHANCE

The manner in which a game is presented includes not only the game title and/or the way in which it is described on the machine's livery but also how the game itself is presented to the player. A business cannot therefore avoid AMLD or restrictions on where machines can be sited by just changing the game title or the manner in which it's described. They would also have to change the way the game is presented to the person playing the game on the machine such that it's no longer presented as involving an element of chance.

IMPLICATIONS

Depending on stake and prize limits, these machines are therefore liable to Amusement Machine Licence Duty.

These machines will also be subject to the requirements for gaming machines under the Gambling Act 2005.

WHAT YOU NEED TO DO

If you provide a machine on any premises offering games presented as games of chance such as bingo, roulette and poker you must hold a valid AMLD licence before you make the machine available for play unless the machine falls within one of the exemptions.

You should also ensure you satisfy the requirements of the Gambling Act 2005 in that the correct permissions are in force to be able to site the machine, the machine entitlement is not exceeded and the stake/prize made available complies with the applicable limits. Manufacturers, suppliers and any entity maintaining the machine should also ensure it complies with the applicable regulations and Commission technical standards for gaming machines.

If you are unsure whether your machine is liable to duty, you should consult HMRC on the Helpline on 0845 010 9000 with full details of the game before making the machine available for play.

If you are unsure as to whether you are permitted to have a gaming machine on your premises please contact the Gambling Commission on 0121 230 6666.

FURTHER INFORMATION

HMRC provides guidance in Notice 454 (October 2007) which can be viewed on www.hmrc.gov.uk under 'Quick Links' click on 'library' then on publications and then on 'Notices, Information Sheets and other reference materials'.

The Gambling Commission provides guidance at www.gamblingcommission.gov.uk.

Gambling Commission December 2009

COMPUTERS IN GAMBLING PREMISES, DUAL-USE COMPUTERS

November 2010

1 INTRODUCTION

6.2634.2 1.1 The Gambling Commission (the Commission) has received a number of enquiries from the gambling industry about whether computers offering access to gambling websites can be sited in gambling premises.

1.2 The purpose of this advice note is to set out a range of indicators you will need to take into account when considering whether a specific arrangement is permitted. This advice is not a comprehensive or a binding interpretation of the law and anyone intending to provide gambling facilities should refer to the Act and if necessary seek independent legal advice.

2 RELEVANT LEGISLATION

2.1 Section 5 of the Gambling Act 2005 (the Act) defines facilities for gambling. If you are providing facilities for gambling as defined in section 5, you will require the appropriate operating licence from the Commission, unless a relevant exemption applies.

2.2 Section 235(1) of the Act defines a gaming machine as a machine that is designed or adapted for use by individuals to gamble (whether or not it can also be used for other purposes). Section 235(2) then lists a number of computers, devices and machines which are not necessarily gaming machines just because they can be used to participate in gambling.

2.3 The Act and relevant regulations provide that gaming machines can only be provided with the appropriate permission (operating and premises licence, permit or alcohol licence as appropriate). In addition, gaming machines must also comply with the relevant requirements[1] regarding the number of gaming machines allowed and the limits on stakes and prizes. Details of these requirements are contained on the Commission's website.

3 COMPUTERS IN GAMBLING PREMISES

3.1 The Commission has received a number of enquiries in relation to the exemptions applying to dual use computers, which are covered in section 235(2)(a) of the Act and relevant regulations[2].

DUAL-USE COMPUTERS

3.2 The regulations state that a computer is a dual-use computer (and therefore not a gaming machine) within the meaning of section 235(2)(a) of the Act if:

(a) it is capable of being used for a purpose that is not related to gambling, and

(b) either-

- (i) it is not knowingly adapted or presented by the owner or a person connected with the owner, in such a way as to facilitate, or to draw attention to the possibility of, its use for gambling, or
- (ii) it is so adapted or presented but only where its use is limited to private use or it is being adapted, maintained or repaired.

1 For further information on gaming machine entitlement for different types of premises go to the Gaming Machine section on the Commission's website www.gamblingcommission.gov.uk

2 The Gambling Act 2005 (Gaming Machines) (Definitions) Regulations 2007 SI 2007/2082

3.3 In short a computer is not a gaming machine merely because there is a possibility of accessing a gambling website via the internet. However, a computer will be considered a gaming machine if it is knowingly adapted or is presented to facilitate or draw attention to the possibility of it being used for gambling.

3.4 It is not possible to provide a definitive list of examples of what constitutes a computer that is knowingly adapted or presented to facilitate or draw attention to the possibility of it being used for gambling. Each case will need to be looked at individually and ultimately the decision regarding whether a machine is a gaming machine is one for the courts to make.

3.5 The precise circumstances in which the facilities are offered - including the environment in which they are offered and the relationship with other gambling facilities provided - will need to be taken into account when assessing the status of those facilities. The Commission has provided the following indicators that may help in making decisions about whether a computer is knowingly adapted or presented to facilitate or draw attention to the possibility of it being used for gambling. This list is not exhaustive, and the presence or absence of any single factor is not necessarily conclusive:

- icons for gambling websites displayed on the desktop screen
- links to gambling websites available via the start menu
- screensavers, desktop wallpapers referring to gambling websites
- internet browsing history or favourites menu containing gambling websites
- promotional material (ie posters/flyers) indicating the use of computers for gambling
- gambling software downloaded onto a computer
- staff informing customers of the existence of the computer for access to gambling websites
- emails or other promotional material sent to customers/individuals referring to the availability of computers on premises for gambling purposes.

3.6 This advice draws on the Commission's experience to date and is designed to assist operators in understanding whether an arrangement involving the use of computers is permitted. Ultimately, it is the responsibility of the operator to ensure that it is acting legally.

Note

Regulatory return forms (October 2011) and guides as to how to complete them (June 2011) are available from the Gambling Commission's website at www.gamblingcommission.gov.uk

ILLEGAL GAMING MACHINES, A QUICK GUIDE FOR LICENSING OFFICERS

August 2011

6.2634.3 In order to site gaming machines some form of authorisation is normally required[1]. Typically this is:

- an operating licence from the Gambling Commission and a gambling premises licence from a licensing authority or
- an alcohol premises licence from a licensing authority or
- a gaming machine permit from a licensing authority.

Depending on the authorisation, there are limits placed on the category of machines than can be sited and, in some cases, on the number of machines that can be made available for use.

ESTABLISHING PREMISES AUTHORISATION

Your public register of gambling premises will confirm whether a licence has been granted. A copy of the licence must be available for inspection.

Qualifying alcohol licensed premises are entitled to two gaming machines of category C or D upon notification to the licensing authority. A gaming machine permit is required if there are more than two category C or D gaming machines sited (see part 26 of the *Guidance to Licensing Authorities – May 2009* for details.

Clubs, miners' welfare institutes and commercial clubs require a club machine permit for gaming machines to be sited within their premises (see table overleaf).

GAMING MACHINE CATEGORY

The gaming machine category should be clearly labelled on the body of the cabinet (see the example illustrations within this guide). If no category label is found, the category:

- may be shown on the video screen
- can be determined by comparing the stated maximum stake and prize on the machine to the statutory stake and prize limits for gaming machines (as summarised below[2]).

Premises and authorisation	Machine category			
	B3	B4	C	D
Adult gaming centre with an operating licence from the Gambling Commission and a premises licence	Maximum of 4 machines in category B3 or B4, or 20% of the total number of gaming machines		No limit on category C or D machines	
Family entertainment centre with a premises licence			No limit on category C or D machines	
Family entertainment centre with a gaming machine permit				No limit on category D machines
Clubs or miners welfare institutes with a club machine permit	Maximum of 3 machines in categories B3A or B4 to D but only one B3A machine can be sited as part of this entitlement			
Commercial club with a club machine permit		A maximum of 3 machines in categories B4 to D		
Qualifying alcohol-licensed premises with an alcohol licence			2 machines of category C or D automatic upon notification to the licensing authority	
Qualifying alcohol licensed premises with a gaming machine permit			Number of category C or D machines as specified on gaming machine permit	
Travelling fair				No limit on category D machines

Maximum stakes and prizes	B3A	B3	B4	C	D (money prize)
Maximum stake	£1	£2	£1	£1	£0.10
Maximum prize	£500	£500	£250	£70	£5

SKILL WITH PRIZES (SWP) MACHINES

In general terms, machines marketed as SWP machines offering games designed to look like recognised games of chance (such as roulette, bingo or poker) are indeed games of chance under the Gambling Act 2005. They are therefore gaming machines and not SWPs.

If the machine offers prizes of more than £50 the Gambling Commission is doubtful whether they can be genuine SWPs.

We issued a joint statement with HMRC in December 2009 which sets out our views in respect of games presented as recognised games of chance.

Our advice not: *Is a prize machine a gaming machine? July 2010*, provides further information including a flow diagram to help determine whether a prize machine is a gaming machine.

WHAT TO DO IF GAMING MACHINES APPEAR TO BE ILLEGALLY SITED

If the premises does not have authorisation to site gaming machine(s) you should:

- advise the premises owner/occupier that they are committing an offence under the Gambling Act 2005 (sections 37 and 242) and are liable to a maximum penalty of imprisonment
- ask the premises owner/occupier to remove the gaming machine(s) from the premises. As the gaming machine(s) may be reliant on an authorisation granted by the licensing authority – for example an alcohol licence, a gambling premises licence or a club permit – other parts of their business could be put in jeopardy if they do not comply. They might, for example, lose their alcohol licence
- contact Her Majesty's Revenue and Customs (HMRC) as experience shows there is the possibility that the relevant duties/taxes applicable to gaming machines might not have been paid. HMRC also has powers under separate legislation to collect monies due and stop illegal machine usage
- inform the Gambling Commission (see below).

Under section 317 of the Gambling Act 2005 an authorised person may 'remove and retain anything if he reasonably believes that it is being used or has been used in the commission of an offence under this Act'. This power has been used by a licensing authority to seize suspected illegal machines. You may wish to obtain advice as to the agreed regulatory processes within your licensing authority.

Under specific circumstances, particularly in relation to illegal machine supply, the Gambling Commission has acted with HMRC and/or the police to seize illegal machines.

PROVIDING INFORMATION TO THE GAMBLING COMMISSION

There is a requirement for those manufacturing and supplying gaming machines to be licensed by the Gambling Commission, as well as those involved in certain aspects of machine maintenance.

Our effort is focused on the illegal supply of gaming machines. Illegal suppliers often conduct their transactions across a number of licensing authorities. Your help in supplying information about illegally sited machines helps us to take action against illegal suppliers and reduce the incidence of illegally sited machines in your area.

Please email intelligencereports@gamblingcommission.gov.uk, enter 'Illegal Gaming Machine Supply' in the subject line and provide:

(1) the name of the manufacturer and game title
(2) the stake and prize stated on the machine (if available)
(3) all available contact details of the supplier.

GAMING MACHINE (FRUIT MACHINE, SLOT MACHINE) MANUFACTURING, SUPPLY, MAINTENANCE, INSTALLATION, AND REPAIR (INFORMATION NOTE)

December 2011

[1] Except if there is no opportunity to win a prize from the machine, or the only prize is another opportunity to play the machine, or the value of the prize does not exceed any payment made to use the machine.

[2] A full list of machine categories, types of premises permitted to site machines, and machine category stakes and prizes if available in appendix A and B of the Guidance to Licensing Authorities (GLA) – May 2009.

6.2634.4 The Gambling Commission frequently receives queries about the types of activities that can be carried out on gaming machines (fruit machines, slot machines) without the requirement for a licence. It is an offence under the Gambling Act 2005 to supply, install, adapt, maintain or repair a gaming machine (or part of a gaming machine) without the appropriate operating licence. However, operators who are licensed or have an appropriate permit (issued by a local licensing authority) to make a gaming machine available for use may carry out certain tasks in relation to the gaming machine, under limited circumstances, as explained below.

This information sets out the types of activity which we consider would not require a licence. This information does not constitute legal advice, nor does it set out our legal opinion. Where any doubt exists it is always recommended that you seek your own advice. It also covers activities which may only be carried out by those with a licence or permit to make a gaming machine available for use. If you do not have an appropriate permit or licence, you cannot legally carry out these activities.

MANUFACTURE AND SUPPLY OF GAMING MACHINES (FRUIT MACHINES, SLOT MACHINES)

Under the Gambling Act 2005 it is an offence to manufacture or supply a gaming machine (fruit machine, slot machine) or part of a gaming machine (including software) without the appropriate licence. 'Supply' in this context includes selling a gaming machine. This prohibition does not apply to parts of a gaming machine which do not affect game outcome (such as fuses, light bulbs and artwork) or part exchanging a machine with a licensed supplier.

MAINTENANCE AND REPAIR OF GAMING MACHINES (FRUIT MACHINES, SLOT MACHINES)

Under the Gambling Act 2005 it is an offence to maintain or repair a gaming machine (fruit machine, slot machine) or part of a gaming machine (including software) without the appropriate licence. There are however certain maintenance and repair activities which may need to be carried out on a day-to-day basis, for which additional licences or permits are not required. These are activities which cannot affect the outcome of the game.

Such activities are likely to include, but are not limited to:

- changing the front display of the gaming machine (including glass or paper artwork but not software modifications for video display)
- changing display notices on the gaming machine
- cleaning the gaming machine
- clearing coin jams and emptying hoppers
- changing fuses/light bulbs
- moving the gaming machine to a new location within the licensed premises
- changing percentage, stake and/or prize settings provided this does not require any software modification.

INSTALLATION OF GAMING MACHINES (FRUIT MACHINES, SLOT MACHINES)

Generally, where the installation is of a type which does not affect the outcome of the game, it may be carried out without a licence. For example, plugging in a network cable, or plugging a gaming machine into an electricity socket, would not require a licence.

The following activities however would require a licence:

- Installing components, either as part of a repair or maintenance schedule, which has an impact upon game outcome.
- Installing a retrofit component which impacts upon game outcome.
- Installing any external component, including that in relation to server-based systems, which impacts upon game outcome.
- Installing software code, security patches, game upgrades or new games.

Where a technician is required to carry out an installation task, they must be licensed appropriately.

ADAPTING A GAMING MACHINE (FRUIT MACHINES, SLOT MACHINES)

All activities which adapt gaming machines require a licence, including:

- making changes which alter the category of machine (unless this involves only a simple switch or dongle change, or changing artwork)
- making modifications to machine security devices (other than external security devices such as locks or security snakes)
- modifying components, as part of a repair or maintenance schedule, which has an impact upon game outcome
- swapping out components that may affect the outcome of the game
- stake/prize changes
- changing percentage, stake and/or prize settings where software modification is required.

WHAT IF I NEED TO DO SOMETHING THAT REQUIRES A LICENCE?

If you already hold a full operating licence which allows you to provide facilities for gaming machines, you may apply for a linked gambling software or supplier licence which is cheaper than a full technical operating licence. This will allow you to supply, install, adapt, maintain or repair your own gaming machines. The cost of carrying out these activities must not exceed £50,000 per year (inclusive of all costs such as wages, parts and other expenses). If this amount is exceeded, a gaming machine technical operating licence will be required.

If you collect gaming machines as a private individual and you want to supply, repair, install or maintain a single machine, you will require a single machine permit. Single machine permits will only be issued in very limited circumstances, and not for commercial reasons. There are limits as to how many single machine permits we will grant to an individual.

If you do not hold a full operating licence and your circumstances mean that a single machine permit is not appropriate, you may choose to contract someone who is licensed to provide the necessary services. Before doing so you should ensure that they are appropriately licensed by us.

If you are considering applying for an operating licence, or if you have a query which is not answered here, you can contact us by telephoning 0121 230 6666 or submit your question online.

IS A LICENCE NEEDED TO REPAIR CIRCUIT BOARDS/PCS USED IN GAMING MACHINES?

August 2012

1 INTRODUCTION

6.2634.5 1.1 This guidance note seeks to clarify the position regarding the third party repair of certain gaming machine components and whether this task may be carried out without the need for a Commission operating licence.

2 LEGISLATION

2.1 The Gambling Act 2005 (the Act) requires that the repair of a gaming machine or part of a gaming machine requires a licence. The Act defines a part of a gaming machine as follows:

Section 235(3)(c) a reference to a part of a gaming machine:

(i) includes a reference to any computer software designed or adapted for use in a gaming machine, but

(ii) does not include a reference to a component of a gaming machine which does not influence the outcome of a game,

3 BACKGROUND

3.1 Gaming machines consist of many different components. Section 235(3)(c) of the Act defines a part of a gaming machine as set out above. Section 243 of the Act makes it an offence to manufacture, supply, install, adapt, maintain or repair a gaming machine or part of a gaming machine without an operating licence or an exception applying.

3.2 However, of the many varied parts of a gaming machine that could undergo repair, the only component that might be considered to influence the outcome of a game is either the bespoke main circuit board, or the personal computer (PC) – depending on the configuration of the gaming machine. It is already considered unnecessary for those manufacturing the basic gaming machine components to hold a Commission licence, whether they manufacture push buttons, note validators, main circuit boards or PCs. It would therefore seem disproportionate to require a third party repairer of those components to require such a licence, provided that any third party repairer is not able to influence the outcome of a game as a result of any repair.

3.3 Components such as main circuit boards and PCs would only normally be identified as gaming machine components when fitted into gaming machines. They would require gaming machine software to be installed onto them to be considered a component that could influence the outcome of a game.
3.4 Bespoke circuit boards and PCs are repaired predominantly without any gaming machine software installed on them. However, even if gaming machine software is installed, then the gaming machine software does not operate either during the repair or the subsequent testing of the hardware since this could inhibit the repair and testing processes.

4 LIMITATIONS OF THIS GUIDANCE

4.1 To remove components from, or reinstall components back into, a gaming machine an appropriate operating licence is required.
4.2 But, once a component has been removed from a gaming machine then the repair of that component can be carried out by a third party (person or company) which is not licensed by the Gambling Commission, providing that all the repairer does is to return the component back to its 'as new' operating condition. The assumption being that the repairer is remote from the entity that installs the repaired component back into the gaming machine and therefore they have no interest in the gambling. Also, their repairs must not be able to influence the outcome of the game. The above will only apply when the entity repairing the component is not the same entity that removes the component from or installs the component back into a gaming machine (they must be an independent third party).
4.3 The Commission will keep this under review to ensure that no risks to the licensing objectives arise from this clarification.

LICENSING AUTHORITY

GAMBLING ACT 2005 PERMITS: TRAINING MATERIALS FOR LICENSING AUTHORITIES
March 2007

INTRODUCTION[1]

6.2635 1. **Purpose of training package**
This is the second package of training materials produced by the Department for Culture, Media and Sport to assist licensing authority officers and councillors in undertaking their new responsibilities under the Gambling Act 2005 (the Act). The first package entitled The Gambling Act 2005: Training Materials for Licensing Authorities dealt with licensing authorities' responsibilities under part 8 of the Gambling Act, which concerned the granting, issuing and maintenance of premises licences. This pack focuses on licensing authorities responsibilities to issue various types of permits.

2. By making these training materials available, the Department hopes that licensing officers and councillors will be able to associate themselves with the principles and processes of the Act before taking on their new responsibilities from 21 May 2007. As a result, the Department hopes that this will increase the levels of confidence within licensing authorities in undertaking their new roles and responsibilities in relation to the licensing and regulation of gambling premises.

3. Similarly, the Department hopes that the quality and consistency of decision-making will be enhanced through the utilisation of this package, providing some assurance to the gambling industry, which is also undergoing a period of significant change.

4. However, these training materials do not constitute a verbatim blueprint for training; they are a flexible learning tool. They condense and refer to a large volume of information from the Act, Gambling Commission Guidance and other sources. Licensing authorities are encouraged to use the information contained in this training pack and adapt them to suit their own needs. If, for example, they wish to deliver less detailed training, they can do so. Furthermore, if a licensing authority wishes to devise its own training, it can do so — none of these training materials are mandatory. They are provided to assist local authorities in whatever way they can.

5. This package is part of an information strategy and should be used together with the relevant guidance and codes of practice issued by the Gambling Commission (eg the Gambling Commission's "Guidance to Licensing Authorities" published in April 2006), DCMS general guides (Local Authorities and Gambling etc.) and material produced by LACORS and the Institute of Licensing. The training should be delivered in conjunction with any existing and subsequent Regulations made by the Secretary of State or Scottish Ministers.

---

1 [*Author's note*: the earlier version of this document is dated 2.8.06.]

6. **Format of training package and target audience**
These training materials will be of most use to **licensing authority officers**, as their principle focus is on permits for low-level gambling. Licensing authorities have greater discretion to grant these without the involvement of outside parties (such as responsible authorities and interested parties, as with premises licences), as they are expected to be less contentious. Consequently, they are less likely to require the intervention of councillors and applications are more likely to be a formality. The training therefore predominately deals with procedural issues. However, councillors may also wish to attend for completeness, depending in some cases, on the level of delegation for various functions determined by the individual authority.

7. **User testing and Endorsements**

The training package has been piloted by licensing officers.

MODULE 1: GENERAL INTRODUCTION TO PERMITS

Key learning objectives:

- *Awareness and understanding of the purpose of permits*
- *Awareness and understanding of the different types of permits*
- *Awareness of generic issues concerning permits*
- *Awareness and understanding of licensing authorities' responsibilities regarding permits*

Reference materials:

- *Gambling Commission Guidance to Licensing Authorities: Part 23*
- *The Gambling Act 2005*

1. **What are permits for?**

Permits are issued to premises that either offer very low-stakes and prizes gambling, or premises whose primary function is not the provision of gambling facilities. Therefore, the only premises eligible to apply to licensing authorities for permits are:

- Unlicensed Family Entertainment Centres
- Alcohol Licensed Premises (under Licensing Act 2003)
- Clubs, both commercial and non-commercial
- Premises wishing to offer commercial prize-gaming

2. In contrast, licensing authorities issue premises licences to premises whose primary function is to provide gambling facilities and, in the case of casinos, bingo and betting shops, offer gambling with comparatively high stakes and prizes. Premises licences form part of a robust licensing regime which includes operating licences and personal licences. Premises licences are issued for:

- Casinos
- Bingo halls
- Betting shops and tracks
- Adult Gaming Centres
- Licensed Family entertainment Centres

3. **Permit types**

Licensing authorities will issue the following permits:

- Family Entertainment Centre Gaming Machine Permits
- Prize Gaming Permits
- Licensed Premises Gaming Machine Permits (licensing authorities will also receive notifications of a licensed premises' intention to exercise its automatic entitlement to two gaming machines)
- Club Gaming Permits
- Club Machine Permits

4. **How are permits different to premises licences?**

In addition to the difference outlined above, there are several key differences between permits and premises licences:

- Permit applicants/holders are not required to have operating licences
- There are no responsible authorities or interested parties in relation to permit applications
- Licensing authorities can only grant or reject permits, they can not attach conditions.
- Gambling Commission have less power and involvement in relation to permits than they do with premises licences.
- With the exception of permits relating to alcohol licensed premises, permits are of limited duration.

5. **Licensing authority role**

- Operators will apply to their licensing authority for all permits.
- Licensing authorities will dictate the form and manner of unlicensed FEC and Prize Gaming permits and stipulate any additional information required.

- The licensing authority will determine applications, which, in some cases, may involve consultation with the police and the Gambling Commission
- In general, the licensing authority has more discretion in the determination of permit application than with premises licences because:

1. there are no interested parties/responsible authorities to make representations(although the case of club permits, the police and Gambling Commission can make objections)
2. ***in the case of unlicensed FECs and prize gaming permits*** licensing authority need not have regard to the licensing objectives when determining applications
3. ***in the case of alcohol licensed premise permits*** licensing authorities can take into account "other matters . . . they think relevant" in addition to the licensing objectives and guidance

- However, in the case of club permits, the Gambling Act imposes limits on a licensing authority's discretion to refuse an application
- Once a permit is issued, licensing authorities will be responsible for the maintenance of permits

6. **Transitional arrangements**

- There is a transitional period before the new legislation comes into force in September 2007
- There is a slightly different application process for operators with existing permissions (ie permissions under the 1968 and 1976 gambling legislation).
- Providing certain conditions are met, most operators with existing permissions will be entitled to an equivalent permission under the new Act.
- The grounds for refusing applications from such operators are severely restricted.
- Alcohol licensed premises and clubs with existing permissions that do not expire until after September 2007 will be treated as though they have an equivalent permit under the Gambling Act 2005 until such time as their existing permission expires.
- In such circumstances, the operator will have to abide by the new rules from 1 September 2007.

MODULE 2: INTRODUCTION TO GAMING MACHINES

Key Learning Objectives:

- *Understanding of what is meant by the term "gaming machine"*
- *Understanding of the role of the Gambling Commission in respect of gaming machines*
- *Understanding of the categories of gaming machines*
- *Awareness of age restrictions*
- *Awareness of difference between skill for prizes and gaming machines*

Reference Materials:

- *Gambling Commission Guidance to Licensing Authorities: Part 16*
- *Gambling Act 2005: Part 10*
- *Gambling Act regulations concerning Gaming Machines*

1. **Key Principles**

- The term "gaming machine" has a broad definition but there are also some important exceptions
- The Gambling Commission licence manufacturers and suppliers of gaming machines, set technical standards for machines and have considerable expertise and powers in relation to machines
- Machines are divided into four categories, only three of these categories (B4, C and D) are permitted by permits (Although the Act only refers to category B machines, regulations will specify that the relevant category of machine for club machine permits is category B4).
- The only determining factor in a machine's categorisation is the level of stakes and prizes, rather than the game that is offered

- Age restrictions apply to categories A,B and C, but not to category D
- Skill game machines are different from gaming machines and are not subject to the Gambling Act

2. **Gaming Machines and Permits**

With the exception of prize gaming permits, all permit types provide permission to make gaming machines available. Some permits limit the number of machines a premises can have, others do not (further details in the next module). It is important to have a basic understanding of gaming machines and the various rules relating to them.

3. **Definition**

Section 235 of the Gambling Act defines the term "gaming machine". It includes all machines on which people can gamble. However, section 235 also outlines several important exceptions. For example, domestic computers, whilst potentially satisfying the definition of "gaming machines" because they can be used to access gambling websites, are exempt from the definition in the Act. The definition of domestic computers will be provided in regulations[1]. There is also a distinction drawn between gaming machines and skill machines (see paragraph 12, below). In their Guidance to Licensing Authorities the Gambling Commission advise licensing authorities to "take legal advice or contact the Commission if they have concerns about the precise legal nature of equipment being used on premises".

[1] See Gaming Machines Dual Use Regulations.

4. **The role of the Gambling Commission**

- The Gambling Commission will licence manufacturers and suppliers of gaming machines.
- The Commission will set technical standards relating to the way in which each category of machine will operate.
- They have power to make arrangements with any person to test the machines for compliance with their standards.
- Concerns over the manufacture, supply or repair of machines, or the manner in which they are operated should be brought to the attention of the Gambling Commission.

5. A condition of operating licences issued by the Gambling Commission requires operators to obtain machines only from licensed suppliers. However, permit holders do not require an operating licence and will not be subject to the Gambling Commission operating licence conditions (but will be subject to any relevant code of practice which is issued by the Commission). Licensing authorities do not have the power to attach a similar condition to permits. Instead, Gambling Commission guidance will advise permit holders to obtain machines only from licensed suppliers.

6. **Categories of machines**

- There are four categories of machines, A,B,C and D.
- Category B is sub-divided into four sub categories.
- The categories of machines are defined are according to their maximum stakes and prizes.
- The categories of machines permitted to be used in premises holding permits are limited to to categories B4, C and D.

7. It should be noted that one type of machine (ie slot machines) could be used as a machine in several categories. The only indicator of category type is the level of stakes and prizes, rather than the "game" that is being offered. Conceivably, a slot machine could be a category B or a category D machine.

8. Common examples of the type of machines being offered in the categories permitted by permits would include fruit machines for categories B4 and C, which can be themed in various ways (Deal or No Deal, Leprechaun, Austin Powers), and crane grabs, penny pushers and mechanised horse races for category D machines.

9. Annex A provides tables showing the **levels of stakes and prizes.**

10. **Age restrictions**

Category A, B and C machines are restricted to over 18's. At present there is no age restriction on category D machines. They are the only machines that children are allowed to play.

11. The permit holder will have to comply with the codes of practice issued by the Commission concerning the location of and access to machines by children and young persons. They will also have to comply with any codes of practice regarding the separation of category C and B machines from those of category D machines where they are located on the same premises.

12. **Skill games**

The Gambling Act 2005 does not cover machines that give prizes (including cash or non-cash) as a result of the application of skill by players. Such machines are often referred to as "skill with prizes" machines. The winning of a prize is determined by the player's skill, there is no element of chance. If there were an element of chance imparted by the machine, it would be a gaming machine. Skills games can include:

- Trivia games
- Racing games
- Shooting games

13. Many Family Entertainment Centres have games where prizes are given by redemption of tickets accumulated. Providing the games rely on skill such as shooting baskets with a basket ball or hoopla, then they are exempt.

ANNEX A
STAKES AND PRIZES BY MACHINE CATEGORY UNDER THE GAMBLING ACT 2005[2]

Category of Machine	Maximum Stake	Maximum Prize
A	Unlimited	Unlimited
B1	£2	£4,000
B2	Maximum single stake £15, maximum multiple stake £100 per game.	£500
B3	£1	£500
B4	£1	£250
C	50p	£35
D	10p 30p when non-monetary	£5 cash or non cash £8 token or non-monetary prize

[2] These figures are subject to Parliamentary approval

MODULE 3: PERMIT AND PREMISES TYPES AND EXEMPTIONS

Key Learning Objectives:

- *Understanding of function of each type of permits*
- *Understanding of what sort of premises each type of permit relates*
- *Awareness of permitted category and number of machines for each permit*
- *Awareness of Exempt Gaming and other provision of prize gaming in reliance on other permissions*

Reference Materials:

- *Gambling Act 2005: Part 10, Part 12, Part 13, Schedule 10, 12,13 and 14*
- *Gambling Commission Guidance to Licensing Authorities: Part 24,25,26 and 27*

- *Gambling Commission Gaming Machines Code of Practice – for Clubs and Alcohol Licensed Premises*
- *Gambling Commission Code of Practice for gaming in clubs and alcohol licensed premises – due to be published July 2007*
- *Relevant Gambling Act regulations*

1. **Key Principles**

- Family Entertainment Centre Gaming Machine Permits allows any number of category D machines to be made available.
- Prize Gaming Permits permit a variety of low stakes and prizes gambling, they do not permit any gaming machines.
- Prize gaming can be offered under the auspices of various other permits and permissions.
- (Alcohol) Licensed Premises Gaming Machine Permits allow category C and D machines to be made available.
- Club Gaming Permits allow "equal chance gaming", specified banker's games and 3 (in total) category B4,C or D machines to be made available.
- Club Machine Permits only permit 3 (in total) category B4,C or D machines to be made available.
- Clubs and Alcohol Licensed Premises can offer Exempt (equal chance) Gaming without a permit.

2. **Family Entertainment Centre Gaming Machine Permit**

- Family Entertainment Centres (FECs) can be either licensed (which means it has a premises licence) or unlicensed (***uFECs*** — which means it has Family Entertainment Centre Gaming Machine permit – referred to as a ***uFEC*** permit in these training materials).
- ***uFECs*** provide category D gaming machines for use by families and unaccompanied children.
- ***uFECs*** are often located at seaside resorts, in airports and at motorway service stations.
- Category D machines only offer low stakes and prizes gambling – maximum stake is 10p cash or 30p non-cash and the maximum prize is £5 cash or £8 non-cash.
- The Gambling Act does not impose a limit on the number of machines that can be made available under their ***uFEC*** permit.
- Under the auspices of their ***uFEC*** permit, ***uFECs*** can offer prize gaming on their premises (described below).
- ***uFEC*** permits replace section 34(1) permits under the 1968 Act.

3. In contrast, a **licensed FEC** can provide both category D and C gaming machines and is subject to the full licensing structure established by the Act (see previous training materials). The operator would also be required to comply with the relevant mandatory conditions. For example, category C machines must be located in areas separated from those to which under 18s may have access[3].

---

[3] For more information see DCMS' training on premises licences.

4. **Prize Gaming Permits**

- Prize gaming is a form of normally low stakes and prizes gambling in which neither the nature nor the size of the prize is determined by the number of persons playing or the amount paid for or raised by the gaming.
- It can comprise a variety of games (eg bingo or roulette), providing that the participation fees and prizes do not exceed the level to be prescribed in regulations.
- The prize can be a cash or non-cash prize.
- Any non-gambling premises (ie one that has not got a premises licence under the Gambling Act 2005) that wishes to provide such gambling would need to apply for a ***prize gaming*** permit.

- Holders of premises licences under the Act and holders of club gaming permits may not apply for prize gaming permits.
- Part 13 of the new Act, which concerns Prize Gaming, replaces and updates Section 21 of the Gaming Act 1968 and Section 16 of the Lotteries and Amusements Act 1976.

5. ***Prize gaming*** permits do not permit the provision of gaming machines. Certain equipment used for prize gaming – for example, mechanised cash bingo equipment — will not be treated as gaming machines by virtue of the exemptions to the general gaming machine definition included in Section 235.

6. Various forms of prize gaming are permitted as part of many of the other permits and premises licences issued under the Gambling Act 2005. Prize gaming is allowed in the following premises without a specific permit (but subject to certain conditions):

- Adult gaming centres
- Licensed family entertainment centres
- Unlicensed family entertainment centres with *uFEC* gaming machine permit
- Travelling fairs
- Bingo halls

7. The conditions under which those with the above permissions can provide prize gaming without a permit are listed in section 293 of the Act.

8. **Licensed Premises Gaming Machines Permit**

- Licensed Premises Gaming Machines permits (referred to in this training as an ***alcohol licensed premises*** permit) apply to premises with a Licensing Act 2003 on-premises alcohol licence that also serve alcohol without the requirement that it accompanies food.
- A pub, restaurant or hotel with a bar will be eligible to apply for an ***alcohol licensed premises*** permit, but hotels and restaurants that serve alcohol only with food will not.
- An ***alcohol licensed premises*** permit entitles a holder to make category C and D machines available for use, in addition to the exempt gaming described in paragraphs 21-25, below.
- There is no prescribed limit on the number of machines, but an applicant must specify the number they are applying for.
- Each permit must specify the number of machines it allows.
- Licensing authorities have discretion to reduce the number or vary the category of machines applied for (further details in the next module).
- Holders must comply with Gambling Commission Gaming Machine Code of Practice for Alcohol Licensed Premises, which concerns the location and operation of machines.

9. In addition, alcohol licensed premises have an **automatic entitlement** to make two category C or D gaming machines available for use without a permit (Section 282). If a premises intends to use this entitlement they must give notice to the licensing authority. They must also comply with the relevant Gambling Commission Code of Practice. The licensing authority does not have discretion to turn a notification down. However under Section 284 of the Act a licensing authority may make an order to remove the automatic entitlement, and therefore stop the premises from making gaming machines available. This power can only be exercised under specific circumstances set out in Section 284(2) generally involving an offence or breach of the licensing objectives. Similar powers exist in relation to exempt gaming on alcohol-licensed premises. The process for these procedures will be described in the next module.

10. **Club Gaming and Club Machine Permits**

There are three types of club recognised under the Gambling Act 2005.

11. **Members' clubs** – these must have at least 25 members and be established or conducted mainly for purposes other than gaming. The club should not be established to make a commercial profit and should be controlled by its members. Examples include most sports clubs, working men's clubs, branches of the Royal British Legion

and politically affiliated clubs. Although members clubs should generally be established or conducted for purposes other than gaming, regulations may permit certain types of gaming clubs.

12. **Commercial clubs** – these have the same characteristics as members clubs, except that they are established to make a profit. An example of such a club would be a snooker club. Certain bridge and whist clubs may operate as commercial clubs if they are established to make a profit.

13. **Miners' welfare institutes** – the definition of this class of club has changed to reflect social and economic changes since their establishment. These are associations established for recreational or social purposes. They are managed by a charitable trust which has received funds from one of a number of mining organisations.

14. **Club Gaming Permits** — Commercial clubs are not eligible for club gaming permits. These can be issued only to members' clubs and miners' welfare institutes and authorise:

- The provision of no more than three gaming machines — these can be from categories B4, C or D.
- The provision of equal chance gaming subject to the conditions for exempt gaming (described below), except that the limit on stakes and prizes is removed
- The provision of games of chance as prescribed in regulations.

15. The provision of gambling at clubs in reliance on a ***club gaming permit*** will be subject to the conditions listed below:

- *For equal chance gaming:*
- The same conditions as for exempt gaming described below apply, with the exception that any limit on stakes and prizes does not apply.
- *For other games of chance:*
- The games offered are limited to those prescribed in regulations.
- There is no participation fee charged otherwise than in accordance with regulations
- That no amount is deducted from sums staked or won otherwise than in accordance with any regulations made by the Secretary of State (current proposals are not to exercise this power at present)
- *For gaming machines:*
- No child or young person (under 18) can use category B or C machines on the premises.
- The permit holder needs to comply with any relevant provision of the Gambling Commission code of practice regarding the location and operation of gaming machines.
- *For all gaming:*
- The public, children and young persons are excluded from any area in which gaming is taking place
- In the case of members' clubs and miners' welfare institutes only, those taking part in the gaming must be a member of the club who applied for, or was nominated for membership at least 48 hours prior to participating, or are a guest of a member.

16. ***Club gaming permits*** replace the permissions provided by Part II registration under the 1968 Act.

17. **Club Machine Permits** – If a club does not wish to have the full facilities permitted by a ***club gaming permit***, or if they are a commercial club not permitted to provide non-machine gaming (other than exempt gaming under section 269), they may apply for a ***club machine permit***. This permits the holder to have up to three machines from the categories B4, C or D in addition to providing exempt gaming (subject to the conditions described below and the limit on stakes and prizes). It does not permit games of chance.

18. Three conditions are automatically attached to a club machine permit, they are:

- Prior membership (as described above) for use of the machines (but not for a commercial club)

- Children and young people must not play category B4 or C machines
- Gambling Commission codes of practice concerning the location and operation of machines (including any associated social responsibility provisions) must be complied with.

19. The club may provide equal chance gaming, as exempt under section 269, providing the conditions listed in that section are met.

20. ***Club Machine Permits*** replace the permissions provided by Part III registration under the 1968 Act.

21. **Exempt Gaming in Pubs and Clubs**

Alcohol licensed premises (which meet the criteria above for an ***alcohol licensed premises*** permit) and Clubs may offer games of equal chance without a permit, providing certain conditions are met.

22. In order to qualify for exemption, the gaming in a **club** must meet the conditions set out in section 269 of the Act:

- It must be equal chance gaming, as defined in Part 1 of the Act (examples would include bingo, poker or bridge)
- Stakes and prizes must be in accordance with any rules or limits prescribed in regulations
- The club must not deduct any amounts from sums staked or won in the gaming
- Any charge for participation must not exceed amounts prescribed in regulations
- The games played may only take place on one set of premises, meaning there may not be any linking of games between premises: Games may be considered linked if the game is split by sites so that part of one game is played elsewhere and:
- The result of one game is, or may be wholly or partly determined by reference to the result of the other game; or
- The amount of winnings is wholly or partly determined by the participation of more than one set of players;
- In the case of members' clubs and miners' welfare institutes only, people may only participate in the gaming if they have been a member (or applied or were nominated for membership) at least 48 hours before playing, or are genuine guests of such a person.

23. For gaming in an **alcohol licensed premises** to qualify for exemption, it must meet the conditions set out in section 279:

- It must be equal chance gaming (traditional examples in a pub may include dominoes and cribbage, although, in fact, there is no difference between the types of games that may be offered in pubs and clubs)
- Stakes and prizes must not exceed the prescribed limits as to value or amount.
- The licensed premises must not deduct any amounts from sums staked or won in the gaming.
- There must be **no charge** for participation.
- The games played may only take place on one set of premises, meaning there may not be any linking of games between premises.
- Children and young persons must be excluded from participation.

24. **High turnover bingo** – providing bingo played on the premises does not exceed £2000 in stakes or prizes in a seven day period (this is known as 'high turnover bingo'), it can be provided as an exempt (equal chance) game in both clubs and licensed premises. However, if high turnover bingo is played, the club or licensed premises will have to (a) notify the Gambling Commission, and (b) if, at the end of the seven days, it wants to continue to offer high turnover bingo in the following twelve months, it must obtain a bingo operating licence.

25. The Gambling Commission are planning to issue an additional Code of Practice under section 24 of the Act for non-machine gaming in clubs and pubs. Whilst the provisions of this code will not be binding on operators and licensees, it will be designed to help them meet their obligations and responsibilities under the Act, and would for example be admissible as evidence in any court proceedings and may be taken into

account by the Commission in the exercise of its functions.

ANNEX A
CATEGORIES OF GAMING MACHINE ENTITLEMENT BY TYPE OF PREMISES

	Machine category						
Premises	**A**	**B1**	**B2**	**B3**	**B4**	**C**	**D**
Clubs and Miner's Welfare Institutes with permit					√	√	√
Premises licensed for alcohol consumption						√	√
Unlicensed Family Entertainment Centre with permit							√
Travelling Fair							√

ANNEX B
NUMBER OF GAMING MACHINES BY PREMISES

	Machine category (x = category of machine not permitted on this type of premises)						
Premises	**A**	**B1**	**B2**	**B3**	**B4**	**C**	**D**
Clubs or Miners' welfare institutes with permits	X	X	X	x	3 in total, any combination of B4, C or D		
Premises licensed for alcohol consumption	X	X	X	x	x	2 in total, automatically, with notification.	
						In addition, as many as allowed by permit.	
Unlicensed FEC with permit	X	X	X	x	x	x	Any number
Travelling Fair	X	X	X	x	x	x	Any number

MODULE 4: APPLICATION, CONSIDERATION, GRANT AND BEYOND

Key Learning Objectives:

- *Understanding of application process for each type of licence*
- *Understanding of consideration process for each type of licence*
- *Awareness of matters that can be taken into account in considering applications*
- *Awareness of limits imposed by the Act in considering applications*
- *Understanding of process for grant and refusal*

- *Understanding and awareness of maintenance issues*

Reference Materials:

- *Gambling Act, especially Schedules 10, 12,13, and 14*
- *Gambling Commission Guidance to Licensing Authorities parts 24,25,26 and 27*
- *Related Gambling Act regulations*

Note that for existing operators (those with permissions under the existing legislation) applying during the transitional phase some of these processes will be slightly different — see Module 6.

APPLYING FOR A PERMIT

1. ***For all permits***

- Applicants are not required to have an operating licence
- An application cannot be made in respect of premises that have been issued a gambling premises licence
- The application must be made to the licensing authority in whose area the premises are wholly or partly situated (in the case of ***alcohol licensed premises*** permits, this will be the authority from which it obtained its on-premises licence)
- The application must be accompanied by the appropriate fee

2. ***Unlicensed FECs and Prize Gaming permits***

Applications for ***uFEC*** or ***prize gaming*** permits:

- can only be made by a person who:

1. Occupies or plans to occupy the premises intended to be used
2. In the case of an individual, is over 18 years of age

- should be made in the form and manner specified by the licensing authority
- should specify the premises to which it relates
- should be accompanied by any additional documentation (such as plans or insurance certificates) required by the authority
- for ***prize gaming*** permits, the application will ask the applicant to specify the nature of the gaming in respect of which the permission is being sought.

3. In addition, Gambling Commission Guidance suggests licensing authorities may wish to consider asking applicants to demonstrate the following during the application process:

4. *For* **uFECs** *permits:*

- That the applicant has a full understanding of the maximum stakes and prizes of the gambling permissible in unlicensed FECs;
- That the applicant has no relevant convictions (as set out in Schedule 7 of the Act); and,
- That staff are trained to have a full understanding of the maximum stakes and prizes

5. *For* **prize gaming** *permits:*

- That the applicant understands the limits to stakes and prizes that are set out in regulations;
- That the gaming offered is within the law

6. ***Alcohol Licensed Premises — Automatic Entitlement***

- Alcohol licensed premises (as described in the previous module) may make up to two category C or D machines available for use without requiring a permit or gambling licence.
- To exercise this entitlement the on-premises licence holder must
  - (a) notify the licensing authority in writing of his intention to make such machines available
  - (b) pay the prescribed fee.
- There is no other prescription regarding the form or content of the notification to be given.
- Licensing authorities have no discretion to turn a notification down.

6: Gambling Act 2005: Additional Material

- Once the operator has notified the licensing authority, he will be able to make the gaming machines available for use.
- The machines must be located and operated in accordance with the Gambling Commission's code of practice for Gaming Machines in Alcohol Licensed Premises.

7. Under Section 284 of the Act a licensing authority may make an order to remove the automatic entitlement from a specified premises, and therefore stop the premises from making gaming machines available, if:

- provision of gaming machines is not reasonably consistent with the licensing objectives
- gaming has taken place on the premises in breach of a condition of section 282 – for example, the gaming machines have been made available in a way that does not comply with requirements concerning their location and operation
- the premises are mainly used or to be used for gaming
- an offence under the Gambling Act has been committed on the premises
- these procedures also apply to the removal of the exempt gaming entitlement under section 279

8. A licensing authority must give the licensee at least 21 days notice of their intention to make such an order and consider any representations they may make. If the licensee requests a hearing, the authority must hold one and comply with any other procedural requirements set out in regulations.

9. If the licensee makes no representations the order can be made no less than 21 days after the notice of intention was given. Licensing authorities can allow a longer notice period but will still have to make the order when the time is up, or after the hearing. The licensee may appeal to the magistrates' court or the sheriff

10. *Alcohol Licensed Premises Permit*

For licensed premises wishing to make available more than two category C or D machines, the person or organisation who holds the "on-premises" alcohol licence for the premises in question must apply to the appropriate licensing authority for an ***alcohol licensed premises*** permit. The form and manner of the application, including any additional information and documentation, is to be decided by the licensing authority but must include the following, as stipulated by the Act:

- the premises for which the permit is sought
- the number and category of gaming machines

11. *Club Gaming/Machine permits*

For a club (as described in the previous module) to obtain a ***club gaming/machine*** permit, the club or institute must make an application to the relevant licensing authority in the format prescribed by the Secretary of State.

NOTICE OF APPLICATION AND REPRESENTATIONS

12. *For all permits*

- There are no interested parties or responsible authorities in relation to permits, as there are in relation to a premises licence.
- There is no requirement for the applicant to give notice of their application.
- There is no provision for representations in relation to an application for a permit.

But:

- Applicants for ***club gaming/machine*** permit must send a copy of their application to the Gambling Commission and Police, who may object to the application (unless the application has been made under the fast track procedure).
- For applications for ***prize gaming*** and ***uFEC*** permits, the licensing authority must consult the police before granting the application.

13. *Club Gaming/Machine permits – Fast-Track procedure*

- The fast track procedure only applies to clubs holding club premises certificates under section 72 of the Licensing Act 2003

- Section 72 of the Licensing Act 2003 authorises the sale or supply of alcohol or provision of regulated entertainments.
- Fast-track applications must be accompanied by the applicants section 72 certificate.
- The provisions for fast-track applications do not apply to Scotland
- The fast-track procedure is not available to clubs holding an alcohol premises licence as opposed to a club premises certificate.

What makes it fast?

- Applicants using the fast track do not need to submit copies of their application to the Gambling Commission or Police.
- The Gambling Commission and the Police cannot make objections in relation to fast tracked applications
- The grounds upon which an authority can refuse a fast track application are reduced (described below).

Why should section 72 certificated clubs benefit from a fast track?

- Because the club or institute will already have been through a licensing process in relation to its club premises certificate under the 2003 Act.
- It is therefore unnecessary to impose the full requirements of Schedule 12.

CONSIDERING AN APPLICATION – PRINCIPLES TO BE APPLIED

14. *For all permits*

- The licensing principles outlined for premises licences detailed in section 153 **do not apply** to applications for permits.
- The delegations outlined in sections 154 and 155 **do apply** (although for ***club gaming/machines*** the section 154 delegation has been amended slightly – see Schedule 12 section 28 (2)).
- Licensing authorities shall have regard to relevant Gambling Commission Guidance.

15. ***uFEC*** **and** ***Prize Gaming*** **permits**

When considering permit applications for ***uFECs*** and ***prize gaming,*** licensing authorities:

- **need not** (but may) have regard to the licensing objectives.
- must have regard to any guidance issued by the Gambling Commission
- can also draw up a statement of principles to be applied in relation to applications for ***uFEC*** and ***prize gaming*** permit applications

16. In particular, the statement may provide details of the factors to be taken into account when determining the suitability of the applicant to hold an ***uFEC*** permit or a ***prize gaming*** permit. This is a matter for the licensing authority rather than the Gambling Commission because ***uFECs*** and ***prize gaming*** operators are not required to have an operator licence. The consideration of child protection issues is likely to play a role in a licensing authority's determination of ***uFEC*** and ***prize gaming*** applications.

17. For ***prize gaming*** applications, the Gambling Commission guidance also indicates the following to be relevant considerations:

- any objections the police may have that relate to the licensing objectives
- any convictions the applicant may have that make them unsuitable to operate prize gaming
- the suitability of the premises in relation to their location and issues about disorder.

18. ***Alcohol Licensed Premises*** **and** ***Club Gaming/Machine*** **permits**

When considering applications for ***alcohol licensed premises*** permits and ***club gaming/machine*** permits licensing authorities:

- **do** need to have regard to the licensing objectives
- have regard to any guidance issued by the Gambling Commission
- in addition, in the case of ***alcohol licensed premises***, licensing authorities can take into consideration "other such matters as they think relevant"

- in addition, in the case of ***club gaming/machine*** permits, the Act restricts the grounds upon which a licensing authority can turn down an application (described below)

GRANTING AND REFUSING A PERMIT

19. ***For most permits:***

- On considering an application, a licensing authority can either grant or refuse it.
- Licensing authorities cannot attach conditions to a permit as with a premises licence.
- **In the case of an *alcohol licensed premises* permit only** — the licensing authorities can also grant a different number and category of machine.
- **For *uFEC, prize gaming*** and ***alcohol licensed premises*** the licensing authority can not refuse without having first given the applicant the opportunity to make representations.
- The Gambling Act does not stipulate a time-limit within which such representations must be made.

20. ***Refusal – uFECs and Prize Gaming***

Licensing authorities may not **refuse *uFEC*** or ***prize gaming*** permit applications unless they:

- notify the applicant of their intention to refuse their application
- give their reasons for refusal
- give the applicant the opportunity to make representations orally, in writing or both.

21. If a licensing authority maintains its decision to refuse an application after following the process above, it must notify the applicant of the refusal and give reasons for it.

22. ***Refusal – Club Gaming/Machines***

The grounds upon which a licensing authority can refuse an application for a ***club gaming/machine*** permit are limited in the Act to one or more of the following:

- the applicant not being a members' club or institute (bearing in mind that the only gaming clubs that meet the statutory definition for a members' club are those established for the purposes of prescribed types of gaming).
- the premises being wholly or mainly used by children or young persons
- an offence or licence breach having been committed in the course of gaming provided by the club
- a permit held by the applicant having been cancelled during the previous ten years
- an objection being made by the Police or Gambling Commission

23. If the licensing authority is minded to refuse an application based on the above, they are required to hold a hearing. However, the licensing authority can dispense with a hearing subject to the agreement of both the applicant and any person who objected to the application.

24. For ***fast-track club gaming/machine*** applications, the grounds for refusal are more limited. A licensing authority must grant an application unless they think they think:

- the club is established or conducted wholly or mainly for the provision of gaming, other than gaming of a prescribed kind (This means that licensing authorities are not obliged to grant the permit under this fast track procedure if they think the club is a gaming club, unless it is gaming of the prescribed kind and the club doesn't provide facilities for other types of non-machine gaming)
- the club is established wholly or mainly for the provision of gaming of a prescribed kind, but also provides gaming of another kind
- that a club gaming/machine permit held by the applicant has been cancelled during the previous ten years

25. A licensing authority is not required to hold a hearing if they decide to refuse a ***fast track club gaming/machines*** permit.

- an offence under the Act has been committed on the premises
- if the holder fails to pay the annual fee licensing authorities are *obliged* to cancel the permit in this case, unless they think the failure to pay is attributable to administrative error.

(For ***alcohol licensed premises*** the licensing authority also has the option to vary the number or category of machines authorised, instead of cancelling the permit)

46. If a licensing authority wishes to cancel (or vary) either a ***club gaming/machine*** permit or an ***alcohol licensed premises*** permit they would first have to

- give the permit holder 21 days notice
- consider any representations made by the holder
- hold a hearing if requested
- The licensing authority also needs to comply with any prescribed requirements for the procedure to be followed in considering whether to cancel (or vary) a permit.

47. The cancellation would not take effect until 21 days after notice of the intention to cancel was given. If an appeal is made the decision would not take effect until the appeal is determined.

RENEWAL

48. Apart from ***alcohol licensed premises*** permits which are of unlimited duration (subject to the premises continuing to hold an on-premises alcohol licence and the permit holder being the licensee), all other permits are of a fixed duration of ten years, unless they cease to have effect because they are surrendered, lapse or are forfeited. If the holder wishes to continue to provide gambling facilities after the permit expires, they will have to have their permit renewed.

49. For ***uFEC*** and ***prize gaming*** permits, an application for renewal must be made at least two months, but no more than six months, before the expiration of the permit. The procedure for renewal is the same as for an application. Whilst the renewal application is being considered, the permit will still have effect, including during the appeal process against a decision not to renew. The operator can only appeal once in respect of the decision – it would be an abuse of process to make multiple appeals in respect of the same decision

50. In the case of ***uFECs***, there are two grounds upon which a licensing authority may refuse to renew a permit.

(1) If a local authority officer has been refused access to the premises without reasonable excuse.

(2) If renewal would not be reasonably consistent with the licensing objectives – to determine this, the licensing authority will be able to consult the police and consider any concerns that may have arisen about the use of the premises during the life of the permit.

51. For ***Prize Gaming*** permit renewals, the statement of principles will have effect.

52. For ***club gaming/machine*** permits, an application for renewal must be made during the period beginning three months before the permit expires and ending six weeks before it expires. As with the other renewals, the procedure is the same as for application and the permit will still have effect during the consideration process and appeal process.

53. The consequence of not meeting these deadlines is that the premises will have to stop operating whilst they apply for a "new" permit?

MAINTENANCE

54. All permits must be kept on the premises and it is an offence not to produce it when requested by a constable, an enforcement officer or an authorised local authority officer.

55. ***Annual Fees***

- There are **no** annual fees for ***uFEC*** or ***prize gaming*** permits
- ***Alcohol licensed premises*** and ***club gaming/machine*** permits **do** have an annual fee.

56. *Change of name*

In the event that the holder of a permit changes their name, they should send their permit to the licensing authority accompanied by the appropriate fee and the authority must make the appropriate amendment and return it.

57. *Copies of permit*

Holders of all permit types can apply to a licensing authority for a replacement permit in the event that the original is lost, stolen or damaged, subject to paying the prescribed fee. The loss or theft of the permit must be reported to the police. Providing the licensing authority is satisfied that the permit has been lost, stolen or damaged, they must grant the application and issue a copy certified as a true copy.

58. *Variations*

Only ***alcohol licensed premises*** permits can be varied at the request of the holder. The holder can request a variation of the number or category of machines. The same processes as for the initial application apply.

59. *Transfers*

- Only ***alcohol licensed premises*** permits can be transferred to another person.
- This can only occur if the person who is seeking the transfer is also seeking to have the premises' Licensing Act 2003 on-premises licence transferred to him.
- The provisions for an application to issue of a permit apply to the application to transfer.
- The applicant must supply the permit, or a statement explaining why it is not practicable to produce the permit, with his application.
- The permit can not be transferred unless the alcohol licence transfer has been approved.
- If the permit transfer has been refused because the alcohol licence transfer is refused, the applicant can not make representations in relation to their permit refusal.

MODULE 5: INSPECTION, COMPLIANCE AND ENFORCEMENT

Key Learning Objectives:

- *Understanding of circumstances under which enforcement officers may enter premises*
- *Understanding of what action licensing authorities can take in relation to permits*

Reference Materials:

- *Gambling Act 2005: Part 15, section 346*
- *Relevant Gambling Act 2005 regulations*

1. **Key Principles**

- Licensing authorities have powers to enter premises with unlicensed FEC, prize gaming and alcohol licensed premises permits but only for specific reasons
- Licensing authorities do not have powers to enter clubs other than in connection with consideration of their application for a club permit
- There are two types of sanction available to licensing authorities: criminal and regulatory
- Licensing authorities can impose criminal sanctions in relation to any permit holding premises if an offence under section 346 has been committed.
- Licensing Authorities do not have regulatory sanctions in relation to unlicensed FECs and Prize Gaming permits
- Licensing authorities can impose regulatory sanctions in respect of clubs and licensed premises

2. **Entering premises:**

Authorised Local Authority Officers (officers designated by the authority) may enter premises as part of the consideration process for a permit application.

3. Once a permit has been issued, enforcement officers have *powers* to enter for specified purposes depending on type of permit issued

4. *For unlicensed FECs*

- A local authority officer may enter to determine whether gaming machines used on the premises, and the arrangements for their use, comply with the requirements of the Act and its regulations.
- For example, they could check that only category D machines are being provided.

5. *For Prize Gaming*

- A local authority officer may enter to determine whether prize gaming on the premises complies with the requirements of the Act and its regulations.
- For example, they could check that the levels of participation fees and prizes comply with regulations

6. *For Alcohol Licensed Premises*

- To check that any gaming taking place complies with the conditions for exempt gaming set out in section 279 (see above),
- For example, they could check that children are excluded from participation
- To check whether any bingo being provided exceeds £2000 in a seven day period, that the Commission has been notified, or that the premises are subject to a bingo operating licence and that the terms and conditions of that licence are being met
- To check the number and category of machines being made available are consistent with the permit issued or the provisions for automatic entitlement

7. *For Club Gaming/Machine permits*

- Licensing authority officers have no *powers* to enter clubs, other than in connection with an application
- Only the police or Gambling Commission enforcement officers have powers to enter a premises once the permit has been issued

8. **Sanctions**

There are two types of sanctions a licensing authority can impose on permit holders who are not operating in compliance with the Act or regulations – criminal or regulatory. There are some instances in which a licensing authority can only impose one type of sanction, for example there are no regulatory sanctions a licensing authority can impose on unlicensed FECs. In other instances, there is an overlap between the types of action a licensing authority may be able to take, for example in relation to breach of a condition of a permit, where it may be open to the authority to prosecute and cancel the permit.

9. Section 346 of the Act lists the offences under the Act in respect of which licensing authorities may institute criminal proceedings. The first of these, is the offence under section 37 of the Act, of using, causing or permitting premises to be used for gambling. Where gambling is offered on premises in breach of any conditions of a permit (or of the Act), it can amount to a breach of section 37, which means licensing authorities have powers to prosecute.

10. If the holder of any permit is convicted of a 'relevant offence' (these are listed in Schedule 7 of the Act and include offences under the Act and under other gambling legislation, as well as numerous other offences such as theft, robbery, and so on), a court has power to order forfeiture of a permit.

11. **Unlicensed FECs**

There is no power to cancel or vary a permit. Permits have a duration of ten years, at which point the permit-holder may apply for their renewal. Licensing authorities may refuse to renew permits, but only if they have been refused access to the premises without a reasonable excuse, or renewal would not be reasonably consistent with pursuit of the licensing objectives.

12. **Prize Gaming**

There is no power to cancel or vary a permit. Permits have a duration of ten years, at which point the permit-holder may apply for their renewal. Licensing authorities have a wide discretion to refuse to renew permits.

13. **Alcohol Licensed Premises**

Licensing authorities may cancel a permit or vary the number or category of machines authorised by it if:

(1) it would not be reasonably consistent with the pursuit of the licensing objectives for the permit to continue to have effect
(2) gaming has taken place on the premises otherwise than in accordance with the permit issued
(3) the premises is mainly used for making gaming machines available
(4) an offence under the Gambling Act has been committed on the premises

14. Compliance with the Gambling Commission's code of practice on the location and operation of gaming machines is effectively a condition of the permit. Therefore, failure to comply would amount to a ground to cancel or vary the permit. Failure to comply could also constitute an offence under the Act and could lead to prosecution. There is also a power under section 284 of the Act for a licensing authority to make an order disapplying the gaming exemption in respect of individual premises.

15. There are no provisions for renewal: a licensed premises gaming machine permit has an indefinite duration and will last as long as the relevant on-premises alcohol licence.

16. **Club gaming and machine permits**

Licensing authorities cannot vary club permits, but they can cancel them in certain circumstances:

- if the premises is wholly or mainly used by children
- if an offence or breach of a permit condition (eg regarding membership or permitted games of chance) has been committed

17. As with licensed premises, compliance with the Gambling Commission's code of practice on the location and operation of gaming machines is effectively a condition of the permit. Therefore, failure to comply would amount to a breach of a permit condition and grounds to cancel the permit. Failure to comply could also constitute an offence under the Act and could lead to prosecution.

18. Club permits have a duration of ten years, at which point the holder may apply for renewal. Licensing authorities have a wide discretion to refuse to renew permits.

MODULE 6: TRANSITIONAL ARRANGEMENTS AND PERMITS

Key Learning Objectives:

- *Understanding of transitional arrangements for each type of permit*
- *Awareness of key deadlines*
- *Understanding of continuation rights and grandfather rights as they apply to each type of premises*
- *Awareness of existing permissions which are rolled over*

Reference Materials:

- *Transitional Order*

1. **Key principles**

- Some of the transitional provisions impact on the processes in Module 4
- There are several key dates concerning transitional arrangements (see annex A)
- Existing operators may qualify for grandfather and continuation rights, but there are differences in the how these rights apply to each type of permit
- "New operators" may qualify for grandfather and continuation rights providing they obtain permissions under the existing legislation (deadlines apply)
- Applications for grandfathered permits can not be turned down (except if there is information missing)
- Licensing justices/licensing authorities will continue to receive applications under the existing legislation until 31 August 2007

- For alcohol licensed premises and clubs, unexpired permissions under the existing legislation will continue to have effect (subject to the new rules) after the 1st September

UNLICENSED FAMILY ENTERTAINMENT CENTRES

2. **Existing Operators**
To operate after 1st September 2007, existing operators, those holding valid permissions under the 1968 Act, will need to apply to the relevant licensing authorities for a Family Entertainment Centre Machines permit under the Gambling Act 2005. They will be able to do this from 21 May 2007. To obtain a permit the operator will need to complete and submit an application form to their licensing authority, as well as any other information that may be required, and pay the prescribed fee. Operators with existing permissions may qualify for grandfather and continuation rights, explained below.

3. **Continuation rights**
To qualify for continuation rights, an operator holding a valid permit issued under Section 34(1) of the 1968 Act, must submit their advance application by 30 July 2007. This will allow them to continue to be able to operate from 1 September 2007, even if their application has not been resolved by that date.

4. It is important to note that, operators operating by virtue of continuation rights will need to abide by the relevant rules and code of practice relating to ***uFEC*** permits that come into force on 1 September 2007. They will also be subject to the review provisions set out in the Act.

5. DCMS are recommending to licensing authorities that they notify operators that their application has been received in time and qualify for continuation rights when they acknowledge receipt of applications.

6. **Grandfather rights**
Operators holding a valid section 34(1) permission will be guaranteed a Gambling Act 05 permit if they apply before 1 September 2007. However, if they did not apply before 30 July, they will not qualify for continuation rights and will have to cease operation if their application is not processed until after 1 September, until their application has been decided.

7. **Grant and refusal**
Providing an operator has applied before 1 September, they are guaranteed a permit and a licensing authority must grant it. The only grounds upon which a licensing authority can refuse to grant are if the applicant fails to submit any of the information requested. However, if an applicant has made a mistake on their application form, the licensing authority will need to notify the applicant of any error or omission and allow them a period of no less than 14 days to rectify the error. If the applicant fails to rectify any error within this period, their continuation rights will lapse. Ultimately, the licensing authority may refuse the application.

8. **New operators**
New operators seeking to begin operating before 31 August 2007 will need to apply to their licensing authority for a Section 34 permit before 27 April 2007. No further applications under the existing legislation will be permitted after this date.

9. Once their application under the existing legislation is underway, and after 21 May, the applicant will be able to apply for permission under the new legislation. Providing they make their advance application under the 2005 Act before 30 July, and their application under the existing legislation is granted before 31 August, they will receive continuation rights in the event that their application under the new act is not resolved by 1 September 2007. They will also benefit from grandfather rights. However, their application under the new legislation can not be resolved until their application under the existing legislation has been. If the licensing authority decides to refuse the application under the existing legislation, the authority will be required to refuse the application for a grandfathered permit.

10. New operators applying for permission after 27 April 2007 will need to make their application under the Gambling Act 2007. They will not be eligible for continuation or grandfather rights and will not be able to commence operating until after 1 September, or once their application has been decided.

PRIZE GAMING

11. Existing holders of permits for commercial provision of amusements with prizes (Section 16 permits) issued under Schedule 3 of the Lotteries and Amusements Act 1976, and who want to continue to offer prize gaming after 1 September 2007 will need to apply to a licensing authority for a Gambling Act 2005 Prize Gaming Permit. The above provisions relating to the application, grant, and continuation rights for existing and new operators also apply to Prize Gaming Permits. There are no grandfather rights in relation to Prize Gaming permits.

LICENSED PREMISES GAMING MACHINES PERMIT

12. **Existing operators**
Alcohol licensed premises that hold a section 34 permission under the 1968 Act that expire **on or before** 31st August 2007 should apply to the licensing authority in the usual way to renew their permission. If successful they will be granted a permission running for 3 years. When the new Act comes into force on 1st September 2007, existing operators will continue to operate under their old permit which will be treated for the purposes of the 2005 Act in the same way as a licensed premises gaming machine permit issued under that Act. The premises will only have to apply for a Gambling Act 2005 permit when their 1968 Act permission expires. Conceivably this could mean that some alcohol licensed premises will not need to apply for their first Gambling Act 2005 permit before August 31 2010, when all section 34 1968 Act permissions will cease to have effect.

13. Those whose permissions expire after the 31st August will be required to either

- Notify the licensing authority of their intention to use their automatic entitlement for two machines prior to their section 34 permission expiring, if they only wish to make two available; *and/or*
- If they wish to make more than two machines available, apply to their licensing authority for permissions under the new legislation

14. **Grandfather rights and continuation rights**
Particular grandfather rights will apply to pubs and other alcohol licensed premises. Holders of a Section 34 permit authorising three or more machines, will be entitled to a licensed premises gaming machine permit which authorises the same number of gaming machines under the new Act.

15. If a premises wishes to provide more machines under the new legislation than it is currently permitted it will need to apply for a new licensed premises gaming machine permit under the new Act. Grandfather rights will not apply. The licensing authority will consider the application for more machines as if it were a new application, on its merits.

16. Holders of Section 34 permit authorising two machines or less will technically not qualify for grandfather rights, as they will anyway have an automatic entitlement to offer up to two gaming machines under the new Act. However, the automatic entitlement means that they will not be disadvantaged in any way.

17. Holders will only lose their grandfather rights in the rare event that their section 34 permit is cancelled or forfeited.

18. To qualify for **grandfather rights** and **continuation rights** existing operators will need to apply for their permit under the new legislation before the expiry of their section 34 permission.

19. The licensing authority can only refuse an application for a grandfathered permit if the applicant has failed to submit any information required as part of the application.

Where the licensing authority write requesting the relevant information they will not be under a duty to grant the application until the information is provided. If the licensing authority specifies a period in the notice (being not less than 14 days), but the applicant fails to comply with the request before the end of that period, continuation rights will be lost. However the licensing authority will still be under a duty to grant the grandfathered permit once the information is supplied.

20. **New operators**

Alcohol licensed premises wishing to apply for a first permit to begin before 1 September 2007 will apply licensing authorities for a Section 34 permit under the old legislation. If successful licensing authorities will normally grant a permission for three years.

21. Licensing authorities will still be able to resolve applications for section 34 permits under the 1968 Act made on or before 31 August 2007, even if it is not able to do so until after 31 August. However, all such permits will cease to have effect on 31 August 2010.

22. Licensing authorities will be able to treat "new operators" like existing operator, as described above.

23. New operators may also apply to their licensing authority for a permit under the new Act from 1 August 2007, but it is important to note that they would not be able to operate by virtue of a 2005 Act permit before 1 September 2007.

24. Alcohol licensed premises applying for first permission on or after 1 September 2007 must make a notification/application to their licensing authority for the appropriate permission under the 2005 Act.

CLUB GAMING/MACHINES PERMITS

25. **Existing operators**

Under the 1968 Act Clubs could provide facilities for gambling by virtue of a Part II or Part III registration. Part II registration roughly equates to a Club Gaming Permit under the new Act and Part III registration is roughly equivalent to a Gambling Act 2005 club machines permit.

26. Clubs that have Part II or Part III permissions under the 1968 Act that expire **on or before** 31st August 2007 should apply to the licensing justices in the usual way to renew their permission. If successful they will be granted a permission running for either 10 years, in the case of a Part II registration, or five years in the case of a Part III registration. When the new Act comes into force on 1st September 2007, these permissions will still be valid; they will roll over.

27. Clubs with Part II permissions will be treated as though they have a ***club gaming*** permit. Those holding Part III permissions will be treated as though they have a ***club machine permit***. The club will have to operate in accordance with the any new rules brought in by the new Act. The club will only have to apply for a Gambling Act 2005 permit when their 1968 Act permission expires, conceivably this could mean that some clubs will not need to apply for their first Gambling Act 2005 permit before 2017.

28. Clubs whose permissions under the 1968 Act expire **on or after** the 1st September 2007 will need to apply to their licensing authority for permission under the new Act. The time by which they are required to apply for new permissions and continuation rights is determined by the expiry date of their original permissions, as described below.

29. **Grandfather and Continuation rights**

Grandfather and continuation rights will be linked to the expiry date of individual permits rather than being subject to an arbitrary date. Providing a club applies for a 2005 Act permit before its 1968 Act permission expires, it will be permitted to continue operating until such time as its application is decided. In the case of clubs whose 1968 Act permission does not expire until several years after the 2005 Act comes into force, this means they will not use their continuation rights for some time.

30. This approach is intended to stagger the application process for club permits so that licensing authorities are not inundated with new applications all at the same time. It is anticipated that this will ease the burden for licensing authorities.

31. The grandfather rights applying to clubs are:
- A club holding a Part II registration will automatically be granted a ***club gaming permit*** under the 2005 Act
- A club holding a Part III registration will automatically be granted a ***club machine permit*** under the 2005 Act.

32. **New operators**

New operators wishing to apply for a first permission before 1 September should apply to licensing justices/sheriffs for the relevant registration under the under the old legislation. If successful, as with new registrations currently, their registration will be granted as follows:
- Part II registration – for one year
- Part III registration — for five years

33. As long as clubs apply on or before 31 August 2007, their application will still be able to be resolved by the licensing justice/sheriff under the old Act, even if it is not able to do so until after 31 August.

34. A successful applicant will then be treated like any other existing operator, will be able to follow the process above to obtain the relevant permit under the new Act.

35. New operators may also apply to their licensing authority for a permit under the new Act from 1 August 2007, but it is important to note that they would not be able to operate by virtue of a 2005 Act permit before 1 September 2007.

Chronology — Transitional Arrangements for Permits

2007

27 April
- Final date for new applications for section 16 permits under the Lotteries and Amusements Act 1976 (which will become Prize Gaming under the Gambling Act 2005)
- Final date for new applications for Section 34 permits under the 1968 Act (which could become Family Entertainment Centre Machines permit under the Gambling Act 2005)

21 May

First date licensing authorities will accept applications for unlicensed FEC and Prize Gaming permits under the Gambling Act 2005

30 July
- Deadline for applications for Prize Gaming permits by existing section 16 permit holders to qualify for continuation rights
- Deadline for applications for an unlicensed FEC permits by existing section 34 permit holders to qualify for continuation rights

1 August
- First date licensing authorities will accept applications for Club Gaming/Machine permits
- First date licensing authorities will accept applications for and Alcohol Licensed Premises permits under the Gambling Act 2005

31 August
- Deadline for applications to **licensing justices** for (new permissions and renewal) Part II and Part III registration for clubs under the 1968 Act
- Deadline for applications for to **licensing authorities** for (new permissions or renewal) for section 34 permits (for alcohol licensed premises) under the 1968 Act

1 SEPTEMBER

- New legislation comes into force
- All permissions under the 1968 and 1976 Act for unlicensed FECs and Prize Gaming operators **cease to have effect**
- Any applications for new unlicensed FEC permits by existing operators received from this date will not receive grandfather rights
- Unexpired permissions under the 1968 Act for Clubs and Alcohol Licensed Premises continue to have effect, but subject to any new rules

CASE STUDIES

Two case studies have been provided. They both follow the same format with the delegates being given initial instructions with additional information to be supplied in envelopes labelled A and B to be opened as directed.
The first case study is relatively straight forward. The second is slightly more complicated. The focus of each is on the consideration and determination process rather than the more functional processes like checking forms.
Feel free to embellish either case study or to develop your own if you wish to address other premises types more suitable to your area.

CASE STUDY 1 – INITIAL INFORMATION

A representative from Bowla-phenia, a new mods and rockers themed bowling alley, which is in the process of being built, telephones you to ask about the provision of gaming machines on their premises. They wish to provide gaming machines but are not sure for which permit to apply.

Q1. To best advise them, what sort of information should you obtain?

Open envelope A

Q2. What would you advise them to do?

A week or two later, the premises submits its application for the permit you suggested. The application has been completed correctly and they have paid the correct fee.

Q3. What can you take into consideration/have regard to when determining the application?

Open envelope B

Q4. Does this seem reasonable? If not, what could you do?

Q5. What steps do you need to take next?

CASE STUDY 1 — ADDITIONAL INFORMATION

Envelope A

- Bowla-phenia have asked for 8 machines of category C or D and has a bar serving alcohol without the requirement that it accompany food

CASE STUDY 1 — ADDITIONAL INFORMATION

Envelope B

- Although Bowla-phenia mentioned 8 gaming machines over the phone, in their application, they have asked for 20 category C and D machines.

CASE STUDY 1 — ANSWERS

Q1. To best advise them, what sort of information should you obtain?

A. Approximately how many gaming machines they wish to provide and of what category. Also, you should ask whether the premises has an on-premises licence.

Q2. What would you advise them to do?

A. Apply for a Licensed Premises permit

Q3. What can you take into consideration/have regard to when determining the application?

A. If the application is for a licensed premises permit:

- The licensing objectives
- Any relevant guidance issued by the Commission
- Other such matters as they think relevant

Q4. Does this seem reasonable? If not, what could you do?

A. If it does not seem reasonable you could:

- Refuse the application
- vary the number and category of machines requested

If you think it does sound reasonable, you can grant the application

Q5. What steps do you need to take next?

A. If the application is refused or varied, you should notify the applicant of the intention to refuse or vary and give them the opportunity to make representations. These can either be written or orally. If the applicant makes representations they should be considered.

Or

If you grant the application you need to issue a permit as soon as is reasonably practicable.

CASE STUDY 2 – INITIAL INFORMATION

You have received an application for a Family Entertainment Centre Machines permit from Mitch Buchannan. The application has been completed correctly and the prescribed fee has been paid.

Q1 What can be taken into consideration when deciding whether to grant or refuse this permit?

Q2 What needs to be done before the application can be granted?

Open envelope A

Q3 How are you going to determine the application?

Q4 What steps do you need to take?

If you have refused the application, open envelope B

Q5 Do you agree with your earlier decision?

CASE STUDY 2 — ADDITIONAL INFORMATION

Envelope A

- The police inform you that the premises has previously been used as an unlicensed FEC. Under the previous owner, the police regularly received complaints that it was a hang-out for children who had been drinking
- In addition, Mr Buchannan has received a caution for possession of marijuana (no intent to supply)

CASE STUDY 2 ADDITIONAL INFORMATION

Envelope B

- Mr Buchannan has made a representation in which he states that the marijuana possession was five years ago and he has subsequently been to drug counselling and has not been in trouble since.
- In his representation, Mr Buchannan also mentions that he will have a zero-tolerance policy towards under-age drinking. He will run his FEC in a completely different way to the previous owner. He is more focused on attracting families to play games together, than children on their own. He also states that it is not in his interest to have rowdy children in his establishment.

CASE STUDY 2 – ANSWERS

Q1. What can be taken into consideration when deciding whether to grant or refuse this permit?

A. Licensing authority can take into consideration:

- Their statement of principles
- The licensing objectives (although do not have to)
- Any guidance issued by the Commission – this is likely to recommend asking applicants to demonstrate during the application process:
- That the applicant has a full understanding of the maximum stakes and prizes of the gambling permissible in unlicensed FECs;
- That the applicant has no relevant convictions (as set out in Schedule 7 of the Act)
- That staff are trained to have a full understanding of the maximum stakes and prizes

Q2. What needs to be done before the application can be granted?

A. The licensing authority needs to be satisfied that the applicant intends to use the premises as an unlicensed FEC. The licensing authority must have consulted the police

Q3. How are you going to determine the application?

A. Either grant or refuse

Q4. What steps do you need to take?

A. Either grant it as soon as is practicable or refuse it and provide notification and reasons for refusal to the applicant. The applicant may then make representations.

Q5. Do you agree with your earlier decision?

A.?

department for culture, media and sport
2-4 Cockspur Street
London SW1Y 5DH
www.culture.gov.uk

ADVICE TO LICENSING AUTHORITIES ON INFORMATION EXCHANGE WITH THE GAMBLING COMMISSION

Second edition, December 2007
Updated April 2008
This edition supersedes the February 2007 document entitled 'Information exchange between the Gambling Commission and licensing authorities'.

1 INTRODUCTION

6.2640 1.1 The interrelationship between the three types of licence[1] introduced by the Gambling Act 2005 (the Act) means that the Gambling Commission (the Commission) and licensing authorities need to share information on a regular basis. As licensing authorities vary in terms of size and expertise it is important to standardise the type of information sought and received.

1.2 The Act empowers the Commission to seek information from licensing authorities, and places an obligation on authorities to comply with information requests. Specifically, section 29 of the Act entitles the Commission to request information from licensing authorities providing it is:

- part of a register or
- in the licensing authority's possession in connection with a provision of the Act.

1.3 The Commission requires up to date information on premises licences and permits from licensing authorities, and will seek to minimise duplication of information in obtaining this.

6: Gambling Act 2005: Additional Material

1.4 The Commission has identified five categories of information that are exchanged between licensing authorities and itself, as follows:

[1] Operating and personal licences issued by the Commission and premises licences issued by licensing authorities.

INFORMATION ON SPECIFIC PREMISES OR LOTTERIES THAT LICENSING AUTHORITIES ARE REQUIRED BY THE ACT TO SEND TO THE COMMISSION

1.5 The Act obliges licensing authorities to provide information to the Commission in relation to premises licences applied for and issued and the small society lotteries that they register. These information requirements are set out in **section two** of this document.

INFORMATION ON SPECIFIC OPERATORS THAT THE COMMISSION MAKES AVAILABLE TO LICENSING AUTHORITIES

1.6 Section 159 of the Act states that applicants for premises licences must have applied for an operating licence from the Commission. The information exchange to support this process is set out in **section two** of this document.

INTELLIGENCE EXCHANGED BETWEEN LICENSING AUTHORITIES AND THE COMMISSION

1.7 To ensure operator compliance with licence conditions, and to make certain that appropriate enforcement action is taken, information on the misconduct of gambling operators and illegal gambling needs to be exchanged. These information requirements are discussed in **section three** of this document.

INFORMATION ON THE INCIDENCE AND CONDUCT OF GAMBLING IN GREAT BRITAIN

1.8 The Commission requires information from licensing authorities to enable it to fulfil the requirements of section 26 of the Act – its duty to advise the Secretary of State on the incidence of gambling, the manner in which gambling is carried on, the effects of gambling and the regulation of gambling. These information requirements are discussed in **section four** of this document.
The Commission is aware that the Department for Culture, Media and Sports (DCMS) aims to rely upon information collated by the Commission rather than approaching local authorities directly for data, in order to minimise duplication of efforts for licensing authorities.

INFORMATION THAT INFORMS THE COMMISSION'S COMPLIANCE AND ENFORCEMENT MODEL

1.9 The compliance and enforcement activity that licensing authorities will undertake in relation to premises licences may impact the Commission's compliance and enforcement model. The information that the Commission requires from licensing authorities is set out in **section five** of this document.

GENERAL INFORMATION ON GAMBLING

1.10 The Commission is collating information of interest to licensing authorities and the wider public on matters related to gambling and will make it available through a number of channels. This is discussed in **section six** of this document. This section also includes details of other relevant documents published by the Commission and confirms its contact details.

1.11 The activities contained within this document that require specific information to be forwarded by licensing authorities to the Commission are summarised in APPENDIX A at the end of the document.

1.12 Please note that this is the second edition of this document, and replaces the first (published in February 2007) entirely. The Commission may publish subsequent editions featuring additions or amended working practices. The arrangements for managing the information exchange outlined in this document will be kept under review, and the Commission will continue to research new methods of facilitating the transfer of knowledge and data between itself and licensing authorities. Future developments will be agreed with the Local Authorities Coordinators of Regulatory Services (LACORS) and other bodies, in order to ensure sufficient timeframe for licensing authorities to make any required local changes.

2 INFORMATION THAT LICENSING AUTHORITIES ARE REQUIRED TO SEND TO THE COMMISSION

2.1 There are a number of separate phases or actions associated with the processing of premises licenses, provisional statements, lottery registrations and some types of permit which result in the transfer of information between licensing authorities and the Commission. These include:

- the consideration and determination of premises licence and provisional statement applications
- a review of a premises licence by the issuing licensing authority
- premises licence variations, transfers, lapses and reinstatements.

2.2 The required formats for many of the notices referred to in this section have been set through regulations, however for some types of permission there is no prescribed format for notices to take (such as for notices relating to club permits).

2.3 Word versions of the notices, with a password for local authority use, are available via LACORS website for authorities in England and Wales.

APPLICATIONS FOR PREMISES LICENCES

Licensing authorities should send their notices of premises licence grants and refusals via email to mailto://localauthority@gamblingcommission.gov.uk or post to the address shown in section six.

Relevant statutory instruments:

- Statutory Instrument 2007/459 – The Gambling Act 2005 (Premises Licences and Provisional Statements) Regulations 2007
- Scottish Statutory Instrument 2007/196 – The Gambling Act 2005 (Premises Licences and Provisional Statements) (Scotland) Regulations 2007

2.4 Applicants for premises licences are required by the regulations listed above to forward notice of their application to the Commission, as a responsible authority[2] under the Act. The Commission would prefer applicants to email their notice of application to info@gamblingcommission.gov.uk although if email is not possible they may post their notice to the Commission's licensing team at the address shown in section seven of this document.

2.5 The Commission will email the applicant to confirm it has received the notice by the next working day following receipt. If the applicant is only contactable by post, a confirmation will be posted to them on the next working day[3] following receipt. The relevant licensing authority will be copied with these exchanges.

2.6 The Commission may make observations on the suitability of the applicant for a premises licence or any other aspect of the application.

[2] Responsible authorities as listed under section 157 of the Act.

[3] "working day" means a day which is not a Saturday, Sunday, Christmas Day, Good Friday or a bank holiday in England and Wales.

CONSIDERATION OF APPLICATION – HEARINGS AND REPRESENTATIONS

2.7 Normally the Commission will not make formal representations on applications for premises licence because the majority of applicants for premises licences will already hold operating licences. However before deciding if it will make a representation it may need to contact the relevant licensing authority on an informal basis, by phone or email, to discuss matters pertaining to the application.

2.8 If representations are made by responsible authorities or interested parties, or if the licensing authority proposes to attach or exclude a condition to the premises licence, then there must be a hearing, unless all the parties involved (applicant, authorities and interested parties making representations) agree it is not necessary, or unless the licensing authority considers the representations to be vexatious or frivolous or ones that will not influence the determination of the application. If the Commission makes a representation it will be a party to the hearing. However it will not attend all hearings as a matter of course, and will notify the authority in question if it will be attend a hearing.

NOTICE OF DECISION

2.9 Following consideration of the application, and completion of any hearings that were required, the licensing authority may decide to:

- grant the licence
- grant the licence subject to conditions or
- refuse the licence

2.10 Sections 164 and 165 of the Act require the licensing authority to notify the Commission of the outcome of each application. Upon receiving a notice of grant for a premises licence, the Commission adds the details of the licence to the Premises Licence Register on its website (www.gamblingcommission.gov.uk).

Reviews

Licensing authorities should send notices relating to reviews via email to localauthority@gamblingcommission.gov.uk or post to the address shown in section six. The prescribed format for notices can be found in:

- Statutory Instrument 2007/2258: The Gambling Act 2005 (Premises Licences)(Review) Regulations 2007
- Scottish Statutory Instrument 2007/394 – The Gambling Act 2005 (Review of Premises Licences)(Scotland) Regulations 2007

2.11 There are two main routes for initiating a review of a premises licence, as follows:

- a responsible authority (including the local police or the Commission) or an interested party can apply to a licensing authority to review a particular premises licence or
- a licensing authority can initiate a review by its own accord (for example if it received complaints from the public about a particular premises or a class of premises).

2.12 The proceedings for undertaking a review are set out in the regulations listed above. If the review is initiated at the request of a responsible authority or an interested party, then the initiating party must notify the premises licence holder of the circumstances of the review, and copy this notice to all responsible authorities, including the Commission. If the review is initiated by a licensing authority, then the licensing authority is required to notify the premises licence holder of the circumstances of the review and to publish notice of its intention to hold the review.

2.13 Following completion of a premises licence review, licensing authorities are required to provide determination of the review to the parties listed under section 203 of the Act, which includes the Commission.

Changes to existing premises licences

Licensing authorities should send any notices referred to in this section via email to localauthority@gamblingcommission.gov.uk or post to the address shown in section six.

The prescribed format for notices can be found in:

- Statutory Instrument 2007/459 – The Gambling Act 2005 (Premises Licences and Provisional Statements) Regulations 2007
- Scottish Statutory Instrument 2007/196 – The Gambling Act 2005 (Premises Licences and Provisional Statements)(Scotland) Regulations 2007

2.14 Once a premises licence has been issued the holder may apply to the licensing authority to make certain changes to it. This could include an application to vary certain licence conditions or change the licence status.

VARIATIONS

2.15 Premises licence holders may seek to make changes to specific details of their licence, such as requesting certain conditions are excluded or amended, and as such may apply to vary their licence. The licence holder is responsible for notifying the Commission of their application to vary, and the licensing authority is required to inform the Commission of the outcome of the application.

TRANSFERS

2.16 If an application to transfer a premises licence to a new person is made, the licensing authority will need to know if the proposed new licensee has an operating licence, or has applied for one (except in the case of tracks premises licences where an operating licence is not required). Licensing authorities can find this out via the Commission's website, as explained in section three of this document. Once a decision has been made whether to grant or reject the application, the licensing authority must give notice to the Commission. Grant notices will include information about any conditions attached to the licence and any representations made.

LICENCE LAPSES AND REINSTATEMENTS

2.17 Premises licences can lapse for various reasons, such as the licence holder dying or becoming bankrupt. The issuing licensing authority is required by section 194 of the Act to inform the Commission as soon as practicable about lapsed premises licenses. There is no prescribed format for informing the Commission about licence lapses, however the details of the premises licence and the circumstances of the lapse should be forwarded to the Commission in writing either by email or by post.

2.18 If the holder of a lapsed premises licence, or some other operating licence holder, applies to reinstate the licence (within 6 months of the date on which the licence lapsed), the applicant must notify the Commission of their application. Where the Commission has concerns about such an application it will contact the relevant licensing authority to discuss the application, and if appropriate make representations and attend any hearing.

2.19 Licensing authorities are required to forward notices of grant and notices of rejection to reinstate to the Commission.

SURRENDERED LICENCES

2.20 Licensing authorities are required to inform the Commission if a premises licence holder chooses to surrender their licence, in accordance with section 192 of the Act. There is no prescribed format for informing the Commission about surrendered licences, however the details of the premises licence and the circumstances of the surrender should be forwarded to the Commission in writing either by email or by post.

Provisional statements

2.21 Applicants for provisional statements are required to send a notice of their application to the Commission, and licensing authorities are required to send the Commission a notice of grant/rejection following their determination of the application.
Licensing authorities should send their notices of provisional statement grants or refusals via email to mailto://localauthority@gamblingcommission.gov.uk or post to the address shown in section six.
The prescribed format for notices can be found in:

- Statutory Instrument 2007/459 – The Gambling Act 2005 (Premises Licences and Provisional Statements) Regulations 2007
- Scottish Statutory Instrument 2007/196 – The Gambling Act 2005 (Premises Licences and Provisional Statements)(Scotland) Regulations 2007

Club permits

Licensing authorities should send notice of the outcome of club permit applications via email to mailto://localauthority@gamblingcommission.gov.uk or post to the address shown in section six.
There is no prescribed format for such notices, however they should contain details of whether the application was granted or rejected, and provide reasons why that decision was reached.
2.22 Schedule 12 of the Act requires applicants for club gaming permits and club gaming machine permits to forward notice of their application to the Commission.
2.23 Licensing authorities must inform the Commission of the outcome of club permit applications within a reasonable timeframe.

Lotteries

Local authorities should send details of small society lottery registrations, cancelled registrations, and incidents of small lotteries exceeding the permitted proceeds, via email to mailto://localauthority@gamblingcommission.gov.uk or post to the address shown in section six.
There is no prescribed format for sending this information, however any information sent should include the society name, and the date of registration / cancellation.
2.24 Schedule 11 of the Act requires local authorities[4] to inform the Commission as soon as is reasonably practicable when they register a society to run small lotteries, and also when they cancel a society's registration to run small lotteries.
2.25 Schedule 11 also requires local authorities to inform the Commission if they believe that a small lottery should be reclassified as a large lottery, which would occur where a small lottery had exceeded the permitted proceeds.
2.26 Detailed information regarding local authority responsibilities towards small society lotteries can be found in part 32 of the Commission's 'Guidance to Licensing Authorities' document[5].
2.27 No other information about small society lotteries (eg lottery returns) are required to be sent to the Commission.

---

[4] Schedule 11 uses the wider term of local authorities, rather than licensing authorities, with reference to small society lotteries

[5] available on the Commission's website at www.gamblingcommission.gov.uk

INFORMATION ON SPECIFIC OPERATORS THAT THE COMMISSION MAKES AVAILABLE TO LICENSING AUTHORITIES

Enquiries about status of applicants for premises licences

2.28 Premises licences can only be issued to holders of operating licences (with the exception of applicants for track premises licences). Licensing authorities will need to verify that applicants for premises licences hold a valid operating licence for the type of premises licence that has been applied for, or have applied for such a licence. There is a regularly updated list on the website of LACORS showing all granted, cancelled and refused operating licences, and operating licence numbers can also be requested by telephoning 0121 230 6666 or emailing localauthority@gamblingcommission.gov.uk.

2.29 The Commission is required by section 106 of the Act to maintain a register of operating licence holders and to make this register publicly accessible. This register is available at www.gamblingcommission.gov.uk, and licensing authorities can check the register to verify if the applicant currently holds an operating licence, or has applied for one.

2.30 Information on the progress of an operating licence application can be requested by telephoning the Commission's licensing team on 0121 230 6666, or emailing them at localauthority@gamblingcommission.gov.uk

2.31 These measures will also assist licensing authorities to screen organisations and individuals who have applied for registration to run small society lotteries, and comply with their duty to refuse an application for registration where the applicant has been refused an operating licence or one has been revoked in the last five years (in accordance with schedule 11 of the Act).

2.32 Licensing authorities need to be made aware of changes made by the Commission to operating licences that may impact the status of related premises licences. Where the Commission revokes an operating licence it will seek to inform any licensing authorities that issue premises licences linked to the operating licence (at the same time as informing the licence holder about the changes made to the status of their licence).

Information about operators' compliance

2.33 The Commission recommends that gambling operators maintain records of regulatory breaches at each of the premises that they use. Whilst not a statutory requirement, it encourages operators to have registers of action taken to remedy such breaches and potential breaches, and recommends these are made available for licensing authorities to inspect at the premises themselves.

2.34 Occasionally the Commission will conduct a regulatory review of operating licences under section 116 of the Act. Local input and knowledge will greatly assist such reviews, and for every review the Commission will therefore assess whether licensing authority input will be beneficial. The number and location of authorities invited to participate in reviews is likely to depend on the size and geographic spread of the operator's estate.

2.35 If such a review raises issues that licensing authorities could usefully take into consideration when determining local premises risk ratings, the Commission will communicate this information to licensing authorities as appropriate. An example of this type of information would include where the social responsibility policies of an operator had been found to be lacking following a review.

Licensing authorities would benefit from being informed of this as it could impact upon the licensing objectives at premises level.

2.36 Each year the Commission visits a proportion of the premises owned by an operator as part of its national inspection programme, some of which are undertaken alongside local authority authorised officers. If the Commission records anything at a premises or set of premises that it believes licensing authorities may benefit from knowing, it will contact them accordingly. For example, this type of scenario could include the discovery, during an inspection at an operator's headquarters, of poor system controls in relation to underage gambling, which could potentially result in age verification not being adequately enforced at their gambling premises. Another example would be identifying that an operator lacked a sufficiently robust social responsibility training programme, which could potentially result in staff at the operators' premises failing to make leaflets and posters on responsible gambling available.

2.37 The process that will govern the circumstances used for exchanging information about non-compliant operators will depend on the nature of the suspected or actual breach.

3 INTELLIGENCE EXCHANGED BETWEEN LICENSING AUTHORITIES AND THE COMMISSION

3.1 The Commission is dependent on information to uncover illegal activity associated with gambling and to monitor the incidence of gambling in Great Britain. The Commission's intelligence unit collates and disseminates information about gambling from a wide range of sources, including the police, the public and licensing authorities. It can use this information to identify areas which need to be inspected and/or reported on to other bodies.

3.2 Information that the Commission is interested in includes (but is not restricted to):

- reports of police activity at premises
- reports of suspected illegal gambling
- reports of underage gambling
- reports of breaches of premises licence conditions
- including breaches of locally applied conditions
- reports of other activity which may cause concern as to the integrity of operating or personal licences
- reports of disorder at or around gambling premises
- surveys undertaken by Crime and Disorder Reduction Partnerships which highlight gambling issues.

3.3 The Commission undertakes intelligence assessments to ascertain the state of the gambling industry in Great Britain and measure how effectively the industry is complying with the provisions of the Act. These assessments also identify what is not known about the industry and inform the intelligence requirements of the Commission. These assessments will develop over time, and information identified during this process that may be of significance to licensing authorities' premises risk ratings will be communicated to authorities accordingly. Extracts from assessments may also be published periodically via the Commission's website.

3.4 From time to time the Commission may solicit information from licensing authorities on specific topics or classes of premises licence. However, in doing so the Commission will not expect authorities to complete arduous statistical exercises within specified timeframes, nor will it enforce participation. Examples may include asking whether authorities had encountered incidents of bingo being offered in pubs in their area, or whether they were aware of numbers of school truants found in family entertainment centres. This type of information will generally be requested by email.

3.5 All intelligence and information on unlicensed gambling should be directed to the Commission's intelligence unit by email to mailto://intelligence@gamblingcommission.gov.uk or by telephoning 0121 230 6666. Intelligence received from licensing authorities may be referred to a regionally based compliance manager who in turn may then contact the licensing authority in question to discuss the matter further.

4 INFORMATION ON THE INCIDENCE AND CONDUCT OF GAMBLING IN GREAT BRITAIN

REGISTERS

4.1 The Act requires licensing authorities to keep a number of registers of the licences and permissions that they issue, as follows:

- Premises licences (section 156)
- Temporary use notices (section 234)
- Family entertainment centre permits (schedule 10 part 23)
- Club gaming and machine permits (schedule 12 paragraph 26)
- Pub machine permits (schedule 13 paragraph 22)
- Prize gaming permits (schedule 14 paragraph 23)
- Registered lotteries (schedule 11 paragraph 44 — not a public register but it is the Commission's view that licensing authorities should make the information they hold on small society lotteries available)

RETURNS

4.2 The information held on licensing authority registers is required by the Commission to inform general surveys of gambling activity in Great Britain. Numbers of new premises licences issued will be communicated to the Commission via notices of grant, but it also needs to access information regarding permits and temporary permissions. Each licensing authority is therefore required to forward returns to the Commission showing the information set out below.

WHEN ARE RETURNS REQUIRED?

4.3 The Commission requires returns from each licensing authority on permits and temporary permissions issued every quarter. If an authority has nil activity to report, it must still submit a return stating this. The periods covered by the returns are:

1 April – 30 June
1 July – 30 September
1 October – 31 December
1 January – 31 March

4.4 Submissions are to be made to the Commission within one month of the end of the period — no later than 31 July, 31 October, 31 January and 30 April. The Commission asks for the first returns to be sent in January 2008, for the period Oct-Dec 2007.

HOW SHOULD RETURNS BE SUBMITTED?

4.5 Licensing authorities can download and complete the returns templates on the Commission's website[6] or use extracts from local databases, provided they are populated with all the data fields required by the Commission. In either case, the return should be emailed to localauthorityreturns@gamblingcommission.gov.uk by the dates specified above in paragraph 4.3. In the event that a return cannot be sent by email, a hard copy can be posted to the Commission using the contact details shown in section six of this document.

6 http://www.gamblingcommission.gov.uk/UploadDocs/publications/Document/Templates %20for%20LAs.doc

WHAT INFORMATION IS REQUIRED FROM LICENSING AUTHORITIES?

4.6 The three tables below show the information that is required by the Commission from each licensing authority, for each quarter, relating to permits and temporary permissions. Please note that the Commission does **not** require to be sent copies of permits and temporary permissions issued.

TABLE 1 — PERMITS[7]

		Total number of permits issued this quarter	**Number of permits cancelled or forfeited this quarter**	**Number of permits refused this quarter**	**Number of permits surrendered this quarter**	**Current total number of active permits**
A	Family entertainment centre gaming machine permits					
B	Alcohol licensed premises (automatic)					
C	Alcohol licensed premises gaming machine permits					
D	Prize gaming permits (pubs)					
E	Prize gaming permits (unlicensed family entertainment centres)					
F	Prize gaming permits (other – specify) (add in type)					

TABLE 2 – TEMPORARY USE NOTICES[8]

2		**Total**
A	Number of notices received this quarter	
B	Number of objections received this quarter	
C	Number counter-noticed this quarter	
D	Number withdrawn this quarter	
E	Number endorsed this quarter	
F	Total number of days for which a temporary use notice is in operation[9]	

TABLE 3 — OCCASIONAL USE NOTICES

3		**Betting premises**
A	Number of notices received this quarter	
B	Total number of days for which an occasional use notice is in operation[10]	

7 The definitions assumed of 'cancellation', 'forfeiture', 'refused' and 'surrendered' are as defined by schedule 12 of the Act.

8 Returns must only report actions that have occurred within the quarter (with the exception of the 'Current total number of active permits' field). For example if an objection is received on the first day of a quarter it must be reported within that quarter's returns, regardless of whether it relates to a notice made in a previous quarter.

9 This row refers to the total number of days covered by all the temporary use notices that were issued during the quarter.

10 This row refers to the total number of days covered by all the occasional use notices that were issued during the quarter.

5 INFORMATION THAT INFORMS THE COMMISSION'S COMPLIANCE AND ENFORCEMENT MODEL

5.1 The Commission's approach to compliance is risk based. This risk based approach involves the operation of a comprehensive risk assessment process of each individual operator to ensure that compliance resources are concentrated in relevant areas and on those operators which pose the greatest risk to the licensing objectives.

5.2 Complaints and comments about gambling activity play a major part in developing the Commission's risk assessment model. Complaints relating to specific premises may be best handled at a local level, and as such may be forwarded on to the relevant licensing authority.

5.3 Periodically, the Commission will issue reports on the work that it is undertaking. These may focus on trends that are emerging and will report the outcomes of thematic reviews, eg into the incidence of illegal gambling dens. These may include recommendations for licensing authorities or examples of good practice in enforcement and compliance.

RETURNS

5.4 Much of the information exchanged between the Commission and licensing authorities will be about crime and disorder associated with gambling or concerns about the activity of licence holders. However it is also important for the Commission to have an appreciation of the overall formal enforcement and compliance activity undertaken by licensing authorities. This knowledge assists the Commission to establish an overview of inspection activity being undertaken within each industry sector, and assists greatly in terms of being able to identify problem areas and trends, such as a particular premises licence being reviewed because of incidents involving crime and disorder.

WHEN ARE RETURNS REQUIRED?

5.5 The Commission requires returns from each licensing authority every quarter on the number of gambling premises inspections, and also on the number and outcomes of reviews. If an authority has no activity to report it must still submit a nil return. The periods covered by the returns are:

1 April – 30 June
1 July – 30 September
1 October – 31 December
1 January – 31 March

5.6 Submissions should be made to the Commission within one month of the end of the period — no later than 31 July, 31 October, 31 January and 30 April. The Commission asks for the first returns to be sent in January 2008, for the period Oct-Dec 2007.

HOW SHOULD RETURNS BE SUBMITTED?

5.7 Licensing authorities can download and complete the returns templates on the Commission's website[11], or use extracts from local databases, provided they are populated with all the data fields required by the Commission. In either case, returns should be emailed to localauthorityreturns@gamblingcommission.gov.uk by the dates specified above.

5.8 In the event that a return cannot be sent by email, a hard copy can be posted to the Commission using the contact details shown in section six of this document.

---

11 http://www.gamblingcommission.gov.uk/UploadDocs/publications/Document/Templates%20for%20LAs.doc

What information is required from licensing authorities?

5.9 The three tables below show the compliance and enforcement information that is required by the Commission from each licensing authority, for each quarter.

5.10 Licensing authorities should note that inspections or reviews undertaken of 'selfcontained' betting premises situated on tracks (ie high street betting shops with their own betting premises licence) are to be recorded under the 'Betting premises' heading.

TABLE 4 – NUMBER OF PREMISES INSPECTIONS UNDERTAKEN DURING THE QUARTER

4		Casino	Bingo	Betting premises	Tracks	Adult gaming centres	Family entertainment centres (with premises licence)	Total
A	Number of pre-planned inspections undertaken as part of authority's inspection programme							
B	Number of inspections undertaken following receipt of a complaint or specific intelligence about a premises							
C	Number of re-inspections (follow-up visits)							

TABLE 5 – REASONS FOR REVIEWS COMPLETED DURING THE QUARTER

5	Reasons for review	Casino	Bingo	Betting premises	Tracks	Adult gaming centres	Family entertainment centres	Total
A	Protection of children/young people							
B	Protection of vulnerable people							
C	Breach of licensing authority additional condition							
D	Breach of mandatory condition							
E	Breach of default condition							
F	Crime and disorder							
G	Other							

TABLE 6 – OUTCOMES OF REVIEWS COMPLETED DURING THE QUARTER

6	Outcomes of reviews	Casino	Bingo	Betting premises	Tracks	Adult gaming centres	Family entertainment centres	Total
A	No change							
B	Licensing authority condition(s) added							
C	Revised licensing authority condition(s)							
D	Removed licensing authority condition(s)							
E	Removed default condition (where replaced by licensing authority condition)							
F	Suspension of licence							
G	Revocation of licence							

6 GENERAL INFORMATION ON GAMBLING

6.1 The Commission is the primary source of general information on gambling in Great Britain. Licensing authorities are encouraged to sign up to the Commission's fortnightly email alert system to be notified of new postings on its website, as information of interest to them will be made available here. This can be done by clicking on the 'Register for Updates' feature at the Commission's website at www.gamblingcommission.gov.uk.
6.2 Licensing authorities should provide advice to all those who make enquiries, whether or not they are licence or permit holders, about the legal responsibilities of those involved in providing premises or holding permits for gambling. Specific enquiries about operating or personal licences should be referred to the Commission.
6.3 The Commission's annual report contains information on licences, permits and temporary permissions that has been received from licensing authorities. The Commission will also publish national trends reports from time to time outlining developments in the industry, major research results and good practice from other jurisdictions. Commission published list of premises licences issued on its website.

FUTURE POLICY DEVELOPMENT

6.4 The Commission's website, www.gamblingcommission.gov.uk, contains information about gambling and the licensing of operators, and has general information and guidance on gambling in Great Britain. Licensing authorities that have specific queries should forward these to the Commission by email to localauthority@gamblingcommission.gov.uk
6.5 Representatives of the Commission will attend appropriate policy forums, including those organised by LACORS, and ensure that developments in the Commission's policy are forwarded to LACORS, the Convention of Scottish Local Authorities (COSLA) and other relevant bodies such as the Institute of Licensing.
6.6 The Commission's 'Guidance to Licensing Authorities' documents will be reviewed regularly and updated with recommendations that may result from information supplied to it, following consultation.

LICENSING AUTHORITY EMAIL CONTACTS

6.7 The Commission will normally use the '*licensing@*' email addresses (or an equivalent) to communicate with licensing authorities. Licensing authorities that would prefer to use an alternative email address should notify the Commission of this using the contact details shown below.

CONTACT DETAILS

6.8 The Commission's postal address is:

Gambling Commission
Victoria Square House
Victoria Square
Birmingham B2 4BP
The main telephone number for all departments is: 0121 230 6666
The main fax number is: 0121 230 6720
Gambling Commission

APPENDIX A

Summary of information required in this document by the Commission from licensing authorities (this summary does not include intelligence reports or ad-hoc requests)

6: Gambling Act 2005: Additional Material

Licensing function	Event requiring information to be sent to Commission	Section to refer to in this document
Premises licences and provisional statements	Licensing authority has granted / rejected an application for a premises licence or provisional statement	Paragraphs 2.9 — 2.10 and 2.21
	A premises licence has lapsed	Paragraphs 2.17 – 2.19
	Licensing authority has granted or rejected an application to reinstate a premises licence	Paragraph 2.17 – 2.19
	Licensing authority has granted or rejected an application to transfer or vary a premises licence	Paragraphs 2.15 and 2.16
	A review of a premises licence has been completed and a decision made	Paragraph 2.11 – 2.13
	A hearing is to be held where the Commission has made a representation	Paragraph 2.7
	A premises licence has been surrendered	Paragraph 2.20
Club permits	A club permit application has been granted / rejected	Paragraphs 2.22 — 2.23
Small society lottery registration	Licensing authority registers a society to operate small lotteries	Paragraph 2.24
	Licensing authority cancels a society's registration to operate small lotteries	Paragraph 2.24
	Where a society has exceeded the permitted proceeds for small lotteries	Paragraph 2.25
Issue of permits and temporary permissions	Quarterly returns	Section 4
Inspections and reviews	Quarterly returns	Section 5

GAMBLING ACT 2005: TRAINING MATERIALS FOR LICENSING AUTHORITIES

INTRODUCTION

PURPOSE OF TRAINING PACKAGE

6.2645 1. The Department for Culture, Media and Sport (the Department) has developed this training package to assist and support Local Authority licensing officers and councillors as they prepare to take on their new responsibilities from 21st May under the Gambling Act 2005 (the Act).

2. These training materials are designed to be a flexible learning tool. They condense and refer to a large volume of information from the Act, Gambling Commission Guidance and other sources. Licensing authorities are encouraged to this training pack and adapt them to suit their own needs.

4. This package should be used together with the "Gambling Commission Guidance to Licensing authorities" (Commission Guidance) published in April 2006, and currently being updated.[1] Material has also been produced by LACORS and the Institute of Licensing. Further guidance can be found on the DCMS website.

[1] See the third edition of May 2009 at para **6.2655** below.

FORMAT OF TRAINING PACKAGE AND TARGET AUDIENCE

6. This training documentation has been developed to assist **licensing authority officers** and **councillors**. The Department is conscious that the parties have different roles under the Act and the package may be delivered to accommodate these differences. To this end, the package may be split into sections:
7. Part 1 is for both officers and councillors and deals with both the principles of licensing as well as some procedural aspects.
8. Part 2 is aimed at officers only (though councillors may also wish to attend for completeness depending, in some cases, on the level of delegation for various functions determined by the individual authority) as it deals predominantly with procedural issues.

USER TESTING AND ENDORSEMENTS

9. The training package has undergone user testing.

GUIDANCE NOTE

10. All the materials presented in this training pack are based regulations laid in February 2007. These materials will be routinely updated by DCMS to reflect any changes.

1.1: LICENSING OBJECTIVES, REGULATORY FRAMEWORK AND LICENSING FRAMEWORK

Key learning objectives:

- *Awareness and understanding of the three licensing objectives*
- *Awareness and understanding of the role of the Gambling Commission*
- *Awareness and understanding of the role of licensing authorities*
- *Awareness and understanding of the different types of licences*

Reference materials:

- *Gambling Commission Guidance to Licensing Authorities: Part 1*
- *The Gambling Act 2005*

1. The Gambling Act 2005 received Royal Assent on 7 April 2005. The Act repeals the Betting, Gaming and Lotteries Act 1963, the Gaming Act 1968 and the Lotteries and Amusements Act 1976 and sets out that gambling will be unlawful in Great Britain unless permitted by the measures contained in the Act or measures contained in the National Lottery etc. Act 1993 or the Financial Services and Markets Act 2000. The Act covers all Great Britain (and where it amends the National Lottery Acts, Northern Ireland too).
2. The Act contains **three licensing objectives** that underpin the entire legislation:

- Preventing gambling from being a source of crime and disorder, being associated with crime or disorder, or being used to support crime;
- Ensuring that gambling is conducted in a fair and open way;
- Protecting children and other vulnerable people from being harmed or exploited by gambling.

3. The Act created a unified regulator for gambling in Great Britain, **the Gambling Commission**, and a new licensing regime for commercial gambling. The Act

transfers all responsibility for granting gaming and betting permissions from licensing justices and grants new powers to licensing authorities in relation to the licensing and regulation of gambling premises.

4. The Gambling Commission will regulate all commercial gambling in Great Britain, except the National Lottery and Spread Betting, which will continue to be the responsibility of the National Lottery Commission and the Financial Services Authority respectively.

5. Under the new regime there will be three types of licence:

(i) **operating** licences (issued to gambling businesses)

(ii) **personal** licences (issued to those who are either in a senior managerial position eg directors or those who have an ability to affect the outcome of the gambling eg croupiers)

(iii) **premises** licences (issued for gambling establishments)

6. The Gambling Commission is responsible for issuing **operating** and **personal** licences under the Act. An operating licence will be required by anyone wishing to provide facilities for gambling and will be the main form of permission for commercial gambling. Operating licences will be issued for an unlimited period. A maintenance fee will be payable on an annual basis. The Commission also has the power to review a licence, amend licence conditions and, ultimately, revoke a licence if it has reason to do so.

7. Personal licences will fall into two categories: management and operational. Management functions will include particular, legally defined roles, such as directors or partners of a company. They will also include roles commonly filled by compliance officers and managers or supervisors of those handling significant amounts of money. Operational functions will include posts where the individual has the ability to influence the outcome of gambling, for example bingo callers or croupiers.

8. Licensing authorities will be responsible for issuing **premises** licences, a role previously undertaken in part by licensing justices. In addition to licences, there are other forms of authorisation that may permit gambling facilities to be provided on particular premises, for example, temporary and occasional use notices, and a number of different permits. Licensing authorities will be responsible for these additional authorisations and permissions. Licensing authorities will exercise their new powers from 21 May 2007. Operators who apply for their new licenses under the Act before 31 July 2007 will receive continuation rights ie automatic renewal subject to the requirements of the new Act.

1.2: APPLICATION AND GRANT

Key learning objectives:

- *Demonstrate understanding of the application of the principles set out in s.153 of the Act*
- *Demonstrate understanding of the application process*
- *Demonstrate understanding of responsible authorities, interested parties, and relevant representations*
- *Demonstrate understanding of Mandatory and Default conditions*
- *Demonstrate understanding of Individual conditions*
- *Demonstrate understanding of Appeals*

Reference materials:

- *Gambling Act 2005: Part 8*
- *The Gambling Act 2005 (Premises Licences and Provisional Statements) Regulations 2007*
- *The Gambling Act 2005 (Mandatory and Default Conditions) (England and Wales) Regulations 2007*
- *The Gambling Act 2005 (Premises Licence Fees) Regulations 2007*
- *Gambling Commission Guidance to Licensing Authorities: Part 4, Part 5, Part 7, Part 8, Part 9*
- *Case Study 1*

- *Case Study 2*
- *Role Play*

KEY PRINCIPLES

1. Section 153 of the Act sets out the principles to be applied by licensing authorities when exercising their functions under Part 8 of the Act (premises licences and provisional statements). This section states that a licensing authority should aim to permit the use of premises for gambling in so far as it thinks it:

(a) in accordance with any relevant code of practice under section 24

(b) in accordance with any relevant guidance issued by the Commission under section 25;

(c) reasonably consistent with the licensing objectives (subject to paragraphs a) and b))and

(d) in accordance with the statement published by the licensing authority under section 349 (subject to paragraphs a) to c).

2. Section 153 also sets out that in exercising its functions under Part 8 of the Act, a licensing authority must **not** have regard to the expected demand for the facilities that are subject to the application. This is a key difference between the 2005 Act and previous legislation on gaming and betting which required potential operators to demonstrate demand.

3. There are a number of points for licensing authorities to be aware of in regard to the key principles to be applied:

(i) The principles set out in s.153 apply **only** in relation to the exercise of functions under Part 8 of the Act[1]

(ii) Different principles apply when exercising functions under other Parts of the Act, ie in relation to different kinds of permits. Authorities will need to be aware of these differences.

(iii) The licensing objectives within the Gambling Act differ from those within the Licensing Act 2003. In particular, there is no objective to prevent public nuisance or to ensure public safety and this must not be considered when undertaking functions under Part 8 of the Gambling Act. Additionally, the licensing objective in the Gambling Act relating to children is explicitly to protect them from being harmed or exploited by gambling, rather than more generally.

PREMISES LICENCES

When is a Premises Licence required?

4. Premises licences are required in respect of specific premises where an individual or company proposes to offer premises based gambling. They are issued by the licensing authority with responsibility for the area in which the premises is located. An application for a premises licence may be made to a licensing authority at the same time as an application for an operating licence is made to the Gambling Commission. A premises licence cannot generally be issued until the Commission has issued an operating licence to the individual or company.

5. A premises licence, once issued, will be of unlimited duration unless and until it ceases to have effect in accordance with a provision of Part 8 (for example, the licence is revoked by the licensing authority, is surrendered by the holder or lapses due to death or bankruptcy).

Which types of gambling qualify?

6. In accordance with section 150 of the Act, premises licences can be issued to the following premises:

- casinos
- bingo halls

- adult gaming centres
- family entertainment centres
- betting premises

Only one premises licence may be issued for any particular premises at any time, although the licence may authorise more than one type of gambling. Tracks have an exemption to this rule, as they may be subject to more than one premises licence, as long as the licence applies to a specific area of the track. In this instance, the owner of the track does not have to apply for an operator's licence.

What are the arrangements for Vessels and vehicles?

7. The Act permits premises licences to be granted for passenger vessels, defined as *anything (other than a seaplane or amphibious vehicle) designed or adapted for use on water, a hovercraft or anything, or part of any place, situated on or in water.* This enables vessels such as pleasure boats and floating restaurants to apply for premises licences. Premises licences may not be issued in respect of vessels that are not passenger vessels.

8. It should be noted that gambling is not a licensable activity if it takes place aboard a vessel engaged on an international journey. This therefore included cross channel ferries. In the case of aircraft, no offence occurs if the gambling takes place in international airspace.

9. Vehicles (trains, aircraft, cars etc.) are not entitled to hold a premises licence and therefore all forms of commercial betting and gaming will be unlawful in a vehicle in Great Britain.

10. The relevant licensing authority which should consider an application for a premises licence for a vessel is the authority in which the vessel is permanently or usually moored or berthed. There are separate applications forms for vessels.

APPLICATION FOR A PREMISES LICENCE

11. An application for a premises licence may only be made by persons:

- who are over 18 years of age (this includes companies and partnerships)
- have a right to occupy the premises
- who hold, or have applied for, an operating licence authorising the proposed activities

12. Track owners who wish to offer betting facilities themselves, rather than through an on course betting operator must apply for an operators licence.

13. Section 159 of the Act sets out that an application must be made to the relevant licensing authority in the form prescribed by the Secretary of State or Scottish Ministers [2]. We have prescribed the forms in Statutory instrument 2007 No. 459-The Gambling Act 2005 (Premises Licences and Provisional statements). Licensing Authorities forms are available through LACORS and can be amended to add a Licensing Authority logo. Forms for applicants can be obtained through the DCMS and Gambling Commission websites.

---

[2] See Gambling Act 2005 (Premises Licences and Provisional Statements) Regulations 2007

14. The application must be accompanied by the prescribed fee and a plan of the premises.

Application for a premises licence

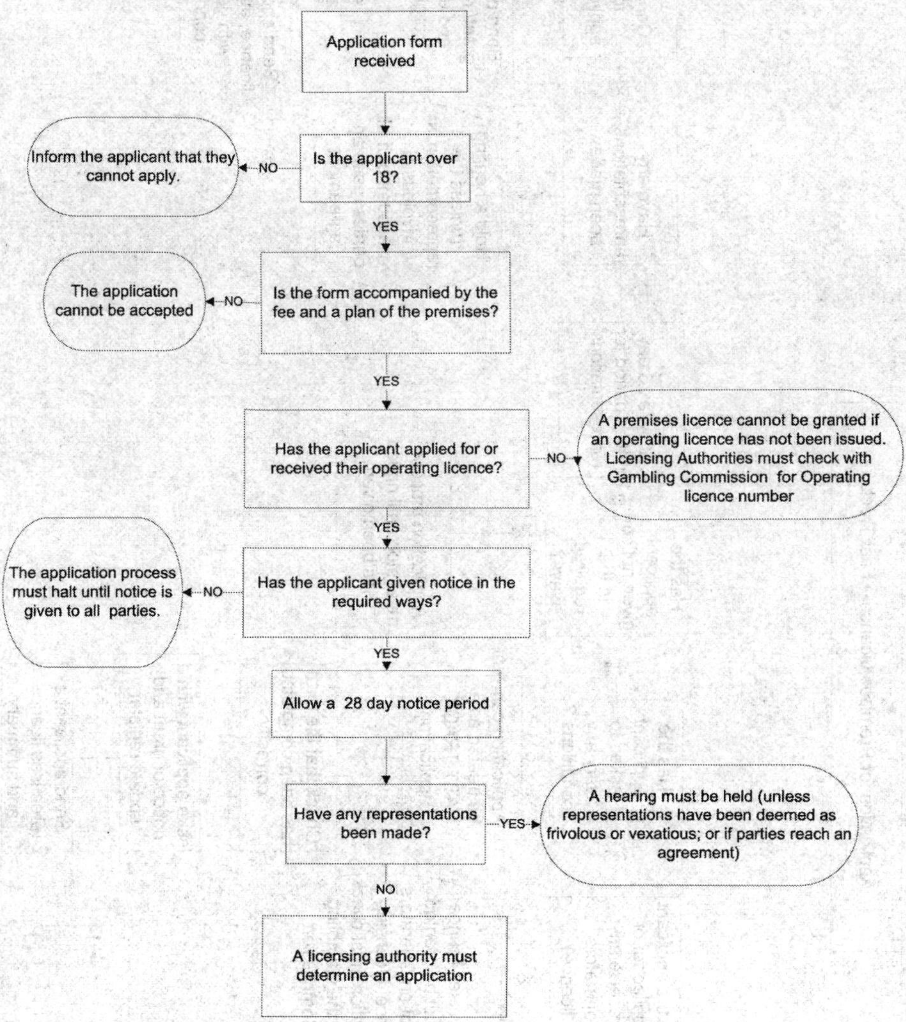

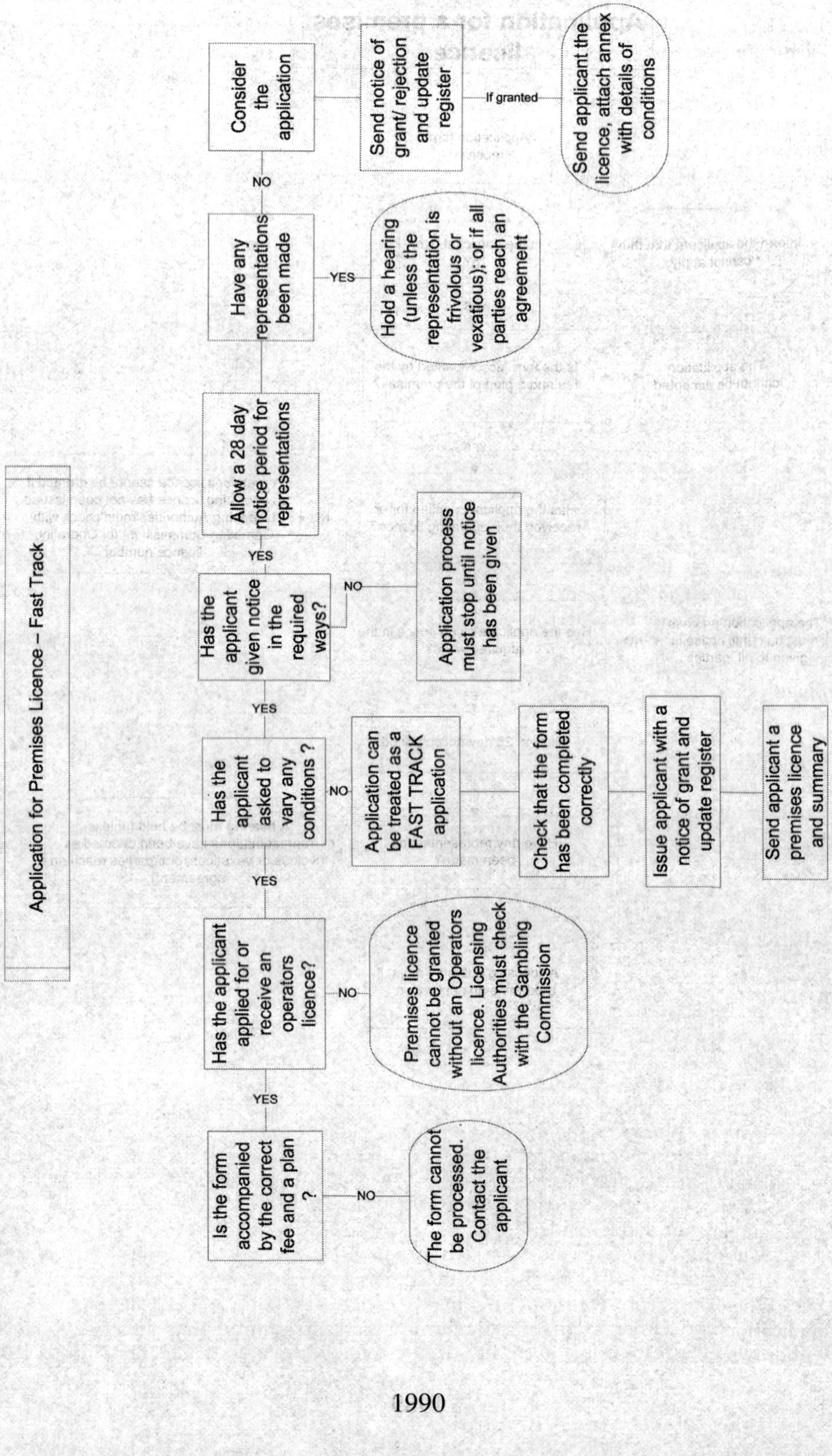
Application for Premises Licence – Fast Track
Is the form accompanied by the correct fee and a plan ?
NO
The form cannot be processed. Contact the applicant
YES
Has the applicant applied for or receive an operators licence?
NO
Premises licence cannot be granted without an Operators licence. Licensing Authorities must check with the Gambling Commission
YES
Has the applicant asked to vary any conditions ?
NO
Application can be treated as a FAST TRACK application
Check that the form has been completed correctly
Issue applicant with a notice of grant and update register
Send applicant a premises licence and summary
YES
Has the applicant given notice in the required ways?
NO
Application process must stop until notice has been given
YES
Allow a 28 day notice period for representations
Have any representations been made
YES
Hold a hearing (unless the representation is frivolous or vexatious); or if all parties reach an agreement
NO
Consider the application
Send notice of grant/ rejection and update register
If granted
Send applicant the licence, attach annex with details of conditions

FEES

15. Licensing authorities are responsible for setting fees on a cost recovery basis. The fee maxima for each type of premises has been prescribed by the Secretary of State[3] in SI 459 The Gambling (Premises Licence Fees) (England and Wales) Regulations 2007. The setting of fees can be delegated to the licensing committee but need not be. The maximum fees are attached in **Annex E** and the Department will be issuing separate guidance on setting fees.

---

[3] See Gambling Act 2005 (Premises Licence Fees) Regulations 2007

PLANS

16. The plan of the premises forms an important part of the application. Regulations stipulate what should be shown on the plan. As well as requiring all premises to show several generic details on their plans, regulations also require each type of premises to provide additional information relating to their particular premises type. Plans must include the following and be drawn to scale.

For all premises:

- The boundary /perimeter of the premises (sides in the case of vessels)
- Internal/ external walls
- Points of entrance/ exit and description of where they lead to
- Where the premises is located if it is part of a larger building

Casinos:

- The principle entrance and where is it leads to
- The table gaming area
- The non gaming areas
- Areas which children can access and any barriers (regional only)

Bingo

- Areas which children can access and any barriers
- Location of category B & C machines

Adult gaming centres

- The location of machines

Family Entertainment centres

- The location of category C machines
- The location of category B machines
- Any barriers

GIVING NOTICE

17. Applicants are also required to publish notice of their application and to notify the responsible authorities and other persons (interested parties) of their application. This process enables representations to be made and considered by the licensing authority. Notice must be given using the notice forms provided in Premises Licence and Provisional statement regulations; and must be given in the following ways:

- Publish notice in a newspaper or newsletter of local relevance, at least once within 10 days of the application being made
- Publish notice outside the premises in a place where it can be conveniently read and is clearly visible
- Notice must be copied to all responsible authorities within 7 days of the application being made.

  The notice period must last for 28 consecutive days, during which time representations can be given to the Licensing Authority in writing.

18. Where no representations are made, a licensing officer may determine the application and either grant or reject it. Where representations are made and not withdrawn by a responsible authority or interested party, a licensing committee must

6: Gambling Act 2005: Additional Material

consider the application at a hearing. However, hearings do not need to be held if representations are frivolous, vexatious, and / or won't influence the licensing authority's determination of the application.

19. The licensing committee hears applications for casino licences, although the consideration of a "no casino" resolution must be done by the whole authority.

RESPONSIBLE AUTHORITIES, INTERESTED PARTIES AND RELEVANT REPRESENTATIONS

20. The Act states that responsible authorities and interested parties have to be informed about an application for a premises licence. Definitions for both parties are below:

21. Responsible authorities are public bodies with an interest to the application. Section 157 of the Act and paragraph 8.2 of the Commission Guidance set out the full list of responsible authorities. An abbreviated list is included below:

- A licensing authority in England and Wales in whose area the premises is wholly or partly situated
- The Gambling Commission
- The Police Authority
- The Fire and Rescue Authority
- The Planning Authority
- The Council constituted under s.2 of the Local Government (Scotland) Act 1994
- Environmental Health (or equivalent)
- A body designated in writing by the licensing authority as competent to advise about the protection of children from harm (eg Social Services.)
- HM Revenue and Customs
- Navigation authorities (Environment Agency, British Waterways Board, Maritime and Coastguard Agency) and the Secretary of State. (for vessels only).

22. Section 158 of the Act defines interested parties as persons who:

- Live sufficiently close to the premises to be likely to be affected by the authorised activities
- Have business interests that might be affected by the authorised activities
- Represent persons in either of these two groups.

23. The Commission Guidance provides further advice regarding the approach to be taken by licensing authorities in determining who is an interested party. Approaches will ultimately differ between authorities and licensing officers and members should ensure that any decisions in relation to interested parties are taken in accordance with any relevant authority policies.

RELEVANT REPRESENTATIONS

24. As part of its consideration, a licensing authority must determine whether or not representations are admissible. A representation is inadmissible if it is not made by a responsible authority or interested party. After this, the authority must determine its relevance. The only representations that are likely to be relevant are those that

- raise issues under the Commission Guidance or codes of practice,
- relate to the three licensing objectives,
- raise issues regarding the authority's own licensing policy statement.

25. The Act contains no obligation for responsible authorities to respond to applications for premises licences if they do not wish to do so. Where relevant representations are made and not withdrawn by a responsible authority or interested party, a licensing committee must consider the application at a hearing.

THE DECISION

26. Licensing committees or officers have a range of options:

(a) grant a licence

(b) refuse an application;
(c) grant a licence with an adjustment to the default condition
(d) grant a licence but with an individual condition attached

LICENCE CONDITIONS

27. The Gambling Act provides for three types of condition to be attached to a premises licence:

- Mandatory conditions
- Default conditions
- Individual conditions

28. **Mandatory conditions** – Gambling Act 2007 (Mandatory and Default conditions) regulations have been made which give details of the conditions for each type of premises licence. These have been made under section 167 of the Act.

29. Mandatory conditions can only be removed by further regulations. A licensing authority has no power to remove or vary conditions that are attached under section 167. (See **Annex F** for a summary of the mandatory and default conditions)

30. **Default conditions** refer to opening hours of each premises only and are attached in the same way as mandatory conditions, however, they can be removed or replaced by licensing authorities (either under section 169 on issue of a licence, or as a result of an application for a variation or review of a premises licence). Licensing authorities are free to limit or exclude them where appropriate, they should only be more rigorous where there is evidence of real need (this is the effect of section 153).

31. There are no default conditions for Adult Gaming Centres or Family Entertainment Centres.

32. Licensing authorities can attach **individual conditions** to a licence. Section 169 gives the licensing authority the power to attach a condition to a licence respond to local situations, for example the need for CCTV. As with all other functions under Part 8, the power to attach individual conditions must be exercised in accordance with the principles set out in section 153.

GRANTING A LICENCE

33. Before an application is granted, either by a licensing officer or following a committee hearing, the Licensing Authority must confirm that the applicant has been issued an operating licence from the Gambling Commission for the activities to which the application for the premises licence relates. The officer must then give notice of the grant, using the form which has been prescribed, to the following:

- the applicant
- the Commission
- any persons who made representations under s.161
- the Chief Officer of Police (in England and Wales)
- the Chief Constable of Police (in Scotland)
- HM Revenue and Customs

34. The Licensing Authority must then issue a premises licence to the applicant and provide the applicant with a summary of the terms and conditions of the licence. Again, both these documents have been prescribed in regulations.

35. The summary of the licence also forms the notice which must be displayed within the premises itself.

36. Where an application is rejected, the officer must give notice of the rejection to those persons listed in paragraph 36, and must give the authority's reasons for rejecting the application. Again, the form of this is prescribed in regulations and are available on the LACORS website.

REGISTERS

37. The register of premises licences must also be updated following the grant of a premises licence, under section 156 of the Act. The Department have not prescribed the form and manner in which the register must be kept, thought the Act allows them the discretion to do so. The manner in which the register is kept and updated will depend on the technological capabilities of each Licensing Authority. Licensing Authorities must bear in mind that the register should be available to the public and must contain information which is relevant to the public.
38. Good practice dictates that the register will be updated regularly and contain details of all premises licences issued by the authority.
39. Licensing Authorities are not required to keep copies of the plan of the premises on the register.

APPEALS

40. Under the Gambling Act 2005, appeals against decisions made by the Gambling Commission (ie decisions made in respect of operating or personal licences) must be made to the Gambling Appeals Tribunal.
41. Appeals against decisions made by licensing authorities in England and Wales in respect of premises licences, permits or other permissions within the Act, must be made to the Magistrates' Court for a local justices area in which the premises is situated. In Scotland, such appeals are to be made to the Sheriff's court in whose sheriffdom the premises are situated.

RIGHTS OF APPEAL

42. Where a licensing authority rejects an application under Part 8 (to issue a premises licence or to vary a premises licence), the applicant may appeal.
43. Where a licensing authority grants an application under Part 8 (ie issues a premises licence in line with the application, issues a premises licence with conditions, varies, transfers, reinstates or reviews a premises licence etc), the applicant and any person who made representations may appeal.
44. Where a licensing authority takes action (including revocation or suspension of a licence, or the addition or removal of conditions) following a review of a premises licence, the following persons may appeal:
(i) the licence holder;
(ii) any person who made representations in relation to the review;
(iii) where relevant, the person who applied for the review;
(iv) The Gambling Commission.

1.3: PROVISIONAL STATEMENTS

Key Learning Objectives:
- *Understanding of what provisional statements are for;*
- *Understanding of the application process, including representations that can be considered;*
- *Understanding of the processes and principles to be applied in respect of a premises licence, once a provisional statement has been issued.*

Reference Materials:
- *Gambling Act 2005: Part 8*
- *Gambling Commission Guidance to Licensing Authorities: Part 11*
- *Gambling (Premises Licences and Provisional Statement) Regulations 2007*

KEY POINTS:

1. Under section 204 of the Act a person may make an application for a provisional statement in respect of premises that they:

(i) expect to be constructed,
(ii) expect to be altered, or
(iii) expect to acquire the right to occupy.

WHAT IS THE PURPOSE OF A PROVISIONAL STATEMENT?

2. A provisional statement is a provisional grant of premises licence. The outcome of the provisional statement application would enable an applicant them to judge whether it would be worth building a premises.
3. The applicant must apply in using the form set out in regulations, which largely asks for similar information to a standard application form, it must be accompanied by a plan of the proposed premises and the fee. The same rules for publishing notice of a premises licence apply to provisional statements and representations can be made.

WHAT MUST A LICENSING AUTHORITY CONSIDER?

4. The licensing authority must apply the same tests for the provisional statement as it would for a premises licence and take into consideration all the same licensing objectives. Conditions can be attached in the same way in which they can be attached to a premises licence and must be included on the notice of grant of an application for a provisional statement.
5. However, a person can apply for a provisional licence without having first obtained or made an application for an operating licence. Nor do they have to have the right to occupy the premises for which they are making their application.

REPRESENTATIONS

6. Once the application is submitted, the process for considering it is the same as with a full premises licence application. Notice must be published and Responsible authorities and interested parties have 28 consecutive days to make representations in the same way as for a premises licence application and there are the same rights of appeal

GRANTING AN APPLICATION FOR A PROVISIONAL STATEMENT

7. Once a provisional statement has been issued, the applicant can be reassured that when the application for the premises licence comes in, no representations can be taken into account of the same, **as long as** there has been no material change in the circumstances of the premises or the area in the vicinity of the premises since the provisional statement was made. The plan of the premises will obviously prove vital to this stage of the application process.
8. Once a provisional statement is granted, if a premises licence application is subsequently made by the statement holder in relation to the premises to which it relates, the application needs to be treated in a different way to one that does not have a provisional statement.

PREMISES LICENCE APPLICATION BY A PROVISIONAL STATEMENT HOLDER

9. Once the premises have been built, altered or acquired, the holder of the provisional statement should then to return to the licensing authority and apply for a premises licence. This application will need to be treated in a different way to an application by someone who doesn't have a provisional statement[4]. Licensing authorities should note that there could be more than one valid provisional statement in respect of the same premises, as the applicants for provisional statements do not need to have right to occupy.

6: Gambling Act 2005: Additional Material

4 See section 205 of the Act

10. When determining whether to grant an application for a premises licence in such circumstances, the licensing authority cannot take into account further representations from responsible authorities or interested parties, unless they concern matters which could not have been addressed at the provisional statement stage, or they reflect a change in the applicant's circumstances.

10. Similarly, the authority may refuse the premises licence (or grant it on terms different to those attached to the provisional statement) only by reference to matters which could not have been addressed in representations at the provisional licence stage, or, in the licensing authority's opinion reflect a change in the operator's circumstances.

11. If the licensing authority does not think that the premises were constructed or altered in accordance with the plans and information submitted with the application for the provisional statement, then the restrictions of the two paragraphs above are no longer applicable.

2.1: TRANSITIONAL PROVISIONS

Key learning objectives:

- *Understand the concepts of Grandfather rights and Continuation Rights*
- *Understand the differences between the transitional application process and new applications under the Act*

Reference materials:

- *DCMS Transitional Arrangements Paper*
- *Transitional provisions orders*

KEY POINTS

1. The transition period runs from 1 September 2006 until 31 August 2007. The new Act comes into force 1 September 2007 (a chronology is at Annex A).

2. All operators must apply for new permissions under the Act if they wish to operate after 1 September 2007, whether this is by continuing an existing business or starting a new operation.

3. Licensing authorities will accept applications from 21 May 2007.

4. Existing operators have two rights under the transitional arrangements:

(i) The right to continue to operate after 1 September 2007(until their new licence is granted), even if the new licence for which they have applied has not yet been granted. To qualify for this entitlement operators need to make their application to operate under the new act by 31st July 2007. These are called **continuation rights**

(ii) The right to be automatically granted the equivalent standard permissions for their premises type under the new legislation. These are called **grandfather rights**. There are two important things to note:

(a) Grandfathering only applies to premises licences, not operating licences.

(b) The new Act applies. The type of licence granted will be the closest equivalent allowed by the new Act, and will permit the operator to continue to carry out the same type of gambling activity, although the rights will not be identical to those under the former Act. At the end of this section there are four diagrams (annexes B-E) illustrating the transitional arrangements for various types of operators. Further information is available in the DCMS Transitional Arrangements guidance on the DCMS website.

EXISTING OPERATORS

5. To qualify as an 'existing operator' an operator will need to have an existing permission immediately before 1 September 2007, or have an outstanding application under existing legislation that is subsequently granted under the new legislation.

6. A new operator would be treated as an existing operator and be entitled to grandfather and/or continuation rights (even if they had not operated before), if they:

(i) Apply for permission under the existing legislation and are granted it (either before or after 1 September 2007).

(ii) Apply for permission under the new legislation by 30 July 2007. In which case (subject to being granted their licence), they would also qualify for continuation rights.

7. Therefore continuation rights and grandfather rights are available for those applicants who make their applications for premises licences under the new Act by the relevant deadline.

GRANDFATHER RIGHTS

8. The term 'grandfather rights' means the entitlement of existing operators, who have applied for a licence under the Gambling Act 2005, to be granted the equivalent type of permission in relation to their premises under the new legislation. For example, a person operating a betting shop under the existing legislation would be entitled to a betting shop premises licence under the new legislation. However, the licence granted would be subject to the standard mandatory and default conditions for a betting shop premises licence under the new legislation.

9. 'Grandfathering' does not entitle an operator to be granted a licence under the new legislation that exactly mirrors the permissions and conditions under which they operated under the existing legislation. However, existing operators would have the option of applying for a licence under the new legislation and request the removal of one or more default conditions.

10. Therefore, existing operators with premises permissions under the existing legislation will have two choices when they apply for grandfathered premises licences:

(i) A fast track application for a "standard" grandfathered premises licence with mandatory and default conditions (as set out in other regulations) attached and nothing more or,

(ii) An application that seeks to vary the standard default conditions. The applicant would still be guaranteed the grandfathered premises licence but, in this case, the licensing authority would consider the licence application fully, in the light of the proposed changes in conditions, and would be able to attach its own conditions.

11. The first option would require a relatively simple process: the applicant would signify on the application form that they wished to receive the "standard" grandfather rights. They would then be entitled to the standard premises licence for their premises type. The licensing authority would not be permitted to attach additional conditions. Responsible authorities and interested parties would not have the right to make representations. There would be no need to provide notice of application and there would be no hearings. Essentially, all that the licensing authority will be doing is checking that the application form has been filled in correctly and the right documents are attached.

12. The second option would require full consideration by the licensing authority, similar to the process for a new applicant. In this instance, the applicant would still be guaranteed a licence but, since changes to the existing conditions are being sought, the licensing authority may also exclude other default or attach specific conditions, if it considers that appropriate. As the applicant is seeking to change the default conditions, he would need to give notice of application to the responsible authorities and interested parties, which may make representations. If representations are made or if the licensing authority attaches conditions to the licence a hearing will be required, unless the parties agree otherwise.

CONTINUATION RIGHTS

13. Continuation rights permit an existing operator who has applied for a premises licence under the new legislation to continue to operate after 1st September 2007, even if their new licence has not been issued. Although they will be permitted to continue operating, their operation will be subject to the mandatory and default conditions. This includes those operators who applied under option two until such time as their application is granted and they receive their new licence with the default conditions altered.

14. To qualify for continuation rights, existing operators must have made their application under the new legislation before 30 July 2007. Applications received after 30 July 2007 will be processed but will not be entitled to continuation rights. If their application is not processed 1 September 2007, they will have to stop operating until their new premises licence is issued.

TRANSITIONAL PROVISIONS

15. Should an existing operator's licence or permit expire before the transition period ie before 1 September 2006 an application for renewal should be made to their issuing institution for a renewal in the normal way (ie according to the prescriptions of the previous Acts). If successful, the new permission will run until 31 August 2007.

16. Should the licence or permit expire during the transition period (ie between 1 September 2006 and 31 August 2007), no action is required as all such existing permissions will automatically be extended until the end of the transition period.

17. In both cases, premises licences under the previous legislation will run until 31 August 2007. Thereafter, all operators must operate with permissions granted under the 2005 Act.

18. In the case of casinos, if an existing operator is granted a premises licence under the 2005 Act, and the licence is granted with continuation rights, the following will apply:

(i) The casino will not be subject to the minimum size requirements which otherwise apply under the 2005 Act

(ii) The casino premises licence will not count against the limit on the number of casino premises licences allowed by the 2005 Act (section 175)

(iii) The casino will be subject to the limit of 20 Category B gaming machines but will be permitted to make available unlimited category C or D machines.

19. New operators who apply after 30 July 2007 will only be able to apply under the 2005 Act and will, therefore, not be permitted to operate until 1st September 2007.

2.2: OTHER APPLICATIONS – VARY, TRANSFER AND REINSTATE

Key Learning Objectives:

- *Understanding of the processes and principles to be applied in respect of variation of a premises licence;*
- *Understanding of the processes and principles to be applied in respect of transfer of a premises licence;*
- *Understanding of circumstances in which premises licences are deemed to have lapsed and the processes and principles to be applied in respect of the reinstatement of a premises licence.*

Reference Materials:

- *Gambling Act 2005: Part 8*
- *Gambling Commission Guidance: Part 10*
- *Gambling Act 2005 (Premises Licences and Provisional Statement) Regulations 2007*

KEY POINTS

1. Once a premises licence has been issued, the holder or another person with an operating licence may apply to a licensing authority to make certain changes to it. These are applications to vary, transfer or reinstate.
2. Again, all the forms associated with these other applications are prescribed by Premises Licences and Provisional Statements Regulations 2007.
3. For applications for transfer and reinstatement, the application and determination process is simpler than for premises licences. In particular, the requirements for notice and representations will not be as robust. This is because the changes to the licence are limited to a change in licensee, rather than a change in the premises or licensable activities.
4. For applications to vary, the application and determination process will be almost exactly the same as for premises licences. This is because the variation could be a substantial change to the premises or the licensable activities. Therefore, such an application could be contentious, which justifies full scrutiny.
5. In each case, the applicant must submit the premises licence to which their application relates or both a statement explaining why it is not possible to produce the licence and an application for a copy of the licence. This is because in each case, the licence will have to be amended and reissued.

Variation

6. If a licensee wishes to change a detail of their premises licence they will have to make an application to vary to the appropriate licensing authority. Section187 of the Act sets out the three ways in which a premises licence can be varied.

- Adding, amending or removing an authorised activity,
- Amending another detail of the licence,
- Excluding a default condition and/or a condition imposed by a licensing authority.
- A licence cannot be varied so that it applies to a different premises.

7. Some of these changes could be quite significant and would justify greater scrutiny. For example, an applicant could be asking to change their premises from a bingo hall to a casino, or they could be seeking to vary their licence because they wish to extend their premises and double its size (which would be a variation seeking to amend a detail of the licence ie the plan).

THE APPLICATION

8. The application must be in the prescribed form and should be accompanied by either the licence or both a statement explaining why it is not possible to produce the licence.
9. If the applicant does not hold a copy of the existing licence, they must request a copy by ticking the relevant box on the application form and pay the relevant fee.
10. The provisions for notice and representations are the same as for an application for a premises licence. The same consideration should be given to representations as with a premises licence application. The same processes for notice of grant or rejection also apply and the applicant should be issued with an updated licence.
11. Should a licensing authority grant an application to vary they should specify a time when the transfer is to take effect on the notice of grant.
12. The application must be accompanied by a revised plan of the premises and the appropriate fee.

Transfer

13. An application can be made to transfer the licence to another name. The person to whom it is transferred must have an operating licence and this must be checked with the Gambling Commission.

THE APPLICATION

14. As before, the application must be made using the prescribed form and the applicant must submit their licence or both a statement explaining why it is not possible to produce the licence.
15. If the applicant does not hold a copy of the existing licence, they must request a copy by ticking the relevant box on the application form and pay the relevant fee.
16. The application form should be accompanied by a written statement from the existing licence holder consenting to the transfer. However if the applicant is unable to contact the licence holder, having taken all reasonable steps to do so, the application may be processed without this statement.
17. An application for transfer should be relatively straightforward, as the premises itself has already been determined as suitable for gambling and the terms and conditions of the licence will not be changed (except if the licensing authority considers an alteration is required). Should the applicant wish to change any of the details of the licence they may make an application to vary once they have submitted their application to transfer, if they have asked to be treated as the licensee during the determination process (see paragraph 14 below), otherwise they will have to wait until the licence has been transferred.

GIVING NOTICE

18. An applicant is required to give notice of an application to transfer but to responsible authorities only as they may make representations. Interested parties may not make representations in this case.
19. If the licensing authority decides to grant an application to transfer, the must issue a notice of grant which specifies the time at which the transfer takes place should and alter the licence to name the applicant as licensee. They may also attach or removing any condition.
20. If they choose not to grant the application, they must issue a notice of rejection, with details of their reasons for rejection.
21. In their application the applicant should have stated when they wish the transfer to take effect. If they wish, they may request to be treated as the licensee from the time when the application is made until it is determined. This allows the gambling business to continue trading without interruption until the determination is made.

LAPSE OF LICENCE

22. Section 194 of the Act stipulates the various circumstances in which a premises licence will be deemed to have lapsed. Generally, a premises licence will lapse if the licensee

- dies
- becomes physically or mentally incapacitated
- declared bankrupt.
- If the licence is held by a company or organisation, a lapse will have taken place in the event of the company ceasing to exist, or becoming insolvent.

23. If a licensing authority becomes aware that a premises licence issued by them has lapsed they should notify the Gambling Commission, the police and HMRC as soon as possible.

Reinstatement

24. An application for reinstatement can only be made in relation to a licence which has lapsed. Reinstatement allows another operator to take over a premises licence and continue operating a gambling business from the premises. Section 195 stipulates that for six months following a licence lapse a person may apply to the licensing authority for the licence to be reinstated in their name.

25. The provisions for reinstatement under this Act differ from those under the Licensing Act 2003, where a person could apply for an interim authority notice of limited duration, or apply for the licence to be transferred to them. The reinstatement is similar to the licence being transferred as there is no time limit on the duration of the licence once reinstated.

THE APPLICATION

26. The application process is similar to that for a premises licence, with a few minor differences, and almost exactly the same as for applications to transfer. All applications should be accompanied by either the licence, or a statement explaining why it is not possible to produce the licence and an application for a copy of the licence

27. If the applicant does not hold a copy of the existing licence, they must request a copy by ticking the relevant box on the application form and pay the relevant fee.

28. Although the applicant is required to give notice, they do not need to give notice to all responsible authorities and interested parties. In this case, responsible authorities may make representations in relations to applications to reinstate, but interested parties are not allowed to make representations in this instance.

29. Applications to reinstate, as with applications to transfer, should be comparatively straightforward. As with transfers, the premises has already been deemed suitable for gambling and the terms and conditions will not be changed (unless the licensing authority thinks it necessary, or the applicant makes a separate application to vary – as above in paragraph 11).

30. The licensing authority should grant applications for reinstatement unless representations made by responsible authorities give them good reason not to do so. The same processes for notice of grant or rejection apply to reinstatements as for premises licences.

31. The application for reinstatement must include a request that the reinstatement takes effect upon the application being granted. In addition, the applicant is treated as being the licensee for the period during which the application is being determined. In such a case, the premises licence is effectively transferred to the applicant for the period between the submission of the application for reinstatement and its determination by the licensing authority. Note the contrast with transfers, where an applicant can request to be so treated, but the conferral of status is not automatic.

ANNEX A
TRANSITIONAL ARRANGEMENTS – CHRONOLOGY FOR PREMISES LICENCES

1 SEPTEMBER 2006

- Transitional period began.
- Operators whose existing permissions expired after 1st September 2006 have had their permissions automatically extended until 31st August 2007 (the end of the transitional period). There is no need for application or fee.

1 JANUARY 2007

- Gambling Commission starts to accept applications for **operating licences**

21 MAY 2007

- Licensing authorities starts to accept advance applications for **premises licences**

30 JULY 2007 – KEY DATE

- This is the deadline for applications for existing operators (or new operators outstanding applications under the existing legislation) wishing to receive **continuation rights**
- Applications received after this date will still be processed but will not receive continuation rights.

- This is also the closing date for new operators to apply for permissions under the existing legislation in order to start operating before 1st September 2007 and/or potentially qualify for **continuation and grandfather rights.**
- After 30 July only Gambling Act 2005 permissions will be granted, which means new operators would not be able to commence operating until 1st September 2007.

31 AUGUST 2007

- Transitional period ends.

1 SEPTEMBER 2007

- Gambling Act 2005 comes into effect along with the new licences and permits granted under that Act.
- Those operators with continuation rights may continue to operate, subject to the mandatory and default conditions.
- Those who do not have continuation rights and have yet to receive their permissions under the new legislation must cease operation.
- Existing legislation is repealed

1 OCTOBER 2007

Payment of the first annual fee must be made before this date by holders of converted licences.

ANNEX B

EXISTING OPERATORS:
1.1 Betting, Bingo, Arcades and External Lottery Managers

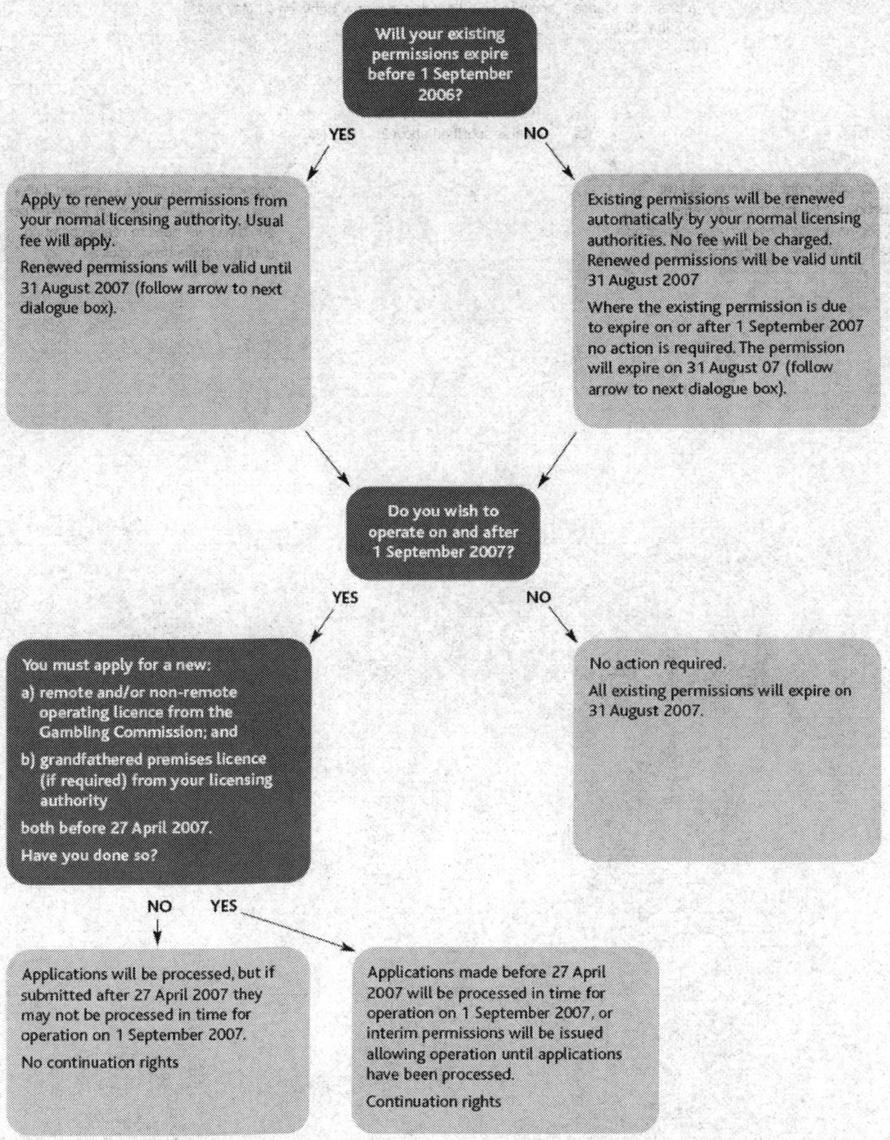

ANNEX C

Summary – for an operator with existing permissions under current legislation

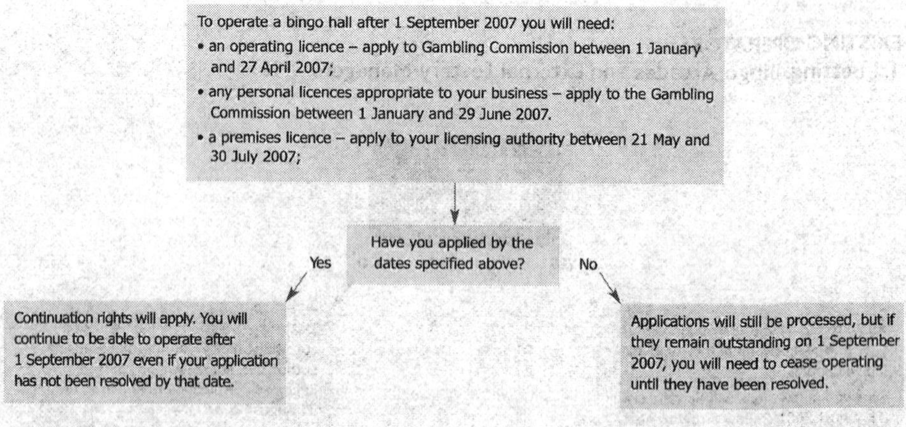

ANNEX D

NEW OPERATORS

2.1 Betting, Bingo, Arcades and External Lottery Managers

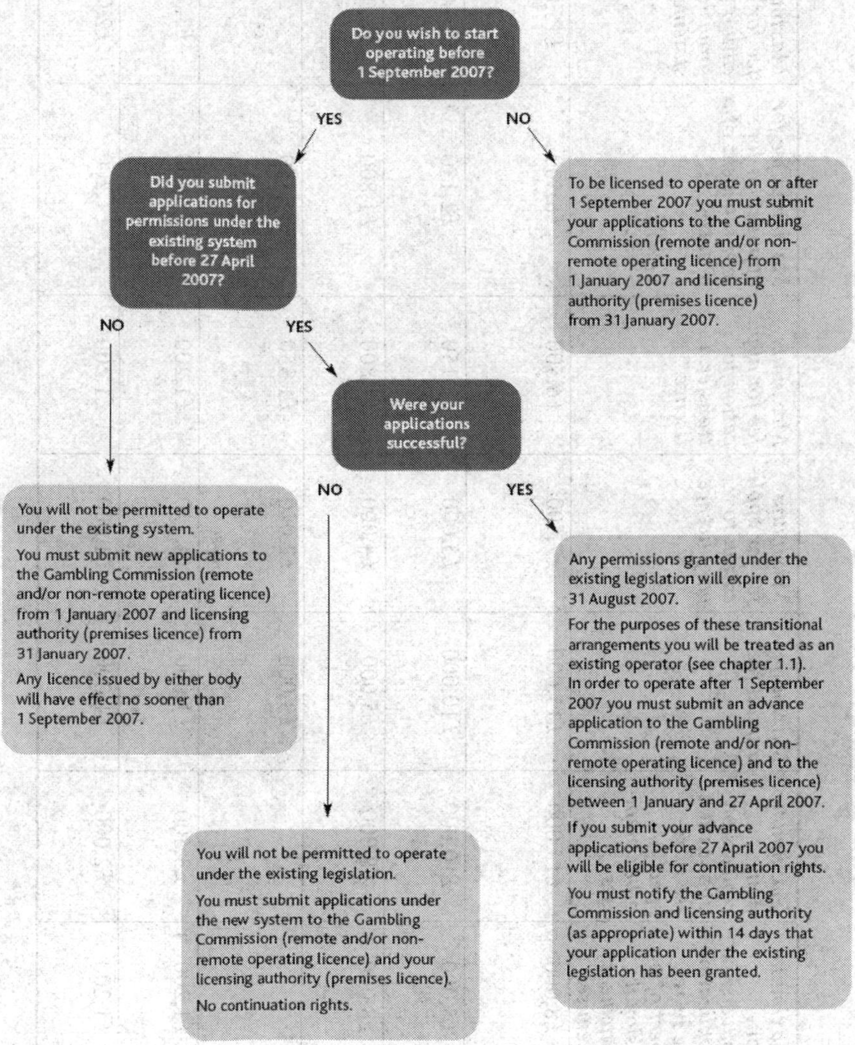

ANNEX E
2007

Classes of premises licence	*Maximum conversion application fee for non-fast track application*	*Maximum non-conversion application fee in respect of provisional statement premises*	*Maximum non-conversion application fee in respect of other premises*	*Maximum annual fee*	*Maximum fee for application to vary licence*	*Maximum fee for application to transfer a licence*	*Maximum fee for application for reinstatement of a licence*	*Maximum fee for application for provisional statement*
Regional casino premises licence		£8,000	£15,000	£15,000	£7,500	£6,500	£6,500	£15,000
Large casino premises licence		£5,000	£10,000	£10,000	£5,000	£2,150	£2,150	£10,000
Small casino premises licence		£3,000	£8,000	£5,000	£4,000	£1,800	£1,800	£8,000
Converted casino premises licence	£2,000			£3,000	£2,000	£1,350	£1,350	
Bingo premises licence	£1,750	£1,200	£3,500	£1,000	£1,750	£1,200	£1,200	£3,500
Adult gaming centre	£1,000	£1,200	£2,000	£1,000	£1,000	£1,200	£1,200	£2,000

Classes of premises licence	*Maximum conversion application fee for non-fast track application*	*Maximum non-conversion application fee in respect of provisional statement premises*	*Maximum non-conversion application fee in respect of other premises*	*Maximum annual fee*	*Maximum fee for application to vary licence*	*Maximum fee for application to transfer a licence*	*Maximum fee for application for reinstatement of a licence*	*Maximum fee for application for provisional statement*
Betting premises (track)	£1,250	£950	£2,500	£1,000	£1,250	£950	£950	£2,500
Family entertainment centre	£1,000	£950	£2,000	£750	£1,000	£950	£950	£2,000
Betting premises (other) licence	£1,500	£1,200	£3,000	£600	£1,500	£1,200	£1,200	£3,000

ANNEX F – SUMMARY OF MANDATORY AND DEFAULT CONDITIONS

MANDATORY CONDITIONS

The following mandatory conditions will apply to gambling premises licences:

- National Lottery products may not be sold on the premises;
- A maximum of 40 separate player positions at wholly automated versions of real games of chance ("automated gaming tables") in any casino;
- ATMs must be positioned so that customers must cease to gamble at tables or gaming machines in order to use them, but we will not specify how this should be done in terms of distance etc.
- A maximum of 40 betting positions at betting machines to be permitted in new casinos.

Access

- There can be no direct access between one premises licensed under the Gambling Act 2005 and another premises licensed under the Gambling Act 2005 with the following exceptions:
  - (i) between bingo premises and alcohol licensed premises / clubs with a club gaming or club gaming machine permit / family entertainment centres (FECs) and tracks;
  - (ii) between tracks and alcohol licensed premises / clubs with a club gaming or club gaming machine permit / (FECs) / betting premises and bingo premises;
  - (iii) between FECs and alcohol licensed premises / bingo halls / clubs with club gaming or club gaming machine permit and tracks;
- Over 18 areas within FECs and bingo halls that admit U18s must be separated by a barrier with notices displayed prominently stating that U18s are not allowed in that area and with adequate supervision in place to ensure that children and young people are not able to access these areas or the Category B or C machines. Supervision may be done either by placing the terminals within the line of sight of an official of the betting operator or via monitored CCTV.
- The principal entrance to a casino should be from the street (defined as any bridge, road, lane, footway, subway, square, court, alley or passage (including passages through enclosed premises such as shopping malls) whether a thoroughfare or not;
- There should be no access to a casino from a premises wholly or mainly used by children and young people;
- The gambling area of the regional casino should not be capable of being seen from any part of the premises to which children or young people have access;
- There should be no access to a betting premises from another premises which undertakes a commercial activity (except from other premises with a betting premises licence including tracks). In addition, the entrance to a betting shop should be from the street (defined as any bridge, road, lane, footway, subway, square, court, alley or passage (including passages through enclosed premises such as shopping malls) whether a thoroughfare or not;

Layout of New Casinos

- Casinos must provide the following minimum table gaming area:
  - small casino: a minimum of $500m^2$;
  - large casino: a minimum of $1000m^2$;
  - regional casinos: a minimum of $1000m^2$
- Only table gaming may take place in the table gaming areas of a casinos;
- No area counting towards the minimum table gaming area may comprise less than 12.5% of the total minimum table gaming area for that category of casino;
- No other gambling facilities may be situated within 2 metres of any ordinary table game;

- For the purposes of these conditions, table games are defined as:
  - ordinary table games – ie gaming tables which facilitate the playing of casino games ie card games, dice games, roulette etc;
  - tables operated by employees but on which customers places stakes on automated terminals;
  - wholly automated tables of the sort permitted by virtue of section 235(2)(i) of the Act.

  The following minimum non-gambling areas must be offered:
  - Regional casinos – 1500m^2;
  - Large casinos – 500m^2;
  - Small casinos – 250m^2
  - No gambling facilities may be offered in the non-gambling areas;
- The non-gambling area may consist of one or more areas;
- The area must be readily available to customers (ie offices, kitchen areas, staff areas will not count);
- The area must include recreational facilities for casino customers which are available for use when the casino is open; where there is more than one area each area must contain recreational facilities;
- The area may include, but should not consist exclusively of lavatories and lobby areas

Converted casino licences

- Casinos with converted licences, and which have a gambling area of over 200m2, must offer a minimum non-gambling area equivalent to at least 10% of its total gambling area.

Adult Gaming Centres (AGCs) and Family Entertainment Centres (FECs)

- The consumption of alcohol in AGCs and FECs is prohibited.

Betting Shops (other than tracks)

- No apparatus for making information or other material available in the form of sounds or visual images may be used on the licensed premises, except where the matter seen or heard is a sporting event and bets may have been affected on the premises in relation to that event. Betting operator owned TV channels will be permitted;
- No music, dancing or other entertainment is permitted;
- The consumption of alcohol is prohibited;
- The only publication that may be sold on the premises are racing periodicals or specialist betting publications;

Information to be displayed

Type of premises	Information to be displayed in a prominent position on the premises
All	A summary of the premises licence.
Casino	A notice displayed at all entrance to casinos (except the non-gambling area of the regional casino) stating no person under the age of 18 will be admitted. The rules of the games that are available to be played in the table gaming area and other gambling area must be displayed in that area.
Bingo	A notice stating that no person under the age of 18 can gamble on the premises. Any admission charges and the charges for playing bingo games.

Type of premises	Information to be displayed in a prominent position on the premises
	The rules of bingo.
AGCs	A notice stating that under 18s are prohibited from entering the premises. A notice stating that the consumption of alcohol on the premises is prohibited.
FECs	A notice stating that the consumption of alcohol on the premises is prohibited.
LBOs	A notice stating that under 18s are prohibited from entering the premises. A notice stating that the consumption of alcohol on the premises is prohibited. Clear and accessible information about the terms on which a bet may be placed.
Tracks	Clear and accessible information about the terms on which a bet may be placed. A notice at every public entrance to the premises stating that no person under the age of 18 is permitted to bet.
O18 area in FECs and bingo halls	A notice stating that under 18s are prohibited from entering this area.

Tracks

- The track operator, who will hold the premises licence, must ensure that all betting operators accepting bets on the track are properly licensed and take reasonable steps to remove unlicensed bookmakers from the track;
- The five times rule will to be attached to betting premises licences for horseracing tracks (only) in relation to the betting rings that are subject to the five times rule on 31 August 2007; this provision will lapse after 31 August 2012;
- Track operators are only permitted to make charges to betting operators who benefit from the five times rule for the reasonable operating costs incurred in respect of permitting betting to operate in the existing betting rings.;
- The totaliser on a licensed dog track can only be operated while the pubic are admitted to the track for the purpose of attending dog races and no other sporting events are taking place on the tracks; and for effecting betting transactions on dog races run on that track
- Under S182 (4) the Secretary of State will add all other sports tracks as premises to be exempted under S182(1) from the requirement to exclude children and young people from betting areas on days when sporting events are taking place.

Default Conditions

- The following hours will apply:

Premises Type	Gambling facilities may be not offered between these hours
Casinos	0600 – 1200 on any day
Betting Offices	2200 – 0700 on any day

Tracks	2200 -0700 – on days when no public sporting event is taking place; No restrictions on days on which a public sporting event is taking place
Bingo Halls	0000 – 0900 – on any day. **NB.** No restrictions on access to gaming machines in bingo halls.
AGCs/FECs	No restrictions

Proposals that will be operating licence conditions rather than premises licence conditions

- A minimum of 4 player positions for any individual automated gaming tables in any casino.
- Betting machines on tracks must be supervised by the betting operator to prevent access by children and young people.
- Gambling Commission Advice to Track Owners will advise that betting track premises licence holders are expected to support the Gambling Act objectives and make every effort to ensure that children and young people are not able to access gambling facilities while on a track.

N.B. These is an abbreviated list, for full details please refer to the Gambling Act 2005 Statutory Instrument No

GAMBLING ACT 2005: GUIDANCE TO LICENSING AUTHORITIES ON SETTING PREMISES LICENCE FEES

SUMMARY

6.2650 1. Licensing authorities are responsible for setting the fees for gambling premises licences. These must be calculated on a cost recovery basis. Fees must not exceed the maximums set out in the Gambling (Premises Licence Fees) (England and Wales) Regulations 2007 (Annex A). The Treasury Guide on Fees and Charges contains useful definitions. Fees for premises licences should include an element for overheads and for dealing with illegal gambling in the area. The fees must not include start up costs. Councils can delegate responsibility for setting fees to their licensing committee or officers. Licensing authorities have discretion to offer discounts on first annual fees and discounts for premises which open on a seasonal basis. Fees cannot be set on the basis of size, rateable value or any other basis. Licensing authorities must be transparent about the assumptions they have made in setting their fees. Fees should be published and reviewed on an annual basis initially. Fees for permits are set centrally by the Department for Culture Media and Sport (the Department).

DETAIL

2. The Gambling Act 2005 (the Act) gives licensing authorities responsibility for licensing gambling premises. The cost of providing this service will be met by application, annual fees and other fees paid by the licensees. A definition of the different types of fees and what each covers is at Annex A.

3. The Secretary of State has made the Regulations which specify the maximum fees a licensing authority can charge for each type of fee (described in Annex A) and each type of premises. In addition, these Regulations give licensing authorities the discretion to determine:

- discounted first annual fees; and
- discounted annual fees for premises which only open on a seasonal basis;

4. Licensing authorities have a duty to set these fees on a cost recovery basis. The Act states (S212 (2) (d)) that licensing authorities "shall aim to ensure that income from fees as nearly as possible equates to the cost of providing the service to which the fee relates

including a reasonable share of expenditure which is referable only partly or only indirectly linked to the provision of the service". Licensing authorities must be transparent about the assumptions they have made in setting their fees.

5. Licensing authorities may find it helpful to refer to the Treasury Fees and Charges Guide. Although this applies to the provision of central government rather than local government fees and services, it is contains relevant definitions and guidance, including on how services are to be costed and forecast and how to deal with accidental surpluses and deficits. This defines full cost as the total cost of all the resources used in providing the service (direct and indirect costs, including a full proportional share of overhead costs and any selling and distribution expenses, insurance, depreciation and cost of capital, both cash and "non-cash" costs). Full cost should be calculated on a accruals basis and use a cost of capital rate of 3.5%.

START UP COSTS

6. Local authorities have already received funding to the cover the cost of preparing for their new responsibilities under the Act. This was included in the EPCS settlement through the revenue support grant for 2004/5 and 2005/6 (DCMS' letter of 21 October 2004). This funding was provided to cover the costs of:

- training existing licensing offices, councillors and administrative staff;
- staff/recruitment costs (where additional staff are required to fulfil gambling premises licence responsibilities;
- additional software/hardware requirements;
- transfer of records from Magistrates to authorities;
- producing and consulting on the three year licensing policy statement.

7. Start up costs should not therefore be included when calculating fees.

ILLEGAL GAMBLING

8. The annual fee will cover the costs of compliance and enforcement work, including the cost of dealing with illegal gambling in a licensing authority's area. The Gambling Commission will shortly publish guidance to licensing authorities on this which advocates a risk based approach. The Gambling Commission will also be taking a risk based approach and will concentrate its resources on those cases which pose greatest risk to the licensing objectives and will pursue appropriate levels of intervention in conjunction with licensing authorities to resolve other cases.

DISCRETIONS

9. Under section 212 (2)(b) of the Act a licensing authority may determine different fees for differing classes of case specified in the Regulations. A licensing authority may not otherwise determine different fees for different cases (for example on the basis of rateable value or size).

10. The Regulations authorise licensing authorities to set different fees for the different classes of premises licence specified in Regulation 3 (for example, bingo premises licence, large casino premises licence etc). In relation to each class of premises licence, licensing authorities may set different fees for the following:

- a fast track conversion application for a licence (Regulation 4);
- a non-fast track conversion application for a licence (Regulation 4);
- a non-conversion application for a licence for premises in respect of which a provisional statement has already been issued (Regulation 5);
- a non-conversion application for any other premises (Regulation 5);
- a first annual fee (which may not exceed the annual fee) (Regulation 6);
- an annual fee (Regulation 8);
- first annual and annual fees for a premises licence that is subject to a seasonal condition (that is, a condition that provides for the premises to be used for part of the year only) (Regulation 9);

- a notification of a change of circumstance (Regulation 10);
- an application to vary a licence (Regulation 11);
- an application to transfer a licence (Regulation 12);
- an application for a copy of a licence (Regulation 13);
- an application for reinstatement of a licence (Regulation 14);
- an application for a provisional statement (Regulation 15).

11. First annual fees are payable within 30 days after the date that a licence is issued or comes into effect (Regulation 7). They cover premises' first year of operation. In determining first annual fees licensing authorities may wish to consider whether it is appropriate to set a lower fee than the "ordinary" annual fee. In making this determination, licensing authorities should consider whether work done by the authority in relation to the application for the licence will reduce the amount of work required in relation to that licence during the first year. For example, inspections carried out in the context of considering an application for a licence may reduce the number of inspections required in the first year of operations.

DELEGATIONS

12. A licensing authority's fee setting functions under section 212 are not automatically delegated to the authority's licensing committee. However, an authority may choose to delegate those functions to its licensing committee (section 154(2) (b) of the Gambling Act).

13. Where a licensing authority chooses to delegate its fee setting function to a licensing committee, section 154(3) of the Gambling Act applies. This section applies section 10 of the Licensing Act 2003 to the fee setting functions delegated to a licensing committee. Section 10 allows the licensing committee to arrange for those functions to be discharged by a sub-committee or an officer of the licensing authority. Under section 10(2), a sub-committee may in turn arrange for the discharge of the functions by an officer of the licensing authority.

SETTING FEES FOR TYPES OF PREMISES NOT IN YOUR AREA?

14. Fees must be determined and published by licensing authorities before the date on which they are payable. Licensing authorities therefore need to have finalised and published their fees for applications for licences and provisional statements by 21 May 2007, which is the first day for advance applications.

15. Licensing authorities should determine licence application and provisional statement application fees for all categories of licence which they may issue, even if they do not currently have any premises of a particular category within their area. This is because those fees have to be in place before a person can apply for a licence or provisional statement, and people may wish to apply to open a category of premises which is new to the area.

16. Licensing authorities can determine when they set the other fees. However, when deciding whether to defer setting fees (for example, the annual fee for a premises type which is not currently established in the area), a licensing authority will wish to consider the efficiency of this approach (in terms of additional administrative burdens) as well as the potential impact on business (in terms of their ability to assess future business costs).

17. Licensing authorities who are not authorised to issue a licence for one of the new casinos do not need to set fees for this type of premises.

REVIEWS

18. Licensing authorities have a duty to ensure that income from fees equates as nearly as possible to the cost of providing the service to which the fee relates. Licensing authorities should therefore review their fees annually to ensure that the income from the premises licence fees in any one accounting period (ie in any full financial year) does not exceed the full costs incurred by the authority in carrying out the relevant functions.

19. We recognised that 2007/8 will be atypical. There will be a large number of conversion applications and the new licensing regime is only coming into effect part way through the financial year. We therefore recognise that this may not give a true picture of the costs of implementing the new regime in future years. We therefore consider that it would be appropriate for licensing authorities to review their fees at the end of 2007/8 and then again at the end of 2008/9 to satisfy themselves that they are charging fees which are as close to the cost of providing the service as possible.

Application Fee	This is a one-off, non-refundable fee payable to the licensing authority upon application for a new gambling premises licence or one under the transitional arrangements for existing operators. The fee will cover the cost to the licensing authority of receiving, considering and determining the application, including staff costs, overheads, IT, legal and other central support costs, initial inspections, Licensing Committee costs and hearing costs and appeals. Under the Transitional Arrangements separate fees will be payable for: Fast-track transitional licence applications, which are made by an existing licence holder who accepts all the default conditions that will attach to the licence; Slow-track transitional licence applications, which are made by an existing licence holder who seeks to, vary the default conditions that would otherwise attach to the licence.
First Annual Fee	This will cover the regulatory costs for the first year (eg processing costs, plus review, inspection and enforcement activity). Licensing authorities have discretion to offer a discount on the first annual fee in recognition of the fact that checks will have been done at time of application, and the costs will be on average lower than in subsequent years. This is consistent with the Gambling Commission's approach to non-remote operating licensing fees. First annual fees for licences issued from 1st September 2007 are due within 30 days after the licence comes into effect or within 12 months after the issue date, whichever is sooner (SI 2007 / 479 paragraph 7). Note that a licence will come into effect on the date it is issued, unless the licence states otherwise. First annual fees for licences issued before 1st September 2007 (which may include conversion applications) are payable within 30 days after 1st September 2007.
Annual Fee	Payable annually by all premises licence holders for the maintenance of their licence. This will cover the regulatory costs for the next year (ie inspection, holding reviews and enforcement activity), the costs associated with processing the annual fee (ie updating computer systems, register of gambling premises licences and processing fee) and annualised periodic costs incurred by the licensing authority in respect of its 3 year licensing policy statements; Under the Act, subsequent annual fees are payable before each anniversary of the date on which the licence is issued. Under the Act, a licensing authority must revoke a premises licence if a licensee fails to pay the annual fee, except where the authority thinks the failure to pay is due to an administrative error.
	MISCELLANEOUS FEES
Change of circumstance fees	Payable by holders of premises licences when they submit a notification of a change of circumstance.

Variation of licence fees	Payable by holders of premises licences when they apply to vary a licence.
Transfer of licence fees	Payable by holders of premises licences when they apply to transfer a licence from one operator to another.
Re-instatement fees	Payable by anyone applying for a licence to be re-instated.
Provisional statement fees	Payable by anyone applying for a provisional statement (a statement from the licensing authority in advance of a full premises licence). An adjusted licence application fee payable subsequently by provisional statement holders.
Copy of licence fees	Payable for the provision of a replacement copy of a premises licence.

GUIDANCE TO LICENSING AUTHORITIES 4TH EDITION

6.2655 September 2012

Contents

This document comprises 36 parts with pages numbered relevant to their section. Future updates will be provided by section without affecting other parts of the guidance

PART 1: BACKGROUND

GAMBLING ACT 2005

1.1 The Gambling Act 2005 ('the Act') contains the regulatory system to govern the provision of all gambling in Great Britain, other than the National Lottery and spread betting. It received Royal Assent on 7 April 2005.

Summary of the Act

1.2 Gambling is unlawful in Great Britain, unless permitted by:

- the measures contained in the Act

- measures contained in the National Lottery etc Act 1993, or pursuant to the Financial Services and Markets Act 2000.

1.3 Two comprehensive offences are established by the Act: providing facilities for gambling or using premises for gambling, in either case without the appropriate permission. Such permission may come from a licence, permit, or registration granted in accordance with the Act or from an exemption given by the Act. Where authority to provide facilities for gambling is granted, it is subject to varying degrees of regulation, depending on the type of gambling, the means by which it is conducted, and the people by whom and to whom it is offered.

1.4 The Gambling Commission (the Commission) is the unified regulator for gambling in Great Britain.

1.5 The Commission does not regulate spread betting, which remains the responsibility of the Financial Services Authority; nor the National Lottery, which is regulated by the National Lottery Commission. However, the National Lottery Commission has been co-located with the Gambling Commission since January 2012 and the Public Bodies Bill includes legislation to merge the two Commissions.

1.6 The Gambling Commission has responsibility for granting operating and personal licences for commercial gambling operators and personnel working in the industry. It also regulates certain lottery managers and promoters. The Act sets out different types of operating licence that cover the full range of commercial gambling activities conducted in Great Britain. It also makes provision for the Commission to have powers of entry and inspection to regulate gambling, with safeguards for those subject to the powers.

1.7 Licensing authorities license gambling premises within their area, as well as undertaking functions in relation to lower stake gaming machines in clubs and miners' welfare institutes. In England and Wales local authorities have these responsibilities; in Scotland they have been given to licensing boards. The Act also provides a system of temporary and occasional use notices. These authorise premises that are not licensed generally for gambling purposes to be used for certain types of gambling, for limited periods.

Licensing objectives

1.8 The Act contains three licensing objectives which underpin the functions that the Commission and licensing authorities will perform. These objectives are central to the Act. They are:

- preventing gambling from being a source of crime or disorder, being associated with crime or disorder, or being used to support crime
- ensuring that gambling is conducted in a fair and open way
- protecting children and other vulnerable persons from being harmed or exploited by gambling.

The Commission has an overriding obligation to pursue and have regard to the objectives, and to permit gambling so far as it thinks is reasonably consistent with them.

Achieving compliance with the Act

1.9 Regulation of gambling in Great Britain is achieved through a variety of measures established under the Act. These include:

- regulations made by the Secretary of State or Scottish Ministers, including mandatory and default licence conditions
- conditions on licences imposed by the Gambling Commission or by licensing authorities
- codes of practice from the Commission
- guidance from the Commission.

GUIDANCE TO LICENSING AUTHORITIES

1.10 Section 25 of the Act requires the Commission to issue guidance on:

- the manner in which local authorities are to exercise their functions under the Act
- in particular, the principles to be applied by local authorities in exercising their functions under the Act.

1.11 Before issuing guidance to local authorities, the Act requires the Commission to consult:

- the Secretary of State
- the Scottish Ministers
- Commissioners for Her Majesty's Revenue & Customs (HMRC)
- representatives of local authorities
- representatives of gambling businesses
- persons with knowledge of social problems that may be associated with gambling.

1.12 Depending on the nature of the guidance, the Act also requires the Commission to consult, if it thinks appropriate, members of the public and representatives of Chief Constables of police forces.

1.13 Licensing authorities licence gambling premises and issue a range of permits to authorise other gambling facilities in their licensing areas. In exercising their functions generally under the Act, licensing authorities must have regard to the Guidance issued by the Commission. Authorities have similar regulatory powers to the Commission with respect to their licensees, including the power to impose conditions and to review licences. However, they are not able to impose financial penalties.

Functions of licensing authorities

1.14 The Act gives licensing authorities a number of important regulatory functions in relation to gambling. Their main functions are to:

- licence premises for gambling activities
- consider notices given for the temporary use of premises for gambling
- grant permits for gaming and gaming machines in clubs and miners' welfare institutes
- regulate gaming and gaming machines in alcohol-licensed premises
- grant permits to family entertainment centres (FECs) for the use of certain lower stake gaming machines
- grant permits for prize gaming
- consider occasional use notices for betting at tracks
- register small societies' lotteries.

1.15 Licensing authorities have an obligation to provide information to the Gambling Commission, including details of licences, permits and registrations issued.

1.16 In addition, licensing authorities are required to prepare and publish, every three years, a statement of the principles which they propose to apply when exercising their functions. The statement, which may also be referred to as a 'policy', can be reviewed and re-published during the three-year period in which it has effect. In preparing the statement, licensing authorities must follow the procedure set out in the Act, including who should be consulted. (See part 6 of this Guidance for more on policy statements.)

Status of this Guidance

1.17 As mentioned previously, in carrying out its functions under the Act a licensing authority must have regard to this Guidance. This general principle applies in relation to a number of the licensing authority's functions, including considering temporary use notices and occasional use notices, and issuing permits. 'Must have regard to' does not mean that the licensing authority must always follow the Guidance to the letter; however, the expectation is that there should be strong and defensible reasons for departing from it.

1.18 However, this Guidance has a particular role and significance in the context of the principles that must be applied by licensing authorities when exercising their functions in relation to Part 8 of the Act, including premises licensing. Section 153 of the Act provides that licensing authorities shall aim to permit the use of premises for gambling in so far as they think it

(a) in accordance with any relevant code of practice under section 24

(b) in accordance with any relevant guidance issued by the Commission under section 25

(c) reasonably consistent with the licensing objectives (subject to (a) and (b) above), and

(d) in accordance with the statement published by the authority under section 349 (hereafter the "Licensing Authority Statement of Policy") (subject to paragraphs (a) to (c) above).

1.19 Therefore a licensing authority has no discretion in exercising its functions under Part 8 of the Act to grant a premises licence where that would mean taking a course which it did not think accorded with the Guidance contained in this document, any relevant Commission code of practice or the Licensing Authority Statement of Policy or to be consistent with the licensing objectives. In reaching a view that a grant would be in accordance with such Guidance, code of practice or Licensing Authority Statement of Policy a licensing authority is of course, as any public authority decision maker, obliged to act fairly and rationally.

1.20 In drafting this Guidance, the Commission's intention is that, where appropriate, there should be consistency across licensing authorities about the manner in which functions under the Act are carried out. That is important in two respects:

- to meet the obligations on the Commission and on licensing authorities to pursue the licensing objectives, the Commission seeks to achieve a consistent standard of regulation and shared priorities
- in accordance with government initiatives on minimising the impact of regulation on businesses and, in particular, the Hampton Review of regulation, it is part of the Commission's role to ensure that operators receive sufficient advice to help them understand and comply with gambling regulation. Part of this requires the Commission to be satisfied that operators know what the requirements of licensing authorities are.

1.21 In seeking to encourage consistency across licensing areas, the Commission does not seek to fetter the discretion that authorities have under the Act. This Guidance is not intended to replace the judgement of a licensing authority in an individual case. Moreover, this Guidance cannot anticipate every set of circumstances that may arise and, except in relation to Part 8 of the Act, as long as it has been understood and taken into account, licensing authorities may depart from it where they consider it would be right to do so. As set out above, there should however be strong and defensible reasons for departing from the Guidance; and these need to be clearly expressed and explained if a licensing authority is to avoid judicial review for failing to take the Guidance into account.

1.22 Licensing authorities should note that interpretation of the Act is ultimately a matter for the Courts and that they should take their own legal advice on the application and interpretation of the Act. This Guidance is not intended to replace that.

1.23 This Guidance should be read in conjunction with the Act, regulations and guidance issued by the Department for Culture, Media and Sport (DCMS) and Scottish Government.

1.24 This Guidance has been prepared in accordance with primary and secondary legislation in place or in draft form as at the time of publication. Further editions of this Guidance will be produced as more regulations come into effect and following further consultation.

PART 2: THE LICENSING FRAMEWORK

2.1 The Gambling Act 2005 provides for three categories of licence:

- operating licences
- personal licences
- premises licences.
- Within these categories, a number of different types of licence may be issued.

2.2 Each type of licence may have conditions attached to it. Conditions may be attached in a number of ways:

- they may attach automatically, having been set out on the face of the Act
- they may attach through regulations made by the Secretary of State or Scottish Ministers
- they may be attached to operating and personal licences by the Commission or
- they may be attached to premises licences by licensing authorities.

Conditions may sometimes be general in nature (ie they attach to all licences or all licences of a particular class) or they may be specific to a particular licence.

OPERATING LICENCES

2.3 Individuals and companies who intend to provide facilities for certain types of gambling must obtain an operating licence from the Gambling Commission. In general, these licences cover the principal commercial forms of gambling operation. Section 65 of the Act sets out the types of licences that may be issued. These are:

- a casino operating licence
- a bingo operating licence
- a general betting operating licence
- a pool betting operating licence
- a betting intermediary operating licence
- a gaming machine general operating licence (for an adult gaming centre)
- a gaming machine general operating licence (for a family entertainment centre)
- a gaming machine technical operating licence (to manufacture, supply, install, adapt, maintain or repair a gaming machine or part of a gaming machine)
- a gambling software operating licence (to manufacture, supply, install or adapt gambling software)
- a lottery operating licence.

2.4 The first five and the tenth of these types of licence may authorise remote or non-remote gambling, and the eighth and ninth activities which may or may not be carried on by means of remote communication. However, a person who wishes to offer gambling, or carry on activities, both remotely and non-remotely will need to obtain both a remote and a non-remote operating licence. A single licence cannot authorise both remote and non-remote activities.

2.5 By virtue of section 68 of the Act some types of operating licence carry additional permissions and a single operating licence may authorise more than one of the activities listed in paragraph 2.3.

2.6 In considering an application, the Commission will have regard to the licensing objectives, and will consider the suitability of applicants to provide facilities for gambling. In particular, the Commission will have regard to the integrity of the applicant, and any others relevant to the application, and to their competence and financial circumstances.

2.7 Conditions covering a range of matters may be attached to operating licences. The Commission's powers are wide. A condition could, for example, contain restrictions on the number of premises that may be operated or minimum requirements for staffing levels. In relation to particular categories of licence, conditions could cover the display of rules or the provision of information to customers. The Act provides that the

Secretary of State may impose conditions on operating licences of a specified description. At the date of this Guidance the Secretary of State has done so only in respect of the minimum number of playing positions at wholly automated roulette tables in casinos and the level of participation fees and money prizes in prize bingo played under the auspices of a bingo operating licence[1]. Therefore, it generally falls to the Commission to determine what licence conditions are necessary, both for particular categories of licence and, where appropriate, for particular licensees. Supporting the licence conditions there are codes of practice issued by the Commission for each sector of the gambling industry.

2.8 The Commission published the latest version of its *Licence Conditions and Codes of Practice* ('the LCCP') in December 2011. This document, and any subsequent update to it, is available from the Commission's website[2],

2.9 Breach of an operating licence condition gives rise to a criminal offence (as the result of the fact that unauthorised gambling is taking place). The Commission also has a range of administrative penalties available to it, separate from taking criminal proceedings. These include warnings, unlimited fines and suspension or revocation of the licence. The Commission has also consulted on its policy in relation to financial penalties (under section 121 of the Act) and published a Statement of Principles, as part of the Licensing, Compliance and Enforcement policy. Some provisions of the Commission's principal code of practice are designated as 'social responsibility' provisions and breaches of these carry the same weight and potential penalties as breaches of licence conditions. Failure to comply with an ordinary code of practice provision will not be a criminal offence, but it may be taken into account in considering licence breaches or criminal prosecutions.

2.10 Operating licences are not transferable. However, there are provisions in the Act which deal with circumstances in which control of a company changes hands.

---

1 The Gambling Act 2005 (Operating Licence Conditions) Regulations 2007 SI 2007 No 2257.

2 Licence conditions and codes of practice available from www.gamblingcommission.gov.uk,

PERSONAL LICENCES

2.11 One of the mandatory conditions that the Commission has placed on operating licences, except in the case of small-scale operators, is to ensure that for each operating licence at least one person holds a specified management office and that person must hold a personal licence from the Commission.

2.12 In addition, the Commission requires key employees in other management offices and those employed to carry out specified operational functions to hold a personal licence as follows:

- people holding management offices including directors, partners, those who are responsible for ensuring compliance with operating licences, marketing, information technology (in so far as it relates to gambling related information technology and software), or have management of employees involved in conducting the gambling
- people carrying out operational functions including those who are able to influence the outcome of gambling, or handle money in relation to the gambling.

2.13 The purpose of the personal licence is to ensure that individuals who control facilities for gambling or are able to influence the outcome of gambling are licensed to ensure that they are suitable to carry out those functions, and that they understand the legal and compliance requirements concerned with the gambling they operate.

2.14 Personal licences are granted to an individual and are not transferable. They cannot be held by a company. Once granted they are portable between posts and employers provided that the same type of personal licence is appropriate. The Commission has imposed licence conditions that are specific to personal licences. These require that the holder takes reasonable steps to avoid causing a breach of an operating licence; keeps up to date with developments in gambling legislation or guidance; and informs the Commission of certain specified key events.

2.15 Small-scale operators are exempt from the obligation to have at least one member of management hold a personal licence.

2.16 The definition of a small-scale operator has been set out in regulations made by the Secretary of State. Individuals or companies are classed as small-scale operators if, in relation to the activity authorised by their operating licence, they have no more than three 'qualifying positions' each of which is occupied by a 'qualified person'.

2.17 Qualifying positions are those whose occupants have the primary responsibility for any of the following:

- management of the licensed activity
- management of financial affairs
- ensuring compliance with the requirements of the Act
- marketing the licensed activity
- management of information technology facilities used in the provision of the licensed activity
- management of the licensed activity for a particular locality or area of Great Britain where there are five or more sets of premises for which a premises licence is held or
- management of a single set of casino or bingo licensed premises.

2.18 Qualified persons are those:

- named on the operating licence as holding a qualifying position or
- who are the subject of an application to vary the licence to add their name as a person holding a qualifying position.

PREMISES LICENCES

2.19 Premises licences will be granted by licensing authorities and may authorise the provision of facilities on:

- casino premises
- bingo premises
- betting premises, including tracks
- adult gaming centres
- family entertainment centres.

2.20 Except in the case of tracks (where the occupier of the track who gets the premises licence may not be the person who actually offers the gambling) premises licences may only be issued to people with a relevant operating licence. For example, to obtain a bingo premises licence the applicant must hold a bingo operating licence. Premises licences are transferable to someone else holding a valid operating licence.

2.21 The Act provides that licensing authorities may attach conditions to premises licences. Part 9 of this Guidance suggests what conditions might be considered in relation to each type of licence.

2.22 In addition to licences, there are other forms of authorisation that a licensing authority may grant, for example, authorisations for the temporary use of premises, occasional use notices and five different sorts of permit for unlicensed family entertainment centres, prize gaming, gaming machines on alcohol-licensed premises and club gaming and club machine permits.

PART 3: THE GAMBLING COMMISSION

3.1 The Act established the Gambling Commission to regulate all commercial gambling in Great Britain (other than spread betting or the National Lottery).

3.2 The Commission was established on 1 October 2005 and has an overriding obligation to pursue and have regard to the licensing objectives as set out in section 1 of the Act, and to permit gambling so far as it thinks is reasonably consistent with them.

3.3 The Commission published its Statement of principles for licensing and regulation in September 2009. The Statement sets out how the Commission would approach its regulatory and other functions under the Gambling Act 2005. This document and any subsequent update to it is available from the Commission's website[3].

---

[3] Statement of principles for licensing and regulation available from www.gamblingcommission.gov.uk

ABOUT THE COMMISSION

3.4 The Commission is headed by a Chairman and other Commissioners appointed by the Secretary of State.

3.5 The Commission keeps in regular contact with representatives of those it licences and with licensing authorities. It aims to meet regularly with representatives of licensing authorities such as the Local Government Association (LGA), the Convention of Scottish Local Authorities (COSLA), Local Authorities Coordinators of Regulatory Services (LACoRS) and the Society of Local Authority Lawyers and Administrators (SOLAR). These meetings provide opportunities to informally review this Guidance and to discuss emerging trends and issues of concern. Changes to this Guidance may be made only after formal consultation, as required by the Act.

OPERATING AND PERSONAL LICENCES

3.6 The Commission issues operating licences under the 2005 Act to organisations and individuals who are providing facilities for gambling. It also issues personal licences to certain categories of people working in the gambling industry.

3.7 The Commission has specified the conditions under which these licences are granted, and issued codes of practice for the provision and management of gambling facilities.

3.8 The Commission has legal powers to monitor licence holders and is able to apply penalties. Penalties for both operating and personal licences may include fines and/or revocation of the licence. The Commission also has the ability to prosecute operating and personal licence holders. It may also investigate and, where appropriate, in consultation with licensing authorities and the police, may prosecute illegal gambling.

ADVICE TO THE SECRETARY OF STATE

3.9 The Commission is required to advise the Secretary of State about the incidence of gambling, the manner in which gambling is carried on, the effects of gambling and the regulation of gambling. Copies of the advice are sent to Scottish Ministers.

3.10 To ensure that the Commission is well placed to provide advice, it monitors developments in gambling in Great Britain and in other jurisdictions. It works closely with a range of stakeholders including the National Lottery Commission, academics, the Department of Health and bodies working in the field of gambling research and problem gambling.

3.11 Licensing authorities have a key role in providing information to the Commission to assist it in carrying out these functions. Part 13 of this Guidance provides information regarding the Commission's advice paper which sets out the requirements on local authorities to provide data on those they licence and on compliance and enforcement action that may be necessary.

3.12 The Commission also requires operators to submit information and, together, these sources of information will allow it to build up a picture of gambling in Great Britain that can be relied upon so the Commission offers advice that is evidence-based.

FURTHER INFORMATION ABOUT THE COMMISSION

3.13 Further information about the Commission can be found on our website www.gamblingcommission.gov.uk

PART 4: LICENSING AUTHORITIES

WHAT ARE LICENSING AUTHORITIES?

4.1 Section 2 of the Act provides that the following are licensing authorities:
(a) in relation to England:
  (i) a district council
  (ii) a county council for a county in which there are no district councils
  (iii) a London borough council
  (iv) the Common Council of the City of London
  (v) the Council of the Isles of Scilly
(b) in relation to Wales:
  (i) a county council
  (ii) a county borough council
(c) in relation to Scotland, a licensing board constituted under section 5 of the Licensing (Scotland) Act 2005.
(d) for the purposes of licensed premises gaming machine permits, the Sub-Treasurer of the Inner Temple and the Under-Treasurer of the Middle Temple.

4.2 It should be noted that the Act uses the definitions of local authority set out in the Local Authority Act 1972. The commonly used term 'unitary authority' is not used in that Act nor in the subsequent Acts that re-organised local government (the Local Government Act 1985 and Local Government Act 1992). These Acts have created single tier unitary authorities in the form of:
(i) London borough councils
(ii) non-metropolitan county councils (for areas in which there are no district councils)
(iii) non-metropolitan district councils (for areas where there are no county councils).

RESPONSIBILITIES OF THE LICENSING AUTHORITY AND DELEGATIONS

4.3 The power of a licensing authority to delegate decision-making is set out below.

(a) England and Wales

Section 154 of the Act provides that all decisions relating to premises licences are delegated to the licensing committee of the authority that has been established under section 6 of the Licensing Act 2003 (referred to in this Guidance as the 'licensing committee'), except:

- a resolution not to issue casino licences, which must be taken by the whole authority (see part 17 of this Guidance for more information)
- functions in relation to the Licensing Authority Statement of Policy, which must be taken by the whole authority (see part 6 for more information)
- setting fees (to the extent that a licensing authority has delegated power in relation to fees) is the responsibility of the full council – the full council can delegate decisions to the licensing committee, but there is no automatic delegation, so each authority must decide its approach to setting fees.

(b) Scotland

Section 155 of the Act provides that all decisions relating to premises licences may be delegated to a committee of the authority, a member or members of the authority, the clerk of the authority, or any person appointed to assist the clerk. The exceptions to this are:

- resolutions by the licensing authority not to issue casino licences

- formulation of the Licensing Authority Statement of Policy under section 349
- the matters listed under paragraph 4.4 below.

The first two categories may not be delegated at all, but the third category may be delegated to a committee of the authority, or to a member or members of the authority.

Delegations

4.4 Decisions that are delegated to a licensing committee may be further delegated to a sub-committee of the licensing committee, which may arrange for them to be taken by an officer of the authority. However, the following decisions may not be made by an officer (ie they must be made by either the sub-committee or the licensing committee):

- determination of an application for a premises licence where representations have been made and not withdrawn
- determination of an application for variation of a premises licence where representations have been made and not withdrawn
- determination of an application for transfer, following representations by the Commission
- determination of an application for a provisional statement where representations have been made and not withdrawn
- review of a premises licence.

4.5 Decisions on temporary use notices (see part 14 of this Guidance) are delegated to the licensing committee, and may be sub-delegated to a sub-committee, or an officer of the licensing authority. Any decision to give a counter-notice cannot be delegated to an officer, so it must be made by the full committee or a sub-committee. In Scotland, the powers mirror those in England and Wales.

4.6 Decisions in relation to permits (see part 23 of this Guidance) are delegated to the licensing committee and may be further delegated to a sub-committee or an officer of the authority. The following decisions may not be made by an officer of the licensing authority:

- determination of an application for a club gaming permit or club machine permit in respect of which objections have been made and not withdrawn (see Schedule 12, para 28(2))
- cancellation of a club gaming or club machine permit.

4.7 It is open to licensing committees to choose not to delegate decisions. An important consideration in determining whether any particular decision should be delegated will be whether delegation might give rise to a risk of judicial review challenge (particularly on the basis of an appearance of bias). A licensing committee should consult the licensing authority lawyers where it considers that concerns of this nature may be raised.

4.8 Table 4.i summarises the lowest level of delegation that is permitted under sections 154 and 155, applicable to England and Wales only. These sections do not, however, apply to certain functions under the Act (for example, the removal of the automatic gaming exemption for alcohol-licensed premises under section 284). Licensing authorities will, in relation to those functions, need to ensure that they are familiar with any changes that have been made to the relevant legislation dealing with the allocation of responsibility for functions between the authority as a whole, and the executive.[4] Any such changes are likely to affect the way that licensing authorities can delegate such functions under other local government legislation.

---

[4] In England this is the Local Authorities (Functions and Responsibilities) (Amendment no 2) (England) Regulations 2007, made by the Department of Communities and Local Government (DCLG) (SI No 2007/1557).

Matter to be dealt with	Full Council	Sub-committee of licensing committee	Officers
Final approval of the Licensing Authority Statement of Policy	X		
Policy not to permit casinos	X		
Fee setting (when appropriate)		X	
		(if delegated by full council)	
Application for premises licences		Where representations have been received and not withdrawn	Where no representations received/ representations have been withdrawn
Application for a variation to a licence		Where representations have been received and not withdrawn	Where no representations received/ representations have been withdrawn
Application for a transfer of a licence		Where representations have been received from the Commission or responsible authority	Where no representations received from the Commission or responsible authority
Application for a provisional statement		Where representations have been received and not withdrawn	Where no representations received/ representations have been withdrawn
Review of a premises licence		X	
Application for club gaming/club machine permits		Where objections have been made and not withdrawn	Where no objections made/objections have been withdrawn
Cancellation of club gaming/club machine permits		X	
Applications for other permits			X
Cancellation of licensed premises gaming machine permits			X
Consideration of temporary use notice			X
Decision to give a counter notice to a temporary use notice		X	

X indicates the lowest level to which decisions can be delegated

LICENSING ACT 2003

4.9 Licensing authorities in England and Wales also have responsibilities under the Licensing Act 2003. There are some inter dependencies between the Licensing Act 2003 and the Gambling Act 2005 in terms of the framework for decision making and the procedures that must be followed. But licensing authorities must take care to ensure that in dealing with applications under the Gambling Act they follow the procedures that this Act requires and only take into account issues that are relevant to this Act. Particular care should be taken to distinguish Gambling Act considerations from those relevant to alcohol licensing, public entertainment or late night refreshments.

LICENSING (SCOTLAND) ACT 2005

4.10 The position in Scotland is similar, with similar procedures for decision making and procedures to be followed under both the Licensing (Scotland) Act 2005 and the Gambling Act 2005. The same care must therefore be taken by licensing authorities in Scotland to distinguish those issues which are relevant to Gambling Act matters in their decision making and to ensure that the procedures prescribed by the Gambling Act and related regulations are followed in Gambling Act matters.

LICENSING COMMITTEE'S DISCRETION TO REGULATE ITS OWN PROCEEDINGS

4.11 In carrying out its functions under this Act a local authority must 'have regard' to Guidance issued by the Commission under section 25. Please note that the definition of 'local authority' in section 25 is synonymous with the definition of 'licensing authorities' set out in section 2.

4.12 However, the Commission's statutory Guidance has a more specific role in the context of the principles that must be applied by licensing authorities when exercising their functions in relation to premises licensing and temporary use notices (under Part 8 of the Act) is more prescriptive. Section 153 provides that licensing authorities shall aim to permit the use of premises for gambling in so far as they think it:

(a) in accordance with any relevant code of practice under section 24
(b) in accordance with any relevant guidance issued by the Commission under section 25
(c) reasonably consistent with the licensing objectives (subject to (a) and (b) above), and
(d) in accordance with the Licensing Authority Statement of Policy (subject to (a) to (c) above).

4.13 Therefore, as explained at paragraph 1.21 above, a licensing authority has no discretion in exercising its functions under Part 8 of the Act to grant a premises licences where that would mean taking a course which it did not think accorded with the guidance contained in this document, any relevant Commission code of practice or the Licensing Authority Statement of Policy.

4.14 The Commission's view is that, whenever appropriate, there should be consistency across licensing authorities in the manner in which functions under the Act are carried out. In seeking to encourage consistency across licensing areas, the Commission does not seek to fetter the discretion that authorities have under the Act. This Guidance is not intended to replace the judgement of a licensing authority in an individual case. Moreover, this Guidance cannot anticipate every set of circumstances that may arise and, except in relation to Part 8 (premises licences) of the Act, as long as it has been understood and taken into account, licensing authorities may depart from it where they consider it would be right to do so. However, as discussed in part 1 of this Guidance, there should be strong and defensible reasons for departing from the Guidance, and these will need to be clearly set out if a licensing authority is to avoid judicial review for failing to take the Guidance into account.

4.15 Licensing authorities should note that interpretation of the Act will ultimately be a matter for the Courts and that they should take their own legal advice on the application and interpretation of the Act. This Guidance is not intended to replace that.

THE APPLICATION OF OTHER LOCAL GOVERNMENT LEGISLATION

4.16 Conditions on premises licences should relate only to gambling, as considered appropriate in the light of the principles to be applied by licensing authorities under section 153 (see paragraph 4.12). Accordingly, if the Commission's *Licence Conditions and Codes of Practice* (LCCP) or other legislation places particular responsibilities or restrictions on an employer or the operator of premises, it is not necessary or appropriate to impose the same or similar duties in conditions on a premises licence issued in accordance with the Gambling Act. Similarly, where other legislation confers powers on inspection and enforcement agencies in relation to separate activities or concerns, the Gambling Act does not affect the continued use of such powers; for example, the powers of an environmental health officer in respect of statutory nuisance under the Environmental Protection Act 1990.

CONFLICTS OF INTEREST

4.17 Councillors in England will be aware that the model code of conduct drawn up by the Standards Board for England will apply in their decision making and that requires that public confidence in the probity of decision making is paramount[5].

4.18 The general principles that apply in decision making to underpin the code of conduct are that members of licensing authorities should:

- serve only the public interest and should never improperly confer an advantage or disadvantage on any person
- not place themselves in situations where their honesty and integrity may be questioned and make decisions on merit
- be accountable to the public for their actions
- reach their own conclusions on the issues before them and act in accordance with those conclusions
- uphold the law and, on all occasions, act in accordance with the trust that the public is entitled to place in them.

4.19 The Standards Commission for Scotland has produced similar guidance for councillors in Scotland. The Code of Conduct for Councillors emphasises the importance of all applications being dealt with fairly, and being seen to be dealt with fairly.

4.20 In Wales, the Local Government Ombudsman will investigate if a councillor has broken the code of conduct for councillors drawn up by their local authority.

---

5 The National Model Code of Conduct established under the Local Government Act 2000 by Statutory Instrument 2001 number 1401 'The Relevant Authorities (General Principles) Order 2001' on 5 November 2001.

WHERE CAN A LICENSING AUTHORITY OBTAIN FURTHER ADVICE?

4.21 The Gambling Commission website contains further and fuller information about the work of the Commission. Please see the website for the latest information on licence conditions, codes of practice and other guidance.

4.22 Please refer to the DCMS website for the latest information on these issues and for details of the regulations issued by the Secretary of State in relation to the Gambling Act. The website address is www.culture.gov.uk. Similar information in Scotland can be accessed on www.scotland.gov.uk/Topics/Justice/Licensing/Gambling

PART 5: PRINCIPLES TO BE APPLIED BY LICENSING AUTHORITIES

PRINCIPLES TO BE APPLIED

5.1 In exercising most of their functions under the 2005 Act, licensing authorities must have regard to the licensing objectives set out in section 1 of the Act. In particular, licensing authorities must have regard to the licensing objectives when exercising their functions in relation to premises licences, temporary use notices and some permits. Those objectives are:

- preventing gambling from being a source of crime or disorder, being associated with crime or disorder or being used to support crime
- ensuring that gambling is conducted in a fair and open way
- protecting children and other vulnerable persons from being harmed or exploited by gambling.

5.2 In considering applications, licensing authorities in England and Wales should take particular care to bear in mind that these objectives are not the same as those in the Licensing Act 2003. In particular, they do not include considerations in relation to public safety or prevention of public nuisance. The requirement in relation to children is explicitly to protect them from being harmed or exploited by gambling.

5.3 Similarly in Scotland the licensing objectives for the Licensing (Scotland) Act 2005 are different. In particular the Gambling Act does not include the objectives of preventing public nuisance and protecting and improving public health.

5.4 Section 153 of the Act provides that in exercising its functions under Part 8 of the Act (premises licensing and provisional statements), a licensing authority shall aim to permit the use of premises for gambling in so far as it thinks it is:

(a) in accordance with any relevant code of practice under section 24 (ie such as that found within the Commission's *Licence Conditions and Codes of Practice* (LCCP))

(b) in accordance with any relevant guidance issued by the Commission under section 25 (ie this document)

(c) reasonably consistent with the licensing objectives (subject to (a) and (b) above), and

(d) in accordance with the Licensing Authority Statement of Policy (subject to (a) and (c) above). (See part 6 of this Guidance.)

5.5 Section 153 applies not only to a licensing authority's relevant functions under Part 8 of the Act (ie applications for the grant, transfer, reinstatement or review of premises licences and provisional statements) but also when it is deciding whether to give a counter notice on receipt of a temporary use notice. Its effect is that, whilst in such circumstances there is a presumption in favour of permitting the relevant premises to be used for gambling, the licensing authority may not do so unless satisfied that such use would be in accordance with the guidance contained in this document, any relevant Commission code of practice and its own statement of licensing policy as well as reasonably consistent with the licensing objectives. In reaching a view that the grant of a licence, or the giving of the temporary use notice, is in accordance with such guidance, code of practice or policy statement, a licensing authority is, in common with all such public authority decision makers, under a duty to act fairly and rationally. In cases where an authority is concerned whether a grant would be in accordance with, for example, the guidance in this document, this can be resolved by the imposition of appropriate licence conditions. In the unlikely event that a licensing authority perceives a conflict between a provision of a Commission code of practice or this Guidance and its own policy statement or view as to the application of the licensing objectives the structure of section 153 makes it plain that the Commission's codes and Guidance take precedence.

5.6 Section 153 also makes it clear that in deciding whether or not to grant a licence a licensing authority must not have regard to the expected demand for gambling premises that are the subject of the application.

5.7 The requirements in section 153 are subject to the licensing authority's power (under section 166) to resolve not to issue casino premises licences. This means that a resolution not to issue a casino premises licence applies regardless of the matters set out in section 153.

5.8 It should be noted that, unlike the Licensing Act, the Gambling Act does not include as a specific licensing objective the prevention of public nuisance. Any nuisance associated with gambling premises should be tackled under other relevant legislation.

MORE ABOUT THE LICENSING OBJECTIVES

Objective 1

PREVENTING GAMBLING FROM BEING A SOURCE OF CRIME OR DISORDER, BEING ASSOCIATED WITH CRIME OR DISORDER OR BEING USED TO SUPPORT CRIME

5.9 The Commission play a leading role in preventing gambling from being a source of crime. It will maintain rigorous licensing procedures that aim to prevent criminals from providing facilities for gambling, or being associated with providing such facilities. The Act provides the Commission with powers to investigate the suitability of applicants for operating and personal licences, and others relevant to the application. This will provide the Commission with the power to make enquiries about and investigate those who are involved in the control of a company or the provision of gambling. In considering applications for operating and personal licences the Commission will, in particular, take a serious view of any offences involving dishonesty committed by applicants or persons relevant to the application.

5.10 As applicants for premises licences (except occupiers of tracks who do not propose to offer gambling themselves) will have to hold an operating licence from the Commission before the premises licence can be issued, licensing authorities will not need to investigate the suitability of an applicant. If during the course of considering a premises licence application, or at any other time, the licensing authority receives information that causes it to question the suitability of the applicant to hold an operating licence, these concerns should be brought to the attention of the Commission without delay.

5.11 Among other matters, licensing authorities may need to consider the location of premises in the context of this licensing objective. If an application for a licence or permit is received in relation to premises that are in an area noted for particular problems with organised crime, for example, licensing authorities should think about what (if any) controls might be appropriate to prevent those premises becoming a source of crime. These might include conditions being put on the licence, such as a requirement for door supervisors.

5.12 A licensing authority will need to consider questions raised by the location of gambling premises when:

- formulating its Licensing Authority Statement of Policy
- receiving relevant representations to an application
- dealing with applications as a responsible authority in its own right
- considering applications before it.

5.13 Regulatory issues arising from the prevention of disorder are likely to focus almost exclusively on premises licensing, rather than on operating licences. (Although if there are persistent or serious disorder problems that an operator could or should do more to prevent, the licensing authority should bring this to the attention of the Commission so that it can consider the continuing suitability of the operator to hold an operating licence.)

5.14 Local authorities are experienced in making judgements in relation to the suitability of premises, particularly those for which they have responsibilities under the Licensing Act 2003, in which context they have wider powers to also take into account measures to prevent nuisance.

5.15 In relation to preventing disorder, licensing authorities have the ability under section 169 of the Act to attach additional conditions to premises licences, and are entitled to include a requirement for door supervision, as provided for in section 178 of the Act. If a person employed on door supervision would be required to hold a licence issued by the Security Industry Authority (SIA), that requirement will have force as though it were a condition on the premises licence. Further information on conditions can be found in part 9 of this Guidance.

5.16 Local authorities should note that in the case of gambling premises licences, disorder is intended to mean activity that is more serious and disruptive than mere nuisance. Factors to consider in determining whether a disturbance was serious enough to constitute disorder would include whether police assistance was required and how threatening the behaviour was to those who could see or hear it. There is not a clear line between nuisance and disorder and the licensing authority should take the views of its lawyers before determining what action to take in circumstances in which disorder may be a factor.

Objective 2

ENSURING THAT GAMBLING IS CONDUCTED IN A FAIR AND OPEN WAY

5.17 The Commission is concerned to ensure that not only is gambling fair in the way it is played, but also that the rules are transparent to players and they know what to expect. It achieves this by working to ensure that:

- operating and personal licences are issued only to those who are suitable to offer gambling facilities or work in the industry
- easily understandable information is made available by operators to players about, for example: the rules of the game, the probability of losing or winning, and the terms and conditions on which business is conducted
- the rules are fair
- advertising is not misleading
- the results of events and competitions on which commercial gambling takes place are made public
- machines, equipment and software used to produce the outcome of games meet standards set by the Commission and operate as advertised.

5.18 Generally the Commission would not expect licensing authorities to become concerned with ensuring that gambling is conducted in a fair and open way as this will be a matter for either the management of the gambling business, and therefore subject to the operating licence, or will be in relation to the suitability and actions of an individual and therefore subject to the personal licence. (However, if licensing authorities suspect that gambling is not being conducted in a fair and open way this should be brought to the attention of the Commission so that it can consider the continuing suitability of the operator to hold an operating licence or of an individual to hold a personal licence.)

5.19 In relation to the licensing of tracks the licensing authority's role will be different from other premises in that track owners will not necessarily have an operating licence. In those circumstances the premises licence may need to contain conditions to ensure that the environment in which betting takes place is suitable. Please see part 20 of this Guidance for more information.

Objective 3

PROTECTING CHILDREN AND OTHER VULNERABLE PERSONS FROM BEING HARMED OR EXPLOITED BY GAMBLING

5.20 With limited exceptions, the intention of the Gambling Act is that children and young persons should not be permitted to gamble and should be prevented from entering those gambling premises which are adult-only environments. The objective refers to protecting children from being 'harmed or exploited by gambling'. That means preventing them from taking part in gambling and for there to be restrictions on advertising so that gambling products are not aimed at children or advertised in such a way that makes them particularly attractive to children, excepting Category D gaming machines.

5.21 In relation to casinos, the Commission has issued a code of practice on access to casino premises by children and young persons, as provided for by section 176 of the Act. The code of practice is available as part of the *Licence Conditions and Codes of Practice* on the Commission website[6]. In accordance with that section, adherence to the code will be a condition of the premises licence. (Please see part 9 of this Guidance for more information.)

5.22 The Act does not seek to prohibit particular groups of adults from gambling in the same way that it prohibits children. The Commission does not seek to define 'vulnerable persons', but it does for regulatory purposes assume that this group includes people who gamble more than they want to; people who gamble beyond their means; and people who may not be able to make informed or balanced decisions about gambling due to mental health needs, learning disability or substance misuse relating to alcohol or drugs.

5.23 Licensing authorities need to consider, in relation to particular premises, whether any special considerations apply in relation to the protection of vulnerable persons. Any such considerations need to be balanced against the authority's objective to aim to permit the use of premises for gambling.

6 LCCP, available from www.gamblingcommission.gov.uk

GOOD PRACTICE IN REGULATION

5.24 Under the Legislative and Regulatory Reform Act 2006, any person exercising a specified regulatory function has a legal duty to have regard to the statutory principles of good regulation[7] in the exercise of the function. These provide that regulatory activities should be carried out in a way which is transparent, accountable, proportionate, and consistent and should be targeted only at cases in which action is needed. The Gambling Commission has regard to these principles in relation to its responsibilities and also has regard to the requirements of the Regulators' Compliance Code[8] ('the Code'). The purpose of the Code is to promote efficient and effective approaches to regulatory inspection and enforcement which improve regulatory outcomes without imposing unnecessary burdens on business.

5.25 The statutory principles of good regulation and the Code also apply to local authorities when they are fulfilling regulatory functions under the Gambling Act 2005 [9] and the Gambling Commission reminds licensing authorities that they are under a statutory duty to have regard to these principles and the Code.

5.26 Guidance produced by the Better Regulation Delivery Office seeks to assist local authorities in interpreting the requirements of the Code, for example in developing their Compliance and Enforcement Policy[10], and in delivering risk-based regulation in relation to age restrictions[11].

7 Legislative and Regulatory Reform Act 2006, section 21.

8 Regulators' Compliance Code, Department for Business, Innovation and Skills (formerly the Department for Business, Enterprise and Regulatory Reform), 2007, issued under section 22 of the Legislative and Regulatory Reform Act 2006.

9 The Legislative and Regulatory Reform (Regulatory Functions) Order 2007, was amended by the Legislative and Regulatory Reform (Regulatory Functions) (Amendment) Order 2009, which, amongst other things, extended the application of the 2007 Order to local authorities in Wales and Scotland exercising regulatory functions under the Gambling Act 2005 – see Parts 3 and 7.

10 Template: Compliance and Enforcement Policy, Better Regulation Delivery Office. This template policy was developed by the Local Better Regulation Office, with local authorities,

to assist local authorities in developing a policy that is in line with the requirements of the Regulators' Compliance Code, or to review their existing policy. It is available on the BRDO website at http://www.bis.gov.uk/brdo/resources/risk- based-regulation/compliance-policy.

11 The Age Restricted Products and Services Framework published in 2011 sets out an agreed set of shared responsibilities and reasonable expectations for young people, their parents and carers, businesses, employees and regulators with regards to access to age restricted products and services. The principles for regulators and enforcers will be underpinned by a Code of Practice for Regulatory Delivery, which is due to be launched for consultation in June 2012.

HUMAN RIGHTS ACT 1998

5.27 The Secretary of State has certified that the Act is compatible with the European Convention on Human Rights. In considering applications, and taking enforcement action, under the Gambling Act licensing authorities should bear in mind that they are subject to the Human Rights Act and in particular:

- Article 1, Protocol 1 – peaceful enjoyment of possessions. A licence is considered a possession in law and people should not be deprived of their possessions except in the public interest
- Article 6 – right to a fair hearing
- Article 8 – respect for private and family life. In particular, removal or restriction of a licence may affect a person's private life
- Article 10 – right to freedom of expression.

Licensing authorities are reminded of their duty when applying their Licensing Authority Statement of Policy to consider whether, in the light of relevant representations made to them, exceptions to those policies should be made in any particular case.

5.28 In deciding to reject an application, a licensing authority should rely on reasons that demonstrate that the licensing objectives are not being, or are unlikely to be, met. Licensing authorities should be aware that other considerations such as moral or ethical objections to gambling are not a valid reason to reject applications for premises licences. This is because such objections do not relate to the licensing objectives. An authority's decision cannot be based on dislike of gambling, or a general notion that it is undesirable to allow gambling premises in an area (with the exception of the casino resolution powers).

PART 6: LICENSING AUTHORITY STATEMENT OF POLICY

6.1 Section 349 of the Act requires all licensing authorities to prepare and publish a statement of the principles that they propose to apply in exercising their functions under the Act during the three-year period to which the policy applies.

6.2 The Licensing Authority Statement of Policy will last for a maximum of three years, but can be reviewed and revised by the authority at any time. The statement must be produced following consultation with those bodies and persons set out in subsection (3) of section 349 of the Act. Regulations made by the Secretary of State, or Scottish Ministers in Scotland, prescribe the form of statements, and the procedure to be followed in relation to them and their publication[12].

12 SI No. 636: The Gambling Act 2005 (Licensing Authority Policy Statement) (England and Wales) Regulations 2006 SSI No. 154: The Gambling Act 2005 (Licensing Authority Policy Statement) (Scotland) Regulations 2006.

FUNDAMENTAL PRINCIPLES

6.3 All Licensing Authority Statements of Policy should begin by stating the three licensing objectives, which the policy will promote. The statement should also state that the licensing authority shall aim to permit the use of premises for gambling as set out in section 153 of the Act.

6.4 Licensing Authority Statements of Policy should include a firm commitment to avoid duplication with other regulatory regimes so far as possible. For example, a range of general duties are imposed on the self-employed, employers and operators of gambling premises, both in respect of employees and of the general public, by legislation governing health and safety at work and fire safety. Therefore such requirements need not be included in the Licensing Authority Statement of Policy.

6.5 In determining its policy, the licensing authority must have regard to this Guidance, and give appropriate weight to the views of those it has consulted. In determining what weight to give particular representations, the factors to be taken into account will include:

- who is making the representations (what is their expertise or interest)
- relevance of the factors to the licensing objectives
- how many other people have expressed the same or similar views
- how far the representations relate to matters that the licensing authority should be including in its policy statement.

6.6 In relation to premises licensing, licensing authorities can only consider matters within the scope of the Guidance, Act and Codes of Practice. Even if there is a large response regarding a certain issue, an authority may be unable to deal with the issue under the Gambling Act. However the issue may be a matter for other legislation, for example planning.

6.7 It will be up to the licensing authority to ensure that it looks at the views of consultees and considers carefully whether they should be taken into account and to what extent (having regard to the above factors). A licensing authority should always be able to give reasons for the decisions it has made following consultation. Having regard to this Guidance will be important for consistency, especially where licensing authority boundaries meet.

6.8 As with the Commission, it is expected that local licensing authorities will regulate gambling in the public interest.

6.9 While statements of policy may set out a general approach to the exercise of functions under the Act, no statement of policy should override the right of any person to make an application under the Act and to have that application considered on its merits. Additionally, a statement of policy must not undermine the right of any person to make representations on an application or to seek a review of a licence where provision has been made for them to do so. However if a 'no-casino' resolution has been passed by an authority it does not have to consider applications for new casino premises licences in its area.

'Demand' for gaming premises

6.10 Previous legislation required that the grant of certain gambling permissions should take account of whether there is unfulfilled demand for the facilities. Absence of unmet demand is not a criterion for a licensing authority in considering an application for a premises licence under the Gambling Act. Each application must be considered on its merits without regard to demand.

6.11 The Licensing Authority Statement of Policy should reflect this situation and not comment on the need for gambling premises.

6.12 However, the licensing authority may comment on the location of premises in so far as the location relates to the licensing objectives. So, for example, a Licensing Authority Statement of Policy could, and should, set out the general principles that the licensing authority will apply when determining whether the location of proposed gambling premises is acceptable (with or without conditions) in light of the licensing objectives. For example, a Licensing Authority Statement of Policy might set out that the authority will consider very carefully whether applications for premises licences in respect of certain gambling premises located very close to a school or a centre for gambling addicts should be granted in light of the third licensing objective. Any such policy must, however, come with the qualification that each case will be decided on its merits, and will depend to a large extent on the type of gambling that it is proposed will be offered on the premises. If an applicant for a premises licence can show how licensing objective concerns can be overcome, that will have to be taken into account.

CONSULTATION

6.13 Section 349(3) requires the licensing authority to consult the following on the Licensing Authority Statement of Policy or any subsequent revision:

- in England and Wales, the chief officer of police for the authority's area
- in Scotland, the Chief Constable of the police force maintained for the police area comprising that area
- one or more persons who appear to the authority to represent the interests of persons carrying on gambling businesses in the authority's area
- one or more persons who appear to the authority to represent the interests of persons who are likely to be affected by the exercise of the authority's functions under this Act.

6.14 The list of persons to be consulted when preparing the Licensing Authority Statement of Policy is deliberately wide. This enables licensing authorities to undertake a comprehensive consultation exercise with anyone who may be affected by or otherwise have an interest in the Licensing Authority Statement of Policy.

6.15 Licensing authorities will develop their own consultation practices but they may like to consider the following:

- consultation with a range of organisations including faith groups, voluntary and community organisations working with children and young people, organisations working with people who are problem gamblers, medical practices or primary care trusts, and advocacy organisations (such as the Citizen's Advice Bureau and trade unions)
- consultation with other tiers of local government (where they exist)
- consultation with businesses that are, or will be, holders of a premises licence
- consultation with the organisations named as responsible authorities in the Act
- using a variety of consultation methods including meetings with gambling businesses in the local authority area and open forums for the public.

6.16 Any written consultation should follow best practice as set out by the Department for Business, Innovation and Skills including allowing 12 weeks for responses to the consultation[13]. Consultation documents could be provided on the licensing authority's website.

---

13 Further information is available at www.bis.gov.uk

FORM AND CONTENT OF THE LICENSING AUTHORITY STATEMENT OF POLICY

6.17 Regulations made by the Secretary of State or Scottish Ministers set out requirements as to the form and publication of Licensing Authority Statements of Policy and subsequent revisions of statements. In addition to the requirements set out by the regulations (below), this Guidance sets out certain information that the Commission considers should be included in all Licensing Authority Statements of Policy.

6.18 The regulations provide for the form of the statement to be determined by the licensing authority subject to the following requirements:

- Licensing Authority Statement of Policy must contain an introductory section summarising the matters contained within the statement, describing the geographical area to which the statement applies, and listing the persons consulted in preparing the statement.

6.19 As required by the regulations, the statement should make clear the geographical area that it covers. This may be achieved by including a plan of the area covered by the statement.

6.20 The statement should also set out the licensable activities that are covered.

6.21 Statements of principles to be applied by the licensing authority in exercising its functions must be contained in four separate sections within the Licensing Authority Statement of Policy as set out below:

(1) Licensing Authority Statements of Policy must contain a section that sets out the principles to be applied by the authority in designating, in writing, a body which is competent to advise the authority about the protection of children from harm.

6.22 Section 157 of the Act sets out the responsible authorities. Within this section, the licensing authority has discretion to determine the most appropriate body competent to advise the authority about the protection of children from harm. Such a body may, but not necessarily, be the Local Safeguarding Children Board in England and Wales, or the Child Protection Committee in Scotland. The licensing authority must consider which body best fulfils this function and the Licensing Authority Statement of Policy should set out this consideration, or the criteria the authority intends to use, in order to designate that body in writing.

(2) Licensing Authority Statements of Policy must contain a section that sets out the principles to be applied by the authority to determine whether a person is an interested party in relation to a premises licence, or in relation to an application for or in respect of a premises licence.

6.23 Section 158 of the Act defines interested parties as persons who:

(a) live sufficiently close to the premises to be likely to be affected by the authorised activities

(b) have business interests that might be affected by the authorised activities or

(c) represent persons who satisfy paragraph a) or b).

6.24 Licensing authorities must consider whether a person is an interested party with regard to particular premises on a case by case basis, judging each on its merits. However, an authority may have regard to a number of factors when making its decision. These factors should be set out in this part of the Licensing Authority Statement of Policy. An authority may take into account, for example, the size of the premises and the nature of the activities taking place. Larger premises may be considered to affect people over a broader geographical area compared with smaller premises offering similar facilities.

6.25 Licensing authorities should include guidance in their Licensing Authority Statements of Policy whom they consider comes within the category of those who represent persons living close to premises, or have business interests that may be affected by it. For example, this category could include trade associations and trade unions and residents' and tenants' associations. It is expected that the types of organisations that may be considered to have business interests will be given a wide interpretation to include, for example, partnerships, charities, faith groups and medical practices etc.

(4) Licensing Authority Statements of Policy must contain a section that sets out the principles to be applied by the authority in exercising the functions under Sections 29 and 30 of the Act with respect to the exchange of information between it and the Commission, and the functions under section 350 of the Act with respect to the exchange of information between it and the other persons listed in Schedule 6 of the Act.

6.26 The Act empowers the Commission to seek information from licensing authorities, and places an obligation on authorities to comply with information requests. Specifically, section 29 of the Act entitles the Commission to request information from licensing authorities and to set out the manner in which the information is compiled, collated and provided, providing it:

- forms part of a register maintained under the Act
- is in the possession of the authority in connection with a provision of the Act.

6.27 Section 350 of the Act allows licensing authorities to exchange information with other persons or bodies listed in Schedule 6(1) for use in the exercise of functions under the Act as follows:

- a constable or police force
- an enforcement officer
- a licensing authority
- HMRC
- the Gambling Appeal Tribunal
- the Secretary of State
- Scottish Ministers.

6.28 The licensing authority must set out how it will approach information exchange with other regulatory bodies under the Act, and whether it intends to establish any protocols in this regard. The statement should also include the authority's approach to data protection and freedom of information. In particular, how information will be protected, whether the confidentiality of those making representations will be maintained, what information will be shared with other agencies or persons and how information can be accessed by data subjects.

6.29 Further information regarding the exchange of information can be found in part 13 of this Guidance.

6.30 For the purposes of their Licensing Authority Statement of Policy, licensing authorities should confirm that they will act in accordance with the relevant legislation and Guidance from the Commission and will adopt the principles of better regulation.

(8) Licensing Authority Statements of Policy must contain a section that sets out the principles to be applied by the authority in exercising the functions under Part 15 of the Act with respect to the inspection of premises; and the powers under section 346 of the Act to institute criminal proceedings in respect of the offences specified in that section.

6.31 Licensing authorities are referred to what has been said at paragraphs 5.23 to 5.25 above concerning the Regulators' Compliance Code.

6.32 Further guidance on licensing authorities' compliance and enforcement responsibilities is available in part 36 of this Guidance. This has been developed following discussions between the Commission, the police, licensing authorities and other law-enforcement and regulatory agencies to agree respective roles in relation to particular types of gambling and licensed premises.

6.33 It is recommended that licensing authorities adopt a risk-based inspection programme. This would include targeting high-risk premises which require greater attention, whilst operating a lighter touch in respect of low-risk premises, so that resources are more effectively concentrated on problem premises. The policy statement should set out the principles to be applied by the authority in respect of such a programme and the criteria the authority is likely to use to determine the level of risk in respect of premises.

6.34 Many licensing authorities in England and Wales will have general enforcement policies which are in accordance with the codes of practice developed with the Crown Prosecution Service. Licensing authorities in England and Wales may wish to include in their Licensing Authority Statements of Policy that they will apply these codes in the management of criminal cases.

6.35 Part 36 of this Guidance covers more detailed issues such as the agreement of protocols with the local police and the Commission on enforcement issues.

OTHER MATTERS TO BE COVERED IN POLICY STATEMENTS

6.36 In addition to these requirements as set out in regulations, a number of other matters should be included in Licensing Authority Statements of Policy.

Consideration of applications

6.37 The authority should set out in its statement what factors it may take into account when considering applications for premises licences, permits and other permissions and matters that it will consider relevant when determining whether to review a licence. This is where considerations such as the proximity of gambling premises to schools and vulnerable adult centres, or to residential areas where there may be a high concentration of families with children, should be detailed. Any such policy must, however, come with the qualification that each case will be decided on its merits, so if an applicant can show how they might overcome licensing objective concerns, that will have to be taken into account.

Statement regarding casino resolution

6.38 Under section 166(5) of the Gambling Act, any resolution not to issue casino licences must be published in the Licensing Authority Statement of Policy. In addition, the Licensing Authority Statement of Policy should include details about how the authority has taken or will take a decision to pass (or not to pass) a casino resolution.

Statement of principles

6.39 If an authority intends to apply a statement of principles when considering applicant suitability for applications for FEC permits under paragraph 7 of Schedule 10, or prize gaming permits under paragraph 8 of Schedule 14 of the Act, it is not obliged to include those statements as part of the Licensing Authority Statement of Policy, but may want to consider doing so to make them available in one place.

Declaration by licensing authority

6.40 Each Licensing Authority Statement of Policy should include a declaration which sets out that in producing the final Licensing Authority Statement of Policy, the authority has had regard to the licensing objectives of the Gambling Act 2005, the Guidance issued by the Commission, and any responses from those consulted on the policy statement. To avoid later challenge, it would be sensible if the licensing authority demonstrated how the licensing objectives and Commission Guidance have been taken into account when drawing up the statement.

6.41 Authorities should note that the regulations and this Guidance do not prevent authorities from including any additional information that the authority considers necessary or helpful.

ADVERTISEMENT OF THE LICENSING AUTHORITY STATEMENT OF POLICY OR REVISIONS

6.42 Before publishing a statement or revision, the regulations made by the Secretary of State or Scottish Ministers require authorities to publish a notice of their intention to publish a statement or revision (this must be done no later than the date on which the statement or revision is to be published). The notice must:

(a) specify the date on which the statement or revision is to be published
(b) specify the date on which the statement or revision will come into effect
(c) specify the internet address where the statement or revision will be published and the address of the premises at which it may be inspected
(d) be published on the authority's website and in/on one or more of the following places:
 - a local newspaper circulating in the area covered by the statement
 - a local newsletter, circular, or similar document circulating in the area covered by the statement
 - a public notice board in or near the principal office of the authority
 - a public notice board on the premises of public libraries in the area covered by the statement.

PUBLICATION OF THE LICENSING AUTHORITY STATEMENT OF POLICY OR REVISIONS

6.43 The regulations stipulate that the Licensing Authority Statement of Policy or any subsequent revision of the statement must be published on the authority's website and be made available at reasonable times for inspection by members of the public either in the principal office of the authority, at one or more public libraries in the area covered by the statement or in other premises situated in that area. The statement or revision must be published at least four weeks before it takes effect.

REVIEW OF THE LICENSING AUTHORITY STATEMENT OF POLICY

6.44 The Licensing Authority Statement of Policy will have effect for three years but the licensing authority may review and alter the policy in that period.

6.45 Licensing authorities will need to consider, in the event of a change of policy, whether a review of the statement is necessary. For example, a change in planning policy could lead to a review and subsequent revision of a statement (if, for example, a change in planning policy led to family entertainment centres (FECs) where previously there were none, the statement may then be required to make reference to FECs where it was previously silent). Where the statement is reviewed and changes made, authorities must consult on any revision.

6.46 Authorities should note that where a statement is revised, it is only the revision that needs to be published and consulted on. So, for example, an authority may consult separately on whether to pass a casino resolution and then subsequently publish the resolution as part of the statement. This can be done without any need to review and reopen consultation on the main body of the statement. Any revisions must be published and advertised in the same way as a new statement.

6.47 Regulations provide for the form and content of revisions to the Licensing Authority Statement of Policy to be determined by the licensing authority, subject to the following requirements:

- revisions to Licensing Authority Statements of Policy must include an introductory section at or near the beginning, summarising the matters dealt with in the statement and listing the persons consulted in preparing the revision.

6.48 Where the revision deals with any of the matters below, these must be presented in separate sections:

(1) the principles to be applied by the authority in exercising the powers under section 157(h) of the Act to designate, in writing, a body which is competent to advise the authority about the protection of children from harm

(2) the principles to be applied by the authority in exercising the powers under section 158 of the Act, to determine whether a person is an interested party in relation to a premises licence, or an application for or in respect of a premises licence

(3) the principles to be applied by the authority in exercising its functions under sections 29 and 30 of the Act with respect to the exchange of information between it and the Gambling Commission, and the functions under section 350 of the Act with respect to the exchange of information between it and the other persons listed in Schedule 6 to the Act or

(4) the principles to be applied by the authority in exercising the functions under Part 15 of the Act with respect to the inspection of premises; and the powers under section 346 of the Act to institute criminal proceedings in respect of the offences specified in that section.

ADDITIONAL INFORMATION TO BE MADE AVAILABLE

6.49 In order to ensure that applicants and persons who wish to make representations have the necessary information to be able to do so, the information set out below should be made available by licensing authorities as part of their communications strategy.

6.50 It should be noted that, unlike the Licensing Act, the Gambling Act does not include as a specific licensing objective the prevention of public nuisance. There is however other relevant legislation which deals with public nuisance. It would be helpful if licensing authorities could explain that objections to new premises or requests for a review should be based on the licensing objectives of the Gambling Act.

6.51 It is open to licensing authorities to include any of this information in their Licensing Authority Statement of Policy. However, authorities might think it more appropriate to make it available in another form, such as on the authority website.

Registers

6.52 Section 156 of the Act requires licensing authorities to maintain a register of the premises licences that it has issued. The register must be made available, at any reasonable time, to the public who may request copies of the entries. Authorities should ensure that information regarding the location of the registers (ie on the website, in the council offices etc), when they can be viewed, and the cost of obtaining copies is made available to the public.

Fees

6.53 Authorities should ensure that information regarding the fees to be charged, including the level of fees, for applications for premises licences and other permissions under the Act is available to the public.

6.54 Separate guidance relating to the calculation of fees and accounting procedures has been produced by the Secretary of State available from the Department for Culture, Media and Sport website (www.culture.gov.uk). In Scotland, all of the equivalent fees will be set centrally by Scottish Ministers[14].

[14] Gambling Act 2005 (Premises Licence Fees) (Scotland) Regulations 2007; Gambling Act 2005 (Fees) (Scotland) Regulations 2007; Gambling Act 2005 (Fees No 2) (Scotland) Regulations 2007; Gambling Act 2005 (Fees No 3) (Scotland) Regulations 2007 and Gambling Act 2005 (Fees No 4) (Scotland) Regulations 2007.

Applications

6.55 Authorities should ensure that information is available on how to make applications for licences and other permissions under the Act. In particular, it would be helpful if authorities ensure that a full list of responsible authorities and their appropriate contact details, is readily available. Application forms, where appropriate, should also be made available. Authorities should note that there will be no prescribed application forms for family entertainment centre, prize gaming or licensed premises gaming machine permits. As such, the authority will need to make clear how applications for these permits should be made and in what form. Additionally, authorities will need to ensure that information regarding making representations, and applying for a review of a premises licence, is also made available.

Delegation

6.56 Information should be provided as to how functions are delegated under the Act (ie whether decisions are to be taken by a licensing officer, licensing sub-committee or full committee etc). A table setting out the scheme of delegation required by the Act may be the most appropriate method for this and is located in part 4 of this Guidance.

Statutory application forms and notices

6.57 There are a range of statutory application forms and notices that licensing authorities are required to use as part of their gambling licensing responsibilities. A summary list of these can be found in Appendix E. The forms and notices can be downloaded from the Department for Culture, Media and Sport website (www.culture.gov.uk).

PART 7: PREMISES LICENCES

7.1 Where an individual or company proposes to offer gambling for which an operating licence is required, and which is premises based, that individual or company will also need to apply for a premises licence.

7.2 Premises licences are issued by the licensing authority with responsibility for the area in which the premises are situated.

7.3 The Act contains no rules about cases where premises lie within more than one authority's area. Such cases are likely to be rare. The Commission would expect an applicant to apply to the licensing authority in whose area the greater or greatest part of the premises is situated. If another authority receives an application it should discuss with the applicant and the neighbouring authority as to which is the appropriate authority. Ultimately, there is nothing in the Act giving an authority the right to turn down an application because it is responsible for a smaller area of the premises than another authority. However, in such circumstances, the other authority will be a 'responsible authority' in relation to the premises (see part 8 of this guidance), and will be able to give a view on the application through these channels. Note, this is not the same as the Licensing Act where an application must be made to the authority in which the greater part of the premises is situated.

7.4 Where the premises are located in two or more areas (equally or otherwise), ultimately the applicant may choose which licensing authority to apply to. In the rare cases where such premises exist, it will be important that the licensing authorities concerned maintain close contact about the grant of the premises licence, and subsequent compliance (including inspection powers) and other licensing functions. The licensing authority to which the premises licence application was made will have jurisdiction and the other(s) will need to pass relevant information about the premises to it.

PRIMARY GAMBLING ACTIVITY

7.5 In accordance with section 150 of the Act, premises licences can authorise the provision of facilities on:

(a) casino premises
(b) bingo premises
(c) betting premises, including tracks and premises used by betting intermediaries
(d) adult gaming centre premises (for category B3, B4, C and D machines)
(e) family entertainment centre premises (for category C and D machines) (note that, separate to this category, the licensing authority may issue a family entertainment centre gaming machine permit, which authorises the use of category D machines only).

7.6 By distinguishing between premises types the Act makes it clear that the primary gambling activity of the premises should be that described. Thus, in a bingo premises, the primary activity should be bingo, with gaming machines as an ancillary offer on the premises. This principle also applies to existing casino licences (but not 2005 Act casinos) and betting premises licences. The latest issue of the *Licence Conditions and Codes of Practice*[15] sets out in full the requirements on operators. Subject to the gaming machine entitlements which various types of licence bring with them (and except in the case of tracks), the Act does not permit premises to be licensed for more than one of the above activities.

7.7 From time to time, the Commission publishes advice notes which whilst they are not legally binding are designed to assist in the understanding of matters such as primary gambling activity. These are updated in light of experience and innovation. Reference to them may assist licensing authorities in establishing compliance with primary gambling activity requirements.
7.8 Please see part 16 of this Guidance for more information about gaming machine categories.

---

[15] The Licence Conditions and Codes of Practice (LCCP) is available from www.gamblingcommission.gov.uk .

CASINO PREMISES

7.9 New casino premises licences issued under the Act will fall into one of two categories:
(a) large casino premises licence
(b) small casino premises licence.
7.10 These premises are subject to separate regulations, involving a two-stage application process. Details of the two stage process can be found in part 17 of this Guidance.
7.11 In addition, there is a third category of casino that is permitted through transitional arrangements under Schedule 18 of the Act. Most of these casinos fall below the size thresholds of the other two categories. Such casinos may operate as card clubs without offering casino games.
7.12 Please see part 17 of this Guidance for more information about the definition of casinos and the licensing of those premises.

MEANING OF PREMISES

7.13 In the Act, 'premises' is defined as including 'any place'. Section 152 therefore prevents more than one premises licence applying to any place. But, there is no reason in principle why a single building could not be subject to more than one premises licence, provided they are for different parts of the building, and the different parts of the building can reasonably be regarded as being different premises. This approach has been taken to allow large, multiple unit premises such as pleasure parks, tracks, or shopping malls to obtain discrete premises licences, where appropriate safeguards are in place. However, licensing authorities should pay particular attention if there are issues about sub-division of a single building or plot and should ensure that mandatory conditions relating to access between premises are observed.
7.14 In most cases the expectation is that a single building/plot will be the subject of an application for a licence, for example, 32 High Street. But that does not mean that 32 High Street cannot be the subject of separate premises licences for the basement and ground floor, if they are configured acceptably. Whether different parts of a building can properly be regarded as being separate premises will depend on the circumstances. The location of the premises will clearly be an important consideration and the suitability of the division is likely to be a matter for discussion between the operator and the licensing officer. However, the Commission does not consider that areas of a building that are artificially or temporarily separated, for example by ropes or moveable partitions, can properly be regarded as different premises.
7.15 We recognise that different configurations may be appropriate under different circumstances but the crux of the matter is whether the proposed premises are genuinely separate premises that merit their own licence with, for example, the machine entitlements that brings and are not an artificially created part of what is readily identifiable as a single premises.
7.16 The Act sets out that the type and number of higher stake gaming machines allowable in premises is restricted according to the type of premises licence or permit

granted. For example, a converted casino licence allows for 20 gaming machines in categories B, C or D, a bingo licence allows for up to eight category B3 machines and an unlimited number of category C and D machines. With the exception of AGCs and FECs, premises are not permitted to be used exclusively for making available gaming machines, but rather to provide the gaming facilities corresponding to the premises licence type. The Licence Conditions and Codes of Practice (LCCP), sets out in full the requirements on operators. The latest version of the LCCP can be found on the Commission's website.

7.17 With the exception of bingo clubs, tracks on race-days and licensed family entertainment centres, children will not be permitted to enter licensed gambling premises. Therefore businesses will need to consider carefully how they wish to configure their buildings if they are seeking to develop multi-purpose sites.

7.18 Licensing authorities should take particular care in considering applications for multiple premises licences for a building and those relating to a discrete part of a building used for other (non-gambling) purposes. In particular they should be aware of the following:

- The third licensing objective seeks to protect children from being harmed by gambling. In practice that means not only preventing them from taking part in gambling, but also preventing them from being in close proximity to gambling. Therefore premises should be configured so that children are not invited to participate in, have accidental access to, or closely observe gambling where they are prohibited from participating.
- Entrances to and exits from parts of a building covered by one or more premises licences should be separate and identifiable so that the separation of different premises is not compromised and people do not 'drift' into a gambling area. In this context it should normally be possible to access the premises without going through another licensed premises or premises with a permit.
- Customers should be able to participate in the activity named on the premises licence.

7.19 In determining whether two or more proposed premises are truly separate, the licensing authority should be aware of factors which could assist them in making their decision. Depending on all the circumstances of the case, these may include:

- Is a separate registration for business rates in place for the premises?
- Is the premises' neighbouring premises owned by the same person or someone else?
- Can each of the premises be accessed from the street or a public passageway?
- Can the premises only be accessed from any other gambling premises?

7.20 Where more than one premises licence is permitted within a building the gaming machine entitlement for the separately licensed premises may not be aggregated and no more than the permitted number and category of machines for the relevant type of premises may be placed in any one of the individual sets of premises within the building.

7.21 The proper application of section 152 means that different premises licences cannot apply in respect of single premises at different times. There is no temporal element to a premises licence. Therefore, premises could not, for example, be licensed as a bingo club on week days and a betting shop at weekends.

DIVISION OF PREMISES AND ACCESS BETWEEN PREMISES

7.22 An issue that may arise when division of a premises is being considered is the nature of the unlicensed area from which a customer may access a licensed gambling premises. For casinos, bearing in mind the wide definition of a street, access might be from a foyer or other area which the public might enter for purposes other than gambling. The precise nature of this public area will depend on the location and nature of the premises. Licensing authorities will need to consider whether the effect of any division is to create a machine shed-type environment with very large banks of machines, which is not the intention of the access conditions, or whether it creates a public environment with gambling facilities being made available. Licensing authorities should, in particular, remember that where they have concerns about the use of premises for gambling, these may be addressed through licence conditions.

7.23 The Gambling Act 2005 (Mandatory and Default Conditions) Regulations[16] set out the access provisions for each type of premises. The broad principle is that there can be no access from one licensed gambling premises to another, except between premises which allow access to those under the age of 18 and with the further exception that licensed betting premises may be accessed from other licensed betting premises. Under-18s can go into family entertainment centres, tracks, pubs and some bingo clubs. So access is allowed between these types of premises.

7.24 It should be noted that the Gambling Act 2005 (Mandatory and Default Conditions) Regulations define street as 'including any bridge, road, lane, footway, subway, square, court, alley or passage (including passages through enclosed premises such as shopping malls) whether a thoroughfare or not'. This is to allow access, for example, to casinos from hotel foyers.

7.25 There is no definition of 'direct access' in the Act or regulations. However, it could be said that there should be an area separating the premises concerned (for example a street or cafe), which the public go to for purposes other than gambling, for there to be shown to be no direct access.

7.26 The relevant access provisions for each premises type is as follows:

Casinos

- the principal entrance to the premises must be from a street (as defined above)
- no entrance to a casino must be from premises that are used wholly or mainly by children and/or young persons
- no customer must be able to enter a casino directly from any other premises which holds a gambling premises licence.

Adult gaming centres

- no customer must be able to access the premises directly from any other licensed gambling premises.

Betting shops

- access must be from a street (as defined above) or from other premises with a betting premises licence
- no direct access from a betting shop to another premises used for the retail sale of merchandise or services. In effect there cannot be an entrance to a betting shop from a shop of any kind and you could not have a betting shop at the back of a cafe
  – the whole area would have to be licensed.

Tracks

- no customer should be able to access the premises directly from:
  - a casino
  - an adult gaming centre.

Bingo premises

- no customer must be able to access the premises directly from:
  - a casino
  - an adult gaming centre
  - a betting premises, other than a track.

Family entertainment centres

- no customer must be able to access the premises directly from:
  - a casino
  - an adult gaming centre
  - a betting premises, other than a track.

16 SI no 1409: The Gambling Act 2005 (Mandatory and Default Conditions) (England and Wales) Regulations 2007 SI no 266: The Gambling Act 2005 (Mandatory and Default Conditions) (Scotland) Regulations 2007.

MANAGEMENT OF AREAS WHERE CATEGORY B AND C GAMING MACHINES ARE LOCATED IN GAMBLING PREMISES THAT ADMIT CHILDREN AND YOUNG PEOPLE

7.27 According to mandatory and default conditions relating to gambling premises that admit under 18s, any area where category B and C gaming machines are located must be:

- separated from the rest of the premises by a physical barrier which is effective to prevent access other than by an entrance designed for that purpose
- supervised (see below) at all times to ensure that under-18s do not enter the area
- arranged in a way that ensures that all parts of the area can be observed
- supervised either by:
  - one or more persons whose responsibilities include ensuring that under-18s do not enter the areas
  - CCTV monitored by one or more persons whose responsibilities include ensuring that under-18s do not enter the areas.

A notice stating that no person under the age of 18 is permitted to enter the area must be displayed in a prominent place at the entrance to the area.

7.28 There are a range of other conditions which attach to each type of premises. These are not covered in this section, but are set out in part 9 and the parts of this document relating to each type of premises.

ACCESS TO GAMBLING BY CHILDREN AND YOUNG PEOPLE

7.29 The Act contains the objective of 'protecting children and other vulnerable persons from being harmed or exploited by gambling'. Children (defined in the Act as under-16s) and young persons (16–17s) may take part in private and non-commercial betting and gaming but the Act contains a number of restrictions on the circumstances in which they may participate in gambling or be on premises where gambling is taking place. An adult is defined as 18 and over. In summary:

- casinos are not permitted to admit anyone under 18
- betting shops are not permitted to admit anyone under 18
- bingo clubs may admit those under 18 but must have policies to ensure that they do not play bingo, or play category B or C machines that are restricted to those over 18
- adult entertainment centres are not permitted to admit those under 18
- family entertainment centres and premises with a liquor licence (for example pubs) can admit under-18s, but they must not play category C machines which are restricted to those over 18
- clubs with a club premises certificate can admit under-18s, but they must have policies to ensure those under 18 do not play machines other than category D machines
- all tracks can admit under-18s, but they may only have access to gambling areas on days where races or other sporting events are taking place, or are expected to take place. This was extended to other sporting venues under the Gambling Act

2005 (Exclusion of Children from Track Areas) Order 2007. Tracks will be required to have policies to ensure that under-18s do not participate in gambling other than on category D machines.

7.30 Licensing authorities should take particular care in considering applications for multiple licences for a building and those relating to a discrete part of a building used for other (non-gambling) purposes. In particular they should be aware that entrances and exits from parts of a building covered by one or more licences should be separate and identifiable so that the separation of different premises is not compromised and that people do not 'drift' into a gambling area. The plan of the premises should clearly denote entrances and exits.

VESSELS AND VEHICLES

7.31 The Act permits premises licences to be granted for passenger vessels. Separate application forms are prescribed for vessels under the Premises Licences and Provisional Statements Regulations. The definition of a vessel in section 353(1) of the Act is:

- anything (other than a seaplane or amphibious vehicle), designed or adapted for use on water
- a hovercraft
- anything, or part of any place, situated on or in water.

7.32 This last part of the definition should be given a normal and sensible interpretation. Structures which are an extension of the land are not vessels, even if they arch over water. Thus, neither a pier nor a bridge is to be considered a vessel. Instead, they remain premises under the Act. This is important because not all forms of permit are available to vessels.

7.33 The Act allows pleasure boats to apply for premises licences. As with multipurpose buildings, the part of the vessel where gambling takes place will be licensed and the usual restrictions on access for children will apply. The Act applies in relation to a vessel that is not permanently moored or berthed as if it were premises situated in a place where it is usually moored or berthed. The relevant licensing authority for considering an application for a premises licence in respect of a vessel is therefore the licensing authority for the area in which it is usually moored or berthed.

7.34 Vehicles (trains, road vehicles, aircraft, sea planes and amphibious vehicles, other than a hovercraft) may not be the subject of a premises licence and therefore all forms of commercial betting and gaming will be unlawful in a vehicle in Great Britain. Certain allowances are made for private and non-commercial gaming or betting to take place in a vehicle, but these are subject to a number of stringent requirements. These ensure that, at no point, can the gambling become a commercial activity.

7.35 Where a premises licence is sought in connection with a vessel which will be navigated while licensable activities take place, the licensing authority should be concerned with the promotion of the licensing objectives on board the vessel. It should not focus on matters relating to safe navigation or operation of the vessel, the general safety of passengers or emergency provision, all of which are subject to regulations which must be met before the vessel is issued with its Passenger Certificate and Safety Management Certificate.

7.36 Licenses are not required for gambling if it takes place aboard a vessel engaged on an international journey. Such gambling is exempted from the offences under the Act if the vessel is on a journey which has taken it, or is intended to take it, into international waters (so this includes cross-channel ferries). In the case of aircraft, no offence takes place if the gambling takes place in international airspace.

7.37 This means that licensing authorities will have jurisdiction over gambling conducted on vessels on all inland waterways, at permanent moorings, and on all aircraft on the ground or in domestic airspace. If an ocean-going vessel is involved, authorities will need to establish where the vessel has been, or is intending to go.

SINGLE AND COMBINED LICENCES

7.38 Only one premises licence may be issued for any particular premises at any time, although the licence may authorise more than one type of gambling. Details of the gambling permissible under each type of licence are set out in the Act and in the premises specific parts of this Guidance.

7.39 There is one exception to this rule, namely a track (that is a horse racing course, dog track or other premises where races or sporting events take place), which may be subject to more than one premises licence, provided each licence relates to a specified area of the track.

7.40 The Act sets out that there will be a main (betting premises) licence for the track, and, in addition, subsidiary premises licences for other gambling activities may be issued. The normal limitations in respect of access by children and young persons will apply, although in relation to a premises licence for a track, children and young persons will be permitted to enter track areas where facilities for betting are provided on days when dog racing and/or horse racing takes place. This is subject to the rule that children and young persons may not enter any area where gaming machines (other than category D machines) are provided.

7.41 In principle there is no reason why multiple types of gambling should not co-exist on a track (with the exception of a casino or adult gaming centre), but authorities will want to think about how the third licensing objective is delivered by the co-location of premises. As with the granting of multiple licences in a single building, licensing authorities will need to ensure that entrances to each type of premises are distinct and that under-18s are excluded from gambling areas where they are not permitted to enter.

WHO CAN MAKE AN APPLICATION?

7.42 An application for a premises licence may only be made by persons (which includes companies or partnerships):

- who have the right to occupy the premises
- who have an operating licence which allows them to carry out the proposed activity, for example a bingo operating licence for a bingo premises, or have applied for an operating licence (the premises licence cannot be determined until an operating licence has been issued).

7.43 The exception to this is an applicant for a premises licence to allow a track to be used for betting, as these applicants are not required to hold an operating licence if they are merely providing space for other people to provide betting (and those other people hold valid betting operating licences). However, if a track owner is also acting as a betting operator or running pool betting he will have to have the relevant type of operating licence.

7.44 An applicant for a premises licence must be 18 or over.

7.45 An application must be made to the relevant licensing authority in the form prescribed in regulations laid down by the Secretary of State or Scottish Ministers.

7.46 The application must be accompanied by:

- the prescribed fee
- the prescribed documents (that is a plan of the premises; the plan needs to be to scale, however, a specific scale has not been prescribed).

7.47 The Secretary of State and Scottish Ministers have made regulations[17] requiring the applicant to publish notice of his application and to notify responsible authorities and other persons about the application. This will allow representations to be made.

7.48 Notice must be given in three ways:

- a notice placed outside the premises for 28 consecutive days in a place where it can be read conveniently
- in a newspaper or newsletter of local relevance, on at least one occasion within ten days of the application being made

- to all responsible authorities within seven days of the application being made (the Commission is one of these responsible authorities).

[17] SI No 459: The Gambling Act 2005 (Premises Licences and Provisional Statements) Regulations 2007 SI No 196: The Gambling Act 2005 (Premises Licences and Provisional Statements) (Scotland) Regulations 2007

REPRESENTATIONS

7.49 In dealing with an application, licensing authorities are obliged to consider representations from two categories of person, referred to in the Act as 'responsible authorities' and 'interested parties'. Please see part 8 of this Guidance for more information on these categories.

7.50 It would be helpful if licensing authorities provide advice in a form that is readily accessible (for example, on their websites) about how representations can be made.

7.51 When considering a representation, the first thing the licensing authority should determine is whether the representation has been made by a responsible authority or interested party. This is very important as only representations from these two categories of person are admissible. If the representation has not been made by a responsible authority or interested party it is inadmissible.

7.52 Licensing authorities should be aware that their decision on this initial issue could be subject to legal challenge in the courts. There is no right of appeal under the Act against a licensing authority's determination that representations are not admissible.

7.53 After determining whether the representation has come from a responsible authority or interested party, and consequently whether it is admissible or inadmissible, the authority must then determine its relevance. The only representations that are likely to be relevant are those that relate to the licensing objectives, or that raise issues under the Licensing Authority Statement of Policy, or the Commission's Guidance or Codes of Practice (that is those matters mentioned in section 153 of the Act).

7.54 The Secretary of State and Scottish Ministers have made regulations under section 160 of the Act concerning notice of application. These require applicants for premises licences to give notice of their application to the responsible authorities. They also stipulate that applicants publish notice of their application in a local newspaper and display it on the premises for the benefit of interested parties. These provisions apply, with one or two necessary modifications, in relation to applications for provisional statements and some ancillary applications that can be made in relation to a premises licence. Responsible authorities will have a legitimate interest in the development of the premises, because of the functions that they will need to carry out in relation to them. But licensing authorities must take care to ensure that the concerns that responsible authorities may have in relation to their own functions are not taken into account if they are not relevant to the application for a premises licence under the Act. Thus, the following examples of possible representations would not likely be relevant:

- that there are already too many gambling premises in the locality (although it may be relevant if it points, as a result, to rising problems in crime, disorder, underage gambling or problem gambling)
- that the proposed premises are likely to be a fire risk
- that the location of the premises is likely to lead to traffic congestion; or that the premises will cause crowds of people to congregate in one area, which will be noisy and create a nuisance.

This list is by no means exhaustive, and each case must be decided on the facts.

7.55 It should be noted that, unlike the Licensing Act, the Gambling Act specifically does not include as a licensing objective the prevention of public nuisance. Any nuisance associated with gambling premises should be tackled under other relevant laws.

7.56 Linked to this is the question of what is a 'frivolous' or 'vexatious' representation. This is a question of fact, and authorities are advised to seek help from their legal advisers in interpreting these phrases. Representations that could be considered 'frivolous' or 'vexatious' are more likely to come from interested parties. However, matters that licensing authorities will want to look at are likely to include:

- who is making the representation, and whether there is a history of making representations that are not relevant
- whether it raises a 'relevant' issue
- whether it raises issues specifically to do with the premises that are the subject of the application.

7.57 The Commission does not routinely make representations on premises licence applications. However, the fact that the Commission has not made a representation on a particular premises licence application should not be taken as indicating the Commission's approval of that application. Exceptionally, where an application for a premises licence, or the operation of a current premises licence, raises matters of wider or national significance, the Commission will consider making representations or requesting a review.

MAKING A DECISION

7.58 As explained earlier in this Guidance, in relation to premises licences, the licensing authority's primary obligation under section 153(1) is to permit the use of premises in so far as it thinks that to do so is:

(a) in accordance with relevant codes of practice issued by the Commission
(b) in accordance with guidance issued by the Commission
(c) reasonably consistent with the licensing objectives (subject to (a) and (b) above), and
(d) in accordance with the Licensing Authority Statement of Policy published by the authority (subject to (a) to (c) above).

7.59 For guidance as to the meaning and effect of section 153, see paragraph 5.5 above. If, in a particular case, a licensing authority were to decide either to grant or to refuse a premises licence in circumstances in which the Commission's Guidance indicated the opposite conclusion the decision could be challenged on appeal or by judicial review.

RELATIONSHIP BETWEEN PLANNING PERMISSION, BUILDING REGULATIONS AND GRANTING OF A PREMISES LICENCE

7.60 In determining applications the licensing authority has a duty to take into consideration all relevant matters and not to take into consideration any irrelevant matters, in effect those not related to gambling and the licensing objectives. One example of an irrelevant matter would be the likelihood of the applicant obtaining planning permission or building regulations approval for their proposal. Licensing authorities should bear in mind that a premises licence, once it comes into effect, authorises premises to be used for gambling. Accordingly, a licence to use premises for gambling should only be issued in relation to premises that the licensing authority can be satisfied are going to be ready to be used for gambling in the reasonably near future, consistent with the scale of building or alterations required before the premises are brought into use. This is why the Act allows a potential operator to apply for a provisional statement if construction of the premises is not yet complete, or they need alteration, or he does not yet have a right to occupy them. See part 11 of this Guidance for more information about provisional statements.

7.61 As the Court has held in a 2008 case[18], operators can apply for a premises licence in respect of premises which have still to be constructed or altered, and licensing authorities are required to determine any such applications on their merits. Such cases should be considered in a two stage process; first, licensing authorities must decide whether, as a matter of substance after applying the principles in section 153 of the Act, the premises ought to be permitted to be used for gambling; second, in deciding whether or not to grant the application a licensing authority will need to consider if appropriate conditions can be put in place to cater for the situation that the premises are not yet in the state in which they ought to be before gambling takes place. An authority is entitled to decide that it is appropriate to grant a licence subject to conditions, but it is not obliged to grant such a licence.

7.62 For example, where the operator has still to undertake final fitting out of the premises but can give a reasonably accurate statement as to when the necessary works will be completed, it may be sufficient to simply issue the licence with a future effective date, as is possible under the Regulations[19]. The application form allows the applicant to suggest a commencement date and the notice of grant allows the licensing authority to insert a date indicating when the premises licence comes into effect. In other cases, it may be appropriate to issue the licence subject to a condition that trading in reliance on it shall not commence until the premises have been completed in all respects in accordance with the scale plans that accompanied the licence application. If changes to the pre-grant plans are made, then parties who have made representations should be able to comment on the changes made. See part 9 of this Guidance for more information about licence conditions.

7.63 If the plans submitted at the time of the application for a premises licence are changed in any material respect during the fitting out of the premises after the grant of the licence, then the applicant will be in breach of the licence. If the applicant wishes to change the proposed plans after grant then, in order to avoid breaching the licence, it will be necessary for the applicant to either make a fresh application under section 159 or seek an amendment to a detail of the licence under section 187 of the Act. If there are substantive changes to the plans then this may render the premises different to those for which the licence was granted. In such a case, variation of the licence under section 187 is not possible. For this reason, and while this is a matter of judgement for the licensing authority, we consider it would be more appropriate in the case of any material post grant change, for the applicant to make a fresh application under section 159 to preserve the rights of interested parties and responsible authorities to make representations in respect of the application.

7.64 The local authority will need to be satisfied in any individual case that the completed works comply with the original, or changed, plan attached to the premises licence. Depending upon circumstances, we consider that this could be achieved either through physical inspection of the premises or written confirmation from the applicant or surveyor that the condition has been satisfied.

7.65 Requiring the building to be complete before trading commences would ensure that the authority could, if considered necessary, inspect it fully, as could other responsible authorities with inspection rights under Part 15 of the Act. Inspection will allow authorities to check that gambling facilities comply with all necessary legal requirements. For example, category C and D machines in a licensed family entertainment centre must be situated so that people under 18 do not have access to the category C machines. The physical location of higher stake gaming machines in premises to which children have access will be an important part of this, and inspection will allow the authority to check that the layout complies with the operator's proposals and the legal requirements.

7.66 If faced with an application in respect of uncompleted premises which it appears are not going to be ready to be used for gambling for a considerable period of time, a licensing authority ought to consider whether, applying the two stage approach advocated in paragraph 7.61 above, it should grant a licence or whether the circumstances are more appropriate to a provisional statement application. For example, the latter would be the case if there was significant potential for circumstances to change before the premises opens for business. In such cases, the provisional statement route would ensure that the limited rights of responsible authorities and interested parties to make representations about matters arising from such changes of circumstance are protected. Licensing authorities may choose to discuss with individual applicants which route is appropriate, to avoid them having to pay a fee for, say, an application that the authority did not think was grantable, when it seems likely at an early stage that a provisional statement might be the better option.

7.67 When dealing with a premises licence application for finished buildings, the licensing authority should not take into account whether those buildings have to comply with the necessary planning or building consents. Nor should fire or health and safety risks be taken into account. Those matters should be dealt with under relevant planning control, building and other regulations, and must not form part of the consideration for the premises licence. Section 210 of the Act prevents licensing authorities taking into account the likelihood of the proposal by the applicant obtaining planning or building consent when considering a premises licence application. Equally, the grant of a gambling premises licence does not prejudice or prevent any action that may be appropriate under the law relating to planning or building.

---

[18] *The Queen (on the application of) Betting Shop Services Limited v Southend-on-Sea Borough Council* [2008] EWHC 105 (Admin)

[19] SI 2007/459 Premises Licensing and Provisional Statements Regulations SI No 196: The Gambling Act 2005 (Premises Licences and Provisional Statements) (Scotland) Regulations 2007.

PART 8: RESPONSIBLE AUTHORITIES AND INTERESTED PARTIES – DEFINITIONS

8.1 The Act sets out two categories of organisations and individuals ('responsible authorities' and 'interested parties') that may feature in applications for and reviews of premises licences.

RESPONSIBLE AUTHORITIES

8.2 Responsible authorities are public bodies that must be notified of applications and that are entitled to make representations to the licensing authority in relation to applications for, and in relation to, premises licences. All representations made by responsible authorities are likely to be relevant representations if they relate to the licensing objectives.

8.3 Section 157 of the Act identifies the bodies that are to be treated as responsible authorities. They are:

(a) a licensing authority in England and Wales in whose area the premises is wholly or partly situated

(b) the Gambling Commission

(c) the chief officer of police or chief constable for the area in which the premises is wholly or partially situated

(d) the fire and rescue authority for the same area

(e)

 (i) in England and Wales, the local planning authority, or

 (ii) in Scotland, the planning authority

(f) the relevant authority as defined in section 6 of the Fire (Scotland) Act 2005

(g) an authority which has functions in relation to pollution to the environment or harm to human health

(h) anybody, designated in writing by the licensing authority as competent to advise about the protection of children from harm

(i) HM Revenue & Customs

(j) any other person prescribed in regulations by the Secretary of State.

8.4 Section 211(4) of the Act provides that in relation to a vessel, but no other premises, responsible authorities also include navigation authorities, within the meaning of section 221(1) of the Water Resources Act 1991, that have statutory functions in relation to the waters where the vessel is usually moored or berthed, or any waters where it is proposed to be navigated at a time when it is used for licensable activities. This would include:

(a) the Environment Agency
(b) the British Waterways Board
(c) the Secretary of State (Note: in practice, the Secretary of State for Transport who acts through the Maritime and Coastguard Agency).

For applications in Scotland, the reference to the Environment Agency can reasonably be taken to refer to the Scottish Environment Protection Agency.

8.5 The Act contains a similar list of responsible authorities to that contained in the Licensing Act 2003, despite the lack of the corresponding licensing objective of public safety, whilst the Licensing (Scotland) Act 2005 does not define responsible authorities at all. The result the Act aims to achieve through the inclusion of a wide range of responsible authorities is one where all relevant regulatory bodies and organisations are made aware of applications for gambling premises licences or other permissions. In many instances comments that responsible authorities make are relevant to the licensing authority's determination.

8.6 Equally, in some cases, representations may not relate to matters that lead to the licensing authority refusing a premises licence. However, a policy of wide dissemination of applications allows responsible authorities to take action under their own legislation and enforcement powers, even if there is no direct role for them in the gambling licence process.

8.7 The Act contains no obligation on responsible authorities to respond to applications for premises licences if they do not wish to do so. The Commission would not wish to second guess what is for the licensing authority to decide and so will not normally comment on an application unless it has particular observations to make about the operator. If no response is received from the Commission, licensing authorities should not assume we have any view (whether supportive or otherwise) on the merits of the particular premises licence application. Licensing authorities will, of course, be aware of the Commission's views on generic issues as set out in this Guidance.

8.8 Licensing authorities are required to set out, in their policy statement made under section 349, their approach to their functions under the Act. One of those functions is to determine who will be competent to advise them about the protection of children from harm. Regulations[20] made by the Secretary of State and Scottish Ministers require licensing authorities to set out their approach in a separate section of the Licensing Authority Statement of Policy.

8.9 In many licensing authority areas, the body recognised by the licensing authority as competent in this regard is the local Safeguarding Children Board in England and Wales, or the Child Protection Committee in Scotland.

8.10 The Secretary of State and Scottish Ministers may prescribe other responsible authorities by means of regulations. For example, Scottish Ministers have prescribed that a responsible authority under the Act includes an enforcing authority under the Fire (Scotland) Act 2005[21].

---

20 SI No 636: The Gambling Act 2005 (Licensing Authority Policy Statement) (England and Wales) Regulations 2006 SSI No 154: The Gambling Act 2005 (Licensing Authority Policy Statement) (Scotland) Regulations 2006

21 SSI No 475: The Fire (Scotland) Act 2005 (Consequential Modifications and Savings) Order 2006

INTERESTED PARTIES

8.11 Section 158 of the Act defines interested parties. To accept a representation from an interested party, the licensing authority must take the view that the person:

(a) lives sufficiently close to the premises to be likely to be affected by the authorised activities
(b) has business interests that might be affected by the authorised activities
(c) represents persons in either of these two groups.

8.12 Interested parties can be people who are democratically elected such as councillors and MPs. Where appropriate, this will include county, parish and town councillors. Other than these persons, authorities should require written evidence that a person 'represents' someone who either lives sufficiently close to the premises to be likely to be affected by the authorised activities and/or business interests that might be affected by the authorised activities. A letter from one of these persons requesting the representation is sufficient.

8.13 The following gives further advice on how licensing authorities can determine whether someone is an interested party.

People living close to the premises

8.14 The approach taken by licensing authorities in determining who is an interested party is also a function that should be dealt with in their Licensing Authority Statement of Policy. As with responsible authorities, regulation[22] requires this information to be in a separate section of the Licensing Authority Statement of Policy.

8.15 The factors that licensing authorities should take into account when determining what 'sufficiently close to the premises' means (in each case) might include:

- the size of the premises
- the nature of the premises
- the distance of the premises from the location of the person making the representation
- the potential impact of the premises (number of customers, routes likely to be taken by those visiting the establishment)
- the circumstances of the complainant. This is not the personal characteristics of the complainant, but the interests of the complainant which may be relevant to the distance from the premises.

For example, it could be reasonable for an authority to conclude that 'sufficiently close to be likely to be affected' could have a different meaning for (a) a private resident, (b) a residential school for children with truanting problems, and (c) a residential hostel for vulnerable adults.

22 SI No 636: The Gambling Act 2005 (Licensing Authority Policy Statement) (England and Wales) Regulations 2006 SSI No 154: The Gambling Act 2005 (Licensing Authority Policy Statement) (Scotland) Regulations 2006

The nature and scope of business interests that could be affected

8.16 It could be argued that any gambling business could be affected by another gambling business expanding into any part of Great Britain. But that is unlikely to be enough to satisfy the test of being 'a person with business interests that might be affected by the premises' under consideration. For example, an operator in a particular sector (be it casino, bingo, betting, etc) should not be able to lodge representations on every application put in by a rival operator anywhere in the country, simply because they are in competition within the same gambling sector. The licensing authority should be satisfied that the relevant business is likely to be affected. In this respect, licensing authorities should bear in mind that the 'demand test' from the 1963 and 1968 Acts is not continued in the 2005 Act. Factors that are likely to be relevant include:

- the size of the premises
- the 'catchment' area of the premises (that is, how far people travel to visit the premises)

- whether the person making the representation has business interests in that catchment area that might be affected.

People representing those in the above categories

8.17 Licensing authorities should include guidance in their Licensing Authority Statement of Policy on whom they consider comes within this category. For example, it should include democratically elected representatives such as local councillors and MPs, and could include bodies such as trade associations and trade unions, and residents' and tenants' associations. In other cases licensing authorities should satisfy themselves on a case by case basis, and possibly request written evidence, that a person does represent interested parties. For example, a school head or governor might act in representing the interests of pupils or parents and a community group might represent vulnerable people living near to the proposed premises.

8.18 Licensing authorities will need to have regard to anything an interested party says about their status to make representations.

PART 9: PREMISES LICENCE CONDITIONS

9.1 The Act provides that conditions may be attached to licences in a number of ways:

- they may attach automatically, having been set out on the face of the Act
- they may attach through regulations made by the Secretary of State or Scottish Ministers
- they may be attached to operating and personal licences by the Commission
- they may be attached to premises licences by licensing authorities.

9.2 Conditions may sometimes be general in nature (in effect they attach to all licences or all licences of a particular class) or they may be specific to a particular licence.

9.3 Conditions on premises licences should relate only to gambling, as considered appropriate in the light of the principles to be applied by licensing authorities under section 153. Accordingly, if the Commission's Licence Conditions and Codes of Practice or other legislation places particular responsibilities or restrictions on an employer or the operator of premises, it is not necessary or appropriate to impose the same or similar duties in conditions on a premises licence issued in accordance with the Gambling Act. Similarly, where other legislation confers powers on inspection and enforcement agencies in relation to separate activities or concerns, the Gambling Act does not affect the continued use of such powers; for example, the powers of an environmental health officer in respect of statutory nuisance under the Environmental Protection Act 1990.

CONDITIONS AND AUTHORISATIONS THAT ATTACH AUTOMATICALLY TO PREMISES LICENCES BY VIRTUE OF PROVISIONS ON THE FACE OF THE ACT

9.4 The following paragraphs discuss the sections of the Act that provide for conditions to be attached automatically to premises licences, or for authorisations to be granted automatically. The Secretary of State may make regulations requiring these conditions to be set out on the premises licence. There is no discretion to decide not to include them, or to modify them.

SECTION 172

9.5 Section 172 provides for premises licences to permit a specified number of gaming machines of particular categories in each type of gambling premises. These permissions are set out in detail in part 16 of this Guidance.

SECTION 173

9.6 Section 173 authorises the holder of a casino premises licence or a betting premises licence to make facilities available for betting on virtual events. This is separate from betting on virtual events by means of a gaming machine. It is intended to cover facilities such as Portman Park, which is currently provided in some betting shops. These are person-to-person transactions, involving virtual images that are not displayed on a machine.

SECTION 174

9.7 Section 174 authorises the holder of a casino premises licence for a small or large casino to make available the following types of gambling in addition to casino games (see part 17 of this document for details of the casino games authorised by the Commission):
- equal chance games
- betting (but not in pre-2005 Act casinos with grandfather rights and only with a betting operating licence)
- bingo (but only in large casinos and only with a bingo operating licence).

9.8 For the purposes of the Act, equal chance games are ones which do not involve playing or staking against a bank and in which the chances are equally favourable to all players. Licensing authorities must not restrict the equal chance gaming available (for example by prohibiting mah-jong) nor permit casino games that have not been approved by the Commission (see part 17 of this document).

SECTION 176

9.9 Section 176 requires the Commission to issue at least one code of practice about access to casino premises for children and young persons. In particular, the code must:
- specify steps that the premises licence holder must take to ensure that under-18s do not enter casino premises, including ensuring that each entrance to the casino is supervised by at least one person ('the supervisor') who is responsible for compliance with the code of practice
- require that, unless the supervisor is certain that a person seeking admittance is an adult, evidence of age must be provided by those seeking to enter the casino or gambling area.

9.10 Section 176 also makes it a condition of the premises licence that the licensee must comply with the code of practice issued under this section. The relevant code of practice has been issued by the Commission and is available along with other codes and conditions on the Commission's website. Licensing authorities should note that the requirement under this section to identify a 'supervisor' is separate from any other condition that may be attached relating to 'door supervision' more generally.

SECTION 177

9.11 Section 177 attaches a condition to casino premises licences and bingo premises licences that prohibits the licensee from:
- giving credit in connection with the gambling taking place on the premises
- participating in, arranging, permitting or knowingly facilitating the giving of credit in connection with the gambling on the premises.

9.12 However, section 177 does not prevent the licensee from contracting a third party to install cash dispensers (ATMs) on their premises, which may accept both credit and debit cards. Such an arrangement is subject to requirements that the premises licence holder has no other commercial connection in relation to gambling with the provider of the ATMs (aside from the agreement to site the machines), does not profit from the arrangement, and does not make any payment in connection with the machines. All premises licences also include a mandatory condition which requires that any ATM made available for use on the premises must be located in a place that requires any customer who wishes to use it to cease gambling in order to do so.

9.13 This part of the Guidance deals only with the issue of credit in the context of section 177. The provision of credit by gambling operators and the use of credit cards are separate matters that are managed through operating licence conditions and codes of practice issued by the Commission.

SECTION 178

9.14 Section 178 relates to door supervision at premises licensed for gambling. It defines a condition for door supervision as one requiring someone to be responsible for 'guarding the premises against unauthorised access or occupation, against outbreaks of disorder or against damage'. Where a licensing authority chooses to attach such a condition, section 178 also provides that if the person carrying out such duties is required to be licensed under the Private Security Industries Act 2001 (PSIA), then that requirement must be treated as though it were a condition of the premises licence. There is, however, an exemption from the PSIA licensing requirement for in-house employees working as door supervisors at casino and bingo premises, details of which can be found in part 33 of this Guidance.

SECTION 179

9.15 Section 179 provides that a track betting premises licence may not authorise pool betting to take place other than in respect of dog or horse racing and only where the acceptance of bets is by the holder of the betting premises licence, or in accordance with arrangements made by him. In the case of dog racing, this preserves the existing arrangements at dog tracks where the totalisator is operated by or on behalf of the occupier of the track. In the case of horse racing, pool betting can only be made available at racetracks by the Betfred following their purchase of the Tote.

SECTION 180

9.16 Section 180 applies to all betting premises licences, except a licence in respect of a dog track. It provides that pool betting on dog racing, for example in a high street betting office, may be offered only in accordance with arrangements made with the occupier of the dog track at which the racing is taking place. This means that the dog track operator controls whether or not pool betting on the races that take place at his track is available outside the track, in other premises where betting is permitted. If he does wish this to happen, he can make arrangements with other betting operating licence holders for them to offer pool betting on the events he holds. This is a transitional measure and it will lapse on 31 December 2012, unless it is repealed before then.

SECTION 182

9.17 Section 182 applies only to betting premises licences in relation to tracks. It requires the licensee to ensure that children and young persons are excluded from any area in which facilities for betting are provided and from any area where a gaming machine (other than a category D gaming machine) is situated. The exception to this, for betting areas only, is on race days (that is, on those days when racing occurs or is expected to take place) at a dog racing track or horse racing track. On race days, on those tracks only, under-18s may have access to betting areas, but licensing authorities should note that this exception does not affect the prohibition on betting by children and young persons.

SECTION 183

9.18 Section 183 applies to all premises licences. It attaches the condition to the premises licence that facilities for gambling must not be provided on Christmas Day. In this context, 'Christmas Day' covers the period of 00.01 hours on 25 December until 00.00 hours on 26 December.

CONDITIONS ATTACHED THROUGH REGULATIONS MADE BY THE SECRETARY OF STATE OR SCOTTISH MINISTERS

9.19 These conditions fall into two categories. The first are mandatory conditions under section 167 of the Act, which provides for the Secretary of State or Scottish Ministers to set out in regulations conditions that must be attached to premises licences.
9.20 The second category relates to default conditions which may be imposed under section 168 of the Act, which provides for the Secretary of State or Scottish Ministers to make conditions that apply, unless the licensing authority decides to exclude them using its powers under section 169.
9.21 Mandatory and default conditions apply to all premises licences.
9.22 The Secretary of State and Scottish Ministers have made regulations setting mandatory and default conditions to be attached to premises licences[23].
9.23 Licensing authorities should note that mandatory conditions are set by the Secretary of State and Scottish Ministers with the intention that no further regulation in relation to that matter is required. Therefore, it is extremely unlikely that licensing authorities will need to impose individual conditions that will lead to a more restrictive regime in relation to matters that are already dealt with by mandatory conditions. Licensing authorities should only consider doing so where there are regulatory concerns of an exceptional nature, and any additional licence conditions must relate to the licensing objectives.
9.24 Licensing authorities have more flexibility in relation to default conditions, and may exclude a default condition and substitute it with one that is either more or less restrictive. Licensing authorities should note, however, that default conditions are intended to be the basic industry norm. While, given the requirements of section 153, the Commission would expect default conditions to be excluded and replaced with less rigid conditions on a relatively regular basis, licensing authorities should ensure that they have clear regulatory reasons for excluding default conditions and replacing them with more restrictive ones.
9.25 In addition to the following conditions the regulations also specify conditions that relate to each category of premises licence. Details of these can be found in parts 17, 18, 19, 20, 21 and 22 of this Guidance.

[23] SI no 1409: The Gambling Act 2005 (Mandatory and Default Conditions) (England and Wales) Regulations 2007 SSI no 266: The Gambling Act 2005 (Mandatory and Default Conditions) (Scotland) Regulations 2007

MANDATORY CONDITIONS ATTACHING TO ALL PREMISES LICENCES

9.26 The following mandatory conditions apply to all premises licences:

- the summary of the terms and conditions of the premises licence issued by the licensing authority must be displayed in a prominent place on the premises
- the layout of the premises must be maintained in accordance with the plan that forms part of the premises licence
- neither National Lottery products nor tickets in a private or customer lottery may be sold on the premises.

There are also mandatory conditions attaching to each type of premises licence controlling access between premises. There can be no direct access between one

premises licensed under the Gambling Act 2005 and another premises licensed under the Gambling Act 2005, with the following exceptions:
- between licensed betting premises
- between bingo premises and alcohol-licensed premises/clubs with a club gaming or club machine permit/FECs and tracks
- between tracks and alcohol-licensed premises/clubs with a club gaming or club machine permit/FECs/betting premises and bingo premises
- between FECs and alcohol-licensed premises/bingo halls/clubs with club gaming or club machine permit and tracks.

CONDITIONS THAT MAY BE IMPOSED ON OR EXCLUDED FROM PREMISES LICENCES BY LICENSING AUTHORITIES

9.27 Section 169 of the Act gives licensing authorities:
- the ability to exclude from premises licences any default conditions that have been imposed under section 168
- the power to impose conditions on the premises licences that they issue.

9.28 Licensing authorities should bear in mind their duty to act in accordance with the principles set out in section 153. Since they must aim to permit the use of premises for gambling, they should not attach conditions that limit the use of premises for gambling, except where that is necessary as a result of the requirement to act:
- in accordance with this Guidance, the Commission's codes of practice or their own Licensing Authority Statement of Policy
- in a way that is reasonably consistent with the licensing objectives.

Conversely, licensing authorities should not turn down applications for premises licences where relevant objections can be dealt with through the use of conditions.

9.29 Conditions imposed by the licensing authority must be proportionate to the circumstances which they are seeking to address. In particular, licensing authorities should ensure that the premises licence conditions are:
- relevant to the need to make the proposed building suitable as a gambling facility
- directly related to the premises and the type of licence applied for
- fairly and reasonably related to the scale and type of premises
- reasonable in all other respects.

9.30 It is the Commission's view that the conditions necessary for the general good conduct of gambling premises are those set as default and mandatory conditions by the Secretary of State and Scottish Ministers. Therefore, a pool of additional conditions published by the Commission is not necessary. Where there are specific, evidenced risks or problems associated with a particular locality, or specific premises or class of premises, a licensing authority will be able to attach individual conditions to address this. That will be a matter for them in the light of local circumstances.

9.31 Licensing authorities should take decisions on individual conditions on a case-by-case basis, although this will be against the background of any general policy set out in this Guidance or their own Licensing Authority Statement of Policy.

CONDITIONS THAT MAY NOT BE ATTACHED TO PREMISES LICENCES BY LICENSING AUTHORITIES

9.32 The Act sets out certain matters that may not be the subject of conditions, as follows:
- section 169(4) prohibits an authority from imposing a condition on a premises licence which makes it impossible to comply with an operating licence condition
- section 172(10) provides that conditions may not relate to gaming machine categories, numbers, or method of operation

- section 170 provides that membership of a club or body cannot be required by attaching a condition to a premises licence (the Act specifically removes the membership requirement for casino and bingo clubs and this provision prevents it being reinstated)
- section 171 prevents an authority imposing conditions in relation to stakes, fees, winnings or prizes.

PART 10: REVIEW OF PREMISES LICENCE BY LICENSING AUTHORITY

10.1 A premises licence may be reviewed by the licensing authority of its own volition or following the receipt of an application for a review, which is essentially a request by a third party to the licensing authority to review a particular licence. Licensing authorities should note that reviews cannot be delegated to an officer of the licensing authority – the lowest level of delegation permitted is to a licensing sub-committee.

INITIATION OF REVIEW BY LICENSING AUTHORITY

10.2 Section 200 of the Act provides that licensing authorities may initiate a review in relation to a particular class of premises licence or in relation to particular premises. Officers may be involved in the initial investigations of complaints leading to a review, or may try informal mediation or dispute resolution techniques prior to a full-scale review being conducted. Licensing authorities may wish to consider in their scheme of delegation who initiates reviews, and whether a 'filter' system should be implemented to prevent unwarranted reviews from being conducted.

10.3 In relation to a class of premises, the licensing authority may review the use made of premises and, in particular, the arrangements that premises licence holders have made to comply with licence conditions. In relation to these general reviews, the authority would most likely be acting as a result of specific concerns or complaints about particular types of premises, which would cause them to want, for example, to look at the default conditions that apply to that category of licence.

10.4 In relation to particular premises, the licensing authority may review any matter connected with the use made of the premises if it has reason to suspect that premises licence conditions are not being observed, or for any other reason (such as a complaint from a third party) which gives them cause to believe that a review may be appropriate.

10.5 A formal review would normally be at the end of a process of ensuring compliance by the operator. If the operator does not meet the requirements then, after a formal review, the licensing authority may impose additional conditions or revoke the licence.

10.6 The licensing authority must give notice in writing to the licence holder that it intends to undertake a review, and must also publish notice of its intention to carry out the review. Regulations[24] for reviews state that the notice should be published in a local newspaper at least once in the ten working days following the day on which the application to review was made to the authority, or should be published on the licensing authority's website and remain there for 28 consecutive days starting from eight days after the application to review was made. In addition, regulations state that the notice must also be displayed outside the premises itself, and remain there for the 28 days referred to above.

[24] SI No 2258: The Gambling Act 2005 (Premises Licences) (Review) Regulations 2007 SSI No 394: The Gambling Act 2005 (Review of Premises Licences) (Scotland) Regulations 2007

APPLICATION FOR A REVIEW

10.7 Section 197 of the Act provides that an application for review may be made by a responsible authority or an interested party (see part 8 of this Guidance). Such applications must be submitted to the licensing authority in the prescribed form and state the reasons why a review is being requested, together with any supporting information and documents. The regulations referred to in paragraph 10.6 require the applicant for a review to provide notice in writing of their application to the premises licence holder, and to all responsible authorities, within seven days of making their application. Failure to do this will mean that the application process is halted until notice is received by all parties.

10.8 Representations must be made within 28 days, commencing seven days after the date on which the application was received. During these seven days the licensing authority is required to publish notice of the application, as per the process set out in the regulations referred to in paragraph 10.6.

DECISION WHETHER TO GRANT AN APPLICATION FOR A REVIEW

10.9 The decision to grant a review must not, and if properly managed will not, amount to pre-judging the outcome of a review.

10.10 Section 199 provides that an authority must grant an application for a review, unless it decides to reject the application under section 198 of the Act. An application for a review may be (but need not be) rejected if the licensing authority thinks that the grounds on which the review is sought:

(a) are not relevant to the principles that must be applied by the licensing authority in accordance with section 153 — so, if the application raises issues that are not relevant to the Commission Guidance/codes of practice, the Licensing Authority Statement of Policy, or the licensing objectives, then the licensing authority may reject it. In addition, if the application raises general objections to gambling as an activity, that is likely to be irrelevant to the principles in section 153, given that a licensing authority is required to permit the use of premises for gambling insofar as it thinks that permission is in accordance with the matters set out in that section. Examples that are likely to be irrelevant include demand for gambling premises, issues relating to planning, public safety, and traffic congestion

(b) are frivolous

(c) are vexatious

(d) 'will certainly not' cause the authority to revoke or suspend a licence or to remove, amend or attach conditions on the premises licence

(e) are substantially the same as the grounds cited in a previous application relating to the same premises. Here the licensing authority must take into account how much time has passed since the earlier application in reaching a judgement about whether it is reasonable to rely on this as a reason not to review the licence

(f) are substantially the same as representations made at the time the application for a premises licence was considered. As with sub-section (e) the licensing authority will need to take into account the period of time that has passed since the representations were made, but the underlying requirement is that the licensing authority should not review the licence on the basis of the same arguments considered on the grant of the premises licence.

10.11 Most applications for a review are likely to be the result of a public complaint or a complaint from the police. It is important that licensing authorities process applications for review without delay, so that both the review applicant and the premises operator know where they stand.

CARRYING OUT A REVIEW

10.12 Having given notice of their intention to initiate a review or having determined that a review initiated by a third party should go ahead, section 201 of the Act requires the licensing authority to carry out the review as soon as possible after the 28 day period for making representations has passed.

10.13 The purpose of the review will be to determine whether the licensing authority should take any action in relation to the licence. If action is justified, the options are to:

(a) add, remove or amend a licence condition imposed by the licensing authority
(b) exclude a default condition imposed by the Secretary of State or Scottish Ministers (relating to, for example, opening hours) or remove or amend such an exclusion
(c) suspend the premises licence for a period not exceeding three months
(d) revoke the premises licence.

In determining what action, if any, should be taken following a review, the licensing authority must have regard to the principles set out in section 153 of the Act, as well as any relevant representations.

10.14 In particular, the licensing authority may take action as described above on the grounds that a premises licence holder has not provided facilities for gambling at the premises. This is to prevent people from applying for licences in a speculative manner without intending to use them.

10.15 The licensing authority must hold a hearing, unless the applicant and any person who has made representations that have not been withdrawn (that are not vexatious, frivolous or irrelevant) consent to the review being conducted without one.

10.16 Once the review has been completed, the licensing authority must, as soon as possible, notify its decision to:

- the licence holder
- the applicant for review (if any)
- the Commission
- any person who made representations
- the chief officer of police or chief constable
- HM Revenue and Customs.

10.17 Please see part 12 of this Guidance for information on rights of appeal.

PART 11: PROVISIONAL STATEMENTS

11.1 Section 204 of the Act provides for a person to make an application to the licensing authority for a provisional statement in respect of premises that he or she:

- expects to be constructed
- expects to be altered
- expects to acquire a right to occupy.

11.2 Developers may wish to apply for provisional statements before they enter into a contract to buy or lease property or land to judge whether a development is worth taking forward in light of the need to obtain a premises licence. It is also possible for an application for a provisional statement to be made for premises that already have a premises licence (either for a different type of gambling or the same type).

11.3 Applicants for premises licences must fulfil certain criteria. They must hold or have applied for an operating licence from the Commission (except in the case of a track), and they must have the right to occupy the premises in respect of which their premises licence application is made. However, these restrictions do not apply in relation to an application for a provisional statement. In circumstances in which an applicant has also applied to the Commission for an operating licence, the Commission will not be able to comment on whether the application is likely to be granted; and the licensing authority should not speculate on or otherwise take into account the likelihood of an operating licence being granted in its consideration of the application for a provisional statement.

11.4 An application for a provisional statement must be accompanied by plans and the prescribed fee. Licensing authorities in England and Wales set their own provisional statement fees up to a pre-determined maximum, whereas licensing authorities in Scotland must use the provisional statement fees set by Scottish ministers[25].

11.5 Subject to any necessary modifications (and the differences already set out in paragraph 11.3), the process for considering an application for a provisional statement is the same as that for a premises licence application. The applicant is obliged to give notice of the application in the same way as applying for a premises licence. Responsible authorities and interested parties may make representations and there are rights of appeal. Please note that the provisions in the Act relating to provisional statements are not the same as those in the Licensing Act 2003 or the references to provisional licences in the Licensing (Scotland) Act 2005.

11.6 Once the premises are constructed, altered, or acquired the holder of a provisional statement can put in an application for the necessary premises licence. A premises licence application for a premises where the applicant already holds a provisional statement for that premises attracts a lower application fee. Section 205 of the Act sets out rules on how the authority must treat this application. Licensing authorities should note that, in the absence of a requirement that an applicant for a provisional licence must have the right to occupy the premises, there may be more than one valid provisional statement in respect of the same premises.

11.7 If a provisional statement has been granted, the licensing authority is constrained in the matters it can consider when an application for a premises licence is made subsequently in relation to the same premises.

11.8 No further representations from relevant authorities or interested parties can be taken into account unless they concern matters which could not have been addressed at the provisional statement stage, or they reflect a change in the applicant's circumstances.

11.9 In addition, the authority may refuse the premises licence (or grant it on terms different to those attached to the provisional statement) only by reference to matters:

- which could not have been raised by way of representations at the provisional licence stage
- which, in the authority's opinion, reflect a change in the operator's circumstances
- where the premises has not been constructed in accordance with the plan and information submitted with the provisional statement application. This must be a substantial change to the plan and licensing authorities should discuss any concerns they have with the applicant before making a decision.

11.10 Section 210 of the Act (which applies to premises licences and provisional statements) makes it clear that a licensing authority must not have regard to whether or not a proposal by the applicant is likely to be permitted in accordance with planning or building law.

[25] SI no 479: The Gambling (Premises Licence Fees) (England and Wales) Regulations 2005 SSI no 197: The Gambling (Premises Licence Fees) (Scotland) Regulations 2005

PART 12: RIGHTS OF APPEAL AND JUDICIAL REVIEW

APPEALS

12.1 This part deals only with appeals relating to premises licensing and other decisions by licensing authorities. Please note that any appeals against decisions made by the Commission (on operating and personal licences) must be made to the First-tier Tribunal (Gambling) (which replaces the Gambling Appeals Tribunal – for more information see the Commission's website, www.gamblingcommission.gov.uk).

12.2 This part is divided into sections dealing with premises licences and permits to provide facilities for gambling. Licensing authorities will be aware that their decisions may be subject to judicial review.

PREMISES LICENCES

12.3 The avenues of appeal against decisions by a licensing authority are set out in sections 206 to 209 of the Act.

WHO MAY APPEAL?

12.4 If an application under Part 8 of the Act is rejected, only the applicant may appeal.
12.5 If an application under Part 8 of the Act is granted, the applicant and a person who made representations may appeal. It does not automatically follow that the person who made the representations will be the appellant. It could be the licensee who is appealing, because he or she considers conditions attached to the licence too onerous. Similar arrangements will apply in appeals against a decision not to take action following a review, and in relation to the grant of temporary use notices. A licensing authority may choose who it has as its witnesses.
12.6 If a licensing authority takes action or determines to take no action (which may include revocation or suspension of the licence, or the removal or addition of licence conditions) after a review of a licence (see part 10 of this Guidance), any of the following may appeal:

- the licence holder
- a person who made representations in relation to the review
- where relevant, the person who applied for the review
- the Commission.

12.7 Where a licensing authority makes a decision in relation to the transfer of a premises licence, which may involve amending licence conditions, the licence holder and the applicant for transfer have a right of appeal.
12.8 Notice of an appeal must be given within 21 days of notice of the decision being received by the appellant. During that period, and until any appeal that has been brought has been finally determined, a determination or other action by the licensing authority under Part 8 of the Act will not have effect unless the authority so directs (see section 208 of the Act).

GIVING REASONS FOR DECISIONS

12.9 In many cases, it is a requirement of the Act that a licensing authority gives clear and comprehensive reasons for a rejection of an application, and it is good practice for reasons to be given in relation to all decisions (see section 165, which is also applied in relation to other applications under Part 8 of the Act). A failure to give reasons may compel a person to appeal, and may suggest that the licensing authority did not make its decision with regard to all the information that it should have had regard to, and in line with its obligation under section 153 (regardless of the decision that was reached). It is particularly important that reasons should address the extent to which the decision has been made with regard to the Licensing Authority's Statement of Policy and the Commission's Guidance. Reasons for decisions should be made available to all of the parties of any process which might give rise to an appeal under the terms of the Act.

APPELLATE AUTHORITIES

12.10 In England and Wales an appeal against a decision of a licensing authority has to be made to the magistrates' court for the local justice area in which the premises concerned are situated. In Scotland, the appeal is made to the local sheriff court in the sheriffdom in which the premises are situated.

HOW TO APPEAL

12.11 An appeal has to be commenced by the giving of a notice of appeal by the appellant to the local magistrates' court/sheriff within a period of 21 days, beginning with the day on which the appellant was notified by the licensing authority of the decision being appealed.
12.12 It should be noted that unless he is the appellant, the licence holder or a person who has made an application for:

- a licence
- the transfer or reinstatement of a licence
- a provisional statement

is a respondent in any appeal, in addition to the licensing authority.

WHAT THE COURT MAY TAKE INTO ACCOUNT

12.13 In hearing an appeal against a decision made by a licensing authority, the magistrates' court or sheriff will have regard to the Licensing Authority Statement of Policy, guidance issued by the Commission, relevant codes of practice issued by the Commission and the licensing objectives (after hearing the evidence).

OUTCOME OF APPEALS

12.14 On determining an appeal, the court or sheriff may:

- dismiss the appeal
- substitute the decision appealed against with any other decision that could have been made by the licensing authority
- remit the case to the licensing authority to dispose of the appeal in accordance with the direction of the court/sheriff.

12.15 The court or sheriff may make such order as to costs as they think fit, but will be required to bear in mind guidance and legislation about the awarding of costs against a public body.
12.16 The court or sheriff, on hearing any appeal, may therefore review the merits of the decision on the facts and consider points of law or address both.
12.17 There is a further right of appeal from the magistrates' court or sheriff to the High Court in England and Wales or the Court of Session in Scotland.

IMPLEMENTING THE DETERMINATION OF THE COURTS

12.18 As soon as the decision of the magistrates' court or sheriff has been notified to all parties, licensing authorities should not delay its implementation. Any attempt to delay such implementation will bring the appeal system into disrepute. Standing orders should therefore be put in place that, on receipt of the decision, necessary action should be taken forthwith unless ordered by the court/sheriff or a higher court to suspend such action (for example, as a result of an on-going judicial review).

PROVISIONAL STATEMENTS

12.19 A provisional statement can be refused on exactly the same grounds as a premises licence (the provisions of Part 8 of the Act which apply to a premises licence apply, by virtue of section 204(2), to a provisional statement). The applicant may appeal against the rejection of an application for a provisional statement under section 206(1); and a person who made representations or the applicant may appeal against the grant of an application.

PERMITS

12.20 The process of appeals in respect of permits is different to that for premises licences and is set out in the relevant Schedules of the Act.

SCHEDULE 10 – FAMILY ENTERTAINMENT CENTRE GAMING MACHINE PERMITS

12.21 Schedule 10, paragraph 22 sets out the processes for appeals for family entertainment centre gaming machine permits. The applicant or holder of a permit may appeal if the licensing authority has rejected an application (for a permit or renewal), given notice that the premises are not being used as an FEC or stated that the holder is incapable of carrying out an FEC business by reason of mental or physical incapacity. The appeal, which must be made within 21 days of receipt of a notice of the decision, must be made to the local magistrates' court, or sheriff court in Scotland.

12.22 In considering an appeal, the court will take into account any statement prepared by the licensing authority which sets out the principles that it applied in making its decision. This statement may specify particular matters for consideration in determining the suitability of the applicant and may include such matters as the authority thinks fit in determining the suitability of an applicant for a lower stake gambling establishment. In addition, the court will take into account the following factors:

- the authority's duty to have regard to the Commission's Guidance and to what extent this duty was discharged
- to what extent, if any, the local authority had regard to the Act's licensing objectives.

12.23 On an appeal, the magistrates' court or sheriff may take the following action: dismiss the appeal, substitute any decision that the licensing authority could have made, restore a permit, or remit it back to the authority to decide in accordance with a determination of the court, and make an order for costs. It should be noted that if the decision is remitted to the authority, the same rights of appeal will apply as for the original decision.

SCHEDULE 11 (PARTS 4 AND 5) – SMALL SOCIETY LOTTERIES

12.24 Schedule 11, paragraph 51 sets out the processes for appeals for small society lotteries. A society may appeal if the local authority in England and Wales (the Act states that local authorities register societies to run lotteries rather than licensing authorities) or the licensing board in Scotland has refused an application for registration or revoked their registered status. The appeal must be made to the local magistrates' court, or sheriff in Scotland, within 21 days of the decision being notified to the society.

12.25 In considering an appeal, the magistrates' court or sheriff may uphold the licensing authority's decision, reverse it, or make any other order. It should be noted that, if the decision is remitted to the authority, the same rights of appeal will apply as for the original decision. In addition, the court will take account of any of the following factors:

- the authority's duty to have regard to Commission Guidance and to what extent this duty has been discharged
- to what extent, if any, the authority had regard to the Act's licensing objectives.

SCHEDULE 12 – CLUB GAMING PERMITS AND CLUB MACHINE PERMITS

12.26 Schedule 12, paragraph 25 sets out the process of appeal for club gaming permits and club machine permits. If the authority rejects an application for the issue or renewal of a permit the applicant may appeal. The holder of a permit may appeal if the permit is cancelled. A person who made an objection to the grant of the permit, or made representations in relation to the cancellation of a permit, may appeal against a grant or refusal to cancel respectively. The appeal must be made to the local magistrates' court, or sheriff in Scotland, within 21 days of the appellant receiving information about the decision.

12.27 The authority may only refuse an application on one or more of the following grounds:

(a)

(i) for a club gaming permit: the applicant is not a members' club/miners' welfare institute

(ii) for a club machine permit: the applicant is not a members' club, miners' welfare institute or commercial club
(b) the premises are used by children or young persons
(c) an offence or a breach of a condition of the permit has been committed by an applicant
(d) a permit held by an applicant has been cancelled during the last ten years
(e) an objection has been made by the Commission or local chief officer of police.

12.28 The authority may only cancel a permit on one of the following grounds:
(a) if the premises are used wholly or mainly by children or young persons
(b) if an offence or breach of condition of the permit has been committed in the course of gaming activities.

12.29 Therefore, in considering an appeal the court will determine whether any of these statutory grounds apply. In addition, the court will take into account the following factors:
(a) any objections made by the Commission or local police chief
(b) the authority's duty to have regard to both the Commission's Guidance and the Act's licensing objectives, and to what extent these duties were discharged.

12.30 In England and Wales only, there is a fast track procedure for holders of a club premises certificate under section 72 of the Licensing Act 2003. In these circumstances the Commission and police do not have to be consulted and therefore the authority will not receive any objections. The permit must be granted unless:
(a) the applicant is established or conducted wholly or mainly for the purposes of the provision of facilities for gaming, other than gaming of a prescribed kind
(b) the applicant is established or conducted wholly or mainly for the purposes of the provision of facilities for gaming of a prescribed kind and also provides facilities for gaming of another kind
(c) a club gaming permit or club machine permit issued to the applicant has been cancelled during the period of ten years ending with the date of the application.

There is no equivalent provision for clubs in Scotland under the Licensing (Scotland) Act 2005.

12.31 On an appeal, the magistrates' court or sheriff may take the following action: dismiss the appeal, substitute any decision that the local authority could have made, restore a permit, remit it back to the authority to decide in accordance with a determination of the court, and make an order for costs. It should be noted that if the decision is remitted to the authority, the same rights of appeal will apply as for the original.

SCHEDULE 13 – LICENSED PREMISES GAMING MACHINE PERMITS

12.32 Schedule 13, paragraph 21 sets out the appeal process for licensed premises gaming machine permits. This applies to England and Wales only. The Scottish Government has set regulations[26] on permits for alcohol-licensed premises in Scotland. An applicant for a permit may appeal if the application is rejected. The holder of a permit may appeal if he is permitted fewer or a different category of machines than applied for, or if the licensing authority gives a notice which cancels or varies the entitlements of the permit. The application has to be made to the local magistrates' court within 21 days of the notice of the decision being received.

12.33 In considering an appeal, the court will take into account the authority's duty to have regard to the Commission's Guidance, the licensing objectives and such other matters as they think relevant, and to what extent these duties were discharged.

12.34 On an appeal, the magistrates' court may take the following action: dismiss the appeal, substitute any decision that the local authority could have made, restore a permit, remit it back to the authority to decide in accordance with a decision of the court, and make an order for costs. It should be noted that if the decision is remitted to the authority, the same rights of appeal will apply as for the original.

[26] SSI no 505: The Licensed Premises Gaming Machine Permits (Scotland) Regulations 2007

SCHEDULE 14 – PRIZE GAMING PERMITS

12.35 Schedule 14, paragraph 22 sets out the appeal process for prize gaming permits. If the licensing authority rejects an application for the issue or renewal of a permit, the applicant may appeal to the magistrates' court or sheriff within 21 days of the decision.

12.36 In considering an appeal, the court will look at any statement of principles prepared by the licensing authority which sets out specific matters for consideration in determining the suitability of an applicant to hold a permit. In addition, the court will take account of the following factors:

- the authority's duty to have regard to Commission Guidance and to what extent this duty has been discharged
- to what extent, if any, the local authority had regard to the licensing objectives.

12.37 On an appeal, the magistrates' court or sheriff may take the following action: dismiss the appeal, substitute any decision that the local authority could have made, remit it back to the authority to decide in accordance with a determination of the court, and make an order for costs. It should be noted that if the decision is remitted to the authority, the same rights of appeal will apply as for the original.

TEMPORARY USE NOTICES

12.38 Appeals in relation to temporary use notices are dealt with in section 226 of the Act. This section grants the right to appeal to the magistrates' court (or sheriff's court in Scotland) to both the applicant and any person entitled to receive a copy of the notice (that is the Commission, local chief of police and HM Revenue & Customs). Appeals must be made within 21 days of receiving notice of the licensing authority's decision. If the appeal is against the decision of the authority not to issue a counter-notice, then the person giving notice must be joined with the licensing authority as a respondent in the case.

12.39 The magistrates' court or sheriff may take the following action: dismiss the appeal, direct the authority to take specified action, remit it back to the authority to decide in accordance with a decision of the court, and make an order for costs. It should be noted that if the decision is remitted to the authority, the same rights of appeal will apply as for the original decision.

12.40 There is no stay of proceedings in relation to temporary use notices (as there are in relation to applications under Part 8 of the Act). However, the time limits are such that the Commission would expect proceedings on an appeal to be heard before the temporary use notice would otherwise take effect.

JUDICIAL REVIEW

12.41 Any party to a decision may apply for judicial review if they believe that the decision taken by the licensing authority is:

- illegal – that is beyond the powers available to the licensing authority
- subject to procedural impropriety or unfairness – which is a failure in the process of reaching the decision, such as not observing the 'rules of natural justice'
- irrational – where a decision is so unreasonable that no sensible person could have reached it (in effect 'perverse' or 'Wednesbury' unreasonable).

12.42 For an application to succeed, the application must show that:

- the applicant has sufficient standing to make that claim
- the actions of the reviewed licensing authority give grounds for review.

But the remedy is a discretionary one and the Court may decline judicial review if, for example, it considers that the applicant has an alternative remedy which is more appropriate to pursue, such as a right of appeal, or has a private law claim against the defendant.

12.43 The applicant can ask the Court to grant a number of orders. A mandatory order compels the reviewed body to do something; a prohibitory order compels it to refrain from doing something; a 'declaration' sets out the court's view on the legality of a particular course of action; and a quashing order nullifies a decision and remits it for reconsideration. In addition, the applicant can seek an injunction (interdict in Scotland) which is, in practice, similar to a mandatory or a prohibitory order.

PART 13: INFORMATION EXCHANGE

INFORMATION EXCHANGE BETWEEN THE COMMISSION AND LICENSING AUTHORITIES

13.1 Under section 26 of the Act, the Commission has a duty to advise the Secretary of State about the incidence of gambling and the manner in which it is conducted. Section 29 of the Act entitles the Commission to seek information from licensing authorities, and places an obligation on authorities to comply with its information requests, providing the information is:

- part of a register
- in the licensing authority's possession in connection with a provision of the Act.

13.2 The purpose of information exchange is not only to fulfil the requirements under the Act, but also to enable both the Commission and the licensing authorities to carry out work related to their regulatory functions in a risk-based manner, using the best available information. It is essential for both parties to establish a framework by which information and knowledge can be exchanged between all parties to the regime.

13.3 In keeping with the Hampton principles and the Regulators Compliance Code, we seek to avoid the risk of duplication or over-regulation and maximise the efficient use of our resources. To accomplish this, we recognise the need to share information about our inspections and compliance activities regularly.

INFORMATION REQUIREMENTS

Premises data

13.4 It is important for the Commission to maintain registers of the various forms of gambling activity to understand the national picture and for licensing authorities to gain a regional and in some cases a national picture. It is therefore important to share this information with each other to effectively work together.

13.5 The Act requires licensing authorities to maintain data on premises licences and to provide this information to the Commission. As part of the application process for a premises licence, applicants will forward notice of the application to the Commission, and licensing authorities subsequently notify the Commission of the outcome of each application - whether it is granted or refused.

13.6 Licensing authorities are also required to inform the Commission of any changes to licences, such as variations, transfers, lapses, reinstatements, and surrenders. It is important that the Commission's national data set for premises licences is accurate as it is used for conducting national compliance work. Accuracy also reduces the need for the Commission to request ad hoc information on particular premises from the licensing authorities, which is time consuming and resource intensive.

13.7 The Commission may make observations and representations on the suitability of the applicant for a premises licence or any other aspect of the application. In such cases, the Commission and licensing authority will discuss matters pertaining to the application, and the appropriate action to take. An example of how this works in practice is provided in the shaded box below. More information on the Commission's role as a responsible authority and its involvement in individual premises licence applications is given in part 8 of this guidance.

Returns

13.8 All licensing authorities are required to submit returns to the Commission on an annual basis, providing information on licensed gambling activity and details of compliance and regulatory work undertaken. This includes providing details of permits and notices issued, premises inspections conducted, and reasons for and outcome of licence reviews.

13.9 The Annual Return is now included in the Single Data List that has been issued by DCLG. The List is a catalogue of all the datasets that local government must submit to central government and such organizations as the Commission in a given year.

13.10 The returns are an important source of information and can assist both the Commission and the licensing authorities in improving their work as risk based regulators. The returns provide the Commission with details of licensing authority compliance and regulatory work. Both parties will work together to ensure that the returns process is managed effectively.

13.11 Licensing authorities will ensure that the information on the returns is accurate and sent to the Commission within agreed timescales. In return, the Commission will ensure that information derived from the returns is analysed and reported to licensing authorities to help identify risks and prioritise work.

13.12 The Commission will minimise the burden imposed on licensing authorities by keeping its data requests to an absolute minimum. The data requirements will be kept under review to ensure that any data requests have a clear and valid regulatory purpose.

List of data requirements

Licensing function	Event requiring information to be sent to Commission
Premises licences and provisional statements	Licensing authority has granted / rejected an application for a premises licence or provisional statement
	A premises licence has lapsed
	Licensing authority has granted or rejected an application to reinstate a premises licence
	Licensing authority has granted or rejected an application to transfer or vary a premises licence
	A review of a premises licence has been completed and a decision made
	A hearing is to be held where the Commission has made a representation
	A premises licence has been surrendered/revoked
Club permits	A club permit application has been granted/ rejected
Small society lottery registration	Licensing authority registers a society to operate small lotteries
	Licensing authority cancels a society's registration to operate small lotteries
	Where a society has exceeded the permitted proceeds for small lotteries
Issue of permits and temporary permissions	LA Returns

Other information requirements

13.13 Small society lotteries: licensing authorities are responsible for registering societies to run small society lotteries and are required to record details of the society on a register and to notify both the applicant and the Commission of this registration.
13.14 Club Gaming Permits: When a licensing authority either grants or rejects an application for a Club Gaming Permit they are required to inform both the applicant and the Commission.
13.15 There are a range of statutory application forms and notices that licensing authorities are required to use as part of their gambling licensing responsibilities. A summary list of these can be found in Appendix E. The forms and notices can be downloaded from the Department for Culture, Media and Sport website (www.culture-.gov.uk).

INFORMATION ON SPECIFIC OPERATORS THAT THE COMMISSION MAKES AVAILABLE TO LICENSING AUTHORITIES

13.16 The Commission is required under section 106 of the Act to maintain a register of operating licence holders and make this publicly available. Where a licensing authority needs to check if an applicant for a premises licence holds an operating licence, verification can be found on the edited register on the Commission's website. An unedited register can be made available upon request.
13.17 The Commission will inform the relevant licensing authorities of any changes to operating licences that may have an impact on the status of related premises licences.

PART 14: TEMPORARY USE NOTICES

14.1 Part 9 of the Act sets out the position in relation to temporary use notices. These allow the use of premises for gambling where there is no premises licence but where a gambling operator wishes to use the premises temporarily for providing facilities for gambling. Premises that might be suitable for a temporary use notice include hotels, conference centres and sporting venues.
14.2 A temporary use notice may only be granted to a person or company holding a relevant operating licence, in effect a non-remote casino operating licence.
14.3 Regulations[27] state that temporary use notices may only be used to permit the provision of facilities for equal chance gaming, where the gaming is intended to produce a single overall winner. However, the facilities may not be provided in circumstances where any person participating in the gaming does so by means of a gaming machine. Equal chance gaming is gaming which does not involve playing or staking against a bank and gives equally favourable chances to all participants. Examples of equal chance gaming include games such as backgammon, mah-jong, rummy, kalooki, dominoes, cribbage, bingo and poker.

27 SI No 3157: The Gambling Act 2005 (Temporary Use Notices) Regulations 2007

MEANING OF PREMISES

14.4 Section 218 of the Act refers to a 'set of premises' and provides that a set of premises is the subject of a temporary use notice if 'any part' of the premises is the subject of a notice. This is not the same as the references to 'premises' in Part 8 of the Act. The reference to 'a set of premises' prevents one large premises from having a temporary use notice in effect for more than 21 days in a year by giving notification in relation to different parts of the premises and re-setting the clock.
14.5 The meaning of 'premises' in Part 8 of the Act is discussed in part 7 of this Guidance. As with 'premises', the definition of 'a set of premises' will be a question of

fact in the particular circumstances of each notice that is given. In the Act 'premises' is defined as including 'any place'. In considering whether a place falls within the definition of 'a set of premises', licensing authorities will need to look at, amongst other things, the ownership/occupation and control of the premises. A large exhibition centre, for example, would be likely to come within the definition as it is properly one premises, and should not be granted a temporary use notice for 21 days in respect of each of its exhibition halls. But in relation to other covered areas, such as shopping centres, the licensing authority will need to consider whether different units are in fact different 'sets of premises', given that they may be occupied and controlled by different people. This is a new permission and licensing authorities should be ready to object to notices where it appears that their effect would be to permit regular gambling in a place that could be described as one set of premises.

PROCEDURE FOR GIVING NOTICE

14.6 The holder of an operating licence must give notice to the licensing authority in whose area the premises are situated. The Secretary of State has prescribed the form of the notice which must specify information including:

- the type of gaming to be carried on
- the premises where it will take place
- the dates and times the gaming will take place
- any periods during the previous 12 months that a temporary use notice has had effect for the same premises
- the date on which the notice is given
- the nature of the event itself.

MAXIMUM PERIOD

14.7 The same set of premises may not be the subject of a temporary use notice for more than 21 days in any 12-month period, but may be the subject of several notices provided that the total does not exceed 21 days.

14.8 If the premises have been the subject of one or more temporary notice for more than a total of 21 days in the past 12 months, the licensing authority must issue a counter-notice that has the effect of stopping the temporary notice coming into effect. Failure to comply with the counter-notice will be an offence. A licensing authority may issue a counter-notice which limits the number of days that the temporary use notice comes into effect, bringing it within the 21-day limit. Such counter-notices require consultation with the applicant to ensure that the restrictions they impose do not result in an unworkable event.

14.9 As notices may be given by different operators in respect of the same premises, the licensing authority will always need to check whether a counter-notice is appropriate.

14.10 A notice may not be given in respect of a vehicle. A notice may be given in respect of a vessel, but only if it is a passenger vessel or a vessel that is situated at a fixed place. A vessel at a fixed place would include a structure on water that is not intended to be able to move (such as an oil rig, or an artificially constructed island in the middle of a lake). Licensing authorities should note that a notice could only be given in respect of a vessel that is moored permanently at a place (ie it could move but it does not) if it is a passenger vessel.

GIVING NOTICE

14.11 A temporary use notice must be lodged with the licensing authority not less than three months and one day before the day on which the gambling event will begin. The application, fee[28] and counter-notices are specified by the Secretary of State and Scottish Ministers. The application must be copied to:

- the Commission
- the police
- HM Commissioners for Revenue and Customs
- if applicable, any other licensing authority in whose area the premises are situated.

14.12 The person who is giving the temporary use notice must ensure that the notice and the copies are with the recipients within seven days of the date of the notice. Where the premises are situated in the area covered by more than one authority, the person giving notice must send the notice to one authority and copy to the other(s). Licensing authorities will have to work closely together in such circumstances to ensure that the 21-day maximum period for temporary notices is not breached.

14.13 When the licensing authority receives a notice, it must send a written acknowledgement as soon as is reasonably practicable. A written acknowledgement may include one sent by electronic mail.

---

[28] The fee for England and Wales can be set by each licensing authority to a maximum of £500, as set out in regulations SI 2007/3157. The fee for Scottish licensing boards has been set as £350 by regulations SSI 2007/461

OBJECTIONS

14.14 The licensing authority and the other bodies to which the notice is copied should consider whether they wish to give notice of objection. In considering whether to do so, they must have regard to the licensing objectives and if they consider that the gambling should not take place, or only with modifications, they must give a notice of objection to the person who gave the temporary use notice. Such a notice must be copied to the licensing authority (unless it is given by the licensing authority). The notice of objection and the copy to the licensing authority must be given within 14 days of the date of the temporary use notice. An objection may be withdrawn by giving written notice to those to whom the notice of objection was sent and copied.

14.15 Licensing authorities should note the timescales set out in the Act. The need to give a notice of objection within 14 days of the date of the temporary use notice means that there must be procedures to ensure that such notices are considered without delay so that, where appropriate, the opportunity to lodge an objection is not missed.

14.16 If objections are received, the licensing authority must hold a hearing to listen to representations from the person who gave the temporary use notice, all the objectors and any person who was entitled to receive a copy of the notice. If all the participants agree that a hearing is unnecessary, it may be dispensed with.

14.17 Those who raise objections may offer modifications to the notice that will alleviate their concerns. Remedies may include a reduction in the number of days when gambling occurs or a restriction on the type of gambling permitted. If the modifications are accepted by the applicant, a new temporary notice must be prepared and the original notice withdrawn. The three-month time limit and fee will not apply to the new notice. The person who made the original objection and proposed the modification may not object to the new notice, but others to whom it is copied may object. If there are no new objections, there will be no need for a hearing.

14.18 If the licensing authority, after a hearing has taken place or has been dispensed with, considers that the temporary use notice should not have effect, it must issue a counter-notice which may:

- prevent the temporary use notice from taking effect
- limit the activities that are permitted
- limit the time period of the gambling
- allow the activity to take place subject to a specified condition.

14.19 The principles that the authority must apply in issuing a counter-notice are the same as those in determining premises licence applications. In particular, the licensing authority should aim to permit the provision of facilities for gambling under a temporary use notice subject to its view as to whether to do so accords with a Commission code, this Guidance, or the Licensing Authority Statement of Policy and is reasonably consistent with the licensing objectives.

14.20 If the licensing authority gives a counter-notice, it must give reasons for doing so and must copy the counter-notice to all those who received copies of the temporary use notice.

14.21 If the licensing authority decides not to issue a counter-notice, the temporary use notice will take effect. The authority must give notice of its decision to the person who gave the temporary use notice and others to whom it was copied.

APPEALS

14.22 An appeal against the licensing authority's decision may be made by the applicant, or any person entitled to receive a copy of the temporary use notice, to the magistrates' court or sheriff's court within 21 days of receiving notice of the authority's decision. There is a further right of appeal to the High Court or Court of Session on a point of law.

ENDORSEMENT OF THE NOTICE

14.23 If no objections are made within 14 days of the date of the notice, the licensing authority must endorse the notice as valid and return it to the person who gave it. If the endorsed copy of the notice is lost, stolen or damaged, the person who gave the notice may request a new endorsed copy from the licensing authority, subject to the payment of a fee.

14.24 Section 228 sets a time limit of six weeks for the completion of all proceedings on a temporary use notice. This includes considering whether to give a notice of objection; holding a hearing, if that is necessary; and giving a counter-notice or notice dismissing the objections.

14.25 The person who gives a temporary notice may notify the authority that it is withdrawn at any time up to and during the time it has effect. In those circumstances the notice will have no effect, and any unlapsed period of time will not count towards the 21-day maximum for a temporary use notice having effect on the premises.

DISPLAYING THE NOTICE

14.26 While the gambling is taking place, a copy of the temporary use notice must be displayed prominently on the premises. It is an offence not to produce the notice endorsed by the authority when requested to do so by a constable, an officer of HM Revenue and Customs, an enforcement officer, or an authorised local authority officer.

PART 15: OCCASIONAL USE NOTICES

15.1 Section 39 of the Act provides that where there is betting on a track on eight days or less in a calendar year, betting may be permitted by an occasional use notice without the need for a full premises licence. Licensing authorities and track operators and occupiers should note that the processes set out in the Act for applying for an occasional use notice are different to those for temporary use notices.

15.2 While tracks are normally thought of as permanent racecourses, authorities should note that the meaning of 'track' in the Act covers not just horse racecourses or dog tracks, but also any other premises on any part of which a race or other sporting event takes place, or is intended to take place (section 353(1)). The Commission's Guidance relating to tracks is contained in part 20 of this document.

15.3 This means that land which has a number of uses, one of which fulfils the definition of track, can qualify for the occasional use notice provisions (for example agricultural land upon which a point-to-point meeting takes place). Land used temporarily as a track can qualify, provided races or sporting events take place or will take place there. The track need not be a permanent fixture.

15.4 The intention behind occasional use notices is to permit licensed betting operators (with appropriate permission from the Commission) to use tracks for short periods for conducting betting, where the event upon which the betting is to take place is of a temporary, infrequent nature. The occasional use notice dispenses with the need for a betting premises licence for the track in these circumstances.

15.5 The Commission is aware of some instances of the apparent misuse of OUNs, by the arrangement of a contrived sporting event at a premises solely in order to apply for an OUN and to permit betting on premises where it would not normally be allowed. We consulted on a new licence condition limiting the betting to bets on the outcomes of a race, competition or other sporting event taking place at the track in question whilst the OUN is in force. We decided that this would be too restrictive but are keeping the situation under review.[29] Further details on this topic can be found on the Commission's website .

15.6 Occasional use notices may not be relied upon for more than eight days in a calendar year. Note that the requirement relates to a calendar year (starting 1 January) and not to any period of 12 months. The Secretary of State has the power to increase or decrease the number of occasional use notices that are permitted, but there are currently no plans to use this power.

15.7 Licensing authorities should keep a record of the number of notices served in relation to each track.

PROCEDURE

15.8 A notice must be served by a person who is responsible for the administration of events on the track or by an occupier of the track. The notice must be served on the licensing authority and copied to the chief officer of police for the area in which the track is located. The notice must specify the day on which it has effect. Notices may be given in relation to consecutive days, so long as the overall limit of eight days is not exceeded in the calendar year.

15.9 Provided that the notice will not result in betting facilities being available for more than eight days in a calendar year, there is no provision for counter-notices or objections to be submitted.

15.10 The Act does not require the applicant or the local authority to notify the Commission that an occasional use notice has been given. However the Commission does require licensing authorities to submit returns showing how many occasional use notices were received during each quarter – more information on this can be found in part 13 of this Guidance document.

15.11 It should be noted that betting operators cannot provide gaming machines at tracks by virtue of an occasional use notice. Gaming machines may be made available by betting operators and this is reliant on a betting premises licence, which refers to a specific licensed area, but does not enable the operator to site gaming machines outside of that area.

PART 16: GAMING MACHINES

16.1 This part of the Guidance describes the categories of gaming machine and the number of such machines that may be permitted in each type of gambling premises as set out in the Act. Licensing authorities should note that the term 'gaming machine' now covers all machines on which people can gamble and the term has been preserved in the Act, because it is one that is readily understood by people.

16.2 Section 235 of the Act sets out the definition of a gaming machine. The definition is wider than those included in previous gaming legislation and covers all types of gambling activity that can take place on a machine, including betting on virtual events. However, the following should be noted:

- there remains a distinction between skill machines and gaming machines, in that skill machines are unregulated
- section 235 contains important exemptions for equipment that is not to be considered a gaming machine, even when gambling can be performed on it – for example, a home PC is not classed as a gaming machine, even though someone could access remote gambling facilities on a home PC.

16.3 Specific guidance on machines that are exempt from the definition laid out in the Act is set out later in this section of the Guidance, although licensing authorities should take legal advice or contact the Commission directly if they have concerns about the precise legal status of equipment being used on premises.

16.4 The Commission is responsible for licensing manufacturers and suppliers of gaming machines and advises operators to obtain machines from Commission-licensed suppliers. Similarly, permit holders and those applying for permits for clubs, alcohol-licensed premises or family entertainment centres will also be advised through Commission guidance to obtain gaming machines from Commission-licensed suppliers.

16.5 The Commission has set Gaming Machine Technical Standards relating to the way in which each category of machine will operate[30]. The Commission has also set out a testing strategy that details the testing arrangements for each category of machine[31]. The Commission has the power to test gaming machines, both before they are supplied and when in operation in premises, to ensure that they are operating as advertised.

16.6 If a licensing authority has concerns relating to the manufacture, supply or repair of gaming machines, or the manner in which they are operating, it should contact the Commission.

16.7 Section 172 of the Act prescribes the number and category of gaming machines that are permitted in each type of gambling premises licensed by authorities. Neither the Commission nor licensing authorities have the power to set different limits or further expand or restrict the categories of machine that are permitted (with the exception of alcohol-licensed premises holding gaming permits where authorities have discretion to specify the number of permitted gaming machines). In addition, limits are set separately in the Act for certain types of permit issued by authorities. Machine limits are summarised at Appendix A of this Guidance.

30 The Gaming Machine Technical Standards is available from www.gamblingcommission.gov.uk

31 The Gaming Machine testing strategy is available from www.gamblingcommission.gov.uk

CATEGORIES OF GAMING MACHINES[32]

16.8 Regulations define four categories of gaming machine (as per section 236 of the Act): categories A, B, C and D, with category B divided into a further five subcategories. The categories and sub-categories have been defined according to the maximum amount that can be paid for playing the machine and the maximum prize it can deliver. Please see Appendix B for a breakdown of machine categories and entitlements.

32 Category C and complex category D gaming machines stakes and prizes are currently under review. Once these have been confirmed the new stakes and prize limits will be incorporated into the Guidance as a codicil.

AGE RESTRICTIONS

16.9 There is a minimum age of 18 for all players for all category A, B and C machines, including category B3A gaming machines offering lottery games. However there is no minimum age for players of category D machines. The holder of any permit or premises licence has to comply with the codes of practice issued by the Commission on the location of and access to gaming machines by children and young persons, and the separation from category C and B machines where those are also located on the same premises.

MAXIMUM NUMBER OF MACHINES BY PREMISES TYPE

16.10 The maximum number of machines permitted, and in the case of casinos the ratios between tables and machines, is set out by premises type below, and is also summarised in Table 16.ii (note that this information includes premises with permit entitlements, as well as licensed premises).

Large casinos

16.11 Section 172(4) provides that large casinos must have at least one gaming table to qualify for gaming machines, and are permitted five machines (of category B, C or D) for each gaming table available for use (see paragraph 17.6). Large casinos therefore need 30 gaming tables available for use to qualify for the maximum 150 machines.

Small casinos

16.12 Section 172(5) provides that small casinos must have at least one gaming table to qualify for gaming machines, and are permitted two machines (of category B, C or D) for each gaming table available for use (see paragraph 17.6). Small casinos therefore need 40 gaming tables available for use to qualify for the maximum 80 machines.

Converted casinos (Schedule 18 of the Act (Part 7))

16.13 Unless an existing casino decides to apply for one of the new casino premises licences (and the application is granted), it will operate under the 2005 Act by virtue of preserved rights for existing casino operators. These casinos will retain the rights to gaming machines equivalent to their entitlements under previous legislation. That means they are permitted no more than 20 machines of category B to D (except B3A machines), or they may elect to have any number of category C or D machines instead (as was previously the case under section 32 of the 1968 Gaming Act[33]).There is no table-to-machine ratio in these casinos.

---

33 Commencement No 6 and Transitional Provisions Order SI 2006/3272 Schedule 4 paragraph 65(6)

Bingo premises

16.14 Section 172(7) provides that the holder of a bingo premises licence may make available for use a number of category B gaming machines not exceeding 20% of the total number of gaming machines which are available for use on the premises and any number of category C or D machines. Premises in existence before 13 July 2011 are entitled to make available eight category B gaming machines, or 20% of the total number of gaming machines, whichever is the greater. The holder of a bingo premises licence granted on or after 13 July 2011 but before 1 April 2014 is entitled to make available a maximum of eight category B gaming machines or 20% of the total number of gaming machines, whichever is the greater; from 1 April 2014 these premises will be entitled to 20% of the total number of gaming machines only. Regulations state that category B machines at bingo premises are restricted to sub-category B3 and B4 machines but not B3A machines.

Betting premises (including track operators with pool betting licence)

16.15 Section 172(8) provides that the holder of a betting premises licence may make available for use up to four gaming machines of category B, C or D. By virtue of section 172(9) this permission extends to tracks, but only those where the licence holder also holds a pool betting operating licence. Regulations state that category B machines at betting premises are restricted to sub-category B2, B3 and B4 machines, but not B3A machines.

Adult gaming centres

16.16 Section 172(1) provides that the holder of an adult gaming centre premises licence may make available for use a number of category B gaming machines not exceeding 20% of the total number of gaming machines which are available for use on the premises and any number of category C or D machines. Premises in existence before 13 July 2011 are entitled to make available four category B gaming machines, or 20% of the total number of gaming machines, whichever is the greater. The holder of an adult gaming centre premises licence granted on or after 13 July 2011 but before 1 April 2014 is entitled to make available a maximum of four category B gaming machines or 20% of the total number of gaming machines, whichever is the greater; from 1 April 2014 these premises will be entitled to 20% of the total number of gaming machines only. Regulations state that category B machines at adult gaming centres are restricted to sub-category B3 and B4 machines, but not B3A machines.

Family entertainment centres (with a Commission operating licence)

16.17 Section 172(2) provides that the holder of a family entertainment centre premises licence may make available for use any number of category C and D machines. However category C machines must be in a separate area to ensure the segregation and supervision of machines that may only be played by adults.

Family entertainment centres (with gaming machine permit)

16.18 Section 247 provides that the holder of a family entertainment centre gaming machine permit may make available for use any number of category D machines. As with the position on licences, there is no power for the licensing authority to set a limit on the number of machines under the permit.

Clubs

16.19 Sections 271 and 273 provide that the holder of a club gaming permit or club machine permit may make available for use on premises operated by a members' club, a commercial club or a miners' welfare institute, up to three machines of category B, C or D (that is, three machines in total). As well as clubs with alcohol licences, premises that are not licensed to sell alcohol, for example, works premises which operate membership-based social clubs, are able to apply for club machine permits or club gaming permits. They need to have 25 members, be permanently established and be for the benefit of the members. Regulations state that category B machines for club machine permits are restricted to sub- category B3A and/or B4 machines, depending on the class of club. Commercial clubs are restricted to B4 machines only whereas members' clubs and miners' welfare institutes may site sub-category B3A and/or B4 machines. CORCA, the trade association representing the majority of members' clubs, entered into a voluntary agreement to site only one B3A machine as part of the allowance of three machines in each of their clubs. CORCA is responsible for ensuring that its 11 member associations and their clubs abide by the agreement.

Pubs and other premises with a qualifying on-premises alcohol licence (or equivalent in Scotland)

16.20 Section 282 provides that certain persons are automatically entitled to make gaming machines available for use by virtue of holding an alcohol licence. Specifically, these are the on-premises alcohol licence holders (or holders of the relevant Scottish licence) for premises which contain a bar at which alcohol is served, but without a requirement that alcohol is served only with food.

16.21 There is an automatic entitlement to two gaming machines of category C or D, subject to the licence holder notifying the licensing authority, paying the prescribed fee and complying with any relevant code of practice issued by the Commission. If the person ceases to be the holder of the on-premises alcohol licence for the premises, the automatic entitlement to the two gaming machines also ceases. In order to retain the entitlement to gaming machines, whoever applies for the new premises alcohol licence would also need to apply under section 282(2), notifying the licensing authority of their intention to make the gaming machines available for use and paying the prescribed fee.

16.22 In addition, in accordance with section 283, an application may be made for a licensed premises gaming machines permit, which allows for further category C or D machines to be made available in alcohol-licensed premises. There is no limit in the Act to the number of additional machines that may be authorised. Note that this is a total figure and is not in addition to the two machines which can be sited automatically. This will be a matter for the licensing authority to determine in each case, and specify on the permit.

Travelling fairs

16.23 Sections 286 and 287 provide that any number of category D machines may be made available for use at travelling fairs, subject to a requirement that the facilities for gambling (including but not confined to gaming machines) amount to no more than an ancillary amusement at the fair. There is no application or notification requirement, but licensing authorities will want to satisfy themselves from time to time that the gambling offered by virtue of these sections is taking place at a travelling fair within the definition contained in section 286. Travelling fairs may be adequately controlled through bye-laws and therefore no additional regulation through the Act is imposed.

Amusement with prizes machines in non-amusement premises

16.24 Permits for amusement with prizes gaming machines (AWPs) granted under section 34 of the 1968 Act in respect of non-amusement premises (such as, chip shops, taxi offices, corner tearooms), are valid only until 31 July 2009. AWPs are no longer permitted in non-amusement premises.

The meaning of 'available for use'

16.25 The offence in section 242 of the Act committed by a person who does not hold an operating licence or other permission covering gaming machines and where no other exemption applies, is that of making a gaming machine 'available for use'. However, the Act does not define what 'available for use' means here. In this section we aim to assist licensing authorities by providing guidance on the meaning of 'available for use'.

16.26 The Commission considers that a gaming machine is 'available for use' if a person can play it. It follows that more than the permitted number of machines may be physically located on a premises, provided the operator has a system in place that ensures no more than the permitted number are 'available for use' at any one time. The operator must control this system. If there is more than one player position, that is two people can play a gaming machine simultaneously, then the machine counts as two machines[34].

16.27 An example of an appropriate system may be a situation where the power supply for machines of a certain category is controlled by the operator (and is not accessible to the player) so that one machine must be unplugged before another machine can be played. An example of an inappropriate system would be where an additional machine was located on premises and there was a spare socket which a player could plug the machine into at will, allowing play on more than the permitted number of machines.

16.28 If an operator does wish to put more than the permitted number of machines in a public area, the onus will be on the operator to demonstrate that no more than the permitted number of machines are 'available for use' at any one time.

16.29 A machine that can operate at more than one category, which is operating at a lower category, does not contribute to the number of machines 'available for use' at a higher category until it switches to that category. However, the operator must also have a system in place for these machines which ensures no more than the permitted number are 'available for use' at any one time.

16.30 The Commission permits systems in which a number of machines network so that the player can select which game and category they play at, but which adhere to any restrictions on the number of machines at a certain category.

---

[34] SI No 2289: The Gaming Machine (Single Apparatus) Regulations 2007

MACHINES OTHER THAN GAMING MACHINES IN GAMBLING PREMISES

Automated roulette

16.31 There are two types of automated casino equipment that are excluded from the definition of a gaming machine established by the Act. The first type is those linked to a live game of chance, for example, roulette. These enable the player to gamble on a live game as it happens, without actually being seated at the table, sometimes referred to as 'electronic roulette'. These are not regulated as gaming machines but as live gaming and there is no limit on the number of items of such equipment. The second type is a machine that plays a live game but is fully automated, that is, it operates without any human intervention. For example, a roulette wheel that is electrically or mechanically operated with an air blower to propel the ball around the wheel. Again, these are not regulated as gaming machines, although casinos are bound by controls on the specification and number of player positions using such equipment. The Act requires that equipment used to play a game of chance, for example, cards, dice and roulette wheels is 'real' and not 'virtual' if it is not to be classed as a gaming machine.

Bet receipt terminals

16.32 Section 235(2)(c) provides that a machine is not a gaming machine by reason only of the fact that it is designed or adapted for use to bet on future real events. Some betting premises may make available for use machines that accept bets on live events, such as a sporting event, as a substitute for placing a bet over the counter. These 'betting machines' are not gaming machines and therefore neither count towards the maximum permitted number of gaming machines, nor have to comply with any stake or prize limits. Such betting machines merely replicate and automate the process that can be conducted in person, and therefore do not require regulation as gaming machines.

16.33 However, a machine made available to take bets on virtual races (that is, images generated by computer to resemble races or other events) is classified as a gaming machine and does, therefore, count towards the maximum permitted number of gaming machines. Accordingly, it must meet the relevant category limitations for the premises.

16.34 Section 181 of the Act contains an express power for licensing authorities to restrict the number of betting machines, their nature and the circumstances in which they are made available, by attaching a licence condition to a betting premises licence or to a casino premises licence (where betting is permitted in the casino). When considering whether to impose a condition to restrict the number of betting machines in these premises, the licensing authority, amongst other things, should take into account the size of the premises, the number of counter positions available for person-to-person transactions, and the ability of employees to monitor the use of the machines by vulnerable people. The authority should also bear in mind that the mandatory conditions set by the Secretary of State for large and small casinos already set a maximum of 40 player positions in relation to betting machines.

Skill games

16.35 The Act does not cover machines that give prizes as a result of the application of pure skill by players. A skill with prizes machine is one on which the winning of a prize is determined only by the player's skill – any element of chance imparted by the action of the machine would cause it to be a gaming machine. An example of a skill game would be trivia game machines, popular in pubs and clubs, which require the player to answer general knowledge questions to win cash prizes. Other examples include racing games, such as F1 simulators, and shooting games. Many family entertainment centres have games that give prizes by redemption of tickets accumulated. Providing these machines give prizes according to the skill of the player, for example getting a high score shooting basketball, they will be exempt.

16.36 Further information on skill with prizes machines, and advice on how to distinguish between these machines and gaming machines, can be found on the Commission's website.

OTHER EXCLUSIONS

16.37 Section 235 of the Act sets out a number of exclusions, covering machines that are not considered gaming machines, even though gambling may take place on them, as follows:

- A domestic or dual use computer is not a gaming machine just because it can be used to take part in remote gambling. Regulations define a 'domestic computer' as one capable of being used for a purpose not related to gambling that is located in a private dwelling and used only on domestic occasions. A 'dual use computer' is also defined as having to be capable of being used for a purpose not related to gambling, but in addition must not be knowingly adapted or presented in such a way as to facilitate or draw attention to the possibility of its use for gambling[35].
- A telephone or other 'machine facilitating communication' that could be used for gambling purposes, for example, a mobile phone via which text message based lotteries can be entered, is not considered to be a gaming machine unless that is its primary purpose. Ordinary mobile phones are therefore exempt from the definition, but telephones designed or adapted for the purpose of enabling gambling would not be.
- Some machines that allow the purchase of lottery tickets are not gaming machines. However, this is intended as an exemption for the sale of tickets in a real lottery with other participants (for example a lottery vending machine), and not a virtual scratch card lottery conducted only by means of the machine. This means, first, that if the results of the lottery are determined by the machine, the machine is not exempt; and, second, if the machine displays the results of the lottery (determined otherwise than by the machine) then the interval between the sale of the ticket and the announcement of the result must comply with the minimum period of time specified by regulations[36]. It should be noted that regulations have created a category of gaming machine that is defined by the fact that it is a lottery machine. These are category B3A machines and can only be sited in members' clubs and miners' welfare institutes.
- A machine operated by virtue of a bingo operating licence for the purpose of playing bingo will be exempt provided it complies with any conditions set by the Commission. This covers what are known as mechanised cash bingo and electronic bingo ticket minders.
- Also exempted are machines used for the playing of bingo by way of prize gaming in Adult Gaming Centres and Family Entertainment Centres, however, the prize gaming regulations must be followed.

35 The regulations defining these terms are SI No 2082: The Gambling Act 2005 (Gaming Machines) (Definitions) Regulations 2007

36 SI No 2495: The Gambling (Lottery Machine Interval) Order 2007

PART 17: CASINOS

17.1 Section 7(1) of the Act states that 'a casino is an arrangement whereby people are given an opportunity to participate in one or more casino games'. Casino games are defined by the Act to mean a game of chance which is not equal chance gaming. Equal chance gaming is gaming which does not involve playing or staking against a bank, and where the chances are equally favourable to all participants. The Act gives the Commission power through conditions attached to operating licences to restrict the types of casino games that may be made available.

17.2 2 In March 2011 the Commission consulted on licence condition 9 of the Licence Conditions and Codes of Practice (LCCP): *Types and rules of casino and other games*. The licence condition was amended with effect from 20 June 2011 and effectively removed the requirement for casino operators in Great Britain to seek approval to trial new games. The Commission now only prescribes a list of games that may not be played (none at present).

17.3 One final edition of the *Rules of casino games in Great Britain* was published (June 2011) to accurately capture all those games, side bets and variations that were available in casinos in Great Britain at the time that the new licence condition came into effect on 20 June 2011. The Commission has published a document entitled *Rules of core casino games in Great Britain – June 2011* which will serve as its replacement, and which outlines the basic rules of the most popular casino games: roulette, blackjack, punto banco, three card poker and dice. Player information on the specific rules and odds applied to these and any other table games by individual operators are displayed in each casino, as required by code of practice 3 of the LCCP.

17.4 Operators who are interested in running a trial of a new game, side bet or variation should contact the industry-led Casino Games Review Group (CGRG) which has been set up to co-ordinate and monitor new games and determine their suitability for the market place ensure that core rules and information is added to a dedicated web site (www.ukcasinotablegames.info) for the information of other operators, the public, regulators and licensing authorities.

17.5 Under the Act, licensing authorities in England and Wales have been given the new role of issuing premises licences for casinos and monitoring those licences. In Scotland the licensing boards become licensing authorities and continue to have responsibilities for granting permissions for casinos in the form of premises licences.

PROTECTION OF CHILDREN AND YOUNG PERSONS

17.6 No-one under the age of 18 is permitted to enter a casino and operators are required to display notices to this effect at all entrances to a casino. Children and young persons are not allowed to be employed at premises with a casino premises licence. Licensing authorities are able to find information about the restrictions that apply in the *LCCP*, which is published on the Commission's website.

NEW CASINOS

17.7 Section 174 of the Act specifies the categories of casino premises licence that may be issued under the Act. These relate to the categories of casino provided for by section 7(5) of the Act. The gaming machines permitted to be made available in new casinos are related to the number of gaming tables available for use[37].

- No more than eight large casino premises licences will be permitted. Large casinos will have a minimum total customer area of 1,500m^2. This category of casino will be able to offer casino games, bingo and/or betting and up to 150 gaming machines in any combination of categories B1 to D (except B3A lottery machines) provided that a maximum ratio of 5:1 gaming machines to gaming tables is met.

- Large casino premises licences may be issued by the following licensing authorities: Great Yarmouth Borough Council; Kingston upon Hull City Council; Leeds City Council; Middlesbrough Borough Council; Milton Keynes Borough Council; Newham London Borough Council; Solihull Metropolitan Borough Council, and Southampton City Council.
- No more than eight small casino premises licences will be permitted. Small casinos will have a minimum total customer area of 750m^2. A small casino will be able to offer casino games, betting and up to 80 gaming machines in any combination of categories B1 to D (except B3A lottery machines) provided that a maximum ratio of 2:1 gaming machines to gaming tables is met.
- Small casino premises licences may be issued by Bath and North East Somerset District Council; East Lindsey District Council; Luton Borough Council; Scarborough Borough Council; Swansea City and County Council; Torbay Borough Council; Wigtown Divisional Licensing Board in the area of Dumfries and Galloway Council; and Wolverhampton City Council.

[37] SI No 1970 The Gambling Act 2005 (Gaming Tables in Casinos) (Definitions) Regulations 2009.

THE PROCESS FOR ISSUING CASINO PREMISES LICENCES

17.8 As a first step in licensing a casino, the licensing authority will have to invite applications for any casino premises licences that it may issue. Regulations set out how the process of inviting applications is to be done.[38]

17.9 It is possible that the number of applications that the relevant licensing authorities will receive will exceed the number of licences available. The Act lays down a framework for a two-stage process for considering applications in these circumstances.

17.10 As with all deliberations in premises licences, the authority should not confuse planning and building regulation considerations with the matter before it.

17.11 Licensing authorities whose areas have been chosen for the new casinos should, in their Licensing Authority Statement of Policy, set out the principles they intend to apply when determining the 'winner' of a premises licence competition.

17.12 Authorities should think carefully before entering into any agreements or arrangements with potential casino operators which might be perceived to affect their ability to exercise their stage two functions objectively and without having prejudged any of the issues. If any such agreements or arrangements are entered into, it will be important that authorities are able to demonstrate (for example, through having obtained independent and impartial advice on the competing applications) that any decision they reach is objectively based and is not affected by the arrangements.

[38] SI No 469; The Gambling (Inviting Competing Applications for Large and Small Casino Premises Licences) Regulations 2008

Stage one

17.13 If more applications are received than the number of available licences, the authority must determine whether each application would be granted a licence if there were no limit on the number of licences that the authority could grant. Each application must be considered separately and no reference made to the other applications received.

17.14 During this process each of the other applicants will be considered an 'interested party' and may make representations. The consideration of representations should be the same as that for normal applications for premises licences (see part 7 of this Guidance).
17.15 This process will result in one or more provisional decisions to grant a premises licence.
17.16 As with other decisions on premises licences, the decision of the authority may be appealed against. Until all appeals are determined the licensing authority may not proceed to stage two.

Stage two

17.17 The second stage of the process only applies where the number of applications which the licensing authority would provisionally grant under the stage one process exceeds the number of available casino premises licences.
17.18 Under the second stage of the process the authority has to decide between the competing applications and grant any available licences to those applications which in their opinion will result in the greatest benefit to its area. The principles which the licensing authority are going to apply in determining the stage two competition must be included in the authority's policy statement and therefore should be available to potential applicants before the authority invites applications for the available casino premises licence(s). The unsuccessful applicants must be informed of the result of the competition.
17.19 There is no right of appeal against the grant or refusal at stage two (other than by way of judicial review).
17.20 The Secretary of State has issued a code of practice about the procedure to be followed by licensing authorities in making determinations at both stage one and stage two, and also about the matters authorities are to take into account in making such determinations. The Act requires licensing authorities to comply with any code of practice issued by the Secretary of State.
17.21 Where an authority invites applications, those applications may be in the form of an application for a provisional statement as well as in the form of an application for the grant of a full casino premises licence. Where an application is made in the form of a provisional statement it is to be treated in the same way as an application for a casino premises licence and included in any two-stage determination process that the authority is required to carry out. If an application for a provisional statement is successful in that process, then it is not necessary for a further two-stage licensing process to be held when a casino premises licence application is eventually made by the operator to whom the statement has been issued.
17.22 Where a licensing authority issues a provisional statement following a two-stage determination process, they may limit the period of time for which the statement has effect. This is so that the authority can control the period within which the full casino premises licence application has to be made. Under Schedule 9 to the Gambling Act the authority is allowed to extend the period for which the provisional statement has effect if the person to whom it is issued applies to have it extended.

CASINO RESOLUTIONS

17.23 Section 166(1) of the Act states that a licensing authority may resolve not to issue casino premises licences.
17.24 The decision to pass such a resolution may only be taken by the authority as a whole and cannot be delegated to the licensing committee. In passing such a resolution the authority may take into account any principle or matter, not just the licensing objectives. Where a resolution is passed, it must be published by the authority in its Licensing Authority Statement of Policy.
17.25 The resolution must apply to casino premises generally, so that the authority cannot limit its effect to geographic areas or categories of casinos. The resolution must

specify the date it comes into effect. The authority may revoke the resolution by passing a counter-resolution (again the whole authority must pass that resolution). The resolution will lapse after three years, so the authority should pass a resolution every three years to keep such a policy in place.

17.26 A resolution not to issue casino premises licences will only affect new casinos. It will not have any effect on casino premises licences issued before the resolution takes effect or on provisional statements issued before that date. Similarly a resolution will not affect the ability of existing casinos with preserved entitlements from the 1968 Act from continuing to operate as casinos.

CONVERTED CASINOS (WITH PRESERVED RIGHTS UNDER SCHEDULE 18 OF THE ACT)

17.27 Casino operators with licences granted under the 1968 Act are eligible to be granted a casino premises licence under 'grandfathering' arrangements. Additionally, special provisions apply to enable these operators to relocate premises by way of a variation to a converted casino premises licence providing those premises are wholly or partly situated in the area of the licensing authority which issued the licence.[39]

17.28 These premises licences are subject to the normal system of review as outlined in part 10 of this Guidance. Where a licensing authority in whose area there are existing casinos has passed a 'no new casinos' resolution, the fact that such a resolution has been passed will not be a relevant factor to take into account in considering whether to review a premises licence.

---

39 SI No 3272; The Gambling Act 2005 (Commencement No 6 and Transitional Provisions) Order 2006; schedule 4, paragraph 65 (12, 13)

CASINO PREMISES LICENCE CONDITIONS

17.29 Part 9 of this Guidance discusses the conditions that may or may not be attached to premises licences, and those that are attached automatically. The Secretary of State and Scottish Ministers have set out in regulations the conditions relating specifically to casino premises. The paragraphs below discuss these conditions, both mandatory conditions – those that must be attached to casino premises; and default conditions – those that will apply unless the licensing authority chooses to exclude them using its powers under section 169.

Mandatory conditions attaching to all casino premises licences

17.30 Access to premises is regulated to add additional safeguards for both the public and industry. Mandatory conditions that must be attached to all casino premises licences require that the principal entrance to the casino should be from a street. A street is defined as including any bridge, road, lane, footway, subway, square, court, alley or passage (including passages through enclosed premises such as shopping centres), whether it is a thoroughfare or not.

17.31 A mandatory condition requires that no customer must be able to enter the casino from any other premises holding a casino, bingo, AGC, FEC or betting premises licence, or from premises where a FEC, club gaming and club machine, or licensed premises gaming machine permit, has effect.

17.32 There should be no access to a casino from premises wholly or mainly used by children and young persons.

17.33 No other gambling equipment may be situated within two metres of any ordinary gaming table. For the purposes of these conditions an ordinary gaming table means one which is not wholly or partially automated.

17.34 A maximum of 40 separate player positions may be made available for use in relation to wholly automated gaming tables at any time.

17.35 All casinos must display the rules of each type of casino game that can be played on the premises in a prominent place within both the table gaming area and other gambling areas to which customers have unrestricted access. Licensees may do this either by displaying clear and legible signs or by making available to customers leaflets or other written material setting out the rules.

17.36 ATMs must be positioned so that customers must cease to gamble at tables or gaming machines in order to use them.

Mandatory conditions attaching to large casino premises licences

17.37 A notice shall be displayed at all entrances to the casino stating that no person under the age of 18 will be admitted.

17.38 Large casinos must provide a minimum table gaming area of 1000m^2. In determining the floor area of the table gaming area, any number of separate areas within the casino may be taken into account. However, no area counting towards the minimum table gaming area may comprise less than 12.5% of the total minimum table gaming area. No gambling shall be permitted in the table gaming area of the premises other than gambling by way of table gaming.

17.39 Large casinos must offer a non-gambling area of a minimum of 500m^2. The non-gambling area may consist of one or more areas within the casino. These areas must be readily available to customers (ie offices, kitchen areas, employee areas will not count). They may include but should not consist exclusively of lavatories and lobby areas. The area must also include recreational facilities for casino customers that are available for use when the casino is open; where there is more than one area each area must contain recreational facilities. No gambling facilities may be offered in the non-gambling areas.

17.40 Clear and accessible information about the terms on which a bet may be placed should be displayed in a prominent position on the premises.

17.41 Any admission charges, the charges for playing bingo games and the rules of bingo must be displayed in a prominent position on the premises. Rules can be displayed on a sign, by making available leaflets or other written materials containing the rules, or running an audio-visual guide to the rules prior to any bingo game being commenced.

17.42 No more than 40 separate betting positions may be made available for use in relation to betting terminals at any time.

17.43 In addition to these conditions the Commission has issued a code of practice relating to access to casinos by children and young people. This can be found in the Commission's *Licence Conditions and Codes of Practice*, which is available on the Commission's website[40].

[35] Licence Conditions and Codes of Practice, available from www.gamblingcommission.gov.uk

Mandatory conditions attaching to small casino premises licences

17.44 A notice shall be displayed at all entrances to the casino stating that no person under the age of 18 will be admitted.

17.45 Small casinos must provide a minimum table gaming area of 500m^2. In determining the floor area of the table gaming area, any number of separate areas within the casino may be taken into account. However, no area counting towards the minimum table gaming area may comprise less than 12.5% of the total minimum table gaming area. No gambling shall be permitted in the table gaming area of the casino other than gambling by way of table gaming.

17.46 Small casinos must offer a non-gambling area of a minimum of 250m^2. The non-gambling area may consist of one or more areas within the premises. These areas must be readily available to customers (ie offices, kitchen areas, employee areas will not count). They may include, but should not consist exclusively of lavatories and lobby areas. The area must also include recreational facilities for casino customers that are available for use when the casino is open; where there is more than one area each area must contain recreational facilities. No gambling facilities may be offered in the non-gambling areas.

17.47 Clear and accessible information about the terms on which a bet may be placed should be displayed in a prominent position on the premises.

17.48 No more than 40 separate betting positions may be made available for use in relation to betting machines at any time.

17.49 In addition to these conditions the Commission has issued a code of practice relating to access to casinos by children and young people. This can be found in the Commission's *Licence Conditions and Codes of Practice*, which is available on the Commission's website.

Mandatory conditions attaching to converted casino premises licences

17.50 A notice shall be displayed at all entrances to the casino stating that no person under the age of 18 will be admitted.

17.51 Casinos with converted licences, and that have a gambling area of over 200m^2, must offer a minimum non-gambling area equivalent to at least 10% of its total gambling area. In determining the floor area of the gambling area, all areas in which facilities for gambling are provided should be taken into account. The non-gambling area may consist of one or more areas within the casino. These areas must be readily available to customers (ie offices, kitchen areas, employee areas will not count). They may include, but should not consist exclusively of, lavatories and lobby areas. The area must also include recreational facilities for casino customers that are available for use when the casino is open; where there is more than one area each area must contain recreational facilities. No gambling facilities may be offered in the non-gambling areas.

17.52 In addition to these conditions the Commission has issued a code of practice relating to access to casinos by children and young people. This can be found in the Commission's *Licence Conditions and Codes of Practice*, which is available on the Commission's website.

Default conditions attaching to all casino premises licences

17.53 The default opening hours of all casinos are noon to 6am.

PRIMARY GAMBLING ACTIVITY

17.54 An operating licence condition provides that gaming machines may be made available for use in casinos only on those days when sufficient facilities for playing casino games or games of equal chance are also available for use.

17.55 In this respect, when a casino exclusively offers fully automated casino games, there must be more individual player positions made available for these games than there are gaming machines made available for use.

17.56 The Licence Conditions and Codes of Practice, sets out in full the requirements on operators which are found in licence condition 16 and in associated code of practice provision 9. This document, and any subsequent update to it, is available from the Commission's website.

PART 18: BINGO

18.1 Bingo is not given a statutory definition in the Act other than that it means any version of the game irrespective of by what name it is described. It is to have its ordinary and natural meaning. Two types of bingo are commonly understood:

- cash bingo, where the stakes paid make up the cash prizes that are won
- prize bingo, where various forms of prizes are won, not directly related to the stakes paid.

18.2 Cash bingo is the main type of bingo played in commercial bingo premises. They also offer prize bingo, largely as interval games. The distinction between the two versions of the game is abolished for commercial operators, and the holder of a bingo operating licence will be able to offer any type of bingo game, whether cash or prize. This means that only premises with a bingo premises licence, or a 2005 Act large casino premises licence (where the operator holds a bingo as well as a casino operating licence), will be able to offer bingo in all its forms.

18.3 Apart from commercial bingo halls, prize bingo is traditionally a game played in arcades, especially seaside amusement arcades, or at travelling funfairs. For these operators, prize bingo is being subsumed within the allowances for prize gaming in the Act. This means that, subject to limits on participation fees and prizes, adult gaming centres, both licensed and unlicensed family entertainment centres, and travelling fairs, (or any premises with a prize gaming permit) are able to offer prize gaming, which includes prize bingo. In this form of gaming, the nature of the prize must not be determined by reference to the number of people playing the game, and the nature or the size of the prize must not be determined by reference to the amount paid for or raised by the gaming. See part 27 of this Guidance for a fuller discussion of prize gaming.

18.4 Licensing authorities need to satisfy themselves that bingo can be played in any bingo premises for which they issue a premises licence. This is a relevant consideration where the operator of an existing bingo premises applies to vary their licence to exclude an area of the existing premises from its ambit and then applies for a new premises licence, or multiple licences, for that or those excluded areas.

PROTECTION OF CHILDREN AND YOUNG PERSONS

18.5 Under the Act, children and young persons (anyone up to the age of 18) cannot be employed in providing any facilities for gambling on bingo premises, and children (under 16) cannot be employed, in any capacity, at a time when facilities for playing bingo are being offered. However, young persons, aged 16 and 17, may be employed in bingo premises (while bingo is being played), provided the activities on which they are employed are not connected with the gaming or gaming machines. Licensing authorities are able to find information about the restrictions that apply in *Licence Conditions and Codes of Practice*.

18.6 Children and young people are allowed into bingo premises; however they are not permitted to participate in the bingo and if category B or C machines are made available for use these must be separated from areas where children and young people are allowed.

GAMING MACHINES

18.7 Section 172(7) provides that the holder of a bingo premises licence may make available for use a number of category B gaming machines not exceeding 20% of the total number of gaming machines which are available for use on the premises. Premises in existence before 13 July 2011 are entitled to make available eight category B gaming machines, or 20% of the total number of gaming machines, whichever is the greater. The holder of bingo premises licence granted on or after 13 July 2011 but before 1 April 2014 is entitled to make available a maximum of eight category B gaming machines or 20% of the total number of gaming machines, whichever is the greater; from 1 April 2014 these premises will be entitled to 20% of the total number of gaming machines only. Regulations state that category B machines at bingo premises should be restricted to sub-category B3 and B4 machines, but not B3A lottery machines.

18.8 The gaming machines must remain within the licensed area covered by the premises licence. In the unusual circumstance that an existing bingo premises covered by one premises licence applies to vary the licence and acquire additional bingo premises licences (so that the area that was the subject of a single licence will become divided between a number of separate licensed premises) it is not permissible for all of the gaming machines to which each of the licences brings an entitlement to be grouped together within one of the licensed premises.

18.9 Equipment operated by a bingo operating licence for the purpose of playing bingo, for example what are currently known as mechanised cash bingo and electronic bingo terminal (EBTs), will be exempt from controls on gaming machines provided they comply with any conditions set by the Commission and (in the case of EBTs) do not hold gaming machine content.

18.10 An EBT that offers gaming machine content in addition to bingo content is considered to be a gaming machine for the purposes of primary gambling activity and would count towards the total number of gaming machines. Correspondingly, that terminal would not count towards the offering of bingo for primary gambling activity purposes. Any EBTs that do not offer gaming machine content would not count towards the number of gaming machines.

PRIMARY GAMBLING ACTIVITY

18.11 An operating licence condition provides that gaming machines may be made available for use in licensed bingo premises only on those days when sufficient facilities for playing bingo are also available for use.

18.12 In this respect, in cases where bingo is exclusively offered by means of electronic bingo terminals or bingo machines, there must be more individual player positions made available for bingo than there are gaming machines made available for use.

18.13 The Licence Conditions and Codes of Practice (LCCP) sets out in full the requirements on operators.

BINGO IN CLUBS AND ALCOHOL-LICENSED PREMISES

18.14 Bingo is a class of equal chance gaming permitted on alcohol-licensed premises, and in clubs and miners' welfare institutes, under the allowances for exempt gaming in Part 12 of the Act. There are regulations setting controls on this form of gaming, to ensure that it remains a low stakes and prizes activity.[41]

18.15 In addition, new rules are laid down in the Act about the playing of bingo specifically in alcohol-licensed premises, clubs and miners' welfare institutes. Where the level of bingo played in these premises reaches a certain threshold, it will no longer be authorised by these rules and a bingo operating licence will have to be obtained from the Commission for future bingo games. The aim of these provisions is to prevent bingo becoming a predominant commercial activity on such non-gambling premises.

18.16 The threshold is reached if the bingo played during any seven-day period exceeds £2,000 (either in money taken or prizes awarded) once in a year, referred to as 'high turnover bingo'. There is a legal duty on the licensee or club to inform the Commission if they offer high turnover bingo in any seven day period. That allows the Commission to monitor the bingo activity on the premises, and discuss with the relevant licensee or club the point at which a bingo operating licence may be needed. A 'high turnover period' begins with the first day of the seven day period in which the threshold was exceeded and lasts for a year. If a second period of high turnover bingo occurs within that year, a bingo operating licence will be required. Where bingo is played in a members club under a bingo operating licence no premises licence will be required.

181.7 If it comes to the attention of licensing authorities that alcohol-licensed premises or clubs or institutes are playing bingo during the course of a week which involves significant stakes and prizes, that makes it possible that the £2,000 in seven days is being exceeded, authorities should inform the Commission. To help clubs and institutes to comply with the full range of statutory requirements for gaming the Commission has developed a statutory code of practice. The *Code of Practice for gaming in clubs and premises with an alcohol licence* is available on the Commission website.

[41] SI No 1940; The Gambling Act 2005 (Exempt Gaming in Alcohol-Licensed Premises) Regulations 2007 SI No 1944; The Gambling Act 2005 (Exempt Gaming in Clubs) Regulations 2007

BINGO IN CASINOS

18.18 The eight large casinos will be able to offer bingo. Bingo will be permitted as part of their casino premises licence and they will not require a separate bingo premises licence, though they will need to obtain a bingo operating licence (which may be combined with their casino licence) in order to offer facilities for bingo at a casino. The standards in this respect will be no lower than for operators seeking only to provide facilities for bingo alone.

BINGO PREMISES LICENCE CONDITIONS

18.19 Part 9 of this Guidance discusses the conditions that may or may not be attached to premises licences, and those that are attached automatically. The Secretary of State and Scottish Ministers have set out in regulations the conditions relating specifically to bingo premises. The paragraphs below discuss these conditions, both mandatory conditions – those that must be attached to bingo premises; and default conditions – those that will apply unless the licensing authority chooses to exclude them using its powers under section 169.

Mandatory conditions attaching to bingo premises licences

18.20 A notice stating that no person under the age of 18 years is permitted to play bingo on the premises shall be displayed in a prominent place at every entrance to the premises.

18.21 No customer shall be able to enter bingo premises directly from a casino, an adult gaming centre or betting premises (other than a track).

18.22 Over 18 areas within bingo halls that admit under-18s must be separated by a barrier with prominently displayed notices stating that under-18s are not allowed in that area and with adequate supervision in place to ensure that children and young people are not able to access these areas or the category B or C machines. Supervision may be done either by placing the terminals within the line of sight of an official of the operator or via monitored CCTV.

18.23 Any admission charges, the charges for playing bingo games and the rules of bingo must be displayed in a prominent position on the premises. Rules can be displayed on a sign, by making available leaflets or other written material containing the rules, or running an audio-visual guide to the rules prior to any bingo game being commenced.

18.24 Any ATM made available for use on the premises shall be located in a place that requires any customer who wishes to use it to cease gambling in order to do so.

Default conditions attaching to bingo premises licences

18.25 Bingo facilities in bingo halls may not be offered between the hours of midnight and 9am. However, there are no restrictions on access to gaming machines in bingo halls.

PART 19: BETTING PREMISES

19.1 The Act contains a single class of licence for betting premises. However, within this single class of licence, there are different types of premises which require licensing. This part of the Guidance discusses off-course betting, that is, betting that takes place other than at a track in what was previously known as a licensed betting office. Tracks are discussed in part 20 of this Guidance. Please note that there are also betting offices on tracks, that have a separate premises licence from the track licence. Those are also discussed in part 20 of this Guidance.

19.2 The Act also permits betting intermediaries to operate from premises, although betting intermediaries usually offer their services via remote communication, such as the internet. In principle, however, there is nothing to stop a betting intermediary applying for a betting premises licence to offer intermediary services upon the premises.

19.3 Under the Gambling Act, licensing authorities are responsible for issuing and monitoring premises licences for all betting premises. The issuing of premises licences is discussed in part 7 of this Guidance.

PROTECTION OF CHILDREN AND YOUNG PERSONS

19.4 Children and young persons are not able to enter premises with a betting premises licence, although special rules apply to tracks, as explained in part 20 of this Guidance. Children and young persons are not allowed to be employed at premises with a betting premises licence unless the premises are shut and any gaming machines are switched off.

BETTING PREMISES LICENCE CONDITIONS

19.5 Part 9 of this Guidance discusses the conditions that may or may not be attached to premises licences, and those that are attached automatically. The Secretary of State and Scottish Ministers have set out in regulations the conditions relating specifically to betting premises. The paragraphs below discuss these conditions, both mandatory – those that must be attached to betting premises; and default – those that will apply unless the licensing authority chooses to exclude them using its powers under section 169.

Mandatory conditions attaching to betting premises licences

19.6 A notice shall be displayed at all entrances to the betting premises stating that no person under the age of 18 will be admitted. The notice should be clearly visible to people entering the premises.

19.7 There must be no access to betting premises from other premises that undertake a commercial activity (except from other premises with a betting premises licence including tracks). Except where it is from other licensed betting premises, the entrance to a betting shop should be from a street (defined as including any bridge, road, lane, footway, subway, square, court, alley or passage – including passages through enclosed premises such as shopping centres – whether a thoroughfare or not).

19.8 Any automated telling machine (ATM) made available for use on the premises shall be located in a place that requires any customer who wishes to use it to leave any gaming machine or betting machine in order to do so.

19.9 No apparatus for making information or any other material available in the form of sounds or visual images may be used on the licensed premises, except where used to communicate:

- information about or coverage of sporting events, including information relating to betting on such events (and incidental information including advertisements); or
- information relating to betting (including results) on any event in connection with which bets may have been effected on the premises.

Betting operator-owned TV channels are permitted.

19.10 No music, dancing or other entertainment is permitted on betting premises. This includes any form of entertainment such as apparatus producing sound or visual images which do not fall within paragraph 19.9 or machines which do not come within the categories of machine explicitly allowed in betting premises under section 172(8) of the Act.

19.11 The consumption of alcohol on the premises is prohibited.

19.12 The only publications that may be sold or made available on the premises are racing periodicals or specialist betting publications.

19.13 A notice setting out the terms on which a bet may be placed must be displayed in a prominent position on the premises.

Default conditions attaching to betting premises licences

19.14 Gambling facilities may not be offered in betting premises between the hours of 10pm on one day and 7am on the next day, on any day.

GAMING MACHINES

19.15 Section 172(8) provides that the holder of a betting premises licence may make available for use up to four gaming machines of category B, C or D. Regulations state that category B machines at betting premises are restricted to sub-category B2, B3 and B4 machines. See part 16 of this Guidance for information on gaming machines.

BETTING MACHINES (BET RECEIPT TERMINALS)

19.16 Section 235(2)(c) provides that a machine is not a gaming machine if it is designed or adapted for use to bet on future real events. Some betting premises may make available machines that accept bets on live events, such as horse racing, as a substitute for placing a bet over the counter. These 'betting machines' are not gaming machines and therefore neither count towards the maximum permitted number of gaming machines, nor have to comply with any stake or prize limits. Such betting machines merely automate the process that can be conducted in person and therefore do not require regulation as a gaming machine.

19.17 However, where a machine is made available to take bets on virtual races (that is, images generated by computer to resemble races or other events) that machine is a gaming machine and does count towards the maximum permitted number of gaming machines, and must meet the relevant category limitations for the premises.

19.18 Section 181 contains an express power for licensing authorities to restrict the number of betting machines, their nature and the circumstances in which they are made available by attaching a licence condition to a betting premises licence or to a casino premises licence (where betting is permitted in the casino). When considering whether to impose a condition to restrict the number of betting machines in particular premises, the licensing authority, amongst other things, should take into account the size of the premises, the number of counter positions available for person-to-person transactions, and the ability of employees to monitor the use of the machines by children and young persons (it is an offence for those under 18 to bet) or by vulnerable people.

PRIMARY GAMBLING ACTIVITY

19.19 It is not permissible for an operator to offer gaming machines on a premises which is licensed for betting but not to offer sufficient facilities for betting. A betting operating licence authorises its holder to 'provide facilities for betting' (section 65(2)(c) of the Act). Likewise, a betting premises licence authorises premises to be used for 'the provision of facilities for betting . . .' (section 150(1)(e) of the Act). The ability to make up to four gaming machines, within categories B2 – D, available is an additional authorisation conferred upon the holder of a betting premises licence (section 172(8) of the Act); it is not a free standing right to make gaming machines available for use. It follows that unless a betting premises operator offers sufficient facilities for betting it should not be making gaming machines available on the premises in question.

19.20 In the Commission's view it is also important, in relation to the licensing objective of protecting vulnerable persons from being harmed or exploited by gambling, that customers should be offered a balanced mix of betting and gaming machines in licensed betting premises. Thus, whilst the Commission recognises that betting premises are permitted to offer gaming machines, including B2 gaming machines, the Commission considers that betting should be the primary element of the gambling facilities being offered to customers in such premises. Betting may be provided by way of betting terminals or over a counter (face to face).

19.21 Accordingly, an operating licence condition provides that gaming machines may be made available for use in licensed betting premises only at times when there are also sufficient facilities for betting available. In this respect, such facilities must include information that enables customers to access details of events on which bets can be made, make such bets, learn of the outcome and collect any winnings.

19.22 The Licence Conditions and Codes of Practice (LCCP) sets out the full requirements on operators in licence condition 16 and code of practice provision 8.

19.23 Should a licensing authority receive an application to vary a premises licence for betting in order to extend the opening hours, the authority should satisfy itself that the reason for the application is in line with the requirements on primary gambling activity. Therefore, the applicant should be able to demonstrate that the extension of the opening hours is not designed solely to benefit from the machine entitlement and activity which is an ancillary to the primary activity of the premises, namely betting.

PART 20: TRACKS

INTRODUCTION TO TRACKS

Definition of a track

20.1 Section 353 of the Act defines a track as a horse racecourse, greyhound track or other premises on any part of which a race or other sporting event takes place or is intended to take place.

20.2 The Act does not give a list of premises that are officially recognised as 'tracks' but there are a number of venues where sporting events do or could take place, and accordingly could accommodate the provision of betting facilities. Examples of tracks include:

- a horse racecourse (referred to in this Guidance as 'racecourses')
- a greyhound track
- a point-to-point horserace meeting
- football, cricket and rugby grounds
- an athletics stadium
- a golf course
- venues hosting darts, bowls, or snooker tournaments
- a premises staging boxing matches
- a section of river hosting a fishing competition
- a motor racing event.

20.3 This list is by no means exhaustive, as, in theory, betting could take place at any venue where a sporting or competitive event is occurring. While many of these venues are not commonly understood to be 'tracks', they fall within the definition of 'track' defined by the Act. Licensing authorities may be of the view that they have few tracks in their administrative area, but the very nature of the Act's definition indicates that most localities are likely to have venues that could be classified as a track for betting purposes.

20.4 The Act also provides for tracks which do not currently offer betting facilities, but may elect to do so at some stage in the future. This means that land which has a number of uses, one of which fulfils the definition of a track, could qualify for a premises licence. Examples could include agricultural land upon which a point-to-point meeting takes place or a theatre, arena or exhibition centre where sporting events such as darts or snooker competitions are held. Under the Act, these may all be classified as tracks.

20.5 The Act does not define what constitutes a sporting event or race and the Commission leaves this to licensing authorities to decide on a case by case basis.

20.6 If an individual or company wants to offer betting facilities on a sporting event then different forms of 'approval' are available, one of which must be obtained if betting is to be provided, irrespective of whether the betting is generally incidental to the main sporting activity. The different types of approval for the provision of betting facilities at premises are:

- a premises licence
- an occasional use notice.

LICENCES AND OTHER PERMISSIONS FOR THE PROVISION OF BETTING FACILITIES

20.7 A track premises licence permits the premises to be used for the provision of facilities for betting, but does not permit the licence holder to provide casino, bingo or other types of gambling on tracks, as these activities must be the subject of separate premises licences.

20.8 As outlined above, sporting events and races take place at many different venues including hotels, conference centres, on agricultural land, and at designated sporting venues such as football grounds. In many cases such venues do not hold sporting events all year round and the number of 'event' days may be limited. The Act provides that if certain conditions are met, a premises licence is not always required to permit betting facilities at such events.

20.9 The Act allows a temporary use notice to be issued to allow premises to be used for gambling where there is no premises licence but where an operator wishes to use the premises temporarily for providing facilities for gambling. Part 14 of this Guidance has already established the process for issuing these notices, which can be issued by a person or company holding an operating licence granted by the Commission, and allow specified gambling facilities to take place for a maximum period of 21 days within any 12 month period.

20.10 Section 39 of the Act provides that where there is betting on a track on eight days[42] or fewer in a calendar year, betting may be permitted by an occasional use notice, as described at part 15 of this Guidance, without the full need for a premises licence. This permits licensed betting operators to use tracks for short periods for conducting betting. An occasional use notice may be suitable for a point-to-point track which holds race meetings eight times a year or less. No conditions are attached to an occasional use notice. However, only licensed betting operators may offer betting facilities at such tracks, otherwise an offence would be committed under section 33 of the Act.

20.11 It is the responsibility of the track owner and/or gambling operator to determine which route is the most appropriate for their particular circumstances.

---

42 The Secretary of State has the power to increase or decrease the number of occasional use notices that an operating licence holder could apply for each calendar year. At the time of going to print, the Secretary of State had no plans to exercise this power. The Commission also understands that 'day' is defined as midnight to midnight, so an event that starts on one calendar day and ends on the following day would count as two days.

BETTING ON TRACKS

20.12 There are various types of betting which take place in relation to tracks, often divided into 'on-course' and 'off-course'.

'On-course' betting

20.13 The 'on-course' betting operator is one who comes onto the track, temporarily, while races or sporting events are taking place, and operates at the track-side. On-course betting operators tend to offer betting only on the events taking place on the track, that day. For example, betting operators attending horserace and greyhound racing meetings will only attend on race days. Similarly, betting operators at cricket and football grounds are only likely to attend on days when matches are taking place.

20.14 Betting on tracks is organised in different ways and can take place in different parts of the track in many different forms. These include the following:

- **Betting rings** (at racecourses and greyhound tracks)
  The ring can be dispersed throughout the track, and can include 'temporary' rings at large meetings, but all different locations form part of the betting ring. On-course betting operators will be located in the betting ring according to a position ('pitch') allocated to them. For greyhound tracks, the betting ring is not an official term but marks that area of the track where track premises licence holders allow betting operators, by virtue of a permit, to provide betting facilities.
- **Betting counters or kiosks** (permanent/temporary)
  A betting counter or booth may be a permanent or temporary stand or a facility where a bookmaker receives or negotiates bets. Examples include manned stands or portacabins located at football grounds on match days, and the temporary erected stands used by bookmakers at cricket grounds during test matches.
- **Mobile betting**
  Mobile betting machines (often hand held) operated by employees of betting operators allow customers to place a bet or receive payouts outside of betting kiosks or the betting ring.
- **Bet receipt terminals**
  A bet receipt terminal is sometimes known as a 'betting machine' and in simple terms is a machine that allows customers to place bets. Unlike gaming machines they do not pay out winnings. The terminals lack the direct human intervention of a betting counter staffed by a cashier, and can be located at different parts of tracks.
- **Pool betting** (also known as totalisator betting)
  This involves the pooling of stakes on a given event, and the splitting of the total pool, less a commission for the operator amongst the winners. This form of betting was often provided by the Horserace Totalisator Board, commonly known as the 'Tote'. In 2011 the Tote was purchased by BetFred. As part of the sale process Betfred received an exclusive seven year licence to operate pool betting operations on all UK racecourses. Pool betting is also offered at greyhound tracks, usually by the owner of the track under a pool betting operating licence or a person authorised to act on their behalf. Tracks may also conduct inter-track pool betting when other tracks are holding races.

'Off-course' betting

20.15 'Off-course' betting operators are those who provide betting facilities other than at a track in betting premises such as those found on the high street. In addition to premises away from the track, betting operators may operate self-contained betting premises or designated areas such as a row of betting kiosks within the track premises. Self-contained premises provide facilities for off-course betting (in effect, the opportunity to bet on other events not just those taking place on the track), although they normally operate only on race days.

20.16 Licensing authorities will need to familiarise themselves with the different types of betting that take place on tracks and the locations where it is intended that betting takes places.

TRACK PREMISES LICENCES – DIFFERENCES FROM OTHER PREMISES LICENCES

20.17 A betting premises licence permits a premises to be used for the provision of facilities for betting, whether by making or accepting bets, by acting as a betting intermediary, or by providing other facilities for the making or accepting of bets.

20.18 While there is no special class of betting premises licence for a track, the Act does contain rules which apply specifically to premises licences granted in respect of a track.

20.19 Premises licences in relation to tracks differ from other types of premises licence in a number of ways. Most importantly, the applicant for the licence need not hold an operating licence from the Commission[43]. That is because, unless the occupier of the track wishes to offer pool betting (or general betting) facilities himself (for which he will need a licence), the betting that is provided upon the track will not be provided by him, but will be provided by other operators who come onto the track. Since those operators will require the necessary operating licences, the Act allows the track premises licence holder to obtain a premises licence, without also having to hold an operating licence.

20.20 The secondary aspect to this rule is that each individual operator coming onto the track on race days does not need to hold a premises licence. Instead they are covered by the umbrella of the premises licence held by the track premises licence holder.

20.21 Tracks may also benefit from rules permitting low-level, infrequent betting activity, under the provisions for occasional use notices as explained above.

20.22 In addition, tracks are the only class of premises that may be subject to more than one premises licence, provided each licence relates to a specified area of the track. The Act sets out that there can be a primary premises licence for the track and, in addition, subsidiary premises licences for other parts of the track[44]. This allows track venues to develop leisure facilities such as a casino and apply for a premises licence for that part of the track.

20.23 Tracks are distinguishable from other betting premises licences as under section 47(4) of the Act, children and young persons are allowed to be present on the track while betting is taking place on those licensed premises.

20.24 There are also a limited number of track premises licence holders who have an operating licence because they operate a pool. An example of these is the 28 greyhound tracks which are approved by the Greyhound Board of Great Britain[45]. In addition to admitting independent fixed-odds betting operators, these tracks may run their own pool betting facilities as permitted by sections 179 and 180 of the Act, and are subject to licence conditions applicable to their status as both betting operators and track premises licence holders.

20.25 Tracks are also recognised as multi-purpose venues having a wide range of facilities that enable them to host various other activities, often on non-event days, including:

- private dinners and parties
- weddings
- retail events (auctions, car boot sales etc)
- concerts
- conferences
- exhibitions.

20.26 The Act recognises that tracks are primarily premises intended for entertainment other than gambling and therefore places no restrictions on offering ancillary entertainment including allowing music, dancing or other entertainment on the premises and the sale of alcohol.

20.27 These provisions outline the difference between track premises licences and most other premises licences. In essence, tracks admit third-party operators to provide betting facilities, whereas other premises licence holders – betting shops, bingo clubs and casinos for instance – provide the gambling facilities themselves and are subject to the conditions of the operating licence as well as the premises licence.

[43] Section 159 (3) (4) of the Act

[44] Section 152 (3) of the Act

[45] A small number of point-to-point track owners also offer pool betting but the Commission expects these will be subject to occasional use notices (see Part 15 for further details)

THE PREMISES

Defining the premises

20.28 Section 151 of the Act requires applicants for premises licences to submit plans of the premises with their application. This ensures that licensing authorities have the necessary information to make an informed judgement about whether the premises are fit for gambling. The plan also informs future premises inspection activity.

20.29 Plans for tracks need not be in a particular scale, but should be drawn to scale and should be sufficiently detailed to include the information required by regulations.

20.30 In the majority of cases, such as greyhound tracks, racecourses, football stadia and cricket grounds, defining the extent of boundaries may be assisted by reference to existing plans already submitted to obtain other permissions. These could include:

- the obtaining of a safety certificate under 'Safety at Sports Ground' legislation (this applies in respect of sports grounds with capacity to accommodate more than 10,000 spectators)
- the approval of a racecourse by the Horserace Betting Levy Board
- the historic boundaries under previous legislation such as, the approval of tracks under Schedule 3 of the Betting, Gaming and Lotteries Act 1963.

20.31 Some tracks may be situated on agricultural land where the perimeter is not defined by virtue of an outer wall or fence, such as point-to-point racetracks. In such instances, where an entry fee is levied, track premises licence holders may erect temporary structures to restrict access to premises.

20.32 In the rare cases where the outer perimeter cannot be defined, it is likely that the track in question will not be specifically designed for the frequent holding of sporting events or races. In such cases betting facilities may be better provided through occasional use notices where the boundary premises do not need to be defined.

20.33 The Commission appreciates that it is sometimes difficult to define the precise location of betting areas on tracks. The precise location of where betting facilities are provided is not required to be shown on track plans, both by virtue of the fact that betting is permitted anywhere on the premises and because of the difficulties associated with pinpointing exact locations for some types of track. Licensing authorities should satisfy themselves that the plan indicates the main areas where betting might take place. For racecourses in particular, any betting areas subject to the 'five times rule' (commonly known as betting rings, and discussed later in this section) must be indicated on the plan.

20.34 As the plan forms part of the licence document, it also needs to be sufficiently flexible to ensure that a relatively small change in the premises layout would not require an operator to submit an application to vary the track premises licence. Only a significant change to the track layout would require a licence variation. For example, moving a category C gaming machine from one end of a bar that had been marked on the plan as a gaming machine area to another may not necessitate a full variation to a tracks premises licence, nor would the establishment of a new betting ring at a racetrack, as neither of these events have any impact on the purpose of the licence or the conditions attached to it. However, relocating category C machines to entirely different parts of a track or relocating an existing betting ring protected by the 'five times rule' would generally need to be the subject of an application to vary the premises licence.

20.35 Some tracks extend across the geographical boundaries of licensing authority areas. In such cases applications can only be made to licensing authorities in whose area the premises is wholly or partly situated, although the Act contains no rules about cases where premises lie across multiple authority areas. In such cases, applicants will note this on the application form, and the application can be made to any of the authorities that the track extends over. The applicant is then required to notify the other licensing authorities covered by the track location about the application (as they would be designated as responsible authorities and therefore entitled to make representations about the application). The Commission expects applicants will apply to the licensing authority in whose area the greater or greatest part of the track site is situated, although ultimately the Act does not entitle an authority to reject an application because it is responsible for a smaller area of the premises than another authority.

Ensuring that premises are fit for the provision of gambling facilities

20.36 Licensing authorities are required to ensure that premises are fit for a specific type of gambling. Premises which meet the conditions required to operate as, for example, a casino may not meet the requirements for offering track betting facilities.

20.37 Track premises that safeguard the achievement of the three licensing objectives may generally be considered fit for gambling, and some general principles whereby licensing authorities can establish whether a track is fit for the provision of gambling facilities are as follows:

Licensing objective	**Issues to consider**	**Reason to consider a track premises unfit for gambling purposes?**	**Part of this Guidance containing specific information**
The protection of children and other vulnerable persons from being harmed or exploited by gambling	Tracks permit access to children.	No — Children are allowed access to tracks on race days.	Part 4
	Bet receipt terminals in areas where there is no supervision which would allow children or young persons to use machines undetected.	No — It is a mandatory condition of the operating licence that operators ensure that bet receipt terminals are supervised. This is not an issue for the premises licence.	Part 6
	Children are allowed access to areas holding category B and C gaming machines.	It is a mandatory condition of the operating licence that operators ensure that children are not allowed access to areas where category B and C gaming machines are provided. However, section 182 of the Act also creates a premises licence condition that children and young persons must be excluded from areas where any gaming machines other than category D are located.	Part 7
	Issues to consider	**Reason to consider a track premises unfit for gambling purposes?**	**Part of this Guidance containing specific information**

Licensing objective	Issues to consider	Reason to consider a track premises unfit for gambling purposes?	Part of this Guidance containing specific information
The protection of children and other vulnerable persons from being harmed or exploited by gambling	Betting areas adjacent to areas where children/young persons are present such as play areas	No — Children are allowed access to tracks on race days and so will be exposed to gambling areas.	Part 9
		It is a mandatory condition of the operating licence that operators do not accept bets from children or young persons.	
		The Commission considers that the location of betting does not generally pose a risk to this licensing objective. Licensing authorities may impose their own local conditions where they perceive problems.	
	Issues to consider	**Reason to consider a track premises unfit for gambling purposes?**	**Part of this Guidance containing specific information**
Ensure gambling is conducted in a fair and open way	The rules of betting are not displayed on the premises.	No (not an issue at application stage) — it is a mandatory condition of the premises licence that the rules of betting are displayed.	Part 8
	Unlicensed betting operators are allowed to operate on tracks.	No (not an issue at application stage) — it is a mandatory condition of the premises licence that licence holders make arrangements to ensure that they only allow licensed operators on track.	Part 8
	Betting takes place out of approved hours.	No (not an issue at application stage) — it is a mandatory condition of the premises licence that betting only takes place within the specified hours.	Part 5

Licensing objective	Issues to consider	Reason to consider a track premises unfit for gambling purposes?	Part of this Guidance containing specific information
Licensing objective	**Issues to consider**	**Reason to consider a track premises unfit for gambling purposes?**	**Part of this Guidance containing specific information**
Prevent gambling from being a source of crime and disorder	Betting is allowed in all parts of a track resulting in greater difficulties for track premises licence holders to identify instances of illegal Betting.	No — the Commission's view is that this does not generally pose a risk to this objective. Licensing authorities may impose their own conditions should they perceive a problem.	Part 9
	No formal exit/entry points allowing easy access for unapproved operators and customers.	No — the Commission's view is that this does not generally pose a risk to this objective. Licensing authorities may impose their own conditions should they perceive a problem.	Part 9

ACCESS

Access to premises and other parts of the track

20.38 Section 152 of the Act provides that premises may not have more than one premises licence authorising a type of activity, with the exception of track premises, whereby a track may be the subject of multiple premises licences.

20.39 Access between premises licensed for gambling and non-gambling areas is an important local licensing consideration, for reasons such as the following:

- to prevent operators from seeking to circumvent the Act by artificially subdividing a premises and securing separate premises licences for its composite parts
- to ensure that operators do not circumvent regulations governing the maximum number of gaming machines applicable to specific premises
- to ensure that people who have entered a premises for one type of gambling are not exposed to another, potentially harder, form of gambling
- to ensure that there is no direct access between gambling premises to which children have access and those which they are prohibited from entering
- to ensure that all gambling premises have publicly accessible entrances
- to ensure that gambling premises are not developed in the backrooms of other commercial premises.

20.40 As tracks may be the subject of multiple premises licences, regulations[46] have been laid to stipulate the access requirements between gambling premises, and when entering or leaving gambling premises. By virtue of the regulations no direct access is allowed from a track to a casino or adult gaming centre. Therefore if, for example, a casino is built on a track premises that is the subject of a track premises licence, clearly defined public thoroughfares should be in place to ensure that customers have to leave one gambling premises, and be aware they have done so, before entering another.

46 SI no 1409: The Gambling Act 2005 (Mandatory and Default Conditions) (England and Wales) Regulations 2007 SSI no 266: The Gambling Act 2005 (Mandatory and Default Conditions) (Scotland) Regulations 2007

Access by children – special dispensation for tracks

20.41 The Act forbids all persons under 18 years old to enter premises when betting facilities are being provided, other than at tracks. This dispensation allows families to attend premises such as greyhound tracks or racecourses on event days, and children to be permitted into areas where betting facilities are provided, such as the betting ring, where betting takes place.

20.42 Licensing authorities should note however that the exemption allowing children access to betting areas on tracks does not extend to areas within a track where category C or above machines are provided, or other premises to which under 18 year olds are specifically not permitted access.

20.43 As under-18s are permitted to enter betting areas on tracks on event days, there are licensing requirements in place at tracks to mitigate the likelihood of underage betting occurring. Licensed betting operators at tracks are bound by their operating licence conditions which prevent them from accepting bets from persons who are under 18 years old. The track premises licence holder is also required through premises licence conditions to display a notice in a prominent place at every public entrance stating that no person under the age of 18 is permitted to bet on the premises.

20.44 Licensing authorities should be aware that there was an anomaly in the Act, wholly prohibiting the employment of children and young people on tracks, which DCMS is taking steps to remedy through the use of a Legislative Reform Order (LRO) under the Legislative and Regulatory Reform Act 2006. This will create an exemption under section 55 of the Gambling Act 2005, allowing the employment of children and young persons in non- gambling roles on tracks (such as racecourses) which hold a betting premises licence. This was the original policy intention; which would allow young people to work for example as jockeys, stable lads, or dog handlers. Section 51 of the Act, which prohibits people under 18 from working in roles related to the provision of facilities for gambling, is not affected by these proposals and would continue to apply. Subject to the outcome of consultation and Parliamentary consideration, DCMS have proposed that the changes are implemented from 1 October 2012.

20.45 Where betting facilities are provided through a self-contained betting office on a track which has a separate betting premises licence, the betting operator of the self-contained premises is expected to exclude under-18s from their premises.

BETTING ON EVENT AND NON-EVENT DAYS

Hours of betting on event days

20.46 Regulations[47] state that gambling facilities may be provided at any time when a sporting event is taking place on a track.

20.47 As such, licensing authorities should establish the upcoming fixtures and events to be held at tracks, at the time of application – a list could be provided by the applicant themselves, or could be retrieved from the applicant's website. While such lists may be subject to change, licensing authorities will need indicative dates to inform local compliance and enforcement activity at tracks (for example, to determine inspection dates). Significant changes to the fixture/events listing have a bearing on the licence conditions in that track premises licence holders will be expected to comply with the mandatory and default conditions applicable to them on both event and non-event days (as discussed below). As such, licensing authorities may wish to establish a local mechanism by which they are made aware of any significant fixture changes. Licensing authorities will not generally need to reassess licence applications as a result of such changes.

47 SI no 1409: The Gambling Act 2005 (Mandatory and Default Conditions) (England and Wales) Regulations 2007 SSI no 266: The Gambling Act 2005 (Mandatory and Default Conditions) (Scotland) Regulations 2007

Hours of betting on non-event days

20.48 On days when no public sporting event is taking place on a track, regulations state that gambling facilities may only be provided on the track between the hours of 7am and 10pm.

20.49 Some tracks have traditionally offered, and will wish to continue to offer, facilities for gambling outside the proposed gambling hours on non-event days. For example, to screen live televised events from other time-zones (which may take place after 10pm or before 7am) and provide betting facilities during those events.

20.50 Tracks will be able to continue to provide these betting facilities on a limited number of days a year by virtue of occasional use notices permitted by section 39 of the Act. This permission enables tracks to offer occasional betting facilities on international events, such as the Superbowl or the Melbourne Cup, without becoming frequent providers of out-of-hours betting facilities, since section 39 limits the number of occasional uses to eight days per calendar year.

20.51 An event running past midnight and ending on the following day accounts for two occasional use days, even though in practice it is one event. At the time of publishing this document, the Secretary of State has no plans to change the definition of 'a day' or to vary the number of occasional use notices that can be issued by betting operators per calendar year.

20.52 Where tracks plan to open and allow provision for betting facilities on non-event days, betting operators will need to either exclude children from the premises on these days or demonstrate that they are able to exclude children and young persons from betting areas[48]. In simple terms, on non-event days, tracks become similar to licensed betting offices on the high street. Tracks may achieve this requirement by:

- locating all betting areas inside an area of the premises that is separated from the remainder of the premises by a physical barrier, thereby preventing access other than through a designated entrance
- only admitting adults to the part of the track where betting areas are located, by establishing procedures for verifying customer ages and refusing entry to adult-only areas for those unable to produce an acceptable form of identification (and taking action where there are unlawful attempts to enter adult-only areas)
- placing prominent notices in front of and inside each entrance stating that access to the area is prohibited to persons under 18.

20.53 Licensing authorities may choose to reduce the default gambling hours, providing any reduction is in line with the principles set out in section 153 of the Act.

48 Section 182 (2) of the Act

BET RECEIPT TERMINALS

20.54 Section 235(2)(c) of the Act provides that a machine is not a gaming machine by reason only of the fact that it is designed or adapted for use to bet on future real events. Betting operators may make available machines that accept bets on live events, such as horseracing, as a substitute for placing a bet over the counter. These 'betting machines' are commonly known as bet receipt terminals and are not gaming machines; they merely automate the process that can be conducted in person and therefore are not regulated as gaming machines. The other difference is that a bet receipt terminal only accepts a bet; it does not pay out winnings (although this situation may develop in the future). Therefore any person under the age of 18 seeking to obtain their winnings will have to speak to one of the betting operator's employees. The betting operator's operating licence requires that any winning bets placed by an underage person are considered void and the stake returned, but not any winnings.

20.55 Licensed operators may install bet receipt terminals on tracks. There is no restriction on the number of bet receipt terminals that may be in use but operators must, by virtue of their operating licence conditions, supervise such terminals to prevent them being used by those under 18 years of age.

20.56 There is no formal requirement on track premises licence holders to involve themselves in the procedures used by betting operators to supervise their bet receipt terminals (unless specific local conditions specifying supervisory arrangements are added to the track premises licence by the licensing authority). Some betting operators may agree supervisory assistance to be provided by employees of the track premises licence holders, but this is a commercial matter between the track owner and betting operators.

20.57 While track premises licence holders have no formal responsibilities in this regard, the Commission has advised them to inform it of instances where they are aware that betting operators are persistently failing to ensure the adequate supervision of their bet receipt terminals.

20.58 At many tracks, betting operators receive bets via hand-held devices, which are also regarded as betting machines by the Act as opposed to gaming machines. These are only operated by employees of the betting operator, and as such are deemed automatically to fulfil the supervision requirement.

GAMING MACHINES

20.59 A track premises licence does not of itself entitle the holder to provide gaming machines, as this type of premises licence can be held without any corresponding operating licence. However, by virtue of section 172(9) of the Act, track owners holding both a track premises licence and a pool betting operating licence issued by the Commission (in effect, greyhound tracks only), may site up to four gaming machines within categories B2 to D on the track.

20.60 Some tracks will also qualify for an alcohol licence and as such they will be automatically entitled under section 282 of the Act to two gaming machines of category C or D. This permission is activated by notifying the licensing authority and paying them the required fee. If a track premises licence holder has both an alcohol licence and a pool betting operating licence, then they will be entitled to a total of six gaming machines (two via the alcohol licence and four via the operating licence). In such scenarios the operating licence entitlement does not take precedence, and each licence has its own requirements that must be complied with.

20.61 Applications for permits to allow additional gaming machines are not permitted where the premises is already covered by a track premises licence[49]. This represents a change to previous legislation whereby betting (track) premises licence holders could hold gaming machine permits authorising in excess of two gaming machines. However, there is special provision for alcohol-licensed premises within tracks in England and Wales which are allowed to continue to hold gaming machine permits or apply for new ones. For these premises, Schedule 13, paragraph 1(2) of the 2005 Act will not apply [50].

20.62 Children and young persons can play category D gaming machines on a track, but are not allowed to play other categories of machine.

20.63 It is a condition of section 282 of the Act that alcohol-licensed premises licence holders (not necessarily the owners) must comply with any relevant provision of a code of practice under section 24 about the location and operation of a gaming machine. The gaming machine permits code of practice can be found on the Commission's website.

Where track premises licence holders possess a pool betting operating licence, the Commission places a mandatory licence condition on such operators that they must:

- have and put into effect documented policies and procedures to prevent underage gambling
- monitor the effectiveness of these.

---

49 Schedule 13, section 1 (2), of the Act

50 SI 2006/3272 — The Gambling Act 2005 (Commencement No 6 and Transitional Provisions) Order 2006 — (C.119), section 30

TRACK ADMINISTRATION

Administration of betting

20.64 Different systems of administrative and quasi-regulatory arrangements are in place to ensure that activities held on tracks run smoothly for paying customers, track operators and betting operators. These administrative arrangements are considered to be outside the remit of the Act unless they affect the licensing objectives.

The role of track premises licence holders

20.65 Track premises licence holders act effectively as landlords, letting out parts of their premises to licensed betting operators. The responsibilities of track premises licence holders are established by the mandatory and default licence conditions attaching to their premises licence. The licensed betting operators authorised by track owners to provide betting facilities at tracks must comply with their operating licence conditions and codes of practice issued by the Commission.

20.66 The Commission has assessed the impact of existing administrative arrangements upon the achievement of the licensing objectives, and some of the existing rules within these arrangements relating to the conduct and administration of licensed betting operators have been incorporated into operating licence or premises licence conditions. The Commission considers all other issues as administrative matters for the premises licence holder and betting operators.

20.67 The Commission expects that track premises licence holders will make their own arrangements for dealing with administrative matters. They may undertake the administration and control of betting areas themselves or they can make arrangements with another body to take on this work. Whichever way, the track premises licence holder retains the responsibility to meet all relevant conditions attached to their premises licence.

20.68 Track premises licence holders have a responsibility to report regulatory breaches or potential breaches relating to the premises itself or to betting operators. The Commission may then liaise with the relevant licensing authorities regarding action taken towards the breaches.

Acceptance of bets

20.69 Under section 33(2) of the Act, only licensed betting operators may accept bets or provide facilities for gambling. The Commission is responsible for issuing betting operating licences, and each betting operator must comply with the conditions of their operating licence. The Commission can invoke penalties or revoke licences if they fail to do so.

20.70 Track premises licences for greyhound tracks and racecourses are subject to mandatory licence conditions requiring access to be offered at the track-side to betting operators generally. This prevents track premises licence holders who are also pool betting operators from becoming a monopoly supplier of betting on tracks. While this

operators generally abide by Tattersall's 'Rules on Betting', and as such the premises licence holder should make this clear to customers. At a sports stadium where betting facilities are provided by a high street operator, the track licence holder may choose to state on the centrally provided notice that the rules followed by the betting operator will apply throughout the track.

20.87 Betting operators offering betting facilities on racecourses and at greyhound tracks are required through the conditions of their operating licence to clearly display any of their own rules that differ from those that the track premises licence holder elects to display, and their rules concerning voids, late bets, and maximum payouts. For racecourses and greyhound tracks, the maximum payout will vary according to the rules of individual on-course operators. The Commission expects track premises licence holders to refer customers to the rules of individual on-course betting operators who are required to display this information on their stands (often referred to as 'bookmaker joints').

20.88 Licensing authorities need not concern themselves with the terms or rules of betting (apart from the requirement to display them), as this is a consideration of the Commission in respect of the licensing of betting operators.

APPROVED BETTING AREAS

Betting areas

20.89 The Secretary of State has determined not to impose any default conditions on tracks restricting where betting can take place. Moreover the Act does not prevent permanent or temporary structures being erected on the track for providing facilities for betting.

20.90 In considering applications, the licensing authority would need to take into account the licensing objectives and assess whether these objectives are compromised by the betting arrangements and the layout being proposed. It is the Commission's view that the location of betting facilities (other than those for gaming machines and bet receipt terminals) does not generally pose a threat to the licensing objectives and that no additional conditions should be imposed by licensing authorities. (What was known as the five time rule no longer exists).

Multiple licences

20.91 Section 152(3) of the Act permits the issuance of more than one premises licence for a track provided that each licence relates to a distinct specified area of the track (although there cannot be more than one premises licence covering the same area of the track.)

20.92 This enables track owners to extend existing facilities to provide other gambling facilities such as a casino on their existing tracks, whereby these additional gambling activities are covered by separate premises licences. In the event that track owners intend to apply for additional premises licences, they will need to take into consideration access issues and in particular whether access to the desired premises will be allowed directly from the track. This is particularly significant as direct access between a track and other betting premises (other than a track betting shop) is not permitted. The track owner would need to make arrangements so that access to a casino or bingo hall would be via a street, not via the track itself.

20.93 The Act permits self-contained parts of tracks, such as a permanent betting office on a racecourse or at a sports stadium, to be the subject of a separate betting premises licence. The effect of this approach would be that the betting premises licence holder would be responsible for upholding the premises licence conditions relating to the self-contained premises. Accordingly this removes premises licence condition responsibilities from the main track premises licence holder towards the self-contained premises. The betting premises licence holder would be responsible for maintaining the conditions associated with the licence (no alcohol consumption, and so on).

20.94 A track betting licence for a track can authorise the entire track premises to be used for providing betting facilities, which would avoid the need for a separate betting premises licence to cover any self-contained betting premises.
20.95 Where a particular area of a track is already subject to a premises licence, and a person wishes to apply for a licence to offer another type of activity in that area, an application must be made to the issuing licensing authority to vary the original premises licence, under section 187 of the Act. The new track premises licence can only be granted at the same time as, or after, the original licence has been varied.
20.96 Licensing authorities may receive applications indicating separate betting areas that may not necessarily have clear physical boundaries, such as walls or fencing. Such areas could still be the subject of a separate betting premises licence provided the area is clearly delineated, both in terms of making it clear to the public that they are entering a 'betting office', and to keep out persons aged under 18. The Commission considers that customers will be aware that they are moving into a separate betting area operated by an independent betting operator by virtue of the fixtures and fittings bearing the betting operator's corporate identity. The delineation of such an area is best achieved through a physical barrier. A licensing authority concerned that such an area cannot be satisfactorily delineated may wish to refuse an application for a separate betting premises licence.
20.97 Conditions applicable to off-track betting premises also apply to self-contained betting premises on tracks that are the subject of their own betting premises licence, which entitles the self-contained premises to offer up to four gaming machines (from categories B2 to D).
20.98 The Commission considers that track owners should decide in conjunction with the betting operators offering facilities at their track which premises licensing arrangement best suits the specific nature and circumstances of their track.

SOCIAL RESPONSIBILITY CONSIDERATIONS FOR TRACKS

20.99 The achievement of the licensing objectives requires betting operators to adopt socially responsible gambling policies and procedures designed both to ensure that gambling is open and fair and that children and other vulnerable people are not harmed or exploited by gambling.
20.100 While betting operators must put into effect policies and procedures to promote socially responsible gambling, there is no equivalent requirement on track premises licence holders. However, section 182(1)(a) of the Act places a condition on the track premises licence that the licensee shall ensure that children and young persons are excluded from any area where facilities for betting are provided (unless on race days at racetracks and at greyhound tracks).
20.101 The Commission considers that track premises licence holders should accept some accountability for promoting socially responsible gambling on their premises, and that the level of responsibility should be commensurate with the volume and intensity of gambling that occurs on their premises. Specific guidance on responsibilities in this area can be found in the '*Advice to track premises licence holders*' document, available on the Commission's website.

PART 21: ADULT GAMING CENTRES

21.1 Persons operating an Adult Gaming Centre (AGC) must hold a gaming machines general operating licence (Adult Gaming Centre) from the Commission and must seek a premises licence from the licensing authority. They will be able to make category B, C and D gaming machines available to their customers.

GAMING MACHINES

21.2 Section 172(1) of the Act provides that the holder of an adult gaming centre premises licence may make available for use a number of category B gaming machines not exceeding 20% of the total number of gaming machines which are available for use on the premises and any number of category C or D machines. Premises in existence before 13 July 2011 are entitled to make available four category B gaming machines, or 20% of the total number of gaming machines, whichever is the greater. The holder of an adult gaming centre premises licence granted on or after 13 July 2011 but before 1 April 2014 is entitled to make available a maximum of four category B gaming machines or 20% of the total number of gaming machines, whichever is the greater; from 1 April 2014 these premises will be entitled to 20% of the total number of gaming machines only. Regulations specify that the category B machines should be restricted to sub-category B3 and B4 machines, but not B3A machines.

21.3 Where the operator of an existing AGC premises licence applies to vary the licence and acquire additional AGC premises licences (so that the area that was the subject of a single licence will become divided between a number of separate licensed premises) each separate licensed premises must only contain the allowed machine entitlement. So for example, where two separate AGC premises have been created adjacent to each other by genuinely splitting a pre-existing premises, it is not permissible to locate eight category B3 gaming machines in one of the resulting premises (with none in the other one), as the gaming machine entitlement for that premises would be exceeded.

PROTECTION OF CHILDREN AND YOUNG PERSONS

21.4 No-one under the age of 18 is permitted to enter an AGC. Licensing authorities will wish to have particular regard to the location of and entry to AGCs to minimise the opportunities for children to gain access. This may be of particular importance in areas where young people may be unsupervised for example, where an AGC is in a complex, such as a shopping centre or airport.

AGC PREMISES LICENCE CONDITIONS

21.5 Part 9 of this Guidance discusses the conditions that may or may not be attached to premises licences, and those that are attached automatically. Currently there are no default conditions specific to AGCs. It was considered unnecessary to set default opening hours for AGCs, leaving the matter to be decided locally by licensing authorities on a case by case basis.
21.6 The Secretary of State and Scottish Ministers have set out in regulations the conditions relating specifically to AGC premises. The paragraphs below discuss these conditions, all of which are mandatory.

Mandatory conditions attaching to adult gaming centre premises licences
21.7 A notice must be displayed at all entrances to AGCs stating that no person under the age of 18 years will be admitted to the premises.
21.8 There can be no direct access between an AGC and any other premises licensed under the Act or premises with an FEC, club gaming, club machine or licensed premises gaming machine permit. There is no definition of 'direct access' in the Act or regulations. However, it could be said that there should be an area separating the premises concerned (for example, a street or cafe), which the public go to for purposes other than gambling, for there to be shown to be no direct access.
21.9 Any ATM made available for use on the premises shall be located in a place that requires any customer who wishes to use it to cease gambling at any gaming machine in order to do so.
21.10 The consumption of alcohol in AGCs is prohibited at any time during which facilities for gambling are being provided on the premises. A notice stating this should

be displayed in a prominent place at every entrance to the premises.

PART 22: LICENSED FAMILY ENTERTAINMENT CENTRES

22.1 The Act creates two classes of family entertainment centre (FEC). This part of the Guidance concerns licensed FECs. Persons operating a licensed FEC must hold a gaming machine general operating licence (Family Entertainment Centre) from the Commission and must seek a premises licence from the licensing authority. They will be able to make category C and D gaming machines available to their customers. Unlicensed FECs provide category D machines only and are regulated through FEC gaming machine permits (see part 24 of this Guidance).

PROTECTION OF CHILDREN AND YOUNG PERSONS

22.2 Children and young persons will be permitted to enter an FEC and may play on the category D machines. They are not permitted to play on category C machines, and it is a requirement that there must be clear segregation between the two types of machine, so that children do not have access to category C machines.

22.3 In the gaming machine general operating licence (Family Entertainment Centre), the Commission has set out conditions that require operators to ensure that employees prevent access to the area containing category C machines by under-18s and challenge children or young persons who do attempt to play the machines. Licensing authorities will find it helpful to refer to the Commission's website to see the conditions that apply. [53] Regulations[54] relevant to the way in which the area containing the category C machines should be set out are specified in the mandatory conditions that apply to premises licences (see below).

[53] Code of Practice on Licensed Family Entertainment Centres, available from www.gambling-commission.gov.uk

[54] SI No 1409: The Gambling Act 2005 (Mandatory and Default Conditions) (England and Wales) Regulations 2007 SSI No 266: The Gambling Act 2005 (Mandatory and Default Conditions) (Scotland) Regulations 2007

LICENSED FEC PREMISES LICENCE CONDITIONS

22.4 Part 9 of this guidance discusses the conditions that may or may not be attached to premises licences, and those that are attached automatically. Currently there are no default conditions specific to FECs. It was considered unnecessary to set default opening hours for FECs, leaving the matter to be decided locally by licensing authorities on a case by case basis.

22.5 The Secretary of State and Scottish Ministers have set out in regulations the conditions relating specifically to FEC premises. The paragraphs below discuss these conditions, all of which are mandatory.

Mandatory conditions attaching to family entertainment centre premises licences

22.6 The summary of the terms and conditions of the premises licence issued by the licensing authority under section 164(1)(c) of the Act must be displayed in a prominent place within the premises.

22.7 The layout of the premises must be maintained in accordance with the plan.

22.8 The premises must not be used for the sale of tickets in a private lottery or customer lottery, or the National Lottery.

22.9 No customer shall be able to enter the premises directly from a casino, an adult gaming centre or betting premises (other than a track). There is no definition of 'direct access' in the Act or regulations. However, it could be said that there should be an area separating the premises concerned (for example, a street or cafe), which the public go to for purposes other than gambling, for there to be shown to be no direct access.

22.10 Any ATM made available for use on the premises must be located in a place that requires any customer who wishes to use it to cease gambling at any gaming machine in order to do so.

22.11 Over-18 areas within FECs that admit under-18s must be separated by a barrier with prominently displayed notices at the entrance stating that under-18s are not allowed in that area and with adequate supervision in place to ensure that children and young persons are not able to access these areas or the category C machines. Supervision may be done either by placing the terminals within the line of sight of an official of the operator or via monitored CCTV.

22.12 The consumption of alcohol in licensed FECs is prohibited at any time during which facilities for gambling are being provided. A notice stating this should be displayed in a prominent position on the premises.

PART 23: INTRODUCTION TO PERMITS

23.1 The Act introduces a range of permits for gambling which are granted by licensing authorities. Permits are required when premises provide a gambling facility but either the stakes and prizes are very low or gambling is not the main function of the premises. The permits regulate gambling and the use of gaming machines in a specific premises.

23.2 Holders of alcohol-licensed premises gaming machine permits and club permits are required to comply with codes of practice, drawn up by the Commission, on the location and operation of machines. Information on this code can be found on the Commission's website[55].

23.3 The following parts of the Guidance discuss the various permits that licensing authorities are responsible for issuing:

- Part 24 – family entertainment centre gaming machine permits (as set out in Schedule 10 of the Act)
- Part 25 – club gaming permits and club machine permits (as set out in Schedule 12)
- Part 26 – alcohol-licensed premises gaming machine permits (as set out in Schedule 13)
- Part 27 – prize gaming permits (as set out in Schedule 14).

23.4 Licensing authorities may only grant or reject an application for a permit. No conditions may be attached to a permit.

23.5 There are different factors to be taken into account by licensing authorities when considering the different types of permit applications. Please see the relevant parts of this Guidance for further information.

23.6 In addition, licensing authorities are responsible for receiving, from holders of alcohol-licensed premises (under the Licensing Act 2003 or the Licensing (Scotland) Act 2005), notifications that they intend to exercise their automatic entitlement to two gaming machines in their premises under section 282 of the Act.

[55] Gaming Machine Permits Code of Practice, available from www.gamblingcommission.gov.uk

PART 24: UNLICENSED FAMILY ENTERTAINMENT CENTRES

24.1 Family entertainment centres (FECs) are commonly located at seaside resorts, in airports and at motorway service stations, and cater for families, including unaccompanied children and young persons. Unlicensed FECs are able to offer only category D machines in reliance on a gaming machine permit. Any number of category D machines can be made available with such a permit subject to other considerations, such as fire regulations and health and safety. Permits cannot be issued in respect of vessels or vehicles.

6: Gambling Act 2005: Additional Material

24.2 If the operator of a family entertainment centre wants to make category C machines available in addition to category D machines, the operator will need to apply for a gaming machine general operating licence (Family Entertainment Centre) from the Commission and a premises licence from the licensing authority (see part 7 of this Guidance).

24.3 Schedule 10 of the Act sets out the application process and regulatory regime for FEC gaming machine permits.

APPLYING FOR A PERMIT

24.4 The application for a permit can only be made by a person who occupies or plans to occupy the premises to be used as an unlicensed FEC and, if the applicant is an individual, he or she must be aged 18 or over. Applications for a permit cannot be made if a premises licence is in effect for the same premises. The application must be made to the licensing authority in whose area the premises are wholly or partly situated.

24.5 The licensing authority must specify the form and manner in which the application should be made, and specify what other information and documents (such as insurance certificates, plans of building, and so on) they require to accompany the application. Applications must also be accompanied by a fee, as prescribed in regulations[56] set by the Secretary of State for England and Wales and Scottish Ministers for Scotland.

24.6 In its Licensing Authority Statement of Policy, a licensing authority may include a statement of principles that it proposes to apply when exercising its functions in considering applications for permits. In particular it may want to set out the matters that it will take into account in determining the suitability of the applicant. Given that the premises will particularly appeal to children and young persons, licensing authorities may want to give weight to matters relating to child protection issues.

[56] SI No 454: The Gambling Act 2005 (Family Entertainment Centre Gaming Machine) (Permits) Regulations 2007 SSI No 309: The Gambling Act 2005 (Fees) (Scotland) Regulations 2007

GRANTING OR REFUSING A PERMIT

24.7 The licensing authority can grant or refuse an application for a permit, but cannot add conditions. An application for a permit may be granted only if the licensing authority is satisfied that the premises will be used as an unlicensed FEC, and if the chief officer of police has been consulted on the application. Unlicensed FECs, by definition, will not be subject to scrutiny by the Commission as no operating (or other) licences will be applied for and issued. Licensing authorities might wish to consider asking applicants to demonstrate:

- a full understanding of the maximum stakes and prizes of the gambling that is permissible in unlicensed FECs
- that the applicant has no relevant convictions (those that are set out in Schedule 7 of the Act)
- that employees are trained to have a full understanding of the maximum stakes and prizes.

24.8 The licensing authority may not refuse an application unless it has notified the applicant of the intention to refuse and the reasons for it, and given them an opportunity to make representations orally or in writing or both. The rights of appeal in relation to permits are discussed in part 12 of this Guidance.

24.9 If a permit is granted, the licensing authority must issue it as soon as is reasonably practicable. The Secretary of State has set out the form of the permit in regulations[57]. The permit must specify the person to whom it is issued, the premises it relates to, the date on which it takes effect, the date on which it expires and the name and address of the licensing authority issuing it.

24.10 The permit will have effect for ten years, unless it ceases to have effect because it is surrendered or lapses or is renewed. There is no annual fee for FEC gaming machine permits.
24.11 If the person to whom the permit is issued changes their name, or wants to be known by another name, they may send the permit to the issuing authority for amendment, together with the appropriate fee. The authority must comply with the request and return the permit to the holder.

---

57 SI No 454: The Gambling Act 2005 (Family Entertainment Centre Gaming Machine) (Permits) Regulations 2007

LAPSE, SURRENDER AND FORFEITURE

24.12 The permit may lapse for a number of reasons, namely:
- if the holder ceases to occupy the premises
- if the licensing authority notifies the holder that the premises are not being used as an unlicensed FEC
- if an individual permit holder dies, becomes incapable by reason of mental or physical incapacity, becomes bankrupt, or sequestration of his estate is ordered
- if the company holding the permit ceases to exist, or goes into liquidation.

24.13 The purpose of the second reason listed in the previous paragraph is to ensure that there is no erosion of the principle that an unlicensed FEC permit should be obtained for premises that are wholly or mainly used for gaming machines. Licensing authorities would need to use this power in circumstances in which, since the grant of the permit, other activities have been introduced in the premises that mean the gaming machines have become ancillary.
24.14 In the last two circumstances listed in paragraph 24.12, the Act provides that the personal representative (in the case of death), trustee of the bankrupt estate or liquidator of the company may rely on the permit for a period of six months as though it had effect and was issued to them.
24.15 The permit may also cease to have effect if the holder surrenders it to the licensing authority. Notice of such surrender must be accompanied by the permit, or by an explanation of why the permit cannot be produced.
24.16 If the permit holder is convicted of a relevant offence (that is, an offence listed in Schedule 7 of the Act) the court may order the forfeiture of the permit. The court may order the holder to deliver the permit to the licensing authority; and it must in any case notify the licensing authority that it has made a forfeiture order as soon as is reasonably practicable after making the order. Such an order may be suspended by a higher court, pending appeal.

RENEWAL

24.17 In accordance with paragraph 18 of Schedule 10 of the Act, an application for renewal of a permit must be made during the period beginning six months before the permit expires and ending two months before it expires. The procedure for renewal is the same as for an application. The licensing authority may only refuse to renew a permit on the grounds that:
- an authorised local authority officer has been refused access to the premises without reasonable excuse
- renewal would not be reasonably consistent with the licensing objectives. In this respect, the licensing authority will have the benefit of having consulted the chief officer of police and will be aware of any concerns that have arisen about the use of the premises during the life of the permit.

24.18 The duration of the permit will not be curtailed while a renewal application is pending, including an appeal against a decision not to renew.

MAINTENANCE

24.19 The permit must be kept on the premises and it is an offence not to produce it when requested to do so by a constable, an enforcement officer, or an authorised local authority officer.

24.20 If a permit is lost, stolen or damaged, the holder may apply for a replacement, subject to paying a fee that has been set by the Secretary of State or Scottish Ministers in regulations. The licensing authority must grant the application if it is satisfied that the permit has been lost, stolen or damaged and a report has been made to the police. The authority should issue a copy and certify it as a true copy of the original permit.

PART 25: CLUBS

25.1 This part of the Guidance covers the following types of premises:

- Members' clubs
- Commercial clubs
- Miners' welfare institutes

25.3 Under section 271 of the Act, a licensing authority may grant members' clubs and miners' welfare institutes (but not commercial clubs) club gaming permits which authorise the establishments to provide gaming machines (as well as equal chance gaming and games of chance, as prescribed in regulations[54]). The club gaming permit has certain conditions, including that, in respect of gaming machines, no child or young person uses a category B or C machine on the premises and that the holder complies with any relevant provision of a code of practice about the location and operation of gaming machines (available on the Commission's website[55]).

25.4 If a club does not wish to have the full range of facilities permitted by a club gaming permit or if they are a commercial club not permitted to provide non-machine gaming (other than exempt gaming under section 269 of the Act), they may apply to the licensing authority for a club machine permit under section 273 of the Act. This authorises the holder to have up to three gaming machines of categories B4, C or D (that is, three machines in total). Members' clubs and miners' welfare institutes (but not commercial clubs) are entitled to site category B3A gaming machines offering lottery games in their clubs. However, the limit of three machines in total remains.

[53] SI No 504/2007: The Club Gaming and Club Machine Permits (Scotland) Regulations 2007

[54] SI No 1945: The Gambling Act 2005 (Club Gaming Permits) (Authorised Gaming) Regulations 2007

[55] Code of Practice on Machine Permits available from www.gamblingcommission.gov.uk

DEFINING CLUBS

25.2 The Act separates gaming in clubs from that in other alcohol licensed premises (commonly known as pubs).

25.3 The Act creates two types of club for the purposes of gaming: members' clubs (including miners' welfare institutes) and commercial clubs. This is an important distinction in respect of the gaming that may take place.

Members' clubs

25.4 A members' club is a club that is not established as a commercial enterprise, and is conducted for the benefit of its members. Examples include working men's clubs, miners' welfare institutes, branches of the Royal British Legion and clubs with political affiliations. Members' clubs may apply to their local licensing authority for club gaming permits and club machine permits. Particular care should be taken when assessing applications for permits by premises that intend to have a heavy emphasis on offering poker, to ensure that a) they remain within the statutory definition of a members' club (which must be established and conducted wholly or mainly for purposes other than the provision of facilities for gaming), b) the club satisfies the conditions attached to a club gaming permit and c) they are not commercial clubs that would then be offering gambling illegally.

25.5 The Act states that members' clubs must have at least 25 members and be established and conducted 'wholly or mainly' for purposes other than gaming, unless the gaming is restricted to bridge and whist. Members' clubs must be permanent in nature, but there is no need for a club to have an alcohol licence.

Miners' welfare institutes

25.6 The definition of a miners' welfare institute has changed since they were first set up. They are associations established for recreational or social purposes. They are managed by representatives of miners or use premises regulated by a charitable trust which has received funds from one of a number of mining organisations. Miners' welfare institutes may also apply for club gaming permits and club machine permits.

Commercial clubs

25.7 A commercial club is a club established for commercial gain (whether or not they are making a commercial gain). Examples include snooker clubs, clubs established as private companies and clubs established for personal profit. There are established tests in respect of determining a club's status (see paragraphs 25.47 to 25.49). In case of doubt, legal advice should be sought. Commercial clubs may only apply for club machine permits.

BINGO IN CLUBS

25.8 Clubs and miners' welfare institutes are able to provide facilities for playing bingo under section 275 of the Act, or in accordance with a permit under section 271, provided that the restrictions in section 275 are complied with. These include that in any seven day period the aggregate stakes or prizes for bingo must not exceed £2,000. If that limit is breached the club must hold a bingo operator's licence and the relevant operating, personal and premises licences must be sought (see part 18 of the Guidance). The bingo must comply with any code issued by the Commission under section 24 of the Act. Information about this code can be found on the Commission's website[58]. Further information about bingo in clubs can be found in paragraphs 18.15 to 18.18.

58 Code of practice for equal chance gaming in clubs and premises with an alcohol licence, available from www.gamblingcommission.gov.uk

BETTING IN CLUBS

25.9 Commercial betting, regardless of the level of stakes, is not allowed in clubs. Those who facilitate such betting in clubs – whether designated premises supervisors or club officials – are providing illegal facilities for gambling and are breaking the law. Even where designated premises supervisors or club officials accept bets on behalf of licensed bookmakers, or just facilitate betting through their own telephone accounts, they are acting as betting intermediaries and could be prosecuted.

25.10 Licensed bookmakers with a full or ancillary remote licence may accept telephone bets from a customer watching an event in a club, as long as that customer has an individual account with them. It is illegal for bookmakers to sit in the club taking bets themselves. Similarly, it is also illegal for operators to put their agent in clubs, for example, in a working men's club on a Saturday, to take bets.

EXEMPT GAMING

25.11 Exempt gaming is equal chance gaming generally permissible in any club. Such gaming should be ancillary to the purposes of the premises. This provision is automatically available to all such premises, but is subject to statutory stakes and prize limits determined by the Secretary of State.

25.12 Equal chance gaming is gaming that does not involve staking against a bank and the chances of winning are equally favourable to all participants. It includes games such as backgammon, mah-jong, rummy, kalooki, dominoes, cribbage, bingo and poker.

25.13 The Secretary of State has set both daily and weekly prize limits for exempt gaming. Different, higher stakes and prizes are allowed for exempt gaming in clubs than are allowed in alcohol-licensed premises[59]. These limits are set out in Appendix C to this Guidance.

25.14 Exempt gaming should be supervised by a nominated gaming supervisor and comply with any code of practice issued by the Commission under section 24 of the Act [60].

25.15 Clubs may levy a charge for participation in equal chance gaming under the exempt gaming rules. The amount they may charge is as prescribed in regulations[61]. See Appendix C for further details.

25.16 In order to qualify as exempt gaming, clubs may not charge a rake on games (a commission or fee deducted from the prize fund), or levy or deduct an amount from stakes or winnings.

25.17 Members' clubs may only be established wholly or mainly for the purposes of the provision of facilities for gaming, if the gaming is of a prescribed kind. The Secretary of State has decided that bridge and whist should be the only prescribed kinds of gaming[62]. So long as it does not provide facilities for other types of non-machine gaming, a bridge or whist club may apply for a club gaming permit. If gaming is the principal reason for attendance at a club (other than a dedicated whist or bridge club), then it is not exempt gaming under section 269 of the Gambling Act 2005. This would include poker clubs and the like established primarily for the purpose of providing poker or other gaming. Such clubs require Commission operating licences and premises licences.

25.18 The gaming offered must not be linked to gaming in other premises and no person under 18 may participate in the gaming.

25.19 Gaming which meets these conditions needs no permission from the licensing authority. However, if an authority believes that these conditions are being breached, it has a power to remove the exemption and ban gaming in a specific pub or club.

25.20 The Commission has issued a code of practice under section 24 of the Act in respect of exempt equal chance gaming. This can be found on the Commission's website[63].

25.21 The code of practice requires owners/licensees to adopt good practice measures for the provision of gaming in general and poker in particular. The code also sets out the stakes and prizes limits and the limits on participation fees laid out in regulations.

25.22 The emphasis of the regulations and the code of practice is on self-regulation by the management of the premises and licensing authorities should take a strong line in cases where breaches are detected.

---

59 SI No 1944/2007: The Gambling Act 2005 (Exempt Gaming in Clubs) Regulations 2007

60 Code of practice for equal chance gaming in clubs and premises with an alcohol licence, available from www.gamblingcommission.gov.uk

61 SI No 1944/2007: The Gambling Act 2005 (Exempt Gaming in Clubs) Regulations 2007

62 SI No 1942/2007: The Gambling Act 2005 (Gaming in Clubs) Regulations 2007

63 Code of practice for equal chance gaming in clubs and premises with an alcohol licence, available from www.gamblingcommission.gov.uk

CLUB PERMITS

25.23 Schedule 12 of the Act sets out the application process and regulatory regime for club gaming permits and club machine permits. Scottish Ministers may, with the consent of the Secretary of State, make separate regulations in relation to club gaming or club machine permits in place of Schedule 12, if the applicant or the holder of the permit is the holder of a relevant Scottish licence. Scottish Ministers have made regulations in this regard[64]. In exercising a function under Schedule 12, the licensing authority must have regard to this Guidance and, subject to the Guidance, the licensing objectives.

25.24 A club gaming permit or club machine permit may not be issued in respect of a vessel or vehicle.

---

64 No 504/2007: The Club Gaming and Club Machine Permits (Scotland) Regulations 2007

CLUB GAMING PERMITS

25.25 Under section 271 of the Act, the licensing authority may grant members' clubs and miners' welfare institutes (but not commercial clubs) club gaming permits which authorise the establishments to provide gaming machines, equal chance gaming (without having to abide by the stake and prize limits which would apply to exempt gaming in the absence of a permit) and games of chance as prescribed in regulations[65], namely pontoon and *chemin de fer*. This is in addition to the exempt gaming authorisation under section 269 of the Act.

25.26 Club gaming permits allow the provision of no more than three gaming machines. These may be from categories B3A, B4, C or D but only one B3A machine can be sited as part of this entitlement. See part 16 of this Guidance for information on machine categories.

25.27 Where a club has gaming machines they are required to comply with the code of practice, which has been issued by the Commission on the location and operation of machines. Information about this code can be found on the Commission's website[66].

25.28 The gaming which a club gaming permit allows is subject to conditions:

(a) in respect of equal chance gaming:
- the club must not deduct money from sums staked or won
- the participation fee must not exceed the amount prescribed in regulations
- the game takes place on the premises and must not be linked with a game on another set of premises.

Two games are linked if:
- the result of one game is, or may be, wholly or partly determined by reference to the result of the other game, or
- the amount of winnings available in one game is wholly or partly determined by reference to the amount of participation in the other game,

and a game which is split so that part is played on one site and another part is played elsewhere is treated as two linked games
- only club members and their genuine guests participate.

(b) in respect of other games of chance:
- the games must be pontoon and chemin de fer only
- no participation fee may be charged otherwise than in accordance with the regulations
- no amount may be deducted from sums staked or won otherwise than in accordance with the regulations.

25.29 There are limits on stakes and prizes for poker played in those clubs and institutes that do not hold a club gaming permit issued by their local licensing authority. The introduction of these limits reflects significant recent growth in the popularity of

6: Gambling Act 2005: Additional Material

poker, and the need to address the particular risks associated with such gaming. The regulations[67] impose a stakes limit of £10 per person per game, within a premises limit of up to £250 in stakes per day and £1,000 per week. The maximum fees that clubs may charge their members for participating in gaming has been set at £1 per day (or £3 if they hold a club gaming permit). Clubs and institutes holding a club gaming permit are also able to provide facilities for specified banker's games.

25.30 To help clubs and institutes to comply with the full range of statutory requirements for gaming, the Commission has issued a statutory code of practice on equal chance gaming in consultation with interested parties. The *Code of Practice for equal chance gaming in clubs and premises with an alcohol licence* is available from the Commission's website[68]. The provisions of the code (which also applies to alcohol-licensed premises) include:

- ensuring that young people and children are protected by excluding them from gaming (even if they are permitted on the premises)
- ensuring that gaming is fair and open by requiring close supervision of the games, record keeping (as appropriate), the need for standard rules and the display of stakes and prizes limits and the rules during play.

25.31 A 48 hour rule applies in respect of all three types of gaming, so that the games may only be played by people who have been members of the club for at least 48 hours, or have applied or been nominated for membership or are genuine guests of a member.

---

65 SI No 1945/2007: The Gambling Act 2005 (Club Gaming Permits) (Authorised Gaming) Regulations 2007

66 www.gamblingcommission.gov.uk

67 SI No 1944: The Gambling Act 2005 (Exempt Gaming in Clubs) Regulations 2007

68 Code of practice for equal chance gaming in clubs and premises with an alcohol licence, available from www.gamblingcommission.gov.uk

Protection of children and young persons

25.32 The gambling provided under the authority of a club gaming permit must also meet the following conditions:

(a) in respect of gaming machines:
   - no child or young person may use a category B or C machine on the premises
   - that the holder must comply with any relevant provision of a code of practice about the location and operation of gaming machines.

(b) the public, children and young persons must be excluded from any area of the premises where the gaming is taking place.

CLUB MACHINE PERMITS

25.33 If a members' club or a miners' welfare institute does not wish to have the full range of facilities permitted by a club gaming permit, they may apply to the licensing authority for a club machine permit under section 273 of the Act. This authorises the holder to have up to three gaming machines of categories B3A, B4, C and D. Commercial clubs are not permitted to provide non-machine gaming (other than exempt gaming under section 269 of the Act) so they should apply for a club machine permit, however, they will not be able to site category B3A gaming machines offering lottery games in their club.

25.34 In England and Wales, there are a number of premises, such as work premises which operate membership-based social clubs, that are not licensed to sell alcohol but are allowed to apply for a club machine permit. Before granting the permit the licensing authority will need to satisfy itself that the premises meet the requirements of a members' club and may grant the permit if the majority of members are over 18 years of age. The permit will allow up to three machines of category B3A, B4, C or D. If under-18s use the club, for example they are apprentices, they may play the category D, but not the B4 or C, machines. This does not apply in Scotland because only a club with a premises licence under the Licensing (Scotland) Act 2005 may apply for a club machine permit[69].

25.35 Holders of licensed premises club machine permits are required to comply with the code of practice, which has been issued by the Commission on the location and operation of machines. Information about this code can be found on the Commission's website[70].

---

[69] See SSI No 504/2007: The Club Gaming and Club Machine Permits (Scotland) Regulations 2007 and SSI No 150/2011: The Licensing (Scotland) Act 2005 (Consequential Provisions) Order 2011

[70] Code of practice for gaming machines in clubs and premises with an alcohol licence, available from www.gamblingcommission.gov.uk

Protection of children and young persons

25.36 Section 273 sets out the conditions that will apply to the club machine permit, including that in respect of gaming machines no child or young person uses a category B or C machine on the premises and that the holder complies with any relevant provision of a code of practice about the location and operation of gaming machines. It should be noted that clubs do not have to have permanent premises or an alcohol licence.

APPLICATIONS FOR CLUB GAMING PERMITS AND CLUB MACHINE PERMITS

25.37 The Secretary of State has made regulations in relation to applications for these permits, and Scottish Ministers have made separate regulations setting out the fees and applications requirements that apply in Scotland.

25.38 Applications must be made to the licensing authority in whose area the premises are located, and must be accompanied by the fee and documents prescribed in regulations[71]. Within a time prescribed in the regulations, the applicant must also copy the application to the Commission and to the chief officer of police. The Commission and the police may object to the permit being granted. The period within which such objections must be lodged and the grounds on which they may be made are set out in regulations. If any objections are made, the authority must hold a hearing (unless consent has been given to dispense with it), otherwise no hearing is necessary.

25.39 A licensing authority may grant or refuse a permit, but it may not attach any conditions to a permit. The authority has to inform the applicant, the Commission and the police of the outcome of the application and of any objections made.

25.40 Licensing authorities may only refuse an application on the grounds that:

(a) the applicant does not fulfil the requirements for a members' or commercial club or miners' welfare institute and therefore is not entitled to receive the type of permit for which it has applied
(b) the applicant's premises are used wholly or mainly by children and/or young persons
(c) an offence under the Act or a breach of a permit has been committed by the applicant while providing gaming facilities
(d) a permit held by the applicant has been cancelled in the previous ten years
(e) an objection has been lodged by the Commission or the police.

25.41 If the authority is satisfied that (a) or (b) is the case, it must refuse the application. Licensing authorities shall have regard to relevant guidance issued by the Commission and (subject to that guidance), the licensing objectives.

25.42 In cases where an objection has been lodged by the Commission or the police, the licensing authority is obliged to determine whether the objection is valid.

[71] SI No 1834: The Gambling Act 2005 (Club Gaming and Club Machine Permits) Regulations 2007, and SI No 2689: The Gambling Act 2005 (Club Gaming and Club Machine Permits) (Amendments) Regulations 2007 SSI No 504: The Club Gaming and Club Machine Permits (Scotland) Regulations 2007

FAST-TRACK PROCEDURE

25.43 There is a fast-track procedure for clubs in England and Wales which hold a club premises certificate under section 72 of the Licensing Act 2003. Under the fast-track procedure there is no opportunity for objections to be made by the Commission or the police, and the grounds upon which an authority can refuse a permit are reduced. This is because the club or institute will already have been through a licensing process in relation to its club premises certificate under the 2003 Act, and it is therefore unnecessary to impose the full requirements of Schedule 12. Commercial clubs cannot hold club premises certificates under the Licensing Act 2003 and so cannot use the fast-track procedure. The fast-track procedure also does not apply in Scotland.

25.44 Those clubs applying for permits by way of conversion of their pre-existing 1968 Act Part II or Part III club registrations do not have the fast track procedure available to them, even if they hold club premises certificates. In these instances, the club must still send a copy of the application to the Commission and chief officer of police. However, the Commission (and the police) may not object to the application and the licensing authority is, in fact, obliged to grant the application. However, care should be taken that the emphasis of the club is not being changed, to become a dedicated poker club for example.

25.45 The grounds on which an application under this process may be refused are that:

(a) the club is established primarily for gaming, other than gaming prescribed by regulations under section 266 of the Act

(b) in addition to the prescribed gaming, the applicant provides facilities for other gaming

(c) a club gaming permit or club machine permit issued to the applicant in the last ten years has been cancelled.

FACTORS TO CONSIDER WHEN GRANTING A CLUB GAMING PERMIT

25.46 The licensing authority has to satisfy itself that the club meets the requirements of the Act to obtain a club gaming permit. It is suggested that applicants for permits should be asked to supply sufficient information and documents to enable the licensing authority to take account of the matters discussed in paragraphs 25.47 to 25.49, at the time they submit their applications to the licensing authority.

25.47 In determining whether a club is a genuine members' club, the licensing authority should take account of a number of matters, such as:

- Is the primary purpose of the club's activities something other than the provision of gaming to its members? This is an indicator that it's a genuine members' club.
- Are the profits retained in the club for the benefit of the members? This is the key difference between a members' club and a commercial club.
- Are there 25 or more members? This is the amount of members a club has to have to qualify.
- Are there genuine domestic addresses on the register of members? Are domestic addresses listed for every member? Are members local to the club? These are all indicators that the member lists are bona fide and are made up of genuine members.

- Do members participate in the activities of the club via the internet? It is less likely to be a genuine members' club if this is the case.
- Do guest arrangements link a member to every guest? Is there evidence of a signing-in register for guests? Guests must be genuine guests of members and not members of the general public.
- Is the 48 hour rule between applying for membership and participating in any gaming properly applied? This is an indication that the club has a proper membership scheme.
- Are there annual accounts for more than one year? This would indicate that the club is permanent in nature, rather than temporary.
- How is the club advertised and listed in directories, including on the internet? If the club is categorised under "gaming" or "poker", it is less likely to be genuine members' club.
- Are children permitted into the club? The more access they have to areas of the premises, the less likely it is that the club is primarily for gambling activities.
- Does the club have a constitution and can it provide evidence that the constitution was approved by the members of the club? This provides further evidence that it is a properly constituted members' club.
- Is there a list of committee members and evidence of their election by the members of the club? Can the club provide minutes of committee and other meetings? These are further evidence that the club is a properly constituted members' club.

25.48 The constitution of the club could also indicate whether it is a legitimate members' club. Amongst the things to consider when examining the constitution are the following:

- Who makes commercial decisions on behalf of the club and what are the governance arrangements? Clubs are normally run by a committee made up of members of the club, rather than individuals or managers, who make decisions on behalf of the members. There will normally be a system (consultation, voting, paper ballots, annual general meetings, special meetings, etc) which allows members to be involved in major decisions concerning the management and running of the club. Such arrangements would normally be spelt out in the constitution.
- Are the aims of the club set out in the constitution? A lack of aims or aims which involve gaming could indicate that it is not a genuine members' club.
- Are there shareholders or members? Shareholders would indicate a business enterprise linked to a commercial club.
- Is the members' club permanently established? Clubs can't be temporary and must be permanent in nature
- Can people join with annual or quarterly membership? This would indicate that the club is permanent in nature.
- Are there long term membership benefits? This would also indicate that the club is permanent in nature and that it is a genuine members' club. The benefits of membership would normally be set out in the rules of membership.

25.49 Other than bridge and whist clubs, which are separately catered for in regulations, a club cannot be established wholly or mainly for purposes of gaming. In applying for a club gaming permit, a club must therefore provide substantial evidence of activities other than gaming. Useful questions which a licensing authority should consider include:

- How many nights is gaming made available? If gaming is available for all or most nights with little other activity, then it is likely that the club is established wholly or mainly for gaming.
- Is the gaming advertised? If gaming is advertised with little or no reference to the other activities of the club, then it is likely that gaming is the main activity of the club and that the gaming is run commercially.

- What are the stakes and prizes offered? The stakes and prizes limits must be complied with. Unlimited stakes and prizes are only available to genuine members' clubs once a club gaming permit has been granted. If high stakes and prizes are offered, this is also likely to indicate that gaming is one of the main activities of the club.
- Is there evidence of leagues with weekly/monthly/annual winners? This could indicate that the club's main activity is gaming.
- Is there evidence of non-playing members? If members participate in gaming exclusively, this is an indication that the main or only activity of the club is gaming.
- Are there teaching sessions to promote gaming, such as poker? This could be evidence that the club's main activity is gaming.
- Is there tie-in with other clubs offering gaming, such as poker, through tournaments or leagues? This is also an indication that gaming is possibly one of the main activities of the club.
- Is there sponsorship by gaming organisations, for example on-line poker providers? Similarly, this could indicate that poker is one of the main activities of the club.
- Are participation fees within limits? The licensing authority could consider club records and adverts for gaming, etc. Fees that exceed the limits could indicate that the gaming is run commercially.

25.50 The Commission advises that a visit to the premises before granting of the permit may assist the licensing authority to understand how the club will operate.

FACTORS TO CONSIDER FOR GAMING UNDER A CLUB MACHINE PERMIT

25.51 The licensing authority should satisfy itself that the gaming on offer meets the conditions set out in the Act and relevant regulations. To do this, the licensing authority may wish to ask questions of the applicant or ensure that the exempt gaming complies with these conditions. The conditions are:

- There must be no rake from the pot (that is, the organiser cannot take any money from the prize fund, or deduct money from the stakes or winnings). Licensing authorities should examine the records for gaming or, if possible, observe or get statements about the pot.
- There must be no side bets. This is probably only going to be possible to verify through observation.
- Participation fees must be within the limits prescribed in the regulations. Is there evidence of excess participation fees in club records, adverts for gaming in or outside of the club or from complaints? Participation fees must not be disguised as charges for dealers, mandatory tipping of dealers, table charges or hire charges. Again, observation of the gaming may be necessary.
- Prizes must be within the limits prescribed in the regulations. Is there evidence that they are excessive from records at the club, in adverts for gaming, etc? Note that daily and weekly limits must be monitored by the operator and that "money or money's worth" (for example, goods) counts towards the prize limits.
- Where the games are poker tournaments or leagues, the licensing authority may find it useful to consult part 29 which sets out how the law applies to poker. This should help the licensing authority to determine whether the gaming is within the law from evidence such as records in the club and adverts for gaming.

FACTORS TO CONSIDER WHEN MONITORING CLUB GAMING PERMITS

25.52 Once the licensing authority has issued a club gaming permit, it is recommended that various aspects need to be considered by licensing authorities in monitoring the club gaming permit. In addition to monitoring whether the club continues to meet the requirements of the Act for a club gaming permit (that is, whether it remains a genuine members' club) and whether the gaming meets the conditions set out in the Act and the relevant regulations, licensing authorities may also wish to consider the issues described in the paragraphs that follow.

25.53 Where clubs have computers available for use by members, licensing authorities should be aware that these may be so-called dual use computers which, among other things, allow club members to access gambling websites via the internet. In certain circumstances, these computers may be taken to be gaming machines. Generally, a computer is not a gaming machine merely because there is a possibility of accessing a gambling website via the internet. However, a computer will be taken to be a gaming machine if it is knowingly adapted or presented to facilitate or draw attention to the possibility of it being used for gambling.

25.54 It is not possible to provide a definitive list of examples of what constitutes a computer that is knowingly adapted or presented to facilitate or draw attention to the possibility of it being used for gambling. Each case will need to be looked at individually and ultimately the decision regarding whether a machine is a gaming machine is one for the courts to make.

25.55 The precise circumstances in which the facilities are offered – including the environment in which they are offered and the relationship with other gambling facilities provided – will need to be taken into account when assessing the status of those facilities. The Commission has provided the following indicators that may help in making decisions about whether a computer is knowingly adapted or presented to facilitate or draw attention to the possibility of it being used for gambling. This list is not exhaustive, and the presence or absence of any single factor is not necessarily conclusive:

- icons for gambling websites displayed on the desktop screen
- links to gambling websites available via the start menu
- screensavers, desktop wallpapers referring to gambling websites
- internet browsing history or favourites menu containing gambling websites
- promotional material (posters, flyers) indicating the use of computers for gambling
- gambling software downloaded onto a computer
- staff informing customers of the existence of the computer for access to gambling websites
- email messages or other promotional material sent to customers/individuals referring to the availability of computers on premises for gambling purposes.

25.56 Licensing authorities should note that permission to advertise gambling in Great Britain is restricted to operators licensed by the Commission, operators from the European Economic Area, Gibraltar and the white-listed jurisdictions (Alderney, Antigua and Barbuda, Isle of Man and Tasmania).

25.57 Club premises, computer terminals in the club or the club website may contain advertising of 'foreign gambling', or clubs may offer seats at overseas poker tournaments as prizes in poker tournaments run on the club premises. In the Commission's view, this amounts to advertising of non-UK gambling, as defined by section 327 of the Act. Unless the overseas tournament is based in the European Economic Area, Gibraltar or the white-listed jurisdictions, this is likely to amount to the advertising of 'foreign gambling', which is an offence under section 331 of the Act.

25.58 Any of the factors mentioned in the preceding paragraphs in this section may give rise to the need to review the club gaming permit or take appropriate enforcement action.

25.59 The Commission provides advice and guidance to licensing authorities on permits and related matters and, on a case-by-case basis, will undertake targeted collaborations with licensing authorities in order to establish principle and precedent, and a clear understanding of the legal requirements.

25.60 An agency that may also be able to assist licensing authority enquiries is HM Revenue and Customs (HMRC). If a club is trading under the auspices of a club gaming permit (as a members' club) but is in fact a commercial club with, for example, their main activity being poker, they would be liable for gaming duty. Licensing authorities should bear in mind that clubs of this nature have premises to maintain, as well as staff and other costs, so the sums involved may be significant. There may also be other aspects of the financing of such clubs that would cause HMRC to become involved.

MAINTENANCE OF PERMITS

25.61 The permit will have effect for ten years, unless it ceases to have effect because it is surrendered or lapses or is renewed. However, a permit granted under the fast-track procedure does not expire, unless it ceases to have effect because it is surrendered, cancelled or forfeited, or it lapses.
25.62 The holder of the permit must pay to the licensing authority the first annual fee, and an annual fee before each anniversary of the issue of the permit, in accordance with regulations.
25.63 Permits may be amended to meet changing circumstances. Licensing authorities may only refuse a variation if on consideration of a completely new application they would refuse the permit.
25.64 The permit, which is to be kept on the premises it relates to, must be in a form specified by the regulations and, if obtained through the fast-track procedure, must identify the appropriate club premises certificate it relates to. It is an offence not to produce the permit when requested to do so by a constable or an enforcement officer.
25.65 If a permit is lost, stolen or damaged, the holder may apply for a replacement, subject to payment of a prescribed fee. The licensing authority must grant the application if it is satisfied that the permit has been lost, stolen or damaged and, where the permit is lost or stolen, a report has been made to the police. It should issue a copy and certify it as a true copy.
25.66 A permit will lapse if the holder of the permit stops being a club or miners' welfare institute, or if it no longer qualifies under the fast-track system for a permit. In addition, a permit will cease to have effect upon being surrendered to the authority. A notice to surrender must be accompanied by the permit or a statement explaining why it cannot be produced. The authority must inform the police and the Commission when a permit has been surrendered or lapsed.

CANCELLATION AND FORFEITURE OF PERMITS

25.67 The licensing authority may cancel the permit if:
- the premises are used wholly by children and/or young persons
- an offence or breach of a permit condition has been committed in the course of gaming activities by the permit holder.

Reference here to 'a permit condition' means a condition in the Act or in regulations that the permit is operating under.
25.68 Before cancelling a permit, the licensing authority must give the permit holder at least 21 days' notice of the intention to cancel and consider any representations that they may make. The authority must hold a hearing if the permit holder so requests and must comply with any other procedural requirements set out in regulations. If there is no appeal, the cancellation will take effect 21 days after notice of the intention to cancel was given. The authority must notify the permit holder, the Commission and the police that the permit has been cancelled and the reasons for the cancellation.

RENEWAL OF PERMITS

25.69 In England and Wales, in accordance with paragraph 24 of Schedule 12 of the Act, an application for renewal of a permit must be made during the period beginning three months before the licence expires and ending six weeks before it expires. The procedure for renewal is the same as for an application. In Scotland, the Licensed Premises Gaming Machine Permits (Scotland) Regulations 2007 apply. Permits granted in terms of these Regulations do not expire, although they can cease to have effect in certain circumstances, can be cancelled and can be varied.

25.70 The duration of the permit will not be curtailed while a renewal application is pending, including an appeal against a decision not to renew.
25.71 If, at the time a permit is renewed, the applicant holds a club premises certificate, the fast track procedure will apply as it does when application is first made for the permit. This does not apply in Scotland.

APPEALS

25.72 The rights of appeal in relation to permits are discussed in part 12 of this Guidance.

COMMISSION CODES OF PRACTICE

25.73 The Commission has issued a code of practice under section 24 of the Act in respect of exempt equal chance gaming. This can be found on the Commission's website[72].
25.74 The code of practice requires clubs and welfare institutes to adopt good practice measures for the provision of gaming. The code also sets out the stakes and prizes limits and the limits on participation fees (as applicable) laid out in regulations.
25.75 The emphasis of the regulations and the code of practice is on self-regulation by the management of the premises and licensing authorities should take a strong line in cases where breaches are detected.
25.76 Additionally, the Commission's code of practice for gaming machines in clubs can be found on the Commission's website[73]. This code includes sections relating to:

- the location and operation of machines, which are a requirement of club permits
- access to gambling by children and young persons, which sets out good practice guidance for permit holders
- customer complaints and disputes, which again sets out good practice for permit holders.

---

72 Code of practice for equal chance gaming in clubs and premises with an alcohol licence, available from www.gamblingcommission.gov.uk

73 Code of practice for gaming machines in clubs and premises with an alcohol licence, available from www.gamblingcommission.gov.uk

POWERS IN RESPECT OF CLUB PREMISES

25.77 Section 312 of the Act provides that:

- a constable or enforcement officer can enter club or miners' welfare institute premises, or premises which they reasonably believe to be used by a club or institute, to determine whether:
  - gaming is taking place on the premises or is about to take place on the premises
  - any gaming that is taking place or is about to take place on the premises meets the requirements for exempt gaming in section 269 of the Act, a club gaming permit or a club machine permit
- an authorised local authority officer can enter premises in respect of which an application for a club gaming permit or club machine permit has been made for a purpose connected with the consideration of the application.

25.78 An enforcement officer is an employee of the Commission designated as an enforcement officer for the purposes of the Act, or a person other than an employee appointed as an enforcement officer for the same purpose. An authorised local authority officer is an officer of a LA designated as an authorised person for the purposes of section 304 of the Act, where the premises are wholly or partly situated in the LA's area.

25.79 As the Act indicates that local licensing officers are not authorised to enter club premises under the Act once the club permit has been issued, this has generally been assumed to mean that the LAs lack all the necessary powers and the Commission is, therefore, the default organisation for enforcement action. However, the necessary powers are available to the police and the Commission suggests that LAs, working in partnership with local police forces, have the ability to enforce compliance by clubs where needed.

25.80 LAs may also want to consider whether their officers have powers under other relevant Acts, such as the Licensing Act or Local Government Act.

PART 26: ALCOHOL-LICENSED PREMISES

26.1 Sections 279 to 284 of the Act only apply to premises in respect of which an on-premises alcohol licence (in England and Wales) or a licence for sale by retail or supply of alcoholic liquor, but excluding an off-sale licence (in Scotland), has been issued and that have a bar at which alcohol is served, without a requirement that alcohol is served only with food. So, any hotel, restaurant or pub that has a bar can offer gambling under Part 12 of the Act, but hotels and restaurants that serve alcohol only with food cannot.

AUTOMATIC ENTITLEMENT TO TWO MACHINES

26.2 Section 282 of the Act provides an automatic entitlement to alcohol licence holders to make available two gaming machines (of category C or D) for use in alcohol-licensed premises. To take advantage of this entitlement, the person who holds the on-premises licence (under the Licensing Act 2003) or relevant Scottish licence must give notice to the licensing authority of their intention to make gaming machines available for use, and must pay the prescribed fee (as set by regulations)[74]. If the person ceases to be the holder of the on- premises alcohol licence for the premises, the automatic entitlement to the two gaming machines also ceases. Whoever applies for the new premises alcohol licence would also need to apply under section 282(2), notifying the licensing authority of their intention to make the gaming machines available for use and paying the prescribed fee.

26.3 This is not an authorisation procedure. Licensing authorities have no discretion to consider the notification or to turn it down. The only considerations to apply are whether the person applying for the automatic gaming machine entitlement is the holder of the alcohol licence and whether the prescribed fee has been paid. There is no statutory requirement for pubs and other alcohol-licensed premises to display a notice of their automatic entitlement to gaming machines.

[74] SI No 1832: The Gaming Machines in Alcohol Licensed Premises (Notification Fee) (England and Wales) Regulations 2007 SSI No 311: The Gambling Act 2005 (Fees No 2) (Scotland) Regulations 2007

Removal of exemption

26.4 Licensing authorities can remove the automatic authorisation in respect of any particular premises by making an order under section 284 of the Act. That section provides for the licensing authority to make such an order if:

- provision of the machines is not reasonably consistent with the pursuit of the licensing objectives
- gaming has taken place on the premises that breaches a condition of section 282 – for example, the gaming machines have been made available in a way that does not comply with requirements on the location and operation of gaming machines
- the premises are mainly used for gaming

- an offence under the Act has been committed on the premises.

26.5 Before making an order, the licensing authority must give the licensee at least 21 days' notice of the intention to make the order and consider any representations that they may make. The authority must hold a hearing if the licensee so requests and must comply with any other procedural requirements set out in regulations. If there is no appeal, the order will take effect 21 days after notice of the intention was given. The authority must give the licensee a copy of the order and written reasons for making it. The licensee may appeal to the magistrates' court or the sheriff.

LICENSED PREMISES GAMING MACHINE PERMITS

26.6 Licensing authorities may issue licensed premises gaming machine permits for any number of category C or D machines in licensed premises. Where a permit authorises the making available of a specified number of gaming machines in particular premises, this will effectively replace, and not be in addition to, any automatic entitlement to two machines under section 282.

26.7 Holders of alcohol-licensed premises gaming machine permits are required to comply with a code of practice, which has been drawn up by the Commission on the location and operation of machines. Information about this code can be found on the Commission's website[75].

26.8 The detail of how to apply for licensed premises gaming machine permits is set out in Schedule 13 of the Act (for England and Wales) and in The Licensed Premises Gaming Machine Permits (Scotland) Regulations 2007 (for Scotland).

26.9 Applications must be made by a person who, or organisation which, holds the 'on-premises' alcohol licence for the premises for which the application is made. An application may not be made if a premises licence under the Gambling Act is in effect at the premises. The application must be made to an authority in whose area the premises are wholly or partly situated. The Act requires an application to include certain information – the premises to which it relates and the number and category of gaming machines sought. Apart from this it is for the authority to direct the form and manner of the application and what additional information and documents are required.

26.10 In determining an application, the authority must have regard to the licensing objectives and to this Guidance. They may also take account of any other matters that are considered relevant to the application. The application does not require notification to the Commission or police before determination. However, licensing authorities are able to specify this as a requirement should they see fit.

26.11 The authority may grant or refuse an application. In granting the application, the authority may vary the number and category of gaming machines authorised by the permit. If the authority grants the application, they must issue the permit as soon as possible after that. Where they refuse the application they must notify the applicant as soon as possible, setting out the reasons for refusal. The authority must not refuse an application, or grant it for a different number or category of machines, unless they have notified the applicant of their intention to do so and given the applicant an opportunity to make representations (orally or in writing, or both).

26.12 The permit must specify the person or organisation to which it is issued, the number of gaming machines for which the permit has effect, the address of the premises and the date on which it takes effect.

26.13 The permit holder can apply to the authority to amend the permit to reflect a change in the holder's name. The authority must comply with the request, provided the prescribed fee is paid.

26.14 The permit holder must keep the permit on the premises, and it must be produced on request for inspection by a constable, enforcement officer or local authority officer (not to do so will be an offence). If the permit is lost, stolen or damaged, the holder may apply to the issuing authority for a copy. The application must be accompanied by the prescribed fee.

26.15 There are no renewal provisions for this class of permit because these permits are indefinite, and continue in force for so long as the premises continues to have an alcohol licence and the holder of the permit continues to hold that licence. The permit can lapse if the holder surrenders it to the licensing authority.

26.16 The holder may apply to vary the permit by changing the number and/or category of machines authorised by it.

26.17 The licensing authority is able to cancel a permit. It may only do so in specified circumstances which include if the premises are used wholly or mainly by children or young persons or if an offence under the Act has been committed. Before it cancels a permit the licensing authority must notify the holder, giving 21 days notice of intention to cancel, consider any representations made by the holder, hold a hearing if requested, and comply with any other prescribed requirements relating to the procedure to be followed. Where the authority cancels the permit, the cancellation does not take effect until the period for appealing against that decision has elapsed, or (where an appeal is made) until the appeal is determined.

26.18 The authority can also cancel a permit if the holder fails to pay the annual fee (unless failure is the result of an administrative error). The court may order forfeiture of the permit if the holder is convicted of a relevant offence.

26.19 Where a person applies to a licensing authority for the transfer of an alcohol premises licence, they will also need to apply separately for the transfer of the licensed premises gaming machine permit. Both applications will require a fee to be paid.

26.20 The applicant may appeal to the magistrates' court against an authority's decision not to issue a permit. The holder can also appeal against a decision to cancel a permit.

---

[75] Code of practice for gaming machines in clubs and premises with an alcohol licence, available fromwww.gamblingcommission.gov.uk

EXEMPT GAMING

26.21 Exempt gaming is equal chance gaming generally permissible in any club or alcohol- licensed premises. Such gaming should be ancillary to the purposes of the premises. This provision is automatically available to all such premises, but is subject to statutory stakes and prize limits determined by the Secretary of State.

26.22 Equal chance gaming is gaming that does not involve staking against a bank and the chances of winning are equally favourable to all participants. It includes games such as backgammon, mah-jong, rummy, kalooki, dominoes, cribbage, bingo and poker.

26.23 The Secretary of State has set both daily and weekly prize limits for exempt gaming in alcohol-licensed premises[76]. These limits are set out in Appendix C to this Guidance.

26.24 Exempt gaming should be supervised by a nominated gaming supervisor and comply with any code of practice issued by the Commission under section 24 of the Act. Information about this code can be found on the Commission's website[77].

26.25 A fee may not be levied for participation in the equal chance gaming offered by an alcohol- licensed premises under the exempt gaming rules. A compulsory charge, such as charging for a meal, may constitute a participation fee, depending on the particular circumstances.

26.26 In order to qualify as exempt gaming, clubs and alcohol-licensed premises may not charge a rake on games or levy or deduct an amount from stakes or winnings.

26.27 The gaming offered must not be linked to gaming in other premises and no person under 18 may participate in the gaming.

26.28 Information about poker in alcohol-licensed premises can be found in Part 29 of this guidance.

[76] SI No 1940/2007: The Gambling Act 2005 (Exempt Gaming in Alcohol Licensed Premises) Regulations 2007

[77] Code of practice for equal chance gaming in clubs and premises with an alcohol licence, available from www.gamblingcommission.gov.uk

Removal of exemption

26.29 Licensing authorities can remove the automatic authorisation for exempt gaming in respect of any particular premises by making an order under section 284 of the Act. That section provides for the licensing authority to make such an order if:

- provision of the gaming is not reasonably consistent with the pursuit of the licensing objectives
- gaming has taken place on the premises that breaches a condition of section 279 – for example, the gaming does not abide by the prescribed limits for stakes and prizes, a participation fee is charged for the gaming or an amount is deducted or levied from sums staked or won
- the premises are mainly used for gaming
- an offence under the Act has been committed on the premises.

26.30 Before making an order, the licensing authority must give the licensee at least 21 days' notice of the intention to make the order and consider any representations that they may make. The authority must hold a hearing if the licensee so requests and must comply with any other procedural requirements set out in regulations. If there is no appeal, the order will take effect 21 days after notice of the intention was given. The authority must give the licensee a copy of the order and written reasons for making it. The licensee may appeal to the magistrates' court or the sheriff.

BINGO

26.31 Alcohol-licensed premises are able to provide facilities for bingo under section 281 of the Act, provided that the restrictions in section 281 are complied with. These include that, in any seven day period, the aggregate stakes or prizes for bingo must not exceed £2,000. If that limit is exceeded, the relevant operating and personal licences must be sought (see part 18 of the Guidance).

26.32 The bingo must comply with any code issued by the Commission under section 24 of the Act. Information about this code can be found on the Commission's website[78].

[78] Code of practice for equal chance gaming in clubs and premises with an alcohol licence, available from www.gamblingcommission.gov.uk

BETTING

26.33 Commercial betting, regardless of the level of stakes, is not permitted in alcohol-licensed premises. Those who facilitate such betting in pubs are providing illegal facilities for gambling and are breaking the law. Even where publicans accept bets on behalf of licensed bookmakers, or just facilitate betting through their own telephone betting accounts, they are acting as betting intermediaries and could be prosecuted.

26.34 Licensed bookmakers who knowingly accept bets from pub customers through a single account are encouraging illegal gambling and may be in breach of the Act and could risk losing their licence.

26.35 Licensed bookmakers with a remote or ancillary licence can accept telephone bets from a customer watching an event in a pub, as long as that customer has an individual account with them. It is illegal for bookmakers or their agents to sit in the pub taking bets themselves.

26.36 It should be noted, however, that the prohibition on commercial betting in alcohol-licensed premises does not apply in relation to tracks, but only in certain circumstances. Where the betting takes place under the authority of a track premises licence, it can take place in an area on the track licensed for the sale of alcohol, provided that the licensing authority has approved the betting area as part of the track premises licence application. However, this does not apply in relation to separate and discrete premises on the track where betting takes place under the authority of a general betting licence. In this case, the consumption of alcohol on those premises is prohibited.

COMMISSION CODES OF PRACTICE

26.37 The Commission has issued a code of practice under section 24 of the Act in respect of exempt equal chance gaming. This can be found on the Commission's website[79].

26.38 The code of practice requires owners/licensees to adopt good practice measures for the provision of gaming in general and poker in particular. The code also sets out the stakes and prizes limits laid out in regulations.

26.39 The emphasis of the regulations and the code of practice is on self-regulation by the management of the premises and licensing authorities should take a strong line in cases where breaches are detected.

26.40 Under section 310(2) of the Act, an authorised licensing authority officer may enter premises with an alcohol licence for the purpose of:

(a) determining whether the gaming satisfies the conditions in section 279 of the Act;
(b) in the case of bingo played on the premises, determining:
    (i) whether the terms and conditions of any relevant operating licence are being complied with;
    (ii) whether section 281 of the Act applies;
(c) ascertaining the number and category of gaming machines being made available for use on the premises.

26.41 Additionally, the Commission's code of practice on gaming machines in alcohol-licensed premises can be found on the Commission's website[80]. This code includes sections relating to:

- the location and operation of machines, which are a requirement of machine permits
- access to gambling by children and young persons, which sets out good practice guidance for permit holders
- customer complaints and disputes, which again sets out good practice for permit holders.

---

79 Code of practice for equal chance gaming in clubs and premises with an alcohol licence, available from www.gamblingcommission.gov.uk

80 Code of practice for gaming machines in clubs and premises with an alcohol licence, available from www.gamblingcommission.gov.uk

SCOTLAND

26.42 The provisions of the Act which relate to gaming and gaming machines in licensed premises also apply to Scotland. In Scotland they apply to premises which have a premises licence granted under the Licensing (Scotland) Act 2005, provided that it is not a licence authorising the sale of alcohol for consumption off the premises only.

26.43 The provisions affecting licensed premises gaming machine permits in Scotland have been set out separately. This is because Schedule 13 of the Act does not apply in Scotland. Instead, Scottish Ministers have power under section 285 of the Act to make regulations about the regime in Scotland. The same also applies to gaming and gaming machine permits for clubs in Scotland. Schedule 12 of the Act does not apply in that case and, instead, Scottish Ministers have the power to make provision in regulations about the regime for club gaming and club machine permits. The Scottish Executive has made separate regulations in this regard[81]. It is also important to note that, in Scotland, Schedule 12 does not apply to clubs licensed to sell alcohol (by virtue of section 274(2) of the Act).

---

81 SSI No 505/2007: The Licensed Premises Gaming Machine Permits (Scotland) Regulations 2007 and SSI No 504/2007: The Club Gaming and Club Machine Permits (Scotland) Regulations 2007.

ALCOHOL-LICENSED PREMISES GAMING MACHINE PERMITS (SECTION 34 PERMITS)

26.44 With effect from 1 September 2007, all old 'section 34' permits issued under the Gaming Act 1968 were renamed 'alcohol-licensed premises gaming machine permits'. With effect from that date, amongst other things, the renamed section 34 permits (alcohol-licensed premises gaming machine permits) could be transferred in accordance with Schedule 13 to the Gambling Act 2005. The alcohol-licensed premises gaming machine permits could only be approved by the licensing authority if the transfer of the relevant on-premises alcohol licence was approved. These permits expired on 31 August 2010.[82]

---

82 SI No 3272/2006: The Gambling Act 2005 (Commencement No. 6 and Transitional Provisions) Order 2006

PROTECTION OF CHILDREN AND YOUNG PERSONS

26.45 The Commission's code of practice relating to the location and operation of gaming machines provides that, in respect of gaming machines in alcohol-licensed premises, the licence holder or permit holder should put into effect procedures intended to prevent underage gambling. This should include procedures for:

- checking the age of apparently underage customers; and
- refusing access to anyone who appears to be underage, and who tries to use category B or C gaming machines and cannot produce an acceptable form of identification.

It requires that all gaming machines situated on the premises must be located in a place within the premises where their use can be supervised, either by staff whose duties include such supervision (including bar or floor staff) or by other means. Alcohol premises licence holders or permit holders must have in place arrangements for such supervision.

26.46 In respect of exempt equal chance gaming, the code requires the gaming supervisor to put into effect procedures designed to prevent underage gambling. These should include:

- holding the gaming in premises or parts of premises which are restricted to adults;
- checking the age of potentially underage players; and
- refusing access to the gaming to anyone apparently underage who cannot produce an acceptable form of age verification and identification.

Procedures should be in place for dealing with cases where an underage person repeatedly attempts to gamble, including verbal warnings and reporting the offence to the Commission and the police. The gaming supervisor should also take reasonable steps to ensure that all employees understand their responsibilities under the code of practice.

PROHIBITED GAMING

26.32 No bankers' games may be played either in commercial clubs or alcohol licensed premises or in members' clubs/miners' welfare institutes unless they have a club gaming permit. With a permit the two bankers' games of pontoon and *chemin de fer* may be played. Otherwise, games such as blackjack, roulette and any others which involve staking against the holder of the bank are unlawful on such premises.

PART 27: PRIZE GAMING AND PRIZE GAMING PERMITS

27.1 Section 288 defines gaming as prize gaming if the nature and size of the prize is not determined by the number of people playing or the amount paid for or raised by the gaming. Normally the prizes are determined by the operator before play commences.
27.2 A prize gaming permit is a permit issued by the licensing authority to authorise the provision of facilities for gaming with prizes on specified premises.

PRIZE GAMING WITHOUT A PRIZE GAMING PERMIT

27.3 Casinos are able to offer any form of prize gaming, other than bingo. That is because a casino operating licence gives authority to provide all games of chance, except any form of bingo, which is excluded from the scope of the casino licence by section 68(3)(b). If a casino wishes to provide bingo generally, it would need to obtain a bingo operating licence, however, this is subject to the constraint that only one premises licence may be issued for any particular premises at any time (see section 152) *and so the premises would have to be distinct.* Only casino premises licences for 2005 Act large casinos permit bingo to be offered *within the casino premises* (see section 174). If a casino wishes to offer prize bingo, it could obtain a prize gaming permit, however, it is more likely that the casino will apply for an operating licence to cover all forms of bingo (subject to the constraint already mentioned).
27.4 Section 291 enables any form of prize gaming to be provided in bingo premises in reliance on their bingo operating licence. This provision allows bingo operators to provide prize gaming in respect of casino games as well as games of equal chance, which they would not otherwise be able to do under the conditions of their operating licence. In the case of bingo operators, the Commission or Secretary of State could impose conditions preventing specified games from being offered, although there are currently no plans to do so. Additionally, limits have been set on individual and aggregated stakes and prizes for prize gaming in bingo premises, the purpose of which is to ensure that such gaming is restricted to low stakes[83].
27.5 Section 290 provides that any type of prize gaming may be provided in adult gaming centres and licensed family entertainment centres, and that unlicensed family entertainment centres may offer equal chance prize gaming under the auspices of their gaming machine permit, without the need for a prize gaming permit.
27.6 Section 292 provides that travelling fairs are also able to offer equal chance prize gaming without a permit, provided that, taken together, the facilities for gambling are an ancillary amusement at the fair.
27.7 Children and young persons may participate in equal chance prize gaming only.
27.8 Section 293 sets out four conditions that permit holders, AGCs, FECs and travelling fairs must comply with to lawfully offer prize gaming. These are:

- the limits on participation fees, as set out in regulations[84], must be complied with
- all chances to participate in the gaming must be allocated on the premises on which the gaming is taking place and on one day; the game must be played and

completed on the day the chances are allocated; and the result of the game must be made public in the premises on the day that it is played
- the prize for which the game is played must not exceed the amount set out in regulations (if a money prize), or the prescribed value (if non-monetary prize)
- participation in the gaming must not entitle the player to take part in any other gambling.

---

83 SI No 2257/2007: The Gambling Act 2005 (Operating Licence Conditions) Regulations 2007 and SI No 774/2010: The Gambling Act 2005 (Operating Licence Conditions) (Amendment) Regulations 2010

84 SI No 1777/2007: The Gambling Act 2005 (Limits on Prize Gaming) Regulations 2007

PRIZE GAMING PERMITS

27.9 Schedule 14 sets out the application process and regulatory regime for prize gaming permits.
27.10 An application for a permit can only be made by a person who occupies or plans to occupy the relevant premises and if the applicant is an individual, he must be aged 18 or over. An application for a permit cannot be made if a premises licence or club gaming permit is in effect for the same premises. The application must be made to the licensing authority in whose area the premises are wholly or partly situated.
27.11 The authority must specify the form and manner in which the application should be made, and specify what information and documents (for example, insurance certificates, plans of building) they require to accompany the application. An application must specify the premises and the nature of the gaming for which the permit is sought.
27.12 In their Licensing Authority Statement of Policy, licensing authorities should include a statement of principles that they propose to apply when exercising their functions in considering applications for permits. In particular, they may want to set out the matters that they will take into account in determining the suitability of the applicant. Given that the premises will particularly appeal to children and young persons, in considering what to take into account in the application process and what information to request from the applicant, licensing authorities will want to give weight to child protection issues. Licensing authorities should ask the applicant to set out the types of gaming that he or she is intending to offer and the applicant should be able to demonstrate that:
- they understand the limits to stakes and prizes that are set out in regulations
- the gaming offered is within the law.

GRANTING OR REFUSING A PERMIT

27.13 The licensing authority can grant or refuse an application for a permit, but cannot add conditions. The licensing authority may grant a permit only if they have consulted the chief officer of police about the application. The licensing authority will want to take account of any objections that the police may wish to make which are relevant to the licensing objectives. Relevant considerations would be the suitability of the applicant in terms of any convictions that they may have that would make them unsuitable to operate prize gaming; and the suitability of the premises in relation to their location and issues about disorder. Licensing authorities need not (but may) have regard to the licensing objectives and shall have regard to this Guidance.
27.14 A permit cannot be issued in respect of a vessel or a vehicle.
27.15 The licensing authority may not refuse an application unless they have notified the applicant of the intention to refuse and the reasons for it, and given them an opportunity to make representations orally or in writing or both.
27.16 If a permit is granted, the licensing authority must issue it as soon as is reasonably practicable. The Secretary of State has set out the form of the permit in

regulations[85]. The permit must specify the person to whom it is issued, the premises to which it relates, the nature of the gaming, the date on which it takes effect, the date on which it expires, and the name and address of the licensing authority issuing the permit. Scottish Ministers have made separate regulations[86] in respect of fees associated with prize gaming permits.

27.17 If the person to whom the permit is issued changes their name, or wants to be known by another name, they may send the permit to the issuing authority for amendment, together with the appropriate fee. The authority must comply with the request and return the permit to the holder.

---

70 SI No 455/2007: The Gambling Act 2005 (Prize Gaming) (Permits) Regulations 2007

71 SSI No 309/2007: The Gambling Act 2005 (Fees) (Scotland) Regulations 2007

DURATION, LAPSE, SURRENDER AND FORFEITURE

27.18 The permit will have effect for ten years, unless it ceases to have effect or is renewed. There is no annual fee for prize gaming permits.

27.19 The permit may lapse for a number of reasons:

- if the holder ceases to occupy the premises
- if an individual permit holder dies, becomes incapable by reason of mental or physical incapacity, becomes bankrupt, or sequestration of his estate is ordered
- if a company holding the permit goes into liquidation
- if the holder (for example a partnership) otherwise ceases to exist.

27.20 Where a permit lapses, the Act provides that the permit may be relied upon for a period of six months after it has lapsed, by the following persons:

- the personal representative of the holder (in the case of death)
- the trustee of the bankrupt estate (in the case of individual bankruptcy)
- the holder's interim or permanent trustee (in the case of an individual whose estate is sequestrated)
- the liquidator of the company (in the case of a company that goes into liquidation).

27.21 The permit may also cease to have effect if the holder surrenders it to the licensing authority. Notice of such surrender must be accompanied by the permit, or by an explanation of why the permit cannot be produced.

27.22 If the permit holder is convicted of a relevant offence (that is an offence listed in Schedule 7 of the Act), the court may order the forfeiture of the permit. The court must order the holder to deliver the permit to the licensing authority, or provide a statement explaining why it is not reasonably practicable to produce it. The court must notify the licensing authority that it has made a forfeiture order as soon as is reasonably practicable after making the order. Such an order may be suspended by a higher court pending appeal against conviction of a relevant offence.

RENEWAL

27.23 In accordance with paragraph 18 of Schedule 14, an application for renewal of a permit must be made during the period beginning six months before the permit expires and ending two months before it expires. The procedure for renewal is the same as for an application.

27.24 A permit will not cease to have effect while a renewal application is pending, including an appeal against a decision not to renew.

MAINTENANCE

27.25 The permit must be kept on the premises and it is an offence not to produce it when requested to do so by a constable, an enforcement officer, or an authorised local authority officer.

27.26 If a permit is lost, stolen or damaged, the holder may apply for a replacement subject to paying the fee set by the Secretary of State and Scottish Ministers. The licensing authority must grant the application if it is satisfied that the permit has been lost, stolen or damaged and a report has been made to the police. It should issue a copy and certify it as a true copy.

APPEALS

27.27 The rights of appeal in relation to permits are discussed in part 12 of this Guidance.

PART 28: NON-COMMERCIAL AND PRIVATE GAMING AND BETTING

28.1 The Act permits gambling without any specific permissions under limited circumstances. In summary these are:

- non-commercial gaming
- incidental non-commercial lotteries (these are discussed in part 32 – small society lotteries)
- private gaming and betting

NON-COMMERCIAL GAMING

28.2 The Act permits non-commercial gaming if it takes place at a non-commercial event, either as an incidental or principal activity at the event. Events are non-commercial if no part of the proceeds is for private profit or gain. The proceeds of such events may benefit one or more individuals if the activity is organised:

- by, or on behalf of, a charity or for charitable purposes
- to enable participation in, or support of, sporting, athletic or cultural activities.

So it would be possible to raise funds for an individual providing the proceeds were, for example, for a wheelchair or to support a sporting endeavour. Additionally, popular events such as race nights or casino nights may be permitted if they comply with the regulations and profits go to a 'good cause'. More details about these can be found later in this part.

28.3 Section 297(3) of the Act defines proceeds as:

(a) the sums raised by the organisers (whether by way of fees for entrance or for participation, by way of sponsorship, by way of commission from traders, or otherwise), minus

(b) amounts deducted by the organisers in respect of costs reasonably incurred in organising the event.

However, sums raised by other persons will not form part of the proceeds of the event and may be appropriated for private gain. An example would be refreshments provided at the event by an independent third party.

28.4 If someone uses any profits from non-commercial gaming for something other than the specified purpose, then they commit an offence under section 301 of the Act. The maximum penalty, upon conviction for such an offence, is a term of imprisonment not exceeding 51 weeks for England and Wales (six months in Scotland), and/or a level five fine.

28.5 The Act identifies two types of permissible non-commercial gaming:

- prize gaming (which must comply with the conditions set out in section 299 of the Act)
- equal chance gaming (which must comply with the conditions set out in section 300 of the Act and the conditions prescribed in regulations).

NON-COMMERCIAL PRIZE GAMING

28.6 Provided that the conditions set out in section 299 are met, the organiser does not need to have an operating or premises licence nor a prize gaming permit. In summary, the conditions are:

- players are told that the purpose of the gaming is to raise money for a specified charitable, sporting, athletic or cultural purpose
- profits are not for private gain
- the event cannot take place in a venue (other than a track) which has a premises licence. If at a track the premises licence cannot be in use (in effect no betting can be taking place) and no temporary use notice can have effect
- the gaming must be on the premises and not be remote gaming.

28.7 In these circumstances, prize gaming occurs if the nature and size of the prize is not determined by the number of people playing or the amount paid for or raised by the gaming. Normally the prizes will be determined by the operator before play commences.

NON-COMMERCIAL EQUAL CHANCE GAMING

28.8 The conditions set out under section 300 are as follows:

- All players must be told what purpose the money raised from the gaming is going to be used for (this must be something other than private gain), and the profits must be applied for that purpose
- The gaming must also comply with regulations[87] made by the Secretary of State:
  - limiting the maximum payment each player can be required to make to participate in all games at an event to £8
  - limiting the aggregate amount or value of prizes in all games played at an event to £600, although where an event is the final one of a series in which all of the players have previously taken part, a higher prize fund of up to £900 is permitted.
- The non-commercial event cannot take place on premises (other than a track) which hold a premises licence, nor on a track at a time when activities are being carried on in reliance on a premises licence, nor on premises at a time when activities are being carried on in reliance on a temporary use notice. There is nothing to stop such premises running charitable or other gambling events to raise money for good causes, but they should do so using the gambling permissions granted to them by their premises licence or use notice. The one exception to this is that a non-commercial event can take place at a track, provided no licensed gambling activities are taking place at the same time. This enables a track to be used for non-commercial gambling when races are not taking place
- The gaming must be non-remote gaming. In other words, the authorisation can only apply to gaming which takes place at events, on premises, and for gaming in person.

---

[87] SI No 2041/2007: The Gambling Act 2005 (Non-Commercial Equal Chance Gaming) Regulations 2007

PRIVATE GAMING

28.9 Private gaming can take place anywhere to which the public do not have access. That would include a workplace, for example. Domestic and residential gaming are two subsets where non-equal chance gaming is allowed:

- Domestic gaming is permitted without the need for permissions if:
  - it takes place in a private dwelling
  - it is on a domestic occasion
  - no charge or levy is made for playing.
- Residential gaming is permitted when:
  - it takes place in a hall of residence or hostel not administered in the course of a trade or business
  - more than 50% of the participants are residents.

28.10 Private gaming can potentially take place on commercial premises in circumstances where a members' club hires a room in, for example, a pub or hotel for a private function where equal chance gaming only is played. However, organisers would need to scrutinise very carefully the arrangements put in place to make sure that the particular area of the pub, hotel or other venue in which the gaming takes place is not, on the occasion of the private function, a place to which the public have access and that those participating are not selected by a process which means that, in fact, they are members of the public rather than members of the club. The law in this area is complex and organisers should be advised to seek their own legal advice before organising events of this nature.

28.11 It is a condition of private gaming that no charge (by whatever name called) is made for participation and Schedule 15 to the Act makes it clear that a deduction from or levy on sums staked or won by participants in gaming is a charge for participation in the gaming. It is irrelevant whether the charge is expressed to be voluntary or compulsory, particularly if customers are prevented from playing if they do not make the "voluntary" donation, or there is strong peer pressure to make the donation. A relevant decided case in another licensing field is that of *Cocks v Mayner* (1893) 58 JP 104, in which it was found that an omnibus said to be available free of charge but whose passengers who were invited to (and in some cases did) make a voluntary contribution was "plying for hire" without the appropriate licence.

28.12 Additionally, the decided cases of *Panama (Piccadilly) Ltd v Newberry* (1962) 1 WLR 610 and *Lunn v Colston-Hayter* (1991) 155 JP 384 are helpful in guiding local authorities in deciding whether a person ceases to be a member of the public merely because they have agreed to become a member of a club.

28.13 In the first of these cases (which related to a strip show), the court said that an applicant for membership of the club and admission to the show was and remained a member of the public, as the whole purpose (of membership) was to get members of the public to see the show and there was no sufficient segregation or selection to cause an applicant to cease to be a member of the public and to acquire a different status as a member of a club on signing his application form and paying the charge. In the second (which related to an acid house party), the judge said that it was impossible, merely because of the existence of a formal scheme of club membership enforced to the extent of requiring tickets to be obtained 24 hours in advance of the event, to regard those who obtained such membership and tickets as having ceased to be members of the public.

28.14 This means that people joining a club to attend and take part in a "private" event are likely to remain members of the public, particularly if "club membership" is acquired only a short time before, and in order to attend the event. The courts will not readily allow "membership" status to be abused in order to circumvent the law in this way.

NON-COMMERCIAL AND PRIVATE BETTING

28.15 The Act also says that betting is private if it is domestic betting or workers' betting. Domestic betting is a betting transaction made on premises in which each party to the transaction habitually resides. Workers' betting is where a betting transaction is made between persons who are employed by the same employer. A person does not commit an offence under section 33 or 37 of the Act if he or she provides facilities for private betting.

Occasional use notices

28.16 Section 39 of the Act provides that where there is betting on a track on eight days or fewer in a calendar year, betting may be permitted by an occasional use notice (OUN), without the need for a full premises licence.

28.17 While tracks are normally thought of as permanent racecourses, the meaning of 'track' in the Act covers not just horse racecourses or dog tracks, but also any other premises on any part of which a race or other sporting event takes place, or is intended to take place (see section 353(1) of the Act). This could include football grounds, cricket grounds, golf courses and the like.

28.18 This also means that land which has a number of uses, one of which fulfils the definition of a track, can qualify for the OUN provisions (for example, agricultural land on which a point- to-point meeting takes place). Land used temporarily as a track can qualify, provided races or sporting events take place or will take place there. The track need not be a permanent fixture.

28.19 The intention of OUNs is to permit licensed betting operators to use tracks for short periods for conducting betting, where the event upon which the betting is to take place is of a temporary, infrequent nature. OUNs dispense with the need for a betting premises licence for the track in these circumstances. OUNs can also potentially be used to facilitate betting at non-commercial or charity events.

28.20 It should be noted that betting operators cannot provide gaming machines at tracks by virtue of an OUN.

28.21 Non-commercial, fund raising race nights can be run as betting events at sporting venues under the authority of an OUN, whether or not the sporting event on which the bets are taken is held at that venue. The sporting event on which the bets are or will be taken also need not be taking place at the same time as the betting under the OUN.

28.22 An OUN must be sent in writing to the relevant local authority in advance of the event and be copied to the chief officer of police for the area in which the venue is located (or, in Scotland, the chief constable of the police force for the area) and specify a day on which it is to have effect. OUNs must be given for each day on which they are to have effect and must be given by the person responsible for the administration of events on the track or the occupier of the track.

28.23 No more that eight OUNs may be issued in a calendar year (that is, for a total of eight days per calendar year), in respect of any one venue. OUNs may be given for consecutive days, so long as the overall limit of eight days is not exceeded in the calendar year.

NON-COMMERCIAL 'CASINO NIGHT'

28.24 A non-commercial casino night is an event where participants stake money on casino-style games, such as poker or roulette, at a non-commercial event, where none of the money the organisers raise from the event is used for private gain.

28.25 Apart from reasonable costs, proceeds (including any entrance fees, sponsorship, the difference between stakes placed and payout made):

- must not be used for private gain
- must all be given to a good cause.

Reasonable costs would include costs incurred by providing the prizes. If third parties are selling goods or services at the event, for example if someone is selling refreshments, this does not count as money raised for the charity or good cause and can be retained by that third party.

28.26 A non-commercial casino night can be run without a licence, or any other form of permission, providing the operation of the gaming falls into one of the three categories discussed below.

28.27 Organisers should note that, under the Act, it is illegal to organise a commercial casino night outside of a licensed casino. As the law stands, only the holder of a valid non-remote casino operating licence can apply to a licensing authority for a temporary use notice (TUN) in respect of other premises to offer gaming on a commercial basis, and then only in respect of equal chance gaming organised on a tournament basis with a single overall winner[88]. There can, however, be more than one competition with a single winner held at the individual event covered by a specific TUN.

[88] 88SI No 3157/2007: The Gambling Act 2005 (Temporary Use Notices) Regulations 2007

Casino night as non-commercial prize gaming

28.28 Casino nights can be held as non-commercial prize gaming. The players must be told what good cause will benefit from the profits of the gaming before placing a bet. The prizes must be advertised in advance and must not depend on the number of people playing or the stakes raised. In non-commercial prize gaming, the casino gaming determines the individual winner or winners, for example by counting who has the most casino chips at a set time. The winners are then awarded the prizes that have been advertised in advance.

Casino night as non-commercial equal chance gaming

28.29 Casino nights can also be run as non-commercial equal chance gaming. Equal chance gaming is gaming where the chances are equally favourable to all participants and players are not competing against a bank. In non-commercial equal chance gaming, the charitable funds are usually raised through an entrance fee, participation fee, or through other payments related to the gaming. The maximum amount that a player may be charged is £8 per day (this includes entrance or participation fees, stakes and any other payments in relation to the gaming). Organisers must ensure that the total amount paid out in prizes remains below £600 in total across all players. However, where an event is the final one of a series in which all of the players have previously taken part, a higher prize fund of up to £900 is allowed.

Casino night as private gaming

28.30 A casino night may also be run under the private gaming provisions in the Act. Private gaming may only occur in a place to which the public does not have access (normally a private dwelling, hostel, hall of residence or similar establishment). No charge may be made for participation in private gaming (and that includes an entrance fee or other charge for admission), nor may any amounts be deducted from stakes or prizes. No profits can be made from private gaming, irrespective of how the organiser intended to use those profits and, thus, even if intended for charitable purposes.

28.31 Private gaming is restricted to equal chance gaming (poker, for example), except where it is domestic or residential gaming.

28.32 Private gaming can potentially take place on commercial premises in circumstances where a members' club hires a room in, for example, a pub or hotel for a private function where equal chance gaming only is played. However, organisers would need to scrutinise very carefully the arrangements put in place to make sure that the particular area of the pub, hotel or other venue in which the gaming takes place is not, on the occasion of the private function, a place to which the public have access and that those participating are not selected by a process which means that, in fact, they are members of the public rather than members of the club. The law in this area is complex and organisers are advised to seek their own legal advice before organising events of this nature.

NON-COMMERCIAL 'RACE NIGHT'

28.33 'Race nights' are permitted for charitable purposes. However, in some circumstances, they can only be undertaken by a licensed betting operator and after the premises owner has notified the local authority.

28.34 A non-commercial race night is an event where participants stake money on the outcome of live, recorded or virtual races. The money the organisers raise from the event is called the proceeds.

28.35 Apart from reasonable costs, proceeds (including any entrance fees, sponsorship, the difference between stakes placed and payout made):

- must not be used for private gain
- must all be given to a good cause.

Reasonable costs would include costs reasonably incurred, for example by providing any prizes and for betting slips. If third parties are selling goods or services at your event, for example if someone is selling refreshments, this does not count as money raised for the charity or good cause and can be retained by that third party.

28.36 Broadly there are three types of race nights which can be organised for charitable purposes.

Race night as non-commercial gaming

28.37 The first type of race night occurs where the selection of a 'horse' by a participant is totally dependent on chance, and where no 'odds' or 'form' are available to assist the gambler's selection. An example would be the use of archive films of horseracing without revealing the details of each race.

28.38 Such nights can be run without a licence, or any other form of permission, providing the operation of the gaming falls into one of the three categories discussed below.

INCIDENTAL NON-COMMERCIAL LOTTERY

28.39 Where the race night is not the only or main purpose of a non-commercial event, it is possible to operate it as an incidental lottery. In this case there are no limits on the amount that players may be charged to participate, but no more than £500 may be deducted from the proceeds of the lottery for the cost of prizes (which may be in cash or in kind), and no more than £100 for other expenses. The organisers can only sell tickets at the event and they have to announce the results at the event. As an example, a 'horse' might be picked at random for each paying customer who is awarded a prize if the horse 'wins'.

RACE NIGHT AS NON-COMMERCIAL PRIZE GAMING

28.40 Race nights can be held as non-commercial prize gaming. The players must be told what good cause will benefit from the profits of the gaming. The prizes must be advertised in advance and must not depend on the number of people playing or the stakes raised. In non-commercial prize gaming, the 'race' determines the individual winner or winners, for example, those who have paid are allocated or select a named horse in the race. The winners are then awarded the prizes that had been advertised in advance.

NON-COMMERCIAL EQUAL CHANCE GAMING

28.41 Race nights can also be run as non-commercial equal chance gaming. Equal chance gaming, which also includes games such as poker or bingo, is gaming where the chances are equally favourable to all participants and players are not competing against a bank.

28.42 The maximum amount that a player may be charged is £8 per day (this includes entrance or participation fees, betting stakes and any other payments in relation to the gaming). Organisers must ensure that the total amount paid out in prizes remains below £600 in total across all players. However, where an event is the final one of a series in which all of the players have previously taken part, a higher prize fund of up to £900 is allowed. This could take place, for example, where each participant pays a fee for a randomly selected 'horse' in each 'race' and the participant with the winning horse or chooser of the winning horse receives a prize commensurate with the stakes placed.

Secretary of State has decided that bridge and whist should be the only prescribed kinds of gaming. So long as it does not provide facilities for other types of non-machine gaming, a bridge or whist club may apply for a club gaming permit. If gaming is the principal reason for attendance at a club (other than a dedicated whist or bridge club), then it is not exempt gaming under section 269 of the Act. This would include poker clubs and the like established primarily for the purpose of providing poker or other gaming. Such clubs require Commission operating licences and premises licences.

---

[90] SI No 1940/2007: The Gambling Act 2005 (Exempt Gaming in Alcohol-Licensed Premises) Regulations 2007

[91] SI No 1944/2007: The Gambling Act 2005 (Exempt Gaming in Clubs) Regulations 2007

[92] SI No 1944/2007: The Gambling Act 2005 (Exempt Gaming in Clubs) Regulations 2007

REMOVAL OF EXEMPTION FOR ALCOHOL-LICENSED PREMISES

29.17 Licensing authorities can remove the automatic authorisation for exempt gaming in respect of any particular alcohol-licensed premises by making an order under section 284 of the Act. That section provides for the licensing authority to make such an order if:

- provision of the gaming is not reasonably consistent with the pursuit of the licensing objectives
- gaming has taken place on the premises that breaches a condition of section 279 – for example, the gaming does not abide by the prescribed limits for stakes and prizes, a participation fee is charged for the gaming or an amount is deducted or levied from sums staked or won
- the premises are mainly used for gaming
- an offence under the Act has been committed on the premises.

29.18 Before making an order, the licensing authority must give the licensee at least 21 days' notice of the intention to make the order and consider any representations that they may make. The authority must hold a hearing if the licensee so requests and must comply with any other procedural requirements set out in regulations. If there is no appeal, the order will take effect 21 days after notice of the intention was given. The authority must give the licensee a copy of the order and written reasons for making it. The licensee may appeal to the magistrates' court or the sheriff.

29.19 This is an important power for licensing authorities where, for example, they discover that poker is being offered in alcohol-licensed premises that consistently breaches the prescribed limits on stakes and prizes, participation fees are being charged for the poker, amounts are deducted from stakes or winnings, or poker (and other gaming) is the main activity offered on the premises.

CODE OF PRACTICE

29.20 The Commission has issued a code of practice under section 24 of the Act in respect of exempt equal chance gaming. This can be found on the Commission's website[93].

29.21 The code of practice requires owners/licensees/clubs/welfare institutes to adopt good practice measures for the provision of gaming in general, and poker in particular. The code also sets out the stakes and prizes limits and the limits on participation fees (for clubs) laid out in regulations.

29.22 The emphasis of the regulations and the code of practice is on self-regulation by the management of the premises and licensing authorities should take a strong line in cases where breaches are detected.

93 Code of practice for equal chance gaming in clubs and premises with an alcohol licence, available from www.gamblingcommission.gov.uk

POKER LEAGUES AND TOURNAMENTS

29.23 Gaming is only covered by the Act if it is played for prizes of money or money's worth. However, since 2004 a number of poker tournaments and leagues have been established in alcohol-licensed premises based on playing for points. In some leagues the organisers offer 'prizes' at the end of a series of weekly games for the players with the most points.

29.24 It is likely that the association of a prize with a monetary value with a game or series of games constitutes gaming, certainly by the latter stages of the competition. If the eventual prize is worth more than the maximum prize set out in regulations then it could be unlawful gaming. For example, if a tournament simply involves a series of straightforward 'knockout' qualifying rounds, culminating in a 'final' game, then the winner's prize in the final - whether it comprises the stakes laid in that game, a separate prize provided by the organiser, or a combination of the two — must not exceed £100. The regulations set a limit of £100 on a prize that may be won in any game of poker. In a knockout tournament, the overall prize is clearly referable to a single game (the 'final') and is therefore won in a game of poker and subject to the prize limit. The stake and prize limits must also, of course, be applied to each game in the tournament.

29.25 In other leagues the prize competed for is the opportunity to play in 'invitational cash tournaments'. Notwithstanding that these 'prizes' may be of an uncertain value, and are likely to be held in mainstream gaming venues under regulated conditions, usually a casino, the Act prohibits gaming in alcohol licensed premises being linked to gaming in any other premises. Players competing across premises for a 'prize' are likely to be engaged in linked gaming, which is unlawful. Consequently, organisers should not host events where players are competing against players in other premises for a prize.

29.26 In some types of tournaments there will be no single 'final' game in which it can be said with certainty that the player won the overall prize. In such circumstances, the Commission's view is that one should look to the individual games played by the overall winner and ensure that the overall prize does not cause any of those individual games to exceed the maximum £100 prize limit per game and the maximum stake of £100 per day.

The overall winner wins the pot in each game and wins an overall prize based on points

If the tournament winner played three games in the whole tournament, and his winnings (from the pot) in each of these games were £100, £70 and £60 respectively, each game would fall under the £100 prize limit. This would leave £0 from the first game, £30 from the second game and £40 from the third game, which could be put towards the winner's overall tournament prize. In these circumstances, the tournament prize could be up to £70 (£0 + £30 + £40). Thus where the pot in individual games is under £100, the tournament winner's overall prize must not exceed the aggregate of the shortfall in each of the games he plays.

The overall winner is only awarded points in each game and wins an overall prize based on points

Let's still assume that the tournament winner plays three games in the whole tournament. If there is no individual prize in any of the three games, then the overall prize can be up to £300 (£100 for each game the winner has played). If, on the other hand, the winner played in only two games, then his overall prize may not exceed £200, and so on. Please note that the relevant number of games is the games in which the winning player participated, and not only the games that they won.

29.27 Organisers of such competitions will therefore need to work out the total value of any overall prize with reference to the number of games to be played by the overall winner and the total pot (if any) in each game.

29.28 While 'non-cash' poker for points leagues can provide harmless and legal entertainment, those promoting such leagues should be aware of the Commission's code of practice on equal chance gaming, and take steps to prevent individual stakes limits being exceeded through side bets or illegal activity such as agreements to 'settle' games outside the gaming area. Where illegal activity is detected, licensing authorities should consider the removal of the alcohol-licensed premises' exemption, which allows poker and other exempt gaming to be played.

The overall winner is only awarded points in each game and wins an overall prize such as the opportunity to participate in a major poker tournament, casino vouchers, holidays, etc

In these circumstances, tournament organisers must ensure that the statutory limits for poker in alcohol-licensed premises and clubs are complied with. In particular, they must carefully consider the value of the prizes offered for games leading up to the tournament final (including money's worth or non-monetary prizes such as holidays, cars, casino vouchers, or buy-ins or seats at the final). In addition, organisers should take into account that where players are competing across premises for an overall prize, they are likely to be engaged in linked gaming, which is not permitted.

29.29 **Free or donated prizes are awarded to players in addition to the maximum prize pools for poker in clubs and alcohol licensed premises**

The Gambling Act 2005 refers to money or money's worth in respect of prizes. This would include free or donated prizes which have an intrinsic value. Any prizes offered in addition to the prize pool must remain within the limits for prizes in games of poker in clubs and alcohol licensed premises. The prize limit is £250 per game in a club and £100 per game in a pub. Therefore, for example, if the prize pool available for a particular game is £80, then any non-monetary prizes must not have a value exceeding £20.

Poker is offered in a members' club or miners' welfare institute with a club gaming permit

29.30 Members' clubs or miners' welfare institutes with club gaming permits may offer poker with unlimited stakes and prizes, but the only persons who may participate in such gaming are club members and their genuine guests. In this regard, the club must be able to demonstrate that it has a genuine and legitimate club membership scheme. Clubs must also ensure that the statutory limits on participation fees are not exceeded. The limit for bridge and whist is £20 and for other gaming is £3. In addition, there is a limit of a maximum of £2,000 per week in stakes and prizes for bingo in a members' club or welfare institute. If it is the intention of the club or institute to exceed these limits, it will be necessary for them to apply for an operating licence.

WHAT CONSTITUTES 'MONEY'S WORTH'?

29.31 Money's worth relates to the realistic value of the prize offered. It includes emoluments, vouchers, goods or other items which have a value.

29.32 A prize such as a 'goody bag' would be considered money's worth and is, therefore, subject to the statutory limits for exempt gaming. Donated prizes would also be considered money's worth. This would include prizes such as the buy-ins at major poker tournaments or the opportunity to participate in poker tournaments at venues such as Monte Carlo, especially as this type of prize is likely to include the cost of the airfare and accommodation.

POKER UNDER A CLUB GAMING PERMIT

29.33 A club gaming permit can only be granted to a members' club (including a miners' welfare institute), but cannot be granted to a commercial club or other alcohol-licensed premises.

29.34 Other than in the case of clubs established to provide the prescribed games of bridge and whist, clubs seeking club gaming permits must be established 'wholly or mainly' for purposes other than gaming. When a club gaming permit is granted there are no limits on the stakes and prizes associated with poker.

29.35 If bridge or whist clubs have a club gaming permit they may not offer any other gaming besides bridge and whist. If they do not have a permit, they may provide exempt gaming. If they wish to offer other non-exempt gaming they will require a Commission casino operating licence and any relevant personal licences.

29.36 The poker which a club gaming permit allows is subject to conditions:

(a) in respect of equal chance gaming:
- the club must not deduct money from sums staked or won
- the participation fee must not exceed the amount prescribed in regulations
- the game takes place on the premises and must not be linked with a game on another set of premises.

Two games are linked if:
- the result of one game is, or may be, wholly or partly determined by reference to the result of the other game, or
- the amount of winnings available in one game is wholly or partly determined by reference to the amount of participation in the other game, and a game which is split so that part is played on one site and another part is played elsewhere is treated as two linked games
- only club members and their genuine guests participate.

(b) in respect of other games of chance:
- the games must be pontoon and chemin de fer only
- no participation fee may be charged otherwise than in accordance with the regulations
- no amount may be deducted from sums staked or won otherwise than in accordance with the regulations.

29.37 To help clubs and institutes to comply with the full range of statutory requirements for gaming, the Commission has issued a statutory code of practice on equal chance gaming in consultation with interested parties. The code of practice is available from the Commission's website[95]. The provisions of the code (which also applies to alcohol-licensed premises) include:
- ensuring that young people and children are protected by excluding them from gaming (even if they are permitted on the premises)
- ensuring that gaming is fair and open by requiring close supervision of the games, record keeping (as appropriate), the need for standard rules and the display of stakes and prizes limits and the rules during play.

29.38 A 48 hour rule applies in respect of all three types of gaming, so that the games may only be played by people who have been members of the club for at least 48 hours, or have applied or been nominated for membership or are genuine guests of a member.

29.39 More information about club gaming permits can be found in Part 25, but there are certain matters we wish to highlight here.

---

[95] Code of practice for equal chance gaming in clubs and premises with an alcohol licence, available from www.gamblingcommission.gov.uk

Factors to consider when granting a club gaming permit

29.40 The LA has to satisfy itself that the club meets the requirements of the Act to obtain a club gaming permit. It is suggested that applicants for permits should be asked to supply sufficient information and documents to enable the LA to take account of the matters discussed in paragraphs 29.41 to 29.43, at the time they submit their applications to the LA.

29.41 In determining whether a club is a genuine members' club, the LA should take account of a number of matters, such as:

- Is the primary purpose of the club's activities something other than the provision of gaming to its members? This is an indicator that it's a genuine members' club.
- Are the profits retained in the club for the benefit of the members? This is the key difference between a members' club and a commercial club.
- Are there 25 or more members? This is the amount of members a club has to have to qualify.
- Are there genuine domestic addresses on the register of members? Are domestic addresses listed for every member? Are members local to the club? These are all indicators that the member lists are bona fide and are made up of genuine members.
- Do members participate in the activities of the club via the internet? It is less likely to be a genuine members' club if this is the case.
- Do guest arrangements link a member to every guest? Is there evidence of a signing-in register for guests? Guests must be genuine guests of members and not members of the general public.
- Is the 48 hour rule between applying for membership and participating in any gaming properly applied? This is an indication that the club has a proper membership scheme.
- Are there annual accounts for more than one year? This would indicate that the club is permanent in nature, rather than temporary.
- How is the club advertised and listed in directories, including on the internet? If the club is categorised under "gaming" or "poker", it is less likely to be genuine members' club.
- Are children permitted into the club? The more access they have to areas of the premises, the less likely it is that the club is primarily for gambling activities.
- Does the club have a constitution and can it provide evidence that the constitution was approved by the members of the club? This provides further evidence that it is a properly constituted members' club.
- Is there a list of committee members and evidence of their election by the members of the club? Can the club provide minutes of committee and other meetings? These are further evidence that the club is a properly constituted members' club.

29.42 The constitution of the club could also indicate whether it is a legitimate members' club. Amongst the things to consider when examining the constitution are the following:

- Who makes commercial decisions on behalf of the club and what are the governance arrangements? Clubs are normally run by a committee made up of members of the club, rather than individuals or managers, who make decisions on behalf of the members. There will normally be a system (consultation, voting, paper ballots, annual general meetings, special meetings, etc) which allows members to be involved in major decisions concerning the management and running of the club. Such arrangements would normally be spelt out in the constitution.
- Are the aims of the club set out in the constitution? A lack of aims or aims which involve gaming could indicate that it is not a genuine members' club.
- Are there shareholders or members? Shareholders would indicate a business enterprise linked to a commercial club.
- Is the members' club permanently established? Clubs can't be temporary and must be permanent in nature.
- Can people join with annual or quarterly membership? This would indicate that the club is permanent in nature.
- Are there long term membership benefits? This would also indicate that the club is permanent in nature and that it is a genuine members' club. The benefits of membership would normally be set out in the rules of membership.

29.43 Other than bridge and whist clubs, which are separately catered for in regulations, a club cannot be established wholly or mainly for purposes of gaming. In applying for a club gaming permit, a club must therefore provide substantial evidence of activities other than gaming. Useful questions which a LA should consider include:

- How many nights is gaming made available? If gaming is available for all or most nights with little other activity, then it is likely that the club is established wholly or mainly for gaming.
- Is the gaming advertised? If gaming is advertised with little or no reference to the other activities of the club, then it is likely that gaming is the main activity of the club and that the gaming is run commercially.
- What are the stakes and prizes offered? The stakes and prizes limits must be complied with. Unlimited stakes and prizes are only available to genuine members' clubs once a club gaming permit has been granted. If high stakes and prizes are offered, this is also likely to indicate that gaming is one of the main activities of the club.
- Is there evidence of leagues with weekly/monthly/annual winners? This could indicate that the club's main activity is gaming.
- Is there evidence of non-playing members? If members participate in gaming exclusively, this is an indication that the main or only activity of the club is gaming.
- Are there teaching sessions to promote gaming, such as poker? This could be evidence that the club's main activity is gaming.
- Is there tie-in with other clubs offering gaming, such as poker, through tournaments or leagues? This is also an indication that gaming is possibly one of the main activities of the club.
- Is there sponsorship by gaming organisations, for example on-line poker providers? Similarly, this could indicate that poker is one of the main activities of the club.
- Are participation fees within limits? The LA could consider club records and adverts for gaming, etc. Fees that exceed the limits could indicate that the gaming is run commercially.

29.44 The Commission advises that a visit to the premises before granting of the permit may assist the licensing officer to understand how the club will operate.

Factors to consider when monitoring club gaming permits

29.45 Once the LA has issued a club gaming permit, it is recommended that various aspects need to be considered by LAs in monitoring the club gaming permit. In addition to monitoring whether the club continues to meet the requirements of the Act for a club gaming permit (that is, whether it remains a genuine members' club) and whether the gaming meets the conditions set out in the Act and the relevant regulations, LAs may also wish to consider the issues described in the paragraphs that follow.

29.46 Where clubs have computers available for use by members, LAs should be aware that these may be so-called dual use computers which, among other things, allow club members to access gambling websites via the internet. In certain circumstances, these computers may be taken to be gaming machines. Generally, a computer is not a gaming machine merely because there is a possibility of accessing a gambling website via the internet. However, a computer will be taken to be a gaming machine if it is knowingly adapted or presented to facilitate or draw attention to the possibility of it being used for gambling.

29.47 It is not possible to provide a definitive list of examples of what constitutes a computer that is knowingly adapted or presented to facilitate or draw attention to the possibility of it being used for gambling. Each case will need to be looked at individually and ultimately the decision regarding whether a machine is a gaming machine is one for the courts to make.

29.48 The precise circumstances in which the facilities are offered – including the environment in which they are offered and the relationship with other gambling facilities provided – will need to be taken into account when assessing the status of those facilities. The Commission has provided the following indicators that may help in making decisions about whether a computer is knowingly adapted or presented to facilitate or draw attention to the possibility of it being used for gambling. This list is not exhaustive, and the presence or absence of any single factor is not necessarily conclusive:

- icons for gambling websites displayed on the desktop screen
- links to gambling websites available via the start menu
- screensavers, desktop wallpapers referring to gambling websites
- internet browsing history or favourites menu containing gambling websites
- promotional material (posters, flyers) indicating the use of computers for gambling
- gambling software downloaded onto a computer
- staff informing customers of the existence of the computer for access to gambling websites
- email messages or other promotional material sent to customers/individuals referring to the availability of computers on premises for gambling purposes.

29.49 LAs should note that permission to advertise gambling in Great Britain is restricted to operators licensed by the Commission, operators from the European Economic Area, Gibraltar and the white-listed jurisdictions (Alderney, Antigua and Barbuda, Isle of Man and Tasmania).

29.50 Club premises, computer terminals in the club or the club website may contain advertising of 'foreign gambling', or clubs may offer seats at overseas poker tournaments as prizes in poker tournaments run on the club premises. In the Commission's view, this amounts to advertising of non-UK gambling, as defined by section 327 of the Act. Unless the overseas tournament is based in the European Economic Area, Gibraltar or the white-listed jurisdictions, this is likely to amount to the advertising of 'foreign gambling', which is an offence under section 331 of the Act.

29.51 Any of the factors mentioned in the preceding paragraphs in this section may give rise to the need to review the club gaming permit or take appropriate enforcement action.

29.52 The Commission provides advice and guidance to LAs on permits and related matters and, on a case-by-case basis, will undertake targeted collaborations with LAs in order to establish principle and precedent, and a clear understanding of the legal requirements.

29.53 An agency that may also be able to assist LA enquiries is HM Revenue and Customs (HMRC). If a club is trading under the auspices of a club gaming permit (as a members' club) but is in fact a commercial club with, for example, their main activity being poker, they would be liable for gaming duty. LAs should bear in mind that clubs of this nature have premises to maintain, as well as staff and other costs, so the sums involved may be significant. There may also be other aspects of the financing of such clubs that would cause HMRC to become involved.

POWERS IN RESPECT OF PREMISES

29.54 Section 310 of the Act prescribes that a constable, enforcement officer or authorised local authority officer can enter alcohol-licensed premises to determine whether any gaming that is taking place satisfies the conditions for exempt gaming in section 279 of the Act.

29.55 Section 312 of the Act prescribes that:

- a constable or enforcement officer can enter club or miners' welfare institute premises, or premises which they reasonably believe to be used by a club or institute, to determine whether:
    - gaming is taking place on the premises or is about to take place on the premises
    - any gaming that is taking place or is about to take place on the premises meets the requirements for exempt gaming in section 269 of the Act, a club gaming permit or a club machine permit

- an authorised local authority officer can enter premises in respect of which an application for a club gaming permit or club machine permit has been made for a purpose connected with the consideration of the application.

29.56 An enforcement officer is an employee of the Commission designated as an enforcement officer for the purposes of the Act, or a person other than an employee appointed as an enforcement officer for the same purpose. An authorised local authority officer is an officer of a LA designated as an authorised person for the purposes of section 304 of the Act, where the premises are wholly or partly situated in the licensing authority's area.

29.57 As the Act indicates that local licensing officers are not authorised to enter club premises under the Act once the club permit has been issued, this has generally been assumed to mean that licensing authorities lack all the necessary powers and the Commission is, therefore, the default organisation for enforcement action. However, the necessary powers are available to the police and the Commission suggests that licensing authorities, working in partnership with local police forces, have the ability to enforce compliance by clubs where needed.

29.58 LAs may also want to consider whether their officers have powers under other relevant Acts, such as the Licensing Act or Local Government Act. In addition, in England and Wales, sections 87, 88 and 89 of the Licensing Act give licensing authorities the ability to review club premises certificates, including suspending and withdrawing certificates, and section 90 allows licensing authorities to withdraw certificates where it appears to the LA that the club does not satisfy the conditions for being a qualifying club.

The position in Scotland

29.59 In Scotland, the relevant licensing authority is called a licensing board. The powers of licensing boards are similar to those of licensing authorities in England and Wales in that they grant, review and cancel club gaming permits and club machine permits.

29.60 However, due to an oversight, sections 310 and 312 have created an anomaly in Scotland. In Scotland the equivalent of a licensing officer is a licensing standards officer (LSO). Although section 304(2) of the Act was intended to provide licensing authorities with the opportunity to empower licensing authority staff already involved in licensing, it does not apply to Scotland because those given responsibility by Scottish licensing authorities (usually the LSOs) are not officers of the licensing authority. The licensing boards are separate and LSOs are deliberately legally separated from the boards.

29.61 Section 304(3) and (4) of the Act was intended to provide licensing authorities with the opportunity to empower staff involved in other regulatory roles, such as trading standards officers and environmental health officers, but because most Scottish licensing authorities have given responsibility to LSOs instead, they are unable to do this.

29.62 However, it must be emphasised that the local police in Scotland have similar powers under the Act to those given to their equivalents in England and Wales. This means that the licensing authorities should approach the police for assistance if needed.

29.63 It should also be noted that police officers have the power to enter and inspect premises licensed under the Licensing (Scotland) Act 2005 at any time.

POKER AS NON-COMMERCIAL GAMING

29.64 The Act permits non-commercial gaming if it takes place at a non-commercial event, either as an incidental or principal activity at the event. Events are non-commercial if no part of the proceeds is for private profit or gain. The proceeds of such events may benefit one or more individuals if the activity is organised:

- by, or on behalf of, a charity or for charitable purposes

- to enable participation in, or support of, sporting, athletic or cultural activities.

So it would be possible to raise funds for an individual providing the proceeds were, for example, for a wheelchair or to support a sporting endeavour. Additionally, popular events such as casino nights or poker nights may be permitted if they comply with the regulations and profits go to a 'good cause'. More details about these can be found later in this Part.

29.65 Section 297(3) of the Act defines proceeds as:

(a) the sums raised by the organisers (whether by way of fees for entrance or for participation, by way of sponsorship, by way of commission from traders, or otherwise), minus

(b) amounts deducted by the organisers in respect of costs reasonably incurred in organising the event.

However, sums raised by other persons will not form part of the proceeds of the event and may be appropriated for private gain. An example would be refreshments provided at the event by an independent third party.

29.66 If someone uses any profits from non-commercial gaming for something other than the specified purpose, then they commit an offence under section 301 of the Act. The maximum penalty, upon conviction for such an offence, is a term of imprisonment not exceeding 51 weeks for England and Wales (six months in Scotland), and/or a level five fine.

29.67 The Act identifies two types of permissible non-commercial gaming: •

- prize gaming (which must comply with the conditions set out in section 299 of the Act)
- equal chance gaming (which must comply with the conditions set out in section 300 of the Act and the conditions prescribed in regulations).

Non-commercial prize gaming

29.68 Provided that the conditions set out in section 299 are met, poker can be offered as non- commercial prize gaming without the need to have an operating or premises licence, nor a prize gaming permit. In summary, the conditions are:

- players are told that the purpose of the gaming is to raise money for a specified charitable, sporting, athletic or cultural purpose
- profits are not for private gain
- the event cannot take place in a venue (other than a track) which has a premises licence. If at a track the premises licence cannot be in use (in effect no betting can be taking place) and no temporary use notice can have effect
- the gaming must be on the premises and not be remote gaming.

29.69 In these circumstances, poker as prize gaming occurs if the nature and size of the prize is not determined by the number of people playing or the amount paid for or raised by the gaming. Normally the prizes will be determined by the organiser before play commences.

Non-commercial equal chance gaming

29.70 Provided that the conditions set out under section 300 are met, poker can be offered as non-commercial equal chance gaming without the need to have an operating or premises licence. In summary, the conditions are:

- All players must be told what purpose the money raised from the gaming is going to be used for (this must be something other than private gain), and the profits must be applied for that purpose.
- The gaming must comply with regulations[96] made by the Secretary of State:
    - limiting the maximum payment each player can be required to make to participate in all games at an event to £8

  - limiting the aggregate amount or value of prizes in all games played at an event to £600, although where an event is the final one of a series in which all of the players have previously taken part, a higher prize fund of up to £900 is permitted.
- The non-commercial event cannot take place on premises (other than a track) which hold a premises licence, nor on a track at a time when activities are being carried on in reliance on a premises licence, nor on premises at a time when activities are being carried on in reliance on a temporary use notice. There is nothing to stop such premises running charitable or other gambling events to raise money for good causes, but they should do so using the gambling permissions granted to them by their premises licence or use notice. The one exception to this is that a non-commercial event can take place at a track, provided no licensed gambling activities are taking place at the same time. This enables a track to be used for non-commercial gambling when races are not taking place.
- The gaming must be non-remote gaming. In other words, the authorisation can only apply to gaming which takes place at events, on premises, and for gaming in person.

[96] SI No 2041/2007: The Gambling Act 2005 (Non-Commercial Equal Chance Gaming) Regulations 2007

Non-commercial 'casino night' or 'poker night'

29.71 A non-commercial casino night or poker night is an event where participants stake money on casino-style games, such as poker, at a non-commercial event, where none of the money the organisers raise from the event is used for private gain.
29.72 Apart from reasonable costs, proceeds (including any entrance fees, sponsorship, the difference between stakes placed and payout made):
- must not be used for private gain
- must all be given to a good cause.

Reasonable costs would include costs incurred by providing the prizes. If third parties are selling goods or services at the event, for example if someone is selling refreshments, this does not count as money raised for the charity or good cause and can be retained by that third party.
29.73 A non-commercial casino night or poker night can be run without a licence, or any other form of permission, providing the operation of the gaming falls into one of the three categories discussed below.
29.74 Organisers should note that, under the Act, it is illegal to organise a commercial casino night or poker night outside of a licensed casino. As the law stands, only the holder of a valid non-remote casino operating licence can apply to a licensing authority for a temporary use notice (TUN) in respect of other premises to offer gaming on a commercial basis, and then only in respect of equal chance gaming organised on a tournament basis with a single overall winner[97].

[97] SI No 3157/2007: The Gambling Act 2005 (Temporary Use Notices) Regulations 2007

Casino night or poker night as non-commercial prize gaming

29.75 Casino nights or poker nights can be held as non-commercial prize gaming. The players must be told what good cause will benefit from the profits of the gaming before placing a bet. The prizes must be advertised in advance and must not depend on the number of people playing or the stakes raised. For example, the individual winner or winners could be determined by counting who has the most casino chips after the game or tournament ends. The winners are then awarded the prizes that have been advertised in advance.

Casino night or poker night as non-commercial equal chance gaming

29.76 Casino nights or poker nights can also be run as non-commercial equal chance gaming. In non-commercial equal chance gaming, the charitable funds are usually raised through an entrance fee, participation fee, or through other payments related to the gaming. The maximum amount that a player may be charged is £8 per day (this includes entrance or participation fees, stakes and any other payments in relation to the gaming). Organisers must ensure that the total amount paid out in prizes remains below £600 in total across all players. However, where an event is the final one of a series in which all of the players have previously taken part, a higher prize fund of up to £900 is allowed.

POKER AS PRIVATE GAMING

29.77 Poker offered as private gaming can take place anywhere to which the public do not have access. That would include a workplace, for example. Domestic and residential gaming are two subsets where non-equal chance gaming is allowed:

- Domestic gaming is permitted without the need for permissions if:
    - it takes place in a private dwelling
    - it is on a domestic occasion
    - no charge or levy is made for playing.
- Residential gaming is permitted when:
    - it takes place in a hall of residence or hostel not administered in the course of a trade or business
    - more than 50% of the participants are residents.

29.78 Private gaming can potentially take place on commercial premises in circumstances where a members' club hires a room in, for example, a pub or hotel for a private function where equal chance gaming only is played. However, organisers would need to scrutinise very carefully the arrangements put in place to make sure that the particular area of the pub, hotel or other venue in which the gaming takes place is not, on the occasion of the private function, a place to which the public have access and that those participating are not selected by a process which means that, in fact, they are members of the public rather than members of the club. The law in this area is complex and organisers should be advised to seek their own legal advice before organising events of this nature.

29.79 It is a condition of private gaming that no charge (by whatever name called) is made for participation and Schedule 15 to the Act makes it clear that a deduction from or levy on sums staked or won by participants in gaming is a charge for participation in the gaming. It is irrelevant whether the charge is expressed to be voluntary or compulsory, particularly if customers are prevented from playing if they do not make the "voluntary" donation, or there is strong peer pressure to make the donation. A relevant decided case in another licensing field is that of *Cocks v Mayner* (1893) 58 JP 104, in which it was found that an omnibus said to be available free of charge but whose passengers who were invited to (and in some cases did) make a voluntary contribution was "plying for hire" without the appropriate licence.

29.80 Additionally, the decided cases of *Panama (Piccadilly) Ltd v Newberry* (1962) 1WLR 610 and *Lunn v Colston-Hayter* (1991) 155 JP 384 are helpful in guiding local authorities in deciding whether a person ceases to be a member of the public merely because they have agreed to become a member of a club.

29.81 In the first of these cases (which related to a strip show), the court said that an applicant for membership of the club and admission to the show was and remained a member of the public, as the whole purpose (of membership) was to get members of the public to see the show and there was no sufficient segregation or selection to cause an applicant to cease to be a member of the public and to acquire a different status as a member of a club on signing his application form and paying the charge. In the second (which related to an acid house party), the judge said that it was impossible, merely because of the existence of a formal scheme of club membership enforced to the extent of requiring tickets to be obtained 24 hours in advance of the event, to regard those who obtained such membership and tickets as having ceased to be members of the public.

29.82 This means that people joining a club to attend and take part in a "private" event are likely to remain members of the public, particularly if "club membership" is acquired only a short time before, and in order to attend the event. The courts will not readily allow "membership" status to be abused in order to circumvent the law in this way.

ADVERTISING

29.83 Section 331 of the Act specifically prohibits the advertising of 'foreign gambling' in the United Kingdom. Foreign gambling in this sense is gambling which takes place outside of the European Economic Area (including Gibraltar and Malta) or white-listed states[98] (the Isle of Man, Alderney, Tasmania and Antigua and Barbuda). Therefore advertising of this nature would be illegal, but if the prize advertised was an all-expenses paid holiday to Las Vegas for example, then the operator would not fall foul of section 331 of the Act, unless it included some form of gaming as part of the prize, for example entry into a poker tournament.

29.84 Many poker websites promote other online gambling websites, usually by the provision of a hyperlink to that website. A hyperlink has been deemed to constitute advertising as it brings facilities for advertising to the attention of the person who clicks on the link. The provision of a hyperlink to a gambling website operating outside of the EEA or white-listed states (the Isle of Man, Alderney, Tasmania and Antigua and Barbuda) by a poker operator will constitute advertising of foreign gambling, which is not permitted.

98 As of July 2012, these are the current white-listed states.

PART 30 TRAVELLING FAIRS

30.1 The Act defines a travelling fair as 'wholly or principally' providing amusements and they must be on a site that has been used for fairs for no more than 27 days per calendar year. The Act does not change the principles on which travelling fairs have been regulated under previous legislation.

30.2 Travelling fairs do not require a permit to provide gaming machines, but must comply with legal requirements about the way the machine operates. They may provide an unlimited number of Category D gaming machines provided that facilities for gambling amount to no more than an ancillary amusement at the fair. Current stakes and prizes can be found on the Commission's website.

30.3 Part 27 of the Guidance discusses the prize gaming that may be provided at travelling fairs.

30.4 Licensing authorities should note that the 27-day maximum is during a calendar year and not in any 12-month period, and applies to the piece of land on which fairs are held, regardless of whether it is the same or different travelling fairs occupying the land. Authorities should therefore monitor the use of land and maintain a record of the dates on which it is used. If the land straddles licensing authority areas, the authorities concerned will need to work together to maintain a central log.

30.5 Local authorities may adopt byelaws to control travelling fairs under a discretionary power set out in section 75 of the Public Health Act 1961, as amended by section 22 of the Local Government (Miscellaneous Provisions) Act 1976.

PART 31: CROWN IMMUNITY AND EXCLUDED PREMISES

31.1 With the exception mentioned below, the Act applies to the Crown. This includes government departments and therefore there is no immunity for establishments such as civil service social clubs, which must apply for club machine permits or other permissions in the normal way.

31.2 However the Act has no effect in relation to anything done on premises occupied, either on a permanent or temporary basis, by the armed forces, in effect Her Majesty's naval, military or air forces.

31.3 The Act enables the Secretary of State to classify a premises as exempt from the Act on the grounds of national security. There are no plans at present for the Secretary of State to use this power.

PART 32: TERRITORIAL APPLICATION OF THE GAMBLING ACT 2005

32.1 The Act only applies to Great Britain (England, Wales and Scotland) except for two main areas which also apply in Northern Ireland. These are:

- Chain gift schemes (see part 35 of this Guidance)
- Offences relating to foreign gambling (see section 331 of the Act).

32.2 A fixed premise such as a building or a track in Great Britain will need the appropriate licences to operate.

VESSELS

32.3 Vessels such as cruise ships, ferries, boats and hovercrafts are required to have a premises licence if commercial gambling is provided at them. However if a vessel is engaged on a journey into or from international waters then no premises licence is required (see part 7 paragraphs 7.31 to 7.37).

VEHICLES

32.4 No premises licences can be issued in respect of a vehicle. A car, lorry or coach is obviously a vehicle, and the Act also provides that 'vehicle' includes a train, aircraft, seaplane and any amphibious vehicle other than a hovercraft. There is no exemption for international travel. Whilst this is ultimately a matter for the courts it is the Commission's view that a vehicle remains a vehicle not only when stationary but also if located permanently at a particular site, perhaps with its wheels removed but capable of being reinstated.

AIRCRAFT

32.5 No offence occurs if gambling is conducted on an aircraft which is in international space. As an aircraft is a vehicle, no premises licences can be granted to aircraft for gambling in domestic airspace.

AIRPORTS

32.6 The Act applies to all parts of an airport including both domestic and international departure halls. Therefore any business that would normally require a premises licence will also require a licence to operate at an airport.

32.7 Due to differences in jurisdictional application, there is an anomaly in respect of granting gaming machine permits to pubs and bars where alcohol is sold airside in airports.

32.8 In England and Wales, the Licensing Act 2003 applies to pubs and bars in the domestic part of the airport and therefore these businesses are able to qualify for the automatic gaming machine entitlement or can apply for a gaming machine permit for more than two gaming machines (see part 26 of this Guidance for more details). The Licensing Act does not apply airside, so pubs and clubs are not required to obtain a licence to serve alcohol. This has created an anomaly which DCMS have taken steps to rectify. DCMS intends to use a Legislative Reform Order (LRO) under the Legislative and Regulatory Reform Act 2006 to reform the Gambling Act 2005 insofar as it governs the gambling entitlements at airside bars and at wharves. The LRO will amend section 278 of the Gambling Act 2005 and will remedy a technical problem caused by a legislative oversight to enable airside bars to continue to provide low-level gambling facilities, as they have been doing for some time without giving rise to any problems.. Subject to the outcome of consultation and Parliamentary consideration, DCMS have proposed that the changes are implemented from 1 October 2012.

32.9 In Scotland, designated airports which currently hold alcohol licences under the Licensing (Scotland) Act 2005, qualify for the automatic gaming machine entitlement and can apply for gaming machine permits. However, a situation also exists in Scotland where the Licensing (Scotland) Act 2005 does not apply to airside pubs. It is expected that DCMS's proposed LRO will also correct this anomaly.

PART 33: DOOR SUPERVISION

33.1 If a licensing authority is concerned that a premises may attract disorder or be subject to attempts at unauthorised access (for example, by children and young persons) then it may require that the entrances to the premises are controlled by a door supervisor, and is entitled to impose a premises licence condition to this effect.

33.2 Section 178 of the Gambling Act 2005 sets out a definition of 'door supervisor', and provides that where a person employed in such a role is required to hold a licence issued by the Security Industry Authority (SIA), that requirement will have force as though it were a condition on the premises licence.

33.3 The SIA regulates the private security industry in England, Wales and Scotland, and is responsible for licensing individuals working within the various industry sectors, by virtue of the Private Security Industry Act 2001 (PSIA). The majority of persons employed to work as door supervisors at premises licensed for gambling, and carrying out the functions listed under Schedule 2 Part 1 of the PSIA, will need to be licensed by the SIA. There are, however, exceptions to this requirement.

33.4 The PSIA requires that all contract staff (those employed under a contract for services) carrying out the functions set out under Schedule 2 Part 1 of the PSIA require licensing by the SIA. However, certain premises also need to have their in-house employees (those employed under a contract of service), who carry out these functions, licensed. These premises include those holding a premises licence for the supply of alcohol or regulated entertainment under the Licensing Act 2003.

33.5 This requirement is relaxed when applied to door supervisors at casino and bingo premises. Where 'contract' staff are employed as door supervisors at casino or bingo premises, such staff will need to be licensed by the SIA. However, 'in-house' employees working as door supervisors at casino and bingo premises are exempt from these requirements.

33.6 In Scotland, the PSIA currently applies in respect of the Licensing (Scotland) Act 2005 by virtue of the Licensing (Scotland) Act 2005 (Consequential provisions) Order 2009, Scottish SSI 2009/248. This ensures that the same requirements in relation to the licensing of staff by the SIA in England and Wales also apply in Scotland.

PART 34: SMALL SOCIETY LOTTERIES

34.1 The Act denotes local authorities as being responsible for registering societies to run small society lotteries, as opposed to licensing authorities. Section 2 of the Act defines licensing authorities, and section 25 defines local authorities, and both are given the same definition. The Commission considers therefore that for the purposes of the Act both terms are broadly the same, and in the interests of consistency with the other areas of guidance contained in this document, we refer throughout this section to licensing authorities, as opposed to local authorities.

THE STATUS OF LOTTERIES UNDER THE ACT

34.2 The Act sets out a definition of a lottery and provides that promoting or facilitating a lottery is illegal, unless it falls into one of two categories of permitted lottery, namely:

- licensed lotteries:
  these are large society lotteries and lotteries run for the benefit of local authorities that are regulated by the Commission and require operating licences
- exempt lotteries:
  there are four types of exempt lottery that are expressly permitted under Schedule 11 of the Act, including the small society lottery.

34.3 The National Lottery is not regulated by the Commission, but continues to be regulated by the National Lottery Commission (NLC). However the NLC has been co-located with the Commission since January 2012 and the Public Bodies Bill includes legislation to merge the two Commissions.

Definition of lottery

34.4 Licensing authorities need to have an understanding of how a lottery is defined. In essence a lottery is an arrangement that satisfies all of the criteria contained within the statutory description of either a simple lottery or a complex lottery, under section 14 of the Act.

34.5 An arrangement is a simple lottery if:

- persons are required to pay to participate
- one or more prizes are allocated to one or more members of a class
- the prizes are allocated by a process which relies wholly on chance.

34.6 An arrangement is a complex lottery if:

- persons are required to pay to participate
- one or more prizes are allocated to one or more members of a class
- the prizes are allocated by a series of processes
- the first of those processes relies wholly on chance.

Definition of society

34.7 Licensing authorities should define 'society' as the society, or any separate branch of such a society, on whose behalf a lottery is to be promoted, and need to understand the purposes for which a society has been established in ensuring that it is a non-commercial organisation. Section 19 of the Act defines a society as such if it is established and conducted:

- for charitable purposes[99]
- for the purpose of enabling participation in, or of supporting, sport, athletics or a cultural activity
- for any other non-commercial purpose other than that of private gain.

34.8 It is inherent in this definition that the society must have been established for one of the permitted purposes, and that the proceeds of any lottery must be devoted to those purposes. It is not permissible to establish a society whose sole purpose is to facilitate lotteries – it must have some other purpose.

---

99 As defined by section 2 of the Charities Act 2006

LOCAL AUTHORITY LOTTERIES

34.9 Local authorities are themselves entitled to operate their own lotteries, but may only do so if licensed by the Commission. Authorities must commit a minimum of 20%

of the proceeds from such lotteries for a purpose for which they have power to incur expenditure, and must also adhere to the other relevant provisions in the Act. They may also need to hold a remote gambling operating licence, in the event that they wish to sell lottery tickets via electronic or technological methods such as over the telephone.

34.10 This document will not focus in detail on this type of lottery, but local authorities wishing to operate their own lotteries can, in the first instance, find relevant information on the Commission's website.

APPLICATION AND REGISTRATION PROCESS FOR SMALL SOCIETY LOTTERIES

34.11 When licensing authorities are approached by societies who want to register with them to operate lotteries, they will need to refer to the Act's definition of a small society lottery, which falls into two distinct areas:

- society status – the society in question must be 'non-commercial'
- lottery size – the total value of tickets to be put on sale per single lottery must be £20,000 or less, or the aggregate value of tickets to be put on sale for all their lotteries in a calendar year must not exceed £250,000. If the operator plans to exceed either of these values then they may need to be licensed with the Commission to operate large lotteries instead.

34.12 The Commission has published a series of advisory documents, which licensing authorities may wish to refer applicants or potential applicants, to enable them to establish which type of lottery they plan to operate. *Promoting society and local authority lotteries* provides information for those seeking to run small and large society lotteries and local authority lotteries. *Organising small lotteries* provides advice on exempt lotteries that do not require a licence or registration. The Commission has also published a leaflet for fundraisers, to help them identify what types of lottery they can run. All documents are available on the Commission's website.

34.13 The promoting society of a small society lottery must, throughout the period during which the lottery is promoted, be registered with a licensing authority. Parts four and five of Schedule 11 of the Act set out the requirements on both societies and licensing authorities with respect to the registration of small society lotteries.

34.14 The licensing authority with which a small society lottery is required to register must be in the area where their principal office is located. If a licensing authority believes that a society's principal office is situated in another area, it should inform the society and the other authority as soon as possible.

34.15 Applications for small society lottery registrations must be in the form prescribed by the Secretary of State and be accompanied by both the required registration fee and all necessary documents required by the licensing authority to assess the application accordingly.

34.16 Licensing authorities may wish to ask new applicants for a copy of their terms and conditions or their constitution to establish that they are a non-commercial society. They may also choose to require applicants to provide a declaration, stating that they represent a bona-fide non-commercial society.

34.17 The Commission has been made aware that some small society lotteries may be avoiding applying for a society lottery operating licence from the Commission by obtaining two or more registrations with the same or different local authorities.

34.18 As set out previously, the Act states that a society lottery is a large lottery if the arrangements for it are such that its proceeds may exceed £20,000, or if the aggregate proceeds in a calendar year exceed £250,000.

34.19 In cases where a society has separate branches with different aims and objectives, it is acceptable for them to hold more than one licence or registration. However, in cases where a society holds more than one registration and the aims and objectives of those societies are the same, this may constitute a breach of the threshold limits for small society lotteries set out in Schedule 11, Part 4 of the Act.

34.20 Local authorities are advised that in a case where a society applies for more than one registration, care should be taken to ensure that the applicant societies have separate and different aims and objectives. Where a society applies for more than one registration, the aims and objectives of the applicant societies are the same and the combined proceeds are likely to exceed the threshold limits for small society lotteries, the applicant should be advised to apply to the Commission for a society lottery operating licence, instead of obtaining society lottery registrations with the local authority.

34.21 Local authorities may also wish to check with the society at the time the annual fee is paid to renew the registration, to ensure that a society does not hold a duplicate registration with them or another local authority where the aims and objectives of the societies are the same. If that is the case and the combined proceeds exceed or are likely to exceed the threshold limits for small society lotteries, the society should be advised to apply to the Commission for a society lottery operating licence. The local authority should also notify the Commission.

34.22 Licensing authorities may delegate the registration of small societies to licensing officers, subject to each authority's own specific process of delegations.

34.23 Licensing authorities are required by paragraph 44 of Schedule 11 of the Act to record details of the society on a register. While it does not have to be a public register, the Commission recommends that licensing authorities make the register available to the public on request.

34.24 Once the application for registration has been accepted and entered on the local register, the licensing authority must then notify both the applicant and the Commission of this registration as soon as practicable (again as required by paragraph 44 of Schedule 11 of the Act). The Commission would prefer to receive this information electronically via email to mailto://info@gamblingcommission.gov.uk, although licensing authorities may also forward this information by post.

34.25 Registrations run for an unlimited period, unless the registration is cancelled. If a licensing authority cancels the registration of a society they are required by paragraph 53 of Schedule 11 of the Act to notify the Commission.

REFUSAL OF AN APPLICATION

34.26 Paragraphs 47 and 48 of Schedule 11 of the Act set out the grounds for licensing authorities to refuse a small society lottery registration application. In summary, licensing authorities may propose to refuse an application for any of the following reasons:

- **An operating licence held by the applicant for registration has been revoked or an application for an operating licence made by the applicant for registration has been refused, within the past five years.** The Commission will be able to advise the details of people and organisations that have been refused an operating licence or have had an operating licence revoked in the past five years. Licensing authorities should consult the Commission as part of their consideration process.
- **The society in question cannot be deemed non-commercial.** Under previous regimes, licensing authorities often required applicants to provide a statement with their application form declaring that they represented a bona-fide non-commercial society, and identifying how the purpose of the society could be established. The Commission considers that a similar approach remains appropriate. However, licensing authorities should also consider whether such a declaration is sufficient in the particular circumstances of each case or whether there are additional determining factors, such as an unusual or novel purpose of the society, which may suggest that further enquiry is needed.
- **A person who will or may be connected with the promotion of the lottery has been convicted of a relevant offence** [100]. Under previous regimes, licensing authorities often required applicants to provide a statement alongside their application form declaring that they had no relevant convictions that would

prevent them from running lotteries. The authority could then verify the accuracy of the statement with the police. The Commission considers that this scenario remains appropriate.

- **Information provided in or with the application for registration is found to be false or misleading.**

34.27 A licensing authority may only refuse an application for registration after the society has had the opportunity to make representations. These can be taken at a formal hearing or via correspondence. Licensing authorities should inform the society of the reasons why it is minded to refuse registration and provide it with at least an outline of the evidence on which it has reached that preliminary conclusion – in order to enable representations to be made. Representations and objections that may result after such a decision should be handled in accordance with local procedures, and in the same way that the authority would handle representations relating to other licensing matters. The Commission considers that, as a matter of good practice, licensing authorities should set out, perhaps on their website, the principles they will apply in such circumstances.

---

100 Relevant offences are listed at Schedule 7 of the Act

REVOCATION OF A SMALL SOCIETY'S REGISTERED STATUS

34.28 A licensing authority may determine to revoke the registration of a society if it thinks that they would have had to, or would be entitled to, refuse an application for registration if it were being made at that time. Revocations cannot take place unless the society has been given an opportunity to make representations at a hearing or via correspondence. In preparation for this, licensing authorities should inform the society of the reasons why it is minded to revoke the registration and provide them with the terms of the evidence on which it has reached that preliminary conclusion. Representations that may result after such a decision should be handled in accordance with local procedures, and in the same way that the authority would handle representations relating to other licensing matters.

APPEALS

34.29 Following the conclusion of any hearings and receipt of representations, paragraph 51 of Schedule 11 of the Act then requires the authority to notify the applicant or the society as soon as possible if their registration is still to be revoked, or if their application for registration has still been rejected.

34.30 The applicant or society may decide to make an appeal against the decision, and has 21 days following receipt of the notice of the decision to lodge an appeal, which must be made directly to the local magistrates' court if in England or Wales, or the sheriff court in Scotland.

34.31 The magistrates' court or sheriff may accordingly choose to affirm the decision of the licensing authority, reverse the decision, or make any other order.

LICENSING AUTHORITY GUIDANCE

34.32 The Commission recommends that licensing authorities consider producing their own guidance for organisations and individuals seeking to operate small society lotteries, to be made available through mediums such as websites and hard copies. The Commission's *Promoting society and local authority lotteries* document[101] may provide a useful starting point for licensing authorities that wish to develop such local guidance. Suggested content includes:

- the forms and documentation needed for registration (as prescribed by regulations)

- the information that societies will need to keep concerning the management and operation of the lottery (to enable it to meet the Act's requirements stipulated by paragraph 39 of Schedule 11)
- the forms and documentation needed for returns following a lottery draw
- details of fees due and when they should be paid (as prescribed by regulations)
- the criteria and evidence that the authority will use when determining whether to register a society or revoke a registration.

---

101 Copies can be downloaded from the Commission's website at www.gamblingcommission.gov.uk

ADMINISTRATION AND RETURNS

34.33 As the purpose of permitted lotteries is to raise money for non-commercial causes, the Act requires that a minimum proportion of the money raised by the lottery is channelled to the goals of the society that promoted the lottery. If a small society lottery does not comply with these limits it will be in breach of the Act's provisions, and consequently be liable to prosecution.

34.34 The limits placed on small society lotteries are as follows:

- at least 20% of the lottery proceeds must be applied to the purposes of the society (Schedule 11, paragraph 33)
- no single prize may be worth more than £25,000 (Schedule 11, paragraph 34)
- rollovers between lotteries are only permitted where every lottery affected is also a small society lottery promoted by the same society, and the maximum single prize is £25,000 (Schedule 11, paragraph 35)
- every ticket in the lottery must cost the same and the society must take payment for the ticket fee before entry into the draw is allowed (Schedule 11, paragraph 37).

34.35 Paragraph 39 of Schedule 11 in the Act sets out the information that the promoting society of a small society lottery must send as returns to the licensing authority with which it is registered, following each lottery held. This information allows licensing authorities to assess, in particular, whether financial limits are being adhered to and to ensure that any money raised is applied for the proper purpose. The information that must be submitted is as follows:

- the arrangements for the lottery – specifically the date on which tickets were available for sale or supply, the dates of any draw and the value of prizes, including any donated prizes and any rollover
- the total proceeds of the lottery
- the amounts deducted by the promoters of the lottery in providing prizes, including prizes in accordance with any rollovers
- the amounts deducted by the promoters of the lottery in respect of costs incurred in organising the lottery
- the amount applied to the purpose for which the promoting society is conducted (this must be at least 20% of the proceeds)
- whether any expenses incurred in connection with the lottery were not paid for by deduction from the proceeds, and, if so, the amount of expenses and the sources from which they were paid.

34.36 Paragraph 39 of Schedule 11 in the Act also requires that returns must:

- be sent to the licensing authority no later than three months after the date of the lottery draw, or in the case of 'instant lotteries' (scratch cards) within three months of the last date on which tickets were on sale
- be signed (electronic signatures are acceptable if the return is sent electronically) by two members of the society, who must be aged eighteen or older, are appointed for the purpose in writing by the society or, if it has one, its governing body, and be accompanied by a copy of their letter or letters of appointment.

34.37 The Commission may inspect a society's returns, although it will not routinely do so. As such licensing authorities are required to retain returns for a minimum period of three years from the date of the lottery draw. They should also make them available for inspection by the general public for a minimum period of 18 months following the date of the lottery draw. Licensing authorities should ensure that information regarding the location of statements (in effect on websites, in council offices etc), when they can be viewed, and the cost of obtaining copies, is made available to the public.

34.38 Licensing authorities should allow for returns to be sent to them both electronically and manually. The Commission recommends that each licensing authority should make details concerning the form of returns required available through appropriate media, such as licensing authority websites and leaflets.

34.39 Where societies run more than one lottery in a calendar year, licensing authorities must monitor the cumulative totals of returns to ensure that societies do not breach the annual monetary limit of £250,000 on ticket values.

34.40 Licensing authorities must notify the Commission if returns reveal that a society's lotteries have exceeded the values permissible for small society lotteries, and such notifications should be copied to the society in question. The Commission will contact the society to determine if they are going to apply for a lottery operator's licence, thereby enabling them to run large society lotteries lawfully, and will inform the licensing authority of the outcome of its exchanges with the society.

34.41 Licensing authorities will also need to be aware of the status of external lottery managers, when monitoring returns. They are an individual, a firm or a company appointed by a society to manage a lottery or lotteries on behalf of the society, and are generally consultants that take their fees from the expenses of the lottery. A maximum of 80% of a lottery's proceeds may be attributed to expenses and prizes, and managers' fees must be included within this total.

EXTERNAL LOTTERY MANAGERS' LICENCE STATUS

34.42 External lottery managers are required to hold a lottery operator's licence issued by the Commission to manage any lottery, including small society lotteries registered with a licensing authority.

34.43 However, individuals or firms can and do provide services to a society or local authority lottery without assuming the role of an external lottery manager. When determining whether a third party is a 'service provider' only, or has assumed the role of external lottery manager, the degree of management undertaken by both the promoter and the sub-contractor will be crucial factors. Key indicators will include:

- who decides how the lottery scheme will operate
- who appoints and manages any sub-contractors
- the banking arrangements for handling the proceeds of the lottery
- who sells the tickets and pays the prizes
- who controls promotional aspects of the lottery.

34.44 Societies employing an unlicensed external lottery manager commit an offence, and they will need to satisfy themselves that any external lottery manager they employ holds an external lottery operator's licence issued by the Commission. This can be achieved by consulting the publicly-accessible register of operating licences held on the Commission's website, at www.gamblingcommission.gov.uk. Licensing authorities should advise societies planning to use, or already using, an external lottery manager that they should do this, and may also wish to verify that it has been done.

34.44 Licensing authorities can refer those seeking further information on external lottery managers to the Commission's website or its publication *Promoting society and local authority lotteries.*[102]

34.45 The Commission has also published a quick guide about ELMs for licensing authorities called *Society lotteries, external lottery managers and service providers*. This is available from the Commission's website.

[102] Available from the Commission's website: www.gamblingcommission.gov.uk

LOTTERY TICKETS

34.46 Lotteries may involve the issuing of physical or virtual tickets to participants (a virtual ticket being non-physical, for example in the form of an email or text message). All tickets must state:

- the name of the promoting society
- the price of the ticket (which must be the same for all tickets)
- the name and address of the member of the society who is designated as having responsibility at the society for promoting small lotteries, or (if there is one) the external lottery manager
- the date of the draw, or information which enables the date to be determined.

The requirement to provide this information can be satisfied by providing an opportunity for the participant to retain the message electronically or print it.

34.47 The Commission recommends that licensing authorities require all registered small society lottery operators to maintain written records of any unsold and returned tickets for a period of one year from the date of the lottery draw. The licensing authority is permitted to inspect the records of the lottery for any purpose related to the lottery.

34.48 The Act requires that lottery tickets may only be sold by persons that are aged 16 or over to persons that are aged 16 or over.

34.49 With regards to where small society lottery tickets may be sold, the Commission recommends that licensing authorities should apply the following criteria to all small society lottery operators:

- tickets should not be sold in a street, where street includes any bridge, road, lane, footway, subway, square, court or passage (including passages through enclosed premises such as shopping malls)
- tickets may, however, be sold in a street from a kiosk, in a shop or door to door.

This approach is consistent with the operating licence conditions imposed upon operators of large lotteries and local authority lotteries.

PRIZES

34.50 Prizes awarded in small society lotteries can be either cash or non-monetary. Licensing authorities need to be aware that the value of prizes declared on returns must not exceed the limits on prizes set out by the Act – in effect that combined with any expenses incurred with the running of the lottery, such as managers' fees, they must not comprise more than 80% of the total proceeds of the lottery. Donated prizes would not be counted as part of this 80% (as no money would be withdrawn from the proceeds to cover their purchase) but is still subject to the limit on a single maximum prize of £25,000 and should be declared on the return following the lottery draw.

34.51 The Commission recommends that licensing authorities should advise small society lottery operators to check with local police if they wish to award items containing alcohol as prizes. This is in order to ensure that licensing law is not breached.

COMPLIANCE AND ENFORCEMENT OF SMALL SOCIETY LOTTERIES

34.52 For information about compliance and enforcement of small society lotteries see part 36 of this Guidance.

SPECIFIC OFFENCES IN RELATION TO LOTTERIES

34.53 The Act sets out a number of offences that apply to lotteries, as follows:

Section of the Act	Offence
s. 258	Promoting a non-exempt lottery without a licence
s. 259	Facilitating a non-exempt lottery without a licence
s. 260	Misusing the profits of a lottery
s. 261	Misusing the profits of an exempt lottery
s. 262	Purporting to operate a small society lottery when not registered, or failing to make the required, or making false or misleading, returns in respect of such lotteries
s. 326	Without reasonable excuse, obstructing or failing to co-operate with an authorised person exercising his/her powers
s. 342	Without reasonable excuse, giving false or misleading information to the Commission or a licensing authority

34.54 If a society running small lotteries fails to comply with any of the conditions of running such lotteries specified in Part 4 of Schedule 11 of the Act, it will be operating in an illegal manner, irrespective of whether it is registered with a licensing authority or not. Under these circumstances small society lottery operators may face prosecution by the Commission, a licensing authority, or the police. The lead organisation for initiating prosecutions will vary depending upon the specific circumstances of the case, but it is expected that licensing authorities will investigate offences in respect of small society lotteries. If necessary the local compliance manager can be asked for advice but the Commission is unlikely to investigate a case unless it has national or regional significance.

34.55 Licensing authorities in Scotland should refer cases where there has been a breach of the Act to the police for investigation, in line with Crown Office and Procurator Fiscal Service[103] guidance on reporting practices for non-police agencies.

103 Refer to website: www.crownoffice.gov.uk

SOCIAL RESPONSIBILITY

34.56 Participation in a lottery is a form of gambling, and as such licensing authorities must be aware that the societies they register are required to conduct their lotteries in a socially responsible manner and in accordance with the Act.

34.57 As the minimum age for participation in a lottery is 16, societies are required to implement effective procedures to minimise the risk of lottery tickets being sold to children, including procedures for:

- checking the age of potentially underage purchasers of lottery tickets
- taking action where there are unlawful attempts to purchase tickets.

34.58 Licensing authorities may wish to refer to the Commission's *Promoting society and local authority lotteries* document for further information regarding social responsibility requirements for lottery operators.

PART 35: CHAIN GIFT SCHEMES

35.1 Section 43 of the Act makes it an offence to invite others to join a chain gift scheme or to participate knowingly in the promotion or administration of a scheme. A person found guilty of the offence could be liable to a fine or imprisonment. This offence was added to the Gambling Act following widespread concern about schemes such as 'Women Empowering Women'. These schemes have most of the relevant features of pyramid selling schemes, but escape the ban on them because they do not involve the sale of any product.

35.2 The Commission is aware that the Office of Fair Trading (OFT) and local authority trading standards officers have considerable relevant experience of dealing with chain gift schemes and are well placed to deal with schemes that arise from time to time. The Commission will keep its role in tackling chain gift schemes, where there is a gambling issue related to the scheme, under review so that if more concerted action is required centrally it can liaise with other bodies to determine what action may be taken.

35.3 The chain gifting offence is part of a suite of consumer protections set out in the Consumer Protection from Unfair Trading Regulations 2008[104]. The main element of consumer protection against these schemes is publicity to prevent people becoming involved in them. Local authorities may wish to use their websites and other publicity tools to educate consumers against participation in such schemes.

35.4 If licensing authorities are contacted by members of the public regarding schemes of this nature, they should in the first instance refer to their trading standards department, or the OFT, as they are likely to have relevant experience of dealing with chain gift schemes, lottery-style scams and similar arrangements.

[104] The Consumer Protection from Unfair Trading Regulations 2008 is available from www.opsi.gov.uk/si/si2008/draft/ukdsi_9780110811574_en_1

STREET COLLECTORS SELLING GAMECARDS

35.5 Licensing authorities may also be aware of street sellers in their areas approaching the public to sell them gamecards, often saying that the cards are being sold to raise money for good causes. If such cards require an element of skill on the part of the player, such as completing a tiebreak question, they may be genuinely distinguishable from a lottery.

35.6 It will be unlikely that the product being sold is a legal lottery. This is because societies running large lotteries are not permitted (by virtue of a condition on their operating licence) to sell lottery tickets in the street, and those running small lotteries are recommended (through this Guidance document) to have a similar restriction imposed upon them by the local authority that registers them.

35.7 The Commission has no comment on products that are't classed as gambling under the Act, but advises authorities with concerns over street sales of such products to contact the trading standards department at the local authority covering the area where sales are being made. They will be able to advise on whether what is being sold amounts to a gambling product, and agree on the best course of action, which may include relying on relevant legislation such as street trading regulations.

PART 36: COMPLIANCE AND ENFORCEMENT

UNDERLYING PRINCIPLES

36.1 For the purposes of this document regulatory action would include informal or formal warnings and licence reviews, issue of simple cautions (warnings) or, in England and Wales only, the prosecution of an offence under the Act. The main objective of the compliance process will be to ensure compliance with the three licensing objectives, including, in particular, compliance with the general licensing conditions (including mandatory and default conditions), specific licence conditions and any applicable codes of practice. Enforcement can be defined as the criminal or regulatory investigation process and any consequent laying of criminal charges or imposition of a regulatory sanction.

36.2 The approach we propose is similar to the approach adopted by most licensing authorities in relation to liquor or other licensing; that is a risk-based approach where the main determinant is the risk posed to the three licensing objectives, as follows:

- preventing gambling from being a source of crime or disorder, being associated with crime or disorder or being used to support crime
- ensuring that gambling is conducted in a fair and open way
- protecting children and other vulnerable persons from being harmed or exploited by gambling.

36.3 Both the Commission and licensing authorities must have regard to the three licensing objectives. However, whilst the Commission generally concentrates on enforcement and compliance relating to the way in which gambling is provided, with a particular focus on regional and national matters, licensing authorities are expected to concentrate more on issues relating to the premises themselves and local instances of illegality and non compliance. In addition licensing authorities are responsible for issuing premises licences, permits, dealing with temporary permissions and the registration of societies running small lotteries.

36.4 The Commission, licensing authorities and the police are all parties to the inspection and enforcement regime created by the Act, and it is important to the effectiveness of this regime that information is readily exchanged and efforts are coordinated. Section 350 and Schedule 6 of the Act establish the principles by which information should be managed between all parties.

36.5 The Commission and licensing authorities will need, during compliance and enforcement activity, to ensure that they act in a proportionate manner reflecting the impact of any breach and the consequences of the breach.

Principles for determining whether it is the Commission or the licensing authority who should act

36.6 It is up to gambling operators, in the first instance, to ensure that their business is compliant with the licences held, including the conditions set out on the face of the Act, in regulations, generic conditions applying to a class of licence or any conditions specific to the operator. The operator should be able to demonstrate to the regulator that their business is compliant.

36.7 The Commission will provide licensing authorities with generic guidance and advice on the steps they should take and approaches they could adopt in dealing with non-compliance. This may take the form of this Guidance or any further guidance, general advice or FAQs published on the Commission's website.

36.8 Licensing authorities are responsible for monitoring compliance with the licences (and permits) that they have issued as well as instances of local illegality. Similarly the Commission is responsible for monitoring the licences that it issues. Where an operator has not demonstrated compliance with the licences the relevant agency will be responsible for taking action against the licence holder. In specific circumstances on a case by case basis the Commission will lead on matters which would normally be best handled by a licensing authority in order to establish principle and precedent and provide operators with a clear understanding of where we regard the bounds of the permissible to lie. Examples have included applications for premises and club gambling permits.

36.9 The Commission, licensing authorities, the police and other agencies who act as co- regulators under the Act have a duty to pursue the licensing objectives and ensure they are not put at risk.

36.10 Licensing authorities are best-placed to monitor and ensure compliance with the Act at a local level. For example, they are generally in the best position to proceed against individual unlicensed premises, although the Commission will be keen to consider compliance activity against operators who have a large regional or national presence. The Commission and licensing authorities should work together to identify and investigate organised or persistent illegal activity.

36.11 The Commission will deal with national operators where their action impacts on more than one premises or where the appropriate sanctions rest with the Commission. The Commission will generally lead on matters relating to businesses with a regional or national presence.

36.12 The provision of facilities for non-remote gambling requires a premises, therefore the first offence is a breach of section 37 of the Act, which is the prime responsibility of the licensing authority. Under most circumstances the licensing authority will take the lead.

36.13 The Commission and licensing authorities should exchange information on non-compliance with licences and permits to ensure that any action taken is coordinated.

---

[83] A new Concordat is due to be published in the Summer of 2009.

Risk-based assessments

36.14 The Commission is pursuing a risk-based approach to compliance and enforcement, as set out in its document *Compliance and Enforcement Policy Statement* the latest version of which can be found on the Commission's website. The basis of the approach is to assess when and where to take action depending on the assessment of how likely it is that the licence conditions or codes of practice may be breached, and with what impact.

36.15 Many licensing authorities already pursue a risk-based approach towards other areas of licensable activity, such as alcohol and taxi licensing.

36.16 As a starting point for developing their local risk-based approach, licensing authorities should undertake a review of existing records and risk assessments. These may include police reports relating to gambling premises, records that the authority may have in relation to alcohol licences, and information held by trading standards and/or environmental health colleagues. This exercise should inform a proposed pattern of visits to premises, planned in connection with the authority's other functions or when reacting to complaints. After any visit undertaken, a licensing authority should review their risk assessments with a view to informing their criteria for undertaking a premises inspection. Complaints, information and intelligence received by the licensing authority relating to gambling premises will also inform the general risk ratings of premises.

Permits

36.17 The Act introduced a range of permits for providing gambling facilities, which are granted and issued by licensing authorities. Permits regulate gambling and the use of gaming machines for non-licensed premises, and generally apply where the stakes and prizes involved in the gambling are very low (with certain exceptions), or gambling is not the main function of the premises (except in the case of family entertainment centre gaming machine permits). The Commission has no specific powers to take action over the misuse of permits other than the general power of prosecution of illegal gambling.

36.18 Codes of Practice on the location and operation of gaming machines are issued by the Commission under section 24 of the Act but compliance with them is a condition of several of the permits that are granted by licensing authorities. Therefore monitoring of compliance with the Codes will fall to licensing authorities as they have the power to withdraw the permit if the Codes are breached. Similarly, if the Commission's Code of Practice is not followed in the case of gaming machines on alcohol licensed premises, licensing authorities have the power to withdraw the automatic entitlement to two machines.

36.19 Licensing authorities are responsible under section 282 of the Act for receiving notifications from owners of alcohol-licensed premises when they intend to exercise their automatic entitlement to two gaming machines in each premises.
36.20 Licensing authorities may grant or reject an application for a permit, but may not attach conditions to it other than limiting the number of machines in limited cases. However, holders of club gaming permits, club gaming machine permits or alcohol-licensed premises permits must abide by the Commission's codes of practice on the location and operation of gaming machines (issued under section 24 of the Act), and licensing authorities may take into account matters set out in the relevant paragraphs of Schedules 10 to 14 of the Act. Permit holders are not normally required to also hold an operating licence, but in all cases a permit cannot be granted for a premises which has already been issued with a valid premises licence.
36.21 Licensing authorities in England and Wales have the power to prosecute if a gaming machine is made available for use in contravention of section 242 of the Act. Licensing authorities in Scotland should refer intentions to prosecute to the Procurator Fiscal.

Small society lotteries

36.22 Licensing authorities will be responsible for ensuring that the provisions of Schedule 11 of the Act in respect of all exempt lotteries are adhered to, with reference to the societies registered with them to operate small lotteries.
36.23 The Act gives licensing authorities in England and Wales the power to prosecute offences relating to the promotion and facilitation of non-exempt lotteries, misusing the proceeds of a lottery and breaching the conditions of a small society lottery.
36.24 The Commission recommends that licensing authorities pursue a risk based approach towards their enforcement responsibilities for small society lotteries.
36.25 Licensing authorities are advised to consider a number of key factors in determining the risk status of small society lottery operators. The Commission considers that the following criteria would be likely to affect the risk status of an operator:

- submission of late returns (returns must be submitted no later than three months after the date on which the lottery draw was held)
- submission of incomplete or incorrect returns
- breaches of the limits for small society lotteries

36.26 Licensing authorities might also consider compiling a list of scenarios that would give reason to investigate the particular circumstances of a society running small society lotteries and feed this into their regime. These scenarios could include:

- making a late return of a statement
- making no returns at all within a year of registration
- failure to pay the annual fee as it becomes due
- reports of sales of lottery tickets to persons under the age of sixteen
- reports of sales of lottery tickets by persons under the age of sixteen
- reports of societies running lotteries without holding registration
- indications that the society has breached permissible limits
- reports of misappropriation of funds.

Temporary use and occasional use permissions

36.27 The Commission has no specific powers in relation to temporary permissions for gambling. It is the function of licensing authorities to record applications for temporary permissions to provide gambling facilities in the form of temporary and occasional use notices.

Premises licences

36.28 Premises licences are issued by licensing authorities to regulate where gambling takes place, and to ensure that the premises are suitable for gambling. To be granted a premises licence the applicant must hold a valid operating licence issued by the Commission (except for track premises licences where the licence holder may not be the actual provider of betting facilities), and the premises licence holder must comply with the Act. A register of those holding an operating licence is available on the Commission's website.

36.29 The inter-relationship between the operating licences issued by the Commission and premises licences issued by licensing authorities and the respective roles of the enforcement agencies (the Commission, licensing authorities and the police) forms the basis of the rest of this section.

PREMISES LICENCE COMPLIANCE

36.30 While enforcement is the regulatory or criminal investigation process which may result in either the imposition of a regulatory sanction or the laying of criminal charges, the compliance process involves gambling operators, individuals working in the industry at all levels, licensing authorities and the Commission. It is aimed at ensuring compliance with all aspects of regulation (the licensing objectives, licence conditions and codes of practice).

36.31 This must be primarily a collaborative process, and the effectiveness of the regulatory regime for the gambling industry depends on the establishment and maintenance of an open, cooperative and effective relationship between operators, individuals, licensing authorities and the Commission.

36.32 The primary responsibility for compliance by any organisation subject to regulation lies with that organisation's senior management, and not the regulator. It is the Commission's role, through the operating and personal licence regime, to ensure that senior management have adequate systems and controls in place to ensure that their business does not pose a regulatory risk, that they are aware of their responsibilities and are carrying them out effectively. The incentive for operators is that better compliance results in less regulatory intervention.

Inspection visits

36.33 Premises licences granted by licensing authorities authorise the provision of facilities for casinos, bingo, betting (including on tracks), adult gaming centres and family entertainment centres.

36.34 Premises licences may only be issued to people with a relevant gambling operating licence issued by the Commission, although as mentioned previously this may not be the case for tracks (where the occupier of the track who gets the premises licence need not be the person who actually offers the facilities for gambling).

36.35 In addition to the mandatory and default conditions attached to premises licences, licensing authorities are entitled to attach local conditions provided they are proportionate and relate to the upholding of the licensing objectives. Part 9 of this Guidance suggests types of conditions that might be applicable. In undertaking inspection activity, licensing authorities should seek to ensure that all relevant conditions attached to a particular premises licence are being complied with and are not at risk of breach.

36.36 The Commission has a legitimate interest in what happens in premises as the operating licence conditions require that the businesses' policies developed centrally are translated into practice at the point of interaction with the customer. To this end, the Commission's compliance regime contains elements of random and programmed premises inspections based on the risks to the operating licence conditions, codes of practice and the licensing objectives. The Commission's local compliance managers will attempt to coordinate such work in order to prevent unnecessary duplication of effort.

36.37 The Act gives licensing authorities, the Commission and the police parallel powers of inspection in respect to premises. In theory a premises licence holder could be subject to inspections from both the Commission and the issuing licensing authority as part of their risk-based compliance programme, and as such the potential for over-regulation exists. The Commission intends to ensure, to the extent that is feasible and cost-effective, that there is no duplication with the relevant bodies visiting the same premises within a short space of time apparently to check the same or similar issues. This can and should be done through regular liaison and cooperation between local Commission compliance managers and licensing authorities.

36.38 This document has already identified that licensing authorities are used to operating in a risk-based environment and that they should adopt a risk-based approach when determining the frequency at which gambling premises are to be inspected. It is open to an authority to visit all of the premises in their area, particularly when considering applications, as this will enable them to risk rate premises. Licensing authorities will receive complaints and observations about premises and these should also be factored into decisions on when to visit specific premises. They may also have a random element in their inspection programme. This combined approach will enable each licensing authority to develop a range of options dependent on the risk assessment model that they adopt.

36.39 The Commission recommends that licensing authorities, in programming their risk-based inspection activity, have particular regard to the need to co-ordinate such activity, both with the Gambling Commission and other agencies that might inspect the business, and between local authority officers (including those employed in a licensing function) that may visit gambling premises for a range of regulatory reasons, for example in relation to an alcohol licence, health and safety regulation or in response to reports of noise nuisance. Such co-ordination can provide opportunities to regulate the premises more efficiently, whilst minimising unnecessary burdens on the operator.

36.40 The Commission will undertake visits to premises in accordance with its risk model to ensure compliance with the relevant operating licence, for example to ensure that the policy and procedures adopted by licence holders are translated into appropriate transactions with customers. Most Commission inspections will be programmed, and the local licensing authority will normally be invited to offer any observations it has on the specific premises in advance of visits. If appropriate the Commission will undertake joint visits with licensing authorities.

Information

36.41 Licensing authorities should provide advice to all those who make enquiries to them, about the legal responsibilities involved in providing premises or holding permits for gambling, whether or not they currently hold a licence or a permit.

36.42 Enquiries relating to operating or personal licences should be handled by consulting the Commission's website, or referring such enquiries directly to the Commission.

36.43 Further details on the Commission's approach to compliance can be found in the document *Compliance and Enforcement Policy Statement*, available through the Commission's website.

TEST PURCHASING AND AGE VERIFICATION

36.44 Test purchasing is one method by which the Commission or Licensing Authorities may, in England and Wales, measure the compliance of licensed operators, or groups of licensed operators, with aspects of the Gambling Act 2005.

36.45 Local authorities are most familiar with the methodology in relation to the sale of age restricted products, and are aware of the importance of following current guidance in this area, in order to ensure that tests are carried out in a manner that is risk-based and fair, with due regard to the welfare of young people involved in the test purchasing.

36.46 As noted above (paragraph 36.6) in the first instance it is up to operators to ensure they are compliant with the Act and the associated regulations. The Commission's approach in relation to test purchasing in general and age verification in particular is set out in our Advice Note[105]. This approach is in line with the responsibilities[106] set out for regulators and enforcers in the Age Restricted Products and Services Framework published by the Better Regulation Delivery Office (formerly the Local Better Regulation Office) in 2011, which applies to England and Wales.

36.47 The Commission encourages operators to manage the business risk associated with both underage access to premises and permitting a young person to gamble. Where an operator takes measures to do this, such as commissioning a third party to test the effectiveness of their policies and procedures, and where the results of the tests are shared with us, we are less inclined to conduct our own test purchasing.

36.48 Local authorities, whether acting as a licensing authority or through another function such as trading standards, should in the first instance consult with operators where they have concerns about the underage access and age verification policies or whose premises they plan to test purchase. This will enable them to discover what programmes they may have in place to manage the business risk and take these into account in planning a test purchase exercise. To do otherwise would not be compliant with the Hampton principles. This approach is analogous to what is sometimes called 'earned recognition'.

36.49 Local authorities should also consult with the Commission before planning such exercises in order to ensure that there is no conflict between any ongoing investigation or enforcement activity related to either the premises or the operator that we have initiated and the test purchase operation.

36.50 However, local authorities will have in place democratically determined priorities and resource allocations as well as the ability to respond to complaints and intelligence related to specific premises. As a result, irrespective of the actions of an operator on their overall estate, test purchasing may be deemed to be an appropriate course of action.

36.51 In December 2011 the Department for Business, Innovation and Skills published the government response to a consultation - Transforming Regulatory Enforcement'. The paper announced the Department's intention to legislate to extend the primary authority scheme to include age related sales in gambling.

---

105 Approach to test purchasing – England and Wales only May 2011, available on the Commission website www.gamblingcommission.gov.uk

106 The principles for regulators and enforcers will be underpinned by a Code of Practice for Regulatory Delivery, which was launched for consultation in June 2012.

ENFORCEMENT

Regulatory sanctions

36.52 If a premises licence or permit holder is found to be at risk of breaching, or is actually in breach of: a premises licence condition; a code of practice, compliance with which is a condition attached to a permit; or otherwise committing an offence under the Act, then licensing authorities may take enforcement action against that licence or permit holder. Such enforcement action may take the form of regulatory action, ranging from informal action through to prosecuting an offence under the Act.

36.53 Informal actions that could be taken include giving oral and written advice, or issuing oral and written warnings. Formal actions that could be taken include conducting interviews under PACE (Police And Criminal Evidence) (or common law in Scotland), reviewing a premises licence, issuing simple cautions and initiating prosecutions. In Scotland, the licensing board will refer the question of interview to the police in the first instance and the decision to initiate a prosecution will be taken by the procurator fiscal.

36.54 If the matter relates to a premises licence, then it may be that the particular circumstances give rise to the possibility of breaching the conditions of both a premises and an operating licence. In such circumstances the Commission will generally take action against the operator (which might include prosecution but would normally be regulatory action) following discussion with the licensing authority, against the operator. However there may be occasions where a licensing authority is better placed to take the lead, particularly where there is a breach of a premises licence condition that is confined to one authority area and is a particular priority for that area, or where the risk of, or impact of, any operating licence breach is isolated rather than systemic. The licensing authority may also be best placed to take the lead if there are additional specific matters that it also wants to take action on that fall outside the scope of the Act's licensing objectives, such as health and safety concerns.

36.55 Licensing authorities will also take the lead if there is a possibility of a breach or an actual breach of a permit, as the Commission does not have powers to undertake enforcement action relating to permits, besides the general power to prosecute illegal gambling.

36.56 Section 197 of the Act requires licensing authorities to inform the Commission when a review into a premises licence is initiated, either as a result of a complaint from another party or if initiated by the licensing authority itself. The Commission will therefore be able to provide an input into any premises licence review and as such requires to be informed of the output of such reviews, as there may be wider implications towards the status of the operating licence.

36.57 Where considered appropriate and necessary, cases that involve offences other than gambling offences should be referred to the appropriate external enforcement agency (for example the police, Advertising Standards Authority, Trading Standards etc), but the Commission will need to be aware of the breach.

36.58 The Commission has established criteria by which it will determine which agency should take the lead on enforcement matters relating to breaches connected to premises licences, permits and temporary use notices, and recommends that licensing authorities should pursue a similar approach. The criteria are as follows:

- The powers available under the Act:
  only licensing authorities can undertake administrative action (suspensions, revocations) in relation to premises licences and permits
- The nature of the breach or risk of breach:
  if it involves permits, temporary permissions or breaches of premises licences conditions with essentially local impacts the local licensing authority should normally deal with them
- The seriousness of the breach or risk of breach:
  where a breach appears to be widespread or stemming from systemic failures on the part of the operator, then the Commission will generally take action. The Commission will also generally take action if the offence is high impact, if there is nationwide deterrence value of enforcement action or if the case will establish a precedent. As noted above the Commission will be notified if a licensing authority starts to review a premises licence and so will have the opportunity to comment and contribute to the review
- The geographical impact of the breach:
  if there is a regional element to the breach, for example a number of pubs in a particular city are offering a similar type of unlicensed gambling, it may be appropriate for licensing authorities to co-ordinate their activity locally and to liaise with the Commission on the regulatory action to be taken
- The frequency of the breach, or risk of breach:
  a 'one off' event may be best dealt with by a licensing authority, whereas repeat offences, or offences in several premises owned by the holder of an operating

licence suggesting systemic breaches of licence conditions, should generally be dealt with by the Commission. Also whether the breach has a seasonal and therefore temporary impact

- The enforcement action that is available:
  for example whether a fine would be a suitable enforcement outcome.

36.59 Generally, if a licensing authority discovers a breach of a premises licence condition or permit in the course of other regulatory activity, it is expected that it will deal with the case. However, when formal enforcement action in relation to suspected breaches of a premises licence is to be taken by a licensing authority, it should inform the Commission that it is taking such action. This enables the Commission to comment on the proposed course of action if it considers it necessary to do so. It will be for the Commission to respond promptly to the notification of the intention to take action, and it is not expected that licensing authorities will wait for agreement from the Commission before taking action.

36.60 If the Commission is preparing a case against an operator and would prefer the local licensing authority not to act, the Commission will advise the authority accordingly of this, and will inform it of the reasons for this request.

Prosecutions

36.61 The Act gives licensing authorities (in England and Wales), the police and the Commission the power to prosecute (among other offences) the offence of using premises for gambling without the requisite permissions. In exceptional circumstances, such as repeated deliberate breaches of premises licence conditions, licensed operators or permit holders may be prosecuted without any prior regulatory action (warnings, suspension or revocation of licence or removal of permit etc). Most prosecutions will be against those illegally providing gambling without a licence or permit.

36.62 In Scotland, licensing authorities are not able to institute criminal proceedings themselves, but are to refer cases where there has been a breach of the Act to the Procurator Fiscal.

36.63 Normally the Commission or the licensing authority would decide when to involve the police, rather than the police initiating any action. The Commission considers that examples of scenarios where the police should be involved include:

- when non-gambling offences are discovered, for example large-scale theft or other serious crime which extends beyond the reach of licence conditions
- assistance with Commission investigations, for example enquiries into other criminal activity.

36.64 There is a distinction between those who conduct gambling operations under a licence or permits but breach the conditions of their licence or permit, and those who seek to profit from providing facilities for gambling without a licence. While both situations result in unlawful gambling, the latter situation is generally considered by the Commission to be more serious.

Illegal gambling

36.65 The Commission views the prevention of illegal gambling as an enforcement priority. Combating illegal gambling is of significant benefit to the licensed community as the provision of illegal unregulated gambling impacts upon the reputation of the industry as a whole. The persistent and widespread existence of illegal gambling also reduces the incentive on operators to be correctly licensed. Those engaged in illegal gambling should expect to be subject to the criminal investigation and prosecution process.

36.66 The Commission will generally take the lead in prosecuting the offence of providing facilities for gambling where it is committed in the context of illegal gambling which appears organised and has a potentially national or regional impact, or where there are deliberate, reckless or significant breaches by a licensed operator.

36.67 The expectation is that licensing authorities will take prosecutions against those providing or facilitating illegal gambling in effect gambling without a licence or permit, where the criminality is contained in one premises.
36.68 The annual premises licence fee is set to cover the costs of compliance and enforcement work undertaken by licensing authorities, including the cost of dealing with illegal gambling in a licensing authority's area.
36.69 The issue of illegal or illegally-sited machines is complex and will need a co-ordinated approach. Licensing officers should contact their local compliance manager in the first instance to agree an approach.

Breaches of licences

36.70 For the licensed industry there are a range of compliance and regulatory tools to ensure that licence holders remain compliant. Enforcement is a highly effective method of ensuring regulatory compliance and deterring regulatory breaches. Therefore the Commission will undertake enforcement cases against those licensed operators and individuals who fall below the required regulatory standard or who fail to take effective remedial action to correct regulatory failings. In serious cases this will mean regulatory or criminal proceedings that may ultimately result in loss of the licence and therefore expulsion from the industry.
36.71 Before commencing criminal proceedings against a licensed operator or his employee without a prior premises licence review (by virtue of which the Commission would be notified), licensing authorities should consult the Commission, as it may be that there have also been related breaches connected to operating and/or personal licences held by the operator, or breaches at premises in other parts of the country.
36.72 If a particular breach is committed by a large national or regional operator, which may have wider implications for the gambling industry as a whole, then the Commission may wish to take primacy. However under such circumstances the Commission will liaise with licensing authorities to establish who should take the lead on a case by case basis.
36.73 In exceptional circumstances, where a licensing authority considers that enforcement action is justified and would normally take primacy, but feels it does not have sufficient investigatory powers or resources to deal with a relevant breach of the Act, it should refer the matter to the Commission to consider whether or not it can either assist the authority by providing resources/expertise or assuming primacy in the investigation and potential prosecution. The authority should contact their local compliance manager in the first instance.
36.74 In the course of an investigation into a breach of licence conditions or codes of practice, a licensing authority may find that other non-gambling offences are being committed on the premises, for example drugs offences or handling of stolen goods. Under these circumstances a multi-agency approach involving the police and the Commission is essential.
36.75 Appendix D sets out a summary of offences under the Gambling Act 2005.

APPENDIX A: SUMMARY OF MACHINE PROVISIONS BY PREMISES

	Machine category						
Premises type	**A**	**B1**	**B2**	**B3**	**B4**	**C**	**D**
Large casino (machine/table ratio of 5-1 up to maximum)		Maximum of 150 machines Any combination of machines in categories B to D (except B3A machines), within the total limit of 150 (subject to machine/table ratio)					
Small casino(machine/table ratio of 2-1 up to maximum)		Maximum of 80 machines Any combination of machines in categories B to D (except B3A machines), within the total limit of 80 (subject to machine/table ratio)					

	Machine category						
Premises type	**A**	**B1**	**B2**	**B3**	**B4**	**C**	**D**
Pre-2005 Act casino(no machine/table ratio)		Maximum of 20 machines categories B to D (except B3A machines), or any number of C or D machines instead					
Betting premises and tracks occupied by pool betting			Maximum of 4 machines categories B2 to D (except B3A machines)				
Bingo premises				Maximum of 20% of the total number of gaming machines which are available for use on the premises categories B3 or B4		No limit on category C or D machines	
Adult gaming centre				Maximum of 20% of the total number of gaming machines which are available for use on the premises categories B3 or B4		No limit on category C or D machines	
Family entertainment centre (with premises licence)						No limit on category C or D machines	
Family entertainment centre (with permit)							No limit on category D machines
Clubs or miners' welfare institute (with permits)					Maximum of 3 machines in categories B3A or B4 to D		
Qualifying alcohol-licensed premises						1 or 2 machines of category C or D automatic upon notification	
Qualifying alcohol-licensed premises (with gaming machine permit)						Number of category C-D machines as specified on permit	
Travelling fair							No limit on category D machines

* It should be noted that members' clubs and miners' welfare institutes are entitled to site a total of three machines in categories B3A to D but only one B3A machine can be sited as part of this entitlement. Commercial clubs are entitled to a total of three machines in categories B4 to D.

** Adult gaming centre and bingo premises are entitled to make available a number of Category B gaming machines not exceeding 20% of the total number of gaming machines which are available for use on the premises. Premises in existence before 13 July 2011 are entitled to make available four (adult gaming centre premises) or eight (bingo premises) category B gaming machines, or 20% of the total number of gaming machines, whichever is the greater. Adult gaming centre premises and bingo premises licences granted on or after 13 July 2011 but before 1 April 2014 are entitled to a maximum of four or eight category B gaming machines or 20% of the total number of gaming machines, whichever is the greater; from 1 April 2014 these premises will be entitled to 20% of the total number of gaming machines only. But not B3A machines.

APPENDIX B: SUMMARY OF GAMING MACHINE CATEGORIES AND ENTITLEMENTS

Category of machine	Maximum stake (from July 2011)	Maximum prize (from July 2011)
A	Unlimited — No category A gaming machines are currently permitted	
B1	£2	£4,000
B2	£100 (in multiples of £10)	£500
B3A	£1	£500
B3	£2	£500
B4	£1	£250
C	£1	£70
D — non-money prize (other than a crane grab machine or a coin pusher or penny falls machine)	30p	£8
D – non-money prize (crane grab machine)	£1	£50
D – money prize (other than a coin pusher or penny falls machine)	10p	£5
D — combined money and non-money prize (other than a coin pusher or penny falls machine)	10p	£8 (of which no more than £5 may be a money prize)
D — combined money and non-money prize (coin pusher or penny falls machine)	10p	£15 (of which no more than £8 may be a money prize)

APPENDIX C: SUMMARY OF GAMING ENTITLEMENTS FOR CLUBS AND ALCOHOL-LICENSED PREMISES

	Members' club or MW institute with club gaming permit	Bridge or whist club	Members' club or commercial club with club machine permit	Members' club, commercial club or MW institute without a club gaming permit or club machine permit	Pubs and other alcohol-licensed premises
Equal chance gaming	Yes	Bridge and/or Whist only	Yes	Yes	Yes

	Members' club or MW institute with club gaming permit	Bridge or whist club	Members' club or commercial club with club machine permit	Members' club, commercial club or MW institute without a club gaming permit or club machine permit	Pubs and other alcohol-licensed premises
Limits on stakes	No limit	No limit	**Poker** £1000 per week £250 per day £10 per person per game **Other gaming** No limit	**Poker** £1000 per week £250 per day £10 per person per game **Other gaming** No limit	**Poker** £100 per premises per day **Other gaming** £5 per person per game **Cribbage & dominoes** No limit
Limits on prizes	No limit	No limit	**Poker** £250 per game **Other gaming** No limit	**Poker** £250 per game **Other gaming** No limit	**Poker** £100 per game **Other gaming** No limit
Maximum participation fees – per person per day	**Bridge and/or whist** £20 **Other gaming** £3	£18 (without club gaming permit) £20 (with club gaming permit)	**Bridge and/or whist** £18 **Other gaming** £3 (commercial club) £1 (members' club)	**Bridge and/or whist** £18 **Other gaming** £1	None permitted
Bankers or unequal chance gaming	Pontoon *Chemin de Fer*	None permitted	None permitted	None permitted	None permitted
Limits on bingo	Maximum of £2,000 per week in stakes/prizes. If more then will need an operating licence.	No bingo permitted	Maximum of £2,000 per week in stakes/prizes. If more then will need an operating licence.	Maximum of £2,000 per week in stakes/prizes. If more then will need an operating licence.	Maximum of £2,000 per week in stakes/prizes. If more then will need an operating licence.

* On a day when no other facilities for gaming are provided

APPENDIX D: SUMMARY OF OFFENCES UNDER THE GAMBLING ACT 2005

GENERAL OFFENCES REGARDING THE PROVISION OF GAMBLING FACILITIES

Providing gambling facilities in Great Britain without a relevant licence, permit, notice, or exemption included under the Act.	Section 33
Using premises to provide gambling facilities from, or causing them to be provided, without a relevant licence, permit, notice or exemption under the Act.	Section 37

OFFENCE REGARDING CHEATING AT GAMBLING

Cheating, attempting to cheat, or assisting another person to cheat at gambling.	Section 42

OFFENCES COMMITTED TOWARDS OR BY UNDER-18S

Inviting, causing or permitting a child (under 16) or young person (16 – 17) to gamble, with the exception of: • private / non-commercial gaming and betting • participating in lotteries • participating in football pools • using a category D gaming machine • participating in equal chance gaming at premises subject of a prize gaming permit or an FEC premises licence • participating in prize gaming at a fair or an unlicensed FEC	Section 46
This offence includes intentional distribution of advertising to under-18s where the intent is to encourage gambling.	
It is also an offence on the part of a young person to gamble with the exception of situations listed above.	Section 48
Inviting or permitting a child or young person to enter: • a casino • a betting premises (except for betting areas of horse and greyhound tracks on race days) • an adult gaming centre • areas of a family entertainment centre where category C gaming machines are situated.	Section 47
This offence is committed at all times when the premises listed above are being used in reliance on the premises licence.	
It is also an offence on the part of a young person to enter the premises listed above.	Section 49
Young person providing facilities for gambling, with the exception of: • private / non-commercial gaming and betting • a lottery • football pools	Section 50

• prize gaming at a travelling fair.	
Employing a child or young person to provide gambling facilities, with the exception of providing the following facilities: • private / non-commercial gaming and betting • prize gaming at a travelling fair.	**Section 51**
Employing a child to provide facilities in connection with: • a lottery • football pools.	**Section 52**
Employing a child for any purposes when bingo is provided or gambling provided in accordance with a club gaming permit or club machine permit.	**Section 53**
Employing a child or young person to perform any function connected to a gaming machine.	**Section 54**
It is also an offence on the part of a young person if they are employed in such a role.	
Employing a child or young person in a casino, an adult gaming centre, or at a betting premises, unless it is at a time when no activity is being carried on in reliance on the premises licence.	**Section 55**
It is also an offence on the part of a young person if they are employed in such a role.	
Inviting, causing or permitting a child to take part in football pools or a lottery with the exception of: • an incidental non-commercial lottery • a private lottery • part of the National Lottery.	**Sections 56 and 57**
Failure to comply with an operating licence condition to return stake to a child or young person.	**Section 58**

OFFENCES CONNECTED TO OPERATING LICENCES

Failure to comply with an operating licence condition to return stake to a child or young person.	**Section 58**
Failing without reasonable excuse to notify the Commission of change in circumstances.	**Section 101**
Licensee failing without reasonable excuse to produce their operating licence when requested by a police officer or enforcement officer.	**Section 108**
Licensee failing to notify the Commission without reasonable excuse and as soon as reasonably practicable about conviction of an offence.	**Section 109**
Licensee failing to notify the court upon conviction of a relevant offence that they are an operating licence holder.	**Section 109**
Licensee failing without reasonable excuse to produce records for the Commission relating to operating licensed activities or information about licensed activities.	**Section 122**
Operating licence holder fails without reasonable excuse to produce the authorisation they have given to someone to accept bets on their behalf, when asked to do so by a police officer or enforcement officer. This offence can also apply to the person that has been authorised to accept bets.	**Section 316**

OFFENCES CONNECTED TO PERSONAL LICENCES

Failure without reasonable excuse to produce a personal licence to a police officer or enforcement officer.	**Section 134**
Licensee failing to notify the Commission as soon as reasonably practicable about a conviction of offence.	**Section 138**
Licensee failing to act within the terms and conditions of their licence.	**Section 139**

GENERAL OFFENCES CONNECTED TO ALL PREMISES LICENCES

Licensee failing without reasonable excuse to keep premises licence on premises and make available for inspection to a police officer, enforcement officer or authorised person.	**Section 185**
Licensee failing to notify without reasonable excuse the licensing authority about change of residential address or other details on the licence.	**Section 186**

OFFENCES CONNECTED TO TEMPORARY USE NOTICES

Failure of premises licence holder to without reasonable excuse prominently display or make available their temporary use notice to a police officer, customs and excise officer, enforcement officer or licensing authority officer.	**Section 229**

OFFENCES CONNECTED TO GAMING MACHINES

Making a gaming machine available for use without a relevant licence or permit, or in contravention of regulations made under section 240 of the Act (SI No 2007/2319).	**Section 242**
Manufacturing, supplying, installing, adapting, maintaining, or repairing a gaming machine without a suitable operating licence, unless:	**Section 243**
• the gaming machine is scrap with no commercial value • the gaming machine is incidental to the sale/letting of previously-licensed property.	
Supplying, installing, adapting, maintaining or repairing a gaming machine (or part of) without complying with regulations made under section 241 of the Act (SI: No. 2007/2320), unless: • the gaming machine is scrap with no commercial value • the gaming machine is incidental to the sale/letting of previously-licensed property.	**Section 243**
Supplying, installing or making available for use a gaming machine allowing payment by credit card.	**Section 245**

OFFENCES CONNECTED TO LOTTERIES

The offences listed here do not apply to lotteries or products forming part of the National Lottery, as the Act does not regulate the National Lottery. Police enquiries regarding offences connected to the National Lottery should be directed to the National Lottery Commission.

Promoting a non-exempt lottery without a suitable operating licence or on behalf of someone with a suitable operating licence.	**Section 258**
Facilitating a non-exempt lottery without holding a suitable operating licence (where facilitating includes functions such as advertising and printing tickets and promotional materials).	**Section 259**
Misusing profits from a lottery, ie using them or causing them to be used for purposes other than the advertised purpose of the lottery.	**Section 260**
Misusing profits from an incidental non-commercial lottery, a private society lottery, or a small society lottery.	**Section 261**
A non-commercial society promoting a lottery without being registered with a licensing authority, or failing to provide the licensing authority with returns (or providing false returns) following a small society lottery.	**Section 262**

OFFENCE CONNECTED TO BINGO PLAYED IN CLUBS AND INSTITUTES

Failing without reasonable excuse to inform the Commission of periods of high turnover bingo if the club or institute does not hold an operating licence (high turnover bingo being where the stakes or prizes of all games of bingo played in a seven day period exceed £2,000).	**Section 275**

OFFENCE CONNECTED TO USE OF PROCEEDS FROM GAMING AT NON-COMMERCIAL EVENTS

Using the profits (or permitting them to be used) from non-commercial prize gaming or equal chance gaming for a purpose other than that specified as the fund-raising purpose of the gaming.	**Section 301**

OFFENCE CONNECTED TO CASINO PREMISES LICENCES

Failure on the part of the casino premises licence holder to produce upon demand (by a police officer or enforcement officer) the authorisation they have given to someone to provide bingo or betting facilities at the casino in question.	**Section 316**
This offence can also be committed by the individual or organisation authorised by the casino premises licence holder if they fail to produce the authorisation.	

OFFENCE OF OBSTRUCTING OR FAILING TO CO-OPERATE DURING AN INSPECTION

Obstructing or failing to cooperate without reasonable excuse with a police officer, enforcement officer or authorised person carrying out inspection activity under Part 15 of the Act.	**Section 326**

OFFENCE OF PROVIDING FALSE OR MISLEADING INFORMATION

Providing false or misleading information to the Commission or a licensing authority regarding any provision of the Act.	**Section 342**

OFFENCES CONNECTED TO ADVERTISING OF GAMBLING FACILITIES

Contravention of any regulations relating to gambling advertising. (nb the Secretary of State for Culture, Media and Sport has chosen not to exercise their reserve powers to make such secondary legislation at this time).	**Section 328**
Knowingly advertising unlawful gambling without reasonable belief otherwise.	**Section 330**
Advertising foreign gambling facilities other than lotteries (in accordance with regulations SI: 2007/2329).	**Section 331**

OFFENCE OF FAILING TO COMPLY WITH A FORFEITURE ORDER

Failure to comply with a court's forfeiture order to surrender named materials to a police officer, or co-operate with steps to comply with the order.	**Section 345**

OFFENCE CONNECTED TO UNLICENSED FAMILY ENTERTAINMENT CENTRES

Occupier of premises failing without reasonable excuse to produce their family entertainment centre gaming machine permit for a police officer, enforcement officer or authorised officer.	**Schedule 10(20)**

OFFENCES CONNECTED TO CLUB GAMING AND CLUB MACHINE PERMITS

Failing without reasonable excuse to produce a club gaming permit or club machine permit for a police officer or enforcement officer.	**Schedule 12(13)**
Failure without reasonable excuse to have club gaming or club machine permits varied by the licensing authority as soon as practicable upon a change of circumstances.	**Schedule 12(15)**

OFFENCE CONNECTED TO ALCOHOL LICENSED PREMISES GAMING MACHINE PERMITS

Failure without reasonable excuse to produce a licensed premises gaming machine permit upon the request of a police officer, enforcement officer or authorised person.	**Schedule 13(10)**

OFFENCE CONNECTED TO PRIZE GAMING PERMITS

Failure without reasonable excuse to produce a prize gaming permit upon the request of a police officer, enforcement officer or authorised person.	**Schedule 14(20)**

OFFENCE CONNECTED TO GAMBLING SOFTWARE

Manufacturing, supplying, installing or adapting gambling software without holding a relevant operating licence.	**Section 41**

OFFENCE CONNECTED TO CHAIN-GIFT SCHEMES

Inviting another person to join chain-gift schemes or participating in the promotion of chain-gift schemes.	**Section 43**

Gambling Commission May 2009

APPENDIX E: SUMMARY OF STATUTORY APPLICATION FORMS AND NOTICES

LIST OF PRESCRIBED FORMS

Application

Application for a premises licence under the Gambling Act 2005 (standard form)
Application for a premises licence under the Gambling Act 2005 (vessel)
Notice of application for a premises licence under the Gambling Act 2005 (to be published)
Notice of application for a premises licence (Form A) (for responsible authorities)
Notice of application for a premises licence (Form B) (for responsible authorities)
Summary of the Terms and Conditions of a premises licence
Premises licence
Notice of a grant of an application for a premises licence
Annex A - form to accompany notice of grant (conditions to be attached)
Annex B – form to accompany notice of grant (conditions to be excluded)
Annex C – form to accompany notice of grant (representations)
Notice of rejection of an application for a premises licence

Variation

Application to vary a premises licence under the Gambling Act 2005
Notice of Application to vary a premises licence under the Gambling Act 2005 (to be published)
Notice of Application to vary a premises licence (Form A) (for responsible authorities)
Notice of Application to vary a premises licence (Form B) (for responsible authorities)
Notice of grant of an application to vary a premises licence
Annex A - form to accompany notice of grant (conditions to be attached)
Annex B – form to accompany notice of grant (conditions to be excluded)
Annex C – form to accompany notice of grant (representations)
Notice of rejection of an application to vary a premises licence

Review

Application for a review of a premises licence under the Gambling Act 2005
Notice of application for a review of a premises licence under the Gambling Act 2005
Notice of application for a review of a premises licence (to the premises licence holder and responsible authorities)
Notice of intention to hold a review of a premises licence under the Gambling Act 2005
Notice of intention to hold a review of a premises licence (to the premises licence holder)
Notice of the decision on a review of a premises licence

Provisional

Application for a provisional statement under the Gambling Act 2005 (standard form)
Notice of application for a provisional statement under the Gambling Act 2005
Application for a provisional statement under the Gambling Act 2005 (vessel)
Notice of application for a provisional statement (Form A) (for responsible authorities)
Notice of application for a provisional statement (Form B) (for responsible authorities)
Provisional statement
Notice of grant of an application for a provisional statement
Annex A - form to accompany notice of grant (conditions to be attached)
Annex B – form to accompany notice of grant (conditions to be excluded)
Annex C – form to accompany notice of grant (representations)
Notice of rejection of an application for a provisional statement

Transfer

Application to transfer a premises licence under the Gambling Act 2005
Notice of application to transfer a premises licence (Form A) (for responsible authorities)
Notice of application to transfer a premises licence (Form B) (for responsible authorities)
Summary of terms and conditions of a premise licence
Premises Licence
Notice of grant of an application to transfer a premises licence
Annex A - form to accompany notice of grant (conditions to be attached)
Annex B – form to accompany notice of grant (conditions to be excluded)
Annex C – form to accompany notice of grant (representations)
Notice of rejection of an application to transfer a premises licence

Reinstatement

Application for the reinstatement of a premises licence under the Gambling Act 2005
Notice of application of the reinstatement of a premises licence (Form A)
Notice of application of the reinstatement of a premises licence (Form B)
Summary of terms and conditions of a premise licence
Premises Licence
Notice of grant of an application for the reinstatement of a premises licence
Annex A - form to accompany notice of grant (conditions to be attached)
Annex B – form to accompany notice of grant (conditions to be excluded)
Annex C – form to accompany notice of grant (representations)
Notice of the rejection of an application for the reinstatement of a premises licence

Temporary Use Notices

Gambling Act 2005 – Temporary Use Notice (for premises other than vessels)
Gambling Act 2005 – Temporary Use Notice (vessel)
Counter Notice (given in response to a temporary use notice)

Permits/lottery

Application Form for Club Gaming Permit or Club Machine Permit
Registration of Small Society Lotteries (Application form for registration of non commercial society)
Club Gaming Permit
Club Machine Permit
Prize Gaming Permit
Family Entertainment Centre Gaming Machine Permit
Licensed Premises Gaming Machine Permit

REVISION TO GUIDANCE TO LICENSING AUTHORITIES (PROVISIONAL STATEMENTS)

Responses document, August 2008

1 INTRODUCTION

6.2656 1.1 In April 2008, The Gambling Commission ("the Commission") issued a consultation paper proposing revisions to the second edition of the Guidance to Licensing Authorities ("the Guidance"). The consultation ended on 30 May 2008. This responses document explains the key issues considered during that consultation and the changes made to the Guidance as a result.

1.2 We received eight responses to the consultation, and we would like to thank those who took part. A list of respondents can be seen at Annex A of this document, and copies of the responses that were not marked as confidential will be available shortly on the Commission's website, www.gamblingcommission.gov.uk.

2 THE ISSUE

2.1 In the recent Judicial Review claim brought by Betting Shop Services Limited against Southend-on-Sea Borough Council (The Queen (on the application of) Betting Shop *Services Limited v Southend*-on-Sea Borough Council [2008] EWHC 105 (Admin)), the Court made an order quashing the licensing authority's original decision and remitted the case to the licensing authority for reconsideration in accordance with the law, including the Judgment of the Court in that case.

2.2 It was clear from the Judgment that paragraphs 7.55, 7.56 and 7.57 of the Commission's current Guidance were based on a misunderstanding of the legal position. The Court declared that a premises licence may lawfully be granted in respect of premises that are not ready to be used for gambling (for example, in respect of premises which are about to be constructed or in the course of construction or alteration), provided that the applicant has a right to occupy the premises and holds an operating licence authorising him to carry on the activity in respect of which the premises licence is sought. We considered that we needed to revise the Guidance to reflect the Court Judgment, and give guidance in situations where an application for a premises licence is made in respect of premises which are not yet ready to be used for gambling.

3 SECTIONS OF THE GUIDANCE FOR REVISION

3.1 We reviewed all sections of the Guidance which look at the definition of premises, which refer to provisional statements and which refer to the process for applying for either a premises licence or a provisional statement. The Commission reviewed paragraphs 7.11, 7.12, 7.55 to 7.58, as well as 11.1 to 11.10, of its Guidance in the light of the judgment. We consider that part 11 of the Guidance requires no further review because this part looks at how licensing authorities consider an application for a provisional statement, but is silent on whether an application for a provisional statement is appropriate.

We felt that paragraphs 7.11 and 7.12 accurately reflect the definition of a 'premises' as set out in the Gambling Act 2005 ("the Act") and we stated that we do not propose to make any changes to them at this stage.
3.2 None of the respondents disagreed with our reasoning or suggested that further sections needed review.

4 COMMENTS ON THE PROPOSED REVISIONS

4.1 Unlike other consultations we did not ask specific questions in the consultation paper. This is because we are reviewing an existing document and suggesting changes for a limited purpose ie to reflect the judgment in the Southend case.
4.2 The remainder of this section sets out the text on which we consulted, a summary of respondents' opinions, the Commission's response and the final text which was imported into the Guidance to Licensing Authorities on 22 August 2008.

PART 7: PREMISES LICENCES.

Relationship between planning permission, building regulations and granting of a premises licence [existing heading]

Text proposed in the consultation document

7.54 The licensing authority should not take into account irrelevant matters, ie those not related to gambling and the licensing objectives. One example of an irrelevant matter would be the likelihood of the applicant obtaining planning permission or building regulations approval for their proposal.

Respondents' comments and Commission views

One trade association noted that the judicial review works both ways ie licensing authorities have a duty to take into consideration all relevant considerations and a duty not to take into consideration all irrelevant considerations. They suggest that the meaning of irrelevant considerations might not just be those which are not related to gambling or the licensing objectives but will depend upon the individual facts. We agree with this point and have amended the paragraph accordingly.

Final text

7.54 In determining applications the licensing authority has a duty to take into consideration all relevant matters and not to take into consideration any irrelevant matters, ie those not related to gambling and the licensing objectives. One example of an irrelevant matter would be the likelihood of the applicant obtaining planning permission or building regulations approval for their proposal. [revised paragraph which is paragraph 7.54 in the current document]

Text proposed in the consultation document

7.55 Licensing authorities should bear in mind that a premises licence, once it comes into effect, authorises premises to be used for gambling. Accordingly, a licence to use premises for gambling should only be issued in relation to premises that the licensing authority can be satisfied are going to be ready to be used for gambling in the reasonably near future, consistent with the scale of building or alterations required before the premises are bought into use. This is why the Act allows a potential operator to apply for a provisional statement if construction of premises is not yet complete, or they need alteration, or he does not yet have a right to occupy them. See Part 11 of this guidance for more information about provisional statements.

Respondents' comments and Commission views

One trade association asked that the Commission offer a definition of 'reasonably near future'. We do not think this is necessary as the length of time for the preparation of a building for gambling purposes will depend on the size and scale of each premises under consideration and we consider that this is a matter for the licensing authority and the operator. The reference is to "issue" not "grant" and, as they point out, the possibility of issue with a delayed effective date where appropriate is dealt with at paragraph 7.57. This paragraph therefore remains unchanged.

Final text

7.55 Licensing authorities should bear in mind that a premises licence, once it comes into effect, authorises premises to be used for gambling. Accordingly, a licence to use premises for gambling should only be issued in relation to premises that the licensing authority can be satisfied are going to be ready to be used for gambling in the reasonably near future, consistent with the scale of building or alterations required before the premises are bought into use. This is why the Act allows a potential operator to apply for a provisional statement if construction of premises is not yet complete, or they need alteration, or he does not yet have a right to occupy them. See Part 11 of this guidance for more information about provisional statements. [revised paragraph which is paragraph 7.55 in the current document]

Text proposed in the consultation document

7.56 As the Court has held in a recent case, operators can apply for a premises licence in respect of premises which have still to be constructed or altered, and licensing authorities are required to determine any such applications as may be made on their merits. Such cases should be considered as a two stage process; first, local authorities must decide whether, as a matter of substance after applying the principles in section 153 of the Act, the application ought to be successful; secondly, in deciding whether or not to grant such an application a licensing authority will need to consider if appropriate conditions can be put in place to cater for the situation that the premises are not yet in the state in which they ought to be before gambling takes place. An authority is entitled to decide that it is appropriate to grant a licence subject to conditions, but it is not obliged to grant such a licence.

Respondents' comments and Commission views

One trade association suggested that this paragraph is confusing because it suggests that an application which ought to succeed could nonetheless be refused. We have revised the second section for greater clarity. One industry operator asked that the last sentence be deleted referring to s164 of the Act, and the duty to issue a licence". A trade association also suggested deletion of the last sentence suggesting that it invited uncertainty.

Final text

As the Court has held in a recent case[1], operators can apply for a premises licence in respect of premises which have still to be constructed or altered, and licensing authorities are required to determine any such applications as may be made on their merits. Such cases should be considered as a two stage process; first, local authorities must decide whether, as a matter of substance after applying the principles in section 153 of the Act, the premises ought to be permitted to be used for gambling; secondly, in deciding whether or not to grant the application a licensing authority will need to consider if appropriate conditions can be put in place to cater for the situation that the premises are not yet in the state in which they ought to be before gambling takes place. An authority is entitled to decide that it is appropriate to grant a licence subject to conditions, but it is not obliged to grant such a licence. [new paragraph]

1 *The Queen (on the application of) Betting Shp Services Ltd v Southend-on-Sea Borough Council* [2008] EWHC 105 (Admin).

Text proposed in the consultation document

7.57 For example, where the operator has still to undertake final fitting out of the premises but can give a reasonably accurate statement as to when the necessary works will be completed, it may be sufficient simply to issue the licence with a future effective date as is possible under the Regulations. The application form allows the applicant to suggest a commencement date and the notice of grant allows the licensing authority to insert a date when the premises licence comes into effect. In other cases, it may be appropriate to issue the licence subject to a condition that trading in reliance on it shall not commence until the premises have been completed in all respects in accordance with the scale plans that accompanied the licence application. See Part 9 of this guidance for more information about licence conditions. If the original plans to the premises are changed in any material respect, during the fitting out of the premises, then the applicant will be in breach of the licence. If the applicant wishes to change the proposed plans then, in order to avoid breaching the licence, it will be necessary for the applicant to either make a fresh application under section 159 or seek a variation under section 187 of the Act. If there are substantive changes to the plans then we consider it would be more appropriate for the applicant to make a fresh application under section 159 to preserve the rights of interested parties and responsible authorities to make representations in respect of the application.

Respondents' comments and Commission views

One trade association asked for a definition of 'material', we do not consider that this is necessary as it will depend on the size and scale of the premises. Another trade association stated that the final sentence of this paragraph also introduces a further condition not present in the Act. They said that it appeared to be the Commission's own opinion rather than anything driven by the Act. We disagree with this view and note that in a number of areas licensing authorities take a practical approach in respect of licensing.

One operator rightly said, there must be room for sensible negotiation over detail of the plans between application and grant. The need for any such change may depend on how detailed the plans were to start with. We agree there is merit in adding to the Guidance something about fairness requiring pre grant changes to be drawn to the attention of those who had notice of the application. The operator also makes the point that one could not, on a variation under s187, change the plans to such an extent that the premises in effect become different premises. We have changed the paragraph accordingly. Due to the length of the paragraph we have split it in two for clarity.

Final text

7.57 For example, where the operator has still to undertake final fitting out of the premises but can give a reasonably accurate statement as to when the necessary works will be completed, it may be sufficient simply to issue the licence with a future effective date as is possible under the Regulations[2]. The application form allows the applicant to suggest a commencement date and the notice of grant allows the licensing authority to insert a date when the premises licence comes into effect. In other cases, it may be appropriate to issue the licence subject to a condition that trading in reliance on it shall not commence until the premises have been completed in all respects in accordance with the scale plans that accompanied the licence application. See Part 9 of this guidance for more information about licence conditions. [new paragraph]

[2] SI 2007/459 Premises Licensing and Provisional Statements Regulations

7.58 If the plans as submitted at the time of the application for a premises licence are changed in any material respect, during the fitting out of the premises after the grant of the licence, then the applicant will be in breach of the licence. If the applicant wishes to change the proposed plans after grant then, in order to avoid breaching the licence, it will be necessary for the applicant to either make a fresh application under section 159 or seek an amendment to a detail of the licence under section 187 of the Act. If there are substantive changes to the plans then this may render the premises different premises to those for which the licence was granted. In such a case variation of the licence under section 187 is not possible. But in any event, and whilst this is a matter of judgement for the licensing authority, we consider it would be more appropriate in the case of any material post grant change, for the applicant to make a fresh application under section 159 to preserve the rights of interested parties and responsible authorities to make representations in respect of the application. [new paragraph]

Text proposed in the consultation document

7.58 The local authority will need to be satisfied in any individual case that the completed works comply with the original, or changed, plan attached to the premises licence. Depending upon circumstances, we consider that this could be achieved either through physical inspection of the premises or written confirmation from the applicant or surveyor that the condition has been satisfied.

Respondents' comments and Commission views

No comments were received on this section so no changes have been made

Final text

7.59 The local authority will need to be satisfied in any individual case that the completed works comply with the original, or changed, plan attached to the premises licence. Depending upon circumstances, we consider that this could be achieved either through physical inspection of the premises or written confirmation from the applicant or surveyor that the condition has been satisfied. [new paragraph]

Text proposed in the consultation document

7.59 Requiring the building to be complete before trading commences would ensure that the authority could, if considered necessary, inspect it fully, as could other responsible authorities with inspection rights under part 15 of the Act. Inspection will allow authorities to check that gambling facilities comply with all necessary legal requirements. For example, category C and D machines in a licensed family entertainment centre must be situated so that people under 18 do not have access to the category C machines. The physical location of the machines will be an important part of this, and inspection will allow the authority to check that the layout complies with the operator's proposals and the legal requirements.

7.60 If faced with an application in respect of uncompleted premises which it appears are not going to be ready to be used for gaming for a considerable period of time, a licensing authority ought to consider whether a provisional statement application would be more appropriate. For example, that would be the case if there was significant potential for circumstances to change before the premises open for business. In such cases, the provisional statement route would ensure that the limited rights of responsible authorities and interested parties to make representations about matters arising from such changes of circumstance are protected. Licensing authorities may choose to discuss with individual applicants which route was appropriate, to avoid them paying a fee for, say, an application that the authority did not think was grantable, when it seems likely at an early stage that a provisional statement might be.

Respondents' comments and Commission views

One trade association and one operator stated that the Guidance cannot fetter applicants' right to take whichever course they wish. While this is correct, it follows from the judicial review judgment that there is no absolute obligation on licensing authorities to grant licences where premises are incomplete and, for example, they see difficulties in framing appropriate conditions. Therefore we have made an alteration to the paragraph to reflect this.

Final text

7.60 Requiring the building to be complete before trading commences would ensure that the authority could, if considered necessary, inspect it fully, as could other responsible authorities with inspection rights under part 15 of the Act. Inspection will allow authorities to check that gambling facilities comply with all necessary legal requirements. For example, category C and D machines in a licensed family entertainment centre must be situated so that people under 18 do not have access to the category C machines. The physical location of higher stake gaming machines in premises to which children have access will be an important part of this, and inspection will allow the authority to check that the layout complies with the operator's proposals and the legal requirements. [new paragraph]

7.61 If faced with an application in respect of uncompleted premises which it appears are not going to be ready to be used for gaming for a considerable period of time, a licensing authority ought to consider whether, applying the two stage approach advocated in paragraph 7.56 above, it should grant a licence or whether the circumstances are more appropriate to a provisional statement application. For example, the latter would be the case if there was significant potential for circumstances to change before the premises open for business. In such cases, the provisional statement route would ensure that the limited rights of responsible authorities and interested parties to make representations about matters arising from such changes of circumstance are protected. Licensing authorities may choose to discuss with individual applicants which route was appropriate, to avoid them paying a fee for, say, an application that the authority did not think was grantable, when it seems likely at an early stage that a provisional statement might be. [new paragraph]

Text proposed in the consultation document

7.61 When dealing with a premises licence application for finished buildings, the licensing authority should not take into account whether those buildings have or comply with the necessary planning or buildings consents. Those matters should be dealt with under relevant planning control and building regulation powers, and must not form part of the consideration for the premises licence. Section 210 of the 2005 Act prevents licensing authorities taking into account the likelihood of the proposal by the applicant obtaining planning or building consent when considering a premises licence application. Equally, the grant of a gambling premises licence does not prejudice or prevent any action that may be appropriate under the law relating to planning or building.

Respondents' comments and Commission views

One trade association stated that it would be helpful to include other matters such as health and safety and fire. We agree with this and have made the changes.

Final Text

7.62 When dealing with a premises licence application for finished buildings, the licensing authority should not take into account whether those buildings have or comply with the necessary planning or buildings consents. Nor should fire or health and safety risks be taken into account. Those matters should be dealt with under relevant planning control, building and other regulations, and must not form part of the consideration for the premises licence. Section 210 of the Act prevents licensing authorities taking into account the likelihood of the proposal by the applicant obtaining planning or building consent when considering a premises licence application. Equally, the grant of a gambling premises licence does not prejudice or prevent any action that may be appropriate under the law relating to planning or building. [revised paragraph which is paragraph 7.58 in the current document]

[The rest of the document remains unchanged]

8 BRINGING THE CHANGES INTO EFFECT

8.1 The Guidance has been updated to reflect the changes outlined in this paper. The Guidance comes into effect immediately and the revised document is available on the Commission's website.

Gambling Commission August 2008

ANNEX A: NON- CONFIDENTIAL RESPONDENTS TO THE CONSULTATION

Association of British Bookmakers (ABB)	Trade Association
Association of Chief Police Officers in Scotland (ACPOS)	Regulatory Authority
Bingo Association	Trade Association
British Amusement and Catering Trades Association (BACTA)	Trade Association
Local Authority Co-ordinators of Regulatory Services (LACORS)	Regulatory Authority
The Noble Organisation	Industry operator
The Rank Group	Industry operator
South Tyneside District Council	Local government

ADVICE TO LICENSING AUTHORITIES ON CLUB GAMING PERMITS AND CLUB MACHINE PERMITS: GAMBLING ACT 2005

Second edition

April 2011

INTRODUCTION

6.2657 The Gambling Act 2005 (the Act) introduced a range of permits for gambling which are granted by licensing authorities (LAs). Permits provide a means to offer gambling where the stakes and prizes are low or where the gambling is not the main function of the premises. The permits regulate gambling and the use of gaming machines in specific premises.

The purpose of this advice note is to set out a number of matters that LAs should consider before a permit is issued and once the permission has been granted. This note should be read in conjunction with:

- Parts 25 and 29 of the Gambling Commission's (the Commission's) *Guidance to Licensing Authorities*
- the Commission's code of practice on equal chance gaming in clubs and premises with an alcohol licence
- the Commission's gaming machine permits code of practice and Schedule 12 to the Act, which contains the provisions relating to club gaming permits and club machine permits.

This advice note does not constitute guidance for the purposes of section 25 of the Act.

1 DEFINING CLUBS, MINERS' WELFARE INSTITUTES AND ALCOHOL-LICENSED PREMISES

1.1 The Act defines alcohol-licensed premises and two types of club for the purposes of gaming, namely members' clubs (including miners' welfare institutes) and commercial clubs. This is an important distinction in respect of the gaming that may take place. In particular, when determining whether a club is able to apply for and be issued with a permit, the LA must consider whether the club is a genuine members' club or a commercial club within their meaning in the Act.

MEMBERS' CLUB

1.2 A members' club is a club that is not established as a commercial enterprise, and is conducted for the benefit of its members. Examples include working men's clubs, branches of the Royal British Legion and clubs with political affiliations. Members' clubs may apply to their local LA for club gaming permits and club machine permits.

1.3 The Act prescribes that members' clubs must have at least 25 members and be established and conducted 'wholly or mainly' for purposes other than gaming, unless the gaming is restricted to bridge and whist. Members' clubs must be permanent in nature, but there is no need for a club to provide alcohol.

1.4 Before granting a club gaming permit which, for example, will permit the playing of poker with unlimited stakes and prizes, LAs must satisfy themselves that the club is not wholly or mainly devoted to gaming (including poker). Even if a club offers other sport and activities, if the majority of the club's activities is gaming judged by income, time spent on activities or some combination of these measures, then the club's purpose will not be 'wholly or mainly' for purposes other than gaming. Those clubs that hold club gaming permits and conduct themselves in such a way that gaming is the main activity, are in breach of the Act and may render themselves liable to prosecution by the LA.

1.5 Clubs that offer poker as the main activity or on a commercial basis must have a casino operating licence and premises licence.

MINERS' WELFARE INSTITUTE

1.6 Miners' welfare institutes are associations established for recreational or social purposes. They are managed by a group of individuals made up of at least two thirds of miners' representatives or use premises regulated by a charitable trust which has received funds from one of a number of mining organisations.

1.7 Miners' welfare institutes may apply for club gaming permits and club machine permits.

COMMERCIAL CLUB

1.8 A commercial club is a club established for commercial gain (whether or not they are making a commercial gain). Examples include snooker clubs, clubs established as private companies and clubs established for personal profit. There are established tests to determine a club's status. In case of doubt, legal advice should be sought. Commercial clubs may only apply for club machine permits.

1.9 The Act prescribes that commercial clubs must have at least 25 members and be established and conducted 'wholly or mainly' for purposes other than gaming, unless the gaming is restricted to bridge and whist. Commercial clubs must be permanent in nature, but there is no need for a club to have an alcohol licence.

1.10 Even if a commercial club offers other activities, if the majority of the club's activities is gaming (including poker) judged by income, time spent on activities or some combination thereof, then the club's purpose will not be 'wholly or mainly' for purposes other than gaming.

1.11 Clubs that offer poker as the main activity or on a commercial basis must have a casino operating licence and premises licence.

ALCOHOL-LICENSED PREMISES

1.12 Premises which are covered by an on-premises alcohol licence authorising the supply of alcohol for consumption on licensed premises under Part 3 of the Licensing Act 2003 or, in Scotland, the Licensing (Scotland) Act 2005 can offer certain types of gaming. The Act stipulates that the premises must contain a bar at which alcohol is sold and, in addition, that there is no condition on the alcohol premises licence which requires that alcohol can only be served with food. This means that the premises must be dedicated bar premises as opposed to restaurant type premises. These premises are referred to as alcohol-licensed premises in this document.

1.13 Gaming and the use of gaming machines is only permitted on these premises during the hours that the premises licence allows the sale of alcohol. Premises which are not clubs, but sell alcohol, are not able to apply for club gaming or club machine permits.

2 PERMITTED AND EXEMPT GAMING IN CLUBS, MINERS' WELFARE INSTITUTES AND ALCOHOL-LICENSED PREMISES

2.1 The Act creates two types of equal chance gaming permissible in clubs, miners' welfare institutes and alcohol-licensed premises: 'permitted gaming' and 'exempt gaming'.

PERMITTED GAMING

2.2 Permitted gaming is equal chance gaming and two bankers' games, pontoon and chemin de fer, permissible through the grant of a club gaming permit. A club gaming permit can only be granted to a members' club or miners' welfare institute. A club gaming permit cannot be granted to a commercial club or other alcohol-licensed premises.

2.3 Other than in the case of clubs established to provide the prescribed games of bridge and whist, clubs seeking club gaming permits must be established 'wholly or mainly' for purposes other than gaming. Where a club gaming permit is granted there are no limits on the stakes and prizes associated with permitted gaming.

EXEMPT GAMING

2.4 Exempt gaming is equal chance gaming generally permissible in any members' club, miners' welfare institute, commercial club or alcohol-licensed premises. Such gaming must be ancillary to the purposes of the premises. This exemption is automatically available to all such premises, but is subject to statutory stakes and prize limits determined by the Secretary of State.

2.5 The Secretary of State has set both daily and weekly prize limits for exempt gaming in alcohol-licensed premises[1]. Different, higher stakes and prizes are allowed for exempt gaming in clubs[2]. These limits are set out in the attached appendix.

2.6 Exempt gaming must be supervised by a nominated gaming supervisor and comply with the Commission's code of practice on equal chance gaming in clubs and premises with an alcohol licence, issued under section 24 of the Act.

3 CONDITIONS ON CLUB GAMING PERMITS

3.1 Club gaming permits are only available to members' clubs and miners' welfare institutes. The Act sets out conditions that a club must meet to get a club gaming permit. They are:

(a) *in respect of equal chance gaming:*
- the club or institute must not deduct or levy money from sums staked or won
- the participation fee must not exceed the amount prescribed in regulations
- the games must take place on the premises and must not be linked with a game on another set of premises. Games are considered to be linked if:
  - the result of one game is, or may be, wholly or partly determined by reference to the result of the other games
  - the amount of winnings is wholly or partly determined by the participation of more than one set of players
  - the game is split by sites so that part of one game is played on one site and another part is played elsewhere
- each person who participates must be:
  - a member of the club or institute who applied for membership, was nominated for membership, or became a member, at least 48 hours before he participates, or
  - a guest of a member of the club or institute[3]
- the holder complies with the Commission's code of practice on equal chance gaming in clubs and premises with an alcohol licence.

(b) *in respect of other games of chance:*
- the games are prescribed in regulations - currently only pontoon and chemin de fer are prescribed
- no participation fee is charged otherwise than in accordance with the regulations
- no amount is deducted or levied from sums staked or won otherwise than in accordance with the regulations
- the public, children and young persons must be excluded from any area of the premises where the gaming is taking place
- each person who participates must be:
  - a member of the club or institute who applied for membership, was nominated for membership, or became a member, at least 48 hours before he participates, or
  - a guest of a member of the club or institute.[4]

(c) *in respect of gaming machines:*
- that no child or young person uses a category B or C machine on the premises
- that the holder complies with any relevant provision of a code of practice about the location and operation of gaming machines.

---

1 The Gambling Act 2005 (Exempt Gaming in Alcohol-Licensed Premises) Regulations 2007 (SI 2007/1940).

2 The Gambling Act 2005 (Exempt Gaming in Clubs) Regulations 2007 (SI 2007/1944).

3 Existing case law may assist in determining whether a person is a "bona fide guest" of a member. The case of *Mackley v Ladup Ltd* (1974) 139 JP Jo 121 sets out guidelines in determining whether a guest is legitimate or not. In particular, if the court finds that (i) the person invited as a guest had no previous acquaintance with the member, and (ii) the sole reason for the invitation was to allow the invitee to take advantage of the gaming facilities,

then the person invited is unlikely to be considered to be a genuine guest of a member.

[4] See footnote 3.

3.2 Applicants for club gaming permits must also agree to abide by the Commission's code of practice on equal chance gaming in clubs and premises with an alcohol licence.

4 FACTORS TO CONSIDER WHEN GRANTING A CLUB GAMING PERMIT

4.1 The LA has to satisfy itself that the club meets the requirements of the Act to obtain a club gaming permit. It is suggested that applicants for permits should be asked to supply sufficient information and documents to enable the LA to take account of the matters discussed in paragraphs 4.2 to 4.4, at the time they submit their applications to the LA.

4.2 In determining whether a club is a genuine members' club, the LA should take account of a number of matters, such as:

- Is the primary purpose of the club's activities something other than the provision of gaming to its members? This is an indicator that it's a genuine members' club.
- Are the profits retained in the club for the benefit of the members? This is the key difference between a members' club and a commercial club.
- Are there 25 or more members? This is the amount a club has to have to qualify.
- Are there genuine domestic addresses on the register of members? Are domestic addresses listed for every member? Are members local to the club? These are all indicators that the member lists are bona fide and are made up of genuine members.
- Do members participate in the activities of the club via the internet? It is less likely to be a genuine members' club if this is the case.
- Do guest arrangements link a member to every guest? Is there evidence of a signing- in register for guests? Guests must be genuine guests of members and not members of the general public.[5]
- Is the 48 hour rule between applying for membership and participating in any gaming properly applied? This is an indication that the club has a proper membership scheme.
- Are there annual accounts for more than one year? This would indicate that the club is permanent in nature, rather than temporary.
- How is the club advertised and listed in directories, including on the internet? If the club is categorised under "gaming" or "poker", it is less likely to be genuine members' club.
- Are children permitted into the club? The more access they have to areas of the premises, the less likely it is that the club is primarily for gambling activities.
- Is there a list of committee members and evidence of their election by the members of the club? Can the club provide minutes of committee and other meetings? These are further evidence that the club is a properly constituted members' club.
- Does the club have a constitution and can it provide evidence that the constitution was approved by the members of the club? This provides further evidence that it is a properly constituted members' club.

4.3 The constitution of the club could also indicate whether it is a legitimate members' club. Amongst the things to consider are the following:

- Who makes commercial decisions on behalf of the club and what are the governance arrangements? Clubs are normally run by a committee made up of members of the club, rather than individuals or managers, who make decisions on behalf of the members. There will normally be a system (consultation, voting, paper ballots, annual general meetings, special meetings, etc) which allows members to be involved in major decisions concerning the management and running of the club. Such arrangements would be spelt out in the constitution.

- Are the aims of the club set out in the constitution? A lack of aims or aims which involve gaming could indicate that it is not a genuine members' club.
- Are there shareholders or members? Shareholders would indicate a business enterprise linked to a commercial club.
- Is the members' club permanently established? Clubs can't be temporary and must be permanent in nature
- Can people join with annual or quarterly membership? This would indicate that the club is permanent in nature.
- Are there long term membership benefits? This would also indicate that the club is permanent in nature and that it is a genuine members' club. The benefits of membership would normally be set out in the rules of membership.

---

5 See footnote 3.

4.4 Other than bridge and whist clubs, which are separately catered for in regulations, a club cannot be established wholly or mainly for purposes of gaming. In applying for a club gaming permit, a club must therefore provide substantial evidence of activities other than gaming. Useful questions which a LA should consider include:

- How many nights is poker made available? If poker is available for all or most nights with little other activity, then it is likely that the club is established wholly or mainly for gaming.
- Is the poker advertised? If poker is advertised with little or no reference to the other activities of the club, then it is likely that gaming is the main activity of the club and that the poker is run commercially.
- What are the stakes and prizes offered? The stakes and prizes limits must be complied with. Unlimited stakes and prizes are only available to genuine members' clubs once a club gaming permit has been granted. If high stakes and prizes are offered, this is also likely to indicate that gaming is one of the main activities of the club.
- Is there evidence of leagues with weekly/monthly/annual winners? This could indicate that the club's main activity is gaming.
- Is there evidence of non-playing members? If members play poker exclusively, this is an indication that the main or only activity of the club is poker.
- Are there teaching sessions to promote poker? This could be evidence that the club's main activity is poker.
- Is there tie-in with other clubs offering poker through tournaments or leagues? This is also an indication that poker is possibly one of the main activities of the club.
- Is there sponsorship by poker organisations, for example on-line poker providers? Similarly, this could indicate that poker is one of the main activities of the club.
- Are participation fees within limits? The LA could consider club records and adverts for gaming, etc. Fees that exceed the limits could indicate that the gaming is run commercially.

4.5 The Commission advises that a visit to the premises before granting of the permit may assist the licensing officer to understand how the club will operate.

5 CONDITIONS ON EXEMPT GAMING AND GAMING UNDER A CLUB MACHINE PERMIT

5.1 The Act allows all clubs and miners' welfare institutes to offer machine gaming under a club machine permit. Section 273 of the Act sets out the conditions that will apply to the club machine permit, including that, in respect of gaming machines, no child or young person uses a category B or C machine on the premises and that the holder complies with the Commission's code of practice about the location and operation of gaming machines. Clubs do not have to have permanent premises or to provide alcohol.

5.2 The Act also permits clubs and premises with an alcohol licence to offer "exempt gaming" under section 279 of the Act. This is non-machine gaming and is subject to the following conditions:

- the gaming must comply with the regulations set by Secretary of State that limit the stakes and prizes
- there must not be a levy on the sums staked or won
- there must be no entry or participation fees
- the gaming offered must not be linked to gaming in other premises
- the gaming complies with the Commission's code of practice on equal chance gaming in clubs and premises with an alcohol licence
- no person under 18 may participate in the gaming.

5.3 The regulations set out the stakes and prizes limits that apply to exempt gaming. These are summarised in the attached appendix. A similar table is attached to the code of practice on equal chance gaming in clubs and premises with an alcohol licence, and the *Guidance to Licensing Authorities*.

6 FACTORS TO CONSIDER FOR EXEMPT GAMING AND GAMING UNDER A CLUB MACHINE PERMIT

6.1 The LA should satisfy itself that the poker on offer meets the conditions set out in the Act and relevant regulations. To do this the LA may wish to ask questions of the applicant or ensure that exempt gaming complies with these conditions. The conditions are:

- There must be no rake from the pot (that is, the organiser cannot take any money from the prize fund, or deduct money from the stakes or winnings). LAs should examine the records for gaming or, if possible, observe or get statements about the pot.
- There must be no side bets. This is probably only going to be possible to verify through observation.
- Participation fees are within the limits prescribed in the regulations (club gaming only). Is there evidence of excess participation fees in club records, adverts for gaming in or outside of the club or from complaints? Participation fees must not be disguised as charges for dealers, mandatory tipping of dealers, table charges or hire charges. Again, observation of the gaming may be necessary.
- Prizes are within the limits prescribed in the regulations. Is there evidence that they are excessive from records at the club or alcohol-licensed premises, in adverts for gaming, etc? Note that daily and weekly limits must be monitored by the operator and that "money or money's worth" (for example, goods) counts towards the prize limits.
- Where the games are tournaments or leagues, the LA may find it useful to consult the Commission's general guidance on poker which sets out how the law applies to such games. This should help the LA to determine whether the gaming is within the law from evidence such as records in the club or alcohol-licensed premises and adverts for gaming.

7 APPEALS ON DECISIONS BY THE LA

7.1 The authority may only refuse an application on one or more of the following grounds:

- (i) for a club gaming permit: the applicant is not a members' club or miners' welfare institute
- (ii) for a club machine permit: the applicant is not a members' club, miners' institute or commercial club
- the premises are used wholly or mainly by children or young persons
- an offence or a breach of a condition of a permit has been committed by an applicant
- a permit held by an applicant has been cancelled during the last ten years

- an objection has been made by the Commission or local chief officer of police.

7.2 The authority may only cancel a permit on one of the following grounds:

- the premises are used wholly or mainly by children or young persons
- an offence or breach of a condition of the permit has been committed in the course of gaming activities.

7.3 Therefore, in considering an appeal the court will determine whether any of these statutory grounds apply. In addition, the court will take into account the following factors:

- any objections made by the Commission or local police chief
- the authority's duty to have regard to both the Commission guidance and the licensing objectives, and to what extent these duties were discharged.

7.4 On an appeal, the magistrates' court or sheriff may take the following action: dismiss the appeal, substitute any decision that the LA could have made, restore a permit, or remit it back to the LA to decide in accordance with a determination of the court; and may make an order for costs. If the decision is remitted to the LA, the same rights of appeal will apply as for the original application.

8 FAST TRACK PROCEDURE FOR PERMITS

8.1 There is a fast track procedure for members' clubs in England and Wales that hold a club premises certificate under section 72 of the Licensing Act 2003 (the Licensing Act). Commercial clubs cannot hold club premises certificates under the Licensing Act and so cannot use the fast track procedure. The fast track procedure also does not apply in Scotland.

8.2 Where the club holds a club premises certificate, there is no opportunity for objections to be made by the Commission or the police, and the grounds on which a LA can refuse a permit are reduced.

8.3 There are three grounds for refusal of a permit by the LA in these circumstances. They are, where:

- the club is established or conducted solely or primarily for gaming (other than bridge or whist)
- the club is established or conducted solely or mainly for bridge or whist, and also provides gaming of another kind
- a club gaming permit or club machine permit issued to the club has been cancelled in the preceding ten years.

9 FACTORS TO CONSIDER WHEN MONITORING CLUB GAMING PERMITS

9.1 Once the LA has issued a club gaming permit, it is recommended that various aspects need to be considered by LAs in monitoring the club gaming permit. In addition to monitoring whether the club continues to meet the requirements of the Act for a club gaming permit (that is, whether it remains a genuine members' club) and whether the gaming meets the conditions set out in the Act and the relevant regulations, LAs may also wish to consider the issues described in the paragraphs that follow.

9.2 Where clubs have computers available for use by members, LAs should be aware that these may be so-called dual use computers which, among other things, allow club members to access gambling websites via the internet. In certain circumstances, these computers may be taken to be gaming machines. Generally, a computer is not a gaming machine merely because there is a possibility of accessing a gambling website via the internet. However, a computer will be taken to be a gaming machine if it is knowingly adapted or presented to facilitate or draw attention to the possibility of it being used for gambling.

9.3 It is not possible to provide a definitive list of examples of what constitutes a computer that is knowingly adapted or presented to facilitate or draw attention to the possibility of it being used for gambling. Each case will need to be looked at individually and ultimately the decision regarding whether a machine is a gaming machine is one for the courts to make.

9.4 The precise circumstances in which the facilities are offered – including the environment in which they are offered and the relationship with other gambling facilities provided – will need to be taken into account when assessing the status of those facilities. The Commission has provided the following indicators that may help in making decisions about whether a computer is knowingly adapted or presented to facilitate or draw attention to the possibility of it being used for gambling. This list is not exhaustive, and the presence or absence of any single factor is not necessarily conclusive:

- icons for gambling websites displayed on the desktop screen
- links to gambling websites available via the start menu
- screensavers, desktop wallpapers referring to gambling websites
- internet browsing history or favourites menu containing gambling websites
- promotional material (posters, flyers) indicating the use of computers for gambling
- gambling software downloaded onto a computer
- staff informing customers of the existence of the computer for access to gambling websites
- emails or other promotional material sent to customers/individuals referring to the availability of computers on premises for gambling purposes.

9.5 LAs should note that permission to advertise gambling in Great Britain is restricted to operators licensed by the Commission, operators from the European Economic Area, Gibraltar and the white-listed jurisdictions (Alderney, Antigua and Barbuda, Isle of Man and Tasmania).

9.6 Club premises, computer terminals in the club or the club website may contain advertising of 'foreign gambling', or clubs may offer seats at overseas poker tournaments as prizes in poker tournaments run on the club premises. In the Commission's view, this amounts to advertising of non-UK gambling, as defined by section 327 of the Act. Unless the overseas tournament is based in the European Economic Area, Gibraltar or the white-listed jurisdictions, this is likely to amount to the advertising of 'foreign gambling', which is an offence under section 331 of the Act.

9.7 Any of the factors mentioned in the preceding paragraphs in this section may give rise to the need to review the club gaming permit or take appropriate enforcement action.

9.8 The Commission provides advice and guidance to LAs on permits and related matters and, on a case-by-case basis, will undertake targeted collaborations with LAs in order to establish principle and precedent, and a clear understanding of the legal requirements.

9.9 An agency that may also be able to assist LA enquiries is HM Revenue & Customs (HMRC). If a club is trading under the auspices of a club gaming permit (as a members' club) but is in fact a commercial club with, for example, their main activity being poker, they would be liable for gaming duty. LAs should bear in mind that clubs of this nature have premises to maintain, as well as staff and other costs, so the sums involved may be significant. There may also be other aspects of the financing of such clubs that would cause HMRC to become involved.

10 POWERS IN RESPECT OF CLUB PREMISES

10.1 Section 312 of the Act prescribes that:

- a constable or enforcement officer can enter club or miners' welfare institute premises, or premises which they reasonably believe to be used by a club or institute, to determine whether:
  - gaming is taking place on the premises or is about to take place on the premises
  - any gaming that is taking place or is about to take place on the premises meets the requirements for exempt gaming in section 269 of the Act, a club gaming permit or a club machine permit

- an authorised local authority officer can enter premises in respect of which an application for a club gaming permit or club machine permit has been made for a purpose connected with the consideration of the application.

10.2 An enforcement officer is an employee of the Commission designated as an enforcement officer for the purposes of the Act, or a person other than an employee appointed as an enforcement officer for the same purpose. An authorised local authority officer is an officer of a LA designated as an authorised person for the purposes of section 304 of the Act, where the premises are wholly or partly situated in the LA's area.

10.3 As the Act indicates that local licensing officers are not authorised to enter club premises under the Act once the club permit has been issued, this has generally been assumed to mean that the LAs lack all the necessary powers and the Commission is, therefore, the default organisation for enforcement action. However, the necessary powers are available to the police and the Commission suggests that LAs, working in partnership with local police forces, have the ability to enforce compliance by clubs where needed.

10.4 LAs may also want to consider whether their officers have powers under other relevant Acts, such as the Licensing Act or Local Government Act. In addition, sections 87, 88 and 89 of the Licensing Act give LAs the ability to review club premises certificates, including suspending and withdrawing permits, and section 90 allows LAs to withdraw certificates where it appears to the LA that the club does not satisfy the conditions for being a qualifying club.

11 PRIVATE GAMING

11.1 Private gaming can only occur in a place to which the public does not have access. While primarily aimed at games occurring in private dwellings, this could potentially also apply where a club hires a room in a pub or hotel for a private function where poker is played.

11.2 However, there must be a meaningful selection process for participation in the gaming to enable a distinction to be made between members of the general public and those permitted to enter the gaming area (that is, members of the club). If there is no real selection process, and anyone who wishes to enter the area or join the club can do so simply by asking or registering to join, the courts are likely to consider that the general public have access. If this is the case, the gaming will not be private and is likely to be illegal.

11.3 LAs are advised that no money can be deducted from any stakes or winnings, and no fee can be charged to take part in the private gaming, regardless of how it is described.

12 CASE STUDIES

12.1 LAs may find the following case studies helpful when considering applications by clubs for club gaming or club machine permits, investigating the misuse of a permit and considering the review thereof, or considering the unlawful provision of gaming in club premises.

CASE STUDY 1: REFUSAL OF A CLUB GAMING PERMIT

The club was sited within commercial premises that operated as a snooker club. The commercial premises held a premises licence under the Licensing Act 2003. When considering an application for a club gaming permit by the club, the LA found that the club:

- did not meet the definition of members' club in the Act as it was established for the purpose of gaming
- did not satisfactorily prove that it was established and conducted for the benefit of its members

- offered activities that could already be accessed through the existing commercial premises on a much larger scale and with no membership fee payable
- was trying to circumvent the requirements of the Licensing Act 2003 by setting up a club within a club
- did not have a satisfactory club constitution with regard to the nomination of new members and election of the committee
- provided financial documentation that was inadequate and showed that the applicant's main activity was gaming (in particular, poker).

On the basis of these findings, the LA refused the club gaming permit because the club had failed to demonstrate that it:

- met the definition of a members' club by being established and conducted for purposes other than the provision of facilities for gaming
- was established and conducted for the benefit of its members (and was not otherwise established or conducted as a commercial enterprise).

The LA subsequently offered the applicant an appeal under paragraph 25(1) of Schedule 12 to the Act.

CASE STUDY 2: REFUSAL OF A CLUB GAMING PERMIT

The Commission received a copy of an application for a club gaming permit and decided to lodge objections to the application on the basis that the club is not a members' club within its meaning in the Act. The LA subsequently held a hearing and heard oral evidence from the applicant. Guided by the Act, the Commission's *Guidance to Licensing Authorities*, the LA's statement of principles for the Act, and the evidence received and heard, the LA decided that the applicant was not entitled to a club gaming permit on the following basis:

- the LA was not satisfied that the club was a members' club as defined under section 266 of the Act
- the rules of membership produced by the applicant did not demonstrate that the club had been constituted as a genuine members' club, specifically that there was no provision for members to participate in the management and running of the club, and that it does not set out the objectives or benefits of membership.

CASE STUDY 3: REVIEW OF A CLUB GAMING PERMIT

The club had been granted a club gaming permit, but intelligence activity had later suggested that the club was in breach of several conditions of its permit. After a joint visit to the club by the LA and the police, the LA found that the club:

- was not established and conducted for the benefit of its members
- appeared to be established and conducted almost solely for the purpose of playing poker.

A letter was sent to the club instructing it to comply with the conditions of the club gaming permit within a set time period. The club failed to comply with the instruction and the LA subsequently withdrew the club gaming permit.

CASE STUDY 4: COOPERATION AND SHARED RESOURCES

This case concerned a poker organiser operating in several local authority areas. In this instance, the relevant LAs set up a working group to deal with the case. Following discussions by the working group, a letter was drafted and sent to all the relevant alcohol premises licensees in each LA area setting out the licensees' personal liability for illegal activities conducted on their premises, making direct reference to poker.

The matter and the action taken were then discussed at the regional licensing and enforcement officers meetings so that the scope of this approach was widened to other LAs facing the same issues. The Commission was kept informed of developments in the case.

APPENDIX: SUMMARY OF GAMING ENTITLEMENTS FORCLUBS AND ALCOHOL-LICENSED PREMISES

	Members' club, commercial club or MW institute without a club gaming permit or club machine permit	**Members' club or commercial club with club machine permit**	**Members' club or MW institute with club gaming permit**	**Bridge or whist club**	**Alcohol-licensed premises**
Equal chance gaming	Yes	Yes	Yes	Bridge and/or whist only	Yes
Limits on stakes	Poker £1000 per week £250 per day £10 per person per game Other gaming No limit	Poker £1000 per week £250 per day £10 per person per game Other gaming No limit	No limit	No limit	Poker £100 per premises per day £5 per person per game Other gaming £5 per person per game Cribbage . . . dominoes No limit
Limits on prizes	Poker £250 per game Other gaming No limit	Poker £250 per game Other gaming No limit	No limit	No limit	Poker £100 per game Other gaming No limit
Maximum participation fees (per person per day)	Bridge and/or whist [6] £18 Other gaming £1	Bridge and/or whist £18 Other gaming £3 (commercial club) £1 (members' club)	Bridge and/or whist [6] £20 Other gaming £3	£18 (without club gaming permit) £20 (with club gaming permit)	None permitted
Bankers or unequal chance gaming	None permitted	None permitted	Pontoon Chemin de fer	None permitted	None permitted

	Members' club, commercial club or MW institute without a club gaming permit or club machine permit	Members' club or commercial club with club machine permit	Members' club or MW institute with club gaming permit	Bridge or whist club	Alcohol-licensed premises
Limits on bingo	Maximum of £2,000 per week in stakes/prizes. If more then will need an operating licence.	Maximum of £2,000 per week in stakes/prizes. If more then will need an operating licence.	Maximum of £2,000 per week in stakes/prizes. If more then will need an operating licence.	No bingo permitted	Maximum of £2,000 per week in stakes/prizes. If more then will need an operating licence.

[6] On a day when no other facilities for gaming are provided

Gambling Commission April 2011

DEFINITION OF PREMISES
25 April 2008
ADV 08/08

6.2658 The Gambling Commission (the Commission) intends to strengthen the guidance it issues to local authorities under section 25 of the Gambling Act 2005 (the Act) relating to the definition of premises. This will include changes to part seven of the 'Guidance to Licensing Authorities (2nd edition June 2007)' document. This has been prompted by increasing numbers of premises licence applications being made to licensing authorities which appear to be in conflict with the intentions of Parliament.

THE INTENTION OF PARLIAMENT REGARDING THE DEFINITION OF PREMISES

Parliament's intention relating to the number of higher category gaming machines available for use in gambling premises is set out on the face of the Act. In particular, section 172 the Act places restrictions on the number and categories of gaming machines that can be made available in casinos, bingo premises, betting premises and adult gaming centres.

Parliament's intention relating to access between different types of gambling premises is set down in regulations, through the Gambling Act 2005 (Mandatory and Default Conditions) (England and Wales) Regulations 2007 (SI 2007/1409) and the Gambling Act 2005 (Mandatory and Default Conditions) (Scotland) Regulations 2007 (SSI 2007/266). The Government's intention behind restricting access between certain gambling premises in this way is set down in the Department for Culture, Media and Sports' document 'Explanatory Memorandum to the Gambling Act 2005 (Mandatory and Default Conditions) (England and Wales) Regulations 2007'. Paragraph 7.6 of this document reads:

"The Act provides that . . . a single premises may not have more than one premises licence authorising a type of gambling activity. There were concerns that some unscrupulous operators might seek to circumvent this by artificially subdividing their premises and securing separate premises licences for its composite parts, which would undermine the different categories of premises licence created by the Act . . . we wanted to ensure that operators do not circumvent the rules governing the maximum number of gaming machines of Category B and above permitted in different premises. And finally, we were determined to ensure that all gambling premises have publicly accessible entrances, and are not developed in the backrooms of other commercial premises. The department decided to address these concerns by proposing conditions which restricted the access between different types of gambling premises."

The full text of the Explanatory Memorandum can be found here. It refers only to the regulations for England and Wales, however the Memorandum also reflects the policy intentions behind the equivalent Scottish regulations.

STRENGTHENING THE GUIDANCE

Currently, the Commission's guidance at paragraphs 7.11 and 7.12 of the 'Guidance to Licensing Authorities (June 2007)' document describes what may be considered as a premises. Paragraph 7.1 states that:

" . . . there is no reason why a single building could not be subject to more than one premises licence, provided they are for different parts of the building, and the different parts of the building can reasonably be regarded as being different premises."

However, this paragraph goes on to describe that this approach has been taken in order to allow large, multiple unit premises to obtain premises licences, as long as appropriate safeguards are in place. Any sub-division of an existing premises must of course comply with the mandatory conditions relating to access between premises. Paragraph 7.12 then suggests that whether different parts of a building can properly be regarded as being separate premises will depend on the circumstances such as its location and the suitability of the separation. The guidance also states that the Commission does not consider that areas of a building that are artificially or temporarily separated can properly be regarded as different premises.

We intend to add a further section to this part of the 'Guidance to Licensing Authorities (June 2007)' document to further emphasise Parliament's intentions of the Act regarding the definition of premises, and to make clear that premises existing under the Act must be genuinely separate with the required access and supervision requirements in place.

The new section will also include guidance on providing the principal gambling activity in all premises licensed under the Act. This is to assist licensing authorities considering applications for multiple premises licences on a single site, where they need to be satisfied that the primary purpose of the premises licence is being fulfilled, ie betting facilities are provided in a betting shop, players can fully participate in bingo at all bingo premises, and so on.

This updated guidance will be based around our position as set out in our open letter to trade associations: first letter, and our follow-up letter which confirms that there needs to be an acceptable balance between the provision of the principal gambling activity and the provision of gaming machines: second letter.

NEXT STEPS

The Commission is committed to full consultation on any changes to the 'Guidance to Licensing Authorities (June 2007)' document. We expect to issue a consultation paper in May 2008 detailing our proposed revisions to our guidance, and will publish a final version during the summer.

The Commission will continue to monitor the way in which operators seek to use the provisions of the Act. If it becomes clear that operators are attempting to provide what are, in effect, higher category machine arcades under the guise of either a betting or bingo premises licence with only token betting or bingo provision we will not hesitate to introduce operating licence conditions and / or recommend to the Department for Culture, Media and Sports and Scottish Ministers that additional regulations are required to underpin the clear policy intentions of the Act.

Licensing authorities that are currently considering premises licence applications to divide an existing premises into multiple premises may wish to refer to the sections of the Explanatory Memorandum highlighted above, and to the Commission's draft revised guidance which we will shortly be consulting on. We will consider also the application of our updated guidance towards premises that have already been divided.

If the premises licence applications refer to bingo premises licences, licensing authorities are reminded that the Commission has published an information paper summarising some considerations, which is available here.
Gambling Commission April 2008

MEMBERS' CLUB OR COMMERCIAL CLUB?

6.2659 The Gambling Act 2005 created a way of regulating gaming in two distinct types of club: **members' clubs** (including miners' welfare institutes) and **commercial clubs,** both of which must be established and conducted wholly or mainly for purposes other than gaming.
The distinction between the two types of club is important as it reflects the type of gaming that is permitted. Only genuine members' clubs, as defined below, can apply for both a club gaming permit and/or a club machines permit, while commercial clubs can only apply for a club machines permit.
Local authorities are responsible for issuing both club gaming permits and club machines permits.

WHAT IS A MEMBERS' CLUB?

It is a club that:
- is not established as a commercial enterprise and is conducted for the benefit of its members
- has at least 25 members
- is established and conducted wholly or mainly for purposes other than gaming (unless gaming is restricted to bridge and whist)
- is permanent in nature.

Examples include working men's clubs, branches of the Royal British Legion and clubs with political affiliations.

WHAT IS A COMMERCIAL CLUB?

It is a club that:
- is established for commercial gain (whether or not they are making a commercial gain)
- has at least 25 members
- is established and conducted wholly or mainly for purposes other than gaming (unless gaming is restricted to bridge and whist)
- is permanent in nature.

Examples include snooker clubs, clubs established as privately owned companies and clubs established for personal profit.

HOW TO DETERMINE WHETHER A CLUB IS A GENUINE MEMBERS' CLUB

In determining whether a club is a genuine members' club, the licensing authority takes account of a number of matters, such as:
- Is the primary purpose of the club's activities something other than the provision of gaming to its members?
- Are profits retained in the club for the benefit of the members? This is the key difference between a members' club and a commercial club.
- Are there 25 or more members? This number is the amount a club has to have to qualify.

- Are there genuine domestic addresses on the register of members?
- Are domestic addresses listed for every member?
- Are members local to the club?
- Do members participate in the activities of the club via the internet? It is less likely to be a genuine member's club if this is the case.
- Do guest arrangements link a member to every guest?
- Is the 48 hour rule between applying and becoming a member properly applied?
- Are there annual accounts for more than one year?

The constitution of the club could also indicate whether it is a legitimate members' club. Amongst the things to consider are the following:

- Who makes commercial decisions on behalf of the club and what are the governance arrangements?
- Are there shareholders or members? Shareholders would indicate a business enterprise linked to a commercial club
- Is the members' club permanently established?
- Can people join with annual or quarterly membership?
- Are there long-term membership benefits?

Full details are included in *Guidance to Licensing Authorities* available on our website www.gamblingcommission.gov.uk

Club Gaming Permit
(available to members' clubs only)

- can offer equal chance gaming such as poker and bingo
- no limits on stakes and prizes except bingo where there is a stakes and prizes limit of £2,000 in any seven day period
- can offer games of chance (pontoon and chemin de fer only)
- limit on participation fees per person per day
  £20 for bridge and or whist
  £3 for other gaming (including poker)
- can offer up to three gaming machines in total of categories B4, C or D but only one machine of category B3A.

Club Machine Permit
(available to members' clubs and commercial clubs)

- can offer equal chance gaming such as poker and bingo – where there is a stakes and prizes limit of £2,000 in any seven day period
- limits on stakes
  poker – £10 per person per game, within a premises limit of £250 in stakes per day and £1,000 per week
- limit on participation fees per person per day
  £18 for bridge/whist
  £1 for other gaming (including poker), £3 where it's a commercial club
- limits on prizes
- can offer up to three gaming machines in total of categories B4, C or D. Members' clubs can also offer one of these three machines as category B3A.

Fast-track procedure for getting a permit

There is a fast-track procedure for clubs in England and Wales that hold a club premises certificate (under section 72 of the Licensing Act 2003).

There is no opportunity for objections to be made by the Gambling Commission or the police, and the grounds upon which an authority can refuse are reduced.

There are three grounds for refusal by a licensing authority, including when the club is established primarily for gaming.

The Commission provides advice and guidance to local authorities and, on a case by case basis, will undertake targeted collaborations in order to establish principle and precedent and a clear understanding of legal requirements.

www.gamblingcommission.gov.uk

LOCAL AUTHORITY CASE STUDIES

REFUSAL OF A CLUB GAMING PERMIT

The club was situated within commercial premises that operated as a snooker club. The commercial premises holds a premises licence under the Licensing Act 2003. The local authority found that the club:

- did not meet the definition of a members' club as it was established for the purpose of gaming
- did not prove it was established and conducted for the benefit of its members
- offered activities that could already be accessed through the existing commercial premises on a much larger scale and with no membership fee
- was trying to circumvent the Licensing Act 2003 by setting up a club within a club
- did not have a satisfactory constitution with regard to the nomination and election of new members and the committee
- provided financial documentation that was inadequate and showed that the applicant's main activities constituted gaming (in particular, poker).

The club gaming permit was refused. The licensing authority has subsequently offered the applicant an appeal under Schedule 12 S25(1) of the Gambling Act 2005.

REVIEW OF A CLUB GAMING PERMIT

The club had been granted a club gaming permit, but intelligence has suggested that the club is in breach of several conditions of its permit. After a joint visit to the club with local police, the local authority found that the club:

- was not established and conducted for the benefit of its members
- appeared to be established and conducted almost solely for the purpose of playing poker.

A letter was sent to the club instructing it to comply with the conditions of its club gaming permit within a set time period.
The club failed to comply and the local authority withdrew the club gaming permit.
Gambling Commission October 2010

PUBS

GAMING MACHINE PERMITS CODE OF PRACTICE – CLUB GAMING PERMITS AND CLUB MACHINE PERMITS – ALCOHOL LICENSED PREMISES PERMITS AND PERMISSIONS

June 2007

INTRODUCTION

6.2660

(i) This is the Gambling Commission's Code of Practice issued under section 24 Gambling Act 2005 (the Act) relating to provision of facilities for gambling in accordance with club gaming, club machine and licensed premises gaming machine permits. This includes:

- registrations under Parts II and III Gaming Act 1968 which, under transitional provisions, are treated as club gaming and club machine permits respectively; and
- alcohol licensed premises gaming machine permits (formerly s34 1968 Act permits).

(ii) The Code will come into force on 1 September 2007.

(iii) Those items marked in bold and shaded are the provisions which are a condition of the permit and must be complied with.

SECTION A: LOCATION AND OPERATION OF MACHINES

ALL PERMIT HOLDERS

Compliance with these provisions is a condition of your permit, and failure to do so could result in revocation of the permit [1].

1 All gaming machines situated on the premises must be located in a place within the premises so that their use can be supervised, either by staff whose duties include such supervision (including bar or floor staff) or by other means.

Permit holders must have in place arrangements for such supervision.

2 All gaming machines situated on the premises shall be located in a place that requires a customer who wishes to use any ATM made available on the premises to cease gambling at the gaming machine in order to do so. 'ATM' means a machine located on the premises, which enables a person using it to obtain cash by use of a credit or debit card.

---

1 Compliance with these provisions is a condition of the relevant permit as a result of the Gambling Act 2005: section 271 for Club Gaming Permits, section 273 for Club Machine Permits, section 282 for alcohol licensed premises using their automatic machine permissions and section 283 for licensed premises Gaming Machine Permits and alcohol licensed premises

SECTION B: ACCESS TO GAMBLING BY CHILDREN AND YOUNG PERSONS

ALL PERMIT HOLDERS

This section sets out the best practice which the Gambling Commission considers should be implemented by permit-holders, compliance with this provision is not a condition of your permit.

3 Permit holders should put into effect procedures intended to prevent underage gambling. This should include procedures for:

- checking the age of apparently underage customers; and

- refusing access to anyone who appears to be underage, and who tries to use category B or C gaming machines and cannot produce an acceptable form of identification.

4 Permit holders should take all reasonable steps to ensure that all relevant employees understand their responsibilities for preventing underage gambling.

5 Permit holders should only accept identification which:

- contains a photograph from which the individual can be identified;
- is valid; and
- is legible and has no visible signs of tampering or reproduction.

(The Commission considers acceptable forms of identification to include any identification carrying the PASS logo (eg Citizencard, Validate and the Government's own Connexions card); driving licence (including a provisional licence) with photocard; and passport).

6 Procedures should be in place for dealing with cases where a child or young person repeatedly attempts to gamble on category B or C machines, including oral warnings, reporting the offence to the Gambling Commission and the police, and making available information on problem gambling.

SECTION C: SELF EXCLUSION

This section sets out the best practice which the Gambling Commission considers should be implemented by permit-holders, compliance with this provision is not a condition of your permit.

CLUB GAMING PERMIT AND CLUB MACHINE PERMIT HOLDERS ONLY

7 Permit holders should put in place procedures for self-exclusion and take all reasonable steps to refuse service or to otherwise prevent an individual who has entered a self-exclusion agreement from participating in gambling.

8 Permit holders should implement procedures designed to ensure that an individual who has self-excluded cannot gain access to gambling; this includes:

- a register of those excluded with appropriate records (name, address, other details, and any membership or account details that may be held by the operator);
- photo identification (where available and in particular where enforcement of the system may depend on photographic ID), and a signature;
- staff training to ensure that relevant staff are able to enforce the systems; and
- the removal of those self-excluded persons found in the gambling area or attempting to gamble from the premises.

9 Self-exclusion procedures should require individuals to take positive action in order to self-exclude. This can be a signature on a self-exclusion form.

10 Before an individual self-excludes, permit holders should provide or make available sufficient information about what the consequences of self-exclusion are. Customers should be given the opportunity to discuss self-exclusion in private, where possible.

11 Permit holders should take all reasonable steps to ensure that:

- the self-exclusion period is a minimum of six months and give customers the option of extending this to a total of at least five years;
- a customer who has decided to enter a self-exclusion agreement is given the opportunity to so do immediately without any cooling off period. However, if the customer wishes to consider the self exclusion further (for example to discuss with problem gambling groups) the customer may return at a later date to enter into self exclusion;
- at the end of the period chosen by the customer (and at least six months later), maintain the self-exclusion in place, unless the customer takes positive action in

order to gamble again. No marketing material may be sent to the individual unless that has taken positive action in order to gamble again, and has agreed to accept such material; and

- where a customer chooses not to renew, and makes a positive request to begin gambling again, give the customer 1 day to cool off before being allowed access to the gambling facilities.

12 Please note that the Commission does not require the permit-holder to carry out an assessment or make any judgement of whether the individual should have access to gambling. The requirement to take positive action in person or over the phone is purely to:

(a) check that the customer has considered the decision to access gambling again and allow them to consider the implications; and

(b) implement the 1 day cooling-off period and explain why this has been put in place.

Gambling Commission June 2007

GAMING AND GAMING MACHINES IN PUBS AND OTHER ALCOHOL-LICENSED PREMISES UNDER THE GAMBLING ACT 2005

WHICH PREMISES ARE ELIGIBLE TO PROVIDE GAMING?

6.2670 Any premises that have an alcohol licence, and which have a bar at which alcohol is served for consumption on the premises without a requirement that alcohol is served only with food.

WHAT ABOUT CLUBS?

There are separate provisions covering gaming in clubs and miners' welfare institutes – please see the separate DCMS fact sheet.

What kind of gaming can pubs and other eligible premises provide?

Section 279 of the Gambling Act allows pubs and other eligible premises to provide what the Act calls "exempt gaming". There are a number of conditions:

- it must be **equal chance gaming** (examples would be bingo, bridge and certain poker games);
- stakes and prizes must comply with the limits prescribed in regulations;
- no amount may be deducted or levied from amounts staked or won;
- no participation fees may be charged;
- the games played may only take place on one set of premises, ie there may not be any linking of games between premises; and
- children and young people must be excluded from participation.

WHAT LIMITS ARE THERE ON STAKES AND PRIZES?

Different limits apply to different types of gaming.

For dominoes and cribbage there are no limits on either stakes or prizes.

For all other types of equal chance gaming there is a limit on stakes of £5 per person, per game.

For **poker**, a stakes limit of £5 per player **per game** (n.b. not per hand) applies, and the aggregate stakes limit for pub poker is £100 per day for each premises. So, for example, a pub could run a daily poker game involving 20 players staking £5 each. The maximum prize for a game of poker played in a pub is also £100.

WHAT ABOUT PUB BINGO?

Pubs that wish to provide facilities for bingo may do so under the Act's exempt gaming provisions. The following rules apply:

- the maximum amount that may be staked by a player in a game of bingo is £5;
- no amounts may be deducted from sums staked or won;
- players may not be charged a fee for taking part;
- there should be no linking of games between premises; and,
- nobody under 18 may participate.

As with clubs, pubs that wish to offer high turnover bingo (ie where stakes or prizes exceed £2000 per week) will require a bingo operating licence from the Gambling Commission. See the Commission's website (details above) for further information.

CAN PUBS CHARGE CUSTOMERS FOR TAKING PART IN GAMING, OR MAKE DEDUCTIONS FROM STAKES OR PRIZES?

No charges or deductions may be made.

CAN A PUB CHARGE A MEMBERSHIP FEE FOR GAMBLING?

No – under section 344(3) of the Act any membership fee charged in these circumstances would be regarded as a participation fee.

DO PUBS NEED A GAMBLING PERMIT OR LICENCE?

No licence or permit is required for pubs or other eligible premises providing gaming under the exempt gaming provisions (see above).

WHAT IF A PUB ONLY WANTS TO PROVIDE GAMING MACHINES?

Under section 282 of the Act alcohol-licensed premises are entitled to a maximum of two gaming machines (each of which may be category C or D) without the need for a permit or licence. To exercise this entitlement the person who holds the relevant alcohol licence should notify their local licensing authority of their intention to make gaming machines available, and pay the required notification fee. If a licensee wishes to make more than two gaming machines available he will need to obtain a **licensed premises gaming machine permit**, once again from the local licensing authority. There are a number of statutory conditions relating to the way in which gaming machines are used, and licensees will also need to ensure compliance with the Gambling Commission's code of practice on the location and operation of gaming machines. See the Commission's website – www.gamblingcommission.gov.uk — for further details.

WHAT IS THE MAXIMUM NUMBER OF GAMING MACHINES THAT A PUB MAY HAVE?

There is no statutory limit on the number of gaming machines that individual premises may apply for, but the licensing authority has the discretion to restrict the number of machines on individual premises (or change the category of the machines), having regard to the licensing objectives of the Gambling Act.

WHAT HAPPENS IF A PUB BREAKS THE RULES?

Licensees will be expected to monitor any gaming that takes place on their premises, and take all reasonable steps to ensure that it complies with the statutory requirements, including the limits on stakes and prizes. Under section 310(2) of the Act, a constable, Gambling Commission enforcement officer or authorised local authority officer may enter premises that hold an on-premises alcohol licence in order to determine whether gaming carried on there satisfies the statutory conditions. Any breach of those conditions in respect of particular premises would leave them liable to the loss of their entitlement to offer gaming and/or gaming machines, and criminal prosecution. Where a breach of the Gambling Act has implications for alcohol licensing objectives it may, as with breaches of other laws, be taken into account by licensing authorities and others in the exercise of their functions under the relevant legislation.

IS PRACTICAL ADVICE AVAILABLE ABOUT HOW TO OPERATE GAMING IN PUBS AND OTHER ELIGIBLE PREMISES?

The Gambling Commission has issued a statutory code of practice on gaming in clubs and alcohol-licensed premises, which is available from its website (see above).

NB. This fact sheet is intended to provide a general explanation of the regulatory regime under the Gambling Act 2005 and its subordinate legislation, and does not deal with every detail of the legislative provisions, or with the individual circumstances of a particular case. This fact sheet does not constitute legal advice and is not a substitute for the relevant legislative provisions. If you are in any doubt about the legality of any gambling activities that you intend to promote or for which you intend to provide facilities, you are strongly advised to seek independent legal advice.

DCMS
August 2007

ADVICE ON GAMING IN CLUBS AND ALCOHOL LICENSED PREMISES: GAMBLING ACT 2005

September 2008
6.2671

1 INTRODUCTION

1.1 This advice replaces the memorandum issued by the Gambling Commission (the Commission) in June 2006 concerning gaming on alcohol licensed premises. In the light of the interest in poker, the Commission has been asked to give advice to licensing authorities (local authorities and Scottish licensing boards) and others on poker games, including tournaments and leagues, bingo and other equal chance gaming in clubs and alcohol licensed premises. It has therefore revised and updated its earlier advice following the full implementation of the Gambling Act 2005 (the Act). This advice has been circulated to licensing authorities in England, Wales and Scotland and to chief officers of police. This advice does not constitute guidance under section 25 of the Gambling Act 2005.

1.2 It is an offence to provide facilities for gambling without the relevant operating licence and premises licence unless the activity is subject to an exception. Part 12 of the Act provides that in pubs and clubs, certain gaming, including poker, is exempt, subject to stakes and prizes limitations or, if correct permissions are held (club gaming permit), then there can be unlimited stakes and prizes.

1.3 Gaming of the type usually provided in clubs and alcohol licensed premises is subject to lesser controls and a code of practice. These are designed to protect both the players and those providing the gaming facilities and ensure that, in general, gaming remains ancillary to the main purpose of the pub or club. While the principles are the same for both pubs and clubs there are different provisions for each sector. It remains the case that the law in this area is complex and each case must be judged according to its facts.

1.4 A summary of gaming entitlements is set out in an appendix at the end of this paper.

2 DEFINING CLUBS AND ALCOHOL LICENSED PREMISES

2.1 The Act separates gaming in clubs from that in other alcohol licensed premises (commonly known as pubs).

2.2 The Act creates two types of club for the purposes of gaming: members' clubs (including miners' welfare institutes) and commercial clubs. This is an important distinction in respect of the gaming that may take place.

MEMBERS' CLUB

2.3 A **members' club** is a club that is not established as a commercial enterprise, and is conducted for the benefit of its members. Examples include working men's clubs, miners' welfare institutes, branches of the Royal British Legion and clubs with political affiliations. Members' clubs may apply to their local licensing authority for club gaming permits and club machine permits.

2.4 The Act states that members' clubs must have at least 25 members and be established and conducted 'wholly or mainly' for purposes other than gaming, unless the gaming is restricted to bridge and whist. Members' clubs must be permanent in nature, but there is no need for a club to have an alcohol licence, if they want to provide gaming.

MINERS' WELFARE INSTITUTE

2.5 The definition of a **miners' welfare institute** has changed since they were first set up. They are associations established for recreational or social purposes. They are managed by representatives of miners or use premises regulated by a charitable trust which has received funds from one of a number of mining organisations. Miners' welfare institutes may also apply for club gaming permits and club machine permits.

COMMERCIAL CLUB

2.6 A **commercial club** is a club established for commercial gain (whether or not they are making a commercial gain). Examples include snooker clubs, clubs established as private companies and clubs established for personal profit. There are established tests in respect of determining a club's status. In case of doubt, legal advice should be sought. Commercial clubs may only apply for club machine permits.

ALCOHOL LICENSED PREMISES

2.7 **Alcohol licensed premises** are premises where there is an 'on-premises alcohol licence'. The Act applies to premises which have a bar and where there is no requirement that alcohol is only served with food, that is, the premises should be dedicated bar premises as opposed to restaurant type premises. Pubs are not able to apply for club gaming or club machine permits, as they do not have membership.

3 PERMITTED AND EXEMPT GAMING IN CLUBS AND ALCOHOL LICENSED PREMISES

3.1 The Act creates two types of gaming permission for clubs and alcohol licensed premises.

PERMITTED GAMING

3.2 **Permitted gaming** is equal chance and other gaming permissible through the grant of a club gaming permit. A club gaming permit can only be granted to a members' club (including a miners' welfare institute). A club gaming permit cannot be granted to a commercial club or other alcohol licensed premises. A club gaming permit will allow a club to offer equal chance gaming with unlimited stakes and prizes, pontoon and chemin de fer (unequal chance gaming), and bingo. There are limits on participation fees (maximum of £20 for bridge and whist and £3 for other gaming) and the maximum for bingo stakes and prizes is £2,000 per week.

3.3 Other than in the case of clubs established to provide the prescribed games of bridge and whist, clubs seeking club gaming permits must, as set out above, be established 'wholly or mainly' for purposes <u>other</u> than gaming. As was the position under the former Gaming Act 1968, when a club gaming permit is granted there are no limits on the stakes and prizes associated with permitted gaming. Permitted gaming also includes two bankers' games: pontoon and chemin de fer.

EXEMPT GAMING

3.4 **Exempt gaming** is equal chance gaming generally permissible in any club or alcohol licensed premises. Equal chance gaming includes games such as backgammon, mah-jong, rummy, kalooki, dominoes, cribbage, bingo and poker. Such gaming should be ancillary to the purposes of the premises. Unlike the position under the Gaming Act 1968, this exemption is automatically available to all club or alcohol licensed premises, but is subject to statutory stakes and prize limits determined by the Secretary of State.
3.5 The Secretary of State has set both daily and weekly prize limits for exempt gaming (ref SI 2007/1940). Different, higher stakes and prizes are allowed for exempt gaming in clubs than in alcohol licensed premises (ref SI 2007/1944). These limits are set out in the Appendix to this advice document.
3.6 Exempt gaming should be supervised by a nominated gaming supervisor and comply with any code of practice issued by the Commission under section 24 of the Act. In this regard, the Commission has issued a code of practice for exempt equal chance gaming. This can be found here: www.gamblingcommission.gov.uk/client/mediadetail.asp
3.7 A fee may not be levied for participation in the equal chance gaming offered by the club or alcohol licensed premises under the exempt gaming rules. A compulsory charge, such as a charge for a meal, would probably constitute a participation fee.
3.8 In order to qualify as exempt gaming, clubs and alcohol licensed premises may not charge a rake on games or levy or deduct an amount from stakes or winnings.
3.9 Members' clubs may only be established wholly or mainly for the purposes of the provision of facilities for gaming *if the gaming is of a prescribed kind*. The Secretary of State has decided that bridge and whist should be the only prescribed kinds of gaming. So long as it does not provide facilities for other types of non-machine gaming, a bridge or whist club may apply for a club gaming permit. If gaming is the principal reason for attendance at a club (*other than a dedicated whist or bridge club*), then it is not exempt gaming under Section 269 of the Gambling Act 2005. This would include poker clubs and the like established primarily for the purpose of providing poker. If the gaming which is provided is not exempt, the operator will need to apply to the Commission for the relevant operating licence.

4 PERMITS

CLUB GAMING PERMITS

4.1 **Club gaming permits** allow the playing of poker for unlimited stakes and prizes and also allow certain bankers games to be played, but may only be issued to members' clubs and miners' welfare institutes.

CLUB MACHINE PERMITS

4.2 **Club machine permits** may be issued to members' clubs, commercial clubs or miners' welfare institutes, but these permits do not allow the playing of poker for unlimited stakes and prizes.
4.3 Before granting club gaming or machine permits, local authorities are required to satisfy themselves that the club is not wholly or mainly devoted to gaming (other than bridge and whist). It will not be sufficient for a club simply to offer other sports and activities with a view to meeting this requirement. Where the majority of the club's activities is gaming (for example, poker), gaming will be considered the main activity of the club. Those clubs which hold club permits and then conduct themselves

in such a way that gaming (for example, poker) is their main activity, will lose their entitlement to a permit and may be in breach of the Act and may render themselves liable to prosecution, unless the gaming offered is exempt gaming.

4.4 Clubs with a gaming permit or a machine permit may have up to a maximum of three gaming machines of categories B4, C or D on their premises. Non-commercial members' clubs and miners' welfare institutes may also have a category B3A as one of their machines, but may not exceed three gaming machines in total. The restriction of one category B3A machine is as a result of the voluntary agreement entered into by CORCA, the trade association representing the majority of members' clubs.

4.5 Pubs and other alcohol licensed premises have an automatic entitlement to two category C or D gaming machines and may apply for more machines to their licensing authority. No conditions are applied to gaming machine permits but all operators offering gaming machines should abide by the Commission's code of practice on gaming machines.

5 GAMBLING COMMISSION CODES OF PRACTICE

5.1 The Commission has issued a code of practice under section 24 of the Act in respect of exempt equal chance gaming. This can be found here: www.gamblingcommission.gov.uk/client/mediadetail.asp

5.2 The guidance requires owners/licensees to adopt good practice measures for the provision of gaming in general and poker in particular. The code also sets out the stakes and prizes limits and the limits on participation fees (as applicable) laid out in regulations.

5.3 The additional advice in respect of poker provided in this document is a result of the nature of the game and it's escalating staking patterns. These can create significant tensions and losses and it is possible for experienced players to collude or manipulate the game to the disadvantage of weaker players.

5.4 There is likely to be limited regulatory scrutiny of the gaming provided in pubs and clubs given that, while licensing authorities will have issued the premises with an alcohol licence, they have limited powers in respect of the inspection of gaming in pubs, and the fee payable for the club gaming permit is low. Therefore, the emphasis of the regulations and the code of practice are on self-regulation by the management of the premises. For this reason, and where breaches are detected, licensees and management can expect a strong line to be taken by both the Commission and licensing authorities.

5.5 The Commission's code of practice on gaming machine permits can be found here:
www.gamblingcommission.gov.uk/client/mediadetail.asp
This code includes sections relating to:

- the location and operation of machines, which are a requirement of the permits
- access to gambling by children and young persons, which sets out best practice guidance for permit-holders
- self-exclusion, which relates only to club gaming permits and club machine permits and which again sets out best practice for permit-holders.

6 POKER LEAGUES AND TOURNAMENTS

6.1 Gaming is only covered by the Act if it is played for prizes of money or money's worth. However, since 2004 a number of poker tournaments and leagues have been established in alcohol licensed premises based on playing for points. In some leagues the organisers offer 'prizes' at the end of a series of weekly games for the players with the most points.

6.2 It is likely that the association of a prize with a monetary value with a game or series of games constitutes gaming, certainly by the latter stages of the competition. If the eventual prize is worth more than the maximum prize set out in regulations then it could be unlawful gaming. For example, if a tournament simply involves a series of straightforward 'knockout' qualifying rounds, culminating in a 'final' game, then the

6: Gambling Act 2005: Additional Material

winner's prize in the final — whether it comprises the stakes laid in that game, a separate prize provided by the organiser, or a combination of the two — must not exceed £100. The regulations set a limit of £100 on a prize that may be won in any game of poker. In a knockout tournament, the overall prize is clearly referable to a single game (the 'final') and is therefore won in a game of poker and subject to the prize limit. The stake and prize limits must also, of course, be applied to each game in the tournament.

6.3 In other leagues the prize competed for is the opportunity to play in 'invitational cash tournaments'. Notwithstanding that these 'prizes' may be of an uncertain value, and are likely to be held in mainstream gaming venues under regulated conditions, usually a casino, the Act prohibits gaming in alcohol licensed premises being linked to gaming in any other premises. Players competing across premises for a 'prize' are likely to be engaged in linked gaming, which is unlawful. Consequently, licensees should not host events where players are competing against players in other premises for a prize.

6.4 In some types of tournaments there will be no single 'final' game in which it can be said with certainty that the player won the overall prize. In such circumstances, our view is that one should look to the individual games played by the overall winner and ensure that the overall prize does not cause any of those individual games to exceed the maximum £100 prize limit per game and the maximum stake of £100 per day.

EXAMPLE 1: THE OVERALL WINNER WINS THE POT IN EACH GAME AND WINS AN OVERALL PRIZE BASED ON POINTS

6.5 If the tournament winner played three games in the whole tournament, and his winnings (from the pot) in each of these games were £100, £70 and £60 respectively, each game would fall under the £100 prize limit. This would leave £0 from the first game, £30 from the second game and £40 from the third game, which could be put towards the winner's overall tournament prize. In these circumstances, the tournament prize could be up to £70 (£0 + £30 + £40). Thus where the pot in individual games is under £100, the tournament winner's overall prize must not exceed the aggregate of the shortfall in each of the games he plays.

EXAMPLE 2: THE OVERALL WINNER IS ONLY AWARDED POINTS IN EACH GAME AND WINS AN OVERALL PRIZE BASED ON POINTS

6.6 Let's still assume that the tournament winner plays three games in the whole tournament. If there is no individual prize in any of the three games, then the overall prize can be up to £300 (£100 for each game the winner has played). If, on the other hand, the winner played in only two games, then his overall prize may not exceed £200, and so on. Please note that, the relevant number of games is the games in which the winning player participated, and not only the games that they won.

6.7 Organisers of such competitions will therefore need to work out the total value of any overall prize with reference to the number of games to be played by the overall winner and the total pot (if any) in each game.

6.8 While 'non-cash' poker for points leagues can provide harmless and legal entertainment, those promoting such leagues should be aware of the Commission's code of practice on equal chance gaming, and take steps to prevent individual stakes limits being exceeded through side bets or illegal activity such as agreements to 'settle' games outside the gaming area. Any such illegal activity would expose the owner or manager of the alcohol licensed premises, the organisers and the participants to risk of prosecution, or lead to the removal of the alcohol licensed premises' exemption, which allows poker to be played.

EXAMPLE 3: THE OVERALL WINNER IS ONLY AWARDED POINTS IN EACH GAME AND WINS AN OVERALL PRIZE SUCH AS THE OPPORTUNITY TO PARTICIPATE IN A MAJOR POKER TOURNAMENT, CASINO VOUCHERS, HOLIDAYS, ETC

6.9 The final of a poker tournament may be held in a licensed casino where high stakes poker may be played. Tournament organisers must nonetheless ensure that the statutory limits for poker in alcohol licensed premises and clubs are complied with. In particular, they must carefully consider the value of the prizes offered for games leading up to the tournament final (including money's worth or non-monetary prizes such as holidays, cars, casino vouchers, or buy-ins or seats at the final).

EXAMPLE 4: FREE OR DONATED PRIZES ARE AWARDED TO PLAYERS IN ADDITION TO THE MAXIMUM PRIZE POOLS FOR POKER IN CLUBS AND ALCOHOL LICENSED PREMISES

6.10 The Gambling Act 2005 speaks about money or money's worth in respect of prizes. This would include free or donated prizes which have an intrinsic value. Any prizes offered in addition to the prize pool must remain within the limits for prizes in games of poker in clubs and alcohol licensed premises. The prize limit is £250 per game in a club and £100 per game in a pub. Therefore, for example, if the prize pool available for a particular game is £80, then any non-monetary prizes must not have a value exceeding £20.

EXAMPLE 5: POKER IS OFFERED IN A MEMBERS' CLUB OR MINERS' WELFARE INSTITUTE WITH A CLUB GAMING PERMIT

6.11 Members' clubs or miners' welfare institutes with club gaming permits may offer poker with unlimited stakes and prizes, but the only persons who may participate in such gaming are club members and their genuine guests. In this regard, the club must be able to demonstrate that it has a genuine and legitimate club membership scheme. Clubs must also ensure that the statutory limits on stakes are not exceeded. The limit for bridge and whist is £20 and for other gaming is £3. In addition, there is a limit of a maximum of £2,000 per week in stakes and prizes for bingo in a members' club or welfare institute. If it is the intention of the club or institute to exceed these limits, it will be necessary for them to apply for an operating licence.

7 WHAT CONSTITUTES 'MONEY'S WORTH'?

7.1 Money's worth relates to the *realistic value of the prize* offered. It includes emoluments, vouchers, goods or other items which have a value.

7.2 A prize such as a 'goodies bag' would be considered money's worth and is hence subject to the statutory limits for exempt gaming. Donated prizes would also be considered money's worth. This would include prizes such as the buy-ins at major poker tournaments or the opportunity to participate in poker tournaments at venues such as Las Vegas, especially as this type of prize is likely to include the cost of the airfare and accommodation.

8 BRIDGE AND WHIST

8.1 Bridge and whist clubs may not offer any other gaming besides bridge and whist if they rely on a club gaming permit. If they do not have a permit, they may provide exempt gaming as set out in paragraphs 3.4 to 3.6 above. If they wish to offer other non-exempt gaming they will require a Commission casino or bingo operating licence and any relevant personal licences.

9 BINGO

9.1 Under the Act, clubs and pubs can offer bingo without a permit or a licence provided that:

- no sums are deducted from sums staked or won – so there can be no 'rake' from the prize pot
- no participation fee is charged in respect of bingo games in pubs and the participation fee is no more than £1 per person per day in respect of bingo games in clubs, or £3 where a club gaming permit is held
- games are held on the premises
- games are not linked with games held on other premises
- the total stakes or prizes for bingo games played in any seven day period does not exceed £2,000 more than once in 12 months, and
- there is a maximum stake per game per player of £5 for bingo in pubs.

9.2 In the case of members' clubs and miners' welfare institutes, bingo may only be played by members and bona fide guests.

9.3 Clubs and pubs will need to apply for a bingo operating licence if they operate bingo on club/pub premises with total stakes or prizes that go above £2,000 in any week and they plan to do so again at any time during the following twelve months. This is known as high turnover bingo. After the first week of high turnover bingo the club will commit an offence if high turnover bingo is played again in the following twelve months, unless a bingo operating licence has been obtained. Provided the conditions outlined in the Act are complied with, the club will not need a premises licence.

10 CHARITY EVENTS

10.1 Organisations that wish to provide casino games or equal chance gaming (such as poker or bingo) for charitable or other non-commercial purposes (for example, to raise funds for a club or society) may do so under the non-commercial gaming provisions in Part 14 of the Act.

10.2 Non-commercial gaming is gaming that takes place at an event where none of the proceeds from the event itself are used for private gain. For these purposes, the proceeds of an event constitute the sums raised by its organisers (including sums raised by way of entrance or participation fees, sponsorship, commission from traders, or otherwise) minus the costs reasonably incurred in organising the event. However, sums raised by other persons will not form part of the proceeds of the event and so may be appropriated for private gain. An example would be refreshments provided at the event by an independent third party.

10.3 The Act lays down different rules depending on whether the non-commercial gaming is prize gaming or equal chance gaming. In both instances, however, the players participating in the gaming must be told what 'good cause' is to benefit from the profits from the gaming.

NON-COMMERCIAL PRIZE GAMING

10.4 There are no statutory limits on stakes, prizes, participation fees or other charges for non-commercial prize gaming. In addition, no licence, permit or other form of permission is required to operate this kind of gaming, provided that the statutory conditions are complied with.

NON-COMMERCIAL EQUAL CHANCE GAMING

10.5 No licence, permit or other form of permission is required to operate non-commercial equal chance gaming, provided that the statutory conditions are complied with, including any limits on participation fees, stakes and prizes.

10.6 In order to participate in each and every game played at an event where non-commercial equal chance gaming is offered, participants must not make or be required to make more than one payment (whether by way of a participation fee, stake or other charge, or a combination of those charges) and this payment must not exceed £8. The participation fee includes any charge for admission to the premises where the gambling takes place.
10.7 In respect of all games played at an event at which non-commercial equal chance gaming is offered, the aggregate amount or value of prizes and awards distributed in respect of those games must not exceed £600.
10.8 Where two or more events at which non-commercial equal chance gaming is offered are promoted on the same premises by the same person on the same day, the limits mentioned in paragraphs 10.6 and 10.7 above apply collectively in relation to those events (as if they were a single event).
10.9 Where a series of events are held (excluding cases where two or more events are promoted on the same premises by the same person on the same day), the limits mentioned in paragraphs 10.6 and 10.7 above apply separately in relation to each event in the series. In these circumstances, the amount or value of prizes and awards distributed in respect of all games played at the final event must also not exceed £900. In this context, an event is a 'final event' if no other event is promoted on the same premises by the same person on the same day as that on which the final event takes place, and each person participating in the event has qualified to do so by reason that they have taken part in games played at another event of the series held on a previous day.

11 PROHIBITED GAMING

11.1 No bankers' games may be played either in commercial clubs or alcohol licensed premises or in members' clubs/miners' welfare institutes unless they have a club gaming permit. This means that games such as pontoon, blackjack, roulette and any others which involve staking against the holder of the bank are unlawful on such premises except as mentioned in paragraph 4.1 above.

12 ADVERTISING

12.1 Section 331 of the Gambling Act 2005 specifically prohibits the advertising of 'foreign gambling' in the United Kingdom. Foreign gambling, in this sense, is gambling which takes place outside of the European Economic Area (including Gibraltar and Malta), the Isle of Man, Alderney and Tasmania. Therefore advertising of this nature would be illegal, but if the prize advertised was an all-expenses paid holiday to Las Vegas, then the operator would not fall foul of Section 331.
12.2 Many poker websites promote other online gambling websites, usually by the provision of a hyperlink to that website. A hyperlink has been deemed to constitute advertising as it brings facilities for advertising to the attention of the person who clicks on the link. Poker operators must, therefore, be mindful that the provision of a hyperlink to a website operating outside of the EEA or white-listed states (the Isle of Man, Alderney and Tasmania) will constitute advertising of foreign gambling which is not permitted.
Gambling Commission August 2008

APPENDIX: SUMMARY OF GAMING ENTITLEMENTS FOR CLUBS AND PUBS

	Members' club or MW institute with club gaming permit	Bridge or whist club	Members' club or commercial club with club machine permit	Members' club, commercial club or MW institute without a club gaming permit	Pubs and other alcohol-licensed premises
Equal chance gaming	Yes	Bridge and/or Whist only	Yes	Yes	Yes
Limits on stakes	No limit	No limit	Poker £1000 per week £250 per day £10 per person per game Other gaming No limit	Poker £1000 per week £250 per day £10 per person per game Other gaming No limit	Cribbage & dominoes No limit Poker £100 per premises per day Other gaming £5 per person per gamec
Limits on prizes	No limit	No limit	Poker £250 per game Other gaming No limit	Poker £250 per game Other gaming No limit	Poker £100 per game Other gaming No limit
Maximum participation fees – per person per day	Bridge and/or Whist [1] £20 Other gaming £3	£18 (without club gaming permit) £20 (with club gaming permit)	Bridge and/or Whist [1] £18 Other gaming £3 (commercial club) £1 (members' club)	Bridge and/or whist [1] £18 Other gaming £1	None permitted

Bankers or unequal chance gaming	Pontoon Chemin-de-Fer	None permitted	None permitted	None permitted	None permitted
Limits on bingo	Maximum of £2,000 per week in stakes/prizes. If more then will need an operating licence.	No bingo permitted	Maximum of £2,000 per week in stakes/prizes. If more then will need an operating licence.	Maximum of £2,000 per week in stakes/prizes. If more then will need an operating licence.	Maximum of £2,000 per week in stakes/prizes. If more then will need an operating licence.

[1] On a day when no other facilities for gaming are provided

BETTING IN PUBS AND CLUBS

FACILITATING BETTING IN PUBS AND CLUBS IS ILLEGAL

6.2672 No commercial betting at all, regardless of the level of stakes, is allowed in pubs and clubs. It is not socially responsible and those who facilitate such betting in pubs and clubs – whether publicans, designated premises supervisors or club officials – are providing illegal facilities for gambling and are breaking the law.

Even where publicans, designated premises supervisors or club officials accept bets on behalf of licensed bookmakers, or just facilitate betting through their own telephone accounts, they are acting as betting intermediaries and could be prosecuted.

Licensed bookmakers who knowingly accept bets from pub customers through a single account are encouraging illegal gambling. They may be in breach of the Gambling Act 2005 and could risk losing their licence.

Licensed bookmakers with a remote or ancillary licence may accept telephone bets from a customer watching an event in a pub or club, as long as that customer has an individual account with them.

It is illegal for bookmakers or their agents to sit in the pub taking bets themselves.

Similarly, it is also illegal for operators to put their agent in clubs, for example, in a working men's club on a Saturday, to take bets.

Licensed bookmakers should be vigilant. Where they suspect an individual telephone account is being used to transact business for a number of pub customers they should be alert to the possibility that it is being used to facilitate betting and where appropriate take steps to close the account.

Individuals who engage in the facilitation of illegal betting risk up to 51 weeks imprisonment (6 months in Scotland) and/or up to a £5,000 fine

QUESTIONS AND ANSWERS ON BETTING IN PUBS AND CLUBS

Q. I am a designated premises supervisor. Can my customers watch sport on the television and engage in betting activities?

A. Yes, as long as they place the bet using their own telephone account or take a betting slip to the bookmaker themselves.

Q. Is it illegal to have betting slips/coupons in a pub or club?

A. No, as long as when the customer completes the slip they take it to the bookmaker themselves.

Q. I am a club official. Can I take all the betting slips that my members have completed along with the stake money to the bookmakers before the event?

A. No. You are acting as a betting intermediary and risk prosecution.

Q. How about if I phone all the bets through to the bookmaker on my own telephone account?

A. No. You are acting as a betting intermediary by providing illegal facilities for gambling and risk prosecution.

Q. I am a licensed bookmaker. Can I, or my employee/agent, take bets in a working men's club?

A. No. You can only take bets in your licensed premises or over the telephone (if you have an ancillary remote or full remote licence).

Anyone betting and drinking alcohol at the same time may lose their inhibitions and place more than they can afford on a bet

It is the responsibility of all licensed bookmakers to ensure gambling is carried out in a socially responsible manner

For further information or advice: call the enquiries line on 0121 230 6666

Or email enquiries@gamblingcommission.gov.uk

Gambling Commission April 2008

CODE OF PRACTICE FOR EQUAL CHANCE GAMING IN CLUBS AND PREMISES WITH AN ALCOHOL LICENCE

March 2012
6.2673

1 GENERAL PROVISIONS

1.1 This is the Gambling Commission's (the Commission) code of practice relating to the provision of facilities for equal chance gaming in pubs and clubs. It is issued in accordance with section 24 of the Gambling Act 2005 (the Act) and in respect of gaming carried out under Part 12 of the Act and the associated regulations. This gaming is known as 'exempt gaming', and may be carried out without a gambling licence or permit. However, the club or alcohol licensed premises can only offer equal chance gaming that does not involve staking against a bank and where there are set daily and weekly prize limits. Where a club holds a club gaming permit additional entitlements are available.

1.2 Compliance with the code of practice should be the responsibility of a designated person:

- in pubs in England and Wales: the designated premises supervisor (which the Licensing Act 2003 requires as a condition of any alcohol premises licence)
- in premises which are licensed to serve alcohol for consumption on the premises under the relevant Scottish licence: the premises manager (which the Licensing (Scotland) Act 2005 requires as a condition of the premises licence)
- in clubs in England and Wales:
  - if an alcohol licence is held, the designated premises supervisor;
  - if no alcohol licence is held, a responsible individual to be nominated by the club management or other governing body elected by the members
- in clubs in Scotland:
  - for a qualifying club under the Licensing (Clubs) (Scotland) Regulations 2007 (SI No 76 of 2007) a person nominated by the club management committee, or other governing body elected by the members, and who is trained in accordance with the Licensing (Training of Staff) (Scotland) Regulations 2007
  - for a qualifying club operating under an occasional licence a responsible person to be nominated by the club management committee or other governing body elected by the members.
  - the name and contact details of the nominated person should be made available to the clerk of the relevant licensing board.

1.3 The regulations place certain limits on stakes and prizes for equal chance gaming. All exempt gaming is expected to be 'low level' and the designated person is expected to take all reasonable steps to ensure that this remains the case. Gaming in pubs and clubs should be ancillary to the main purpose of the premises – the gaming should not be the main reason to go to the premises. The statutory limits on stakes, prizes and, for clubs, participation fees, are set out in the attached table. Pubs may not charge participation fees. All gaming in pubs (other than dominoes and cribbage) has a stakes limit of £5 per person per game. Neither clubs nor pubs may impose levies or deductions on stakes or prizes.

1.4 All gaming carried out on the premises must be in a place where it can be supervised by staff whose duties include supervision of gaming (including bar or floor staff).

1.5 The designated person should put into effect procedures designed to prevent under age gambling. This should include:

- holding the gaming in premises or parts of premises which are restricted to adults;
- checking the age of potentially under age players and

- refusing access to the gaming to anyone apparently under age who cannot produce an acceptable form of age verification and identification.

1.6 Permit holders should only accept identification which:

- contain a photograph from which the customer can be identified
- states the individual's date of birth
- is valid
- is legible and has no visible signs of tampering or reproduction.

1.7 The Commission considers acceptable forms of identification to include: any identification carrying the PASS logo (for example Citizencard or Validate); a driving licence (including provisional licence) with photocard; or a passport.

1.8 Procedures should be in place for dealing with cases where an under age person repeatedly attempts to gamble including verbal warnings and reporting the offence to the Commission and the police.

1.9 The designated person should take reasonable steps to ensure that all employees understand their responsibilities under this code.

1.10 All payments in respect of the gaming covered by this code (including, in the case of clubs, any participation fees) should be paid for in cash before the commencement of the game. No credit may be offered to customers by the designated person. All players should be notified of any stakes limits that apply.

1.11 All equipment used in the gaming should be supplied by the premises and the equipment should be secured when not in use. The equipment should be replaced when damaged or marked. No player should supply his/her own equipment.

1.12 For all organised games, the rules of the game being played should be displayed or otherwise made available to all players before and during the game, for example by providing the rules on a laminated card.

1.13 The designated person should ensure a pleasant atmosphere and deny participation to customers who cheat or collude with other players or employees, threaten other players or employees, create a disturbance or damage equipment.

1.14 In Scotland care will need to be taken to ensure that the provision of facilities for equal chance gaming is provided for in the premises licence operating plan.

2 SPECIFIC PROVISIONS FOR POKER

2.1 To ensure that the stake and prize limits are not breached, it is strongly advised that cash games should not be permitted. Where cash games are allowed, the sum of money wagered (known as the 'pot') should be kept in sight so that it can be viewed by the designated person at all times.

2.2 In any event, all games organised by, or on behalf of, the management of the premises should not be cash games but tournament poker played in chips supplied by the premises.

2.3 The maximum stakes and prizes set out in the regulations are for a game and not a hand of poker. In the context of the code a game is what is generally considered to be an established and conventional game.

2.4 The designated person is to keep a record of:

- the number of games played
- the number of players and
- the amount staked
- the amount won

to ensure that the individual, daily and weekly stake and prize limits are not exceeded.

2.5 The designated person should take all reasonable steps to ensure that individual stakes limits are not exceeded through side bets, additional raises, re-buys or other ways of increasing the pot. Where this is discovered to be the case, the game should be stopped immediately and stakes returned to the individual players.

3 SPECIFIC PROVISIONS FOR BINGO

3.1 Separate provisions apply in respect of bingo. The designated person should contact the Commission if the total stakes or prizes for bingo games played in any seven day period exceeds £2,000 (either in money taken or prizes awarded).

4 SPECIFIC PROVISIONS FOR CLUBS

4.1 Clubs must ensure that appropriate membership records are completed for each member with a record of subscriptions paid. Records of daily participation fees should be kept separately. The club should demonstrate it has a bona fide club membership scheme.

4.2 Clubs that hold a club gaming permit may offer two kinds of banker's game only: pontoon and chemin de fer.

5 COMPLAINTS AND DISPUTES

5.1 The designated person should put into effect a written procedure for handling customer complaints and disputes regarding equal chance gambling.

5.2 A 'complaint' means a complaint about any aspect of the permit holder's conduct of their permissible activities, and a 'dispute' is any complaint which:

- is not resolved at the first stage of the complaints procedure and
- relates to the outcome of the complainant's gambling transaction.

5.3 The designated person should ensure that:

- customers are told the name and status of the person to contact about their complaint
- customers are given a copy of the complaints procedure on request or on making a complaint
- all complaints are handled in accordance with the procedure.

APPENDIX: SUMMARY OF GAMING ENTITLEMENTS FOR CLUBS AND ALCOHOL-LICENSED PREMISES

	Members' club, commercial club or MW institute without a club gaming permit or club machine permit	**Members' club or commercial club with club machine permit**	**Members' club or MW institute with club gaming permit**	**Bridge or whist club**	**Alcohol-licensed premises**
Equal chance gaming	Yes	Yes	Yes	Bridge and/or whist only	Yes
Limits on stakes	Poker £1,000 per week £250 per day £10 per person per game Other gaming	Poker £1,000 per week £250 per day £10 per person per game Other gaming	No limit	No limit	Poker £100 per premises per day £5 per person per game Other gaming £5 per person per game

	No limit	No limit			Cribbage & dominoes
					No limit
Limits on prizes	Poker £250 per game Other gaming No limit	Poker £250 per game Other gaming No limit	No limit	No limit	Poker £100 per game Other gaming No limit
Maximum participation fees – per person per day	Bridge and/or whist [1] £18 Other gaming £1	Bridge and/or whist [1] £18 Other gaming £3 (commercial club) £1 (members' club)	Bridge and/or whist [1] £20 Other gaming £3	£18 (without club gaming permit) £20 (with club gaming permit)	None permitted
Bankers or unequal chance gaming	None permitted	None permitted	Pontoon Chemin de fer	None permitted	None permitted
Limits on bingo	Maximum of £2,000 per week in stakes/prizes. If more then will need an operating licence.	Maximum of £2,000 per week in stakes/prizes. If more then will need an operating licence.	Maximum of £2,000 per week in stakes/prizes. If more then will need an operating licence.	No bingo permitted	Maximum of £2,000 per week in stakes/prizes. If more then will need an operating licence.

[1] On a day when no other facilities for gaming are provided

Gambling Commission March 2012

POKER IN PUBS
Advice on allowing poker in alcohol licensed premises

6.2674

CAN I ALLOW POKER IN MY PUB?

Poker can be played in a pub, but you must take account of the conditions that apply to any gaming in pubs, including limits on stakes and prizes. Licensing authorities can take action against licence holders who do not comply with these conditions.

STAKES AND PRIZES

There is a maximum value to both the amount that can be staked and the prize that can be offered when playing poker in a pub.
The maximum prize is £100 per game. This maximum includes money, payments in-kind, vouchers, goods, donated items, goody- bags, buy-ins at other poker tournaments and other items which have a value.
Additionally, you cannot charge a participation fee, including for example by having entrants pay a compulsory charge for a meal.

CAN I RUN A POKER TOURNAMENT?

The Gambling Commission recommends you take legal advice before you run a tournament or league.
A document called *Advice on gaming in clubs and alcohol-licensed premises: Gambling Act 2005* is available on our website and has some examples of ways a tournament might be structured which you may find helpful.

CAN I HOST A POKER LEAGUE?

Yes; provided it is not linked gaming. The Gambling Act 2005 says that a game of poker played on one set of premises cannot be linked to a game played on another set of premises
Games of poker are linked if:

- players in more than one pub are competing in the same game of poker across premises and the winner of that game of poker gets a prize, or
- the amount of the prize is determined by the number of people playing in different games of poker in different pubs.

Poker tournaments where the winners of games or top players in a series of games from various pub venues go through to play in a tournament final would not be linked gaming, even if the final was held at another venue, for example a licensed casino.
The amount each entrant can win depends on the number of games they have played in the tournament. See the example on the back of this leaflet.
You should always keep to the stakes and prizes limits discussed on the previous page,

6: Gambling Act 2005: Additional Material

in particular the limit of £100 per day in combined stakes for the premises.

HOW FINAL PRIZE LIMITS ARE WORKED OUT

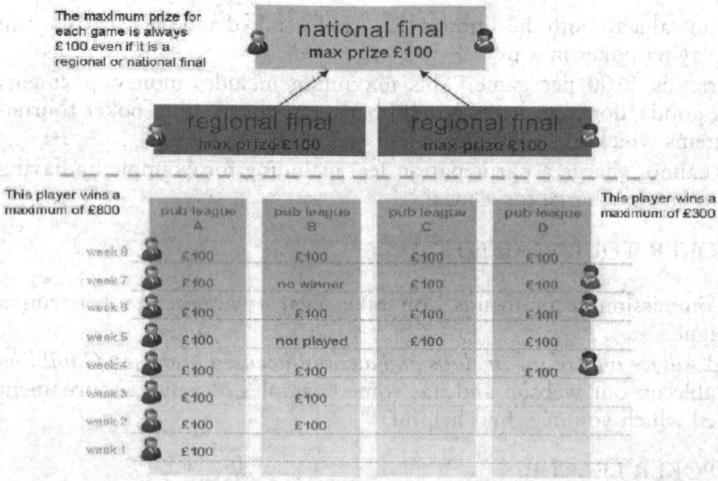

For example, if the player in pub league A reaches a tournament final by playing eight games in the league, the total prize can be no larger than £800 at the pub league level. The player can then win a maximum of £100 at the regional final and another £100 at the national final. If the player in pub league D only plays in three games in the league out of five games available, his or her total prize can be no larger than £300 at the pub league level. Again, the player can then win a maximum of £100 at the regional final and another £100 at the national final.

Gambling Commission July 2009

CLUBS

GAMING MACHINE PERMITS CODE OF PRACTICE – CLUB GAMING PERMITS AND CLUB MACHINE PERMITS – ALCOHOL LICENSED PREMISES PERMITS AND PERMISSIONS

To avoid duplication this document has not been reproduced here but can be found at para 6.2660 above.

GAMING AND GAMING MACHINES IN CLUBS AND MINERS' WELFARE INSTITUTES UNDER THE GAMBLING ACT 2005

WHAT IS A CLUB?

6.2685 The Gambling Act 2005 ("the Act") defines three categories of clubs: members' clubs, commercial clubs and miners' welfare institutes.

Members' clubs (section 266 of the Act) must have at least 25 members and be established and conducted wholly or mainly for purposes other than gaming (unless the gaming is of a prescribed kind – see below). They must be established and conducted for the benefit of their members, and with the intention of operating on an ongoing basis. Examples of such clubs are sports clubs, local political associations, working men's clubs and branches of the Royal British Legion.

Commercial clubs (section 267 of the Act) are subject to the same requirements as members' clubs, except that they may operate on a commercial basis rather than for the benefit of their members. These clubs are sometimes referred to as *proprietary clubs*. An example of a commercial club would be a snooker club. Like members' clubs, they may not be gaming clubs, unless the gaming is of a type prescribed in regulations.

Miners' welfare institutes (see section 268 of the Act) are associations established for social or recreational purposes, where the association is either managed by a group of miners' representatives or uses premises regulated under a charitable trust, where the trust has, at some time, received funds from one of a number of mining related organisations. They too enjoy the same gaming entitlements as members' clubs.

MUST A CLUB HAVE AN ALCOHOL LICENCE OR PERMIT IN ORDER TO PROVIDE GAMING?

No, as long as the above requirements are met any club may provide gaming under the Act, whether or not an alcohol licence or permit is held.

WHAT GAMING PERMISSIONS ARE AVAILABLE TO CLUBS UNDER THE ACT?

There are three types of permission: exempt gaming, club gaming permits and club machine permits. Exempt gaming and club machine permits are available to all three categories of club. Club gaming permits are available only to members' clubs and miners' welfare institutes. Further details about each of these can be found below.

CAN A CLUB BE FORMED SOLELY TO PROVIDE FACILITIES FOR GAMING?

Any club established wholly or mainly for gaming may operate under the exempt gaming provisions in section 269 of the Act. The Act also gives the Secretary of State powers to specify particular kinds of gaming, thereby allowing members' clubs established for the purposes of providing such gaming to take advantage of further gaming rights by applying for a club gaming permit. The Secretary of State has decided that **bridge** and **whist** should be the only prescribed kinds of gaming and, so long as they don't provide facilities for other types of non-machine gaming, a bridge or whist club may apply for a club gaming permit (see further details below).

WHAT IS EXEMPT GAMING?

Section 269 of the Act allows clubs and institutes (including clubs established and conducted for the purposes of gaming, and which otherwise meet the requirements for a members' or commercial club – see above) to provide certain facilities for gaming without the need for a licence or a permit. In order to qualify for this exemption the gaming must meet a number of conditions:

- it must be **equal chance gaming** (examples would be bingo, bridge and certain poker games);
- stakes and prizes must comply with any limits set in regulations;
- the club must not deduct any amounts from sums staked or won;
- any charge for participation must not exceed amounts set by the Secretary of State;
- the games played may only take place on one set of premises, so there may not be any linking of games between premises; and
- **in the case of members' clubs and miners' welfare institutes only, people may only participate in the gaming if they have been a member (or applied or were nominated for membership) at least 48 hours before playing, or are genuine guests of such a person.**

WHAT ARE THE LIMITS ON STAKES AND PRIZES FOR EXEMPT GAMING?

Although there are, at present, no limits in the legislation on stakes and prizes for most types of gaming in clubs and institutes, it should be noted that the exempt gaming provisions are intended to facilitate low stakes, low scale gaming activity. Clubs and institutes should therefore take steps to ensure that any gaming permitted on club premises remains at a low-level.

There are, however, regulations setting limits on **poker** played in all clubs and institutes under the exempt gaming provisions. There is a stakes limit of £10 per player per game (n.b. the limit applies to a **game of poker**, not a single hand), as well as aggregate stakes limits of £250 per day and £1000 per week for each individual club or institute. So, for example, a club could run a poker game for 25 players paying £10 each, four times per week. The maximum prize in a game of poker is also £250. Further information is available in the separate DCMS fact sheet on poker, and from the Gambling Commission's website: www.gamblingcommission.gov.uk.

WHAT ABOUT BINGO?

There are no limits on stakes and prizes for games of bingo played in clubs. **However,** clubs or institutes that wish to offer high turnover bingo (ie where stakes or prizes exceed £2000 per week) will require a bingo operating licence from the Gambling Commission. See the Gambling Commission's website (details above) for further information.

DO CLUBS AND INSTITUTES NEED A PERMIT OR LICENCE?

No licence or permit is required for clubs that operate solely under the exempt gaming provisions. Members' clubs and institutes (but not commercial clubs) that wish to provide additional facilities for gaming may apply for a **club gaming permit** from their local licensing authority.

WHAT ARE THE ADVANTAGES OF A CLUB GAMING PERMIT?

These permits allow clubs to provide facilities for two specific banker's games — chemin de fer and pontoon (**not blackjack**) – and to charge higher participation fees (up to £3 per person per day). In addition, gaming in a club or institute that holds a club gaming permit is not subject to the stake and prize limits that apply to exempt gaming. Club gaming permits also allow clubs to provide a **total** of 3 gaming machines in the following categories:

- B3A: a maximum stake of £1 and prize of £500
- B4: a maximum stake of £1 and prize of £250
- C: a maximum stake of 50p and prize of £35
- D: a maximum stake of 10p and prize of £5 cash; or 30p stake and £8 prize in a non-money prize machine

The use of these machines is subject to certain statutory conditions, and the holder of the permit must comply with the Gambling Commission's code of practice on the location and operation of gaming machines. See the Commission's website (details above) for further information.

WHICH CLUBS CAN APPLY FOR A CLUB GAMING PERMIT?

Members' clubs (including bridge or whist clubs) and miner's welfare institutes may apply to their local licensing authority for a club gaming permit.

CAN CLUBS CHARGE MEMBERS FOR TAKING PART IN GAMING?

Clubs and institutes operating under the exempt gaming provisions may make a charge of up to £1 per person per day for participating in gaming. Where a club gaming permit (or in the case of a commercial club, a club machine permit) is held a charge of up to £3 may be made.

WHAT IF A CLUB ONLY WANT TO PROVIDE GAMING MACHINES?

Members' clubs (including bridge and whist clubs), miners' welfare institutes and commercial clubs that wish to provide machine gaming may apply for a **club machine permit** from their local licensing authority. This type of permit authorises the same gaming machine allowance as that described immediately above, and use of the machines is subject to similar statutory conditions and the same code of practice. See the Commission's website (details above) for further information.

WHAT HAPPENS IF A CLUB BREAKS THE RULES?

Clubs will be expected to monitor any gaming that takes place on their premises, and take all reasonable steps to ensure that it complies with the statutory conditions. Under section 312 of the Act, a constable or Gambling Commission enforcement officer may enter club premises in order to determine whether gaming carried on there is in accordance with the statutory conditions or the terms of any club gaming or club machine permit. Any breach of the statutory conditions would render those providing the premises or facilities liable to prosecution under section 33 or 37 of the Act. Any breach of a permit could lead to its cancellation by the licensing authority, and might also constitute an offence under section 33 or 37 of the Act.

IS PRACTICAL ADVICE AVAILABLE ABOUT HOW TO OPERATE GAMING IN CLUBS AND INSTITUTES?

The Gambling Commission has issued a statutory code of practice on gaming in clubs and alcohol-licensed premises, which is available from its website (see above).

NB. This fact sheet is intended to provide a general explanation of the regulatory regime under the Gambling Act 2005 and its subordinate legislation, and does not deal with every detail of the legislative provisions, or with the individual circumstances of a particular case. This fact sheet does not constitute legal advice and is not a substitute for the relevant legislative provisions. If you are in any doubt about the legality of any

gambling activities that you intend to promote or for which you intend to provide facilities, you are strongly advised to seek independent legal advice.

DCMS
August 2007

ADVICE ON GAMING IN CLUBS AND ALCOHOL LICENSED PREMISES

To avoid duplication this document has not been reproduced here but can be found at para 6.2671 above.

ADVICE TO LICENSING AUTHORITIES ON CLUB GAMING PERMITS AND CLUB MACHINE PERMITS: GAMBLING ACT 2005

To avoid duplication this document has not been reproduced here but can be found at para 6.2657 above.

BETTING IN PUBS AND CLUBS

To avoid duplication this document has not been reproduced here but can be found at para 6.2672 above.

CODE OF PRACTICE FOR EQUAL CHANCE GAMING IN CLUBS AND PREMISES WITH AN ALCOHOL LICENCE

To avoid duplication this document has not been reproduced here but can be found at para 6.2673 above.

MEMBERS' CLUB OR COMMERCIAL CLUB

To avoid duplication this document has not been reproduced here but can be found at para 6.2659 above.

POKER IN CLUBS

ADVICE ON ALLOWING POKER IN CLUBS

Can we allow poker in our club?

6.2686 Poker can be played in a members' club or commercial club, but you must take account of the conditions that apply to any gaming in clubs, including limits on stakes and prizes. Action can be taken against clubs that do not comply with these conditions.

What is a members' club?
It is a club that:

What is a commercial club?
It is a club that:

What is a members' club?	**What is a commercial club?**
■ is not established as a commercial enterprise and is conducted solely for the benefit of its members	■ is established for commercial gain (whether or not it is making a commercial profit)
■ has at least 25 members	■ has at least 25 members
■ is established and conducted wholly or mainly for purposes other than gaming (unless the gaming is restricted to bridge and whist)	■ is established and conducted wholly or mainly for purposes other than gaming (unless the gaming is restricted to bridge and whist)
■ is permanent in nature.	■ is permanent in nature.
Examples include working men's clubs, branches of the Royal British Legion and clubs with political affiliations.	Examples include snooker clubs, clubs established as privately owned companies and clubs established for personal profit.

What are the stakes and prizes?

There may be a maximum value to both the amount that can be staked and the prize that can be offered when playing poker in a club, depending on whether it is a members' club or commercial club, and the type of permit held, if any.

The maximum prizes include money, payments-in-kind, vouchers, goods, donated items, goody bags, buy-ins at other poker tournaments and other items which have a value.

Members' clubs and commercial clubs (with or without club machine permits)

The maximum stake per player is £10 per game, and the combined stakes for your premises must not exceed £250 per day and £1,000 per week.

The maximum prize is £250 per game.

A maximum participation fee of £1 per person per day can be charged by a members' club, with or without a club machine permit. A commercial club with a club machine permit can charge £3 per person per day, but only £1 otherwise.

6: Gambling Act 2005: Additional Material

Members' clubs (with club gaming permits)
Members' clubs with club gaming permits are allowed to offer their members poker with unlimited stakes and prizes.
A maximum participation fee of £3 per person per day can be charged.
Commercial clubs are not entitled to club gaming permits, so they cannot offer poker with unlimited stakes and prizes. There are important tests to determine whether a club is a genuine members' club. Any club which offers poker as the primary or only activity of the club, or on a commercial basis, does not qualify as a members' club under the Gambling Act 2005 and, therefore, cannot have a club gaming permit. For further information, see the separate quick guide called ***Members' club or commercial club?*** which is available on our website.
Money must not be deducted from any stakes or winnings, and no fee can be charged to take part in the poker, other than the participation fees mentioned earlier in this guide.

www.gamblingcommission.gov.uk

Can I run a poker tournament?

The Gambling Commission recommends you take legal advice before you run a poker tournament or league.
A document called ***Advice on gaming in clubs and alcohol-licensed premises: Gambling Act 2005*** is available on our website and has some examples of ways a tournament might be structured which you may find helpful.

Can I host a poker league?

Yes, provided it is not linked gaming. The Gambling Act 2005 says that a single game of poker cannot be played across a number of different premises.
Games of poker are linked if:

- players in more than one club or pub are competing in the same game of poker across premises, and the winner of that game of poker gets a prize
- the amount of the prize is determined by the number of people playing in different games of poker in different clubs or pubs.

Poker tournaments where the winners of games, or top players in a series of games, from various club and pub venues go through to play in a tournament final, would not be linked gaming even if the final was held at another venue, for example a licensed casino. The amount each entrant can win depends on the number of games they have played in the tournament. See the example at the end of this guide.
You should always keep to the stakes and prizes limits already discussed, in particular the limit of £250 per day and £1,000 per week in combined stakes for the premises.

How final prize limits are worked out

The maximum prize for each game is always £250, even if it is a regional or national final. They are regarded as separate and distinct games and cannot be linked to the league games.
For example, if the player in poker league A reaches a tournament final by playing eight games in the league, the total prize can be no larger than £2000 at the club league level. The player can then win a maximum of £250 at the regional final and another £250 at the national final, if played in a club. If the player in league D only plays in three games in the league out of five games available, his or her total prize can be no larger than

£750 at the club league level. Again, the player can then win a maximum of £250 at the regional final and another £250 at the national final.

Gambling Commission January 2011

SOFTWARE

CONDITIONS AND CODES OF PRACTICE APPLICABLE TO: NON-REMOTE GAMING MACHINE TECHNICAL: FULL LICENCES; NON-REMOTE GAMING MACHINE TECHNICAL: SUPPLIER LICENCES; NON-REMOTE GAMING MACHINE TECHNICAL: SOFTWARE LICENCES; NON-REMOTE GAMBLING SOFTWARE LICENCES

To avoid duplication this document has not been reproduced here but can be found at paras 6.2590 – 6.2595 above.

Note

Regulatory return forms (October 2011) and guides as to how to complete them (June 2011) are available from the Gambling Commission's website at www.gamblingcommission.gov.uk

GAMING MACHINE PERMITS CODE OF PRACTICE – CLUB GAMING PERMITS AND CLUB MACHINE PERMITS – ALCOHOL LICENSED PREMISES PERMITS AND PERMISSIONS

To avoid duplication this document has not been reproduced here but can be found at para 6.2660 above.

CODE OF PRACTICE FOR EQUAL CHANCE GAMING IN CLUBS AND PREMISES WITH AN ALCOHOL LICENCE

To avoid duplication this document has not been reproduced here but can be found at para 6.2673 above.

CONDITIONS AND CODES OF PRACTICE APPLICABLE TO: REMOTE GAMING MACHINE TECHNICAL: FULL LICENCES; REMOTE GAMING MACHINE TECHNICAL: SUPPLIER LICENCES; REMOTE GAMING MACHINE TECHNICAL: SOFTWARE LICENCES; REMOTE GAMBLING SOFTWARE LICENCES; REMOTE GAMING MACHINE TECHNICAL: FULL ANCILLARY LICENCES; REMOTE GAMING MACHINE TECHNICAL: SUPPLIER ANCILLARY LICENCES; REMOTE GAMING MACHINE TECHNICAL: SOFTWARE ANCILLARY LICENCES; REMOTE GAMBLING SOFTWARE ANCILLARY LICENCES

To avoid duplication this document has not been reproduced here but can be found at para 6.2600 above.

PERSONAL LICENCES

CONDITIONS AND CODES OF PRACTICE APPLICABLE TO:
PERSONAL MANAGEMENT LICENCES
PERSONAL FUNCTIONAL LICENCES

October 2010

6.2710 Your licence is subject to certain conditions and codes of practice, these are detailed in the following pages

STATUTORY CONDITIONS ATTACHED BY VIRTUE OF THE ACT

SOCIAL RESPONSIBILITY

Statutory Conditions applicable to performing management functions

By virtue of section 82 of the Act as modified by The Gambling (Personal Licences) (Modification of Part 5 of the Gambling Act 2005) Regulations 2006, this licence is subject to a condition that the licensee and persons for whom the licensee is responsible ensure compliance with any relevant social responsibility provision of a code of practice issued by the Commission.

The licensee is responsible for a person if the licensee is required, by the terms of their appointment, to take or share responsibility for the conduct of that person and that person performs an operational function in connection with an activity performed in reliance on an operating licence in connection with which the licensee performs the functions authorised by this licence.

The social responsibility provisions that are relevant to the activities authorised by this licence are set out in the Commission's publication "Licence Conditions and Codes of Practice" available on the Commission's website.

Statutory Conditions applicable to performing operational functions

By virtue of section 82 of the Act, as modified by The Gambling (Personal Licences) (Modification of Part 5 of the Gambling Act 2005) Regulations 2006, this licence is subject to a condition that the licensee ensures compliance with any relevant social responsibility provision of a code of practice issued by the Commission.

The social responsibility provisions that are relevant to the activities authorised by this licence are set out in the Commission's publication "Licence Conditions and Codes of Practice" available on the Commission's website.

RETURN OF STAKES TO CHILDREN

By virtue of section 83 of the Act, as modified by The Gambling (Personal Licences) (Modification of Part 5 of the Gambling Act 2005) Regulations 2006, this licence is subject to a condition that if the licensee becomes aware that a child or young person is using or has used facilities for gambling provided in reliance on an operating licence and in connection with the provision of which the licensee is authorised to perform a specified operational function, the licensee:

(a) must return any money paid in respect of the use of those facilities (whether by way of fee, stake or otherwise) by the child or young person as soon as is reasonably practicable, and

(b) may not give a prize to the child or young person.

The above paragraph does not apply where the licensee does not have authority under the terms and conditions of their employment to act in the way required by that paragraph; but in such a case the licensee must take all reasonable steps to inform a person having the appropriate authority of the relevant matters relating to the child or young person concerned.

This condition does not apply to use of a Category D gaming machine.

SUITE OF GENERAL CONDITIONS TO BE ATTACHED TO PERSONAL LICENCES UNDER SECTION 75 OF THE GAMBLING ACT 2005

(1) Personal licence holders must take all reasonable steps to ensure that the way in which they carry out their responsibilities in relation to licensed activities does not place the holder of the operating or any relevant premises licence in breach of their licence conditions.

(2) Personal licence holders must keep themselves informed of developments in gambling legislation, codes of practice and any Commission guidance (whether issued on the Commission website or communicated direct to licence holders) relevant to their role. Holders of personal functional licences must keep their technical competence in respect of their licensed activities up to date.

(3) Personal licence holders must notify the Commission of the occurrence of any of the following key events within five working days, or as soon as reasonably practicable after the licensee becomes aware of the event's occurrence[1]:

- the imposition of a disciplinary sanction against them, including dismissal, for gross misconduct
- their resignation from a position for which a personal licence is required following commencement of disciplinary proceedings in respect of gross misconduct
- their disqualification from acting as a company director
- the entry of any court judgment against them
- the presentation of a petition for their bankruptcy or sequestration or their entering into an individual voluntary agreement
- their conviction for any criminal offence or receipt of a formal police caution or any other out-of-court disposal
- the imposition of any sanction or penalty against them following an investigation by any professional, statutory, regulatory or government body
- a change in their name or address.

---

[1] Key events can be reported securely online at the Commission's website at www.gamblingcommission.gov.uk or by email to key.events@gamblingcommission.gov.uk or posted to Key Events, Compliance Administration Team, Gambling Commission, Victoria Square House, Victoria Square, Birmingham, B2 4BP

SECRETARY OF STATE GENERAL CONDITIONS

None at present
Gambling Commission October 2010

BANKRUPTCY OF PERSONAL LICENCE HOLDERS

6.2711 November 2008
Dear trade associations,
It has come to our attention that some operators may not be aware of the provisions of the Gambling Act 2005 regarding bankruptcy of personal licence holders.
Section 114 of the Act provides that an operating licence issued to an individual will lapse if the licensee becomes bankrupt. The provisions of this section are applied to personal licence holders by sections 128 and 131 of the Act.
This applies to Personal Management Licence and Personal Function Licence holders. It also applies to bankruptcy of holders of section 19 Gaming Act 1968 certificates employed in Casinos and Bingo clubs, who have been made bankrupt after 1 September

2007. If a section 19 certificate holder was made bankrupt prior to this date, the Commission may still review that certificate under the 2005 Act.
(In Scotland, it is the sequestration of the licensee's estate (under section 12(1) of the Bankruptcy (Scotland) Act 1985), which is the event triggering the lapse of the licence.)
Once the licence lapses, the former personal licence holder will be unable to carry out any of the functions for which a personal licence is required.
The former personal licence holder may apply to the Commission for a new licence, but will need to explain the circumstances of the bankruptcy. The Commission will give due consideration to the application, taking into account all the circumstances, including the financial circumstances of the applicant.
In addition, with effect from 1 January 2009, a personal licence holder, or a partner in a partnership, must notify the Commission where a petition is presented for their bankruptcy (or sequestration in Scotland) or where they enter into an individual voluntary agreement (IVA). This is in effect the start of the bankruptcy process and is not the same as a final bankruptcy order being made. This is in section 15.2 of the October 2008 Licence Conditions and Codes of Practice document (LCCP). For the avoidance of doubt, the licence does not automatically lapse until the bankruptcy order is actually made. The Commission will decide what action to take as a result of being notified of a key event.
I would be grateful if this letter could be brought to the attention of your members. If you have any questions regarding this, please contact me.
Yours sincerely
Hazel Canter
Gambling Commission November 2008

LICENCE CONDITIONS AND CODES OF PRACTICE SUPPLEMENT 11: SUITE OF GENERAL CONDITIONS TO BE ATTACHED TO PERSONAL LICENCES UNDER SECTION 75 OF THE GAMBLING ACT 2005

May 2012

INTRODUCTORY NOTES

6.2712 1.1 The Gambling Commission (the Commission) conducted a consultation in November 2006 to consider the requirement to hold personal licences. The Commission stated at that time that the requirement would be kept under review. The five year maintenance point provides an opportunity to conduct the review and to ensure that this part of the regulatory regime is compliant with the principles of the Hampton Report[1].
1.2 The Commission recently held a consultation with the aim of seeking views and establishing whether the existing requirements as set out in the Licence Conditions and Codes of Practice (LCCP) at 1.2 for personal management licences (PMLs) and personal functional licences (PFLs) remain appropriate and serve to protect the licensing objectives of the Gambling Act 2005 in ways which operators would be unable to do themselves.
1.3 The consultation also sought views on aspects of the maintenance process itself, the Commission's existing approach to disciplinary and regulatory sanctions for personal licence holders (PLs) and an enhancement to the online personal licence register.
1.4 As a result of this consultation the Commission has made some changes to the Suite of general conditions to be attached to personal licences under Section 75 of the Gambling Act 2005 as specified in the LCCP. The resultant change to the LCCP is shown below, where deletions are indicated by use of strikethrough and new text is <u>underlined</u>. A clean text version is also reproduced below with all changes incorporated.

1.5 The amended licence condition will take effect from 15 August 2012.

1 Reducing administrative burdens: effective inspection and enforcement HM Treasury 2005

SUITE OF GENERAL CONDITIONS TO BE ATTACHED TO PERSONAL LICENCES UNDER SECTION 75 OF THE GAMBLING ACT 2005

1 Personal licence holders must take all reasonable steps to ensure that the way in which they carry out their responsibilities in relation to licensed activities does not place the holder of the operating or any relevant premises licence in breach of their licence conditions.
2 Personal licence holders must keep themselves informed of developments in gambling legislation, codes of practice and any Commission guidance (whether issued on the Commission's website or communicated directly to licence holders) relevant to their role. Holders of personal functional licences must keep their technical competence in respect of their licensed activities up to date.
3 Personal licence holders must notify the Commission of the occurrence of any of the following key events within five working days, or as soon as reasonable practicable after the licensee becomes aware of the event's occurrence[2]:

- their subjection to any criminal investigation which is listed under Schedule 7 Relevant Offences of the Gambling Act 2005;
- their conviction of any offence listed under Schedule 7 – Relevant Offences of the Gambling Act 2005;
- any current or pending investigation by a professional, statutory, regulatory or government body in Great Britain or abroad;
- the imposition of any sanction or penalty against them following an investigation by any professional, statutory, regulatory or government body in Great Britain or abroad;
- the imposition of a disciplinary sanction against them, including dismissal, for gross or serious misconduct;
- their resignation from a position for which a personal licence is required following commencement of disciplinary proceedings in respect of gross misconduct;
- their disqualification from acting as a company director;
- *the entry of any court judgment against them;*
- the presentation of a petition for their bankruptcy or sequestration or their entering into an individual voluntary agreement;
- *their conviction of any criminal offence or receipt of a formal police caution or any other out-of-court disposal;*
- a change in their name or address.

2 Key events may be reported securely on-line using the Commission's website at www.gamblingcommission.gov.uk. Or by email to key.events@gamblingcommission.gov.uk or posted to Key Events, Compliance Administration Team, Gambling Commission, Victoria Square House, Victoria Square, Birmingham, B2 4BP

SUITE OF GENERAL CONDITIONS TO BE ATTACHED TO PERSONAL LICENCES UNDER SECTION 75 OF THE GAMBLING ACT 2005

1 Personal licence holders must take all reasonable steps to ensure that the way in which they carry out their responsibilities in relation to licensed activities does not place the holder of the operating or any relevant premises licence in breach of their licence conditions.
2 Personal licence holders must keep themselves informed of developments in gambling legislation, codes of practice and any Commission guidance (whether issued

on the Commission's website or communicated directly to licence holders) relevant to their role. Holders of personal functional licences must keep their technical competence in respect of their licensed activities up to date.

3 Personal licence holders must notify the Commission of the occurrence of any of the following key events within five working days, or as soon as reasonable practicable after the licensee becomes aware of the event's occurrence[3]:

- their subjection to any criminal investigation which is listed under Schedule 7 Relevant Offences of the Gambling Act 2005;
- their conviction of any offence listed under Schedule 7 – Relevant Offences of the Gambling Act 2005;
- any current or pending investigation by a professional, statutory, regulatory or government body in Great Britain or abroad;
- the imposition of any sanction or penalty against them following an investigation by any professional, statutory, regulatory or government body in Great Britain or abroad;
- the imposition of a disciplinary sanction against them, including dismissal, for gross or serious misconduct;
- their resignation from a position for which a personal licence is required following commencement of disciplinary proceedings in respect of gross misconduct;
- their disqualification from acting as a company director;
- the presentation of a petition for their bankruptcy or sequestration or their entering into an individual voluntary agreement;
- a change in their name or address.

---

[3] Key events may be reported securely on-line using the Commission's website at www.gamblingcommission.gov.uk. Or by email to key.events@gamblingcommission.gov.uk or posted to Key Events, Compliance Administration Team, Gambling Commission, Victoria Square House, Victoria Square, Birmingham, B2 4BP

MISCELLANEOUS

CASINO NIGHTS UNDER THE GAMBLING ACT 2005

6.2715 Casino gaming includes games like roulette and blackjack where players compete against the "house" or a banker, rather than against one another on equal terms.

COMMERCIAL CASINO GAMING

Commercial casino gaming is licensed and regulated by the Gambling Commission. If you wish to provide casino gaming on a commercial basis you should consult the Commission: www.gamblingcommission.gov.uk.

CASINO GAMING IN CLUBS

Clubs and miners' welfare institutes that hold a club gaming permit issued by their local licensing authority may provide facilities for two specific types of "banker's" game: chemin de fer and pontoon (blackjack is not permitted). A maximum participation fee of £3 per person, per day may be charged for this gaming, but no amounts may be deducted from either stakes or prizes. See the separate fact sheet on "Gaming in clubs" for further details.

NON-COMMERCIAL CASINO GAMING

Organisations that wish to provide casino games for charitable or other non-commercial purposes (eg to raise funds for a club or society) may do so under the prize gaming provisions in Part 14 of the Act. Non-commercial gaming of this kind may only take place at events where none of the proceeds from the event itself are used for private gain. For these purposes, the proceeds of an event constitute the sums raised by its *organisers* (including sums raised by way of participation fees, sponsorship, commission from traders, or otherwise) minus the costs reasonably incurred in organising the event. However, sums raised by other persons will not form part of the proceeds of the event and so may be appropriated for private gain. An example would be refreshments provided at the event by an independent third party.

Non-commercial gaming may be an ancillary activity or the only or principal purpose of the event. To qualify as prize gaming, the prizes (whether in cash or in kind) should be put up in advance, and must not be dependent on the number of players taking part or the amount of money staked. The players participating in non-commercial gaming must also be told what "good cause" is to benefit from the profits from the gaming. There are no statutory limits on stakes, prizes, participation fees or other charges for this type of non-commercial gaming. No licence, permit or other form of permission is required to operate this kind of gaming provided that the statutory conditions are complied with.

PRIVATE CASINO GAMING

Private casino gaming may take place in two sets of circumstances.

Domestic gaming: in a private dwelling, on a domestic occasion.

Residential gaming: in a hostel, hall of residence or similar establishment (but not on premises operated as a trade or business) provided that the majority of those taking part are residents.

No charge may be made for participation in private gaming (and that includes an entrance fee or other charge for admission), nor may any amounts be deducted from stakes or prizes. Private gaming may not be provided in any place to which the public have access, and no profits may be made from it, regardless of the purpose to which they may be put.

NB. This fact sheet is intended to provide a general explanation of the circumstances in which "casino nights" can be operated under the Gambling Act 2005. It does not deal with every detail of the legislative provisions, or with the individual circumstances of a particular case. This fact sheet does not constitute legal advice and is not a substitute for the relevant legal provisions. If you are in any doubt about the legality of any gambling activities that you intend to promote or for which you intend to provide facilities, you are strongly advised to seek independent legal advice.
Department for Culture Media and Sport
August 2007

RACE NIGHTS UNDER THE GAMBLING ACT 2005

DEFINITION OF A RACE NIGHT

6.2720 "Race nights" are events in which participants stake money on the outcome of recorded or virtual races, where the selection is totally dependent on chance, and where no "odds" or "form" are available to assist the selection. As a general principle, "race nights" may only take place at non-commercial events where none of the proceeds from the event itself are used for private gain. For these purposes, the proceeds of an event constitute the sums raised by its organisers (including sums raised by way of participation fees, sponsorship, commission from traders, or otherwise) minus the costs reasonably incurred in organising the event. However, sums raised by other persons will not form part of the proceeds of the event and so may be appropriated for private gain. An example would be refreshments provided at the event by an independent third party. All participants must be told what "good cause" is to benefit from the profits from the gaming, but no licence, permit or other form of permission is required to operate a race night provided that the statutory conditions are complied with.

Depending on how an event is structured, a "race night" may be operated under either the non-commercial gaming provisions in Part 14 of the Act, or as an incidental non-commercial lottery under Part 1 of Schedule 11. In all cases the prizes may be paid out in cash or in kind.

PRIZE GAMING

To qualify as prize gaming under section 299 of the Act, the prizes should be put up in advance, and must not be dependent on the number of players taking part or the amount of money staked. There are, however, no statutory limits on stakes, prizes, participation fees or other charges for this type of non-commercial gaming, which may be an incidental activity or the only or principal purpose of the event.

EQUAL CHANCE GAMING

Where the prizes awarded are dependent on the number of players taking part, or on the amount of money staked on a race, the non-commercial equal chance gaming provisions in section 300 of the Act apply. Once again, gaming may be either an incidental activity or the only or principal purpose of the event, provided that none of the proceeds are used for private gain. However, for this type of gaming there are limits on the amounts that players may be charged to take part, and on the amount or value of the prizes. The maximum amount that a player may be charged is £8 per day (and this includes entrance or participation fees, stakes and any other payments in relation to the gaming). The total amount paid out in prizes may not exceed £600, although where an event is the final one of a series in which all of the players have previously taken part, a higher prize fund of up to £900 is permitted.

INCIDENTAL LOTTERY

Where the "race night" is not the only or main purpose of a non-commercial event, it may be possible to operate it as an incidental lottery under Schedule 11 to the Act. In this case there are no limits on the amount that players may be charged to participate, but no more than £500 may be deducted from the proceeds of the lottery for the cost of prizes (which may be in cash or in kind), and no more than £100 for other expenses.

PRIVATE GAMING

A "race night" may also be run as equal chance gaming under the private gaming provisions in Schedule 15 to the Act. Private gaming may only occur in a place to which the public does not have access (eg a private dwelling, hostel or hall of residence). No charge may be made for participation in private gaming (and that includes an entrance fee or other charge for admission), nor may any amounts be deducted from stakes or prizes. No profits can be made from private gaming, irrespective of the purpose to which such profits may be put.

NB. This fact sheet is intended to provide a general explanation of the circumstances in which "race nights" can be played under the Gambling Act 2005. It does not deal with every detail of the legislative provisions, or with the individual circumstances of a particular case. This fact sheet does not constitute legal advice and is not a substitute for the relevant legal provisions. If you are in any doubt about the legality of any gambling activities that you intend to promote or for which you intend to provide facilities, you are strongly advised to seek independent legal advice.

Department for Culture Media and Sport
August 2007

POKER UNDER THE GAMBLING ACT 2005

WHAT IS POKER?

6.2725 Poker is a card game which, like bridge, involves elements of both chance and skill. It is therefore classified as a game of chance under the Gambling Act 2005. There are many variations on the game of poker, but the information in this fact sheet relates to **equal chance** poker games, like "Texas Hold 'Em", where players compete against each other, on equal terms. In most forms of the game players bet or stake progressively into a communal pot or kitty, with the player holding the best hand at the end of the betting winning the accumulated stakes. Unequal chance poker (eg "Casino stud poker" where the banker or dealer participates in the game and holds a mathematical edge over the other players) may only be played in licensed casinos or, if it is 'domestic' or 'residential', under the Act's private gaming provisions (see below).

WHERE CAN POKER BE PLAYED?

- In **licensed casinos**, usually in dedicated card rooms or salons – there are no statutory limits on stakes, prizes or other charges for poker played in casinos.
- In **clubs and miners' welfare institutes** – but unless a club or institute holds a club gaming permit from their local licensing authority there are statutory limits on stakes, prizes and participation fees for poker played in these types of premises.
- In **pubs** – once again there are limits on stakes and prizes; no participation fee or other charge may be made.
- At **non-commercial events** where none of the proceeds of the event are used for private gain.

- **On a private occasion** – for example, in a private house or on residential premises, such as a hostel, to which the public do not have access.

POKER IN CLUBS AND INSTITUTES

Members' clubs, commercial clubs and miners' welfare institutes may provide facilities for equal chance poker for their members under the exempt gaming provisions in Part 12 of the Gambling Act. There is a stakes limit of £10 per player per game (n.b. the limit applies to a **game of poker**, not a single hand), as well as aggregate stakes limits of £250 per day and £1000 per week for each individual club or institute. So, for example, a club could run a poker game for 25 players paying £10 each four times per week. The maximum prize in a game of poker is also £250. The maximum charge that a club or institute may make for participating in poker is £1 per player per day, and no deductions or levies are permitted from either stakes or prizes. Where a club holds a club gaming permit issued by their local licensing authority (or, in the case of a commercial club, a club machine permit) the maximum participation fee is £3. Where a club gaming permit is held there are no statutory limits on stakes or prizes. The Gambling Commission has issued a statutory code of practice on gaming in clubs and pubs, which is available from its website: www.gamblingcommission.gov.uk. See also the separate DCMS fact sheet on "Gaming in clubs and miners' welfare institutes" for further details.

POKER IN PUBS

A limited amount of low stakes, social poker may be played in pubs. There is a stakes limit of £5 per player **per game** (not per hand), and the aggregate stakes limit for pub poker is £100 per day for each premises. So, for example, a pub could run a daily poker game involving 20 players staking £5 each. The maximum prize for a game of poker played in a pub is also £100. No charge or entry fee may be made for participating in pub poker and, as with clubs, no deductions or levies may be made from either stakes or prizes. The Gambling Commission has issued a statutory code of practice on gaming in clubs and pubs, which is available from its website: www.gamblingcommission.gov.uk. See also the separate DCMS fact sheet on "Gaming in pubs and other alcohol-licensed premises" for further details.

POKER AT NON-COMMERCIAL EVENTS

Poker may be played at non-commercial events under section 300 of the Gambling Act. Poker, or equal chance gaming more generally, may be the main or sole purpose of the event, but none of the proceeds of a non-commercial event may be used for private gain. These provisions are intended to be used by charities and other non-commercial societies for fund-raising purposes. There are limits on the amounts that players may be charged to take part, and on the amount or value of the prizes. The maximum amount that a player may be charged is £8 per day (and this includes entrance fees, stakes and any other charges in relation to the gaming). The total amount paid out in prizes may not exceed £600, although where an event is the final one of a series in which all of the players have previously taken part, a higher prize fund of up to £900 is permitted (please note that the earlier events must have taken place on a different day to the final).

PRIVATE POKER

Equal chance poker may be played under the private gaming provisions in section 296 of, and Schedule 15 to, the Act. Private gaming may only occur in a place to which the public does not have access (eg a private dwelling, hostel or hall of residence). No charge may be made for participation in private gaming (and that includes an entrance fee or other charge for admission), nor may any amounts be deducted from stakes or prizes.

If private gaming is domestic or residential, the above conditions will apply, but unequal chance poker may also be played. Private gaming is 'domestic' if it takes place in a private dwelling and on a domestic occasion. Private gaming is 'residential' if it takes place in a hostel, hall of residence or similar establishment which is not administered in the course of a trade or business, and more than half of the participants are residents of that hostel, hall of residence or establishment.

NB. This fact sheet is intended to provide a general explanation of the regulatory regime under the Gambling Act 2005 and its subordinate legislation, and does not deal with every detail of the legislative provisions, or with the individual circumstances of a particular case. This fact sheet does not constitute legal advice and is not a substitute for the relevant legislative provisions. If you are in any doubt about the legality of any gambling activities that you intend to promote or for which you intend to provide facilities, you are strongly advised to seek independent legal advice.

DCMS August 2007

CAN I HOLD A RACE NIGHT, CASINO NIGHT OR POKER NIGHT?

6.2726 A non-commercial race night is an event where participants stake money on the outcome of live, recorded or virtual races. And a non-commercial casino night is an event where participants stake money on casino-style games, such as poker or roulette. The money raised from the event is called the proceeds.

Apart from reasonable costs, proceeds:

- must not be used for private gain
- must all be given to a good cause (including any entrance fees, sponsorship, the difference between stakes placed and payout made).

Reasonable costs would include costs reasonably incurred, for example by providing any prizes and for betting slips.

If third parties are selling goods or services at your event, for example if someone is selling refreshments, this does not count as money raised for the charity or good cause and can be retained by that third party.

RACE NIGHTS

Race nights can be permitted for charitable purposes. However, in some circumstances, they can only be undertaken by a licensed betting operator and after the premises owner has notified the local authority. Broadly there are three types of race night. Type one and two can be organised for charitable purposes.

TYPE ONE: NON-COMMERCIAL GAMING

The selection of a 'horse' by a participant is totally dependent on chance, and no 'odds' or 'form' are available to assist the gambler's selection.An example would be the use of archive films of horseracing without revealing the details of each race.

Such nights can be run without a licence, or any other form of permission, providing the operation of the gaming falls into one of the three categories described on the next page.

Incidental non-commercial lottery

Where the race night is not the only or main purpose of a non-commercial event, it is possible to operate it as an incidental lottery.

In this case there are no limits on the amount that players may be charged to participate, but no more than £500 may be deducted from the proceeds of the lottery for the cost of prizes (which may be in cash or in kind), and no more than £100 for other expenses. The organisers can only sell tickets at the event and they have to announce the results at the event. As an example, a 'horse' might be picked at random for each paying customer who is awarded a prize if the horse'wins'.

Non-commercial prize gaming

The players must be told what good cause will benefit from the profits of the gaming. The prizes must be advertised in advance and must not depend on the number of people playing or the stakes raised.
In non-commercial prize gaming, the'race' determines the individual winner or winners, for example, those who have paid are allocated or select a named horse in the race. The winners are then awarded the prizes that had been advertised in advance.

Non-commercial equal chance gaming

Equal chance gaming, which also includes games such as poker or bingo, is gaming where the chances are equally favourable to all participants and players are not competing against a bank.
The maximum amount that a player may be charged is £8 per day (this includes entrance or participation fees, betting stakes and any other payments in relation to the gaming). Organisers must ensure that the total amount paid out in prizes remains below £600 in total across all players.
However, where an event is the final one of a series in which all of the players have previously taken part, a higher prize fund of up to £900 is allowed.
This could take place, for example, where each participant pays a fee for a randomly selected 'horse' in each 'race' and the participant with the winning horse or chooser of the winning horse receives a prize commensurate with the stakes placed.'

TYPE TWO: OCCASIONAL USE NOTICES

This type of race night relies on bets being taken by a licensed betting operator on events, including cases where odds and form are available to gamblers.
It can only be organised at sporting venues under the authority of an occaisional use notice (OUN). It does not matter whether the sporting event on which the bets are taken is held at that venue. The sporting event on which the bets are taken also need not be taking place at the same time as the betting under the OUN.
An OUN must be sent in writing to the relevant local authority in advance of the event and be copied to the chief officer of police for the area in which the venue is located (or, in Scotland, the chief constable of the police force for the area). OUNs may not be used for more than eight days in a calendar year in respect of any one venue.
The person administering the betting under an OUN must have a Gambling Commission operating licence (that is, must be a licensed bookmaker). For further information about betting under an OUN see section 39 of the Gambling Act 2005.

TYPE THREE: PRIVATE GAMING

Private gaming may only occur in a place to which the public does not have access (a private dwelling, hostel, hall of residence or similar establishment).
No charge may be made for participation in private gaming (and that includes an entrance fee or other charge for admission), nor may any amounts be deducted from stakes or prizes. No profits can be made from private gaming, irrespective of how the organiser intended to use those profits **even if intended for charitable purposes.**

CASINO NIGHTS

A non-commercial casino night can be run without a licence, or any other form of permission, providing the operation of the gaming falls into one of the three types:

TYPE ONE: NON-COMMERCIAL PRIZE GAMING

The players must be told what good cause will benefit from the profits of the gaming before placing a bet. The prizes must be advertised in advance and must not depend on the number of people playing or the stakes raised.
The casino gaming determines the individual winner or winners, for example by counting who has the most casino chips at a set time. The winners are then awarded the prizes that have been advertised in advance.

TYPE TWO: NON-COMMERCIAL EQUAL CHANCE GAMING

Casino nights can be held as non-commercial equal chance gaming. Equal chance gaming includes games such as poker or bingo, where the chances are equally favourable to all participants and players are not competing against a bank.
In non-commercial equal chance gaming the charitable funds are usually raised through an entrance fee, participation fee, or through other payments related to the gaming. The maximum amount that a player may be charged is £8 per day (this includes entrance or participation fees, stakes and any other payments in relation to the gaming).
Organisers must ensure that the total amount paid out in prizes remains below £600 in total across all players. However, where an event is the final one of a series in which all of the players have previously taken part, a higher prize fund of up to £900 is allowed.

TYPE THREE: PRIVATE GAMING

Private gaming may only occur in a place to which the public does not have access (a private dwelling, hostel, hall of residence or similar establishment).
No charge may be made for participation in private gaming (and that includes any entrance fee or other charge for admission), nor may any amounts be deducted from stakes or prizes. No profits can be made from private gaming, irrespective of how the organiser intends to use those profits **even if intended for charitable purposes.**

POKER NIGHTS

Poker is equal chance gaming. You do not need a licence, permit or any other form of permission to run a non-commercial equal-chance gaming night (for example, a poker night organised to raise money for charity), as long as you comply with the statutory conditions, including any limits on participation fees, and stakes and prizes.
The players must be told what good cause is to benefit from the profits of the gaming.

STAKES AND PRIZES

No matter how many games you run or a participant expects to play in, they must not make more than one payment (whether as an admission or participation fee, stake or other charge, or a combination of those charges), and this payment must not exceed £8 (per person). The total amount or value of prizes for all the games played at your event must not exceed £600. If you are running more than one event on the same premises and on the same day, you must still comply with the £8 participation fee and £600 total prize limit.
If you are running a series of events held on separate days, the limits of £8 and £600 apply separately to each event. In the final event of a series, where people have qualified by playing at previous events, the total amount or value of prizes for all the games played at the final event can be up to £900.

MONEY'S WORTH

Please be aware that for stakes and prizes, the maximum values include both money and money's worth. Money's worth is the fair or full equivalent of the money that is

paid and includes: payment in-kind, vouchers, goods, donated items, goody-bags, buy-ins at other poker tournaments, or other items which have a value.
Gambling Commission February 2010

Part 7

Miscellaneous Statutes, Statutory Instruments and Forms

Section 1

Betting

NOTE: Although it was originally intended that save for very limited transitional purposes (as to which see the Gambling Act 2005 (Commencement No 6 and Transitional Provisions) Order 2006, SI 2006/3272) at para **10.1537** on accompanying CD) the Betting, Gaming and Lotteries Act 1963 would be repealed in its entirety, the failure to find any method of providing funding to horseracing other than via the Levy has resulted in the need to keep it and the Levy Board alive for the foreseeable future. Although the Tote was sold in July 2011 and as a result various statutory instruments have amended some provisions as noted below, it seems that a number of relevant enactments which one would have expected to be deleted/amended have surprisingly remained as they were. Accordingly, as a result of SI 2007/2102 and SI 2007/2159 ss 12, 14 (as modified), 15 and 24–31 and as a result of Art 2(3) SI 2007/2159, s 55(1) of the 1963 Act remain in force.

We include below only those provisions which are not merely of transitional effect; the complete text of the Act is included on the disc which will accompany this edition.

STATUTES

BETTING, GAMING AND LOTTERIES ACT 1963

(1963 c 2)

Arrangement of sections

PART I

BETTING

AN ACT to consolidate certain enactments relating to betting, gaming, lotteries and connected matters.

[28 February 1963]

Repeal

Repealed by the Gambling Act 2005, s 356(3)(f), (4), Sch 17 from 1 September 2007: see SI 2006/3272, art 3(1); for savings and transitional provisions in relation to the Totalisator Board and the Levy Board, see SI 2007/2102 and SI 2007/2159.

PART I
BETTING

The Totalisator Board and pool betting on horse races[1]

7.1 12 Horserace Totalisator Board

(1) There shall be a Horserace Totalisator Board (in this Act referred to as 'the Totalisator Board') which shall be a body corporate and have perpetual succession and a common seal.

(2) The Totalisator Board shall consist of [a chairman and such number of other members as the Secretary of State may determine, all of whom][1A] shall be appointed by the Secretary of State and hold and vacate office in accordance with the terms of the respective instruments under which they are appointed.

(3) The Totalisator Board may pay to any member of the Board such remuneration, and travelling, subsistence or other allowances at such rates, as the Board may with the approval of the Secretary of State determine:

Provided that the Board shall not by virtue of this subsection have power to pay remuneration to any member of the Board who is for the time being a member of, or nominated as a candidate for election to, the House of Commons.

[(3A) The Board may pay such pension or gratuity to or in respect of any member of the Board as the Board may, with the approval of the Secretary of State, determine.][2]

(4) The Totalisator Board may appoint officers, servants and agents on such terms as to remuneration, pensions or otherwise as the Board may determine.

(5) The Totalisator Board may regulate their own procedure and make standing orders governing the conduct of their business.

(6) No act or proceeding of the Totalisator Board shall be questioned on account of any vacancy in the number of the members thereof or on account of the appointment of any member having been defective.

(7) Except where the context otherwise requires, any reference in any Act or other document to the Racecourse Betting Control Board[3] shall be construed as a reference to the Totalisator Board.[4]

Previous corresponding enactment: Racecourse Betting Act 1928, s 2; Betting Levy Act 1961, s 7.

1 Cross-heading: words deleted by virtue of the Horserace Betting and Olympic Lottery Act 2004, s 1(1). Date in force: 13 July 2011: see SI 2011/1704, art 2.

1A Sub-s (2) amended by the Horserace Totalisator and Betting Levy Boards Act 1972, s 2.

2 Sub-s (3A) inserted by the Social Security Act 1985, s 25(1).

3 This was the original name of the Board under the Racecourse Betting Act 1928, before its reconstitution under the Betting Levy Act 1961, s 7(1).

4 See the National Lottery etc Act 1993, s 17, for extensions of the powers of the Horserace

Totalistator Board.

7.2
13 [*Repealed by the Gambling Act 2005, s 356(3)(f), (4), Sch 17.*]

7.3 14 Functions of Totalisator Board with respect to betting on horse races

(1) The Totalisator Board [shall have the exclusive right] to do, and to authorise other persons to do, either of the following things, that is to say—

(a) to carry on pool betting business[1] in any form on a recognised horse race; 1 and

(b) by way of business to receive or negotiate bets on a recognised horse race on terms that the winnings or any part thereof shall be calculated or regulated directly or indirectly by reference to the amounts or rates of any payments or distributions in respect of winning bets on that race made by way of sponsored pool betting;[1]

and in giving any authority under this subsection the Board may do so on such terms, including terms as to payments to the Board, as the Board may think fit.

(2) Any infringement of the right conferred on the Totalisator Board by the foregoing subsection shall be actionable at the suit of the Board; and in any action for such an infringement all such relief, by way of damages, injunction, accounts or otherwise, shall be available to the Board as is available to the plaintiff in any corresponding proceedings in respect of infringements of proprietary rights and, notwithstanding anything to the contrary in any enactment or rule of law relating to the jurisdiction of county courts, a county court may, on the application of the Board, grant an injunction restraining an infringement or apprehended infringement of the right aforesaid whether or not any other relief is claimed; and for the purposes of this subsection the right aforesaid is infringed by any person who, without the authority of the Board—

(a) does or authorises any other person to do any thing such as is mentioned in subsection (1)(a) or (b) of this section; or

(b) by way of business holds himself out as willing to enter into any pool betting transaction on a recognised horse race, whether by way of sponsored pool betting or otherwise, or to receive or negotiate a bet on a recognised horse race on such terms as are mentioned in the said subsection (1)(b).

(3) Where bets on a race[2] or combination of races are made by way of sponsored pool betting, the Totalisator Board shall—

(a) cause to be deducted from the aggregate amount staked either—

(i) such percentage of that amount as may be determined from time to time by the Board, either generally or with respect to any particular racecourse;[3] or

(ii) if so determined as aforesaid, such percentage of such part of that amount as may be determined as aforesaid; and

(b) cause the whole of the remainder of that amount to be distributed among the persons making such of those bets as are winning bets.

(4) Where facilities for sponsored pool betting are being provided on an approved racecourse by the persons having the management of that racecourse, any amount deducted by those persons under subsection (3)(a) of this section shall be paid to the Totalisator Board,[4] but the Board may pay to those persons the amount of the expenses shown to the satisfaction of the Board to have been properly incurred by those persons in connection with the provision of those facilities.

(5) Without prejudice to section 12(4) of this Act, the Totalisator Board may remunerate any person, by the payment of commissions or otherwise, in respect of the negotiation, receipt or transmission by that person—

(a) of bets to be made by way of sponsored pool betting; or

(b) of bets such as are mentioned in subsection (1)(b) of this section to be made with the Board or, under the authority of the Board, with the persons having the management of an approved horse racecourse

and may provide facilities on any such racecourse for persons engaged in receiving bets to be so made.[5]

(6) Nothing in this Act shall be construed as restricting the betting transactions which may be effected by way of sponsored pool betting to betting transactions upon the result of a single race, or upon the results of races run on a particular racecourse or on a particular day, or as preventing the Totalisator Board from giving credit in any betting transaction.

Previous corresponding enactments: Racecourse Betting Act 1928, s 3(3); Betting and Lotteries Act 1934, s 18; Betting and Gaming Act 1960, s 11.

Note:

see SI 2007/2102 which provides special definitions for some of the expressions used in s 14.

Sub-ss (1) and (3)(a)(i) are printed as amended by the Horserace Totalisator and Betting Levy Boards Act 1972, s 1(3)(b), (5).

Words omitted from sub-s (2) apply to Scotland.

---

1 See the definition in BGLA 1963, s 55(1).

2 Or, in the case of pool betting by means of facilities provided by the Board, any event other than a race; see the HTBLBA 1972, s 1(3)(a).

3 In relation to pool betting by means of facilities provided by the Board, for the word 'racecourse' substitute 'case or class of cases'; see the HTBLBA 1972, s 1(3)(b).

4 Where the facilities are provided with the authority of the Board, the Board may allow the amount deducted or part of it to be retained; see the HTBLBA 1972, s 4(1).

5 This sub-s does not limit the powers of the Board under s 15(1)(d); see the HTBLBA 1972, s 1(4).

7.4 15 Additional powers and duties of Totalisator Board

(1) The Totalisator Board shall have power—

(a) to acquire and hold such land as may be reasonably required for the purposes of any of their functions and to sell or lease any land held by them which is not required for those purposes;

(b) to borrow for the purposes of any of their functions and to give security for any moneys borrowed by them;

(c) to make such loans or investments as they judge desirable for the proper conduct of their affairs, being loans or investments either—

(i) such as, under the enactments for the time being in force, a trustee would be authorised to make out of trust funds; or

(ii) approved, or of a description approved, by the Secretary of State;

(d) to do all such things as are incidental to, or conducive to the attainment of the purposes of, any of their functions.

(2) Subject to section 14(3) to (5) of this Act, the Totalisator Board shall apply any moneys from time to time available in their hands—

(a) in providing for the payment of rates, taxes, charges, expenses and other outgoings;

(b) in making provision for the payment of any contribution for the time being payable by them under section 30 of this Act;

(c) in making such other provision in connection with any of their functions as they think proper.

Previous corresponding enactments: Betting and Gaming Act 1960, s 11(3); Betting Levy Act 1961, s 7(6), (7).

Contributions for benefit of horse racing by bookmakers and Totalisator Board

7.5 24 Horserace Betting Levy Board

(1) There shall be a Horserace Betting Levy Board (in this Act referred to as 'the Levy Board') which shall be charged with the duty of assessing and collecting in accordance with the subsequent provisions of this Part of this Act, and of applying, subject to those provisions, for purposes conducive to any one or more of the following, that is to say—

(a) the improvement of breeds of horses;

(b) the advancement or encouragement of veterinary science or veterinary education;

(c) the improvement of horse racing,

monetary contributions from bookmakers and the Totalisator Board.

(2) The Levy Board shall consist of a chairman and seven other members of whom—

(a) the chairman and two other members shall be appointed by the Secretary of State and be persons who the Secretary of State is satisfied have no interests connected with horse racing which might hinder them from discharging their functions as members of the Board in an impartial manner;

[(b) three members shall be appointed by the Jockey Club (incorporating the National Hunt Committee);][1]

(d) one member shall be the chairman for the time being of the Bookmakers' Committee; and

(e) one member shall be the chairman for the time being of the Totalisator Board.

(3) Any person appointed to be a member of the Levy Board under subsection (2)(a) of this section shall hold and vacate office in accordance with the terms of the instrument under which he was appointed; and any person appointed to be a member of the Board under [subsection (2)(b)][1] of this section may be removed from the Board at any time by the body by whom he was appointed.

(4) The Jockey Club [(incorporating the National Hunt Committee)][1], the Bookmakers' Committee and the Totalisator Board respectively may from time to time appoint a person to act in the place of such a member of the Levy Board as is mentioned in [subsection (2)(b), (d) or (e)][1,2], as the case may be, of this section at any meeting of the Levy Board at which that member is unable to be present, and while so acting any such person shall be deemed for the purposes of any act or proceeding of the Levy Board to be a member of that Board.

(5) The Levy Board shall be a body corporate and shall have perpetual succession and a common seal.

(6) The Levy Board may pay to the chairman and the two other members appointed by the Secretary of State such remuneration, and to any member of the Board travelling, subsistence or other allowances at such rates, as the Board may with the approval of the Secretary of State determine.

[(6A) The Levy Board may pay such pension or gratuity as the Board may, with the approval of the Secretary of State, determine, to or in respect of the chairman and any other members appointed by the Secretary of State.][3]

(7) The Levy Board may appoint officers, servants and agents on such terms as to remuneration, pensions or otherwise as the Board may determine.

(8) The Levy Board may regulate their own procedure and make standing orders governing the conduct of their business.

(9) No act or proceeding of the Levy Board shall be questioned on account of any vacancy in the number of the members thereof or on account of the appointment of any member having been defective.

Previous corresponding enactment: Betting Levy Act 1961, s 1.

---

1 Amended by the Horserace Betting and Olympic Lottery Act 2004, s 13, Sch 2, paras 1, 12. Date in force: 13 July 2011: see SI 2011/1704, art 2.

2 Sub-ss (2)–(4) are printed as amended by the Horserace Betting Levy Act 1969, s 6(2)–(4).

3 Sub-s (6A) inserted by the Social Security Act 1985, s 25(2).

7.6 25 General powers and duties of Levy Board

(1) The Levy Board shall have power—

(a) with the approval of, and subject to any conditions imposed by, the Secretary of State, to engage in any activity connected with any of the matters specified in section 24(1)(a) to (c) of this Act;

(b) to acquire and hold such land as may be reasonably required for the purposes of any of their functions and to sell or lease any land held by them which is not required for those purposes;

(c) to borrow for the purposes of any of their functions and to give security for any moneys borrowed by them;

(d) to lend or invest money for the purposes of or in connection with any activity in which they have power under paragraph (a) of this subsection to engage;

[(e) to make such other investments as—

(i) they judge desirable for the proper conduct of their affairs, and

(ii) a trustee would be able to make under the general power of investment in section 3 of the Trustee Act 2000 (as restricted by sections 4 and 5 of that Act);][1]

(f) to do all such things as are incidental to, or conducive to the attainment of the purposes of, any of their functions.

(2) The Levy Board shall apply any moneys from time to time available in their hands—

(a) in providing for the payment of rates, taxes, charges, expenses and other outgoings, including any sums which they are required or authorised to pay by virtue of [any enactment];[2]

(b) in retaining such sums and making provision for such matters as they think proper in connection with any of their functions.

(c) in making such payments as they think fit for charitable purposes;

(d) subject to the foregoing paragraphs of this subsection, in making payments, in accordance with schemes from time to time prepared by the Levy Board and approved with or without modifications by the Secretary of State, for such purposes as are mentioned in section 24(1) of this Act. [3]

---

1 Sub-s (1)(e) is substituted by the Trustee Act 2000, s 40(1), Sch 2, Pt II, para 34.

2 Sub-s (2)(a) is printed as amended by the Horserace Betting Levy Act 1969, s 7(3).

3 These purposes include the provision on approved horse racecourses of facilities for sponsored pool betting; see the Horserace Totalisator and Betting Levy Boards Act 1972, s 4(2).

7.7 26 Bookmakers' Committee

(1) For the purposes of the contributions such as are mentioned in section 24(1) of this Act to be made by bookmakers, there shall be a committee, which shall be known as the Bookmakers' Committee, constituted in such manner as the Secretary of State may, after consultation with any body appearing to him to be representative of the interests[1] of bookmakers generally, by regulations made by statutory instrument provide.

(2) Provision may be made, and from time to time varied, by a scheme under this subsection for the payment of remuneration to all or any of the members of the Bookmakers' Committee, and for the provision of secretarial and other facilities for that committee; and such a scheme—

(a) may be made at any time by agreement between the committee and the Levy Board; or

(b) on any occasion on which proposals for such a scheme are made by the committee or by the Levy Board but the committee and the Board cannot agree thereon, may be made by the three persons for the time being appointed to be members of the Levy Board by the Secretary of State.

(3) The Levy Board shall pay—

(a) any amounts payable by virtue of any scheme under subsection (2) of this section;

(b) any other expenses incurred by the Bookmakers' Committee for the purposes of this Act with the approval, whether general or special, of the Levy Board;

(c) any travelling and other expenses reasonably incurred by any person as a member of the Bookmakers' Committee.

(4) The Bookmakers' Committee may regulate their own procedure and make standing orders governing the conduct of their business.

(5) No act or proceeding of the Bookmakers' Committee shall be questioned on account of any vacancy in the number of the members thereof or on account of the appointment of any person as a member thereof having been defective.

Previous corresponding enactment: Betting Levy Act 1961, s 3(3), Sch 1.

[1] See the Horserace Betting Levy (Bookmakers' Committee) Regulations 2003, SI 2003/1909.

7.8 27 Bookmakers' levy schemes

(1) The contributions such as are mentioned in section 24(1) of this Act to be made by bookmakers shall be paid by way of a levy in respect of each levy period in accordance with a scheme having effect for that period under this section; and in this Act the expression 'levy period' means a period of twelve months beginning with 1st April in any year.

(2) Any such scheme shall include provision—

(a) for securing that the levy shall be payable only by a bookmaker who carries on on his own account a business which includes the effecting of betting transactions on horse-races, and only in respect of so much of the business of the bookmaker as relates to such betting transactions;

(b) for bookmakers to be divided for the purposes of the levy into different categories;

(c) for the amount, if any, payable by way of the levy by any particular bookmaker to be determined by reference to the category into which he falls;

(d) as to the method of the promulgation of the scheme by the Levy Board;

(e) for the submission to the Levy Board by each bookmaker before a specified date of a declaration as to the category into which he falls;

(f) for the issue by the Levy Board of notices of assessment to, and certificates of exemption from, the levy.

(3) Not later than such date before the beginning of any levy period as the Levy Board may determine, the Bookmakers' Committee shall make recommendations to the Levy Board with respect to the scheme to have effect under this section for that period, and those recommendations shall take the form either of a draft scheme or of a recommendation that the current scheme shall continue to have effect without amendment or with specified amendments.

(4) If the Levy Board approve the recommendations aforesaid, or those recommendations as revised by the Bookmakers' Committee in the light of any observations thereon made to the committee by the Board, the scheme so recommended and approved shall have effect accordingly for the levy period in question.[1]

(5) . . .[2]

Previous corresponding enactment: Betting Levy Act 1961, s 3.

---

1 For the position in the event of non-approval by the Board, see the Horserace Betting Levy Act 1969, s 1.

2 Sub-s (5): repealed by the Horserace Betting Levy Act 1969, s 7(4).

7.9 28 Assessment of or exemption from bookmakers' levy

(1)–(4) . . .[1]

(5) An assessment notice issued by the Levy Board in the case of any bookmaker for any levy period shall be conclusive as to his liability to the levy for that period and the amount payable by him by way thereof unless not later than twenty-eight days after the notice is served on him he gives to the Board notice in writing of appeal therefrom.

(6) On receiving any notice of appeal under the last foregoing subsection, the Levy Board shall refer the appeal to an appeal tribunal established in pursuance of section 29 of this Act, which shall have power to confirm, increase or reduce the assessment, or grant the appellant a certificate of exemption from the levy, according to the tribunal's opinion as to the category into which he falls, but which—

(a) shall not reduce the assessment or grant the appellant a certificate of exemption unless the appellant has afforded the tribunal all the facilities it may have required for the investigation of his case;

(b) shall confirm the assessment unless the tribunal is satisfied that, on all the evidence made available to it, the assessment should be varied or rescinded;

and any decision of the tribunal as to the category into which the appellant falls for the purposes of the levy for the levy period in question shall be final.[2]

(7) Any amount assessed as payable by any bookmaker by way of the levy in respect of any levy period shall [(except to the extent of any payments on account)][3] become due twenty-eight days after notice of the assessment has been served on the bookmaker or, if he appeals therefrom in pursuance of the foregoing provisions of this section, on the determination or abandonment of the appeal, and shall be recoverable by the Levy Board as a debt due to them.

(8) Upon the discharge by a bookmaker of his liability by way of the levy in respect of any levy period [in accordance with the notice of assessment issued in his case],[4] the Levy Board shall issue to him a certificate in writing to the effect that he has done so, and any such certificate shall be conclusive evidence of the facts stated therein.

(9) An assessment notice may be served on any bookmaker either by serving it on him personally or by sending it to him by post at his usual or last-known residence or place of business in the United Kingdom or, if the bookmaker is a company, at the company's registered office.

(10) If, otherwise than with the consent in writing of the bookmaker concerned or—

(a) for the purposes of this section [or section 2 of the Horserace Betting Levy Act 1969][5] or of a report of any proceedings before an appeal tribunal thereunder; or

(b) for the purposes of, or of a report of—

(i) proceedings for the recovery from that bookmaker of any amount due from him [under this section][6] by way of the levy; or

(ii) proceedings relating to that bookmaker before an appropriate authority within the meaning of Schedule 1 to this Act, or before any court on an appeal from any such authority; or

(iii) any criminal proceedings,

any person who is a member, officer or servant of the Levy Board, the Bookmakers' Committee or an appeal tribunal established in pursuance of section 29 of this Act, or who is consulted by the Bookmakers' Committee in pursuance of subsection (4) of this section [or by members of the Levy Board in pursuance of section 2(4) of the said Act of 1969],[5] discloses to any other person in such a manner as to identify the bookmaker concerned any declaration by or assessment on any bookmaker for the purposes of the levy, or any other information concerning that bookmaker obtained through the exercise of any functions under this section [or under section 2 of the said Act of 1969],[6] or any ruling of the Bookmakers' Committee or an appeal tribunal as to the category into which any bookmaker falls, he shall be liable on summary conviction to a fine not exceeding [level 5 on the standard scale].[7, 8]

Previous corresponding enactment: Betting Levy Act 1961, s 4.

---

1 Sub-ss (1)–(4) repealed by the Horserace Betting Levy Act 1969, s 7(4).

2 As to the expenses of the Levy Board, see the HBLA 1969, s 3.

3 Words in square brackets inserted by the HBLA 1981, s 4(6), Schedule, para 1(a).

4 Words in square brackets inserted by the HBLA 1981, para 1(b).

5 Words in square brackets inserted by the HBLA 1969, s 2(5).

6 Words in square brackets inserted by the HBLA 1981, s 4(6), Schedule, para 1(c).

7 £500 was substituted for £100 in pursuance of the Criminal Justice Act 1982, s 39(2), Sch 3 and the new figure replaced by the words in square brackets in pursuance of the CJA 1982, s 46. See also note 6 to BGLA 1963, s 1.

8 See SI 2007/2159, art 2(2) which makes specific provision to disapply s 28(10) in the case of certain communications between the Levy Board and the Gambling Commission.

7.10 29 Levy Appeal Tribunals

(1) There shall be established for the purposes of section 28 of this Act [and section 2 of the Horserace Betting Levy Act 1981]—

(a) one or more appeal tribunals for England and Wales; and

(b) one or more appeal tribunals for Scotland;

and an appeal under section 28(5) of this Act [or section 2(1) of the said Act of 1981] shall be referred to a tribunal established for Scotland if the appellant is the holder of a bookmaker's permit which was last granted or renewed by an authority in Scotland.

(2) Each such tribunal shall consist of a chairman and two other members of whom—

(a) the chairman, who shall be

[[(i) a person who satisfies the judicial-appointment eligibility condition on a 5-year basis; or]

(ii) an advocate or solicitor in Scotland of at least [5] years' standing,]

shall be appointed by the Lord Chancellor or, in the case of a tribunal established for Scotland, by the Lord President of the Court of Session; and

(b) the other members shall be appointed by the Secretary of State;

and each member of any such tribunal shall hold office in accordance with the terms of the instrument under which he was appointed[, but subject, in the case of the chairman, to subsection (2A) of this section].

[(2A) The chairman of any such tribunal shall vacate his office on the day on which he attains the age of seventy years; but this subsection is subject to section 26(4) to (6) of the Judicial Pensions and Retirement Act 1993 (power to authorise continuance in office up to the age of seventy-five years).]

(3) The procedure of any such tribunal shall be such as the Lord Chancellor or, in the case of a tribunal established for Scotland, the Lord President of the Court of Session may by rules prescribe; and any such rules shall be made by statutory instrument, which shall be subject to annulment in pursuance of a resolution of either House of Parliament.

(4) The Levy Board shall pay to the members of any such tribunal such remuneration as the Board may with the approval of the Secretary of State determine and any travelling and other expenses reasonably incurred by them as members of the tribunal.

(5) The Levy Board shall provide any such tribunal with such secretarial and other facilities as may appear to the Board to be necessary or expedient, and, without prejudice to subsection (7) of this section, shall pay any expenses incurred by the tribunal for the purposes of their functions with the approval, whether general or special, of the Levy Board.

(6) If any such tribunal thinks it just so to direct in allowing any appeal by a bookmaker, the Levy Board shall pay to that bookmaker such amount as the tribunal may specify towards expenses appearing to the tribunal to have been reasonably incurred by the bookmaker in connection with the appeal.

(7) If any such tribunal, in dismissing any appeal by a bookmaker, or on the abandonment of any appeal after the tribunal has taken some action towards its determination, thinks it just that the bookmaker should make a payment towards expenses incurred by the tribunal in connection with the appeal, the tribunal may certify accordingly and the Levy Board shall be entitled to recover from the bookmaker as a debt due to them the amount specified in the certificate.

7.11 30 Contributions by Totalisator Board[1]

(1) Subject to subsection (2) of this section, the contribution such as is mentioned in section 24(1) of this Act to be paid by the Totalisator Board in respect of any levy period shall be such as may be determined before the beginning of that period by the Levy Board after consultation with the Totalisator Board.

(2) . . . [2]

Previous corresponding enactment: Betting Levy Act 1961, s 6.

---

1 Heading and sub-s(1) amended and new sub-s (1A) inserted by the Horserace Betting and Olympic Lottery Act 2004, s 13, Sch 2, paras 1, 13. Date in force: 13 July 2011: see SI 2011/1704, art 2.

2 Sub-s (2), which dealt with objections and their determination, repealed by the Horserace Betting Levy Act 1969, s 7(4). In relation to such matters see now the HBLA 1969, s 5.

Accounts and reports of Levy Board and Totalisator Board

7.12 31 Accounts of, and reports by, Levy Board and Totalisator Board

(1) The Levy Board and the Totalisator Board shall each keep proper accounts and proper records in relation to those accounts and prepare proper statements of account in respect of each levy period; and the accounts of each of the Boards for each such period shall be audited by qualified accountants appointed for the purpose by the Board in question for that period.[1]

(2) As soon as the accounts of the Totalisator Board for any levy period have been audited, that Board shall submit a copy of their statements of account and the auditor's report thereon for that period, together with a report of their proceedings during that period, to the Levy Board; and the Levy Board shall submit to the Secretary of State a report of the proceedings during that period both of the Levy Board and of the Totalisator Board, which shall include the statements of account and the auditor's report for that period of each of the Boards; and the Secretary of State shall cause a copy of the Levy Board's report to be laid before each House of Parliament.

(3) The Levy Board shall cause copies of any report submitted by them under the last foregoing subsections to be made and kept available at their offices for inspection by the public without charge during reasonable hours and for supply on demand to any member of the public upon payment of such reasonable charge in respect of each copy as the Board may determine.

Previous corresponding enactment: Betting Levy Act 1961, s 8.

---

1 Sub-s (1) amended and sub-s (2) substituted by the Horserace Betting and Olympic Lottery Act 2004, s 13, Sch 2, paras 1, 14 from a date to be appointed.

7.12A 55 Interpretation, etc—general

(1) In this Act, except where the context otherwise requires, the following expressions have the following meanings respectively, that is to say—

'approved horse racecourse' means any ground in respect of which there is for the time being in force a certificate of approval of that ground as a horse racecourse issued by the [Levy Board] under section 13 of this Act;[1]

['bet' does not include any bet made or stake hazarded in the course of, or incidentally to, any gaming;]

'betting agency permit' has the meaning assigned by section 9(2) of this Act;

'betting office licence' has the meaning assigned by section 9(1) of this Act;

'betting transaction' includes the collection or payment of winnings on a bet and any transaction in which one or more of the parties is acting as a bookmaker;[1]

'bookmaker' means any person other than the Totalisator Board who—

(a) whether on his own account[2] or as servant or agent to any other person, carries on, whether occasionally or regularly, the business of receiving or negotiating bets or conducting pool betting operations; or

(b) by way of business in any manner holds himself out, or permits himself to be held out, as a person who receives or negotiates bets or conducts such operations,

so, however, that a person shall not be deemed to be a bookmaker by reason only of the fact—

(i) that he carries on, or is employed in, sponsored pool betting business; or[1]

(ii) that he operates, or is employed in operating, a totalisator;

and the expression 'bookmaking' shall be construed accordingly;

'Bookmakers' Committee' means the committee established in accordance with section 26 of this Act;

'bookmaker's permit' has the meaning assigned by section 2(1) of this Act;

'contravention', in relation to any requirement, includes a failure to comply with that requirement, and cognate expressions shall be construed accordingly;

'dog race' means a race in which an object propelled by mechanical means is pursued by dogs, and 'dog racecourse' shall be construed accordingly;

['game of chance'[3] and 'gaming' have the same meanings as in the Gaming Act 1968;][1]

['inter-track betting scheme' means a scheme for the pooling of bets made by means of totalisators on different licensed tracks, being bets on a dog race run on a track participating in the scheme or on a combination of dog races run on the same participating track;]

'the Levy Board' means the Horserace Betting Levy Board established in accordance with section 24 of this Act;

'levy period' has the meaning assigned by section 27(1) of this Act;

'licensed betting office' means premises in respect of which a betting office licence is for the time being in force;

['licensed inter-track betting scheme' means an inter-track betting scheme in respect of which a licence under Schedule 5ZA to this Act is for the time being in force;]

'licensed track' means a track in respect of which a track betting licence is for the time being in force;

'licensee' in relation to a licensed betting office, means the holder of the betting office licence for the time being in force in respect of that office;

'money' includes a cheque, banknote, postal order or money order;

. . .

'player', in relation to a game of chance, includes any person taking part in the game against whom other persons taking part in the game stake, play or bet;[1]

'pool betting' has the same meaning as for the purposes of [the Betting and Gaming Duties Act 1981];

'pool betting business' means business involving the receiving or negotiating of bets made by way of pool betting;

'premises' includes any place and, in sections 1, 32 and 33 of this Act, also includes any vessel;

'prescribed' means prescribed by regulations made by the Secretary of State by statutory instrument,[4] which shall be subject to annulment in pursuance of a resolution of either House of Parliament, and any such regulations may make different provision for different circumstances;

['qualified accountant' means a person who is eligible for appointment as a company auditor under section 25 of the Companies Act 1989;]

'recognised horse race' means a horse race run on an approved horse racecourse on a day when horse races and no other races take place on that racecourse;

'registered pool promoter' has the meaning assigned by section 4(2) of this Act;

'sponsored pool betting' means pool betting by means of facilities provided by the Totalisator Board or provided on an approved horse racecourse with the authority of that Board by the persons having the management of that racecourse;

'ticket', in relation to any lottery or proposed lottery, includes any document evidencing the claim of a person to participate in the chances of the lottery;

'totalisator' means the contrivance for betting known as the totalisator or pari mutuel, or any other machine or instrument of betting of a like nature, whether mechanically operated or not;

'the Totalisator Board' means the Horserace Totalisator Board established in accordance with section 12 of this Act;

'track' means premises on which races of any description, athletic sports or other sporting events take place;

'track betting licence' has the meaning assigned by section 6(1) of this Act;

'winnings' includes winnings of any kind and any reference to the amount or to the payment of winnings shall be construed accordingly.

(2), (3) . . .

(4) [*Applies to Scotland only*.]

(5) Save where the context otherwise requires, any reference in this Act to any enactment shall be construed as a reference to that enactment as amended by or under any other enactment.

Previous corresponding enactments: Racecourse Betting Act 1928, s 1(3); Betting and Lotteries Act 1934, ss 20(1), 28; Pool Betting Act 1954, ss 1(5), 11(1), 12(4); Small Lotteries and Gaming Act 1956, s 2(3); Betting and Gaming Act 1960, s 28, Sch 1, para 22, Sch 3, para 7, Sch 5, paras 6–8; Betting Levy Act 1961, s 8(5), Sch 2, para 3(2).

Words in square brackets in definition 'approved horse racecourse' substituted by the Horserace Totalisator and Betting Levy Boards Act 1972, s 5(1).

Definition 'bet' inserted by the Gaming Act 1968, s 53, Sch 11, Pt I.

Definitions 'game of chance' and 'gaming' substituted by the Gaming Act 1968, s 53, Sch 11, Pt I.

Definitions 'inter-track betting scheme' and 'licensed inter-track betting scheme' inserted by the Deregulation (Greyhound Racing) Order 1995, SI 1995/3231, art 5(4).

Words omitted between definitions 'money' and 'player' repealed by the Lotteries and Amusements Act 1976, s 25, Sch 5.

Words in square brackets in definition 'pool betting' substituted by the Betting and Gaming Duties Act 1981, s 34(1), Sch 5, para 1.

Word and figures in italics in the definition of 'premises' no longer have effect (due to the repeal of the BGLA 1963, ss 32, 33 by the Gaming Act 1968, s 53(1)(c), Sch 12) and should, therefore, be disregarded. As a consequence of that repeal the word 'sections' in this definition should read as 'section'.

Definition 'qualified accountant' substituted by the Companies Act 1989 (Eligibility for Appointment as Company Auditor) (Consequential Amendments) Regulations 1991, SI 1991/1997, reg 2, Schedule, para 11. For transitional provisions as to termination and resignation of appointments, see SI 1991/1997, reg 4 of those Regulations.

Sub-s (2) repealed by the Lotteries and Amusements Act 1976, s 25, Sch 5.

Sub-s (3) repealed by the Administration of Justice Act 1964, s 41(8), Sch 5.

---

1 A betting transaction takes place whenever a substantial part of the transaction, eg the handing in of a betting slip or coupon with the stake, takes place; see *Stovell v Jameson* [1940] 1 KB 92, [1939] 4 All ER 76; *Zeidman v Owen* [1950] 1 KB 593, [1950] 1 All ER 290.

2 Each partner in a partnership who acts as a bookmaker does so 'on his own account'; see *Dungate v Lee* [1969] 1 Ch 545, [1967] 1 All ER 241.

3 In order for there to be a game of chance there must be a game played by players who do something; see *Director of Public Prosecutions v Regional Pool Promotions Ltd* [1964] 2 QB 244, [1964] 1 All ER 65, and *Armstrong v Director of Public Prosecutions* [1965] 1 All ER 1012; affd [1965] AC 1262, [1965] 2 All ER 745, HL.

4 Regulations made under corresponding repealed provisions are continued in force by BGLA 1963, s 57(3). See the Betting (Licensing) Regulations 1960, SI 1960/1701, the Betting (Bookmakers' Agents) Regulations 1960, SI 1960/2333, and the Betting Levy (Particulars of Bookmakers' Permits) Regulations 1961, SI 1961/1547; the Licensed Betting Offices Regulations 1986, SI 1986/103, as amended by SI 1993/51, SI 1995/578, SI 1997/1071, were made

in pursuance of BGLA 1963, s 10(6). See also the notes to BGLA 1963, Sch 5, para 3.

HORSERACE BETTING LEVY ACT 1969

(1969 c 14)

AN ACT to make further provision with respect to the contributions to be made under Part I of the Betting, Gaming and Lotteries Act 1963, by bookmakers and the Totalisator Board to the Horserace Betting Levy Board; and to amend section 24 of the said Act of 1963 with respect to the appointment and removal of members of the last-mentioned Board.

[27 March 1969]

7.13 1 Determination of annual scheme for bookmakers' levy

(1) In section 27 of the Act of 1963 (settlement of annual scheme for levy to be paid by bookmakers to the Horserace Betting Levy Board), the provisions of subsection (5) (which requires a scheme to be settled, in the absence of agreement between the Bookmakers' Committee and the Board, by the members of the Board appointed by the Secretary of State) shall, in relation to the levy period beginning with 1st April 1970 and any subsequent levy period, be replaced by those of the following subsection.

(2) If [five months][1] before the beginning of a levy period the Levy Board have not approved recommendations or revised recommendations of the Bookmakers' Committee with respect to the scheme to have effect under section 27 for that period (or if no such recommendations have been received by the Levy Board), then—

(a) the Levy Board shall forthwith report the circumstances to the Secretary of State; and

(b) the Secretary of State shall determine the scheme to have effect as aforesaid.

(3) The Secretary of State may under subsection (2) of this section either—

(a) determine a new scheme for the said period; or

(b) direct that the current scheme shall continue to have effect for that period also, subject to such modifications (if any) as he may specify.

(4) A scheme determined by members of the Levy Board for the levy period beginning with 1st April 1969 shall not have effect unless confirmed by the Secretary of State, who may in confirming it direct that it shall have effect with such modifications as he may specify.

(5) Before determining a scheme under subsection (2) of this section, or confirming a scheme under subsection (4) thereof, the Secretary of State may appoint one or more persons to enquire into, and report to him their opinion on, any matter appearing to him to be relevant to the form or content of the scheme.

(6) The Secretary of State may require the Levy Board to pay to a person appointed by him under subsection (5) of this section such remuneration as the Secretary of State may specify and any travelling and other expenses reasonably incurred by that person in doing that which he was appointed by the Secretary of State to do.

(7) The period of months specified in subsection (2) of this section may be varied by order of the Secretary of State substituting, in relation to any levy period beginning after the date on which the order comes into force, a different period, whether longer or shorter, but not longer than fifteen months.[1]

Provided that where the effect of an order is to increase the said period of months, the order shall not be made so as to come into force later than three months before the beginning of the increased period.

(8) The power of the Secretary of State to make an order under subsection (7) of this section shall be exercisable by statutory instrument and include power to vary or revoke the order by a subsequent order.

1 Words in square brackets in sub-s (2) substituted by the Horserace Betting Levy Schemes (Variation of Settlement Period) Order 1981, SI 1981/753, made in pursuance of sub-s (7) (superseding an earlier variation from the original period of six months).

7.14 2 Assessment to levy of individual bookmakers

(1) [*Spent in consequence of repeal under s 7.*]

(2) A bookmaker shall, whether or not he submits a declaration in accordance with the scheme having effect for any such period, be assessed to, or exempted from, levy in accordance with such opinion as the Government-appointed members of the Levy Board may form as to the category into which he falls for the purposes of the [levy].[1]

(3) In this section, references to the Government-appointed members of the Levy Board are to the three persons for the time being appointed to be members of the Board by the Secretary of State.

(4) In considering the category into which a bookmaker falls for the purposes of a [levy],[1] the said members of the Board may consult the Bookmakers' Committee and such other persons, if any, as those members of the Board think proper.

(5) [*Amends the Betting, Gaming and Lotteries Act 1963, s 28(10).*]

1 Word in square brackets substituted by the Horserace Betting Levy Act 1981, s 4(6), Schedule, para 4.

7.15 3 Levy Board's costs on appeal by bookmaker against assessment of levy

(1) The following subsection shall have effect where, under section 28 of the Act of 1963 (assessment of individual bookmakers to levy) [or under section 2 of the Horserace Betting Levy Act 1981 (appeals against notices of determination of liability to make payments on account)],[1] a bookmaker appeals in respect of an assessment notice [or a notice of determination][1] issued by the Levy Board in his case, and the appeal, having been referred to a tribunal under section 29 of that Act, is either dismissed by the tribunal or abandoned by the bookmaker.

(2) If the tribunal thinks it just that the bookmaker should make a payment towards expenses appearing to it to have been reasonably incurred by the Levy Board in connection with the appeal, the tribunal may certify accordingly and the Board shall be entitled to recover from the bookmaker as a debt due to them the amount specified in the certificate.

1 Words in square brackets inserted by the Horserace Betting Levy Act 1981, s 4(6), Schedule, para 5.

7.16 4 Non-renewal of bookmaker's permit in case of failure to pay levy

(1) Subject to this section, where an application is made to the appropriate authority under Schedule 1 to the Act of 1963 for the renewal of a bookmaker's permit and the authority, at the time when they determine the application, are satisfied—

(a) that the applicant is in default in respect of bookmakers' levy and has been so for at least three months; and

(b) that on a previous occasion (not before the passing of this Act, nor before the period of five years ending with the date of the application), being an occasion on which the permit was renewed (whether by the same or another authority), he was so in default and had been so for at least three months,

the authority shall refuse the application.

[(2A) In subsection (2), "authorised person" means a person (other than counsel or a solicitor) who, for the purposes of the Legal Services Act 2007, is an authorised person in relation to an activity which constitutes the exercise of a right of audience or the conduct of litigation (within the meaning of that Act).][1]

(2) Subsection (1) of this section shall apply only where the Levy Board appear, by counsel[, a solicitor or an authorised person][2], at the hearing of the application and maintain an objection duly made by them in accordance with Schedule 1 to the Act of 1963, being an objection to the renewal of the permit on the ground (either alone or among other grounds) that the applicant has failed to discharge his liabilities by way of the bookmakers' levy.

(3) For the purposes of subsection (1) of this section, a person is in default in respect of bookmakers' levy if—

(a) there has become due from him under section 28(7) of the Act of 1963 an amount assessed as payable by him by way of levy; and

(b) the whole or any part of that amount remains unpaid.

(4) . . . [3]

(5) Nothing in this section shall be taken as prejudicing paragraph 16(2) of Schedule 1 to the Act of 1963 (under which an authority dealing with an application for the renewal of a bookmaker's permit have a discretion to refuse the application on the ground of the character or conduct of the applicant, including his failure to pay levy).

---

1 Sub-s (2A): inserted by the Legal Services Act 2007, s 208(1), Sch 21, para 24(b). Date in force: 1 January 2010: see SI 2009/3250, art 2(h).

2 Sub-s (2): words ", a solicitor or an authorised person" in square brackets substituted by the Legal Services Act 2007, s 208(1), Sch 21, para 24(a). Date in force: 1 January 2010: see SI 2009/3250, art 2(h).

3 Sub-s (4): adds BGLA 1963, Sch 1, para 15(ee); see the para printed as so amended.

7.17 5 Annual contribution by [successor company to the][1] Totalisator Board

(1) If, in the case of the levy period beginning with 1st April 1970 or any subsequent levy period, the [successor company to the][2] Totalisator Board [objects][3] to the contribution determined by the Levy Board under section 30(1) of the Act of 1963, the contribution payable by the Totalisator Board in respect of that period shall instead be determined by the Secretary of State.

[(1A) Subsection (1) does not apply to any contribution which the successor company to the Totalisator Board is liable to make—

(a) in respect of a time when the exclusive licence does not have effect, and

(b) as a bookmaker.][4]

(2) If the contribution payable by the Totalisator Board in respect of the levy period beginning with 1st April 1969 falls, or has before the passing of this Act fallen, to be determined under section 30(2) of the Act of 1963 by the three members of the Levy Board referred to in that subsection, their determination shall not have effect unless confirmed by the Secretary of State; and if the Secretary of State decides not to confirm it, he shall himself determine the contribution.

(3) Before determining a contribution under this section, or confirming a determination under subsection (2) thereof, the Secretary of State may appoint one or

more persons to enquire into, and report to him their opinion on, any matter appearing to him to be relevant to the subject matter of his determination.

(4) The Secretary of State may require the Levy Board to pay to a person appointed by him under subsection (3) of this section such remuneration as the Secretary of State may specify and any travelling and other expenses reasonably incurred by that person in doing that which he was appointed by the Secretary of State to do.

---

1 Section heading: words "successor company to the" in square brackets inserted by the Horserace Betting and Olympic Lottery Act 2004, s 13, Sch 2, para 19(a). Date in force: 13 July 2011: see SI 2011/1704, art 2.

3 Sub-s (1): words "successor company to the" in square brackets in both places they occur inserted by the Horserace Betting and Olympic Lottery Act 2004, s 13, Sch 2, para 19(a). Date in force: 13 July 2011: see SI 2011/1704, art 2.

4 Sub-s (1): word "objects" in square brackets substituted by the Horserace Betting and Olympic Lottery Act 2004, s 13, Sch 2, para 19(b). Date in force: 13 July 2011: see SI 2011/1704, art 2.

5 Sub-s (1A): inserted by the Horserace Betting and Olympic Lottery Act 2004, s 13, Sch 2, para 19(c). Date in force: 13 July 2011: see SI 2011/1704, art 2.

6 . . . [1]

---

1 This section amended the Betting, Gaming and Lotteries Act 1963, s 24 to take account of the amalgamation of the Jockey Club and the National Hunt Committee, and contained a consequential provision now spent. See the section printed as amended.

7.18 7 Citation, interpretation, repeal and extent

(1) This Act may be cited as the Horserace Betting Levy Act 1969.

(2) In this Act 'the Act of 1963' means the Betting, Gaming and Lotteries Act 1963; and the expressions 'bookmaker', 'Bookmakers' Committee', 'bookmaker's permit', 'Levy Board', 'levy period' and 'Totalisator Board' have the same meanings as in that Act.

(3) . . . [1]

(4) . . . [2]

(5) This Act shall not extend to Northern Ireland.

---

1 Sub-s (3) amends the Betting, Gaming and Lotteries Act 1963, s 25(2)(a). See that section reproduced as so amended ante.

2 Sub-s (4) repealed the BGLA 1963, ss 27(5), 28(1), (4), 30(2), except in relation to a levy period beginning with or before 1 April 1969.

HORSERACE TOTALISATOR AND BETTING LEVY BOARDS ACT 1972

(1972 c 69)

AN ACT to extend the corporate powers of the Horserace Totalisator Board; to remove the limit on the number of members of that Board; to make provision with respect to applications by that Board for betting office licences; to transfer the functions of that Board with respect to the approval of horse racecourses to the Horserace Betting Levy Board; to facilitate the exercise of the functions of the government-appointed members of the Horserace Betting Levy Board; and for other purposes related to the activities of those Boards.

[17 October 1972]

7.19 1 New corporate powers for Totalisator Board

(1) The Totalisator Board shall have power—

(a) to carry on pool betting business in any form—

(i) on any horse race;

(ii) on any other event approved by the Secretary of State for the purposes of this paragraph;

[(b) by way of business to receive or negotiate bets on any event made otherwise than by way of pool betting, except bets on the outcome of any lottery forming part of the National Lottery for the purposes of Part I of the National Lottery etc Act 1993.][1]

(2) Any approval for the purposes of paragraph (a) . . . [2] of subsection (1) of this section shall be given by order made by statutory instrument which shall be subject to annulment in pursuance of a resolution of either House of Parliament; and the power to make orders under this subsection shall include power to vary or revoke a previous order under this subsection.

(3) In its application to pool betting by means of facilities provided by the Totalisator Board, section 14(3) of the Act of 1963 (which requires the Board when bets on a race or races are made by way of sponsored pool betting to cause the whole of the aggregate amount of the stake money to be distributed after deducting a percentage determined by the Board either generally or with respect to any particular racecourse) shall have effect as if—

(a) references to a race included references to any event other than a race; and

(b) for the words 'either generally or with respect to any particular racecourse' there were substituted the words 'either generally or with respect to any particular case or class of cases'.

(4) Nothing in section 14(5) of the Act of 1963 (which gives the Board power to remunerate and provide facilities for persons who negotiate, receive or transmit bets on behalf of the Board) shall be construed as limiting the power which the Board have under section 15(1)(d) of that Act (general incidental powers) to make arrangements of any kind for the performance of any of their functions with the assistance of, or in conjunction with, any other person.

(5) . . . [3]

(6) . . . [4]

---

1 Sub-s (1)(b) substituted by the Horserace Totalisator Board Act 1997, s 1(2).

2 Words omitted from sub-s (2) repealed by the Horserace Totalisator Board Act 1997, s 1(3).

[3] Sub-s (5): amends the Betting, Gaming and Lotteries Act 1963, s14(1).

[4] Sub-s (6): repealed by the Betting and Gaming Duties Act 1981, s 34(2), Sch 7.

2 [*Amends the Betting, Gaming and Lotteries Act 1963, s 12(2).*]

7.20 3 Applications by Totalisator Board for betting office licences

(1) Paragraph 19(b)(ii) of Schedule 1 to the Act of 1963 (which enables the appropriate authority to refuse an application for the grant or renewal of a betting office licence on the ground that the grant or renewal would be inexpedient having regard to the demand in the locality and the number of betting offices already available) shall not apply to an application by the Totalisator Board for the grant of a betting office licence, but such an application may be refused on the ground that reasonably adequate facilities exist in the locality for betting at licensed betting offices of the Board.

(2) Paragraph 19(b)(ii) shall also cease to apply to any application for the renewal of such a licence, or to any application for the grant of such a licence by way of transfer of one that is in force for the same premises at the time of the application; and accordingly in paragraph 19(b)(ii) for the words 'or renewal' there shall be substituted the words '(if the application is for that, and the applicant is not the Totalisator Board nor applying for the grant of a licence by way of transfer of one that is in force for the same premises at the time of the application)'.

(3) This section shall not come into force unless and until the Secretary of State so directs by order made by statutory instrument of which a draft has been laid before Parliament.

7.21 4 Financing of totalisators on approved horse racecourses

(1) Where facilities for sponsored pool betting are, with the authority of the Totalisator Board, being provided on an approved horse racecourse by the persons having the management of that course, any amount deducted by those persons under section 14(3)(a) of the Act of 1963 from the aggregate amount staked may, to such extent as the Totalisator Board may allow, be retained by those persons instead of being paid to the Board as required by section 14(4).

(2) It is hereby declared that the purposes for which the Levy Board have power under section 25(2)(d) of the Act of 1963 to make payments (in accordance with schemes prepared by them and approved by the Secretary of State) as purposes conducive to the improvement of horseracing include the provision on approved horse racecourses of facilities for sponsored pool betting, whether provided by the Totalisator Board or by the persons having the management of the course.

7.22 5 Transfer to Levy Board of Totalisator Board's functions with respect to approval of horse racecourses

(1) The functions of the Totalisator Board under section 13 of the Act of 1963 (grant and revocation of certificates of approval of horse racecourses) are hereby transferred to the Levy Board; and accordingly in the said section 13 and in the definition of 'approved horse racecourse' in section 55(1) of that Act for any reference to the Totalisator Board there shall be substituted a reference to the Levy Board.

(2) This section does not affect the validity of any certificate under the said section 13 which is in force at the passing of this Act, and any such certificate shall thereafter be treated for the purposes of the said section 13 as if it had been granted by the Levy Board.

7.23 6 Exercise of functions of government-appointed members of Levy Board

Any functions of the government-appointed members of the Levy Board may be exercised by any two of those members.

7.24 7 Remission of contributions due from Totalisator Board to Levy Board

The Levy Board shall have power to remit in whole or in part any sums outstanding at the passing of this Act in respect of the contributions payable to that Board by the Totalisator Board as mentioned in section 24(1) of the Act of 1963.

7.25 8 Short title, interpretation and extent

(1) This Act may be cited as the Horserace Totalisator and Betting Levy Boards Act 1972.

(2) In this Act 'the Act of 1963' means the Betting, Gaming and Lotteries Act 1963, and any expression in this Act which is also used in that Act has the same meaning as in that Act.

(3) In this Act references to the government-appointed members of the Levy Board are references to the three persons for the time being appointed to be members of the Board by the Secretary of State.

(4) Except where the context otherwise requires, any reference in this Act to any enactment shall be construed as a reference to that enactment as amended by or under any other enactment.

(5) This Act shall not form part of the law of Northern Ireland.

HORSERACE BETTING LEVY ACT 1981

(1981 c 30)

AN ACT to make provision for and in connection with the making of payments on account of the levy payable under section 27 of the Betting, Gaming and Lotteries Act 1963 by bookmakers to the Horserace Betting Levy Board.

[2 July 1981]

7.26 1 Payments on account of bookmakers' levy

(1) A bookmakers' levy scheme to which this section applies may include provision requiring bookmakers within the scheme to make payments on account of the levy in advance of assessment to the levy.

(2) This section applies to any bookmakers' levy scheme under which the amounts payable by way of the levy by one or more categories of bookmakers are determined by reference to the amounts staked with them during the levy period for which the scheme has effect.

(3) Where a scheme provides for payments on account to be made the scheme shall specify the basis on which the amount to be so paid is to be determined and the times during the levy period at which the payments are to be made and may, for those purposes, make different provision for different categories of bookmaker.

(4) The categories into which bookmakers may be divided for the purposes of payments on account of the levy may, but need not, be the same as the categories into which they are required to be divided for the purposes of the levy.

(5) It shall be for the Government-appointed members of the Levy Board to determine in accordance with the scheme—

(a) the amounts to be paid on account of the levy by bookmakers within the scheme; and

(b) the times at which the payments on account are to be made;

and they may, in making any such determination, consult the Bookmakers' Committee and such other persons, if any, as those members of the Board think proper.

(6) Where a determination is made under subsection (5) above that an amount is payable on account by a bookmaker the Levy Board shall, except as provided in

subsection (7) below, issue a notice of the determination made in his case and cause it to be served on the bookmaker.

(7) The Levy Board shall, if they are of the opinion that payments on account should not be required in the case of any bookmaker within the scheme, refrain from issuing a notice of determination under subsection (6) above or withdraw a notice which they have issued.

(8) In this section—

'bookmakers' levy scheme' means a scheme for the payment of a levy by bookmakers under section 27 of the Act of 1963;

'Government-appointed', with reference to members of the Levy Board, means appointed for the time being by the Secretary of State;

and for the purposes of this section a bookmaker is 'within the scheme' for any levy period if in that period he carries on on his own account a business which includes the effecting of betting transactions on horse races.

7.27 2 Appeals

(1) A notice of determination issued by the Levy Board (and not withdrawn) under section 1 above requiring a bookmaker to make payments on account shall be conclusive as to his liability to make the payments specified in the notice unless, not later than twenty-eight days after the notice is served on him, he gives to the Board notice in writing of appeal therefrom on the grounds that the determination was not in accordance with the scheme.

(2) On receiving any notice of appeal under subsection (1) above, the Levy Board shall refer the appeal to an appeal tribunal established in pursuance of section 29 of the Act of 1963.

(3) The appeal tribunal shall have power to confirm or rescind the determination or to increase or reduce the amount which is payable by the bookmaker under the determination according to the tribunal's opinion as to what amount (if any) is payable on account by him in accordance with the scheme, but the tribunal—

(a) shall not rescind the determination or reduce the amount so payable unless the appellant has afforded the tribunal all the facilities it may have required for the investigation of his case;

(b) shall confirm the determination of the amount unless the tribunal is satisfied that, on all the evidence made available to it, the amount should be varied or the determination rescinded.

(4) The decision of the appeal tribunal as to the amount to be paid on account under the scheme shall be final.

7.28 3 Relief from payments

(1) A bookmaker on whom a notice of determination has been served may apply in writing to the Levy Board to be excused from making payments on account in accordance with the notice on the grounds that his circumstances make it unjust that he should do so.

(2) It shall be for the Government-appointed members of the Levy Board to consider applications under subsection (1) above and, for the purpose of disposing of them, they may consult the Bookmakers Committee and such other persons, if any, as those members of the Board think proper.

(3) If on an application under subsection (1) above the Government-appointed members are of the opinion that a reduction ought to be made in the payments on account to be made by a bookmaker they shall give either of the following directions with respect to payments becoming due as from a date specified in the direction, that is to say—

(a) a direction that those payments shall cease to be payable; or

(b) a direction that those payments shall be reduced to such amount or amounts as they may specify;

but otherwise the Government-appointed members shall dismiss the application.

(4) Where the Government-appointed members give a direction under subsection (3) above then—

(a) in the case of a direction under paragraph (a), they shall issue a notice cancelling the notice of determination with respect to which the application was made so far as that notice relates to payments on account becoming due on or after the specified date;

(b) in the case of a direction under paragraph (b), they shall issue a revised notice of determination which shall have effect as from the specified date in place of the notice with respect to which the application was made so far as that notice relates to payments on account becoming due on or after the specified date;

and they shall cause the notice of cancellation or the revised notice of determination to be served on the bookmaker.

(5) A revised notice of determination issued under subsection (4) above shall, subject to subsection (7) below, have effect as if it were a notice of determination issued in accordance with the scheme under section 1 above.

(6) More than one application may be made by a bookmaker under subsection (1) above in any levy period but only where there has been a change in his circumstances since his last application.

(7) If an application is made under this section with respect to a notice of determination no appeal shall lie under section 2 above with respect to that notice or any revised notice of determination issued in place of it under this section and if a bookmaker gives notice of appeal under the said section 2 he shall not make an application under this section until after the appeal has been determined or abandoned.

(8) In this section references to the Government-appointed members of the Levy Board are to be construed in accordance with section 1(8) above.

7.29 4 Supplementary provisions

(1) Payments on account shall become due on the date or dates specified in the notice of determination and shall be recoverable by the Levy Board as a debt due to the Board, save that—

(a) where the date or first date specified in the notice of determination falls within the period allowed for appealing under subsection (1) of section 2 above, the payment or first payment shall become due at the expiration of that period; and

(b) where the bookmaker appeals under that subsection, any payments which become due before the determination or abandonment of the appeal shall become due on the determination or abandonment of the appeal.

(2) Where the amount paid on account of the levy by a bookmaker in any levy period exceeds the amount assessed by the Levy Board as payable by him by way of the levy in respect of that period, the Board shall repay the excess to the bookmaker when they issue the notice of assessment and, if a further excess arises on a reduction of the assessment on appeal, shall repay that further excess to the bookmaker within fourteen days of the determination of the appeal.

(3) If, otherwise than with the consent in writing of the bookmaker concerned or—

(a) for the purposes of this Act or of a report of any proceedings before an appeal tribunal under section 2 above; or

(b) for the purposes of, or of a report of—

(i) proceedings for the recovery of any payment on account from that bookmaker; or

(ii) proceedings relating to that bookmaker before an appropriate authority within the meaning of Schedule 1 to the Act of 1963, or before any court on appeal from any such authority; or

(iii) any criminal proceedings,

any person to whom this subsection applies discloses to any other person in such a manner as to identify the bookmaker concerned any information concerning that bookmaker obtained through the exercise of any functions under this Act, he shall be liable on summary conviction to a fine not exceeding [level 4 on the standard scale][1].

(4) Subsection (3) above applies to any person who is a member, officer or servant of the Levy Board, the Bookmakers' Committee or an appeal tribunal established in pursuance of section 29 of the Act of 1963, or who is consulted by the members of the Levy Board in pursuance of this Act.

(5) Any notice issued under this Act in the case of any bookmaker may be served on him either by serving it on him personally or by sending it to him by post at his usual or last known residence or place of business in the United Kingdom or, if the bookmaker is a company, at the company's registered office.

(6) The Act of 1963 and the Act of 1969 shall have effect subject to the amendments specified in the Schedule to this Act, being amendments consequential upon the provisions of this Act.

---

1 Substituted for £500 in pursuance of the Criminal Justice Act 1982, s 46. CJA 1982, s 37(2), which sets out the amounts of the standard scale, was substituted by the CJA 1991, s 17(1), as from 1 October 1992. The scale for level 4 as so substituted is £2,500.

7.30 5 Citation, interpretation and extent

(1) This Act may be cited as the Horserace Betting Levy Act 1981.

(2) In this Act—

'the Act of 1963' means the Betting, Gaming and Lotteries Act 1963;

'the Act of 1969' means the Horserace Betting Levy Act 1969;

and 'betting transaction', 'bookmaker', 'Bookmakers' Committee', 'the Levy Board' and 'levy period' have the same meanings as in the Act of 1963.

(3) This Act does not extend to Northern Ireland.

SCHEDULE

[*The amendments of the Betting, Gaming and Lotteries Act 1963 and the Horserace Betting Levy Act 1969 set out in this Schedule have been incorporated in those Acts as printed.*]

BETTING AND GAMING DUTIES ACT 1981

(1981 c 63)

Arrangement of sections

PART I

BETTING DUTIES

General betting duty

AN ACT to consolidate certain enactments[1] *concerning the duties of excise relating to betting and gaming.*

[30 October 1981]

[1] For the derivation of the provisions consolidated in this Act see the 97th edition of this work.

PART I
BETTING DUTIES

[General betting duty]

7.31 [1 The duty

A duty of excise to be known as general betting duty shall be charged in accordance with sections 2 to 5D.][1]

[1] Inserted by the Finance Act 1987, s 3(1)(a), with respect to bets made on or after 27 March 1987. Substituted, together with ss 2–5, 5A–5D, for ss 1–5 as originally enacted, by the Finance Act 2001, s 6(1), Sch 1, para 1 (in relation to spread bets made on or after that date and in relation to other bets irrespective of when those bets were or are made): see SI 2001/3089, art 2.

7.32 [2 Bookmakers: general bets

(1) General betting duty shall be charged on a bet made with a bookmaker who is in the United Kingdom.

(2) Subsection (1) does not apply to—

(a) an on-course bet,

(b) a spread bet,

(c) a bet made by way of pool betting, . . . [2]

(d) a bet made using a gaming machine, within the meaning of section 23 of the Value Added Tax Act 1994].

(3) The amount of duty charged in respect of bets made with a bookmaker in an accounting period shall be 15 per cent of the amount of his net stake receipts for that period.][1]

[1] Substituted as noted to s 1.

[2] Para (d) inserted by the Finance Act 2006, s 9(1).

7.33 [3 Bookmakers: spread bets]

[(1) General betting duty shall be charged on a spread bet made with a bookmaker who—

(a) is in the United Kingdom, . . . [1]

(b) . . . .[1]

[(2) A bet is a spread bet if it constitutes a contract the making or accepting of which is a regulated activity within the meaning of section 22 of the Financial Services and Markets Act 2000.][2]

(3) The amount of duty charged under subsection (1) in respect of spread bets made with a bookmaker in an accounting period shall be—

(a) 3 per cent of the amount of his net stake receipts in respect of financial spread bets for that period (if any), plus

(b) 10 per cent of the amount of his net stake receipts in respect of other spread bets for that period (if any).

(4) A "financial spread bet" is a spread bet the subject of which is a financial matter.

(5) The Commissioners may by order provide that a specified matter—

(a) shall be treated as a financial matter for the purpose of subsection (4), or

(b) shall not be treated as a financial matter for that purpose.][3]

[1] Sub-s (1): para (b) and word omitted immediately preceding it repealed by the Finance Act 2007, ss 105, 114, Sch 25, Pt 2, paras 3, 4(1), (2), Sch 27, Pt 6(3).

[2] Sub-s (2): substituted by the Finance Act 2007, s 105, Sch 25, Pt 2, paras 3, 4(1), (3).

[3] Substituted, together with ss 1, 2, 4, 5, 5A–5D, for ss 1–5 as originally enacted, by the Finance Act 2001, s 6(1), Sch 1, para 1.

7.34 [4 Pool betting on horse and dog races]

[(1) General betting duty shall be charged on pool betting which —

(a) relates only to horse racing or dog racing, and

(b) is not on-course betting.

(2) But subsection (1) does not apply to pool betting if—

(a) the promoter is outside the United Kingdom, and

(b) it is conducted otherwise than by means of a totalisator situated in the United Kingdom.

(3) The amount of duty charged under subsection (1) in respect of bets made by means of facilities provided by a person in an accounting period shall be 15 per cent of the amount of his net stake receipts for the period.][1]

---

1 Substituted by the Finance Act 2004, s 15(1), (2).

7.35 [5 Net stake receipts]

[(1) For the purposes of a charge under a provision of sections 2 to 4 in respect of the class of bets to which the provision applies, the amount of a person's net stake receipts for an accounting period is X minus Y, where—

(a) X is the aggregate of amounts which fall due to that person in the accounting period in respect of bets of that class made with him, and

(b) Y is the aggregate of amounts paid by the person in that period by way of winnings to persons who made bets of that class with him (irrespective of when the bets were made or determined).

(2) Where—

(a) a person makes a bet other than a spread bet, and

(b) the sum which he will lose if unsuccessful is known when the bet is made,

that sum shall be treated for the purposes of subsection (1)(a) as falling due when the bet is made (irrespective of when it is actually paid or required to be paid).

(3) Where the amount of a person's net stake receipts is zero or a negative amount, it shall be disregarded for the purposes of sections 2 to 4 [except as provided for by section 5AA][2].

(4) In calculating an amount due to a person in respect of a bet, no deduction shall be made in respect of—

(a) any other benefit secured by the person who makes the bet as a result of paying the money,

(b) a person's expenses, whether in paying duty or otherwise, or

(c) any other matter.

(5) Where a person makes a bet in pursuance of an offer which permits him to pay nothing or less than the amount which he would have been required to pay without the offer, he shall be treated for the purposes of this section as being due to pay that amount—

(a) to the person with whom the bet is made, and

(b) at the time when the bet is made.

(6) For the purpose of subsection (1)(b)—

(a) the reference to paying an amount to a person includes a reference to holding it in an account if the person is notified that the amount is being held for him in the account and that he is entitled to withdraw it on demand,

(b) the return of a stake shall be treated as a payment by way of winnings, and

(c) only payments of money shall be taken into account.

(7) In the application of this section to a charge under [section 4(1)][2], a reference to bets made with a person shall be treated as a reference to bets made by means of facilities provided by him.][3]

---

1 Sub-s (3): words "except as provided for by section 5AA" in square brackets inserted by the Finance Act 2003, s 6(1), (2).

2 Sub-s (7): words "section 4(1)" in square brackets substituted by the Finance Act 2004, s 15(1), (3).

3 Substituted, together with ss 1–4, 5A–5D, for ss 1–5 as originally enacted, by the Finance Act

2001, s 6(1), Sch 1, para 1.

7.36 [5AA Relief for losses

(1) This section applies where the amount of a person's net stake receipts for an accounting period in respect of a class of bets (calculated in accordance with section 5(1)) is a negative amount.

(2) That amount shall be carried forward to the following accounting period and, to the extent that it does not exceed it, deducted from the amount of the person's net stake receipts in respect of the same class of bets for that period.

(3) If the amount of those net stake receipts for that following accounting period—

(a) is not a positive amount, or

(b) is less than the amount carried forward,

the amount carried forward or, as the case may be, the balance of it shall be treated for the purposes of this section as if it were a negative amount of net stake receipts for that period in respect of the same class of bets.][1]

---

1 Inserted by the Finance Act 2003, s 6(1), (3): applies in relation to any accounting period beginning on or after 1 September 2003 for which the net stake receipts in respect of a particular class of bets, or (as the case may be) the net pool betting receipts, is a negative amount.

7.37 [5AB Betting exchanges

(1) This section applies where—

(a) one person makes a bet with another person using facilities provided by a third person in the course of a business, and

(b) that business is one that does not involve the provision of premises for use by persons making or taking bets.

(2) General betting duty shall be charged on the amounts ('commission charges') that the parties to the bet are charged, whether by deduction from winnings or otherwise, for using those facilities.

(3) No deductions shall be allowed from commission charges.

(4) The amount of duty charged under this section in respect of bets determined in an accounting period shall be 15 per cent of the commission charges relating to those bets.

(5) For the purposes of this section, and section 5B(4) so far as relating to this section, a person who arranges for facilities relating to a bet to be provided by another person shall be treated as providing them himself (and the other person shall not).][1]

---

1 Inserted by the Finance Act 2003, s 7(1), (2): applies in relation to any accounting period beginning on or after 1 June 2003 (but does not apply in relation to a 'straddling bet' made, using facilities provided by a broker, in an accounting period of the broker beginning before that date, but not determined until an accounting period of the broker beginning on or after that date).

5A *[Repealed by the Finance Act 2003, ss 6(1), (4), 216, Sch 43, Pt 1(1) in relation to any accounting period beginning on or after 1 September 2003 for which the net stake receipts in respect of a particular class of bets, or (as the case may be) the net pool betting receipts, is a negative amount.]*

7.38 [5B Liability to pay

[[(1) All general betting duty chargeable in respect of—

(a) bets made in an accounting period, or

(b) in the case of duty chargeable under section 5AB, bets determined in an accounting period, shall become due at the end of that period.][1]

(2) In the case of bets made with a bookmaker in an accounting period the general betting duty shall be paid—

(a) when it becomes due, and
(b) by the bookmaker.

(3) But general betting duty which is due to be paid by a bookmaker in respect of bets may be recovered from the following persons as if they and the bookmaker were jointly and severally liable to pay the duty—

(a) the holder of a [general betting operating licence (in Great Britain), or a bookmaker's permit (in Northern Ireland),][2] for the business in the course of which the bets were made;
(b) a person responsible for the management of that business;
(c) where the bookmaker is a company, a director.

(4) In the case of bets made in an accounting period by means of facilities provided by a person as described in [section 4(1)][3] [or 5AB][4] the general betting duty shall be paid—

(a) when it becomes due, and
(b) by the person who provides the facilities.

(5) This section is without prejudice to paragraph 2 of Schedule 1 to this Act or regulations made under it.][5]

---

1 Sub-s (1): substituted by the Finance Act 2003, s 7(1), (3)(a).

2 Sub-s (3): in para (a) words "general betting operating licence (in Great Britain), or a bookmaker's permit (in Northern Ireland)," in square brackets substituted by the Finance Act 2007, s 105, Sch 25, Pt 2, paras 3, 5.

3 Sub-s (4): words "section 4(1)" in square brackets substituted by the Finance Act 2004, s 15(1), (3).

4 Sub-s (4): words "or 5AB" in square brackets inserted by the Finance Act 2003, s 7(1), (3)(b).

5 Substituted, together with ss 1–5, 5A, 5C, 5D, for ss 1–5 as originally enacted, by the Finance Act 2001, s 6(1), Sch 1, para 1.

7.39 [5C Bet-brokers]

[(1) This section applies where—

(a) one person (the "bettor") makes a bet with another person (the "bet-taker") using facilities provided in the course of a business[, other than a betting-exchange business,][1] by a third person (the "bet-broker"), or
(b) one person (the "bet-broker") in the course of a business makes a bet with another person (the "bet-taker") as the agent of a third person (the "bettor") (whether the bettor is a disclosed principal or an undisclosed principal).

[In paragraph (a) "betting-exchange business" means a business such as is mentioned in section 5AB(1).][2]

(2) . . .[3]

(3) . . .[3]

(4) . . . [4]For the purposes of sections 2 to 5B—

(a) the bet shall be treated as if it were made separately by the bettor with the bet-broker and by the bet-broker with the bet-taker,
(b) the bet-broker shall be treated as a bookmaker in respect of the bet,
(c) the aggregate of amounts due to be paid by the bettor in respect of the bet shall be treated as being due separately to the bet-broker and to the bet-taker (and any amount due to be paid by the bet-broker to the bet-taker shall be disregarded), and

(d) a sum paid by the bet-taker by way of winnings in respect of the bet shall be treated as having been paid separately by the bet-taker and by the bet-broker at that time and for that purpose (and any sum paid by the bet-broker shall be disregarded).

(5) This section does not apply—

(a) to bets made by way of pool betting, . . . [5]

(b) . . . .[5]

(6) Where there is any doubt as to which of two persons is the bettor and which the bet-taker for the purposes of subsection (1)(a), whichever of the two was the first to use the facilities of the bet-broker to offer the bet shall be treated as the bet-taker.]
1

---

1 Sub-s (1): in para (a) words ", other than a betting-exchange business," in square brackets inserted by the Finance Act 2003, s 7(1), (4)(a).

2 Sub-s (1): words from "In paragraph (a)" to "section 5AB(1)." in square brackets inserted by the Finance Act 2003, s 7(1), (4)(b).

3 Sub-ss (2), (3): repealed by the Finance Act 2003, ss 7(1), (4)(c), 216, Sch 43, Pt 1(1).

4 Sub-s (4): words omitted repealed by the Finance Act 2003, ss 7(1), (4)(d), 216, Sch 43, Pt 1(1).

5 Sub-s (5): para (b) and word omitted immediately preceding it repealed by the Finance Act 2007, ss 105, 114, Sch 25, Pt 2, paras 3, 6, Sch 27, Pt 6(3).

6 Substituted, together with ss 1–5, 5A, 5B, 5D, for ss 1–5 as originally enacted, by the Finance Act 2001, s 6(1), Sch 1, para 1.

7.40 [5D Accounting period

(1) For the purposes of sections 2 to 5C—

(a) each calendar month is an accounting period, but

(b) the Commissioners may provide in regulations under paragraph 2 of Schedule 1 to this Act for some other specified period to be an accounting period.

(2) Regulations made by virtue of subsection (1)(b) may—

(a) make provision which applies generally or only in relation to a specified person or class of person;

(b) make different provision for different purposes;

(c) make transitional provision.][1]

---

1 Substituted as noted to s 1.

Pool betting duty

7.41 [6 The duty

A duty of excise to be known as pool betting duty shall be charged in accordance with sections 7 to 8C.][1]

---

1 Sections 6, 7, 7A–7F, 8, 8A–8C substituted for ss 6–8 as originally enacted, by the Finance Act 2002, s 12(1), Sch 4, Pt 1, paras 1, 2. This amendment has effect for the purposes of accounting periods beginning on or after 31 March 2002: see the Finance Act 2002, s 12(3).

7.42 [7 Duty charged on net pool betting receipts

(1) If the amount of a person's net pool betting receipts for an accounting period is greater than zero, pool betting duty is charged on those receipts.

(2) The amount of that duty is 15 per cent of the amount of the receipts.][1]

---

1 See note 1 to s 6.

7.43 [7ZA Relief for losses

(1) This section applies where the amount of a person's net pool betting receipts for an accounting period is a negative amount.

(2) That amount shall be carried forward to the following accounting period and, to the extent that it does not exceed it, deducted from the amount of the person's net pool betting receipts for that period.

(3) If the amount of the net pool betting receipts for that following accounting period—

(a) is not a positive amount, or

(b) is less than the amount carried forward,

the amount carried forward or, as the case may be, the balance of it shall be treated for the purposes of this section as if it were a negative amount of net pool betting receipts for that period.][1]

---

1 Inserted by the Finance Act 2003, s 6(1), (5). Amendment applies in relation to any accounting period beginning on or after 1 September 2003 for which the net stake receipts in respect of a particular class of bets, or (as the case may be) the net pool betting receipts, is a negative amount.

7.44 [7A Calculating net pool betting receipts

For the purposes of section 7, the amount of a person's net pool betting receipts for an accounting period is—

$$S + E - W$$

where—

S is the aggregate of amounts falling due to the person in the accounting period in respect of dutiable pool bets,

E is the aggregate of expenses and profits falling within section 7E(2) that are attributable to the accounting period, and

W is the aggregate of amounts paid by the person in the accounting period by way of winnings on dutiable pool bets (irrespective of when the bets were made or determined).][1]

---

1 See note 1 to s 6.

7.45 [7B Net pool betting receipts: meaning of "dutiable pool bet"

[(1) For the purposes of a calculation under section 7A of the amount of a person's net pool betting receipts for any accounting period, a bet (wherever made) is a "dutiable pool bet" if—

(a) the bet is made by way of pool betting, and

(b) the following conditions are satisfied.

(2) The first condition is that—

(a) the bet is made by means of a totalisator situated in the United Kingdom and that person is the operator, or

(b) . . . [2] that person is the promoter and is in the United Kingdom.

(3) The second condition is that the bet is not—

[(a) made wholly in relation to horse racing or dog racing.][3]

(c) made for community benefit.

(4) The third condition is that if the bet was made before 31st March 2002, at least one event to which it relates takes place on or after that date.][1]

1 See note 1 to s 6.

2 Sub-s (2): in para (b) words omitted repealed by the Finance Act 2004, ss 15(1), (4)(a), 326, Sch 42, Pt 1(2).

3 Sub-s (3): para (a) substituted, for paras (a), (b), by the Finance Act 2004, s 15(1), (4)(b).

7.46 [7C Net pool betting receipts: calculating stake money

(1) This section applies for the purpose of calculating S in a calculation under section 7A.

(2) Any payment that entitles a person to make a bet shall, if he makes the bet, be treated as stake money on the bet.

(3) All payments made—

(a) for or on account of or in connection with bets that are dutiable pool bets for the purposes of the calculation,

(b) in addition to the stake money, and

(c) by the persons making the bets,

shall be treated as amounts due in respect of the bets except in so far as the contrary is proved by the person whose net pool betting receipts are being calculated.][1]

1 See note 1 to s 6.

7.47 [7D Net pool betting receipts: when stakes etc fall due

(1) Subsections (2) to (5) apply for the purpose of calculating S in a calculation under section 7A but have effect subject to any regulations under subsection (6).

(2) Where—

(a) a person makes a bet, and

(b) the bet relates to a single event, or to two or more events all taking place on the same day,

any sum due to a person in respect of the bet shall be treated as falling due on the day on which the event or events take place.

(3) Where—

(a) a person makes a bet, and

(b) subsection (2) does not apply,

any sum due to a person in respect of the bet shall (subject to subsection (5)) be treated as falling due when the bet is made.

(4) Subsections (2) and (3) have effect in relation to a sum irrespective of when it is actually paid or required to be paid (even where a sum that those subsections require to be treated as falling due on or after 31st March 2002 was actually paid, or required to be paid, before that date).

(5) As respects a bet made before 31st March 2002 that relates to events at least one of which takes place before that date and at least one of which takes place on or after that date, any sum paid on or after that date in respect of the bet shall be treated as falling due when it is paid.

(6) The Commissioners may by regulations make provision as to when any sum due to a person in respect of a bet is to be treated as falling due for the purpose of calculating S in a calculation under section 7A.

(7) Provision made by regulations under subsection (6) may not provide for a sum due to a person in respect of a bet to be treated as falling due—

(a) earlier than when the bet is made, or

(b) later than when the bet is determined.

(8) Regulations made under subsection (6) may—

(a) make provision that applies generally or only in relation to a specified description of bet;

(b) make different provision for different purposes;

(c) make provision relating to bets made before the regulations are made (including bets made before the passing of the Finance Act 2002);

(d) make transitional provision.][1]

---

1 See note 1 to s 6.

7.48 [7E Net pool betting receipts: expenses and profits

[(1) Subsections (2) and (3) apply for the purpose of calculating E in a calculation under section 7A.

(2) The expenses and profits falling within this subsection are (subject to subsection (3))—

(a) those of the person whose net pool betting receipts are being calculated, and

(b) those of any other person concerned with or benefiting from the promotion of the betting concerned.

(3) Expenses and profits do not fall within subsection (2) so far as they are—

(a) provided out of amounts due, in respect of bets that are dutiable pool bets for the purposes of the calculation, to the person whose net pool betting receipts are being calculated, or

(b) referable to matters other than—

(i) the promotion or management of the betting concerned, or

(ii) activities ancillary to, or connected with, such promotion or management.]

(4) The Commissioners may by regulations make provision as to the accounting period to which expenses and profits falling within subsection (2) are to be treated as attributable for the purpose of calculating E in a calculation under section 7A.

(5) Regulations made under subsection (4) may—

(a) make provision that applies generally or only in relation to a specified description of bet;

(b) make different provision for different purposes;

(c) make provision applying in respect of expenses incurred, and profits accruing, before the regulations are made (including any incurred or accruing before the passing of the Finance Act 2002);

(d) make transitional provision.][1]

---

1 See note 1 to s 6.

7.49 [7F Net pool betting receipts: calculating winnings

(1) Subsections (2) to (5) apply for the purpose of calculating W in a calculation under section 7A.

(2) The reference to paying an amount to a person includes a reference to holding it in an account if the person is notified that the amount is being held for him in the account and that he is entitled to withdraw it on demand.

(3) The return of a stake shall be treated as a payment by way of winnings.

(4) Only payments of money shall be taken into account.

(5) Where a bet made before 31st March 2002 relates to events at least one of which takes place before that date and at least one of which takes place on or after that date, no account shall be taken of any payment by way of winnings on the bet.

(6) The Commissioners may by regulations make provision as to when amounts paid by way of winnings are to be treated as being paid for the purposes of calculating W in a calculation under section 7A.

(7) Regulations made under subsection (6) may—

(a) make provision that applies generally or only in relation to a specified description of bet;

(b) make different provision for different purposes;

(c) make provision applying in respect of amounts paid before the regulations are made (including amounts paid before the passing of the Finance Act 2002);

(d) make transitional provision.][1]

1 See note 1 to s 6.

7.50 [8 Payment and recovery

(1) Pool betting duty charged on a person's net pool betting receipts for an accounting period—

(a) becomes due at the end of the period,

(b) shall be paid by the person, and

(c) shall, subject to any regulations under subsection (3) ...[2], be paid when it becomes due.

(2) Pool betting duty that is due to be paid may be recovered from the following persons as if they were jointly and severally liable to pay the duty—

(a) the person on whose net pool betting receipts the duty is charged ('the primary payer');

(b) a person responsible for the management of any business in the course of which any bets have been made that are dutiable pool bets for the purposes of calculations under section 7A of the amount of the primary payer's net pool betting receipts for any accounting period;

(c) a person responsible for the management of any totalisator used for the purposes of any such business;

(d) where a person within any of paragraphs (a) to (c) is a company, a director.

(3) The Commissioners may by regulations—

(a) make provision as to when pool betting duty is to be paid (including provision repealing paragraph 3 of Schedule 1 to this Act and the reference to that paragraph in subsection (1)(c));

(b) make provision as to how pool betting duty is to be paid.

(4) Regulations made under subsection (3) may—

(a) make provision that applies generally or only in relation to a specified person or class of person;

(b) make different provision for different purposes;

(c) make transitional provision.][1]

1 See note 1 to s 6.

2 Sub-s (1): in para (c) words omitted repealed by SI 2010/1783, reg 3(1)(a). Date in force: 26 September 2010 (except when the time for payment of pool betting duty pursuant to a direction under Sch 1, para 3 hereto fell before that date): see SI 2010/1783, regs 1, 3(2).

7.51 [8A Meaning of 'bet made for community benefit' in sections 6 to 8

(1) For the purposes of sections 6 to 8 (but subject to any direction under subsection (3)), a bet is made 'for community benefit' if—

(a) the promoter of the betting concerned is a community society or is bound to pay all benefits accruing from the betting to such a society, and

(b) the person making the bet knows, when making it, that the purpose of the betting is to benefit such a society.

(2) In the case of a bet made by means of a totalisator, the reference in subsection (1) to the promoter of the betting concerned is a reference to the operator.

(3) The Commissioners may direct that any bet specified by the direction, or of a description so specified, is not a bet made for community benefit.

(4) The power conferred by subsection (3) may not be exercised unless the Commissioners consider that an unreasonably large part of the amounts paid in respect of the bets concerned will, or may, be applied otherwise than—

(a) in the payment of winnings, or

(b) for the benefit of a community society.

(5) In this section 'community society' means—

(a) a society established and conducted for charitable purposes only, or

(b) a society established and conducted wholly or mainly for the support of athletic sports or athletic games and not established or conducted for purposes of private gain.

(6) In this section 'society' includes any club, institution, organisation or association of persons, by whatever name called.][1]

---

1 See note 1 to s 6.

7.52 [8B Meaning of 'accounting period' in sections 6 to 8

(1) For the purposes of sections 6 to 8—

(a) each period that ends with the last Saturday in a calendar month, and begins with the Sunday immediately following the previous such Saturday, is an accounting period, but

(b) the Commissioners may by regulations make provision for some other specified period to be an accounting period.

(2) Regulations made under subsection (1)(b) may—

(a) make provision that applies generally or only in relation to a specified person or class of person;

(b) make different provision for different purposes;

(c) make transitional provision.][1]

---

1 See note 1 to s 6.

7.53 [8C Meaning of 'bet' in sections 6 to 8A

(1) For the purposes of sections 6 to 8A, 'bet' does not include the taking of a ticket or chance in a lottery.

(2) Where payments are made for the chance of winning any money or money's worth on terms under which the persons making the payments have a power of selection that may (directly or indirectly) determine the winner, those payments shall be treated as bets for the purposes of sections 6 to 8A notwithstanding that the power is not exercised.

(3) Subsection (2) has effect subject to section 12(3).

(4) Where any payment entitles a person to take part in a transaction that is, on his part only, not a bet made by way of pool betting by reason of his not in fact making any stake as if the transaction were such a bet, the transaction shall be treated as such a bet for the purposes of pool betting duty (and section 7C(3) shall apply to any such payment).][1]

1 See note 1 to s 6.

General

7.54

9 [*Repealed by the Gambling Act 2005, ss 340, 356(4), Sch 17 from 1 September 2007: see SI 2006/3272, art 2(4); for transitional provisions see art 6, Sch 4 thereto.*]

7.55

9A [*Repealed by the Gambling Act 2005, ss 340, 356(4), Sch 17 from 1 September 2007: see SI 2006/3272, art 2(4); for transitional provisions see art 6, Sch 4 thereto.*]

9B [*Repealed by the Gambling Act 2005, ss 340, 356(4), Sch 17 from 1 September 2007: see SI 2006/3272, art 2(4); for transitional provisions see art 6, Sch 4 thereto.*]

7.56 10 Definition of pool betting

(1) For the purposes of this Part of this Act, a bet shall be deemed to be made by way of pool betting unless it is a bet at fixed odds, and, in particular, bets shall be held to be made by way of pool betting wherever a number of persons make bets—

(a) on terms that the winnings of such of those persons as are winners shall be, or be a share of, or be determined by reference to, the stake money paid or agreed to be paid by those persons, whether the bets are made by means of a totalisator, or by filling up and returning coupons or other printed or written forms, or in any other way, or

(b) on terms that the winnings of such of those persons as are winners shall be, or shall include, an amount (not determined by reference to the stake money paid or agreed to be paid by those persons) which is divisible in any proportions among such of those persons as are winners, or

(c) on the basis that the winners or their winnings shall, to any extent, be at the discretion of the promoter or some other person.

(2) A bet is a bet at fixed odds within the meaning of this section only if each of the persons making it knows or can know, at the time he makes it, the amount he will win, except in so far as that amount is to depend on the result of the event or events betted on, or on any such event taking place or producing a result, or on the numbers taking part in any such event, or on the starting prices or totalisator odds for any such event, or on there being totalisator odds on any such event, or on the time when his bet is received by any person with or through whom it is made.

In this subsection—

"starting prices" means, in relation to any event, the odds ruling at the scene of the event immediately before the start, and

["totalisator odds" means the odds paid on bets made—

(a) by means of a totalisator, and

(b) at the scene of the event to which the bets relate].[1]

(3) A bet made with or through a person carrying on a business of receiving or negotiating bets, being a bet made in the course of that business, shall be deemed not to be a bet at fixed odds within the meaning of this section if the winnings of the person by whom it is so made consist or may consist wholly or in part of something other than money.

(4) Where a person carries on a business of receiving or negotiating bets and there is or has been issued in connection with that business any advertisement or other publication calculated to encourage in persons making bets of any description with or through him a belief that the bets are made on the basis mentioned in subsection (1)(c) above, then any bets of that description subsequently made with or through him in the

course of that business shall be deemed for the purposes of this section to be made on that basis.

---

1 Sub-s (2): definition "totalisator odds" substituted by the Finance Act 2004, s 15(1), (6).

7.57
11 [*Repealed by the Finance Act 2002, ss 12(1), 141, Schs 4 and 40.*]

7.58 **12 Supplementary provisions**

(1) Where particulars of an intended bet on which general betting duty or pool betting duty would be chargeable and the stake on that bet are collected for transmission to the person by whom that duty would fall to be paid by some other person, whether or not a bookmaker, who holds himself out as available for so collecting and transmitting them, but are in fact not so transmitted, the bet shall be deemed to have been made but the duty in respect of it shall be paid by that other person.

(2) The provisions of Schedule 1 to this Act (supplementary provisions as to betting duties) shall have effect.

(3) In sections 1 to 10 above . . . [1], in subsection (1) above and in paragraph 10 of Schedule 1 to this Act, "bet" does not include any bet made or stake hazarded in the course of, or incidentally to, any gaming.

(4) In this Part of this Act—

["betting office licence"—

(a) . . . [2]

(b) in Northern Ireland, means a bookmaking office licence as defined in Article 2(2) of the Betting, Gaming, Lotteries and Amusements (Northern Ireland) Order 1985;

["bookmaker" means a person who—

(a) carries on the business of receiving or negotiating bets or conducting pool betting operations (whether as principal or agent and whether regularly or not), or

(b) holds himself out or permits himself to be held out, in the course of a business, as a person within paragraph (a);][3]

"bookmaker's permit"—

(a) . . . [4]

(b) in Northern Ireland, means a bookmaker's licence as defined in Article 2(2) of the said Order of 1985;][5]

["general betting operating licence" has the same meaning as in Part 5 of the Gambling Act 2005 (see section 65(2)(c));][6]

. . . [7]

["on-course bet" has the meaning given by subsection (4A);][8]

"operator", in relation to bets made by means of a totalisator, means the person who, as principal, operates the totalisator;

"promoter", in relation to any betting, means the person to whom the persons making the bets look for the payment of their winnings, if any;

[. . .

. . .

. . .][9], [10], [11]

"winnings" includes winnings of any kind, and references to amount and to payment in relation to winnings shall be construed accordingly;

. . . [12]

[(4A) A bet is an on-course bet for the purposes of this Part of this Act if it—

(a) is made by a person present at a horse or dog race meeting or by a bookmaker,
(b) is not made through an agent of an individual making the bet or though an intermediary, and
(c) is made—
(i) with a bookmaker present at the meeting, or
(ii) by means of a totalisator situated in the United Kingdom, using facilities provided at the meeting by or by arrangement with the person operating the totalisator.][13]

(5) In this Part of this Act references to this Part of this Act include Schedule 1 to this Act.

---

1 Sub-s (3): words omitted repealed by the Finance Act 2002, ss 12(1), 141, Sch 4, Pt 1, paras 1, 9, Sch 40, Pt 1(4).

2 Sub-s (4): in definition "betting office licence" para (a) repealed by the Finance Act 2007, ss 105, 114, Sch 25, Pt 2, paras 3, 7(1), (2), Sch 27, Pt 6(3).

3 Sub-s (4): definition "bookmaker" substituted by the Finance Act 2004, s 15(1), (7)(a).

4 Sub-s (4): in definition "bookmaker's permit" para (a) repealed by the Finance Act 2007, ss 105, 114, Sch 25, Pt 2, paras 3, 7(1), (3), Sch 27, Pt 6(3).

5 Sub-s (4): definitions "betting office licence", "bookmaker" and "bookmaker's permit" inserted by the Finance Act 1986, s 6, Sch 4, Part I, para 4(a).

6 Sub-s (4): definition "general betting operating licence" inserted by the Finance Act 2007, s 105, Sch 25, Pt 2, paras 3, 7(1), (4).

7 Sub-s (4): definition "meeting" (omitted) repealed by the Finance Act 2007, ss 105, 114, Sch 25, Pt 2, paras 3, 7(1), (5), Sch 27, Pt 6(3).

8 Sub-s (4): definition "on-course bet" substituted by the Finance Act 2004, s 15(1), (7)(b).

9 Sub-s (4): definition "sponsored pool betting" (omitted) repealed by the Finance Act 2004, ss 15(1), (7)(c), 326, Sch 42, Pt 1(2).

10 Sub-s (4): definition "totalisator" (omitted) repealed by the Finance Act 2007, ss 105, 114, Sch 25, Pt 2, paras 3, 7(1), (5), Sch 27, Pt 6(3).

11 Sub-s (4): definition "track" (omitted) repealed by the Finance Act 2007, ss 105, 114, Sch 25, Pt 2, paras 3, 7(1), (5), Sch 27, Pt 6(3).

12 Sub-s (4): words omitted repealed by the Finance Act 1986, ss 6, 114, Sch 4, Part I, para 4(c), Sch 23, Part III.

13 Sub-s (4A): inserted by the Finance Act 2004, s 15(1), (8).

[The provisions of this Act which are not reproduced in this Part are considered in Section 2, Gaming.]

PART III
GENERAL

7.59 27 Offences by bodies corporate

Where an offence under section . . . [1] above, paragraph 13(1) or (3) or 14(1) of Schedule 1, . . . [2] paragraph 16 of Schedule 3 or paragraph 16 of Schedule 4 to this Act has been committed by a body corporate, every person who at the date of the commission of the offence was a director, general manager, secretary or other similar officer of the body corporate, or was purporting to act in any such capacity, shall be deemed to be guilty of that offence unless he proves—

(a) that the offence was committed without his consent or connivance, and
(b) that he exercised all such diligence to prevent the commission of the offence as he ought to have exercised having regard to the nature of his functions in that capacity and in all the circumstances.

1 Words omitted repealed by the Finance Act 1997, s 113, Sch 18, Pt II, with effect in relation to any gaming on or after 1 October 1997.

2 Words omitted repealed by the FA 1997, s 113, Sch 18, Pt II, with effect in relation to any gaming on or after 1 October 1997.

28, 29 [*Repealed by the Finance Act 1997, s 113(1), Sch 18, Pt V(2).*]

7.60 [29A Evidence by certificate, etc

(1) A certificate of the Commissioners—

(a) that any notice required by or under this Act to be given to them had or had not been given at any date, or

(b) that any permit, licence or authority required by or under this Act had or had not been issued at any date, or

(c) that any return required by or under this Act had not been made at any date, or

(d) that any duty shown as due in any return [made in pursuance of this Act or in any assessment made under section 12 of the Finance Act 1994][2] had not been paid at any date,

shall be sufficient evidence of that fact until the contrary is proved.

(2) A photograph of any document furnished to the Commissioners for the purposes of this Act and certified by them to be such a photograph shall be admissible in any proceedings, whether civil or criminal, to the same extent as the document itself.

(3) Any document purporting to be a certificate under subsection (1) or (2) above shall be deemed to be such a certificate until the contrary is proved.][1]

1 Inserted by the Finance Act 1986, s 7.

2 Words in square brackets substituted by the FA 1994, s 18(5).

30 [*Repealed by the Insolvency Act 1985, s 235, Sch 10, Pt IV; see now the Insolvency Act 1986, ss 175, 176, 327, 328, Sch 6, para 5.*]

7.61 31 Protection of officers

Where an officer takes any action in pursuance of instructions of the Commissioners or a Collector of Customs and Excise given in connection with the enforcement of the enactments relating to general betting duty, bingo duty [, remote gaming duty][1] or the duty on . . . [2] [amusement machine licences][3] and, apart from the provisions of this section, the officer would in taking that action be committing an offence under the enactments relating to betting or gaming, he shall not be guilty of that offence.

1 Words ", remote gaming duty" in square brackets inserted by the Finance Act 2007, s 8(1), Sch 1, Pt 2, para 4.

2 Words omitted repealed by the Finance Act 1997, s 113, Sch 18, Pt II.

3 Words in square brackets substituted, in relation to machines provided on or after 1 November 1995 and to licences for periods beginning on or after that date and the duty on such licences, by the Finance Act 1995, s 14, Sch 3, para 9(1).

7.62 32 Orders and regulations

(1) Any power conferred by any provision of this Act to make an order or regulations shall be exercisable by statutory instrument.

(2) . . . [1] Any statutory instrument made under any power conferred by this Act shall be subject to annulment in pursuance of a resolution of the House of Commons.

(3) But in the case of an order under section 26H(4) which has the effect of adding to the class of activities in respect of which remote gaming duty is chargeable—

(a) subsection (2) above shall not apply, and

(b) the order may not be made unless a draft has been laid before and approved by resolution of the House of Commons.][2]

(3) . . . [3]

---

1 Sub-s (2): words omitted repealed by the Finance Act 1997, s 113, Sch 18, Pt II.

2 First sub-s (3): inserted by the Finance Act 2007, s 8(1), Sch 1, Pt 2, para 5.

3 Second sub-s (3): repealed by the Finance Act 1997, s 113, Sch 18, Pt II.

7.63 [32A Application to limited liability partnerships

(1) This Act applies to limited liability partnerships as it applies to companies.

(2) In its application to a limited liability partnership, references to a director of a company are references to a member of the limited liability partnership.][1]

---

1 Inserted by the Limited Liability Partnerships Regulations 2001, SI 2001/1090, reg 9, Sch 5, para 8.

7.64 33 Interpretation

(1) In this Act—

"the Commissioners" means the Commissioners of Customs and Excise;

["gaming" means playing a game of chance for a prize . . . [1];][2]

"the prescribed sum" in relation to the penalty provided for an offence, means—

(a) if the offence was committed in England or Wales, the prescribed sum within the meaning of section 32 of the Magistrates' Courts Act 1980 (£1,000 or other sum substituted by order under section 143(1) of that Act); and

(b) *if the offence was committed in Scotland, the prescribed sum within the meaning of [subsection (8) of section 225 of the Criminal Procedure (Scotland) Act 1995 (£5,000 or other sum substituted by order under subsection (4) of that section)] [and*

(c) if the offence was committed in Northern Ireland, the prescribed sum within the meaning of Article 4 of the Fines and Penalties (Northern Ireland) Order 1984.]

[(1A) In the definition of "gaming" in subsection (1)—

(a) "game of chance" has the meaning given by section 6(2) of the Gambling Act 2005,

(b) "playing a game of chance" is to be read in accordance with section 6(3) of that Act, and

(c) "prize" does not include the opportunity to play the game again.][3]

(2) For the avoidance of doubt it is hereby declared that the imposition by this Act of general betting duty, pool betting duty, bingo duty[, remote gaming duty][4] or the duty on [amusement machine licences][5] does not make lawful anything which is unlawful apart from this Act.

---

1 Sub-s (1): in definition "gaming" words omitted repealed by the Finance Act 2009, s 116(1), (6)(a).

2 Sub-s (1): definition "gaming" substituted by the Finance Act 2007, s 105, Sch 25, Pt 2, paras 3, 10.

3 Sub-s (1A): inserted by the Finance Act 2009, s 116(1), (6)(b)..

4 Sub-s (2): words ", remote gaming duty" in square brackets inserted by the Finance Act 2007, s 8(1), Sch 1, Pt 2, para 6.

5 Sub-s (2): words "amusement machine licences" in square brackets substituted, in relation to

machines provided on or after 1 November 1995 and to licences for periods beginning on or after that date and the duty on such licences, by the Finance Act 1995, s 14, Sch 3, para 9(1).

7.65 34 Consequential and transitional provisions and repeals

(1) Schedule 5 (consequential amendments) and Schedule 6 (transitional and saving provisions) to this Act shall have effect, but without prejudice to the operation of sections 15 to 17 of the Interpretation Act 1978 (which relate to the effect of repeals).

(2) The enactments specified in Schedule 7 to this Act are hereby repealed to the extent mentioned in the third column of that Schedule.

7.66 35 Short title, construction, commencement and extent

(1) This Act may be cited as the Betting and Gaming Duties Act 1981.

(2) This Act shall be construed as one with the Customs and Excise Management Act 1979.

[(3) The following provisions of this Act do not extend to Northern Ireland—

(a) . . . [1]

(b) sections 29 and 30;

(c) . . . [1]

(d) paragraph 15 of Schedule 4;

. . . .][2], [1]

[(4) . . .][3]

---

[1] Sub-s (3): substituted by the Finance Act 1986, s 6, Sch 4, Part I.

[2] Sub-s (3): paras (a), (c) and the words after para (d) repealed by the Finance Act 1997, s 113, Sch 18, Pt II.

[3] Sub-s (4): inserted by the Finance Act 1985, s 8, Sch 5, Part I; repealed by the Finance Act 1986, s 114, Sch 23, Part III.

SCHEDULES

SCHEDULE 1
BETTING DUTIES
Section 12

Definitions

7.67

1 In this Schedule—

'general betting business' means a business the carrying on of which involves or may involve any sums becoming payable by the person carrying on the business by way of general betting duty [or would or might involve such sums becoming so payable if on-course bets were not excluded from that duty][1];

'general betting operations' means betting operations which do not involve liability to pool betting duty;

'pool betting business' means a business the carrying on of which involves or may involve any sums becoming payable by the person carrying on the business by way of pool betting duty [or would or might involve such sums becoming so payable if receipts from bets made for community benefit (as defined by section 8A of this Act) were not excluded from that duty][2].

---

[1] Words in square brackets inserted by the Finance Act 1987, s 3(3)(a) on 29 March 1987 (FA 1987, s 3(4)).

Books, records, accounts, etc

6 (1) Any person for the time being carrying on a general betting business or a pool betting business shall—

(a) keep in relation to the business such books, records and accounts in such form as the Commissioners may direct,

(b) for at least six months or such shorter or longer period as the Commissioners may direct, preserve any books, records and accounts directed to be kept by him under paragraph (a) above and any other books, records, accounts or documents relating to the business, on premises specified in sub-paragraph (2) below,

(c) permit any officer authorised in that behalf by the Commissioners to enter on any premises used for the purposes of the business, and, where the business is a general betting business, to remain on the premises at any time while they are being used, or when the officer has reasonable cause to believe that they are likely to be used, for the conduct of betting operations, and

(d) permit any officer so authorised to inspect any totalisator used for the purposes of the business, and to inspect and take copies of any books, records, accounts or other documents in his possession or power or on any premises used for the purposes of the business, being books, records, accounts or documents which relate or appear to relate to the business.

(2) The premises on which a person is to preserve any books, records, accounts or other documents under sub-paragraph (1)(b) above are—

(a) in the case of books, records, accounts and other documents relating to general betting operations, such of the premises used for the purposes of the business as the Commissioners may direct;

(b) . . . [1]

(c) in any other case, premises of which entry has been made in accordance with paragraph 4(2) above.

(3) The power of the Commissioners under sub-paragraph (1)(b) above to give directions as to the period for which a person is to preserve any books, records, accounts or documents relating to the business carried on by him shall be exercisable either in any particular case or in relation to any particular class of such books, records, accounts or documents.

---

1 Para 6: sub-para (2)(b) repealed by the Finance Act 2002, ss 12(1), 141, Sch 4, Pt 1, paras 1, 10(1), (10).

7 . . . [1]

---

1 Para 7: repealed by the Finance Act 2007, ss 105, 114, Sch 25, Pt 2, paras 3, 11(1), (2), Sch 27, Pt 6(3).

8 . . . [1]

---

1 Para 8: repealed by the Finance Act 2002, ss 12(1), 141, Sch 4, Pt 1, paras 1, 10(1), (11), Sch 40, Pt 1(4)

9 (1) The provisions of this paragraph shall apply to a bookmaker at any time when any person is for the time being, or has at any time during the immediately preceding two months been, authorised by that bookmaker to act as his agent for receiving or negotiating bets or otherwise conducting betting operations, other than such bets or operations as involve liability only to pool betting duty.

(2) The bookmaker shall maintain at any of his premises to which bets received by any such person as aforesaid as the bookmaker's agent are or were transmitted, or, if in the case of any such premises the Commissioners think fit, at such other places as the Commissioners may allow, a record in such form and containing such particulars as the Commissioners may direct in respect of any such person who is for the time being, and any such person who has at any time during the said two months been but is no longer authorised as aforesaid, being in either case a person by or on whose behalf bets received as aforesaid are or were transmitted to those premises.

(3) A bookmaker shall not be guilty of contravening or failing to comply with the provisions of sub-paragraph (2) above by reason of a failure to make an entry or alteration in the record if that entry or alteration is made before six o'clock in the evening of the day after that on which the happening which necessitated the entry or alteration took place.

Powers to enter premises and obtain information

10 (1) Where in the case of any track or other premises an officer has reason to believe that bookmaking on events taking place thereon is being or is to be carried on . . . [1] or that a totalisator is being or is to be operated in connection with those events, at a place on those premises or on any ground or premises adjacent thereto, he shall be entitled for the purpose of exercising the powers conferred by this paragraph to be admitted without payment to that place, and he may require—

- (a) any person who appears to him to be or intend carrying on bookmaking, providing such facilities or operating a totalisator there to give such information as he may demand and to produce to him any accounts, records, or other documents which appear to him to be connected with the business of bookmaking or with the provision of those facilities or the operation of that totalisator or which it appears to him will establish the identity of that person; and
- (b) any person who appears to him to have made a bet there with any bookmaker, or through the persons providing any such facilities, or by means of a totalisator, to give such information with respect to the bet as he may demand and to produce to him any document in connection with the bet supplied to that person by the bookmaker, the persons providing those facilities, or the operator of that totalisator, as the case may be,

and any such person as aforesaid shall comply with any such requirement.

(2) Where an officer—

- (a) has reason to believe that any person who is not a bookmaker is holding himself out as mentioned in section 12(1) of this Act at any place, and
- (b) has reason to suspect that person to have become liable by virtue of that section to pay an amount by way of general betting duty or pool betting duty,

the officer shall have the like powers with respect to that place as if the person so holding himself out were a bookmaker and that place were such a place as is mentioned in sub-paragraph (1) above.

---

[1] Para 10: in sub-para (1) words omitted repealed by the Finance Act 2004, ss 15(1), (9), 326, Sch 42, Pt 1(2).

Power of Commissioners to estimate general betting duty payable

11 . . . [1]

[(5) Subject to sub-paragraph (6) below, where under sub-paragraph (1) above a court orders that a betting office licence held by a person in respect of premises . . . [10] shall be forfeited and cancelled, no court of summary jurisdiction shall entertain an application by that person for the grant (or provisional grant) of a new betting office licence in respect of those premises or any other premises situated in the same petty sessions district as those premises made less than twelve months after that forfeiture and cancellation.

(6) Sub-paragraph (5) above—

(a) shall not prejudice the right of such a person as is mentioned in that sub-paragraph to seek the renewal of any betting office licence (other than that which is forfeited) which he holds; and

(b) applies notwithstanding anything in Article 12 of the Betting, Gaming, Lotteries and Amusements (Northern Ireland) Order 1985.][11]

---

1 Para 15: sub-para (A1) inserted by the Finance Act 2007, s 105, Sch 25, Pt 2, paras 3, 11(1), (3)(a).

2 Para 15: in sub-para (1) words "paragraph 13(3) above" in square brackets substituted by the Finance Act 1994, s 9(9), Sch 4, para 62(3)(a), in accordance with s 19 thereof.

3 Para 15: in sub-para (1) words omitted repealed by the Finance Act 1994, ss 9(9), 258, Sch 4, para 62(3)(a), Sch 26, Pt III, in accordance with s 19 thereof.

4 Para 15: in sub-para (a)(ii) words from "or a penalty" to "(penalties for errors)" in square brackets inserted by SI 2009/571, art 8, Sch 1, paras 5, 6.

5 Para 15: in sub-para (1)(a) words from "there has been" to "conduct taking place" in square brackets substituted by the Finance Act 1994, s 9(9), Sch 4, para 62(3)(b), in accordance with s 19 thereof.

6 Para 15: in sub-para (2) words omitted repealed by the Finance Act 2007, ss 105, 114, Sch 25, Pt 2, paras 3, 11(1), (3)(b), Sch 27, Pt 6(3).

7 Para 15: sub-paras (3), (4) repealed by the Finance Act 2007, ss 105, 114, Sch 25, Pt 2, paras 3, 11(1), (3)(c), Sch 27, Pt 6(3).

8 Para 15: sub-para (4A) inserted by the Access to Justice Act 1999, s 90(1), Sch 13, paras 119, 120(1), (3).

9 Para 15: sub-para (4A) repealed by the Finance Act 2007, ss 105, 114, Sch 25, Pt 2, paras 3, 10(1), (3)(c), Sch 27, Pt 6(3).

10 Para 15: in sub-para (5) words omitted repealed by the Finance Act 2007, ss 105, 114, Sch 25, Pt 2, paras 3, 11(1), (3)(d), Sch 27, Pt 6(3).

11 Para 15: sub-paras (5), (6) inserted by the Finance Act 1986, s 6, Sch 4, Pt I, para 11.

16 (1) If a justice of the peace . . . [1] is satisfied on information on oath that there is reasonable ground for suspecting that an offence in connection with general betting duty is being, has been, or is about to be committed on any premises, he may issue a warrant in writing authorising any officer to enter those premises (if necessary by force) at any time within [one month][2] from the time of the issue of the warrant and search them.

(2) An officer who enters premises under the authority of such a warrant may—

(a) seize and remove any records, accounts or other documents, money or valuable thing, instrument or other thing whatsoever found on the premises which he has reasonable cause to believe may be required as evidence for the purposes of proceedings in respect of such an offence, and

(b) search any person found on the premises whom he has reasonable cause to believe to be carrying on bookmaking on the premises.

---

1 Words omitted apply to Scotland only.

2 Words in square brackets substituted by the Police and Criminal Evidence Act 1984, s 119,

Sch 6, Pt I, para 39(b).

[*The provisions of this Act which are not reproduced in this Part are considered in Section 2, Gaming.*]

SCHEDULE 5

7.68 [*This Schedule contained consequential amendments to the Betting, Gaming and Lotteries Act 1963, the Gaming Act 1968 and the Customs and Excise Management Act 1979.*]

SCHEDULE 6

7.68.1 [*This Schedule contained consequential amendments to the Betting, Gaming and Lotteries Act 1963, the Gaming Act 1968 and the Customs and Excise Management Act 1979.*]

SCHEDULE 7

7.68.2 [*This Schedule contained consequential amendments to the Betting, Gaming and Lotteries Act 1963, the Gaming Act 1968 and the Customs and Excise Management Act 1979.*]

HORSERACE BETTING AND OLYMPIC LOTTERY ACT 2004

(2004 c 25)

Arrangement of sections

An Act to make provision for the sale of the Tote; to make provision for the abolition of the horserace betting levy system; to make provision for the establishment of National Lottery games designed to raise money in connection with the hosting by London of the Olympic Games in 2012; and for connected purposes.

[28th October 2004]

BE IT ENACTED by the Queen's most Excellent Majesty, by and with the advice and consent of the Lords Spiritual and Temporal, and Commons, in this present Parliament assembled, and by the authority of the same, as follows:—

PART 1
SALE OF THE TOTE

Dissolution, and transfer of assets

7.69 1 Dissolution of the Tote

(1) On the appointed day the Horserace Totalisator Board shall by virtue of this section cease to exist.

(2) In this Part 'the appointed day' means a day appointed for the purposes of this section by the Secretary of State by order made by statutory instrument.

Appointment

Appointment: 25 February 2011: see SI 2011/462, art 2.

Appointed Day

Appointed day (for the purposes of sub-s (1)): 13 July 2011: see SI 2011/1703, art 2.

7.70 2 Successor company: transfer

(1) All property, rights and liabilities to which the Horserace Totalisator Board was entitled or subject immediately before the appointed day shall on that day vest in the successor company by virtue of this section.

(2) In this Part 'the successor company' means a company which—

(a) is nominated for the purposes of this section by the Secretary of State in writing before the appointed day, and

(b) on the appointed day is—

(i) a company formed and registered under the [Companies Act 2006][1] as a company limited by shares, and

(ii) wholly owned by the Crown.

Appointment

Appointment: 25 February 2011: see SI 2011/462, art 2.

[1] Sub-s (2): in para (b)(i) words "the Companies Act 2006" in square brackets substituted by SI 2009/1941, art 2(1), Sch 1, para 221(1), (2). Date in force: 1 October 2009: see SI 2009/1941, art 1(2).

7.71 3 Sections 1 and 2: supplemental

(1) Anything done by or in relation to the Horserace Totalisator Board which has effect immediately before the appointed day shall continue to have effect as if done by or in relation to the successor company.

(2) Anything (including any legal proceedings) which immediately before the appointed day is in the process of being done by or in relation to the Board may be continued by or in relation to the successor company.

(3) So far as necessary or appropriate in consequence of section 2, on and after the appointed day—

(a) a reference to the Board in an agreement (whether written or not), instrument or other document shall be treated as a reference to the successor company, and

(b) a reference in an agreement (whether written or not), instrument or other document to a member or officer of the Board shall be treated as a reference either—

(i) to a person appointed for the purpose in writing by the successor company, or

(ii) where no person is appointed under sub-paragraph (i), to the person who most nearly corresponds in relation to the successor company to that member or officer of the Board.

(4) The successor company shall provide information on request about an appointment under subsection (3)(b)(i).

(5) Section 2(1) shall operate in relation to property, rights or liabilities—

(a) whether or not they would otherwise be capable of being transferred by the Board,

(b) without any instrument or other formality being required, and

(c) irrespective of any requirement for consent that would otherwise apply.

(6) In so far as section 2 transfers to the successor company liabilities under contracts of employment—

(a) nothing in that section or this section shall affect the operation of the [Transfer of Undertakings (Protection of Employment) Regulations 2006] [1], and

(b) the Secretary of State shall not appoint the appointed day unless satisfied that sufficient notice has been given to enable compliance with any applicable requirement of those regulations.

(7) An order under section 1 may include consequential, incidental or transitional provision.

(8) The Secretary of State shall consult the Board before nominating the successor company.

(9) The Secretary of State shall consult the Board and the successor company before appointing the appointed day.

(10) A nomination under section 2(2)(a) may be revoked (and replaced) before the appointed day.

Appointment

Appointment: 25 February 2011: see SI 2011/462, art 2.

[1] Sub-s (6): in para (a) words in square brackets substituted by SI 2006/246, reg 20(3), Sch 2, para 1(j).

7.72 4 Tax

(1) For the purposes of any enactment about income tax, corporation tax or capital gains tax—

(a) the successor company and the Horserace Totalisator Board shall be treated as the same person, and

(b) in particular, the transfer effected by section 2 shall be disregarded.

(2) The transfer effected by section 2—

(a) shall be disregarded for the purpose of section 12 of the Finance Act 1895 (c 16) (duty on property vested by Act, &c), and

(b) shall not give rise to liability under an enactment about stamp duty or stamp duty land tax in respect of anything done (by any person) before the transfer.

(3) Nothing in this Part constitutes arrangements for the purposes of—

(a) section 42(2) of the Finance Act 1930 (c 28) (relief from stamp duty),

(b) section 27(3) of the Finance Act 1967 (c 54) (stamp duty), or

(c) paragraph 2 of Schedule 7 to the Finance Act 2003 (c 14) (relief from stamp duty land tax).

Appointment

Appointment: 25 February 2011: see SI 2011/462, art 2.

Operation of successor company

7.73 5 Pre-sale issue of shares, &c to government

(1) The successor company shall comply with any request of the Secretary of State to issue securities to—

(a) the Secretary of State, or

(b) a person nominated by the Secretary of State.

(2) A request under subsection (1) may include provision about—

(a) the nature and nominal value of securities to be issued;

(b) timing;

(c) terms of issue.

(3) A request under subsection (1) requiring the issue of shares shall specify the nominal value of the shares to be issued; and the shares—

(a) shall be issued as fully paid,

(b) shall be treated for the purposes of the [the Companies Act 2006][1] (c 6) as having been paid up by virtue of payment of their nominal value in cash, and

(c) shall be treated for the purposes of the Corporation Tax Acts as if they had been issued wholly in consideration of a subscription of an amount equal to their nominal value.

(4) A debenture issued in accordance with a request under subsection (1) shall be treated for the purposes of the Corporation Tax Acts as if it had been issued wholly in consideration of a loan of an amount equal to the principal sum payable under the debenture.

(5) A request under subsection (1)—

(a) may be made before, on or after the appointed day, but
(b) may not be made after the successor company has ceased to be wholly owned by the Crown.

(6) The Secretary of State shall not make a request under subsection (1) without the consent of the Treasury.

(7) Where a security is issued in accordance with a request under subsection (1) to the Secretary of State or his nominee, neither the Secretary of State nor his nominee may dispose of the security without the consent of the Treasury.

Appointment

Appointment: 25 February 2011: see SI 2011/462, art 2.

1 Sub-s (3): in para (b) words "the Companies Act 2006" in square brackets substituted by SI 2009/1941, art 2(1), Sch 1, para 221(1), (3). Date in force: 1 October 2009: see SI 2009/1941, art 1(2).

7.74 6 Accounts

(1) This section applies for the purposes of statutory accounts prepared by the successor company.

(2) The transfer effected by section 2(1) shall be treated as having—
(a) occurred immediately after the end of the last complete accounting year of the Horserace Totalisator Board, and
(b) transferred all property, rights and liabilities to which the Board was entitled or subject immediately before the end of that year.

(3) For the purpose of subsection (2)(b) in its application to accounts of the successor company the value of an asset, or the amount of a liability, on transfer shall be taken as the value or amount assigned for the purposes of the corresponding accounts of the Board for its last complete accounting year.

(4) The amount to be included in the accounts in respect of an asset or liability shall be determined as if anything done by the Board had been done by the successor company.

(5) An amount included in the accounts for the Board's last complete accounting year as accumulated realised profits retained by the Board shall be treated as if realised and retained by the successor company.

(6) Before the preparation of the successor company's first set of statutory accounts for a complete accounting year, [sections 836 to 840 of the Companies Act 2006][1] (distribution: justification by reference to accounts) shall apply as if the successor company had prepared accounts for the relevant period in accordance with the preceding provisions of this section.

(7) In this section 'statutory accounts' means accounts prepared for the purpose of a provision of the [the Companies Act 2006][2].

Appointment

Appointment: 25 February 2011: see SI 2011/462, art 2.

1 Sub-s (6): words "sections 836 to 840 of the Companies Act 2006" in square brackets substituted by SI 2008/948, arts 3(1)(b), 6, Sch 1, Pt 2, para 231(1), (2)(a). Date in force: 6 April 2008: see SI 2008/948, art 2(2); for transitional provisions and savings see arts 6, 12 thereof.

2 Sub-s (7): words "the Companies Act 2006" in square brackets substituted by SI 2008/948, arts 3(1)(b), 6, Sch 1, Pt 2, para 231(1), (2)(b). Date in force: 6 April 2008: see SI 2008/948, art 2(2); for transitional provisions and savings see arts 6, 11, 12 thereof.

7.75 7 Shadow directors

While the successor company is wholly owned by the Crown, neither the Secretary of State nor the Treasury shall be treated as a shadow director of the successor company for the purpose of any provision of [the Companies Acts (as defined in section 2 of the Companies Act 2006)][1].

Appointment

Appointment: 25 February 2011: see SI 2011/462, art 2.

[1] Words "the Companies Acts (as defined in section 2 of the Companies Act 2006)" in square brackets substituted by SI 2007/2194, art 10(1), (2), Sch 4, Pt 3, para 103. Date in force: 1 October 2007: see SI 2007/2194, art 1(3)(a); for savings see art 12 thereof.

Post-transfer control of horserace pool betting

7.76 8 Exclusive licence

(1) The Gaming Board shall, if the Secretary of State so requires, issue to the successor company a licence (referred to in this Part as 'the exclusive licence') granting the successor company the right—

(a) to carry on pool betting business (in any form) in connection with horse races on approved horse racecourses,

(b) by way of business to receive or negotiate bets in connection with horse races on approved horse racecourses on terms that all or part of the winnings shall be calculated or regulated directly or indirectly by reference to the amounts or rates of payments or distributions in respect of winning bets made by way of pool betting, and

(c) to provide facilities in relation to a matter mentioned in paragraph (a) or (b).

(2) The exclusive licence shall, unless revoked under subsection (7), have effect for the period of seven years beginning with the date of issue.

(3) In requiring the issue of the exclusive licence the Secretary of State may specify terms or conditions of the licence.

(4) The Secretary of State—

(a) may require the issue of the exclusive licence before, on or after the appointed day,

(b) may require the issue of the exclusive licence after the successor company has ceased to be wholly owned by the Crown, and

(c) may not require the issue of the exclusive licence more than once.

(5) While the exclusive licence has effect—

(a) the successor company may authorise one or more other persons to do anything that the successor company is authorised to do by the exclusive licence, and

(b) a person other than the successor company may not do anything that the successor company is authorised to do by the exclusive licence, except in accordance with an authorisation under paragraph (a).

(6) An authorisation under subsection (5)(a) may be given on terms and conditions; which may, in particular, include provision—

(a) for payment to or by the successor company;

(b) for agency or commission;

(c) about facilities to be provided by the successor company under subsection (1)(c).

(7) The Gaming Board—

(a) may make an order revoking the exclusive licence if they think that a term or condition of the licence has been breached, and
(b) shall make an order revoking the exclusive licence if the Secretary of State so directs.

(8) A direction of the Secretary of State under subsection (7)(b) shall specify the reasons for the direction.

(9) An order revoking the exclusive licence—
(a) must specify the reasons for the revocation (or, in the case of revocation pursuant to a direction under subsection (7)(b), the reasons for the direction specified under subsection (8)), and
(b) shall take effect at such time as the order may specify.

(10) The Secretary of State may require revocation under subsection (7)(b) only while the successor company is wholly owned by the Crown.

(11) The exclusive licence may not be—
(a) renewed, or
(b) issued or revoked otherwise than in accordance with subsection (1) or (7).

Appointment

Appointment: 25 February 2011: see SI 2011/462, art 2.

7.77 9 Section 8: supplemental

(1) In considering whether to require the Gaming Board to issue or revoke the exclusive licence the Secretary of State shall consider whether the issue or revocation—
(a) would be in the best interests of members of the public who are in the habit of placing bets on horse races;
(b) would be in the best interests of the sport of horse racing;
(c) would promote the objectives of—
(i) preventing betting from being a source of crime or disorder, being associated with crime or disorder or being used to support crime,
(ii) ensuring that betting is conducted in a fair and open way, and
(iii) protecting children and other vulnerable persons from being harmed or exploited by betting.

(2) While the exclusive licence has effect—
(a) sections 4(1) and 4A(1) of the Betting, Gaming and Lotteries Act 1963 (c 2) (restriction on pool betting) (as substituted by section 10 of this Act) shall not apply in relation to anything done—
(i) by the successor company in pursuance of the exclusive licence, or
(ii) in accordance with an authorisation under section 8(5)(a) above, and
(b) nothing in section 4 or 4A of that Act shall prejudice the generality of section 8(5)(b) above.

(3) While the exclusive licence has effect—
(a) the successor company or a person authorised under section 8(5)(a) above may apply under section 9(2) of that Act for the grant or renewal of a betting office licence authorising the use of premises for carrying on activity in accordance with the exclusive licence,
(b) a betting office licence under section 9(2) of that Act shall not authorise the use of premises for doing anything prohibited by section 8(5)(b), and
(c) section 9(1) of that Act disapplies section 1(1) of that Act only in relation to activity authorised by a betting office licence.

(4) While the exclusive licence has effect—

(a) the successor company shall not be treated as a bookmaker for the purposes of that Act by virtue of anything done in accordance with the exclusive licence, and

(b) a person authorised under section 8(5)(a) above shall not be treated as a bookmaker for the purposes of that Act by virtue of anything done in accordance with the authorisation.

(5) A person who acts in contravention of section 8(5)(b) above shall be treated as having committed an offence under—

(a) section 4(1) of that Act, in the case of anything done on a track, or

(b) section 4A(1) of that Act, in the case of anything done otherwise than on a track,

whether or not he otherwise would have committed the offence.

(6) If a person commits or threatens a breach of section 8(5)(b), the successor company may (whether or not criminal proceedings are instituted against him by virtue of subsection (5) above) proceed against him in the High Court or a county court for damages or such other relief as the court thinks appropriate.

(7) Subsection (6) is subject to—

(a) Civil Procedure Rules, and

(b) section 1 of the Courts and Legal Services Act 1990 (c 41) (allocation of business between High Court and county courts).

Appointment

Sub-ss (1), (4), (6), (7): Appointment: 25 February 2011: see SI 2011/462, art 2.

7.78 10 Control when no exclusive licence

(1) For section 4 of the Betting, Gaming and Lotteries Act 1963 (c 2) (restriction on pool betting) substitute—

> **'4 Restriction on pool betting on track**
>
> (1) A person commits an offence if he carries on pool betting business on a track unless subsection (2), (3) or (5) applies.
>
> (2) This subsection applies to pool betting business which is in connection with horse racing and which is carried on—
>
> (a) by the holder of a bookmaker's permit,
>
> (b) on an approved horse racecourse,
>
> (c) on a day on which one or more horse races take place on the racecourse, and
>
> (d) in accordance with Part 2 of Schedule 1A.
>
> (3) This subsection applies to pool betting business in connection with horse racing carried on—
>
> (a) on an approved horse racecourse, and
>
> (b) in accordance with a notice (to be known as a 'point-to-point exemption notice') issued by the Gaming Board under this subsection.
>
> (4) A point-to-point exemption notice—
>
> (a) may be issued by the Gaming Board in response to an application in writing,
>
> (b) must relate to horse racing to be carried on along a single course specified in the notice,
>
> (c) must specify a maximum number of days, not exceeding 7, on which horse racing may be carried on in reliance on the notice,
>
> (d) may specify other conditions which relate to—
>
> (i) the operation of a totalisator,

(ii) the publication of terms on which pool bets may be made (and a condition may, in particular, relate to minimum stakes, or deductions), or

(iii) compliance with terms published under sub-paragraph (ii),

(e) must specify a calendar year during which the notice has effect, and

(f) must be issued before the beginning of that year.

(5) This subsection applies to pool betting business which is in connection with dog racing and which is carried on—

(a) on a dog racecourse which is a licensed track, and

(b) by means of a totalisator operated—

(i) in accordance with section 16, and

(ii) by the occupier of the track or by a person authorised by him in writing.

4A Restriction on pool betting off track

(1) A person commits an offence if he carries on pool betting business otherwise than on a track, unless subsection (2), (3) or (4) applies.

(2) This subsection applies to pool betting business which is in connection with horse racing and which is carried on—

(a) by the holder of a bookmaker's permit, and

(b) in accordance with Part 2 of Schedule 1A.

(3) This subsection applies to pool betting business which is carried on by a person registered for the purpose of this subsection (in this Act referred to as a 'registered pool promoter'); and Schedule 2 to this Act (registration and conduct of business) shall have effect.

(4) This subsection applies to pool betting business carried on in accordance with a licensed inter-track betting scheme.

4B Regulation of horserace pool betting

(1) Schedule 1A (which provides for the regulation of pool betting business in connection with horse racing) shall have effect.

(2) Subsection (3) applies where—

(a) a condition imposed by Part 2 of that Schedule requires or may require a person to act after the conclusion of a race or set of races in relation to which he conducts pool betting business, and

(b) the person fails, in respect of a matter wholly or partly relating to that race or set of races, to comply with the condition after that conclusion.

(3) The pool betting business carried on by the person in relation to the race or set of races shall be treated as not having been carried on in accordance with Part 2 of that Schedule.

(4) Subsection (5) applies where a person who has received or negotiated bets made by way of pool betting in connection with horse racing fails to comply with a requirement of Part 3 of that Schedule.

(5) Any pool betting business which was carried on by the person and to which the requirement was or might have been relevant shall be treated as not having been carried on in accordance with Part 2 of that Schedule.'

(2) After Schedule 1 to that Act (bookmakers' permits, &c) insert the Schedule 1A set out in Schedule 1 to this Act (regulation of horserace pool betting).

(3) Sections 281 and 282 of the Criminal Justice Act 2003 (c 44) (increases in maximum terms of imprisonment) shall apply to the Betting, Gaming and Lotteries Act 1963 (c 2) as amended by this section.

General

7.79 11 Preparatory work by the Tote

(1) The Horserace Totalisator Board may do anything that it or the Secretary of State thinks necessary or expedient in connection with—

(a) a provision of this Part,

(b) the operation of the successor company on or after the appointed day, or

(c) the listing, issue, sale or other disposal of securities of the successor company or a company associated with it.

(2) The Board shall so far as is reasonably practicable comply with—

(a) any request of the Secretary of State to provide information or assistance in connection with a matter specified in subsection (1)(a) to (c), and

(b) any direction of the Secretary of State made in connection with a matter specified in subsection (1)(a) to (c).

(3) Before making a request or giving a direction under subsection (2) the Secretary of State shall consult the Board.

7.80 12 Interpretation

(1) In this Part 'the Gaming Board' means the Gaming Board for Great Britain (established under section 10 of the Gaming Act 1968 (c 65)).

(2) For the purposes of this Part a company is wholly owned by the Crown if all its shares are held by the Crown.

(3) For the purposes of subsection (2) shares are held by the Crown if they are held—

(a) by a Minister of the Crown,

(b) by the nominee of a Minister of the Crown, or

(c) by a company of which all the shares are held by the Crown.

(4) In this Part 'securities' means shares (including stock), debentures, bonds and other securities, whether constituting a charge on the assets of a company or not.

(5) An expression used in this Part which is given a meaning by [the Companies Acts (as defined in section 2 of the Companies Act 2006)][1] for general purposes of that Act shall have the same meaning for the purposes of this Part.

(6) An expression used in this Part and in the Betting, Gaming and Lotteries Act 1963 (c 2) shall have the same meaning in this Part as in that Act.

---

1 Sub-s (5): words "the Companies Acts (as defined in section 2 of the Companies Act 2006)" in square brackets substituted by SI 2008/948, arts 3(1)(b), 6, Sch 1, Pt 2, para 231(1), (3). Date in force: 6 April 2008: see SI 2008/948, art 2(2); for transitional provisions and savings see arts 6, 11, 12 thereof.

7.81 13 Consequential amendments

Schedule 2 (consequential amendments) shall have effect.

Appointment

Appointment (for certain purposes): 13 July 2011: see SI 2011/1704, art 2.

7.82 14 Extent

This Part shall not extend to Northern Ireland.

PART 2
ABOLITION OF THE HORSERACE BETTING LEVY SYSTEM

7.83 15 Abolition of levy

(1) The Secretary of State may by order made by statutory instrument—

(a) repeal any of sections 24 to 30 of the Betting, Gaming and Lotteries Act 1963 (levy);
(b) repeal a provision of the Horserace Betting Levy Act 1969 (c 14);
(c) repeal a provision of the Horserace Betting Levy Act 1981 (c 30);
(d) provide for the Horserace Betting Levy Board to cease to exist.

(2) An order under subsection (1) may—
(a) repeal different provisions at different times;
(b) repeal a provision generally or only to a specified extent;
(c) make consequential provision (which may include provision amending or repealing an enactment, in addition to the provision made by section 17 and Schedule 4).

(3) An order under subsection (1) may make transitional provision or savings, which may include provision—
(a) modifying the effect of a provision pending its repeal;
(b) about the conduct of the Horserace Betting Levy Board pending the repeal of section 24 of the Betting, Gaming and Lotteries Act 1963;
(c) about the conduct of the Bookmakers' Committee pending the repeal of section 26 of that Act;
(d) about the conduct of an appeal tribunal pending the repeal of section 29 of that Act.

(4) An order under subsection (1) shall be subject to annulment in pursuance of a resolution of either House of Parliament.

7.84 16 Property of the Levy Board

(1) In this Part 'transfer scheme' means a scheme providing for the transfer of specified property, rights and liabilities of the Horserace Betting Levy Board—
(a) to a person specified in the scheme, and
(b) at a time specified in the scheme.

(2) If the Secretary of State directs the Board to make and submit to the Secretary of State a transfer scheme—
(a) the Board shall comply with the direction,
(b) the Secretary of State may approve the scheme with or without modification, and
(c) if approved, the scheme shall have effect.

(3) A direction of the Secretary of State under subsection (2)—
(a) shall specify a date by which the transfer scheme is to be made;
(b) may specify property, rights or liabilities to be transferred by the transfer scheme;
(c) may specify to whom property, rights or liabilities are to be transferred by the transfer scheme.

(4) The Secretary of State may make a transfer scheme if—
(a) the Board fails to comply with a direction under subsection (2), or
(b) the Secretary of State decides not to approve a scheme submitted under that subsection.

(5) A transfer scheme made under subsection (4) shall have effect.

(6) The Secretary of State shall not make or approve a transfer scheme under this section unless satisfied that any property or rights transferred will be used or exercised for the purpose of—
(a) the improvement of breeds of horses,
(b) the advancement or encouragement of veterinary science or veterinary education, or
(c) the improvement of horse racing.

(7) Schedule 3 (which makes supplementary provision in connection with directions and schemes under this section) shall have effect.

7.85 17 Consequential amendments

(1) The Secretary of State—

(a) may bring this section into force by provision included in an order made under section 15(1), and

(b) shall not make an order under section 15(1)(d) providing for the Horserace Betting Levy Board to cease to exist unless the order also makes provision, or an earlier order under section 15(1) has made provision, bringing this section into force at or before the time when that Board ceases to exist.

(2) Schedule 4 (consequential amendments) shall have effect.

(3) A certificate of approval issued under section 13 of the Betting, Gaming and Lotteries Act 1963 (c 2) before the coming into force of this section ('commencement')—

(a) shall continue to have effect after commencement as if issued by the Gaming Board for Great Britain under that section as amended by Schedule 4,

(b) may be revoked by the Gaming Board for Great Britain, and

(c) shall expire at the end of the period of three years beginning with the date of commencement (but without prejudice to the power to issue a new certificate).

7.86 18 Tax

(1) The Treasury may make regulations providing—

(a) for a tax provision not to apply, or to apply with modifications, in respect of anything done under or in consequence of a transfer scheme;

(b) for anything done under or in consequence of a transfer scheme to have or not have a specified consequence, or to be treated in a specified way, for the purposes of a tax provision;

(c) for anything done in connection with, or done by a person with rights in connection with, anything that was at any time transferred under a transfer scheme, to have or not have a specified consequence, or to be treated in a specified way, for the purposes of a tax provision;

(d) for a tax provision not to apply, or to apply with modifications, in respect of anything transferred under a transfer scheme;

(e) for anything transferred under a transfer scheme to be treated in a specified way for the purposes of a tax provision;

(f) for the withdrawal of relief (whether or not granted by virtue of the regulations), and the charging of tax, in connection with anything done under or in consequence of a transfer scheme where a specified event occurs, or specified conditions are satisfied, whether on or after the commencement of the scheme;

(g) for a power under this Part, or anything done in exercise of a power under this Part, to have or not have a specified consequence, or to be treated in a specified way, for the purposes of a tax provision.

(2) In subsection (1) 'tax provision' means a provision of an enactment about income tax, corporation tax, capital gains tax, stamp duty, stamp duty land tax or stamp duty reserve tax.

(3) Regulations under this section—

(a) shall be made by statutory instrument, and

(b) shall be subject to annulment in pursuance of a resolution of either House of Parliament.

7.87 19 Interpretation: 'enactment'

In this Part 'enactment' includes an Act of the Scottish Parliament.

7.88 20 Extent

This Part shall not extend to Northern Ireland.

PART 4
GENERAL

7.89 38 Repeals

The enactments listed in Schedule 6 are hereby repealed to the extent specified.

Appointment

Appointment (for certain purposes): 8 April 2005: see SI 2005/1134, art 2.
Appointment (for certain purposes): 13 July 2011: see SI 2011/1704, art 2.

7.90 39 Money

There shall be paid out of money provided by Parliament—

(a) any expenditure of the Secretary of State in connection with this Act,
(b) any expenditure of the National Debt Commissioners in connection with this Act, and
(c) any increase attributable to this Act in the sums payable out of money provided by Parliament under another enactment.

7.91 40 Commencement

(1) The preceding provisions of this Act shall come into force in accordance with provision made by order of the Secretary of State.

(2) An order under subsection (1)—

(a) may make provision that has effect generally or only for specified purposes,
(b) may make different provision for different purposes,
(c) may include incidental, consequential or transitional provision, and
(d) shall be made by statutory instrument.

(3) Section 29 shall not be brought into force unless the Secretary of State has made an order under section 22(2).

7.92 41 Extent

(1) An amendment effected by this Act shall have the same extent as the enactment amended (or as the relevant part of the enactment amended).

(2) Sections 14, 20 and 37 are subject to subsection (1) above.

7.93 42 Short title

This Act may be cited as the Horserace Betting and Olympic Lottery Act 2004.

7.94

SCHEDULE 1
NEW SCHEDULE 1A TO THE BETTING, GAMING AND LOTTERIES ACT 1963
Section 10

'SCHEDULE 1A

REGULATION OF HORSERACE POOL BETTING

PART 1
INTRODUCTION

1

Part 2 of this Schedule specifies the conditions to be complied with, for the purposes of sections 4(2)(d) and 4A(2)(b), in relation to pool betting business.

2

Part 3 of this Schedule makes provision for the supervision of pool betting business.

3

In this Schedule 'pool betting business' means pool betting business in connection with horse racing.

PART 2
CONDITIONS

4 **Totalisator**

Any totalisator being used must—

(a) be in proper working order, and
(b) be properly operated.

5 **Publicity for arrangements**

(1) A person receiving or negotiating bets in relation to a race or set of races must display in a conspicuous position a notice stating, prominently and in easily legible print—

(a) the minimum amount (if there is one) that he will accept as a stake,
(b) the amounts or percentage of the aggregate of the stakes that he will distribute by way of winnings,
(c) the principles that he will apply in calculating winnings (including any rules for rounding sums up or down),
(d) the arrangements that he will make for enabling persons to claim winnings,
(e) the arrangements that he will make in respect of winnings not claimed, and
(f) the arrangements that he will make if there is no winning bet.

(2) Where a person receives or negotiates bets by the use of remote communication of a kind that does not permit the display of a notice, sub-paragraph (1) shall not apply but the person must—

(a) have prepared a notice of the kind required by sub-paragraph (1),
(b) inform the person making the bet, or arrange for him to be informed, of a method by which he can see a copy of the notice, and
(c) if the person making the bet asks to be supplied with a copy of the notice, comply with the request.

(3) In sub-paragraph (2) 'remote communication' means communication using—

(a) the internet,
(b) telephone,
(c) television,
(d) radio, or
(e) any other kind of electronic or other technology for facilitating communication.

(4) Nothing in sub-paragraph (1)—
(a) provides a defence to an offence under section 10, or
(b) excuses compliance with a provision of regulations under paragraph 3 of Schedule 4.

(5) The Secretary of State may by regulations—
(a) provide that a specified system or method of communication is or is not to be treated as a form of remote communication for the purposes of sub-paragraph (2) (and sub-paragraph (3) is subject to any regulations under this paragraph);
(b) provide that a specified system or method of communication is or is not to be treated for the purposes of sub-paragraph (2) as being of a kind that does not permit the display of a notice.

(6) Regulations under sub-paragraph (5)—
(a) may make different provision for different circumstances,
(b) shall be made by statutory instrument, and
(c) shall be subject to annulment in pursuance of a resolution of either House of Parliament.

6

(1) Where a person makes statements in accordance with paragraph 5 in respect of a race or set of races—
(a) he may not alter any of the statements in respect of that race or set of races, and
(b) he must act in accordance with the statements.

(2) But sub-paragraph (1) does not apply to a person before he has received or negotiated a bet in respect of the race or set of races to which the statements relate.

7

Where a person receives or negotiates bets in respect of a race or set of races, as soon as is reasonably practicable after the conclusion of the race or set he must make reasonable arrangements to announce or display details of the amounts payable by way of winnings.

8 Compliance with supervision

A person who receives or negotiates bets must—
(a) comply with any requirement imposed by or under Part 3 of this Schedule,
(b) co-operate with the supervising accountant appointed under that Part,
(c) co-operate with the technical adviser appointed under that Part, and
(d) co-operate with any person authorised by the supervising accountant or the technical adviser under paragraph 11(2)(e) or 13(2)(f).

9 Annual fee

(1) A person who carries on pool betting business in a calendar year must have paid the prescribed fee in respect of that year.

(2) In sub-paragraph (1) 'prescribed' means prescribed by order of the Secretary of State.

(3) An order under sub-paragraph (2)—

(a) shall include provision about the timing and manner of payment,

(b) shall provide for fees to be paid (by the person who receives them in accordance with arrangements prescribed by virtue of paragraph (a)) into the Consolidated Fund,

(c) may make different provision for different circumstances,

(d) shall be made by statutory instrument, and

(e) shall be subject to annulment in pursuance of a resolution of either House of Parliament.

(4) In prescribing fees under this paragraph the Secretary of State shall aim, so far as is reasonably practicable, to ensure that the amount paid by way of fees in respect of a calendar year equals the expenditure incurred during that year in respect of—

(a) the performance of the functions of the supervising accountant and technical adviser under Part 3, and

(b) the activities of the Gaming Board in relation to pool betting business.

PART 3
SUPERVISION

10 Supervising accountant

(1) The Gaming Board shall appoint a person who is eligible for appointment as a company auditor (in accordance with section 25 of the Companies Act 1989 (c 40)) to carry out such activities as he thinks necessary or expedient for the purpose of determining whether the conditions in Part 2 of this Schedule are complied with by persons carrying on pool betting business.

(2) The person appointed under sub-paragraph (1) is referred to in this Part as the 'supervising accountant'.

11

(1) The supervising accountant may do anything that he thinks necessary or expedient for the purpose of determining whether the conditions in Part 2 of this Schedule have been complied with.

(2) In particular, the supervising accountant—

(a) may require access to premises on which pool betting business is being or has been carried on,

(b) may require any person to produce for examination any accounts or other document,

(c) may require any person to permit the supervising accountant to examine a record (whether held on computer or otherwise),

(d) may require any person to supply a copy of any accounts or other document,

(e) may authorise a person in writing to do anything that the supervising accountant could do by virtue of this paragraph, and

(f) may delegate a function under this Part.

12 Technical adviser

(1) The Gaming Board shall appoint a person to advise the supervising accountant on the working condition of totalisators ('the technical adviser').

(2) Before appointing an adviser under this paragraph the Gaming Board shall consult the supervising accountant.

13

(1) The technical adviser may do anything that he thinks necessary or expedient for the purpose of advising the supervising accountant whether the conditions in Part 2 of this Schedule have been complied with.

(2) In particular, the technical adviser—

(a) may require access to premises on which a totalisator is or has been in operation in relation to pool betting business,

(b) may carry out a process for the purposes of examining the operation of a totalisator,

(c) may require any person to produce a document for examination,

(d) may require any person to permit the technical adviser to examine a record (whether held on computer or otherwise),

(e) may require any person to supply a copy of a document,

(f) may authorise a person in writing to do anything that the technical adviser could do by virtue of this paragraph, and

(g) may delegate a function under this Part.

14 Submission of accounts

(1) A person who carries on pool betting business in any month shall send to the supervising accountant a statement of the person's accounts for pool betting business carried on by him in that month.

(2) A statement submitted under sub-paragraph (1) must, in particular—

(a) specify any amounts carried over from one race or set of races to another in accordance with arrangements of a kind described in paragraph 5(1)(f), and

(b) give such other information as the supervising accountant may require for the purpose of determining whether the conditions in Part 2 of this Schedule have been complied with.

(3) The requirement under sub-paragraph (1) must be complied with before the end of the period of 28 days beginning with the last day of the month to which the accounts relate.

(4) Where the supervising accountant imposes a requirement under sub-paragraph (2)(b)—

(a) he may impose the requirement in relation to accounts for any month, whether ending before or after the requirement is imposed and whether or not accounts for that month have been submitted, and

(b) if he imposes the requirement in relation to accounts for a month ending before the requirement is imposed—

(i) a person who has already submitted accounts for that month must re-submit them, and

(ii) in relation to a person obliged to re-submit accounts, sub-paragraph (3) shall have effect as if the period of 28 days began with the day on which the requirement came to his notice.

15

Where accounts are submitted to the supervising accountant under paragraph 14 he shall—

(a) examine them, and

(b) arrange for their retention for a period of at least two years.

16 Annual audit

(1) This paragraph applies to a person who submits accounts to the supervising accountant under paragraph 14 during a calendar year.

(2) As soon as is reasonably practicable after the end of the calendar year the supervising accountant shall, in relation to each person to whom this paragraph applies—

(a) audit the person's accounts for pool betting business in that year (as submitted under paragraph 14),

(b) certify whether, so far as he is reasonably able to ascertain—

(i) the person has complied with paragraph 14,

(ii) the accounts are complete and accurate, and

(iii) the pool betting business carried on by the person during that year has been carried on in accordance with Part 2 of this Schedule.

(3) Having audited and certified a person's accounts under sub-paragraph (2) the supervising accountant shall as soon as is reasonably practicable send the audited accounts and the certificate to the person.

(4) As soon as is reasonably practicable after receiving audited accounts and a certificate under sub-paragraph (3) a person must send two copies of each to the Gaming Board.

(5) The Gaming Board shall make one copy of any accounts and certificate received under sub-paragraph (4) available for inspection by the public—

(a) at all reasonable times, and

(b) without charge.

17 Report to Gaming Board

If the supervising accountant suspects that pool betting business has been carried on otherwise than in accordance with Part 2 of this Schedule, he shall report the matter to the Gaming Board.

18

The supervising accountant and the technical adviser shall on request make available to the Gaming Board any accounts or other document supplied or provided under paragraph 11, 13 or 14.

19 Offences

A person commits an offence if he obstructs the supervising accountant or the technical adviser in the exercise of a function under this Part.

20

A person commits an offence if without reasonable excuse he fails to co-operate with the supervising accountant or the technical adviser in the exercise of a function under this Part.

21

A person commits an offence if he supplies to the supervising accountant or the technical adviser information which the person knows to be—

(a) false, or

(b) misleading.

22

In paragraphs 19 to 21 'person' does not mean only a person who carries on or has carried on pool betting business.

23

A person commits an offence if he fails to comply with paragraph 14(1) or 16(4).

24

(1) A person guilty of an offence under any of paragraphs 19 to 21 shall be liable on summary conviction to a fine not exceeding level 3 on the standard scale.

(2) A person guilty of an offence under paragraph 23 shall be liable on summary conviction to—

(a) imprisonment for a term not exceeding six months,

(b) a fine not exceeding level 5 on the standard scale, or

(c) both.'

SCHEDULE 2

SALE OF THE TOTE: CONSEQUENTIAL AMENDMENTS

Section 13

7.95 1 **Betting, Gaming and Lotteries Act 1963 (c 2)**

The Betting, Gaming and Lotteries Act 1963 shall be amended as follows.

2 In section 1 (restriction on using premises for betting)—

(a) in subsection (1)(a) for 'section 4(1)' substitute 'section 4(2), (3) or (5)', and

(b) in subsection (5)(a) omit 'but no other races'.

3 In section 3 (authorisation of agents)—

(a) in subsection (1) omit—

(i) 'or to the Totalisator Board',

(ii) 'or, as the case may be, by the said Board', and

(iii) 'or by the said Board',

(b) in subsection (2) omit—

(i) 'or to the said Board', and

(ii) 'or, as the case may be, the Board', and

(c) in subsection (3) omit—

(i) 'The said Board and', and

(ii) 'by that Board or, as the case may be,'.

4 In section 5(3) (restriction of betting on tracks) omit—

(a) 'by the Totalisator Board or, with the authority of that Board, by the persons having the management of that racecourse', and

(b) 'by that Board or, as the case may be, by those persons'.

5 In section 6(1) (restriction of bookmaking on tracks) omit 'only'.

6 In section 9 (betting office licences and betting agency permits)—

(a) in subsection (1) omit the words from 'Provided that' to the end,

(b) subsection (2)(b) shall cease to have effect, and

(c) in subsection (2)(c)(i) omit—

(i) 'or by the Totalisator Board', and

(ii) 'or, as the case may be, with or through that Board'.

7 In section 11(1) (bookmaker's permit and betting agency permit: cancellation and disqualification) after ', 4(1)' insert ', 4A(1)'.

8 Section 12 (which establishes the Horserace Totalisator Board) shall cease to have effect.

9 Section 14 (Tote's monopoly in relation to pool betting) shall cease to have effect.

10 Section 15 (Tote's additional powers and duties) shall cease to have effect.

11 In section 16(1) (totalisators on licensed tracks) for '4(1)(b)' substitute '4(5)'.

12 (1) Section 24 (Horserace Betting Levy Board) shall be amended as follows.

(2) In subsection (1) for 'the Totalisator Board' substitute ', while the exclusive licence under section 8 of the Horserace Betting and Olympic Lottery Act 2004 (sale of

the Tote) has effect, the successor company nominated for the purposes of section 2 of that Act'.

(3) In subsection (2)—

(a) for 'seven other members' substitute 'six other members', and

(b) omit subsection (2)(e).

(4) In subsection (4)—

(a) for ', the Bookmakers' Committee and the Totalisator Board respectively' substitute 'or the Bookmakers' Committee', and

(b) for 'subsection (2)(b), (d) or (e)' substitute 'subsection (2)(b) or (d)'.

13 In section 30 (contributions by Totalisator Board)—

(a) in each place (including in the heading) before 'Totalisator Board' insert 'successor company to the', and

(b) after subsection (1) insert—

'(1A) Subsection (1) does not apply to any contribution which the successor company to the Totalisator Board is liable to make—

(a) in respect of a time when the exclusive licence does not have effect, and

(b) as a bookmaker.'

14 In section 31 (accounts and reports)—

(a) in subsection (1)—

(i) for 'and the Totalisator Board shall each' substitute 'shall',

(ii) for 'proper statements' substitute 'a proper statement',

(iii) omit 'of each of the Boards', and

(iv) omit 'in question', and

(b) for subsection (2) substitute—

'(2) As soon as reasonably practicable after its accounts for a levy period have been audited, the Levy Board shall submit to the Secretary of State a report of its proceedings during that period which shall include the statement of account and the auditor's report for that period; and the Secretary of State shall lay before Parliament a copy of each report received by him under this subsection.'

15 In section 52(1) (penalties) after '4,' insert '4A,'.

16 In section 55(1) (interpretation)—

(a) in the definition of 'bookmaker' omit—

(i) 'other than the Totalisator Board', and

(ii) for 'sponsored pool betting business' substitute 'pool betting business on an approved racecourse in accordance with a point-to-point exemption notice',

(b) after the definition of 'game of chance' and 'gaming' insert—

'"the Gaming Board" means the Gaming Board for Great Britain;',

(c) after the definition of 'player' insert—

'"point-to-point exemption notice" has the meaning given by section 4(3)(b) of this Act;',

(d) omit the definition of 'recognised horse race',

(e) in the definition of 'registered pool promoter' for 'section 4(2)' substitute 'section 4A(3)', and

(f) omit the definitions of—

(i) 'sponsored pool betting', and

(ii) 'the Totalisator Board'.

17 In paragraph 19(a)(i) of Schedule 1 (permits) omit 'in the case of an applicant other than the Totalisator Board,'.

18 Gaming Act 1968 (c 65)

In paragraph 6 of Schedule 1 to the Gaming Act 1968 (Gaming Board: remuneration of staff, &c) after '(including the inspectors appointed under section 43 of this Act' insert 'and the supervising accountant and technical adviser appointed under Schedule 1A to the Betting, Gaming and Lotteries Act 1963 (c 2) and anyone acting under the authority of the supervising accountant or technical adviser)'.

19 Horserace Betting Levy Act 1969 (c 14)

In section 5 of the Horserace Betting Levy Act 1969 (annual contribution by Totalisator Board)—

(a) in each place in subsection (1) (and the heading) before 'Totalisator Board' insert 'successor company to the',

(b) in subsection (1) for 'object' substitute 'objects', and

(c) after subsection (1) insert—

'(1A) Subsection (1) does not apply to any contribution which the successor company to the Totalisator Board is liable to make—

(a) in respect of a time when the exclusive licence does not have effect, and

(b) as a bookmaker.'

20 Race Relations Act 1976 (c 74)

In Part II of Schedule 1A to the Race Relations Act 1976 (persons subject to statutory duty) omit—

'The Horserace Totalisator Board.'

21 National Lottery etc Act 1993 (c 39)

Section 17 of the National Lottery etc Act 1993 (extension of powers of Tote) shall cease to have effect.

22 Freedom of Information Act 2000 (c 36)

In Part VI of Schedule 1 to the Freedom of Information Act 2000 (public authorities) omit—

'The Horserace Totalisator Board.'

SCHEDULE 3

HORSERACE BETTING LEVY BOARD: TRANSFER OF PROPERTY

Section 16

7.96 1 Introductory

In this Schedule—

'the Board' means the Horserace Betting Levy Board,

'transfer direction' means a direction of the Secretary of State under section 16(2), and

'transfer scheme' means a transfer scheme under section 16.

2 Board to assist Secretary of State

The Board shall on request give the Secretary of State information or assistance in connection with—

(a) a transfer direction which the Secretary of State has given or may give, or

(b) a transfer scheme which the Secretary of State has made or may make.

3 Ancillary powers of Board

(1) The Board may do anything that it thinks necessary or appropriate in connection with a transfer direction or a transfer scheme.

(2) In particular, the Board may enter into an agreement which confers or imposes on the Board rights or liabilities in respect of anything which has been or is to be transferred by a transfer scheme; and those rights and liabilities may include—

(a) rights to receive payments by way of consideration for transfer or otherwise, and

(b) liabilities to make payments.

(3) But the Board may enter into an agreement by virtue of sub-paragraph (2) only with the consent of—

(a) the Secretary of State, and

(b) the Treasury.

4 Ancillary powers of Secretary of State

The Secretary of State may with the consent of the Treasury enter into an agreement which confers or imposes on the Secretary of State rights or liabilities in respect of anything which has been or is to be transferred by a transfer scheme.

5 Content of transfer scheme

A transfer scheme—

(a) may transfer property, rights or liabilities whether or not they would otherwise be capable of being transferred,

(b) may dispense with a formality in relation to a transfer (whether or not it would otherwise be required by virtue of an enactment or instrument),

(c) may dispense with a requirement for consent (whether arising under an enactment, an instrument or an agreement),

(d) may provide for a transfer not to have an effect which it would otherwise have by virtue of an enactment, instrument or agreement, and

(e) may provide for a transfer to have an effect different to that which it would otherwise have by virtue of an enactment, instrument or agreement.

6 In specifying property, rights or liabilities to be transferred a transfer scheme—

(a) may use any manner of description (which may include reference to criteria specified in the scheme or to be determined in accordance with the scheme),

(b) may provide for exceptions, and

(c) may provide for the division of property, rights or liabilities in a manner specified in the scheme or to be determined in accordance with the scheme.

7 A transfer scheme may transfer property, rights or liabilities which—

(a) do not exist when the scheme is made but do exist when the transfer takes effect, or

(b) become property, rights or liabilities of the Board after the scheme is made and before the transfer takes effect.

8 A transfer scheme may transfer property, rights or liabilities to more than one person; and a scheme making provision under this paragraph may provide for property, rights or liabilities—

(a) to vest jointly in a manner specified by the scheme or determined in accordance with the scheme, or

(b) to be divided in a manner specified by the scheme or determined in accordance with the scheme.

9 A transfer scheme—

(a) may impose obligations on a person to whom property, rights or liabilities are transferred,

(b) may require a person to whom property, rights or liabilities are transferred to enter into an agreement of a specified kind or for a specified purpose,

(c) may make provision for the enforcement of an obligation imposed by virtue of this paragraph (which may, in particular, provide for an obligation to be treated as if it arose under a contract between specified persons), and

(d) may make provision for the enforcement of a requirement included in a scheme by virtue of this paragraph.

10 (1) A transfer scheme may include provision for the payment of compensation in a case where—

(a) as a result of a provision of the scheme—

(i) a third-party right becomes enforceable partly against one transferee and partly against another, or

(ii) a third-party liability becomes enforceable partly by one transferee and partly by another, and

(b) an effect of that result is to reduce the value of—

(i) property of the third party, or

(ii) a right of the third party.

(2) Provision included under this paragraph may, in particular—

(a) provide for compensation to be paid by a transferee;

(b) provide for compensation to be paid by the transferor;

(c) provide for compensation to be paid by the Secretary of State;

(d) provide for arbitration (as to liability or quantum).

(3) In this paragraph—

(a) a reference to a third-party right, in relation to a provision of a transfer scheme, is a reference to a right of a person who under that provision is neither the transferor nor a transferee,

(b) a reference to a third-party liability, in relation to a provision of a transfer scheme, is a reference to a liability of a person who under that provision is neither the transferor nor a transferee,

(c) a reference to a right's being enforceable includes a reference to its being enforceable if certain events occur or circumstances appertain,

(d) 'transferee' means a person to whom property, rights or liabilities are transferred under a transfer scheme, and

(e) 'transferor' means the Board.

11 A transfer scheme may make consequential, incidental or transitional provision; in particular, a transfer scheme—

(a) may provide for anything done by or in relation to the Board to have effect as if done by or in relation to another person,

(b) may permit anything (which may include legal proceedings), which is in the process of being done by or in relation to the Board when a provision of a transfer scheme takes effect, to be continued by or in relation to another person, and

(c) may provide for a reference to the Board in an agreement (whether written or not), instrument or other document to be treated as a reference to another person.

12 Transfer of undertakings

(1) Nothing in a transfer scheme shall affect the operation of the [Transfer of Undertakings (Protection of Employment) Regulations 2006][1].

(2) The Secretary of State shall not approve, make or modify a transfer scheme unless satisfied that sufficient notice has been given to enable compliance with any applicable requirement of those regulations.

13 Certificate of title

(1) The Secretary of State may certify that specified property, rights or liabilities vest in a specified person by virtue of a transfer scheme.

(2) A certificate under this paragraph shall be conclusive.

14 Modification of scheme

(1) This paragraph applies where—

(a) a transfer scheme provides for the transfer of specified property, rights or liabilities, and

(b) the transfer has not yet taken effect (whether or not another transfer under the scheme has taken effect).

(2) The Secretary of State may modify the scheme in so far as it relates to the transfer.

15 (1) This paragraph applies where—

(a) a transfer scheme provides for the transfer of specified property, rights or liabilities, and

(b) the transfer has taken effect.

(2) The Secretary of State may modify the scheme in so far as it relates to the transfer.

(3) Modification under this paragraph must be made by order of the Secretary of State made by statutory instrument.

(4) An order under this paragraph may not be made without the consent of—

(a) the person to whom the transfer is made, and

(b) any other person specified in or in relation to the provision to be modified.

(5) An order under this paragraph shall not be made unless a draft has been laid before Parliament.

16 Consultation and consent

The Secretary of State shall consult the Board before—

(a) giving a transfer direction,

(b) modifying a transfer scheme under section 16(2)(b) or paragraph 14 or 15,

(c) approving a transfer scheme, or

(d) making a transfer scheme.

17 The Secretary of State shall not approve or make a transfer scheme which provides for the transfer to a person of property, rights or liabilities unless satisfied that the person has consented to—

(a) the transfer, and

(b) the terms of the scheme relevant to the transfer.

18 Accounts

If the Secretary of State directs the Board to prepare accounts in respect of a specified period ending with the day on which a transfer scheme comes into force—

(a) the Board shall comply with the request,

(b) the Board shall arrange for the accounts to be audited by qualified accountants,

(c) the Board shall submit the accounts and the auditors' report to the Secretary of State, and

(d) the Secretary of State shall lay a copy of the accounts and the auditors' report before Parliament.

[1] Para 12: in sub-para (1) words in square brackets substituted by SI 2006/246, reg 20(3), Sch 2, para 1(j).

SCHEDULE 4
ABOLITION OF THE HORSERACE BETTING LEVY SYSTEM: CONSEQUENTIAL AMENDMENTS
Section 17

7.97 1 **Betting, Gaming and Lotteries Act 1963 (c 2)**

The Betting, Gaming and Lotteries Act 1963 shall be amended as follows.

2 (1) Section 13 (approval of horse-race courses) shall be amended as follows.

(2) In subsections (1) and (2) for 'The Levy Board' substitute 'The Gaming Board'.

(3) In subsection (1) omit ', and the Board may at any time revoke any such certificate issued by them'.

(4) At the end add—

'(3) The Gaming Board shall grant a certificate of approval requested in respect of any ground if satisfied that the arrangements for the management of the ground are reasonably consistent with pursuit of the objectives of—

(a) preventing betting from being a source of crime or disorder, being associated with crime or disorder or being used to support crime,

(b) ensuring that betting is conducted in a fair and open way, and

(c) protecting children and other vulnerable persons from being harmed or exploited by betting.

(4) In particular, the Gaming Board shall consider whether—

(a) the place mentioned in subsection (2) will be clearly delineated,

(b) the terms on which members of the public are invited to make bets will be clearly displayed, and

(c) satisfactory arrangements will be made—

(i) to control the conduct of persons receiving or negotiating bets on the ground, and

(ii) to address complaints made by members of the public about the conduct of persons receiving or negotiating bets on the ground.

(5) If the Gaming Board would be satisfied in respect of the matters specified in subsections (3) and (4) if the certificate of approval were granted on conditions, the Gaming Board shall—

(a) grant the certificate of approval, and

(b) impose the conditions.

(6) The Gaming Board shall not grant a certificate of approval unless the prescribed fee has been paid for the certificate; and subsections (3) and (5) are subject to this subsection.

(7) The Gaming Board may revoke a certificate of approval if not satisfied that the arrangements for the management of the ground are reasonably consistent with pursuit of the objectives specified in subsection (3)(a) to (c) (having regard, in particular, to the matters specified in subsection (4)).

(8) A certificate of approval shall, unless earlier revoked, expire at the end of the period of three years beginning with the date of issue (but without prejudice to the power to issue a new certificate).

(9) If the Gaming Board refuse a request for a certificate of approval, or revoke a certificate of approval, they shall give their reasons in writing.

(10) In subsection (6) 'prescribed' means prescribed by order of the Secretary of State.

(11) An order under subsection (10)—
- (a) shall include provision about the timing and manner of payment,
- (b) shall provide for fees to be paid into the Consolidated Fund,
- (c) may make different provision for different circumstances,
- (d) shall be made by statutory instrument, and
- (e) shall be subject to annulment in pursuance of a resolution of either House of Parliament.'

3 In section 55(1) (interpretation)—
- (a) in the definition of 'approved horse racecourse' for 'issued by the Levy Board' substitute 'issued by the Gaming Board for Great Britain', and
- (b) omit the entries for—
  - (i) 'Bookmakers' Committee',
  - (ii) 'the Levy Board', and
  - (iii) 'levy period'.

4 In Schedule 1 (bookmaker's permits, betting agency permits and betting office licences)—
- (a) paragraph 25A shall cease to have effect, and
- (b) paragraph 36 shall cease to have effect.

5 Parliamentary Commissioner Act 1967 (c 13)

In Schedule 2 to the Parliamentary Commissioner Act 1967 (departments, &c subject to investigation) omit—

'Horserace Betting Levy Board.'

6 Finance Act 1969 (c 32)

Section 59 of the Finance Act 1969 (disclosure of information by Customs and Excise to Levy Board) shall cease to have effect.

7 House of Commons Disqualification Act 1975 (c 24)

In Part III of Schedule 1 to the House of Commons Disqualification Act 1975 (other disqualifying offices) omit—

'Member appointed by the Secretary of State of the Horserace Betting Levy Board.'

8 Race Relations Act 1976 (c 74)

In Part II of Schedule 1A to the Race Relations Act 1976 (persons subject to statutory duty) omit—

'The Horserace Betting Levy Board.'

9 Freedom of Information Act 2000 (c 36)

In Part VI of Schedule 1 to the Freedom of Information Act 2000 (public authorities) omit—

'The Horserace Betting Levy Board.'

SCHEDULE 6
REPEALS
Section 38

7.98

Short title and chapter	*Extent of repeal*
Betting, Gaming and Lotteries Act 1963 (c 2)	In section 1(5)(a), 'but no other races'.
	In section 3(1)— (a) 'or to the Totalisator Board', (b) 'or, as the case may be, by the said Board', and (c) 'or by the said Board'.
	In section 3(2)— (a) 'or to the said Board', and (b) 'or, as the case may be, the Board'.
	In section 3(3)— (a) 'The said Board', and (b) 'by that Board or, as the case may be,'.
	In section 5(3)— (a) 'by the Totalisator Board or, with the authority of that Board, by the persons having the management of that racecourse', and (b) 'by that Board or, as the case may be, by those persons'.
	In section 6(1) 'only'.
	In section 9— (a) in subsection (1) the words from 'Provided that' to the end, (b) subsection (2)(b), (c) in subsection (2)(c)(i) 'or by the Totalisator Board', and (d) in subsection (2)(c)(i) 'or, as the case may be, with or through that Board'.
	Section 12.
	Section 17.
	Section 15.
	Section 24(2)(e).
	In section 31(1)— (a) 'and the Totalisator Board', (b) 'of each of the Boards', and (c) 'in question'.
	In section 55(1)— (a) in the definition of 'bookmaker', 'other than the Totalisator Board', and (b) the definitions of 'recognised horse race', 'sponsored pool betting' and 'the Totalisator Board'. In paragraph 19(a)(i) of Schedule 1, 'in the case of an applicant other than the Totalisator Board,'.

(b) in the case of a document directed to any other person, to his last known address,

and, if sent or given to the authorised representative of the appellant or the Board, shall be deemed to have been sent or given to him or it, as the case may be.

Time

7.113

15 The tribunal may, if it thinks fit, extend the time appointed by these rules for doing any act and may do so notwithstanding that the time appointed has already expired.

Miscellaneous

7.114

16 The tribunal may, if it thinks fit, postpone the day or time fixed for, or adjourn, the hearing of any appeal.

7.115

17 Any act, other than the consideration of an appeal or of an application for expenses, required or authorised by these rules to be done by the tribunal, may be done by, or on the direction of, the chairman.

7.116

18 Subject to the provisions of these rules, the tribunal may regulate its own procedure.

SCHEDULE

[*The forms prescribed in this Schedule (as amended) are printed in the Forms section of this Part.*]

GENERAL BETTING DUTY REGULATIONS 2001

(SI 2001/3088)

Made . . . . .11th September 2001
Laid before the House of Commons . . . . .13th September 2001
Coming into force . . . . .6th October 2001

The Commissioners of Customs and Excise, in exercise of the powers conferred upon them by sections 5D and 12(2) of, and paragraph 2 of Schedule 1 to, the Betting and Gaming Duties Act 1981 and of all other powers enabling them in that behalf, hereby make the following regulations:

Citation and commencement

7.117

1 [(1) These Regulations may be cited as the General Betting Duty Regulations 2001 and come into force on 6th October 2001.[1]

(2) Their provision, however, for pool betting duty forming part of regulations 3, 5, 6, 10 and 11 starts having effect on 26th September 2010][2].

---

1 Para (1): numbered as such by SI 2010/1783, reg 2(1), (2).

2 Para (2): inserted by SI 2010/1783, reg 2(1), (2).

Revocation and amendment

7.118

2 (1) The General Betting Duty Regulations 1987 and the General Betting Duty (Amendment) Regulations 2000 are revoked.

(2) Regulation 2 of the Betting and Gaming Duties (Payment) Regulations 1995 is omitted.

Interpretation

7.119

3 In these Regulations—

'accounting period', subject to [regulations 8, 10 and 11][1] below, has the meaning given in section 5D(1)(a) of the Act [(for general betting duty) or section 8B(1)(a) of the Act (for pool betting duty)][2];

'the Act' means the Betting and Gaming Duties Act 1981;

'bookmaker' [is used in relation to general betting duty only, and][3] includes—

(a) a person who is a bet-broker (as defined in section 5C(1) of the Act), and

(b) a person who is liable to pay duty by virtue of section 5B(4) of the Act,

and 'bookmaking' includes the betting related activities of those persons;

'duty' [, in places where the one in question is not mentioned,][4] means general betting duty charged in accordance with sections 2 to 5D of the Act [and, but only in regulations 5, 6, 10 and 11, pool betting duty charged in accordance with sections 7 to 8C of the Act][5];

'off-course bet' means a bet that is not an on-course bet;

'on-course bookmaker' [is used in relation to general betting duty only, and][6] means a person who intends to carry on or is carrying on bookmaking at a [horse or dog race][7] meeting,

. . . [8]

---

1 In definition "accounting period" words "regulations 8, 10 and 11" in square brackets substituted by SI 2003/2631, reg 3(a)(i); for transitional provisions in relation to this amendment not affecting accounting periods that end on or before 31 December 2003 see reg 4 thereof.

2 In definition "accounting period" words from "(for general betting" to "pool betting duty)" in square brackets inserted by SI 2010/1783, reg 2(1), (3)(a).

3 In definition "bookmaker" words "is used in relation to general betting duty only, and" in square brackets inserted by SI 2010/1783, reg 2(1), (3)(b).

4 In definition "duty" words ", in places where the one in question is not mentioned," in square brackets inserted by SI 2010/1783, reg 2(1), (3)(c)(i).

5 In definition "duty" words from "and, but only" to "of the Act" in square brackets inserted by SI 2010/1783, reg 2(1), (3)(c)(ii).

6 In definition "on-course bookmaker" words "is used in relation to general betting duty only, and" in square brackets inserted by SI 2010/1783, reg 2(1), (3)(d).

7 In definition "on-course bookmaker" words "horse or dog race" in square brackets inserted by SI 2003/2631, reg 3(a)(ii); for transitional provisions in relation to this amendment not affecting accounting periods that end on or before 31 December 2003 see reg 4 thereof.

8 Words omitted revoked by SI 2003/2631, reg 3(a)(iii); for transitional provisions in relation to this revocation not affecting accounting periods that end on or before 31 December 2003 see reg 4 thereof.

Accepting bets

7.120

4 (1) A bookmaker must not accept a bet unless he immediately makes a record of that bet in such form as, in accordance with paragraph 6 of Schedule 1 to the Act, the Commissioners have directed.

(2) In the case of a bet placed by a person who is present, a bookmaker must immediately issue to that person a voucher bearing a record number.

(3) Where paragraph (2) above applies, the record number must be the same as the number used to identify the bet in the record referred to in paragraph (1) above.

(4) Subject to paragraph (5) below, an on-course bookmaker is not required to comply with paragraphs (1) and (2) above.

(5) An on-course bookmaker who accepts an off-course bet must in relation to that bet—

(a) comply with paragraphs (1) and (2) above, and

(b) except where paragraph (6) below applies, within 7 days of accepting it notify the Commissioners that he has accepted it.

(6) An on-course bookmaker who has—

(a) notified the Commissioners that he intends to accept off-course bets, and

(b) has not subsequently notified the Commissioners that he does not intend to accept off-course bets,

is not required to comply with paragraph (5)(b) above.

Returns

7.121

5 (1) For the purpose of accounting for duty every bookmaker [and every primary payer][1] must furnish the Commissioners with a return by the fifteenth day following the end of the accounting period to which it relates [(for general betting duty), or by the fifteenth day of the calendar month following the calendar month in which the accounting period to which it relates ends (for pool betting duty); and in these Regulations "primary payer", as described in section 8(2)(a) of the Act, is used in relation to pool betting duty only][2].

(2) A return must be furnished—

(a) in a form specified in a notice published by the Commissioners and not withdrawn by a further notice, or

(b) in such form to the like effect as the Commissioners may approve.

(3) A return must be furnished—

(a) at the address specified on the form, or

(b) by such means as the Commissioners may approve.

(4) Subject to paragraph (5) below, an on-course bookmaker is not required to furnish returns.

(5) An on-course bookmaker who accepts an off-course bet in an accounting period must furnish a return for that accounting period and, subject to paragraph (6) below, for every subsequent accounting period.

(6) An on-course bookmaker who has accepted off-course bets is not required to furnish a return for an accounting period if—

(a) he did not accept an off-course bet in that accounting period,

(b) when furnishing his return in relation to an earlier accounting period he notified the Commissioners that he does not intend to accept off-course bets, and

(c) since he so notified the Commissioners he has not accepted an off-course bet.

---

1 Para (1): words "and every primary payer" in square brackets inserted by SI 2010/1783, reg 2(1), (4)(a).

2 Para (1): words from "(for general betting" to "betting duty only" in square brackets inserted by SI 2010/1783, reg 2(1), (4)(b).

Payment

7.122

6 (1) Not later than the fifteenth day following the end of an accounting period a bookmaker or primary payer][1] must pay to the Commissioners the duty due from him in respect of that accounting period [(for general betting duty) or the fifteenth day of the calendar month following the calendar month in which an accounting period ends (for pool betting duty)][2].

(2) Payment must be made—

(a) in such manner as is specified in a notice published by the Commissioners and not withdrawn by a further notice, or

(b) in such manner as the Commissioners may approve.

(3) Where the manner of payment involves the collection of the duty due to the Commissioners by means of a direct debit, the bookmaker [or primary payer][3] must ensure that he has sufficient funds in his account to satisfy the payment.

---

1 Para (1): words "or primary payer" in square brackets inserted by SI 2010/1783, reg 2(1), (6).

2 Para (1): words from "(for general betting" to "pool betting duty)," in square brackets inserted by SI 2010/1783, reg 2(1), (5).

3 Para (3): words "or primary payer" in square brackets inserted by SI 2010/1783, reg 2(1), (6).

Non-standard accounting periods

7.123

7 . . . [1]

---

1 Revoked by SI 2003/2631, reg 3(b); for transitional provisions in relation to this revocation not affecting accounting periods that end on or before 31 December 2003 see reg 4 thereof.

7.124

8 (1) Subject to the provisions of this regulation, a bookmaker may give the Commissioners written notice that the twelve consecutive periods set out in his notice will be his accounting periods.

(2) The notice required by paragraph (1) above must—

(a) be given to the Commissioners at least twenty-eight days before the day on which the first accounting period set out in the notice begins,

(b) specify the day on which each accounting period begins, and

(c) specify the day on which the twelfth accounting period ends,

and the day on which the twelfth accounting period ends must be no later than fifty-three weeks after the day on which the first accounting period begins.

(3) Each accounting period must be a period of not less than 27 consecutive days and not more than 35 consecutive days.

(4) Where the Commissioners receive a bookmaker's notice complying with this regulation—

(a) his accounting period immediately preceding the first accounting period set out in his notice will end when that first accounting period begins,

(b) the twelve consecutive periods set out in his notice will be his accounting periods, and

(c) his accounting period immediately following the twelfth accounting period set out in his notice will begin when that twelfth accounting period ends.

(5) Unless in compliance with this regulation the Commissioners have received a notice that a bookmaker's accounting periods will be the further twelve consecutive accounting periods beginning when the twelfth accounting period mentioned in paragraph (4)(c) above ends, the accounting period immediately following that twelfth accounting period ends at the end of the month in which it began.

7.125

9 . . . [1]

[1] Revoked by SI 2003/2631, reg 3(b); for transitional provisions in relation to this revocation not affecting accounting periods that end on or before 31 December 2003 see reg 4 thereof.

7.126

10 (1) Subject to the provisions of this regulation, a [qualifying][1] bookmaker [or qualifying primary payer][2] may give the Commissioners written notice that consecutive periods each comprising three consecutive months [(for a qualifying bookmaker), or each comprising three consecutive periods individually meeting the description in section 8B(1)(a) of the Act (for a qualifying primary payer)][3] will be his accounting periods . . . [4]

(2) The notice required by paragraph (1) above must be given to the Commissioners at least twenty-eight days before the day on which the first [such] [5] accounting period begins and must specify the first calendar month of that accounting period [(for general betting duty), or a Sunday immediately following the last Saturday in a calendar month as the first day of that accounting period (for pool betting duty)][6].

(3) A bookmaker [or primary payer][7] must not give notice under paragraph (1) above if [, in relation to the duty in question][8]—

(a) he has in the twelve months immediately preceding the date of his notice been convicted of an offence under paragraph 13(3) of Schedule 1 to the Act, or

(b) he has failed to furnish any return that he was, in accordance with regulation 5 above . . . [9], required to furnish in the twelve months immediately preceding the date of his notice, or

(c) (subject to regulation 11(3) below) any duty due from him in accordance with regulation 6 above . . . [10] is outstanding at the date of his notice.

(4) Any notice that does not comply with the requirements of this regulation or that is given in contravention of paragraph (3) above is ineffective.

(5) . . . [11]

(6) A bookmaker [or primary payer][12] is a qualifying bookmaker [or qualifying primary payer][13] if in the twelve months immediately preceding the date of his notice the aggregate of the amounts that were due to him in respect of bets . . . [14] [(for a bookmaker) or dutiable pool bets (for a primary payer)][15]14 did not exceed [£660,000][16].

[1] Para (1): word "qualifying" in square brackets inserted by SI 2003/2631, reg 3(c)(i); for transitional provisions in relation to this amendment not affecting accounting periods that end on or before 31 December 2003 see reg 4 thereof.

2 Para (1): words "or qualifying primary payer" in square brackets inserted by SI 2010/1783, reg 2(1), (7)(a).

3 Para (1): words from "(for a qualifying" to "qualifying primary payer)," in square brackets inserted by SI 2010/1783, reg 2(1), (7)(b).

4 Para (1): words omitted revoked by SI 2003/2631, reg 3(c)(i); for transitional provisions in relation to this revocation not affecting accounting periods that end on or before 31 December 2003 see reg 4 thereof.

5 Para (2): word "such" in square brackets substituted by SI 2010/1783, reg 2(1), (8)(a).

6 Para (2): words from "(for general betting" to "pool betting duty)" in square brackets inserted by SI 2010/1783, reg 2(1), (8)(b).

7 Para (3): words "or primary payer" in square brackets inserted by SI 2010/1783, reg 2(1), (9)(a).

8 Para (3): words ", in relation to the duty in question" in square brackets inserted by SI 2010/1783, reg 2(1), (9)(b).

9 Para (3): in sub-para (b) words omitted revoked by SI 2003/2631, reg 3(c)(ii); for transitional provisions in relation to this revocation not affecting accounting periods that end on or before 31 December 2003 see reg 4 thereof.

10 Para (3): in sub-para (c) words omitted revoked by SI 2003/2631, reg 3(c)(ii); for transitional provisions in relation to this revocation not affecting accounting periods that end on or before 31 December 2003 see reg 4 thereof.

11 Para (5): revoked by SI 2003/2631, reg 3(c)(iii); for transitional provisions in relation to this revocation not affecting accounting periods that end on or before 31 December 2003 see reg 4 thereof.

12 Para (6): words "or primary payer" in square brackets inserted by SI 2010/1783, reg 2(1), (10)(a).

13 Para (6): words "or qualifying primary payer" in square brackets inserted by SI 2010/1783, reg 2(1), (10)(b).

14 Para (6): words omitted revoked by SI 2003/2631, reg 3(c)(iv); for transitional provisions in relation to this revocation not affecting accounting periods that end on or before 31 December 2003 see reg 4 thereof.

15 Para (6): words "(for a bookmaker) or dutiable pool bets (for a primary payer)" in square brackets inserted by SI 2010/1783, reg 2(1), (10)(c).

16 Para (6): sum "£660,000" in square brackets substituted by SI 2004/768, reg 2(a).

7.127

11 (1) Where a bookmaker's [or primary payer's][1] accounting periods are specified under regulation . . . [2] 10 above and [in relation to the duty in question,][3] he—

(a) is convicted of an offence under paragraph 13(3) of Schedule 1 to the Act,

(b) fails to furnish a return by the due date in accordance with regulation 5 above, or

(c) fails to pay duty due from him in accordance with regulation 6 above, each calendar month [(for a bookmaker) or period in section 8B(1)(a) of the Act (for a primary payer)][4] following the accounting period in which he was convicted or in respect of which that failure occurred is an accounting period.

(2) If—

(a) a bookmaker's [or primary payer's][5] accounting periods are specified under regulation 10 above, and

(b) in the twelve months immediately preceding the end of [any such specified][6] accounting period the aggregate of the amounts that were due to that bookmaker [or primary payer][7] in respect of bets . . . [8] [(for a bookmaker) or dutiable pool bets (for a primary payer)][9] exceeded [£825,000][10], his accounting periods . . . [11] cease to be those specified under regulation 10 above; and each calendar month [(for a bookmaker) or period in section 8B(1)(a) of the Act (for a primary payer)][12] following the end of [that specified][13] accounting period is an accounting period.

(3) For the purposes of—

(a) [regulation][14] 10(3)(c) above, and

(b) paragraph (1)(c) of this regulation,

if the Commissioners have agreed to accept late payment of any duty that duty is not to be treated as outstanding from a bookmaker [or primary payer][15] unless he fails to pay it by the time for payment agreed with the Commissioners.

---

1 Para (1): words "or primary payer's" in square brackets inserted by SI 2010/1783, reg 2(1), (11)(a).

2 Para (1): words omitted revoked by SI 2003/2631, reg 3(d)(i); for transitional provisions in relation to this revocation not affecting accounting periods that end on or before 31 December 2003 see reg 4 thereof.

3 Para (1): words ", in relation to the duty in question," in square brackets inserted by SI 2010/1783, reg 2(1), (11)(b).

4 Para (1): in sub-para (c) words from "(for a bookmaker)" to "a primary payer)" in square brackets inserted by SI 2010/1783, reg 2(1), (11)(c).

5 Para (2): in sub-para (a) words "or primary payer's" in square brackets inserted by SI 2010/1783, reg 2(1), (12)(a).

6 Para (2): in sub-para (b) words "any such specified" in square brackets substituted by SI 2010/1783, reg 2(1), (12)(b).

7 Para (2): in sub-para (b) words "or primary payer" in square brackets inserted by SI 2010/1783, reg 2(1), (12)(c).

8 Para (2): in sub-para (b) words omitted revoked by SI 2003/2631, reg 3(d)(ii); for transitional provisions in relation to this revocation not affecting accounting periods that end on or before 31 December 2003 see reg 4 thereof.

9 Para (2): in sub-para (b) words "(for a bookmaker) or dutiable pool bets (for a primary payer)" in square brackets inserted by SI 2010/1783, reg 2(1), (12)(d).

10 Para (2): in sub-para (b) sum "£825,000" in square brackets substituted by SI 2004/768, reg 2(b).

11 Para (2): words omitted revoked by SI 2003/2631, reg 3(d)(ii); for transitional provisions in relation to this revocation not affecting accounting periods that end on or before 31 December 2003 see reg 4 thereof.

12 Para (2): words from "(for a bookmaker)" to "a primary payer)" in square brackets inserted by SI 2010/1783, reg 2(1), (12)(e).

13 Para (2): words "that specified" in square brackets substituted by SI 2010/1783, reg 2(1), (12)(f).

14 Para (3): in sub-para (a) word "regulation" in square brackets substituted by SI 2003/2631, reg 3(d)(iii); for transitional provisions in relation to this amendment not affecting accounting periods that end on or before 31 December 2003 see reg 4 thereof.

15 Para (3): words "or primary payer" in square brackets inserted by SI 2010/1783, reg 2(1), (13).

Protection of the revenue

7.128

12 (1) The Commissioners may require a bookmaker to provide security (by means of deposit or otherwise) for the payment of any duty that is or may become due from him.

(2) Where—

(a) a person provides facilities for bookmaking at the place where any event is to be held, and
(b) it comes to his attention that a bookmaker at that place is not complying with regulation 4, 5 or 6 above,

he must notify the Commissioners of the circumstances without delay.

HORSERACE BETTING LEVY (BOOKMAKERS' COMMITTEE) REGULATIONS 2003

(SI 2003/1909)

Made . . . . *17th July 2003*
Coming into force . . . . *28th July 2003*

The Secretary of State, in exercise of the powers conferred upon her by section 26(1) of the Betting, Gaming and Lotteries Act 1963, and after consultation with such bodies as appear to her to be representative of the interests of bookmakers generally, hereby makes the following Regulations:

7.129

1 These Regulations may be cited as the Horserace Betting Levy (Bookmakers' Committee) Regulations 2003 and shall come into force on 28th July 2003.

7.130

2 The Bookmakers' Committee shall consist of thirteen members of whom—

(a) two shall be appointed by Coral Racing Ltd;
(b) two shall be appointed by Ladbroke Racing Ltd;
(c) two shall be appointed by William Hill Organisation Ltd;
(d) two shall be appointed by the National Association of Bookmakers Ltd from amongst persons nominated for the purpose by associations for the time being affiliated to the National Association of Bookmakers Ltd;
(e) four shall be appointed by the Association of British Bookmakers Ltd to represent the interests of the members of that body other than those listed in paragraphs (a) to (c) above; and
(f) one shall be appointed by the Sporting Exchange Ltd.

7.131

3 The appointment of the Committee shall be for a term of three years, but a person ceasing to be a member on the expiry of his term of office shall not on that account be ineligible for reappointment.

7.132

4 A person may be removed at any time from membership of the Committee by the body by which he was appointed.

7.133

5 Where any vacancy occurs in the membership of the Committee, the body by which the person whose office has been vacated was appointed shall, as soon as practicable, make a fresh appointment to the Committee (that is to say an appointment for a term of three years).

7.134

6 The members of the Committee shall appoint one of their number to be the chairman of the Committee and, subject to his remaining a member of the Committee,

he shall hold office as chairman for such period as they may determine and shall be eligible for reappointment as such.

7.135

7 Seven members present (or such larger number of members as the Committee may from time to time determine) shall be a quorum at any meeting of the Committee.

7.135.1

8 The Horserace Betting Levy (Bookmakers' Committee) Regulations 1999 are hereby revoked.

REMOTE GAMBLING (DOUBLE TAXATION RELIEF) REGULATIONS 2012

(SI 2012/1900)

Made .... *18th July 2012*
Laid before Parliament .... *19th July 2012*
In Operation .... *9th August 2012*

The Commissioners for Her Majesty's Revenue and Customs, in exercise of the powers conferred by section 26IC of and paragraphs 2(5) and 2A(4) of Schedule 1 to the Betting and Gaming Duties Act 1981, make the following Regulations:

7.135.2 1 Citation and commencement

These Regulations may be cited as the Remote Gambling (Double Taxation Relief) Regulations 2012 and come into force on 9th August 2012.

7.135.3 2 Interpretation

In these Regulations—

"the Act" means the Betting and Gaming Duties Act 1981;

"the Commissioners" means the Commissioners for Her Majesty's Revenue and Customs;

"qualifying foreign tax" has the meaning given by section 10A or 26IB of the Act (definition of qualifying foreign tax) as appropriate;

"relevant claim" means a claim under sections 5E, 8ZA or 26IA, (double taxation relief), of the Act; and "claimant" shall be construed accordingly.

7.135.4 3 Amount and form of relief

(1) In relation to any relevant claim, the amount of relief shall be calculated in accordance with the provisions of Schedule A1 or Schedule 4B to the Act (rules for determining whether credit is allowed for qualifying foreign tax).

(2) Relief claimed under these Regulations shall be in the form of a repayment by the Commissioners to the claimant.

7.135.5 4 Claim periods

(1) A relevant claim can only be made in relation to—

(a) quarterly accounting periods,

(b) in the case of a person who accounts for duty under the Act on a monthly basis, periods of 3 months in which a relevant claim arises, or

(c) in the case of a person who accounts for duty under the Act on any other basis, periods of such number of accounting periods as would produce a claim period as near as possible to 91 days.

(2) In any case falling within paragraph (1), the first accounting period for which a claim can be made is the accounting period ending on or after 1st April 2012.

7.135.6 5 Application for relief

(1) Any relevant claim must—

(a) by reference to such documentary evidence as is in the possession of the claimant, state the amount of the claim and the method by which that amount was calculated, and

(b) contain evidence of payment of the qualifying foreign tax giving rise to that claim.

(2) Any relevant claim must—

(a) be made on a form specified by the Commissioners for the purpose, and

(b) contain the information specified in that form.

(3) The claimant must sign and date the form and declare that the information provided on it is true and complete.

7.135.7 6 Time limit for claim

A relevant claim must be made within one year of the later of—

(a) the end of the accounting period in which the entitlement to make that claim arose, or

(b) the date on which the qualifying foreign tax was paid.

7.135.8 7 Payment of claim

A repayment under regulation 3(2) must be made—

(a) within 30 days of the later of—

(i) the receipt by the Commissioners of a relevant claim, or

(ii) the receipt of such evidence or information as may be required under regulation 8;

(b) by electronic means.

7.136 8 Further evidence and information

Every claimant must furnish such certificates, documents, information and evidence in connection with the claim, or any question arising out of it, as may be required by the Commissioners and shall do so within 30 days of being required to do so or such longer period as the Commissioners may consider reasonable.

FORMS

[The following forms are prescribed by the Betting Levy Appeal Tribunal (England and Wales) Rules 1963, SI 1963/748 (as amended).]

[7.136.1]

1 Notice of reference

[Form 1 in Schedule to Regs.]

Betting, Gaming and Lotteries Act 1963

The Horserace Betting Levy Board hereby refers to the Horserace Betting Levy Appeal Tribunal for England and Wales the appeal of [*name and address of appellant*).

Notice of the appeal, of which a copy is attached, was received by the Board on 20.

Dated 20. (Signed]

On behalf of the Board.

To the Horserace Betting Levy Appeal Tribunal for England and Wales.

[7.136.2]

2 Notice requiring facilities for investigation

[Form 2 in Schedule to Regs.]

Betting, Gaming and Lotteries Act 1963

The Horserace Betting Levy Appeal Tribunal for England and Wales, to which your appeal has been referred, requires the following facilities [*or* further facilities] for the investigation of your appeal, which was referred to the tribunal on 20:—

[Here state facilities required]

If you object to affording the facilities mentioned above on the grounds that they are unnecessary or unreasonable, you should so inform the tribunal immediately. You will then be given an opportunity of making your representations to the tribunal which may, if it thinks fit, after having considered your representations, modify or withdraw this notice.

Note.—BGLA 1963, s 28(6) provides that the tribunal 'shall not reduce the assessment or grant the appellant a certificate of exemption unless the appellant has afforded the tribunal all the facilities it may have required for the investigation of his case'.

Dated 20. (Signed)

On behalf of the tribunal.

To [name of appellant].

[7.136.3]

3 Decision of the Tribunal

[Form 3 in Schedule to Regs.]

Betting, Gaming and Lotteries Act 1963

The Horserace Betting Levy Appeal Tribunal for England and Wales, to which the appeal against notice of assessment of [*name of appellant*] was referred by the Horserace Betting Levy Board by notice dated 20, having heard the said appeal, has determined that, in respect of the levy period commencing on 1st April 20.

*(1) the appellant falls for the purposes of the relevant scheme into the following categories:

*(2) the following special provisions of the said scheme apply to the appellant:

*(3) the appellant is exempt from payment of a levy under the said scheme.

The tribunal accordingly directs that—

*(1) the notice of assessment issued by the Board in respect of the appellant and dated 20 shall be confirmed [*or* shall be amended by substituting for the amount therein stated an amount of]

*(2) the appellant shall, in respect of the levy period aforesaid, be granted a certificate of exemption.

Dated 20.
(*Signed*)

Chairman.

On behalf of the tribunal.

* Delete if inapplicable.

[7.136.4]

4 Notice of reference

[Form 4 in Schedule to Regs.]

Horserace Betting Levy Act 1981

The Horserace Betting Levy Board hereby refers to the Horserace Betting Levy Appeal Tribunal for England and Wales the appeal of [*name and address of appellant*].

Notice of the appeal, of which a copy is attached, was received by the Board on 20.

Dated 20.

(Signed)

On behalf of the Board.

To the Horserace Betting Levy Appeal Tribunal for England and Wales.

[7.136.5]

5 Notice requiring facilities for investigation

[Form 5 in Schedule to Regs.]

Horserace Betting Levy Act 1981

The Horserace Betting Levy Appeal Tribunal for England and Wales, to which your appeal has been referred, requires the following facilities [*or* further facilities] for the investigation of your appeal, which was referred to the tribunal on 20:—

[Here state facilities required]

If you object to affording the facilities mentioned above on the grounds that they are unnecessary or unreasonable, you should so inform the tribunal immediately. You will then be given an opportunity of making representations to the tribunal which may, if it thinks fit, after having considered your representations, modify or withdraw this notice.

Note.—Horseracing Betting Levy Act 1981, s 2(3)(a) provides that the tribunal 'shall not rescind the determination or reduce the amount so payable unless the appellant has afforded the tribunal all the facilities it may have required for the investigation of his case'.

Dated 20.

(Signed)

On behalf of the tribunal.

To [name of appellant].

[7.136.6]

6 Decision of the tribunal

[Form 6 in Schedule to Regs.]

Horserace Betting Levy Act 1981

The Horserace Betting Levy Appeal Tribunal for England and Wales, to which the appeal against notice of determination of [*name of appellant*] was referred by the Horserace Betting Levy Board by notice dated 20, having heard the said appeal, has determined that, in respect of the levy period commencing on 1st April 20.

*(1) the appellant falls for the purposes of the relevant scheme into the following categories for payments on account of the levy:

*(2) the following special provisions of the said scheme requiring payments on account of the levy apply to the appellant:

*(3) the appellant is not liable under the said scheme to make any payments on account of the levy.

The tribunal accordingly directs that—

*(1) the notice of determination issued by the Board in respect of the appellant and dated 20 shall be confirmed [*or* shall be amended by substituting for the amounts to be paid on account the following amounts] [*and/or* shall be amended by substituting for the times specified therein as the times during the levy period at which payments on account are to be made the following times].

*(2) the notice of determination issued by the Board in respect of the appellant shall be rescinded.

Dated 20.

(Signed)

Chairman

On behalf of the tribunal.

* Delete if inapplicable.

Section 2

Gaming

NOTE: The Gaming Act 1968 has now been repealed save for very limited transitional purposes (as to which see art 4 of the Gambling Act 2005 (Commencement No 6 and Transitional Provisions) Order 2006, SI 2006/3272 at para **6.1537** above). The complete text of the Act is included on the CD which will accompany this edition.

STATUTES

BETTING AND GAMING DUTIES ACT 1981

(1981 c 63)

Arrangement of sections

[*The provisions of this Act not mentioned above are considered in Section 1, Betting.*]

Bingo duty

7.137 [17 Bingo duty]

[(1) A duty of excise, to be known as bingo duty, shall be charged—

(a) on the playing of bingo in the United Kingdom, and

(b) at the rate of [20][2] per cent of a person's bingo promotion profits for an accounting period.

(2) Subsection (1) is subject to the exemptions specified in Part 1 of Schedule 3 to this Act.

[(2A) Bingo duty is not charged on the playing of bingo which is not licensed bingo if remote gaming duty is charged on the provision of facilities for playing it.][3]

(3) The amount of a person's bingo promotion profits for an accounting period is—

(a) the amount of the person's bingo receipts for the period (calculated in accordance with section 19), minus

(b) the amount of his expenditure on bingo winnings for the period (calculated in accordance with section 20).

(4) Bingo duty charged in respect of a person's bingo promotion profits shall be paid by him.

(5) Where the amount that would be charged in respect of a person's bingo promotion profits for an accounting period is less than £1, no duty shall be charged.][1]

1 Substituted, together with ss 18–20, 20A–20C, for ss 17–20 as originally enacted, by the Finance Act 2003, s 9(1).

2 Sub-s (1): in para (b) sum "20" in square brackets substituted by the Finance Act 2010, s 19(1).

3 Sub-s (2A): inserted by the Finance Act 2009, s 115(1), (2).

7.138 [18 Accounting period

[(1) For the purposes of section 17 an accounting period ends, and another begins, at the end of the last Sunday in each calendar month.

(2) But regulations under paragraph 9 of Schedule 3 to this Act may make provision in place of subsection (1) for the purposes of the application of section 17 to specified persons or in specified circumstances.

(3) Regulations made by virtue of subsection (2) may make transitional provision.][1]

1 Substituted as noted to s 17: see para **7.137** above.

7.139 [19 Bingo receipts

(1) A person has bingo receipts for an accounting period if payments fall due in the period in respect of entitlement to participate in bingo promoted by him.

(2) The amount of the person's bingo receipts for the accounting period is the aggregate of those payments.

(3) For the purposes of subsections (1) and (2)—

(a) an amount in respect of entitlement to participate in a game of bingo is to be treated as falling due in the accounting period in which the game is played,

(b) . . . [1]

(c) it is immaterial whether an amount falls due to be paid to the promoter or to another person,

(d) it is immaterial whether an amount is described as a fee for participation, as a stake, or partly as one and partly as the other, and

(e) where a sum is paid partly in respect of entitlement to participate in a game of bingo and partly in respect of another matter—

(i) such part of the sum as is applied to, or properly attributable to, entitlement to participate in the game shall be treated as an amount falling due in respect of entitlement to participate in the game, and

(ii) the remainder shall be disregarded.][2]

[1] Sub-s (3): para (b) repealed by the Finance Act 2009, s 113(5)(a).

[2] Substituted as noted to s 17: see para 7.137 above.

7.140 [20 Expenditure on bingo winnings

(1) A person's expenditure on bingo winnings for an accounting period is the aggregate of the values of prizes provided by him in that period by way of winnings at bingo promoted by him.

(2) Where a prize is obtained by the promoter from a person not connected with him, the cost to the promoter shall be treated as the value of the prize for the purpose of subsection (1).

(3) Where a prize is a voucher which—

(a) may be used in place of money as whole or partial payment for benefits of a specified kind obtained from a specified person,

(b) specifies an amount as the sum or maximum sum in place of which the voucher may be used, and

(c) does not fall within subsection (2),

the specified amount is the value of the voucher for the purpose of subsection (1).

(4) Where a prize is a voucher (whether or not it falls within subsection (2)) it shall be treated as having no value for the purpose of subsection (1) if—

(a) it does not satisfy subsection (3)(a) and (b), or

(b) its use as described in subsection (3)(a) is subject to a specified restriction, condition or limitation which may make the value of the voucher to the recipient significantly less than the amount mentioned in subsection (3)(b).

(5) In the case of a prize which—

(a) is neither money nor a voucher, and

(b) does not fall within subsection (2),

the value of the prize for the purpose of subsection (1) is—

(i) the amount which the prize would cost the promoter if obtained from a person not connected with him, or

(ii) where no amount can reasonably be determined in accordance with sub-paragraph (i), nil.

(6) For the purpose of this section—

(a) a reference to connection between two persons shall be construed in accordance with [section 1122 of the Corporation Tax Act 2010][2] (connected persons), and

(b) an amount paid by way of value added tax on the acquisition of a thing shall be treated as part of its cost (irrespective of whether or not the amount is taken into account for the purpose of a credit or refund).][1]

---

1 Substituted as noted to s 17: see para **7.137** above.

2 Sub-s (6): words in square brackets substituted by the Corporation Tax Act 2010, s 1177, Sch 1, Pt 2, paras 173, 174; for transitional provisions and savings see s 1180(1), Sch 2, Pts 1, 2 thereto.

7.141 [20A Combined bingo

(1) A game of bingo is 'combined bingo' if—

(a) . . .[1]

(b) it is played in more than one place and promoted by more than one person.

(2) Payments made in respect of entitlement to participate in combined bingo shall be treated for the purposes of section 19(1) as bingo receipts only of the first promoter to whom (or at whose direction) they are paid.

(3) Where money representing stakes hazarded at combined bingo is paid in an accounting period by one promoter of the bingo ('the first promoter') to another ('the second promoter')—

(a) the money shall not be treated as a bingo receipt of the second promoter for the purposes of section 19(1),

(b) the payment shall be treated as expenditure of the first promoter on bingo winnings for the accounting period for the purposes of section 20(1), and

(c) no subsequent payment of all or part of the money shall be treated as expenditure on bingo winnings for the purposes of section 20(1) (whether paid by the second promoter to another person, by the first promoter having received it from the second promoter, or otherwise).

(4) Subsections (2) and (3) shall apply only where the combined bingo is played entirely in the United Kingdom.][2]

---

1 Sub-s (1): para (a) repealed by the Finance Act 2007, ss 105, 114, Sch 25, Pt 2, paras 3, 8, Sch 27, Pt 6(3).

2 Substituted as noted to s 17: see para **7.137** above.

7.142 [20B Carrying losses forward

(1) Where the calculation of a person's bingo promotion profits for an accounting period results in a negative amount ('the loss')—

(a) no bingo duty shall be chargeable in respect of that accounting period, and

(b) for the purpose of section 17(3), the amount of the person's expenditure on bingo winnings for the next accounting period shall be increased by the amount of the loss.

(2) Subsection (1) applies to an accounting period whether or not the loss results wholly or partly from the previous application of that subsection.][1]

(ii) the maximum value of the prize for winning a single game does not exceed £500.

Category B3—a gaming machine which is not within a lower category and in respect of which—

(i) the cost of a single game does not exceed [£2][9], and

(ii) the maximum value of the prize for winning a single game does not exceed £500.

Category B4—a gaming machine which is not within a lower category and in respect of which—

(i) the cost of a single game does not exceed £1, and

(ii) the maximum value of the prize for winning a single game does not exceed £250.

Category C—

(i) a gaming machine in respect of which the cost of a single game does not exceed 5p, and

(ii) a gaming machine in respect of which—

(a) the cost of a single game does not exceed [£1][3], and

(b) the maximum value of the prize for winning a single game does not exceed [£70][4].

(4) Where a machine offers more than one class of game, it falls within a category only if it satisfies the requirements of that category in respect of each class.

(5) . . . [5]

(6) For the purposes of subsection (3) Category A is the highest category and Category C is the lowest.][6]

[(7) The Commissioners may by order substitute for a sum for the time being specified in subsection (3) such higher sum as they consider appropriate.]][7, 8]

1 Sub-s (1): words "an amusement machine licence" in square brackets substituted, in relation to machines provided on or after 1 November 1995 and to licences for periods beginning on or after that date and the duty on such licences, by the Finance Act 1995, s 14, Sch 3, para 4(1).

2 Sub-s (2): table substituted by the Finance Act 2011, s 18(1). Date in force: this amendment has effect in relation to cases where the application for the amusement machine licence is received by the Commissioners for Her Majesty's Revenue and Customs after 4 pm on 25 March 2011: see the Finance Act 2011, s 18(2).

3 Sub-s (3): in definition "Category C" in para (ii)(a) sum "£1" in square brackets substituted by the Finance Act 2009, s 22(1), (8), (9)(a).

4 Sub-s (3): in definition "Category C" in para (ii)(b) sum "£70" in square brackets substituted by the Finance Act 2009, s 22(1), (8), (9)(b).

5 Sub-s (5): repealed by the Finance Act 2009, s 22(1), (8), (10).

6 Sub-ss (2)–(6): substituted, for sub-ss (2), (3), by the Finance Act 2006, s 12(3).

7 Substituted, in relation to gaming machine licences granted for any period beginning on or after 1 May 1994, by the Finance Act 1994, s 6, Sch 3, para 1(4), (9); for further provision as to the application of this amendment see Sch 3, paras 4(3), 5(5) thereof.

8 Sub-s (7): inserted by the Finance Act 2007, s 9(1), (3).

9 Sub-s (3): in the definition of Category B3 gaming machine, in paragraph (i), word in square brackets substituted by SI 2011/1753, art 2. Date in force: 11 August 2011: see SI 2011/1753, art 1.

7.148 24 Restrictions on provision of gaming machines

(1), (2) . . . [1, 2]

(3) [Amusement machines][3] chargeable at a particular rate shall not be provided on any . . . [4] premises in excess of the number authorised by the licence [or licences][5] authorising the provision of [amusement machines][3] chargeable at that rate . . . [6]

(4) Where a licence which authorises the provision of [amusement machines][3] chargeable at one rate only is in force in respect of any . . . [4] premises, [amusement machines][3] chargeable at any other rate shall not be provided [for play][3] on those premises unless another licence authorising the provision of [amusement machines][3] chargeable at that other rate is also in force in respect of the premises . . . [7] [or the machines][8].

(5) If any [amusement machine][3] is provided [for play][3] on any premises in contravention of [section 21(1) above or][9] this section, [the provision of the machine shall attract a penalty under section 9 of the Finance Act 1994 (civil penalties) and, for the purposes of the application of that section to the conduct attracting the penalty, the provision of the machine shall be treated as the conduct of each of the persons who, at the time when the [amusement machine][3] is provided][10]—

(a) is the owner, lessee or occupier of the premises, or

(b) is for the time being responsible to the owner, lessee or occupier for the management of the premises, or

[(c) is a person responsible for controlling the use of any amusement machine on the premises, or][11]

(d) is for the time being responsible for controlling the admission of persons to the premises or for providing persons resorting thereto with any goods or services, or

(e) is the owner or hirer of the machine, or

(f) is a party to any contract under which [an amusement machine][3] may, or is required to, be on the premises at that time . . . [12]

(6) If any [amusement machine][3] is provided [for play][3] on any premises in contravention of [section 21(1) above or][9] this section and any such person as is mentioned in subsection (5) above knowingly or recklessly brought about the contravention or took any steps with a view to procuring it he shall be guilty of an offence and liable—

[(a) on summary conviction to a penalty—

(i) of the prescribed sum,[13] . . . [14] or to imprisonment for a term not exceeding six months or to both such penalty and imprisonment;][15] or

(b) on conviction on indictment to a penalty of any amount or to imprisonment for a term not exceeding two years or to both.

---

1 Sub-s (1) repealed by the Finance Act 1984, ss 7, 128(6), Sch 3, paras 1, 6(a), Sch 23, Pt II.

2 Sub-s (2) repealed by the FA1994, ss 6, 258, Sch 3, para 1(5)(a), Sch 26, Pt II.

3 Words in square brackets substituted by the FA 1995, s 14, Sch 3, paras 1, 5.

4 Words omitted repealed by the FA 1994, ss 6, 258, Sch 3, para 1(5)(b), Sch 26, Pt II.

5 Words in square brackets substituted by the FA 1984, s 7, Sch 3, Pt I, para 6.

6 Words omitted repealed by the FA 1994, ss 6, 258, Sch 3, para 3(4), Sch 26, Pt II.

7 See note 4 ante.

8 Words in square brackets added by the FA 1996, s 12(4).

9 Words in square brackets inserted by FA 1996, s 12(4), paras 1, 6(e).

10 Words in square brackets substituted by the FA 1994, s 9(9), Sch 4, Pt V, paras 60, 61(a).

11 Substituted by the Finance Act 2003, s 12(1).

12 Words omitted repealed by the FA 1994, s 9(9), Sch 4, Pt V, paras 60, 61(b).

13 See note 7 to BGDA 1981, s 9.

14 Words omitted repealed by the FA 1994, ss 6, 258, Sch 3, para 1(5)(c), Sch 26, Pt II.

15 Substituted by the FA 1982, s 8, Sch 6, para 12 for original sub-para.

7.149 [24A Unlicensed machines: duty chargeable

Schedule 4A to this Act (which provides for the recovery of amusement machine licence duty in relation to unlawfully unlicensed machines) shall have effect.][1]

---

1 Inserted by the Finance Act 2000, s 17, Sch 2, paras 1, 9.

7.150 25 Meaning of "gaming machine"

[(1) A machine is an amusement machine for the purposes of this Act if it is—

(a) a gaming machine, and

(b) a prize machine.

[(1A) In this Act "gaming machine" means a machine which is designed or adapted for use by individuals for gambling (whether or not it can also be used for other purposes).[1]

(1B) But a machine is not a gaming machine to the extent that—

(a) it is designed or adapted for use to bet on future real events,

(b) it is designed or adapted for the playing of bingo and bingo duty is, or but for paragraphs 1 to 5 of Schedule 3 would be, charged under section 17 on the playing of the bingo, or

(c) it is designed or adapted for the playing of a real game of chance and the playing of the game is dutiable gaming for the purposes of section 10 of the Finance Act 1997, or would be dutiable gaming but for subsections (3) and (4) of that section.]][1, 2]

(1C) For the purposes of this Act [a machine is a prize machine][3] unless it is [designed][4] or adapted so that a person playing it once and successfully either receives nothing or receives only—

(a) an opportunity, afforded by the automatic action of the machine, to play again (once or more often) without paying, or

(b) a prize, determined by the automatic action of the machine and consisting in either—

(i) money of an amount not exceeding the sum payable to play the machine once, or

(ii) a token which is, or two or more tokens which in the aggregate are, exchangeable for money of an amount not exceeding that sum.][5]

[(4) A machine which has a number of individual playing positions allowing persons to play simultaneously (whether or not participating in the same game) shall be treated for the purposes of sections 21 to 24 as that number of separate machines.][6]

---

1 Sub-ss (1), (1A): further substituted, for sub-ss (1), (1A), (1B) (as substituted as noted above), by the Finance Act 2006, s 11(1).

2 Sub-s (1A), (1B): further substituted, for sub-s (1A) (as substituted as noted above), by the Finance Act 2009, s 116(1)–(3).

3 Sub-s (1C): words "a machine is a prize machine" in square brackets substituted by the Finance Act 2006, s 11(2).

4 Sub-s (1C): word "designed" in square brackets substituted by the Finance Act 2009, s 116(1), (2), (4)

5 Sub-ss (1), (1A)–(1C): substituted for sub-ss (1)–(3), as originally enacted, in relation to machines provided on or after 1 November 1995 and to licences for periods beginning on or after that date and the duty on such licences, by the Finance Act 1995, s 14, Sch 3, para 6(1).

6 Sub-s (4): substituted, for sub-ss (4), (5), (5A), (6), (7), by the Finance Act 2006, s 12(4).

(Sub-s (4), as originally enacted, was substituted by new sub-ss (4)–(9) by the Finance Act 1993, s 16(6), (9), and sub-ss (5)–(9) were further substituted by new sub-ss (5), (5A), (6), (7) by the Finance Act 1995, s 14, Sch 3, para 6(3).)

7.151 [25A . . .
[. . .][1]

---

1 Repealed by the Finance Act 2006, ss 12(5), 178, Sch 26, Pt 1(2).

7.152 26 Supplementary provisions as to gaming machine licence duty

(1) The provisions of Part II of Schedule 4 to this Act (supplementary provisions as to [amusement machine licence duty][1]) shall have effect.

(2) In sections 21 to 25 above and in Schedule 4 to this Act—

...[2]

["United Kingdom" includes the territorial waters of the United Kingdom;][3]

[. . .

"prize machine" has the meaning given by section 25(1C) above;][4, 5]

["small-prize machine" has the meaning given by section 22(2) above];[6]

["two-penny machine" means an amusement machine in relation to which the cost for each time a game is played on it—

(a) does not exceed 2p, or

(b) where the machine provides differing numbers of games in different circumstances, cannot exceed 2p,

. . . [7];][8]

[. . .][9, 10] and

"premises" includes any place whatsoever and any means of transport.

[(2A) References in sections 21 to 25 above and in this section and Schedule 4 to this Act to a game, in relation to any machine, include references to a game in the nature of a quiz or puzzle and to a game which is played solely by way of a pastime or against the machine, as well as one played wholly or partly against one or more contemporaneous or previous players.][11]

(3) A machine is provided [for play][12] on any premises if it is made available on those premises in such a way that persons resorting to them can play it; and [subject to subsection (3A) below][12] where on any premises one or more [amusement machines][12] are so made available, any such machine anywhere on the premises shall be treated as provided [for play][12] on those premises, notwithstanding that it is not so made available or is not in a state in which it can be played.

[(3A) The Commissioners may by regulations make provision for the purpose of enabling spare [amusement machines] to be kept on premises for use in the case of the breakdown of other [amusement machines] on those premises; and such regulations may provide that, in such circumstances and subject to such conditions as may be specified in the regulations, [an amusement machine] on any premises which is not made available as mentioned in subsection (3) above, or is not in a state in which it can be played, shall not be treated by virtue of that subsection as provided [for play] on those premises.][13]

[(4) . . .][14, 15]

---

1 Sub-s (1): words in square brackets substituted, in relation to machines provided on or after 1 November 1995 and to licences for periods beginning on or after that date and the duty on such licences, by the Finance Act 1995, s 14, Sch 3, para 8(1).

2 Sub-s (2): definition "coin" (omitted) repealed by the Finance Act 2003, ss 11(1), 216, Sch 43, Pt 1(3).

3 Sub-s (2): definition "United Kingdom" substituted by the Finance Act 1985, s 8, Sch 5, Pt I.

4 Sub-s (2): definitions "video machine" (omitted) and "prize machine" inserted, in relation to machines provided on or after 1 November 1995 and to licences for periods beginning on or after that date and the duty on such licences, by the Finance Act 1995, s 14, Sch 3, para 8(2).

5 Sub-s (2): definition "video machine" (omitted) repealed by the Finance Act 2006, ss 12(6)(a), 178, Sch 26, Pt 1(2).

6 Sub-s (2): definition "small-prize machine" substituted by the Finance Act 1985, s 8, Sch 5, Pt I.

7 Sub-s (2): in definition "two-penny machine" words omitted repealed by the Finance Act 2006, ss 12(6)(b), 178, Sch 26, Pt 1(2).

8 Sub-s (2): definition "two-penny machine" substituted, for definitions "two-penny machine", "five-penny machine" (inserted by the Finance Act 1993, s 16(7), (9)) and "ten-penny machine" (inserted by the Finance Act 2000, s 17, Sch 2, paras 1, 6) by the Finance Act 2003, s 10(3).

9 Sub-s (2): definition "thirty-five penny machine" (omitted) inserted, in relation to machines provided on or after 1 November 1995 and to licences for periods beginning on or after that date and the duty on such licences, by the Finance Act 1995, s 14, Sch 3, para 8(2).

10 Sub-s (2): definition "thirty-five penny machine" (omitted) repealed by the Finance Act 2002, s 141, Sch 40, Pt 1(3).

11 Sub-s (2A): inserted, in relation to machines provided on or after 1 November 1995 and to licences for periods beginning on or after that date and the duty on such licences, by the Finance Act 1995, s 14, Sch 3, para 8(3).

12 Sub-s (3): first, third and final words in square brackets substituted, in relation to machines provided on or after 1 November 1995 and to licences for periods beginning on or after that date and the duty on such licences, by the Finance Act 1995, s 14, Sch 3, para 8(1); second words in square brackets inserted by the Finance Act 1987, s 5(2), (3).

13 Sub-s (3A): inserted by the Finance Act 1987, s 5(2), (3); words in square brackets substituted, in relation to machines provided on or after 1 November 1995 and to licences for periods beginning on or after that date and the duty on such licences, by the Finance Act 1995, s 14, Sch 3, para 8(1).

14 Sub-s (4): inserted by the Finance Act 1982, s 8, Sch 6, Pt V, para 14, in relation to licences for any period beginning after 30 September 1982.

15 Sub-s (4): repealed by the Finance Act 2003, s 216(1), Sch 43, Pt 1(3).

7.153 [26A Interpretation]

[(1) For the purposes of remote gaming duty "remote gaming" means gaming in which persons participate by the use of—

(a) the internet,

(b) telephone,

(c) television,

(d) radio, or

(e) any other kind of electronic or other technology for facilitating communication.

(2) For the purposes of remote gaming duty the expressions listed below shall be construed (for the whole of the United Kingdom) in accordance with the Gambling Act 2005.

Expression	Defining provision of Gambling Act 2005
Provision of facilities	Section 5(1) to (3)
Remote gambling equipment	Section 36(4) and (5)
Remote operating licence	Section 67

(3) In relation to remote gaming duty "P" means a person who provides facilities for remote gaming.

(4) The Treasury may by order amend the definition of "remote gaming" in subsection (1) (and an order may include incidental, consequential or transitional provision).][1]

1 Inserted by the Finance Act 2007, s 8(1), Sch 1, Pt 1.

7.154 [26B The duty]

[A duty of excise to be known as remote gaming duty shall be charged on the provision of facilities for remote gaming if—

(a) the facilities are provided in reliance on a remote operating licence, or

(b) at least one piece of remote gambling equipment used in the provision of the facilities is situated in the United Kingdom (whether or not the facilities are provided for use wholly or partly in the United Kingdom).][1]

1 Inserted by the Finance Act 2007, s 8(1), Sch 1, Pt 1. Date in force: this amendment has effect in respect of the provision of facilities for remote gaming on or after 1 September 2007: see SI 2007/2172, art 2.

7.155 [26C The rate]

[(1) Remote gaming duty is chargeable at the rate of 15% of P's remote gaming profits for an accounting period.

(2) P's remote gaming profits for an accounting period are—

(a) the amount of P's remote gaming receipts for the period (calculated in accordance with section 26E), minus

(b) the amount of P's expenditure for the period on remote gaming winnings (calculated in accordance with section 26F).][1]

1 Inserted by the Finance Act 2007, s 8(1), Sch 1, Pt 1. Date in force: this amendment has effect in respect of the provision of facilities for remote gaming on or after 1 September 2007: see SI 2007/2172, art 2.

7.156 [26D Accounting periods]

[(1) The following are accounting periods for the purposes of remote gaming duty—

(a) the period of three months beginning with 1st January,

(b) the period of three months beginning with 1st April,

(c) the period of three months beginning with 1st July, and

(d) the period of three months beginning with 1st October.

(2) The Commissioners may agree with P for specified periods to be treated as accounting periods, instead of those described in subsection (1), for purposes of remote gaming duty relating to P.

(3) The Commissioners may by direction make transitional arrangements for the periods to be treated as accounting periods where—

(a) P becomes registered, or ceases to be registered, under section 26J, or

(b) an agreement under subsection (2) begins or ends.][1]

1 Inserted by the Finance Act 2007, s 8(1), Sch 1, Pt 1. Date in force: this amendment has effect in respect of the provision of facilities for remote gaming on or after 1 September 2007: see SI 2007/2172, art 2.

7.157 [26E Remote gaming receipts]

[(1) The amount of P's remote gaming receipts for an accounting period is the aggregate of—

(a) amounts falling due to P in that period in respect of entitlement to use facilities for remote gaming provided by P, and

(b) amounts staked, or falling due to be paid, in that period by a user of facilities for remote gaming provided by P, if or in so far as responsibility for paying any amount won by the user falls on P (or a person with whom P is connected or has made arrangements).

(2) . . . [1]

(3) The Treasury may by order provide that where a person who uses facilities (U) relies on an offer which waives payment or permits payment of less than the amount which would have been required to be paid without the offer, U is to be treated for the purposes of this section as having paid that amount.][2]

---

1 Sub-s (2): repealed by the Finance Act 2009, s 113(5)(a). Date in force: 27 April 2009: see the Finance Act 2009, s 113(6).

2 Inserted by the Finance Act 2007, s 8(1), Sch 1, Pt 1. Date in force: this amendment has effect in respect of the provision of facilities for remote gaming on or after 1 September 2007: see SI 2007/2172, art 2.

7.158 [26F Remote gaming winnings]

[(1) The amount of P's expenditure on remote gaming winnings for an accounting period is the aggregate of the value of prizes provided by P in that period which have been won (at any time) by persons using facilities for remote gaming provided by P.

(2) Prizes provided by P to one user on behalf of another are not to be treated as prizes provided by P.

(3) A reference to providing a prize to a user (U) includes a reference to crediting money in respect of gaming winnings by U to an account if U is notified that—

(a) the money is being held in the account, and

(b) U is entitled to withdraw it on demand.

(4) The return of a stake is to be treated as the provision of a prize.

(5) Where P participates in arrangements under which a number of persons who provide facilities for remote gaming contribute towards a fund which is wholly used to provide prizes in connection with the use of those facilities (sometimes described as arrangements for "linked progressive jackpot games")—

(a) the making by P of a contribution which relates to the provision by P of facilities for remote gaming shall be treated as the provision of a prize, and

(b) the award of a prize from the fund shall not be treated as the provision of a prize by P.

(6) Where P credits the account of a user of facilities provided by P (otherwise than as described in subsection (3)), the credit shall be treated as the provision of a prize; but the Commissioners may direct that this subsection shall not apply in a specified case or class of cases.

(7) Subsections (2) to (6) of section 20 shall apply (with any necessary modifications) for the purpose of remote gaming duty as for the purpose of bingo duty.][1]

---

1 Inserted by the Finance Act 2007, s 8(1), Sch 1, Pt 1. Date in force: this amendment has effect in respect of the provision of facilities for remote gaming on or after 1 September 2007: see SI 2007/2172, art 2.

7.159 [26G Losses]

[Where the calculation of P's remote gaming profits for an accounting period produces a negative amount, it may be carried forward in reduction of the profits of one or more later accounting periods.][1]

---

1 Inserted by the Finance Act 2007, s 8(1), Sch 1, Pt 1. Date in force: this amendment has effect in respect of the provision of facilities for remote gaming on or after 1 September 2007: see SI 2007/2172, art 2.

7.160 [26H Exemptions]

[(1) Remote gaming duty shall not be charged in respect of the provision of facilities for remote gaming if and in so far as—

(a) the provision is charged with another gambling tax, or

(b) the use of the facilities is charged with another gambling tax.

(2) Remote gaming duty shall not be charged in respect of the provision of facilities for remote gaming if and in so far as—

(a) the provision would be charged with another gambling tax but for an express exception, or

(b) the use of the facilities would be charged with another gambling tax but for an express exception.

[(2A) Subsection (2) does not prevent remote gaming duty being charged in respect of the provision of facilities for the playing of bingo which is not licensed bingo (as to the meaning of which terms see section 20C).][1]

(3) In this section "gambling tax" means—

(a) amusement machine licence duty,

(b) bingo duty,

(c) gaming duty,

(d) general betting duty,

(e) lottery duty, and

(f) pool betting duty.

(4) The Treasury may by order—

(a) confer an exemption from remote gaming duty, or

(b) remove or vary (whether or not by textual amendment) an exemption under this section.

(5) In calculating P's remote gaming profits for an accounting period, no account shall be taken of amounts or prizes if, or in so far as, they relate to the provision of facilities to which an exemption applies under or by virtue of this section.][2]

---

1 Sub-s (2A): inserted by the Finance Act 2009, s 115(1), (3). Date in force: this amendment has effect in relation to games of bingo that begin to be played on or after 1 July 2009: see the Finance Act 2009, s 115(4).

2 Inserted by the Finance Act 2007, s 8(1), Sch 1, Pt 1. Date in force: this amendment has effect in respect of the provision of facilities for remote gaming on or after 1 September 2007: see SI 2007/2172, art 2.

7.161 [26I Liability to pay]

[(1) P is liable for any remote gaming duty charged on P's remote gaming profits for an accounting period.

(2) If P is a body corporate, P and P's directors are jointly and severally liable for any remote gaming duty charged on P's remote gaming profits for an accounting period.

(3) The Commissioners may make regulations about payment of remote gaming duty; and the regulations may, in particular, make provision about—

(a) timing;
(b) instalments;
(c) methods of payment;
(d) when payment is to be treated as made;
(e) the process and effect of assessments by the Commissioners of amounts due.

(4) Subject to regulations under subsection (3), section 12 of the Finance Act 1994 (assessment) shall apply in relation to liability to pay remote gaming duty.][1]

---

1 Inserted by the Finance Act 2007, s 8(1), Sch 1, Pt 1. Date in force: this amendment has effect in respect of the provision of facilities for remote gaming on or after 1 September 2007: see SI 2007/2172, art 2 and see SI 2007/2192.

7.162 [26J Registration]

[(1) The Commissioners shall maintain a register of persons who provide facilities for remote gaming in respect of which remote gaming duty may be chargeable.

(2) A person may not provide facilities for remote gaming in respect of which remote gaming duty may be chargeable without being registered.

(3) The Commissioners may make regulations[1] about registration; in particular, the regulations may include provision (which may include provision conferring a discretion on the Commissioners) about—

(a) the procedure for applying for registration;
(b) the timing of applications;
(c) the information to be provided;
(d) notification of changes;
(e) de-registration;
(f) re-registration after a person ceases to be registered.

(4) The regulations may require a registered person to give notice to the Commissioners before applying for a remote operating licence.

(5) The regulations[1] may permit the Commissioners to make registration, or continued registration, of a foreign person conditional; and the regulations may, in particular, permit the Commissioners to require—

(a) the provision of security for payment of remote gaming duty;
(b) the appointment of a United Kingdom representative with responsibility for discharging liability to remote gaming duty.

(6) In subsection (5) "foreign person" means a person who—

(a) in the case of an individual, is not usually resident in the United Kingdom,
(b) in the case of a body corporate, does not have an established place of business in the United Kingdom, and
(c) in any other case, does not include an individual who is usually resident in the United Kingdom.

(7) The regulations[1] may include provision for the registration of groups of persons; and may provide for the modification of the provisions of this Part about remote gaming duty in their application to groups.

(8) The regulations[1]—

(a) may make provision which applies generally or only for specified purposes, and
(b) may make different provision for different purposes.][2]

---

1 See SI 2007/2192.

2 Inserted by the Finance Act 2007, s 8(1), Sch 1, Pt 1. Date in force: this amendment has effect in respect of the provision of facilities for remote gaming on or after 1 September 2007: see

SI 2007/2172, art 2.

7.163 [26K Returns]

[(1) The Commissioners may make regulations[1] requiring persons who provide facilities for remote gaming in respect of which remote gaming duty may be chargeable to make returns to the Commissioners in respect of their activities.

(2) The regulations[1] may, in particular, make provision about—

(a) liability to make a return;
(b) timing;
(c) form;
(d) content;
(e) method of making;
(f) declarations;
(g) authentication;
(h) when a return is to be treated as made.

(3) The regulations[1]—

(a) may make provision which applies generally or only for specified purposes, and
(b) may make different provision for different purposes.][2]

---

1 See SI 2007/2192.

2 Inserted by the Finance Act 2007, s 8(1), Sch 1, Pt 1. Date in force: this amendment has effect in respect of the provision of facilities for remote gaming on or after 1 September 2007: see SI 2007/2172, art 2.

7.164 [26L Enforcement]

[(1) Contravention of a provision made by or by virtue of sections 26I to 26K—

(a) is conduct to which section 9 of the Finance Act 1994 applies (penalties), and
(b) attracts daily penalties under that section.

(2) A person who is knowingly concerned in, or in taking steps with a view to, the fraudulent evasion of remote gaming duty commits an offence.

(3) A person guilty of an offence under subsection (2) shall be liable on summary conviction to—

(a) a penalty of—
  (i) the statutory maximum, or
  (ii) if greater, three times the duty which is unpaid or the payment of which is sought to be avoided,
(b) imprisonment for a term not exceeding six months, or
(c) both.

(4) A person guilty of an offence under subsection (2) shall be liable on conviction on indictment to—

(a) a penalty of any amount,
(b) imprisonment for a term not exceeding seven years, or
(c) both.][1]

---

1 Inserted by the Finance Act 2007, s 8(1), Sch 1, Pt 1. Date in force: this amendment has effect in respect of the provision of facilities for remote gaming on or after 1 September 2007: see SI 2007/2172, art 2.

7.165 [26M Review and appeal]

[(1) Sections [13A to 16][1] of the Finance Act 1994 (review and appeal) shall apply in relation to liability to pay remote gaming duty [as they apply to the decisions mentioned in section 13A(2)(a) to (h) of that Act][2].

(2) Sections [13A to 16][3] of that Act shall also apply to the decisions listed in subsection (3) below.

(3) Those decisions are—

(a) a decision to refuse a request for an agreement under section 26D(2),

(b) a decision to give a direction under section 26D(3),

(c) a decision not to give a direction under section 26D(3),

(d) a decision to direct that section 26F(6) shall not apply in a specified case,

(e) a decision under regulations by virtue of section 26J(3), and

(f) a decision about security by virtue of section 26J(5)(a).

(4) A decision of a kind specified in subsection (3) shall be treated as an ancillary matter for the purposes of sections 14 to 16 of the Finance Act 1994.][4]

---

1 Sub-s (1): words "13A to 16" in square brackets substituted by SI 2009/56, art 3(1), Sch 1, paras 96, 97(1), (2)(a). Date in force: 1 April 2009: see SI 2009/56, art 1(2); for transitional and savings provisions see art 6, Sch 3, paras 1, 6–8, 12, 13 thereto.

2 Sub-s (1): words "as they apply to the decisions mentioned in section 13A(2)(a) to (h) of that Act" in square brackets inserted by SI 2009/56, art 3(1), Sch 1, paras 96, 97(1), (2)(b). Date in force: 1 April 2009: see SI 2009/56, art 1(2); for transitional and savings provisions see art 6, Sch 3, paras 1, 6–8, 12, 13 thereto.

3 Sub-s (2): words "13A to 16" in square brackets substituted by SI 2009/56, art 3(1), Sch 1, paras 96, 97(1), (3). Date in force: 1 April 2009: see SI 2009/56, art 1(2); for transitional and savings provisions see art 6, Sch 3, paras 1, 6–8, 12, 13 thereto.

4 Inserted by the Finance Act 2007, s 8(1), Sch 1, Pt 1. Date in force: this amendment has effect in respect of the provision of facilities for remote gaming on or after 1 September 2007: see SI 2007/2172, art 2.

[General][1]

7.166 2[1] [[26N][2] Amounts in currencies other than sterling]

[(1) Any reference in this Part of this Act to a amount in sterling, in the context of—

(a) the cost of playing a game, or

(b) the amount of the prize for a game,

includes a reference to the equivalent amount in another currency.

(2) The equivalent amount in another currency, in relation to any day, shall be determined by reference to the London closing exchange rate for the previous day.

(3) For the purposes of determining what duty is payable on an amusement machine licence in a case where this section applies, the equivalent in another currency of an amount in sterling shall be taken to be its equivalent on the day on which the application for the licence is received by the Commissioners, or the due date in the case of a default licence.

(4) In subsection (3) above—

"default licence" means a licence granted under paragraph 3(1) of Schedule 4A to this Act;

"due date" has the meaning given by paragraph 2(4) of that Schedule.][3]

---

1 Cross-heading: inserted by the Finance Act 2007, s 8(1), Sch 1, Pt 2, para 3. Date in force: this amendment has effect in respect of the provision of facilities for remote gaming on or after 1 September 2007: see SI 2007/2172, art 2.

[2] Section renumbered as s 26N by the Finance Act 2007, s 8(1), Sch 1, Pt 1, para 1. Date in force: this amendment has effect in respect of the provision of facilities for remote gaming on or after 1 September 2007: see SI 2007/2172, art 2.

[3] Inserted by the Finance Act 2003, s 11(2). Date in force: 10 July 2003 (except in relation to any amusement machine licence granted before that date or to anything done under such a licence): see the Finance Act 2003, s 11(3).

PART III
GENERAL

7.167 27 Offences by bodies corporate

Where an offence under section . . . [1] 24 above, paragraph 13(1) or (3) or 14(1) of Schedule 1, . . . paragraph 16 of Schedule 3 or paragraph 16 of Schedule 4 to this Act has been committed by a body corporate, every person who at the date of the commission of the offence was a director, general manager, secretary or other similar officer of the body corporate, or was purporting to act in any such capacity, shall be deemed to be guilty of that offence unless he proves—

(a) that the offence was committed without his consent or connivance, and
(b) that he exercised all such diligence to prevent the commission of the offence as he ought to have exercised having regard to the nature of his functions in that capacity and in all the circumstances.

[1] Words omitted repealed by the Finance Act 1997, s 113, Sch 18, Pt II.

7.168
28 [*Repealed by the Finance Act 1997, s 113(1), Sch 18, Pt V(2).*]

7.169
29 [*Repealed by the Finance Act 1997, s 113(1), Sch 18, Pt V(2).*]

7.170 [29A Evidence by certificate, etc]

[(1) A certificate of the Commissioners—

(a) that any notice required by or under this Act to be given to them had or had not been given at any date, or
(b) that any permit, licence or authority required by or under this Act had or had not been issued at any date, or
(c) that any return required by or under this Act had not been made at any date, or
(d) that any duty shown as due in any return [made in pursuance of this Act or in any assessment made under section 12 of the Finance Act 1994][1] had not been paid at any date,

shall be sufficient evidence of that fact until the contrary is proved.

(2) A photograph of any document furnished to the Commissioners for the purposes of this Act and certified by them to be such a photograph shall be admissible in any proceedings, whether civil or criminal, to the same extent as the document itself.

(3) Any document purporting to be a certificate under subsection (1) or (2) above shall be deemed to be such a certificate until the contrary is proved.][2]

[1] Sub-s (1): in para (d) words in square brackets substituted by the Finance Act 1994, s 18(5), in accordance with s 19 thereof.

[2] Inserted by the Finance Act 1986, s 7.

7.171
30 [*Repealed by the Insolvency Act 1985, s 235(3), Sch 10, Pt IV.*]

7.172 31 Protection of officers

Where an officer takes any action in pursuance of instructions of the Commissioners or a Collector of Customs and Excise given in connection with the enforcement of the enactments relating to general betting duty, bingo duty[, remote gaming duty][1] or the duty on . . . [2] [amusement machine licences][3] and, apart from the provisions of this section, the officer would in taking that action be committing an offence under the enactments relating to betting or gaming, he shall not be guilty of that offence.

1 Words ', remote gaming duty' in square brackets inserted by the Finance Act 2007, s 8(1), Sch 1, Pt 2, para 4.

2 Words omitted repealed by the Finance Act 1997, s 113, Sch 18, Pt II.

3 Words in square brackets substituted, in relation to machines provided on or after 1 November 1995 and to licences for periods beginning on or after that date and the duty on such licences, by the Finance Act 1995, s 14, Sch 3, para 9(1).

7.173 35 Short title, construction, commencement and extent

(1) This Act may be cited as the Betting and Gaming Duties Act 1981.

(2) This Act shall be construed as one with the Customs and Excise Management Act 1979.

[(3) The following provisions of this Act do not extend to Northern Ireland—

(a) . . . [1]

(b) sections 29 and 30;

(c) . . . [1]

(d) paragraph 15 of Schedule 4;

. . . .][1]][2]

[(4) . . .][3]

1 Sub-s (3): paras (a), (c) and the words after para (d) repealed by the Finance Act 1997, s 113, Sch 18, Pt II.

2 Sub-s (3): substituted by the Finance Act 1986, s 6, Sch 4, Part I.

3 Sub-s (4): inserted by the Finance Act 1985, s 8, Sch 5, Part I; repealed by the Finance Act 1986, s 114, Sch 23, Part III.

[*The provisions of this Act not reproduced in this Part are considered in Section 1, Betting.*]

SCHEDULE 3
BINGO DUTY
sections 17, 20

PART I
EXEMPTION FROM DUTY

Domestic bingo

7.174

1 [In calculating liability to bingo duty no account shall be taken of][1] bingo played both in a private dwelling and on a domestic occasion.

1 Para 1: words "In calculating liability to bingo duty no account shall be taken of" in square brackets substituted by the Finance Act 2003, s 9(2). Date in force: this amendment shall have effect in relation to bingo played on or after 27 October 2003 (being the first day of the accounting period for the purposes of s 17 hereof): see the Finance Act 2003, s 9(10).

[Small-scale bingo

2 (1) This paragraph applies where entitlement to participate in non-licensed bingo depends on a person's being—

(a) a member of a group or organisation,

(b) a guest of a member of a group or organisation, or

(c) a guest of a group or organisation.

(2) Payments in respect of entitlement to participate in the non-licensed bingo shall not be brought into account in relation to any person for the purpose of section 19.

(3) Winnings at the non-licensed bingo shall not be brought into account in relation to any person for the purpose of section 20.

2A (1) In the case of non-licensed bingo to which paragraph 2 does not apply—

(a) payments in respect of entitlement to participate in the non-licensed bingo shall not be brought into account in relation to any person for the purpose of section 19 (subject to sub-paragraphs (2) to (5) below), and

(b) winnings at the non-licensed bingo shall not be brought into account in relation to any person for the purpose of section 20 (subject to sub-paragraphs (2) to (5) below).

(2) If on a day winnings at non-licensed bingo promoted by a person exceed £500, sub-paragraph (1) shall not apply in relation to the person in respect of the accounting period in which that day falls and the next two accounting periods.

(3) If stakes exceeding in aggregate £500 are hazarded on a day at non-licensed bingo promoted by a person, sub-paragraph (1) shall not apply in relation to the person in respect of the accounting period in which that day falls and the next two accounting periods.

(4) If in an accounting period winnings at non-licensed bingo promoted by a person exceed £7,500, sub-paragraph (1) shall not apply in relation to the person in respect of that accounting period and the next two accounting periods.

(5) If stakes exceeding in aggregate £7,500 are hazarded in an accounting period at non-licensed bingo promoted by a person, sub-paragraph (1) shall not apply in relation to the person in respect of that accounting period and the next two accounting periods.

(6) For the purposes of this paragraph winnings at bingo shall be valued in accordance with section 20(2) to (6).][1]

---

1 Paras 2, 2A: substituted, for para 2 (which had previously been substituted for paras 2–4 as originally enacted by the Finance Act 1982, s 8, Sch 6, Pt IV, para 5(2)) by the Finance Act 2003, s 9(3). Date in force: this amendment shall have effect in relation to bingo played on or after 27 October 2003 (being the first day of the accounting period for the purposes of s 17 hereof): see the Finance Act 2003, s 9(10).

[Non-profit-making bingo

2B (1) In calculating liability to bingo duty no account shall be taken of non-profit making bingo.

(2) "Non-profit making bingo" means bingo—

(a) in respect of the playing of which no charge in money or money's worth is made, and

(b) in respect of which no levy is charged on any of the stakes or on the winnings of any of the players (irrespective of the means by which the levy is charged),

and it does not matter whether the charge or levy is compulsory, customary or voluntary.

(3) In sub-paragraph (2)(a) "charge" includes an admission charge, but does not include—

(a) any payment of the whole or any part of an annual subscription to a club,

(b) any payment of an entrance subscription for membership of a club, or

(c) any stakes hazarded.

(4) In sub-paragraph (3)—

"club" means a club which is so constituted and conducted, in respect of membership and otherwise, as not to be of a temporary character, and

"membership of a club" does not include temporary membership of a club.][1]

---

1 Para 2B (inserted by the Finance Act 2003, s 9(4)): substituted by the Finance Act 2007, s 105, Sch 25, Pt 2, paras 3, 12(1), (2). Date in force: 1 September 2007: see SI 2007/2532, art 2.

Small-scale amusements provided commercially

5 (1) [In calculating liability to bingo duty no account shall be taken of][1] bingo played in compliance with the conditions of this paragraph—

(a) on any [family entertainment centre within the meaning of the Gambling Act 2005 (see section 238)][2];

[(aa) on any premises in Northern Ireland in respect of which an amusement permit under Article 111 of the Betting, Gaming, Lotteries and Amusements (Northern Ireland) Order 1985 or a pleasure permit under Article 157 of that Order has been granted;][3]

(b) on any premises in respect of which there is for the time being in force both [an amusement machine licence][4] under this Act and [an adult gaming centre premises licence issued under Part 8 of the Gambling Act 2005 (see section 150(1)(c))][5]; or

(c) at any pleasure fair consisting wholly or mainly of amusements provided by travelling showmen, which is held on any day of a year on premises not previously used in that year for more than twenty-seven days for the holding of such a pleasure fair.

(2) The conditions of this paragraph are that—

(a) the amount payable by any person for a card for any one game of bingo does not exceed [£1][6];

(b) the total amount taken as payment by players for their cards for any one game does not exceed [£500][7];

(c) no money prize exceeding [£70][8] is distributed or offered;

(d) the winning of, or the purchase of a chance to win, a prize does not entitle any person (whether subject to a further payment by him or not) to any further opportunity to win money or money's worth by taking part in any gaming or in any lottery; and

(e) in the case of such a pleasure fair as is described above, the opportunity to play bingo is not the only, or the only substantial, inducement to persons to attend the fair.

---

1 Para 5: in sub-para (1) words "In calculating liability to bingo duty no account shall be taken of" in square brackets substituted by the Finance Act 2003, s 9(5). Date in force: this amendment shall have effect in relation to bingo played on or after 27 October 2003 (being the first day of the accounting period for the purposes of s 17 hereof): see the Finance Act 2003, s 9(10).

2 Para 5: in sub-para (1)(a) words "family entertainment centre within the meaning of the Gambling Act 2005 (see section 238)" in square brackets substituted by the Finance Act 2007, s 105, Sch 25, Pt 2, paras 3, 12(1), (3)(a). Date in force: 1 September 2007: see SI 2007/2532, art 2; for transitional provisions see art 6(1), (2) thereof.

3 Para 5: sub-para (1)(aa) inserted by the Finance Act 1986, s 6, Sch 4, Pt I, para 12(2).

4 Para 5: in sub-para (1)(b) words "an amusement machine licence" in square brackets substituted, in relation to machines provided on or after 1 November 1995 and to licences for periods beginning on or after that date and the duty on such licences, by the Finance Act 1995, s 14, Sch 3, para 10(a).

5 Para 5: in sub-para (1)(b) words "an adult gaming centre premises licence issued under Part 8 of the Gambling Act 2005 (see section 150(1)(c))" in square brackets substituted by the Finance Act 2007, s 105, Sch 25, Pt 2, paras 3, 12(1), (3)(b). Date in force: 1 September 2007: see SI 2007/2532, art 2; for transitional provisions see art 6(1), (3) thereof.

6 Para 5: in sub-para (2)(a) sum "£1" in square brackets substituted by SI 1995/2374, art 5.

7 Para 5: in sub-para (2)b) sum "£500" in square brackets substituted by SI 2007/2152, art 2(1). Date in force: 1 September 2007: see SI 2007/2152, art 1.

8 Para 5: in sub-para (2)(c) sum "£70" in square brackets substituted by the Finance Act 2009, s 20(1), (3). Date in force: this amendment has effect in relation to bingo played on or after 1 June 2009: see the Finance Act 2009, s 20(5).

. . . [1]

6 . . . [1]

---

1 Para 6: repealed by the Finance Act 2006, ss 11(3), 178, Sch 26, Pt 1(2). Date in force: this repeal has effect in relation to accounting periods beginning on or after 1 August 2006: see the Finance Act 2006, s 11(5).

Power to increase limits of exemptions

7 The Commissioners may by order provide that any provision of this Part of this Schedule which is specified in the order and which mentions a sum shall have effect (whether as from a date so specified or in relation to events taking place on or after a date so specified) as if for that sum there were substituted such larger sum as may be specified in the order.

PART II
SUPPLEMENTARY PROVISIONS

Definitions

7.175

8 In this Part of this Schedule—

"bingo-promoter" means a person who promotes the playing of bingo chargeable with bingo duty;

"prescribed" means prescribed by regulations;

"regulations" means regulations of the Commissioners made under this Part of this Schedule.

General administration

9 (1) Bingo duty shall be under the care and management of the Commissioners and shall be accounted for by such persons, and accounted for and paid at such times and in such manner, as may be required by or under regulations.

(2) Without prejudice to any other provision of this Schedule, regulations may provide for any matter for which provision appears to the Commissioners to be necessary for the administration or enforcement of bingo duty, or for the protection of the revenue in respect of that duty.

Notification to Commissioners by, and registration of, bingo-promoters

10 (1) Any person who intends to promote the playing of bingo [in connection with which bingo duty may be chargeable][1] shall, not less than fourteen days before the first day on which bingo is to be played, notify the Commissioners of his intention, specifying the premises on which the bingo is to be played, and applying to be registered as a bingo-promoter.

[(1A) Any person who is a bingo-promoter but is not registered as such and is not a person to whom sub-paragraph (1) above applies shall within five days of the date on which he became a bingo-promoter (disregarding any day which is a Saturday or a Sunday or a Bank Holiday) notify the Commissioners of that fact and of the place where the bingo was and (if he intends to continue to promote the playing of bingo which will or may be chargeable with duty) is to be played and apply to be registered as a bingo-promoter.][2]

(2) Where a person [gives notice to the Commissioners under sub-paragraph (1) or (1A) above][3], he shall be entitled to be registered by the Commissioners, except that the Commissioners may, where it appears to them to be requisite for the security of the revenue to do so, impose as a condition of a person's registration, or may subsequently impose as a condition of the continuance in force of his registration, a requirement that he shall give such security (or further security) by way of deposit or otherwise for any bingo duty which he is, or may become, liable to pay as the Commissioners may from time to time require.

[Conditions shall not be imposed under this sub-paragraph if the premises at which the bingo in question is or is to be played are not licensed under [a bingo premises licence][4] [or under Chapter II of Part III of the Betting, Gaming, Lotteries and Amusements (Northern Ireland) Order 1985][5].][6]

(3) Where, in the case of a person who is for the time being registered as a bingo-promoter, the Commissioners exercise their power under sub-paragraph (2) above to impose, as a condition of the continuance in force of his registration, a requirement that he shall give security or further security, and he does not give it, the Commissioners may cancel his registration but without prejudice to his right to apply again to be registered.

---

1 Para 10: in sub-para (1) words "in connection with which bingo duty may be chargeable" in square brackets substituted by the Finance Act 2003, s 9(7). Date in force: this amendment shall have effect in relation to bingo played on or after 27 October 2003 (being the first day of the accounting period for the purposes of s 17 hereof): see the Finance Act 2003, s 9(10).

2 Para 10: sub-para (1A) inserted by the Finance Act 1982, s 8, Sch 6, Pt IV, para 5.

3 Para 10: in sub-para (2) words "gives notice to the Commissioners under sub-paragraph (1) or (1A) above" in square brackets substituted by the Finance Act 1982, s 8, Sch 6, Pt IV, para 5.

4 Para 10: in sub-para (2) words "a bingo premises licence" in square brackets substituted by the Finance Act 2007, s 105, Sch 25, Pt 2, paras 3, 12(1), (4). Date in force: 1 September 2007: see SI 2007/2532, art 2.

5 Para 10: in sub-para (2) words "or under Chapter II of Part III of the Betting, Gaming, Lotteries and Amusements (Northern Ireland) Order 1985" in square brackets inserted by the Finance Act 1986, s 6, Sch 4, Pt I, para 12(3).

6 Para 10: in sub-para (2) words in square brackets beginning with the words "Conditions shall not" inserted by the Finance Act 1982, s 8, Sch 6, Pt IV, para 5.

. . .

11 . . .

12 . . .[1]

1 Paras 11, 12: repealed by the Finance Act 2003, ss 9(8)(a), (b), 216, Sch 43, Pt 1(2). Date in force: this repeal shall have effect in relation to bingo played on or after 27 October 2003 (being the first day of the accounting period for the purposes of s 17 hereof): see the Finance Act 2003, s 9(10).

Powers to enter premises and obtain information

13 (1) Any officer may, without paying, enter on any premises where bingo is played or on which he has reasonable cause to suspect that bingo has been or is about to be played, and inspect the premises and anything whatsoever which he finds there; and he may further—

- (a) require any person concerned with the management of the premises to provide him with information with respect to activities carried on there;
- (b) require any person on the premises who appears to him to be, or to have been, playing any game to provide him with information with respect to the game and, in particular, to produce to him any document or thing in his possession which is or was used in connection with the playing of the game.

(2) An officer who enters any premises in the exercise of powers conferred by this paragraph shall be permitted to remain there at any time when the premises are being used for gaming, or when he has reasonable cause to suspect that they are about to be so used.

14 < . . . >[1]

1 Para 14: repealed by the Finance Act 1994, s 258, Sch 26, Part III, in accordance with s 19 thereof.

. . .

15 . . . [1]

1 Para 15: repealed by the Finance Act 2003, ss 9(8)(c), 216, Sch 43, Pt 1(2). Date in force: this repeal shall have effect in relation to bingo played on or after 27 October 2003 (being the first day of the accounting period for the purposes of s 17 hereof): see the Finance Act 2003, s 9(10).

16 (1) Any person who is knowingly concerned in or in taking steps with a view to the fraudulent evasion by him or any other person of bingo duty shall be guilty of an offence and liable—

- (a) on summary conviction to a penalty of the prescribed sum or, if greater, treble the amount of the duty payment of which is sought to be evaded or to imprisonment for a term not exceeding six months or to both, or
- (b) on conviction on indictment to a penalty of any amount or to imprisonment for a term not exceeding [seven years][1] or to both.

(2) Any person who—

- (a) is knowingly concerned with the promotion of bingo [(being bingo in connection with which bingo duty may be chargeable)][2] where the promoter is not registered by the Commissioners in accordance with paragraph 10 above . . .
- (b) ...[3]

shall be guilty of an offence and liable—

- (i) on summary conviction to a penalty of the prescribed sum or to imprisonment for a term not exceeding six months or to both; or

(ii) on conviction on indictment, to a penalty of any amount or to imprisonment for a term not exceeding two years or to both.

(3) [Where any person][4]—

(a) contravenes or fails to comply with any provision of this Part of this Schedule or of regulations, or

(b) fails to comply with any requirement made of him by or under any such provision,

[his contravention or failure to comply shall attract a penalty under section 9 of the Finance Act 1994 (civil penalties)].[4]

(4) < . . . >[5]

---

1 Para 16: in sub-para (1)(b) words "seven years" in square brackets substituted, in relation to offences committed after 29 July 1988, by the Finance Act 1988, s 12(1)(c).

2 Para 16: in sub-para (2)(a) words "(being bingo in connection with which bingo duty may be chargeable)" in square brackets substituted by the Finance Act 2003, s 9(9)(a). Date in force: this amendment shall have effect in relation to bingo played on or after 27 October 2003 (being the first day of the accounting period for the purposes of s 17 hereof): see the Finance Act 2003, s 9(10).

3 Para 16: sub-para (2)(b) and word omitted immediately preceding it repealed by the Finance Act 2003, ss 9(9)(b), 216, Sch 43, Pt 1(2). Date in force: this repeal shall have effect in relation to bingo played on or after 27 October 2003 (being the first day of the accounting period for the purposes of s 17 hereof): see the Finance Act 2003, s 9(10).

4 Para 16: in sub-para (3) words "Where any person" and "his contravention or failure to comply shall attract a penalty under section 9 of the Finance Act 1994 (civil penalties)." in square brackets substituted by the Finance Act 1994, s 9, Sch 4, para 64(1), in accordance with s 19 thereof.

5 Para 16: sub-para (4) repealed by the Finance Act 1994, ss 9, 258, Sch 4, para 64(2), Sch 26, Pt III, in accordance with s 19 thereof.

17 . . . [1]

---

1 ara 17: repealed by the Finance Act 2007, ss 84(4), 114, Sch 22, Pt 2, paras 3, 6(b), Sch 27, Pt 5(1). Date in force: 1 December 2007: by virtue of SI 2007/3166, art 3(a).

7.176

SCHEDULE 4
[AMUSEMENT MACHINE][1] LICENCE DUTY

---

1 Words in square brackets substituted, in relation to machines provided on or after 1 November 1995 and to licences for periods beginning on or after that date and the duty on such licences, by the Finance Act 1995, s 14, Sch 3, para 11(1).

sections 21, 24, 26

PART I
EXEMPTION FROM REQUIREMENT OF EXCISE LICENCE

Charitable entertainments, etc

1 (1) [An amusement machine][1] licence shall not be required in order to authorise the provision of [an amusement machine][1] at an entertainment (whether limited to one day or extending over two or more days), being a bazaar, sale of work, fete, dinner, dance, sporting or athletic event or other entertainment of a similar character, where the conditions of this paragraph are complied with in relation to the entertainment.

(2) The conditions of this paragraph are that—

(a) the whole proceeds of the entertainment (including the proceeds [from any amusement machines][1]) after deducting the expenses of the entertainment, including any expenses incurred in connection with the provision of [amusement machines][1] and of prizes to successful players of the machines will be devoted to purposes other than private gain; and

(b) the opportunity to win prizes by playing the machine (or that machine [and any other amusement machines provided][1] at the entertainment) does not constitute the only, or the only substantial, inducement for persons to attend the entertainment.

[(3) In construing sub-paragraph (2)(a) above, proceeds of an entertainment promoted on behalf of a society falling within this sub-paragraph which are applied for any purpose calculated to benefit the society as a whole shall not be held to be applied for purposes of private gain by reason only that their application for that purpose results in benefit to any person as an individual.

(4) A society falls within sub-paragraph (3) above if it is established and conducted either—

(a) wholly for purposes other than purposes of any commercial undertaking, or

(b) wholly or mainly for the purpose of participation in or support of athletic sports or athletic games;

and in this paragraph "society" includes any club, institution, organisation or association of persons, by whatever name called, and any separate branch or section of such a club, institution, organisation or association.][2]

1 Para 1: in sub-paras (1), (2) words in square brackets substituted, in relation to machines provided on or after 1 November 1995 and to licences for periods beginning on or after that date and the duty on such licences, by the Finance Act 1995, s 14, Sch 3, para 11(1), (2).

2 Sub-paras (3), (4) substituted for sub-para (3), as originally enacted, by the Finance Act 1983, s 5(2).

. . .

2 . . .

3 . . . [1]

1 Paras 2, 3: repealed by the Finance Act 2006, ss 12(7), 178, Sch 26, Pt 1(2). Date in force: this repeal has effect in relation to the grant of an amusement machine licence on or after 1 August 2006: see the Finance Act 2006, s 12(8); for further effect see sub-ss (9)–(11) thereof.

[Seasonal licences

4 (1) If at any time during March of any year there has previously been granted a seasonal licence for that year authorising the provision of any number of [relevant machines][1] on any premises and that licence has not been surrendered, it shall be treated for the purposes of this Act as authorising the provision at that time of that number of [relevant machines][1] on the premises.

(2) Where a seasonal licence is granted for any year authorising the provision of any number of [relevant machines][1] on any premises, and the licence is not surrendered, it shall be treated for the purposes of this Act as authorising [the provision of that number of relevant machines on the premises during the period in that year—

(a) beginning with 1st October; and

(b) ending with the Sunday before the first Monday in November][2].

(3) Subject to sub-paragraph (4) below, in this Schedule "seasonal licence", in relation to any year, means [an amusement machine] licence expressed to authorise only the provision of [relevant machines][1] on any premises for the period of six months beginning with 1st April in that year.

(4) A licence in respect of any premises is not a seasonal licence in relation to any year if any [amusement machine] licence has been granted in respect of those premises for any period which includes the whole or any part of the preceding winter period.

(5) If in relation to any year—

(a) a seasonal licence is granted in respect of any premises, and

(b) another [amusement machine] licence is granted (whether before or after the grant of the seasonal licence or after the surrender of the seasonal licence) in respect of those premises for any period which includes the whole or any part of the following winter period (and does not include the whole or any part of the preceding winter period),

there shall (unless an amount has already become payable under this sub-paragraph in respect of the seasonal licence) be payable on the seasonal licence on the relevant date an additional amount of duty.

(6) The additional amount is the difference between the duty payable (apart from this paragraph) on that licence at the time it was granted and the amount that would have been so payable if the licence had been granted for a period of eight months or, in a case where the seasonal licence has been surrendered before the beginning of September, seven months.

(7) In sub-paragraph (5) above, the "relevant date" means—

(a) the date on which the seasonal licence is granted, or

(b) the date on which the other licence is granted,

whichever is the later.

[(7AA) Sub-paragraphs (4) and (5) above shall have effect where—

(a) an amusement machine is provided on any premises at any time in a winter period, and

(b) the provision of that machine on those premises at that time is authorised by a special amusement machine licence,

as if an amusement machine licence had been granted in respect of those premises for that winter period.][3]

[(7A) An amusement machine is a relevant machine for the purposes of this paragraph unless it is a gaming machine which is not a small-prize machine.][4]

(8) In this paragraph "winter period" means [the period beginning with the first Monday in November and ending with the last day of February][5].][6]

---

1 Para 4: in sub-paras (1)–(5) words "relevant machines" in square brackets, in each place they occur, substituted, in relation to machines provided on or after 1 November 1995 and to licences for periods beginning on or after that date and the duty on such licences, by the Finance Act 1995, s 14, Sch 3, para 11(1), (4).

2 Para 4: in sub-para (2) words from "the provision of" to the end of the sub-para substituted by the Finance Act 2000, s 17, Sch 2, paras 1, 8(1), (2). Date in force: this amendment applies in relation to any licence expressed to be granted for a period beginning with 1 April in 2000 or any subsequent year: see the Finance Act 2000, Sch 2, para 8(4).

3 Para 4: sub-para (7AA) inserted by the Finance Act 1996, s 12(5).

4 Para 4: sub-para (7A) inserted, in relation to machines provided on or after 1 November 1995 and to licences for periods beginning on or after that date and the duty on such licences, by the Finance Act 1995, s 14, Sch 3, para 11(1), (4).

5 Para 4: in sub-para (8) words from "the period beginning" to "last day of February" in square brackets substituted by the Finance Act 2000, s 17, Sch 2, paras 1, 8(3). Date in force: this amendment has effect for determining what was comprised in the winter period beginning in 1999, and for determining what is comprised in any subsequent winter period: see the Finance Act 2000, Sch 2, para 8(5).

6 Para 4: substituted, in relation to gaming machine licences granted for any period beginning on or after 1 April 1994, by the Finance Act 1994, s 6, Sch 3, para 4(1), (4).

PART II
SUPPLEMENTARY PROVISIONS

General administration

7.177

5 [(1)] [1]The duty on [amusement machine][2] licences shall be under the care and management of the Commissioners, who may (without prejudice to any other provision of this Schedule) make regulations providing for any matter for which provision appears to them to be necessary for the administration or enforcement of the duty, or for the protection of the revenue in respect thereof; and in this Schedule—

(a) "regulations" means regulations of the Commissioners made thereunder; and

(b) "prescribed" means prescribed by regulations.

[(2) Regulations may provide for this Schedule to have effect in relation to special amusement machine licences with such exceptions, adaptations and modifications as may be prescribed.

(3) Without prejudice to the generality of sub-paragraphs (1) and (2) above, regulations may include provision requiring—

(a) a special amusement machine licence to be displayed on such premises and in such manner, and

(b) the machine to which such a licence relates to bear such labels and marks,

as may be determined by directions given, in accordance with the regulations, by the Commissioners.][1]

1 Para 5: sub-para (1) numbered as such, and sub-paras (2), (3) inserted, by the Finance Act 1996, s 12(6).

2 Words in square brackets substituted, in relation to machines provided on or after 1 November 1995 and to licences for periods beginning on or after that date and the duty on such licences, by the Finance Act 1995, s 14, Sch 3, para 11(1), (8).

Applications for and duration of licence

[6 An application for [an amusement machine][1] licence shall be made to the Commissioners in such form and manner as they may require.

7 The period for which [an amusement machine][1] licence is granted shall begin with the day on which application for the licence is received by the Commissioners or, if a later day is specified for that purpose in the application, with that day; and the licence shall expire at the end of that period.][2]

1 Paras 6, 7: substituted, in relation to gaming machine licences granted for any period beginning on or after 1 May 1994, by the Finance Act 1994, s 6, Sch 3, para 1(7), (9).

2 Words in square brackets substituted, in relation to machines provided on or after 1 November 1995 and to licences for periods beginning on or after that date and the duty on such licences, by the Finance Act 1995, s 14, Sch 3, para 11(1).

[Payment of duty by instalments

7A (1) The Commissioners may make and publish arrangements setting out the circumstances in which, and the conditions subject to which, a person to whom an amusement machine licence is granted for a period of twelve months may, at his request and if the Commissioners think fit, be permitted to pay the duty on that licence by regular instalments during the period of the licence, instead of at the time when it is granted.

(2) Arrangements under this paragraph shall provide for the amount of each instalment to be such that the aggregate amount of all the instalments to be paid in respect of any licence is an amount equal to 105 per cent of what would have been the duty on that licence apart from this paragraph.

(3) Sub-paragraph (4) below applies if a person who has been permitted, in accordance with arrangements under this paragraph, to pay the duty on any amusement machine licence by instalments—

(a) fails to pay any instalment at the time when it becomes due in accordance with the arrangements; and

(b) does not make good that failure within seven days of being required to do so by notice given by the Commissioners.

(4) Where this sub-paragraph applies—

(a) the licence shall be treated as having ceased to be in force as from the time when the instalment became due;

(b) the person to whom the licence was granted shall become liable to any unpaid duty to which he would have been liable under paragraph 11(1C) below if he had surrendered the licence at that time; and

(c) any amusement machines found on the premises to which the licence related shall be liable to forfeiture.

(5) Sections [13A to 16][1] of the Finance Act 1994 [(meaning of relevant decision, reviews and appeals to a tribunal)][2] shall have effect in relation to any decision of the Commissioners refusing an application for permission to pay duty by instalments in accordance with arrangements under this paragraph as if that decision were a decision of a description [falling within section 13A(2)(j)][3] to that Act.][4]

---

1 Para 7A: in sub-para (5) words "13A to 16" in square brackets substituted by SI 2009/56, art 3(1), Sch 1, paras 96, 98(1), (2)(a). Date in force: 1 April 2009: see SI 2009/56, art 1(2); for transitional and savings provisions see art 6, Sch 3, paras 1, 6–8, 12, 13 thereto.

2 Para 7A: in sub-para (5) words "(meaning of relevant decision, reviews and appeals to a tribunal)" in square brackets substituted by SI 2009/56, art 3(1), Sch 1, paras 96, 98(1), (2)(b). Date in force: 1 April 2009: see SI 2009/56, art 1(2); for transitional and savings provisions see art 6, Sch 3, paras 1, 6–8, 12, 13 thereto.

3 Para 7A: in sub-para (5) words "falling within section 13A(2)(j)" in square brackets substituted by SI 2009/56, art 3(1), Sch 1, paras 96, 98(1), (2)(c). Date in force: 1 April 2009: see SI 2009/56, art 1(2); for transitional and savings provisions see art 6, Sch 3, paras 1, 6–8, 12, 13 thereto.

4 Para 7A: inserted, in relation to machines provided on or after 1 November 1995 and to licences for periods beginning on or after that date and the duty on such licences, by the Finance Act 1995, s 14, Sch 3, para 11(5).

Transfer of licence

8 (1) The proper officer may, in such manner as the Commissioners may direct, and without any additional payment, [transfer [an amusement machine][1] licence in respect of any premises to a successor in title to the interest in those premises of the person to whom the licence was granted.][1]

(2) Where the holder of [an amusement machine][2] licence . . . [3] dies, the proper officer may transfer the licence, in such manner as the Commissioners may direct and without any additional payment, to some other person for the remainder of the period for which the licence was granted.

1 Para 8: in sub-para (1) first words in square brackets substituted by the Finance Act 1994, s 6, Sch 3, para 3(5), (11), words in square brackets therein substituted, in relation to machines provided on or after 1 November 1995 and to licences for periods beginning on or after that date and the duty on such licences, by the Finance Act 1995, s 14, Sch 3, para 11(1).

2 in sub-para (2) words in square brackets substituted, in relation to machines provided on or after 1 November 1995 and to licences for periods beginning on or after that date and the duty on such licences, by the Finance Act 1995, s 14, Sch 3, para 11(1).

3 Words omitted repealed by the Finance Act 1984, ss 7, 128(6), Sch 3, Part I, Sch 23, Part II.

Amendment of licence

9, 10 . . . [1]

1 Paras 9, 10: repealed by the Finance Act 1994, ss 6, 258, Sch 3, para 5(2), Sch 26, Part II; for provision as to the application of these provisions at any time before 1 May 1994 in relation to gaming machine licences granted for any period beginning on or after 1 May 1994, see Sch 3, para 1(8), (9) thereof.

Surrender of licence

11 [(1) The holder of [an amusement machine][1] licence may surrender it to the proper officer at any time.

(1A) On the surrender of the licence the holder shall be entitled to repayment of duty of the following amount.

(1B) That amount is the difference between—

(a) the amount of duty actually paid on the licence, and

(b) the amount (if less) that would have been paid if the period for which the licence was granted had been reduced by the number of complete months in that period which have not expired,

and for the purposes of this paragraph a seasonal licence is to be treated as granted for the period of eight months beginning with 1st March.][2]

[(1C) Where, in a case where duty is being paid in accordance with arrangements made under paragraph 7A above, the amount of duty actually paid on a licence that is surrendered is less than the amount which would have been paid on that licence if the period for which it was granted had been reduced by the number of complete months in that period which have not expired when the licence is surrendered, the difference between those amounts shall be treated as unpaid duty.][1]

(2) . . . [3]

(3) [Sub-paragraph (1)][4] above shall not apply if any person has been convicted of an offence under section 24 of this Act in respect of a contravention of [section 21(1) or 24 of this Act][3] which occurred between the grant of the licence and the date of surrender; and where at the date of surrender proceedings for such an offence are pending against any person, the right to repayment under this paragraph shall not arise until the proceedings are terminated, nor unless every person charged in those proceedings with such an offence has been acquitted thereof.

1 Words in square brackets in sub-para (1) substituted, and sub-para (1C) inserted, in relation to machines provided on or after 1 November 1995 and to licences for periods beginning on or after that date and the duty on such licences, by the Finance Act 1995, s 14, Sch 3, para 11(1), (6).

2 Para 11: sub-paras (1)–(1B) substituted for existing sub-para (1) by the Finance Act 1994, s 6, Sch 3, para 5(3).

3 Sub-para (2) repealed by the Finance Act 1994, s 6, Sch 3, para 3(6), (11).

4 Words in square brackets in sub-para (3) substituted by the Finance Act 1984, s 7, Sch 3, Part I; for provision as to the application of this provision at any time before 1 May 1994 in relation to gaming machine licences granted on or after 1 May 1994, see the Finance Act 1994, Sch 3, para 1(8), (9).

[11A . . . [1]

1 Para 11A: inserted by the Finance Act 1984, s 7, Sch 3, Part I; repealed by the Finance Act 1994, ss 6, 258, Sch 3, para 5(4), (6), Sch 26, Part II; for provision as to the application of this provision at any time before 1 May 1994 in relation to gaming machine licences granted for any period beginning on or after 1 May 1994, see Sch 3, para 1(8), (9) thereof.

Requirements to be observed by licence-holder

12 The holder of [[an amusement machine][1] licence][2] in respect of any premises shall secure that the licence is displayed on the premises at such times and in such manner as may be prescribed, and shall on demand by an officer at any time produce the licence for the officer's inspection.

1 Para 12: first words in square brackets substituted by the Finance Act 1994, s 6, Sch 3, para 3(7), (11).

2 Words in square brackets therein substituted, in relation to machines provided on or after 1 November 1995 and to licences for periods beginning on or after that date and the duty on such licences, by the Finance Act 1995, s 14, Sch 3, para 11(1).

[13 . . . [1]

1 Para 13: substituted, in relation to licences for any period beginning on or after 1 November 1993, by the Finance Act 1993, s 16(8), (9); repealed, in relation to machines provided on or after 1 November 1995 and to licences for periods beginning on or after that date and the duty on such licences, by the Finance Act 1995, s 14, Sch 3, para 11(7).

Power to enter premises and obtain information

14 Any officer may (without payment) enter on any premises on which he knows or has reasonable cause to suspect that [amusement machines][1] are or have been provided [for play][2] and inspect those premises and require any person who is concerned in the management of the premises, or who is on the premises and appears to the officer to have any responsibility whatsoever in respect of their management or of the control of the admission of persons thereto—

(a) to produce or secure the production of any [amusement machine][3] licence for the time being in force in respect of the premises, or

(b) to provide information with respect to any use to which the premises are or have been put, or to any machine which is or has been on the premises and any game which may have been played by means of such a machine or to the way in which the machine works, or to the amount which is or has been payable to play it.

1 Para 14: words "amusement machines" in square brackets substituted, in relation to machines provided on or after 1 November 1995 and to licences for periods beginning on or after that date and the duty on such licences, by the Finance Act 1995, s 14, Sch 3, para 11(1)(a).

2 Para 14: words "for play" in square brackets substituted, in relation to machines provided on or after 1 November 1995 and to licences for periods beginning on or after that date and the duty on such licences, by the Finance Act 1995, s 14, Sch 3, para 11(8).

3 Para 14: in para (a) words "amusement machine" in square brackets substituted, in relation

to machines provided on or after 1 November 1995 and to licences for periods beginning on or after that date and the duty on such licences, by the Finance Act 1995, s 14, Sch 3, para 11(1)(a).

. . .

15 . . . [1]

[1] Para 15: repealed by the Finance Act 2006, s 178, Sch 26, Pt 1(2). Date in force: this repeal came into force on 19 July 2006 (date of Royal Assent of the Finance Act 2006) in the absence of any specific commencement provision.

Enforcement

16 (1) If any person contravenes or fails to comply with any provision of this Part of this Schedule or regulations, or fails or refuses to comply with any requirement lawfully made of him under this Part of this Schedule or regulations, [his contravention, failure to comply or refusal shall attract a penalty under section 9 of the Finance Act 1994 (civil penalties)].[1]

[(1A) This paragraph does not apply to any contravention or failure to comply with arrangements under paragraph 7A above or to any failure or refusal to comply with a requirement made under or for the purposes of any such arrangements.][2]

(2) ...[3]

[1] Para 16: in sub-para (1) words in square brackets substituted by the Finance Act 1994, s 9, Sch 4, para 65(1), in accordance with s 19 thereof.

[2] Sub-para (1A) inserted, in relation to machines provided on or after 1 November 1995 and to licences for periods beginning on or after that date and the duty on such licences, by the Finance Act 1995, s 14, Sch 3, para 11(9).

[3] Sub-para (2) repealed by the Finance Act 1994, ss 9, 258, Sch 4, para 65(2), Sch 26, Part III, in accordance with s 19 thereof.

17 . . . [1]

[1] Para 17: repealed by the Finance Act 2007, ss 84(4), 114, Sch 22, Pt 2, paras 3, 6(c), Sch 27, Pt 5(1). Date in force: 1 December 2007: by virtue of SI 2007/3166, art 3(a).

18 Where an officer finds [amusement machines][1] provided on any premises in such circumstances that [an amusement machine][1] licence is required so as to authorise them so to be provided and [the officer is satisfied, having regard to the number and description of [those machines which are authorised by the [amusement machine][1] licence or licences produced to him][1] that there has been a contravention of section 21(1) or 24 of this Act,] all [amusement machines][1] found on the premises shall be liable to forfeiture.

[1] Para 18: third words in square brackets substituted by the Finance Act 1984, s 7, Sch 3, Part I, first words in square brackets therein substituted by the Finance Act 1994, s 6, Sch 3, para 3(9), (11). Other words in square brackets substituted, in relation to machines provided on or after 1 November 1995 and to licences for periods beginning on or after that date and the duty on such licences, by the Finance Act 1995, s 14, Sch 3, para 11(1).

7.178

[SCHEDULE 4A
UNLICENSED AMUSEMENT MACHINES
Section 24A

[Application

1 This Schedule applies where it appears to the Commissioners that an amusement machine is or was provided for play on premises in contravention of section 21(1) or 24(3) or (4) of this Act.

Default notice requesting production of licence

2 (1) The Commissioners may give a notice which complies with the requirements of sub-paragraphs (3) and (4) below.

(2) In this Schedule such a notice is referred to as a "default notice".

(3) The notice shall state that one or more amusement machines appear to have been provided for play on specified premises ("relevant premises") during a specified period (the "alleged default period")—

- (a) the first day of which falls not more than [4 years][8] before the date of the notice, and
- (b) the last day of which falls on or before the date of the notice.

(4) The notice shall request the production to the Commissioners on or before a specified date (the "due date") of every relevant amusement machine licence.

(5) For the purposes of sub-paragraph (4) above an amusement machine licence is a relevant licence if, at any time during the alleged default period, it was in force in relation to an amusement machine provided for play on the relevant premises at that time.

(6) A single default notice may relate to—

- (a) different alleged default periods, or
- (b) different relevant premises.

(7) A default notice shall be deemed to have been given if it is—

- (a) left at, or posted to, the relevant premises, or
- (b) given to, or posted to or left at the proper address of one or more persons falling within sub-paragraph (8) below.

(8) Those persons are—

- (a) one or more of the persons who are or appear to be, or who at any time during the alleged default period were or appear to have been, responsible persons in relation to the relevant premises or an amusement machine provided for play on those premises, or
- (b) any person who is the representative of such a person.

Failure to produce a licence: grant of default licence

3 (1) In any case where—

- (a) the Commissioners give a default notice,
- (b) the due date specified in the notice passes, and
- (c) it appears to the Commissioners that at some time during the alleged default period specified in the notice one or more amusement machines were provided for play on the relevant premises so specified without an amusement machine licence being in force in relation to the machines,

the Commissioners may grant, in accordance with this paragraph, one or more licences in relation to each of the machines.

(2) In this Schedule—

"default licence" means a licence granted by the Commissioners under sub-paragraph (1) above;

"unlicensed machine" means a machine in relation to which a default licence is granted by the Commissioners.

(3) The Commissioners may grant a separate default licence for each period of consecutive days—

(a) which falls within the alleged default period, and

(b) for which no amusement machine licence in force in relation to the unlicensed machine was produced.

(4) The Commissioners may grant a default licence in relation to an unlicensed machine even though the period of that licence would include a day or days when the unlicensed machine was provided for play in contravention of section 21(1) or 24(3) or (4) of this Act on premises other than the relevant premises specified in the applicable default notice.

(5) In a case where the Commissioners grant a default licence in accordance with sub-paragraph (4) above, references in this Schedule to the relevant premises shall be construed in relation to any particular time as references to the premises on which the machine was provided for play at that time.

(6) The Commissioners may grant a default licence even though no application has been made for it.

(7) A default licence may be granted for a period of any length (whether or not a licence under Schedule 4 to this Act could be granted for a period of that length).

Assessment of amount equivalent to duty

4 (1) This paragraph applies where a default licence is granted in relation to an unlicensed machine.

(2) The Commissioners may, subject to the following provisions of this paragraph, assess to the best of their judgement the amount which would have been payable under this Act as amusement machine licence duty if the default licence had been an amusement machine licence granted under Schedule 4 to this Act.

(3) The Commissioners shall make the assessment using the rates of amusement machine licence duty which apply in relation to amusement machine licences granted in consequence of applications received by the Commissioners on the due date.

(4) If the period of the licence is 12 months or less, the assessment shall be made as if an amusement machine licence had been granted in relation to the unlicensed machine for that period.

(5) If the period of the licence is longer than 12 months, the assessment shall be made as if—

(a) a separate amusement machine licence had been granted in relation to the unlicensed machine for each complete period of 12 months falling wholly within the period of the licence, and

(b) a further amusement machine licence had been granted in relation to the unlicensed machine for any remaining part of the period of the licence.

(6) Sub-paragraphs (7) and (8) below shall apply in relation to an assessment to be made in any case where—

(a) the period of a licence mentioned in sub-paragraph (4) above, or

(b) the part of the period mentioned in sub-paragraph (5)(b) above,

is not a period of complete months.

(7) Any period of less than a month comprised in the period or the part of the period shall be treated as a complete month; and accordingly the period or the part of the period in question shall be treated as if it consisted of a complete month or, as the case may be, complete months.

(8) The amusement machine licence treated as granted for such a period, or for such a part of a period, shall be treated as having been—

(a) granted for that period, or that part of the period, as extended in accordance with sub-paragraph (7) above, and

(b) surrendered at the end of the last day of the period mentioned in sub-paragraph (4) above or, as the case may be, of the part of the period mentioned in sub-paragraph (5)(b) above.

Liability to pay

5 (1) Where an amount has been assessed under paragraph 4 above and notified to a responsible person or his representative, that amount—

(a) shall be deemed to be an amount of duty charged in accordance with section 22 of this Act on an amusement machine licence within the meaning of section 21 of this Act,

(b) shall be due from the responsible person, and

(c) may be recovered accordingly unless, or except to the extent that, the assessment has subsequently been withdrawn or reduced.

(2) The responsible persons to whom an assessment may be notified are any one or more of the persons who are or appear to be, or at any time during the period to which the assessment relates were or appear to have been, responsible persons in relation to the unlicensed machine or the relevant premises.

(3) An assessment shall be deemed to have been notified to a person if it is—

(a) given to him, or

(b) left at or posted to his proper address.

(4) But an assessment shall not be deemed to have been notified to a person unless and until—

(a) the default licence in relation to which the assessment has been made, or

(b) a copy of that licence,

has been given to him, or left at or posted to his proper address.

(5) Where an amount has been assessed and notified to more than one responsible person (or his representative), that amount shall be recoverable jointly and severally from any or all of the responsible persons.

(6) Arrangements made in accordance with paragraph 7A of Schedule 4 to this Act do not apply in relation to an amount assessed and notified in accordance with this paragraph.

Reviews and time limits on recovery

6 (1) Section [13A to 16][1] of the Finance Act 1994 [(meaning of relevant decision, reviews and appeals to a tribunal)][2] shall apply to so much of any decision by the Commissioners as is of any of the kinds mentioned in sub-paragraph (2) below, [as they apply to the decisions mentioned in section 13A(2)(a) to (h) of that Act][3].

(2) Those decisions are—

(a) any decision that a default licence should be granted,

(b) any decision contained in an assessment under paragraph 4 above that a person is liable to pay an amount of duty, and

(c) any decision contained in an assessment under paragraph 4 above as to the amount of a person's liability.

(3) Sub-paragraph (4) below applies where the Commissioners—

(a) have given a default notice, and

(b) in consequence of so doing have granted a default licence.

(4) An assessment made under paragraph 4 above in relation to the default licence may not be notified to a responsible person (or his representative) at any time after the end of the period of one year beginning with the due date specified in the default notice.

(5) The reference to *three years* [4 years][4] in paragraph 2(3)(a) above shall have effect as if it were a reference to twenty years in any case where sub-paragraph (6) *or (7)*[5] below applies.

[(6) This sub-paragraph applies where—

(a) a loss of amusement machine licence duty is brought about deliberately by the responsible person or anyone acting on the responsible person's behalf (including a representative), or

(b) the responsible person has participated in a transaction knowing that it was part of arrangements of any kind (whether or not legally enforceable) intended to bring about a loss of amusement machine licence duty.][6]

(7) This sub-paragraph applies where an amusement machine has been provided for play in circumstances where proceedings for an offence under section 24(6) of this Act would have been commenced or continued against a person (whether or not the person assessed), but for their having been compounded under section 152(a) of the Customs and Excise Management Act 1979.[7]

---

1 Para 6: in sub-para (1) words "13A to 16" in square brackets substituted by SI 2009/56, art 3(1), Sch 1, paras 96, 99(1), (2)(a). Date in force: 1 April 2009: see SI 2009/56, art 1(2); for transitional and savings provisions see art 6, Sch 3, paras 1, 6–8, 12, 13 thereto.

2 Para 6: in sub-para (1) words "(meaning of relevant decision, reviews and appeals to a tribunal)" in square brackets substituted by SI 2009/56, art 3, Sch 1, paras 96, 99(1), (2)(b). Date in force: 1 April 2009: see SI 2009/56, art 1(2); for transitional and savings provisions see art 6, Sch 3, paras 1, 6–8, 12, 13 thereto.

3 Para 6: in sub-para (1) words "as they apply to the decisions mentioned in section 13A(2)(a) to (h) of that Act" in square brackets substituted by SI 2009/56, art 3(1), Sch 1, paras 96, 99(1), (2)(c). Date in force: 1 April 2009: see SI 2009/56, art 1(2); for transitional and savings provisions see art 6, Sch 3, paras 1, 6–8, 12, 13 thereto.

4 Para 6: in sub-para (5) words "three years" in italics repealed and subsequent words in square brackets substituted by the Finance (No 3) Act 2010, s 29, Sch 13, Pt 2, para 6(1), (3)(a). Date in force: to be appointed: see the Finance (No 3) Act 2010, s 29(2).

5 Para 6: in sub-para (5) words "or (7)" in italics repealed by the Finance (No 3) Act 2010, s 29, Sch 13, Pt 2, para 6(1), (3)(b). Date in force: to be appointed: see the Finance (No 3) Act 2010, s 29(2).

6 Para 6: sub-para (6) substituted by the Finance (No 3) Act 2010, s 29, Sch 13, Pt 2, para 6(1), (4). Date in force: 1 April 2011: see SI 2011/777, art 2.

7 Para 6: sub-para (7) repealed by the Finance (No 3) Act 2010, s 29, Sch 13, Pt 2, para 6(1), (5). Date in force: 1 April 2011: see SI 2011/777, art 2.

8 Para 2: in sub-para (3)(a) words "4 years" in square brackets substituted by the Finance (No 3) Act 2010, s 29, Sch 13, Pt 2, para 6(1), (2). Date in force: 1 April 2011: see SI 2011/777, art 2; for transitional provisions see art 6 thereof.

General interpretation

7 (1) The following provisions of this paragraph apply for the purposes of this Schedule.

(2) A person is a responsible person in relation to an amusement machine at a particular time if, at that time, he is or was—

(a) the owner or hirer of the machine, or

(b) a party to any contract under which the machine may be, or may have been, or is or was required to be, on the relevant premises at that time.

(3) A person is a responsible person in relation to relevant premises at a particular time if, at that time, he is or was—

(a) the owner, lessee or occupier of the premises, or

(b) responsible to the owner, lessee or occupier for the management of the premises, or [(c) responsible for controlling the use of any amusement machine on the premises, or][1]

(d) responsible for controlling the admission of persons to the premises or for providing persons resorting to the premises with any goods or services.

(4) A person's representative is—

(a) his personal representative,

(b) his trustee in bankruptcy,

(c) any receiver or liquidator appointed in relation to him or any of his property, or

(d) any other person acting in a representative capacity in relation to him.

(5) The proper address of a person is—

(a) in the case of a body corporate, its registered office or principal office, and

(b) in any other case—

(i) his last known place of abode or business, or

(ii) any vessel or aircraft to which he may belong or have lately belonged.

(6) An item is only to be treated as posted to an address or place if it has been sent there by registered post or the recorded delivery service.

---

1 Para 7: sub-para (3)(c) substituted by the Finance Act 2003, s 12(2). Date in force: this amendment came into force on 10 July 2003 (date of Royal Assent of the Finance Act 2003) in the absence of any specific commencement provision.

Saving for liability

8 The grant of a default licence in relation to an unlicensed machine shall be without prejudice to any liability arising under section 24 of this Act in relation to the machine.][1]

---

1 Inserted by the Finance Act 2000, s 17, Sch 2, paras 1, 10. Date in force: this amendment has effect in relation to amusement machines which appear to the Commissioners of Customs and Excise to have been provided for play on premises in contravention of the Betting and Gaming Duties Act 1981, ss 21(1) or 24(3) or (4), on or after 28 July 1997: see the Finance Act 2000, Sch 2, para 10(2).

STATUTORY INSTRUMENTS

AMUSEMENT MACHINE LICENCE DUTY REGULATIONS 1995

(SI 1995/2631)

Made ....*10th October 1995*
Laid before the House of Commons ....*10th October 1995*
Coming into force ....*1st November 1995*

The Commissioners of Customs and Excise, in exercise of the powers conferred on them by section 26(3A) of, and paragraph 5 and 12 of Schedule 4 to the Betting and Gaming Duties Act 1981 and of all other powers enabling them in that behalf, hereby make the following Order:

Citation and commencement

7.179

1 These Regulations may be cited as the Amusement Machine Licence Duty Regulations 1995 and shall come into force on 1st November 1995.

Revocation

7.180

2 The Gaming Machine Licence Duty Regulations 1988 are hereby revoked.

Display of licence

7.181

3 The holder of an amusement machine licence shall display it at all times in a prominent position in the premises to which it relates.

As of 1st November 2008, this does not apply when the licence is with the Commissioners or in transit to or from them.[1]

---

1 Second paragraph inserted by the Amusement Machine Licence Duty, etc (Amendments) Regulations 2008 (SI 2008/2693).

Spare amusement machines

7.182

4 (1) A spare or broken down amusement machine shall not be treated by virtue of s 26(3) of the Betting and Gaming Duties Act 1981 as provided for play on any premises where—

(a) the machine is of the same type for duty purposes as [another machine][1] licensed on the premises; and

(b) there is a licence in force in respect of at least two other machines; and

(c) either—

(i) the machine is kept in a place to which persons resorting to those premises have no access, or

(ii) the machine is installed so that it cannot be played at the same time as those licensed on the premises, but [(subject to paragraph (1A) below)][1] this regulation shall not apply to more than one machine at any premises other than an arcade.

[(1A) Where the number of machines licensed on the premises exceeds three paragraph (1) above shall apply as if for the words 'one machine' there were substituted 'two machines'; but this paragraph shall not apply unless for each machine that is spare or broken down there is licensed on the premises another machine of the same type for duty purposes.][1]

(2) In this regulation, 'arcade' means premises used wholly or mainly for the playing of games by means of machines.

---

[1] In para (1) words in first pair of square brackets substituted and words in second pair of square brackets inserted, and para (1A) inserted by the Amusement Machine Licence Duty (Amendment) Regulations 1997, SI 1997/859, reg 2.

Licences combined in single document

7.182.1

5 Amusement machine licences need only be combined in a single document if each of the following is true—

(a) their expiry dates are the same;
(b) their holder is the same;
(c) the premises with respect to which each of them is in force is the same;
(d) each of them authorises the provision of only one amusement machine for play on those premises, but is not a special amusement machine licence (see section 21(2) of the Betting and Gaming Duties Act 1981 – licence granted with respect to a machine rather than premises);
(e) none of them is a seasonal licence (licence for 6 months beginning 1st April – see Schedule 4 paragraphs 4(3), 4(4) and 4(8) to the Betting and Gaming Duties Act 1981);
(f) at least one of them was granted for 12 months;
(g) at least one of them was first granted on 1st November 2008 or later.[1]

---

[1] Regulation 5 inserted by theAmusement Machine Licence Duty, etc (Amendments) Regulations 2008 (SI 2008/2693).

AMUSEMENT MACHINE LICENCE DUTY (SPECIAL LICENCES) REGULATIONS 1996

(SI 1996/1423)

Made .... *5th June 1996*
Laid before the House of Commons .... *7th June 1996*
Coming into force .... *1st July 1996*

The Commissioners of Customs and Excise, in exercise of the powers conferred upon them by section 21(3AA) of, and paragraph 5 of Schedule 4 to the Betting and Gaming Duties Act 1981 and of all other powers enabling them in that behalf, hereby make the following Regulations—

Citation and commencement

7.183

1 These Regulations may be cited as the Amusement Machine Licence Duty (Special Licences) Regulations 1996 and shall come into force on 1st July 1996.

Interpretation

7.184

2 In these Regulations—

'the Act' means the Betting and Gaming Duties Act 1981;

'qualified applicant' has the meaning given in regulation 3 below;

'special licence' means a special amusement machine licence.

Qualified applicants

7.185

3 (1) No person shall apply for a special licence unless he is a qualified applicant.

(2) A person is a qualified applicant if—

(a) he is applying for at least ten special licences that will all take effect on the same day; or

(b) he is the holder of one or more special licences and will be the holder of at least ten special licences that will all be in force on the day when any special licence he is applying for takes effect.

Directions concerning special licences

7.186

4 The Commissioners may by a notice they publish that has not been withdrawn by a further notice direct the holder of a special licence—

(a) to display it in such manner and on such premises as the Commissioners see fit; and

(b) to mark any machine to which it relates with such labels and marks as the Commissioners may require.

Application of Schedule 4 to the Act

7.187

5 (1) Except as otherwise provided by this regulation, Schedule 4 to the Act shall apply to special licences as it applies to amusement machine licences granted with respect to premises.

(2) Paragraphs 8(1) and 12 of that Schedule shall not apply to special licences.

(3) Paragraph 11(1) of that Schedule shall not apply unless, if the special licence is surrendered, its holder will (having regard to any other special licences surrendered at the same time) hold at least ten, or cease to hold any, special licences.

GAMING DUTY REGULATIONS 1997

(SI 1997/2196)

Made ....*9th September 1997*
Laid before Parliament ....*10th September 1997*
Coming into force ....*1st October 1997*

The Commissioners of Customs and Excise, in exercise of the powers conferred upon them by sections 11(5), 12(3) and (4), and 14(1) of, and paragraph 11 of Schedule 1 to the Finance Act 1997, and of all other powers enabling them in that behalf, hereby make the following Regulations:

PART I
PRELIMINARY

Citation and commencement

7.188

1 These Regulations may be cited as the Gaming Duty Regulations 1997 and shall come into force on 1st October 1997.

Interpretation

7.189

2 In these Regulations—
'the Act' means the Finance Act 1997;
'duty' means gaming duty;
'gross gaming yield' has the meaning given in section 11(8) of the Act;
'quarter' means the first three months of an accounting period;
'registered provider' means a person who is, in accordance with section 12(2) of the Act, presumed to be the provider of premises.

PART II
PAYMENTS ON ACCOUNT

Application of Part II

7.190

3 The obligations imposed by this Part of these Regulations apply to any person who is a registered provider.

The obligation to make payments on account

7.191

4 For every quarter every registered provider shall make a payment on account of the duty that is likely to be chargeable on any premises of which he is the provider.

The amount

7.192

5 (1) Subject to regulation 6 below, the amount of any payment on account of duty shall be calculated in accordance with this regulation.

(2) The gross gaming yield for the quarter shall be calculated, treating the quarter as an accounting period.

(3) The rates specified in the following Table shall be applied to the parts so specified of the gross gaming yield in that quarter from the premises and the results shall be aggregated.

(4) That aggregate shall be the amount of the payment on account.

Part of gross gaming yield	*Rate*
[The first £1,087,500	15 per cent
The next £749,750	20 per cent
The next £1,313,000	30 per cent
The next £2,771,250	40 per cent
The remainder	50 per cent]

Amendment

Reg (5): Table substituted by SI 2012/1897, reg 4.

Gaming that does not take place throughout a quarter

7.193

6 (1) This regulation applies where dutiable gaming takes place on any premises during a quarter but that gaming does not take place throughout that quarter.

(2) In any quarter the duration of the dutiable gaming shall be treated as being the number of days from the first day on which dutiable gaming took place in that quarter until the last day on which it took place, including both the first day and last day.

(3) If dutiable gaming did not take place on the last day of the preceding accounting period the first day on which it shall be treated as taking place shall be the first day on which it actually took place.

(4) In any other case the first day on which the dutiable gaming shall be treated as taking place shall be the first day of the quarter.

(5) The dutiable gaming shall be treated as ceasing on the last day on which it actually took place.

(6) For the purpose of determining the amount of the payment on account each of the parts of the gross gaming yield specified in the first column of the Table in regulation 5 above, other than the last, shall be reduced by multiplying that part by the duration of the dutiable gaming (determined in accordance with this regulation) and dividing the result by the number of days in the quarter.

PART III
GAMING THAT DOES NOT TAKE PLACE THROUGHOUT AN ACCOUNTING PERIOD

Application of Part III

7.194

7 (1) This Part of these Regulations applies where dutiable gaming takes place on any premises during an accounting period but that gaming does not take place throughout that period.

(2) This Part of these Regulations does not apply to any case where section 11(3) of the Act applies.

The duration of the dutiable gaming

7.195

8 (1) In any accounting period the duration of the dutiable gaming shall be treated as being the number of days from the first day on which dutiable-gaming took place in that period until the last day on which it took place, including both the first day and last day.

(2) If dutiable gaming did not take place on the last day of the preceding accounting period the first day on which it shall be treated as taking place shall be the first day on which it actually took place.

(3) In any other case the first day on which the dutiable gaming shall be treated as taking place shall be the first day of the accounting period.

(4) The dutiable gaming shall be treated as ceasing on the last day on which it actually took place.

(5) If the dutiable gaming ceased at any time between midnight and four o'clock in the morning of the last day on which it actually took place it shall be treated as having ceased on the day before that day.

The amount

7.196

9 For the purpose of determining the amount of duty which is to be charged on the premises each of the parts of the gross gaming yield specified in the first column of the Table in section 11 of the Act, other than the last, shall be reduced by multiplying that part by the duration of the dutiable gaming (determined in accordance with regulation 8 above) and dividing the result by the number of days in the accounting period.

PART IV
APPORTIONING THE LIABILITY FOR DUTY

Application of Part IV

7.197

10 This Part of these Regulations applies where during an accounting period the registered provider of any premises changes.

The apportionment

7.198

11 (1) For any accounting period each registered provider—

(a) shall be liable for the duty charged on the premises from the time that he first becomes a provider of the premises, and
(b) shall cease to be liable for any further duty charged on the premises from the time that another person becomes the registered provider of the premises in substitution for him.

(2) The amount of duty charged on the premises for which each registered provider is liable shall be determined in accordance with regulation 9 above; but the period for which each registered provider is liable shall be treated as the duration of the dutiable gaming.

PART V
DIRECTIONS

Directions as to the making of returns

7.199
12 The Commissioners shall give directions under paragraph 10 of Schedule 1 to the Act in a notice published by them and not withdrawn by a further notice.

Directions concerning premises

7.200
13 (1) This regulation applies to any direction given under section 11(6) of the Act.

(2) The Commissioners shall give any direction in writing to a person who appears to them to be a provider of the premises.

(3) In the case of a registered provider, any direction shall be sent to him at his address shown in the gaming duty register.

(4) In any other case, any direction shall be sent to a provider at one of the premises to which it relates.

(5) A direction shall take effect from the first day of the next accounting period following the day on which it was given.

(6) Subject to section 11(7) of the Act, a direction shall remain in force until it is revoked by the Commissioners.

AMUSEMENT MACHINE LICENCE DUTY (SMALL-PRIZE MACHINES) ORDER 1998

(SI 1998/2207)

Made ....*7th September 1998*
Laid before Parliament ....*8th September 1998*
Coming into force ....*1st October 1998*

The Commissioners of Customs and Excise, in exercise of the powers conferred upon them by section 22(3) of the Betting and Gaming Duties Act 1981 and of all other powers enabling them in that behalf, hereby make the following Order—

7.201
1 This Order may be cited as the Amusement Machine Licence Duty (Small-prize Machines) Order 1998 and shall come into force on 1st October 1998.

7.202

2 The Amusement Machine Licence Duty (Small-prize Machines) Order 1996 is hereby revoked.

7.203

3 In section 22(2) of the Betting and Gaming Duties Act 1981 for '£10' there shall be substituted '£15'.

AMUSEMENT MACHINE LICENCE DUTY (MEDIUM-PRIZE MACHINES) ORDER 2001

(SI 2001/4028)

Made ....*17th December 2001*
Laid before Parliament ....*20th December 2001*
Coming into force ....*14th January 2002*

The Commissioners of Customs and Excise, in exercise of the powers conferred upon them by section 22(3) of the Betting and Gaming Duties Act 1981, and of all other powers enabling them in that behalf, hereby make the following Order:

7.204

1 This Order may be cited as the Amusement Machine Licence Duty (Medium-prize Machines) Order 2001 and comes into force on 14th January 2002.

7.205

2 In section 22(2)(b) of the Betting and Gaming Duties Act 1981 for '£15' substitute '£25'.

BINGO DUTY REGULATIONS 2003

(SI 2003/2503)

Made ....*29th September 2003*
Laid before the House of Commons ....*30th September 2003*
Coming into force ....*27th October 2003*

The Commissioners of Customs and Excise, in exercise of the powers conferred upon them by paragraph 9 of Schedule 3 to the Betting and Gaming Duties Act 1981 hereby make the following regulations:

Citation and commencement

7.206

1 These Regulations may be cited as the Bingo Duty Regulations 2003 and come into force on 27th October 2003.

Interpretation

7.207

2 In these Regulations—

'accounting period' means, subject to regulation 5 below, a period beginning at the end of the last Sunday of each month and ending at the end of the last Sunday of the next month;

'bingo-promoter' means a person who promotes the playing of bingo that is not exempt from bingo duty;

'business day' has the meaning given in section 92 of the Bills of Exchange Act 1882.

Revocation and saving

7.208

3 (1) Subject to paragraph (2) below, the Bingo Duty Regulations 1988 and the Betting and Gaming Duties (Payment) Regulations 1995 are revoked.

(2) The Bingo Duty Regulations 1988 continue to apply to bingo played before these Regulations came into force.

Bingo-promoters

7.209

4 (1) The notification and application for registration required by paragraph 10(1) or (1A) of Schedule 3 to the Act (notification and application for registration by a person who intends to promote, or has begun to promote, the playing of chargeable bingo) must be made on an application form provided by the Commissioners.

(2) An application form must contain such information as the Commissioners think is necessary for the administration of bingo duty and the protection of the revenue from that duty.

(3) The Commissioners may provide different application forms for different purposes; in particular, they may provide application forms that are suitable for electronic transmission.

(4) If there is any change in the information contained in his application form, or subsequently notified to the Commissioners in accordance with this paragraph, a registered bingo-promoter must, within seven days of that change, notify the Commissioners in writing.

(5) A registered bingo-promoter who ceases to promote the playing of chargeable bingo must, within seven days of that cessation, notify the Commissioners in writing.

(6) In this regulation—

'the Act' means the Betting and Gaming Duties Act 1981;

'chargeable bingo' means bingo that is not subject to an exemption specified in Part 1 of Schedule 3 to the Act; and

'registered bingo-promoter' means a person registered as a bingo-promoter under paragraph 10 of Schedule 3 to the Act.

Non-standard accounting periods

7.210

5 (1) Subject to the provisions of this regulation, a bingo-promoter may give the Commissioners written notice that the twelve consecutive periods set out in his notice will be his accounting periods.

(2) The notice required by paragraph (1) above must—

(a) be given to the Commissioners at least twenty-eight days before the day on which the first accounting period set out in the notice begins,

(b) specify the day on which each accounting period begins, and

(c) specify the day on which the twelfth accounting period ends, and the day on which the twelfth accounting period ends must be no later than fifty-three weeks after the day on which the first accounting period begins.

(3) Each accounting period must be a period of not less than 27 consecutive days and not more than 35 consecutive days.

(4) Where the Commissioners receive a bingo-promoter's notice complying with this regulation—

(a) his accounting period immediately preceding the first accounting period set out in his notice will end when that first accounting period begins,

(b) the twelve consecutive periods set out in his notice will be his accounting periods, and

(c) his accounting period immediately following the twelfth accounting period set out in his notice will begin when that twelfth accounting period ends.

(5) Unless in compliance with this regulation the Commissioners have received a notice that a bingo-promoter's accounting periods will be the further twelve consecutive accounting periods beginning when the twelfth accounting period mentioned in paragraph (4)(c) above ends, the accounting period immediately following that twelfth accounting period ends at the end of the last Sunday of the month in which it began.

(6) Before 1 January 2004, the Commissioners may treat a notice under paragraph (1) above as complying with paragraph (2)(a) or (3) above if—

(a) it is given to them at least twenty-one days before the day on which the first accounting period set out in it begins,

(b) only the first accounting period is a period of less than 27 days or more than 35 days, and

(c) the first accounting period is a period of not more than 50 consecutive days.

Bingo cards

7.211

6 (1) This regulation does not apply to a bingo card that forms part of a machine.

(2) A bingo card must be marked with a unique identifying number in a numbered series.

(3) Bingo cards that can only be used once must be issued in numerical order.

(4) If there is more than one issuing point, the bingo cards issued at each point must be from different series.

(5) The Commissioners may require bingo cards to be marked with the amount due for entitlement to participate in the game or games of bingo to which they relate.

(6) In this regulation, 'bingo card' means the set of numbers or symbols that a player uses to play bingo.

Bingo returns

7.212

7 (1) A bingo-promoter must furnish the Commissioners with a bingo return by the fifteenth day following the end of every accounting period.

(2) A bingo return is a return furnished on a form provided by the Commissioners containing the information specified in the Schedule below.

(3) The Commissioners may provide different forms of bingo return for different purposes; in particular, they may provide forms that are suitable for electronic transmission.

(4) A bingo return must be furnished—

(a) at the address specified on the form, or

(b) by such means as the Commissioners may approve.

(5) If the fifteenth day following the end of an accounting period is not a business day, a bingo return must be furnished by the last business day before that day.

Payment of bingo duty

7.213

8 (1) Not later than the fifteenth day following the end of an accounting period, a bingo-promoter must pay to the Commissioners the bingo duty due from him in respect of that accounting period.

(2) Payment must be made—

(a) in such manner as is specified in a notice published by the Commissioners and not withdrawn by a further notice, or

(b) in such manner as the Commissioners may approve.

(3) Where the manner of payment involves the collection of the bingo duty due to the Commissioners by means of direct debit, the bingo-promoter must ensure that he has sufficient funds in his account to satisfy the payment.

(4) If the fifteenth day following the end of an accounting period is not a business day, the bingo duty must be paid by the last business day before that day.

7.214

SCHEDULE

INFORMATION CONTAINED IN A BINGO RETURN

Regulation 7

Information that must be contained in a bingo return—

(a) the name and address of the bingo-promoter;

(b) any bingo registration number allocated by the Commissioners to the bingo-promoter;

(c) the accounting period to which the return relates;

(d) the day by which the return must be furnished;

(e) the amount of the bingo-promoter's bingo receipts for the accounting period;

(f) the amount of the bingo-promoter's expenditure on bingo winnings for the accounting period;

(g) the amount of any losses the bingo-promoter has carried forward from the last accounting period;

(h) the aggregate of the amounts referred to in paragraphs (f) and (g) above;

(i) the amount of the bingo-promoter's bingo promotion profits for the accounting period;

(j) the amount of bingo duty due from the bingo-promoter for the accounting period;

(k) the amount of any bingo duty due from the bingo-promoter for earlier accounting periods that has not been included in an earlier return; and

(l) the net amount of bingo duty due to the Commissioners.

MONEY LAUNDERING REGULATIONS 2003

(SI 2003/3075)

Casinos

7.215
8 (1) A person who operates a casino by way of business in the United Kingdom must obtain satisfactory evidence of identity of any person before allowing that person to use the casino's gaming facilities.

(2) A person who fails to do so is to be treated as having contravened regulation 3.

REMOTE GAMING DUTY REGULATIONS 2007

(SI 2007/2192)

Made .... *26th July 2007*
Laid before the House of Commons .... *26th July 2007*
Coming into force .... *1st September 2007*

The Commissioners for Her Majesty's Revenue and Customs make the following Regulations in exercise of the powers conferred by sections 26I(3), 26J(3), 26J(5), 26J(7), 26J(8), 26K(1), 26K(2) and 26K(3) of the Betting and Gaming Duties Act 1981:

7.215A 1 Citation and commencement

These Regulations may be cited as the Remote Gaming Duty Regulations 2007 and come into force on 1st September 2007.

7.215B 2 Interpretation

In these Regulations—

"the Act" refers to the Betting and Gaming Duties Act 1981;

"GD 120" or "GD 121" includes a version of the form with minor revisions;

"registered person" refers to a person on the Commissioners' register of those who provide facilities for remote gaming in respect of which remote gaming duty may be chargeable (see section 26J(1) of the Act).

7.215C 3 Registration

(1) Registration of a person (P) in relation to P's provision of facilities for remote gaming in respect of which remote gaming duty may be chargeable is conditional on a successful application by P to the Commissioners.

(2) The Commissioners need not register P as of earlier than the fourteenth day after the one on which they receive that application.

But if P is a foreign person (see section 26J(6) of the Act), they need not register P as of any day in the month that starts on the day they receive that application.

(3) Any application must be made on the form GD 120 as provided to the applicant by the Commissioners (reproduced in the Schedule—Application for registration), and must provide all the relevant information sought by that form.

This includes the signing of the declaration, if appropriate, that the other information on the form and in any accompanying document is true and complete.

(4) A person whom the Commissioners have registered in relation to the provision of such facilities must notify them of any change to that information, and in this context "change" includes failing or ceasing to provide such facilities.

The notification must be in writing.

It must be delivered to the Commissioners no later than the fourteenth day after the change in question.

(5) A person whom the Commissioners have registered in relation to the provision of such facilities may be de-registered by them for failing or ceasing to provide such facilities.

(6) The Commissioners may make the registration or continued registration of a foreign person (see section 26J(6) of the Act) conditional on that person (P)—

(a) providing what the Commissioners consider adequate security for payment of any remote gaming duty for which P is or may become liable (see section 26I(1) of the Act);

(b) appointing a person other than a foreign person (and whom the Commissioners otherwise consider suitable for the purpose) as a representative with responsibility for discharging P's liability for payment of remote gaming duty.

The expression "foreign person" in sub-paragraph (b) carries the meaning described by section 26J(6), but disregarding the reference to section 26J(5), of the Act.

7.215D

4 (1) Two or more bodies corporate are eligible to be treated as members of a group for the purposes of their being registered as mentioned in regulation 3(1) if each of them provides such facilities in reliance on a remote operating licence (see sections 26A(2) and 26B(a) of the Act), and—

(a) one of them controls each of the others;

(b) one person (whether a body corporate or an individual) controls all of them; or

(c) two or more individuals carrying on a business in partnership control all of them.

(2) Such treatment is conditional on a written application to the Commissioners for this purpose.

(3) Unless under paragraph (5) the Commissioners refuse the application, the bodies corporate shall be treated as members of a group as mentioned in paragraph (1) from such date as is specified in the application.

The representative member of the group shall be the one specified as such in the application.

(4) Where any bodies corporate are treated as members of a group as mentioned in paragraph (1) and a written application for the purpose is made to the Commissioners and not refused by them under paragraph (5), then, from such time as is specified in the application—

(a) a further body eligible to be so treated shall be included among the bodies so treated; or

(b) a body corporate shall be excluded from the bodies so treated; or

(c) another member of the group shall be substituted as the representative member; or

(d) the bodies corporate shall no longer be treated as members of the group.

(5) The Commissioners may refuse an application under paragraph (3) or (4), but only if it appears to them necessary to do so for the protection of the revenue from remote gaming duty.

(6) Where—

(a) a body corporate is treated as a member of a group under this regulation by virtue of being controlled by any person, and

(b) the Commissioners consider that it has ceased to be so controlled,

that treatment is terminated from such date as the Commissioners specify in a notice they give to that body corporate or that person.

(7) Where—

(a) a notice under paragraph (6) is given to a body corporate which is the representative member of the group,

(b) there are two or more other bodies corporate who will continue to be treated as members of the group after the time when that notice takes effect, and

(c) none of those bodies corporate is substituted from that time, or from before that time, as the representative member of the group in pursuance of an application under paragraph (4)(c),

the representative member is the body corporate substituted as such by the Commissioners in a notice they give to such one of the bodies corporate mentioned in sub-paragraph (b) as they think fit, and from that time.

(8) Where a notice under paragraph (6) is given to one member of a group of which there is only one other member, then (subject to any further application under this regulation) the other member shall also cease, from the time specified in the notice, to be treated for the purposes of this regulation as a member of the group.

(9) An "application" under this regulation with respect to any bodies corporate refers only to—

(a) one made by one of those bodies or by the person controlling them; and

(b) one made not less than ninety days before the date from which it is to take effect, unless the Commissioners have at their discretion accepted less time.

(10) For the purposes of this regulation a body corporate shall be taken to control another body corporate if—

(a) it is empowered by statute to control that body's activities; or

(b) it is that body's holding company within the meaning of section 1159 of the Companies Act 2006;

and an individual or individuals is or are taken to control a body corporate if (were that individual or those individuals a company) that individual or those individuals would be that body's holding company within the meaning of that Act.

7.215E 5 Returns and payment

(1) A registered person must make a return to the Commissioners in respect of that person's activities in each of that person's accounting periods (see section 26D of the Act).

The representative member of a group must do this instead of the other members, and for every such member's activities in each of their accounting periods (see regulation 4(3)).

(2) That return must be on the form GD 121 as provided to that registered person by the Commissioners (reproduced in the Schedule—Return) and must provide all the relevant information sought by that form.

This includes the signing of the declaration, if appropriate, that the other information on the form is true and complete.

(3) That return must be delivered to the Commissioners at the address specified on the form.

The time that return is treated as made for the purposes of this regulation is when it is received by them at that address.

(4) That return must be delivered there no later than the thirtieth day after the end of the relevant accounting period.

If the thirtieth day is not a business day, it must be delivered there no later than the most recent business day before then.

For these purposes, a "business day" is any day except—

(a) Saturday, Sunday, Good Friday or Christmas Day;

(b) a bank holiday under the Banking and Financial Dealings Act 1971;

(c) a day appointed by Royal proclamation as a public fast or thanksgiving day;

(d) a day declared by an order under section 2(1) of the Banking and Financial Dealings Act 1971 to be a non-business day.

7.215F

6 (1) That registered person (P) must pay to the Commissioners any remote gaming duty charged on P's remote gaming profits for each accounting period (see sections 26C and 26I(1) of the Act).

The representative member of a group must do this instead of the other members, and for every such member's remote gaming profits for each of their accounting periods (see regulation 4(3)).

(2) That payment must be made no later than when the return for the corresponding accounting period must be made (see regulations 5(3) and 5(4)).

(3) If that payment is by cheque or cash, it must be delivered to the address specified for payments by cheque on the relevant form GD 121 (the Greenock Accounting Centre, see regulations 5(2) and 5(3) and the Schedule).

(4) If that payment is by the Bankers Automated Clearing System or the Clearing House Automated Payment Centre, it must credit such bank account as the Commissioners nominate and publicise for these purposes.

(5) If that payment is by other reasonable means, it must be as earlier arranged with the Commissioners.

(6) The time that a payment is treated as made for the purposes of paragraphs (3) and (5) is when it is received by the Commissioners, and for the purposes of paragraph (4) when it is credited to the account in question.

7.215G
SCHEDULE
Regulations 3(3) and 5(2)

HM Revenue & Customs

Application for registration Remote Gaming duty

Use this form to apply for registration for Remote Gaming duty. Write in capital letters and use black ink.

Please make sure that this form is received by us at least 14 days before you intend to start business. If you are not resident in the UK you should allow at least one month for your application to be processed.

For further information on Remote Gaming duty go to **www.nas.gov.uk** or phone the National Advice Service on **0845 010 9000**.

Have you received your licence from the Gambling Commission?

No ☐ If No, please give the date you applied for it below

Yes ☐ If Yes, please give your licence number below

Date you intend to make dutiable supplies *DD MM YYYY*

Estimated gaming yield for the next 12 months

£ · 0 0

Do you require a group registration?

No ☐ Yes ☐

Your business

Business name
If you are a limited company, give company's name
If you are in a partnership, give names of all partners

Trading name *If different from above*

Business address *Give your principal place of business*

Postcode

If not UK, Country

Phone number

Email address

UK VAT registration number

Legal status of your business *Put 'X' in one box*

Sole proprietorship ☐

Partnership ☐

Limited company ☐

Other ☐ If Other, give details below

If you are a limited company, give further details below

Certificate number

Date of certificate *DD MM YYYY*

If the address given aside is outside the UK, do you have a fixed establishment within the UK?

No ☐ Yes ☐

If Yes, give address below

Postcode

GD120 v0.10 Page 1 HMRC 07/07

Declaration

Please complete and sign this declaration. You may be prosecuted if you give a false statement

Name

Capacity
Give full title, for example sole proprietor, partner or director

I declare that the information given on this form and in any accompanying document is true and complete.

Signature

Date *DD MM YYYY*

Send this form to
HM Revenue & Customs
National Registration Unit
Portcullis House
21 India Street
Glasgow
G2 4PZ

How we use your information
HM Revenue & Customs is a Data Controller under the Data Protection Act 1998. We hold information for the purposes specified in our notification to the Information Commissioner, including the assessment and collection of tax and duties, the payment of benefits and the prevention and detection of crime, and may use this information for any of them.

We may get information about you from others, or we may give information to them. If we do, it will only be as the law permits to:

- check the accuracy of information
- prevent or detect crime
- protect public funds.

We may check information we receive about you with what is already in our records. This can include information provided by you, as well as by others, such as other government departments or agencies and overseas tax and customs authorities. We will not give information to anyone outside HM Revenue & Customs unless the law permits us to do so. For more information go to **www.hmrc.gov.uk** and look for *Data Protection Act* within the *Search* facility.

Page 2

HM Revenue & Customs

Return
Remote Gaming Duty

This return is for the period from ☐☐ ☐☐ ☐☐☐☐ **to** ☐☐ ☐☐ ☐☐☐☐

These dates must not be altered, unless agreed by us

Reference number

Date of issue

You must ensure that this return is completed and sent back to us with any payment due no later than

Please allow for delays in the post.

You may be charged a penalty if you do not send in this return or pay duty by the due date. *Nil returns must be submitted.*

Calculation of the duty

Total amount of remote gaming receipts in the period

£ ☐☐☐☐☐☐☐☐☐ · 0 0

Total amount of winnings paid out in the period

£ ☐☐☐☐☐☐☐☐☐ · 0 0

Net amount of remote gaming profits (or losses) *(box 1 minus box 2)*

£ ☐☐☐☐☐☐☐☐☐ · 0 0

Amount of any losses carried forward from previous period

£ ☐☐☐☐☐☐☐☐☐ · 0 0

Net amount of remote gaming profits on which remote duty due (or loss to be carried forward) *(box 3 minus box 4)*

£ ☐☐☐☐☐☐☐☐☐ · 0 0

Remote gaming duty due

£ ☐☐☐☐☐☐☐☐☐ · 0 0

Any amount under declared from previous returns

£ ☐☐☐☐☐☐☐☐☐ · 0 0

Total amount payable *(box 6 plus box 7)*

£ ☐☐☐☐☐☐☐☐☐ · 0 0

Declaration

You may be prosecuted if you give a false statement

Full name *Use capital letters*

I declare that I am an authorised signatory and that the information given above is true and complete.
If any duty is due, payment is enclosed.

Signature

Date *DD MM YYYY*

What to do next

Send this Return with your payment in the envelope provided.

Make your cheque payable to 'The Commissioners of HM Revenue & Customs' followed by your reference number.
If your cheque is not already crossed 'Account Payee', cross the cheque 'Not transferable'.

If you do not have the envelope, send the form to:
HM Revenue & Customs
Greenock Accounting Centre
Custom House
Custom House Quay
Greenock
PA15 1EQ

GD121 v0.6 Page 1 HMRC 07/07

REMOTE GAMBLING (DOUBLE TAXATION RELIEF) REGULATIONS 2012

(SI 2012/1900)

These Regulations are set out at para **7.135.2** above.

AN ACT to authorise lotteries to be promoted as part of a National Lottery; to make provision with respect to the running and regulation of that National Lottery and with respect to the distribution of its net proceeds; to increase the membership and extend the powers of the Trustees of the National Heritage Memorial Fund; to amend section 1 of the Revenue Act 1898 and the Lotteries and Amusements Act 1976; to amend the law relating to pool betting; and for connected purposes.

[21 October 1993]

PART I
AUTHORISATION AND REGULATION OF THE NATIONAL LOTTERY

Preliminary

7.216 1 The National Lottery

(1) In this Act 'the National Lottery' means all the lotteries that form part of the National Lottery, taken as a whole.

(2) A lottery forms part of the National Lottery if the following conditions are satisfied.

(3) The lottery must be promoted or proposed to be promoted—

(a) by the [person][1] licensed to run the National Lottery under section 5, or

(b) in pursuance of an agreement that has been made between that [person] 1 and the lottery's promoter or proposed promoter.

(4) The promotion of the lottery must be authorised by a licence that has been granted to its promoter or proposed promoter under section 6.

Substitution

Paras 1 and 2 to be substituted by the National Lottery Act 2006, s 6, Sch 1, from a date to be appointed.

1 Words in square brackets substituted by the National Lottery Act 2006, s 3(a).

7.217 2 Legality of lotteries forming part of the National Lottery

(1) A lottery that forms part of the National Lottery shall not be unlawful.

(2) Schedule 1 contains amendments consequential on subsection (1).

Repeal

Repealed, in relation to England, Wales and Scotland, by the Gambling Act 2005, s 356(4), Sch 17 from 1 September 2007: see SI 2006/3272, art 2(4); for transitional provisions see art 6, Sch 4 thereto.

3 [*Repealed by the National Lottery Act 1998, ss 1(2), 26, Sch 5, Pt I*].

7.218 [3A The National Lottery Commission

(1) There shall be a body corporate known as the National Lottery Commission.

(2) Schedule 2A makes provision in relation to the Commission.][1]

1 Inserted by the National Lottery Act 1998, s 1(3).

7.219 4 Overriding duties of the Secretary of State and Director General

(1) The Secretary of State and (subject to any directions he may be given by the Secretary of State under section 11) the Director General shall each exercise his functions under this Part in the manner he considers the most likely to secure—

(a) that the National Lottery is run, and every lottery that forms part of it is promoted, with all due propriety, and

(b) that the interests of every participant in a lottery that forms part of the National Lottery are protected.

(2) Subject to subsection (1), the Secretary of State and the Director General shall each in exercising those functions do his best to secure that the net proceeds of the National Lottery are as great as possible.

(3) In subsection (2) 'the net proceeds of the National Lottery' means the sums that are paid to the Secretary of State by virtue of section 5(6).[1]

---

1 Amended by the National Lottery Act 2006, s 6, Sch 1, paras 1, 3 from a date to be appointed.

7.220 [4A Consultation with Gambling Commission

(1) If in the course of the exercise of its functions the National Lottery Commission becomes aware of a matter about which the Gambling Commission is likely to have an opinion, the National Lottery Commission shall consult the Gambling Commission.

(2) The National Lottery Commission shall comply with any direction of the Secretary of State (which may be general or specific) to consult the Gambling Commission.][1]

---

1 Inserted by the Gambling Act 2005, s 15(5), Sch 3, para 2.

7.220.1 [4B Disclosure of information

(1) The Commissioners for Her Majesty's Revenue and Customs may disclose information to the National Lottery Commission.

(2) The National Lottery Commission may disclose information to the Commissioners for Her Majesty's Revenue and Customs.

(3) Information disclosed under this section shall not be further disclosed except in accordance with subsection (4).

(4) Information may be further disclosed—

(a) for the purpose of complying with an enactment,

(b) in pursuance of an order of a court,

(c) for the purpose of legal proceedings connected with the operation of an enactment relating to lotteries,

(d) with the consent of the Commissioners for Her Majesty's Revenue and Customs,

(e) with the consent of each person to whom the information relates, or

(f) to [the Comptroller and Auditor General] for the purposes of the exercise of functions under Part II of the National Audit Act 1983 (c 44).

(5) This section has effect despite any prohibition or restriction that would otherwise prevent disclosure of information.]

Amendment

Inserted by the National Lottery Act 2006, s 2. Sub-s (4): in para (f) words 'the Comptroller and Auditor General' in square brackets substituted by the Budget Responsibility and National Audit Act 2011, s 26(2), Sch 5, Pt 2, para 17.

7.220.2 [4C Wrongful disclosure

(1) This section applies to a person—

(a) who is or was an officer or employee of the National Lottery Commission, or

(b) who acts or acted on behalf of the National Lottery Commission.

(2) A person to whom this section applies commits an offence if he discloses information received from the Commissioners for Her Majesty's Revenue and Customs in contravention of section 4B(3) and the information relates to a person whose identity—

(a) is specified in the disclosure, or

(b) can be deduced from it.

(3) It is a defence for a person charged with an offence under this section of disclosing information to prove that he reasonably believed—

(a) that the disclosure was lawful, or

(b) that the information had already and lawfully been made available to the public.

(4) A person guilty of an offence under this section shall be liable—

(a) on conviction on indictment, to imprisonment for a term not exceeding two years, to a fine or to both, or

(b) on summary conviction, to imprisonment for a term not exceeding 12 months, to a fine not exceeding the statutory maximum or to both.

(5) In relation to a conviction occurring before the commencement of section 282 of the Criminal Justice Act 2003 (c 44) (short sentences) the reference in subsection (4)(b) to 12 months shall have effect as if it were a reference to six months.

(6) In the application of this section to Scotland or Northern Ireland the reference in subsection (4)(b) to 12 months shall be taken as a reference to six months.][1]

---

1 Inserted by the National Lottery Act 2006, s 2.

The licensing system

7.221 5 Licensing of a [person][3] to run the National Lottery[1]

(1) The Director General may by licence authorise a [person][3] corporate to run the National Lottery.

(2) Only one [person][3] may be licensed under this section at any one time.

(3) The Director General shall not grant a licence under this section unless an application in writing, containing such information as he has specified as necessary for enabling him to determine whether to grant it, has been made to him by such date as he has specified.

(4) The Director General shall not grant such a licence unless he is satisfied that the applicant is a fit and proper [person][3] to run the National Lottery.

(5) In determining whether to grant such a licence, the Director General may consider—

(a) whether any person who appears to him to be likely to manage the business or any part of the business of running the National Lottery under the licence is a fit and proper person to do so, and

(b) whether any person who appears to him to be likely to be a person for whose benefit that business would be carried on is a fit and proper person to benefit from it.

[(6) A licence under this section shall include a condition requiring the licensee to pay into the National Lottery Distribution Fund sums out of the proceeds of lotteries forming part of the National Lottery.

(6A) A licence under this section shall include provision for determining—

(a) the amount of payments under subsection (6), and

(b) the timing of payments under subsection (6).][2]

(7) A licence under this section may include a condition requiring the licensee to make such arrangements as may be determined by or under the licence for securing

that, in circumstances specified in the licence, such sums as may be so determined are paid to the Director General for distribution to participants in lotteries forming part of the National Lottery.

---

1 Section substituted by the National Lottery Act 2006, s 6, Sch 1, paras 1, 4 from a date to be appointed.

2 Sub-ss (6), (6A) substituted, for sub-s (6) as originally enacted, by the Horserace Betting and Olympic Lottery Act 2004, s 34(1), (3), (4).

3 Words in square brackets substituted by the National Lottery Act 2006, s 3(b).

7.222 6 Licensing of [persons][2] to promote lotteries

(1) The Director General may by licence authorise a [persons][2] corporate to promote lotteries as part of the National Lottery.

(2) A licence under this section shall specify the lotteries, or descriptions of lottery, the promotion of which it authorises.

(3) The Director General shall not grant such a licence unless an application in writing, containing such information as he has specified as necessary for enabling him to determine whether to grant it, has been made to him.

(4) The Director General shall not grant such a licence unless he is satisfied that the applicant is a fit and proper [persons][2] to promote lotteries under the licence.

(5) In determining whether to grant such a licence, the Director General may consider—

(a) whether any person who appears to him to be likely to manage the business or any part of the business of promoting lotteries under the licence is a fit and proper person to do so, and

(b) whether any person who appears to him to be likely to be a person for whose benefit that business would be carried on is a fit and proper person to benefit from it.

(6) A licence under this section may include a condition requiring the licensee to obtain the Director General's approval of the rules of any lottery before the lottery is promoted under the licence.[1]

---

1 Section substituted and new s 6A inserted by the National Lottery Act 2006, s 6, Sch 1, paras 1, 4 from a date to be appointed.

2 Words in square brackets substituted by the National Lottery Act 2006, s 3(c).

7.223 7 Licences under sections 5 and 6: further provisions

(1) A licence granted under section 5 or 6 shall be in writing and shall specify the period for which (subject to being revoked or suspended) it is to have effect.

[(1A) The period specified under subsection (1) must—

(a) begin with the date of grant of the licence, and

(b) not exceed 15 years.

(1B) A licence granted under section 5 or 6 may (subject to the restriction in subsection (1A)(b)) include—

(a) provision enabling the period specified under subsection (1) to be extended by the Commission;

(b) provision enabling the period specified under subsection (1) to be extended by agreement between the Commission and the licensee.][2]

(2) [A licence granted under section 5 or 6][3] may include such conditions (in addition to those required or authorised by section 5 or 6) as the Director General considers appropriate and in particular may include conditions requiring the licensee—

(a) to obtain the consent of the Director General before doing anything specified, or of a description specified, in the licence;

(b) to refer matters to the Director General for approval;
(c) to ensure that such requirements as the Director General may from time to time determine or approve are complied with;
(d) to provide the Director General at times specified by him with such information as he may require (including, if the information is of a description specified in the licence, information for publication by him);
(e) to allow the Director General to inspect and take copies of any documents of the licensee, including any information kept by the licensee otherwise than in writing, relating to the National Lottery or a lottery forming part of it;
(f) where such information is kept by means of a computer, to give the Director General such assistance as he may require to enable him to inspect and take copies of the information in a visible and legible form or to inspect and check the operation of any computer, and any associated apparatus or material, that is or has been in use in connection with the keeping of the information;
(g) to do such things (and, in particular, to effect such transfers of property or rights) as the Director General may require in connection with the licence ceasing to have effect and the grant of a licence to another [body][1].

(3) In subsection (2)(e) and (f) 'the Director General' includes any representative of the Director General, as well as any member of his staff, who has been authorised by him (whether generally or specially) to make such an inspection.

(4) Conditions in a licence granted under section 5 or 6 may impose requirements to be complied with by the licensee after the licence has ceased to have effect.

(5) . . . [4]

(6) . . . [4]

---

1 Words in square brackets substituted by the National Lottery Act 2006, s 3(d).

2 Sub-ss (1A), (1B) inserted by the National Lottery Act 2006, s 4(1).

3 Words in square brackets substituted by the National Lottery Act 2006, s 4(2).

4 Sub-ss (5), (6) repealed by the National Lottery Act 2006, ss 5(2), 21, Sch 3.

7.223.1 [7A Annual fee

(1) The holder of a licence under section 5 or 6—
(a) shall pay a first annual fee to the Commission within such period after the issue of the licence as may be prescribed[2], and
(b) shall pay an annual fee to the Commission before each anniversary of the issue of the licence.

(2) In this section—
"annual fee" means a fee of such amount as may be prescribed, and
"prescribed" means prescribed by regulations made by the Secretary of State.

(3) Subsection (1)(b) does not apply in relation to an anniversary of the issue of a licence on or immediately before which the licence ceases, by virtue of its terms, to have effect.

(4) The Commission shall pay fees received by virtue of this section into the Consolidated Fund."][1]

---

1 Inserted by the National Lottery Act 2006, s 5(1).

2 See the National Lottery (Annual Licence Fees) Regulations 2010, s.i. 2010/17 at para 7.437.

7.224 8 Variation of conditions in licences

(1) The Director General may vary any condition in a licence granted under section 5 or 6 if the licensee consents.

(2) Subject to subsection (3), the Director General may vary any condition in such a licence without the licensee's consent if the licensee has been given a reasonable opportunity of making representations to the Director General about the variation.

(3) Subsection (2) does not apply—

(a) where the variation would result in a condition requiring the licensee to transfer any property or rights, or

(b) in the case of a licence granted under section 5, in relation to a condition that the licence provides may only be varied with the consent of the licensee.

(4) Where the Director General varies a condition in a licence under subsection (2)—

(a) he shall serve a notice on the licensee informing the licensee of the variation, and

(b) the variation shall take effect at the end of such period as may be specified in the notice.

(5) The period specified in the notice shall be a period of at least twenty-one days beginning with the date of the notice.

(6) The Director General's power to vary a condition in a licence under subsection (1) or (2) includes power to add a condition to the licence or omit a condition from it (and references in this section to the variation of a condition are to be read accordingly).

7.225 9 Enforcement of conditions in licences

(1) If, on an application made by the Director General, the court is satisfied—

(a) that there is a reasonable likelihood that a person will contravene a condition in a licence granted under section 5 or 6,

(b) that a person has contravened such a condition and there is a reasonable likelihood that the contravention will continue or be repeated, or

(c) that a person has contravened such a condition and there are steps that could be taken for remedying the contravention,

the court may grant an injunction restraining the contravention or, in Scotland, an interdict prohibiting the contravention or (as the case may be) make an order requiring the licensee, and any other person who appears to the court to have been party to the contravention, to take such steps as the court may direct to remedy it.

(2) In subsection (1) 'the court' means the High Court or, in Scotland, the Court of Session.

[(3) Where a sum is due to be paid to the National Lottery Distribution Fund by virtue of section 5(6)—

(a) the sum shall be recoverable by the Secretary of State as a debt due to the Fund, and

(b) the licensee's liability to pay shall not be affected by his licence ceasing to have effect.][1, 2]

---

1 Sub-s (3) substituted by the Horserace Betting and Olympic Lottery Act 2004, s 34(1), (5).

2 Section amended by the National Lottery Act 2006, s 6, Sch 1, paras 1, 8 from a date to be appointed.

7.226 10 Revocation of licences

(1) The Director General shall revoke a licence granted under section 5 if he is satisfied that the licensee no longer is, or never was, a fit and proper [person][1] to run the National Lottery.

(2) The Director General shall revoke a licence granted under section 6 if he is satisfied that the licensee no longer is, or never was, a fit and proper [person][1] to promote lotteries under the licence.

(3) The Director General may revoke a licence granted under section 5 or 6—

(a) if it appears to him that any of the grounds for revocation set out in Part I of Schedule 3 applies, or

(b) if the licensee consents.

[(3A) The Commission shall revoke a licence granted under section 5 or 6 if the licensee fails to pay the annual fee in accordance with section 7A; but the Commission may disapply this subsection if it thinks that a failure to pay is attributable to administrative error.][2]

(4) Part II of Schedule 3 shall have effect in relation to the revocation of a licence under this section, other than a revocation with the licensee's consent [or under subsection (3A)].[3]

---

1 Words in square brackets substituted by the National Lottery Act 2006, s 3(e).

2 Sub-s (3A) inserted by the National Lottery Act 2006, s 5(3)(a).

3 Words in square brackets substituted by the National Lottery Act 2006, s 5(3)(b).

7.227 [10A Financial penalties for breach of conditions in licences

(1) If the Director General is satisfied that a person has contravened a condition in a licence under section 5 or 6, he may impose a financial penalty on that person in respect of the contravention.

(2) The matters to which the Director General may have regard in imposing a financial penalty include the desirability of both—

(a) deterring persons from contravening conditions in licences under section 5 or 6, and

(b) recovering any diminution in the sums paid to the Secretary of State under section 5(6) which is attributable to the contravention.

(3) If the Director General proposes to impose a financial penalty on a person, he shall serve on that person a notice—

(a) stating that the person has contravened conditions in the licence,

(b) identifying the contraventions in question,

(c) stating that the Director General proposes to impose a financial penalty,

(d) specifying the amount of the financial penalty,

(e) stating the Director General's reasons—

(i) for the imposition of a financial penalty, and

(ii) for the amount of the financial penalty,

(f) stating the person to whom the financial penalty is to be paid and the manner in which, and place at which, payment may be made, and

(g) stating the effect of subsections (5) and (12).

(4) A notice under subsection (3) must state that the person may, within the period of 21 days beginning with the date of the notice, either—

(a) make written representations about the matter to the Director General, or

(b) notify the Director General in writing of the person's intention to make oral representations,

and that the right of appeal conferred by section 10B is dependent on the person having made such written or oral representations.

(5) If, within the period mentioned in subsection (4), the Director General receives neither—

(a) written representations, nor

(b) written notification of the person's intention to make oral representations,

the financial penalty shall become payable at the end of that period.

(6) The Secretary of State may make regulations as to the procedure to be followed where a person's intention to make oral representations is notified to the Director General as mentioned in subsection (4).

(7) The regulations may in particular make provision—

(a) for the financial penalty to become payable if the person fails to comply with any requirements imposed by or under the regulations, and

(b) as to the hearing by the Director General of oral representations.

(8) If—

(a) any written representations against the imposition of the financial penalty are made as mentioned in subsection (4), or

(b) any oral representations against the imposition of the financial penalty are made in accordance with regulations under subsection (6),

subsection (9) shall apply.

(9) Where this subsection applies, the Director General shall after taking the representations into account—

(a) decide whether or not to impose a financial penalty, and

(b) serve a further notice on the person informing the person of the decision.

(10) Where the decision is to impose a financial penalty, the further notice must—

(a) identify the contraventions in question,

(b) specify the amount of the financial penalty imposed,

(c) state the Director General's reasons—

(i) for the imposition of a financial penalty, and

(ii) for the amount of the financial penalty,

(d) state the person to whom the financial penalty is to be paid and the manner in which, and place at which, payment may be made, and

(e) state the effect of subsections (11) and (12).

(11) A financial penalty imposed by virtue of a decision under subsection (9) becomes payable on the date of the further notice.

(12) A person on whom a financial penalty is imposed is required to pay the penalty within the period of fourteen days beginning with the date on which the financial penalty becomes payable.

(13) If the whole or any part of a financial penalty is not paid within the period mentioned in subsection (12), then as from the end of that period the unpaid balance from time to time shall carry interest at the rate for the time being specified in section 17 of the Judgments Act 1838.

[(14) Where under this section one person ("the debtor") becomes liable to pay a penalty to another person ("the creditor")—

(a) the penalty and any interest accrued under subsection (13) shall be recoverable by the Secretary of State from the debtor as a debt due to the creditor, and

(b) the debtor's liability to pay shall not be affected by his licence ceasing to have effect.

(15) A penalty under this section may be payable partly to the National Lottery Distribution Fund and partly to the Olympic Lottery Distribution Fund.]][1, 2, 3]

---

1 Inserted by the National Lottery Act 1998, s 2(1).

2 Sub-s (14) substituted, by new sub-ss (14), (15), by the Horserace Betting and Olympic Lottery Act 2004, s 34(1), (6).

3 Section amended by the National Lottery Act 2006, s 6, Sch 1, paras 1, 10 from a date to be

appointed.

7.228 [10B Appeals against financial penalties

(1) Where the Director General decides under subsection (9) of section 10A to impose a financial penalty on a person, the person may appeal against the decision on the grounds specified in subsection (2) or, as the case may be, subsection (3).

(2) To the extent that an appeal under this section is against a finding by the Director General that a person contravened a condition of a licence, the grounds for the appeal are—

- (a) that the Director General made an error as to the facts,
- (b) that there was a material procedural error, or
- (c) that the Director General made some other error of law.

(3) To the extent that an appeal under this section is against the amount of a financial penalty, the grounds for the appeal are—

- (a) that the amount of the penalty is unreasonable,
- (b) that there was a material procedural error, or
- (c) that the decision was based on a manifest material misapprehension as to the facts.

(4) Where on an appeal under this section a court reduces the amount of a financial penalty, the powers of the court shall include power to make such orders as to interest on the penalty as the court considers just and equitable in all the circumstances of the case.

(5) The power conferred by subsection (4) includes power to make orders as to—

- (a) the rates of interest which are to apply, and
- (b) the date from which interest is to run.

(6) An appeal under this section lies to the High Court or, in Scotland, to the Court of Session.

(7) Any appeal under this section to the Court of Session shall be heard in the Outer House.][1]

---

1 Inserted by the National Lottery Act 1998, s 3.

7.229 [10C Annual levy

(1) The Secretary of State may make regulations requiring holders of licences under *section 5 or 6* to pay an annual levy to the Gambling Commission.

(2) The regulations shall, in particular, make provision for—

- (a) timing of payment of the levy, and
- (b) the amount of the levy.

(3) The regulations may, in particular, make provision—

- (a) determining the amount of the levy by reference to a percentage of specified receipts of the holder of a licence under *section 5 or 6* [2],
- (b) determining the amount of the levy by reference to a percentage of specified profits of the holder of a licence under *section 5 or 6* [2],
- (c) providing for the determination of the amount of the levy according to a specified formula, or
- (d) providing for the determination of the amount of the levy in some other way.

(4) Any sum due by way of levy by virtue of this section shall be treated for the purposes of this Act as if its payment were a condition of the licence under *section 5 or 6* [2].

(5) The Gambling Commission shall, with the consent of the Treasury and of the Secretary of State, expend money received by way of levy for purposes related to, or by providing financial assistance for projects related to—

(a) addiction to gambling,

(b) other forms of harm or exploitation associated with gambling, or

(c) any of the licensing objectives for the purposes of the Gambling Act 2005.

(6) In subsection (5) the reference to financial assistance is a reference to grants, loans and any other form of financial assistance, which may be made or given on terms or conditions (which may include terms and conditions as to repayment with or without interest).

(7) The Secretary of State may make regulations under this section only if—

(a) he has made regulations under the Gambling Act 2005 requiring holders of operating licences to pay an annual levy to the Gambling Commission, and

(b) he has consulted the National Lottery Commission.

(8) The Gambling Commission shall consult the National Lottery Commission before incurring expenditure under subsection (5).][1]

1 Inserted by the Gambling Act 2005, s 15(5), Sch 3, para 1 from 1 September 2007: see SI 2006/3272, art 2(4); for transitional provisions see art 6, Sch 4 thereto.

2 Section amended by the National Lottery Act 2006, s 6, Sch 1, paras 1, 11 from a date to be appointed.

Control by the Secretary of State

7.230 11 Directions to the Director General

(1) The Director General shall in exercising his functions under [sections5 to 10A] 1 comply with any directions that he may be given by the Secretary of State.

(2) Such directions may deal in particular—

(a) with the matters that the Director General should take into account in deciding whether or not to grant licences;

(b) with the conditions that licences should contain.

1 Sub-s (1): words in square brackets substituted by the National Lottery Act 1998, s 2(2).

7.231 12 Regulations as to the promotion of lotteries

(1) The Secretary of State may by regulations make such provision in relation to the promotion of lotteries that form part of the National Lottery as he considers necessary or expedient.

(2) Such regulations may in particular impose requirements or restrictions as to—

(a) the minimum age of persons to whom or by whom tickets or chances may be sold;

(b) the places, circumstances or manner in which tickets or chances may be sold or persons may be invited to buy them;

(c) the information that must appear in an advertisement for a lottery;

(d) the places, circumstances or manner in which signs relating to a lottery may be displayed.

(3) In subsection (2) 'tickets' includes any document providing evidence of a person's claim to participate in the chances of a lottery.

(4) Regulations under this section may make different provision for different areas.

7.232 13 Contravention of regulations an offence

(1) If any requirement or restriction imposed by regulations made under section 12 is contravened in relation to the promotion of a lottery that forms part of the National Lottery—

(a) the promoter of the lottery shall be guilty of an offence, except if the contravention occurred without the consent or connivance of the promoter and the promoter exercised all due diligence to prevent such a contravention,

(b) any director, manager, secretary or other similar officer of the promoter, or any person purporting to act in such a capacity, shall be guilty of an offence if he consented to or connived at the contravention or if the contravention was attributable to any neglect on his part, and

(c) any other person who was party to the contravention shall be guilty of an offence.

(2) A person guilty of an offence under this section shall be liable—

(a) on summary conviction, to a fine not exceeding the statutory maximum;

(b) on conviction on indictment, to imprisonment for a term not exceeding two years, to a fine or to both.

(3), (4) [*Apply to Scotland only.*]

Provision of information by the Director General

7.233 14 Annual report

(1) As soon as possible after the end of every financial year, the Director General shall make a report on the exercise of his functions during that year to the Secretary of State.

(2) In subsection (1) 'financial year' means—

(a) . . . [1]

[(aa) the period beginning with the date on which section 3A comes into force and ending with the next 31st March, and][1]

(b) each successive period of twelve months ending with 31stMarch.

(3) The Secretary of State shall lay a copy of every report received by him under this section before Parliament.

The functions of the Secretary of State under this section shall be treated as exercisable in or as regards Scotland and may be exercised separately; see the Scotland Act 1998 (Modification of Functions) Order 1999, SI 1999/1756, art 2, Schedule, para 15(1).

---

1 Para (a) repealed and para (aa) inserted by the National Lottery Act 1998, ss 1, 26, Sch 1, para 13, Sch 5, Pt I.

7.234 15 Power of the Secretary of State to require information

The Director General shall provide the Secretary of State with such information relating to the National Lottery or a lottery forming part of it as the Secretary of State may direct.

Miscellaneous and supplementary

7.235 16 False representations as to the National Lottery

(1) If a person advertising, or offering the opportunity to participate in, a lottery, competition or game of another description gives, by whatever means, a false indication that it is a lottery forming part of, or is otherwise connected with, the National Lottery, he shall be guilty of an offence.

(2) A person guilty of an offence under this section shall be liable—

(a) on summary conviction, to a fine not exceeding the statutory maximum;

(b) on conviction on indictment, to imprisonment for a term not exceeding two years, to a fine or to both.

7.236 **17** . . .

. . . [1]

---

[1] Repealed by the Horserace Betting and Olympic Lottery Act 2004, ss 13, 38, Sch 2, para 21, Sch 6. Date in force: 13 July 2011: see SI 2011/1704, art 2.

18 [*The amendments made by this section to the Betting, Gaming and Lotteries Act 1963 have been incorporated into the text of that Act.*]

7.237 19 Restriction of enactments relating to the rehabilitation of offenders

(1) Neither section 4(1) of the Rehabilitation of Offenders Act 1974 nor Article F5(1) of the Rehabilitation of Offenders (Northern Ireland) Order 1978 (exclusion of evidence and questions relating to an individual's previous convictions) shall apply in relation to any proceedings—

(a) before the Director General in respect of the grant or revocation of a licence, or

(b) by way of appeal to the Secretary of State against the revocation of a licence by the Director General.

(2) A conviction shall not be regarded as spent for the purposes of section 4(2) of that Act or Article 5(2) of that Order (restrictions in respect of such questions put otherwise than in proceedings) if the question is put by the Director General and the following conditions are satisfied.

(3) The question must be put for the purpose of determining whether to grant or revoke a licence.

(4) The question must relate to an individual—

(a) who manages the business or any part of the business carried on under the licence (or who is likely to do so if the licence is granted), or

(b) for whose benefit that business is carried on (or is likely to be carried on if the licence is granted).

(5) When the question is asked, the person questioned must be informed that by virtue of this section all the individual's previous convictions are to be disclosed. [1]

---

[1] Repealed by the Police Act 1997, s 133(d), 134(2), Sch 10, as from a day to be appointed.

7.238 20 Interpretation of Part I

In this Part—

['the Commission' means the National Lottery Commission;][1]

['lottery' has the same meaning as in the Gambling Act 2005;][2]

'contravention', in relation to a condition or requirement, includes a failure to comply with that condition or requirement (and 'contravened' is to be read accordingly);

. . . [1]

'participant', in relation to a lottery, means a person who has bought a ticket or chance in the lottery;

'promote' includes conduct (and 'promotion' is to be read accordingly);

and any reference to a lottery forming part of the National Lottery is to be read in accordance with section[1].

1 Definition 'the Commission' inserted and definition 'the Director General' repealed by the National Lottery Act 1998, ss 1, 26, Sch 1, para 14, Sch 5, Pt I.

2 Definition 'lottery' inserted by the Gambling Act 2005, s 15(5), Sch 3, para 3 from 1 September 2007: see SI 2006/3272, art 2(4); for transitional provisions see art 6, Sch 4 thereto.

PART II
DISTRIBUTION OF THE NET PROCEEDS OF THE NATIONAL LOTTERY

The distribution system

7.239 21 The National Lottery Distribution Fund

(1) There shall be a fund maintained under the control and management of the Secretary of State and known as the National Lottery Distribution Fund.

(2) *Repealed by the Horserace Betting and Olympic Lottery Act 2004, ss 34(1), (8), 38, Sch 6.*

7.240 22 Apportionment of money in Distribution Fund

(1) Every sum that is paid into the Distribution Fund [by virtue of section 5(6) or 10A][1] shall be apportioned as follows.

(2) So much of the sum as the Secretary of State considers appropriate shall be allocated for making payments under section 31 and held in the Distribution Fund for that purpose.

(3) Of the balance—

(a) [20 per cent][2] shall be allocated for expenditure on or connected with the arts,

(b) [20 per cent][2] shall be allocated for expenditure on or connected with sport,

(c) [20 per cent][2] shall be allocated for expenditure on or connected with the national heritage, [and]

[(d) [40 per cent][8] shall be allocated for prescribed expenditure that is—

(i) charitable, or

(ii) connected with health, or

(iii) connected with education or

(iv) connected with the environment.][3]

[(including, in each case, for establishing or contributing to endowments in connection with such expenditure)].[4]

[(3A) In subsection (3)(d) "prescribed expenditure" means expenditure of a description prescribed by order of the [Minister for the Cabinet Office][7].

(3B) A description of expenditure under subsection (3A) may, in particular, refer to expenditure in relation to—

(a) England,

(b) Wales,

(c) Scotland,

(d) Northern Ireland,

(e) any of the Channel Islands, or

(f) the Isle of Man;

and expenditure described by virtue of this subsection is referred to in this Act as "devolved expenditure".

(3C) Before making an order under subsection (3A) the [Minister for the Cabinet Office][7] shall consult—

(a) the Big Lottery Fund,

(b) the National Assembly for Wales,
(c) the Scottish Ministers,
(d) the Northern Ireland Department of Culture, Arts and Leisure, and
(e)such other persons (if any) as he thinks appropriate."][6]

[(4) This section has effect subject to section 19 of the National Lottery Act 1998 [and to section 25 of the Horserace Betting and Olympic Lottery Act 2004][4A].][5]

[1A] Words in square brackets substituted by the Horserace Betting and Olympic Lottery Act 2004, s 34(1), (9)(a).

[2] Sub-s (3): in paras (a), (b) and (c) words in square brackets inserted by SI 2010/2863, art 3(1), (2). Date in force: this amendment has effect from 1 April 2012: see SI 2010/2863, art 3(1).

[3] Sub-s (d) substituted for (d), (f) by the National Lottery Act 2006, s 7(2)(b).

[4] Words in square brackets inserted by the National Lottery (Funding of Endowments) Act 2003, s 1. This amendment is deemed always to have had effect.

[4A] Sub-s (4): words in square brackets inserted by the Horserace Betting and Olympic Lottery Act 2004, s 34(1), (9)(c).

[5] Inserted by the National Lottery Act 1998, s 19(7).

[6] Sub-ss (3A), (3B) (3C)inserted by the National Lottery Act 2006, s 7(3).

[7] Sub-s (3A) and (3C): words "Minister for the Cabinet Office" in square brackets substituted by SI 2011/739, arts 2(1)(a), 4, Schedule, paras 1, 2; for supplementary provision see art 3 thereof. Date in force: 13 April 2011: see SI 2011/739, art 1.

[8] Sub-s (3): in para (d) words in square brackets inserted by SI 2010/2863, art 3(1), (5). Date in force: this amendment has effect from 1 April 2012: see SI 2010/2863, art 3(1).

7.241 23 The distributing bodies

(1) So much of any sum paid into the Distribution Fund as is allocated for expenditure on or connected with the arts shall be held in the Distribution Fund—

[(a) as to [69.78 per cent][1A], for distribution by the Arts Council of England,
[(b) [(b) as to 8.9 per cent, for distribution by Creative Scotland,][2B]
(c) as to 5 per cent., for distribution by the Arts Council of Wales, . . . [2A]
(d) as to 2.8 per cent., for distribution by [the Arts Council of Northern Ireland][2]][1][. . . [2B]
(e) as to [13.52 per cent][1A], for distribution by [The British Film Institute][6] [. . .
(f) . . .][7]

(2) So much of any sum paid into the Distribution Fund as is allocated for expenditure on or connected with sport shall be held in the Distribution Fund—

(a) as to [62 per cent][3A], for distribution by [the English Sports Council][4],
(b) as to [8.1 per cent.][3], for distribution by the Scottish Sports Council,
(c) as to [4.5 per cent.][3], for distribution by the Sports Council for Wales, and
(d) as to [2.6 per cent.][3], for distribution by the Sports Council for Northern Ireland [and
(e) as to [22.8 per cent][3A], for distribution by the United Kingdom Sports Council.][3],

(3) So much of any sum paid into the Distribution Fund as is allocated for expenditure on or connected with the national heritage shall be held in the Distribution Fund for distribution by the Trustees of the National Heritage Memorial Fund.

[(4) So much of any sum paid into the Distribution Fund as is allocated under section 22(3)(d) shall be held by the Distribution Fund for distribution by the Big Lottery Fund (established under section 36A).][5]

1 Sub-s (1)(a)–(d) substituted for original sub-s (1)(a), (b), by the National Lottery etc Act 1993 (Amendment of Section 23) Order 1994, SI 1994/1342.

1A Words in square brackets by substituted by the by the National Lottery etc Act 1993 (Amendment of Section 23) Order 2007, SI 2007/743, art 2(1), (2).

2 Words in square brackets substituted by the National Lottery etc Act 1993 (Amendment of Section 23) Order 1995, SI 1995/2088.

2A In sub-s (1)(c) words omitted repealed by the National Lottery etc Act 1993 (Amendment of Section 23) (No 2) Order 1999, SI 1999/2090, art 2.

2B Sub-s (1): para (b) substituted by SSI 2010/223, art 2(1), (2). Date in force: 1 July 2010: see SSI 2010/223, art 1.

3 Words in square brackets substituted by the National Lottery etc Act 1993 (Amendment of Section 23) Order 1999, SI 1999/1563, art 2.

3A 3A Words in square brackets by substituted by the by the National Lottery etc Act 1993 (Amendment of Section 23) Order 2007, SI 2007/743, art 2(1), (2).

4 Words in square brackets substituted by the National Lottery etc Act 1993 (Amendment of Section 23) Order 1996, SI 1996/3095.

5 Sub-s (4): substituted by the National Lottery Act 2006, s 15(1).

6 Sub-s (1): in sub-para (e) words "The British Film Institute" in square brackets substituted by SI 2011/685, art 2. Date in force: 1 April 2011: see SI 2011/685, art 1.

7 Sub-s (1): para (f) and word omitted immediately preceding it inserted, in relation to Scotland, by SSI 2000/78, art 2(1), (3). Date in force: 7 April 2000: see SSI 2000/78, art 1(1). Sub-s (1): para (f) and word omitted immediately preceding it repealed by SSI 2010/223, art 2(1), (4). Date in force: 1 July 2010: see SSI 2010/223, art 1.

7.242 24 Payments from Distribution Fund to distributing bodies

At such times as the Secretary of State thinks appropriate, payments of such amounts as he thinks appropriate may be made to a body specified in section 23 [or in an order under section 29A][2] out of so much of any money in the Distribution Fund as is held for distribution by that body.[1]

1 Section amended by the National Lottery Act 2006, s 8 from a date to be appointed.

2 Words in square brackets inserted by the National Lottery Act 2006, s 8(2).

7.243 25 Application of money by distributing bodies

(1) Subject to the provisions of this Part, a body shall distribute any money paid to it under section 24 for meeting expenditure of the relevant description mentioned in section 22(3).

[(1A) The manner in which a body may distribute any money paid to it under section 24 includes making or entering into arrangements for or in connection with meeting expenditure (including arrangements with respect to vouchers); and this subsection shall apply notwithstanding anything to the contrary in any enactment or instrument relating to the functions of the body.][1]

(2) A body shall not under subsection (1) distribute money for any purpose or in any manner if it does not have power to distribute money for that purpose or in that manner apart from subsection (1).

[(2A) A body which distributes money under subsection (1) shall have power to solicit applications from other bodies or persons for any of the money which the body so distributes, notwithstanding anything to the contrary in any enactment or instrument relating to the functions of the body.

(2B) In determining whether a decision of a body concerning its distribution of money under subsection (1) was unlawful, it shall be immaterial whether or not the body, or any person acting on behalf of the body, solicited an application from a body or person for such money.][1]

[(2C) In determining how to distribute money in accordance with subsection (1) a body may—

(a) consult any person;

(b) take account of opinions expressed to it or information submitted to it.][4]

(3) A body may defray out of any money paid to it under section 24 any expenses incurred by the body in consequence of this Act.

(4) The Trustees of the National Heritage Memorial Fund may apply any money paid to them under section 24 for any purpose for which they have power to apply money under section 4 of the National Heritage Act 1980 [(other expenditure out of the fund)][2].

[(5) References in this section (however expressed) to the distribution of money for meeting expenditure are to be construed as including distribution of money for the purpose of establishing, or contributing to, endowments in connection with expenditure of the description concerned.][3]

[(6) A reference in this section to meeting expenditure includes a reference to meeting expenditure which relates to—

(a) the Isle of Man, or

(b) any of the Channel Islands.][5]

---

1 Inserted by the National Lottery Act 1998, ss 9(1), 10.

2 Words in square brackets substituted by the National Heritage Act 1997, s 3, Schedule, Pt I, para 4.

3 Inserted by the National Lottery (Funding of Endowments) Act 2003, s 1. This amendment is deemed always to have had effect.

4 Sub-s (2C) inserted by the National Lottery Act 2006, s 10.

5 Sub-s.(6) inserted by the National Lottery Act 2006, s 13(1).

7.244 [25A Delegation by distributing bodies of their powers of distribution

(1) A body which distributes money under subsection (1) of section 25 may appoint any other body or person to exercise on its behalf any of its functions relating to, or connected with, the distribution of money under that subsection (including its function of making decisions as to the persons to whom such distributions are to be made)—

(a) in any particular case, or

(b) in cases of any particular description.

(2) The persons who may be appointed by a body under subsection (1) include a member, employee or committee of the body itself.

(3) A body which makes an appointment under subsection (1) may defray out of any money paid to it under section 24 any expenses incurred by the appointee in consequence of the appointment.

(4) Power to accept any such appointment as is mentioned in subsection (1) is conferred by this subsection on the following bodies—

(a) any body which distributes money under section 25(1),

(b) any charity or any charitable, benevolent or philanthropic institution,

(c) any body established by or under an enactment, and

(d) any body established by Royal Charter.

(5) A body appointed by virtue of subsection (1) to exercise a function on behalf of another may itself appoint any of its members or employees, or a committee, to exercise the function in its stead, but only if—

(a) the terms of the body's appointment by virtue of subsection (1) so permit, and

(b) the body has power apart from this section to appoint a member or, as the case may be, an employee or committee of the body to exercise some or all of its functions.

(6) Subject to the following provisions of this section—

(a) a body which distributes money under section 25(1) may establish a committee for the purpose of exercising on behalf of the body any such function as is mentioned in subsection (1), and

(b) a body falling within any paragraph of subsection (4) may establish a committee for the purpose of exercising on behalf of any body which distributes money under section 25(1) any such function as is mentioned in subsection (1).

(7) A committee established under subsection (6)—

(a) must consist of or include one or more members, or one or more employees, of the body establishing the committee, but

(b) may include persons who are neither members nor employees of that body.

(8) Any power conferred on a body by subsections (1) to (7) is so conferred—

(a) to the extent that the body would not have the power apart from this section, and

(b) notwithstanding anything to the contrary in any enactment or instrument relating to the functions of the body.

(9) In this section—

'charity' means a body, or the trustees of a trust, established for charitable purposes only;

'charitable, benevolent or philanthropic institution' means a body, or the trustees of a trust, which is established for charitable purposes (whether or not those purposes are charitable within the meaning of any rule of law), benevolent purposes or philanthropic purposes, and which is not a charity.

(10) For the purposes of this section—

(a) the trustees of a trust shall be regarded as a body, and

(b) any reference to a member of a body shall, in the case of a body of trustees, be taken as a reference to any of the trustees,

and references to a committee shall be construed accordingly.

(11) Any reference in this section to a member of a body includes a reference to the chairman or deputy chairman of (or the holder of any corresponding office in relation to) the body.][1]

[(12) A body established under the law of the Isle of Man may be the subject of an appointment under this section in connection with expenditure which relates to the Isle of Man.

(13) A body established under the law of any of the Channel Islands may be the subject of an appointment under this section in connection with expenditure which relates to that Island.][2]

1 Inserted by the National Lottery Act 1998, s 11(1).

2 Sub-ss (12), (13) inserted by the National Lottery Act 2006, s 13(2).

7.245 [25B Joint schemes for distribution of money by distributing bodies

(1) A body which distributes money under subsection (1) of section 25 may, in accordance with the following provisions of this section, participate with one or more other such bodies in a joint scheme for the distribution of money under that subsection.

(2) A body may participate in a joint scheme if the principal purposes of the joint scheme include purposes for which the body has power to distribute money under subsection (1) of section 25, notwithstanding that the body would not, apart from this section, have power to distribute money under that subsection for meeting expenditure on some of the particular projects for which money may be distributed under the scheme.

(3) Money shall not, under a joint scheme, be distributed for meeting expenditure on any particular project unless the expenditure is such that—

(a) at least one of the bodies participating in the joint scheme has power, acting alone, to distribute money under section 25(1) for meeting the expenditure, or

(b) two or more of the bodies participating in the joint scheme, taken together, have power between them to distribute money under section 25(1) for meeting the expenditure.

(4) Nothing in subsection (3) affects the liability of each body participating in a scheme in relation to the distribution of any money under section 25(1) under the scheme.

(5) Schedule 3A contains supplementary provision in relation to joint schemes.][1]

[(6) References in this section (however expressed) to distribution under section 25(1) of money for meeting expenditure are to be construed in accordance with section 25(5).][2]

1 Inserted by the National Lottery Act 1998, s 12(1).

2 Inserted by the National Lottery (Funding of Endowments) Act 2003, s 1. This amendment is deemed always to have had effect.

7.246 [25C Strategic plans for distributing bodies

(1) If the Secretary of State instructs it do so, a body which distributes money under section 25(1) shall, in accordance with the following provisions of this section—

(a) prepare and adopt a strategic plan, or

(b) review and modify any strategic plan which it has adopted, or

(c) replace any strategic plan which it has adopted by preparing and adopting another.

(2) In this section 'strategic plan', in the case of any body, means a statement containing the body's policies for the distribution of the money likely to be available to it for distribution under section 25(1).

(3) A strategic plan must also contain—

(a) a statement of any directions given to the body by the Secretary of State [or the Minister for the Cabinet Office][3] under section 26(1) [or 36E][2],

(b) a statement of the estimate given to the body by the Secretary of State of the money likely to be available for distribution by the body under section 25(1),

(c) a statement of the body's assessment of the needs which the body has power to deal with, in whole or in part, by distributing money under section 25(1), and

(d) a statement of the body's priorities in dealing with those needs by the distribution of money under section 25(1).

(4) A strategic plan must be such as to demonstrate how the body is taking into account or, as the case may be, complying with the directions mentioned in subsection (3)(a).

(5) Before adopting a strategic plan, a body shall—

(a) consult such other bodies as it thinks fit for the purpose of identifying the needs mentioned in subsection (3)(c) and formulating the policies to be adopted for dealing with those needs,
(b) prepare a draft of the proposed plan,
(c) send a copy of the draft to the Secretary of State, and
(d) after consultation with the Secretary of State, make such modifications to the draft as it considers necessary or expedient.

(6) Where a body adopts a strategic plan—
(a) the body shall send copies of the document containing the plan to the Secretary of State, and
(b) the Secretary of State shall lay a copy of the document before each House of Parliament.

(7) Nothing in this section applies in relation to any body which distributes under section 25(1) money allocated under section 22(3)(e).][1].

---

1 Inserted by the National Lottery Act 1998, s 13.

2 Sub-s (3): in para (a) words "or 36E" in square brackets substituted by the National Lottery Act 2006, s 19(1), (2). Date in force: 1 December 2006: see SI 2006/3201, art 2(d).

3 Sub-s (3): in para (a) words "or the Minister for the Cabinet Office" in square brackets inserted by SI 2011/739, art 4, Schedule, paras 1, 3. Date in force: 13 April 2011: see SI 2011/739, art 1.

7.247 [25D Strategic plans for distributing bodies in or as regards Scotland

The functions of the Secretary of State—
(a) under section 25C(1) shall, as regards instructions to—
  (i) any body specified in section 23(1) whose functions exclusively or mainly relate to the arts in Scotland; or
  (ii) any body specified in section 23(2) whose functions exclusively or mainly relate to sport in Scotland; and
(b) under section 25C(5)(c) and (d) and (6) shall, as regards strategic plans prepared by any body other than—
  (i) any body specified in section 23(1) whose functions relate exclusively or mainly to the arts in any one of England, Wales or Northern Ireland; or
  (ii) any body specified in section 23(2) whose functions relate exclusively or mainly to sport in any one of England, Wales or Northern Ireland,

be treated as exercisable in or as regards Scotland and may be exercised separately.][1, 2]

---

1 Inserted by the Scotland Act 1998 (Modification of Functions) Order 1999, SI 1999/1756, art 2, Schedule, para 15(2).

2 Section amended by the National Lottery Act 2006, s 13 from a date to be appointed.

7.247.1 [25E Distribution of funds: publicity

A body which distributes money under section 25(1) may make or participate in arrangements for—
(a) publishing information relating to the effect of a provision of this Act,
(b) publishing information relating to the distribution of money under this Act or the expenditure of money distributed under this Act, or
(c) encouraging participation in activities relating to the distribution of money under this Act.][1]

[1] Inserted by the National Lottery Act 2006, s 11.

Control by the Secretary of State

7.248 26 Directions to distributing bodies

(1) A body shall comply with any directions given to it by the Secretary of State as to the matters to be taken into account in determining the persons to whom, the purposes for which and the conditions subject to which the body distributes any money under section 25(1).

(2) The Trustees of the National Heritage Memorial Fund shall comply with any directions given to them by the Secretary of State as to the matters to be taken into account in determining the purposes for which and the conditions subject to which the Trustees apply any money under section 25(4).

(3) A body shall comply with any directions that the Secretary of State considers it appropriate to give the body for securing the proper management and control of money paid to the body under section 24.

[(3A) In exercising any power under section 25A, a body which distributes money under section 25(1) shall comply with any directions given to it by the Secretary of State.][1]

(4) Directions under subsection (3) [or (3A)][2] may in particular require a body—

- (a) to obtain the consent of the Secretary of State before doing anything specified, or of a description specified, in the directions;
- (b) to provide the Secretary of State at times specified by him with such information as he may require.

[(4A) Directions under subsection (3A) may in particular—

- (a) impose limits on the amount of money which may be distributed by a body under section 25(1) by virtue of decisions made on its behalf by bodies or persons not falling within section 25A (2), and
- (b) require a body, before appointing any body or person not falling within section 25A (2) to exercise on its behalf any function of making decisions concerning the distribution of money under section 25(1), to obtain the approval of the Secretary of State to its plans for making such appointments.][3]

(5) The Secretary of State shall consult a body before giving any directions to it under this section.

[(6) This section does not apply to the Big Lottery Fund.][4]

[1] Sub-s (3A): inserted by the National Lottery Act 1998, s 11(2).

[2] Sub-s (4): words in square brackets inserted by the NLA 1998, s 11(3).

[3] Sub-s (4A): inserted by the NLA 1998, s 11(4).

[4] Sub-s (6) inserted by the National Lottery Act 2006, s 19 (3).

7.249 [26A Directions to distributing bodies in or as regards Scotland

(1) The functions of the Secretary of State—

- (a) under section 26(1), (3), (3A) (4) and (5) shall, as regards directions to—
  - (i) any body specified in section 23(1) whose functions exclusively or mainly relate to the arts in Scotland; or
  - (ii) any body specified in section 23(2) whose functions exclusively or mainly relate to sport in Scotland; and
- (b) under section 26(3A) shall, as regards directions to any other body except—

(i) any body specified in section 23(1) whose functions relate exclusively or mainly to the arts in any one of England, Wales or Northern Ireland; or

(ii) any body specified in section 23(2) whose functions relate exclusively or mainly to sport in any one of England, Wales or Northern Ireland,

be treated as exercisable in or as regards Scotland and may be exercised separately.

(2) Directions given to the National Lottery Charities Board or the New Opportunities Fund under section 26(1) or to the Trustees of the National Heritage Memorial Fund under section 26(2) may be made—

(a) to apply to the whole of the United Kingdom and provide for all matters other than those to be provided specifically for Scotland in accordance with subsection (3); or

(b) to apply only to Scotland and provide for the matters specified in subsection (3).

(3) Directions given in accordance with subsection (2)(b) may, in relation to any distribution made for a purpose which does not concern reserved matters, provide for priorities and other matters to be taken into account in determining the persons to whom and the purposes for which the money available for distribution in Scotland is distributed and in determining conditions of distribution for the purpose of specific cases but may not provide for—

(a) the total allocation of resources to Scotland or between Scotland and other parts of the United Kingdom; or

(b) except in relation to any initiative specified in an order made under section 43B which applies only in Scotland, the general conditions subject to which lottery money is distributed in accordance with directions applying to the whole of the United Kingdom.][1]

---

1 Inserted by the Scotland Act 1998 (Modification of Functions) Order 1999, SI 1999/1756, art 2, Schedule, para 15(3).

7.250 27 Power to prohibit distribution in certain cases

(1) Where subsection (2) applies, the Secretary of State may by order prohibit a body from distributing money under section 25(1) to a person specified in the order.

(2) This subsection applies if at the time the order is made—

(a) the person specified is a company of which the body, or a wholly-owned subsidiary of the body, is a member, or

(b) the Secretary of State considers that the body is able (whether directly or indirectly) to control or materially to influence the policy of the person specified in carrying on any undertaking or performing any functions.

(3) In subsection (2)—

(a) 'company' means a company formed and registered under [the Companies Act 2006][2] or a company to which [any provisions of the Companies Acts (as defined in section 2(1) of that Act)][3] apply as they apply to a company so formed and registered, and

(b) 'wholly-owned subsidiary' has the meaning given by [section 1159 of that Act][4].

(4) Where subsection (5) applies, the Secretary of State may give directions to a body—

(a) prohibiting it from distributing money under section 25(1) to a person in Northern Ireland specified in the directions, or

(b) requiring it to secure that any money distributed by it under section 25(1) to such a person is not applied for a purpose specified in the directions.

(5) This subsection applies if at the time the directions are given the Secretary of State considers that—

(a) a proscribed organisation for the purposes of the Northern Ireland (Emergency Provisions) Act 1991, or

(b) any other organisation that appears to him to be concerned in terrorism in Northern Ireland or in promoting or encouraging it,

might directly or indirectly derive benefit from the distribution of money to the person specified.

(6) In subsection (5) 'benefit' includes benefit of a non-financial nature and, in particular, an enhancement of reputation.

(7) A body may not disclose to any other person either the identity of any person specified in directions given to it under subsection (4) or any information that might lead to the identification of such a person.

(8) A body shall provide the Secretary of State with such information as he may require for the purpose of exercising his powers under this section in relation to the body.

[(9) The function of the Secretary of State—

(a) under subsection (1) to prohibit a body from distributing money; or

(b) under subsection (8) to require information,

may, in relation to—

(i) any body specified in section 23(1) whose functions exclusively or mainly relate to the arts in Scotland; or

(ii) any body specified in section 23(2) whose functions exclusively or mainly relate to sport in Scotland,

be exercised separately.][1]

---

1 Sub-s (9): inserted by the Scotland Act 1998 (Modification of Functions) Order 1999, SI 1999/1756, art 2, Schedule, para 15(4).

2 Sub-s (3): in para (a) words "the Companies Act 2006" in square brackets substituted by SI 2009/1941, art 2(1), Sch 1, para 142(a)(i).

3 Sub-s (3): in para (a) words "any provisions of" to "of that Act)" in square brackets substituted by SI 2009/1941, art 2(1), Sch 1, para 142(a)(ii).

4 Sub-s (3): in para (b) words "section 1159 of that Act" in square brackets substituted by SI 2009/1941, art 2(1), Sch 1, para 142(b).

7.251 28 Power to amend section 22

(1) The Secretary of State may by order amend section 22(3) so as to substitute different percentages for any of the percentages for the time being specified there.

(2) Any amendment made under this section shall be such that—

(a) no percentage lower than 5 per cent. is specified in section 22(3), and

(b) the percentages specified in section 22(3) amount in total to 100 per cent.

(3) Without prejudice to the generality of section 60(5), an order under this section may provide for sums that apart from the order would be held in the Distribution Fund for distribution by a particular body to be held in the Distribution Fund for distribution by another body specified in section 23.

7.252 29 Power to amend section 23

(1) The Secretary of State may by order amend subsection (1), (2), (3) or (4) of section 23 so as—

(a) to substitute a different body for any body for the time being specified in that subsection;

(b) to add another body to the bodies or body for the time being specified in it;

(c) to omit any body for the time being specified in it;

(d) to substitute different percentages for any percentages for the time being specified in it.

(2) Any amendment made under subsection (1) shall be such that the amended subsection—

(a) provides for the whole of the sum mentioned in that subsection to be held for distribution by the one body specified in that subsection, or

(b) provides for the whole of that sum to be held for distribution by the two or more bodies specified in that subsection and specifies, in relation to each of those bodies, what percentage of that sum is to be held for distribution by that body.

(3) The Secretary of State may by order provide that subsection (1), (2), (3) or (4) of section 23 shall, pending the making of an order amending that subsection under subsection (1),—

(a) cease to have effect, or

(b) have effect as if any of the bodies for the time being specified in it were omitted.

(4) Without prejudice to the generality of section 60(5)—

(a) an order made under subsection (1) may provide for sums that apart from the order would be held in the Distribution Fund for distribution by a particular body to be held in the Distribution Fund for distribution by another body (being a body that on the coming into force of the order is specified in the subsection amended by the order);

(b) an order made under subsection (3) may provide for sums that apart from the order would be held in the Distribution Fund for distribution by a particular body to be held in the Distribution Fund in the name of the Secretary of State, pending being held for distribution by another body in accordance with the order to be made under subsection (1).

(5) Without prejudice to the generality of subsection (1), the Secretary of State may exercise his powers under that subsection so as to remove from section 23 any body that has contravened or failed to comply with a requirement or prohibition imposed on it by or under section 26 or 27.

[(6) The functions of the Secretary of State under this section shall, in so far as they relate to—

(a) substitution of a different body for, or addition of another body to, the body specified in section 23(3) or (4) or omission of a body specified in either of those subsections; or

(b) substitution of a different percentage for the total aggregate percentage specified as held in the Distribution Fund for—

(i) any body or bodies specified in section 23(1) whose functions exclusively or mainly relate to the arts in Scotland, or

(ii) any body or bodies specified in section 23(2) whose functions exclusively or mainly relate to sport in Scotland;

(c) substitution of a different body for, or addition of another body to, any such body specified in section 23(1) or (2) as is mentioned in paragraph (b) above or omission of any such body specified in section 23(1) or (2); or

(d) where more than one such body is specified in section 23(1) or (2), specification of the particular percentage held in the Distribution Fund for distribution by any one of those bodies,

be treated as exercisable in or as regards Scotland and may be exercised separately.][1]

[1] Sub-s (6): inserted by the Scotland Act 1998 (Modification of Functions) Order 1999, SI 1999/1756, art 2, Schedule, para 15(5).

7.252.1 [29A Reallocation of funds

(1) This section applies where money is—

(a) allocated for a purpose under section 22(3), and

(b) held for distribution by a body under section 23.

(2) The Secretary of State may by order provide for the money to be held for distribution by a different body specified in the order (without altering the purpose for which the money is allocated).

(3) Before making an order under this section the Secretary of State shall consult—

(a) each body mentioned in the order,

(b) the National Assembly for Wales,

(c) the Scottish Ministers,

(d) the Northern Ireland Department of Culture, Arts and Leisure, and

(e) such other persons (if any) as he thinks appropriate.][1]

[1] Inserted by the National Lottery Act 2006, s 8(1).

7.253 30 Winding up of fund allocated under section 22(3)(e)

Repealed by the Horserace Betting and Olympic Lottery Act 2004, ss 34(1), (10), 38, Sch 6.

Distribution Fund: further provisions

7.254 31 Payments from Distribution Fund in respect of expenses

(1) At such times as the Secretary of State with the approval of the Treasury determines to be appropriate, payments shall be made into the Consolidated Fund out of so much of any money in the Distribution Fund as is held under section 22(2).

(2) The payments shall be of such amounts as the Secretary of State with the approval of the Treasury determines to be appropriate for—

(a) . . . [1]

[(aa) meeting payments made or to be made under paragraph 10 of Schedule 2A,][1]

(b) defraying expenses incurred or to be incurred by the [or the Minister for the Cabinet Office][2] in exercising his functions under this Act, and

(c) defraying expenses incurred or to be incurred by the National Debt Commissioners in making investments under section 32.

(3) . . . [1]

[(4) In determining what amounts are appropriate for meeting the payments referred to in subsection (2)(aa), the Secretary of State shall take into account sums paid or to be paid into the Consolidated Fund under section 7(6).][1]

[1] Sub-ss (2)(a), (3) repealed and sub-ss (2)(aa), (4) inserted by the National Lottery Act 1998, ss 1, 26, Sch 1, para 15.

[2] Sub-s (2): in para (b) words "or the Minister for the Cabinet Office" in square brackets inserted by SI 2011/739, art 4, Schedule, paras 1, 4. Date in force: 13 April 2011: see SI 2011/739, art 1.

7.255 32 Investment of Distribution Fund

(1) So much of any money in the Distribution Fund as is neither held under section 22(2) nor immediately required for making payments under section 24 may be paid over to the National Debt Commissioners and invested by them in accordance with such directions as may be given by the Treasury.

(2) The proceeds of any investment made under subsection (1) or this subsection may be re-invested by the National Debt Commissioners in accordance with such directions as may be given by the Treasury.

(3) The proceeds of any investment made under subsection (1) or (2) shall, if they are not re-invested under subsection (2), be paid into the Distribution Fund and [treated as if paid into the Fund by virtue of *section 5(6)*][1].

(4) In this section 'proceeds', in relation to an investment, means any interest or dividends received in respect of the investment and any sums received on the realisation of the investment.

(5) . . . [1]

---

1 Sub-s (3): words in square brackets substituted by the National Lottery Act 2006, s 9(a) from 1 April 2007; words in italics substituted by words "section 5(2)(c)" by the National Lottery Act 2006, s 6, Sch 1, paras 1, 13 from a date to be appointed. Sub-s (5): repealed by the the National Lottery Act 2006, ss 9(b), 21, Sch 3.

7.256 33 Accounts of the Secretary of State and National Debt Commissioners

(1) The Secretary of State shall prepare accounts in respect of the Distribution Fund in such form, and in such manner and at such times, as the Treasury may direct.

(2) The National Debt Commissioners shall prepare accounts in respect of any investments under section 32 in such form, and in such manner and at such times, as the Treasury may direct.

(3) Each account prepared under subsection (1) or (2) shall be sent to the Comptroller and Auditor General who shall examine, certify and report on it and shall lay copies of it and of his report before Parliament.

[(4) For the purpose of exercising his examination function in relation to any accounts prepared under subsection (1), the Comptroller and Auditor General—

(a) shall have a right of access at all reasonable times to any documents which he reasonably requires which are in the custody or under the control of any section 5 licensee; and

(b) shall have a right to require from any officer or employee of any section 5 licensee, or from the auditors of any section 5 licensee, an explanation of, or information relating to, any such documents;

but a section 5 licensee shall not, by virtue only of this subsection, be a body to which section 6 of the National Audit Act 1983 applies.

(5) For the purpose of—

(a) exercising his examination function in relation to any accounts prepared under subsection (1), or

(b) deciding whether, or to what extent, to exercise any right conferred by subsection (4),

the Comptroller and Auditor General shall have regard to any information which the Director General has obtained from any section 5 licensee and which is relevant to the exercise of that function.

(6) Where, in exercising his examination function in relation to any accounts prepared under subsection (1), the Comptroller and Auditor General obtains any information which gives him grounds to believe that a section 5 licensee has, or may have, contravened any of the conditions of its licence under section 5, the Comptroller and Auditor General shall as soon as practicable disclose that information to the Director General.

(7) A section 5 licensee shall be under a duty—

(a) to permit the Comptroller and Auditor General to exercise the right conferred by subsection (4)(a); and

(b) to do all that may be reasonably practicable to secure that any person who under subsection (4)(b) is required to provide an explanation of, or information relating to, any document complies with that requirement;

and any breach of that duty shall be actionable at the suit of the Comptroller and Auditor General.

(8) The right of access to documents conferred by subsection (4)(a) includes a right to take copies of or make extracts from documents.

(9) In this section any reference to documents includes a reference to information held by means of a computer or in any other electronic form; and in the case of information so held the right of access conferred by subsection (4)(a) includes a right of access to, and to take copies of, that information in a visible and legible form.

(10) In this section—

'examination function', in relation to the Comptroller and Auditor General, means his function under subsection (3);

'section 5 licensee' means a body which holds or has held a licence under section 5.][1]

---

1 Sub-ss (4)–(10): inserted, in relation to accounts prepared under sub-s (1) above so far as they relate to periods beginning on or after 1 April 1999, by the National Lottery Act 1998, s 5.

Reports and accounts of distributing bodies

7.257 34 Annual reports by distributing bodies . . . [4]

(1) As soon as possible after the end of every financial year, each body that in that year was paid any money under section 24 or distributed or applied any money under section 25 shall make a report to the Secretary of State on the exercise during that year of its functions under this Act.

(2) The report shall set out any directions given to the body under section 26 that had effect during the financial year to which the report relates.

[(2A) The report shall set out the body's policy and practice in relation to the principle that proceeds of the National Lottery should be used to fund projects, or aspects of projects, for which funds would be unlikely to be made available by—

(a) a Government department,

(b) the Scottish Ministers,

(c) a Northern Ireland department, or

(d) the National Assembly for Wales.][2]

(3) The Secretary of State shall lay a copy of every report received by him under this section before Parliament.

(4) . . . [3]

[(5) The functions of the Secretary of State under this section shall, in so far as they relate to any body other than—

(a) any body specified in section 23(1) whose functions relate exclusively or mainly to the arts in any one of England, Wales or Northern Ireland; or

(b) any body specified in section 23(2) whose functions relate exclusively or mainly to sport in any one of England, Wales or Northern Ireland,

be treated as exercisable in or as regards Scotland and may be exercised separately.][1]

[(6) Where a report is made under subsection (1) to the Scottish Ministers (by virtue of provision made under section 63 of the Scotland Act 1998), the Scottish Ministers shall lay a copy of the report before the Scottish Parliament.][5]

[(7) See the Transfer of Functions (Big Lottery Fund) Order 2011 for provision under which the functions of the Secretary of State under this section, so far as they relate to the Big Lottery Fund, are transferred to the Minister for the Cabinet Office.] 6

---

1 Sub-s (5): inserted by the Scotland Act 1998 (Modification of Functions) Order 1999, SI 1999/1756, art 2, Schedule, para 15(6).

2 Sub-s (2A): inserted by the National Lottery Act 2006, s 12.

3 Sub-s (4) repealed by the National Lottery Act 2006, ss 19(4)(a), 21, Sch 3.

4 Words in heading repealed by by the National Lottery Act 2006, ss 19(4)(b).

5 Sub-s (6): inserted by SI 1999/1750, art 6(1), Sch 5, para 12(1), (3). Date in force: 1 July 1999: see SI 1999/1750, art 1(1), and SI 1998/3178, art 3.

6 Sub-s (7): inserted by SI 2011/739, arts 2(1)(b), 4, Schedule, paras 1, 5; for supplementary provision see art 3 thereof. Date in force: 13 April 2011: see SI 2011/739, art 1.

7.258 35 Accounts of distributing bodies other than [the Big Lottery Fund][3]

(1) A body shall keep proper accounts in respect of any money paid to it under section 24 and proper records in relation to the accounts.

(2) A body shall prepare a statement of accounts in respect of each financial year in which it was paid any money under section 24 or distributed or applied any money under section 25.

(3) The statement shall comply with any directions that may be given by the Secretary of State as to the information to be contained in such a statement, the manner in which such information is to be presented or the methods and principles according to which such a statement is to be prepared.

(4) Copies of the statement shall be sent to the Secretary of State and the Comptroller and Auditor General within such period after the end of the financial year to which the statement relates as the Secretary of State may direct.

(5) The Comptroller and Auditor General shall examine, certify and report on the statement and shall lay copies of the statement and of his report before Parliament.

(6) The Secretary of State shall not give a direction under this section without the Treasury's approval.

(7) This section does not apply to the [the Big Lottery Fund].[1]

[(8) The functions of the Secretary of State—

(a) under subsection (3) to give directions shall, in so far as they relate to—

(i) any body specified in section 23(1) whose functions exclusively or mainly relate to the arts in Scotland; or

(ii) any body specified in section 23(2) whose functions exclusively or mainly relate to sport in Scotland; and

(b) under subsection (4) to receive copies of the statement shall, in so far as they relate to any body other than—

(i) any body specified in section 23(1) whose functions relate exclusively or mainly to the arts in any one of England, Wales or Northern Ireland; or

(ii) any body specified in section 23(2) whose functions relate exclusively or mainly to sport in any one of England, Wales or Northern Ireland,

be treated as exercisable in or as regards Scotland and may be exercised separately.][2]

---

1 Sub-s (7): words in square brackets substituted by the National Lottery Act 2006, s 19(5)a.

2 Sub-s (8): inserted by the Scotland Act 1998 (Modification of Functions) Order 1999, SI 1999/1756, art 2, Schedule, para 15(7).

3 Words in heading substituted by the National Lottery Act 2006, s 19(5)(b).

The Trustees of the National Heritage Memorial Fund

7.258.1 36 Amendment of the National Heritage Act 1980

The National Heritage Act 1980 shall have effect with the amendments set out in Schedule 4.

The Big Lottery Fund

7.258.2 [36A The Fund

(1) There shall be a body corporate known as the Big Lottery Fund.

(2) Schedule 4A (which makes provision in relation to the Fund) shall have effect.][1]

1 Inserted by the National Lottery Act 2006, s 15(2).

7.258.3 [36B Power to distribute funds

(1) The Big Lottery Fund may make grants or loans, or make or enter into other arrangements, for the purpose of complying with section 25(1).

(2) A grant or loan may be subject to conditions (which may, in particular, include conditions as to repayment with interest).

(3) The [Minister for the Cabinet Office][2] may by order make provision limiting the amounts distributed under subsection (1).

(4) An order under subsection (3) may in particular—

(a) specify a maximum amount that may be distributed during a specified period for expenditure of a description prescribed under section 22(3A);

(b) specify a minimum amount that must be distributed during a specified period for expenditure of a description prescribed under section 22(3A);

(c) make provision by reference to the aggregate of amounts distributed, to a percentage of amounts available for distribution or otherwise;

(d) make provision (which may, in particular, confer a power on the Fund) for the treatment of expenditure which satisfies more than one prescribed description.

(5) Before making an order under subsection (3) the [Minister for the Cabinet Office][2] shall consult—

(a) the Fund,

(b) the National Assembly for Wales,

(c) the Scottish Ministers,

(d) the Northern Ireland Department of Culture, Arts and Leisure, and

(e) such other persons (if any) as he thinks appropriate.][1]

1 Inserted by the National Lottery Act 2006, s 15(2).

2 Sub-s (3) and (5): words "Minister for the Cabinet Office" in square brackets substituted by SI 2011/739, arts 2(1)(c), 4, Schedule, paras 1, 6; for supplementary provision see art 3 thereof. Date in force: 13 April 2011: see SI 2011/739, art 1.

7.258.4 [36C Non-lottery funds

(1) The Fund may enter into an arrangement with a person under which—

(a) the person pays money to the Fund, and

(b) the Fund distributes the money to a third party.

(2) An arrangement under subsection (1) may, in particular—

(a) identify the third party, or

(b) otherwise limit the Fund's freedom of action in relation to the distribution of the money paid under the arrangement.

(3) The Fund shall distribute money received under subsection (1) for meeting expenditure that is—

(a) charitable,

(b) connected with health,

(c) connected with education, or

(d) connected with the environment.

(4) The reference in subsection (3) to the distribution of money received under subsection (1) is a reference to doing anything of a kind that the Fund can do under section 36B.

(5) A reference in this Act to payment under section 25(1) shall include a reference to payment under subsection (3) above.][1]

1 Inserted by the National Lottery Act 2006, s 15(2).

7.258.5 [36D Power to give advice

The Big Lottery Fund may give advice about—

(a) the distribution of money under any provision of this Act;

(b) inviting, making or considering applications for grants and loans under any provision of this Act;

(c) the use of money paid under any provision of this Act.][1]

1 Inserted by the National Lottery Act 2006, s 15(2).

7.258.6 [36E Directions

[(1) In exercising any of its functions the Big Lottery Fund shall comply with any direction given to it by

(a) the Secretary of State in relation to a direction given by virtue of subsection (3), or

(b) (subject to subsection (4) the Minister for the Cabinet Office in relation to any other direction][2].

[(2) A direction under subsection (1)(b) may, in particular—

(a) specify matters to be taken into account in determining the persons to whom, the purposes for which and the conditions subject to which the Fund distributes money;

(b) relate to the employment of staff;

(c) in so far as it relates to the employment of staff—

(i) relate to the persons to whom or the terms on which the Fund delegates functions;

(ii) require the Fund to obtain the Minister for the Cabinet Office's consent before taking action of a specified kind;

(iii) require the Fund to provide information to that Minister.][3]

(3) A direction under [subsection (1)(a) may][4]

(a) relate to the management and control of money received by the Fund;

(b) [. . .][5]

(c) with the consent of the Treasury, relate to—

(i) the form of accounts, or

(ii) methods and principles for the preparation of accounts;

(d) in so far as it relates to a matter specified in [paragraph (a) or (c)][6]

(i) relate to the persons to whom or the terms on which the Fund delegates functions;
(ii) require the Fund to obtain the Secretary of State's consent before taking action of a specified kind;
(iii) require the Fund to provide information to the Secretary of State.

(4) A direction under [subsection (1)(b), other than a direction given by virtue only of subsection (2)(b) or (c), may not be given by the Minister for the Cabinet Office][7] in relation to Welsh, Scottish or Northern Ireland devolved expenditure, but—

(a) may be given by the National Assembly for Wales in relation to Welsh devolved expenditure,
(b) may be given by the Scottish Ministers in relation to Scottish devolved expenditure, and
(c) may be given by the Northern Ireland Department of Culture, Arts and Leisure in relation to Northern Ireland devolved expenditure.

(5) A direction under [subsection (1)(b), other than a direction given by virtue only of subsection (2)(b) or (c), may not be given by the Minister for the Cabinet Office][8] in relation to Welsh, Scottish or Northern Ireland devolved expenditure, but—

(a) the Fund,
(b) the National Assembly for Wales,
(c) the Scottish Ministers, and
(d) the Northern Ireland Department of Culture, Arts and Leisure.

(6) But subsection (5)(b) to (d) shall not apply to a direction which relates only to English devolved expenditure.

(7) A direction under [subsection (1)(b), other than a direction given by virtue only of subsection (2)(b) or (c), may not be given by the Minister for the Cabinet Office][9] in relation to Welsh, Scottish or Northern Ireland devolved expenditure, but—

(8) Before giving a direction to the Fund by virtue of subsection (4)(a) to (c) the person giving the direction shall—

(a) consult the Fund, and
(b) obtain the consent of the [Minister for the Cabinet Office].[10]

(9) A report of the Fund under section 34 shall set out any directions given to the Fund under subsection (1) that had effect during the financial year to which the report relates.][1]

---

1 Inserted by the National Lottery Act 2006, s 15(2).

2 Sub-s (1): words from "by— (a)" to "any other direction" in square brackets substituted by SI 2011/739, arts 2(1)(d), (2), 4, Schedule, paras 1, 7(1), (2); for supplementary provision see art 3 thereof. Date in force: 13 April 2011: see SI 2011/739, art 1.

3 Sub-s (2): substituted by SI 2011/739, arts 2(1)(d), (2), 4, Schedule, paras 1, 7(1), (3); for supplementary provision see art 3 thereof. Date in force: 13 April 2011: see SI 2011/739, art 1.

4 Sub-s (3): words "subsection (1)(a) may" in square brackets substituted by SI 2011/739, arts 2(1)(d), (2), 4, Schedule, paras 1, 7(1), (4)(a); for supplementary provision see art 3 thereof. Date in force: 13 April 2011: see SI 2011/739, art 1.

5 Sub-s (3): para (b) repealed by SI 2011/739, arts 2(1)(d), (2), 4, Schedule, paras 1, 7(1), (4)(b); for supplementary provision see art 3 thereof. Date in force: 13 April 2011: see SI 2011/739, art 1.

6 Sub-s (3): in para (d) words "paragraph (a) or (c)" in square brackets substituted by SI 2011/739, arts 2(1)(d), (2), 4, Schedule, paras 1, 7(1), (4)(c); for supplementary provision see art 3 thereof. Date in force: 13 April 2011: see SI 2011/739, art 1.

7 Sub-s (4): words from "subsection (1)(b), other" to "the Cabinet Office" in square brackets substituted by SI 2011/739, arts 2(1)(d), (2), 4, Schedule, paras 1, 7(1), (5); for supplementary provision see art 3 thereof. Date in force: 13 April 2011: see SI 2011/739, art 1.

8 Sub-s (5): words from "subsection (1)(b), other" to "the Cabinet Office" in square brackets

substituted by SI 2011/739, arts 2(1)(d), (2), 4, Schedule, paras 1, 7(1), (6); for supplementary provision see art 3 thereof. Date in force: 13 April 2011: see SI 2011/739, art 1.

9 Sub-s (7): words from "under subsection (1)(a)," to "the Cabinet Office" in square brackets substituted by SI 2011/739, arts 2(1)(d), (2), 4, Schedule, paras 1, 7(1), (7); for supplementary provision see art 3 thereof. Date in force: 13 April 2011: see SI 2011/739, art 1.

10 Sub-s (8): in para (b) words "Minister for the Cabinet Office" in square brackets substituted by SI 2011/739, arts 2(1)(d), (2), 4, Schedule, paras 1, 7(1), (8); for supplementary provision see art 3 thereof. Date in force: 13 April 2011: see SI 2011/739, art 1.

The National Lottery Charities Board

7.259

37 . . . [1]

1 Repealed by the National Lottery Act 2006, ss 19(6)(a), 21, Sch 3.

7.260

38 . . . [1].

1 Repealed by the National Lottery Act 2006, ss 19(6)(a), 21, Sch 3

7.261

39 . . . [1]

1 Repealed by the National Lottery Act 2006, ss 19(6)(a), 21, Sch 3

The Millennium Commission

7.262

40 . . . [1]

1 Repealed by the National Lottery Act 2006, ss 19(6)(b), 21, Sch 3.

7.263

41 . . . [1]

1 Repealed by the National Lottery Act 2006, ss 19(6)(b), 21, Sch 3.

7.264

42 . . . [1]

1 Repealed by the National Lottery Act 2006, ss 19(6)(b), 21, Sch 3.

7.265

43 . . . [1]

1 Repealed by the National Lottery Act 2006, ss 19(6)(b), 21, Sch 3.

[The New Opportunities Fund

7.266
43A . . . [1]

---

[1] Repealed by the National Lottery Act 2006, ss 19(6)(c), 21, Sch 3.

7.267
[43B . . . [1]

---

[1] Repealed by the National Lottery Act 2006, ss 19(6)(c), 21, Sch 3.

7.268
[43C . . . [1]

---

[1] Repealed by the National Lottery Act 2006, ss 19(6)(c), 21, Sch 3.

7.269
[43CC . . . [1]

---

[1] Repealed by the National Lottery Act 2006, ss 19(6)(c), 21, Sch 3.

7.270
[43D . . . [1]

---

[1] Repealed by the National Lottery Act 2006, ss 19(6)(c), 21, Sch 3.

Supplementary

7.271 44 Interpretation of Part II

(1) In this Part—

["charitable" in relation to expendeture, means expenditure for a charitable, benevolent or philanthropic purpose.][8]

. . . [7]

'the Distribution Fund' means the National Lottery Distribution Fund;

['education' includes training and the provision of activities for children;

['endowment' includes permanent endowment;][6]

'the environment' includes the living and social environment;][1]

'expenditure on or connected with the national heritage' [means expenditure for any purpose for which expenditure may be incurred under sections 3, 3A or 4 of the National Heritage Act 1980];[2]

'financial year', in relation to a body, means—

(a) the period beginning with the date on which the body is established and ending with the next 31st March, and

(b) each successive period of twelve months ending with 31st March.

['joint scheme' means a joint scheme under section 25B;][3]

(2) For the purposes of the definition of 'expenditure on or connected with the national heritage' in subsection (1), any reference in section 3 [3A or 4][4] of the National Heritage Act 1980 to the opinion of the Trustees shall be read, in relation to

any body other than the Trustees of the National Heritage Memorial Fund that is for the time being specified in section 23(3), as a reference to the opinion of that body.

[(3) A project or arrangement shall be regarded for the purposes of this Part as concerned or connected with health, education or the environment notwithstanding that it contains incidental provision—

(a) which is not concerned or connected with any of those matters; but

(b) which is necessary or expedient for the purposes of the project or arrangement.[5]]

(4) Any reference in this Part to the distribution of money shall be construed as including the making or entering into of arrangements in accordance with section 25(1A) [. . .][7]; and related expressions used in this Part shall be construed accordingly.][5]

---

1 Definitions in square brackets inserted, in relation to sums paid into the National Lottery Distribution Fund under NLA 1993, s 21(2) above on or after 14 October 1997, by the National Lottery Act 1998, s 6(8).

2 Words in square brackets substituted by the National Heritage Act 1997, s 3, Schedule, Pt 1, para 5.

3 Definition 'joint scheme' inserted by the National Lottery Act 1998, s 12(2).

4 Words in square brackets inserted by the National Heritage Act 1997, s 3, Schedule, Pt 1, para 5.

5 Sub-ss (3), (4): added by the National Lottery Act 1998, ss 8(2), 9(2).

6 Definition 'endowment' inserted by the National Lottery (Funding of Endowments) Act 2003, s 1. This amendment is deemed always to have had effect.

7 Repealed by the National Lotteries Act 2006, s 19(7).

8 Substituted by the National Lotteries Act 2006, s 20.

9 Words in square brackets repealed by the National Lotteries Act 2006, s 21, Sch 3.

PART III
MISCELLANEOUS AMENDMENTS RELATING TO LOTTERIES

Preliminary

Repeal

Part III repealed by the Gambling Act 2005, s 356(4), Sch 17 from 1 September 2007: see SI 2006/3272, art 2(4); for transitional provisions see art 6, Sch 4 thereto.

7.272 45 Interpretation of Part III

In this Part 'the 1976 Act' means the Lotteries and Amusements Act 1976.

Importation and exportation restrictions

7.273 46 Importation and exportation restrictions

[*This section amends the Revenue Act 1898, s 1, the Lotteries and Amusements Act 1976, s 2(1), and the Betting, Gaming, Lotteries and Amusements (Northern Ireland) Order 1985, SI 1985/1204, art 132(1). Repealed in part by the Gambling Act 2005, s 356(4), Sch 17 from 1 September 2007: see SI 2006/3272, art 2(4); for transitional provisions see art 6, Sch 4 thereto.*]

Private lotteries

47–55 [*Sections 47–55 amend the Lotteries and Amusements Act 1976, as noted thereto. Repealed by the Gambling Act 2005, s 356(4), Sch 17 from 1 September 2007: see SI 2006/3272, art 2(4); for transitional provisions see art 6, Sch 4 thereto.*]

PART IV
POOL BETTING

56–59 [*Sections 56–59 amend the Betting, Gaming and Lotteries Act 1963, as noted thereto. Repealed by the Gambling Act 2005, s 356(4), Sch 17 from 1 September 2007: see SI 2006/3272, art 2(4); for transitional provisions see art 6, Sch 4 thereto.*]

PART V
SUPPLEMENTARY

7.274 60 Orders and regulations

(1) Any power to make an order or regulations under this Act shall be exercisable by statutory instrument.

(2) An order shall not be made under

[(a) section 22(3A)28 or 36B(3), ",and][3]

[(aa) section 29A][2] [or][1]

[(b) paragraph 2(5) of Schedule 3A,][1]

unless a draft of the statutory instrument containing it has been laid before, and approved by a resolution of, each House of Parliament.

[(2A) Subsection (2) does not apply to an order which contains only provision revoking an order under [section 22(3A) or 36B(3)][4].][1]

(3) A statutory instrument containing any order or regulations under this Act, other than

[(a) an order to which subsection (2) applies, or

(b) an order under section 65,][1]

shall be subject to annulment in pursuance of a resolution of either House of Parliament.

[(3A) Subsection (3) does not apply to a statutory instrument which contains only provision revoking an order under paragraph 2(1) of Schedule 3A.

(3B) A statutory instrument which contains only provision revoking an order under paragraph 2(1) of Schedule 3A shall be laid before each House of Parliament.][1]

(4) Any order or regulations under this Act may make different provision for different cases or circumstances.

(5) Any order or regulations under this Act may make such incidental, supplemental and transitional provision as the person making the order or regulations thinks appropriate.

[(6) Any reference in this section to an order is a reference to an order of the Secretary of State [or the Minister for the Cabinet Office][5].][1]

---

1 In sub-ss (2), (3) paras (a), (b) substituted, and sub-ss (2A), (3A), (3B), (6) inserted, by the National Lottery Act 1998, s 15.

2 Sub-s(2)(aa) inserted by the National Lottery Act 2006, s 8(3).

3 Sub-s(2)(a) substituted by the National Lottery Act 2006, s 19(8)(a).

4 Words in square brackets substituted by the National Lottery Act 2006, s 19(8)(b).

5 Sub-s (6): words "or the Minister for the Cabinet Office" in square brackets inserted by SI 2011/739, art 4, Schedule, paras 1, 8. Date in force: 13 April 2011: see SI 2011/739, art 1.

Remuneration and allowances

5 (1) The Commission may pay such remuneration, and such travelling and other allowances, to a member of the Commission as the Secretary of State may determine in the case of the member.

(2) Where the Secretary of State so determines in the case of a member of the Commission, the Commission shall—

(a) pay to or in respect of him such pension, allowances or gratuities, or

(b) make such payments towards the provision of a pension, allowances or gratuities to or in respect of him,

as the Secretary of State may determine.

(3) If the Secretary of State determines that there are special circumstances that make it right for a person ceasing to be a member of the Commission to receive compensation, the Commission may pay to him such compensation as the Secretary of State may determine.

Staff

6 (1) There shall be a Chief Executive of the Commission, who shall be appointed by the Commission as an employee of theirs.

(2) The Chief Executive shall be responsible to the Commission for the general exercise of the Commission's functions.

(3) Subject to any directions given to them by the Secretary of State with respect to the number of persons who may be employed by the Commission, the Commission may appoint such other employees as they think fit.

(4) Subject to any directions given to the Commission by the Secretary of State, the Chief Executive and any other employees shall be employed on such terms and conditions (including terms and conditions as to remuneration) as the Commission think fit.

(5) Service as an employee of the Commission shall be included in the kinds of employment to which a scheme under section 1 of the Superannuation Act 1972 can apply.

(6) Accordingly, in the Superannuation Act 1972, in Schedule 1 (kinds of employment etc referred to in section 1) the following entry shall be inserted at the appropriate place among the entries under the heading 'Royal Commissions and other Commissions'—

'National Lottery Commission'.

(7) The Commission shall pay to the Minister for the Civil Service, at such times as that Minister may direct, such sums as that Minister may determine in respect of the increase attributable to sub-paragraphs (5) and (6) in the sums payable out of money provided by Parliament under the Superannuation Act 1972.

[6A (1) The Secretary of State may appoint the Chief Executive of the Commission as a member.

(2) Where the Chief Executive is appointed as a member—

(a) paragraph 5 shall not apply to him, and

(b) if he ceases to be Chief Executive he ceases to be a member.

(3) Where the Chief Executive is appointed as a member the Secretary of State may, on the recommendation of the Commission, appoint another employee of the Commission as a member; and—

(a) paragraph 5 shall not apply to a person appointed by virtue of this sub-paragraph,

(b) the Secretary of State may suspend or terminate an appointment made by virtue of this sub-paragraph if the Chief Executive ceases to be a member, and

(c) if a person appointed by virtue of this sub-paragraph ceases to be an employee of the Commission he shall cease to be a member.][4]

Proceedings

7 (1) The Commission may regulate their own procedure and that of any of their committees (and in particular may specify a quorum for meetings).

(2) The validity of any proceedings of the Commission shall not be affected—

(a) by any vacancy among the members or in the office of chairman, or

(b) by any defect in the appointment or selection of any person as a member or as chairman of the Commission.

Delegation

8 (1) Anything authorised or required by or under any enactment to be done by the Commission may be done—

(a) by any member or employee of the Commission who has been authorised for the purpose, whether generally or specially, by the Commission; or

(b) by any committee of the Commission which has been so authorised and whose membership consists of—

(i) members of the Commission; or

(ii) one or more members of the Commission and one or more employees of the Commission.

(2) In exercising their functions under sub-paragraph (1), the Commission shall comply with any directions given to them by the Secretary of State.

Duty to give reasons for decisions

9 (1) It shall be the duty of the Commission to give to any person affected a written statement of their reasons for any decisions which they may make in the exercise of their functions under sections 5 to 10 or Schedule 3.

(2) It shall be the duty of the Commission to arrange for the publication, in such manner as they think fit, of a written statement of their reasons—

(a) for any decision which they may make to grant, or not to grant, to any particular applicant a licence under section 5;

(b) for any decision which they may make to revoke a licence granted under section 5; and

(c) for any other decision which they may make in the exercise of their functions under sections 5 to 10A or Schedule 3 and which they consider likely to be of interest to the public.

(3) Sub-paragraphs (1) and (2) do not apply if or to the extent that the giving, or (as the case may be) the publication, of reasons would involve disclosure of information in breach of—

(a) a restriction imposed by or under any other enactment; or

(b) an obligation of confidence.

Finance

10 There shall be paid out of money provided by Parliament such sums as are necessary to defray any expenditure of the Commission.

Accounts

11 (1) The Commission shall—

(a) keep proper accounts and proper records in relation to the accounts, and

(b) prepare a statement of accounts in respect of each financial year.

(2) The statement shall comply with any directions that may be given by the Secretary of State as to the information to be contained in such a statement, the manner in which such information is to be presented or the methods and principles according to which such a statement is to be prepared.

(3) Copies of the statement shall be sent to the Secretary of State and the Comptroller and Auditor General within such period after the end of the financial year to which the statement relates as the Secretary of State may direct.

(4) The Comptroller and Auditor General shall examine, certify and report on the statement and shall lay copies of the statement and of his report before Parliament.

(5) The Secretary of State shall not give a direction under this paragraph without the Treasury's approval.

(6) In this paragraph 'financial year' means—

(a) the period beginning with the coming into force of section 3A and ending with the next 31st March, and

(b) each successive period of twelve months ending with 31st March.

Application of seal and evidence

12 The application of the seal of the Commission shall be authenticated by the signature—

(a) of any member of the Commission, or

(b) of any other person who has been authorised by the Commission (whether generally or specially) for that purpose.

13 A document purporting to be duly executed under the seal of the Commission, or to be signed on behalf of the Commission, shall be received in evidence and, unless the contrary is proved, taken to be so executed or signed.

14 Paragraphs 12 and 13 do not extend to Scotland.][1]

---

1 Inserted by the National Lottery Act 1998, s 1, Sch 1, para 7.

2 Substituted by the National Lottery Act 2006, s 1(2).

3 Substituted by the National Lottery Act 2006, s 1(3).

4 Inserted by the National Lottery Act 2006, s 1(4).

7.282

SCHEDULE 3
REVOCATION OF LICENCES
Section 10

PART I
DISCRETIONARY GROUNDS FOR REVOCATION

7.283

1 A condition in the licence has been contravened.

2 Any information given by the licensee to the Director General—

(a) in or in connection with the application for the licence,

(b) in pursuance of a condition in the licence, or

(c) in making representations under section 8(2) or Part II of this Schedule,

was false in a material particular.

3 (1) A proposal for a voluntary arrangement under Part I of the Insolvency Act 1986 or Part II of the Insolvency (Northern Ireland) Order 1989 has been made in relation to the licensee.

(2) A petition . . . [1] for the winding up of the licensee has been presented to the court.

(3) A resolution for the voluntary winding up of the licensee has been passed.

(4) A receiver or manager of the whole or any part of the licensee's property has been appointed.

[(5) An administration application has been made or a notice of intention to appoint an administrator or a notice of an appointment of an administrator under paragraph 14 or 22 of Schedule B1 to the Insolvency Act 1986 (c 45) has been filed.] 2

---

1 Words omitted repealed by SI 2003/2096, art 4, Schedule, Pt 1, para 21(a). In force 15 September 2003 (except in relation to any case where a petition for an administration order was presented before that date).

2 Inserted by SI 2003/2096, art 4, Schedule, Pt 1, para 21(b). In force 15 September 2003 (except in relation to any case where a petition for an administration order was presented before that date).

4 In the case of a licence granted under section 5—

(a) the licensee is not providing or proposing to provide facilities that are necessary or desirable for running the National Lottery;

(b) any person who is managing the business or any part of the business of running the National Lottery under the licence is not a fit and proper person to do so;

(c) any person for whose benefit that business is carried on is not a fit and proper person to benefit from it.

5 In the case of a licence granted under section 6—

(a) the licensee is not taking or proposing to take steps that are necessary or desirable for preventing the commission of fraud by participants in any lottery promoted under the licence;

(b) a person who is managing the business or any part of the business of promoting lotteries under the licence is not a fit and proper person to do so;

(c) a person for whose benefit that business is carried on is not a fit and proper person to benefit from it.

PART II
PROCEDURE AND APPEALS

Notice of proposed revocation

7.284

6 (1) Where the Director General proposes to revoke a licence, he shall serve a notice on the licensee stating—

(a) that he proposes to revoke the licence,

(b) the ground or grounds for revocation,

(c) that the licensee may within the period of twenty-one days beginning with the date of the notice either make written representations about the matter to him or notify him in writing of the licensee's intention to make oral representations, . . . [1]

[(cc) that the right of appeal conferred by paragraph 11 is dependent on the licensee having made such written or oral representations, and][1]

(d) the effect of sub-paragraph (2).

(2) If, within the period mentioned in sub-paragraph (1)(c), the Director General receives neither written representations nor written notification of the licensee's intention to make oral representations, the revocation shall take effect at the end of that period.

Suspension of licence

7 (1) The Director General may suspend a licence as from the date of any notice served in respect of it under paragraph 6 if—

(a) he reasonably believes that the ground or any of the grounds specified in the notice involves fraud by the licensee, or

(b) the ground or one of the grounds specified in the notice is the ground set out in paragraph 5(a).

(2) Where a licence is suspended under this paragraph—

(a) the suspension shall last until the revocation takes effect or the Director General decides not to revoke the licence [or an appeal against the revocation is allowed][2], and

(b) the notice shall inform the licensee accordingly.

Decision by the Director General

8 (1) The Secretary of State may make regulations as to the procedure to be followed where a licensee's intention to make oral representations is notified to the Director General as mentioned in paragraph 6(1)(c).

(2) The regulations may in particular make provision—

(a) for the revocation of the licence to take effect if the licensee fails to comply with any requirements imposed by or under the regulations, and

(b) as to the hearing by the Director General of oral representations.

9 (1) If any written representations against the revocation of a licence are made as mentioned in paragraph 6(1)(c) or any oral representations against the revocation of a licence are made in accordance with regulations under paragraph 8, the Director General shall after taking the representations into account—

(a) decide whether or not to revoke the licence, and

(b) serve a further notice on the licensee informing the licensee of his decision and (if the case so requires) of the effect of sub-paragraph (2).

(2) Where the decision is to revoke the licence, the revocation shall not take effect—

(a) until the end of such period as may be specified in the further notice, or

[(b) if the licensee appeals within that period against the revocation and the court makes an order under paragraph 11(2), until such time as is specified in the order,

whichever is the later.][3]

(3) The period specified in the further notice shall be a period of at least twenty-eight days beginning with the date of that notice.

Appeals to the Secretary of State

10 . . . [4]

[Appeals

11 (1) Where the Director General decides under paragraph 9 to revoke a licence, the licensee may appeal against the decision on the grounds—

(a) that the Director General made an error as to the facts,

(b) that there was a material procedural error, or

(c) that the Director General made some other error of law.

(2) Where a licensee appeals under this paragraph, the powers of the court pending the withdrawal or final disposal of the appeal shall include power, on the application of the licensee or the Director General, to make an order, if the court considers it just and equitable to do so in all the circumstances of the case, preventing the revocation taking effect until such time as may be specified in the order.

(3) An appeal under this paragraph lies to the High Court or, in Scotland, to the Court of Session.

(4) Any appeal under this paragraph to the Court of Session shall be heard in the Outer House.][5]

---

1 Words omitted repealed and para (cc) inserted by the National Lottery Act 1998, s 4(2).

2 Words in square brackets substituted by the NLA 1998, s 4(3).

3 Para (b) substituted by the NLA 1998, s 4(4).

4 Para 10 repealed by the NLA 1998, ss 4(5), 26, Sch 5, Pt II.

5 Para 11 inserted by the NLA 1998, s 4(6).

7.285

[SCHEDULE 3A
JOINT SCHEMES: SUPPLEMENTARY PROVISIONS
Section 25B

Interpretation

1 In this Schedule 'year' means any period of twelve months.

Authorisation or approval by Secretary of State

2 (1) Where the maximum amount of money which could be distributed under section 25(1) under a particular joint scheme in any year exceeds £15 million, the joint scheme shall not have effect unless the Secretary of State makes an order authorising the scheme.

(2) Where the maximum amount of money which could be distributed under section 25(1) under a particular joint scheme in any year does not exceed the amount for the time being specified in sub-paragraph (1), the joint scheme shall not have effect unless the Secretary of State gives his written approval.

(3) In determining for the purposes of this Schedule the maximum amount of money which may be distributed under section 25(1) in any year under a joint scheme, any administrative expenses incurred in distributing such money under the scheme shall be brought into account.

(4) The Secretary of State shall only—

(a) make an order under sub-paragraph (1) authorising a joint scheme, or

(b) give his approval under sub-paragraph (2) to a joint scheme,

on an application made for the purpose by the bodies proposing to participate in the joint scheme.

(5) The Secretary of State may by order amend sub-paragraph (1) so as to increase the amount for the time being specified in that sub-paragraph.

[(6) The Secretary of State's functions under sub-paragraphs (1) and (2) shall, in relation to any particular joint scheme applying—

(a) only in Scotland; or

(b) in one or more parts of the United Kingdom, including Scotland,

be treated as exercisable in or as regards Scotland and may be exercised separately.][1]

---

1 Para 2(6) inserted by the Scotland Act 1998 (Modification of Functions) Order 1999, SI 1999/1756, art 2, Schedule, para 15(12).

Contents of authorisations and approvals

3 An order under paragraph 2(1) or an approval under paragraph 2(2) shall—

(a) contain a brief description of the nature and purposes of the joint scheme,
(b) identify the area within the United Kingdom to which the scheme applies,
(c) specify the maximum amount of money which may be distributed under section 25(1) in any year under the scheme,
(d) identify the bodies participating in the scheme,
(e) state the proportions in which the money to be distributed under section 25(1) under the scheme is attributable to each of those bodies, and
(f) state the duration of the scheme, if its duration is limited.

Effect of increasing annual limit on schemes authorised by order

4 Where—
(a) a joint scheme is authorised by an order under sub-paragraph (1) of paragraph 2, and
(b) that sub-paragraph is amended by an order under sub-paragraph (5) of that paragraph, and
(c) the maximum amount of money which may be distributed under section 25(1) in any year under the scheme does not exceed the amount specified in paragraph 2(1) as so amended,

the scheme shall be treated for the purposes of this Schedule as if the maximum amount of money which may be distributed under section 25(1) in any year under the scheme continued to exceed the amount for the time being specified in paragraph 2(1).

Powers

5 (1) The powers conferred by section 25A may, in particular, be exercised by a body for the purpose of running or otherwise participating in a joint scheme.

(2) The powers conferred on a body by section 25B and this Schedule are in addition to, and shall not derogate from, any powers which the body has apart from that section and this Schedule.

Modification

6 (1) A joint scheme may be modified by the bodies participating in the scheme, but if any such modifications—
(a) in the opinion of the Secretary of State, substantially alter the nature or purposes of the scheme,
(b) alter the area within the United Kingdom to which the scheme applies,
(c) increase the maximum amount of money which may be distributed under section 25(1) in any year under the scheme,
(d) vary the proportions in which the money to be distributed under section 25(1) under the scheme is attributable to each of the bodies participating in the scheme, or
(e) extend the duration of the scheme,

the scheme shall not have effect with those modifications unless the Secretary of State makes an order under paragraph 2(1) or, as the case may require, gives his approval under paragraph 2(2) in relation to the scheme as so modified.

(2) In determining for the purposes of sub-paragraph (1) whether the case requires an order under paragraph 2(1) or approval under paragraph 2(2), paragraph 4 shall be disregarded.

Termination

7 (1) If, in the case of a joint scheme authorised by an order under paragraph 2(1), the Secretary of State revokes the order, the scheme shall terminate on the date on which the revocation takes effect.

(2) If, in the case of a joint scheme approved under paragraph 2(2), the Secretary of State gives notice of withdrawal of his approval to each body participating in the scheme, the scheme shall terminate on the date on which the withdrawal of approval takes effect.

(3) The Secretary of State may terminate a joint scheme in accordance with sub-paragraph (1) or (2)—

(a) of his own motion, or

(b) on the application of one or more of the bodies participating in the scheme.

Orders under s 29(1): participant ceasing to be distributing body

8 (1) This paragraph applies in any case where an order under section 29(1) affects a body which, immediately before the order comes into force, is participating in a joint scheme.

(2) In any such case, the Secretary of State may by order under section 29(1)—

(a) make provision amending the joint scheme, or

(b) revoke the joint scheme.

(3) The provision that may be made by virtue of sub-paragraph (2)(a) includes—

(a) provision varying the bodies participating in the joint scheme;

(b) provision varying the proportions in which the money to be distributed under section 25(1) under the scheme is attributable to each of the bodies participating in the joint scheme; and

(c) provision for all or any of the actual or contingent rights or liabilities of a body which are attributable to the joint scheme to become rights or liabilities of another body participating in the scheme as amended.

(4) No provision shall be made by virtue of sub-paragraph (2)(a) without the written agreement of the bodies which, if the provision were made, would be the participants in the joint scheme as amended.

(5) This paragraph is without prejudice to section 60(5) or paragraph 9.

Authorisation to continue payments despite occurrence of certain events

9 (1) This paragraph applies in any case where—

(a) on an application for a distribution of money under section 25(1), a decision under a joint scheme to make such a distribution has been notified to the applicant, but

(b) an event falling within sub-paragraph (2) ('the relevant event') occurs before the whole of the distribution has been made.

(2) The events which fall within this sub-paragraph are—

(a) that, by virtue of an order under section 29(1), any of the bodies participating in the scheme ceases to be specified in subsection (1), (2), (3) or (4) (as the case may be) of section 23,

(b) that the joint scheme terminates under paragraph 7, or

(c) that the joint scheme is revoked under paragraph 8(2)(b).

(3) Where this paragraph applies, the Secretary of State may authorise any of the bodies which were participating in the joint scheme immediately before the relevant event occurred to continue making distributions of money under section 25(1) in pursuance of the decision mentioned in sub-paragraph (1)(a) as if the relevant event had not occurred.

(4) Where the Secretary of State gives an authorisation under sub-paragraph (3) in relation to any distributions of money under section 25(1), the other provisions of this Act shall have effect in relation to those distributions as if the relevant event had not occurred.

(5) An authorisation under this paragraph accordingly extends to the defrayal of any administrative expenses incurred in making the distributions concerned.

(6) This paragraph is without prejudice to section 60(5) or paragraph 8.

(7) Any authorisation under this paragraph must be in writing.][1]

---

1 Inserted by the National Lottery Act 1998, s 12(3), Sch 3.

* * * * *

7.285.1

[SCHEDULE 4A
THE BIG LOTTERY FUND

PART 1
CONSTITUTION

Membership

1 (1) The Big Lottery Fund shall consist of [between 9 and 12][4] appointed by the [Minister for the Cabinet Office][2].

(2) The [Minister for the Cabinet Office][2] shall appoint one of the members as Chairman.

(3) The [Minister for the Cabinet Office][2] shall ensure that at any time—

(a) one of the members is appointed to represent the interests of England,

(b) one of the members is appointed to represent the interests of Wales,

(c) one of the members is appointed to represent the interests of Scotland, and

(d) one of the members is appointed to represent the interests of Northern Ireland.

(4) In complying with paragraphs (a) to (d) of sub-paragraph (3) the Secretary of State—

(a) may not appoint a member for the purpose of satisfying more than one of those paragraphs,

(b) may appoint the Chairman for the purpose of satisfying one of those paragraphs,

(c) shall obtain the agreement of the National Assembly for Wales before appointing a person to satisfy paragraph (b),

(d) shall obtain the agreement of the Scottish Ministers before appointing a person to satisfy paragraph (c), and

(e) shall obtain the agreement of the Northern Ireland Department of Culture, Arts and Leisure before appointing a person to satisfy paragraph (d).

(5) The [Minister for the Cabinet Office][2] may by order vary the number specified in sub-paragraph (1).

(6) Before making an order under sub-paragraph (5) the [Minister for the Cabinet Office][2] shall consult—

(a) the National Assembly for Wales,

(b) the Scottish Ministers, and

(c) the Northern Ireland Department of Culture, Arts and Leisure.

Tenure

2 A person shall hold and vacate office as Chairman or other member of the Fund in accordance with the terms of his appointment (subject to this Schedule).

3 The Chairman or another member may resign his office by notice in writing to the [Minister for the Cabinet Office][2].

4 (1) The Chairman or another member may be removed from office by the [Minister for the Cabinet Office][2] on the grounds that—

- (a) a bankruptcy order has been made against him, his estate has been sequestrated or he has made a composition or arrangement with, or granted a trust deed for, his creditors, or
- (b) he is, in the opinion of the [Minister for the Cabinet Office][2], unable, unfit or unwilling to discharge the functions of his office.

(2) Before exercising the power under sub-paragraph (1) in respect of a person appointed for the purpose of satisfying paragraph 1(3)(b), (c) or (d) the [Minister for the Cabinet Office][2] shall consult—

- (a) the National Assembly for Wales, in the case of a person appointed for the purpose of satisfying paragraph 1(3)(b),
- (b) the Scottish Ministers, in the case of a person appointed for the purpose of satisfying paragraph 1(3)(c), and
- (c) the Northern Ireland Department of Culture, Arts and Leisure, in the case of a person appointed for the purpose of satisfying paragraph 1(3)(d).

5 A person who ceases, otherwise than by virtue of paragraph 4, to be Chairman or another member may be re-appointed.

Staff

6 The Fund may appoint staff (subject to any directions under section [36E(2)(b)][3])

Committees

7 (1) The Fund shall establish—

- (a) a committee, chaired by the member appointed under paragraph 1(3)(a), for the purpose of exercising the Fund's functions in relation to English devolved expenditure,
- (b) a committee, chaired by the member appointed under paragraph 1(3)(b), for the purpose of exercising the Fund's functions in relation to Welsh devolved expenditure,
- (c) a committee, chaired by the member appointed under paragraph 1(3)(c), for the purpose of exercising the Fund's functions in relation to Scottish devolved expenditure, and
- (d) a committee, chaired by the member appointed under paragraph 1(3)(d), for the purpose of exercising the Fund's functions in relation to Northern Ireland devolved expenditure.

(2) Before appointing the members of a committee established under sub-paragraph (1) the Fund shall obtain the consent of—

- (a) in the case of the committee concerned with England, the [Minister for the Cabinet Office][2];
- (b) in the case of the committee concerned with Wales, the National Assembly for Wales;
- (c) in the case of the committee concerned with Scotland, the Scottish Ministers;
- (d) in the case of the committee concerned with Northern Ireland, the Northern Ireland Department of Culture, Arts and Leisure.

(3) A committee established under sub-paragraph (1) shall carry on its activities under such name as the committee may determine with the consent of the [Minister for the Cabinet Office][2] and—

(a) in the case of the committee concerned with Wales, with the consent of the National Assembly for Wales;

(b) in the case of the committee concerned with Scotland, with the consent of the Scottish Ministers;

(c) in the case of the committee concerned with Northern Ireland, with the consent of the Northern Ireland Department of Culture, Arts and Leisure.

8 Nothing in paragraph 7 or section 25A(6) shall prevent the Fund from—

(a) establishing a committee otherwise than in accordance with that paragraph or section, or

(b) authorising a committee (whether or not established in accordance with that paragraph or section) to exercise a function of the Fund.

9 Section 25A(7) shall apply in relation to any committee of the Fund as it applies in relation to a committee established under section 25A(6).

Status

10 The Fund shall not be regarded as the servant or agent of the Crown or as enjoying any status, immunity or privilege of the Crown.

Supervision

11 In Schedule 2 to the Parliamentary Commissioner Act 1967 (c 13) (departments, &c. subject to investigation) insert at the appropriate place—

"The Big Lottery Fund."

Disqualification

12 In Part III of Schedule 1 to the House of Commons Disqualification Act 1975 (c 24) (other disqualifying offices) insert at the appropriate place—

"Chairman, or member in receipt of remuneration, of the Big Lottery Fund. "

13 In Part III of Schedule 1 to the Northern Ireland Assembly Disqualification Act 1975 (c 25) (other disqualifying offices) insert at the appropriate place—

"Chairman, or member in receipt of remuneration, of the Big Lottery Fund. "

PART 2
PROCEEDINGS

Self-regulation

14 The Fund may, subject to this Schedule, regulate its procedure and the procedure of its committees (and may, in particular, make provision for a quorum).

Records

15 In Schedule 1 to the Public Records Act 1958 (definition of public records) the following entry shall be inserted at the appropriate place in Part II of the Table at the end of paragraph 3—

"The Big Lottery Fund."

Saving

16 The validity of proceedings of the Fund or a committee shall not be affected by—

(a) a vacancy among its members, or

(b) a defect in the appointment of a person as Chairman or member.

PART 3
MONEY

Remuneration, &c

17 (1) The Fund may pay to the Chairman, another member or a member of a committee—

(a) such remuneration as the [Minister for the Cabinet Office][2] may determine, and

(b) such travelling and other allowances as the [Minister for the Cabinet Office][2] may determine.

(2) The Fund may pay to or in respect of the Chairman or another member such sums as the [Minister for the Cabinet Office][2] may determine by way of, or in respect of, pensions, allowances or gratuities.

(3) If the [Minister for the Cabinet Office][2] thinks that there are special circumstances that make it right for a person ceasing to hold office as Chairman or member to receive compensation, the Fund may pay him such compensation as the [Minister for the Cabinet Office][2] may determine.

18 (1) The Fund may (subject to any directions under section [36E(2)(b)][3]) pay sums to or in respect of a member or former member of staff by way of or in respect of—

(a) remuneration,

(b) allowances,

(c) pensions,

(d) gratuities, or

(e) compensation for loss of employment.

(2) In Schedule 1 to the Superannuation Act 1972 (c 11) (employment to which superannuation schemes may extend) in the list of other bodies insert at the appropriate place—

"The Big Lottery Fund."

Payments

19 The Fund may make payments in respect of expenditure (which may include expenditure of a capital nature) of—

(a) the Fund, or

(b) a person to whom it delegates a function under section 25A(1).

Investment

20 (1) The Fund may deposit money in an interest-bearing account (but may not otherwise invest).

(2) The proceeds of money received by the Fund and invested under sub-paragraph (1) shall be treated for the purposes of Part II of this Act as part of that money.

Accounts

21 (1) The Fund shall—

(a) keep proper accounting records, and

(b) prepare a statement of accounts in respect of each financial year.

(2) The Fund shall send a copy of a statement under sub-paragraph (1)(b)—

(a) to the [Minister for the Cabinet Office][2],

(b) to the National Assembly for Wales,
(c) to the Scottish Ministers,
(d) to the Northern Ireland Department of Culture, Arts and Leisure, and
(e) to the Comptroller and Auditor General.

(3) A copy of a statement must be sent under sub-paragraph (2) within such period, beginning with the end of the financial year to which the statement relates, as the [Minister for the Cabinet Office][2] may, with the consent of the Treasury, direct.

(4) The Comptroller and Auditor General shall—
(a) examine, certify and report on a statement received under this paragraph, and
(b) lay a copy of the statement and his report before Parliament."][1]

---

1 Inserted by the National Lottery Act 2006, s 14(2), Sch 2.

2 Words "Minister for the Cabinet Office" in square brackets substituted by SI 2011/739, arts 2(1)(e), 4, Schedule, paras 1, 9(1), (2); for supplementary provision see art 3 thereof. Date in force: 13 April 2011: see SI 2011/739, art 1.

3 Reference to "36E(2)(b)" in square brackets substituted by SI 2011/739, art 4, Schedule, paras 1, 9(1), (3). Date in force: 13 April 2011: see SI 2011/739, art 1.

4 Para 1: in sub-para (1) words "between 9 and 12" in square brackets substituted by SI 2011/2385, art 2. Date in force: 2 November 2011: see SI 2011/2385, art 1.

7.286

SCHEDULE 5

. . .[1]

---

1 Repealed by the National Lottery Act 1998, ss 19(9)(a), 21 Sch 3.

7.287

SCHEDULE 6

. . .[1]

---

1 Repealed by the National Lottery Act 1998, ss 19(9)(b), 21, Sch 3.

7.288

[SCHEDULE 6A

. . .[1]

---

1 Repealed by the National Lottery Act 1998, ss 19(9)(c), 21, Sch 3.

SCHEDULE 7
REGISTRATION OF SOCIETIES
Section 48

[*The amendments made by this Schedule to the Lotteries and Amusements Act 1976, Sch 1, have been incorporated into the text of that Act. Schedule repealed by the Gambling Act 2005, s 356(4), Sch 17 from 1 September 2007: see SI 2006/3272, art 2(4); for transitional provisions see art 6, Sch 4 thereto.*]

SCHEDULE 8
Section 49
[*The amendments made by this Schedule to the Lotteries and Amusement Act 1976, Sch 2, have been incorporated into the text of that Act. Schedule repealed by the Gambling Act 2005, s 356(4), Sch 17 from 1 September 2007: see SI 2006/3272, art 2(4); for transitional provisions see art 6, Sch 4 thereto.*]
SCHEDULE 9
Section 50
[*This Schedule inserts the Lotteries and Amusements Act 1976, Sch 2A, which insertion has been incorporated into the text of that Act*). *Schedule repealed by the Gambling Act 2005, s 356(4), Sch 17 from 1 September 2007: see SI 2006/3272, art 2(4); for transitional provisions see art 6, Sch 4 thereto.*]
7.289

SCHEDULE 10
REPEALS
Section 64

Chapter	Short title	Extent of repeal
61 & 62 Vict c 46	The Revenue Act 1898	Section 1 so far as it applies in the British Islands outside the United Kingdom and section 6(2).
* * * * *		
1980 c 17	The National Heritage Act 1980	In section 3(6)(d), the words from 'acting' to '1979'.

NATIONAL LOTTERY ACT 1998

(1998 c 22)

Arrangement of sections

PART I
PROVISIONS RELATING TO THE NATIONAL LOTTERY

An Act to make further provision in relation to the National Lottery; to make provision for and in connection with the establishment of a body corporate to be endowed out of the National Lottery Distribution Fund and to be known as the National Endowment for Science, Technology and the Arts; and for connected purposes.

[2nd July 1998]

PART I
PROVISIONS RELATING TO THE NATIONAL LOTTERY

The Director General and the National Lottery Commission

7.290 1 Replacement of Director General by National Lottery Commission

(1) There shall cease to be an office of Director General of the National Lottery.

(2) In consequence of subsection (1) above, in the National Lottery etc Act 1993 (in this Act referred to as 'the 1993 Act') section 3 and Schedule 2 (which relate to the Director General of the National Lottery) shall cease to have effect.

(3) After section 3 of the 1993 Act there shall be inserted—

'3A The National Lottery Commission

(1) There shall be a body corporate known as the National Lottery Commission.

(2) Schedule 2A makes provision in relation to the Commission.'

(4) On the day on which this subsection comes into force under section 27(3) below, the functions conferred or imposed on the Director General of the National Lottery by or under the 1993 Act (including any functions so conferred or imposed by virtue of this Act) shall, by virtue of this subsection, be transferred to the National Lottery Commission.

(5) Schedule 1 to this Act (which makes provision supplemental to, or consequential on, this section) shall have effect.

Licensees

7.291 2 Financial penalties for breach of conditions in licences

(1) After section 10 of the 1993 Act (revocation of licences) there shall be inserted—

'10A Financial penalties for breach of conditions in licences

(1) If the Director General is satisfied that a person has contravened a condition in a licence under section 5 or 6, he may impose a financial penalty on that person in respect of the contravention.

(2) The matters to which the Director General may have regard in imposing a financial penalty include the desirability of both—

(a) deterring persons from contravening conditions in licences under section 5 or 6, and

(b) recovering any diminution in the sums paid to the Secretary of State under section 5(6) which is attributable to the contravention.

(3) If the Director General proposes to impose a financial penalty on a person, he shall serve on that person a notice—

(a) stating that the person has contravened conditions in the licence,

(b) identifying the contraventions in question,

(c) stating that the Director General proposes to impose a financial penalty,

(d) specifying the amount of the financial penalty,

(e) stating the Director General's reasons—

(i) for the imposition of a financial penalty, and

(ii) for the amount of the financial penalty,

(f) stating the person to whom the financial penalty is to be paid and the manner in which, and place at which, payment may be made, and

(g) stating the effect of subsections (5) and (12).

(4) A notice under subsection (3) must state that the person may, within the period of 21 days beginning with the date of the notice, either—

(a) make written representations about the matter to the Director General, or

(b) notify the Director General in writing of the person's intention to make oral representations,

and that the right of appeal conferred by section 10B is dependent on the person having made such written or oral representations.

(5) If, within the period mentioned in subsection (4), the Director General receives neither—

(a) written representations, nor

(b) written notification of the person's intention to make oral representations,

the financial penalty shall become payable at the end of that period.

(6) The Secretary of State may make regulations as to the procedure to be followed where a person's intention to make oral representations is notified to the Director General as mentioned in subsection (4).

(7) The regulations may in particular make provision—

(a) for the financial penalty to become payable if the person fails to comply with any requirements imposed by or under the regulations, and

(b) as to the hearing by the Director General of oral representations.

(8) If—

(a) any written representations against the imposition of the financial penalty are made as mentioned in subsection (4), or

(b) any oral representations against the imposition of the financial penalty are made in accordance with regulations under subsection (6),

subsection (9) shall apply.

(9) Where this subsection applies, the Director General shall after taking the representations into account—

(a) decide whether or not to impose a financial penalty, and

(b) serve a further notice on the person informing the person of the decision.

(10) Where the decision is to impose a financial penalty, the further notice must—

(a) identify the contraventions in question,

(b) specify the amount of the financial penalty imposed,

(c) state the Director General's reasons—

(i) for the imposition of a financial penalty, and

(ii) for the amount of the financial penalty,

(d) state the person to whom the financial penalty is to be paid and the manner in which, and place at which, payment may be made, and

(e) state the effect of subsections (11) and (12).

(11) A financial penalty imposed by virtue of a decision under subsection (9) becomes payable on the date of the further notice.

(12) A person on whom a financial penalty is imposed is required to pay the penalty within the period of fourteen days beginning with the date on which the financial penalty becomes payable.

(13) If the whole or any part of a financial penalty is not paid within the period mentioned in subsection (12), then as from the end of that period the unpaid balance from time to time shall carry interest at the rate for the time being specified in section 17 of the Judgments Act 1838.

(14) A financial penalty imposed on any person, and any interest accrued under subsection (13) in respect of the penalty, shall be recoverable from that person as a debt due to the Secretary of State from that person (and the person's liability to pay it shall not be affected by the person's licence ceasing for any reason to have effect).'

(2) In section 11 of the 1993 Act (directions to the Director General in respect of his functions under sections 5 to 10) for 'sections 5 to 10' there shall be substituted 'sections 5 to 10A'.

(3) In section 21 of the 1993 Act, in subsection (2) (Secretary of State to pay into the National Lottery Distribution Fund all the sums paid to him by virtue of section 5(6)) after 'section 5(6)' there shall be inserted 'or 10A'.

(4) . . .[1]

(5) Subsection (1) above has effect in relation to any contravention, after the coming into force of that subsection, of a condition in a licence under section 5 or 6 of the 1993 Act, whenever granted.

---

1 Sub-s (4): repealed by the National Lottery Act 1998, s 26, Sch 5, Pt I.

7.292 3 Appeals against financial penalties

After section 10A of the 1993 Act (financial penalties for breach of conditions of licences) there shall be inserted—

'10B Appeals against financial penalties

(1) Where the Director General decides under subsection (9) of section 10A to impose a financial penalty on a person, the person may appeal against the decision on the grounds specified in subsection (2) or, as the case may be, subsection (3).

(2) To the extent that an appeal under this section is against a finding by the Director General that a person contravened a condition of a licence, the grounds for the appeal are—

(a) that the Director General made an error as to the facts,
(b) that there was a material procedural error, or
(c) that the Director General made some other error of law.

(3) To the extent that an appeal under this section is against the amount of a financial penalty, the grounds for the appeal are—

(a) that the amount of the penalty is unreasonable,
(b) that there was a material procedural error, or
(c) that the decision was based on a manifest material misapprehension as to the facts.

(4) Where on an appeal under this section a court reduces the amount of a financial penalty, the powers of the court shall include power to make such orders as to interest on the penalty as the court considers just and equitable in all the circumstances of the case.

(5) The power conferred by subsection (4) includes power to make orders as to—

(a) the rates of interest which are to apply, and
(b) the date from which interest is to run.

(6) An appeal under this section lies to the High Court or, in Scotland, to the Court of Session.

(7) Any appeal under this section to the Court of Session shall be heard in the Outer House.'

7.293 4 Appeals against revocation of licences

(1) Part II of Schedule 3 to the 1993 Act (which relates to procedure and appeals in connection with the revocation, under section 10, of licences under section 5 or 6) shall be amended as follows.

(2) In paragraph 6(1) (which specifies what a notice of proposed revocation must state) the word 'and' at the end of paragraph (c) shall be omitted and after that paragraph there shall be inserted—

'(cc) that the right of appeal conferred by paragraph 11 is dependent on the licensee having made such written or oral representations, and'.

(3) In paragraph 7(2)(a) (duration of suspension of licence) for 'or the Secretary of State allows an appeal against the revocation' there shall be substituted 'or an appeal against the revocation is allowed'.

(4) In paragraph 9(2) (time at which revocation takes effect) for paragraph (b) (determination of appeal to Secretary of State) there shall be substituted—

'(b) if the licensee appeals within that period against the revocation and the court makes an order under paragraph 11(2), until such time as is specified in the order,

whichever is the later.'

(5) Paragraph 10 (appeals to the Secretary of State) shall cease to have effect.

(6) After paragraph 10 there shall be inserted—

'*Appeals*

11

(1) Where the Director General decides under paragraph 9 to revoke a licence, the licensee may appeal against the decision on the grounds—

(a) that the Director General made an error as to the facts,
(b) that there was a material procedural error, or
(c) that the Director General made some other error of law.

(2) Where a licensee appeals under this paragraph, the powers of the court pending the withdrawal or final disposal of the appeal shall include power, on the application of the licensee or the Director General, to make an order, if the court

considers it just and equitable to do so in all the circumstances of the case, preventing the revocation taking effect until such time as may be specified in the order.

(3) An appeal under this paragraph lies to the High Court or, in Scotland, to the Court of Session.

(4) Any appeal under this paragraph to the Court of Session shall be heard in the Outer House.'

7.294 5 Access by Comptroller and Auditor General to documents etc

(1) Section 33 of the 1993 Act (accounts of Secretary of State and National Debt Commissioners) shall be amended as follows.

(2) After subsection (3) there shall be inserted—

'(4) For the purpose of exercising his examination function in relation to any accounts prepared under subsection (1), the Comptroller and Auditor General—

(a) shall have a right of access at all reasonable times to any documents which he reasonably requires which are in the custody or under the control of any section 5 licensee; and

(b) shall have a right to require from any officer or employee of any section 5 licensee, or from the auditors of any section 5 licensee, an explanation of, or information relating to, any such documents;

but a section 5 licensee shall not, by virtue only of this subsection, be a body to which section 6 of the National Audit Act 1983 applies.

(5) For the purpose of—

(a) exercising his examination function in relation to any accounts prepared under subsection (1), or

(b) deciding whether, or to what extent, to exercise any right conferred by subsection (4),

the Comptroller and Auditor General shall have regard to any information which the Director General has obtained from any section 5 licensee and which is relevant to the exercise of that function.

(6) Where, in exercising his examination function in relation to any accounts prepared under subsection (1), the Comptroller and Auditor General obtains any information which gives him grounds to believe that a section 5 licensee has, or may have, contravened any of the conditions of its licence under section 5, the Comptroller and Auditor General shall as soon as practicable disclose that information to the Director General.

(7) A section 5 licensee shall be under a duty—

(a) to permit the Comptroller and Auditor General to exercise the right conferred by subsection (4)(a); and

(b) to do all that may be reasonably practicable to secure that any person who under subsection (4)(b) is required to provide an explanation of, or information relating to, any document complies with that requirement;

and any breach of that duty shall be actionable at the suit of the Comptroller and Auditor General.

(8) The right of access to documents conferred by subsection (4)(a) includes a right to take copies of or make extracts from documents.

(9) In this section any reference to documents includes a reference to information held by means of a computer or in any other electronic form; and in the case of information so held the right of access conferred by subsection (4)(a) includes a right of access to, and to take copies of, that information in a visible and legible form.

(10) In this section—

'examination function', in relation to the Comptroller and Auditor General, means his function under subsection (3);

'section 5 licensee' means a body which holds or has held a licence under section 5.'

(3) This section has effect in relation to accounts prepared under section 33(1) of the 1993 Act so far as they relate to periods beginning on or after 1st April 1999.

The new good cause

7.295 6 The new good cause and the re-allocation of lottery money

(1) Section 22 of the 1993 Act (apportionment of money in Distribution Fund) shall be amended in accordance with subsections (2) to (6) below.

(2) After subsection (3)(e) (20 per cent of balance of sums paid into National Lottery Distribution Fund to be allocated for expenditure on projects to mark the year 2000 and the beginning of the third millennium) there shall be inserted—

'and

(f) 13 ⅓ per cent shall be allocated for expenditure on or connected with health, education or the environment.'

(3) In subsection (3)(a) (20 per cent to be allocated for expenditure on or connected with the arts) for '20 per cent' there shall be substituted '16 ⅔ per cent'.

(4) In subsection (3)(b) (20 per cent to be allocated for expenditure on or connected with sport) for '20 per cent' there shall be substituted '16 ⅔ per cent'.

(5) In subsection (3)(c) (20 per cent to be allocated for expenditure on or connected with the national heritage) for '20 per cent' there shall be substituted '16 ⅔ per cent'.

(6) In subsection (3)(d) (20 per cent to be allocated for charitable expenditure) for '20 per cent' there shall be substituted '16 ⅔ per cent'.

(7) In section 30 of the 1993 Act (winding up of fund allocated under section 22(3)(e)) in subsection (1)(b) (substitution of higher percentages for the percentages which on 31st December 2000 are specified in section 22(3)(a) to (d)) after '(a) to (d)' there shall be inserted 'and (f)'.

(8) In subsection (1) of section 44 of the 1993 Act (interpretation of Part II) after the definition of 'the Distribution Fund' there shall be inserted—

"education' includes training and the provision of activities for children;

'the environment' includes the living and social environment;'.

(9) This section shall apply in relation to sums paid into the National Lottery Distribution Fund under section 21(2) of the 1993 Act on or after 14th October 1997.

(10) The Secretary of State shall make such re-allocations of—

(a) the money held in the National Lottery Distribution Fund at the commencement of this section,

(b) the money invested by the National Debt Commissioners under section 32 of the 1993 Act as at the commencement of this section, and

(c) the proceeds (as defined in section 32(4) of the 1993 Act) of the money mentioned in paragraph (b) above,

as are designed by the Secretary of State to give effect to the provisions of this section.

7.296 7 The New Opportunities Fund

(1) In section 23 of the 1993 Act (the distributing bodies) after subsection (5) there shall be inserted—

'(6) So much of any sum paid into the Distribution Fund as is allocated for expenditure on or connected with health, education or the environment shall be held in the Distribution Fund for distribution by the New Opportunities Fund (established under section 43A).'

(2) After section 43 of the 1993 Act there shall be inserted—

'The New Opportunities Fund

43A The New Opportunities Fund

(1) There shall be a body corporate known as the New Opportunities Fund.

(2) Schedule 6A makes provision in relation to the New Opportunities Fund.

43B Functions of the New Opportunities Fund

(1) The New Opportunities Fund—

(a) may make grants out of any money they receive to fund or assist in the funding of projects, or

(b) may make or enter into arrangements,

which are designed to give effect to such initiatives concerned or connected with health, education or the environment as may from time to time be specified in an order made by the Secretary of State.

(2) In making a grant under this section, the New Opportunities Fund may impose such conditions as they think fit, including conditions requiring the amount of a grant to be repaid forthwith on breach of any condition.

(3) The New Opportunities Fund may do anything that they consider desirable for enabling them to determine—

(a) the projects in respect of which grants under this section are to be made; or

(b) the arrangements which are to be made or entered into under this section.

(4) The New Opportunities Fund may for the purpose of enabling them to exercise their functions acquire and dispose of land.

43C Provisions supplemental to section 43B

(1) In exercising their functions under section 43B the New Opportunities Fund shall comply with any directions given to them by the Secretary of State.

(2) The Secretary of State shall consult the New Opportunities Fund before giving any directions to them under this section.

(3) An initiative may be so framed that it applies—

(a) throughout the whole of the United Kingdom; or

(b) in one or more areas of the United Kingdom.

(4) Before making an order under section 43B in respect of a particular initiative the Secretary of State shall consult such persons as appear to him to be appropriate.

(5) Before revoking an order under section 43B the Secretary of State shall consult the New Opportunities Fund.

(6) Any reference in this section to an initiative is a reference to an initiative specified in an order made under section 43B.

(7) The report for any financial year of the New Opportunities Fund under section 34 shall set out any directions given to the Fund under this section that had effect during that year.

43D Accounts

(1) The New Opportunities Fund shall—

(a) keep proper accounts and proper records in relation to the accounts, and

(b) prepare a statement of accounts in respect of each financial year.

(2) The statement shall comply with any directions that may be given by the Secretary of State as to the information to be contained in such a statement, the manner in which such information is to be presented or the methods and principles according to which such a statement is to be prepared.

(3) Copies of the statement shall be sent to the Secretary of State and the Comptroller and Auditor General within such period after the end of the financial year to which the statement relates as the Secretary of State may direct.

(4) The Comptroller and Auditor General shall examine, certify and report on the statement and shall lay copies of the statement and of his report before Parliament.

(5) The Secretary of State shall not give a direction under this section without the Treasury's approval.'

(3) After Schedule 6 to the 1993 Act there shall be inserted the Schedule 6A set out in Schedule 2 to this Act.

7.297 8 Provisions supplemental to section 7

(1) In section 35 of the 1993 Act (accounts of certain distributing bodies) in subsection (7) (section not to apply to the National Lottery Charities Board or to the Millennium Commission) for 'or to the Millennium Commission' there shall be substituted ', the Millennium Commission or the New Opportunities Fund'.

(2) In section 44 of the 1993 Act (interpretation of Part II) after subsection (2) there shall be inserted—

'(3) A project or arrangement shall be regarded for the purposes of this Part as concerned or connected with health, education or the environment notwithstanding that it contains incidental provision—

(a) which is not concerned or connected with any of those matters; but
(b) which is necessary or expedient for the purposes of the project or arrangement.'

(3) In the House of Commons Disqualification Act 1975, in Part III of Schedule 1 (other disqualifying offices) the following entry shall be inserted at the appropriate place—

'Chairman of the New Opportunities Fund and, if in receipt of remuneration, any other member of that Fund;'.

(4) The same entry as is set out in subsection (3) above shall be inserted at the appropriate place in Part III of Schedule 1 to the Northern Ireland Assembly Disqualification Act 1975.

(5) Any consultation undertaken before the commencement of section 7 above in connection with an initiative proposed to be specified in an order made under section 43B of the 1993 Act shall be as effective, in relation to that initiative, as if section 7 above had been in force at the time the consultation was undertaken.

(6) Where any consultation has been undertaken before the commencement of section 7 above in connection with one or more initiatives proposed to be specified in an order made under section 43B of the 1993 Act, a statutory instrument containing an order under section 43B of that Act which specifies only that or those initiatives shall, notwithstanding the provisions of section 60(2) of the 1993 Act, be subject to annulment in pursuance of a resolution of either House of Parliament.

(7) The payments which may be made under section 31 of the 1993 Act (payments from Distribution Fund into Consolidated Fund in respect of expenses) shall include a payment of such amount as the Secretary of State with the approval of the Treasury determines to be appropriate for defraying expenses incurred by the Secretary of State before the commencement of section 7 above for the purpose of facilitating the establishment of the New Opportunities Fund.

Distributing bodies

7.298 9 Manner of distribution

(1) In section 25 of the 1993 Act (application of money by Manner of distributing bodies) after subsection (1) there shall be inserted—

'(1A) The manner in which a body may distribute any money paid to it under section 24 includes making or entering into arrangements for or in connection with meeting expenditure (including arrangements with respect to vouchers); and this subsection shall apply notwithstanding anything to the contrary in any enactment or instrument relating to the functions of the body.'

(2) In section 44 of the 1993 Act (interpretation of Part II) after subsection (3) (which is inserted by section 8 above) there shall be inserted—

'(4) Any reference in this Part to the distribution of money shall be construed as including the making or entering into of arrangements in accordance with section 25(1A) or 43B; and related expressions used in this Part shall be construed accordingly.'

7.299 10 Power of distributing bodies to solicit applications

In section 25 of the 1993 Act (application of money by distributing bodies) after subsection (2) there shall be inserted—

'(2A) A body which distributes money under subsection (1) shall have power to solicit applications from other bodies or persons for any of the money which the body so distributes, notwithstanding anything to the contrary in any enactment or instrument relating to the functions of the body.

(2B) In determining whether a decision of a body concerning its distribution of money under subsection (1) was unlawful, it shall be immaterial whether or not the body, or any person acting on behalf of the body, solicited an application from a body or person for such money.'

7.300 11 Delegation by distributing bodies of their powers of distribution

(1) After section 25 of the 1993 Act there shall be inserted—

'25A Delegation by distributing bodies of their powers of distribution

(1) A body which distributes money under subsection (1) of section 25 may appoint any other body or person to exercise on its behalf any of its functions relating to, or connected with, the distribution of money under that subsection (including its function of making decisions as to the persons to whom such distributions are to be made)—

(a) in any particular case, or

(b) in cases of any particular description.

(2) The persons who may be appointed by a body under subsection (1) include a member, employee or committee of the body itself.

(3) A body which makes an appointment under subsection (1) may defray out of any money paid to it under section 24 any expenses incurred by the appointee in consequence of the appointment.

(4) Power to accept any such appointment as is mentioned in subsection (1) is conferred by this subsection on the following bodies—

(a) any body which distributes money under section 25(1),

(b) any charity or any charitable, benevolent or philanthropic institution,

(c) any body established by or under an enactment, and

(d) any body established by Royal Charter.

(5) A body appointed by virtue of subsection (1) to exercise a function on behalf of another may itself appoint any of its members or employees, or a committee, to exercise the function in its stead, but only if—

(a) the terms of the body's appointment by virtue of subsection (1) so permit, and

(b) the body has power apart from this section to appoint a member or, as the case may be, an employee or committee of the body to exercise some or all of its functions.

(6) Subject to the following provisions of this section—
(a) a body which distributes money under section 25(1) may establish a committee for the purpose of exercising on behalf of the body any such function as is mentioned in subsection (1), and
(b) a body falling within any paragraph of subsection (4) may establish a committee for the purpose of exercising on behalf of any body which distributes money under section 25(1) any such function as is mentioned in subsection (1).

(7) A committee established under subsection (6)—
(a) must consist of or include one or more members, or one or more employees, of the body establishing the committee, but
(b) may include persons who are neither members nor employees of that body.

(8) Any power conferred on a body by subsections (1) to (7) is so conferred—
(a) to the extent that the body would not have the power apart from this section, and
(b) notwithstanding anything to the contrary in any enactment or instrument relating to the functions of the body.

(9) In this section—

'charity' means a body, or the trustees of a trust, established for charitable purposes only;

'charitable, benevolent or philanthropic institution' means a body, or the trustees of a trust, which is established for charitable purposes (whether or not those purposes are charitable within the meaning of any rule of law), benevolent purposes or philanthropic purposes, and which is not a charity.

(10) For the purposes of this section—
(a) the trustees of a trust shall be regarded as a body, and
(b) any reference to a member of a body shall, in the case of a body of trustees, be taken as a reference to any of the trustees,

and references to a committee shall be construed accordingly.

(11) Any reference in this section to a member of a body includes a reference to the chairman or deputy chairman of (or the holder of any corresponding office in relation to) the body.'

(2) In section 26 of the 1993 Act (directions to distributing bodies) after subsection (3) there shall be inserted—

'(3A) In exercising any power under section 25A, a body which distributes money under section 25(1) shall comply with any directions given to it by the Secretary of State.'

(3) In subsection (4) of that section, after 'Directions under subsection (3)' there shall be inserted 'or (3A)'.

(4) After subsection (4) of that section there shall be inserted—

'(4A) Directions under subsection (3A) may in particular—
(a) impose limits on the amount of money which may be distributed by a body under section 25(1) by virtue of decisions made on its behalf by bodies or persons not falling within section 25A(2), and
(b) require a body, before appointing any body or person not falling within section 25A(2) to exercise on its behalf any function of making decisions concerning the distribution of money under section 25(1), to obtain the approval of the Secretary of State to its plans for making such appointments.'

(5) In Schedule 5 to the 1993 Act (the National Lottery Charities Board) in paragraph 2 (committees) sub-paragraphs (4) to (6) (which are superseded by amendments made by this section) shall cease to have effect, and after sub-paragraph (6) there shall be inserted—

'(7) Subsection (7) of section 25A shall apply in relation to any committee of the Charities Board as it applies in relation to a committee appointed under subsection (6) of that section.'

(6) In paragraph 3 of that Schedule (tenure of office) in sub-paragraph (4)(a) (removal on grounds of absence from meetings) for 'or (as the case may be) from meetings of the committee without the committee's consent' there shall be substituted 'or from meetings of a committee of the Board without the committee's consent'.

7.301 12 Joint schemes for distribution of money by distributing bodies

(1) After section 25A of the 1993 Act there shall be inserted—

'25B Joint schemes for distribution of money by distributing bodies

(1) A body which distributes money under subsection (1) of section 25 may, in accordance with the following provisions of this section, participate with one or more other such bodies in a joint scheme for the distribution of money under that subsection.

(2) A body may participate in a joint scheme if the principal purposes of the joint scheme include purposes for which the body has power to distribute money under subsection (1) of section 25, notwithstanding that the body would not, apart from this section, have power to distribute money under that subsection for meeting expenditure on some of the particular projects for which money may be distributed under the scheme.

(3) Money shall not, under a joint scheme, be distributed for meeting expenditure on any particular project unless the expenditure is such that—

(a) at least one of the bodies participating in the joint scheme has power, acting alone, to distribute money under section 25(1) for meeting the expenditure, or

(b) two or more of the bodies participating in the joint scheme, taken together, have power between them to distribute money under section 25(1) for meeting the expenditure.

(4) Nothing in subsection (3) affects the liability of each body participating in a scheme in relation to the distribution of any money under section 25(1) under the scheme.

(5) Schedule 3A contains supplementary provision in relation to joint schemes.'

(2) In section 44 of the 1993 Act (interpretation of Part II) the following definition shall be inserted at the appropriate place in subsection (1)—

'"joint scheme" means a joint scheme under section 25B;'.

(3) After Schedule 3 to the 1993 Act there shall be inserted the Schedule 3A set out in Schedule 3 to this Act.

7.302 13 Strategic plans for distributing bodies

After section 25B of the 1993 Act there shall be inserted—

'25C Strategic plans for distributing bodies

(1) If the Secretary of State instructs it do so, a body which distributes money under section 25(1) shall, in accordance with the following provisions of this section,—

(a) prepare and adopt a strategic plan, or

(b) review and modify any strategic plan which it has adopted, or

(c) replace any strategic plan which it has adopted by preparing and adopting another.

(2) In this section 'strategic plan', in the case of any body, means a statement containing the body's policies for the distribution of the money likely to be available to it for distribution under section 25(1).

(3) A strategic plan must also contain—

(a) a statement of any directions given to the body by the Secretary of State under section 26(1) or 43C (1),

(b) a statement of the estimate given to the body by the Secretary of State of the money likely to be available for distribution by the body under section 25(1),

(c) a statement of the body's assessment of the needs which the body has power to deal with, in whole or in part, by distributing money under section 25(1), and

(d) a statement of the body's priorities in dealing with those needs by the distribution of money under section 25(1).

(4) A strategic plan must be such as to demonstrate how the body is taking into account or, as the case may be, complying with the directions mentioned in subsection (3)(a).

(5) Before adopting a strategic plan, a body shall—

(a) consult such other bodies as it thinks fit for the purpose of identifying the needs mentioned in subsection (3)(c) and formulating the policies to be adopted for dealing with those needs,

(b) prepare a draft of the proposed plan,

(c) send a copy of the draft to the Secretary of State, and

(d) after consultation with the Secretary of State, make such modifications to the draft as it considers necessary or expedient.

(6) Where a body adopts a strategic plan—

(a) the body shall send copies of the document containing the plan to the Secretary of State, and

(b) the Secretary of State shall lay a copy of the document before each House of Parliament.

(7) Nothing in this section applies in relation to any body which distributes under section 25(1) money allocated under section 22(3)(e).'

7.303 14 The National Lottery Charities Board

(1) In section 38 of the 1993 Act (grants to charities etc by the National Lottery Charities Board) after subsection (2) there shall be inserted—

'(3) The Charities Board may for the purpose of enabling them to exercise their functions acquire and dispose of land.'

(2) Paragraph 4 of Schedule 5 to the 1993 Act (remuneration and allowances etc of members of the Board) shall be amended in accordance with subsections (3) to (6) below.

(3) In sub-paragraph (1)(a) (which permits the payment of remuneration to the chairman of the Board and the chairman of any committee of the Board) for 'the chairman of any committee of theirs' there shall be substituted 'any other member of the Board'.

(4) In sub-paragraph (2) (which permits provision to be made in respect of pensions for the chairman of the Board or the chairman of any committee of the Board) for 'or chairman of a committee of the Charities Board,' there shall be substituted ', or in the case of any other member of the Charities Board,'.

(5) In sub-paragraph (3) (which permits the payment of compensation for loss of office to the chairman of the Board or the chairman of any committee of the Board) for 'or of a committee of the Charities Board' there shall be substituted ', or ceasing to be a member of the Charities Board,'.

(6) Sub-paragraph (4) (approval of Treasury required) shall cease to have effect.

(7) Paragraph 5 of that Schedule (staff of the Board) shall be amended in accordance with subsections (8) to (10) below.

(8) For sub-paragraph (1) (Board may appoint such staff as they may determine with the Secretary of State's approval as to numbers and terms and conditions of service) there shall be substituted—

'(1) Subject to any directions under section 26(3), the Charities Board may appoint such staff as they think fit, on such terms and conditions of service as they think fit.'

(9) In sub-paragraph (2) (provision may be made in relation to pensions etc with the Secretary of State's approval)—

(a) at the beginning there shall be inserted 'Subject to any directions under section 26(3),'; and

(b) the words 'with the Secretary of State's approval' shall cease to have effect.

(10) Sub-paragraph (4) (consent of Treasury required) shall cease to have effect.

(11) In Schedule 1 to the Public Records Act 1958 (definition of public records) the following entry shall be inserted at the appropriate place in Part II of the Table at the end of paragraph 3—

'National Lottery Charities Board.'

(12) In the entry relating to the National Lottery Charities Board—

(a) in Part III of Schedule 1 to the House of Commons Disqualification Act 1975 (other disqualifying offices), and

(b) in Part III of Schedule 1 to the Northern Ireland Assembly Disqualification Act 1975 (other disqualifying offices),

for 'and any chairman of a committee of that Board' there shall be substituted 'and, if in receipt of remuneration, any other member of that Board'.

Supplemental provision

7.304 15 Orders and regulations

(1) Section 60 of the 1993 Act (orders and regulations) shall be amended as follows.

(2) In subsection (2) (affirmative procedure for orders under specified provisions) for 'section 28 or 30' there shall be substituted the following paragraphs—

'(a) section 28, 30 or 43B, or

(b) paragraph 2(5) of Schedule 3A,'.

(3) After subsection (2) there shall be inserted—

'(2A) Subsection (2) does not apply to an order which contains only provision revoking an order under section 43B.'

(4) In subsection (3) (negative procedure for statutory instruments containing orders and regulations other than orders under specified provisions) for 'an order under section 28, 30 or 65' there shall be substituted the following paragraphs—

'(a) an order to which subsection (2) applies, or

(b) an order under section 65,'.

(5) After subsection (3) there shall be inserted—

'(3A) Subsection (3) does not apply to a statutory instrument which contains only provision revoking an order under paragraph 2(1) of Schedule 3A.

(3B) A statutory instrument which contains only provision revoking an order under paragraph 2(1) of Schedule 3A shall be laid before each House of Parliament.'

(6) After subsection (5) there shall be inserted—

'(6) Any reference in this section to an order is a reference to an order of the Secretary of State.'

PART III
SUPPLEMENTAL PROVISIONS

7.305 26 Repeals

The enactments mentioned in Schedule 5 to this Act are hereby repealed to the extent specified in the third column of that Schedule.

7.306 27 Short title, interpretation, commencement and extent

(1) This Act may be cited as the National Lottery Act 1998.

(2) In this Act 'the 1993 Act' means the National Lottery etc Act 1993.

(3) The following provisions of this Act, namely—

(a) section 1,

(b) Schedule 1, and

(c) Part I of Schedule 5 and section 26 so far as relating to that Part of that Schedule,

shall come into force on such day as the Secretary of State may appoint by order made by statutory instrument; and different days may be so appointed for different purposes.[1]

(4) The following provisions of this Act, namely—

(a) this section,

(b) sections 6 to 12 and 15 to 25,

(c) Schedules 2 to 4, and

(d) section 26 and Part II of Schedule 5, so far as relating to the repeals in section 22 of, and paragraphs 2, 3 and 6 of Schedule 5 to, the 1993 Act,

shall come into force on the day on which this Act is passed.

(5) The remaining provisions of this Act shall come into force at the end of the period of two months beginning with the day on which this Act is passed.

(6) The power conferred by subsection (3) above to make an order includes power to make incidental, consequential, supplemental or transitional provision or savings (including power to amend enactments).

(7) This Act extends to Northern Ireland.

---

1 The provisions of this Act specified in sub-s (3) were brought into force on 1 April 1999 (SI 1999/650).

SCHEDULES

7.307

SCHEDULE 1
REPLACEMENT OF DIRECTOR GENERAL BY COMMISSION: SUPPLEMENTARY PROVISIONS
Section 1

PART I
TRANSFERS ETC

Interpretation

7.308

1 In this Part of this Schedule—

'the appointed day' means the day on which subsection (4) of the principal section comes into force under section 27(3) of this Act;

'the Commission' means the National Lottery Commission;

'the Director General' means the Director General of the National Lottery;
'instrument' includes orders, rules, regulations, schemes, licences, agreements and other documents;
'the principal section' means section 1 of this Act.

Transfer of property, rights and liabilities

2 On the appointed day, there shall by virtue of this paragraph be transferred to the Commission any property, rights or liabilities to which, immediately before that day, the Director General was entitled or subject in connection with any functions transferred to the Commission by the principal section.

Transfer of staff

3 (1) This paragraph applies to any person who, immediately before the appointed day, is employed by virtue of paragraph 3 of Schedule 2 to the 1993 Act.

(2) Any contract of employment under which a person to whom this paragraph applies is so employed shall have effect as from the appointed day as if it had originally been made between him and the Commission.

(3) Without prejudice to sub-paragraph (2) above—

(a) all the rights, powers, duties and liabilities of the employer under or in connection with a contract to which that sub-paragraph applies shall by virtue of that sub-paragraph be transferred to the Commission on the appointed day, and

(b) anything done before that day by or in relation to the employer in respect of that contract or the employee shall be deemed from that day to have been done by or in relation to the Commission.

(4) Sub-paragraphs (2) and (3) above are without prejudice to any right of an employee to terminate his contract of employment if his working conditions are changed substantially to his detriment; but such a change shall not be taken to have occurred by reason only of the change in employer effected by sub-paragraph (2) above.

(5) In sub-paragraph (4) above, the reference to an employee's working conditions includes a reference to any rights (whether accrued or contingent) under any pension or superannuation scheme of which he was a member by virtue of his employment immediately before the appointed day.

Construction of references to the Director General

4 Any enactment or instrument passed or made before the appointed day shall have effect, so far as necessary for the purposes of, or in consequence of, the transfers effected by the principal section and paragraphs 2 and 3 above, as if any reference to the Director General were a reference to the Commission.

Continuing validity of past acts

5 (1) Nothing in any other provision of the principal section or this Schedule shall affect the validity of anything done by or in relation to the Director General before the coming into force of that provision.

(2) Anything (including legal proceedings) which immediately before the appointed day is in the process of being done by or in relation to the Director General may, if it relates to any of the functions, property, rights or liabilities transferred by the principal section or paragraph 2 or 3 above, be continued by or in relation to the Commission.

(3) Any approval, authorisation, consent, delegation, direction, licence or appointment given, granted or made or other thing whatever done by the Director General for the purposes of any of the functions transferred by the principal

section shall, if in force immediately before the appointed day, continue in force and have effect as if similarly given, granted, made or done by the Commission.

Final report and accounts of the Director General

6 (1) As respects any time on or after the appointed day, the duties imposed on the Director General in relation to—

(a) accounts, and

(b) the making of a report under section 14 of the 1993 Act,

in respect of his last financial year, or any preceding financial year for which those duties have not been discharged, shall be discharged by the Commission.

(2) Any reference in this paragraph to the Director General's last financial year is a reference to the financial year beginning with the 1st April last preceding the appointed day.

(3) The duties imposed on the Commission by sub-paragraph (1) above shall be discharged by them as if the Director General's last financial year ended with the day preceding the appointed day (if it would not in fact do so).

(4) The property transferred to the Commission by virtue of paragraph 2 above shall include the records of the Director General.

(5) For the purposes of this paragraph, the amendments of section 14 of the 1993 Act made by paragraph 13 below shall be disregarded.

(6) In this paragraph 'financial year' means the twelve months beginning with 1st April in any year and ending with the 31st March next following.

PART II
CONSTITUTION OF THE COMMISSION

7.309

7 After Schedule 2 to the 1993 Act there shall be inserted—

'SCHEDULE 2A

THE NATIONAL LOTTERY COMMISSION

Section 3A

Status and capacity

1

(1) The Commission shall not be regarded as the servant or agent of the Crown or as enjoying any status, immunity or privilege of the Crown.

(2) The members and employees of the Commission shall not be regarded as civil servants and the Commission's property shall not be regarded as property of, or held on behalf of, the Crown.

(3) The Commission may for the purpose of enabling them to exercise their functions acquire and dispose of land.

(4) It shall be within the capacity of the Commission as a body corporate created by statute to do such things and enter into such transactions as are incidental or conducive to the discharge of their functions under this Act.

Membership

2

(1) The Commission shall consist of five members, all of whom shall be appointed by the Secretary of State.

(2) Before appointing a person to be a member, the Secretary of State shall satisfy himself that that person will have no such financial or other interest as is likely to affect prejudicially the discharge by him of his functions as a member.

(3) The Secretary of State shall also satisfy himself from time to time with respect to every member that he has no such interest as is mentioned in sub-paragraph (2).

(4) Any person who is, or whom the Secretary of State proposes to appoint to be, a member shall, whenever requested by the Secretary of State to do so, furnish him with such information as the Secretary of State considers necessary for the performance by him of his duties under sub-paragraphs (2) and (3).

Tenure of office

3

(1) Members shall hold and vacate office in accordance with their terms of appointment, subject to the following provisions.

(2) Any appointment of a member shall be for a term no longer than five years.

(3) A member may resign his membership by giving written notice to the Secretary of State.

(4) A person who ceases to be a member shall be eligible for re-appointment.

(5) The Secretary of State may by notice in writing to the member concerned remove from office a member who—

(a) has been absent from three or more consecutive meetings of the Commission without their prior approval,

(b) has become bankrupt, has made an arrangement with his creditors, has had his estate sequestrated, has granted a trust deed for his creditors or has made a composition contract with his creditors, or

(c) is, in the opinion of the Secretary of State, unable or unfit to perform his duties as a member.

Chairman

4

(1) The members of the Commission shall select one of their number to be the chairman of the Commission.

(2) A person's term of office as chairman shall be no longer than twelve months.

(3) A person may resign as chairman by giving written notice to the other members.

(4) If the chairman ceases to be a member he shall also cease to be chairman.

(5) A member who ceases to be the chairman shall again become eligible for selection as chairman after the expiration of a period equal to that for which he was last chairman.

Remuneration and allowances

5

(1) The Commission may pay such remuneration, and such travelling and other allowances, to a member of the Commission as the Secretary of State may determine in the case of the member.

(2) Where the Secretary of State so determines in the case of a member of the Commission, the Commission shall—

(a) pay to or in respect of him such pension, allowances or gratuities, or

(b) make such payments towards the provision of a pension, allowances or gratuities to or in respect of him,

as the Secretary of State may determine.

(3) If the Secretary of State determines that there are special circumstances that make it right for a person ceasing to be a member of the Commission to receive compensation, the Commission may pay to him such compensation as the Secretary of State may determine.

Staff

6

(1) There shall be a Chief Executive of the Commission, who shall be appointed by the Commission as an employee of theirs.
(2) The Chief Executive shall be responsible to the Commission for the general exercise of the Commission's functions.
(3) Subject to any directions given to them by the Secretary of State with respect to the number of persons who may be employed by the Commission, the Commission may appoint such other employees as they think fit.
(4) Subject to any directions given to the Commission by the Secretary of State, the Chief Executive and any other employees shall be employed on such terms and conditions (including terms and conditions as to remuneration) as the Commission think fit.
(5) Service as an employee of the Commission shall be included in the kinds of employment to which a scheme under section 1 of the Superannuation Act 1972 can apply.
(6) Accordingly, in the Superannuation Act 1972, in Schedule 1 (kinds of employment etc referred to in section 1) the following entry shall be inserted at the appropriate place among the entries under the heading '*Royal Commissions and other Commissions*'—

'*National Lottery Commission*'

(7) The Commission shall pay to the Minister for the Civil Service, at such times as that Minister may direct, such sums as that Minister may determine in respect of the increase attributable to sub-paragraphs (5) and (6) in the sums payable out of money provided by Parliament under the Superannuation Act 1972.

Proceedings

7

(1) The Commission may regulate their own procedure and that of any of their committees (and in particular may specify a quorum for meetings).
(2) The validity of any proceedings of the Commission shall not be affected—
- (a) by any vacancy among the members or in the office of chairman, or
- (b) by any defect in the appointment or selection of any person as a member or as chairman of the Commission.

Delegation

8

(1) Anything authorised or required by or under any enactment to be done by the Commission may be done—
- (a) by any member or employee of the Commission who has been authorised for the purpose, whether generally or specially, by the Commission; or
- (b) by any committee of the Commission which has been so authorised and whose membership consists of—

(i) members of the Commission; or

(ii) one or more members of the Commission and one or more employees of the Commission.

(2) In exercising their functions under sub-paragraph (1), the Commission shall comply with any directions given to them by the Secretary of State.

Duty to give reasons for decisions

9

(1) It shall be the duty of the Commission to give to any person affected a written statement of their reasons for any decisions which they may make in the exercise of their functions under sections 5 to 10 or Schedule 3.

(2) It shall be the duty of the Commission to arrange for the publication, in such manner as they think fit, of a written statement of their reasons—

(a) for any decision which they may make to grant, or not to grant, to any particular applicant a licence under section 5;

(b) for any decision which they may make to revoke a licence granted under section 5; and

(c) for any other decision which they may make in the exercise of their functions under sections 5 to 10A or Schedule 3 and which they consider likely to be of interest to the public.

(3) Sub-paragraphs (1) and (2) do not apply if or to the extent that the giving, or (as the case may be) the publication, of reasons would involve disclosure of information in breach of—

(a) a restriction imposed by or under any other enactment; or

(b) an obligation of confidence.

Finance

10

There shall be paid out of money provided by Parliament such sums as are necessary to defray any expenditure of the Commission.

Accounts

11

(1) The Commission shall—

(a) keep proper accounts and proper records in relation to the accounts, and

(b) prepare a statement of accounts in respect of each financial year.

(2) The statement shall comply with any directions that may be given by the Secretary of State as to the information to be contained in such a statement, the manner in which such information is to be presented or the methods and principles according to which such a statement is to be prepared.

(3) Copies of the statement shall be sent to the Secretary of State and the Comptroller and Auditor General within such period after the end of the financial year to which the statement relates as the Secretary of State may direct.

(4) The Comptroller and Auditor General shall examine, certify and report on the statement and shall lay copies of the statement and of his report before Parliament.

(5) The Secretary of State shall not give a direction under this paragraph without the Treasury's approval.

(6) In this paragraph 'financial year' means—

(a) the period beginning with the coming into force of section 3A and ending with the next 31st March, and

(b) each successive period of twelve months ending with 31st March.

Application of seal and evidence

12

The application of the seal of the Commission shall be authenticated by the signature—

(a) of any member of the Commission, or

(b) of any other person who has been authorised by the Commission (whether generally or specially) for that purpose.

13

A document purporting to be duly executed under the seal of the Commission, or to be signed on behalf of the Commission, shall be received in evidence and, unless the contrary is proved, taken to be so executed or signed.

14

Paragraphs 12 and 13 do not extend to Scotland.'

PART III
MINOR AND CONSEQUENTIAL AMENDMENTS

The Public Records Act 1958

7.310

8 In Schedule 1 to the Public Records Act 1958 (definition of public records) the following entry shall be inserted at the appropriate place in Part II of the Table at the end of paragraph 3—

'National Lottery Commission.'

The Parliamentary Commissioner Act 1967

9 In the Parliamentary Commissioner Act 1967, in Schedule 2 (departments and authorities subject to investigation)—

(a) the following entry shall be inserted at the appropriate place—

'National Lottery Commission.'; and

(b) the entry relating to the Office of the Director General of the National Lottery shall be omitted.

The House of Commons Disqualification Act 1975

10 In the House of Commons Disqualification Act 1975—

(a) in Part II of Schedule 1 (bodies of which all members are disqualified) the following entry shall be inserted at the appropriate place—

'The National Lottery Commission;'; and

(b) in Part III of that Schedule (other disqualifying offices) the entry relating to the Director General of the National Lottery shall be omitted.

The Northern Ireland Assembly Disqualification Act 1975

11 In the Northern Ireland Assembly Disqualification Act 1975—

(a) the same entry as is set out in paragraph 10(a) above shall be inserted at the appropriate place in Part II of Schedule 1; and

(b) in Part III of that Schedule, the entry relating to the Director General of the National Lottery shall be omitted.

The Tribunals and Inquiries Act 1992

12 (1) The Tribunals and Inquiries Act 1992 shall be amended as follows.

(2) In section 7 (which restricts Ministers' powers to remove members of tribunals listed in Schedule 1 to that Act) in subsection (2) (tribunals to which that section does not apply)—

(a) after '33(a),' there shall be inserted '33AA,'; and

(b) the words '33A,' shall be omitted.

(3) In Schedule 1 (tribunals under the supervision of the Council on Tribunals) paragraph 33A (which relates to the Director General) shall be omitted and after paragraph 33 there shall be inserted—

'National Lottery	33AA The National Lottery Commission in respect of their functions under sections 10 and 10A of, and Schedule 3 to, the National Lottery etc Act 1993 (c 39), and any member, employee or committee of that Commission authorised under paragraph 8 of Schedule 2A to that Act to exercise any of those functions.'

The 1993 Act

13 In section 14 of the 1993 Act (annual report) in subsection (2)—

(a) paragraph (a) (which relates to the first report of the Director General) shall be omitted; and

(b) after that paragraph there shall be inserted—

'(aa) the period beginning with the date on which section 3A comes into force and ending with the next 31st March, and'.

14 In section 20 of the 1993 Act (interpretation of Part I)—

(a) before the definition of 'contravention' there shall be inserted—

"the Commission' means the National Lottery Commission;'; and

(b) the definition of 'the Director General' shall be omitted.

15 (1) Section 31 of the 1993 Act (payments from Distribution Fund in respect of expenses) shall be amended as follows.

(2) In subsection (2)—

(a) paragraph (a) (meeting payments made or to be made under paragraph 5 of Schedule 2) shall cease to have effect; and

(b) after that paragraph there shall be inserted—

'(aa) meeting payments made or to be made under paragraph 10 of Schedule 2A,'.

(3) Subsection (3) (which relates to subsection (2)(a)) shall be omitted.

(4) At the end of the section there shall be added—

'(4) In determining what amounts are appropriate for meeting the payments referred to in subsection (2)(aa), the Secretary of State shall take into account sums paid or to be paid into the Consolidated Fund under section 7(6).'

7.311

SCHEDULE 2
THE NEW OPPORTUNITIES FUND: SCHEDULE 6A TO THE 1993 ACT
Section 7

'SCHEDULE 6A
THE NEW OPPORTUNITIES FUND

Section 43A

Membership

1

(1) The New Opportunities Fund shall consist of a chairman and not less than 8 nor more than 12 other members, all of whom shall be appointed by the Secretary of State.

(2) Four of the members of the New Opportunities Fund (other than the chairman) shall be persons who appear to the Secretary of State to be suited to make the interests of England, Scotland, Wales and Northern Ireland, respectively, their special care.

(3) The Secretary of State may by order amend sub-paragraph (1) so as to vary any number for the time being specified in that sub-paragraph.

Committees

2

Subsection (7) of section 25A shall apply in relation to any committee of the New Opportunities Fund as it applies in relation to a committee appointed under subsection (6) of that section.

Tenure of office

3

(1) Subject to the following provisions of this paragraph, a person shall hold and vacate office as chairman or other member of the New Opportunities Fund in accordance with the terms of his appointment.

(2) The Secretary of State shall not appoint a person to hold office as a member of the New Opportunities Fund for a term of more than five years.

(3) A chairman or member of the New Opportunities Fund may at any time resign his office by notice in writing addressed to the Secretary of State.

(4) A member of the New Opportunities Fund may be removed from office by the Secretary of State on the ground that—

(a) he has been absent for a period longer than three consecutive months from meetings of the Fund without the Fund's consent,

(b) a bankruptcy order has been made against him, or his estate has been sequestrated, or he has made a composition or arrangement with, or granted a trust deed for, his creditors, or

(c) he is unable or unfit to discharge the functions of his office.

(5) If a chairman of the New Opportunities Fund ceases to be a member of the Fund he shall also cease to be chairman.

(6) A person who ceases, otherwise than by virtue of sub-paragraph (4), to be a member or chairman of the New Opportunities Fund shall be eligible for re-appointment.

Remuneration and allowances

4

(1) The New Opportunities Fund may pay—

(a) such remuneration to their chairman and any other member of the Fund, and

(b) such travelling and other allowances to their chairman, any other member of the Fund and any member of a committee of theirs,

as the Secretary of State may determine.

(2) Where the Secretary of State so determines in the case of a holder of the office of chairman of the New Opportunities Fund, or in the case of any other member of the Fund, the Fund shall—

(a) pay to or in respect of him such pension, allowances or gratuities, or

(b) make such payments towards the provision of a pension, allowances or gratuities to or in respect of him,

as the Secretary of State may determine.

(3) If the Secretary of State determines that there are special circumstances that make it right for a person ceasing to hold office as chairman of the New Opportunities Fund, or ceasing to be a member of the Fund, to receive compensation, the Fund may pay to him such compensation as the Secretary of State may determine.

Staff

5

(1) Subject to any directions under section 26(3), the New Opportunities Fund may appoint such staff as they think fit, on such terms and conditions of service as they think fit.

(2) Subject to any directions under section 26(3), the New Opportunities Fund may—

(a) pay such pensions, allowances or gratuities to or in respect of any persons who have been or are members of their staff as they may determine;

(b) make such payments as they may determine towards the provision of pensions, allowances or gratuities to or in respect of any such persons;

(c) provide and maintain such schemes as they may determine (whether contributory or not) for the payment of pensions, allowances or gratuities to or in respect of any such persons.

(3) Any reference in sub-paragraph (2) to pensions, allowances or gratuities to or in respect of any such persons as are mentioned in that sub-paragraph includes pensions, allowances or gratuities by way of compensation to or in respect of any members of the New Opportunities Fund's staff who suffer loss of office or employment.

Proceedings

6

(1) Subject to the provisions of this Schedule, the New Opportunities Fund may regulate their own procedure and that of any of their committees (and in particular may specify a quorum for meetings).

(2) The validity of any proceedings of the New Opportunities Fund shall not be affected by any vacancy among their members, or by any defect in the appointment of any person as chairman or a member.

Application of seal and evidence

7

The application of the seal of the New Opportunities Fund shall be authenticated by the signature—

(a) of any member of the Fund, or
(b) of any other person who has been authorised by the Fund (whether generally or specially) for that purpose.

8

A document purporting to be duly executed under the seal of the New Opportunities Fund or to be signed on their behalf shall be received in evidence and, unless the contrary is proved, taken to be so executed or signed.

Status of New Opportunities Fund

9

The New Opportunities Fund shall not be regarded as the servant or agent of the Crown or as enjoying any status, immunity or privilege of the Crown.

10

In Schedule 1 to the Public Records Act 1958 (definition of public records) the following entry shall be inserted at the appropriate place in Part II of the Table at the end of paragraph 3—

'New Opportunities Fund.'

Application to Scotland

11

Paragraphs 7 and 8 do not extend to Scotland.'

7.312

SCHEDULE 3

JOINT SCHEMES: SCHEDULE 3A TO THE 1993 ACT

Section 12

'SCHEDULE 3A

JOINT SCHEMES: SUPPLEMENTARY PROVISIONS

Section 25B

Interpretation

1

In this Schedule 'year' means any period of twelve months.

Authorisation or approval by Secretary of State

2

(1) Where the maximum amount of money which could be distributed under section 25(1) under a particular joint scheme in any year exceeds £15 million, the joint scheme shall not have effect unless the Secretary of State makes an order authorising the scheme.

(2) Where the maximum amount of money which could be distributed under section 25(1) under a particular joint scheme in any year does not exceed the

amount for the time being specified in sub-paragraph (1), the joint scheme shall not have effect unless the Secretary of State gives his written approval.

(3) In determining for the purposes of this Schedule the maximum amount of money which may be distributed under section 25(1) in any year under a joint scheme, any administrative expenses incurred in distributing such money under the scheme shall be brought into account.

(4) The Secretary of State shall only—

(a) make an order under sub-paragraph (1) authorising a joint scheme, or

(b) give his approval under sub-paragraph (2) to a joint scheme,

on an application made for the purpose by the bodies proposing to participate in the joint scheme.

(5) The Secretary of State may by order amend sub-paragraph (1) so as to increase the amount for the time being specified in that sub-paragraph.

Contents of authorisations and approvals

3

An order under paragraph 2(1) or an approval under paragraph 2(2) shall—

(a) contain a brief description of the nature and purposes of the joint scheme,

(b) identify the area within the United Kingdom to which the scheme applies,

(c) specify the maximum amount of money which may be distributed under section 25(1) in any year under the scheme,

(d) identify the bodies participating in the scheme,

(e) state the proportions in which the money to be distributed under section 25(1) under the scheme is attributable to each of those bodies, and

(f) state the duration of the scheme, if its duration is limited.

Effect of increasing annual limit on schemes authorised by order

4

Where—

(a) a joint scheme is authorised by an order under sub-paragraph (1) of paragraph 2, and

(b) that sub-paragraph is amended by an order under sub-paragraph (5) of that paragraph, and

(c) the maximum amount of money which may be distributed under section 25(1) in any year under the scheme does not exceed the amount specified in paragraph 2(1) as so amended,

the scheme shall be treated for the purposes of this Schedule as if the maximum amount of money which may be distributed under section 25(1) in any year under the scheme continued to exceed the amount for the time being specified in paragraph 2(1).

Powers

5

(1) The powers conferred by section 25A may, in particular, be exercised by a body for the purpose of running or otherwise participating in a joint scheme.

(2) The powers conferred on a body by section 25B and this Schedule are in addition to, and shall not derogate from, any powers which the body has apart from that section and this Schedule.

Modification

6

(1) A joint scheme may be modified by the bodies participating in the scheme, but if any such modifications—

(a) in the opinion of the Secretary of State, substantially alter the nature or purposes of the scheme,

(b) alter the area within the United Kingdom to which the scheme applies,

(c) increase the maximum amount of money which may be distributed under section 25(1) in any year under the scheme,

(d) vary the proportions in which the money to be distributed under section 25(1) under the scheme is attributable to each of the bodies participating in the scheme, or

(e) extend the duration of the scheme,

the scheme shall not have effect with those modifications unless the Secretary of State makes an order under paragraph 2(1) or, as the case may require, gives his approval under paragraph 2(2) in relation to the scheme as so modified.

(2) In determining for the purposes of sub-paragraph (1) whether the case requires an order under paragraph 2(1) or approval under paragraph 2(2), paragraph 4 shall be disregarded.

Termination

7

(1) If, in the case of a joint scheme authorised by an order under paragraph 2(1), the Secretary of State revokes the order, the scheme shall terminate on the date on which the revocation takes effect.

(2) If, in the case of a joint scheme approved under paragraph 2(2), the Secretary of State gives notice of withdrawal of his approval to each body participating in the scheme, the scheme shall terminate on the date on which the withdrawal of approval takes effect.

(3) The Secretary of State may terminate a joint scheme in accordance with sub-paragraph (1) or (2)—

(a) of his own motion, or

(b) on the application of one or more of the bodies participating in the scheme.

Orders under s 29(1): participant ceasing to be distributing body

8

(1) This paragraph applies in any case where an order under section 29(1) affects a body which, immediately before the order comes into force, is participating in a joint scheme.

(2) In any such case, the Secretary of State may by order under section 29(1)—

(a) make provision amending the joint scheme, or

(b) revoke the joint scheme.

(3) The provision that may be made by virtue of sub-paragraph (2)(a) includes—

(a) provision varying the bodies participating in the joint scheme;

(b) provision varying the proportions in which the money to be distributed under section 25(1) under the scheme is attributable to each of the bodies participating in the joint scheme; and

(c) provision for all or any of the actual or contingent rights or liabilities of a body which are attributable to the joint scheme to become rights or liabilities of another body participating in the scheme as amended.

(4) No provision shall be made by virtue of sub-paragraph (2)(a) without the written agreement of the bodies which, if the provision were made, would be the participants in the joint scheme as amended.

(5) This paragraph is without prejudice to section 60(5) or paragraph 9.

Authorisation to continue payments despite occurrence of certain events

9

(1) This paragraph applies in any case where—

(a) on an application for a distribution of money under section 25(1), a decision under a joint scheme to make such a distribution has been notified to the applicant, but

(b) an event falling within sub-paragraph (2) ('the relevant event') occurs before the whole of the distribution has been made.

(2) The events which fall within this sub-paragraph are—

(a) that, by virtue of an order under section 29(1), any of the bodies participating in the scheme ceases to be specified in subsection (1), (2), (3) or (4) (as the case may be) of section 23,

(b) that the joint scheme terminates under paragraph 7, or

(c) that the joint scheme is revoked under paragraph 8(2)(b).

(3) Where this paragraph applies, the Secretary of State may authorise any of the bodies which were participating in the joint scheme immediately before the relevant event occurred to continue making distributions of money under section 25(1) in pursuance of the decision mentioned in sub-paragraph (1)(a) as if the relevant event had not occurred.

(4) Where the Secretary of State gives an authorisation under sub-paragraph (3) in relation to any distributions of money under section 25(1), the other provisions of this Act shall have effect in relation to those distributions as if the relevant event had not occurred.

(5) An authorisation under this paragraph accordingly extends to the defrayal of any administrative expenses incurred in making the distributions concerned.

(6) This paragraph is without prejudice to section 60(5) or paragraph 8.

(7) Any authorisation under this paragraph must be in writing.'

7.313

SCHEDULE 5
ENACTMENTS REPEALED
Section 26

PART I
ENACTMENTS RELATING TO REPLACEMENT OF DIRECTOR GENERAL BY COMMISSION

7.314

Chapter	**Short title**	**Extent of repeal**
1967 c 13	The Parliamentary Commissioner Act 1967.	In Schedule 2, the entry relating to the Office of the Director General of the National Lottery.
1975 c 24	The House of Commons Disqualification Act 1975.	In Schedule 1, in Part III, the entry relating to the Director General of the National Lottery.
1975 c 25	The Northern Ireland Assembly Disqualification Act 1975.	In Schedule 1, in Part III, the entry relating to the Director General of the National Lottery.
1992 c 53	The Tribunals and Inquiries Act 1992.	In section 7(2), the words '33A,'.
1993 c 39	The National Lottery etc Act 1993.	In Schedule 1, paragraph 33A. Section 3. Section 14(2)(a). In section 20, the definition of 'the Director General'. Section 31(2)(a) and (3). Schedule 2.
1998 c 22	The National Lottery Act 1998.	Section 2(4).

PART II
OTHER ENACTMENTS

7.315

Chapter	**Short title**	**Extent of repeal**
1993 c 39	The National Lottery etc Act 1993.	In section 22(3), the word 'and' at the end of paragraph (d).
		In Schedule 3, in paragraph 6(1), the word 'and' at the end of paragraph (c), and paragraph 10.

Chapter	Short title	Extent of repeal
		In Schedule 5, paragraph 2(4) to (6); in paragraph 3, in sub-paragraph (1) the words 'or a committee of theirs', in sub-paragraph (2) the words 'or a committee of theirs', in sub-paragraph (3) the words 'or a person appointed to a committee of theirs by the Secretary of State', in sub-paragraph (4) the words 'or a person appointed to a committee of theirs by the Secretary of State', in sub-paragraph (5) the words 'or a committee of theirs' and in sub-paragraph (6) the words 'or a committee of theirs'; paragraph 4(4); in paragraph 5, in sub-paragraph (2), the words 'with the Secretary of State's approval', and sub-paragraph (4); and paragraph 6(3).

NATIONAL LOTTERY ACT 2006

2006 c 23

An Act to make provision about the National Lottery.

[11th July 2006]

Be it enacted by the Queen's most Excellent Majesty, by and with the advice and consent of the Lords Spiritual and Temporal, and Commons, in this present Parliament assembled, and by the authority of the same, as follows:—

National Lottery Commission

7.316 1 Constitution

(1) Schedule 2A to the National Lottery etc Act 1993 (c 39) (National Lottery Commission) shall be amended as follows.

(2) For paragraph 2(1) substitute—

"(1) The Commission shall consist of at least five members, appointed by the Secretary of State."

(3) For paragraph 4 substitute—

"4

(1) The Secretary of State shall appoint a member of the Commission as chairman.

(2) A member of the Commission who is also an employee of the Commission may not be appointed as chairman.

(3) The chairman shall hold and vacate office in accordance with the terms of his appointment; but—

(a) sub-paragraphs (2) to (5) of paragraph 3 shall apply to the office of chairman as they apply to the office of member, and

(b) if the chairman ceases to be a member he shall cease to be chairman."

(4) After paragraph 6 insert—

"6A

(1) The Secretary of State may appoint the Chief Executive of the Commission as a member.

(2) Where the Chief Executive is appointed as a member—

(a) paragraph 5 shall not apply to him, and

(b) if he ceases to be Chief Executive he ceases to be a member.

(3) Where the Chief Executive is appointed as a member the Secretary of State may, on the recommendation of the Commission, appoint another employee of the Commission as a member; and—

(a) paragraph 5 shall not apply to a person appointed by virtue of this sub-paragraph,

(b) the Secretary of State may suspend or terminate an appointment made by virtue of this sub-paragraph if the Chief Executive ceases to be a member, and

(c) if a person appointed by virtue of this sub-paragraph ceases to be an employee of the Commission he shall cease to be a member."

7.317 2 Disclosure of information

After section 4A of the National Lottery etc Act 1993 (c 39) (consultation with Gambling Commission: inserted by the Gambling Act 2005) insert—

"4B Disclosure of information

(1) The Commissioners for Her Majesty's Revenue and Customs may disclose information to the National Lottery Commission.

(2) The National Lottery Commission may disclose information to the Commissioners for Her Majesty's Revenue and Customs.

(3) Information disclosed under this section shall not be further disclosed except in accordance with subsection (4).

(4) Information may be further disclosed—

(a) for the purpose of complying with an enactment,

(b) in pursuance of an order of a court,

(c) for the purpose of legal proceedings connected with the operation of an enactment relating to lotteries,

(d) with the consent of the Commissioners for Her Majesty's Revenue and Customs,

(e) with the consent of each person to whom the information relates, or

(f) to the National Audit Office for the purposes of the exercise of functions under Part II of the National Audit Act 1983 (c 44).

(5) This section has effect despite any prohibition or restriction that would otherwise prevent disclosure of information.

4C Wrongful disclosure

(1) This section applies to a person—

(a) who is or was an officer or employee of the National Lottery Commission, or

(b) who acts or acted on behalf of the National Lottery Commission.

(2) A person to whom this section applies commits an offence if he discloses information received from the Commissioners for Her Majesty's Revenue and Customs in contravention of section 4B(3) and the information relates to a person whose identity—

(a) is specified in the disclosure, or

(b) can be deduced from it.

(3) It is a defence for a person charged with an offence under this section of disclosing information to prove that he reasonably believed—

(a) that the disclosure was lawful, or

(b) that the information had already and lawfully been made available to the public.

(4) A person guilty of an offence under this section shall be liable—

(a) on conviction on indictment, to imprisonment for a term not exceeding two years, to a fine or to both, or

(b) on summary conviction, to imprisonment for a term not exceeding 12 months, to a fine not exceeding the statutory maximum or to both.

(5) In relation to a conviction occurring before the commencement of section 282 of the Criminal Justice Act 2003 (c 44) (short sentences) the reference in subsection (4)(b) to 12 months shall have effect as if it were a reference to six months.

(6) In the application of this section to Scotland or Northern Ireland the reference in subsection (4)(b) to 12 months shall be taken as a reference to six months."

Licensing System

7.318 3 Licensees

In the following provisions of the National Lottery etc Act 1993 (c 39) for "body corporate" or "body" substitute "person" (and for "bodies" substitute "persons")—

(a) section 1(3)(a) and (b) (promotion of lottery),

(b) section 5(1), (2) and (4) (and the heading) (licence to run National Lottery),

(c) section 6(1) and (4) (and the heading) (licence to promote lotteries),

(d) section 7(2)(g) (supplemental), and

(e) section 10(1) and (2) (revocation).

7.319 4 Length of licence

(1) In section 7 of the National Lottery etc Act 1993 (c 39) (licensing: supplemental) after subsection (1) insert—

"(1A) The period specified under subsection (1) must—

(a) begin with the date of grant of the licence, and

(b) not exceed 15 years.

(1B) A licence granted under section 5 or 6 may (subject to the restriction in subsection (1A)(b)) include—

(a) provision enabling the period specified under subsection (1) to be extended by the Commission;

(b) provision enabling the period specified under subsection (1) to be extended by agreement between the Commission and the licensee."

(2) In section 7(2) of that Act for "Such a licence" substitute "A licence granted under section 5 or 6".

7.320 5 Fees

(1) After section 7 of the National Lottery etc Act 1993 (c 39) (licences: supplemental) insert—

"**7A Annual fee**

(1) The holder of a licence under section 5 or 6—

(a) shall pay a first annual fee to the Commission within such period after the issue of the licence as may be prescribed, and

(b) shall pay an annual fee to the Commission before each anniversary of the issue of the licence.

(2) In this section—

"annual fee" means a fee of such amount as may be prescribed, and

"prescribed" means prescribed by regulations made by the Secretary of State.

(3) Subsection (1)(b) does not apply in relation to an anniversary of the issue of a licence on or immediately before which the licence ceases, by virtue of its terms, to have effect.

(4) The Commission shall pay fees received by virtue of this section into the Consolidated Fund."

(2) Section 7(5) and (6) of that Act (fee on grant of licence) shall cease to have effect.

(3) In section 10 of that Act (revocation of licence)—

(a) after subsection (3) insert—

"(3A) The Commission shall revoke a licence granted under section 5 or 6 if the licensee fails to pay the annual fee in accordance with section 7A; but the Commission may disapply this subsection if it thinks that a failure to pay is attributable to administrative error.", and

(b) at the end of subsection (4) add "or under subsection (3A)."

7.321 6 Licensing structure

(1) The Secretary of State may by order provide for Schedule 1 (which amends the licensing structure of the National Lottery) to have effect.

(2) Before making an order under subsection (1) the Secretary of State must consult the National Lottery Commission.

(3) An order under subsection (1)—

(a) may make transitional or incidental provision,

(b) may bring all or part of Schedule 1 into force,

(c) may make different provision for different purposes,

(d) shall be made by statutory instrument, and

(e) shall be subject to annulment in pursuance of a resolution of either House of Parliament.

Distribution of Lottery Funds

7.322 7 National Lottery Distribution Fund: apportionment

(1) Section 22 of the National Lottery etc Act 1993 (c 39) (apportionment of money in Distribution Fund) shall be amended as follows.

(2) In subsection (3)—

(a) at the end of paragraph (c) add "and", and

(b) for paragraphs (d) and (f) substitute—

"(d) 50 per cent shall be allocated for prescribed expenditure that is—

(i) charitable, or

(ii) connected with health, or

(iii) connected with education, or

(iv) connected with the environment."

(3) After subsection (3) insert—

"(3A) In subsection (3)(d) "prescribed expenditure" means expenditure of a description prescribed by order of the Secretary of State.

(3B) A description of expenditure under subsection (3A) may, in particular, refer to expenditure in relation to—

(a) England,

(b) Wales,

(c) Scotland,

(d) Northern Ireland,
(e) any of the Channel Islands, or
(f) the Isle of Man;

and expenditure described by virtue of this subsection is referred to in this Act as "devolved expenditure".

(3C) Before making an order under subsection (3A) the Secretary of State shall consult—

(a) the Big Lottery Fund,
(b) the National Assembly for Wales,
(c) the Scottish Ministers,
(d) the Northern Ireland Department of Culture, Arts and Leisure, and
(e) such other persons (if any) as he thinks appropriate."

7.323 8 Reallocation of funds

(1) After section 29 of the National Lottery etc Act 1993 (c 39) (variation of percentages for allocation of funds) insert—

"29A Reallocation of funds

(1) This section applies where money is—

(a) allocated for a purpose under section 22(3), and
(b) held for distribution by a body under section 23.

(2) The Secretary of State may by order provide for the money to be held for distribution by a different body specified in the order (without altering the purpose for which the money is allocated).

(3) Before making an order under this section the Secretary of State shall consult—

(a) each body mentioned in the order,
(b) the National Assembly for Wales,
(c) the Scottish Ministers,
(d) the Northern Ireland Department of Culture, Arts and Leisure, and
(e) such other persons (if any) as he thinks appropriate."

(2) In section 24 of that Act (payments from Distribution Fund) after "section 23" insert "or in an order under section 29A".

(3) In section 60(2) of that Act (orders and regulations: affirmative resolution) after paragraph (a) (and before the word "or" immediately after that paragraph) insert—

"(aa) section 29A,".

7.324 9 Investment income

In section 32 of the National Lottery etc Act 1993 (National Lottery Distribution Fund: investment)—

(a) for subsection (3)(a) and (b) substitute "treated as if paid into the Fund by virtue of section 5(6).", and
(b) omit subsection (5).

7.325 10 Distributing bodies: consultation

After section 25(2B) of the National Lottery etc Act 1993 (application of money by distributing bodies) insert—

"(2C) In determining how to distribute money in accordance with subsection (1) a body may—

(a) consult any person;
(b) take account of opinions expressed to it or information submitted to it."

7.326 11 Distributing bodies: publicity

After section 25D of the National Lottery etc Act 1993 (c 39) (strategic plans) insert—

> **"25E Distribution of funds: publicity**
>
> A body which distributes money under section 25(1) may make or participate in arrangements for—
>
> (a) publishing information relating to the effect of a provision of this Act,
>
> (b) publishing information relating to the distribution of money under this Act or the expenditure of money distributed under this Act, or
>
> (c) encouraging participation in activities relating to the distribution of money under this Act."

7.327 12 Distributing bodies: annual reports

In section 34 of the National Lottery etc Act 1993 (annual reports) after subsection (2) insert—

> "(2A) The report shall set out the body's policy and practice in relation to the principle that proceeds of the National Lottery should be used to fund projects, or aspects of projects, for which funds would be unlikely to be made available by—
>
> (a) a Government department,
>
> (b) the Scottish Ministers,
>
> (c) a Northern Ireland department, or
>
> (d) the National Assembly for Wales."

7.328 13 Isle of Man and Channel Islands

(1) After section 25(5) of the National Lottery etc Act 1993 (application of money by distributing bodies) add—

> "(6) A reference in this section to meeting expenditure includes a reference to meeting expenditure which relates to—
>
> (a) the Isle of Man, or
>
> (b) any of the Channel Islands."

(2) After section 25A(11) (delegation by distributing bodies) add—

> "(12) A body established under the law of the Isle of Man may be the subject of an appointment under this section in connection with expenditure which relates to the Isle of Man.
>
> (13) A body established under the law of any of the Channel Islands may be the subject of an appointment under this section in connection with expenditure which relates to that Island."

The Big Lottery Fund

7.329 14 Establishment

(1) After section 36 of the National Lottery etc Act 1993 (c 39) insert—

"The Big Lottery Fund

> **36A The Fund**
>
> (1) There shall be a body corporate known as the Big Lottery Fund.
>
> (2) Schedule 4A (which makes provision in relation to the Fund) shall have effect."

(2) After Schedule 4 to that Act insert the Schedule 4A set in out in Schedule 2 to this Act.

7.330 15 Functions

(1) In section 23 of the National Lottery etc Act 1993 (the distributing bodies) for subsections (4), (5) and (6) substitute—

"(4) So much of any sum paid into the Distribution Fund as is allocated under section 22(3)(d) shall be held by the Distribution Fund for distribution by the Big Lottery Fund (established under section 36A)."

(2) After section 36A of that Act (inserted by section 14 above) insert—

"36B Power to distribute funds

(1) The Big Lottery Fund may make grants or loans, or make or enter into other arrangements, for the purpose of complying with section 25(1).

(2) A grant or loan may be subject to conditions (which may, in particular, include conditions as to repayment with interest).

(3) The Secretary of State may by order make provision limiting the amounts distributed under subsection (1).

(4) An order under subsection (3) may in particular—

(a) specify a maximum amount that may be distributed during a specified period for expenditure of a description prescribed under section 22(3A);

(b) specify a minimum amount that must be distributed during a specified period for expenditure of a description prescribed under section 22(3A);

(c) make provision by reference to the aggregate of amounts distributed, to a percentage of amounts available for distribution or otherwise;

(d) make provision (which may, in particular, confer a power on the Fund) for the treatment of expenditure which satisfies more than one prescribed description.

(5) Before making an order under subsection (3) the Secretary of State shall consult—

(a) the Fund,

(b) the National Assembly for Wales,

(c) the Scottish Ministers,

(d) the Northern Ireland Department of Culture, Arts and Leisure, and

(e) such other persons (if any) as he thinks appropriate.

36C Non-lottery funds

(1) The Fund may enter into an arrangement with a person under which—

(a) the person pays money to the Fund, and

(b) the Fund distributes the money to a third party.

(2) An arrangement under subsection (1) may, in particular—

(a) identify the third party, or

(b) otherwise limit the Fund's freedom of action in relation to the distribution of the money paid under the arrangement.

(3) The Fund shall distribute money received under subsection (1) for meeting expenditure that is—

(a) charitable,

(b) connected with health,

(c) connected with education, or

(d) connected with the environment.

(4) The reference in subsection (3) to the distribution of money received under subsection (1) is a reference to doing anything of a kind that the Fund can do under section 36B.

(5) A reference in this Act to payment under section 25(1) shall include a reference to payment under subsection (3) above."

36D Power to give advice

The Big Lottery Fund may give advice about—

(a) the distribution of money under any provision of this Act;

(b) inviting, making or considering applications for grants and loans under any provision of this Act;

(c) the use of money paid under any provision of this Act.

36E Directions

(1) In exercising any of its functions the Big Lottery Fund shall comply with any direction given to it by the Secretary of State (subject to subsection (4)).

(2) A direction under this section may, in particular, specify matters to be taken into account in determining the persons to whom, the purposes for which and the conditions subject to which the Fund distributes money.

(3) A direction under this section may, in particular—

(a) relate to the management and control of money received by the Fund;

(b) relate to the employment of staff;

(c) with the consent of the Treasury, relate to—

(i) the form of accounts, or

(ii) methods and principles for the preparation of accounts;

(d) in so far as it relates to a matter specified in paragraphs (a) to (c)—

(i) relate to the persons to whom or the terms on which the Fund delegates functions;

(ii) require the Fund to obtain the Secretary of State's consent before taking action of a specified kind;

(iii) require the Fund to provide information to the Secretary of State.

(4) A direction under this section, other than a direction given by virtue only of subsection (3), may not be given by the Secretary of State in relation to Welsh, Scottish or Northern Ireland devolved expenditure, but—

(a) may be given by the National Assembly for Wales in relation to Welsh devolved expenditure,

(b) may be given by the Scottish Ministers in relation to Scottish devolved expenditure, and

(c) may be given by the Northern Ireland Department of Culture, Arts and Leisure in relation to Northern Ireland devolved expenditure.

(5) Before giving a direction under this section, other than by virtue only of subsection (3), the Secretary of State shall consult—

(a) the Fund,

(b) the National Assembly for Wales,

(c) the Scottish Ministers, and

(d) the Northern Ireland Department of Culture, Arts and Leisure.

(6) But subsection (5)(b) to (d) shall not apply to a direction which relates only to English devolved expenditure.

(7) Before giving a direction to the Fund by virtue only of subsection (3) the Secretary of State shall consult the Fund.

(8) Before giving a direction to the Fund by virtue of subsection (4)(a) to (c) the person giving the direction shall—

(a) consult the Fund, and

(b) obtain the consent of the Secretary of State.

(9) A report of the Fund under section 34 shall set out any directions given to the Fund under subsection (1) that had effect during the financial year to which the report relates."

Dissolution of old distributors

7.331 16 Dissolution

(1) The Secretary of State may by order provide that one or more of the following shall cease to exist—

(a) the National Lottery Charities Board,

(b) the Millennium Commission, and

(c) the New Opportunities Fund.

(2) An order under subsection (1) may include consequential, incidental or transitional provision (which may include provision amending an enactment, whether by removing a reference to a body, by substituting a reference to the Big Lottery Fund, or otherwise).

(3) An order under subsection (1)—

(a) shall be made by statutory instrument,

(b) if it contains provision amending an enactment, shall not be made unless a draft has been laid before and approved by each House of Parliament, and

(c) in any other case, shall be subject to annulment in pursuance of a resolution of either House of Parliament.

7.332 17 Transfer of property, &c

(1) In this section—

"old lottery distributor" means a body dissolved by section 16, and

"the appointed day" means the day appointed under section 16(1).

(2) The property, rights and liabilities to which an old lottery distributor was entitled or subject immediately before the appointed day shall on that day vest in the Big Lottery Fund by virtue of this subsection.

(3) Anything done by or in relation to an old lottery distributor which has effect immediately before the appointed day shall, so far as necessary for continuing its effect after that day, have effect as if done by or in relation to the Fund.

(4) Anything (including any legal proceedings) which immediately before the appointed day is in the process of being done by or in relation to an old lottery distributor may be continued by or in relation to the Fund.

(5) So far as necessary or appropriate in consequence of subsection (2), on and after the appointed day—

(a) a reference to an old lottery distributor in an agreement (whether written or not), instrument or other document shall be treated as a reference to the Fund, and

(b) a reference in an agreement (whether written or not), instrument or other document to a member or officer of an old lottery distributor shall be treated as a reference to a person appointed for the purpose in writing by the Fund.

(6) The Fund must provide information on request about an appointment under subsection (5)(b).

(7) Subsection (2) shall operate in relation to property, rights or liabilities—

(a) whether or not they would otherwise be capable of being transferred,

(b) without any instrument or other formality being required, and

(c) irrespective of any requirement for consent that would otherwise apply.

(8) In so far as subsection (2) transfers liabilities under contracts of employment—

(a) nothing in this section shall affect the operation of the Transfer of Undertakings (Protection of Employment) Regulations 1981 (SI 1981/1794), and

(b) the Secretary of State shall not appoint the appointed day unless satisfied that sufficient notice has been given to enable compliance with any applicable requirement of those regulations.

(9) Without prejudice to the generality of subsections (3) and (4), the Big Lottery Fund may do anything it thinks necessary or expedient for the purpose of giving effect to a decision, agreement or undertaking of an old lottery distributor (whether in respect of a grant or loan or otherwise) irrespective of whether the Big Lottery Fund would have the power under the National Lottery etc Act 1993 (c 39), as amended by this Act, to make that decision or agreement or to give that undertaking.

7.333 18 Outstanding balances

(1) Money that immediately before the appointed day is held in the National Lottery Distribution Fund for distribution by an old lottery distributor shall on that day be treated as—

(a) allocated under section 22(3)(d) of the National Lottery etc Act 1993 (as substituted by section 7 above), and

(b) held in the Distribution Fund for distribution by the Big Lottery Fund in accordance with section 23(4) of that Act (as substituted by section 15 above).

(2) Money transferred under section 17(2) to the Big Lottery Fund having been paid to an old lottery distributor under section 24 of the National Lottery etc Act 1993 shall be treated as having been paid to the Fund under that section.

(3) In this section—

"old lottery distributor" means a body dissolved by section 16, and

"the appointed day" means the day appointed under section 16(1).

7.334 19 Consequential amendments

(1) The National Lottery etc Act 1993 shall be amended as follows.

(2) In section 25C(3)(a) for "or 43C(1)," substitute "or 36E,".

(3) At the end of section 26 (directions to distributing bodies) add—

"(6) This section does not apply to the Big Lottery Fund."

(4) In section 34 (annual reports)—

(a) omit subsection (4), and

(b) in the heading omit "other than Millennium Commission".

(5) In section 35 (accounts)—

(a) in subsection (7) for "the National Lottery Charities Board, the Millennium Commission or the New Opportunities Fund" substitute "the Big Lottery Fund", and

(b) in the heading for "Charities Board and Millennium Commission" substitute "the Big Lottery Fund".

(6) The following shall cease to have effect—

(a) sections 37 to 39 (the National Lottery Charities Board),

(b) sections 40 to 43 (the Millennium Commission), and

(c) sections 43A to 43D (the New Opportunities Fund).

(7) In section 44(1) (interpretation) omit the entry for "the Charities Board".

(8) In section 60 of that Act (orders and regulations)—

(a) in subsection (2) for paragraph (a) substitute—

"(a) section 22(3A), 28 or 36B(3),",and

(b) in subsection (2A) for "section 43B." substitute "section 22(3A) or 36B(3)."

(9) The following shall cease to have effect—

(a) Schedule 5 (National Lotteries Charities Board),

(b) Schedule 6 (the Millennium Commission), and

(c) Schedule 6A (the New Opportunities Fund).

(10) In Schedule 5 to the Government of Wales Act 1998 (c 38) (persons who may be compelled to attend proceedings of or provide documents to the National Assembly for Wales) after paragraph 7 insert—

"7A

The Big Lottery Fund."

National Lottery etc Act 1993: interpretation

7.335 20 Meaning of "charitable expenditure"

In section 44(1) of the National Lottery etc Act 1993 (c 39) (interpretation) for the definition of "charitable expenditure" substitute—

""charitable", in relation to expenditure, means expenditure for a charitable, benevolent or philanthropic purpose."

General

7.336 21 Repeals

The enactments listed in Schedule 3 are hereby repealed to the extent specified.

7.337 22 Commencement

(1) The preceding provisions of this Act, other than sections 6 and 16 and Schedule 1, shall come into force in accordance with provision made by order of the Secretary of State under this subsection.

(2) An order under subsection (1)—

(a) may make transitional or incidental provision,

(b) may make different provision for different purposes, and

(c) shall be made by statutory instrument.

7.338 23 Extent

This Act extends to Northern Ireland.

7.339 24 Short title

This Act may be cited as the National Lottery Act 2006.

7.340

SCHEDULE 1

NATIONAL LOTTERY LICENSING[1]

Section 6

The National Lottery etc Act 1993 (c 39)

1 The National Lottery etc Act 1993 shall be amended as follows.

2 For section 1 (the National Lottery) substitute—

"1 The National Lottery

(1) A lottery forms part of the National Lottery if it is promoted in accordance with a licence under section 5.

(2) A reference to the National Lottery is a reference to the lotteries forming part of the National Lottery in accordance with subsection (1)."

3 In section 4(3) (overriding duties) for "the sums that are paid to the Secretary of State by virtue of section 5(6)." substitute "the sums paid into the National Lottery Distribution Fund under section 5(2)(c)."

4 For sections 5 and 6 (licence to run the National Lottery and licence to promote lottery) substitute—

"5 Licence to promote lottery

(1) The Commission may by licence authorise a person to promote a lottery.

(2) A licence—

(a) may make provision about any matter connected with the promotion of a lottery (including, in particular, arrangements for advertising, for the sale of tickets, for the distribution of prizes or for compliance with a provision of this Act),

(b) may, in particular, require the licensee to—

(i) obtain in advance the Commission's approval of the rules of a lottery, and

(ii) pay a fee of such amount as may be prescribed by regulations made by the Secretary of State in respect of an application for approval of the rules of a lottery,

(c) shall include a condition requiring the licensee to pay into the National Lottery Distribution Fund sums out of the proceeds of any lottery promoted in reliance on the licence,

(d) shall include provision for determining—

(i) the amount of payments under paragraph (c), and

(ii) the timing of payments under paragraph (c), and

(e) may include provision requiring the licensee to make arrangements (which may include payments to the Commission) for securing the payment of prizes in certain circumstances.

(3) No more than one licence may be issued in relation to any one lottery; but—

(a) a licence may relate to one or more specified lotteries or to lotteries of a specified description,

(b) a person may hold more than one licence at a time, and

(c) a licence may require or permit the holder to make arrangements with another person for the performance of specified functions.

6 Section 5 licence: procedure

(1) The Commission may issue a licence under section 5 to a person only if—

(a) he has applied in writing for the licence,

(b) he has supplied such information or documents in or with the application as the Commission directs,

(c) having considered the application the Commission is satisfied that the applicant is a suitable person to promote the lottery or lotteries to which the licence relates, and

(d) the Commission has complied with any relevant regulations under section 6A (but this paragraph is subject to section 6A(3)).

(2) For the purposes of subsection (1)(c) the Commission may, in particular, have regard to—

(a) the integrity of the applicant or of a person relevant to the application;

(b) the competence of the applicant or of any person relevant to the application;

(c) the financial and other circumstances of the applicant or of a person relevant to the application.

(3) A person is relevant to an application under section 5 for the purposes of this section if, in particular—

(a) he is likely to exercise a function in connection with the promotion of a lottery in reliance on the licence applied for, or

(b) he is likely to have an interest in a lottery promoted in reliance on the licence applied for.

6A Competition for licences

(1) The Commission may not issue a licence under section 5 unless it has complied, in relation to the licence, with regulations of the Secretary of State about inviting competing applications for licences.

(2) The regulations shall, in particular, make provision—

(a) about the publication of invitations (including provision as to the manner and timing of publication and the matters to be published), and

(b) about the timing of responses.

(3) Where an application for a licence under section 5 relates to a lottery already licensed the Commission may issue the licence without complying with the regulations (whether or not compliance has begun) if the Commission thinks it—

(a) is likely to be in the interests of compliance with the duty under section 4(2), or

(b) is necessary in order to prevent the lapse of the lottery.

(4) Where a licence is issued in reliance on subsection (3)(b), the period specified for the duration of the licence under section 7(1A) shall be no longer than the Commission thinks necessary to enable a further licence to be issued having complied with the regulations.

(5) This section applies to a variation of a licence which expands the class of authorised activities as it applies to the issue of a licence.

(6) Before making regulations under subsection (1) the Secretary of State shall consult the Commission."

5 (1) Section 7 (licensing: supplemental) shall be amended as follows.

(2) For subsections (1) and (1A) substitute—

"(1) A licence under section 5 must be in writing.

(1A) A licence under section 5 must specify a period during which it has effect (unless revoked or suspended)—

(a) beginning with the date of issue, and

(b) not exceeding 15 years."

(3) In subsection (1B) for "section 5 or 6" substitute "section 5".

(4) In subsection (2)—

(a) for "A licence granted under section 5 or 6" substitute "A licence under section 5", and

(b) for "by section 5 or 6" substitute "by section 5".

(5) After subsection (3) insert—

"(3A) Conditions under subsection (2), or requirements under subsection (2)(c), may, in particular, require the holder of a licence under section 5—

(a) to provide information in connection with the licensed activities to—

(i) the holder of another licence under section 5,

(ii) a person who is applying, or considering whether to apply, for a licence under section 5, or

(iii) such other person as the condition or requirement may specify or may enable the Commission to specify;

(b) to make facilities in connection with the licensed activities available to—

(i) the holder of another licence under section 5,

(ii) a person who is applying, or considering whether to apply, for a licence under section 5, or

(iii) such other person as the condition or requirement may specify or may enable the Commission to specify;

(c) to co-operate with the holder of another licence under section 5 in a specified matter;

(d) to participate in or co-operate with arrangements designed for the purposes of—

(i) holders of section 5 licences generally, or

(ii) a class of holders of section 5 licences generally;

(e) not to enter into an arrangement of a specified kind that would or might be harmful to the interests of the holder of another licence under section 5."

(6) In subsection (4) for "section 5 or 6" substitute "section 5".

(7) In the heading of the section for "sections 5 and 6" substitute "section 5".

6 In section 7A(1) (annual fee) (inserted by section 5 above) for "section 5 or 6" substitute "section 5".

7 In section 8 (variation of licence conditions)—

(a) in subsection (1) for "section 5 or 6" substitute "section 5", and

(b) in subsection (3)(b) omit "in the case of a licence granted under section 5".

8 In section 9 (enforcement of licence conditions)—

(a) in subsection (1) for "section 5 or 6" substitute "section 5", and

(b) in subsection (3) for "section 5(6)" substitute "section 5(2)(c)".

9 In section 10 (revocation of licence)—

(a) in subsection (1) for "a fit and proper body to run the National Lottery." substitute "a suitable person to promote the lottery or lotteries to which the licence relates",

(b) omit subsection (2),

(c) in subsection (3) for "section 5 or 6" substitute "section 5", and

(d) in subsection (3A) for "section 5 or 6" substitute "section 5".

10 In section 10A (financial penalties for breach of licence condition)—

(a) in subsections (1) and (2)(a) for "section 5 or 6" substitute "section 5", and

(b) in subsection (2)(b) for "paid to the Secretary of State under section 5(6)" substitute "payable under section 5(2)(c)".

11 In section 10C (annual levy) in subsections (1), (3)(a) and (b) and (4) for "section 5 or 6" substitute "section 5".

12 In section 22 (apportionment of National Lottery Distribution Fund: saving) for "section 5(6)" substitute "section 5(2)(c)".

13 In section 32 (distribution fund: investment) for "section 5(6)" substitute "section 5(2)(c)".

14 In Schedule 3 (revocation of licences) for paragraphs 4 and 5 substitute—

"4

(1) The licensee is not providing or proposing to provide facilities that are necessary or desirable in connection with the operation of a lottery.

(2) The licensee is not taking or proposing to take steps that are necessary or desirable for preventing the commission of fraud by participants in a lottery.

(3) A person who is exercising a function in connection with the promotion of a lottery is unsuitable.

(4) A person who has an interest in a lottery is unsuitable."

Other Acts

15 For section 115(5)(d) of the Police Act 1997 (c 50) (enhanced criminal record certificates) substitute—

"(d) a licence under section 5 of the National Lottery etc Act 1993 (c 39) (licence to promote lottery);".

16 (1) The Horserace Betting and Olympic Lottery Act 2004 (c 25) shall be amended as follows.

(2) In section 21 (designation of Olympic Lotteries)—

(a) in subsection (1) for "section 6" substitute "section 5", and

(b) subsections (2) and (3) shall cease to have effect.

(3) In section 22(1) (timing) for "section 6" substitute "section 5".

(4) For section 24(1) (payments into Olympic Lottery Distribution Fund) substitute—

"(1) Where a sum is required by virtue of section 5(2)(c) of the National Lottery etc Act 1993 (c 39) to be paid into the National Lottery Distribution Fund out of proceeds of lotteries promoted in reliance on a licence, such proportion of that sum as is attributable to Olympic Lotteries shall be paid instead into the Olympic Lottery Distribution Fund.".

(5) In section 26(4)(a) (payments out of Olympic Lottery Distribution Fund) for "section 5(6)" substitute "section 5(2)(c)".

(6) In section 28(3)(a) (winding up of Olympic Lottery Distribution Fund) for "section 5(6)" substitute "section 5(2)(c)".

(7) In section 32(3)(a) (distribution of Olympic Lottery Distributor) for "section 5(6)" substitute "section 5(2)(c)".

---

[1] To be appointed: see s 6(1).

7.341

SCHEDULE 2
NEW SCHEDULE 4A TO THE NATIONAL LOTTERY ETC ACT 1993
Section 14

'SCHEDULE 4A
THE BIG LOTTERY FUND

PART 1
CONSTITUTION

Membership

1

(1) The Big Lottery Fund shall consist of 12 members appointed by the Secretary of State.

(2) The Secretary of State shall appoint one of the members as Chairman.

(3) The Secretary of State shall ensure that at any time—

(a) one of the members is appointed to represent the interests of England,

(b) one of the members is appointed to represent the interests of Wales,

(c) one of the members is appointed to represent the interests of Scotland, and

(d) one of the members is appointed to represent the interests of Northern Ireland.

(4) In complying with paragraphs (a) to (d) of sub-paragraph (3) the Secretary of State—

(a) may not appoint a member for the purpose of satisfying more than one of those paragraphs,

(b) may appoint the Chairman for the purpose of satisfying one of those paragraphs,

(c) shall obtain the agreement of the National Assembly for Wales before appointing a person to satisfy paragraph (b),

(d) shall obtain the agreement of the Scottish Ministers before appointing a person to satisfy paragraph (c), and

(e) shall obtain the agreement of the Northern Ireland Department of Culture, Arts and Leisure before appointing a person to satisfy paragraph (d).

(5) The Secretary of State may by order vary the number specified in sub-paragraph (1).

(6) Before making an order under sub-paragraph (5) the Secretary of State shall consult—

(a) the National Assembly for Wales,

(b) the Scottish Ministers, and

(c) the Northern Ireland Department of Culture, Arts and Leisure.

Tenure

2

A person shall hold and vacate office as Chairman or other member of the Fund in accordance with the terms of his appointment (subject to this Schedule).

3

The Chairman or another member may resign his office by notice in writing to the Secretary of State.

4

(1) The Chairman or another member may be removed from office by the Secretary of State on the grounds that—

(a) a bankruptcy order has been made against him, his estate has been sequestrated or he has made a composition or arrangement with, or granted a trust deed for, his creditors, or

(b) he is, in the opinion of the Secretary of State, unable, unfit or unwilling to discharge the functions of his office.

(2) Before exercising the power under sub-paragraph (1) in respect of a person appointed for the purpose of satisfying paragraph 1(3)(b), (c) or (d) the Secretary of State shall consult—

(a) the National Assembly for Wales, in the case of a person appointed for the purpose of satisfying paragraph 1(3)(b),

(b) the Scottish Ministers, in the case of a person appointed for the purpose of satisfying paragraph 1(3)(c), and

(c) the Northern Ireland Department of Culture, Arts and Leisure, in the case of a person appointed for the purpose of satisfying paragraph 1(3)(d).

5

A person who ceases, otherwise than by virtue of paragraph 4, to be Chairman or another member may be re-appointed.

Staff

6

The Fund may appoint staff (subject to any directions under section 36E(3)(b)).

Committees

7

(1) The Fund shall establish—

(a) a committee, chaired by the member appointed under paragraph 1(3)(a), for the purpose of exercising the Fund's functions in relation to English devolved expenditure,

(b) a committee, chaired by the member appointed under paragraph 1(3)(b), for the purpose of exercising the Fund's functions in relation to Welsh devolved expenditure,

(c) a committee, chaired by the member appointed under paragraph 1(3)(c), for the purpose of exercising the Fund's functions in relation to Scottish devolved expenditure, and

(d) a committee, chaired by the member appointed under paragraph 1(3)(d), for the purpose of exercising the Fund's functions in relation to Northern Ireland devolved expenditure.

(2) Before appointing the members of a committee established under sub-paragraph (1) the Fund shall obtain the consent of—

(a) in the case of the committee concerned with England, the Secretary of State;

(b) in the case of the committee concerned with Wales, the National Assembly for Wales;

(c) in the case of the committee concerned with Scotland, the Scottish Ministers;

(d) in the case of the committee concerned with Northern Ireland, the Northern Ireland Department of Culture, Arts and Leisure.

(3) A committee established under sub-paragraph (1) shall carry on its activities under such name as the committee may determine with the consent of the Secretary of State and—

(a) in the case of the committee concerned with Wales, with the consent of the National Assembly for Wales;

(b) in the case of the committee concerned with Scotland, with the consent of the Scottish Ministers;

(c) in the case of the committee concerned with Northern Ireland, with the consent of the Northern Ireland Department of Culture, Arts and Leisure.

8

Nothing in paragraph 7 or section 25A(6) shall prevent the Fund from—

(a) establishing a committee otherwise than in accordance with that paragraph or section, or

(b) authorising a committee (whether or not established in accordance with that paragraph or section) to exercise a function of the Fund.

9

Section 25A(7) shall apply in relation to any committee of the Fund as it applies in relation to a committee established under section 25A(6).

Status

10

The Fund shall not be regarded as the servant or agent of the Crown or as enjoying any status, immunity or privilege of the Crown.

Supervision

11

In Schedule 2 to the Parliamentary Commissioner Act 1967 (c 13) (departments, &c. subject to investigation) insert at the appropriate place—

"The Big Lottery Fund."

Disqualification

12

In Part III of Schedule 1 to the House of Commons Disqualification Act 1975 (c 24) (other disqualifying offices) insert at the appropriate place—

"Chairman, or member in receipt of remuneration, of the Big Lottery Fund."

13

In Part III of Schedule 1 to the Northern Ireland Assembly Disqualification Act 1975 (c 25) (other disqualifying offices) insert at the appropriate place—

"Chairman, or member in receipt of remuneration, of the Big Lottery Fund."

PART 2
PROCEEDINGS

Self-regulation

14

The Fund may, subject to this Schedule, regulate its procedure and the procedure of its committees (and may, in particular, make provision for a quorum).

Records

15

In Schedule 1 to the Public Records Act 1958 (definition of public records) the following entry shall be inserted at the appropriate place in Part II of the Table at the end of paragraph 3—

"The Big Lottery Fund."

Saving

16

The validity of proceedings of the Fund or a committee shall not be affected by—

(a) a vacancy among its members, or

(b) a defect in the appointment of a person as Chairman or member.

PART 3
MONEY

Remuneration, &c

17

(1) The Fund may pay to the Chairman, another member or a member of a committee—

(a) such remuneration as the Secretary of State may determine, and

(b) such travelling and other allowances as the Secretary of State may determine.

(2) The Fund may pay to or in respect of the Chairman or another member such sums as the Secretary of State may determine by way of, or in respect of, pensions, allowances or gratuities.

(3) If the Secretary of State thinks that there are special circumstances that make it right for a person ceasing to hold office as Chairman or member to receive compensation, the Fund may pay him such compensation as the Secretary of State may determine.

18

(1) The Fund may (subject to any directions under section 36E(3)(b)) pay sums to or in respect of a member or former member of staff by way of or in respect of—

(a) remuneration,
(b) allowances,
(c) pensions,
(d) gratuities, or
(e) compensation for loss of employment.

(2) In Schedule 1 to the Superannuation Act 1972 (c 11) (employment to which superannuation schemes may extend) in the list of other bodies insert at the appropriate place—

"The Big Lottery Fund."

Payments

19

The Fund may make payments in respect of expenditure (which may include expenditure of a capital nature) of—

(a) the Fund, or
(b) a person to whom it delegates a function under section 25A(1).

Investment

20

(1) The Fund may deposit money in an interest-bearing account (but may not otherwise invest).

(2) The proceeds of money received by the Fund and invested under sub-paragraph (1) shall be treated for the purposes of Part II of this Act as part of that money.

Accounts

21

(1) The Fund shall—

(a) keep proper accounting records, and
(b) prepare a statement of accounts in respect of each financial year.

(2) The Fund shall send a copy of a statement under sub-paragraph (1)(b)—

(a) to the Secretary of State,
(b) to the National Assembly for Wales,
(c) to the Scottish Ministers,
(d) to the Northern Ireland Department of Culture, Arts and Leisure, and
(e) to the Comptroller and Auditor General.

(3) A copy of a statement must be sent under sub-paragraph (2) within such period, beginning with the end of the financial year to which the statement relates, as the Secretary of State may, with the consent of the Treasury, direct.

(4) The Comptroller and Auditor General shall—

(a) examine, certify and report on a statement received under this paragraph, and

(b) lay a copy of the statement and his report before Parliament.'

7.342

SCHEDULE 3

REPEALS

Section 21

Short title and chapter	***Extent of repeal***
Public Records Act 1958 (c 51)	In Schedule 1, in Part II of the Table at the end of paragraph 3, the entries for the National Lottery Charities Board, the Millennium Commission and the New Opportunities Fund.
Parliamentary Commissioner Act 1967 (c 13)	In Schedule 2, the entries for the National Lottery Charities Board, the Millennium Commission and the New Opportunities Fund.
Superannuation Act 1972 (c 11)	In Schedule 1, the references to employment by—
	(a) the National Lottery Charities Board, and
	(b) the New Opportunities Fund.
House of Commons Disqualification Act 1975 (c 24)	In Schedule 1, in Part III, the entries for the Chairman and members of—
	(a) the National Lottery Charities Board, and
	(b) the New Opportunities Fund.
Northern Ireland Assembly Disqualification Act 1975 (c 25)	In Schedule 1, in Part III, the entries for the Chairman and members of—
	(a) the National Lottery Charities Board, and
	(b) the New Opportunities Fund.
Race Relations Act 1976 (c 74)	In Schedule 1A, in Part II, the entries for the National Lottery Charities Board, the Millennium Commission and the New Opportunities Fund.
Charities Act 1993 (c 10)	In Schedule 2, paragraph (zb).
National Lottery etc Act 1993 (c 39)	Section 7(5) and (6).
	Section 32(5).
	Section 34(4).
	Sections 37 to 43D.
	In section 44(4), "or 43B".
	Schedules 5 to 6A.
National Lottery Act 1998 (c 22)	In section 6, subsections (2) to (7) and (9) to (10).
	Section 7.

Short title and chapter	*Extent of repeal*
	In section 8, subsections (1) and (3) to (7).
	Section 11(5) and (6).
	Section 14.
	Schedule 2.
Government of Wales Act 1998 (c 38)	In Schedule 5, paragraph 34.
Freedom of Information Act 2000 (c 36)	In Schedule 1, in Part VI, the entries for the National Lottery Charities Board, the Millennium Commission and the New Opportunities Fund.
National Lottery (Funding of Endowments) Act 2003 (c 23)	In section 1, subsections (5) to (7).

HORSERACE BETTING AND OLYMPIC LOTTERY ACT 2004

(2004 c 25)

Arrangement of sections

An Act to make provision for the sale of the Tote; to make provision for the abolition of the horserace betting levy system; to make provision for the establishment of National Lottery games designed to raise money in connection with the hosting by London of the Olympic Games in 2012; and for connected purposes.

[28th October 2004]

BE IT ENACTED by the Queen's most Excellent Majesty, by and with the advice and consent of the Lords Spiritual and Temporal, and Commons, in this present Parliament assembled, and by the authority of the same, as follows:—

Dates in force

Sections 21–24, 33, 34(1)–(5), (7), (8), (9)(a), (9)(b), (10), (11), 35–37, 38 (for certain purposes), 39 and Sch 6 (in part) in force 8 April 2005: Horserace Betting and Olympic Lottery Act 2004 (Commencement No 2) Order 2005, SI 2005/1134.

Sections 25–32, 34(6), (9)(c) and Sch 5 in force 8 July 2005: SI 2005/1831 Horserace Betting and Olympic Lottery Act 2004 (Commencement No 3) Order 2005.

PART 3
NATIONAL LOTTERY: OLYMPIC LOTTERIES

Olympic Lotteries

7.343 21 Licensing of Olympic Lotteries

(1) A licence under section 6 of the National Lottery etc Act 1993 (c 39) (licence authorising a body to promote lotteries as part of the National Lottery) may designate a lottery to which the licence relates as an Olympic Lottery.

(2) A licence under section 5 of that Act (licence to run the National Lottery) must include provision—

(a) for determining in respect of any period the proportion of proceeds of lotteriesforming part of the National Lottery that is attributable to Olympic Lotteries, or

(b) enabling the National Lottery Commission to determine that proportion in respect of any period.

(3) A designation under subsection (1) may be made only while provision under subsection (2) has effect.

(4) In respect of a licence under section 5 of that Act that has effect when this section comes into force—

(a) the Commission shall, after consulting the licensee, vary the licence so as to introduce provision of a kind specified in subsection (2)(a) or (b) above, and

(b) the variation shall take effect at such time as the Commission shall specify (whether or not the licensee consents).

7.344 22 Timing

(1) This section applies to a licence under section 6 of the National Lottery etc Act 1993 (c 39) which designates a lottery to which the licence relates as an Olympic Lottery.

(2) A licence to which this section applies must include a condition prohibiting the promotion of an Olympic Lottery unless the Secretary of State has by order declared that the International Olympic Committee has elected London as the host city for the 2012 Olympic Games.

(3) Subsection (4) applies if the Secretary of State by order declares—

(a) that the International Olympic Committee has elected a city other than London as the host city for the 2012 Olympic Games, or

(b) that the election of London by the International Olympic Committee as the host city for the 2012 Olympic Games has been revoked.

(4) Where this subsection applies—

(a) a licence to which this section applies shall cease to have effect in so far as it relates to an Olympic Lottery on such date as may be specified in the order under subsection (3), and

(b) the National Lottery Commission may not grant a licence to which this section applies.

(5) If the Secretary of State by order specifies a date as the termination date for the purposes of this section—

(a) any licence to which this section applies that has effect immediately before the termination date shall cease to have effect on that date in so far as it relates to an Olympic Lottery, and

(b) the National Lottery Commission may not grant a licence to which this section applies in respect of a period of time falling wholly or partly on or after the termination date.

Olympic Lottery Distribution Fund

7.345 23 The Fund

There shall be a fund maintained under the control and management of the Secretary of State and known as the Olympic Lottery Distribution Fund.

7.346 24 Payments into Fund from lottery proceeds

(1) Where a sum is required by virtue of section 5(6) of the National Lottery etc Act 1993 (c 39) (as substituted by section 34 of this Act) to be paid into the National Lottery Distribution Fund out of proceeds of lotteries in respect of a period, such proportion of that sum as is determined in accordance with section 21(2) or (4) of this Act to be attributable to Olympic Lotteries shall be paid instead into the Olympic Lottery Distribution Fund.

(2) Section 9(3) of that Act (as substituted by section 34 of this Act) shall have effect in relation to the Olympic Lottery Distribution Fund and sums due to be paid into it as it has effect in relation to the National Lottery Distribution Fund and sums due to be paid into it.

7.347 25 Payments into Fund from National Lottery Distribution Fund

(1) The Secretary of State may make an order permitting the Secretary of State to make payments from the National Lottery Distribution Fund into the Olympic Lottery Distribution Fund.

(2) A payment by virtue of an order under subsection (1) shall be treated as if paid out of money allocated for such of the purposes listed in section 22(3) of the National Lottery etc Act 1993 (apportionment of money in Distribution Fund) as the order shall specify.

(3) Before making an order under subsection (1) the Secretary of State shall consult each of the bodies for the time being mentioned in section 23 of that Act.

7.348 26 Payments out of Fund

(1) The Secretary of State may pay sums from the Olympic Lottery Distribution Fund to the Olympic Lottery Distributor.

(2) The Secretary of State may make regulations[1] permitting payments from the Olympic Lottery Distribution Fund—

(a) in respect of expenses of the Secretary of State in connection with functions under this Part;

(b) in respect of expenses incurred or to be incurred by the National Debt Commissioners in making investments under section 27;

(c) into the National Lottery Distribution Fund;
(d) to the Greater London Authority;
(e) to the National Olympic Committee;
(f) into the Consolidated Fund for the purpose of meeting payments made or to be made under paragraph 10 of Schedule 2A to the National Lottery etc Act 1993 (expenses of National Lottery Commission).

(3) Regulations by virtue of subsection (2)(a) and (b) shall permit payment only with the consent of the Treasury.

(4) Regulations by virtue of subsection (2)(c) shall in respect of each payment specify, or enable the Secretary of State to specify, whether it is to be—
(a) treated as having been paid into the National Lottery Distribution Fund by virtue of section 5(6) of the National Lottery etc Act 1993 (c 39) (general payments into fund), or
(b) allocated entirely for expenditure on or connected with sport and held in accordance with section 23(2) of that Act (distributing bodies for sports).

(5) Regulations by virtue of subsection (2)(c) may, in respect of a payment allocated in accordance with subsection (4)(b) provide, or enable the Secretary of State to provide, for section 23(2) of that Act to apply with specified modifications (which may, in particular, include modifications reducing a distributor's share to nil).

(6) Money paid to the Greater London Authority by virtue of subsection (2)(d) may be used by the Authority for any purpose for which it is authorised to incur expenditure.

---

1 The Olympic Lotteries (Payments out of Fund) Regulations 2006, SI 2006/655 have been made.

7.349 27 Investment

(1) Money in the Olympic Lottery Distribution Fund may be paid to the National Debt Commissioners and invested by them.

(2) Proceeds of an investment under this section—
(a) may be re-invested by the National Debt Commissioners, and
(b) unless re-invested, shall be paid into the Olympic Lottery Distribution Fund.

(3) In exercising a function under this section the National Debt Commissioners shall comply with any direction of the Treasury.

7.350 28 Winding up

(1) The Secretary of State [. . .][1] may by order make provision for the winding up of the Olympic Lottery Distribution Fund.

(2) An order under this section shall provide, in particular, for any money in or due to the Olympic Lottery Distribution Fund to be paid into the National Lottery Distribution Fund.

(3) An order under this section shall in respect of any payment specify, or enable the Secretary of State [. . .][2] to specify, whether it is to be—
(a) treated as having been paid into the National Lottery Distribution Fund by virtue of section 5(6) [section 5(2)(c)][3] of the National Lottery etc Act 1993 (general payments into fund), or
(b) allocated entirely for expenditure on or connected with sport and held in accordance with section 23(2) of that Act (distributing bodies for sports).

(4) Provision by virtue of subsection (3)(b) may provide for section 23(2) of that Act to apply with specified modifications (which may, in particular, include modifications reducing a distributor's share to nil).

1 Sub-s (1): words omitted repealed by SI 2010/1551, art 11, Schedule, Pt 1, para 4(d).

2 Sub-s (3): words omitted repealed by SI 2010/1551, art 11, Schedule, Pt 1, para 4(d).

3 Sub-s (3): in para (a) words 'section 5(6)' in italics repealed and subsequent words in square brackets substituted by the National Lottery Act 2006, s 6, Sch 1, para 16(1), (6).

Olympic Lottery Distributor

7.351 29 The Olympic Lottery Distributor

(1) There shall be a body corporate known as the Olympic Lottery Distributor.

(2) Schedule 5 (which makes provision in relation to the Distributor) shall have effect.

7.352 30 Distribution

(1) The Olympic Lottery Distributor shall distribute money received, whether under section 26 or otherwise, by way of grant or loan (subject to Part 3 of Schedule 5).

(2) The Distributor may make a grant or loan only if it considers it necessary or expedient for the purpose of or in connection with—

(a) the provision of facilities which are necessary or expedient if London is to be the host city of the 2012 Olympic games, or

(b) any other service or function which it is necessary or expedient to provide or undertake if London is to be the host city of the 2012 Olympic Games.

(3) In exercising its functions under this section the Distributor shall have regard to—

(a) the Olympic Charter, and

(b) any agreement entered into by or on behalf of the International Olympic Committee in the course of or in connection with the election of London as the host city for the 2012 Olympic Games.

(4) A grant or loan may, in particular, fund expenditure related to the provision of—

(a) facilities outside London;

(b) cultural and other events held in accordance with a provision of the Olympic Charter or in accordance with an agreement entered into by or on behalf of the International Olympic Committee.

(5) A grant or loan may be subject to conditions which may, in particular, include conditions—

(a) as to repayment (with or without interest);

(b) providing for payments to be made only with the consent of a specified person.

(6) The Secretary of State [. . .][1] may by regulations provide that a specified class of expenditure is to be treated as—

(a) satisfying the requirements of subsection (2), or

(b) not satisfying those requirements.

1 Sub-s (6): words omitted repealed by SI 2010/1551, art 11, Schedule, Pt 1, para 4(e).

7.353 31 Distribution policy

(1) The Olympic Lottery Distributor shall comply with any requirement of the Secretary of State [. . .][1] to—

(a) prepare a policy for the distribution of money under section 30, or

(b) review and revise the policy.

(2) A policy must, in particular—

(a) estimate the Distributor's annual income,

(b) specify the sources of the income estimated,

(c) specify matters in respect of which the Distributor thinks that it will or may make grants or loans, and

(d) estimate, where possible, the amount of grants or loans that the Distributor will or may make.

(3) A requirement under subsection (1) may include provision (which may supplement or amplify subsection (2)) about—

(a) the form of the policy;

(b) the content of the policy.

(4) Before preparing or revising a policy the Distributor—

(a) shall submit a draft of the policy or revision to the Secretary of State [. . .][2], and

(b) shall consult—

(i) the National Lottery Commission,

(ii) the Mayor of London,

(iii) the National Olympic Committee, and

(iv) the British Paralympic Association.

(5) The Distributor shall as soon as is reasonably practicable send a copy of a policy or revision under this section to—

(a) the Secretary of State [. . .][3],

(b) the Mayor of London,

(c) the National Olympic Committee, and

(d) the British Paralympic Association.

(6) Where the Secretary of State [. . .][4] receives a copy of a policy or revision under subsection (5) he shall lay it before Parliament.

---

1 Sub-s (1): words omitted repealed by SI 2010/1551, art 11, Schedule, Pt 1, para 4(f).

2 Sub-s (4): in para (a) words omitted repealed by SI 2010/1551, art 11, Schedule, Pt 1, para 4(f).

3 Sub-s (5): in para (a) words omitted repealed by SI 2010/1551, art 11, Schedule, Pt 1, para 4(f).

4 Sub-s (6): words omitted repealed by SI 2010/1551, art 11, Schedule, Pt 1, para 4(f).

7.354 32 Dissolution

(1) The Secretary of State [. . .][1] may by order make provision for the dissolution of the Olympic Lottery Distributor.

(2) An order under this section may, in particular—

(a) provide for the transfer of property, rights or liabilities of the Distributor to—

(i) the Secretary of State, or

(ii) any other person;

(b) make provision enabling a person to receive anything transferred under paragraph (a) (and that provision shall have effect despite any other enactment or instrument);

(c) establish a body corporate;

(d) make consequential, incidental or transitional provision which may, in particular—

(i) provide for anything done by or in relation to the Distributor to have effect as if done by or in relation to another person;

(ii) permit anything (which may include legal proceedings) which is in the process of being done by or in relation to the Distributor when a transfer takes effect, to be continued by or in relation to another person;

(iii) provide for a reference to the Distributor in an instrument or other document to be treated as a reference to another person.

(3) An order transferring a sum of money to the Secretary of State under subsection (2)(a)(i) may require the Secretary of State to pay the sum into the National Lottery Distribution Fund; and an order containing such provision shall specify whether the payment is to be—

(a) treated as having been paid into the National Lottery Distribution Fund by virtue of section 5(6) [section 5(2)(c)][2] of the National Lottery etc Act 1993 (c 39) (general payments into fund), or

(b) allocated entirely for expenditure on or connected with sport and held in accordance with section 23(2) of that Act (distributing bodies for sports).

(4) Provision by virtue of subsection (3)(b) may provide for section 23(2) of that Act to apply with specified modifications (which may, in particular, include modifications reducing a distributor's share to nil).

(5) [The Secretary of State may not][3] make an order under this section providing for the transfer of property, rights or liabilities to a person unless the person has consented to the transfer.

(6) An order under this section—

(a) may transfer rights and liabilities relating to employees, but

(b) shall not affect the operation of the [Transfer of Undertakings (Protection of Employment) Regulations 2006][4].

(7) [The Secretary of State may not][5] make an order by virtue of subsection (6)(a) unless satisfied that sufficient notice has been given to enable compliance with any applicable requirement of those regulations.

---

1 Sub-s (1): words omitted repealed by SI 2010/1551, art 11, Sch, Pt 1, para 4(g).

2 Sub-s (3): in para (a) words 'section 5(6)' in italics repealed and subsequent words in square brackets substituted by the National Lottery Act 2006, s 6, Sch 1, para 16(1), (7).

3 Sub-s (5): words 'The Secretary of State may not' in square brackets substituted by SI 2010/1551, art 11, Sch, Pt 1, para 5.

4 Sub-s (6): in para (b) words in square brackets substituted by SI 2006/246, reg 20(3), Sch 2, para 1(j).

5 Sub-s (7): words 'The Secretary of State may not' in square brackets substituted by SI 2010/1551, art 11, Sch, Pt 1, para 5.

Miscellaneous

7.355 33 Interpretation

(1) In this Part—

(a) a reference to the 2012 Olympic Games is a reference to—

(i) the Games of the Olympiad that are to take place in the year 2012, and

(ii) except where the context otherwise requires, the Paralympic Games that are to take place in that year,

(b) 'the National Olympic Committee' means the National Olympic Committee of the United Kingdom,

(c) 'the Organising Committee' means the Organising Committee established by the National Olympic Committee,

(d) 'the Paralympic Games' means the events known by that name and in connection with which the Organising Committee has functions by virtue of an agreement between that committee and the International Olympic Committee,

(e) 'the Olympic Charter' means the Olympic Charter of the International Olympic Committee, and

(f) any expression used in connection with the Olympic Games (including an expression mentioned in this section) shall have the meaning which it has in or in accordance with the Olympic Charter of the International Olympic Committee (as it has effect from time to time).

(2) A reference in this Part to the making of a loan includes a reference to the provision of any other kind of financial assistance.

7.356 34 Consequential amendments, &c

(1) The National Lottery etc Act 1993 (c 39) shall have effect subject to this section.

(2) In section 4 (overriding duties)—

(a) a reference to functions under Part I of that Act shall be treated as including a reference to functions under this Part of this Act, . . .[1] [and][2]

[(aa) . . .][3]

(b) the definition in subsection (3) of 'the net proceeds of the National Lottery' shall be treated as including a reference to sums paid into the Olympic Lottery Distribution Fund by virtue of section 24 of this Act.

(3) For section 5(6) (payments by licensee) substitute—

'(6) A licence under this section shall include a condition requiring the licensee to pay into the National Lottery Distribution Fund sums out of the proceeds of lotteries forming part of the National Lottery.

(6A) A licence under this section shall include provision for determining—

(a) the amount of payments under subsection (6), and

(b) the timing of payments under subsection (6).'

(4) In the case of a licence granted under section 5 before the coming into force of subsection (3) above, the condition included in accordance with section 5(6) shall, after that time, be construed as if any sum required to be paid by that condition were required to be paid into the National Lottery Distribution Fund (subject to section 24 of this Act).

(5) For section 9(3) (enforcement of conditions) substitute—

'(3) Where a sum is due to be paid to the National Lottery Distribution Fund by virtue of section 5(6)—

(a) the sum shall be recoverable by the Secretary of State as a debt due to the Fund, and

(b) the licensee's liability to pay shall not be affected by his licence ceasing to have effect.'

(6) For section 10A(14) (breach of licence condition: financial penalty: recovery) substitute—

'(14) Where under this section one person ("the debtor") becomes liable to pay a penalty to another person ("the creditor")—

(a) the penalty and any interest accrued under subsection (13) shall be recoverable by the Secretary of State from the debtor as a debt due to the creditor, and

(b) the debtor's liability to pay shall not be affected by his licence ceasing to have effect.

(15) A penalty under this section may be payable partly to the National Lottery Distribution Fund and partly to the Olympic Lottery Distribution Fund.'

7.365

SCHEDULE 5
THE OLYMPIC LOTTERY DISTRIBUTOR
Section 29

PART 1
CONSTITUTION

7.366 1 **Membership**

(1) The Secretary of State [. . .][1]—

(a) shall appoint the members of the Olympic Lottery Distributor, and

(b) shall appoint one of the members as Chairman.

(2) The Secretary of State [. . .][1] shall aim to ensure that the Distributor has at least 5 members at any time.

(3) Before making an appointment under sub-paragraph (1) the Secretary of State [. . .][1] shall consult—

(a) the Mayor of London, and

(b) the National Olympic Committee.

2 **Tenure**

A person shall hold and vacate office as Chairman or other member of the Distributor in accordance with the terms of his appointment (subject to this Schedule).

3 [The Secretary of State shall not][2] appoint a person to hold office as Chairman or other member of the Distributor for a term of more than five years.

4 The Chairman or another member of the Distributor may resign his office by notice in writing to the Secretary of State [. . .][3].

5 The Chairman or another member of the Distributor may be removed from office by the Secretary of State [. . .][4] on the grounds that—

(a) a bankruptcy order has been made against him, his estate has been sequestrated or he has made a composition or arrangement with, or granted a trust deed for, his creditors, or

(b) he is, in the opinion of the Secretary of State [. . .][4], unable, unfit or unwilling to discharge the functions of his office.

6 A person who ceases, otherwise than by virtue of paragraph 5, to be Chairman or another member of the Distributor may be re-appointed.

7 **Staff**

The Distributor may appoint staff.

8 **Committees**

(1) The Distributor may establish a committee.

(2) A committee—

(a) must include a member or employee of the Distributor, but

(b) may also include persons who are neither members nor employees of the Distributor.

9 **Status**

The Distributor shall not be regarded as the servant or agent of the Crown or as enjoying any status, immunity or privilege of the Crown.

10 **Supervision**

In Schedule 2 to the Parliamentary Commissioner Act 1967 (c 13) (departments, subject to investigation) insert at the appropriate place—

'Olympic Lottery Distributor.'

11 Disqualification

In Part III of Schedule 1 to the House of Commons Disqualification Act 1975 (c 24) (other disqualifying offices) insert at the appropriate place—

'Chairman, or member in receipt of remuneration, of the Olympic Lottery Distributor'.

12 In Part III of Schedule 1 to the Northern Ireland Assembly Disqualification Act 1975 (c 25) (other disqualifying offices) insert at the appropriate place—

'Chairman, or member in receipt of remuneration, of the Olympic Lottery Distributor.'

PART 2
PROCEEDINGS

7.367 **13 Delegation**

(1) The Distributor may delegate a function to—

(a) a member,
(b) an employee,
(c) a committee, or
(d) any other person.

(2) The following provisions of section 25A of the National Lottery etc Act 1993 (c 39) (delegation) shall apply (with any necessary modifications) for the purposes of this paragraph as they apply for the purposes of that section—

(a) subsection (4) (power to accept delegation),
(b) subsections (5) to (7) (sub-delegation), and
(c) subsections (8) to (11) (general).

14 Directions of the Secretary of State

(1) In exercising its functions the Distributor shall comply with any direction given to it by the Secretary of State.

(2) A direction under this paragraph may, in particular—

(a) relate to the management and control of money received by the Distributor,
(b) relate to the terms and conditions on which grants or loans are made under section 30,
(c) require the Distributor to obtain the Secretary of State's consent before taking action of a specified kind,
(d) require the Distributor to provide information,
(e) relate to the employment of staff, or
(f) with the consent of the Treasury, relate to—
    (i) the form of accounts, or
    (ii) methods and principles for the preparation of accounts.

(3) Before giving a direction under this paragraph the Secretary of State shall consult the Distributor.

15 Self-regulation

The Distributor may, subject to this Schedule, regulate its own procedure and that of its committees (and in particular may specify a quorum for meetings).

16 Records

In Schedule 1 to the Public Records Act 1958 (c 51) (definition of public records) the following entry shall be inserted at the appropriate place in Part II of the Table at the end of paragraph 3—

'Olympic Lottery Distributor.'

17 Annual report

(1) As soon as is reasonably practicable after the end of each financial year the Distributor shall send to the Secretary of State a report on the exercise of the Distributor's functions during the year.

(2) A report under sub-paragraph (1) shall, in particular, specify any directions given to the Distributor under paragraph 14 that had effect during the financial year to which the report relates.

(3) The Secretary of State shall lay before Parliament a copy of each report received by him under this paragraph.

18 Saving

The validity of proceedings of the Distributor shall not be affected by—

(a) a vacancy among its members, or

(b) a defect in the appointment of a person as Chairman or member.

PART 3
MONEY

7.368 19 Remuneration, &c

(1) The Distributor may pay to the Chairman, another member or a member of a committee—

(a) such remuneration as the Secretary of State may determine, and

(b) such travelling and other allowances as the Secretary of State may determine.

(2) The Distributor may pay to or in respect of the Chairman or another member such sums as the Secretary of State may determine by way of, or in respect of, pensions, allowances or gratuities.

(3) If the Secretary of State thinks that there are special circumstances that make it right for a person ceasing to hold office as Chairman or member of the Distributor to receive compensation, the Distributor may pay to him such compensation as the Secretary of State may determine.

20 (1) The Distributor may pay sums to or in respect of a member or former member of staff by way of or in respect of—

(a) remuneration,

(b) allowances,

(c) pensions,

(d) gratuities, or

(e) compensation for loss of employment.

(2) In Schedule 1 to the Superannuation Act 1972 (c 11) (employment to which superannuation schemes may extend) in the list of other bodies insert at the appropriate place—

'The Olympic Lottery Distributor.'

21 Payments

The Distributor may make payments in respect of expenditure (which may include expenditure of a capital nature) by—

(a) the Distributor, or

(b) a person to whom it delegates functions under paragraph 13.

22 Investment

The Distributor may deposit money in an interest-bearing account (but may not otherwise invest).

23 Miscellaneous receipts

(1) The Secretary of State may pay money to the Distributor for the purpose of enabling it to meet expenditure.

(2) A payment under sub-paragraph (1)—

(a) may not be used to make grants or loans under section 30,

(b) may be made only where the Secretary of State thinks the Distributor's income is or is likely to be insufficient to meet the expenditure to which the payment relates, and

(c) may be made on conditions (which may include conditions about repayment).

24 The Distributor may accept gifts.

25 Accounts

(1) The Distributor shall—

(a) keep proper accounting records, and

(b) prepare a statement of accounts in respect of each financial year.

(2) The Distributor shall send a copy of a statement under sub-paragraph (1)(b)—

(a) to the Secretary of State, and

(b) to the Comptroller and Auditor General.

(3) A copy of a statement must be sent under sub-paragraph (2) within such period, beginning with the end of the financial year to which the statement relates, as the Secretary of State may, with the consent of the Treasury, direct.

(4) The Comptroller and Auditor General shall—

(a) examine, certify and report on a statement received under this paragraph, and

(b) lay a copy of the statement and his report before Parliament.

26 Financial year

(1) The financial year of the Distributor shall be the period of 12 months ending with the 31st March.

(2) But the first financial year of the Distributor shall be the period—

(a) beginning with the coming into force of section 29, and

(b) ending with the following 31st March.

7.369

SCHEDULE 6
REPEALS
Section 38

Short title and chapter	*Extent of repeal*
Betting, Gaming and Lotteries Act 1963 (c 2)	In section 1(5)(a), 'but no other races'.
	In section 3(1)— (a) 'or to the Totalisator Board', (b) 'or, as the case may be, by the said Board', and (c) 'or by the said Board'. In section 3(2)— (a) 'or to the said Board', and (b) 'or, as the case may be, the Board'. In section 3(3)— (a) 'The said Board', and (b) 'by that Board or, as the case may be,'. In section 5(3)—

Short title and chapter	*Extent of repeal*
	(a) 'by the Totalisator Board or, with the authority of that Board, by the persons having the management of that racecourse', and (b) 'by that Board or, as the case may be, by those persons'. In section 6(1) 'only'. In section 9— (a) in subsection (1) the words from 'Provided that' to the end, (b) subsection (2)(b), (c) in subsection (2)(c)(i) 'or by the Totalisator Board', and (d) in subsection (2)(c)(i) 'or, as the case may be, with or through that Board'. Section 12. Section 14. Section 15. Section 24(2)(e). In section 31(1)— (a) 'and the Totalisator Board',[1] (b) 'of each of the Boards', and (c) 'in question'. In section 55(1)— (a) in the definition of 'bookmaker', 'other than the Totalisator Board', and (b) the definitions of 'recognised horse race', 'sponsored pool betting' and 'the Totalisator Board'. In paragraph 19(a)(i) of Schedule 1, 'in the case of an applicant other than the Totalisator Board,'.
Horserace Totalisator and Betting Levy Boards Act 1972 (c 69)	The whole Act.
Race Relations Act 1976 (c 74)	In Part II of Schedule 1A, 'The Horserace Totalisator Board'.
National Lottery etc Act 1993 (c 39)	Section 17. Section 21(2). Section 22(3)(e). Section 30.
Horserace Totalisator Board Act 1997 (c 1)	The whole Act.
Trustee Act 2000 (c 29)	Paragraph 34 of Schedule 2.
Freedom of Information Act 2000 (c 36)	In Part VI of Schedule 1, 'The Horserace Totalisator Board'.

Appointment

Appointment (in part): 8 April 2005: see SI 2005/1134, art 2.

Appointment (in part): 13 July 2011: see SI 2011/1704, art 2.

Miscellaneous

It is understood that amendment (a) to the Betting, Gaming and Lotteries Act 1963, s 31(1) above contradicts an amendment made by Sch 2, para 14(a)(i) hereof. The relevant Government Department has confirmed that this is an oversight and that it is unlikely to be brought into force.

TRIBUNALS, COURTS AND ENFORCEMENT ACT 2007

(2007 c 15)

Arrangement of sections

PART I

TRIBUNALS AND INQUIRIES

An Act to make provision about tribunals and inquiries; to establish an Administrative Justice and Tribunals Council; to amend the law relating to judicial appointments and appointments to the Law Commission; to amend the law relating to the enforcement of judgments and debts; to make further provision about the management and relief of debt; to make provision protecting cultural objects from seizure or forfeiture in certain circumstances; to amend the law relating to the taking of possession of land affected by compulsory purchase; to alter the powers of the High Court in judicial review applications; and for connected purposes.

[19th July 2007]

BE IT ENACTED by the Queen's most Excellent Majesty, by and with the advice and consent of the Lords Spiritual and Temporal, and Commons, in this present Parliament assembled, and by the authority of the same, as follows:—

PART 1
TRIBUNALS AND INQUIRIES

CHAPTER 1
TRIBUNAL JUDICIARY: INDEPENDENCE AND SENIOR PRESIDENT

7.369.1 Senior President of Tribunals

(1) Her Majesty may, on the recommendation of the Lord Chancellor, appoint a person to the office of Senior President of Tribunals.

(2) Schedule 1 makes further provision about the Senior President of Tribunals and about recommendations for appointment under subsection (1).

(3) A holder of the office of Senior President of Tribunals must, in carrying out the functions of that office, have regard to—

- (a) the need for tribunals to be accessible,
- (b) the need for proceedings before tribunals—
  - (i) to be fair, and
  - (ii) to be handled quickly and efficiently,
- (c) the need for members of tribunals to be experts in the subject-matter of, or the law to be applied in, cases in which they decide matters, and
- (d) the need to develop innovative methods of resolving disputes that are of a type that may be brought before tribunals.

(4) In subsection (3) "tribunals" means—

- (a) the First-tier Tribunal,
- (b) the Upper Tribunal,

(c) employment tribunals, [and]
(d) the Employment Appeal Tribunal, . . .
(e) . . . .

CHAPTER 2
FIRST-TIER TRIBUNAL AND UPPER TRIBUNAL

Establishment

7.369.2 3 The First-tier Tribunal and the Upper Tribunal

(1) There is to be a tribunal, known as the First-tier Tribunal, for the purpose of exercising the functions conferred on it under or by virtue of this Act or any other Act.

(2) There is to be a tribunal, known as the Upper Tribunal, for the purpose of exercising the functions conferred on it under or by virtue of this Act or any other Act.

(3) Each of the First-tier Tribunal, and the Upper Tribunal, is to consist of its judges and other members.

(4) The Senior President of Tribunals is to preside over both of the First-tier Tribunal and the Upper Tribunal.

(5) The Upper Tribunal is to be a superior court of record.

Members and composition of tribunals

7.369.3 4 Judges and other members of the First-tier Tribunal

(1) A person is a judge of the First-tier Tribunal if the person—
(a) is a judge of the First-tier Tribunal by virtue of appointment under paragraph 1(1) of Schedule 2,
(b) is a transferred-in judge of the First-tier Tribunal (see section 31(2)),
(c) is a judge of the Upper Tribunal,
(d) . . . or
(e) is a member of a panel of chairmen of employment tribunals.

(2) A person is also a judge of the First-tier Tribunal, but only as regards functions of the tribunal in relation to appeals such as are mentioned in subsection (1) of section 5 of the Criminal Injuries Compensation Act 1995 (c 53), if the person is an adjudicator appointed under that section by the Scottish Ministers.

(3) A person is one of the other members of the First-tier Tribunal if the person—
(a) is a member of the First-tier Tribunal by virtue of appointment under paragraph 2(1) of Schedule 2,
(b) is a transferred-in other member of the First-tier Tribunal (see section 31(2)),
(c) is one of the other members of the Upper Tribunal, or
(d) is a member of a panel of members of employment tribunals that is not a panel of chairmen of employment tribunals.

(4) Schedule 2—
contains provision for the appointment of persons to be judges or other members of the First-tier Tribunal, and
makes further provision in connection with judges and other members of the First-tier Tribunal.

7.369.4 5 Judges and other members of the Upper Tribunal

(1) A person is a judge of the Upper Tribunal if the person—
(a) is the Senior President of Tribunals,
(b) is a judge of the Upper Tribunal by virtue of appointment under paragraph 1(1) of Schedule 3,
(c) is a transferred-in judge of the Upper Tribunal (see section 31(2)),
(d) . . .

(e) is the Chief Social Security Commissioner, or any other Social Security Commissioner, appointed under section 50(1) of the Social Security Administration (Northern Ireland) Act 1992 (c 8),

(f) is a Social Security Commissioner appointed under section 50(2) of that Act (deputy Commissioners),

(g) is within section 6(1),

(h) is a deputy judge of the Upper Tribunal (whether under paragraph 7 of Schedule 3 or under section 31(2)), or

(i) is a Chamber President or a Deputy Chamber President, whether of a chamber of the Upper Tribunal or of a chamber of the First-tier Tribunal, and does not fall within any of paragraphs (a) to (h).

(2) A person is one of the other members of the Upper Tribunal if the person—

(a) is a member of the Upper Tribunal by virtue of appointment under paragraph 2(1) of Schedule 3,

(b) is a transferred-in other member of the Upper Tribunal (see section 31(2)), [or]

(c) is a member of the Employment Appeal Tribunal appointed under section 22(1)(c) of the Employment Tribunals Act 1996 (c 17) . . .

(d) . . .

(3) Schedule 3—

contains provision for the appointment of persons to be judges (including deputy judges), or other members, of the Upper Tribunal, and

makes further provision in connection with judges and other members of the Upper Tribunal.

7.369.5 6 Certain judges who are also judges of First-tier Tribunal and Upper Tribunal

(1) A person is within this subsection (and so, by virtue of sections 4(1)(c) and 5(1)(g), is a judge of the First-tier Tribunal and of the Upper Tribunal) if the person—

(a) is an ordinary judge of the Court of Appeal in England and Wales (including the vice-president, if any, of either division of that Court),

(b) is a Lord Justice of Appeal in Northern Ireland,

(c) is a judge of the Court of Session,

(d) is a puisne judge of the High Court in England and Wales or Northern Ireland,

(e) is a circuit judge,

(f) is a sheriff in Scotland,

(g) is a county court judge in Northern Ireland,

(h) is a district judge in England and Wales or Northern Ireland, or

(i) is a District Judge (Magistrates' Courts).

(2) References in subsection (1)(c) to (i) to office-holders do not include deputies or temporary office-holders.

7.369.6 7 Chambers: jurisdiction and Presidents

(1) The Lord Chancellor may, with the concurrence of the Senior President of Tribunals, by order make provision for the organisation of each of the First-tier Tribunal and the Upper Tribunal into a number of chambers.

(2) There is—

(a) for each chamber of the First-tier Tribunal, and

(b) for each chamber of the Upper Tribunal,

to be a person, or two persons, to preside over that chamber.

(3) A person may not at any particular time preside over more than one chamber of the First-tier Tribunal and may not at any particular time preside over more than

one chamber of the Upper Tribunal (but may at the same time preside over one chamber of the First-tier Tribunal and over one chamber of the Upper Tribunal).

(4) A person appointed under this section to preside over a chamber is to be known as a Chamber President.

(5) Where two persons are appointed under this section to preside over the same chamber, any reference in an enactment to the Chamber President of the chamber is a reference to a person appointed under this section to preside over the chamber.

(6) The Senior President of Tribunals may (consistently with subsections (2) and (3)) appoint a person who is the Chamber President of a chamber to preside instead, or to preside also, over another chamber.

(7) The Lord Chancellor may (consistently with subsections (2) and (3)) appoint a person who is not a Chamber President to preside over a chamber.

(8) Schedule 4 (eligibility for appointment under subsection (7), appointment of Deputy Chamber Presidents and Acting Chamber Presidents, assignment of judges and other members of the First-tier Tribunal and Upper Tribunal, and further provision about Chamber Presidents and chambers) has effect.

(9) Each of the Lord Chancellor and the Senior President of Tribunals may, with the concurrence of the other, by order—

(a) make provision for the allocation of the First-tier Tribunal's functions between its chambers;

(b) make provision for the allocation of the Upper Tribunal's functions between its chambers;

(c) amend or revoke any order made under this subsection.

7.369.7 8 Senior President of Tribunals: power to delegate

(1) The Senior President of Tribunals may delegate any function he has in his capacity as Senior President of Tribunals—

(a) to any judge, or other member, of the Upper Tribunal or First-tier Tribunal;

(b) to staff appointed under section 40(1).

(2) Subsection (1) does not apply to functions of the Senior President of Tribunals under section 7(9).

(3) A delegation under subsection (1) is not revoked by the delegator's becoming incapacitated.

(4) Any delegation under subsection (1) that is in force immediately before a person ceases to be Senior President of Tribunals continues in force until varied or revoked by a subsequent holder of the office of Senior President of Tribunals.

(5) The delegation under this section of a function shall not prevent the exercise of the function by the Senior President of Tribunals.

Review of decisions and appeals

7.369.8 9 Review of decision of First-tier Tribunal

(1) The First-tier Tribunal may review a decision made by it on a matter in a case, other than a decision that is an excluded decision for the purposes of section 11(1) (but see subsection (9)).

(2) The First-tier Tribunal's power under subsection (1) in relation to a decision is exercisable—

(a) of its own initiative, or

(b) on application by a person who for the purposes of section 11(2) has a right of appeal in respect of the decision.

(3) Tribunal Procedure Rules may—

(a) provide that the First-tier Tribunal may not under subsection (1) review (whether of its own initiative or on application under subsection (2)(b)) a decision of a description specified for the purposes of this paragraph in Tribunal Procedure Rules;

(b) provide that the First-tier Tribunal's power under subsection (1) to review a decision of a description specified for the purposes of this paragraph in Tribunal Procedure Rules is exercisable only of the tribunal's own initiative;

(c) provide that an application under subsection (2)(b) that is of a description specified for the purposes of this paragraph in Tribunal Procedure Rules may be made only on grounds specified for the purposes of this paragraph in Tribunal Procedure Rules;

(d) provide, in relation to a decision of a description specified for the purposes of this paragraph in Tribunal Procedure Rules, that the First-tier Tribunal's power under subsection (1) to review the decision of its own initiative is exercisable only on grounds specified for the purposes of this paragraph in Tribunal Procedure Rules.

(4) Where the First-tier Tribunal has under subsection (1) reviewed a decision, the First-tier Tribunal may in the light of the review do any of the following—

(a) correct accidental errors in the decision or in a record of the decision;

(b) amend reasons given for the decision;

(c) set the decision aside.

(5) Where under subsection (4)(c) the First-tier Tribunal sets a decision aside, the First-tier Tribunal must either—

(a) re-decide the matter concerned, or

(b) refer that matter to the Upper Tribunal.

(6) Where a matter is referred to the Upper Tribunal under subsection (5)(b), the Upper Tribunal must re-decide the matter.

(7) Where the Upper Tribunal is under subsection (6) re-deciding a matter, it may make any decision which the First-tier Tribunal could make if the First-tier Tribunal were re-deciding the matter.

(8) Where a tribunal is acting under subsection (5)(a) or (6), it may make such findings of fact as it considers appropriate.

(9) This section has effect as if a decision under subsection (4)(c) to set aside an earlier decision were not an excluded decision for the purposes of section 11(1), but the First-tier Tribunal's only power in the light of a review under subsection (1) of a decision under subsection (4)(c) is the power under subsection (4)(a).

(10) A decision of the First-tier Tribunal may not be reviewed under subsection (1) more than once, and once the First-tier Tribunal has decided that an earlier decision should not be reviewed under subsection (1) it may not then decide to review that earlier decision under that subsection.

(11) Where under this section a decision is set aside and the matter concerned is then re-decided, the decision set aside and the decision made in re-deciding the matter are for the purposes of subsection (10) to be taken to be different decisions.

7.369.9 10 Review of decision of Upper Tribunal

(1) The Upper Tribunal may review a decision made by it on a matter in a case, other than a decision that is an excluded decision for the purposes of section 13(1) (but see subsection (7)).

(2) The Upper Tribunal's power under subsection (1) in relation to a decision is exercisable—

(a) of its own initiative, or

(b) on application by a person who for the purposes of section 13(2) has a right of appeal in respect of the decision.

(3) Tribunal Procedure Rules may—

(a) provide that the Upper Tribunal may not under subsection (1) review (whether of its own initiative or on application under subsection (2)(b)) a decision of a description specified for the purposes of this paragraph in Tribunal Procedure Rules;

(b) provide that the Upper Tribunal's power under subsection (1) to review a decision of a description specified for the purposes of this paragraph in Tribunal Procedure Rules is exercisable only of the tribunal's own initiative;

(c) provide that an application under subsection (2)(b) that is of a description specified for the purposes of this paragraph in Tribunal Procedure Rules may be made only on grounds specified for the purposes of this paragraph in Tribunal Procedure Rules;

(d) provide, in relation to a decision of a description specified for the purposes of this paragraph in Tribunal Procedure Rules, that the Upper Tribunal's power under subsection (1) to review the decision of its own initiative is exercisable only on grounds specified for the purposes of this paragraph in Tribunal Procedure Rules.

(4) Where the Upper Tribunal has under subsection (1) reviewed a decision, the Upper Tribunal may in the light of the review do any of the following—

(a) correct accidental errors in the decision or in a record of the decision;

(b) amend reasons given for the decision;

(c) set the decision aside.

(5) Where under subsection (4)(c) the Upper Tribunal sets a decision aside, the Upper Tribunal must re-decide the matter concerned.

(6) Where the Upper Tribunal is acting under subsection (5), it may make such findings of fact as it considers appropriate.

(7) This section has effect as if a decision under subsection (4)(c) to set aside an earlier decision were not an excluded decision for the purposes of section 13(1), but the Upper Tribunal's only power in the light of a review under subsection (1) of a decision under subsection (4)(c) is the power under subsection (4)(a).

(8) A decision of the Upper Tribunal may not be reviewed under subsection (1) more than once, and once the Upper Tribunal has decided that an earlier decision should not be reviewed under subsection (1) it may not then decide to review that earlier decision under that subsection.

(9) Where under this section a decision is set aside and the matter concerned is then re-decided, the decision set aside and the decision made in re-deciding the matter are for the purposes of subsection (8) to be taken to be different decisions.

7.369.10 11 Right to appeal to Upper Tribunal

(1) For the purposes of subsection (2), the reference to a right of appeal is to a right to appeal to the Upper Tribunal on any point of law arising from a decision made by the First-tier Tribunal other than an excluded decision.

(2) Any party to a case has a right of appeal, subject to subsection (8).

(3) That right may be exercised only with permission (or, in Northern Ireland, leave).

(4) Permission (or leave) may be given by—

(a) the First-tier Tribunal, or

(b) the Upper Tribunal,

on an application by the party.

(5) For the purposes of subsection (1), an "excluded decision" is—

(a) any decision of the First-tier Tribunal on an appeal made in exercise of a right conferred by the Criminal Injuries Compensation Scheme in compliance with section 5(1)(a) of the Criminal Injuries Compensation Act 1995 (c 53) (appeals against decisions on reviews), [(aa) any decision of the First-tier Tribunal on an appeal made in exercise of a right conferred by the Victims of Overseas Terrorism Compensation Scheme in compliance with section 52(3) of the Crime and Security Act 2010,]

(b) any decision of the First-tier Tribunal on an appeal under section 28(4) or (6) of the Data Protection Act 1998 (c 29) (appeals against national security certificate),

(c) any decision of the First-tier Tribunal on an appeal under section 60(1) or (4) of the Freedom of Information Act 2000 (c 36) (appeals against national security certificate),

(d) a decision of the First-tier Tribunal under section 9—

(i) to review, or not to review, an earlier decision of the tribunal,

(ii) to take no action, or not to take any particular action, in the light of a review of an earlier decision of the tribunal,

(iii) to set aside an earlier decision of the tribunal, or

(iv) to refer, or not to refer, a matter to the Upper Tribunal,

(e) a decision of the First-tier Tribunal that is set aside under section 9 (including a decision set aside after proceedings on an appeal under this section have been begun), or

(f) any decision of the First-tier Tribunal that is of a description specified in an order made by the Lord Chancellor.

(6) A description may be specified under subsection (5)(f) only if—

(a) in the case of a decision of that description, there is a right to appeal to a court, the Upper Tribunal or any other tribunal from the decision and that right is, or includes, something other than a right (however expressed) to appeal on any point of law arising from the decision, or

(b) decisions of that description are made in carrying out a function transferred under section 30 and prior to the transfer of the function under section 30(1) there was no right to appeal from decisions of that description.

(7) Where—

(a) an order under subsection (5)(f) specifies a description of decisions, and

(b) decisions of that description are made in carrying out a function transferred under section 30,

the order must be framed so as to come into force no later than the time when the transfer under section 30 of the function takes effect (but power to revoke the order continues to be exercisable after that time, and power to amend the order continues to be exercisable after that time for the purpose of narrowing the description for the time being specified).

(8) The Lord Chancellor may by order make provision for a person to be treated as being, or to be treated as not being, a party to a case for the purposes of subsection (2).

7.369.11 Proceedings on appeal to Upper Tribunal

(1) Subsection (2) applies if the Upper Tribunal, in deciding an appeal under section 11, finds that the making of the decision concerned involved the making of an error on a point of law.

(2) The Upper Tribunal—

(a) may (but need not) set aside the decision of the First-tier Tribunal, and

(b) if it does, must either—

(i) remit the case to the First-tier Tribunal with directions for its reconsideration, or

(ii) re-make the decision.

(3) In acting under subsection (2)(b)(i), the Upper Tribunal may also—

(a) direct that the members of the First-tier Tribunal who are chosen to reconsider the case are not to be the same as those who made the decision that has been set aside;

(b) give procedural directions in connection with the reconsideration of the case by the First-tier Tribunal.

(4) In acting under subsection (2)(b)(ii), the Upper Tribunal—

(a) may make any decision which the First-tier Tribunal could make if the First-tier Tribunal were re-making the decision, and

(b) may make such findings of fact as it considers appropriate.

7.369.12 13 Right to appeal to Court of Appeal etc

(1) For the purposes of subsection (2), the reference to a right of appeal is to a right to appeal to the relevant appellate court on any point of law arising from a decision made by the Upper Tribunal other than an excluded decision.

(2) Any party to a case has a right of appeal, subject to subsection (14).

(3) That right may be exercised only with permission (or, in Northern Ireland, leave).

(4) Permission (or leave) may be given by—

(a) the Upper Tribunal, or

(b) the relevant appellate court,

on an application by the party.

(5) An application may be made under subsection (4) to the relevant appellate court only if permission (or leave) has been refused by the Upper Tribunal.

(6) The Lord Chancellor may, as respects an application under subsection (4) that falls within subsection (7) and for which the relevant appellate court is the Court of Appeal in England and Wales or the Court of Appeal in Northern Ireland, by order make provision for permission (or leave) not to be granted on the application unless the Upper Tribunal or (as the case may be) the relevant appellate court considers—

(a) that the proposed appeal would raise some important point of principle or practice, or

(b) that there is some other compelling reason for the relevant appellate court to hear the appeal.

(7) An application falls within this subsection if the application is for permission (or leave) to appeal from any decision of the Upper Tribunal on an appeal under section 11.

(8) For the purposes of subsection (1), an "excluded decision" is—

(a) any decision of the Upper Tribunal on an appeal under section 28(4) or (6) of the Data Protection Act 1998 (c 29) (appeals against national security certificate),

(b) any decision of the Upper Tribunal on an appeal under section 60(1) or (4) of the Freedom of Information Act 2000 (c 36) (appeals against national security certificate),

(c) any decision of the Upper Tribunal on an application under section 11(4)(b) (application for permission or leave to appeal),

(d) a decision of the Upper Tribunal under section 10—

(i) to review, or not to review, an earlier decision of the tribunal,

(ii) to take no action, or not to take any particular action, in the light of a review of an earlier decision of the tribunal, or

(iii) to set aside an earlier decision of the tribunal,

(e) a decision of the Upper Tribunal that is set aside under section 10 (including a decision set aside after proceedings on an appeal under this section have been begun), or

(f) any decision of the Upper Tribunal that is of a description specified in an order made by the Lord Chancellor.

(9) A description may be specified under subsection (8)(f) only if—

(a) in the case of a decision of that description, there is a right to appeal to a court from the decision and that right is, or includes, something other than a right (however expressed) to appeal on any point of law arising from the decision, or

(b) decisions of that description are made in carrying out a function transferred under section 30 and prior to the transfer of the function under section 30(1) there was no right to appeal from decisions of that description.

(10) Where—

(a) an order under subsection (8)(f) specifies a description of decisions, and

(b) decisions of that description are made in carrying out a function transferred under section 30,

the order must be framed so as to come into force no later than the time when the transfer under section 30 of the function takes effect (but power to revoke the order continues to be exercisable after that time, and power to amend the order continues to be exercisable after that time for the purpose of narrowing the description for the time being specified).

(11) Before the Upper Tribunal decides an application made to it under subsection (4), the Upper Tribunal must specify the court that is to be the relevant appellate court as respects the proposed appeal.

(12) The court to be specified under subsection (11) in relation to a proposed appeal is whichever of the following courts appears to the Upper Tribunal to be the most appropriate—

(a) the Court of Appeal in England and Wales;

(b) the Court of Session;

(c) the Court of Appeal in Northern Ireland.

(13) In this section except subsection (11), "the relevant appellate court", as respects an appeal, means the court specified as respects that appeal by the Upper Tribunal under subsection (11).

(14) The Lord Chancellor may by order make provision for a person to be treated as being, or to be treated as not being, a party to a case for the purposes of subsection (2).

(15) Rules of court may make provision as to the time within which an application under subsection (4) to the relevant appellate court must be made.

7.369.13 14 Proceedings on appeal to Court of Appeal etc

(1) Subsection (2) applies if the relevant appellate court, in deciding an appeal under section 13, finds that the making of the decision concerned involved the making of an error on a point of law.

(2) The relevant appellate court—

(a) may (but need not) set aside the decision of the Upper Tribunal, and

(b) if it does, must either—

(i) remit the case to the Upper Tribunal or, where the decision of the Upper Tribunal was on an appeal or reference from another tribunal or some other person, to the Upper Tribunal or that other tribunal or person, with directions for its reconsideration, or

(ii) re-make the decision.

(3) In acting under subsection (2)(b)(i), the relevant appellate court may also—

(a) direct that the persons who are chosen to reconsider the case are not to be the same as those who—

(i) where the case is remitted to the Upper Tribunal, made the decision of the Upper Tribunal that has been set aside, or

(ii) where the case is remitted to another tribunal or person, made the decision in respect of which the appeal or reference to the Upper Tribunal was made;

(b) give procedural directions in connection with the reconsideration of the case by the Upper Tribunal or other tribunal or person.

(4) In acting under subsection (2)(b)(ii), the relevant appellate court—

(a) may make any decision which the Upper Tribunal could make if the Upper Tribunal were re-making the decision or (as the case may be) which the other tribunal or person could make if that other tribunal or person were re-making the decision, and

(b) may make such findings of fact as it considers appropriate.

(5) Where—

(a) under subsection (2)(b)(i) the relevant appellate court remits a case to the Upper Tribunal, and

(b) the decision set aside under subsection (2)(a) was made by the Upper Tribunal on an appeal or reference from another tribunal or some other person,

the Upper Tribunal may (instead of reconsidering the case itself) remit the case to that other tribunal or person, with the directions given by the relevant appellate court for its reconsideration.

(6) In acting under subsection (5), the Upper Tribunal may also—

(a) direct that the persons who are chosen to reconsider the case are not to be the same as those who made the decision in respect of which the appeal or reference to the Upper Tribunal was made;

(b) give procedural directions in connection with the reconsideration of the case by the other tribunal or person.

(7) In this section "the relevant appellate court", as respects an appeal under section 13, means the court specified as respects that appeal by the Upper Tribunal under section 13(11).

"Judicial review"

7.369.14 15 Upper Tribunal's "judicial review" jurisdiction

(1) The Upper Tribunal has power, in cases arising under the law of England and Wales or under the law of Northern Ireland, to grant the following kinds of relief—

(a) a mandatory order;

(b) a prohibiting order;

(c) a quashing order;

(d) a declaration;

(e) an injunction.

(2) The power under subsection (1) may be exercised by the Upper Tribunal if—

(a) certain conditions are met (see section 18), or

(b) the tribunal is authorised to proceed even though not all of those conditions are met (see section 19(3) and (4)).

(3) Relief under subsection (1) granted by the Upper Tribunal—

(a) has the same effect as the corresponding relief granted by the High Court on an application for judicial review, and

(b) is enforceable as if it were relief granted by the High Court on an application for judicial review.

(4) In deciding whether to grant relief under subsection (1)(a), (b) or (c), the Upper Tribunal must apply the principles that the High Court would apply in deciding whether to grant that relief on an application for judicial review.

(5) In deciding whether to grant relief under subsection (1)(d) or (e), the Upper Tribunal must—

(a) in cases arising under the law of England and Wales apply the principles that the High Court would apply in deciding whether to grant that relief under section 31(2) of the [Senior Courts Act 1981] (c 54) on an application for judicial review, and

(b) in cases arising under the law of Northern Ireland apply the principles that the High Court would apply in deciding whether to grant that relief on an application for judicial review.

(6) For the purposes of the application of subsection (3)(a) in relation to cases arising under the law of Northern Ireland—

(a) a mandatory order under subsection (1)(a) shall be taken to correspond to an order of mandamus,

(b) a prohibiting order under subsection (1)(b) shall be taken to correspond to an order of prohibition, and

(c) a quashing order under subsection (1)(c) shall be taken to correspond to an order of certiorari.

7.369.15 16 Application for relief under section 15(1)

(1) This section applies in relation to an application to the Upper Tribunal for relief under section 15(1).

(2) The application may be made only if permission (or, in a case arising under the law of Northern Ireland, leave) to make it has been obtained from the tribunal.

(3) The tribunal may not grant permission (or leave) to make the application unless it considers that the applicant has a sufficient interest in the matter to which the application relates.

(4) Subsection (5) applies where the tribunal considers—

(a) that there has been undue delay in making the application, and

(b) that granting the relief sought on the application would be likely to cause substantial hardship to, or substantially prejudice the rights of, any person or would be detrimental to good administration.

(5) The tribunal may—

(a) refuse to grant permission (or leave) for the making of the application;

(b) refuse to grant any relief sought on the application.

(6) The tribunal may award to the applicant damages, restitution or the recovery of a sum due if—

(a) the application includes a claim for such an award arising from any matter to which the application relates, and

(b) the tribunal is satisfied that such an award would have been made by the High Court if the claim had been made in an action begun in the High Court by the applicant at the time of making the application.

(7) An award under subsection (6) may be enforced as if it were an award of the High Court.

(8) Where—

(a) the tribunal refuses to grant permission (or leave) to apply for relief under section 15(1),

(b) the applicant appeals against that refusal, and

(c) the Court of Appeal grants the permission (or leave),

the Court of Appeal may go on to decide the application for relief under section 15(1).

(9) Subsections (4) and (5) do not prevent Tribunal Procedure Rules from limiting the time within which applications may be made.

7.369.16 17 17 Quashing orders under section 15(1): supplementary provision

(1) If the Upper Tribunal makes a quashing order under section 15(1)(c) in respect of a decision, it may in addition—

(a) remit the matter concerned to the court, tribunal or authority that made the decision, with a direction to reconsider the matter and reach a decision in accordance with the findings of the Upper Tribunal, or

(b) substitute its own decision for the decision in question.

(2) The power conferred by subsection (1)(b) is exercisable only if—

(a) the decision in question was made by a court or tribunal,

(b) the decision is quashed on the ground that there has been an error of law, and

(c) without the error, there would have been only one decision that the court or tribunal could have reached.

(3) Unless the Upper Tribunal otherwise directs, a decision substituted by it under subsection (1)(b) has effect as if it were a decision of the relevant court or tribunal.

7.369.17 18 Limits of jurisdiction under section 15(1)

(1) This section applies where an application made to the Upper Tribunal seeks (whether or not alone)—

(a) relief under section 15(1), or

(b) permission (or, in a case arising under the law of Northern Ireland, leave) to apply for relief under section 15(1).

(2) If Conditions 1 to 4 are met, the tribunal has the function of deciding the application.

(3) If the tribunal does not have the function of deciding the application, it must by order transfer the application to the High Court.

(4) Condition 1 is that the application does not seek anything other than—

(a) relief under section 15(1);

(b) permission (or, in a case arising under the law of Northern Ireland, leave) to apply for relief under section 15(1);

(c) an award under section 16(6);

(d) interest;

(e) costs.

(5) Condition 2 is that the application does not call into question anything done by the Crown Court.

(6) Condition 3 is that the application falls within a class specified for the purposes of this subsection in a direction given in accordance with Part 1 of Schedule 2 to the Constitutional Reform Act 2005 (c 4).

(7) The power to give directions under subsection (6) includes—

(a) power to vary or revoke directions made in exercise of the power, and

(b) power to make different provision for different purposes.

(8) Condition 4 is that the judge presiding at the hearing of the application is either—

(a) a judge of the High Court or the Court of Appeal in England and Wales or Northern Ireland, or a judge of the Court of Session, or

(b) such other persons as may be agreed from time to time between the Lord Chief Justice, the Lord President, or the Lord Chief Justice of Northern Ireland, as the case may be, and the Senior President of Tribunals.

(9) Where the application is transferred to the High Court under subsection (3)—

(a) the application is to be treated for all purposes as if it—

(i) had been made to the High Court, and

(ii) sought things corresponding to those sought from the tribunal, and

(b) any steps taken, permission (or leave) given or orders made by the tribunal in relation to the application are to be treated as taken, given or made by the High Court.

(10) Rules of court may make provision for the purpose of supplementing subsection (9).

(11) The provision that may be made by Tribunal Procedure Rules about amendment of an application for relief under section 15(1) includes, in particular, provision about amendments that would cause the application to become transferrable under subsection (3).

(12) For the purposes of subsection (9)(a)(ii), in relation to an application transferred to the High Court in Northern Ireland—

(a) an order of mandamus shall be taken to correspond to a mandatory order under section 15(1)(a),

(b) an order of prohibition shall be taken to correspond to a prohibiting order under section 15(1)(b), and

(c) an order of certiorari shall be taken to correspond to a quashing order under section 15(1)(c).

7.369.18 19 Transfer of judicial review applications from High Court

(1) In the [Senior Courts Act 1981] (c 54), after section 31 insert—

"31A Transfer of judicial review applications to Upper Tribunal

(1) This section applies where an application is made to the High Court—

(a) for judicial review, or

(b) for permission to apply for judicial review.

(2) If Conditions 1, 2, 3 and 4 are met, the High Court must by order transfer the application to the Upper Tribunal.

(3) If Conditions 1, 2 and 4 are met, but Condition 3 is not, the High Court may by order transfer the application to the Upper Tribunal if it appears to the High Court to be just and convenient to do so.

(4) Condition 1 is that the application does not seek anything other than—

(a) relief under section 31(1)(a) and (b);

(b) permission to apply for relief under section 31(1)(a) and (b);

(c) an award under section 31(4);

(d) interest;

(e) costs.

(5) Condition 2 is that the application does not call into question anything done by the Crown Court.

(6) Condition 3 is that the application falls within a class specified under section 18(6) of the Tribunals, Courts and Enforcement Act 2007.

(7) Condition 4 is that the application does not call into question any decision made under—

(a) the Immigration Acts,

(b) the British Nationality Act 1981 (c 61),

(c) any instrument having effect under an enactment within paragraph (a) or (b), or

(d) any other provision of law for the time being in force which determines British citizenship, British overseas territories citizenship, the status of a British National (Overseas) or British Overseas citizenship."

(3) Where an application is transferred to the Upper Tribunal under 31A of the [Senior Courts Act 1981] (c 54) or section 25A of the Judicature (Northern Ireland) Act 1978 (transfer from the High Court of judicial review applications)—

(a) the application is to be treated for all purposes as if it—

(i) had been made to the tribunal, and
(ii) sought things corresponding to those sought from the High Court,

(b) the tribunal has the function of deciding the application, even if it does not fall within a class specified under section 18(6), and

(c) any steps taken, permission given, leave given or orders made by the High Court in relation to the application are to be treated as taken, given or made by the tribunal.

(4) Where—

(a) an application for permission is transferred to the Upper Tribunal under section 31A of the [Senior Courts Act 1981] (c 54) and the tribunal grants permission, or

(b) an application for leave is transferred to the Upper Tribunal under section 25A of the Judicature (Northern Ireland) Act 1978 (c 23) and the tribunal grants leave,

the tribunal has the function of deciding any subsequent application brought under the permission or leave, even if the subsequent application does not fall within a class specified under section 18(6).

(5) Tribunal Procedure Rules may make further provision for the purposes of supplementing subsections (3) and (4).

Miscellaneous

7.369.19 22 Tribunal Procedure Rules

(1) There are to be rules, to be called "Tribunal Procedure Rules", governing—

(a) the practice and procedure to be followed in the First-tier Tribunal, and

(b) the practice and procedure to be followed in the Upper Tribunal.

(2) Tribunal Procedure Rules are to be made by the Tribunal Procedure Committee.

(3) In Schedule 5—

Part 1 makes further provision about the content of Tribunal Procedure Rules,

Part 2 makes provision about the membership of the Tribunal Procedure Committee,

Part 3 makes provision about the making of Tribunal Procedure Rules by the Committee, and

Part 4 confers power to amend legislation in connection with Tribunal Procedure Rules.

(4) Power to make Tribunal Procedure Rules is to be exercised with a view to securing—

(a) that, in proceedings before the First-tier Tribunal and Upper Tribunal, justice is done,

(b) that the tribunal system is accessible and fair,

(c) that proceedings before the First-tier Tribunal or Upper Tribunal are handled quickly and efficiently,

(d) that the rules are both simple and simply expressed, and

(e) that the rules where appropriate confer on members of the First-tier Tribunal, or Upper Tribunal, responsibility for ensuring that proceedings before the tribunal are handled quickly and efficiently.

(5) In subsection (4)(b) "the tribunal system" means the system for deciding matters within the jurisdiction of the First-tier Tribunal or the Upper Tribunal.

7.369.20 23 Practice directions

(1) The Senior President of Tribunals may give directions—

(a) as to the practice and procedure of the First-tier Tribunal;

(b) as to the practice and procedure of the Upper Tribunal.

(2) A Chamber President may give directions as to the practice and procedure of the chamber over which he presides.

(3) A power under this section to give directions includes—

(a) power to vary or revoke directions made in exercise of the power, and

(b) power to make different provision for different purposes (including different provision for different areas).

(4) Directions under subsection (1) may not be given without the approval of the Lord Chancellor.

(5) Directions under subsection (2) may not be given without the approval of—

(a) the Senior President of Tribunals, and

(b) the Lord Chancellor.

(6) Subsections (4) and (5)(b) do not apply to directions to the extent that they consist of guidance about any of the following—

(a) the application or interpretation of the law;

(b) the making of decisions by members of the First-tier Tribunal or Upper Tribunal.

(7) Subsections (4) and (5)(b) do not apply to directions to the extent that they consist of criteria for determining which members of the First-tier Tribunal or Upper Tribunal may be chosen to decide particular categories of matter; but the directions may, to that extent, be given only after consulting the Lord Chancellor.

7.369.21 24 Mediation

(1) A person exercising power to make Tribunal Procedure Rules or give practice directions must, when making provision in relation to mediation, have regard to the following principles—

(a) mediation of matters in dispute between parties to proceedings is to take place only by agreement between those parties;

(b) where parties to proceedings fail to mediate, or where mediation between parties to proceedings fails to resolve disputed matters, the failure is not to affect the outcome of the proceedings.

(2) Practice directions may provide for members to act as mediators in relation to disputed matters in a case that is the subject of proceedings.

(3) The provision that may be made by virtue of subsection (2) includes provision for a member to act as a mediator in relation to disputed matters in a case even though the member has been chosen to decide matters in the case.

(4) Once a member has begun to act as a mediator in relation to a disputed matter in a case that is the subject of proceedings, the member may decide matters in the case only with the consent of the parties.

(5) Staff appointed under section 40(1) may, subject to their terms of appointment, act as mediators in relation to disputed matters in a case that is the subject of proceedings.

(6) In this section—

"member" means a judge or other member of the First-tier Tribunal or a judge or other member of the Upper Tribunal;

"practice direction" means a direction under section 23(1) or (2);

"proceedings" means proceedings before the First-tier Tribunal or proceedings before the Upper Tribunal.

7.369.22 25 Supplementary powers of Upper Tribunal

(1) In relation to the matters mentioned in subsection (2), the Upper Tribunal—

(a) has, in England and Wales or in Northern Ireland, the same powers, rights, privileges and authority as the High Court, and

(b) has, in Scotland, the same powers, rights, privileges and authority as the Court of Session.

(2) The matters are—
(a) the attendance and examination of witnesses,
(b) the production and inspection of documents, and
(c) all other matters incidental to the Upper Tribunal's functions.

(3) Subsection (1) shall not be taken—
(a) to limit any power to make Tribunal Procedure Rules;
(b) to be limited by anything in Tribunal Procedure Rules other than an express limitation.

(4) A power, right, privilege or authority conferred in a territory by subsection (1) is available for purposes of proceedings in the Upper Tribunal that take place outside that territory (as well as for purposes of proceedings in the tribunal that take place within that territory).

7.369.23 26 First-tier Tribunal and Upper Tribunal: sitting places

Each of the First-tier Tribunal and the Upper Tribunal may decide a case—
(a) in England and Wales,
(b) in Scotland, or
(c) in Northern Ireland,
even though the case arises under the law of a territory other than the one in which the case is decided.

7.369.24 27 Enforcement

(1) A sum payable in pursuance of a decision of the First-tier Tribunal or Upper Tribunal made in England and Wales—
(a) shall be recoverable as if it were payable under an order of a county court in England and Wales;
(b) shall be recoverable as if it were payable under an order of the High Court in England and Wales.

(2) An order for the payment of a sum payable in pursuance of a decision of the First-tier Tribunal or Upper Tribunal made in Scotland (or a copy of such an order certified in accordance with Tribunal Procedure Rules) may be enforced as if it were an extract registered decree arbitral bearing a warrant for execution issued by the sheriff court of any sheriffdom in Scotland.

(3) A sum payable in pursuance of a decision of the First-tier Tribunal or Upper Tribunal made in Northern Ireland—
(a) shall be recoverable as if it were payable under an order of a county court in Northern Ireland;
(b) shall be recoverable as if it were payable under an order of the High Court in Northern Ireland.

(4) This section does not apply to a sum payable in pursuance of—
(a) an award under section 16(6), or
(b) an order by virtue of section 21(1).

(5) The Lord Chancellor may by order make provision for subsection (1) or (3) to apply in relation to a sum of a description specified in the order with the omission of one (but not both) of paragraphs (a) and (b).

(6) Tribunal Procedure Rules—
(a) may make provision as to where, for purposes of this section, a decision is to be taken to be made;
(b) may provide for all or any of subsections (1) to (3) to apply only, or not to apply except, in relation to sums of a description specified in Tribunal Procedure Rules.

7.369.25 28 Assessors

(1) If it appears to the First-tier Tribunal or the Upper Tribunal that a matter before it requires special expertise not otherwise available to it, it may direct that in

dealing with that matter it shall have the assistance of a person or persons appearing to it to have relevant knowledge or experience.

(2) The remuneration of a person who gives assistance to either tribunal as mentioned in subsection (1) shall be determined and paid by the Lord Chancellor.

(3) The Lord Chancellor may—

(a) establish panels of persons from which either tribunal may (but need not) select persons to give it assistance as mentioned in subsection (1);

(b) under paragraph (a) establish different panels for different purposes;

(c) after carrying out such consultation as he considers appropriate, appoint persons to a panel established under paragraph (a);

(d) remove a person from such a panel.

7.369.26 29 Costs or expenses

(1) The costs of and incidental to—

(a) all proceedings in the First-tier Tribunal, and

(b) all proceedings in the Upper Tribunal,

shall be in the discretion of the Tribunal in which the proceedings take place.

(2) The relevant Tribunal shall have full power to determine by whom and to what extent the costs are to be paid.

(3) Subsections (1) and (2) have effect subject to Tribunal Procedure Rules.

(4) In any proceedings mentioned in subsection (1), the relevant Tribunal may—

(a) disallow, or

(b) (as the case may be) order the legal or other representative concerned to meet,

the whole of any wasted costs or such part of them as may be determined in accordance with Tribunal Procedure Rules.

(5) In subsection (4) "wasted costs" means any costs incurred by a party—

(a) as a result of any improper, unreasonable or negligent act or omission on the part of any legal or other representative or any employee of such a representative, or

(b) which, in the light of any such act or omission occurring after they were incurred, the relevant Tribunal considers it is unreasonable to expect that party to pay.

(6) In this section "legal or other representative", in relation to a party to proceedings, means any person exercising a right of audience or right to conduct the proceedings on his behalf.

(7) In the application of this section in relation to Scotland, any reference in this section to costs is to be read as a reference to expenses.

CHAPTER 3
TRANSFER OF TRIBUNAL FUNCTIONS

7.369.27 30 Transfer of functions of certain tribunals

(1) The Lord Chancellor may by order provide for a function of a scheduled tribunal to be transferred—

(a) to the First-tier Tribunal,

(b) to the Upper Tribunal,

(c) to the First-tier Tribunal and the Upper Tribunal with the question as to which of them is to exercise the function in a particular case being determined by a person under provisions of the order,

(d) to the First-tier Tribunal to the extent specified in the order and to the Upper Tribunal to the extent so specified,

(e) to the First-tier Tribunal and the Upper Tribunal with the question as to which of them is to exercise the function in a particular case being determined by, or under, Tribunal Procedure Rules,
(f) to an employment tribunal,
(g) to the Employment Appeal Tribunal,
(h) to an employment tribunal and the Employment Appeal Tribunal with the question as to which of them is to exercise the function in a particular case being determined by a person under provisions of the order, or
(i) to an employment tribunal to the extent specified in the order and to the Employment Appeal Tribunal to the extent so specified.

(2) In subsection (1) "scheduled tribunal" means a tribunal in a list in Schedule 6 that has effect for the purposes of this section.

(3) The Lord Chancellor may, as respects a function transferred under subsection (1) or this subsection, by order provide for the function to be further transferred as mentioned in any of paragraphs (a) to (i) of subsection (1).

(4) An order under subsection (1) or (3) may include provision for the purposes of or in consequence of, or for giving full effect to, a transfer under that subsection.

(5) A function of a tribunal may not be transferred under subsection (1) or (3) if, or to the extent that, the provision conferring the function—
(a) would be within the legislative competence of the Scottish Parliament if it were included in an Act of that Parliament, or
(b) would be within the legislative competence of the Northern Ireland Assembly if it were included in an Act of that Assembly.

(6) Subsection (5) does not apply to—
(a) the Secretary of State's function of deciding appeals under section 41 of the Consumer Credit Act 1974 (c 39),
(b) functions of the Consumer Credit Appeals Tribunal,
(c) the Secretary of State's function of deciding appeals under section 7(1) of the Estate Agents Act 1979 (c 38), or
(d) functions of an adjudicator under section 5 of the Criminal Injuries Compensation Act 1995 (c 53) (but see subsection (7)).

(7) Functions of an adjudicator under section 5 of the Criminal Injuries Compensation Act 1995 (c 53), so far as they relate to Scotland, may be transferred under subsection (1) or (3) only with the consent of the Scottish Ministers.

(8) A function of a tribunal may be transferred under subsection (1) or (3) only with the consent of the Welsh Ministers if any relevant function is exercisable in relation to the tribunal by the Welsh Ministers (whether by the Welsh Ministers alone, or by the Welsh Ministers jointly or concurrently with any other person).

(9) In subsection (8) "relevant function", in relation to a tribunal, means a function which relates—
(a) to the operation of the tribunal (including, in particular, its membership, administration, staff, accommodation and funding, and payments to its members or staff), or
(b) to the provision of expenses and allowances to persons attending the tribunal or attending elsewhere in connection with proceedings before the tribunal.

7.369.28 31 Transfers under section 30: supplementary powers

(1) The Lord Chancellor may by order make provision for abolishing the tribunal by whom a function transferred under section 30(1) is exercisable immediately before its transfer.

(2) The Lord Chancellor may by order make provision, where functions of a tribunal are transferred under section 30(1), for a person—
(a) who is the tribunal (but is not the Secretary of State), or

(b) who is a member of the tribunal, or

(c) who is an authorised decision-maker for the tribunal,

to (instead or in addition) be the holder of an office specified in subsection (3).

(3) Those offices are—

(a) transferred-in judge of the First-tier Tribunal,

(b) transferred-in other member of the First-tier Tribunal,

(c) transferred-in judge of the Upper Tribunal,

(d) transferred-in other member of the Upper Tribunal, and

(e) deputy judge of the Upper Tribunal.

(4) Where functions of a tribunal are transferred under section 30(1), the Lord Chancellor must exercise the power under subsection (2) so as to secure that each person who immediately before the end of the tribunal's life—

(a) is the tribunal,

(b) is a member of the tribunal, or

(c) is an authorised decision-maker for the tribunal,

becomes the holder of an office specified in subsection (3) with effect from the end of the tribunal's life (if the person is not then already the holder of such an office).

(5) Subsection (4) does not apply in relation to a person—

(a) by virtue of the person's being the Secretary of State, or

(b) by virtue of the person's being a Commissioner for the general purposes of the income tax;

and a reference in subsection (4) to the end of a tribunal's life is to when the tribunal is abolished or (without being abolished) comes to have no functions.

(6) For the purposes of this section, a person is an "authorised decision-maker" for a tribunal if—

(a) the tribunal is listed in column 1 of an entry in the following Table, and

(b) the person is of the description specified in column 2 of that entry.

(1) ***Tribunal***	*(2)* ***Authorised decision-maker***
Adjudicator to Her Majesty's Land Registry	Member of the Adjudicator's staff who is authorised by the Adjudicator to carry out functions of the Adjudicator which are not of an administrative character
The Secretary of State as respects his function of deciding appeals under section 41 of the Consumer Credit Act 1974 (c 39)	Person who is a member of a panel under regulation 24 of the Consumer Credit Licensing (Appeals) Regulations 1998 (SI 1998/1203)
The Secretary of State as respects his function of deciding appeals under section 7(1) of the Estate Agents Act 1979 (c 38)	Person appointed, at any time after 2005, under regulation 19(1) of the Estate Agents (Appeals) Regulations 1981 (SI 1981/1518) to hear an pappeal on behalf of the Secretary of State

(7) Where a function of a tribunal is transferred under section 30(1), the Lord Chancellor may by order provide for procedural rules in force immediately before the transfer to have effect, or to have effect with appropriate modifications, after the transfer (and, accordingly, to be capable of being varied or revoked) as if they were—

(a) Tribunal Procedure Rules, or

(b) employment tribunal procedure regulations, or Appeal Tribunal procedure rules, within the meaning given by section 42(1) of the Employment Tribunals Act 1996 (c 17).

(8) In subsection (7)—

"procedural rules" means provision (whether called rules or not)—

(a) regulating practice or procedure before the tribunal, and
(b) applying for purposes connected with the exercise of the function;

"appropriate modifications" means modifications (including additions and omissions) that appear to the Lord Chancellor to be necessary to secure, or expedient in connection with securing, that the procedural rules apply in relation to the exercise of the function after the transfer.

(9) The Lord Chancellor may, in connection with provision made by order under section 30 or the preceding provisions of this section, make by order such incidental, supplemental, transitional or consequential provision, or provision for savings, as the Lord Chancellor thinks fit, including provision applying only in relation to cases selected by a member—

(a) of the First-tier Tribunal,
(b) of the Upper Tribunal,
(c) of the Employment Appeal Tribunal, or
(d) of a panel of members of employment tribunals.

(10) Subsections (1), (2) and (7) are not to be taken as prejudicing the generality of subsection (9).

7.369.29 32 Power to provide for appeal to Upper Tribunal from tribunals in Wales

(1) Subsection (2) applies if—

(a) a function is transferred under section 30(1)(a), (c), (d) or (e) in relation to England but is not transferred under section 30(1) in relation to Wales, or
(b) a function that is not exercisable in relation to Wales is transferred under section 30(1)(a), (c), (d) or (e) in relation to England and, although there is a corresponding function that is exercisable in relation to Wales, that corresponding function is not transferred under section 30(1) in relation to Wales.

(2) The Lord Chancellor may by order—

(a) provide for an appeal against a decision to be made to the Upper Tribunal instead of to the court to which an appeal would otherwise fall to be made where the decision is made in exercising, in relation to Wales, the function mentioned in subsection (1)(a) or (as the case may be) the corresponding function mentioned in subsection (1)(b);
(b) provide for a reference of any matter to be made to the Upper Tribunal instead of to the court to which a reference would otherwise fall to be made where the matter arises in exercising, in relation to Wales, the function mentioned in subsection (1)(a) or (as the case may be) the corresponding function mentioned in subsection (1)(b).

(3) The Lord Chancellor may by order provide for an appeal against a decision of a scheduled tribunal to be made to the Upper Tribunal, instead of to the court to which an appeal would otherwise fall to be made, where the decision is made by the tribunal in exercising a function in relation to Wales.

(4) In subsection (3) "scheduled tribunal" means a tribunal in a list in Schedule 6 that has effect for the purposes of that subsection.

(5) An order under subsection (2) or (3)—

(a) may include provision for the purposes of or in consequence of, or for giving full effect to, provision made by the order;
(b) may include such incidental, supplemental, transitional or consequential provision or savings as the Lord Chancellor thinks fit.

7.369.30 35 Transfer of Ministerial responsibilities for certain tribunals

(1) The Lord Chancellor may by order—

(a) transfer any relevant function, so far as that function is exercisable by a Minister of the Crown—

(i) to the Lord Chancellor, or

(ii) to two (or more) Ministers of the Crown of whom one is the Lord Chancellor;

(b) provide for any relevant function that is exercisable by a Minister of the Crown other than the Lord Chancellor to be exercisable by the other Minister of the Crown concurrently with the Lord Chancellor;

(c) provide for any relevant function that is exercisable by the Lord Chancellor concurrently with another Minister of the Crown to cease to be exercisable by the other Minister of the Crown.

(2) In this section "relevant function" means a function, in relation to a scheduled tribunal, which relates—

(a) to the operation of the tribunal (including, in particular, its membership, administration, staff, accommodation and funding, and payments to its members or staff), or

(b) to the provision of expenses and allowances to persons attending the tribunal or attending elsewhere in connection with proceedings before the tribunal.

(3) In subsection (2) "scheduled tribunal" means a tribunal in a list in Schedule 6 that has effect for the purposes of this section.

(4) A relevant function may not be transferred under subsection (1) if, or to the extent that, the provision conferring the function—

(a) would be within the legislative competence of the Scottish Parliament if it were included in an Act of that Parliament, or

(b) would be within the legislative competence of the Northern Ireland Assembly if it were included in an Act of that Assembly.

(5) Subsection (4) does not apply to any relevant function of the Secretary of State—

(a) under section 41 of the Consumer Credit Act 1974 (c 39) (appeals), or

(b) under section 7 of the Estate Agents Act 1979 (c 38) (appeals).

(6) Any reference in subsection (1) to a Minister of the Crown includes a reference to a Minister of the Crown acting jointly.

(7) An order under subsection (1)—

(a) may relate to a function either wholly or in cases (including cases framed by reference to areas) specified in the order;

(b) may include provision for the purposes of, or in consequence of, or for giving full effect to, the transfer or (as the case may be) other change as regards exercise;

(c) may include such incidental, supplementary, transitional or consequential provision or savings as the Lord Chancellor thinks fit;

(d) may include provision for the transfer of any property, rights or liabilities of the person who loses functions or whose functions become shared with the Lord Chancellor.

(8) An order under subsection (1), so far as it—

(a) provides under paragraph (a) for the transfer of a function, or

(b) provides under paragraph (b) for a function to become exercisable by the Lord Chancellor, or

(c) provides under paragraph (c) for a function to cease to be exercisable by a Minister of the Crown other than the Lord Chancellor,

may not, after that transfer or other change has taken place, be revoked by another order under that subsection.

(9) Section 1 of the 1975 Act (power to transfer Ministerial functions) does not apply to a function of the Lord Chancellor—

(a) so far as it is a function transferred to the Lord Chancellor under subsection (1)(a),

(b) so far as it is a function exercisable by the Lord Chancellor as a result of provision under subsection (1)(b), or

(c) so far as it is a function that has become exercisable by the Lord Chancellor alone as a result of provision under subsection (1)(c).

(10) In this section—

"Minister of the Crown" has the meaning given by section 8(1) of the 1975 Act but includes the Commissioners for Her Majesty's Revenue and Customs;

"the 1975 Act" means the Ministers of the Crown Act 1975 (c 26).

7.369.31 36 Transfer of powers to make procedural rules for certain tribunals

(1) The Lord Chancellor may by order transfer any power to make procedural rules for a scheduled tribunal to—

(a) himself, or

(b) the Tribunal Procedure Committee.

(2) A power may not be transferred under subsection (1) if, or to the extent that, the provision conferring the power—

(a) would be within the legislative competence of the Scottish Parliament if it were included in an Act of that Parliament, or

(b) would be within the legislative competence of the Northern Ireland Assembly if it were included in an Act of that Assembly.

(3) Subsection (2) does not apply to—

(a) power conferred by section 40A(3) . . . of the Consumer Credit Act 1974 (c 39) (power to make provision with respect to appeals), or

(b) power conferred by section 7(3) of the Estate Agents Act 1979 (c 38) (duty of Secretary of State to make regulations with respect to appeals under section 7(1) of that Act).

(4) An order under subsection (1)(b)—

(a) may not alter any parliamentary procedure relating to the making of the procedural rules concerned, but

(b) may otherwise include provision for the purpose of assimilating the procedure for making them to the procedure for making Tribunal Procedure Rules.

(5) An order under subsection (1)(b) may include provision requiring the Tribunal Procedure Committee to make procedural rules for purposes notified to it by the Lord Chancellor.

(6) An order under this section—

(a) may relate to a power either wholly or in cases (including cases framed by reference to areas) specified in the order;

(b) may include provision for the purposes of or in consequence of, or for giving full effect to, the transfer;

(c) may include such incidental, supplementary, transitional or consequential provision or savings as the Lord Chancellor thinks fit.

(7) A power to make procedural rules for a tribunal that is exercisable by the Tribunal Procedure Committee by virtue of an order under this section must be exercised by the committee with a view to securing—

(a) that the system for deciding matters within the jurisdiction of that tribunal is accessible and fair,

(b) that proceedings before that tribunal are handled quickly and efficiently,

(c) that the rules are both simple and simply expressed, and

(d) that the rules where appropriate confer on persons who are, or who are members of, that tribunal responsibility for ensuring that proceedings before that tribunal are handled quickly and efficiently.

(8) In this section—

"procedural rules", in relation to a tribunal, means provision (whether called rules or not) regulating practice or procedure before the tribunal;

"scheduled tribunal" means a tribunal in a list in Schedule 6 that has effect for the purposes of this section.

7.369.32 37 Power to amend lists of tribunals in Schedule 6

(1) The Lord Chancellor may by order amend Schedule 6—

(a) for the purpose of adding a tribunal to a list in the Schedule;

(b) for the purpose of removing a tribunal from a list in the Schedule;

(c) for the purpose of removing a list from the Schedule;

(d) for the purpose of adding to the Schedule a list of tribunals that has effect for the purposes of any one or more of sections 30, 32(3), 35 and 36.

(2) The following rules apply to the exercise of power under subsection (1)—

(a) a tribunal may not be added to a list, or be in an added list, if the tribunal is established otherwise than by or under an enactment;

(b) a tribunal established by an enactment passed or made after the last day of the Session in which this Act is passed must not be added to a list, or be in an added list, that has effect for the purposes of section 30;

(c) if any relevant function is exercisable in relation to a tribunal by the Welsh Ministers (whether by the Welsh Ministers alone, or by the Welsh Ministers jointly or concurrently with any other person), the tribunal may be added to a list, or be in an added list, only with the consent of the Welsh Ministers;

(d) a tribunal may be in more than one list.

(3) In subsection (2)(c) "relevant function", in relation to a tribunal, means a function which relates—

(a) to the operation of the tribunal (including, in particular, its membership, administration, staff, accommodation and funding, and payments to its members or staff), or

(b) to the provision of expenses and allowances to persons attending the tribunal or attending elsewhere in connection with proceedings before the tribunal.

(4) In subsection (1) "tribunal" does not include an ordinary court of law.

(5) In this section "enactment" means any enactment whenever passed or made, including an enactment comprised in subordinate legislation (within the meaning of the Interpretation Act 1978 (c 30)).

7.369.33 38 Orders under sections 30 to 36: supplementary

(1) Provision in an order under any of sections 30 to 36 may take the form of amendments, repeals or revocations of enactments.

(2) In this section "enactment" means any enactment whenever passed or made, including an enactment comprised in subordinate legislation (within the meaning of the Interpretation Act 1978).

(3) Any power to extend enactments to a territory outside the United Kingdom shall have effect as if it included—

(a) power to extend those enactments as they have effect with any amendments and repeals made in them by orders under any of sections 30 to 36, and

(b) power to extend those enactments as if any amendments and repeals made in them under those sections had not been made.

CHAPTER 4
ADMINISTRATIVE MATTERS IN RESPECT OF CERTAIN TRIBUNALS

7.369.34 39 The general duty

(1) The Lord Chancellor is under a duty to ensure that there is an efficient and effective system to support the carrying on of the business of—

(a) the First-tier Tribunal,

(b) the Upper Tribunal,

(c) employment tribunals, [and]

(d) the Employment Appeal Tribunal . . .

(e) . . .

and that appropriate services are provided for those tribunals (referred to in this section and in sections 40 and 41 as "the tribunals").

(2) Any reference in this section, or in section 40 or 41, to the Lord Chancellor's general duty in relation to the tribunals is to his duty under subsection (1).

(3) The Lord Chancellor must annually prepare and lay before each House of Parliament a report as to the way in which he has discharged his general duty in relation to the tribunals.

7.369.35 40 Tribunal staff and services

(1) The Lord Chancellor may appoint such staff as appear to him appropriate for the purpose of discharging his general duty in relation to the tribunals.

(2) Subject to subsections (3) and (4), the Lord Chancellor may enter into such contracts with other persons for the provision, by them or their sub-contractors, of staff or services as appear to him appropriate for the purpose of discharging his general duty in relation to the tribunals.

(3) The Lord Chancellor may not enter into contracts for the provision of staff to discharge functions which involve making judicial decisions or exercising any judicial discretion.

(4) The Lord Chancellor may not enter into contracts for the provision of staff to carry out the administrative work of the tribunals unless an order made by the Lord Chancellor authorises him to do so.

(5) Before making an order under subsection (4) the Lord Chancellor must consult the Senior President of Tribunals as to what effect (if any) the order might have on the proper and efficient administration of justice.

(6) An order under subsection (4) may authorise the Lord Chancellor to enter into contracts for the provision of staff to discharge functions—

(a) wholly or to the extent specified in the order,

(b) generally or in cases or areas specified in the order, and

(c) unconditionally or subject to the fulfilment of conditions specified in the order.

7.369.36 41 Provision of accommodation

(1) The Lord Chancellor may provide, equip, maintain and manage such tribunal buildings, offices and other accommodation as appear to him appropriate for the purpose of discharging his general duty in relation to the tribunals.

(2) The Lord Chancellor may enter into such arrangements for the provision, equipment, maintenance or management of tribunal buildings, offices or other accommodation as appear to him appropriate for the purpose of discharging his general duty in relation to the tribunals.

(3) The powers under—

(a) section 2 of the Commissioners of Works Act 1852 (c 28) (acquisition by agreement), and

(b) section 228(1) of the Town and Country Planning Act 1990 (c 8) (compulsory acquisition),

to acquire land necessary for the public service are to be treated as including power to acquire land for the purpose of its provision under arrangements entered into under subsection (2).

(4) In this section "tribunal building" means any place where any of the tribunals sits, including the precincts of any building in which it sits.

7.369.37 42 Fees

(1) The Lord Chancellor may by order prescribe fees payable in respect of—

(a) anything dealt with by the First-tier Tribunal,
(b) anything dealt with by the Upper Tribunal,
(c) . . .
(d) anything dealt with by an added tribunal, and
(e) mediation conducted by staff appointed under section 40(1).

(2) An order under subsection (1) may, in particular, contain provision as to—

(a) scales or rates of fees;
(b) exemptions from or reductions in fees;
(c) remission of fees in whole or in part.

(3) In subsection (1)(d) "added tribunal" means a tribunal specified in an order made by the Lord Chancellor.

(4) A tribunal may be specified in an order under subsection (3) only if—

(a) it is established by or under an enactment, whenever passed or made, and
(b) is not an ordinary court of law.

(5) Before making an order under this section, the Lord Chancellor must consult—

(a) the Senior President of Tribunals, and
(b) the Administrative Justice and Tribunals Council.

(6) The making of an order under subsection (1) requires the consent of the Treasury except where the order contains provision only for the purpose of altering amounts payable by way of fees already prescribed under that subsection.

(7) The Lord Chancellor must take such steps as are reasonably practicable to bring information about fees under subsection (1) to the attention of persons likely to have to pay them.

(8) Fees payable under subsection (1) are recoverable summarily as a civil debt.

(9) Subsection (8) does not apply to the recovery in Scotland of fees payable under this section.

(10) Until the Administrative Justice and Tribunals Council first has ten members appointed under paragraph 1(2) of Schedule 7, the reference to that council in subsection (5) is to be read as a reference to the Council on Tribunals.

7.369.38 43 Report by Senior President of Tribunals

(1) Each year the Senior President of Tribunals must give the Lord Chancellor a report covering, in relation to relevant tribunal cases—

(a) matters that the Senior President of Tribunals wishes to bring to the attention of the Lord Chancellor, and
(b) matters that the Lord Chancellor has asked the Senior President of Tribunals to cover in the report.

(2) The Lord Chancellor must publish each report given to him under subsection (1).

(3) In this section "relevant tribunal cases" means—

(a) cases coming before the First-tier Tribunal,
(b) cases coming before the Upper Tribunal,
(c) cases coming before the Employment Appeal Tribunal, . . . [and]

(d) cases coming before employment tribunals[. . .
(e) . . .].

CHAPTER 5
OVERSIGHT OF ADMINISTRATIVE JUSTICE SYSTEM, TRIBUNALS AND INQUIRIES

7.369.39 44 The Administrative Justice and Tribunals Council

(1) There is to be a council to be known as the Administrative Justice and Tribunals Council.

(2) In Schedule 7—

Part 1 makes provision about membership and committees of the Council,

Part 2 makes provision about functions of the Council,

Part 3 requires the Council to be consulted before procedural rules for certain tribunals are made, confirmed etc, and

Part 4 contains interpretative provisions.

Judicial review

7.369.40 141 Judicial review: power to substitute decision

In section 31 of the [Senior Courts Act 1981] (c 54) (application for judicial review), for subsection (5) substitute—

"(5) If, on an application for judicial review, the High Court quashes the decision to which the application relates, it may in addition—

(a) remit the matter to the court, tribunal or authority which made the decision, with a direction to reconsider the matter and reach a decision in accordance with the findings of the High Court, or

(b) substitute its own decision for the decision in question.

(5A) But the power conferred by subsection (5)(b) is exercisable only if—

(a) the decision in question was made by a court or tribunal,

(b) the decision is quashed on the ground that there has been an error of law, and

(c) without the error, there would have been only one decision which the court or tribunal could have reached.

(5B) Unless the High Court otherwise directs, a decision substituted by it under subsection (5)(b) has effect as if it were a decision of the relevant court or tribunal."

STATUTORY INSTRUMENTS

LOTTERY DUTY REGULATIONS 1993

(SI 1993/3212)

Made . . . .*21st December 1993*
Laid before the House of Commons . . . .*4th January 1994*
Coming into force . . . .*1st February 1994*

Arrangement of regulations

The Commissioners of Customs and Excise, in exercise of the powers conferred on them by sections 24(1) and (2), 26(2), 27(2), 28(2), 29(3) and (4) and 38 of the Finance Act 1993 and of all other powers enabling them in that behalf, hereby make the following Regulations:

PART I
PRELIMINARY

Citation and commencement

7.370

1 These Regulations may be cited as the Lottery Duty Regulations 1993 and shall come into force on 1st February 1994.

Interpretation

7.371

2 In these Regulations—

'accounting period' means—

(a) a period ending on the last Saturday of each month; or

(b) where payment is deferred, such period as the Commissioners may require;

'the Act' means the Finance Act 1993;

'the 1979 Act' means the Customs and Excise Management Act 1979;

'applicant' means any person who makes an application to be registered under section 29 of the Act;

'business day' means a day which is a business day within the meaning of section 92 of the Bills of Exchange Act 1882;

'chargeable lottery' means a lottery in respect of which lottery duty is chargeable (or, on the taking of a ticket or chance, will be chargeable) in accordance with section 24 of the Act;

'the National Lottery' has the meaning given by section 1 of the National Lottery etc Act 1993;

'registered promoter' means a person registered under section 29 of the Act.

PART II
REGISTRATION OF PROMOTERS

Application for registration by promoters etc

7.372

3 (1) Every person required to be registered under section 29 of the Act shall make application to the Commissioners for registration on a form provided by the Commissioners for that purpose and shall provide with his application a copy of any licence issued to him under the National Lottery etc Act 1993.

(2) An application shall contain the particulars specified in Schedule 1.

(3) Every application shall be made at least fifteen days before the day on which the applicant begins or, if earlier, intends to begin to promote a chargeable lottery.

(4) For the purposes of paragraph (3) above a person begins to promote a chargeable lottery on the first day on which any ticket or chance is taken in that lottery.

Requirements to be satisfied as a condition of registration

7.373

4 Every applicant must satisfy the requirements set out in Schedule 2 as a condition of his registration and every registered promoter must satisfy those requirements as a condition of his continued registration.

Requirements to be observed by registered promoters

7.374

5 Every registered promoter must observe the requirements set out in Schedule 3 while he remains registered.

PART III
PAYMENT OF LOTTERY DUTY

Deferred payment

7.375

6 (1) A registered promoter may defer payment of lottery duty which has become due and payable upon his complying with such conditions or requirements as the Commissioners think fit to impose.

[(2) Where payment of any lottery duty is deferred—

(a) it must be paid using either the Clearing House Automated Payment System (CHAPS) or the Bankers' Automated Clearing Services (BACS), and

(b) payment must be credited to such bank account as the Commissioners may require on or before the day by which the return showing that duty must be furnished.][1]

---

1 Subs (2) substituted by the Lottery Duty (Amendment) Regulations 2001, SI 2001/4021, regs 2, 3, as from 27 January 2002 (except in relation to duty which became due before that date): see SI 2001/4021, regs 1, 10.

Refunds

7.376

7 (1) This regulation shall apply to any lottery which did not take place but in which tickets or chances were taken.

(2) A person ('the claimant') may make written application to the Commissioners for duty he has paid to be refunded (a 'refund application') in respect of a lottery promoted by him provided that—

(a) it is a lottery to which this regulation applies;

(b) at the time he promoted the lottery he was a registered promoter;

(c) his refund application is received by the Commissioners within six months of the day upon which the lottery would have taken place; and

(d) he has refunded to any person who took a ticket or chance in that lottery the amount of consideration given for it, or, if this is not the case, he has refunded the consideration given for every ticket or chance in respect of which he claims a refund of duty.

(3) A refund application shall be made—

(a) if the claimant is a registered promoter, as part of a return furnished in accordance with regulation 14 [or 14A][1] below; or

(b) in any other case, in a letter addressed to the Commissioners which shall, for the purpose of regulation 15 below, be treated as if it were a return.

(4) A refund application shall contain the particulars specified in Schedule 4.

(5) No refund shall be paid until the claimant has complied with the provisions of this regulation and the Commissioners shall cancel any entitlement to refund, or reduce the amount of that entitlement, if it appears to them that a refund application is untrue in any material particular.

(6) If the Commissioners cancel any entitlement to refund in accordance with paragraph (5) above and that refund has, at the time of cancellation, already been paid they shall be entitled to recover the amount of that refund from the claimant as if that amount was an amount of lottery duty due and payable on the date of cancellation.

---

1 Words in square brackets inserted by the Lottery Duty (Amendment) Regulations 2001, SI 2001/4021, regs 2, 4, as from 27 January 2002 (except in relation to duty which became due before that date): see SI 2001/4021, regs 1, 10.

The National Lottery

7.377

8 Any lottery duty payable in respect of the National Lottery shall be paid by the [person][1] licensed under section 5 of the National Lottery etc Act 1993 instead of by the promoter.

---

1 Word in square brackets substituted by the Lottery Duty (Amendment) Regulations 2007, SI 2007/870, reg 2.

PART IV
TICKETS OR CHANCES TAKEN ABROAD

The taking outside the United Kingdom of a ticket or chance

7.378

9 Where any ticket or chance is taken outside the United Kingdom in the National Lottery the taking of that ticket or chance shall be treated as having occurred—

(a) at the principal place of business within the United Kingdom of the registered promoter; and

(b) at the time that—

(i) the ticket or chance is taken; or

(ii) payment for the ticket or chance is made,

whichever is the earlier.

PART V
ADMINISTRATION AND PROTECTION OF THE REVENUE DERIVED FROM LOTTERY DUTY

Information on tickets

7.379

10 The price of every ticket shall be stated on the ticket.

Price of chances

7.380

11 The price of every chance shall be stated on any document which evidences the taking of that chance and which is given to the person taking that chance.

Unique referencing of tickets and chances

7.381

12 (1) In every lottery every ticket or chance shall be allocated a unique reference which shall be stated—

(a) on the ticket; and

(b) on any document which evidences the taking of the chance and which is given to the person taking that chance.

(2) References allocated in accordance with paragraph (1) above shall be arranged in a sequence or sequences in such a way as to enable—

(a) the number of tickets or chances already taken; and

(b) the number of tickets or chances remaining untaken,

in any lottery to be ascertained at any time both whilst that lottery is being promoted and so long thereafter as the registered promoter is required, by or under any enactment, to keep and preserve records relating to that lottery.

Destruction of tickets

7.382

13 Except in the case of tickets which are not printed and allocated unique references until the time they are taken, a registered promoter who intends to destroy lottery tickets shall give seven clear days notice to the Commissioners of the unique references of the tickets to be destroyed.

Returns

7.383

14 (1) Every registered promoter shall, not later than the [thirteenth day][1] of the month next following the end of every accounting period furnish to the Commissioners a return in such form as they may approve containing the particulars specified in Schedule 5; provided that where the last day for furnishing a return would (if determined in accordance with the foregoing provisions) fall on a day which is not a business day the return shall be furnished not later than the last business day before that day.

[(2) Returns must be furnished to the Commissioners at their accounting centre for lottery duty.

(3) The Commissioners must give the address of their accounting centre for lottery duty to every registered promoter.][2]

---

1 Words in square brackets substituted by the Lottery Duty (Amendment) Regulations 2001, SI 2001/4021, regs 2, 5, as from 27 January 2002 (except in relation to duty which became due before that date): see SI 2001/4021, regs 1, 10.

2 Paras (2), (3) substituted, for para (2) as originally enacted, by the Lottery Duty (Amendment) Regulations 2001, SI 2001/4021, regs 2, 6, as from 27 January 2002 (except in relation to duty which became due before that date): see SI 2001/4021, regs 1, 10.

7.384

[14A (1) A registered promoter may furnish a return required by regulation 14(1) above using electronic communications.

(2) Such a method of furnishing a return shall be referred to in this regulation as an 'electronic return system'.

(3) A registered promoter may furnish a return by way of an electronic return system only on condition that—

(a) the electronic return system in question takes a form approved by the Commissioners in a specific or general direction; and

(b) that promoter remains authorised by the Commissioners in accordance with paragraph (7) below.

(4) No return shall be treated as having been furnished under paragraph (1) above unless the conditions imposed by paragraph (3) above are satisfied.

(5) An electronic return system shall incorporate an electronic validation process.

(6) Subject to paragraph (4) above—

(a) the use of an electronic return system shall be proved to have resulted in the furnishing of the return to the Commissioners only if this has been successfully recorded as such by the relevant electronic validation process;

(b) the time of furnishing the return to the Commissioners using an electronic return system shall be conclusively presumed to be the time recorded as such by the relevant electronic validation process; and

(c) the person furnishing the return to the Commissioners shall be presumed to be the person identified as such by any relevant feature of the electronic return system.

(7) The Commissioners may on application authorise a registered promoter to furnish returns using an electronic return system and may revoke such authorisation.

(8) The Commissioners shall pay proper regard to the following factors before authorising a registered promoter or revoking an authorisation under paragraph (7) above—

(a) the state of development of any relevant electronic return system;

(b) the protection of the revenue;

(c) the degree of compliance with these Regulations of the promoter concerned; and

(d) any other relevant factor.][1]

---

1 Inserted by the Lottery Duty (Amendment) Regulations 2001, SI 2001/4021, regs 2, 7, as from 27 January 2002 (except in relation to duty which became due before that date): see SI 2001/4021, regs 1, 10.

Signature and declaration on relevant documents

7.385

15 (1) This regulation applies to every application for registration and every return made in accordance with these regulations ('relevant document').

(2) Every relevant document shall contain a declaration that the particulars and statements contained in it are true and complete and that any statement or other document which accompanies that relevant document is also true and complete.

(3) Subject to [paragraphs (4) and (5)][1] below, every application for registration shall be signed by the applicant and every return shall be signed by the registered promoter who makes it.

(4) If the person required to sign a relevant document in accordance with paragraph (3) above—

(a) is a partnership, that relevant document shall be signed by a partner; or

(b) is a body corporate, that relevant document shall be signed by a director of that body,

and where a relevant document is so signed by a partner or director the person signing it shall state beneath his signature the capacity in which he signs it.

[(5) The requirement in paragraph (3) above that every return shall be signed by the registered promoter shall not apply to a return furnished in accordance with regulation 14A above.][2]

---

1 Words in square brackets substituted by the Lottery Duty (Amendment) Regulations 2001, SI 2001/4021, regs 2, 8, as from 27 January 2002 (except in relation to duty which became due before that date): see SI 2001/4021, regs 1, 10.

2 Inserted by the Lottery Duty (Amendment) Regulations 2001, SI 2001/4021, regs 2, 9, as from 27 January 2002 (except in relation to duty which became due before that date): see SI 2001/4021, regs 1, 10.

7.386

SCHEDULE 1
PARTICULARS OF A REGISTERED PROMOTER APPLICATION
Regulation 3

(a) the name and address of the applicant;
(b) the address of the applicant's principal place of business;
(c) whether the applicant is a partnership or body corporate;
(d) if the applicant is a partnership, the name and address of each of the partners;
(e) if the applicant is a body corporate
  (i) the address of its registered office;
  (ii) its registered number;
  (iii) its date of incorporation; and
  (iv) the name and address of each of the directors of that body;
(f) if the applicant is registered for value added tax purposes, his registration number;
(g) the date from which the applicant intends to begin to promote any chargeable lottery;
(h) whether the applicant is licensed under section 5 of the National Lottery etc Act 1993.

Notes of interpretation

1 'Address' in relation to a partner or director means that person's usual place of residence in the United Kingdom.

2 'Registered Office', 'registered number' and 'date of incorporation' bear the same meanings as they bear in the Companies Act 1985 in relation to companies registered under that Act and, in the case of any other body corporate, shall be taken to mean the nearest equivalent of those terms applicable to the body corporate in question.

7.387

SCHEDULE 2
REQUIREMENTS TO BE SATISFIED AS A CONDITION OF REGISTRATION
Regulation 4

(a) if the lottery forms part of the National Lottery, the promoter must be licensed pursuant to section 5 of the National Lottery etc Act 1993;

(b) the promoter must, when the Commissioners by notice in writing so require, give security or further security (by means of a deposit or otherwise) for any lottery duty that may become due;

(c) when registered, the promoter must comply fully with the requirements of regulations 6 and 14 above and with any directions made in accordance with section 116 of the 1979 Act.

7.388

SCHEDULE 3
REQUIREMENTS TO BE OBSERVED BY REGISTERED PROMOTERS
Regulation 5

A registered promoter shall notify the Commissioners within one month of the change of—

(a) any change of address;
(b) any change of the address of his principal place of business;
(c) if he is a partnership, any change of
  (i) the membership of the partnership (including the name and address of any new member of the partnership);
  (ii) address of any partner;
(d) if he is a body corporate, any change of
  (i) the name of the body;
  (ii) the directors of the body (including the name and address of any new director);
  (iii) address of any director.

Note of interpretation

'Address' in relation to a partner or director means that person's usual place of residence in the United Kingdom.

7.389

SCHEDULE 4
PARTICULARS OF A REFUND APPLICATION
Regulation 7

(a) the claimant's name and address;
(b) the date upon which the lottery would have taken place;
(c) a declaration that the claimant has refunded the consideration given for every ticket or chance taken in the lottery in question or, if this is not the case, that he has refunded the consideration given for every ticket or chance in respect of which he claims a refund of duty;
(d) the number of tickets or chances taken, the value of the consideration received for them and the amount of duty actually paid to the Commissioners in respect of them;
(e) the amount of duty which he claims should be refunded.

7.390

SCHEDULE 5
PARTICULARS OF A RETURN
Regulation 14

(a) the name and address of the registered promoter and any registration number allocated to him for purposes connected with lottery duty;
(b) the accounting period to which the return relates;
(c) the value of the consideration given for tickets or chances in that accounting period;
(d) the amount of lottery duty due in that accounting period (calculated in accordance with section 25 of the Act);
(e) the amount of any lottery duty due from any earlier accounting period unless that amount has been shown on an earlier return;
(f) the amount of any refund claimed;
(g) the amount of any lottery duty shown in error as due on any earlier return;
(h) the net amount of lottery duty due and payable in that accounting period;

(i) where payment is deferred, such other particulars as the Commissioners may require.

NATIONAL LOTTERY REGULATIONS 1994

(SI 1994/189)

Made ....*31st January 1994*
Laid before Parliament ....*9th February 1994*
Coming into force ....*1st April 1994*

The Secretary of State, in exercise of the powers conferred by section 12 of the National Lottery etc Act 1993 and of all other powers enabling him in that behalf, hereby makes the following Regulations—

Citation, commencement and extent

7.391

1 (1) These Regulations may be cited as the National Lottery Regulations 1994 and shall come into force on 1st April 1994.

(2) These Regulations extend to Northern Ireland.

Interpretation

7.392

2 In these Regulations—

'the Act' means the National Lottery etc Act 1993; and

'National Lottery ticket' means a ticket or chance in a lottery that forms part of the National Lottery.

Age restriction on sales of National Lottery tickets

7.393

3 No National Lottery ticket shall be sold by or to a person who has not attained the age of 16 years.

Prohibition on sales of or invitations to purchase National Lottery tickets in a street

7.394

4 (1) Subject to paragraph (2) below no National Lottery ticket shall be sold to a person, nor shall a person be invited to purchase a National Lottery ticket, in any street.

(2) Paragraph (1) above shall not have effect in relation to the sale of or invitation to purchase a National Lottery ticket by a person present in a kiosk or shop premises having no space for the accommodation of customers.

(3) In this regulation 'street' includes any bridge, road, lane, footway, subway, court, alley or passage, whether a thoroughfare or not, which is for the time being open to the public without payment.

Prohibition of sales of or invitations to purchase National Lottery tickets on certain premises

7.395

5 (1) No National Lottery ticket shall be sold to a person, nor shall a person be invited to purchase a National Lottery ticket—

(a) in any licensed betting office within the meaning of the 1963 Act or licensed office within the meaning of the 1985 Order;

(b) on any approved racecourse within the meaning of the 1963 Act on a day on which horse races take place thereon;

(c) on any licensed track within the meaning of the 1963 Act on any day on which under sections 5, 6 and 20 of that Act bookmaking may lawfully be carried out on the track or on any licensed track within the meaning of the 1985 Order on any day on which under articles 36, 47 and 48 of that Order betting may lawfully be carried out on the track;

(d) in any premises used wholly or mainly for providing amusements in the form of amusements with prizes or of amusements by means of slot machines or both; or

(e) in any bingo or other gaming club, that is to say, in any premises in respect of which a licence under the Gaming Act 1968 is for the time being in force or in any bingo club premises within the meaning of the 1985 Order.

(2) In paragraph (1) above—

(a) 'the 1963 Act' means the Betting, Gaming and Lotteries Act 1963; and

(b) 'the 1985 Order' means the Betting, Gaming, Lotteries and Amusements (Northern Ireland) Order 1985.

Restriction on sales of National Lottery tickets by vending machines

7.396

6 (1) No National Lottery ticket shall be sold by means of a vending machine unless such machine is, at all times when tickets can be sold by means of it, attended by a person authorised by either—

(a) the holder of the licence under section 5 of the Act; or

(b) the holder of a licence under section 6 of the Act which authorises the promotion of the lottery, the tickets or chances of which are being sold by means of the vending machine.

(2) A vending machine shall not be treated as attended for the purposes of this regulation unless the person attending the vending machine is in a position where he can control the operation of the machine and in particular take action to prevent the purchase of tickets by any person whom he believes has not attained the age of 16 years.

Restriction on sales of or invitations to purchase National Lottery tickets at a person's home

7.397

7 No National Lottery ticket shall be sold, nor shall a person be invited to purchase a National Lottery ticket, by a person when visiting any other person at his home in the discharge of any official, professional or commercial function (including the function of selling National Lottery tickets).

Sums held in the National Lottery Distribution Fund

7.406

3 Sums that apart from this Order would be held in the Distribution Fund for distribution by the Sports Council shall be held in the Distribution Fund for distribution by the English Sports Council.

NATIONAL LOTTERY (IMPOSITION OF PENALTIES AND REVOCATION OF LICENCES) PROCEDURE REGULATIONS 1999

(SI 1999/137)

Made .... *25th January 1999*
Laid before Parliament .... *26th January 1999*
Coming into force .... *27th January 1999*

The Secretary of State, in exercise of the powers conferred on him by sections 10A(6) and 60(5) of, and paragraph 8(1) of Schedule 3 to, the National Lottery etc Act 1993, after consultation with the Council on Tribunals in accordance with section 8 of the Tribunals and Inquiries Act 1992, hereby makes the following Regulations:

PART I
GENERAL

Citation, commencement and revocation

7.407

1 These Regulations may be cited as the National Lottery (Imposition of Penalties and Revocation of Licences) Procedure Regulations 1999 and shall come into force on 27th January 1999.

7.408

2 The National Lottery (Revocation of Licences) Procedure Regulations 1994 are revoked.

Interpretation

7.409

3 In these Regulations:

'the Director General' means the Director General of the National Lottery or any member of his staff who has been authorised by him (whether generally or specifically) for the purpose;

'hearing' means a hearing at which oral representations may be heard;

'the licensee' means:—

(a) in Part II of these Regulations the holder of the licence in respect of which the Director General proposes to impose a financial penalty; and

(b) in Part III of these Regulations the licensee whose licence the Director General proposes to revoke;

'Schedule 3' means Schedule 3 to the National Lottery etc Act 1993; and

'section 10A' means section 10A of the National Lottery etc Act 1993.

PART II
PROCEDURE IN RELATION TO ORAL REPRESENTATIONS TO THE DIRECTOR GENERAL IN RELATION TO THE IMPOSITION OF A PENALTY

Application of Part II

7.410

4 This Part of these Regulations applies in a case where the licensee has notified the Director General in consequence of section 10A(4)(b) of its intention to make oral representations.

Notice of hearing

7.411

5 The Director General shall send a written notice to the licensee of the date, time and place fixed for the holding of the hearing; such notice shall be sent at least seven days before the date so fixed.

Power to require particulars

7.412

6 The Director General may at any time direct the licensee to furnish any particulars which appear to him to be requisite in connection with the hearing within such time as the Director General may allow, being not less than seven days.

Admission to a hearing

7.413

7 (1) Subject to the provisions of this regulation, a hearing shall be held in public.

(2) The Director General may direct that the whole or any part of a hearing be held in private if he is satisfied that by reason of—

- (a) the likelihood of disclosure of intimate personal or financial circumstances;
- (b) the likelihood of disclosure of commercially sensitive information or information obtained in confidence; or
- (c) exceptional circumstances not falling within sub-paragraph (a) or (b) above,

it is just and reasonable for him to do so.

(3) Where the hearing is in private the Director General may admit such persons as he considers appropriate.

(4) Notwithstanding the provisions of paragraph (2) and (3) above, a member of the Council on Tribunals or of the Scottish Committee of that Council is entitled to be present in his capacity as such even though the hearing or part of the hearing is not in public.

Appearance at hearing

7.414

8 The licensee shall appear at the hearing and may be represented by any person whom it may appoint for the purpose.

Procedure at hearing

7.415

9 (1) Except as otherwise provided in these Regulations, the Director General shall determine the procedure at the hearing.

(2) The licensee shall be entitled to give evidence, call witnesses and address the Director General both on the evidence and generally on the proposal to impose a penalty.

(3) The Director General may from time to time adjourn the hearing.

Imposition of Penalty

7.416

10 If the licensee has notified the Director General in writing of its intention to make oral representations and having been duly notified of the hearing pursuant to regulation 5 above does not comply with the requirement in regulation 8 above to appear at the hearing, the financial penalty specified in the notice served by the Director General pursuant to section 10A(3) becomes payable on the seventh day after the day fixed for the hearing specified in the notice referred to in regulation 5 above.

PART III
PROCEDURE IN RELATION TO ORAL REPRESENTATIONS TO THE DIRECTOR GENERAL IN RELATION TO THE REVOCATION OF A LICENCE

Application of Part III

7.417

11 This Part of these Regulations applies in a case where the licensee has notified the Director General pursuant to paragraph 6(1)(c) of Schedule 3 of its intention to make oral representations.

Notice of hearing

7.418

12 The Director General shall send a written notice to the licensee of the date, time and place fixed for the holding of the hearing; such notice shall be sent at least seven days before the date so fixed.

Power to require particulars

7.419

13 The Director General may at any time direct the licensee to furnish any particulars which appear to him to be requisite in connection with the hearing within such time as the Director General may allow, being not less than seven days.

Admission to a hearing

7.420

14 (1) Subject to the provisions of this regulation, a hearing shall be held in public.

(2) The Director General may direct that the whole or any part of a hearing be held in private if he is satisfied that by reason of—

(a) the likelihood of disclosure of intimate personal or financial circumstances;

(b) the likelihood of disclosure of commercially sensitive information or information obtained in confidence; or

(c) exceptional circumstances not falling within sub-paragraph (a) or (b) above,

it is just and reasonable for him to do so.

(3) Where the hearing is in private the Director General may admit such persons as he considers appropriate.

(4) Notwithstanding the provisions of paragraph (2) and (3) above, a member of the Council on Tribunals or of the Scottish Committee of that Council is entitled to be present in his capacity as such even though the hearing or part of the hearing is not in public.

Appearance at hearing

7.421

15 The licensee shall appear at the hearing and may be represented by any person whom it may appoint for the purpose.

Procedure at hearing

7.422

16 (1) Except as otherwise provided in these Regulations, the Director General shall determine the procedure at the hearing.

(2) The licensee shall be entitled to give evidence, call witnesses and address the Director General both on the evidence and generally on the proposal to revoke its licence.

(3) The Director General may from time to time adjourn the hearing.

Revocation of licence

7.423

17 If the licensee has not made any written representations pursuant to paragraph 6(1)(c) of Schedule 3 and having been duly notified of the hearing pursuant to regulation 12 above does not comply with the requirement in regulation 15 above to appear at the hearing, the revocation of its licence shall take effect on the seventh day after the day fixed for the hearing specified in the notice referred to in regulation 12 above.

Reasons

7.424

18 The Director General shall, except where regulation 17 above applies, send to the licensee a written statement of reasons (in summary form) for his decision whether or not to revoke the licence.

PART IV
MISCELLANEOUS

Giving of notices

7.425

19 (1) Any notice or other document required or authorised to be sent to the licensee under these Regulations shall be duly sent if—

(a) it is sent by post in a registered letter or by recorded delivery to, or delivered to, or left for, the secretary of the licensee at its registered or principal office in the United Kingdom or at the address stated in the notice of intention to make oral representations; or

(b) it is transmitted by electronic means to an address stated as being for the purpose of receiving notices or other documents in the notice of intention to make oral representations and is in legible form capable of being used for subsequent reference.

(2) If a notice of intention to make oral representations is sent by registered post or recorded delivery, it shall be treated as if it had been received on the date on which it is received for despatch by the [postal operator (within the meaning of the Postal Services Act 2000) concerned].[1]

(3) If a notice of intention to make oral representations is transmitted by electronic means, it shall be treated as received on the date on which it was transmitted.

(4) In this regulation 'the licensee' has the same meaning as in Part II of these Regulations or, as the case may be, Part III of these Regulations.

1 Words in square brackets substituted by the Postal Services Act 2000 (Consequential Modifications No 1) Order 2001, SI 2001/1149, art 3(1), Sch 1, para 125.

APPORTIONMENT OF MONEY IN THE NATIONAL LOTTERY DISTRIBUTION FUND ORDER 1999

(SI 1999/344)

Made .... *14th February 1999*
Coming into force .... *15th February 1999*

Whereas a draft of this Order has been laid before, and approved by resolution of each House of Parliament pursuant to section 60(2) of the National Lottery etc Act 1993; Now, therefore, the Secretary of State, in exercise of the powers conferred on him by section 28(1) of the National Lottery etc Act 1993, hereby makes the following Order:

Citation and commencement

7.426

1 This Order may be cited as the Apportionment of Money in the National Lottery Distribution Fund Order 1999 and shall come into force on the day after the day on which it is made.

Apportionment of Money in the National Lottery Distribution Fund

7.427

2 (1) With effect from 15th February 1999 section 22(3) of the National Lottery etc Act 1993 (apportionment of money in Distribution Fund) shall be amended in accordance with paragraphs (2) to (6) below.

(2) In subsection (3)(a) (16 $^2/_3$ per cent, to be allocated for expenditure on or connected with the arts) for '16 $^2/_3$ per cent' there shall be substituted '5 per cent'.

(3) In subsection (3)(b) (16 $^2/_3$ per cent to be allocated for expenditure on or connected with sport) for '16 $^2/_3$ per cent' there shall be substituted '5 per cent'.

(4) In subsection (3)(c) (16 $^2/_3$ per cent to be allocated for expenditure on or connected with the national heritage) for '16 $^2/_3$ per cent' there shall be substituted '5 per cent'.

(5) In subsection (3)(d) (16 $^2/_3$ per cent to be allocated for charitable expenditure) for '16 $^2/_3$ per cent' there shall be substituted '5 per cent'.

(6) In subsection (3)(f) (13 $^1/_3$ per cent to be allocated for expenditure on or connected with health, education or the environment) for '13 $^1/_3$ per cent' there shall be substituted '60 per cent'.

7.428

3 (1) With effect from 17th May 1999 section 22(3) of the National Lottery etc Act 1993 (apportionment of money in Distribution Fund) shall be amended in accordance with paragraphs (2) to (6) below.

(2) In subsection (3)(a) (5 per cent to be allocated for expenditure on or connected with the arts) for '5 per cent' there shall be substituted '16 $^2/_3$ per cent'.

(3) In subsection (3)(b) (5 per cent to be allocated for expenditure on or connected with sport) for '5 per cent' there shall be substituted '16 $^2/_3$ per cent'.

(4) In subsection (3)(c) (5 per cent to be allocated for expenditure on or connected with the national heritage) for '5 per cent' there shall be substituted '16 $^2/_3$ per cent'.

(5) In subsection (3)(d) (5 per cent to be allocated for charitable expenditure) for '5 per cent' there shall be substituted '16 $^2/_3$ per cent'.

(6) In subsection (3)(f) (60 per cent to be allocated for expenditure on or connected with health, education or the environment) for '60 per cent' there shall be substituted '13 $^1/_3$ per cent'.

NATIONAL LOTTERY (LICENCE FEES) ORDER 2001

(SI 2001/2506)

Made .... *11th July 2001*
Laid before Parliament .... *12th July 2001*
Coming into force .... *9th August 2001*

The Secretary of State, in exercise of the powers conferred on her by sections 7(5) and 60(4) of the National Lottery etc Act 1993 and of all other powers enabling her in that behalf, hereby makes the following Order:

Citation and commencement

7.429

1 This Order may be cited as the National Lottery (Licence Fees) Order 2001 and shall come into force on the 9th August 2001.

Fees for licences under section 5

7.430

2 The fee to be paid by the licensee to the National Lottery Commission on the granting of a licence under section 5 of the National Lottery etc Act 1993 (licensing of a body to run the National Lottery) shall be—

(a) in the case of a licence specified to have effect (subject to being revoked or suspended) for a period not exceeding 6 months, £11,000; and
(b) in any other case, £70,000.

Fees for licences under section 6

7.431

3 [(1)] [1] [Subject to [the following provisions of this article][2]][1] the fee to be paid by the licensee to the National Lottery Commission on the granting of a licence under

section 6 of that Act (licensing of bodies to promote lotteries as part of the National Lottery) shall be—

(a) in the case of a licence that—

(i) takes effect on the expiry of a licence under section 6 that was held by the same licensee, and

(ii) is in substantially the same terms as the licence mentioned in paragraph (i),

£1,000; and

(b) in any other case, £20,000.

[(2) [Subject to paragraph (3)][2], where a licence granted under section 6 of that Act authorises the promotion by the licensee of an unrestricted number of lotteries which fall within a particular description specified in the licence, the fee shall be £100,000.][1]

[(3) Where a licence granted under section 6 of that Act authorises the promotion by the licensee of a lottery pursuant to an agreement, entered into between the licensee and the promoters of other lotteries in other countries of the European Union, under which lotteries falling within the agreement share a common game structure and prizes, the fee shall be £150,000.

(4) In the case of a licence that—

(a) takes effect on the expiry of a licence mentioned in paragraphs (2) or (3) that was held by the same licensee, and

(b) is in substantially the same terms as the licence mentioned in paragraphs (2) or (3), the fee shall be £20,000.][3]

---

1 Sub-para (1) numbered as such, words in square brackets and sub-para (2) inserted by the National Lottery (Licence Fees) (Amendment) Order 2002, SI 2002/3124.

2 Words in square brackets substituted or inserted by inserted by the National Lottery (Licence Fees) (Amendment) Order 2003, SI 2003/2771.

3 Paras (3), (4) inserted by the National Lottery (Licence Fees) (Amendment) Order 2003, SI 2003/2771, art 2(1), (4).

Revocation

7.432

4 The National Lottery (Licence Fees) Order 1994 is hereby revoked.

NATIONAL LOTTERY DISTRIBUTORS DISSOLUTION ORDER 2006

(SI 2006/2915)

Made .... 5th November 2006
Laid before Parliament .... 7th November 2006
Coming into force in accordance with Article 1

The Secretary of State makes the following Order in exercise of the powers conferred by section 43B of, paragraph 1 of Schedule 5, paragraph 2 of Schedule 6 and paragraph 1 of Schedule 6A to, the National Lottery etc Act 1993 and section 16 of the National Lottery Act 2006.

In accordance with section 17(8)(b) of the National Lottery Act 2006, the Secretary of State is satisfied that, in relation to the dissolution of the National Lottery Charities Board, the Millennium Commission and the New Opportunities Fund and the transfer of their rights and liabilities to the Big Lottery Fund, sufficient notice has been given to enable compliance with any applicable requirement of the Transfer of Undertakings (Protection of Employment) Regulations 2006.

7.433 1 Citation, commencement and interpretation

(1) This Order may be cited as the National Lottery Distributors Dissolution Order 2006.

(2) This Order shall come into force only if the Prescribed Expenditure Order is made, and shall do so on the day that Order comes into force.

(3) If the Prescribed Expenditure Order is not made before 31st December 2006, this Order is revoked with effect from that date.

(4) In this article "the Prescribed Expenditure Order" means the Big Lottery Fund (Prescribed Expenditure) Order 2006 laid in draft before Parliament on 11th October 2006.

7.434 2 Dissolution

The National Lottery Charities Board, the Millennium Commission and the New Opportunities Fund shall cease to exist on the day this Order comes into force.

7.435 3 Revocation

The Orders listed in the Schedule are hereby revoked.

7.436

SCHEDULE

REVOCATIONS

Article 3

1 The National Lottery Charities Board (Increase in Membership) (Revocation) Order 1999 (No 1878).

2 The Millennium Commission (Substitution of a Later Date) Order 2000 (No 3355).

3 The New Opportunities Fund (Increase in Membership) Order 2003 (No 2869).

4 The Millennium Commission (Reduction in Membership) Order 2003 (No 3033).

5 The New Opportunities Fund (Specification of Initiative) Order 2005 (No 1102).

6 The Millennium Commission (Reduction in Membership) Order 2005 (No 2470).

7 The New Opportunities Fund (Specification of Initiatives) (No 2) Order 2005 (No 3235).

NATIONAL LOTTERY (ANNUAL LICENCE FEES) REGULATIONS 2010

(SI 2010/17)

Made . . . .*6th January 2010*
Laid before Parliament . . . .*7th January 2010*
Coming into force . . . .*28th January 2010*

The Secretary of State makes the following Regulations in exercise of the powers conferred by sections 7A and 60(4) of the National Lottery etc Act 1993.

7.437 1 Citation, commencement and interpretation

These Regulations may be cited as the National Lottery (Annual Licence Fees) Regulations 2010 and shall come into force on 28th January 2010.

7.438

2 In these Regulations—

"the 1993 Act" means the National Lottery etc Act 1993,

"the Commission" means the National Lottery Commission.

7.439 3 Annual fee for licence under section 5 (Licensing of a person to run the National Lottery)

The holder of a licence under section 5 of the 1993 Act shall pay—

(a) a first annual fee of £35,000 to the Commission within 12 months after the issue of the licence,

(b) an annual fee of £3,900 to the Commission before the first anniversary and before each subsequent anniversary of the issue of the licence.

7.440 4 Annual fees for licences under section 6 (Licensing of persons to promote lotteries as part of the National Lottery)

Subject to regulations 5 and 6, the holder of a licence under section 6 of the 1993 Act to promote lotteries shall pay—

(a) a first annual fee of £2,500 to the Commission within 12 months after the issue of the licence, and

(b) an annual fee of £2,500 to the Commission before the first anniversary and before each subsequent anniversary of the issue of the licence.

7.441

5 Subject to regulation 6, the holder of a licence under section 6 of the 1993 Act authorising the promotion of an unrestricted number of lotteries which fall within a particular description specified in the licence, shall pay—

(a) a first annual fee of £8,000 to the Commission within 12 months after the issue of the licence, and

(b) an annual fee of £8,000 to the Commission before the first anniversary and before each subsequent anniversary of the issue of the licence.

7.442

6 The holder of a licence under section 6 of the 1993 Act authorising the promotion of a lottery pursuant to an agreement, entered into between the licencee and the promoters of other lotteries in other countries of the European Union, under which lotteries falling within the agreement share a common game structure and prizes, shall pay—

(a) a first annual fee of £16,000 to the Commission within 12 months after the issue of the licence, and

(b) an annual fee of £16,000 to the Commission before the first anniversary and before each subsequent anniversary of the issue of the licence.

2338

2 In these Regulations—

the "1993 Act" means the National Lottery etc. Act 1993;

"the Commission" means the National Lottery Commission.

2339 3 Annual fee for licence under section 5 (licensing of a person to run the National Lottery)

The holder of a licence under section 5 of the 1993 Act shall pay—

(a) a first annual fee of £[illegible] to the Commission within 12 months after the issue of the licence;

(b) an annual fee of £3,700 to the Commission before the first anniversary and before each subsequent anniversary of the issue of the licence.

2340 4 Annual fees for licences under section 6 (licensing of persons to promote lotteries as part of the National Lottery)

Subject to regulations 5 and 6, the holder of a licence under section 6 of the 1993 Act to promote lotteries shall pay—

(a) a first annual fee of £2,500 to the Commission within 12 months after the issue of the licence; and

(b) an annual fee of £2,500 to the Commission before the first anniversary and before each subsequent anniversary of the issue of the licence.

2341

5 Subject to regulation 6, the holder of a licence under section 6 of the 1993 Act authorising the promotion of an unrestricted number of lotteries which fall within paragraph [illegible] of that section, shall pay—

(a) a first annual fee of £[illegible] to the Commission within 12 months after the issue of the licence; and

(b) an annual fee of £[illegible] to the Commission before the first anniversary and before each subsequent anniversary of the issue of the licence.

2342

6 The holder of a licence under section 6 of the 1993 Act authorising the promotion of a lottery pursuant to an agreement entered into between the licence holder and the promoter of other lotteries in other countries of the European Union, in which lotteries falling within the agreement share a common game structure and prizes, shall pay—

(a) a first annual fee of £[illegible] to the Commission within 12 months after the issue of the licence; and

(b) an annual fee of £[illegible] to the Commission before the first anniversary and before each subsequent anniversary of the issue of the licence.

Part 8

Gambling Appeals, Applications and Procedure

Section 1

Commentary

PART A: APPEALS UNDER THE GAMBLING ACT 2005

Appeals to the First-tier Tribunal

8.1 Under Part 7 of the Gambling Act 2005 appeals in respect of operating and personal licences and, in the case of the decision to void a bet under s 336, are to be made to a newly-established body, the First-tier Tribunal which has, since January 2010 assumed all the powers of the defunct Gambling Appeals Tribunal. Thereafter an appeal on a point of law can only be made if permission has been granted to the High Court. Such an appeal will be a statutory appeal within CPR r 52. There is also a very limited right to appeal further to the Court of Appeal. For a more detailed examination of Part 7 see paras **6.130–6.135** above.

Appeals to and from the magistrates' court

8.2

(a) a licensing authority decision under GA 2005, Pt 8 (re premises licences and provisional statements) can be appealed in accordance with ss 206–208. The appeal is to the local magistrates' court and will be by way of a rehearing. A dissatisfied party can then appeal solely on a point of law to the High Court under s 209. This is a statutory appeal under CPR, Pt 52. For a more detailed examination of the relevant provisions see paras **6.184–6.185** above;

(b) appeals in respect of GA 2005, Pt 9 concerning the temporary use of premises are to the local magistrates' court under s 226 and will be a rehearing. A further appeal solely on a point of law can be brought under s 226(8) to the High Court. This is a statutory appeal under CPR Pt 52;

(c) appeals in respect of GA 2005, Sch 10 concerning Family Entertainment Centre Gaming Machine Permits are to the local magistrates' court under para 22(2) of the Schedule and will be a rehearing. Although the GA 2005 itself makes no mention of any further appeal, the application of the Magistrates' Courts Act 1980, s 111 (see also the Senior Courts Act 1981, s 28A) produces the result that an appeal by way of case stated can be brought;

(d) appeals in respect of Sch 11, Pt 5, concerning registration of small society lotteries are to the local magistrates' court under para 51(2) of the Schedule and will be a rehearing. Although the GA 2005 itself makes no mention of any further appeal, the application of the

Magistrates' Courts Act 1980, s 111 (see also the Senior Courts Act 1981, s 28A) produces the result that an appeal by way of case stated can be brought;

(e) appeals in respect of GA 2005, Sch 12 concerning Club Gaming Permits and Club Machine Permits are to the local magistrates' court under para 25(5) of the Schedule and will be a rehearing. Although the GA 2005 itself makes no mention of any further appeal, the application of the Magistrates' Courts Act 1980, s 111 (see also the Senior Courts Act 1981, s 28A) produces the result that an appeal by way of case stated can be brought;

(f) appeals in respect of GA 2005, Sch 13 concerning Licensed Premises Gaming Machine Permits are to the local magistrates' court under para 21(2) of the Schedule and will be a rehearing. Although the GA 2005 itself makes no mention of any further appeal, the application of the Magistrates' Courts Act 1980, s 111 (see also the Senior Courts Act 1981, s 28A) produces the result that an appeal by way of case stated can be brought;

(g) appeals in respect of GA 2005, Sch 14 concerning Prize Gaming Permits and Club Machine Permits are to the local magistrates' court under para 22(2) of the Schedule and will be a rehearing. Although the GA 2005 itself makes no mention of any further appeal, the application of the Magistrates' Courts Act 1980, s 111 (see also the Senior Courts Act 1981, s 28A) produces the result that an appeal by way of case stated can be brought.

Unlike an application for judicial review, none of the appeals to the High Court under (a)–(g) above requires permission from the High Court.

In relation to appeals under the Licensing Act, the Court of Appeal has confirmed in two cases *R (on the application of Hope and Glory Public House Ltd) v City of Westminster Magistrates' Court (Lord Mayor and Citizens of the City of Westminster, interested party)*[1] and *R (on the application of Khan) v Coventry Magistrates' Court*[2] that appeals to the magistrates are by way of re-hearing. The same reasoning would apply to appeals to the magistrates under the Gambling Act 2005.

In the *Hope and Glory* case, the Court of Appeal also considered, in the context of an appeal to the magistrates from a decision of the Licensing Authority made under the Licensing Act, to what extent is the appellate court entitled to have regard to the decision appealed from. The Court of Appeal set out to answer three questions:

(1) How much weight was the district judge entitled to give to the decision of the licensing authority?

(2) More particularly, was he right to hold that he should only allow the appeal if satisfied that the decision of the licensing authority was wrong?

(3) Was the district judge's ruling compliant with art 6?

The court answered both questions 2 and 3 'yes' but gave no definitive answer to question 1. What the court did say by way of guidance is to be found at para 45 of the judgement:

> 'It is right in all cases that the magistrates' court should pay careful attention to the reasons given by the licensing authority for arriving at the decision under appeal, bearing in mind that Parliament has chosen to place responsibility for making such

decisions on local authorities. The weight which the magistrates should ultimately attach to those reasons must be a matter for their judgment in all the circumstances, taking into account the fullness and clarity of the reasons, the nature of the issues and the evidence given on the appeal.'

The court also made clear that it was for the appellant to present his case first as it is for the appellant to persuade the court that the original decision was wrong. The court approved the statement of Burton J in his judgement at first instance.

'It means that the task of the district judge — having heard the evidence which is now before him, and specifically addressing the decision of the court below — is to give a decision whether, because he disagrees with the decision below in the light of the evidence before him, it is therefore wrong'.

It seems to us that the practical effect of all this is that the burden of proving the case on the balance of probabilities is on the appellant on the evidence called on the appeal. This seems to be the way that the issue has been approached in two further cases under the Licensing Act which have reached the Administrative Court since *Hope and Glory* was decided in the Court of Appeal. They are *R (on the application of Developing Retail Ltd) v East Hampshire Magistrates' Court*[3] and *R (on the application of Townlink Ltd) v Thames Magistrates' Court*[4]. Unhappily in both these cases the applications were unopposed and only one party was represented. In those circumstances the cases can only be cited as authority if the judge agrees that his or her decision has advanced the law in some way and allows their decision to be quoted. In the Hampshire case the judge (Claire Montgomery QC sitting as a Deputy High Court Judge) was not asked and in the other case Lindblom J refused to allow it to be cited as he said that he was simply following *Hope and Glory*. However the way they both approached the question must we suggest be right. The appellant does not have to demonstrate that the decision of the Licensing Authority was irrational or an unreasonable conclusion to have reached on the evidence that the committee heard. What the appellant has to do is satisfy the magistrates on the evidence that they hear that the decision of the Licensing Authority was wrong. The ruling in the *Hope and Glory* appeal would seem to apply equally to appeals to magistrates under the Gambling Act.

While in most cases the only respondent to the appeal will be the Licensing Authority, it was held by a Divisional Court in *R (on the application of the Chief Constable of Nottinghamshire Police) v Nottingham Magistrates' Court*[5] that the magistrates had an implied power under the statute to allow a party who had appeared to oppose the application in front of the licensing authority to appear on the appeal and call evidence if that would further the licensing objectives. That should not be allowed if this would simply lead to duplication and extend the length of the hearing. The court should also consider protecting the appellant from having to pay two sets of costs where there has been duplication between the cases. This was again an appeal from a decision taken by the Licensing Authority under the Licensing Act, there seems no reason why the same principles should not apply to appeals to magistrates under the Gambling Act.

---

1 [2011] EWCA Civ 31, [2011] 3 All ER 579, [2011] PTSR 868.
2 [2011] EWCA Civ 751, [2011] All ER (D) 226 (Jun).
3 [2011] EWHC 618 (Admin), [2011] All ER (D) 29 (Apr).

4 [2011] EWHC 898 (Admin).
5 [2009] EWHC 3182 (Admin), [2010] 2 All ER 342, [2011] PTSR 92.

Judicial review

8.3–8.11 In each case, if appropriate, a dissatisfied party will be able to seek permission to apply for judicial review; see Part B below (para **8.12** ff below).

PART B: APPEALS AND APPLICATIONS TO THE HIGH COURT

Introduction

8.12 A party dissatisfied with a decision in a betting or gaming case may in certain cases appeal under Part 52 CPR 1998 to the Administrative Court by way of case stated or apply to that court for judicial review under Pt 54 CPR 1998. In some cases the applicant can choose either route. In others however he must decide whether to appeal or to seek judicial review (see for example *Tehrani v Rostron*[1]) or risk that his case will be rejected for failure to adopt the correct procedure. Analysis of the relevant case law indicates that the matters set out in **8.13–8.18** below should be borne in mind when deciding which route is appropriate. This does not, however, prevent an appeal by way of judicial review. Where the dissatisfied party has a right to appeal to the magistrates he should normally exercise that right of appeal. Judicial review is a remedy of last resort. In *R (on the application of JD Wetherspoon plc) v Guildford Borough Council*[2], a liquor licensing case, the point was taken that Wetherspoons should have exercised its right to appeal to the magistrates rather than proceed by judicial review. Beatson J reviewed the authorities and said that the test was whether the real issue to be decided could be determined by an appeal to the magistrates. In that case he said that, as the issue concerned a matter of principal where uniformity of approach was required, that could only properly be determined by the High Court and the application for judicial review was appropriate. This is likely only to be the case on relatively rare occasions. Normally the High Court will insist that there is an appeal to the magistrates before any appeal to the High Court.

1 [1972] 1 QB 182 at 187–8, Lord Denning MR.
2 [2006] EWHC 815 (Admin), [2007] 1 All ER 400, [2006] LGR 767.

Exclusions/lack of statutory provision

8.13 Judicial review, being a public law remedy, cannot be used to challenge decisions which exclusively affect an individual's private law rights. Therefore traditionally, in order for a decision to be challenged by judicial review, two conditions had to be satisfied. First, the decision had to be that of a public body, that is a person or entity empowered by statute, statutory instrument or royal prerogative to perform a public function. Second, the actual decision complained of had to be made by the public law entity whist operating in its public law capacity[1]. However, the first of these traditional preconditions has been eroded by common law development from around the Commonwealth, culminating in the landmark case of *Datafin*[2]. In that case the Court of Appeal held that the workings of the private non-statutory body; the Takeover and Mergers Panel, was susceptible to judicial review. The court took a pragmatic approach, accepting that despite its non-public origin it, 'operates wholly in the public domain . . . performing a public duty and an important one . . . '. It seems, therefore, that whilst it can no longer be said that a non-public body cannot automatically be subjected to judicial review, decisions of a body which does not operate in the public domain or a particular decision which does not affect public law rights and duties remains immune to judicial review proceedings[3]. However bodies which are not susceptible to judicial review but who are alleged to have acted, in effect, unfairly, may be (depending on the facts and usually depending on the relevant contractual terms) sued in the Civil Courts. For a recent example see *Flaherty v NGRC Ltd*[4]. Judicial review proceedings are substantially based on the common law. Subject to the principles set out below it is possible for an applicant to seek judicial review in respect of a decision of the magistrates' court. However, in contrast, an appeal by way of case stated is statute-based; unless a relevant provision exists in a statute no such appeal can be taken. Section 111 of the Magistrates' Courts Act 1980 enables a case to be stated from the justices although, by contrast, no such power exists in the case of other bodies exercising powers under the Gambling Act 2005

1 *R v Panel of Takeovers and Mergers, ex p Datafin plc* [1987] QB 815.
2 *R v Panel of Takeovers and Mergers, ex p Datafin plc* [1987] QB 815 per Sir John Donaldson MR.
3 See also *R (Boyle) v Haverhill Pub Watch and the Chief Constable of Suffolk etc* [2009] EWHC 2441 (Admin); [2010] LLR 93 a decision regarding a pub watch scheme, in which despite the involvement of public bodies in the scheme it was held not to be subject to judicial review.
4 [2005] LLR 70, Ch D.

Jurisdiction

8.14 Where a party successfully contends that the inferior tribunal had no jurisdiction to entertain and determine an application, the appropriate remedy for the aggrieved party is to seek judicial review in the form of a mandatory order from the Administrative Court directing the inferior court to hear the matter[1].

Where however the inferior court accepts jurisdiction, the aggrieved party has a choice of which avenue to follow. One method is an appeal by way of case stated against the decision by the court to accept jurisdiction. The appropriate time for instituting such an appeal is after the conclusion of the substantive hearing[2].

Alternatively, the aggrieved party has a concurrent right to apply to the Administrative Court for leave to seek judicial review in the nature of a prohibitory order preventing the inferior tribunal from entertaining the substantive hearing. If the latter course is adopted, the tribunal will in the interests of justice and the public purse invariably adjourn the hearing of the substantive proceedings until after the conclusion of the judicial review hearing[3].

1 *Streames v Copping* [1985] QB 920 at 928.
2 Ibid.

[3] *R v Wimbledon Justices, ex p Derwent* [1953] 1 QB 380; *R v Crown Court at Maidstone, ex p Harris* [1994] COD 514.

Points of law

8.15 The appropriate time for stating a case on a point of law is after the conclusion of the substantive hearing. Where a tribunal has made an interlocutory ruling which is challenged it is inappropriate for a case to be stated. The aggrieved party should seek permission to obtain judicial review[1].

[1] *R v Greater Manchester Justices, ex p Aldi GmbH* (1994) 159 JP 717.

Post decision

8.16 Following the initial decision by the lower tribunal any application which will involve disputed or complex facts should be by way of case stated (if available) rather than judicial review[1].

This is because the actual facts as found by the relevant tribunal will be clearly set out in the stated case, together with the evidence purportedly supporting such findings.

Similarly, and for the same reason, case stated is the appropriate mode of appeal where the challenge to the decision of the lower tribunal is based on an allegation that there was no or insufficient evidence to support a material factual finding by it[2].

However, where the complaint is not that the decision was based on scarcity of evidence, but rather that a party was refused the opportunity of giving evidence at the hearing, or indeed any other breach of the rules of natural justice, the challenge should be by way of judicial review[3].

Judicial review is also the most appropriate mode of challenge where the complaint is that the inferior court misunderstood its role or functions[4], including where a public body based its judgment on a fundamental misunderstanding as to the true factual position[5].

Subject to the above limitations (and to the point made in para **8.17** below), any decision of an inferior tribunal expressed to be 'final' by Parliament is still open to challenge by either case stated or judicial review:

> '. . . When Parliament says that a decision of an inferior tribunal is to be "final" it does so on the assumption that the tribunal will observe the law. Parliament only gives the impression of "finality" to the decision on the condition that it is read in accordance with law: and the Queen's courts will see to it that this condition is fulfilled. Accordingly if a tribunal goes wrong in law and the error appears on the face of the record, the High Court will interfere by certiorari to quash the decision . . . if a point of law can be resolved by certiorari or declaration, I do not see why it should not also be resolved by case stated'[6].

[1] *R v Ipswich CC, ex p Baldwin* [1981] 1 All ER 596.

[2] *Stubbings v Beaconsfield Justices and S Bucks DC* (1987) 152 JP 17.

[3] *R v Wandsworth Justices, ex p Read* [1942] 1 KB 281.

[4] *R v Chief Commons Commissioner, ex p Winnington* (1982) Times, 26 November.

[5] *R (on the application of Lunt) v Liverpool City Council* [2009] EWHC 2356 (Admin), [2010] 1 CMLR 431.

6 *Tehrani v Rostron* [1972] 1 QB 182 at 187–8, per Lord Denning MR.

Specific statutory provision

8.17 Section 28A(4) of the Senior Courts Act 1981 provides that in case stated proceedings from a magistrates' court in non-criminal proceedings the decision of the High Court is final. Section 18 states that no appeal shall lie to the Court of Appeal from any High Court order which is final. This factor must be taken into account when deciding which route to choose; it provides a great incentive in those cases in which either option is open to the applicant to adopt judicial review rather than case stated.

Challenges to awards of costs

8.18 As the case of the *Chief Constable of Derbyshire v Goodman and Newton*[1] makes plain there is an advantage in proceeding by way of case stated in cases where the challenge is to a costs order made in the lower tribunal. As Collins J pointed out in *R (Chief Constable of Sussex) v Chichester Crown Court and Stoner*[2], the High Court has greater theoretical latitude in costs appeals by way of case stated in comparison with judicial review cases; in the former it can exercise the discretion afresh on broad grounds whereas in the latter case it must conclude that the award was perverse before it can intervene.

1 [2001] LLR 127.
2 [2003] LLR 312, AC at para 17.

Further differences between judicial review and case stated

8.19 In order to make a fully informed choice between the two routes of challenge when none of the above principles applies, it is important to bear in mind the different procedural rules and regimes between the two competing routes as well as their differing 'raison d'être'.

An important procedural difference is that whilst an applicant for judicial review requires permission from the High Court in order to take his case to a full hearing, there is no such requirement for appeals by way of case stated.

The basis of judicial review proceedings is to provide a legal challenge to administrative or executive decisions which affect a person's public law rights. It is not concerned with the merits of a decision but rather the way in which the decision was reached:

> 'Judicial review, as the words imply, is not an appeal from a decision, but a review of the manner in which the decision was made . . . judicial review is concerned not with the decision, but with the decision-making process. Unless that restriction on the power of the court is observed, the court will, in my view, under the guise of presenting the abused power, be itself guilty of usurping power'[1].

Traditionally, any challenge to such a decision has been under one of three heads: that the decision was illegal; that the decision was irrational; or that the procedure adopted in reaching the decision was fundamentally flawed:

> 'Judicial review has I think developed to a stage today when . . . one can conveniently classify under three heads the grounds upon which administrative

action is subject to control by judicial review. The first ground I would call "illegality", the second "irrationality" and the third "procedural impropriety"[2]'.

The first head covers three main areas: a decision made ultra vires, that is in excess of power or authority; a decision based upon an error of law or fact; and a decision flawed by the failure of the decision maker to take account of relevant considerations or conversely, the taking into account of irrelevant matters:

> 'by "illegality" as a ground for judicial review I mean that the decision maker must understand correctly the law that regulates his decision making power and must give effect to it'[3].

A challenge under the second head of 'irrationality' is based squarely upon the perversity or unreasonableness of a decision:

> 'By "irrationality" I mean what can now succinctly be referred to as "Wednesbury unreasonableness" (*Associated Provincial Picture Houses Ltd v Wednesbury Corpn* [1948] 1 KB 223). It applies to a decision which is so outrageous in its defiance of law or accepted moral standards that no sensible person who had applied his mind to the question to be decided could have arrived at it'[4,5].

In recent years the ground of 'irrationality' also seems to have consumed the idea of proportionality, ie that legal principle requires a reasonable and proportionate relationship between the measures taken and the objective hoped to be achieved by those methods. Although the House of Lords in *Ex p Brind* rejected the idea of proportionality in that particular case and Lords Ackner and Lowry were dismissive of such a principle; Lords Bridge, Templeman and Roskill did not go so far as to dismiss the idea of proportionality as a legitimate principle of English law, although it is perhaps wise to view it as an aspect of the broader concept of Lord Diplock's second category of 'unreasonableness' or 'irrationality'. Proportionality also exists as a basic principle of the European Convention on Human Rights under which there must be a 'reasonable relationship of proportionality between the means employed and the legitimate objectives pursued by the contested limitation'[6]. The third broad head of challenge to an administrative decision, 'procedural impropriety', contemplates the disregard of an express procedural requirement or the violation of general common law principles of natural justice:

> 'I have described the third head as "procedural impropriety" rather than failure to observe basic rules of natural justice or failure to act with procedural fairness towards the person who will be affected by the decision. This is because susceptibility to judicial review under this head covers also failure by an administrative tribunal to observe procedural rules that are expressly laid down in the legislative instrument by which its jurisdiction is conferred, even where such failure does not involve any denial of natural justice'.

Following *Schmidt* it was thought that the idea of 'legitimate expectation' was a new and separate head on which to launch the judicial review proceedings. However, it is clear from the speech of Lord Diplock in *CCSU v Minister for the Civil Service* and in subsequent cases which emphasise the significance of reliance and detriment that the better view is to regard it as an aspect of 'procedural impropriety'.

In a series of cases in the House of Lords, it has been decided that, where it is alleged that human rights under the European Convention of Human Rights have been breached, it is for the Court on appeal to decide whether there has been a breach. This proposition was applied to a licensing case in *Miss Behavin' Ltd v Belfast City Council*[7]. At para 31 Baroness Hale said 'the first and most straightforward question is who decides whether or not a claimant's convention rights have been infringed. The answer is that it is the court before which the issue is raised. The role of the court in human rights adjudication is quite different from the role of the courts in an ordinary judicial review of administrative action. In human rights adjudication the court is concerned with whether the human rights of the claimant have been infringed, not with whether the administrative decision maker properly took them into account'. As many licensing cases involve human rights, this will be the proper approach of the court in many licensing judicial reviews. It requires an 'intense focus' on those matters which are said to amount to a breach of human rights.

In contrast to judicial review proceedings, appeals by case stated, not being an exclusively public law remedy, are not confined to questions of public law and can encompass questions of private law. Under the case stated procedure, the decision of any inferior court or tribunal may be challenged on the ground that the decision is either wrong in law or in excess of jurisdiction[8]. An aggrieved party may also challenge a factual finding of an inferior court or tribunal on the basis that it is unsupported by the preponderance of evidence and as such constitutes a gross mistake of fact amounting to an error of law[9]. The rationale behind stating a case is to provide a procedure for the High Court to exercise a supervisory role over magistrates' and Crown Courts, as well as ministers and tribunals when exercising a judicial function. The spectrum covered by case stated in therefore narrower than judicial review proceedings, as the former does not cover challenges based on the consideration of relevant or irrelevant material, unreasonable or irrational decisions, or those based on proportionality; or on breaches of natural justice or legitimate expectation.

One matter which should be borne in mind when deciding whether to start proceedings by case stated or judicial review is that there is no appeal to the Court of Appeal from a case stated appeal whereas there is on judicial review (see *Paterson* vol 1, para **5.54** for commentary on the case of *Westminster City Council v O'Reilly*).

1 *Chief Constable of North Wales Police v Evans* [1982] 1 WLR 1155 at 1174.

2 *CCSU v Minister for the Civil Service* [1985] AC 374 at 410 and 411 per Lord Diplock.

3 *R v Secretary of State for the Home Department, ex p Brind* [1991] 1 AC 696.

4 *Schmidt v Secretary of State for Home Affairs* [1969] 2 Ch 149, [1968] 3 All ER 795. How long the rationale of *Wednesbury* will survive is currently in doubt given the opinions of Lords Cooke and Steyn in *R (Daly) v Secretary of State for the Home Department* [2001] 3 All ER 433, HL. A consequence of the ECHR may be to substitute for the very high *Wednesbury* hurdle a more limited obstacle or even to supplant it entirely by an analysis of the merits of the case.

5 For recent licensing cases in this area see: *R (on the application of Thompsett) v Croydon Crown Court* [2001] LLR 714, QBD; *Macdonald v The Western Isles Licensing Board* [2001] LLR 655, Ct Sess; and *White and Gibbenson v South East Cornwall Justices* [2001] LLR 729, QBD.

6 *Fayed v United Kingdom* (1994) 18 EHRR 393, 432, ECtHR, para 71.

7 [2007] UKHL 19, [2007] All ER (D) 219 (Apr).

8 Magistrates' Courts Act 1980, s 111(1) and Senior Courts Act 1981, s 28.

9 *Cababe v Walton-upon-Thames District Council* [1914] AC 102.

8.20 Locus standi A party wishing to pursue judicial review proceedings must show 'sufficient interest'[1] in that decision and its consequences. The conditions of locus applies both on the application for permission to apply for judicial review and also at the substantive hearing itself. 'Sufficient interest' does not necessarily mean that the applicant must have a direct financial interest in the decision, and is usually satisfied by a direct personal or professional or representative interest in the relief sought[2]. In *R v Horsham Justices, ex p Farquharson*[3], the Divisional Court held an individual journalist as well as the National Union of Journalists both had locus standi to seek a writ of certiorari quashing a decision of the Horsham magistrates prohibiting the publication of events at the committal stage of any proceedings until the commencement of the actual trial. However, 'sufficient interest' does imply something more than a feeling of sympathy or injustice on the part of a public spirited applicant. The question of locus standi is not resolved by simply having regard to the individual facts of the case then before the court. Rather, it is a mixed question of fact and law to be decided on legal principles although the threshold for satisfying the test is not necessarily the same in all cases[4]. Since October 2000 and the application of the new Pt 54 CPR, apart from the claimant and defendant an interested 'party', ie a person directly affected by the claim, may also become involved in the proceedings[5].

Similar grounds for satisfying locus standi apply to cases stated by the magistrates' court, namely any person who was a party to any proceedings before the magistrates' court or any person 'who is aggrieved by a conviction, order, determination or other proceedings of such a court'[6]. However, slightly narrower grounds apply when a case is to be stated by the Crown Court. In such circumstances only a person who was a 'party to the proceedings'[7] before the Crown Court has sufficient locus standi to have a case stated questioning 'any order, judgment or other decision of the Crown Court'.

---

1 Senior Courts Act 1981, s 31(3).

2 *R v Inspectorate of Pollution, ex p Greenpeace Ltd (No 2)* [1994] 4 All ER 329.

3 [1982] QB 762.

4 *IRC v National Federation of Self Employed and Small Businesses* [1982] AC 617 at 631 per Lord Wilberforce.

5 CPR Part 54.1(2)(f).

6 Magistrates' Courts Act 1980, s 111(1).

7 Senior Courts Act 1981, s 28(1).

PART B1: JUDICIAL REVIEW – SUMMARY OF THE CURRENT PROCEDURE

Introduction

8.21 Applications for permission to seek leave to obtain judicial review are governed by Pt 54 CPR. They are made to the Administrative Court. An applicant needs to familiarise himself with the terms of Pt 54. He must also be aware of a number of other rules (in particular Pts 8 and 10), the Pre-Action Protocol and the Practice Direction relevant to Pt 54 and the Practice Statement issued on 1 February 2002. The administrative court is now located in Cardiff, Birmingham, Manchester and Leeds as well as London and applications local to those courts should be commenced there (see Practice Direction 54D). The regional offices have been a great success and in addition to providing single judge administrative courts, they have the capacity also to sit divisional courts when necessary. Many members of the public may have an interest in a licensing appeal and it is important if possible that the hearing should be heard locally. The regional courts have a significantly smaller workload and as a result cases are heard quicker. The court will also sit in other court buildings around the region if the matter is of sufficient local interest. In 2009 there were also some amendments made to the Pre-Action Protocol.[1]

The most commonly sought remedies available have been renamed (no doubt out of some bizarre belief that by doing so they have become more 'user friendly' or even relevant) as a prohibiting order, a quashing order and a mandatory order.[2] If any of these remedies or a declaration or injunction as well is required the procedure set out in Part 54 must be used.[3] However, if only a declaration or injunction is sought the procedure is not mandatory but permissive.[4]

NOTE

Under the Tribunals, Courts and Enforcement Act 2007, ss 15–21 the Upper Tribunal is to have jurisdiction over judicial review applications transferred to it from the High Court although it seems from the terms of s 11 and the Direction made by the Lord Chief Justice under s 18(6) that such jurisdiction does not apply in Gambling Act cases.

---

1 [2002] 1 All ER 633.
2 Part 54.1(2) CPR.
3 Part 54.2 CPR.
4 Part 54.3 CPR.

Pre-action protocol

8.22 On 4 March 2002 a pre-action protocol in judicial review cases came into force. In most licensing cases the protocol should be used – only in urgent cases can it be ignored, although even then a claimant is encouraged to fax a draft Claim Form to the defendant. Failure to use it in non-urgent cases can have ramifications later, especially in relation to costs.

The essentials of the protocol are that:

(1) the claimant should, prior to making the claim, send a letter to the defendant identifying the issues and seeking to establish whether litigation can be avoided. The claimant is expected to use a standard form of the letter set out at Annex A to the protocol. The letter should contain the date and details of the decision, act or omission being challenged and a clear summary of the facts on which the claim is based. It should also contain the details of any relevant information that the claimant is seeking and an explanation of why this is considered relevant. The letter should normally contain the details of any interested parties known to the claimant. They should be sent a copy of the letter before claim for information. The claim should not normally be made until the proposed reply date given in the letter before claim has passed, unless the circumstances of the case require more immediate action to be taken;

(2) the defendant should normally respond within 14 days using the standard form set out at Annex B to the protocol. Failure to do so will be taken into account by the court and sanctions may be imposed unless

there are good reasons. Where it is not possible to reply within the proposed time limit the defendant should send an interim reply and propose a reasonable extension. Where an extension is sought, reasons should be given and, where required, additional information requested. This will not affect the time limit for making a claim for judicial review, nor will it bind the claimant where he or she considers this to be unreasonable. However, where the court considers that a subsequent claim is made prematurely it may impose sanctions. If the claim is being conceded in full, the reply should say so in clear and unambiguous terms. If the claim is being conceded in part or not being conceded at all, the reply should say so in clear and unambiguous terms, and:

(a) provide a fuller explanation for the decision, if considered appropriate to do so;
(b) address any points of dispute, or explain why they cannot be addressed;
(c) enclose any relevant documentation requested by the claimant, or explain why the documents are not being enclosed; and
(d) where appropriate, confirm whether or not they will oppose any application for an interim remedy.

The response should be sent to all interested parties identified by the claimant and should contain details of any other parties who the defendant considers also have an interest.

Permission to seek judicial review

8.23 As before under RSC Ord 53, an applicant must first seek permission (formerly 'leave') to seek judicial review. This he now does by filing a claim form in the Administrative Court Office (formerly the Crown Office). In urgent applications the procedure can no doubt, for good reason, be abbreviated, at least as to time periods, under the inherent jurisdiction of the court.

Urgent cases procedure

8.24 CPR Pt 54 makes no express provision for urgent applications for permission to apply for judicial review to be made orally. As the result of users' concerns, on 1 February 2002 guidance on the procedure to be applied for urgent applications and for interim injunctions was issued as Annex B to a practice statement.[1] Advocates must comply with this guidance, and where a manifestly inappropriate application is made, consideration will be given to a wasted costs order. In summary, this states:

(1) Where a claimant makes an application for the permission application to be heard as a matter of urgency and/or seeks an interim injunction, he must complete a prescribed form which states:
(a) the need for urgency;
(b) the timescale sought for the consideration of the permission application, eg within 72 hours or sooner if necessary (see para (5) below); and
(c) the date by which the substantive hearing should take place.
(2) Where an interim injunction is sought, a claimant must, in addition, provide:

(a) a draft order; and
(b) the grounds for the injunction.

(3) The claimant must serve (by fax and post) the claim form and application for urgency on the defendant and interested parties, advising them of the application and that they may make representations.

(4) Where an interim injunction is sought, the claimant must serve (by fax and post) the draft order and grounds for the application on the defendant and interested parties, advising them of the application and that they may make representations.

(5) A judge will consider the application within the time requested and may make such order as he considers appropriate.

(6) If the judge directs that an oral hearing take place within a specified time the representatives of the parties and the Administrative Court will liaise to fix a permission hearing within the time period directed.

1 [2002] 1 All ER 633.

The claim form

8.25 The claim form must comply with Pt 8.2 CPR, Pt 54.6 and the Practice Direction dated 20 July 2000. The appropriate claim form is Form N461. Apart from the usual formal parts, the form must state:

- that Pt 8 applies;
- the question which the court is to be asked to decide or the remedy sought and its legal basis – if there is a claim for interim relief this should be made in the claim form;
- which enactment (eg Gaming Act 1968) is relevant to the claim;
- the name and address of any person the claimant considers to be an interested party;
- that he is requesting permission to proceed with a claim for judicial review;
- a detailed statement of the grounds for bringing the claim;
- a statement of the facts relied upon;
- if any application for an extension of time is sought;
- if any application for directions is necessary – this would include, for example, an application for a stay;[1]
- a time estimate for the substantive hearing of the JR application if permission is granted.

The claim form must be accompanied by two paginated and indexed copies of:

(a) any written evidence in support of the claim and of any application to extend the time-limit for filing the claim form;
(b) any order which is sought to be quashed;
(c) an approved copy of the reasons given by the court/tribunal in reaching its decision;
(d) any documents upon which the claimant proposes to rely and other relevant documents;
(e) copies of all relevant statutory provisions; and
(f) a list of essential reading.

There is a general duty of full and frank disclosure.

---

[1] See Part 54.10 CPR. Such an application was made (but refused) in *R (Embelle Leisure Ltd) v Bristol City Council* [2004] LLR 322, AC, a case concerning the cancellation of a public entertainments licence.

Service of the claim form

8.26 Having filed it in the Administrative Court Office, the claim form must be served by the claimant within seven days on the defendant and any other person the claimant considers to be an interested party.

Delay at the permission stage

8.27 The claim form must be filed promptly[1] and in any event within three months after the grounds for making the claim first arose.[2] This time period cannot be extended by agreement between the parties. An extension of time may be granted by the court[3] if the claimant can provide a good reason[4] for the delay and that extending the time limit will not cause substantial hardship or substantial prejudice or be detrimental to good administration[5].

---

[1] As the overriding requirement is one of promptness a claimant may, if he has unreasonably delayed his claim, fail even if he starts his case within the 12-week period: see *R v Independent Television Commission, ex p TVNI Ltd* (1991) Times 30 December.

[2] Part 54.5 CPR 1998. Note that unlike under the Limitation Act 1980 there is no formal provision for time limits only starting to run from when the claimant first discovering his claim or having adequate information to bring the claim. See also para 4.1 Practice Direction – Judicial Review which states that if the claim is for a quashing order in respect of a judgement or order time runs from that date of judgment or order.

[3] Under Part 3.1(2)(a) CPR 1998.

[4] For example if the claim raises issues of general public importance: see *R v Secretary of State for the Home Department, ex p Ruddock* [1987] 1 WLR 1482; *Re S* [1998] COD 52. However, if the delay is attributable to the claimant's lawyers that may not be sufficient reason; see *R v Secretary of State for Health, ex p Furneaux* [1994] 2 All ER 652 cf *R v London Borough of Newham, ex p Gentle* (1993) 26 HLR 466, QBD and *R v Secretary of State for the Home Department, ex p Oyeleye* [1994] Imm AR 268, QBD. See also *R (on the application of Camelot UK Lotteries Ltd) v Gambling Commission* [2012] EWHC 2391 (Admin).

[5] An interesting recent case in which the applicant for judicial review felt unable, because of delay, to apply for a quashing order but was effectively driven to seek solely declarations is *R (on the application of Crew (Chief Constable of West Midlands Police)) v Birmingham Licensing Justices* [2002] LLR 293, QBD.

Delay at the hearing stage

8.28 Even if an applicant persuades the court that despite the existence of delay he should be given permission, that is not necessarily the end of the significance of delay because s 31(6) of the Senior Courts Act 1981 still applies. That provides:

> 'Where the High Court considers that there has been undue delay in making an application for judicial review, the court may refuse to grant–
> (a) leave for making of the application; or
> (b) any relief sought on the application,

if it considers that the granting of the relief sought would be likely to cause substantial hardship to, or substantially prejudice the rights of, any person or would be detrimental to good administration.'

The construction of the subsection and its relationship to the provisions in the CPR, which require that an application be made promptly and in any event within three months, have been the subject of two cases before the House of Lords: *Caswell v Dairy Produce Quota Tribunal for England and Wales*;[1] and *R v Criminal Injuries Compensation Board, ex p A.*[2] The upshot of those authorities is that if 'leave', ie permission, to apply for judicial review out of time has been granted – or has been granted within time – then the question whether leave should have been granted cannot be reopened at the substantive hearing, and it is not open to a judge at that hearing to reconsider the question of an extension of time and whether good grounds have been shown under the CPR. What can be done at the substantive hearing is to consider whether relief should be refused if the granting of such relief would be likely to cause hardship or prejudice within the meaning of s 31(6), or would be detrimental to good administration. That issue is still open, but delay must have had the effect mentioned in s 31(6) to disable the court on that ground from granting relief that it would otherwise have been prepared to grant.

In *R (on the application of the British Beer and Pub Association) v Canterbury City Council* [3] Richards J found that although the applicant had delayed he had good reason for it but that the respondent had established that prejudice existed. He concluded that although the issue of prejudice was not sufficient to persuade him not to grant an extension of time it was important enough for him to refuse to grant a quashing order.

1 [1990] 2 AC 738.
2 [1999] 2 AC 330, [1999] 2 WLR 974, [1999] COD 244, 143 Sol Jo LB 120, HL.
3 [2005] EWHC 1318 (Admin), 169 JP 521, Times, 11 July, [2005] All ER (D) 285 (Jun), [2005] LLR 353 Admin, DC.

Acknowledgement of service

8.29 If any person wishes to participate in the judicial review he must file such an acknowledgement within 21 days of the service on him of the claim form and serve it as soon as practicable and in any event within seven days after filing on the claimant and any other person named in the claim form. The acknowledgement must summarise any grounds upon which the claim is contested and state the name and address of any person whom the filing party considers to be an interested party. It may seek directions. A failure to file an acknowledgement of service has the effect of disqualifying that party from participating in any hearing to decide whether permission should be granted unless the court expressly allows such participation although in certain circumstances he may take part in any judicial review hearing.[1]

1 Part 54.9 CPR 1998. There may however be costs implications.

Procedure for determining applications for permission

8.30 Unlike under the previous RSC Ord 53 procedure, the claimant has no right to seek in the first instance that his application for permission be dealt with at an oral hearing. The new procedure assumes in most cases that a single judge having considered the claim form and attached documents together with the acknowledgement of service and any accompanying documents will then decide on the papers alone whether to grant or refuse permission or to grant it subject to conditions or on limited grounds. However there is no rule which prevents him inviting oral argument whether at his own volition or at the request of any party.

The test for granting permission

8.31 Permission will only be granted if the court is satisfied that the papers disclose that there is an arguable case that a ground for seeking judicial review exists[1] which merits full investigation[2]. Delay may cause permission to be refused as will the availability of an adequate alternative remedy[3].

1 See para **8.19** above.

2 However if the court has all or most of the initial documents before it a higher test may be applied and the applicant may need to show that he is likely to succeed before being granted permission: see *Mass Energy Ltd v Birmingham City Council* [1994] Env LR 298 at 307–8, 311 and 318; *R v Docklands Development Corporation, ex p Sister Christine Frost* (1996) 73 PCR 203; *R v Liverpool City Council, ex p Barry* [2001] LLR 310 at 314–15.

3 See *R v Chief Constable of Merseyside Police, ex p Calveley* [1986] QB 424; *R v Secretary of State for the Home Department, ex p Swati* [1986] 1 WLR 477.

Permission granted

8.32 If permission is given the court may also then give directions and a stay[1]. The order giving permission is served on all parties[2]. Neither the defendant nor any other person served with the claim form may apply to set aside the order giving permission[3]. Thereafter the case will proceed to a full oral hearing (see paras **8.35–8.38** below for the procedure prior to that hearing).

1 Part 54.10 CPR 1998.

2 Part 54.11 CPR 1998.

3 Part 54.13 CPR 1998. There appears to exist a residual inherent jurisdiction to set aside but it is generally thought that it will be rarely exercised.

Permission to proceed considered without a hearing and refused or granted on conditions or in a more limited form than that claimed

8.33 In such a case the court will serve its reasons on all parties. Whilst the claimant may not appeal he may request that the decision be reconsidered at a hearing[1] but must do so within seven days of service of the reasons[2]. All parties will be given at least two days' notice of the hearing date[3]. The oral hearings will usually be very short[4]. If after the hearing permission is still refused[5] the claimant may apply to the Court of Appeal for permission to appeal. He must do so within seven days of the refusal by the High Court. In practice if the Court of Appeal is sympathetic it will probably grant permission to apply for judicial review rather than mere permission to appeal[6]. The case is initially considered by a single Lord Justice on paper only. Should he refuse permission the applicant can renew his application orally to two Lord Justices.

In such a case he must file his request for reconsideration within seven days after service of the refusal and must comply with para 4.14A of the Practice Direction under CPR Part 52.

---

1 Part 54.12(3) CPR 1998.

2 Part 54.12(4) CPR 1998.

3 Part 54.12(5) CPR 1998.

4 Under RSC Ord 53 they were usually only 20 minutes long; longer hearings required special notification. It is expected that these norms will apply under the new procedure.

5 It seems from the wording of Pts 52.15 and 54.12 that this avenue is only open to a claimant if there has been an outright refusal of permission rather than a limited or conditional permission only.

6 Part 52.15(3) CPR 1998.

Permission and costs

8.34 Whilst it is difficult to anticipate precisely how the courts will deal with this topic, it seems that the following costs orders will be reasonable in most cases:

(a) permission granted without a hearing – no order at permission stage of hearing unless defendant then takes action which renders a judicial review hearing otiose[1];

(b) permission granted with a hearing – the result should be the same as above. Paragraph 8.6 of the Practice Direction states that if the defendant attends the hearing and permission is granted costs will not be awarded against the claimant;

(c) permission refused without a hearing – in such a case the defendant should normally recover costs incurred in producing the acknowledgement of service[2]. After all his involvement at this stage is mandatory according to Pt 54.8(1) CPR 1998.

(d) permission refused after a hearing which the defendant attended on a voluntary basis – the costs implications in such a case have recently been considered by the Court of Appeal in *R (on the application of Mount Cook Land Ltd) v Westminster City Council*[3]. There Auld LJ stated:

> '(1) The effect of paragraph 8.6, when read with paragraph 8.5, of the Practice Direction, in conformity with the long-established practice of the courts in judicial review and the thinking of the Bowman Report giving rise to the CPR 54 procedure, is that a defendant who attends and successfully resists the grant of permission at a renewal hearing should not generally recover from the claimant his costs of and occasioned by doing so.
>
> (2) A court, in considering an award against an unsuccessful claimant of the defendant's and/or any other interested party's costs at a permission hearing, should only depart from the general guidance in the Practice Direction if he considers there are exceptional circumstances for doing so.
>
> (3) A court considering costs at the permission stage should be allowed a broad discretion as to whether, on the facts of the case, there are exceptional

circumstances justifying the award of costs against an unsuccessful claimant;

(4) Exceptional circumstances may consist in the presence of one or more of the features in the following non-exhaustive list:
 (a) the hopelessness of the claim:
 (b) the persistence in it by the claimant after having been alerted to facts and/or of the law demonstrating its hopelessness;
 (c) the extent to which the court considers that the claimant, in the pursuit of his application, has sought to abuse the process of judicial review for collateral ends – a relevant consideration as to costs at the permission stage, as well as when considering discretionary refusal of relief at the stage of substantive hearing, if there is one; and
 (d) whether, as a result of the deployment of full argument and documentary evidence by both sides at the hearing of a contested application, the unsuccessful claimant has had, in effect, the advantage of an early substantive hearing of the claim.

(5) A relevant factor for a court, when considering the exercise of its discretion on the grounds of exceptional circumstances, may be the extent to which the unsuccessful claimant has substantial resources which it has used to pursue the unfounded claim and which are available to meet an order for costs.

(6) The Court of Appeal should be slow to interfere with the broad discretion of the court below in its identification of factors constituting exceptional circumstances and in the exercise of its discretion whether to award costs against an unsuccessful claimant.'

(e) permission refused after a hearing which the defendant attended at the request of the court – such a situation was not considered in the *Mount Cook* case. It is submitted that in such a case the defendant should usually be awarded his costs; the bases for this view are a combination of general fairness, s 51 of the Senior Courts Act 1981 and Pt 44.3(2) CPR 1998. The provisions of paras 8.5 and 8.6 of the Practice Direction do not appear to undermine this proposition.

---

1 See for example *R v Kensington and Chelsea Royal London Borough Council, ex p Ghebregiogis* (1994) 27 HLR 602.

2 *R (on the application of Leach) v Local Administration Comr* [2001] EWHC Admin 455, [2001] CP Rep 97, [2001] 4 PLR 28 approved in *R (on the application of Mount Cook Land Ltd) v Westminster City Council* [2004] 2 P & CR 22, 405, [2003] 43 EG 137 (CS), 147 Sol Jo LB 1272, [2003] All ER (D) 222 (Oct).

3 [2003] EWCA Civ 1346, [2004] 2 P & CR 405, [2003] 43 EG 137 (CS), 147 Sol Jo LB 1272, [2003] All ER (D) 222 (Oct).

Protected Costs Orders

8.34A A claimant can apply for a protected costs order in certain limited circumstances. The effect of such an order will be either that an unsuccessful claimant will not have to pay the costs of a successful defendant or that the amount of costs that he will be liable to pay will be limited. The Court of Appeal in *R (on the application of Corner House Research) v Secretary of State for Trade and Industry*[1] laid down the circumstances in which such an order should be made:

> 'The court set out the following principles governing the making of protective costs orders in public law cases raising issues of general public importance to allow claimants of limited means access to the court without the fear of substantial

orders for costs being made against them: A protective costs order may be made at any stage of the proceedings, on such conditions as the court thinks fit, provided that the court is satisfied that:

(i) the issues raised are of general public importance;

(ii) the public interest requires that those issues be resolved;

(iii) the applicant has no private interest in the outcome of the case;

(iv) having regard to the financial resources of the applicant and the respondent(s) and to the amount of costs that are likely to be involved, it is fair and just to make the order;

(v) if the order is not made the applicant will probably discontinue the proceedings and will be acting reasonably in so doing.

(2) If those acting for the applicant are doing so pro bono, that will be likely to enhance the merits of the application for a protective costs order.

(3) It is for the court, in its discretion, to decide whether it is fair and just to make a protective costs order and what form such an order should take, depending on what is appropriate and fair. An order capping the claimant's costs is likely to be required in all cases, except where the claimant's lawyers are acting pro bono and the effect of the protective costs order is to prescribe in advance that there should be no order as to costs in the substantive proceedings whatever the outcome.'

1 [2005] EWCA Civ 192, [2005] 4 All ER 1,[2005] 1 WLR 2600.

Procedure post the granting of permission

8.35 Within 35 days after the service of the order giving permission a defendant or any other person served with the claim form and who wishes to contest it or support it on additional grounds must serve both detailed grounds for so doing and any written evidence[1]. The claimant himself may with express permission from the courts rely on grounds additional to those advanced by him at the permission stage[2]. At the hearing[3] of the judicial review application no written evidence may be relied upon unless it has been served in accordance with Pt 54 or a direction of the court or unless the court gives permission[4]. Disclosure is unusual in judicial review proceedings[5], and when it is ordered it is invariably limited to specific documents. There is power to allow any person eg an intervenor to be heard[6].

1 Part 54.14(1) CPR 1998. This may have been done wholly or in part at the permission stage although the current procedure makes no express provision for it.
2 Part 54.15 CPR 1998.
3 Although there is power for the court to decide the judicial review application without a hearing if all parties agree: Pt 54.18 CPR 1998.
4 Part 54.16 CPR 1998.
5 See para 12.1 Practice Direction – Judicial Review.
6 Part 54.17 CPR 1998 and see para 13 Practice Direction – Judicial Review.

Alternative dispute resolution

8.36 The lawyers in a public law dispute have a heavy obligation to consider alternatives to litigation and, if necessary, to devise dispute resolution procedures to meet the situation even when such proceedings may not fulfill all the functions of judicial review[1].

[1] *Cowl v Plymouth City Council* [2001] EWCA Civ 1935, [2002] 1 WLR 803.

Bundles and skeleton arguments

8.37 The claimant must file and serve a skeleton argument not less than 21 working days before the hearing or warned date[1]. Other parties must file and serve skeleton arguments not less than 14 days before the hearing or warned date[2]. Each skeleton argument must contain:[3]

(a) a time estimate for the hearing, including delivery of judgment;
(b) a list of issues;
(c) a list of the legal points to be taken (together with any relevant authorities with page references to the passages relied on);
(d) a chronology of events with page references to the bundle of documents;
(e) a list of essential documents for the advance reading of the court with page references to the passages relied on (if different from that filed with the claim form) and a time estimate for that reading;
(f) a list of persons referred to.

[1] See para 15.1 Practice Direction – Judicial Review.
[2] See para 15.2 Practice Direction – Judicial Review.
[3] See para 15.3 Practice Direction – Judicial Review.

8.38 The bundle of documents must be filed by the claimant when he files his skeleton argument; it is a paginated and indexed bundle of all relevant documents required for the hearing[1] and must include those required by the defendant and any other party[2].

[1] See para 16.1 Practice Direction – Judicial Review.
[2] See para 16.2 Practice Direction – Judicial Review.

Powers exercisable if a quashing order made

8.39 If a quashing order is made the court may remit the matter to the decision-maker directing it to reconsider the matter and reach a decision in accordance with the court's judgment or subject to any statutory provision and if the court considers that no purpose is served in remitting the matter it can take the decision itself[1]. In practice in licensing cases there seems little if, any scope, for the court to take the latter course; remission will invariably happen.

[1] Part 54.19 CPR 1998.

8.40 The Administrative Court has power to award costs *inter partes* when dealing either with an appeal by way of case stated (when that route is available) or on an application for judicial review in respect of either a decision of licensing justices or the Crown Court[1]. The new regime governing costs is to be found in CPR Parts 43–48 and the relevant Practice Directions. In many cases summary assessment will be made under Part 44.

The High Court has a wide discretion as to costs[2] but as a general rule costs should follow the event[3]. The High Court also has power to award costs in respect of the proceedings in the court below[4].

In appeals by way of case stated magistrates should not have costs awarded against them[5]. There have, however, been several examples of costs awarded against magistrates where they have appeared in the Divisional (now Administrative) Court[6]. If magistrates have failed to state the case fairly costs may be awarded against them[7].

If magistrates are represented and appear at the hearing of an application for a prerogative order, instead of adopting the procedures open to them under the Review of Justices' Decisions Act 1872, they will become liable for an order for costs[8]. Even though they are successful in opposing an application they may not recover their costs unless they were justified in appearing because of an attack on their bona fides or the way in which they conducted the proceedings[9]. It has been recognised for a long time that if magistrates act capriciously they are liable to be ordered to pay the costs of an application[10] and in recent years there has been a tendency to award costs against magistrates who are found to have acted *ultra vires*.

---

1 Summary Jurisdiction Act 1857, s 6 and Senior Courts Act 1981, s 51.

2 See CPR Part 44.3(1).

3 See CPR Part 44.3(2) and *Chief Constable of Leicestershire Police v Tatam* [2005] EWHC 912 (Admin), 169 JP 485, [2005] All ER (D) 159 (Jul) Admin, [2005] LLR 384, Admin Ct where Mitting J ordered the Chief Constable to pay the respondent's costs in a stated case which 'never stood any prospect of success. It should not have been brought.'

4 See *Turner & Son Ltd v Owen* [1956] 1 QB 48, [1955] 3 All ER 565n.

5 Summary Jurisdiction Act 1857, s 6 and *R v Surrey Justices, ex p Witherick* [1932] 1 KB 450.

6 See *R v Llanidloes Licensing Justices, ex p Davies* [1957] 2 All ER 610n, [1957] 1 WLR 809.

7 See *Edge v Edwards* (1932) 48 TLR 449 on an application for mandamus to state the case fairly.

8 See *R v Camborne Justices, ex p Pearce* [1955] 1 QB 41, [1954] 2 All ER 850.

9 See *R v Marlow (Bucks) Justices, ex p Schiller* [1957] 2 QB 508, [1957] 2 All ER 783.

10 See *R v Boteler* (1864) 4 B & S 959.

PART B2: CASE STATED – SUMMARY OF CURRENT PROCEDURE

Case stated from the magistrates' court

8.41 The starting point is s 111(1) of the Magistrates' Courts Act 1980, which states:

> 'Any person who was a party to any proceeding before a magistrates' court or is aggrieved by the conviction, order, determination or other proceeding of the court may question the proceeding on the ground that it is wrong in law or is in excess of jurisdiction by applying to the justices composing the court to state a case for the opinion of the High Court on the question of law or jurisdiction involved; but a person shall not make an application under this section in respect of a decision against which he has a right of appeal to the High Court'.

The application to state a case must be made within 21 days after the day on which the decision of the court was given[1]. The application must be in writing and signed, and it must identify the question of law on which the opinion of the High Court is sought. It is sent to the clerk of the relevant magistrates' court. The justices may refuse to state a case if they consider that the application to do so is frivolous[2]. However such a refusal is susceptible to judicial review[3]. In such a case the claimant for judicial review will usually seek a mandatory order to state the case and/or a quashing order in respect of the original decision which he sought to appeal by way of case stated. Although it is possible for there to be a stated case in respect of an interlocutory decision, the justices have no relevant mandatory power but may do so in the exercise of their discretion. However, such discretionary power is to be exercised sparingly and only in exceptional cases[4].

1 MCA 1980, s 111(2).

2 MCA 1980, s 111(5): 'frivolous' means futile, misconceived, hopeless or of academic interest only.

3 *Sunworld Ltd v Hammersmith and Fulham London Borough Council* [2000] 2 All ER 837, DC; *R v Licensing Justices of East Gwent, ex p Chief Constable of Gwent* [2001] LLR 693, QBD.

4 *R v Chesterfield Justices, ex p Kovacs* [1992] 2 All ER 325; although not a licensing case it seems likely that its principles and dictum in *Streames v Copping* [1985] 2 All ER 122, [1985] QB 920, [1985] 2 WLR 993 DC will apply in the licensing field.

8.42 The procedure for stating a case is to be found in rr 76–81 of the Magistrates' Court Rules 1981[1].

1 See paras **8.1519–8.1524** below.

Procedure once a case has been stated

8.43–8.44 Once the case has been stated, the governing procedure is found in Pt 52 CPR 1998. In the case of appeals by way of case stated from justices no permission is required[1]. The appellant must file an appellant's notice at the High Court within 10 days after he receives the finalised stated case[2]. The notice must be in form N161 and it must, inter alia, set out the basis on which the decision of the lower court is said to be wrong in law or in excess of jurisdiction. The notice can only be amended with the leave of the court[3]. The appellant must lodge with the notice: (1) the stated case; (2) a copy of the judgment, order or decision in respect of which the case has been stated; and (3) where the judgment, order or decision in respect of which the case has been stated was itself given or made on appeal, a copy of the judgement etc appealed from[4]. Within four days of filing/lodging the appellant must serve the notice and accompanying documents on all respondents. Within 14 days of filing the notice a skeleton argument must be lodged and served[5]. If a respondent wishes to uphold the lower court decision for reasons different or additional to those given by it he must file a respondent's notice within 14 days of having been served with the appellant's notice[6], which must be served on the appellant and all other respondents as soon as practicable and in any event not later than seven days after it has been filed[7]. In every case in which a respondent 'proposes to address arguments to the court'[8] he must provide a skeleton argument. He must lodge and serve it no later than 21 days after he receives the appellant's skeleton argument[9].

1 See para 18.3 Practice Direction – Appeals and see also CPR 52.3(1)(a), which does not encompass case stated appeals, and the Senior Courts Act 1981, s 28A.

2 See para 18.4 Practice Direction – Appeals. This is obviously a different time scale from that set out in Pt 52.4(2) CPR 1998.

3 Part 52.8 CPR 1998.

4 Para 18.5 Practice Direction – Appeals.
5 Para 5.9 Practice Direction – Appeals. For the contents of the skeleton argument see paras 5.10 and 5.11 Practice Direction – Appeals.
6 Part 52.5(4) CPR 1998 unless the lower court has directed a different period.
7 Part 52.5(6) CPR 1998.
8 Para 7.6 Practice Direction – Appeals. This phrase is surely wide enough to compel a respondent to serve a skeleton argument if he wishes to address the court even though he is merely adopting the reasons given by the lower court. In such a situation there is no duty on him to serve a respondent's notice although he is free to do so under Part 52.5(1) CPR 1998 (quaere recovery of costs).
9 See para 7.7 Practice Direction – Appeals. Para 7.8 sets out the content of the respondent's skeleton argument.

Further points

8.45 The parties have no power to extend any time limit set out in Pt 52 or the relevant practice direction or ordered by the lower or appeal court[1]. Specific provision is made in Pt 52 only for an application to the appeal court for a variation of the time limit for filing an appeal notice[2], however presumably that court would have an inherent jurisdiction to vary time limits applicable to the filing/lodging/service of all documents.

Unless the appeal court or the lower court orders otherwise, an appeal does not operate as a stay of any order or decision of the lower court[3]. An appeal notice can be struck out, but only in exceptional circumstances[4].

The powers of the appeal court in relation to the whole or part of an order of the lower court are very wide. Apart from having all the powers of the lower court it can affirm, set aside or vary an order or judgment made or given by the lower court; it may refer any claim or issue for determination by the lower court; it may order a new trial or hearing and it may make a costs order[5]. In most cases the appeal is a review of the lower court decision based on the evidence called in that court[6].

See para **8.36** above re alternative dispute resolution. This is applicable to case stated.

1 Part 52.6(2) CPR 1998.
2 Part 52.6(1) CPR 1998. Note that the application for an extension of time must be made in the appeal notice itself; a respondent has a right to be heard on this matter but is subject to costs risk if he unreasonably opposes the application; see paras 5.2 and 5.3 Practice Direction – Appeals.
3 Part 52.7 CPR 1998.
4 Part 52.9 CPR 1998.
5 Part 52.10 CPR 1998. See also Senior Courts Act 1981, s 28A.
6 Part 52.11 CPR 1998.

Recent Cases on Costs Applications in Licensing matters

8.46 We set out below detailed citations from a number of cases which deal with the question of awards of costs. As arguments on the topic are often made without much time for reflection we have decided to provide extensive details of the cases in order to give the practitioner the opportunity to deal with the matter with some degree of confidence without (we hope) the need for further research.

A useful starting point is the decision by Roch J in *R v Totnes Licensing Justices, ex p Chief Constable of Devon and Cornwall.*[1] In that case he said:

'There can be no doubt that in civil proceedings between litigants, be it in the High Court or county court, the principle is that costs follow the event. The winning party obtains an order for costs against the losing party unless there are exceptional circumstances or reasons why this should not be so.

Mr Barrie has pointed out that the basis of that principle is this: the losing litigant should not have contested the matter before the court. In my judgment it was wrong for the justices to treat this matter as civil proceedings between two private litigants and to ignore the factor urged upon them by the solicitor appearing for the police authority, namely, that the police have a function which they are required to perform. They are required to supervise the proper conduct of the licensed premises and to object in those cases where there are good grounds for objecting to the renewal of the licence. That that is the police's function is clearly demonstrated by the provisions in the Licensing Act which give the police power to enter licensed premises whether at the invitation of the licensee or not.

In addition, in my view, the police authority must also bring to the attention of the licensing justices matters of which the police know and which can fairly and properly be said to amount to misconduct by the licensee or those for whom he is responsible.

Such factors emphasise the importance of the police being able to discharge their functions with regard to the licensing laws fairly and properly. Of course, if the evidence indicated that an objection by a police authority to the renewal of the justices' on-licence was misconceived, that it was without foundation or born of malice or some improper motive, then it would be just and reasonable for the police to be ordered to pay the costs of the successful licensee . . .

. . . Where, as in this case, the objector is the police authority who in good faith is discharging its function in relation to the proper conduct of licensed premises and the justices, as in this case, fully accept that the objection has been properly made, then the justices must take account of both these factors in deciding what order is just and reasonable . . .

In my judgment, that is still sound advice which the justices should follow when seeking to make orders for costs under s 193B(1) of the Licensing Act 1964. Their duty is to take into account all the relevant circumstances. In cases such as the present, the justices must remind themselves that the police are performing the role which is required of them, namely, to supervise the proper conduct of licensed premises.'

1 (1990) 156 JP 587, (1990) Times, 28 May; cited with approval in *Chief Constable of Derbyshire v Goodman and Newton* [2001] LLR 127, DCS, *R v Merthyr Tydfil County Council, ex p Chief Constable of Dyfed Powys Police* [2001] LLR 133 DC.

8.47 A rash of more recent cases have followed the *Totnes* case and demonstrate how difficult it is for a successful applicant/appellant to obtain/maintain costs orders against public authorities.

In *Chief Constable of Derbyshire v Goodman and Newton*[1] the court was asked to review a costs order made against the applicant by the Crown Court in a case concerning the partial revocation by him of a firearms certificate. Although the Crown Court found that the Chief Constable had acted in good faith and in reliance on a Home Office circular when making his decision as it also found that the decision had been incorrect it ordered him to pay the certificate holders' costs on appeal. The Divisional Court quashed that decision primarily because the Chief Constable was simply performing a statutory licensing function. It concluded that generally speaking a costs order adverse to a party discharging a statutory duty should not be made unless there was some good reason for doing so. The fact that the other party had succeeded was not sufficient reason to abrogate the general rule. If, however, the Chief Constable had not acted in good faith or had run a case without foundation, or borne of malice or of some improper motive that could provide good reason for ignoring the general approach[2] Lightman J reached a similar conclusion in *R v Merthyr Tydfil Crown Court, ex p Chief Constable of Dyfed Powys Police*[3] in which he quashed an order for costs made against the police by a Crown Court on appeal. The facts were that in September 1996 W was granted a protection order. The police did not object to the application because there was no ground on which to do so. However, before a transfer of the licence was considered certain incidents occurred at the licensed premises which gave the police serious cause for concern. They involved the sale of intoxicating liquor outside permitted hours, allowing children in the bar and leaving the premises in the control of someone who was not a fit and proper person. The police objected to the transfer and in April 1997 the licensing justices refused to transfer the licence to W. An appeal to the Crown Court followed at which the police were the only respondent. In August 1997 the Crown Court found that the objections of the police were well founded and related to serious breaches of the licensing laws but that since the time of those breaches W had undergone extensive training and now understood her duties and responsibilities and the court felt disposed to give the appellant the benefit of the doubt.

W asked for costs and costs were ordered against the police on the basis that costs follow the event. The Chief Constable sought judicial review of the decision as to costs.

Lightman J stated that the same principle applies before the Crown Court as before licensing justices. The language of the relevant rules is for all practical purposes identical. That is reinforced by the consideration that the proceedings before the Crown Court take place by way of a rehearing. In the same way as the justices need the assistance of the police in respect of the provision of any information which may assist them in deciding whether or not an applicant is a fit person to hold a licence, the Crown Court requires that assistance. No order can properly be made against the police simply on the basis that costs follow the event. The Crown Court can only make such an order if it can be shown that the police's position has been totally unreasonable or prompted by some improper motive.

In *Chief Constable of the West Midlands Police v Coventry Crown Court and Tubman*[4] Munby J quashed an order for costs made in the Crown Court against the applicant. The relevant facts were that in October 1999 the licensing justices for Coventry revoked the on-licence for a public house held by Mr Tubman. The police had applied for revocation following the execution of a search warrant when drugs were found and Mr Tubman's wife and children were cautioned, as were a customer and an employee. The ground for revocation was that Mr Tubman was not a fit and proper person to hold a justices' licence in that he had either ignored the use and exchange of drugs on his premises or he was insufficiently diligent as a publican.

Mr Tubman appealed to the Crown Court which found that he was a fit and proper person and allowed his appeal. There was no criticism of the police by the Crown Court which nevertheless ordered the Chief Constable to pay Mr Tubman's costs. No reason was given for making the order. The Chief Constable applied for judicial review of the decision as to costs. After permission to apply had been given the Crown Court provided a note to the High Court stating that the reasons for the costs order were that although it accepted that the police had believed, on information, that there was drug dealing taking place at the premises and were bound to act on such information, a raid involving some 67 officers organised some 3–4 months later was an unreasonable response which in any event had failed to provide any evidence of dealing or any involvement or knowledge by Mr Tubman who had been ill in bed at the time of the raid. Further the Crown Court, bearing in mind the result of the raid, did not find that the police were bound to oppose the licence. The note went on to say: 'We did not give separate reasons for awarding costs as we were concerned that the police have a difficult job and did not want to criticise them publicly when there was no real need to do so'.

Munby J found that:

(a) in circumstances where an order for costs can only be made on the court being satisfied that certain conditions are met at least some indication should be given as to the reasoning which underlies the court's decision and why it is that the court finds that those conditions are met;

(b) the note suggested that the Crown Court was allowing its discretion as to how the costs of proceedings should be borne to be affected by matters which did not relate to the police's conduct of proceedings, but rather to the steps previously taken by the police to enforce the criminal law;

(c) this was not a case in which costs could properly have been awarded against the police. The police behaved entirely properly at all stages of these proceedings both before the justices and before the Crown Court.

---

1 [2001] LLR 127 DC. Applied in *R (Chief Constable of Sussex) v Chichester Crown Court and Stoner* [2003] EWHC 267 (Admin), [2003] LLR 312, [2003] All ER (D) 245 (Jul): the court concluded that the Chief Constable had acted in good faith, accordingly no order for costs against him should have been made in favour of a successful appellant.

2 See also a number of other cases on which the court relied: *R v Uxbridge Justices, ex p Commissioner of Police of the Metropolis* [1981] QB 829; *Enfield London Borough Council v Mahoney* [1983] 1 WLR 749; *R v Totnes Licensing Justices, ex p Chief Constable of Devon and Cornwall* (1990) 156 JP 587, (1990) Times, 28 May; *Hussain v Singh* (unreported, 3 November 1997), DC.

3 [2001] LLR 133.

4 [2001] LLR 144.

8.48 *City of Bradford Metropolitan District Council v Booth*[1] concerned the power of a magistrates' court to award costs to a successful appellant under s 64 of the Magistrates' Courts Act 1980[2]. The respondent to an appeal by case stated operated a private car hire business. The local authority granted him a licence with conditions. One condition was that not more than one private hire vehicle should be run from his home address. Upon forming the view that that condition had been broken the local authority refused to renew the licence. B appealed to the magistrates' court by way of complaint (following the statutory procedure). It found that B was not in breach of the condition and, allowing his appeal, renewed the licence. B asked for costs against the local authority on the basis that costs follow the event. The justices ordered the local authority to pay costs of £750 + VAT a sum they considered to be 'just and reasonable' under s 64 of the Magistrates' Court Act 1980. The local authority appealed to the High Court. The questions posed by the justices in the case stated were: (1) Were we correct in finding that the principle that costs follow the event apply against local authorities which make decisions on licensing functions which they are required to perform?; and (2) Were we correct in law in finding that there was no requirement that we be satisfied that the local authority had acted unreasonably or in bad faith before we could order costs against the local authority?

In allowing the appeal the court stated that the justices were wrong to rely on the principle that costs follow the event. It stated that the proper approach to questions of costs in cases such as this is:

(a) s 64(1) confers a discretion upon a magistrates' court to make such orders as to costs as it thinks just and reasonable. That provision applies both to the quantum of the costs (if any) to be paid, but also to the party (if any) which should pay them;

(b) what the court will think just and reasonable will depend on the relevant facts and circumstances of the case before the court. The court may think it just and reasonable that costs should follow the event, but need not think so in all cases covered by the subsection;

(c) when a complainant has successfully challenged before justices an administrative decision made by a police authority or regulatory authority acting honestly, reasonably, properly and on grounds that reasonably appeared to be sound, in the exercise of its public duty, the court should consider, in addition to any other relevant facts or circumstances both: (i) the financial prejudice to the particular complainant in the particular circumstances if an order for costs is not made in his favour; and (ii) the need to encourage public authorities to make and stand by honest, reasonable and apparently sound administrative decisions made in the public interest without fear of exposure to undue financial prejudice if the decision is successfully challenged.

For a case which applied *Booth* but in so doing reached a different result see *Powell v City and County of Swansea*[3], in which at first instance the magistrates had found that a local authority had treated a renewal application for a taxi licence as a new application the consequence of which was that certain policies had been incorrectly applied to the application. Notwithstanding that the court declined to award costs to Mr Powell; in doing so it purported to follow *Booth*. In the High Court Pitchford J found that the *Booth* test of whether the regulatory authority had acted 'reasonably . . . on grounds that reasonably appeared to be sound' had not been met; accordingly he concluded that an award of costs to Mr Powell should have been made. However see also *R (Borough of Telford and Wrekin Borough Council) v Crown Court at Shrewsbury*[4] in which a costs' order made by the Crown Court in favour of a taxi driver was quashed on the basis that the court has misdirected itself on the point on which it then made the costs award. A similar approach was taken in *R (Chief Constable of Hampshire Constabulary) v Oldring*[5].

In two cases decided under the new Licensing Act 2003, the Administrative Court has applied the *Booth* principles although on the individual facts it reached different conclusions[6].

Under the Gambling Act 2005, it is possible to judicially review a decision of the licensing authority. Judicial review rather than appeal to the Magistrates is only likely to be appropriate where a principle of general importance is involved which can only properly be decided by the High Court (see *R (on the application of JD Wetherspoon plc) v Guildford Borough Council*[7]). Judicial review may be refused because the Applicant has failed to exhaust an alternative suitable avenue of appeal.

1 [2001] LLR 151, DC. Note that *Booth* has been upheld by the Court of Appeal in *Baxendale-Walker v Law Society* [2007] EWCA Civ 233, [2008] 1 WLR 46 and followed in *R (Prinpanathan) v City of Westminster Magistrates Court and the Metropolitan Police Commissioner* [2010] EWCA Civ 40, [2010] LLR 514.

2 This applies only to the award of costs made on an application made by way of complaint; nonetheless the principles set out in the judgement are clearly of general application to licensing cases.

3 [2004] LLR 145, AC.

4 [2003] EWHC 230 (Admin), [2004] LLR 291, [2003] All ER (D) 58 (Feb), AC.

5 [2003] EWHC 1807 (Admin), [2004] LLR 531, [2003] All ER (D) 246 (Jul), AC.

6 *Crawley Borough Council v Attenborough* [2006] EWHC 1278 (Admin), 170 JP 593, [2006] All ER (D) 104 (May), DC; *Cambridge City Council v Alex Nestling Ltd* [2006] EWHC 1374 (Admin), 170 JP 539, (2006) Times, 11 July, [2006] All ER (D) 252 (May), DC.

7 [2006] EWHC 815 (Admin), [2006] 16 EG 147 (CS), (2006) Times, 14 April, [2006] All ER (D) 147 (Apr).

8.49–8.54 Lest it be thought that it is automatically much easier to obtain valid costs orders against trade objectors (as opposed to public authorities). *R v Stafford Crown Court, ex p Wilf Gilbert (Staffs) Ltd*[1] serves to remind us otherwise. Although this case concerned an application for a betting shop licence there is every reason to assume that the principles contained in it will apply generally to all licensing cases. The facts were that in January 1997 the Betting Licensing Committee refused the applicant company a betting office licence. In October 1997 the Crown Court allowed an appeal and granted the licence but refused to order the trade objectors to pay the costs. No reason was given for that refusal. Legal representatives for the objectors, William Hill and Ladbrokes, had argued that the parties were commercial entities; there was a significant financial advantage to the party which succeeded in the appeal; and that the losers (respondents) were simply advancing the licensing committee's reasons for refusing the application. The licence holders applied for judicial review contending that it was a generally rule of practice that costs should follow the event and that in any event on any of the grounds put forward by the trade objectors in the Crown Court the decision not to award costs was *Wednesbury* unreasonable.

Scott Baker J refused the application stating that Betting Licensing Appeals are a very special jurisdiction. They are neither civil proceeding nor criminal proceedings. The court is exercising an administrative jurisdiction that goes back to the day of Quarter Sessions. It would be wrong to import a rule of practice of either the civil or the criminal courts. If anything the position is closer to the position in planning appeals where the unsuccessful party is only ordered to pay costs if he has behaved unreasonably. There is no rule of practice that costs do or do not follow the outcome of an appeal in betting licensing cases. In some cases unsuccessful objectors will be ordered to pay the successful appellants costs; in other they will not. It will depend on what seems to the court to be just on the particular facts of the particular case. Amongst other things the court will wish to consider the nature of the proceedings and the status and behaviour of the parties.

He also decided that there was no general obligation for a court to give any reasons for its decision on costs[2].

In the subsequent case of *Crawley Borough Council v Attenborough*[3] Scott Baker LJ doubted whether this part of the decision should now be followed because of changes introduced by the Civil Procedure Rules.

The current editors of *Paterson* feel that Scott Baker J's judgment needs to be considered very carefully and that it does not give anything approaching immunity on costs to unsuccessful trade objectors. The planning appeal analogy is phrased somewhat tentatively. Moreover, it would surely be very surprising if a trade objector should generally enjoy the same position on costs as a public authority as in reality in nearly all cases he is defending a purely commercial position – despite how the matter is dressed up by him. Further in cases in which a public authority (for example the police or the justices on appeal) take an active role in responding to an application the unsuccessful trade objector must surely face a much stiffer task in resisting an application for costs from a successful party. In such a case it will usually be very difficult for him to assert that his presence is necessary from the public point of view.

1 [2001] LLR 138, DC.

2 This seems wrong in the light of *Tubman* [2001] LLR 144: see para **8.47** above. See *R (Chief Constable of Sussex) v Chichester Crown Court and Stoner* [2003] EWHC 267 (Admin), [2003] LLR 312, [2003] All ER (D) 245 (Jul), AC at para 28 where Collins J stated 'reasons ought to be given by courts in relation to contested applications for costs. The reasons need not . . . be in the least elaborate'. See also *R (Cunningham) v Crown Court at Exeter* [2003] EWHC 184 (Admin), [2003] 2 Cr App Rep (S) 374, 167 JP 93, [2003] All ER (D) 248 (Jan), [2003] LLR 325, AC; the court should give the reasons for its decision on costs. These need not be long and can be very short where the circumstances make the decision obvious. Moreover, a court surely cannot refuse to give reasons if requested to do so.

3 [2006] EWHC 1278 (Admin), 170 JP 593, [2006] All ER (D) 104 (May), DC.

PART C: HUMAN RIGHTS

Introduction

8.55 On 2 October 2000 the Human Rights Act 1998 (HRA 1998) came into force in its entirety. From that date the European Convention on Human Rights was incorporated into the law of England and Wales[1]. The primary effect of the Act is that Convention rights can now be enforced in domestic courts. Previously such enforcement could only be achieved by taking a case to the European Human Rights Court in Strasbourg. Convention rights may be relied on both by individuals and, for example, companies. Indeed there has been an increasing development of 'commercial rights' under the Convention.

1 Incorporation in Scotland had occurred earlier.

8.56 The scheme of the Act A court, tribunal or public body determining a question concerning a Convention right must take into account the relevant decisions/opinions of various bodies including, most importantly, those of the European Court of Human Rights[1]. They are not however bound by them. The principle of stare decisis does not apply to decisions of the court or commission because the Convention organs interpret the Convention as a living instrument to be interpreted in the light of modern standards.

So far as it is possible primary and subordinate legislation must[2] be read and given effect to in a way which is compatible with Convention rights[3].

However there is a critical difference between the status of primary and some subordinate legislation should the court not be able to 'read down' the provision so as to make it Convention compatible. Legislation may be characterised as: (a) primary; (b) subordinate simpliciter; or (c) subordinate but related to primary legislation. Provisions falling within the primary category which a court is unable to read as Convention compatible are still valid, have continuing operation and are enforceable until amended[4] although certain higher courts only have the power to make a declaration of incompatibility[5]. Legislation falling into the third category set out above is to be treated in the same way as primary legislation if primary legislation prevents removal of the incompatibility[6]. Only if the provisions fall within the second category set out above ie it is subordinate legislation which is not prevented by any relevant primary legislation from having removed from it any Convention incompatible parts that any court, tribunal or public body is free to disregard the provision. An example in which this has occurred is the *Gosling* case (at various levels)[7].

It is generally[8] unlawful for a public authority (including a court or tribunal[9] and any person who carries out functions of a public nature[10]) to act or fail[11] to act in a way which is incompatible with a Convention right[12]. It follows from the definition of 'public authority' in the HRA 1998 that 'licensing authorities' as defined by s 3(1) of the Licensing Act 2003 are public authorities for the purposes of the HRA 1998. Accordingly, they will be under a duty to act compatibly with Convention rights in the exercise of their functions. Other public authorities involved in licensing will be under a similar duty, including magistrates' courts hearing appeals from licensing authorities under Sch 5 to the Licensing Act 2003 and chief officers of police in the exercise of their functions under that Act.

Although the duty to act in ways compatible with the Convention is placed on, for example, a bench of licensing justices, points under the Convention will most likely be raised by the private parties appearing before them[13]; the bench, as it is a public authority is obliged to enforce the Convention by protecting persons against breaches of their Convention rights.

Section 7 of the HRA 1998 allows a person who claims that a public authority has acted or proposes to act in a way which is made unlawful by s 6(1) can bring proceedings against the authority in respect of the act and can rely on the Convention. In order to bring proceedings the applicant must be a 'victim of an unlawful act'. For the purposes of the Act a person is a victim of an unlawful act only if he would be a victim for the purposes of art 34 of the Convention if proceedings were brought in the European Court of Human Rights in respect of that act[14]. What this means is that a person is a victim for the purposes of article 34 if he/she is 'directly affected' by an actual or threatened breach of the Convention. Representative actions by those wholly unconnected with the breach and not representing anyone so affected are not allowed in Strasbourg. On an application for judicial review a person will be taken to have a 'sufficient interest' only if he/she would be a 'victim': HRA 1998, s 7(3).

It is possible for a party to bring a civil action against a public authority which is claimed to have acted in breach of art 6(1) for remedies such as damages[15]. However if the public authority was exercising a judicial function the claimant will not be awarded any damages unless he can show bad faith[16].

1 Human Rights Act 1998, s 2(1). An opinion of the Commission in a report adopted under art 31 of the Convention, a decision of the Commission in connection with art 26 or 27(2) thereof or a decision of the Committee of Ministers taken under art 46 are also to be taken account of.

2 The combination of the words 'possible' and 'must' in effect means that interpretation compatible with the Convention is mandatory unless the legislation itself is so clearly incompatible with the Convention that this is impossible.

3 HRA 1998, s 3(1).

4 See HRA 1998, ss 3(2)(a) and 10.

5 See HRA 1998, s 4. The relevant courts include the High Court, Court of Appeal and House of Lords, see HRA 1998, s 4(5). Clearly the Crown Court and lower courts have no such power.

6 See HRA 1998, s 3(2)(c).

7 [2001] LLR 274, Crown Court and [2002] 1 WLR 1332, [2002] LLR 14, QBD. This case is discussed in more detail at para **8.61** below.

8 See HRA 1998, s 6(2) for exceptions.

9 See HRA 1998, s 6(3)(a). This even includes a court from which an appeal lies if such a court is integrated into the standard judicial machinery in the relevant country. See *De Cubber v Belgium* (1984) 7 EHRR 236 and the discussion on this topic in *Gosling* [2002] LLR 14, QBD at paras 41–43.

10 See HRA 1998, s 6(3)(b).

11 See HRA 1998, s 6(6).

12 See HRA 1998, s 6(1).

13 See HRA 1998, s 7(1)(b).

14 See HRA 1998, s 7(7).

15 See HRA 1998, ss 7(1)(a) and 8.

16 See HRA 1998, s 9(3).

8.56A A fair balance and the principle of proportionality Interpretation of the Human Rights Act 1998 should strive to give effect to the general principle, 'inherent in the whole Convention', that it is seeking to strike a 'fair balance . . . between the demands of the general interest of the community and the requirements of the protection of the individual's fundamental rights'[1]. Central to the principle of a 'fair balance' is the doctrine of proportionality. A restriction on the freedom guaranteed by the Convention must be 'proportionate to the legitimate aim pursued'[2]. There must be 'a reasonable relationship of proportionality between the means employed and the legitimate objectives pursued by the contested limitation'[3]. A measure will satisfy the proportionality test only if three criteria are satisfied:

(1) the legislative objective must be sufficiently important to justify limiting a fundamental right;

(2) the measures deigned to meet the legislative objective must be rationally connected to that objective – they must not be arbitrary, unfair or based on irrational considerations;

(3) the means used to impair the right or freedom must be no more than is necessary to accomplish the legitimate object – the more severe the deleterious effects of a measure, the more important the objective must be if the measure is to be justified in a democratic society[4].

For an example of the application of the principle of proportionality in the licensing context see *Bushell* at para **8.59** below[5].

1 *Sporrong and Lonroth v Sweden* (Applications 7151/75, 7152/75) (1982) 5 EHRR 35 at 52, ECtHR, para 59. See also *Soering v United Kingdom* (Application 14038/88) (1989) 11 EHRR 439 at 468, ECtHR, para 89.

2 *Handyside v United Kingdom* (Application 5493/72) (1976) 1 EHRR 737 at 754, ECtHR, para 49.

3 *Fayed v United Kingdom* (Application 17101/90) (1994) 18 EHRR 393, 432, ECtHR, para 71.

4 See *De Freitas v Permanent Secretary of Ministry of Agriculture, Fisheries, Lands and Housing* [1998] 3 WLR 675, PC per Lord Clyde at 684A–F.

5 See also, for example, *Crompton (t/a David Crompton Haulage) v Department of Transport North Western Area* [2003] EWCA Civ 64, [2003] RTR 517, [2003] LLR 426, [2003] All ER (D) 311 (Jan), CA.

8.57 The licensing context – overview The parts of the Convention most relevant to licensing matters are likely to be the right to a fair trial (art 6), the right to respect for private and family life (art 8) and the protection of property (art 1 of the First Protocol).

In a small minority of cases a dissatisfied party who claims that the tribunal has wrongly failed to uphold his Convention Rights may decide to bring proceedings against it. He will need to prove bad faith in order to obtain damages. He will rarely be able to do so.

In many cases taking a Convention point at first instance may be difficult in the light of the principle that if there is a right of appeal to a tribunal which has full jurisdiction the lower tribunal may not need to be Convention compliant. This point was made clear in, for example, *Albert and Le Compte v Belgium*[1] which in an art 6 case stated that it is sufficient under the Convention if the tribunal adjudicating either complies with the requirements of art 6(1), or if it does not so comply it is subject to subsequent control by a judicial body that has full jurisdiction and does provide the guarantees of art 6(1).

It is likely that an appeal to a to the Crown Court will fulfil this requirement. Moreover, as is illustrated by *R (Brogan) v Metropolitan Police*[2] the availability of review by the High Court will usually satisfy art 6.1.

1 (1983) 5 EHRR 533.

2 [2002] All ER (D) 66 (Oct), [2003] LLR 107.

The Convention

8.58 Article 6 This article guarantees the right of applicants[1] to a fair trial and provides as a minimum the following as of right:

(a) a fair and public hearing with a public judgment;

(b) an independent and impartial tribunal established by law;

(c) a reasoned judgment.

1 In *R (Chief Constable of Lancashire) v Preston Crown Court* [2002] 1 WLR 1332 it was conceded by the Chief Constable, and accepted by Laws LJ (para 17), that the right to apply for a on-licence under the Licensing Act 1964 fell within the scope of 'civil rights and obligations' in article 6(1) because it related to the applicant's right to make a living and pursue commercial activity. Therefore applicants for such licences had the right to have their application determined fairly in accordance with the guarantees contained within article 6(1). The editors of *Paterson* believe that the same principles will apply to the forms of permit or licence created by BGLA 1963 or GA 1968.

8.59 However it is not only applicants but also objectors who may enjoy the rights set out in art 6.

Where the grant of a licence may affect the interests of local residents or others in a significant way then art 6(1) will be engaged. In *R (Friends Provident Life Office) v Secretary of State for the Environment, Transport and the Regions*[1] developers applied for planning permission for a proposed major shopping centre to be built in Norwich. The claimant, who was the owner of an existing shopping centre in Norwich city centre, formally objected to the application on the basis that the proposed development would have adverse consequences for its shopping centre and the city centre as a whole. The claimant requested the Secretary of State to call in the application for determination by him pursuant to s 77 of the Town and Country Planning Act 1990, so that the application could be considered by an independent inspector at a public inquiry, but the Secretary of State refused. The claimant sought judicial review of the Secretary of State's refusal on the ground, inter alia, that determination of the application by the local planning authority, even though its decision would be subject to the High Court's power of review, would constitute a breach of the claimant's right guaranteed by art 6(1) to have its civil rights determined by an independent and impartial tribunal, while determination of the application by the Secretary of State would make the whole process compliant with art 6[2], so that by refusing to call in the application the Secretary of State had acted in a way which was incompatible with the claimant's Convention rights, contrary to s 6(1) of the Human Rights Act 1998. Although the claim was dismissed, the court rejected the developer's argument that no right of the claimant's recognised by art 6(1) was involved[3]. The right involved is the right to use, enjoy and own land[4].

In *Ortenburg v Austria*[5] the applicant wished to object to building works close to her land on the grounds *inter alia* that they would affect the value of her own land. Her objections were rejected by the domestic courts, and she complained that she had not received a fair hearing in accordance with art 6(1). The government raised as a preliminary objection the argument that art 6 did not apply to third parties where the issue concerned the grant of planning permission by a public authority. The Commission and the court rejected this submission because of the close link between the proceedings which the applicant brought and the impact which the result of those proceedings would have on her property.

In a liquor licensing case, *R (Bushell) v Newcastle Licensing Justices, Ultimate Leisure plc*[6] Owen J, having found that a special removal of a licence was capable by reason of evidence of noise and nuisance infringing the Convention rights of neighbours of the proposed licensed premises, also found that it followed that art 6 become engaged. He went on to find however that it was not possible to interpret ss 12 and 15 of the Licensing Act 1964 so as to make them comply with art 6; accordingly he then examined whether the interference with the claimant's rights under art 6 was proportionate. He found that it was and in so doing he said:

> '48. The justices were right to focus their attention on the other means by which the claimants' rights under art 8 and art 1 of Protocol 1 can be protected. The state, as represented by the police and the local authority are under a positive duty to take reasonable and appropriate measures to protect the claimants' convention rights, see *Hatton v United Kingdom* (2002) 34 EHRR 1. If the premises do create a nuisance or lead to disorder, there are a number of steps that can be taken namely:
>
> 1. a closure order under ss 170A–K of the Act, at the instigation of the police,
> 2. the revocation of the licence by the Justices under s 20A of the Act on the application of the police, the Claimants, the local authority, or of their

own motion,

3. the exercise by the local authority of its statutory powers under the Environmental Protection Act 1990.

It would of course also be open to the claimants to take proceedings for nuisance, seeking injunctive relief if appropriate.

49. In incorporating ss 12 and 15 in the 1964 Act, Parliament clearly intended to limit the circumstances in which licensing justices could refuse to transfer an old on-licence from one premises to another. That was a perfectly legitimate objective. Such a transfer does not of itself infringe convention rights. In the light of the protection of convention rights that are otherwise available, the special removal provisions are proportionate to the end that Parliament sought to achieve, and are not therefore incompatible with the ECHR. Accordingly the Justices did not err in their conclusion that ss 12 and 15 of the Act are compatible with the HRA 1998.'

It is important to note that objectors' rights under art 6(1) will not automatically be triggered merely because they wish to object. The question of whether they have a sufficient interest to engage art 6(1) is ultimately a question of fact. In *R (Spearing) v London Borough of Hammersmith and Fulham*[7] Sullivan J rejected the trade objector claimants' submissions that the Council had violated their art 6(1) rights on the ground, inter alia, that there was no evidence that their interests would be affected by the proposed grant of a permit under s 34 of the Gaming Act 1968.

1 [2002] 1 WLR 1450.

2 *R (Alconbury Developments Ltd) v Secretary of State for the Environment, Transport and the Regions* [2001] 2 WLR 1389.

3 Paras 54–63.

4 *R (Alconbury Developments Ltd) v Secretary of State for the Environment, Transport and the Regions* [2001] 2 WLR 1389, para 68.

5 (1994) 19 EHRR 524. See also *Balmer-Schafroth v Switzerland* (1997) 25 EHRR 598.

6 [2003] LLR 775, AC.

7 [2002] LLR 401, QBD.

8.60 A fair and public hearing The right to a fair hearing in art 6(1) is primarily concerned with procedural fairness. In *Kraska v Switzerland*[1], the European Court of Human Rights said that the purpose of art 6(1) was, *inter alia*:

> . . . to place the tribunal under a duty to conduct a proper examination of the submissions, arguments and evidence adduced by the parties, without prejudice to its assessment of whether they are relevant to its decision.

The requirements inherent in the concept of 'fair hearing' are not the same in cases concerning the determination of civil rights and obligations as they are in cases concerning the determination of a criminal charge. This is shown by the absence of detailed provisions such as art 6(2) and 6(3), which only apply in criminal cases[2]. On its face, art 6(1) merely requires that civil hearings be fair and be held in public (unless there are good reasons not to do so) within a reasonable time[3]. However, certain principles concerning the notion of a fair hearing in cases concerning civil rights and obligations emerge from the court's case-law on civil cases[4] and these have application to licensing hearings under the 2003 Act given that they engage article 6(1). Particular examples of the constitutents of the right to a fair hearing are:

- *There must be 'equality of arms' between the parties.* This means that each party must be afforded a reasonable opportunity to present his case—including his evidence—under conditions that do not place him at a substantial disadvantage vis-à-vis his opponent[5]. Whilst it is acknowledged in the current system that an applicant for a licence should know of the objections he has to face, it would appear that he has no right to demand that the objectors be present at the hearing and available for cross-examination.

  In the case of *R v Licensing Justices of East Gwent*[6], licensing justices refused to consider written statements of objectors which the police authority wished to have put before them on the basis that the applicant licensee did not have the opportunity to cross-examine them. The High Court found that the justices were obliged to consider such evidence, but how much weight they attached to it was a matter for them taking into account the fact that the makers had not given oral evidence and that such evidence had not been tested by cross-examination.
- *The hearing must be properly adversarial*[7]. This requires that both sides should have adequate notice of their opponents' case and proper time to consider and address the issues relevant to the case[8].
- *There must be full and proper disclosure of relevant material.* In *McMichael v United Kingdom*[9] the European Court read into the adversarial principle a requirement for full disclosure. The court considered that without such disclosure it would be impossible for the parties to know and comment about the evidence adduced.

Application of these principles to the betting and gaming fields is likely to lead to major changes in practice: we believe that these are highly desirable. In our view licensing procedures must be reformed so that they not only convention compliant but also so that the tribunal is in a position to make the best decision on the evidence presented to it. This goal is not assisted by not serving evidence in advance. Justices should insist that proper advance disclosure should occur. Many Crown Court judges are going further and insisting on a complete exchange of witness statements well before the hearing and even that witness statements stand as evidence in chief. We applaud these developments. They show that licensing is not immune to the approach now adopted in civil proceedings; given the commercial background to most licensing cases this must be right.

1 (1993) 18 EHRR 188, para 30.
2 *Dombo Beheer v Netherlands* (1994) 18 EHRR 213, paras 32–33.
3 For the principles applicable to the 'reasonable time' guarantee see: *König v Federal Republic of Germany* (1978) 2 EHHR 170, 197, para 99.
4 *Porter v Macgill* [2002] 2 AC 357 paras 86, 87 per Lord Hope of Craighead.
5 *De Haes and Gijsels v Belgium* (1997) 25 EHRR 1.
6 (1999) 154 JP 339.
7 *Brandstetter v Austria* (1993) 15 EHRR 378, para 66; *Ruiz-Mateos v Spain* (1993) 16 EHRR 505, para 63.
8 *Lombo Machado v Portugal* (1997) 23 EHRR 79, para 31; *Niderost-Huber v Switzerland* (1998) 25 EHRR 709, para 24.
9 (1995) 20 EHRR 205.

8.61 An independent and impartial tribunal The tribunal which determines the license application has to be 'independent and impartial' within the meaning of art 6(1). These two concepts are closely related[1]. In testing whether a tribunal is impartial the European Court of Human Rights has adopted a two stage approach. First, it considers the subjective question and endeavours to ascertain the judge's own personal convictions in order to determine whether there was actual bias. In applying this test the personal impartiality of a judge is presumed until there is proof to the contrary[2]. If no actual bias is shown the court goes on to consider the objective question, namely, whether the judge offered guarantees sufficient to exclude any legitimate doubt about his impartiality[3].

The common law test for bias and the article 6(1) approach are now the same. In *Porter v Macgill*[4] the House of Lords stated the correct approach:

> The court must first ascertain all the circumstances which have a bearing on the suggestion that the judge was biased. It must then ask whether those circumstances would lead a fair-minded and informed observer to conclude that there was a real possibility . . . that the tribunal was biased.

In order to be independent, the tribunal must be independent both of the parties to the dispute and of the executive. It follows that licensing authorities established under the Licensing Act 2003 may not be independent for the purposes of art 6(1) because they are, or may be, part of the executive. This is not to say, however, that the new system of licensing created by the 2003 Act necessarily fails to comply with art 6(1). As pointed out at para 8.57 above, this is because the European Court has said that where the initial determination of 'civil rights' within the meaning of art 6(1) is made by an administrative or professional authority which does not comply with the right to a fair trial, art 6(1) is satisfied if there is an appeal to a body with full jurisdiction which does comply with it[5]. Accordingly, the right to appeal to the magistrates' court conferred by Sch 5, and the right to appeal to the High Court thereafter[6], may be sufficient to secure compliance with art 6(1). (See further para 8.57 above.)

The requirements of independence and impartiality in practice are likely to overlap (as they clearly did in *Gosling* and *Smith*[7]) although it seems that each is separate as a matter of construction of art 6(1).

According to *Bryan v United Kingdom*[8] when asking whether a tribunal is independent consideration must be given inter alia to the manner of appointment of its members and to their term of office, to the existence of guarantees against outside pressure and to the question whether the tribunal presents an appearance of independence. In a recent Scottish case[9] the short length of tenure of Scottish Temporary Sheriffs caused there to be a failure to comply with this part of art 6[10].

The concept of an impartial tribunal has recently been considered by the Court of Appeal in *Director General of Fair Trading v Proprietary Association of Great Britain*[11]. Lord Phillips MR set out the following principles:

(a) if a judge is shown to have been influenced by actual bias, his decision must be set aside;

(b) where actual bias has not been established, the personal impartiality of the judge is to be presumed;

(c) the court then has to decide whether, on an objective appraisal, the material facts give rise to a legitimate fear that the judge might not have been impartial. If they do, the decision of the judge must be set aside;

(d) the material facts are not limited to those which were apparent to the applicant. They are those which are ascertained upon examination by the court;

(e) an important consideration in making an objective appraisal of the facts is the desirability that the public should remain confident in the administration of justice.

The most interesting recent decisions for licensing practitioners in respect of art 6(1) are the joined cases of *Gosling* and *Smith* in which appellants to the Crown Court from a refusal to grant a new justices' licence challenged as incompatible with art 6(1), r 3(2) Crown Court Rules 1982 which provides that two of the justices hearing a Crown Court appeal must originate from the petty sessional area in which the premises to which the appeal relates are situated. The two Crown Courts differed in their conclusions and each case became the subject of judicial review proceedings. Preston Crown Court found that the rule was incompatible with the appellant's right to fair trial by an independent and impartial tribunal and having severed the offending part of r 3(2) it ordered that the appeal should be heard by a judge and four justices none of whom came from the relevant area. It appears that the following arguments found favour with it[12]:

(a) The system by which licensing justices are appointed. Although magistrates are appointed for life and generally have security of tenure the licensing bench is elected annually by all magistrates in the petty session division. The judge described their position as 'highly precarious' and found that they may have an 'unconscious desire not to offend others by allowing appeals against their decisions'.

(b) Licensing justices attend informal and private meetings to discuss general policy and decision making. A published policy document may emerge as a product of such discussions however 'often there may be a shared perception or understanding, falling short of a policy statement, that may colour or condition their approach to any particular application'. It may be that in this case the justices sitting on the appeal had discussed the case at such a meeting and whilst there was no evidence that this had taken place the judge found that there was no verifiable guarantee that no such discussion had occurred.

(c) The appointment of justices sitting on the appeal was carried out, unsupervised, by the justices' clerk. He had complete discretion in deciding who to appoint. The judge concluded 'This system hardly presents the appearance of impartiality or independence'.

(d) There were no checks or safeguards to ensure that the advice set out in the *Good Practice Guide* at paragraph 8.4 concerning the desirability of justices sitting on an appeal approached it with an open mind and without interference from colleagues. The judge stated in a passage, which is admirable for its candour and which will confirm the suspicions of many, that in his experience it was common for the two local justices to seek to uphold the decision of their colleagues and that many appellants were correct in thinking that they were 'two down' even before the case started[13].

The judge went on to dismiss the justification of having two local justices present in order for them to impart their local knowledge. He said that such knowledge could be articulated in the reasons given by the lower court, moreover the justices could be legally represented on appeals and could make the points about locality in open court. In this way those points were amenable to debate and challenge.

It seems to the current editors that even if the justices did not have the power to be represented the 'local knowledge' point is entirely irrelevant to the aims enshrined in art 6(1) of the Convention and indeed as the judge pointed out the ability of justices to be represented may cause a further problem which did not arise in his case but might in others, ie given that the local bench is a respondent to the appeal (and may choose to be legally represented at it) the two local justices appear to be sitting in judgment in a case in which they are representatives of a party.

A two-judge administrative court upheld the decision of the Crown Court in *Gosling* and quashed the decision in *Smith*. In the leading judgment (of Laws LJ) primary importance appears to have been attached to:

(a) the system of appointing licensing justices; ie the annual election of the licensing bench by the whole bench; and

(b) the fact that members of a licensing committee sitting on appeal in the Crown Court were expected to pass objective judgment on their colleagues who are members of the same committee and who made the first instance decision and against whom they might be asked to order costs.

Laws LJ may have attached some importance to the fact that the clerk to licensing justices decides who to invite to sit on appeals. The court concluded that as there was a risk of apparent bias or an apparent lack of that degree of impartiality and independence which art 6 requires coupled with an inability to put in place any objective or substantial safeguards to counteract those risks, then CCR r 3(2) was not compatible with art 6(1). It also went on to decide that the availability of judicial review as a means to remedy the decision of the Crown Court did not save the procedure under rule 3(2) at the Crown Court stage. Particular emphasis was placed here on the fact that an appreciation of local conditions was often central to the decision whether to allow the appeal or not. This factor could not adequately be second guessed at the judicial review stage, which was not well equipped to consider matters of apparent bias.

The court was divided in its views on one point however. Laws LJ expressed misgivings as to whether the court in *Gosling* should have given judgment on the convention point at a preliminary hearing or whether it should have only done so only if Mr Gosling's appeal to the Crown Court had failed. Crane J expressly differed on this point. His view was that once the matter had been raised with the court, it was necessary for it to be ruled upon in the light of s 7 of the Human Rights Act 1998. It is submitted that Crane J's view is to be preferred.

It will be interesting to see whether this case has any further ramifications. Laws LJ was very careful to restrict the decision to the arrangements in place concerning appeals. He specifically reserved the question whether the system of appointment of licensing justices could be attacked if they were sitting at first instance. Policy factors suggest to the current editors that there will be great reluctance to find the election procedure incompatible with art 6, although it may, objectively, be so. For example, what if the bench has a policy on a certain matter and a particular justice frequently decides that it should not be followed. Isn't it more likely than not that the individual will not be re-elected?

This likelihood and the short tenure (12 months) may combine to produce a licensing bench which is more than likely to toe the line. Perhaps to counteract a suggestion of this type, the current edition of the Good Practice Guide, at para 1.4, recommends that there should be an expectation that an incumbent will in fact sit for a period of at least three years. Whether this attempt to provide a safeguard is sufficient is a moot point: the annual election is still in existence.

However in a betting case, *In the matter of an appeal by Jack Brown (Bookmakers) Ltd against a decision of the Betting Licensing Committee for the petty sessional division of Cardiff*[14], Richards J rejected claims that two justices from the division which had refused the licence application at first instance should not sit on the appeal. The provision which sets out the constitution of the Crown Court in such cases is CCR r 3(3). This bears much similarity to r 3(2), the rule considered in *Gosling* although in one respect, as Richards J decided, it is different; critically under r 3(3) the two local justices are drawn from the whole panel of justices in the division and not, as under r 3(2), from the relevant licensing committee. It was this factor in particular which enabled the judge to reach a different conclusion from that in *Gosling*. Such issues as the lack of security of tenure and collegiate loyalty were, he found, of little importance in betting cases as were questions of licensing policy. Nor was he impressed by the dangers to impartialty allegedly posed by the ability of the justices to be legally represented at the appeal or by the claimed reluctance to allow an appeal because of the potential costs ramifications for the justices sitting at first instance.

The Court of Appeal in *R (on the application of Hope and Glory Public House Ltd) v City of Westminster Magistrates' Court* (see above) ruled that there was no breach of art 6 if the magistrates placed weight on the fact that the democratically elected council by its licensing committee had made the decision being appealed against. The magistrates were still an independent and impartial tribunal within the terms of art 6.

1 *Porter v Macgill* [2002] 2 AC 597, para 489 per Lord Hope of Craighead. For recent applications of the principles see *Georgiou v Enfield London Borough Council (Cygnet Healthcare Ltd, interested parties)* [2004] EWHC 779 (Admin), [2004] LGR 497, [2004] 2 P & CR 380, [2004] 17 LS Gaz R 33, [2004] All ER (D) 135 (Apr), [2004] LLR 453, AC and *Flaherty v National Greyhound Racing Club Ltd* [2005] LLR 70, ChD; [2005] EWCA Civ 1117, [2005] All ER (D) 70 (Sep), CA.

2 *De Cubber v Belgium* (1984) 7 EHRR 236, para 25.

3 *Piersack v Belgium* (1982) 5 EHRR 169, para 30; *Gregory v United Kingdom* (1997) 25 EHRR 577 at para 45.

4 [2002] 2 AC 597, paras 102–103, per Lord Hope of Craighead.

5 Cf *R (Alconbury Developments Ltd) v Secretary of State for the Environment, Transport and the Regions* [2001] 2 WLR 1389; *Preiss v General Dental Council* [2001] 1 WLR 1926.

6 *R (Alconbury Developments Ltd and others) v Secretary of State for the Environment, Transport and the Regions* [2001] 2 WLR 1389.

7 *R (on the application of the Chief Constable of Lancashire) v Preston Crown Court and Gosling*; *R (on the application of Smith) v Lincoln Crown Court* [2002] 1 WLR 1332, [2002] LLR 14, QBD.

8 [1996] 21 EHRR 342.

9 *Starrs and Chalmers v Ruxton* [2000] UKHRR 78, HC (SC).

10 This case also led to the abolition of the Office of Assistant Recorder in England and Wales.

11 [2001] EWCA Civ, [2001] NJLR 17. See also *Locabail (UK) Ltd v Bayfield Properties Ltd* [2000] 1 All ER 65, CA, *R v Bow Street Metropolitan Stipendiary Magistrate, ex p Pinochet Ugarte (No 2)* [2000] 1 AC 119.

12 The Crown Court decision in *Gosling* (only) is reported at [2001] LLR 274.
13 Crane J, a former circuit judge, confirmed this view in his judgment on the judicial review application: see [2002] LLR 14 at 26.
14 (11 February 2002, unreported) Cardiff Crown Court.

8.62 A reasoned judgment Article 6(1) obliges domestic courts to give reasons for their decisions[1] so that the parties and the public know the basis of the decision[2]. The reasons must be sufficiently detailed so that they address the essential issues[3]. Where a submission is relevant and potentially decisive then it must be specifically addressed[4]. In accordance with these principles the Licensing Act 2003 contains a requirement that reasons be given for granting or refusing licences[5].

There has in the past been an unwillingness among some local authority licensing committees and even justices and Crown Courts to provide a full justification for the decisions they make. Article 6 means that this will have to change; this principle has already been recognised by domestic courts in the case of a disciplinary tribunal in *Stefan v General Medical Council*[6]. Here it was stated that the provisions of art 6 'will require closer attention to be paid to the duty to give reasons, at least in relation to those cases where a person's civil rights and obligations are being determined'.

The particular reluctance of tribunals in licensing cases to give reasons as to costs orders must now be consigned to history: see para **8.9** above.

This requirement will lead to the decision-making body being liable to challenge from both applicants for licences and objectors if either believe their arguments have not been properly considered and balanced.

1 *Van de Hurk v Netherlands* (1994) 18 EHRR 481, para. 61.
2 *Hadjianastassiou v Greece* (1993) 16 EHRR 219.
3 *Helle v Finland* (1997) 26 EHRR 159, para. 60.
4 *Toriga (Ruiz) v Spain* (Application 18390/91) (1994) 19 EHRR 553, para 60.
5 Sections 23(2) and (3) (premises licenses), 77(2) and (3) (clubs) and 122(1) and (2) (personal licences).
6 [1999] 1 WLR 1293, PC.

8.63–8.64 Articles 8 and 10; article 1 of the First Protocol The rights guaranteed by these articles are not absolute. The state is entitled to interfere with them in accordance with the qualifications set out in the second paragraph of each article, each of which are in similar terms. The rights themselves must be broadly and purposively construed[1], and the exceptions to the rights must be narrowly interpreted[2]. In deciding whether the refusal of a licence[3] will result in a violation of the applicant's rights two questions in particular have to be considered:

(1) Is the conduct protected by one of the articles of the Convention? If so,
(2) Would the refusal of the licence be justified under the terms of that article?

In most cases the first question will present little difficulty. For example, art 10(1) protects all modes of artistic expression including films, plays and dancing[4] and a refusal to grant a licence which has the effect of preventing or restricting the applicant's rights to perform or show will therefore almost certainly infringe his rights (or those of the performers) under this provision. In *Miss Behavin' Ltd v Belfast City Council*[5], a majority of the House of Lords decided that art 10 was engaged at a low level on an application for a sex shop licence.

Although the right to sell alcohol is not per se conduct protected by the Convention, a licence is a 'possession' for the purposes of article 1 of Protocol 1 and a decision to revoke it amounts to an interference which has to be justified within the terms of that article which protects disproportionate state interference with property rights[6].

The second question generally presents more difficulty. As has been explained, where there is a prima facie interference with one of these rights, it is for the state to show that any restriction on the exercise of the right concerned is justified according to the conditions set out under the second paragraph of each article. This can raise difficult issues of judgment.

For an interference to be permissible, the first condition which must be satisfied is that the measure taken was 'prescribed by law' or 'in accordance with law'. This requires that the interference have a basis in domestic law[7], and that the domestic law itself must be accessible and formulated with sufficient precision to be foreseeable in its consequences[8]. The provisions of English licensing law plainly meet these criteria.

Second, the interference must be 'necessary in a democratic society' in pursuit of one of the legitimate aims set out in the text of the Article itself. The adjective 'necessary' implies the existence of a 'pressing social need' for the interference[9]. In addition, there must be a reasonable relationship of 'proportionality' between the means employed and the aim pursued[10]. The principle of proportionality involves the striking of a fair balance between the demands of the general interest of the community and the requirements of the protection of the individual's fundamental rights[11]. The three questions the court should ask when considering whether an interference is proportionate are:

(i) whether the legislative objective is sufficiently important to justify limiting a fundamental right;

(ii) whether the measures designed to meet the legislative objective are rationally connected to it; and

(iii) whether the means used to impair the right or freedom are no more than is necessary to accomplish that objective[12].

---

1 *Niemietz v Germany* 16 EHRR 97, para 31.

2 *Sunday Times v United Kingdom* 2 EHRR 245, para 65.

3 Imposition of conditions may also raise Convention issues.

4 Including erotic and lap-dancing where it can be classified as expressive conduct and is not obscene: *Barnes v Glen Theatre, Inc* (1991) 501 US 560; *City of Erie v PAP's AM dba Kandyland* (2000) 529 US 277.

5 [2007] UKHL 19, [2007] All ER (D) 219 (Apr).

6 *Tre Traktorer v Sweden* (1989) 13 EHRR 309; *Fredin v Sweden* (1991) 13 EHRR 784; *Catscratch Limited v City of Glasgow Licensing Board* [2001] LLR 610.

7 *Silver v United Kingdom* 5 EHRR 347 at para 86.

8 *Sunday Times v United Kingdom* (1979) 2 EHRR 245, para 49

9 *Sunday Times v United Kingdom* (1979) 2 EHRR 245 at para 59; *Handyside v United Kingdom* 1 EHRR 737, para 48; *Goodwin v United Kingdom* 22 EHRR 123, para 40.

10 *Handyside v United Kingdom* at para 49.

11 *Sporrong and Lonroth v Sweden* 5 EHRR 35, para 69; *Soering v United Kingdom* 11 EHRR 439, para 89.

12 *De Freitas v Permanent Secretary of Ministry of Agriculture, Fisheries, Lands and Housing* [1999] 1 AC 69, 80; *R v A (No 2)* [2002] 1 AC 45, para 38.

8.65 Article 8 This article states:

'1 Everyone has the right to respect for his private and family life, his home and his correspondence.

2 There shall be no interference by a public authority with the exercise of this

> right except such as is in accordance with the law and is necessary in a democratic society in the interests of national security, public safety or the economic well-being of the country, for the prevention of disorder or crime, for the protection of health or morals, or for the protection of the rights and freedoms of others.'

This article has the potential to feature prominently in licensing applications where objectors allege that their Convention right to respect for their private, home and family life is being or will be affected by the granting or renewal of a licence, either due to noise nuisance or some other interference.

The 'right' is, however, subject to the qualification set out in art 8(2) discussed above.

8.66 It might be thought that a decision to grant a licence which might result in noise and disturbance to local residents would violate their rights under article 8(1). However the current Strasbourg approach severely restricts the circumstances in which objectors will be able to show a violation in these circumstances. In *Asselbourg v Luxembourg*[1] the applicants complained that the grant of licenses for a steelworks would result in pollution, release of toxic gases and noise and, therefore, that the grant of the licenses infringed their art 8 rights. The court held the application to be inadmissible because:

> From the terms 'victim' and 'violation' in Article 34 of the Convention, like the underlying philosophy of the obligation to exhaust all domestic remedies imposed by Article 35, it can be deduced that, in the system for the protection of human rights as envisaged by the framers of the Convention, exercise of the right of individual petition cannot have the aim of preventing a violation of the Convention. It is only in wholly exceptional circumstances that the risk of a future violation may nevertheless confer the status of 'victim' on an individual applicant, and only then if he or she produces reasonable and convincing evidence of the probability of the occurrence of a violation concerning him or her personally: mere suspicions or conjectures are not enough in that respect.

In *R (Vetterlein) v Hampshire County Council*[2] the applicants challenged the grant of planning permission for a waste disposal site *inter alia* on the grounds that it violated their article 8 rights. Sullivan J was prepared to assume without deciding that the grant of a license by itself could result in the violation of a Convention right but rejected the claimants' case because their complaints amounted to no more than 'generalised environmental concerns' which did not engage art 8.

The same approach was taken by Maurice Kay J in *R (Westminster City Council) v Mayor of London*[3], where he held that potential increases in traffic (and hence noise and pollution) which would allegedly be caused by the Mayor of London's Congestion Charging Scheme did not engage art 8(1).

However, in *R (Bushell) v Newcastle Licensing Justices, Ultimate Leisure plc*[4] Owen J found that it was reasonable to infer from the evidence as to the behaviour of those resorting to licensed premises in a particular road that the grant of an on-licence to other premises in the same road would result in some increase of such behaviour both in and in the immediate vicinity of the claimants' properties; this would have direct effect on their enjoyment of their properties.

It follows that the decision to grant a licence will, by itself, infringe the rights of objectors only in a wholly exceptional case where the evidence shows the decision to grant a licence will lead to an inevitable and serious violation of their Convention rights.

The European Commission and the European Court of Human Rights has considered a number of applications concerning nuisance suffered by individuals of member States which may be relevant in licensing cases.

In *Powell and Rayner v United Kingdom*[5] the applicants complained of noise pollution from Heathrow Airport. The court held that art 8 was material as:

> 'The quality of the applicant's private life and the scope for enjoying the amenities of his home had been adversely affected by the noise generated by aircraft using Heathrow Airport. Article 8 is therefore a material provision in relation to both Mr Powell and Mr Rayner.'

The court then considered whether the interference was justifiable,

> ' . . . regard must be had to the fair balance that has to be struck between the competing interests of the individual and of the community as a whole . . . '

They then considered the benefits derived from having an airport and the steps undertaken by the airport to minimise its impact:

> ' . . . the existence of large international airports, even in densely populated urban areas . . . have without question become necessary in the interests of a country's economic well-being.
>
> A number of measures have been introduced . . . to control, abate and compensate for aircraft noise . . . including restrictions on night jet movements, noise monitoring . . . and runway alteration'.

On that basis the court concluded:

> ' . . . there is no serious ground for maintaining that either the policy approach to the problem or the content of the particular regulatory measures adopted by the United Kingdom authorities gives rise to a violation of art 8 . . . '

Thus, the operation of the airport was a legitimate aim and it was accepted that, despite the government having taken certain measures, one could not entirely eliminate negative repercussions on the environment.

---

1 Unreported, Application 29121/95.
2 [2001] EWHC Admin 560, [2001] All ER D 146 (Jun).
3 [2002] EWHC 2440 (Admin), paras 111–115.
4 [2003] LLR 775, AC.
5 (1990) 12 EHRR 355, ECtHR. See also *Lopez Ostra v Spain* (1994) 20 EHRR 277, ECtHR (air pollution) and *Guerra v Italy* (1998) 26 EHRR 357, ECtHR (toxic pollution).

8.67 From that case and the Spanish and Italian cases referred to in para **8.66** above, note 5, it seems that the following points may be relevant in licensing cases.

(a) First it is clear that a public authority may interfere with the right to respect for family life and home under certain circumstances including economic well-being and 'for the protection of the rights and freedoms of others'. This may include the consideration by the licensing authority of the effect upon the applicant of a failure to grant or a revocation.

(b) One could use the decision in *Powell and Rayner* to argue that it is for the public authority to decide policy in relation to issues such as land-use and whether premises should be licensed, especially where there are procedures in place to mitigate any interference, for example by way of conditions.

(c) The only cases that have been successful before the European Court for Human Rights are those where there has been significant damage. In the *Lopez Ostra* case local residents were evacuated from their homes and in the *Guerra* case 150 persons were affected by arsenic poisoning. Thus for an objector to be successful under art 8 the disturbance or threat of disturbance would have to be major.

(d) The *Lopez Ostra* case suggests the possibility of a new cause of action for what would effectively be damage sustained due to a breach of convention rights, for example, where a licensing authority failed to take action to require the abatement of a nuisance either through the statutory nuisance regime or by way of conditions.

This is an interesting issue as currently the UK courts do not recognise the right in nuisance for damages due to failure to act (*R v Lam and Brennan and Torbay Borough Council*[1]).

Whether this will encourage objectors to take actions against licensing authorities for damages for the loss of enjoyment of their home due to the authority granting or renewing a licence is open to debate. To justify such awards the objectors would have to show, it is suggested, a major interference with their right under art 8 together with the authority being unable to justify that such interference fell within art 8(2) in that it was protecting the rights and freedoms of others. It is therefore unlikely that such actions will be common especially when the limitation in the HRA 1998, s 9(3) concerning judicial acts is also taken into account.

1 [1997] 3 PLR 22.

8.68 Article 10 Licensing authorities' power to control the activities specified in s 1(1) of the LA 2003 engages the Convention to the extent that they consist of conduct protected by the Convention. For example, the definition of 'regulated entertainment' in LA 2003, Sch 1, para 1(1) includes plays and films, and these are forms of expression which fall within the rights protected by art 10(1)[1].

1 *Wingrove v United Kingdom* (1996) 24 EHRR 1 (British Board of Film Classification's decision to refuse to certify 'Visions of Ecstasy' on grounds of its potential blasphemy did not violate article 10(1) because it was a proportionate interference with the director's freedom of expression and was therefore justified under article 10(2)).

8.69 Article 1 First Protocol This article provides a right to the peaceful enjoyment of one's possessions. However, it is important to realise that the article protects only existing rights and certain legitimate expectations. It does not guarantee a right to acquire what one does not already have[1]. In *Di Ciacca v Scottish Ministers*[2] Lord Reid decided that a decision to refuse to remove a condition attached to an existing grant of planning permission (allowing its use as a shop only and thereby not as a wine bar) did not engage the article. There is no doubt however that an existing licence is a possession[3] for these purposes as of course are homes near licensed premises. However, this is a qualified right in that both deprivation and control of the possession are expressed in the article to be permissible in specified situations:

> 'No one shall be deprived of his possessions except in the public interest and subject to the conditions provided for by law and by the general principles of international law.

> The proceeding provisions shall not however, in any way impair the right of a state to enforce such laws as it deems necessary to control the use of property in accordance with the general interest or to secure the payment of taxes or other contributions or penalties'.

Should a licensing authority attempt to interfere with the right to the peaceful enjoyment of, for example, the licence by the licence-holder, the authority must be able to justify it by recognising that a balance should be drawn between the requirements and demands of the general population and the protection of the licence-holder's individual rights. In other words, in balancing the interest of the community against the interest of the licence-holder, has the licence-holder who has been deprived of his licence or whose licence is being controlled by conditions suffered an excessive burden? For a discussion as to the extent that a hackney carriage licence is a possession for the purposes of the First Protocol, art 1 see *R (on the application of Royden) v Wirral Metropolitan Council*[4].

---

1 *Pine Valley Developments Ltd v Ireland* (Application 12742/87) (1992) 14 EHRR 319, ECtHR, para 51; *ISKCON v United Kingdom* (1994) 18 EHRR CD 133.

2 [2003] LLR 426, 2003 SLT 1031, Ct of Sess.

3 *Crompton (t/a David Crompton Haulage) v Department of Transport North Western Area* [2003] EWCA Civ 64, [2003] RTR 517, [2003] LLR 426, [2003] All ER (D) 311 (Jan), CA.

4 [2002] EWHC Admin 2484,[2003] LGR 290, [2002] All ER (D) 256 (Oct).

8.70 One of the factors to be considered when deciding whether an excessive burden has been imposed is whether compensation is available.

Tre Traktörer v Sweden[1] concerned the removal of a licence to sell alcohol from premises in Sweden. The licence-holders made an application to the European Court of Human Rights on a number of grounds including an allegation of violation of art 1 of the First Protocol.

The state initially argued that the licence was not a possession within the article. The court disagreed, stating:

> ' . . . the economic interests connected with the running of (the premises) were possessions for the purposes of art 1 of the Protocol. Indeed, the court has already found that the maintenance of the licence was one of the principal conditions for the carrying on of the applicant company's business, and that its withdrawal had adverse affects on the goodwill and value of the restaurant. Such withdrawal thus constitutes . . . interference with (the applicants) right to the peaceful enjoyment of its possessions'.

The court then went on,

> 'Severe though it may have been, the interference at issue does not fall within the ambit of the second sentence of the first paragraph (namely deprivation of possessions). The applicant company, although it could no longer open as a restaurant business, kept some economic interest represented by the leasing of the premises and the property assets contained therein which it finally sold in June 1984. There was accordingly no deprivation of property in terms of art 1 of the Protocol.
>
> The court finds, however, that the withdrawal of the licence to serve alcoholic beverages constituted a measure of control of the use of the property which falls to be considered under the second paragraph of art 1 of the Protocol'.

The court then considered whether the control of the premises was in 'the general interest' and 'proportionate' to the effect on the licence holder. Unfortunately for the applicants the court concluded,

> '. . . having regard to the legitimate aim of Swedish social policy concerning the consumption of alcohol . . . the state did not fail to strike a fair balance between the economic interest of the applicant company and the general interest of Swedish society'.

The licence holder's claim under art 1 of the First Protocol was therefore dismissed.

---

1 (1989) 13 EHRR 309, ECtHR. See also *Catscratch Ltd and Lettuce Holdings Ltd v City of Glasgow Licensing Board* [2001] LLR 610.

8.71 Another case concerning the deprivation/control of licences is *Fredin v Sweden*[1]. In this case the applicant owned a number of gravel pits that had been licensed and exploited for a number of years. The state served notice of its intention to revoke the permit thereby effectively closing the business. Whilst finding that the permit was a possession, the court held that its removal was 'control' and not 'deprivation', and that as 'in today's society the protection of the environment is an increasingly important consideration', the steps taken were justifiable and there was no violation of the article. Importantly the court bore in mind the fact that a three-year notice period had been given to the applicant.

What these decisions mean in a UK licensing context is difficult to discern. Each case is likely to turn on its own facts.

What is clear however, is that due to the broadness of the qualifying provision within the article which allows the licensing authority to 'control' the use of the premises in the public interest and where the balance of interference is in favour of the general public, this article may be of limited assistance to licence-holders who have had their licence revoked or curtailed in some way, especially if the public interest has a firm foundation and is applied in a reasonable manner.

Having said that there have been cases, albeit extreme ones, where the interference was found to be disproportionate to the general public benefit achieved.

In *Sporrong and Lönnroth v Sweden*[2] Mr Sporrong owned substantial property in Stockholm that had a rateable value of some 600,000 Swedish Crowns.

The city council obtained the Swedish equivalent of Compulsory Purchase Orders on the land together with orders preventing any construction taking place on the land. The orders and the construction bans were in force for over 20 years on Mr Sporrong's property. He complained that as he had been unable to sell or do anything worthwhile on the site during the period of the order and construction ban, this was equivalent to depriving him of his right to property contrary to the First Protocol.

The Swedish government argued that such orders and prohibitions were an intrinsic feature of town planning and did not impair Mr Sporrong's right to the peaceful enjoyment of his possessions.

The European Court rejected the government's contention finding that the orders and prohibitions did impair Mr Sporrong's right to peaceful enjoyment. However, the real question was whether the interference was justified. As the court, said the issue was whether

> 'a fair balance was struck between the demands of the general interests of the community and the requirements of the protection of the individual's fundamental

rights . . . the search for this balance is inherent in the whole of the Convention and is also reflected in the structure of art 1.'

The court held that there had been a violation of the First Protocol, art 1. The construction prohibitions were characterised as matters which 'controlled' the use of the property, whilst the Compulsory Purchase Orders (although being accepted to be an interference with the applicants possessions) were determined not to fall within the definition of 'deprivation' as they could, in theory, still be sold. The fair balance between the protection of the right of property and requirements of general interest had been upset by the prolonged extension of the orders and prohibitions.

An award equivalent to £100,000 was provided. In this case it was the time period which offended rather than the control itself.

1 (1991) 13 EHRR 784, ECtHR.
2 (1982) 5 EHRR 35.

8.72 Equating the principles of these cases to a licensing situation, it appears that:

(a) revocation of a licence would be seen as control rather than deprivation if the premises could continue to be used for some other purpose;
(b) there is no guarantee compensation will be required to be paid in such circumstances;
(c) any such controls must be seen as being in the public interest objectively determined and not disproportionate to the aim to be achieved;
(d) accordingly, only where the existence of the public interest is not objectively demonstrated or is insubstantial or where the interference is extreme will the licence-holder be successful in an action under this article.

rights ... the search for this balance is inherent in the whole of the Convention and is also reflected in the structure of art 1.

The court held that there had been a violation of the First Protocol, art 1. The construction prohibitions were characterised as measures which controlled the use of the property, whilst the Compulsory Purchase Orders (although being accepted to be an interference with the applicants possessions) were determined not to fall within the definition of deprivation as they could in theory still be sold. The fair balance between the protection of the right of property and requirements of general interest had been upset by the prolonged extension of the orders and prohibitions.

An award equivalent to £100,000 was provided. In this case it was the time period which offended rather than the control itself.

(1993) 18 EHRR 384, ECtHR.

(1982) 5 EHRR 35.

8.72 Applying the principles of these cases to a licensing situation, it appears that—

(a) revocation of a licence would be seen as a control rather than deprivation if the premises could continue to be used for some other purpose;
(b) there is no guarantee compensation will be required to be paid in such circumstances;
(c) any such controls must be seen as being in the public interest objectively determined and not disproportionate to the aim to be achieved;
(d) accordingly, only where the existence of the public interest is not objectively demonstrated or is insubstantial or where the interference is extreme will the licence-holder be successful in an action under this article.

Statutes

LOCAL GOVERNMENT ACT 1972

(1972 c 70)

AN ACT to make provision with respect to local government and the functions of local authorities in England and Wales; to amend Part II of the Transport Act 1968; to confer rights of appeal in respect of decisions relating to licences under the Home Counties (Music and Dancing) Licensing Act 1926; to make further provision with respect to magistrates' courts committees; to abolish certain inferior courts of record; and for connected purposes.

[26 October 1972]

PART XI
GENERAL PROVISIONS AS TO LOCAL AUTHORITIES

Documents and notices, etc

8.420 231 Service of notices on local authorities, etc

(1) Subject to subsection (3) below, any notice, order or other document required or authorised by any enactment or any instrument made under an enactment to be given to or served on a local authority or the chairman or an officer of a local authority shall be given or served by addressing it to the local authority and leaving it at, or sending it by post to, the principal office of the authority or any other office of the authority specified by them as one at which they will accept documents of the same descriptions as that document.

(2) Any notice, order or other document so required or authorised to be given to or served on a parish meeting, or the chairman of the parish meeting, shall be given or served by addressing it to the chairman of the parish meeting and by delivering it to him, or by leaving it at his last known address, or by sending it by post to him at that address.

(3) The foregoing provisions of this section do not apply to a document which is to be given or served in any proceedings in court,[1] but except as aforesaid the methods of giving or serving documents provided for by those provisions are in substitution for the methods provided for by any other enactment or any instrument made under an enactment so far as it relates to the giving or service of documents to or on a local authority, the chairman or an officer of a local authority or a parish meeting or the chairman of a parish meeting.

[(4) In this section 'local authority' includes a joint authority [and a police authority established under [section 3 of the Police Act 1996]][3], [and the Metropolitan Police Authority][5] [. . .][4] . . .][2]

---

1 Notices of applications to licensing justices under the Licensing Act 1964 are not (it is submitted) 'given or served in proceedings in court' and may accordingly be served under the provisions of this section.

2 Sub-s (4) added by the Local Government Act 1985, s 84, Sch 14, Pt I, para 27; words omitted repealed by the Education Reform Act 1988, s 237(2), Sch 3, Pt I.

3 Words in first pair of square brackets in sub-s (4) inserted by the Police and Magistrates' Courts Act 1994, s 43, Sch 4, Pt I, para 14(b). Words in square brackets therein substituted by the Police Act 1996, s 103(1), Sch 7, Pt I, para 1(2)(h).

4 Words in square brackets omitted inserted by the Police Act 1997, s 88, Sch 6, para 9 and

subsequently repealed by the Criminal Justice and Police Act 2001, ss 128(1), 137, Sch 6, Pt 2, paras 22, 31(b), Sch 7, Pt 5(1).

5 Words in square brackets inserted by the Greater London Authority Act 1999, s 325, Sch 27, para 32.

MAGISTRATES' COURTS ACT 1980

(1980 c 43)

Arrangement of sections

AN ACT to consolidate certain enactments relating to the jurisdiction of, and the practice and procedure before, magistrates' courts and the functions of justices' clerks, and to matters connected therewith, with amendments to give effect to recommendations of the Law Commission.

[1 August 1980]

PART IV
WITNESSES AND EVIDENCE

EVIDENCE GENERALLY

8.484 98 Evidence on oath

Subject to the provisions of any enactment or rule of law authorising the reception of unsworn evidence, evidence given before a magistrates' court shall be given on oath.

PART V
APPEAL AND CASE STATED

APPEAL

8.485 109 Abandonment of appeal

(1) Where notice to abandon an appeal has been duly given by the appellant—

(a) the court against whose decision the appeal was brought may issue process for enforcing that decision, subject to anything already suffered or done under it by the appellant; and

(b) the said court[1] may, on the application of the other party to the appeal, order the appellant to pay to that party such costs as appear to the court to be just and reasonable in respect of expenses properly incurred by that party in connection with the appeal before notice of the abandonment was given to that party.

(2) In this section 'appeal' means an appeal from a magistrates' court to the Crown Court, and the reference to a notice to abandon an appeal is a reference to a notice shown to the satisfaction of the magistrates' court to have been given in accordance with [rules of court][2,3]

---

1 See the notes to the Licensing Act 1964, s 22 and to the Crown Court Rules 1982, SI 1982/1109, r 11, as to the meaning of this expression in relation to an appeal against a refusal by licensing justices to grant a licence.

2 Words in square brackets substituted for 'Crown Court rules' by the Courts Act 2003, s 109(1), Sch 8, para 234, from 1 September 2004 (except in relation to the operation of this section in relation to rules of court other than Criminal Procedure Rules during the period between that date and the coming into force of the first Criminal Procedure Rules made under the Courts Act 2003, s 69): see SI 2004/2066.

3 See SI 1982/1109.

8.486 110 Enforcement of decision of the Crown Court

After the determination by the Crown Court of an appeal from a magistrates' court the decision appealed against as confirmed or varied by the Crown Court, or any decision of the Crown Court substituted for the decision appealed against, may, without prejudice to the powers of the Crown Court to enforce the decision, be enforced—

(a) by the issue by the court by which the decision appealed against was given of any process that it could have issued if it had decided the case as the Crown Court decided it;[1]

(b) so far as the nature of any process already issued to enforce the decision appealed against permits, by that process;

and the decision of the Crown Court shall have effect as if it had been made by the magistrates' court against whose decision the appeal is brought.

---

1 Where an appeal against a refusal by licensing justices to grant a licence (as to which see the Licensing Act 1964, s 21) is allowed it is expedient for the sake of administrative convenience for the Crown Court to direct the licensing justices to issue the licence.

CASE STATED

8.487 111 Statement of case by magistrates' court

(1) Any person who was a party to any proceeding before a magistrates' court[1] or is aggrieved by the conviction, order, determination or other proceeding of the court may question the proceeding on the ground that it is wrong in law or is in excess of jurisdiction by applying to the justices composing the court to state a case for the opinion of the High Court on the question of law or jurisdiction involved; but a person shall not make an application under this section in respect of a decision against which he has a right of appeal to the High Court or which by virtue of any enactment passed after 31st December 1879 is final.

(2) An application under subsection (1) above shall be made within 21 days after the day on which the decision of the magistrates' court was given.

(3) . . . [2]

(4) On the making of an application under this section in respect of a decision any right of the applicant to appeal against the decision to the Crown Court shall cease.

(5) If the justices are of opinion that an application under this section is frivolous, they may refuse to state a case, and, if the applicant so requires, shall give him a

certificate stating that the application has been refused; but the justices shall not refuse to state a case if the application is made by or under the direction of the Attorney General.

(6) Where justices refuse to state a case, the High Court may, on the application of the person who applied for the case to be stated, make an order of mandamus requiring the justices to state a case.

[(7) This section does not apply in relation to family proceedings within the meaning of section 111A of this Act.][3]

1 See MCA 1980, s 148 (para 8.488 below). It is clear that licensing justices are included within the phrase 'magistrates' court': *R v East Riding Quarter Sessions, ex p Newton* [1968] 1 QB 43, [1967] 3 All ER 118.

2 Not relevant to *Paterson's*.

3 Sub-s (7): inserted by SI 2009/871, art 4(1), (2).

PART VII
MISCELLANEOUS AND SUPPLEMENTARY

INTERPRETATION

8.488 148 'Magistrates' court'

(1) In this Act the expression 'magistrates' court' means any justice or justices of the peace acting under any enactment or by virtue of his or their commission or under the common law.

(2) Except where the contrary is expressed, anything authorised or required by this Act to be done by, to or before the magistrates' court by, to or before which any other thing was done, or is to be done, may be done by, to or before any magistrates' court acting [in the same local justice][1] area as that court.

1 Words in square brackets substituted by the Courts Act 2003, s 109(1), Sch 8, para 248.

SCHEDULES

SCHEDULE 6[1]
FEES
section 137

[PART I
FEES TO BE TAKEN BY [JUSTICES' CHIEF EXECUTIVES][2]

8.489

* * * * *

Certificate:—	
Every certificate not otherwise charged	8.00
* * * * *	
Duplicate:—	
For the duplicate of any document	5.00
* * * * *	
Licences:—	
For every licence, consent or authority not otherwise provided for, to include registration when necessary	8.00
Application for the revocation of a licence not otherwise provided for	30.00][3]

1 Schedule repealed by the Courts Act 2003, s 109(1), (3), Sch 8, para 254, Sch 10, from a date to be appointed: see the Courts Act 2003, s 110(1).

2 In the heading words in square brackets substituted by the Access to Justice Act 1999, s 90(1), Sch 13, paras 95, 117.

3 Substituted by the Magistrates' Courts Fees (Amendment) Order 1993, SI 1993/1889, art 2, Schedule.

PART III
MATTERS TO WHICH PART I DOES NOT APPLY

1. . . . [1]

2. . . . [2]

3. *Licences under [section 1 of the Cinemas Act 1985].*[3,4]

5. *Matters in respect of which fees are authorised to be charged by section 29 of the Licensing Act 1964.*[4]

---

1 Repealed by the Billiards (Abolition of Restrictions) Act 1987, s 1, Schedule.

2 Repealed by the Local Government (Miscellaneous Provisions) Act 1982, s 47, Sch 7, Pt I.

3 Words in square brackets substituted for a reference to the Cinematograph Act 1909 by the Cinemas Act 1985, s 24(1), Sch 2, para 12. This item appears to have been retained per incuriam; the power of cinematograph licensing authorities to delegate their licensing jurisdiction to justices sitting in petty sessions under the Cinemas Act 1985; the CA 1909, s 5 was abolished in 1972 and has not been reinstated.

4 Once para 74, Sch 6 of the Licensing Act 2003 comes into force paras 3 and 5 will be omitted.

8: Appeals Applications and Procedure

SENIOR COURTS ACT 1981

(1981 c 54)

Arrangement of sections

AN ACT to consolidate with amendments the Supreme Court of Judicature (Consolidation) Act 1925 and other enactments relating to the Supreme Court in England and Wales and the administration of justice therein; to repeal certain obsolete or unnecessary enactments so relating; to amend Part VIII of the Mental Health Act 1959, the Courts-Martial (Appeals) Act 1968, the Arbitration Act 1979 and the law relating to county courts; and for connected purposes.

[28 July 1981]

PART I
CONSTITUTION OF SUPREME COURT

THE CROWN COURT

8.519 8 The Crown Court

(1) The jurisdiction of the Crown Court shall be exercisable by—

(a) any judge of the High Court; or

(b) any Circuit judge[, Recorder or District Judge (Magistrates' Courts)][1]; or

(c) subject to and in accordance with the provisions of sections 74 and 75(2), a judge of the High Court, Circuit judge or Recorder sitting with not more than four justices of the peace,

and any such persons when exercising the jurisdiction of the Crown Court shall be judges of the Crown Court.

[(2) A justice of the peace is not disqualified from acting as a judge of the Crown Court merely because the proceedings are not at a place within the local justice area to which he is assigned or because the proceedings are not related to that area in any other way.][2]

(3) When the Crown Court sits in the City of London it shall be known as the Central Criminal Court; and the Lord Mayor of the City and any Alderman of the City shall be entitled to sit as judges of the Central Criminal Court with any judge of the High Court[, Circuit judge, Recorder or District Judge (Magistrates' Courts)][3].

1 Words in square brackets substituted by the Courts Act 2003, s 65(1).

2 Substituted by the Courts Act 2003, s 109(1), Sch 8, para 259(1), (2).

3 Words in square brackets substituted by the Courts Act 2003, s 109(1), Sch 8, para 259.

8.519A 28 Appeals from Crown Court and inferior courts

(1) Subject to subsection (2), any order, judgment or other decision of the Crown Court may be questioned by any party to the proceedings, on the ground that it is wrong in law or is in excess of jurisdiction, by applying to the Crown Court to have a case stated by that court for the opinion of the High Court.

(2) Subsection (1) shall not apply to—

(a) a judgment or other decision of the Crown Court relating to trial on indictment; or

(b) any decision of that court under the *Betting, Gaming and Lotteries Act 1963*[4], . . .[3][, *the Gaming Act 1968*[4] or the Local Government (Miscellaneous Provisions) Act 1982][1] which, by any provision of any of those Acts, is to be final.

(3) Subject to the provisions of this Act and to rules of court, the High Court shall, in accordance with section 19(2), have jurisdiction to hear and determine—

(a) any application, or any appeal (whether by way of case stated or otherwise), which it has power to hear and determine under or by virtue of this or any other Act; and

(b) all such other appeals as it had jurisdiction to hear and determine immediately before the commencement of this Act.

[(4) In subsection (2)(a) the reference to a decision of the Crown Court relating to trial on indictment does not include a decision relating to an order under section 17 of the Access to Justice Act 1999.][2]

---

1 Words in square brackets substituted by the Local Government (Miscellaneous Provisions) Act 1982, s 2, Sch 3, para 27(6).

2 Inserted by the Access to Justice Act 1999, s 24, Sch 4, paras 21, 22.

3 Words in italics repealed by the Licensing Act 2003, s 199, Sch 7.

4 Words in italics repealed by the Gambling Act 2005, s 356(4), Sch 17 from 1 September 2007.

8.519B [28A Proceedings on case stated by magistrates' court or Crown Court

(1) This section applies where a case is stated for the opinion of the High Court—

(a) by a magistrates' court under section 111 of the Magistrates' Courts Act 1980; or

(b) by the Crown Court under section 28(1) of this Act.

(2) The High Court may, if it thinks fit, cause the case to be sent back for amendment and, where it does so, the case shall be amended accordingly.

(3) The High Court shall hear and determine the question arising on the case (or the case as amended) and shall—

(a) reverse, affirm or amend the determination in respect of which the case has been stated; or

(b) remit the matter to the magistrates' court, or the Crown Court, with the opinion of the High Court,

and may make such other order in relation to the matter (including as to costs) as it thinks fit.

(4) Except as provided by the Administration of Justice Act 1960 (right of appeal to *House of Lords*[1] in criminal cases), a decision of the High Court under this section is final.][2]

---

1 Words 'Supreme Court' substituted for words in italics by the Constitutional Reform Act 2005, s 40(4), Sch 9, Pt 1, para 36(1), (4) from a date to be appointed.

2 Inserted by the Statute Law (Repeals) Act 1993, s 1(2), Sch 2, para 9 and substituted by the Access to Justice Act 1999, s 61. The effect of this provision is that the Court of Appeal has no jurisdiction to entertain an appeal in case stated proceedings: *Ryan, Hulme and Henderson v Rees* [2002] LLR 742.

8.519C 29 [Mandatory, prohibiting and quashing orders][1]

[(1) The orders of mandamus, prohibition and certiorari shall be known instead as mandatory, prohibiting and quashing orders respectively.

(1A) The High Court shall have jurisdiction to make mandatory, prohibiting and quashing orders in those classes of case in which, immediately before 1st May 2004, it had jurisdiction to make orders of mandamus, prohibition and certiorari respectively.]

(2) Every such order shall be final, subject to any right of appeal therefrom.

(3) In relation to the jurisdiction of the Crown Court, other than its jurisdiction in matters relating to trial on indictment, the High Court shall have all such jurisdiction to make orders of [mandatory, prohibiting or quashing orders][1] as the High Court possesses in relation to the jurisdiction of an inferior court.

[(3A) The High Court shall have no jurisdiction to make orders of [mandatory, prohibiting or quashing orders][1] in relation to the jurisdiction of a court-martial in matters relating to—

(a) trial by court-martial for an offence, or

(b) appeals from a Standing Civilian Court;

and in this subsection 'court-martial' means a court-martial under the Army Act 1955, the Air Force Act 1955 or the Naval Discipline Act 1957.][2]

(4) The power of the High Court under any enactment to require justices of the peace or a judge or officer of a county court to do any act relating to the duties of their respective offices, or to require a magistrates' court to state a case for the opinion of the High Court, in any case where the High Court formerly had by virtue of any enactment jurisdiction to make a rule absolute, or an order, for any of those purposes, shall be exercisable by [mandatory order][1].

[(5) In any statutory provision—

(a) references to mandamus or to a writ or order of mandamus shall be read as references to a mandatory order;

(b) references to prohibition or to a writ or order of prohibition shall be read as references to a prohibiting order;

(c) references to certiorari or to a writ or order of certiorari shall be read as references to a quashing order; and

(d) references to the issue or award of a writ of mandamus, prohibition or certiorari shall be read as references to the making of the corresponding mandatory, prohibiting or quashing order.][1]

[(6) In subsection (3) the reference to the Crown Court's jurisdiction in matters relating to trial on indictment does not include its jurisdiction relating to orders under section 17 of the Access to Justice Act 1999.]

1 Words in square brackets substituted by SI 2004/1033.

2 Inserted by the Armed Forces Act 2001, s 23(1), (3). Substituted by the Armed Forces Act 2006, s 378(1), Sch 16, para 93 from a date to be appointed.

3 Sub-s (6): inserted by the Access to Justice Act 1999, s 24, Sch 4, paras 21, 23.

8.519D 31 Application for judicial review

(1) An application to the High Court for one or more of the following forms of relief, namely—

[(a) a mandatory, prohibiting or quashing order;][1]

(b) a declaration or injunction under subsection (2); or

(c) an injunction under section 30 restraining a person not entitled to do so from acting in an office to which that section applies,

shall be made in accordance with rules of court by a procedure to be known as an application for judicial review.

(2) A declaration may be made or an injunction granted under this subsection in any case where an application for judicial review, seeking that relief, has been made and the High Court considers that, having regard to—

(a) the nature of the matters in respect of which relief may be granted by [mandatory, prohibiting or quashing orders][1];
(b) the nature of the persons and bodies against whom relief may be granted by such orders; and
(c) all the circumstances of the case,

it would be just and convenient for the declaration to be made or of the injunction to be granted, as the case may be.

(3) No application for judicial review shall be made unless the leave of the High Court has been obtained in accordance with rules of court; and the court shall not grant leave to make such an application unless it considers that the applicant has a sufficient interest in the matter to which the application relates.

[(4) On an application for judicial review the High Court may award to the applicant damages, restitution or the recovery of a sum due if—
(a) the application includes a claim for such an award arising from any matter to which the application relates; and
(b) the court is satisfied that such an award would have been made if the claim had been made in an action begun by the applicant at the time of making the application.][1]

[(5) If, on an application for judicial review, the High Court quashes the decision to which the application relates, it may in addition—
(a) remit the matter to the court, tribunal or authority which made the decision, with a direction to reconsider the matter and reach a decision in accordance with the findings of the High Court, or
(b) substitute its own decision for the decision in question.

(5A) But the power conferred by subsection (5)(b) is exercisable only if—
(a) the decision in question was made by a court or tribunal,
(b) the decision is quashed on the ground that there has been an error of law, and
(c) without the error, there would have been only one decision which the court or tribunal could have reached.

(5B) Unless the High Court otherwise directs, a decision substituted by it under subsection (5)(b) has effect as if it were a decision of the relevant court or tribunal.][2]

(6) Where the High Court considers that there has been undue delay in making an application for judicial review, the court may refuse to grant—
(a) leave for the making of the application; or
(b) any relief sought on the application,

if it considers that the granting of the relief sought would be likely to cause substantial hardship to, or substantially prejudice the rights of, any person or would be detrimental to good administration.

(7) Subsection (6) is without prejudice to any enactment or rule of court which has the effect of limiting the time within which an application for judicial review may be made.

---

1 Words in square brackets substituted by SI 2004/1033.

2 Sub-ss (5), (5A), (5B): substituted, for sub-s (5) as originally enacted, by the Tribunals, Courts and Enforcement Act 2007, s 141.

PART II
JURISDICTION

THE CROWN COURT

8.520 45 General jurisdiction of Crown Court

(1) The Crown Court shall be a superior court of record.

(2) Subject to the provisions of this Act, there shall be exercisable by the Crown Court—

- (a) all such appellate and other jurisdiction as is conferred on it by or under this or any other Act; and
- (b) all such other jurisdiction as was exercisable by it immediately before the commencement of this Act.

(3) Without prejudice to subsection (2), the jurisdiction of the Crown Court shall include all such powers and duties as were exercisable or fell to be performed by it immediately before the commencement of this Act.

(4) Subject to section 8 of the Criminal Procedure (Attendance of Witnesses) Act 1965 (substitution in criminal cases of procedure in that Act for procedure by way of subpoena) and to any provision contained in or having effect under this Act, the Crown Court shall, in relation to the attendance and examination of witnesses, any contempt of court, the enforcement of its orders and all other matters incidental to its jurisdiction, have the like powers, rights, privileges and authority as the High Court.

(5) The specific mention elsewhere in this Act of any jurisdiction covered by subsections (2) and (3) shall not derogate from the generality of those subsections.

8.521 48 Appeals to Crown Court

(1) The Crown Court may, in the course of hearing any appeal, correct any error or mistake in the order or judgment incorporating the decision which is the subject of the appeal.

(2) On the termination of the hearing of an appeal the Crown Court—

- (a) may confirm, reverse or vary [any part of the decision appealed against, including a determination not to impose a separate penalty in respect of an offence][1]; or
- (b) may remit the matter with its opinion thereon to the authority whose decision is appealed against; or
- (c) may make such other order in the matter as the court thinks just, and by such order exercise any power which the said authority might have exercised.

(3) Subsection (2) has effect subject to any enactment relating to any such appeal which expressly limits or restricts the powers of the court on the appeal.

(4) . . . [2]

(5) This section applies whether or not the appeal is against the whole of the decision.

(6)–(8) . . . [2]

---

1 Sub-s (2): words in square brackets substituted by the Criminal Justice Act 1988, s 156.

2 Sub-ss (4), (6)–(8): not relevant to *Paterson's*.

GENERAL PROVISIONS

Costs

8.521A [51 Costs in civil division of Court of Appeal, High Court and county courts [1]

(1) Subject to the provisions of this or any other enactment and to rules of court, the costs of and incidental to all proceedings in—

- (a) the civil division of the Court of Appeal;
- (b) the High Court; and
- (c) any county court,

shall be in the discretion of the court.

(2) Without prejudice to any general power to make rules of court, such rules may make provision for regulating matters relating to the costs of those proceedings including, in particular, prescribing scales of costs to be paid to legal or other representatives [or for securing that the amount awarded to a party in respect of the costs to be paid by him to such representatives is not limited to what would have been payable by him to them if he had not been awarded costs].[2]

(3) The court shall have full power to determine by whom and to what extent the costs are to be paid.

(4) In subsections (1) and (2) 'proceedings' includes the administration of estates and trusts.

(5) . . . [3]

(6) In any proceedings mentioned in subsection (1), the court may disallow, or (as the case may be) order the legal or other representative concerned to meet, the whole of any wasted costs or such part of them as may be determined in accordance with rules of court.

(7) In subsection (6), 'wasted costs' means any costs incurred by a party—

(a) as a result of any improper, unreasonable or negligent act or omission on the part of any legal or other representative or any employee of such a representative; or

(b) which, in the light of any such act or omission occurring after they were incurred, the court considers it is unreasonable to expect that party to pay.

(8)–(12) . . . [3]

(13) In this section 'legal or other representative', in relation to a party to proceedings, means any person exercising a right of audience or right to conduct litigation on his behalf.]

---

1 Substituted by the Courts and Legal Services Act 1990, s 4.

2 Words in square brackets inserted by the Access to Justice Act 1999, s 31.

3 Sub-ss (5), (8)–(12): not relevant to *Paterson's*.

8.522 52 Costs in Crown Court

(1) [Rules of court][1] may authorise the Crown Court to award costs and may regulate any matters relating to costs of proceedings in that court, and in particular may make provision as to—

(a) any discretion to award costs;

(b) the taxation of costs, or the fixing of a sum instead of directing a taxation, and as to the officer of the court or other person by whom costs are to be taxed;

(c) a right of appeal from any decision on the taxation of costs, whether to a Taxing Master of the *Supreme Court*[1A] or to any other officer or authority;

(d) a right of appeal to the High Court, subject to any conditions specified in the rules, from any decision on an appeal brought by virtue of paragraph (c);

(e) the enforcement of an order for costs; and

(f) the charges or expenses or other disbursements which are to be treated as costs for the purposes of the rules.

(2) The costs to be dealt with by rules made in pursuance of this section may, where an appeal is brought to the Crown Court from the decision of a magistrates' court, or from the decision of any other court or tribunal, include costs in the proceedings in that court or tribunal.

[(2A) Subsection (6) of section 51 applies in relation to any civil proceedings in the Crown Court as it applies in relation to any proceedings mentioned in subsection (1) of that section.][2]

(3) Nothing in this section authorises the making of rules about the payment of costs out of central funds, whether under [Part II of the Prosecution of Offences Act 1985][3] or otherwise, but rules made in pursuance of this section may make any such provision as, [in relation to costs of proceedings in the Crown Court, is contained in section 18 of that Act or in regulations made under section 19 of that Act (awards of party and party costs in criminal proceedings].[3]

(4) Rules made in pursuance of this section may amend or repeal all or any of the provisions of any enactment about costs between party and party in criminal or other proceedings in the Crown Court, being an enactment passed before, or contained in, [Part II of the Prosecution of Offences Act 1985].[4]

(5) Rules made in pursuance of this section shall have effect subject to the provisions of section 41 of, and Schedule 9 to, the Administration of Justice Act 1970 (method of enforcing orders for costs).

---

1 Words in square brackets substituted by the Courts Act 2003 (Consequential Amendments) Order 2004, SI 2004/2035, from 1 September 2004.

1A Words 'Senior Courts' substituted for words in italics by the Constitutional Reform Act 2005, s 59(5), Sch 11, Pt 4, para 26(1), (2) from a date to be appointed.

2 Sub-s (2A): inserted by the Courts and Legal Services Act 1990, s 4(2).

3 Words in square brackets substituted by the Prosecution of Offences Act 1985, s 30(5), Sch 1, para 7.

4 Words in square brackets substituted by the POA 1985, s 30(5), Sch 1, para 8.

PART III
PRACTICE AND PROCEDURE

THE CROWN COURT
COMPOSITION OF COURT

8.523 73 General provisions

(1) Subject to the provisions of section 8(1)(c), 74 and 75(2) as respects courts comprising justices of the peace, all proceedings in the Crown Court shall be heard and disposed of before a single judge of that court.

(2) [Rules of court][1] may authorise or require a judge of the High Court, Circuit judge or Recorder, in such circumstances as are specified by the rules, at any stage to continue with any proceedings with a court from which any one or more of the justices initially constituting the court has withdrawn, or is absent for any reason.

(3) Where a judge of the High Court, Circuit judge or Recorder sits with justices of the peace he shall preside, and—

(a) the decision of the Crown court may be a majority decision; and

(b) if the members of the court are equally divided, the judge of the High Court, Circuit judge or Recorder shall have a second and casting vote.

---

1 Words in square brackets substituted by the Courts Act 2003 (Consequential Amendments) Order 2004, SI 2004/2035, from 1 September 2004.

8.524 74 Appeals and committals for sentence

(1) On any hearing by the Crown Court—

(a) of any appeal; . . .[1]

(b) . . .[1]

the Crown Court shall consist of a judge of the High Court or a Circuit judge or a Recorder who, subject to the following provisions of this section, shall sit with not less than two nor more than four justices of the peace.

(2) [Rules of court][2] may, with respect to hearings falling within subsection (1)—

(a) prescribe the number of justices of the peace constituting the court (within the limits mentioned in that subsection); and

(b) prescribe the qualifications to be possessed by any such justices of the peace;

and the rules may make different provision for different descriptions of cases, different places of sitting or other different circumstances.

(3) [Rules of court] may authorise or require a judge of the High Court, Circuit judge or Recorder, in such circumstances as are specified by the rules, to enter on, or at any stage to continue with, any proceedings with a court not comprising the justices required by subsections (1) and (2).

(4) The Lord Chancellor may from time to time, having regard to the number of justices, or the number of justices with any prescribed qualifications, available for service in the Crown Court, give directions providing that, in such descriptions of proceedings as may be specified by the Lord Chancellor, the provisions of subsections (1) and (2) shall not apply.

(5) Directions under subsection (4) may frame descriptions of proceedings by reference to the place of trial, or by reference to the time of trial, or in any other way.

3

[(5A) Before exercising any functions under subsection (4), the Lord Chancellor must consult the Lord Chief Justice.][3]

(6) No decision of the Crown Court shall be questioned on the ground that the court was not constituted as required by or under subsections (1) and (2) unless objection was taken by or on behalf of a party to the proceedings not later than the time when the proceedings were entered on, or when the alleged irregularity began.

(7) [Rules of court][2] may make provision as to the circumstances in which—

(a) a person concerned with a decision appealed against is to be disqualified from hearing the appeal;

(b) . . . [1]

(c) proceedings on the hearing of an appeal . . . [1] are to be valid notwithstanding that any person taking part in them is disqualified.[3]

[(8) The Lord Chief Justice may nominate a judicial office holder (as defined in section 109(4) of the Constitutional Reform Act 2005) to exercise his functions under this section.][3]

---

1 Words omitted repealed by the Access to Justice Act 1999, ss 79, 106, Sch 15, Pt V(4).

2 Words in square brackets substituted by the Courts Act 2003 (Consequential Amendments) Order 2004, SI 2004/2035, from 1 September 2004.

3 Sub-ss (5A) and (8) inserted by the Constitutional Reform Act 2005, s 15(1), Sch 4, Pt 1, paras 114, 133.

SITTINGS

8.525 78 Sittings

(1) Any Crown Court business may be conducted at any place in England or Wales, and the sittings of the Crown Court at any place may be continuous or intermittent or occasional.

(2) Judges of the Crown Court may sit simultaneously to take any number of different cases in the same or different places, and may adjourn cases from place to place at any time.

(3) The places at which the Crown Court sits, and the days and times at which the Crown Court sits at any place, shall be determined in accordance with directions given by the Lord Chancellor [after consulting the Lord Chief Justice][1].

[(4) The Lord Chief Justice may nominate a judicial office holder (as defined in section 109(4) of the Constitutional Reform Act 2005) to exercise his functions under this section.][1]

---

1 Words in square brackets in sub-s (3), and sub-s (4) inserted by the Constitutional Reform Act 2005, s 15(1), Sch 4, Pt 1, paras 114, 134.

OTHER PROVISIONS

8.526 79 Practice and procedure in connection with indictable offences and appeals

(3) The customary practice and procedure with respect to appeals to the Crown Court, and in particular any practice as to the extent to which an appeal is by way of rehearing of the case, shall continue to be observed.[1]

---

1 In licensing cases appeals to the Crown Court are always by way of a rehearing: see *Sagnata Investments Ltd v Norwich Corporation* [1971] 2 QB 614, CA.

RULES OF COURT

8.527 87 Particular matters for which rules of court may provide

* * * * *

(5) [Rules of court made under section 84] may amend or repeal any statutory provision about appeals to the Crown Court so far as it relates to the practice and procedure with respect to such appeals [(except so far as relating to criminal causes or matters)][1].

---

1 Words in square brackets substituted by the Courts Act 2003 (Consequential Amendments) Order 2004, SI 2004/2035, from 1 September 2004.

* * * * *

PART VI
MISCELLANEOUS AND SUPPLEMENTARY

SUPPLEMENTARY

8.528 151 Interpretation of this Act, and rules of construction for other Acts and documents

(1) In this Act, unless the context otherwise requires—

* * * * *

'jurisdiction' includes powers:

* * * * *

'party', in relation to any proceedings, includes any person who pursuant to or by virtue of rules of court or any other statutory provision has been served with notice of, or has intervened in, those proceedings;

* * * * *

CRIMINAL JUSTICE ACT 1982

(1982 c 48)

AN ACT to make further provision as to the sentencing and treatment of offenders (including provision as to the enforcement of fines and the standardisation of fines and of certain other sums specified in enactments relating to the powers of criminal courts); to make provision for the prescribing of criteria for the placing and keeping of children in different descriptions of accommodation in community homes; to amend the law of Scotland relating to the mode of trial of certain offences and the recall of witnesses; to amend the law of England and Wales relating to the remand in custody of accused persons and to the grant of bail to persons convicted or sentenced in the Crown Court; to abolish (subject to savings) the right of a person accused in criminal proceedings under the law of England and Wales to make an unsworn statement; and for connected purposes.

[28 October 1982]

Introduction of standard scale of fines

8.558 37 The standard scale of fines for summary offences

(1) There shall be a standard scale of fines for summary offences, which shall be known as 'the standard scale'.

[(2) The standard scale is shown below.

Level on the scale	*Amount of fine*
1	£200
2	£500
3	£1,000
4	£2,500
5	£5,000][1]

(3) Where any enactment (whether contained in an Act passed before or after this Act) provides—

(a) that a person convicted of a summary offence shall be liable on conviction to a fine or a maximum fine by reference to a specified level on the standard scale; or

(b) confers power by subordinate instrument to make a person liable on conviction of a summary offence (whether or not created by the instrument) to a fine or maximum fine by reference to a specified level on the standard scale,

it is to be construed as referring to the standard scale for which this section provides as that standard scale has effect from time to time by virtue either of this section or of an order under section 143 of the Magistrates' Courts Act 1980[2].

1 Sub-s (2) substituted by the Criminal Justice Act 1991, ss 17(1), 101(1), Sch 12, para 6.

2 See the Criminal Penalties etc (Increase) Order 1984, SI 1984/447.

8.559 75 Construction of reference to 'the standard scale'

In any enactment (whether contained in an Act passed before or after this Act) 'the standard scale'—

(a) *in relation to England and Wales, has the meaning given by section 37 of this Act;*[1]

---

[1] Repealed, except in relation to the Channel Islands and the Isle of Man, by the Criminal Justice Act 1988, s 170(2), Sch 16; the same definition of 'the standard scale' is now to be found in the Interpretation Act 1978, s 1.

HUMAN RIGHTS ACT 1998

(1998 c 42)

An Act to give further effect to rights and freedoms guaranteed under the European Convention on Human Rights; to make provision with respect to holders of certain judicial offices who become judges of the European Court of Human Rights; and for connected purposes.

[9th November 1998]

Introduction

8.705 1 The Convention Rights

(1) In this Act 'the Convention rights' means the rights and fundamental freedoms set out in—

(a) Articles 2 to 12 and 14 of the Convention,

(b) Articles 1 to 3 of the First Protocol, and

(c) [Article 1 of the Thirteenth Protocol],[1]

as read with Articles 16 to 18 of the Convention.

(2) Those Articles are to have effect for the purposes of this Act subject to any designated derogation or reservation (as to which see sections 14 and 15).

(3) The Articles are set out in Schedule 1.

(4) The [Secretary of State][2] may by order make such amendments to this Act as he considers appropriate to reflect the effect, in relation to the United Kingdom, of a protocol.

(5) In subsection (4) 'protocol' means a protocol to the Convention—

(a) which the United Kingdom has ratified; or

(b) which the United Kingdom has signed with a view to ratification.

(6) No amendment may be made by an order under subsection (4) so as to come into force before the protocol concerned is in force in relation to the United Kingdom.

---

[1] Words in square brackets substituted by SI 2004/1574, art 2(1).

[2] Words in square brackets substituted by SI 2003/1887, art 9, Sch 2, para 10(1).

8.706 2 Interpretation of Convention rights

(1) A court or tribunal determining a question which has arisen in connection with a Convention right must take into account any—

(a) judgment, decision, declaration or advisory opinion of the European Court of Human Rights,

(b) opinion of the Commission given in a report adopted under Article 31 of the Convention,

(c) decision of the Commission in connection with Article 26 or 27(2) of the Convention, or

(d) decision of the Committee of Ministers taken under Article 46 of the Convention,

whenever made or given, so far as, in the opinion of the court or tribunal, it is relevant to the proceedings in which that question has arisen.

(2) Evidence of any judgment, decision, declaration or opinion of which account may have to be taken under this section is to be given in proceedings before any court or tribunal in such manner as may be provided by rules.

(3) In this section 'rules' means rules of court or, in the case of proceedings before a tribunal, rules made for the purposes of this section—

(a) by . . . [1] [the Lord Chancellor or][2] the Secretary of State, in relation to any proceedings outside Scotland;

(b) by the Secretary of State, in relation to proceedings in Scotland; or

(c) by a Northern Ireland department, in relation to proceedings before a tribunal in Northern Ireland—

(i) which deals with transferred matters; and

(ii) for which no rules made under paragraph (a) are in force.

---

1 Words omitted repealed by SI 2003/1887, art 9, Sch 2, para 10(2).

2 Words in square brackets inserted by SI 2005/3429, art 8, Schedule, para 3.

Legislation

8.707 3 Interpretation of legislation

(1) So far as it is possible to do so, primary legislation and subordinate legislation must be read and given effect in a way which is compatible with the Convention rights.

(2) This section—

(a) applies to primary legislation and subordinate legislation whenever enacted;

(b) does not affect the validity, continuing operation or enforcement of any incompatible primary legislation; and

(c) does not affect the validity, continuing operation or enforcement of any incompatible subordinate legislation if (disregarding any possibility of revocation) primary legislation prevents removal of the incompatibility.

8.708 4 Declaration of incompatibility

(1) Subsection (2) applies in any proceedings in which a court determines whether a provision of primary legislation is compatible with a Convention right.

(2) If the court is satisfied that the provision is incompatible with a Convention right, it may make a declaration of that incompatibility.

(3) Subsection (4) applies in any proceedings in which a court determines whether a provision of subordinate legislation, made in the exercise of a power conferred by primary legislation, is compatible with a Convention right.

(4) If the court is satisfied—

(a) that the provision is incompatible with a Convention right, and

(b) that (disregarding any possibility of revocation) the primary legislation concerned prevents removal of the incompatibility,

it may make a declaration of that incompatibility.

(5) In this section 'court' means—

(a) *the House of Lords*[1];

(b) the Judicial Committee of the Privy Council;

(c) the *Courts-Martial Appeal Court*[2];

(d) in Scotland, the High Court of Justiciary sitting otherwise than as a trial court or the Court of Session;
(e) in England and Wales or Northern Ireland, the High Court or the Court of Appeal.[3]

(6) A declaration under this section ('a declaration of incompatibility')—
(a) does not affect the validity, continuing operation or enforcement of the provision in respect of which it is given; and
(b) is not binding on the parties to the proceedings in which it is made.

---

1 Substituted by the Constitutional Reform Act 2005, s 40(4), Sch 9, Pt 1, para 66(1), (2) from a date to be appointed.

2 Words in italics substituted by the Armed Forces Act 2006, s 378(1), Sch 16, para 156 from a date to be appointed.

3 New para (f) inserted by the Mental Capacity Act 2005, s 67(1), Sch 6, para 43, from a date to be appointed.

> '[(f) the Court of Protection, in any matter being dealt with by the President of the Family Division, the Vice-Chancellor or a puisne judge of the High Court.]'

8.709 5 Right of Crown to intervene

(1) Where a court is considering whether to make a declaration of incompatibility, the Crown is entitled to notice in accordance with rules of court.

(2) In any case to which subsection (1) applies—
(a) a Minister of the Crown (or a person nominated by him),
(b) a member of the Scottish Executive,
(c) a Northern Ireland Minister,
(d) a Northern Ireland department,

is entitled, on giving notice in accordance with rules of court, to be joined as a party to the proceedings.

(3) Notice under subsection (2) may be given at any time during the proceedings.

(4) A person who has been made a party to criminal proceedings (other than in Scotland) as the result of a notice under subsection (2) may, with leave, appeal to the *House of Lords*[1] against any declaration of incompatibility made in the proceedings.

(5) In subsection (4)—

'criminal proceedings' includes all proceedings before the *Courts-Martial Appeal Court*[2]; and

'leave' means leave granted by the court making the declaration of incompatibility or by the *House of Lords*[1].

---

1 Words in italics substituted by the Constitutional Reform Act 2005, s 40(4), Sch 9, Pt 1, para 66(1), (3) from a date to be appointed.

2 Words in italics substituted by the Armed Forces Act 2006, s 378(1), Sch 16, para 157 from a date to be appointed.

Public authorities

8.710 6 Acts of public authorities

(1) It is unlawful for a public authority to act in a way which is incompatible with a Convention right.

(2) Subsection (1) does not apply to an act if—
(a) as the result of one or more provisions of primary legislation, the authority could not have acted differently; or

(b) in the case of one or more provisions of, or made under, primary legislation which cannot be read or given effect in a way which is compatible with the Convention rights, the authority was acting so as to give effect to or enforce those provisions.

(3) In this section 'public authority' includes—

(a) a court or tribunal, and

(b) any person certain of whose functions are functions of a public nature,

but does not include either House of Parliament or a person exercising functions in connection with proceedings in Parliament.

(4) *In subsection (3) 'Parliament' does not include the House of Lords in its judicial capacity.*[1]

(5) In relation to a particular act, a person is not a public authority by virtue only of subsection (3)(b) if the nature of the act is private.

(6) 'An act' includes a failure to act but does not include a failure to—

(a) introduce in, or lay before, Parliament a proposal for legislation; or

(b) make any primary legislation or remedial order.

---

1 Repealed by the Constitutional Reform Act 2005, ss 40(4), 146, Sch 9, Pt 1, para 66(1), (4), Sch 18, Pt 5 from a date to be appointed.

8.711 7 Proceedings

(1) A person who claims that a public authority has acted (or proposes to act) in a way which is made unlawful by section 6(1) may—

(a) bring proceedings against the authority under this Act in the appropriate court or tribunal, or

(b) rely on the Convention right or rights concerned in any legal proceedings,

but only if he is (or would be) a victim of the unlawful act.

(2) In subsection (1)(a) 'appropriate court or tribunal' means such court or tribunal as may be determined in accordance with rules; and proceedings against an authority include a counterclaim or similar proceeding.

(3) If the proceedings are brought on an application for judicial review, the applicant is to be taken to have a sufficient interest in relation to the unlawful act only if he is, or would be, a victim of that act.

(4) If the proceedings are made by way of a petition for judicial review in Scotland, the applicant shall be taken to have title and interest to sue in relation to the unlawful act only if he is, or would be, a victim of that act.

(5) Proceedings under subsection (1)(a) must be brought before the end of—

(a) the period of one year beginning with the date on which the act complained of took place; or

(b) such longer period as the court or tribunal considers equitable having regard to all the circumstances,

but that is subject to any rule imposing a stricter time limit in relation to the procedure in question.

(6) In subsection (1)(b) 'legal proceedings' includes—

(a) proceedings brought by or at the instigation of a public authority; and

(b) an appeal against the decision of a court or tribunal.

(7) For the purposes of this section, a person is a victim of an unlawful act only if he would be a victim for the purposes of Article 34 of the Convention if proceedings were brought in the European Court of Human Rights in respect of that act.

(8) Nothing in this Act creates a criminal offence.

(9) In this section 'rules' means—

(a) in relation to proceedings before a court or tribunal outside Scotland, rules made by . . . [1] [the Lord Chancellor or][2] the Secretary of State for the purposes of this section or rules of court,

(b) in relation to proceedings before a court or tribunal in Scotland, rules made by the Secretary of State for those purposes,

(c) in relation to proceedings before a tribunal in Northern Ireland—

(i) which deals with transferred matters; and

(ii) for which no rules made under paragraph (a) are in force,

rules made by a Northern Ireland department for those purposes,

and includes provision made by order under section 1 of the Courts and Legal Services Act 1990.

(10) In making rules, regard must be had to section 9.

(11) The Minister who has power to make rules in relation to a particular tribunal may, to the extent he considers it necessary to ensure that the tribunal can provide an appropriate remedy in relation to an act (or proposed act) of a public authority which is (or would be) unlawful as a result of section 6(1), by order add to—

(a) the relief or remedies which the tribunal may grant; or

(b) the grounds on which it may grant any of them.

(12) An order made under subsection (11) may contain such incidental, supplemental, consequential or transitional provision as the Minister making it considers appropriate.

(13) 'The Minister' includes the Northern Ireland department concerned.

---

1 Words in omitted repealed by SI 2003/1887, art 9, Sch 2, para 10(1).

2 Words in square brackets inserted by SI 2005/3429, art 8, Schedule, para 3.

8.712 8 Judicial remedies

(1) In relation to any act (or proposed act) of a public authority which the court finds is (or would be) unlawful, it may grant such relief or remedy, or make such order, within its powers as it considers just and appropriate.

(2) But damages may be awarded only by a court which has power to award damages, or to order the payment of compensation, in civil proceedings.

(3) No award of damages is to be made unless, taking account of all the circumstances of the case, including—

(a) any other relief or remedy granted, or order made, in relation to the act in question (by that or any other court), and

(b) the consequences of any decision (of that or any other court) in respect of that act,

the court is satisfied that the award is necessary to afford just satisfaction to the person in whose favour it is made.

(4) In determining—

(a) whether to award damages, or

(b) the amount of an award,

the court must take into account the principles applied by the European Court of Human Rights in relation to the award of compensation under Article 41 of the Convention.

(5) A public authority against which damages are awarded is to be treated—

(a) in Scotland, for the purposes of section 3 of the Law Reform (Miscellaneous Provisions) (Scotland) Act 1940 as if the award were made in an action of damages in which the authority has been found liable in respect of loss or damage to the person to whom the award is made;

(b) for the purposes of the Civil Liability (Contribution) Act 1978 as liable in respect of damage suffered by the person to whom the award is made.

(6) In this section—

'court' includes a tribunal;

'damages' means damages for an unlawful act of a public authority; and

'unlawful' means unlawful under section 6(1).

8.713 9 Judicial acts

(1) Proceedings under section 7(1)(a) in respect of a judicial act may be brought only—

(a) by exercising a right of appeal;

(b) on an application (in Scotland a petition) for judicial review; or

(c) in such other forum as may be prescribed by rules.

(2) That does not affect any rule of law which prevents a court from being the subject of judicial review.

(3) In proceedings under this Act in respect of a judicial act done in good faith, damages may not be awarded otherwise than to compensate a person to the extent required by Article 5(5) of the Convention.

(4) An award of damages permitted by subsection (3) is to be made against the Crown; but no award may be made unless the appropriate person, if not a party to the proceedings, is joined.

(5) In this section—

'appropriate person' means the Minister responsible for the court concerned, or a person or government department nominated by him;

'court' includes a tribunal;

'judge' includes a member of a tribunal, a justice of the peace . . . [1] and a clerk or other officer entitled to exercise the jurisdiction of a court;

'judicial act' means a judicial act of a court and includes an act done on the instructions, or on behalf, of a judge; and

'rules' has the same meaning as in section 7(9).

---

[1] Words omitted apply to Northern Ireland only.

Sections 10–20 not reproduced in this work.

8.714 21 Interpretation, etc

(1) In this Act—

'amend' includes repeal and apply (with or without modifications);

'the appropriate Minister' means the Minister of the Crown having charge of the appropriate authorised government department (within the meaning of the Crown Proceedings Act 1947);

'the Commission' means the European Commission of Human Rights;

'the Convention' means the Convention for the Protection of Human Rights and Fundamental Freedoms, agreed by the Council of Europe at Rome on 4th November 1950 as it has effect for the time being in relation to the United Kingdom;

'declaration of incompatibility' means a declaration under section 4;

'Minister of the Crown' has the same meaning as in the Ministers of the Crown Act 1975;

'Northern Ireland Minister' includes the First Minister and the deputy First Minister in Northern Ireland;

'primary legislation' means any—

(a) public general Act;

(b) local and personal Act;

(c) private Act;
(d) Measure of the Church Assembly;
(e) Measure of the General Synod of the Church of England;
(f) Order in Council—
  (i) made in exercise of Her Majesty's Royal Prerogative;
  (ii) made under section 38(1)(a) of the Northern Ireland Constitution Act 1973 or the corresponding provision of the Northern Ireland Act 1998; or
  (iii) amending an Act of a kind mentioned in paragraph (a), (b) or (c);

and includes an order or other instrument made under primary legislation (otherwise than by the *National Assembly for Wales*[1], a member of the Scottish Executive, a Northern Ireland Minister or a Northern Ireland department) to the extent to which it operates to bring one or more provisions of that legislation into force or amends any primary legislation;

'the First Protocol' means the protocol to the Convention agreed at Paris on 20th March 1952;

. . .[2]

["the Thirteenth Protocol" means the protocol to the Convention (concerning the abolition of the death penalty in all circumstances) agreed at Vilnius on 3rd May 2002;][2]

'the Eleventh Protocol' means the protocol to the Convention (restructuring the control machinery established by the Convention) agreed at Strasbourg on 11th May 1994;

'remedial order' means an order under section 10;

'subordinate legislation' means any—

(a) Order in Council other than one—
  (i) made in exercise of Her Majesty's Royal Prerogative;
  (ii) made under section 38(1)(a) of the Northern Ireland Constitution Act 1973 or the corresponding provision of the Northern Ireland Act 1998; or
  (iii) amending an Act of a kind mentioned in the definition of primary legislation;
(b) Act of the Scottish Parliament[1];
(c) Act of the Parliament of Northern Ireland;
(d) Measure of the Assembly established under section 1 of the Northern Ireland Assembly Act 1973;
(e) Act of the Northern Ireland Assembly;
(f) order, rules, regulations, scheme, warrant, byelaw or other instrument made under primary legislation (except to the extent to which it operates to bring one or more provisions of that legislation into force or amends any primary legislation);
(g) order, rules, regulations, scheme, warrant, byelaw or other instrument made under legislation mentioned in paragraph (b), (c), (d) or (e) or made under an Order in Council applying only to Northern Ireland;
(h) order, rules, regulations, scheme, warrant, byelaw or other instrument made by a member of the Scottish Executive,[1] a Northern Ireland Minister or a Northern Ireland department in exercise of prerogative or other executive functions of Her Majesty which are exercisable by such a person on behalf of Her Majesty;

'transferred matters' has the same meaning as in the Northern Ireland Act 1998; and

'tribunal' means any tribunal in which legal proceedings may be brought.

(2) The references in paragraphs (b) and (c) of section 2(1) to Articles are to Articles of the Convention as they had effect immediately before the coming into force of the Eleventh Protocol.

(3) The reference in paragraph (d) of section 2(1) to Article 46 includes a reference to Articles 32 and 54 of the Convention as they had effect immediately before the coming into force of the Eleventh Protocol.

(4) The references in section 2(1) to a report or decision of the Commission or a decision of the Committee of Ministers include references to a report or decision made as provided by paragraphs 3, 4 and 6 of Article 5 of the Eleventh Protocol (transitional provisions).

(5) Any liability under the Army Act 1955, the Air Force Act 1955 or the Naval Discipline Act 1957 to suffer death for an offence is replaced by a liability to imprisonment for life or any less punishment authorised by those Acts; and those Acts shall accordingly have effect with the necessary modifications.[3]

---

1 Sub-s (1): in definition 'primary legislation' words in italics substituted, in definition 'subordinate legislation' paras (ba), (bb) and words in para (h) inserted by the Government of Wales Act 2006, s 160(1), Sch 10, para 56. These amendments come into force immediately after the ordinary election (under the Government of Wales Act 1998, s 3) held in 2007: see the Government of Wales Act 2006, s 161(1); for further effect

2 Sub-s (1): definition omitted repealed and definition in square brackets inserted by SI 2004/1574, art 2(2).

3 Sub-s (5): repealed by the Armed Forces Act 2006, s 378(2), Sch 17 from a date to be appointed.

Section 22 not reproduced in this work.

8.715

SCHEDULE 1
THE ARTICLES
Section 1(3)

PART I
THE CONVENTION

RIGHTS AND FREEDOMS

8.716 *Articles 1–5 not reproduced in this work.*

Article 6
Right to a fair trial

1 In the determination of his civil rights and obligations or of any criminal charge against him, everyone is entitled to a fair and public hearing within a reasonable time by an independent and impartial tribunal established by law. Judgment shall be pronounced publicly but the press and public may be excluded from all or part of the trial in the interest of morals, public order or national security in a democratic society, where the interests of juveniles or the protection of the private life of the parties so require, or to the extent strictly necessary in the opinion of the court in special circumstances where publicity would prejudice the interests of justice.

2 Everyone charged with a criminal offence shall be presumed innocent until proved guilty according to law.

3 Everyone charged with a criminal offence has the following minimum rights:

(a) to be informed promptly, in a language which he understands and in detail, of the nature and cause of the accusation against him;

(b) to have adequate time and facilities for the preparation of his defence;

(c) to defend himself in person or through legal assistance of his own choosing or, if he has not sufficient means to pay for legal assistance, to be given it free when the interests of justice so require;

(d) to examine or have examined witnesses against him and to obtain the attendance and examination of witnesses on his behalf under the same conditions as witnesses against him;

(e) to have the free assistance of an interpreter if he cannot understand or speak the language used in court.

Article 7 not reproduced in this work.

Article 8
Right to respect for private and family life

1 Everyone has the right to respect for his private and family life, his home and his correspondence.

2 There shall be no interference by a public authority with the exercise of this right except such as is in accordance with the law and is necessary in a democratic society in the interests of national security, public safety or the economic well-being of the country, for the prevention of disorder or crime, for the protection of health or morals, or for the protection of the rights and freedoms of others.

Remainder of Part I not reproduced in this work.

PART II
THE FIRST PROTOCOL

Article 1
Protection of property

8.717 Every natural or legal person is entitled to the peaceful enjoyment of his possessions. No one shall be deprived of his possessions except in the public interest and subject to the conditions provided for by law and by the general principles of international law.

The preceding provisions shall not, however, in any way impair the right of a State to enforce such laws as it deems necessary to control the use of property in accordance with the general interest or to secure the payment of taxes or other contributions or penalties.

Remainder of Act not reproduced in this work.

Section 3

Statutory Instruments

MAGISTRATES' COURTS RULES 1981

(SI 1981/552)

Arrangement of rules

Appeal to Crown Court

8.1517 74 Documents to be sent to Crown Court

(1) A [[designated officer][2] for][1] a magistrates' court shall as soon as practicable send to the appropriate officer of the Crown Court any notice of appeal to the Crown Court given to the [[designated officer][2] for][1] the court.

(2) The [[designated officer][2] for][1] a magistrates' court shall send to the appropriate officer of the Crown Court, with the notice of appeal, a [copy of the extract of the magistrates' court register relating to that decision][3] and of the last known or usual place of abode of the parties to the appeal.

Paras (1) and (2) only reproduced: remainder not relevant to *Paterson's*.

---

1 Words in square brackets in both places they occur substituted by SI 2001/610, rr 2, 3.

2 Words 'designated officer' in square brackets further substituted by SI 2005/617, art 2, Schedule, para 85.

3 Words in square brackets substituted by SI 1993/1183, r 3(e).

8.1518 75 Abandonment of appeal

Where notice to abandon an appeal has been given by the appellant, any recognizance conditioned for the appearance of the appellant at the hearing of the appeal shall have effect as if conditioned for the appearance of the appellant before the court from whose decision the appeal was brought at a time and place to be notified to the appellant by the [[designated officer][2] for][1] that court.

---

1 Words in square brackets substituted by SI 2001/610, rr 2, 3.

2 Words 'designated officer' in square brackets further substituted by SI 2005/617, art 2, Schedule, para 85.

Case Stated

8.1519 76 Application to state case

(1) An application under section 111(1) of the Act of 1980 shall be made in writing and signed by or on behalf of the applicant and shall identify the question or questions of law or jurisdiction on which the opinion of the High Court is sought.

(2) Where one of the questions on which the opinion of the High Court is sought is whether there was evidence on which the magistrates' court could come to its decision, the particular finding of fact made by the magistrates' court which it is claimed cannot be supported by the evidence before the magistrates' court shall be specified in such application.

(3) Any such application shall be sent to the [[designated officer][2] for][1] the magistrates' court whose decision is questioned.

---

1 Words in square brackets substituted by SI 2001/610, rr 2, 3.

2 Words 'designated officer' in square brackets further substituted by SI 2005/617, art 2, Schedule, para 85.

8.1520 77 Consideration of draft case

(1) Within 21 days after receipt of an application made in accordance with rule 76, the [[designated officer][2] for][1] the magistrates' court whose decision is questioned shall, unless the justices refuse to state a case under section 111(5) of the Act of 1980, send a draft case in which are stated the matters required under rule 81 to the applicant or his solicitor and shall send a copy thereof to the respondent or his solicitor.

(2) Within 21 days after receipt of the draft case under paragraph (1), each party may make representations thereon. Any such representations shall be in writing and signed by or on behalf of the party making them and shall be sent to [the [designated officer][2]][3].

(3) Where the justices refuse to state a case under section 111(5) of the Act and they are required by the High Court by order of mandamus under section 111(6) to do so, this rule shall apply as if in paragraph (1)—

- (a) for the words 'receipt of an application made in accordance with rule 76' there were substituted the words 'the date on which an order of mandamus under section 111(6) of the Act of 1980 is made'; and
- (b) the words 'unless the justices refuse to state a case under section 111(5) of the Act of 1980' were omitted.

---

1 Words in square brackets substituted by SI 2001/610, rr 2, 3.

2 Words 'designated officer' in square brackets further substituted by SI 2005/617, art 2, Schedule, para 85.

3 Words in square brackets substituted by SI 2001/610, rr 2, 5.

8.1521 78 Preparation and submission of final case

(1) Within 21 days after the latest day on which representations may be made under rule 77, the justices whose decision is questioned shall make such adjustments, if any, to the draft case prepared for the purposes of that rule as they think fit, after considering any such representations, and shall state and sign the case.

(2) A case may be stated on behalf of the justices whose decision is questioned by any 2 or more of them and may, if the justices so direct, be signed on their behalf by their clerk.

(3) Forthwith after the case has been stated and signed the [[designated officer][2] for][1] the court shall send it to the applicant or his solicitor, together with any statement required by rule 79.

---

1 Words in square brackets substituted by SI 2001/610, rr 2, 3.

2 Words 'designated officer' in square brackets further substituted by SI 2005/617, art 2, Schedule, para 85.

8.1522 79 Extension of time limits

(1) If the [[designated officer][2] for][1] a magistrates' court is unable to send to the applicant a draft case under paragraph (1) of rule 77 within the time required by that paragraph, he shall do so as soon as practicable thereafter and the provisions of that rule shall apply accordingly; but in that event [the [designated officer][2] shall][3] attach to the draft case, and to the final case when it is sent to the applicant or his solicitor under rule 78(3), a statement of the delay and the reasons therefor.

(2) If the [[designated officer][2] for][1] a magistrates' court receives an application in writing from or on behalf of the applicant or the respondent for an extension of the time within which representations on the draft case may be made under paragraph (2) of rule 77, together with reasons in writing therefor, [the clerk of the magistrates' court may by notice in writing][4] sent to the applicant or respondent as the case may be [by the [designated officer][2]][4] extend the time and the provisions of that paragraph and of rule 78 shall apply accordingly; but in that event [the [designated officer][2] shall][3] attach to the final case, when it is sent to the applicant or his solicitor under rule 78(3), a statement of the extension and the reasons therefor.

(3) If the justices are unable to state a case within the time required by paragraph (1) of rule 78, they shall do so as soon as practicable thereafter and the provisions of that rule shall apply accordingly; but in that event [the [designated officer][2]][5] shall attach to the final case, when it is sent to the applicant or his solicitor under rule 78(3), a statement of the delay and the reasons therefor.

---

1 Words in square brackets substituted by SI 2001/610, rr 2, 3.

2 Words 'designated officer' in square brackets further substituted by SI 2005/617, art 2, Schedule, para 85.

3 Words in square brackets substituted by SI 2001/610, rr 2, 7.

4 Words in square brackets substituted by SI 2001/610, rr 2, 17.

5 Words in square brackets substituted by SI 2001/610, rr 2, 5.

8.1523 80 Service of documents

Any document required by rules 76 to 79 to be sent to any person shall either be delivered to him or be sent by post in a registered letter or by recorded delivery service and, if sent by post to an applicant or respondent, shall be addressed to him at his last known or usual place of abode.

8.1524 81 Content of case

(1) A case stated by the magistrates' court shall state the facts found by the court and the question or questions of law or jurisdiction on which the opinion of the High Court is sought.

(2) Where one of the questions on which the opinion of the High Court is sought is whether there was evidence on which the magistrates' court could come to its decision, the particular finding of fact which it is claimed cannot be supported by the evidence before the magistrates' court shall be specified in the case.

(3) Unless one of the questions on which the opinion of the High Court is sought is whether there was evidence on which the magistrates' court could come to its

decision, the case shall not contain a statement of evidence.

CROWN COURT RULES 1982

(SI 1982/1109)

Made ....*27th July 1982*
Laid before Parliament ....*16th August 1982*
In Operation ....*1st October 1982*

Arrangement of rules

* * * * *

We, the Crown Court Rule Committee, in exercise of the powers conferred upon us by section 9(3) of the Juries Act 1974, sections 5(1) and 8(4) of the Bail Act 1976 and sections 52, 73(2), 74(2), (3) and (7), 88, 81(2), 84(1) and (2), 86 and 87(5) of the Supreme Court Act 1981, hereby make the following Rules:—

PART I
INTRODUCTION

8.1527 1. Citation, commencement, revocations and transitionals

(1) These Rules may be cited as the Crown Court Rules 1982 and shall come into operation on 1st October 1982.

(2) Subject to paragraph (3), the instruments specified in Schedule 1 are hereby revoked.

(3) The transitional provisions in Schedule 2 shall have effect.

8.1528 2. Interpretation

(1) In these Rules, unless the context otherwise requires, any reference to a judge is a reference to a judge of the High Court or a Circuit judge or a Recorder; 'justice' means a justice of the peace; and 'Taxing Master' means a Master of the Supreme Court (Taxing Office).

(2) In these Rules any reference to a Rule or Schedule shall be construed as a reference to a Rule contained in these Rules or, as the case may be, to a Schedule thereto; and any reference in a Rule to a paragraph shall be construed as a reference to a paragraph of that Rule.

PART II
JUSTICES AS JUDGES OF CROWN COURT

8.1529 3. Number and qualification of justices

(1) Subject to the provisions of Rule 4 and to any directions under section 74(4) of the *Supreme Court Act 1981*[1], on any proceedings to which a subsequent paragraph of this Rule applies, the number of justices sitting to hear the proceedings and the qualification of those justices shall be as specified in that paragraph.

(2) On the hearing of an appeal against a decision of licensing justices under the Licensing Act 1964 the Crown Court shall consist of a judge sitting with four justices, each of whom is a member of a licensing committee appointed under Schedule 1 to that Act [and two (but not more than two) of whom are justices for the [local justice area][2] in which the premises to which the appeal relates are situated.][3,4,5]

(3) On the hearing of an appeal against a decision of any authority under the Betting, Gaming and Lotteries Act 1963 or the Gaming Act 1968, the Crown Court shall consist of a judge sitting with four justices, two (but not more than two) of whom are justices for the [local justice area][2] in which the premises to which the appeal relates are situated.[6]

* * * * *

---

1 Words 'Supreme Court Act 1981' substituted for the words in italics by the Constitutional Reform Act 2005, s 59(5), Sch 11, Pt 1, para 1(2) from a date to be appointed.

2 Words in square brackets substituted by SI 2005/617, art 2, Schedule, para 88.

3 See, however, SI 1982/1109, r 5.

4 See *Gosling v Preston Licensing Justices and the Chief Constable of Lancashire* [2001] LLR 27, Crown Ct and *R (on the application of the Chief Constable of Lancashire) v Preston Crown Court and Gosling*; *R (on the application of Smith) v Lincoln Crown Court* [2002] LLR 14, QBD discussed at para **8.61**.

5 The square brackets show that these words are to be deleted following the decision in *Gosling* and *Smith*.

6 See *In the matter of an appeal by Jack Brown (Bookmakers) Ltd against a decision of the Betting Licensing Committee for the petty sessional division of Cardiff*, the decision of Richards J, (11 Februray 2002, unreported) Cardiff Crown Court, noted at para **8.61** above. This reached a different conclusion on the facts from *Gosling*.

8.1530 4. Dispensations for special circumstances

(1) The Crown Court may enter on any appeal . . . [1] notwithstanding that the Court is not constituted as required by section 74(1) of the *Supreme Court Act 1981*[2] or Rule 3 if it appears to the judge that the Court could not be so constituted without unreasonable delay and the Court includes—

(a) in a case to which paragraph (2) of that Rule applies, at least two justices each of whom is a member of a committee specified in that paragraph, provided that the Court includes a justice for the [local justice area][3] so specified and a justice for some other area;

(b) in a case to which paragraph (3) of that Rule applies, at least two justices including a justice for the petty sessions area so specified and a justice for some other area;

(c)–(e) . . . [4]

Provided that the judge may sit without one or both of the justices required by sub-paragraphs (a) and (b) above if the parties appearing at the hearing of the appeal agree.

(2) . . . [5]

(3) The Crown Court may at any stage continue with any proceedings with a Court from which any one or more of the justices initially comprising the Court has withdrawn, or is absent for any reason.

1 Words omitted from para (1) revoked by the Crown Court (Amendment) Rules 1999, SI 1999/2838, r 2(2).

2 Words 'Senior Courts Act' substituted for words in italics by the Constitutional Reform Act 2005, s 59(5), Sch 11, Pt 1, para 1(2) from a date to be appointed.

3 Words in square brackets substituted by SI 2005/617, art 2, Schedule, para 88.

4 Paras (1)(c)–(e) not relevant to *Paterson's*.

5 Para 4(2) revoked by SI 1999/2838, r 2(3).

8.1531 5. Disqualifications

A justice of the peace shall not sit[1] in the Crown Court on the hearing of an appeal in a matter on which he adjudicated . . .[2].

1 The fact that a justice sitting in contravention of this rule takes no part in the hearing or in influencing or arriving at the decision is immaterial; see *R v Lancashire JJ* (1906) 70 JP 337.

2 Words omitted revoked by the Crown Court (Amendment) Rules 1999, SI 1999/2838, r 2(4).

PART III
APPEALS TO THE CROWN COURT

8.1532 6. Application of Part III

(1) Subject to the following provisions of this Rule, this Part of these Rules shall apply to every appeal which by or under any enactment lies to the Crown Court from any court, tribunal or person [except any appeal against a decision of a magistrates' court under section 22(7) or (8) of the Prosecution of Offences Act 1985][1] [or under section 1 of the Bail (Amendment) Act 1993][2].

(2) Without prejudice to rule 7(5), this Part of these Rules shall have effect subject to the provisions of the enactments specified in Part I of Schedule 3 (being enactments

which make special procedural provisions in respect of certain appeals), and those enactments shall have effect subject to the amendments set out in Part II of that Schedule (being amendments reproducing amendments made by Rule 6(2) of, and Part II of Schedule 1 to, the Crown Court Rules 1971).

---

1 Words in square brackets inserted by the Crown Court (Amendment) (No 3) Rules 1988, SI 1988/1635, r 2.

2 Words in square brackets inserted by the Crown Court (Amendment) Rules 1994, SI 1994/1480, r 3.

8.1533 7. Notice of appeal

(1) An appeal shall be commenced by the appellant's giving notice of appeal in accordance with the following provisions of this Rule.

[(2) The notice required by the preceding paragraph shall be in writing and shall be given—

- (a) in a case where the appeal is against a decision of a magistrates' court, to the [[designated officer][5] for][4] the magistrates' court;
- (b) in the case of an appeal under section [67B or][1] 81B of the Licensing Act 1964 against a decision of licensing justices, to the [designated officer for] 5 the justices;
- (c) in any other case, to the appropriate officer of the Crown Court; and
- (d) . . . [3]
- (e) in any case, to any other party to the appeal.][2]

(3) Notice of appeal shall be given not later than 21 days after the day on which the decision appealed against is given and, for this purpose, where the court has adjourned the trial of an information after conviction, that day shall be the day on which the court sentences or otherwise deals with the offender.

Provided that, where a court exercises its power to defer sentence under section 1(1) of the Powers of Criminal Courts Act 1973, that day shall, for the purposes of an appeal against conviction, be the day on which the court exercises that power.

(4) A notice of appeal shall state—

- (a) in the case of an appeal arising out of a conviction by a magistrates' court, whether the appeal is against conviction or sentence or both; and
- (b) in the case of an appeal under an enactment listed in Part III of Schedule 3, the grounds of appeal.

(5) The time for giving notice of appeal (whether prescribed under paragraph (3), or under an enactment listed in Part I of Schedule 3) may be extended, either before or after it expires, by the Crown Court, on an application made in accordance with paragraph (6).

(6) An application for an extension of time shall be made in writing, specifying the grounds of the application and sent to the appropriate officer of the Crown Court.

(7) Where the Crown Court extends the time for giving notice of appeal, the appropriate officer of the Crown Court shall give notice of the extension to—

- (a) the appellant;
- (b) in the case of an appeal from a decision of a magistrates' court, to the [[designated officer for][5] for][4] that court;
- (c) in the case of an appeal under section [678B or][1] 81B of the Licensing Act 1964 from a decision of licensing justices, to the [designated officer for][5] to the justices,

and the appellant shall give notice of the extension to any other party to the appeal . . . [3]

1 Words in square brackets inserted by the Crown Court (Amendment) (No 2) Rules 1988, SI 1988/1322, r 2, Schedule, para 1.

2 Para (2) substituted by the Crown Court (Amendment) Rules 1988, SI 1988/952, r 2(1), Schedule, para 1.

3 Words omitted not relevant to *Paterson's*.

4 Words in square brackets substituted by the Crown Court (Amendment) Rules 2001, SI 2001/614, r 2(1)–(3).

5 Words in square brackets substituted by SI 2005/617, art 2, Schedule, para 88.

8.1534 8. [Entry of appeal and notice of hearing

On receiving notice of appeal, the appropriate officer of the Crown Court shall enter the appeal and give notice of the time and place of the hearing to—

(a) the appellant;

(b) any other party to the appeal;

(c) in the case of an appeal from a decision of a magistrates' court, to the [[designated officer for] for][4] that court;

(d) in the case of an appeal under section [67B or][2] 81B of the Licensing Act 1964 from a decision of licensing justices, to the [chief executive][4] to the justices.

* * * * *[3]][1]

1 Substituted by the Crown Court (Amendment) Rules 1988, SI 1988/952, r 2(1), Schedule, para 3.

2 Words in square brackets inserted by the Crown Court (Amendment) (No 2) Rules 1988, SI 1988/1322, r 2, Schedule, para 1.

3 Paras (e) and (f) omitted as not relevant to *Paterson's*.

4 Words in square brackets substituted by the Crown Court (Amendment) Rules 2001, SI 2001/614, r 2(1)–(3).

8.1535 11. Abandonment of appeal

(1) Without prejudice to the power of the Crown Court to give leave for an appeal to be abandoned, an appellant may abandon an appeal by giving notice in writing, in accordance with the following provisions of this Rule, not later than the third day before the day fixed for hearing the appeal.

(2) The notice required by the preceding paragraph shall be given—

(a) in a case where the appeal is against a decision of a magistrates' court, to the [justices' chief executive for][4] the magistrates' court;

(b) in the case of an appeal under section 21 of the Licensing Act 1964, or in the case of an appeal under section [67B or][1] 81B of that Act against a decision of licensing justices to the [chief executive][4] to the licensing justices;

(c) in any other case, to the appropriate officer of the Crown Court; and

[(d) in any case, to any other party to the appeal . . . [3];][2]

and, in the case of an appeal mentioned in sub-paragraph (a) or (b), the appellant shall send a copy of the notice to the appropriate officer of the Crown Court.

(3) For the purposes of determining whether notice of abandonment was given in time there shall be disregarded any Saturday, Sunday and any day which is specified to be a bank holiday in England and Wales under section 1(1) of the Banking and Financial Dealings Act 1971.

No order for costs can be made by the Crown Court on the abandonment of an appeal by giving notice under this rule (see SI 1982/1109, r 12(3)). The

Magistrates' Courts Act 1980, s 109(1) as applied by the Licensing Act 1964, s 22(4) (or, as the case may be, LA 1964, s 81B(4)) enables an application to be made to 'the court against whose decision the appeal was brought' for an order for costs incurred before the notice of abandonment was given. There seems no room for doubt that in the case of an appeal against a decision of licensing justices where they are respondents as provided by the LA 1964, s 22(3) they may be the 'other party to the appeal' for the purposes of the MCA 1980, s 109. There is now no provision (as used to be the case before the jurisdiction of the Crown Court was excluded by the provision now contained in SI 1982/1109, r 12(3)(a)) for justices who cannot recover their costs in such a case to obtain payment out of central funds (cf the Licensing Act 1964, s 25(1)(b) in relation to an award by the Crown Court).

---

1 Words in square brackets inserted by the Crown Court (Amendment) (No 2) Rules 1988, SI 1988/1322, r 2, Schedule, para 2.

2 Para (2)(d) substituted by the Crown Court (Amendment) Rules 1988, SI 1988/952, r 2(1), Schedule, para 8.

3 Words omitted not relevant to *Paterson's*.

4 Words in square brackets substituted by the Crown Court (Amendment) Rules 2001, SI 2001/614, r 2(1)–(3).

PART IV
COSTS BETWEEN PARTIES IN CROWN COURT

8.1537 12. Jurisdiction to award costs

(1) Subject to the provisions of section 109(1) of the Magistrates' Courts Act 1980 (power of magistrates' courts to award costs on abandonment of appeals from magistrates' courts) and sections 22(4) and 81B(4) of the Licensing Act 1964 (application of section 109(1) of the Act of 1980 to appeals under sections 21 and 81B of the Act of 1964), no party shall be entitled to recover any costs of any proceedings in the Crown Court from any other party to the proceedings except under an order of the Court.

(2) Subject to the Prosecution of Offences Act 1985, Part II and to the following provisions of this Rule, the Crown Court may make such order for costs as it thinks just.

(3) In the case of an appeal under section 21 [or 67B][4] of the Licensing Act 1964—

- (a) no order for costs shall be made on the abandonment of an appeal by giving notice under Rule 11;[1]
- (b) no order for costs shall be made against a person who appeared before the licensing justices and opposed the grant of the justices' licence unless he appeared at the hearing of the appeal and opposed the appeal;
- (c) if the appeal, not being an appeal against the grant of a justices' licence, is dismissed, the Court shall order the appellant to pay to the justices against whose decision he has appealed, or such person as those justices may appoint,[2] such sum by way of costs as is, in the opinion of the Court, sufficient to indemnify the justices from all costs and charges to which they have been put in consequence of his having given notice of appeal.[3]

(4) In the case of an appeal under section 81B of the Licensing Act 1964 against a decision of licensing justices, no order for costs shall be made on the abandonment of an appeal by giving notice under Rule 11.[1]

(5) No order for costs shall be made on the abandonment of an appeal from a magistrates' court by giving notice under Rule 11.[1]

(6) Without prejudice to the generality of paragraph (2), the Crown Court may make an order for costs on dismissing an appeal where the appellant has failed to proceed with the appeal or on the abandonment of an appeal not being an appeal to which paragraph (3), (4) or (5) applies.

---

1 As to such costs, see the note to SI 1982/1109, r 11.

2 Before an order is made to pay such costs to the justices' clerk or some other named person, care should be taken to see that he has been 'appointed' to receive them (*cf R v Winder* [1900] 2 QB 666). The appointment must be signed by all the licensing justices whose decision is appealed against (per Bigham J, the Licensing Act 1964). See further, as to orders directing payment of costs to a wrong person, *R v Binney* (1853) 1 E&B810; *R v Ely JJ* (1855) 5 E&B 489; *R v Huntley* (1854)3 E&B 172; *R v Peek, etc Devonport JJ* (1869) 33 JP 614; *R v Davidson* (1871) 35 JP 500; *R v Goodall* (1874) LR 9 QB 557.

3 This provision does not apply in the case of an appeal against the grant of a licence, because the justices are not respondents (Licensing Act 1964, s 22(2)). Where an order is made under this para, and an item of costs is disallowed as not having been properly incurred, the justices cannot obtain an order for payment of such item under the LA 1964, s 25, inasmuch as the same principle is to be applied under both provisions with regard to the indemnity to which the justices are entitled (*R v West Riding of Yorkshire JJ* [1918] 1 KB 362). In this case ten guineas were taxed off an item of twenty-five guineas paid to King's Counsel. The court disapproved of the taxation, but was unable to interfere.

The costs to which the justices are entitled are solicitor and own clients' costs, which is more extensive than as between solicitor and client (*R v West Riding JJ*). The order for costs to be paid under this section is 'the widest order known to the law for the payment of costs' . . . and 'means costs properly incurred by the justices in defending the appeal' (per Lord Reading CJ (LA 1964)), and (per Sharman J), 'The appellant is to pay a proper indemnity and prevent the justices from being out of pocket. But such an order is not without a limit. No one is entitled to be extravagant either against a litigant or against a public fund, but subject to that, the costs should be taxed so that the justices are not out of pocket, and so that they are to have anything expended within reason and prudence. That is the highest scale known to the law' (*cf* also *Giles v Randall* [1915] 1 KB 290).

The amount of the costs, if not ascertained by the court itself, must be ascertained by the taxation of the appropriate officer. For detailed provisions dealing with the procedure on taxation see SI 1982/1109, rr 12ff.

Several other cases decided under the old law may still be relevant in relation to matters not specifically provided for in the Crown Court Rules 1982, SI 1982/1109. In one of these it was held that an order to pay costs 'to be taxed by the clerk of the peace' was bad, and that the amount must be specified by the court in its order (*R v Winder* [1900] 2 QB 666; *Sellwood v Mount* (1841) 1 QB 726); but the court could adopt his taxation as theirs, and this has been the usual practice.

4 Words in square brackets inserted by the Crown Court (Amendment) (No 2) Rules 1988, SI 1988/1322, r 2, Schedule, para 3.

8.1538 13. Costs in proceedings from which appeal is brought

Where an appeal is brought to the Crown Court from the decision of a magistrates' court or a tribunal and the appeal is successful, the Crown Court may make an order as to the costs of the proceedings in the magistrates' court or tribunal which that court or tribunal had power to make.

8.1539 14. Taxation

(1) Where under these Rules the Crown Court has made an order for the costs of any proceedings to be paid by a party and the Court has not fixed a sum, the amount of the costs to be paid shall be ascertained as soon as practicable by the appropriate officer of the Crown Court (hereinafter referred to as the taxing authority).

(2) On a taxation under the preceding paragraph or under the Prosecution of Offences Act 1985, Part II, there shall be allowed the costs reasonably incurred in or about the prosecution and conviction or the defence, as the case may be.

8.1540 15. Review by taxing authority

(1) Any party dissatisfied with the taxation of any costs by the taxing authority under the Prosecution of Offences Act 1985, Part II or Rule 14 may apply to the taxing authority to review his decision.

(2) The application shall be made by giving notice to the taxing authority and to any other party to the taxation within 14 days of the taxation, specifying the items in respect of which the application is made and the grounds of objection.

(3) Any party to whom notice is given under the preceding paragraph may within 14 days of the service of the notice deliver to the taxing authority answers in writing to the objections specified in that notice to the taxing authority and, if he does, shall send copies to the applicant for the review and to any other party to the taxation.

(4) The taxing authority shall reconsider his taxation in the light of the objections and answers, if any, of the parties and any oral representations made by or on their behalf and shall notify them of the result of his review.

8.1541 16. Further review by Taxing Master

(1) Any party dissatisfied with the result of a review of taxation under Rule 15 may, within 14 days of receiving notification thereof, request the taxing authority to supply him with reasons in writing for his decision and may within 14 days of the receipt of such reasons apply to the Chief Taxing Master for a further review and shall, in that case, give notice of the application to the taxing authority and to any other party to the taxation, to whom he shall also give a copy of the reasons given by the taxing authority.

(2) Such application shall state whether the applicant wishes to appear or be represented, or whether he will accept a decision given in his absence and shall be accompanied by a copy of the notice given under Rule 15, of any answer which may have been given under paragraph (3) thereof and of the reasons given by the taxing authority for his decision, together with the bill of costs and full supporting documents.

(3) A party to the taxation who receives notice of an application under this Rule shall inform the Chief Taxing Master whether he wishes to appear or be represented at the further review, or whether he will accept a decision given in his absence.

(4) The further review shall be conducted by a Taxing Master and if the applicant or any other party to the taxation has given notice of his intention to appear or be represented, the Taxing Master shall inform the parties (or their agents) of the date on which the further review will take place.

(5) Before reaching his decision the Taxing Master may consult the judge who made the order for costs and the taxing authority and, unless the Taxing Master otherwise directs, no further evidence shall be received on the hearing of the further review; and no ground of objection shall be valid which was not raised on the review under Rule 15.

(6) In making his review, the Taxing Master may alter the assessment of the taxing authority in respect of any sum allowed, whether by increase or decrease.

(7) The Taxing Master shall communicate the result of the further review to the parties and to the taxing authority.

8.1542 17. Appeal to High Court judge

(1) Any party dissatisfied with the result of a further review under Rule 16 may, within 14 days of receiving notification thereof, appeal by originating summons to a judge of the Queen's Bench Division of the High Court if, and only if, the Taxing Master certifies that the question to be decided involves a point of principle of general importance.

(2) On the hearing of the appeal the judge may reverse, affirm or amend the decision appealed against or make such other order as he thinks appropriate.

8.1543 18. Supplementary provisions

(1) On a further review or an appeal to a judge of the High Court the Taxing Master or judge may make such order as he thinks just in respect of the costs of the hearing of the further review or the appeal, as the case may be.

(2) The time prescribed by Rule 15, 16 or 17 may be extended by the taxing authority, Taxing Master or judge of the High Court on such terms as he thinks just.

PART V
MISCELLANEOUS

* * * * *

8.1544 26. Application to Crown Court to state case

(1) An application under section 28 of the Supreme Court Act 1981 to the Crown Court to state a case for the opinion of the High Court shall be made in writing to the appropriate officer of the Crown Court within 21 days after the date of the decision in respect of which the application is made.

(2) The application shall state the ground on which the decision of the Crown Court is questioned.

(3) After making the application, the applicant shall forthwith send a copy of it to the parties to the proceedings in the Crown Court.

(4) On receipt of the application, the appropriate officer of the Crown Court shall forthwith send it to the judge who presided at the proceedings in which the decision was made.

(5) On receipt of the application, the judge shall inform the appropriate officer of the Crown Court as to whether or not he has decided to state a case and that officer shall give notice in writing to the applicant of the judge's decision.

(6) If the judge considers that the application is frivolous, he may refuse to state a case and shall in that case, if the applicant so requires, cause a certificate stating the reasons for the refusal to be given to him.

(7) If the judge decides to state a case, the procedure to be followed shall, unless the judge in a particular case otherwise directs, be the procedure set out in paragraphs (8) to (12).

(8) The applicant shall, within 21 days of receiving the notice referred to in paragraph (5), draft a case and send a copy of it to the appropriate officer of the Crown Court and to the parties to the proceedings in the Crown Court.

(9) Each party to the proceedings in the Crown Court shall, within 21 days of receiving a copy of the draft case under paragraph (8), either—

(a) give notice in writing to the applicant and the appropriate officer of the Crown Court that he does not intend to take part in the proceedings before the High Court; or

(b) indicate in writing on the copy of the draft case that he agrees with it and send the copy to the appropriate officer of the Crown Court; or

(c) draft an alternative case and send it, together with the copy of the applicant's case, to the appropriate officer of the Crown Court.

(10) The judge shall consider the applicant's draft case and any alternative draft case sent to the appropriate officer of the Crown Court under paragraph (9)(c).

(11) If the Crown Court so orders, the applicant shall, before the case is stated and delivered to him, enter before an officer of the Crown Court into a recognizance, with or without sureties and in such sum as the Crown Court considers proper, having regard to the means of the applicant, conditioned to prosecute the appeal without delay.

(12) The judge shall state and sign a case within 14 days after either—

(a) the receipt of all the documents required to be sent to the appropriate officer of the Crown Court under paragraph (9); or

(b) the expiration of the period of 21 days referred to in that paragraph, whichever is the sooner.

(13) A case stated by the Crown Court shall state the facts found by the Crown Court, the submissions of the parties (including any authorities relied on by the parties during the course of those submissions), the decision of the Crown Court in respect of which the application is made and the question on which the opinion of the High Court is sought.

(14) Any time limit referred to in this Rule may be extended either before or after it expires by the Crown Court.

(15) If the judge decides not to state a case but the stating of a case is subsequently required by the High Court by order of mandamus, paragraphs (7) to (14) shall apply to the stating of the case save that—

(a) in paragraph (7) the words 'If the judge decides to state a case' shall be omitted; and

(b) in paragraph (8) for the words 'receiving the notice referred to in paragraph (5)' there shall be substituted the words 'the day on which the order of mandamus was made'.

8.1545 27. Business in chambers

(1) The jurisdiction of the Crown Court specified in the following paragraph may be exercised by a judge of the Crown Court sitting in chambers.

(2) The said jurisdiction is—[1]

(a), (b) . . . [1]

(c) hearing any application relating to procedural matters preliminary or incidental to proceedings in the Crown Court, . . . [1]

[(d) jurisdiction under rule 7(7), 9, 23, 25, 26 or 39;][1A]

[(dd) . . . [1B]

[(e) hearing applications under subsection (3) of section 22 of the Prosecution of Offences Act 1985 for the extension or further extension of a time limit imposed by regulations made under subsection (1) of that section;

(f) hearing an appeal brought by an accused under subsection (7) of the said section 22 against a decision of a magistrates' court to extend, or further extend, such a time limit or brought by the prosecution under subsection (8) thereof against a decision of a magistrates' court to refuse to extend, or further extend, such a time limit.][2]

[(g) hearing appeals under section 1 of the Bail (Amendment) Act 1993.][3]

[(h) jurisdiction under Rule 24ZA.][4]

1 Words omitted from para (2) not relevant to *Paterson*.

1A Para (d) substituted by Crown Court (Amendment) (No 3) Rules 2003, SI 2003/1664, r 2.

1B Para (dd) omitted as not relevant to *Paterson*.

2 Paras (e), (f) inserted by the Crown Court (Amendment) (No 3) Rules 1988, SI 1988/1635, r 4.

3 Para (g) inserted by the Crown Court (Amendment) Rules 1994, SI 1994/1480, r 5.

4 Para (h) added by the Crown Court (Amendment) (No 3) Rules 2000, SI 2000/3362, r 2(1), (6).

8.1546 27A. [Appeals relating to time limits

(1) This rule applies—

(a) to any appeal brought by an accused, under subsection (7) of section 22 of the Prosecution of Offences Act 1985, against a decision of a magistrates' court to extend, or further extend, time limit imposed by regulations made under subsection (1) of that section; and

(b) to any appeal brought by the prosecution, under subsection (8) of the said section 22, against a decision of a magistrates' court to refuse to extend, or further extend, such a time limit.

(2) An appeal to which this rule applies shall be commenced by the appellant's giving notice in writing of appeal—

(a) to the [justices' chief executive for][2] the magistrates' court which took the decision;

(b) if the appeal is brought by the accused, to the prosecutor and, if the prosecution is to be carried on by the Crown Prosecution Service, to the appropriate Crown Prosecutor;

(c) if the appeal is brought by the prosecution, to the accused; and

(d) to the appropriate officer of the Crown Court.

(3) The notice of an appeal to which this rule applies shall state the date on which the time limit applicable to the case is due to expire and, if the appeal is brought by the accused under section 22(7) of the Prosecution of Offences Act 1985, the date on which the time limit would have expired had the court decided not to extend or further extend the time limit.

(4) On receiving notice of an appeal to which this rule applies, the appropriate officer of the Crown Court shall enter the appeal and give notice of the time and place of the hearing to—

(a) the appellant;

(b) the other party to the appeal; and

(c) the [justices' chief executive for][2] the magistrates' court which took the decision.

(5) Without prejudice to the power of the Crown Court to give leave for an appeal to be abandoned, an appellant may abandon an appeal to which this rule applies by giving notice in writing to any person to whom notice of the appeal was required to be given by paragraph (2) not later than the third day preceding the day fixed for the hearing of the appeal:

Provided that, for the purpose of determining whether notice was properly given in accordance with this paragraph, there shall be disregarded any Saturday and Sunday and any day which is specified to be a bank holiday in England and Wales under section 1(1) of the Banking and Financial Dealings Act 1971.][1]

---

[1] Inserted by the Crown Court (Amendment) (No 3) Rules 1988, SI 1988/1635, r 5.

[2] Words in square brackets substituted by the Crown Court (Amendment) Rules 2001, SI 2001/614, r 2(1), (2).

8.1547 28. Service of documents

Any notice or other document which is required by these Rules to be given to any person may be served personally on that person or sent to him by post at his usual or last known residence or place of business in England or Wales or, in the case of a company, at the company's registered office in England or Wales.

SCHEDULE 1

REVOCATIONS

Rule 1(2)

[*Effect has been given to these revocations in the preceding pages.*]

SCHEDULE 2
TRANSITIONAL PROVISIONS
Rule 1(3)

[*For the text of these transitional provisions (the effect of which seems no longer of practical importance) see the 1985 and earlier editions of* Paterson.]

SCHEDULE 3
ENACTMENTS RELATING TO APPEALS TO CROWN COURT
Rules 6 and 7

PART I
ENACTMENTS MAKING SPECIAL PROVISIONS ABOUT PROCEDURE ON APPEALS TO CROWN COURT

8.1548

Chapter	Act	Section or Schedule
	* * * * *	
1963 c 2.	The Betting, Gaming and Lotteries Act 1963	Schedule 1, paragraphs 21, 28.
		Schedule 2, paragraph 6.
		Schedule 3, paragraph 13.
1963 c 33.	The London Government Act 1963	Schedule 12, paragraph 19(4).
1964 c 26.	The Licensing Act 1964	Sections 22, 50, [67B,] 81B, 146, 154.
	* * * * *	
1968 c 54.	The Theatres Act 1968	Section 14(4).
1968 c 65.	The Gaming Act 1968	Schedule 2, paragraphs 29, 31, 45, 46, 50, 61.
		Schedule 3, paragraphs 12, 13, 15, 16.
		Schedule 7, paragraphs 11, 20.
		Schedule 9, paragraph 11.
	* * * * *	
1976 c 32.	The Lotteries and Amusements Act 1976	Schedule 3, paragraph 8.
	* * * * *	

PART II
AMENDMENTS TO ENACTMENTS SPECIFIED IN PART I
[*Effect has been given to these amendments in the preceding pages.*]

PART III
APPEALS IN WHICH THE NOTICE OF APPEAL IS TO STATE THE GROUNDS OF APPEAL

8.1549

Chapter	Act	Section or Schedule
	* * * * *	
1963 c 2	The Betting, Gaming and	Schedule 1, paragraphs 21, 28.
	Lotteries Act 1963	Schedule 2, paragraph 6.
		Schedule 3, paragraph 13.
1963 c 33.	The London Government Act	Schedule 12, paragraph 19(2).
1964 c 26.	The Licensing Act 1964	Sections 22, 50, [67B,] 81B, 146,
	1963	154.
	* * * * *	
1968 c 54.	The Theatres Act 1968	Section 14(4).
1968 c 65.	The Gaming Act 1968	Schedule 2, paragraphs 29, 31, 45, 46, 50, 61.
		Schedule 3, paragraphs 12, 13, 15, 16.
		Schedule 7, paragraphs 11, 20.
		Schedule 9, paragraph 11.

Chapter	Act	Section or Schedule
1976 c 32.	The Lotteries and	Schedule 1, paragraph 5.
	Amusements Act 1976	Schedule 3, paragraph 8.
1982 c 30.	The Local Government	Schedule 5.
	(Miscellaneous Provisions)	Schedule 1, paragraph 17.
	Act 1982	Schedule 3, paragraph 27.
	* * * * *	
1982 c 33.	The Cinematograph	Section 4.
	(Amendment) Act 1982	
	* * * * *	

LOCAL AUTHORITIES (FUNCTIONS AND RESPONSIBILITIES) (ENGLAND) REGULATIONS 2000

(SI 2000/2853)

Made ....*19th October 2000*
Laid before Parliament ....*26th October 2000*
Coming into force ....*16th November 2000*

The Secretary of State for the Environment, Transport and the Regions, in exercise of the powers conferred on him by sections 13 and 105 of the Local Government Act 2000 hereby makes the following Regulations:

8.1569 1 Citation, commencement, application and interpretation

(1) These Regulations may be cited as the Local Authorities (Functions and Responsibilities) (England) Regulations 2000 and shall come into force on 16th November 2000.

(2) These Regulations apply in relation to local authorities in England.

(3) In these Regulations—

"the 1972 Act" means the Local Government Act 1972;

"the 1998 Act" means the School Standards and Framework Act 1998[; . . . [1]

"the 2004 Act" means the Planning and Compulsory Purchase Act 2004][2];

["the 2005 Act" means the Gambling Act 2005 (c 19)][3][; and

"the 2006 Act" means the Health Act 2006][4].

1 Definition "the 1998 Act" word omitted revoked by SI 2007/1557, reg 2(1), (2)(a).

2 Definition "the 2004 Act" and word omitted immediately preceding it inserted by SI 2005/929, reg 2(1), (2).

3 Definition "the 2005 Act" inserted by SI 2006/886, reg 2(1), (2).

4 Definition "the 2006 Act" and word "; and" immediately preceding it inserted by SI 2007/1557, reg 2(1), (2)(b).

8.1570 2 Functions not to be the responsibility of an authority's executive

(1) The functions of a local authority specified in column (1) of Schedule 1 to these Regulations by reference to the enactments, directions and circulars specified in relation to those functions in column (2) are not to be the responsibility of an executive of the authority.

(2) The functions of—

(a) imposing any condition, limitation or other restriction on an approval, consent, licence, permission or registration granted—

(i) in the exercise of a function specified in column (1) of Schedule 1; or

(ii) otherwise than by an executive of the authority, in the exercise of any function under a local Act; and

(b) determining any other terms to which any such approval, consent, licence, permission or registration is subject,

are not to be the responsibility of an executive of the authority.

(3) The function of determining whether, and in what manner, to enforce—

(a) any failure to comply with an approval, consent, licence, permission or registration granted as mentioned in paragraph (2)(a);

(b) any failure to comply with a condition, limitation or term to which any such approval, consent, licence, permission or registration is subject; or

(c) any other contravention in relation to a matter with regard to which the function of determining an application for approval, consent, licence, permission or registration would not be the responsibility of an executive of the authority,

is not to be the responsibility of an executive of the authority.

(4) The function of—

(a) amending, modifying or varying any such approval, consent, licence, permission or registration as is mentioned in paragraph (2), or any condition, limitation or term to which it is subject; or

(b) revoking any such approval, consent, licence, permission or registration,

is not to be the responsibility of an executive of the authority.

(5) The function of making any scheme authorised or required by regulations under section 18 (schemes for basic, attendance and special responsibility allowances for local authority members) of the Local Government and Housing Act 1989, or of amending, revoking or replacing any such scheme, is not to be the responsibility of an executive of the authority.

(6) The function of determining—

(a) the amount of any allowance payable under—

(i) subsection (5) of section 3 (chairman's expenses) of the 1972 Act;

(ii) subsection (4) of section 5 (vice-chairman's expenses) of that Act;

(iii) subsection (4) of section 173 (financial loss allowance) of that Act;

(iv) section 175 (allowances for attending conferences and meetings) of that Act;

(b) the rates at which payments are to be made under section 174 (travelling and subsistence allowances) of that Act;

(c) the amount of any allowance payable pursuant to a scheme under section 18 of the Local Government and Housing Act 1989, or the rates at which payments by way of any such allowance are to be made;

(d) whether a charge should be made for any approval, consent, licence, permit or registration the issue of which is not the responsibility of an executive of the authority; and

(e) where a charge is made for any such approval, consent, licence, permit or registration, the amount of the charge,

is not to be the responsibility of an executive of the authority.

[(6A) The function of making a request under section 14A(1) (requests for single-member electoral areas) of the Local Government Act 1992 for single-member electoral areas is not to be the responsibility of an executive of the authority.

(6B) The function of passing a resolution to change a scheme for elections under section 32(1), 37(1) or 39(1) (resolutions for schemes for elections) of the 2007 Act is not to be the responsibility of an executive of the authority.

(6C) The functions of—

(a) deciding whether to make proposals for a change in governance arrangements of the kind set out in sections 33A and 33B of the 2000 Act;

(b) deciding whether a change of the kind set out in section 33A of the 2000 Act should be subject to approval in a referendum under section 33E(5) of the Act; and

(c) passing a resolution to make a change in governance arrangements under section 33F of that Act,

are not to be the responsibility of an executive of the authority.

(6D) The functions of—

(a) including provision in executive arrangements for the council to remove the executive leader by resolution under section 44C(1) of the 2000 Act; and

(b) passing a resolution to remove the executive leader under 44C(2) of that Act,

are not to be the responsibility of an executive of the authority.

(6E) The function of making an order giving effect to recommendations made in a community governance review under section 86 (reorganisation of community governance) of the 2007 Act is not to be the responsibility of an authority's executive.

(6F) The duty to make a change in governance arrangements under paragraph 3 or 8 of Schedule 4 to the 2007 Act is not to be the responsibility of an authority's executive.][1]

(7) Section 101 (arrangements for discharge of functions by local authorities) of the 1972 Act shall not apply with respect to the discharge of any function mentioned in paragraph (5) or (6)(a) to (c).

(8) Subject to any provision of regulations under section 20 (joint exercise of functions) of the Local Government Act 2000, the function of—

(a) making arrangements for the discharge of functions by a committee or officer under section 101(5) of the 1972 Act; and

(b) making appointments under section 102 (appointment of committees) of the 1972 Act,

is not to be the responsibility of an executive of the authority.

(9) The functions of York City Council in relation to the management of the Yorkshire Museum and Gardens pursuant to an agreement dated 30th December 1960 between that Council and the Yorkshire Philosophical Society are not to be the responsibility of an executive of that Council.

(10) The functions of South Lakeland District Council in relation to the management of land at Lake Windermere pursuant to an agreement dated 1st April 1975 between that Council, Windermere Parish Council and Lakes Parish Council are not to be the responsibility of an executive of the District Council.

(11) Unless otherwise provided by any other provision of these Regulations, a function of a local authority which, by virtue of any enactment passed or made before the making of these Regulations, may be discharged only by an authority, is not to be the responsibility of an executive of the authority.

(12) In paragraphs (1) and (11), "enactment" includes an enactment contained in a local Act or comprised in subordinate legislation (within the meaning of the Interpretation Act 1978).

[1] Paras (6A)–(6F): inserted by SI 2008/516, regs 2, 4(b). Date in force: 31 March 2008: see SI 2008/516, reg 1(1)(a).

8.1571 3 Functions which may be the responsibility of an authority's executive

(1) The functions specified in Schedule 2 to these Regulations may be (but need not be) the responsibility of an executive of the authority.

(2) The functions of Hastings Borough Council in relation to the management of the Hastings and Saint Leonards Museum may be (but need not be) the responsibility of an executive of the Council.

(3) Where the functions mentioned in paragraph (2) are the responsibility of the Council's executive, the Hastings and Saint Leonards Museum Association may appoint persons who are for the time being members of the Association to attend any meeting of an overview and scrutiny committee of that Council, or of a sub-committee of any such committee ("the relevant committee or sub-committee"), at which the management of the Museum is the subject of consideration; and the persons so appointed shall, subject to paragraph (4), be entitled to speak and vote at the meeting on any question relating to the management of the Museum which falls to be decided at the meeting.

(4) The number of persons appointed as mentioned in paragraph (3) shall, as nearly as may be, bear to the number for the time being of members of the relevant committee or sub-committee, the same proportion as 2 bears to 5, but the number of persons representing the Association at any such meeting as is referred to in that paragraph as are entitled to vote shall not exceed the number of members of the relevant committee or sub-committee present at that meeting.

8.1572 4 Functions not to be the sole responsibility of an authority's executive

(1) In connection with the discharge of the function—

(a) of formulating or preparing a plan or strategy of a description specified in column (1) of Schedule 3 to these Regulations;

[(b) of formulating a plan or strategy for the control of the authority's borrowing, investments or capital expenditure; or][1]

(c) of formulating or preparing any other plan or strategy whose adoption or approval is, by virtue of regulation 5(1), a matter for determination by the authority,

the actions designated by paragraph (3) ("the paragraph (3) actions") shall not be the responsibility of an executive of the authority.

(2) Except to the extent of the paragraph (3) actions, any such function as is mentioned in paragraph (1) shall be the responsibility of such an executive.

(3) The actions designated by this paragraph are—

(a) the giving of instructions requiring the executive to reconsider any draft plan or strategy submitted by the executive for the authority's consideration;

(b) the amendment of any draft plan or strategy submitted by the executive for the authority's consideration;

[(bb) the approval, for the purposes of public consultation in accordance with regulation 10 or 22 of the Town and Country Planning (Development Plans) (England) Regulations 1999, of draft proposals associated with the preparation of alterations to, or the replacement of, a development plan;][2]

(c) the approval, for the purpose of its submission to the Secretary of State or any Minister of the Crown for his approval, of any plan or strategy (whether or not in the form of a draft) of which any part is required to be so submitted; . . . [3]

8: Appeals Applications and Procedure

[(ca) the approval, for the purpose of its submission to the Secretary of State for independent examination under section 20 (independent examination) of the 2004 Act, of a development plan document; and][4]

(d) the adoption (with or without modification) of the plan or strategy.

(4) The function of amending, modifying[, revising][5], [varying, withdrawing or revoking][6] any plan or strategy of a description referred to in paragraph (1), (whether approved or adopted before or after the coming into force of these Regulations)—

(a) shall be the responsibility of an executive of the authority to the extent that the making of the amendment, modification[, revision][7], [variation, withdrawal or revocation][8]—

(i) is required for giving effect to requirements of the Secretary of State or a Minister of the Crown in relation to a plan or strategy submitted for his approval, or to any part so submitted;

. . .

[(ia) is recommended by the person carrying out, under section 20 of the 2004 Act, an independent examination of a development plan document; or][10]

(ii) is authorised by a determination made by the authority when approving or adopting the plan or strategy, as the case may be; and

(b) shall not be the responsibility of such an executive to any other extent.

[(4A) In connection with the discharge of functions under any of sections 28 to 31 (joint local development documents and joint committees) of the 2004 Act, the actions designated by paragraph (4C) ("the paragraph (4C) actions") shall not be the responsibility of an executive of the authority.

(4B) Except to the extent of the paragraph (4C) actions, any such function as is mentioned in paragraph (4A) shall be the responsibility of such an executive.

(4C) The actions designated by this paragraph are—

(a) the making of an agreement to prepare one or more joint development plan documents;

(b) the making of an agreement to establish a joint committee to be, for the purposes of Part 2 (local development) of the 2004 Act, the local planning authority;

(c) where the authority is a constituent authority to a joint committee, the making of an agreement that the joint committee is to be, for the purposes of Part 2 of the 2004 Act, the local planning authority for any area or matter which is not the subject of an order under section 29 of the 2004 Act or an earlier agreement under section 30 of the 2004 Act; and

(d) the making of a request to the Secretary of State for the revocation of an order constituting a joint committee as the local planning authority for any area or in respect of any matter.][11]

(5) Except to the extent mentioned in paragraph (6), the function of making an application—

(a) under subsection (5) of section 135 (programmes for disposals) of the Leasehold Reform, Housing and Urban Development Act 1993, or [for the inclusion of a disposal in a disposals programme][12]

(b) [for consent to that disposal][13] under section 32 (power to dispose of land held for the purposes of Part II) or section 43 (consent required for certain disposals not within section 32) of the Housing Act 1985,

shall be the responsibility of an executive of the authority.

(6) The extent mentioned in this paragraph is the authorisation of the making of the application.

(7) The function of making such an application as is referred to in paragraph (5), to the extent mentioned in paragraph (6), shall not be the responsibility of an executive of the authority.

(8) Section 101 of the 1972 Act shall not apply with respect to the discharge—

(a) of a function specified in paragraph (1) to the extent that, by virtue of that paragraph, it is not the responsibility of an executive of the authority;

[(b) of the functions specified in paragraphs (4), (4A) and (5) to the extent that they are not the responsibility of an executive of the authority][14].

(9) In connection with the discharge of the function of—

(a) making a calculation in accordance with any of sections 32 to 37, 43 to 49, 52I, 52J, 52T and 52U of the Local Government Finance Act 1992, whether originally or by way of substitute; or

(b) issuing a precept under Chapter IV of Part I of that Act,

the actions designated by paragraph (11) ("the paragraph (11) actions") shall be the responsibility of an executive of the authority.

(10) Except to the extent of the paragraph (11) actions, any such function as is mentioned in paragraph (9) shall not be the responsibility of such an executive.

(11) The actions designated by this paragraph are—

(a) the preparation, for submission to the authority for their consideration, of—

(i) estimates of the amounts to be aggregated in making the calculation or of other amounts to be used for the purposes of the calculation and estimates of the calculation; or

(ii) the amounts required to be stated in the precept;

(b) the reconsideration of those estimates and amounts in accordance with the authority's requirements;

(c) the submission for the authority's consideration of revised estimates and amounts.

[(12) The function, pursuant to an order under section 70 (functions of local authorities) of the Deregulation and Contracting Out Act 1994, of authorising a person to exercise a function to which that section applies ("section 70 function")—

(a) shall be the responsibility of an executive of the authority to the extent that the section 70 function is the responsibility of that executive; and

(b) shall not be the responsibility of such an executive to any other extent.

(13) The function of revoking such an authorisation as is referred to in paragraph (12)—

(a) shall be the responsibility of an executive of the authority to the extent that the section 70 function is the responsibility of the executive; and

(b) shall not be the responsibility of such an executive to any other extent.][15]

---

1 Sub-para (b) substituted by SI 2004/1158, reg 2.

2 Sub-para (bb) inserted by SI 2001/2212, reg 2(a)(i).

3 In sub-para (c) word omitted revoked by SI 2005/929, reg 2(1), (3)(a).

4 Sub-para (ca) inserted by SI 2005/929, reg 2(1), (3)(a).

5 Word ", revising" in square brackets inserted by SI 2005/929, reg 2(1), (3)(b)(i).

6 Words "varying, withdrawing or revoking" in square brackets substituted by SI 2005/929, reg 2(1), (3)(b)(ii).

7 In sub-para (a) word ", revision" in square brackets inserted by SI 2005/929, reg 2(1), (3)(b)(iii)(aa).

8 In sub-para (a) words "variation, withdrawal or revocation" in square brackets substituted by SI 2005/929, reg 2(1), (3)(b)(iii)(bb).

9 In sub-para (a)(i) word omitted revoked by SI 2005/929, reg 2(1), (3)(b)(iii)(cc).

10 Sub-para (a)(ia) inserted by SI 2005/929, reg 2(1), (3)(b)(iii)(cc).

11 Paras (4A)–(4C): inserted by SI 2005/929, reg 2(1), (3)(c).

12 In sub-para (a) words "for the inclusion of a disposal in a disposals programme" in square brackets inserted by SI 2001/2212, reg 2(a)(ii).

13 In sub-para (b) words "for consent to that disposal" in square brackets inserted by SI 2001/2212, reg 2(a)(iii).

14 Sub-para (b) substituted by SI 2005/929, reg 2(1), (3)(d).

15 Paras (12), (13): inserted by SI 2001/2212, reg 2(a)(iv).

8.1573 5 Discharge of executive functions by authorities

(1) Subject to paragraph (2), a function of any of the descriptions specified in column (1) of Schedule 4 to these Regulations (which, but for this paragraph, might be the responsibility of an executive of the authority), shall not be the responsibility of such an executive in the circumstances specified in column (2) in relation to that function.

(2) Paragraph (1) shall not apply in relation to the discharge of a function of the description specified in paragraph 3 of column (1) of Schedule 4 where—

(a) the circumstances which render necessary the making of the determination may reasonably be regarded as urgent; and

(b) the individual or body by whom the determination is to be made has obtained from the chairman of a relevant overview and scrutiny committee or, if there is no such person, or if the chairman of every relevant overview and scrutiny committee is unable to act, from the chairman of the authority or, in his absence, from the vice-chairman, a statement in writing that the determination needs to be made as a matter of urgency.

(3) In paragraph (2) "relevant overview and scrutiny committee" means an overview and scrutiny committee of the authority concerned whose terms of reference include the power to review or scrutinise decisions or other actions taken in the discharge of the function to which the determination relates.

(4) The individual or body by whom a determination is made pursuant to paragraph (2) shall, as soon as reasonably practicable after the making of the determination, submit to the authority a report which shall include particulars of—

(a) the determination;

(b) the emergency or other circumstances in which it was made; and

(c) the reasons for the determination.

(5) Section 101 of the 1972 Act shall not apply with respect to the discharge of a function referred to in paragraph (1) which, by virtue of that paragraph, is not the responsibility of an executive of the authority.

SCHEDULE 1

FUNCTIONS NOT TO BE THE RESPONSIBILITY OF AN AUTHORITY'S EXECUTIVE

Regulation 2(1)

8.1574

(1)	(2)
Function	**Provision of Act or Statutory Instrument**
[A Functions relating to town and country planning and development control[1]	
1 . . .	. . .
2 . . .	. . .

(1)		(2)
Function		**Provision of Act or Statutory Instrument**
3	. . .	. . .
4	. . .	. . .[2]
5	Power to determine application for planning permission.	Sections 70(1)(a) and (b) and 72 of the Town and Country Planning Act 1990 (c 8).
6	Power to determine applications to develop land without compliance with conditions previously attached.	Section 73 of the Town and Country Planning Act 1990.
7	Power to grant planning permission for development already carried out.	Section 73A of the Town and Country Planning Act 1990.
8	Power to decline to determine application for planning permission.	Section 70A of the Town and Country Planning Act 1990.
9	Duties relating to the making of determinations of planning applications.	Sections 69, 76 and 92 of the Town and Country Planning Act 1990 and Articles 8, 10 to 13, 15 to 22 and 25 and 26 of the Town and Country Planning (General Development Procedure) Order 1995 (SI 1995/419) and directions made thereunder.
10	Power to determine application for planning permission made by a local authority, alone or jointly with another person.	Section 316 of the Town and Country Planning Act 1990 and the Town and Country Planning General Regulations 1992 (SI 1992/1492).
11	Power to make determinations, give approvals and agree certain other matters relating to the exercise of permitted development rights.	Parts 6, 7, 11, 17, 19, 20, 21 to 24, 26, 30 and 31 of Schedule 2 to the Town and Country Planning (General Permitted Development) Order 1995 (SI 1995/418).
12	Power to enter into agreement regulating development or use of land.	Section 106 of the Town and Country Planning Act 1990.
13	Power to issue a certificate of existing or proposed lawful use or development.	Sections 191(4) and 192(2) of the Town and Country Planning Act 1990.
14	Power to serve a completion notice.	Section 94(2) of the Town and Country Planning Act 1990.
15	Power to grant consent for the display of advertisements.	Section 220 of the Town and Country Planning Act 1990 and the Town and Country Planning (Control of Advertisements) Regulations 1992 (SI 1992/666).
16	Power to authorise entry onto land.	Section 196A of the Town and Country Planning Act 1990.
17	Power to require the discontinuance of a use of land.	Section 102 of the Town and Country Planning Act 1990.
18	Power to serve a planning contravention notice, breach of condition notice or stop notice.	Sections 171C, 187A and 183(1) of the Town and Country Planning Act 1990.
[18A	Power to issue a temporary stop notice.	Section 171E of the Town and Country Planning Act 1990.][3]
19	Power to issue an enforcement notice.	Section 172 of the Town and Country Planning Act 1990.

8: Appeals Applications and Procedure

(1) Function		(2) Provision of Act or Statutory Instrument
20	Power to apply for an injunction restraining a breach of planning control.	Section 187B of the Town and Country Planning Act 1990.
21	Power to determine applications for hazardous substances consent, and related powers.	Sections 9(1) and 10 of the Planning (Hazardous Substances) Act 1990.
22	Duty to determine conditions to which old mining permissions, relevant planning permissions relating to dormant sites or active Phase I or II sites, or mineral permissions relating to mining sites, as the case may be, are to be subject.	Paragraph 2(6)(a) of Schedule 2 to the Planning and Compensation Act 1991 (c 34), paragraph 9(6) of Schedule 13 to the Environment Act 1995 (c 25) and paragraph 6(5) of Schedule 14 to that Act.
23	Power to require proper maintenance of land.	Section 215(1) of the Town and Country Planning Act 1990.
24	Power to determine application for listed building consent, and related powers.	Sections 16(1) and (2), 17, 27(2) and 33(1) of the Planning (Listed Buildings and Buildings in Conservation Areas) Act 1990 (c 9).
25	Power to determine applications for conservation area consent.	Section 16(1) of the Planning (Listed Buildings and Buildings in Conservation Areas) Act 1990, as applied by section 74(3) of that Act.
26	Duties relating to applications for listed building consent and conservation area consent.	Sections 13(1) and 14(1) and (4) of the Planning (Listed Buildings and Buildings in Conservation Areas) Act 1990 and regulations 3 to 6 and 13 of the Town and Country Planning (Listed Buildings and Buildings in Conservation Areas) Regulations 1990 and paragraphs 8, 15 and 22 of the Department of the Environment Circular 14/97.
27	Power to serve a building preservation notice, and related powers.	Sections 3(1) and 4(1) of the Planning (Listed Buildings and Buildings in Conservation Areas) Act 1990.
28	Power to issue enforcement notice in relation to demolition of unlisted building in conservation area.	Section 38 of the Planning (Listed Buildings and Buildings in Conservation Areas) Act 1990.
29	Powers to acquire a listed building in need of repair and to serve a repairs notice.	Sections 47 and 48 of the Planning (Listed Buildings and Buildings in Conservation Areas) Act 1990.
30	Power to apply for an injunction in relation to a listed building.	Section 44A of the Planning (Listed Buildings and Buildings in Conservation Areas) Act 1990.
31	Power to execute urgent works.	Section 54 of the Planning (Listed Buildings and Buildings in Conservation Areas) Act 1990.]
B Licensing and registration functions (in so far as not covered by any other paragraph of this Schedule)		
1	Power to issue licences authorising the use of land as a caravan site ("site licences").	Section 3(3) of the Caravan Sites and Control of Development Act 1960 (c 62).

(1)		(2)
Function		**Provision of Act or Statutory Instrument**
2	Power to license the use of moveable dwellings and camping sites.	Section 269(1) of the Public Health Act 1936 (c 49).
3	Power to license hackney carriages and private hire vehicles.	(a) as to hackney carriages, the Town Police Clauses Act 1847 (10 & 11 Vict c 89), as extended by section 171 of the Public Health Act 1875 (38 & 39 Vict c 55), and section 15 of the Transport Act 1985 (c 67); and sections 47, 57, 58, 60 and 79 of the Local Government (Miscellaneous Provisions) Act 1976 (c 57); (b) as to private hire vehicles, sections 48, 57, 58, 60 and 79 of the Local Government (Miscellaneous Provisions) Act 1976.
4	Power to license drivers of hackney carriages and private hire vehicles.	Sections 51, 53, 54, 59, 61 and 79 of the Local Government (Miscellaneous Provisions) Act 1976.
5	Power to license operators of hackney carriages and private hire vehicles.	Sections 55 to 58, 62 and 79 of the Local Government (Miscellaneous Provisions) Act 1976.
6	Power to register pool promoters.	Schedule 2 to the Betting, Gaming and Lotteries Act 1963 (c 2).
7	Power to grant track betting licences.	Schedule 3 to the Betting, Gaming and Lotteries Act 1963.
8	Power to license inter-track betting schemes.	Schedules 5ZA to the Betting, Gaming and Lotteries Act 1963.
9	Power to grant permits in respect of premises with amusement machines.	Schedule 9 to the Gaming Act 1968 (c 65).
10	Power to register societies wishing to promote lotteries.	Schedule 1 to the Lotteries and Amusements Act 1976 (c 32).
11	Power to grant permits in respect of premises where amusements with prizes are provided.	Schedule 3 to the Lotteries and Amusements Act 1976.
12	Power to issue cinema and cinema club licences.	Section 1 of the Cinema Act 1985 (c 13).
13	Power to issue theatre licences.	Sections 12 to 14 of the Theatres Act 1968 (c 54).
14	Power to issue entertainments licences.	Section 12 of the Children and Young Persons Act 1933 (c 12), section 52 of, and Schedule 12 to, the London Government Act 1963 (c 33), section 79 of the Licensing Act 1964 (c 26), sections 1 to 5 and 7 of, and Parts I and II of the Schedule to, the Private Places of Entertainment (Licensing) Act 1967 (c 19) and Part I of, and Schedules 1 and 2 to, the Local Government (Miscellaneous Provisions) Act 1982 (c 30).

(1)		(2)
Function		**Provision of Act or Statutory Instrument**
[14A	Functions relating to licensing.	Sections 5 to 8 of the Licensing Act 2003 (c 17).][4]
[14B	Power to resolve not to issue a casino premises licence.	Section 166 of the 2005 Act.][5]
[14C	Power to designate officer of a licensing authority as an authorised person for a purpose relating to premises.	Section 304 of the 2005 Act.][6]
[14D	Power to institute criminal proceedings for offences under section 342 of the 2005 Act.	Section 346 of the 2005 Act.][7]
[14E	Power to exchange information.	Section 350 of the 2005 Act.][8]
[14F	Functions relating to the determination of fees for premises licences.	The Gambling (Premises Licence Fees) (England and Wales) Regulations 2007 (SI 2007/479).][9]
[14G	Functions relating to the registration and regulation of small society lotteries.	Part 5 of Schedule 11 to the 2005 Act.][25]

[FA Functions relating to smoke-free premises, etc[10]

(1)		(2)
Function		**Function**
1	Power to enforce offences relating to the display of no-smoking signs.	Section 6(5) of the 2006 Act.
2	Power to enforce offences relating to smoking in smoke-free places.	Section 7(4) of the 2006 Act.
3	Power to enforce offence of failing to prevent smoking in smoke-free places.	Section 8(4) of the 2006 Act.
4	Power to transfer enforcement functions to another enforcement authority.	Smoke-free (Premises and Enforcement) Regulations 2006 (SI 2006/3368).]
15	Power to license sex shops and sex cinemas.	The Local Government (Miscellaneous Provisions) Act 1982, section 2 and Schedule 3.
16	Power to license performances of hypnotism.	The Hypnotism Act 1952 (c 46).
17	Power to license premises for acupuncture, tattooing, ear-piercing and electrolysis.	Sections 13 to 17 of the Local Government (Miscellaneous Provisions) Act 1982.
18	Power to license pleasure boats and pleasure vessels.	Section 94 of the Public Health Acts Amendment Act 1907 (c 53).
19	Power to register door staff.	Paragraphs 1(2) and 9 of Schedule 12 to the London Government Act 1963 (c 33) and Part V of the London Local Authorities Act 1995 (c x).

(1) Function		(2) Provision of Act or Statutory Instrument
20	Power to license market and street trading.	Part III of, and Schedule 4 to, the Local Government (Miscellaneous Provisions) Act 1982, Part III of the London Local Authorities Act 1990 (c vii) and section 6 of the London Local Authorities Act 1994 (c xii).
21	Power to license night cafes and take-away food shops.	Section 2 of the Late Night Refreshment Houses Act 1969 (c 53), Part II of the London Local Authorities Act 1990 and section 5 of the London Local Authorities Act 1994.
22	Duty to keep list of persons entitled to sell non-medicinal poisons.	Sections 3(1)(b)(ii), 5, 6 and 11 of the Poisons Act 1972 (c 66).
23	Power to license dealers in game and the killing and selling of game.	Sections 5, 6, 17, 18 and 21 to 23 of the Game Act 1831 (c 32); sections 2 to 16 of the Game Licensing Act 1860 (c 90), section 4 of the Customs and Inland Revenue Act 1883 (c 10), sections 12(3) and 27 of the Local Government Act 1874 (c 73), and section 213 of the Local Government Act 1972 (c 70).
24	Power of register and license premises for the preparation of food.	Section 19 of the Food Safety Act 1990 (c 16).
25	Power to license scrap yards.	Section 1 of the Scrap Metal Dealers Act 1964 (c 69).
26	Power to issue, amend or replace safety certificates (whether general or special) for sports grounds.	The Safety of Sports Grounds Act 1975 (c 52).
27	Power to issue, cancel, amend or replace safety certificates for regulated stands at sports grounds.	Part III of the Fire Safety and Safety of Places of Sport Act 1987 (c 27).
28	Power to issue fire certificates.	Section 5 of the Fire Precautions Act 1971 (c 40).
29	Power to license premises for the breeding of dogs.	Section 1 of the Breeding of Dogs Act 1973 (c 60) and section 1 of the Breeding and Sale of Dogs (Welfare) Act 1999 (c 11).
30	Power to license pet shops and other establishments where animals are bred or kept for the purposes of carrying on a business.	Section 1 of the Pet Animals Act 1951 (c 35); section 1 of the Animal Boarding Establishments Act 1963 (c 43); the Riding Establishments Acts 1964 and 1970 (1964 c 70 and 1970 c 70); section 1 of the Breeding of Dogs Act 1973 (c 60), and sections 1 and 8 of the Breeding and Sale of Dogs (Welfare) Act 1999.
31	Power to register animal trainers and exhibitors.	Section 1 of the Performing Animals (Regulation) Act 1925 (c 38).
32	Power to license zoos.	Section 1 of the Zoo Licensing Act 1981 (c 37).
33	Power to license dangerous wild animals.	Section 1 of the Dangerous Wild Animals Act 1976 (c 38).

(1) Function		(2) Provision of Act or Statutory Instrument
34	Power to license knackers' yards.	Section 4 of the Slaughterhouses Act 1974. *See also* the Animal By-Products Order 1999 (SI 1999/646).
35	Power to license the employment of children.	Part II of the Children and Young Persons Act 1933 (c 33), byelaws made under that Part, and Part II of the Children and Young Persons Act 1963 (c 37).
36	Power to approve premises for the solemnisation of marriages.	Section 46A of the Marriage Act 1949 (c 76) and the Marriages (Approved Premises) Regulations 1995 (S I 1995/510).
37	Power to register common land or town or village greens, except where the power is exercisable solely for the purpose of giving effect to— (a) an exchange of lands effected by an order under section 19(3) of, or paragraph 6(4) of Schedule 3 to, the Acquisition of Land Act 1981 (c 67) or (b) an order under section 147 of the Inclosure Act 1845 (c 8 & 9 Vict c 118).	Regulation 6 of the Commons Registration (New Land) Regulations 1969 (SI 1969/1843).
38	Power to register variation of rights of common.	Regulation 29 of the Commons Registration (General) Regulations 1966 (SI 1966/1471).
39	Power to license persons to collect for charitable and other causes.	Section 5 of the Police, Factories etc (Miscellaneous Provisions) Act 1916 (c 31) and section 2 of the House to House Collections Act 1939 (c 44).
40	Power to grant consent for the operation of a loudspeaker.	Schedule 2 to the Noise and Statutory Nuisance Act 1993 (c 40).
41	Power to grant a street works licence.	Section 50 of the New Roads and Street Works Act 1991 (c 22).
42	Power to license agencies for the supply of nurses.	Section 2 of the Nurses Agencies Act 1957 (c 16).
43	Power to issue licences for the movement of pigs.	Article 12 of the Pigs (Records, Identification and Movement) Order 1995 (SI 1995/11).
44	Power to license the sale of pigs.	Article 13 of the Pigs (Records, Identification and Movement) Order 1995.
45	Power to license collecting centres for the movement of pigs.	Article 14 of the Pigs (Records, Identification and Movement) Order 1995.
46	Power to issue a licence to move cattle from a market.	Article 5(2) of the Cattle Identification Regulations 1998 (SI 1998/871).
[46A	Power to grant permission for provision, etc of services, amenities, recreation and refreshment facilities on highway, and related powers.	Sections 115E, 115F and 115K of the Highways Act 1980.

(1)		(2)
Function		**Provision of Act or Statutory Instrument**
47A	Duty to publish notice in respect of proposal to grant permission under section 115E of the Highways Act 1980.	Section 115G of the Highways Act 1980.]
47	Power to permit deposit of builder's skip on highway.	Section 139 of the Highways Act 1980 (c 66).
48	Power to license planting, retention and maintenance of trees etc in part of highway.	Section 142 of the Highways Act 1980.
49	Power to authorise erection of stiles etc on footpaths or bridleways.	Section 147 of the Highways Act 1980.
50	Power to license works in relation to buildings etc which obstruct the highway.	Section 169 of the Highways Act 1980.
51	Power to consent to temporary deposits or excavations in streets.	Section 171 of the Highways Act 1980.
52	Power to dispense with obligation to erect hoarding or fence.	Section 172 of the Highways Act 1980.
53	Power to restrict the placing of rails, beams etc over highways.	Section 178 of the Highways Act 1980.
54	Power to consent to construction of cellars etc under street.	Section 179 of the Highways Act 1980.
55	Power to consent to the making of openings into cellars etc under streets, and pavement lights and ventilators.	Section 180 of the Highways Act 1980.
56	Power to sanction use of parts of buildings for storage of celluloid.	Section 1 of the Celluloid and Cinematograph Film Act 1922 (c 35).
57	Power to approve meat product premises.	Regulations 4 and 5 of the Meat Products (Hygiene) Regulations 1994 (SI 1994/3082).
58	Power to approve premises for the production of minced meat or meat preparations.	Regulation 4 of the Minced Meat and Meat Preparations (Hygiene) Regulations 1995 (SI 1995/3205).
59	Power to approve dairy establishments.	Regulations 6 and 7 of the Dairy Products (Hygiene) Regulations 1995 (SI 1995/1086).
60	Power to approve egg product establishments.	Regulation 5 of the Egg Products Regulations 1993 (SI 1993/1520).
61	Power to issue licences to retail butchers' shops carrying out commercial operations in relation to unwrapped raw meat and selling or supplying both raw meat and ready-to-eat foods.	Schedule 1A to the Food Safety (General Food Hygiene) Regulations 1995 (SI 1995/1763).
62	Power to approve fish products premises.	Regulation 24 of the Food Safety (Fishery Products and Live Shellfish) (Hygiene) Regulations 1998 (SI 1998/994).
63	Power to approve dispatch or purification centres.	Regulation 11 of the Food Safety (Fishery Products and Live Shellfish) (Hygiene) Regulations 1998.

8: Appeals Applications and Procedure

(1) Function		(2) Provision of Act or Statutory Instrument
64	Power to register fishing vessels on board which shrimps or molluscs are cooked.	Regulation 21 of the Food Safety (Fishery Products and Live Shellfish) (Hygiene) Regulations 1998.
65	Power to approve factory vessels and fishery product establishments.	Regulation 24 of the Food Safety (Fishery Products and Live Shellfish) (Hygiene) Regulations 1998.
66	Power to register auction and wholesale markets.	Regulation 26 of the Food Safety (Fishery Products and Live Shellfish) (Hygiene) Regulations 1998.
67	Duty to keep register of food business premises.	Regulation 5 of the Food Premises (Registration) Regulations 1991 (SI 1991/2828).
68	Power to register food business premises.	Regulation 9 of the Food Premises (Registration) Regulations 1991.
[69	Power to issue near beer licence.	Sections 16 to 19 and 21 of the London Local Authorities Act 1995 (c x) and, to the extent that it does not have effect by virtue of regulation 2(3), section 25 of that Act.
70	Power to register premises or stalls for the sale of goods by way of competitive bidding	Section 28 of the Greater London Council (General Powers) Act 1984 (c xxvii).][12]
[71	Power to register motor salvage operators.	Part I of the Vehicles (Crime) Act 2001 (c 3).][13]
C Functions relating to health and safety at work		
Functions under any of the "relevant statutory provisions" within the meaning of Part I (health, safety and welfare in connection with work, and control of dangerous substances) of the Health and Safety at Work etc Act 1974, to the extent that those functions are discharged otherwise than in the authority's capacity as an employer.		Part I of the Health and Safety at Work etc Act 1974 (c 37).
D Functions relating to elections		
1	Duty to appoint an electoral registration officer.	Section 8(2) of the Representation of the People Act 1983 (c 2).
2	Power to assign officers in relation to requisitions of the registration officer.	Section 52(4) of the Representation of the People Act 1983.
3	Functions in relation to parishes and parish councils.	Part II of the Local Government and Rating Act 1997 (c 29) and subordinate legislation under that Part.
4	Power to dissolve small parish councils.	Section 10 of the Local Government Act 1972.
5	Power to make orders for grouping parishes, dissolving groups and separating parishes from groups.	Section 11 of the Local Government Act 1972.
6	Duty to appoint returning officer for local government elections.	Section 35 of the Representation of the People Act 1983.

(1)		(2)
Function		**Provision of Act or Statutory Instrument**
7	Duty to provide assistance at European Parliamentary elections.	Paragraph 4(3) and (4) of Schedule 1 to the European Parliamentary Elections Act 1978 (c 10).
8	Duty to divide constituency into polling districts.	Section 18 of the Representation of the People Act 1983.
9	Power to divide electoral divisions into polling districts at local government elections.	Section 31 of the Representation of the People Act 1983.
10	Powers in respect of holding of elections.	Section 39(4) of the Representation of the People Act 1983.
11	Power to pay expenses properly incurred by electoral registration officers.	Section 54 of the Representation of the People Act 1983.
12	Power to fill vacancies in the event of insufficient nominations.	Section 21 of the Representation of the People Act 1985.
13	Duty to declare vacancy in office in certain cases.	Section 86 of the Local Government Act 1972.
14	Duty to give public notice of a casual vacancy.	Section 87 of the Local Government Act 1972.
15	Power to make temporary appointments to parish councils.	Section 91 of the Local Government Act 1972.
16	Power to determine fees and conditions for supply of copies of, or extracts from, elections documents.	Rule 48(3) of the Local Elections (Principal Areas) Rules 1986 (SI 1986/2214) and rule 48(3) of the Local Elections (Parishes and Communities) Rules 1986 (SI 1986/2215).
17	Power to submit proposals to the Secretary of State for an order under section 10 (pilot schemes for local elections in England and Wales) of the Representation of the People Act 2000.	Section 10 of the Representation of the People Act 2000 (c 2).
E Functions relating to name and status of areas and individuals		
1	Power to change the name of a county, district or London borough.	Section 74 of the Local Government Act 1972.
2	Power to change the name of a parish.	Section 75 of the Local Government Act 1972.
3	Power to confer title of honorary alderman or to admit to be an honorary freeman.	Section 249 of the Local Government Act 1972.
4	Power to petition for a charter to confer borough status.	Section 245b of the Local Government Act 1972.
[F Power to make, amend, revoke, re-enact or enforce byelaws][14]		Any provision of any enactment (including a local Act), whenever passed, and section 14 of the Interpretation Act 1978 (c 30).
G Power to promote or oppose local or personal Bills		Section 239 of the Local Government Act 1972.
H Functions relating to pensions etc		

8: Appeals Applications and Procedure

(1) Function		(2) Provision of Act or Statutory Instrument
1	Functions relating to local government pensions, etc	Regulations under section 7, 12 or 24 of the Superannuation Act 1972 (c 11).
[2	Functions under the Fire-fighters' Pension Scheme relating to pensions, etc as respects persons employed by fire and rescue authorities pursuant to section 1 of the Fire and Rescue Services Act 2004	Sections 34 and 36 of the Fire and Rescue Services Act 2004 (c 21).][15]

[I Miscellaneous functions[16]

(1) Function		(2) Provision of Act or Statutory Instrument
Part I: functions relating to public rights of way		
1	Power to create footpath[, bridleway or restricted byway][17] by agreement.	Section 25 of the Highways Act 1980 (c 66).
2	Power to create footpaths[, bridleways and restricted byways].[18]	Section 26 of the Highways Act 1980.
3	Duty to keep register of information with respect to maps, statements and declarations.	Section 31A of the Highways Act 1980.
4	Power to stop up footpaths[, bridleways and restricted byways].[19]	Section 118 of the Highways Act 1980.
5	Power to determine application for public path extinguishment order.	Sections 118ZA and 118C(2) of the Highways Act 1980.
6	Power to make a rail crossing extinguishment order.	Section 118A of the Highways Act 1980.
7	Power to make a special extinguishment order.	Section 118B of the Highways Act 1980.
8	Power to divert footpaths[, bridleways and restricted byways].[20]	Section 119 of the Highways Act 1980.
9	Power to make a public path diversion order.	Sections 119ZA and 119C(4) of the Highways Act 1980.
10	Power to make a rail crossing diversion order.	Section 119A of the Highways Act 1980.
11	Power to make a special diversion order.	Section 119B of the Highways Act 1980.
12	Power to require applicant for order to enter into agreement.	Section 119C(3) of the Highways Act 1980.
13	Power to make an SSSI diversion order.	Section 119D of the Highways Act 1980.
14	Duty to keep register with respect to applications under sections 118ZA, 118C, 119ZA and 119C of the Highways Act 1980.	Section 121B of the Highways Act 1980.
15	Power to decline to determine certain applications.	Section 121C of the Highways Act 1980.

(1)		(2)
Function		**Provision of Act or Statutory Instrument**
16	Duty to assert and protect the rights of the public to use and enjoyment of highways.	Section 130 of the Highways Act 1980.
17	Duty to serve notice of proposed action in relation to obstruction.	Section 130A of the Highways Act 1980.
18	Power to apply for variation of order under section 130B of the Highways Act 1980.	Section 130B(7) of 0the Highways Act 1980.
19	Power to authorise temporary disturbance of surface of footpath[, bridleway or restricted byway].[21]	Section 135 of the Highways Act 1980.
20	Power temporarily to divert footpath[, bridleway or restricted byway].[22]	Section 135A of the Highways Act 1980.
21	Functions relating to the making good of damage and the removal of obstructions.	Section 135B of the Highways Act 1980.
22	Powers relating to the removal of things so deposited on highways as to be a nuisance.	Section 149 of the Highways Act 1980.
23	Power to extinguish certain public rights of way.	Section 32 of the Acquisition of Land Act 1981 (c 67).
24	Duty to keep definitive map and statement under review.	Section 53 of the Wildlife and Countryside Act 1981 (c 69).
25	Power to include modifications in other orders.	Section 53A of the Wildlife and Countryside Act 1981.
26	Duty to keep register of prescribed information with respect to applications under section 53(5) of the Wildlife and Countryside Act 1981.	Section 53B of the Wildlife and Countryside Act 1981.
27	. . .	. . .[23]
28	Power to prepare map and statement by way of consolidation of definitive map and statement.	Section 57A of the Wildlife and Countryside Act 1981.
29	Power to designate footpath as cycle track.	Section 3 of the Cycle Tracks Act 1984 (c 38).
30	Power to extinguish public right of way over land acquired for clearance.	Section 294 of the Housing Act 1981 (c 68).
[30A	Power to authorise stopping up or diversion of highway.	Section 247 of the Town and Country Planning Act 1990 (c 8).][24]
31	Power to authorise stopping-up or diversion of footpath[, bridleway or restricted byway].[25]	Section 257 of the Town and Country Planning Act 1990.
32	Power to extinguish public rights of way over land held for planning purposes.	Section 258 of the Town and Country Planning Act 1990.
33	Power to enter into agreements with respect to means of access.	Section 35 of the Countryside and Rights of Way Act 2000 (c 37).
34	Power to provide access in absence of agreement.	Section 37 of the Countryside and Rights of Way Act 2000.

8: Appeals Applications and Procedure

(1)		(2)
Function		**Provision of Act or Statutory Instrument**
Part II: other miscellaneous functions		
35	Functions relating to sea fisheries.	Sections 1, 2, 10 and 19 of the Sea Fisheries Regulation Act 1966 (c 38).
36	Power to make standing orders.	Section 106 of, and paragraph 42 of Schedule 12 to, the Local Government Act 1972 (c 70).
37	Power to appoint staff, and to determine the terms and conditions on which they hold office (including procedures for their dismissal).	Section 112 of the Local Government Act 1972.
38	Power to make standing orders as to contracts.	Section 135 of the Local Government Act 1972.
39	Duty to make arrangements for proper administration of financial affairs etc.	Section 151 of the Local Government Act 1972.
40	Power to appoint officers for particular purposes (appointment of "proper officers").	Section 270(3) of the Local Government Act 1972.
41	Power to make limestone pavement order.	Section 34(2) of the Wildlife and Countryside Act 1981 (c 69).
42	Power to make closing order with respect to take-away food shops.	Section 4 of the Local Government (Miscellaneous Provisions) Act 1982 (c 30).
43	Duty to designate officer as the head of the authority's paid service, and to provide staff, etc.	Section 4(1) of the Local Government and Housing Act 1989 (c 42).
44	Duty to designate officer as the monitoring officer, and to provide staff, etc.	Section 5(1) of the Local Government and Housing Act 1989.
[44A	Duty to provide staff, etc to person nominated by monitoring officer.	Sections 82A(4) and (5) of the Local Government Act 2000.
44B	Powers relating to overview and scrutiny committees (voting rights of co-opted members).	Paragraphs 12 and 14 of Schedule 1 to the Local Government Act 2000.] 26
45	Duty to approve authority's statement of accounts, income and expenditure and balance sheet, or record of payments and receipts (as the case may be).	The Accounts and Audit Regulations 1996 (SI 1996/590).
46	Powers relating to the protection of important hedgerows.	The Hedgerows Regulations 1997 (SI 1997/1160).
47	Powers relating to the preservation of trees.	Sections 197 to 214D of the Town and Country Planning Act 1990, and the Trees Regulations 1999 (SI 1999/1892).
[47A	Powers relating to complaints about high hedges.	Part 8 of the Anti-Social Behaviour Act 2003.][27]
48	Power to make payments or provide other benefits in cases of maladministration etc.	Section 92 of the Local Government Act 2000.

(1)		(2)
Function		**Provision of Act or Statutory Instrument**
[49	Power to make an order identifying a place as a designated public place for the purposes of police powers in relation to alcohol consumption.	Section 13(2) of the Criminal Justice and Police Act 2001 (c 16).][28]
[50	Power to make or revoke an order designating a locality as an alcohol disorder zone.	Section 16 of the Violent Crime Reduction Act 2006 (c 38).]
[51	Power to apply for an enforcement order against unlawful works on common land.	Section 41 of the Commons Act 2006.]
[52	Power to protect unclaimed registered common land and unclaimed town or village greens against unlawful interference.	Section 45(2)(a) of the Commons Act 2006.]
[53	Power to institute proceedings for offences in respect of unclaimed registered common land and unclaimed town or village greens.	Section 45(2)(b) of the Commons Act 2006.][30]

1 Para A (Functions relating to town and country planning and development control) substituted by SI 2004/2211, reg 2, Schedule.

2 In para A (Functions relating to town and country planning and development control) entries "1–4" (omitted) revoked by SI 2005/929, reg 2(1), (4)(a).

3 In para A (Functions relating to town and country planning and development control) entry "18A" inserted by SI 2005/929, reg 2(1), (4)(b), (c).

4 In para B (Licensing and registration functions) entry "14A" inserted by SI 2004/2748, reg 2(a), Schedule, Pt 1, para 1(1).

5 In para B (Licensing and registration functions) entry "14B" inserted by SI 2006/886, reg 2(1), (3), Schedule, Pt 1, para 1.

6 In para B (Licensing and registration functions) entry "14C" inserted by SI 2007/1284, reg 2(1), (2)(a), (b).

7 In para B (Licensing and registration functions) entry "14D" inserted by SI 2007/1284, reg 2(1), (2)(c), (d).

8 In para B (Licensing and registration functions) entry "14E" inserted by SI 2007/1284, reg 2(1), (2)(e), (f).

9 Table: in para B (Licensing and registration functions) entry "14F" inserted by SI 2007/1284, reg 2(1), (2)(g), (h).

10 Para FA (Functions relating to smoke-free premises, etc) inserted by SI 2007/1557, reg 2(1), (3), Schedule.

11 In para B (Licensing and registration functions) entries "46A" and "47A" inserted by SI 2004/2748, reg 2(a), Schedule, Pt 1, para 1(2).

12 In para B (Licensing and registration functions) entries "69" and "70" inserted by SI 2001/2212, reg 2(b), Schedule, Pt I, para 1.

13 In para B (Licensing and registration functions) entry "71" inserted by SI 2002/1916, reg 6.

14 Para F (Power to make, amend, revoke, re-enact or enforce byelaws) heading substituted by SI 2006/886, reg 2(1), (3), Schedule, Pt 1, para 2.

15 In para H (Functions relating to pensions etc) entry 2 substituted by SI 2004/3168, art 53.

16 Para I (Miscellaneous functions) substituted by SI 2001/2212, reg 2(b), Schedule, Pt I, para 2.

17 In para I (Miscellaneous functions) in entry "1" words ", bridleway or restricted byway" in square brackets substituted by SI 2006/1177, reg 2, Schedule, Pt II.

18 In para I (Miscellaneous functions) in entry "2" words ", bridleways and restricted byways"

in square brackets substituted by SI 2006/1177, reg 2, Schedule, Pt II.

19 In para I (Miscellaneous functions) in entry "4" words ", bridleways and restricted byways" in square brackets substituted by SI 2006/1177, reg 2, Schedule, Pt II.

20 In para I (Miscellaneous functions) in entry "8" words ", bridleways and restricted byways" in square brackets substituted by SI 2006/1177, reg 2, Schedule, Pt II.

21 In para I (Miscellaneous functions) in entry "19" words ", bridleway or restricted byway" in square brackets substituted by SI 2006/1177, reg 2, Schedule, Pt II.

22 In para I (Miscellaneous functions) in entry "20" words ", bridleway or restricted byway" in square brackets substituted by SI 2006/1177, reg 2, Schedule, Pt II.

23 In para I (Miscellaneous functions) entry "27" revoked by SI 2006/1177, reg 2, Schedule, Pt II.

24 In para I (Miscellaneous functions) entry "30A" inserted by SI 2004/2748, reg 2(a), Schedule, Pt 1, para 2(1).

25 In para I (Miscellaneous functions) in entry "31" words ", bridleway or restricted byway" in square brackets substituted by SI 2006/1177, reg 2, Schedule, Pt II.

26 In para I (Miscellaneous functions) entries "44A" and "44B" inserted by SI 2004/2748, reg 2(a), Schedule, Pt 1, para 2(2).

27 In para I (Miscellaneous functions) entry "47A" inserted by SI 2005/714, reg 2.

28 In para I (Miscellaneous functions) entry "49" (as inserted by SI 2001/2831, reg 10) substituted by SI 2007/806, reg 10.

29 Table: in para B (Licensing and registration functions) entry "14G" inserted by SI 2007/1950, reg 2(1), (3)(p), (q).

30 Table: in para I (Miscellaneous functions) entry 50 inserted by SI 2008/1430, reg 25 and entries 51 to 53 inserted by SI 2008/2787, reg 2.

SCHEDULE 2
FUNCTIONS WHICH MAY BE (BUT NEED NOT BE) THE RESPONSIBILITY OF AN AUTHORITY'S EXECUTIVE
Regulation 3(1)

8.1575

1 Any function under a local Act other than a function specified or referred to in regulation 2 or Schedule 1.

2 The determination of an appeal against any decision made by or on behalf of the authority.

3 The appointment of review boards under regulations under subsection (4) of section 34 (determination of claims and reviews) of the Social Security Act 1998.

[**4** The making of arrangements in relation to appeals against the exclusion of pupils from maintained schools.

5 The making of arrangements pursuant to sections 94(1), (1A) and (4) of the 1998 Act (admissions appeals).

6 The making of arrangements pursuant to section 95(2) of the 1998 Act (children to whom section 87 applies: appeals by governing bodies).][1]

7 The making of arrangements under section 20 (questions on police matters at council meetings) of the Police Act 1996 for enabling questions to be put on the discharge of the functions of a police authority.

8 The making of appointments under paragraphs 2 to 4 (appointment of members by relevant councils) of Schedule 2 (police authorities established under section 3) to the Police Act 1996.

9 The conducting of best value reviews in accordance with the provisions of any order for the time being having effect under section 5 (best value reviews) of the Local Government Act 1999.

10 Any function relating to contaminated land.

11 The discharge of any function relating to the control of pollution or the management of air quality.

12 The service of an abatement notice in respect of a statutory nuisance.

13 The passing of a resolution that Schedule 2 to the Noise and Statutory Nuisance Act 1993 should apply in the authority's area.

14 The inspection of the authority's area to detect any statutory nuisance.

15 The investigation of any complaint as to the existence of a statutory nuisance.

16 The obtaining of information under section 330 of the Town and Country Planning Act 1990 as to interests in land.

17 The obtaining of particulars of persons interested in land under section 16 of the Local Government (Miscellaneous Provisions) Act 1976.

18 The making of agreements for the execution of highways works.

19 The appointment of any individual—

- (a) to any office other than an office in which he is employed by the authority;
- (b) to any body other than—
  - (i) the authority;
  - (ii) a joint committee of two or more authorities; or
- (c) to any committee or sub-committee of such a body,

and the revocation of any such appointment.

[**20** The making of agreements with other local authorities for the placing of staff at the disposal of those other authorities.

Any function of a local authority in their capacity as a harbour authority (to the extent that the function does not fall within paragraph 1 of this Schedule.][2]

[1] Paras 4–6: substituted by SI 2004/2748, reg 2(b), Schedule, Pt 2.

[2] Paras 20, 21: inserted by SI 2001/2212, reg 2(c), Schedule, Pt II.

SCHEDULE 3

FUNCTIONS NOT TO BE THE SOLE RESPONSIBILITY OF AN AUTHORITY'S EXECUTIVE

Regulation 4(1)

8.1576

(1) *Plans and strategies*	(2) *Reference*
Annual Library Plan	Section 1(2) of the Public Libraries and Museums Act 1964 (c 75).
Best Value Performance Plan	Section 6(1) of the Local Government Act 1999 (c 27).
[Children and Young People's Plan	Children and Young People's Plan (England) Regulations 2005.][1]
. . .	. . . [2]
Community Strategy	Section 4 of the Local Government Act 2000 (c 22).
Crime and Disorder Reduction Strategy	Sections 5 and 6 of the Crime and Disorder Act 1998 (c 37).
[Development plan documents	Section 15 of the 2004 Act.][3]
[Licensing Authority Policy Statement	Section 349 of the 2005 Act.][4]
. . .	. . . [5]

(1) *Plans and strategies*	(2) *Reference*
[Local Transport Plan	Section 108(3) of the Transport Act 2000 (c 38).][6]
Plans and alterations which together comprise the Development Plan	(a) for Greater London and the metropolitan counties, section 27 of the Town and Country Planning Act 1990 (c 8); (b) for districts outside Greater London and the metropolitan counties, section 54 of that Act.
[Sustainable Community Strategy	Section 4 of the 2000 Act.][7]
Youth Justice Plan	Section 40 of the Crime and Disorder Act 1998 (c 37).

1 Entry "Children and Young People's Plan" substituted, for entry "Children's Services Plan" as originally enacted, by SI 2006/886, reg 2(1), (4), Schedule, Pt 2, para 3(a), (b).

2 Entry "Community Care Plan" (omitted) revoked by SI 2006/886, reg 2(1), (4), Schedule, Pt 2, para 3(c), (d).

3 Entry "Development plan documents" inserted by SI 2005/929, reg 2(1), (5).

4 Entry "Licensing Authority Policy Statement" substituted, for entry "Early Years Development Plan" as originally enacted, by SI 2006/886, reg 2(1), (4), Schedule, Pt 2, para 3(e), (f).

5 Entry "Education Development Plan" (omitted) revoked by SI 2006/886, reg 2(1), (4), Schedule, Pt 2, para 3(g), (h).

6 Entry "Local Transport Plan" inserted by SI 2001/2212, reg 2(d), Schedule, Pt III.

7 Entry "Sustainable Community Strategy" inserted by SI 2008/516, regs 2, 6(2)(e), (f).8.1577

SCHEDULE 4

CIRCUMSTANCES IN WHICH FUNCTIONS ARE NOT TO BE THE RESPONSIBILITY OF AN AUTHORITY'S EXECUTIVE

Regulation 5(1)

(1) *Function*	(2) *Circumstances*
1 The adoption or approval of a plan or strategy (whether statutory or non-statutory), other than a plan or strategy of a description referred to in regulation 4(1)(b) or Schedule 3.	The authority determines that the decision whether the plan or strategy should be adopted or approved should be taken by them.
2 The determination of any matter in the discharge of a function which—	The individual or body by whom, by virtue of any of sections 14 to 17 of the Local Government Act 2000 or provision made under section 18 or 20 of that Act, the determination is to be made—
(a) is the responsibility of the executive; and	(a) is minded to determine the matter contrary to, or not wholly in accordance with—

(1) *Function*	(2) *Circumstances*
(b) is concerned with the authority's budget, or their borrowing or capital expenditure.	(i) the authority's budget; or (ii) the plan or strategy for the time being approved or adopted by the authority in relation to their borrowing or capital expenditure; and (b) is not authorised by the authority's executive arrangements, financial regulations, standing orders or other rules or procedures to make a determination in those terms.
3 The determination of any matter in the discharge of a function—	The individual or body by whom, by virtue of any of sections 14 to 17 of the Local Government Act 2000 or provision made under section 18 or 20 of that Act, the determination is to be made, is minded to determine the matter in terms contrary to the plan or, as the case may be, the strategy adopted or approved by the authority.
(a) which is the responsibility of the executive; and (b) in relation to which a plan or strategy (whether statutory or non-statutory) has been adopted or approved by the authority.	

(2) Circumstances	(1) [illegible]
(a) [illegible] the authority's budget [illegible] (i) [illegible] the form of strategy for [illegible] than one being approved or adopted by the authority in relation to that borrowing or capital expenditure; and (b) is not authorised by the authority's executive arrangements, financial regulations, standing orders or other rules or procedures to make a determination in those circumstances.	(ii) [illegible] contained in the [illegible] authority's budget [illegible]
The individual or body [illegible] by virtue of section [illegible] of the Local Government Act 2000 or [illegible] provision made under section 20 of that Act, the determination is minded to determine the matter [illegible] contrary to the plan or strategy [illegible] the authority [illegible] approved by the authority.	5. The determination of any matter in the discharge of a function— (a) which is the responsibility of the executive; and (b) in relation to which a plan or strategy (whether statutory or non-statutory) has been adopted or approved by the authority [illegible]

Section 4

Additional Material

CIVIL PROCEDURE RULES 1998

1998/3132

PART 52
APPEALS 8.2000

PART 52
APPEALS

I
GENERAL RULES ABOUT APPEALS

8.2000 52.1 Scope and interpretation

[8.2001]

[(1) The rules in this Part apply to appeals to—

(a) the civil division of the Court of Appeal;
(b) the High Court; and
(c) a county court.

[(2) This Part does not apply to an appeal in detailed assessment proceedings against a decision of an authorised court officer.]

(Rules [47.20] to [47.23] deal with appeals against a decision of an authorised court officer in detailed assessment proceedings)

(3) In this Part—

(a) "appeal" includes an appeal by way of case stated;
(b) "appeal court" means the court to which an appeal is made;
(c) "lower court" means the court, tribunal or other person or body from whose decision an appeal is brought;
(d) "appellant" means a person who brings or seeks to bring an appeal;
(e) "respondent" means—
  (i) a person other than the appellant who was a party to the proceedings in the lower court and who is affected by the appeal; and
  (ii) a person who is permitted by the appeal court to be a party to the appeal; and
(f) "appeal notice" means an appellant's or respondent's notice.

(4) This Part is subject to any rule, enactment or practice direction which sets out special provisions with regard to any particular category of appeal.

Amendment

Inserted by SI 2000/221, r 19, Sch 5.

Para (2): substituted by SI 2000/2092, r 20; words omitted revoked by SI 2000/2092, r 21; references to '47.20' and '47.23' in square brackets substituted by SI 2005/3515, r 11(a).

8.2002 Rule 52.2 Parties to comply with [Practice Direction 52]

All parties to an appeal must comply with [Practice Direction 52].

Amendment

Provision heading: words 'Practice Direction 52' in square brackets substituted by SI 2009/3390, r 28(b)(i).

Words 'Practice Direction 52' in square brackets substituted by SI 2009/3390, r 28(c).

8.2003 Rule 52.3 Permission

(1) An appellant or respondent requires permission to appeal—

(a) where the appeal is from a decision of a judge in a county court or the High Court, except where the appeal is against—
  (i) a committal order;
  (ii) a refusal to grant habeas corpus; or
  (iii) a secure accommodation order made under section 25 of the Children Act 1989; or
(b) as provided by [Practice Direction 52].[1]

(Other enactments may provide that permission is required for particular appeals)

(2) An application for permission to appeal may be made—

(a) to the lower court at the hearing at which the decision to be appealed was made; or
(b) to the appeal court in an appeal notice.

(Rule 52.4 sets out the time limits for filing an appellant's notice at the appeal court. Rule 52.5 sets out the time limits for filing a respondent's notice at the appeal court. Any application for permission to appeal to the appeal court must be made in the appeal notice (see rules 52.4(1) and 52.5(3))

(Rule 52.13(1) provides that permission is required from the Court of Appeal for all appeals to that court from a decision of a county court or the High Court which was itself made on appeal)

(3) Where the lower court refuses an application for permission to appeal, a further application for permission to appeal may be made to the appeal court.

(4) [Subject to paragraph (4A), where] the appeal court, without a hearing, refuses permission to appeal, the person seeking permission may request the decision to be reconsidered at a hearing.

[(4A) Where the Court of Appeal refuses permission to appeal without a hearing, it may, if it considers that the application is totally without merit, make an order that the person seeking permission may not request the decision to be reconsidered at a hearing. . . .

(4B) Rule 3.3(5) will not apply to an order that the person seeking permission may not request the decision to be reconsidered at a hearing made under paragraph (4A).]

(5) A request under paragraph (4) must be filed within 7 days after service of the notice that permission has been refused.

(6) [Permission to appeal may be given only where]—

(a) the court considers that the appeal would have a real prospect of success; or

(b) there is some other compelling reason why the appeal should be heard.

(7) An order giving permission may—

(a) limit the issues to be heard; and

(b) be made subject to conditions.

(Rule 3.1(3) also provides that the court may make an order subject to conditions)

(Rule 25.15 provides for the court to order security for costs of an appeal)

Amendment

Inserted by SI 2000/221, r 19, Sch 5. Para (1): in sub-para (b) words 'Practice Direction 52' in square brackets substituted by SI 2009/3390, r 28(c).

Para (4): words 'Subject to paragraph (4A), where' in square brackets substituted by SI 2006/1689, r 7(1)(a).

Paras (4A), (4B): inserted by SI 2006/1689, r 7(1)(b).

Para (4A): first words omitted revoked by SI 2008/2178, r 26(a).

Parenthesis below para (4A) (omitted): revoked by SI 2008/2178, r 26(b).

Para (6): words 'Permission to appeal may be given only where' in square brackets substituted by SI 2005/3515, r 11(b).

8.2004 Rule 52.4 Appellant's notice

(1) Where the appellant seeks permission from the appeal court it must be requested in the appellant's notice.

(2) The appellant must file the appellant's notice at the appeal court within—

(a) such period as may be directed by the lower court [(which may be longer or shorter than the period referred to in sub-paragraph (b))]; or

(b) where the court makes no such direction, [21] days after the date of the decision of the lower court that the appellant wishes to appeal.

(3) [Subject to paragraph (4) and unless] the appeal court orders otherwise, [an appellant's notice] must be served on each respondent—

(a) as soon as practicable; and

(b) in any event not later than 7 days,

after it is filed.

[(4) Where an appellant seeks permission to appeal against a decision to refuse to grant an interim injunction under section 41 of the Policing and Crime Act 2009 the appellant is not required to serve the appellant's notice on the respondent.]

Amendment

Inserted by SI 2000/221, r 19, Sch 5.

Para (2): in sub-para (a) words '(which may be longer or shorter than the period referred to in sub-paragraph (b))' in square brackets inserted by SI 2005/3515, r 11(c)(i); in sub-para (b) reference to '21' in square brackets substituted by SI 2005/3515, r 11(c)(ii).

Para (3): words 'Subject to paragraph (4) and unless' in square brackets substituted by SI 2010/1953, r 6(a); words 'an appellant's notice' in square brackets substituted by SI 2005/3515, r 11(c)(iii).

Para (4): inserted by SI 2010/1953, r 6(b).

8.2005 Rule 52.5 Respondent's notice

(1) A respondent may file and serve a respondent's notice.

(2) A respondent who—

(a) is seeking permission to appeal from the appeal court; or

(b) wishes to ask the appeal court to uphold the order of the lower court for reasons different from or additional to those given by the lower court,

must file a respondent's notice.

(3) Where the respondent seeks permission from the appeal court it must be requested in the respondent's notice.

(4) A respondent's notice must be filed within—

(a) such period as may be directed by the lower court; or

(b) where the court makes no such direction, 14 days after the date in paragraph (5).

(5) The date referred to in paragraph (4) is—

(a) the date the respondent is served with the appellant's notice where—

(i) permission to appeal was given by the lower court; or

(ii) permission to appeal is not required;

(b) the date the respondent is served with notification that the appeal court has given the appellant permission to appeal; or

(c) the date the respondent is served with notification that the application for permission to appeal and the appeal itself are to be heard together.

(6) Unless the appeal court orders otherwise a respondent's notice must be served on the appellant and any other respondent—

(a) as soon as practicable; and

(b) in any event not later than 7 days,

after it is filed.

[(7) This rule does not apply where rule 52.4(4) applies.]]

Amendment

Inserted by SI 2000/221, r 19, Sch 5.

Para (7): inserted by SI 2010/1953, r 6(c).

8.2006 Rule 52.6 Variation of time

(1) An application to vary the time limit for filing an appeal notice must be made to the appeal court.

(2) The parties may not agree to extend any date or time limit set by—

(a) these Rules;

(b) [Practice Direction 52]; or

(c) an order of the appeal court or the lower court.

(Rule 3.1(2)(a) provides that the court may extend or shorten the time for compliance with any rule, practice direction or court order (even if an application for extension is made after the time for compliance has expired))

(Rule 3.1(2)(b) provides that the court may adjourn or bring forward a hearing)

Amendment

Inserted by SI 2000/221, r 19, Sch 5.

Para (2): in sub-para (b) words 'Practice Direction 52' in square brackets substituted by SI 2009/3390, r 28(c).

8.2007 Rule 52.7 Stay

Unless—

(a) the appeal court or the lower court orders otherwise; or

(b) the appeal is from the [Immigration and Asylum Chamber of the Upper Tribunal],

an appeal shall not operate as a stay of any order or decision of the lower court.

Amendment

Inserted by SI 2000/221, r 19, Sch 5.

In para (b) words 'Immigration and Asylum Chamber of the Upper Tribunal' in square brackets substituted by SI 2009/3390, r 28(d).

8.2008 Rule 52.8 Amendment of appeal notice

An appeal notice may not be amended without the permission of the appeal court.

Amendment

Inserted by SI 2000/221, r 19, Sch 5.

8.2009 Rule 52.9 Striking out appeal notices and setting aside or imposing conditions on permission to appeal

(1) The appeal court may—

(a) strike out the whole or part of an appeal r ice;

(b) set aside permission to appeal in whol or in part;

(c) impose or vary conditions upon ich an appeal may be brought.

(2) The court will only exercise its po rs under paragraph (1) where there is a compelling reason for doing so.

(3) Where a party was presn the hearing at which permission was given he may not subsequently apply order that the court exercise its powers under sub paragraphs (1)(b) or (1)

Amendment SI 2000/221, r 19, Sch 5.

Inse

Rule 52.10 Appeal court's powers

(1) In relation to an appeal the appeal court has all the powers of the lower court.

(Rule 52.1(4) provides that this Part is subject to any enactment that sets out special provisions with regard to any particular category of appeal—where such an enactment gives a statutory power to a tribunal, person or other body it may be the case that the appeal court may not exercise that power on an appeal)

(2) The appeal court has power to—

(a) affirm, set aside or vary any order or judgment made or given by the lower court;

(b) refer any claim or issue for determination by the lower court;

(c) order a new trial or hearing;

(d) make orders for the payment of interest;

(e) make a costs order.

(3) In an appeal from a claim tried with a jury the Court of Appeal may, instead of ordering a new trial—

(a) make an order for damages; or

(b) vary an award of damages made by the jury.

(4) The appeal court may exercise its powers in relation to the whole or part of an order of the lower court.

(Part 3 contains general rules about the court's case management powers)

[(5) If the appeal court—

(a) refuses an application for permission to appeal;

(b) strikes out an appellant's notice; or

(c) dismisses an appeal,

and it considers that the application, the appellant's notice or the appeal is totally without merit, the provisions of paragraph (6) must be complied with.

(6) Where paragraph (5) applies—

(a) the court's order must record the fact that it considers the application, the appellant's notice or the appeal to be totally without merit; and

(b) the court must at the same time consider whether it is appropriate to make a civil restraint order.]

Amendment

Inserted by SI 2000/221, r 19, Sch 5.
Paras (5), (6): inserted by SI 2004/2072, r 13.

8.2011 Rule 52.11 Hearing of appeals

(1) Every appeal will be limited to a review of the decision of the lower court unless—

(a) a practice direction makes different provision for a particular category of appeal; or

(b) the court considers that in the circumstances of an individual appeal it would be in the interests of justice to hold a re-hearing.

(2) Unless it orders otherwise, the appeal court will not receive—

(a) oral evidence; or

(b) evidence which was not before the lower court.

(3) The appeal court will allow an appeal where the decision of the lower court was—

(a) wrong; or

(b) unjust because of a serious procedural or other irregularity in the proceedings in the lower court.

(4) The appeal court may draw any inference of fact which it considers justified on the evidence.

(5) At the hearing of the appeal a party may not rely on a matter not contained in his appeal notice unless the appeal court gives permission.

Amendment

Inserted by SI 2000/221, r 19, Sch 5.

8.2012 Rule 52.12 Non-disclosure of Part 36 offers and payments

[(1) The fact that a Part 36 offer or payment into court has been made must not be disclosed to any judge of the appeal court who is to hear or determine-

(a) an application for permission to appeal; or

(b) an appeal,

until all questions (other than costs) have been determined.]

(2) Paragraph (1) does not apply if the Part 36 offer [or payment into court] is relevant to the substance of the appeal.

(3) Paragraph (1) does not prevent disclosure in any application in the appeal proceedings if disclosure of the fact that a Part 36 offer [or payment into court] has been made is properly relevant to the matter to be decided.

[(Rule 36.3 has the effect that a Part 36 offer made in proceedings at first instance will not have consequences in any appeal proceedings. Therefore, a fresh Part 36 offer needs to be made in appeal proceedings. However, rule 52.12 applies to a Part 36 offer whether made in the original proceedings or in the appeal.)]

Amendment

Inserted by SI 2000/221, r 19, Sch 5.

Para (1): substituted by SI 2003/3361, r 10; words 'or payment into court' in square brackets substituted by SI 2006/3435, r 13(a).

Para (2): words 'or payment into court' in square brackets substituted by SI 2006/3435, r 13(b).

Para (3): words 'or payment into court' in square brackets substituted by SI 2006/3435, r 13(c).

Words from '(Rule 36.3 has' to 'in the appeal.)' in square brackets inserted by SI 2006/3435, r 13(d).

8.2012A [Rule 52.12A Statutory appeals—court's power to hear any person

(1) In a statutory appeal, any person may apply for permission—

(a) to file evidence; or

(b) to make representations at the appeal hearing.

(2) An application under paragraph (1) must be made promptly.]

Amendment

Inserted by SI 2007/2204, r 18(c).

II

SPECIAL PROVISIONS APPLYING TO THE COURT OF APPEAL

8.2013 Rule 52.13 Second appeals to the court

(1) Permission is required from the Court of Appeal for any appeal to that court from a decision of a county court or the High Court which was itself made on appeal.

(2) The Court of Appeal will not give permission unless it considers that—

(a) the appeal would raise an important point of principle or practice; or

(b) there is some other compelling reason for the Court of Appeal to hear it.

Amendment

Inserted by SI 2007/2204, r 18(c).

8.2014 Rule 52.14 Assignment of appeals to the Court of Appeal

(1) Where the court from or to which an appeal is made or from which permission to appeal is sought ("the relevant court") considers that—

(a) an appeal which is to be heard by a county court or the High Court would raise an important point of principle or practice; or

(b) there is some other compelling reason for the Court of Appeal to hear it,

the relevant court may order the appeal to be transferred to the Court of Appeal.

(The Master of the Rolls has the power to direct that an appeal which would be heard by a county court or the High Court should be heard instead by the Court of Appeal—see section 57 of the Access to Justice Act 1999)

(2) The Master of the Rolls or the Court of Appeal may remit an appeal to the court in which the original appeal was or would have been brought.

Amendment

Inserted by SI 2007/2204, r 18(c).

8.2015 Rule 52.15 Judicial review appeals

(1) Where permission to apply for judicial review has been refused at a hearing in the High Court, the person seeking that permission may apply to the Court of Appeal for permission to appeal.

(2) An application in accordance with paragraph (1) must be made within 7 days of the decision of the High Court to refuse to give permission to apply for judicial review.

(3) On an application under paragraph (1), the Court of Appeal may, instead of giving permission to appeal, give permission to apply for judicial review.

(4) Where the Court of Appeal gives permission to apply for judicial review in accordance with paragraph (3), the case will proceed in the High Court unless the Court of Appeal orders otherwise.

Amendment

Inserted by SI 2007/2204, r 18(c).

8.2016 Rule 52.16 Who may exercise the powers of the Court of Appeal

(1) A court officer assigned to the Civil Appeals Office who is—

(a) a barrister; or

(b) a solicitor

may exercise the jurisdiction of the Court of Appeal with regard to the matters set out in paragraph (2) with the consent of the Master of the Rolls.

(2) The matters referred to in paragraph (1) are—

(a) any matter incidental to any proceedings in the Court of Appeal;

(b) any other matter where there is no substantial dispute between the parties; and

(c) the dismissal of an appeal or application where a party has failed to comply with any order, rule or practice direction.

(3) A court officer may not decide an application for—

(a) permission to appeal;

(b) bail pending an appeal;

(c) an injunction;

(d) a stay of any proceedings, other than a temporary stay of any order or decision of the lower court over a period when the Court of Appeal is not sitting or cannot conveniently be convened.

(4) Decisions of a court officer may be made without a hearing.

(5) A party may request any decision of a court officer to be reviewed by the Court of Appeal.

(6) At the request of a party, a hearing will be held to reconsider a decision of—

(a) a single judge; or

(b) a court officer,

made without a hearing.

[(6A) A request under paragraph (5) or (6) must be filed within 7 days after the party is served with notice of the decision.]

(7) A single judge may refer any matter for a decision by a court consisting of two or more judges.

(Section 54(6) of the [Senior Courts Act 1981] provides that there is no appeal from the decision of a single judge on an application for permission to appeal)

(Section 58(2) of the [Senior Courts Act 1981] provides that there is no appeal to the [Supreme Court] from decisions of the Court of Appeal that—

(a) are taken by a single judge or any officer or member of staff of that court in proceedings incidental to any cause or matter pending before the civil division of that court; and

(b) do not involve the determination of an appeal or of an application for permission to appeal,

and which may be called into question by rules of court. Rules 52.16(5) and (6) provide the procedure for the calling into question of such decisions)

Amendment

Inserted by SI 2000/221, r 19, Sch 5. Para (6A): inserted by SI 2003/3361, r 11.

Para (7): words 'Senior Courts Act 1981' in square brackets in both places they occur substituted by the Constitutional Reform Act 2005, s 59(5), Sch 11, Pt 1, para 1(2); words 'Supreme Court' in square brackets substituted by SI 2009/2092, r 10.

III
PROVISIONS ABOUT REOPENING APPEALS

8.2017 Rule 52.17 Reopening of final appeals

(1) The Court of Appeal or the High Court will not reopen a final determination of any appeal unless—

(a) it is necessary to do so in order to avoid real injustice;

(b) the circumstances are exceptional and make it appropriate to reopen the appeal; and

(c) there is no alternative effective remedy.

(2) In paragraphs (1), (3), (4) and (6), "appeal" includes an application for permission to appeal.

(3) This rule does not apply to appeals to a county court.

(4) Permission is needed to make an application under this rule to reopen a final determination of an appeal even in cases where under rule 52.3(1) permission was not needed for the original appeal.

(5) There is no right to an oral hearing of an application for permission unless, exceptionally, the judge so directs.

(6) The judge will not grant permission without directing the application to be served on the other party to the original appeal and giving him an opportunity to make representations.

(7) There is no right of appeal or review from the decision of the judge on the application for permission, which is final.

(8) The procedure for making an application for permission is set out in [Practice Direction 52].]

Amendment

Inserted by SI 2003/2113, r 14.

Para (8): words 'Practice Direction 52' in square brackets substituted by SI 2009/3390, r 28(b)(ii).

IV
STATUTORY RIGHTS OF APPEAL

8.2017.1 52.18 Appeals under the Law of Property Act 1922

An appeal lies to the High Court against a decision of the Secretary of State under paragraph 16 of Schedule 15 to the Law of Property Act 1922.

Amendment

Inserted by SI 2007/2204, r 18(d).

8.2017.2 52.19 Appeals from certain tribunals

(1) A person who was a party to proceedings before a tribunal referred to in section 11(1) of the Tribunals and Inquiries Act 1992 and is dissatisfied in point of law with the decision of the tribunal may appeal to the High Court.

(2) The tribunal may, of its own initiative or at the request of a party to the proceedings before it, state, in the form of a special case for the decision of the High Court, a question of law arising in the course of the proceedings.

Amendment

Inserted by SI 2007/2204, r 18(d).

8.2017.3 52.20 Appeals under certain planning legislation

(1) Where the Secretary of State has given a decision in proceedings on an appeal under Part VII of the Town and Country Planning Act 1990 against an enforcement notice—

(a) the appellant;

(b) the local planning authority; or

(c) another person having an interest in the land to which the notice relates,

may appeal to the High Court against the decision on a point of law.

(2) Where the Secretary of State has given a decision in proceedings on an appeal under Part VIII of that Act against a notice under section 207 of that Act—

(a) the appellant;

(b) the local planning authority; or

(c) any person (other than the appellant) on whom the notice was served,

may appeal to the High Court against the decision on a point of law.

(3) Where the Secretary of State has given a decision in proceedings on an appeal under section 39 of the Planning (Listed Buildings and Conservation Areas) Act 1990 against a listed building enforcement notice—

(a) the appellant;

(b) the local planning authority; or

(c) any other person having an interest in the land to which the notice relates,

may appeal to the High Court against the decision on a point of law.

Amendment

Inserted by SI 2007/2204, r 18(d).

PRACTICE DIRECTION 52A—APPEALS: GENERAL PROVISIONS

THIS PRACTICE DIRECTION SUPPLEMENTS PART 52

CONTENTS OF THIS PRACTICE DIRECTION

8.2018 This Practice Direction is divided into the following sections—

SECTION 1: PRACTICE DIRECTIONS SUPPLEMENTING PART 52

1.1 There are five Practice Directions supplementing Part 52—

PD 52A — Appeals: General Provisions
PD 52B — Appeals in the county courts and the High Court
PD 52C — Appeals to the Court of Appeal
PD 52D — Statutory appeals and Appeals subjec to specific provision
PD 52E — Appeals by way of case stated

SECTION 2: INTRODUCTION

2.1 These Practice Directions apply to all appeals to which Part 52 applies.

2.2 Part 52 complements the provisions of sections 54 to 57 of the Access to Justice Act 1999 and provides a uniform procedure for appeals in the county courts and the High Court and a modified procedure for the Civil Division of the Court of Appeal. Part 52 does not apply to—

(a) family proceedings in the High Court or county courts but does apply to appeals to the Court of Appeal from decisions made in family proceedings with such modifications as may be required;

(b) appeals in detailed assessment proceedings against the decision of an authorised court officer.

SECTION 3: DESTINATIONS OF APPEAL

3.1 Section 56 of the Access to Justice Act 1999 enables the Lord Chancellor by Order to specify the destinations of appeal in different cases. The Access to Justice Act 1999 (Destination of Appeals) Order 2000, SI 2000/1071 made under section 56, specifies the general destinations of appeal which apply subject to any statutory provision to the contrary. The destinations of appeal provided by that Order are explained in the following paragraphs of this section of this Practice Direction.

3.2 "Statutory appeals" and "Appeals by way of case stated" are dealt with in PD52D— refer to those provisions for the appropriate court to which such an appeal may lie.

3.3 The court or judge to which an appeal is to be made (subject to obtaining any necessary permission) is set out in the tables below—

Table 1 deals with appeals in proceedings other than family and insolvency proceedings;
Table 2 deals with appeals in insolvency proceedings; and
Table 3 deals with appeals in family proceedings which may be heard in the Family Division and to which the CPR may apply.
3.4 Definitions of terms and abbreviations used in Tables 1, 2 and 3:
"Destination": the court to which the appeal lies.
"Pt 7 Claim (not MT)": Part 7 Claim, other than a claim allocated to the multi-track.
"Pt 7 Claim (MT)": Part 7 Claim, allocated to the multi-track.
"Pt 8 Claim (not MT)": Part 8 Claim, other than a claim allocated to the multi-track.
"Pt 8 Claim (MT)": Part 8 Claim, allocated to the multi-track.
"DJ": District judge.
"CJ": Circuit judge including a recorder or a district judge who is exercising the jurisdiction of a Circuit judge with the permission of the Designated Civil Judge in respect of the case.
"CJ (CC)": Circuit judge in the county court.
"Master": Master, district judge sitting in a district registry or any other judge referred to in article 2 of the Destination of Appeals Order
"Final": A final decision within the meaning of paragraphs 3.6 to 3.8 of this Practice Direction.
"Interim": A decision that is not a final decision within the meaning of paragraphs 3.6 to 3.8 of this Practice Direction.
"HCJ": single judge of the High Court.
"HCJ (FD): single judge of the family Division of the High Court.
"CA": Court of Appeal.
"Other": Claims or originating or pre-action applications started otherwise than by a Part 7 or Part 8 claim (for example an application under Part 23).
"Specialist": Specialist proceedings (under the Companies Act 1985 or the Companies Act 1989 or to which Sections I, II or III of Part 57 or any of Parts 58,59,60, 62 or 63 apply).
(Note: Tables 1, 2 and 3 do not include so-called "leap frog" appeals either to the Court of Appeal pursuant to section 57 of the Access to Justice Act 1999 or to the Supreme Court pursuant to section 13 of the Administration of Justice Act 1969.)
3.5 The destinations in the tables set out below apply whether the decision is interim or final. For the meaning of "final decision" for the purposes of this table see paragraphs 3.6 to 3.8 below.

TABLE 1: PROCEEDINGS OTHER THAN FAMILY OR INSOLVENCY PROCEEDINGS

Court	Deciding judge	Nature of claim	Interim / final	Destination
County	DJ	Pt 7 Claim	Interim	CJ (CC)
		Pt 7 Claim (not MT)	Final	
		Pt 7 Claim (MT)	Final	CA
		Pt 8 Claim	Interim / final	CJ (CC)
		Other	Interim / final	
		Specialist	Interim	
			Final	CA
		Pt 7 Claim	Interim	HCJ
		Pt 7 Claim (not MT)	Final	
		Pt 7 Claim (MT)	Final	CA

Court	Deciding judge	Nature of claim	Interim / final	Destination
	CJ	Pt 8 Claim	Interim / final	HCJ
		Other	Interim / final	
		Specialist	Interim	
			Final	CA
High	Master	Pt 7 Claim	Interim	HCJ
		Pt 7 Claim (not MT)	Final	
		Pt 7 Claim (MT)	Final	CA
		Pt 8 Claim	Interim / final	HCJ
		Other	Interim / final	
		Specialist	Interim	
			Final	C.A.
	HCJ	Any	Interim / final	CA

TABLE 2: INSOLVENCY PROCEEDINGS

Court	Deciding judge	Destination
County	DJ or CJ	HCJ
High	Registrar	
	HCJ	CA

TABLE 3: FAMILY PROCEEDINGS IN THE PRINCIPAL REGISTRY OF THE FAMILY DIVISION AND TO WHICH THE CPR WILL APPLY

The proceedings to which this table applies include proceedings under the Inheritance (Provision for Family and Dependants) Act 1975 and proceedings under the Trusts of Land and Appointment of Trustees Act 1996.

Deciding judge	Nature of claim	Decision under appeal	Destination
DJ	Part 7 Claim (not MT)	Any decision other than a final decision	HCJ (FD)
	Pt 7 Claim (MT)	Final decision	CA
	Part 8 Claim (not MT)	Any decision	HCJ (FD)
	Part 8 Claim (MT)	Any decision	HCJ (FD)
HCJ (FD)	Any	Any decision	CA

3.6 A "final decision" is a decision of a court that would finally determine (subject to any possible appeal or detailed assessment of costs) the entire proceedings whichever way the court decided the issues before it.

3.7 A decision is to be treated as a final decision for destination of appeal purposes where it:-

(a) is made at the conclusion of part of a hearing or trial which has been split into parts; and
(b) would, if it had been made at the conclusion of that hearing or trial, have been a final decision.

3.8

(1) The following are examples of final decisions:-
- a judgment on liability at the end of a split trial;
- a judgment at the conclusion of an assessment of damages following a judgment on liability.

(2) The following are examples of decisions that are not final:-
- a case management decision (within the meaning of paragraph 5.6);
- a grant or refusal of interim relief;
- summary judgment;
- striking out a claim or statement of case;
- a summary or detailed assessment of costs;
- an order for the enforcement of a final decision.

FILING APPELLANT'S NOTICE IN WRONG COURT

3.9

(1) Where a party attempts to file an appellant's notice in a court which does not have jurisdiction to issue the notice, a court officer may notify that party in writing that the appeal court does not have jurisdiction in respect of the notice
(2) Before notifying a person under paragraph (1) the court officer must confer–
 (a) with a judge of the appeal court; or
 (b) where the Court of Appeal is the appeal court, with a court officer who exercises the jurisdiction of that Court under rule 52.16.
(3) Where a court officer, in the Court of Appeal, notifies a person under paragraph (1), rule 52.16(5) and (6) shall not apply.

SECTION 4: OBTAINING PERMISSION TO APPEAL

WHERE TO APPLY FOR PERMISSION

4.1 An application for permission to appeal may be made:-

(a) to the lower court at the hearing at which the decision to be appealed against is given (in which case the lower court may adjourn the hearing to give a party an opportunity to apply for permission to appeal); or
(b) where the lower court refuses permission to appeal or where no application is made to the lower court, to the appeal court in accordance with rule 52.4.

FORM

4.2 An application for permission to appeal to the appeal court must be made using an appellant's notice (Form N161 or N164 (small claims track)).

APPEALS FROM MASTERS AND DISTRICT JUDGES OF HIGH COURT

4.3 In relation to appeals from Masters or district judges of the High Court: appeals, applications for permission and any other applications in the appeal may be heard and directions in the appeal may be given by a High Court Judge or by any person authorised under section 9 of the Senior Courts Act 1981 to act as a judge of the High Court.

WHERE THE LOWER COURT IS A COUNTY COURT

4.4 Where the lower court is a county court:-

(a) subject to paragraph (2), appeals and applications for permission to appeal will be heard by a High Court Judge or by a person authorised under paragraphs (1), (2) or (4) of the Table in section 9(1) of the Senior Courts Act 1981 to act as a judge of the High Court;

(b) an appeal or application for permission to appeal from the decision of a recorder may be heard by a Designated Civil Judge who is authorised under paragraph (5) of the Table in section 9(1) of the Senior Courts Act 1981 to act as a judge of the High Court; and

(c) other applications in the appeal may be heard and directions in the appeal may be given either by a High Court Judge or by any person authorised under section 9 of the Senior Courts Act 1981 to act as a judge of the High Court.

4.5 The Designated Civil Judge in consultation with the Presiding Judge has responsibility for allocating appeals from decisions of district judges to circuit judges.

APPEAL IN RELATION TO CASE MANAGEMENT DECISION

4.6 Where the application is for permission to appeal from a case management decision, the court dealing with the application may take into account whether:

(a) the issue is of sufficient significance to justify the costs of an appeal;

(b) the procedural consequences of an appeal (e.g. loss of trial date) outweigh the significance of the case management decision;

(c) it would be more convenient to determine the issue at or after trial.

Case management decisions include decisions made under rule 3.1(2) and decisions about disclosure, filing of witness statements or experts' reports, directions about the timetable of the claim, adding a party to a claim and security for costs.

SECOND APPEAL

4.6 An application for permission to appeal from a decision of the High Court or a county court which was itself made on appeal is a second appeal and must be made to the Court of Appeal. If permission to appeal is granted the appeal will be heard by the Court of Appeal.

SECTION 5: SKELETON ARGUMENTS

5.1

(1) The purpose of a skeleton argument is to assist the court by setting out as concisely as practicable the arguments upon which a party intends to rely.

(2) A skeleton argument must:

- be concise;
- both define and confine the areas of controversy;
- be set out in numbered paragraphs;
- be cross-referenced to any relevant document in the bundle;
- be self-contained and not incorporate by reference material from previous skeleton arguments;
- not include extensive quotations from documents or authorities.

(3) Documents to be relied on must be identified.

(4) Where it is necessary to refer to an authority, a skeleton argument must:-

(a) state the proposition of law the authority demonstrates; and

(b) identify the parts of the authority that support the proposition.

If more than one authority is cited in support of a given proposition, the skeleton argument must briefly state why.

(5) The cost of preparing a skeleton argument which –

(a) does not comply with the requirements set out in this paragraph; or

(b) was not filed within the time limits provided by this Practice Direction (or any further time granted by the court),

will not be allowed on assessment except as directed by the court.

5.2 The appellant should consider what other information the appeal court will need. This may include a list of persons who feature in the case or glossaries of technical terms. A chronology of relevant events will be necessary in most appeals.

5.3 Any statement of costs must show the amount claimed for the skeleton argument separately.

SECTION 6: DISPOSING OF APPLICATIONS AND APPEALS BY CONSENT

DISMISSAL OF APPLICATIONS OR APPEALS BY CONSENT

6.1 An appellant who does not wish to pursue an application or appeal may request the appeal court to dismiss the application or the appeal. If such a request is granted it will usually be subject to an order that the appellant pays the costs of the application or appeal.

6.2 If the appellant wishes to have the application or appeal dismissed without costs, his request must be accompanied by a letter signed by the respondent stating that the respondent so consents.

6.3 Where a settlement has been reached disposing of the application or appeal, the parties may make a joint request to the court for the application or appeal to be dismissed by consent. If the request is granted the application or appeal will be dismissed.

ALLOWING UNOPPOSED APPEALS OR APPLICATIONS ON PAPER

6.4 The appeal court will not normally make an order allowing an appeal unless satisfied that the decision of the lower court was wrong or unjust because of a serious procedural or other irregularity. The appeal court may, however, set aside or vary the order of the lower court by consent and without determining the merits of the appeal if it is satisfied that there are good and sufficient reasons for so doing. Where the appeal court is requested by all parties to allow an application or an appeal the court may consider the request on the papers. The request should set out the relevant history of the proceedings and the matters relied on as justifying the order and be accompanied by a draft order.

DISPOSAL OF APPLICATIONS AND APPEALS INVOLVING CHILDREN OR PROTECTED PARTIES

6.5 Where one of the parties is a child or protected party, any disposal of an application or the appeal requires the court's approval. A draft order signed by the parties' solicitors should be sent to the appeal court, together with an opinion from the advocate acting on behalf of the child or protected party and, in the case of a protected party, any relevant documents prepared for the Court of Protection.

SECTION 7: REOPENING APPEALS (RULE 52.17)

7.1 A party applying for permission to reopen an appeal or an application for permission to appeal must apply for such permission from the court whose decision the party wishes to reopen.

7.2 The application for permission must be made by application notice and be supported by written evidence, verified by a statement of truth. A copy of the application for permission must not be served on any other party to the original appeal unless the court so directs.

7.3 Where the court directs that the application for permission is to be served on another party, that party may, within 14 days of the service on him of the copy of the application, file and serve a written statement either supporting or opposing the application.

7.4 The application for permission will be considered on paper by a single judge.

SECTION 8: TRANSITIONAL PROVISIONS

8.1 This Practice Direction and Practice Directions 52B, 52C, 52D and 52E shall come into force on 1 October 2012 and shall apply to all appeals where—
(a) the appeal notice was filed; or
(b) permission to appeal was given
on or after that date.

8.2 The appeal court may at any time direct that, in relation to any appeal, one or more of Practice Directions 52A, 52B, 52C, 52D or 52E shall apply irrespective of the date on which the appeal notice was filed or permission to appeal was given.

CIVIL PROCEDURE RULES 1998

1998/3132

PART 54
JUDICIAL REVIEW AND STATUTORY REVIEW

8.2030

I
JUDICIAL REVIEW

8.2031 Rule 54.1 Scope and interpretation

(1) [This Section of this Part] contains rules about judicial review.
(2) [In this Section]—

(a) a "claim for judicial review" means a claim to review the lawfulness of—
  (i) an enactment; or
  (ii) a decision, action or failure to act in relation to the exercise of a public function.
(b) . . .
(c) . . .
(d) . . .
(e) 'the judicial review procedure' means the Part 8 procedure as modified by [this Section];
(f) "interested party" means any person (other than the claimant and defendant) who is directly affected by the claim; and
(g) "court" means the High Court, unless otherwise stated.

(Rule 8.1(6)(b) provides that a rule or practice direction may, in relation to a specified type of proceedings, disapply or modify any of the rules set out in Part 8 as they apply to those proceedings)

Amendment

Inserted by SI 2000/2092, r 22, Schedule.

Para (1): words 'This section of this part' in square brackets substituted by SI 2003/364, r 5(a).

Para (2): words 'In this Section' in square brackets substituted by SI 2003/364, r 5(b)(i); sub-paras (b)–(d) revoked by SI 2003/3361, r 12; in sub-para (e) words 'this Section' in square brackets substituted by SI 2003/364, r 5(b)(ii).

8.2032 Rule 54.2 When this [Section] must be used

The judicial review procedure must be used in a claim for judicial review where the claimant is seeking—
(a) a mandatory order;
(b) a prohibiting order;
(c) a quashing order; or
(d) an injunction under section 30 of the [Senior Courts Act 1981] (restraining a person from acting in any office in which he is not entitled to act).]

Amendment

Inserted by SI 2000/2092, r 22, Schedule.

Provision heading: word 'Section' in square brackets substituted by SI 2003/364, r 5(c).

In para (d) words 'Senior Courts Act 1981' in square brackets substituted by the Constitutional Reform Act 2005, s 59(5), Sch 11, Pt 1, para 1(2).

8.2033 Rule 54.3 When this Section may be used

(1) The judicial review procedure may be used in a claim for judicial review where the claimant is seeking—
(a) a declaration; or
(b) an injunction.

(Section 31(2) of the [Senior Courts Act 1981] sets out the circumstances in which the court may grant a declaration or injunction in a claim for judicial review)

(Where the claimant is seeking a declaration or injunction in addition to one of the remedies listed in rule 54.2, the judicial review procedure must be used)

(2) A claim for judicial review may include a claim for damages[, restitution or the recovery of a sum due] but may not seek [such a remedy] alone.

(Section 31(4) of the [Senior Courts Act 1981] sets out the circumstances in which the court may award damages[, restitution or the recovery of a sum due] on a claim for judicial review)

Amendment

Inserted by SI 2000/2092, r 22, Schedule.

Provision heading: word 'Section' in square brackets substituted by SI 2003/364, r 5(c).

Para (1): words 'Senior Courts Act 1981' in square brackets substituted by the Constitutional Reform Act 2005, s 59(5), Sch 11, Pt 1, para 1(2).

Para (2): words ', restitution or the recovery of a sum due' in square brackets in both places they occur inserted by SI 2003/3361, r 13(a)(i), (b); words 'such a remedy' in square brackets substituted by SI 2003/3361, r 13(b); words 'Senior Courts Act 1981' in square brackets substituted by the Constitutional Reform Act 2005, s 59(5), Sch 11, Pt 1, para 1(2).

8.2034 Rule 54.4 Permission required

The court's permission to proceed is required in a claim for judicial review whether started under this [Section] or transferred to the Administrative Court.

Amendment

Inserted by SI 2000/2092, r 22, Schedule.

Word 'Section' in square brackets substituted by SI 2003/364, r 5(d).

8.2035 Rule 54.5 Time limit for filing claim form

(1) The claim form must be filed—

(a) promptly; and

(b) in any event not later than 3 months after the grounds to make the claim first arose.

(2) The time limit in this rule may not be extended by agreement between the parties.

(3) This rule does not apply when any other enactment specifies a shorter time limit for making the claim for judicial review.

Amendment

Inserted by SI 2000/2092, r 22, Schedule.

Word 'Section' in square brackets substituted by SI 2003/364, r 5(d).

8.2036 Rule 54.6 Claim form

(1) In addition to the matters set out in rule 8.2 (contents of the claim form) the claimant must also state—

(a) the name and address of any person he considers to be an interested party;

(b) that he is requesting permission to proceed with a claim for judicial review; and

(c) any remedy (including any interim remedy) he is claiming.

(Part 25 sets out how to apply for an interim remedy)

(2) The claim form must be accompanied by the documents required by [Practice Direction 54A].

Amendment

Inserted by SI 2000/2092, r 22, Schedule.

Para (2): words 'Practice Direction 54A' in square brackets substituted by SI 2009/3390, r 29(b).

8.2037 Rule 54.7 Service of claim form

The claim form must be served on—

(a) the defendant; and

(b) unless the court otherwise directs, any person the claimant considers to be an interested party, within 7 days after the date of issue.

Amendment

Inserted by SI 2000/2092, r 22, Schedule.

8.2038 Rule 54.8 Acknowledgement of service

(1) Any person served with the claim form who wishes to take part in the judicial review must file an acknowledgment of service in the relevant practice form in accordance with the following provisions of this rule.

(2) Any acknowledgment of service must be—

(a) filed not more than 21 days after service of the claim form; and

(b) served on—

(i) the claimant; and

(ii) subject to any direction under rule 54.7(b), any other person named in the claim form,

as soon as practicable and, in any event, not later than 7 days after it is filed.

(3) The time limits under this rule may not be extended by agreement between the parties.

(4) The acknowledgment of service—

(a) must—

(i) where the person filing it intends to contest the claim, set out a summary of his grounds for doing so; and

(ii) state the name and address of any person the person filing it considers to be an interested party; and

(b) may include or be accompanied by an application for directions.

(5) Rule 10.3(2) does not apply.

Amendment

Inserted by SI 2000/2092, r 22, Schedule.

8.2039 Rule 54.9 Failure to file acknowledgement of service

(1) Where a person served with the claim form has failed to file an acknowledgment of service in accordance with rule 54.8, he—

(a) may not take part in a hearing to decide whether permission should be given unless the court allows him to do so; but

(b) provided he complies with rule 54.14 or any other direction of the court regarding the filing and service of—

(i) detailed grounds for contesting the claim or supporting it on additional grounds; and

(ii) any written evidence,

may take part in the hearing of the judicial review.

(2) Where that person takes part in the hearing of the judicial review, the court may take his failure to file an acknowledgment of service into account when deciding what order to make about costs.

(3) Rule 8.4 does not apply.

Amendment

Inserted by SI 2000/2092, r 22, Schedule.

8.2040 Rule 54.10 Permission given

(1) Where permission to proceed is given the court may also give directions.

[(2) Directions under paragraph (1) may include—

(a) a stay (GL) of proceedings to which the claim relates;
(b) directions requiring the proceedings to be heard by a Divisional Court.]

Amendment

Inserted by SI 2000/2092, r 22, Schedule.
Para (2): substituted by SI 2010/2577, r 3.

8.2041 Rule 54.11 Service of order giving or refusing permission

The court will serve—

(a) the order giving or refusing permission; and
(b) any directions,

on—

(i) the claimant;
(ii) the defendant; and
(iii) any other person who filed an acknowledgement of service.

Amendment

Inserted by SI 2000/2092, r 22, Schedule.

8.2042 Rule 54.12 Permission decision without a hearing

(1) This rule applies where the court, without a hearing—

(a) refuses permission to proceed; or
(b) gives permission to proceed—
(i) subject to conditions; or
(ii) on certain grounds only.

(2) The court will serve its reasons for making the decision when it serves the order giving or refusing permission in accordance with rule 54.11.

(3) The claimant may not appeal but may request the decision to be reconsidered at a hearing.

(4) A request under paragraph (3) must be filed within 7 days after service of the reasons under paragraph (2).

(5) The claimant, defendant and any other person who has filed an acknowledgment of service will be given at least 2 days' notice of the hearing date.

[(6) The court may give directions requiring the proceedings to be heard by a Divisional Court.]

Amendment

Inserted by SI 2000/2092, r 22, Schedule.
Para (6): inserted by SI 2010/2577, r 4.

8.2043 Rule 54.13 Defendant etc may not apply to set aside

Neither the defendant nor any other person served with the claim form may apply to set aside an order giving permission to proceed.

Amendment

Inserted by SI 2000/2092, r 22, Schedule.

8.2044 Rule 54.14 Response

(1) A defendant and any other person served with the claim form who wishes to contest the claim or support it on additional grounds must file and serve—

(a) detailed grounds for contesting the claim or supporting it on additional grounds; and

(b) any written evidence,

within 35 days after service of the order giving permission.

(2) The following rules do not apply—

(a) rule 8.5(3) and 8.5(4) (defendant to file and serve written evidence at the same time as acknowledgement of service); and

(b) rule 8.5(5) and 8.5(6) (claimant to file and serve any reply within 14 days).

Amendment

Inserted by SI 2000/2092, r 22, Schedule.

8.2045 Rule 54.15 Where claimant seeks to rely on additional grounds

The court's permission is required if a claimant seeks to rely on grounds other than those for which he has been given permission to proceed.

Amendment

Inserted by SI 2000/2092, r 22, Schedule.

8.2046 Rule 54.16 Evidence

(1) Rule 8.6[(1)] does not apply.

(2) No written evidence may be relied on unless—

(a) it has been served in accordance with any—

(i) rule under this [Section]; or

(ii) direction of the court; or

(b) the court gives permission.

Amendment

Inserted by SI 2000/2092, r 22, Schedule.

Para (1): reference to '(1)' in square brackets inserted by SI 2002/2058, r 21.

Para (2): in sub-para (a)(i) word 'Section' in square brackets substituted by SI 2003/364, r 5(d).

8.2047 Rule 54.17 Court's powers to hear any person

(1) Any person may apply for permission—

(a) to file evidence; or

(b) make representations at the hearing of the judicial review.

(2) An application under paragraph (1) should be made promptly.

Amendment

Inserted by SI 2000/2092, r 22, Schedule.

8.2048 Rule 54.18 Judicial review may be decided without a hearing

The court may decide the claim for judicial review without a hearing where all the parties agree.

Amendment

Inserted by SI 2000/2092, r 22, Schedule.

8.2049 54.19 Court's powers in respect of quashing orders

(1) This rule applies where the court makes a quashing order in respect of the decision to which the claim relates.

[(2) The court may—

(a)
  (i) remit the matter to the decision-maker; and
  (ii) direct it to reconsider the matter and reach a decision in accordance with the judgment of the court; or

(b) in so far as any enactment permits, substitute its own decision for the decision to which the claim relates.

(Section 31 of the Supreme Court Act 1981 enables the High Court, subject to certain conditions, to substitute its own decision for the decision in question.)]

(3) . . .

Amendment

Inserted by SI 2000/2092, r 22, Schedule.
Para (2): substituted by SI 2007/3543, r 7(b).
Para (3): revoked by SI 2007/3543, r 7(c).

8.2050 Rule 54.20 Transfer

The court may—

(a) order a claim to continue as if it had not been started under this [Section]; and

(b) where it does so, give directions about the future management of the claim.

(Part 30 (transfer) applies to transfers to and from the Administrative Court)

Amendment

Inserted by SI 2000/2092, r 22, Schedule.
In para (a) word 'Section' in square brackets substituted by SI 2003/364, r 5(e).

III

APPLICATIONS FOR STATUTORY REVIEW UNDER SECTION 103A OF THE NATIONALITY, IMMIGRATION AND ASYLUM ACT 2002

[*Revoked.*]

PRACTICE DIRECTION 54A—JUDICIAL REVIEW

8.2060 THIS PRACTICE DIRECTION SUPPLEMENTS CPR PART 54

SECTION I—GENERAL PROVISIONS RELATING TO JUDICIAL REVIEW

1.1 In addition to Part 54 and this practice direction attention is drawn to:
(1) section 31 of the Senior Courts Act 1981; and
(2) the Human Rights Act 1998

THE COURT

2.1 Part 54 claims for judicial review are dealt with in the Administrative Court.
(Practice Direction 54D contains provisions about where a claim for judicial review may be started, administered and heard.)
[revoked]

RULE 54.5 – TIME LIMIT FOR FILING CLAIM FORM

4.1 Where the claim is for a quashing order in respect of a judgment, order or conviction, the date when the grounds to make the claim first arose, for the purposes of rule 54.5(1)(b), is the date of that judgment, order or conviction.

RULE 54.6 – CLAIM FORM

INTERESTED PARTIES

5.1 Where the claim for judicial review relates to proceedings in a court or tribunal, any other parties to those proceedings must be named in the claim form as interested parties under rule 54.6(1)(a) (and therefore served with the claim form under rule 54.7(b)).

5.2 For example, in a claim by a defendant in a criminal case in the Magistrates or Crown Court for judicial review of a decision in that case, the prosecution must always be named as an interested party.

HUMAN RIGHTS

5.3 Where the claimant is seeking to raise any issue under the Human Rights Act 1998, or seeks a remedy available under that Act, the claim form must include the information required by paragraph 15 of Practice Direction 16.

DEVOLUTION ISSUES

5.4 Where the claimant intends to raise a devolution issue, the claim form must:

(1) specify that the applicant wishes to raise a devolution issue and identify the relevant provisions of the Government of Wales Act 2006, the Northern Ireland Act 1998 or the Scotland Act 1998; and

(2) contain a summary of the facts, circumstances and points of law on the basis of which it is alleged that a devolution issue arises.

5.5 In this practice direction 'devolution issue' has the same meaning as in paragraph 1, Schedule 9 to the Government of Wales Act 2006, paragraph 1, Schedule 10 to the Northern Ireland Act 1998; and paragraph 1, Schedule 6 to the Scotland Act 1998.

CLAIM FORM

5.6 The claim form must include or be accompanied by-

(1) a detailed statement of the claimant's grounds for bringing the claim for judicial review;

(2) a statement of the facts relied on;

(3) any application to extend the time limit for filing the claim form;

(4) any application for directions.

5.7 In addition, the claim form must be accompanied by-

(1) any written evidence in support of the claim or application to extend time;

(2) a copy of any order that the claimant seeks to have quashed;

(3) where the claim for judicial review relates to a decision of a court or tribunal, an approved copy of the reasons for reaching that decision;

(4) copies of any documents on which the claimant proposes to rely;

(5) copies of any relevant statutory material;

(6) a list of essential documents for advance reading by the court (with page references to the passages relied on); and

5.8 Where it is not possible to file all the above documents, the claimant must indicate which documents have not been filed and the reasons why they are not currently available.

BUNDLE OF DOCUMENTS

5.9 The claimant must file two copies of a paginated and indexed bundle containing all the documents referred to in paragraphs 5.6 and 5.7.

5.10 Attention is drawn to rules 8.5(1) and 8.5(7).

RULE 54.7–SERVICE OF CLAIM FORM

6.1 Except as required by rules 54.11 or 54.12(2), the Administrative Court will not serve documents and service must be effected by the parties.

6.2 Where the defendant or interested party to the claim for judicial review is—

(a) the Immigration and Asylum Chamber of the First-tier Tribunal, the address for service of the claim form is Official Correspondence Unit, PO Box 6987, Leicester, LE1 6ZX or fax number 0116 249 4240;

(b) the Crown, service of the claim form must be effected on the solicitor acting for the relevant government department as if the proceedings were civil proceedings as defined in the Crown Proceedings Act 1947.

(Practice Direction 66 gives the list published under section 17 of the Crown Proceedings Act 1947 of the solicitors acting in civil proceedings (as defined in that Act) for the different government departments on whom service is to be effected, and of their addresses.)

(Part 6 contains provisions about the service of claim forms.)

RULE 54.8–ACKNOWLEDGMENT OF SERVICE

7.1 Attention is drawn to rule 8.3(2) and the relevant practice direction and to rule 10.5.

RULE 54.10–PERMISSION GIVEN

DIRECTIONS

8.1 Case management directions under rule 54.10(1) may include directions about serving the claim form and any evidence on other persons.

8.2 Where a claim is made under the Human Rights Act 1998, a direction may be made for giving notice to the Crown or joining the Crown as a party. Attention is drawn to rule 19.4A and paragraph 6 of Practice Direction 19A.

PERMISSION WITHOUT A HEARING

8.4 The court will generally, in the first instance, consider the question of permission without a hearing.

PERMISSION HEARING

8.5 Neither the defendant nor any other interested party need attend a hearing on the question of permission unless the court directs otherwise.

8.6 Where the defendant or any party does attend a hearing, the court will not generally make an order for costs against the claimant.

RULE 54.11–SERVICE OF ORDER GIVING OR REFUSING PERMISSION

9.1 An order refusing permission or giving it subject to conditions or on certain grounds only must set out or be accompanied by the court's reasons for coming to that decision.

RULE 54.14–RESPONSE

10.1 Where the party filing the detailed grounds intends to rely on documents not already filed, he must file a paginated bundle of those documents when he files the

8: Appeals Applications and Procedure

detailed grounds.

RULE 54.15–WHERE CLAIMANT SEEKS TO RELY ON ADDITIONAL GROUNDS

11.1 Where the claimant intends to apply to rely on additional grounds at the hearing of the claim for judicial review, he must give notice to the court and to any other person served with the claim form no later than 7 clear days before the hearing (or the warned date where appropriate).

RULE 54.16–EVIDENCE

12.1 Disclosure is not required unless the court orders otherwise.

RULE 54.17–COURT'S POWERS TO HEAR ANY PERSON

13.1 Where all the parties consent, the court may deal with an application under rule 54.17 without a hearing.
13.2 Where the court gives permission for a person to file evidence or make representations at the hearing of the claim for judicial review, it may do so on conditions and may give case management directions.
13.3 An application for permission should be made by letter to the Administrative Court office, identifying the claim, explaining who the applicant is and indicating why and in what form the applicant wants to participate in the hearing.
13.4 If the applicant is seeking a prospective order as to costs, the letter should say what kind of order and on what grounds.
13.5 Applications to intervene must be made at the earliest reasonable opportunity, since it will usually be essential not to delay the hearing.

RULE 54.20–TRANSFER

14.1 Attention is drawn to rule 30.5.
14.2 In deciding whether a claim is suitable for transfer to the Administrative Court, the court will consider whether it raises issues of public law to which Part 54 should apply.

SKELETON ARGUMENTS

15.1 The claimant must file and serve a skeleton argument not less than 21 working days before the date of the hearing of the judicial review (or the warned date).
15.2 The defendant and any other party wishing to make representations at the hearing of the judicial review must file and serve a skeleton argument not less than 14 working days before the date of the hearing of the judicial review (or the warned date).
15.3 Skeleton arguments must contain:

(1) a time estimate for the complete hearing, including delivery of judgment;
(2) a list of issues;
(3) a list of the legal points to be taken (together with any relevant authorities with page references to the passages relied on);
(4) a chronology of events (with page references to the bundle of documents (see paragraph 16.1);
(5) a list of essential documents for the advance reading of the court (with page references to the passages relied on) (if different from that filed with the claim form) and a time estimate for that reading; and
(6) a list of persons referred to.

BUNDLE OF DOCUMENTS TO BE FILED

16.1 The claimant must file a paginated and indexed bundle of all relevant documents required for the hearing of the judicial review when he files his skeleton argument.

16.2 The bundle must also include those documents required by the defendant and any other party who is to make representations at the hearing.

AGREED FINAL ORDER

17.1 If the parties agree about the final order to be made in a claim for judicial review, the claimant must file at the court a document (with 2 copies) signed by all the parties setting out the terms of the proposed agreed order together with a short statement of the matters relied on as justifying the proposed agreed order and copies of any authorities or statutory provisions relied on.
17.2 The court will consider the documents referred to in paragraph 17.1 and will make the order if satisfied that the order should be made.
17.3 If the court is not satisfied that the order should be made, a hearing date will be set.
17.4 Where the agreement relates to an order for costs only, the parties need only file a document signed by all the parties setting out the terms of the proposed order.

SECTION II—APPLICATIONS FOR PERMISSION TO APPLY FOR JUDICIAL REVIEW IN IMMIGRATION AND ASYLUM CASES—CHALLENGING REMOVAL

18.1
(1) This Section applies where—
  (a) a person has been served with a copy of directions for his removal from the United Kingdom by the UK Border Agency of the Home Office and notified that this Section applies; and
  (b) that person makes an application for permission to apply for judicial review before his removal takes effect.
(2) This Section does not prevent a person from applying for judicial review after he has been removed.
(3) The requirements contained in this Section of this Practice Direction are additional to those contained elsewhere in the Practice Direction.
18.2
(1) A person who makes an application for permission to apply for judicial review must file a claim form and a copy at court, and the claim form must—
  (a) indicate on its face that this Section of the Practice Direction applies; and
  (b) be accompanied by—
    (i) a copy of the removal directions and the decision to which the application relates; and
    (ii) any document served with the removal directions including any document which contains the UK Border Agency's factual summary of the case; and
  (c) contain or be accompanied by the detailed statement of the claimant's grounds for bringing the claim for judicial review; or
  (d) if the claimant is unable to comply with paragraph (b) or (c), contain or be accompanied by a statement of the reasons why.
(2) The claimant must, immediately upon issue of the claim, send copies of the issued claim form and accompanying documents to the address specified by the UK Border Agency.

(Rule 54.7 also requires the defendant to be served with the claim form within 7 days of the date of issue. Rule 6.10 provides that service on a Government Department must be effected on the solicitor acting for that Department, which in the case of the UK Border Agency is the Treasury Solicitor. The address for the Treasury Solicitor may be found in the Annex to Part 66 of these Rules.)
18.3 Where the claimant has not complied with paragraph 18.2(1)(b) or (c) and has provided reasons why he is unable to comply, and the court has issued the claim form, the Administrative Court—

(a) will refer the matter to a Judge for consideration as soon as practicable; and
(b) will notify the parties that it has done so.

18.4 If, upon a refusal to grant permission to apply for judicial review, the Court indicates that the application is clearly without merit, that indication will be included in the order refusing permission.

SECTION III—APPLICATIONS FOR PERMISSION TO APPLY FOR JUDICIAL REVIEW OF DECISIONS OF THE UPPER TRIBUNAL

19.1 A person who makes an application for permission to apply for judicial review of the decision of the Upper Tribunal refusing permission to appeal must file a claim form which must—

(a) state on its face that the application is made under Rule 54.7A;
(b) set out succinctly the grounds on which it is argued that the criteria in Rule 54.7A(7) are met; and
(c) be accompanied by the supporting documents required under Rule 54.7A(4).

19.2 If the Upper Tribunal or any interested party wishes there to be a hearing of the substantive application under Rule 54.7A(9), it must make its request in writing (by letter copied to the claimant) for such a hearing no later than 14 days after service of the order granting permission.

PRACTICE DIRECTION 54D—ADMINISTRATIVE COURT (VENUE)

8.2061 THIS PRACTICE DIRECTION SUPPLEMENTS PART 54.

SCOPE AND PURPOSE

1.1 This Practice Direction concerns the place in which a claim before the Administrative Court should be started and administered and the venue at which it will be determined.

1.2 This Practice Direction is intended to facilitate access to justice by enabling cases to be administered and determined in the most appropriate location. To achieve this purpose it provides flexibility in relation to where claims are to be administered and enables claims to be transferred to different venues.

VENUE – GENERAL PROVISIONS

2.1 The claim form in proceedings in the Administrative Court may be issued at the Administrative Court Office of the High Court at—

(1) the Royal Courts of Justice in London; or

(2) at the District Registry of the High Court at Birmingham, Cardiff, Leeds, or Manchester unless the claim is one of the excepted classes of claim set out in paragraph 3 of this Practice Direction which may only be started and determined at the Royal Courts of Justice in London.

2.2 Any claim started in Birmingham will normally be determined at a court in the Midland region (geographically covering the area of the Midland Circuit); in Cardiff in Wales; in Leeds in the North-Eastern Region (geographically covering the area of the North Eastern Circuit); in London at the Royal Courts of Justice; and in Manchester, in the North-Western Region (geographically covering the Northern Circuit).

EXCEPTED CLASSES OF CLAIM

3.1 The excepted classes of claim referred to in paragraph 2.1(2) are—

(1) proceedings to which Part 76 or Part 79 applies, and for the avoidance of doubt—
   - (a) proceedings relating to control orders (within the meaning of Part 76);
   - (b) financial restrictions proceedings (within the meaning of Part 79);
   - (c) proceedings relating to terrorism or alleged terrorists (where that is a relevant feature of the claim); and
   - (d) proceedings in which a special advocate is or is to be instructed;

(2) proceedings to which RSC Order 115 applies;

(3) proceedings under the Proceeds of Crime Act 2002;

(4) appeals to the Administrative Court under the Extradition Act 2003;

(5) proceedings which must be heard by a Divisional Court; and

(6) proceedings relating to the discipline of solicitors.

3.2. If a claim form is issued at an Administrative Court office other than in London and includes one of the excepted classes of claim, the proceedings will be transferred to London.

URGENT APPLICATIONS

4.1 During the hours when the court is open, where an urgent application needs to be made to the Administrative Court outside London, the application must be made to the judge designated to deal with such applications in the relevant District Registry.

4.2 Any urgent application to the Administrative Court during the hours when the court is closed, must be made to the duty out of hours High Court judge by telephoning

020 7947 6000.

ASSIGNMENT TO ANOTHER VENUE

5.1 The proceedings may be transferred from the office at which the claim form was issued to another office. Such transfer is a judicial act.

5.2 The general expectation is that proceedings will be administered and determined in the region with which the claimant has the closest connection, subject to the following considerations as applicable—

(1) any reason expressed by any party for preferring a particular venue;
(2) the region in which the defendant, or any relevant office or department of the defendant, is based;
(3) the region in which the claimant's legal representatives are based;
(4) the ease and cost of travel to a hearing;
(5) the availability and suitability of alternative means of attending a hearing (for example, by videolink);
(6) the extent and nature of media interest in the proceedings in any particular locality;
(7) the time within which it is appropriate for the proceedings to be determined;
(8) whether it is desirable to administer or determine the claim in another region in the light of the volume of claims issued at, and the capacity, resources and workload of, the court at which it is issued;
(9) whether the claim raises issues sufficiently similar to those in another outstanding claim to make it desirable that it should be determined together with, or immediately following, that other claim; and
(10) whether the claim raises devolution issues and for that reason whether it should more appropriately be determined in London or Cardiff.

5.3

(1) When an urgent application is made under paragraph 4.1 or 4.2, this will not by itself decide the venue for the further administration or determination of the claim.
(2) The court dealing with the urgent application may direct that the case be assigned to a particular venue.
(3) When an urgent application is made under paragraph 4.2, and the court does not make a direction under sub-paragraph (2), the claim will be assigned in the first place to London but may be reassigned to another venue at a later date.

5.4 The court may on an application by a party or of its own initiative direct that the claim be determined in a region other than that of the venue in which the claim is currently assigned. The considerations in paragraph 5.2 apply.

5.5. Once assigned to a venue, the proceedings will be both administered from that venue and determined by a judge of the Administrative Court at a suitable court within that region, or, if the venue is in London, at the Royal Courts of Justice. The choice of which court (of those within the region which are identified by the Presiding Judge of the circuit suitable for such hearing) will be decided, subject to availability, by the considerations in paragraph 5.2.

5.6. When giving directions under rule 54.10, the court may direct that proceedings be reassigned to another region for hearing (applying the considerations in paragraph 5.2). If no such direction is given, the claim will be heard in the same region as that in which the permission application was determined (whether on paper or at a hearing).

ADMINISTRATIVE COURT NOTES FOR GUIDANCE ON APPLYING FOR JUDICIAL REVIEW

SECTION 1
GENERAL INTRODUCTION

8.2062 1. These notes are not intended to be exhaustive but are designed to offer an outline of the procedure to be followed when seeking to make an application for judicial review in the Administrative Court. For further details of the procedure to be followed you and your representatives/legal advisers should consult Part 54 of the Civil Procedure Rules (CPR) and the Practice Directions accompanying Part 54.

SECTION 2
WHAT IS JUDICIAL REVIEW?

2.1 Judicial review is the procedure by which you can seek to challenge the decision, action or failure to act of a public body such as a government department or a local authority or other body exercising a public law function. If you are challenging the decision of a court, the jurisdiction of judicial review extends only to decisions of inferior courts. It does not extend to decisions of the High Court or Court of Appeal. Judicial review must be used where you are seeking:

- a mandatory order (i.e. an order requiring the public body to do something and formerly known as an order of mandamus);
- a prohibiting order (i.e. an order preventing the public body from doing something and formerly known as an order of prohibition); or
- a quashing order (i.e. an order quashing the public body's decision and formerly known as an order of certiorari)
- a declaration
- HRA Damages

2.2 Claims will generally be heard by a single Judge sitting in open Court. The Administrative Court sits at:

The Royal Courts of Justice in London – Room C315, Royal Courts of Justice, Strand, London, WC2A 2LL;
Birmingham Civil Justice Centre – Priory Courts, 33 Bull Street, Birmingham, B4 6DS;
Cardiff Civil Justice Centre – 2 Park Street, Cardiff, CF10 1ET;
Leeds Combined Court Centre – 1 Oxford Row, Leeds, LS1 3BG;
Manchester Civil Justice Centre – 1 Bridge Street West, Manchester, M3 3FX

Where a case is directed to be heard by a Divisional Court (a court of two judges) the hearing will usually be in London.

SECTION 3
WHAT IS THE PRE-ACTION PROTOCOL?

3.1 The protocol sets out a code of good practice and contains the steps which parties should generally follow before making a claim for judicial review. The objective of the pre-action protocol is to avoid unnecessary litigation.

3.2 Before making your claim for judicial review, you should send a letter to the defendant. The purpose of this letter is to identify the issues in dispute and establish whether litigation can be avoided. The letter should contain the date and details of the decision, act or omission being challenged and a clear summary of the facts on which the claim is based. It should also contain the details of any relevant information that the claimant is seeking and an explanation of why this is considered relevant. A claim should not normally be made until the proposed reply date given in the letter before claim has passed, unless the circumstances of the case require more immediate action to be taken.

3.3 Defendants should normally respond to that letter within 14 days and sanctions may be imposed unless there are good reasons for not responding within that period.

8: Appeals Applications and Procedure

NB- The protocol does not affect the time limit specified by CPR Part 54.5(1) namely that an application for permission to apply for judicial review must be made promptly and in any event not later than 3 months after the grounds upon which the claim is based first arose.

NB- You should seek advice as to whether the protocol is appropriate in the circumstances of your case. Use of the protocol will not be appropriate where the defendant does not have the legal power to change the decision being challenged. It also may not be appropriate in circumstances where the application is urgent.

NB- A letter before claim will not automatically stop the implementation of a disputed decision.

NB- Even in emergency cases, it is good practice to fax the draft claim form that you are intending to issue to the defendant. You will also normally be required to notify a defendant when you are seeking an interim order; i.e. an order giving some form of relief pending the final determination of the claim.

3.4 Any claim for judicial review must indicate whether or not the protocol has been complied with. If the protocol has not been complied with, the reasons for failing to do so should be set out in the claim form.

SECTION 4
WHERE SHOULD I COMMENCE PROCEEDINGS?

4.1 Claims for judicial review under CPR Part 54 are dealt with in the Administrative Court.

4.2 Claims may be issued at the District Registry of the High Court at Birmingham, Cardiff, Leeds or Manchester as well as at the Royal Courts of Justice in London. Cases started in Birmingham will normally be determined at a court in the Midland region; in Cardiff in Wales; in Leeds in the North-Eastern Region; in London at the Royal Courts of Justice and in Manchester, in the North-Western Region.

4.3 The general expectation is that proceedings will be administered and determined in the region with which the claimant has the closest connection, subject to the following considerations as applicable—

(1) any reason expressed by any party for preferring a particular venue;
(2) the region in which the defendant, or any relevant office or department of the defendant, is based;
(3) the region in which the claimant's legal representatives are based;
(4) the ease and cost of travel to a hearing;
(5) the availability and suitability of alternative means of attending a hearing (for example, by videolink);
(6) the extent and nature of media interest in the proceedings in any particular locality;
(7) the time within which it is appropriate for the proceedings to be determined;
(8) whether it is desirable to administer or determine the claim in another region in the light of the volume of claims issued at, and the capacity, resources and workload of, the court at which it is issued;
(9) whether the claim raises issues sufficiently similar to those in another outstanding claim to make it desirable that it should be determined together with, or immediately following, that other claim; and
(10) whether the claim raises devolution issues and for that reason whether it should more appropriately be determined in London or Cardiff.

CAN I GET LEGAL SERVICES COMMISSION FUNDING (LEGAL AID) FOR MY APPLICATION?

4.4 Neither the Court nor the Administrative Court Offices have power to grant funding (previously legal aid). The responsibility for the provision of public funding is held by the Legal Services Commission.

4.5 Further information on the type(s) of help available and the criteria for receiving that help may be found in the Legal Services Commission Manual Volume 3: "The Funding Code". This may be found on the Legal Services Commission website at http://www.legalservices.gov.uk/.

4.6 A list of contracted firms and Advice Agencies may be found on the Community Legal Services website at http://www.justask.org.uk/. The Legal Services Commission can also provide you with a list of solicitors in your area if you telephone them on 0845 345 4345.

SECTION 5
WHEN SHOULD I LODGE MY APPLICATION FOR PERMISSION TO APPLY FOR JUDICIAL REVIEW?

5.1 The claim form must be filed promptly and in any event not later than three months after the grounds upon which the claim is based first arose (CPR Part 54.5).

5.2 The court has the power to extend the period for the lodging of an application for permission to apply for judicial review but will only do so where it is satisfied there are very good reasons for doing so.

NB - The time for the lodging of the application may not be extended by agreement between the parties.

NB - If you are seeking an extension of time for the lodging of your application, you must make the application in the claim form, setting out the grounds in support of that application to extend time (CPR Part 54.5).

SECTION 6
IS THERE A FEE TO PAY AND IF SO, WHEN SHOULD I PAY IT?

6.1 A fee of £50.00 is payable when you lodge your application for permission to apply for Judicial Review. A further £180.00 is payable if you wish to pursue the claim if permission is granted (Civil Proceedings Fees (Amendment) Order 2008).

NB - If you are in receipt of certain types of benefits you may be entitled to remission of any fee due as part of judicial review proceedings. If you believe you may be entitled to fee remission you should apply to the relevant Administrative Court Office using Form EX160 (Application for Remission of a Fee) and lodge the application with your claim form.

NB - Cheques should be made payable to HMCS. If you lodge your claim form at the court office in person, personal cheques must be supported by a cheque guarantee card presented at the time the claim form is lodged.

SECTION 7
HOW DO I APPLY FOR JUDICIAL REVIEW?

7.1 An application for permission to apply for judicial review must be made by claim form (Form N461).

7.2 The claim form must include or be accompanied by -

- a detailed statement of the claimant's grounds for bringing the claim for judicial review;
- a statement of the facts relied on;
- any application to extend the time limit for filing the claim form; and
- any application for directions.

7.3 Where you are seeking to raise any issue under the Human Rights Act 1998, or a remedy available under that Act, the claim form must include the information required by paragraph 16 of the Practice Direction supplementing Part 16 of the Civil Procedure Rules.

7.4 Where you intend to raise a devolution issue, the claim form must specify that you (a) wish to raise a devolution issue (b) identify the relevant provisions of the Government of Wales Act 1998, and (c) contain a summary of the facts, circumstances and points of law on the basis of which it is alleged that a devolution issue arises. Cases involving Welsh devolution issues are expected to be lodged at the Administrative Court Office in Wales.

7.5 The claim form must also be accompanied by

- any written evidence in support of the claim or application to extend time;
- a copy of any order that you are seeking to have quashed;
- where the claim for judicial review relates to a decision of a court or tribunal, an approved copy of the reasons for reaching that decision;
- copies of any documents upon which you propose to rely;
- copies of any relevant statutory material;
- a list of essential documents for advance reading by the court (with page references to the passages relied upon). Where only part of a page needs to be read, that part should be indicated, by side-lining or in some other way, but not by highlighting.

NB - Where it is not possible for you to file all the above documents, you must indicate which documents have not been filed and the reasons why they are not currently available. The defendant and/or the interested party may seek an extension of time for the lodging of its acknowledgement of service pending receipt of the missing documents.

WHAT DOCUMENTS DO I NEED TO LODGE?

7.6 You must file the original claim form and witness statement, together with a set of paginated and indexed copy documents for the courts use containing the documents referred to in paragraph 7.5 above (CPR Part 54.6 and Practice Direction 54). You should also file a complete set of copy documents (including a copy claim form and witness statement) in a paginated and indexed set for the courts use. Please ensure you paginate in consecutive page number order throughout your bundle. Also ensure that each page has a page number on it and provide an index, which lists the description of documents contained in your bundle together with their page reference numbers.

7.7 Please note that if your case is of a criminal nature then the Court will require you to lodge two paginated and indexed bundles of copy documents.

7.8 You must also lodge sufficient additional copies of the claim form for the court to seal them (i.e. stamp them with the court seal) so that you can serve them on the defendant and any interested parties. The sealed copies will be returned to you so that you can serve them on the defendant and any interested parties.

7.9 If you are represented by solicitors they must also provide a paginated, indexed bundle of the relevant legislative provisions and statutory instruments required for the proper consideration of the application. If you are acting in person you should comply with this requirement if possible.

NB - Applications that do not comply with the requirements of CPR Part 54 and Practice Direction 54 will not be accepted, save in exceptional circumstances. In this context a matter will be regarded as exceptional where a decision is sought from the Court within 14 days of the lodging of the application. In such circumstances an undertaking will be required to provide compliance with the requirements of the CPR within a specified period.

NB - If the only reason given in support of urgency is the imminent expiry of the three month time limit for lodging an application, the papers will nonetheless be returned for compliance with Part 54 and Practice Direction 54. In those circumstances you must seek an extension of time and provide reasons for the delay in lodging the papers in proper form.

WHOM SHOULD I SERVE MY APPLICATION ON?

7.10 The sealed copy claim form (and accompanying documents) must be served on the defendant and any person that you consider to be an interested party (unless the court directs otherwise) within 7 days of the date of issue (i.e. the date shown on the court seal). The Administrative Court Office will not serve your claim on the defendant or any interested party.

NB - An interested party is a person who is likely to be directly affected by your judicial review application.

NB - Please note that under the provisions of the Crown Proceedings Act 1947 service must be upon the Department responsible for the Defendant.

NB - Where the claim for judicial review relates to proceedings in a court or tribunal, any other parties to those proceedings must be named in the claim form as interested parties and served with the claim form (CPR 54 PD.5). For example, in a claim by a defendant in a criminal case in the Magistrates' or Crown Court for judicial review of a decision in that case, the prosecution must always be named as an interested party.

7.11 You should lodge a Certificate of Service in Form N215 in the relevant Administrative Court Office within 21 days of serving the defendant and other interested parties.

7.12 The date of deemed service is calculated in accordance with CPR part 6.14 (see methods of service below).

Method	Deemed day of service	
First class post (or other service which provides for delivery on the next business day).	The second day after it was posted, left with, delivered to or collected by the relevant service provider, eg:	
	Posted	Deemed service
	Monday	Wednesday
	Tuesday	Thursday
	Wednesday	Friday
	Thursday	Monday
	Friday	Monday
	Please note: If the service date falls on a Public Holiday the deemed service date is the first working day following the Public Holiday.	
Delivering the document to or leaving it at a permitted address	Where it is delivered to or left at the relevant place before 12.00 midnight on the second business day after that day.	
Fax	The second business day after completing the transmission of the fax (eg if the fax is sent at 10.30pm on Monday, it will be demed served on Wednesday).	
Other electronic method, eg e-mail	The second business day after sendingthe email or other electronic transmission.	
Personal Service	The second business day after completing the relevant step required by CPR 6.5(3).	

NB - The time for the lodging of the defendant and any interested party's acknowledgement of service (21 days) commences from the date that the claim is deemed served upon them.

SECTION 8
WHAT DO I DO IF MY APPLICATION IS URGENT?

8.1 If you want to make an application for your application for permission to be heard/considered by a Judge as a matter of urgency and/or to seek an interim injunction, you must complete a Request for Urgent Consideration, Form N463, which can be obtained from the HMCS website or the relevant Administrative Court Office. The form sets out the reasons for urgency and the timescale sought for the consideration of the permission application, e.g. within 72 hours or sooner if necessary, and the date by which the substantive hearing should take place.

8.2 Where you are seeking an interim injunction, you must, in addition, provide a draft order; and the grounds for the injunction. You must serve the claim form, the draft order and the application for urgency on the defendant and interested parties (by FAX and by post), advising them of the application and informing them that they may make representations directly to the Court in respect of your application.

8.3 A judge will consider the application within the time requested and may make such order as he/she considers appropriate.

NB - The judge may refuse your application for permission at this stage if he/she considers it appropriate, in the circumstances, to do so.

8.4 If the Judge directs that an oral hearing must take place within a specified time the Administrative Court Office will liaise with you and the representatives of the other parties to fix a permission hearing within the time period directed.

8.5 Where a manifestly inappropriate urgency application is made, consideration may, in appropriate cases, be given to making a wasted costs order.

SECTION 9
WHAT IS AN ACKNOWLEDGEMENT OF SERVICE?

9.1 Any person who has been served with the claim form and who wishes to take part in the judicial review should file an acknowledgment of service (Form N462) in the Administrative Court Office, within 21 days of the proceedings being served upon him.

NB - Whilst there is no requirement upon you to serve the defendant and any interested party with a Form N462 for completion by them, it is good practice to do so.

9.2 The acknowledgement of service must set out the summary of grounds for contesting the claim and the name and address of any person considered to be an interested party (who has not previously been identified and served as an interested party).

9.3 The acknowledgement of service must be served upon you and the interested parties no later than 7 days after it is filed with the court.

NB - Failure to file an acknowledgement of service renders it necessary for the party concerned to obtain the permission of the court to take part in any oral hearing of the application for permission.

SECTION 10
WHAT HAPPENS AFTER THE DEFENDANT AND/OR THE INTERESTED PARTY HAS LODGED AN ACKNOWLEDGEMENT OF SERVICE, OR THE TIME FOR LODGING SUCH HAS EXPIRED?

10.1 Applications for permission to proceed with the claim for judicial review are considered by a single judge on the papers. The purpose of this procedure is to ensure that applications are dealt with speedily and without unnecessary expense.

10.2 The papers will be forwarded to the judge by the Administrative Court Office upon receipt of the Acknowledgement of Service or at the expiry of the time limit for lodging such acknowledgement – whichever is earlier.

10.3 The judge's decision and the reasons for it (Form JRJ) will be served upon you, the defendant and any other person served with the claim form.

10.4 If the judge grants permission and you wish to pursue the claim, you must lodge a further fee of £180.00 (or a further Application for Remission of Fee (Form EX160) with the relevant Administrative Court Office within 7 days of service of the judge's decision upon you.

NB - If you do not lodge the additional fee, your file will be closed.

SECTION 11
WHAT HAPPENS AFTER PERMISSION IS GRANTED IF MY APPLICATION FOR PERMISSION IS REFUSED OR IF PERMISSION IS GRANTED SUBJECT TO CONDITIONS OR IN PART ONLY?

11.1 If permission is refused, or is granted subject to conditions or on certain grounds only, you may request a reconsideration of that decision at an oral hearing.

11.2 Request for an oral hearing must be made on the Notice of Renewal, Form 86b, (a copy of which will be sent to you at the same time as the judge's decision) and must be filed within 7 days after service of the notification of the judge's decision upon you (CPR Part 54.11 & 54.12).

11.3 Where the judge directs an oral hearing or you renew your application after refusal following consideration on paper, you may appear in person or be represented by an advocate (if you are legally represented). If you are not legally represented you may seek the court's permission to have someone speak on your behalf at the hearing.

NB - Any application for permission to have someone speak on your behalf should be made to the judge hearing the application who will make such decision as he considers appropriate in all of the circumstances.

11.4 Notice of the hearing is given to you, the defendant and any interested party by the Administrative Court List Office. An oral hearing is allocated a total of 30 minutes of court time. If it is considered that 30 minutes of court time is insufficient, you may provide a written estimate of the time required for the hearing and request a special fixture.

11.5 Neither the defendant nor any other interested party need attend a hearing on the question of permission unless the court directs otherwise.

SECTION 12
WHAT HAPPENS WHEN MY CASE IS READY FOR HEARING?

12.1 On granting permission the court may make case management directions under CPR 54.10(1) for the progression of the case. Case management directions may include directions as to venue, as to the service of the claim form and any evidence on other persons and as to expedition.

12.2 Where a claim is made under the Human Rights Act 1998, a direction may be made for the giving of notice to the Crown or joining the Crown as a party. In that regard you attention is drawn to the requirements of Civil Procedure rule 19.4A and paragraph 6 of the Practice Direction supplementing Section I of Part 19.

WHEN SHOULD THE DEFENDANT/INTERESTED PARTY LODGE ITS EVIDENCE FOLLOWING THE GRANT OF PERMISSION?

12.3 A party upon whom a claim form has been served and who wishes to contest the claim (or support it on additional grounds) must, within 35 days of service of the order granting permission, file and serve on the Court and all of the other parties

- Detailed grounds for contesting the claim or supporting it on additional grounds and
- Any written evidence relied upon.

12.4 Any party who has done so may be represented at the hearing.

12.5 Where the party filing the detailed grounds intends to rely on documents not already filed, a paginated bundle of those documents must be filed at the Court when the detailed grounds are filed.

12.6 The Court has power to extend or abridge the time for lodging evidence.

SECTION 13
WHAT HAPPENS WHEN MY CASE IS READY FOR HEARING?

13.1 When the time for lodging of evidence by the parties has expired, the case enters a warned list and all parties are informed of this by letter.
13.2 Where a direction has been given for expedition, the case will take priority over other cases waiting to be fixed and enters an expedited warned list.

WHAT IS THE PROCEDURE FOR THE LISTING OF A CASE FOR HEARING?

NB - The procedure is the same whether you act in person or are legally represented.
13.3 Where advocate's details have been placed on the court record, the parties will be contacted by the relevant Administrative Court List Office in order to seek to agree a date for the hearing. You and advocate's clerks will be offered a range of dates and will have 48 hours to take up one of the dates offered. If the parties fail to contact the List Office within 48 hours, the List Office will fix the hearing on one of the dates offered without further notice and the parties will be notified of that fixture by letter. Where a hearing is listed in this way the hearing will only be vacated by the Administrative Court Office if both parties consent and good reason is provided for the need to vacate the fixture, using the adjournment form available from Administrative Court Listing Offices.
13.4 There may be circumstances where you are unable to attend at court on the date fixed to hear your application, i.e. as a result of illness or accident. If you are unlikely to be able to attend court on the hearing date you must notify the relevant List Office immediately. You should contact the other parties to seek their consent to the adjournment using the adjournment form. If illness is the cause of your inability to attend, a medical certificate should also be provided. Your application for an adjournment will be considered by the Appropriate Officer of the relevant Administrative Court Office. Please note that there is a fee payable for any application to adjourn made within 14 days of the hearing date, unless you are entitled to fee remission, in which case you must lodge an Application for a Remission of Fee (Form Ex160) with your adjournment form.
13.5 Where agreement to an adjournment cannot be reached, a formal application for adjournment must be made to the Court (on notice to all parties) using Form PF244-Administrative Court Office. Please note that there is a fee payable for any application to adjourn made within 14 days of the hearing date, unless you are entitled to fee remission, in which case you must lodge an Application for a Remission of Fee (Form Ex160) with your application.
13.6 There are occasions when circumstances, outside the control of the List Office, may necessitate them having to vacate a hearing at very short notice. Sometimes this can be as late as 4.30pm the day before the case is listed. This could be as a result of a case unexpectedly overrunning, a judge becoming unavailable, or other reasons. The List Office will endeavour to re-fix the case on the next available date convenient to the parties.

WHAT IS THE SHORT WARNED LIST?

13.7 Whilst the Administrative Court usually gives fixed dates for hearings, there is also a need to short warn a number of cases to cover the large number of settlements that occur in the list. Parties in cases that are selected to be short warned will be notified that their case is likely to be listed from a specified date, and that they may be called into the list at less than a day's notice from that date. If the case does not get on during that period, a date as soon as possible after that period will be fixed in consultation with the parties.

13.8 There may be circumstances where you are unable to attend at court on the date fixed to hear your application, i.e. as a result of illness or accident. If you are unlikely to be able to attend court on the hearing date you must notify the relevant List Office immediately in writing to seek an adjournment of the hearing, setting out the reasons why you are unable to attend Court. If illness is the cause of your inability to attend, a medical certificate should be provided. Your application for an adjournment will be considered by the Appropriate Officer of the relevant Administrative Court Office. The views of the other parties to the proceedings will be sought and it is good practice to notify the parties of your intention to seek an adjournment of the hearing and ask them to notify the court of their views.

WHAT IS A SKELETON ARGUMENT AND DO I NEED TO LODGE ONE?

13.9 A skeleton argument is a document lodged with the court by a party prior to the substantive hearing of any application for judicial review.
13.10 Whilst there is no requirement for a litigant in person to lodge a skeleton argument there is nothing to prevent you from doing so if you wish and if you consider that it would assist the Court.
13.11 If you wish to lodge a skeleton argument you must file it with the Court and serve it on the other parties not less than 21 working days before the date of the hearing of the judicial review or the short warned date, where a case has been "short warned".
13.12 The defendant and any other party wishing to make representations at the hearing of the judicial review must file and serve a skeleton argument not less than 14 working days before the date of the hearing of the judicial review (or the short warned date).
13.13 The skeleton argument must contain:

- A time estimate for the complete hearing, including delivery of judgment;
- A list of issues;
- A list of the legal points to be taken (together with any relevant authorities with page references to the passages relied on);
- A time estimate for the complete hearing, including delivery of judgment;
- A chronology of events (with page references to the bundle of documents);
- A list of essential documents for the advance reading of the court (with page references to the passages relied on) (if different from that filed with the claim form) and a time estimate for that reading; and
- A list of persons referred to.

WHAT IS A TRIAL BUNDLE AND WHEN SHOULD I LODGE IT?

13.14 You must file a paginated and indexed bundle of all relevant documents required for the hearing of the judicial review whether or not you file a skeleton argument. The bundle must be filed with the court and served on the other parties not less than 21 working days before the hearing.
NB – Two copies of the bundle are required by the Court when the application is to be heard by a Divisional Court in London.
NB – The bundle must also include those documents required by the defendant and any other party who is to make representations at the hearing.

SECTION 14
WHAT IF I NEED TO MAKE AN APPLICATION TO THE COURT FOR FURTHER ORDERS/DIRECTIONS AFTER THE GRANT OF PERMISSION?

14.1 Where case management decisions or directions are sought after permission has been granted, application should be made by way of an application under CPR Part 23, using Form PF244 – Administrative Court Office. You will be required to pay a fee for such application (currently £75.00, or £40.00 if all parties provide their written consent to the order being made), unless you are entitled to fee remission (in which case you should complete and submit a form EX160 with you application).

SECTION 15
CAN MY SUBSTANTIVE APPLICATION BE DETERMINED WITHOUT THE NEED FOR A HEARING?

15.1 The court may decide a claim for judicial review without a hearing where all parties agree (CPR Part 54.18).

SECTION 16
WHAT DO I NEED TO DO IF THE PROCEEDINGS SETTLE BY CONSENT PRIOR TO THE SUBSTANTIVE HEARING OF THE APPLICATION?

16.1 If you reach agreement with the other parties as to the terms of the final order to be made in your claim, you must file at the court a document (with 2 copies) signed by all the parties setting out the terms of the proposed agreed order.
NB – There is a fee of £40.00 payable on lodging the consent order, unless you are entitled to fee remission (in which case you should complete and submit a form EX160 with you application).
NB – If you agree with the other parties that a mandatory order etc. is required, the draft order should be accompanied by a statement of reasons (i.e. a short statement of the matters relied on as justifying the proposed agreed order) and copies of any authorities or statutory provisions relied on. If settlement is reached before permission is considered, the draft consent order must include provision for permission to be granted.
NB - Such a statement is not required where the agreement as to disposal (usually by way of withdrawal of the application) requires an order for costs or a detailed assessment of the Claimant's Legal Services Commission costs - in those circumstances the parties should file a draft consent order setting out the terms of settlement signed by all parties.
16.2 The court will consider the documents submitted and will make the order if it is satisfied that the order should be made. If the court is not satisfied that the order should be made, the court will give directions and may direct that a hearing date be set for the matter to be considered further.

SECTION 17
WHAT IF I WANT TO DISCONTINUE THE PROCEEDINGS AT ANY STAGE?

<u>Before service</u> of the claim form etc. on the other parties,
17.1 If you have not yet served any of the parties with the sealed claim form and accompanying documents you may discontinue the proceedings by notifying the Court in writing of your intention to do so. The Court will accept a letter of withdrawal provided that you confirm in writing that you have not effected service on the parties.
<u>After service</u> of the claim form etc. on the other parties,
17.2 Discontinuance of a claim is governed by CPR Part 38. Discontinuance renders you liable for the costs incurred by the other parties until the date of discontinuance.
17.3 There is a right to discontinue a claim at any time, except where:

- An interim injunction has been granted or an undertaking has been given – in those circumstances the permission of the court is required to discontinue the proceedings (an example of this would be where bail had been granted pending determination of the application for judicial review)
- Interim payment has been made by defendant - in those circumstances the consent of the defendant or the permission of the court is required to discontinue the proceedings
- There is more than one claimant - in those circumstances the consent of every other claimant or the permission of the court is required to discontinue the proceedings.

17.4 If you wish to discontinue the proceedings at any stage after the service of those proceedings upon the other parties you must file a Notice of Discontinuance in the requisite form (N279) at the relevant Administrative Court Office and serve a copy on every other party.
17.5 A defendant may apply to set aside the Notice of Discontinuance, within 28 days of being served with it (CPR Part 38.4).
NB - If the parties require any order for costs, then a draft order setting out the terms of the order sought is required. A Notice of Discontinuance would not be appropriate in those circumstances.

SECTION 18
WILL I BE RESPONSIBLE FOR THE COSTS OF THE DEFENDANT AND/OR THE INTERESTED PARTIES IF MY APPLICATION IS UNSUCCESSFUL?

18.1 The general rule is that the party losing a substantive claim for judicial review will be ordered to pay the costs of the other parties. However, the Judge considering the matter has discretion to deal with the issue of costs as he/she considers appropriate in all of the circumstances.
NB – Costs may be awarded in respect of an unsuccessful paper application. Any application by the defendant/interested party for costs will normally be made in the Acknowledgment of Service.

SECTION 19
WHAT CAN I DO IF I AM UNHAPPY WITH THE JUDGE'S DECISION?

CIVIL MATTERS

Appeal after refusal of permission

19.1 If you are unhappy with the Court's decision in a civil matter you can appeal to the Court of Appeal Civil Division (with permission of the Court of Appeal (CPR Part 52.15)). Application to the Court of Appeal for permission to Appeal must be made within 7 days of the refusal by the Administrative Court of permission to apply for judicial review.

Appeal after substantive hearing

19.2 In substantive applications, permission to appeal may be sought from the Administrative Court when it determines the claim for judicial review. If an application for permission to appeal is not made at the conclusion of the case, the application for permission to appeal must be made to the Court of Appeal Civil Division within 21 days (CPR Part 52.3 & 52.4).
19.3 Guidance as to procedure should be sought from the Civil Appeals Office, Royal Courts of Justice, Strand, London, WC2A 2LL.

Appeal after refusal of permission

19.4 There is no further remedy in the domestic courts after a refusal of permission by the Administrative Court.

Appeal after substantive hearing

19.5 If you are unhappy with the Court's decision in a substantive claim for judicial review in a criminal matter, you can appeal to the Supreme Court but only with the leave of the Administrative Court or the Supreme Court and such leave may only be granted if: (a) The Administrative Court certifies that a point of law of general public importance is involved in its decision; and (b) It appears to the Administrative Court or the Supreme Court that the point is one which ought to be considered by the

Supreme Court. (see The Administration of Justice Act 1960 s.1).

SECTION 20
WHERE CAN I GET ADVICE ABOUT PROCEDURAL MATTERS?

20.1 If in doubt about any procedural matter you can contact the relevant Administrative Court Office, telephone numbers below. Court staff cannot give legal advice as to the merits of a case.

Birmingham Civil Justice Centre – 0121 681 3043 or 0121 681 3181;
Cardiff Civil Justice Centre – 029 2037 6400;
Leeds Combined Court Centre – 0113 306 2578;
Manchester Civil Justice Centre – 0161 240 5313 or 0161 240 5314;
The Royal Courts of Justice in London – 020 7947 6205 or 020 7947 6655.

PRACTICE STATEMENT—ADMIN COURT

8.2063 PRACTICE—ADMINISTRATIVE COURT—PROCEDURE FOR URGENT APPLICATIONS—LISTING POLICY

ANNEX B
THE PROCEDURE FOR URGENT APPLICATIONS TO THE ADMINISTRATIVE COURT

1. In October 2000 CPR Part 54 was introduced which makes no express provision for urgent applications for permission to apply for judicial review to be made orally.
2. The Administrative Court is now issuing the following guidance on the procedure to be applied for urgent applications and for interim injunctions. It is the duty of the advocate to comply with this guidance; and where a manifestly inappropriate application is made, consideration will be given to a wasted costs order.
3. The Administrative Court currently allocates paper applications for judicial review on a daily basis and one judge also act as the "Urgent Judge".
4. Where a claimant makes an application for the permission application to be heard as a matter of urgency and/or seeks an interim injunction, he must complete a prescribed form which states:
- the need for urgency;
- the timescale sought for the consideration of the permission application, eg within 72 hours or sooner if necessary (see para 8 below); and
- the date by which the substantive hearing should take place.

5. Where an interim injunction is sought, a claimant must, in addition, provide:
- a draft order; and
- the grounds for the injunction.

6. The claimant must serve (by fax and post) the claim form and application for urgency on the defendant and interested parties, advising them of the application and that they may make representations.
7. Where an interim injunction is sought, the claimant must serve (by fax and post) the draft order and grounds for the application on the defendant and interested parties, advising them of the application and that they may make representations.
8. A judge will consider the application within the time requested and may make such order as he considers appropriate.
9. If the judge directs that an oral hearing take place within a specified time the representatives of the parties and the Administrative Court will liaise to fix a permission

hearing within the time period directed.

ANNEX C
LISTING POLICY IN THE ADMINISTRATIVE COURT
FEBRUARY 2002

FIXING SUBSTANTIVE HEARINGS

Where a case is ready to be heard substantively, it enters a warned list and all parties are informed of this by letter. Some cases require an early hearing date and take priority over other cases waiting to be fixed – these enter the expedited warned list.
Where counsel has been placed on the court record, their chambers are contacted by the Administrative Court list office in order to agree a convenient date for the hearing. Counsel's clerks are offered a range of dates and have 48 hours to take up one of the dates offered. If counsel's clerk fails to contact the list office within 48 hours, the list office will fix the hearing on one of the dates that was offered, without further notice and the parties will be notified of that fixture by letter. Where a hearing is listed in this way the hearing will only be vacated by the Administrative Court Office if both parties consent. Failing that, a formal application for adjournment must be made (on notice to all parties) to the court. The same procedure is followed where a claimant is in person.

SHORT WARNED LIST

Whilst the Administrative Court usually gives fixed dates for hearings, there is also a need to short warn a number of cases to cover the large number of settlements that occur in the list. Parties in cases that are selected to be short warned will be notified that their case is likely to be listed from a specified date, and that they may be called into the list at less than a days notice from that date. Approximately six cases are short warned for any specified week. If the case does not get on during that period, a date as soon as possible after that period will be fixed in consultation with the parties.

VACATING FIXTURES

There are occasions when circumstances, outside the control of the List Office, may necessitate them having to vacate a hearing at very short notice. Sometimes this can be as late as 4.30 pm the day before the case is listed. This could be as a result of a case unexpectedly overrunning, a judge becoming unavailable, or other reasons. In deciding which hearing has to be vacated, the list office will assess the cases listed for the following day and take the following factors into consideration.

- Which case/s, if removed, will cause the least disruption to the list (the aim is to adjourn as few cases as possible, ideally one).
- How many cases need to be adjourned given the reduced listing time available.
- Have any matters previously been adjourned by the court.
- The urgency and age/s of the matter/s listed.
- Where the parties and/or their representatives are based (this is relevant as in some cases the parties travel to London the day before the hearing).
- Whether it is appropriate to "float" the case in the event of another listed matter going short (cases will not be floated without the consent of the parties).
- The likelihood of a judge becoming available to hear a floated case.

After taking these factors into account, the list office decide upon the case(s) which will have to be refixed and will inform the parties concerned that their hearing has been vacated. The case record will be noted that the matter is not to be adjourned by the court again. The court will also endeavour to refix the case on the next available date convenient to the parties.

In the High Court of Justice CO Ref no: CO

Queens Bench Division
Administrative Court

In the matter of a claim for Judicial Review

The Queen on the application of
. . . .
Versus
. . . .

Notice of RENEWAL of claim for permission to apply for Judicial Review (CPR 54.12)
1. This notice must be lodged in the Administrative Court Office and served upon the defendant (and interested parties who were served with the claim form) within 7 days of the service on the claimant or his solicitor of the notice that the claim for permission has been refused.
2. If this form has not been lodged within 7 days of service (para 1 above) please set out below the ***reasons for delay:***
3. Set out below the grounds for renewing the application:
4. Please supply
COUNSEL'S NAME:
COUNSEL'S TELEPHONE NUMBER:

Signed Dated

Claimant's Ref No. Tel.No. Fax No.

To the Master of the Crown Office, Royal Courts of Justice, Strand, London, WC2A 2LL
FORM 86B

PRACTICE STATEMENT (ADMINISTRATIVE COURT: UNCONTESTED PROCEEDINGS) (4 APRIL 2008)

8.2070 This direction replaces the practice note of 12 May 1997 [1997] 2 All ER 799

1.DETERMINATION OF PROCEEDINGS

Where the parties are agreed as to the terms on which proceedings in the Administrative Court can be disposed of and require an order of the court to put those terms into effect they should lodge with the Administrative Court Office a document (with one copy thereof) signed by the parties setting out the terms of the proposed agreed order and a short statement of the matters relied on as justifying the making of the order, authorities and statutory provisions relied on being quoted.
The Administrative Court Office will then submit the document to the Master or Deputy Master of the Crown Office and, if the court is satisfied that the order should be made, the order will be made without the need for attendance by the parties or their representatives. The making of the order will be publicised on the HMCS website.
If the court is not satisfied on the information originally provided or subsequently provided at the court's request, that the order can properly be made, the proceedings

Index

[all references are to paragraph number in volume 2]

Please note all references to paragraphs in Parts 9, 10 and 11 can be found on the CD that accompanies this edition.

B

C

G

H

I

J

n

P

u

y

GENERAL TERMS AND CONDITIONS
FOR USE OF THE COMPACT DISC GOODS AND MATERIALS CONTAINED THEREIN

This Licence Agreement is between Reed Elsevier (UK) Limited trading as LexisNexis ("**we or us**") and the individual or company ("**you**") to whom LexisNexis has agreed to supply the Compact Disc Goods ("the **Goods**") and the Materials and content contained therein ("the **Materials**"). The following terms and conditions govern your use of the Goods supplied by LexisNexis and the Materials available therein:

1. LICENCE; RESTRICTIONS ON USE

1.1 You are granted a non-exclusive, non-transferable, limited licence to access and use the Goods and the Materials from time to time made available to you for the purposes only of (i) research or study, (ii) providing professional services to your clients, and (iii) providing academic services to students. This licence is subject to the following limitations:

(a) The right to electronically display the Materials retrieved from the Goods is limited to the display of such the Materials primarily to one person at a time;

(b) The right to obtain a printout of the Materials is limited to single printout of the Materials downloaded (collectively, "**Authorised Printouts**"). You are not permitted to sell these Authorised Printouts; and

(c) The right to retrieve and store machine-readable copies of the Materials is limited to the retrieval of a single copy of the Materials included in the Goods and storage of that copy in machine readable form primarily for one person's exclusive use. You are not permitted to transfer the Goods or the Materials electronically or via any other medium for commercial profit or for resale.

1.2 To the extent expressly permitted by applicable copyright law, you may make copies of Authorised Printouts and distribute Authorised Printouts and copies.

1.3 Except as specifically provided in Sections 1.1 and 1.2, you are otherwise prohibited from downloading, storing, reproducing, transmitting, displaying, printing, copying, distributing, or using the Materials retrieved from the Goods.

1.4 All right, title, and interest (including all copyrights and other intellectual property rights) in the Goods and the Materials (in both print and machine-readable forms) belong to us or our third party suppliers. You acquire no ownership of copyright or other intellectual property rights or proprietary interest in the Goods, the Materials, or copies thereof.

1.5 Except as specifically provided herein, you may not use the Goods or the Materials retrieved from the Goods in any fashion that infringes the copyright or proprietary interests therein.

1.6 You may not remove or obscure the copyright notice or other notices contained in the Materials retrieved from the Goods.

2. ACCESS TO SERVICES

2.1 Only you shall be entitled to access and use the Goods and the Materials ("**Authorised Users**").

2.2 Except for use incidental to occasional, short-term travel, you may not access the Goods and the Materials from outside the country for which it was issued.

2.3 Materials and features may be added to or withdrawn from the Goods and the Goods otherwise changed without notice.

2.4 You must ensure that each person having access to the Goods and the Materials:

(a) is an Authorised User; and

(b) is using those Goods and the Materials only in accordance with these General Terms and Conditions.

3. LIMITED WARRANTY

3.1 We represent and warrant that we have the right and authority to make the Goods and the Materials available pursuant to these General Terms and Conditions.

3.2 EXCEPT AS OTHERWISE PROVIDED IN SECTION 3.1, THE GOODS AND THE MATERIALS ARE PROVIDED ON AN "AS IS", "AS AVAILABLE" BASIS AND WE MAKE NO EXPRESS WARRANTIES UNDER THIS AGREEMENT, INCLUDING WITHOUT LIMITATION THAT THE GOODS AND THE MATERIALS ARE OR WILL BE COMPLETE OR FREE FROM ERRORS OR THAT INFORMATION WILL CONTINUE TO BE AVAILABLE TO US TO ENABLE US TO KEEP THE GOODS AND THE MATERIALS UP-TO-DATE.

4. LIMITATION OF LIABILITY

4.1 To the maximum extent permitted by law, a Covered Party (as defined below) shall not be liable for any loss, injury, claim, liability, or damage of any kind resulting in any way from (a) any errors in or omissions from the

Goods or any Materials available or not included therein, (b) the unavailability or interruption to the supply of the Goods or any features thereof or any Materials, (c) Any Authorised Users use or misuse of the Goods or Materials (regardless of whether you received any assistance from a Covered Party in using or misusing the Goods), (d) your use of any equipment in connection with the Goods, (e) the content of Materials, (f) any delay or failure in performance of the Goods, or (g) any negligence of a Covered Party or its employees, contractors or agents in connection with the performance of our obligations under this agreement.

4.2 "Covered Party" means (a) us, our affiliates, and any officer, director, employee, subcontractor, agent, successor, or assign of us or our affiliates; and (b) each third party supplier of the Materials, their affiliates, and any officer, director, employee, subcontractor, agent, successor, or assign of any third party supplier of the Materials or any of their affiliates.

4.3 Our liability to you for breach of any condition or warranty implied under any law which cannot be lawfully modified or excluded by this agreement shall, to the extent permitted by law, be limited at our option to supplying the Goods or the Materials again or paying for their re-supply. Nothing in this Agreement is intended to exclude liability for death or personal injury resulting from any negligence by us.

4.4 Our liability to you for loss or damage of any kind (including loss or damage caused by negligence) is reduced to the extent that you caused or contributed to that loss or damage.

4.5 SUBJECT TO CLAUSE 4.3, THE AGGREGATE LIABILITY OF THE COVERED PARTIES IN CONNECTION WITH ANY OTHER CLAIM ARISING OUT OF OR RELATING TO THE GOODS OR THE MATERIALS SHALL NOT EXCEED THE AMOUNT OF YOUR ACTUAL DIRECT DAMAGES. YOUR RIGHT TO MONETARY DAMAGES IN THAT AMOUNT SHALL BE IN LIEU OF ALL OTHER REMEDIES WHICH YOU MAY HAVE AGAINST ANY COVERED PARTY.

4.6 SUBJECT TO CLAUSE 4.3, THE COVERED PARTIES SHALL NOT BE LIABLE FOR ANY SPECIAL, INDIRECT, INCIDENTAL, OR CONSEQUENTIAL DAMAGES OF ANY KIND WHATSOEVER (INCLUDING, WITHOUT LIMITATION, LEGAL FEES) IN ANY WAY DUE TO, RESULTING FROM, OR ARISING IN CONNECTION WITH THE GOODS, THE MATERIALS, OR THE FAILURE OF ANY COVERED PARTY TO PERFORM ITS OBLIGATIONS, REGARDLESS OF ANY NEGLIGENCE OF ANY COVERED PARTY.

4.7 The Materials are provided for reference purposes only and are not intended, nor should they be used, as a substitute for professional advice or judgement or to provide legal advice with respect to particular circumstances.

4.8 Whilst reasonable efforts are made to make sure the Materials are up to date, you should obtain independent verification or advice before relying upon any piece of information in circumstances where loss or damage may result.

5. MISCELLANEOUS

5.1 These General Terms and Conditions may be changed from time to time as described below or by written agreement.

5.2 The failure of us or any third party supplier of the Materials to enforce any provision hereof shall not constitute or be construed as a waiver of such provision or of the right to enforce it at a later time.

5.3 You may not assign your rights or delegate your duties under these General Terms and Conditions without our prior written consent.

5.4 These General Terms and Conditions shall be governed by and construed in accordance with the laws of England.

5.5 Each third party supplier of the Materials has the right to assert and enforce these provisions directly on its own behalf as a third party beneficiary.

5.6 We will use personal information collected about Authorised Users for the purposes of (a) providing access to and use of the Goods to Authorised Users, (b) providing customer support, billing and other similar activities related to the Goods, and (c) keeping Authorised Users informed about products, services, offers and upcoming events and to improve our services. We may also provide personal information about Authorised Users to third parties for the purpose of providing Authorised Users with direct marketing offers which we think may be of interest. If you do not wish to receive information about other products, services, offers and events, notify us in writing.

5.7 In accordance with the Data Protection Act 1998 we will provide and export personal information about Authorised Users to other members of our company group, including Reed Elsevier Inc. in the United States, for the purposes of (a) providing access to and use of the Goods to Authorised Users, and (b) providing customer support, billing and other similar activities related to the Goods.

5.8 Save for the owners of any intellectual property supplied by us, no third parties shall acquire any rights under this Agreement and the provisions of the Contracts (Rights of Third Parties) Act 1999 are excluded.